# The technology
## to move the world

Rotem's technology leads the world in the manufacturing safe, hi-tech, hi-speed trains. Our goal is to bring people together safely and quickly, all over the world.

**Rotem**

Rolling stock- Hi-tech Rolling Stock System, Hi-Speed Train, Maglev Vehicle, Light Rail Transit etc. **Plant**- Steel Making Facilities, Press, Crane, Airport Equipment etc. **Defense System**- Main Battle Tank(K1A1), Armored Recovery Vehicle, Armored Vehicle Launched Bridge etc.
#231, Yangjae-dong, Seocho-ku, Seoul, Korea Representative TEL : +82 2 3464 4114  FAX : +82 2 3464 4795

# HITACHI
## Inspire the Next

## We don't just want to be the choice of rail professionals

How do you know when a train manufacturer is here to stay? When it's not just on the shopping list of the rail networks, but on the wish list of the rail enthusiasts.

Hitachi has the design and engineering skills to help provide rail transportation solutions for years to come. And because we're in the UK for the long term, we'll be solving present-giving problems for generations too.

Our proven capabilities include a wide range of trains in operation outside the UK. Now we're ready to prove ourselves in one of the most technically and commercially demanding markets of all.

Soon a verification version of the traction equipment for our A-Train will begin UK trials. So, for anyone who wants a leading technology train, it looks like they've now got their wish.

**Hitachi Europe Ltd**
Old Change House, 128 Queen Victoria Street, London EC4V 4BJ
Tel: 020 7970 2711   Fax: 020 7970 2799
www.hitachi-rail.com

# Jane's
# WORLD RAILWAYS

Edited by Ken Harris
Contributing Editor, Manufacturers: Jackie Clarke

---

Forty-fourth Edition
## 2002-2003

---

Total Number of Entries 3,084  New and Updated Entries 1,252
Total Number of Images 1,132  New Images 302

---

**Bookmark Jane's homepage on**
**http://www.janes.com**

Jane's award-winning web site provides you with continuously updated news and information.
As well as extracts from our world renowned magazines, you can browse the online catalogue,
visit the Press Centre, discover the origins of Jane's, use the extensive glossary,
download our screen saver and much more.

Jane's now offers powerful electronic solutions to meet the rapid changes in your
information requirements. All our data, analysis and imagery are available on CD-ROM
or via a new secure web service – Jane's Online at http://www.janes.com.

Tailored electronic delivery can be provided through Jane's Data Services.
Contact an information consultant at any of our international offices to
find out how Jane's can change the way you work or e-mail us at

info@janes.co.uk *or* info@janes.com

---

ISBN 0 7106 2453 0
"Jane's" is a registered trade mark

Copyright © 2002 by Jane's Information Group Limited, Sentinel House, 163 Brighton Road, Coulsdon, Surrey CR5 2YH, UK

In the USA and its dependencies
Jane's Information Group Inc, 1340 Braddock Place, Suite 300, Alexandria, Virginia 22314-1651, USA

# Acting Global

Take a closer look and you'll see a global force at work. Wherever you go in Asia, Europe or the United States, you'll find we're already there, using our experience and expertise to create successful projects. We're right where you need us to be – all around the world.

We're in China, for example, where the Transrapid will be transporting passengers between Pudong International Airport and downtown Shanghai at speeds of up to 430 km/h by the year 2003.

And we're in Spain, where the RENFE rail authority has opted for the ICE 3. It runs at speeds of up to 350 km/h, making it Europe's fastest series-production train – and making the 650 km trip between Madrid and Barcelona a convenient, short journey of just over 2 hours.

Siemens Transportation Systems. A global player for a global market.

www.siemens.com/ts

## SIEMENS

efficient rail solutions

# Contents

| | |
|---|---|
| **How to use** *Jane's World Railways* | [6] |
| **Glossary** | [8] |
| **Alphabetical list of advertisers** | [11] |
| **Users' Charter** | [18] |
| **Foreword** | [21] |

**Railway Systems**

| | |
|---|---|
| Afghanistan | 3 |
| Albania | 3 |
| Algeria | 4 |
| Angola | 5 |
| Argentina | 7 |
| Armenia | 17 |
| Australia | 18 |
| Austria | 43 |
| Azerbaijan | 50 |
| Bangladesh | 51 |
| Belarus | 52 |
| Belgium | 53 |
| Benin | 57 |
| Bolivia | 58 |
| Bosnia-Herzegovina | 59 |
| Botswana | 60 |
| Brazil | 61 |
| Bulgaria | 72 |
| Burkina Faso | 74 |
| Cambodia | 75 |
| Cameroon | 76 |
| Canada | 76 |
| Chile | 93 |
| China, People's Republic | 97 |
| Colombia | 106 |
| Congo | 108 |
| Congo, Democratic Republic | 108 |
| Costa Rica | 109 |
| Côte d'Ivoire | 110 |
| Croatia | 111 |
| Cuba | 113 |
| Czech Republic | 114 |
| Denmark | 122 |
| Dominican Republic | 131 |
| Ecuador | 131 |
| Egypt | 132 |
| El Salvador | 134 |
| Eritrea | 135 |
| Estonia | 135 |
| Ethiopia | 137 |
| Finland | 138 |
| France | 140 |
| Gabon | 151 |
| Georgia | 151 |
| Germany | 152 |
| Ghana | 177 |
| Greece | 178 |
| Guatemala | 181 |
| Guinea Republic | 182 |
| Honduras | 182 |
| Hungary | 183 |
| India | 186 |
| Indonesia | 197 |

*Contents continued on page [5]*

# Quality Policy

Jane's Information Group is the world's leading unclassified information integrator for military, government and commercial organisations worldwide. To maintain this position, the Company will strive to meet and exceed customers' expectations in the design, production and fulfilment of goods and services.

Information published by Jane's is renowned for its accuracy, authority and impartiality, and the Company is committed to seeking ongoing improvement in both products and processes.

Jane's will at all times endeavour to respond directly to market demands and will also ensure that customer satisfaction is measured and employees are encouraged to question and suggest improvements to working practices.

Jane's will continue to invest in its people through training and development, to meet the Investor in People standards and changing customer requirements.

# Jane's

---

## SELECONTROL® MAS Traffic

**Transport Division**

## Tailor-Made Solutions for Rail Vehicles

We can offer:
- Complete I&C solutions
- Hardware and engineering for vehicle subsystems
- I&C and controller modules
- Technical support, engineering, service

**Selectron**

*a company of*
**Schneider Electric**

Selectron Systems AG
Bernstrasse 70
CH-3250 Lyss
Phone +41 32 387 61 51
Fax +41 32 387 61 00

transport@selectron.ch
www.selectron.ch

# CONTENTS

|  |  |
|---|---|
| Iran | 199 |
| Iraq | 202 |
| Ireland | 203 |
| Israel | 205 |
| Italy | 207 |
| Jamaica | 221 |
| Japan | 222 |
| Jordan | 246 |
| Kazakhstan | 248 |
| Kenya | 249 |
| Kyrgyzia | 250 |
| Korea, North | 250 |
| Korea, South | 251 |
| Kosovo | 254 |
| Laos | 254 |
| Latvia | 254 |
| Lebanon | 256 |
| Liberia | 256 |
| Libya | 257 |
| Lithuania | 257 |
| Luxembourg | 259 |
| Macedonia | 261 |
| Madagascar | 262 |
| Malawi | 263 |
| Malaysia | 264 |
| Mali | 267 |
| Mauritania | 268 |
| Mexico | 268 |
| Moldova | 271 |
| Mongolia | 272 |
| Morocco | 273 |
| Mozambique | 275 |
| Myanmar (Burma) | 276 |
| Namibia | 277 |
| Nepal | 278 |
| Netherlands | 279 |
| New Zealand | 286 |
| Nicaragua | 289 |
| Nigeria | 289 |
| Norway | 290 |
| Pakistan | 293 |
| Panama | 296 |
| Paraguay | 296 |
| Peru | 297 |
| Philippines | 299 |
| Poland | 300 |
| Portugal | 303 |
| Puerto Rico | 306 |
| Romania | 306 |
| Russian Federation | 309 |
| Saudi Arabia | 316 |
| Senegal | 317 |
| Slovakia | 318 |
| Slovenia | 323 |
| South Africa | 324 |
| Spain | 327 |
| Sri Lanka | 337 |
| Sudan | 338 |
| Swaziland | 339 |
| Sweden | 340 |
| Switzerland | 349 |
| Syria | 365 |
| Taiwan | 366 |
| Tajikistan | 368 |
| Tanzania | 369 |
| Thailand | 370 |
| Togo | 373 |
| Tunisia | 373 |
| Turkey | 375 |
| Turkmenistan | 377 |
| Uganda | 378 |
| Ukraine | 379 |
| United Kingdom | 381 |
| United States of America | 408 |
| Uruguay | 453 |
| Uzbekistan | 454 |
| Venezuela | 455 |
| Vietnam | 457 |
| Yugoslavia, Federal Republic | 459 |
| Zambia | 460 |
| Zimbabwe | 462 |

**Operators of international rail services in Europe** ... 467

**Manufacturers**

| | |
|---|---|
| Locomotives and powered/non-powered passenger vehicles | 473 |
| Diesel engines, transmission and fuelling systems | 531 |
| Electric traction equipment | 549 |
| Passenger coach equipment | 559 |
| Freight vehicles and equipment | 587 |
| Brakes and drawgear | 605 |
| Bogies and suspension, wheels and axles, bearings | 619 |
| Simulation and training systems | 639 |
| Signalling and communications systems | 643 |
| Passenger information systems | 669 |
| Revenue collection systems and station equipment | 679 |
| Electrification contractors and equipment suppliers | 691 |
| Cables and cable equipment | 703 |
| Permanent way components, equipment and services | 709 |
| Freight yard and terminal equipment | 757 |
| Vehicle maintenance equipment and services | 765 |
| Turnkey systems contractors | 783 |
| Information technology systems | 789 |

**Rolling stock leasing companies** ... 797

**International railway associations and agencies** ... 805

**Consultancy services** ... 815

**Index** ... 853

---

# DON'T LET OVERRUNS RUIN YOUR DAY!

**CHOOSE RELIABLE BUFFER STOPS FROM**
**RAWIE®**

OVER 39 000 units have been fitted to track ends in METROS, PEOPLE MOVERS, TRAM SYSTEMS and of course MAIN LINE RAILWAYS in order to **save lives** and also protect **vehicles and installations**. Our standard and especially custom made BUFFER STOPS have been delivered to operators in major cities and countries al over the world.

For full information please write to the following address:
A.Rawie GmbH & Co. ● Dorniestr. 11 ● D-49090 Osnabrueck, Germany
Tel: +49 541 91207-0 ● Fax: +49 541 91207-36
email: info@rawie.de Internet: http://www.rawie.de

# How to use *Jane's World Railways*

In order to help our readers, this page gives details of the different sections in this book and an explanation of the 'Entry Tags' we have introduced.

*Jane's World Railways* is designed to give the reader data on railway systems and railway equipment manufacturers across the globe. A companion volume, *Jane's Urban Transport Systems*, gives details on metro, light rail and bus operations in the world's larger cities. Also available in this field is a special report, 'Locomotives and Rolling Stock Forecasts', detailing traction and rolling stock on order and giving a forecasting model for future orders.

*Jane's World Railways* is divided into two main sections. The first half of the book is a country-by-country listing of the railway systems of the world. For most countries, basic data is given on the transport ministry, including key personnel and contact details. System operators then follow, with address, telephone and fax numbers, website, key personnel, track gauge, route length and, where appropriate, length of track electrified and electrification system.

The text description of each system is broken down into a number of standard subheadings: Political background, Finance, Passenger operations, Freight operations, Intermodal operations, New lines, Improvements to existing lines, Major new stations, Traction and rolling stock, Signalling and telecommunications, Electrification and Track. Motive power details are given in tables. The smaller systems do not necessarily have entries for each standard subheading, while for the larger systems the standard subheadings are broken down with italicised subheads on individual subjects.

This section is followed by a list of operators of international rail services in Europe.

The second half of the book concentrates on the manufacturing industry; it is broken into a number of chapters, detailing firms active in different sectors such as locomotive manufacture, permanent way equipment and so on. At the front of each chapter are three company listings: an alphabetical listing, a listing by country and a classified listing. The classified listing allows the reader to look up firms involved in a specific activity within the section: for example, those companies in the 'Locomotives and powered passenger vehicles' section which undertake locomotive remanufacture.

Each entry gives details of the manufacturer including address, telephone, fax, website, key personnel, product information, recent contracts and, where appropriate, recent corporate developments.

After the Systems and Manufacturers sections are sections on rolling stock leasing companies, international railway associations and agencies, information technology systems and consultancy services.

---

*To help users of this title evaluate the published data, Jane's Information Group has divided entries into three categories.*

● **VERIFIED** The editor has made a detailed examination of the entry's content and checked it's relevancy and accuracy for publication in the new edition to the best of his ability.

● **UPDATED** During the verification process, significant changes to content have been made to reflect the latest position known to Jane's at the time of publication.

● *NEW ENTRY* Information on new equipment and/or appearing for the first time in the title.

All new pictures are dated with the year of publication. New pictures this year are dated 2002. Some are followed by a seven digit number for ease of identification by our image library.

Total Number of Entries 3,084    New and Updated Entries 1,252
Total Number of Images 1,132    New Images 302

**DPA** DIRECTORY & DATABASE PUBLISHERS ASSOCIATION MEMBER

All rights reserved. No part of this publication may be reproduced, stored in retrieval systems or transmitted in any form or by any means, electronic, mechanical, photocopying, recording or otherwise, without the prior written permission of the Publishers. Licences, particularly for use of the data in databases or local area networks are available on application to the Publishers. Infringements of any of the above rights will be liable to prosecution under UK or US civil or criminal law.

Copyright enquiries
Contact: Keith Faulkner, Tel/Fax: +44 (0) 1342 305032, e-mail: keith.faulkner@janes.co.uk

British Library Cataloguing-in-Publication Data.
A catalogue record for this book is available from the British Library.

Printed and bound in Great Britain by Bath Press, Bath and Glasgow

---

**DISCLAIMER** This publication is based on research, knowledge and understanding, and to the best of the author's ability the material is current and valid. While the authors, editors, publishers and Jane's Information Group have made reasonable effort to ensure the accuracy of the information contained herein, they cannot be held responsible for any errors found in this publication. The authors, editors, publishers and Jane's Information Group do not bear any responsibility or liability for the information contained herein or for any uses to which it may be put.

While reasonable care has been taken in the compilation and editing of this publication, it should be recognised that the contents are for information purposes only and do not constitute any guidance to the use of the equipment described herein. Jane's Information Group cannot accept any responsibility for any accident, injury, loss or damage arising from the use of this information.

# www.janes.com

## Total access.
## Total content.
## Total control.

Log on to the ultimate online resource providing improved access to Jane's free and subscription information.

Connect from anywhere in the world!

**Jane's**
www.janes.com

---

# METCALFE
## RAILWAY PRODUCTS LIMITED

**Products**

Complete Locomotive Brake Systems. Complete Passenger Coach, and Freight Wagon systems. These are all Oerlikon Type and UIC approved. Brake Cylinders 6" to 18" all UIC approved, Rigging Regulators all types, Tread Brake Units, Brake Actuators, Air Brake Distributor Valves to meet all applications, Distributor Carrier Brackets S2, S3, and S4, Compressor Overhaul Kits, Coupling Heads, Drivers Brake Valves, Drivers Straight Air Brake Valves, EP Valves, Locomotive Operating Valves, Pressure Relay Valves, Brake Accelerator Valves, Passive Values, Changeover Boxes, De-rail Detectors, Cylinder Regulators, Pressure Regulators, Safety Valves, Check Valves, None return Valves, Air Reservoirs, Discharge Valves, Air Filter, Oil & Water Separators, Alcohol Sprayers, Change over Mechanism, Indicators, Levelling Valves, Changeover "Empty-Load" Valves, Wheel slide Protection system, Emergency Brake system, Automatic Train stop system, End Cock, Various Ball cock, Coupling Hoses, Unloading equipment, Pipe Fitting, Walter Bushes, Air Dryers, Windscreen Wiper & Washer systems, Flange Lubrication Systems, Static Test Benches, Mobile Test Benches, A full range of Vacuum Brake equipment is available, and AAR approved Air Brake equipment. We also supply a complete range of spare parts for all of the above systems such as Diaphragms, Seal, "O" Rings, Inserts, Valves, Valve Steams, Springs, Circlips, Antifreeze Units etc. All parts are of European manufacture and UIC approved where applicable. Detailed technical information provided on request. All assemblies are supplied with Test Certificates.

**Key Personnel**

Chairman and Managing Director Mr. Richard H Metcalfe.
Sales Director: Mr Neil Pointon

**Company**

Metcalfe Railways Products Ltd incorporating Metcalfe's Brakes Limited was established in its present format in 1994. The company is ISO 9002 accredited, and are suppliers of UIC railway brake equipment world-wide. All components supplied are manufactured to UIC specification where applicable. We supply a full range of Oerlikon type UIC approved Air Brake Equipment. The company holds a sole distributor agreement with MZT-Hepos A.D and also has sales agreements with other specialised companies of all rail equipment. All goods are of european manufacture unless stated.

**Training**

We are able to offer on site training for the commissioning of equipment, and for the maintenance and overhaul of Air Brake Equipment. This type of training allows you to give your customers confidence in your products and workmanship.

**Steam**

The company also offers the facility to supply and overhaul various types of Injectors & Ejectors together with a full range of Boiler fittings and associated equipment for Steam Locomotives

Tolletts Farm, Leek Old Road, Sutton, Macclesfield, Cheshire SK11 0HZ.
Tel: 0044 (0)1260 252329  Fax: 0044(0)1260 253413  Web: www.metcalfeprodltd.co.uk

# Glossary

| | |
|---|---|
| **AAR** | Association of American Railroads |
| **AC** | Alternating current |
| **ACI** | Automatic car identification |
| **AFC** | Automatic fare collection |
| **APTA** | American Public Transit Association |
| **ATC** | Automatic train control |
| **ATO** | Automatic train operation |
| **ATP** | Automatic train protection. System which takes control of train in event of failure of driver to respond to adverse signals. |
| **AVE** | *Alta Velocidad Española*. Spanish name given to French design of high-speed train. |
| **AVI** | Automatic vehicle identification |
| **BOT** | Build, operate, transfer |
| **CAD** | Computer-aided design |
| **CKD** | Completely knocked down |
| **CRT** | Cathode ray tube |
| **CTC** | Centralised traffic control |
| **cwr** | Continuously welded rail |
| **DBOM** | Design, build, operate and maintain |
| **DC** | Direct current |
| **demu** | Diesel-electric multiple-unit: a dmu with electric transmission. |
| **dmu** | Diesel multiple-unit: a self-powered diesel train. |
| **DPTAC** | Disabled Persons Transport Advisory Committee |
| **DVMD** | Distance/velocity measurement device |
| **EC** | EuroCity. European international intercity passenger service conforming to predetermined levels of quality. |
| **E & M** | Electrical and mechanical |
| **EMD** | Electro Motive Division (former name of locomotive manufacturing division of General Motors) |
| **emu** | Electric multiple-unit: a self-powered electric train. |
| **EuroCity** | European international passenger service meeting predetermined standards for performance and accommodation. |
| **GDP** | Gross domestic product, a measure of national output. |
| **GE** | General Electric |
| **GIS** | Geographical Information System |
| **GM** | General Motors |
| **GNP** | Gross national product, a measure of national income, counting GDP plus income from foreign investments. |
| **GPS** | Global positioning system (satellite tracking technology) |
| **GTO** | Gate turn-off thyristor employed in traction control systems |
| **HVAC** | Heating, ventilation and air conditioning |
| **Hz** | Hertz (unit of measurement of the electrical frequency of AC power systems) |
| **IC** | InterCity. European domestic intercity passenger service conforming to predetermined levels of quality. |
| **ICE** | InterCity Express. The German design of high-speed train. |
| **ICN** | InterCity Night. Brand name for German Rail's overnight services. |
| **ICT** | InterCity Tilt. The German design of intercity tilting train. |
| **IGBT** | Integrated gate bipolar transistor. Leading edge technology for control of electric traction systems. |
| **Indusi** | German driver vigilance system |
| **kV** | Kilovolts. 1 kV = 1,000 V |
| **kW** | Lilowatts. 1 kW = 1,000 W |
| **LCD** | Liquid crystal display |
| **LED** | Light-emitting diode |
| **LGV** | *Ligne à Grande Vitesse*. French high-speed line |
| **LIM** | Linear induction motor |
| **LRT** | Light rapid transit (modern tram system) |
| **LRV** | Light rail vehicle, for operations on urban systems (a modern tram) |
| **LZB** | *Linienzugbeeinflussung* (ATP) |
| **Maglev** | Magnetic levitation |
| **MW** | Megawatts. 1 MW = 1,000 kW |
| **NBS** | *Neubaustrecke*. Newly constructed line, usually for high-speed services, in Germany |
| **OEM** | Original equipment manufacturer |
| **ppa** | Passengers per annum |
| **Pendolino** | Italian tilting train, designed by Fiat. |
| **RoLa** | *Rollende Landstrasse*. 'Rolling highway' piggyback system for conveying lorries. |
| **S-Bahn** | High-frequency heavy rail suburban passenger service in Austria, Germany and Switzerland. |
| **Shinkansen** | Japanese high-speed railway system |
| **TAV** | *Treno Alta Velocita*. The Italian design of high-speed train. |
| **TEU** | foot equivalent units (standard method of measuring container capacity/traffic) |
| **TGV** | *Train à Grande Vitesse*. The French design of high-speed train. |
| **TOC** | Train Operating Company |
| **TVM** | French-designed cab-signalling system, as used on the TGV network |
| **UIC** | Union Internationale de Chemin de Fer. International trade association and lobying organisation for railway operating companies, based in Paris. |
| **UIRR** | International Union of Road-Rail Transport Companies. Formed to develop and operate combined transport in Europe. |
| **UNIFE** | International trade association for European railway equipment manufacturers, based in Brussels. |
| **VVVF** | Variable voltage, variable frequency. Leading edge technology for the control of electric traction systems |
| **X2000** | Swedish tilting train, designed by Adtranz (now Bombardier Transportation) |

**Locomotive wheel arrangement**

A classification system is used whereby the number of driven axles on a bogie or frame is denoted by a letter (A = 1, B = 2, C = 3) and the number of undriven axles is noted by a number. The letter 'o' after a letter indicates that each axle is powered individually.

The most common types are Co-Co, two three-axle bogies, all axles individually powered, and Bo-Bo, a similar machine but with two-axle bogies rather than three-axle ones. In the former Soviet bloc, many double and triple unit locomotives exist, such as Bo-Bo+Bo-Bo.

# italferr
## engineering on the move

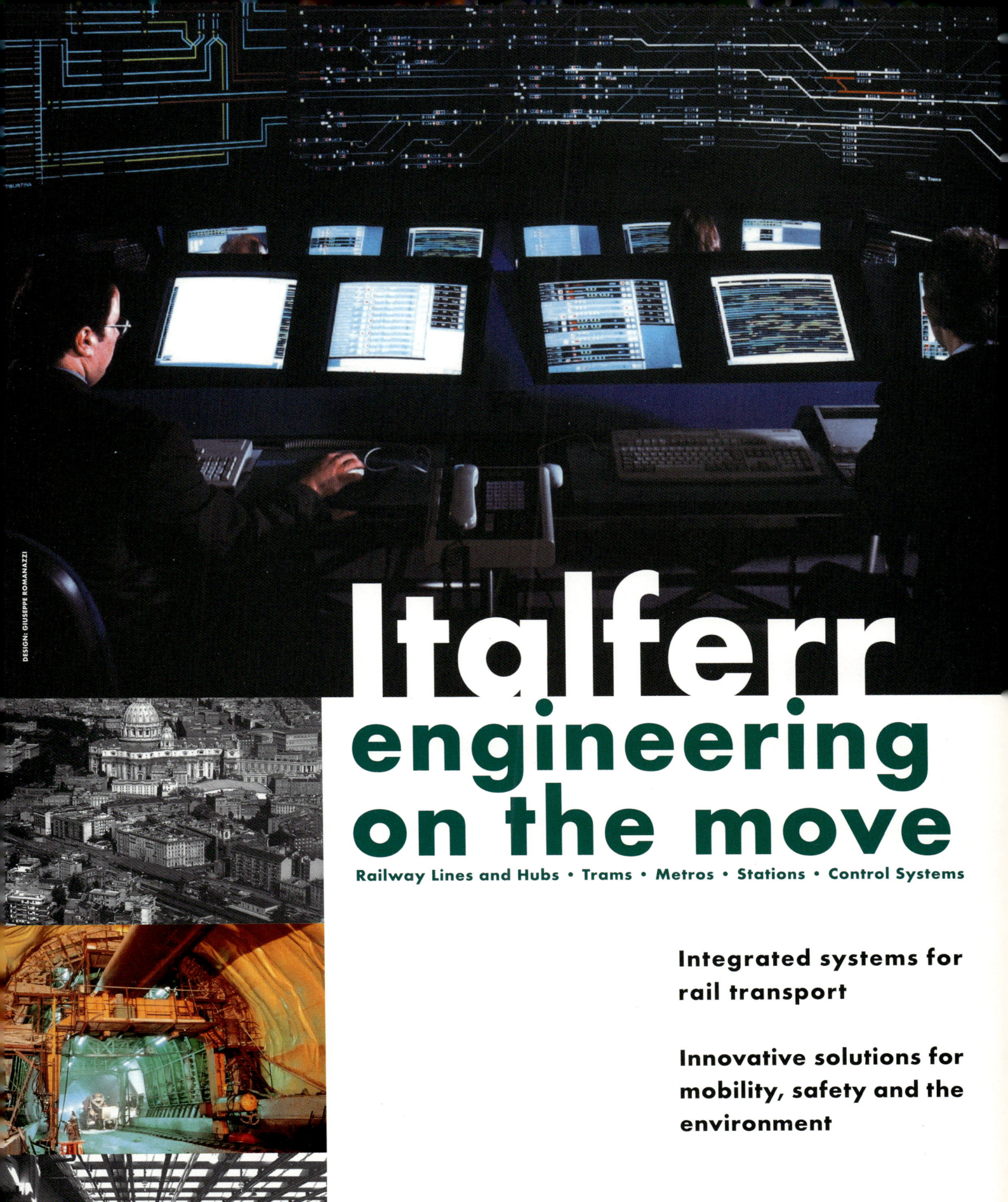

Railway Lines and Hubs • Trams • Metros • Stations • Control Systems

Integrated systems for rail transport

Innovative solutions for mobility, safety and the environment

DESIGN: GIUSEPPE ROMANAZZI

**ITALFERR S.p.A.**
via Marsala 53 • 00185 Roma • Italy
tel. +39.06.49751 • fax +39.06.49752437
web site: www.italferr.it
e.mail: italferr@mail.italferr.it

Engineering company of the Ferrovie dello Stato

ITALFERR

**AVAILABLE IN HARDCOPY • CD-ROM • ONLINE**

# Transport
## family of titles

### Jane's Airports, Equipment and Services
The indispensable guide to the world's airport suppliers, manufacturers and their products. With details of more than 1,500 specialised contractors this is an essential tool for efficient airport management.

### Jane's Airports and Handling Agents
A unique planning tool that enables pilots and operations centres to research the facilities available at over 1,600 airports throughout the world and puts you in contact with more than 2,700 handling agents/FBOs.

### Jane's Air Traffic Control
An extensive review of ATC manufacturers and equipment, allowing you to analyse all the latest developments and technologies from around the world. You will discover systems in use, who manufactures them and what plans are in place for the next millennium.

### Jane's Urban Transport Systems
Used by transport professionals, this comprehensive guide provides unrivalled information on transportation systems in place, and planned, in over 400 cities from 115 countries worldwide.

You will also find details of more than 1,000 manufacturers, consultants and contracting services — complete with full contact details.

### Jane's World Airlines
An invaluable source of information and analysis of over 500 of the world's leading airlines. The extensive coverage includes fleet details, profit and loss and balance sheet figures, key personnel, traffic statistics, overhaul and maintenance, reservation systems and more.

### Jane's World Railways
The foremost source of information on railway operators and manufacturers, providing you with in-depth market intelligence of more than 450 railway systems operating in 120 countries worldwide. In excess of 1,400 manufacturers, suppliers and service companies are listed, with concise descriptions and specifications of their products and services.

## Other Jane's titles

**Magazines**
Jane's Airport Review
Jane's Asian Infrastructure
Jane's Defence Industry
Jane's Defence Upgrades
Jane's Defence Weekly
Jane's Foreign Report
Jane's Inner Circle
Jane's Intelligence Digest
Jane's Intelligence Review
Jane's International Defense Review
Jane's Islamic Affairs Analyst
Jane's Missiles and Rockets
Jane's Navy International
Jane's Terrorism and Security Monitor
Jane's Transport Finance
Police Review

**Security**
Jane's Chem-Bio Handbook
Jane's Chemical-Biological Defense Guidebook
Jane's Copcase
Jane's Counter Terrorism
Jane's Facility Security Handbook
Jane's Intelligence Watch Report
Jane's Police and Security Equipment
Jane's School Safety Handbook
Jane's Sentinel Security Assessments
Jane's Terrorism Watch Report
Jane's World Insurgency and Terrorism

**Industry**
Jane's International ABC Aerospace Directory
Jane's International Defence Directory
Jane's World Defence Industry

**Systems**
Jane's C$^4$I Systems
Jane's Electronic Mission Aircraft
Jane's Electro-Optic Systems
Jane's Military Communications
Jane's Radar and Electronic Warfare Systems
Jane's Simulation and Training Systems
Jane's Strategic Weapon Systems

**Land**
Jane's Ammunition Handbook
Jane's Armour and Artillery
Jane's Armour and Artillery Upgrades
Jane's Explosive Ordnance Disposal
Jane's Infantry Weapons
Jane's Land-Based Air Defence
Jane's Military Biographies
Jane's Military Vehicles and Logistics
Jane's Mines and Mine Clearance
Jane's Nuclear, Biological and Chemical Defence
Jane's Personal Combat Equipment
Jane's World Armies

**Air**
Jane's Aero-Engines
Jane's Aircraft Component Manufacturers
Jane's Aircraft Upgrades
Jane's Air-Launched Weapons
Jane's All the World's Aircraft
Jane's Avionics
Jane's Helicopter Markets and Systems
Jane's Space Directory
Jane's Unmanned Aerial Vehicles and Targets
Jane's World Air Forces

**Sea**
Jane's Amphibious and Special Forces
Jane's Exclusive Economic Zones
Jane's Fighting Ships
Jane's High-Speed Marine Transportation
Jane's Marine Propulsion
Jane's Merchant Ships
Jane's Naval Construction and Retrofit Markets
Jane's Naval Weapon Systems
Jane's Survey Vessels
Jane's Underwater Technology
Jane's Underwater Warfare Systems

# www.janes.com

# Alphabetical list of advertisers

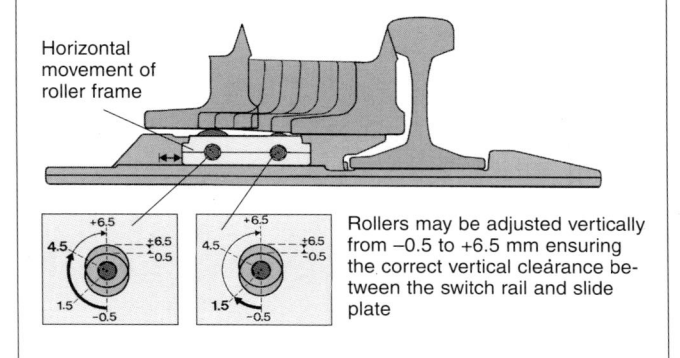

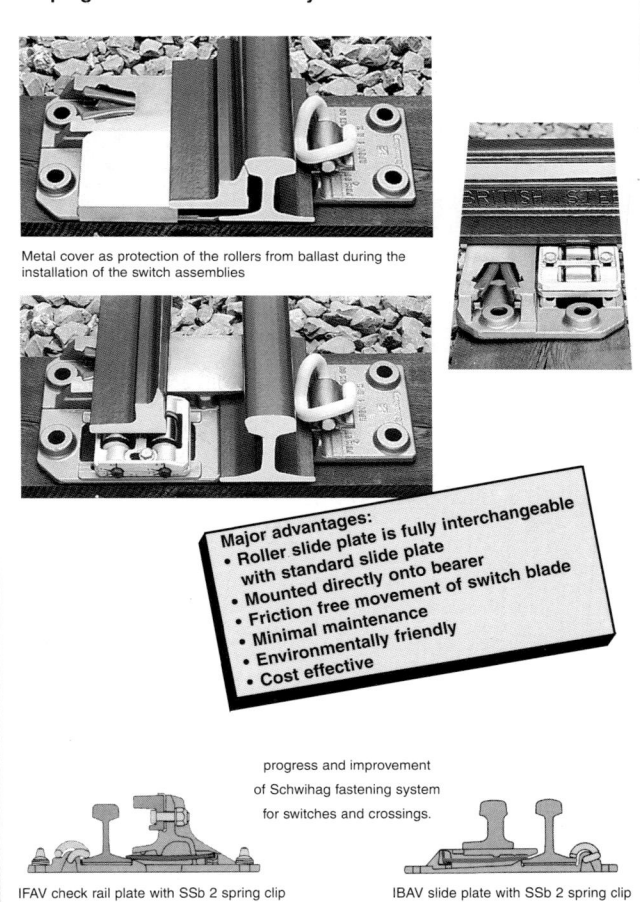

## A

**Alcatel TAS**
Building S, 1st floor, 10 rue Latécoère BP57,
F-78141 Vélizy Cedex, France .............................. 647

**Alstom**
48 rue Albert Dhalenne, F-93482 Saint-Ouen Cedex,
France ................................................................. *Spine*

**Ansaldobreda Spa**
Via Argine 425, I-80147 Napoli,
Italy ............................................... *Outside front cover*

**APS electronic Ltd**
Bahnhofstrasse 135, CH-4626 Niederbuchsiten,
Switzerland ........................................................... 549

## B

**Behr Industrietechnik GmbH & Co**
Heilbronner Strasse 380, D-70469 Stuttgart, Germany ........ 537

**Bochumer Verein, Verkehrstechnik GmbH**
Alleestrasse 70, D-44793 Bochum, Germany ....................... 623

**Gebr Bode & Co GmbH**
Ochshäuser Strasse 14, D-34123 Kassel,
Germany ................................................ 581 and 583

**Bombardier Transportation GmbH**
Saatwinkler Damm 43, D-13627 Berlin,
Germany ....................................... *Inside front cover*

## D

**DEUTA-Werke GmbH**
Paffrather Strasse 140, D-51465 Bergisch Gladbach,
Germany ........................................ *Facing page* 642

## F

**Walter Finkbeiner GmbH**
Alte Postrasse 9, D-72250 Freudenstadt, Germany ............. 767

**Freudenberg Schwab GmbH**
Postplatz 3, D-16761 Hennigsdorf, Germany ....................... 584

**Furrer + Frey AG**
Thunstrasse 35, PO Box 182, CH-3000 Berne 6,
Switzerland ........................................................... 691

## ALPHABETICAL LIST OF ADVERTISERS

### G

**G E Transportation Systems**
1300 Jefferson Court, Blue Springs, Missouri 64015,
USA .................................................................... *Facing page* 643

**Gottwald Port Technology GmbH**
PO Box 180343, D-40570 Düsseldorf, Germany ................. 715

**Gummi Metall Technik GmbH**
Liechtersmatten 5, D-77815 Bühl, Germany ....................... 585

### H

**Hitachi Europe Ltd**
Old Change House, 128 Queen Victoria Street,
London EC4V 4BJ, UK .............................. *Opposite title page*

### I

**International Technical Services**
400 Queens Avenue, London, Ontario N6B 1X9,
Canada ................................................................................ 819

**Italferr S.p.A.**
via Marsala 53, I-00185 Rome, Italy ..................................... [9]

### K

**KLW-Wheelco SA**
Via Calloni 1, PO Box 45, CH-6907 Lugano,
Switzerland ........................................................................ 631

**Knorr-Bremse AG**
Moosacher Strasse 80, D-80809 Munich,
Germany .......................................................... *Facing page* 604

### L

**LAF**
55 rue du Bois Chaland, CE 2928, F-91090 Lisses,
France ................................................................................ 611

**Lahmeyer International GmbH**
Friedberger Strasse 173, D-61118 Bad Vilbel, Germany ..... 817

**Lucchini SpA**
Via Paglia 45, I-24065 Lovere, Italy ............ *Outside back cover*

### M

**Metcalfe Railway Products Limited**
Tolletts Farm, Leek Old Road, Sutton, Macclesfield,
Cheshire SK11 0HZ, UK ..................................................... [7]

**Miba Gleitlager GmbH**
Dr-Mitterbauer-Strasse 3, A-4663 Laakirchen, Austria ........ 629

### N

**Nabco Ltd**
9-18 Kaigan-1-chome, Minatoku, Tokyo 105-0022,
Japan ................................................................................. 615

### O

**Orx**
One Park Avenue, Tipton, Pennsylvania 16684,
USA ................................................... *Facing pages* 618 and 619

### P

**Parsons Brinkerhoff**
One Penn Plaza, New York, New York 10119-0061,
USA .................................................................................. [13]

**Pfleiderer**
Ingolstaedter Strasse 51, D-92318 Neumarkt,
Germany ................................................................. 711 and 739

**Plasser & Theurer GmbH**
Johannesgasse 3, A-1010 Vienna, Austria ....... *Facing page* 709

### Q

**QR Consulting Services**
GPO Box 1429, Brisbane, Queensland 4001, Australia ....... 829

### R

**Radsatzfabrik Ilsenburg GmbH**
Schmiedestrasse 16/17, D-38871, Ilsenburg, Germany ....... [23]

**Rail Services International**
38 rue de la Convention, F-94270 Le Kremlin-Bicetre,
France ................................................................................ 477

---

**DISCLAIMER**

Jane's Information Group gives no warranties, conditions, guarantees or representations, express or implied, as to the content of any advertisements, including but not limited to compliance with description and quality or fitness for purpose of the product or service. Jane's Information Group will not be liable for any damages, including without limitation, direct, indirect or consequential damages arising from any use of products or services or any actions or omissions taken in direct reliance on information contained in advertisements.

# ALPHABETICAL LIST OF ADVERTISERS

**A Rawie GmbH & Co**
Dornierstrasse 11, D-49090 Osnabruck, Germany ................ [5]

**Robel Bahnbaumaschinen GmbH**
Industriestrasse 31, D-83395 Freilassing, Germany ............. [3]

**Rotem**
231 Yangjae-dong, Seocho-ku, Seoul,
South Korea ......................... *Facing inside front cover*

## S

**Schwihag Gesellschaft für Eisenbahnoberbau mbH**
Lebernstrasse 3, CH-8274 Tägerwilen, Switzerland ............ [11]

**Sécheron SA**
14 Avenue de Secheron, CH-1211 Geneva, Switzerland ..... [15]

**Selectron Systems AG**
Bernstrasse 70, CH-3250 Lyss, Switzerland .......................... [4]

**Siemens AG**
PO Box 3240, D-91052 Erlangen, Germany ......................... [2]

**Speno International SA**
26 Parc Château-Banquet, CH-1211 Geneva 21,
Switzerland ..................................................... *Facing page* 708

**SwedeRail AB**
S-10550 Stockholm, Sweden ................................................. 825

## V

**Voith Turbo GmbH**
Alexanderstrasse 2, D-89522 Heidenheim,
Germany ........................................................ *Facing page* 531

**VSFT Vossloh Schienenfahrzeugtechnik GmbH**
PO Box 9293, D-24159 Kiel, Germany ................................ 473

---

## Leaders in Rail Engineering for Over a Century

Beginning with the original New York City subway, designed by William Barclay Parsons in the 1890s, to our current role on the Taiwan High Speed Rail project, Parsons Brinckerhoff has been a world leader in rail engineering.

w w w . p b w o r l d . c o m

**PB** 100 YEARS

## EDITORIAL AND ADMINISTRATION

**Publishing Director:** Alan Condron, e-mail: Alan.Condron@janes.co.uk

**Managing Editor:** Simon Michell, Simon.Michell@janes.co.uk

**Group Content Manager:** Anita Slade, e-mail: Anita.Slade@janes.co.uk

**Content Editing Manager:** Jo Agius, e-mail: Jo.Agius@janes.co.uk

**Pre-Press Manager:** Christopher Morris, Christopher.Morris@janes.co.uk

**Team Leaders:** Sharon Marshall, e-mail: Sharon.Marshall@janes.co.uk
Neil Grace, e-mail: Neil.Grace @janes.co.uk

**Production Editor:** Melanie Rovery, e-mail: Melanie.Rovery @janes.co.uk

**Production Controller:** Victoria Powell, Victoria.Powell@janes.co.uk

**Content Update:** Jacqui Beard, Information Collection Co-Ordinator
Tel: (+44 20) 87 00 38 08 Fax: (+44 20) 87 00 39 59
e-mail: yearbook@janes.co.uk

Jane's Information Group Limited, Sentinel House, 163 Brighton Road, Coulsdon, Surrey CR5 2YH, UK
Tel: (+44 20) 87 00 37 00 Fax: (+44 20) 87 00 37 88
e-mail: jwr@janes.co.uk

## SALES OFFICES

**Send Europe, Middle East and Africa enquiries to:** *Mike Gwynn – Head of Information Sales*
Jane's Information Group Limited, Sentinel House, 163 Brighton Road, Coulsdon, Surrey CR5 2YH, UK
Tel: (+44 20) 87 00 37 00 Fax: (+44 20) 87 63 10 06
e-mail: info@janes.co.uk

Send USA enquiries to: *Robert Loughman – Sales Director*
Jane's Information Group Inc, 1340 Braddock Place, Suite 300, Alexandria, Virginia 22314-1651, USA
Tel: (+1 703) 683 37 00 Fax: (+1 703) 836 02 97 Telex: 6819193
Tel: (+1 800) 824 07 68 Fax: (+1 800) 836 02 971
e-mail: info@janes.com

Send Asia enquiries to: *David Fisher – Group Business Manager*
Jane's Information Group Asia, 5 Shenton Way , #01-01 UIC Building, Singapore 068808
Tel: (+65) 6410 1240 Fax: (+65) 6226 1185
e-mail: info@janes.com.sg

Send Australia/New Zealand enquiries to: *Pauline Roberts – Business Manager*
Jane's Information Group, PO Box 3502, Rozelle Delivery Centre, New South Wales 2039, Australia
Tel: (+61 2) 85 87 79 00 Fax: (+61 2) 85 87 79 01
e-mail: info@janes.thomson.com.au

---

## ADVERTISEMENT SALES OFFICES

**(Head Office)**
**Jane's Information Group**
Sentinel House, 163 Brighton Road,
Coulsdon, Surrey CR5 2YH
Tel: (+44 20) 87 00 37 00
Fax: (+44 20) 87 00 38 59/37 44
e-mail: transadsales@janes.co.uk

**Robert Sitch,** Advertisement Sales Manager – Transport
Tel: (+44 20) 87 00 37 41
Fax: (+44 20) 87 00 38 59/37 44
e-mail: robert.sitch@janes.co.uk

**USA/Canada**

**Jane's Information Group**
1340 Braddock Place, Suite 300,
Alexandria, Virginia 22314-1651, USA
Tel: (+1 703) 683 37 00
Fax: (+1 703) 836 55 37
e-mail: transadsales@janes.com

Katie Taplett, US Advertising Sales Director
Tel: (+1 703) 683 37 00
Fax (+1 703) 836 55 37
e-mail: katie.taplett@janes.com

Sean Fitzgerald, Account Executive
Tel: (+1 703) 683 37 00
Fax: (+1 703) 836 55 37
e-mail: sean.fitzgerald@janes.com

**Northern USA and Eastern Canada**
Harry Carter, Advertising Sales Manager
Tel: (+1 703) 683 37 00
Fax: (+1 703) 836 55 37
e-mail: harry.carter@janes.com

**South Eastern USA**
Kristin D Schulze, Advertising Sales Manager
PO Box 270190, Tampa, Florida 33688-0190
Tel: (+1 813) 961 81 32
Fax: (+1 813) 961 96 42
e-mail: kristin@intnet.net

**Australia:** *The Falsten Partnership (see Scandinavia)*

**Benelux:** *The Falsten Partnership (see Scandinavia)*

**RFAS, Eastern Europe, France, Germany and Austria:** *Robert Sitch (UK Head Office)*

**Hong Kong:** *The Falsten Partnership (see Scandinavia)*

**Israel:** *Oreet – International Media*
Tel: (+972 3) 570 65 27
Fax: (+972 3) 570 65 26
e-mail: liat_h@oreet-marcom.com

**Italy and Switzerland:** *Ediconsult Internazionale Srl*
Tel: (+39 010) 58 36 84
Fax: (+39 010) 56 65 78
e-mail: genova@ediconsult.com

**Japan:** Skynet Media, Inc
Contact: Mr Osamu Yoneda
Tel: (+81 3) 54 74 78 35
Fax: (+81 3) 54 74 78 37
skynetme@wonder.ocn.ne.jp

**Middle East:** Robert Sitch (see UK Head Office)

**Russia:** Vladimir N Usov
Tel/Fax 007 (3435) 329-623
e-mail: uvn125@uraltelecom.ru

**Scandinavia:** *The Falsten Partnership*
Tel: (+44 20) 88 06 23 01
Fax: (+44 20) 88 06 81 37
e-mail: sales@falsten.com

**Singapore:** *The Falsten Partnership (see Scandinavia)*

**South Africa:** *The Falsten Partnership (see Scandinavia)*

**South Korea:** *JES Media Inc*
*Contact*: Mr. Young-Seoh Chinn, President
Tel: (+82 2) 481 34 11/3
Fax: (+82 2) 481 34 14
e-mail: jesmedia@unitel.co.kr

**Spain:** *Via Exclusivas, SL*
*Contact:* Julio de Andres
C/Viriato no 69SC, E-28010 Madrid
Tel: (+34 91) 448 76 22
Fax: (+34 91) 446 0214
e-mail: j.a.deandres@viaexclusivas.com

For all other areas, contact Robert Sitch (UK Head Office)

**ADVERTISING COPY**
Linda Letori (Jane's UK Head Office)
Tel: (+44 20) 87 00 38 56
Fax: (+44 20) 87 00 38 59; 37 44
e-mail: linda.letori@janes.co.uk

**For North America, South America and Caribbean only:**
Shanee Johnson (Jane's USA address)
Tel: (+1 703) 683 37 00
Fax: (+1 703) 836 55 37
e-mail: shanee.johnson@janes.com

# Take stock of new market opportunities...

## Locomotive and Rolling Stock Forecasts – Edition 2

### A Jane's Special Report

An essential report for anyone involved in strategic decision making in the locomotive and rolling stock industry, this in-depth guide provides you with expert insight into current and future trends in the locomotive and rolling stock industry around the world.

Contents include:
- Survey of current locomotive markets
- Survey of current passenger vehicle markets
- Survey of current urban passenger vehicle markets
- Structure of the rail manufacturing industry
- Thumbnail sketches of principal manufacturers
- Projected demand for:
  locomotives and multiple- unit passenger coaches main line passenger coaches
  urban locomotives and passenger rail vehicles
  freight wagons
- Glossary of terms and abbreviations

For further information, please visit our online catalogue at www.janes.com

**Jane's**
www.janes.com

---

## LET US HELP YOU FIND THE RIGHT SOLUTION

Everyday throughout the world millions of people travel on trains, trams, subways or trolleybuses. This demand for public transport systems will continue to grow over the years to come and will require higher levels of security and quality.

Sécheron has been a leader in the field of electrical transportation engineering for over a century. Our innovative approach to the design of high performance and high quality products guarantees efficient protection and an optimal level of safety for the passengers as well as high reliability for the end-users. With our complete range of **protection switches** and **breakers**, **electronic control devices** for Rolling Stock and/or Fixed Installations (**DC Switchgear**), and **speed measuring** and **data acquisition systems**, we are sure that Sécheron can certainly fulfil one of your requirements.

*Assembly of a line of DC High Speed Circuit Breakers, one of the key elements in the protection system.*

**Sécheron**
*Technology Designed for Performance*

ISO 9001

Sécheron SA
P.O. Box 116
1211 Geneva 21
Switzerland

Tel: +41 (0)22 739 41 11
Fax: +41 (0)22 738 73 05
E-mail: info@secheron.com
www.secheron.com

**JANE'S ONLINE • CD-ROM • DATA SERVICE • CONSULTANCY**

# Information Services & Solutions

Jane's is the leading unclassified information provider for military, government and commercial organisations worldwide, in the fields of defence, geopolitics, transportation and law enforcement.

We are dedicated to providing the information our customers need, in the formats and frequency they require. Read on to find out how Jane's information in electronic format can provide you with the best way to access the information you require.

## Jane's Online

**Why not choose the online format for your Jane's information?**

Choosing to subscribe to Jane's information online will allow you to get the maximum use of the detailed information, as you will have:
- Instant access 24-hours a day.
- Advanced power search tools to take you directly to the information you are seeking.
- The opportunity to browse the information section-by-section and copy and paste the information for use in your own internal presentations.
- High quality colour JPEG images to support recognition and for use in your internal presentations.
- Active interlinking allows you to navigate via hyperlinks in records, within the viewed documents, to other related information, thus reducing your search time down to minutes.
- Regular monthly updates to ensure you always have the most current information available.

Jane's information is accessible by IP address for networking within your organisation or by unique username and password, allowing you access from anywhere in the world.

Check out this site today: http://www.janes.com

## Jane's CD-ROM Libraries

**Quickly pinpoint the information you require from Jane's**

Choose from nine powerful CD-ROM libraries for quick and easy access to the defence, geopolitical, space, transportation and law enforcement information you need. Take full advantage of the information groupings and purchase the entire library.

Libraries available:
Jane's Air Systems Library
Jane's Defence Equipment Library
Jane's Defence Magazines Library
Jane's Geopolitical Library
Jane's Land and Systems Library
Jane's Market Intelligence Library
Jane's Police and Security Library
Jane's Sea and Systems Library
Jane's Transport Library

**Key benefits of Jane's CD-ROM include:**
- Quick and easy access to Jane's information and graphics
- Easy-to-use Windows interface with powerful search capabilities
- Online glossary and synonym searching
- Search across all the titles on each disc, even if you do not subscribe to them, to determine whether you would like to add them to your library
- Export and print out text or graphics
- Quarterly updates
- Full networking capability
- Supported by an experienced technical team

## Jane's Data Service – Intranet Solution

**Get Jane's Data behind your intranet**

**Access over 200 sources of defence, security, law enforcement and transport data, integrated behind your intranet or closed network**

When you need mission-critical information, searching across multiple sources retrieves your answers quickly and easily. Integrate Jane's data with your own intelligence sources and your users can rely on the impartiality, accuracy and authority of Jane's information as a benchmark. With more users able to access Jane's directly from their desktop, you can centrally streamline your information requirements to better monitor and respond to needs as they arise.

- Flexibility of choice with your selection of Jane's data
- Full integration of data into a secure environment
- Frequent updates via e-mail or ftp
- All data can be exported into other desktop applications
- High quality JPEG images for recognition training, internal briefing or analysis

For further information contact your local Jane's office or e-mail: jds@janes.co.uk

## Jane's Consultancy

Jane's Consultancy draws on a unique international network of experts to undertake special research on your behalf, to your specifications. Simply contact us, in confidence, with your requirements and we will provide the expert and authoritative research you need.
- Unrivalled access to hard-to-find information
- Impartial expert analysis
- Unique global reach providing a balanced view
- Cost and time effective solutions
- Complete confidentiality

Visit consultancy.janes.com today and put our experts to work for you. Alternatively contact your nearest Jane's office or e-mail: consultancy@janes.com

**The information you require, delivered in a format to suit your needs.**

# www.janes.com

# FREE ENTRY/CONTENT IN THIS PUBLICATION

Having your products and services represented in our titles means that they are being seen by the professionals who matter – both by those involved in procurement and by those working for the companies that are likely to affect your business. We therefore feel that it is very much in the interests of your organisation, as well as Jane's, to ensure your data is current and accurate.

- **Don't forget** – You may be missing out on business if your entry in a Jane's book, CD-ROM or Online product is incorrect because you have not supplied the latest information to us.

- **Ask yourself** – Can you afford not to be represented in Jane's printed and electronic products? And if you are listed, can you afford for your information to be out of date?

- **And most importantly** – The best part of all is that your entries in Jane's products are TOTALLY FREE OF CHARGE.

**Please provide (using a photocopy of this form) the information on the following categories where appropriate:**

1. Organisation name: _____
2. Division name: _____
3. Location address: _____
   _____
4. Mailing address if different: _____
   _____
5. Telephone (please include switchboard and main department contact numbers, for example Public Relations, Sales, and so on):
   _____
6. Facsimile: _____
7. E-mail: _____
8. Web sites: _____
9. Contact name and job title: _____
   _____
10. A brief description of your organisation's activities, products and services: _____
    _____
    _____
11. Jane's publications in which you would like to be included: _____
    _____

**Please send this information to:**
Jacqui Beard, Information Collection, Jane's Information Group,
Sentinel House, 163 Brighton Road, Coulsdon, Surrey, CR5 2YH, UK
Tel: (+44 20) 87 00 38 08
Fax: (+44 20) 87 00 39 59
E-mail: yearbook@janes.co.uk

**Copyright enquiries:**
Contact: Keith Faulkner
Tel/Fax: (+44 1342) 30 50 32
E-mail: keith.faulkner@janes.co.uk

Please tick this box if you do not wish your organisation's staff to be included in Jane's mailing lists ☐

JWR

# Users' Charter

This publication is brought to you by Jane's Information Group, a global company with more than 100 years of innovation and an unrivalled reputation for impartiality, accuracy and authority.

Our collection and output of information and images is not dictated by any political or commercial affiliation. Our reportage is undertaken without fear of, or favour from, any government, alliance, state or corporation.

We publish information that is collected overtly from unclassified sources, although much could be regarded as extremely sensitive or not publicly accessible.

Our validation and analysis aims to eradicate misinformation or disinformation as well as factual errors; our objective is always to produce the most accurate and authoritative data.

In the event of any significant inaccuracies, we undertake to draw these to the readers' attention to preserve the highly valued relationship of trust and credibility with our customers worldwide.

If you believe that these policies have been breached by this title, you are invited to contact the editor.

A copy of Jane's Information Group's Code of Conduct for its editorial teams is available from the publisher.

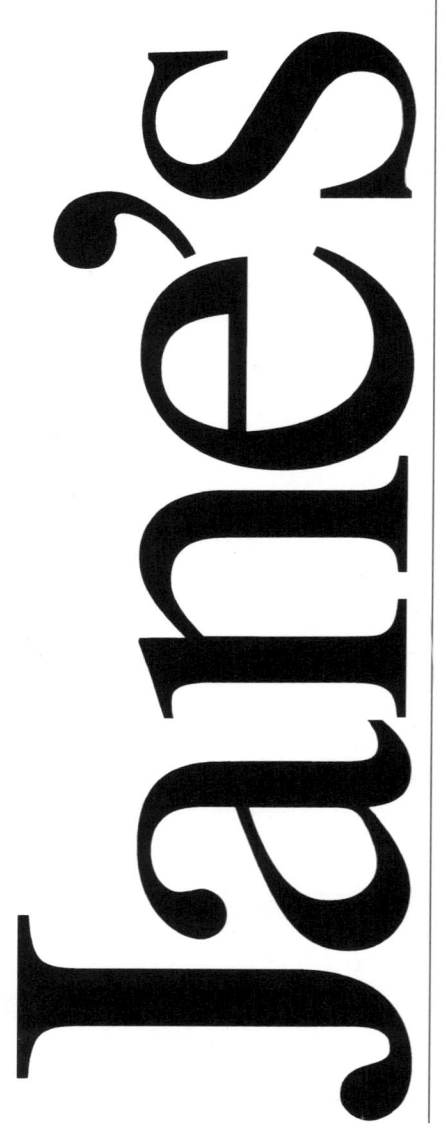

INVESTOR IN PEOPLE

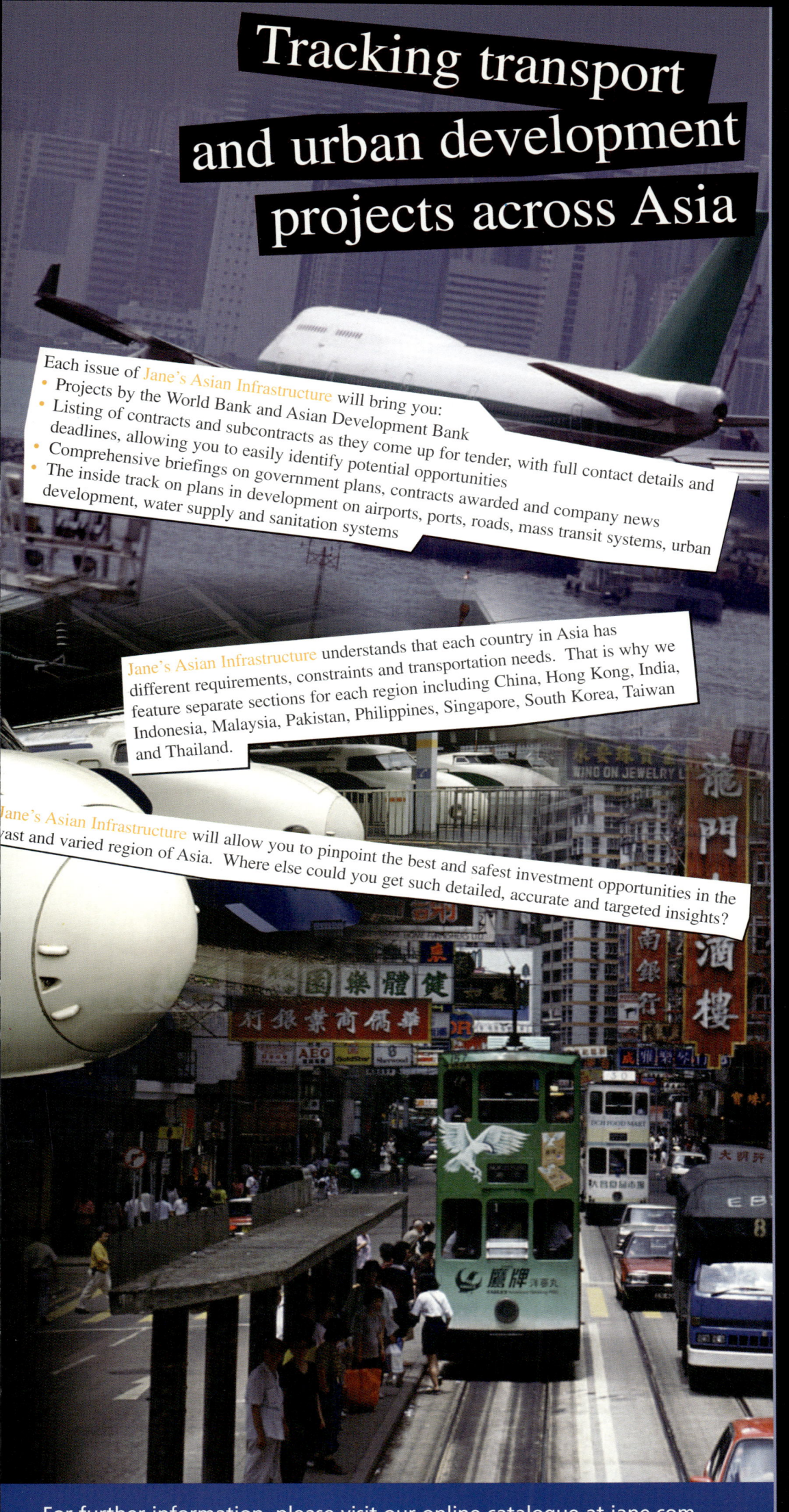

# Tracking transport and urban development projects across Asia

Each issue of *Jane's Asian Infrastructure* will bring you:
- Projects by the World Bank and Asian Development Bank
- Listing of contracts and subcontracts as they come up for tender, with full contact details and deadlines, allowing you to easily identify potential opportunities
- Comprehensive briefings on government plans, contracts awarded and company news
- The inside track on plans in development on airports, ports, roads, mass transit systems, urban development, water supply and sanitation systems

*Jane's Asian Infrastructure* understands that each country in Asia has different requirements, constraints and transportation needs. That is why we feature separate sections for each region including China, Hong Kong, India, Indonesia, Malaysia, Pakistan, Philippines, Singapore, South Korea, Taiwan and Thailand.

*Jane's Asian Infrastructure* will allow you to pinpoint the best and safest investment opportunities in the vast and varied region of Asia. Where else could you get such detailed, accurate and targeted insights?

For further information, please visit our online catalogue at jane.com or telephone your local sales office using one of the numbers below

## Jane's ASIAN INFRASTRUCTURE

**Europe, Middle East and Africa**
Jane's Information Group
Sentinel House
163 Brighton Road
Coulsdon, Surrey CR5 2YH
United Kingdom
Tel: (+44 20) 8700 3700
Fax: (+44 20) 8763 1006
e-mail: info@janes.co.uk

**London**
Jane's Information Group
The Quadrangle
180 Wardour Street, 1st Floor
London W1F 8FY
United Kingdom
Tel: (+44 20) 8700 3700
Fax: (+44 20) 8763 1006
e-mail: info@janes.co.uk

**North/Central/South America**
Jane's Information Group
1340 Braddock Place
Suite 300
Alexandria, Virginia 22314-1657
United States
Tel: (+1 703) 683 3700
    (+1 800) 824 0768
Fax: (+1 703) 836 0297
    (+1 800) 836 0297
e-mail: info@janes.com

**USA West Coast**
Jane's Information Group
201 East Sandpointe Avenue
Suite 370
Santa Ana, California 92707
United States
Tel: (+1 714) 850 0585
Fax: (+1 714) 850 0606
e-mail: janeswest@janes.com

**Canada**
Jane's Information Group
220 Laurier Avenue West
Suite 550
Ottawa, Ontario K1P 5Z9
Canada
Tel: (+1 613) 288 0189
Fax: (+1 613) 288 0190
e-mail: geoff.mizen@janes.com

**Asia**
Jane's Information Group Asia
5 Shenton Way
#01-01, UIC Building
Singapore 068808
Tel: (+65) 6 410 1240
Fax: (+65) 6 226 1185
e-mail: info@janes.com.sg

**India**
Jane's Information Group
Post Box No. 3806
New Delhi 110049
India
Tel: (+91 11) 651 6105
Fax: (+91 11) 651 6105
e-mail: janesindia@sify.com

**Japan**
Jane's Information Group
Palaceside Building, 5F,
1-1-1, Hitotsubashi
Chiyoda-ku, Tokyo 100-0003
Japan
Tel: (+81 3) 5218 7682
Fax: (+81 3) 5222 1280
e-mail: norihisa.fukuyama@janes.jp

**Australia and New Zealand**
Jane's Information Group
PO Box 3502
Rozelle Delivery Centre
New South Wales 2039
Australia
Tel: (+61 2) 8587 7900
Fax: (+61 2) 8587 7901
e-mail: janesinfo@janes.thomson.com.au

## Jane's
www.janes.com

*One of Siemens Transportation Systems' latest products is its Hercules diesel-electric locomotive, 70 examples of which were under delivery in 2002 to Austrian Federal Railways, where the type is designated Class 2016*

# Foreword

**Railtrack collapse precipitates major UK rail rethink**

In the UK, the always questionable government policy of placing the national railway infrastructure in the hands of the private sector in the form of Railtrack plc has come to an end. In October 2002, Railtrack plc, and with it the British rail network, was acquired for some £500 million by Network Rail, a not-for-dividend 'company limited by guarantee', the shares of which are owned by the state. The new company has a remit still to make profits, but these will be put back into the railway rather than contributing to shareholder dividends. The government denied that the creation of Network Rail was in effect renationalisation but to a large degree this is what this move means. It followed the refusal of the government in October of the previous year to provide a further funding package to Railtrack, which had seen its business severely damaged by a fatal high-speed crash at Hatfield, on the East Coast Main Line. That derailment, in which four people died, was attributed to serious rail flaws and led to the widespread imposition of speed restrictions throughout the system, severely disrupting services.

Under the new structure, Network Rail is responsible for day-to-day operations and for the upkeep of the system, including track maintenance and renewals. However, in a significant change, the government's Strategic Rail Authority (SRA) assumes control of major new or upgrading projects in its role of sponsor and specifier. At the top of the list of such schemes is the troubled upgrading of the electrified West Coast Main Line (WCML), the 1,255 km key artery that links London with the West Midlands, Manchester, Merseyside and Scotland. Why 'troubled'? Because the estimated cost of the project, which was intended to allow 225 km/h running with high-speed tilting trainsets, has risen from £2.1 billion to nearly £10 billion. Moreover, in mid-2002 work was about two years behind schedule. None of this helped Railtrack, which had been responsible for WCML modernisation. In a bid to bring matters under control, the SRA moved swiftly on taking over leadership of the scheme. In October 2002, it unveiled a package of proposals intended in its own words 'to get a grip on this project'. A key feature of the new strategy was the deferral of 225 km/h operations, which would have necessitated the provision of still unproven transmission-based signalling, until 2013 at the very earliest, rather than by 2005 as originally planned – and only then after what the SRA described as 'further analysis and examination'. Now, under these latest plans, the maximum speed of WCML services will be 200 km/h, with 2004 stated as the launch date for the first of these. This will still deliver capacity for around 80 per cent more passenger trains than the WCML currently carries and will still cut journey times substantially.

The SRA's plan certainly went some way towards easing government anxieties over the project's costs and was generally well received by the UK railway industry. But where does this leave the private-sector train operators which use the WCML? The route's principal intercity service provider is Virgin Trains. In 1996, this company signed a contract with Railtrack which would see it bearing a substantial share of the investment cost of the WCML upgrade in return for a guaranteed number of paths for a new fleet of Alstom-built Class 390 Pendolino high-speed tilting trainsets operating at up to 225 km/h. Forecasts of resulting increased passenger numbers and revenue formed the backbone of Virgin Trains' successful bid for the 15-year franchise that it signed with the (then) Office of Passenger Rail Franchising (OPRAF). Under the terms of the franchise agreement, Virgin Trains was to receive subsidies totalling £350 million for the first five years, but thereafter would pay 'premiums' to OPRAF (now the SRA) eventually totalling £1.4 billion. The failure of Railtrack to deliver early phases of the scheme on schedule had already led Virgin Trains in June 2002 to negotiate an additional SRA subsidy payment of £106 million. As this edition of *Jane's World Railways* closed for press, the announcement of the intended abandonment for the foreseeable future of plans for 225 km/h running was set to trigger further lively negotiations between Virgin Trains and the SRA, including a likely exploration of funding options

*Currently under delivery by ALSTOM Transport to Virgin Trains for West Coast Main Line Services, the 53 nine-car Pendolino tilting trainsets will for the foreseeable future be limited to 200 km/h rather than the planned 225 km/h (Milepost 92«)*     *2002*/0114314

# FOREWORD

for extra trains needed to meet the capacity shortfall created by slower running.

However, not all WCML operators are unhappy at the way the upgrading project has unfolded. The deal that Virgin Trains signed to secure capacity for its planned intensive services – 11 in each direction into and out of London's Euston station – limited track access for other companies, not least because of the scheduling impact of running 225 km/h trains over sections of line shared with slower traffic. Freight operators, especially English Welsh & Scottish Railway, had already expressed concern at the restricted number of pathways that would be available to them, especially on sections of the WCML in northern England and southern Scotland which are double- rather than quadruple-track, and on the intensively used lines at the route's southern end. They argued that imposing such constraints on one of the system's principal rail freight arteries was unacceptable at a time when government policy is substantially to increase goods transport by this mode. Therefore it was no surprise that the SRA, when announcing the proposed abandonment for the present of work to allow 225 km/h running, was stressing that one major benefit of the revised WCML upgrade strategy would be the creation of some 60 to 70 per cent more capacity for freight traffic than is presently available. Achieving growth of this order will also be assisted by a more strategic approach to timetabling. This will provide higher frequencies for passenger services in peak periods but more freight paths between peaks and in the evening.

Few disagree that the structure adopted for the privatisation of the former British Rail network was radical and many in the industry opposed the plan when it was tabled in the 1990s. These recent interlinked episodes witnessing the failure of Railtrack and the emergence of a single authoritative body in the shape of the SRA to provide leadership, are therefore instructive. The policy centrepiece of placing ownership of a complex multi-user national railway infrastructure in the hands of the private sector is, in the view of this writer, deeply flawed. Reconciling the maintenance of shareholder value with effective stewardship of the network and investment in its long-term development would always prove problematic, especially when one of the government's aims in privatising the system was to reduce the call on public subsidy. Transferring ownership of the British railway infrastructure to Network Rail will at least see surpluses reinvested in the system and promises a fresh focus on tackling the maintenance issues that have led to poor network reliability and increasing public concern about safety.

The solution proposed for unravelling the troubled WCML upgrade has also provided an opportunity for the SRA to play the greater leadership role in the running of the country's railway system that has been long overdue. In its new role as specifier and sponsor of major infrastructure projects, the authority has encouragingly achieved the kind of compromise between leading participants that is essential to ensure that network improvements are for the benefit of all rail operators and users. Indeed, under its new chairman, Richard Bowker, the SRA also appeared to be moving towards a more co-ordinated, prescriptive approach to passenger service provision that cast doubts over the future of the franchise system. Such a move, together with the creation of Network Rail, would rein in many of the policy excesses of UK rail privatisation and should lead to the optimisation of a network under pressure.

---

## Responding to Europe's rail freight challenge

In mid-2002, IKEA, the Swedish-based furnishings and homecare retail chain, launched its international rail service, which it claimed to be the first own-account, privately operated cross-border rail freight operation in Europe. Linking the company's distribution centre at Älmhult, Sweden, and Duisburg, Germany, and running five times a week, the train was the first of a network of similar services planned by IKEA Rail AB. Such an operation must have been very much in the minds of European Commission policy makers in the 1980s when plans were drawn up to open up the rail networks of all EU member companies to any operator licensed to run trains on them. However, despite the apparent success of the

*A new locomotive design for a new freight operator: At InnoTrans 2002 in Berlin, VSFT unveiled this G 1000 BB diesel-hydraulic locomotive for Connex Cargo Logistics in Germany (Ken Harris)*

# FOREWORD

Swedish company's initiative, progress has been slow, and shippers wishing to launch international services face major obstacles that competing road transport operators do not. As well as having to meet operational requirements governing traction, signalling and communications systems compatibility and crewing, a new rail operator has to obtain licences and the necessary insurance coverage for each railway network over which it intends to run services. Added to that is the process of negotiating paths through often heavily used stretches of line, each managed by its own capacity allocating authority.

To overcome some of these problems and give a much-needed boost to international freight traffic, rail infrastructure operators in 16 countries have formed RailNetEurope (RNE). Launched at the 2002 InnoTrans rail industry exhibition in Berlin by the Chairman of Deutsche Bahn AG, Hartmut Mehdorn, RNE has been developed from the UIC-led Trans-European Rail Freight Network (TERFN) initiative to improve the performance of cross-border rail traffic. It pledges to simplify and stimulate international movements by reducing those operational and administrative barriers that have led to protracted transit times and levels of customer service that fall short of those offered by other modes. RNE is based on a concept introduced in 1998 on some international rail freight corridors, such as the North-South Freight Freeways and Belifret, and will provide so-called 'One-Stop-Shops' (OSSs) in each participating country. Each OSS will act as the point of contact for intending operators or shippers, handling all aspects of a traffic flow, from initial inquiry to invoicing, and will co-ordinate the roles of other rail infrastructure authorities which carry the traffic. RNE will be charged with drawing up contracts more quickly and making these more comprehensive. Infrastructure companies participating in RNE include those in all EU member countries in mainland Europe and Great Britain, as well as GySEV in Hungary, JBV in Norway and BLS Lötschbergbahn and SBB in Switzerland.

Liberalisation of the EU's rail networks is also beginning to have an impact on domestic operations, with open access operators emerging as competitors to national carriers. While for political reasons some countries have been slow to face up to the reality that Community legislation now requires them to open up their networks to competent operators, progress elsewhere has been impressive. This is especially true in Germany. Here, significant rail freight flows are now carried by start-up companies which have taken advantage of open access legislation to compete with DB Cargo. Good progress is also being made in the Netherlands and open access operators are entering the market in Italy.

The emergence of new operators, coupled with a trend for existing companies to broaden their operations, has had a favourable impact on the supply market. Certainly one underlying theme at InnoTrans 2002 was the response by diesel locomotive manufacturers to what they interpret as new business opportunities from operators wishing to buy, or lease, small numbers of standard, proven products.

# FOREWORD

Models on display ranged from VSFT's medium-powered diesel-hydraulics to Bombardier Transportation's 2,460 kW Blue Tiger and the promise of a 3,200 kW collaboration from ALSTOM Transport and General Motors. Power plant manufacturers Cummins and MTU also displayed new engine models in the 2,600 to 2,700 kW range. These leading suppliers clearly see business opportunities ahead.

There are compelling reasons why a start-up or small-scale operator in Europe might favour diesel traction, despite much of the continent's railway system being electrified, albeit using a variety of voltages. Many of the secondary lines or industrial sidings on which freight traffic originates or terminates are not electrified and the employment of electric traction for the core haul requires locomotive changes. Modern diesel engines are highly efficient and satisfy demanding requirements governing emissions. And the issue of residual value has become increasingly important – the ease with which a new customer can be found for a serviceable machine should traffic or business circumstances change. In theory there should be a wider future market for a diesel locomotive than for system-specific electric machine.

This matter of residual value gives a clue to another significant trend to emerge as a result of the emergence of open access operators, especially in the freight market: the growth of traction leasing. Two of the rolling stock leasing companies that were established as a result of UK rail privatisation, Angel Trains and Porterbrook, have entered the market in mainland Europe. Some major locomotive builders are also responding to this new business environment. Siemens Transportation Systems has taken the step of creating its Dispolok business, hiring both diesel and electric locomotives from its own product range, and at InnoTrans 2002 ALSTOM Transport president Michel Moreau did not discount the possibility of his company entering the leasing market.

Clearly, the railway supply industry is playing its part by providing operators with the necessary equipment to enable them to enter the European rail freight market. Now, with increasing pressure at national and EU levels to harness the environmental benefits of rail freight, the RNE initiative has to succeed. Shippers wishing to use the rail network in an international economic community that is increasingly integrated should not face obstacles of types that do not impede other transport modes. And those countries in Europe that have been slow to respond to EU Directives on open access need to play their full role in ensuring the success and growth of rail freight.

**Acknowledgements**

It gives us pleasure again to acknowledge with our usual gratitude the contributors, correspondents and friends who have assisted in various way in the preparation of this latest edition of *Jane's World Railways*. Their specialised skills, knowledge and photographic contributions are an essential feature of this book.

For this edition, Jackie Clarke, Contributing Editor, Manufacturers, has been responsible for coverage of the railway supply industry. Her much valued efforts have resulted in a significant improvement and expansion of our coverage of the rail industry's suppliers. Special thanks are also due again to Mary Webb, editor of our sister publication, *Jane's Urban Transport Systems*, and her predecessor, Tony Pattison, for their contributions to the Manufacturers section.

Thanks for information and illustrations in this edition are especially due to numerous friends, contributors and correspondents around the world. They include Edward Barnes, Colin Boocock, Chris Bushell, Roger Carvell, Tom Ellett, Bruce Evans, Angel Ferrer, Aharon Gazit, K K Gupta, David Haydock, Tony Heywood, Flávio Francesconi Lage, Michal Málek, Brian Perren, Milan Šrámek, Frank Valoczy, Wolfram Veith, Marcel Vleugels, Quintus Vosman, Brian Webber and John Westwood. The efforts of many other photographic contributors are also acknowledged, as are those of our graphic artist, Barrie Compton, who has undertaken the often complex task of updating the maps.

Processing the substantial volume of material that makes up *Jane's World Railways* is very much a team effort involving many people in our Coulsdon offices in the UK, but special mention should be made of Melanie Rovery, who without complaint has handled the difficult task of copy processing on this edition in advance long-anticipated production changes, and of Diana Barrick and Sharon Marshall whose efforts have all enhanced this year's publication.

*Jane's World Railways* is available via the Internet as a *Jane's Online* product. As a consequence, updating is a year-round activity. Even before this printed version was published, substantial updates and additions had already been made to our data resource. Thanks are due to Belinda Dodman and Jacqui Beard, who oversee our data-gathering mailing activities and for many companies in the rail industry are often the first point of contact in *Jane's*.

Updating *Jane's World Railways* would also be impossible without the co-operation of the railway undertakings and companies featured in it. We therefore acknowledge and thank the many industry organisations which have responded so generously to our requests for the data that enables *Jane's World Railways* to provide such extensive coverage of the railway industry worldwide.

Ken Harris, Editor
Brighton, October 2002

# RAILWAY SYSTEMS

# RAILWAY SYSTEMS

## AFGHANISTAN

### Ministry of Transport

PO Box 2509, Ansari Walt, Kabul
Tel: (+93) 210 15

**Key personnel**
Minister of Transport: Syed Anwari

**Political background**
In 1982 the first railway tracks appeared in Afghanistan with completion, after three years' work by Afghan and Soviet labour, of an 816 m combined rail and road bridge over the Abu Darja river, the border with the former USSR, now Uzbekistan, and the projection over it of a rail link from the Bukhara–Dushanbe line near Termez to Hairaton in Afghanistan. This penetration was to be continued into Afghanistan, beginning with a 200 km line to Pali-Khumri, some 160 km north of Kabul, but progress was blocked by the mountainous terrain, the long annual periods in which the area is blanketed by heavy snow and the unstable political situation within the country.

A new prospect that would place Afghanistan astride a Central Asian railway was opened up in 1992 when Pakistan's Economics Minister offered the Central Asian republics aid for the construction of a railway through Afghanistan to an emergent Arabian Sea port in Baluchistan at Pasni. Later, a revised plan emerged for an 800 km trans-Afghan line linking the existing Pakistan Railways route at Chaman with Kushka in Turkmenistan, via Herat and Kandahar. This has been accorded priority by the Pakistan government, and was the subject of an accord signed in March 1994 between the Pakistan, Afghan and Turkmenistan governments. A World Bank-funded US$1.5 million feasibility study into the scheme was published in 2000. Construction cost of the line is estimated at US$600 million.

---

## ALBANIA

### Ministry of Industry, Trade & Transport

Rruge Myslym Shyri 42, Tirana

**Key personnel**
Minister: Maqo Lakrori

*UPDATED*

### Albanian Railways (HSH)

Hekurudhat Shqiptare
Drejitoria e Pergjithshle e Hekurudhave Shqiptare, Rue Skenderbeg, Durrës
Tel: (+355 52) 223 11   Fax: (+355 52) 220 37

**Key personnel**
Director General: Leonard Burnaci
Assistant Director General: Petraq Pano
Directors
  Finance: Petrit Tafili
  Rolling Stock: Nderim Kasa
  Commercial: Dhimiter Karanxha
  Infrastructure: Cesk Radovani
  Passenger: Fadil Kaja
  Planning, Personnel: Shkelzen Xava
  International Relations: Miranda Jani

Gauge: 1,435 mm
Route length: 447 km

**Political background**
Following deposition of the hardline Communist government, consideration was given in the early 1990s to abandonment of the badly rundown state railway system. However, after a study on the future of the railway by CIE Consult of Ireland under World Bank auspices, it was decided that efforts would be made to revitalise HSH. Since then, funding for improvements has been provided by the World Bank, the European Union and the governments of the United States and Italy. In spite of this, political instability has continued to hamper revitalisation of the system, while the conflict in Kosovo in 1999 placed new demands on HSH.

In mid-1998, a co-operation agreement between the governments of Albania and Austria provided for the supply to HSH of second-hand passenger coaches, communications equipment and track materials, as well as technical assistance and training in connection with the rehabilitation of principal routes.

**Organisation**
Following the CIE Consult report, HSH was restructured into two business units (passenger and freight) and two service units (infrastructure and rolling stock).

**Passenger operations**
Passenger services are operated on the Tirana–Durrës, Tirana–Vlorë, Tirana–Pogradec, Tirana–Shkodër (Durrës) and Fier–Ballsh routes. Only one class of accommodation is provided. A regular interval between Durrës and Tirana is proposed. Passenger services were withdrawn in 1996 from the Milot–Rrëshen line, which was closed in early 1998.

**Freight operations**
In 1998 HSH carried 305,000 tonnes of freight, an increase of 10 per cent on the 1997 figure. Principal commodities handled were petroleum products, construction materials, coal and chrome.

**New lines**
A link from the northern Albanian railhead at Shkodër into Montenegro was finished in 1986. This was Albania's first rail connection with a foreign railway, but it fell foul of the United Nations 1991 embargo on trade with Yugoslavia. Although subsequently reinstated, the line was not available for traffic during 1997 due to track damage. Restoration of services looked likely to follow a decision in early 1998 by the South Balkan Development initiative to provide US$10 million to modernise the corridor. Reconstruction of the line north of Shkodër to Hani i Hotit, on the border with Montenegro, was reported to have started in late 2001.

An agreement is in place to extend the line from Pogradec via Korce to Flórina in Greece; design work was completed in 1995, but no physical construction has taken place. A further international link is planned from Qanë-e-Thanes to Struga in Macedonia, which would form part of a future rail route from the Adriatic to the Black Sea. Also projected is a freight line from Lezhë to the port of Shengjin.

The Milot–Rrëshen line has been closed and plans to extend it to Klos have been suspended. Rails from the closed line were to be used to restore track between Shkodër and Hani i Hotit.

**Improvements to existing lines**
Italy has financed upgrading of the 40 km route from the capital, Tirana, to the port at Durrës, with a Lit6 billion credit supplementing a government contribution of US$2 million. The work, undertaken by Italian contractor Fersalente, involves upgrading the line and improving signalling and telecommunications systems. Renewal of the 28.2 km from Durrës to Kashar to 70 km/h standards was completed in early 1997, and work on the Kashar–Tirana section was completed in January 1998 with the help of World Bank funding.

Reconstruction of the Rrogozhinë–Fier–Vlorë and Fier–Ballsh sections is planned at an estimated cost of US$67 million. It was expected that the project would be completed by 2002.

**Traction and rolling stock**
The only serviceable locomotives are 29 Czech-built 1,007 kW (1,350 hp) T669 Co-Co diesels, operational survivors of 61 delivered by CKD Praha between 1968 and 1990.

During 1998 talks were reported to have taken place between Albanian government ministers and General Motors regarding the supply of locomotives, some of which would be funded by Japanese government loans.

In 1998 HSH's serviceable passenger coach fleet totalled 50 vehicles, mostly of Chinese, Italian or Polish origin. The co-operation agreement signed by the Albanian and Austrian governments in mid-1998 (see 'Political background') included the supply to HSH of 80 second-hand passenger coaches and other vehicles, although in early 1999 there were no reports of these having arrived.

Total freight vehicle stock is around 2,100, but only about 400 wagons are serviceable.

**Signalling and telecommunications**
Colourlight signalling is in place between Durrës and Tirana, Durrës and Elbasan, and Durrës and Laç. As there is a problem with theft of exposed cables, all stations are equipped with radios and are in contact with the control office in Durrës. Train order tickets are given to drivers. An underground cable is planned for the main line between Tirana and Durrës.

**Track**
Rail: 38, 43, 48, 49 kg/m in 12 to 24 m lengths
Sleepers: Wood, duo-bloc concrete
Min curve radius: 300 m
Max axleload: 21-24 tonnes
Max speed: 60 km/h

*UPDATED*

# ALGERIA

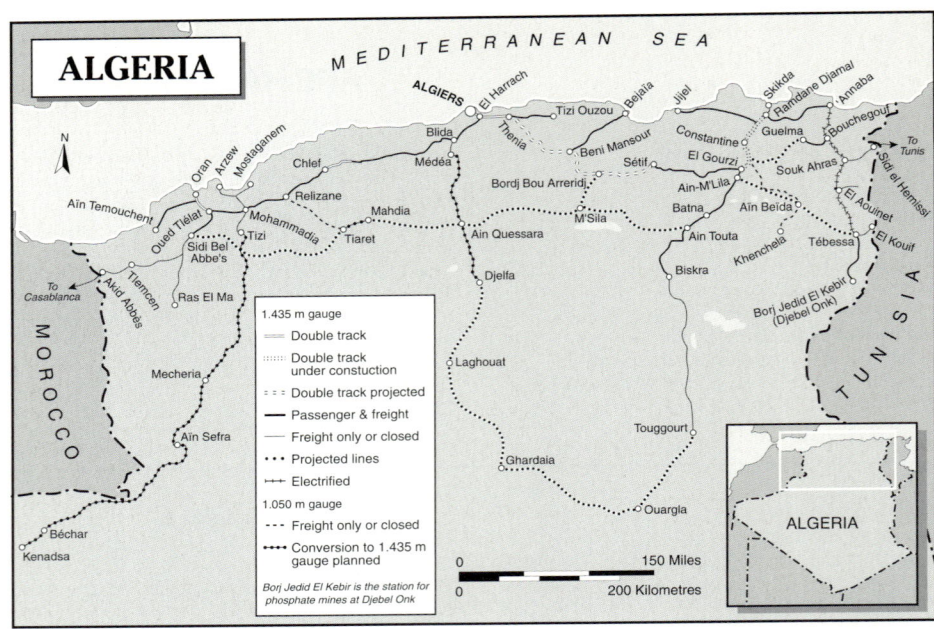

## Ministry of Transport

Algiers

### Key personnel
Minister: Essaid Bendakir
Secretary-General: A Brachemi
Director, Infrastructure and Rail Transport:
  A Benallegue

## Algerian National Railways (SNTF)

Société Nationale des Transports Ferroviaires
21 Boulevard Mohamed V, Algiers
Tel: (+213 2) 71 15 10   Fax: (+213 2) 63 32 98

### Key personnel
Director General: Ing Abdelhamid Lalaimia
Secretary General: Ahmed Halfaoui
Directors
  Operating: Ali Leulmi
  Human Resources: Abderrahmane Belkadi
  Infrastructure: Mourad Soliman Benameur
  Rolling Stock: Lakhdar Saadi
  Finances: Djamel Djenas
  Planning: El Berkenou
  Purchasing: Abdelhamid Moudjebeur
  Studies: Tahar Bouifrou
  Audit: Moukhtar Rahal
Regional Directors
  Algiers: Kerdel Ramdane
  Annaba: Abdelhamid Benboudjemaa
  Constantine: Mohammed Chérif Handel
  Oran: Yacine Bendjaballah
Working Directors
  Algiers: Zaki Fouad Azzouz
  Constantine: Mustapha Makhloufi
  Mohammadia: Abderrahmane Belkacemi
  Sidi-Bel-Abbès: Mohammed Boumaaza
Director of Freight Vehicle Operations:
  Abdelmalek Hamzaoui
External Relations Manager: Ms Houriadib

Gauges: 1,432 mm; 1,055 mm
Route length: 2,888 km; 1,085 km
Electrification: 283 km at 3 kV DC

### Organisation
The network consists primarily of two standard-gauge coastal lines running east and west from Algiers: about 550 km westward to the railhead at Akid Abbès (where a connection with Moroccan Railways, broken in 1976, was reactivated in 1989), and about 370 km eastwards to a connection with the 520 km north-south line at El Guerrah. In addition to standard-gauge spur lines, a 300 km (partly electrified) 1,435 mm gauge line runs parallel with the Tunisian border, providing international connecting services at Souk-Ahras with Tunisian National Railways (SNCFT) from the port of Annaba to Djebel Onk. Major narrow-gauge lines run from Tizi to Béchar and Blida to Djelfa; conversion to standard gauge is proposed.

In 1987 a number of subsidiaries were formed to free the railway's management for full attention to transport. Setirail and Estel are the infrastructure and signalling/telecommunications subsidiaries; the others include Infrafer and Infrarail, new construction and tracklaying; Restau-Rail, on-train catering; Rail-Express, small freight consignments door-to-door; and STIM, multimodal transport.

The railway is managed by nine central divisions and four regional administrations. In 2000 12,510 staff were employed.

### Passenger operations
SNTF operates long-distance locomotive-hauled passenger services on nine main routes, the best served being Algiers–Chlef–Oran (422 km), with five daily services in each direction. Three classes of accommodation are provided: luxury (air conditioned), first class and second class. A suburban network also serves Algiers.

In 1999 32 million passenger journeys were made, nearly 90 per cent of these on suburban and commuter services.

*Class 040 YDA General Motors 1,055 mm gauge diesel-electric locomotive (Marcel Vleugels)*

*Newly laid trackwork in the industrial suburbs of Algiers*

### Freight operations
Petroleum products form SNTF's principal freight traffic, in 2000 generating over one quarter of the 8 million tonnes lifted. Volumes of phosphates from the mines at Djebel Onk are also significant, much of the output conveyed over the electrified line to Annaba for export. Also carried is traffic for the El Hadjar steel complex, which gets its ore in 1,500 tonne trains from mines at Quenza and Bou Khedra, about 190 km south of Annaba (whence the imported coal for its coking plant is also ferried by unit train).

SNTF employs bogie-changing to facilitate the transfer of rail vehicles from standard to 1,055 mm gauge tracks.

| Traffic (million) | 1998 | 1999 | 2000 |
|---|---|---|---|
| Passenger journeys | 34.1 | 31.4 | 28.3 |
| Passenger-km | 1,163 | 1,069 | 1,142 |
| Freight tonnes | 8.29 | 7.8 | 7.8 |
| Freight tonne-km | 2,174 | 2,057 | 2,029 |

### New lines
A joint Algerian-Indian study group developed plans for a first section of the High Plateau route, the 146 km from Ain Touta, on the line south from Constantine to Biskra, to M'Sila, location of an aluminium plant. Construction of this line was in progress in 2000, although less than one quarter of the scheme was reported to be completed. The line is being engineered for 160 km/h with long-welded 54 kg/m rail on twin-block sleepers, the latter manufactured in a plant established at Ain Touta.

SNTF contemplates extension of its standard-gauge system across the heart of the Sahara, looping southward from Touggourt in the southeast, through Ouargla then northwest via Ghardaia and Laghouet to Ain Quessara, on the projected High Plateau route. The first section of this project, from Touggourt 210 km south to Hassi Messaoud features in SNTF's network development programme.

### Improvements to existing lines
SNTF has an extensive programme of network development which includes track doubling and upgrading, renewals, and realignments and reconstruction. However, progress has been hampered by Algeria's economic and political difficulties.

Among large-scale projects completed is the double-tracking of the line between Ramdane Djamal, 67 km north of Constantine and El Gourzi, 38 km south of Constantine. This vital link between Algiers and the petrochemical port of Skikda, as well as Annaba, has been doubled throughout the 67 km from Ramdane Djamal to Constantine and the 20.6 km south from El Gourzi to El Khroub, along with realignments.

In conjunction with installation of heavier UIC 54 welded rail on concrete sleepers of SL Type U (1,722 per km), this scheme has raised permissible freight speed from 60 to 90 km/h and wagon axleload from 18 to 28 tonnes. Following installation of modern automatic signalling, the line's train operating capacity has doubled and a throughput of 7 million tonnes a year is possible.

Also completed is doubling of the 43.5 km from El Harrach, on the outskirts of Algiers, to Thénia, a project funded by an Austrian loan.

Track renewals are in progress between Ramdane Djamal and Annaba. To create a relief route between Constantine and Annaba, resuscitation of the 95 km El Khroub–Guelma connection, abandoned in the 1950s, is under way. Upgrading and conversion to standard-gauge is planned for the 600 km metre-gauge line between Mohammadia and Bechar.

### Traction and rolling stock
On 1,432 mm gauge SNTF operates 19 electric and 194 diesel locomotives, 59 locotractors and 12 twin-unit diesel railcars. Coaching stock totals 422, and there are 10,118 wagons. The narrow-gauge traction fleet comprises 30 diesel locomotives and there are 33 coaches.

A new fleet of electric locomotives came into service in 1996 on the Djebel Onk–Annaba ore haul. Alstom supplied 14 Co-Cos rated at 2,400 kW, designed to haul trains of up to 2,700 tonnes.

On the diesel front, General Motors has supplied 10 Co-Cos rated at 2,400 kW, the first of which was delivered in 1994. A further 50 units of various types were supplied by GM through to 1996, some as kits for assembly locally.

Three diesel shunting locomotives rated at 448 kW were supplied in 1995 by local manufacturer Ferrovial. An order was also anticipated for a new fleet of 10 diesel multiple-units for Algiers suburban services.

### Signalling and telecommunications
Automatic block signalling is installed on the Algiers–Thénin (50 km) and El Harrach–El Affroun (50 km) sections. Resignalling and a complete renewal of the telecommunications network ranks high. Among other things, the railway aims to make track-to-train radio communication a standard feature on its principal routes. Electrically operated mechanical signals are gradually being replaced by colourlight displays throughout the system. On new lines and upgraded tracks automatic signalling is being installed. SNTF has signed an agreement in principle with Siemens for formation of a joint company to manufacture and install signalling equipment. As a result, a programme of installing modern interlocking systems has been undertaken at 33 stations between El Affroun and Oued Tlelat.

### Track
**Rail:** UIC 54 has been adopted as the standard for main line renewals
**Sleepers:** Concrete twin-block installed on 1,732 km
**Max gradient:** 3.2%
**Max axleload:** 20 tonnes

*SNTF employs bogie changing facilities such as these lifting jacks at Relizane to enable wagons to move between standard and 1,055 mm gauge networks (Marcel Vleugels)* 2002/0524891

### Diesel locomotives

| Class | Builder's type | Wheel arrangement | Output kW | Speed km/h | Weight tonnes | No in service | First built | Mechanical | Builders Engine | Transmission |
|---|---|---|---|---|---|---|---|---|---|---|
| **Standard gauge** | | | | | | | | | | |
| 060 DD | GT 26 W | Co-Co | 2,400 | 120 | 120 | 27 | 1971 | GM | GM | E GM |
| 060 DF | GT 26 W | Co-Co | 2,400 | 120 | 120 | 25 | 1973 | GM | GM | E GM |
| 060 DG | GT 26 W | Co-Co | 2,400 | 120 | 120 | 15 | 1976 | GM | GM | E GM |
| 060 DH | GT 22 W | Co-Co | 1,600 | 120 | 120 | 24 | 1976 | GM | GM | E GM |
| 060 DL | GT 26 W | Co-Co | 2,400 | 120 | 120 | 25 | 1982 | GM | GM | E GM |
| 060 WDK | GL 18 M | Co-Co | 800 | 100 | 78 | 5 | 1977 | GM | GM | E GM |
| 060 DJ | U 18 C | Co-Co | 1,400 | 100 | 96 | 25 | 1977 | GE | GE | E GE |
| 060 DM | GT 26 HCW-2A | Co-Co | 2,400 | 125 | 125 | 10 | 1985 | GM | GM | E GM |
| 040 DH | GL 18 B | Bo-Bo | 800 | 80 | 80 | 5 | 1990 | GM | GM | E GM |
| 040 DH | GL 18 B | Bo-Bo | 800 | 80 | 80 | 8 | 1993 | GM | GM | E GM |
| 060 DP | GT 26 HCW-2A | Co-Co | 2,400 | | | | 1994 | GM | GM | E GM |
| **1,050 mm gauge** | | | | | | | | | | |
| 040 YDA | GL 18 M | A1A-A1A | 800 | 80 | 72 | 24 | 1977 | GM | GM | E GM |
| 060 YDD | GL 18 2C/2M | Co-Co | 1,200 | 80 | 80 | 5 | 1989 | GM | GM | E GM |

### Diesel railcars

| Class | Builder's type | Cars per unit | Motor cars per unit | Power/car kW | Speed km/h | No in service | First built | Mechanical | Builders Engine | Transmission |
|---|---|---|---|---|---|---|---|---|---|---|
| ZZN 200 | ALN 668 | 2 | 2 | 286 | 120 | 14 | 1972 | Fiat (Iveco) | Fiat (Iveco) | Fiat (Iveco) |

### Electric locomotives

| Class | Wheel arrangement | Power kW | Speed km/h | Weight tonnes | No in service | First built | Mechanical | Builders Electrical |
|---|---|---|---|---|---|---|---|---|
| 6CE | Co-Co | 1,492 | 80 | 130 | 17 | 1972 | LEW | Škoda |
| 6FE | Co-Co | 2,400 | - | 132 | 14 | 1995 | GEC Alsthom Transporte | ACEC |

*UPDATED*

# ANGOLA

## Ministry of Transport and Communications

PO Box 1250-C, Luanda
Tel: (+244 2) 33 77 93; 33 77 44
Tx: 3108 Mitrans AN

### Key personnel
Minister of Transport: André Luis Brandao
Deputy Minister, Transport: Dr A de Sousa e Silva

## Direcçao Nacional dos Caminhos de Ferro

PO Box 1250-C, Luanda
Tel: (+244 2) 33 97 94; 33 02 33
Fax: (+244 2) 33 99 76
Tx: 3108 Mitrans AN

### Key personnel
Director: R M da C Junior

Gauge: 1,067 mm; 600 mm
Route length (four railways combined): 2,648 km; 123 km

### Organisation
Three previously independent railways (the Amboim, Luanda and Namibe Railways) are now amalgamated in a national system, while the Benguela Railway is supervised by the Ministry of Transport but retains its own administration. Because of the country's continuing guerrilla warfare, the four railways have so far been unable

# RAILWAY SYSTEMS/Angola

to integrate operations fully or handle international traffic consistently.

### Freight and passenger operations
Despite operating difficulties, in 1991 the four railways carried a total of 3.6 million tonnes of freight, 45.3 million tonne-km. Passenger journeys amounted to 5 million, for 246 million passenger-km. Passenger traffic held up well through to 1993, but freight was 20 per cent down at 2.8 million tonnes.

| Traffic | 1991 | 1993 |
|---|---|---|
| (All four railways) | | |
| Passenger journeys (million) | 5.0 | 5.0 |
| Passenger-km (million) | 246.2 | n/a |
| Freight tonnes (million) | 3.6 | 2.8 |
| Freight tonne-km (million) | 45.3 | n/a |

*2001*/0114277

## Amboim Railway

Caminho de ferro do Amboim
Estaçao Puerto Amboim

### Key personnel
General Manager: A Guia

Gauge: 600 mm
Route length: 123 km

### Organisation
The railway is a single line between the port of Amboim and the coffee-growing region at Gabela. The first 40 km out of Amboim is fully operational, the remainder intermittently so.

### Passenger and freight operations
Steam-hauled mixed trains are run when circumstances permit. The main freight commodities carried are timber, agricultural products and coffee. A railcar-operated service also operates intermittently between Amboim and Gabela.

### Improvements to existing lines
A partial rehabilitation has been accorded priority, and a new telecommunications system is urgently required.

### Traction and rolling stock
There are six steam locomotives, 12 wooden-bodied coaches and 60 freight wagons, around 50 per cent of which are operational. A Wickham-built railcar is also in service.

## Benguela Railway

Companhia do Caminho de ferro de Benguela
Praça 11 de Novembro no 3, Lobito
Tel: (+244 72) 226 45   Fax: (+244 72) 401 33
e-mail: CFB/LOBITO-rocha@ebonet.net

### Key personnel
Chairman: Dr Guilherme Magaihães Pratas
Administrator and General Manager:
  Dr Daniel João Quipaxe
Administrator and Commercial Director:
  Eng Enesto Alpoim Ferreira da Rocha
Administrators:
  Eng José Manuel Miranda Vaz de Carvalho
  Eng Carlos dos Santos Braz
  Cristiano Reis d'Almeida

Gauge: 1,067 mm
Route length: 1,301 km

### Organisation
The Benguela Railway should be a major traffic route to the sea for Zambian and Congolese copper, but the connection from the port of Lobito across Angola to the Congo Democratic Republic border at Dilolo, where it is connected with SNCC, has been disrupted by guerrilla action since 1975.

In late 1996, an Italian company, Tor di Valle, won a contract to reconstruct the out-of-use section of the railway. The company was to be paid by the exploitation of eucalyptus forests. A further move to rehabilitate the line came in 1997, with the awarding of a contract to remove landmines from the Cubal-Kuito section. Work on this started in 1998.

**Benguela Railway diesel locomotives**

| Class | Wheel arrangement | Power kW | Speed km/h | Weight tonnes | No in service | First built | Mechanical | Builders Engine | Transmission |
|---|---|---|---|---|---|---|---|---|---|
| D.101-D.314 | Co-Co | 1,582 | 109 | 90 | 6 | 1973 | GE USA/ GE Brazil | GE 7FDL12 | E GE |
| D.20-D.25 | Bo-Bo | 493 | 46 | 60 | - | 1988 | GE Brazil | Cummins NT 855L | E GE |
| D.11-D.12 | C | 313 | 40 | 42 | - | 1972 | Barclay | Paxman | H Barclay |
| D.1-D.4 | C | 313 | 27 | 41 | - | 1962 | North British | Paxman | H Voith/NBL |
| - | B | 309 | 50 | 44 | - | 1960 | Moyse | Poyaud | E Moyse |

At the end of 1998 the Benguela Railway employed 2,146 staff.

### Passenger and freight operations
Regular passenger trains operate over the 33 km coastal line between Lobito and Benguela. In 1998 mixed train operation resumed on a usually weekly basis over the 957 km section between Benguela and Luena. If circumstances permitted, a mixed train was also running between Luena and Luau, near the border with Congo, Democratic Republic, but international services remained suspended.

| Traffic | 1997 | 1998 |
|---|---|---|
| Passenger journeys (000) | 5.8 | 2.8 |
| Passenger-km (million) | 141.9 | 69.6 |
| Freight tonnes (000) | 101.5 | 57.4 |
| Freight tonne-km (million) | 0.69 | 0.42 |

### Traction and rolling stock
In 1998 the active fleet comprised six main line diesel locomotives and two shunters, with the remainder of the tractive stock unserviceable. The line-haul diesels are GE Type U20C. The 10 passenger cars are survivors of 12 second-hand vehicles supplied from South Africa in 1992-93. The railway owns 750 wagons.

**Type of coupler in standard use:** AAR M201/10A
**Type of braking in standard use:** Vacuum

### Track
**Rail:** BS 60A/N 30 kg/m, BS 80A 40 kg/m, BS 20A 45 kg/m, CFB 60 30 kg/m
**Sleepers:** Wood 2,000 × 250 × 140 mm, spaced 1,460/km in plain track, 1,491/km in curves; steel
**Fastenings:** Elastic spike
**Min curve radius:** 100 m
**Max gradient:** 2%
**Max axleload:** 15 tonnes

## Luanda Railway

Caminho de ferro de Luanda
PO Box 1250-C, Luanda
Tel: (+244 2) 700 61; 732 70

**Key personnel**
Director: A Alvaro Agante

Gauge: 1,067 mm
Route length: 479 km

**Organisation**
The line runs from the port of Luanda to Malanje, serving an iron, cotton and sisal producing region. A branch runs 55 km south from Zenza to Itombe and Dondo. The 600 mm gauge line from Canhoca to Golungo Alto has been closed. Efforts to rehabilitate the system were reported in late 1997, with a US$15 million funding being sought for second-hand locomotives and track work.

**Passenger and freight traffic**
The main freight flow is of agricultural produce to Luanda, which amounted to 2.5 million tonnes in 1993. Passenger traffic is also of some importance, in particular a suburban service into Luanda from Viana and Baia (36 km).

**Improvements to existing lines**
Rehabilitation of the line started in 1989, but only a few short sections have been completed. Poor track conditions and inoperable signalling render train working problematic to the east of N'dalatando.

**Traction and rolling stock**
Of the 35 steam locomotives, only one-third is available at any time; these work the Luanda suburban service. The diesel situation is worse, with no more than a few of the 50-strong fleet in operating condition. All four Fiat diesel railcars are out of service. In addition, there are 50 coaches and about 1,800 wagons.

## Namibe Railway

Caminho de ferro do Namibe
Caixa Postal 130, Sá de Bandeira, Namibe

**Key personnel**
General Manager: J Salvador

Gauge: 1,067 mm
Route length: 858 km

**Organisation**
The Namibe Railway consists of a 756 km line running from Namibe inland to Menongue via Lubango, Matala and Entroncamento. A line of some 150 km linking Lubango with Chiange was destroyed in the war.

**Passenger and freight operations**
In normal times the Cassinga ore fields yielded traffic of some 6 million tonnes annually, but, at last report in late 1994, only the 424 km from Namibe to Matala was in operation and trains were still being affected by military action. Only some 500,000 passengers were carried in 1993, plus less than 100,000 tonnes of freight.

**Traction and rolling stock**
In 1993 only six or eight diesel locomotives were in operational condition. The programme announced in 1990, under which 11 locomotives, 59 passenger cars and 50 freight wagons were to be rehabilitated, had still not been completed. Currently about 20 coaches are in working order, along with 60 wagons.

# ARGENTINA

## Ministry of Infrastructure

Secretariat of Transport
Hipólito Irigoyen 200, Piso 12, Oficina 1209, C1086 AAB, Buenos Aires
Tel: (+54 11) 43 81 89 11   Fax: (+54 11) 48 14 18 23

**Key personnel**
Minister: Nicolás Gallo
Secretary: Ignacio Alfonso
Under-Secretary: Alba Thomas Hatti

*UPDATED*

## Comisión Nacional de Regulación de Transporte (CNRT)

Avenida Maipú 88 – piso 5°, 1084 Buenos Aires
Tel: (+54 11) 43 18 35 48   Fax: (+54 11) 43 18 36 62

**Key personnel**
President: Jose Emilio Bernasconi

Formerly the Unidad de Coordinación del Programa de Reestructuración Ferroviaria, and incorporating functions of the former Ferrocarriles Metropolitanos, this organisation now oversees all concessions for interurban and suburban passenger and freight networks in Argentina.

With the transfer in December 1998 of Ferrocarril Belgrano Cargas to the private sector, all of the former Argentine Railways network, which totalled nearly 34,000 km before the start of privatisation, passed out of central government ownership.

The number of passengers using metropolitan rail services grew from 212 million in 1993 to 456.1 million in 1997, while the figure for interurban passengers declined from 11 million in 1990 to just 2.6 million in 1997. Freight tonnage, which in 1993 stood at 9.5 million tonnes, doubled to 18.9 million tonnes in 1997. Tonne-km increased from 5 billion to 9.8 billion in the same period.

## América Latina Logística (ALL Central)

Avenida Santa Fe 4636 – piso 3°, C1425BHV Buenos Aires
Tel: (+54 11) 47 78 24 00   Fax: (+54 11) 47 78 24 08

**Key personnel**
President: Alexandre Behring
Operations Manager: Rubén Chaparro

Gauge: 1,676 mm
Route length: 5,350 km

**Organisation**
On 5 June 1992 the Consorcio Ferrocarril Central group was awarded the 30 year concession to operate 5,400 km of the General San Martín railway and 706 km of the Sarmiento railway (both 1,676 mm gauge). This network, which became the Buenos Aires al Pacífico/San Martín (BAP) system, was the third freight concession to be granted, and was considered to be potentially very profitable.

The CFC consortium was headed by Industries Metalúrgicas Pescarmona (IMPSA), which held a 60 per cent stake and whose main manufacturing plant in Mendoza is connected to BAP lines. IMPSA was also the main partner in the CFM consortium later awarded the Urquiza concession. Other members of CFC were Román Marítima (25 per cent), Transapelt and Hugo G Bunge. Railroad Development Corporation (which controls the Iowa Interstate Railroad between Chicago and Omaha, USA) was chosen as operator, with Conrail as technical consultant.

In 1997 BAP unified operations with Ferrocarril Mesopotámico General Urquiza (qv), where there are overlapping shareholding interests. In August 1998 the IMPSA-led consortium announced its intention to sell its share in BAP, along with its interests in the Ferrocarril Mesopotámico General Urquiza (qv), to a Brazilian consortium, América Latina Logística, which operates that country's Ferrocarril Centro-Atlantico and Ferrovia Sul-Atlantico networks. This resulted in the adoption of a new name for the system, ALL Central. Investments of US$300 million are planned and in the longer term it is intended to increase tonnage by 50 per cent.

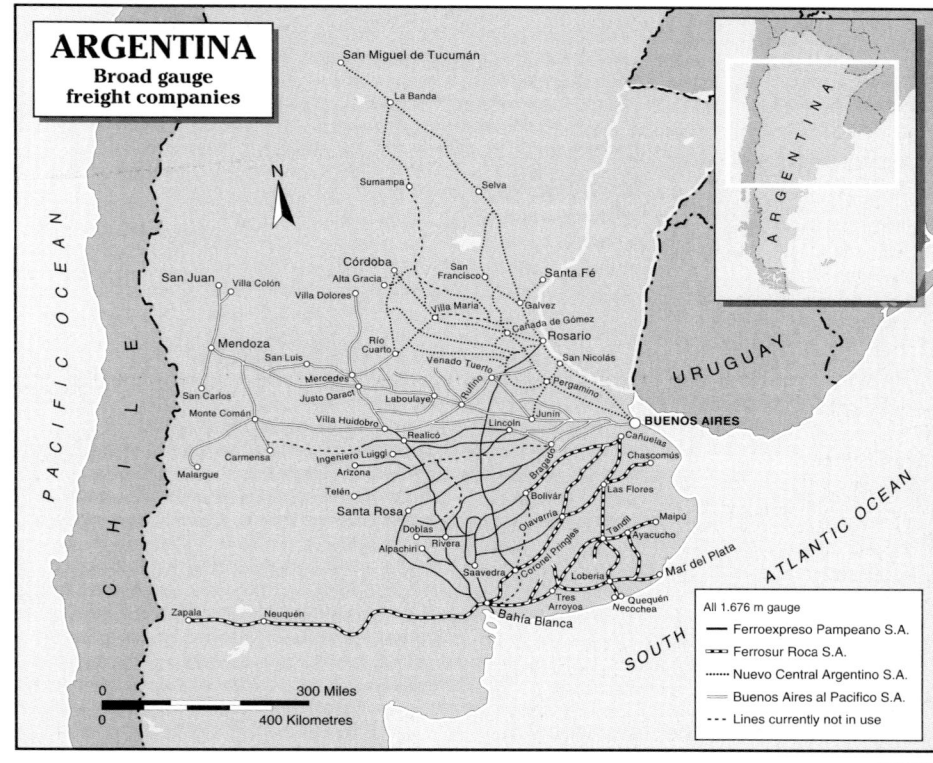

# RAILWAY SYSTEMS/Argentina

*ALL train of cereal hoppers loaded with soya beans for export at Ludueña Junction, Rosario, behind a former Spanish National Railways Class 321 Alco diesel locomotive* (Angel Ferrer)    2000/0089089

### Freight operations
Operations as the Buenos Aires al Pacífico commenced on 26 August 1993, several months later than planned due to problems with the transfer of staff from FA. The lines covered by the concession link the provinces of Mendoza and San Juan in the Andean foothills to Buenos Aires, crossing the provinces of San Luís, Córdoba and Santa Fe in the process. In 1996 BAP began direct services to the Río de la Plata terminal in the port of Buenos Aires following completion of a new link.

The traffic base inherited from FA consisted mainly of trainload movements of petroleum, coke and stone. The new operators have made efforts to develop wagonload, intermodal (both container and piggyback) and door-to-door services and to broaden the range of commodities carried.

Traffic flows, especially of containers, from Mendoza to the port of Buenos Aires have become especially significant, with trains assembled at Palmira yard, near Mendoza. The majority of BAP's traffic is eastward to Buenos Aires and the port and industrial centre of Rosario.

In 2000, diversions due to severe flooding were in force on the main line east of Rufino, in Santa Fe province, with trains to Buenos Aires taking NCA lines to Empalme Villa Constitución and thence to the capital. Permanent way staff were working to reopen other BAP/SM branch lines adjacent to their own main line to reduce running over other operator's tracks. At some locations, water levels rose to 2 m above the rail head.

Trains are operated by a crew of two and have end-of-train telemetry devices.

| Traffic (million) | 1998-99 |
|---|---|
| Freight tonnes | 3.42 |
| Freight tonne-km | 2,562 |

### Improvements to existing lines
At the commencement of BAP operations the maximum permitted speed on the San Martín east-west main line was 120 km/h, although many branch lines were only suitable for speeds of 12 km/h. Of the US$150 million BAP intended to invest in the first five years of the 30 year concession period, US$45 million was to be spent on track improvements and a continuous-rail welding programme. An infrastructure analysis matrix has been deployed to assess the commercial desirability of infrastructure improvements and to determine those which should take priority over others.

In 1997 the loss of oil traffic led to closure of the Malargue branch, although expanding cement traffic led to the reopening of the Justo Daract–San Luis branch.

### Traction and rolling stock
In 1997 the locomotive fleet totalled 97, including 19 shunting units. Main line traction included 20 Alco-engined Class 321 Co-Co diesel-electric locomotives acquired from Spanish National Railways (RENFE).

At the start of 1997, BAP operated 5,271 freight wagons, of which 1,314 were unserviceable. Recent acquisitions included 46 high-capacity wagons for palletised goods, 130 container wagons and 148 general purpose freight wagons.

### Signalling and telecommunications
The old British semaphore and staff block signalling system has been replaced by a North American radio-based track warrant system. In Mendoza province, a 185 km section of CTC dating from the 1960s and expanded in the 1980s was removed by BAP during the IMPSA tenure.

*ALL freight at Rosario yard en route to Puerto San Martín, with a former Spanish National Railways Class 321 locomotive as motive power* (Angel Ferrer)    2000/0089090

### Diesel locomotives

| Class | Builder's type | Wheel arrangement | Output kW | Speed km/h | Weight tonnes | No in service | First built | Builders Mechanical | Engine |
|---|---|---|---|---|---|---|---|---|---|
| Alco RSD 16 | Alco USA | Co-Co | 1,380 | 90 | 118 | 21 | 1968 | Alco 321-B | E GE |
| Alco RSD 35 | Alco Canada | Co-Co | 930 | 90 | 98 | 50 | 1962 | Alco 321 | E GE |
| Alco 321 | Alco Spain | Co-Co | 1,570 | 120 | 119 | 20 | 1979 | Alco 321-C | E GE |
| Gaia | Argentina | Co-Co | 1,380 | 75 | 99 | 4 | 1968 | Alco 321-B | E GE |
| Loco Tractor | Argentina | | 520 | 40 | 50 | 9 | | Detroit Diesel | M |

## América Latina Logística (ALL Mesopotámico)

Avenida Santa Fe 4636 – piso 3°, C1425 BHV Buenos Aires
Tel: (+54 11) 47 78 24 00  Fax: (+54 11) 47 78 24 08

### Key personnel
President: Alexandre Behring
Operations Manager: Rubén Chaparro

Gauge: 1,435 mm
Route length: 2,739 km

### Organisation
In January 1993 the Consorcio Ferrocarril Mesopotámico (CFM) consortium was awarded a 30-year concession to operate FA's Urquiza railway, taking over in October 1993. The majority partner in the CFM consortium with a 71 per cent holding is IMPSa, which also heads the CFC group (see entry for América Latina Logística (ALL Central)). Other companies involved in the CFM consortium are Pescarmona, Alesia, Olmatic SA, and Petersen Thieley Cruz. As with BAP, US Class I railroad Conrail was chosen as operator, assisted by Railroad Development Corporation. FMGU began operations on 12 October 1993.

In 1997 operations were unified with those of the Buenos Aires al Pacifico (see América Latina Logística (ALL Central)), in which FMGU shareholders have interests. In August 1998 the owning consortium announced its intention to sell its share in BAP, along with its interests in the Ferrocarril Mesopotámico General Urquiza, to a Brazilian consortium, América Latina Logística, which operates that country's Ferrocarril Centro-Atlantico and Ferrovia Sul-Atlantico networks. The Argentine government authorised the transaction and ALL took over the system on 26 May 1999.

Combined staff for ALL Central and ALL Mesopotámico totalled 920 in 2000.

### Freight operations
ALL Mesopotámico comprises the former FA 1,435 mm gauge network in the east of the country and by far the best maintained, still carrying acceptable levels of traffic at the time of privatisation. It extends from Buenos Aires north to Encarnación, where it connects with FCPCAL of Paraguay via the Roque González de Santa Cruz bridge over the River Paraná. ALL Mesopotámico also connects with AFE of Uruguay across the Salto dam.

The traffic base consists mainly of soya beans, forestry products, containers, moved largely as wagonloads. Some trainload stone traffic has also been handled. Crews of two and end-of-train devices have replaced FA work practices and brake vans. In 1998-99, the network carried 1.01 million tonnes of freight for 47.1 million tonne-km.

A major priority is to reduce delivery times and ALL Mesopotámico has set a target of nine days for São Paulo–Buenos Aires freight traffic. This requires faster customs formalities at border stations, where three or four days are usually needed to clear traffic between Argentina and Brazil.

### Intermodel operations
The use of a 250 tonne breakdown crane has allowed the company to start handling containers at Mendoza, resulting in intermodal services now being offered to customers. Future strategy is to concentrate on more logistics-oriented services.

### Improvements to existing lines

During the 30-year period of the concession, CFM has undertaken to invest US$166 million. Whilst ALL Mesopotámico infrastructure generally does not demand the attention given to that of ALL Central, the 130 km branch to Corrientes and the 110-year-old truss bridge at Agua Pey will require attention in the near future.

### Traction and rolling stock

At the end of 1996 56 locomotives were in operation. The locomotive fleet consists of some of the more recent General Motors deliveries to FA and some older General Electric locomotives. ALL Central's Mendoza facility was being used in preference to the Urquiza locomotive works at Paraná, with running repairs undertaken at Alianza. A consolidated wagon repair works has been established at Alianza, on the outskirts of Buenos Aires, to serve both the ALL fleets.

At the end of 1996 2,139 wagons were in use. The fleet has been receiving airbrakes and knuckle couplers.

To improve its intermodal operations, ALL has acquired 20 'Roadrailers', which it has tested in Brazil. The introduction of similar equipment in Argentina is expected.

### Signalling and telecommunications

Computer-assisted radio train dispatching with track warrants has been introduced. A microwave system has replaced a semaphore signalling system and also provides business communications in the place of the unreliable Argentine telephone network.

## Cooperativa de Trabajo Ferroviario Urquiza de Paraná

Paraná, Entre Rios

### Key personnel

President: Ramón Ismael Claria

Gauge: 1,435 mm
Route length: 120 km

### Organisation

After a delay of eight months, Cooperativa de Trabajo Ferroviario Urquiza de Paraná introduced regular passenger services on the 120 km Paraná–Nogoyá line in Entre Rios province on 23 December 1998. The line was owned by freight operator Ferrocarril Mesopotámico General Urquiza (FMGU) (see América Latina Logística (ALL Mesopotámico)), which initially was not taking any track access fee for the use of its infrastructure. Following the takeover by ALL from IMPSA of the FMGU system, the new concessionaire stated that it wished to discuss track access fees with Cooperativa de Trabajo Ferroviario Urquiza for its passenger services. However, a derailment in July 1999 of a Paraná–Nogoyá passenger train due to poor track conditions brought services to a halt.

The co-operative consists of 120 staff, mostly former Argentine Railways employees who were not taken on when FMGU took up its concession in 1993.

### Passenger operations

Until March 1999, the service was intended to run twice weekly in each direction, becoming daily therafter. Nine intermediate stations are served in an area of 300,000 inhabitants. Train accommodation includes first and tourist class coaches.

Under the Proyecto Ferroviario Provincial scheme, Entre Rios province was working with FMGU and the Cooperativa to explore reopening the 314 km Paraná–Concordia main line for passenger operations, and some track repairs may be carried out under a state-financed employment arrangement. The line has seen no regular passenger trains since 1992, but it is felt that restoration of services would provide a valuable east-west social and tourist link across Entre Rios province.

### Traction and rolling stock

The Cooperativa owns three diesel locomotives (two GE U13s and one General Motors G22), and 15 passenger coaches, including Pullman, first and tourist class vehicles and luggage vans.

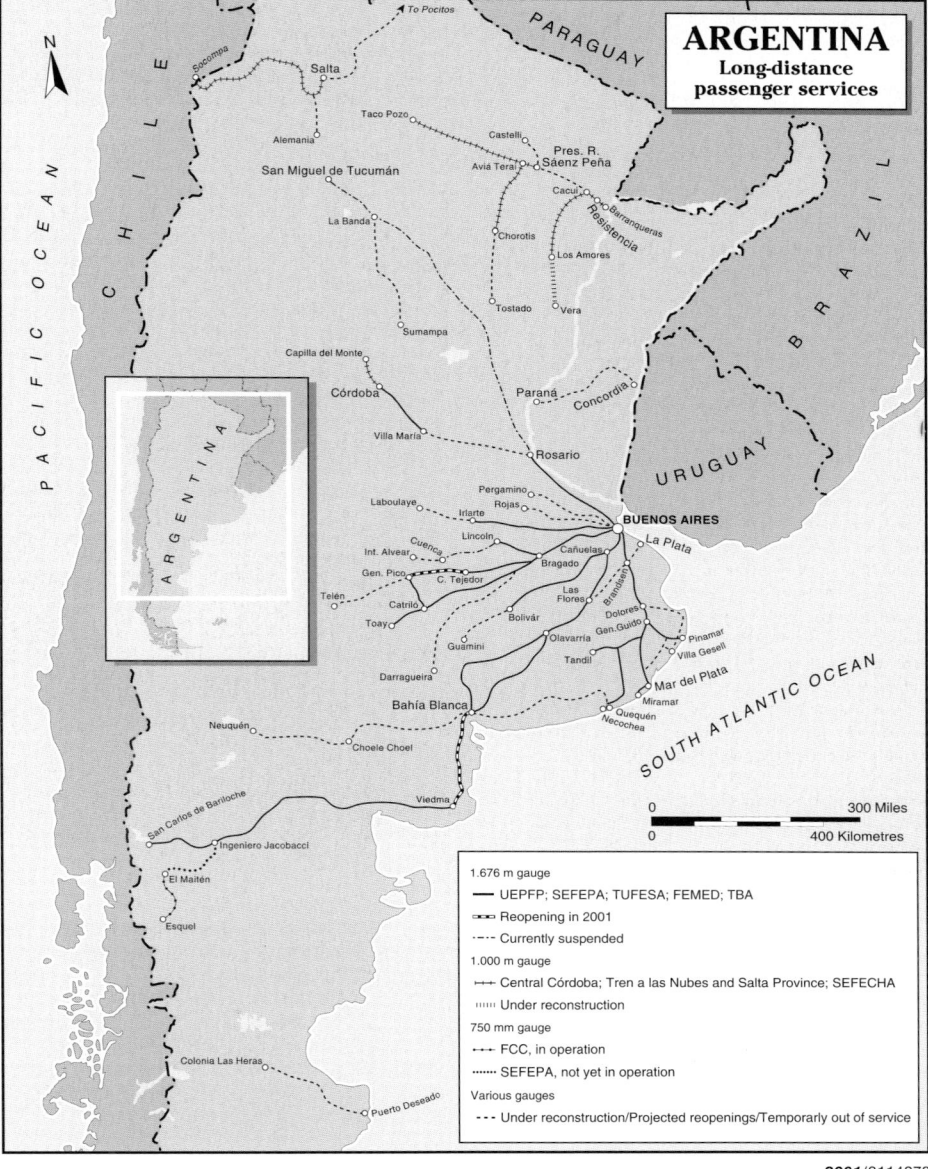

## Ferrocarril Austral Fueguino (FAF) (Tranex Turismo SA)

Avenida Corrientes, 538 – piso 5°, 1043 Buenos Aires
Tel: (+54 11) 43 25 06 81   Fax: (+54 11) 43 26 35 40

### Key personnel

President: Enrique Díz

### Passenger operations

FAF runs a 7.2 km 500 mm gauge tourist line linking Ushuaia and the Tierra del Fuego National Park. It is the world's most southerly railway. Passenger numbers have grown from 7,000 in its first season to 23,000 in the summer of 1996/97, with a 33 per cent increase reported in December 1997.

### Improvements to existing lines

A further 700 m track extension is under construction, and the company has announced its intention eventually to serve Ushuaia.

### Traction and rolling stock

FAF owns two steam locomotives, three diesel locomotives, 16 passenger coaches and 10 service wagons.

## Ferrocarril Belgrano Cargas SA (FBC)

Padre Mugica 426, 1104 Buenos Aires
Tel: (+54 11) 451 00 35 00   Fax: (+54 11) 48 06 35 44

### Key personnel

Chairman: Luis B Schiappori
Vice-President: Omar Vazquez
Director and General Manager: Graciela Coria
Head of Commercial Department: Alberto Paolini

Gauge: 1,000 mm
Route length: 9,800 km

### Political background

The metre-gauge General Belgrano system, now FBC, serves the far northwest of Argentina with routes to the Chilean and Bolivian borders. On 18 December 1998 FBC became the last portion of the former Argentine Railways system to be privatised, with a 30-year concession awarded to a consortium comprising the railway staff union, Unión Ferroviaria (51 per cent), Industrial Laguna Paiva (48 per cent) and the Argentine government (1 per cent), which had been operating the network on a temporary basis since 1997. A formal takeover of operations took place in February 1999. The privatisation mode applied was the same as that for the Metropolitanos lines, with some financial contribution from the national government. This provides annual state financial support for investments of 50 million pesos during the first five years, followed by a total of 142 million pesos during the following ten years. Transurb will assist FBC technically, and will be responsible for operations.

## RAILWAY SYSTEMS/Argentina

Under the terms of a revised agreement, the governments of nine northern provinces obtained the right to operate freight and passenger services throughout their territory (3,313 km), with international connections at border stations. Tenders were called in April 2000, with successful bidders intended to provide their own motive power and rolling stock. The northern provinces generate about 80 per cent of FBC traffic.

The incoming Secretary of Transport stated that the Treasury was unable to provide the subsidy of US$50 million for the first five years of the concession granted by former President Carlos Menem's government to the railway union that took over FBC in 1998. Some congressmen also expressed objections to the subsidy. In response, the chairman of FBC stated that US$145 million required to rehabilitate the system and refurbish equipment would come from revenue and from loans applied for.

### Passenger operations

The Salta–Socompa line is the only section on which FBC operates a passenger service, which is subsidised by Salta province. Other parts of the metre-gauge network have been transferred or leased to Chaco and Santa Fé provinces for the operation of passenger services (see entry for Servicios Ferroviarios Chaqueños (SEFECHA)).

### Freight operations

In 1994 around 1.1 million tonnes were carried. By 1997 this had risen to 1.7 million tonnes, and FBC is expected to carry 2 million tonnes in 1999, increasing to 3 million in 2004. The main commodities handled are mining and ore products, grain and container traffic, the latter playing an important role in movements to and from Chile.

### Improvements to existing lines

The 10,000 km network needs extensive repairs on many sections. Some track renewals have been carried out since 1994, including the section between Güemes and Pocitos in the north of the country, where the line has been partially rebuilt. Attention has also been given to the Salta–Socompa corridor, which is currently the only link with Chile, and where traffic has grown significantly. The aim is to allow train speeds of 50 km/h over the entire network, which will call for investments of 100,000 pesos per km. It is estimated that around 20 per cent of all rail and 50 per cent of all sleepers may need to be replaced.

### Traction and rolling stock

At the beginning of 1999, FBC was operating 84 diesel locomotives, many of them General Motors G22s, with another 38 expected to be rebuilt shortly. A further 15 locomotives were expected to be purchased by 2015.

The freight wagon fleet numbered some 4,000 at the beginning of 1999, with another 1,800 due to be rebuilt. A requirement for a further 700 new vehicles was foreseen to meet future traffic growth.

### Signalling and telecommunications

In 1999 an order was placed with US-based Comsat Mobile Communications to supply a satellite-based communications system to handle train movements from FBC's control centre at Salta.

*FBC General Motors Type GT-22 diesel-electric locomotive at Rosario yard and former running shed in Santa Fe province (Peter Lais)*

Argentina/**RAILWAY SYSTEMS** 11

## Ferrocarril Córdoba Central (FCC)

Estación R del Busto, 5009 Córdoba, CBA
Tel: (+54 351) 482 22 52   Fax: (+54 351) 482 22 52

**Key personnel**
Director: Horacio Cao

*Elderly General Electric locomotive re-engined with an Alco power plant heading an FCC passenger train at Cosquín* (Peter Lais)   0058586

Gauge: 1,000 mm
Length: 158 km

**Organisation**
FCC operates freight and passenger (including the *Tren de las Sierras* tourist operation) services between the city of Córdoba and Cruz del Eje, on a route closed by FA in 1977.

FCC came into being in response to the call for tenders issued by the province of Córdoba, and began operations on 5 December 1993. Services on the final 43 km stretch of line, from Capilla del Monte to Cruz del Eje, were reported as temporarily suspended in early 1998.

| Passenger traffic | 1997 | 1998 | 1999* |
|---|---|---|---|
| Passenger journeys | 24,806 | 25,251 | 17,893 |

(* January-October)

**Passenger operations**
Services are operated on Saturdays and Sundays all year round, with additional trains during the summer period and during school holidays in winter. In 1997 24,806 passengers were carried compared with 27,919 in 1996.

Delivery in 2000 of a Zanello-built railcar was reported as likely to be used for a daily return journey on the Córdoba–Capilla del Monte line.

**Improvements to existing lines**
Between July 1997 and June 1998 US$2.5 million were spent on infrastructure and rolling stock improvements. In 1999 a sleeper replacement programme was under way and in a subsequent phase of improvement work tunnels and bridges may undergo major repairs.

**Traction and rolling stock**
FCC owns three diesel locomotives (two unserviceable), three diesel railcars (two unserviceable) and 14 passenger coaches (nine unserviceable). In 1999 a refurbished Alco RSD-35 diesel locomotive was acquired from Córdoba workshops for use on the passenger service and a twin-unit Zanello railcar was delivered and due to enter revenue service in July 2000.

## Ferrocarriles Del Chubut (FdeC)

Carlos Pellegrini 841, 9210 El Maitén, Chubut
Tel: (+ 54 29 45) 49 51 90   Fax: (+54 29 45) 49 51 90

**Passenger operations**
This company operates one weekly regular service between El Maitén and Esquel on a 750 mm gauge branch line. Other steam-hauled services are run for tourists, including a daily Esquel–Nahuel Pan (20 km) train during summer months.

**Traction and rolling stock**
FdeC operates 6 steam locomotives and 10 passenger coaches.

## Ferrocarriles Mediterráneos (FeMed)

Boulevard Perón 101, 5000 Córdoba
Tel: (+54 351) 42 82 14   Fax: (+54 351) 42 82 14

**Key personnel**
President: Julio Badra

Gauge: 1,676 mm

**Organisation**
This provincially supported regional passenger operator initiated services over Nuevo Central Argentina (qv) tracks between Córdoba and Villa María (140 km) in October 1997. Passenger services on this route had been withdrawn four years earlier.

**Passenger operations**
Two trains each day are provided between Córdoba and Villa Maria (142 km), in 1999 carrying more than 60,000 passengers. A proposal for a first class overnight service between these communities had still not been implemented in 2000, nor had a plan for a service class overnight train between Rosario and Buenos Aires. In 2000 a service between Córdoba and Alta Gracia (48 km) was expected to commence shortly, as were trains on other lines radiating from Córdoba.

**Improvements to existing lines**
FeMed has renovated Córdoba Mitre station, which is to form the hub of the city's rail and road public transport system. However, poor track conditions are reported to be hampering the development of FeMed services. Poor track, especially between Villa Maria and Rosario, has prevented the restoration of passenger services between Córdoba and Buenos Aires, with line speeds at some locations as low as 15 to 25 km/h. Córdoba province was expected to provide funding of peso1.2 million for track improvements in 2000 to raise line speeds to 60 to 70 km/h.

**Traction and rolling stock**
FeMed owns seven diesel locomotives (three unserviceable) and 60 passenger coaches, including six Pullman cars, sleeping and restaurant cars and some car-carrying wagons. Of these, 42 have been refurbished by FeMed and up to 12 more may be similarly treated.

## Ferrocoop

Cooperativa de Trabajo de Olavarría Limitada
Pringles 3100, 7400 Olavarría
Tel: (+54 22 84) 44 05 15   Fax: (+54 22 84) 44 62 60
Gauge: 1,676 mm

**Organisation**
On 19 December 1996, Servicios Ferroviarios Patagónicos (SEFEPA) (qv) signed an agreement with the Ferrocoop co-operative to permit the latter to operate passenger services on the Bahía Blanca–Neuquén line for 30 years. Three services were envisaged: Cipolletti–Neuquén, Villa Regina–Plottier, and a daily train to Cinco Saltas. The co-op would assume responsibility for all costs and was expected initially to transport 4,800 passengers/day.

**Traction and rolling stock**
Initially services were to be provided by four three-car air conditioned dmus built by local supplier Zanello SA. Each is powered by two 360 kW Cummins engines. Ordered from Spanish National Railways in 1998 were four second-hand Class 593 dmus.

## FerroExpreso Pampeano SA (FEPSA)

Avenida Córdoba 320, piso 4, C1054AAP Buenos Aires
Tel: (+54 11) 45 10 49 00
Fax: (+54 11) 45 10 49 30; 49 45

**Key personnel**
General Manager: Rodolfo Glattstein

Gauge: 1,676 mm
Route length: 4,953 km

**Organisation**
FEPSA was the first private enterprise to complete a major takeover of FA operations. FEPSA is 80 per cent owned by Coinfer, an Argentine/US investment consortium comprising four Argentine companies – Techint Compañía Técnica, Sociedad Comercial del Plata, Gesiemes and Riobank Internacional – and the Iowa Interstate Railroad. Iowa Interstate, which has a 2 per cent stockholding, is providing technical advice on operation, traction and rolling stock. The Union Pacific Railroad of the US is serving as technical consultant on telecommunications and computerisation. Argentine Railways retains a 16 per cent stockholding in FEPSA. The residual 4 per cent is held by FEPSA employees.

## RAILWAY SYSTEMS/Argentina

On 1 November 1991, FEPSA took over 5,094 route-km of FA's 1,676 mm gauge grain-carrying lines centred on the routes between Rosario (northwest of Buenos Aires) and Bahía Blanca and between Huinca Renancó and Bahía Blanca; the routes formed part of the Mitre, Sarmiento and Roca railways. FEPSA has an option to extend the 30-year concession by 10 years. In 1998, the company initiated renegotiation of its existing concession with the aim of restructuring its investment programme.

In 1997 FEPSA employed 994 staff.

### Freight operations

FEPSA's principal cargoes include wheat, maize, soya beans, sorghum, sunflower seeds and the pellets and oils derived from them.

The US grain company Cargill has completed a rail-served grain storage facility at the port of Bahía Blanca with a storage capacity of 60,000 short tons. Improvement to warehousing facilities at Bahía Blanca should allow FEPSA to begin importing fertiliser, thereby ensuring return loads for trains discharging export grain.

Experiments with double heading of 60-wagon block grain trains (formerly single-headed trains of 30 wagons were the norm) have shown that it is now possible for FEPSA to operate 4,700 tonne trains. Future traction policy will involve using small switching locomotives on branch lines and concentrating large wagon movements between a limited number of hub yards. In 1996, a co-operation agreement was signed with Ferrosur Roca (qv) to integrate and co-ordinate freight services. Steel traffic is also handled jointly with Nuevo Central Argentino. Door-to-door services have also been developed.

| Traffic (million) | 1997 | 1998-99 |
|---|---|---|
| Freight tonnes | 3.428 | 2.606 |
| Freight tonne-km | 1,375,000 | 938,257 |

### Traction and rolling stock

In 1997 FEPSA operated 47 diesel locomotives and around 1,600 wagons.

### Signalling and telecommunications

Signalling is by cab radio and fax via a microwave network, permitting a track warrant system of train control and operation, replacing the former station-to-station staff, or rod, train movement authority. Communication between Bahía Blanca and Buenos Aires is by satellite.

---

## Ferrosur Roca SA (FR)

Bouchard 680 – piso 8°, 1106 Buenos Aires
Tel: (+54 11) 43 19 39 00   Fax: (+54 11) 43 19 39 01
e-mail: ferrosur@impsat1.com.ar

### Key personnel

General Manager: Sergio do Rego
Directors
  Commercial: Mario Casasco
  Administration and Finance: Ricardo Wagner
  Human Resources: Carlos Sánchez Obertello
  Operations: Gustavo Romera
  Operations Resources: Elbio Armanazqui

Gauge: 1,676 mm
Route length: 3,110 km

### Organisation

In December 1992, the concession to operate the General Roca railway was awarded to the Ferrosur Roca consortium; it was the sole bidder. Cement manufacturer Loma Negra owns 65 per cent of the new company, with other members being Acindar, Petroquímica Comodoro Rivadavia, Decavial, Banco Francés and the Asociación de Cooperativas Agrarias. Operations began on 11 March 1993. Although initial management of the company was Canadian, local managers have since taken over. At the end of 1998 FR employed 720 staff.

The Roca railway extends due south from Buenos Aires and serves the country's main agricultural belt. Three deep water ports, Bahía Blanca, Quequén and San Antonio Oeste, are also served by the railway. There is an inland branch which runs due west of Bahía Blanca and crosses the important fruit-growing area located in the upper valley of the Río Negro, terminating at Zapala.

In 1996, FR and FEPSA decided to co-ordinate their activities, with FEPSA personnel moving into FR's modern headquarters building. FR closed its own workshops in Bahía Blanca and switched all activities to FEPSA's own facilities in the same city. Motive power now moves freely between the two networks, as do wagons, while radio frequencies have been harmonised.

### Freight operations

FR traffic has maintained a steady climb since it took over the concession in 1993, and in August 1997 for the first time lifted over 400,000 tonnes of freight. The main traffic base consists of construction materials, which account for around 75 per cent of total tonnage, petroleum, petrochemicals and hazardous cargos, such as caustic soda, and grain. Polyethylene traffic between Bahía Blanca and Buenos Aires will reach 270,000 tonnes in 2000 and FR plans to increase this figure to 370,000 tonnes in two years. However, aggregates traffic has fallen from 400,000 to 255,000 tonnes per month. The company has a contract to move 120,000 tonnes of cement and 250,000 tonnes of clinker annually for Loma Negra, Argentina's main cement producer. Grain is conveyed to the port of Quequén and to flour mills.

In February 1996 FR initiated its Frigotren service, conveying fresh fruit from the Alto Valle del Río Negro to Buenos Aires for both domestic consumption and for export. The train formation includes a generator vehicle to provide refrigeration power during the train's 40 hour journey.

FR also carries intermodal traffic destined for Chile via the Pino Hachado Pass 'Corredor Bioceánico' route.

Two-person locomotive crews, consisting of a driver and conductor (the latter to handle all point work), operate all trains.

| Traffic (million) | 1997 | 1998 | 1999 |
|---|---|---|---|
| Freight tonnes | 4.500 | 4.125 | 4.364 |
| Freight tonne-km | 1,635 | 1,547 | 1,708 |

### New lines

FR is providing technical project management services for the Argentine section of the Southern Trans-Andean Rail Link (STAR) scheme. STAR involves the construction of a new 220 km link between the 1,676 mm gauge railheads at Lonquimay in Chile and Zapala in Argentina. Construction of the 160 km Argentine section is to be undertaken using public funds, while the Chilean government has attempted to attract private finance (principally in Europe) for the 60 km section of the link that would lie within its borders. In 1994 the Argentine province of Neuquén contracted consulting engineers Bechtel to produce a revised scheme for the link; Neuquén provided US$60,000 towards the study, with the US Trade Development Agency contributing US$380,000.

It is hoped that the completion of the Lonquimay–Zapala link would create a freight route linking Talcahuano on the Pacific with Bahía Blanca on the Atlantic. Annual freight traffic between Chile and Argentina across the southern Andes has been reckoned to be in the order of 1.7 million tonnes.

### Improvements to existing lines

FR plans to invest US$173 million in the first 15 years of its concession, although it will have to pay a total of US$47 million to the government in fees during the full 30-year life of the concession. Eventual maximum speed on trunk routes has been pitched at 68 to 77 km/h. Investment in track improvements will total US$86 million.

Track improvements to the main line in the province of Buenos Aires were well advanced in 2000, with initial sections already completed. The line carries around 80 per cent of its traffic.

### Traction and rolling stock

At the end of 1998 the FR locomotive fleet comprised 57 units, including 25 GM 1,687 kW GT22CW machines built 1972-86. A further three refurbished locomotives have been procured, and in 2000 four additional 1,640 kW locomotives were delivered by Gevisa. These were to be deployed on cement and chemicals traffic.

At the end of 1998 FR operated 2,200 freight wagons. Recent fleet developments included the refurbishment of 84 tank wagons for bulk petroleum products, conversion of existing vehicles into 300 cement wagons and 120 container flat wagons, and the conversion of six covered wagons for the secure transport of hazardous materials. Refurbishment and conversion of an initial batch of 100 cement wagons was in progress in 2000.

### Signalling and telecommunications

The previous station-to-station staff authority system of operation has been replaced by one of track warrants, developed by CN. To make this possible, much initial investment has gone into train radio, end-of-train telemetry, microwave communications and computer data processing to permit use of a Computer-Assisted Manual Block System (CAMBS). Dispatching takes place at Olavarría.

### Track

The main trunk route between Buenos Aires and Bahía Blanca has stone-ballasted track with continuous welded rail. Much of the rest has been poorly maintained in recent years.

**Rail:** Some 2,700 km of track is laid with 49 and 50 kg/m rail, while 1,370 km is 42 kg/m. The remainder of the network uses 28-36 kg/m
**Sleepers:** Timber and steel
**Spacing:** 1,394-1,722/km on plain track; 1,474-1,722 on curves
**Min curve radius:** 160 m
**Max gradient:** 1.4%
**Max axleload:** 20 tonnes

*Ferrosur Roca's Frigotren service for fresh fruit includes a generator car in the train formation to provide power for refrigeration units*
0010762

## Ferrovías

Avenida Ramos Mejia 1430 – piso 4°, 1104 Buenos Aires
Tel: (+54 11) 45 11 88 33   Fax: (+54 11) 45 11 88 43

**Key personnel**
President: Dr Gabriel Romero
Vice-President: Osvaldo R Aldao
General Manager: Felix Imposti
Company Accountant: Hector S Cimo

Gauge: 1,000 mm
Route length: 132.6 km

**Organisation**
The concession for FEMESA's diesel-operated Belgrano North line from Buenos Aires' Retiro station to Villa Rosa was awarded to the Ferrovías consortium, led by Leddevi Construcciones, which had Portuguese Railways (CP) and Barcelona Metro as operators. CP was subsequently forced to withdraw, due to budgetary cutbacks at home; a 1 per cent share in Ferrovías was acquired by Transurb Consult of Belgium, the new technical advisor to the group. Other members of the consortium include Seminara Constructores and the bus operator Cooperativa de Transportes Automotores de Cuyo.

On 3 February 1994 a 10-year operating contract was signed by government and Ferrovías for the Belgrano North route. Operations began on 30 April 1994. In 1998-99 Ferrovías renegotiated its concession with a view to obtain a 20-year extension in return for extensive investment (see 'Improvements to existing lines').

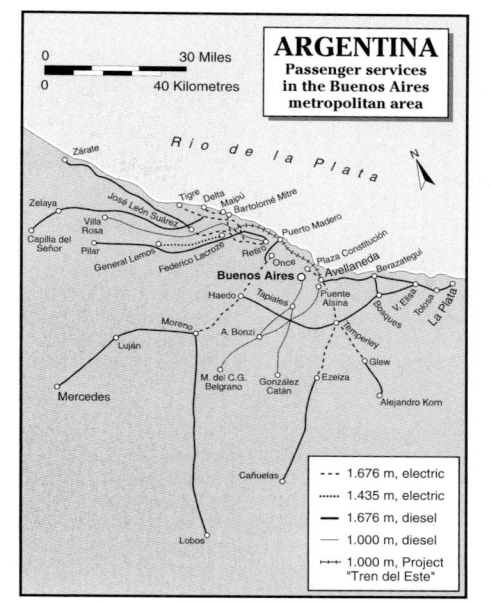

**Passenger operations**
Initial efforts to improve service quality focused on reducing the number of cancellations, improving passenger security and providing the travelling public with cleaner and better-lit trains. Ferrovías claims to have reduced fare evasion by some 30 to 40 per cent by carrying out more ticket inspections, and plans to introduce a closed-station system. Ticketing was to switch to preprinted tickets issued by PCs, with electronic/magnetic tickets to work barriers planned for the long term.

In 1997 Ferrovías carried 32.3 million fare-paying passengers.

**Improvements to existing lines**
A subsidy of US$196 million was negotiated for the concession period, the bulk of which was earmarked for infrastructure improvements. Track, level crossings, signalling and telecommunications were felt to be areas of particular concern.

In 1995, a contract worth US$23 million was signed with local companies for the renewal of 18 route-km of double track between Buenos Aires and Carapachay. Ferrovías has also undertaken a refurbishment programme covering the 22 stations it serves, financed by its own resources to the tune of US$1.5 million.

Under the terms of a renegotiated concession, Ferrovías plans to electrify the 62 km Retiro—Villa Rosa line, on the Belgrano North system, reconstructing all 22 stations and providing a fleet of new emus.

**Traction and rolling stock**
Ferrovías operates a fleet of 21 General Motors G22 CU diesel-electric locomotives. At the end of 1997, the Ferrovías passenger fleet comprised 101 coaches.

**Signalling and telecommunications**
The Ferrovías system is equipped with automatic colour-light signalling.

## Metropolitano

Avenida Santa Fe 4636 – piso 2, C1425BHV Buenos Aires
Tel: (+54 11) 47 78 58 00   Fax: (+54 11) 47 78 58 78

**Key personnel**
Managing Director: Carlos R Beltrán Simó

Gauge: 1,676 mm, 1,000 mm
Route length: 316.3 km, 66.3 km; 119 stations
Electrification: 47.5 km at 25 kV 50 Hz AC

**Organisation**
The 10-year concessions to operate suburban services on the Roca, San Martín and Belgrano South routes were awarded in January 1993 to the Trainmet consortium, consisting of Empresa Argentina de Construcciones, Ormas SA, Román SA, DGT Electronica and 63 independent bus operators. US operator BART and JARTS of Japan were to act as partners. Trainmet, which subsequently changed its name to Transportes Metropolitanos, began operating the three franchises as TMS, TMB and TMR between April 1994 and January 1995. Subsequently, the company has operated under the name Metropolitano. Trainmet now owns 51 per cent of the capital stock but in mid-2000 a legal case was in progress with Ormas SA.

In 1999 Metropolitano began renegotiating its concession to obtain a 20-year extension to 2023 in return for an investment programme amounting to an estimated US$1.5 billion.

**Passenger operations**
*TMS*
Trainmet began operating San Martín suburban services as Transportes Metropolitanos San Martín (TMS) on 1 April 1994. The TMS system comprises a diesel-worked 1,676 mm gauge route (56.3 route-km) between Buenos Aires (Retiro) and Pilar.

*TMB*
Operation of Belgrano South suburban services as Transportes Metropolitanos Belgrano (TMB) began on 1 May 1994. The TMB system comprises 66.3 route-km of diesel-worked 1,000 mm gauge lines.

*TMR*
Operation of Roca suburban services as Transportes Metropolitanos Roca (TMR) began on 1 January 1995.

The system comprises 259 route-km of 1,676 mm gauge lines, only 202 km of which carry passenger services, radiating from Buenos Aires' Plaza Constitución terminus. Electrified routes serve Temperley, Glew and Ezeiza, and services to Cañuelas, Alejandro Korn, Berazategui, La Plata and Haedo are diesel-worked.

Combined ridership on the three systems rose from 88 million passenger journeys in 1994 to 207 million in 1997.

**Traction and rolling stock**
In 1997 the Metropolitano fleet comprised 68 1,676 mm and 20 1,000 mm gauge diesel locomotives mostly of General Electric and General Motors designs, 295 1,676 mm gauge coaches, plus 58 baggage cars, and a further 91 metre-gauge coaches. The Roca system emu fleet totalled 187 units, and a dmu was also in operation on the metre-gauge system.

In 1997, Metropolitano received 10 Canadian-built General Motors diesel locomotives, of which five were for broad-gauge operation and five for metre-gauge. Other broad-gauge diesel locomotives were procured by leasing. More recently, two new U20C units for the metre-gauge Belgrano Sur section were supplied by Gevisa.

## Metrovías SA

Bartolomé Mitre 3342, 1201 Buenos Aires
Tel: (+54 11) 49 59 68 00   Fax: (+54 11) 48 66 30 37
e-mail: info@metrovias.com.ar
Web: http://www.metrovias.com.ar

**Key personnel**
General Manager: Roberto Macías
Planning Manager: José A Barbero

Gauge: 1,435 mm
Route length: 25.6 km
Electrification: 25.6 km at 600 V DC

**Organisation**
In 1993, the Metrovías consortium was awarded a 20-year concession to run electric suburban services on the Urquiza line as well as the 36.5 km Buenos Aires metro system. Headed by Roggio SA (a construction company based in Córdoba), Metrovías originally included Cometrans (an association of 30 independent bus companies in Buenos Aires), with Burlington Northern and Morrison Knudsen of the USA providing technical assistance.

Metrovías, in the guise of Trenes de Buenos Aires (TBA) (qv), was also awarded concessions to operate electric suburban services on the Mitre and Sarmiento lines; it had originally been hoped that TBA operations would start in June 1994. Following a change in TBA's corporate structure, which involved Morrison Knudsen selling its holding in Metrovías to Roggio SA (giving the latter a 72 per cent stake), TBA operations on the Mitre and Sarmiento lines began on 29 May 1995. With Burlington Northern Santa Fe now a member of the TBA consortium, Metrovías has received technical assistance from Transurb Consult of Belgium.

In early 1999, Metrovías was renegotiating its contract with a view to a 20-year extension.

**Finance**
The company is to receive US$130 million in annual subsidies to operate both the Urquiza service and that of the metro system. It was hoped that cost reduction and control of rampant fare evasion would permit the subsidy to be eventually used to upgrade the service on offer. The concession contract allows for fare rises of 3 per cent per year once service and quality targets have been met.

**Passenger operations**
Having begun operations on the Urquiza route on 1 January 1994, Metrovías recorded a total of 22.53 million paying passengers in that year as a whole, with 9.23 million train-km operated. The number of passengers carried was 35 per cent up on 1993. In 1995, 23.26 million paying passengers were recorded and 9.67 million train-km operated, with demand 39 per cent up on 1993. In 1997, 25.2 million passengers were carried.

**Improvements to existing lines**
Metrovías is to provide US$436 million of investment for the Urquiza route and the metro system over the lifetime of the concession. Major infrastructure work on the Urquiza route required by the concession contract includes track renewal, level crossing elimination and improvements to the third-rail electrification system and its cabling. By the start of 1996, Metrovías had begun track renewal, cabling and third-rail work costing US$8.2 million, US$1.9 million and US$0.4 million respectively.

**Traction and rolling stock**
Metrovías trains are usually formed of three two-car emu trainsets, with each trainset comprising one motor and one trailer car. As from November 1996, Spanish rolling stock builder CAF assumed all responsibility for the maintenance of emu cars, using workshops at Lynch and Rubén Dário.

Metrovías also operates three diesel locomotives.

## Nuevo Central Argentino SA (NCA)

Avenida Alberdi 50, 2000 Rosario, Santa Fe
Tel: (+54 341) 437 65 61   Fax: (+54 341) 439 23 77
e-mail: info@nca.com.ar

**Key personnel**
President: Miguel Acevedo
General Manager: Horacio Díaz Hermelo
Operations Manager: Ernesto Gutierrez
Infrastructure and Track Maintenance: Daniel Zurbriggen
Logistics Manager: Hugo Zanelli

Gauge: 1,676 mm
Route length: 4,836 km

**Organisation**
On 2 July 1992 control of Argentine Railways' General Mitre railway passed to Nuevo Central Argentino for a period of 30 years; it was the second concession to be granted. The Mitre network connects three industrial cities in the North Central region (Tucumán, Córdoba and Rosario) with Buenos Aires. It also serves Argentina's most fertile grain-producing area, the Pampa Húmeda, providing access to several bulk-commodity ports on the Paraná river.

The concessionaire is a consortium of two Argentine companies headed by Aceitera General Deheza (AGD), an oil and seed producer which is also one of the NCA's main customers; and the Asociación de Cooperativas Agrarias Argentinas, a major grain co-operative.

Originally, the US-based regional railroad Montana Rail Link (a Burlington Northern Santa Fe subsidiary), the Washington company RBC Associates and the transport management company Anacostia & Pacific were associates.

In 2002 NCA employed 1,221 staff.

**Passenger services**
While NCA is a freight railway, passenger services provided by other companies operate over its tracks. Ferrocarriles Mediterráneos runs two trains each day over NCA tracks between Córdoba and Villa Maria (142 km). Trenes de Buenos Aires (TBA) also runs two trains a week over NCA lines between Retiro (Buenos Aires) and Rosario, the Zárate–Retiro portion operating under TBA's own concession.

A service over NCA tracks linking Tucumán and Buenos Aires was active until 1996, then discontinued until 1997, resuming again until March 2000. A single weekly train in each direction commenced operation in January 2002.

**Freight operations**
NCA ran its first train on 23 December 1992. In 1997 4.8 million tonnes were carried.

Traffic growth has continued, and by 1999 some 5.5 million tonnes annually were being carried. Grain products are the most important commodity handled: 1999 was the third consecutive year in which more than 1.2 million tonnes were transported, an achievement assisted by the rehabilitation of previously unserviceable wagons. Other recent traffic developments include: a new flow of copper concentrate for Minera Alumbrera, a new commodity for NCA which in 1999 was generating 70,000 tonnes of traffic per month; the transport of imported car components to assembly plants in Córdoba; and the movement of raw materials for the cement industry from Córdoba to the Campana plant in Buenos Aires. Possible future traffic flows being studied in 2000 covered cars, fertiliser, bagged soda and copper concentrate from Noroeste Argentino.

NCA has also been pursuing a policy of upgrading yards and improving access to its network via new branches and sidings, as well as focusing on the reliability of its services and equipment.

| Traffic (million) | 1999 | 2000 | 2001 |
|---|---|---|---|
| Freight tonnes | 5.496 | 5.521 | 6.187 |
| Freight tonne-km | 2,445 | 2,491 | 2,928 |

*NCA mixed freight service powered by an Alco locomotive*   2002/0122591

*NCA train of hopper wagons*   2002/0122592

**Improvements to existing lines**
A 1,470 km core network consisting of main lines linking Buenos Aires to Rosario and Tucumán, and Rosario to Córdoba, now have stone ballast, while many wooden sleepers and sections of rail have been replaced. NCA has been pursuing a programme of renewing or rehabilitating branch lines and yards.

**Traction and rolling stock**
The fleet available for line service at December 1999 comprised 63 locomotives. Several GAIA 970 kW diesel-electric locomotives have been refurbished for shunting operations at main yards and terminals.

The NCA wagon fleet amounted to 5,254 vehicles at the end of 1999, comprising grain hoppers (around half the fleet), tank wagons, bulk cement and flat wagons, and mineral hoppers, reflecting the system's diversified traffic base. The refurbishment of unserviceable wagons inherited at the time the concession was won has continued.

Heavy repair shops are located at Villa Diego near Rosario, where a further two smaller shops also handle minor repairs. Other smaller shops are also to be found at Córdoba and Tucumán.

NCA provides a total logistics service that takes into account the needs of production processes, warehousing, port facilities and export requirements. In its ninth year of operation, the railway continued to achieve traffic growth, with an all-time high tonnage in 2001 of 6.187 tonnes. For the fifth year, the volume of grain carried exceeded 1.2 million tonnes. Movements of copper concentrate for a major customer, Minera Alumbrera, totalled 70,000 tonnes per month during 2001, representing 11.5 per cent of NCA traffic. Other major commodities handled include aggregates, slag and clinker, which accounts for 13 per cent of traffic.

In 2002, the company was pursuing contracts to carry new cars, imported fertiliser, bagged soda and additional flows of copper concentrate from northwest Argentina.

**Signalling and telecommunications**
Before assuming operational control of the Mitre railway in 1992, NCA installed a VHF cab-signalling system on its main lines to Tucumán and Córdoba, boosted by repeater stations across the network. Two-person locomotive crews handle 2,000-tonne trains consisting of 40 wagons, and all movements are controlled from a computer-aided dispatching centre located in Rosario. An IBM AS/400-based wagon tracking system is also in operation.

*UPDATED*

---

## Servicios Ferroviarios Chaqueños (SEFECHA)

García Meron 5800, 3514 Fontana, Chaco
Tel: (+54 37 22) 47 55 50   Fax: (+54 37 22) 47 55 50

**Key personnel**
President: Ing Manuel Emilio Vecchi
Vice-President: Sergio Gabriel Peyrano
Chief Engineer: Mario Acevedo

**Organisation**
SEFECHA was set up in 1997 to provide passenger services over some 500 km of metre-gauge routes in Chaco province, mostly operating over track owned by Ferrocarril Belgrano Cargas (qv).

Argentina/**RAILWAY SYSTEMS** 15

**Passenger operations**
SEFECHA's initial daily service between Cacuí and La Sabana (117 km) proved successful and in 1998 new services were added from Presidencia Roque Saenz Peña to Chorotis (188 km) and to Taco Pozo (311 km). The latter is operated three times weekly in each direction, serving communities in the extreme northeast of Santiago del Estero province. In 1999, the La Sabana service was extended to Los Amores, in the extreme north of Santa Fe province and an extension south to Gobernador Vera was likely in 2000. A suburban service from Puerto Barranqueras via the Chaco provincial capital, Resistencia, to Cacuí, Puerto Tiros (16.5 km) was also introduced in 1999 with 11 trains daily in each direction. SEFECHA expected to increase this to 16 in each direction to create virtually a metropolitan service. The largest obstacle to the reintroduction of services is reported to be numerous unmanned level crossings on the track, which is owned by Ferrocarril Belgrano Cargas (qv).

**Improvements to existing lines**
SEFECHA has funded the installation of automatic barriers at two level crossings in Resistencia and in 1999 ordered similar equipment for an additional 26 sites within the city's boundaries. Plans exist to upgrade the 10.5 km section of line between Resistencia and Puerto Barranqueras in collaboration with FBC, and additional passing loops are planned at two intermediate stations.

Two stations and 15 stops have been created for the Puerto Barranqueras—Cacuí service.

**Traction and rolling stock**
Four two-car MAN dmus and six Ferrostaal railcar-trailer sets have been acquired second-hand from Spanish local operator SFM in Mallorca and refurbished by Igarreta in Buenos Aires. The Ferrostaal units have been equipped with air conditioning and audio passenger information systems.

## Servicios Ferroviarios Patagónicos (SeFePa)

Laprida 240, 8500 Viedma, Rio Negro
Tel: (+54 29 20) 42 21 30   Fax: (+54 29 20) 42 74 13

**Key personnel**
Managing Director: German Jalabert

Gauge: 1,676 mm, 750 mm
Route length: 817 km, 237 km

**Political background**
SeFePa was established by the province of Rio Negro to operate passenger services within its boundaries upon the withdrawal of federal support for intercity passenger trains.

Freight services are also operated over SeFePa's southern region, particulary to San Carlos de Bariloche. In late 1997 it was announced that through freight services were to be reintroduced between Buenos Aires and Bariloche. These are operated by Ferrocargas del Sur.

During 1999 SeFePa passenger operations were to be taken over for a 10-year period by Ferrotransportes Patagónicos SA (FTP), a subsidiary of Mar del Plata-based bus operator Platamar. Initially SeFePa's ex-FA rolling stock will be used, but this is expected to be replaced by Zanello-built railcars and dmus based at Córdoba. Service frequencies are to be increased and line speeds will be raised after infrastructure improvements have been carried out. The journey time for the 819 km San Carlos de Bariloche—Viedma service is expected to be reduced from 17 to 12 hours after infrastructure rehabilitation. At a later date FTP is also expected to take over SeFePa freight services, leaving SeFePa responsible only for infrastructure maintenance.

**Passenger operations**
There is no longer a through service between Plaza Constitución (Buenos Aires) and San Carlos de Bariloche. UEPFP trains run as far as Carmen de Patagones and SeFePa provides services from this latter point to San Carlos de Bariloche with its own equipment.

SeFePa has taken over responsibility for the Ingeniero Jacobacci—El Maiten portion of the 750 mm gauge route from Ingeniero Jacobacci to Esquel, although the 'Old Patagonian Train' remains out of service in Rio Negro province. There are plans to transfer provision of tourist train services to a private-sector operator but no potential candidates have expressed an interest. Ingeniero Jacobacci is also on SeFePa's Viedma—San Carlos de Bariloche 1,676 mm gauge route. Operated between El Maiten and Esquel by the province of Chubut, the 402 km steam-operated Ingeniero Jacobacci—Esquel line both attracts tourists and provides essential transport services in a very remote part of Argentina.

SeFePa was reported to be enjoying healthy traffic in 1996, with ridership up 50 per cent on Ingeniero Jacobacci—Bariloche trains, and 100 per cent between Bariloche and Viedma.

In December 1999, SeFePa obtained a national government subsidy of US$280,000 for upgrading permanent way and rolling stock refurbishment. In 2000, the company was operating a twice-weekly passenger train between Viedma, on the Atlantic coast, and San Carlos de Bariloche, receiving an annual subsidy of US$100,000 from the provincial Finance Ministry to maintain services.

**Traction and rolling stock**
In 2000, SeFePa was still seeking motive power and rolling stock from former state-owned railways. Nine diesel locomotives and some 200 freight wagons were due to be transferred to provincial systems.

In 1994 Rio Negro purchased for Pta312 million a batch of used rolling stock from RENFE. Three Class 321 Alco diesel-electric locomotives, four sleeping cars, six first-class coaches, three luggage/generator vans and two diesel multiple-units were purchased.

*Former Spanish National Railways Class 321 diesel-electric locomotive in service with SeFePa at San Carlos de Bariloche (Bryan Philpott)* 0023712

## Trenes de Buenos Aires (TBA)

Avenida Ramos Mejía 1358 – piso 2°, 1104 Buenos Aires
Tel: (+54 11) 43 17 44 00   Fax: (+54 11) 43 17 44 16

**Key personnel**
President: S C Cirigliano
Vice-President: J Crawford
General Manager: Roberto Agosta
Director, Operations: H Payne

Gauge: 1,676 mm
Route length: 419 km
Electrification: 93.9 km at 800 V DC

**Organisation**
Trenes de Buenos Aires (TBA) was formed by the members of the Metrovías consortium (qv), which had been awarded the concessions for suburban services on the Mitre and Sarmiento systems in 1993. TBA's shareholders are Morrison Knudsen (41.65 per cent), Cometrans (41.65 per cent) and Burlington Northern Santa Fe (16.7 per cent).

In 1998 TBA was granted a 20-year extension to its current concession, which runs until 2005. The new agreement provided for investments of US$2.2 billion in

*Refurbished Toshiba-built TBA Mitre line emu (Peter Lais)* 0058588

# RAILWAY SYSTEMS/Argentina

the Mitre and Sarmiento lines and an elimination of government subsidy by 2000.

### Passenger operations
TBA began operating the Mitre and Sarmiento systems on 29 May 1995. FEMESA had carried 37.8 million fare-paying passengers on the Mitre system and 59.9 million on the Sarmiento system in 1994. However, by 1996, TBA had boosted patronage on the Mitre line to 69.8 million passengers and on the Sarmiento route to 99.3 million. In 1997, combined ridership on the two systems had risen to 192.3 million.

In 1997 a US$25 million magnetic ticketing system was introduced.

Also in 1997 TBA launched a three-class daily service between Retiro (Buenos Aires) and Rosario Sur (294 km). Since February 2000, these trains have been running into Rosario Norte station and lightweight dmus have been substituted for locomotive-hauled stock during weekdays.

### Improvements to existing lines
Under its original 10-year concession, TBA was to invest US$405 million. Rolling stock was the immediate priority, but TBA also made provision for track renewal, an extensive programme to eliminate level crossings, and station modernisation. World Bank funding was secured by the government in 1995 for the rebuilding of the Caballito–Liniers section of the Sarmiento system to eliminate 18 level crossings.

Under the concession-extension agreement finalised in 1998, TBA was to electrify the Bancalari–General Rodriguez and Mariano Acosta branches on the Sarmiento system and extend Mitre line electrification to Maquinista Savio. Track improvements were also planned between Buenos Aires and Rosario, and a major station refurbishment programme was to be undertaken.

TBA signed a US$95 million contract with Siemens Argentina in 1995 for the renewal and maintenance of traction power supply equipment, including substations at Floresta and Morón on the Sarmiento network.

In October 1997 TBA reopened a 26 km line linking the city terminal at Castelar and Puerto Madero, including a restored 5 km underground link with two intermediate stations. The service is dmu-operated, and is part of a TBA strategy to develop a regional express network in the Buenos Aires area by linking the Mitre and Sarmiento networks via a cross-city tunnel link.

### Traction and rolling stock
TBA inherited 367 electric multiple-unit cars, 43 hauled passenger coaches and 96 diesel multiple-units from FEMESA. Refurbishment of 362 emu cars and 43 coaches had been made an investment priority, with 130 emu cars to be refurbished by the end of 1997. These include Toshiba-built emus used on the Mitre electrified network. Work on these commenced at TBA's Castelar workshops in 1997. Now known as UMAP (Unidad Múltiple Argentina de Pasajeros) units, each three-car set has been fitted with streamlined cab-ends, new seating and air conditioning.

In 1997 the TBA fleet comprised 29 diesel locomotives (25 serviceable), 78 coaches, 418 emu cars 374 serviceable), 11 dmus. Recent locomotive acquisitions include 15 Class 313 Co-Co diesel-electric locomotives purchased from RENFE of Spain in 1995.

Future rolling stock procurement planned under TBA's 1998 concession extension agreement included 492 emu cars and new vehicle for diesel-operated routes.

Second-hand dmus have been ordered from Spanish National Railways and some of these were thought likely to work on the Retiro–Rosario Norte route.

### Signalling and telecommunications
TBA drivers have been issued with radios to communicate with dispatchers, and on lightly used diesel-operated routes track warrant control has replaced manual block signalling. From 1997, TBA hoped to replace semaphore signals on 5 km of the Mitre main line from Retiro to Empalme Maldonado and carry out signalling improvements at Once, Caballito, Flores, Floresta, Liniers and Moreno on the Sarmiento system.

*Lightweight diesel trainset comprising two power cars and a trailer at Rosario Norte with the daily return working to Retiro (Buenos Aires) (Angel Ferrer)*  
2000/0089092

---

## Trenes & Turismo SA

Caseros 441, 4000 Salta, STA  
Tel: (+54 387) 421 63 94   Fax: (+54 387) 431 12 64  
Buenos Aires office:  
Esmerelda 1008, 1007 Buenos Aires (CF)  
Tel: (+54 11) 431 88 71

### Key personnel
Chairman: Julio Ruiz de los Llanos  
Vice-President: Corina Lewin  
Directors: Miguel Desimone, Eduardo Lewin

Gauge: 1,000 mm  
Route length: 218 km

### Organisation
Trenes & Turismo SA is a consortium comprising La Veloz del Norte and Dinar, both of which are involved in tourism and road transport. It previously traded as Movitren SA. The company operates the famous 'Tren a las Nubes' (Train to the Clouds) tourist service between Salta and the Viaducto La Polvorilla, 4,197 m above sea level, on the Salta-Socompa line owned by Ferrocarril Belgrano Cargas (FBC) (qv). FBC operates freight trains and one weekly passenger service over the entire 570 route-km to and from Socompa. As well as the Tren a las Nubes, which has been operating throughout the year since the summer 1998/99 timetable, Trenes & Turismo also runs the 'Tren a la Quebrada del Inca' (Train to the Valley of the Incas) several times during winter months between Salta and Gobernador M Sola (92 km), on the second zigzag of the line.

As Movitren, the company received its first concession to run the Tren a las Nubes service from Argentine Railways in 1992. In mid-1997 a renewal of the concession until 2026 was granted.

The company employs 60 staff.

### Passenger operations
In 1999, 27,890 passengers were carried, compared with 24,000 in 1996. Both Tren a las Nubes and Tren a la Quebrada del Inca services convey first class coaches and a restaurant car and are staffed with hostesses and medical personnel, the latter necessary to deal with altitude sickness among passengers.

A third tourist train, the 'Tren al Portal Andino' (Train to the Gateway to the Andes), is planned over part of the line to Viaducto la Polvorilla between Salta and Campo Quijano (41km), but in early 1999 a date for its introduction had yet to be announced. Also on Trenes & Turismo's agenda is the introduction of the long-planned international service, the 'Tren del Sol' (Train to the Sun), from Salta to Santa Cruz de la Sierra, in eastern Bolivia, but Ferrocarril Oriental of Bolivia is reportedly also keen to start a similar service. Trenes & Turismo is understood also to be planning to bid for a suburban service from Cerillos through Salta to a station to the south of the provincial capital.

### Traction and rolling stock
Trenes & Turismo owns 14 coaches, including two baggage cars, an air conditioned restaurant car and a Pullman bar coach. The locomotive usually employed is a GM GT-22CU owned and maintained by FBC and leased by Trenes & Turismo. The procurement of new locomotives and coaches has been considered, as well as railcars or railbuses for local services.

---

## Tucumán Ferrocarriles SA (TuFeSA)

Corrientes 1075, 4000 San Miguel de Tucumán, Tucumán  
Tel: (+54 381) 430 38 95   Fax: (+54 381) 430 19 09

### Key personnel
General Manager: Viviana Totongi

### Political background
Owned and funded by regional government, TuFeSA in October 1997 reinstated passenger services between Buenos Aires and Tucumán (1,170 km) after a one-year suspension. Trains ran over 1,676 mm gauge tracks owned by Nuevo Central Argentino (qv), and were to operate without subsidy.

However, following the death in November 1998 of its President, David Giménez, TuFeSA ran into serious financial difficulties and in March 2000 the provincial authority withdrew the concession. Services ceased and their resumption was expected to be delayed. By April 2000, four consortia had expressed an interest in taking over the concession but no agreement had been concluded.

### Improvements to existing lines
TuFeSA planned to take over the long-disused Tucumán–Juan Bautista Alberdi line (100 km) to rehabilitate it for local services.

### Traction and rolling stock
TuFeSA invested in the refurbishment of a fleet of 36 coaches taken over from Tucumán province. Some of these were destroyed in an accident in January 1998, leaving TuFeSA with 24 serviceable vehicles.

TuFeSA also owns six diesel locomotives (four unserviceable) and planned to lease two GT-22 machines from Ferrocarril Belgrano Cargas and equip them with broad-gauge bogies.

Argentina—Armenia/**RAILWAY SYSTEMS**

## Unidad Ejecutora del Programa Ferroviario Provincial (UEPFP)

General Hornos 11 – piso 4°, 1154 Buenos Aires
Tel: (+54 11) 43 05 51 74   Fax: (+54 11) 43 05 59 33

**Key personnel**
General Manager: Guillermo Crespo
General Co-ordinator: Dr Alberto Trezza

Gauge: 1,676 mm
Route length: 793 km

**Political background**
UEPFP was established by Eduardo Duhalde, governor of the province of Buenos Aires, after the federal government ceased to support long-distance passenger services in March 1993. The company initially contracted Ferrocarriles Argentinos to run services, and on 27 August 1993 began operations itself with a fleet of ex-FA locomotives and coaches.

UEPFP now runs services supported by Buenos Aires and La Pampa provinces. It owns the Buenos Aires—Mar del Plata and General Guido—Pinamar lines, totalling 412 km.

| Traffic (million) | 1997 | 1998 | 1999* |
|---|---|---|---|
| Passenger journeys | 2.4 | 1.87 | 1.7 |

* 1 Jan – 31 Oct

**Passenger operations**
UEPFP passenger operations are marketed as 'Ferrobaires' and comprise the Atlantic and Pampas zones. The Atlantic zone comprises services from Buenos Aires to Mar del Plata, Pinamar, Tandil, Quequén, Necochea, Bahía Blanca, Carmen de Patagones and Bolivar; the Pampas zone comprises services from Buenos Aires to Darregueira, Santa Rosa-Toay, General Pico, Pasteur, Cuenca, Iriarte and Rojas.

The Atlantic zone is considered to be potentially profitable, serving coastal resorts south of Buenos Aires and attracting much holiday traffic. To serve the principal resort of Mar del Plata, UEPFP operates 'El Marplatense' featuring refurbished air conditioned rolling stock. By late 1994, eight trains were in operation daily (with an extra return service at weekends) in each direction between Buenos Aires and Mar del Plata, covering the 400 km in 4 hours 50 minutes. In 1999 it was reported that UEPFP had ordered Talgo coaches for service on this route. After completion of track improvements, these vehicles would allow speeds to be raised to 160-170 km/h, cutting the end-to-end journey time to under three hours.

On 21 May 1994 UEPFP reopened the 72 km General Guido—General Madariaga route, closed in 1978. A new branch to Pinamar opened in 1996 and the company also reintroduced services on the General Madariaga—Vivoratá line using 80 km/h dmus. Ferrobaires declare the Pinamar service a great success, exceeding all expectations, with 27,000 tickets sold in January 1997 alone. Buenos Aires—Pinamar intercity services resumed in November 1997 following a programme to reinstate track on the final 21 km of the 101 km General Guido—Pinamar line. In 1997/98 a service of two return trains a day was scheduled to complete the 346 km journey in 4 hours 35 minutes.

**New lines**
In 1996, UEPFP and Spanish National Railways began conversations regarding the creation of a high-speed rail link between Rosario and Mar del Plata using the 'ring' line around western and southwestern Buenos Aires. Similar plans have also been advanced by Japanese, Italian and German interests. In a first phase of this project UEPFP plans to introduce tilting rolling stock to cut journey times.

A new line from Dolores towards Bahía Blanca featured in 1998 proposals to upgrade the Buenos Aires—Mar del Plata line (see below).

A branch line from Pinamar to the coastal resort of Villa Gesell is under construction and further branches from the Buenos Aires-Mar del Plata main line are under consideration.

**Improvements to existing lines**
In 1998 and 1999, plans were being developed to upgrade for 160 km/h running the line from Buenos Aires to Mar del Plata at an estimated cost of US$600 million. The project would include resignalling, some double-tracking, and the elimination of level crossings.

**Traction and rolling stock**
In 1998 the UEPFP fleet comprised 70 diesel locomotives and 302 passenger coaches. Most of the latter have been refurbished in UEPFP workshops, although in 2000 work commenced on the modernisation of 34 vehicles in the Chascomús workshops of Emepa. In addition, seven diesel multiple-units (each seating 170 passengers) have been purchased from RENFE of Spain for US$1.3 million, for use on routes with low traffic levels.

In July 1995 an agreement was signed with GEC Alsthom Transporte and RENFE of Spain to form a company to maintain traction and rolling stock at La Plata.

In 1999 UEPFP was reported to have ordered around 60 Talgo coaches under a leasing arrangement for 160 km/h services on the Buenos Aires—Mar del Plata line. The vehicles were to be built locally.

**Signalling and telecommunications**
The agreement signed with RENFE in 1995 also made provision for Spanish assistance with the resignalling of the Buenos Aires—Mar del Plata route.

*UEPFP's 'El Bahiense' overnight service at Bahía Blanca Sud station behind a General Motors locomotive (Peter Lais)*   0058590

---

## Yacimientos Carboníferos Río Turbio SA (RFIRT)

Gdor Lista 790, 9400 Río Gallegos, Santa Cruz
Tel: (+54 29 66) 42 08 74   Fax: (+54 29 66) 42 08 74

**Passenger operations**
Plans for the operation of a tourist train have been announced by the mayor of Río Turbino. This would be steam-hauled using wooden-bodied coaches currently in store. The scheme has provincial government support.

**Freight operations**
RFIRT is a privately owned company running coal trains on 750 mm track between the Andes Australes mines and the ports of Río Gallegos and Loyola. Two return services a day are operated using four Faur diesel-hydraulics acquired second-hand from Bulgaria in 1996, replacing former steam traction, which had held sway for more than 40 years. Two of the 1,000 hp locomotives have been remotored using Caterpillar D379 traction motors, while the other two retain their Romanian originals. A fifth Faur has been cannabilised.

The service is operated by fewer than 100 workers. Attempts to introduce radio signalling were defeated by the topography; and crews are now contacted by cell phone.

---

# ARMENIA

## Ministry of Transport and Communications

10 ul Zakian, 375015 Yerevan
Tel: (+374 2) 52 88 10   Fax: (+374 2) 56 05 28

**Key personnel**
Minister: Andranik Manoukyan

*UPDATED*

## Armenian Railways

Tigrana velikogo ul 50, 375005 Yerevan
Tel: (+374 2) 52 04 28   Fax: (+374 2) 15 13 95

**Key personnel**
President: A Khrimyan

Gauge: 1,520 mm
Route length: 852 km
Electrification: 779 km at 3 kV DC

**Political background**
In recent years traffic has been effectively paralysed due to a suspension of services into Azerbaijan via Nakhichevan, and into Turkey via the border crossings at Erazhkh (closed in 1989) and Akuryan (closed in 1993).

In 1999, plans were announced to invest US$50 million in Armenia's transport network, with some funding going to rail. Eighty per cent of the finance was to come from the World Bank and the government of Japan, the remainder from domestic funds.

**Organisation**
The rail network has existed as a separate entity since January 1992. It comprises a southern portion of the former SZhD's Trans-Caucasus Railway and is fully electrified. Backbone of the system is the 295 km single-track line from the capital, Yerevan, through Gyurmi (formerly Leninakan) and Vanadzor (formerly Kirovakan)

to the border with Georgia at Ayrum. This currently forms the only international connection, with a Yerevan–Tbilisi through passenger service reintroduced in July 1997.

A few sections of the Yerevan—Ayrum line were doubled in response to a heavy increase in traffic following the disastrous 1988 earthquake which struck the country, but the second track has since been removed following a substantial fall in demand for capacity resulting from the break-up of the Soviet Union.

The line south of Erazkhh leading the Azerbaijani republic of Nakhichevan has been closed since 1990. In February 1996 passenger services ceased on the 84 km electrified route between Yerevan and Sevan. Also out of use are the electrified lines from Sevan eastwards along Lake Sevan to Zod (121 km, closed 1995) and northwards to Idzhevan (48 km, closed 1990). The latter line includes the 8 km Megradzhorsk tunnel.

In 1997 discussions took place aimed at restoring cross-border operations into Turkey via the closed Akuryan–Dogukapi line. It was reported that the Turkish position on this proposal was that restoration of services would be possible, but only for freight traffic.

### Passenger and freight traffic

In 1991, the railway carried 29.1 million tonnes of freight for 4,200 million tonne-km, while passenger traffic amounted to 2.8 million journeys and 300 million passenger-km. Unrest in the area prompted dramatic declines in subsequent years: in 1996, 1.7 million tonnes were carried for 351 million tonne-km, and passenger traffic was 1.9 million journeys, 84 million passenger-km.

In 1999, 0.58 million tonnes were carried for 320 million tonne-km, while passenger traffic amounted to 1.3 million journeys for 46 million passenger-km.

All import and export freight traffic is carried over the main line via Ayrum and Tbilisi to the Georgian ports of Batumi and Poti. In June 1998 Georgian Railways reduced tariffs for transit traffic to and from Armenia by 25 per cent. This was expected to accelerate traffic recovery.

### Traction and rolling stock

Electric locomotive classes include the VL8, VL10, and derivatives (46 in service), while main line diesels include the M62 and TEM3 types (11 in service). There are 28 emus, 134 coaches and 1,250 wagons in use, and large amounts of rolling stock stored unserviceable.

### Electrification

The Armenian Railways network is fully electrified using the 3 kV DC system except for a short cross-border section between Karzhyvan and Nyuvedi, which provides a link with the country's isolated republic of Nakhichevan.

*2000*/0088711

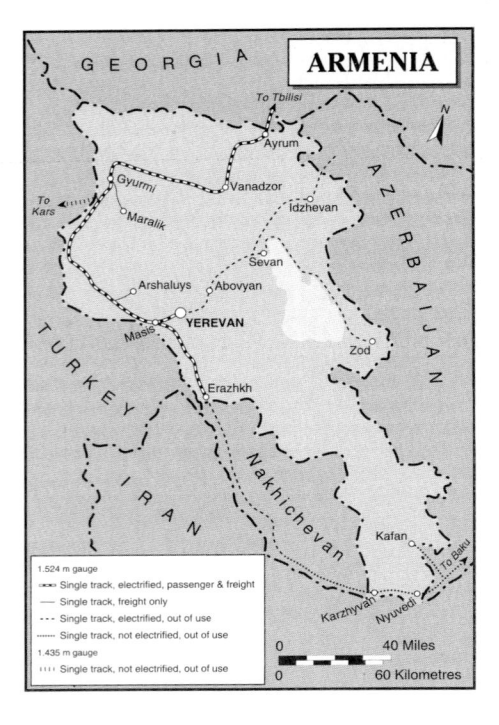

---

# AUSTRALIA

## Department of Transport and Regional Development

PO Box 594, Canberra, ACT, 2601
Tel: (+61 6) 274 71 11   Fax: (+61 6) 257 25 05

### Key personnel
Minister: Hon John Anderson, MP

### Political background

The Australian railway industry continues its evolution from a number of government departments to many privately owned competing transport organisations operating across state borders and on tracks often not owned by themselves.

Railways in Australia were built initially by state governments (to four different gauges) to serve local needs. When it was necessary to connect Western Australia with South Australia by rail, the Commonwealth government built the line across the Nullarbor Plain (as standard gauge but isolated from that gauge elsewhere). As the tracks extended to state borders, there arose the problem of the break of gauge. Although interstate trade grew, each state had a vested interest in retaining as much industry and trade as possible within its state boundaries.

The Second World War showed the folly of a change of gauge each time a border was reached. Post war, efforts were slowly made to convert track (or provide new track as between Albury and Melbourne) to standard gauge. It was only in 1995 that all state capitals were directly connected by standard gauge, although they had been connected via Broken Hill since 1970.

While much of the difficulty of not having one standard gauge has been overcome, the disadvantage of having geographically based railways all with different standards is just beginning to be addressed. In 1991, the National Rail Corporation Ltd was established to provide interstate (only) freight services over the tracks of the state systems. All governments have now agreed (to a greater or lesser degree) to introduce competition to their rail activities.

By 1997, a few private-sector organisations were operating services over the tracks of others. Each state is working towards providing third-party access to its tracks while the Commonwealth government and State governments have established a body to regulate interstate standard-gauge third-party access, Australian Rail Track Corporation (ARTC) (qv). So it is now theoretically possible for a company (which meets acceptable standards) to run train services on any government organisation's tracks.

Each state is dividing its passenger, freight and track businesses into discrete operations, though the problem of freight trains getting rail access at commuting times is yet to be addressed. There has been movement towards the standardisation of safe-working practices and radio systems. Fortunately, the physical train aspects (coupler height, braking systems, locomotive multiple-unit compatibility) have, by chance, been uniform. There are 22 different signalling regimes and 18 different radio systems, with some drivers having to be conversant with 11 different safe-working systems.

In 2001 there were the following permutations of railways:
(a) Railways that provided everything including track, locomotive, crew and wagons (some State railways and private mine-to-port railways)
(b) Railways that provided locomotive, crew and wagons but ran on another's track (for example NR, WCR)
(c) Operators that provided wagons but hired locomotives and crews and ran on another's tracks (for example SCT)
(d) Operators that provided locomotives and crews but hauled others' wagons over another's tracks (operators providing terminal shunting only).

Commonwealth government has promised A$250 million over four years from 1998-99 for rail. Victoria and the Commonwealth government have agreed, as a first step to providing a 'one-stop shop', to operators bringing their Wodonga– and Broken Hill–Kalgoorlie tracks under ARTC management.

It has been suggested that throughout Australia there is a track maintenance shortfall of A$3.2 billion: 535 km of the inter-capital track was subject to speed restrictions in 1997. There has been no indication how that shortfall might be funded. Obviously those entering the market now will not wish to pay towards the 'unfunded debt' incurred previously. A Commonwealth parliamentary enquiry, the Neville Report, has recommended significantly increased government funding to catch up the shortfall from the past and to get rail to the stage where it is on equal terms with road operators. Between 1974 and 1999 the Commonwealth government spent A$4 billion on the highway and A$40 million on the railway between Sydney and Melbourne. Rail's share of freight business on the Sydney–Melbourne corridor has fallen from 48.5 per cent in 1971 to about 22 per cent in 1996. Melbourne–Perth rail freight services across the Nullarbor Plain now carry 77 per cent of available traffic.

The rail industry has been stressing the imbalance between government support for road and rail transport. It is claimed that rail access costs five times more than road for a similar transport task. Several months after tabling of the Neville Report there had been no response from either level of government. Australian governments have been reducing or minimising expenditure on all their activities for most of the 1990s in line with current political wisdom. In this climate, any expansion of expenditure to help what is now regarded as a non-government function is unlikely to get priority over hospitals and other functions of government generally thought to be underfunded.

The six State and Commonwealth Transport Ministers envisage that the interstate network should provide the following levels of service by 2002:
(a) Less than 2 per cent of track to be subject to speed restriction.
(b) At axleloads to 21 tonnes, maximum speed to be 115 km/h, with average speed of 80 km/h.
(c) At axleloads between 21 and 25 tonnes, maximum speed to be 80 km/h, with average speed of 60 km/h.
(d) Crossing loops to accommodate train lengths of 1,800 m on the east-west route and 1,500 m on the Melbourne—Brisbane route.

They also wish to establish a protocol whereby on-time operations are rewarded.

Apart from the government public transport rail segment mentioned above there is a thriving private rail freight sector in Australia, mainly serving the Queensland sugar industry and in the Pilbara region of Western Australia.

### Organisation

Australian rail operations are hindered by the historic situation where three gauges were used in the 1800s and gauge standardisation has seldom been financially possible for the state governments. Today there are about 4,000 km of 1,600 mm gauge (mainly in Victoria), 19,000 km of 1,067 mm gauge (mainly in Queensland, Western Australia and Tasmania) and 16,300 km of standard gauge (1,435 mm).

A feature of recent years has been the move away from operators staying within their home state's boundaries. To give a continental view of the following operator listings, we summarise the national and state situations (clockwise).

Australia: The Commonwealth government-owned freight operator National Rail provides services in New South Wales, Victoria, South Australia and Western Australia. It is expected to be sold in the near future. Non-government operators include Specialized Container Transport and Toll. The national passenger service is provided by Great Southern Railway.

Queensland: The state government-owned QR is vertically integrated, and there are no plans to sell. Airtrain Citylink operates the airport railway in Brisbane.

New South Wales: The state government owns separate freight (FreightCorp), urban passenger (CityRail), rural passenger (Countrylink) and track owners (Rail Access Corporation). There are also non-government freight haulers (for example Austrac, Freight Australia, Silverton).

Victoria: The (previous) government privatised most activities previously thought to be the province of government, including railway operations: suburban passenger operators (Bayside Trains, Connex Trains Melbourne), rural passenger operator (V/Line Passenger) and country freight operator (Freight Australia). The government retains ownership of the track and right of way, though responsibility for access rests with the private operators (without their having the power to reject competition).

South Australia: The state government owns the urban passenger operator (TransAdelaide). All freight is privately operated and track privately owned (Australia Southern Railroad). The government has called for Registration of Interest from operators to standardise the present unused broad-gauge track in the southeast of the state and then operate services. The routes are from the Victorian border to Mount Gambier and towards Naracoorte.

Western Australia: The state government owns the passenger operator. Freight operations have been sold to Australian Railroad Group. Track is leased to Westnet.

Tasmania: The privately owned freight operator and track owner is Tasrail.

The Australian Rail Operations Unit is a non-statutory body established within the department on 1 January 2000 under an intergovernment agreement on rail operational uniformity.

### Finance
Australian rail productivity is believed by economists to be only half that of the USA, though with different characteristics, while freight rates are about twice those of Canada and the USA.

### Freight operations
Statistics show that interstate rail freight volumes rose from 8.4 million tonnes in 1991 to 12 million tonnes in 2000. The total tonnage of rail freight in Australia, including that of mineral lines, increased from 340 million tonnes in 1991 to over 500 million tonnes in 2000.

### New lines
Schemes for new lines are regularly promoted. These currently include the Alice Springs–Darwin route, a new line to link Victoria through western New South Wales with Brisbane and Darwin, a high-speed route between Sydney, Canberra and Melbourne, and schemes to link capital city airports with the rail network. Although these proposals have corporate supporters with good credentials, only the Brisbane and Sydney airport schemes have, to date, been able to move to the construction phase. Both lines have opened, though initial patronage has been disappointing. In 2001, a similar link in Melbourne was the subject of studies. Costs of between A$200 million and A$400 million have been estimated, depending on the route selected.

On 17 July 2001, the Prime Minister turned the first 'sod' of the Alice Springs–Darwin railway. Darwin's population is only 100,000 but its position in relation to southeast Asia could lead to its development as the prime entry/exit port for trade between Australia and the region. Traffic predictions for the 1,420 km line initially foresee just one freight train per day and two weekly passenger services. The project's total cost of A$1.3 billion will include A$560 million from the Northern Territory, South Australia and Commonwealth governments. The earlier 1,067 mm gauge railway between Larrimah and Darwin saw its last train in 1976.

### Improvements to existing lines
Victoria: the government plans to inject A$550 million to upgrade existing tracks for fast train operations from Melbourne to Ballarat (119 km), Bendigo (162 km), Traralgon (158 km) and Geelong (73 km). The government expects private operators to inject a further A$160 million to complete the task. The faster trains would run about 20 km/h faster than at present, reducing travelling times by one third. An economic feasibility study was in progress in 2001 to investigate the benefits of converting most of the state's broad gauge track to standard gauge. At present, only 29 per cent of the network is standard gauge.

*UPDATED*

## Airtrain Citylink Limited

PO Box 53, Roma Street, Brisbane, Queensland 4003
Tel: (+61 7) 32 11 28 55   Fax: (+61 7) 32 11 23 45
e-mail: airtraincitylink@primus.com.au

### Key personnel
Chairman: James Cutts
General Manager: Ken Devencorn

Gauge: 1,067 mm
Route length: 8.5 km
Electrification: 8.5 km at 25 kV AC 50 Hz

### Political background
In May 1996, the Queensland government granted the company authority to build and operate a passenger railway between Toombul and Brisbane's airport for 35 years. Between Toombul and Brisbane City trains will use existing QR tracks. Contracts were signed in February 1999.

### Organisation
The company has the support of Transfield, a major construction company, Macquarie Bank, and other appropriate organisations.

### Finance
The construction of the line cost A$190 million. The company has based its strategy on obtaining about 15 per cent of the existing airport traffic. This is the first project in Australia where the developer has accepted the patronage risk.

### Passenger operations
Services commenced on schedule on 7 May 2001, with QR operating trains under contract. Patronage was forecast to start at about 2.5 million per annum rising to 5 million per annum after 5 years. Brisbane airport has experienced continuing rises in the volume of operations in recent years, with all forecasts showing this trend continuing for many years to come. Initial patronage was disappointing but long-term forecasts remain as projected.

*QR SMU emu at Airtrain's International station at Brisbane airport (Brian Webber)*   2002/0121161

### New lines
The 8.5 km long, elevated single-track branch line required about 2 years to construct. Design work was complete in mid-1999 and construction started in July of that year. QR was contracted to provide track, overhead catenary and signalling for A$11.7 million.

The single-track line runs on the longest bridge construction in Australia, with two stations serving Domestic and International air terminals.

### Traction and rolling stock
A contract was placed in mid-1999 with Walkers-Adtranz, manufacturers of all Queensland Rail's Brisbane passenger emu fleet, for four 3-car emus at a cost of A$38 million. These will work with QR units to provide the service between the airport and Brisbane City, with certain services extended to Robina on the Gold Coast.

### Signalling and telecommunications
These are to the same standards as those for a QR line.

### Track
The line was built to current Queensland Rail standards though with fairly steep grades for grade separation with roads and a future airport runway. While it is expected only passenger emus will use the line, it could be used by freight trains in the future if that became desirable. Cwr and concrete sleepers are used. The 8.5 route-km of track is supported on a viaduct comprising 2,300 piled foundations with 258 concrete columns and headstocks spaced between 30 and 45 m apart. The initial 500 m are double track, as is the section between the two stations. Total track length is 11 km.

*UPDATED*

## Asia Pacific Freight Consortium Pty Ltd

### Key personnel
See AustralAsia Railway Corporation.

Gauge: 1,435 mm
Track length: 1,420 km

### Organisation
This organisation will build, own and operate the Alice Springs–Darwin railway until 2051. It won the rights from the government organisation AustralAsia Railway Corporation (qv), to which the railway will revert after 50 years. The construction will be arranged by an associated company, ADrail. Shareholders include engineering and construction companies and Australian Railroad Group Pty Ltd (qv).

The publicity name Freightlink has been used for the future rail/port operation, though it is not clear at this stage whether this organisation will run trains.

### Passenger operations
Great Southern Railway, operator of 'The Ghan' service to Alice Springs has indicated its intention of extending the service to Darwin when the line opens.

### Freight operations
During the construction phase, 10 locomotives and 154 wagons will be used. When the line is completed it is expected that Australian Railroad Group Pty Ltd and others will operate trains.

### Signalling and telecommunications
It is likely that systems will be similar to ARTC standards.

### Track
150,000 tonnes of rail, 7.8 million rail clips and 2 million sleepers will be required. Each day, 5,000 tonnes of material will be moved to the railheads.

*NEW ENTRY*

# RAILWAY SYSTEMS/Australia

## Austrac Rail Ltd

PO Box 297, Botany, New South Wales 1455
Tel: (+61 2) 93 16 45 17  Fax: (+61 2) 93 16 62 91
e-mail: service@austrac.com.au
Web: http://www.austrac.com.au

### Key personnel
Chief Executive: John Ross

Gauge: 1,435 mm

### Political background
Austrac is one of a number of non-government operators which have entered the rail industry since the various governments decided to allow competition in the industry.

### Organisation
The company is based in southern New South Wales, and has a workforce of about 25 employees.

### Freight operations
The company provides freight services between Griffith, Young, Cowra and Sydney. It has entered a partnership with V/Line Freight for hauls between Sydney and Melbourne which started in August 1998.

Austrac was the first private operator to serve Canberra and has also developed export log traffic from Junee to Port Kembla.

### Traction and rolling stock
The company has purchased a small number of locomotives previously operated by major state systems. From Westrail it has obtained two NB Class locomotives and from the NSWSRA two 48 Class. Other locomotives are being rebuilt or are hired when required. Most rolling stock is leased.

### Track
Austrac operates by agreement over the tracks of others.

*VERIFIED*

---

## AustralAsia Railway Corporation

GPO Box 4796, Darwin, Northern Territory 0801
Tel: (+61 8) 89 46 95 95  Fax: (+61 8) 89 46 95 78
e-mail: rail@aarc.com.au
Web: http://www.aarc.com.au
http://www.nt.gov.au/railway

### Key personnel
Chairman: Richard H Allert
Chief Executive Officer: Paul Tyrrell

### Political background
In 1911, the Federal government promised to construct a railway linking South Australia with Darwin as part of their agreement to take over responsibility of the Northern Territory from that state. However, no timescale was set. The Tarcoola–Alice Springs line was built between 1975 and 1980 and following completion the Federal government pledged A$10 million for a route survey between Alice Springs and Darwin.

### Finance
By 1995, the governments of Australia, Northern Territory and South Australia had agreed to contribute large sums if private enterprise provided the majority of the funds. The result has been that the governments are contributing A$165 million each, together with A$80 million of stand-by funding. The Federal government is to lease the 830 km Tarcoola–Alice Springs railway for a nominal rental fee, while a consortium of private interests will contribute the remainder (about A$800 million) as a build/own/operate/transfer back (BOOT) venture.

### Organisation
To facilitate the process of awarding the concession, the Northern Territory and South Australia governments have jointly established AustralAsia Railway Corporation (AARC). The Corporation will ultimately receive back the railway at the end of the concession period.

Asia Pacific Transport Consortium was named as the preferred bidder to take the concession and the date of April 2000 was set to finalise the financial arrangements before construction would begin later in the year, to be completed by mid-2003. The consortium comprises six companies, all experienced in civil engineering or rail transport operation. They are: Brown and Root Engineering and Construction; Genesee and Wyoming Australia Pty Ltd; Barclay Mowlem Construction Ltd; John Holland Group Ltd; Macmahon Holdings; and MPG Logistics.

### Passenger operations
It is anticipated that a daily passenger service will be provided, most likely by the operators of the Ghan service, Great Southern Railway.

### Freight operations
It is expected that initially the line will sustain one or two freight services daily in each direction.

### Intermodal operations
The new railway is seen as part of the transport link between Australia and Asia, with Darwin port being upgraded to handle an expected boom in traffic when the railway opens.

### New lines
The new line, to be about 1,412 km, will cost A$1 billion. The project includes 17 million $m^3$ of earthworks, 120 bridges, including a very substantial one over the Elizabeth River, and 1,220 culverts. Buildings and workshops will cost a further A$26 million.

In 2001, construction had started at both Katherine and Tennant Creek with two Australian Northern Railroad 22 Class locomotives at each location to haul work trains.

### Traction and rolling stock
These will be provided by train operators.

### Signalling and telecommunications
It is assumed that train order will be the safe-working system used, similar to the Adelaide–Kalgoorlie and Alice Springs lines.

### Track
Construction requirements include: 155,000 tonnes of steel rail; 2.3 million sleepers; 9.2 million spring steel rail fastenings; 15 km of culverts; and 2.2 million $m^3$ of ballast.

*UPDATED*

---

## Australia Northern Railroad

Web: http://www.arg.net.au

### Key personnel
See Australian Railroad Group Pty Ltd.

### Organisation
This railway is a subsidiary of Australian Railroad Group, formed to be associated with the construction of the Alice Springs–Darwin Railway.

### Freight operations
The company was expected to haul construction material from the south to Alice Springs for the new railway construction.

### Traction and rolling stock
The company has four 22 Class diesel-electric locomotives painted with its logo, with two based at Katherine and two at Tennant Creek in the Northern Territory to haul work trains during the construction period of the new line.

*NEW ENTRY*

---

## Australian Railroad Group Pty Ltd

Westrail Centre, West Parade, East Perth, Western Australia
PO Box S1422, Perth, Western Australia 6845
Tel: (+61 8) 93 26 22 22  Fax: (+61 8) 93 26 25 89
Web: http://www.arg.net.au

### Key personnel
Chief Executive Officer: Charles W Chabot
Deputy Chief Executive Officer: Martin Larcombe
Chief Financial Officer: Murray Vitlich

Route length: approximately 10,000 km

### Political background
The group was formed when Westrail was privatised and this corporate structure was established.

### Organisation
Australian Railroad Group Pty Ltd is jointly and equally owned by Wesfarmers, a public corporation, and Genesee & Wyoming Inc (GWI) of USA. It acquired Westrail Freight in December 2000 from the state government of Western Australia for A$323 million. To complete the transaction GWI contributed Australia Southern Railroad and its interest in the Asia Pacific Transport Consortium, which has been selected to construct and operate the Alice Springs–Darwin line. The Group is the largest private rail owner/operator in Australia, although it has, to date, had minimal involvement in the major market in the eastern states. ASR (qv) has recently commenced a weekly service between Sydney and Adelaide via Broken Hill.

### Freight operations
Three subsidiaries, Australia Northern Railroad, Australia Southern Railroad and Australia Western Railroad provide day-to-day operations in their geographic areas.

### Traction and rolling stock
Rolling stock is held by the three operating subsidiaries with some interchange possible where the gauge is identical.

### Signalling and telecommunications
Australia Southern Railroad is responsible for some train control and safe working in South Australia.

### Track
Australia Southern Railroad is responsible for some track in South Australia.

*NEW ENTRY*

Australia/**RAILWAY SYSTEMS** 21

## Australian Transport & Energy Corridor Limited (ATEC)

14 Argyle Place, Argyle Street, Albion, Queensland 4010
Tel: (+61 7) 32 62 81 77   Fax: (+61 7) 32 62 81 99
Web: http://www.aire.com.au

### Key personnel
Chairman: Everard Compton, AM

### Political background
ATEC is the promoter of a proposed standard-gauge double-track inland rail link, initially between Melbourne and Brisbane but ultimately continuing to Darwin via western Queensland. The organisation is privately owned and was formed in 1996. The route would use existing lines between Melbourne, Cootamundra and Dubbo and between Gunnedah and Boggabilla, north of Moree. (There is an indirect route via Merrygoen currently available between these towns.) New construction would be required between those two sections. Between Boggabilla and Brisbane new construction will follow existing QR narrow-gauge corridors with some dual-gauge track. Construction of the 10 km missing link between Boggabilla (NSW) and Carrington (Queensland) is planned to commence in early 2002.

### Organisation
ATEC has been given government grants to arrange studies of their proposal but claim that they will not need government financial support with their project. Several bodies who stand to gain from the project are offering support, such as local authorities and corporate backers.

The promoters use the name Australian Inland Rail Expressway in their publicity.

### Freight operations
The scheme envisages several trains daily running over the route, with some diversion of traffic from the existing interstate track.

### Traction and rolling stock
These would be provided by operators granted access.

*NEW ENTRY*

## Australian Transport Network Ltd (ATN Access)

Level 29, 459 Collins Street, Melbourne, Victoria 3000
Tel: (+61 3) 96 12 55 00   Fax: (+61 3) 96 12 55 55

### Key personnel
Operations Manager: Mark Rosner

Gauge: 1,435 mm

### Organisation
This organisation is the owner of Tasrail and is connected with New Zealand's Tranz Rail. It holds contracts to haul grain from the Junee area of New South Wales and from Dimboola in Victoria.

### Traction and rolling stock
The company purchased seven ex-Westrail L Class locomotives in July 1999 and arranged their overhaul by NREC at Whyalla, South Australia. It also purchased three 830 Class locomotives from Australia Southern Railroad (qv) for use on light axleload lines. ATN Access also imported 44 new 92 tonne capacity grain wagons from China.

### Track
The company operates on track owned by others.

## Australia Southern Railroad (ASR)

PO Box 2086, Regency Park, South Australia 5942
Tel: (+61 8) 83 43 54 55   Fax: (+61 8) 83 43 54 54

### Key personnel
Chief Executive Officer: Wayne James
Chief Financial Officer: Ian Jamieson
General Managers
    Transportation: Anthony Mogytych
    Business Development: Colin Turner

Gauge: 1,067 mm; 1,435 mm; 1,600 mm
Route length: 748 km; 325 km; 288 km

### Political background
When the Commonwealth government sold Australian National in August 1997, the freight operations in South Australia were purchased by a consortium of Genesee & Wyoming Inc and its partners Clyde and Transfield to form Australia Southern Railroad (ASR). The company forms part of the Australian Railroad Group Pty Ltd (ARG).

### Organisation
Genesee & Wyoming Inc is North America's second largest regional freight operator. It has made 14 other major acquisitions around the world over the past 16 years. The consortium includes Clyde, which will maintain the locomotive fleet, and Transfield, which will be responsible for track maintenance.

The consortium paid A$57.4 million for the South Australian freight and maintenance business. Over the first five years, it is committed to inject a further A$62 million into locomotives, track and rolling stock. It plans to merge Dry Creek, Islington and Port Augusta facilities. ASR has about 600 employees.

### Freight operations
With the purchase came 89 locomotives, 1,300 km of track, seven wagon maintenance facilities and some maintenance rolling stock. The business, which generated A$230 million revenue in 1996, is complicated by having three different gauges. ASR has increased its share of the grain haul from 35 to 40 per cent.

In 1997/98 ASR hauled 6,400,000 tonnes of freight comprising: 2.7 million tonnes of coal; 1.7 million tonnes of ore/minerals; and 2 million tonnes of grain.

It won a five-year contract to manage and operate the BHP narrow-gauge ore railway at Whyalla, and purchased the eight diesel locomotives in use there. The operation has 180 km of track and employs 110 wagons hauling 3 million tonnes annually to a steelworks.

ASR is contracted to provide locomotives, crews and 70 wagons for Patrick's Melbourne–Adelaide services for 2 years.

In May 2001, ASR commenced a weekly return Sydney–Adelaide via Cootamundra and Broken Hill service. This gave the ARG group an entry into markets in the eastern states.

*Broad (1,600 mm) gauge*
Traffic comprises limestone and grain. Limestone traffic is 500,000 tonnes annually railed seven days a week from Penrice Quarry to suburban Adelaide in a 22-wagon consist. Grain is hauled from the Balaklava, Burra and Kapunda branches.

*Standard (1,435 mm) gauge*
From north of Adelaide about 250,000 tonnes of grain are hauled to port annually, while significant tonnages are hauled on the Loxton and the recently standardised Pinaroo line in the east of the state. New grain sheds built at Roseworthy will probably see the 29 km branch from there to Kapunda carrying few trains.

*Narrow (1,067 mm) gauge*
The isolated Eyre Peninsula network transports about 1.3 million tonnes of gypsum from Kevin to the port at Thevenard, 60 km, and up to a million tonnes of grain annually to Port Lincoln following a good season.

### Diesel locomotives

| Class | Wheel arrangement | Power kW | Speed km/h | Weight tonnes | No in service | First built | Mechanical | Builders Engine | Transmission |
|---|---|---|---|---|---|---|---|---|---|
| ALF | Co-Co | 2,460 | | 130 | 8 | 1994* | Clyde | GM 16-645E3 | E GM |
| CLF | Co-Co | 2,460 | 130 | 128.5 | 7 | 1993* | Clyde | GM 16-645E3 | E GM |
| CLP | Co-Co | 2,460 | 140 | 131 | 10 | 1993* | Clyde | GM 16-645E3 | E GM |
| 700 | Co-Co | 1,490 | | 115 | 5 | 1970 | A E Goodwin | Alco 251C | E |
| GM | A1A-A1A | 1,390 | | 110 | 9 | 1967 | Clyde | GM 16-567B | E GM |
| 830/DA | Co-Co | 671 | | 76 | | 1960 | A E Goodwin | Alco 251C | E |
| 500 | Bo-Bo | 373 | 64 | 57 | 4 | 1964 | SAR | EE 45RKT | E |
| CK** | Bo-Bo | 708 | 100 | 70 | 6 | 1960 | Clyde | GM 8-567/8-645E | E GM |
| 22 | Co-Co | 1,490 | 124 | 110 | 16† | 1969 | Clyde | GM 16-645E | E GM |

*Rebuilt
**Formerly V/Line T Class
† Includes locomotives requiring overhaul before entering service

### Traction and rolling stock
ASR purchased a collection of some 50 mainly elderly locomotives of the following Classes: GM, CLF, CLP, ALF, 830, DA, 600, 500, CK. The more modern locomotives of the previous Australian National fleet are in traffic with National Rail (qv). The 1,067 mm gauge Eyre Peninsula network fleet comprises six NJ Class, three DA Class and eight 830 Class, all over 30 years old.

In mid-2000, ASR purchased 16 withdrawn 422 Class locomotives from FreightCorp (qv). Most required overhaul before entering traffic.

ASR has contracted with EDI Rail to overhaul four ex-FreightCorp 422 Class locomotives and four ex-Westrail L Class locomotives and to build 65 ballast wagons which will be used initially on the Alice Springs–Darwin construction.

### Signalling and telecommunications
ASR is responsible for train control on non-ARTC lines.

### Track
The purchasers bought a track infrastructure which could only be described as tired. The Tailem Bend-Pinaroo line was converted from broad-gauge to standard-gauge in late 1998, ending the need to tranship grain at Tailem Bend.

ASR currently operates in the state of South Australia only.

*UPDATED*

## Australian Rail Track Corporation Limited (ARTC)

PO Box 10343, Gouger Street, Adelaide, South Australia 5035
Tel: (+61 8) 82 17 43 66   Fax: (+61 8) 82 17 45 78
e-mail: Track@arcom.com.au
Web: http://www.artc.com.au

### Key personnel
Managing Director: David Marchant
Directors: Dale Budd; Robert Maher; Martine Pop
General Managers:
    Engineering and Infrastructure: Malcolm Owens
    Finance and Administration: Geoff Atkinson
    Safety and Operations: Kent Donaldson

Gauge: 1,435 mm
Route length: 4,400 km

### Political background
The federal government-owned Corporation was established in February 1998 following inter-governmental agreement to establish an organisation

# RAILWAY SYSTEMS/Australia

solely to manage access to and infrastructure development of the interstate standard-gauge network. It had become apparent to the various governments that the continuation of state control of the network was untenable and only an organisation with overall responsibility could enable the rail industry to compete with road transport, which deals with only one government agency, and to a lesser degree, the shipping industry.

The Corporation is negotiating to establish equitable and transparent access pricing arrangements on the standard-gauge network and is aiming to introduce common standards, including for safe working, throughout Australia.

In 2001, there were 11 operators with access agreements with ARTC: Australia Southern Railroad; Countrylink; FreightCorp; Freight Australia; Great Northern Rail Services; Great Southern Railway; National Rail; Patrick Rail; Silverton Tramway; Specialised Container Transport; and Toll Rail.

ARTC has become the agent for the sale of paths between Kalgoorlie and Perth, providing a single point of access for the line between Melbourne and Perth.

## Organisation

In November 1997 Australia's Transport Ministers signed an agreement to establish a single company, Australian Rail Track Corporation (ARTC), to manage the interstate standard-gauge rail network. The agreement operates until June 2003 and covers track previously owned by Australian National. It will also manage and control Victoria's interstate track (Wolseley-Melbourne-Albury) under a lease arrangement. Access to other systems' track will be by agreement with those organisations. It is intended that ARTC will become a 'one-stop shop' for interstate rail operators.

## Improvements to existing lines

An audit of track condition in 2001 revealed upgrading estimated at A$507 million to be necessary. This figure was twice the government's funding commitment but well short of the A$1 billion identified by a government committee in 1995. Most of the work required is in New South Wales but on interstate routes on which that state's government will not invest. The audit suggested A$398 million was needed on the Melbourne—Sydney—Brisbane corridor, of which ARTC controls only the Melbourne—Albury section. A figure of A$146 million was identified as necessary to start on the Sydney Freight Priority Project. The Sydney commuter rail network is a critical bottleneck which causes many hours of delay to vital freight movements, with a block on freight traffic in effect at peak hours. No commitment to funding has been made.

The A$3.5 million Port Augusta track upgrading project has been completed. An additional track bypassing the existing station provides a faster route and a 1.8 km crossing loop. The area has been provided with improved signalling, controlled by ARTC rather than ASR.

ARTC has implemented a national Code of Practice for operations and safe working on its track and it is expected that the code will later be extended to the tracks of other owners to standardise everyday activities associated with train running.

## Traction and rolling stock

ARTC has purchased seven ballast hoppers from CFCLA in the USA to replace unserviceable vehicles.

## Signalling and telecommunications

Train control previously in Melbourne has been centralised in Adelaide. The aim is for 96 per cent of services to arrive on time. Safe-working systems include CTC in the Melbourne and Adelaide metropolitan areas and between Adelaide and the Victorian border, train order between Adelaide, Alice Springs and Kalgoorlie, and Section Working Authority (similar to train order) in Victoria country areas.

ARTC is providing train control facilities for FreightCorp's Port Augusta—Leigh Creek operation.

Replacement of the signalling system on the approach to Melbourne has improved efficiency and reduced transit times.

## Track

ARTC-controlled track comprises: standard-gauge (1,435 mm) main lines from Broken Hill (NSW) via Port Augusta (South Australia) to Kalgoorlie (Western Australia) (2,173 km), with a connecting line from Crystal Brook to Adelaide (197 km) and on to the Victorian border (313 km); the Central Australia Railway from Tarcoola to Alice Springs (831 km); and the important branch line from Port Augusta to Whyalla (75 km).

The 1,600 mm gauge branches between Wolseley and Mount Gambier (183 km), and Snuggery and the Victorian border, which were isolated by conversion to standard gauge of the Melbourne—Adelaide track in April 1995, remain unused.

Self-restoring points have been installed at 42 locations, while 19 crossing loops in South Australia and Western Australia have been extended to 1.8 km. In 2000, A$7.6 million has been budgeted to extend five loops between Adelaide and Melbourne to 1.5 km and provide two new loops at Laverton (Victoria) and Mount Barker (South Australia).

**Standard rail:** Flat bottom throughout, weighing 60, 53, 47, and on some branch lines 40, 31.2, 30 and 25kg/m
**Joints:** Fishplates, bolts: but all main lines are cwr
**Rail fastening:** Dog and screw spikes, Pandrol and McKay Safelok elastic rail spikes and clips, T-headed bolts and nuts
**Crossties (sleepers):** untreated hardwood 2,500 × 230 × 115 mm; CR2 prestressed concrete 2,514 × 264 × 211 mm; AN3/AN4 prestressed concrete 2,500 × 264 × 211 mm; AN6 prestressed concrete 2,500 × 264 × 240 mm
**Spacing:** 1,600 to 1,300 per km
**Filling:** Crushed stone and gravel ballast
**Min curve radius:** 14.5°
**Max gradient:** 2.5%; between Mitcham (Adelaide) and Mount Lofty (22.4 km) the grade averages 1 in 53
**Longest straight:** 477 km – Nullarbor Plain
**Max axleload:** 23 tonnes (permissible axleloads in Victoria have been raised from 20 to 21 tonnes as a result of track upgrading)
**Highest station:** Peterborough, South Australia (532 m)

*UPDATED*

---

# Australia Western Railroad

Tel: (+61 8) 93 26 23 47  Fax: (+61 8) 93 26 21 91
Web: http://www.arg.net.au

## Key personnel

General Manager: John Goodall
Marketing and Customer Service Manager:
    Ron Dagostino

## Political background

This railway organisation is a subsidiary of Australian Railroad Group and was formed to take over the operations previously conducted by the state government-owned Westrail.

## Finance

Revenue exceeds A$250 million.

## Freight operations

AWR operates over WestNet track carrying about 30 million tonnes of bulk intrastate freight.

## Traction and rolling stock

AWR obtained 57 narrow-gauge and 35 standard-gauge locomotives and 2,200 wagons in the Westrail purchase.

## Track

AWR operates over track accessed from Westnet Rail (qv).

### Diesel locomotives: 1,067 mm gauge

| Class | Wheel arrangement | Power kW | Speed km/h | Weight tonnes | No in service | First built | Builders Mechanical | Engine | Transmission |
|---|---|---|---|---|---|---|---|---|---|
| A | Co-Co | 1,063/977 | 100 | 89.2 | 3 | 1960 | Clyde | EMD 12-567C | E EMD D25-D29 |
| AB | Co-Co | 1,230/1,120 | 100 | 96 | 4 | 1969 | Clyde | EMD 12-645E | E EMD D32-D29 |
| DA | Co-Co | 1,640/1,490 | 90 | 96.7 | 7 | 1972 | Clyde | EMD 16-645E | E EMD D32-D29 |
| DB | Co-Co | 1,640/1,490 | 90 | 110 | 13 | 1982 | Clyde | EMD 16-645E | E EMD AR6-D29 |
| P | Co-Co | 2,000/1,830 | 90 | 100.5 | 17 | 1989 | Goninan | GE 7 FDL 12 | E 5GNMG 191A1 |
| S | Co-Co | 2,424/2,260 | 90 | 118.5 | 11 | 1998 | Clyde | EMD 710 G3B-ES | E EMD AR8-D43 |

### Diesel locomotives: 1,435 mm gauge

| Class | Wheel arrangement | Power kW | Speed km/h | Weight tonnes | No in service | First built | Builders Mechanical | Engine | Transmission |
|---|---|---|---|---|---|---|---|---|---|
| K | Co-Co | 1,454/1,338 | 130 | 114 | 6 | 1966 | EE | EE 12 CSVT | E EE 822/16J-538 |
| L | Co-Co | 2,386/2,162 | 134 | 134 | 10 | 1967 | Clyde | EMD 16-645E3 | E EMD AR10-D77 |
| Q | Co-Co | 3,095/2,862 | 115 | 133.5 | 19 | 1997 | Clyde | EMD 710G3B-ES | E AR11-D87 |

*NEW ENTRY*

---

# Bayside Trains (M > Trains)

Reply Paid 5343, Melbourne, Victoria 3000
Web: http://www.nationalexpressgroup.com

## Key personnel

Managing Director: Colin Andrews

Gauge: 1,600 mm
Route length: 237 km
Electrification: 1.5 kV DC overhead

## Political background

The Melbourne suburban passenger train network was state government-owned and -operated until 1999, when the government privatised the system by the unusual method of offering two franchises, each of roughly half the system. The two successful franchises therefore do not compete although there are a few inner city stations served by both. The two franchises, called Bayside Trains and Hillside Trains (now Connex Trains Melbourne (qv)) are for 15 years. The UK-based National Express Group won the Bayside Trains franchise (as well as V/Line Passenger (qv)).

## Organisation

When the present operator took over its 15-year contract on 29 August 1999, it had 1,589 employees. The contract provides a subsidy from the state government for the first year of A$84.8 million, reducing regularly until the final year when the company will pay A$18.5 million. It is committed to an investment of A$497 million over the contract, of which A$400 million is to replace about one third of the fleet, starting in late 2002; A$70 million is to refurbish the remainder of the fleet, with A$9 million to be spent on station improvements and A$18 million to improve accessibility for disabled passengers.

The company is progressively adopting the M > Trains brand name to coincide with the introduction of a new identity and rolling stock colour scheme and with a programme of station improvements.

### Finance
A condition of the contract is that fares cannot be increased above rate of inflation. In 1998/99, revenue was A$242.9 million while expenditure was A$226.4 million.

### Traffic
In 2000, the company's trains covered 9.6 million km and in 2000-01 carried 74 million passengers. The company expects traffic to grow by 84 per cent over the 15-year contract.

### Passenger operations
Bayside Trains is responsible for providing services on the Sandringham, Frankston/Stony Point, Pakenham, Cranbourne, Upfield, Broadmeadows, St Albans, Werribee and Williamstown lines. On weekdays in 2001, 1,054 services were provided. This nine-line network covers 237 route-km, with 118 stations, of which 34 are known as 'Premium Stations' and are attended for all trains. They have toilets, improved lighting and waiting room facilities. About 14,000 free car-parking spaces are provided at stations.

### Traction and rolling stock
The company operates a fleet of 78 three-car trains. In mid-2000 it let a contract to Siemens, Austria, to supply and maintain 62 new three-car emus partly to replace existing vehicles from early 2003. In 2001, refurbishment of the existing fleet was under way, including provision of improved lighting and information displays, more comfortable seats and CCTV in each carriage.

### Signalling and telecommunications
A contract has been let for supply of a 'Position of Train' system to enable employees to establish the location of rolling stock and the service it is working.

### Electrification
A$30 million is to be spent to extend suburban electrification from St Albans to Sydenham, a distance of 4 km. The project includes relocating Sydenham station and provision of a car park and bus interchange there. The improvement is expected to attract an additional 1.5 million passengers annually to the network.

### Track
A$3.5 million is being spent on track improvements at North Melbourne to equalise the usage of the existing six tracks.

*UPDATED*

## BHP Iron Ore Railroad

PO Box 231, Nelson Point, Port Hedland, Western Australia 6721
Tel: (+61 8) 91 73 67 13   Fax: (+61 8) 91 73 67 89

### Key personnel
Vice-President, Railways: Mike Darby
Managers
    Operations: Lindsay Morrison
    Track and Signal: Euginuo Alvarez
    Rolling Stock: Russell Donnelly

Gauge: 1,435 mm
Route length: 699 km

### Organisation
The railway has two operations: the Mount Newman mine operation and the Yarrie mine operation. These lines were once operated as separate entities but are now amalgamated with common management.

### Freight operations
One line runs from Jimblebar and Mount Newman to Port Hedland, on the northwest coast (489 km), with 35 tonne axleloadings, one of the highest figures in the world. Trains are of 240 wagons, but the company has operated trains of up to 300 wagons.

The single-track route has two 1.64 km and twelve 3 km passing loops. Normal operations see nine loaded trains daily hauled either by three 4,476 kW GE locomotives or four 2,984 kW GE Dash 8 locomotives hauling 224 hopper wagons. Maximum speed of a fully loaded train is 75 km/h. The sophisticated facilities at the Mount Newman railhead allow a train to be fully loaded in only 70 minutes, so that a trainset can be turned, loaded and remanned within 120 minutes. Each return journey over the 426 km route from Port Hedland to Mount Newman and back is scheduled to take less than 19 hours; ore dumping at the port takes 4-5 hours for a 240-wagon train.

The other line is from Yarrie to Finucane Island (near Port Hedland) over a route length of 217 km. Three train-rakes of 88 wagons each (6,700 tonnes per train) run daily.

The railway hauls about 65 million tonnes of ore annually.

### Improvements to existing lines
An impressive marshalling yard has been built at Jimblebar Junction to enable trains to be uncoupled and combined. The yard is 8.5 km long and is believed to be the longest in the southern hemisphere.

A new crossing loop, 3.7 km long, has been commissioned at Shaw, in the Chichester Range, to improve train operations.

### Traction and rolling stock
The company operates 48 diesel locomotives, 2,224 ore wagons and 66 other freight wagons on the Newman line, and eight diesel locomotives and 282 wagons on the Goldsworthy line. Also owned is a lounge/dining car. The locomotive fleet replacement programme has been completed. There are now 40 2,984 kW Dash 8 locomotives and eight Dash 7 locomotives.

Goninan has won contracts worth A$70 million to provide a further six GE AC6000 locomotives and 231 iron ore wagons each with a capacity of 115 tonnes. Three of these locomotives will haul 240 wagons instead of the four currently required on the Newman line. They are the first 4,475 kW/6,000 hp machines ordered in Australia and the first to use AC traction motors. They are being imported from the USA and completed at Perth. Delivery will allow eight of 27 GE Dash 8 units to be transferred to the Goldsworthy/Yarrie line to permit retirement of eight GE Dash 7 units currently employed on that line.

The company is to convert to electronic train braking, where each wagon receives an electronic signal from the locomotive. This system will improve the speed of application and release of braking effort.

The railway has beaten its previous record by running a train of eight AC6000 locomotives and 682 hoppers carrying 82,000 tonnes of iron ore. Gross weight of the train was 99,732 tonnes while the length was 7.35 km. The train, run on 21 June 2001, tested the latest version of Locotrol remote-control equipment.

### Signalling and telecommunications
The railway is controlled by CTC, supplemented by track-to-train radio, from a control centre at Port Hedland. Interlockings can function automatically in the event of any failure in the CTC telemetry.

Eight hot box detectors, three hot wheel detectors and 39 dragging equipment detectors are used on the main line.

Automatic Car Identification (ACI) transponders are fitted to each ore wagon and readers are located at two positions on the track.

Nineteen Dash 8 locomotives have been equipped with Harmon ATP equipment, EPIC electronic air brakes and Locotrol 3 equipment.

*Dash 8 locomotives marshalled mid-train in an empty iron ore train returning from Port Hedland to Newman (Wolfram Veith)*
2002/0121162

### Track
A contract has been signed with Barclay Mowlem to replace 250 km of rail and 500,000 sleepers over a four-year period. The Newman line will comprise concrete sleepers when the contract is completed.

Daily and weekly inspections are made of the complete length of the main line in special-purpose hi-rail vehicles. Analysis of track geometry is provided by a Plasser EM80 recorder car and an ultrasonic rail testing car. Track maintenance crews are based at Port Hedland and Newman, as well as at the Redmont Track Centre, about 200 km south of Port Hedland, which acts as a base for about 25 permanent employees.

**Rail:** 66 and 68 kg/m continuous welded rail in 400 m lengths (standard carbon on tangent and head-hardened on curves and some tangents)
**Sleepers:** Concrete: 300 wide × 240 deep × 2,600 mm long
Steel: 120 mm deep × 9 or 10 mm thick
**Spacing:** Steel/concrete 1,667/km
**Fastenings:** Concrete : Pandrol
Steel : Traklok
**Min curvature radius:** 528 m
**Max gradient:** Newman line: 1.5% (empty); 0.55% (loaded); Yarrie line: 1.04%
**Max axleload:** 35 tonnes

**Type of brake:** Air
**Type of coupling:** Alliance automatic

*UPDATED*

# CityRail

PO Box K349, Haymarket, New South Wales 1238
Tel: (+61 2) 93 79 30 00   Fax: (+61 2) 93 79 53 10
Web: http//www.cityrail.nsw.gov.au

### Key personnel
General Manager, CityRail Stations: Bob Irving

Gauge: 1,435 mm

### Organisation
CityRail is a business group of SRA. It operates an extensive rail network and provides suburban and regional passenger services from Sydney to Lithgow in the Blue Mountains (156 km), Goulburn (225 km) in the Southern Highlands, Nowra (184 km) in the Illawarra, and South Coast areas, and to Scone (315 km) and Dungog (245 km) in the north. It provides around 2,500 services each weekday, carrying approximately 750,000 passengers. These services operate between 306 stations over some 2,060 km of track.

### Finance
Farebox revenue of A$509.3 million in 1999-2000, compared with A$449 million the previous year.

Fares covered 41 per cent of operating costs, other commercial sources 2 per cent, the remainder being a state government community service obligation contract payment.

### Passenger operations
Patronage continues to rise, to 278.7 million journeys in 1999-2000, compared with 270.5 million in 1998-99. Two security guards now travel on all services after 19.00.

During the 2000 Olympic Games, CityRail carried 29.5 million passengers over a two-week period during which it would normally convey 13.8 million. Some 80 per cent of spectators visiting the Olympic Park travelled by rail. Technological support introduced to back up this operation included systems to assist train planning processes, featuring simulation of timetables before implementation and automation of crew rostering.

### New lines
The 10 km underground double-track New Southern Railway opened May 2000, serving Sydney's main airport with through running to other lines to the north and south. Trains take 9 minutes, half the time of bus trips. The Bondi extension mentioned in previous editions of *Jane's World Railways* has been abandoned.

### Improvements to existing lines
Preparations for CityRail's key role in moving large volumes of passengers during the 2000 Olympic Games included a significant programme to modernise facilities. The programme involved the completion of five new stations at Ashfield, Lidcombe, Liverpool, Penrith and St Leonards, a major upgrade of Central Station, the installation of 'easy access' facilities at Central, Town Hall and Wynyard, and at the new stations detailed above. Also included was the introduction of real-time passenger information displays at 15 main stations in the central business district and on the main Olympic routes, and the upgrading of station signage at nine stations.

### Traction and rolling stock
CityRail operates 1,457 double-deck emu cars (Tangara suburban 367; other suburban 770; outer suburban 80; interurban 240). Currently 1,312 are rostered in peak-hour service. Additionally 30 Endeavour and 16 620 Class railcars are used.

The system is to get its first new trains in a decade with the construction of 20 double-deck 'Millennium Trains' of four coaches. The contract was let in October 1998 to Evans Deakin Industries, whose Sydney subsidiary Clyde Engineering will build the trains. The first is to be delivered in early 2001 with the remainder by 2003. The contractor is to be responsible for maintenance until 2016. The four-car trains will have driving trailer cars at each end, with the motor cars in the centre. Each set seats 464 in 'walkover' seats, with standing space for a further 620.

The seven two-car 620/720 railcars have been refurbished with improved cab facilities and repaints. They run services west from Newcastle.

As part of CityRail's preparations for the 2000 Olympic Games, 151 intercity and 679 suburban coaches were refurbished.

In 2001, the New South Wales government announced that it intended to invite tenders to supply new batches of dmus and emus. The dmus will comprise 14 cars in two-car sets for the Hunter Region, these to be operationally compatible with the existing Endeavour dmus. A contract was expected to be signed by October 2002, with the first set delivered by mid-2004. The tender invitation for emus called for 10 four-car double-deck sets for Central Coast,

### Double-deck electric multiple-units

| Class | Cars per unit | Motor cars per unit | Motors per car | Power/motor kW | Speed km/h | Cars in service | First built | Builders Mechanical | Builders Electrical |
|---|---|---|---|---|---|---|---|---|---|
| **Suburban** | | | | | | | | | |
| C | 2/4/6 | 1/2/3 | 4 | 135 | 115 | 201 | 1972 | Comeng | Mitsubishi |
| C | 4/6 | 2/3 | 4 | 135 | 115 | 79 | 1978 | Goninan | Mitsubishi |
| C | 2/4 | 1/2 | 4 | 135 | 115 | 80 | 1981 | Goninan | Mitsubishi |
| C | 6 | 3 | 4 | 150 | 115 | 28 | 1986 | Goninan | Mitsubishi |
| T | 4/6 | 2/3 | - | - | 115 | 56 | 1964 | Tullochs | - |
| T | 4/6 | 2/3 | - | - | 115 | 138 | 1974 | Comeng | - |
| T | 4/6 | 2/3 | - | - | 115 | 70 | 1978 | Goninan | - |
| T | 4 | 2 | - | - | 115 | 76 | 1981 | Goninan | - |
| T | 6 | 3 | - | - | 115 | 28 | 1986 | Goninan | - |
| D | 2 | 1 | - | - | 115 | 10 | 1979 | Comeng | - |
| D | 2 | 1 | - | - | 115 | 4 | 1981 | Goninan | - |
| D | 4 | 2 | - | - | 115 | 184 | 1988 | Goninan | - |
| N | 4 | 2 | 4 | 170 | 115 | 184 | 1988 | Goninan | Mitsubishi |
| **Outer suburban** | | | | | | | | | |
| ON | 4 | 2 | 4 | 170 | 115 | 20 | 1994 | Goninan | Mitsubishi |
| ONL | 4 | 2 | 4 | 170 | 115 | 20 | 1994 | Goninan | Mitsubishi |
| OD | 4 | 2 | - | - | 115 | 40 | 1994 | Goninan | - |
| **Interurban** | | | | | | | | | |
| DCM | 4/6 | 2/3 | 4 | 140 | 130 | 10 | 1977 | Comeng | Mitsubishi |
| DTM | 2/4/6 | 1/2/3 | 4 | 140 | 130 | 5 | 1978 | Comeng | Mitsubishi |
| DIM | 4/6 | 2/3 | 4 | 140 | 130 | 53 | 1981 | Comeng | Mitsubishi |
| DJM | 4/6 | 2/3 | 4 | 140 | 130 | 45 | 1986 | Comeng | Mitsubishi |
| DKM | 4/6 | 2/3 | 4 | 140 | 130 | 7 | 1989 | Comeng | Mitsubishi |
| DKT | 4/6 | 2/3 | - | - | 130 | 7 | 1989 | Comeng | - |
| DTD | 2 | 1 | - | - | 130 | 5 | 1977 | Comeng | - |
| DCT | 2/4/6 | 1/2/3 | - | - | 130 | 9 | 1977 | Comeng | - |
| DMT | 4/6 | 2/3 | - | - | 130 | 7 | 1970 | Comeng | - |
| DDT | 4/6 | 2/3 | - | - | 130 | 4 | 1970 | Comeng | - |
| DFT | 4/6 | 2/3 | - | - | 130 | 4 | 1970 | Comeng | - |
| DIT | 4/6 | 2/3 | - | - | 130 | 84 | 1981 | Comeng | - |

### Diesel railcars or multiple-units

| Class | Cars per unit | Motor cars per unit | Motored axles/car | Power/motor kW | Speed km/h | Cars in service | First built | Builders Mechanical | Builders Engine | Builders Transmission |
|---|---|---|---|---|---|---|---|---|---|---|
| **620 Class** | | | | | | | | | | |
| NPF | 2 | 1 | 2 | 227 × 2 | 122 | 7 | 1961 | NSWGR | Cummins NTA855 R4 | H Voith |
| NTC | 2 | 1 | - | - | 122 | 7 | 1961 | NSWGR | | |
| **Endeavour** | | | | | | | | | | |
| TE | 2 | 2 | 2 | 353 | 145 | 15 | 1994 | ABB | Cummins KTA 19R | H Voith |
| LE | 2 | 2 | 2 | 353 | 145 | 15 | 1994 | ABB | Cummins KTA 19R | H Voith |

*CityRail Tangara double-deck emu at Sydney Terminal (Brian Webber)*

Illawarra and Blue Mountain outer suburban services. Contract signature was expected in late 2002, with a target date for delivery of the first set of the second half of 2004 to enable it to commence timetabled services in June 2005.

### Electrification
In 2001, a further section of the Illawarra Line was being electrified between Dapto and Kiama. Signalling had also been upgraded, with remote operation from Woollongong.

**Type of coupler in standard use:** Passenger, automatic; Endeavour, Scharfenberg

**Type of braking in standard use:** Westinghouse air; Endeavour air and hydrodynamic

UPDATED

*CityRail 'V' set double-deck emu at Sydney Terminal (Brian Webber)*

## Comalco Railway

Post Office, Weipa, North Queensland 4874
Tel: (+61 7) 40 69 89 69   Fax: (+61 7) 40 69 83 21

### Key personnel
Railway Superintendent: R Dickson

Gauge: 1,435 mm
Route length: 19 km

### Freight operations
Owned by Comalco Minerals and Alumina, the railway connects Andoom (mine) with Weipa (port). Operations commenced in 1972 and the line carries some 10 million tonnes of bauxite ore annually.

### Traction and rolling stock
The railway is operated with one Clyde-EMD GT26C and one Clyde-EMD JT42C 3,000 hp/2,240 kW diesel-electric locomotives, 120 bottom-discharge ore (124 tonne gross) wagons and nine freight wagons.

### Track
Rails are 67.5 kg/m on hardwood sleepers at 2,020/km spacing. The line includes a 1 km long concrete bridge.

UPDATED

*Comalco Railway workshops at Weipa (Wolfram Veith)*

## Connex Trains Melbourne

589 Collins Street, Melbourne, Victoria 3000
Tel: (+61 3) 96 19 11 11   Fax: (+61 3) 96 19 23 43
Previously part of Victoria Public Transport Corporation

### Key personnel
Chief Executive: Dale Larkin
Managing Director: Roger Mendes

Gauge: 1,600 mm
Route length: 129 km
Electrification: 1.5 kV DC overhead

### Political background
The Melbourne passenger train network was government-owned and -operated until 1999, when it was privatised by the novel method of granting two franchises, each of roughly half the system. The two successful franchises Bayside trains (qv) and Hillside Trains (now Connex Trains Melbourne) only compete in a minor way at a few stations in the inner city. The Hillside Trains contract was won by MTE Melbourne Transport Enterprises associated with CGEA Transport Asia Pacific, part of the global Vivendi group of France. In July 2000, it was announced that Hillside Trains would have a new company name, Connex Trains Melbourne.

### Organisation
In the first year Connex Trains Melbourne received a government subsidy of A$91 million but this gradually reduces over the 15-year life of the contract to A$25 million in the final year. It is to invest A$389 million over the term of the contract, with A$314 million for 29 new six-car emus in 2002 and A$75 million to refurbish the remainder.

At takeover Connex Trains Melbourne employed 1,254 staff.

*Comeng-built suburban emu at Richmond on the Connex Trains Melbourne network (Brian Webber)*

| Finance (A$ million) | 1998/99 |
|---|---|
| Passenger revenue | 70.4 |
| Other revenue | 16.1 |
| Subsidy | 117.3 |
| Total revenue | 203.8 |
| Expenses | 186.7 |
| Operating surplus | 17.1 |

It is a condition of the contract that fares cannot be increased above rate of inflation.

### Traffic
There were 50.4 million passenger journeys in 1997/98, increasing to 52 million in 1998/99. The company plans to increase patronage by 64 per cent.

# RAILWAY SYSTEMS/Australia

### Passenger operations
Connex Trains Melbourne provides services on the Glen Waverley, Alamein, Belgrave, Lilydale, Hurstbridge and Epping lines, all to the east of the city centre, and a short line to the Showgrounds and Flemington Racecourse. About 750-850 services are provided daily, achieving peak period punctuality of 90.6 per cent in 1997/98. Additional services have been provided since the contract commenced. Of the 90 stations, 31 are known as 'Premium Stations' and are attended for all trains. They have superior facilities. Free parking is provided for about 14,000 cars at Connex Trains Melbourne stations, with an additional 800 spaces to be provided in 2000.

In June 2000, almost all services ran with 95 per cent running within 5 minutes of the timetable. Additional services have been provided and it is intended to ad more to ease overcrowding.

### Improvements to existing lines
A$27 million has been spent upgrading the busiest station at Flinders Street in the city centre used by 100,000 people daily. The result has been a design making it an impressive facility, with an open concourse with emphasis on natural light.

### Traction and rolling stock
Connex Trains Melbourne operates a fleet of 75 six-car sets comprising 45 built by Comeng and 29 by Hitachi. There is also one double-deck set. Annual train-km totalled 6.3 million in 1998/99. The Hitachi trains are to be replaced by 2004 by trains equipped with CCTV cameras and help points, similar to the Comeng trains.

### Signalling and telecommunications
Asset management of Connex Trains Melbourne's infrastructure is being carried out by Alstom. The system includes 240 km of track, 27 substations, 60 km of 22 kV transmission lines, 739 signals, 90 stations, 176 bridges and various communications systems.

*UPDATED*

---

## Countrylink

Level 1, Sydney Central Station, Sydney, New South Wales 2000
PO Box K349, Haymarket, New South Wales 1238
Tel: (+61 2) 93 79 12 98   Fax: (+61 2) 93 79 48 36

### Key personnel
General Manager Countrylink: Tim Poulter

Gauge: 1,435 mm

### Political background
Under the restructure of railways in New South Wales, Countrylink is a business group of the State Rail Authority (qv).

### Organisation
Countrylink operates long-distance passenger services (train and connecting coach) to 334 destinations, primarily in New South Wales but also across borders into Queensland, Victoria and the Australian Capital Territory. The New South Wales services are provided under a community service obligations contract arrangement with the state government.

### Passenger operations
Countrylink services operate a daily average of more than 14,000 km. Return train services operate between Sydney and 10 destinations:
Daily services to Brisbane (990 km), Murwillumbah (935 km), Grafton (700 km), Armidale (579 km), Moree (666 km) and Dubbo (462 km)
Three times daily to Canberra (330 km)
Twice daily (daylight and overnight) to Melbourne
Weekly services to Broken Hill (1,125 km) and Griffith (640 km).

Traffic remains stable at some 2.4 million passenger journeys annually.

The weekly weekend Sydney–Griffith return services previously run by a locomotive-hauled train were replaced by an Xplorer set in May 2000. At the same time, the Broken Hill weekly service was withdrawn, with Countrylink arranging travel for its customers on Great Southern Railway trains.

### Traction and rolling stock
Countrylink's all-diesel fleet consists of:
XPT trains with a power car at each end of a set of trailers.
Xplorer railcars which can be coupled and uncoupled en route to allow a train to separate and serve two destinations.

Countrylink operates 19 XPT power cars, 52 XPT cars for seated passengers, eight XPT sleeping cars, 21 Xplorer railcars and nine locomotive-hauled cars.

The XPT power cars are being re-engined with new VP185 Paxman engines.

The New South Wales government has announced that it intends to call tenders for a three-car diesel passenger set for a Sydney–Broken Hill service, to be delivered early 2005 and in service mid-2005. This set will include some first class seating, buffet facilities and onboard entertainment.

**Diesel railcars or multiple-units**

| Class | Cars per unit | Motor cars per unit | Motored axles/car | Power/motor kW | Speed km/h | Units in service | First built | Mechanical | Builders Engine | Transmission |
|---|---|---|---|---|---|---|---|---|---|---|
| XPT | 7-9 | 2 | 4 | 1,500 | 160 | * | 1981 | Comeng/ABB | Paxman Valenta | E Brush |
| Xplorer | 2-6 | 2-6 | 2 | 353 | 145 | 21 | 1994 | ABB | Cummins KTA-19-R | H Voith |

*19 power cars, 60 trailers

*Countrylink Xplorer dmu at Uralla (Brian Webber)* 2002/0121165

*Countrylink XPT south of Casino (Brian Webber)* 2001/0099112

**Type of coupler:** XPT, automatic; Xplorer, Scharfenberg
**Type of braking:** XPT, Westinghouse air; Xplorer, air and hydrodynamic

*UPDATED*

---

## Freight Australia

PO Box 1646N, Melbourne, Victoria 3001
Tel: (+61 3) 96 19 13 11   Fax: (+61 3) 96 19 45 55
e-mail: inquiries@freightaustralia.com.au
Web: http://www.freightaustralia.com.au

### Key personnel
Chief Executive Officer: Marinus van Onselen
General Manager, Commercial: Garry Molloy

Gauge: 1,600 mm; 1,435 mm
Track access: 3,458 km; 454 km of track in Victoria

### Political background
With the reorganisation of Victoria's rail operators, V/Line Freight was corporatised on 1 July 1997 and in February 1999 the government announced the privatisation of the business via a consortium wholly owned by RailAmerica Inc of the USA. The consortium bid A$163 million for the purchase of V/Line Freight's assets and the 15-year lease of access to the track involved.

### Organisation
Staff numbers grew from 570 to nearly 700 in the first two years since privatisation, reflecting business growth. The purchasers have indicated that they will pay particular

attention to the relationship between administrative and maintenance costs and the income generated by a particular section of track.

Freight Victoria changed its name to Freight Australia better to reflect its business intentions geographically.

### Finance
In the first 20 months following the acquisition of the former V/Line Freight business for A$163 million and the transfer of A$27 million of liabilities, FA provided an extra A$53 million in additional capital. Earnings before interest, tax, depreciation and amortisation for the calendar year 2000 were A$45.3 million, a considerable turn-round from the A$11.6 million loss reported in the final year of government ownership.

In the first 20 months of privatisation, FA increased locomotive-km by 20 per cent and wagon-km by 54 per cent. Productivity has been improved by a policy of ignoring state borders to capture profitable business wherever it can. Locomotives have been hired from other operators to handle additional traffic.

### Freight operations
Freight Australia provides freight services on two gauges and resources for services run by other operators. Reference to the map accompanying Victoria Rail Track Corporation shows that effectively there are two independent systems, broad gauge and standard gauge. In 1998-99, 6.9 million tonnes of freight were carried. About 4 million tonnes of grain, 370,000 tonnes of cement, 550,000 tonnes of minerals/quarry and a million tonnes of containers are hauled annually. The Australian Wheat Board has signed a five-year contract with Freight Australia to haul most of the state's grain to Melbourne for domestic use or to Geelong or Portland for export. At the peak of the 2001 export season, FA was hauling 17,000 tonnes of grain daily to ports. There has been strong growth in container traffic at several provincial centres. The two lines into southern New South Wales carry a considerable number of wheat or rice containers.

The broad-gauge lines west from Ouyen and Heywood into South Australia see no trains. The new standard-gauge line via Wolseley provides an alternative for any available traffic.

FA won a five-year contract to provide hook-and-pull services for SCT between Melbourne and Adelaide and across the Nullarbor Plain to Perth. To avoid refuelling stops, an innovative in-line fuelling system has been introduced, enabling locomotives to receive fuel from a tank car as the journey progresses.

Freight Australia provides safe working, crews or locomotives for other operators, including West Coast Railway, SCT, and Toll (qv).

### New lines
The purchasers have committed to extending the standard-gauge rails the few kilometres from the existing track at North Geelong into the Geelong port complex.

*G Class diesel-electric locomotive on a grain train*

**Diesel locomotives: 1,600 mm or 1,435 mm gauge**

| Class | Builder's type | Wheel arrangement | Power kW | Speed km/h | Weight tonnes | No in service | First built | Mechanical | Builders Engine | Transmission |
|---|---|---|---|---|---|---|---|---|---|---|
| A | AAT22C-2R | Co-Co | 1,840 | 115 | 121 | 7 | 1983* | Clyde | GM 12-645E3B | E GM |
| G | JT26C-255 | Co-Co | 2,460 | 115 | 127 | 31 | 1984 | Clyde | GM 16-645E3B | E GM |
| H | G188 | Bo-Bo | 820 | 100 | 81 | 5 | 1968 | Clyde | GM 8-645E | E GM |
| P | G18HB-R | Bo-Bo | 826 | 100 | 77 | 5 | 1984* | Clyde | GM 8-645E | E GM |
| S | - | Co-Co | 1,450/1,340 | 133 | 123 | 4 | 1957 | Clyde | GM 16-567C | E GM |
| T | G88 | Bo-Bo | 710/826 | 100 | 69 | 12 | 1959 | Clyde | GM 8-567CR or 8-645E | E GM |
| X | - | Co-Co | 1,450/1,640 | 115 | 118 | 22 | 1966/1974 | Clyde | GM 16-567E or 16-645E | E GM |
| Y | - | Bo-Bo | 480 | 64 | 68 | 18 | 1963 | Clyde | GM 6-567C or 6-645E | E GM |

* Rebuilt

### Improvements to existing lines
FA has reopened a 74 km freight-only line between Sale and Bairnsdale to capture timber products traffic.

### Traction and rolling stock
The V/Line Freight traction fleet at sale comprised 86 diesel-electric locomotives, of which 15 are standard gauge (11 G Class, three H Class, and one X Class). While most date from the 1960s and 1980s, the three S Class units are over 40 years old.

In 2001, FA was rebuilding six G Class locomotives with 2,600 kW GM 645F3B engines and repowering six X Class to 2,235 kW. Seven A Class units are to be equipped with Super Series control equipment. EDI/Clyde was building one 2,984 kW V Class unit.

V/Line Freight owned 655 grain wagons, 489 container wagons, 162 gypsum wagons, 130 cement wagons, 74 rice hopper wagons, 49 briquette wagons, 48 petroleum tankers, 33 super phosphate wagons, 27 quarry hopper wagons and nine other wagons reflecting the traffics carried.

In 2001, 700 grain wagons were being rebuilt to increase their capacity from 76 to 100 tonnes, install improved loading and discharge systems and equip them with bogies allowing their operating speed to be increased to 115 km/h.

### Track
Freight Australia holds a sub-lease of most country track in the state of Victoria. It must grant access to any other operator of both passenger and freight services.

The Victoria state government is investigating the desirability of converting some or all broad-gauge track to standard gauge. It seems likely that most broad-gauge country track will be converted, perhaps over a five-year timespan.

**UPDATED**

---

## FreightCorp

Locked Bag 90, Parramatta, New South Wales 2124
Tel: (+61 2) 98 93 25 00   Fax: (+61 2) 98 93 25 01
Web: http://www.freightcorp.com.au

### Key personnel
Managing Director: Lucio Di Bartolomeo
Deputy Managing Director: Terry Kearney
General Managers
   Coal Services: Peter Winder
   Freight Services: Neil Matthews
   Operations: Tom Stuber
   Strategy and Corporate Affairs: Gary Pedersen
   Engineering Services: Bob Clague
   Human Resources: Elizabeth Harrison
   Finance: David Lamb
   Risk and Assurance: Robert Sullivan

Gauge: 1,435 mm
Route access: 7,469 route-km

### Political background
Following the restructure of the previous (New South Wales) State Rail Authority at 1 July 1996, FreightCorp became responsible for 'above rail' freight operations. Responsibility for track rests with Rail Access Corporation (qv).

At the end of January 2002, the Australian government announced that FreightCorp was to be sold to National Rail Consortium Pty Ltd (NRC Pty) in a combined sale with National Rail Corporation Ltd (qv). The value of the transaction, which was completed at the end of February 2002, was A$1.172 billion. NRC Pty is owned jointly by Lang Corporation and Toll Holdings. The company announced plans to upgrade the Melbourne–Perth via Parkes line to accommodate trains of double-stack containers and to reduce journey times between Sydney and Brisbane, subject to the conclusion of track access arrangements with Australian Rail Track Corporation.

### Organisation
FreightCorp conducts two core businesses: the transport of commodities and the provision of services. Bulk

*FreightCorp 82 and 81 Class locomotives (Brian Webber)*

commodities such as coal, grain and minerals are transported in unit trains and general freight train services carry a range of products including cement, petroleum and export containers. FreightCorp provides services to other rail operators including locomotive and wagon maintenance and hire, train crew hire and terminal services.

In order to capture more business, FreightCorp is moving towards providing total logistics solutions, which will build on its capability as a rail operator with an expanded service to include storage and short-haul road operations. Joint venture initiatives with private-sector companies are being pursued. With the organisation now maturing into its role, it is vigorously embracing competition from road and other rail operators.

A new integrated train management Customer Service Centre has commenced operation with a new management information computer system. A real-time train operating system has been implemented to integrate train planning, programming, monitoring and rolling stock control. FreightCorp has an access contract with Rail Access Corporation in New South Wales, and access to 250 km of private track in South Australia and into Queensland and Victoria on the interstate network.

As at June 2000, FreightCorp employed 2,200 staff, a reduction of 45 per cent since 1996.

### Finance
Total revenue for 1999-2000 was A$638.5 million, compared with A$688 million the previous year. Profit before tax was A$55.5 million, up from A$33.7 million the previous year. Coal traffic accounted for nearly 48 per cent of revenue in 1999-2000, with grain contributing 30 per cent.

### Freight operations
In 1998/1999 a record 85.5 million tonnes were carried including: 72.5 million tonnes of coal to Newcastle or Port Kembla; 3.2 million tonnes of ores and minerals; 6.3 million tonnes of grain and 0.6 million tonnes of cement; and 2.1 million tonnes of intermodal and general freight.

Export coal from the Hunter Valley and Southern coalfields was FreightCorp's largest business, with 57.4 million tonnes hauled. Haul distances range from 20 km to 320 km, with coal conveyed from 30 loading points. Totals of 6.2 million tonnes were hauled to Port Kembla, Wollongong and 61.6 million tonnes to Newcastle. FreightCorp's largest trains are Ulan Mine—Newcastle coal trains which comprise three 90 Class locomotives and 91 coal wagons grossing 10,920 tonnes.

FreightCorp is also the preferred tenderer for haulage of up to 6 million tonnes of coal for 10 years from the Blackwater area, Queensland, to Stanwell Power Station or Gladstone. This is subject to track access charges and purchase of suitable rolling stock. If the contract comes to fruition, it will be FreightCorp's initial entry onto Queensland's 1,067 mm gauge.

Important recent contracts include an agreement to transport 180,000 tonnes annually of copper concentrate from the North Parkes Mine to Newcastle and a five-year contract to haul 2 million tonnes annually of limestone and clinker between plants. FreightCorp has also signed contracts to haul 130,000 tonnes of sugar annually from Grafton to Sydney and containerised rice from the Griffith area to Sydney. FreightCorp intends to target port container traffic as currently only 12 per cent is moved by rail.

The state government has announced that it has adopted an open access policy to infrastructure, which allows any company which can meet the standards of the 1993 Rail Safety Act to run trains over tracks previously used exclusively by FreightCorp. This has introduced competition in the very important Hunter Valley coal haulage market. The rail freight component of coal costs is significant and is seen by the coal industry as having a potential for cost reduction.

FreightCorp commenced an occasional service between New South Wales and the Brisbane port at Fisherman Islands in late 1998. A daily service is now also provided between Sydney and Melbourne for a freight forwarding company. Both these routes could provide considerable traffic in the future.

The company won a contract to haul 2.7 million tonnes of coal annually from Leigh Creek to Port Augusta power station in South Australia from February 1999. The haul of about 250 km is for 10 years. Most trains comprise three 82 Class locomotives and 150 NHKF hoppers. This was FreightCorp's first major interstate contract.

### Intermodal operations
FreightCorp's intermodal strategy has seen the development of a network of terminals around New South Wales. The company is experiencing significant growth in container traffic, especially conveying export and import products. A new Freight Centre was opened at Tamworth to handle traffic to/from the ports of Sydney and Newcastle in a joint venture with truck operators Hills Transport Pty Ltd.

FreightCorp is providing transport for containers between ports and freight yards in Sydney to reduce truck congestion in the port area and surrounding suburbs. Some of these services are being operated as push-pull shuttles by PL Class locomotives (formerly 48 Class). These initiatives have seen 22 per cent of containers passing through the port carried by rail, considerably higher than at any other port in Australia.

| Traffic (million) | 1996-97 | 1997-98 | 1998-99 |
|---|---|---|---|
| Freight tonnes | 72.6 | 82.0 | 85.5 |

### Improvements to existing lines
The first stage of redevelopment of the large Enfield marshalling yard in Sydney is in use after four years' work. A$60 million was spent providing an appropriate layout for longer (1.2 km) trains. The yard track will remain under FreightCorp control for the present.

In March 1997 a new A$7.8 million locomotive depot was commissioned at Port Waratah, in the Newcastle area. It incorporates the first fully automated locomotive washing plant.

### Traction and rolling stock
FreightCorp has about 430 diesel locomotives of which about 400 are in use regularly. There are also 36 electric locomotives which receive minimal use and are mostly stored. About 6,200 wagons are in traffic.

Six 48 Class locomotives have been altered to PL Class to enable them to work new push-pull freight services between Sydney's several freight yards and the port.

Maintenance of the new 82 and 90 Class locomotives is the responsibility of Clyde Engineering under a Ready Power agreement, the first of its kind in Australia. The agreement requires 100 per cent availability of 84 locomotives. To meet this requirement 89 locomotives were built. These are all based at Clyde Engineering's Newcastle Ready Power facility.

In April 1996, FreightCorp owned 1,935 coal wagons, 1,429 grain wagons, 326 mineral wagons, 1,512 general freight/container wagons, and 1,018 service wagons.

Novacoal, a business unit of a coal mining company in the Hunter Valley, has placed in traffic 98 120-tonne PHCH coal wagons built by ABB/ANI Bradken. FreightCorp is contracted to haul the coal but, by owning the wagons, Novacoal is able to change to another haulier should it wish.

Four hundred NHPH 110 tonne coal wagons have been delivered from Goninan and 385 NHSH coal wagons have had their frames strengthened and have been coupled into sets of three to reduce the noise associated with coupler slack. The current wagon acquisition programme will provide an annual coal-carrying capacity of 92 million tonnes.

FreightCorp has ordered 25 cement wagons of 75 tonne capacity from Australian National Workshops.

A new 110 tonne capacity mobile recovery crane, built by Clarke Chapman Ltd of Carlisle, has been commissioned. The crane can be hauled at 120 km/h and run on 30 kg/m track, if required.

**Type of coupler:** Freight cars, AAP
**Type of braking:** Air

*UPDATED*

### Diesel locomotives

| Class | Builder's type | Wheel arrangement | Power kW | Speed km/h | Weight tonnes | No in service | First built | Mechanical | Builders Engine | Transmission |
|---|---|---|---|---|---|---|---|---|---|---|
| 48/PL | DL531G | Co-Co | 710 | 120 | 75 | 114 | 1959 | Goodwin | Alco 6-251 B | E GE/AEI |
| 80 | CE615A | Co-Co | 1,492 | 130 | 121 | 10 | 1978 | Comeng | Alco 12-251 CE | E Mitsubishi |
| 81 | JT26C-2SS | Co-Co | 2,240 | 125 | 129 | 84 | 1982 | Clyde | EMD 16-645E3 B | E EMD |
| 82 | JT42C | Co-Co | 2,259 | 115 | 132 | 55 | 1994 | EMD | EMD 710G3A | E EMD |
| 90 | GT46CW-M | Co-Co | 2,836 | 115 | 165 | 31 | 1994 | EMD | EMD 710G3A | E EMD |

### Electric locomotives

| Class | Wheel arrangement | Output kW continuous/one-hour | Speed km/h | Weight tonnes | No in service | First built | Mechanical | Builders Electrical |
|---|---|---|---|---|---|---|---|---|
| 86 | Co-Co* | 2,700/2,880 | 130 | 119 | 36 | 1983 | Comeng | Mitsubishi |

* One locomotive is Bo-Bo-Bo

## Great Northern Rail Services Pty Ltd

Box 14608, Melbourne City Mail Centre, Victoria 8001
Tel: (+61 3) 96 19 63 23  Fax: (+61 3) 96 19 63 31
e-mail: gnrs@greatnorthernrail.com.au
Web: http://www.greatnorthernrail.com.au

### Key personnel
Manager, Commercial Operations: Andrew Bridger

**Gauge:** 1,435 mm; 1,600 mm

### Organisation
The family-owned company was formed in 1993 and has established itself as a quality provider of motive power in Victoria. It has strategic relationships with National Rail and other operators to provide locomotives for terminal shunts, trip working, infrastructure and ballast operations. The company also offers in-field servicing and maintenance of locomotives and rolling stock and is currently leasing a heavy locomotive maintenance facility in South Australia for the overhaul of its own and other operator's rolling stock.

During 1998 the company expanded into the provision of train crew and is currently crewing its own trains and providing crewed 'hook and pull' services for operators in three states (Victoria, New South Wales and South Australia). A staff of 22 is employed.

### Freight operations
The company has purchased Bendigo locomotive depot for use as a maintenance facility.

Since October 1999, it has provided track audit and infrastructure maintenance operations throughout Victoria.

### Traction and rolling stock
The company owns five ex-V/Line T Class and three former Westrail J Class locomotives, providing motive power on both 1,435 mm and 1,600 mm gauges. During 1998, the company purchased 12 unserviceable GM Class from Australia Southern Railroad (ASR) (qv), of which three have been returned to service. The company also owns six former TransAdelaide diesel-hydraulic railcars.

The company has also purchased eight 44/45 Class withdrawn locomotives from Rail Services Australia. For its infrastructure contract it acquired 64 51 tonne air discharge ballast wagons.

### Track
The company operates on the tracks of other operators in the vicinity of Melbourne.

*UPDATED*

## Great Southern Railway (GSR)

PO Box 445, Marleston Business Centre, Marleston, South Australia 5033
Tel: (+61 8) 82 13 44 44   Fax: (+61 8) 82 13 44 80
e-mail: stationmaster@gsr.com.au
Web: http://www.trainways.com.au

### Key personnel
Chief Executive Officer: Stephen Bradford
Director, Finance: Ian Rhodes
Director, Sales: Alan Stuart
Director, Operations: Brian Duffy
Director, Marketing and Guest Services:
   Anthony Kirchner
General Manager: Keith Hunt

Gauge: 1,435 mm

### Background
Following its decision to sell off the assets of the Australian National Railway Commission, the Commonwealth Government of Australia executed a contract with the Great Southern Railway Consortium for the acquisition of the passenger rail business in November 1997. The company became a wholly owned subsidiary of Serco Group Pty Ltd in October 1999.

### Passenger operations
Carrying some 250,000 passengers annually, Great Southern Railway is a leading provider of long distance rail services in Australia and the owner of the country's three celebrated tourist trains, The Indian Pacific, The Ghan and The Overland. The company also operates its 'Trainways' programme of holiday packages that include rail travel, accommodation, tours and one-way air tickets.

The Ghan runs twice-weekly from Sydney, Melbourne and Adelaide to Alice Springs, in Australia's heartland. Three classes of accommodation are provided: Gold Kangaroo, with private sleeping cabins and en suite facilities; Red Kangaroo Sleeper, with shared twin sleeping accommodation and private washing facilities; and Red Kangaroo Daynighter, providing reclining seat accommodation. Dining and lounge cars are provided for Gold and Red Kangaroo services. The Ghan is to be extended to Darwin when the rail link from Alice Springs is completed in 2004.

The twice-weekly Indian Pacific runs 4,352 km from Perth to Sydney via the Nullarbor Plain and Adelaide, with accommodation provided in two classes, Gold Kangaroo and Red Kangaroo and restaurant, bar and sleeping facilities.

The Overland is operated four times a week in each direction between Adelaide and Melbourne, running during daytime from Adelaide and overnight from Melbourne. Gold and Red Kangaroo levels of service are provided.

*GSR's 'Indian Pacific' service passes Parramatta, Sydney, hauled by a National Rail NR Class locomotive (Brian Webber)* 2002/0121167

### Traction and rolling stock
GSR is the owner of 111 passenger cars and 14 motorail wagons, which are maintained under contract by United Goninan.

The company does not own any locomotives: traction is hired from Pacific National (formerly National Rail Corporation) and primarily consists of 2,984 kW NR Class machines, but with limited use of 2,238 kW BL Class locomotives on The Overland.

### Track
GSR does not own any track. Track access fees are paid to Australian Rail Track Corporation (South Australia and Victoria), Rail Infrastructure Corporation (New South Wales) and WestNet Rail (Western Australia).

*UPDATED*

---

## Hamersley Iron Ore Railway

PO Box 21, Dampier, Western Australia 6713
Tel: (+61 8) 91 43 63 00   Fax: (+61 8) 91 43 63 45
e-mail: alan.watling@hi.riotinto.com.au

### Key personnel
General Manager: G Rowley
Manager, Railway Operations: A Watling

Gauge: 1,435 mm
Route length: 638 km

### Organisation
The railway operates solely to convey iron ore from the mines to the port at Dampier in the remote Pilbara area of Western Australia. The original section of 280 km to Mount Tom Price opened in 1966, with the line being extended a further 100 km to Paraburdoo in 1972. Since then 56 km have been duplicated and a 40 km spur was constructed to serve Brockman Mine in 1991. In 1994, another spur line was constructed to a new mine at Marandoo.

The parent mining operation, Hamersley Iron, is a wholly owned subsidiary of Rio Tinto.

Hamersley has reached an agreement with the Robe River Iron Associates joint venture for use of its rail infrastructure. A new Pilbara Rail Company will operate and maintain the rail assets of both companies. Instead of Robe River having to build a separate parallel line to West Angelas, Hamersley's line will be used, with about 50 km of additional dual track added, increasing efficiency.

### Freight operations
Trains from the mines at Tom Price, Brockman and Marandoo consist of two diesel-electric locomotives hauling 226 wagons each of 105 tonnes nominal capacity. This results in gross train weights of 29,000 tonnes. Wagons are coupled in pairs by a solid drawbar with rotary couplings connecting each pair. A train is approximately 2.3 km in length and is the heaviest and longest employing head-end locomotive power operating anywhere in the world. The main line configuration permits following train movements at 15 minutes headway.

The maximum opposing grade to loaded trains on the Mount Tom Price to Dampier section is 0.33 per cent whilst empty trains returning to the mine negotiate a maximum adverse grade of 2 per cent. These grades and the gross loads of trains permit an exact balance of locomotive power. On the Mount Tom Price to Paraburdoo section, there is a constant compensated grade of 0.42 per cent against the loaded trains. Three banker locomotives are required by loaded trains for the 100 km journey between Paraburdoo and Mount Tom Price to overcome this adverse grade. At Dampier, trains are unloaded in rotary dumpers at either the Parker Point or the Ell terminal. At Parker Point pairs of wagons are uncoupled from the train prior to dumping.

When the tare weights of wagons and work trains are added, the single-line railway sees about 85 million tonnes of traffic annually, making it one of the heaviest tonnage single-line railways in the world.

While tonnages hauled over recent years have shown small falls due to export contract variations, contracts signed recently will see higher tonnages hauled in future years.

| Traffic | 1997 | 1998 | 1999 |
|---|---|---|---|
| Freight tonnes (million) | 57.3 | 56.6 | 55.4 |

### New lines
A new branch leaving the main line at Rosella, 250 km from the port of Dampier, has been opened to a new mine at Marandoo. The branch is currently 60 km long but work was under way on a 145 km extension towards a new mine at Yandicoogina.

### Traction and rolling stock
A fleet comprising 29 main line diesel locomotives, 2,430 ore wagons and 126 maintenance vehicles is available. The General Electric Dash 9 locomotives, the most

*Dash 9 locomotives on loaded and empty trains at Dampier (Wolfram Veith)* 2002/0121168

powerful in Australia, have microwave ovens and CD players for crew comfort.

The company sold five SD50 and three C36-7 redundant locomotives to USA leasing company NRE.

To cater for increased projected tonnages, the company is purchasing 240 iron ore wagons from Bradken for A$25 million, with delivery from September 2000.

### Signalling and telecommunications

A Centralised Traffic Control (CTC) system, using motorised point operations and block signalling, controls traffic. Radio communication is maintained with train crews and track personnel and provides an emergency back-up service should the CTC fail. The communication system consists of a microwave bearer and UHF mobiles.

Hamersley Iron, in conjunction with Union Switch Co and AT Signal Systems of Sweden, is currently installing a cab signalling system to replace lineside signals. This will be the first entirely cab-signalled system in Australia and will control trains on about 600 km of track.

### Track

The main line is predominantly single-track with passing sidings at approximately 20 km intervals. Heavy-duty 68 kg/m rail, continuously welded, is used throughout, with alloy and head-hardened steels utilised for high-wearing curve sections.

**Rail:** 68 kg/m
**Crossties (sleepers):** Concrete, 2,590 × 265 × 211 mm
**Spacing:** 1,640/km + 1,539/km

### Diesel locomotives

| Class | Wheel arrangement | Power kW | Speed km/h | Weight tonnes | No in service | First built | Mechanical | Builders Engine | Transmission |
|---|---|---|---|---|---|---|---|---|---|
| Dash 9 | Co-Co | 3,280 | 80 | 197 | 29 | 1995 | GE | GE7FDL16 | E GE |

**Fastenings:** Pandrol clips
**Max speeds**
Loaded train 80 km/h
Empty train 70 km/h
Freight train 80 km/h
Light engines 100 km/h
**Max gradients**
Against empty 2.03%
Against loaded ex-Tom Price 0.33%
Against loaded ex-Paraburdoo 0.42%
**Max altitude:** About 750 m near Tom Price

*UPDATED*

---

## National Rail Corporation Ltd (NR)

PO Box 1419, Parramatta, New South Wales 2124
Tel: (+61 2) 96 85 25 55   Fax: (+61 2) 96 87 18 08
e-mail: information@nrc.com.au
Web: http://www.nationalrail.com.au

### Key personnel

Chairman: Peter Young
Managing Director: Vince Graham
Company Secretary: Ian Roxburgh
Chief Financial Officer: Aidan Hughes
Chief Operating Officer: John Fullerton

Gauge: 1,435 mm; 1,600 mm
Route access: Rail Access Corporation (New South Wales) – 2,865 km; ARTC (Victoria, South Australia, Western Australia) – 4,490 km; QR (Queensland) – 131 km; Westnet (West of Kalgoorlie, Western Australia) – 710 km

### Political background

National Rail Corporation Ltd was formed in September 1991 to create a competitive and commercially viable rail freight business. Its shareholders are the Commonwealth Government of Australia and the states of New South Wales and Victoria. The company commenced commercial operations in April 1993.

The company took over all of the interstate rail freight business conducted by five separate state-based rail authorities, including the assets predominantly used in that business.

The company purchases access to track owned by five rail authorities and obtains a large part of its business through freight forwarding companies. It is legally prevented under its memorandum of association from carrying interstate rail freight in any state without the approval of the relevant state government.

At the end of January 2002, the Australian government announced that NR was to be sold to National Rail Consortium Pty Ltd (NRC Pty) in a combined sale with FreightCorp (qv). The value of the transaction, which was completed at the end of February 2002, was A$1.172 billion. NRC Pty is owned jointly by Lang Corporation and Toll Holdings. The company announced plans to upgrade the Melbourne–Perth via Parkes line to accommodate trains of double-stack containers and to reduce journey times between Sydney and Brisbane, subject to the conclusion of track access arrangements with Australian Rail Track Corporation.

### Organisation

NR uses its own employees to operate its own intermodal terminals and trains, using wagons and locomotives it owns, leases or hires. Access to track is obtained through contracts with authorities owned by state and commonwealth governments, which also provide all train control. Having begun operations in 1993, NR is now the country's largest carrier of long-distance freight by rail.

The number of employees is around 1,200. By 1999, driver-only operation of shunting locomotives and some shortline-haul tasks had commenced.

| Finance (A$ million) | 1997-98 | 1998-99 | 1999-2000 |
|---|---|---|---|
| Revenue | 485.2 | 429.7 | 460 |
| Expenses | 505.6 | 465.7 | - |

*National Rail NR Class locomotives at Fisherman Islands (Brian Webber)*   2002/0121169

### Diesel locomotives

| Class | Builder's type | Wheel arrangement | Power kW | Speed km/h | Weight tonnes | No in service | First built | Mechanical | Builders Engine | Transmission |
|---|---|---|---|---|---|---|---|---|---|---|
| BL | JT26C-2SS | Co-Co | 2,240 | 150 | 128 | 10 | 1983 | Clyde | GM 16-645E3B | E GM |
| 81 | JT26C-2SS | Co-Co | 2,240 | 133 | 129 | 13 | 1982 | Clyde | GM 16-645E3B | E GM |
| C | GT26C | Co-Co | 2,240 | 133 | 132 | 2* | 1977 | Clyde | GM 16-645E3 | E GM |
| DL | AT42C | Co-Co | 2,240 | 150 | 122 | 14 | 1988 | Clyde | GM 12-710 G3A | E GM |
| AN | JT46C | Co-Co | 2,860 | 150 | 130 | 9 | 1992 | Clyde | GM 16-710 G3A | E GM |
| NR | CV40-9i | Co-Co | 3,000 | 115 | 132 | 120 | 1996 | Goninan | GE 7FDL-16 | E GE |

* 8 C Class locomotives are in storage

### Passenger operations

While NR does not operate passenger services, its locomotives are seen at the head of Great Southern Railways' (qv) interstate 'Indian Pacific', 'Ghan' and 'Overland' services as NR provides 'hook and pull' services for GSR.

### Freight operations

In 1999-2000, NR achieved 16.2 billion net tonne-km, an increase of 7.3 per cent on the previous year. The completion of the Melbourne–Adelaide standard-gauge link has enabled diversion of most freight trains from Sydney to the west from running via Broken Hill to the route via Melbourne. Only five freights a week each way now run via Broken Hill. Two trains a day service Whyalla and a daily concentrate train runs from Broken Hill to Port Pirie. NR's market share ranges between 15 per cent on the Sydney–Melbourne route to 40 per cent on the long-haul east coast–Perth corridor (across the Nullarbor Plain).

NR increased coal traffic between Hunter Valley mines and power stations from 1.4 million tonnes in 1999/2000 to 3 million tonnes in 2000/2001. The trains are unusual in that they operate in push/pull mode to facilitate reversals at trailing junctions.

NR has signed a contract with BHP worth A$1.5 billion over eight and a half years to provide transport between manufacturing and distribution centres. A daily train of blue metal is now provided from Dunmore Quarry, south of Sydney, to Cooks River, Sydney.

The heaviest train yet run was a Broken Hill–Port Pirie ore train of 9,320 tonnes with one NR and two AN locomotives hauling 120 wagons.

Following improvements to track, speeds on the Melbourne–Adelaide link have increased and 21 tonne axleloads are now allowed. Maximum train length on that route is now 1,500 m with loads to 5,000 tonnes.

Between Adelaide and Perth, clearances have been improved to 6.7 m to enable the regular double-stacking of containers on well wagons. On this route, NR now has competition from Patrick Stevedores, Specialized Container Transport (qv) and Toll Rail.

NR trains up to 1,800 m long are now operating in the east-west corridor and trains up to 1,300 m in the north-south corridor. Infrastructure improvements to permit 1,500 m operations are progressing.

A large challenge in 2000 was the rescheduling of services in the Sydney area during the Olympic Games period so that CityRail passenger services could have total track occupancy at appropriate times. NR was allowed to operate trains only between 01.00 and 04.00 for three weeks. Extra locomotives were added to all services in the Sydney district to cover any failures.

| Traffic (million) | 1997 | 1998 | 1999 |
|---|---|---|---|
| Freight tonnes | 9.4 | 9.3 | 8.4 |

### Intermodal operations

In 2001, NR was carrying some 600,000 containers annually.

New business initiatives have had promising results on the east coast. A service operated jointly with Queensland Rail, NQ Direct, provides excellent connections for freight to and from far north Queensland. Since the start up of a new faster timetable, total TEUs carried by this service have more than tripled.

The Internet-based FreightWeb e-commerce system, on line since August 1997, is a first for rail in Australia. FreightWeb provides customers with secure access to book and trace containers across the network, and has received strong market acceptance.

*SeaTrain*
Four weekly SeaTrain container services run between Brisbane and Sydney port areas. Mayne Logistics (Boxcar) now gives all its business to NR.

*Trailerail*
Trailerail has been operated by NR since 1 July 1996. This unit's freight is carried in road/rail trailers of three types: dry or refrigerated pantechnicons or curtain-sided trailers. Two trains are operated weekly between Melbourne, Adelaide and Perth and return, offering services which compete directly with road transport. NR introduced a Sydney–Perth service in February 1999.

### Improvements to existing lines
Although National Rail is not responsible for track conditions, the operator has benefited by the continued reduction in the number of speed restrictions across the standard-gauge network. A new Y connection at Parkes, New South Wales, which cost only A$2 million, has resulted in substantial time savings, sometimes of up to three hours.

A new operating yard to accommodate 1,500 m trains was opened adjacent to Sydney freight terminal in time for the 2000 Olympic Games. The A$15 million project provided stabling for three trains.

NR reports that track access reliability (percentage of trains exiting on time that entered each authority's network on time) was only 59 per cent in late 1999.

### Traction and rolling stock
The NR Class locomotives have a fuel capacity of 12,500 litres, allowing them to run through between Brisbane and Melbourne at 115 km/h, where track permits. One locomotive can haul 1,780 tonnes in Victoria. The type features a variable horsepower system which allows drivers to conserve fuel when the locomotives are running on sections not requiring full power or with light loads. Crews participate in a competition aimed at minimising fuel consumption.

Supplementing the NR Class now are some 81, AN, BL, and DL Class locomotives used as trailing or shunting units. Four BL Class are used on broad gauge for Long Island (Melbourne area) steel traffic.

NR purchased 32 120 tonne coal wagons from Adtranz for a Macquarie Generation contract in the Hunter Valley of New South Wales. The operator has also spent A$10 million for 73 wagons of three permanently coupled skeletal platforms to haul steel products, from ANI Engineering, Mittagong, New South Wales.

NR Class maintenance is contracted to Goninan, which provides all services except refuelling throughout Australia. Each locomotive visits the Spotswood, Melbourne maintenance depot every 122 days, and continuous computer links to the locomotives provide diagnostic analysis.

In total 4,602 freight wagons are available within NR's fleet. A fleet of 150 new articulated skeletal '5-Pack' wagons is now in service. The award-winning design is claimed by NR to be the lightest of its type in the world, exceeding North American best practice for container transport.

NR has also introduced a triple-deck two-pack fully enclosed Type RMEY wagon which carries 27 cars. The company expects to haul 23,000 cars annually between Adelaide and Perth.

### Signalling and telecommunications
Train control and signalling functions are provided by the owners of track on which NR trains operate.

NR's need to monitor its train operations across all mainland Australian states has seen the use of mobile telephones pioneered for communication between locomotives and the company's control centre. NR has also developed a truly national train radio system, which provides transparent and seamless communication across all states and track owners.

A computer system is being installed to enhance further NR's ability to track its trains and customers' freight and to manage freight resources. Supported by AEI readers in and near terminals, the system will handle operational train and marshalling yard management, as well as locomotive and wagon deployment and management.

**UPDATED**

---

## Northern Rivers Railroad Pty Ltd (NRR)
9 Armada Crescent, Currumbin Waters, Queensland 4223
Tel: (+61 7) 55 98 60 99   Fax (+61 7) 55 98 60 88
e-mail: nrrail@bigpond.com.au
Web: http://www.northernriversrailroad.com.au
   http://www.ritzrail.com.au

### Key personnel
General Manager: Warren Judd

Gauge: 1,435 mm

### Organisation
Northern Rivers Railroad Pty Ltd is a private company incorporated on 1 July 1996. As well as haulage operations, the company has won a contract to maintain certain FreightCorp wagons and to provide 'rescue' facilities to operators in northern New South Wales.

### Passenger operations
NRR introduced a tourist passenger service, known as Ritz Rail, from April 1999. Services operate from Murwillumbah at weekends and at other times, often in conjunction with horse race meetings or local festivals. Annual trips venture interstate to Brisbane, Queensland.

### Freight operations
The company has formed a strategic alliance with FreightCorp to provide services to that organisation. NRR commenced operations in September 1997 when it took over haulage of existing fly ash traffic between Grafton and Murwillumbah, and cement traffic to Old Casino. A freight train operates several days weekly. The company intends to develop a freight service from Northern New South Wales across the state border to Brisbane.

This was the first privately operated service under the new Rail Access regime, although NRR was operating by arrangement with FreightCorp.

### Traction and rolling stock
The company owns four ex-NSWSRA 421 Class GM 1,850 hp locomotives and 10 carriages. It also offers train maintenance and restoration services under contract.

*Two NRR 421 Class locomotives on a Ritz Rail service near Bangalow (Brian Webber)* 2002/0121170

NRR has also acquired and renovated locomotive 42206 from FreightCorp (qv) for Ritz Rail services and to release its 421 Class locomotives for freight tasks. By 2001 it had also purchased four additional second-hand locomotives for restoration and anticipated hire to other operators.

### Track
The company operates by agreement over the tracks of others.

**UPDATED**

---

## QR
PO Box 1429, 305 Edward St, Brisbane, Queensland 4001
Tel: (+61 7) 32 35 22 22   Fax: (+61 7) 32 35 17 99
e-mail: qrati.bit.net.au
Web: http://www.qr.com.au

### Key personnel
Chairman, Railways Board: Bronwyn Morris
Chief Executive: Bob Scheuber
General Managers:
  Passenger Services: Mike Scanlan
  Coal and Freight Services: David George
  Infrastructure Services: Tony Drake
  Network Access: Steve Cantwell
  Workshops: Brian Bock
  Corporate Services: Michael Goode

Gauge: 1,435 mm (interstate line); 1,067 mm; dual-gauge
Route length (owned): 99 km; 9,072 km; 35 km. An additional 293 km of 1,067 mm gauge route see no services
Route length (not owned): 35 km of 1,067 mm gauge; 875 km of 1,435 mm gauge
Electrification: 1,877 route-km; 2,453 track-km of 1,067 mm gauge at 25 kV 50 Hz AC

### Political background
QR is a government-owned corporation established under the state Queensland Transport Infrastructure Act. All shares are held on behalf of the state by the state Treasurer and the Minister for Transport and Main Roads. Of the 12 members of the government-appointed QR board, 11 were new in 1997.

### Organisation
QR is Australia's largest rail network and one of Australia's major transport businesses. The change of name from Queensland Rail has been introduced to reflect the company's future direction in not restricting its activities either to its home state or to Australia. Operations currently consist of the following groups: Coal and Main Line Freight; Metropolitan and Regional Services; Infrastructure Services; Network Access; Workshops; Business Services. This new structure has separated commercial operations from those dependent on government Community Service Obligation grants whilst remaining as one integrated organisation. It has also placed Network Access at arm's length from QR operator groups. QR will be able to invite the private sector to participate in joint venture operations, particularly where there are opportunities for expansion. QR intends to remain an integrated organisation keeping train operations and infrastructure together. Unlike other Australian railways, QR believes that, worldwide, this is the structure of the most successful operators.

QR has commenced running its prestige passenger service, Great South Pacific Express, outside the state and has indicated an interest in operating freight services outside Queensland when a suitable opportunity presents.

In June 2000, QR employed 14,728 staff.

# RAILWAY SYSTEMS/Australia

| Finance (A$ million) | 1997-98 | 1998-99 | 1999-2000 |
|---|---|---|---|
| Operating revenue | 1,895.5 | 1,902.1 | 2,347.3 |
| Profit before interest and tax | 542.8 | 422.4 | 439.7 |
| Profit after interest and tax | 187.3 | 104.2 | 186.0 |
| Dividend to government | 100.0 | 95.0 | 101.0 |

QR has a new financial structure and a requirement to pay income tax equivalent to the Queensland government.

## Passenger operations
*Citytrain (urban)*

QR operates eight suburban and three interurban routes in Brisbane and adjoining cities with most routes provided with half-hourly services. Patronage in 1999-2000 was 42.3 million journeys. About 150,000 people are carried each weekday with 4,848 services provided weekly. A new, more robust timetable has provided many stations with a 15 minute off-peak weekday service. Punctuality improved to 97 per cent on-time to within three minutes. Patronage on the newly opened Robina line serving the Gold Coast exceeded expectations, with 1.17 million boardings in the first full year.

QR has provided all stations with mini-computers and ticket vending machines, contributing to a 15 per cent increase in revenue.

Some 90 stations have been equipped with closed circuit television and 12 trains have been equipped with video surveillance cameras in an effort to combat anti-social behaviour. Each evening two or three services on each line are advertised as 'Guardian trains' and carry two security guards to improve passenger security and confidence.

Delivery of 30 sets of new SMU units has led to the withdrawal of locomotive-hauled sets, a feature of Brisbane region passenger services for over 100 years.

*Traveltrain (country)*

QR provides air conditioned passenger services between Brisbane and:
Rockhampton (622 km; 'Tilt Train' daily)
Cairns (1,654 km; 'Sunlander' three times weekly)
Cairns (1,654 km; 'Queenslander' weekly)
Townsville (1,319 km; 'Spirit of the Tropics' weekly)
Longreach (1,325 km; 'Spirit of the Outback' twice weekly)
Charleville (777 km; 'Westlander' twice weekly)
and between Townsville and
Mount Isa (977 km; 'Inlander' twice weekly).

These trains are enjoying an unprecedented resurgence in popularity. They carried 452,000 passengers in 1998-99.

Unlike most other Australian rail systems, which have scaled down long-distance passenger services because of increasing road and air competition, Traveltrain has upgraded rolling stock, focused on travel through scenic areas and actively marketed its products through its travel centres, travel agents and wholesalers.

A high-profile QR activity is the running of 15-carriage Kuranda Scenic Railway tourist trains from Cairns, ascending a range with spectacular views, 15 tunnels and passing two waterfalls. The two daily services carry about 450,000 passengers each year. The locomotives run freight services overnight.

The 'Savannahlander' railcar service, introduced in April 1995 between Mount Surprise and Forsayth, has been extended to start from Cairns. The 421 km tourist journey is spread over four days with stops along the way to view historic sites and wildlife and to handfeed rock-wallabies. Whilst patronage is low, the service brings tourists to a remote area in need of the assistance.

The unique rail motor (built in 1950) called the 'Gulflander' continues to run its weekly 153 km service on the isolated Normanton—Croydon line, attracting tourists to the remote Gulf of Carpentaria region.

The two electric Tilt Trains commenced running the daylight services between Brisbane and Rockhampton from November 1998, replacing ICE units which have been cascaded to Citytrain Nambour line services. Additional Tilt Train services between Brisbane and Bundaberg commenced in July 1999. The services operated by the Tilt Trains have proved very popular and even resulted in competing airlines reducing their fares. A Tilt Train servicing depot has been established at Gracemere, near Rockhampton. Contracts have been signed for two diesel Tilt Trains to run between Brisbane and Cairns.

The prestigious A$35 million 'Great South Pacific Express' has celebrated a successful first year with travellers on the luxury train drawn mainly from USA, Japan and other overseas countries. It operates on 1,067 mm gauge between Brisbane, Proserpine for a Barrier Reef helicopter excursion, Cairns and Kuranda weekly and on 1,435 mm gauge (following a bogie change) between Brisbane and Canberra fortnightly.

| Passenger traffic Journeys (million) | 1997-98 | 1998-99 | 1999-2000 |
|---|---|---|---|
| Traveltrain | 0.84 | 0.90 | 1.04 |
| Citytrain | 39.9 | 41.1 | 42.3 |

## Freight operations
The general traffic wagon fleet has the capacity to haul three million tonnes of grain, 1.7 million tonnes of raw

*New SMU emu for Brisbane area services (Brian Webber)*

*QR Tilt Train at Beerburrum (Brian Webber)*

## Australia/RAILWAY SYSTEMS

*2300 and 2170 Class locomotives lead the 'Great South Pacific Express' at Murphy's Creek* (Brian Webber)
*2002*/0121171

*2800 Class locomotive on a containerised freight train near Bundaberg* (Brian Webber) *2002*/0121172

sugar and 800,000 head of cattle annually. QR is the only Australasian system now hauling cattle; 600,000 head are carried in most years.

With the recommencement of the Phosphate Hill project, QR is preparing to haul a million tonnes of fertiliser to the coast with a similar volume of acid being hauled west from Townsville.

New container terminals have been provided at Cloncurry and Ayr.

With the growth of coal exports, QR again hauled record tonnages during 1999-2000. For the first time, coal hauls exceeded 100 million tonnes in a year. The coal haul is expected to rise to 114 million tonnes in 2000-2001. New traffics include sulphuric acid between Mount Isa and Phosphate Hill and fertiliser from Phosphate Hill to Townsville.

| Freight traffic (millions) | 1997-98 | 1998-99 | 1999-2000 |
|---|---|---|---|
| **1,067 mm gauge** | | | |
| Tonnes carried | | | |
| Coal | 96.0 | 104.5 | 114.4 |
| Minerals | 5.6 | 7.4 | 7.5 |
| Other | 8.8 | 8.6 | 9.6 |
| Total | 110.4 | 120.5 | 131.5 |
| Gross tonne-km | 59,871 | 63,015 | 66,407 |

### New lines
Further development of Queensland coal and mineral deposits has prompted expansion of the existing network to service new mines and associated processing industries.

Pacific Coal has indicated it is to open a new coal mine at Hail Creek which will require a 52 km connection to QR's Goonyella line. Production should reach 5.5 million tonnes annually after four years. A 5.1 km branch was opened on 9 January 1999 from McArthur Mine to McArthur Junction for the movement of coal. The junction is near Coppabella on the electrified line west from Hay Point in central Queensland. A 7.2 km balloon loop has been provided for Sun Metals refinery near Townsville.

### Improvements to existing lines
*Citytrain network*
A fourth track has been provided between Mayne and Northgate, while a third track has also opened between Northgate and Lawnton which includes one 18-span and one six-span bridge.

Additional platforms and track have been provided at Park Road on Brisbane's Citytrain network at a cost of A$13 million. With bidirectional signalling from there to the central business district stations, it is now possible to run more peak hour services.

*Country network*
A turning triangle has been provided at Meadowvale, north of Bundaberg, to facilitate turning of the Tilt Trains.

A major regrading of the track at The Leap, north of Mackay, has been completed to enable a larger through load to be hauled.

A 7 km deviation has been completed on the Drummond Range (Central line) to improve the present 100 m radius curvature and reduce the grade.

Most coal lines have now been approved for 80 km/h operation by block trains and for 100 km/h when other trains run.

The 977 km line between Townsville and Mount Isa is being upgraded to allow increased axleloads (20 tonnes) and higher operating speeds (80 km/h for mineral trains). Works completed include the replacement or upgrading of bridges, steel resleepering of the 590 km between Hughenden and Mount Isa and commencement of heavy-duty turnouts to all main line loops. A programme to replace all timber sleepers between Townsville and Hughenden with prestressed concrete sleepers and to install heavier rail cascaded from other lines was completed by late 1998.

Tenders have been invited for a new passenger station at Townsville. Expected cost is A$24 million.

### Traction and rolling stock
QR's locomotive fleet at June 2000 comprised 328 diesel locomotives and 184 electric locomotives, while 11,474 (mainly coal and container) wagons and 1,261 service vehicles were available.

The passenger fleet comprised 407 urban emu cars, 12 Tilt Train cars and 203 Traveltrain locomotive-hauled coaches. On order in 2001 were five power cars for the air conditioned Traveltrain fleet to replace older vehicles.

The Maxi overhaul programme to upgrade and renumber locomotives as they pass through the workshops has seen the number of 2300 Class diesel-electric locomotives increase to 24.

The introduction of the 4000 Class has enabled the cascading of 2600 Class from Newlands coal hauls to general freight traffic following rebuilding, while displaced 2800 Class now run to Brisbane, releasing six 3900 Class electric locomotives to assist the increasing Blackwater area coal traffic.

Ten 2100 Class have been sold and shipped to FCAB, Chile.

*Newly built 4000 Class diesel-electric locomotive for coal and mineral haulage* (Brian Webber) *2001*/0099111

*Coal trains headed by QR's latest diesel type, the 4000 Class, and 3500 and 3300 Class electric locomotives at Callemondah* (Brian Webber)
*2002*/0121173

Thirty sets of improved SMU units have entered service on Brisbane Region passenger services, replacing the remaining locomotive-hauled sets.

An electric locomotive exceeded 200,000 km, while a diesel-electric exceeded 170,000 km, both in coal haulage, during 1998-99.

QR has changed from tippler emptying of coal wagons to bottom discharge. In addition, wagons are being converted to KWIK DROP doors to speed unloading at the ports.

One of the Tilt Trains was run up to 210 km/h on a special run on 23 May 1999. This broke the Australian speed record previously held by a standard-gauge Countrylink XPT. It is not a narrow-gauge world record but, with the train in standard condition (although certain overspeed controls were disconnected) and running on its normal track, it shows that the Tilt Train is world class.

A$122 million has been allocated to Walkers to design and build two seven-car diesel Tilt Trains which, like the two existing electric Tilt Trains, will be able to run at 160 km/h where track conditions permit.

Recently 400 new container flat wagons have been delivered and a further 319 existing wagons have been upgraded for heavier loads and 100 km/h running.

## Signalling and telecommunications

Safe-working systems in use are:
Remote-controlled signalling (CTC): 3,119 km
Train order: 6,382 km
Ordinary staff: 643 km
Electric staff: 75 km (1,435 mm line)

Radio is used extensively, with a UHF system on suburban electric stock providing continuous driver-to-control communications, VHF for driver wayside communications in country areas, a variety of UHF yard systems for shunting applications in major marshalling yards, and VHF and UHF car-to-base systems. All electric and most diesel locomotives are at least VHF radio-fitted and have direct access with train controllers while en route.

Centralised Traffic Control is in use between Brisbane and Townsville and between Ipswich and Toowoomba, allowing improved running times and withdrawal of employees from remote crossing loops. Train Order (by radio to the driver) has been introduced on many lightly trafficked lines. Direct Traffic Control, a train order type system involving computers on locomotives, was extended to the Cairns and Mareeba section during 1998. The impressive Universal Traffic Control, a PC-based signalling system for the Brisbane suburban area has been commissioned. It has allowed fewer staff to control 268 km of track, allowing for 1,916 routes with 1,069 signals and 669 points.

The former standard-gauge track between South Brisbane and Yeerongpilly has been relaid as dual gauge and equipped with computer-controlled signalling via a solid state interlocking, the first such installation on QR.

A$85 million is being spent providing a fibre optic cable along the 1,680 km North Coast line between Brisbane and Cairns.

QR has an agreement with a telecommunications company which uses QR's spare communications capacity.

## Electrification

Most Brisbane suburban services (over six million kilometres annually) are run by emus, while most passenger and freight services between Brisbane and Rockhampton are hauled by electric locomotives. Central Queensland coal services from the Blackwater and Goonyella areas are hauled by up to five electric locomotives, including two or three mid-train controlled by the driver with Locotrol remote equipment.

Several short sections have been electrified in connection with the opening of additional trackage and the McArthur branch.

*39 Class electric locomotive crosses the North Pine River with a livestock train (Brian Webber)*

## Track

Double track is provided in the Brisbane area between Caboolture and Helidon, Sandgate, Mitchelton, Ormeau and Manly, with further additional tracks between Lawnton and Lindum, Salisbury and Corinda. In Central Queensland, double track extends from Gladstone to Rocklands (112 km) and from Jilalan to Broadlea (130 km) with a few other shorter sections. In North Queensland, Nome to Townsville (20 km) is double track.

The Cairns—Mareeba branch and to Arriga (25 km further west) is being strengthened at a cost of A$13.2 million to allow 90 tonne locomotives to haul sugar juice; traffic started in 1999.

A A$42 million re-equipping of the on-track maintenance fleet is at an advanced stage with deliveries of three new high production continuous action tampers, ballast regulators, sleeper inserting machines and on-track welders. A new A$8 million 72 tonne rail grinder was supplied by Speno Australia in August 1997. QR estimates the Speno Star 40 M1 self-propelled rail grinder will save A$50 million in five years.

A new A$14 million Plasser ballast cleaning machine has been acquired. It weighs 245 tonnes empty and is 88.5 m long. The impressive machine is similar to units in use in Europe and the USA but is the first in the world on 1,067 mm gauge. With three ballast storage wagons, it represents the largest single contract for track maintenance machinery ever in Australia. It will be used on the Goonyella Line.

A major A$240 million programme to relay the Rockhampton—Townsville (702 km) section of the North Coast line with 60 kg/m rail on concrete sleepers has been started. Some 1.5 million sleepers and 310 turnouts will be required.

**Standard rail:** Flat bottom 60, 53, 50, 47, 41, 40, 31, 30 and 20 kg/m rail has been used throughout the state, dependent on line class. New construction has been standardised to 60 kg/m rail for heavy-haul lines, 50 kg/m as the normal main line standard and 41 kg/m for lighter trafficked lines.

**Joints:** 6-hole bar fishplates

**Welded rail:** Rails are purchased in 27.4 m lengths and flashbutt welded at depot into lengths up to 110 m. Long-welded rails are laid in lengths up to 220 m on unplated track and to unrestricted lengths on plated track. Heavy-haul lines and other lines with prestressed concrete sleepers are continuously welded. Site welding is generally by the thermite process though extensive work using a mobile flashbutt welding machine has been undertaken.

**Tracklaying:** Relaying of track is predominantly carried out by tracklaying machine. In 1997/98 170 km was relaid, well over budget, with the machine laying a record 12.63 km in one week. Some 350,000 prestressed concrete sleepers worth A$22.1 million are being inserted in the Townsville to Hughenden section over two years.

**Sleepers:** Mostly unimpregnated local hardwood timber 2,150 × 230 × 115 mm or 150 mm thick on the older heavy-haul lines. Prestressed concrete sleepers are used extensively for new construction including heavy-haul lines. Steel sleepers are being installed on a continuous face for over 450 km between Hughenden and Mount Isa and on shorter sections of other lines. They are also replacing timber sleepers on a 1 in 3 or 1 in 4 pattern for almost 1,000 km between Rockhampton and Cairns. Extensive installation of treated timber sleepers has also been undertaken in recent years.

**Sleeper spacing:** Normally 610 mm in main line or heavy-haul tracks for timber, 685 mm for concrete and steel

### Electric railcars

| Class | Cars per unit | Motor cars per unit | Motored axles/car | Power/motor kW | Speed km/h | Units in service | First built | Builders Mechanical | Electrical |
|---|---|---|---|---|---|---|---|---|---|
| 1979 emu | 3 | 2 | 4 | 135 | 100 | 68 | 1979 | Walkers | ASEA |
| 1982 emu | 3 | 1.5 | 4 | 135 | 100 | 20 | 1983 | Walkers | ASEA |
| 1988 ICE | 2 | 2 | 4 | 135 | 120 | 8* | 1988 | Walkers | ASEA |
| 1994 SMU | 3 | 2 | 4 | 180 | 100** | 42 | 1994 | Walkers | ABB |
| 1995 IMU | 3 | 2 | 4 | 180 | 140 | 14† | 1995 | Walkers | ABB |
| 1998 Tilt | 3 | 2 | 2 |  | 160 | 4 | 1998 | Walkers | ABB |

* plus 4 trailers  ** some 115 km/h  † includes four on order in 2001

### Electric locomotives

| Class | Wheel arrangement | Output kW | Speed km/h | Weight tonnes | No in service | First built | Builders Mechanical | Electrical |
|---|---|---|---|---|---|---|---|---|
| 3100/3200 | Bo-Bo-Bo | 2,900 | 80 | 110 | 84 | 1986 | Comeng | Hitachi/GEC |
| 3300/3400 | Bo-Bo-Bo | 2,900 | 80 | 113 | 22 | 1994 | Clyde | Hitachi/GEC |
| 3500/3600 | Bo-Bo-Bo | 2,900 | 80 | 110 | 50 | 1986 | Walkers/ASEA | ASEA/Clyde |
| 3900 | Bo-Bo-Bo | 2,900 | 100 | 110 | 29 | 1988 | Walkers/ASEA | ASEA/Clyde |

### Diesel locomotives

| Class | Builder's type | Wheel arrangement | Power kW | Speed km/h | Weight tonnes | No in service | First built | Builders Mechanical | Engine | Transmission |
|---|---|---|---|---|---|---|---|---|---|---|
| 1502 | G 22C | Co-Co | 1,119 | 80 | 91 | 10* | 1967 | Comeng/Clyde | GM 12-645 E | E EMD/Clyde |
| 1550 | GL 22C | Co-Co | 1,119 | 80 | 91 | 6 | 1975 | Comeng/Clyde | EMD 12-645 E | E EMD/Clyde |
| 2400 | GL 22C | Co-Co | 1,119 | 80 | 91 | 14 |  | Comeng/Clyde | EMD 12-645 E | E EMD/Clyde |
| 2450 | GL 22C | Co-Co | 1,119 | 80 | 91 | 9 |  | Comeng/Clyde | EMD 12-645 E | E EMD/Clyde |
| 2470 | GL 22C | Co-Co | 1,119 | 80 | 91 | 34 |  | Comeng/Clyde | EMD 12-645 E | E EMD/Clyde |
| 1700 | GL 8C | Co-Co | 652 | 80 | 60 | 4* | 1963 | Comeng/Clyde | EMD 8-557CR | E EMD/Clyde |
| 1720 | GL 18C | Co-Co | 746 | 80 | 62.5 | 44 | 1966 | Comeng/Clyde | EMD 8-645E | E Clyde |
| 2100 | GL 26C | Co-Co | 1,492 | 80 | 93-97 | 10 | 1970 | Comeng/Clyde | EMD 16-645E | E EMD/Clyde |
| 2130 | GL 26C | Co-Co | 1,492 | 80 | 93-97 | 9 | 1974 | Comeng/Clyde | EMD 16-645E | E EMD/Clyde |
| 2141 | GL 26C | Co-Co | 1,492 | 80 | 93-97 | 5 | 1973 | Comeng/Clyde | EMD 16-645E | E EMD/Clyde |
| 2150 | GL 26C | Co-Co | 1,492 | 80 | 93-97 | 5 | 1978 | Comeng/Clyde | EMD 16-645E | E EMD/Clyde |
| 2170 | GL 26C | Co-Co | 1,492 | 80 | 93-97 | 40 | 1982 | Comeng/Clyde | EMD 16-645E | E EMD/Clyde |
| 2300** | GL 22C | Co-Co | - | 80 | 97 | 39 | 1998 | Clyde/QR | EMD 12-645E | E EMD |
| 2600 | U 22C | Co-Co | 1,640 | 80 | 109 | 13 | 1983 | Goninan, Qld | GE FDL12 | E GE |
| 2800 | CM 30-8 | Co-Co | 2,240 | 110 | 117 | 50 | 1995 | Goninan, Qld | GE 7CDL12 | E GE |
| 4000 | GT 42CU | Co-Co | 2,260 | 100 | 120 | 38 | 2000 | Walkers/Clyde | EMD12N710G | E EMD/Siemens |

* stored   ** rebuilt from 1550/2400/2450/2470 Classes

Australia/**RAILWAY SYSTEMS** 35

**Fastenings:** Normal standard 16 mm square dogspikes and springspikes with 115 mm thick timber sleepers; 19 mm square dogspikes used with 150 mm thick timber sleepers and indirect fasteners on curves used on older heavy-haul lines. The use of elastic rail spikes has now been discontinued. Indirect fastenings are used with concrete and steel sleepers.
**Ballast:** Mainly crushed rock in new work but river gravel used on some branch lines
**Max curvature:** Generally minimum radius of 100 m though new construction to 300 m radius at least

**Max gradient:** Generally not exceeding 1 in 50, recently 1 in 90
**Max altitude:** 925 m at The Summit, Southern line
**Max permitted speed:** Freight trains – 80 km/h; long-distance passenger trains – 100 km/h for the 'Lander' services and 80 km/h for other services; suburban emus – 100 km/h; interurban ICE units – 120 km/h; interurban IMUs – 140 km/h. Tilt emus operate at 160 km/h where allowed on the North Coast line
**Max axleload:** 26 tonnes on some mineral lines, 20 tonnes on North Coast line and electrified tracks, 15.75 or 10.6 tonnes elsewhere

**Bridge loading:** All bridges on important lines can carry loading equivalent to Coopers E25-E30. Many equivalent to Coopers E35 and most new construction to this standard. Heavy-haul mineral lines have bridges built to carry Coopers E50 loading. QR's longest pre-stressed concrete bridge is the 856 m Coomera River bridge on the Gold Coast line, opened in 1996.
**Tunnels:** 51
**Electric railcars**

*Class Cars*

## Rail Access Corporation (New South Wales)

GPO Box 47, Level 16, 55 Market St, Sydney, New South Wales 2000
Tel: (+61 2) 92 24 30 00   Fax: (+61 2) 92 24 39 00

### Key personnel
Chief Executive Officer: John Cowling
Chief Financial Officer: Michael Taylor
Group General Managers
  Metropolitan Division: Jim Holt
  Freight Division: Peter Hicks
  Safety Division: Owen Henry

Gauge: 1,435 mm
Route length: 7,310 km
Track length: 8,797 km operational
Electrification: route length: 618 km, track length: 1,784 km at 1.5 kV DC overhead

### Political background
Following the further restructuring of government rail organisations after just five years of the previous structure, this organisation is now a division of Rail Infrastructure Corporation (NSW) (qv).

After a period when its track maintenance contracts were put out to open tender, the state government has now required that contracts be granted to RSA (qv).

### Organisation
The Corporation has five divisions: Assets, Finance, Marketing, Operations and Telecommunications. The Corporation owns essential rail-related infrastructure and facilitates the opening of the network to competition among train operators. It sets standards for operators and funds the upkeep of track. The Corporation employs about 350 staff.

The Assets Division is responsible for rail corridors (track, signals and communication equipment and overhead wiring) but not facilities required by one operator (for example station buildings). Construction and maintenance work was contracted initially with Rail Services Australia but this work is progressively to be put out to competitive tender.

The Marketing Division is required by the New South Wales government to generate adequate revenue to cover its operating costs. All train operators are guaranteed access to track on individually negotiated confidential pricing terms. Passenger trains have priority over freight trains. New freight operators have commenced running trains in New South Wales, an indication that the new Corporation is achieving one of its aims of encouraging new operators into the rail market. The government has also changed the law so that 'access purchasers', not only operators, can negotiate access with the Corporation.

At June 1999, RAC employed 392 staff.

### Finance
Revenue in 1998-99 was A$888 million, generating an operating profit of A$79 million.

### New lines
The Parramatta Rail Link involves construction of a new 29 km long line between Westmead/Parramatta on the Western line and Chatswood on the North Shore line. This A$15 billion project is to provide a passenger bypass of the lines through Sydney's central business district to relieve capacity constraints on the inner Western line. The new line, which will be mainly underground, will provide commuters with a direct link between the west of Sydney, the Macquarie Park business district and the Lower North Shore.

In 2001, the state government announced a four-year commitment to fund A$1 billion of rail improvements including a start of planning and preconstruction on the Chatswood–Epping section of the link to Parramatta.

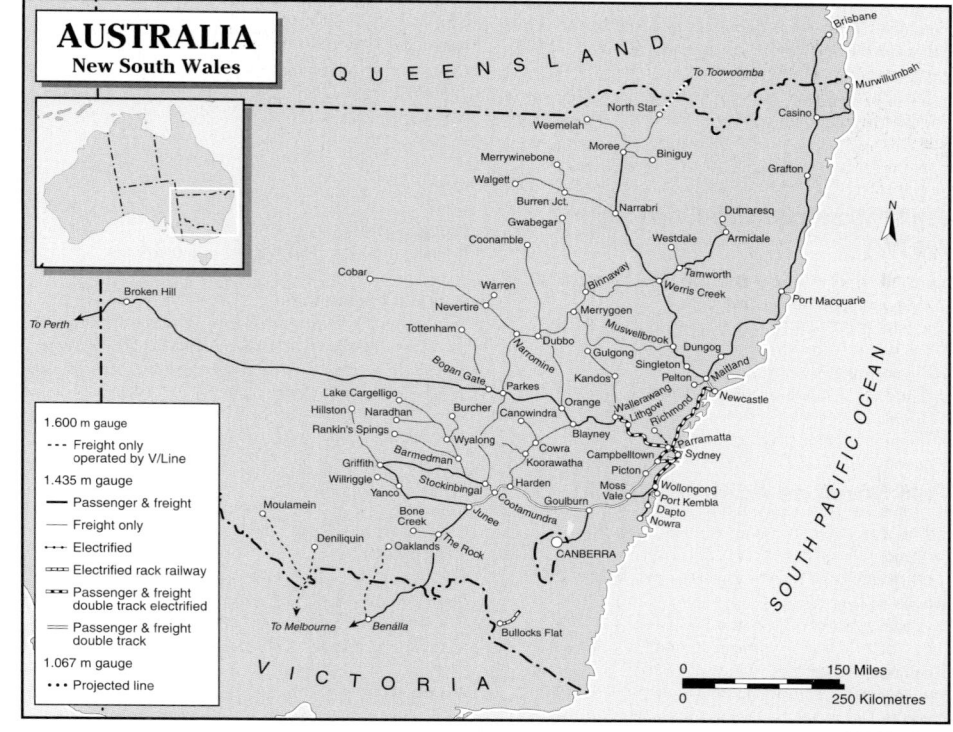

### Improvements to existing lines
An 1896 cast-iron lattice bridge over the Parramatta River on the suburban Carlingford branch has been replaced by a 199 m fully welded continuous truss bridge, the first in New South Wales.

Additional track and grade separation was provided between Flemington and Rhodes in Sydney's busy western suburbs area to enable segregation of freight and passenger services running between the west and north, easing one of Australia's worst rail bottlenecks.

A newly commissioned 6.6 km third bidirectional track between Glenfield and Ingleburn in Sydney's south-western suburbs provides paths for freight services amongst the heavy passenger traffic.

Several crossing loops on the North Coast line and south of Junee have been extended to about 1,500 m, and a new refuge loop is being provided at Cowan at cost of A$1.8 million to enable Sydney–Newcastle passenger services to overtake freights. Between Parkes and Broken Hill, trains 2 km in length are now allowed.

The NSW government has announced a A$273 million package to boost safety and reliability across the network. This funding package includes A$90 million additional for track maintenance, A$30 million to accelerate the amplification of track on the East Hills line between Turella and Kingsgrove in suburban Sydney, and A$25 million for an additional track on the Richmond line by 2002.

Station improvements are programmed at 19 stations.

After an expenditure of A$15 million, the Kandos–Gulgong connection was reopened but has found no regular traffic.

RAC is aiming to increase rail's freight market share from Sydney from 15 per cent to 25 per cent by 2008, which will require continuing expansion of the track network.

### Traction and rolling stock
The corporation has built 25 new ballast wagons at its Goulburn workshops, with an additional 25 to be built under an extended contract.

### Signalling and telecommunications
Signalling systems in use as at 31 December 1998 were:
Ordinary train staff: 2,915 km
Electric train staff: 1,350 km
Automatic track block: 1,805 km
Centralised traffic control (CTC): 1,000 km
Train order: 600 km
Manual block telegraph: 55 km.

Work in progress at that date included:
Upgrading of the busy suburban Hornsby and Blacktown signalboxes
Bidirectional signalling: Picton-Mittagong: 45 km
CTC: Mt Owen and Stratford balloon loops: 7 km.

Train-to-ground radio is being provided on 400 locomotives and 530 CityRail and Countrylink electric trainsets. A$22 million has been expended on improved train radio facilities.

A new screen-based PC operating system interlocking has been introduced between Wallerawang and Tarana (West line) where the previous double track has been singled following diversion of much of the route's freight traffic via the Southern line. The system was supplied by Union Switch and Signal, marking a change to North American practice from the British practice previously followed.

A significant improvement in train operation has resulted from the provision of bidirectional signalling between Cowan and Hawkesbury River on the North line. The section involves a steep climb with several tunnels.

Bidirectional signalling has been provided on both tracks between Heathcote and Helensburgh on the Illawarra line and between Branxton and Whittingham (22 km) in the Hunter Valley to facilitate maintenance and train operations.

Signalling renewals have been completed at Hornsby, a major northern suburbs junction and at Blacktown, a western suburbs junction, which now controls a new crossing loop at Clarendon, on the Richmond branch.

Train order working from Orange control centre has been introduced between Parkes and Broken Hill in the west, replacing staff and ticket working and reducing train running times by 75 minutes.

Train control operates from Sydney, Newcastle, Junee and Orange. The system uses most forms of safe-working

# RAILWAY SYSTEMS/Australia

from ordinary staff to train order and double line track block, as is appropriate for traffic levels. Surprisingly, there is no large signalling centre in Sydney.

## Electrification
Overhead extends from Newcastle in the north to Bowenfels in the west, Glenlee in the south and to Dapto, in the Illawarra. It is planned to extend electrification to the end of the Illawarra line at Nowra.

## Track
At the time of the reorganisation of the previous SRA all track maintenance was performed by the Authority's employees, with assistance from outside contractors and machinery suppliers as necessary. This maintenance task has been divided into 13 'bundles'. Each bundle is being progressively put to tender.

Double track extends from Muswellbrook (289 km) in the north to Junee (486 km) in the south, Wallerawang (171 km) in the west, and Unanderra (88 km) in the Illawarra. Quadruple (or more) track is provided between Newcastle and Maitland in the north, between Sydney and St Marys in the west and between Sydney and Hurstville (Illawarra Line).

A third track has been provided between Turella and Kingsgrove on the East Hills line in Sydney.

The Sydney Harbour bridge, though not owned by a rail company, has the longest span (503 m) of any railway bridge in Australia and carries the tracks 60 m above the water.

Concrete sleepers are being laid between Maitland and Muswellbrook; 54 km have been completed, with the remaining 18 km programmed for 1998/99.

**Rail:** Type to AS1085: 30, 36, 40, 47, 53 and 60 kg/m.
**Crossties (sleepers):** Timber or concrete, 230 × 130 × 2,440 mm, spaced 1,666/km in plain track, 1,818/km in curves.

**Fastenings:** Resilient
**Min curvature:** 160 m (10.9°)
**Max axleload:** 25 tonnes
**Max gradient:** 1 in 30 (3.3%)
**Spirals:** two, at Bethungra (South line) and at Border Loop (North Coast)
**Highest altitude:** 1,092 m at Bell (Western line)
**Longest single-track tunnel:** Cox's Gap, 2.03 km
**Longest double-track tunnel:** Woy Woy, 1.8 km
**Longest bridge:** Hawkesbury River, 843 m
**Recent bridge standard:** Coopers E60
**Bridges:** about 1,700, totalling about 22 km

*UPDATED*

## Rail Infrastructure Corporation (NSW)

Level 14, Pacific Power Building, 201 Elizabeth Street, Sydney, New South Wales 2000
Tel: (+61 2) 92 24 37 02   Fax: (+61 2) 92 24 39 00

### Key personnel
Acting Chief Executive Officer: John Cowling

Gauge: 1,435 mm
Route length: 7,310 km

### Political background
This corporation commenced operations in January 2001 and is a merger of Rail Services Australia and Rail Access Corporation, which remain as divisions, and a new division, Safety, Standards and Safeworking. It operates and maintains the NSW rail network on behalf of the state government and grants access to passenger and freight operators.

For details, refer to Rail Access Corporation and Rail Services Australia.

*NEW ENTRY*

## Rail Services Australia (RSA)

Locked box A4090, South Sydney, New South Wales 1235
Tel: (+61 2) 92 24 37 02   Fax: (+61 2) 92 24 26 00
e-mail: rsa@railservices.com.au
Web: http://www.railservices.com.au

### Key personnel
Chief Executive: Terry Ogg
Chief Financial Officer: Frank Morrison
General Managers
  Safety: Paul Poynton
  Workshops: Michael Peter
  Corporate Services: Irina White

### Political background
This corporatised Authority (of the New South Wales government) has been created as an independent unit following the restructure of the previous State Rail Authority from 1 July 1996.

Following corporatisation, RSA is better designed to operate under a more autonomous and commercial framework for competing in the open market. Corporatisation has also created a new framework of obligations and risks. Its major client, Rail Access Corporation, is also partner in Rail Infrastructure Corporation and all are owned by the New South Wales state government.

### Organisation
RSA provides track and infrastructure maintenance and rolling stock maintenance and construction services. It continues activities under way at June 1996 but is also free to compete for projects for other undertakings. RSA now looks beyond New South Wales for work and has already obtained a major contract with Indonesian Railways to recondition traction motors. The original workforce of 6,500 employed by the Authority has been reduced by a thousand as activities have passed to the private sector.

RSA has opened offices in Melbourne, Adelaide and Perth as it moves outside its home state.

The organisation is reinforcing safety as a primary focus with a policy of 'Zero Injuries Zero Incidents'.

### Finance
Following its first year as a statutory state-owned corporation, RSA made a profit of A$10.3 million. In the first year, new work worth A$98.5 million was won and the corporation now has contracts in all mainland states and also in Asia. Some 3,400 staff work directly on these contracts. The immediate challenges for the future are the financial viability of its workshop business and the reintroduction of competition for NSW rail infrastructure maintenance contracts.

### New lines
RSA was the successful tenderer for the fit-out (track, signalling and overhead) of the 10 km New Southern Railway between Sydney central business district and Sydney's airports.

RSA in a joint venture has also won a contract to design and construct 54 km of trackwork in Hong Kong.

### Improvements to existing lines
RSA has won a major contract outside its original state base to provide signal and communication maintenance for 3,585 km of track between Wolseley (Victoria/South Australia border) and Kalgoorlie, including the lines to Alice Springs and Broken Hill. The five year contract with Australian Rail Track Corporation (qv) is worth about A$30 million.

RSA was awarded a contract to maintain and enhance the signalling system on the Australian Rail Track Corporation's interstate track from the Victorian border with South Australia to Tarcoola in the far north of South Australia and Kalgoorlie in Western Australia.

RSA was also awarded a contract to upgrade and re-signal level crossings in Western Australia and won a contract to construct crossing loops in Victoria for the Australian Rail Track Corporation.

The Rail Access Corporation's Country North rail infrastructure contract was awarded to RSA in recognition of the major reforms undertaken since the beginning of the government's rail maintenance contestability moratorium.

RSA established commercial ventures with a number of compatible and strategically placed companies to complement its core competencies. For example, ventures have been formed with Leighton (Asia) for contracts in Hong Kong; Plasser and Theurer for mechanised track maintenance; Thiess Contractors for specific contracts in New South Wales; and Victoria and Transfield in New South Wales.

In a joint venture with Thiess Contractors, the Authority is responsible for infrastructure maintenance and management for Bayside Trains (qv) in Melbourne. The 15-year contract includes 533 km track, 118 stations, 207 route-km of traction overhead and 358 bridges.

### Traction and rolling stock
Fifty new NDFF class ballast wagons with pneumatically operated doors have been supplied by ABB Construction Pty Ltd at a cost of A$4.5 million to enable improved productivity during track upgrading. They were the first wagons to carry the new organisation's colour scheme. A 48 Class locomotive used to shunt at Chullora Workshops has also been painted in the Authority's colour scheme.

*UPDATED*

## Robe River Iron Associates (Railroad)

PO Box 21, Wickham, Western Australia 6720
Tel: (+61 8) 91 59 23 78   Fax: (+61 8) 91 59 24 08
e-mail: robe.railroad@north.com.au
Web: http://www.roberiver.com.au

### Key personnel
Manager, Operations: Derek Brown
Manager, Railroad: E E Girdler
Superintendent, Rail Operations and Track Maintenance:
  Lindsay Morrison

Gauge: 1,435 mm
Route length: 203 km

### Organisation
RRIA is an unincorporated joint venture widely regarded as the world's most cost-effective and reliable supplier of consistent quality iron ore. Joint venture participants are North Limited, which owns 53 per cent of the project and three Japanese companies. North Limited is fully owned by Rio Tinto.

### Freight operations
The railway provides transport of ore from Pannawonica to Cape Lambert port. Ore tonnage totalled a record 31.2 million tonnes in 1999-2000. The first haul was in August 1972 and the 400 millionth tonne was hauled in May 1997.

Single-operator trains of about 160 to 200 wagons travel between the mine and port in under four hours. The railway has the capacity to carry well over 32 million tonnes annually.

The railway operated Australia's longest train when it ran a 3.8 km long ore consist of 350 wagons controlled by one driver using Locotrol equipment to control remote locomotives. Seven GE Dash 8 locomotives were required, with a train configuration comprising: two locomotives, 120 wagons, two locomotives, 115 wagons, two locomotives, 115 wagons, one locomotive. Gross load was 45,465 tonnes and average speed was about 40 km/h.

### New lines
The mining company is planning a major new development at West Angelas, near Paraburdoo, which could require a 340 km line. An alternative that may be negotiated is joint use of Hamersley Iron Ore Railways track.

Development is taking place at a new West Angelas mine, which is expected to rail 7 million tonnes in 2002-03 increasing to 20 million tonnes within several years. Agreement has been reached with Hamersley Iron (qv) to use its track, with an additional 50 km of second track added. This will save A$220 million compared with RRIA building its own branch to the area. A new company, Pilbara Rail Company, will be formed to operate and maintain the rail assets of both companies. Should exports reach 15 million tonnes, then the Japanese venture partners can require an independent branch to be built.

### Improvements to existing lines
Replacement of timber with concrete sleepers throughout the main line was completed in 1991.

During 1992-93 the main line track was extended, a new loadout facility installed and a new rail yard constructed to service a new ore deposit.

### Traction and rolling stock
In 2000 the railroad used 12 General Electric Dash 8 CM40-8M 2,983 kW locomotives and six Alco/MLW M636 2,700 kW locomotives, 822 rotary dump gondola wagons and 21 service vehicles. In 2001, RRIA was purchasing 366 ore wagons from Bradken.

*Four Dash 8 locomotives lead a loaded iron ore train across the Hamersley Iron Ore Railway on the descent to Port Lambert (Wolfram Veith)*
*2002/0121174*

### Diesel locomotives

| Class | Wheel arrangement | Power kW | Speed km/h | Weight tonnes | No in service | First built | Builders Mechanical | Engine | Transmission |
|---|---|---|---|---|---|---|---|---|---|
| GE Dash 8 CM40-8M | Co-Co | 2,983 | 110 | 190 | 18 | - | GE | GE7FDL16 E | GE |

The new traffic from West Angelas mine will require eight new locomotives to supplement the existing fleet.

### Signalling and communications
Trains are controlled by train order using UHF radio.

**Couplers in standard use:** Fixed and rotary
**Braking in standard use:** Westinghouse air

### Track
Three crossing loops are provided in the 200 km between Mesa J load point and Cape Lambert port unloading centre.

**Standard rail:** Head-hardened 1,130 mpc 68 kg/m
**Crossties (sleepers):** Concrete 2,600 × 280 × 235 mm
**Spacing:** Concrete 1,538/km
**Fastenings:** Concrete, Mackay Safelock
**Min curvature radius:** 3°
**Max gradient:** 1.29% (empty); 0.50% (loaded)
**Max axleload:** 36 tonnes

*UPDATED*

## The Silverton Tramway Company Limited

Level 5, 99 St Kilda Road, Melbourne, Victoria 3004
Tel: (+61 3) 98 66 76 72   Fax: (+61 3) 98 66 76 41
e-mail: clements@silverton.net.au

### Key personnel
Managing Director: Graham Clements
Regional Managers:
  Parkes: Gerry Truswell
  Broken Hill: Doug Aikins

Gauge: 1,435 mm

### Organisation
Now a subsidiary of Transcorp Pty Ltd, the company originated as the connecting railways between Broken Hill (New South Wales) and Silverton (South Australia), hauling minerals and supplies for the mines of Broken Hill. With the conversion to standard gauge of the railway through Broken Hill, the company remained as a provider of shunting services in Broken Hill. With the governments of Australia allowing third-party operators onto the tracks of the government systems, Silverton has expanded its activities into the niche market of leasing of locomotives and wagons to other operators.

### Freight operations
The company is responsible to National Rail for a Cobar–Newcastle ore haul and containerised grain hauls from Lyngon.

### Traction and rolling stock
The company owns six 442 Class and ten 48 Class locomotives and 120 wagons.

*UPDATED*

## Specialized Container Transport

7 Westlink Court, Laverton, Victoria 3018
Tel: (+61 3) 99 31 53 33   Fax: (+61 3) 93 69 97 47
Web: http://www.sct.net.au

### Key personnel
Chairman: Peter J Smith
Chief Executive Officer: Martin A Svikis

Gauge: 1,435 mm

### Political background
Specialized Container Transport decided that it should operate its own trains after experiencing difficulties dealing with existing operators. It introduced a private weekly freight service between Melbourne, Adelaide and Perth in July 1995, breaking 100 years of government monopoly of rail services. Today it operates three weekly services between those three cities.

### Freight operations
Patronage has necessitated that trains be run three times each week. SCT built an A$9 million rail freight terminal in Perth in 1998; in 1999 a new terminal in Melbourne was commissioned at a cost of A$20 million and a A$7 million facility was opened in Adelaide in 2001.

SCT claims to have continually broken records, notably introducing Australia's first refrigerated rail service and achieving trailing loads of 4,400 tonnes in 53-wagon formations through the Adelaide Hills and 6,300 tonne 74-wagon trains elsewhere, operating at speeds of up to 110 km/h.

### Traction and rolling stock
SCT has purchased three H Class locos from Westrail for shunting at Forrestfield (Perth). The company has invested considerably in rolling stock, with a fleet of over 250 vehicles. Locomotives and crews are provided by other operators. SCT also has a substantial fleet of road vehicles in most states of Australia to complement its rail operations.

### Track
The company's trains operate by agreement over track managed by the Australian Rail Transport Corporation.

*UPDATED*

## State Rail Authority/SRA (New South Wales)

Level 2, Sydney Central Station, Sydney, New South Wales 2000
PO Box K349, Haymarket, New South Wales 1238
Tel: (+61 2) 93 79 30 00   Fax: (+61 2) 93 79 53 10
Web: http://www.staterail.nsw.gov.au

### Key personnel
Board Chairman: Michael Sexton
Chief Executive: Howard Lacy
Chief Operations Manager: Arthur Smith
General Managers
  Corporate Services: Dominic Staun
  Rail Development: Dick Day
  CityRail Stations: Bob Irving
  Countrylink: Gail Gregory
  Station Management: Kim Finnimore
  Management Review & Audit: David Spedding

Gauge: 1,435 mm

### Political background
On 1 July 1996, the New South Wales government initiated a reform programme to improve public transport services by separating the infrastructure and train management functions of the former State Rail Authority and establishing four separate entities.

From that date, SRA became responsible for the operation of all passenger services of the CityRail and Countrylink business units (qv) and retained those assets essential to its business, including rolling stock and stations.

All rail freight services were established under the separate FreightCorp organisation (qv); the Railway Services Authority (now Rail Services Australia) was established to supply goods and services to the rail industry including infrastructure, while the Rail Access

# RAILWAY SYSTEMS/Australia

Corporation became responsible for ownership and management of the New South Wales rail permanent way.

## Organisation
SRA employs approximately 8,900 staff. The revenue-raising businesses are supported by a corporate group which provides centralised services.

## Finance
In 1998/99, revenue was A$627.7 million, including a state government Community Service Obligation grant of A$483.7 million. An operating deficit of A$38.1 million after abnormal items resulted in a surplus of A$13.5 million.

## Passenger operations
Details of operations and traction and rolling stock appear under headings CityRail and Countrylink.

*UPDATED*

---

# Tasrail

Tasrail Services Pty Ltd
Trading name of Australian Transport Network (ATN)
PO Box 140, Newstead, Launceston, Tasmania 7250
Tel: (+61 3) 63 37 22 00   Fax: (+61 3) 63 37 22 10

### Key personnel
ATN Executive Manager: David Crispin
General Manager: Robert Evetts
Marketing Manager: Mike Ward
Operations Manager: Mark Rosner

Gauge: 1,067 mm
Track length: 890 km

## Political background
Tasrail was a component of Australian National (qv) which was auctioned in August 1997.

## Organisation
Tasrail was purchased by a consortium led by Wisconsin Central Transportation Corporation, Berkshire Partners, and Fay Richwhite and Company (of New Zealand), which has also bought into rail operations resulting from privatisation in New Zealand and the United Kingdom. The group paid A$22 million for the Tasmanian rail freight business including track and infrastructure, 30 locomotives, rolling stock and modern maintenance workshops. Ownership of Tasrail land passed to state government control to be leased to ATN.

A requirement of purchase was a commitment to spend A$20 million over four years improving track and rolling stock. The purchaser also will consider reopening the Burnie-Wiltshire line (northwest), last used in November 1996; and branches to Scottsdale (northeast), and beyond Boyer to Maydena.

ATN is a long-term investor committed to developing growth in transport businesses, with a six-point business strategy focusing on: customer service; revenue growth; upgrading the asset base; operational efficiency; motivating employees; and improving occupational health and safety.

The company intends to explore untapped rail freight opportunities to provide growth: pulp and paper, limestone, gypsum and agricultural supplies such as fertiliser have been identified as possible sources of traffic.

The new owners took over at midnight on 14 November 1997, commencing operations with 177 employees.

In April 1998 ATN acquired the Pasminco Emu Bay Railway for a purchase price of A$7.8 million.

## Freight operations
The island of Tasmania does not represent an ideal market for rail, as distances are short and there is little bulk traffic available. The distance between the two major cities, Hobart and Launceston, is only about 150 km. Additionally, the railway now competes with B-double trucks, which have been allowed to operate on the state's major roads.

Most trains require two or three locomotives, with most track seeing two or three trains on weekdays. About a third of the traffic is bulk cement from Railton. New workshop facilities for wagon and locomotive maintenance at East Tamar Junction, Launceston, were completed in September 1993, resulting in improvements in productivity and maintenance efficiency, and reducing delays in returning locomotives and rolling stock to traffic.

Prior to the sale of the company by AN, limestone traffic was lost to road competition, though it may have been unprofitable. Haulage of woodchip logs has also virtually ceased. This traffic was a major part of Tasrail's task for many years.

With the closing of the Hellyer Mine, traffic from the mine to Burnie along the former Emu Bay Railway ceased. The 11.5 km branch opened in April 1989 and closed in June 2000 after about 15 million tonnes had been hauled over it.

## New lines
A feasibility study is being conducted into construction of a 32 km branch line to serve a magnesium processing plant at West Takone in the northwest of the state.

The North Western line is likely to be reconstructed from Wiltshire to the former terminus at Smithton at a cost of A$20 million. The line was closed in 1987.

## Traction and rolling stock
Included in the purchase were 30 locomotives and nine GM locomotives have been provided from New Zealand to supplement the existing fleet.

*Tasrail Clyde/GM diesel-electric locomotive acquired from Tranz Rail, New Zealand, at East Tamar depot, Launceston (Brian Webber)* 0058615

### Diesel locomotives

| Class | Wheel arrangement | Power kW | Weight tonnes | No in service | First built | Builders Mechanical | Builders Engine | Transmission |
|---|---|---|---|---|---|---|---|---|
| 2150 | Bo-Bo | 597 | 58.4 | 2 | 1961 | TGR[1] | EE 6SRKT | E EE |
| 2140 | Co-Co | 1,339 | 89.5 | 6 | 1967 | EE, Rocklea | EE 12CSVT | E EE[2] |
| 2110 | Co-Co | 1,380 | 97.5 | 4 | 1972 | EE, Rocklea | EE 12CSVT 11 | E EE |
| 2114 | Co-Co | 1,752 | 97.5 | 5 | 1973 | EE, Rocklea | EE 12CSVT 111 | E EE |
| 2120 | Co-Co | 1,752 | 92 | 9 | 1973 | EE, Rocklea | EE 12CSVT 111 | E EE[3] |
| 2100 | Co-Co | 1,339 | | 1 | 1996 | EE, Rocklea | EE 12CSVT 111 | E EE[4] |
| 2101 | Co-Co | 1,339 | | 1 | 1997 | EE, Rocklea | EE 12CSVT 111 | E EE[4] |
| DH | Bo-Bo | 522 | | 11 | 1963 | Walkers | Caterpillar | H[5] |
| 22 | 0-6-0 | | | 1 | 1953 | Vulcan Drewry | | H[5] |
| 2000 | Co-Co | 1,119 | 91 | 5 | 1964 | Clyde | GM 12-645E | E EMD[6] |
| QR | Co-Co | 1,119 | 91 | 3 | 1964 | Clyde | GM 12-645E | E EMD[6] |
| DC | A1A-A1A | 1,230 | 82.75 | 1 | 1978 | Clyde | GM 12-645E | E EMD[6] |

[1] Tasmanian Government Railways, Launceston
[2] Acquired from Queensland Rail 1988
[3] Acquired from Queensland Rail 1987
[4] Rebuilt from 2120 Class
[5] Purchased with Emu Bay Railway
[6] From Tranz Rail (New Zealand)

Tasrail recently received from Tranz Rail, New Zealand, two D Class originally owned by Westrail. Unusually the Clyde-GM locomotives were to be fitted with overhauled English Electric traction motors before entering traffic.

Locomotives are often refuelled from road tankers during stabling periods at terminating stations.

There are about 610 wagons available for revenue traffic and another 60 for maintenance use. Twelve Tranz Rail container wagons were received from New Zealand.

## Signalling and communications
A communications upgrade has been completed, with cellular telephones and UHF radios now installed in all locomotives and track maintenance vehicles.

Train order safe-working was replaced in 2000 by the similar Track Warrant Control system.

## Track
The track west of Burnie sees no traffic following damage.

Tunnels: 3

*UPDATED*

---

# Toll

Level 8, 380 St Kilda Road, Melbourne, Victoria 3004
Tel: (+61 3) 96 94 28 88   Fax: (+61 3) 96 94 28 80
Web: http://www.toll.com.au

### Key personnel
Rail Business Managers
  Melbourne: David Fishburn
  Perth: Steve Gabovec
  Perth: Bill Jordan

## Organisation
Toll Ltd, formerly TNT, is one of Australia's major transport organisations. To complement its extensive road transport operations it introduced a private rail freight service between Melbourne and Perth in June 1996. The company wished to gain control of its customers' freight over the entire movement from pick-up to delivery.

## Freight operations
Toll operates a thrice-weekly freight service between Melbourne and Perth.

Toll plans to open dual-gauge terminals in Perth and Brisbane to provide seamless transfer of freight between the national standard-gauge network and local narrow-gauge trains.

## Traction and rolling stock
The company leases wagons, locomotives and crews from major rail operators.

*VERIFIED*

Australia/**RAILWAY SYSTEMS**

## TransAdelaide

136 North Terrace, Adelaide, South Australia 5000
Postal: GPO Box 2351, Adelaide, South Australia 5001
Tel: (+61 8) 82 18 22 59   Fax: (+61 8) 82 18 22 06
e-mail: Sandford.Jim@transadelaide.sa.gov.au
Web: http://www.transadelaide.sa.gov.au

### Key personnel
Minister for Transport: Hon Diana Laidlaw
General Manager: Roy Arnold

Gauge: 1,600 mm
Length: 119.63 route-km

### Political background
Following the dissolution of the State Transport Authority, TransAdelaide was launched on 4 July 1994. It operates bus, train and tram services under contract to the Passenger Transport Board, which has responsibility for policy and planning aspects of public transport. The state government's reform agenda requires a reduction of costs. To provide a more efficient, effective and responsive transit system, a competitive tendering process has been devised.

### Organisation
The Authority controls only the metropolitan passenger railway system of Adelaide. Some track is used by freight services to and from the country system as well as by suburban rail services.

At the end of December 1997 TransAdelaide employed 328 staff in railway operations.

### Passenger operations
The Authority operates five suburban rail routes serving 84 stations to termini at Outer Harbour, Gawler, Noarlunga, Grange and Belair, providing 30 minute off-peak/20 minute peak frequency railcar services. The contract for these services is for two years, with an option to renew for a further three years. The years of steady decline in public transport patronage in Adelaide, a city of about one million residents, has been arrested. A survey has revealed that school and tertiary level students form the largest group of travellers, with 60 per cent using rail services five days per week.

The Authority continues to encourage passengers to purchase tickets 'off-board' from licensed ticket vendors. However, in an acknowledgement that this is not convenient for all travellers, in 1996 TransAdelaide awarded a contract to Camms Systems Pty Ltd to manufacture 130 ticket vending machines for fitting to railcars. Only seven stations are staffed.

In 1996-97 on-time running reached 89 per cent to within three minutes and 96 per cent to within five minutes.

**Diesel railcars or multiple-units**

| Class | Cars per unit | Motor cars per unit | Power/car kW | Speed km/h | Vehicles in service | First built | Builders Mechanical | Engine | Transmission |
|---|---|---|---|---|---|---|---|---|---|
| 2000 | 2/3 | 1 | 395 × 2 | 130 | M12 | 1980 | Comeng | Cummins KTA 19R | H Voith |
| 2100 | 2/3 | 1 | - | - | T18 | 1980 | Comeng | - | - |
| 3000 | 1 | 1 | 354 | 100 | M30 | 1988 | Comeng/Clyde | MTU 12V 183 TER | E ABB |
| 3100 | 2 | 2 | 354 | 100 | M40 | 1988 | Comeng/Clyde | MTU 12V 183 TER | E ABB |

*Adelaide Central station, with 3000/3100 Class railcars (Marcel Vleugels)* 0010778

| Passenger traffic (million) | 1997-98 | 1998-99 | 1999-2000 |
|---|---|---|---|
| Journeys | 8.0 | 7.4 | 7.44 |

### Improvements to existing lines
TransAdelaide has accelerated work across its rail system to comply with the Disabled Discrimination Act. Work has focused on wheelchair access, ramps, platform condition, access to pedestrian mazeways, and new signage.

Following market research that revealed that one of the biggest issues concerning train customers is that of safety, TransAdelaide has employed an additional 44 Passenger Service Assistants to improve security and reduce fare evasion. A private security company provides guards on all services after 19.00. Three-quarters of the railcar fleet is now equipped with CCTV, with similar equipment also provided at many stations and stabling areas.

### Traction and rolling stock
In 2000, the fleet comprised 100 railcars. During 1995-96 railcars were equipped with ticket vending machines, security cameras and closed circuit TV to allow drivers to observe passengers boarding and alighting.

AGoninan & Co Ltd has been awarded a contract to maintain the railcar fleet.

### Signalling and telecommunications
The principal signalling system is CTC.

**Coupler in standard use:** Scharfenberg fully automatic

### Track
Between Adelaide and Woodville 17,000 gauge-convertible concrete sleepers were installed to replace aged timber sleepers at a cost of A$4 million. A further 15,000 sleepers are to be installed between Port Adelaide and Draper.

**Rail:** Australian Standard 47 kg/m (177 km); 53 kg/m (45 km)
**Crossties (sleepers):** Hardwood timber 2,800 × 260 × 130 mm; steel (BHP M7-5 section) 2,595 × 260 × 127/146 mm
**Spacing:** 1,335/km plain track and curves
**Fastenings:** 19 mm$^2$ dogspike with sleeper plates. Elastic fastenings on steel sleepers, points and crossings
**Min curvature radius:** 200 m
**Max gradient:** 1 in 45
**Max axleload:** 21 tonnes
**Max line speed:** 90 km/h

*UPDATED*

## V/Line Passenger

Transport House, 589 Collins Street, Melbourne, Victoria 3000
PO Box 5343BB, Melbourne, Victoria 3001
Tel: (+61 3) 96 19 88 81   Fax: (+61 3) 96 19 26 80

### Key personnel
Chief Executive Officer: Geoff Tighe

Gauge: 1,600 mm
Service network: 1,152 km

### Political background
When the government privatised V/Line Passenger, it was bought by National Express Group Australia, which also won the Bayside Trains contract (qv).

### Organisation
The 10-year contract will see a government subsidy of A$77.4 million in the first year reducing to A$49.3 million in the final year. The company has guaranteed investment of A$165 million over the term of the contract with A$158 million for new trains, A$1.5 million to upgrade existing trains and A$5.5 million to be spent on station facilities. The company plans to increase patronage by 74 per cent during the contract period.

V/Line Passenger employs 800 staff, including about 200 drivers.

### Finance
In 1998-99, revenue was A$164.6 million while expenditure was A$168.0 million. Fares cannot be increased above rate of inflation.

### Passenger operations
V/Line operates country passenger services between Melbourne and South Geelong, Ballarat, Bendigo, Echuca, Traralgon, Stony Point, Albury, Shepparton, and Swan Hill. Sprinter railcars work many services.

In 1998-99 passenger journeys totalled 7.3 million and trains ran about 6 million km. In 1997-98 the Sprinter railcars ran 2.1 million km and the locomotive-hauled trains ran 3.6 million km.

General station facelifts and upgrading of passenger facilities have been completed at 11 smaller country centres.

135 extra services were introduced from May 2000.

The state government has been negotiating with V/Line Passenger and other possible operators to reintroduce services on the Ararat, Bairnsdale, Leongatha and Mildura lines. All had passenger services in the past and the government is budgeting A$32.7 million

*V/Line Sprinter dmu and A Class locomotive at Melbourne Spencer Street (Brian Webber)* 2002/0121175

# RAILWAY SYSTEMS/Australia

to upgrade the track and A$12 million a year as a subsidy.

### Traction and rolling stock
The locomotive fleet comprises 41 units, all of Clyde/General Motors origin.

At 30 June 1998, V/Line used 151 passenger carriages, 22 Sprinter railcars, and owned an eight-car 1,435 mm gauge XPT train, which is used in a pool with Countrylink vehicles for Sydney–Melbourne services.

In November 2001, Bombardier Transportation signed a contract to build 29 two-car dmus, with an option for an additional 10 similar units. Deliveries are scheduled to take place between October 2004 and July 2006. The contract includes maintenance provision for 15 years.

**Diesel locomotives: 1,600 mm gauge**

| Class | Builder's type | Wheel arrangement | Power kW | Speed km/h | Weight tonnes | No in service | First built | Mechanical | Builders Engine | Transmission |
|---|---|---|---|---|---|---|---|---|---|---|
| A | AAT22C-2R | Co-Co | 1,840 | 115 | 121 | 4 | 1983* | Clyde | GM 12-645E3B | E GM |
| N | JT22C HC-2 | Co-Co | 1,840 | 115 | 124 | 25 | 1985 | Clyde | GM 12-645E3B | E GM |
| P | G18HB-R | Bo-Bo | 826 | 100 | 77 | 8 | 1984* | Clyde | GM 8-645E | E GM |
| Y | G-6B | Bo-Bo | 480 | 64 | 68 | 4 | 1963 | Clyde | GM 6-567C or 6-645E | E GM |

\* Rebuilt

**Diesel railcars: 1,600 mm gauge**

| Class | Cars per unit | Motored axles | Power/motor kW | Speed km/h | No in service | First built | Mechanical | Builders Engine | Transmission |
|---|---|---|---|---|---|---|---|---|---|
| Sprinter | 1 | 4 | 235 | 130 | 22 | 1993 | Goninan | Deutz | H Voith |

**UPDATED**

---

## Victorian Rail Track Corporation (VRT)

Level 17, Transport House, 589 Collins St, Melbourne, Victoria 3000
Tel: (+61 3) 96 19 88 50   Fax: (+61 3) 96 19 88 51

### Key personnel
Chairman: Tom Quirk
Chief Executive: John Sutton

Gauge: 1,600 mm; 1,435 mm
Route length: 4,582 km
Track length: 5,648 km

### Political background
In the reorganisation of Victoria's rail system, the VRT (also known as VicTrack Access) was created to provide arm's-length control of the state's track infrastructure excluding The Met system.

### Organisation
VRT commenced operations on 1 July 1997 as an independent business unit responsible for the provision of access to and asset management of the non-electrified rail infrastructure. It is intended that VRT remain in government ownership.

VRT's remit is that train control should become 'commercial and efficient', ultimately not requiring government funding. Ten operators had network access approval at the commencement of operations. The two-gauge issue is one for the organisation to contemplate. As a first step, the Victoria and Commonwealth governments agreed to bring their Wodonga–Kalgoorlie and Broken Hill–Kalgoorlie tracks under single management from mid-1998.

At 1 July 1997, the assets of the Corporation were valued at A$772 million.

### Improvements to existing lines
Former 1,600 mm gauge lines in the west of the state (Murtoa–Hopetoun; Dimboola–Yaapeet; Ararat–Portland), isolated by the standard-gauging of the Geelong–Adelaide route, have been converted to standard gauge at a cost of A$20.4 million to enable continued haulage of grain. Ararat–Maryborough (88 km) was converted to standard gauge in April 1996, while Maryborough–Dunolly (22 km) is to be dual-gauged. The former broad-gauge main line between Ballarat and Ararat now has siding status.

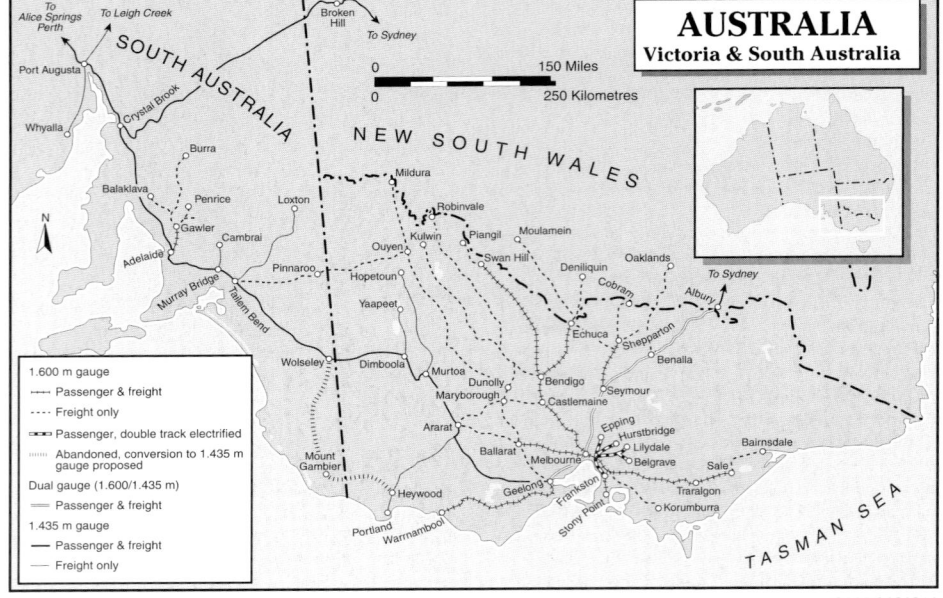

Redevelopment of Jolimont Yard (central Melbourne) is being undertaken, with 41 stabling sidings being removed, leaving 12 running lines realigned for 80 km/h operation.

Approval has been given for five standard-gauge crossing loops between Melbourne and Albury to be lengthened to 1,500 m to cater for the longer trains that constitute a full load for more powerful locomotives recently introduced.

A$30 million is being contributed by the Victorian government to electrify 6 km of track beyond St Albans, currently a terminus of Bayside/M > Trains (qv) suburban passenger service. An additional station is to be provided, while the existing Sydenham stations, served only by V/Line Bendigo line trains, will be replaced by a new station at a more convenient site adjacent to a new shopping centre.

Remedial work worth A$2.5 million has been programmed on the historic (1886) Melton Reservoir Viaduct, an iron superstructure on wrought-iron lattice piers, to enable speed to be raised from 80 km/h to 115 km/h and to extend its life by 25 years.

The 200 km Geelong–Warrnambool section has had its 47 kg rails welded.

### Signalling and communications
From August 1997, VRT took over responsibility for train control of services using its track.

Most of the V/Line system is controlled by a simple train order working system. Other systems in use are CTC (577 km), staff and ticket (336 km), automatic block signalling (322 km), electric staff (318 km), double line block (240 km) and automatic and track control (194 km).

### Track
The standard-gauge track between Albury, Melbourne and Wolseley sees between eight and ten daily freights, run by various operators, and one passenger service.

Melbourne–South Australian Border is 47 kg/m or 60 kg/m rail on timber or concrete sleepers. Speeds are more conservative than those allowed on other systems.

The 35-year-old standard-gauge line between Albury and Melbourne, with its 47 kg/m rail and old timber sleepers is worn out and costly to maintain. About 20 per cent of this line has been upgraded to current standards with 60 kg/m rail suitable for 25 tonne axleloads and 115 km/h speeds. About 170,000 sleepers are replaced annually.

Geelong line track circuits were altered in 1997 to allow 130 km/h running by Sprinters and 120 km/h operation by passenger trains (up from 115 km/h).

The country 1,600 mm gauge lines to Bendigo and Geelong and the suburban network are mainly double track.

*This track-recording car supplied by Plasser Australia is available to the 1,600 mm gauge network in Victoria (Brian Webber)*   0010780

**Standard rail:** Flat-bottomed 47, 53 and 60 kg/m rail rolled in 13.72 m lengths
**Crossties (sleepers)**
**Timber:** Non-treated Australian hardwoods (Red Gum, Ironbark, Box Stringbark and Messmate)
**Dimensions:** 1,600 mm gauge 2,705 × 250 × 125 mm; 1,435 mm gauge 2,590 × 250 × 125 mm
**Spacing:** 685 mm centres
**Concrete:** Prestressed concrete with cast-iron shoulders to take Pandrol rail clips
**Dimensions:** 2,670 × 275 × 145 mm at midspan (208 mm deep at ends). Rail seat canted at 1 in 20
**Spacing:** 670 mm centres
**Fastenings**
**Timber:** Most track fastened with dogspikes. Sleeper plates used on all tracks except 60 lb/yd branch lines, double-shouldered and canted at 1 in 20. 'Fair' deep bow one-piece rail anchors used instead of pads. Approximately 150 km of track relaid in 60 kg/m rail on rolled double-shoulder sleeper plates with Pandrol clips and three lock spikes per rail foot
**Concrete:** Pandrol rail clips, rail pads and insulators used on 53 and 60 kg/m rail laid on concrete sleepers
**Ballast:** Generally broken stone, usually basalt, but granite, rhyodicite and diabase also used. For rail lengths up to 27 m, 250 mm bearing depth with 50 mm shoulder width. For long or continuously welded rail, 300 mm deep with 405 mm shoulder width
**Trackwork design standards:** Curves of less than 2,400 m radius transitioned. Main line curves for 100 km/h traffic to be 830 m radius minimum, while for 50 km/h main line traffic minimum radius should be 400 m
**Welded rail:** Standard 13.72 m rail lengths welded into 27.5 to 82 m lengths at the central flashbutt welding depot, Spotswood. Once laid, rails Thermit-welded into 328 m lengths or continuously welded rail. Stress-control measures taken during field welding to ensure the continuously welded rail is in an unstressed condition within the temperature range of 33 to 38°C
**Maximum gradient**
**Main line:** 2.08% = 1 in 48
**Branch line:** 3.33% = 1 in 30
**Max speeds:** 130 km/h – Sprinter railcars, 115 km/h – locomotives
**Max axleload:** 22.6 tonnes
**Max altitude:** 591.3 m near Wallace, Melbourne—Ballarat line
**Longest straight:** 38.3 km between Glenorchy and Murtoa, Western line
**Tunnels:** 3

*UPDATED*

## West Coast Railway

The Victorian Railway Company Pty Ltd
PO Box 1936, Geelong, Victoria 3220
Level 3, 75-77 Moorabool Street, Geelong, Victoria 3220
Tel: (+61 3) 52 22 59 00  Fax: (+61 3) 52 22 59 66
e-mail: wcr@wcr.com.au
Web: http://www.wcr.com.au

### Key personnel
Director/General Manager, Corporate: Donald M Gibson
Director/General Manager, Operations, Rolling Stock and Maintenance: Gary McDonald

Gauge: 1,600 mm
Route km: 267 km

### Political background
In January 1993, the state government of Victoria called tenders for private operation of most of the long-distance passenger services throughout rural Victoria. West Coast Railway (the trading name of The Victorian Railway Company Pty Ltd) was the successful tenderer for the operation of the Melbourne—Geelong—Warrnambool service, becoming Victoria's first privately owned passenger rail service for more than a century. The contract is with the Department of Infrastructure, Victoria, and was initially for eight years from 1993. This was subsequently extended to 2004.
The French-owned company Connex has taken a 50 per cent share in the company.

### Finance
Government contracts prohibit publication of revenue statistics.

### Passenger operations
The railway provides the rail passenger service of 37 services weekly between Melbourne and Warrnambool, a distance of 267 km. Trains, usually comprising four or five vehicles, ran some 500,000 km and carried 324,000 passengers in 1999-2000, as well as 6,000 during special events. Passenger-km rose from 52.44 million in 1996-97 to 54.75 in 1997-98. Some 55 staff are employed, with drivers contracted from V/Line Freight but others directly employed in connection with new train operations, particularly steam-hauled excursions.

*A West Coast Railway service and a V/Line Sprinter dmu pass at Footscray (Brian Webber)* 2002/0121176

In addition to connecting with National Express Group Australia (V/Line Passenger) trains at Geelong and Melbourne, WCR trains connect with road coach services providing travel to locations throughout south-western Victoria and to Mount Gambier in South Australia.
The company also operates a locomotive and maintenance business at Ballarat East and Warrnambool. As part of that business, the company supplies on hire to other operators, locomotives, crews and heritage access to the network for historic trains by contract.

| Passenger traffic | 1999 | 2000 | 2001 |
|---|---|---|---|
| Passenger journeys | 321,000 | 319,000 | 310,300 |
| Passenger-km (millions) | 55.0 | 54.63 | 53.62 |

### Traction and rolling stock
West Coast Railway has purchased 13 diesel and four steam locomotives, 34 carriages, 12 luggage vans and seven freight wagons. Nine diesel locomotives and 19 carriages were available for service in 2000, plus two steam locomotives and three excursion cars. Maintenance staff carry out heavy maintenance and overhaul in workshops at Ballarat East, while a servicing facility has been established at Warrnambool where routine checks and the servicing of rolling stock occurs. Two North British-built R Class 4-6-4 steam locomotives have been rebuilt and introduced for tourist traffic.

### Signalling and telecommunications
Some safe-working and signalling duties are carried out by WCR staff at Colac, Camperdown and Winchelsea, and some by Freight Australia (the trading name of Freight Victoria Ltd) staff at Colac and Warrnambool. WCR employees staff stations at Winchelsea, Colac, Camperdown and Warrnambool. Train conductors carry mobile phones for emergency use. Fees are paid to Freight Australia and Bayside Trains (the trading name of National Express Group Australia Pty Ltd) for the use of their train control and for operation at their stations between Melbourne and Geelong.

### Track
West Coast Railway runs its trains over the tracks of Bayside Trains and Freight Australia (qv).
WCR has a heritage train access agreement with Freight Australia and Connex Group Australia Pty Ltd.

*UPDATED*

#### Diesel locomotives

| Class | Builder's type | Wheel arrangement | Power kW | Speed km/h | Weight tonnes | No in service | First built | Mechanical | Builders Engine | Transmission |
|---|---|---|---|---|---|---|---|---|---|---|
| B | ML2 | Co-Co | 1190/1120 | 133 | 123 | 3 | 1952 | Clyde | EMD16-567BC | E EMD |
| S | A7 | Co-Co | 1450/1340 | 133 | 123 | 3 | 1957 | Clyde | EMD 16-567C | E EMD |
| T | G8B | Bo-Bo | 710/650 | 100 | 70 | 3 | 1962 | Clyde | EMD 8-567CR | E EMD |

## Western Australian Government Railways

Westrail Centre, West Parade, Perth, Western Australia 6000
PO Box S1422, GPO Perth, Western Australia 6845
Tel: (+61 9) 83 26 22 22  Fax: (+61 9) 83 26 26 59
e-mail: westrail@westrail.wa.gov.au
Web: http://www.westrail.wa.gov.au

### Key personnel
Minister for Transport: Hon M J Criddle, MLC
Commissioner of Railways (Acting): G Wayne James
Urban Passenger: Hugh Smith
Finance Director: Dick Collister

### Political background
The Western Australian Government Railways Commission was established under the (State) Government Railways Act 1904. Westrail, the previously state government-owned freight operator in Western Australia, was privatised in December 2000 and its haulage task is now performed by the Australian Railroad Group Pty Ltd subsidiary, Australia Western Railroad (qv). The overview of track access is now performed by WestNet Rail (qv). Following the sale of the freight business, WAGR's remaining role is that of operator of passenger services in the state.

# RAILWAY SYSTEMS/Australia

It is also responsible for provision of electric suburban railway services in the state capital, Perth, under contract to Transperth.

## Passenger operations

WAGR operates two country passenger rail services: the 11 per week standard-gauge 'Prospector' railcar service between Perth and Kalgoorlie and the twice-daily 1,067 mm gauge 'Australind' service between Perth and Bunbury (183 km). The 'Prospector' railcars have been refurbished and a contractor is now responsible for catering. The 'Prospector' cars also provide a commuter service (AvonLink) between Perth and Northam (109 km). The 'Australind' service attracted increased patronage and a Sunday service was introduced. The railcars (of both gauges) have been overhauled to improve their reliability and government approval has been obtained to replace the standard-gauge 'Prospector' railcars with 200 km/h trains capable of reducing travel time to Kalgoorlie by 2 hours.

WAGR provides suburban passenger services on the 95 km electrified Transperth urban network on four routes serving 56 stations. Patronage each year continues to grow. Some 93 per cent of trains arrive within three minutes of their scheduled time; better than most other Australian metropolitan rail systems. The interior of one train has been reconfigured to provide only longitudinal seating to increase standing space; it is rostered for Whitford-Perth all-stations services.

A successful trial has been conducted at two metropolitan stations to create secure car parks and it is now proposed to extend this concept to further stations.

In 1999-2000, urban passenger patronage rose 2.2 per cent to a record 29.5 million journeys. Country rail passengers totalled 258,000, 1 per cent down on the previous year.

## New lines

Legislation to permit extension of electric passenger services from Currambine to Clarkson (4 km) to the north and from Kenwick to Mandurah via Jandalot and Rockingham has passed Parliament. Eathworks started on the Clarkson extension in May 2001. The extension is expected to open in September 2003.

Plans have been developed for a new 77 km addition to the Perth electrified suburban network, from the city centre to Rockingham and Mandurah in the south. This will run from Fitzgerald Street, on the Joondalup line, via a tunnel under the city centre, serving Perth Central and Busport. Two park and ride stations are to serve Rockingham. The project is due to be completed by the end of 2006.

## Improvements to existing lines

In connection with a major urban development, Subiaco station on the Fremantle line was completely rebuilt at a lower level to enable retail construction above. The track has been lowered for nearly a kilometre with the developer providing most of the cost.

A new station is to be built at Greenwood on the Northern Suburbs line. Parking will be provided for 660 cars. The popularity of the line and its service has exceeded all expectations.

## Traction and rolling stock

At the end of June 1998, Westrail operated, on 1,067 mm, five 'Australind' diesel railcars and 48 electric railcar units. On standard gauge it operated eight 'Prospector' diesel railcars.

During 1999, five two-car emus were delivered by Walkers Adtranz. They have video surveillance cameras and LED passenger information displays.

In late 2001, a consortium of EDI Rail and Bombardier Transportation was named preferred bidder to supply 31 three-car emus to serve extensions to the electrified Perth suburban network. Deliveries were expected to commence in early 2004. The contract was to include vehicle maintenance for a 15-year period.

Goninans was selected as the preferred tenderer to build two two-car and one three-car dmus for 'Prospector' (Kalgoorlie) services and one two-car dmu for 'Avonlink' Northam service. The standard-gauge vehicles are to be in service during 2003.

**UPDATED**

### Diesel railcars

| Class | Cars per unit | Motor cars per unit | Motored axles/car | Output/motor kW | Speed km/h | Units in service | First built | Mechanical | Builders Engine | Transmission |
|---|---|---|---|---|---|---|---|---|---|---|
| WCA | 5 | 5 | 2 | 335 | 144 | 5 | 1972 | Comeng | Cummins K19 | H Voith T113r |
| WCE | 3 | - | - | - | 144 | 3 | 1972 | Comeng | - | - |
| ADP | 3 | 3 | 2 | 406 | 110 | 3 | 1987 | Comeng | Cummins K19 | H Voith T311r |
| ADQ | 3 | 2 | 2 | 406 | 110 | 2 | 1987 | Comeng | Cummins K19 | H Voith T311r |

### Electric railcars or multiple-units

| Class | Cars per unit | Motor cars per unit | Motored axles/car | Output/motor kW | Speed km/h | Units in service | First built | Builders Mechanical | Electrical |
|---|---|---|---|---|---|---|---|---|---|
| AEA | 1 | 1 | 4 | 195 | 110 | 48 | 1990 | Walkers | ABB |
| AEB | 1 | 1 | 2 | 195 | 110 | 48 | 1990 | Walkers | ABB |

*Midland-bound WAGR emu leaving Perth on dual-gauge track (Wolfram Veith)*

*Perth-bound Westrail 'Australind' dmu at Brunswick Junction (Wolfram Veith)*

## WestNet Rail

West Parade, Perth, Western Australia 6000
Tel: (+61 8) 93 26 24 52   Fax: (+61 8) 93 26 25 70

### Key personnel
General Manager: Tim Ryan

Gauge: 1,067 mm (74 per cent); 1,453 mm (22 per cent); dual-gauge (4 per cent)
Route length: 5,335 km (including some closed lines)
Track length: 6,401 km
Electrification: 95 km of 1,067 mm gauge at 25 kV 50 Hz AC – Perth suburban passenger network

### Political background
With the privatisation of Westrail, a 50-year lease to manage the Western Australian intrastate rail network was granted to WestNet Rail, a subsidiary of Australian Railroad Group Pty Ltd. WestNet Rail is responsible for track maintenance, train control and setting track access charges. Network ownership remains with the state. A regulatory overview and arbitration mechanism is provided by the Office of the Western Australian Independent Rail Access Regulator, established under the Railways (Access) Act 1998 to ensure access to the network on fair commercial terms.

### Improvements to existing lines
Track upgrading between Perth and Kalgoorlie will see eight loops extended and concrete replacing wooden sleepers over 100 km between Koolyanobbing and Kalgoorlie.

### Signalling and communications
A A$52 million signalling upgrade has enabled all signals and points between Koolyanobbing and Kalgoorlie to be remotely controlled from Merredin.

*NEW ENTRY*

---

# AUSTRIA

## Ministry of Transport

Radetzkystrasse 2, A-1031 Vienna
Tel: (+43 1) 711 62   Fax: (+43 1) 713 78 76

### Key personnel
Minister: Matthias Reichhold
Head of Railways: Dr K Bauer

*UPDATED*

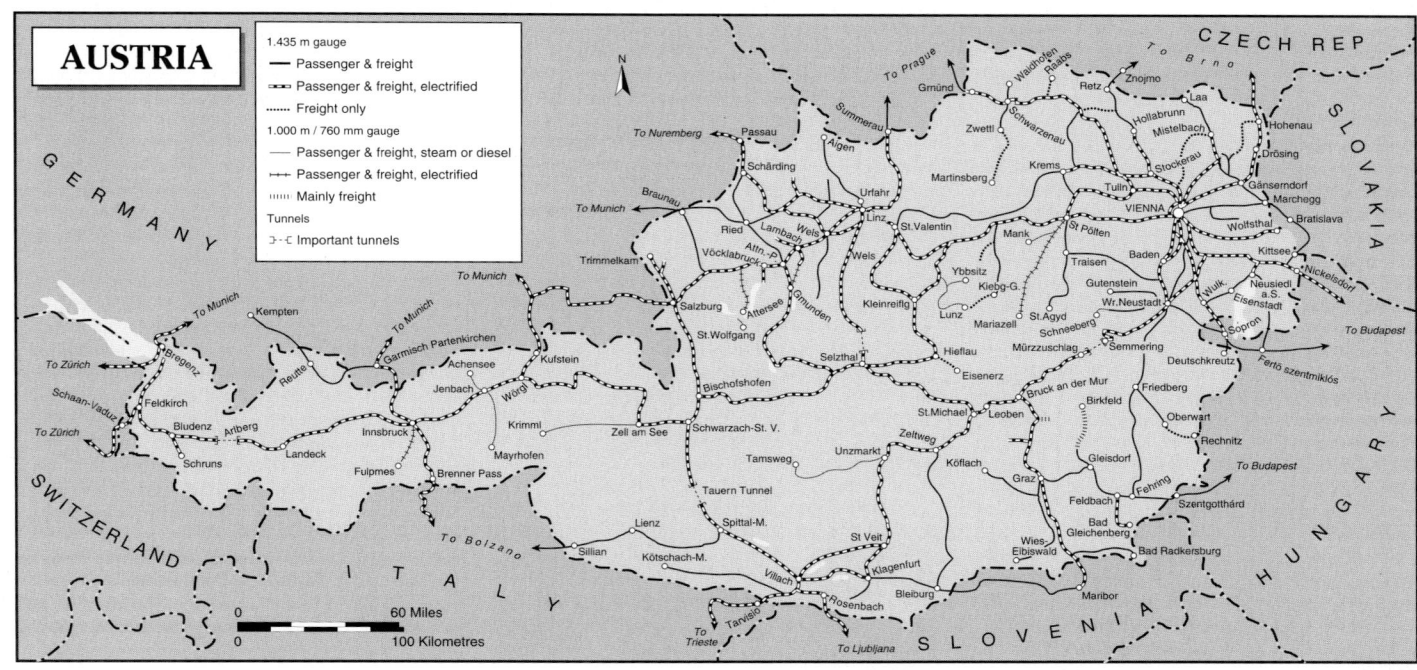

## Austrian Federal Railways (ÖBB)

Österreichische Bundesbahnen
Elisabethstrasse 9, A-1010 Vienna
Tel: (+43 1) 580 00   Fax: (+43 1) 580 02 50 01
Web: http://www.oebb.au

### Key personnel
Chairman of the Supervisory Board:
  KR Franz R Rottmeyer

Members of the Board of Management
  Director General: Rüdiger vorm Walde
  Deputy Director General: Dipl-Ing Helmut Hainitz
  Director: Ferdinand Schmidt
Directors of Business Units
  Freight Traffic: Mag Anton Hoser
  Passenger Traffic: Dr Gerhard Stindl
  Traction: Dipl-Ing Herwig Wiltberger
  Technical Services: Dipl-Ing Dr Alfred Zimmermann

Operations and Capacity Management:
  Dipl-Ing Peter Klugar
Planning and Engineering: Dipl-Ing Thomas Türinger
Infrastructure: Dipl-Ing Michael Zuzic
Building Works and Maintenance:
  Dipl-Ing Christian Fuchs
Signalling and Systems Engineering:
  Dipl-Ing Helmut Steindl

# RAILWAY SYSTEMS/Austria

Telecommunications: Dipl-Ing Ewald Hladky
Energy: Dipl-Ing Manfred Irsigler
Directors of Central Services
  Planning, Control and Accounting:
    Mag Rudolf Wotruba
  Personnel: Dr Wolfgang Moldaschl
  Purchasing and Materials Management:
    Mag-Ing Johann Göbel
  Informatics: Walter Linn
  Finance: Mag Gerhard Leitner
  Estate Management: Ing Mag Heinz Redl
Directors of Staff Units
  Audit Office: Mag Norbert Wagner
  Communications: Dr Viktoria Kickinger
  Equity Holdings and International Relations:
    Mag Edmund Hauswirth
  Change Management: Mag Erich Pirkl
  Legal Affairs: Mag Andrea Ergert

Gauge: 1,435 mm; 1,000 mm; 760 mm
Route length: 5,294 km standard gauge; 5.8 km 1,000 mm gauge; 334.6 km 760 mm gauge
Electrification: 1,435 mm: 3,263 km at 15 kV 16⅔ Hz AC, 2.2 km at 3 kV DC, 760 mm: 84 km at 6.5 kV 25 Hz AC

## Political background

A new Bundesbahngesetz (Railways Act/BBG) reorganised ÖBB from 1 January 1993. The railway became a company (combining elements of public (AG) and private (GmbH) status) with a distinct legal personality and subject to normal company law.

The state pays for new infrastructure and contributes five-eighths of the cost of track maintenance, as agreed in 1987, but it neither covers deficits nor makes any statutory grant to the railway. ÖBB as operator pays a track-access charge. Loss-making but socially necessary local services are grant-supported at a level set by the Ministers of Transport and Finance jointly. Any services over and above the basic specification must be 'purchased' by the Länder governments, which received significant extra federal funding out of oil tax revenues to this end. The Länder were slow to conclude their contracts with the railway, being unwilling to pay the state-owned carrier for its services and desirous of using the tax-money for other transport services they had long bought in, thus freeing their own money for use elsewhere. After the Minister of Transport intervened in 1994, cuts were postponed, thus causing a requirement for additional state support. The contracts were all eventually signed, that with Vienna being the last, at the end of 1998. In 2001 these contracts were under review.

## Organisation

ÖBB meets European Union Directive 91/440 in separating for accountancy purposes infrastructure from transport services, thus creating a framework for third-party access. An infrastructure sector and a commercial sector are each divided into a number of business-units, each with its own bottom-line responsibility. There are also central services and central staffs. The Board of Management, increased from three members to five in August 1997, was reduced again to three in May 2001. Dipl-Ing Hainitz, the only member of the old board to have his contract renewed, continues to be responsible for infrastructure, and Ferdinand Schmidt, who joined the railway from Lauda-Air, took on responsibility for passenger traffic. There is no longer a board member for freight traffic.

The number of employees has continued to fall to approximately 49,000 at the end of 2000. Since 1993 productivity had risen to 66 per cent by the end of 2000.

## Finance

**Table 1: Transport Operations Sector: Profit & Loss Account** (Sch billion)

|  | 1997 | 1998 | 1999 |
|---|---|---|---|
| Sales | 26.6 | 27.3 | 27.6 |
| Other income | 5.2 | 6.3 | 6.0 |
| Total income | 31.8 | 33.6 | 33.6 |
| Personnel costs | 14.5 | 14.9 | 15.2 |
| Depreciation | 3.9 | 4.0 | 3.3 |
| Expenses on property, plant & equipment | 9.0 | 9.6 | 9.8 |
| Infrastructure user charges | 3.4 | 3.5 | 3.7 |
| Total expenditure | 30.8 | 32.0 | 32.0 |
| Operating profit | 1.0 | 1.6 | 1.6 |
| Financial result | –0.7 | - | - |
| Profit | 0.3 | - | - |

**Table 2: Rail Cargo Austria: Sales** (Sch million)

|  | 1997 | 1998 | 1999 |
|---|---|---|---|
| Express-Cargo | 1,573 | - | - |
| Complet-Cargo | 8,316 | - | - |
| Combi-Cargo | 1,084 | - | - |
| Public Benefit Service Income | 2,049 | 2,062 | 2,084 |
| Total | 13,022 | 12,800 | 14,100 |

**Table 3: Passenger Business** (Sch million)

|  | 1997 | 1998 | 1999 |
|---|---|---|---|
| Rail business | 5,742 | 5,416 | 5,525 |
| Bus operations | 1,318 | 1,330 | 1,354 |
| Navigation | 39 | 39 | 39 |
| Public Benefit Service income | 6,100 | 6,458 | 6,292 |
| Total | 13,199 | 13,243 | 13,210 |

## Passenger operations

*Long-distance*

Following the introduction of the first stage of a national fixed-interval passenger timetable, *Neuer Austrotakt 1991* (NAT91), a second stage was planned between 1995 and 1997, and a third and final stage for 2000. NAT91 focused on ÖBB's seven InterCity (IC) routes, offering an hourly service pattern between Vienna and Graz, Villach, Selzthal, and Innsbruck via Salzburg and Zell am See, and 2-hourly services over other routes. Additionally, peak-hour InterCity services on the Vienna–Salzburg–Bregenz, Vienna–Innsbruck, and Vienna–Villach–Salzburg routes featured 'SuperCity' train-pairs, timed to facilitate day-return business trips and offering enhanced facilities, and subject, like EuroCity (EC) services running through Austria, to a supplementary fare.

Although the new fixed-interval service increased train-km by 30 per cent and costs by 20.4 per cent, passenger receipts rose only by 6.8 per cent. Despite a reduction from 94 million to 92 million train-km in 1995, services in that year covered only 73 per cent of their costs, making a loss of Sch1,537 million. In 1996 train-km were further cut, to 85 million. The fixed-interval principle stayed, but the 'SuperCity' trains and a number of the more lightly loaded early and late services were withdrawn, and on some routes through trains were replaced by connections.

The 1996 timetable also brought a major change in on-board service provision. Wagons-Lits, the long-standing provider, lost the on-train contract (though retaining station restaurants and sleeper services) to the Austrian company Trainristo, and the number of trains with full restaurant-car service was reduced from 152 to 60 (with another 76 running with foreign restaurant cars). At-seat service, delivered by ÖBB staff, was extended.

Both the number of passengers and the load-factor rose steadily in 1999 and 2000, with the latter reaching 2.02 passengers per train-km operated. In 2000 ÖBB joined its German and Swiss counterparts DB and SBB in establishing the Trans Europe Excellence Rail Alliance (TEE), which aims to offer a unified cross-border rail service in Central Europe. It was originally planned that 116 tilting trains would be ordered by the alliance, of which 32 would belong to ÖBB. However, in late 2001, DB withdrew from the planned joint procurement of rolling stock, although it was to retain its marketing role in the alliance. Meanwhile, 2001 saw major accelerations on the routes between Graz and Linz, Salzburg, and Innsbruck.

Since 1 January 2001 it has been possible to buy tickets for domestic journeys online, paying for them by credit card and printing them on a domestic printer. This represents a world first for Austria. The VorteilsCard, which can already be used for payment at stations, was due to be made usable for payment on the Internet in mid-2001.

ÖBB now accepts electronic payment at its principal stations, and the equipment in use is capable of working with all current cards and with the future *Quick* electronic purse. The *VorteilsCard,* which replaced the old Half Price Pass in 1996, was made available with a *Eurocard* function in mid-1997, becoming the first Austrian credit card to carry the holder's photograph.

*Suburban and urban*

At the end of 1995 a 10-year Sch30,000 million investment programme in S-Bahn and U-Bahn facilities in the Vienna area began. The S-Bahn works include greatly increased park-and-ride provision at principal stations, a better link to Vienna International Airport, and extension of the line to Heiligenstadt to run southeastwards along the Handelskai on the Danube west bank.

The airport link is being provided by development of the Pressburger Bahn as S-Bahn line S7. In late 1997 the annual investment in this project was doubled to Sch840 million to allow completion for 2002 instead of for 2006. The work is now expected to be finished in 2003, and the city section of the route was closed in mid-2001 to allow major engineering works to take place.

The S70 is also being planned. This involves a link from a rebuilt Südtiroler Platz station past the Schweizer Garten and the Ostbahn and then curving to the Donauländebahn and running on to a junction with the S7 at Klein Schwechat.

Salzburg and Graz are also to have S-Bahns. Salzburg's plans involve four new city stations and a 15-minute service on the core (common) route section between Salzburg and Freilassing, where a third line is also to be provided. Cost of the stations and this widening will be Sch38.55 million, split between city, *Land,* and federal government. Completion is envisaged for about 2005.

The developments being considered by the Styrian *Länder* and the city of Graz for the Graz area, which envisage the provision of S-Bahn services on existing lines, follow the cancellation of plans for a Karlsruhe-type network. In addition to ÖBB, the city transport services and the various minor railways operating in the area are involved. Where ÖBB cannot provide an economic rail service, it will, in consultation with the states, propose a bus or group taxi service as an alternative and will also support the states if they wish to find an alternative rail operator. Seven lines were closed to passenger traffic on 10 June 2001 and five others were being assessed.

| **Traffic** (million) | 1998 | 1999 | 2000 |
|---|---|---|---|
| Passenger journeys | 179.1 | 181.7 | 182.7 |
| Passenger-km | 7,971 | - | - |
| Freight tonnes | 76.5 | 78.0 | 84.7 |
| Freight tonne-km | 15,348 | - | - |

## Freight operations

Since 1993 the freight business has traded as Rail Cargo Austria, in three divisions: Complet-Cargo (wagonload traffic), Combi-Cargo (intermodal traffic), and Express-Cargo (less-than-wagonload business).

*Three-car emu on the 760 mm gauge Mariazellerbahn (D Trevor Rowe)*

*Class 1014 dual-voltage electric locomotive in the Vienna suburbs with empty coal wagons returning to the Czech Republic* (Ken Harris)  
2001/0109841

Freight operations have seen considerable growth in recent years, though pressure on rates has meant that the increase in traffic has not been matched by a similar growth in profits. The 1997 freight record was exceeded in 1998, again in 1999, and rose further to 84.7 million tonnes in 2000.

Rail Cargo Austria is investing heavily in the expansion of its Logistik Centres in the period up to 2004. The investment will see expansion of 19 centres, construction of a new freight centre in Vienna, and an enlargement of the Linz goods station. The three new Logistik Centres, at Bischofshofen, Wels, and Wörgl, awarded ISO 9001 quality management certification at the beginning of 1997 at the end of a one-year assessment period, are all flourishing. Austria's transit significance is likely to grow, and substantial improvements to cross-border routes are planned to meet developing needs.

To improve freight operation in the Vienna area and to free up line capacity for additional S-Bahn services, the Floridsdorfer Hochbahn, a 4 km line built in 1916 and abandoned after the Second World War, was restored to provide a new freight route between the northern main lines and the Kledering marshalling yard. Diversion of goods traffic, primarily from Retz, Gmünd, and Krems, to this electrified single line linking Jedlersdorf with Leopoldau has allowed the very busy line through Vienna Mitte to be freed almost entirely of freight trains and has also relieved the heavily used section of the Franzjosefbahn between Tulln and Vienna of some of its traffic.

In 1998, the Wieselburg–Gresten line was converted from narrow gauge to standard gauge in order to facilitate the working of goods traffic.

ÖBB has joined with DB in establishing a locomotive pool, EuroTraction, to which each railway is contributing 25 new high-performance locomotives in a first step. The aim is to reach a figure of 1,500 machines by 2005, thus making modern freight locomotives available in the free market for operators requiring haulage.

### Intermodal operations
Much of the recent growth in intermodal traffic stems from political moves to restrict heavy lorries. In 1989 the Transport Minister barred all freight vehicles above 7.5 tonnes, domestic and foreign, from night-time use of Austrian roads and the government underwrote a six-month cut in ÖBB piggyback rates over the Brenner Pass, on which route intermodal services were vigorously expanded.

A by-product of the European Union Schengen open frontiers policy has been a switch back to road by significant numbers of ÖKOMBI customers on the Brenner route (of whom 50 per cent come from third countries), and, in an attempt to counter this, two additional trains were put on each way from 1 February 1998 to give a two-hourly interval service throughout the 24 hours and prices were significantly reduced for a trial period, by up to 41 per cent for day-transits and up to 24 per cent for night-transits. New Class 1012 locomotives have been brought into use on the Brenner route.

### New lines
ÖBB is pursuing a major capital programme to increase capacity and raise speeds on its principal network. In 1987 government approved the *Neue Bahn* ('New Railway') plan in principle, and execution and funding of the first phase were agreed in 1989, when the High Performance Lines Act was passed. The high-performance network is essentially five major axes: the Donauachse (Regensburg–Passau/Salzburg–Vienna–Nickelsdorf(-Budapest)); the Pyhrn–Schoberachse (Regensburg–Passau–Wels–Pyhrn–Schoberpass–Graz–Spielfeld(–Marburg)); the Brennerachse ((Munich–)Kufstein–Brenner(–Verona)); the Tauernachse ((Munich–)Salzburg–Rosenbach(–Laibach)); and the Südbahnachse (or Pontebbana) ((Warsaw–)Hohenau–Vienna–Tarvis(–Trieste)) — broadly the network of lines making up the main trunk routes for international traffic.

The first phase envisaged commitment of Sch44 billion up to 1998, on a mixed-funding basis as used in Austria for motorway construction. A state-owned company, Eisenbahn-Hochleistungsstrecken-AG (HL-AG), was created on 3 April 1989 to manage the planning and execution of new infrastructure and upgrading projects. HL-AG reports directly to the Ministry of Economics and Transport, and the scope of its work is determined exclusively by orders issued by that ministry in collaboration with the Ministry of Finance. Legislation, in the form of a Treaty of Co-operation with ÖBB, sets out the framework for collaboration with the federal railways. While HL-AG deals with most of the new construction, ÖBB is handling major route improvement schemes and planning the Brenner corridor improvements either side of the new Innsbruck avoiding line. Between 1988 and 1994 some Sch22 billion were spent on the elimination of a number of significant bottlenecks, a prerequisite for achieving the high freight traffic growth rates of recent years.

The Rail Infrastructure Financing Act of July 1996 allocated Sch60 billion to be spent at a rate of Sch12 billion per year over the following five years. This was the first time ever that investment funds have been allocated on a long-term basis, and the figure represents a continuation of the level of spending of 1995.

The 2000 expenditure on the principal routes was: Donauachse Sch1,600 million, Tauernschse Sch700 million, Brenner Sch200 million, Arlberg Sch1,400 million, Pontebbana Sch1,200 million, Pyhrn-Schober Sch1,200 million, Vienna area Sch900 million, other lines Sch3,900 million.

### The Brenner line
The Brenner route, linking Munich with Innsbruck and Verona, now ranks first of the 14 principal trans-European infrastructure projects supported by the European Union. The principal attraction for Austria of the planned base tunnel is the elimination of a substantial amount of lorry traffic known to be causing significant environmental damage. The existing line has already been extensively upgraded. Although clearance work on the Austrian section to accept RoLa piggyback road vehicles of up to 4.05 m in height was finished in 1989, enlargement of tunnel clearances on the Italian side is not yet complete, so RoLa trains terminate at Brenner.

ÖBB opened the 15 km Innsbruck avoiding line (12.7 km in Austria's longest tunnel) in 1994. In 1995, work was begun on quadrupling between the German frontier at Kufstein and the start of the Innsbruck avoiding line at Baumkirchen. Also begun was installation of automatic block signalling and reversible working on both tracks of the northern ramp of the Brenner.

No firm date for a start on the 65 km base tunnel, which will reach deep into Italy, has been reached. In late 1994 Austria, Germany and Italy agreed that an optimal scheme for the Brenner route would see new infrastructure on the whole 400 km between Munich and Verona at a total cost of €12.5 billion, the tunnel taking €4.5 billion, works north of it €2.8 billion, and works south of it €5.2 billion. Up to 400 trains daily, double the current figure, could be run.

### Südbahn and Semmering base tunnel
Work is proceeding to improve the capacity of the Südbahn; this is the Semmering Pass route from Vienna to Bruck an der Mur, Graz, and Villach. To permit more local services between Vienna and Wiener Neustadt (about 50 km out), Südbahn main line traffic will eventually be rerouted over the Ostbahn main line to Grammatneusiedl, where a new spur will take trains on through Wampersdorf to Wiener Neustadt over a doubled and upgraded branch line. The rerouteing will also improve Südbahn access to the Kledering marshalling yard.

ÖBB's scheme to bypass the steep and curvaceous Semmering Pass section of the Südbahn, which it describes as the sole section of the main European network with branch line characteristics, received the go-ahead in 1993. Gradients of 1:40 and curves down to a radius of only 170 m, a distance twice that of a direct line, tight tunnel clearances, problems in the use of banking locomotives, and high maintenance costs all conspire to make the historic Ghega line unsuitable for today's traffic and unavailable for RoLa operations.

The Sch6.1 billion solution will provide by 2002 a new double-track railway between Gloggnitz and Mürzzuschlag with a summit tunnel more than 12 km long and several smaller tunnels. The ruling grade will be 1 in 91, distance will be reduced by some 19 km, capacity on this very busy route will be greatly enhanced, and passenger trains will save 30 minutes.

However, in April 1998 a provisional stop to the plans was announced. At the end of September a commission of experts appointed to review the Semmering Base Tunnel Project reported, recommending not only a delay of at least two years for the tunnel scheme (to await a constitutional court decision) but also bringing forward plans for a Vienna–Schwechat–Eisenstadt–Sopron line. The commission held that the basic case for a high-capacity north-south link remained convincing, but it felt that as a consequence of the 1989 opening up of Eastern Europe, the traffic projections that had been made were too high and that sufficient capacity could be found on the Semmering line till 2015 and on the Aspang line till 2025. It also noted that the base tunnel project would bring with it a need for further additional and expensive projects, and it suggested other measures for consideration in the meantime. In particular, it noted that Hungary's possible accession to the European Union could mean that an alternative and very attractive 'plains' solution would become possible, also taking the place of the *Süd-Ost Spange* long-term proposals. The Semmering line itself was declared a UNESCO World Heritage Site in December 1998.

Another complication was that the *Land* of Niederösterreich argued before the Austrian Constitutional Court that the Semmering base tunnel plans were unconstitutional because they contravened its environmental protection law, but on 25 June 1999 the court dismissed this claim and gave the *Land* until the end of the year to lodge a new complaint (which cannot prevent the building of the line but can only ask for conditions to be set, such an application to be considered in the light of public interest).

Mid-April 2000 saw the go-ahead for the first stage of the Koralmbahn, between Klagenfurt and Grafenstein. The last consent required was that of the Defence Minister, needed because the line will cross land belonging to the Gradnitz ammunition store. The 14 km of new railway will cost Sch2,000 million and will be financed by the rail infrastructure company. The Hochleistungsstrecken AG is responsible for the planning and the execution of the project and was expected to begin the tendering process in mid-2000.

### Improvements to existing lines
*Environmental measures*
The first agreement on railway noise-protection measures for an entire *Land* was signed in August 1997 in Salzburg by the federal transport minister, those responsible for transport and environment in the *Land* Salzburg, and ÖBB. This formally regulates the planning and realisation of noise-protection measures for the whole of the *Land,* the cost of projects being met half from government railway funds, a quarter by the *Land,* and a quarter by the local authority affected.

*Westbahn*
The Westbahn is the main east-west transversal connecting Vienna with St Pölten, Linz, and Salzburg. Westbahn modernisation for 200 km/h speeds began before the opening up of the east and Austria's accession to the European Union. The changed situation requires a capacity increase that can be obtained only by full quadrupling between Vienna and Wels (and possibly later on to Salzburg).

Two twin-track, mixed-traffic lines are envisaged throughout, linked every 25 to 30 km, one of them a high-speed railway. The new concept builds on the old. Thus, for example, where major realignments are planned, four-tracking will be obtained by retaining the (modernised) original route. Work so far has raised capacity by 10 per cent; the first accelerations came in 1996.

Working westwards from the Austrian capital, between Vienna and St Pölten there is to be a new high-speed line on the north side of the Danube, and there will also be a 25.7 km St Pölten freight avoiding line (with a 3.9 km tunnel). Much of the work between St Pölten and Attnang-Puchheim is now complete, with a mixture of upgrading of the historic line and new construction. The existing Attnang-Puchheim to Salzburg line will for the time being be maintained as it is but HL-AG was commissioned in early 1990 to plan a new line at a possible cost of Sch12 billion.

According to the Hochleistungsstrecken AG, progress on the upgrading of the Westbahn at the end of 1998 was as follows:

| Work completed (35.2 km) | km |
|---|---|
| Melk (in part) (May 1997) | 7.0 |
| Krummnussbaum–Säusenstein (March 1994) | 7.0 |
| Pyhrnbahn connection (Marchtrenk–Traun) (May 1994) | 13.2 |
| Lambach (January 1995) | 3.9 |
| Breitenschützing–Schwanenstadt (June 1997) | 4.1 |
| St Peter–Seitenstetten | 6.2 |
| Haag–St Valentin | 13.3 |
| **Work in progress (49.2 km)** | |
| St Pölten–Prinzersdorf | 7.5 |
| Loosdorf | 4.7 |
| Melk | 12.1 |
| Sarling–Ybbs | 4.3 |
| Kottingburgstall | 1.1 |
| **Work at the planning stage (203.1 km)** | |
| Vienna–St Pölten | 49.1 |
| St Pölten goods avoiding line | 24.8 |
| Prinzersdorf–Gross Sierning | 4.5 |
| Rohr node | 2.1 |
| Pöchlarn–Krummnussbaum Junction | 4.7 |
| Ybbs/D–Hubertendorf | 4.5 |
| Hubertendorf–Blindenmarkt | 4.2 |
| Blindenmarkt–Amstetten | 6.3 |
| Aschbach–Krenstetten | 8.2 |
| St Valentin station reconstruction | 2.5 |
| Enns avoiding line | 10.8 |
| Asten–Linz Hauptbahnhof | 11.4 |
| Attnang/Puchheim–Salzburg | 70.0 |

Early in 2000 it was announced that the Austrian and German governments and the two national railways had signed agreements for the development of the main railway lines linking Austria with Bavaria. There is to be a step-by-step improvement of the Munich–Mühldorf–Freilassing–Salzburg–Wels–Linz line and of the line from Nuremberg through Passau to Wels. On the Mühldorf–Simbach–Neumarkt–Kallham line there will be capacity guarantees.

*Ostbahn*
The Ostbahn is the main line into Hungary, crossing the border at Nickelsdorf/Hegyeshalom. It was upgraded between 1990 and 1996 for 140/160 km/h operation,

*Class 1014 electric locomotive leaving the Hungarian border station at Hegyeshalom with a Vienna–Budapest express (Eddie Barnes)*

with major renewals, alterations to stations, and modernisation of signalling and safety equipment, and there were significant accelerations to the Vienna–Budapest services in the 1997 timetable.

Together, the Westbahn and Ostbahn form the 'Donauachse'. These two routes are being linked by a new connecting line in Vienna through the Lainzer tunnel and the new Vienna station (see 'Major new stations').

*Schober Pass*
The north-south Schober Pass line between Selzthal and St Michael is the central link in the (Germany–)Linz–Graz (–Slovenia) route. Until recently largely single track, the route would have been unable to provide sufficient operating capacity for the regular-interval passenger timetable and the planned increase from 90 to 150 freight trains daily. The case for this and other north-south increased operating capacity projects was further strengthened by events in eastern Europe.

There has been an extensive double-tracking, realignment, and resignalling programme, which has allowed a major acceleration of passenger services in the 2001-02 timetable. A new curve at Selzthal to save Graz–Salzburg trains reversal there will contribute to faster timings. Total cost of all the works, including elimination of level crossings, is put at Sch4.7 billion.

South of the Schober Pass, the 28 km section between St Michael and Bruck an der Mur, over which north-south Schober Pass trains share the route with east-west Südbahn trains, is being quadrupled. Boring of a 5.4 km Galgenberg Tunnel for a Leoben avoiding line is the first step. North of the pass, the Pyhrnbahn from Selzthal north to Linz is due to be doubled and resignalled before the end of the century.

A 13-km single-track Linz avoiding line, linking the Pyhrnbahn at Traun with the Westbahn at Marchtrenk, at the approach to Wels, was opened in 1994.

*Tauern line*
The trans-Alpine north-south line from Salzburg through the Tauern Tunnel to Rosenbach on the Slovenian border, where trains can go on further south via the Karawanken Tunnel route, is being doubled at a cost of Sch600 million.

Enlargement of the 280 m Untersberg Tunnel near Schwarzach St Veit in a Sch46 million scheme has permitted Tauern route piggybacking of 4.05 m high road vehicles.

Long-term plans cover improvements to the north of the Tauern route between Salzburg and Schwarzach St Veit (already double-track, but where curves are being eased) and to the south of it between Spittal-Millstättersee and Rosenbach. Realignments where feasible will lift maximum speed to 130 km/h, 140 km/h over parts of the southern section. The aim is to raise freight train capacity from 110 to 150 a day.

*Arlberg line*
The Arlberg is the key east-west trans-Alpine route in the west of Austria, linking Innsbruck and points to the east with Switzerland. Progressive double-tracking continues, with attention now focused on the 25 km segment between Ötztal and Landeck on the eastern approaches to the Arlberg Tunnel. Associated work aims to raise line-speed to 140 km/h, provide extra capacity for an S-Bahn service, and eliminate the railway's division of some communities by rerouteing, principally in the Ötztal to Kronburg section. Given the steep sides of the valley, this necessitates tunnelling, and eventually 12 km of the 25 km section will be underground. Preliminary work on the Schnann to St Jakob section has begun and plans are under way for the Langen to Klösterle section.

The two-track Arlberg Tunnel has had its clearances enlarged to allow RoLa piggybacking with 4.05 m high road-vehicles.

*Links with Eastern Europe*
In 1995 the governments of Austria, the Czech Republic and Germany agreed a programme to upgrade the Vienna–Prague–Berlin corridor, and a further agreement was signed between ÖBB and ČD in October 1997.

Studies have been commissioned by ÖBB and its Hungarian counterpart MÁV into electrification of the line between Graz, Szentgotthard and Szombathely.

Three lines will improve links with the Slovak capital, Bratislava. The Pressburger Bahn is being developed as far as Schwechat as the S7 link to Vienna International Airport (see above). Beyond the airport, more double-tracking and some new construction will extend the line beyond its present terminus at Wolfsthal to Kittsee and a junction with the line from Parndorf, extension of which to Bratislava began in late 1994.

The Parndorf route uses the Budapest main line as far as Parndorf, whence the existing single-track branch to Kittsee has been rebuilt for 160 km/h speeds and later doubling. A 2.5 km extension suitable for 140 km/h leads on to the border, and on the Slovak side the line is linked to Petržalka, across the Danube from Bratislava. The full service, of both D-trains and local trains, began running on 1 August 1999 and loadings soon rose above expectations. Plans to work the route with ÖBB Class 1014 bi-current locomotives had to be dropped because there was no opportunity for Slovakian Railways to provide the necessary kilometre exchange. On the Austrian side Class 1046s are being used, and through trains change to a ŽSR Class 240 at Petržalka (where three tracks are divided in the middle by isolating sections).

The third route into Slovakia runs from Vienna via Marchegg to Bratislava. This has now lost its fast trains to the new route via Parndorf.

### Major new stations
In Vienna, the Südbahn at Meidling (where there will also be a junction with the Donauländebahn for freight traffic use) is being linked by a 14 km new line, with all but 2 km in tunnel, under the Lainzer Tiergarten and the city's southwestern residential area, with the Westbahn and with the new high-speed line at Purkersdorf Sanatorium. A new Vienna station on the site of the present Südbahnhof is planned, with a major urban redevelopment as well as the station works.

In 1997 ÖBB began work on a Sch6.2 billion programme for the modernisation and redevelopment of its principal stations, the aim being to create a more attractive environment for the customer, with many more service and trading outlets. Private capital will be involved wherever possible. This follows on from the *Neue Bahn* plan to spend Sch650 million on 32 stations to create public transport interchanges, provide parking space and station garages, and offer a wide range of other passenger services and amenities. The stations involved are: Vienna West, South, North, Rennweg, Floridsdorf,

*Siemens-built Class 1016 Taurus electric locomotive leaving Vienna Kledering marshalling yard with a wagonload of freight (Ken Harris)* 2001/0109842

Hütteldorf, and Heiligenstadt; Baden, Wiener Neustadt, Bruck an der Mur, Graz; Leoben, Klagenfurt; Krems; St Polten, Linz, Wels, Attnang-Puchheim, Salzburg, Bischofshofen, Schwarzach St Veit, Innsbruck, and Feldkirch. This last will be the first station in western Austria to be totally renovated. The aim was to complete the project in 2000 at a total cost of Sch62.6 million (in collaboration with the local authority). For Linz a planning company (formed by ÖBB, the city of Linz, and the Raiffeisenlandesbank Oberösterreich) has been set up to manage a project with a total value of Sch3-4 billion for station improvement, Sch1 billion for development of the station as a local traffic hub for rail, and Sch1.6 billion for development of offices for the *Land* (federal state) government of Oberösterreich, along with flats and shops.

## Traction and rolling stock

At the end of 1998 ÖBB had 715 electric locomotives, 465 diesel locomotives and 17 steam locomotives. There were also 226 emus and 129 dmus.

In early 1997 ÖBB opened a new depot at Villach, where 110 staff look after 160 locomotives, 250 passenger coaches and 4,000 freight wagons. This is a third major modern installation, alongside Knittelfield and Linz. The Linz works are being extensively modernised and will, in future, look after all ÖBB's high-performance passenger equipment. The railway aims in the future to exploit its modern facilities more extensively by tendering for international work.

*Locomotives*
The last Class 1044 locomotive was delivered in 1995. The first three locomotives of Class 1012, the 82 tonne, 6,000 kW, Bo-Bo successor to Class 1044, were due to be delivered in June 1996 but they were not actually acquired until December 1996, after considerable negotiation about costs, the price paid being Sch70 million per machine instead of the Sch90 million originally asked. They are used in place of Class 1044s on domestic services, so they have only been authorised for 160 km/h operation instead of the design speed of 230 km/h.

For through freight working between Germany and Italy via the Brenner, an Adtranz-Siemens-SGP consortium has delivered five prototypes of a dual-voltage (15 kV AC/3 kV DC) 82 tonne Class 1822 Bo-Bo rated at 4,300 kW with a top speed of 140 km/h. Since June 1997 these locomotives have been deployed on passenger workings over the Brenner in an integrated ÖBB/FS service running in timings laid down for FS electric traction which the previous Austrian diesels could not maintain.

In 1997 ÖBB sought tenders for 200 high-performance locomotives, with installed power of 6.5 MW and a top speed of 230 km/h, to be used on both fast passenger and heavy freight services. In view of the fall in prices of recent years, it hoped to be able to obtain a purchase price of only Sch40 million per locomotive. By the end of 2000 orders for 400 of the type had been placed with Siemens AG Österreich. Deliveries of these 'Taurus' locomotives began early in 2000. The locomotives, designated Classes 1116 (dual-voltage) and 1016, will be able to work not only in Germany and Austria but also, in the case of Class 1116, in Hungary, the Czech Republic, Slovakia, France, and Belgium. Rated at 6.4 MW, they have a maximum tractive effort of 300 kN and a maximum speed of 230 km/h. They weigh 86 tonnes, and their length is 19.28 m. In freight traffic they are able to work trains of between 1,600 and 2,000 tonnes at speeds of up to 120 km/h. A major share of the construction work is being carried out in Austria – some components are bought from ÖBB workshops and final assembly is in Linz Works.

In 2001, ÖBB sold its nine surviving ASEA-built Class 1043 electric locomotives to Swedish operator Tågab (qv).

In 2001, Elin EBG was awarded a contract to equip 10 Class 1044 electric locomotives with radio remote-control equipment for mid-train working.

As part of it plans to build up a new fleet of standard locomotives, in 1998 ÖBB ordered 40 new main line diesel locomotives and 60 diesel shunters, with options on a further 200 locomotives.

The main line locomotives are being supplied by Siemens Austria, with first deliveries due in early 2002. Designated Class 2016 and also known as the 'Hercules' type, they are diesel-electric units with three-phase traction motors and are intended for both freight and passenger services. An option has been confirmed on 30 additional locomotives to the 40 originally ordered, and further options exist on 80 more.

The Class 2070 'Hector' B-B diesel-hydraulic shunting locomotives are being supplied by Vossloh Schienenfahrzeugtechnik, forming the company's G800 model. Deliveries commenced in 2001 and options exist on 90 additional units.

Pending the availability of the new main line diesel locomotives, ÖBB is leasing a small number of Soviet-built Class 232 high-powered diesel locomotives from DB AG to work freight services between the Slovak border and Vienna.

Also on order from Bombardier Transportation/Elin in 2001 were 11 three-car Talent emus for the Salzburg area and 40 four-car Talent emus for the Vienna S-Bahn. ÖBB is also to obtain a number of new dmus.

*Passenger vehicles*
The ÖBB stock of passenger coaches fell from 3,436 at the end of 1995 to 3,287 at the end of 1996, and then rose to 3,583 at the end of 1998.

The first phase of *Neue Bahn* investment earmarks Sch1.6 billion for new traction and rolling stock (though over the whole *Neue Bahn* programme forecast expenditure in this area totals Sch12.5 billion). Most of the first-phase money is going on development and evaluation of new 200 km/h passenger car prototypes with sophisticated amenities. ÖBB aims eventually to have trains in international service capable of using the 300 km/h new lines in neighbouring states. SGP has developed an SGP-300 range of guided-wheelset bogie designs including a model with 300 km/h capability.

In September 1995 the railway works at St Pölten rolled out ÖBB's first push-pull driving trailer, designated Class 80-75. After the initial production run of 14 vehicles, 75 were built by 1999 by conversion of 26.4 m Jenbacher vehicles built between 1982 and 1987 at a total cost in the order of Sch615 million.

Tenders were sought in 1994 for 50 bilevel coaches and 10 bilevel driving coaches. The contract went to ARGE Doppelstockwagen (a consortium of Siemens Verkehrstechnik/SGP and Jenbacher) in March 1995 for a sum of roughly Sch700 million. Add-on orders took the total number of vehicles on order to 240, to be formed as 40 six-car push-pull sets and branded 'City Shuttles'. The bilevel cars began to enter service in May 1998 on the Südbahn and then came into use on the Ostbahn in October 1998.

ÖBB's latest SGP Class Rh 4090 narrow-gauge electric (6.5 kV AC 25 Hz) multiple-units can be used in three- or four-car formations, two powered vehicles and two trailers, or a power-car, a trailer, and a driving trailer. Two sets can be coupled. Maximum speed is 70 km/h. They have modern seating, enclosed gangways, and closed-system toilets.

ÖBB is also spending Sch2,800 million on 660 refurbished City Shuttle cars. This stock is for use in Carinthia, Styria, Upper Austria, Tirol, and Salzburg. The work of refurbishment includes making the vehicles suitable for mobile telephones, providing power supplies for PCs, installing new general purpose power supply equipment and fitting modular air conditioning systems.

*Bilevel City Shuttle push-pull set powered by a Class 1142 electric locomotive forming a Vienna S-Bahn service at Simmering Ostbahn (Ken Harris)* 2001/0109843

# RAILWAY SYSTEMS/Austria

The first vehicles entered service in 2001 and the work is scheduled for completion in 2004.

ÖBB is also in the course of renewing its BahnBus fleet, with the purchase of 440 new buses at a cost of Sch1,100 million.

Twenty new couchette coaches, costing Sch300 million, were brought into service in 2001 on trains to Berlin, Hamburg and Paris, thus completing the modernisation of ÖBB's night stock.

In 2001 tenders were invited for 116 dual-voltage 200-230 km/h tilting trainsets to be ordered jointly by ÖBB, German Rail and Swiss Federal Railways to equip the three companies' Trans Europe Excellence Rail Alliance (TEE) (see Passenger operations, Long-distance). Of these, 32 were to be procured by ÖBB, with the first examples entering service in 2004.

## Signalling and telecommunications

Electronic signalling installations are being developed by two companies, Alcatel Austria and Siemens AG. Each is pursuing its own software technology.

With the commissioning of new signalling and LZB (the German form of automatic train protection) in March 1993 over the 25 km between Linz and Wels, 200 km/h running became possible for the first time in Austria. Later that year LZB was commissioned from Wels to Lambach and Attnang-Puchheim. The new Salzburg electronic signalling control centre was brought into use in May 1996. This is an Alcatel installation replacing five previous signalboxes.

Between mid-October and mid-November 1999 the first trials of European Train Control System (ETCS) took place on the Parndorf—Hungarian border section of the Vienna—Budapest main line (which will be ÖBB's first main line to be equipped with the system). The line was fitted with transponders, and two locomotives were appropriately adapted (1014.015 from ÖBB and V63.156 from MÁV).

## Track

**Standard rail**
Standard-gauge: 60.34, 53.81, 49.43 kg/m
Narrow-gauge: 35.65 kg/m

**Length**
Standard-gauge: 30 and 60 m
Narrow-gauge: 20 m

**Crossties (sleepers)**
Standard-gauge: impregnated wood 2,600 × 260 × 160 mm; concrete 2,600 × 300 max × 200 mm max; also some steel
Narrow-gauge: impregnated wood 1,600 × 200 × 130 mm; concrete 1,500 × 200 max × 160 mm max

**Crossties spacing**
Standard-gauge: 600-700 mm (1,667-1,429 per km)
Narrow-gauge: 700-810 mm (1,429-1,235 per km)

**Rail fastening**
Standard-gauge: resilient fastening, ribbed slabs, clips and bolts
Narrow-gauge: ribbed plates and elastic clips

**Filling**
Standard-gauge: broken stone ballast 30-65 mm
Narrow-gauge: broken stone ballast 25-35 mm

**Thickness under sleepers**
Standard-gauge: 200-300 mm
Narrow-gauge: 150 mm

**Min or sharpest curvature**
Standard-gauge: 9.7° = min radius of 180 m
Narrow-gauge: 29.1° = min radius of 60 m

**Max gradient compensated**
Standard-gauge: 4.6 per cent
Narrow-gauge: 2.5 per cent

**Gauge width with max curvature**
Standard-gauge: 20 mm
Narrow-gauge: 20 mm

**Max super elevation**
Standard-gauge: 160 mm
Narrow-gauge: 60 mm

**Max axleload**
Standard-gauge: 22.5 tonnes
Narrow-gauge: 12 tonnes

### Diesel locomotives

| Class | Wheel Arrangement | Power KW | Speed km/h | Weight Tonnes | No in service | First built | Mechanical | Builders Engine | Transmission |
|---|---|---|---|---|---|---|---|---|---|
| **1,435 mm gauge** | | | | | | | | | |
| 2043 | B-B | 1,035 | 110 | 70 | 72 | 1964 | JW | JW 400 (01-4) LM 1500 (5+) | H Voith |
| 2143 | B-B | 1,035 | 110 | 68 | 75 | 1965 | SGP | SGP T 12c | H Voith |
| 2048 | B-B | 808 | 100/65 | 64 | 34 | 1991 | MAK | CAT3512DI | H Voith |
| 2050 | Bo-Bo | 1,140 | 100 | 75 | 12 | 1958 | Henschel | GM 12-567c | E GM |
| 2016 | Bo-Bo | 2,150 | 140 | 80 | 70* | 2002 | Siemens | MTU 16V 4000 R41 | E Siemens |
| **Shunting locomotives** | | | | | | | | | |
| 2060 | B | 129 | 30/60 | 27 | 16 | 1954 | JW | JW 200 | H Voith |
| 2062 | B | 250 | 40/60 | 32 | 48 | 1958 | JW | JW 400 | H Voith |
| 2067 | C | 398 | 65 | 49 | 111 | 1959 | SGP | S 12a/S12na | H Voith |
| 2068 | B-B | 820 | 50/100 | 68 | 60 | 1989 | JW | JW 480D | H Voith |
| 2070 | B-B | 740 | 100 | 72 | 60* | 2001 | Vossloh | — | H Voith |
| **760 mm gauge** | | | | | | | | | |
| 2090 | Bo | 72 | 40 | 13 | 1 | 1930 | SGP | Saurer BXD | E Syst Gebus |
| 2190 | Bo | 86 | 45 | 13 | 1 | 1934 | SGP | SGP SU8 | E Syst Gebus |
| 2091 | 1-Bo-1 | 114 | 50 | 22 | 4 | 1936 | SGP | SGP R 8 | E Syst Gebus |
| 2092 | C | 88 | 20 | 17 | 3 | 1943 | | Deutz ABM 517 | H Voith |
| 2095 | B-B | 405 | 60 | 32 | 15 | 1958 | SGP | S 12a | H Voith |

* Includes locomotives on order

### Electric locomotives

| Class | Wheel arrangement | Output kW Continuous/One-hour | Speed km/h | Weight tonnes | No in service | First built | Mechanical | Builders Electrical |
|---|---|---|---|---|---|---|---|---|
| 1010 | Co-Co | 3,260/3,990 | 130 | 110 | 18 | 1955 | SGP | ABES |
| 1110 | Co-Co | 3,260/3,990 | 110 | 110 | 28 | 1956 | SGP | ABES |
| 1014/1114 | Bo-Bo | 3,000/3,400 | 160 | 74 | 18 | 1993 | SGP | BES |
| 1016/1116* | Bo-Bo | 6,400 | 230 | 86 | 400** | 1999 | Siemens/ÖBB | Siemens |
| 1040 | Bo-Bo | 1,980/2,020 | 80 | 80 | 12 | 1950 | Lofag | ABES |
| 1041 | Bo-Bo | 1,980/2,020 | 80 | 83 | 20 | 1952 | SGP | ABES |
| 1141 | Bo-Bo | 2,100/2,400 | 110 | 80 | 28 | 1955 | SGP | ABES |
| 1042 | Bo-Bo | 3,336/3,600 | 130 | 84 | 198 | 1963 | SGP | BES |
| 1042.5 | Bo-Bo | 3,808/4,000 | 150 | 84 | | 1966 | SGP | BES |
| 1142 | Bo-Bo | 3,336/3,600 | 130 | 84 | 54 | 1963 | SGP | BES |
| 1044 | Bo-Bo | 5,000/5,310 | 160 | 84 | 122 | 1974 | SGP | BES |
| 1044.2 | Bo-Bo | 5,000/5,310 | 160 | 84 | 88 | 1989 | SGP | BES |
| 1245 | Bo-Bo | 1,504/1,780 | 80 | 83 | 2 | 1934 | Lofag | ABES |
| 1046 | Bo-Bo | 1,360/1,550 | 125 | 67 | 13 | 1956 | Lofag | ABES |
| 1146 | Bo-Bo | 2,400 | 140 | 73 | 2 | 1987 | Lofag | Elin |
| 1163 | Bo-Bo | -/1,600 | 120 | 80 | 20 | 1994 | Graz | Adtranz |
| 1822 | Bo-Bo | 4,400/- | 140 | 83 | 5 | 1991 | SGP | ABB |
| **Shunting locomotives** | | | | | | | | |
| 1063 | Bo-Bo | 1,520/2,000 | 100 | 82 | 50 | 1983 | SGP | BES |
| 1064 | Co-Co | 1,520 | 100 | 113 | 10 | 1985 | SGP | BES |
| **760 mm gauge, 6.5 kV 50 Hz** | | | | | | | | |
| 1099 | C-C | 310/405 | 45 | 50 | 15 | 1911 | Krauss | Siemens |

* Class 116 is dual-voltage (15 kV AC 16⅔ Hz/25 kV AC 50 Hz)
** Includes units on order

### Diesel railcars or multiple-units

| Class | Cars per unit | Motor cars per unit | Motored axles/car | Power/motor KW | Speed km/h | Units in service | First Built | Mechanical | Builders Engine | Transmission |
|---|---|---|---|---|---|---|---|---|---|---|
| **1,435 mm gauge** | | | | | | | | | | |
| 5047 | 1 | 1 | 2 | 419 | 120 | 100 | 1987 | JW | OM444LA | H Voith |
| 5147 | 2 | 1 | 4 | 838 | 120 | 10 | 1992 | JW | OM444LA | H Voith |
| 8081 | - | - | - | - | 90 | 3 | 1964 | - | - | - |
| **760 mm gauge** | | | | | | | | | | |
| 5090 | 1 | 1 | 4 | 235 | 70 | 17 | 1986 | Knotz | MAN-D 2,866 LUE | E BBC |

### Electric railcars or multiple-units

| Class | Cars per unit | Motor cars per unit | Motored Axles/car | Output/motor KW | Speed km/h | Units in Service | First built | Mechanical | Builders Electrical |
|---|---|---|---|---|---|---|---|---|---|
| **1,435 mm gauge** | | | | | | | | | |
| 4010 | 6 | 1 | 4 | 620 | 150 | 29 | 1964 | SGP | BBC |
| 4020 | 3 | 1 | 4 | 300 | 120 | 120 | 1978 | SGP | BES |
| 4030.1/2 | 3 | 1 | 4 | 250 | 100 | 50 | 1956 | SGP | BES |
| 4030.2 | 3 | 1 | 4 | 315 | 120 | 22 | 1962 | SGP | BES |
| 4130 | 3 | 1 | | 315 | 120 | 2 | 1958 | SGP | Siemens |
| 4855* | 1 | 1 | | 480 | 120 | 2 | 1989 | | Elin |
| **760 mm gauge** | | | | | | | | | |
| 4090 | 3/4 | 1/2 | | | | 2 | 1994 | SGP | Elin |

*15 kV/800 V DC

**UPDATED**

---

## Graz—Köflach Railway

Graz—Köflacher Eisenbahn GmbH (GKE)
Köflacher Gasse 35-41, A-8020 Graz
Tel: (+43 316) 598 70   Fax: (+43 316) 59 87 16
e-mail: sales@gke.at
Web: http://www.gke.at

### Key personnel
Managing Director: Franz Weintögl

Gauge: 1,435 mm
Length: 96.5 km

### Organisation
The railway, which is operated as an autonomous entity, heads south from its own station at Graz to Lieboch, where it branches northwest to Köflach and south to Wies. In addition, the company operates 28 bus routes in West Steiermark. There are 467 staff.

# Austria/RAILWAY SYSTEMS

A subsidiary company, Logistik Transport GmbH, has been established by GKE as an open access freight operator. Operations commenced in August 2001, hauling cement traffic between Marchegg and Vienna Liesing. Initially, locomotives from the Vossloh hire pool were used, pending delivery from the same company of two Type G1209 diesel-hydraulics in late 2001.

### Passenger operations
The GKE operates a diesel railcar and commuter push-pull services. In 1999, 3.96 million passenger journeys were made.

### Freight operations
Total freight tonnage in 1999 was 576,717 compared with 525,923 in 1998. Tonne-km was 10.2 million in 1997, compared with 9.9 million in 1998.

### Improvements to existing lines
In 1988 a modernisation plan was formulated. Its main aims were double-tracking, an increase in maximum speed to 100 km/h, introduction of track-to-train radio, signalling renewal, acquisition of bilevel passenger cars, and electrification from Graz to Köflach and Lieboch to Wies/Eibiswald.

### Traction and rolling stock
The company operates two steam locomotives, 13 diesel locomotives, 13 VT70 diesel trainsets, three VT10 diesel railcars and three trailers, 27 passenger coaches, including 15 bilevel passenger cars, 15 two-axle passenger cars, and 125 freight wagons. The VT70 dmus are articulated twin-units with MTU engines and ABB electric transmissions, built by Simmering-Graz-Pauker to Linke-Hofmann-Busch design under licence.

### Signalling and telecommunications
Track-to-train radio communication, supplied by AEG-Westinghouse, became operational in 1992.

**Type of coupling:** UIC-coupler, railcars and railbuses excepted
**Type of braking:** Compressed air

#### Diesel line-haul locomotives

| Class | Wheel arrangement | Power kW | Speed km/h | Weight tonnes | No in service | First built | Builders Mechanical | Builders Engine | Transmission |
|---|---|---|---|---|---|---|---|---|---|
| 1500.1-6 | B-B | 1,103 | 100 | 64-72 | 6 | 1975 | Jenbacher/Henschel | Jenbacher LM1500 | H Voith L720rU2 |
| 700 | C | 515 | 48 | 6 | 1 | 1977 | MaK | MaK | H Voith L4r4U2 |
| 600 | C | 441 | 60 | 48 | 3 | 1973 | Jenbacher | Jenbacher JW600 | H Voith L26StV |
| 1500.7 | B-B | 1,120 | 90 | 72 | 1 | 1992 | MaK | MTU 12V 396 TC14 | H Voith HDHL4r425tvz |
| 1100 | B-B | 808 | 100 | 64 | 2 | 1961 | Henschel | Caterpillar 3512DI-TA | H Voith HDHL 216rs |

#### Diesel railcars

| Class | Cars per unit | Motor cars per unit | Motored axles/car | Power/motor kW | Speed km/h | Units in service | First built | Mechanical | Builders Engine | Transmission |
|---|---|---|---|---|---|---|---|---|---|---|
| VT70 | 2 | 2 | 2 | 228 | 90 | 5 | 1980 | SGP/LHB | Büssing BTYUE | E BBC AC-DC |
| VT70 | 2 | 2 | 2 | 237 | 90 | 8 | 1985 | SGP/LHB | Büssing D2866 LUE | E BBC AC-DC |
| VT10 | 1 | 1 | 2 | 2 × 110 | 90 | 2 | 1953 | Uerdingen | Büssing U10 | M ZF-Gmeinder |

### Track
**Rail:** (B) (S49) 49.43 kg/m
**Crossties (sleepers):** Wood, thickness 160 mm
Concrete, thickness 200 mm
**Spacing:** 1,538/km plain track and curves
**Fastening:** Rippenplatte and Pandrol
**Min curvature radius:** 181.25 m
**Max gradient:** 0.015%
**Max axleload:** 20 tonnes

*UPDATED*

## Stern & Hafferl Light Railways

Stern & Hafferl Verkehrs Gesellschaft mbH
PO Box 122, A-4810 Gmunden
Tel: (+43 7612) 79 52 07  Fax: (+43 7612) 79 52 02
e-mail: sekretariat@stern-verkehr.at
Web: http://www.stern-verkehr.at

### Key personnel
President: Dipl-Ing Jochen Döderlein

### Organisation
The group operates the following railways:

*Gauge: 1,435 mm*
Linz–Eferding–Waizenkirchen–Neumarkt–Kallham/Peuerbach, 58.9 km, electrified at 750 V DC (Linzer Lokalbahn)
Lambach–Vorchdorf, 15.5 km, electrified at 800 V DC
Lambach–Haag am Hausruck, 26.3 km, electrified at 800 V DC and 15 kV 16⅔ Hz

*Gauge: 1,000 mm*
Gmunden–Vorchdorf, 14.7 km, electrified at 800 V DC
Vöcklamarkt–Attersee, 13.4 km, electrified at 800 V DC

In 2000 there were some 470 employees. Turnover was Sch550 million.

*Type GTW 2/6 electric railcars used on Linzer Lokalbahn services, which are operated by Stern & Hafferl Light Railways (Milan Šrámek)* 2001/0109844

### Traction and rolling stock
The group owns 11 electric locomotives, one diesel locomotive, 29 passenger cars, 40 light rail vehicles and 53 freight wagons. Also operated are eight Stadler GTW 2/6 lightweight electric railcars, one equipped for dual-voltage (750 V DC/15 kV AC 16⅔Hz) operation, the remainder DC only. These are used on the Linzer Lokalbahn.

## Styrian Provincial Railways

Steiermärkische Landesbahnen
PO Box 893, Radeyzkystrasse 31, A-8010 Graz
Tel: (+43 316) 812 58 10  Fax: (+43 316) 81 25 81 25
e-mail: direktion@stlb.co.at
Web: http://www.stlb.co.at

### Key personnel
General Manager: F Brünner
Managers
 Finance: H Wittmann
 Traffic: A Pint

Chief Engineers
 Mechanical and Electrical: R Zeller
 Track: F Brünner

### Organisation
The group operates the following railways:

*Gauge: 1,435 mm*
Feldbach–Bad Gleichenberg, 21 km, electrified at 1.8 kV DC
Gleisdorf–Weiz, 15 km
Peggau–Übelbach, 10 km, electrified at 15 kV AC

*Gauge: 760 mm*
Weiz–Anger, 13.5 km
Unzmarkt–Tamsweg, 65 km
Mixnitz–St Erhard, 10 km, electrified at 800 V DC.

### Traction and rolling stock
The group owns five steam, five electric and 17 diesel locomotives, four electric and seven diesel railcars, six trailers, 34 passenger cars, five baggage and postal cars, and 194 freight wagons. The most recent traction acquisitions were two 1,100 kW B-B diesel-hydraulic locomotives from Gmeinder.

## Vienna—Baden Railway (WLB)

Wiener Lokalbahnen AG
PO Box 73, Eichenstrasse 1, A-1121 Vienna
Tel: (+43 1) 55 49 10/55 49 09  Fax: (+43 1) 55 49 10 50
Web: http://www.wlb.at

### Key personnel
General Managers: R Köhler, G Zimmerl

Gauge: 1,435 mm
Length: 28 km
Electrification: 28 km at 850 V DC

### Traction and rolling stock
The railway operates four diesel locomotives, 31 electric railcars and 10 other passenger cars.

In 2000 the first of eight three-section light rail vehicles was delivered by Bombardier Transportation.
In 2001 WLB ordered three former DR Type V100.4 B-B diesel-hydraulic locomotives from Bombardier Transportation, which would first refurbish them. This would enable older machines to be withdrawn.

# AZERBAIJAN

## Azerbaijani Railways (AZR)

ul Mustofaeva 230, 370010 Baku
Tel: (+994 12) 98 44 67    Fax: (+994 12) 98 85 47

### Key personnel
President: V M Nadirli
Director General: Z A Mamedov
Deputy Director: M S Panakhov
Manager, International Affairs: R T Zeinalov

Gauge: 1,520 mm
Route length: 2,122 km
Electrification: 1,278 km at 3 kV DC

### Political background
Having borders with Russia, Georgia, Armenia and Iran, Azerbaijan gained independence from the USSR in 1991. The dispute with Armenia concerning the territory of Nagorno-Karabakh, and the cutting of both links with Russia in Abkhazia and Chechnya, had a serious effect on traffic levels. The Russian construction of a Chechnya avoiding line in 1997 restored confidence, and in late 1997 there were six pairs of cross-frontier trains daily.

In 1999 228 route-km in the country's southeastern area were reported to be controlled by Armenian military forces, preventing through operations via Nakhichevan to Iran.

Privatisation of AZR was reported to be a possibility following the introduction of enabling legislation in 1999-2000.

### Organisation
The network comprises the whole of the former SZhD's Azerbaijani Railway. Two main lines extend from the capital, Baku: the northern runs along the Caspian coast to Makhachkala in Russia, the other heads south to Alat before turning inland to serve Kyurdamir, Yevlakh, Kirovabad and Akstafa before reaching Tbilisi in Georgia. Both lines are double-track and electrified.

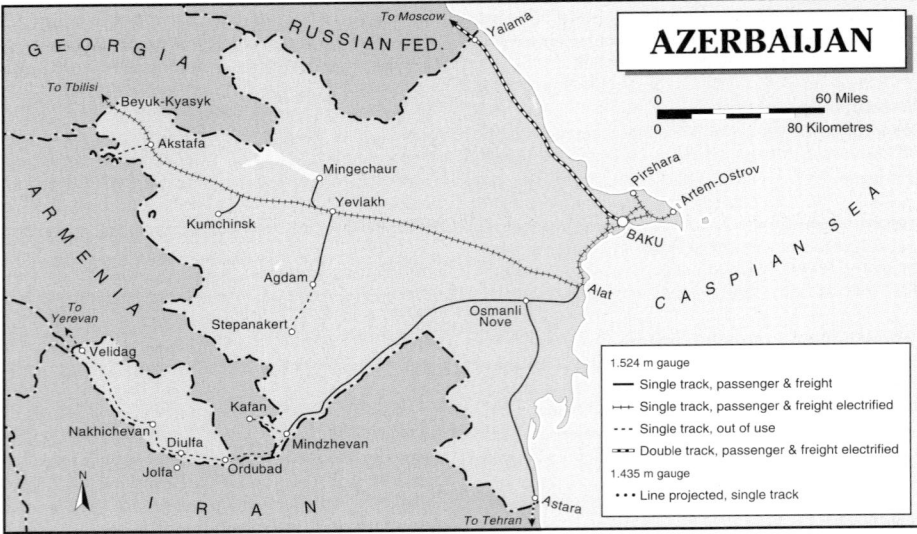

A third main line, only partially electrified, follows the Iranian border to Nakhichevan, from where there is an electrified link to Iran at Jolfa.

AZR operates a cross-Caspian ferry from Baku to Krasnovodsk in Turkmenistan.

In April 1997 agreement was reached between the governments of Azerbaijan, Georgia, and Ukraine to establish a joint international company to run rail and train ferry services linking the three countries.

### Passenger operations
In 1989, traffic stood at 2,020 million passenger-km. By 1999, this had declined to 422 million passenger-km.

In May 1997 the Baku–Moscow service was restored after a 33-month break, and in late 1997 the Baku–Rostov service was reinstated. In March 1998 a daily luxury passenger train from Baku into the disputed and Armenian-held territory of Nagorno-Karabakh was advertised; however, it could operate only as far as the *de facto* frontier, terminating at the wayside station of Barda.

A weekly service between Nakhichevan and Tabriz was also restored in February 1997, linking Azerbaijan and Iran after a nine-year break.

### Freight operations
The country is rich in oil, ore and other resources, and agrarian produce and chemicals have also been important in freight shipments. The collapse of the Soviet Union hit traffic levels hard: down from 92 million tonnes (44,900 million tonne-km) in 1989 to 7 million tonnes (2,100 million tonne-km) in 1996. Traffic then rose sharply in 1997, thanks to which the railway was able to contribute 12 billion manat to the state budget. Freight shipments were 9.1 million tonnes in 1997, 10.6 million in 1998, and 11.7 million in 1999, 5.1 billion tonne-km being recorded in 1999. Oil and petroleum products accounted for 85.9 per cent of this tonnage, with most of the remainder consisting of building materials.

### New lines
A second route into Iran has been long planned from the Astara port terminus of the line south from Baku. Its immediate goal is a mere 7 km across the border, to a site where customs and warehousing facilities are to be provided for Iranian imports which currently languish awaiting clearance at Astara. Preliminary works started in early 1993, and some construction was undertaken in 1994-95.

### Traction and rolling stock
At the end of 1996 the fleet comprised 152 electric and 142 diesel locomotives, 44 emus, 300 coaches. Among the main line electric classes are the VL8, VL10 and VL15, while diesel designs include the 3TE3, 2M62, and ChME3 types. Large amounts of stock in addition to those listed above were stored unserviceable, and in 1997 it was estimated that half the locomotive fleet was in need of replacement.

In late 1997 the railway owned 25,000 freight wagons. New and refurbished oil tank wagons were also required, both for export of Azerbaijani oil and for transit oil from Turkmenistan and Kazakhstan.

To restore the Baku–Rostov service, passenger stock had to be leased from Russia's North Caucasus Railway.

### Electrification
Azerbaijan was one of the pioneers of Soviet electrification, with the 33 km from Baku to Sabunchi and Surachami energised at 1.2 kV DC in 1926. Conversion to 1.5 kV followed in 1940, and to 3 kV in the 1960s. The most recent project was the Jolfa–Nopachen line, energised in 1989. Electric traction is responsible for 80 per cent of all traffic.

*AZR yard scene, with TEM2 and VL11 locomotives in evidence (Norman Griffiths)*

# BANGLADESH

## Ministry of Communications

Rail Bhavan, Abdul Ghani Road, 1000 Dhaka
Tel: (+880 2) 83 16 65   Fax: (+880 2) 86 43 70

**Key personnel**
Minister: Anwar Hossain

## Bangladesh Railway (BR)

Rail Headquarters, Chittagong
Tel: (+880 31) 50 01 20; 50 01 39

**Key personnel**
Director-General: M A Manaf
Additional Directors-General
  Infrastructure: M A Matin
  Marketing and Corporate Planning: A H Khan
  Rolling Stock: M A Rahim
  Operations: M A Alim
  Finance: A I M Habibur Rahman
Joint Directors-General
  Finance: Abduhu Mahmood Khan
  Operations: P C Biswas
  Engineering: A T M Nurul Islam
  Mechanical: A Z M Sazzadur Rahman
  Passenger Marketing: N M Khurshid Anwar
  Freight Marketing: Sultan Ahmed Talukder
  Personnel: MD Saifur Rahman
  Chief Planning Officer: A T M Nurul Islam
EAST ZONE
General Manager: M Farhad Reza
Additional General Manager: A M M Yahya
Chief Commercial Manager: M A Alim
Chief Mechanical Engineer: MD Shamsuddin Habibullah
Chief Engineer: M A Hashem
Chief Signals and Telecommunications Engineer:
  M Mokhlesur Rahman
Chief Electrical Engineer: M Anisur Rahman
Chief Estate Officer: Iqbal Mollah
Chief Traffic Manager: SK Habibullah
Chief Accounts Officer: R Das
Stores Controller: MD Shahjahan
WEST ZONE
General Manager: M Syed Hossain
Additional General Manager: Q A Fida
Chief Operating Superintendent: A Ahmad
Chief Accounts Officer: Shaktipati Moitra
Stores Controller: M Ahsan Habib
Chief Engineer: MD Nurul Amin Khan
Chief Mechanical Engineer: S M A Razzaque
Chief Signals and Telecommunications Engineer:
  M Aktharuzzaman
Chief Electrical Engineer: Syed Faruk Ahmed
Chief Estate Officer: Habib Ahmed
Chief Executive, Central Locomotive Workshops:
  Ahsan Zakir
PROJECT ORGANISATION
Additional General Manager: A K M Rezaul Karim
Financial Adviser: R S Devnath

Gauge: 1,676 mm; 1,000 mm
Total route length: 883.6 km; 1,822 km

## Organisation

The system is under the overall control of a Director General who heads the Railway Division of the Ministry of Communications. For day-to-day operational management the railway is partitioned into two administrative zones. The West Zone is mainly broad-gauge, the East metre-gauge. In 1994 an Asian Development Bank loan of US$80 million was granted to fund costs associated with a restructure of the railway's management and financial sectors, initiating a new 15-year investment programme.

Railway-owned shipping services operate on two routes: Jagannathganj-Serajganj Ghat (passenger ferry) and Bahadurabad-Phulchhari Ghat (passenger and wagon).

At the end of FY95-96 BR employed 41,364 staff, compared with 42,475 the previous year.

## Finance

In early 1995, the Canadian International Development Agency made BR a grant of C$150 million towards various projects, including rail investment. Expenditure of some 2.6 billion taka was planned for 1995-96, more than one-third of which was allocated to the purchase of 10 metre-gauge diesel-electrics.

| Traffic (million) | 1995 | 1996 |
|---|---|---|
| Passenger journeys | 39.6 | 32.7 |
| Passenger-km | 4,037 | 3,333 |
| Freight tonnes | 2.73 | 2.55 |
| Freight tonne-km | 760 | 689 |

## Passenger operations

Early 1995 saw systemwide implementation of a computerised seat reservation and ticketing scheme. This was installed by local company Techno Haven, under a 1991 build-operate-transfer deal. Equipment has been installed at 33 major stations which handle the bulk of BR's originating journeys. Techno Haven was managing the scheme for four years, during which time it was allowed to levy a commission on each ticket sold to recover its investment.

Further privatisation of the passenger business's commercial aspects was foreshadowed in 1998 when tenders were invited for the provision of ticketing and onboard services on selected routes in the north of the network. In the same year a private sector company, Agngur Enterprise, commenced operation of passenger services between Santahar and Lamonirhat, paying BR an annual fee. Bids were invited for similar arrangements on the Dhaka-Chittagong and Dhaka-Mymenshing routes.

Current works are aimed at raising the top speed of existing metre-gauge services from 75 to 95 km/h. Instrumental to this was the delivery of 10 diesel locomotives from India's DLW in 1996. A new fleet of coaches is also proposed (see below).

Early in 1997, India and Bangladesh reached agreement in principle on the restoration of passenger services between the two countries, which have been suspended since the war of 1965. First priority will be a Calcutta-Jessore route.

## Freight operations

BR's principal freight task is now hauling containers between the port of Chittagong and Dhaka, using box wagons converted into flats. In 1993, to cope with planned expansion of the Dhaka terminal to handle 25,000 containers a year, China's LORIC supplied 80 container flat wagons for this traffic. A second daily container train was inaugurated in early 1994.

In this sector, too, the emphasis is on long-haul traffic. General freight haulage has declined on account of poor-quality service, with many non-containerised imported goods arriving at Chittagong now being distributed by road.

## New lines

At present the only link between the East and West networks is a metre-gauge freight wagon ferry across the Jamuna River. The crossing adds 18 hours to transits. BR is to construct a 100 km metre-gauge rail connection between the two zones, from Bogra on its Santahar-Bonarpara line to Boria on the Jamalpur-Jagannathganj Ghat branch. Centrepiece of the new link is the long-planned US$696 million, 4.8 km road-rail bridge over the Jamuna River; this was due to open in mid-1998. In early 1997, BR shortlisted eight groups for construction of 99 km of new railway to link up with the new bridge and for reconstruction of 250 km of existing track. Construction supervision contracts for these related track projects were awarded to Canarail and Systra in early 1998.

Feasibility studies for three new lines and a Dhaka-Laksam direct line have been completed, but the latter project has been shelved despite the obvious benefit to Dhaka-Chittagong trains.

## Improvements to existing lines

BR intends to renew track and bridges over its chief broad-gauge route, the 475 km from Parbatipur to Khulna. On the metre-gauge, similar work covering 489 km is planned on the Bhairab Bazar-Dewangonj Bazar, Bonapara-Kanchan and Akhaura-Chhatak Bazar lines.

Indian aid has been sought for the doubling of a 32 km section of the Dhaka-Chittagong main line, while a further 65 km section, from Tongi to Bhairab Bazar, is to be doubled with funding from the German government.

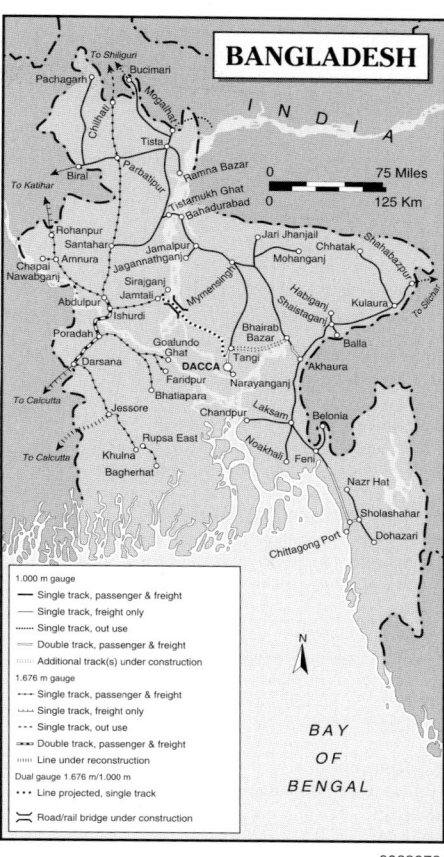

Mechanised track maintenance has been introduced on the Dhaka-Chittagong main line and BR plans to introduce such techniques more widely.

In 1998 consultants were appointed to oversee a two-year programme of flood damage repair.

## Traction and rolling stock

In mid-1996 BR was operating 225 diesel-electric (55 broad-gauge and 170 metre-gauge) and 47 diesel-hydraulic (13 broad-gauge and 34 metre-gauge) locomotives. Coaching stock comprised 288 broad-gauge and 1,142 metre-gauge vehicles; 3,601 broad-gauge and 12,450 metre-gauge freight wagons were also owned. Motive power includes units of British, Canadian, US, Hungarian and Japanese manufacture. BR also operates seven single-unit diesel railcars.

The equipment of wagon stock with vacuum brakes is a high priority, with the objective of continuously braking at least half the vehicles in all freight trains.

In early 1995, metre-gauge operations benefited from the delivery of nine Type DE 1650 diesel-electrics ordered from ABB Henschel. These were funded by a grant from the German government. Other rolling stock purchases approved for 1995 included 66 metre-gauge coaches from Iran's Wagon Pars, delivered mid-1998, 18 broad-gauge coaches (air conditioned) and eight generator cars. A deal was also concluded with India's RITES for supply of 10 metre-gauge diesel-electrics built by DLW, which were delivered in early 1996. In addition, BR has procured 223 passenger coaches and 34 67-tonne freight wagons from the Pakistan Railways Carriage Factory.

In the longer term, complete renewal of the traction fleet is planned, with 77 broad-gauge and 197 metre-gauge locomotives required. Substantial purchases of passenger stock would be necessary to uplift the quality of intercity service.

## Signalling and telecommunications

A 1,700 km fibre optic network has been constructed along routes connecting the East and West zones of the railway with a radio link across the Jamuna River. The work included the supply and installation of digital automatic telephone exchanges and telephone instruments. This provides an automatic telephone service between BR

# BELARUS

## Ministry of Transport and Communications

ul Lenina 17, 220030 Minsk
Tel: (+375 172) 68 74 07   Fax: (+375 172) 27 56 48

### Key personnel
Minister: A V Lukashov
Head of Presidential Cabinet: V I Rakhmanko

### Political background
In mid-1996, a governmental decree transferred control of the national railway from the Ministry of Transport and Communications to direct oversight by the Presidential Cabinet.

## Belarussian Railways (BCh)

ul Lenina 17, 220745 Minsk GSP
Tel: (+375 172) 96 44 63   Fax: (+375 172) 27 56 48

### Key personnel
President: V I Rakhmanko
Directors
  Passengers: V M Kochanov
  Freight: A I Stankevich
  Infrastructure: G M Pankov
  Strategy: G V Brychkina
  Operations: N A Dichtienko
  Traction and Rolling Stock: V V Nasarenko
  Research and Development: V I Stepouk
  Personnel: S G Chilov
  Information Technology: G V Novik
  Finance: P M Babich
  Supplies: V F Chentsov
  Law: I I Zariedskaja
Manager, International Affairs: G A Talay
Manager, Communications: V I Ring

Gauge: 1,520 mm
Route length: 5,523 km
Electrification: 875.2 km at 25 kV 50 Hz

### Political background
Belarus, now an independent state, signed wide-ranging Union Treaties with Russia in 1996 and 1997. Belarus straddles the Berlin–Moscow main line and, in conjunction with Poland, potentially provides, from a Russian point of view, a more reliable form of access from Lithuania to the Russian enclave of Kaliningrad on the Baltic coast. In March 1998 a permanent Belarussian/Russian working group for railway co-operation was set up.

In 1998, a Railway Law, four years in the making, was passed. Previously, Soviet-era procedures had been preserved, although many of these had no legal foundation. The new law, among other things, defines railway property and thereby makes more difficult piecemeal appropriation under the guise of privatisation. The wearing of railway uniforms and the name of the railway itself are now legalised.

Unlike in some other eastern European countries, privatisation has not become an issue for BCh.

### Organisation
BCh was formed after the break-up of the former Soviet Railways (SZhD) in 1992 and comprises SZhD's Belarussian Railway. It is mainly a transit railway. Workers engaged in the 'main activity' totalled 78,526 at end-1999. Those directly engaged in operations totalled 55,783.

### Finance
Despite a precipitous collapse, freight traffic remains profitable, especially transit traffic, for which the tariffs are about six times higher than domestic rates. The surplus is used to offset losses on passenger services, but in September 1997 an overall loss was recorded. The government no longer provides financial support, so the subsequent recovery depended on cost-cutting and the marketing of auxiliary services. Thirty per cent of foreign currency earnings have to be sold to the government at a rate fixed by the latter. Belarus reportedly has the lowest tariff rates in the Russian Federation and Associated States (CIS). Some 15 per cent of railway income is assigned to the Railway Investment Fund and is treated for tax purposes as an operating cost.

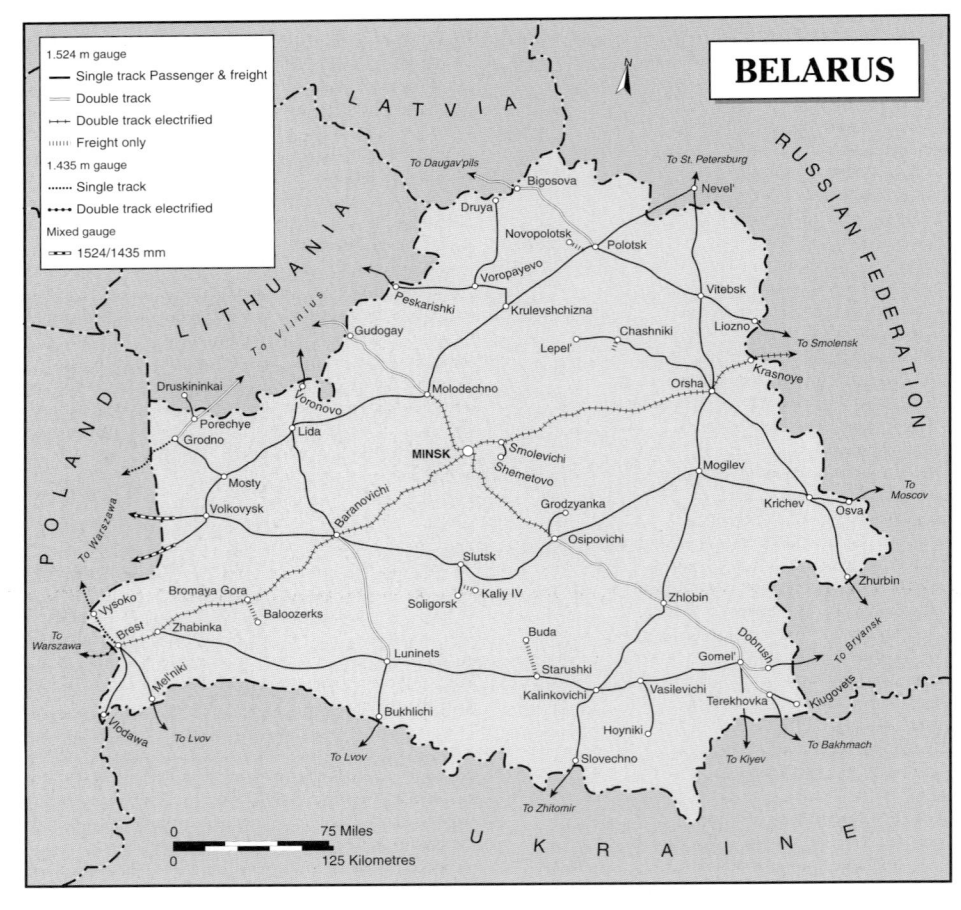

| Traffic | 1998 | 1999 |
|---|---|---|
| Passenger journeys (million) | 147 | 165 |
| Passenger-km (billion) | 13.3 | 16.9 |
| Freight tonnes (million) | 52.3 | 51.6 |
| Freight tonne-km (billion) | 30.4 | 30.5 |

### Passenger operations
At the time of the break up of SZhD, Belarus was recording over 18 billion rail passenger-km annually. The subsequent decline resulted in a figure of 12.5 billion passenger-km for 1995.

Whereas international services are profitable, internal services return only 23 per cent of their costs. The railway's Dortura travel agency is seeking to develop long-distance traffic and operates trains to Bulgarian holiday resorts.

### Freight operations
Traffic in 1991 was recorded at 65.6 billion tonne-km, but by 1995 this had dropped to 25.5 billion. Up to half of this volume is international traffic and the 1995 figure represented an increase of 50 per cent over 1994, partly encouraged by certain tariff cuts. The freight agency Belintertrans has captured some east-west traffic from Ukrainian routes.

BCh signed an agreement with Russia's Gazprom gas company to build a terminal for exports of compressed gas to Europe, with construction starting in 1996. The location is near the Belarus-Poland border in the vicinity of Vaukavysk, the cost is put at US$800,000 and there are interchange facilities with 1,435 mm gauge tanker wagons.

### Improvements to existing lines
Electrification began in the 1960s on the Minsk–Molodechno and Minsk–Pukhovchi lines. Now two double-track routes form the core of the system: a line from Minsk to Vilnius, Lithuania, which is electrified as far as Molodechno; and a northeast to southwest line crossing the country from the Russian Federation to Poland, passing through Orsha, Minsk, Baranovichi and Brest, which is electrified throughout.

Station improvements have been undertaken at Minsk, Gomel, Glubokoe, Brest, Vitebsk and Mogilev.

BCh has begun planning track, signalling and other improvements to raise the maximum speed of passenger traffic on its part of the Berlin–Moscow 'corridor' — the Orsha–Brest section — to 160 km/h by 2005. Thanks partly to the import of Austrian track manufacturing, the Orsha–Minsk section is now rated as top grade. Meanwhile, a new dedicated high-speed Berlin–Moscow line (300-350 km/h) has been proposed for the future. The European Union is helping to fund the design phase, but further work awaits extra funds, which are being sought from the European Investment Bank, the European Bank for Reconstruction and Development and the World Bank. Part of the project could be a Talgo-type automatic gauge-changing system.

### Traction and rolling stock
In 1994 the number of active main line locomotives was reduced from 317 to 128 in response to falling traffic. The stock includes ChS4t electrics plus ChME3, M62 family

and TEP60 diesels, together with DR1P, DR1A and ER9 family multiple-units. To preserve the advantages of standardisation and in view of the close operational links with Russian Federal Railways, it is intended that future locomotives will be imported from Russia. The Russian EP200 electric locomotive design will be imported for use on the Moscow—Berlin through passenger trains.

BCh has embarked on a rolling stock modernisation programme which is due to be completed in 2000, the main aim of which is to exploit domestic resources. In 1999, BCh took delivery of a prototype diesel Class DDB1 trainset from the Demikhovo dmu plant in Russia. The train is formed of two M62 diesel locomotives and 10 refurbished trailers in a push-pull configuration.

In addition to existing locomotive overhaul facilities in Baranovichi, Vitebsk and Zhlobin, a new maintenance shop for diesel multiple-units is to be built in Lida. This will allow the Baranovichi workshops to be responsible exclusively for overhauls of Class ChS4T electric locomotives, Mogilev for Class ChME3 diesels and Brest for Classes M62 and 2M62. Power units and spare parts will be supplied by Brest, Orsha and Polotsk depots, while axles will be provided by Baranovichi and Lida.

# BELGIUM

## Ministry of Transport

63-65 Rue de la Loi, B-1040 Brussels
Tel: (+32 2) 237 67 00  Fax: (+32 2) 231 19 12

**Key personnel**
Minister: Isabelle Durant
Secretary-General: R de Borger

*UPDATED*

## DL Cargo

Velodoomstrat 121, B-2850 Boom
Tel: (+32 3) 844 97 02  Fax: (+32 3) 844 97 03
e-mail: jeroen.lejeune@dlcargo.com
Web: http://www.dlcargo.com

**Key personnel**
Director: Jeroen Le Jeune

**Organisation**
DL Cargo was the first open access operator to run freight trains in Belgium, commencing services on 3 April 2002. It operates a three times-weekly train of BMW car components for export from Regensburg, Germany, to Antwerp. The company, of which 40 per cent is owned by Hupac (qv), has stated its intention to expand its operations in Europe.

**Traction and rolling stock**
Within Belgium DL Cargo uses a General Motors JT42CWR diesel-electric locomotive ('Class 66') hired from Porterbrook and one electric and diesel locomotive, both hired, in Germany.

*NEW ENTRY*

## Société Nationale des Chemins de fer Belges (SNCB) Nationale Maatschappij der Belgische Spoorwegen (NMBS)

85 Rue de France, B-1060 Brussels
Tel: (+32 2) 525 20 34  Fax: (+32 2) 525 40 45
Web: http://www.sncb.be/www.nmbs.be/www.b-rail.be

**Key personnel**
Chairman of the Board of Administration: Alain Deneef
Chief Executive: Karel Vinck
Managing Director: (vacant)
Deputy Managing Director: (vacant)
Director: Jean-Marie Raviart
Public and Press Relations: (vacant)

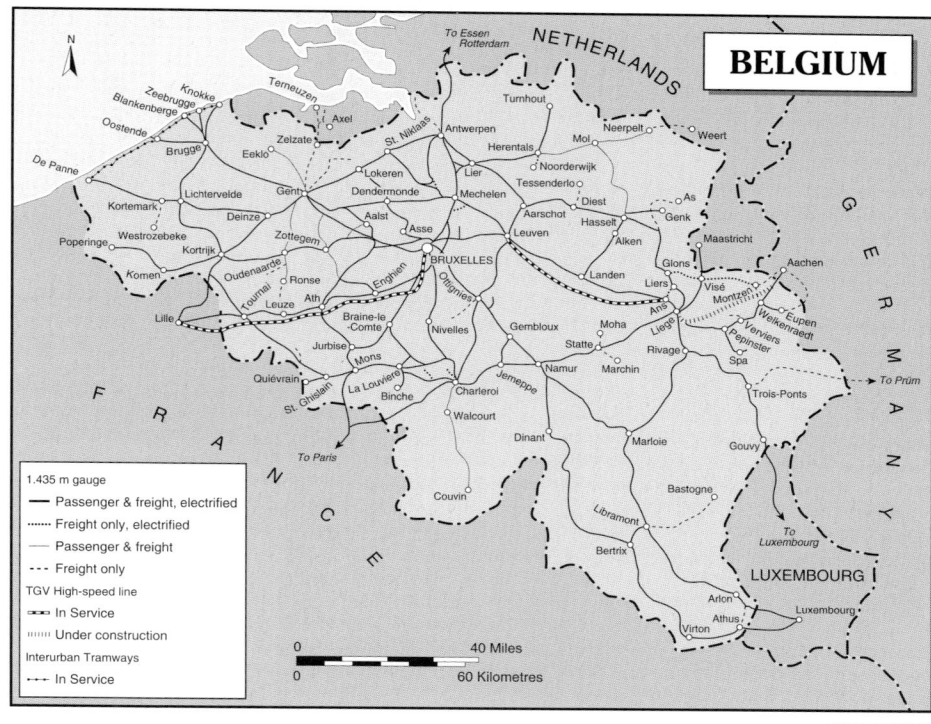

Gauge: 1,435 mm
Route length: 3,471 km
Electrification: 2,631 km at 3 kV DC, 74 km at 25 kV 50 Hz AC

**Political background**
In October 1992 SNCB was statutorily reconstituted as a public limited company with the state holding all shares. New financial arrangements were concluded at this time, under which international passenger traffic and all wagon and part-load freight operations were excluded from state support; in these sectors SNCB is required to be fully commercial.

The early 1990s economic recession hit SNCB hard and prompted a series of economising measures in 1994-95. This resulted in a severe bout of labour unrest in late 1995, which led to a tripartite agreement between SNCB, government and unions to put the corporation on a fresh financial footing. The agreement, reached in January 1996, was to see €9.2 billion invested in the railway over the period 1996-2005. About a third of this would go to high-speed line construction, the rest to upgrading the historic network.

The state undertook to provide €396-570 million annually towards the investment plan. In addition, the state reimburses the railway for the cost of meeting its social obligations.

The Belgian government has created a special fund for financing new infrastructure, consisting of both public and private contributions; interest will be paid on investments with the fund. The fund will invest €3.1 billion in the high-speed line project.

SNCB's Board of Directors approved an action plan, 'Target 2005', based on the tripartite agreement, in February 1996. On 1 January 1998, the enterprise was restructured as ten 'activity centres', five 'service centres' and seven 'central co-ordination units'. This will include the separation of infrastructure management according to EU rules.

In May 2001, a new 12-year investment plan was agreed. Over this period €16 billion will be invested to cope with forecast traffic growth of 50 per cent. The main priorities will be:
- purchase of new stock (€3.4 billion);
- completion of the TGV network (€2.38 billion);
- modernisation of main lines;
- creation of a Brussels RER system (€3.3 billion);
- development of rail links to Brussels airport;
- development of rail links to ports.

This sum does not include rolling stock for the Brussels RER. The new plan includes a call for investment from the private sector, the most likely source being the port authorities.

At the same time, the board of SNCB was reduced from 18 to 10 members. The trade unions lose representation but are part of a new 'strategic council', together with regional transport operators.

Approval of several major schemes and reorganisation plans were delayed by top management changes. Several key posts remained vacant in mid-2002.

In 2000, SNCB's total staff was 41,384.

*Alstom-built Class 41 dmu for regional services at Hasselt (Marcel Vleugels)* 2002/0524917

# RAILWAY SYSTEMS/Belgium

**Finance** (million €)

| Revenue | 2000 | 2001 |
|---|---|---|
| Passenger | 887.3 | 917.7 |
| Freight | 344.5 | 323.0 |
| ABX | 133.1 | 114.5 |
| Infrastructure management | 628.6 | 642.9 |
| Other | 192.5 | 173.2 |
| Total operating revenue | 2,186.0 | 2171.3 |
| Other revenue | 1,450.7 | 1,456.5 |
| Total revenue | 3,636.7 | 3,634.8 |

| Expenditure | 2000 | 2001 |
|---|---|---|
| Materials | 211.9 | 223.8 |
| Services | 672.2 | 641.8 |
| Personnel | 2,306.8 | 2,392.0 |
| Depreciation | 454.6 | 474.1 |
| Provision for risk | −147.7 | −160.8 |
| Other | 11.2 | 25.8 |
| Total expenditure | 3,509.0 | 3,596.7 |

SNCB reported a surplus of €38 million in 2001 compared with €128 million in 2000. Turnover was down 0.7 per cent to €3,634.8 million but operating costs rose 2.5 per cent to €3,596.7 million. Passenger traffic was up 5.4 per cent.

| Traffic (million) | 1999 | 2000 | 2001 |
|---|---|---|---|
| Passenger journeys | 147.3 | 153.3 | 160.3 |
| Passenger-km | 7,354 | 7,754 | 8,117 |
| Freight tonnes | 59.1 | 61.3 | 57.1 |
| Freight tonne-km | 7,392 | 7,674 | 7,080 |

## Passenger operations

Passenger revenue overall rose by 3.4 per cent in 2001, to reach €917.7 million. International revenue, at €201.6 million, made up an increasing proportion of the total.

International passenger traffic grew by 3 per cent and revenue by 1 per cent in 2001.

*Eurostar*

Eurostar trains to London via the Channel Tunnel introduced in November 1994 (for details see United Kingdom entry) and TGV services to Paris in January 1995 (for details see France entry), have dramatically improved international rail services to and from Brussels.

Eurostar has become market leader on this route. In March 1999, a centralised management structure – Eurostar Group – was implemented to determine commercial policy and the development of all Eurostar activities.

Eurostar traffic has been slower to develop than on the Paris–London route and the basic service remains every two hours. The opening of the Belgian high-speed line on 14 December 1997 cut journey times to London by 40 minutes to 2 hours 40 minutes. This will be reduced further to 2 hours 20 minutes in 2003 with the opening in the UK of the Channel Tunnel Rail Link. Eurostar traffic fell by 4.5 per cent in 2001.

*Thalys*

SNCB and SNCF (French National Railways) created a joint venture company, Westrail International, to manage Thalys services over the new Paris–Brussels high-speed route. Westrail International was renamed Thalys International (qv) in May 1999 and was expected subsequently to include the participation of Netherlands and German Railways.

In June 1996, the Paris TGVs, marketed as Thalys, began using the first section of the Belgian high-speed line. Frequencies were improved to hourly, with the journey taking 2 hours between the French and Belgian capitals. The opening of the complete line cut the journey time to 85 minutes and was accompanied by an increase in frequency. Success has been such that the service frequency was to be increased to half-hourly in September 2002.

Six weekday Thalys services from Paris run beyond Brussels to Amsterdam. Seven of the Paris trains run beyond Brussels via Liège and Aachen to Cologne on a basic two-hour frequency. One pair of return Thalys services per day run from Ostend to Paris via Bruges and Ghent and one pair between Namur and Paris via Charleroi and Mons.

A Thalys service from Amsterdam to Disneyland, Paris, operates during summer months and in November 1999, Thalys introduced four pairs of trains between Brussels and Disneyland, with some calling at Charles de Gaulle/Roissy airport. From May 2001, Thalys introduced an Amsterdam–Marseille service. In 2001 Thalys traffic grew by 4.4 per cent and revenue by 9.2 per cent, with 5.8 million passengers carried.

*TGV*

A Brussels–Nice through TGV introduced in 1995 proved successful: this prompted the introduction of additional through TGVs to Bordeaux, Lyon, Marseille, Perpignan and Grenoble. Almost all of these trains run via Lille, where they attach a second unit. In winter, direct TGV services to the Alps have been introduced.

In early 2001, Air France decided to withdraw its Brussels–Paris service. Air France passengers are now carried in dedicated coaches on the Thalys Brussels–Roissy CDG service, which has been increased to six train pairs daily.

*Domestic services*

Domestic traffic rose by 4.7 per cent in 2001. Traffic is dominated by travel to and from the Brussels area. A regular-interval domestic timetable, carefully designed to facilitate interchange, provides connections between internal InterCity (IC) and InterRegional (IR) routes. The services are among the most intensive in Europe. International expresses fit into this pattern at less-frequent intervals and the basic service is supplemented by large numbers of direct trains, mainly to/from Brussels during Monday-Friday peak periods. At weekends, additional direct trains run to/from tourist areas, particularly coastal resorts.

The IC/IR system was completely revised in May 1998. The main features were more through services to Brussels, Brussels Airport and Lille, and improved co-ordination with the TGV system.

*Brussels RER*

The 1980s STAR 21 plan for Belgian Railways foresaw the creation of a Brussels RER (Regional Express) network of nine routes. Most of them should converge on the cross-city Brussels Junction railway, while the others will provide important orbital connections.

In 2001 the government approved the quadrupling of lines from Brussels to Nivelles and Ottignies to allow more frequent RER stopping services.

SNCB has also proposed construction of a new high-speed line from the outskirts of Brussels to Namur with a branch to Charleroi. This would free capacity on existing lines. In May 2000, the government asked SNCB to add a third track to the Brussels–Denderleeuw line. SNCB is studying the design of a new double-deck emu type for RER services.

SNCB wishes to create a second high-speed terminal for the Brussels area at Schaerbeek, north of the city centre. The new station would become a major interchange for RER and other domestic services and would include a terminal for services to Brussels airport.

In May 1998, a larger station opened at Brussels airport on a new alignment of the branch line from Zaventem. This was part of the work on expanding the airport passenger terminal. The new alignment will eventually allow a spur off the Brussels–Antwerp line to the airport and a further spur to the Brussels–Leuven–Liège line. Total cost of this work is €74 million. The second of these was under construction in 2001.

Also planned is a tunnel connection between the Brussels–Ottignies line at Schuman and Schaerbeek–Josaphat. This will create a second north-south RER route, possibly for direct services between the European Union headquarters complex at Schumann and the airport station.

## Freight operations

SNCB's freight services are now marketed under the 'B-Cargo' logo, using the stylised 'B' that is the railway's trademark. B-Cargo's strategy is based on creating group synergies with SNCB's IFB and ABX subsidiaries.

Rail freight traffic is dominated by Antwerp, which generates around half of all traffic, either in the port or its hinterland. The ports of Gent and Zeebrugge also generate large volumes. The other main traffic generator is heavy industry, particularly steel production, concentrated around Liège and Charleroi. This traffic is likely to decline and B-Cargo is therefore seeking to diversify its activities. In 2000 B-Cargo lost all coal traffic to power stations after the generating company Electrabel switched to barge transport. Transit traffic between the Netherlands and southern Europe via France is important.

SNCB now reviews private sidings served on a biannual basis. The number of marshalling yards has been reduced to four: Gent Zeehaven, Antwerp Nord, Kinkempois (Liège) and Monceau (Charleroi). Minor yards still open include Schaerbeek (Brussels), Stockem and Montzen.

In 2001, freight volume fell by 7 per cent and revenue by 6.2 per cent.

The ABX parcels subsidiary saw volume rise by 1.4 per cent but turnover fell by 14 per cent. Early in 2000, ABX formed a joint subsidiary with the Belgian post office with the aim of offering an express parcels service. The subsidiary's joint turnover is €2.5 billion.

In January 1998 SNCB, in conjunction with SNCF, established Europe's first 'freight corridor' with the aim of providing faster transits and more train paths plus a 'one-stop-shop' for the creation of new services. The route runs from Muizen, Leuven and Namur to Luxembourg, then to Lyon, France with a branch to Spain (Barcelona and Valencia) and to Italy (Gioia Tauro). In the first two years, the corridor generated 1.1 million tonnes or 29,000 wagonloads, the equivalent of two trains a day.

International services, particularly 'Eurailcargo' wagonload services, are increasingly important to SNCB, Antwerp–Munich traffic growing by 29 per cent in 1997 and Antwerp to Malaczewicze (Poland) by 60 per cent.

## Intermodal operations

SNCB sees intermodal freight as a growth area, both for maritime containers and for inland swapbodies.

A domestic shuttle 'Railbarge' service for containers operates between Antwerp and Zeebrugge, the 'Port Express' service links Antwerp with Rotterdam on a daily basis and a Zeebrugge–Dunkerque service is also provided.

A new intermodal terminal, known as 'Main Hub,' near Antwerp Noord marshalling yard, opened in late 2000. Capacity is 600,000-700,000 TEU annually and this can eventually be doubled.

In 1998, SNCB created a subsidiary, InterFerryBoats (IFB), through the merger of Interferry and Ferryboats. IFB specialises in operating terminals for intermodal traffic and logistics. It operates five terminals in Belgium and recently opened a facility in Dunkerque, France. It also organises the operation of intermodal shuttles via its hub at Muizen.

*Class 21 and 27 electric locomotives heading a Zeebrugge–Antwerp 'Rail Barge' intermodal service (John C Baker)*

*Class 13 electric locomotive on an Eupen—Ostend intercity service at Oostkamp* (John C Baker)

## New lines

### Paris—Brussels high-speed line
The complete Belgian section of the Brussels—Paris high-speed line, from Fretin near Lille (France) to Lembeek, opened on 14 December 1997. The new line cut Brussels—Paris and Brussels—London journey times by around 40 minutes. Upgrading work continues on the classic line between Lembeek and Brussels Midi station. A six-track cut-and-cover tunnel through Halle was completed in 1999 and 220 km/h operation will soon be possible most of the way from Lembeek to Brussels. A flyover at the mouth of Midi station is to be completed by 2004.

### Brussels—Antwerp upgrading
At an estimated cost of €116 million, two tracks of the existing quadruple line from Brussels to Antwerp are being upgraded for 160 km/h by 2005. The work includes: complete track renewal, including increase of inter-track space to 2.25 m to simplify mechanised maintenance; resignalling for reversible working and accompanying installation of crossovers; and renewal of the electric traction current supply system.

From Berchem, on the southern outskirts of Antwerp, construction of a through line in tunnel under the city began in 1998. The new line will serve an underground station beneath the Antwerp Central terminus before joining the Roosendaal line near Antwerp Dam. Thus, services to and from the Netherlands will avoid their present reversal in Antwerp Central, saving more than 10 minutes. Completion is scheduled in 2005.

Construction started in 2000 of the new high-speed line from Antwerp to Schiphol, Amsterdam; completion date is estimated at 2006.

### Brussels—Liège—Aachen—Cologne
Tracklaying on the new 300 km/h line from Leuven to Liège started in September 2000. The line will open in December 2002. Liège Guillemins station is to be completely rebuilt (see below). The line from Brussels to Leuven will be widened and upgraded for 220 km/h running by 2005. From Brussels Midi to Liège, 105 km, the transit time will be 39 minutes when the project is completed. From Liège to Aachen, 41.5 km, a mix of new line and upgrading will bring the travel time down from 42 to 28 minutes.

SNCB has created three subsidiary companies to manage construction of the Belgian elements of the high-speed lines: TUC Rail SA for the infrastructure; Eurostation SA for the works at Brussels Midi and Antwerp Central stations; and Euro-Liège TGV, for the new station in Liège.

## Improvements to existing lines
In 2000, 74 km were approved for 300 km/h running, 116 km for 160 km/h, 621 km for 140 km/h, 239 km for 130 km/h, 1,117 km for 120 km/h and 1,247 km for less than 120 km/h.

The lines from Brussels to Antwerp, Halle and Leuven are being upgraded as part of the high-speed lines programme (see section above).

Other parts of the network are being upgraded for 160 km/h speeds. Routes being tackled include Charleroi to Antoing; Brussels to Namur; and Brussels to Ostend. Parts of the last named route will be improved for speeds of up to 200 km/h. In most cases, the spacing between tracks has to be widened from 140 to 160 cm during track renewal work.

SNCB is to study an increase in speeds on the Brussels—Luxembourg line, on which trains are currently limited to 130 km/h. Given the nature of the route, tilting stock may be used.

The 1996-2005 plan for freight concentrates investment on raising limits to 22.5 tonnes per axle and speeds to 120 km/h, plus standardisation on a large loading gauge for intermodal traffic. In addition, there will be investment in extra tracks on the approaches to Antwerp and Zeebrugge.

Agreement was reached in 2000 on the reopening of the 'Iron Rhine' route between Antwerp and the Ruhr region of Germany. This will lead to increased use of the non-electrified Antwerp—Neerpelt line, and SNCB is considering an order for heavy freight diesel locomotives for this route.

It has also been agreed that a new freight line east of Antwerp should be built to link Antwerp Noord yard and Lier to bypass the congested city area. Another new line from the port to the Roosendaal—Vlissingen line in the Netherlands is at the planning stage. A line from the port to the Gent line awaits finance.

The SNCB infrastructure department is to reorganise its maintenance activities around 22 'infrastructure logistics centres' (CLIs) by 2006.

## Major new stations
A mammoth reconstruction of Brussels Midi (South) station is under way. To be executed in four phases, the project had to be carried out in stages because of the need to keep the busy 22-platform station fully operational throughout the rebuilding. When complete the station will form part of a major urban redevelopment project embracing 120,000 m² of offices and conference facilities, and 20,000 m² of retail space. A new underground parking area for 2,500 cars was completed in 2001.

The first three phases of the scheme are concerned with completion of a terminal and platforms for high-speed train services on the west side of the station. As all passengers for Eurostar services to London must first pass through security checks, an airport-style enclosed departure area for terminal platforms 1 and 2 has been created, with its own bar and toilet facilities.

Through platforms are used mainly by Thalys (Paris—Brussels—Cologne/Amsterdam) TGV trains. The main concourse, a wide gallery with the usual offices and facilities along each flank, including a travel centre with 32 open counters, has been rebuilt to more spacious proportions. Overall roofing has been provided for all platforms.

Liège Guillemins station is being completely rebuilt as part of SNCB's high-speed plans. There will be a major remodelling of the track layout and a new building designed by the Spanish architect, Santiago Calatrava.

Antwerp Centraal station is being rebuilt. The former terminal with 10 platforms is being expanded to provide 14 platforms on three levels. Capacity will be doubled by 2005 by the provision of through tracks below street level.

## Traction and rolling stock
At the end of 2001 SNCB traction and rolling stock comprised 408 electric locomotives, 634 diesel locomotives, 1,235 emu vehicles, four Eurostar trainsets, seven Thalys trainsets, 120 dmu vehicles, 27 cars, 1,650 passenger coaches and 13,867 freight wagons.

*Vossloh-built Class 77 B-B diesel-hydraulic locomotive at Bruges* (Marcel Vleugels)

*15-road yard built to handle expanding traffic at the port of Zeebrugge* (David Haycock)

# RAILWAY SYSTEMS/Belgium

SNCB is investing heavily in both new rolling stock and refurbishment at present. In December 1995 SNCB and CFL (Luxembourg Railways) ordered a total of 80 3 kV DC/25 kV AC locomotives from Alstom. Designated Class 13 by SNCB, the locomotives cost €3.48 million each and deliveries were completed in late 2001. The locos will be managed in a pool with the 19 CFL machines. Main duties will be freight on the Antwerp–Luxembourg corridor plus Ostend–Antwerp, Ostend–Eupen (at speeds up to 200 km/h) and Liège–Luxembourg passenger trains. In June 2001 these locomotives started to operate through to Metz, in France. SNCB is considering ordering 60 additional locomotives.

In the short term, SNCB foresees the need for around 140 new electric locomotives to replace older types and is consulting neighbouring countries over the need for multi-voltage designs. A specification for a four-voltage locomotive design is being drawn up.

In June 1997, SNCB ordered 90 Class 77 B-B 1150 kW diesel-hydraulic locomotives from Siemens (now Vossloh) for €1.5 million each. These will have ABC power units manufactured in Belgium. The locomotives will be used mainly to replace a heterogeneous fleet used for shunting and short-distance freight duties. Delivery started in late 1999. In 2001, SNCB ordered 90 additional locomotives and was considering an order for 90 more of the class to replace its entire main line diesel fleet.

At the same time, SNCB ordered 80 Class 41 two-car dmus seating 150 passengers from Alstom Transporte of Spain at a cost of €1.76 million each. In 2001, SNCB ordered 16 additional units of this type. The units were being delivered from late 2000 to 2003, replacing all remaining diesel locomotive-hauled passenger trains. In 2002, SNCB was modifying six Class 55 Co-Co diesel electric locos for operation on the 'Iron Rhine' route from Antwerp to Mönchengladbach, Germany. This involves adding Dutch and German signalling equipment.

In 1999, deliveries of 163 Type I11 air conditioned cars, capable of 200 km/h were completed. They were constructed by Bombardier Transportation (BN) in Bruges.

Also placed with Bombardier was an order for 120 three-car air conditioned 160 km/h Type AM96 emus with three-phase AC drives by ACEC, regenerative braking and comprehensive diagnostics. Delivery began early in 1996 and ran to May 2000. Each unit has a single power car, motored on all axles, for a total output of 1,240 kW. Cab design follows that of Danish IC-3 trains. For operation from Antwerp and Liège to Lille, 50 of the AM96 units are dual-voltage (3 kV DC/25 kV 50 Hz AC) versions.

In 1999, an order was placed with Bombardier Transportation for 210 Type M6 double-deck coaches for push-pull commuter services. They will be air conditioned and equipped to a much higher standard than previous stock. Delivery is planned for 2002-2004.

SNCB is carrying out refurbishment work on its fleet of 578 Type M4 hauled coaches and 181 two-car AM66-79 emus.

In the freight sector, B-Cargo has recently introduced 200 type Shimns bogie covered wagons for carrying steel coil, built by Costamasnaga in Italy, and has unveiled the prototype of the future type Rils covered wagon for the carriage of pallets, steel coils or rolls of paper. This has a new fast load blocking system known as 'Easy Clamp'. In 2000 SNCB started to receive 700 Lgnss 500 Sgnss wagons for container transport from Astra, Romania.

New traction maintenance depots have opened at Antwerp Noord and Charleroi, while in 2001 a third facility was under construction at Ostend. New wagon repair works have opened at Kinkempois and Monceau.

### High-speed rolling stock

SNCB owns four of the 38 Eurostar trainsets used jointly with SNCF and Eurostar UK Ltd for the London–Paris/Brussels high-speed operation (for details see the United Kingdom entry).

Seventeen four-voltage Thalys sets are jointly operated for the Paris–Brussels–Cologne service by SNCB, NS, SNCF, and DB. A maintenance depot for Eurostar and Thalys sets has been built at Brussels-Forest. Two NS and two DB sets as well as the seven Belgian sets are maintained there by SNCB.

## Signalling and telecommunications

SNCB is progressively installing a track-to-train radio system, employing equipment supplied by Alcatel-Bell. Because of the country's dual language and the need for drivers to use the system with facility in both French- and Flemish-speaking territory, the system uses

### Diesel locomotives

| Class | Wheel arrangement | Power hp | Speed km/h | Weight tonnes | No in service | First built | Mechanical | Builders Engine | Transmission |
|---|---|---|---|---|---|---|---|---|---|
| 51 | Co-Co | 1,950 | 120 | 117 | 49 | 1961 | Cockerill-Ougrée | Cockerill-Ougrée (licence Baldwin) | E ACEC/SEM |
| 59 | Bo-Bo | 1,750 | 120 | 87 | 5 | 1955 | Cockerill/B&M | Cockerill | E ACEC (licence Westinghouse) |
| 52/53/54 | Co-Co | 1,720 | 120 | 108 | 28 | 1955 | AFB | GM | E GM/Smit |
| 55 | Co-Co | 1,950 | 120 | 110 | 38 | 1961 | BN | GM | E ACEC/SEM (licence GM) |
| 62 | Bo-Bo | 1,425 | 120 | 80 | 107 | 1961 | BN | GM | E GM |
| 91 | B | 335 | 35 40 | 36 | 45 | 1961 | Cockerill/BN ABC | GM | H Twin-Disc Q Cockerill |
| 84 | C | 550 | 30 50 | 55.8 | 24 | 1958 | ABR/B&M | ABC 6 DUS | H Voith L37U |
| 85 | C | 550 | 30 50 | 57.3 | 8 | 1956 | Haine St Pierre | ABC 6 DXS | H Voith L37U/ SEMT.B.122 |
| 80 | C | 650 | 30 60 | 52.1 | 34 | 1960 | BN/ABR | Maybach GTO 6A | H Voith L37 |
| 82 | C | 650 | 60 | 57 | 75 | 1965-66 | BN/ABR | ABC 6 DXS | H Voith L217U |
| 73 | C | 750 | 60 | 56 | 95 | 1965-68 | BN | Cockerill-Ougrée 6 TH 695 SA | H Voith L217U |
| 74 | C | 750 | 60 | 59 | 10 | 1977 | BN | ABC 6 DXS | H Voith L217U |
| 76 | B-B | 660 | 100 | 72 | 23 | 1955 | Allan | Storelf | H Heemaf |
| 77 | B-B | 1,540 | 60/100 | 90 | 57* | 1999 | Vossloh | ABC 60 ZC-1000 | H Voith L4 |

B&M = Baume & Marpent    * of 180 on order

### Electric locomotives

| Class | Wheel arrangement | Output kW continuous/ one-hour | Speed km/h | Weight tonnes | No in service | First built | Builders Mechanical | Electrical |
|---|---|---|---|---|---|---|---|---|
| 22 | Bo-Bo | 1,740/1,880 | 130 | 87 | 49 | 1954 | BN | ACEC/SEM |
| 23 | Bo-Bo | 1,740/1,880 | 130 | 93.3 | 82 | 1955 | AM | ACEC/SEM |
| 25 | Bo-Bo | 1,740/1,880 | 130 | 83.9 | 14 | 1960 | BN | ACEC/SEM |
| 25.5[1] | Bo-Bo | 1,740/1,880 | 130 | 85 | 8 | modified 1973 | BN | ACEC/SEM |
| 26 | B-B | 2,240/2,355* 2,470/2,590 | 130 | 82.4 | 34 | 1964 | BN | ACEC |
| 16[3] | Bo-Bo | 2,620/2,780 | 160 | 82.6 | 7 | 1966 | BN | ACEC |
| 20 | Co-Co | 5,130/5,150 | 160 | 110 | 24 | 1975 | BN | ACEC |
| 27 | Bo-Bo | 4,150/4,250 | 160 | 85 | 60 | 1981 | BN | ACEC |
| 21 | Bo-Bo | 3,130/3,310 | 160 | 84 | 60 | 1984 | BN | ACEC |
| 11[1] | Bo-Bo | 3,130/3,310 | 160 | 84 | 12 | 1985 | BN | ACEC |
| 12[4] | Bo-Bo | 3,130/3,310 | 160 | 84 | 12 | 1986 | BN | ACEC |
| 13 | Bo-Bo | 5,000 | 200 | 90 | 60 | 1998 | Alstom | Alstom |
| 15[2] | Bo-Bo | 2,780 | 160 | 78 | 3 | 1962 | BN | ACEC |

* First five locomotives only
[1] Dual-voltage 1.5 kV/3 kV DC
[2] Tri-voltage 1.5 kV/3 kV DC/25 kV AC
[3] Quadri-voltage 1.5 kV/3 kV DC/15 kV 16⅔Hz/25 kV 50 Hz
[4] Dual-voltage 3 kV DC/25 kV AC 50 Hz

### Electric multiple-units

| Class | Cars per unit | Motor cars per unit | Motored axles per car | Power/car kW | Speed km/h | Units in service | First built | Builders Mechanical | Electrical |
|---|---|---|---|---|---|---|---|---|---|
| AM62 | 2 | 2 | 2 | 310 | 130 | 114 | 1962 | BN/Ragheno | ACEC |
| AM66 | 2 | 2 | 2 | 340 | 140 | 188 | 1970 | BN/SNCB | ACEC |
| AM75 | 4 | 2 | 4 | 1,360 | 140 | 44 | 1975 | BN | ACEC |
| AM80 | 3 | 1 | 4 | 1,240 | 160 | 138 | 1981 | BN | ACEC |
| AM86 | 2 | 1 | 4 | 680 | 120 | 52 | 1988 | BN | ACEC |
| AM96 | 3 | 1 | 4 | 1,400 | 160 | 105* | 1996 | Bombardier | Alstom |

*Includes 50 dual-voltage 3 kV DC/25 kV

*Two Class 62 diesel-electric locomotives with a train of coal imported via Gent and destined for France (David Haydock)*

illuminated cab displays of pictogram codes rather than telephonic communication between control centre and train crew.

SNCB is in the course of replacing its traditional Automatic Train Control (ATC) system, based on contact between brushes mounted beneath traction units and track-mounted 'crocodiles', with an inductive transponder system known as Train-Balise-Locomotive (TBL). The TBL system – being installed first on the new high-speed lines – brakes the train automatically if the authorised speed is exceeded. The existing Brussels—Lille high-speed line is equipped with TVM 430 cab-signalling but Leuven—Liège will be equipped with TBL as it will be used by both TGVs at 300 km/h and locomotive-hauled trains at 200 km/h.

SNCB promised to accelerate both programmes after a head-on crash near Leuven in March 2001.

Signalling and track circuits are gradually being modified on main routes to allow trains with three-phase drive to operate over these lines.

Modernisation of switching technology for Antwerp marshalling yard has been carried out by Siemens and the Duisburg-Wanheim unit of Thyssen AG. The work included delivery of the MSR32 guidance system (a radio-controlled system for shunting locomotives) as well as systems installation.

### Electrification
78 per cent of the SNCB network is electrified, and 93 per cent of passenger trains and 72 per cent of freight trains are electrically hauled.

While the Belgian network has thus far used the 3 kV DC system, new high-speed lines are being electrified on the 25 kV AC system. The 142 km Dinant—Athus 'Athus—Meuse' line – an important freight artery between Antwerp and Luxembourg – is also being electrified at 25 kV. Work began on this project in 1995; it is due to be finished in December 2002.

Electrification of the 58 km from Rivage (24 km south of Liège) to Gouvy was finished in May 2000, completing electrification of the Liège—Luxembourg route. Like CFL's network, the Belgian section's electrification is at 25 kV 50 Hz AC. Cost was divided, the European Union bearing €10 million, SNCB €7.3 million and CFL €3.72 million. SNCB is to electrify the remaining 7 km from Montzen to the German border by 2005, completing the Antwerp/Liège—Aachen corridor.

### Track
77 per cent of the SNCB network has been laid with continuously welded rail (cwr). Some 182 km of cwr were installed in 1997.

**Standard rail:** Flat bottom, 50 and 60 kg/m main track, 50 kg/m secondary track
**Length:** Main track: 243 m rails long-welded. Secondary track: jointed 28 m rails
**Joints:** 4-hole fishplates
**Rail fastenings:** Sole plates and screws, mostly K-fastenings on wood sleepers. New track Pandrol fastenings. Pads are inserted under the rail when concrete sleepers are used.

**Crossties (sleepers):** Existing track: generally oak, 2,600 × 280 × 140 mm. Sections of welded-rail track have been laid with three types of concrete sleeper: Type RS (two blocks joined by a steel bar) with Type RN flexible rail fastenings; Type VDH (two blocks joined by a steel bar) with Pandrol fastenings; and Type DMD (monobloc prestressed) with Pandrol fastenings.
**Spacing:** 1,667/km on main line track; 1,370-1,590/km secondary routes
**Filling:** Broken stone or slag
**Min curvature radius**
Main line: 2.18° = 800 m
Secondary line: 3.5° = 500 m
Running lines: 8.75° = 200 m
Sidings: 11.7° = 150 m
**Max gradient:** 2.5%
**Max altitude:** 536 m at Hockai on Pepinster-Trois Ponts line
**Max axleload:** Certain locomotives have axleloads of 24 tonnes. Except for certain bridges they can operate anywhere on the system, subject to speed restriction.

*UPDATED*

---

# BENIN

## Ministry of Public Works and Transport

PO Box 16, Cotonou
Tel: (+229) 31 33 80

### Key personnel
Minister: Joseph Sourou Attin
Director General: A Glele

## Organisation Commune Benin-Niger des Chemins de Fer et des Transports (OCBN)

PO Box 16, Cotonou
Tel: (+229) 31 33 80   Fax: (+229) 31 41 50
Tx: 5210

### Key personnel
Director General: Raphael Bonou
Director of Motive Power and Rolling Stock:
  Edmond Agbla
Director of Way and Works: Alzouma Younsa
Director of Operations: Gabriel Alaye
Director of Supplies: J Hinson
Director of Finance: M Ousseini
Director of Personnel: A Sonon

Gauge: 1,000 mm
Route length: 578 km

### Organisation
OCBN operates, on behalf of Niger and Benin, a single-track metre-gauge railway consisting of the Northern line from Cotonou to Parakou via Pahou (438 km), the Eastern line from Cotonou to Pobé (107 km), and the Western line linking Pahou and Ségboroué   km). From Parakou freight traffic is transported by road to the Niger capital of Niamey.

### Passenger operations
In 1994 the railway carried 600,000 passengers (107 million passenger-km).

### Freight operations
In 1994 OCBN carried 250 million tonne-km of freight.

### New lines
A cherished project is the extension of the Northern line from Parakou to Niamey, Niger's capital, a distance of 650 km. At present, Niger traffic has to be road-hauled to Parakou. An agreement was signed in 1976 between Niger and Benin for construction of a rail link, since three-quarters of Niger's exports are channelled through Cotonou, and work was started in 1978 but made scant progress. Neither the World Bank nor any other aid agency has been prepared to help finance the scheme.

### Improvements to existing lines
A successful application was made in 1991 to France's Fund for International Co-operation (CCCE) for a loan worth US$8.6 million. It was applied to rehabilitation of the Benin segment of the Cotonou-Parakou Northern line, a project which has since been completed.

Further rehabilitation work was undertaken using fresh supplies of new rail delivered from British Steel in 1994.

OCBN has so far been unsuccessful in gaining external finance for modernisation of the Cotonou-Pobé Eastern line and its extension to a cement factory at Onigbulo with a projected output of 500,000 tonnes a year. Half the output would be for Nigeria, and Belgian finance has been offered for construction of a railway from the cement plant to Ilaro, northwest of Lagos, in Nigeria.

### Traction and rolling stock
At last report, locomotives in operation totalled eight Alsthom BB500 and 12 Alsthom BB600 diesel-electrics, plus six shunting tractors. Soulé railcars totalled seven and other stock consisted of 31 Soulé passenger coaches and trailers and 296 freight wagons.

In 1999, it was reported that a credit from the West African Development Bank was being sought to purchase several new locomotives and freight wagons.

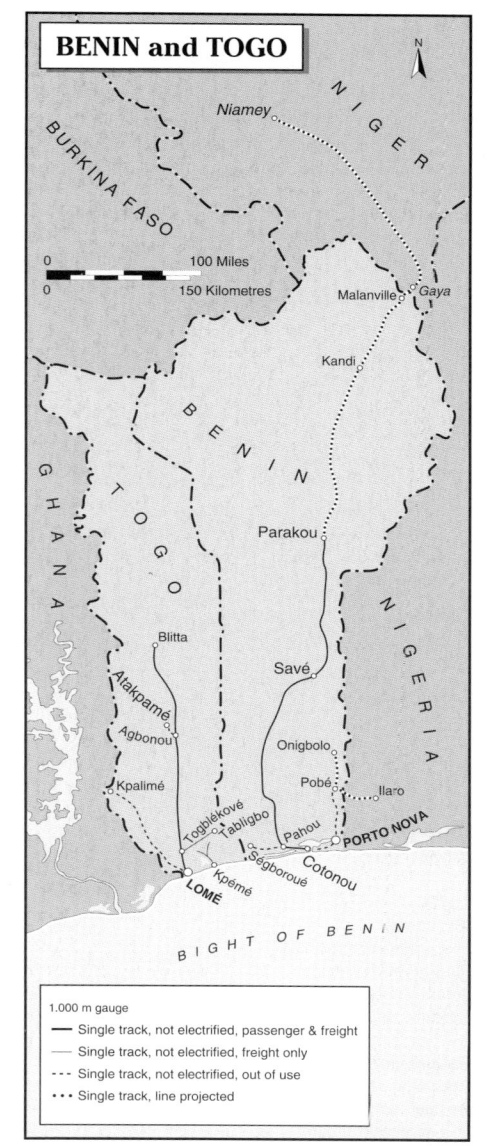

*Benin & Togo*
0058497

# BOLIVIA

## Ministry of Economic Development
Palacio de Comunicaciones, piso 18, Avenida Mariscal Santa Cruz, La Paz
Tel: (+591 2) 37 73 20   Fax: (+591 2) 37 13 47

**Key personnel**
Secretary of Transport: A Revollo

## Bolivian National Railways
Empresa Nacional de Ferrocarriles (ENFE)
Empresa Ferroviaria Andina (FCA) (former ENFE Andean network)
PO Box 428, Estación Central, Plaza Zalles, La Paz
Tel: (+591 2) 35 12 03   Fax: (+591 2) 39 21 06

**Key personnel**
President: Abraham Monasterios Castro
General Manager: José Taborga
Empresa Ferroviaria Oriental (FCO) (former ENFE Eastern network)
PO Box 108, Santa Cruz
Tel: (+591 33) 34 84 67   Fax: (+591 33) 32 75 07

**Key personnel**
General Manager: Ing Fernando Marticorena Zillerulo

Gauge: 1,000 mm
Route length: (FCA) 2,275 km; (FCO) 1,244 km

## Political background
All rail services in Bolivia are now run by the private sector. In 1995 the Ministry of Capitalisation invited bids for a 50 per cent shareholding in a new public/private corporation holding ENFE's assets. Of the seven bidders which came forward, Cruz Blanca – now CB Transportes – was successful, paying US$39 million for a 40-year operating concession. The remaining 50 per cent of ENFE has been retained by the government to form the basis of private pension funds for the country's citizens. The money paid by Cruz Blanca is being invested in the rail network.

Under the terms of the concession, the company was required to invest US$25 million in the network over seven years. However, Santa Cruz has decided to spend US$32 million in just five years, much of which will finance infrastructure upgrades to increase line speeds.

In 1996 Antofagasta and Bolivia Holdings, parent of Chile's Antofagasta, Chili and Bolivia Railway (FCAB), purchased a 73 per cent stake in Cruz Blanca's share of ENFE's Andean network and 23 per cent of its share of the Eastern network. FCAB connects with the Andean network at Ollagüe.

## Organisation
Bolivia is a landlocked country and lack of communications has made virtually impossible the sort of economic development which the country needs. The country's two railways, the Andean (2,275 km) and Eastern networks (1,244 km) connect only via Argentina. They are of major importance as a means of access to ports on the Pacific and Atlantic oceans via neighbouring countries. These international railway connections, some of which have fallen into disrepair, are as follows: with Chile to the Pacific ports of Arica and Antofagasta; with Argentina to the Atlantic ports of Rosario and Buenos Aires; with Brazil to the Atlantic port of Santos; with Peru (by ship across Lake Titicaca to Puno) to the Pacific port of Matarani.

## Traffic

| (EFO only) | 1996 | 1997 |
|---|---|---|
| Passenger journeys (000) | 303.9 | 324.2 |
| Passenger-km (million) | 132.9 | 136.7 |
| Freight tonnes (000) | 869.8 | 894.7 |
| Freight tonne-km (million) | 513.2 | 524.2 |

## Passenger operations
Passenger operations were progressively run down during the final years of state ownership of the ENFE network and now represent around 6 to 7 per cent of total revenue. Although the Eastern network concession requires FCO to provide minimal passenger services, CB Transportes has invested in this area. All existing passenger rolling stock has been refurbished and 11 second-hand coaches have been

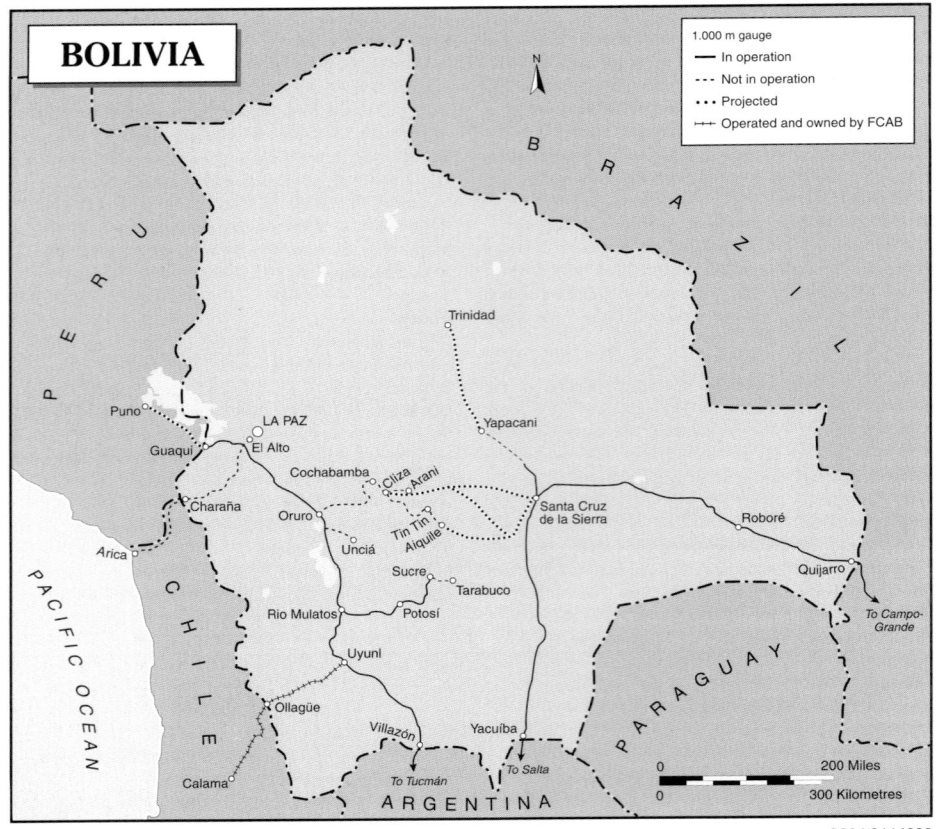

### Diesel locomotives

| Class | Wheel arrangement | Power kW | Speed km/h | Weight tonnes | No in service | First built | Builders Mechanical | Engine | Transmission |
|---|---|---|---|---|---|---|---|---|---|
| 950 | Bo-Bo-Bo | 970 | 70 | 81.6 | 9 | 1968 | Hitachi/Mitsubishi | MAN VGV 22/30 ATL | E Hitachi/Mitsubishi |
| 1000 | Bo-Bo-Bo | 1,550 | 100 | 90 | 7 | 1978 | Hitachi/Mitsubishi | MTU 12 V 956TB 11 | E Hitachi/Mitsubishi |
| 521 | Bo-Bo | 280 | 25 | 30 | 1 | 1968 | Hitachi | Hitachi MAN RGV 18/12 TL | H Hitachi |
| 841 | Bo-Bo | 395 | 40 | 55 | 1 | 1980 | Hitachi/Mitsubishi | MTU V396 TC 12 | H Hitachi |
| U 20C | Co-Co | 1,550 | 103 | 89.9 | 6 | 1977 | GE | FDL 12 GE | E GE |
| U 10B | Bo-Bo | 590 | 103 | 50.8 | 7 | 1977 | GE | Caterpillar 398 | DE GE |
| 980 | Bo-Bo | 551 | 60 | 66.5 | 1 | 1987 | Sulzer | MTU | E Sulzer |
| 846 | Bo-Bo | 480 | 60 | 66.4 | 2 | 1950 | Sulzer | Sulzer | EM Sulzer |

### Diesel railbuses

| Cars per unit | Motor cars per unit | Motored axles/car | Power hp per motor | Speed km/h | No in service | First built | Builders Mechanical | Engine | Transmission |
|---|---|---|---|---|---|---|---|---|---|
| 2 | 1 | 2 | 340/240 | 80 | 8 | 1967/78 | Ferrostaal | Cummins NHHRTO-6 | M Zahnfabrik |
| 2 | 1 | 2 | 335/240 | 90 | 3 | 1978 | Ferrostaal | Cummins | H Voith T 211 R |

*Santa Cruz Estacion on Bolivia's Eastern Network*

bought from the Ferrocarril Arica-La Paz (FCALP). Services are operated between Santa Cruz de la Sierra and Corumbá and between Santa Cruz de la Sierra and Yacuiba.

In 1999 FCA was only operating services between Oruro and Villazón.

### Freight operations
In 1998 FCO was reported to have carried over 1 million tonnes of freight. The company planned to develop domestic intermodal traffic to link FCO and FCA networks and was seeking to increase cross-border traffic with Argentina and Brazil.

### New lines
A technical assistance agreement with the US Federal Railroad Administration was signed in December 1998 aimed at reopening studies into a rail link between the FCA and FCO networks. The new 388 km line would connect Aiquile and Santa Cruz de la Sierra.

### Traction and rolling stock
In 1997 FCO operated 22 diesel locomotives, two diesel railbuses, 51 passenger coaches and 727 freight wagons. At last report, the Andean network operated 27 locomotives, seven railbuses, 53 passenger coaches and 727 freight wagons.

In 1997 FCO invited tenders for 200 box wagons, 75 flat wagons and 45 high-sided wagons.

### Signalling and telecommunications
Recent investments have concentrated on communications and control systems, including GPS train-positioning technology.

### Track
**Rail:** ASCE 29.76, 37.2 and 39 kg/m
BSS 32.24 and 37.2 kg/m
**Crossties (sleepers):** Wood and steel
**Spacing:** 1,400-1,640/km
**Min curvature radius:** 15°
**Max gradient:** 3% compensated on curves
**Max axleload:** 18 tonnes

---

# BOSNIA-HERZEGOVINA

## Bosnia-Herzegovina Railways Public Corporation

Bosnia-Herzegovina Railways Public Corporation (BHŽJK)
Željeznice Bosne i Hercegovine (ŽBH)
Musala 1, 71000 Sarajevo
Tel: (+387 71) 61 84 48  Fax: (+387 71) 144 62 55

### Key personnel
Director of Traction and Maintenance:
   Miroslav Mehmedbasič
Željeznice Republike Srpske (ŽRS)
Svetog Save 71, 74000 Doboj, Republika Srpska
Tel: (+381 53) 22 40 50  Fax: (+381 53) 22 40 50

### Key personnel
Director General: Dipl Ing Marinko Biljanovič

Gauge: 1,435 mm
Route length (1991): 1,021 km
Electrification (1991): 795 km at 25 kV 50 Hz AC

### Political background
Under the terms of the 1995 Dayton Peace Agreement an accord to form the Bosnia-Herzogovina Railways Public Corporation (BHŽJK) was signed in April 1998. The role of the corporation is to co-ordinate the activities of the railway companies which emerged as a result of the ethnic divisions which formed the basis of the Dayton Agreement. These were ŽBH, responsible for lines and services in the Federation (Bosnian Croats and Bosnian Muslims) and ŽRS, which operates lines in Republika Srpska (Bosnian Serbs). Subsequently, a third organisation ŽHB emerged to manage Federation routes where there was Bosnian Croat dominance, although this body has not received official recognition. In late 1998 it appeared probable that ŽBH and ŽHB would merge to form a new Federation Railway (ŽFBH) organisation.

### Passenger operations
By 1998, ŽBH commenced running local services from Sarajevo to Konjic and Zenica and some freight trains, while ŽHB was operating local trains south from Mostar. The revival of passenger services continued in 1999-2000. By early 2000, ŽBH was running services on nine routes. The Sarajevo–Mostar–Capljina saw the highest frequency, with four trains daily each way. The international 'Bosna Ekspres' was running once daily in each direction between Sarajevo, Mostar and Ploče, Croatia. ŽRS was providing a higher level of service, with trains operating on 13 routes. In general, trains do not cross inter-entity borders; passengers are required to change trains at these points.

It was expected that the following services would be reintroduced during 2000: Sarajevo–Bihač; Sarajevo–Doboj–Zagreb; Doboj–Zagreb–Ljubljana; and Banja Luka–Doboj–Tuzla–Žvornik–Belgrade. In addition, ŽBH planned to introduce a Tuzla–Brcko service.

*ŽBH Class 1141.1 electric locomotive on the operator's only international service, the Sarajevo–Ploče 'Bosna Ekspres', at Zenica (Frank Valoczy)*

### Freight operations
During the NATO-Yugoslav war, ŽRS freight traffic fell drastically to about 10 per cent of pre-war levels, as most movements had previous been to and from the Federal Republic of Yugoslavia. During 2000, there was a revival of this traffic. ŽBH freight loadings were less affected by the war. Freight trains regularly cross all border points, both inter-entity and international. A large volume of ŽBH traffic and a fair part of that of ŽRS is SFOR-related.

### Improvements to existing lines
Restoration of heavily damaged infrastructure, including the reconstruction of many damaged bridges, began in 1995/96. Italian and British military railway engineers have played a prominent role in this process, while funding has been provided by the United States Agency for International Development and the Swedish International Development Co-operation Agency, among others.

### Traction and rolling stock
ŽBH traction in early 2000 comprised: 29 Class 441 and two ex-Croatian Railways Class 1141.1 25 kV electric locomotives; eight Class 661, 28 Class 642, one Class 643 and five ex-German Rail Class 232 diesel-electrics; four ex-German Rail Class 212 diesel-hydraulics; and eight Class 732 and two Class 733 shunters. The Class 1141.1 machines were acquired to

# RAILWAY SYSTEMS/Bosnia–Herzegovina–Botswana

work 'Bosna Ekspres' services between Sarajevo and Ploče, Croatia.

Also owned were six Class 411 emus (four serviceable) and 31 steam locomotives.

ŽRS traction in regular use in early 2000 comprised: 11 Class 441 electric locomotives; seven Class 661, two Class 642 and two Class 643 diesel-electrics; and five ex-German Rail Class 212 diesel-hydraulics. One Class 734 diesel-hydraulic shunter was also reported to be active.

### Signalling and telecommunications
In 1999, signalling on most ŽRS lines was reported to be inoperable and trains were being controlled by radio despatching.

ŽBH also uses radio despatching on all lines except Sarajevo–Konjič, where colourlight signalling is in use.

# BOTSWANA

## Ministry of Works, Transport and Communication

Private Bag 007, Gaborone
Tel: (+267) 35 85 00  Fax: (+267) 31 33 03

### Key personnel
Minister: D N Magang
Permanent Secretary: A V Lionjanga
Deputy Permanent Secretary: M J M Moatshe

## Botswana Railways (BR)

Private Bag 0052, Mahalapye
Tel: (+267) 41 13 75  Fax: (+267) 41 13 85
e-mail: botrail@info.bw

### Key personnel
General Manager: A Ramji
Assistant General Manager (Finance): P K Sengupta
Assistant General Manager (Human Resources): Batlhatswi S Tsayang
Assistant General Manager (Infrastructure): S S Kapoor
Assistant General Manager (Rolling Stock): Bennet M Katai
Assistant General Manager (Business Management): C B Botana
Number of staff employed (1999): 1,168

Gauge: 1,067 mm
Route length: 888 km

### Political background
The country is traversed by 640 km of main line between Ramatlabama (north of Mafikeng, South Africa) and Bakaranga (south of Plumtree, Zimbabwe) with three branch lines, formerly managed by National Railways of Zimbabwe. Botswana Railways took over operation of the railway in 1986 and the following year took control of the assets and administrative services. The 175 km branch from Francistown to serve soda ash deposits at Sua Pan was opened in 1991.

In 1999, serious concern was expressed in Botswana regarding the impact on BR traffic, and therefore financial viability, of the Bulawayo–Beitbridge line in Zimbabwe, which opened during the year.

### Finance (million pula)

| Revenue | 1996-97 | 1997-98 | 1998-99 |
|---|---|---|---|
| Passengers | 10.0 | 10.5 | 10.3 |
| Freight | 73.4 | 97.8 | 109.4 |
| Other income | 7.1 | 10.2 | 13.2 |
| Total | 90.5 | 118.5 | 132.9 |

| Expenditure | | | |
|---|---|---|---|
| Total | 74.8 | 104.8 | 115.0 |

| Traffic | 1996-97 | 1997-98 | 1998-99 |
|---|---|---|---|
| Passenger journeys (000) | 574 | 496 | 360 |
| Freight tonnes (million) | 1.97 | 2.57 | 2.81 |
| Freight tonne-km (million) | 795 | 1,111 | 1,282 |

### Passenger operations
Passenger numbers recorded a significant fall in 1998-99 to 360,000 compared with 496,000 the previous year. This was mainly a result of fierce competition from road transport. Revenue held up due to increases in promotional fares.

Through-running to South Africa was resumed in early 1995 when the Bulawayo–Lobatse train was extended to Mafikeng.

### Freight operations
Freight traffic achieved modest growth to 2.81 million tonnes in 1998-99, compared with 2.57 million tonnes in the previous year. Domestic traffic increased by 12 per cent, mainly due to a growth in coal hauled for Soda Ash Plant. The development of intermodal facilities at Gabcon, an inland port and container terminal in Gabarone, and a similar facility, Francon, serving the north of Botswana, also contributed to domestic traffic growth. Gabcon handled 2,894 TEU in 1997-98, a figure higher than the terminal's design capacity.

Import traffic fell by 2 per cent to 0.79 million tonnes in 1998-99. Transit traffic increased by 22 per cent to 1.15 million tonnes, mainly as a result of a routing policy and favourable haulage rates agreed with South African operator, Spoornet, which was intended to provide a sound long-term basis for stable cross-border traffic.

### New lines
In a bid to regain traffic levels lost following opening of the Bulawayo–Beitbridge line in Zimbabwe, BR has proposed the construction of a direct line to Zambia to provide an alternative corridor for freight between South Africa and Zambia and Congo, Democratic Republic.

### Improvements to existing lines
Track rehabilitation between Mahalapye and Radisele has been completed. This is the first such project undertaken by Botswana Railways using its own planning, design and engineering resources. In 1999 a similar scheme was in progress between Serule and Linchwe. Scheduled for completion by June 2000, this will complete the rehabilitation of BR's main line.

### Traction and rolling stock
Botswana Railways operates 10 Krupp diesel-electrics, 20 Type GT22LC-2 diesel-electrics and 10 short-haul/shunting diesel locomotives. Freight wagon stock totals 1,025; there are 52 passenger coaches and one Cummins-powered railcar supplied by Union Carriage in 1993.

The GE-built Class BD 3 locomotives have been uprated from 1,120 kW to 1,340 kW under a re-engineering programme.

Recent deliveries include: 330 wagons for soda ash traffic over the Sua Pan line and coal haulage from Morupule; and 41 air conditioned passenger cars, including five buffet and six sleeping cars. The wagon contract was awarded to China National Machinery Import & Export Corporation and the passenger car contract to Mitsui (but the vehicles were built in South Africa). Generator cars have been subject to a re-engining programme.

BR plans to install solid state event recorders in its locomotives.

### Signalling and telecommunications
The Radio Electronic Token Block system now controls 698 km of line. A modification and improvement plan was

*Class BD 2 GM-built diesel locomotives at Lobatse with a train of chemical salt destined for Durban and shipment to Argentina (Marcel Vleugels)*

### Diesel locomotives

| Class | Builder's type | Wheel arrangement | Power kW | Speed km/h | Weight tonnes | No in service | First built | Builders Mechanical | Builders Engine | Builders Transmission |
|---|---|---|---|---|---|---|---|---|---|---|
| BD 1 | UM 20C | Co-Co | 1,500 | 103 | 96 | 10 | 1982 | Krupp | GE 7FDL 12 | E GE |
| BD 2 | GT22LC-2 | Co-Co | 1,700 | 107 | 96.6 | 20 | 1986 | GM | GM 645E3B-12 | E GM |
| BD 3 | U15C | Co-Co | 1,340 | 107 | 97.9 | 10 | 1991 | GE | GE FDL8 | E GE |

implemented in 1993 and work continues to improve reliability. A back-up VHF radio system has been installed to help keep trains moving when there is a communications breakdown. An automatic block signalling scheme has been installed between Rakhuna and Mafikeng, a distance of 10 km.

A network of microcomputers has been installed using Novell Netware. A vehicle control system has been written 'in house', primarily to calculate vehicle hire charges and produce operational statistics, and the first phase of a personnel management system has been implemented. Systems to monitor vehicle utilisation, schedule preventive maintenance and automate the daily operating diary have been developed by the railway as an adjunct to the vehicle control system. A new stock control system was implemented in 1994.

BR has suffered from theft of copper wire from communications lines, necessitating the provision of back-up facilities from the national telecommunications company.

**Type of coupler in standard use**
Passenger cars: Alliance 8X6 vacuum
Freight cars: Alliance 8X6

**Type of braking in standard use, locomotive-hauled stock:** Vacuum

**Track**
Rail type and weight: Flat-bottom 40 kg/m (378 km), 50 kg/m (510 km)
Sleepers: Concrete, spaced 1,430/km in 50 kg/m cwr plain track, 1,500/km in curves; steel, spaced 1,430/km in 40 kg/m plain jointed track, 1,500/km in curves
Fastenings: Fist on concrete sleepers, clip bolt on steel
Min curvature radius: 200 m
Max gradient: 1.6%
Max permissible axleload: 17.2 tonnes

# BRAZIL

## Ministry of Transport

Esplanada dos Ministérios, Bloco R, 6° Andar, 70044-900
Brasilia DF
Tel: (+55 61) 224 01 85  Fax: (+55 61) 225 09 15

**Key personnel**
Minister of Transport: Eliseu Padilha
Surface Transportation Secretary:
  Luiz Henrique Teixeira Baldez

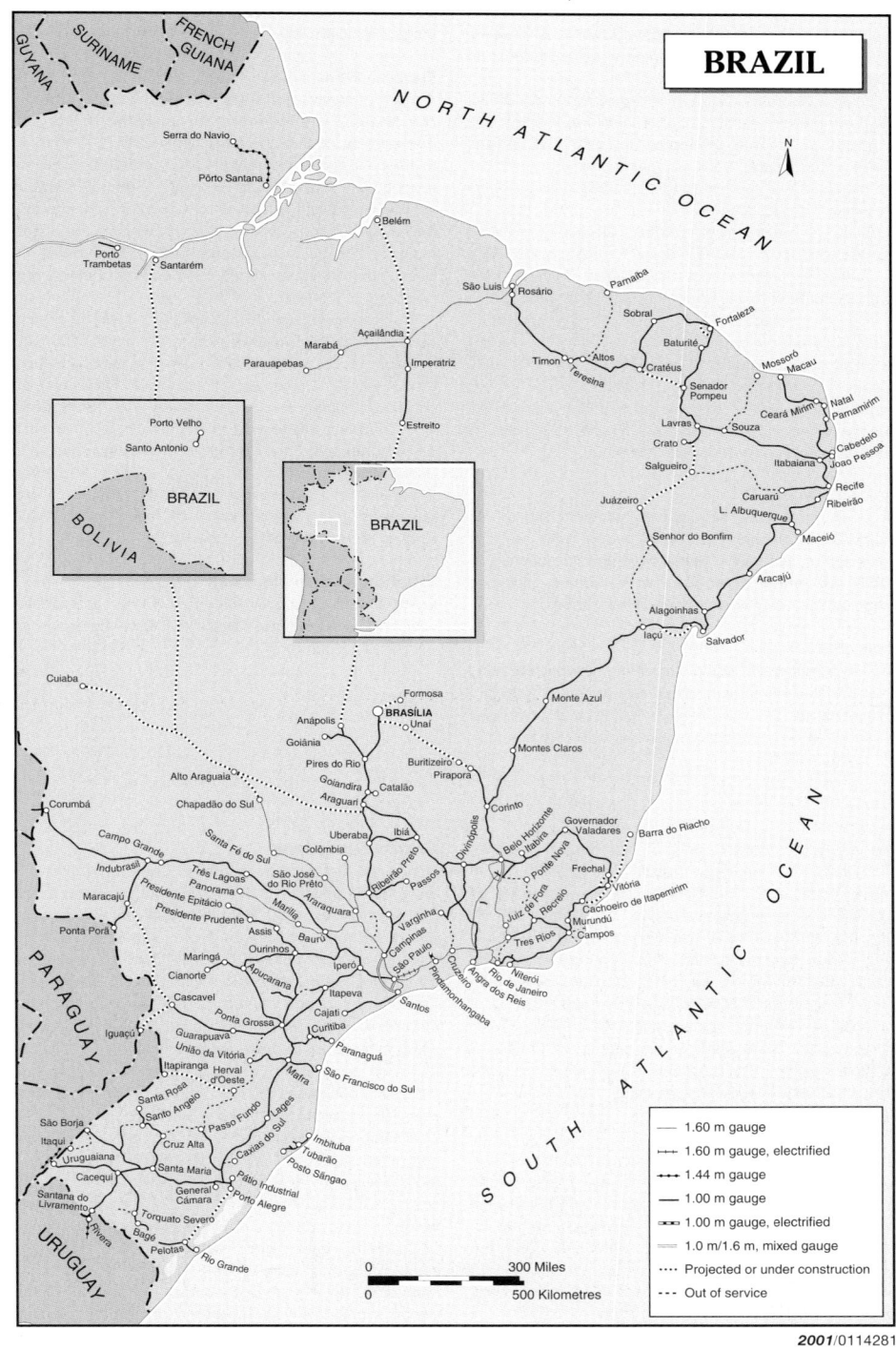

## Carajás Railway (EFC)

Estrada de Ferro Carajás
Avenida dos Portugueses s/n, Praia do Boqueirão, São Luís, Maranhão, CEP 65085-850
Tel: (+55 98) 218 44 05  Fax: (+55 98) 218 45 20

**Key personnel**
Director, Northern System: Jayme Nicolato Corrêa
General Managers
  Railway Operation: Carlos Eduardo Fontenelle Carriero
  Mechanical and Electrical Maintenance:
    Ronaldo José Costa

Gauge: 1,600 mm
Route length: 892 km

### Organisation

EFC is owned by the mining group Companhia Vale do Rio Doce (CVRD), which also owns the 1,000 mm gauge Vitória a Minas Railway (EFVM) (qv). Brazil's largest holder of mineral rights, CVRD is the world's largest producer of iron ore and pellets. The company also mines maganese, kaolin and potash, and has a significant presence in the aluminium and woodpulp markets. EFC and EFVM are operated as the company's Northern System and Southern System respectively. As well as its railway operations, the CVRD portfolio also includes ports.

CVRD's Northern System has implemented a policy of forming partnerships to create multimodal transport links covering rail, road, river and ports, including collaborations with other rail operators.

**Finance** (US$ million)

| Revenue | 1998 | 1999 |
|---|---|---|
| Passengers | 3.56 | 1.99 |
| Freight* | 43.89 | 31.87 |
| Total | 47.40 | 33.86 |

| Expenditure | | |
|---|---|---|
| Staff/personnel | 39.33 | 23.83 |
| Materials and services | 78.54 | 50.62 |
| Total | 117.87 | 74.45 |

| Traffic (million) | 1998 | 1999 |
|---|---|---|
| Passenger journeys | 0.538 | 0.459 |
| Passenger-km | 191 | 163 |
| Freight tonnes | 50.13 | 47.74 |
| Freight tonne-km | 42,117 | 40,090 |

\* General cargo, excluding iron ore

### Passenger operations

Principally a freight railway, EFC operates three trains (of around 16 coaches including executive and standard classes) a week in each direction between São Luís and Parauapebas (861 km).

### Freight operations

EFC's principal traffic is iron ore, moved from the mine at Carajás to Ponta da Madeira in trains comprising 204 ore wagons with a total capacity of 20,910 tonnes, hauled by two locomotives. A return trip, including crew changes, refuelling, loading and unloading, usually takes 58 hours and on average six loaded and six empty trains are in operation each day.

Other freight traffic in 1999 amounted to around 4.6 million tonnes. Soya products, fertiliser, pig iron, petroleum products, cement, road vehicles and other commodities are carried on freight trains composed of around 80 wagons.

### Traction and rolling stock

At the end of 1999 the rolling stock fleet comprised 83 diesel-electric locomotives, 37 passenger coaches (including two buffet cars and three luggage vans), 3,528 ore wagons and 728 other freight wagons.

### Signalling and telecommunications

Since 1989 EFC's main line operation has been supported by a comprehensive CTC system, including wayside equipment such as power point motors, track circuits, cab signalling and hotbox detectors, onboard equipment including ATC and event recorders, and a control centre.

To increase capacity, EFC has installed solid state interlocking, constant warning time grade crossings, new hotbox hot wheel detectors and electrocode equipment. The analogue communications network is being replaced by a fibre optic system.

EFC is studying the development and implementation of a CTC system which will support GPS for train-position and locomotive health monitoring systems and an integrated maintenance centre, and an auxiliary traffic control system for train working optimisation and meet/pass planning which will be introduced to increase capacity.

### EFC diesel locomotives

| Builder's type | Wheel arrangement | Power kW | Speed km/h | Weight tonnes | No in service | First built | Mechanical | Builders Engine | Transmission |
|---|---|---|---|---|---|---|---|---|---|
| C30-7B | Co-Co | 2,465 | 80 | 180 | 6 | 1984 | GE | GE 7FDL16 | E GE |
| C40-8 | Co-Co | 3,018 | 80 | 180 | 4 | 1989 | GE | GE FDL16 | E GE |
| SD40-2 | Co-Co | 2,429 | 80 | 180 | 27 | 1985 | GM | EMD 645E3C | E EMD |
| SD60M | Co-Co | 3,056 | 80 | 180 | 2 | 1991 | GM | EMD 16-710G3A | E EMD |
| GT26-CU2 | Co-Co | 2,208 | 80 | 180 | 2 | 1984 | GM | EMD-16-645E3B | E EMD |
| C36-7B | Co-Co | 2,720 | 80 | 180 | 33 | 1984 | GE | GE 7FDL | E GE |
| C44-9 | Co-Co | 3,350 | 80 | 180 | 7 | 1997 | GE | GE 7FDL | E GE |
| SL80 | Bo-Bo | 898 | 42 | 65 | 2 | 1993 | GE | GE | E GE |

### Track

**Rails:** 68 kg/m long-welded
**Fastenings:** Pandrol or Denik
**Crossties (sleepers):** Timber, creosote-treated, thickness 170 mm, spaced 540 mm between centres
**Min curve radius:** 860 m
**Max gradient:** 0.4% loaded trains, 1% empty trains
**Max axleload:** 31.5 tonnes

## Companhía Brasilera de Trens Urbanos (CBTU)

Estrada Velha da Tijuca 77, CEP 20531-080 Rio de Janeiro, RJ
Tel: (+55 21) 288 19 92  Fax: (+55 21) 571 61 49

### Key personnel

President: Luiz Otavia Mota Valadares
Finance and Administration: Jorge Miguel Felippe

### Organisation

For many years, CBTU was the operator of nearly all suburban passenger rail networks in major Brazilian cities. Progressively, these systems have been transferred to control by the states: São Paulo took over CBTU lines serving the city and integrated them with CPTM; Rio de Janeiro's Flumitrens has been transferred to SuperVia; the systems of Fortaleza and Salvador were transferred to state ownership in 1998 and 1999 respectively; and Recife's suburban systems were taken over by Metrorec and Companhía Pernambucana de Trans. This has left CBTU with the Demetrô system in Belo Horizonte and networks serving João Pessoa, Maceió, Natal and Teresina. It was expected that Demetrô would be transferred to Minas Gerais state during 2000, and studies were in progress to explore how the remaining systems could be similarly handed over to their states.

### Passenger operations

*Belo Horizonte (Minas Gerais)*
The 21.3 km Demetrô 1,600 mm gauge suburban system is double-track and electrified at 3 kV DC overhead. It runs from Eldorado via Calafate, Central and Santa Terza to Minas Shopping, with 14 stations open to passenger traffic. Around 25 million passengers were carried in 1999.

In April 1999, prequalification bids were invited for a 6.5 km extension from São Gabriel to Vía Norte. Estimated to cost US$99 million, this will feature two tunnels and two of the five stations will provide bus transfer facilities. Also under construction in 2000 was a 10 km branch from Entroncamento/Rodoviário to Barreiro.

Later extensions planned include: Eldorado—Betim (29 km); Barreiro—Ibirité (12 km); Vía Norte—Santa Luzia (13 km); and Minas Shopping to Venda Nova and Ribeirao das Neves. When completed, the entire network is expected to carry around 125 million passengers annually.

Of the original series of 15 emus, five were refurbished in 1999 and 10 more were ordered for delivery in 2000.

In August 1999, a new maintenance centre at São Gabriel, north of Minas Shopping, was commissioned.

*Joao Pessoa (Paraíba)*
A 32 km line running from Santa Rita via João Pessoa to Cabedelo is operated by CBTU. The single-track line has eight stations and is operated by two Alco RS-8 diesel locomotives and 17 coaches (14 serviceable). Around 1.5 million passengers are carried annually.

*Maceió (Alagoas)*
A 32 km single-track line runs from Maceió to Utinga, Rio Largo and Lourenço de Albuquerque, with services provided by two diesel locomotives and 21 coaches. In 1999, 2.3 million passengers were carried, excluding 'account' passengers travelling on free passes.

*Natal (Rio Grande do Norte)*
CBTU operates an 18-station 56 km network radiating from Natal to Parnamirim and Ceará Mirim. In 1998, 1.4 million passengers were carried. Rolling stock comprises three Alco RS-8 diesel locomotives and 20 coaches.

It is expected that responsibility for the system will be transferred to Rio Grande do Norte within the next few years. Parts of the Northern Line, between Ribiera and Soledade (11.3 km) may be doubled and electrified to convert it to light rail.

*Teresina (Piauí)*
A short line traversing Teresina city centre to reach Timon, Maranhao (8 km) is served by suburban trains and marketed as 'Sistema de Trens Urbanos (STU) Teresina'. In 1998, 1.8 million passengers were carried. The present system was operated by Brazilian Federal Railways (RFFSA) as 'Metro Teresina' from 1990 until 1996, when CBTU took it over. Rolling stock comprises five Ganz-Mavag diesel trainsets transferred from Rio Grande do Sul. Three of these units are serviceable but only one is operating at any time.

Projects have been developed to construct a 9 km branch from Centro to Bela Vista, in the south of the city, and another branch would run from Frei Serafim to Bela Vista (7 km). These two lines would generate an additional 30,000 passengers a day, five times the current level of traffic. In the east of the city, completion of a 1.2 km branch to Bandeirante still awaited completion in 2000, construction having commenced in 1992. Proposals have been made to convert the system to light rail operation but financial problems faced by Piauí state have so far prevented these being implemented.

### Traction and rolling stock

In 2000, CBTU was refurbishing 20 'Pidner' coaches for use on the Joao Pessoa, Maceió and Natal systems.

## Companhia Ferroviária do Nordeste (CFN)

Avenida Francisco Sá 4829, CEP 70 310-002, Fortaleza, Ceará
Tel: (+55 85) 286 25 25  Fax: (+55 85) 286 61 56

### Key personnel

President: Wagner Bittencourt de Oliveira
Directors
 Operations: Lauro Fassarella
 Commercial: Carlos Kopiptke
 Finance: Martiniano Dias

Gauge: 1,000 mm
Route length: 4,633 km

### Political background

The CFN network was the poorest of the former Brazilian Federal Railways (RFFSA) regions. It combines the former subdivisions of Fortaleza, Recife and São Luis and connects with the Carajás Railway at São Luis and with Ferrovia Centro Atlántico at Proporia, south of Maceió. Of the 4,633 km network, only 557 km are in operable condition; the remainder needs varying amounts of rehabilitation work. A deficit of Cr50 million was recorded in 1994, when the workforce totalled more than 5,000. By January 1997, this figure had been reduced to 2,027 in preparation for privatisation. This occurred in January 1998, when the system was taken over by a consortium led by Taquari, part of the Vicunha group, with 40 per cent of the equity. Other consortium members are CSN, CVRD and Bradesco, each with a 20 per cent stake. In spite of modest freight traffic prospects, early indications were that privatisation had been successful.

### Passenger operations

In 1999, the following passenger services continued over CFN tracks: suburban services around Fortaleza, João Pessoa, Maceió, Natal, Recife and on a short stretch of line through Terezina. All these services were run by CBTU or by local state-owned companies. Only the Recife—Cabo—Ribeirão service could be considered interurban. Services between Recife and Caruarú are still operated for special events.

### Freight operations

During the first year under private ownership, CFN was expected to achieve 1.2 billion tonne-km thanks to a new commercial strategy. Through daily freight services branded 'Expressos' and running to fixed schedules have been introduced on the Fortaleza—São Luis, Fortaleza—Recife and Recife—Maceió corridors and a 30 per cent discount has been offered to new customers. Main commodities carried include alcohol, sugar, cement, scrap metal, steel products and aluminium. In 1998 CFN launched a bid to win oil products traffic back to rail, potentially generating 70 million tonne-km annually, and it was also expecting to introduce container services.

In 1999, traffic increased to around 1 billion tonne-km, compared with 640 million in 1998, and revenue increased by 49 per cent to Cr26.2 million. Manufactured products have been the main contributor to this increase, which was the highest of all Brazilian railways. Tonnages of cement, beer and coke increased especially significantly, with rises of 317, 164 and 113 per cent respectively in the amounts loaded in 1999 compared with the previous year. Loadings of cereals are also

# Brazil/RAILWAY SYSTEMS

increasing significantly. Because of the poor condition of many freight wagons, which are unable to accept palletised goods, much freight is loaded manually.

### New lines
A new line, projected in the 1980s, was the Transnordestina Railway. As its name suggests, this would traverse the country's far northeast inland, linking up to three metre-gauge lines that head inland from the Atlantic coast between Salvador and Fortaleza. The Transnordestina scheme is divided into three segments: the first, on which some construction work has been carried out during the 1990s, would connect Petrolina, in southwest Pernambuco, with Salgueiro (231 km); the second, for which detailed planning has been completed, will provide a 113 km link between Salgueiro and Missão Velha; the third line will connect Piquet Carneiro, on the Fortaleza–Missão Velha–Crato line, with Crateús, on the Fortaleza–Terezina line (178 km). In conjunction with this project, several existing lines are to be upgraded or rehabilitated. These include: Salgueiro–Caruarú (468 km); Missão Velha–Fortaleza (580 km); and Crateús–Terezina (290 km). Also likely is a new bridge from Petrolina to Juázeiro, including a 6 km link to provide a connection with the Ferrovia Centro Atlántico (qv). Connecting lines south of Juázeiro could also be upgraded.

The entire Transnordestina system would be single-track and has been estimated to cost US$815 million. Between 1991 and 1994, US$7.17 million was spent on the Petrolina–Salgueiro section and CFN has reached agreement with the federal government to raise US$322 million for this stretch of line, with this funding being found by CFN and the Northeast Development Agency (SUDENE). Work started in early 1999 and this first phase of the project was expected to be completed by 2001.

CFN also plans to build a new line diverging from the existing system and the planned Transnordestina at Salgueiro, running 120 km west to Araripina, a town at the centre of a gypsum-producing region in the extreme west of Pernambuco state. At Araripina, between 1.5 and 2 million tonnes of gypsum are produced annually and a potential export contract with a US-based company could add an additional 1.5 million tonnes of production. Construction will be simplified by the flat and dry terrain, with the project costed at an estimated Cr78 million. Construction was expected to start in 2000 or 2001 and take less than one year.

At Uniao dos Palmares, in Alagoas state, a short branch line is to be built, at an estimated cost of Cr300,000, to provide a connection to Usina Santa Clotilde, which serves several sugar cane mills producing over 200 million litres of fuel-alcohol annually. CFN aims to capture 10 to 20 per cent of this traffic.

### Improvements to existing lines
In February 2000, CFN received a 15-year loan of Cr62 million from the National Bank for Social and Economic Development (BNDES) to help modernise its network. This forms part of a Cr569 million programme to modernise the entire CFN system, and was to be complemented by a contribution of Cr39 million from the railway's own resources. The money was intended to be spent during 2000 to eliminate critical bottlenecks, especially the repair of several bridges. The largest rehabilitation projects include the 453 km Terezina–São Luis and 468 km Caruarú–Salgueiro lines, and it has also been decided to reconstruct the 243 km Souza–Mossoró line.

In May 1999, construction was started of a 16 km bypass line southwest of Fortaleza to divert freight trains from the city centre, reducing traffic on lines used by Metrofor suburban services. The line runs from Aracapé to Caucaia. At a later stage, a new freight terminal and marshalling yard may be built at Aracapé and the freight line from the port of Mucuripe to Aracapé and Vila des Flores could be separated from the existing suburban line. The bypass could also be used in future by diesel-hauled suburban passenger services (see entry for Metrofor). Completion was expected in December 2001.

On the outskirts of São Luis, a new container terminal is to be built, possibly also with 1,600 mm gauge tracks to enable intermodal traffic to be exchanged with CVRD's Carajás Railway.

### Traction and rolling stock
With the help of 20 General Motors G12 diesel-electrics procured form other parts of Brazil, CFN commenced operations with 71 locomotives, of which 55 were serviceable. The average age of the locomotive fleet in 1998 was 33 years, and failures were frequent. The freight wagon fleet comprised 2,302 vehicles, including 441 transferred by RFFSA from other regions. In 1998, 1,861 wagons were available for traffic. Any passenger vehicles have been transferred to regional operators.

Rolling stock maintenance workshops are located at Fortaleza and Recife.

### Signalling and telecommunications
Train despatching is generally by radio. As a result, the number of staffed stations has been reduced from 108 to 34 and the number of train control centres from six to two.

### Track
Most parts of the network are laid with 25 or 30 kg/m rail. Sleepers are generally timber, spaced 1,500 to 1,666 per km.

## Companhia Paulista de Trens Metropolitanos (CPTM)

Avenida Paulista 402, 5° andar, 01310-903 São Paulo, SP
Tel: (+55 11) 33 71 15 30; 15 31; 15 85
Fax: (+55 11) 288 22 24
e-mail: oliver@cptm.sp.gov.br
Web: http://www.cptm.com.br

### Key personnel
President: Oliver Hossepian Salles de Lima
Directors
  Operations and Maintenance: João Roberto Zaniboni
  Administration and Finance:
    Benedito Dantas Chiaradia
  Planning: Pedro Pereira Benvenuto
  Engineering: Ademir Venâncio de Araújo

Gauge: 1,600 mm; 1,000 mm; dual 1,600 mm/1,000 mm
Route length: 192 km; 18 km; 60 km
Electrification: 270 km at 3 kV DC; 9.4 km at 1.5 kV DC (under construction)

### Political background
CPTM was created by the São Paulo state government on 2 July 1993 to run the city of São Paulo's suburban passenger services, with a view to better integration with the city's metro system. CPTM began operation of FEPASA's (see separate entry) suburban routes in August 1993 and took over the former Companhia Brasiliera de Trens Urbanos (CBTU) system on 27 May 1994.

The CPTM system is due to be privatised in 2003 by a process of concessioning operations on individual lines and major infrastructure investments are being made in preparation for this (see *Improvements to existing lines* and *New lines*). Studies to determine the privatisation model were in progress in 2001.

### Finances (Cr million)
| | 1999 | 2000 |
|---|---|---|
| **Revenue** | | |
| Passengers | 212 | 233 |
| Other income | 4 | 23 |
| Operating subsidy | 192 | 194 |
| Total | 408 | 450 |
| **Operating expenditure** | | |
| Staff/personnel | 210 | 225 |
| Materials and services | 140 | 149 |
| Depreciation | 60 | 224 |
| Other | 236 | 189 |
| Total | 646 | 787 |

### Traffic (million)
| | 1997 | 1999 | 2000 |
|---|---|---|---|
| Passenger journeys | 249.9 | 235.0 | 271.0 |
| Passenger-km | 4,631 | 4,187 | 4,900 |

### Passenger operations
Initially, the former FEPASA and CBTU systems were known as the West System and the East System respectively. Operations are now organised as six routes, Lines A to F. A seventh line, Line G, is under construction (see New lines).
Lines currently operated are:
Line A (Luz–Jundiaí, 57 km), comprising 16 stations with metro and Line B interchange at Barra Funda.
Line B (Julio Preste–Amador Bueno, 42 km), comprising 24 stations with Line C interchange at Osasco and Presidente Altino.
Line C (Osasco–Varginha, 36 km), comprising nine stations.
Line D (Luz–Paranapiacaba, 52 km), comprising 16 stations.
Line E (Brás–Mogi das Cruzes, 50 km), comprising 19 stations with metro interchanges at three.
Line F (Brás–Calmon Viana, 33 km), with Line E interchanges at Brás, Tatuapé and Sebastião Gualberto.

*Ex-RENFE Class 2100 emu at Pinheiros Station (Line C)* (Flávio Francesconi Lage)

# RAILWAY SYSTEMS/Brazil

## Improvements to existing lines
Modernisation investments in progress in 2001 include:
Line C: in 2001 modernisation was taking place between Osasco and Jurubatuba and a 24 km seven-station extension was under construction along the route of the Pinheiros river. The scheme includes modernisation of power supply, signalling and telecommunications systems and the provision of a new fare collection system. New rolling stock was being supplied by Siemens.
Line E: improvements include the construction of four new stations.
Line I (Brás—Luz—Barra Funda, 5 km): to integrate Lines A to F, this section in central São Paulo will remain under CPTM control and be provided with four additional tracks to allow concessionaires to run through services from different city-centre stations in return for track access fees. The project includes remodelling of Brás and Luz stations and provision of a new control and train supervision centre, providing 90 second headways. CPTM anticipates completion by 2002.

## New lines
Line G (Capão Redondo—Santo Amaro—Largo Treze, 9.4 km): this line is currently under construction and is being built to metro standards, but it may be operated as a suburban line until a connection with another projected metro line can be made. With six stations, it will be standard gauge, claimed by CPTM to be the first of this gauge in Brazil, and will be electrified with a 1.5 kV DC rigid overhead catenary. Completion is scheduled for 2002 at a cost of US$517.7 million.

A link with private sector funding has been proposed to Guarulhos airport. The line would commence near Ermelino Matarazzo station on Line F and run 10.3 km north to the airport. Construction cost, including the provision of 20 emus, is estimated at US$177 million. At a later stage, Congonhas and Campo de Marte airports could also be provided with rail links, necessitating the construction of an additional 13 km of lines, although this is not expected to occur before 2010.

CPTM is also expecting to expand its network over existing lines before also including them in the privatisation project. Suburban services could be operated over the Barra Funda—Campinas (105 km), Barra Funda—Sorocaba (102 km) and São Paulo Luz—São José dos Campos (110 km) lines.

## Traction and rolling stock
In 1999, CPTM operated a fleet of 801 electric multiple-unit cars. The Class 400M and Class 160 emus have been the subject of refurbishment programmes.

In 2000, CPTM received the last of 30 new Class 2000 emus for Line 6 in a transaction financed through a Eurobond issue. The new trainsets have been built by a Franco-Spanish consortium (including CAF, GEC Alsthom and Adtranz) known as COFESBRA, to a design similar to the Class 447 for RENFE of Spain.

In early 1998, CPTM took delivery of the first of 48 refurbished ex-Spanish National Railways (RENFE) Class 440 emus. These became CPTM Class 2100.

In 2000, deliveries commenced of 10 new emus from Siemens for Line C modernisation. Orders for eight new units for Line G were also likely in 2000, while refurbishment of the entire existing fleet was also reported to be a possibility.

*Budd-type emu at Rio Grande da Serra (Line D) (Flávio Francesconi Lage)*       2001/0062495

### CPTM electric multiple-units

| Class | Cars per unit | Motor cars per unit | Motored axles/car | Output/motor kW | Speed km/h | Units in service | First built | Builders Mechanical | Electrical |
|---|---|---|---|---|---|---|---|---|---|
| 1100 | 3 | 1 | 4 | 306 | 100 | 20 | 1956 | Budd/Mafersa/Cobrasma | Toshiba/Hitachi/Sepsa |
| 1400 | 3 | 1 | 4 | 344 | 90 | 16 | 1976 | Mafersa | GE |
| 1600 | 3 | 1 | 4 | 344 | 100 | 15 | 1978 | Mafersa | GE |
| 1700 | 4 | 2 | 4 | 315 | 120 | 15 | 1987 | Mafersa | Hitachi/Toshiba |
| 2000 | 4 | 1 | 4 | 300 | 90 | 30 | 1999 | CAF/Alstom | Adtranz |
| 2100 | 3 | 1 | 4 | 290 | 140 | 43 | 1964 | CAF | Toshiba/Sepsa |
| 3000 | 4 | 2 | - | - | 90 | 10 | 2000 | Siemens | Siemens |
| 4400 | 3 | 1 | 4 | 315 | 100 | 26 | 1964 | FNV/Cobrasma | Hitachi/Toshiba |
| 4800 | 3 | 1 | 4 | 168 | 90 | 6 | 1958 | Nippon/Kawasaki/Kinki | Toshiba |
| 5000 | 3 | 1 | 4 | 207 | 90 | 86 | 1978 | Cobrasma | Brown Boveri/MTE |
| 5500 | 3 | 1 | 4 | 250 | 90 | 24 | 1981 | Mafersa/Sorefame | Villares/ACEC |

### CPTM diesel locomotives

| Class | Wheel arrangement | Power kW | Speed km/h | Weight tonnes | No in service | First built | Builders Mechanical | Engine | Transmission |
|---|---|---|---|---|---|---|---|---|---|
| 6011 | Bo-Bo | 716 | 90 | 74 | 7 | 1968 | LEW | MGO V12 BSHR | E LEW |
| 6031 | Bo-Bo | 522 | 65 | 57 | 2 | 1967 | GE | Caterpillar D-379BV8 | E GE |
| 6021 | Co-Co | 1,492 | 103 | 110 | 2 | 1976 | GE | GE 7FDL | E GE |
| 6001 | Bo-Bo | 1,193 | 100 | 109 | 8 | 1952 | Alco/GE | Alco 244 | E GE |

### Signalling and telecommunications
ATC is in use on Lines A, B, C and D (187 km); ATS is used on Lines E and F (83 km).

### Track
**Rail**
**Type:** TR 57 (57 kg/m) (201 km); TR 57 (67 kg/m) (20 km); TR 68 (50 kg/m) (79 km)
**Sleepers**
**Wood:** 2,800 × 240 × 170 mm; 2,000 × 220 × 160 mm
**Spacing:** 1,833/km; 1,660/km
**Concrete:** 2,800 × 300 × 250
**Spacing:** 1,833/km or 1,660/km (wood); 1,667/km (concrete)
**Fastenings:** Pandrol or Denik elastic
**Min curve radius:** 200 m
**Max gradient:** 2.43%
**Max axleload:** 32 tonnes

*UPDATED*

---

# Estrada de Ferro Do Amapá (EFA)

Macapá, Território do Amapá
Gauge: 1,440 mm
Route length: 194 km

## Organisation
The EFA is the only standard-gauge railway in Brazil. It extends over 194 km from the River Amazon port of Pôrto Santana to Serra do Navio, in central Amapá. The northernmost railway in Brazil, the line was originally built to carry manganese deposits mined at Serra do Navio and was inaugurated in January 1955 with the assistance of the US-based Bethlehem Steel and Eximbank of Washington. Passenger operations began in 1957. The line is privately owned and operated by Indústria e Comércio de Minérios SA (Icomi), which holds the mining concession until 2003, when the railway will be transferred to the state government of Amapá. After that date, the line is to continue to operate under state government administration, assisting the development of agriculture along its route. Passenger services are also likely to continue both for tourism and social purposes. The financial position of the railway is reported as sound and it operates without deficit.

## Passenger operations
Services are provided three times a week in each direction, carrying about 150,000 passengers annually. The line is served by 15 stations and halts.

## Freight operations
The main traffic is manganese, of which more than 600,000 tonnes are carried annually. Over 5,000 tonnes of general freight, mostly agricultural products including tapioca, are also conveyed, with rail providing an essential means of transport in a region poorly served by roads. An expansion of agricultural traffic is foreseen.

## Traction and rolling stock
The locomotive fleet comprises five GM SW-1200 diesel-electrics, three acquired in 1955 and two in 1966, and an SW-1500 from the same manufacturer, delivered in 1971. There are 130 freight wagons, including 108 open wagons for manganese transport. Passenger services employ one small railcar and five coaches, plus a composite passenger/baggage car and two brakes. Other vehicles are used as mobile accommodation for track maintenance crews and the railway boasts an ambulance car for use in emergencies. Maintenance is undertaken at EFA's workshops at Pôrto Santana.

## Track
**Rail type and weight:** 90-AS of 44.64 kg/m
**Sleepers:** wood
**Ballast:** crushed stone
**Max gradient:** 1.5%
**Min curve radius:** 305.6 m

## Estrada de Ferro Trombetas (EFT/MRN)

Mineração Rio do Norte (MRN), Porto Trombetas, Municipality of Oriximiná, Pará

### Key personnel
Manager: Reginaldo Pedriera Lapa

Gauge: 1,000 mm
Route length: 30 km

### Organisation
The line commences at Porto Trombetas on the river Trombetas in the northwest of Pará state, some 80 km from Oriximiná and more than 300 km northwest of Santarém, and extends to the Rio do Norte bauxite mines. The railway employs 65 people for train operation and maintenance in a community that exists purely to exploit bauxite reserves and is considered to be highly profitable. Major shareholders in MRN are Companhía do Rio Doce (CVRD) (46 per cent), Grupo Votorantim (10 per cent) and Alcan (24 per cent).

### Freight operations
Bauxite is the railway's sole traffic, amounting to 9 to 11 million tonnes annually, Up to 15 22-wagon trains are run daily in each direction. Unloading is undertaken by a Viardor wagon-tippler and the wagons are equipped with automatic centre couplers.

### Traction and rolling stock
The locomotive fleet comprises five GM G-12 970 kW diesel-electrics. There are 90 freight wagons, all high-sided four-axle vehicles with a payload capacity of 70 tonnes.

### Track
**Rail type and weight:** TR-68 welded
**Sleepers:** CD 50 concrete
**Fastenings:** Pandrol E 209
**Ballast:** crushed stone
**Max gradient:** 1%
**Min axleload:** 32 tonnes

---

## Ferrovia Centro-Atlântica (FCA)

Rua Sapucai 383, CEP 30150-904, Floresta, Belo Horizonte
Tel: (+55 31) 218 27 46    Fax: (+55 31) 218 27 11
Web: http://www.centro-atlantica.com.br

Gauge: 1,000 mm
Route length: 7,080 km

### Key personnel
Director General: Thiers Manzano Barsotti

### Political background
In June 1996, the second concession under the government's privatisation programme for RFFSA (qv), for the Centre-East Network, was sold for the minimum price of Cr317 million. The so-called Tacumã Consortium, which bought the concession, consisted of CVRD subsidiary Tacumã Mining, Valia (the CVRD pension fund), intermodal operator Interférrea, local steel and cement producers, plus Judori Administração Empreendimentos e Participações. From the US came shortline operator Railtex, the Bank of Boston and investment group Ralph Partners. The buyer was the only bidder at the auction. The new company took over operations on 1 September 1996.

In February 2000, CVRD acquired the Railtex shareholding for US$6.4 million to become FCA's major shareholder. This step was undertaken because FCA largely depends on CVRD's EFVM line for traffic.

### Organisation
FCA operates all former RFFSA metre-gauge lines in the states of Espírito Santo, Minas Gerais, Goiás, Bahía, Sergipe, Rio de Janeiro and the south of Alagoas, serving such major centres as Belo Horizonte, Brasília, Rio de Janeiro and Salvador. It connects with the EFVM system at Belo Horizonte and Vitória, with Ferroban at Uberaba and Araguari and with CFN at Maceió, all of which are also 1,000 mm gauge. At Belo Horizonte, Rio de Janeiro, Tres Rios, Barra Mansa and Cuzeiro, connections are made with the broad gauge lines of MRS Logística. If the Transnordestina line is built, FCA will make a connection with it at Juázeiro, in the far north of Bahía state.

In 2000, measures were implemented to rehabilitate many lines that were in such poor condition that operations were not possible. In particular, lines in Bahía were in a bad state of repair and the Migule Burnier–Ponte Nova–Recreio section was out of use, leaving parts of the network in southeast Minas Gerais, Rio and Espírito Santo isolated from the rest of the system. The Três Coraçoes–Cruzeiro line was also out of service.

| Traffic (million) | 1998 | 1999 | 2000 |
|---|---|---|---|
| Freight tonnes | 18.1 | 18.3 | 19.6 |
| Freight tonne-km | 7,019 | 7,429 | 7,651 |

### Freight operations
The main commodities carried by FCA are cement from various producers in northern Minas Gerais and Bahía, chemicals from Bahía and agricultural products from various locations in Minas Gerais and Goiás. On the Belo Horizonte–Uberaba line, fertiliser from Araferíl is also transported, while in Minas Gerais steel and iron ore are also important commodities. Petroleum products are also a major source of traffic. Increasing volumes of transit freight from CFN are handled, especially on manufactured goods such as beer, sugar and cement to centres of consumption in central southern Brazil.

A customer support centre (CAC) has been established to provide improved service to shippers.

### Passenger operations
FCA does not operate passenger services but the company shares tracks with SuperVía (formerly Flumitrens) in the Rio de Janeiro and Niterói regions. Similar arrangements are in place around Salvador, while between Lourenço de Albuquerque and Maceió, FCA shares tracks with neighbouring freight operator CFN and with CBTU, which runs some suburban passenger services.

### Improvements to existing lines
Initially, lines in Bahía radiating from the Salvador region to Brumado in the south, to Juázeiro in the northwest and to Aracajú in Sergipe state were repaired as an emergency measure. In 1999-2000 the 800 km line through Sergipe was re-sleepered and track joints were welded.

Further track improvements were undertaken during 2000.

### Traction and rolling stock
In 2001, FCA's fleet comprised 270 locomotives and 8,400 wagons. In 1999, FCA invested Cr12.2 million in heavy repairs to locomotives and wagons and an additional Cr11.2 million was spent in routine maintenance aimed at increasing availability. This included the overhaul of 40 General Electric U20 locomotives and the refurbishment of more than 1,400 wagons. FCA has also acquired 22 new locomotives.

All locomotives are equipped with satellite tracking equipment.

*FCA General Electric U20C locomotives at Horto Florestal* (Flávio Francesconi Lage)

---

## Ferroeste

Estrada de Ferro Paraná Oeste SA
Avenida Iguaçu 420, 7° Andar, Curitiba PR, CEP 80230-902
Tel: (+55 41) 322 18 11    Fax: (+55 41) 233 21 47
e-mail: ferroest@pr.gov.pr
Web: http://www.pr.gov.br/ferroeste

### Key personnel
President Director: José Haraldo Carneiro Lobo
Works and Maintenance Director:
  Leo Casella Bittencourt
Finance and Administration Director: Edmond Fatuch

Gauge: 1,000 mm
Route length: 248 km

### Political background
Ferroeste is owned by the government of the state of Paraná, one of the most prosperous states in Brazil due to

*The Ferroeste line features major civil engineering works*

its highly developed agriculture and growing agro-industrial activity. The railway runs through an area with substantial agricultural production requiring efficient transport of both produce and materials such as fertiliser.

The first phase of the line, the Guarapuava–Cascavel section, required an investment of US$212.7 million. This enabled commercial operations to begin in the first quarter of 1996. However, at the end of 1996, a 30-year concession (with a possible 30-year extension) was awarded to the Ferropar (Ferrovia Paraná SA) consortium comprising Brazilian companies Gemon, FAO, and Pound SA. Ferropar began operations on 1 March 1997.

### Freight traffic
In 1999 Ferropar carried 1 million tonnes of freight. Grain predominates, with the state of Paraná responsible for some 25 per cent of Brazil's production, but soya beans, bran, wheat, corn, cement and fertilisers are also carried in significant quantities, with much of the agricultural produce destined for the port of Paranagua.

### New lines
As well as controlling the performance of its subcontracted concessionaire, Ferroeste is conducting studies and undertaking projects related to the railway's extension to Foz do Iguaçu and Guaíra, a development considered necessary to integrate Brazil into the continent's rail transport market and one greatly encouraged by Mercosul.

The 171 km link from Cascavel to Foz do Iguaçu will be started as soon as funding of US$130 million can be raised from private sector sources, feasibility studies having determined the level of state grants necessary to render the scheme attractive to investors. Additional investment will be need to fund the fleet of 70 locomotives and 1,052 wagons needed to operate the line. Once operational, the Cascavel–Foz do Iguaçu line will have capacity to handle 4.52 million tonnes annually.

Expansion of the network to Guaíra (169 km), close to the border with Paraguay, is seen as a way of funnelling the agricultural output for export from the neighbouring parts of Paraguay and the Brazilian states of Mato Grosso and Mato Grosso Sul via Ferroeste to the port of Paranagua.

### Track
The Ferroeste system employs 45 kg/m rail on a mixture of concrete (main line) and wooden (yards) sleepers. Minimum curve radius is 250 m. Maximum gradient is 1.5 per cent for export traffic and 1.8 per cent for import flows.

## Ferronorte

Gauge: 1,600 mm
Route length: 430 km; additional 608 km under construction or planned

### Organisation
A soya farming magnate in the states of Mato Grosso and Goiás who also fronts one of the country's major banks, Olacyr Francisco de Moraes, formed a company, Ferronorte, to build a line from the Ferroban system at Santa Fé do Sul, northwest of São Paulo, into Mato Grosso. The new railway would eventually be 4,000 km long and two-pronged, forking at Cuiabá (Mato Grosso) into lines heading northwest to Porto Velho and north to Santarém, on the Amazon. In early 1995 Ferronorte's founder announced further plans to construct a railway from Santarém to the western extremity of the Carajás Railway (EFC). The distance from Santa Fé do Sul to Cuiabá will be 1,038 km. En route, at Alto Araguaia, a 550 km branch will run to Uberlandia, where there are soya processing plants.

Services on an initial 310 km from Santa Fé do Sul to Aparecida do Taboado commenced in May 1999, followed by the opening in August 1999 of the 120 km Chapado do Sul–Alto Taquari. During 1999, work commenced on the 390 km section from Alto Taquari to Rodonópolis. It was anticipated that this would be completed in 2001, before that year's harvest. By this time, Ferronorte expects to be carrying between 10 and 12 million tonnes annually.

Since 1998, ownership of Ferronorte has been held by the Ferronorte Participações SA (Ferropasa) consortium, in which the Itamarati group, whose president is Mr de Moraes, owns 16.05 per cent. Ferropasa also holds a 36 per cent share of Ferroban (qv). In 1999, Ferropasa was awarded a grant of Cr200 million towards the Cr850 million construction cost of the Alto Taquari–Rodonópolis section by the Amazonia Investment Fund (Finam), a sum that by law had to be matched by Ferroban.

Ferronorte's purpose is the movement of rice, soya and grain for export to the Atlantic ports of Santos (near São Paulo) and Rio de Janeiro. Soya production in particular is expanding fast in Mato Grosso and at present its only outlet is by road transport, which is markedly more expensive than rail for bulk movement.

Ferronorte is one of four railways which in 2000 jointly took over the 200 km network in the port of Santos from port authority Codesp. Ferroban, Ferrovia Novoeste and MRS Logística are also participants in a company established to replace Codesp's own rail operations.

### Traction and rolling stock
In 1999, leasing arrangements were announced covering the acquisition of 50 GE Dash 9-44CW diesel-electric locomotives.

In December 1998, Trinity Industries Inc, based in Dallas, announced that its Brazilian subsidiary, Trinity Rail do Brasil, had entered a consortium with Companhia Comércio e Construcoes to build 300 grain hopper wagons for Ferronorte. Production commenced early in 1999. Additional wagons were ordered from Johnstown to provide a total initial fleet of 600.

## Ferrovías Bandeirantes SA (Ferroban)

Praça Marechal Floriano Peixoto s/n°, Centro, CEP 13013-120 Campinas, São Paulo

### Key personnel
President: José Carlos Nunes Marreco
Director, Administration & Finance: Sérigo Suney Gabizo
Director, Operations and Infrastructure:
  Joao Gouveia Ferrao Neto
Managers
  Permanent Way: Alvaro Delmont
  Mechanical Department: Joao Carlos Novaes
  Commercial: Pedro A Cutini
  Control: Pedro F Theberge
  Finance: Floriano P da Costa Neto
  Human Resources: José Homero B Elias
  Information Technology: Joarez Casagrande
  Contracts: Fernando Soria Henriquez

Gauge: 1,600 mm; 1,000 mm; dual 1,600/1,000 mm
Route length: 1,491 km; 2,517 km; 336 km (total route length 4,855 km)
Electrification: 463 km of 1,600 mm gauge, 581 km of 1,000 mm gauge and 78 km of dual gauge, all at 3 kV DC

### Political background
After several attempts to privatise the former São Paulo State Railways (FEPASA) network, the federal government decided early in 1998 to incorporate it into the residual Brazilian Federal Railways (RFFSA) to speed up its transfer to the private sector. This move allowed São Paulo state to reduce its debt to the federal government.

RFFSA managed and operated FEPASA's freight and passenger operations for nearly 12 months under the name Malha Paulista. On 10 November 1998, Malha Paulista was sold at the Rio de Janeiro stock exchange to the Ferrovías consortium, led by Ferropasa Participações, formed by the neighbouring Ferrovia Novoeste (qv) and Ferronorte (qv) railways, and including Companhia do Rio Doce and several banks and investment companies. Ferrovías took over operations under the name Ferrovías Bandeirantes SA on 1 January 1999, having paid Cr245 million for the network.

Ferrovia Sul Atlántico/América Latina Logística has acquired track access on most metre-gauge lines in the São Paulo–Presidente Epitácio corridor. Ferronorte had trackage rights to run over the entire line from Santa Fé to the port of Santos. Similar trackage rights are expected to be granted to Novoeste as soon as the Baurú–Santos metre-gauge corridor is upgraded.

Ferroban is one of four railways which in 2000 jointly took over the 200 km network in the port of Santos from port authority Codesp. Ferronorte, Ferrovia Novoeste and MRS Logística are also participants in a company established to replace Codesp's own rail operations.

### Finance
In 1999, Ferroban invested Cr75 million in an emergency programme to rehabilitate infrastructure and repair rolling stock, including some expenditure on improvements to workshops. In 2000, Cr156 million is to be spent on the purchase of new locomotives, the refurbishment of existing machines and the overhaul of freight wagons. In the same year, an additional Cr65 million was to be spent on rehabilitation of two lines: Sante Fé do Sul–São Paulo and Campinas–Santos. In its first five years, Ferroban plans to invest Cr500 million in improvements to infrastructure and rolling stock.

### Passenger operations
Ferroban took over some long-distance services from RFFSA but all were suspended in February 1999 after safety concerns were voiced by the São Paulo state authorities. Until then, these services were self-supporting. Some services were reinstated in August 1999 but only as a short-term step to fulfil contractual obligations. These included services three times weekly on Campinas–Panorama, Itirapina–São José do Rio Preto and Sorocaba–Apiaí routes, all without first class accommodation or catering vehicles. Four months later, these services were reduced to twice-weekly and further slowed, with very poor punctuality. With rarely more than 50 per cent occupancy during the peak travel period of

*FEPASA freight at Campinas headed by four General Electric U20C locomotives (F F Lage)* 0010790

January and February, these services look increasingly unlikely to undergo projected privatisation.

### Freight operations
In 1998, Malha Paulista, then under RFFSA control, carried 9.7 million tonnes of freight, well under the figure of 13.8 million tonnes initially claimed early in 1999. In 1999, a slight upturn was achieved with 10.28 million tonnes carried, but an additional 12.8 million tonnes offered to Ferroban could not be carried due to a lack of locomotives and rolling stock. Loadings of around 15 million tonnes were thought likely for 2000.

### Intermodal operations
Despite several past studies having been undertaken into possible container services to and from the port of Santos, intermodal operations have not been developed on the former FEPASA Malha Paulista system. Cnaga, a private-sector transport operator, has been studying the possibility of using the Ferroban network to move road-rail trailers from a terminal at Boa Vista, near Campinas, to Pelotas, in Rio Grande do Sul state. Paper would be conveyed northbound and rice southbound.

FSA/ALL has reinstated a weekly São Paulo–Uruguayana–Buenos Aires container service, which was first run by RFFSA prior to privatisation, and the same company is also undertaking trials with road-railers in this corridor. Neighbouring Ferronorte and Novoeste also plan to convey containers over Ferroban tracks.

### New lines
Late in 1998, the connection between Santa Fé do Sul and the new Ferronorte railway was put into operation, completing a project involving a new 2,600 m double-deck road bridge over the River Paraná between Rubinéia and Santa Fé do Sul.

### Improvements to existing lines
A priority for Ferroban is to improve access to the port of Santos for the neighbouring systems Ferronorte and Novoeste, both of which hold shares in Ferroban. Consequently, almost all infrastructure investment is made on the broad-gauge Campinas–Itirapina–Santa Fé do Sul and the metre-gauge Mairink–Botucatú–Baurú lines, including the Campinas–Mairink–Santos line.

On the broad-gauge corridor, some 200 locations requiring urgent repair or improvements have been identified. Axleloads are to be increased to 30 tonnes and crossing points will be lengthened to 1,500 m. In 1999, 200,000 sleepers were replaced on the Itirapina–Santa Fé do Sul line. On the Mairink–Santos section, additional tracks are being provided at the station yards at Embú Guaçú, Aldeinha and Caucaia and the marshalling yards at Paratinga and Perequê were to be remodelled in 2000. When completed in 2002, these improvements should allow Ferroban to run trains of 6,000 tonnes gross.

After these improvements, a key remaining problem will be the over-utilisation of the port of Santos, although privatisation of this facility was underway in 2000. Also to be resolved is the high rate of accidents on Ferroban lines, with an increase in trespass and the violation of level crossing regulations since the virtual disappearance of fast passenger trains. Some local authorities have started to play a role in attempting to cut the number of such incidents.

An additional problem facing Ferroban is the poor condition of some branch lines, resulting in a reduction of even suspension of services. Such measures have resulted in pressure from customers to make the necessary investments to improve or restore such services.

### Traction and rolling stock
At the beginning of 2000, Ferroban owned 84 diesel and 45 electric locomotives for its broad-gauge network and 207 diesel and 72 electric locomotives for metre gauge. The fleet also contained four broad-gauge diesel railcars and two demotorised units on metre gauge, and 7,551 broad-gauge and 3,317 metre-gauge wagons. Of the combined wagon fleet of 10,868, some 7,900 were serviceable. The combined passenger vehicle fleet for both gauges comprised 252 coaches, including 46 recently refurbished. Around 150 were reported to need urgent repairs.

The average age of the diesel locomotive fleet was 39 years, while that of Ferroban electric locomotives was over 40 years. Some electric locomotives have been withdrawn because of their age and the planned de-electrification of the network. Locomotive availability at the end of 1999 stood at 52 per cent.

In 2000, 60 GE Class 3800 U20 locomotives were due to be overhauled and re-engined. It was also reported that 20 new metre-gauge locomotives could be acquired, possibly from China. Also planned was the rebuilding of 550 unserviceable freight wagons by private contractors and the overhaul of 400 to 500 operational vehicles in Ferroban's own workshops.

### Signalling and telecommunications
A modern telecommunications system has been installed across much of the network in conjunction with Embratel.

A new operations control centre at Campinas was to be commissioned in 2000, with a capability to track every train and freight wagon from loading to unloading points. Train despatching was being upgraded by Engesis to enable GPS tracking via Omnisat to be implemented. New end-of-train devices have been installed by Linksat on 130 locomotives.

### Track
**Rail**
**Type:** TR 37, TR 45, TR 50, TR 55, TR 57, TR 68
**Weight:** 37, 45, 50, 55, 57, 68 kg/m
**Crossties (sleepers)**
**Wood:** 1,000 mm gauge 2,000 × 220 × 160 mm; 1,600 mm gauge 2,800 × 240 × 170 mm
**Spacing:** 1,000 mm gauge 1,600/km; 1,600 mm gauge 1,667/km
**Rail fastenings:** GEO or K; ML
**Concrete block:** 1,000 mm gauge 680 × 290 × 211 mm; 1,600 mm gauge 680 × 290 × 239 mm
**Spacing:** 1,500/km
**Fastenings:** FN
**Concrete (monobloc):** (1,000 mm gauge only) 2,000 × 220 × 210 mm to 2,000 × 320 × 242 mm
**Spacing:** 1,500/km
**Fastenings:** RN
**Min curve radius:** Main lines 150 m; branches 90 m
**Max gradients:** Main lines 2%; branches 3%
**Max axleload:** 1,000 mm gauge 20 tonnes; 1,600 mm gauge 25 tonnes

*Three GE-built metre-gauge electric locomotives on FEPASA freight service at Mayrink (Günter Sieg) 0023713*

**Diesel-electric locomotives**

| Class | Wheel arrangement | Power kW | Speed km/h | Weight tonnes | No in service | First built | Mechanical | Builders Engine | Transmission |
|---|---|---|---|---|---|---|---|---|---|
| 3100 | Co+Co | 447 | 80 | 64 | 8 | 1948 | GE | CB | GE |
| 3200 | Bo-Bo | 894 | 138 | 71.2 | 13 | 1957 | GE | CB | GE |
| 3500 | Co-Co | 671 | 95 | 68.1 | 7 | 1957 | GE | Alco | GE |
| 3600 | Bo-Bo | 652 | 100 | 56.7 | 13 | 1961 | GM | GM | GM |
| 3600 | Bo-Bo | 652 | 100 | 60.5 | 14 | 1960 | GM | GM | GM |
| 3650 | Bo-Bo | 976 | 100 | 74.9 | 21 | 1957 | GM | GM | GM |
| 3700 | Bo-Bo | 574 | 90 | 70 | 16 | 1969 | LEW | SACM | LEW |
| 3750 | Bo-Bo | 835 | 100 | 74 | 9 | 1968 | LEW | SACM | LEW |
| 3800 | Co-Co | 1,491 | 103 | 108 | 106 | 1974 | GE | GE | GE |
| 7000* | Bo-Bo | 1,304 | 105 | 110.6 | 16 | 1958 | GM | GM | GM |
| 7050* | Bo-Bo | 976 | 124 | 80 | 17 | 1958 | GM | GM | GM |
| 7760* | Bo-Bo | 574 | 90 | 74 | 25 | 1967 | LEW | SACM | LEW |
| 7800* | Co-Co | 1,491 | 103 | 108 | 26 | 1977 | GE | GE | GE |

* Broad gauge

**Electric locomotives**

| Class | Wheel arrangement | Output kW | Weight tonnes | No in service | First built | Builders Mechanical | Electrical |
|---|---|---|---|---|---|---|---|
| 2000 | 1-Co+Co-1 | 1,729 | 130 | 22 | 1943 | GE | GE |
| 2050 | 1-Co+Co-1 | 1,729 | 108 | 18 | 1943 | Westinghouse | Westinghouse |
| 2100 | Bo-Bo | 1,371 | 72.7 | 30 | 1968 | GE | GE |
| 6100* | 2-Co+Co-2 | 2,846 | 122 | 19 | 1982 | Westinghouse | rebuilt FEPASA |
| 6150* | 2-Co+Co-2 | 2,846 | 122 | 8 | 1982 | Westinghouse | rebuilt FEPASA |
| 6350* | Co-Co | 3,269 | 144 | 10 | 1967 | GE Brasil | GE Brasil |
| 6370* | 2-Co+Co-2 | 2,846 | 165 | 3 | 1940 | GE | GE |
| 6450* | 2-Do+Do-2 | 3,470 | 184 | 5 | 1951 | GE | GE |
| EC362 | Bo-Bo | 2,480 | 98 | 2 | 1984 | 50 c/s Gp | 50 c/s Gp |

* Broad gauge

## Ferrovía Norte-Sul (North-South Railway)

Operated by Companhia Vale do Rio Doce (CVRD)
Gauge: 1,000 mm
Route length: 226 km (additional 1,974 km planned)

### Organisation
The Brazilian government projected this line during the 1980s to create a new transport corridor from central Brazil to the north coast at São Luiz and to Belém on the mouth of the Amazon. When complete, the line will follow an existing highway and the Tocantins river to run from Goiânia, in Goiás state, via Miracema do Norte and Estreito, in Tocantins state, Porto Franco and Imperatriz to Açailândia (Maranhão state), and then north to Belém.

The project is divided into three phases. The first brings the line from an interchange with the Carajás Railway (EFC) at Açailândia into Tocantins state; the second

# RAILWAY SYSTEMS/Brazil

foresees the construction of a line from Senador Canedo, near Goiânia; and the third covers the 600 km line from Açailândia to Belém.

In 1989, the first 106 km from Açailândia to Imperatriz were put into service, and EFC operates and maintains this section. Work on the section south of Imperatriz began in 1989 using labour from the Brazilian army, but this ended after a few months for financial reasons. In 1994 and again in 1996 some earthworks were undertaken by the army, but a major obstacle has been the need for a 1,300 m bridge over the Tocantins river at the border between the states of Maranhão and Tocantins. In 1999, Valec, the state concessionaire for the line, recommenced work between Imperatriz and Estreito using Cr100.4 million of public funds. Opening of this section took place on 29 October 1999. Completion of the entire 2,200 km line, which will traverse some 1.8 million km$^2$ of fertile agricultural land, could require an investment estimated at US$1.6 billion and take five years. In 2000, Cr49 million was budgeted for infrastructure work on the scheme.

Privatisation of the Norte-Sul project was under discussion in 2000 because the Federal government foresees little prospect of funding completion of the project with public funds.

### Passenger operations
A passenger service is run three times weekly between Açailândia and Estreito, providing a connection to and from São Luiz via EFC's broad-gauge service.

### Freight operations
Freight consists mainly of agricultural products grown in the Imperatriz area, including soya beans and cereals. Fertiliser, general freight and fuel are also carried. In 1999, around 2.2 million tonnes were carried, 18 per cent more than the previous year. From 2000, a new fertiliser plant at Imperatriz was expected to generate an additional 300,000 tonnes of traffic annually. Once the entire line is completed, it is expected to handle around 14 million tonnes of freight annually, including soya, cereals, cellulose and timber. It will also improve the movement of freight to Belém and other Amazonian destinations.

All freight has to be transhipped to EFC's broad-gauge trains at Açailândia.

### Traction and rolling stock
All rolling stock is owned by CVRD, which transferred equipment from its Vitória a Minas Railway.

### Track
**Sleepers:** wood (Açailândia–Imperatriz); concrete (Imperatriz–Estreito)
**Ballast:** crushed stone
**Max gradient:** 1.5%
**Min curve radius:** 385 m

## Ferrovia Novoeste (New West Railway)

**Key personnel**
Director: Glen Michael
Transport Director: Sergio Julian Cardoso
Administration and Finance: Homero Boretti Elias
Logistics and Permanant Way: Edmundo Dias do Amaral
Marketing: Ricardo Lopes
Engineering: Melvin Jones

Gauge: 1,000 mm
Route length: 1,600 km

### Political background
The privatisation of the RFFSA network as seven 30-year regional freight operating concessions (including FEPASA) began in earnest in 1996. The concession for the route from Bauru to Corumbá and its branch to Ponta Porã (known as the Western Network) was auctioned at the Rio de Janeiro stock exchange on 5 March. The concession was acquired for Cr62.36 million (US$63.4 million) by a consortium of Brazilian and US investors, led by the Noel Group (owners of Illinois Central) and including Chemical Bank, Bank of America, Brazil Railway Partners and Western Rail Investors. Operations under the new ownership began in June 1996.

The concession for the Western Network is renewable for a further 30 years, with the concessionaire leasing infrastructure and rolling stock from RFFSA. As of March 1996, the Western Network's rolling stock fleet comprised 88 diesel-electric locomotives and 2,600 freight wagons, with half of the locomotives and some 7 per cent of the wagons out of service for want of maintenance and spare parts. Under the terms of the concession, the government requires some Cr359 million to be invested in the Western Network, with rolling stock, track maintenance and the upgrading of structures and communications regarded as priorities.

Ferrovia Novoeste is one of four railways which in 2000 jointly took over the 200 km network in the port of Santos from port authority Codesp. Ferroban, Ferronorte, and MRS Logística are also participants in a company established to replace Codesp's own rail operations.

| Traffic (million) | 1997 | 1998 |
|---|---|---|
| Freight tonnes | 2.54 | 2.88 |
| Freight tonne-km | 1,490 | 1,579 |

### Freight operations
In 1998 Ferrovia Novoeste carried 2.88 million tonnes for 1.58 billion tonne-km, the principal commodities carried include petroleum products, ores, grain and fertiliser and manufactured products bound for Bolivia via Corumbá.

## Ferrovia Sul-Atlantico (South Atlantic Railway)

Ferrovia Sul-Atlantico (FSA)

**Key personnel**
President: José Paulo Oliveira Alves

Gauge: 1,000 mm
Route length: 6,349 km

### Political background
In December 1996, RFFSA's (qv) Southern Network was sold for US$208 million, 37 per cent higher than the reserve price, to a consortium of Railtex and Ralph Partners of the US and Banco Garantia, Judore and Interferrea of Brazil. The consortium took over operations on 1 March 1997. Cr300 million was to be invested within the first two years of the concession period, aimed at boosting revenue by 50 per cent. Some 100 locomotives were to be rebuilt in this period. Oil traffic would account for 45 per cent of the total hauled.

The new railway operates in the states of Paraná, Santa Catarina and Rio Grande do Sul and carries 50 per cent of all RFFSA traffic.

| Traffic (million) | 1997 | 1998 |
|---|---|---|
| Freight tonnes | 11.7 | 15.58 |
| Freight tonne-km | 6,250 | 8,534 |

## Ferrovia Tereza Cristina (FTC)

Ferrovia Tereza Cristina SA
Rua dos Ferroviários 100, Oficinas, Tubarão, SC
Tel: (+55 48) 626 47 77  Fax: (+55 48) 626 43 25
e-mail: ftc@matrix.com.br

**Key personnel**
General Manager: Benony Schmitz Filho

Gauge: 1,000 mm
Route length: 164 km

### Political background
A concession to operate RFFSA's former Tuberão division, in Santa Catarina province in the extreme south of Brazil, was awarded in January 1997 to a consortium of Gemon, Interfinance SA Participações and Santa Lúcia Agro-Indústria e Comércio. The isolated metre-gauge network serves a coal-producing region, with access to the port of Imbituba.

### Freight operations
FTC mainly conveys coal from deposits near Siderópolis. Most is supplied to Gerasul, an energy producer. Agricultural products and containerised traffic are also handled. Tonnages carried in 1999 increased by nearly 30 per cent compared with the previous year.

| Traffic (million) | 1997 | 1998 | 1999 |
|---|---|---|---|
| Freight tonnes | 2,070 | 2,255 | 2,900 |
| Freight tonne-km | 149 | 166 | 230 |

### Improvements to existing lines
In 1999, FTC invested Cr4 million in infrastructure and rolling stock. Work included completion of resleepering 82 km of track under a programme started in 1998 and the construction of a 2 km branch from Siderópolis to coal mines at Rio Deserto and Beluno. The Cr700,000 cost of this project is being borne jointly by FTC and the coal producers.

### Traction and rolling stock
FTC owns 10 diesel locomotives, all of which were operational in 2000. Freight wagons consist mainly of coal hoppers, together with general freight vehicles and flatcars for container transport. The railway owns some steam locomotives and passenger coaches, but none of these were in service in 2000. In April 2000, Santa Catarina state began to develop plans for tourist services using this stock.

## Flumitrens

Companhia Fluminense de Trens Urbanos
Praça Cristiano Ottoni, Sala 445, Rio de Janeiro RJ, CEP 20221
Tel: (+55 21) 233 85 94  Fax: (+55 21) 253 30 89

**Key personnel**
President: Murilo Siqueira Junqueira
Production Director: Jose Carlos Martins Lopes
Administrative Director: Gilberto Martins Velloso
Engineering Director: Ronaldo da Silva Cotrim
Human Resources Director: Marluce M S M Tavares

Gauge: 1,600 mm; 1,000 mm
Route length: 228 km; 152 km (total route length 380 km)
Electrification: 167 km of 1,600 mm gauge at 3 kV DC

### Political background
The suburban network serving the city of Rio de Janeiro passed from the control of Companhia Brasiliera de Trens Urbanos to the state of Rio de Janeiro on 22 December 1994. Services are now marketed under the name Flumitrens. In 1996, it was decided to initiate privatisation of the network based on the Buenos Aires model and in early 1999 the Supervía consortium took over the network under a 25-year concession. A three-year programme to upgrade the network commenced in 1999 with a loan from the Inter-American Development Bank.

In 1997 Flumitrens employed 4,602 staff.

Brazil/**RAILWAY SYSTEMS** 69

### Passenger operations
Flumitrens operates the largest suburban system in Brazil, with electrified 1,600 mm gauge routes from two city-centre termini, Dom Pedro II and Barão de Mauá, to Santa Cruz, Paracambi, Belford Roxo, and Gramacho. The Santa Cruz-Itaguaí section is diesel-worked. The 1,000 mm gauge network comprises routes from Gramacho to Vila Inhomirim and Guapimirim and from Barreto on the east side of Guanabara Bay to Visconde de Itaboraí.

In 1997 Flumitrens recorded 71 million passenger journeys for 2.9 billion passenger-km.

Fare evasion is a major problem, with passengers often riding outside vehicles.

### Traction and rolling stock
At the end of 1997, the 1,600 mm gauge fleet comprised 38 diesel-electric locomotives (24 unserviceable) and 253 electric multiple-units. The 1,000 mm gauge fleet comprised 19 diesel-electric locomotives and 57 passenger coaches.

Twelve Class 900 emus have been refurbished, with IGBT chopper equipment supplied by Adtranz Switzerland replacing the original camshaft control system.

### Signalling and telecommunications
At the end of 1995, Centralised Traffic Control (CTC) was in operation on 150.1 route-km of the Flumitrens system, with train staff operation in place on 75 route-km. CTC has subsequently been installed on the Dom Pedro II-Lauro Muller (2.3 km), Marechal Hermes-Deodoro (1.5 km) and Mesquita-Japeri (29.8 km) sections of the 1,600 mm gauge network, and Automatic Train Control (ATC) on the Dom Pedro II-Deodoro (22 km), Deodoro-Japeri (39.7 km) and Deodoro-Santa Cruz (32.7 km) sections.

**Flumitrens electric multiple-units**

| Class | Cars per unit | Motor cars per unit | Motored axles/car | Output/motor kW | Speed km/h | No in service | First built | Builders Mechanical | Electrical |
|---|---|---|---|---|---|---|---|---|---|
| 400M | 3 | 1 | 4 | 315 | 90 | 50 | 1964 | FNV/Cobrasma | Hitachi/Toshiba |
| 400 | 3 | 1 | 4 | 255 | 90 | 12 | 1964 | FNV/Cobrasma | GE |
| 500 | 4 | 2 | 4 | 315 | 90 | 28 | 1977 | Nippon Sharyo | Hitachi/Toshiba |
| 700 | 4 | 2 | 4 | 315 | 90 | 29 | 1980 | Mafersa | Hitachi/Toshiba |
| 800 | 4 | 2 | 4 | 280 | 90 | 55 | 1980 | Santa Matilde | GE |
| 900 | 4 | 2 | 4 | 279 | 90 | 60 | 1980 | Cobrasma | MTE |
| 1000 | 3 | 1 | 4 | 315 | 90 | 22 | 1954 | Metro-Vick | Hitachi/Toshiba/Villares |

## Metrofor

Autarquia de Região Metropolitana de Fortaleza
Rua Jose Laurenço, Aldeota, Fortaleza 60000, Ceará
Tel: (+55 85) 212 40 34

Gauge: 1,000 mm
Route length: 45 km

### Political background
In 1998, Ceará state took over responsibility for the former CBTU suburban network in Fortaleza. This development unlocked investments of US$511 million, including a US$268 million loan from Japan's Eximbank which had been frozen since 1992. The state of Ceará is also making a contribution of US$58 million.

### Organisation
The network consists of two separate metre-gauge lines. The southern line runs from the city's João Felipe main station via Paragaba, Mondubim, Aracapé and Maracanaú to Vila das Flores (25 km). The western line runs from João Felipe via Alvaro Wayne and Antônio Bezerra to Caucáia (20 km).

### Passenger operations
Both lines are served by diesel locomotive-hauled trains operating at regular intervals on the southern line and irregularly on the western line. In 2000, Metrofor was carrying some 30,000 passengers daily. Fares covered only 18 per cent of operating costs.

### Improvements to existing lines
The US$511 million mentioned above is to be used to boost the capacity of the Metrofor system to 185,000 passengers daily. In a first phase, the southern line is to be remodelled and electrified for operation by emus. Existing stations are to be rebuilt and new ones created. A new maintenance facility is to be built at Vila das Flores. Rail access to João Felipe station will be taken underground, eliminating the use of busy level crossings in the city centre. Also in the first phase, a new line will be built from Aracapé to Caucáia to divert freight trains from the city centre (see entry for Companhia Ferroviária do Nordeste).

The western line will be remodelled but not electrified. Services to Caucáia will be provided by refurbished diesel trains operating at a 20 min frequency. Existing stations will receive a facelift and some new ones are to be built.

In a later phase, freight lines from Vila das Flores to Parangaba, junction of the line from the port of Mucuripé, will be separated from Metrofor's suburban line. This phase also foresees the construction of a new 6 km branch from Jereissati to Maranguape, replacing a long-disused line from Maracanaú.

### Traction and rolling stock
Services are provided by a fleet of six diesel locomotives and 45 coaches. Under plans to electrify the southern line, 10 four-car emus are to be acquired.

## Metrorec

Trem Metropolitano de Recife
Rua José Natario 478, 50900-000 Recife
Tel: (+55 81) 251 09 33   Fax: (+55 81) 251 48 44

Gauge: 1,600 mm; 1,000 mm
Route length: 22 km; 32 km
Electrification: 22 km at 3 kV DC

### Organisation
Formerly operated by CBTU (qv), Metrorec operates a suburban passenger network in and around Recife. The majority shareholding is by Pernambuco state.

### Passenger operations
Metrorec operates an electrified 1,600 mm gauge double-track line from Recife to Ipiranga, Coqueiral and Jabatao (17 km) and from Coqueiral to Terminal Intermodal de Passageiros (TIP) (5 km). There are 17 stations. Also operated is a 32 km diesel-operated metre-gauge line from Recife south to Cajueiro Seco and Cabo. Together, the two systems carry around 120,000 passengers daily, the broad-gauge lines accounting for around three-quarters of these.

A second ex-CBTU state-owned operator, Companhía Pernumbaca de Trens (CPT), provides one weekday return service on the metre-gauge line between Recife and Ribeirao via Cabo (88 km) as well as occasional long-distance trains between Recife and Caruarú (146 km) via CFN's Salgueiro line. It was expected that CBT would take over diesel-operated services on the line to Cabo once electrification of the Recife–Cajueiro Seco section was complete (see below).

### Improvements to existing lines
Early in 1998, upgrading commenced of the metre-gauge line, including regauging and electrifying the 21 km Recife–Cajueiro Seco section. Eleven new stations are to be provided. The scheme includes provision of a third metre-gauge track alongside the newly converted section to enable diesel-hauled passenger and freight trains to continue to reach Recife Central station. On the original electrified network, a 4.5 km extension is planned from TIP to Timbi. Funded jointly by the World Bank and the Brazilian federal government, the US$204 million project is scheduled for completion by the end of 2001.

### Traction and rolling stock
On broad-gauge electrified lines, services are provided by 25 four-car emus supplied in 1984 by Brazilian manufacturer San Matilde. Metre-gauge rolling stock comprises seven diesel locomotives and 41 coaches.

## MRS Logística

MRS Logística S/A

*Headquarters*
Praia de Botafogo, 228/sala 1201-E, Botafogo 22359-900, Rio de Janeiro – RJ
Tel: (+55 21) 551 14 50   Fax: (+55 21) 552 26 35
e-mail: cgi@mrs.com.br
Web: http://www.mrs.com.br

*Operations and administration*
Avenida Brasil, 2001, Centro 36060-010, Juiz de Fora – MG
Tel: (+55 32) 239 26 00   Fax: (+55 32) 239 36 09

### Key personnel
Chief Executive Officer: Mauro R F Knudsen
Chief Financial Officer: Alberto Régis Távora
Development Director: Henrique Aché Pilar
Production Director: Rinaldo Bastos Vieira Filho

Gauge: 1,600 mm
Route length: 1,674 km
Electrification: 8 km at 3 kV DC

### Political background
MRS was established in August 1996 by the MRS Consortium, which was formed with the aim of acquiring from the Brazilian government a concession to operate RFFSA's (qv) 1,674.1 km South-Eastern Network (the former Regions 3 and 4). MRS' main shareholders are its main customers: MBR and Ferteco Mineração, and four steel-producing companies, Companhia Siderúgica Nacional (CSN), Usinas Siderúgicas de Minas Gerais (Usiminas), Companhia Siderúrgica Paulista (Cosipa) and Gerdau S/A Siderúrgica. Other shareholders include Ultrafértil, ABS Empreendimentos Imobiliáros, Participações e Serviços, Celto Intergração Multimodal. In addition, former RFFSA employees were granted rights to subscribe up to ten per ecnt of the company's shares.

In November 1996 MRS was granted a 30-year concession by the federal government to be the exclusive provider of freight transport on the network and was also granted a lease by RFFSA for the same term to use its operational assets. The consortium paid the auction price of US$870 million for the concession and on 1 December 1996, now in the form of a corporation named MRS Logística S/A, took over operations.

At the end of 1998, the company employed 3,299 staff.

# RAILWAY SYSTEMS/Brazil

## Finance

| Revenue (Cr million) | 1997 | 1998 |
|---|---|---|
| Freight | 397.8 | 444.2 |
| Total | 397.8 | 444.2 |

| Expenditure | 1997 | 1998 |
|---|---|---|
| Staff/personnel | 147.0 | 116.8 |
| Materials and services | 132.0 | 140.3 |
| Depreciation | 3.9 | 13.1 |
| Asset/leasing | 54.9 | 63.0 |
| Total | 337.8 | 333.2 |

| Traffic (million) | 1997 | 1998 |
|---|---|---|
| Freight tonnes | 51.0 | 52.8 |
| Freight tonne-km | 20,400 | 21,400 |

## Freight operations

The MRS network is located in the most developed region of Brazil, which accounts for some 65 per cent of the country's GDP. Its lines provide the most direct transport link between the iron ore producing region in Minas Gerais state and the Atlantic ports of Guaíba, Rio de Janeiro, Santos and Sepetiba.

In 1998 iron ore both for export and for the domestic market was responsible for approximately 70 per cent of the railway's traffic, with 36.6 million tons carried, while other steel-related products accounted for another 13 per cent. Total haulage was 52.8 million tonnes for 21.4 billion tonne/km, resulting in a gross revenue of Cr444.2 million.

The MRS network includes an 8 km electrified section which incorporates the rack-operated Old Serra Incline (10.7%), for which a small fleet of specialised Hitachi-built 3 kV DC electric locomotives is retained.

## New lines

Two of MRS Logística's customers have built branch lines to connect their facilities to the network. BASF has built a 3 km spur to the MRS Logística line at Guaratinguetá (São Paulo state) and fertiliser and a chemicals producer is investing in similar facilities at its Santos terminal.

## Traction and rolling stock

At the end of 1998 the MRS Logística traction fleet comprised 286 diesel locomotives and nine electric locomotives. The freight wagon fleet consisted of 9,305 vehicles; a further 1,699 wagons owned by the railway's clients were in use on the network. In 1999, 450 wagons for mineral traffic were ordered from Maxion (270) and T'Trans (180). Since it took over the network in 1996, MRS Logística has given investment priority to rehabilitation and modernisation of the motive power and rolling stock fleets.

## Signalling and telecommunications

CTC covers 1,290 route-km of the MRS network. Since 1996 MRS Logística has invested in improvements to its signalling and telecommunications systems and has also introduced a satellite communications system. The company has also procured a train operations simulator.

## Track

**Weight:** 68 kg/m (1,072/km); 57 kg/m (602 km)
**Sleepers**
**Wood:** 280 × 24 × 17 cm
**Spacing:** 1,850/km
**Concrete:** twin-block
**Spacing:** 1,493/1,667/km
**Fastenings:** Pandrol clips, coach screws and RN System
**Min curve radius:** 300 m
**Max gradient:** 2%
**Max axleload:** 30 tonnes

### Diesel locomotives

| Class | Wheel arrangement | Power kW | Speed km/h | Weight tonnes | No in service | First built | Builders Mechanical | Engine | Transmission |
|---|---|---|---|---|---|---|---|---|---|
| SD18 | Co-Co | 1,340 | 104 | 163 | 16 | 1961 | GM | GM 567 | E GM |
| SD38 | Co-Co | 1,493 | 97 | 163 | 34 | 1967 | GM | GM 645E | E GM |
| SD40-2M | Co-Co | 2,238 | 104 | 180 | 38 | 1980 | GM | GM 645E3 | E GM |
| U20C | Co-Co | 1,493 | 104 | 120 | 23 | 1981 | GE | GE 7FDL 12 | E GE |
| U23C | Co-Co | 1,680 | 112 | 180 | 76 | 1975 | GE | GE 7FDL 12 | E GE |
| U23C1 | Co-Co | 1,680 | 112 | 165 | 13 | 1975 | GE | GE 7FDL 12 | E GE |
| U23CA | Co-Co | 1,940 | 112 | 180 | 27 | 1987 | GE | GE 7FDL 12 | E GE |
| U23CE | Co-Co | 1,680 | 112 | 180 | 16 | 1995 | GE | GE 7FDL 12 | E GE |
| 720 | Bo-Bo | 537 | 90 | 80 | 17 | 1956 | GE | Alco 251 6K | E GE |
| RSD12 | Co-Co | 1,493 | 104 | 163 | 2 | 1986 | Alco | Alco 251 | E GE |
| U5B | Bo-Bo | 448 | 64 | 51 | 9 | 1961 | GE | Caterpillar D379 | E GE |
| U6B | Bo-Bo | 522 | 64 | 53 | 7 | 1967 | GE | Caterpillar D379 | E GE |
| EFCB | Bo | 201 | 30 | 20 | 3 | 1969 | EFCB | Detroit Diesel 401 | E Leece Leville |
| RS3 | Bo-Bo | 1,194 | 104 | 109 | 3 | 1952 | Alco | Alco 251 | E GE |
| Hitachi | Bo-Bo | 746 | 25 | 115 | 2 | 1980 | Hitachi | Alco 251B | E Hitachi |

### Electric locomotives

| Class | Wheel arrangement | Power kW continuous | Speed km/h | Weight tonnes | No built | First built | Builders Mechanical | Electrical |
|---|---|---|---|---|---|---|---|---|
| Hitachi | B-B | 2,460 | 45 | 118 | 9 | 1980 | Hitachi | Hitachi |

*MRS Logística GE-built diesel-electric locomotive on a container train at Piaçaguera*

*MRS Logística handles large volumes of iron ore traffic*

# Brazil/RAILWAY SYSTEMS

## Rede Ferroviaria Federal SA (RFFSA)

Praça Procópio Ferreira 86, 20224-900 Rio de Janeiro
Tel: (+55 21) 233 57 95  Fax: (+55 21) 263 31 28

**Key personnel**
President: I Popoutchi

**Political background**
The state-owned operator RFFSA has been privatised in the form of six 30-year freight operating concessions. By the end of 1997, all six RFFSA regions had been transferred to the private sector. Also in 1997, Ferrovia Paulista SA (FEPASA) was transferred to RFFSA allowing it to be privatised (see Ferrovías Bandeirantes SA). A concession was awarded for this system in November. RFFSA retains ownership and responsibility for the infrastructure of the railways which have been the subject of concessions. The new operators therefore have to enter into contracts for infrastructure use and maintenance with RFFSA.

**Finance**
Privatisation of RFFSA was prompted by the withdrawal of most former subsidies and compensations as desperate efforts were made in the early 1990s to stabilise the national economy, driving the railway into technical bankruptcy in the process. By 1991 the daily loss had soared to US$1 million and accumulated debt stood at US$1.2 billion. The latter had reached US$1.84 billion in 1994 and was expected to rise to some US$2.56 billion in 1995, when the intention was that funds generated by the auction of operating concessions would go towards settling RFFSA's accumulated debt. The enabling law was passed in 1995.

## Trensurb

Empresa de Trens Urbanos de Porto Alegre SA
Av Ernesto Neugebauer 1985, Bairro Dona Teodora, Porto Alegre RS, CEP 90250-140
Tel: (+55 51) 371 50 00  Fax: (+55 51) 371 51 27
e-mail: seapobib@trensurb.com.br
Web: http://www.trensurb.com.br

**Key personnel**
President: Pedro Bisch Neto
Director, Operations: R Guimarães de Oliveira
Director, Administration and Finance:
  Mário Rache Freitas
Expansion and Development Superintendent:
  Nelson Lídio Nunes

Gauge: 1,600 mm
Route length: 31.5 km
Electrification: 31.5 km at 3 kV DC

**Political background**
Trensurb was founded in 1980 to create and operate a suburban rail system in Porto Alegre. Its principal shareholder is the Brazilian federal government (96 per cent), with remaining shares held by the Rio Grande do Sul state government and Porto Alegre city council. Fares cover 33 per cent of operating costs. A further 6 per cent is provided by other commercial sources and the remaining 61 per cent by subsidies and grants.

**Organisation**
Trensurb provides high-capacity suburban rail transport in Porto Alegre. It is managed by an executive directorate comprising: the Presidency; a Directorate of Administration and Finance; and a Directorate of Operations. Staff levels stood at 1,032 in December 1999.

**Passenger operations**
Trensurb operates a 16-station electrified route linking Unisinos in the northern suburbs of Porto Alegre with the city centre. The line was opened from Mercado to Sapucaia do Sul in 1985 and subsequently extended by 3.9 km to Unisinos in São Leopoldo.

Trains operate at 4- to 5-minute intervals under ATC and CTC control. Eighteen trains are in operation at peak periods.

### Trensurb electric multiple-units

| Class | Cars per unit | Motor cars per unit | Motored axles/car | Output/motor kW | Speed km/h | Units in service | First built | Builders Mechanical | Builders Electrical |
|---|---|---|---|---|---|---|---|---|---|
| 100 | 4 | 2 | 4 | 315 | 90 | 25 | 1984 | Nippon Sharyo/ Hitachi-Kawasaki | Japanese Consortium |

| Traffic (million) | 1997 | 1998 | 1999 |
|---|---|---|---|
| Passenger journeys | 31.4 | 35.4 | 36.3 |

**New lines**
By September 2000, completion is expected of a 2.4 km elevated extension to São Leopoldo, generating an increased demand of some 20,000 passengers daily. In February 2000, Trensurb signed engineering contracts covering an additional 9 km extension northwards to Novo Hamurgo. Also proposed is a 14 km line from Mercado to Triângulo, as well as a 17.5 km mostly underground route from Sarandi to Praç Isabela.

**Traction and rolling stock**
Trensurb operates a fleet of 25 four-car air conditioned emus built by a Japanese consortium of Hitachi, Nippon Sharyo, Seizo Kaisha and Mitsui. The purchase was financed by a World Bank loan.

## Vitória a Minas Railway (EFVM)

Vitória-Minas Railway (EFVM)
Avenida Dante Michelini 5500, Ponta de Tubarão
PO Box 8001, Vitória 29090-900, Espírito Santo
Tel: (+55 27) 335 34 20  Fax: (+55 27) 335 33 50
Web: http://www.cvrd.com.br

**Key personnel**
Southern System Director: Juarez Saliva de Avelar
General Managers
  Commercial: Mauro Oliviera Dias
  Control: Sílvio Renato Ribiero Louro
  Permanent Way: Antonio José Cuzzol
  Logistics: Elías David Nigri
  Sales: Cleber Cordeiro Lucas
Marketing: Flávio Barbosa Montenegro
Programming: Paulo Afonso Polese
Railway Operations: Jayme Nicolatto
Traffic Control and Train Operations:
  Arnaldo Soares Silva
Rolling Stock Maintenance:
  Lidemberg José Rosa Cesário

Gauge: 1,000 mm
Route length: 898 km

**Organisation**
EFVM is owned by the mining group Companhia Vale do Rio Doce (CVRD), the world's largest producer of iron ore, which also owns the Carajás Railway (EFC) (qv).

At the end of 1998 EFVM employed 2,846 staff.

**Passenger operations**
EFVM operates daily trains between Vitória and Belo Horizonte and on its Desembargador Drumond—Itabira branch line. First, second and a superior air conditioned class are provided and main line trains also include a restaurant car. It is reported that there are plans to introduce a peak-season Vitória—Belo Horizonte overnight service.

**Freight operations**
The railway's principal role is to transport iron ore from mines at Itibara, east of Belo Horizonte, to Port Tubarão, Vitória. This accounts for around 78 per cent of freight traffic. Steel, steel products, coal, chalk, soya products, cellulose and cereals are also carried, as are cars, containers, manufactured goods and just-in-time goods. General freight traffic amounts to around 5.3 million tonnes annually.

| Traffic (million) | 1997 | 1998 | 1999 |
|---|---|---|---|
| Passenger journeys | 1.488 | 1.175 | 1.255 |
| Passenger-km | 358.6 | 287.1 | n/a |
| Freight tonnes | 104.7 | 104.8 | 101.2 |
| Freight tonne-km | 56,599 | 55,443 | 52,691 |

**New lines**
Jointly with the government of Espírito Santo, EFVM plans to build a new 17.5 km line from Frechal, the first station out of Vitória on the Belo Horizonte line, to Viana, on the FCA line to Rio de Janeiro. This would carry freight trains around Vitória, easing access to its port, and could also serve as a feeder to the planned new Vitória—Cachoeira do Itapemirim line, which will follow the coast to avoid the mountainous region south of Viana, easing the flow of freight traffic from southern Espírito Santo to Rio de Janeiro. The first 10 km of the new line may be electrified to be used as the first section of a 45 km light rail system in and around Vitória.

**Improvements to existing lines**
Double-tracking of the 62 km Desembargador Drumond—Costa Lacerda line was expected to be completed in July 2000 at a cost of Cr115 million. Construction of the second part of the 28 km Capitao Eduardo—Costa

*Four Macosa-built General Motors GT26CU2s at General Carneiro (F F Lage)* 0010791

Lacerda deviation was also nearing completion in 2000. This scheme has cost Cr143.5 million. With these improvements, most of the 705 km Vitória–Belo Horizonte line will be double-track.

### Traction and rolling stock

In 2000, EFVM operated 218 diesel locomotives, the most recent additions being 10 GE Dash-9 WC units with Bo-Bo-Bo-Bo axle arrangement delivered in 1997. In 2000, an additional batch of 15 similar Dash-9 locomotives was on order from GE's Brazilian licensee, GEVISA. The railway's rolling stock fleet comprised 64 passenger coaches, including six restaurant cars, and 13,117 wagons.

During 2000, it was planned to equip 100 locomotives with GE Harris Locotrol remote control equipment at a cost of US$5.5 million, enabling EFVM to increase train lengths from 160 to 258 cars. This was intended to alleviate pressures on line capacity, which can average a train every 72 mins during a 24 hour period.

### Signalling and telecommunications

CTC is used on 540 km of double-track main line and 185 km of branches. Train despatching is employed on a non-signalled 134 km branch line. Signal aspects are reproduced in locomotive cabs. Each signal block has the added protection of derailment detectors, supplemented by hot box and broken wheel detectors.

**Braking in standard use:** Locomotives, 26L (AAR); hauled stock, ABD mechanical empty/load

### EFVM diesel locomotives

| Class | Wheel arrangement | Power kW | Speed km/h | Weight tonnes | No in service | First built | Builders Mechanical | Builders Engine | Transmission |
|---|---|---|---|---|---|---|---|---|---|
| G12 | Bo-Bo | 1,063 | 60 | 76 | 7 | 1956 | GM | GM 12-567C | E GM |
| G12 | Bo-Bo | 1,063 | 60 | 76 | 18 | 1956 | GM | GM 12-645E3 | E GM |
| G16 | Co-Co | 1,455 | 60 | 101 | 38 | 1962 | GM | GM 16-645E3 | E GM |
| GT-GM | Co-Co | 2,240 | 60 | 121 | 4 | 1973 | GM | GM 16-645E3 | E GM |
| GT-MAC | Co-Co | 2,240 | 60 | 121 | 28 | 1978 | GM/Macosa | GM 16-645E3 | E GM |
| U26C | Co-Co | 2,126 | 60 | 120 | 1 | 1981 | GE Brasil | GE 7FDL12 | E GE Brasil |
| GT-VIL | Co-Co | 2,462 | 60 | 138 | 6 | 1982 | GM/Villares | GM 16-645E3B | E GM |
| MATE* | Bo-Bo+Bo-Bo | 1,063 | 28 | 125 | 1 | 1987 | GM | GM 12-567C | E GM |
| DDM-45 | Do-Do | 2,910 | 60 | 162 | 72 | 1989 | GM | GM 20-645E3 | E GM |
| GT-MP | Co-Co | 2,462 | 60 | 138 | 6 | 1991 | GM/Villares | GM 16-645E3B | E GM |
| Dash-8 | Bo-Bo-Bo-Bo | 3,085 | 60 | 160 | 6 | 1991 | GE Brasil | GE 7FDL16 | E GE Brasil |
| DDM-MP** | Do-Do | 2,910 | 60 | 162 | 6 | 1993 | GM | GM 20-645E3B | E GM |
| Dash-9 | Bo-Bo-Bo-Bo | 3,085 | 60 | 160 | 12 | 1996 | GE | GE 7FDL16 efi | E GE |
| Dash-9 WC | Bo-Bo-Bo-Bo | 3,085 | 60 | 160 | 10 | 1997 | GE | GE 7FDL16 efi | E GE |

* EFVM conversion based on two G12s
** Rebuilt from DDM-45s with new engines, generators, traction motors and computerised instrumentation

### Track

**Rail type:** 136 RE 68kg/m (2,494 km)

**Sleepers**

**Wood:** 2,300 × 240 × 170 mm
**Spacing:** 1,852/km in plain track and in curves
**Fastenings:** Denick

**Steel:** 2,200 × 260 × 200 mm
**Spacing:** 1,667/km in plain track and in curves
**Fastenings:** Denick

**Concrete:** 2,300 × 260 × 200 mm
**Spacing:** 1,667/km in plain track and in curves
**Minimum curve radius:** 12° 40′ (90.47 m)
**Max gradient:** 2.7%
**Max axleload:** 25 tonnes

## Other Brazilian railway projects

Many projects for new lines in Brazil await realisation. In many instances, these were developed during state ownership of Brazilian Federal Railways (RFFSA) but not taken forward due to a lack of finance. Some of the more significant projects are listed below.

### Rio de Janeiro—São Paulo—Campinas high-speed line

Under a technical co-operation agreement between Brazil and Germany, a plan to build a high-speed passenger line in the Rio de Janeiro–Campinas corridor has been drawn up. The 500 km railway would serve an area which accounts for some 20 per cent of the population of Brazil. A decision on whether to build the line was expected in 2000.

### Ferrovía Norte do Espírito Santo

This proposed 336 km line would run from Barra do Riacho at Aracruz, near Vitória (Espírito Santo state) to Taquarí (southern Bahía state). It would be used for transporting timber from Bahía to Aracruz for cellulose and paper production and paper and cellulose from a plant near Taquarí for export via the port of Vitória. Some 8.6 million tonnes of freight annually have been forecast. Construction cost is estimated at around US$300 million. Companhia Vale do Rio Doce (CVRD) would be the line's operator, but private investors are sought as no public funds are available for its construction.

### Ferrovía Litorânea Sul

A 147 km railway has been proposed to connect Vitória and Cachoeiro do Itapemirim, both in Espírito Santo state, to create a coastal route which would replace the existing inland line. The latter is in poor condition and is unable to carry more than 400,000 tonnes of freight annually. Traffic demand between the two locations could be as high as 6 million tonnes. The cost of the line is estimated at US$113 million.

Another significant proposal is for an 18 km line around Cachoeiro do Itapemirim from Cobiça via Moro Grande to Monte Cristo, taking rail traffic out of the city centre, where street running is currently necessary. RFFSA and the city council commenced construction of this line in 1989 and two years later the central 8 km had been completed. Completion of the remaining 10 km is still required.

### Variante do Paraguaçu

The existing railway from Iaçu to Salvador passes through the streets of the historic towns of São Felix and Cachoeira, with curve radii down to 60 m. A combined rail and road bridge between the two communities is in poor condition, preventing the operation of heavy trains, and steep gradients are encountered to reach towns on the river Paraguaçu. A proposed new line is intended to eliminate this bottleneck, beginning at Salvador Pinto and running south of the existing line for 76 km, compared with the current 123 km, to Candeias, also replacing the existing line between Santo Amaro and Candeias. Work commenced in 1990 and 7 km of earthworks from Salvador Pinto to Baragogipe were completed, with 2.5 km of track laid. Some US$12 million of an estimated total cost of US$120 million have already been spent but work has been suspended until additional funds can be secured.

### Ramal Pirapora—Unaí

The state government of Minas Gerais and Companhia Vale do Rio Doce (CVRD) have undertaken studies into this 285 km line, which would open up a fertile agricultural region in the northwest of the state. Traffic forecasts suggested that some 3 million tonnes of agricultural products annually could be carried by the line. State funding of US$200 million has been proposed for the US$432 million project, the remainder to come from CVRD, which would also operate the line. However, Federal government pressure in 1996 prevented Minas Gerais state from making its contribution to the scheme and construction was postponed. CVRD has also drawn up plans for connecting lines from Unaí to Luziânia, where a connection with the former RFFSA main line to Brasilia would be made. From Brasilia, a 65 km branch northeast to Formosa has also been proposed.

### Ferrofrango

The government of Santa Catarina state has developed proposals to build a 170 km branch line from Herval d'Oeste through Concórdia, Seara and Chapecó to Itapiranga, a chicken-rearing region. As well as meat products in refrigerated containers, other agricultural products could be carried. Private investors are being sought to participate in this scheme.

# BULGARIA

## Ministry of Transport

9 Levski Str, Sofia
Tel: (+359 2) 87 28 62  Fax: (+359 2) 88 50 94

**Key personnel**
Minister: Antoni Slavinskí

## Bulgarian State Railways (BDZ)

Ivan-Vazov Str 3, 1080 Sofia
Tel: (+359 2) 981 11 10  Fax: (+359 2) 987 71 51

**Key personnel**
Director General: Vladimir Duntchev
Assistant Directors General
  Infrastructure: Ivan Kovatchev
  Operations: Alexander Kamenov
  Commercial: Vladimir Duntchev
  Strategic Development and Reforms: Yordan Mirtchev
  Rolling Stock: Stoyan Vladov
Directors
  Strategic Development: Simeon Evtimov
  Passenger Service: Peter Panov
  Freight Service: Aspassia Vatralova
  Traffic: Hristo Monov
  Traction: Bogomil Kovatchev
  Rolling Stock: Dimitre Stoitchkov
  Fixed Installations: Lyubomir Tangalov
  Signalling and Telecommunications: Ivanka Stoyanova
  Electrification and Catenary: Gueorgui Hristov
  Investment: Tzvetan Ivanov
  Research and Development: Lyubomir Pomakov
  Supplies: Zdravko Ivanov
Manager, International Relations: Vassil Hinov
Manager, Press and Public Relations: Ioto Krastev
Manager, UIC Relations: Dimitri Boev

**Gauge:** 1,435 mm; 760 mm
**Route length:** 4,049 km; 245 km
**Electrification:** 2,710 km at 25 kV 50 Hz AC

### Political background

With the collapse of Communism, BDZ found itself in radically altered economic circumstances: instead of functioning as part of a command economy, the railway had to adjust to a market system and a 30 per cent cut in

# Bulgaria/RAILWAY SYSTEMS

the country's gross domestic product. BDZ has suffered a dramatic decline in traffic, labour productivity has suffered as a consequence and the railway has been losing money; the loss in 1995 was Lv2.7 billion (approximately US$34 million). Bulgaria's poor economic record in the 1990s, compared to its former Comecon partners, has hampered recovery efforts on the railway.

In early 1995, BDZ announced a radical action programme, involving the closure of rural branch lines, the raising of fares and freight rates, asset sales and the establishment of joint ventures with foreign partners. Progress has been made in slimming staff numbers (down nearly 40 per cent since 1990 to 48,700 in 1996) and reducing sparsely used passenger and freight services.

One of the first joint ventures was between a Sofia plant producing railway points and the Austrian engineering company VAE Eisenbahnsysteme. Another joint venture was planned for a plant producing sleepers, but this ran into problems and was delayed.

In early 1997, BDZ received a US$170 million loan from the World Bank to fund modernisation projects over the coming year.

| Traffic (million) | | 1996 |
|---|---|---|
| Passenger journeys | | 66.1 |
| Passenger-km | | 5,065 |
| Freight tonnes | | 30.1 |
| Freight tonne-km | | 7,500 |

| Revenue (Lv) | 1993 | 1994 |
|---|---|---|
| Passengers | 768,552 | 1,363,068 |
| Freight | 4,137,151 | 6,485,323 |
| Parcels and mail | 18,373 | 65,433 |
| Other income | 1,122,940 | 579,405 |
| Total | 6,047,016 | 8,493,229 |

| Expenditure (Lv) | 1993 | 1994 |
|---|---|---|
| Passengers | 4,043,363 | 5,319,634 |
| Materials and service | 3,069,515 | 3,996,860 |
| Depreciation | 196,810 | 211,303 |
| Other | 2,367,459 | 3,456,926 |
| Total | 9,677,147 | 12,984,723 |

## Passenger operations
Passenger traffic has not shown such a sharp decline as freight traffic. In 1996, total journeys amounted to 66.1 million, compared to the 1986 figure of 109 million.

As part of the Restructuring Action Plan, lightly used services on some 1,000 km of lines – a quarter of the network – are being targeted for closure or disposal. About a third of this total – 340 km – is proposed for closure, while 185 km of branch lines are set to be transferred to the industrial plants which they serve. BDZ proposes that local authorities take over responsibility for passenger services on another 540 km, with the railway operating them under contract.

## Freight operations
In 1996 the tonnage carried was only 30.1 million tonnes – much below the capacity of the railway.

In 1995, Bulgaria signed an agreement with Russia to develop a train ferry service from Varna, in the east of Bulgaria, across the Black Sea to Novorossisk.

## New lines
Capital for extending the network is scarce, but the Bulgarian government is considering construction of a new rail/road bridge over the river Danube between Lom (Bulgaria) and Rastu (Romania) and construction of a line between Gyueshevo and the Macedonian border as part of an international Adriatic-Black Sea link.

## Improvements to existing lines
The length of double-track line is currently no more than 964 km, less than a quarter of the network. Track doubling is currently under way between Karnobat and Syndel, on the route from Sofia to Burgas and Varna.

In 1998, BDZ sought tenders to renew 65 km of track on the Kakarel-Verinsko and Zimnitza-Tzerkovski routes.

## Traction and rolling stock
At the end of 1996 BDZ was operating 335 electric and 476 diesel locomotives, 1,835 carriages, 83 electric multiple-units, three dmus and 28,341 wagons. Main line diesels have been built in Romania and the former Soviet Union with Hungarian and East German industry supplying shunters. Electric locomotives are mostly from Škoda-Plzen (Czech Republic), although some have also been procured from Romania.

To replace older types of main line electric locomotives, BDZ plans to purchase new thyristor-controlled four-axle machines from Škoda. A contract for 30 3,060 kW 130 km/h 85-tonne machines, similar to Czech Railways' and Slovakian Republic Railways' Class 263, was placed as long ago as 1989 but this was cancelled in 1991 due to a lack of funds.

In early 1997, a deal was struck with Adtranz UK whereby that company would re-equip BDZ's Dryanovo workshops with modern equipment, allowing them to undertake coach refurbishment. As part of the deal, the Adtranz/MÁV Dunakeszi joint venture workshops are providing plant, equipment, components and project management for refurbishment of 50 BDZ coaches, plus spares to enable another 50 to be tackled.

In the wagon fleet, many of the vehicles are in good condition, as much of the fleet is under 10 years old. However, the fleet size far exceeds current needs: the western European consultants estimated that the wagon fleet could be cut to just 15,000 and meet likely demand.

*Škoda-built Class 43.000 electric locomotive at Sofia depot (Michal Málek)*

*Soviet-built BDZ Class 07.000 diesel-electric locomotive leaves Giugiu, Romania, for Bulgaria with an international passenger service (Eddie Barnes)*

# RAILWAY SYSTEMS/Bulgaria–Burkina Faso

Massive scrapping of surplus rolling stock is planned under the Restructuring Action Plan. Half the electric locomotive fleet, 70 per cent of the diesel and shunting fleets, 30 per cent of the passenger coaches and 40 per cent of the freight wagon fleet are to be withdrawn.

### Signalling and telecommunications
Automatic Train Protection (ATP) has been installed on the 156 km Sofia-Plovdiv line. Centralised Traffic Control (CTC) exists between Sofia and Plovdiv and on the single track Sofia-Karlovo line. Automatic Train Stop (ATS) equipment has been fitted to 103 locomotives.

BDZ's communications system comprises about 80 per cent cable, with the rest on aerial poles. There are 112 telephone exchanges serving about 25,000 extensions. Train radio covers about 1,200 km of trunk lines. Improved communication systems, replacement of aerial wires and extension of the train radio system are needed.

In 1999, Alcatel was awarded a contract to provide a communications-based train control system for the 200 km Stara Zagora-Burgas line. Commissioning was scheduled for mid-2000.

### Electrification
Over 62 per cent of BDZ's network is electrified at 25 kV AC 50 Hz. In January 1996, BDZ called for tenders to electrify a further two lines: Volujak-Dragoman-Yugoslav border (the section up to Dragoman was energised in August 1997); and Dupnitsa-Kulata, on the international line to Greece. Electrification of the important Plovdiv-Dimitrovgrad-Svilengrad-Turkish/Greek border transit corridor has been postponed due to a lack of funds.

Also planned is the wiring of a single-track line between Radomir and Kjustendil, which would complete electrification of BDZ's main line network.

### Track
At present 49 kg/m rail predominates and only on high-density lines are there rails of 60 kg/m. The rail is laid on timber or prestressed concrete sleepers secured with K-type fastenings. Maximum permissible axleload is 22.5 tonnes, minimum curve radius 300 m and maximum gradient 2.8 per cent.

### Electric locomotives

| Class | Wheel arrangement | Output kW | Speed km/h | Weight tonnes | No in service | First built | Builders |
|---|---|---|---|---|---|---|---|
| 41.000[1] | Bo-Bo | 2,800 | 110 | 88 | 1 | 1962 | Škoda |
| 42.000[2] | Bo-Bo | 2,800 | 110 | 88 | 59 | 1965 | Škoda |
| 43.000[3] | Bo-Bo | 3,020 | 130 | 84 | 46 | 1971 | Škoda |
| 43.300[4] | Bo-Bo | 3,020 | 130 | 84 | 10 | 1992 | Škoda |
| 44.000 | Bo-Bo | 3,040 | 130 | 84 | 87 | 1975 | Škoda |
| 45.000 | Bo-Bo | 3,040 | 110 | 84 | 59 | 1982 | Škoda |
| 46.000 | Co-Co | 5,100 | 130 | 126 | 44 | 1986 | Electroputere |
| 60.000[5] | Bo-Bo | 800 | 65 | 80 | 4 | 1982 | Stara Zagora |
| 61.000 | Bo-Bo | 960 | 80 | 74 | 20 | 1991 | Škoda |

[1] Originally Class 41.000, refurbished in 1980s
[2] Some refurbished and redesignated Class 42.100 since 1992
[3] Two re-geared for 110 km/h (Class 43.500)
[4] Refurbished Classes 43.000 and 44.000
[5] Rebuilt in BDZ workshops from Škoda 1.5 kV DC mining locomotive

### Diesel locomotives

| Class | Wheel arrangement | Power kW | Speed km/h | Weight tonnes | No in service | First built | Builders |
|---|---|---|---|---|---|---|---|
| 04.000 | Bo-Bo | 1,620 | 120 | 81 | 10 | 1963 | H SGP |
| 06.000 | Co-Co | 1,540 | 100 | 117 | 92 | 1966 | E Electroputere |
| 07.000 | Co-Co | 2,205 | 100 | 119 | 90 | 1972 | E Lugansk |
| 51.000 | Bo-Bo | 442 | 80 | 62 | 43 | 1960 | E VEB Hennigsdorf |
| 52.000 | D | 442 | 30/60 | 60 | 108 | 1965 | H Ganz-Mávag |
| 55.000 | Bo-Bo | 920 | 60/100 | 68 | 151 | 1969 | H Faur |
| **760 mm gauge** | | | | | | | |
| 75.000 | Bo-Bo | 810 | 70 | 48 | 9 | 1966 | H Henschel |
| 76.000 | Bo-Bo | 810 | 70 | 52 | 13 | 1975 | H 23 August |
| 77.000 | Bo-Bo | 810 | 70 | 52 | 10 | 1988 | H 23 August |
| 80.000 | C | 283 | 30 | 36 | 1 | 1967 | H Henschel |
| 81.000 | Bo-Bo | 294 | 50 | 24 | 3 | 1982 | H Kambarsg |

### Electric railcars or multiple-units

| Class | Builder's type | Cars per unit | Motor cars per unit | Motored axles/car | Output/motor kW | Speed km/h | Units in service | First built | Builders Mechanical | Electrical |
|---|---|---|---|---|---|---|---|---|---|---|
| 32.000 | (CE)P-25 | 4 | 2 | 4 | 165/210 | 130 | 77 | 1970 | RVZ | RVZ |
| 33.000 | (CE)P-33 | 4 | 2 | 4 | 170/210 | 120 | 6 | 1990 | RVZ | RVZ |

### Diesel railcars or multiple-units

| Class | Cars per unit | Motor cars per unit | Motored axles/car | Power/motor kW | Speed km/h | Units in service | First built | Builders Mechanical | Engine | Transmission |
|---|---|---|---|---|---|---|---|---|---|---|
| 18.000 | 3 | 2 | 2 | 600 | 100 | 3 | 1967 | | Ganz-Mávag | M |

---

# BURKINA FASO

## Ministry of Transport & Communications
PO Box 162, Ouagadougou
Tel: (+226) 30 62 11

**Key personnel**
Minister: Salvador Yameogo

*UPDATED*

## SOPAFER-B
Société de gestion du patrimoine ferroviaire du Burkina
PO Box 192, Ouagadougou 01
Tel: (+226) 31 35 99   Fax: (+226) 31 35 94

**Key personnel**
Director General: Oumar Zongo

Gauge: 1,000 mm
Route length: 622 km

### Political background
The country was long-served by the Abidjan-Niger Railway under a joint arrangement with neighbouring Ivory Coast (qv). In 1986, following a disagreement over the wisdom of embarking on the 375 km Tambao extension in Burkina Faso, the railway was split. This move did little to help performance in either country and much freight traffic deserted to the roads.

By 1992, both railways were in a poor physical state and carrying little traffic. After considering total abandonment, the two countries decided that the railways should be managed as a single entity once again and bids were sought from private operators to form a joint holding

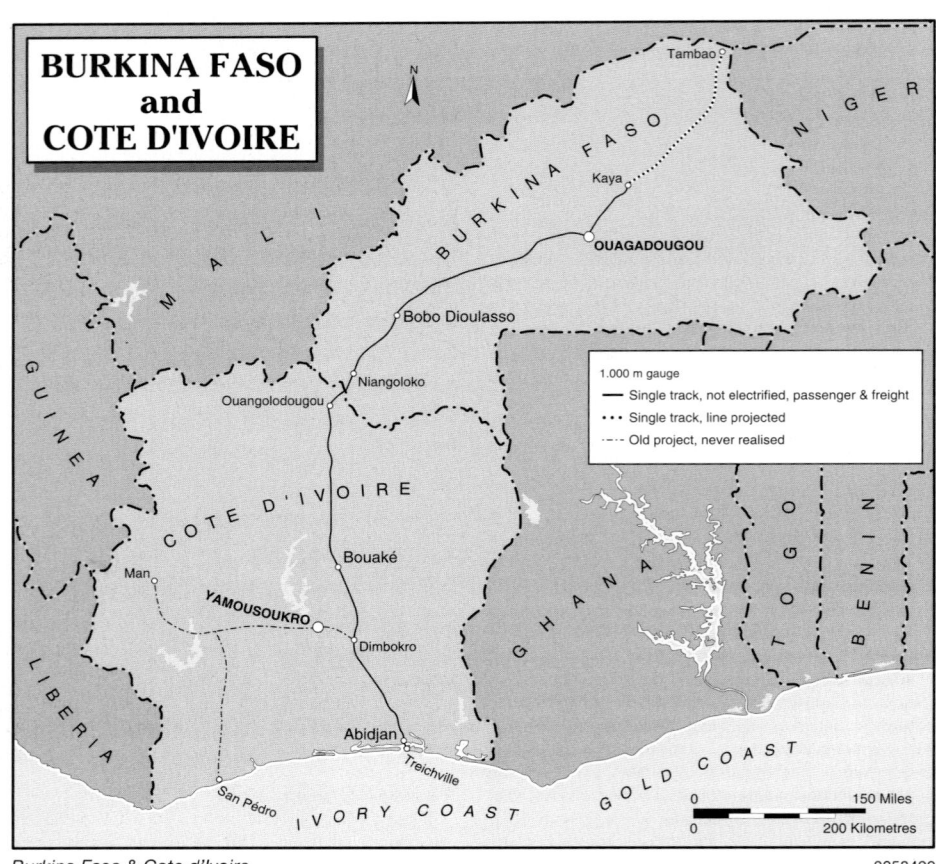

*Burkina Faso & Cote d'Ivoire*

company, acting as concessionaire. In 1993, a contract was awarded to the Sitarail group, a consortium comprising private investors (holding 67 per cent of the capital), the Burkina and Ivorian governments (15 per cent each) and Sitarail staff (3 per cent). The Sofrerail arm of French consultant Systra is the operating partner of the consortium. Private sector operation of the railway started in August 1995.

All fixed installations, infrastructure and rolling stock remain state-owned in the hands of two companies, SIPF and Sopafer, but Sitarail will maintain the infrastructure and rolling stock for the 15-year duration of the contract. For full details of the Sitarail operation in both countries, see the Ivory Coast entry.

### Passenger operations
Operations in January 1998 consisted of: a daily passenger service between Ouagadougou and Abidjan, in Ivory Coast; a Saturday-only round-trip offered on the Ouagadougou and Kaya extension; and a daily 'luxury' (first class) railcar introduced between Ouagadougou and Bobo Dioulasso. However, due to a lack of spare parts to maintain locomotives and rolling stock in serviceable condition, by June 1998 the frequency of the Ouagadougou-Abidjan train had again been reduced to three times a week. A few weeks later the first class railcar on the Ouagadougou-Bobo Dioulasso route was also suspended.

### Freight operations
There was some growth in imported oil traffic in the early 1990s, accounting for much of the meagre freight business, and trial hauls were made of manganese ore brought by road from Tambao to the Kaya railhead for forwarding to Abidjan. Freight carried in Burkina in 1995 amounted to about 200,000 tonnes, about 92 million tonne-km. Early indications were that tonnage was on the increase as a result of the concessioning agreement.

Sitarail's freight plans are based on development of the export manganese traffic and exploitation of zinc mined at Perkoa, some 30 km from the railway at Koudougou.

### New lines
Construction of the Tambao extension has begun, with the aim of tapping rich manganese deposits in the region. The government bought 6,000 tonnes of used rail from Canadian National and in 1989 funds were obtained from the UN Development Programme for engagement of consultants to manage work on the initial 105 km from Ouagadougou to Kaya, which was opened in 1993.

The Burkina Faso government then advanced CFAFr6.2 billion for construction of the remaining 271 km from Kaya to Tambao. In 1990 Canac International of Canada was contracted by the UN Development Programme to oversee the first stage and assist in planning the second.

Earlier, in 1988, Canac International had secured a C$2.3 million turnkey contract to supply and install a telecommunications network over the new line. The work included installation of five microwave sites between Ouagadougou and Kaya. In addition, a VHF/FM communications network would be installed to link train stations and train crews.

These works are currently in abeyance on account of the need to concentrate on rehabilitation of the existing line. Finance totalling some US$5 million for this was agreed by the West African Development Bank in 1996 (see Ivory Coast entry).

### Improvements to existing lines
In late 1995, Sitarail invited tenders for supply of rail and sleepers to begin a programme of upgrading throughout the railway. Spare parts to refurbish GM locomotives were also sought.

### Traction and rolling stock
At the start of 1996, the Sitarail combined operation had available 20 diesel locomotives, 17 shunters, 40 coaches and 600 wagons. Burkina's 1994-96 plan provided for purchase of three diesel-electric locomotives and 30 mineral wagons, while 60 tank wagons were acquired through the national oil company Sonabhy.

A deal has been agreed with Projects & Equipment Corporation of India for launch of local freight wagon production. The Indians are to set up a manufacturing plant at Bobo Dioulasso, get it going with a supply of wagon kits for assembly, then oversee transition to local manufacture from scratch.

---

# CAMBODIA

## Ministry of Public Works and Transport

PO Box 65, Phnom Penh
Tel: (+855 23) 72 36 15

### Key personnel
Minister: Khy Teng Lim

**NEW ENTRY**

## Royal Railway of Cambodia

Chemin de fer du Cambodge
Central Railway Station, Sangkat Srach Chak, Khan Daun Penh, Phnom Penh
Tel: (+855 23) 72 41 43   Fax: (+855 23) 72 58 97

### Key personnel
Director: Pich Kim Sreang

Gauge: 1,000 mm
Route length: 602 km

### Organisation
Because of the country's internal unrest, most of the rail network was out of use during the 1970s and 1980s, but in 1993 trains were operating on all sections except for the 48 km between Sisophon and the Thai border at Poipet. There are two main lines. The Old line runs westwards from Phnom Penh to Sisophon (339 km), whence the route to Poipet was removed in the 1970s. The New line, opened in 1969, links Phnom Penh with the country's only deep water port at Kompong Som, 263 km distant.

At the end of 1998 1,732 staff were employed.

| Traffic (million) | 1997 | 1998 |
|---|---|---|
| Passenger journeys | 0.530 | 0.438 |
| Passenger-km | 49.3 | 43.9 |
| Freight tonnes | 0.170 | 0.294 |
| Freight tonne-km | 36.1 | 75.7 |

### Passenger and freight operations
In 1999 passenger services were operated on the Phnom Penh-Sisophon and Phnom Penh-Sianoukville lines, with passenger coaches also being added to some freight services. Freight traffic has shown growth following some rehabilitation of the railway's infrastructure and an improved economic environment. However, a shortage of freight wagons and the considerable age of existing vehicles was claimed by the railway in 1997 to be hampering traffic development.

### New lines
A 450 km line linking Phnom Penh and Ho Chi Minh City (formerly Saigon) has been projected for a number of years but consistently cancelled owing to hostilities. The line would fill one of the missing links in the Trans Asian Railway Project. In 1996, Malaysia offered to finance and carry out a feasibility study for this route and reopening from Sisophon to Poipet; the two projects would close the missing links in a 5,500 km Singapore-Beijing dual-gauge route.

### Improvements to existing lines
In 1999 government plans were announced to restore the line between Sisophon and Aranyaprathet, on the Thai border.

### Traction and rolling stock
In 1998 the railway's serviceable fleet amounted to 18 diesel locomotives. Backbone of the diesel-electric fleet were nine Alsthom-built B-B 900 kW Class BB 1050 units fitted with MGO-V12 BZSHR engines, delivered in 1967-69. Between 1990 and 1994, ČKD Praha of the Czech Republic supplied four Class BB 1010 736 kW Bo-Bo diesel-electrics. The shunting locomotive fleet comprises two French-built machines delivered in 1957 and two ČKD-built 310 kW two-axle units with MTU engines, supplied in 1994.

In 1998 the passenger fleet comprised 12 coaches and a German-built railbus dating from 1969; there were 167 wagons.

### Signalling and telecommunications
Both the former telegraph and radio signalling systems were destroyed and the current service is manually signalled.

### Track
Rail of 30 kg/m (329 km) and 43 kg/m (264 km) on a mixture of steel and wooden sleepers is in use. Maximum permissible axleload is 20 tonnes for upgraded lines and 13 tonnes for older lines. Minimum curve radius is 300 m.

# CAMEROON

## Ministry of Transport

PO Box 8043, Yaoundé
Tel: (+237) 23 22 36

**Key personnel**
Minister: Issa Tchiroma
Director of Land Transport: M Mundi Kengnjisu

## Cameroon Railways (Camrail)

Gare Centrale de Bessengue, PO Box 766, Douala
Tel: (+237) 340 60 45; 340 99 61   Fax: (+237) 40 82 52
e-mail: camrail.dg@iccnet2000.com

**Key personnel**
Administrator and Director General: Patrick Claes
Directors
  Finance: Raymond Constansa
  Operations: Claude Kontcho
  Rolling Stock: Marcel Ekoka
  Human Resources: Jean-Pierre Moudourou
  Fixed Installations: Georges Lomre
  Co-ordinator of Investments: Emmanuel Adiang
Chief of Division for Economic and Commercial Studies:
  Stéphane Ekoko
Chief of Economic Studies: Rose Asongwe

Gauge: 1,000 mm
Route length: 1,016 km

### Political background
Moves towards privatisation of the former Regifercam railway system started in 1994, when 15 state enterprises were considered for sale into the private sector. Bidding closed at the end of May 1996 for prequalification for a 20-year operating concession which would also demand investment in modernisation and maintenance of the infrastructure. Those bidding included Comazar, a joint venture between Spoornet, South Africa and Belgian National Railways, and a consortium which included Systra of France. Railway equipment suppliers and construction companies were prohibited from bidding. In 1998 it was announced that the concession was to be split between two of the rival bidders, Saga, a subsidiary of the French Bolloré group, which now formally holds the concession, and Comazar, which operates the system. The two organisations were reported to share a 51 per cent stake in Camrail, with local investors holding 34 per cent and the government retaining 15 per cent. Operations under the concession started in April 1999.

### Organisation
The Cameroon system consists of two single-track lines: the West line running from Bonaberi to Kumba and Nkongsamba; and the much longer Transcameroon line, opened in 1974, between Douala and Ngaoundéré.
In March 2002, Camrail employed 2,643 staff.

| Traffic (000s) | 2000-01 | 2001-02* |
|---|---|---|
| Passenger journeys | 1,411.5 | 923.7 |
| Passenger-km | 350,700 | 237,800 |
| Freight tonnes | 1,755.9 | 1,402.9 |
| Freight tonne-km | 1,062.7 | 854.6 |

* 9 months to 31 March 2002

### Freight operations
Principal commodities carried include: bulk petroleum products; logs and timber products; cotton; fertiliser; bulk alumina; and bagged cement.

### New lines
A new port is proposed for Grand Batanga, and in 1988 the Transcameroon Authority commissioned from French consultants a feasibility study of a 136 km freight line from the Regifercam main line near Eséka to Grand Batanga and Kribi, on the coast some 20 km north of the new port's site. Kribi is the starting point of a proposed 1,100 km new line running east to the Central African Republic. No decision to build has yet been taken.

### Improvements to existing lines
Following completion of the Transcameroon line to Ngaoundéré (935 km from Douala), it was decided to realign the Douala–Yaoundé section to match the standard of the Yaoundé–Ngaoundéré extension. The work was phased in four stages.
The most difficult stretch, the 27 km from Eséka to Maloumé, which entailed construction of three tunnels aggregating 3,295 m in length and five viaducts with a total length of 875 m, took much longer than expected. It was not until 1991 that the project was completed. The works doubled the line's capacity to 40 services a day, raised single-locomotive trainloads to 1,000 tonnes and increased annual throughput potential to over 14 million tonnes.

### Traction and rolling stock
In April 2002, Camrail operated 69 diesel locomotives, including three hired from Spoornet, South Africa, 1,359 freight wagons, including 145 privately owned, and 76 passenger coaches. In addition, the fleet included 19 diesel railcars.

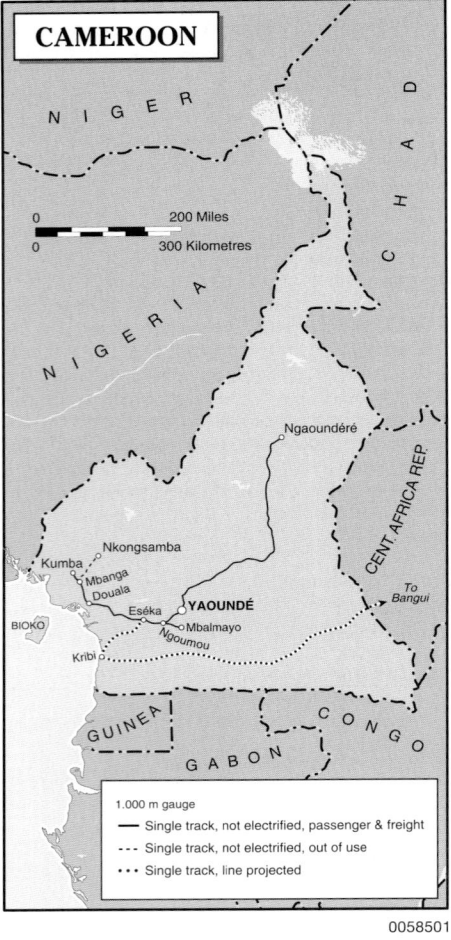

### Signalling and telecommunications
The Yaourndé–Ngaoundéré section (521.3 km) is operated using track-to-train radio. An additional 263 km are controlled by solar-powered colourlight signalling with interlocking at intermediate stations.

### Track
**Rail:** Vignole 30 kg/m (637 km) and 36 kg/m (275 km); 54 kg/m (45 km)
**Crossties (sleepers):** Timber and steel, thickness 130 mm
**Spacing:** 1,500/km plain track; 1,714/km curves
**Fastenings:** Sleeper screw (stiff); sleeper screw and Nabla (elastic)
**Min curvature radius:** 120 m
**Max gradient:** 1.6%
**Max axleload:** 20 tonnes

### Diesel locomotives

| Class | Wheel arrangement | Power kW | Speed km/h | Weight tonnes | No in service | First built | Builders Mechanical | Engine | Transmission |
|---|---|---|---|---|---|---|---|---|---|
| 2200 | Co-Co | 1,540 | 107 | 101 | 28 | 1980 | Bombardier | Alco V12 251 C4 | E CGE |
| 1200 | Bo-Bo | 700 | 70 | 56 | 8 | 1969 | Alsthom | SACM MGO V16 ASHR | E Alsthom/MTE |
| 1100 | Bo-Bo | 600 | 60 | 68 | 20 | 1981 | Alsthom | SACM MGO V12 ASHR | E Alsthom/MTE |
| 1000 | Bo-Bo | 600 | 60 | 68 | 4 | 1978 | Moyse | SACM MGO V12 ASHR | E Moyse |
| ST35200* | Co-Co | 1,065 | 100 | 83 | 9 | 1975 | General Motors | EMD V8 645 | E General Motors |

* on hire from Spoornet, South Africa from October 1999

*UPDATED*

---

# CANADA

## Transport Canada

Rail Policy Branch, Surface Policy, Place de Ville, Tower C, Ottawa, Ontario K1A 0N5
Tel: (+1 613) 998 29 85   Fax: (+1 613) 998 26 86

Rail Safety Branch
Tel: (+1 613) 998 29 85   Fax: (+1 613) 990 77 67

**Key personnel**
Minister: David M Collenette
Deputy Minister: Margaret Bloodworth
Assistant Deputy Minister, Policy: Louis Ranger
Director General, Surface Policy: Guylaine Roy
Assistant Deputy Minister, Safety and Security:
  Ron Jackson
Director General, Rail Safety: Terry M Burtch

### Political background
The federal department responsible for transport in Canada is Transport Canada. Its mission is to develop and administer policies, regulations and services for the best possible transport system for Canada and Canadians. The Department's role is to develop up-to-date, relevant policies and legislation and to maintain the highest possible levels of safety and security.

### Rail Policy Branch
The Canada Transportation Act, 1996 (CTA) is the main legislation governing general rail freight and passenger transportation in Canada. The emphasis of the CTA has been on enhancing trade and the viability and competitiveness of the Canadian transport system, reducing regulatory intervention and encouraging more innovative services. Further, with the enactment of the CTA in 1996, the federal government did its part to ensure the preservation of rail service wherever it can be continued on a commercial basis. The Act was in large measure motivated by a desire to preserve as much rail infrastructure as possible, particularly by encouraging the creation of shortline railways, without federal investment or subsidy. The new rail line discontinuance procedure has fostered the creation of shortline rail operations on lines with low traffic density that otherwise would have been abandoned under the National Transportation Act, 1987. In addition to commercial sales, the process has allowed provinces and communities to intervene in the public interest to acquire uneconomic rail lines important to local economies as an alternative to road and highway investment.

The new policy has proved a major success. Since July 1996, 8,900 km of low-density rail lines have been transferred by CN and CPR to new owners while only 1,700 km have been discontinued. Thus significant volumes of traffic that would have otherwise been converted to road have been retained on rail. Rail traffic levels have exhibited strong growth and in 1997 aggregate tonnage levels for the rail sector in general reached historic highs. In addition, shortlines have been able to recapture traffic that, over the years, had been lost to road.

*CTA Review*
Due to statutory requirements, the Canada Transportation Act was scheduled to be reviewed in July 2000. The Minister of Transport was to appoint one or more persons to conduct a comprehensive review of the CTA, and any other Act under the Minister's responsibility that provides economic regulation of a transport mode or activity. The review, with the subsequent report to the Minister, must be completed within one year. The purpose of the review is to assess whether the existing legislation provides Canadians with an efficient, effective, flexible and affordable transport system; and, where necessary or desirable, recommend amendments to the national transport policy as established in the legislation, and to any of the statutes covered by the review.

*Proposed Merger of Canadian National Railway (CN) and the Burlington Northern/Santa Fe Railway (BNSF)*
On 20 December 1999, CN and BNSF (a US-based railway) filed a notice of intent with the US Surface Transportation Board (STB) to file on approximately 20 March 2000 an application seeking STB authorisation to bring CN and BNSF together under common control. The new proposed railway would be called the North American Railway. The relevant agencies within both the Canadian (Competition Bureau) and United States (Surface Transportation Board) federal governments were in early 2000 examining the planned combination to determine whether the new railway will lessen competition in the railway industry.

*Passenger rail services: VIA Rail*
VIA ended the 1990s with its best performance in 10 years. Passenger numbers reached 3.8 million and passenger-km 1,498 billion, the latter representing a 9 per cent increase over 1998.

VIA and Transport Canada spent 18 months working on strategic options to revitalise rail passenger services. The Minister of Transport presented the plan to Cabinet and on 12 April 2000 announced an infusion of C$400 million over five years for capital expenditure in addition to the annual C$170 million subsidy provided to the passenger railway by the federal government.

VIA has also made a variety of infrastructure improvements in recent years including the renovation of Montreal Central Station in Québec and the opening of a new VIA station in Edmonton, Alberta. In addition, in an effort to improve passenger services, VIA has increased the frequency of trains along its more popular routes.

**Rail Safety Branch**
The Rail Safety and Security Branch is responsible for developing and enforcing regulatory aspects of rail safety and transport of dangerous goods. Headquarters is responsible for policy and programme design, standards, regulations and quality assurance. Five regional offices, located in Vancouver, Winnipeg, Toronto, Montreal and Moncton, apply Transport Canada's programmes, policies and standards in their geographical area and are the central points of contact in each region for the department's stakeholders.

As the regulator, Transport Canada continues to play the leading role in overseeing safety in the rail transport industry. To this end, its stated mission is to further advance the safety and security of an efficient, accessible and sustainable rail transport system through: awareness and education; establishment and implementation of policies, legislation and standards; and monitoring and enforcement.

The Railway Safety Act (RSA) came into force in 1989 to address the many changes that had taken place in the rail transport industry in recent years. The 1999 amendments to the RSA have been made to enhance further the legislation and to make the railway system even safer. These amendments are designed to modernise fully the legislative and regulatory framework of Canada's rail transport system. Railways are more responsible for managing their operations safely, while the general public and interested parties have a greater say on issues of rail safety.

A key initiative is the establishment of the Railway Safety Consultative Committee (RSCC), comprising the Department, railway industry, labour and the Federation of Canadian Municipalities. It was obvious that there was a need for continuing dialogue among all parties involved in rail transport activities and this committee offers an excellent forum for discussion of ways to meet the challenge of improving rail safety in Canada.

## Canadian Transportation Agency (CTA)

Ottawa, Ontario K1A 0N9
Tel: (+1 888) 222 25 92  Fax: (+1 819) 953 83 53
Web: http://www.cta-otc.gc.ca

**Key personnel**
Chairman: Marian Robson
Vice-Chair: Jean Patenaude
Members: Keith Penner, Richard Cashin, Michael Sutton, Gilles Dufault, Mary-Jane Bennett
Director General, Air and Accessible Transport: Gavin Currie
Director General, Rail and Marine Transportation: Seymour Isenberg
Director General, Corporate Management: Joan McDonald
General Counsel and Secretary: Marie-Paule Scott
Director, Communications: Michel Hébert

The CTA was created in 1996 with the issuance of the Canada Transportation Act, succeeding the National Transportation Agency. The CTA is a quasi-judicial federal agency that provides economic regulation over rail (as well as certain air and maritime) operations.

With respect to railway matters, federal regulation normally applies to railways that operate across national or provincial boundaries. The Rail and Maritime Branch of the CTA acts as a dispute resolution mechanism for shipper-carrier and carrier-carrier disputes involving service and competitive access, as well as disputes involving railway interaction with highways, utility companies, municipalities and landowners.

Other regulatory activities include railway line transfer and discontinuance, railway line construction, and monitoring the insurance adequacy of federally regulated railways. The Branch also undertakes statutory costing activities, including preparation of an annual (maximum) rate scale for the rail movement of western Canadian grain, and maintains an audit and compliance function.

## L'Agence Métropolitain de Transport (AMT)

500 Place d'Armes, Suite 2525, Montreal, Quebec H2Y 2W2
Tel: (+1 514) 287 24 64  Fax: (+1 514) 287 24 60
Web: http://www.amt.qc.ca

**Key personnel**
President and Director General: Florence Junca-Adenot
Director, Suburban Trains: Pierre Dorval

Gauge: 1,435 mm
Route length: 91 km
Electrification: 27 km at 25 kV AC

**Political background**
From the beginning of 1996, the two commuter lines connecting Montréal with Rigaud and Deux-Montagnes were taken over by L'Agence Métropolitain de Transport, a newly created body co-ordinating public transport in the greater Montreal area. Services are operated under contract by SNC-Gesproex under a three-year contract awarded in December 1996.

**Passenger operations**
The electrified Canadian National route from Montréal's Gare Centrale to Deux-Montagnes (27 km) was re-commissioned in 1995 after a three-year modernisation project. As part of the modernisation, the line was extended 5.3 km at its outer end from Deux-Montagnes to Autoroute 640.

Diesel push-pull services are operated on three routes: Montreal Windsor–Rigaud and Dorion; Montreal Windsor–Blainville; and Montreal Central–McMasterville. The last of these commenced in June 2000 as a

*Bombardier-built emu car for AMT's Deux-Montagnes line* 0019560

**Diesel locomotives**

| Class | Wheel arrangement | Power kW | Speed km/h | Weight tonnes | No in service | First built | Builders |
|---|---|---|---|---|---|---|---|
| FP7 | Bo-Bo | 1,500 | 105 | 113 | 1 | 1951 | E GM |
| FP7 | Bo-Bo | 1,500 | 105 | 113 | 6 | 1952 | E GM |
| GP9u | Bo-Bo | 1,800 | 105 | 112 | 4 | 1959 | E GM/AMF |
| F59PH | Bo-Bo | 2,400 | - | - | 7 | 2000 | E GM |

**Electric multiple-units**

| Class | Cars per Unit | Motor cars per unit | Motored axles/car | Output/motor kW | Speed km/h | No in service | First Built | Builders Mechanical | Electrical |
|---|---|---|---|---|---|---|---|---|---|
| MR 90 | 2 | 1 | 4 | 284 | 120 | 29 | 1994 | Bombardier | GE |

# RAILWAY SYSTEMS/Canada

temporary measure during road works but is to become permanent, with an extension to St Hilaire. A full service was expected to begin in 2001. In 2000, AMT was studying the introduction of services on a fifth route, from Windsor station to Iberville, southeast of Montreal, as well as network extensions to the Blainville line. Options were also being studied to provide a direct rail link to Dorval International Airport.

### Traction and rolling stock
The Deux-Montagnes line is served by 29 two-car emus built by Bombardier from 1994. Initially, non-electric operations were handled by conventional and double-deck coaches hauled by seven FP7 and four GP9u diesel-electric locomotives. The latter are ex-CN GP9 units remanufactured by CN's Pointe St Charles workshops (later AMF Technotransport, now Alstom) and operate with head-end power generator vans converted from standard box cars. For the Blainville service, launched in 1997, and the McMasterville/St Hilaire line, AMT has returned to service refurbished examples of a fleet of 80 coaches acquired from GO Transit in Toronto. Similar equipment will be used on the proposed Iberville route.

In 2000, AMT took delivery of seven new F59PH locomotives from General Motors.

## Alberta RailNet Inc

9808 96 Street, Grand Prairie, Alberta T8V 7T9
Tel: (+1 780) 831 04 07   Fax: (+1 780) 539 17 11
e-mail: railnet1@telusplanet.net
Web: http://www.albertarailnet.com

### Key personnel
Vice-President and General Manager: Greg Pichette
Directors of Operations: Joe Gizanich, Bruce Whiteman

Chief Mechanical Officer: Dan Sparks
Market Development Officer: Wendy Kemper
Administration Manager: Char Cote

Gauge: 1,435 mm
Route length: 588 km

### Organisation
ARN is a subsidiary of North American RailNet (qv in USA section) which in June 1999 took over the operation of three former CN subdivisions in northwestern Alberta. Trackage begins 58 km northeast of Jasper and runs north to Grande Prairie, from where lines go northwest to Hythe and northeast to Tangent. The railway handles approximately 40,000 carloads annually, including coal, forest and industrial products and grain.

*NEW ENTRY*

## Algoma Central Railway

Algoma Central Railway Inc
PO Box 9500, Sault Ste Marie, Ontario P6A 6Y1
Tel: (+1 705) 541 28 50

### Key personnel
President: Edward A Burkhardt
Vice-President, Marketing: William R Schauer
Marketing Director, ACRI: Domenic A Palumbo

Gauge: 1,435 mm
Route length: 518 km

### Organisation
Following approval in December 1994 from Canada's National Transportation Agency, the rail assets of the Algoma Central Corporation were purchased by Wisconsin Central Transportation Company (WCTC) (qv in the US section) through a wholly owned subsidiary WC Canada Holdings Inc. Algoma Central Railway Inc has been the operating subsidiary since February 1995.

### Finance
In acquiring the Algoma Central, WCTC paid US$16.1 million for property and rolling stock, including 23 locomotives and 879 passenger coaches and freight wagons. Additionally, WCTC paid US$8.2 million for the rights of way in a partnership transaction involving the province of Ontario. Algoma Central's financial results are now consolidated with those of parent WCTC.

### Passenger operations
ACRI provides the thrice-weekly passenger service each way between Sault Ste Marie and Hearst, complemented by seasonal tourist trains (of which the best known is the Agawa Canyon service).

### Freight operations
Under WCTC management, daily freight service operates between Sault Ste Marie and Oba, and on the Michipicoten branch. Service north of Oba to Hearst is Monday-Friday only. Marketing and customer service functions are now integrated with WCTC. Iron ore, steel and forest products are the dominant commodities.

### Traction and rolling stock
The 23 diesel locomotives absorbed into WCTC ownership comprised a mix of EMD 2,200 kW Type SD40, EMD 1,500 kW Type GP38-2, EMD 1,100 kW Type GP7 and one switcher. Several of the higher-power locomotives have been redeployed; 11 ex-VIA steam-generator-equipped EMD FP9 units have been acquired for the passenger trains and seven are in service.

**Coupler in standard use**
Passenger cars: AAR Type E, F, H
Freight cars: AAR Type E, F, H
Braking in standard use, locomotive-hauled stock: Air Type 26

**Track**
Rail type: 115 RE, 100 RE, 85 CPR, 80 ASCE
Sleepers: Wood
Spacing: 1,822/km
Fastenings: Splice bars
Min curve radius: 1°
Max gradient: 1.7%
Max axleload: 30.4 tonnes

## BC Rail

BC Rail Ltd
PO Box 8770, Vancouver, British Columbia V6B 4X6
Tel: (+1 604) 986 20 12   Fax: (+1 604) 984 52 01
Web: http://www.bcrail.com/bcr

### Key personnel
President and Chief Executive Officer: Paul McElligott
Vice-Presidents
  Finance and Information Technology: J Roger Clarke
  Human Resources and Strategic Planning: Eric A Lush
  Marketing and Sales: Dale R MacLean
  Operations and Maintenance: Mark G Mudie

Gauge: 1,435 mm
Route length: 2,314 km
Electrification: 129 km at 50 kV 60 Hz

### Organisation
BC Rail Ltd is the railway operating unit of the BCR Group of companies; the BCR Group is a crown corporation, wholly owned by the province of British Columbia, and has five business units including BC Rail. One unit, British Columbia Railway Company, owns 25 per cent of BC Rail. Another, BCR Properties Ltd, which is the property-owning unit of the Group, owns the other 75 per cent. In 1995 the Group added a unit called BCR Ventures for the purpose of developing business and pursuing a diversification strategy since several major coal contracts are up for renegotiation in 1998 and 1999, plus projections for traffic from the forest products industry show few growth prospects.

The railway's principal yard facilities are at North Vancouver, Squamish, Lillooet, Williams Lake, Quesnel, Prince George, Fort St James, Mackenzie and Fort St John. Rail-served industrial parks are situated at Williams Lake, Prince George, Mackenzie, Fort St John, Dawson Creek, Fort St James and Fort Nelson.

At the end of 1999, BC Rail employed 2,088 staff, compared with 2,249 in 1998.

*Subsidiaries*
BC Rail formed a wholly owned subsidiary known as Westel Telecommunications Ltd in 1993; the subsidiary operates as a facilities-based carrier in the long-distance, voice and data telecommunications market in British Columbia.

BCR Ventures is involved with two partners, Mitsui-Matsushima and Globaltex Industries Inc, in exploring potential for a new open-cast coal mine 50 km west of Chetwynd. BC Rail would be the transport provider and Pine Valley Coal Company, which is one-third owned by the Ventures unit, would be the operator. Start-up plan is for 600,000 tonnes/year (approximately one unit train weekly) with a future plan to double that volume.

In October 1998, the BCR Group acquired Canadian Stevedoring Company Ltd and its subsidiaries Casco Terminals and Casco Forwarding, British Columbia's leading stevedoring firm and a major marine terminal operator. In July 1999, the new acquisition was integrated with Vancouver Wharves Ltd (VWL) to form BCR Marine Company. Within this structure, VWL, Canadian Stevedoring and Casco Terminals continue to operate as independent business units.

VWL is a deep-sea storage and handling facility owned by BC Rail since 1993. Situated at the entrance to the Port of Vancouver and adjacent to BC Rail's North Vancouver yard, the facility ships about 5 million tonnes of bulk commodities annually. Products handled include sulphur, potash, fertilisers, mineral concentrates, methanol, wood pulp, and specialised agricultural products. Some 50,000 wagons are handled at the facility annually.

BCR Properties provides property management services to all group member companies, as well as managing a real estate portfolio on its own account.

International Rail Consultants (IRC) is a joint venture formed in 1985 between BC Rail and Sandwell Inc. During 1997, it hosted visitors from Bangladesh, China, Korea, Romania, South Africa, Tanzania, and Tunisia. Projects were undertaken in Bangladesh, China, Indonesia, and Thailand.

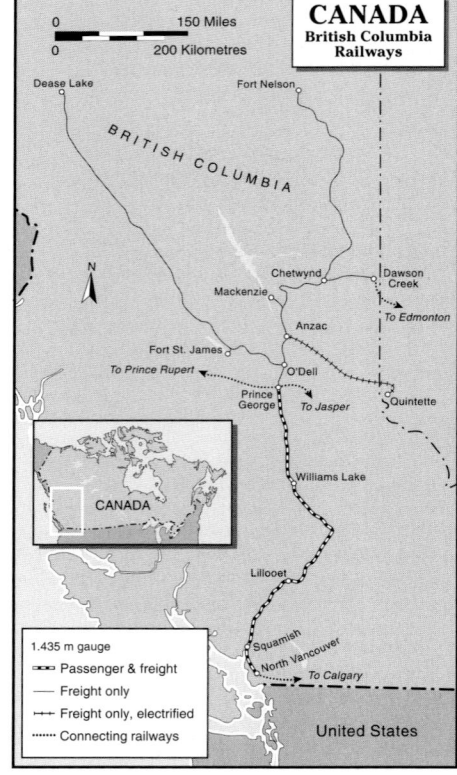

*BC Rail is upgrading its GE Dash 8 locomotives to 3,300 kW, with Dash 9 electronics* 0019553

*Passenger services between North Vancouver and Prince George are provided by Budd RDCs* 0019559

## Passenger operations
BC Rail's scheduled passenger service, 'The Cariboo Prospector', operates a year-round daily return service between North Vancouver and Lillooet, and is extended three days each week to Prince George. Regularly scheduled services are provided with trains composed of Budd RDC diesel railcars.

BC Rail runs excursions to Squamish in the summer season using the 'Royal Hudson' steam locomotive, owned by the province of British Columbia. Also in summer months BC Rail operates 'The Pacific Starlight', a dinner train formed of period coaches running between North Vancouver and Porteau Cove.

## Freight operations
BC Rail serves some 800 shippers (150 on BCR Properties sites) in the province of British Columbia. The railway's traffic volume for 1998 totalled 16.2 million gross revenue tonnes compared with 17.9 million in 1997.

## Intermodal operations
In addition to rail services, BC Rail's Intermodal Division operates a trucking fleet and also provides a warehousing and timber reload facility.

## Improvements to existing lines
During 1999, BCR Marine upgraded rail access to the bulk loading facility in North Vancouver. The installation of dual-nested rail loops allows more efficient unloading of sulphur and grain unit trains without the need for switching.

## Traction and rolling stock
In early 2000 BC Rail rostered seven electric, two steam, and 118 diesel locomotives (including 10 'slugs'); nine Budd diesel railcars; 23 passenger coaches; and 9,846 freight wagons. No new locomotives were purchased in 1998 or 1999, but six second-hand GE model C36-7 and three GE model B39-8 machines were acquired in 1998-99. These are being rebuilt at a rate of four per year.

The GEF40 Dash 8 locomotives are being overhauled and upgraded to 3,300 kW with Dash 9 electronics. A seven-year remanufacturing programme of 27 Alco-engined yard/transfer locomotives has been completed.

Major wagon repairs and rebuilding are undertaken by BC Rail's Squamish workshop facility, which performs similar work on locomotives. Lighter running repairs are undertaken by workshops at Prince George.

## Signalling and telecommunications
During 1996/97 BC Rail installed eight new crossings and six new power switches. The communication system that provides remote control and monitoring was expanded to additional locations.

## Electrification
Development of British Columbia's northeast coalfields prompted construction in 1983 of the 129 km Tumbler Ridge branch line into the coalfield area. It was the fourth line in the world to be electrified at 50 kV AC.

Seven Type GF6C 4,400 kW Co-Co electric locomotives were built by General Motors of Canada, using ASEA (now Adtranz) licensed technology to operate in back-to-back pairs. The standard operation is for 13,000 tonne trains of export coal (Japan is a major customer), consisting of 102 rotary-coupler-fitted 118 tonne hopper wagons, to travel 720 km to the deep-water port at Ridley Island, near Prince Rupert. BC Rail shares the operation with CN, employing CN diesels from the end of the electrification at Tacheeda Junction (Anzac). At Prince George, CN crews take over for the remainder of the journey over CN trackage to Ridley Island. BC Rail provided one-third of the 913-car fleet. The operating plan in 2000 provided for three trains to be in use, each on a 75 hour cycle for the round trip.

## Track
**Rail:** 50, 60 and 68 kg/m
**Crossties (sleepers):** Softwood, 178 × 228 × 2,400 mm; steel, 130 × 300 × 2,500 mm
**Spacing:** Wood 510 mm; steel 610 mm
**Fastenings:** Cut spikes and anchors on timber sleepers, elastic clips on steel sleepers
**Min curve radius:** 110 m
**Max gradient:** 2.2%
**Max axleload:** 29.9 tonnes

### Diesel locomotives

| Class | Wheel arrangement | Power kW | Speed km/h | Weight tonnes | No in service | First built | Mechanical | Builders Engine | Transmission |
|---|---|---|---|---|---|---|---|---|---|
| M420 | Bo-Bo | 1,500 | 105 | 112.5 | 4 | 1973 | MLW | MLW Alco 251-12 | *E* GE |
| C420 | Co-Co | 1,500 | 105 | 119.3 | 2 | 1966 | Alco | Alco 251-16 | *E* GE |
| SD40 | Co-Co | 2,200 | 105 | 192.5 | 23 | 1978 | GM | EMD 645-16 | *E* EMD |
| Slug | Bo-Bo | 1,200 | 105 | 109 | 10 | 1981 | MLW | - | *E* GE |
| CRS20 | Bo-Bo | 1,500 | 105 | 113.6 | 27 | 1990 R | MLW/BCR | Caterpillar 3516 | *E* KATO/GE |
| GEF36 | Bo-Bo | 2,700 | 105 | n/a | 15 | 1980 | GE | GE 7FDL16 | *E* GE |
| GEF36 | Co-Co | 2,700 | 105 | 192.5 | 6 | 1981 | GE | GE 7FDL16 | *E* GE |
| GEF39 | Bo-Bo | 2,900 | 105 | 130 | 3 | 1988 | GE | GE 7FDL16 | *E* GE |
| GEF40 | Co-Co | 3,000 | 105 | 192.5 | 26 | 1990 | GE | GE 7FDL16 | *E* GE |
| GEF44 | Co Co | 3,000 | 105 | 192.5 | 4 | 1995 | GE | GE 7FDL16 | *E* GE |

### Diesel railcars

| Class | Cars per Unit | Power kW | Speed km/h | Weight tonnes | No in service | First built | Mechanical | Builders Engine | Transmission |
|---|---|---|---|---|---|---|---|---|---|
| RDC1 | 1 | 520 | 129 | 53.5 | 6 | 1956 | Budd | Cummins | Twin Disc |
| RDC3 | 1 | 520 | 129 | 53.5 | 3 | 1956 | Budd | Cummins | Twin Disc |

### Electric locomotives

| Class | Wheel Arrangement | Output kW continuous/one hour | Speed km/h | Weight tonnes | No in service | First built | Builders Mechanical | Electrical |
|---|---|---|---|---|---|---|---|---|
| GF6C | Co-Co | 4,400/6,480 | 90 | 178 | 7 | 1983 | GMC | ASEA |

# Canadian American Railroad

Canadian American Railroad Co
RR2, Box 45, North Maine Junction Park, Bangor, Maine 04401-9602, USA
Tel: (+1 207) 848 42 40   Fax: (+1 207) 484 43 43

## Key personnel
Senior Operating Officer: Ted Michon

Gauge: 1,435 mm
Route length: 461 km

## Organisation
The Canadian American Railroad Co (CARC) began operating in November 1994; the company works the former Canadian Pacific Rail System (CPRS) route from Sherbrooke, Québec, into the US state of Maine. The 293 km line is a part of what was previously operated by CPRS as the Canadian Atlantic Railway, and since March 1995 has been owned by Iron Road Railways Inc of Washington DC (qv in US short line section).

The eastern 168 km of the former Canadian Atlantic from Brownville Junction, Maine, to St John in New Brunswick is owned by J D Irving Ltd, under the name of the Eastern Maine Railway in the USA and the New

# RAILWAY SYSTEMS/Canada

Brunswick Southern Railway on the Canadian side of the border. CARC has access to customers on the Irving-owned segment in the US.

The St Lawrence & Hudson Railway (St L & H) sold substantial trackage to Iron Road Railways in September 1996. The latter bought 391 km east from St Jean, Québec, to the CARC at Sherbrooke, together with short branches, and named these the Québec Southern. A 196 km line south from Farnham into the state of Vermont, US, is now the Vermont Northern Railroad, also in the IRR portfolio.

### Traction and rolling stock
CARC operates 31 locomotives, comprising General Motors GP35, GP38 and GP40 types.

## Canadian National

Canadian National Railway Company
935 de la Gauchetière Street Ouest, Montréal, Quebec
H3B 2M9
PO Box 8100, Montréal, Quebec H3C 3N4
Tel: (+1 514) 399 54 30   Fax: (+1 514) 399 54 79
Web: http://www.cn.ca

### Key personnel
President and Chief Executive Officer: Paul Tellier
Executive Vice-President and Chief Operating Officer:
  E Hunter Harrison
Executive Vice-President and Chief Financial Officer:
  Claude Mongeau
Executive Vice-President, Sales and Marketing:
  James M Foote
Senior Vice-President, Chief Legal Officer and Corporate
  Secretary: Sean Finn
Senior Vice-President, Corporate Services: Les Dakens
Senior Vice-President, Eastern Canada Division:
  Keith Heller
Senior Vice-President, Operations: Jack T McBain
Senior Vice-President, Public Affairs: William J (Bill) Fox
Vice-Presidents
  Financial Planning: Ami Haasz
  Intermodal: William K Berry
  Commercial Development: Cliff L Carson
  Risk Management: John Dalzell
  Labour Relations and Employment Legislation:
    Richard Dixon
  Pacific Division: David P Edison
  Grains and Fertilisers (Canada):
    S Ross Goldsworthy
  Forest Products: Stan Jablonski
  Human Resources (US Operation): Kim Madigan
  Midwest Division: Peter C Marshall
  Network Transportation: J Paul Mathieson
  Gulf Division: Terry McManaman
  Wisconsin Central Division: Gordon Trafton
  Prairie Division, Operations: Keith Creel
  Corporate Development: François Hebert
  US Legal Affairs: Myles L Tobin
  Supply Management: Sameh Fahmy
  Investor Relations: Robert E Noorigian
  e-Business, Sales and Marketing: Anita Ernesaks
  Sales and Market Development: Janice Murray
  Automotive: Andy Gonta
  Chemicals and Petroleum: Jean-Jacques Ruest
  Government Affairs: Karen B Phillips
  Sales, Gulf: Howard L Vaughters
  Engineering/Mechanical: Dennis E Waller
  Chief Information Officer: Fred Grigsby
  Corporate Comptroller: Serge Pharand
  Treasurer: Ghislain Houle

Gauge: 1,435 mm
Route length: 29,000 km in Canada and the USA.

### Background
Incorporated in 1919 as a state-owned corporation, CN became a publicly traded company on 18 November 1995 when the government of Canada sold all its shares to private investors in Canada, USA and overseas. The privatisation, the largest in Canadian history, involved the sale of 83.8 million common shares, generating gross proceeds to the government of C$2.28 billion. It followed management's implementation of an aggressive business plan three years before, which had produced a dramatic improvement in CN's financial performance and operational efficiency. While exposing the company to greater market discipline, privatisation unleashed a dynamic, entrepreneurial spirit throughout the organisation, prompting a steadily improving performance as CN focused on business growth, cost containment, competitive advantage for customers, and shareholder value.

### Organisation
CN operates a network of approximately 29,000 route-km of track in Canada and the United States, generating revenues of C$5.652 billion in 2001 from the movement of a diversified and balanced traffic mix. It is the only railroad in North America with a network spanning both Canada and mid-America and connecting three coasts, the Atlantic, the Pacific and the Gulf of Mexico. CN serves the ports of Vancouver, Prince Rupert, Montreal, Halifax, New Orleans, and Mobile, Alabama, and the key cities of Toronto, Buffalo, Chicago, Detroit, Duluth/Superior, Green Bay, Minneapolis/St Paul, Memphis, St Louis, and Jackson, Mississippi, with connections to all points in North America, including Mexico.

In 1999 CN acquired the Illinois Central Corporation (IC), which operated a 5,400-km network in the US Midwest. The acquisition fulfilled CN's 'three-coast' strategy, adding to its Pacific-to-Atlantic network a north-south corridor to the Gulf of Mexico. CN finalised the integration of IC operations with its own in 2001, a process that involved the co-ordination of network operations, traction distribution and rolling stock allocation, and information technology systems. In particular, CN modified and upgraded its Service Reliability Strategy (SRS) information system for tracking shipments and enabling scheduled service, extending

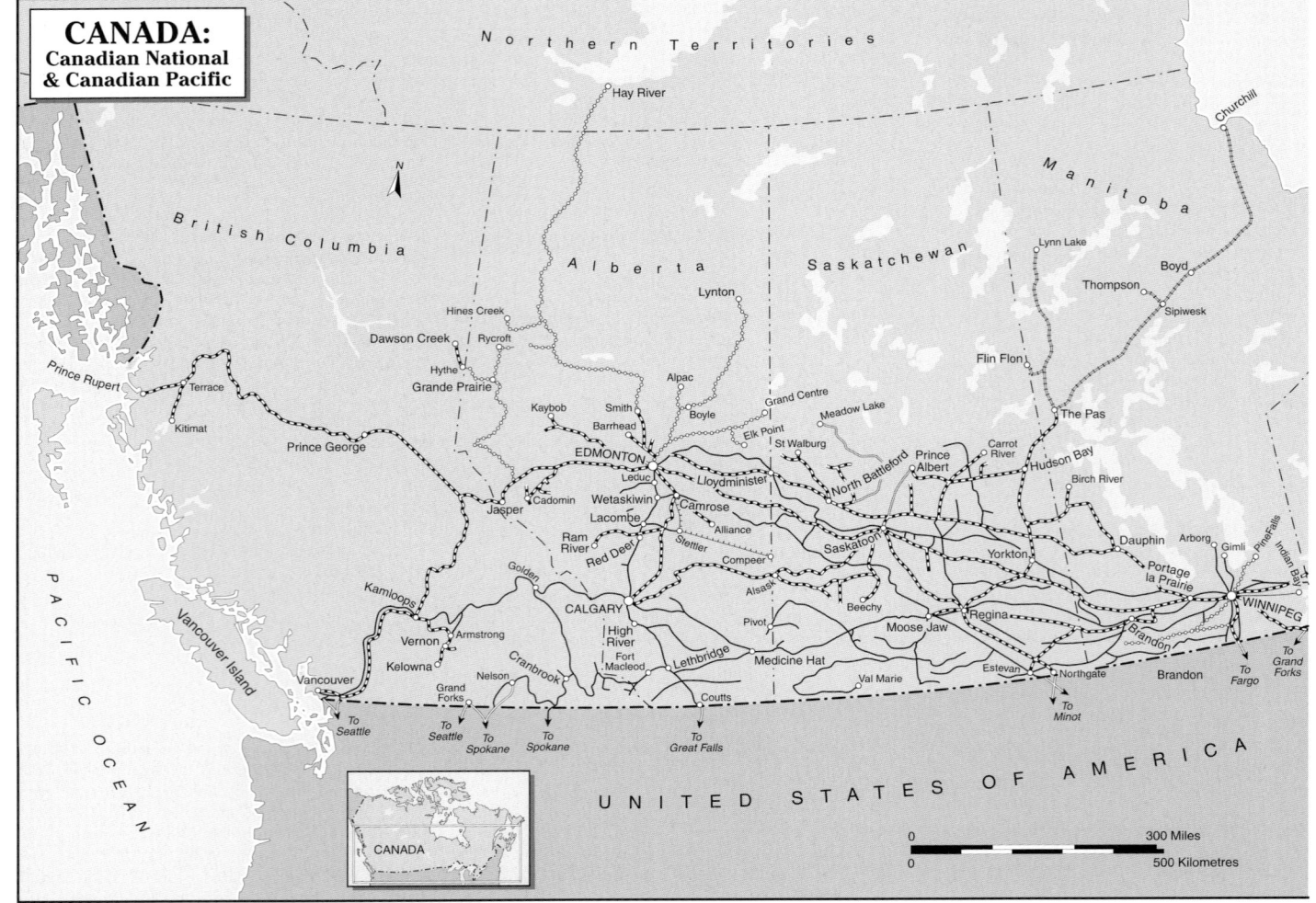

# Canada/RAILWAY SYSTEMS

*General Motors SD75I locomotive leading a train of aluminium-bodied coal wagons from Smokey River mine, at Grande Cache, Alberta*
0058672

SRS to the entire former IC territory in October 2000. The transfer to a single system proceeded smoothly, and tracking accuracy rate has reached 99.8 per cent.

Targeting growth through further strategic acquisitions, CN purchased the Wisconsin Central Transportation Corporation (WC) for C$1.297 billion in 2001, adding 4,500 km and 2,200 employees to the CN system. After the US Surface Transportation Board unanimously approved the transaction on 7 September, formal integration of WC into CN began on 9 October. The acquisition represented a logical move for CN: WC's trackage in Wisconsin and Michigan lay at the very heart of CN's three-coast network, and for a number of years the two railroads had been co-operating under a long-term haulage agreement. With ownership of WC's network, CN was able to secure the link between its eastern and western routes. The acquisition reinforced CN's position as North America's leading carrier of forest products, the dominant element in WC's traffic mix. CN also assumed ownership of WC's investment in three overseas transportation concerns: 40.9 per cent of English Welsh and Scottish Railway in the UK; 33 per cent of Australian Transport Network Ltd in Tasmania, Australia (which CN intends to sell within a year of the acquisition); and 23.7 per cent of Tranz Rail of New Zealand (sold in February 2002 for C$70 million).

The acquisition of IC and WC prompted modifications to CN's corporate structure, beginning with the establishment of five new geographic divisions in mid-1999: Eastern Canada; Prairie; and Pacific in Canada; and Midwest and Gulf in the US. Aimed at bringing CN closer to customers and promoting quicker response and stronger relationships, the new structure strikes a balance between activities better managed centrally with those best managed at a more local level. Network operations, marketing, and management of the largest customer accounts remains centralised, but each division has full responsibility for local operations, sales, and financial performance. When WC joined the CN system, its territory became a sixth division, named Wisconsin Central.

At the end of 2001, CN employed approximately 23,000 people.

## Finance

CN revenues totalled C$5.65 billion in 2001, an increase of 4 per cent over C$5.43 billion the year before and 46 per cent higher than revenues in 1995, the year CN was privatised. Operating expenses (excluding a special workforce adjustment charge) increased by 2 per cent, from C$3.78 billion in 2000 to C$3.87 billion. CN's operating ratio (expenses as a proportion of revenues) continued to improve, dropping from 69.6 per cent in 2000 to 68.5 per cent, once again the best performance of all North American Class I railroads and 14 points better than the industry average. Net income rose to C$978 million, 11 per cent higher than C$879 million in 2000.

Despite less than favourable economic conditions, revenues grew in all but one of CN's seven business units in 2001. Increases were recorded in petroleum and chemicals (3 per cent), metals and minerals (17 per cent), forest products (8 per cent), coal (3 per cent), grain and fertilisers (2 per cent), and intermodal (5 per cent), while revenues from the automotive sector declined by 7 per

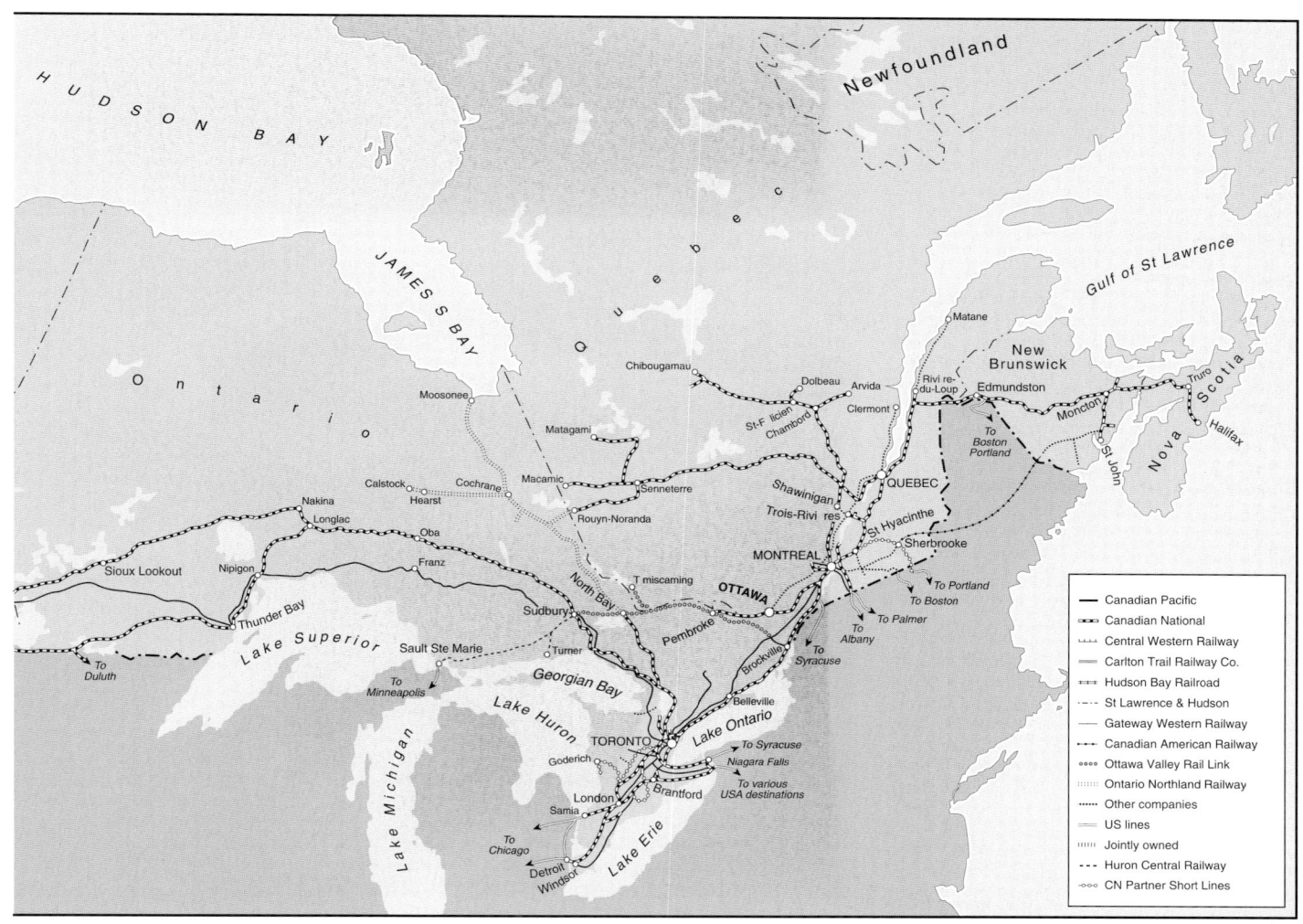

# RAILWAY SYSTEMS/Canada

cent. Carloads increased slightly from 3.796 million to 3.821 million.

The financial and statistical information detailed above includes data relating to WC from 9 October 2001.

### Freight operations

CN markets its freight transportation services through seven business units based on major commodity groups. In 2001 the petroleum and chemicals unit generated 17 per cent of CN's freight revenue, metals and minerals 8 per cent, forest products 20 per cent, coal 6 per cent, grain and fertilisers 21 per cent, intermodal 18 per cent, and automotive 10 per cent. Fifty-three per cent of this revenue comes from US domestic and crossborder traffic, 21 per cent from overseas traffic, and 26 per cent from Canadian domestic traffic.

CN pursues business growth for the company and competitive advantage for customers by offering high-quality service and single-line access to a greater range of markets as a result of acquisitions and alliances with other carriers. With its innovative service plan, unique in the industry, and SRS information technology, CN operates North America's first true 'scheduled railroad', with regularly scheduled trains and a trip plan for each car or container that directs the shipment from origin to destination. The service plan and scheduled operations enable CN to meet customers' demands for faster transit times and better on-time performance. At the same time, they help CN to control costs through more efficient use of its assets. Performance compliance with the service plan exceeded 90 per cent in 2001.

Marketing alliances and operational agreements with other carriers enable CN to offer customers greater reach as well as shorter transit times to markets. In 2000 CN and Canadian Pacific (CP) initiated an agreement on train operations along a 262 km stretch of the Fraser Canyon in British Columbia. With westbound trains using CN trackage and eastbound trains running along CP's, the arrangement has speeded service on both railroads. A haulage agreement with Burlington Northern Santa Fe (BNSF) for Illinois and Iowa agricultural products has resulted in improved transit times since it was implemented in October 2000, while an interline service agreement with BNSF gave shippers of new carload traffic extended access to markets in western Canada and the US when it went into effect in November the same year.

As a result of better asset utilisation and as part of a drive to achieve even greater efficiency, CN introduced a Guaranteed Car Supply programme in 2000, expanding it to cover about half of the railcar fleet the following year. Under the programme, CN guarantees the delivery of the appropriate number of empty cars to customers on specific dates, and the customer agrees to load them within a certain period. During 2002 CN will make it possible for 50 per cent of the car orders under the programme to be conducted over the Internet.

### Intermodal operations

Intermodal business accounted for more than 18 per cent of CN's freight revenues in 2001. The company's intermodal business unit includes two market segments, domestic and international. The domestic segment handles consumer products and manufactured goods moving within Canada and the United States and generated 58 per cent of intermodal revenues in 2001. It offers two sales channels: retail, which supplies full door-to-door service through CN's trucking group, and wholesale, which provides service to trucking companies, carload freight forwarders, and intermodal marketing companies supplying their own transportation service packages to shippers. The international segment transports import-export containers for ocean shipping companies and contributed 42 per cent of the business unit's revenues in 2001.

The intermodal group has a strong base of strategic alliances with numerous trucking companies and other transportation service providers to supply seamless service throughout North America. An agreement with CSX Intermodal, initiated in 2001, led to new truck-competitive services between Vancouver and New York, Toronto and markets in Florida, and Toronto and New York. Also in 2001, CN and Union Pacific implemented an agreement covering NAFTA traffic moving between Canada, New England, and the Detroit area and south Texas, with connections to Mexico via Grupo Transportación Ferroviaria Mexicana.

CN operates 20 strategically located intermodal hubs and satellites in Canada and the United States, including the 52-hectare Gateway Terminal near Chicago. The

*General Motors GP40-2L locomotive leading a mixed freight including three-level auto-racks east of Jasper, Alberta*

*CN locomotive against the Chicago skyline*

*CN coal train at Windy Point, Alberta. The company handles coal for export, primarily for steelmaking in Japan, but also for utilities in North America and abroad*

## Diesel locomotives: Canadian operations

| Class | Builder | Model | No in service | First built | Modified | Rating kW | Speed km/h |
|---|---|---|---|---|---|---|---|
| **Road** | | | | | | | |
| GR-12w | GM | GMD-1 | 1 | 1959 | 1983-87* | 895 | 105 |
| GR-12z | GM | GMD-1 | 1 | 1960 | 1987-90* | 895 | 105 |
| GR-12zc | GM | GMD-1 | 1 | 1959 | 1986-90* | 895 | 105 |
| GR-12u | GM | SW-1200RS | 2 | 1959 | | 895 | 105 |
| GR-12y | GM | SW-1200RS | 5 | 1960 | | 895 | 105 |
| GR-412a | GM | GMD-1B | 39 | 1989 (Rebuilds) | | 895 | 105 |
| GR-418a | GM | GP-9RM | 7 | 1981-82 (Remanufactured) | 1987† | 1,343 | 105 |
| GR-418b | GM | GP-9RM | 9 | 1982-83 (Remanufactured) | 1987† | 1,343 | 105 |
| GR-418c | GM | GP-9RM | 12 | 1984 (Remanufactured) | 1987† | 1,343 | 105 |
| GR-418d | GM | GP-9RM | 12 | 1984 (Remanufactured) | | 1,343 | 105 |
| GR-418e | GM | GP-9RM | 7 | 1989-90 (Remanufactured) | | 1,343 | 105 |
| GR-418f | GM | GP-9RM | 12 | 1991 (Remanufactured) | | 1,343 | 105 |
| GR-420b | GM | GP-38-2 | 34 | 1972-73 | 1982-83† | 1,492 | 105 |
| GR-420c | GM | GP-38-2 | 45 | 1973-74 | 1982-83† | 1,492 | 105 |
| **Road Freight** | | | | | | | |
| EF-640a | GE | 8-40CM | 30 | 1990 | | 2,984 | 105 |
| EF-640b | GE | 8-40CM | 25 | 1992 | | 2,984 | 105 |
| EF-644a | GE | 9-44CWL | 23 | 1994 | | 3,282 | 105 |
| EF-644b | GE | 9-44CW | 40 | 1997 | | 3,282 | 105 |
| EF-644c | GE | 9-44CW | 40 | 1997-98 | | 3,282 | 105 |
| EF-644d | GE | 9-44CW | 40 | 2000 | | 3,282 | 105 |
| GF-30c | GM | SD-40 | 1 | 1967 | | 2,238 | 105 |
| GF-30d | GM | SD-40 | 6 | 1967-68 | | 2,238 | 105 |
| GF-30e | GM | SD-40 | 3 | 1969 | | 2,238 | 105 |
| GF-30k | GM | SD-40 | 2 | 1971 | | 2,238 | 105 |
| GF-30m | GM | SD-40 | 4 | 1971 | | 2,238 | 105 |
| GF-30n | GM | SD-40-2 | 20 | 1975 | | 2,238 | 105 |
| GF-30p | GM | SD-40-2 | 16 | 1975 | | 2,238 | 105 |
| GF-30q | GM | SD-40-2 | 15 | 1976 | | 2,238 | 105 |
| GF-30r | GM | SD-40-2 | 19 | 1978 | | 2,238 | 105 |
| GF-30s | GM | SD-40-2 | 10 | 1979 | | 2,238 | 105 |
| GF-30t | GM | SD-40-2 | 30 | 1980 | | 2,238 | 105 |
| GU-30u-y | GM | SD-40-2 | 34 | 1980 | | 2,238 | 105 |
| GF-636a | GM | SD-50F | 40 | 1985-86 | | 2,685 | 105 |
| GF-636b | GM | SD-50F | 20 | 1987 | | 2,685 | 105 |
| GF-638a | GM | SD-50DAF | 4 | 1986 | | 2,835 | 105 |
| GF-638b | GM | SD-60F | 58 | 1989 | | 2,835 | 105 |
| GF-640a | GM | SD-70I | 26 | 1995 | | 3,000 | 70 |
| GF-643a | GM | SD75I | 104 | 1996 | | 3,208 | 112 |
| GF-643b | GM | SD75I | 34 | 1997 | | 3,208 | 105 |
| GF-643c | GM | SD75I | 35 | 1999 | | 3,208 | 105 |
| GF-620a | GM | SD-38-2 | 4 | 1976 | | 1,492 | 105 |
| GF-630a-c | GM/CN | SD-40Q | 29 | 1992-95 (Remanufactured) | | 2,238 | 105 |
| GF-430a | GM | GP-40-2L | 25 | 1974 | | 2,238 | 105 |
| GF-430b | GM | GP-40-2L | 9 | 1974 | | 2,238 | 105 |
| GF-430c | GM | GP-40-2L | 27 | 1975 | | 2,238 | 105 |
| GF-430d | GM | GP-40-2 | 2 | 1977 | | 2,238 | 105 |
| GF-430e | GM | GP-40-2 | 3 | 1974** | 1991-2 | 2,238 | 130 |
| GF-430f | GM | GP-40-2 | 3 | 1974** | 1991-2 | 2,238 | 130 |
| GF-430g | GM | GP-40-2 | 4 | 1975** | 1991-2 | 2,238 | 130 |
| **Switchers** | | | | | | | |
| GS-418a | GM/CN | GP-9RM | 9 | 1985 (Remanufactured) | | 1,343 | 105 |
| GS-418b/c | GM/CN | GP-9RM | 63 | 1990-93 (Remanufactured) | | 1,343 | 105 |
| GY-418a | GM/CN | GP-9RM | 14 | 1985-86 (Remanufactured) | | 1,343 | 105 |
| GY-418b | GM/CN | GP-9RM | 18 | 1986 (Remanufactured) | | 1,343 | 105 |
| GY-418c | GM/CN | GP-9RM | 8 | 1987/90 (Remanufactured) | | 1,343 | 105 |
| GY-418d-f | GM/CN | GP-9RM | 39 | 1988-90 (Remanufactured) | | 1,343 | 105 |
| GS-412a | GM/CN | SW-1200RB | 11 | 1987 (Rebuild) | | 895 | 105 |
| GH-20b | GM | GP-38-2 | 27 | 1973 | 1977-85 | 1,492 | 105 |
| **Boosters** | | | | | | | |
| GY-00b | GM | YBU-4M | 8 | 1980 | 1985-86 | - | 105 |
| GY-00c | GM/CN | YBU | 4 | 1986 (Remanufactured) | | - | 105 |
| GY-00d | GM/CN | YBU | 18 | 1986 (Remanufactured) | | - | 105 |
| GY-00e/f/g | GM/CN | YBU | 42 | 1987-90 (Remanufactured) | | - | 105 |
| GH-00a | GM | HBU-4 | 19 | 1978 | | - | 105 |
| GH-00b | GM | HBU-4 | 4 | 1980 | | - | 105 |
| GH-00c | GM | HBU-4M | 4 | 1980 | 1986 | - | 105 |

\* Rebogied from A1A-A1A to B-B
† Weight reduced
\*\* Former GO Transit locos converted for freight haulage

## Diesel locomotives: US operations

| Class | Builder | Model | No in service | First built | Rating kW | Speed km/h |
|---|---|---|---|---|---|---|
| EF-640 | GE | D8-40C | 12 | 1994 | 2,984 | 105 |
| GF-30 | GM | SD40R | 99 | 1975-79 | 2,238 | 105 |
| GF-30 | GM | SD40 | 1 | 1970 | 2,238 | 105 |
| GF-30 | GM | SD40-2 | 5 | 1973 | 2,238 | 105 |
| GF30F | EMD | SD40 | 8 | 1969 | 2,238 | 105 |
| GF30G | EMD | SD40 | 6 | 1970 | 2,238 | 105 |
| GF30J | EMD | SD40 | 5 | 1970 | 2,238 | 105 |
| GF30Y | EMD | SD40 | 8 | 1975 | 2,238 | 105 |
| GF-430 | GM | GP40R | 17 | 1987-81 (Remanufactured) | 2,238 | 105 |
| GF-636 | GM | SD45 | 94 | 1965-71 | 2,685 | 105 |
| GF-636 | GM | FP45 | 1 | 1967 | 2,685 | 105 |
| GF-640 | GM | SD70 | 40 | 1995-99 | 3,000 | 105 |
| GPA-17a | GM | FP9A | 4 | 1983 (Remanufactured) | 1,343 | 105 |
| GPA-24a | GM | E9A | 4 | 1949-52 | 1,492 | 125 |
| GPD-15a | GM | FP7A | 1 | 1953 | 1,305 | 105 |
| GR-15a | GM | GP7 | 7 | 1969-71 (Remanufactured) | 1,343 | 105 |
| GR20 | EMD | GP38-2 | 35 | 1972 | 1,492 | 105 |
| GR20A | EMD | GP38AC | 3 | 1971 | 1,492 | 105 |
| GR20D | EMD | GP38-2 | 20 | 1978 | 1,492 | 105 |
| GR20E | EMD | GP38-2 | 5 | 1979 | 1,492 | 105 |
| GR20F | EMD | GP38-2 | 6 | 1979 | 1,492 | 105 |
| GR20G | EMD | GP38-2 | 12 | 1978 | 1,492 | 105 |
| GR20 | EMD | GP38 | 1 | 1966 | 1,492 | 105 |
| GR20 | EMD | GP38AC | 2 | 1969/70 | 1,492 | 105 |
| GR20 | EMD | GP38-2 | 8 | 1975 | 1,492 | 105 |
| GR30 | EMD | GP40 | 1 | 1968 | 2,238 | 105 |
| GR30 | EMD | GP40-2 | 4 | 1972 | | |
| GR-417 | GM | EMD/GTW | 36 | 1989 | 1,305 | 105 |
| GR-420 | GM | GP38-2 | 52 | 1972-74 | 1,492 | 105 |
| GR-420 | GM | GP38-2 | 6 | 1981 | 1,492 | 105 |
| GR-430 | GM | GP40-2 | 21 | 1970 | 2,238 | 105 |
| GR-620 | GM | SD20 | 17 | 1959 | 1,492 | 105 |
| GR-625a | GM | SD35 | 1 | 1965 | 2,100 | 105 |
| GS-412c | GM | SW7 | 28 | 1971 (Remanufactured) | 895 | 105 |
| GS-415 | GM | SW1500 | 15 | 1969-71 | 1,305 | 105 |

company is also a partner in the Deltaport Terminal at Vancouver. In 2001 CN invested C$50 million in new terminals at Edmonton (completed in 2001) and Montreal (due for completion in 2002). The company is currently implementing a new gate technology system, Speed Gate, which provides truckers with self-serve entry to terminals, thus increasing throughput while virtually eliminating queuing at entry points.

RoadRailer service, introduced on the busy Montreal-Toronto corridor in 1999, continues to make inroads in this competitive marketplace, attracting a number of major accounts. The service uses unique dual-mode technology whereby highway trailers can be easily transferred to specially designed rail bogies and hauled as a train. RoadRailer combines the flexibility of highway transport with the efficiency of rail, enhancing CN's ability to compete with trucking for time-sensitive shipments in short-haul markets. CN has also initiated new expedited train services with redesigned schedules, cutting transit times between Toronto or Chicago and western points by as much as 24 hours and between Toronto and eastern centres by up to six hours.

### Traction and rolling stock

CN's 15-year Locomotive Upgrade Program, now in its eighth year, aims at increased fleet utilisation and efficiency through the retirement of less productive units, the acquisition of more efficient ones, and a range of process improvements. The programme continues to move ahead rapidly, thanks in part to efficiencies created by the new service plan and the CN-developed Locomotive Distribution Model, a computer-based system that assigns motive power in the most effective manner.

Over the past four years, CN has been able to reduce its locomotive fleet significantly even while moving more freight. The active locomotive fleet dropped from 2,300 units in early 1998 to 1,500 at the end of 2001. Acquisitions of high-power units also serve to upgrade the efficiency of the fleet. In 2000, CN acquired 40 new GE 4,400 hp locomotives and in 2002 ordered a further 60 units for delivery by the end of 2004. Motive power efficiency, measured in terms of gross ton-miles per available horsepower (gtm/hp), increased by 40 per cent from 1998 to 2001.

In 2002, as part of the ongoing motive power renewal programme, CN awarded a six-year contract to General Motors Electro-Motive Division to remanufacture the engines of 300 high-horsepower locomotives. Ranging from 2,835 to 2,984 kW (3,800 to 4,000 hp), the units represent almost 30 per cent of the 1,100-unit main line fleet with horsepower of 3,000 or more. The remanufactured engines will add to the locomotives' efficiency and reliability and contribute significantly to CN's goal of optimum asset utilisation. The company is also working to achieve further efficiency gains by combining smaller trains into longer ones hauled by the new, more powerful locomotives.

Operational efficiencies have also enabled CN to make significant reductions to its wagon fleet in recent years. The active railcar fleet dropped from 82,900 units in early 1998 to 61,500 at the end of 2001. Fleet productivity in terms of railcar velocity rose by 25 per cent during the same period.

### Track

**Rail:** Currently, sections are being bought in four categories: 136 CN (a special section for head-hardened rail used only in curves), 136 RE, 132 RE (limited amounts for maintenance) and 115 RE.

**Welded rail**
Sections are electric pressure flash-butt welded into strands of about 1,480 ft (451 m) in central plants. After unloading at a laying site, rail may be electric pressure flash-butt field welded by portable plants into longer lengths before laying, or welded by aluminothermic process after laying.

**Crossties (sleepers)**
**Thickness**
**Wood:** Main lines: 7 or 6 in (180 or 150 mm)
Branch lines: 6 in (150 mm)
**Concrete (CN 60B):** 8 in (200 mm) at rail seat
**Spacing**
**Wood:** Main lines: 1,932/km
**Concrete:** 1,640/km
**Rail fastenings**
**Wood:** 6 or 5½ × ⅝ in (150 or 140 × 16 mm)
**Concrete:** Pandrol

***UPDATED***

## Canadian Pacific

Canadian Pacific Railway Company
Suite 500, Gulf Canada Square, 401 9th Avenue SW, Calgary, Alberta T2P 4Z4
Tel: (+1 403) 218 70 00   Fax: (+1 403) 205 90 00
Web: http://www.cprailway.com

### Key personnel
President and Chief Executive Officer: R J Ritchie
Executive Vice-Presidents
   Operations: E V Dodge
   Commercial: J H McDiarmid
   Finance: G C Halatsis
Vice-Presidents
   Legal Services: Ms M M Szel
   Mechanical Services: N R Foot
   Information Services: A H Foster
   Intermodal and Auto: L M Allen
   Resource Products: F J Green
   Agricultural Products & Coal: R A Sallee
   St Lawrence & Hudson: J Coté
   Engineering Services: E J Rewucki
   Government and Public Affairs: D W Flicker
   Human Resources: R A Shields
   Field Operations: P A Pender
   Transport Services: W P Bell
Director, Commuter Rail: R O'Meara

Gauge: 1,435 mm
Route length: 25,000 km

### Soo Line Railroad Company
Soo Line Building, PO Box 530, Minneapolis, Minnesota 55440, USA
Tel: (+1 612) 347 80 00   Fax: (+1 612) 347 80 59

### St Lawrence & Hudson Railway Company Limited
PO Box 6042, Station Centre-Ville, Montréal, Québec H3C 3E4
Tel: (+1 514) 395 51 51   Fax: (+1 514) 395 77 54

### Key personnel
President: Jacques Coté
Commercial Director: Mary McCarthy
Chief Operating Officer: Paul Gilmore

### Organisation
Canadian Pacific Railway Company is currently the fifth largest railway system in North America based on route-kilometres. The railway is a wholly owned subsidiary of Canadian Pacific Limited, which also owns CP Hotels, Fording Coal, CP Ships, and is a majority shareholder in PanCanadian Petroleum.

In 1996 CPRC renamed its former eastern operating unit the St Lawrence & Hudson Railway to include the Delaware & Hudson Railway in the USA. At the same time it effectively scrapped its western operating unit. CPRC also introduced a new concept, the internal short line, on StL&H territory in Ontario, with separate labour agreements and management techniques adopted to operate a 140 km branch line northeast of Toronto. The relationship with CP Limited has also changed in that CPRC is now a stand-alone corporation rather than an operating division of the parent.

CPRC is undergoing a major restructuring which has included, *inter alia,* the relocation of its head office from Montréal to Calgary during 1996, bringing the administrative functions closer to the operations heart of the business, that is into the western provinces, and involving the relocation of 700+ employees. By eliminating a further 1,750 administrative positions the company has generated an annual saving of C$100 million from the reorganisation. Overall, 11 management levels have been compressed into six since 1995.

The declared design for CPRC is a 'wishbone' network consisting of Vancouver-Winnipeg plus Winnipeg-Toronto and Winnipeg-Chicago.

At the end of 1997 the company employed 19,776 staff, a fall of 6.6 per cent over the previous year.

The three core management functions within CPRC are now:

(1) *Commercial:* to market and sell the railway
(2) *Operations:* to run trains
(3) *Support services:* to maximise company effectiveness and performance.

*Soo Line Railroad*
The Soo Line company, based in Minneapolis, Minnesota, continues to operate as a separate entity because of different laws and labour contracts which apply in the USA. It operates in 11 US states: Illinois, Indiana, Iowa, Kansas, Kentucky, Michigan, Minnesota, Missouri, North Dakota, South Dakota and Wisconsin. The Shoreham workshops in the Twin Cities support a fleet of 350 locomotives (252 road units and 98 yard/transfer units).

In 1996, CPRC entertained bids from 15 potential purchasers of the Chicago-Kansas City main line, as well as various grain lines in northern Iowa and southern Minnesota. In April 1997, it was announced that a new company, I&M Rail Link (qv in USA section), with a controlling interest held by the Washington Companies (see Montana Rail Link in USA) would start up operation on these lines with 25 locomotives and 1,000 cars from CP as part of the undisclosed sale price. CPRC retains a minority equity position.

*Delaware and Hudson Railway*
This northeastern US rail operation was purchased out of bankruptcy proceedings in 1991. Since then, CP has invested more than C$80 million to upgrade the railway. It is now part of the CP-owned St Lawrence & Hudson Railway. In addition to its intermodal business, traffic on the D&H includes fertiliser, clay, grain, food products, machinery, coal and forest products.

*St Lawrence & Hudson Railway*
The St Lawrence & Hudson Railway was formerly CP's Eastern Operating Unit, a Montréal-based management structure responsible for all lines and operations in the Montréal-Toronto-Chicago traffic lane, plus all CP lines in the northeastern USA. It competes in the area historically challenged by topographic constraints on rail operations, a dense highway network and abundant truck competition. In part this new creation was the response to the privatisation of CN and came into effect in December 1995; industry observers see a stand-alone condition in the near future. Presently, the operating unit has two management layers: Operations (to address service reliability and cost-effectiveness of running trains) and Commercial (to focus on customer service, accounts management and traffic growth). CPRC provides the third management area, namely Support Services. The 434 power units that CPRC identifies as property of the St Lawrence & Hudson are maintained at St Luc (Montréal), Toronto and Brighamton, New York.

*E&N Railfreight*
CPRC created a separate business unit, called E&N Railfreight, to serve 275 km of line on Vancouver Island. E&N is a freight-only operator but offers leases to passenger (VIA) or tourist interests.

*Line sales*
CPRC has pressed ahead with its rationalisation plan, filing its first three-year plan in August 1996 and its first update of same in April 1997. The St Lawrence & Hudson also has a three-year plan. By mid-1995 CP had disposed of all routes in the provinces of New Brunswick and Nova Scotia and the USA state of Maine.

In January 1995, CP sold the 670 km Sherbrooke-St John route to three newly established short line operators. The portion between Sherbrooke, Québec, and Brownville Junction, Maine, passed to the Canadian American Railroad Company (qv); the remainder was made into two contiguous railways (Eastern Maine in the US; New Brunswick Southern in Canada) formed by the Irving Group of New Brunswick. Earlier, in 1994, CP had abandoned 381 km of lines in eastern Québec and sold 92 km in Nova Scotia, now operated as the Windsor & Hantsport. During 1996 CP sold a further 384 km in southern Québec and the US state of Vermont to Iron Road Railways (qv in USA).

In November 1996, 615 km were leased to the newly formed Northern Plains Railroad (qv in the USA section). Called 'the Wheat Lines', the many branches fan out across North Dakota. Connection with CP is made at Thief River Falls, Minnesota, at the east end, and Kenmare, North Dakota, at the west end.

In the April 1997 three-year plan, 1,655 km of branch lines in the prairie provinces have been marked for rationalisation. CP anticipates 595 km are prospective short lines and the balance may be abandoned after proceedings are exhausted. In total, 7,000 km (including the St Lawrence & Hudson) were identified as underperforming. Some 3,240 km in 31 segments across Canada, ranging from 5 to 291 km in length, have been advertised for expressions of interest.

### Finance
In 1996, CPRC had a fourth consecutive profitable year before restructuring charges, reporting net operating income of C$405.4 million and an operating ratio (expenses as a percentage of income) of 85.9, a four point improvement over a year earlier. Gross revenues were C$3,772.1 billion, essentially unchanged from 1995.

| **Finances** (C$ million) | 1994 | 1995 | 1996 |
| --- | --- | --- | --- |
| Revenues | 3,665.1 | 3,779.4 | 3,772.1 |
| Expenses | 3,621.8 | 4,540.1 | 3,241.3 |
| **Net income (loss)** | 43.3 | (760.7) | 530.8 |
| Net income from real estate/other | 21.0 | 15.9 | (125.4)* |
| Net income after taxes, from railway | 64.3 | (744.8)‡ | 405.4 |

*Includes interest expense
‡In 1995, a C$1.1 billion restructuring charge was booked

Unaudited figures for 1997 indicated revenue of C$3,718.7 million, up 4.4 per cent on a restated 1996 figure of C$3,559.4 million. Freight revenue in 1997 accounted for C$3,428.7 million, the greatest growth being in grain, which produced a 13.2 per cent increase to C$844.8 million. Operating income was up 32.7 per cent to C$802.1 million. Asset rationalisation, including disposals of uneconomic lines, generated proceeds of C$450 million. Capital expenditure totalled some C$700 million, a new record for CPRC.

*CP grain train near Lake Louise, Alberta*

*Transcontinental double-stack container train leaving Vancouver for Toronto and Montreal* 0001839

## Freight operations
Salient statistics on the scale of freight operations on CPRC in 1997 are: 300 billion gross tonne-km, up 1.3 per cent over 1996; revenue tonne-km at 178.8 billion, up 2.4 per cent; gross tonne-km per employee at 14,892, an improvement of 9.3 per cent.

Overall, traffic rose slightly in 1997 from 1996, with grain and coal, sulphur and fertiliser traffic all showing revenue-tonne-km growth of over 10 per cent.

## Intermodal operations
CPRC offers both domestic and import/export intermodal services, although without a port in the Maritimes (far eastern provinces) following recent line disposals, CPRC appears now to be excluded from a major traffic lane. CPRC has an interline service agreement with Conrail to expedite movements of containers between Montréal/Toronto and the ports of New York and New Jersey. The company operates 24 intermodal terminals in Canada and the USA.

In Vancouver CPRC is building a C$37 million replacement terminal, while a new C$27 million facility is being constructed in Calgary: both were scheduled to open in 1999. In Toronto, the Vaughan terminal is the subject of a C$17.8 million expansion scheme.

### TOFC
To meet fierce competition on the Montreal-Toronto corridor, StL&H has introduced its drive-on/drive-off 'Iron Highway' service, which eliminates the need to lift trailers onto rail vehicles, and operates on a slot reservation system accessible by telephone or the Internet.

### RoadRailer
In addition to trailer and container on flat car (TOFC/COFC) traffic, CP hauls RoadRailer bimodal units. Triple Crown Service Inc, the RoadRailer operating subsidiary of the US railway Norfolk Southern, has extended its network into Canada with a Detroit-Toronto service which is operated by CPRC.

### Triple-stack potatoes
In a joint venture involving Soo Line Railroad, container manufacturer Stoughton Composites, Thermo King and logistics company C H Robinson, the last tested a triple-stack container configuration in 1995. Three stacked 6 ft 4 in boxes (equal to the usual pair of 9 ft 6 in boxes) have been used to transport potatoes from Thief River Falls, Minnesota, to a processing plant at Frankfort, Indiana. The 6 ft 4 in containers are designed to 'weigh out' and 'cube out' simultaneously and avoid what would be dead space in a 9ft 6in container.

## Improvements to existing lines
In recent years, CP has spent in the range of C$600-885 million annually to maintain its roadbed and equipment. The three-year projection for 1997-1999 is C$1.8 billion. Included are C$14.2 million for a new locomotive shop in St Paul; C$50 million for a rebuilt Bensenville (Chicago) Yard; and C$40 million for a new intermodal yard at Pitt Meadows (Vancouver). Among the improvements that have been undertaken recently include C$15 million spent on enlarging 47 tunnels, which has allowed CP to introduce double-stack container services between Vancouver and Chicago and on its principal route across Canada. The last job completed was the 13 km Connaught Tunnel in Rogers Pass, in 1995.

The company spent C$27.5 million to enlarge the Detroit River Tunnel connecting Windsor, Ontario, with Detroit, Michigan (USA). Work has also been undertaken on rehabilitation of the Niagara River Bridge, linking Ontario with the US state of New York. Enlargement work on the Detroit River Tunnel was completed in April 1994, with the first double-stack container train between Montréal and Chicago running on 6 May 1994 via the newly enlarged tunnel. By April 1995 CP recorded a 30 per cent increase in traffic through the tunnel following completion of the project. Another project in 1995 involved the installation of 5 km of double-track east out of Moose Jaw, Saskatchewan, to relieve queueing.

## Traction and rolling stock
At the end of 1996 the CPRC locomotive fleet (that is with Soo Line and St Lawrence & Hudson Railway not included, and after dispositions) comprised 821 diesel locomotives. To alleviate a major motive power shortage in 1995, units were leased from EMD, Helm, Conrail, GATX and rebuilders such as Precision National and National Railway Engineering. The 'loaner' fleet peaked at 240, was reduced to 135 by the first quarter of 1996 and then in early 1997 CP experienced a renewed shortage and leased 140 more units; 60 came from Norfolk Southern and 11 from Montana Rail Link.

Over 600 units (close to 40 per cent) are SD40, SD40-2 and SD40-2F models, delivered between 1970 and 1989 and these are shared by all the CP operating units. CP has retired all its high-horsepower MLW locomotives with the exception of one unit re-engined with a Caterpillar diesel; CP has assigned most of its lower-horsepower MLW units to the St Lawrence & Hudson Railway and this fleet is also in decline due to its age and maintenance costs.

By using a new asset management programme featuring enhanced preventive maintenance and quick response repairs, CP has been able to add 60 locomotives to its available fleet, the equivalent of power for 15-20 trains. CP's capital investment programme for 1995 included major expansion of its Moose Jaw, Saskatchewan, locomotive workshops with the doubling of the number of staff employed there.

### Recent locomotive purchases
Having decided to invest C$200 million in its locomotive fleet in 1994, CPRC ordered 40 AC4400CW diesel-electric locomotives from GE in November 1994, the railway's first units with AC drives. The order was increased to 83 in early 1995, and deliveries continued through the end of 1995 and early 1996. The AC4400CW units are all assigned to Calgary, Alberta, for western coal and other bulk commodity service; three new locomotives are replacing five existing DC drive units.

CP subsequently ordered a further 181 of the AC4400CW class for delivery 1997-98, and 60 SD90/43MACs from EMD to be supplied during 1998.

### Freight wagons
At the beginning of 1996, CPRC's revenue freight wagon fleet exceeded 50,000 owned or leased, 21,000 of which were covered hoppers for the transport of bulk commodities such as grain, potash and fertiliser. Recent orders have concentrated on this type of wagon, which has proved to be in short supply at times of peak grain traffic. In common with other Canadian carriers, CPRC has the potential to acquire a share of the fleet of 10,000 hoppers which have yet to be disposed of by the Canadian government. During 1996, 1,400 covered hopper cars were added at a cost of C$105 million. Also, the last tranche of steel coal cars (397 cars in 1996) were remodelled to increase payload by eight tonnes per car.

**Diesel locomotives before assignment to operating units**

| Class | Power kW | First built | No in service | Builder (Rebuilder) | Engine |
|---|---|---|---|---|---|
| **Road Freight** | | | | | |
| SD40; 40A; 40B | 2,238 | 1966-71 | 112 | EMD-MK | GM16-645E3 |
| SD40M-2 | 2,238 | 1995* | 10 | EMD-MK | GM16-645E3 |
| SD40-2, [2F] | 2,238 | 1972-89 | 589 | EMD [AMF] | GM16-645E3 |
| GP40 | 2,238 | 1966-67 | 28 | EMD | GM16-645E3 |
| SD60 | 2,835 | 1987-89 | 58 | EMD | GM16-710G3 |
| SD60M | 2,835 | 1989 | 5 | EMD | GM16-710G3 |
| SD80MAC | 3,730 | 1998 | 10 | EMD | GM20-710G3 |
| M630 | 2,238 | 1969-70 | 1 | MLW | MLW16-251E |
| M636 | 2,238** | 1970-71 | 4 | MLW | MLW16-251F |
| AC4400CW | 3,283 | 1995 | 83 | GE | GE 16V 7FDL16 |
| AC4400CW | 3,283 | 1997-98 | 91 | GE | GE 16V 7FDL16 |
| **Road Switchers** | | | | | |
| GP9 | 1,305 | 1981-88* | 49 | EMD/CP | GM16-645C |
| GP30; 35 | 1,680 | 1963-66 | 25 | EMD | GM16-645D3 |
| GP30C | 1,492 | 1963 | 3 | EMD | GM16-645D3 |
| GP38 | 1,492 | 1970-71 | 21 | EMD | GM16-645E |
| GP38-2 | 1,492 | 1983-86 | 185 | EMD | GM16-645E3 |
| GP39-2 | 1,715 | 1978 | 2 | EMD | GM16-645 |
| SD39 | 1,715 | 1968 | 2 | EMD | GM16-645 |
| RSD17 | 1,790 | 1959 | 1 | MLW | MLW16-251B |
| RS18R | 1,343 | 1989-90* | 67 | MLW/CP | MLW12-251C |
| RS23 | 746 | 1959-60 | 20 | MLW | MLW6-251B |
| C-424 | 1,790 | 1963-66 | 50 | MLW | MLW16-251B |
| **Yard Switchers** | | | | | |
| SW8 | 596 | 1984* | 2 | EMD/CP | GM8-567B |
| SW9 | 671 | 1982-83* | 12 | EMD/CP | GM8-567B |
| SW900 | 671 | 1984-85* | 3 | EMD/CP | GM8-567C |
| SW1200RS | 895 | 1981-85* | 90 | EMD/CP | GM12-567B, C |
| SW1500 | 1,120 | 1966 | 2 | EMD | GM12-645E |
| GP7 | 1,120 | 1987-88* | 24 | EMD/CP | GM16-645B, C |
| GP9 | 1,305 | 1980-87* | 184 | EMD/CP | GM16-645C |
| GP9M | 1,305 | 1954 | 5 | EMD | GM16-645C |
| GP15C | 1,120 | 1990-91 | 7 | EMD | CAT3512 |
| MP15AC | 1,120 | 1975-76 | 32 | EMD | GM12-645E |
| SD10 | 1,343 | 1952-54 | 3 | EMD | GM16-567C, E |
| F7B | 1,120 | 1983* | 1 | EMD | GM16-567B |
| Slugs | n/a | | 7 | EMD | n/a |

*Date of rebuild
**1 rated at 2,312 kW (Caterpillar 3,608 engine)

# RAILWAY SYSTEMS/Canada

## Cando Contracting Ltd

830 Douglas Street, Brandon, Manitoba R7A 7B2
Tel: (+1 204) 725 26 27   Fax: (+1 204) 725 41 00
e-mail: info@candoltd.com
Web: http://www.candoltd.com

### Key personnel
President: Gordon Peters
Controller: Colleen MacCarl
Asset Manager: Doug Phillips
Sales Manager: Brent Montague
Abandonment Manager: Alex Burr
Installation Manager: Jerry Lovas

*Alberta office*
35D Rayborn Crescent, St Albert, Alberta T8N 5B6
Tel: (+1 780) 418 23 53   Fax: (+1 780) 418 23 65
e-mail: don.barr@candoltd.com
General Manager: Don Barr

*Ontario office*
160 Edward Street, St Thomas, Ontario N5P 1Z3
Tel: (+1 519) 637 87 56   Fax: (+1 519) 637 13 62
e-mail: doug.peters@candoltd.com
General Manager: Doug Peters

Cando operates four shortlines totalling some 560 km in Canada:

Athabasca Northern Railway Ltd (323 km), established in October 2000 to operate the former CN line between Boyle and Linton, Alberta, with three locomotives;

Barrie/Collingwood Railway (101 km), municipally owned by the Ontario communities it serves and operated by Cando since January 1998;

Central Manitoba Railway Inc (81 km), former CN lines in Manitoba linking Winnipeg–Pine Falls and Winnipeg–Graysville, operated with a fleet of four locomotives;

Orangeville Brampton Railway (55 km), municipally owned via the Orangeville Railway Development Corporation and operated by Cando with a twice-weekly service.

In addition, Cando provides rail switching and freight handling services for industrial concerns.

*NEW ENTRY*

## Cape Breton & Central Nova Scotia Railway

121 King Street, PO Box 2240, Stellarton, Nova Scotia B0K 1S0
Tel: (+1 902) 752 33 57   Fax: (+1 902) 752 66 65
Web: http://www.railamerica.com

### Key personnel
General Manager: Peter Touesnard

Gauge: 1,435 mm
Route length: 394 km

### Organisation
The Cape Breton & Central Nova Scotia Railway (CBNS) was acquired by RailTex in October 1993. When RailTex was taken over by RailAmerica, the railway became part of that company's North American Rail Group in February 2000. It operates 394 km of ex-Canadian National trackage east from its CN connection at Truro, across Nova Scotia to Sydney, where there is a steel works.

### Freight operations
Carloadings in 2001 were approximately 26,000. Principal commodities carried are scrap iron, limestone, forest products and grain.

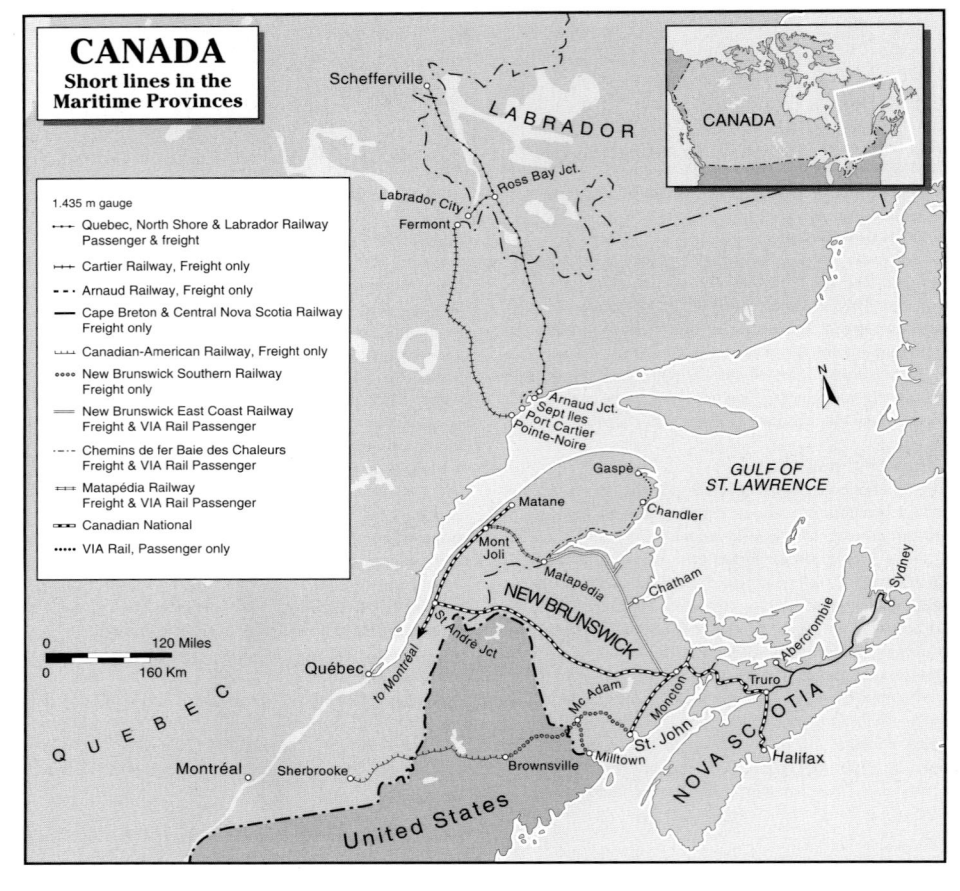

## Cartier Railway

Cie Minière Québec Cartier
Port Cartier, Duplessis County, Québec G5B 2H3
Tel: (+1 418) 766 23 21   Fax: (+1 418) 768 24 28
Web: http://www.qcmines.com

### Key personnel
President and Chief Executive Officer: Guy Dufresne
Vice-Presidents
  Operations Technology: Gaston Morin
  Operations Management: François Pelletier
  Finance: J Roy
General Manager, Railway: Serge A Michaud
Divisional Manager, Mechanical Maintenance:
  Gérard Sirois

Gauge: 1,435 mm
Route length: 416 km

### Organisation
Cartier Railway is a wholly owned subsidiary of Québec Cartier Mining.

### Freight operations
The 307 km railroad built to convey iron ore concentrate from Lac Jeannine (mine and concentrator site) to Port Cartier (harbour site) was completed in 1960. In 1972 a 138 km extension was built to Mont Wright where a second concentrator was built for another iron ore mine.

In 1975-76 a 4.8 km bypass was constructed to transport crude ore from Fire Lake (which was opened to compensate for the closing of the Lac Jeannine mine). However, Fire Lake mining ended in 1985 and today only Mont Wright workings are exploited.

The ore is hauled in unit trains of 156 wagons operated with three 3,600 hp locomotives on the head end, a two-person crew and no caboose. The railroad normally operates five such trains daily throughout the year to match the concentrator production.

Train size best matches the cycle time of the fixed installations, which provide continuous loading and discharge at the port, the latter by a double-car Strachan & Henshaw rotary dumper which works at the rate of 3,800 tonnes per hour. In recent years the annual volume of ore transported and dumped has been 14 to 15 million tonnes.

### Traction and rolling stock
The fleet consists of 32 diesel-electric line-haul locomotives (including 24 MLW 3,600 hp units of model C636/M636) and 985 ore wagons and 380 miscellaneous vehicles.

### Signalling and telecommunications
Computerised control has been superimposed on the Centralised Traffic Control (CTC) system, which is supplemented by centrally controlled hot box detectors and switch-point heaters. Radio communication with crews is employed for dispatch of train orders.

### Track
Main line track is entirely cwr, employing 132 lb rail until 1988, but since then 136 lb has been adopted as the standard weight.
**Rail:** Standard carbon in tangents, low alloy in curves
**Crossties (sleepers)**
**Type:** Hardwood 2,590 × 228 × 177 mm
**Spacing:** 1,851/km
**Fastenings:** Cut spikes
**Min curvature radius:** 250 m
**Max gradient:** 1.35% against empty trains; 0.4% compensated against loaded trains
**Max axleload:** 31 tonnes
**Type of braking:** Wabco 26L
**Type of coupler:** CF70HT

### Diesel locomotives

| Class | Wheel arrangement | Power kW | Speed km/h | Weight tonnes | First built | Builders Mechanical | Engine | Transmission |
|---|---|---|---|---|---|---|---|---|
| C630 | Co-Co | 2,238 | 104.6 | 192 | 1966 | Alco | Alco 251-EV-16*E* | Alco |
| M636 | Co-Co | 2,685 | 104.6 | 183 | 1970-73 | MLW | Alco 251-FV-16*E* | MLW |
| C636 | Co-Co | 2,685 | 104.6 | 192 | 1968 | Alco | Alco 251 V-16 *E* | Alco |
| RS18 | Bo-Bo | 1,343 | 104.6 | 110 | 1959 | MLW | Alco 251-IV | *E* GE |

*UPDATED*

Canada/**RAILWAY SYSTEMS** 87

## Central Western Railway

5220 51 Avenue, PO Box 1030, Stettler, Alberta T0C 1L0
Tel: (+1 403) 742 25 03   Fax: (+1 403) 742 14 77
Web: http://www.railamerica.com

**Key personnel**
General Manager: Vern Hein
Business Development Manager: John Yorke

Gauge: 1,435 mm
Route length: 166 km

**Organisation**
A subsidiary of RailAmerica, the CWR comprises former CN and CP lines in southern Alberta between Stettler and Consort and Morrin and Munson. Approximately 2,800 carloads are handled each year, with grain the main commodity carried.

*NEW ENTRY*

## E&N Railway Company (1998) Ltd

PO Box 581, 23 Esplanade, Nanaimo, British Columbia V9R 5L3
Tel: (+1 250) 754 92 22   Fax: (+1 250) 754 53 18
Web: http://www.railamerica.com

**Key personnel**
General Manager: Anne Venema

Gauge: 1,435 mm
Route length: 291 km

**Organisation**
Operated by RailAmerica, the ENR serves Vancouver Island, linking Victoria in the south with Courtenay via a line running along the island's east coast. The railway handles approximately 8,500 carloads annually, mostly of forest and paper products, minerals and chemicals. Interchange is made with CP via a Wellcox–Vancouver train ferry.

*NEW ENTRY*

## Essex Terminal Railway Company

1601 Lincoln Road, PO Box 24025, Windsor, Ontario N8Y 4Y9
Tel: (+1 519) 973 82 22   Fax: (+1 519) 973 72 34
e-mail: bmckeown@etr.ca
Web: http://www.etr.ca

**Key personnel**
President: Brian G McKeown
Vice-President: Terry J Berthiaume
Controller: Teresa Boutet

Operations Superintendent: Edward G Clough
Road Master: Bill Comboye
Car Foreman: Robert Bulmer
Locomotive Foreman: Robert Woods

Gauge: 1,435 mm
Route length: 35 km

**Organisation**
The ETR provides industrial switching services between the east side of Windsor and Amhertsburg, Ontario, and is strategically located close to one of the key border crossings into the USA. Commodities carried include forest products, agricultural and chemical products, machinery, steel, grain, salt and scrap. Interchange is made with CN, CP, CSXT and NS.

**Traction and rolling stock**
The ETR operates five diesel-electric switching locomotives.

*NEW ENTRY*

## Genesee-Rail-One

6650 rue Durocher, Building 1, Outremon, Quebec H2V 3Z3
Tel: (+1 514) 273 57 39   Fax: (+1 514) 273 99 38
Web: http://www.gwrr.com

**Key personnel**
President: Mario Brault
General Manager, HCR: Garth Rushton
Manager, Marketing, HCR/QGR: Bill Sclater

**Organisation**
A subsidiary of Genesee & Wyoming Inc (qv in USA section), Genesee-Rail-One operates two former Canadian Pacific Rail lines in eastern Canada: the Huron Central Railway (HCR) resulted from the acquisition from CP Rail in July 1997 of the line between Sudbury and Sault Ste Marie, in northern Ontario; the Québec–Gatineau Railway (QGR) began operating in November 1997 and links Quebec, Montreal, Gatineau and Hull, Quebec. The QGR handles some 49,000 carloads annually.

**Traction and rolling stock**
In 2002, the HCR was operating 13 locomotives, all of General Motors design and comprising GP9, SD45 and GP40 types. The QGR fleet totalled 23, a mix of General Motors GP35, GP38, GP40, SD45 and SW1500 types.

*NEW ENTRY*

## Goderich-Exeter Railway

126 Weber Street West, Building #2, Kitchener, Ontario N2H 3Z9
Tel: (+1 519) 749 80 00   Fax: (+1 519) 749 80 88
Web: http://www.railamerica.com

**Key personnel**
General Manager: Ken Monture
Business Development Manager: Cheryl Grigg

Gauge: 1,435 mm
Route length: 256 km

**Organisation**
Based on the former CN Goderich and Exeter subdivisions, the GEXR was initially acquired by RailTex, and was that company's first acquisition outside the USA. RailAmerica took over operations in February 2000 following its acquisition of the interests of RailTex.

The railway links Goderich with Silver, with branches to Centralia and London. Interchange with CN is made at London and McMillan Yard, Toronto, and with CP at Kitchener and Guelph. Approximately 19,000 carloads annually are handled. Principal commodities carried are limestone, food and farm products, plastics, forest products and automotive components.

## GO Transit

20 Bay Street, Suite 600, Toronto, Ontario M5J 2W3
Tel: (+1 416) 869 36 00   Fax: (+1 416) 869 35 25
Web: http://www.gotransit.com

**Key personnel**
Chairman: Eldred R King
Managing Director: Gary W McNeil
Administration Director: Jean M Norman
Finance and Marketing Director: Frances Chung

Gauge: 1,435 mm
Route length: 361 km

**Political background**
GO Transit, set up in 1967, was Canada's first inter-regional transport system created and funded by a provincial government. GO Transit is now under the general direction and control of a new Greater Toronto Services Board (GTSB) in the municipal sector. Funding responsibility was transferred to the municipalities in January 1998. The GTSB came into being in January 1999, and GO Transit transferred to the municipal sector in August 1999, ending over 30 years of direct affiliation with the provincial government.

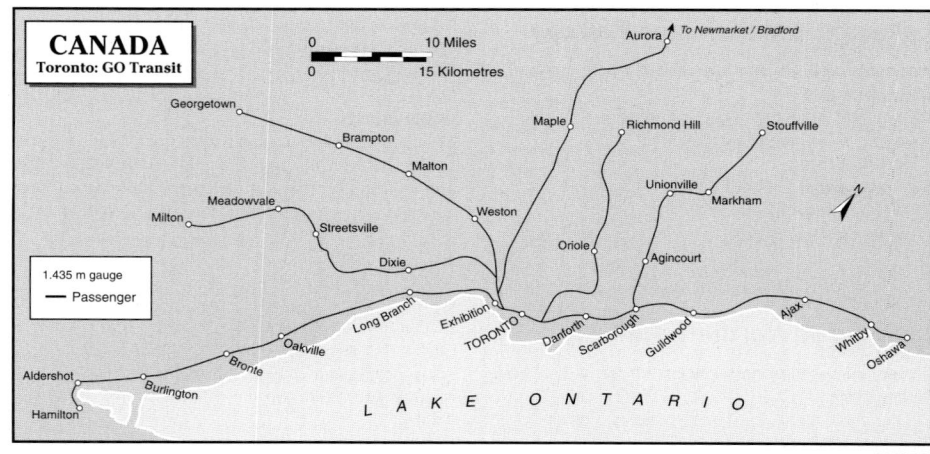

GO (originally an abbreviation of Government of Ontario) Transit serves a territory of over 8,000 km$^2$ with a population of 4.9 million, which continues to increase. It runs an integrated bus and rail passenger network with a total annual ridership of more than 38 million.

**Finance**
In 1999 rail passenger journeys rose (including related bus services) rose to 31.06 million. Operating cost recovery rose to 92.4 per cent.

## RAILWAY SYSTEMS/Canada

### Passenger operations

Starting with a single rail route along Lake Ontario, GO now operates seven lines (taking into account that the Lakeshore line has been split into East and West lines), with Toronto's Union station as the system's hub. In addition to 153 trains run daily, in July 2000 GO Transit operated 1,160 bus trips.

Train services are run under contract over Canadian National tracks (in six corridors) and St Lawrence & Hudson Railway — Canadian Pacific's eastern operating division (one corridor) — by CN and StL&H crews to GO Transit specification, but GO Transit owns the infrastructure of the Lakeshore East line between Pickering and Whitby.

In July 2000, GO Transit took ownership of the platforms at Toronto's Union Station. A CAN$100 million 10-year investment programme is planned to increase capacity and improve facilities at the terminal.

### Traction and rolling stock

GO Transit operates a standardised fleet consisting of 45 F59PH diesel-electrics from GM-Canada (jointly designed by GM and GO Transit) and a 319-strong passenger coach fleet exclusively composed of double-deck vehicles, built by UTDC (now Bombardier). Bombardier also holds a contract to maintain GO's rolling stock.

In May 2000 GO Transit placed an order with Bombardier for an additional 16 double-deck coaches for delivery by July 2002.

**Coupler in standard use (passenger cars):** H-tightlock
**Braking in standard use (locomotive-hauled stock):** 26L, 26LUM and 26C

*GO Transit service at North Bathurst (Marcel Vleugels)*

## Greater Vancouver Transportation Authority (GVTA) – Translink

West Coast Express
Suite 295, 601 West Cordova Street, Vancouver, British Columbia V6C 1B4
Tel: (+1 604) 689 36 41   Fax: (+1 604) 689 38 96

### Key personnel
President and Chief Executive Officer: Doug Kelsey

### Passenger operations
In May 1994 BC Transit, the responsibilities of which were taken over by GVTA in April 1999, entered into an agreement with CP Rail to undertake development work for the introduction of a commuter rail service serving Vancouver. Marketed as West Coast Express (WCE), services began on 1 November 1995 over a 65 km CP route which is now all double-track and equipped with CTC (centralised traffic control) between Mission and central Vancouver. Journey time (with six intermediate stops) is 73 minutes, comparing favourably with two hours by bus. WCE research indicates that 75 per cent of riders were previously motorists. The service contract was awarded to CP Rail and the maintenance contract to VIA Rail.

Service frequency is five trains in the direction of peak flow only. Opening daily ridership was 5,000. WCE carried its five millionth passenger in January 1999, by which time it was operating near maximum capacity. In the first quarter of 2000, daily ridership was over 7,800, a 56 per cent increase since its opening. New rolling stock arriving in late 2000 was expected to ease capacity constraints.

All fare/ticket types have provision for passengers to transfer to other transit modes (bus; Sea Bus; SkyTrain); 60 per cent of train riders make a transfer. WCE issues a smartcard usable for any ticket purchase.

### Traction and rolling stock
WCE is operating with five 2,200 kW GM model F59PHI locomotives in push-pull mode with 31 bilevel cars, three of which have been leased from Tri-Rail in Florida. In late 2000, WCE was due to add nine new bilevel cars to its fleet and return the three Tri-Rail cars, to leave a net total of 37 vehicles. In 1998 a global positioning satellite (GPS) system was installed to monitor adherence to schedules and train location.

## Huron Central Railway

See entry for Genesee-Rail-One

*NEW ENTRY*

## Lakeland & Waterways Railway

Suite 165 Weber Center, 5555 Calgary Trail, Edmonton, Alberta T6H 5P9
Tel: (+1 780) 448 58 55   Fax: (+1 780) 439 56 58
Web: http://www.railamerica.com

### Key personnel
General Manager: Tim Husel
Business Development Manager: Angela Bourbonnais

Gauge: 1,435 mm
Route length: 164 km

### Organisation
Operated by RailAmerica, the LWR comprises a network of four shortlines running north and east from Edmonton. The railway handles approximately 10,500 carloads annually, commodities carried including petroleum coke, grain, forest products and petroleum products. Interchange is made with CN at Edmonton and with the ANY at Boyle.

*NEW ENTRY*

## Mackenzie Northern Railway

Roma Junction Yard Office, PO Box 7648, Peace River, Alberta T8S 1T2
Tel: (+1 780) 332 64 00   Fax: (+1 780) 332 29 04
Web: http://www.railamerica.com

### Key personnel
General Manager: Clayton Jones
Business Development Manager: John Yorke

Gauge: 1,435 mm
Route length: 1,046 km

### Organisation
Operated by RailAmerica since July 1999, the MNR is a former CN line which runs north from Smith, Alberta, to Hay River, Northwest Territories. The railway handles approximately 26,500 carloads annually, mainly of fuel, grain pulp, forest products and chemicals. Interchange with CN is made at Smith.

*NEW ENTRY*

## New Brunswick Southern

New Brunswick Southern Railway Co Ltd
11 Gifford Road, PO Box 5666, Saint John, New Brunswick E2L 5B6
Tel: (+1 506) 632 47 12   Fax: (+1 506) 632 58 18
Web: http://www.nbsouthern.com

### Key personnel
General Manager: B L Bourgeois

Gauge: 1,435 mm
Route length: 190.5 km

### Organisation
As part of the January 1995 disposal of the Canadian Atlantic Railroad by Canadian National, 190.5 km located in New Brunswick were acquired by the J D Irving Company and are now operated as the NBSR using six GP9 units overhauled either by OmniTrax (qv in the USA section) or by AMF Technotransport. The property consists of a 136 km line from the border at McAdam to Saint John, plus a 55 km branch from McAdam to Saint Stephen. The line continues as the Eastern Maine Railroad (also owned by Irving but served by the Candian American Railway (qv) for 168 km into the US from McAdam to Brownville Junction, where it connects with the Bangor and Aroostook Railway.

NB Southern Railway and road operator Sunbury Transport collaborate with CP Rail and Canadian American Railroad to provide intermodal services.

*UPDATED*

## Ontario Midwestern Railway Company

### Organisation
This company was formed in the first half of 1997 to buy or lease 175 km of CP track within Ontario, from Mississauga to Owen Sound.

## Ontario Northland

555 Oak Street E, North Bay, Ontario P1B 8L3
Tel: (+1 705) 472 45 00   Fax: (+1 705) 476 55 98
e-mail: info@ontc.on.ca
Web: http://www.ontc.on.ca

### Key personnel
President and Chief Executive Officer (of the ONTC):
   K J Wallace
Vice-Presidents
   Finance and Administration: S G Carmichael
   Telecommunications: R S Hutton
   Transportation Services: R G Leach
Superintendent, Train Operations: J Thib

Gauge: 1,435 mm
Route length: 1,211 km

### Organisation
Ontario Northland is a component of the multimodal Ontario Northland Transport Commission's operations. The system lies at the eastern rim of the province. It runs from North Bay, where it connects with Canadian National and CPRC routes westward from Ottawa, to Moosonee on James Bay, the southward-probing neck of Hudson Bay.

Trading as Rail Contract Shop, Ontario Northland's repair and maintenance facility at North Bay offers its services to industrial customers in North America.

In addition to rail services, ONTC offers bus services, ferry services on the Great Lakes, and telecommunications. It left the air passenger business in March 1996.

In 1991 agreement was reached for the transfer to Ontario Northland of 240 km of CN line between Cochrane and Calstock. This section connects with Ontario Northland at Cochrane. The Ontario Northland main line has four additional short branches.

### Diesel locomotives

| Class | Wheel arrangement | Power kW | Speed km/h | Weight tonnes | No in service | First built | Mechanical | Builders Engine | Transmission |
|---|---|---|---|---|---|---|---|---|---|
| SD40-2 | C-C | 2,237.1 | 104.6 | 170.7 | 8 | 1973 | GM | 645E3 | E GM Main Gen |
| GP38-2 | B-B | 1,492.5 | 104.6 | 115.67 | 10 | 1974 | GM | 645E | E GM Main Gen |
| FP7A | B-B | 1,529 | 113.0 | 117.11 | 3 | 1994* | GM | Cat 3516 | E GM Main Gen |
| GP-9 | B-B | 1,304.97 | 104.6 | 117.34 | 6 | 1956 | GM | 567C | E GM Main Gen |

* Repowered

### Passenger operations
Ontario Northland runs the Northlander passenger service from Cochrane to Toronto Union station daily except Saturdays, travelling over 367 km of CN track between Toronto and North Bay. North of Cochrane, to Moosonee, a mixed train, the Little Bear, runs three times a week September-June and twice-weekly in July and August when it is augmented by a tourist train, the Polar Bear Express.

In February 1999, ON's seasonal 'Snow Train' service commenced operations, carrying passengers and their snowmobiles between Toronto and Cochrane.

### Freight operations
Freight, chiefly lumber, pulp, newsprint, chemicals, petroleum products and ores, is the backbone of Ontario Northland's business. Express freight services are provided between Cochrane and Moosonee.

### Traction and rolling stock
The railway rosters 30 line-haul and six switching diesel-electric locomotives, 46 passenger coaches and 810 freight wagons. The passenger fleet includes 26 single-level commuter coaches acquired from GO Transit (the last six were purchased in 1994) and comprehensively renovated as first-class long-haul coaches in Ontario Northland workshops.

Three FP7A locomotives have been rebuilt with Caterpillar 3516 engines rated at 1,529 kW. Seven diesel locomotives without cabs have been acquired for conversion to provide head-end power for ON's refurbished passenger coaches.

### Signalling and telecommunications
Ontario Northland employs radio despatching.

### Track
**Rail:** 125.77 kg/m
**Crossties (sleepers)**
**Wood:** Thickness: 180 mm
Spacing: 1,886/km
**Fastenings:** 4 spikes per sleeper on tangent, 8 spikes per sleeper on curves
**Min curvature radius:** 300 m
**Max gradient:** 1.5%
**Max axleload:** 29.5 tonnes (65,000 lb)

*UPDATED*

## O-Train

OC Transpo
Ottawa-Carleton Regional Transit Commission
1500 St Laurent Boulevard, Ottawa, Ontario K1G 0Z8
Tel: (+1 613) 741 64 40   Fax: (+1 613) 741 73 59
Web: http://www.octranspo.com

### Organisation
Established in 1972, OC Transpo has exclusive rights to operate within the area of the 741,000 population Regional Municipality of Ottawa-Carleton, operating extensive bus services in the region.

### Passenger operations
In October 2001, OC Transpo commissioned its O-Train service, running at a 20 min frequency between Bayview and Greenboro (8 km). Serving five stations, at which services are closely integrated with bus operations, the system uses European-style lightweight diesel railcars running over an existing CP freight line. A park and ride facility is provided at Greenboro. The project is viewed as a pilot for a possible larger future network.

### New lines
Possible future extensions under study in 2002 include a route across the Prince of Wales river bridge from Bayview to Place du Portage in Hull, a line from Greenboro to Ottawa International Airport and a link to Ottawa's downtown district.

### Traction and rolling stock
For the Bayview–Greenboro line, OC Transpo acquired three three-car Talent lightweight diesel railcars built in Germany by Bombardier Transportation. Bombardier also undertakes maintenance.

*NEW ENTRY*

## Ottawa Valley Railway

445 Oak Street East, North Bay, Ontario P1B 1A3
Tel: (+1 705) 472 62 00   Fax: (+1 705) 472 25 27
Web: http://www.railamerica.com

### Key personnel
General Manager: Grant Bailey
Business Development Manager: Colleen Fenton

Gauge: 1,435 mm
Route length: 626 km

### Organisation
Operated by RailAmerica, the OVR provides services over CN lines between Smiths Falls and Coniston, Ontario, and on a branch from Mattawa, Ontario, to Temiscaming, Quebec. The railway handles approximately 56,700 carloads annually. Principal commodities carried are chemicals, ores, metal products and wood pulp. Express intermodal services are also operated. Interchange is made with CP at Cartier, Smiths Falls and Sudbury, with Ontario Northland at North Bay and with CN at Pembroke and North Bay.

*NEW ENTRY*

## Québec–Gatineau Railway

See entry for Genesee-Rail-One

*NEW ENTRY*

## Québec North Shore & Labrador Railway

Québec North Shore & Labrador Railway Co
100 rue Retty, Sept-Iles, Québec G4R 3E1
Tel: (+1 418) 968 74 95    Fax: (+1 418) 968 74 98

**Key personnel**
President and Chief Executive Officer: M D Walker
General Manager: Marc Duclos
Manager, Materials and Services: John Turnbull
Superintendents
    Transport and Traffic: Michel Lamontagne
    Equipment Maintenance: Gilbert Sarazin
    Maintenance of Way, Signals and Communications:
        Louis Gravel

Gauge: 1,435 mm
Route length: 639 km

**Organisation**
Begun in 1950 by its then newly formed owners, the Iron Ore Company of Canada (IOCC), with the shareholding support of several US steelmakers, the 573 km main line of the Québec North Shore & Labrador (QNS&L) runs from Schefferville south to Sept-Iles on the St Lawrence River. Schefferville, the railhead for the Ungava ore tract in the Labrador peninsula, is just inside the Québec border, but otherwise the northern half of the route is enclosed by Newfoundland. Within this section a 58 km branch was run from Ross Bay westward to Labrador City in 1960.

**Passenger operations**
Using ex-VIA Rail Budd RDC diesel railcars, QNSL operates passenger services weekly from Sept-Iles to Schefferville and twice-weekly from Sept-Iles to Labrador City. Additional services are operated according to demand during summer months. Car-carrier wagons are attached on most services to convey passengers' cars to locations lacking road access.

**Freight operations**
IOCC stopped mining in the Schefferville area in 1982, but still serves the railhead as there are no roads north of Sept-Iles. Mining is now concentrated in the Carol Lake area, at the extremity of the Labrador City branch.

Despite the savage winters in the region, QNS&L functions all year round. In winter, however, it only moves processed (beneficiated) ore in pellets, because of raw ore's propensity to freeze.

QNS&L runs loaded ore trains varying in length from 117 to 265 wagons; the latter trail about 3.3 km behind their lead locomotives and gross over 33,700 short tons, but a 117-wagon train weighs at least 14,000 short tons. Normal power is two 2,200 kW GM-EMD SD40 locomotives at the front end, but when a train is made up to 165 wagons or more, mid-train helper units, radio-controlled by the Locotrol system from the lead locomotive, are added. Twenty-two of the type SD40-2 units were Locotrol-equipped by AMF Technotransport in 1994 and redesignated SD40-2CLCs. In 1997, IOCC announced a C$14 million contract with GE/Harris Railway Electronics for a train control system aimed at enhancing performance of a train powered by multiple locomotives.

**Traction and rolling stock**
Resources consist of 55 diesel-electric locomotives, 2,400 freight wagons, 11 passenger coaches and six Budd RDC diesel railcars bought used from VIA in 1994. In 1994 the QNS&L acquired its first GE locomotives, three Dash 8-40C units bought new. In 1998, the railway ordered 11 General Electric C44-9W locomotives.

**Signalling and telecommunications**
Centralised Traffic Control (CTC) is in operation on 416 km of QNS&L's 573 km main line. The railway is controlled from Sept-Iles.

**Track**
**Rail:** 65.5 kg/m
**Crossties (sleepers)**
**Treated hardwood:** 177.8 × 228.6 × 2,743.2 mm
**Spacing:** 2,080/km
**Fastenings:** Standard track, 165 mm (5½ in)
**Min curvature radius:** 220 m
**Max gradient:** 1.32%
**Max axleload:** 32.5 tonnes

### Diesel locomotives

| Class | Wheel arrangement | Power kW | Speed km/h | Weight tonnes | No in service | First built | Mechanical | Builders Engine | Transmission |
|---|---|---|---|---|---|---|---|---|---|
| SD40/40-2 | C-C | 2,238 | 114 | 174 | 48 | 1968 | GM | GM | E GM |
| GP-9 | B-B | 1,305 | 114 | 109 | 4 | 1954 | GM | GM | E GM |

## Québec Railway Corporation

1130 Sherbrooke Street West, Suite 310, Montréal, Québec, H3A 2M8
Tel: (+1 514) 982 99 44    Fax: (+1 514) 849 23 19
Web: http://www.domino-hq01.cn.ca

**Key personnel**
President: Serge Belzile
Vice President, Operations: Gilles Richard
Vice President, Finance: Alain Tessier

Gauge: 1,435 mm
Route length: 1,064 km

**Freight operations**
Through acquisitions from CN, QRC has established a network of lines on the north and south shores of the St Lawrence River in eastern Québec and New Brunswick. Wagons are transferred between the two shores and into the North American rail network via the Cogéma train ferry.

The QRC bought 144 km of line linking Limoilou and Clermont from CN in 1994. It is operated as the Chemin de Fer Charlevoix Inc.

In December 1996, the company bought CN's line between Matapédia and Chandler (235 km) which it operates as the Chemin de Fer Baie des Chaleurs.

In December 1997, QRC acquired from CN the 168 km Matapedia Railway, linking Mont-Joli, Quebec and Campbellton, New Brunswick. In March 1999, it acquired from CN the Rivière-du-Loup—Mont-Joli and Mont-Joli—Matane lines (360 km). Together these are operated as the Matapedia and Gulf Railway (CFMG). At Matapedia, connection is made with the Chemin de Fer Baie des Chaleurs. VIA Rail uses the Rivière-du-Loup line at Campbellton for its Maritime service.

In October 1998, QRC purchased the 157 km Pembroke, Ontario-Coteau, Québec line and gained operating rights over VIA Rail trackage between Coteau and Ottawa. It operates this line as the Ottawa Central Railway.

*UPDATED*

## RailAmerica, Inc

RailAmerica operates several regional railroads and shortlines in Canada. See entry in United States of America section

*NEW ENTRY*

## RaiLink Ltd

In 1999 RaiLink was purchased by RailAmerica Inc (qv in USA section) for C$73.2 million.

## RailTex Canada Inc

This company was a wholly owned subsidiary of RailTex Inc, which was acquired in February 2000 by RailAmerica Inc (qv in the USA section).

Canada/**RAILWAY SYSTEMS** 91

## Rocky Mountaineer Railtours

1150 Station Street, 1st Floor, Vancouver, British Columbia V6A 2X7
Tel: (+1 604) 606 72 45   Fax: (+1 604) 606 72 50
Web: http://www.rockymountaineer.com

**Key personnel**
President and Chief Executive Officer: Peter Armstrong
Executive Vice President and Chief Operating Officer: James E Terry
Executive Vice President, Finance and Corporate Development: Glenn Munro

**Passenger operations**
Rocky Mountain Railtours commenced operations in 1990 as the Great Canadian Railtour Company, following the privatisation of VIA Rail's daylight service through the Canadian Rockies, initiated in 1988. The company operates a range of Rocky Mountaineer tourist passenger services over CN and CP lines, offering a total of 148 departures in 2000. Services are provided in both directions between Vancouver, British Columbia and Jasper, Banff and Calgary, Alberta, running from mid-April to mid-October, as well as in December.

**Traction and rolling stock**
Rocky Mountain Railtours operates five General Motors GP40-2 locomotives. Rolling stock includes eight GoldLeaf Service bilevel dome cars built by Colorado Railcar. The company's operations and maintenance facility is located at Kamloops, British Columbia.

*NEW ENTRY*

## Southern Ontario Railway

PO Box 593, Hamilton, Ontario L8N 3P9
Tel: (+1 905) 777 12 34   Fax: (+1 905) 777 01 85
Web: http://www.railamerica.com

**Key personnel**
General Manager: Stuart Thomas
Business Development Manager: Colleen Fenton

Gauge: 1,435 mm
Route length: 87 km

**Organisation**
Operated by RailAmerica, the SOR provides freight services over CN lines linking Nanticoke, Caledonia, and Brantford, Ontario. The railway handles approximately 45,000 carloads annually, mainly of fuel, grain and steel. Interchange with CN is made at Brantford and Hamilton, Ontario.

*NEW ENTRY*

## Southern Railway of British Columbia

Southern Railway of British Columbia Ltd
2102 River Drive, New Westminster, British Columbia V3M 6S3
Tel: (+1 604) 521 19 66   Fax: (+1 604) 526 09 14
e-mail: kdoiron@sryraillink.com
Web: http://www.sryraillink.com

**Key personnel**
President: John F Van Der Burch
Vice President, Marketing and Sales: Ken W Doiron
Chief Mechanical Officer: Don Irwin
Manager Maintenance of Way: Bob Ewanchuck
Controller: Paul Tompkins

Gauge: 1,435 mm
Route length: 200 km

**Organisation**
Formerly the property of the British Columbia Hydro & Power Authority, the Southern Railway of British Columbia (SRY) assumed its current name in September 1988 when it was sold to the Itel Rail Corporation. In October 1994 it was acquired by an Alberta company controlled by Washington Companies, a natural resources and transport conglomerate that owns the US I&M Rail Link and Montana Rail Link systems (qv).

SRY's main line connects Vancouver (New Westminster) and Chilliwack, a distance of 130 km. There are several branches, including one to the industrial centre of Annacis Island. More than half of SRY's current 53,500 annual wagonloads of traffic is made up of cars imported through Annacis. Interchange is made with CN, CP, the Burlington Northern, Santa Fe, Union Pacific and BC Rail.

**Traction and rolling stock**
SRY has 23 locomotives, which are mostly switchers and over 1,100 freight wagons.

SRY also undertakes rolling stock engineering projects for other customers.

*UPDATED*

## St Lawrence & Atlantic Railroad (Quebec) Inc

Chemin de Fer St-Laurent Atlantique (Quebec) Inc
415 Rodman Road, Auburn, Maine 04210, USA
Tel: (+1 207) 782 56 80   Fax: (+1 207) 782 58 57
Web: http://www.gwrr.com

Gauge: 1,435 mm
Route length: (with SLR) 416 km

**Organisation**
Together with the St Lawrence & Atlantic Railroad Company (SLR) in Maine, the St Lawrence & Atlantic Railroad (Quebec) Inc (SLQ) forms a contiguous 416 km route linking Ste Rosalie, Quebec and Portland, Maine, crossing the border at Norton, Vermont. The two companies formed part of the US-based Emons Transportation Group, which in February 2002 was acquired by Genesse & Wyoming Inc (qv in the USA section). SLQ connects directly with the CN system and indirectly with CP Rail via the Iron Road System.

Intermodal services are offered via a subsidiary company, Maine Intermodal Transportation. Together, SLQ and SLR claim to have the only route in Northern New England cleared for hi-cube, double-stack intermodal operations.

*NEW ENTRY*

## Toronto Terminals Railway Company Ltd

Suite 402, Union Station, Toronto, Ontario M5J 1E6
Tel: (+1 416) 864 34 40   Fax: (+1 416) 864 34 87
Web: http://www.ttrly.com

**Key personnel**
Director of Operations: Sam Spares
Supervisor, Rail Operations: Joe Fenech
Manager, Real Estate: Pio Mammone

**Organisation**
A wholly owned subsidiary of Canadian National and Canadian Pacific, TTR operates Toronto's municipally owned Union Station under a management contract with the city. The company's operations cover all tracks within a 5.8 km section in the vicinity of the station, handling some 40 intercity and 152 GO Transit commuter trains daily. Associated operations and through freight services result in some 350 train movements daily.

In 1983, a 600 m dive-under was constructed to reduce conflicting movements by freight services.

In February 2000, TTR announced that by 2003 it intended to transfer its lines and operating interest by sale, lease or transfer.

*NEW ENTRY*

## VIA Rail Canada

VIA Rail Canada Inc
PO Box 8116, Station A, Montréal, Québec H3B 2C9
Tel: (+1 514) 871 60 00   Fax: (+1 514) 871 62 27
Web: http://www.viarail.ca

**Key personnel**
Chairman: Jean Pelletier
President and Chief Executive Officer: Marc LeFrançois
Chief Strategy Officer: Christena Keon Sirsly
Chief Operating Officer: Paul Côté
Chief Financial Officer: J Roger Paquette
Vice-Presidents
  Marketing: Steve Del Bosco
  Procurement and Real Estate: Mike Greenberg
  Operations Support: Mike Gushue
  Capital Program and Business Development: John Marginson
General Counsel and Corporate Counsel: Carole Mackay
Director, Public Affairs: Paul Raynor

Gauge: 1,435 mm
Route length operated: 6,524 km

**Political background**
VIA Rail Canada Inc came into being as a Crown Corporation in January 1977 as a creation of the then Trudeau administration. At that time it took over management of all rail passenger services previously operated by CN and CP Rail, except commuter services. Since then its fortunes have been inextricably tied to the cabinet of the government in office because the law requires only an order in council rather than a vote in parliament to alter VIA's future. The current mandate is clearly to apply private industry principles to administration of the corporation with the intent of determining how close it can come to self-sufficiency. For all its performance gains in the last few years, VIA is still considered expendable in some quarters of Canada's political spectrum.

VIA contracts with the Canadian government for the provision of those rail passenger services specified by the Minister of Transport. In turn, VIA contracts with railway companies for the operation of these services and with non-railway companies for the provision of incidental goods and services; 92 per cent of track used is contracted from CN.

In April 2000 the government announced a C$400 million five-year investment programme in VIA Rail. Projects covered by this funding include: signalling

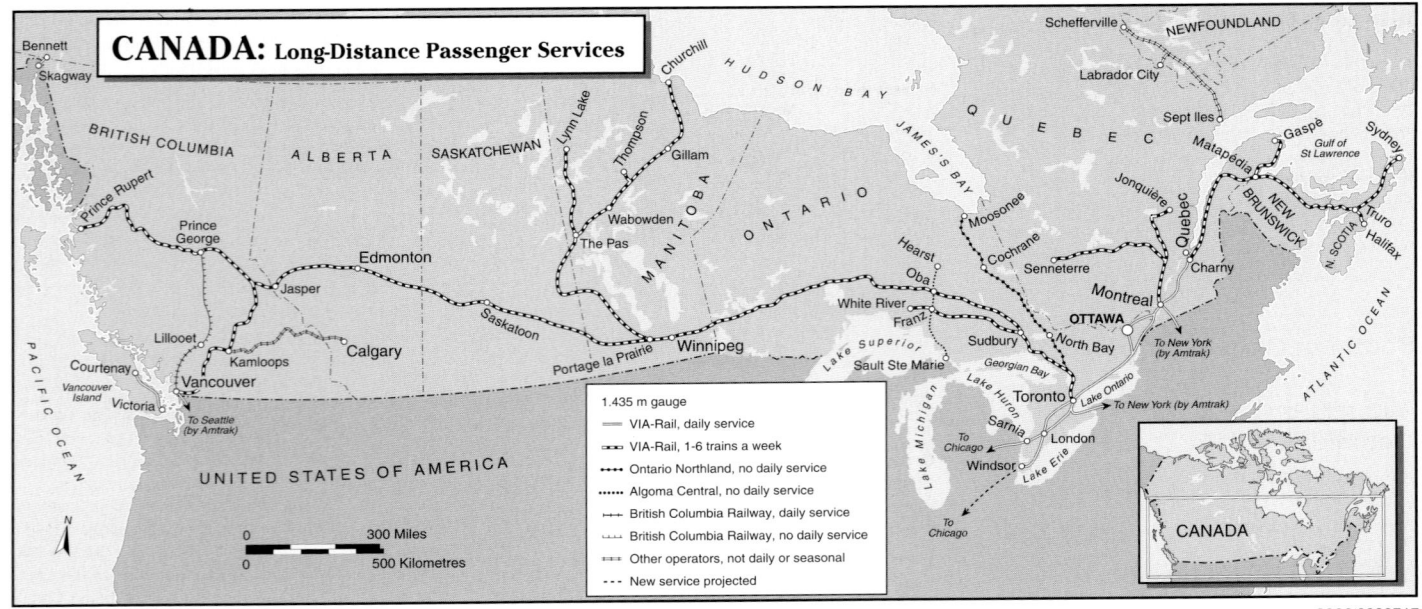

**CANADA: Long-Distance Passenger Services**

improvements, level crossing protection and track upgrades for the Montreal–Ottawa route; a major upgrade of London, Ontario station and other stations; and the development of new waste management procedures, initially on the Quebec City–Windsor corridor and later on other parts of the VIA Rail Canada network.

### Finance
At the end of 2000, the company's workforce stood at 2,958, compared with 2,909 in 1999.

Revenues in 2000 were C$240.7 million, up 9 per cent on 1999, while expenses totalled C$404.7 million, a rise of 1.6 per cent; the Canadian government made a total contribution of C$164.4 million for operating deficits, capital improvements and reorganisation charges. The revenue/cost ratio in 2000 was 59.5 per cent, up from 56.7 per cent a year earlier.

| Traffic | 1998 | 1999 | 2000 |
|---|---|---|---|
| Passenger journeys (000) | 3,646 | 3,757 | 3,957 |
| Passenger-km (million) | 1,378 | 1,498 | 1,516 |

### Passenger operations
The VIA Rail network comprises four main groups of services totalling some 460 trains per week: the Quebec City–Windsor corridor, which accounts for 85 per cent of the corporation's ridership and 70 per cent of its revenue; Western services between Toronto and Vancouver, which primarily serve the tourism market; Eastern services, linking the Atlantic regions with central Canada via the Montreal–Halifax and Montreal–Gaspé routes; and Northern services in British Columbia, Ontario, Quebec and Saskatchewan, providing rail transport in regions where alternative modes are very limited or non-existent.

In 1996 the company introduced VIA Resernet, an on-line interactive booking service claimed to be the first of its type in the world, and launched a frequent-traveller programme, VIA Préference.

In 1997 VIA initiated its New Era Passenger Operation (NEPO) reorganisation of train crewing to merge the functions of locomotive driver and conductor/assistant conductor, and to separate operational and customer service functions. Annual cost savings were estimated to be C$15 million. Improved onboard services were also introduced in 1997, with a catering contract for Québec City-Windsor corridor services awarded to Cara Operations Ltd, and a partnership agreement reached with Second Cup Ltd to provide coffee on all VIA services.

### Diesel locomotives

| Class | Builder's type | Wheel arrangement | Power kW | Speed km/h | Weight tonnes | No in service | First built | Mechanical | Builders Engine | Transmission |
|---|---|---|---|---|---|---|---|---|---|---|
| GPA30a | F40PH2 | Bo-Bo | 2,238 | 153 | 129 | 20 | 1986 | GMD | 16-645E3C | E GMD |
| GPA30b | F40PH2 | Bo-Bo | 2,238 | 145 | 129 | 10 | 1987 | GMD | 16-645E3C | E GMD |
| GPA30c | F40PH2 | Bo-Bo | 2,238 | 145 | 129 | 29 | 1989 | GMD | 16-645E3C | E GMD |
| MPA27 | LRC | Bo-Bo | 2,760 | 153 | 125 | 7 | 1978 | B/MLW | 16 Cyl 251-F | E CGE |
| - | P42 | Bo-Bo | 2,985 | 175 | 112 | 21 | 2001 | GE | 7FDL16 | E GE |

GMD General Motors Diesel (Canada)   CGE Canadian General Electric   B/MLW Bombardier/Montréal Locomotive Works
GE General Electric

A C$5 million refurbishment of Montréal Central station was completed in 1998, while work started on new station facilities in Edmonton, improving interchanges with other transport modes. In November 2001, plans were unveiled to renovate passenger facilities at Toronto's Union Station at a cost of C$10 million.

In 1999 VIA Rail Canada launched a pilot project in partnership with Amtrak to test the viability of carrying express packages between Toronto and Chicago.

In October 2001, integration of ticketing was introduced for passengers using VIA Rail Canada and GO Transit services in the Greater Toronto Area.

### Traction and rolling stock
In 1999 VIA Rail's main line locomotive fleet consisted of 59 GM F40PH diesel-electric locomotives and seven LRC power cars.

In October 2000 VIA Rail ordered seven Type F59PHI diesel locomotives from General Motors.

In 2001 21 Type P42 diesel locomotives were ordered from General Electric to replace LRC-2 and LRC-3 power cars. The first of these was handed over in November 2001.

The LRC coach fleet consists of 99 vehicles: 50 LRC-2 coaches, delivered between 1978-80; and 49 LRC-3 cars, delivered in 1982-83; 10 LRC-1 cars were in store. VIA's coaching stock is 214 stainless steel long-distance cars and five Budd RDC diesel railcars. These have been the subject of a refurbishment programme by Industrial Rail Services, Moncton, with the first unit returned to traffic in November 2001. Four of the RDCs are in use on the 'Malahat' service on Vancouver Island; the fifth is used between Sudbury and White River, Ontario.

Traction and rolling stock maintenance is undertaken at depots at Montreal, Vancouver and Winnipeg.

In December 2000 VIA Rail Canada announced that it was to purchase from Alstom 139 UK-built passenger coaches originally ordered by a consortium of operators for subsequently abandoned international overnight services between Great Britain and the European mainland. None of the vehicles had operated in service and some were incomplete at the time of the sale. Valued at C$125 million, the fleet comprises 47 conventional coaches, 72 sleeping cars and 20 service and catering vehicles. VIA Rail Canada has branded these vehicles Renaissance cars. Delivery was made in 2001.

*Class GPA30c (Type F40PH2) diesel locomotive at Vancouver* (Marcel Vleugels)

**UPDATED**

## Windsor & Hantsport Railway

Windsor & Hantsport Railway Co Ltd
PO Box 578, 2 Water Street, Windsor, Nova Scotia
ON 2TO
Tel: (+1 902) 798 07 98   Fax: (+1 902) 798 08 16

**Key personnel**
General Manager: James Taylor
Chief Mechanical Officer: Peter Johnstone

Gauge: 1,435 mm
Route length: 96 km

**Organisation**
The Windsor & Hantsport began operations in August 1994 after CP Rail sold 96 km of line, eight RS23 diesel locomotives and 76 80-ton hopper wagons to Iron Road Railways (qv in USA short line section). Connection is made with the CN system at Windsor Junction, Nova Scotia. The Windsor & Hantsport is the last working vestige of CP Rail in Nova Scotia and had previously formed part of CP's Dominion Atlantic Railway subsidiary.

# CHILE

## Ministry of Transport & Communications

Amunategui 139, Santiago
Tel: (+56 2) 672 65 03   Fax: (+56 2) 699 51 38

**Key personnel**
Minister of Transport: N Irueta

## Antofagasta (Chili) and Bolivia Railway plc (FCAB)

Ferrocarril de Antofagasta a Bolivia
Bolívar 255, Casilla ST, Antofagasta
Tel: (+56 55) 20 67 00   Fax: (+56 55) 20 62 20
e-mail: webmaster@fcab.cl
Web: http://www.fcab.cl

**Key personnel**
General Manager: Miguel V Sepúlveda
Planning and Development Manager:
  Marcelo F Contreras
Services (Traffic) Manager: L Bernardo Schmidt
Sales Manager: Carlos Yanine
Commercial Manager: Carlos E Acuña
Financial Manager: Pablo E Ribbeck
Human Resources Manager: Victor F Maldonado
Manager, Infrastructure: Juan Pavez
Manager, Engineering Maintenance: José Brown
Manager, Workshop: Carlos Bastías

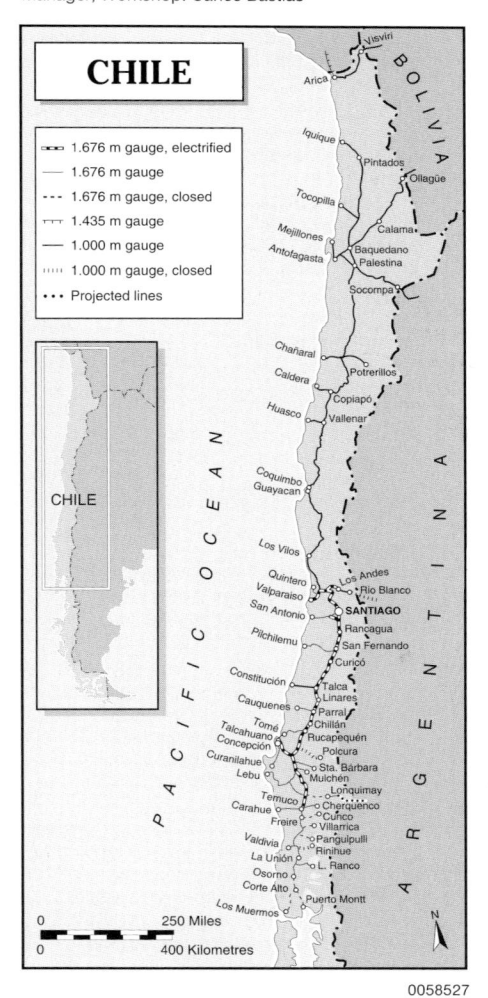

*FCAB Class 1400 locomotive with a train of copper cathodes*  2002/0134132

Gauge: 1,000 mm
Route length: 911.33 km

**Organisation**
FCAB is entirely self-supporting financially. Founded in 1888, the company is listed on the London Stock Exchange. The railway runs from the Pacific port of Antofagasta to the Argentine border at Socompa on one route (over Ferronor track between Augusta Victoria and Socompa), and to the Bolivian border at Ollagüe on the second. FCAB has become the principal transport company in northern Chile, responding to customer needs with three types of service: a door-to-door bimodal service that complements the company's rail transport activities with those of its own truck services; the design and construction of wagons to meet customers' specific requirements; and the provision of complete storage and shipment services.

In March 2002, FCAB employed 562 staff. Personnel development has been achieved through the establishment of 'quality circles' and an internal intranet has been created to enhance employee communications, with each part of the company provided with its own website.

**Passenger operations**
In 2001, a passenger service was operating weekly in both directions between Calama, Chile, and Uyuni in Bolivia via Ollagüe jointly with the neighbouring Andina Railway, which it also controlled by FCAB. In total 1.121 million passenger-km were recorded in 2001, some 20 per cent down on the figure for 1998.

**Freight operations**
In conjunction with FCAB's bulk trainload and wagonload business, door-to-door service has been offered since 1988 in conjunction with the company's road haulage subsidiary, TRAIN Company Ltd. TRAIN is a major truck operator in northern Chile, with more than 100 vehicles active in the mining, industrial and service markets.

The year 2001 proved exceptionally significant for FCAB, when the company transported its highest freight volume since its founding in 1888, with 3.53 million tonnes handled, an increase of 7 per cent on the figure achieved in the previous year. As well as being Chile's leading company in the transport of sulphuric acid and other hazardous materials, FCAB is also the main carrier of copper and mining products in the north of the country.

Recent contracts include one with the Tesoro mine (Antofagasta Minerals) to move 70,000 tonnes of copper cathodes and 180,000 tonnes of sulphuric acid annually and another with El Abra mine to transport 400,000 tonnes of sulphuric acid per year.

| Traffic | 1999 | 2000 | 2001 |
|---|---|---|---|
| Freight tonnes (million) | 3.12 | 3.3 | 3.53 |
| Freight tonne-km (million) | 840 | 868 | 926.2 |

**Traction and rolling stock**
At the end of 2001, the FCAB fleet comprised 48 diesel-electric locomotives (including seven Class 600/900 units for yard service). Three 1,492 kW 2100 Class locomotives were acquired from QR, Australia, in 2001, followed by seven more in 2002. The freight wagon fleet totalled 1,200, of which 600 were in service. The fleet has been progressively reduced in size since 1998 as older vehicles are retired and replaced with new equipment offering increased capacity. Recent additions include 75 acid tank cars for the Tesoro and El Ambra contracts and 10 'porta cátodos' copper plate carriers for traffic from Tesoro.

*FCAB sulphuric acid tank wagons*  2002/0134131

*Former QR 2100 Class diesel-electric locomotive leaving Redbank, Queensland, en route to Chile for use on the FCAB network (Brian Webber)*  2002/0137765

## Diesel locomotives

| Class | Builder's type | Wheel arrangement | Power kW | Speed km/h | Weight tonnes | No in service | First built | Builders Mechanical | Engine | Transmission |
|---|---|---|---|---|---|---|---|---|---|---|
| 600 | | Bo-Bo | 373 | 55 | 45 | 2 | 1958 | GM | Cummins NT.855 | E EMD |
| 900 | GA 8 | Bo-Bo | 708 | 55 | 52 | 3 | 1965 | GM | EMD 8-567C | E EMD |
| 900 | GA 18 | Bo-Bo | 820 | 57 | 54 | 1 | 1969 | GM | EMD 8-645-E | E EMD |
| 900 | G 18U | Bo-Bo* | 820 | 96 | 72 | 1 | 1977 | GM | EMD 8-645-E | E EMD |
| 1400 | GR 12U | Co-Co | 1,063 | 95 | 90 | 6 | 1961 | GM | EMD 12-567C | E EMD |
| 1400 | GR 12UD | Co-Co | 1,063 | 95 | 90 | 4 | 1962 | GM | EMD 12-567C | E EMD |
| 1400 | G 22CU | Co-Co | 1,230 | 97 | 90 | 1 | 1969 | GM | EMD 12-645E | E EMD |
| 1400 | GR 12 | Co-Co | 1,063 | 95 | 90 | 2 | 1962 | GM | EMD 12-567C | E EMD |
| 1400 | NF210 | Co-Co | 1,044 | 96 | 103 | 17 | 1957 | GM | EMD 12-567C | E EMD |
| ** | GL 26C | Co-Co | 1,492 | 80 | 97 | 10 | 2001 | Comeng/Clyde | EMD 16-645E | E EMD/Clyde |

\* Formerly A1A-A1A; centre axles removed
\*\* Acquired from QR, Australia, built 1970

FCAB uses the Q Tron QES 1000 computerised control system for its locomotives, achieving increases in haulage capacity and improved maintenance planning.

**Coupler in standard use, freight and passenger cars:** AAR automatic

**Braking in standard use, locomotive-hauled stock:** 26L and 65L with straight control

### Signalling and telecommunications
Train control is by VHF radio throughout the system. FCAB employs a computerised communications (Intranet) and control system linked to customers. In 2002, studies were in progress by FCAB into the possible use of a VHF radio positioning for its locomotives.

In the field of information technology, FCAB has two interconnected Local Area Networks (LANs) in Antofagasta and another in Calama, together forming a Wide Area Network (WAN). Some 250 PCs are connected to the WAN.

### Track
**Rail:** 24.83 kg/m, 177.77 km; 32.24 kg/m, 306.19 km; 37.2 kg/m, 204.17 km; 37.22 kg/m, 3.02 km; 42.16 kg/m, 6.42 km; 42.21 kg/m, 188.99 km
**Crossties (sleepers):** Wood (Coigüe) 188 × 254 × 1,027 mm
**Spacing:** In plain track: 1,422/km; in curves: 1,422/km, 1,490/km
**Fastenings:** Screw spikes, Pandrol clips
**Min curvature radius:** Main line 10°, branches 15°
**Max gradient:** 3.4%
**Max permissible axleload:** 15 tonnes

*UPDATED*

## Chilean State Railways (EFE)

Empresa de los Ferrocarriles del Estado
Avenida Libertador Bernardo O'Higgins 3322, Santiago
Tel: (+56 2) 779 07 07   Fax: (+56 2) 776 26 09

### Key personnel
President: Hugo Trevelli
Vice President: Guilleromo Artria
General Manager: Jaime Moncada
Managers
  Human Resources: Patricio Corvalan
  Legal Affairs: Patricio Morales
  Operations and Passenger: Jaime Contreras
  Merval: Andres Link
  Rehabilitiation Plan: Fernando Verbal
Comptroller: Ernesto Opazo

Gauge: 1,676 mm; 1,000 mm
Route length: 2,831 km; 402 km
Electrification: 1,317 km at 3 kV DC

### Political background
Under legislation passed in 1992 which established the company in its present form, EFE was granted some measure of autonomy and allowed to meet its objectives by means of contracts, concessions and joint ventures with third parties. Under this legislation, EFE's objectives were to be set out in three-year development plans agreed with the Chilean government, the first of which was approved in August 1993.

As required by the 1993-96 plan, a controlling 51 per cent interest in EFE's freight subsidiary FEPASA (qv) was sold to the Transportes del Pacífico consortium in January 1995. As well as disposing of its non-core activities, EFE has been charged with increasing the involvement of the private sector in the railway system it currently operates. This was to take the form of concessions to operate passenger services, and concessions to upgrade and maintain sections of track to specified standards. It was expected that concessions for passenger services and track maintenance on a particular route could, if advantageous, be awarded to the same bidder.

EFE invited bids for a track maintenance concession on the Santiago—Chillán (to allow speeds of 140 km/h) and Chillán—Temuco/Concepción—Valdivia sections of its Santiago—Puerto Montt main line in 1996, so that work could begin in 1997. FEPASA was to undertake maintenance on those lines and branches where there are no passenger services.

The long-planned privatisation of EFE passenger services was deferred due to global economic conditions, especially in Asia. However, in May 1997 the Ministry of Transport and Telecommunications announced plans to invest US$300 million in EFE. Half of this was to be directed at the Santiago-Puerto Montt line, for which an operating concession had been due to be awarded in early 1998, although no contract has been reported. It was hoped that a state investment in infrastructure upgrades would provide the impetus for a private-sector operator to emerge. Track conditions south of Temuco, some 700 km south of Santiago, have led to a temporary withdrawal of services, with a lack of rolling stock also a factor.

Maintenance concessionaires were to receive subsidy where the track standard required by EFE was above that which could be funded through access charges. It was reported that EFE was to retain responsibility for electrification, major bridges, signalling and dispatching.

Overseeing the project is the state-appointed Transport Investment Infrastructure Planning Commission (Sectra), which sets standards for track maintenance on all routes. Sectra will also determine minimum passenger services, covering such aspects as speed, frequency, capacity and standards of accommodation.

### Organisation
On 29 September 1995 EFE reorganised its activities as six subsidiary limited companies; a property management company was later established on 3 October 1995. With the exception of Ferrocarril de Arica-La Paz SA, all are concerned with the trunk 1,676 mm gauge Valparaíso—Santiago—Puerto Montt route and its 1,000 mm and 1,676 mm gauge branches. Most of the trunk route is electrified, as far south as Temuco.

The separate 1,000 mm gauge system extending from La Calera, near Valparaíso, north to Iquique has been operated by a separate state-owned company, Ferronor (qv), since 1990.

With the exception of some 900 route-km placed under the responsibility of FEPASA, infrastructure maintenance and management on the core EFE system has been undertaken since September 1995 by Infraestructura y Tráfico Ferroviario SA (Infrastructure and Railway Traffic Ltd). Suburban passenger services are operated in the Valparaíso area by Merval (Metro Regional de Valparaíso SA – Valaparaíso Regional Metro Ltd) and in the Santiago area by Ferrocarriles Suburbanos SA (Suburban Railways Ltd) and marketed as 'Metrotren'. Long-distance passenger services between Santiago and Puerto Montt are operated by Ferrocarril de Pasajeros SA (Passenger Railway Ltd), which is marketed as 'Via Sur'. In turn, it was split into separate units in 1999, including Largo Recorrido (long-distance) and Servicios Regionales (regional). On 2 December 1999, Tren Regional del Bio-Bio (Biotren) came into existence, providing regional services around Concepción.

| Traffic | 1997 | 1998 | 1999 |
|---|---|---|---|
| Passenger journeys (million) | | | |
| Merval | 5.434 | 6.352 | 5.268 |
| Metrotren | 1.847 | 2.667 | 3.343 |
| Biotren | – | – | 0.028* |
| Other EFE | 0.981 | 0.949 | 1.341 |
| Total | 8.262 | 9.968 | 9.980 |

\* Services introduced 2 December 1999

### Passenger operations
After years of declining traffic, EFE is now handling growing numbers of passengers. A downturn in traffic on the Merval system, which provides suburban services between Puerto station, Valparaíso, and Limache (43 km), was attributed to modernisation work which led to train cancellations. Since completion of most of this work in November 1999, journey times have been reduced and service frequencies increased. Services continued to be provided by Class AEL emus, but replacements in the form of refurbished ex-RENFE Class 444 units from Spain were expected in 2001.

Since 1998, the number of services on the Metrotren system between Santiago and Rancagua (85 km) has increased steadily to 15 each way on weekdays and 17 on Sundays. All are provided by refurbished ex-RENFE Class 444 emus.

Metrotren services are now administered jointly by EFE and Metro de Santiago, with the possibility of a private-sector partner being sought in the future.

*EFE metre-gauge diesel railcar at Talca (Marcel Vleugels)*

Servicios Regionales comprises Renaico– and Laja–Concepción–Talcahuano services and a metre-gauge Talco–Constitución railbus operation, while Largo Recorrido covers Santiago–Temuco overnight trains (one all-year and a second economy-class service in summer months) and three daytime trains between Santiago and Chillán.

Since December 1999, Biotren has provided suburban services on the Chiguayante–Concepción–Talcahuano route, with 14 services in each direction on weekdays and six on Sundays, all provided by refurbished Class AEL emus. The introduction of this service and the extension of regional services from Renaico and Laja to Talcahuano necessitated reopening the 5 km Concepción–Talcahuano branch to passenger traffic.

Despite enthusiasm from some politicians, there appears little prospect of reinstating passenger services on lines south of Temuco, due to poor track conditions. However, there are plans to revive services on the Santiago–Melipilla line to become part of the Metrotren system. Electrification and modernisation of this section could be carried out by an eventual concessionaire for the service.

### Freight operations
Freight operations on the main EFE network passed out of state ownership in January 1995 with the privatisation of FEPASA, while those undertaken by its Arica–La Paz Railway subsidiary passed to private-sector operator Ferrocarril de Bolivia al Pacífico (qv) in November 1997.

### New lines
In April 1999, the Chilean and Argentine governments agreed each to contribute funding of US$140 million towards a proposed 220 km rail link from Lonquimay to Zapala in Argentina, which would complete the so-called Transandino del Sur route. The Ferrocarril del Pacífico (qv) would be responsible for upgrading the Talcahuano–Lonquimay line feeding the new route, while Ferrosur Roca would undertake similar improvements on the Argentine side.

### Improvements to existing lines
At the start of 1996, branches from the Valparaíso–Santiago–Puerto Montt trunk route, totalling 418 route-km of 1,676 mm gauge and 73 route-km of 1,000 mm gauge, were out of use. Reports from late 1997 say that on some double-track lines only one is in use due to track condition.

EFE has received US$120 million from the government for a three-year investment programme. Most of this is being spent on the Merval and Metrotren corridors. In 2000, modernisation work between Santiago and Rancagua was in progress and was expected to be completed early in 2001, enabling trains to run at speeds of up to 140 km/h.

### Traction and rolling stock
In 1997 the EFE broad-gauge fleet comprised: 22 steam locomotives (2 serviceable); 39 diesel locomotives; 45 electric locomotives; 5 diesel railcars; 29 emus; 131 passenger coaches (plus 96 in private ownership); and 347 freight wagons (including metre-gauge). The metre-gauge fleet comprised: 2 steam locomotives; 21 diesel locomotives; 5 electric locomotives; 9 diesel railcars; and 18 passenger coaches. Large sections of each fleet were unserviceable.

An initial batch of five Class 440 emus procured from Spanish National Railways (RENFE) was joined by a further five examples in late 1998. Further rolling stock procurement from Spain was announced in April 1999. By 2002 EFE will acquire from RENFE 22 Class 440R and five Class 444 emus, one Class 308 diesel-electric locomotive, and two sets of coaching stock. The Class 444 units were expected to be used to improve journey standards on Santiago–Chillán long-distance services.

**Coupler:** Automatic
**Braking:** Air

### Signalling and telecommunications
At the start of 1996, the following signalling systems were in use on the EFE network: Alameda–Puerto (187 km), mechanical signalling with electromechanical interlocking and track circuits; Alameda–Talca (249 km), mechanical signalling and interlocking, track circuits; Talca–Cabrero (208 km), mechanical signalling with electrical interlocking, track circuits; Cabrero–Temuco (233 km), electric signalling and interlocking, train staff working; San Rosendo–Talcahuano (83 km), electrical interlocking and train staff working; Temuco–Puerto Montt (389 km) and various branches (971 km), train staff working.

Under EFE's 1994-97 rehabilitation plan, signalling was to receive investment totalling US$3,52 million and telecommunications US$5.62 million. EFE and Chilesat (a private communications company) were to install an optical fibre network between Santiago and Temuco and San Rosendo and Concepción. The scheme was to receive US$1.75 million from EFE's rehabilitation budget and was to be used for ground-to-ground and later ground-to-train communication.

### Electrification
A total of US$5.27 million was to be spent on EFE's 3 kV DC electrification system under the company's 1994-97 rehabilitation plan. This investment was intended to compensate for several years of deferred maintenance, rather than fund any further electrification. Reports from late 1997 suggest that electrically powered operation north of Santiago is confined to the Merval commuter service. Some removal of overhead power supply equipment north of the capital has been undertaken by EFE.

Overhead power supply equipment on the Santiago–Nós section of the Metrotren system has been modernised and in 2000 similar work was in progress on the Paine–Talagante line.

### Track

| Rails (kg/m) | Lengths laid 1995 (km) |
|---|---|
| 60 | 563.3 |
| 50 | 972.9 |
| 40 | 1,453.7 |
| 30 | 457.1 |

**Crossties (sleepers):** Wood
**Cross-section:** 250 × 150 mm
**Spacing:** 1,800/km
**Min curvature radius, main lines:** 1,000 mm gauge, 80 m; 1,676 mm gauge, 180 m
**Max gradient:** Adhesion, 6%; rack, 8%
**Max permissible axleloading:** 18 tonnes (1,000 mm gauge), 25 tonnes (1,676 mm gauge)

*Class AEL Japanese-built four-car Metrotren emu at Rancagua (Marcel Vleugels)* 0058677

### Diesel locomotives

| Class | Builder's type | Wheel arrangement | Power kW | Speed km/h | Weight tonnes | No in service | First built | Builders Mechanical | Builders Engine | Builders Electrical |
|---|---|---|---|---|---|---|---|---|---|---|
| D-16 00 | 253/253 | Co-Co | 1,305 | 120 | 114.5 | 5 | 1954 | GE | Alco 244 | E GE USA |
| Dt-13 100 | U-13-C | Co-Co | 1,063 | 95 | 85 | 5 | 1967 | GE | GE FDL-8 | E GE USA |
| D-7100 | 040 DE | Bo-Bo | 615 | 90 | 72 | 5 | 1963 | B&L | SACM-MGO 12V-175-A5 | Various European builders |
| Dt-6000 | – | Co-Co | 492 | 80 | 64 | 3 | 1954 | GE | CB FWL-6T | E GE USA |
| D-5100 | U-5-B | Bo-Bo | 447 | 70 | 50 | 2 | 1963 | GE | Caterpillar D-379 | E GE USA |
| Dt-3000 | – | Bo-Bo | 223 | 48 | 40 | 1 | 1953 | GE | Cummins HBI-600 | – |

### Electric railcars or multiple-units

| Class | Cars per unit | Motor cars per unit | Motored axles/car | Output/motor kW | Speed km/h | No in service | First built | Builders Mechanical | Builders Electrical |
|---|---|---|---|---|---|---|---|---|---|
| AEZ | 4 | 2 | 4 | 225 | 160 | 4 | 1973 | Kawasaki | Toshiba |
| AEL | 4 | 2 | 4 | 310 | 130 | 3 | 1973 | Kawasaki | Toshiba/Hitachi |
| AES | 2 | 1 | 4 | 190 | 130 | 12 | 1977 | Fiat-Concord | SEL/Siam di Tella |

### Electric locomotives

| Class | Wheel arrangement | Output kW | Speed km/h | Weight tonnes | No in service | First built | Builders Mechanical | Builders Electrical |
|---|---|---|---|---|---|---|---|---|
| E-32 | Co-Co | 3,400 | 130 | 136 | 4 | 1962 | Breda | Marelli |
| E-30 | Bo-Bo | 2,265 | 130 | 98 | 5 | 1962 | Breda | Ansaldo-Marelli |
| E-17 | Bo-Bo | 1,950 | 90 | 76 | 2 | 1973 | Breda | Ansaldo-Marelli |

## 96 RAILWAY SYSTEMS/Chile

## FEPASA

Ferrocarril del Pacífico SA
La Concepción 331, Providencia, Santiago
Tel: (+56 2) 235 16 86   Fax: (+56 2) 235 09 20

### Key personnel
General Manager: E Valdatta
Chief Operating Officer: Paul Victor
Chief Mechanical Officer: David L Powell
Director, Operations: Robert G Muilenberg
Transportation Superintendent, Southern Division:
   J David Wallace

Gauge: 1,676 mm; 1,000 mm
Route length: 2,085 km; 37 km
Electrification: 841 km

### Political background
FEPASA was created in 1993 to operate freight services on EFE routes, excluding the Arica-La Paz Railway. It was initially a 99 per cent-owned EFE subsidiary, with the Chilean government holding the remaining 1 per cent. In January 1994 a 51 per cent stake in FEPASA (including the government's 1 per cent) was sold to the Transportes del Pacífico consortium for US$30 million. The consortium formally took control of FEPASA on 23 January 1995 under a 20-year concession.

Transportes del Pacífico comprised the Chilean holding company Cruz Blanca, Estrella Americana (a Chilean pension fund company) and San Pablo Bay Railway Company. The last is an affiliate of the US Anacostia and Pacific Company, which was to provide financial, technical and operating expertise.

### Organisation
FEPASA operates freight services over EFE infrastructure, excluding the Arica-La Paz Railway. Responsiblity for scheduling and track maintenance remains with EFE for the core Valparaíso-Puerto Montt route, its branch to Concepción and between San Rosendo and Talcahuano, Paine and Talagante and Santiago and San Antonio. On these routes, FEPASA pays track access fees to EFE. On some 900 km of routes where no EFE passenger trains operate, FEPASA is responsible for scheduling and track maintenance.

### Finance
Bidders for the 51 per cent stake in FEPASA were required to provide details of the development strategies, operational and investment plans as far as 2000, commercial and financial policy and equipment maintenance programmes they intended to implement. Transportes del Pacífico has undertaken to invest US$88 million in FEPASA by 2000, with US$28 million earmarked for freight wagons, US$20 million for locomotives and US$28 million for track improvements.

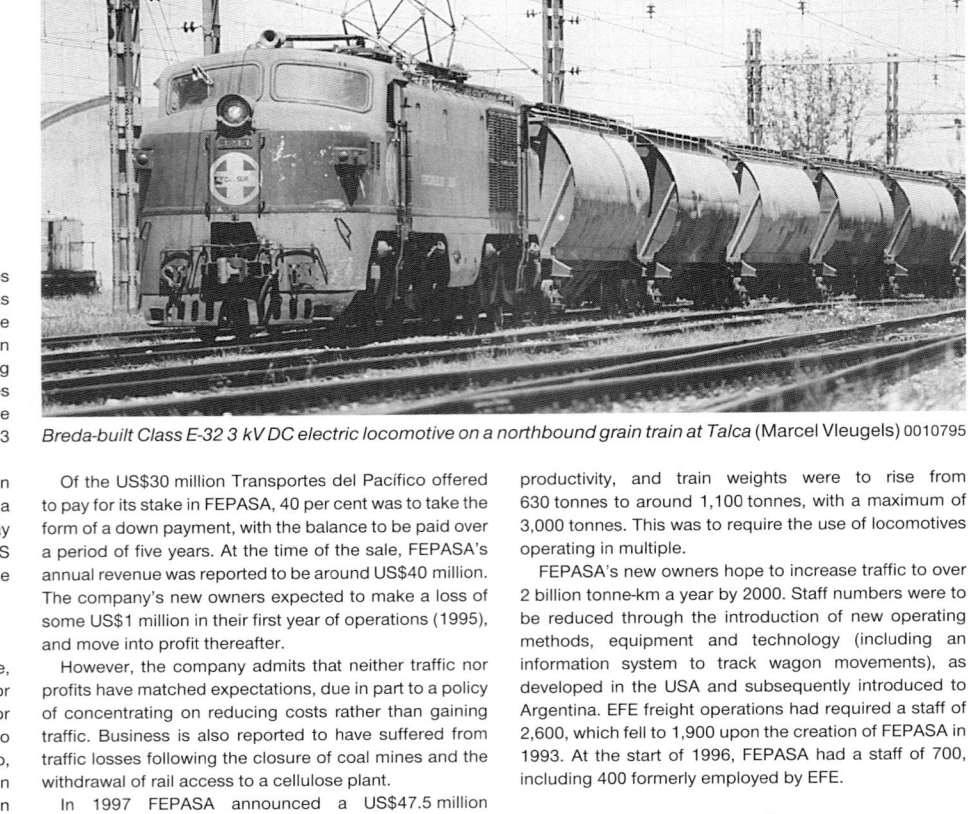

*Breda-built Class E-32 3 kV DC electric locomotive on a northbound grain train at Talca (Marcel Vleugels) 0010795*

Of the US$30 million Transportes del Pacífico offered to pay for its stake in FEPASA, 40 per cent was to take the form of a down payment, with the balance to be paid over a period of five years. At the time of the sale, FEPASA's annual revenue was reported to be around US$40 million. The company's new owners expected to make a loss of some US$1 million in their first year of operations (1995), and move into profit thereafter.

However, the company admits that neither traffic nor profits have matched expectations, due in part to a policy of concentrating on reducing costs rather than gaining traffic. Business is also reported to have suffered from traffic losses following the closure of coal mines and the withdrawal of rail access to a cellulose plant.

In 1997 FEPASA announced a US$47.5 million programme of investment in infrastructure upgrades, locomotive acquisitions, and wagon refurbishment.

### Freight operations
In 1994, prior to privatisation, FEPASA carried 5.132 million tonnes of freight on the EFE system and recorded 1.104 billion tonne-km. In total 4.2 million tonnes were carried in 1998, when 920 million tonne-km were recorded.

Bulk products, such as minerals (copper) and forest products (cellulose), form the principal component of FEPASA traffic base, but major growth in intermodal traffic is also foreseen. The new owning consortium aimed in the short term to cut operating costs and raise productivity, and train weights were to rise from 630 tonnes to around 1,100 tonnes, with a maximum of 3,000 tonnes. This was to require the use of locomotives operating in multiple.

FEPASA's new owners hope to increase traffic to over 2 billion tonne-km a year by 2000. Staff numbers were to be reduced through the introduction of new operating methods, equipment and technology (including an information system to track wagon movements), as developed in the USA and subsequently introduced to Argentina. EFE freight operations had required a staff of 2,600, which fell to 1,900 upon the creation of FEPASA in 1993. At the start of 1996, FEPASA had a staff of 700, including 400 formerly employed by EFE.

### Improvements to existing lines
The raising of train weights in the short term was to require the lengthening of some passing loops. In the long term, conversion of the 1,000 mm gauge Los Andes-Río Blanco branch (the remaining 34 km of the former Transandine Railway to Argentina via Juncal) to 1,676 mm gauge was projected. This would eliminate the present transhipment of copper concentrate containers at Los Andes.

### Traction and rolling stock
FEPASA passed into private ownership with 19 electric locomotives, 90 diesel locomotives (of 13 different models) and 4,800 wagons. Due to financial constraints, EFE had been deferring maintenance for some years and FEPASA's new owners intended to rationalise and modernise the locomotive fleet with a view to obtaining 100,000 km a year from each unit.

Abandonment of electric operation has been suggested to lower track-access charges paid to EFE, which in 1995 began trials of a microprocessor-based onboard system to measure and record traction current consumption by electric locomotives and multiple-units.

In January 1996 FEPASA signed a contract with National Railway Equipment Company, USA, for the supply of eight remanufactured General Motors SD39-2M Co-Co diesel-electric locomotives. In 1997 the company announced plans to acquire 15 rebuilt General Motors SD40 locomotives and to refurbish 1,600 wagons as part of a US$47.5 million investment programme.

### Signalling and telecommunications
Responsible for regulating train movements on routes with no EFE passenger service, FEPASA's new owners intend to convert to a train warrant system, install train radio and replace brake vans with end-of-train devices.

*GE-built Alco-engined FEPASA Class D-1600 dating from the mid-1950s on southbound freight at Chillán (Marcel Vleugels) 0010796*

---

## Ferrocarril de Bolivia al Pacífico

### Key personnel
President: José Saavedí Banzer

Gauge: 1,000 mm
Route length: 206 km

### Political background
A concession to operate the Chilean section of the former 209 km Ferrocarril de Arica-La Paz SA was awarded to a new company on 1 August 1997 in return for half-year royalties of 46.5 million pesos. The successful bid for the 25-year concession came from C B Transportes, part of the Cruz Blanca group, whose subsidiary Ferrocarril Oriental de Bolivia operates the 248 km section of the line in Bolivia. The consortium also includes Metropolitana Bolivia Ltda, Panamerican Securities SA, and Bolivian businessman José Saavedí Banzer. Operations under new ownership began in November 1997.

A 1904 treaty requires the Bolivian government to retain ownership of the infrastructure of its portion of the line

Jane's World Railways 2002-2003   www.janes.com

between Charaña and Alto de La Paz. However, the government is reported to have suggested the FBP should pay US$300,000 per year to lease the Bolivian section for 10 years, the lease including the use of 80 wagons, as well as container-handling facilities.

### Organisation
The new company operates with around 20 commercial and traffic management staff. Locomotive and wagon maintenance has been outsourced from a separate company, Maestranza AG, which was reported to be creating a subsidiary to provide train crew.

### Freight operations
Since being concessioned, the railway has witnessed a significant increase in traffic, with a 45 per cent rise to 183,000 tonnes recorded in the first year of operation under new ownership.

### Traction and rolling stock
The operational fleet available in November 1997 comprised eight diesel locomotives and 350 wagons. In 1998 a rehabilitation programme for traction and rolling stock was started.

## Ferronor

Empresa de Transporte Ferroviario SA
Avenida Alessandri 042, Casilla 62, Coquimbo
Tel: (+56 51) 32 11 51   Fax: (+56 51) 31 34 60
Web: http://www.railamerica.com

### Key personnel
General Manager: Angel Gajardo

Gauge: 1,000 mm
Route length: 2,235 km

### Political background
Privatisation of Ferronor was undertaken in 1997 when the Andrés Pirazzoli construction and transport company bought Ferronor for US$12 million, double the bid of its nearest rival. The Chilean company subsequently sold a 55 per cent equity stake to US short line operator RailAmerica, which assumed operational control in February 1997.

### Organisation
Ferronor's La Calera–Iquique main line crosses the Antofagasta (Chili) and Bolivia Railway (FCAB) at Palestina and Baquedano. Ferronor's route from Augusta Victoria to Socompa and Belgrano Cargas of Argentina is connected to its main line at Palestina via FCAB.

In January 2002, Ferronor took over the operation of the Ferrocarril Portrerillos, linking Portrerillos with Diego Almagro and Barquitos (91 km), under a 15-year agreement with copper producer Codelco.

### Freight operations
Ferronor carries approximately 110,700 carloads annually, including iron ore, potassium chloride, copper ore, limestone, LPG and food products.

A new policy implemented by RailAmerica concentrates on Ferronor's core copper and iron ore traffic, as well as on international business with Argentina.

Copper concentrates and iron ore are moved from mines at the northern end of the system to the Pacific ports of Chañaral, Caldera, Huasco and Coquimbo. Traffic levels are subject to fluctuation in line with the market price of these commodities, but the temporary closure of the Cerro Colorado iron ore mine was offset by a contract to carry 2,000 tonnes/month of El Melón cement from La Calera to Copiapó and limestone in the reverse direction. A subsequent rise in iron ore prices and the reopening of the Cerro Colorado and Copiapó mines have recently boosted Ferronor traffic levels, with a 20-year contract signed with Compañia Minera Huasco (CMH) in 1996 to transport ore from Los Colorades mine to a pellet plant at Huasco. Shipments commenced in the third quarter of 1998.

In March 1998 a US$68 million contract was won from SQM Nitratos SA to transport some 500,000 tonnes annually of potassium chloride and potassium sulphite from the Minsal Salt Flats mine to Coya Sur and Tocopilla. In November 1998, the scope of this contract was expanded, increasing its value to US$80 million over 11 years.

International traffic interchanged with FGB of Argentina at Socompa amounted to 0.112 million tonnes (31.249 million tonne-km) in 1995 and generated 28 per cent of Ferronor's total freight revenue. A 1996 contract should see 38,000 tonnes per year of liquefied gas transported from Socompa to Baquedano. Tolls charged to FCAB for the use of the Augusta Victoria-Socompa route totalled US$1.675 million in 1995, 16 per cent of freight revenue. FCAB bridge traffic over the Ferronor system was 1.278 milion tonnes (34.879 million tonne-km).

### Traction and rolling stock
At the end of 1995, Ferronor's fleet comprised 31 diesel locomotives (including nine for yard service) and 550 wagons. Ferronor's workshops at Coquimbo carry out repairs for other railways as well as non-railway work. In 1998 the company announced that project financing associated with its 20-year CMH contract (see 'Freight operations') would fund the acquisition of six locomotives, 66 freight wagons and the construction of a new maintenance facility.

Ferronor's takeover of operations on the Ferrocarril Portrerillos in January 2002 led to the transfer of nine diesel locomotives and 186 wagons.

*General Electric diesel locomotive on Ferronor iron ore train at Vallenar* (Marcel Vleugels)   0010797

---

# CHINA, PEOPLE'S REPUBLIC

## Chinese Railways (CR)

Ministry of Railways, 10 Fuxing Men, Beijing 100844
Tel: (+86 10) 63 24 69 15   Fax: (+86 10) 63 98 10 65

### Key personnel
Minister of Railways: Fu Zhihuan
Vice-Ministers of Railways: Sun Yong Fu,
  Cai Qinghua, Liu Zhijun
Chairman: Hua Maokun
General Manager: Zhang Zhengqing
Chief Economist: Wang Zhaocheng
Technical Director: Zhou Yumin
Planning Director: Cao Qing
Operations Director: Chang Guozhi
Workshops Director: Tan Datong
Manager, International Co-operation:
  Mrs Tang Wensheng

Gauge: Almost entirely 1,435 mm, some 1,000 mm and 750 mm
Route length:
  National railways: 58,500 km (end 1998)
  Joint-venture railways: 4,900 km (end 1998)
  Local railways: 4,800 km (end 1999)
Electrification: 13,632 km at 25 kV 50 Hz AC (end 1999)
Multiple track: 19,700 route-km (end 1998)

### Political background
The Ministry of Railways controls 14 geographically based railway administrations, as well as most of the country's rail manufacturing and supply industries via five corporations: China National Railway Locomotive & Rolling Stock Industry Corporation (LORIC); the Railway Engineering Corporation; the Railway Construction Corporation; the Railway Materials Corporation; and the China National Railway Signal & Communications Corporation. The railway administrations are Beijing, Chengdu, Guangzhou, Harbin, Hohhot, Lanzhou, Liuzhou, Jinan, Kunming, Nanchang, Shanghai, Shenyang, Urumqi and Zhengzhou.

At the end of 1997 CR employed some 3.4 million staff. However, in April 1998 the government stated its intention to separate the five ministry-run corporations and implement other structural change, with the aim of cutting core rail network staff numbers. Behind this move was a bid to stem heavy losses sustained by the network in recent years.

This decision was implemented by the Ministry of Railways in late 2000 when the five corporations and ten universities and colleges were officially placed under the administration of other non-railway government departments. This structural change reduced the number of Ministry of Railways workers to 2.4 million of which 1.5 million are directly engaged in railway transportation.

The Ministry of Railways has also indicated its intention to gradually undertake more reforms from 2001 by splitting freight business, passenger business and network management into independent divisions. The Ministry will concentrate more on safety and regulation aspects.

Current policy is for progressive devolution of authority to individual railway regions, and joint-stock ownership of non-trunk routes is being encouraged. In 1993 the Guangzhou area administration was reconstituted as the first autonomous railway organisation – the Guangzhou Railway Corporation – with almost 4,000 route-km and 172,000 staff.

In a further move in 1993, it was announced that the state railway monopoly would be ended, and new operating standards and pricing structures introduced to enable the railway to gear itself more closely to the needs of a fast growing economy. Five regions were selected in 1996 as the first batch of autonomous railways.

A separate administration, the Guangshen Railway Company, runs the Chinese section of the Kowloon-Canton Railway, the 147 km line from Guangzhou (Canton) to the Hong Kong border's end-on junction with the former British section. This railway was allowed to produce its own timetables and set its fares independently in April 1996, prior to the offer of shares on the Hong Kong stock market and in the USA the following

# RAILWAY SYSTEMS / China

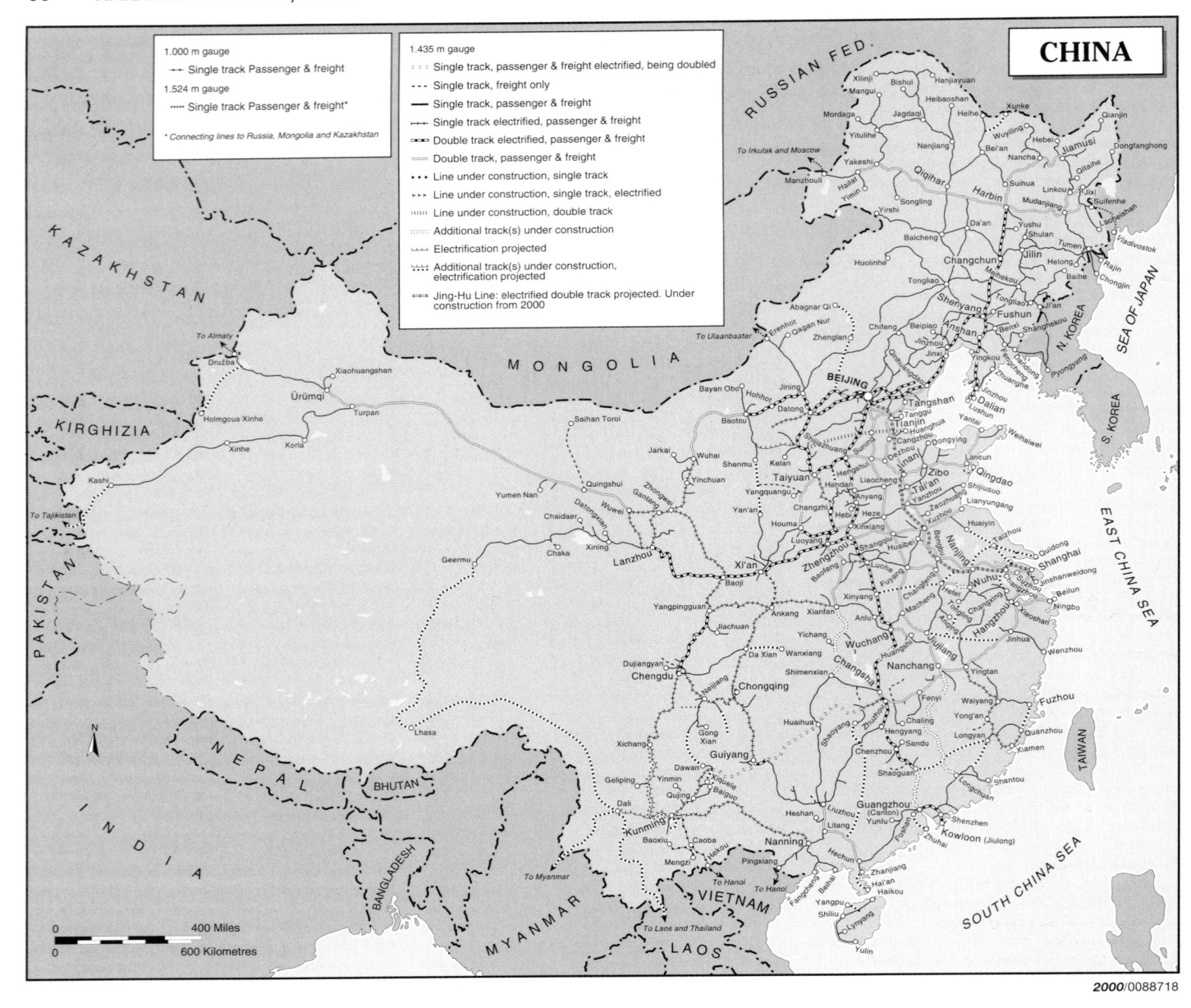

## CHINA

*Adtranz X2000 power car at Guangzhou East station during a test run to Hong Kong* (Tim Runnicles)

month. Funds raised by the flotation will finance purchase of high-speed trains for the Guangzhou-Kowloon route; an X2000 tilting train from Adtranz arrived in early 1998 for a two-year test period.

The demand for new secondary lines in China, often for coal-hauling purposes, has stimulated the development of the joint-venture method of financing. Joint-venture partners are often provinces and autonomous regions, coal mining enterprises and the Ministry of Railways. By the end of 2000 it was expected that some 6,500 km of such railways would be in operation, including some electrified lines.

The government has also encouraged local authorities to build and operate their own railways of up to 2,000 km length, where such investment would stimulate regional economic development. By the end of 1999 there were approximately 75 local railways with a total route length of 4,800 km. Additional lines and extensions, totalling 1,700 km, were under construction. Narrow-gauge railways of 762 mm gauge made up 30 per cent of the total route length at the end of 1999 but many of these are being closed or rebuilt to standard gauge.

In January 1999 the government indicated that foreign investment in the Chinese rail network, hitherto not permitted, would be encouraged on a trial basis from 2000.

| Traffic (million) | 1997 | 1998 | 1999 |
|---|---|---|---|
| Passenger journeys | 918 | 930 | 976 |
| Passenger-km | 352,000 | 369,000 | 405,000 |
| Freight tonnes | 1,618 | 1,532 | 1,569 |
| Freight tonne-km | 1,304,000 | 1,226,000 | 1,258,000 |

### Passenger operations

Demand for passenger and freight transport considerably outstrips both infrastructure and rolling stock capacity. Between 1968 and 1989 passenger traffic quadrupled, whereas the number of trains run rose by only 1.7 per cent. Consequently, severe overcrowding was common. To relieve this congestion, fares were abruptly doubled in 1989, while a 50 per cent rise was implemented in October 1995. The daily average of passenger journeys has dropped sharply from 3.5 million at the end of the 1980s to 2.7 million. From 1995 to 1997 passenger journeys declined but since then have reverted to an increasing trend. In 1999, 976 million passenger journeys were recorded.

The decline in passenger traffic experienced in the mid-1990s was attributed primarily to the growth in competition from road-based transport. China's network of intercity highways is expanding rapidly with over 10,000 km of dual-carriageway highway now in use. This infrastructure is allowing the development of significantly improved intercity bus and coach services that present a major threat to railway passenger services.

To counter the threat posed by expanding road (and air) passenger transport, the national railways embarked on a massive improvement strategy from the mid-1990s. A key development in passenger operations has been the introduction of 160 km/h quasi-high-speed and other accelerated services. Initially attention was focused on four key routes: Beijing–Shanghai; Beijing–Guangzhou; Beijing–Shenyang and Harbin–Dalian. In October 2000, quasi-high-speed services were also introduced on the Wuwei–Urumuqi line in the west of the country. Associated with this have been significant improvements to many adjoining sections of the network and the introduction of more powerful locomotives to allow higher average speeds on these sections where a limit of 120 km/h still applies. Around 260 DF11 and 50 improved DF4D diesel-electric and 240 SS8 electric locomotives capable of hauling the 160 km/h trains and around 580 DF4D and 60 SS7C electric locomotives for other accelerated services were operating by the end of 2000. Production of these types is continuing. Over 1,500 passenger coaches designed for maximum service speeds of 140 or 160 km/h as well as a small number of diesel push-pull trains capable of 160 or 180 km/h are also now in service.

The expansion of the improved passenger services is a major continuing programme. On the key trunk routes the numbers of quasi-high-speed and accelerated trains are being increased and efforts are being made to remove the remaining obstacles to 160 km/h operation on sections where this speed is presently not permitted. On main lines radiating from major cities along the trunk routes accelerated services are being introduced, in many cases in the form of short-distance intercity services.

Separate series of locomotive-hauled passenger rolling stock are being delivered for 120, 140 and 160 km/h service and around 25 per cent of new stock is of double-deck layout, with versions for long-distance overnight travel and for shorter distance intercity services. Several types of diesel push-pull trains, of single- and double-deck layout, and electric push-pull trains are either under development or in trial operation on intercity services. In late 2000 production double-deck diesel-electric NZJ class push-pull trains capable of 170 km/h were introduced on several Beijing Tianjin services, augmenting existing locomotive-hauled trains.

Separation of passenger and freight traffic is now put forward as the solution to congestion on the busiest axes. Consequently, studies began of a pilot scheme for a 200 km/h line reserved for passenger trains. The two routes reviewed for the experiment were Beijing-Tianjin (137 km) and Guangzhou to the Hong Kong border at Shenzhen (143 km). Upgrading of the latter route for 160 km/h running was completed in 1994, and public service at that speed was inaugurated in March 1995.

An intensive passenger train service with many trains travelling at up to 160 km/h is now in operation between Guangzhou and Shenzhen. Several experimental and pre-production Chinese-built 200 km/h electric push-pull trains are being tested on this route.

Construction of China's first dedicated passenger main line railway is now under way between Qinhuangdao and Shenyang. This 400 km double-track electrified line is designed for 200 km/h operation and when opened to traffic in 2004 will help to eliminate the freight bottleneck on the existing line, one of China's busiest. Construction and operation of the new line, which will initially only have six stations along its length, will provide opportunities for technical advances in many aspects of railway engineering in China.

Plans outlined under China's 10th Five-Year Plan (2001-2005) will see the route-length of line on which 140 km/h or 160 km/h trains can be operated steadily increased to a projected total of around 14,000 km by 2005. The network will comprise the Beijing–Shenyang, Beijing–Shanghai, Beijing–Nanchang–Shenzhen, Xuzhou–Lanzhou–Urumuqi, Shanghai–Chongqing–Chengdu and Guangzhou–Shenzhen lines. 200 km/h services will be operated between Guangzhou and Shenzhen in the south and between Beijing and Shenyang in the north. For the latter operation the new dedicated passenger line between Qinhuangdao and Shenyang will be used and the existing Beijing–Qinhuangdao line will be upgraded to permit the higher speed.

### Freight operations

Rapid economic growth in China resulted in freight transported on the national railway system rising from 1,405 million tonnes and 986,019 million tonne-km in 1988 to 1,618 million tonnes and 1,304,000 million tonne-km by 1997. The past five years however have been characterised by a levelling-off of the growth, possibly due to the effects of an economic downturn and the impact of a rapidly expanding high-quality road network. Approximately 40 per cent of the freight traffic carried on the railway is coal.

The Ministry of Railways has been raising individual train weights by up to a third with 3,000 to 4,000 tonnes now the norm on many main lines. On the key trunk lines, on which 160 km/h quasi-high-speed passenger services are being operated, many freight trains of 5,000 tonnes are now being operated to maximise capacity on these lines. These developments have been fraught with several problems, such as restricted yard siding and loop capacities. The historic problem of freight speeds being restricted by rolling stock equipped with plain bearings has largely been eliminated: most vehicles in service are now fitted with roller bearings.

The maximum speed of freight trains in China is restricted to 75 to 85 km/h due to limitations presented by factors such as bogie, coupler and brake system design. Intensive research and development efforts are being made to find ways to eliminate these obstacles to increased freight train speeds. Among the projects being undertaken are several aimed at developing high-stability freight bogies. Specialist engineering organisations from several foreign countries including the USA and South Africa are assisting in these projects.

Average point-to-point freight train speed on important lines is being increased by the use of more powerful locomotives allowing higher speeds on adverse grades.

Plans for increasing maximum freight train speeds are initially focused on parcels and container traffic on the busy trunk lines. Two types of wagon with a maximum designed speed of 120 km/h are now in production. These are the P65 boxcar for parcels traffic, equipped with type 2D cross-braced bogies, and the X1k container flat wagon, with type Zk3 bogies with independently sprung axles.

Another significant technical advance relating to freight train operation now being incorporated in series production of freight rolling stock is the increase of maximum axle-load from 21 to 25 tonnes. As could be expected, initial production is of open coal wagons for unit-train operation on the special purpose Datong Qinhuangdao coal line. Prototypes of a 25 tonne axle-load development of the standard general purpose open wagon for coal, coke and ore transport have also been built.

In both new line construction and electrification, expansion of coal-carrying capacity is of paramount importance. China's domestic energy needs are 70 per cent met by coal and at the same time exports are rising steadily. The principal coalfields are found in Shaanxi, Inner Mongolia, Henan, Shandong, Ningxia, Guizhou, Anhui and Heliongjiang provinces. Coal flows are predominantly north-to-south and west-to-east, and form over half the traffic on some main lines.

A 10-year programme, aimed to raise rail coal-carrying capacity to over 600 million tonnes a year, has involved the upgrading of 12 existing coal routes and construction of eight more, plus a lift of maximum trainloads on key routes from 3,500 to 5,000 tonnes. On the special Da-Qin coal line, trains of up to 10,000 tonnes are being operated. Coal traffic requirements dominated much of the railway expansion and electrification programmes executed in the 1980s and 1990s.

Completion of double-tracking of the 1,800 km lateral route from Lanzhou to the port of Lianyungan, electrification between Lanzhou and Zhengzhou and completion in 1996 of the 502 km Zhongwei-Baoji line, opened up export opportunities for coal from the Gansu and Ningxia fields. Provincial governments provided part of the investment in this scheme, as it brings substantial benefits to their coalfields.

China's second major coal line, which forms part of the Shenhua Project for developing the huge 225 billion tonne Shenfu Dongsheng coalfield in Shaanxi and Inner Mongolia, is rapidly taking form. The electrification of the 270 km western section of this line, between Shenmubei and Shuozhou has been completed and the first part of the 600 km eastern section from Shenchi to the new harbour at Huanghua, south of Tianjin, was opened to

*Class DF4D diesel locomotive on a Shanghai–Harbin express passenger service* (Lennox MacEwan) 0058679

*Class DF8 and DF4 diesel-electric locomotives double-head a heavy freight service* (Lennox MacEwan) 0058680

*Twin-section Class SS4 electric locomotive with '5,000 tonne' freight at Wuhan* (Bruce Evans)

traffic during 2000. The third phase of the overall project, which also includes the development of the mines, the coal terminal at the harbour, a large power station and provision of a shipping fleet for transporting coal, is due for completion in 2005, when production and shipping capacity is planned to reach 60 million tonnes per year.

## Intermodal operations

Following the launch of through service on the Alatau Pass route to Russia in 1992, nine container terminals for landbridge traffic have been established by the Chinese. These are at the port of Lianyungang, and at Tanggu, Hohhot, Erlianhot, Zhengzhou, Xi'an, Lanzhou, Urumqi and Druzhba. Using this route, transits to European destinations from Japan are 2,700 km shorter than via the Trans-Siberian. Japanese industry has access to the new international route via the ports at Lianyungang and Shanghai. Lianyungang port is being extended to raise capacity from 14 to 18.5 million tonnes a year, financed by a loan from the Japanese government.

Collaboration with Japan intensified during 1997 with the establishment of International Freight Railway Systems Co Ltd, a joint venture agreement between China Railway Foreign Service Corporation and JR Freight. This foresaw the establishment of maritime links from Japan feeding intermodal traffic (and general freight) into the CR network for onward rail distribution both in China and to neighbouring countries. Intermodal traffic for Europe was to be handled on new services using the China Land Bridge in a Japanese bid to establish a rail alternative to maritime links.

Intermodal traffic is also the focus of a feasibility study, started in 1997 and funded by the United Nations and the Asian Development Bank, into the Euro-Asia Continental Bridge project, linking east coast ports in China with northwest Europe via Xinjiang province in western China and Kirghizia.

There has been rapid growth in domestic container transport. In recent years for the first time block loads of domestic containers have become a more familiar sight, boosted by production of a number of types of wagon to cater for this traffic. The latest design of container wagon now being produced is the Type X1k designed to operate at speeds up to 120 km/h.

## New lines

New lines are coming on stream all the time, partly to relieve pressure on the heavily occupied trunk routes in the east of the country, where the bulk of the network is concentrated, and partly to extend railways into the western and southern provinces, which are poorly provided with rail transport. In 1999, 1,040 km of new lines were put into operation.

The ninth Five-Year Plan, covering the period 1996-2000, was to see 8,100 km of new lines completed at a cost of Y330 billion. The total includes several routes already under construction; the remaining lines will further improve access to the Shanxi and Inner Mongolia coalfields, and to the Tarim Basin oil deposits. The greater portion of new construction (6,100 km) will be funded by the state, while 2,000 km will be paid for by regional authorities.

The tenth Five-Year Plan, announced in late 2000 for the period 2001 to 2005, shows that the expansion of China's railway system is planned to continue at a rapid pace. Under the new plan China plans to invest US$42 billion in railway construction over the next five years. Construction would include around 6,000 km of new lines, 3,000 km of double-tracking, 5,000 km of electrification and improvements to many of the key main lines to permit 160 km/h passenger train operation. By 2005 the national railway network, including joint-venture lines, is expected to total 75,000 km, of which 20,000 km would be electrified and 25,000 km would be double-track.

Major new line construction projects in progress in 2000 included:
Xi'an–Ankang (Shaanxi Province) (245 km)
Shenmu–Yan'an (Shaanxi) (390 km)
Shenchi–Huanghuagang (Shaanxi and Hebei) (590 km)
Liupanshui–Baiguo (Guizhou) (120 km)
Daxian–Wanxian (Sichuan) (160 km)
Anbian–Meihuashan (Sichuan and Yunnan) (370 km)
Meizhou–Kanshi (Guangdong and Fujian) (150 km)
Xinyi–Changxing (Jiangsu) (640 km)
Zhanjiang–Hai'an (Guangdong) (140 km)
Qinhuangdao–Shenyang (Hebei and Liaoning) (420 km)
Xi'an–Hefei (Shaanxi, Henan, Hubei and Anhui) (955 km)
Chongqing–Huaihua (Chongqing, Sichuan, Guizhou, Hunan) (625 km)
Jixian–Tianjin (Tianjin) (120 km)
Yangquan–Shexian (Shanxi and Hebei) (140 km)
Changjiabu–Jingmen (Hubei) (180 km)

Major new railway construction projects scheduled to start between 2000 and 2002 include:
Golmud–Lhasa (Qinghai and Tibet) (1,120 km)
Jiaozhou–Xinyi (Shandong and Jiangsu) (300 km)
Wenzhou–Fuzhou (Zhejiang and Fujian) (360 km)
Changde–Luodi (Hunan) (160 km)
Shanghai–Nanjing (Jiangsu) (300 km)
Hefei–Nanjing (Jiangsu) (145 km)
Shaoyang–Lengshuitun (Hunan and Guangxi) (100 km)
Lengshuitun–Yulin (Guangxi) (420 km)
Tongling–Jiujiang (Anhui and Jiangxi) (220 km)
Chongqing–Suining (Chongqing and Sichuan) (150 km)
Ganzhou–Longyan (Fujian and Jiangxi) (220 km)

These projects fall essentially into two groups: new lines in existing high-traffic corridors primarily for passenger traffic and involving higher train speeds and thus more advanced technology than presently in general use on existing lines; and projects aimed at creating major new high-capacity rail corridors in various parts of the country to overcome bottlenecks and to assist with economic development.

Two new passenger lines will extend from Beijing to Shanghai and from Qinhuangdao, northeast of Beijing, to Shenyang, Liaoning Province. The existing lines in these corridors are among the busiest double-track lines in China, and the aim for both projects is to construct new lines to carry the long-distance passenger traffic, freeing capacity on the existing lines for additional freight.

The 420 km Qinhuangdao–Shenyang line (the Qin-Shen line), now under construction, has been designed as an electrified double-track quasi-high-speed line, initially for 160 km/h operation. It is planned that the maximum permissible speed on this new line will be increased, in due course, to 200 km/h and eventually to 250 km/h. Work has recently begun on further upgrading of the existing Beijing–Qinhuangdao line to increase the maximum permissible speed to above 160 km/h. Completion of these two projects will allow a significant speeding up of passenger services on the busy Beijing–Shenyang axis.

The new 1,300 km Beijing–Shanghai line has been designated China's first true high-speed line, intended initially for 300 km/h but eventually for an ultimate maximum speed of 350 km/h. Construction had been expected to start in 2000, but reports from China in April 1999 suggested that this might be delayed until as late as 2006.

The second group of new line construction projects in China is aimed at the expansion of the grid of high-capacity corridors. Many of these will focus on the following three corridors: Dalian–Changxing (west of Shanghai); Shimenxian (Hunan)–Zhanjiang (Guangdong); and Nanjing–Xi'an (Jiangsu, Anhui, Henan, Shaanxi and Hubei).

A key proposal of the planning for the new corridor between Dalian and Changxing, which will ease the flow of rail traffic between the southern tip of Liaoning Province and the southern and central parts of China, is the introduction of train ferries between Dalian and Yantai, eliminating a long detour via Tianjin.

The Shimenxian–Zhanjiang scheme, the southern section of the existing north-south corridor linking Luoyang, Liuzhou and Zhanjiang, includes some new construction and doubling of existing tracks.

Improvements to the east-west corridor between Nanjing and Xi'an are required to augment the existing busy route via Xuzhou and to provide a more direct route for coal traffic between the Ningxia and Shaanxi coal-mining areas and the industrialised and developed eastern coastal areas.

On the basis of China's tenth Five-Year Plan (2001-2005), the national railway system, including joint-venture public railways, is projected to total 75,000 km. In the longer term, the public railway network is projected to exceed 120,000 route-km by 2050. Some of the major projected lines include:

A line linking Lhasa, the capital of Tibet, with the national railway network. Tibet remains the last province of China to be connected to the national system. Two routes have been proposed, one an extension of the new Guangtong–Dali line in Yunnan Province and the other an extension of the existing 815 km Xining–Golmud line in Qinghai. In October 2000 the Chinese government formally announced the decision to proceed with the 1,100 km line from Golmud to Lhasa.

A line in Xinjiang linking Korla and Kashi, but following a much more southerly alignment to the recently opened direct link. A connection from this line to Golmud is also envisaged.

A line in Xinjiang linking Kashi, at the end of the recently completed Korla–Kashi line, with the Kirghizia border town of Torugart. New lines would be constructed within Kirghizia to provide international links to Kazakhstan and Uzbekistan.

*Type X1k container-carrying wagon* (Bruce Evans)

A line south from Kunming to the borders with Thailand and Myanmar.

A line from Zhongwei (Ningxia Autonomous Region) eastwards towards Taiyuan.

A line from Shizuishan eastwards to Dongsheng. A new east-west corridor would be created as a new line is presently under construction between Dongsheng and Jungar Qi, the present terminal of an electrified line from Datong.

A line from Xining (Qinghai) to Chengdu, the capital of Sichuan Province.

A new 360 km line along the eastern coast between the cities of Wenzhou in Zhejiang and Fuzhou in Fujian.

A new line from Chongqing to Nanjing generally following the course of the Yangtze River.

The construction of the Golmud to Lhasa railway will be one of the greatest railway construction challenges engineers have faced. Much of the 1,100 km line will be at altitudes of around 4,000 m, with the highest point at 5,070 m, and it will traverse extremely rugged and inhospitable terrain with many areas of permafrost. Preparatory engineering work is now in progress along the route and officials have indicated that they hope to complete this massive engineering task in six to eight years. A related project is also underway to increase capacity on the existing Xining–Golmud line.

In recent years China has greatly increased the rate of development of railway infrastructure in the poorer and more remote western areas of the country. The tenth Five-Year Plan covering the period from 2001 to 2005 will see about 40 per cent of the total planned investment for large and medium railway projects directed to projects in the west involving new lines and improvements to existing lines.

China's second major coal railway is being created to exploit the great Shenfu Dongsheng coalfield straddling the Inner Mongolia/Shaanxi provincial border. This coalfield is one of the eight largest coalfields in the world and is being developed by the state-owned Shenhua Group Corporation. The 270 km double-track western section of the new joint-venture line, between Shenmubei and Shuozhou, was completed several years ago and has recently been electrified. The first part of the 600 km eastern section from Shenchi to the new harbour at Huanghua was opened to traffic during 2000.

Another new route has been created out of the great Shanxi coalfield by construction of an electrified double-track line 270 km eastward from Shenmu, south of Baotou, to Suzhou, on the main north-to-south route from Datong to Taiyuan. The aim is to give direct access from the developing Shenmu coalfield to the port of Huanghua.

A 150 km single-track link between Meizhou in Guangdong and Kanshi in Fujian was recently opened to traffic. This is the first direct rail connection between these two provinces and is a valuable link in the network gradually forming along the coast south of Hangzhou.

Completion was achieved in 2000 of the 10.6 km combined road/rail bridge across the Yangtze River to replace the Wuhu train ferry. Construction of this bridge began in 1997. The bridge's completion has helped to ease traffic on the heavily utilised Nanjing–Shanghai line, as some trains for Hangzhou and points further south now use the route via Wuhu.

During the 1980s and 1990s there was a steady increase in the proportion of new lines constructed as joint-venture railways where the Ministry of Railways, local governments and authorities share the investment costs.

By the end of 2000 more than 20 joint-venture railways, totalling about 6,500 km, were operating with many more under construction or in planning. In addition, on a number of the operating systems extensions, branches and capacity increasing works were under construction. During the ninth Five-Year Plan for the national railways (1996-2000) joint-venture railways were expected to account for over 45 per cent of the total new route-length constructed. It is expected that during the period of the tenth Five-Year Plan, from 2001 to 2005, development of joint-venture railways will account for a similar proportion of total route-length constructed. Approximately 40 per cent of the capital investment in the joint-venture lines has come from provincial authorities, major cities and other organisations.

The joint-venture model for railway development and operation was introduced to speed up the expansion of the railway system, to reform the investment system and to open up new funding channels. Prior to the introduction of this model, funding for public railway development had come almost entirely from the Ministry of Railways.

Joint-venture railways are run as corporations using market-orientated systems for construction and management. Many joint-venture railways are set up as limited liability or joint stock companies. The standardised management system developed for the joint-venture railways includes requirements for establishing boards of directors and supervisors for the company. The companies are required to be managed independently and to have full responsibility for their own financial affairs.

Joint-venture railways are required to use competitive bidding for activities such as railway construction and for acquisition of rolling stock. This is to control costs through market competition. The contract systems for this are gradually being adapted to conform to international practice.

New lines being constructed as joint-venture railways include the following:

Yan'an–Shenmubei (Shaanxi Province)
Shenchinan–Huanghuagang (Shaanxi and Hebei Provinces)
Xinhe–Changxing (Jiangsu Province)
Shuicheng–Baiguo (Guizhou Province)
Tongling–Jiujiang (Anhui and Jiangxi Provinces)
Xi'an–Angkang (Shaanxi Province)
Yangquan–Shexian (Shanxi and Hebei Provinces)
Anbian–Meihuashan (Sichuan and Yunnan Provinces)
Jixian–Tianjin (Tianjin City)
Wenzhou–Fuzhou (Zhejiang and Fujian Provinces)
Changjiabu–Jingmen (Hubei Province)
Qingding–Luling (Anhui Province).

Recently completed projects using investment systems similar to the joint-venture railway model include the new Yangtze River bridge at Wuhu and the doubling of CR's Xiaoshan–Ningbo railway. Various extension and double-tracking work is also being undertaken on several of the operating joint-venture railways.

The rate of construction of local railways, public railways in which there is no investment by the Ministry of Railways, has increased in recent years as local authorities, provincial governments and other bodies such as mining concerns have sought to encourage economic development. At the end of 1999, there were about 75 local railways totalling 4,800 km in operation with around 20 more totalling 1,800 km under construction. About 30 per cent of the local railway route-length at the end of 1999 was narrow-gauge (762 mm) but many of these lines are now being closed.

### Improvements to existing lines

Current improvements to existing lines in China focus on three main areas: track-doubling to improve line capacity; electrification (see 'Electrification' section); and improvements to raise line speeds. In 1999 major track-doubling schemes for completion by 2002 covered over 3,000 route-km. In some cases, where difficult terrain is encountered, such as Chengdu-Yangpingguan (400 km), track-doubling involves extensive engineering such as new tunnels and major viaducts. The recent rate of track-doubling in China has been around 1,000 km each year. China expects to complete about 1,200 km of double-tracking in 2001 and about 5,000 km during the course of the tenth Five-Year Plan extending to the end of 2005. Lines in the process of being doubled in 2000 include the following:

Xiangtang–Longchuan on the Beijing–Kowloon line (Jiangxi and Guangdong Provinces)
Xiangtan–Liupanshui on the Zhuzhou–Kunming line (Hunan and Guizhou Provinces)
Xinxiang–Yanzhou (Henan and Shandong Provinces)
Tianshui–Lanzhou (Gansu Provinces)

*New Class SS6B and SS8 electric locomotives at the Zhuzhou locomotive-building plant* (Bruce Evans)

*Although the use of steam traction is much reduced, it still plays a key role, as in this November 2000 view of a 3,500 tonne coal train on the Badtou–Shenmu joint-venture railway, with two Class QJ locomotives providing haulage and a third member of the same type banking at the rear* (Bruce Evans)

*Class DF5B diesel-electric locomotive for shunting and local duties* (Bruce Evans) 2001/0114231

Shimenxian—Huaihua (Hunan Province)
Xiaoshan—Ningbo (Zhejiang Province)
Yanzhou—Rizhao (Shandong Province)
Yakeshi—Hailaer (Inner Mongolia)
Litang—Nanning (Guangxi Province)

Under the ninth Five-Year Plan, the Ministry of Railways has been implementing improvements to raise line speeds for passenger services on main trunk routes (see 'Passenger operations' section). Work has included: bridge strengthening; replacement of level crossings with grade-separated structures; easing of curves; installation of high-speed turnouts; and some replacement of rail and sleepers. Some similar work is also being done on lines feeding the trunk routes.

### Traction and rolling stock

At the end of December 1997, the railway had 15,335 locomotives in operation, of which 2,931 were steam, 9,583 were diesel and 2,821 electric.

Around 800 new diesel locomotives and 250 electric locomotives are delivered to the national railways annually and this is quickly eliminating steam traction, which is expected to end on the 14 national railway administrations by 2002. On less important joint-venture and local railways the transition will be more prolonged. In addition to the new units supplied to the public railways, approximately 120 new diesel and electric locomotives are delivered to mining and industrial concerns each year. Small numbers of the standard SY type steam shunting locomotive are still constructed to order for Chinese coal mining concerns and occasionally for foreign tourist railways.

New locomotive construction for the four years to 1999 by the factories until recently administered by the Ministry of Railways was as follows:

|  | 1996 | 1997 | 1998 | 1999 |
|---|---|---|---|---|
| Diesel | 892 | 852 | 697 | 671 |
| Electric | 157 | 196 | 255 | 295 |

The Ministry of Railways expects that from 2001 to 2005 more than 50 per cent of the locomotives constructed for the national railways will be electric. To meet the targeted requirement for electric locomotives new production lines have been established at the hitherto diesel-only factories at Dalian and Ziyang, and these will augment production at Zhuzhou and Datong, the two plants that have supplied most of China's electric locomotives. The first locomotives from the new production lines were due to be delivered in late 2000 and were to be of Types SS3B and SS4, both standard mainline designs.

Around 5,000 of the locally produced 2,430 kW DF4/4A/4B (Dong Feng 4) Co-Co diesel-electrics in both freight and passenger versions are now in service. Although DF4B production is continuing, the principal general-purpose main line diesel locomotive type presently being delivered is the 2,650 kW DF4C. The other main production version in this family is the 2,940 kW DF4D, most examples of which are geared for a maximum speed of 132 km/h and are used for improved passenger services. An improved version of the DF4D geared for higher maximum speed entered production in 1999. Around 600 passenger-service DF4Ds have been delivered since 1996.

Other standard Chinese-built types are the Beijing-built DF7 family general-purpose locomotive and the Sifang-built DF5, a heavy shunter which also handles local passenger and freight haulage. The high-powered DF8B freight locomotive produced by the Qishuyan and Ziyang works is the most powerful freight type in domestic production, at 3,680 kW. This is China's first main line diesel designed for a 25 tonne axleload as against the 23 tonne standard. Qishuyan's main production locomotive type at present is the DF11 for quasi-high-speed services. By the end of 2000, about 270 of these units were in traffic.

Development of high-power diesel engines of 4,000 to 5,000 kW is taking place at several of the diesel locomotive plants. At Dalian, work is being undertaken with USA specialist assistance and the first locomotives with the new engines are to be tested in the near future. China is developing diesel locomotives with AC motors and prototype AC-motored versions of the standard mainline DF4D and secondary service DF5 types are now being tested.

In recent years several of the Chinese locomotive and rolling stock works have designed and built diesel multiple-unit/push-pull passenger train sets as part of the massive efforts to improve intercity passenger services on key main lines. Several of these designs are now on test with prototypes and, in some cases, preproduction batches in service. Most of these sets are designed for 160 or 200 km/h operation.

As part of a strategy to develop high-speed passenger services on selected routes, China has been developing its own trainset design for operation at speeds of up to 220 km/h. A prototype unit designed by Changchun Railway Car Works, formed of two power cars, eight single-deck trailers and two double-deck trailers, was due to be completed during 1998. The prototype unit is a joint project of the Zhuzhou Electric Locomotive Works, the Changchun Car Company, the Puzhen Locomotive and Rolling Stock Works and the Tangshan Rolling Stock Works. The unit is formed of a locomotive, a single double-deck passenger coach, four single-deck passenger coaches and a single-deck passenger coach with a driver's cab at one end. The unit was completed in the first half of 1999 and was due to be introduced into trial service on the Guangzhou–Shenzen line, which has been designated as China's 200 km/h test line.

In addition to the 200 km/h experimental train, several types of emu are in use or on trial on various lines. China's first domestically developed modern emu was handed over for revenue-earning services in April 1999. The 'Spring City' trainset was produced jointly by the Changchun Car Plant, The Zhuzhou Electric Locomotive Research Institute and the Kunming Railway Administration. It is in use for tourist services between Kunming and the nearby 'Stone Forest'.

In September 2000, a prototype 25kV AC high-speed trainset was rolled out at the Zhuzhun Electric Locomotive works. The 'Blue Arrow' unit comprises a 4,800 kW power car, fire trailers and a driving trailer, although it was expected that longer versions with two power cars would be produced. Eight trains of the type were reported to have been ordered for the Guangzhou-Kowloon route.

To cater for the increased rate of electrification the Zhuzhou Electric Locomotive Works and the Datong Locomotive Works have expanded output and two new electric locomotive production lines are being established at the Dalian Locomotive and Rolling Stock Works and Ziyang Diesel Locomotive Works. The Shaoshan SS3B Co-Co, a development of the preceding SS1 and SS2 designs offering enhanced adhesion and equipped with single-arm pantographs, remained in production in 2000, having succeeded the SS3, of which over 700 are in service.

A Bo-Bo+Bo-Bo development of the SS3 Co-Co, the SS4, is in batch production at the Zhuzhou and Datong plants and is also to be built at the Dalian plant from which 20 are expected to be delivered in 2001. It weighs 184 tonnes, is rated at 6,400 kW and has a top speed of 100 km/h. Small numbers of the technically improved SS4B have been supplied to the joint-venture railways being constructed as part of the Shenhua coal project. A further version, the SS4C, with axleload increased from 23 to 25 tonnes has also been developed. The 4,800 kW SS6 and SS6B Co-Co emerged in 1992 and 1993 and feature Hitachi traction equipment. At the Zhuzhou works the SS6B has since replaced the SS3B as the main general-purpose electric locomotive built by the plant. The Bo-

*Class DJ1 two-section electric locomotive built by STEZ, a joint venture between Siemens Transportation Systems, Zhuzhou Electric Locomotive Works and Zhuzhou Electric Locomotive Research Institute* 2001/0116570

Bo-Bo SS7, also rated at 4,800 kW, is designed for heavy haulage on steeply graded and sharply curved routes. The SS7B is a freight version with 25 tonne axleload, while the SS7C is in production for 120 km/h passenger service. A further version, the SS7D, has been developed for 160 m/h services. The SS8 Bo-Bo, rated at 3,600 kW, remains the standard electric type in production for 160 km/h quasi-high-speed services, with over 240 units now operating. This type set a Chinese rail speed record on 24 June 1998, when a member of the class attained a maximum speed in excess of 240 km/h on a section of the Beijing–Guangzhou main line south of Zhengzhou. Other passenger electric types, the 4,800 kW Co-Co 160 km/h SS9 type and 200 km/h Bo-Bo type, are presently at prototype stage. China's first domestically produced electric locomotive featuring three-phase AC traction motors, the 4,000 kW AC4000 produced by the Zhuzhou plant, commenced trials in 1997.

In 1999 Siemens Transportation Systems established STEZ, a joint-venture company with the Zhuzhou Electric Locomotive Works and the Zhuzhou Electric Locomotive Research Institute to produce locomotives and traction components in China. The first products of the new company, Siemens Traction Equipment Ltd, Zhuzhou, were to be 20 Class DJ1 three-phase 6,400 kW eight-axle AC electric freight locomotives. The first three of 14 type were built at Siemens' Graz plant in Austria, with deliveries commencing in September 2001. The remaining 17 locomotives were to be constructed at Zhuzhou. Production by the new company is expected to grow to 70 to 100 locomotives per year with export production also planned for the future.

The most high-profile agreement with a western company in recent years was a deal signed in November 1996 with Adtranz, whereby China was to rent a 25 kV AC version of the Swedish X2000 tilting high-speed train for two years, possibly purchasing it thereafter. This arrived in China in March 1998, and in 2000 was running between Guangzhou, Shenzhen and Kowloon.

The country's four coach manufacturing plants have recently been manufacturing about 2,500 vehicles a year. Most of the passenger vehicles now being supplied to the national railways by the four coach manufacturing plants in China are based on the standard Type 25 coach initially developed at Changchun with Brel assistance. A wide selection of variants, of both single-deck and double-deck format, is now being produced for 120, 140 and 160 km/h running. These coaches are produced in soft- and hard-sleeper and soft- and hard-seat configurations with hard-seat being the predominant form. Baggage vans, power cars and dining cars, the last in single- and double-deck format, are also produced.

The joint-venture Changchun Adtranz Railway Co Ltd was established in January 1997, and planned an annual output of 160 vehicles. At the beginning of 1995, DWA in Germany was building 100 passenger coaches for CR, while in 1996 South Korea's Hanjin Heavy Industries Co Ltd supplied 30 coaches suitable for 200 km/h running.

Coach production at a new plant works in Qingdao is set to expand following establishment of a joint venture between the China National Railway Locomotive and Rolling Stock Industry Corporation (LORIC), Canadian manufacturer Bombardier and Power Corp.

Approximately 30,000 freight wagons are produced in China annually, most of which are supplied to CR. The main production types are the C64 general purpose open gondola, the P64A and P65 covered wagons and the XN17A, X6B, X6C and X1k container wagons. Of these the P65 and X1k types are the first 120 km/h freight types to enter large-scale production. A wide variety of other types is also produced including various tank wagons, hopper wagons and car transporters. Special purpose open coal wagons designed for a 25 tonne axleload are now being built for use in unit-trains on the Datong–Qinhuangdao coal line. An enlarged 25 tonne axleload version of the C64 general purpose gondola has also been developed and should soon enter production for the transport of ores and coal.

At the end of 1997, rolling stock comprised 34,346 passenger cars and 437,686 wagons.

On the approximately 75 local railways, rolling stock in 1998 amounted to 231 steam and 155 diesel locomotives, 200 passenger cars and 3,317 wagons.

## Signalling and telecommunications

Overall control of all signalling and telecommunications systems and projects is in the hands of the China National Railway Signal & Communications Corporation, with a staff of 23,000. Nevertheless the scale of work has led to joint ventures and contracts with foreign suppliers. Elin of Austria has supplied a track-to-train radio system embracing some 600 route-km south of Beijing. The country's first solid-state interlocking is being supplied by GEC-General Signal; it will be installed at Xiao Li Zhang, on the Zhengzhou-Wuchang line.

Ansaldo and its US subsidiary Union Switch & Signal are installing computerised interlockings for 13 stations on the new Beijing-Guangzhou line, along with a hump computer process control system for a marshalling yard on the route.

In 1997, the China Academy of Railway Sciences signed a co-operation agreement with Japan's Railway Technical Research Institute covering the joint development of automatic train control for a possible Chinese high-speed line. Japanese suppliers Nippon Sharyo, Keisan and Daido will equip a test track near Beijing.

During 1998-1999 Siemens commissioned China's first electronic interlocking at Fuyang marshalling yard, Anhui Province.

In October 1998 Shanghai GPT, a joint venture between GEC Marconi and Shanghai Railway Communications, won a US$10 million contract from the Ministry of Railways to upgrade Chinese Railways' communications system.

## Electrification

The Ministry of Railways is planning to maintain the rate of electrification during the period of the tenth Five-Year Plan extending to 2005 at about 1,000 km per year.

Electrification at 25 kV 50 Hz has been a high priority since the early 1980s. Total route-km under wires amounted to 13,630 km by the end of 1999. When joint venture railways in major coal-producing regions are added, the total route-km under wires amounts to some 16,000 route-km.

In pursuit of electric traction over the whole length of the 2,313 km north-to-south corridor from Beijing to Guangzhou and Shenzhen, energisation of the 547 route-km from Zhengzhou to Wuhan has been completed, with the backing of a World Bank loan. This scheme embodies CTC, fibre optic cabling, jointless track circuits and computerised interlockings. Wiring began at the northern end of the route, between Beijing and Zhengzhou (697 km) in 1991, and was completed in 1998. The completion of the electrification of the entire

### Diesel locomotives (National railways, including joint-venture railways)

| Class | Wheel arrangement | Power kW | Speed km/h | Weight tonnes | No in service 12/2000 | First built | Mechanical | Builders Transmission |
|---|---|---|---|---|---|---|---|---|
| DF | Co-Co | 1,325 | 100 | 126 | 350 | 1964 | Dalian, Qishuyan, Chengdu, Datong | E |
| DF2 | Co-Co | 790 | 95 | 113 | 80 | 1964 | Qishuyan | E |
| DF4 | Co-Co | 2,430 | 100/120 | 138 | 390 | 1969 | Dalian, Ziyang [2] | E |
| DF4A | Co-Co | 2,430 | 100 | 138 | 360 | 1976 | Dalian | E |
| DF4B | Co-Co | 2,430 | 100/120 | 138 | 4,250 | 1984 | Dalian, Datong, Sifang, Ziyang | E |
| DF4C | Co-Co | 2,650 | 100 | 138 | 920 | 1985 | Dalian, Datong, Sifang, Ziyang | E |
| DF4D | Co-Co | 2,940 | 100/140/170 | 138 | 700 | 1996 | Dalian | E |
| DF4E | Co-Co+Co-Co | 4,860 | 100 | 276 | 16 | 1994 | Sifang | E |
| DF5 [1] | Co-Co | 1,210 | 80/100 | 138 | 750 | 1984 | Dalian, Sifang | E |
| DF5D | Co-Co | 1,210 | 100 | 138 | 10 | 1999 | Dalian | E |
| DF6 | Co-Co | 2,940 | 118 | 138 | 4 | 1989 | Dalian | |
| DF7 | Co-Co | 1,470 | 100 | 135 | 250 | 1982 | Beijing 7 Feb | |
| DF7B | Co-Co | 1,840 | 100 | 135 | 190 | 1990 | Beijing 7 Feb | E |
| DF7C | Co-Co | 1,470 | 100 | 135 | 290 | 1991 | Beijing 7 Feb | E |
| DF7D | Co-Co | 1,840 | 100 | 138 | 210 | 1995 | Beijing 7 Feb | E |
| DF8 | Co-Co | 3,310 | 100 | 138 | 140 | 1984 | Qishuyan | E |
| DF8B | Co-Co | 3,680 | 100 | 138/150 | 130 | 1997 | Qishuyan, Ziyang | E |
| DF9 | Co-Co | 3,610 | 140 | 138 | 2 | 1990 | Qishuyan | E |
| DF10F | Co-Co+Co-Co | 4,400 | 160 | 240 | 5 | 1996 | Dalian | E |
| DF11 | Co-Co | 3,610 | 160 | 138 | 270 | 1992 | Qishuyan | E |
| DF12 | Co-Co | 2,430 | 100 | 138/150 | 5 | 1997 | Ziyang | E |
| ND2 | Co-Co | 1,540 | 120 | 120 | 270 | 1974 | Electroputere | E |
| ND3 | Co-Co | 1,540 | 100 | 126 | 88 | 1985 | Electroputere | E |
| ND5 | Co-Co | 2,940 | 120 | 138 | 400 | 1984 | GE | E |
| BJ [1] | B-B | 1,985 | 90/120 | 92 | 340 | 1970 | Beijing 7 Feb | H |
| DFH2 | B-B | 920 | 60 | 60 | 20 | 1973 | Ziyang | H |
| DFH3 | B-B | 1,980 | 120 | 92 | 250 | 1972 | Sifang | H |
| DFH5 | B-B | 790 | 40/80 | 86 | 260 | 1976 | Ziyang | H |
| DFH21 [2] | B-B | 810 | 50 | 60 | 100 | 1977 | Sifang | H |
| NY6 | C-C | 3,160 | 105 | 138 | 5 | 1972 | Henschel | H |
| NY7 | C-C | 3,680 | 110 | 138 | 10 | 1972 | Henschel | H |

[1] Some built for 1,520 mm gauge
[2] 1,000 mm gauge

### Electric locomotives (National railways, including joint-venture railways)

| Class | Wheel arrangement | Power kW | Speed km/h | Weight tonnes | No in service 12/2000 | First built | Builders |
|---|---|---|---|---|---|---|---|
| SS1 | Co-Co | 3,780 | 93 | 138 | 810 | 1968 | Zhuzhou |
| SS3 | Co-Co | 4,350 | 100 | 138 | 725 | 1978 | Zhuzhou, Datong |
| SS3B | Co-Co | 4,350 | 100 | 138 | 600 | 1992 | Zhuzhou, Datong |
| SS4 | Bo-Bo+Bo-Bo | 6,400 | 100 | 184 | 570 | 1985 | Zhuzhou |
| SS4B | Bo-Bo+Bo-Bo | 6,400 | 100 | 184 | 30 | 1999 | Zhuzhou |
| SS6 | Co-Co | 4,800 | 100 | 138 | 53 | 1991 | Zhuzhou (Hitachi) |
| SS6B | Co-Co | 4,800 | 100 | 138 | 70 | 1992 | Zhuzhou (Hitachi) |
| SS7 | Bo-Bo-Bo | 4,800 | 100 | 138 | 100 | 1992 | Datong |
| SS7C | Bo-Bo-Bo | 4,800 | 120 | 132 | 50 | 1998 | Datong |
| SS8 | Bo-Bo | 3,600 | 170 | 88 | 220 | 1996 | Zhuzhou |
| 6G | Co-Co | 4,800 | 112 | 138 | 5 | 1971 | Alsthom |
| 8G | Bo-Bo+Bo-Bo | 6,400 | 100 | 184 | 100 | 1987 | Novocherkassk |
| 6K | Bo-Bo-Bo | 4,800 | 100 | 132 | 84 | 1987 | Kawasaki, Mitsubishi |
| 8K | Bo-Bo+Bo-Bo | 6,400 | 100 | 184 | 148 | 1986 | 50 Hz Group |

Beijing–Guangzhou–Shenzhen route is expected by the end of 2001.

Further south, the transversal from Kunming in the far southwest to Hangzhou, south of Shanghai, is in course of electrification. The 1,538 km from Kunming to Guiyang was energised throughout in 1993, along with the route northwards through Guiyang to Chongqing. Electric services over the 821 km from Guiding, just outside Guiyang, to Zhuzhou were inaugurated in April 1997. World Bank credits are supporting the double-tracking and wiring of the 892 km onwards from Zhuzhou to Hangzhou. Double-tracking has been completed between Hangzhou and Shanghai.

In 1999 electrification projects in progress for completion by 2002 covered nearly 5,300 route-km, a mixture of new and existing lines or works associated with track-doubling. Electrification projects at the end of 2000 included:

Wuhan–Chenzhou (Hubei and Hunan) (700 km existing double line)
Shaoguan–Guangzhou (Hunan and Guangdong) (200 km existing double line)
Harbin–Dalian (Liaoning, Jilin and Heilongjiang) (950 km existing double line)
Xi'an–Ankang (Shaanxi) (270 km new single line)
Liupanshui–Baiguo (Guizhou) (120 km new single line)
Loudi–Liupanshui (Hunan and Guizhou) (870 km track-doubling)
Qinhuangdao–Shenyang (Hebei and Liaoning) (400 km double-track new line)
Tianshui–Lanzhou (Gansu) (335 km doubling of existing line)
Neijiang–Yibin (Sichuan) (121 km existing single line)
Shouzhou–Daliuta (Shanxi and Shaanxi) (170 km new single line)
Shenchinan–Huanghuagang (Shanxi and Hebei) (588 km new heavy-haul coal line, mostly double-track)
Fuzhou–Nanping (Sichuan) (190 km existing single line)
Xi'an–Nanyang (Shaanxi and Henan) (407 km new single line)
Chongqing–Huaihua (Chongqing, Sichuan, Guizhou, Hunan) (625 km new single line)
Zhanyi–Hongguo–Liupanshui (Yunnan, Guizhou) (140 km existing single line, 120 km new single line)

Electrification projects programmed to start during the course of the tenth Five-Year Plan include many sections of the key heavily utilised double-track lines in the eastern part of China. Sections to be wired include the full length of the Beijing Shanghai line, the Tianjin Qinhuangdao line and the Jinan Qingdao line.

### Track
The standard rail section now in use in China is 60 kg/m and by 1998 this accounted for over 50 per cent of the rail in use on national railway lines. 50 kg/m rail is also in use while the old standard of 43 kg/m is rapidly being eliminated. 75 kg/m rail is also in use on a few sections of line. The use of long-welded track has also rapidly increased with around 26,000 km in place by 1998.

The use of prestressed concrete sleepers with elastic fastenings for main lines is now standard. Concrete sleepers with bolted fastenings are used for less important tracks. Timber sleepers are used for most turnouts, at locations in main lines where the use of concrete sleepers is not appropriate, and on many less important tracks.

The massive efforts made in recent years to speed up and otherwise improve passenger services on many main lines has required a huge programme of turnout replacement and other track upgrading work. To suit the higher speeds more sophisticated turnouts, many with movable frogs and supported on concrete bearers, have been installed. This programme is continuing.

## Kowloon—Canton Railway Corporation

KCRC House, 9 Lok King Street, Fo Tan, Sha Tin, New Territories, Hong Kong
Tel: (+852) 26 88 13 33   Fax: (+852) 26 88 09 83
Web: http://www.kcrc.com

### Key personnel
Chairman: Michael Tien Puk-sun
Directors
Chief Executive: Kai-yin Yeung
Senior Director, Capital Projects: James Blake
Senior Director, Finance and Management: Samuel Lai
Director, East Rail Extensions: K K Lee
Director, Light Rail: Jonathan Yu
Director, East Rail: Y T Li
Director, West Rail: Ian Thoms
Director, Property: Daniel Lam
Director, New Railway Projects: Kenneth Leung

*East Rail*
Gauge: 1,435 mm
Route length: 34 km
Electrification: 34 km at 25 kV 50 Hz AC

*Light Rail*
Gauge: 1, 435 mm
Route length: 31.75 km
Electrification: 31.75 km at 750 V DC overhead

### Organisation
Wholly owned by the Hong Kong Special Administrative Region Government, KCRC operates two rail systems. One is the 34 km East Rail, a suburban mass transit railway with 13 stations linking Kowloon with Shenzhen in mainland China. It began as a single-track system in 1910, and was completely electrified and doubled by 1983. In the North West New Territories, KCRC also operates the Light Rail system, linking the suburban towns of Yuen Long, Tuen Mun and Tin Shui Wai. KCRC also operates feeder buses, freight and intercity passenger services to major cities in mainland China. Additional business carried out by KCRC includes property development and related commercial activities.

KCRC is carrying out a major expansion of its network. Construction of West Rail, Phase 1, commenced in September 1998. At an estimated capital cost of HK$46.4 billion, the 30.5 km line will provide a swift and convenient commuter service between the North West New Territories and urban Kowloon when completed in late 2003. The Corporation is also working on three extensions to East Rail and will spend HK$2.3 billion over the next few years on improving the Light Rail system and building new extensions.

In June 2002, KCRC was awarded the right to build and operate the Sha Tin to Central Link. It is also planning to build the Kowloon Southern Link, which is a natural extension of the KCRC network and will link up East Rail with West Rail.

At the end of 2001 KCRC employed a total of 5,170 staff, of which 1,883 were with the East Rail Division, 839 with West Rail, 350 with East Rail extensions, 910 with Light Rail, 321 with bus, 104 with freight, 75 with property and 680 with corporate and other services.

### Passenger operations
Since electrification in 1983, East Rail's patronage has increased from about 40,000 to 799,000 passenger trips per day in 2001.

East Rail operates intercity passenger services to cities in mainland China, including Dongguan, Foshan, Zhaoqing, Guangzhou, Shanghai and Beijing, services to the last two having been introduced in May 1997. In August 1998, the first double-deck 'Ktt' through train was launched between Kowloon and Guangzhou (181 km). Operated push-pull style by Adtranz electric locomotives at each end of a 12-car double-deck two-class trailer formation, this train runs at up to 160 km/h to complete the journey in 1 hour 40 minutes. In June 1999, the frequency of this service was increased from four to seven round trips a day. In June 2001, a direct through train service was introduced between Donggang (Changping) and Kowloon, running on Fridays, Saturdays and Sundays.

Phase 1 of the Light Rail system was opened in September 1988 and has subsequently been extended to create the present 31.75 km 57-stop network. Eight routes are operated. At peak hours, services run as frequently as every 92 seconds at stops in the busiest section. Daily patronage in 2001 was 319,500.

| Traffic (million) | 1999 | 2000 | 2001 |
|---|---|---|---|
| *East Rail* | | | |
| Passenger journeys | 275 | 288 | 292 |
| Passenger-km | 4,263 | 4,466 | 4,487 |
| *Light Rail* | | | |
| Passenger journeys | 115 | 118 | 117 |
| Passenger-km | 482 | 506 | 501 |

### Freight operations
About 16 freight trains operate daily, including eight inbound and eight outbound. In 2001 total breakbulk freight volume decreased by 24.1 per cent to 16,683 wagons. The total number of containers conveyed, however, went up by 11.9 per cent to 14,925 TEUs in 2000.

Freight traffic is exclusively conveyed in wagons belonging to mainland railway authorities. The Freight Department operates five goods yard at Hung Hom, Mong Kok, Sha Tin, Sheung Shui and Fo Tan, plus a marshalling yard at Lo Wu. It also runs six freight representative offices in mainland China.

Container shuttle services are available to various cities in mainland China, including Changsha, Chengdu, Chongqing, Dongguan, Kunming, Lanzhou, Nanjing, Shanghai, Shenzhen, Shijiazhuang, Ulaanbaatar, Urumqi, Wuhan, Xi'an and Zhengzhou.

### New lines
*West Rail, Phase 1*
According to the government's 1998 projections, Hong Kong's population is forecast to grow from 6.2 million in 1996 to 8.1 million by 2011. The same projections forecast that the population of the North West New Territories will grow by some 70 per cent during the same period, from around 800,000 to 1.35 million. This has created a demand for a new, high-capacity rail system. The West Rail, Phase 1 scheme has been devised to meet the demand for effective commuter transport linking the North West New Territories and urban Kowloon.

In January 1995 the government invited KCRC to submit a proposal for the design, construction and operation of West Rail, and this was submitted in November 1995. In December 1996 the government announced that KCRC's proposal should be adopted.

West Rail, Phase 1, is a domestic line from urban Kowloon to Tuen Mun. The line will run from Nam Cheong in west Kowloon and terminate in the North West New Territories at Tuen Mun. There will be seven intermediate stops. The journey time along the entire alignment will take just 30 mins, a saving of 30 mins compared with road.

West Rail will be integrated with KCRC's existing Light Rail system in the North West New Territories and will provide interchanges with the MTRC system in urban Kowloon. It will also offer an interchange at Nam Cheong

*First examples of a 250-car fleet supplied by the Japanese IKK consortium for both East Rail and West Rail services*
2002/0122539

*KCRC Kowloon—Guangzhou 'Ktt' intercity trainset formed of 12 double-deck trailers and powered by an Adtranz-built 5,000 kW electric locomotive at each end* 2000/0089556

with MTRC's Tung Chung Line and a second interchange at Mei Foo with MTRC's Tsuen Wan Line. Public transport interchanges will be provided to allow passengers to use feeder services such as buses, minibuses and taxis. Ridership is estimated at 340,000 per day when the system opens in 2003, rising to 500,000 per day by 2011.

At an estimated cost of HK$46.4 billion, West Rail, Phase 1, is the single largest infrastructure project currently being undertaken in Hong Kong, comprising nine stations, a depot and a headquarters building housing a central operations control centre. Construction has been packaged into some 20 systems and 17 civil construction contracts. Work commenced in September 1998 and all civil contracts were awarded by the end of March 2000. At the end of 2001, the project was more than 60 per cent complete. Civil works were due to be completed by mid-2002. Initial testing of rolling stock will begin in 2002. Final testing, commissioning and pre-revenue operations are planned for 2003 in readiness for full opening by the end of that year. KCRC remained confident that the railway would be commissioned ahead of schedule and within budget.

*East Rail extensions*
In 2000, the government authorised two extensions to East Rail, Ma On Shan Rail and the Tsim Sha Tsui Extension. It also authorised the third extension, the Lok Ma Chau Spur Line, in June 2002.

Ma On Shan Rail will serve the growing population of the Ma On Shan area in the North East New Territories. The 11.4 km railway will have nine stations located within easy walking distance of large residential developments. It will interchange with East Rail at Tai Wai station, which will be rebuilt to cope with increased passenger flows.

The Tsim Sha Tsui Extension will extend the existing East Rail line southwards from the Hung Hom terminus to East Tsim Sha Tsui. The 1 km extension will be built in tunnel. The new underground station will be connected with the MTRC station in Tsim Sha Tsui and to adjoining developments by a comprehensive subway system. The KCRC/MTR interchange at Tsim Sha Tsui will relieve congestion now prevalent at the Kowloon Tong interchange.

Both Ma On Shan Rail and the Tsim Sha Tsui Extension are due for completion in 2004.

The 7.4 km Lok Ma Chau Spur Line will provide a second passenger rail crossing to the mainland to relieve congestion at the Lo Wu boundary crossing. It will run from Sheung Shui to a new station at Lok Ma Chau.

*Light Rail extensions*
Over the next few years KCRC will spend over HK$2.3 billion on improving the Light Rail system and building new extensions to serve the growing population in the North West New Territories. The projects will also transform Light Rail into an efficient feeder service for West Rail. These projects cover the construction of two new extensions in Tin Shui Wai, upgrading three stations to provide interchanges with West Rail, the installation of a new signalling system and grade separation at several rail and road junctions.

*Other railway lines*
In June 2002, the Government announced the awarding of the right to build and operate the Sha Tin to Central Link to KCRC. The new 17.1 km line will enable commuters to travel between Hong Kong Island and the New Territories on one railway network. It will be combined with Ma On Shan Rail, enabling passengers from Ma On Shan to travel to and from Central without interchange.

The Sha Tin to Central Link will run from Tai Wai to Central West and have 10 stations. The total cost of the project is estimated to be HK$31 billion in money-of-the-day prices. Civil works are planned to begin in 2004 following detailed design and studies on the project's environmental impact. The project was originally planned to be completed in 2008, but the schedule might be affected because the government's award has been delayed by six months.

In June 2001, the Corporation submitted proposals to the government to build and operate the Kowloon Southern Link, which has been identified in the government's Railway Development Strategy 2000 as a natural extension of the KCRC network. The Kowloon Southern Link will connect East Rail and West Rail at the southern end via Tsim Sha Tsui to provide the travelling public with a convenient and direct transfer between these two railway corridors.

## Traction and rolling stock
A HK$1.3 billion three-year mid-life rolling stock refurbishment programme was completed in 1999, enabling the whole fleet of 348 cars to carry 15 per cent more passengers.

In March 1999, KCRC awarded a HK$3.1 billion contract for the design, supply, testing and commissioning of 250 emu cars to a Japanese consortium of Itochu-Kinki-Kawasaki (IKK). Of these, 154 cars will be configured as 22 seven-car trains for West Rail, Phase 1. The remaining 96 cars will be used on the existing East Rail line. Delivery of the cars for East Rail commenced in March 2001. Delivery of the 154 West Rail cars was due to start in April 2002. All 96 cars for East Rail were commissioned by May 2002.

East Rail also has 12 diesel locomotives for freight operations.

At the beginning of 1998, 20 additional vehicles for the Light Rail system were put into service, bringing the fleet total to 119 and increasing the network's carrying capacity by over 20 per cent.

In October 2001, KCRC placed an order with Siemens Transportation Systems for five Eurorunner diesel-electric locomotives. These are similar to the Class 2016 'Hercules' machines supplied from 2002 by Siemens to Austrian Federal Railways.

## Signalling and telecommunications
*East Rail*
The East Rail signalling and telecommunication system is an integrated computerised system designed to comply with the Automatic Train Protection (ATP) principles. It comprises a Traffic Control System (TCS), a Centralised Solid State Interlocking System (CSSI), a Power Control System (PCS) and a Voice Control System (VCS).

Operated on screen-based workstations, the TCS provides a complete range of train control and monitoring functions. The signalling system is centralised at the East Rail Control Centre, which provides manual and automatic route setting and allows bidirectional working in both up and down tracks. The PCS system controls and monitors the 25 kV power supply to the trains and the VCS allows effective voice communications between operation parties by employing the Pulse Code Modulation (PCM) and Fibre Optic Distribution techniques.

In general, the Integrated Communications and Control System provides control and monitoring of the railway systems, including train control, traction power control, long line public address, passenger information, miscellaneous equipment, voice communications and integrated radio.

## Coupler in standard use
Passenger cars: AAR coupler between units; bar coupler between cars
Freight wagons: AAR coupler
**Braking in standard use, locomotive-hauled stock:** Air

## Track
**Rail:** UIC 54 (54 kg/m)
**Crossties (sleepers):** Prestressed concrete, 203 mm thick, spaced 700 mm centre to centre
**Rail fastenings:** Pandrol rail clip, Type PR429A with Pandrol glass-reinforced nylon insulators
**Min curvature radius:** Main line 270 m; sidings 150 m
**Max gradient:** 1 in 100
**Max speed:** 120 km/h throughout
**Max axleload:** 25 tonnes

*UPDATED*

### KCRC electric multiple-units

| Cars per unit | Motor cars per unit | Motored axles/car | Output/motor kW | Speed km/h | Units in service | First built | Builders Mechanical | Builders Electrical |
|---|---|---|---|---|---|---|---|---|
| 3 | 1 | 4 | 228 | 120 | 117 | 1981-91 | Met-Cam | GEC Traction |
| 4/2 | 2/0 | 4 | 240 | 120 | 32 | 2001 | IKK | IKK |
| 7 | | | | 130 | 22* | 2002 | IKK | IKK |

* includes units on order 2002

### KCRC diesel locomotives

| Builder's type | Wheel arrangement | Power kW | Speed km/h | Weight tonnes | No in service | First built | Mechanical | Builders Engine | Transmission |
|---|---|---|---|---|---|---|---|---|---|
| G12 | Bo-Bo | 840 | 80 | 66 | 1 | 1954 | Clyde | GM 567 | *E* GM |
| G12 | Bo-Bo | 977 | 80 | 67 | 3 | 1957 | Clyde | GM 567 | *E* GM |
| G16 | Co-Co | 1,342 | 80 | 94 | 3 | 1961 | GM | GM 567 | *E* GM |
| G16 | Co-Co | 1,342 | 80 | 94 | 1 | 1965 | Clyde | GM 567C | *E* GM |
| G26-CU | Co-Co | 1,492 | 80 | 94 | 1 | 1973 | Clyde, GM | GM 645E | *E* GM |
| G26-CU | Co-Co | 1,492 | 80 | 92 | 2 | 1976 | GM | GM 645E | *E* GM |

### KCRC electric locomotives

| Class | Wheel arrangement | Power kW continuous | Speed km/h | Weight tonnes | No built | First built | Builders Mechanical | Builders Electrical |
|---|---|---|---|---|---|---|---|---|
| TLN001/ TLS002 | Bo-Bo | 5,000 | 160 | 84 | 2 | 1997 | SLM | Adtranz |

## MTR Corporation

Airport Express
GPO Box 9916, MTR Tower, Telford Plaza, Kowloon Bay, Hong Kong
Tel: (+852) 29 93 21 11    Fax: (+852) 27 98 88 22
Web: http://www.mtr.com.hk

### Key personnel
Directors
  Chairman and Chief Executive: Jack So Chak-kwong
  Operations Director: Phil Gaffney
  Project Director: Russell Black
  Property Director: Thomas Ho Hang-kwong
  Finance Director: Lincoln Leong Kwok-kuen
  Legal Director and Secretary: Leonard Turk
  Human Resources Director: William Chan Fu-keung
  Head of Operations: Eric Hui Yip-hung

Gauge: 1,435 mm
Route length: 34.8 km
Electrification: 34.8 km at 1.5 kV DC, overhead

### Political background
In October 2000, partial privatisation of MTR Corporation (MTRC) was achieved when trading in the corporation's shares commenced on the Stock Exchange of Hong Kong. This reduced the government's shareholding to 77 per cent.

### Organisation
The Airport Railway (AR) was developed and built by the MTR Corporation, Hong Kong's metro operator, to provide a direct rail link between Chek Lap Kok airport on Lantau Island via Kowloon to Central, on Hong Kong island. The line was also designed to provide a fast Tung Chung Line suburban service to North Lantau. Tung Chung Line operations started on 22 June 1998, while Airport Express services followed on 6 July, coinciding with the commissioning of the new airport.
Details of MTRC's metro network may be found in *Jane's Urban Transport Systems*.

### Passenger operations
Airport Express services are scheduled to run every 10 minutes, completing the 34.8 km journey in 23 minutes. In-town check-in facilities managed by MTRC are provided at Hong Kong Station in Central District and

*Airport Express services are operated by a fleet of 11 seven-car emus supplied by an Adtranz/CAF joint venture; 12 similar seven-car units were delivered for Tung Chung Line commuter services*    0058681

Kowloon. Initial loadings of 39,000 passengers per day were projected for 1998, growing to 75,000 per day by 2011. However, economic conditions in Asia contributed to an average of only 22,000 per day being carried during 1998. In 1999, the line's first full year of operation, passenger numbers rose to an average of 28,500 per day, representing a 32 per cent share of traffic to and from the airport. In 2000, the average daily number of passengers fell slightly to 28,000 and the market share to 28 per cent. Total passenger journeys in 2000 and 2001 were 10.35 million and 9 million respectively.

A 10 minute service frequency is provided on the Tung Chung Line. During the morning peak period, frequency is increased to an average of 8 minutes, with alternate trains turning back at an intermediate station at Tsing Yi.

### New lines
In 2000, MTRC submitted to government a proposal to build a 3.5 km spur from Yam O, on the Tung Chun line, to a planned Disney theme park at Penny's Bay on Lantau Island.

Construction of the Penny's Bay Link is planned to start in 2002. The cost of the scheme, which includes the construction of two new stations, is estimated at HK$2.6 billion. Opening is scheduled for 2005.

### Improvements to existing lines
A second platform for Airport Express services is planned at Hong Kong station to provide anticipated capacity for airport traffic and additional Tung Chung Line capacity.

### Traction and rolling stock
Emus of a common basic design but with different access and interior layouts have been supplied by an Adtranz/CAF joint venture. Initially 11 seven-car Airport Express and 12 seven-car Tung Chung Line trains were ordered, both types with a 135 km/h capability. Airport Express units incorporate one baggage car to convey containerised checked-in baggage. Train design and infrastructure provide for the addition of extra cars up to ten- and eight-car formations respectively as traffic grows.

***UPDATED***

---

# COLOMBIA

## Ministry of Transport

Avenida Eldorado, CAN Edificio Minobras, Santa Fe de Bogotá
Tel: (+57 1) 222 44 11; 75 77
Fax: (+57 1) 222 16 47; 11 21

### Key personnel
Minister: J Bendex Olivella
Deputy Minister: J A Latorre Uriza

## El Cerrejon Coal Railway

Cra 54 No 72-80, AA52499, Barranquilla
Tel: (+57 5) 877 78 98    Fax: (+57 5) 877 78 98

### Key personnel
Superintendent: M Mendoza
Senior Operations Supervisor: R Stand
Senior CTC Supervisor: J Gonzalez
Senior Maintenance of Way Supervisor: F Acuña

Gauge: 1,435 mm
Route length: 150 km

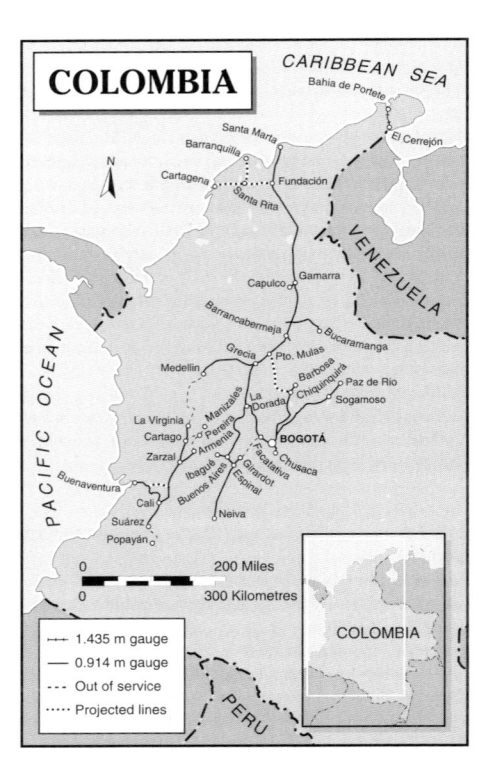

*Coal hoppers built by Johnstown America Corporation for the El Cerrejon system employ 3CR12 stainless steel from Cromweld*    0021530

## Organisation

Constructed by Morrison Knudsen in several months less than the originally scheduled timescale, this railway was built at a cost of US$300 million for Carbocol, the national coal-mining corporation, and Intercor, an Exxon affiliate. These two organisations have jointly developed South America's biggest coal-producing project in an opencast operation in the northeastern province of Guajira. The railway employs 117 people.

## Freight operations

The railway moves some 15 million tonnes of coal annually (12.7 million tonnes/88,400 million tonne-km in 1992; 13.5 million tonnes in 1993) from the El Cerrejon complex to a shipment port close to the Venezuelan border at Bahia de Portete. The line was laid with 61.8 kg/m rail, continuously welded, on timber sleepers. The route is through scrubland, which helped to restrict ruling gradients to 0.3 per cent against loaded trains, 1 per cent in the reverse direction.

At the El Cerrejon mine complex, where trains are overhead-loaded from a pair of 10,000 tonne-capacity silos, and at the port, where the 91 tonne coal wagons are bottom door-discharged, track layouts are in loop form to allow merry-go-round operation of the trains. Thus, each 93-wagon train is planned to achieve three return trips within the 24 hours.

In 1999 coal traffic was promised a boost of up to 6 million tonnes a year by an agreement with other mining companies to move their increased production to Bahia de Portete.

## Traction and rolling stock

The railway operates with 244 hopper wagons supplied by Ortner and 164 Autoflood II automatic discharge wagons manufactured by Johnstown America Corporation. The locomotives are eight General Electric Type B36-7 2,685 kW Bo-Bos.

# Ferrovias

Empresa Colombiana De Vias Ferreas
Calle 31 No 6-41, Piso 20, Santa Fe de Bogotá
Tel: (+57 1) 287 98 88   Fax: (+57 1) 287 25 15

## Key personnel

President: Luis Diego Monsalve Hoyos
General Secretary: Nelson Morse Santos
Vice-Presidents
   Finance and Administration:
      Clara Inés Renjifo Saavedra
   Operations: Eric Morris
   Infrastructure: Jorge Enrique Hincapie

Gauge: 914 mm
Route length: 3,154 km

## Political background

The national railway company FNC was liquidated in 1992, with a wholly state-owned company, Ferrovias, taking over responsibility for the rehabilitation, maintenance and development of the remunerative parts of the FNC infrastructure.

The government intended trains to be operated by a mix of private and joint public-private companies. Of the latter type, the Sociedad Colombiana de Transporte Ferroviario SA (STF) was formally established in 1991 to run a public rail freight service over the core main line from Lenguazaque and Bogotá to Santa Marta, and from Chiriguana to Santa Marta.

Other operators included STFO, offering public freight service on the Pacific line between Buenaventura and Cali; and Tren Metropolitano de Cali, providing passenger service around Cali. Tourist trains were established between Bogotá and Nemocón and around Medellín.

It was also intended to privatise workshop and repair facilities.

A Spanish consortium of RENFE, engineering consultancy Ineco and investment bank Socimer, was awarded a 12 month contract in September 1995 to develop and implement a programme for the private sector to upgrade, maintain and operate key routes via a system of concessions. Tenders were called in 1997 for a 30-year concession to rehabilitate and also operate the so-called Atlantic Network. This consists of the Bogotá-Santa Marta trunk route (969 km) and a further 400 km of branches: Bogotá-Belencito; Espinal-Neiva; and Puerto Berrió-Medellín. In February 1998 the concession was awarded to the 13-member Fepaz consortium, headed by the Colombian company Emcarbón and Dragados FCC International of Spain. However, the award was subsequently withdrawn from Fepaz for contractual reasons.

In mid-1999 it was announced that a consortium led by Dragados and including Spanish National Railways (RENFE) had been selected as preferred bidder. After restoring the main line, the concessionaires expect to handle some 20 million tonnes of freight annually.

Bids for a second concession were invited in May 1998 for the 650 km Pacific network, the main line of which connects Buenaventura, Cali and La Felisa, with a branch from Zarzal to Tebaida and Armenia. The concession will be for 30 years, and will cover renovation and operation of the line. Investments of up to US$190 million were reported to be needed in infrastructure upgrades, with the government expected to contribute US$120 million.

A sole bid was received from a consortium led by a Spanish company, Actividades de Construcción y Servicios, and in late 1998 this was being reviewed by the government.

## Finance

Ferrovias is financed by 10 per cent of national petrol tax revenue and by tolls from rail infrastructure users. The investment budget for 1996 totalled 124.56 billion Colombian pesos, with 110.01 billion pesos allocated to major track improvements, 13.55 billion pesos for signalling and 1 billion for telecommunications.

## New lines

There are two long-planned new line schemes which have remained on the back burner as attention has focused on the rehabilitation of the trunk Bogotá-Santa Marta and Medellín-Buenaventura routes and the recovery of traffic volume. One is a cut-off between Ibague and Armenia that would obviate the circuitous journey from Bogotá to the Pacific port of Buenaventura via Puerto Berrio. The proposed new 85 km cut-off would entail driving a 22 km-long tunnel. Achievement would reduce the rail distance from Bogotá to Buenaventura by no less than 500 km.

The other project is a 180 km link between Saboya and Puerto Carare, known as the Carare Railway. This line would cut the transport distance between the Caribbean port of Santa Marta and Bogotá by 350 km. Ruling gradient would be 2.4 per cent, with the route climbing from a point 100 m above sea level to an altitude of 2,560 m at Saboya. Minimum curve radius would be 200 m, with 56 kg/m rails to sustain 20 tonne axleloads in moving coal traffic from the Checua and Lenguazaque deposits. Construction would entail some 90 tunnels aggregating over 30 km in length and about 50 significant bridges or viaducts.

A new 93 km alignment of the Cali-Medellín line's section between La Pintada and Caldas, derelict since flooding and landslides in 1976, is also being reconsidered. Another proposal involves the construction of 240 km of new railway to connect the northern ports of Cartagena and Barranquilla with the Santa Marta line at Fundación.

Proposals for a new 1,435 mm gauge route for export coal from Cúcuta, west of Gamarra, to La Concha and La Ceiba on Lake Maracaibo in Venezuela were announced by Ferrovias in May 1996. The 16 km Colombian section of the 126 km route was costed at US$33 million, and it was hoped to put a construction concession out to tender by mid-1997.

## Improvements to existing lines

Ferrovias launched an emergency programme of rehabilitation in 1990. An immediate aim was to reduce the frequency of derailments caused by poor track, which had prompted many customers to switch to road transport, and raise average operating speeds from the nadir of 15 km/h on key routes. The programme of track work, well under way by 1991, covered 1,100 track-km, and was raising maximum permissible speed on level track to 40 km/h, and in mountain territory to 25 km/h.

Under a long-term plan costed at US$357.2 million and scheduled for completion by 2000, track was to be thoroughly renewed, using 45 kg/m rail and concrete sleepers except in the mountain territory, in the following route-by-route order of priority: Bogotá-Santa Marta (965 km); Medellín-Grecia/Puerto Berrio (187 km); La Caro-Belencito (181 km); Bogotá-La Caro-Lenguazaque (110 km); and Yumbo-Buenaventura (158 km).

However, by 1995, it was apparent that Ferrovias would, henceforth, be looking to the private sector to undertake comprehensive route upgrades. In May 1996 it was reported that upgrading was under way on the La Loma-Santa Marta and Grecia-San Rafael sections of the network, with completion expected in 1997. The operation of unit coal trains between La Loma and Santa Marta has been proposed by Drummond Mining (see below).

*Oil and coal traffic*

According to forecasts, oil industry development was likely to generate up to 11,000 tonnes of freight a day in the northeast of the country by the end of the 1990s and local state governors have joined with commercial interests in pressing for rehabilitation of the 258 km Bogotá-Belencito route. The oil industry has also pressed for US$2 million to be spent on the renovation of the 618 km south-north line from workings at Neiva to Barrancabermeja, whence oil could be piped to a Caribbean port.

Colombia has developed a major coal export trade, and route upgrades have been mooted to cater for such traffic. Drummond Mining Corporation, USA, has stated its intention to develop mines around La Loma and has proposed operating unit coal trains to the Caribbean port of Ciénaga, near Santa Marta. Track access fees paid by Drummond trains could generate some US$12 million for Ferrovias; initial movements of some 3 million tonnes of coal a year have been forecast, rising to 13 million tonnes by 2000.

## Track

**Rail:** ASCE 37 kg/m
**Crossties (sleepers):** Wood, 1.82 × 0.15 × 0.20 m; concrete, 1.90 m x 0.12 m x 0.22 m
**Fastenings:** Track spikes, drive spikes Deenik and Pandrol
**Spacing:** In plain track 1,666/km in curves 2,000/km
**Min curvature radius:** 80 m
**Max gradient:** 4.3%
**Max speed:** 62 km/h
**Max axleload:** 16 tonnes
**Max altitude:** 2,900 m

# STF

Sociedad Colombiana de Transporte Ferroviario SA
Calle 72 No 13-23, Piso 2, Santa Fe de Bogotá
Tel: (+57 1) 255 86 84   Fax: (+57 1) 255 87 04

## Key personnel

President: Dr Luis Fernando Zea Llano
Vice-Presidents: J G Arango Arango, J E Rojas, L F Vélez

## Organisation

STF took over rail operations from the liquidated FNC in 1992, providing freight service over the core main line from Lenguazaque and Bogotá to Santa Marta, and from Chiriguana to Santa Marta. The Antofagasta (Chili) and Bolivia Railway provided assistance in determining methods of operation. The state owns 51 per cent of STF's capital. The intention was that the company's private partners would help fund renovation and new purchases, as well as provide STF working capital.

## Freight operations

In 1997, 0.7 million tonnes of freight were carried, generating 346 million tonne-km. STF employed 236 staff at the end of that year.

## Traction and rolling stock

In 1997 STF operated 43 diesel-electric locomotives and 1,079 wagons.

## STFO

Sociedad de Transporte Férreo de Occidente SA
23-47, Estación Ferrrocarril 2° Piso, Cali
Tel: (+57 23) 660 33 14   Fax: (+57 23) 660 33 20
e-mail: trapacif@cali.cetcol.net.co

**Key personnel**
General Manager: Robert Antonio Guzman

**Freight operations**
STFO provides freight service between Buenaventura on the Pacific coast to Cali and Cartago, operating as Transpacífico. Five diesel locomotives carried 233,000 tonnes for 30.5 million freight tonne-km in 1996.

## Transferreos

Transferreos Ltda
Terminal de Transporte, Medellín
Tel: (+57 4) 267 11 57; 70 78

**Key personnel**
General Manager: John Jairo Castañeda

**Passenger operations**
Transferreos commenced passenger operations between Medellín and Barrancabermeja in 1992. In 1993, a tourist train was introduced between Medellín and Cisneros.

# CONGO

## Ministry of Transport & Civil Aviation

PO Box 2148, Brazzaville
Tel: (+242) 81 43 34   Fax: (+242) 83 09 16

**Key personnel**
Minister: Isidore Mvouda

## Chemin de Fer Congo-Océan (CFCO)

PO Box 651, Pointe Noire
Tel: (+242) 94 05 61   Fax: (+242) 94 12 30

**Key personnel**
General Manager: J Kidzouani
Technical Manager: J Koutoundou
Directors
  Operations: G Goma-Boukoulou
  Traction and Rolling Stock: B Nykoulou
  Track and Buildings: J Kimbatsa-Koudimba
  Supplies: J-P Niazaire
  Personnel: Joachim Ndebeka
  Finance and Accounting: Jean Claude Tchibassa
  Information Systems: Pierre Boussi
  Research and Development:
    Joseph Yongolo-Tchizinga
  Legal: Ted Nguimbi-Manitou

Gauge: 1,067 mm
Route length: 609 km

**Political background**
The Congo-Océan Railway extends from Pointe Noire to Brazzaville. At Mont Belo it connects with the Comilog Railway (qv), over which it also operates services. CFCO is a department within the Agence Transcongolaise des Communications (ATC) which controls intermodal transport by sea, river and rail.

In 1997, the Ministry of Economics, Finance and Planning retained Canadian consultants CPCS to advise on privatisation of the railway by way of a 20-year concession. The Comilog Railway (qv) would be included in this process. The successful bidder would be required to undertake infrastructure improvements and renew the traction and rolling stock fleet. Moves towards privatisation were subsequently suspended due to political instability, but the process was to be restarted with a new call for expressions of interest.

**Passenger operations**
In 1991 passenger-km totalled 547 million. By 1995, however, passenger-km had declined to 302 million.

**Freight operations**
Freight tonne-km stood at around 400 million in the early 1990s, but by 1995 had declined to 267 million, with 713,000 tonnes carried. Main commodities handled are timber, petroleum products and cement.

**New lines**
In the long term it is hoped to bridge the Congo river and connect CFCO with the Kinshasa–Matadi line in the Democratic Republic of Congo. Tecsult International of Canada has studied a combined road and double-track rail bridge. The plan includes double-tracking of 33 km between Loubomo and Mont Belo, where the 285 km Comilog line diverges to the border of Gabon; and between M'Filou and Brazzaville.

**Improvements to existing lines**
The first 91 km realignment of the Pointe Noire–Brazzaville line, between Loubomo and Bilingua, was completed in 1985. As a result, speed ceilings were raised to 60 km/h for freight and 80 km/h for passenger trains and transit times were reduced by an hour for passenger trains, two hours for Comilog manganese trains and three hours for other freight. This scheme, which was funded by the World Bank and over a dozen other agencies, raised the line's freight-operating capacity beyond its previous 21 trains daily to 31.

Following studies by Tecsult, further realignment and track with welded 46 kg instead of 30 kg rail has progressed between Bilingua and Tahitondi.

Restoration work by SNCF International following the civil war in 1998-99 enabled services to be resumed between Brazzaville and Pointe Noire in August 2000.

**Traction and rolling stock**
At the start of 1998 the fleet comprised 40 locomotives, one diesel railcar, 71 passenger cars and 1,118 freight wagons.

A new fleet of eight dual-purpose diesel-hydraulics went into service in 1994. These are Type DGH 1000 B-B units built by ABB Henschel and powered by 800 kW SACM engines. Top speed is 90 km/h in line-haul mode and 45 km/h when shunting.

In 2001, CFCO received six GM Type GT26MC diesel-electric locomotives second-hand from Spoornet, South Africa.

*UPDATED*

## Comilog Railway

Gauge: 1,067 mm
Route length: 285 km

**Organisation**
Built by the Compagnie Minière de l'Ogooue (Comilog), this railway connects the Congo-Océan Railway's Mont Belo station (200 km from Pointe Noire) with M'Binda, in Gabon. Public service over this line is now provided by the Congo-Océan Railway (qv). Privatisation plans initiated in 1997 for the Congo-Océan Railway would also affect the Comilog system.

**Freight operations**
Until the late 1980s the Comilog Railway was moving some two million tonnes of manganese ore per annum, but since the 1987 completion of the Transgabon Railway most of the traffic has been switched to that route, for shipment through the Gabonese port of Owendo.

# CONGO, DEMOCRATIC REPUBLIC

## National Office of Transport & Communications (ONATRA)

BP 98, Kinshasa 1
Tel: (+243 12) 247 61; 224 21   Fax: (+243 12) 248 92
Gauge: 1,067 mm
Route length: 366 km

**Organisation**
Under the Mobutu regime which was deposed in May 1997, ONATRA had been operating the Kinshasa-Matadi line on a lease from the national railway company SNCZ. Little is known about its operations under the new Kabila regime.

The Kinshasa-Matadi line is a vital part of the so-called Voie Nationale, an export-import route wholly within the former Zaïre which avoided the political problems of reaching the sea by way of railway lines running through the country's frequently unstable neighbours. The Voie Nationale consists of a rail segment from Sakania to Ilebo, then river transport to Kinshasa, and finally use of the isolated rail segment from Kinshasa to the port of Matadi. In 1991, it carried 0.5 million tonnes of freight, for 158 million tonne-km, and 0.6 million passengers.

## Société Nationale des Chemins de Fer Congolais (SNCC)

PO Box 297, Place de la Gare, Lubumbashi, Shaba Region
Tel: (+243 2) 22 34 30   Fax: (+243 2) 70 34 42 33

**Key personnel**
President and Chief Executive Officer (acting):
  Muzinga Ilunga

Gauge: 1,067 mm; 1,000 mm; 600 mm
Route length: 3,621 km; 125 km; 1,026 km

# CONGO, Democratic Republic

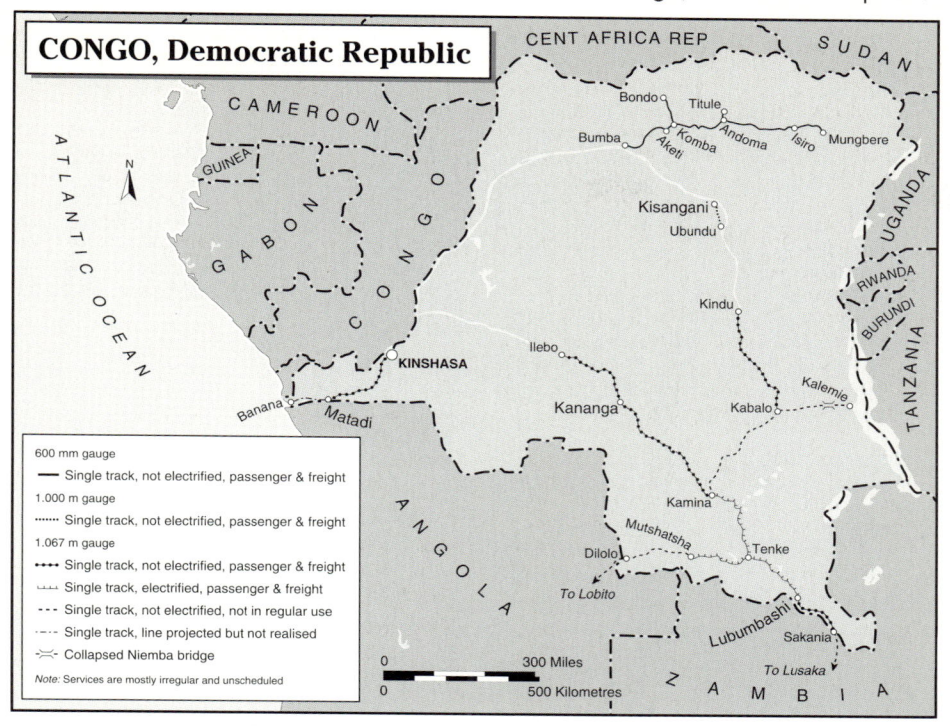

Electrification: 858 km of 1,067 mm gauge at 25 kV 50 Hz AC

## Political background
The National Railway Company is a state-owned organisation set up in May 1997 when forces loyal to new president Laurent-Desire Kabila, who had just deposed the former president Mobutu, seized the assets of Sizarail, a mixed public/private organisation owned by South African, Belgian and local interests. The South Africans had a 51 per cent stake in Sizarail, held by the Comazar joint venture company; the South African railway company Spoornet was a majority shareholder in Comazar, with Belgian National Railways also holding a stake. At least 14 locomotives and some wagons belonging to Spoornet were taken by the new regime, and the total value of assets involved was put at around US$70 million. The seizure led to the cessation of international traffic, cutting the southern and eastern sides of the country off from the outside world; however, later in 1997, there were signs that SNCC was prepared to reach accommodations with its neighbours, and was seeking co-operation with Sizarail. At the same time it was reported that government approval had been given for a US$300 million upgrading programme.

Sizarail had been created in 1995 to take over operation of the former state-owned railway Société Nationale des Chemins de Fer Zaïrois (SNCZ) and had been revitalising the rundown system.

## Organisation
Sizarail's predecessor organisation, SNCZ, had been created in 1974 by the merger of five railways: La Compagnie des Chemins de Fer Kinshasa–Dilolo–Lubumbashi (KDL); Les Chemins de Fer des Grands Lacs (CFL); Matadi–Kinshasa (CFMK); Mayumbe (CFM); and Chemins de Fer Vicinaux Zaïrois (CVZ).

The former KDL railway serves the important mining centres of Shaba province (now renamed Katanga), Likasi, Kolwezi and Mososhi, and other mining and industrial areas such as the manganese mine at Kisenge, cement works at Lubudi, collieries at Leuna, and diamond mines at Mbuji-Mayi. Expanding agricultural and forest product industries have developed along the line of its route. The electrified territory is the 606 km of ex-KDL line from Lubumbashi to Kamina, and part of the branch from the line's mid-point at Tenke to the Angolan border at Dilolo, 252 km.

The isolated Ubundu–Kisangani line is metre-gauge. The 600 mm gauge, also isolated, is found on the Bumba-Mungbere line and its Bondo branch. Both these sections are in the east of the country.

Internationally, the system connects at Dilolo with the CF de Benguela (CFB) in Angola for access to the Atlantic port of Lobito; at Sakania with Zambia Railways and further on, Zimbabwe Railways and South Africa's Spoornet; and via Zambia with the TAZARA railway for access to Dar es Salaam.

In 1999, SNCC and National Railways of Zimbabwe signed agreements covering technical co-operation on the rehabilitation of track, infrastructure and rolling stock. This was particularly aimed at providing a more effective rail freight corridor from Congo to Zimbabwe via Zambia.

## Traction and rolling stock
At last report, for 1,067 mm gauge operation, SNCZ owned 86 line-haul and 59 shunting diesel locomotives, 51 electric locomotives, 282 passenger cars, 30 railcars and 4,793 freight wagons. Metre-gauge stock comprised three diesel locomotives, 9 passenger cars and 78 freight wagons; and 600 mm gauge stock, 14 diesel locomotives, five diesel railcars, 16 passenger cars and 329 freight wagons.

In 1999, SNCC reached agreement with National Railways of Zimbabwe (NRZ) to lease 20 refurbished passenger coaches for two years, with an option to extend the contract.

## Track
**Standard rail:** 29.3 and 40 kg/m on KDL; 24.4 and 29.3 kg/m on CFL; 33.4 and 40 kg/m on ONATRA CFMK; 18 kg/m on ONATRA CFM; 9 to 33.4 kg/m elsewhere
**Joints:** Fishplates and bolts
**Crossties (sleepers):** Chiefly steel, also wood and concrete
**Spacing:** 1,250/km plain track, 1,500 km in curves
**Rail fastenings:** By clips and bolts to steel sleepers. RN flexible fastenings to concrete sleepers
**Min curvature:** 100 m
**Max gradient:** 15%
**Max altitude:** 1,614 ft at Dilongo-Yulu near Tenke on Bukama line
**Max permitted speed**
Electrified lines: 52 km/h
All other lines: 45 km/h
**Max axleload:** 15 tons nominal; 20 tons in special cases

### Diesel locomotives

| Class | Wheel arrangement | Power hp | Weight tonnes | First Built | Builders Mechanical | Transmission |
|---|---|---|---|---|---|---|
| **Line-haul** | | | | | | |
| 1200 | A1A-A1A | 1,500 | 80 | 1968 | Hitachi | E |
| 1300 | Co-Co | 1,650 | 87.3 | 1969 | General Electric | E |
| 1400 | Co-Co | 1,650 | 87.3 | 1969 | General Electric | E |
| 1500 | Bo-Bo | 1,310 | 56.5 | 1967 | Krupp Krauss-Maffei | E |
| 61/63 | 0-6-0 | 250 | 13.5 | 1955 | Atelier Metallurgique Tubize | H |
| 81-85 | B-B | 510 | 31 | 1969 | Nippon Sharyo | H |
| 86-92 | B-B | 510 | 32 | 1974 | Nippon Sharyo | H |
| **Shunters** | | | | | | |
| 71/73 | 0-4-0 | 335 | 16 | 1958 | Cockerill | H |
| 1161-1173 | 0-4-0 | 320 | 30 | 1965-68 | Cockerill | H |
| 1201-1241 | B-B | 510 | 45 | 1968-69-72 | Hitachi Kawasaki | H |
| 501-510 | B-B | 660 | 40 | 1973 | Thyssen-Henschel | H |
| 1011 | 0-8-0 | 1,000 | 58 | 1959 | ARB FUF/HSP | - |
| 21/22/25 | 0-6-0 | 110 | 16 | 1958 | SA Moteur Moes | - |
| 506-508 | Bo-Bo | 60 | 40 | 1980 | Waremme | - |

### Electric locomotives

| Class | Wheel arrangement | Output kW | Speed km/h | Weight tonnes | First built | Builders |
|---|---|---|---|---|---|---|
| 2200 | Bo-Bo | 1,620 | 65 | 76 | 1956 | ACEC |
| 2300 | Bo-Bo | 1,505 | 65 | 73.7 | 1958 | ACEC |
| 2400 | Bo-Bo | 1,620 | 70 | 60 | 1960 | ACEC |
| 2450 | Bo-Bo | 1,620 | 75 | 60 | 1964 | ACEC |
| 2500 | Bo-Bo | 1,600 | 70 | 62 | 1969 | Hitachi |
| 2600 | Bo-Bo | 2,400 | 60 | 93 | 1976 | Hitachi |

*UPDATED*

---

# COSTA RICA

### Ministry of Public Works and Transport
San José
Tel: (+506) 222 86 81    Fax: (+506) 255 02 42

**Key personnel**
Minister: Rodolfo Silva
Director, Transport Division: H Blanco

### Costa Rica Railways (Incofer)
Instituto Costarricense de Ferrocarriles
PO Box 1, 1009 F E al P Estación, Zona 3, San José
Tel: (+506) 221 07 77    Fax: (+506) 222 34 58
Telex: 2393 fecosa cr

**Key personnel**
President: F Bolaños

Gauge: 1,067 mm
Route length: 950 km
Electrification: 128 km at 15 kV 20 Hz AC, 132 km at 25 kV 50 Hz AC

## Political background
Incofer was created in 1985 to undertake the modernisation of the system created by the merger of the National Atlantic and Pacific railways (Incofer's Atlantic

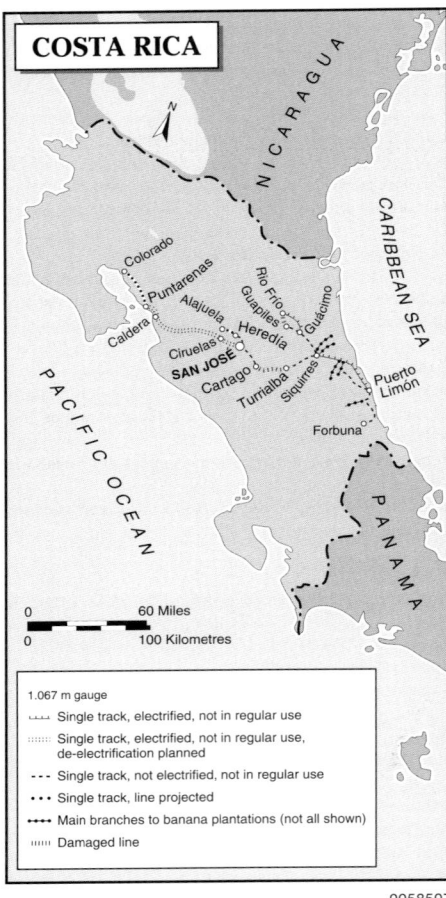

… and Pacific divisions) in 1977. In 1987 it took over the 250 km Ferrocarril del Sur network formerly operated by the Compañía Bananera de Costa Rica. Passenger services on the Ferrocarril del Sur ceased about 1990 and freight services followed around one year later, with the whole network dismantled between 1992 and 1994.

Due to its worsening finances, the government ordered Incofer to cease operations in June 1995 and put the railway into a care and maintenance regime while private-sector participation was sought.

In November 1996, the government invited bids to operate and maintain parts of the national rail network, with concessions to be granted based on promised levels of private-sector investment. However, no award was made. A second call for bids with broadly similar conditions was made in August 1997, and an award had been expected during the first half of 1998. However, none was made due to a lack of potential investors.

In July 2000, the Costa Rican National Council for Concessions (CNC) announced its intention during the following month to initiate a new round of bidding for concessions to operate the system by publishing a request for qualifications. Prequalified firms or consortia would then be invited to respond to a request for proposal prior to submitting a bid.

The government is also being pressurised to implement suburban services in four cities, including San José. The World Bank has made funding available to future concession holders to buy new equipment or improve infrastructure. Incofer's property may be ceded to concessionaires for use as security on loans.

### Passenger operations
At the beginning of 2000, Incofer reinstated Saturday and Sunday round-trips on the San José–Puntarenas line for a trial period of three months. The trial proved highly popular and often failed to offer sufficient capacity for passenger demand. Reports suggested that the service was to become permanent.

### Freight operations
In 1994 Incofer carried a total of 661,349 tonnes of freight, having carried 739,000 tonnes in 1993. The Atlantic division carried 360,711 tonnes in 1994, mostly bananas produced by Standard Fruit for export, with smaller amounts of inbound fertiliser and packaging materials. Wheat and maize accounted for over 50 per cent of the 300,638 tonnes carried on the Pacific division in 1994, with iron, steel and fertiliser making up the bulk of the remainder.

### New lines
A major outstanding project, discussed for some time past, is the construction of an effective link between the Atlantic and Pacific divisions, latterly connected only by a steeply graded line through the streets of San José. At Alajuela, close to the country's international airport, the two divisions are only 3 km apart and an elevated single-track connection has been proposed at an estimated cost of US$70 million, including rolling stock for suburban passenger services.

### Traction and rolling stock
When Incofer operations ceased in June 1995, the traction and rolling stock fleet included three diesel-electric locomotives formerly employed on Canadian National's Newfoundland system; two 14 tonne railbuses with 200 hp Cummins engines assembled by Incofer in its own workshops; a Romanian-built diesel-hydraulic B-B shunter converted to a 15 kV 20 Hz electrohydraulic unit by Incofer; and a pair of two-car diesel multiple-units acquired from FEVE of Spain in 1993.

The initial 15 kV 20 Hz AC electric system was operated by AEG locomotives of 1929 and Siemens locomotives of 1956. The diesel locomotive fleet was chiefly General Electric, with the newest 825 and 1,100 hp units dating from 1979, but including some 950 hp diesel-hydraulic units supplied by the 23 August works of Romania in 1971.

Incofer had received 13 diesel locomotives and some 500 freight wagons when it took over the Ferrocarril del Sur system in 1987.

| | |
|---|---:|
| Electric locomotives | 16 |
| Diesel locomotives | 22 |
| Diesel railcars | 19 |
| *Rolling stock* | |
| Passenger coaches | 82 |
| Freight wagons | 1,331 |

**Type of coupler:** Standard
**Type of braking in standard use:** Westinghouse air

### Signalling and telecommunications
Incofer had hoped to install automatic block signalling throughout the main routes of the Pacific and Atlantic divisions. A new operating control centre was also planned to replace Incofer's radio dispatching system.

### Electrification
The former Pacific Railway running 128 km from San José to Puntarenas was electrified at 15 kV 20 Hz AC in 1929-30. Between 1977 and 1982 modernisation and electrification of the Atlantic Railway was put in hand; the 132 km Limón-Río Frío main line was completely relaid with 43 kg/m long-welded rail on concrete sleepers, new yards were installed at both ends, bridges strengthened for 16 tonne axleloads, and electrification at 25 kV 60 Hz AC executed.

A fleet of 12 dual-voltage (25 kV 60 Hz/15 kV 20 Hz AC), 62 tonne 1,200 kW Bo-Bo electric locomotives was supplied by electrification contractors 50 c/s Group. It was hoped eventually to convert the former Pacific Railway to 25 kV 60 Hz AC operation when its generating plant became due for renewal.

### Track
**Rail:** ASCE 42.5
**Sleepers:** Wood or concrete spaced 1,600/km
**Fastenings:** Pandrol, Nabla RN, spikes
**Min curve radius:** 80 m
**Max gradient:** 4.25%
**Max permissible axleload:** 18 tonnes

---

# CÔTE D'IVOIRE

## Ministry of Public Works Transport and Communications

PO Box V6, Abidjan 01, Ivory Coast
Tel: (+225) 34 73 15    Fax: (+225) 211 73 29

### Key personnel
Minister: Ezan Akele
Director of Land Transport: Y B Quattara

For map see entry for **Burkina Faso**.

## Ivory Coast Railway – SIPF

Société Ivoirienne de gestion du Patrimoine Ferroviaire
1 rue du chemin de fer, PO Box 1415, Abidjan 16
Tel: (+225) 21 96 24    Fax: (+225) 21 39 62

### Key personnel
President: Youssouf Bakayoko
Director General: Bernard Tra Bi
Technical Director: Joseph N'da Ezoa
Director, Finance and Administration: Edouard Bahi Kore

### Political background
SIPF is the shell corporation administering railway assets, both infrastructure and rolling stock. Operations are now run by Sitarail (qv), which leases the assets from SIPF.

## Sitarail

Transport Ferroviaire de Personnel et de Marchandises
PO Box 1216, Abidjan 16, Côte d'Ivoire
Tel: (+225) 21 62 93    Fax: (+225) 21 28 58
e-mail: sitarail@africaonline.co.ci

### Key personnel
Chief Executive: A A Thiam

Gauge: 1,000 mm
Route length: 660 km

### Political background
The railway is the Côte d'Ivoire portion of the former Abidjan-Niger Railway that was jointly owned and managed by Côte d'Ivoire and Burkina Faso (formerly Upper Volta). In 1986 the partnership broke up. In 1988 the countries seemed to settle their differences, but this rapprochement was short-lived, and each country managed its part of the railway separately until 1993.

The former operator SICF, created in 1989, was immediately in serious financial difficulty, unable to meet its costs from revenue. Local analysis estimated that the railway was in urgent need of CFAFr1.2 billion to keep going, and of at least CFAFr14 billion for rehabilitation. Services to Burkina Faso continued to run, but operating difficulties on both sides of the border persuaded the two governments that a common management was perhaps the better option after all. At the end of 1992 it was decided to call tenders for private-sector operation of the railway.

Two groups put forward proposals, and those of the Sitarail joint venture consortium were preferred. Sitarail comprises various local industrial groups including Saga, SDV and Société Ivoirienne de Café et Cacao working with French consultants Systra (Sofrerail), Transurb Consult and others. These hold 67 per cent of the capital, the remainder being held by the two countries' governments (15 per cent each) and Sitarail staff (3 per cent). Two state-owned companies, SIPF and Sopafer, retain ownership of railway assets, including infrastructure, property and rolling stock.

After a long period of negotiation, Sitarail took over operation of the railway as a single entity in August 1995 with some 1,800 of the original staff complement of 3,600. The World Bank and Caisse Française de Développement provided funding to pay off the redundant workforce.

The concession was let for 15 years, but after seven years Sitarail must be prepared to grant track access to third party operators.

In November 2001, the governments of Burkina Faso and Côte d'Ivoire signed an agreement to establish a joint railway infrastructure investment fund. The fund was to be administered by representatives of each government and of Sitarail.

### Passenger operations

Sitarail abandoned unprofitable local services when it took over the concession, but retained a vestigial long-distance passenger service. The company carried some 0.4 million passengers in 1996. Service provision was severely limited by the amount of rolling stock available, with no more than a thrice-weekly Abidjan-Ouagadougou express being operated in early 1996.

### Freight operations

Despite a good network of permanent roads the railway is a vital link with Burkina Faso, which particularly relies on it for transport of freight to and from the coast.

Some 85 per cent of traffic to Burkina Faso consists of petroleum products, containers, fertiliser and clinker. In the reverse direction, cotton, agricultural produce and livestock are the principal commodities carried.

Under the nationalised operator, the railway declined in importance, reaching a low point of 250 million tonne-km in 1994, down from over 600 million in the early 1980s. Prospects for recapturing freight lost during the years of decline are thought to be favourable: in 1996 492 million tonnes were carried for 428 million tonne-km. Two potential traffic flows are manganese and zinc from mines in Burkina Faso for export from Abidjan.

### Improvements to existing lines

The new operator immediately sought bids for rail and other track components to inaugurate an upgrading programme over the entire route in both countries. CFAFr17.6 billion has been allocated to infrastructure improvements in the period 1996-2000. In 1999, funding to upgrade the Abidjan-Ouagadougou line was obtained from the International Development Association.

### Traction and rolling stock

At the start of 1997 the Sitarail fleet comprised 13 diesel locomotives, 17 shunting locotractors, 2 railcars, 17 coaches and 443 wagons. A further 114 private-owner wagons were in service. In late 1995, priority was being given to obtaining spare parts for rehabilitation of the remaining five GM diesel-electrics out of the original fleet of 25. In the company's five-year plan, some CFAFr13.7 billion will be spent on overhauling rolling stock; in late 1996, Sitarail went out to tender for 20 bogie hopper wagons.

### Signalling and telecommunications

A total of 21 stations have been equipped with colourlight signalling and power point operation based on SNCF's NSI relay system. Installation was by a French subsidiary of ABB. Sitarail plans to spend CFAFr1 billion on upgrading the telecommunications system.

In 1999 Sitarail invited tenders for the supply of a fibre optic telecommunications system to replace existing equipment between Abidjan and Ouagadougou.

### Track

**Rail:** 30 and 36 kg/m
**Ballast:** Granite, 800-1,200 litres/m, hard sandstone, 700 litres/m
**Sleepers:** Metal, 1,550/km; concrete monobloc (Blochet), 1,357/km
**Min curvature radius:** 500 m, being raised to 800 m
**Ruling gradient:** 10%
**Max axleload:** 17 tonnes

***UPDATED***

---

# CROATIA

## Ministry of Maritime Affairs, Transport and Communications

Prisavlje 14, 41000 Zagreb
Tel: (+385 1) 51 70 00   Fax: (+385 1) 61 06 91

### Key personnel
Minister: Mario Kovač

***UPDATED***

## Croatian State Railway

Hrvatske Željeznice (HŽ)
Mihanovićeva 12, 10000 Zagreb
Tel: (+385 1) 457 71 11   Fax: (+385 1) 378 33 26

### Key personnel
Director General: Marijan Drempetic
Deputy Director: Damir Zmegac
Directors
   Commercial: Zvonko Podvorac
   Finance: Mirjana Pejkovic
   Traction and Rolling Stock: Damir Toth
Infrastructure: Drazen Ratkovic
Electrification: Ivica Kucan
Development and Informatics: Srećko Krec
International Affairs: Maja Stepcevic
Public Relations: Vlatka Skoric

Gauge: 1,435 mm
Length: 2,296 km
Electrification: 983 km, of which 847 km at 25 kV AC, and 136 km at 3 kV DC

### Political background

A week after Croatia declared its independence from Yugoslavia in October 1991 the new republic severed its railway system from Yugoslav Railways (JŽ).

The railway sustained serious damage in the war in the region in the early 1990s; full reparations are expected to take many years to complete. However, HŽ benefits from its advantageous position between central and western Europe and the Balkan region. It is intersected by the two important transit corridors: Munich-Zagreb-Belgrade-Athens and Rijeka-Zagreb-Budapest-Lvov.

In response to financial pressures, staff have been shed. HŽ had 22,973 employees at the end of December 1996, down from over 36,000 five years previously.

In May 2001, the European Investment Bank announced a €40 million loan for modernisation of the Croatian section of the line linking Hungary and Bosnia Herzegovina, part of Pan-European Corridor Vc.

### Organisation

At the beginning of 1995, infrastructure and operations within HŽ were separated. Infrastructure is still managed by HŽ, but the government takes financial responsibility for it.

In early 1999 the World Bank and the European Bank for Reconstruction and Development granted HŽ loans of US$101 million and US$35 million respectively to assist with network modernisation. Part of this funding was to allow the railway to implement cuts in staff numbers in a bid to raise productivity.

| Finance (US$ million) | | |
|---|---|---|
| **Revenue** | *1995* | *1996* |
| Passengers | 38.9 | 41.1 |
| Freight | 90.2 | 77.3 |
| Other income | 293.3 | 313.6 |
| Total | 422.4 | 432.0 |
| | | |
| **Expenditure** | *1995* | *1996* |
| Staff/personnel | 164.2 | 192.2 |
| Materials and services | 141.3 | 153.3 |
| Depreciation | 87.6 | 85.1 |
| Other expenditure | 55.4 | 52.2 |
| Total | 448.5 | 482.8 |
| | | |
| **Traffic** (million) | *1995* | *1996* |
| Passenger journeys | 28.6 | 29.1 |
| Passenger-km | 1,139 | 1,205 |
| Freight tonnes | 13.3 | 11.0 |
| Freight tonne-km | 1,974 | 1,717 |

### Passenger operations

In 1996, 29.1 million passenger journeys were made (a 1.7 per cent increase on the year before); passenger-km stood at 1,205 million (5.8 per cent up). Cross-border services between Croatia and Yugoslavia resumed in November 1997, with fast Munich—Zagreb—Belgrade and Zurich—Zagreb—Belgrade services planned.

In 1996 HŽ held nearly 25 per cent of the domestic passenger transport market.

### Freight operations

In 1996, freight tonnage stood at 11.0 million tonnes, 17.3 per cent down on the year before. Freight tonne-km were

# RAILWAY SYSTEMS/Croatia

*HŽ Class 2043 diesel-electric locomotive at Zagreb Glavni Kolodvor (Frank Valoczy)* 2001/0099116

13.1 per cent down, standing at 1,717 million. The railway accounted for some 65 per cent of Croatia's total freight traffic. Main commodities carried are iron ore and other minerals, timber and wood products, fertilizers, oil and petroleum products and cereals.

Freight volumes between Croatia and Hungary have doubled since 1994 following an agreement signed in 1995 by HŽ and its Hungarian counterpart MÁV covering traffic flow improvements.

### Intermodal operations
HŽ operates five container terminals in Zagreb, Našice, Osijek, Rijeka and Split, and owns a fleet of around 400 container flat wagons. In 1995, HŽ was admitted as a shareholder member of the Intercontainer international intermodal group. Hungary and Italy are the two most important countries with which container traffic is exchanged. Total intermodal traffic on HŽ in 1996 was estimated at 34,000 TEU, comprising 7,000 TEU imports, 3,000 TEU exports and 24,000 TEU transit traffic; this was down from a high of 41,000 TEU in 1994.

### New lines
A new 23 km route is being studied from Jurdani, west of Rijeka, to Lupoglav Novi, on the Istrian peninsula. At present HŽ's Istrian network is isolated from the core system and traffic has to pass through Slovenian territory, increasing the Croation network's costs. The main construction challenge would be a 14.4 km tunnel under the Učka range at Čičarija.

### Improvements to existing lines
In 1998 248 route-km were double-track. HŽ plans to double-track three further sections of line: Dugo Selo–Koprivnica–Hungarian border; Zagreb–Sisak–Novska; and Zagreb–Krapina.

In August 1995 the 108 km Split–Knin route was reopened and one month later through operations between Zagreb and Split were reinstated following extensive rehabilitation of the 232 km Oštarije–Knin section, which was heavily damaged during the civil war.

The 41 km war-damaged Vinkovci–Tovarnik–Šid cross-border section into Serbia was restored in June 1996. Full operation with diesel traction began in December 1997 following an agreement signed by HŽ and its Yugoslav counterpart, JŽ, on 20 October 1997. Renewal of overhead catenary was completed in late 1998.

International operation into Hungary over the Osijek–Beli Manastir–Pécs line was reintroduced in August 1997.

All but three war-damaged lines were operational by 1999. Political reasons hamper reopening of the 129 km line from Knin northwards towards Bihać in Bosnia-Herzogovina, as the route crosses the Croatian-Bosnian border in the Una valley at seven locations, although reconstruction was completed in September 1998 by Italian military railway engineers forming part of the SFOR peace-keeping force. In 1999, agreement was reached that the HŽ station at Martin Brod would mark the border despite the community of that name being in Bosnia-Herzogovina. The 102 km Karlovac–Sisak line suffered extreme damage during the war and will probably never be reinstated. The Sunja–Novska line also remained out of use due to heavy war damage.

### Traction and rolling stock
At the beginning of 2000, HŽ was operating 263 diesel and 120 electric locomotives, 90 dmus, and 33 emus. At the start of 1996 the hauled coaching stock fleet stood at 798 vehicles and there were 11,543 wagons.

Part of a package of loans from the World Bank (US$101 million) and the European Bank for Reconstruction and Development (US$35 million) granted in early 1999 was intended to fund locomotive and emu refurbishment, the upgrading of 120 passenger coaches for international services, and improvements to 100 freight wagons.

In 2000 HŽ commenced a programme to refurbish its Ansaldo-built Class 1061 electric locomotives. Class 6011 emus were also undergoing refurbishment.

In 2001, HŽ was reported to be negotiating the purchase from Italian Railways of eight Class ALn 668 Fiat-built diesel railcars.

### Electrification
The single-track line from Moravice via Rijeka to Šapjane on the Slovenian border is energised at 3 kV DC, while the remainder of HŽ electrifcation is at 25 kV AC 650 Hz. Conversion of this pocket of DC electrification to the standard 25 kV AC is HŽ's current main electrification project.

In 2001, plans were announced to electrify the line between Strizivojna and Osijek (48 km), in eastern Croatia, to enable IC services to run from Zagreb without a traction change.

### Signalling and telecommunications
In May 1997, HŽ invited tenders for a ground-to-train radio system along the Lika line. Radio exchanges would be located at Ostarije, Gospic, Knin and Split.

*Continuing evidence of war damage at the station at Sunja (Frank Valoczy)* 2001/0099117

### Diesel locomotives

| Class | Wheel arrangement | Transmission | Power kW | Speed km/h | Weight tonnes | No in service | First built | Builders Mechanical | Engine |
|---|---|---|---|---|---|---|---|---|---|
| 2041 | Bo-Bo | DE | 606 | 80 | 64 | 18 | 1962 | B&L/Daković | SACM |
| 2042 | Bo-Bo | DE | 680 | 80 | 64 | 3 | 1966 | B&L/Daković | SACM |
| 2043 | A1A-A1A | DE | 1,454 | 124 | 100 | 6 | 1960 | General Motors | General Motors |
| 2044 | A1A-A1A | DE | 1,820 | 124 | 103 | 31 | 1981 | GM/Daković | General Motors |
| 2061 | Co-Co | DE | 1,454 | 124 | 114 | 24 | 1960 | General Motors | General Motors |
| 2062 | Co-Co | DE | 1,640 | 124 | 103 | 54 | 1973 | General Motors | General Motors |
| 2063 | Co-Co | DE | 2,461 | 124 | 120.1 | 13 | 1973 | General Motors | General Motors |
| 2131 | C | DH | 294 | 60 | 42.5 | 23 | 1963 | Jenbacher Werke | Jenbacher Werke |
| 2132 | C | DH | 441 | 60 | 44 | 88 | 1986 | Jenbacher Werke | Jenbacher Werke |
| 2133 | C | DH | 511 | 60 | 54 | 5 | 1957 | MaK | MaK |
| 2141 | B-B | DH | 1,176 | 120 | 68.2 | 1 | 1977 | Duro Daković | SACM |

B&L = Brissoneau & Lotz

### Electric locomotives

| Class | Wheel arrangement | Output kW | Speed km/h | Weight tonnes | No in service | First built | Builders Mechanical | Electrical |
|---|---|---|---|---|---|---|---|---|
| 1061* | Bo-Bo-Bo | 2,640/3,150 | 120 | 108-112 | 23 | 1960 | Ansaldo | Ansaldo |
| 1141-000† | Bo-Bo | 4,080 | 120 | 78 | 46 | 1970 | SGP | ASEA/Rade Končar |
| 1141-100† | Bo-Bo | 4,080 | 120 | 82 | 8 | 1987 | Gredelj/Daković | Rade Končar |
| 1141-200† | Bo-Bo | 4,080 | 140 | 82 | 28 | 1981 | Gredelj/Thyssen | Rade Končar |
| 1142† | Bo-Bo | 4,400 | 160 | 82 | 13 | 1981 | Gredelji/Daković | Rade Končar |
| 1143 | Bo-Bo | 4,080 | 120 | - | 1 | - | SGP | Rade Končar |
| 1161† | Bo-Bo-Bo | 4,080 | 120 | 129 | 2 | 1988 | Ansaldo/Gredelj | Ansaldo/Uljanik |

*3 kV  † 25 kV

Modernisation of signalling and communications between St Samac and Beli Manastir and between Metkovič and Ploče are planned, with financial support from the EBRD, the EIB and the World Bank.

### Track
**Rail:** 60 UIC, S 49, and some 35-45 kg/m
**Sleepers:** Beechwood, prestressed concrete
**Fastenings:** Elastic SKL1 and SKL2, Fixed-K
**Minimum curve radius:** 150m
**Max gradient:** 2.7%
**Max permissible axleload:** 22.5 tonnes

### Diesel railcars or multiple-units

| Class | Cars per unit | Motor cars per unit | Motored axles/car | Transmission | Power/motor kW | Speed km/h | No in service | First built | Builders Mechanical | Engine |
|---|---|---|---|---|---|---|---|---|---|---|
| 7021 | 5 | 2 | 4 | DE | 386 | 120 | 12 | 1973 | B&L | SACM |
| 7121 | 2 | 1 | 4 | DH | 106 | 120 | 37 | 1981 | Macosa | MAN |
| 7221 | 2 | 1 | 1 | DM | 110 | 90 | 21 | 1959 | Uerdingen | MAN |
| 7122* | 1 | 1 | 2 | DH | 147 | 130 | 20 | 1979 | Fiat/Kalmar | Fiat |

*Purchased second-hand from Swedish State Railways in 1995

### Electric railcars or multiple-units

| Class | Cars per unit | Motor cars per unit | Motored axles/car | Power/motor kW | Speed km/h | No in service | First built | Builders Mechanical | Electrical |
|---|---|---|---|---|---|---|---|---|---|
| 6011* | 4 | 2 | 4 | 145 | 110 | 9 | 1964 | Pafawag | Pafawag |
| 6111† | 3 | 1 | 4 | 300 | 120 | 24 | 1977 | Ganz-Mavag | Ganz-Mavag |

*3 kV  † 25 kV

**UPDATED**

---

# CUBA

## Ministry of Transport

Avenida Rancho Boyeras y Tulipán, Havana
Tel: (+53 7) 81 45 05/81 47 80   Fax: (+53 7) 33 51 18

### Key personnel
Minister of Transport: Álvaro Pérez

## Cuban Railways (UFC)

Unión de Ferrocarriles de Cuba
Edificio Estación Central, Egido y Arsenal, Havana
Tel: (+53 7) 62 15 30   Fax: (+53 7) 33 86 28

### Key personnel
Director General: Ing Pastor Pérez Fleites
Directors
   Locomotives and Rolling Stock: J Noya
   Finance: N Marrero
   Commercial: Dr C M Caballer
   Traffic: R Boffil
   Permanent Way: J C Miranda
   Signalling: R Morales
   Personnel: L Pereda

Gauge: 1,435 mm
Route length: 3,442 km
Electrification: 142 km at 1.2 kV DC

### Organisation
The UFC network is operated as a fully integrated state enterprise by the Ministry of Transportation. A divisional operational structure is in place, covering nine divisions.

In 1998, UFC signed an agreement with the Catalan and Spanish governments covering technological development and the creation of a training plan. Studies were to be undertaken into the development of both passenger and freight traffic, with an action plan established for each sector.

*USSR-built Type M62-K diesel locomotive and domestically built 'Taino' coaches at Calimete (Lennox MacEwan)* 0058682

At the end of 1997 UFC employed 24,525 staff compared with 27,370 in 1996.

| Traffic (million) | 1996 | 1997 |
|---|---|---|
| Passenger journeys | 11.7 | 13.7 |
| Passenger-km | 1,487.6 | 1,684 |
| Freight tonnes | 4.42 | 4.64 |
| Freight tonne-km | 769.5 | 821.5 |

### Passenger operations
Since 1992, passenger traffic is reckoned to have increased by some 20 per cent due to the rationing of petrol for road vehicles, a measure resulting from the end of Comecon trading arrangements and the US blockade. However, services suffer from outdated equipment and poor reliability.

### Freight operations
Freight traffic comprises mostly sugar and its by-products of rum and molasses, tobacco and citrus fruit. Traffic levels have fallen considerably since the 1980s, when some 13 million tonnes were carried annually, compared with the 1997 figure of 4.4 million. However, there has recently been a revival in sugar traffic, which has recovered from low production in the mid-1990s.

### Improvements to existing lines
Reconstruction of the Havana–Santiago de Cuba line is believed to have been brought to a halt by the worsening economic situation, having been undertaken as far as Camaguey. The total length of new track to be installed under this project was 1,170 km, comprising 837 km of main line, 224 km of sidings and passing loops and 109 km of feeder branch lines. The line has been laid with Soviet-supplied Type P50 (50-48 kg/m) rail; sidings have been laid with 43 kg/m rail, also from the Soviet Union. Sleepers are prestressed monobloc concrete.

Improvements have been made to track and bridges on the electrified Havana–Matanzas line to coincide with the introduction of emus procured second-hand from Spain in 1998 (see 'Traction and rolling stock' section).

In 1997 a major new station at Santiago de Cuba was brought into use, and in 1998 improved rail facilities were commissioned at the port of Matanzas, from which much of Cuba's sugar production is shipped.

### Traction and rolling stock
At the end of 1997 UFC's active traction fleet was estimated at 211 diesel and 12 electric locomotives, 42 diesel and 14 electric railcars, 544 passenger cars and 5,074 freight wagons. Large parts of the rolling stock fleet were out of service for want of spare parts.

UFC diesel traction is an eclectic assortment of French, East German, Hungarian, Canadian and, more recently, Soviet types. The Canadian machines are 20 Bombardier-

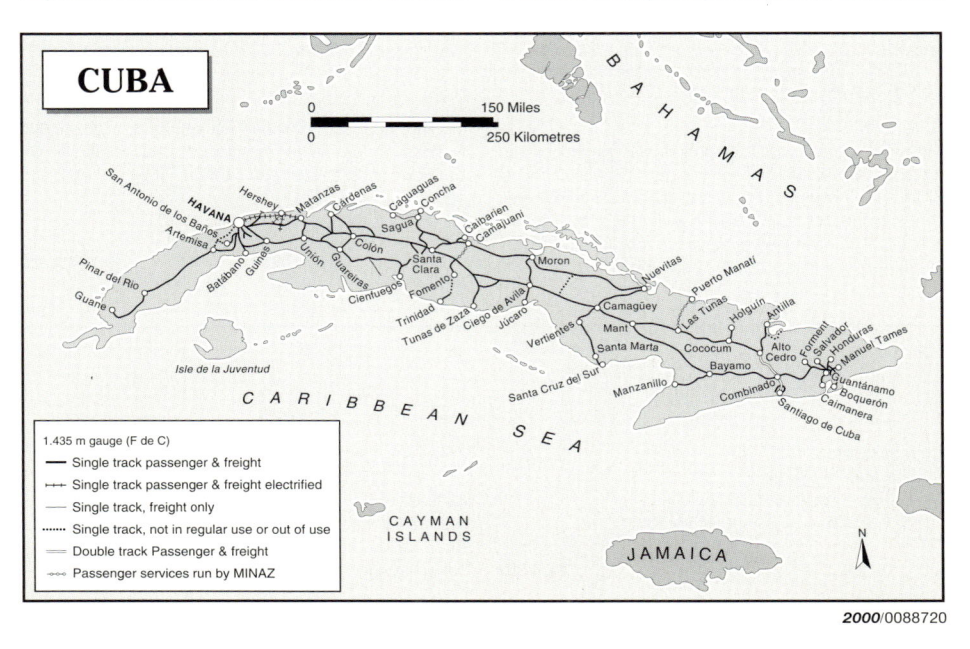

# 114  RAILWAY SYSTEMS/Cuba—Czech Republic

MLW Type MX 624 supplied in the mid-1970s. Dominant model is the Soviet 1,912 kW Type TE-114K Co-Co, of which the stock is 96, although many of these are unserviceable. In 1998 UFC's Camagüey workshops commenced a re-engining and refurbishment programme on this type as part of a wider effort to raise traction availability. The most recent locomotive acquisitions are 16 T-458 Bo-Bo machines obtained second-hand from the Czech Republic.

UFC's 12 vintage electric locomotives are used on the 1.2 kV DC Havana–Matanzas line, the former Hershey Railway.

The diesel railcars are mostly of Fiat design with 409 kW engines, built in the mid-1970s by Concord of Argentina under licence. UFC is now required by national policy (and economic and political circumstance) to seek local rolling stock manufacture and a local company, Empresa Productora de Equipos Ferroviarios of Cardenas, began supply of diesel railbuses based on the Ganz-Mávag design. The plant's first 85 passenger cars have been delivered to UFC. The Ministry of Steel, Iron & Machine Industry has produced two 'Taino' trains at its Cardenas works; these have run in Las Tunas province and can carry 300 passengers.

In 1998 Catalan Railways (FGC) in Spain sold to UFC five three-car and three four-car standard-gauge 1950s-built emus for the electrified Havana–Matanzas line. The Pta315 million acquisition cost was financed by the International Commerce Bank of Cuba and Banco Bilbao Vizcaya in Spain.

In 1998 UFC procured five Budd RDC diesel railcars from VIA Rail, Canada, while a major purchase of second-hand rolling stock was supplied from France in the form of 44 former Trans-Europe-Express (TEE) stainless steel-bodied coaches. All were overhauled before shipment and the contract also covered supplies of spare parts and training for UFC staff.

It was expected that up to 30 Class X 2800 diesel railcars and 60 Class X 6000 railcar trailers would also be supplied upon their retirement by SNCF.

In 2001, UFC also acquired some 150 locomotive-hauled coaches from DB in Germany, together with 30 Class 771 and 772 railbuses and two breakdown cranes.

**Type of coupler in standard use:** Semi-automatic
**Type of brake in standard use:** Air (50% Matrosov, 30% Westinghouse and 20% DAKO)

## Signalling and telecommunications
On the main Havana–Santiago da Cuba line, replacement has proceeded of its almost exclusively manual point and block-telephone operation. Hitherto only nine of some 100 stations have had central point working, but track-to-train and train-to-train radio has been provided. Installation of a semi-automatic block system and relay interlockings has been completed on the 16-station section between Havana and Santa Clara (207 km) and in 1991 was continuing to Santiago de Cuba.

## Electrification
The 147 km 1.2 kV DC electrified section on UFC links Havana with Matanzas. In 1999, agreement was reached with Catalan Railways in Spain to assist planning of a 12 km extension of this electrification to allow operations into Havana Central station.

## Track
**Rail:** P50 51 kg/m
**Sleepers:** Prestressed concrete: 2,460 mm, spaced 1,520-1,840/km; creosoted pine: 2,750 mm, spaced 1,520-1,840/km
**Fastenings:** Elastic and rigid with track rails and screw bolts
**Min curvature radius:** 150 m
**Max gradient:** 3.0%
**Max permissible axleload:** 22 tonnes over 230 km

*Former Catalan Railways emu in service on the Havana–Matanzas 1.2 kV DC line (Lennox MacEwan)* 0058683

### Diesel locomotives

| Class | Wheel arrangement | Power kW | Speed km/h | Weight tonnes | No delivered | First built | Builders Mechanical | Engine | Transmission |
|---|---|---|---|---|---|---|---|---|---|
| TE114K | Co-Co | 1,912 | 120 | 121 | 102 | 1978 | Voroshilovgrad | 5D49 | E Jaricov |
| MX-624 | Co-Co | 1,912 | 135 | 112 | 50 | 1975 | Bombardier | Alco 251E | E GE Canada |
| M62-K | Co-Co | 1,234 | 100 | 120 | 32 | 1974 | Voroshilovgrad | 14D4DT2 PDIT | E Kharkov |
| TEM-4K | Co-Co | 735 | 100 | 120 | 40 | 1964 | Bryansk | | |
| TEM-2K | Co-Co | 757 | 100 | 120 | 60 | 1974 | Bryansk | PDITM | E Kharkov |
| TEM-15K | Co-Co | 757 | 100 | 108 | 25 | 1988 | (Russia) | - | E - |
| DVM-9 | Bo-Bo | 735 | 90 | 76 | 70 | 1969 | Ganz-Mávag | 16VCE17/24 | E Ganz Electric |
| GM-900 | Bo-Bo | 662 | 90 | 72 | 58 | 1955 | GM | 8-567C | E GM |
| BB63000 | Bo-Bo | 606 | 90 | 72 | 32 | 1965 | B&L | MG0V12BSH 22 | E B&L |
| T-458 | Bo-Bo | 492 | 80 | 74 | 16 | 1964 | ČKD | ČKD 6S 310 DR | E ČKD |
| TGM-25 | C | 294 | 50 | 46 | - | 1970 | Voroshilovgrad | - | H - |

B&L = Brissoneau & Lotz

### Electric locomotives

| Class | Wheel arrangement | Output kW | Speed km/h | Weight tonnes | No in service | First built | Builders |
|---|---|---|---|---|---|---|---|
| GE 7230B | Bo-Bo | 588/882 | 60 | 55 | 12 | 1920 | GE |

### Diesel railcars or multiple-units

| Class | Cars per unit | Motor cars per unit | Power/motor kW | Speed km/h | No in service | First built | Builders Mechanical | Engine | Transmission |
|---|---|---|---|---|---|---|---|---|---|
| Fiat Concord | 2 | 1 | 2 × 184 | 110 | 15 | 1976 | Fiat Concord | Fiat 8217 | H Fiat |
| Budd | 1 | 1 | 2 × 184 | 128 | 2 | 1957 | Budd | Leyland | H Leyland |
| Brill | 1 | 1 | 132 | 70 | 10 | 1930 | Brill | Taino | M Taino |

### Electric railcars or multiple-units

| Class | Cars per unit | Motor cars per unit | Output/motor kW | Speed km/h | No in service | First built | Builders |
|---|---|---|---|---|---|---|---|
| Brill | 1 | 1 | 4 × 55 | 70 | 16 | 1923 | Brill |
| M400 | 4 | 3 | 4 × 110 | 80 | 3 | 1943* | FGC/Cenemesa |
| M500 | 3 | 2 | 4 × 110 | 80 | 5 | 1943* | FGC/Cenemesa |

* Ex-Catalan Railways, modernised 1985

## Sugar railways
The numerous railways linking the sugar plantations and factories are in sum of greater extent than UFC and at latest report totalled 7,742 km. Of the total, some 65 per cent is standard-gauge. Serving over 100 of the island's 154 sugar plants, these railways are mostly operated by the Ministry for Sugar (MINAZ) and employ around 900 locomotives, 380 of them steam, and over 30,000 wagons. The diesel fleet mainly comprises locomotives of USSR origin, with over 440 supplied between 1977 and 1990.

*UPDATED*

# CZECH REPUBLIC

## Ministry of Transport and Communications
Nábřeží Ludvíka Svobody 12, CZ-110 15 Prague 1 – Nové Město
Tel: (+420 2) 51 43 11 11

### Key personnel
Minister: Jaromír Schling
Under-Secretary, Railways: Pavel Stoulil
Director, Railways: Václav Nováček

*UPDATED*

## Czech Railways (ČD)
České Dráhy
Nábřeží Ludvíka Svobody 12/1222, CZ-110 15 Prague 1 – Nové Město
Tel: (+420 2) 51 43 24 39; 51 43 30 30; 51 43 11 11

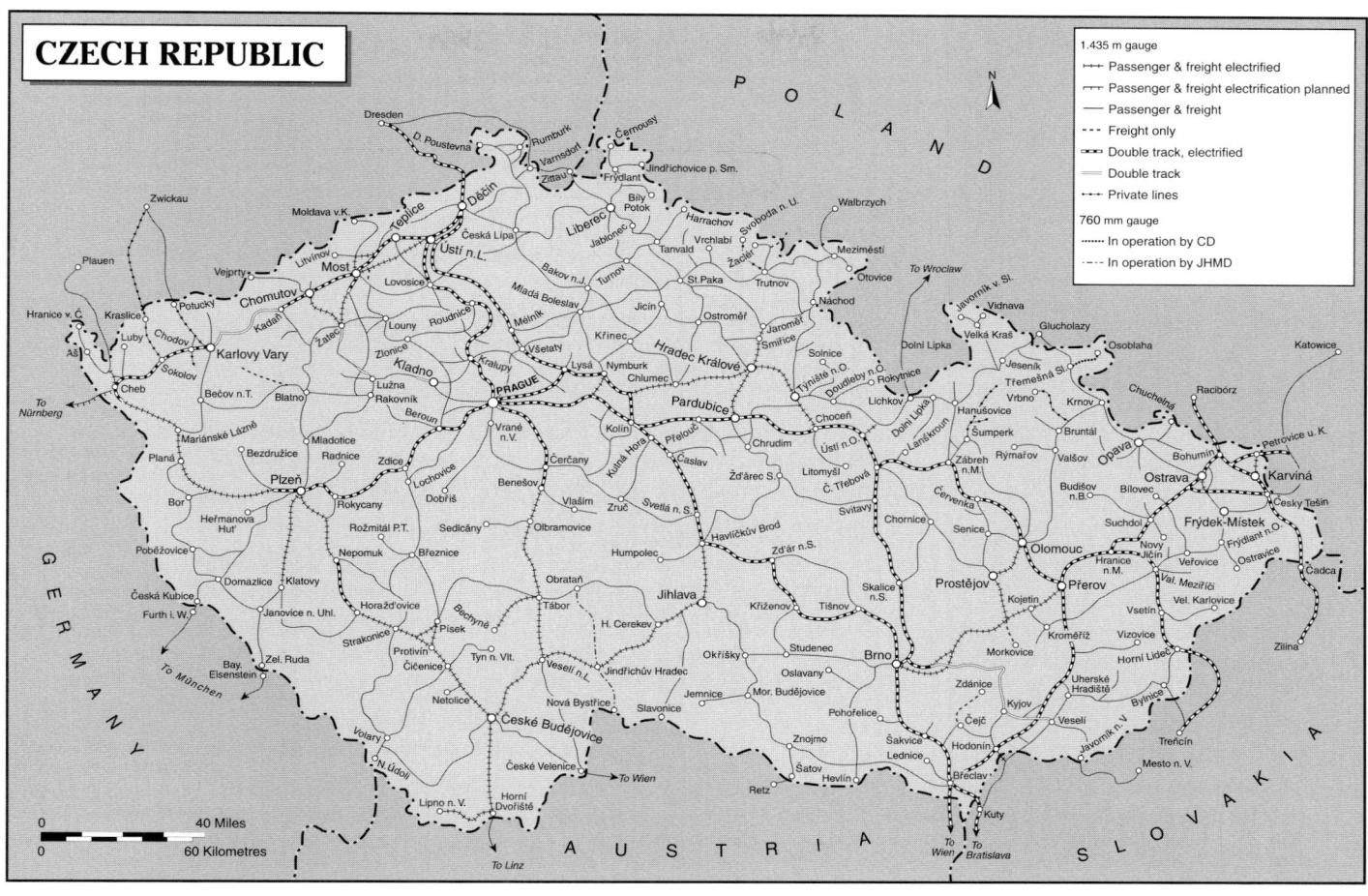

# Czech Republic/RAILWAY SYSTEMS

Fax: (+420 2) 51 43 31 20; 51 43 26 30
e-mail: GROZYPHAsek@gropha.cdrail.cz
Web: http://www.cdrail.cz

**Key personnel**
Chairman of Executive Committee: Pavel Stoulil
General Manager: Dalibor Zelený
General Supervisor: Zdeněk Žák
General Manager's Office
   Director: Mrs Anna Nováková
   First Under-Secretary and Under-Secretary for
   Personnel and International Affairs: Ivo Malina
   Under-Secretary for Economy: Jan Bukač
Management Board
   Strategy: Zdeněk Zouhar
   Personnel: Vojtěch Zelenka
   Economy and Finance: Miroslav Jára
   Privatisation: Jaromír Urban
   Law: Jan Čermák
   Defence, Protection and Ecology: Jiří Fiala
   Technical Development: Jan Bartek
   Permanent Way: Václav Svoboda
   Passenger Traffic: Jan Hanzlik
   Freight Traffic: Pavel Lamacz
   Traction and Rolling Stock: Emil Efler
   Signalling and Telecommunications:
      Tomaš Neugebauer
   Construction and Maintenance: Mojmír Nejezchleb
   Control: Jan Mrkva
   Human Resources: Oldřich Zatbukal
   Public Relations: Radovan Havra'nek
   International: Jiří Havlíček
Divisional Managers
   Commercial and Operations (DOP): Jaroslav Kocourek
   Infrastructure (DDC): Jan Komárek
Regional Managers
   Prague: Jaromír Kadlec
   Plzeň: Josef Chaloupek
   Ústi nad Labem: Jiří Kolář
   Brno: František Raška
   Ostrava: Miroslav Klich
   Pardubice: Jan Grebík

Gauge: 1,435 mm; 760 mm
Route length: 9,336 km standard-gauge; 20.2 km narrow-gauge
Electrification: 1,745 km at 3 kV DC; 46 km at 1.5 kV DC; 1,193 km at 25 kV 50 Hz AC

**Political background**
Mirroring the severance of Slovakia from the Czech Republic, the Czechoslovak railway system was formally divided on 1 January 1993. Three of the former State Railways' four regions, the Midland based on Olomouc, the Northeastern based on Prague and the Southwestern based on Plzeň, are embodied in the new Czech Republic Railways (ČD), which has taken over 72 per cent of the State Railways' network. Slovak Railways (ŽSR) is essentially the old Eastern region based on Bratislava. An agreement ending all disputes relating to the break-up of the former Czechoslovak State Railways was signed by the General Managers of ČD and Slovakian Railways (ŽSR) in October 1999.

On 1 April 1999, ČD became an affiliate member of the Community of European Railways.

*Privatisation*
The proposed break-up and sale of parts of the Czech Railways network has been cancelled following the election in July 1998 of a Social Democratic government. While some branch lines may be leased out to private operators, the new government favours retaining the whole rail network under unified state ownership.

On 26 February 2001 the Czech government ratified a new reform programme for ČD. After being referred back for revision several times during 2001, the programme was finally approved by parliament on 5 February 2002. Signed by President Václav Havel on 19 February, the legislation proposes splitting ČD's infrastructure management from operations and the creation of two separate operating businesses from 1 January 2003. This therefore abandons the initial intention of splitting the operating company into several independent businesses. The existing České dráhy as, joint stock company, would become purely an operating company and a railway infrastructure authority, Správa železniční dopravní cesty (SŽDC), would be formed to own and manage the entire railway infrastructure. The railway's total assets, estimated at some Kcs83.1 billion, would be divided between the two bodies and SŽDC would be given responsibility to sell ČD's non-core property to repay the railway's accumulated debt of Kcs36.6 billion.

The property portfolio includes some potentially lucrative sites in Prague, plus track and machinery centres, repair shops, staff training centres, holiday and convalescent resorts, hospital facilities in six cities and staff quarters throughout the network. The list of assets to be sold include three rural lines abandoned in the 1970s. Some Kcs3.5 billion will be required for severance payments among staff as a result of the planned redundancy of 16 per cent of the 86,000-strong workforce by 2004.

ČD's results for 2000 show that the company remains in a poor financial condition, with a loss of Kcs4.86 billion, mainly the result of unremunerative passenger operations. Attempts to transform ČD into a profitable company which is able to survive in a strongly competitive environment without state subsidy, have been high on the government's agenda since the railway was created out of the former Czechoslovak system in 1993. Earlier plans to split ČD into several independent businesses were abandoned in the face of strong political opposition and objections from the railway trade unions.

The creation of a joint-stock company is expected to broaden ČD's entrepreneurial activities, possibly leading to the establishment of joint ventures with private sector companies and the admittance of a strong strategic partner through the sale of shares.

Since mid-1998, the incoming Minister of Transport and Communications has implemented fundamental changes in ČD's management board, with the replacement of most of its members and the appointment of a new general manager. A priority task for the new board has been to stabilise the company, which had four general managers between 1995 and 1998.

The previous Czech government had continued to examine ways of introducing private capital to the running of the railways, with the aim of rectifying an investment backlog, rendering ČD more competitive against other modes and reducing the level of state support. ČD's electrification (Elektrizace Železnice Praha a s), intermodal (ČSKD-Intrans) and dining and sleeping car (JLV a s) divisions have already been privatised, in addition to nine major workshops and fringe activities such as restaurants and the railway health service. During the first phase, privatisation earned Kcs3.6 billion.

Under legislation passed in 1994 ending the monopoly of the state railways, private companies holding a licence from the Ministry of Transport's Railway Authority were able to bid to operate closed or unprofitable sections of the ČD network. A new organisation, the Railway Authority (DU – Drážni Úřad), was established under the Ministry of Transport in April 1994, charged with awarding operating licences to private sector companies and harmonising their operations with those of ČD.

By 1998, after five years of discussion, privatisation of ČD rural routes was well under way with the support of the railway, which regards the sale of loss-making lines as a route to increasing efficiency and releasing funds for more important projects such as upgrading international corridors and modernising rolling stock to meet wider European standards. In 1996 regional lines carried 13.3 million passengers and some 13 million tonnes of freight. This accounted for less than 5 per cent of the network's output, and generated revenue of Kcs824 million against expenditure of Kcs2.54 billion. Disposal of these lines was estimated to save Kcs5.2 billion annually, an amount roughly comparable with ČD's annual passenger subsidy.

An historic agreement was signed by the National Property Fund and private operator Jindřichův Hradec Local Railways (JHMD) in February 1998, when the latter took over operation of two 760 mm local lines radiating from Jindřichův Hradec in southern Bohemia. JHMD had leased the lines from ČD since March 1997 after their abandonment by the national operator two months earlier, and rapidly recorded substantial increases in freight and passenger traffic.

Under the previous government, a revised programme of ČD regional route privatisation was submitted for government approval in June 1999. This would have seen 117 regional lines, totalling 2,966 km and valued at Kcs3.7 billion, sold off in two stages starting in January 1999 and 2001 respectively. This process was not pursued by the new government.

Also initiated in 1998 was the process of leasing ČD lines to private operators. By February 1999 five rural lines covering 100 route-km had been leased: Trutnov-Svoboda nad Úpou (10 km), Nové Sedlo u Lokte-Krásný Jez (24 km), and Sokolov-Kraslice (23 km), all to private operator Viamont Ústí nad Labem; Milotice-Vrbno pod Pradědem to OKD Doprava; and Šumperk-Petrov nad Desno-Sobotín (29 km) to Železnice Desná.

An Association of Railway Companies (SŽS) was founded in October 1995 representing organisations wishing to purchase or operate over ČD lines or to obtain access to the state network. By 1998 membership had risen to 24, and expressions of interest had come from France and the United Kingdom.

### Organisation

ČD is controlled by the Ministry of Transport and Communications through an Executive Committee.

Management of infrastructure has been divorced from that of operations and there are now two divisions: Commercial and Operations (Divize Obchodněpřepravní - DOP) and Infrastructure (Divize dopravní cesty - DDC). On a territorial basis, ČD is now divided into six regional directorates (OPŘ), following the establishment of the latest of these, covering the Pardubice region, on 1 July 2001.

In mid-2001, ČD's staff numbered 84,873, down by 7 per cent since 1998.

| **Finances (Kcs billion)** | | | |
|---|---|---|---|
| Revenue | *1998* | *1999* | *2000* |
| Passengers | 4.323 | 4.642 | 4.869 |
| Freight | 20.975 | 19.323 | 17.539 |
| Other | 11.668 | 13.422 | 15.979 |
| Total | 36.966 | 37.387 | 38.387 |
| Expenditure | 40.356 | 41.351 | 43.248 |
| Result | (3.390) | (3.964) | (4.861) |
| Budget support to cover passenger losses | 6.031 | 6.658 | 7.541 |

| **Traffic** (million) | *1998* | *1999* | *2000* |
|---|---|---|---|
| Passenger journeys | 181.98 | 175.02 | 182.55 |
| Passenger-km | 7,001 | 6,929 | 7,266 |
| Freight tonnes | 93.52 | 82.16 | 89.77 |
| Freight tonne-km | 19,529 | 17,625 | 18,183 |

### Passenger operations

Passenger traffic has suffered both from economic recession and competition from private bus companies offering cheaper fares and faster timings over routes such as Prague-Brno and Prague-Ústí nad Labem. ČD now accounts for only 7.4 per cent of passenger journeys in the Czech Republic. The response to this position has been to attempt to strengthen services on the main lines, while cutting back on unprofitable branch line services.

In the period of the 2001-02 timetable, ČD was operating 7,261 passenger trains daily: 27 EuroCity; two SuperCity; 18 InterCity; 14 expresses; 217 fast trains; 160 semi-fast; and 6,823 local stopping services. With the introduction of the 2000-01 timetable, ČD accelerated express services on the Prague-Brno main line, authorising for the first time 160 km/h running over upgraded sections of Corridor 1 (see *Improvements to existing lines* section). Diverted via Pardubice and Česka Třebová instead of the traditional route via Havlíčkův Brod, EuroCity trains cover the 257 km line in 2 hours 42 minutes at an average speed of 94.4 km/h, the fastest-ever rail connection between the two cities. Further journey-time reductions will follow completion of Corridor 1 upgrading in 2003 and the introduction of new Class 680 tilting trainsets (see *Traction and rolling stock* section).

Daily EuroCity services now connect Prague with Vienna, Budapest, Warsaw, Dresden, Berlin, Hamburg, Košice, Nuremberg and Zvolen. Two Vienna-Warsaw EuroCity services serves the east of the Czech Republic.

Internally, service on the Prague-Bohumín route has been improved with introduction of InterCity services Nos 500/501 'Ostravan' and Nos 504/505 'Jan Perner', using refurbished coaches. IC 520/521 connects Prague with Zlín in central Moravia. ČD is attempting to attract more passengers to these routes, which as yet have no firm highway competition.

In January 1997, ČD introduced a high-quality service, the 'Manažer', on the route between Prague and Bohumín (366 km). Hauled by Class 162 3 kV DC electric locomotives, SuperCity (SC) train 502/503 consists of three first-class coaches and a restaurant car. Due to speed restrictions on the route caused by extensive works on ČD's Corridor 1 upgrading, the train now completes the journey in 4 hours 22 minutes, a commercial speed of 83.8 km/h. Free at-seat refreshment, newspapers and free parking at Ostrava's main station area are provided. By May 2000, 'Manažer' had carried 120,000 passengers. Another 1997/98 timetable innovation was the provision to carry accompanied private cars on the 'Hornád' international overnight service between Prague and Poprad, in Slovakia's High Tatras region. By the end of 2000, 'Hornád' had carried 1,184 accompanied cars, of which 568 were in 2000.

### Freight operations

ČD forms the Czech Republic's principal means of transporting bulk commodities, mainly coal (32.2 per cent of ČD's total freight volume), steel products (9.23 per cent), ores (8.1 per cent), raw materials (6.23 per cent), forest products (5.83 per cent), cereals and other foodstuffs (4.25 per cent) and chemical products (3.55 per cent). Given ČD's advantageous geographical location at the heart of Europe, transit traffic is very important to the railway and accounts for two-thirds of freight revenues. In 2001, ČD carried 7.1 million tonnes of transit cargo, the best result since the company's creation in 1993.

ČD operated 2,650 regular daily freight services during 2001, 112 of these block trains. Electric traction accounted for 89.2 per cent of freight tonnage moved.

There was a serious loss of traffic after the demise of communism - in 1989 railways now in the Czech Republic carried 226 million tonnes - and the decline continued after Czechoslovakia was split in two; by 1997 rail accounted for just 14.4 per cent of the country's freight tonnage.

ČD has attempted to make itself more competitive by maximising opportunities for block train operation and leasing modern wagons from neighbouring railways, and drop-off in traffic slowed in the mid-1990s. In 1995, revenue rose slightly and ČD's freight operations were profitable for the first time for some years.

In 2001, private companies operating over ČD tracks under licences granted by the Railway Authority (DÚ), principally Viamont and OKD Doprava, accounted for around nine per cent of the country's total rail freight volume. This was carried in 92 daily freight services and generated revenues exceeding Kcs0.5 billion.

On 17 March 1999, ČD signed an accord with Austrian Federal Railways to create a common freight rates policy. A similar agreement was signed in early March with Slovenian Railways and Polish State Railways. Through this harmonisation of tariffs, the four railways hoped to capture much lucrative north-south freight traffic from Railion, the joint freight company formed by Germany's and the Netherlands' national operators.

ČD's domestic express parcels service, 'ČD-Kurýr', is now available at 66 stations in 63 cities and towns (2001).

### Intermodal operations

Intermodal traffic in the Czech Republic is increasing sharply, accounting for 6.4 per cent of ČD's freight volume in 2000 (2.5 per cent in 1997). During the same year, 3.1 million tonnes were carried on RoLa piggyback trains and 2.6 million in containers.

There are two companies operating container trains from their own terminals. The operation of container shuttles to and from northern German ports is mostly in the hands of Metrans Praha, which operates the daily 'Metrans Shutle' and 'Metrans Expres' services between its terminal at Praha-Uhříněves and Hamburg Waltershof/Süd, as well as the weekly 'Metrans Rapid' service between the Czech capital and Bremerhaven Seehafen. Metrans also operates inland container shuttles between Praha-Uhříněves and Zlín-Želechovice and Dunajská Streda, Slovakia. Hamburg port operator HHLA is the majority shareholder in Metrans, while 34.1 per cent of the shares were acquired by DB Cargo in early 1999. Praha-Uhříněves is the country's largest container terminal; the company also operates facilities at Zlín-Želechovice in Moravia and at Dunajská Streda in Slovakia, the latter through its subsidiary Metrans Danubia.

A second private intermodal company, ČSKD-Intrans, formerly a subsidiary of Czechoslovak State Railways, now operates six pairs of container shuttle services from its major terminal at Praha-Žižkov in close collaboration with the Rotterdam-based company, European Rail Shuttle (ERS), and incorporating the major shipping companies Maersk-Sealand and P+O Nedlloyd. The 'Hansa-Prague Shuttle' runs four times a week between Praha-Žižkov and Hamburg Waltershof/Süd and the 'Weser-Prague Shuttle' makes three trips a week between Praha-Žižkov and Bremerhaven-Nordhafen. The 'Bohemia Express' operates six times a week between Praha-Žižkov and Rotterdam Maasvlakte Delta/Waalhaven RSC. Between July 1999 and January 2002, ČSKD-Intrans and ERS launched three continental container feeder services to and from Praha-Žižkov, serving: Bratislava-UNS (three times weekly from July 1999); Budapest-Jozsefváros (twice weekly from November 2001); and Bucuresti-Sud (weekly from January 2002). Another inland container service between Praha-Žižkov and Plzeň-Křimice has been suspended. ČSKD-Intrans is owned by the Port of Rotterdam and also operates terminals at Brno, Ostrava, Pardubice, Plzeň and Přerov and as well as three facilities in Slovakia at Bratislava, Košice and Zilina.

Ten pairs of trains each week carrying swap-bodies containing automotive components run between Mladá Boleslav and Kobylnica, Poland. These are operated by Bohemiakombi, Polkombi and Rösner.

In a bid to boost traffic, the Czech government in 2000 provided a grant of Kcs443.4 million (Kcs250 million in the previous year) to support the development of intermodal transport. The grant was mainly used to fund the purchase of type Sgnss container wagons (see *Traction and rolling stock* section), of which around 300 have been introduced since 1996. Part of the grant was also used to support *Rollende Ländstrasse* piggyback services.

An agreement was signed on 12 June 2001 by Czech transport minister Jaromír Schling and Russia's minister of railways, Nikolai Aksyonenko, covering the construction of a multi-modal international logistics and trans-shipment terminal at Bohumín-Vrbice in northern Moravia. Valued at US$200 million, the project also involves the construction of a new 70 km 1,520 mm gauge extension to the existing Polish State Railways LHS broad-gauge line built in the 1970s and running 394 km from the Ukrainian border at Hrubieszów to Slawków, near Katowice. Tracklaying commenced in October 2001, bringing the 1,520 mm gauge system to the Czech Republic for the first time.

The Israel-based company, Shiran General Trade AG, which is providing 30 per cent of the total cost of the scheme, expects to reduce journey times by two weeks between China, Japan and other countries in Asia and Central Europe by using the Trans-Siberian rail land-bridge and to cut transit costs by 20 per cent. The lowest traffic forecasts for the Bohumín terminal, which is due to open in 2003, are for 100,000 containers annually and approximately 15 million tonnes of raw materials, mostly iron ore.

An international piggyback service was introduced in September 1994 on the 118 km route between Lovosice and Dresden, Germany; 12 pairs of trains each carrying 25 trucks are in operation daily, and journey time is 2 hours 19 minutes. Haulage is provided by ČD/DBAG Class 372/180 dual-voltage locomotives. This service is operated by Bohemiakombi and Kombiverkehr. In 2000, 103,433 lorries were carried, compared with 93,684 in 1999, and by the end of 2001, a total of 650,000 vehicles had been carried. Overall utilisation of the service rose by 10 per cent to 79.6 per cent in 2000. The service is likely to stay in place until at least 2005, when a new international highway is due to be completed.

An agreement has been reached between ČD and DB Cargo over the operation of this service. From 14 February 2002, ČD drivers operate throughout without a crew change at the Děčín/Bad Schandau border crossing. This follows intensive training of ČD drivers based at Děčín depot in DB operating practices and the German language. In turn, DB Cargo drivers were to commence operating trains as far as Lovosice during the first half of 2002. The move is seen as a prelude to a future expansion of through operations by ČD and DB drivers on general cargo and international passenger services.

## New lines

A re-examination has taken place of plans formulated in 1988 for a high-speed (VRT) network. The move was prompted by claims that ČD's projected investment programme for its four principal corridors (see below) will be less than adequate, aiming as it does to raise line speeds to 160 km/h. The VRT network would be some 700 km long, engineered for 250-300 km/h operation and electrified at 25 kV AC. Total cost is estimated at up to Kcs180 billion.

The first section of the VRT network would be the Czech part of the Berlin-Prague-Vienna route. The Prague-Vienna via Gmünd route was one of three that was the subject of a trilateral agreement between the Czech minister of transport and his German and Austrian counterparts in July 1995, providing for construction of high-speed lines in future. The other routes in the agreement were the Prague-Nuremberg and Prague-České Budějovice-Linz lines.

At the start of 1994 a private company, PRaK, was formed to construct a Kcs8.37 billion railway between Prague and Kladno, a distance of 35.7 km. Two route models for the line were being assessed in 2002: one favouring a classic double-track electrified railway roughly following the existing route, the other a newly built S-Bahn-type light railway. Despite the project having suffered several postponements and the absence of a final decision on the nature of the line, it is assumed that construction will take place in conjunction with extensive remodelling of the capitals rail junction in 2002-05. The line would both provide commuter services and serve the international airport at Ruzyně, where an expansion programme was finished in 1997.

In March 2000, construction began on a new alignment between Březno and Chomutov on the Prague-Chomutov main line to replace existing infrastructure affected by mining subsidence. Built by Metrostav Praha, the new single-track alignment will be 7.1 km with a new station at Droužkovice. Construction will entail boring a 1.758 km tunnel, which will be the longest on the ČD network. The alignment is designed for a maximum speed of 100 km/h and it is proposed to electrify the section at 3 kV DC along with electrification of the Kadaň-Karlovy Vary main line in 2005-10. Trial operations using the new alignment are planned for January 2004. The Kcs1.18 billion cost of the project is to be met by the mining company active in the area.

*Class 151 3 kV DC electric locomotive refurbished for 160 km/h operation on the Prague-Košice route (Milan Šrámek)*

## Improvements to existing lines

*Corridor 1*

In February 1994 the Czech government announced the formal inauguration of track renewal on Corridor 1, the country's key rail route. This forms the largest investment of the century on the national rail network, and is being carried out without interrupting regular services.

The 454 km Corridor 1 is double-track throughout and fully electrified, part at 3 kV DC and part at 25 kV AC 50 Hz. It runs from the German border at Děčín through Prague, Kolín, Česká Třebová and Brno to the Austrian border at Břeclav. It forms part of a proposed Central European 160 km/h rail link between Berlin and Vienna, which after completion of upgrading should reduce the journey time between both capitals from the current best of 10 hours 16 minutes to 6 hours 30 minutes. The domestic journey time between the Czech Republic's two largest cities, Prague and Brno, will be cut from 3 hours 10 minutes to 2 hours 30 minutes. Work on the scheme started in 1993 and is now scheduled for completion in 2003. The project is divided into 24 sections, and incorporates 697 bridges and 14 tunnels.

The Czech government approved a funding scheme for Corridor 1 in November 1994, with Kcs9 billion coming directly from the budget and Kcs15.43 billion to be paid from credits guaranteed by the government. Finance for the project has come in the form of credits and loans from the European Bank for Reconstruction and Development, the European Investment Bank, Japan's EXIM Bank, the Kreditanstalt für Wiederaufbau in Germany, and non-guaranteed loans from the domestic Česká spořitelna and Komerční banka institutions. However, it has since become clear that the cost of upgrading will rise by 48 per cent to Kcs36.5 billion due to environmental demands and inflation, and an additional Kcs1.57 billion of funding was approved in December 2001.

The Koridor consortium was established in 1994 by Czech construction and rail industry companies to promote domestic capabilities against foreign competition. In 1995 the group was renamed the Association of Czech Companies for the Modernisation of Rail Corridors.

A Czech-German memorandum was signed on 1 March 1996 to promote modernisation of the Prague-Berlin section of Corridor 1. By 2002 the journey time between the two capitals should be cut by 100 minutes to 3 hours 10 minutes. A similar Czech-Slovak memorandum covering the important Prague-Bratislava axis was signed on 28 October 2000. By 2006, the entire route should be upgraded to 160 km/h for passenger services and 120 km/h for freight operations, with the best journey time cut from the current 4 hours 19 minutes to 3 hours 48 minutes. By 2012, major stations and junctions on the route will also have been modernised.

By the end of 2001, 18 Corridor 1 projects had been completed, covering 280 route-km. During 2001, four sections were completed at a total cost of Kcs4.75 billion: Prelouc-Pardubice (10.3 km) in January; Vranany-Hnevice (17.2 km) and Lovosice-Ustí nad Labem (18.9 km) in April; and Pardubice-Uhersko (16.9 km) in October. In 2002, an additional four sections were scheduled for completion: Lovosice-Hrobce (15.5 km); Kralupy-Vranany (10.3 km); Kolín-Prelouc (24.3 km); and Ustí nad Labem-Decín (16.8 km). Outside the Corridor 1 project proper, but under way since early 2001, is modernisation of the major border station at Decín, scheduled for completion in April 2004 at a cost of Kcs1.45 billion.

In 2000, Kcs5.76 billion were spent on Corridor 1 works, compared with Kcs3.841 billion in the previous year.

*Corridor 2*

In August 1995, the government announced the go-ahead for a similar upgrade of ČD's Corridor 2, which forms part of European rail corridor E65 from Gdynia to Rijeka. In the Czech Republic, this links Břeclav-Přerov-Ostrava-Petrovice u Karviné with a branch from Přerov to Česká Třebová, a total of 323 km. Top speed will be 160 km/h.

Of ČD's four corridors, this north-south link is regarded as the most lucrative, accounting for some 40 per cent of freight transit traffic across the country and 22 per cent of the railway's total revenue, but with competition from Slovak Republic Railways' parallel Bratislava-Trnava-Žilina-Čadca route. The ČD route received European Union support at the Pan-European Transport Conference in Helsinki in June 1997, and the same month also saw the signing of an agreement between the Czech Republic and Poland covering mutual assistance in developing the corridor.

By 2004 the core Corridor 2 route of 215 km, which forms part of the international Vienna-Warsaw route, will have been upgraded for 160 km/h running, while upgrading the 108 km branch between Přerov and Česká Třebová, which provides a link with Corridor 1, will be completed by 2005.

The government approved financing of the corridor in March 1996. The cost of the project is now expected to be

*Bridge improvements in progress between Česká Třebová and Pardubice as part of ČD's extensive Corridor 1 upgrading programme (Milan Šrámek)*

# RAILWAY SYSTEMS/Czech Republic

Kcs36.4 billion, compared with an original estimate of Kcs25 billion. Funding arrangements will be similar to those adopted for Corridor 1, with Kcs7 billion coming directly from the government. A further Kcs11.5 billion will be provided by government-guaranteed credits (from the European Investment Bank and Germany's Kreditanstalt für Wiederaufbau) and Kcs6.5 billion by non-guaranteed credits (from Česká spořitelna, Deutsche Bank, the European Bank for Reconstruction and Development, and the Kuwait Fund for Arab Economic Development). Sources of funding for the Kcs12 billion increase in cost were still to be found in early 2000.

In November 1994 an Association for the Modernisation of Corridor 2 was founded, and now incorporates 29 companies.

The project is divided into 14 sections. Work on the first section, the 20.4 km between Hodonín and Moravský Písek, began in September 1997. Completion was achieved in December 1999. Work on a second section, Břeclav-Hodonín (20 km), was completed in November 2000. In 1999, a total of Kcs5.838 billion was allocated to Corridor 2, compared with Kcs2.364 in 1998, with Kcs1.441 coming from the state budget. During 1999 work started on three sections: Otrokovice-Huštěnovice (11.8 km, completed January 2001); Moravský Písek-Huštěnovice (18.5 km, completed November 2001); and Přerov-Hranice na Moravě (28.2 km, completion November 2002).

In 2000, a total of Kcs5.76 billion was secured for Corridor 2 modernisation, with work starting in June on the 24.1 km Otrokovice-Přerov section for completion in November 2002. By the end of 2001, upgrading for 160 km/h operations was completed on the entire 70.2 km level route between Breclav and Otrokovice. During the same year, work on the remaining three sections to the Polish border were started: Hranice nad Morave-Studénka (32.5 km), commenced in March for completion in June 2004; Ostrava-Petrovice u Karviné (23.8 km), commenced in April for completion in November 2002; and Studénka-Ostrava (23.4 km), commenced in June for completion in October 2003.

The 108 km branch between Prerov and Ceská Trebová is divided into five sections, with work on the first, Ceská Trebová-Krasíkov (18.3 km) due to be started in 2002. Modernisation of the tortuous 17.6 km section between Krasíkov and Zábreh nad Morave, which includes two tunnels, is due to follow in 2003.

In May 1998, ČD, Austrian Federal Railways and Polish State Railways signed a Memorandum of Understanding on modernisation of the Vienna-Břeclav-Ostrava-Warsaw route. By 2005, a total of Euro1.58 billion is to be invested in upgrading the 677 km route, cutting 2 hours from the present best Vienna-Warsaw journey time of 7 hours 48 minutes. The current 2 hours 30 minutes domestic journey time between Ostrava and Břeclav will be cut by 45-60 minutes.

*Corridors 3 and 4*

It is estimated that work on the Cheb-Prague (220 km) and Dětmarovice-Mosty u Jablunkova-Slovak border (56 km) sections of the west-east Corridor 3 could start in 2004, with completion expected in 2010 at an estimated cost of Kcs42.3 billion. Work on Corridor 4, linking Děčín-Prague-České Budějovice-Horní Dvořiště/České Velenice, was stated as a priority by the government in July 1999 and finally approved in December 2001. Work is expected to begin in 2003, with completion expected around 2008 at a cost of Kcs38.6 billion, generated from the state budget, EU funds and private loans. Modernisation will reduce by 32 minutes the present best timings for conventional trains of 2 hours 28 minutes between Prague and České Budějovice.

After completion of the Ceské Budejovice-Horní Dvoriste electrification in June 2001 (see *Electrification*), Corridor 4 is completely under the wires but only 26 per cent of the route is double-track. With feasibility studies completed, modernisation is divided into five sections: Horní Dvoriste-Ceské Budejovice (58 km); Ceské Budejovice-Veselí nad Luznicí (39 km); Veselí nad Luznicí-Tábor (27 km); Tábor-Benesov (54 km); and Benesov-Praha-Hostivar (49 km). Unlike Corridors 1 and 2, the project will involve both upgrading the existing line and the construction of seven new cut-offs (Nemanice-Sevetín; Horusice-Veselí nad Luznicí; Sobselav-Doubí; Sudomerice-Hermanicky; Chotoviny-Sudomerive; Votoce-Olbramovice; and Olbramovice-Tomice.

A Memorandum of Understanding covering modernisation of the Prague-Cheb-Nuremberg corridor was signed in July 1999 by ČD General Manager Dalibor Zeleny and the Chairman of German Rail (DB AG) Johannes Ludewig. The project includes track upgrading, resignalling and full electrification of the 371 km route. The 150 km German portion of the corridor, from Nuremberg to Schirding via Pegnitz and Marktredwitz, is due to be electrified by 2002 and equipped for tilting train operation by 2004.

*Border crossing reopenings*

Since 1991, several cross-border routes, closed under the communist regime, have been reopened to traffic. These include routes into Germany (Železná Ruda-Bayerische Eisenstein; Potůčky-Johanngeorgenstadt; Jiříkov-Ebersbach; Vejprty-Bärenstein/Cranzahl), Austria (Šatov-Retz) and Poland (Bohumín-Chalupki; Meziměstí-Mieroszów; Černousy-Zawidów; Královec-Lubawka; Český Těšín-Cieszyn). Also likely to reopen if sufficient finance can be found is Kořenov-Szklarska Poreba, Poland. The Kraslice-Klingenthal, Germany line reopened in June 2000 (see entry for Viamont). Bavaria's ministry of transport has expressed interest in restoring service on the closed line between Haidmühle and Nové Údol.

## Traction and rolling stock

At the start of 2001, ČD operated 1,027 electric locomotives (643 DC; 248 AC; 145 dual voltage), 1,666 diesel locomotives, 797 diesel railcars, 86 emus, 5,006 passenger cars and around 47,768 freight wagons.

In 2002, CD planned to spend Kcs1.68 billion on the modernisation of its freight wagon fleet, an increase of 28 per cent over the previous year. A total of 153 wagons were scheduled for modernisation, while 150 new vehicles were to be procured, compared with figures of 411 and 101 respectively in 2001. A budget of Kcs250 million was allocated for the refurbishment of locomotives and rolling stock in 2002.

*Pendolinos ordered*

In August 1995, ČD ordered 10 seven-car Class 680 tilting trains for use on the Berlin-Prague-Vienna route; with the new trains, the German and Austrian capitals will be 6 hours 35 minutes apart. The Kcs4.37 billion financial package for the acquisition of the trains was put together by a consortium comprising ČSOB of the Czech Republic, Creditanstalt Finanziaria Milano of Italy, Kreditanstalt für Wiederaufbau Frankfurt of Germany, Česká spořitelna, Creditanstalt Bankverein Wien, and Creditanstalt Praha.

In 1998, ČD cut the order from 10 sets to seven as a result of increased manufacturing costs attributed to unpredicted construction problems, inflation and devaluation of the Czech koruna.

Late in 2000, Alstom undertook to deliver the prototype trainsets for revenue operation by April 2003, with the remainder to be supplied in January 2004. The trainsets will also be deployed on Corridor 4, Prague-České Budějovice-Linz on its completion, scheduled for 2008. There remained a possibility that the Czech government might fund the procurement of the three cancelled sets after 2002.

The trains will be based on the ETR460 Pendolino trains in use in Italy. The Czech trains, to be known as 'Integral', will be tri-voltage versions, capable of operating on 25 kV 50 Hz AC, 15 kV 16⅔Hz AC and 3 kV DC; output will be 4,000 kW and maximum speed 230 km/h. Axle loads will be limited to 13.5 tonnes; bodies will be made from aluminium profiles. The active tilt system will tilt the cars at up to eight degrees.

Initially, construction was to be undertaken by a consortium led by ČKD Dopravni systémy, with final assembly taking place at ČKD's plant at Prague-Zličín. In September 1999, however, ČD expelled ČKD for financial reasons. Consequently the trains are to be partially assembled by Alstom (formerly Fiat Ferroviaria) in Italy under a revised contract signed in January 2000, with traction equipment provided by Siemens. Alstom agreed the 40 per cent of construction would be carried out domestically, particularly by ČKD Vagónka, part of ČKD Holding, at its Vítkovice facility, where aluminium bodyshells will be manufactured and final fittings and interiors installed. On 26 October 2000 the contract was ratified by the consortium of funding banks which is providing ČD with a credit not guaranteed by the state.

*Locomotives*

ČD has identified a need to refurbish a large number of electric locomotives to adapt them for higher speeds, resulting in a programme to upgrade some principal types for 160 km/h operation, the planned maximum speed in main corridors.

In 1992 a Class 150 3 kV DC 4,000 kW locomotive was refurbished for 160 km/h operation and later redesignated Class 151. Series modernisation started in 1995 and by January 2002, 11 locomotives of the 26-strong fleet had been treated. Two additional machines were due to be converted during 2002. Modifications include upgraded bogies, spring suspension and train protection equipment.

A similar programme is being implemented for the dual-voltage (3 kV DC/15 kV 16⅔Hz) 3,060 kW Class 372 machines, which will become Class 371. These share Prague-Dresden services with Deutsche Bahn's similar Class 180 locomotives. A prototype conversion in 1996 was followed by two more in 1997. An additional three locomotives had been modified by June 2001 at a cost of Kcs53 million, with a seventh conversion scheduled for 2002. From the 2000-01 timetable, Class 371 locomotives took over haulage of all EuroCity trains on the Prague-Dresden route. Reconstruction is carried out by Škoda Plzeň together with ČMŽO Přerov.

Due for rollout during 2002 were three former Class 240 25 kV AC electric locomotives converted also to operate under the 15 kV 16 2/3 AC system as dual-voltage machines to handle cross-border services on the newly electrified line between Horní Dvořiště and Summerau, Austria (see *Electrification*). Designated Class 340, conversion was taking place at ČD's České Budějovice depot in close collaboration with Škoda Plzeň.

For future traffic requirements, Škoda Plzeň has developed proposals for two new electric locomotive classes. The 5,000 kW Class 355 would be a 200 km/h 80 tonne machine for use on international corridors such as Prague-Vienna, Linz-Prague-Dresden and Petrovice u Karviné-Vienna. Featuring asynchronous traction motors, this type would be able to operate under 3 kV DC, 25 kV AC 50 Hz and 15 kV AC 16 ⅔ Hz power supplies. Class 319 would be a 1,600 kW machine weighing 76 tonnes and capable of operating at 100 km/h and destined for operation on local international services between Břeclav

*Class 714 diesel-electric locomotive, rebuilt from a Class 735 machine for secondary and shunting duties (Milan Šrámek)*

*Class 812 Liaz-engined diesel railcar, converted from a Class 810 vehicle* (Michal Málek) 2002/0132660

and Vienna and from České Budějovice to Linz. They would be dual voltage (3 kV DC and 25 kV AC 50 Hz). In early 2000, procurement by ČD of both types awaited funding.

ČD has embarked upon a programme to rationalise and modernise its diesel fleet, disposing of obsolete designs and locomotives made redundant by falling freight traffic. Older shunting types have been replaced with new Class 704 and Class 731 locomotives. Class 781 heavy-haul units have been progressively withdrawn since 1989, with just 19 examples retained in reserve in 2000. Twenty Class 781 machines were sold to private operators in Germany in 2001.

Recent modernisation programmes have included the refurbishment in the period 1991-94 of 119 Class 753 diesel locomotives to create Class 750, and a similar modernisation of 60 Class 751 and 753 locomotives into a new Class 749 between 1992 and 1995. Steam heat equipment in these machines has been replaced by electric heating.

Refurbishment of Slovak-built Class 735 locomotives into a new Class 714 has also been completed, with 29 Class 714 and 23 Class 714.2 examples returned to service by the end of 1997. A notable feature of these machines is dynamic braking rated at 1,020 kW.

Two prototypes of a new two-axle 300 kW diesel-electric locomotive design for local services, the Class 708, emerged in the second half of 1995. They are fitted with a Type M1.2C engine from Liaz and a 472 kW electric brake. Ten were manufactured in 1996, entering ČD service in February 1997.

*Multiple-units and railcars*
Electric multiple-units form the most obsolete part of ČD's traction pool, with 83 per cent of the fleet considered life-expired in 2001.

In September 1995, ČD placed a Kcs2.3 billion order for 10 3 kV DC emus for Prague suburban services to replace Class 451 and 452 units. Designated Class 471, these double-deck units with aluminium bodyshells are manufactured by ČKD Vagónka with some components made in Switzerland. Power bogies and electrical equipment, including IGBT control systems, are produced by Škoda Plzeň.

Four two-car (Class 471 power car plus Class 971 driving trailer) and six three-car (Class 471 plus Class 071 trailer plus Class 971) units have been ordered, and these can be coupled into eight-car formations. Both versions are rated at 2,000 kW, with an electric brake capacity of 1,700 kW.

The first power car was completed in 1997, and by the end of 1999, one two-car unit and one three-car set were completed. They were put into revenue operation on the Prague-Kolín line in late July 2000. Credit secured in August 2000 enabled the purchase of three more three-car units by the end of 2000 for Kcs519 million. Some slippage in delivery of the vehicles occured due to the transfer of ČKD Vagónka's plant to Vítkovice. On 20 August 2001, the first three-car unit was rolled out of the new workshops and by the end of 2001 two additional vehicles had followed. Five three-car units were ordered for delivery in 2002 under a Kcs930 million state guarantee secured in December 2001. Under development is a Class 675 dual-voltage (3 kV DC/25 kV AC) 'Interregio' version. It is expected that five of these 160 km/h six-car double-deck units will be employed on Prague-České Budějovice and Brno-Ostrava intercity routes. A prototype is expected to emerge in 2004, with the remaining four units following in 2005-06.

In late 1995, ČD ordered 30 Class 843 diesel-electric railcars; all these were due to be delivered by the end of 1997. In addition, 11 Class 943 driving cars and 32 Class 043 trailers were ordered; preproduction vehicles emerged in 1996, and the entire fleet was in service by the end of 1997.

In 1997, the private sector maintenance company Pars Nova Šumperk completed the refurbishment of a Class 853 diesel-hydraulic railcar, which became the new Class 854. Modernisation work featured the installation of a new Caterpillar diesel engine, a new Intelo Lokel control system, new seats, thermal windows and upgraded toilets. Revenue operation with the prototype began in January 1998. In March 1999, a second railcar was similarly treated. The excellent operational results led ČD in late 2000 to order a series batch of 10 refurbished vehicles, seven of which were operational by the end of 2001. ČD foresees similar refurbishment of the entire fleet of Class 853 railcars.

In September 2001, Pars Nova Šumperk completed the refurbishment of a Class 810 two-axle diesel-mechanical railcar to become new Class 812. The vehicle is powered by a new Liaz M640SE engine rated at 240 kW with Voith DIWA hydro-mechanical transmission. Main structural features are new front-ends of aluminium and a strengthened bodyshell. Other new features include Intelo automatic train control equipment, electro-pneumatic plug doors, driver's cab air conditioning and new seats and windows. Multiple-unit operation is possible with railcars of Classes 811, 843 and 854.

*Passenger coaches*
At the end of 2000, ČD's passenger vehicle fleet stood at 4,960, including non-powered railcar trailers. Of these, only 461 were capable of 160 km/h operation and 45 for 200 km/h.

In 1995, ČD ordered 45 new 200 km/h coaches from a consortium of MSV Studénka and Siemens Austrian subsidiary SGP for EC and IC services, mainly over the Corridor 1 Berlin-Prague-Vienna artery. The Kcs2 billion order comprises 26 Type Bmz second-class and nine Type Ampz first-class coaches, along with 10 Type WRRmz dining cars. MSV is responsible for manufacture of bodyshells, underframes and seats. Final assembly takes place at the Siemens SGP plant in Vienna. The first Type WRRmz car was rolled out in September 1997, with all completed by the year-end. The first two Type Ampz cars were completed in December 1997 and the remainder were operational by October 1999. Production of Type Bmz second class coaches began in 1998. The whole fleet of 26 coaches had been handed over to ČD by

*Class 471 three-car double-deck emu built by Škoda and MSV Studénka for Prague suburban services* (Milan Šrámek) 2001/0062500

*Class 371 dual-voltage electric locomotive for use on Prague-Dresden international passenger services* (Milan Šrámek) 2002/0132661

the end of 2000. Financing has been arranged by a consortium of domestic banks, led by Konsolidační Banka.

Refurbishment of 100 Type Bh Hungarian-built coaches from the 1960s and early 1970s began in March 1996 under a Kcs1.7 billion programme being implemented in close collaboration with DVJ Dunakeszi in Hungary, where the bodyshells and underframes are modernised. Completion took place in mid-1998, creating four vehicle types: 40 second-class compartment (Type Beel); 35 second-class saloon (Bhee); 15 first-class compartment (Aeel); and 10 first-class saloon (Ahee). Improvements include new bogies for 160 km/h running, replacement of brake blocks by discs, new doors from IFE, and new seats from Temoinsa.

During 2000, nine original Type Bmee second class coaches built in East Germany in 1986-7 were rebuilt as Type WLAB couchette cars at a cost of Kcs147 million. They are equipped with disc brakes, air conditioning, vacuum toilets and automatic plug doors to meet RIV standards for international operation on fast overnight trains from Prague to Bucharest, Kosice, Stuttgart and Warsaw.

*Freight wagons*
In response to changes in the rail freight market, especially a continuing decline in volumes carried of bulk products such as coal and iron ore and an increase in the transport of more sophisticated cargo, ČD has been obliged to restructure its freight wagon fleet to cope with customer needs and to operate to international (RIV) standards at speeds of up to 100 km/h.

ČD expects to invest Kcs8 billion in freight wagons in the period from 1998 to 2003, with purchase of new stock, except that required for intermodal operations, funded entirely from the railways' own limited resources.

In 1997, orders were placed for a further 150 Type Tdns two-axle hoppers (Kcs165 million) and 200 Type Hbbillnss sliding-wall two-axle wagons (Kcs422 million), built by Vagónka Česká Lípa in collaboration with DWA (now Bombardier). They were delivered by February 1999 and the end of 1997 respectively. Also ordered were a further 53 Type Sgnss container wagons (Kcs115 million).

In 1998, contracts were placed for an additional 62 Type Sgnss four-axle container flats (delivered in 2001) and 100 Type Habbillns four-axle high-capacity sliding-wall wagons, due for delivery in the first half of 2002; 90 Type Zans four-axle tank wagons; and 8,140 Type Gagns four-axle covered wagons under a long-term programme. By the end of 1998 1,520 of the last-named type were operational. In 1999, a further 100 Type Sgnss container flats were due to be delivered.

During 2000-01, several types of freight wagon were upgraded to RIV international standards: 2,000 Type Falls four-axle coal hoppers; 50 Type Smmps four-axle flats; Type Rils four-axle tarpaulin roof wagons rebuilt from Type Res; and Type Tams four-axle hoppers rebuilt from Type Eas-u.

During 2000, ČD planned to withdraw up to 13,000 freight wagons of older types which have been made redundant by falling traffic volumes. For the same reason, some 2,000 wagons were withdrawn in 1999, generating revenue from their sale or scrap value.

In April 2000, ČD and Ahaus-Alstätter-Eisenbahn Holding AG of Switzerland announced plans to establish a joint venture to overhaul ČD freight wagons. Around 1,000 vehicles are to be upgraded for use on the European rail network.

### Signalling and telecommunications
Automatic block signalling has been installed on almost 26 per cent (2,399 route-km) of the ČD system. Between 1995 and 2000, 2,166 route-km were equipped with train radio at a cost of Kcs540 million. This system now covers 3,694 route-km. Optical cables were laid on 535 route-km.

In August 1999, an agreement was signed with Mannesmann Eurokom of Germany for the purchase of an 85 per cent shareholding in ČD-Telekomunikace, the ČD subsidiary responsible for telecommunications.

### Electrification
Electric traction is available over 30 per cent of ČD route-mileage and hauls 89.2 per cent of all traffic (2001). The north operates at 3 kV DC, the south at 25 kV AC. There are six junctions of the electrification systems: at Kutná Hora, 73 km east of Prague; Králův Dvůr on the Prague-Plzeň route; Nedakonice on the Přerov-Břeclav route; Benešov on the Prague-Tabor route; Nezamyslice on the Přerov-Brno route; and Svitavy on the Česká Třebová-Brno route. Local routes between Tábor and Bechyně (24 km) and Rybník and Lipno nad Vltaron (22 km) are energised at 1.5 kV DC.

In the 1980s, little electrification took place due to plentiful supplies of cheap oil from the Soviet Union favouring diesel haulage. In 1991, the government of the then Czechoslovakia endorsed a rolling programme of electrification that would have seen 347 km electrified by 1995. Some slippage has taken place on this timetable due to a shortage of finance, but a number of projects have proceeded, principally the electrification of main lines in central Moravia.

The largest single electrification project since the 1980s has seen the wiring of the 91 km route between Brno and Česká Trebová via Svitavy and Blansko, a project started in April 1996. Commissioned on 21 January 1999 at a cost of Kcs1.319 billion, this double-track route has been electrified partly at 25 kV AC 50 Hz and partly at 3kV DC, with new substations at Blansko, Svitavy and Opatov, and completes the wiring of Corridor 1 (see 'Improvements to existing lines').

On 7 June 2001, the first electric train ran over the 58.6 km single-track route from Ceské Budejovice to the Austrian border at Horní Dvořiště. Electrification of this route at 25 kV AC 50 Hz began in December 1998 and included extensive track upgrading, installation of new signalling equipment, the construction of two substations and the modernisation of eight stations, including that at Horní Dvořiště. Some funding for the Kcs2.8 billion project was provided by the European Union's Phare programme. On 10 December 2001, the entire corridor between the Adriatic and the Baltic became electrified on completion of a scheme by Austrian Federal Railways to install overhead power supply equipment on its 5.1 km section between the border with the Czech Republic near Horní Dvořiště and Summerau. By 2010, the project will also include conversion from 1.5 kV DC to 25 kV AC of the 22 km Lipno Railway, linking Rybník and Lipno nad Vltavou.

In October 2000, ČD and ÖBB agreed in principle the need to electrify two other important routes in the area,

*Class 363 dual-voltage electric locomotive heading an inaugural train at Kaplice to mark the electrification of the České Budějovice-Horní Dvořiště line on 7 June 2001 (Michal Málek)* 2002/0132662

**Principal diesel locomotives**

| Class | Wheel arrangement | Power kW | Speed km/h | Weight tonnes | No in service | First built | Builders Mechanical | Engine | Transmission |
|---|---|---|---|---|---|---|---|---|---|
| 701 | B | 147 | 40 | 22 | 9 | 1957 | ČKD | Tatra 930-51 | M ČKD |
| 702 | B | 147 | 40 | 24 | 15 | 1968 | ZTS Martin | Tatra 930-51 | M ČKD |
| 703 | B | 170 | 40 | 24 | 26 | 1969 | ZTS Martin | Tatra 930-51 | HM ČKD |
| 704 | B | 250 | 65 | 28 | 20 | 1988 | ČKD | Liaz M2-650 | E ČKD |
| 710 | C | 302 | 60/30 | 40 | 3 | 1961 | ČKD | ČKD 12V 170 DR | HD ČKD |
| 714/714.2* | Bo-Bo | 520/600 | 80 | 64/60 | 52 | 1992 | ČKD | Liaz 6Z 135 M1.2C T | E ČKD |
| 720 | Bo-Bo | 551 | 60 | 61 | 16 | 1958 | ČKD | ČKD 6S 310 DR | E ČKD |
| 726 | B-B | 625 | 70/35 | 56.6 | 2 | 1963 | ZTS Martin | ČKD K12 170 DR | HD ČKD |
| 730 | Bo-Bo | 600 | 80 | 69.5 | 19 | 1978 | ČKD | ČKD K6S 230 DR | E ČKD |
| 721 | Bo-Bo | 551 | 80 | 74 | 35 | 1963 | ČKD | ČKD K6S 310 DR | E ČKD |
| 735 | Bo-Bo | 926 | 90 | 64 | 132 | 1973 | ZTS Martin | Pielstick 12PA 4185 | E ČKD |
| 742 | Bo-Bo | 883 | 90 | 64 | 354 | 1977 | ČKD | ČKD K6S 230 DR | E ČKD |
| 751 | Bo-Bo | 1,102 | 100 | 75 | 105 | 1964 | ČKD | ČKD K6S 310 DR | E ČKD |
| 751.3† | Bo-Bo | 1,102 | 100 | 74 | 19 | 1969 | ČKD | ČKD K6S 310 DR | E ČKD |
| 752‡ | Bo-Bo | 1,213 | 100 | 71 | 2 | 1996 | ČKD | ČKD K6S 310 DR | E ČKD |
| 753 | Bo-Bo | 1,325 | 100 | 73.2 | 126 | 1968 | ČKD | ČKD K12V 230 DR | E ČKD |
| 750** | Bo-Bo | 1,325 | 100 | 72 | 116 | 1991 | ČKD | ČKD K12V 230 DR | E ČKD |
| 754 | Bo-Bo | 1,460 | 100 | 74.4 | 58 | 1975 | ČKD | ČKD K12V 230 DR | E ČKD |
| 770 | Co-Co | 993 | 90 | 114.6 | 49 | 1963 | ČKD, SMZ | ČKD K6S 310 DR | E ČKD |
| 771 | Co-Co | 993 | 90 | 115.8 | 102 | 1968 | SMZ Dubnica | ČKD K6S 310 DR | E ČKD |
| 781 | Co-Co | 1,472 | 100 | 116 | 19 | 1966 | KMZ Lugansk | VSZ 14 D 40 | E CHZE |
| 731 | Bo-Bo | 880 | 70 | 72 | 51 | 1988 | ČKD | ČKD K6S 230 DR | E ČKD |
| 749*** | Bo-Bo | 1,102 | 100 | 75 | 60 | 1992 | ČKD | ČKD K6S 310 DR | E ČKD |
| 743 | Bo-Bo | 800 | 90 | 66 | 10 | 1987 | ČKD | K6S 230 DR | E ČKD |
| 708 | B | 300 | 80 | 34 | 13 | 1995 | ČKD | Liaz M1.2C M640D | E ČKD |
| 799††† | B | 37 | 10 | 22 | 41 | 1992 | ČKD | Zetor 5301 | Battery/DE ČKD |

\* Rebuilt from Class 735   \*\* Rebuilt from Class 753   \*\*\* Rebuilt from Class 751 and 752   † Ex-Class 752
‡ Rebuilt from Class 751, with electronic control   ††† Rebuilt from Class 700-703

**Diesel railcars or multiple-units**

| Class | Motored axles/car | Power/motor kW | Speed km/h | No in service | First built | Builders Mechanical | Engine | Transmission |
|---|---|---|---|---|---|---|---|---|
| 809/810/811 | 1 | 156 | 80 | 534 | 1975 | Studénka | Liaz ML634 | HM/Praga |
| 812* | 1 | 240 | 80 | 1 | 2001 | Pars Sumperk | Liaz M640SE | HM Voith DIWA |
| 820 | 2 | 206 | 70 | 9 | 1963 | Studénka | Tatra T 930-4 | HD ČKD |
| 830 | 2 | 301 | 90 | 48 | 1949 | Studénka | ČKD 12V 170 DR | E ČKD |
| 831** | 2 | 308 | 90 | 37 | 1952 | Studénka | 6L 150 PV-3 | E ČKD |
| 842 | 2 | 408 | 100 | 37 | 1988 | Studénka | Liaz ML640F | HM Allison 4TB 741R |
| 843 | 2 | 600 | 110 | 30 | 1995 | Studénka | Liaz M1.2C-ML640D | E ČKD |
| 850 | 2 | 515 | 110 | 15 | 1962 | Studénka | ČKD 12V 170 DR | HD ČKD |
| 851 | 2 | 588 | 110 | 16 | 1967 | Studénka | ČKD 12V 170 DR | HD ČKD |
| 852 | 2 | 588 | 120 | 17 | 1968 | Studénka | ČKD 12V 170 DR | HD ČKD |
| 853 | 2 | 588 | 120 | 23 | 1969 | Studénka | ČKD 12V 170 DR | HD ČKD |
| 854*** | 2 | 596 | 120 | 9 | 1997 | Studénka | Caterpillar 3412 | HD ČKD |
| 860 | 4 | 442 | 100 | 2 | 1975 | Studénka | 6PA 4 H 185 | E ČKD |

\* Refurbished Class 810   \*\* Re-engined Class 830 (1981-91)   \*\*\* Rebuilt Class 853

# Czech Republic/RAILWAY SYSTEMS

České Budějovice-České Velenice and České Velenice-Veselí nad Lužnicí, but a lack of funds will postpone these projects until around 2010.

Funds from the Phare programme totalling Kcs193 million allowed completion of the 25 kV AC electrification of the 11 km international single-track line from Cheb to the German border at Pomezí. Total cost of the project is Kcs260 million. Work began in August 1998 and was completed in May 2000.

The largest ČD electrification scheme of the first decade of the new millennium should see the double-track Kadaň-Karlovy Vary route (46 km) wired at 25 kV AC in 2003-04. By 2010, three short sections will be energised at 3 kV DC: Letohrad-Lichkov-Polish Border (23 km); Ostrava Kunčice-Ostrava hlavní (8 km); and Lysá nad Labem-Milovice (5 km).

## Track

Main lines are generally laid with 49 kg/m rail, secondary lines with 30 to 40 kg/m. However, almost 10 per cent of all route-km has been relaid with 65 kg/m rail, since the lines concerned, carrying freight trains of increasing weight, are recording 60 to 80 million tonne-km of traffic a year. Most of the system allows maximum axleloads of 20 tonnes.

Rail is welded in long sections, fastened to wood or concrete sleepers spaced 1,450 to 1,500 per km. New Type B-91 200 km/h sleepers have been laid on upgraded sections since 1993. On main lines, minimum curve radius is 300 m and maximum speed 160 km/h.

The Corridor 1 upgrade is being laid with UIC 60 rail supplied by Moravia Steel Třinec and Voest-Alpine on concrete sleepers from ŽPSV Uherský Ostroh, with Vossloh fastenings. UIC GC clearances are being adopted, with a maximum axleload of 22.5 tonnes.

**Type of rails:** S49, R65, UIC60
**Sleepers:** SB8, U94, B91, B915, B90
**Fastenings:** Vossloh, Pandrol

### Principal electric locomotives

| Class | Wheel arrangement | Line voltage | Output kW continuous/ one hour | Speed km/h | Weight tonnes | No in service | First built | Builders Mechanical | Electrical |
|---|---|---|---|---|---|---|---|---|---|
| 100 | Bo-Bo | 1.5 kV | 360/440 | 50 | 48 | 3 | 1956 | Škoda | Škoda |
| 113 | Bo-Bo | 1.5 kV | 400/960 | 50 | 64 | 6 | 1973 | Škoda | Škoda |
| 110 | Bo-Bo | 3 kV | 800/960 | 80 | 72 | 26 | 1971 | Škoda | Škoda |
| 110.1* | Bo-Bo | 1.5 kV | 400/960 | 80 | 72 | 2 | 1971 | Škoda | Škoda |
| 111 | Bo-Bo | 3 kV | 800/880 | 80 | 72 | 34 | 1981 | Škoda | Škoda/ČKD |
| 121 | Bo-Bo | 3 kV | 2,032/2,344 | 90 | 88 | 40 | 1960 | Škoda | Škoda |
| 122 | Bo-Bo | 3 kV | 1,990/2,340 | 90 | 85 | 49 | 1967 | Škoda | Škoda |
| 123 | Bo-Bo | 3 kV | 1,990/2,340 | 90 | 85 | 29 | 1971 | Škoda | Škoda |
| 130 | Bo-Bo | 3 kV | 2,040/2,340 | 100 | 86.8 | 40 | 1977 | Škoda | Škoda |
| 140 | Bo-Bo | 3 kV | 2,032/2,344 | 120 | 82 | 6 | 1953 | Škoda | Škoda-Sécheron |
| 141 | Bo-Bo | 3 kV | 2,032/2,344 | 120 | 84 | 29 | 1957 | Škoda | Škoda |
| 150 | Bo-Bo | 3 kV | 4,000/4,200 | 140 | 82 | 15 | 1978 | Škoda | Škoda |
| 151** | Bo-Bo | 3 kV | 4,000/4,200 | 160 | 82 | 11 | 1978 | Škoda | Škoda |
| 163 | Bo-Bo | 3 kV | 3,060/3,400 | 120 | 85 | 88 | 1984 | Škoda | Škoda/ČKD |
| 163.2** | Bo-Bo | 3 kV | 3,060/3,480 | 120 | 85 | 12 | 1991 | Škoda | Škoda/ČKD |
| 162 | Bo-Bo | 3 kV | 3,060/3,480 | 140 | 85 | 26 | 1991 | Škoda | Škoda/ČKD |
| 181 | Co-Co | 3 kV | 2,790/2,890 | 90 | 120 | 92 | 1961 | Škoda | Škoda |
| 182 | Co-Co | 3 kV | 2,790/2,890 | 90 | 120 | 74 | 1963 | Škoda | Škoda |
| 210 | Bo-Bo | 25 kV | 880/984 | 80 | 72 | 37 | 1973 | Škoda | Škoda |
| 230 | Bo-Bo | 25 kV | 3,080/3,200 | 110 | 88 | 93 | 1966 | Škoda | Škoda |
| 242.2 | Bo-Bo | 25 kV | 3,080/3,200 | 120 | 84 | 86 | 1975 | Škoda | Škoda |
| 240 | Bo-Bo | 25 kV | 3,080/3,200 | 120 | 85 | 32 | 1968 | Škoda | Škoda |
| 263 | Bo-Bo | 25 kV | 2,930/3,060 | 120 | 85 | 2 | 1984 | Škoda | Škoda/ČKD |
| 362*** | Bo-Bo | 3 kV/25 kV | 3,060/3,400 | 140 | 87 | 13 | 1980 | Škoda | Škoda/ČKD |
| 363 | Bo-Bo | 3 kV/25 kV | 3,060/3,400 | 120 | 87 | 117 | 1980 | Škoda | Škoda/ČKD |
| 371† | Bo-Bo | 3 kV/15 kV | 3,060/3,400 | 160 | 84 | 6 | 1997 | Škoda | Škoda/ČKD |
| 372 | Bo-Bo | 3 kV/15 kV | 3,060/3,400 | 120 | 84 | 9 | 1991 | Škoda | Škoda/ČKD |

* Rebuilt 1998 from Class 110   ** Reconstructed from Class 150 for 160km/h operation 1994-2002
*** Bogies exchanged 1993-2000   † Class 372 rebuilt for 160 km/h operation

### Electric multiple-units

| Class | Cars per unit | Line voltage | Motor cars per unit | Motored axles/car | Output/motor kW | Speed km/h | No in service | First built | Builders Mechanical | Electrical |
|---|---|---|---|---|---|---|---|---|---|---|
| 451 | 4 | 3 kV | 2 | 4 | 165/190 | 100 | 37 | 1961 | Studénka | MEZ |
| 452 | 4 | 3 kV | 2 | 4 | 165/190 | 100 | 9 | 1974 | Studénka | MEZ |
| 460 | 5 | 3 kV | 2 | 4 | 250/270 | 110 | 25 | 1974 | Studénka | MEZ |
| 470 | 5 | 3 kV | 2 | 4 | 240/260 | 120 | 2 | 1990 | Studénka | MEZ |
| 560 | 5 | 25 kV | 2 | 4 | 420/465 | 110 | 9 | 1966 | Studénka | MEZ |
| 471 | 2/3 | 3 kV | 1 | 4 | 500 | 140 | 8 | 1997 | Studénka | Škoda |

*UPDATED*

## Desná Railway (ŽD)

Železniční stanice Petrov nad Desnou
pošta Rapotín, CZ-788 14
Tel: (+420 649) 37 60 30/ 24 22 37

### Key personnel
Chairman: Ondřej Kopp
Director, Operations: Karel Mičunek

### Organisation
Železnice Desná, a federation of River Desná valley municipalities, began operation of the 9 km Šumperk–Petrov nad Desnou–Sobotín local railway in northwest Moravia on 1 May 1998. The line forms a section of the Czech Railways (ČD) route from Šumperk to Kouty nad Desnou, where operations were interrupted in July 1997 due to extensive flood damage. Restoration of the line, which ČD had refused to operate, was undertaken by Bohumín-based private construction company Stavební obnova železnic (SOŽ) using funds from the EU's Phare programme. SOŽ was also appointed to operate the line.

However, in 2002, the possibility emerged of ČD once again taking over ownership of the system.

The missing 13 km section between Petrov nad Desnou and Kouty nad Desnou was reopened in May 1999 at a cost of Kcs68.5 million, with the 5 km leg to Velké Losiny opened in December 1998.

ŽD operates 11 daily pairs of passenger services and caries some 5,000 tonnes of freight each month.

### Traction and rolling stock
Rolling stock comprises four Class 810 diesel-hydraulic railcars and three Class 010 trailers, all leased from ČD. Freight services are handled by SOŽ's own fleet of one Class 730 and two Class 742.5 diesel-electric locomotives.

The procurement of four new railcars to replace the Class 810 vehicles in 2001-02 has been proposed.

*UPDATED*

## Jindřichův Hradec Local Railways (JHMD)

Jindřichohradecké místní dráhy as
Nádražní 203/II, CZ-377 01 Jindřichův Hradec
Tel: (+420 331) 36 29 01   Fax: (+420 331) 36 11 65

### Key personnel
Chairman of Administrative Council: Jan Šatava
Deputy Chairman: Jan Hruška
Director of Operations: Jiří Kolář
Head of Freight and Passenger Traffic:
  Miloslava Váchová
Head of Infrastructure: Petr Zoubek

Gauge: 760 mm
Route length: 79 km

### Organisation
JHMD is a private-sector rail company providing passenger and freight services on the former Czech Railways (ČD) Jindřichův Hradec–Nová Bystřice and Jindřichův Hradec–Obrataň narrow-gauge lines in southern Bohemia. These were bought from ČD for a symbolic fee of Kc1 after the national operator ceased operation in January 1997 following heavy losses (see 'Political background – Privatisation' under Czech Railways).

In 1999, JHMD carried 270,000 passengers.

### Traction and rolling stock
The JHMD fleet comprises nine ex-ČD Class 705.9 diesel-electric locomotives built by ČKD, one steam locomotive, 13 passenger coaches and 169 support bogies for carrying ČD standard-gauge wagons.

*VERIFIED*

*JHMD Class 705.9 760 mm gauge diesel-electric locomotive running over dual-gauge track with a passenger service formed of a single railcar trailer (Milan Šrámek)*

# RAILWAY SYSTEMS/Czech Republic—Denmark

## OKD Doprava

OKD Doprava, as
Nádražní 93, CZ-702 62 Ostrava 1-Moravská Ostrava
Tel: (+420 69) 616 62 30   Fax: (+420 69) 611 67 48

**Key personnel**
General Director: Oldřich Faiman
Deputy Director: Milan Hodeček
Director, Railway Transport: Ludvík Semerák

**Organisation**
OKD Doprava is the transport arm of Northern Moravia-based mining company OKD, and is the Czech Republic's largest private rail operator, running freight trains throughout the ČD network. It also owns more than 400 route-km of lines in the Ostrava-Karviná coal basin. Coal is the principal commodity carried.

In December 1997 OKD restored traffic on the 20.5 km rural line from Milotice to Vrbno pod Pradědem, which it leases from ČD. The company has invested over Kcs30 million in rehabilitiation of the line after it sustained heavy flood damage during 1997. Passenger traffic resumed on 25 January 1998 with one Class 810 railcar and a Class 010 trailer leased from ČD. Freight services are operated by OKD's own Class 740 diesel-electric locomotives.

**UPDATED**

*OKD Doprava Class 740 diesel-electric locomotive (Michal Málek)*   2002/0132663

## Viamont

Viamont as
Železničářská 1385/29, CZ-400 03 Ústí nad Labem-Střekov
Tel: (+420 47) 530 01 11   Fax: (+420 47) 530 01 00

**Key personnel**
Chairman of Administrative Council: Aleš Řebíček
General Manager: Miroslav Plíhal
Commercial Director: Martin Blažek
Director, Rail Traffic: Vladimír Trtík

**Organisation**
Viamont is a private-sector company founded in August 1992, with headquarters at Ústí nad Labem, in northern Bohemia. Its main activities include railway operations, rolling stock overhaul and refurbishment, and track modernisation. In 1997, the company recorded revenues of Kcs750 million, and employed 280 staff.

**Passenger operations**
In December 1997 Viamont restored passenger services on the 10 km local line between Trutnov and Svoboda nad Úpou, introducing 16 pairs of trains each day. The line had been closed by Czech Railways (ČD) in the previous September due to heavy losses, and is now leased to Viamont.

In February 1998, Viamont was also selected to operate two more ČD rural lines in western Bohemia, Nové Sedlo u Lokte—Krásný Jez (24 km) and Sokolov—Kraslice (23 km). Viamont operations on the Sokolov—Kraslice route commenced in May 1998, with 12 pairs of trains daily. Services were extended up to Hraničná on the German border in July 1998. The cross-border line to Klingenthal in Germany was reopened in early June 2000 at a cost of Kcs18 million and DM7.5 million respectively, with the support of the European Union. In October 1999, work started on restoration of the 52 m border bridge which was removed during the partition of Germany. The new bridge was installed in September 2000. The route now forms part of the Egronet Czech-German frontier regional railway system. Operations on the Nové Sedlo u Lokte—Krásný Jez still awaited reinstatement in early 2000. The company has also been reported to be seeking to take over 238 km of local lines in southern Bohemia.

**Freight operations**
Since November 1995 the company has been operating one or two pairs of coal trains daily over 211 km of the ČD network from a loading point at Březno u Chomutova to a power station at Dolní Beřkovice, carrying some 130,000 tonnes each month. Other commodities, such as construction materials, are also carried. In 1998, Viamont carried 2.8 million tonnes of freight, accounting for 3 per cent of all rail freight in the Czech Republic. However, in 1999 a decrease to 1.6 million tonnes was anticipated due to a decline in the consumption of coal, which accounts for 90 per cent of Viamont's traffic and revenues.

Freight operations on the Trutnov—Svoboda nad Úpou line began on 1 April 1999.

**Traction and rolling stock**
The Viamont traction fleet comprises seven diesel-electric locomotives of Classes 720, 740 and 742.5 and three Class 710 diesel-hydraulics. Also operated are two electric locomotives of Classes 121 and 130 leased from ČD and mining company DNT, and five diesel-electrics leased from ČD. A fleet of 220 Type Wap coal hoppers is hired from ČD.

For local passenger services on the Trutnov—Svoboda nad Úpou line, Viamont has leased from a private company, Lokotrans, two Class 830 and one Class 810 railcars and one Class 010 trailer. Operations on the Sokolov—Kraslice—Hraničná route employ two Class 714.2 and one Class 720 diesel-electric locomotives and eight Class 020 trailers, all leased out from ČD.

**UPDATED**

# DENMARK

## Ministry of Transport

Frederiksholms Kanal 27, DK-1220 Copenhagen K
Tel: (+45) 33 92 33 55   Fax: (+45) 33 12 38 93

**Key personnel**
Minister: Flemming Hansen

**UPDATED**

## Banestyrelsen

Banestyrelsen – Danish National Railway Agency
Pakhusvej 10, DK-2100 Copenhagen Ø
Tel: (+45) 82 34 00 00
e-mail: bane@bane.dk
Web: http://www.bane.dk

**Key personnel**
Director General: Jens Andersen
Divisional Directors
 Network Management: Eigil Sabroe
 Planning: Ulrik Winge
 Construction: Erik Haldbæk
 Infrastructure Services: Jesper Toft
 Resources: Anne Jøker
Central Service Managers
 Internal Auditor: Henning H Larsen
 Management Secretariat and Public Relations:
  Ellen Andersen Alstrup
 Safety and Quality: Johan K Stranddorf
Business Efficiency Manager: Henrik Jørgensen

Gauge: 1,435 mm
Route length: 2,323 km
Electrification: 165 route-km at 1.5 kV DC (Copenhagen suburban system), 430 route-km at 25 kV 50 Hz AC

**Political background**
As a result of legislation in the Danish parliament, DSB (Danish State Railways) was split in two on 1 January 1997: DSB continued to operate trains, while Banestyrelsen, comprised essentially of the old DSB Infrastructure Management Division, took over responsibility for the infrastructure. Banestyrelsen is responsible for traffic control and capacity management, as well as infrastructure management and development. From 1 January 1999, freight operators have been allowed 'open access' to Banestyrelsen's network and similar rights have been available to passenger operators to compete with DSB since 1 January 2000.

Under the Act, Banestyrelsen was required to open tenders for work on the infrastructure to outside companies. Two contracting units within Banestyrelsen – Consulting Engineers and Infrastructure Services – were set up at 'arm's length' from the main company. The Consulting Engineers unit was sold to WS Atkins in mid-2001 but the Infrastructure Services unit continues to compete with outside organisations for work. Between 2001 and 2005, Banestyrelsen will ask for tenders to carry out routine maintenance throughout its network.

From 1 March 2001, adjustments were made to legislation to place all railway infrastructure owners in Denmark on an equal basis.

**Organisation**
Banestyrelsen is divided into four independent divisions: Construction; Infrastructure Services; Network Management; and Planning. Infrastructure Services competes for tenders for its work, while the other three divisions are responsible for offering tenders. A fifth division, Resources, provides support for the other four,

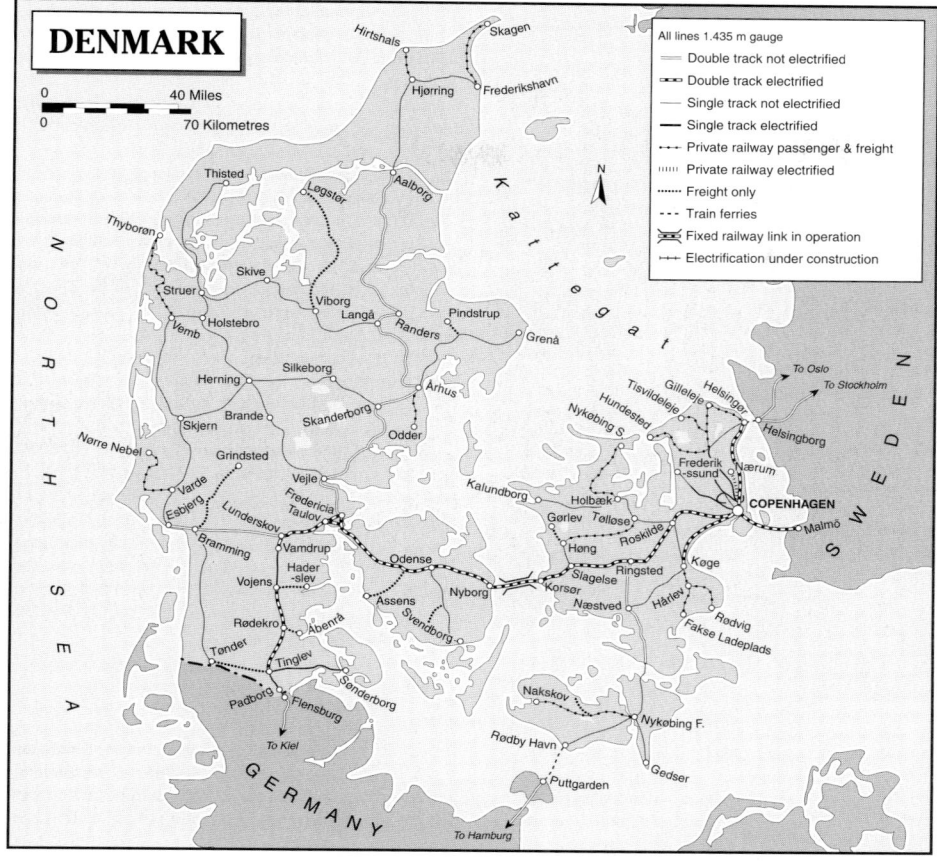

## Denmark/RAILWAY SYSTEMS

*Rødby—Puttgarden fixed link*
In 1992 the German, Danish and Swedish Railways published a stategic plan for traffic links between Scandinavia and the Continent. The plan describes a number of successive improvements, coupled to opening of the Great Belt link in 1997, the Øresund link in 2000 and the proposed fixed link across the Fehmarn Belt between Rødby and Puttgarden, to open at some time in the new century.

The new link would provide a direct Copenhagen–Hamburg route of 345 km, as opposed to 550 km via the Great Belt link, Fredericia and Padborg. The distance could be further shortened, given the intent of the railways to create 250 km/h approaches to the proposed underwater tunnel. On the Danish side, new infrastructure may be proposed that would cut the distance between Vordingborg, at the southern tip of Zealand, and Køge, south of Copenhagen, by 25 km. Ultimately, a two hour journey time between Copenhagen and Hamburg is proposed for passenger trains; most freight traffic would continue to be routed via Padborg, Fredericia and the Great Belt.

A working group under the Danish and German Departments of Transport has studied different models for the link, ranging from a Channel Tunnel-style rail link with an auto-transporter shuttle and classic passenger trains, to an Øresund-style combined rail/road link. Another working group has made a detailed analysis of the expected traffic growth; in 2002, the project was still under consideration.

*Copenhagen—Ringsted capacity expansion*
In May 1997, the Danish parliament decided to investigate ways of increasing capacity between Copenhagen and Ringsted, the busiest section of line in Denmark. Banestyrelsen produced a report evaluating three options: expanding the existing line to four main line tracks throughout (only Høje Taastrup to Roskilde currently has four main line tracks); constructing a new double-track line between Copenhagen and Ringsted via Køge; or a combination of these two options, with the new line starting near Høje Taastrup. In March 1999, the Minister of Transport decided not to proceed with either of the options involving a new line and asked for further examination of ways of expanding the capacity of the existing line.

From early 2000, the study considered extending the S-Train network and in October 2000 a decision was made to adopt this strategy, taking the S-Train system to Roskilde using dual-voltage emus, and at a later date to construct an additional single line over the most heavily used section of line (Hvidovre—Høje Taastrup).

In January 2001, DKr800 million was allocated by the Danish parliament for the extension of the S-Train system and parliamentary authority for the work to start was granted in May 2001. Planning restrictions on the land required for the additional line have been retained, as have restrictions on areas that may be required by a future line from Copenhagen to Ringsted via Køge. Completion of the extension of S-Train services to Roskilde was expected in 2006 and consideration was being given to introducing an S-Train service from Roskilde to Copenhagen Airport avoiding Copenhagen Central station. However, in late May 2002 the project was postponed indefinitely on technical grounds.

### Improvements to existing lines
To take advantage of the opening of the Great Belt and Øresund fixed links, Banestyrelsen, like DSB before it, intends to provide a double-track electrified route through Denmark from the Swedish to the German borders. Although not the shortest route, the opportunities for through working will improve the competitiveness of freight traffic. An east-to-south curve was opened south of Fredericia in 1993 to obviate reversal there and 36 km of the 71 km of single track between Vamdrup and Padborg was doubled in 1996; the remainder is to be doubled at a later date.

In 2001, Banestyrelsen started work to raise capacity through the centre of Copenhagen and to improve facilities for terminating trains at Østerport station. Work is also under way to upgrade the Odense—Svendborg line and to provide new stations for the regional suburban services that feature in DSB's 'Good Trains for All' project.

Banestyrelsen is upgrading the section of the Tønder—Niebüll (Germany) cross-border line that lies within Denmark in preparation for a year-round service.

On the S-Train network, Banestyrelsen will complete the doubling of the Frederikssund line and open a new interchange station at Flintholm in 2002. The

---

while three central services units give support to the company as a whole. The 'Business Efficiency' project has been set up to improve competitiveness and efficiency throughout the company and is responsible to the board of directors. The board consists of the Director General and the directors of the five divisions.

### Finance
Banestyrelsen receives financial support from the Danish Ministry of Transport for its management and modernisation of the network under a four-year agreement covering the period 2001-04. Banestyrelsen has entered into contracts with all the operators on the network.

In 2001, Banestyrelsen had a turnover of approximately DKr1,480 million and employed 2,699 staff.

### New lines
*Great Belt fixed link*
The long-cherished scheme for a fixed crossing of the 18 km *Storebælt* (Great Belt) waterway between Copenhagen on the island of Zealand and the rest of the country, opened to trains in June 1997. The fixed link features both road and rail, with the rail link opened in advance of the road link. The link features three elements: *West Bridge*, a 6.6 km low bridge shared by the railway and the motorway, running from Funen to the island of Sprogø; *East Tunnel*, an 8 km twin-bore railway tunnel between Zealand and Sprogø; and *East Bridge*, a 6.8 km elevated motorway bridge between Zealand and Sprogø. Completion of East Bridge in mid-1998 allows road vehicles to use the link.

The cost of the fixed link escalated almost 50 per cent beyond original estimates. Banestyrelsen was not directly involved in the construction cost, but as administrator of the link pays an annual fee which, from 1999 onwards, amounts to approximately Dkr500 million. This fee is financed by access charges paid by train operating companies.

*Fixed link with Sweden*
After many years of debate, an agreement to create a fixed crossing of the Øresund waterway was signed by the Danish and Swedish Transport Ministers in 1991. Completion was achieved in July 2000, at an estimated cost of some DKr18 billion.

A Danish-Swedish consortium, Øresund Consortium (qv) was formed to design, build and operate the link; by 1995, construction work was well under way on the Danish side between Copenhagen and the city's airport on the Øresund coast.

Like the Great Belt link, the 16 km Øresund crossing combines double-rail tracks and a four-lane motorway. The centrepiece is an 8 km-long bridge lifting the railway and road 57 m above the waterway at its 1.1 km-wide centre span.

This has inclined bridge approaches totalling 6.4 km in length. On the Danish side, rail and road cross artificial islands connected by a 3.85 km-long bridge designed especially to improve water flow and circulation in the low-water areas south of the island of Saltholm. The link enters a 3.5 km submerged tunnel under the eastern channel of the Sound before surfacing immediately east of Copenhagen's Kastrup airport, on an artificial peninsula.

Here the line divides into a northerly cut-off for freight services and a southern branch for passenger services – the latter passes through a two-platform subsurface airport station built under a new airport terminal building, financed and built by the Copenhagen airport authorities. West of the station the branches rejoin to run mainly on the surface for a further 10 km into Copenhagen's Central station.

A 4 km-long cut-off allows freight trains to avoid the city centre on their way to Jutland and central Europe, via the Great Belt link.

DSB and SJ now run a joint interregional train service linking not only the centres of Copenhagen and Malmö but also the other larger towns in the region such as Elsinore and Roskilde in Denmark and Lund and Helsingborg in Sweden.

The journey time from Copenhagen Central to Malmö Central via Kastrup airport takes 25 minutes.

The connection from Copenhagen Central to Kastrup airport was completed ahead of the project as a whole, reducing the journey time between the two to only 10-12 minutes. DSB serves Kastrup with limited-stop express train services from the rest of Denmark, as well as the Øresund Regional trains. SJ has extended X2000 services from Oslo/Gothenburg and Stockholm to Malmö across the link to Copenhagen.

The fixed link is electrified at Banestyrelsen's 25 kV AC 50 Hz. This gives way to the Swedish 15 kV AC 16 Hz immediately west of a new Malmö South station, which also is the limit for the Malmö suburban services (Påga trains) through the new tunnel being built under Malmö in conjunction with the Øresund link.

The Danish and Swedish railways pay a fixed annual rental, amounting to DKr300 million each per year, for unlimited use of the fixed link. This is not enough to cover the construction costs of the railway part of the link; the motorway side of the link is cross-subsidising the railway side, as part of the two governments' policy of promoting rail transport.

# RAILWAY SYSTEMS/Denmark

*Høje Taastrup station, on the busy section of line between Copenhagen and Roskilde, which is the subject of capacity enhancement studies (John C Baker)* — 2002/0137756

Copenhagen Ring Line will be extended from Flintholm to a new station at Ny Ellebjerg by 2005.

## Signalling and traffic control

By early 1999 automatic traffic control had been commissioned on 522 km of Banestyrelsen main lines. The 'silent' element of passenger information is also managed by this system.

Traffic control is handled by three control centres, at Copenhagen Central, Roskilde, and Fredericia, and in event of failure can also be taken over by the Network Control Centre in Copenhagen. There is also a control centre at Copenhagen Central for the city's suburban network, although this cannot be taken over by the Network Control Centre in event of failure. In addition, the line from Copenhagen Central station to Copenhagen airport, which opened in mid-1998, and the Danish part of the fixed link with Sweden are controlled by this automatic system.

A new automatic traffic control system was to have been commissioned on the Copenhagen S-Train network in 2001-02, but in late 2000 the contract was cancelled.

In 1994, DSB started commissioning an Automatic Train Protection (ATP) system that permits 180 km/h running on its network and this has now ben extended to over 800 km of main lines. The installation is based on the Siemens ZUB123 system and mobile units are now required on all motive power running on main lines. A simpler system for use on secondary lines is under evaluation.

## Electrification

The 165 route-km Copenhagen suburban S-Train system operates on 1.5 kV DC overhead supply.

DSB started main line electrification at 25 kV AC 50 Hz east of the Great Belt in the early 1980s. It was extended to the German border at Padborg to coincide with the opening of the Great Belt link. The branch line from Tinglev to Sønderborg, near the German border, and the lines into Fredericia were electrified at the same time. The line from Copenhagen to Copenhagen Airport was electrified from its opening, as was the Øresund link. No further electrification is planned.

## Track

**Rail:** Flat-bottom, 60 kg/m (1,641 km), 45 kg/m (1,199 km), 37 kg/m (52 km)
**Crossties (sleepers):** twin-block concrete 2,328 × 209 × 290 mm with Sonneville fastenings. Monobloc concrete sleepers 2,500 × 206 × 280 mm with Vossloh fastenings have been used as standard since 1989
**Spacing:** 1,600/km
**Min curvature radius:** 300 m
**Max gradient:** 1.25% (1.56% in the Great Belt tunnels)
**Max axleload:** 22.5 tonnes

*UPDATED*

## Danish State Railways (DSB)

Danske Statsbaner
Sølvgade 40, DK-1349 Copenhagen K
Tel: (+45) 33 14 04 00   Fax: (+45) 33 14 04 40
e-mail: dsbkomm@dsbkomm.dsb.dk
Web: http://www.dsb.dk

### Key personnel

Chief Executive Officer: Keld Sengeløv
Chief Financial Officer: Carsten K Thomsen
Chief Operating Officer: Johannes A Pedersen
Division Directors:
  Passenger Services: Bjørn Wahlsten
  S-Train: Benny Würtz
  Rolling Stock: Johannes A Pedersen
  Sales and Stations: Jørn Webler
  Freight (Railion Denmark): Hans Winther
Corporate and service functions:
  Corporate Secretariat: Lone Lindsby
  Public Relations Manager: Anna Vinding
  Chief Administrator: Eilert Løvborg
  Design Manager: Pia Bech Mathiesen
  Corporate Controller: Bartal Kass
  Financial Manager: Søren Skovdal
  Information Technology Manager: Peter Lundsteen
  Corporate Staff Manager: Peter Vesterheden
  Corporate Purchasing Manager: Lars N Pedersen
  Corporate Business Development Director:
    Henrik Nørgaard
  Environment Manager: John Sørensen
  Planning Manager: Ove Dahl Kristensen
  Safety Manager: Per Ingemann Nielsen
  Chief Auditor: Leif Frandsen

### Political background

On 1 January 1997, DSB was split in two: infrastructure was allocated to a new company, Banestyrelsen (qv), while DSB continues to operate trains. Since the sale of its DSB Vognladning (Full Loads) freight division to the Railion Group (qv) in 2001, DSB has been entirely a passenger operator, accounting for 95 per cent of total Danish passenger traffic; the remainder is carried by smaller local railway companies. Earlier, in August 2000, the DSB Stykgods (Part Loads) freight business was sold to DF Logistik A/S.

A bill establishing DSB SV (special-status public company) with effect from 1 January 1999 was passed by the Danish parliament on 25 June 1998. Earlier in 1998, on 7 May, a bill on railway operations in Denmark was also passed. Both pieces of legislation are intended to strengthen the competitiveness of the railway and are therefore both very important for DSB and its efforts to develop into a modern, commercially oriented company. Since 1 January 1999 DSB has been an independent publicly owned corporation and will receive no further public funds. The same bill also saw DSB S-Train become a public company wholly owned by DSB, DSB S-tog A/S, also from 1 January 1999. Services are purchased by the Minister of Transport from DSB under transport contracts,

*IR/4 emus at Tinglev (Marcel Vleugels)* — 2002/0137757

while costs and investments are financed by DSB from operating income and loans, which the company's new status allows it to raise.

In December 1998 DSB and the Ministry of Transport concluded two one-year contracts for public transport service provision in 1999, one covering DSB, the other DSB S-Train (qv). In December 1999, a five-year contract for the period 2000-04 was agreed by DSB and the Ministry of Transport: DSB receives DKr2.9 billion a year for long distance and local services, and in return DSB must achieve agreed standards of frequency and quality.

The DSB Ferries and DSB Buses businesses were separated from DSB in 1995, to form wholly owned subsidiaries.

In a further move to introduce competition on the national rail network, the Danish government in

November 1997 announced that from January 2000 private companies would be able to provide passenger services in competition with DSB, subject to network capacity. The legislation enabling competition distinguishes between two types of passenger transport carried out as a public service: 'negotiated' transport and 'tendered' transport. All services not offered for tender are handled as negotiated transport (see also entry for Ministry of Transport).

The first phase of the Ministry of Transport's plans to invite tenders for 15 per cent of DSB's services covered six sections of line in Jutland. At the end of December 2001, it was announced that Arriva had won the tender, taking over services from 1 January 2003.

### Organisation

DSB has been an independent public corporation since 1 January 1999, with the Ministry of Transport its sole owner.

The DSB Group is managed by a Supervisory Board consisting of nine members and an Executive Board consisting of four members: a chief executive officer; a deputy chief executive officer; a chief financial officer; and a chief operating officer. Since 1 January 2001, DSB has been divided into four divisions, each headed by a director: DSB S-tog A/S (DSB S-Train), which is responsible for all aspects of this business; Passenger Services, responsible for the revenue budget and the daily provision, development and marketing of DSB passenger products, excluding S-Trains; Sales & Stations, responsible for the development and operation of DSB stations and other property assets; and Operations, covering the acquisition, maintenance, servicing and running of rolling stock and the management of DSB operations, excluding S-Trains. The last three of these divisions are all function-based.

A Business Development Unit was established in 2001 to pursue business opportunities outside Denmark.

### Finance

DSB income comes largely from two sources: operating revenue and the government contract payments that replaced operating subsidy. The company can also raise loans. In 2001, DSB achieved a profit of DKr1,215 million, an increase of 56 per cent on the figure for 2000.

**Finances** (DKr million)

| Revenue | 1999 | 2000 | 2001 |
|---|---|---|---|
| Operating income | 5,249 | 5,235 | 4,704 |
| Contract payments | 3,296 | 3,460 | 3,820 |
| Total | 8,545 | 8,695 | 8,524 |

| Operating expenditure | 1999 | 2000 | 2001 |
|---|---|---|---|
| Staff/personnel | 3,059 | 2,915 | 2,588 |
| Other | 4,769 | 4,911 | 4,586 |
| Total | 7,828 | 7,826 | 7,174 |
| Financial costs | −122 | −92 | −135 |
| Result | 595 | 777 | 1,215 |

| Traffic (million) | 1999 | 2000 | 2001 |
|---|---|---|---|
| Passenger journeys | 149 | 154 | 156 |
| Passenger-km | 5,141 | 5,328 | 5,548 |
| Freight tonnes | 7 | 8 | - |
| Freight tonne-km | 1,938 | 2,086 | - |

*IC/3 dmu at Høje Taastrup* (John C Baker)

### Passenger operations

DSB's passenger operations are based around a regular interval timetable, with more than three-quarters of its stations served by at least one train an hour in each direction. Main line InterCity services consist of a core route from Copenhagen via Odense to Århus and Aalborg; most other major towns have a through train from Copenhagen every two hours. East of the Great Belt, most stations have a regular interval local service to Copenhagen, the majority of which run through the centre of Copenhagen to terminate at Østerport station on the north side of the city centre. The Copenhagen–Helsingør line now sees six trains an hour in the peaks; the basic service is now part of the Øresund service and is worked by Øresund trainsets. West of the Great Belt, local services run between regional centres, but there are limited suburban services around Århus, Esbjerg and Odense.

The opening of the fixed link across the Great Belt in 1997 resulted in an increase of 60 per cent in traffic via this route; 10 per cent of this increase was lost when the road link opened a year later. Following the opening of the link, DSB recast its services, introducing limited stop 'Lyntog' trains on main routes and starting regular 180 km/h operation, but it was forced to make many timetable adjustments over the next year to cope with the increased traffic.

On 27 September 1998, the Copenhagen–Kastrup Airport line was opened, served by frequent local trains to Copenhagen and Lyntogs to destinations west of the Great Belt; the latter were later replaced by InterCity services. Few changes were made in 1999, although the Odense–Svendborg line and some local services in Jutland saw improvements.

The major event of 2000 was the opening on 1 July of the fixed link across the Øresund, which is used by a 20 minute frequency Copenhagen–Malmö shuttle, long distance services to destinations in Sweden and DSB trains to Ystad, where connections are made with a fast ferry to the island of Bornholm. From June 2001, the Øresund shuttle was extended northwards from Copenhagen to Helsingør, replacing the Copenhagen–Helsingør services. Trains have also been extended beyond Malmö on the Swedish side.

Since the mid-1990s, DSB has been working on the 'Good Trains for All' (GTA) project. The main elements of this are: an increase in the number of trains operated (by 2006, an increase of 25 per cent compared with 2000 service levels is planned); faster services; extension of the regular interval timetable; and operation of all except a handful of services by new or recently built rolling stock. There will also be new or improved services around Aalborg, Århus, Esbjerg and Odense, as well as improvements to local services, with better connections and more frequent services. The plan should be complete by 2006, but the first step took place in 2001, when an hourly limited stop Lyntog service was introduced between Copenhagen and Århus: there are now two trains an hour between Copenhagen and Århus and three between Copenhagen and Odense.

In 1997, the Danish internal sleeping car service ceased running, although an overnight passenger service still runs using IC/3 trainsets. In 1999, overnight services running south from Copenhagen were combined into a single train serving three destinations and the opening of the Øresund link in 2000 saw the end of overnight services to Stockholm and Oslo. However, DSB retains a small fleet of couchette cars for use on charters and for trains to ski resorts.

### Traction and rolling stock

As a result of the divestment in 2001 of its freight operation to Railion Denmark, the composition of the traction fleet changed significantly. In 2002, the fleet comprised: 12 Class EA line-haul electric locomotives; 47 Class ME and MZ line-haul diesel-electric locomotives; 16 Class MK diesel shunting locomotives and tractors; 241 passenger coaches; 92 IC/3 (Class MFA/FF/MFB) diesel-mechanical trainsets; 96 Class MR/MRD diesel-hydraulic trainsets; 44 IR/4 (Class ER/FR) 25 kV four-car emus; and 24 Class ET/FT 'Øresund' 25 kV/15 kV three-car emus. An additional 18 emus of the Class ET design are owned by operators in Sweden, where they are designated Class X31K.

The IC/3 diesel trainsets are used for most InterCity services and a handful are fitted with either German or Swedish ATC equipment: those with the former work the Copenhagen–Hamburg service. The IR/4 emus are used for local services between Copenhagen and Fredericia and on the InterCity service to Odense and Sønderborg; IC/3 and IR/4 trainsets are capable of being worked in multiple. The line-haul diesel and electric locomotives are mostly used on local and suburban services east of the Great belt and on peak hour and weekend reliefs. The MR/MRD dmus are mostly used on local services in Jutland.

DSB's 'Good Trains for All' programme requires the present fleet of dmus and emus to be enlarged with vehicles of modern design. In 1999, DSB took delivery of the first three-car emus from Adtranz for use on the Øresund link. An initial order for 27 units (17 for DSB and 10 for Swedish State Railways) was increased to 56

*Class ET/FT dual-voltage emu at Ørestad, forming a Copenhagen Østerport–Malmö service via the Øresund link* (John C Baker)

examples, of which DSB was to take 25. For DSB, the main phase of this joint project closed in 2002 when deliveries of its 42 examples were completed, although the last of the additional 14 trains ordered by Swedish companies, including a new X32K variant, was not due to be delivered until 2003.

In December 2000, DSB signed an agreement with the Italian manufacturer, AnsaldoBreda to purchase 83 four-car high-speed diesel-mechanical trainsets for main line services. To be designated Class MG (IC/4), the trains will provide seats for 208 passengers and will feature a low-floor entrance in one car to improve access for passengers with special needs. Each articulated trainset will be powered by four Iveco 560 kW Euro III engines driving through ZF 16 AS 2603 gearboxes. Maximum service speed will be 180 km/h, although the trains' design allows for upgrading for 200 km/h operation. Deliveries are to take place from 2003 to 2005. There is an option for 67 similar units.

In late 2000, DSB hired three two-car Siemens Desiro dmus from Angel Trains for use on the Odense–Svendborg line, designating them Class MQ. In mid-2002, these units were returned as part of a deal that brought to Denmark 12 units if improved specification. In 2002, DSB was considering offers to supply 20 dmus for local services to be improved or introduced as part of the Good Trains for All project; delivery will be required in 2004.

Following the experimental hire of a rake of double-deck coaches from Swiss Federal Railways from September 1999 to April 2001, DSB is to hire 67 double-deck coaches from Porterbrook Leasing from late 2002 to the end of 2006. The coaches, of three types and including 14 driving trailers, will be built by Bombardier Transportation at its Görlitz plant in Germany and will be to the standard design used in that country. They will be used on non-electrified lines on Zealand and Lolland-Falster. East of the Great Belt, and will be powered by 15 Class ME diesel locomotives equipped with push-pull equipment to suit these vehicles.

### Diesel locomotives

| Class | Wheel arrangement | Power kW | Speed km/h | Weight tonnes | No in service | First built | Builders Mechanical | Engine | Transmission |
|---|---|---|---|---|---|---|---|---|---|
| MZ | Co-Co | 2,270 | 143 | 120 | 11 | 1967 | N&H, Frichs | GM 16-645-E3 | E Thrige |
| ME | Co-Co | 2,270 | 175 | 115 | 37 | 1981 | Thyssen-Henschel/Scandia | GM 16-645-E3B | E BBC H Voith |
| Tractor | B | 94 | 45 | 17 | 17 | 1966 | Frichs | Leyland UE 680 | H Voith |
| MK | B | 390 | 60 | 40 | 1 | 1996 | Siemens | MTU 8V183TD13 | |

N&H: Nydqvist & Holm

### Electric locomotives

| Class | Wheel arrangement | Line voltage | Output kW continuous | Speed km/h | Weight tonnes | No in service | First built | Builders Mechanical | Electrical |
|---|---|---|---|---|---|---|---|---|---|
| EA | Bo-Bo | 25 kV | 4,000 | 175 | 80 | 12 | 1984 | Thyssen-Henschel/Scandia | BBC |

### Diesel railcars or multiple-units

| Class | Cars per unit | Motor cars per unit | Motored axles/car | Power/motor kW | Speed km/h | No in service | First built | Builders Mechanical | Engine | Transmission |
|---|---|---|---|---|---|---|---|---|---|---|
| MR/MRD | 2 | 2 | 2 | 191 | 130 | 96 | 1979 | Duewag/Scandia | KHD F12L413F | H Voith |
| MFA/FF/MFB (IC/3) | 3 | 2 | 2 | 250 | 180 | 92 | 1989 | Ascan-Scandia/Duewag | KHD BFBL-513-CP | H ZF 5HP600 |
| MQ | 2 | 2 | 1 | 315 | 120 | 12 | 2000 | Siemens | - | H Voith |

### Electric multiple-units (main lines) 25 kV

| Class | Cars per unit | Motor cars per unit | Motored axles/car | Output/motor kW | Speed km/h | No in service | First built | Builders Mechanical | Electrical |
|---|---|---|---|---|---|---|---|---|---|
| ER/FR FR/ER | 4 | 2 | 4 | 480 | 180 | 44 | 1992 | ABB Scandia | ABB Traction |
| ET/FT/ET* | 3 | 2 | 4 | 290 | 180 | 24 | 1999 | Bombardier | Bombardier |

* dual-voltage (25 kV AC 50 Hz/15 kV AC 16⅔ Hz)

**UPDATED**

## DSB S-Train

DSB S-Tog A/S
Sølvgade 40, DK-1349 Copenhagen K
Tel: (+45) 33 14 04 00   Fax: (+45) 33 14 04 40
e-mail: s-tog@s-tog.dsb.dk
Web: http://www.dsb.dk/s-tog

### Key personnel
Managing Director: Benny Würtz

Gauge 1,435 mm
Route length: 165 km

### Organisation
S-Train is a wholly owned subsidiary of DSB that provides suburban passenger services over 165 km of independent 1.5 kV DC lines in the Greater Copenhagen area. The division also operates the Hillerød–Helsingør 'Lille Nord' line, but this is due to pass to the local council at the end of 2004. Fare levels are set by the Greater Copenhagen Transport Authority (HT). A one-year contract for provision of S-Train services during 1999 was signed by DSB and the Ministry of Transport in December 1998, followed in December 1999 by a five-year contract for the period 2000-04. The contract stipulates targets for service levels and punctuality and also specifies the amount of support to be paid by the Ministry. In 2001, this was DKr702 million, rising to DKr1.1 billion in 2004. DKr1,559 million was invested in new trains in 2001.

In 2002, S-Train employed 1,750 staff.

### DSB S-Train electric multiple-units (1.5 kV)

| Class | Cars per unit | Motor cars per unit | Motored axles/car | Output/motor kW | Speed km/h | No in service | First built | Builders Mechanical | Electrical |
|---|---|---|---|---|---|---|---|---|---|
| MM/FS | 2 | 1 | 4 | 147 | 100 | 77 | 1966 | Scandia | GEC |
| MM/FU/MU/FS/ | 4 | 2 | 4 | 147 | 100 | 63 | 1975 | Scandia | GEC |
| FC/MC/MC/FC | 4 | 2 | 4 | 150 | 100 | 8 | 1986 | Scandia | ASEA |
| SA/SB/SC/SD | 8 | 6 | 8 | 180 | 120 | 46 | 1995 | Alstom (LHB) | Siemens |

### DSB S-Train diesel multiple-units

| Class | Cars per unit | Motor cars per unit | Motored axles/car | Power/motor kW | Speed km/h | No in service | First built | Builders Mechanical | Engine | Transmission |
|---|---|---|---|---|---|---|---|---|---|---|
| ML/FL/FL/ML | 4 | 2 | 2 | 132 | 80 | 3 | 1984 | Duewag/Scandia | Daimler Benz OM407W | H Voith |

### Passenger operations
In 2001, the S-Train system carried 90.6 million passengers for 1,168 million passenger-km. The timetable is based on a 20 minute interval service on each of 10 routes, with most lines served by more than one route for much of the day.

The S-Train division in partnership with Banestyrelsen is doubling the line between Veksø and Frederikssund, the last single-track section on the network, and building a new interchange station at Flintholm, on the western side of Copenhagen. Both of these projects were to be completed late in 2002. The line between Frederiksberg and Vanløse was closed in two stages in 1998 and 2000 to enable the formation to be used for the Copenhagen Metro. The shuttle service from Hellerup was cut back from Vanløse in April 2001 while the line was refurbished by Banestyrelsen; most of the line was reopened in February 2002, but the final section was operating to a temporary terminus replacing Vanløse until its diversion to Flintholm late in 2002. By 2005 this service will be extended from Flintholm to a new station at Ny Elleberg in the south of the city to create the 'Ring Line'.

A programme to improve access to all S-Train stations was completed in 2001.

In 2001, work started on a scheme to extend S-Train services westwards to Roskilde using dual-voltage (25 kV AC 50 Hz/1.5 kV DC) emus but the project was indefinitely postponed in May 2002 for technical reasons.

### Traction and rolling stock
In 1999, delivery commenced of 112 eight-car single-axle articulated emus ordered in 1997 from Linke-Hoffmann-Busch (now Alstom) and Siemens. These are similar to eight units delivered in 1995-97 and are intended to replace all two- and four-car emus built by Scandia and Frichs between 1966 and 1978; scrapping of the two-car sets was underway in 2002. Seven four car sets built by Scandia in 1986 are to remain in service.

The Hillerød–Helsingør line is operated by seven diesel motor coaches and five trailers built by Duewag and Scandia in 1984 to the standard design used on Danish local lines.

*S-Train single-axle articulated emus forming a Køge–Østerport service at Ishoj* (John C Baker) 2002/0137760

**NEW ENTRY**

## Øresund Consortium

Øresundskonsortiet
Vester Søgade 10, DK-1601 Copenhagen V
Tel: (+45) 33 41 60 00   Fax: (+45) 33 41 61 02
e-mail: info@oeresundsbron.com
Web: http://www.oeresundsbron.com

**Key personnel**
Chief Executive Officer: Sven Landelius
Technical Director: Peter Lundhus
Chief Financial Officer: Teddy Jacobsen
Head of Communications: Anna Holm

**New lines**
Øresundskonsortiet is responsible for building the fixed link between Denmark and Sweden. After completion in 2000 Øresundskonsortiet will own the railway and infrastructure management will be shared between Banestyrelsen (Denmark) and Banverket (Sweden). (For details see 'New lines' section in Banestyrelsen entry.)

*UPDATED*

## Arriva Tog

Herstedvang 7C, DK-2620 Albertslund
Tel: (+45) 72 13 96 00   Fax: (+45) 72 13 96 99
Web: http://www.arriva.dk

**Key personnel**
Managing Director: Ernst V Frendsen
Traffic Manager: Keld Højgaard
Customer Services Manager: Karsten German Pedersen
Engineering Manager: Ivan Skødt Andersen
Safety Manager: Mikael Tittel Langager

**Organisation**
In December 2001, Arriva was awarded two franchises to operate local services over 583 km of lines in west and central Jutland from January 2003. The operator will receive an average annual subsidy of DKr156 million. In May 2002, an additional contract was agreed with the Ministry of Transport to provide more peak hour services than Arriva's draft timetable had originally proposed.

Arriva Danmark took over operation of the Western Railway (qv) on 1 June 2002.

**Traction and rolling stock**
In June 2002, an order was placed with Alstom by the leasing company Angel Trains Ltd to supply 30 two-car Coradia LINT regional diesel trainsets for use by Arriva Tog. Production of the new trains was to be undertaken at Alstom's Salzgitter, Germany, plant, with deliveries commencing in 2004. Until then, services were to be operated by Class MR/MRD diesel railcars hired from DSB; after the arrival of the new stock, Class MR/MRD units were still to be used for the additional peak hour services.

*NEW ENTRY*

## Århus-Odder Railway

Hads-Ning Herreders Jernbanen (HHJ)
Banegårdsgade 3, DK-8300 Odder
Tel: (+45) 86 54 09 44   Fax: (+45) 86 54 41 70
e-mail: hhj@hhj.dk
Web: http://www.odderbanen.dk

**Key personnel**
Director: Ove Nygaard
Manager: Henning Møller

Gauge: 1,435 mm
Route length: 26.5 km

**Organisation**
HHJ runs from the DSB station in Denmark's second largest city, Århus, south to the town of Odder.

**Passenger operations**
In 2001, HHJ carried 1 million passengers for 13 million passenger-km.

A plan to interwork the HHJ with DSB's Århus–Hornslet–Grenå line was under consideration in 2002.

**Freight operations**
No freight is carried.

**Traction and rolling stock**
HHJ owns one diesel-hydraulic locomotive, six Duewag motor coaches and seven trailer coaches.

*UPDATED*

*HHJ Duewag railcar at Århus (Marcel Vleugels)*
2002/0137107

## Eastern Railway

Østbanen (ØSJS)

Gauge: 1,435 mm
Route length: 49.6 km

**Organisation**
The Østbanen starts from a junction with DSB at Køge, which is served by Copenhagen S-Bane services. The line runs from Køge to Hårlev where it divides, with one line going to Fakse Ladeplads on the south Zealand coast and the other to Rødvig.

Following the assumption on 1 January 2001 by the Greater Copenhagen Development Authority (HUR) of responsibility for local railways in its area, ownership of the Eastern Railway's infrastructure and rolling stock passed to Greater Copenhagen Local Railways (HL) (qv) and operation of the line was taken over by the Local Railway (qv). Both organisations are wholly owned subsidiaries of HUR.

*UPDATED*

## Greater Copenhagen Local Railways

Hovedstadens Lokalbaner A/S (HL)
Gammel Køge Landevej 3, DK-2500 Valby
Tel: (+45) 36 13 20 61   Fax: (+45) 36 13 20 96
e-mail: nkv@hl-as.dk

**Key personnel**
Managing Director: Niels Munch Christensen

Gauge: 1,435 mm
Route length: 184 km

*Siemens Desiro railcar operating on the Helsingør–Hornbæk–Gilleleje line at Helsingør (John C Baker)*
2002/0137761

### Organisation

On 1 January 2001, the Greater Copenhagen Development Authority (HUR) took over responsibility for the local railways within its area: the jointly managed Gribskov Railway (42 km) and the Hillerød—Hundested Railway (39 km) in north Zealand; the Helsingør—Hornbæk—Gilleleje Railway (24.5 km) along the north Zealand coast; the Lyngby—Nærum Railway (8 km) in Copenhagen's northern suburbs; and the Eastern Railway (50 km) to the south of Køge. The last-named line is geographically only partially within HUR's area of responsibility but agreement has been reached for it to fall within the organisation's authority. On 17 May 2002, HUR set up two companies: Greater Copenhagen Local Railways (HL), which owns the infrastructure and rolling stock; and the Local Railway (Lokalbanen A/S), which is to operate the lines. The infrastructure of the 21 km of the Hillerød—Helsingør line not shared with DSB's Copenhagen—Helsingør line was taken over.

### Traction and rolling stock

HL owns seven former DSB diesel electric locomotives, one tractor, 11 two-car diesel trainsets (including six Adtranz Flexliners and one Siemens Desiro), 28 diesel motor coaches and 34 trailer cars. All were taken over from the absorbed lines and are operated by the Local Railway.

*NEW ENTRY*

*Gribskov line Flexliner railcar at Slotsparillou (John C Baker)* 2002/0137762

## Gribskov Railway

Gribskovbanen (GDS)

Gauge: 1,435 mm
Route length: 42 km

The Gribskovbanen starts from a junction with DSB at Hillerød, which is served by S-Bane services from Copenhagen. The line runs north to Kagerup where it divides into branches to the seaside towns of Tisvildeleje and Gilleleje.

Following the assumption on 1 January 2001 by the Greater Copenhagen Development Authority (HUR) of responsibility for local railways in its area, ownership of the Gribskov Railway's infrastructure and rolling stock passed to Greater Copenhagen Local Railways (HL) (qv) and operation of the line was taken over by the Local Railway (qv). Both organisations are wholly owned subsidiaries of HUR.

*UPDATED*

## Helsingør-Hornbæk-Gilleleje Railway

Helsingør-Hornbæk-Gilleleje Banen (HHGB)

Gauge: 1,435 mm
Route length: 24.5 km

The line starts from Helsingør, terminus of DSB's coast line. It runs via several seaside towns to Gilleleje, terminus of the Gribskov Railway.

It is purely a passenger railway; in summer, it hosts Sunday steam services run by a local museum.

Following the assumption on 1 January 2001 by the Greater Copenhagen Development Authority (HUR) of responsibility for local railways in its area, ownership of the Helsingør—Hornbæk—Gilleleje Railway's infrastructure and rolling stock passed to Greater Copenhagen Local Railways (HL) (qv) and operation of the line was taken over by the Local Railway (qv). Both organisations are wholly owned subsidiaries of HUR.

*UPDATED*

## Hillerød—Hundested Railway

Hillerød-Frederiksvaerk-Hundested Jernbane (HFHJ)

Gauge: 1,435 mm
Route length: 39 km

The line runs from the DSB station at Hillerød west to Frederiksvaerk and Hundested.

Following the assumption on 1 January 2001 by the Greater Copenhagen Development Authority (HUR) of responsibility for local railways in its area, ownership of the Hillerød—Hundested Railway's infrastructure and rolling stock passed to Greater Copenhagen Local Railways (HL) (qv) and operation of the line was taken over by the Local Railway (qv). Both organisations are wholly owned subsidiaries of HUR.

*UPDATED*

## Hjørring—Hirsthals Railway

See entry for Nordjyske Jernbaner (NJ).

*UPDATED*

## Høng—Tølløse Railway

Høng—Tølløse Jernbane A/S (HTJ)
Jernbaneplads 6, DK-4300 Holbæk
Tel: (+45) 59 48 50 00 Fax: (+45) 59 44 23 40
e-mail: post@ohj-htj.dk
Web: http://www.ohj-htj.dk

### Key personnel

Managing Director: Finn B Henningsen

Gauge: 1,435 mm
Route length: 50 km

### Organisation

HTJ runs between a junction with DSB at Slagelse, on the main line from Copenhagen to Jutland via the Storebælt, and Tølløse, on the Copenhagen—Kalundborg line. The 12.5 km of line between Høng and Slagelse was acquired from DSB in 1995 as it was used only by HTJ trains. The company is jointly managed with the Odsherreds Railway.

### Passenger and freight operations

An hourly service is operated between Slagelse and Tølløse, where there connections towards Copenhagen and to Holbæk; a few trains run through to Holbæk and to Nykøbing, over the Odsherreds Railway. In 2001, 600,000 passengers were carried but freight traffic is minimal.

### Traction and rolling stock

HTJ shares a fleet of five diesel locomotives, 13 two- or three-car diesel trainsets (including three Adtranz-built Flexliners), one tractor and six coaches with the Odsherreds Railway.

*UPDATED*

## The Local Railway

Lokalbanen A/S
Nordre Jernbanevej 36, DK-3400 Hillerød

Tel: (+45) 48 29 88 00 Fax: (+45) 48 29 88 30
e-mail: post@lokalbanen.dk
Web: http://www.lokalbanen.dk

### Key personnel

Managing Director: Claus Klitholm
Administration Manager: Lars Aa Jensen
Traffic Manger: Ole D Johansen

# Denmark/RAILWAY SYSTEMS

## Organisation

Having taken over the local railways lying within its area at the beginning of 2001, the Greater Copenhagen Development Authority (HUR) set up two new companies on 17 May 2002: Greater Copenhagen Local Railways (HL) (qv), which owns the infrastructure and rolling stock of five absorbed railways; and the Local Railway, which was to operate the five lines. The Local Railway is wholly owned by HUR.

## Operations

Commuter traffic linking the communities served with Copenhagen forms the main activity on all four lines. In 2001, the total of passengers carried was 6.5 million. On four of the lines, freight traffic is minimal or non-existent, but remains considerable on the former Hillerød—Hundested Railway. The Local Railway will take over operation of the Hillerød—Helsingør line when the current operating contract with DSB S-Train expires in December 2004. Motive power and rolling stock is owned by HL.

*NEW ENTRY*

## Lolland Railway

Lollandsbanen A/S (LJ)
Banegårdspladsen 5, DK-4930 Maribo
Tel: (+45) 54 79 17 00   Fax: (+45) 54 79 17 60
e-mail: lj@lollandsbanen.dk

### Key personnel
General Manager: Benny E Jensen
Manager: Claus Pedersen

Gauge: 1,435 mm
Route length: 50 km

The Lolland Railway runs east-west across the island of Lolland from Nykøbing Falster on the main Copenhagen–Hamburg via Rødby line, to Nakskov, an industrial town in the west. The line also owns a 7.5 km infrequently used freight line, from Maribo to the port of Bandholm; this line is used by a railway museum.

### Traction and rolling stock
The fleet was strengthened in 1997 with the arrival of four Adtranz-built Flexliner RL2D dmus. LJ also owns 11 diesel locomotives, seven Duewag motor coaches, 14 trailer coaches and 27 wagons.

*UPDATED*

*Lolland Railway Flexliner RL2D dmu at Nykøbing (Marcel Vleugels)* 2000/0085566

## Lyngby—Nærum Railway

A/S Lyngby—Nærum Banen

Gauge: 1,435 mm
Route length: 8 km

The Lyngby—Nærum Railway links Nærum with the Copenhagen S-Bane service at Jaegersborg.

Following the assumption on 1 January 2001 by the Greater Copenhagen Development Authority (HUR) of responsibility for local railways in its area, ownership of the Lyngby—Nærum Railway's infrastructure and rolling stock passed to Greater Copenhagen Local Railways (HL) (qv) and operation of the line was taken over by the Local Railway (qv). Both organisations are wholly owned subsidiaries of HUR.

*UPDATED*

## Nordjyske Jernbaner A/S (NJ)

PO Box 37, Sct Laurentiivej 22, DK-9990 Skagen
Tel: (+45) 98 44 10 15   Fax: (+45) 98 44 18 37
e-mail: skagensbanen@post.tele.dk

### Key personnel
Managing Director: Preben Vestergaard

Gauge: 1,435 mm
Route length: 56.2 km

NJ was formed in January 2001 by the merger of the Hjørring—Hirsthals Railway (HP) and the Skagen Railway (SB).

Located in northern Jutland, the 16.5 km former HP line links Hjørring, where a connection with DSB services is made, with the coastal town of Hirsthals. The former SB system is a 39.7 km line from Frederikshavn to Skagen. As well as continuing to operate passenger and freight services over these lines, NJ also handles freight traffic north of Aalborg.

### Traction and rolling stock
The NJ fleet combines equipment of both its constituents, totalling eight diesel locomotives, including three ex-DSB Class Mx machines of 1,047 or 1,064 kW, and nine Class Ym powered dmu cars plus intermediate and driving trailers built by Duewag/Scandia or Uerdingen.

*NEW ENTRY*

*Former Skagensbanen railcar, now part of the NJ fleet* 0058689

## Odsherreds Railway

Odsherreds Jernbane A/S (OHJ)
Jernbaneplads 6, DK-4300 Holbæk
Tel: (+45) 59 48 50 00   Fax: (+45) 59 44 23 40
e-mail: post@ohj-htj.dk
Web: http://www.ohj-htj.dk

### Key personnel
Managing Director: Finn B Henningsen

Gauge: 1,435 mm
Route length: 50 km

### Organisation
OHJ is jointly managed with the Høng—Tølløse Railway.

### Passenger and freight operations
An hourly service is operated between Nykøbing (Sjælland) and Holbæk, where connections are made with services to and from Copenhagen; a few trains run through to Slagelse over the Høng—Tølløse Railway. In 2001, 1.2 million passengers were carried but freight traffic is minimal.

### Traction and rolling stock
OHJ shares a fleet of five diesel locomotives, 13 two- or three-car diesel trainsets (including three Adtranz-built Flexliners), one tractor and six coaches with the Høng—Tølløse Railway.

*UPDATED*

## Privatbanen Sønderjylland ApS (PBS)

Formed in 1997 as Denmark's first open access freight operator, PBS ceased trading in March 2001.

**UPDATED**

## Railion Denmark

Railion Denmark A/S
Bernstorffsgade 50, DK-1577 Copenhagen V
Tel: (+45) 33 54 18 00   Fax: (+45) 33 54 18 54
e-mail: railion@railion.dk
Web: http://www.railion.dk

### Key personnel
Managing Director: Hans Winther
Finance Director: Leif Kepp
Human Resources Director: Erik Schmidt
Operations Director: Erik O Jensen
Sales and Service Director: Anne-Lise Bach Sorensen
Administration Manager: Marianne Bagge Johansen
Business Development Manager: Per Tendstrand
Management Services Manager: Lotte Sørensen
Safety Manager: Preben Jorgensen

### Political background
Following the change of DSB's status to that of an independent publicly owned corporation on 1 January 1999, a requirement was placed on DSB's freight division to be in surplus by the end of 2002. From January 199, it also faced competition on the Danish network and was forced to rationalise to remain competitive. Following the failure on November 1998 of negotiations to form a joint freight companies with the Norwegian and Swedish state railway companies, DSB started to look for other operators with which the freight division could be amalgamated or to which it could be sold. After lengthy negotiations, agreement was reached on 15 December 2000 to sell the company to Railion, a subsidiary of German Rail (DB AG), but it was not until 27 June 2001 that the sale was finalised, although it was backdated to 1 January 2001. The agreement entailed the division being sold to Railion for DKr170 million, which DSB then used to purchase 2 per cent of Railion. Only wagonload, intermodal and international traffic passed to Railion, as the sundries traffic had been sold to a consortium of road hauliers in May 2000 and most of this business has since been lost to rail.

### Organisation
Railion Denmark is divided into four divisions: Finance; Human Resources; Operations; and Sales and Service. Information technology and purchasing functions are overseen by the Finance Division, while training and staff administration are the responsibility of Human Resources. Operations is responsible for all aspects of the operation of trains and terminals, including train planning.

### Freight operations
There are intermodal terminals at: Aalborg; Århus; Copenhagen; Esbjerg; Hoje Taastrup; and Taulov. The facility at Taulov was being extended during 2002. Overnight intermodal services operate between Hoje Taastrup and Aalborg, Århus, Esbjerg and Taulov. International services include trains to France and Italy and special services from Sweden conveying timber and paper products. The Scandinavian Maritime Express runs from Århus and Copenhagen to Bremerhaven conveying containers destined for overseas shipment. Wagonload traffic has been substantially reduced to a core network serving the most important terminals, but some private lines provide feeder services.

### Traction and rolling stock
Railion operates 13 dual-voltage and 10 AC-only line-haul electric locomotives of Classes EG and EA; 20 Class MZ line-haul diesel-electric locomotives; 42 Class MK diesel shunting locomotives and tractors; and 1,760 wagons. The Class EG locomotives are capable of operating into both Germany and Sweden.

*Railion Siemens-built Class EG 6,500 kW dual-voltage electric locomotive at Ørestad with a freight service for Sweden (John C Baker)*
2002/0137763

*Railion Class MK diesel-hydraulic shunting locomotive (Marcel Vleugels)*
2002/0137764

#### Diesel locomotives

| Class | Wheel arrangement | Power kW | Speed km/h | Weight tonnes | No in service | First built | Builders Mechanical | Engine | Transmission |
|---|---|---|---|---|---|---|---|---|---|
| MZ | Co-Co | 2,270 | 143 | 116.5 | 7 | 1967 | N&H, Frichs | GM 16-645E3 | E Thrige |
| MZ | Co-Co | 2,865 | 165 | 123 | 13 | 1977 | N&H, Frichs | GM 20-645E3 | E GM |
| MK | B | 390 | 60 | 40 | 21 | 1996 | Siemens | MTU 8V 183TD13 | H Voith |
| Tractor | B | 94 | 45 | 17 | 21 | 1966 | Frichs | Leyland 680 | H Voith |

#### Electric locomotives

| Class | Wheel arrangement | Power kW continuous | Speed km/h | Weight tonnes | No in service | First built | Builders Mechanical | Electrical |
|---|---|---|---|---|---|---|---|---|
| EA | Bo-Bo | 4,000 | 175 | 80 | 10 | 1984 | Thyssen-Henschel/Scandia | BBC |
| EG* | Co-Co | 6,500 | 140 | 129 | 13 | 1999 | Siemens | Siemens |

* Dual-voltage (25 kV AC 50 Hz/15 kV AC 16⅔ Hz)

**NEW ENTRY**

## Skagen Railway

See entry for Nordjyske Jernbaner (NJ).

**UPDATED**

Denmark—Ecuador/**RAILWAY SYSTEMS** 131

## TraXion

TraXion A/S
Jernbanegade 7, DK-6330 Padborg
Tel: (+45) 73 67 11 10   Fax: (+45) 73 67 11 20
e-mail: mail@traxion.dk
Web: http://www.traxion.dk

**Key personnel**
Director: Erik Panduro

**Organisation**
TraXion operates freight services over the Banestyrelsen network and also provides motive power and drivers for Banestyrelsen's own trains. It is also part of Rail Transport Team (RTT) and was to be responsible for the haulage within Denmark of Älmhult—Dortmund trains operated by the Swedish retail chain, IKEA.

**Traction and rolling stock**
TraXion owns three former DSB A1A-A1A diesel-electric locomotives.

*NEW ENTRY*

## Vemb—Thyborøn Railway

Vemb—Lemvig—Thyborøn Jernbane (VLTJ)
Banegårdsvej 2, DK-7620 Lemvig
Tel: (+45) 97 82 32 22   Fax: (+45) 97 81 08 10
e-mail: vltj@lemvigbanen.dk
Web: http://www.lemvigbanen.dk

**Key personnel**
Managing Director: Knud Vigsø
Manager: Kurt Petersen

Gauge: 1,435 mm
Route length: 58 km

The line runs from the DSB station at Vemb on the remote western Jutland coast line to the town of Thyborøn; a chemical works south of Thyborøn and a fishmeal factory in the town generate freight traffic.

**Traction and rolling stock**
The Vemb—Thyborøn Railway owns two diesel locomotives: one ex-DSB Mx Class machine and one ex-DSB My Class. It has five Duewag diesel trainsets.

*UPDATED*

## Western Railway

Vestbanen A/S (VNJ)
Svinget 11, DK-6800 Varde
Tel: (+45) 76 95 21 00   Fax: (+45) 76 95 21 10
e-mail: vestbanen@vestbanen.dk
Web: http://www.vestbanen.dk

**Key personnel**
Managing Director: Mikael Tittel Langager

Gauge: 1,435 mm
Route length: 38 km

VNJ runs from a junction with DSB at Varde on the west Jutland coastline to Nørre Nebel; the military training camp at Oksbøl generates freight traffic for the line, but in 2001 the company started operating trains between Tønder and Grenå, both on the DSB network. On 1 June 2002, VNJ was taken over by Arriva Danmark.

**Traction and rolling stock**
VNJ owns two former DSB diesel-electric locomotives and three Duewag/Scandia and Uerdingen two-car diesel trainsets.

*UPDATED*

*VNJ railcar at Varde (Marcel Vleugels)*
0063487

---

# DOMINICAN REPUBLIC

## Ministry of Works and Communications

Avenida San Cristobal, Santo Domingo

**Key personnel**
State Secretary: E Williams

## Central Romana Railroad

Central Romana, La Romana

**Key personnel**
President: C Morales T
Vice-President and General Superintendent: R J Rivera
Director, Purchases: B R Grullon

Gauge: 1,435 mm
Route length: 375 km

**Freight operations**
The railway operates 13 locomotives and 950 freight wagons for the transport of sugar cane.

A further 240 km of 558 mm, 762 mm and 1,067 mm gauge track is operated by the private Angelina, CAEI and Cristobal Colon sugar cane systems.

## Dominica Government Railway

Santo Domingo
Gauge: 762 mm
Route length: 142 km

**Freight operations**
The railway operates four locomotives and 72 freight wagons. The main freight traffic comprises bananas from Guayubin moved to the port of Pepillo for export.

A total of eight sugar cane systems are operated by the semi-nationalised CEA group, totalling 986 km on 762 mm, 889 mm and 1,067 mm gauges.

---

# ECUADOR

## Ministry of Public Works & Communications

1184 Avenida 6 de Diciembre y Wilson, Quito
Tel: (+593 2) 24 26 66

**Key personnel**
Minister: P J López T
Under-Secretary: G Uzcátegui P

## State Railways of Ecuador (ENFE)

Empresa Nacional de los Ferrocarriles del Estado
PO Box 159, Calle Bolivar 443, Quito
Tel: (+593 2) 21 61 80

**Key personnel**
Director General: Mario Arias Salazar
Traffic Manager: Vicente Cevallos Cazar
Directors
  Administration: S Gudino C
  Finance: G Vintimilla
  Technical: M Herrera R
Motive Power Superintendent: E Benavides
Transport and Telecommunications Engineer: W Idrovo
Permanent Way Engineer: Marco Redrobán A
Managers
  Quito-San Lorenzo Division: G Gallo
  Sibambe-Cuenca Division: M Montalvo

Gauge: 1,067 mm
Route length: 965.5 km

**Political background**
In September 1999, Ecuador's National Modernisation Council (CONAM) presented proposals for privatising the national rail network. CONAM expected to sell three lines for the following prices: Quito—Guayaquil for US$97 million; Ibarra—San Lorenzo for US$10 million; and Ibarra—Cajas for US$1.5 million. A technical and economic study was to have been drawn up by CONAM but was still not available in April 2000. The change from the sucre to the US dollar as national currency is reported to have caused economic difficulties which would have an impact on the proposed privatisation.

**Organisation**
ENFE is composed of three divisions. The main line (the 446.7 km Guayaquil—Quito Division) connects Durán,

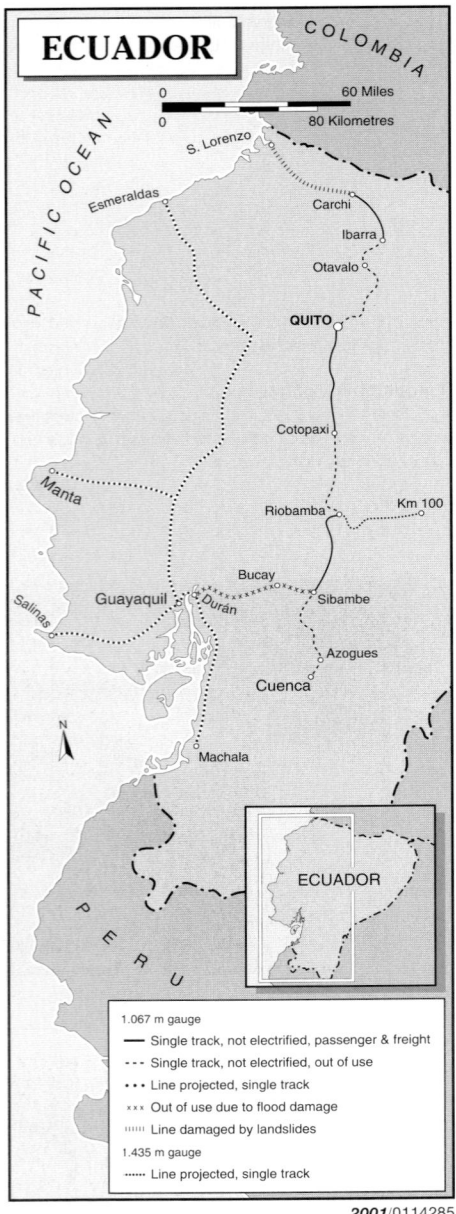

# RAILWAY SYSTEMS/Ecuador–Egypt

**ECUADOR**

located on the opposite bank of the river from Ecuador's main port of Guayaquil, with Quito, which lies at some 2,800 m altitude in the the Andes. From Durán the line runs across low-lying plains for 87 km to Bucay, at the foot of the western slopes of the Andes. Over the next 79 km the line climbs 2,940 m at an average grade over the whole section of 3.7 per cent (1 in 27). The line strikes many sharp curves, and several stretches are laid on a grade of 5.5 per cent (1 in 18), including a double zigzag which was required to negotiate a particularly awkward mountain outcrop known as the *Nariz del Diablo* (Devil's Nose). Once the summit of this section is reached at Palmira, 3,238 m in altitude and 166 km from Durán, the line remains in the high Sierra, never falling below 2,500 m, and rising to 3,609 m at the overall summit of Urbina, 264 km from Durán.

After severe floods in 1992 and 1994 the line was completely relocated and rebuilt near Tixan (from Alausí down to the *Nariz del Diablo* to avoid future breaches). In 1992 floods and high waters of the Rio Chanchán destroyed many bridges on the Sibambe–Huigra–Bucay section, and they have mostly been replaced by new steel structures. Floods during the El Niño weather phenomenon washed away several parts of the lowland line between Durán and Bucay and also some stretches between Bucay and Huigra, making any use of the lower sections of this line impossible. Some repairs have been carried out by ENFE near Huigra. In 1999, ENFE estimated the cost of rebuilding the Durán–Bucay–Sibambe line at US$1 million, with work expected to be completed by October 2000.

In late 1999, a weekly round trip by a mixed train between Quito and Riobamba was introduced, in addition to the three times-weekly railbus between Riobamba and Sibambe and the Sunday Quito–Cotopaxi excursion train.

The 373.4 km Quito–San Lorenzo Division runs northwest from Quito to the coastal town of San Lorenzo, near the border with Colombia. The Quito–Ibarra section of this Division has been out of regular service since the mid-1980s, and subsequently a short section was made inoperable when a parallel road was widened. In the early 1990s a railcar service was introduced between Ibarra and Otavalo to convey tourists to the Otavalo Indian market, but rolling stock problems have since led to its withdrawal. The Ibarra–San Lorenzo section has also suffered from landslides after heavy rainfall and has been repaired on several occasions. The most vulnerable section is around Carchi.

Until 1997 the railway had an effective monopoly in both passenger and freight transport in this part of the country, but the construction of a road on a generally parallel route has had a severe impact on traffic. Heavy rains in early 1999 again disrupted traffic and by May 1999 no signs of reconstruction had been reported.

ENFE's Sibambe–Cuenca Division links Sibambe, 131 km from Durán on the main line, with Cuenca, an important provincial capital in the southern part of the country. On its northernmost section, near Sibambe, the line has been blocked on several occasions due to landslides and in the mid-1990s only sporadic traffic was operated on the southernmost part of the line between Azogues and Cuenca. However, in 1996 the line was closed completely near Cuenca when the track was covered in asphalt as part of a road improvement scheme.

In December 1999, 517 km of line were reported to be open for services.

Late in 1999, staff members were reduced to fewer than 400.

### Passenger and freight operations
Passenger traffic has fallen from some 1.5 million passenger journeys in 1993 to around 110,000 in 1998. Freight traffic fell from 37,000 tonnes to 5,000 tonnes over the same period.

### New lines
The principal ambition of ENFE has been to build a new north-south axis connecting the oil port of Esmeraldas, in the north of the country on the Pacific coast, with Machala, the inland centre of banana plantations south of Guayaquil. It would not entail difficult civil engineering. There would be a case for up to three branches to the line, one to serve a major economic development area based on prawn farms at Manta.

ENFE has also undertaken studies to improve rail access to Guayaquil. Both transhipment by either lorry or river barge and a new rail barge were considered. In 1996 US oil company Occidental Exploration & Production commissioned a feasibility study for a new 100 km 1,435 mm gauge route to bring freight and passengers to oilfields under development in the Amazon basin. This would have 300 tonne freight trains running at 50 km/h.

### Improvements to existing lines
In April 1994, the ENFE board approved a Su212 billion investment programme which included track improvements and resleepering on the San Lorenzo–Ibarra and Riobamba–Durán sections of the system, as well as station modernisation.

### Traction and rolling stock
The nine new Bo-Bo-Bo locomotives ordered from GEC Alsthom in 1991 with French aid began trials in Ecuador in August 1992. Designated Class 2400, each machine cost US$3.3 million; they are powered by SEMT Pielstick Type 12 PA4 V200 VG engines with a UIC rating of 1,780 kW.

ENFE's other motive power comprises a mix of Alco DL535B Co-Cos and GEC Alsthom 960 hp B-B-Bs, steam locomotives and a handful of diesel railcars. Much of the fleet is unserviceable and many items of equipment are marooned by severed rail connections.

In December 1999 the fleet stood at:
Locomotives and rolling stock: 13 diesel-electric (4 reported serviceable), 9 steam (none serviceable); 15 railcars (4 serviceable); 50 passenger coaches (less than half serviceable); 120 freight wagons (fewer than 100 serviceable).

**Type of coupler in standard use:** Automatic
**Type of brake in standard use:** Air

### Track
**Rails:** 35, 30, 27.5 and 22.5 kg/m
**Sleepers:** Wood, 2,000 × 200 × 180 mm
**Spacing:** 1,700/km
**Max curve radius:** 20°
**Max gradient:** 5.5%
**Max axleload:** 15 tonnes

---

# EGYPT

## Ministry of Transport and Communications
Cairo
Tel: (+20 2) 355 55 66   Fax: (+20 2) 355 55 64

**Key personnel**
Minister: Soliman Metwali

## Egyptian National Railways (ENR)
Station Building, Ramses Square, Cairo
Tel: (+20 2) 575 10 00; 577 13 88
Fax: (+20 2) 574 00 00

**Key personnel**
Chairman: Eng Mohamed Arafa Al-Newaem
Deputy Chairmen
  Regions: Eng Harrafee Mahmoud Abdelqaoui
  Permanent Way and Signalling:
    Eng Aschraf Salamee Abu Zeid
  Technical, Purchasing and Stores:
    Magdee El-Ezb Amine Shalabee
  Construction: Eng Nawal Taha Mahmoud
  Financial and Administration Affairs:
    Rushdy Mahmoud El-Khatib
  Operations and Commercial Affairs:
    Eng Eid Abd El Kader Metwalli Awad

Gauge: 1,435 mm
Route length: 5,105 km
Electrification: 62 km at 1.5 kV DC

### Organisation
Egyptian National Railways extends from the Mediterranean up the Nile Valley, serving the Nile Delta, Cairo, Alexandria, Port Said, Ismailia, Suez and connecting at Sadd el Ali, its southernmost point, with the river steamers of Sudan Railways. From El Quantara, on the Port Said–Ismailia line, a branch runs east following the coast and connects with Israel Railways; it has been disused for many years. A significant recent expansion of the network was the opening in 1996 of an west-east line in Upper Egypt, from Abu Tartour to the Red Sea port of Safaga.

At the end of 2000 ENR employed 93,200 staff.

| Traffic (million) | 1999 | 2000 |
|---|---|---|
| Passenger journeys | 842 | 842 |
| Passenger-km | 60,040 | 60,052 |
| Freight tonnes | 10.84 | 12.5 |
| Freight tonne-km | - | - |

### Passenger operations
In modern times ENR has been primarily a passenger railway. Passenger traffic grew to some 462 million journeys by 1990 (compared with 313 million journeys in 1980) and jumped substantially thereafter to reach 775 million journeys in 1997 (60.62 billion passenger-km). This growth continued into 2000, when 842 million passenger journeys were recorded. This was due largely to the huge success of the cross-city tunnel linking Cairo's two busiest commuter lines.

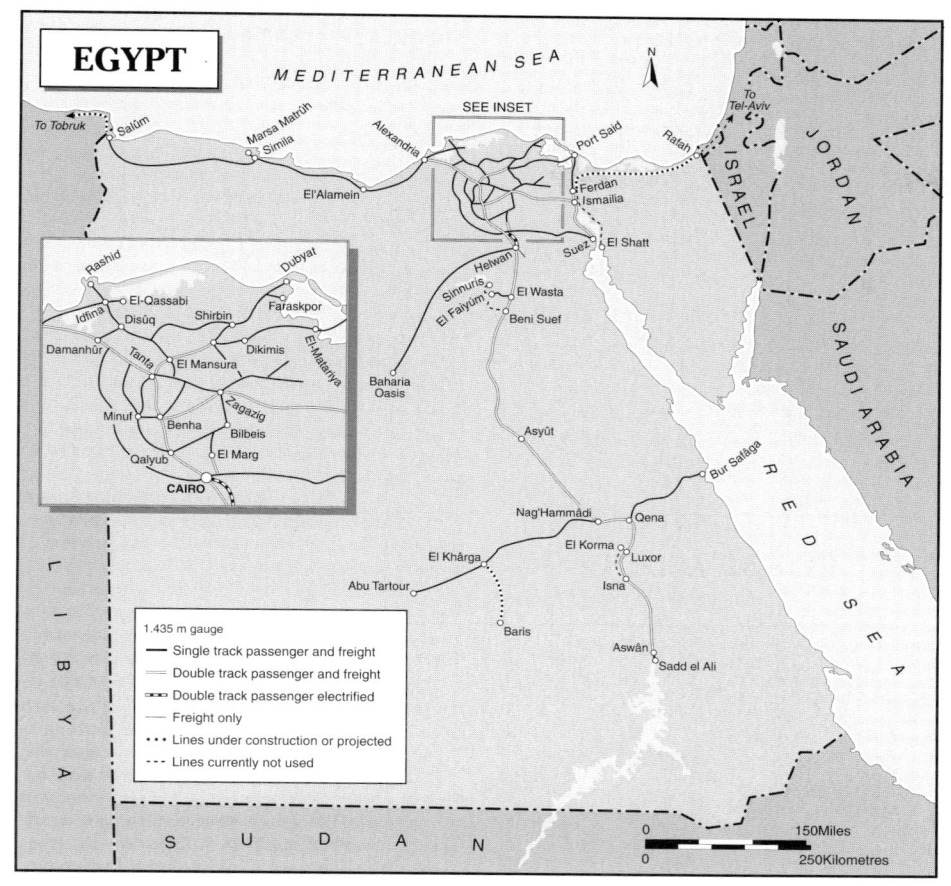

# Egypt/RAILWAY SYSTEMS

130 km alignment have been made by ENR and in 1996 it was announced that Libya would build the line to Salûm from Tobruk with technical assistance from Egypt. This would connect the ENR system to a proposed 3,170 km network in Libya.

The long-closed link across the Sinai peninsula to Rafah, close to the Gaza border was re-established in November 2001 following the opening of a new rail/road swing bridge across the Suez Canal at El Ferdan. At 340 m, this is the world's longest swing bridge. It was built by Consortium El Ferdan Bridge, led by Krupp Stahlbau of Hannover. The line to Rafah has been built for 160 km/h running, and will be CTC-controlled.

In 1998 ENR undertook preliminary studies into a 500 km line to Sudan, linking Aswan with the northern Sudanese town of Wadi Halfa. Other projects studied or developed include: a new branch line to serve iron ore deposits near Aswan; a branch from the Cairo–Suez line to serve a proposed new port on the Gulf of Suez; and a branch from the planned Ismailia–Rafah line to serve a new port east of Port Said.

In 2000, a contract was signed with Spanish consultants to conduct a study into a high-speed line between Alexandria and Cairo, including a possible extension to Aswan.

### Improvements to existing lines

A recent priority has been renovation of the 345 km line built shortly after the Second World War with Soviet aid from Helwan to Baharia, which is primarily an ore and coal carrier. Improvements included complete track renewal and protective measures to prevent service interruptions caused by drifting sand. CTC is managed from a control centre in Cairo.

Much of ENR's track maintenance and renewal is undertaken by private-sector contractors, with both Franco-Egyptian and German-Egyptian joint venture companies active.

### Traction and rolling stock

At the beginning of 2000, rolling stock totalled 787 diesel locomotives, three 10-car turbotrains, 50 multiple-units, 3,476 passenger cars, 38 diesel railcars and 12,724 freight wagons.

On main line services, ENR has expanded train lengths substantially, with the aid of 700 main line day cars and 605 suburban cars acquired since the mid-1970s.

Three 10-car turbotrain sets built by ANF Industrie provide prime service over the 208 km between Cairo and Alexandria. It is hoped eventually to exploit this equipment's 160 km/h capability to achieve a Cairo–Alexandria transit in 1 hour 30 minutes, with each of the trains completing three round trips daily. At present, however, they are confined to 140 km/h, and that only over certain sections. In the Cairo area speed cannot exceed 60 km/h for some 25 km distance.

Luxury air conditioned overnight trains using refurbished stock operate on the Cairo–Luxor–Aswan route. Infrastructure upgrading on this popular tourist route has included double-tracking and resignalling. Daytime services have benefited considerably from the track upgrading, permitting operation at 140 km/h of four trainsets supplied by ABB Henschel (now Adtranz) and Hyundai.

ENR long-term projections for passenger traffic volumes foresee growth of over 250 per cent in the 15 years from 1997 to 2012.

### Freight operations

Freight too has advanced, though ENR has a market share of only around 12 per cent. In 1990, 8.6 million tonnes were hauled for 2,827 million tonne-km, but this had increased to 12.5 million tonnes by 2000. The main constituent is ore carried on the Baharia–Helwan line, with wheat and oil next in importance. Container traffic has also experienced substantial growth, sufficient to encourage ENR to commission studies into the establishment of intermodal terminals, or 'dry ports', in major towns and cities.

### New lines

Freight carryings are expected to receive a further boost of some 7 million tonnes annually with the opening of the long-planned line to tap phosphate deposits at Abu Tartour. The 235 km initial section of this export corridor, linking the Cairo–Aswan main line at Qena with the Red Sea port of Safaga, was opened in 1984, but construction of the western portion up to Abu Tartour was not started until much later. Work on this difficult project, which includes a crossing of the Nile at Nag'Hammadi, was completed in October 1996. A 46 km branch south from El Kharga to Baris is planned.

The infrastructure of a 70 km line from Port Said to the Nile Delta has been completed.

Another longstanding project is that for construction of a line into neighbouring Libya from ENR's northwestern terminal at Salûm, now revived as a joint venture between Egyptian and Libyan interests. Feasibility studies of the

*ENR local service headed by a Henschel/GM AA22T locomotive at Luxor (Colin Boocock)*

*Adtranz/General Motors Type DE2550 for passenger service*

A fleet of 700 bottom-discharge wagons for the Abu Tartour phosphates traffic has been supplied by local manufacturer Semaf. They are hauled by 45 DE2250 single-cab GM-powered diesel-electrics delivered during 1995-96 by Adtranz Germany. These Co-Cos are rated at 1,845 kW. A further 23 similar locomotives, but in a dual-cab configuration, have been delivered for more general duties in the Nile Delta area.

From 1997, 30 1,230 kW diesel-electric locomotives were supplied by General Electric of the USA, ENR's first machines from this manufacturer. Funding for the project was to be provided by the US Agency for International Development.

In December 1997 Bombardier Transportation signed a contract to undertake mid-life refurbishment of 80 ENR Turbotrain bogies. Semaf has received a contract to construct 100 non-air conditioned coaches, and has embarked on a refurbishment programme covering 100 second- and third-class vehicles.

In 2000 ENR commenced a programme to refurbish 63 coaches to luxury standards for Cairo–Alexandria and Cairo–Aswan services.

Upgrading of the existing freight wagon fleet is being undertaken under a programme started at the beginning of 1998.

### Diesel locomotives

| Class | Wheel arrangement | Power kW | Speed km/h | Weight tonnes | First built | Mechanical | Builders Engine | Transmission |
|---|---|---|---|---|---|---|---|---|
| JT22MC | Co-Co | 2,238 | 140 | 111 | 1983 | EMD | 645E3-12 | E EMD |
| AA22T | Co-Co | 2,238 | 140 | 121 | 1983 | Henschel | 645E3-12 | E EMD |
| AA22T | Co-Co | 2,238 | 120 | 121 | 1975-84 | Henschel | 645E3-12 | E EMD |
| G26CW | Co-Co | 2,163 | 140 | 98 | 1973-76 | EMD | 645E-16 | E EMD |
| G22W/AC | Bo-Bo | 1,641 | 105 | 80 | 1980 | EMD | 645E-12 | E EMD |
| G22W | Bo-Bo | 1,641 | 105 | 80 | 1978 | EMD | 645E-12 | E EMD |
| AA22T/DB | Co-Co | 2,238 | 80 | 122 | 1979 | Henschel/EMD | 645E3-12 | E EMD |
| DE2250 | Co-Co | 1,845 | 80 | 132 | 1995 | Adtranz | 645E3-12 | E EMD |

### Electrification
The double-track suburban main line from Cairo to Helwan (42 km) is electrified at 1.5 kV DC, and forms Line 1 of the Cairo metro system.

*UPDATED*

# EL SALVADOR

## Ministry of Public Works
1a Avenida Sur 630, San Salvador
Fax: (+503) 271 01 63

### Key personnel
Minister: Jorge Alberto Sansivirini
Deputy Minister: Roberto Bara Osegueda

## El Salvador National Railways (FENADESAL)
Ferrocarriles Nacionales de El Salvador
PO Box 2292, Avenida Peralta 903, San Salvador
Tel: (+503) 71 56 32  Fax: (+503) 71 56 50

### Key personnel
President (CEPA): C H Figueroa
Managers
 General (CEPA): A German Martinez
 Operations (CEPA): J A Nunez
  Jose Eriberto Erquicia
 General (FENADESAL): Tulio Omar Vergara
 Purchasing: Luis Antonio Guzmán
 Finance: Fredy Antonio Mayora
 Traffic: R Marín
 Personnel: Wilfredo Ciudad Real
 Transportation: L A Carballo
 Rolling Stock and Equipment: Julio Fernando Pienda
 Maintenance of Way: Andres Abelino Cruz

Gauge: 914 mm
Route length (operational): 283 km

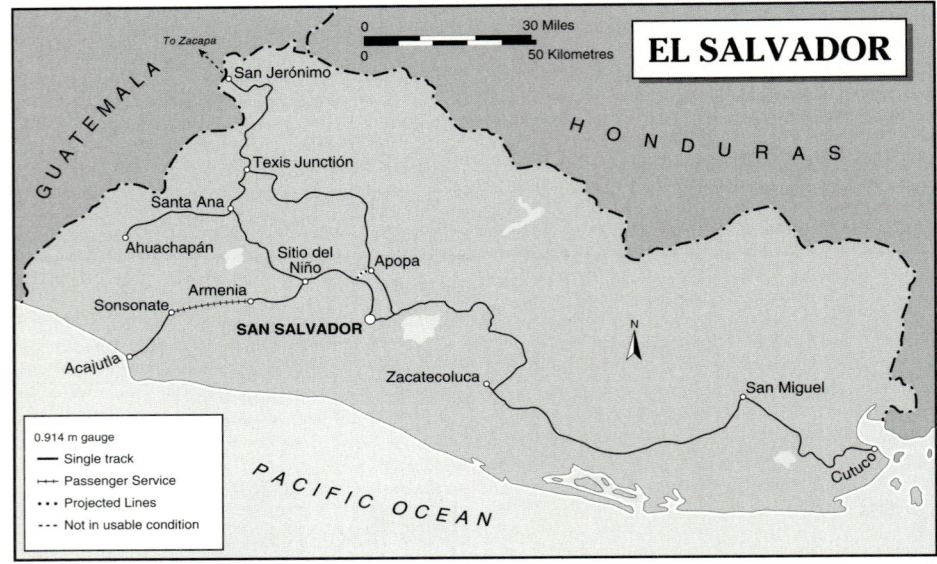

### Organisation
FENADESAL was formed from two railways which were formerly the property of overseas companies: the Salvador Railway, which passed to the state in 1965 under the name of Ferrocarril de El Salvador (FES); and the International Railways of Central America (IRCA), a railway undertaking that included the railway system and port at Cútuco, which was nationalised in 1974 under the name of Ferrocarril Nacional de El Salvador (FENASAL).

The two undertakings were merged under state control in May 1975 (together with the port of Cútuco) and became FENADESAL, which is administered by the port authority CEPA.

The railway is divided into three districts: District No 1 which comprises San Salvador (the capital) to the port of Cutúco in the east of the country (252 km); District No 2 which runs from San Salvador to the frontier of El Salvador with Guatemala (146 km), and a branch to Santa Ana, in the west of the country (20 km); District No 3 which runs from San Salvador to the port of Acajutla, on the Pacific Ocean (104 km), and includes a branch from Sitio del Niño to Santa Ana in the west (40 km).

### Finance
The railway is heavily subsidised. In 1997 its revenues from passenger and freight traffic and other sources totalled c11.9 million, against total expenditure of c48.1 million.

Investment totalling c3.07 million was planned for 1996, with c1.25 million to be spent on major track improvements, c0.28 million on telecommunications, c0.24 million on computer systems and c1.3 million on a locomotive fuelling facility.

| Traffic (million) | 1996 | 1997 |
|---|---|---|
| Passenger journeys | 0.313 | 0.460 |
| Passenger-km | 4.8 | 7.1 |
| Freight tonnes | 0.161 | 0.313 |
| Freight tonne-km | 17.3 | - |

### Passenger operations
By the start of 1996 FENADESAL had ceased to operate passenger services, with the exception of over a short stretch of line between Armenia and Sonsonate, which received some attention by introducing a refurbished railbus which operates four times daily in each direction. On market days in Armenia the railbus is replaced by a mixed train. Occasional services hauled by either steam or diesel traction, mostly for tourist groups, operate between Sonsonate, Armenia and Sitio del Niño.

### Diesel locomotives

| Class | Builder's type | Wheel arrangement | Power kW | Speed km/h | Weight tonnes | No in service | First built | Mechanical | Builders Engine | Transmission |
|---|---|---|---|---|---|---|---|---|---|---|
| 850 | GA-8 | Bo-Bo | 595 | 57 | 61 | 10 | 1965 | GM | GM 567 CR | E EMD |
| 700 | U6B | B-B | 280 | 60 | 47 | 2 | 1956 | GE | Caterpillar D-397 | E GE |

### Improvements to existing lines
A group from Taiwan has expressed interest in upgrading existing track to allow international trains to run through to the port of Cortés in neighbouring Honduras. Ferrovías Guatemala is studying the possibility of reconstructing the international link from San Jerónimo to Zacapa in Guatemala to provide a corridor for international traffic to Mexico, the USA and the port of Puerto Barrios in Guatemala.

### Traction and rolling stock
Operational resources at the end of 1997 totalled: 10 diesel-electric locomotives (plus 2 unserviceable); 1 steam locomotives (plus 1 awaiting restoration); 2 railcars; 16 passenger coaches; 370 freight wagons.

### Track
**Rail:** ASCE 54, 60, 70 and 75 lb/yd
**Sleepers:** Hardwood 7 ft x 6 in by 8 in
**Fastenings:** Standard, spike and angle bar
**Spacing:** 1,725/km in plain track 1,850/km in curves
**Min curvature radius:** 328 ft
**Max gradient:** 3%
**Max axleloading:** 12.5 tonnes

# ERITREA

## Ministry of Transport

PO Box 204, Asmera
Tel: (+291 1) 11 43 07  Fax: (+291 1) 12 70 48

**Key personnel**
Minister: Dr Giorgis Teklemikael

## Eritrean Railways

PO Box 569, Asmera
Tel: (+291 1) 11 43 07  Fax: (+291 1) 12 70 48
Gauge: 950 mm
Route length: 306 km

**Key personnel**
Director: Amanuel Ghébrésélassié

### Political background
Following achievement of independence from Ethiopia in 1993, the government moved to revive parts of the former Northern Ethiopia Railway. This 306 km line, linking Ak'ordat with the capital Asmera and the Red Sea port of Mits'iwa has been out of use since 1978. Consultants have determined that the original alignment could be rehabilitated, and a small fleet of rolling stock rebuilt using existing spare parts.

By the end of 2000, the Mits'iwa–Ghinda section had been reopened and rehabilitation had been completed as far as Embatkala, 13 km west of Ghinda. Reopening of the remaining section to Asmera, 118 km from Mits'iwa was expected to be achieved by the end of 2001. The work is being undertaken by military personnel and reservists.

Plans exist to continue reconstruction west of Asmera to Bisha and to create a new international link to Kassala, Sudan.

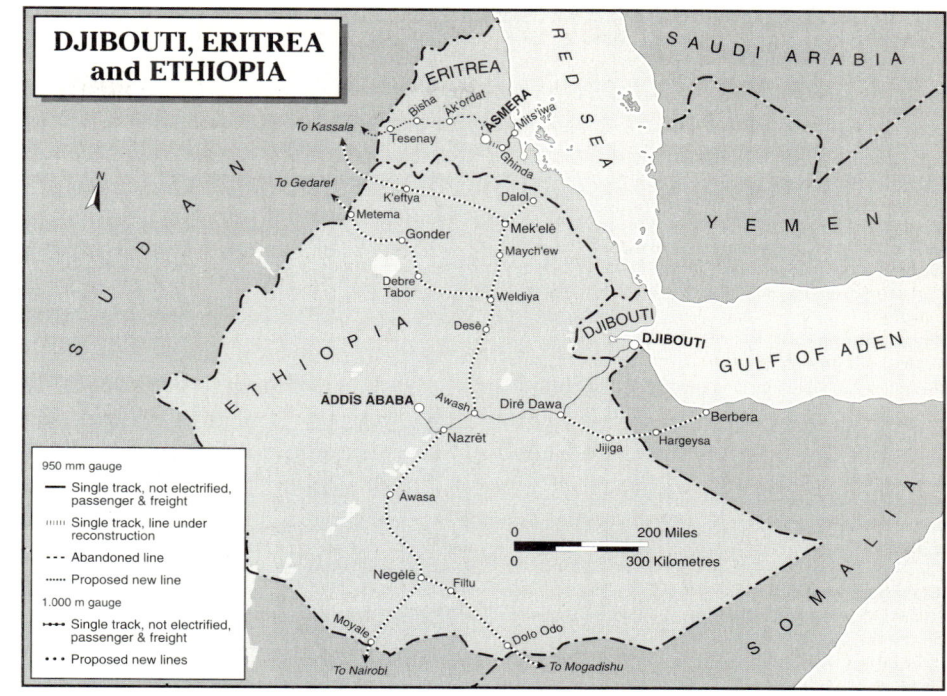

### Passenger and freight operations
A railcar-operated passenger service and tourist trains operate between Mits'iwa and Ghinda. A daily freight service is provided between Damas and Ghinda.

### Traction and rolling stock
Serviceable traction at the end of 2000 comprised one Krupp-built diesel-hydraulic locomotive, five steam locomotives of Italian origin and a Fiat railcar. Two Soviet-built road-rail vehicles were also in use.

---

# ESTONIA

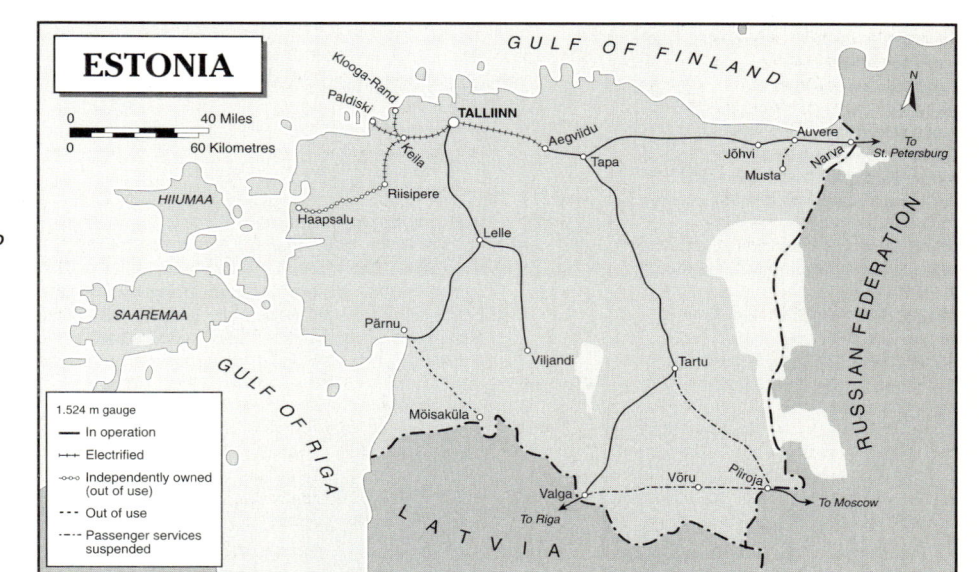

## Ministry of Transport and Communications

Viru 9, EE0 100, Tallinn
Tel: (+372 6) 39 76 13  Fax: (+372 6) 39 76 06

**Key personnel**
Minister: Liina Tönisson

*UPDATED*

## Edelaraudtee AS

Kaare 25, EE-72213 Türi
Tel: (+372 38) 571 23  Fax: (+372 38) 571 21
e-mail: edel@edel.ee
Web: http://www.edel.ee

Gauge: 1,520 mm
Route length: 265 km

**Key personnel**
Chairman: Jyri Kuusik

### Political background
Edelaraudtee (South West Railway) commenced operations as an independent business in January 1997 in anticipation of rail privatisation legislation approved by parliament during the same year. In 2000 Edelaraudtee, which also owns the South Western narrow-gauge lines and runs passenger trains elsewhere, was sold to the British company GB Railways via its subsidiary GB Railways Eesti AS, which agreed to make substantial investment over five years. It soon discovered that the passenger subsidy had become doubtful, and began to withdraw services. This dispute was still not settled in spring 2001.

### Passenger operations
Edelaraudtee provides diesel-operated domestic passenger services on the Tallinn–Lelle–Pärnu/Viljandi

*Edelaraudtee DR1A diesel trainset at Rakvere (Eddie Barnes)*

# RAILWAY SYSTEMS/Estonia

routes. In 2001 there was a suggestion that GB Railways would withdraw all services because of the threat to the operating subsidy, but it later became clear that some services would be maintained until the end of 2001, and would be perpetuated if a subsidy agreement was reached.

### Freight operations
Freight services are provided on the Tallinn–Lelle–Pärnu/Viljandi routes.

### New lines
In 1999 Edelaraudtee announced plans to construct a cross-border freight line from Mõisaküla into Latvia.

### Traction and rolling stock
Edelaraudtee operates a fleet of 11 diesel-electric locomotives of ChME3 and M62 types. DR1A diesel trainsets are used for passenger services.

---

## Elektriraudtee AS

Vabadse pst 176, EE-10917 Tallinn
Tel: (+372 6) 615 88 00   Fax: (+372 6) 615 71 70
e-mail: info@elektriraudtee.ee
Web: http://www.elektriraudtee.ee

### Key personnel
Chairman: Jaanus Paas
Managers: Arnold Knuut; Ilme Lääne; Lauri Reinhold

### Political background
A wholly owned subsidiary of Estonian Railways, Elektriraudtee commenced operations as an independent business on 1 January 1999 in response to rail privatisation legislation approved by parliament in 1997.

### Passenger operations
Elektriraudtee provides suburban commuter services on the 132 km electrified network around Tallinn and in Harju county.

### Traction and rolling stock
Services are provided by a fleet of 84 emu cars built by Riga, Latvia.

*Elektriraudtee Type ER2S four-car emu at Tallinn Balti Jaam (Eddie Barnes)*
2001/0059395

### Electric railcars or multiple-units

| Class | Builder's Type | Cars per unit | Line voltage | Motor cars per unit | Motored axles/car | Output/motor kW | Speed km/h | Units in service | Builders Mechanical | Builders Electrical |
|---|---|---|---|---|---|---|---|---|---|---|
| ER1 |  | 4/6 | 3.3 kV | 2/3 | Bo-Bo | 200 | 130 | 7 | M: Riga (RVR) T, P: Kalinin | Riga (RER) |
| ER2 | 62-61 | 4/6 | 3.3 kV | 2/3 | Bo-Bo | 200 | 130 | 4 | Riga (RVR) | Riga (RER) |
| ER12 | 62-251 | 4/6 | 3.3 kV | 2/3 | Bo-Bo | 200 | 130 | 3 | Riga (RVR) | Riga (RER) |

---

## Estonian Railways (EVR)

AS Eesti Raudtee
Pikk Str 36, EE-15073 Tallinn
Tel: (+372 6) 15 86 10   Fax: (+372 6) 15 87 10
e-mail: raudtee@evr.ee
Web: http://www.evr.ee

### Key personnel
Chairman: Edward A Burkhardt
Deputy Chairman: Guido Sammelselg
Managing Director and Chairman of the Management Board: Earl J Currie
Deputy Managing Director (acting): Mark A Rosner
Infrastructure Director: David Douglas

Gauge: 1,520 mm; 1,524 mm; 750 mm
Route length: 693 km
Electrification: 132 km at 3.3 kV DC

### Diesel locomotives

| Class | Wheel arrangement | Power kW | Speed km/h | Weight tonnes | No in Service | Builders Mechanical | Builders Engine | Transmission |
|---|---|---|---|---|---|---|---|---|
| 2TE116 | Co-Co × 2 | 4,500 | 100 | 276 | 10 | Lugansk | 2 × IA5D49 | E ETM |
| M62 | Co-Co | 1,470 | 100 | 116 | 19 | Lugansk | Kolomna 14D40 | E Kharkov |
| 2M62 | Co-Co × 2 | 1,470 × 2 | 100 | 240 | 29.5 | Lugansk | Kolomna 14D40 | E Kharkov |
| ČME3 | Co-Co | 1,000 | 95 | 123 | 34 | ČKD-Sokolovo | ČKD K65310DR | E ČKD-Trakce |

### Political background
Following the declaration of independence by the three Baltic states of the former USSR in 1991, each country set up its own railway organisation. Estonian Railways became functional at the start of 1992, and its subsequent performance and planning have been in the context of Estonia's rapid drive towards a market economy and proposed eventual membership of the European Union.

In June 1995 EVR signed up to the Baltrail-2000 project, which proposed higher line speeds, better rolling stock, and co-ordinated timetables and marketing.

In 1997 the government approved plans to restructure EVR in preparation for privatisation. This followed studies by Belgian, Finnish and Irish consultancies. By the end of the last century, EVR remained a joint-stock state-owned holding company with shareholdings in a number of subsidiaries that were in process of privatisation, which was being handled by the Estonian Privatisation Agency. As part of this process three additional companies have been established covering parts of the former state system: Edelaraudtee; Elektriraudtee and EVR Ekspress (all qv). This has enabled EVR to focus on its core business, primarily freight, as privatisation of it was pursued. A shareholding of two-thirds of EVR was to be sold, making it the first Eastern European state railway company to be privatised. Ownership of infrastructure is retained by EVR, maintaining vertical integration.

A preferred bidder for EVR was no sooner announced than challenged, the alleged dubious character of a main participant being one arm of the challenge. In March 2001 a new preferred bidder was announced, Baltic Rail Services (BRS), a consortium of UK-based Jarvis International (25.5 per cent), US-based Railroad Development Corporation (5 per cent), Rail World (25.5 per cent) and Estonian investment company Ganiger OU (44 per cent). The transaction was completed in August 2001. At the end of 2001, the AIG Emerging Europe Infrastructure Fund joined the BRS consortium.

*Class 2TE116 two-section diesel locomotives at Tallinn (Eddie Barnes)*
2001/0059394

| Traffic (million) | 1998 | 1999 | 2000 |
|---|---|---|---|
| Freight tonnes | 31.6 | 37.1 | 39.5 |
| Freight tonne-km | 5,750 | 6,992 | 7,829 |

### Freight operations
Freight traffic is mainly concentrated on through routes to/from Moscow and St Petersburg. Principal commodities carried by international services include oil products, cereals, chemicals and fertilisers. Development of this transit traffic is regarded as a key priority. The main commodities carried by domestic services are oil shale and oil products from the Kohtla-Jarva and Johvi mines eastwards to Narva, and forest products.

In 2000 EVR carried 39.5 million tonnes of freight, a growth in volume of 6.5 per cent on the previous year. Transit traffic represented 73 per cent of freight volume and increased by 13.7 per cent compared with 1999.

From the late 1990s EVR implemented its KVIS system which, as well as controlling freight movements, also enables shippers to track the progress of their consignments.

The section of line in the northwest of the country between Haapsalu and Riisipere has been sold to a local businessman for freight operation. Passenger services have been withdrawn on this section.

### Improvements to existing lines
A priority for EVR has been the reconstruction and upgrading of the crucial Tallinn–Narva line, which handles transit traffic to/from the Russian Federation. This was started in 1997 and has received funding from the European Investment Bank, the European Bank for Reconstruction and Development, the EU's Phare programme, the Estonian state and EVR. Ongoing work has included doubling single-line sections and renewing track with long welded rail, concrete sleepers and modern fastenings. During renewal, track is laid to 1,524 mm gauge rather than the prevalent 1,520 mm, to reduce both wheel and rail wear. The project also includes modernisation of border facilities. In March 1998 EVR signed a supervision contract with UK consultants GIBB covering much of this work.

To accommodate heavier US-built diesel locomotives, the EVR main line network was being upgraded in 2002 to accept an axleload of 31 tonnes. Passing loops on single-line sections, especially linking Russia's October Railway and Tapa, were being lengthened to enable longer trains to be run, and widespread improvements to the railway's signalling system were anticipated.

### Traction and rolling stock
At the beginning of 2001 the EVR locomotive fleet comprised 129 diesel locomotives, of which 29 were shunters. The freight fleet comprised 4,154 wagons. Additions to the fleet in 1998 included four new 2TE116 two-section locomotives for Narva–Muuga freight traffic. Despite enabling trailing loads to be increased from 3,500 to 4,700 tonnes, these proved insufficient for traffic demand and additional locomotives of the same type have been hired from Russia. In addition, five diesel locomotives were acquired from Ukraine in December 2001, financed via Hansa Leasing.

Recent moves towards self-sufficiency in locomotive maintenance include procuring technology from Nymburk in the Czech Republic to enable EVR to undertake overhauls on Type ChME3 diesels and upgrading Muuga depot to allow the two-section 2M62 and 2TE116 machines to be serviced.

As part of its upgrading strategy, the BRS consortium was to introduce 74 refurbished General Electric C36-7 diesel-electric locomotives during 2002 to replace Russian- and Ukrainian-built machines.

### Track
**Rail type:** R43, R59, R65, UIC 60
**Sleepers:** wood; concrete (1,840/km)
**Min curvature radius:** 600 m
**Max gradient:** 1.6%
**Max permissible axleload:** 31 tonnes on main lines; 22.5 tonnes elsewhere

*UPDATED*

## EVR Ekspress AS
Telliskivi 62, Tallinn
Tel: (+372 6) 615 67 22   Fax: (+372 6) 631 12 30

### Key personnel
Chairman: Vahur Karniol
Management Board: Tarmo Jürisson; Anti Selge

### Political background
EVR Ekspress commenced operations as an independent business on 1 April 1999 in response to rail privatisation legislation approved by parliament in 1997. Following an international bidding competition, a majority shareholding of 51 per cent was acquired by a private company, the Fraser Group. The remaining share is held by Estonian Railways.

### Passenger operations
EVR Ekspress took over the international passenger services of Estonian Railways. The main routes are to Moscow, St Petersburg and Warsaw.

# ETHIOPIA

## Ministry of Transport and Communications
PO Box 1238, Addis Ababa
Tel: (+251 1) 51 61 66   Fax: (+251 1) 15 80 45

### Key personnel
Minister: Dr A Hussein
For map see entry for **Eritrea**.

## Chemins de Fer Djibouti-Ethiopien (CDE)
PO Box 1051, Addis Ababa
Tel: (+251 1) 51 72 50   Fax: (+251 1) 51 39 97

### Key personnel
President: A Waberi Gedie
General Manager: B Hussien
Deputy General Manager: M Farah Bader
Directors
   Technical: M K Roble
   Commercial: A D Absie
   Finance: Ms F Asrat

Gauge: 1,000 mm
Route length: 781 km

### Organisation
The railway runs from the port of Djibouti to Addis Ababa, a route length of 781 km, of which 100 km are in Djibouti. Since 1982 the railway has been under joint control of the republics of Djibouti and Ethiopia, with headquarters in Addis Ababa. The transport ministers of the two countries occupy the positions of president and vice-president.

### Traffic
Both rail and highway traffic and development have been severely affected by guerrilla activity since the 1970s. Rail traffic volumes have also been depressed by economic factors and poor availability of traction.

### Improvements to existing lines
Since 1987 a rehabilitation programme has been under way with aid from several European countries, notably Italy. It features re-laying with 36 kg/m rail over 80 km, with the aim of raising maximum axleload to 17.2 tonnes, increasing maximum freight train speed to 70 km/h and improving traffic regulation (at present affected by telephone dispatching). Before this work was begun only the first 171 km of the route were laid with 30 kg/m rail; the objective now is to install 36 kg/m over 300 route-km.

### Traction and rolling stock
Line-haul diesel locomotive stock consists of Alsthom units delivered between 1955 and 1985. In 1997 these were supplemented by four second-hand Alsthom locomotives procured from FEVE in Spain. There are also seven locotractors and six 400-700 kW diesel railcars, all supplied from France, two by Soulé in 1984-85. At last report around 30 passenger coaches and some 500 wagons featured in the railway's stock.

In 2000 it was reported that Spoornet, South Africa, was expected to order rolling stock to modernise the CDE fleet.

### Track
**Rail type:** 20 kg, 25 kg, 30 kg
**Sleepers:** Metalbloc
**Fastenings:** Clips and bolts
**Max axleloading:** 13.7 tonnes

# FINLAND

## Ministry of Transport & Communications

PO Box 31, FIN-00023 Government
Tel: (+358 9) 16 02   Fax: (+358 9) 16 02 85 96
Web: http://www.mintc.fi

### Key personnel
Minister: Kimmo Sasi
Permanent Secretary: Juhani Korpela
Head of Railway Affairs: Jaakko Pohjola

**UPDATED**

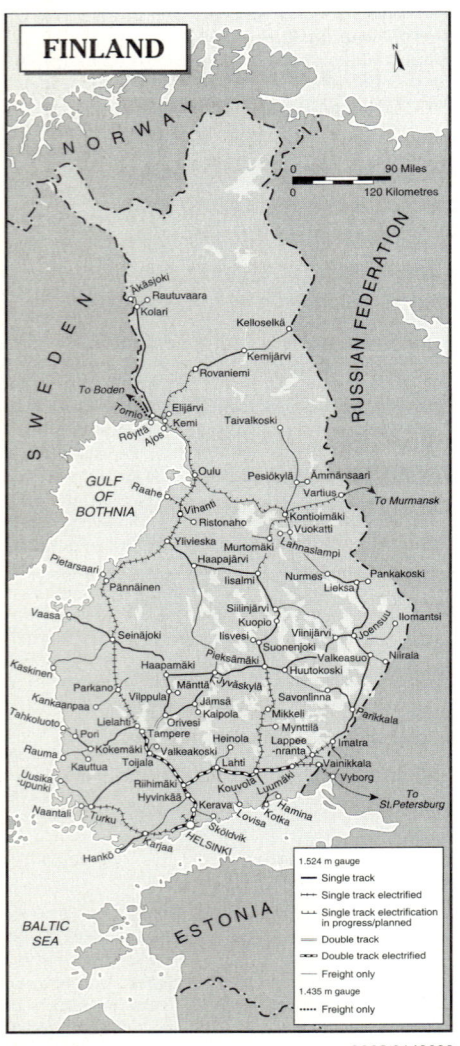

## Finnish Rail Administration (RHK)

Ratahallintokeskus
Kaivokatu 6, PO Box 185, FIN-00101 Helsinki
Tel: (+358 9) 58 40 51 11   Fax: (+358 9) 58 40 51 00
e-mail: info@rhk.fi
Web: http://www.rhk.fi/english/index.html

### Key personnel
Chief Director: Ossi Niemimuukko
Directors
 Traffic System: Anne Herneoja
 Safety: Kari Alppivuouri
 Maintenance: Markku Nummelin
 Project Management: Kari Ruohonen
Head of International Affairs: Kari Konsin
Communications Manager: Timo Saarinen
Financial Manager: Airi Kivelä
Environmental Manager: Arto Hovi

Gauge: 1,524 mm
Route length: 5,850 km
Electrification: 2,400 km at 25 kV 50 Hz AC

### Political background
Under the Rail Network Act 1994, ownership of Finland's railway infrastructure rests with the Finnish Rail Administration, which started operations on 1 July 1995 as a government agency reporting to the Ministry of Transport and Communications.

The Finnish Rail Administration is a small supervisory body, with a headquarters staff of about 60. It has overall responsibility for network development, railway safety, operator licensing and type approvals, and awards contracts (annual value €336 million) for track maintenance, construction work and traffic control. The main supplier is VR-Track Ltd (a division of the national railway company, Finnish Railways (qv)), but all infrastructure work became subject to competitive tendering in 1997.

The Administration is funded by an annual budget allocation and by charges levied for use of the infrastructure. The track fees paid by VR Ltd (see entry for Finnish Railways) equate to €54 million annually. VR Ltd remains the sole train operator at present, but the Rail Network Act includes provision for other operators to apply to run services.

The Administration's assets are valued at €6.7 billion, which includes all permanent way and fixed installations, 28,100 hectares of land, and 2,777 buildings.

### New lines
Plans have been drawn up for a 70 km direct line between Kerava (north of Helsinki) and Lahti, to supplement the present route via Riihimäki. The twin aims of the project are to improve rail connections to eastern Finland and to cater for projected traffic growth on the Helsinki–St Petersburg corridor. Construction is due to take place between 2003 and 2006. The project is costed at €336 billion.

### Improvements to existing lines
The Helsinki–Tampere–Seinäjoki lines are being upgraded for operation at speeds of up to 200 km/h. The project involves track renewal, capacity improvements, elimination or upgrading of level crossings, and installation of new safety equipment.

Track superstructures are being renewed on the Kouvola–Pieksämäki, Oulu–Tornio, Varkaus–Joensuu, Kuopio–Murtomäki, Lappeenranta–Parikkala and Kouvola–Kotka lines.

A fourth track for suburban services between Helsinki and Tikkurila (on the Tampere line) opened in 1996 and will be extended to Kerava in 2002-04. Third and fourth tracks between Helsinki and Leppävaara (on the Turku line) opened in August 2001. These new tracks allow local traffic to be separated from long-distance traffic, permitting a significant increase in local train capacity.

### Signalling and telecommunications
At the end of 2001 a total of 2,278 route-km was equipped with automatic block systems, and 2,159 km with Centralised Traffic Control (CTC).

Automatic Train Protection (ATP) is to be introduced throughout the network by 2005, with the exception of a few lightly used freight-only lines. Lines with ATP totalled 2,399 km at the end of 2001. During the year ATP was installed on 717 route-km, completing coverage of main lines.

### Electrification
At the end of 2001 a total of 2,400 route-km was under catenary, approximately 40 per cent of the network. More than 70 per cent of all traffic is now hauled by electric traction, and the long-term aim is to raise this to over 80 per cent.

Electrification of the Kokemäki–Pori branch (47 km) was completed in 1999, with the Toijala–Turku line (130 km) following in June 2000. The first electrification scheme in northern Finland, between Tuomioja and Raahe (28 km), was completed in 2001. Electrification of the Oulu–Rovaniemi line (208 km) is scheduled for completion in 2004, and the Oulu–Kontiomäki–Iisalmi/Vartius line in 2006.

### Track
**Rail type:** K 30 (30 kg/m), K 43 (43.567 kg/m), K 60 (59.74 kg/m), 54E1 (54.43 kg/m), 60E1 (60.34 kg/m)
**Sleepers:** Concrete 2,600 × 300 × 220 mm; wood 2,700 × 240 × 160 mm
**Spacing:** 1,640/km
**Rail fastenings:** Pandrol for concrete sleepers; Hey-back for wooden sleepers
**Min curve radius:** 300 m
**Max gradient:** Normally 1.25% (9 route-km with gradients up to 2%)
**Max permissible axleload:** 24.5 tonnes Russian wagons; 22.5 tonnes Finnish wagons

**UPDATED**

## Finnish Railways – VR-Group Ltd

VR-Yhtymä Oy
Vilhonkatu 13, PO Box 488, FIN-00101 Helsinki
Tel: (+358) 307 10   Fax: (+358) 30 72 17 00
Web: http://www.vr.fi

### Key personnel
VR-Group Ltd
Chairman: Martin Granholm
Chief Executive: Henri Kuitunen
Group Directors
 Finance: Veikko Vaikkinen
 Administration: Pertti Saarela
 Development: Mirja Mutikainen
 Corporate Communications: Martti Mäkinen
VR Ltd
Managing Director: Juhani Kopperi
Freight Services Director: Kari Hassinen
Passenger Services Director: Pekka Söderling
Technical Director: Markku Pesonen
Operations Director: Risto Kahri
VR-Track Ltd

*Class Sm3 Pendolino tilting trainset at Helsinki station, where a new roof has been added as part of an upgrading programme (Ken Harris)*

Managing Director: Teuvo Sivunen
Planning Director: Harry Harjula
Production Director: Arto Kukkola
Chief Electrical Engineer: Lassi Matikainen

Gauge: 1,524 mm (see entry for RHK)

## Organisation

Since 1 July 1995 the Finnish State Railways (Valtionrautatiet, VR) have been a limited-liability company, with all shares owned by the state. On the same date ownership of rail infrastructure was transferred to the Finnish Rail Administration (qv).

The parent company, VR-Group Ltd (VR-Yhtymä Oy), has about 300 staff providing financial, administrative, information technology and property management services. Its two principal subsidiaries are transport operator VR Ltd (VR Osakeyhtiö), with 9,100 staff, and VR-Track Ltd (Oy VR-Rata Ab), with 2,800 employees engaged in infrastructure construction and renewal work.

## Finance

In 2001, the VR Group recorded a net profit of €42 million on a turnover of €1.15 billion. The train-operating subsidiary, VR Ltd, had a turnover of €617 million, of which freight accounted for €335 million and passenger traffic €282 million.

Socially necessary passenger services receive an annual state subsidy of €37 million. The Finnish Rail Administration purchases infrastructure maintenance from VR-Track Ltd and traffic control services from VR Ltd.

**Finances** (FMk 1,000)

| Profit and loss account | 1998 | 1999 | 2000 |
|---|---|---|---|
| Net turnover | 6,753,212 | 6,772,838 | 6,795,681 |
| Other operating Income | 407,940 | 326,207 | 334,000 |
| Costs | 6,169,703 | 6,130,721 | 6,138,088 |
| Depreciation | 498,413 | 539,182 | 602,447 |
| Operating profit | 493,037 | 429,142 | 389,156 |
| Financial income | 81,559 | 62,860 | 65,152 |
| Direct taxes, etc | −179,243 | −139,100 | −140,748 |
| Minority interests | −9,598 | −10,366 | −6,910 |
| Net profit | 385,755 | 396,039 | 306,650 |

| Balance sheet | 1998 | 1999 | 2000 |
|---|---|---|---|
| Fixed assets | 5,110,855 | 5,747,119 | 5,986,922 |
| Current assets, Stocks | 640,134 | 397,755 | 370,898 |
| Debtors | 744,682 | 759,117 | 741,866 |
| Securities | 2,144,164 | 1,722,529 | 1,765,319 |
| Cash at bank and in hand | 47,455 | 52,068 | 49,203 |
| Total assets | 8,687,290 | 8,678,587 | 8,914,208 |
| Shareholders' equity | 6,572,626 | 6,846,512 | 6,986,773 |
| Long-term liabilities | 578,812 | 640,183 | 679,136 |
| Current liabilities | 1,535,853 | 1,191,893 | 1,248,299 |
| Total liabilities and equity | 8,687,290 | 8,678,587 | 8,914,208 |

| Traffic (million) | 1998 | 1999 | 2000 |
|---|---|---|---|
| Passenger journeys | 51.4 | 53.2 | 54.8 |
| Passenger-km | 3,377 | 3,415 | 3,405 |
| Freight tonnes | 40.7 | 40.0 | 40.5 |
| Freight tonne-km | 9,885 | 9,753 | 10,107 |

## Passenger operations

VR Ltd operates long-distance and local rail services throughout Finland. In total 55 million journeys were made in 2001, 43.4 million commuter journeys and 11.6 million long-distance journeys. Commuter journeys increased by 3 per cent while long-distance journeys fell by 2 per cent. Passenger-km totalled 3.3 billion.

VR plans to introduce tilting high-speed trains on all main intercity routes by 2010, under the brand name Pendolino S220. Two prototype sets entered trial service on the 194 km Helsinki–Turku route in late 1995 (see 'Traction and rolling stock'), and full commercial operation at up to 200 km/h began in mid-1997, cutting journey time from 2 hours to 1 hour 45 minutes. Eight more trainsets were to be delivered by the end of 2002. The first of these was introduced on the Helsinki–Turku line in September 2001, enabling the prototype sets to undergo overhaul. New Pendolino services were introduced from Helsinki to Jyväskylä in October 2001 and to Oulu and Kuopio in June 2002.

*Class Sr2 electric locomotive at Helsinki with an intercity service* (Ken Harris)

Current plans also envisage Pendolino services from Helsinki to Pori and Joensuu, and on the Turku–Tampere route.

The introduction of 220 km/h links between major centres forms part of a wider plan by VR and the government for a nationwide integrated transport system, Vali 2012. The other elements of the plan are conventional locomotive-hauled expresses, operating at 120-160 km/h with stops every 50-100 km, and local services operated by multiple-units or railbuses, with a maximum speed of 120-160 km/h and stops every 5-30 km. These rail services will be complemented by bus and shared taxi connections to stations. A regular-interval service with clock face departures and improved connections was introduced on the busiest intercity routes in southern Finland in June 2002.

VR has purchased 92 double-deck intercity coaches, all of which were in service by mid-2002. By the end of 2000, 61 were already in traffic. The 200 km/h air conditioned vehicles provide facilities which include provision for passengers with impaired mobility, bicycle stowage, a family compartment and children's play area.

In the long term VR also aims to run international Pendolino services between Helsinki and St Petersburg (443 km) once the necessary infrastructure improvements are in place. The present journey time of 6 hours 30 minutes could be cut to as little as 3 hours if the infrastructure is fully upgraded on both sides of the border.

Three daily through trains currently link Helsinki with Russia. The 'Repin' day train to St Petersburg and the 'Tolstoi' night train to Moscow are formed of Russian rolling stock, while the 'Sibelius' day train to St Petersburg employs VR stock. Passenger journeys to and from Russia increased by 16 per cent in 2001.

Within Finland a comprehensive network of overnight services, conveying sleeping cars and car-carriers, links the main cities of Helsinki, Turku and Tampere with the north and east of the country.

*Class Sm4 emu supplied by Fiat for Helsinki suburban services, seen at Helsinki* (Ken Harris)

Since 1996 the entire train fleet has been equipped with a passenger announcement system, which uses satellite positioning to determine where each train is at any time and to synchronise multilingual station and connection announcements accordingly.

### Freight operations
Marketed under the brand name VR Cargo, freight traffic has boomed in recent years. In 2001 the volume of rail freight totalled 41.7 million tonnes, including 17.7 tonnes of international traffic. The total volume increased by 2.9 per cent compared with 2000.

Eastern traffic between Finland and Russia fell by 0.6 per cent and amounted to 12.6 million tonnes. Transit traffic from Russia to the west via Finland grew by 50 per cent in 2001, amounting to 4 million tonnes. Western traffic fell slightly and totalled just over 1 million tonnes. Most of this traffic was on rail ferries to Germany and Sweden.

The rapid growth in container traffic on the Trans-Siberian route continued in 2001. Some 50,000 TEU of containers were carried between Finland and the Asia-Pacific region, a 20 per cent increase from the previous year's figure. The route from Vainikkala through Siberia to Nakhodka on the Pacific Ocean offers an alternative to conventional sea transport. Freight reaches Vainikkala from Nakhodka in 12 days. Consumer goods from the Asia-Pacific region are imported into Finland and stored in transit warehouses, while exports from Finland to the Asia-Pacific region are carried along this route.

### Traction and rolling stock
At the end of 2000 VR deployed in commercial traffic 130 electric locomotives, 299 line-haul diesel locomotives, 194 diesel shunters, two six-car Pendolino emus, 110 two-car suburban emus, 1,047 locomotive-hauled passenger coaches (including 123 sleeper and 62 catering cars), 24 car-carriers and 12,319 freight wagons.

By the end of 2001, VR had taken delivery of the first 29 members of orders for 46 Class Sr2, a 6,000 kW electric locomotive based on the Swiss Federal Railways Class 460. The 230 km/h locomotives were built by the Adtranz/SLM consortium, with Finnish manufacturer Rautaruukki Oy (subsequently acquired by Patentes Talgo of Spain) producing the bodies and undertaking final assembly.

Patentes Talgo is also supplying 92 bilevel intercity coaches to VR, 82 of which were in service by the end of 2001. The first batch of 42 comprised 30 second-class cars, each seating 113, and 12 low-floor service cars with 83 seats; business and children's compartments; wheelchair, pram and cycle accommodation; and self-service minibar. The second batch comprises 50 standard-class vehicles and 10 service cars; the latter will feature some modifications to interior layout compared with the initial batch of service cars. The aluminium vehicles are built for 160 km/h operation initially, though the design allows subsequent adaptation for speeds up to 200 km/h.

Fiat Ferroviaria (now Alstom) has supplied 10 two-car Class Sm4 emus for Helsinki suburban services, all of which had been delivered by the end of 1999. The units are of aluminium low-floor construction, giving platform-level access throughout. Each air conditioned unit seats 180 and stands 100, with wheelchair, pram and cycle space. Maximum speed is 160 km/h. The order includes an option on up to 40 more units. A follow-on order for 20 of these was placed in June 2002 for delivery in 2004-05.

In August 2001 VR placed an order with ČKD Vagónka to supply 16 railbuses for regional lines. The 63-seat vehicles will be equipped for driver-only operation and up to three units can be operated in multiple. Delivery is due to start in 2005. The contract includes an option for an additional 20 similar vehicles.

A programme to refurbish the 50 Class Sm1 emus used on Helsinki suburban services was completed in 2001. Technical upgrading and complete interior modernisation will extend the life of the units, built in 1968-73, by at least 15 years. Next in line for refurbishment are the 50 newer aluminium-bodied Class Sm2 emus. The first refurbished example of this type entered trial service in June 2002, with series refurbishment scheduled for 2003-10.

*Pendolino S220 units – Class Sm3*
In 1995 VR took delivery of two prototype six-car electric trainsets to a 220 km/h design based on the Fiat Pendolino tilt-body units of Italian Railways (FS). Assembled in Finland by Rautaruukki Oy, designated Class Sm3 and branded Pendolino S220, they entered full commercial service in mid-1997.

The Sm3 features Fiat's modified bogie design used in the ETR460 second-generation tilt-body trainsets for FS, in which all tilt and lateral active suspension apparatus is contained within the bogie. Unlike the Italian units, the Sm3 has electromagnetic brakes on each bogie and is equipped for multiple working.

Following experience with the two prototypes, VR placed an order for eight production units with Fiat Ferroviaria in December 1997. The production sets have a higher seating capacity (309) and an improved air conditioning system, and were manufactured entirely at Fiat's Savigliano plant. Five of the eight sets were in service by the end of 2001. An additional eight sets were ordered in 2002 for delivery in 2004-06 and VR has an option on a further seven trains.

**Type of coupler in standard use:** Screw on locomotive-hauled stock; automatic coupler on emus, Pendolino trainsets and some locomotive types

**Type of braking in standard use, locomotive-hauled stock:** KE-GP; KE-GP-A; KE-GP + Mg; KE-PR; KE-PR + Mg

*UPDATED*

### Diesel locomotives

| Class | Wheel arrangement | Power KW | Speed km/h | Weight tonnes | No in service | First built | Builders Mechanical | Engine | Transmission |
|---|---|---|---|---|---|---|---|---|---|
| Dv 12 | B-B | 1,000 | 125 | 64 | 192 | 1964 | Lokomo/Valmet | Tampella-MGO | H Voith L 216 rs V 16 BSHR |
| Dv 12 | B-B | 1,000 | 125 | 68 | | 1974 | Valmet | Tampella-MGO | H Voith L 216 rs V 16 BSHR |
| Dv 12 | B-B | 1,000 | 125 | 66 | | 1965 | Lokomo/Valmet | Tampella-MGO V 16 BSHR | H Voith L 216 rs |
| Dv 15 | D | 620 | 75 | 60 | 26 | 1958 | Lokomo/Valmet | Tampella-MAN W8V 22/30 AmA | H Voith L 217 U |
| Dv 16 | D | 700 | 85 | 60 | 28 | 1962 | Lokomo/Valmet | Tampella-MAN W8V 22/30 AmAuL | H Voith L 217 U |
| Dr 14 | B-B | 875 | 75 | 86 | 23 | 1969 | Lokomo | Tampella-MAN R8V 22/30 ATL | H Voith L 206 rsb |
| Dr 16 | Bo-Bo | 1,500 | 140 | 84 | 2 | 1987 | Valmet | Wärtsilä Vasa 8 V22 | E Strömberg |
| Dr 16 | Bo-Bo | 1,677 | 140 | 84 | 21 | 1987 | Valmet | Pielstick 12 PA4-V-200 VG | E Strömberg |

### Electric locomotives

| Class | Wheel arrangement | Power kW Continuous/One-hour | Speed km/h | Weight tonnes | No in service | First built | Builders Mechanical | Electrical |
|---|---|---|---|---|---|---|---|---|
| Sr 1 | Bo-Bo | 3,100/3,280 | 140/160 | 84 | 108 | 1973 | Novocherkassky | Strömberg |
| Sr 1 | Bo-Bo | 3,100/3,280 | 160 | 84 | 2 | 1993 | Hyvinkää | Strömberg |
| Sr 2 | Bo-Bo | 5,000/6,000 | 230 | 82 | 46* | 1996 | SLM/Transtech | Adtranz |

* Includes examples on order in 2002

### Electric railcars or multiple-units

| Class | Cars per unit | Motor cars per unit | Motored axles/car | Output/motor kW | Speed km/h | Units in service | First built | Builders Mechanical | Electrical |
|---|---|---|---|---|---|---|---|---|---|
| Sm 1 | 2 | 1 | 4 | 215 | 120 | 50 | 1968 | Valmet | Strömberg |
| Sm 2 | 2 | 1 | 4 | 155 | 120 | 50 | 1975 | Valmet | Strömberg |
| Sm 3 | 6 | 4 | 2 | 500 | 220 | 7 | 1994 | Fiat/Transtech/Alstom | Parizzi |
| Sm 4 | 2 | 2 | - | - | 160 | 10 | 1999 | Fiat | Parizzi |

---

# FRANCE

## Ministry of Capital Works, Transport and Housing

La Grande Arche de la Défense, F-92055 Paris La Défense Cedex 04
Tel: (+33 1) 40 81 21 22   Fax: (+33 1) 40 81 39 97

### Key personnel
Minister: Gilles de Robien
Press Relations Officer: Guénola du Couëdic
Tel: (+33 1) 40 81 31 59   Fax: (+33 1) 40 81 31 64

*UPDATED*

## French Railways Infrastructure Authority (RFF)

Réseau Ferré de France
Tour Pascal A F-92045 Paris La Défense Cedex

Tel: (+33 1) 46 96 90 72   Fax: (+33 1) 46 96 90 73
Web: http://www.rff.fr

### Key personnel
President: Claude Martinand
Director General: J-F Benard
Director, Development: Hervé de Tréglodé
Director, Finance: Olivier Debains
Director, Network: Jean-Michel Richard
Communications: Luc Roger

Gauge: 1,435 mm; 1,000 mm
Route length: 32,515 km (of which 1,286 km high-speed lines); 167 km
Electrification: 5,798 km at 1.5 kV DC; 8,195 km at 25 kV 50 Hz AC; 111 km at other voltages

### Organisation
RFF was established at the beginning of 1997 as a 'Public Establishment of Industrial and Commercial Character' (EPIC) to assume the management and development of, and investment in, the national rail infrastructure. It took over from SNCF control of all track, bridges and other structures, station platforms, intermodal freight terminals, marshalling yards, electrification infrastructure, signalling and telecommunications.

These assets are valued at €30.7 billion. The new EPIC will have to balance its accounts from year to year, receiving revenue from SNCF €1.63 billion in 2001 – and other operators for access to the network plus an infrastructure grant from central government and subsidies from national and local government for individual projects.

## France/RAILWAY SYSTEMS

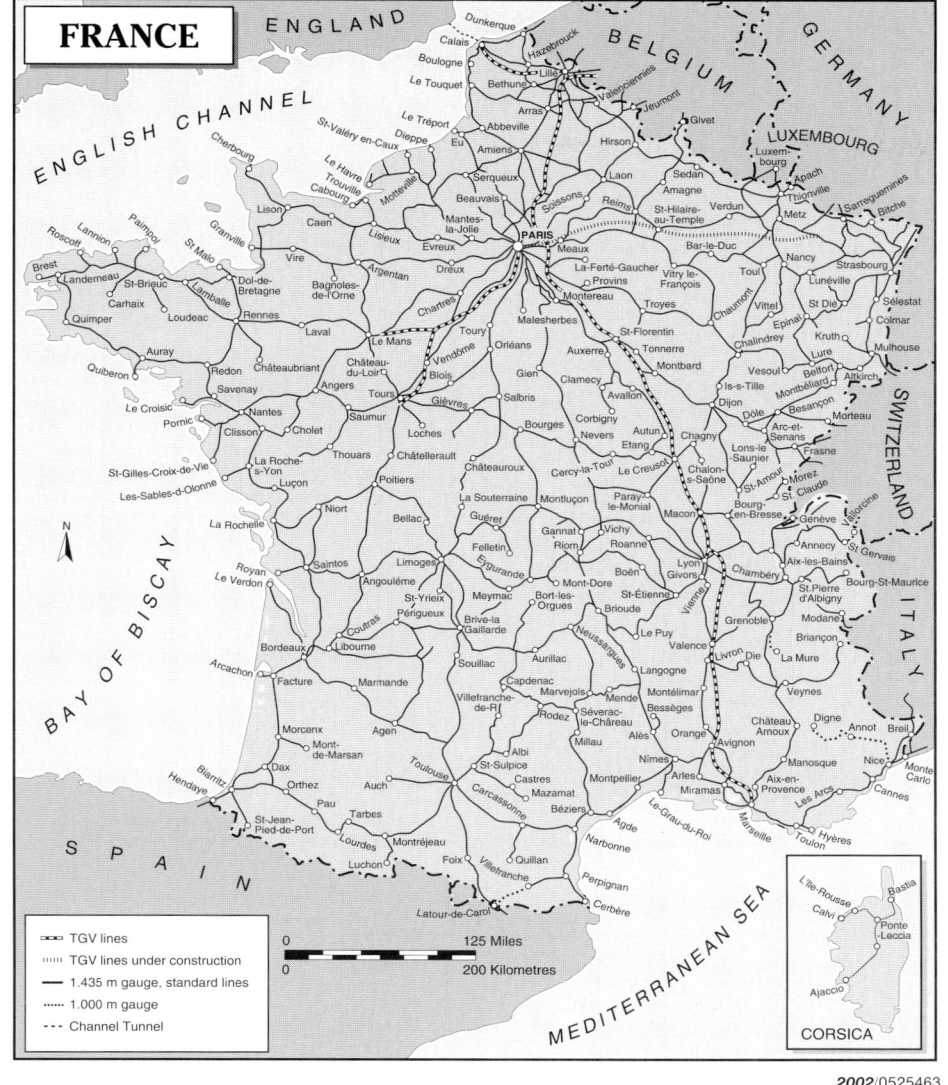

*[Map of France showing railway network, legend: TGV lines, TGV lines under construction, 1.435 m gauge standard lines, 1.000 m gauge, Channel Tunnel]*

2002/0525463

In 2001, RFF's investment totalled €1,327 million, of which €299 million was committed to extensions to the TGV network, €183 million to development of the classic network and €775 on maintenance of the system. SNCF was paid €2,633 million in management charges. In 2002, RFF was pressing the French government to write off the majority of its debt, which stood at €23.25 billion. Debt servicing costs in 2001 were €2,514 million. Maintenance and operation is, initially, subcontracted to SNCF which prepares the timetable and manages traffic movements as well as monitoring, maintaining and repairing installations. In this aspect, the situation in France differs from that in several other European countries where infrastructure has been completely separated from operations. RFF was to receive €1,702 million from central government for servicing the debt in 2001.

Following worries, particularly from trade unions, that the split of RFF/SNCF was a prelude to privatisation, the French government created the *Conseil Supérieur du Service Public Ferroviaire* (CSSPF), a consultative body which will give its opinion on major changes in rail policy and co-ordinate RFF and SNCF.

SNCF has created a new department to manage stations, improve the passenger environment and enhance interchanges with other transport modes. Investment has been doubled to €305 million by 2003.

*Access charges*
RFF introduced a provisional track access charging system in 1997 which has since been revised with higher prices. Charges vary according to the route taken and time of day on busy lines, but are highest in peak periods (06.30-09.00 and 17.00-20.00). The network is divided into four categories of line with different charges. Congested lines around large cities have the highest charges, with prices falling on high-speed lines, less again on interurban lines, and lowest on the rest of the network, which charge €0,23 per km. This system favours freight traffic. The charge is split into a right of access, reservation of a path and use of the path. In 2001 RFF was proposing to reduce the right of access charge in order to favour new operators while increasing charges for use of a path. There are other charges for using marshalling yards and 'stabling' wagons. RFF raised charges to SNCF in 1999 from €930 million to €1,464 million. In order not to endanger SNCF's recovery, the difference was initially financed by the state.

At the end of 2000, RFF was still being set up, having only 250 staff.

A guarantee of open access to outside rail companies operating international services was made law in 1995, with the French state providing licences. However, this is being implemented in a very restricted fashion. SNCF and the government have promoted co-operation rather than competition. By mid-2002, the only open access services on RFF metals were a daily pair of intermodal trains between Paris and Italy operated by TAB but hauled by SNCF traction and a BASF train from Germany to Lauterbourg, 2 km across the border. In January 1998, RFF, SNCF, CFL and SNCB launched Europe's first 'freight freeway' between Muizen, Belgium and Lyon, France via Luxembourg. This was quickly extended to Gioia Tauro in southern Italy, Marseilles in France, and Spain. A second corridor was launched in March 1999 from Glasgow via the Channel Tunnel, France, Germany and Austria to Sopron in Hungary. The aim is to reduce waiting time for existing trains and create new, fast paths to allow capacity expansion. A 'one-stop-shop' for each corridor acts for railways in co-ordinating, allocating and charging for paths.

### Finances
RFF reported a loss of €1,646 million in 2001 compared with €1,700 million in 2000. In Spring 2001, the company asked the French government to write off half its €23 billion debt.

| Expenditure (€) | 1999 | 2000 | 2001 |
| --- | --- | --- | --- |
| Management payment to SNCF | 2,513 | 2,508 | 2,522 |
| Electricity | 383 | 134 | 137 |
| Depreciation | 749 | 784 | 860 |
| Other | 195 | 277 | 327 |
| Total operating expenses | 3,840 | 3,703 | 3,846 |
| Financial expenses | 1,865 | 2,360 | 2,502 |
| Exceptional charges | 38 | 41 | 27 |
| Total expenditure | 5,743 | 6,104 | 6,376 |

| Revenue | | | |
| --- | --- | --- | --- |
| Track access charges | 1,457 | 1,499 | 1,630 |
| Sales of electricity | 383 | 134 | 137 |
| State contribution | 1,648 | 1,633 | 1,606 |
| Other | 675 | 1,138 | 1,357 |
| Total operating revenue | 4,163 | 4,404 | 4,730 |
| Profit/loss | −1,580 | −1,700 | −1,646 |

| Investment | | | |
| --- | --- | --- | --- |
| Renewal of existing infrastructure | 646 | 636 | 678 |
| New development projects | | | |
| - TGV | 797 | 551 | 299 |
| - Other lines | 386 | 157 | 183 |
| Modification of network | 27 | 148 | 167 |
| Total | 1,856 | 1,492 | 1,327 |

### New lines
France's first high-speed line, TGV-Paris Sud-Est (TGV-PSE), from the suburbs of Paris to Lyon, opened in two stages in 1981 and 1983 and was extended to Valence in 1994. It was followed by the Atlantique line opened in

*Interior of Avignon station, one of three newly constructed for TGV-Méditerranée services (David Haydock)*
2001/0114235

1989-90, the Nord Europe in 1993, and the Jonction (Interconnexion) linking lines north and south of Paris in 1994-96. The TGV-Méditerranée opened on 10 June 2001, and the TGV-Est Européen was approved in 1999.

The 'TGV Routes' map shows the current extent of existing routes and of plans at an advanced stage. See earlier editions of JWR for full details of the background.

*TGV-Méditerranée*

The TGV-Med line, which extends southward from Valence to L'Estaque (218.7 km) on the approach to Marseille (3 hours from Paris), and from Avignon to Manduel-Redessan near Nîmes (32.7 km) opened on 10 June 2001. The line has three new stations, at Valence, Avignon and Aix-en-Provence. The route was revised several times and cut back from Lunel near Montpellier, but costs increased – from €2.71 billion to €3.69 billion (this sum includes the upgrade of the Paris Sud-Est line to 300 km/h standards, see below) – reducing the project's estimated rate of return from 12 to 6.4 per cent, below the 8 per cent limit that SNCF put on financing projects entirely from its own funds. The state therefore contributed €366 million towards the project. The European Investment Bank has made loans totalling €396 million for the line.

There are now more than 1,050 km of uninterrupted high-speed lines from Calais to the outskirts of Marseille. On 27 May 2001, SNCF carried out an 'endurance run' with a standard TGV Réseau set and completed this journey in exactly 3 hours 30 minutes, achieving an average speed of almost 305 km/h.

RFF now sees a possible TGV Côte d'Azur, taking high-speed running to Toulon and the French Riviera, as a high priority.

*TGV L-R*

The TGV-Languedoc-Roussillon is a 325 km extension of the Nîmes branch of the TGV-Méditerranée to Perpignan, linking into new lines to Barcelona and Madrid. This line will now be built in stages. A new 60.5 km line from Manduel to the west side of Nîmes, avoiding Nîmes and Montpellier, with new stations serving each city, is to be built by 2008. This will be a mixed TGV and freight line and will cost €905 million. The other section to be built quickly will be from Perpignan to Le Perthus, (24.6 km) continuing to Figueras in Spain. This will also be a mixed-use line and will include a 7.3 km tunnel under the Pyrenees. Cost of the latter will be €549 million plus €122 million for installations in Perpignan. Completion is scheduled for 2005. The central section has yet to find full financing. In the interim €122 million will be invested in extra capacity on the Montpellier—Perpignan classic line. RFF is carrying out feasibility studies of the line but completion is not expected before 2008.

*TGV-Est Européen*

A new 406 km line from Paris to Strasbourg received its 'Declaration of Public Utility' in 1996 but the stumbling block for this project was its low estimated rate of return – of only 1.08 per cent. Savings have been achieved by limiting the first stage of construction to the 300 km Vaires—Baudrecourt (Paris—Metz) section, at a cost of €3,125 million. This will mean projected travel times would be achieved to Reims, Metz and Nancy but that Strasbourg would be 2 hours 20 minutes from Paris rather than 1 hour 50 minutes as planned, although still an improvement on the present best of 4 hours. Construction is being supported by the EU, Luxembourg and the regions and *départements* served en route. Construction started in early 2002. Completion will be in 2006. Extension to Strasbourg is expected in 2010. There will be three new stations on the line: Champagne-Ardenne, near Reims; Meuse, near Verdun; and Lorraine, between Nancy and Metz. The Lorraine station was originally planned near the local airport and motorway but RFF and SNCF have agreed it should now be built where the LGV crosses the existing Metz—Nancy line to provide interchange with regional trains.

The line is to be designed for operation at 350 km/h although, initially, TGV sets will be limited to 320 km/h. Trains employed will be refurbished TGV Réseau sets and German ICEs.

Frankfurt (Main) will be 3 hours 35 minutes from Paris (6 hours at present), Basle 3 hours 30 minutes (4 hours 45 minutes) and Munich 5 hours 30 minutes (8 hours 20 minutes). Plans to extend the high-speed line from the Strasbourg area into Germany were still under discussion in 2002.

*TGV Rhin-Rhône*

The first, eastern branch of this line will run 190 km from Genlis, east of Dijon to Lutterbach on the outskirts of Mulhouse with new stations at Auxon near Besançon and at Meroux near Belfort. Cost is put at €1,875 billion. The route of the line was approved in 2001 and declared of public utility in 2002. Construction of an initial section is expected to start in 2004 for completion in 2008. At a later date, a western branch will link Dijon to the Paris—Lyon LGV.

A southern branch, costing €2,287 billion, from a point near Dole to the outskirts of Lyon, with a new station in the Bresse area, will allow much faster services between Germany/Strasbourg and Lyon/south of France. As the line will not be heavily used by passenger trains, it is SNCF's intention to use it to divert freight traffic from congested lines in the Dijon area. This has complicated the exact choice of route, with five variations under study.

*LGV Ouest*

The route for the 197 km LGV Ouest from Le Mans to Rennes was chosen in late 2000. A new line will avoid Le Mans to the north then continue south of the existing line to the outskirts of Rennes. A branch to Sablé-sur-Sarthe will link to the existing Le Mans—Nantes line, already largely upgraded for 220 km/h, and another will serve Laval. On completion Paris—Rennes times will be cut from 2 hours to 1 hour 20 minutes. The line will cost €1.6 billion. Construction may be staged with Laval served by 2010 and Rennes by 2015. Tilting TGV sets are to be used to reduce journey times to the west of Rennes, allowing Paris to Quimper and Brest journey times of 3 hours.

*Other TGV schemes*

Work is advancing on the TGV-Aquitaine scheme, extending high-speed running over the 343 km from Tours to Bordeaux at a cost of €3 billion. This will cut the Paris—Bordeaux journey time from 3 hours to 2 hours 12 minutes. A route close to the existing line via Poitiers and Angoulême has been confirmed. Studies are taking place into the upgrading of the Bordeaux—Dax line for 220 km/h.

Most of the remainder of the 1991 TGV Master Plan for 16 projects totalling 3,442 km of new lines was abandoned in early 1999. Instead, some classic routes will be upgraded to carry tilting TGVs.

*Liaison Transalpine*

In March 2000, work started on the construction of a 52.7 km base tunnel on the Lyon—Turin route, with completion planned by 2015 at a cost of €10 billion. The tunnel is to have bores sufficiently large to allow its use by shuttle trains carrying complete lorries. Full details appear in the entry for Italy. The French will also build a new high-speed line from Lyon to Chambéry and from Chambéry to the base tunnel.

Prior to opening of the Alpine base tunnel, the line from Ambérieu to Modane via Chambéry and the Fréjus tunnel to Italy will be upgraded, with the tunnel enlarged to B+ loading gauge by 2004-5. A shuttle service carrying complete lorries will be introduced between France and Italy in 2002.

*EOLE*

A new underground route for Paris with main line clearances, known as EOLE (East-West Express Link) or RER line E, opened in July 1999 and now routes some Gare de l'Est local trains via new subterranean stations at Magenta (between Gares de l'Est and Nord) to Haussmann, near the St Lazare terminus. The line will later be extended to Pont Cardinet, where it will connect with suburban lines in the west of Paris. EOLE services will be extended to Tournan by 2006.

*Liaison Normandie-Val de Seine*

In order to link Normandy with Roissy-Charles de Gaulle airport and the TGV network, studies were taking place in 2001 into the use of the EOLE line by TGVs. A link with EOLE and capacity improvements between Epône and Achères and in Mantes-la-Jolie were being studied.

**Improvements to existing lines**

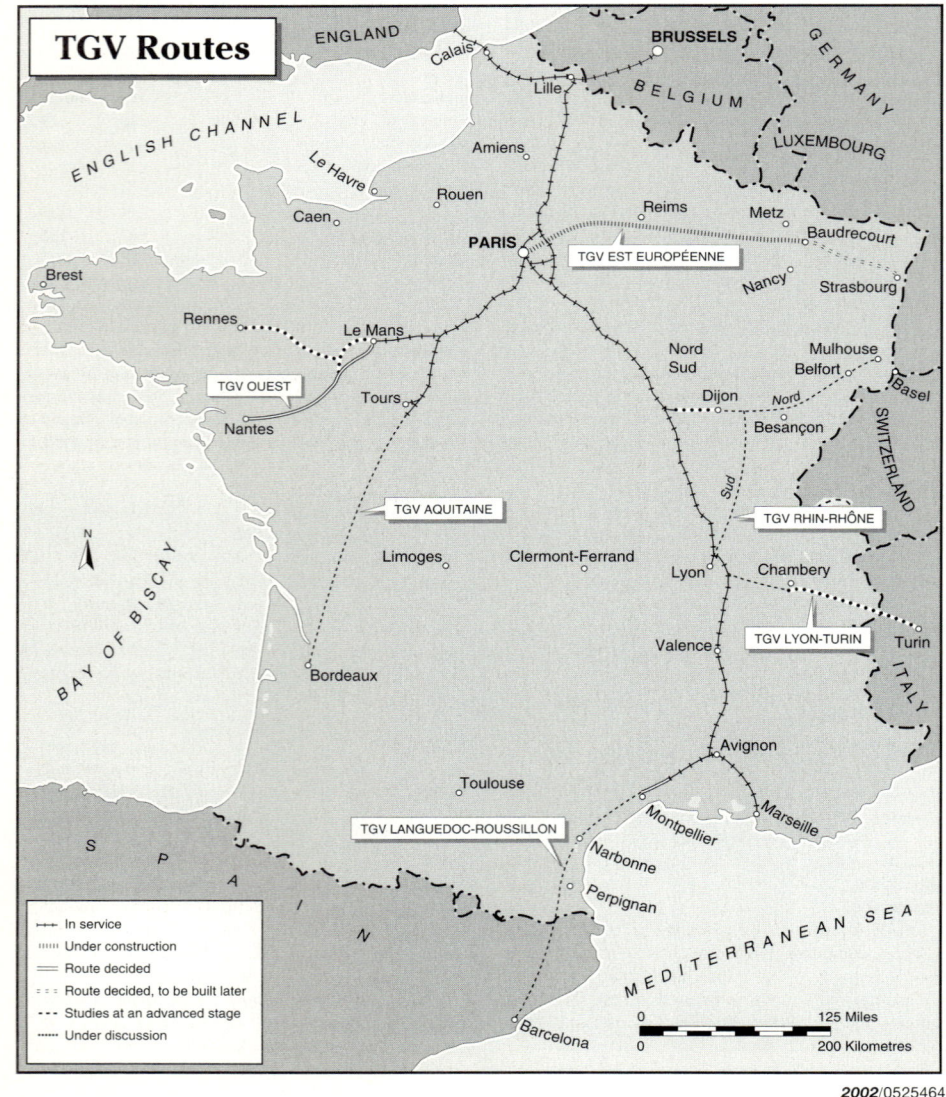

Between 1996 and 2001 the LGV Paris Sud-Est, opened in 1981, was completely upgraded. Renewal work involved the upgrading of the line's signalling system to TVM 300

standards and provision of new track and ballast. This allowed train headways to be reduced from 5 to 4 minutes (later to 3 minutes) and maximum speed raised from 270 to 300 km/h for the opening of the TGV-Méditerranée line.

SNCF and Swiss Federal Railways have agreed to share the cost of reopening and upgrading the La Cluse to Bellegarde line which will reduce Paris–Geneva TGV journey times from 3 hours 30 minutes to 3 hours. Cost is estimated at up to €270 million, with completion due by 2006. The Dole–Pontarlier line will also be upgraded at a cost of €61 million, cutting 25 minutes from Paris–Lausanne timings.

*Paris region master plan*
A 2000-2006 plan places the emphasis on development of orbital routes. An increase in population of 15 per cent, mostly in the outer suburbs, will heighten demand for transport by 60 per cent. Journeys between outer suburbs are expected to grow by 70 per cent.

To respond to demand for inter-suburb travel, existing lines will be adapted and linked by new sections of line. By 2006, the Grande Ceinture freight-only line from Sartrouville to Noisy-le-Sec (first phase of the 'Tangentielle Nord') is to reopen at a cost of €335 million, with a branch from Pontoise to Epinay-sur-Seine at a later stage. This will involve widening from two to four tracks over some sections. 'Tangentielle Sud-Ouest' will create a line from Cergy new town in the northwest to Melun in the southeast, also by 2006. This will use existing lines from Cergy to Achères, the reopened and electrified western Grande Ceinture to Versailles, existing lines to Epinay-sur-Orge, a new line from Epinay to Evry, then existing lines to Melun. This will cost €381 million.

Extensions to the RER network also include extension of line C from Montigny-Beauchamp to Pontoise, opened in August 2000 and the elimination of certain congestion 'black spots'.

On the Mediterranean coast, the 17 km Cannes–Grasse line is being rebuilt and electrified for passenger trains as part of a plan for a Cannes–Nice RER-type system.

*Removing freight congestion*
A special effort will be made during the period 2000-10 to eliminate bottlenecks, in particular to enable freight traffic to grow. Specific projects include: quadrupling the river Garonne bridge in Bordeaux at a cost of €300 million; adding a fourth track between Toury and Cercottes (Paris–Orléans route); reopening and electrification of the Rouen avoiding line; widening Dunkerque–Hazebrouck–Douai; providing a third track on the Sucy–Benneuil–Valenton line (Paris Orbital); and laying a fourth track between Metz and Woippy.

An eastern bypass line for Lyon is being considered but in the meantime a western bypass will be created by refurbishing existing lines at a cost of €439 million.

RFF is also refurbishing the mountainous Béziers–Neussargues line (280 km) and electrifying the 111 km Clermont Ferrand–Neussargues line as a relief route for north-south freight traffic.

The French and Spanish governments have agreed to the reopening of the Pau–Canfranc line and to conversion of the Canfranc–Zaragoza line to 1,435 mm gauge to create a relief route for freight.

*Regional upgrading*

*Paris–Limoges–Toulouse*
RFF, SNCF and the regions concerned are to finance an upgrade of this line to allow tilting train operations by 2006. Cost is €242 million, of which €96 million is for infrastructure. Work will include eliminating level crossings and reinforcing the 1,500 V DC supply. Speeds of up to 220 km/h will be possible north of Vierzon, 170 to 220 km/h from Vierzon to Limoges and 160 km/h south of Limoges.

The Centre region is to finance reopening of the 76 km Chartres–Orléans line by 2006 at a cost of €64 million, the Pays de Loire region the Niort–Fontenay-le-Combe line and the PACA region the Grasse–Cannes line, all by 2006. See also Electrification.

RFF, SNCF and the Basse Normandie region are financing a €109 million upgrade of the cross-country Caen–Rennes line, including electrification at 25 kV AC from Lison to Saint Lô and construction of a new 8 km branch to the Mont St Michel, France's premier tourist site outside Paris.

## Signalling and telecommunications

SNCF has installed an automatic train protection system, a version of the L M Ericsson automatic train and speed control system developed jointly with MTE-Alsthom. SNCF designates the system as KVB (*Contrôle de Vitesse par Balises*). The system, employing track-mounted transponders, identifies temporary speed restrictions as well as signal aspects. All 5,000 main line locomotives and around three-quarters of the network's 16,000 signals have been equipped.

*ETCS*
SNCF is participating in the validation of the EIRENE digital radio standard for European railways which is part of the European Train Control System (ETCS). EIRENE will be tested until 1999 on a 32 km section of the Jonction high-speed line and 55 km of the Nord Europe line.

### Electrification

All main passenger and freight lines in France, except for Paris–Troyes–Mulhouse, are now electrified. In general, lines north and east of Paris are electrified at 25 kV AC and those south of Paris at 1.5 V DC. Almost all recent projects, including fill-ins in the 1.5 V DC area, have been at 25 kV AC necessitating the use of dual-voltage traction and rolling stock.

Electrification of the 42 km Persan-Beaumont to Beauvais line north of Paris was completed in November 1999. Plouaret to Lannion was completed in May 2000.

New schemes to go ahead in the period 2000-06 include: Gretz–Troyes; Tours–Vierzon; Lison–St Lô; Nantes–Les Sables d'Olonne; Rennes–St Malo; Quimper–Landerneau; St-Etienne–Firminy; and Lutterbach–Thann. All these schemes also include upgrading for higher speeds. Electrification of branches from Nancy to Remiremont (78 km) and St Dié (51 km) plus Reims–Chalons-sur-Marne is included in the TGV-Est project.

Other electrification schemes under study include: Morcenx to Mont-de-Marsan in the southwest; Bourges–Saincaize; Marseilles–Aix-en-Provence; Laroche–Migennes–Auxerre; and Gières–Montmélian.

### Track

**Rails:** 60 kg/m where traffic exceeds 30,000 tonnes/day; 50 kg/m elsewhere; UIC 60 on LGVs
**Sleepers:** Wood (oak or tropical wood) 150 mm thick; concrete (mono- or duo-block) 220 mm thick
**Spacing:** 1,600-1,722/km
**Fastenings:** Wooden sleepers: rigid or screw or elastic (Types NR and NABLA); concrete sleepers: elastic or NR or NABLA type
**Min curve radius:** 150 m (in depots)
**Max gradient:** 4%
**Max axleloading:** (on selected routes): 22.5 tonnes

*UPDATED*

---

## French National Railways (SNCF)

Société Nationale des Chemins de Fer Français
34 rue du Commandant Mouchotte, F-75699, Paris Cedex 14
Tel: (+33 1) 53 25 60 00
Web: http://www.sncf.fr

### Key personnel
President: Louis Gallois
Director (President's Cabinet): Gerard Gibot
Director (Strategy): Philippe Citroen
Director (European Affairs): Marie-Pierre Meynard
Director (Research and Technology):
  Philippe Renard
Secretary, Council of Administration: Michèle Audibet
Directors
  Finance: Claire Dreyfus-Cloarec
  Human Resources: Pierre Izard
  Operating: Jacques Couvert
  Station Developments: Pascal Lupo
  Traction & Rolling Stock: Roland Bonnepart
  International Development: Pierre-Louis Rochet
Secretary General: Paul Mingasson
Business Directors
  Long-distance Passenger: Guillaume Pepy
  Press Service: Michel Pronost
  Tel: (+33 1) 53 25 73 88
  Ile de France Passenger: Deny Dartigues
  Press Service: Pierre Yaouanq
  Tel: (+33 1) 53 25 70 60
  Urban and Regional Passenger: Christian Cochet
  Press Service: Fabienne Constance
  Tel: (+33 1) 53 25 86 09
  Freight: Francis Rol-Tanguy
  Press Service: Claude Biarotte
  Tel: (+33 1) 53 25 78 93
  Sernam: Christian Rivet

Director of Communications: Jean-Marie Gerbaux
Head of Press Service: Jean-Paul Boulet

### Political background
SNCF is a 'Public Establishment of an Industrial and Commercial Character' or EPIC, being entirely state-owned but with a legally autonomous status.

Under arrangements to separate SNCF's operations from infrastructure management, the government accepted future responsibility for infrastructure finance and €25.6 billion of SNCF's debt, the part linked to infrastructure investment and past infrastructure losses, leaving €762-930 million which corresponds to other investment, such as that in traction and rolling stock. The infrastructure debt has been transferred to a new EPIC, known as *Réseau Ferré de France* (RFF, qv). RFF now owns all SNCF rail infrastructure as defined by European Union rules. SNCF remains sole manager of the network, having responsibility for allocating train paths and approving new operators. SNCF's own trains will receive first priority for train paths.

Another feature of the new arrangements is the transfer of greater organisational powers to regional government. Following a period of trials, all regions took over full responsibility for planning and finance of local rail transport from 2002. This leaves SNCF merely as a supplier of trains and staff, for which it retains its monopoly. Most regions are investing in new and refurbished rolling stock and boosting service frequencies.

As a consequence of the passage of a law on air quality, all local authorities have produced a study of local transport needs (PDU). Most have opted to improve public transport and some will invest in freight infrastructure as part of state/region contracts in the period 2000-2006.

SNCF put together a new strategy in 1996 under a new president, Louis Gallois.

Following a major public opinion survey in early 1996, a series of 47 action programmes were drawn up. In general, Louis Gallois has adopted a strategy of consolidation without the sort of massive investment seen in recent years and reducing losses by increasing business volumes within existing resources. This will be done by improving passenger services by increasing frequencies, improving stations and information, simplifying and cutting fares. On freight services, SNCF aims to respond more quickly to customer demand and increase utilisation of its trains. Customers were surveyed again in late 1997 with results showing SNCF had improved its image.

Although still state-owned, SNCF now bids for contracts to manage rail services within and outside France, particularly in Europe through its SNCF Participations subsidiary and Keolis (see below). SNCF has also shown interest in the acquisition of EWS in the UK and the freight activity of Polish State Railways. Through Keolis (formerly VIA-GTI) SNCF jointly manages some passenger operations abroad.

### Organisation
SNCF is divided into four businesses, each of which has its own budget and bottom-line responsibility: Long-Distance Passenger (Grandes Lignes); Urban and Regional Passenger (Transports de Proximité Régionaux et Locaux); Paris Region Passenger (Ile de France); and Freight (Fret SNCF). Each Business Director contracts with the other departments for the means of production and back-up services. Regional and Paris Region passenger services are heavily subsidised while other activities are required to break even.

SNCF has moved slowly to assigning dedicated resources to each division, although less strictly than in other European countries. A plan to allocate staff more closely to activity sector, known as Cap Clients, was shelved in April 2001 after a two-week strike.

Apart from the rail core in France, SNCF has full or part ownership of over 400 other companies connected with transport throughout the world, including road hauliers, hotels, travel agencies and ferry operators. Indeed, through its subsidiaries, SNCF is the main road haulier in France. In 1997 73 per cent of turnover came from, and 84 per cent of staff were employed in, the core business.

An early decision taken by Louis Gallois after his appointment to the SNCF presidency was to move out of the historic railway headquarters near Paris St Lazare and to reduce the number of managers considerably. Staff in the Paris HQ number 10,900 out of 177,000 staff – around 6 per cent of SNCF staff compared with 1-2 per cent in comparable industries. The eventual aim will be to move more staff to regional headquarters and to bring more management in contact with the customers.

| Traffic (million) | 1996 | 1997 | 1998 |
|---|---|---|---|
| Passenger journeys | 786 | 807 | 823 |
| of which Paris suburban | 510 | 519 | 528 |
| Passenger-km | 59,770 | 61,830 | 64,460 |
| of which Paris suburban | 8,870 | 9,020 | 9,130 |
| Freight tonnes | 123.8 | 132.2 | 133.8 |
| Freight tonne-km | 48,310 | 52,630 | 52,660 |

### Finance

A major strike at the end of 1995 resulted in a record deficit of €2,53 billion, precipitating the resignation of the SNCF President and leading to the already-mentioned reorganisation. Results since 1997 have shown major growth.

Following several years in which ambitious growth forecasts proved wide of the mark, SNCF produced less ambitious predictions for the five years 1995-1999. Revenue was predicted to rise from €8.37 billion to between €8.64 and 9.04 billion. This took account of a drop of FFr1.3 billion annual loss of revenue once compulsory military service ends.

SNCF recorded a loss of €134 million in 2001, compared with a surplus of €68 million in 2000. The main reason was a collapse in freight traffic. Long-distance passenger traffic was up 3.2 per cent and revenue by 5.0 per cent. Regional passenger traffic was up 5 per cent and revenue by 2.1 per cent. Passenger traffic in the Paris region rose by 2.8 per cent and revenue by 2.1 per cent. Freight traffic rose 6 per cent in 2000.

| Finances (FFr million) | 1997 | 1998 |
|---|---|---|
| **Revenue** | | |
| Grandes Lignes | 20,490 | 22,455 |
| TER | 2,959 | 3,012 |
| Ile de France | 4,067 | 4,126 |
| Fret | 12,519 | 12,492 |
| Sernam | 3,598 | 3,585 |
| State compensation | 10,555 | 11,274 |
| Total operating revenue | 54,188 | 56,944 |
| Other production revenue | 3,499 | 3,521 |
| Transfer from RFF | 16,800 | 16,600 |
| Work for RFF | 4,997 | 5,535 |
| Own work capitalised | 3,495 | 2,991 |
| State contribution | 7,033 | 7,454 |
| Other operating revenue | 2,380 | 1,522 |
| Financial revenue | 11,425 | 12,686 |
| Exceptional items | 5,581 | 5,020 |
| Surplus/Loss | –959 | –649 |
| Total revenue | 110,357 | 112,922 |
| **Expenditure** | | |
| Materials, supplies, services | 15,537 | 15,206 |
| Subcontractors | 13,336 | 13,958 |
| Infrastructure charges | 6,008 | 6,205 |
| Staff | 44,729 | 45,333 |
| Other | 3,857 | 4,024 |
| Depreciation | 7,843 | 7,878 |
| Financial charges | 13,144 | 14,191 |
| Exceptional charges | 5,903 | 6,127 |
| Total costs | 110,357 | 112,922 |

### Passenger operations

SNCF's passenger operations are divided into three sectors:
Grandes Lignes for long-distance services including TGV;
Transports de Proximité Régionaux et Locaux for local semi-fast and stopping trains;
Ile de France for Paris region suburban trains.
Grandes Lignes and Ile de France have their own directors but responsibility for regional services is delegated to local managers who negotiate directly with regional councils, albeit with co-ordination by the Transports de Proximité Regionaux et Locaux support service. SNCF has reorganised the boundaries of several of its regions to correspond more closely to the territory of regional government.

*Long-distance services*
Grandes Lignes (GL) is SNCF's main activity, in terms of turnover and the contribution made to infrastructure from the surplus of revenue over direct costs. This surplus has exceeded €450 million in most recent years. In 1999, Grandes Lignes traffic was 49.3 billion passenger-km. TGV services, which extend well beyond the limits of the new infrastructure, produce a growing proportion of GL revenue – reaching 58 per cent in 2001. Passenger-km on TGV services rose from 10.49 billion in 1988 to 34 billion in 2001 but fell on 'classic' services from 37 billion to 17 billion.

SNCF is carrying out improvements line-by-line to long-distance services with the aim of improving market share and countering air competition and new motorways. Services have been recast on the following routes, mainly producing frequency increases within existing resources: Paris-Limoges, where competition is coming from a new motorway; Paris-Strasbourg and Paris-Basle, where air competition is increasing.

In 1998, SNCF introduced its first-ever strict clock-face interval timetable on a major route from Paris to Lyon. This was followed by Paris-Lille. Success was such that further lines are benefiting, including Paris-Nantes in May 1999 and Paris-Rennes in December 2000.

The LGV Méditerranée opened on 10 June 2001, allowing a three-hour timing for the 250 km from Paris to France's second city, Marseille. Following the success of regular interval timetables elsewhere, the service is exactly hourly off-peak and half-hourly in the peaks. Services are operated mainly by TGV Duplex sets. Most other cities south of Lyon saw major cuts in journey times. In its first year, rail travel on the corridor rose by 35 per cent.

A major part of plans on non-TGV routes has been the modernisation of 710 of SNCF's 3,300 Corail day coaches, which on average are 17 years old. Series refurbishment, at a cost of €50,000 per coach, started in 1995 and modernised vehicles have been introduced on services from Paris to Cherbourg, Limoges, Metz, Strasbourg, Basle, Le Havre and Clermont-Ferrand. SNCF is now to undertake a more profound refurbishment of Corail stock from 2001.

Poorly used services will continue to be pruned or transferred to regional responsibility. Cross-country services such as Bordeaux-Lyon have been drastically reduced in recent years.

SNCF relaunched overnight services in May 2000 with air conditioned stock, fixed train formations, a 'reception area', improved facilities in couchette coaches and much-increased security. Scheduled stops between midnight and 06.00 have been abolished. Usage of overnight trains is rising slowly and reached about 4 million passengers in 1999.

*International services*
To improve management of international passenger services and to stem the general decline in their use, SNCF has moved to create joint ventures (*Groupement d'Intérêt Economique* or GIE) with other national operators. GL was aiming to increase the proportion of revenue from international services from 14 per cent in 1998 to 24 per cent by 2000.

Apart from Eurostar services, the first joint venture, concerning Paris-Lausanne/Bern TGV services, was created in 1993 with Swiss Federal Railways. The first benefit from this agreement was the extension from December 1995 of one Paris-Lausanne service to Brig in order to tap the winter sports market. The GIE has extended the Bern service to Zürich and refurbished the nine three-voltage TGV sets capable of operation into Switzerland. In January 2000, the status of the GIE was changed and the organisation renamed Rail France Suisse SAS (see entry in Operators of international rail services in Europe section) and in 2002, the service was renamed Lyria. In 2001, these services carried 900,000 passengers and turnover rose by 5.5 per cent.

In 1994, SNCF and Italian Railways (FS) created a GIE known as 'Alpetunnel', a company which will study the future TGV Lyon-Turin. At the same time, SNCF and FS agreed on measures designed to boost passenger figures on France-Italy services by 50 per cent. The result was a direct daytime TGV service from September 1996 between Paris and Milan via Turin. At the same time FS ETR.460 'Pendolino' tilting trainsets took over the Milan-Turin-Lyon service. In September 1997, SNCF and FS relaunched overnight services between Paris and Italy under the new 'Artesia' branding. In 2001, Artesia night services carried 932,000 passengers. Turnover rose by 7 per cent.

In 1994, SNCF and Belgian Railways signed a similar agreement with the aim of developing Paris-Brussels services, as well as extensions to Antwerp and Liège. The

*TGV Duplex bilevel high-speed trainset arriving at Lyon Part Dieu from Paris* (David Haydock)

*BB15000 electric locomotive near Courcelles with the Brussels—Milan 'Vauban' EuroCity service* (John C Baker)

company Westrail International was formed to market Thalys TGV services to Amsterdam and Cologne (see entry on Belgium). In May 1999, this company was renamed Thalys International.

On 14 December 1997, the new Belgian high-speed line was opened in its entirety (see Belgium entry for details), and four-voltage PBKA Thalys TGVs were introduced on a new two-hourly Paris-Brussels-Cologne service.

In 1995, SNCF created two GIEs in conjunction with Spanish Railways (RENFE). The first is charged with studying the proposed TGV line between Narbonne and Barcelona. The second aims to develop night services between Paris and Madrid/Barcelona. The latter became a limited company named Elipsos in 2001. From 1996 to 2001, traffic grew by 52 per cent and revenue by 87 per cent on these routes.

In 2000, in partnership with German Rail, Luxembourg Railways and Swiss Federal Railways, SNCF established a joint venture limited company, Rhealys SA, to develop the market for services linking the four countries. In the lead-up to the opening of the TGV-Est Européen in 2006, the company will undertake market studies to define the pattern of future high-speed services, develop a specification for rolling stock requirements and address technical issues relating to interoperability over the four networks.

In order to reinforce its presence abroad, SNCF in 1997 acquired British Rail International, a subsidiary of British Rail specialising in selling rail travel abroad and rail holidays in Britain. This is now managed as Rail Europe.

*Loss-making services*
SNCF has had political problems dealing with uneconomic transversal express services, such as Caen–Rennes, which receive no specific subsidy and lose around €604 million per year. SNCF is gradually negotiating the transfer of responsibility to regional government.

In 1996, SNCF decided that it would no longer subsidise train catering, which was losing €46 million per year. At the end of 1997, Wagons-Lits won a six-year concession covering 95 per cent of Grandes Lignes catering, beating former caterer Servair. Wagons-Lits has promised to break even by 2002.

*Ticketing*
SNCF introduced the Socrate electronic reservation system, based on American Airlines' Sabre system, in 1992-93 (see earlier editions of *Jane's World Railways* for details). Socrate has allowed SNCF to introduce a flexible market pricing system, with fares no longer linked to the number of kilometres travelled. Socrate manages the allocation of reduced price fares in order to maximise revenue per train, basing decisions on historical data on loadings and the progression of reservations. All TGVs have compulsory reservations.

SNCF has the most successful Internet site in France, with an average of 150,000 connections per day. Tickets can be ordered by credit card and are posted free. SNCF hopes to earn 4 per cent of long-distance passenger revenue through its site in 2001. In 2002, the site was achieving annual sales of €220 million.

*Paris region (Ile de France) suburban services*
SNCF services in the Paris region achieved about 10 billion passenger-km from 1991 to 1993. This had fallen to 9.38 billion in 1999 despite extensions to the RER system.

Transport provision in the Paris region is governed by five-year contracts (*contrats de plan*) between the Ile de France region and the state. The 1994-98 plan budgeted for spending of €5.25 billion over the period, of which €1,765 billion went to public transport; 68 per cent of the total was financed by the region and 32 per cent by the state. Specific projects are outlined in the 'Improvements to existing lines' section.

Major developments of the Paris network centre on the RER (Regional Express) network, started in 1969, which links suburban lines across the centre of the city. The network consists of five lines, A, B, C, D and E. The RER is operated by the SNCF, in the case of Lines A and B jointly with the Paris transport authority RATP; SNCF now has 1,282 route-km of suburban operation in the region. All are electrified.

Three-quarters of the traffic is with discounted fares. Operating costs are met 40 per cent by fares (but employers pay half the cost of their employees' annual tickets or Orange Card monthly/weekly tickets); 40 per cent by the *Versement Transport*, the payroll tax levied from employers; and 20 per cent by public authorities (the state, 70 per cent; departmental authorities, 30 per cent).

*Class Z23500 double-deck emus at Ventimiglia, forming a service to Cannes sponsored by the Pyrenées-Alpes-Côte d'Azur region, photographed at Lille Flandres station (Quintus Vosman) 2002/0524920*

*Regional services*
Regional services (*Train Express Régional* - TER) achieved 7.85 billion passenger-km in 1999.

Following an inquiry by the government Haenel commission, new powers over public transport are to be transferred to regional government. Regions will establish public transport plans, then negotiate five-year contracts for train services with SNCF, which will retain the monopoly over operations. Regions will take over complete responsibility for financing all train services.

To finance regional service deficits, the state will transfer €1.5 billion per year to the 20 regions, approximately double the previous subsidy.

The new organisation has been tested in seven regions – Alsace, Centre, Limousin, Nord-Pas-de-Calais, Pays-de-la-Loire, Provence-Alpes-Côte d'Azur and Rhône-Alpes. Participating regions have reported traffic and revenue growth double that in other regions and further regions are now likely to adopt the new system. Full powers of organisation was to be handed to the regions in 2002.

Rolling stock for TER services is now being developed in consultation with the regions (see 'Traction and rolling stock' section).

In 2000 SNCF took a 43 per cent share in French urban transport operator VIA-GTI. The company was then merged with SNCF bus and coach operator Cariane and the resulting company was renamed Keolis in 2001. Through Keolis SNCF is now seeking contracts for joint urban and regional transport operations both in France and abroad.

SNCF has appointed a manager charged with developing short-distance 'peri-urban' services around large towns. The first fruit of this will be the conversion of the Paris region Aulnay-Bondy line to light rail standards. Fifteen light rail vehicles were ordered from Siemens for this line in 2002, with an option for 64 more. Karlsruhe-style projects to run LRVs on tramway and RFF systems are under development for Lyon, Mulhouse, Strasbourg, Grenoble and Toulouse.

The Nord-Pas de Calais region introduced limited TGV services in 2000, taking advantage of local high-speed lines and TGV sets in marginal time. Development of these services depends on the purchase of new sets and the availability of LGV capacity.

## Freight operations

SNCF published separate figures for freight for the first time in 1999, recording a loss of €137 million, compared with €85 million in 1998.

The losses of the rail freight activity rose to €300 million in 2001, more than 10 per cent of turnover. Fret SNCF aims to cut losses through traffic increases and improvements in productivity. Breakdown is expected by 2005.

Fret SNCF registered 50.4 billion tonne-km in 2001, down 9.1 per cent on 2000. In both 2000 and 2001, Fret SNCF was forced to cancel trains due to shortages of locomotives and drivers. This trend has reduced as traffic has fallen, new locomotives arrive and staff duties undergo reorganisation.

*Class BB66400 diesel-electric locomotives on a ballast train at Auxerre St Gervais (Marcel Vleugels) 2001/0099120*

Rail accounts for only 29 per cent of SNCF's freight business, which includes Sernam and road haulage companies.

In 1999, the government set SNCF the target of doubling traffic to 100 billion tonne-km by 2010. Growth is mainly expected in intermodal, cereals and automotive traffic, and is to be achieved using existing resources.

In order to improve service quality, Fret SNCF is to be reorganised around four activities: wagon provision; traction provision; terminal operations; the organisation of complete logistics packages.

In commercial terms, the freight business is divided into business sectors: coal and steel; oil, chemicals and metals; manufactured goods; agricultural products; automobile, exceptional loads and military; and wood, paper and building materials.

SNCF is at present concentrating on developing international traffic which now represents 50 per cent of tonne-km, although cross-border market shares are well below domestic market shares in adjoining. Particular points of action are the establishment of SNCF delegations abroad, concentration of traffic for certain countries on 'hub' freight yards and 'one-stop shops' for the sale and tracking of capacity on cross-border services. In 2001, SNCF and Trenitalia set up common subsidiary, Sideuropa, to develop steel traffic between France and Italy. In the same year, SNCF and DB agreed procedures for the cross-border operation of locomotives and crews.

Rail's share of the French freight market has fallen from 46 to around 25 per cent since 1974, but is still the highest in the European Union, where the average is 14 per cent. A significant rise from 24.8 to 26.7 per cent took place from 1995 to 1997. However, revenue per tonne-km is falling regularly – by 2.5 per cent in 1997. To resolve its difficulties, SNCF is increasingly calling on the state to enforce road transport laws effectively.

Fret SNCF employs approximately 25,000 staff.

### Electric locomotives: principal classes

| Class | Wheel arrangement | Line voltage | Output kW | Speed km/h | Weight tonnes | No in service | First built | Builders Mechanical | Electrical |
|---|---|---|---|---|---|---|---|---|---|
| BB8100 | Bo-Bo | 1.5 kV | 2,100 | 105 | 92 | 24 | 1949 | Alsthom | Alsthom |
| BB8500/8700† | B-B | 1.5 kV | 2,940 | 100/140 | 78 | 141 | 1963 | Alsthom | Alsthom |
| BB7200 | B-B | 1.5 kV | 4,360 | 160* | 84 | 238 | 1977 | Alsthom | MTE |
| BB9200 | Bo-Bo | 1.5 kV | 3,850 | 160 | 82 | 130** | 1957 | MTE | MTE |
| BB9300 | Bo-Bo | 1.5 kV | 3,850 | 160 | 82 |  |  | MTE | MTE |
| BB9700 | Bo-Bo | 1.5 kV | 3,850 | 160 | 82 |  |  | MTE | MTE |
| BB9600 | B-B | 1.5 kV | 2,210 | 140 | 59 | 39 | 1959 | Fives-Lille | CEM |
| CC6500† | C-C | 1.5 kV | 5,900 | 100/220 | 115 | 76 | 1970 | Alsthom | MTE |
| CC7100 | Co-Co | 1.5 kV | 3,490 | 140 | 105 | 6 | 1951 | Alsthom/Fives-Lille | Alsthom/CEM |
| BB16000 | Bo-Bo | 25 kV | 4,130 | 160 | 84 | 58††† | 1958 | MTE | MTE |
| BB16100 | Bo-Bo | 25 kV | 4,130 | 160 | 84 |  |  | MTE | MTE |
| BB15000 | B-B | 25 kV | 4,360 | 160 | 88 | 62 | 1971 | Alsthom | MTE |
| BB16500† | B-B | 25 kV | 2,580 | 100/140 | 74 | 291 | 1958 | Alsthom | Alsthom |
| BB17000† | B-B | 25 kV | 2,940 | 90/140 | 78 | 105 | 1964 | Alsthom | Alsthom |
| BB20200† | B-B | 25/15 kV | 2,940 | 100/140 | 80 | 13 | 1969 | Alsthom | Alsthom |
| BB22200 (2-current) | B-B | 25/1.5 kV | 4,360 | 160†† | 89 | 202 | 1977 | Francorail | Francorail |
| BB25100 (2-current) | Bo-Bo | 25/1.5 kV | 4,130 / 3,400 | 130 | 84 | 70 | 1963 | MTE | MTE |
| BB25200 (2-current) | Bo-Bo | 25/1.5 kV | 4,130 / 3,400 | 160‡ | 84 | 51 | 1964 | MTE | MTE |
| BB25500† (2-current) | B-B | 25/1.5 kV | 2,940 | 100/140 | 78 | 191 | 1963 | Alsthom | Alsthom |
| BB26000 (2-current) | B-B | 25/1.5 kV | 5,600 | 200 | 90 | 233 | 1988 | GEC Alsthom | GEC Alsthom |
| BB27000 | Bo-Bo | 25/1.5 kV | 4,200 | 140 | - | 470‡‡‡ | 2000 | Alstom | Alstom |
| BB36000 (3-current) | B-B | 25/3/1.5 kV | 5,600 | 200 | 90 | 59*** | 1997 | GEC Alsthom | GEC Alsthom |
| BB37500 | Bo-Bo | 25/3/1.5 kV | 4,200 | 140 | - | 30‡‡‡ | - | Alstom | Alstom |
| Class 92 (2-current) | Co-Co | 25 kV/750V | 5,000 | 140 | 126 | 9 | 1994 | Brush | ABB |

\* 102 units geared for higher tractive effort and 100 km/h maximum; 3 units geared for 200 km/h maximum
\*\* Total for BB9200, BB9300 and BB9700
\*\*\* 1 further unit on order
† Monomotor bogies – 2 gear ratios
†† 8 units geared for 200 km/h maximum
††† Total for BB16000 and BB16100
‡ 33 locomotives reduced to 130 km/h
‡‡‡ Includes locomotives on order/option

### Wagonload traffic

The wagonload network was rationalised considerably in the 1980s. Although its traffic declined from 31.8 billion tonne-km in 1980 to 15.9 billion in 1993, it accounts for 28 per cent of all freight and almost half total freight revenue. However, the number of terminals served has been halved to 1,250, and service to some 2,800 private sidings was withdrawn between 1989 and 1993. In addition, since 1993, the number of major marshalling yards was cut from 27 to 19, of which Achères in western Paris specialises in automotive traffic. Only some 239 principal terminals (*Gare Principal Fret*, or GPF), generating at least 10 wagonloads daily, now have direct connection with a marshalling yard. Some major GPFs are linked by through trains avoiding the main marshalling yards. The plan has obtained Day-A-Day-B transits for 70 per cent of wagonload traffic. All freight trains now run at a top speed of at least 100 km/h where track alignment permits. All SNCF main lines are passed for axleloads of 22.5 tonnes, so that four-axle wagons can gross up to 90 tonnes, which means payloads can reach at least 60 tonnes. By 2000 SNCF had acknowledged that wagonload services play an important role and was seeking to 'fill' trains better. Expansion in wagonload traffic led to the reopening of Châlons-en-Champagne marshalling yard in late 2000.

### Block trains

This traffic is relatively stable. Despite a general downward trend in movement of heavy products, SNCF is aiming for a 5 to 10 per cent increase in traffic, mainly through better service. To improve productivity, in the early 1990s the carriage of timber was concentrated on 250 to 300 terminals, served by a dedicated network of trains. This was cut to 150 better-equipped points by 1999. Aggregates traffic is to be rationalised in a similar way.

In 1995, Fret SNCF began an experiment aimed at improving utilisation of traction, information to customers and train punctuality. Known as TENOR, this involves operating block trains over the Dunkerque-Thionville heavy freight route with a fleet of locomotives and team of drivers dedicated solely to this traffic and controlled from a single office.

Fret SNCF is hoping to lengthen freight trains which are normally limited by traction and infrastructure to 750 m. Together with DB Cargo, Fret SNCF has selected Alstom and SAB WABCO to develop a future European Freight Intelligent System (EFIS), a standard electronic brake control and communication system for freight trains. This may allow trains to be extended to 2,250 m. Trials with pairs of coupled freight trains, with the centre locomotive controlled from the leading one, were due to begin in late 2002.

In 2001 SNCF started operating 900 m container trains from the port of Fos to Lyon and 800 m trains of empty ore wagons from Lorraine to Dunkerque.

### Automatic Vehicle Identification

Fret SNCF is now using an AVI system on some 2,200 wagons carrying loads such as bottled beverages or household appliances which may suffer damage during transit. The system employs Amtech vehicle-mounted transponders which incorporate shock detectors and trackside interrogators.

Fret SNCF equipped 43 Class BB16500 electric locomotives with GPS satellite tracking in 1996 and 24 TGV sets in 2001. Fret SNCF plans to equip all 2,600 of its main line locomotives and most of its shunters.

### Sernam

Sernam (*Service Nationale de Messageries*) is SNCF's 100 per cent-owned parcels carrier which uses 600 of its own rail wagons and a fleet of 4,940 road vehicles. Sernam lost €110 million on a turnover of €518 million in 2000 despite continuous reorganisations in recent years. Sernam was expected to be absorbed by SNCF's road haulage subsidiary Geodis in 2001.

In October 1998, Sernam freight services started operating at 200 km/h, the first trains of this type in the world to do so. Trains between Paris and Orange operate partially over the Paris Sud-Est high-speed line, using Class BB22200 electric locomotives with TVM 430 cab signalling. These haul covered bogie vans which have been tested at up to 279 km/h.

### Intermodal operations

Intermodal traffic now accounts for 25 per cent of SNCF freight. Traffic is stable at around 13.8 billion tonne-km. As part of the plan to double freight traffic by 2010, intermodal traffic levels are required to triple in 10 years to 37.2 billion tonne-km by 2010.

Domestic traffic is managed and marketed by two companies, Novatrans (the French UIRR company) and CNC, with the swapbody figuring in the businesses of both. Novatrans is 60 per cent owned by road haulage interests, 40 per cent by SNCF. CNC is 71 per cent owned by SNCF Participations. CNC is open to all users, while Novatrans deals exclusively with road hauliers. Novatrans operates 23 terminals and 1,600 wagons and runs 100 trains daily. CNC runs 100 trains daily, operates some 40 terminals in France, 5,500 flat wagons, and 9,000 containers and swapbodies. It is associated with 150 hauliers deploying some 2,000 road vehicles. To promote intermodal traffic via the Channel Tunnel, SNCF and

*Class BB36000 electric locomotive at Douai with a London–Milan intermodal train* (David Haydock) 2001/0114239

Novatrans respectively take part in the joint ventures ACI and CTL (see Intercontainer-Interfrigo and UIRR SC entries in the 'Operators of International Rail Services in Europe' section for contact details).

Most intermodal traffic is by direct overnight trains running at 120 to 160 km/h, but CNC also operates a service known as 'Combi 24' – a network of evening trains converging on a hub near Paris then, after shunting, departing and giving morning arrivals. Novatrans also has a hub operation centred on Noisy-le-Sec near Paris. Intercontainer operates an international hub at Metz, on the Luxembourg-Strasbourg route, for trains operating under the 'Qualitynet' name between the Benelux countries and Germany, Switzerland, Italy and Spain.

SNCF, CNC and Novatrans have all been losing money on existing traffic because of falling real road haulage rates. To promote fairer competition and intermodal services, a 'council for intermodal transport' was created in 1995. The council includes members from SNCF, CNC and Novatrans, as well as road and canal transport operators. In 2000, SNCF, Novatrans and French road haulier organisations signed an agreement in which 200,000 tonnes of traffic would be transferred to rail if punctuality was 95 per cent or better.

The government is paying SNCF a yearly grant of around €76 million towards new terminals. Investment includes €457 million in terminals and enlarging loading gauges on the Paris–Le Havre and Kehl–Dijon–Modane routes. During the period 2001-03, 17 new or extended terminals will be brought into operation. Bordeaux Hourcade came into service in December 2001. The largest of the terminals will be at Dourges, near Lille, and will open in 2003.

Fret SNCF has developed some intermodal enterprises independent of Novatrans and CNC. One is Chronofroid, with which SNCF aims to recover some of the two million tonnes of refrigerated perishables traffic it has lost to road since 1980. In 1990 a similar operation was launched with tank swapbodies for chemical products, in this case with international service over distances of more than 500 km as an objective. Hence its title of TransEuroChem.

As a trial, SNCF and RFF are to give higher priority to freight services on the Metz–Dijon–Modane route through reorganisation of pathing and track maintenance. This route carries many intermodal services which are particularly time-sensitive.

*Alpine Piggyback*
Following a fire in the Mont Blanc road tunnel in which 39 people died, and increasing concern about the congestion and pollution of Alpine valleys by growing lorry traffic, the French authorities have moved to promote the carriage of complete lorries by train. The types of wagon used elsewhere in Europe have been rejected in favour of a new design, Modalohr, which does not require small wheels. An initial service using two trains, each carrying 18 trucks and operating four train pairs per day, will be introduced in December 2002 from Aiton, France, and Turin, Italy. In mid-2002, the two new transfer terminals were under construction and Modalohr wagons were being tested prior to approval.

*Bimodal systems*
Several bimodal systems have been tested in France since 1990 and CNC has acquired 30 of the US RoadRailer-type trailers. After numerous modifications, CNC hoped to gain approval for the vehicles in 2002.

### Traction and rolling stock
At the beginning of 2001, SNCF owned 356 TGV trainsets, 2,000 electric, 1,766 diesel and 1,221 tractor locomotives, eight five-car RTG gas-turbine trainsets, 1,013 emus (3,575 cars, TGV sets excluded), 1,368 diesel railcars/trailers and 7,663 hauled passenger cars. Freight stock totalled 51,344 SNCF-owned and 65,877 privately owned.

*Current TGV orders*
Deliveries of the current fleet of TGVs were completed in 1998 with the last of 30 TGV-Duplex double-deck sets for the Paris–Lyon route. At the end of 2001, the TGV fleet consisted of 107 eight-car TGV Sud-Est, 105 10-car TGV Atlantique, 79 eight-car TGV Réseau and 33 eight-car TGV Duplex. In addition, there are three postal TGVs.

In 2000/1 SNCF ordered an additional 52 TGV Duplex sets for use on services between Paris and the south of France, freeing PSE and Réseau sets for other services. TGV Est services from 2006 will be launched with 40 heavily refurbished TGV Réseau sets, 10 three-voltage sets and 10 ICE sets. In order to upgrade Paris-Limoges services in 2006, six TGV Atlantique sets will be fitted with tilt equipment.

Other TGV derivatives which are jointly owned are 27 eight-car Thalys sets (10 tri-voltage, 17 quadri-voltage) and 38 Eurostar sets (31 18-car and 7 14-car).

*Eurostar*
Details of the 38 SNCF trains in the jointly owned three-voltage Eurostar fleet for operation between London and Paris/Brussels via the Channel Tunnel and TGV-NE will be found in the United Kingdom entry.

Of the Eurostar fleet, nine sets belonging to SNCF have been modified for operation under 1.5 kV DC in order to allow operation from London to the French Alps over the Paris Sud-Est LGV. They are used for a winter sports service linking London with Bourg St Maurice in about 8 hours during the skiing season. Lower than expected traffic levels on Eurostar have led SNCF to use three sets between Paris and Lille, thus freeing six TGV Réseau sets.

*Future TGV development*
A major project to develop a new generation of TGV has been abandoned. Instead, a variety of tests are being carried out in order to improve the TGV design. These concern eddy current brakes to allow higher speeds and measures such as adding valances to bogies to reduce noise. In 2001, Alstom started tests with an 'AGV' part rake.

Alstom and SNCF have also tested a TGV prototype with automatic body tilting supplied by Fiat. The train, converted from a TGV-PSE set, ran trials from April 1998 to April 2000. Of the development budget, €4.7 million was financed by the French government PREDIT project, €12.8 million by Alstom and €8.4 million by SNCF.

In 2000, SNCF and DB announced that they would work together on future high-speed train design, while Alstom and Siemens created a consortium to work together on this project.

*Locomotives*
Following difficulties in supplying enough locomotives for the freight activity, SNCF divided the main line locomotive fleet by activity sector at the beginning of 1999. Locomotives are allocated to: Grandes Lignes (352 electric, 77 diesel); Fret SNCF (1,310 electric, 578 diesel); Action Régionale (261 electric, 222 diesel); Ile de France (141 electric); and Infrastructure (5 electric, 172 diesel). Use of one activity's locomotives on another's services is

### TGV trainsets

| | TGV-PSE | TGV-PSE | TGV-A | TGV-R | TGV-R | TGV-Duplex (TGV-2N) | Thalys (TGV-PBKA) |
|---|---|---|---|---|---|---|---|
| | Dual-voltage dual-class | Tri-voltage dual-class | Dual-voltage dual-class | Dual-voltage dual-class | Tri-voltage dual-class | Dual-voltage double-deck | Four-voltage dual-class |
| Length over couplers | 200.19 m | 200.19 m | 237.6 m | 200.19 m | 200.19 m | 200.19 m | 200.19 m |
| Tare weight in working order | 386 tonnes | 386 tonnes | 490 tonnes | 383 tonnes | 385 tonnes | 380 tonnes | 380 tonnes |
| Weight available for adhesion | 194 tonnes | 194 tonnes | 136 tonnes | 136 tonnes | 136 tonnes | 137 tonnes | 135 tonnes |
| Continuous power rating | | | | | | | |
| At 25 kV 50 Hz | 6,450 kW | 6,450 kW | 8,800 kW | 8,800 kW | 8,800 kW | 8,800 kW | 8,800 kW |
| At 1.5 kV DC | 3,100 kW | 3,100 kW | 3,880 kW | 3,880 kW | 3,880 kW | 3,880 kW | 3,680 kW |
| At 15 kV 16⅔Hz | - | 2,800 kW | - | - | - | - | - |
| Max speed | 270 km/h | 270 km/h | 300 km/h | 300 km/h | 300 km/h | 300 km/h | 300 km/h |
| Seating capacity | | | | | | | |
| 1st class | 69/110 | 110 | 116 | 120 | 120 | 197 | 120 |
| 2nd class | 276/240 | 240 | 369 | 257 | 257 | 348 | 257 |

### Electric multiple-unit power cars: principal classes

| Class | Cars per unit | Line voltage | Motor cars per unit | Motored axles/car | Output/unit kW | Speed km/h | Units in service | First built | Builders Mechanical | Builders Electrical |
|---|---|---|---|---|---|---|---|---|---|---|
| Z5300 | 3/4 | 1.5 kV | 1 | 4 | 1,180 | 130 | 141 | 1965 | Fives-Lille/ CFL-CIMT/ De Dietrich | Jeumont |
| Z5600 | 4/6 | 1.5 kV | 2 | 4 | 2,700 | 140 | 52 | 1982 | ANF-CIMT | TCO |
| Z7100 | 2/4 | 1.5 kV | 1 | 2 | 940 | 130 | 24 | 1960 | Decauville/ De Dietrich | Jeumont/ Oerlikon |
| Z7300 Z7500 | 2 | 1.5 kV | 1 | 4 | 1,275 | 160 | 90 | 1980 | Francorail | MTE |
| Z6100 | 3 | 25 kV | 1 | 2 | 615 | 120 | 75 | 1964 | SFAC-CFL/ De Dietrich | CEM-SW/ Alsthom |
| Z6300 | 3 | 25 kV | 1 | 2 | 615 | 120 | 33 | 1965 | CFL-Fives Lille/ De Dietrich | CEM-SW/ Alsthom |
| Z6400 | 4 | 25 kV | 2 | 4 | 2,350 | 120 | 75 | 1976 | CFL | Alsthom/ TCO |
| Z8100 | 4 | 1.5/25 kV | 2 | 4 | 2,500 | 140 | 51 | 1979 | SFB-ANF | TCO |
| Z8800 | 4 | 25 kV | 2 | 4 | 2,800 | 140 | 58 | 1985 | Alsthom/ ANF-CIMT | TCO |
| Z9500 Z9600 | 2 | 1.5/25 kV | 1 | 4 | 1,275 | 160 | 56 | 1982 | Francorail | MTE |
| Z11500 | 2 | 25 kV | 1 | 4 | 1,275 | 160 | 22 | 1987 | Alsthom | Alsthom |
| Z20500 | 4/5 | 25/1.5 kV | 2 | 4 | 2,800 | 140 | 194+ | 1988 | GEC Alsthom/ ANF | GEC Alsthom |
| Z20900 | 4 | 25/1.5 kV | 2 | 4 | 2,800 | 140 | 13 | 1988 | Alstom | Alstom |
| Z92050 | 4 | 25/1.5 kV | 2 | 4 | 2,800 | 140 | 6 | 1988 | GEC Alsthom/ ANF | GEC Alsthom |
| Z22500 | 5 | 25/1.5 kV | 2 | 4 | 3,000 | 140 | 53 | 1995 | GEC Alsthom | GEC Alsthom |
| Z23500 | 2 | 25/1.5 kV | 1 | 4 | 1,700 | 140 | 80 | 1998 | Alstom/ Bombardier | Alstom |
| TGV-PSE 23000 | 10 | 25/1.5 kV | 2 | 4 + 2 | 6,450 3,100 | 270 | 98 | 1978 | Alsthom/ Francorail | Alsthom/ Francorail |
| TGV-PSE 33000 | 10 | 25/15/ 1.5 kV | 2 | 4 + 2 | 6,450 3,100 2,800 | 270 | 9 | 1981 | Alsthom/ Francorail | Alsthom/ Francorail |
| TGV-A | 12 | 25/1.5 kV | 2 | 4 | 8,800 3,880 | 300 | 105 | 1989 | GEC Alsthom/ ANF/ De Dietrich | GEC Alsthom |
| TGV-R | 10 | 25/1.5 kV | 4 | 4 | 8,800 3,800 | 300 | 49 | 1992 | GEC Alsthom/ De Dietrich | GEC Alsthom |
| TGV-R | 10 | 25/1.5 kV + 3 kV | 4 | 4 | 8,800 3,800 | 300 | 40 | 1994 | GEC Alsthom/ De Dietrich | GEC Alsthom |
| TGV-Duplex | 10 | 25/1.5 kV | 4 | 4 | 8,800 3,800 | 300 | 32* | 1996 | GEC Alsthom/ De Dietrich | GEC Alsthom |
| Thalys PBKA | 10 | 25/1.5 kV 3/15 kV | 4 | 4 | 8,800 3,800 | 300 | 17 | 1996 | GEC Alsthom/ De Dietrich | GEC Alsthom |

* 32 more on order
+ 31 Class Z20900 also on order

still common but will be gradually reduced. Fret SNCF is to reorganise operations to increase locomotive productivity to allow withdrawal of the oldest units. Locomotives are increasingly organised in small, dedicated fleets to increase reliability for targeted customers. In 2001, 40 locomotives were dedicated to CNC intermodal services from the Villeneuve hub. Transports de Proximité Régionaux et Locaux locomotives and rolling stock are now nominally allocated region by region and are increasingly based closer to their area of operation.

During 1998, Alstom completed an order for 234 dual-voltage, 200 km/h 5,600 kW synchronous-motored class BB26000 'Sybic' locomotives. The last 30 of the original order are being built with asynchronous motors and triple-voltage capability (equipped to run on 3 kV DC); these are known as Class BB36000 and are nicknamed 'Astride'. Two prototypes were delivered in March and June 1996 and underwent an extensive series of tests before delivery of series locomotives began in early 1997. Delivery was delayed by technical problems and a change in the original contract to allow the class to operate into Italy. The class is used on intermodal services from the Channel Tunnel and Belgium via Dijon and Modane to Turin in Italy. Delivery of a second batch of 30 locomotives was completed in 2002.

SNCF placed an order with Alstom for 120 new 'Prima' electric locomotives for freight services in July 1998. Fret SNCF has specified a relatively simple 4,200 kW design, most to be designated Class BB27000 with dual-voltage capability for use throughout France, with asynchronous motors, IGBT technology and a maximum speed of 140 km/h. In tendering, the accent has been placed on low cost and reliability.

During 2001, subsequent orders were placed with Alstom for 180 and 120 locomotives and an option taken for 80 more. This will bring the total fleet to 500 examples. The confirmed orders were for Class BB27000 dual-system (25 kV AC 50 Hz/1.5 kV DC) units, while the option for 80 includes 30 Class BB37500 three-system machines additionally equipped to operate under Belgian and Italian 3 kV DC power supplies. Deliveries of the type are expected to continue until 2007.

In late 2000, Fret SNCF called for tenders for 69 Co-Co diesel locomotives rated at around 3,000 kW and 55 Bo-Bo diesels rated at around 2,000 kW for delivery from 2003 to 2006.

Fret SNCF suffered a severe locomotive shortage in 2000, with many trains stopped for lack of traction. To help solve the shortage of diesel traction, SNCF hired six Vossloh G1206 locomotives from mid-2001 and three more in 2002. They are designated Class 461.

In order to reduce emissions and fuel consumption, SNCF is to re-engine all 525 Class Y8000 and Y8400 shunters with Renault engines by 2007. In addition, around 25 Class CC72000 locomotives will be re-engined.

*Paris suburban stock*
SNCF Paris suburban rolling stock at the start of 1998 totalled 2,867 emu cars (696 sets) and 1,125 push-pull trainset cars. Of the combined fleet, 2,222 cars were double-deck.

At the beginning of 1999 SNCF ordered a further 32 double-deck dual-voltage emus for RER line C, followed by 12 more in 2001 and 10 in 2002; 194 sets are already in service; 94 sets are five-car formations in operation on RER line D. Most four-car units operate on RER line C. The newer units are classified Z20900 and have air conditioning and enhanced passenger security equipment.

A joint RATP/SNCF order for a new type of double-deck emu known as MI 2N (RATP) for RER line A or Class Z22500 (SNCF) for the EOLE line (see 'New lines' section under RFF above) was completed in 2000. RATP units have 12 out of 20 axles powered whilst SNCF rakes have eight out of 20 motored. MI 2N also differs from previous double-deck emus in having shorter vehicles and having the inner rather than the outer vehicles motored. For flexibility, all units are dual-voltage. The new units differ from previous SNCF designs in having three entrance doors per coach instead of two. Initial orders with Alstom were for 53 SNCF units plus 50 on option, plus 17 RATP units, 23 on option.

*Trains for the regions*
The majority of contracts signed by the SNCF and the regions have featured funding from the latter for the purchase of new rolling stock, which has been distinctively liveried to mark its regional affinity.

The regions participated in design of a new two-car diesel trainset from Alstom, classified X72500 and

*Fret SNCF's latest electric locomotive type, the dual-voltage Class BB27000, photographed at Alstom's Belfort works* (David Haydock)

*Class Z11500 emu forming a Metz–Strasbourg service near Courcelles* (John C Baker)

*Two Class Z22500 five-car double-deck emus for service on the new EOLE RER line in Paris* (David Haydock)

**Diesel locomotives: principal classes**

| Class | Wheel arrangement | Power kW | Speed km/h | Weight tonnes | No in service | First built | Builders Mechanical | Engine | Transmission |
|---|---|---|---|---|---|---|---|---|---|
| 68000 | A1A-A1A | 1,660 | 130 | 106 | 61 | 1963 | CAFL | Sulzer 12LVA 24 | E CEM |
| 68500 | A1A-A1A | 1,645 | 130 | 105 | 28 | 1963 | CAFL | SACM-AGO V12 DSHR | E CEM |
| 72000† | C-C | 2,250 | 160 | 110 | 91 | 1967 | Alsthom | SACM-AGO V16 ESHR | E Alsthom |
| 63000 | Bo-Bo | 355 | 80 | 68 | 45 | 1953 | B&L | Sulzer 6LDA22C | E B&L |
| 63100 | Bo-Bo | 435 | 80 | 68 | 51 | 1957 | B&L | Sulzer 6LDA22D | E B&L |
| 63400 | Bo-Bo | 450 | 80 | 68 | 569** | 1956 | B&L | SACM-MGO V12 SH | E B&L |
| 63500 | Bo-Bo | 450 | 80 | 68 | | | B&L | SACM-MGO V12 SH | E B&L |
| 66000 | Bo-Bo | 830 | 120 | 70 | 406*** | 1959 | Alsthom | SACM-MGO V16 BSHR | E CEM |
| 66400 | Bo-Bo | 830 | 120 | 70 | | | Alsthom | SACM-MGO V16 BSHR | E CEM |
| 66700 | Bo-Bo | 830 | 120 | 70 | | | Alsthom | SACM-MGO V16 BSHR | E CEM |
| 67000† 67200* | B-B | 1,440 | 90 | 80 | 102 | 1963 | B&L MTE | SEMT-Pielstick 16PA4 | E MTE |
| 67300† | B-B | 1,440 | 90/140 | 80 | 87 | 1967 | B&L MTE | SEMT-Pielstick 16PA4 | E MTE |
| 67400 | B-B | 1,525 | 140 | 83 | 228 | 1969 | B&L | SEMT-Pielstick 16PA4 | E MTE |
| Y7100 | B | 130 | 54 | 32 | 207 | 1958 | Billiard/Decauville | Poyaud 6PYT | H Voith |
| Y7400 | B | 130 | 60 | 32 | 489 | 1963 | Decauville/De Dietrich/Moyse | Poyaud 6 PYT | M BV Asynchro |
| Y8000 Y8400†† (2 gears) | B | 215 | 30/60 | 36 | 525 | 1977 | Arbel-Fauvet Rail | Poyaud V12-520NS | H Voith |

\* 67200 as 67000 but with TVM cab signal for LGV
\*\* Total for 63400 and 63500
\*\*\* Total for 66000, 66400 and 66700
† Monomotor bogies (2 gears)
†† As Y8000 but with remote control

capable of 160 km/h. Features include the use of two 'disposable' 300 kW MAN lorry engines per power car, with Voith hydraulic transmission, low-floor entrances, air conditioning and a streamlined nose. A tilting version of the design was tested in mid-1999.

The cost per two-car unit is €4.12 million. Central government has given a €12.2 million subsidy to lower the cost of these trains. In total 105 units, fully financed by the regions, were delivered from 1997 to 2000. Units are used mainly on medium-distance limited-stop services, many of them inter-regional. Units are two-car, both of them powered, except for the 15 units for the Paris-Granville line which have an unpowered centre car. An additional 12 three-car sets were subsequently ordered.

Deliveries of a three-car Class Z21500 electric version of the design capable of 200 km/h commenced in mid-2002. The design has been ordered by the Centre (15 sets), Bretagne (17), Pays-de-la-Loire (14) and Poitou-Charentes (5) regions. Alstom has also produced a three-car dual-voltage electric version of the X72500 design capable of 200 km/h. A total of 51 of the units, also known as Class Z21500 or ZTER, have been ordered by four regions, mainly in Britanny.

Delivery was completed in 2000 of 80 two-car double-deck emus of a new design for regional services from Alstom and ANF Industrie, now Bombardier Transportation. Each unit is valued at €4.42 million. SNCF financed only 30 per cent of the total cost, the rest coming from regional government. Thirty sets are operating in Provence-Alpes-Côte d'Azur, 34 in the Nord-Pas-de-Calais and 16 in the Rhône-Alpes region. Known as TER2N, the units were designed in consultation with the regions and feature air conditioning and access for passengers with restricted mobility. Units seat 206 passengers and have a maximum speed of 140 km/h. SNCF has ordered 72 examples of a new generation of double-deck emu (TER2N NG) from Alstom. 203 vehicles will be delivered as two-, three- or four-car sets. There is an option for 426 additional vehicles.

In order to provide economical operation on minor lines, SNCF and DB put a joint order (40 each) for 80 light single railcars with De Dietrich and LHB in October 1996. The French railcars, costing €1.45 million each, are classified X73500, and are powered by two engines totalling 456 kW. They have a 140 km/h maximum speed, seating for 61 passengers, with a low-floor centre section, and are built for one-person operation. The initial order had grown to 300 units by 2002 as the regions have added their own requirements. The first went into service in November 1999 in the Tours and Strasbourg areas.

In September 2001, SNCF named Bombardier Transportation preferred bidder to supply a new fleet of up to 500 160 km/h multiple-units for services which it operates on behalf of regional authorities. Designated *Autorail à Grande Capacité* (AGC), the new trains are intended to replace Class X2720, X4300, X4500, X4630 and X4750 dmus. Contracts for 192 units were placed by the end of 2001, leading to first deliveries in January 2004. The AGC units will be articulated, with a partial low floor, and will be built in two-, three- and four-car versions. Transmission will be electric. Both dmu and emu versions will be supplied and some will be supplied as dual-mode vehicles capable of operating either as dmus or as emus on electrified lines. Construction will be undertaken at Bombardier's Crespin plant, near Valenciennes. SNCF is also receiving five new metre-gauge dmus from Soulé for its Blanc–Argent line and has ordered two emus from Stadler for the Villefranche–La Tour de Carol line.

The regional authorities are increasingly financing refurbishment of existing trains to render them more attractive and increase their useful life.

*France Wagons*
In 1993 SNCF created a subsidiary, France Wagons (FW), charged with management of its fleet of 59,000 wagons. The wagon fleet, worth €762 million, plus the accompanying €213 million debt, was transferred to the wholly owned subsidiary which rents back the wagons to SNCF. SNCF hopes to improve its wagon productivity, which is much lower than that of French private wagons. SNCF wagons made an average of only 15 loaded journeys carrying 501 tonnes over a total of 5,500 km in 1993. Wagon numbers were cut from 76,000 in 1993 to 54,000 in 2000, while traffic rose. There is an increasing trend towards the dedication of wagons to specific traffic flows. One such case concerns wagons conveying tobacco, increasing productivity by 50 per cent.

**UPDATED**

*TGV Réseau high-speed trainset at Hazebrouck forming a Dunkirk–Paris service* (John C Baker)  2002/0524919

*Class X72500 two-car regional dmu at Paris Austerlitz* (Eddie Barnes)  2001/0099121

*Class X73500 railcar at Tours* (David Haydock)  2001/0114238

**Diesel and gas-turbine multiple-units**

| Class | Cars per unit | Motor cars per unit | Motored axles/car | Power kW | Speed km/h | No in service | First built | Mechanical | Builders Engine | Transmission |
|---|---|---|---|---|---|---|---|---|---|---|
| T2000 (RTG*) | 5 | 2 | 2 | 1,970 | 160 | 6 | 1973 | ANF | Turboméca Turmo IIIH Turmo XIIC | H Voith |
| X2100 | 1 | 1 | 2 | 440 | 140 | 54 | 1980 | ANF | SFAC/Saurer | H Voith |
| X2200 | | | | | | 58 | 1985 | | SJS-S 1DHR | |
| X2800 | 1 | 1 | 2 | 426 | 120 | 66 | 1957 | Decauville/ RNUR | SACM-MGO V12 SH | HM Maybach |
| X2720 | 2 | 2 | 2 | 605 | 140 | 16 | 1955 | De Dietrich | SACM-MGO V12 SH | H Maybach |
| X4300 X4500 | 2 | 1 | 2 | 295 | 120 | 185 | 1963 | ANF | Poyaud/ SFAC/Saurer SDHR | M De Dietrich |
| X4630 | 2 | 1 | 2 | 295 | 120 | 115 | 1971 | ANF | SFAC/Saurer SDHR | H Voith |
| X4750 | 2 | 1 | 2 | 440 | 140 | 54 | 1975 | ANF | SFAC/Saurer S1DHR | H Voith |
| X4900 | 3 | 2 | 2 | 590 | 140 | 13 | 1975 | ANF | SFAC/Saurer SDHR | H Voith |
| X72500 | 2/3 | 2 | 2 | 1,200 | 160 | 105† | 1997 | Alstom | MAN | H Voith |
| X73500 | 1 | 1 | 2 | 456 | 140 | 142** | 1999 | Alstom | MAN | H Voith |

\* Gas turbine
† 12 more on order
\*\* of 300 on order

## CDG Express

40 rue d'Alsace, F-75475 Paris Cedex 10
Tel: (+33 1) 40 18 83 80    Fax: (+33 1) 40 18 60 52
e-mail: xavier.duclairoir@gie-cdgexpress.fr
Web: http://www.cdgexpress.org

### Key personnel
President: Thierry Mignauw
Director, External Relations: Pierre-Henri Gronier

### Background
CDG Express is a European economic interest group (GIE) formed jointly by Aéroports de Paris (ADP), Réseau Ferré de France (RFF), the Paris city transport authority (RATP) and French National Railways (SNCF) to develop plans for a fast rail link between Roissy-Charles de Gaulle airport and central Paris. The project consists of a 25 km electrified line from the city's Gare de l'Est to the airport, including 14 km of new line. A service frequency of four trains an hour is foreseen with a non-stop 15 minute journey time.

At Gare de l'Est, complete redevelopment is planned to coincide with the commissioning in 2006 of the TGV Est service. This will include improvements intended to treat Gare de l'Est, Gare du Nord and Magenta (RER 'EOLE' Line E) stations, together with access to five Métro lines, as a single transport hub. A city air terminal at platform level with 28 desks for in-town check-in is to be provided for CDG Express services, which will use two dedicated tracks. At Roissy-Charles de Gaulle, CDG Express services will terminate at the existing TGV station, where track layout modifications will be carried out and passenger and baggage handling facilities provided.

Projected rolling stock requirements are seven 160 km/h six-car emus, each providing capacity for around 400 passengers. Initial traffic projections suggest at least 6 million passengers a year. Costs are estimated at €610 million for infrastructure and €110 million for rolling stock. Completion of the scheme is expected in 2008.

**VERIFIED**

## CFD Industrie

Cie des Chemins de Fer Départementaux
9-11 rue Benoît-Malon, F-92150 Suresnes
Tel: (+33 1) 45 06 44 00    Fax: (+33 1) 47 28 48 84

### Key personnel
President: F de Coincy

### Organisation
CFD Industrie builds small diesel locomotives and railcars at Bagnières-de-Bigare (the former Soulé plant) and has a repair workshop at Montmirail.

In early 2000, SNCF took a 65 per cent shareholding in the company. VFLI, a subsidiary of SNCF, formed a joint venture with CFD to operate the 87 km Autun–Avallon line in central France.

CFD also owns workshops which repair and overhaul rolling stock at Noyon and Liège, Belgium.

**UPDATED**

## CFTA

Société Générale de Chemin de Fer et de Transports Automobiles
Parc des Fontaines, 169 avenue Georges Clemenceau, F-92735 Nanterre Cedex
Tel: (+33 1) 46 69 30 00    Fax: (+33 1) 46 69 30 01

### Key personnel
Chairman: François Peter
Director General: Jean Pierre Fremont

### Organisation
CFTA is a railway operating subsidiary of Connex, the transport business of the French conglomerate Vivendi. CFTA has existed in one form or another for 110 years, with particular experience of operating rural branch lines. In France, CFTA operates several lines on behalf of SNCF, providing station, traction and track maintenance staff. CFTA staff drive both SNCF locomotives and CFTA's fleet of diesel locomotives and multiple-units.

CFTA is bidding for further operating contracts as these come up for renewal but may lose historic contracts to other operators. The company has recently won the contract to operate the Chemin de Fer de la Mure from Saint Georges-de-Commiers to La Mure (25 km), near Grenoble, and the Chemin de Fer de la Rhune, a rack line in the Pyrenees mountains. CFTA also manages the metre-gauge Chemin de Fer de La Provence line from Nice to Digne (151 km).

### Passenger operations
CFTA operates passenger services over the Carhaix–Guingamp–Paimpol lines in Brittany plus Longueville–Provins east of Paris. On the Provins line, SNCF passenger stock is used whilst CFTA supplies a locomotive for freight. In the case of the Brittany lines, CFTA uses two-axle, driver-only-operated railbuses in conjunction with the local regional council.

### Freight operations
CFTA operates freight trains on behalf of SNCF over 11 lines, mainly in central and eastern France. In 2000, CFTA lost the contract for 100 km of lines in the Nevers area to SNCF.

*Diesel railcars at Annot, on the metre-gauge Chemin de Fer de La Provence, which is operated by CFTA*
(David Haydock)    2001/0114242

CFTA also manages private sidings. In 1994, the company took over Socorail, a company specialising in sidings for the oil industry, acquiring 80 shunting locomotives.

### Traction and rolling stock
CFTA operates 25 main line diesel locomotives, 100 shunting locomotives and 10 diesel railcars.

**VERIFIED**

## TAB

### Organisation
In October 2000, French road haulier TAB, which is 35 per cent owned by Connex, launched an intermodal rail service between the river port of Bonneuil in the Paris suburbs and Lungavilla in northern Italy.

### Traction and rolling stock
TAB has hired 120 double wagons from AAE for the service. Traction is provided by the domestic national operators, SNCF and FS.

**NEW ENTRY**

## Voies Ferrées Locales et Industrielles (VFLI)

6 rue d'Amsterdam, F-75009 Paris
Tel: (+33 1) 55 07 81 00    Fax: (+33 1) 55 07 82 48
e-mail: siege.paris@vfli.fr

### Key personnel
General Manager: Yves Bayle

### Organisation
VFLI is a subsidiary of SNCF holding SCETA, which was set up in 1998 to manage local freight lines and industrial branches on a low-cost basis. VFLI operates 14 industrial branches and has two bigger subsidiaries, Voies Ferrées des Landes, which works certain lines around Mont-de-Marsan, and the MDPA potash mine network near Mulhouse. In 2000, VFLI formed a joint venture with CFD Industrie (qv) to operate the 87 km Avallon–Autun line.

In July 2001, VFLI won a contract to operate the rail system of Houllières du Bassin de Lorraine (HBL), a 210 km network serving coal mines in northeast France. VFLI intends to create a wagon maintenance facility and a rail test centre there.

In 2000 VFLI recorded a turnover of €23.6 million.

### Traction and rolling stock
VFLI has 39 shunters and 88 main line diesel locomotives.

**UPDATED**

# GABON

**Ministry of Tourism, National Parks and Transport**

PO Box 3974, Libreville
Tel: (+241) 70 11 62/76 32 40

**Key personnel**
Minister: A M Miyakou

## Gabon State Railways (OCTRA)

Office du Chemin de Fer Transgabonais
PO Box 2198, Libreville
Tel: (+241) 70 07 24; 70 09 74; 70 24 78
Fax: (+241) 70 20 38

**Key personnel**
President: A Ayo Barro
Director-General: Célestin Ndolia-Nhaud
Directors
    Administration and Personnel: Firmin Pascal Ikabanga
    Operations: Samuel Ndoba
    Planning and Development: Jean Daniel M'Bore
Financial Controller: Urmilla Akoumbou
Managers
    Civil Engineering: Ferdinand Mbo Edou
    Operations: M Namry
    Rolling Stock: D Yembit
    Signalling, Telecommunications and Energy: Suzanne Mengome
    Commercial: Guillaume Opaga Okouma
    Privatisation: Marie-Thérèse Ngandji
International Relations: Isabelle Bâ-Oumar

Gauge: 1,435 mm
Route length: 814 km

### Political background
Construction of the Trans-Gabon Railway from Libreville/Owendo to Booué started in 1974 and the first section between Owendo and N'Djolé (183 km) opened in 1979. Plans originally called for construction first of the main Owendo-Booué section, and later extensions south to Franceville and north to iron ore fields at Belinga. However, the economic case for continuous construction of the Booué-Franceville line was found to be overwhelming, as there are large deposits of manganese ore at Moanda in the Haut-Ogooué as well as extensive reserves of timber.

Services were inaugurated over the 162 km from N'Djolé to Booué in 1983, and the Booué-Franceville section was completed in 1986.

OCTRA is burdened by serious debt, attributable to a number of factors, ranging from the costs of its construction to high operating costs as a result of climatic conditions, and its obligation to carry out social projects that are not strictly railway related. As a result, there is a backlog of investment in track and rolling stock.

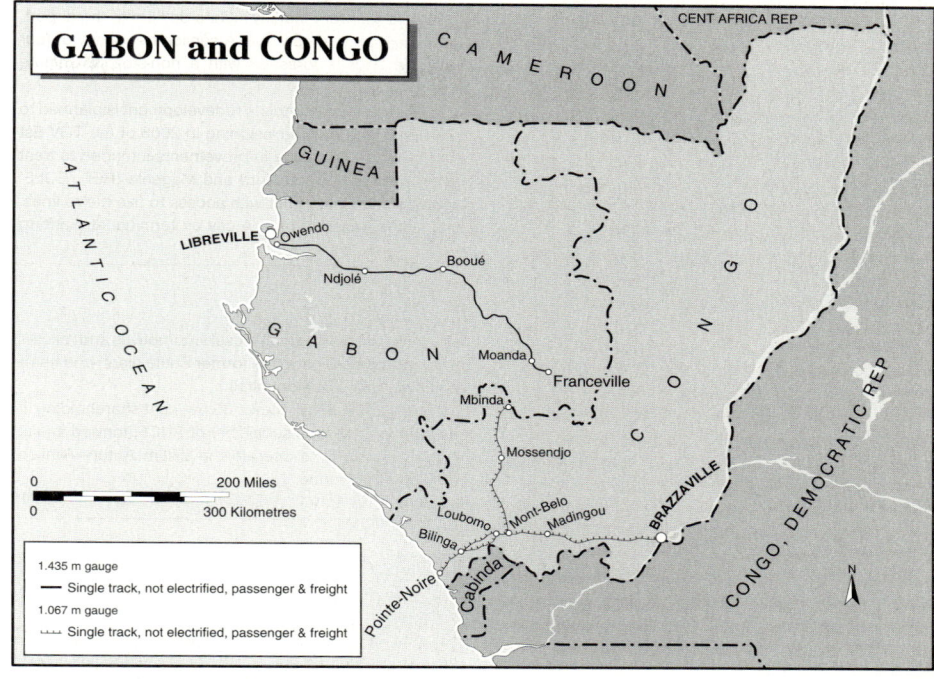

Partial privatisation has been initiated, and two consortia bidding to take a 51 per cent share in OCTRA were due to submit final offers by the end of 1998.

### Passenger operations
Passenger traffic on OCTRA is modest. There were 191,000 journeys in 1996, 85 million passenger-km.

### Freight operations
In 1995 OCTRA carried 2.9 million tonnes (3 million in 1995) for 493 million tonne-km (503 million in 1995), compared to 2.1 million tonnes in 1991. Timber is the principal commodity hauled, generating half the railway's revenue; containers and manganese are also important.

### New lines
The 230 km branch northwards from Booué to Belinga, where vast iron ore and manganese deposits are awaiting exploitation, will not be built until there is an upturn in world demand for manganese. If the line is built, it could generate about 3 million tonnes of freight each year.

### Traction and rolling stock
Diesel locomotive stock comprises 12 Bombardier 2,685 kW MX636, designated locally CC200; 22 Alsthom BB100; six Krupp-MaK 760 kW diesel-hydraulic locomotives based on the company's Type G1203, but with Cummins engines; six 760 kW diesel-hydraulic locomotives from Cockerill; five Brush 90-tonne 820 kW Bo-Bos with Cummins engines and Brush alternator transmission; and 12 other diesel shunters, including a pair from Hyundai of South Korea. In 1996 more than two-thirds of the fleet was reported to be under repair or out of service.

Passenger cars total 16 and there are 935 wagons.

### Track
**Rail:** 50 kg/m
**Crossties (sleepers):** Wood, 1,670/km
**Max gradient:** 0.5%
**Max axleload:** 23 tonnes

---

# GEORGIA

**Ministry of Transport**

Kazbegi ul 12, 380012 Tbilisi
Tel: (+995 32) 93 25 46    Fax: (+995 32) 93 91 45

**Key personnel**
Minister: Merab Adeishvili

## Georgian Railways (GRZhD)

Gruzinskaya Zhelezneya Doroga
Avenue Carica, Tamara 15, 380012 Tbilisi
Tel: (+995 32) 95 25 27    Fax: (+995 32) 95 25 27
e-mail: webmaster@georail.org.ge
Web: http://www.railway.ge

**Key personnel**
President: Akakii Chkhaidze

Gauge: 1,520 mm, 912 mm
Route length: 1,575 km, 37 km
Electrification: Mostly at 3 kV DC; 37 km at 1.5 kV DC

# RAILWAY SYSTEMS/Georgia—Germany

*Class VL8 3 kV DC electric locomotive on freight service at Borjomi* (Norman Griffiths) 2000/0088216

## Political background
Civil unrest since Georgia's independence in 1991 has led to army control of the principal routes and caused much disruption to normal operations.

Traffic to/from Russia was halted in 1992 when the Abkhaz secessionist conflict erupted. Russian-Georgian and Russian-Abkhaz protocols for the resumption of traffic were signed in September and October 1995.

Armenia and Azerbaijan, beneficiaries of such a restoration (on the main line between Zestafoni and the Azerbaijan border, 90 per cent of freight is in transit between Black Sea ports, Armenia and Azerbaijan), will help Georgian Railways rehabilitate this route. However, work is unlikely to start before the Abkhazian problem finds a political solution. Meanwhile a secessionist Abkhazian State Railway has been founded, *de facto* rather than *de jure*, to operate a few trains inside Abkhazia.

## Organisation
The network comprises the greater part of the Caucasian Railway of the former SZhD. Its principal route is the electrified double-track running from the border point with Russia on the Black Sea coast at Sochi/Veseloe, via Sukhumi, Ochamchire, Samtredia, Zestafoni, Khashuri and Gori to Tbilisi, where it divides. One line runs to Baku in Azerbaijan, the other to Yerevan in Armenia.

Much of the terrain is inhospitable. There are severe gradients on the Zestafoni—Khashuri route, which rises 2,000 m in 60 km (2.8 per cent ruling gradient); there are radii as tight as 160 m. Train weights are restricted to 2,500-3,000 tonnes with three locomotives.

Workers employed in railway trades totalled 15,662 in 2001. Operating staff totalled 12,404.

## Passenger and freight operations
The Georgian Railways began a perceptible recovery in 1996, with the restoration of old schedules and a reduction of freight tariffs. Freight trains now take one day to cross from Batumi to Baku, compared to 13 in 1994. Five million tonnes of freight were carried in 1996 and by 2000 the figure had risen to 11.5 million tonnes (for comparison, 36.2 million tonnes were carried in 1989). From late 1996 a container service has been provided between the Black Sea port of Poti and Baku, Azerbaijan. In 2000 more than 70 per cent of freight tonnage was transit traffic.

Passenger revenue in 1996 grew fivefold over the previous year; in 1995, 371 million passenger-km were travelled rising to 572 million in 1997 and then relapsing to 355 million in 1999.

In August 1997 the Tbilisi—Moscow passenger service was restored after four years' cessation; it operates via Baku.

The narrow-gauge Borzhomi—Bakuriany line serves tourism and skiing traffic.

## New lines
The long-projected Arkhot Railway connection across the Caucasus mountains from Tbilisi to Ordzhonkidze in Russia came back on to the agenda when the country gained independence. Three routes have been canvassed for the tortuous ascent from the Tbilisi area to the Arkhot pass, that favoured being a direct line from Gori, some 80 km west of Tbilisi, up the valley of the Liakhvi river to Tskhinvali. The alignment would then strike northeast through a summit tunnel in the Kazbegi area to reach Tarskoye in the Terek valley, thence following the river to Ordzhonkidze.

The proposed double-track and electrified route would extend to some 180 km and would require substantial lengths of bridging and tunnelling. The summit bore alone would exceed 20 km in length. Six intermediate stations are planned.

In 1995, Georgia and Turkey agreed to build a new line between Kars and Tbilisi via Akhalkalaki to replace the existing line via Armenia. This would involve an upgrade of the existing 190 km from Tbilisi to Akhalkalaki and a new 32 km link to the Turkish border. Bids for a build-operate-transfer concession, which could also include the Turkish section of the US$700 million electrified double-track line, were invited in 1998. The cost of the project will be shared equally by the two countries. However, in 1998 tenders to build the Turkish section were cancelled due to reported difficulties funding the Georgian portion of the line. In 1999, the governments of the two countries established a joint commission to handle the tendering process for the scheme.

## Improvements to existing lines
The completion of work on the river bridge at Natanebi has reconnected the Black Sea port of Batumi with the railway network. The Marelisi—Zestafoni section of the main line is being slowly reconstructed.

## Traction and rolling stock
In 2001 the electric locomotive stud, mainly of Classes VL8, VL10, VL11 and VL22, numbered 226, including examples stored out of use. The diesel locomotive fleet totalled 154, including examples stored out of use.

The passenger coach fleet numbered 590 vehicles and the freight fleet 20,000 wagons, of which 5,000 were in service.

An initial batch of four DR1A dmus has been modernised with MTU engines in place of the original Russian units.

## Electrification
The network is fully electrified at 3 kV DC, the 37 km stretch at 1.5 kV DC being the steeply graded 912 mm gauge branch from Borzhomi to Bakuriani (possibly the only remaining line at this gauge in the former USSR).

*912 mm gauge 1.5 kV DC electric locomotive at Tsagveri* (Norman Griffiths) 2000/0088215

---

# GERMANY

## Ministry of Transport
Krausenstrasse 17-20, D-10117 Berlin

**Key personnel**
Minister: Kurt Bodewig
Secretary of State: M Henke
Parliamentary Secretary: Manfred Carstens
Railways Department Manager: H G Gern

## Federal Railway Administration (EBA)
Eisenbahn-Bundesamt
Vorgebirgsstrasse 49, D-53119 Bonn
Tel: (+49 228) 98 26; 0   Fax: (+49 228) 98 26; 199
Web: http://www.bund.de

**Key personnel**
President: Horst Stuchly
Vice-President and Head of Division 1: Ralf Schweinsberg
Head of Division 2: Dr-Ing Jens Böhlke
Head of Division 3: (vacant)
Head of Division 4: Peter Schäfer

The Restructuring of the Railways Act 1993 (*Eisenbahnneuordungsgesetz (ENeuOG)*), provided for the creation of the Federal Railway Administration (*Eisenbahn-Bundesamt (EBA)*) as an independent body under the Federal Ministry of Transport to exercise the rights and duties of the state other than those specifically within the sphere of the Federal Ministry with respect to the restructured railway industry. The EBA came into existence on 1 January 1994. It is based in Bonn, and there are 15 branch offices, one in each of the former DB/DR regional divisions.

The EBA is made up of a President's office and four divisions. Each of the 15 branch offices mirrors the organisation of the headquarters. At presidential level there is also a Preliminary Investigation Bureau, upon the work of which the Federal Audit Office bases its instructions.

The divisions are:
Division 1 : Legal Matters, Approval of Plans, Central Services (four departments)
Division 2 : Infrastructure, Operations, MAGLEV (four departments)
Division 3 : Rolling stock, plants (five departments)
Division 4 : Infrastructure investment (four departments)

Division 1 deals with legal questions relating to the supervision of the railways and with the central services of the EBA. The railway supervisory authorities in the federal states base their regulations for regional railways on those applied at federal level by this division of the EBA. Division 2 deals with all matters of safety connected with infrastructure and operation and with all matters of approval and exemption under the EBO and the signalling regulations, and Division 3 deals with similar questions affecting rolling stock. Division 4 deals with the rationing of the funds assigned by the federal government to the EBA for investment in infrastructure (some DM10 billion a year).

Loans are normally provided interest-free, repayable on a depreciation basis within 40 years. Non-repayable grants are occasionally given, however, on the basis of economic considerations verified by this division. Each project involving federal funds is the subject of a specific agreement covering full details of the scheme, funding methods, and the amount to be spent, and each agreement is based on a specified set of rules.

*2001*/0114289

## Federal Railways Fund (BEV)

Bundeseisenbahnvermögen
Kurt-Georg-Kiesinger Allee 2, D-53175 Bonn
Tel: (+49 228) 307 70   Fax: (+49 228) 307 71 60
e-mail: info@bev-bahnimmobilien.de
Web: http://www.bev-bahnimmobilien.de

### Key personnel
President: Herr Heine
Head, Division 1: Herr Schilling
Head, Division 2: Herr von Niebelschütz
Head, Division 3: Herr Linder
Head of Public Affairs: Herr Scheuber

The *Bundeseisenbahnvermögen* (BEV) (Federal Railways Fund) is the third of the trio of organisations established by the *Eisenbahnneuordnungsgesetz (EneuOG)* 1993. Its functions are the administration and management of non-operational railway estate (currently valued at over DM11.3 billion), co-operation with the Federal Debt Administration in the management of transferred accumulated debt of the former state railways, management of some 70,000 personnel in civil service grades assigned to DB AG, responsibility for the pensions of railway staff in such grades and operation of staff welfare schemes (principally the provision of railway housing).

The BEV has no independent legal capacity – it is technically a *Sondervermögen* (special asset) of the Federal Republic, as DB and DR were previously – although it can act, sue and be sued under its own name. It has its own economic management and accounting functions, and is authorised to raise funds by the issue of debt securities and treasury bills or by taking up loans. Any proper expenditure not covered through income is borne by the federal budget. The total financing requirement is up to DM15 billion a year.

The headquarters of the BEV are in Bonn. Organisationally, there is a two-tier structure: three divisions (and a number of special departments) report to the president, and between five and seven *Referate* report to the head of each division. The First Division deals with personnel matters, education, organisation and central services; the Second Division handles all legal affairs, medical matters, property and housing; and the Third Division is responsible for finances, information technology and telecommunications. There are regional offices in Berlin, Cologne, Essen, Frankfurt am Main (with an outpost in Saarbrücken), Hannover (with an outpost in Hamburg), Karlsruhe (with an outpost in Stuttgart), Munich and Nuremberg.

## AKN Railway

AKN Eisenbahn AG
Rudolf-Diesel Strasse 2, D-24568 Kaltenkirchen
Tel: (+49 4191) 93 30   Fax: (+49 4191) 93 33 09
Web: http://www.akn.de

### Key personnel
Managing Director: Johannes Krusznski
Operations Manager: Dr Ing Klaus Franke

Gauge: 1,435 mm
Route length: 204 km (131 km owned, 73 km operated and maintained for third parties)

### Organisation
The present company was created by the merger of several local government-owned lines in and around Hamburg.

### Passenger operations
The main line from Hamburg to Eidelstedt via Kaltenkirchen to Neumünster runs in its southern section effectively as a diesel-operated S-Bahn. It connects with the electrified S-Bahn at Hamburg-Eidelstedt. Through services via DB tracks to Hamburg Hbf are planned. The line from Norderstedt to Ulzburg is operated on behalf of Verkehrsgesellschaft Norderstedt and connects with the Hamburg metro at Norderstedt. The Neumünster–Heide line (61 km) is operated under contract for DB.

In 2000 AKN secured a contract to operate services on the Heide–Büsum line (20 km) for three years from November of that year. From December 2001 AKN was to take over the operation of the Neumünster–Bad Segeberg–Bad Oldesloe route in a joint venture with Hamburger Hochbahn.

Traffic statistics for all lines in 1999 were 5.9 million passengers and 66.4 million passenger-km.

## 154 RAILWAY SYSTEMS/Germany

**Freight operations**
Traffic statistics for 1999 were 101,000 tonnes and 2.9 million tonne-km.

**Traction and rolling stock**
The AKN fleet comprises 30 two-car dmus, two diesel railcars and six diesel locomotives.

In 2000 AKN ordered five LINT lightweight dmus from Alstom for delivery in 2001.

*Type VT66.1 dmu at Ulzburg Süd (Marcel Vleugels)*
*2001/0109845*

# Albtalbahn (AVG)

Albtal-Verkehrs-Gesellschaft mbH (AVG)
Tullastrasse 71, D-76131 Karlsruhe
Tel: (+49 721) 610 70  Fax: (+49 721) 61 07 50 09
e-mail: avg@karlsruhe.de
Web: http://www.kvv.de

**Key personnel**
Managing Director and Operations Manager:
 Dr-Ing E h Dipl-Ing Dieter Ludwig
Assistant Operating Manager: Dipl-Ing Siegfried Lorenz

Gauge: 1,435 mm
Route length: 301 km (operated, includes duplication of routes)
Electrification: 750 V DC and 15 kV 16⅔Hz AC

**Organisation**
AVG is affiliated with the municipal transport company of Karlsruhe.

**Passenger operations**
The original AVG line ran from Karlsruhe via Ettlingen to Bad Herrenalb/Ittersbach. Since 1966 operations have been extended over DB lines which have been either bought or leased or are operated under contract by AVG. AVG services now extend from Karlsruhe to Bruchsal-Menzingen/Odenheim, Bretten—Eppingen, Pforzheim, Baden-Baden and Wörth. AVG regional routes penetrate the centre of Karlsruhe via tramway tracks. AVG trains run more frequently than former DB services and the number of passengers has more than doubled on some lines. Traffic statistics for 1999 are 44.3 million passengers and 272 million passenger-km, compared with 40.7 million passengers in 1998. These figures include bus operations with a fleet of 27 buses.

**Freight operations**
Traffic statistics for 1999 were 62,724 tonnes and 645,782 tonne-km, compared with 87,744 tonnes in 1998.

**Improvements to existing lines**
The line from Eppingen to Heilbronn has been leased from DB and electrified. Work on an extension to Heilbronn city centre as a tramway was completed in September 1999. In 2000, lines from Pforzheim to Bad Wildbad and from Rastatt to Freudenstadt, both at the limits of the existing network, were leased from DB. After electrification they will extend the system served by dual-voltage light rail vehicles.

**Traction and rolling stock**
A fleet of 211 electric light rail vehicles, owned by AVG, Verkehrsbetriebe Karlsruhe and DB, are operated in a pool. Out of these 69 are equipped for dual-voltage operation. Also in the fleet in 1999 were four diesel locomotives and five diesel railcars (stored).

# Augsburger Localbahn

Augsburger Localbahn GmbH
Friedberger Strasse 43, D-86161 Augsburg
Tel: (+49 821) 56 09 70  Fax: (+49 821) 560 97 45

**Key personnel**
Managing Director: Dipl-Ing Dietrich Neumann
Operating Manager: Georg Konetzki

Gauge: 1,435 mm
Route length: 27 km

**Organisation**
Public freight line serving the city of Augsburg and its environs. The company is mainly owned by its clients, with the city of Augsburg holding a minority share.

**Freight operations**
Connects with DB at Augsburg-Ring and serves many private sidings. Now also operates freight services over DB lines. Carries approximately 430,000 tonnes annually.

**Traction and rolling stock**
Seven diesel locomotives, including two ex-Deutsche Reichsbahn Class 201 to work trains over DB lines.

# BASF

BASF AG
Gebäude B818, Carl-Bosch-Strasse 38, D-67056, Ludwigshafen, Germany
Tel: (+49 621) 605 52 96

**Key personnel**
Logistics Manager: Bernd Flickinger

Gauge: 1,435 mm
Route length: 209 km

**Organisation**
Railway operations undertaken by the chemicals company BASF.

**Freight operations**
As well as operating its own internal rail system, BASF in 1997 commenced services conveying its own products over parts of the DB network and beyond, including a Ludwigshafen—Antwerp service. In early 2001 BASF, two other German companies, Hoyer and VTG, and Bertschi in Switzerland, combined to form rail4chem, a jointly owned company set up to operate chemicals trains in Europe.

**Traction and rolling stock**
In 1999, BASF undertook a one-year lease of the Adtranz Class 250 'Blue Tiger' prototype diesel-electric locomotive. Also in 1999, the company leased from Adtranz two new electric locomotives of a design similar to the DB Class 145.

For its internal operations BASF has 20 diesel locomotives. It also owns some 900 wagons.

# Bayer AG

Eisenbahn Köln—Mulheim—Leverkusen der Bayer AG (EKML)
Bayerwerk ZL VKB SH LEV Schiene, Gebäude X6, D-51368 Leverkusen
Tel: (+49 214) 30 85 24  Fax: (+49 214) 307 24 75

**Key personnel**
Operating Manager: Dipl-Ing Bernd Lauhoff

Gauge: 1,435 mm
Route length: 5 km

**Organisation**
Industrial line of the Bayer chemical works which also carries limited quantities of other freight traffic.

**Freight operations**
Traffic statistics for 1999 were 540,000 tonnes and 3.2 million tonne-km.

**Traction and rolling stock**
Four diesel locomotives.

Jane's World Railways 2002-2003

# Germany/RAILWAY SYSTEMS

## Bayerische Oberlandbahn (BOB)

Bayerische Oberlandbahn GmbH
Bahnhofplatz 1, D-83607 Holzkirchen
Tel: (+49 8024) 99 71 71   Fax: (+49 8024) 99 71 10
e-mail: auskunft@bayerischeoberlandbahn.de
Web: http://www.bayerischeoberlandbahn.de

**Key personnel**
Managing Director: Heino Seeger

Gauge: 1,435 mm
Route length: 204 km

**Organisation**
This company is a joint venture of Connex (formerly DEG) (75 per cent) and Bayerische Zugspitzbahn (25 per cent). A 15-year contract has been awarded to BOB by Bayerische Eisenbahngesellschaft, an executive agency of the state of Bavaria, to run passenger services over the Munich–Holzkirchen–Bayrischzell, Munich–Schaftlach–Tegernsee and Munich–Lenggries lines, a network of 120 km.

*Bayerische Oberlandbahn IVT-built ID5 'Integral' dmu (Milan Šrámek)* 2000/0093219

**Traction and rolling stock**
The fleet comprises 17 five-section dmus built by IVT. These returned to service in 2001 after remedial attention by their builders aimed at improving reliability.

## Behala

Berliner Hafen- und Lagerhausbetriebe AÖR
Westhafenstrasse 1, D-13353 Berlin
Tel: (+49 30) 39 09 50   Fax: (+49 30) 39 90 51 39

**Key personnel**
Chairman: Dipl-Ing Rainer Frohne
Rail Operations Manager: Günter Klein

Gauge: 1,435 mm
Track length: 27 km

**Organisation**
Not a public carrier, the Berlin port railway serves the Westhafen in the former western part of the city.

**Freight operations**
Traffic statistics for 1999 were 1.1 million tonnes.

**Traction and rolling stock**
Four diesel locomotives.

## Bentheimer Eisenbahn (BE)

Bentheimer Eisenbahn AG (BE)
Bahnhofstrasse 24, D-48455 Bad Bentheim
Tel: (+49 5922) 75 0   Fax: (+49 5922) 75 55

**Key personnel**
Managing Director: Dipl.-Betr wirt Peter Hoffmann
Operations Manager: Dipl-Ing Ulrich Walther

Gauge: 1,435 mm
Route length: 76 km

**Freight operations**
The only German regional railway of which the service extends across the border to Coevorden, the Netherlands. BE operates container terminals at Nordhorn and Coevorden and connects with DB at Bad Bentheim and with NS at Coevorden. Also runs freight trains over DB tracks.

Traffic statistics for 1999 were 581,000 tonnes and 31.7 million tonne-km.

**Traction and rolling stock**
In 1999 the fleet comprised 13 diesel locomotives and 67 freight wagons.

## Bodensee—Oberschwaben—Bahn GmbH (BOB)

Kornblumenstrasse 7/1, D-88046 Friedrichshafen
Tel: (+49 7541) 50 50   Fax: (+49 7541) 50 52 21
e-mail: info@bob-fn.de
Web: http://www.bob-fn.de

**Key personnel**
Managing Director: Dipl-Betr.wirt Peter Turkowski

Gauge: 1,435 mm
Route length: 42 km (entirely over DB tracks)

**Organisation**
Owned by city and local authorities. Services started in 1993. Operated by Hohenzollerische Landesbahn (HzL) (qv).

**Passenger operations**
Traffic statistics for 1999 were 805,000 passengers and 12.2 million passenger-km.

**Traction and rolling stock**
Seven diesel railcars.

## BSL – Olefinverbund GmbH

PO Box I163, D-06217 Merseburg
Tel: (+49 3461) 49 21 92   Fax: (+49 3461) 49 80 18

**Key personnel**
Managing Directors: Bart Groot; Heino Zell
Operating Managers
 Schkopau plant: Dipl-Ing Jürgen Jahnke
 Böhlen plant: Dipl-Ing Michael Landgraf
Logistics, rail traffic: Dipl-Wirtsch-Ing Peter Ludwig

Gauge: 1,435 mm
Track length: 94.5 km

**Organisation**
Industrial railway.

**Freight operations**
Traffic statistics for 1997 were 6.1 million tonnes and 20.6 million tonne-km, compared with 5.6 million tonnes and 16.2 million tonne-km in 1996.

**Traction and rolling stock**
15 locomotives, 86 freight wagons.

## Butzbach—Licher Eisenbahn AG (BLE)

Himmrichsweg 3, D-35510 Butzbach
Tel: (+49 6033) 961 50   Fax: (+49 6033) 96 15 15
e-mail: mail@ble-online.de
Web: http://www.ble-online.de

**Key personnel**
Chief Executive: Dipl-Ing Peter Berking
Operating Manager, Rail: Wolfgang Köhler

Gauge: 1,435 mm
Route length: 24 km (owned, freight only)

**Organisation**
Owned and operated by Hessische Landesbahn (qv).

**Passenger operations**
In 1998 the company took over operation of the Friedberg—Friedrichsdorf line (16 km) from DB and in 1999 operations on the lines from Friedberg to Hungen and Nidda from DB.
 From January 2001 BLE took over services on the Gelnhausen—Nidda—Hungen Giessen line.

**Freight operations**
Limited services continue over two unconnected sections of the original network, connecting with DB at Butzbach and Bad Nauheim respectively. Traffic statistics for 1999 were 67,000 tonnes and 409,000 tonne-km.

**Traction and rolling stock**
One diesel locomotive, with passenger equipment initially leased ad hoc. Traffic has subsequently been handled by some of the 70 GTW 2/6 railcars ordered by Hessische Landesbahn and delivered by Stadler in 2000/01.

## DEG

DEG-Verkehrs-GmbH
Rödelheimer Bahnweg 31, D-60489 Frankfurt-am-Main
Tel: (+49 69) 78 90 00 03    Fax: (+49 69) 789 00 01 91

### Key personnel
Managing Directors
  Dipl-Ing Ulrich Homburg (chair); Arthur-Iren Martini;
  Dipl-Kfm Günther Zobel
Director: Frank Sennhenn

### Organisation
Since 1997 this company has been controlled by Vivendi of France, with a 40 per cent minority stake held by a Baden-Württemberg state-owned public utility company.

DEG owns and/or operates the following railways: Eisenbahn Bremen–Thedinghausen (to be disposed of); Farge–Vegesacker Eisenbahn (FVE); Gross Bieberau–Reinheimer Eisenbahn; Teutoburger Wald Eisenbahn (TWE); Hörseltalbahn; Württembergische Eisenbahn Gesellschaft (WEG); Regiobahn Bitterfeld (qv); Industriebahn Berlin; Regiobahn Bitterfeld; and the Bayerische Oberlandbahn.

DEG is also involved in the following new start-up railways, usually as a joint venture with local government interests: Nord-Ostsee Bahn (in Schleswig-Holstein); Nordwestbahn (Niedersachsen); Ost Mecklenburgische Eisenbahn (OME); Regiobahn Kaarst–Düsseldorf–Mettmann; Wieslauftalbahn (Baden–Württemberg, through WEG); Schönbuchbahn (Baden–Württemberg, through WEG).

By 1999, DEG was operating 511 route-km in Germany. The takeover of services on additional routes was expanded to increase to 1,000 route-km the network operated by DEG.

### Traction and rolling stock
Two diesel locomotives directly owned, leased to associated railways as required.

## Dortmunder Eisenbahn (DE)

Dortmunder Eisenbahn GmbH (DE)
Speicherstrasse 23, D-44147 Dortmund
Tel: (+49 231) 983 95    Fax: (+49 231) 983 96 02

### Key personnel
Managing Director, Technical and Operating Manager:
  Dipl-Ing Heinrich Brod
Managing Director, Commercial: Reiner Woermann

Gauge: 1,435 mm
Route length: 20 km (excluding industrial lines and sidings)

### Organisation
Public freight line serving the port of Dortmund. Also acts as industrial railway for the Hoesch and Krupp steelworks. DE is jointly owned by the city of Dortmund and Krupp-Hoesch AG. Provides third-party maintenance services.

### Freight operations
DE freight trains also run over DB lines. Traffic statistics for 1999 were 30.3 million tonnes. These figures include both public and non-public traffic.

### Traction and rolling stock
43 diesel locomotives, 1,116 freight wagons.

## Duisburg Hafen AG

Alte Ruhrorter Strasse 42-52, D-47119 Duisburg
Tel: (+49 203) 80 31    Fax: (+49 203) 80 32 32

### Key personnel
Chairman: Dipl-Ing Martin Schlegel

Gauge: 1,435 mm
Track length: 92 km, including sidings

### Organisation
Industrial railway of Duisburg public port, operated by DB.

### Freight operations
Traffic statistics for 1999 were 7 million tonnes and 69.3 million tonne-km.

### Traction and rolling stock
One diesel locomotive (owned).

## Dürener Kreisbahn GmbH (DKB)

Kölner Landstrasse 271, D-52351 Düren
Tel: (+49 2421) 390 10    Fax: (+49 2421) 39 01 86

### Key personnel
Managing Director: Dipl-Ing Reinhold Alfter
Assistant Operating Manager, Rail:
  Dipl-Betr wirt Hans-Peter Niessen

Gauge: 1,435 mm
Route length: 71 km, of which 45 km with passenger service

### Organisation
Was a small local freight line until 1993, when it took over the former DB branches from Düren to Heimbach and Jülich. These lines were rehabilitated and a frequent passenger service with Siemens Duewag lightweight railcars has since been established.

In 2001, Connex Gruppe acquired a 51 per cent shareholding in DKB, with the remaining 49 per cent held by Landkreis Düren, the local authority in the region in which services are operated.

### Passenger operations
In addition to its own lines, DKB operates the Mönchengladbach–Dalheim line under contract for DB. In 1999 DKB as a company carried 11.2 million passengers for 105.5 million passenger-km, although these figures include extensive bus operations.

*Dürener Kreisbahn Siemens-built RegioSprinter diesel railcars at Düren* (Eddie Barnes)    2000/0089083

In December 2002, DKB plans to extend some Düren–Heimbach/Jülich services to Cologne.

### Freight operations
Traffic statistics for 1999 were 104,000 tonnes and 737,000 tonne-km. In 1999, the company announced plans to reconstruct its freight terminal at Düren.

### Improvements to existing lines
The Jülich–Linnich line has been rehabilitated for reintroduction of passenger services, which commenced in June 2001. It is also planned to relay the line from Linnich to Baal, which has already been lifted.

### Traction and rolling stock
16 Siemens Duewag RegioSprinter lightweight railcars, 2 diesel locomotives.

*UPDATED*

## Eisenbahn und Hafen GmbH (EH)

Franz-Lenze-Str 15, D-47166 Duisburg
Tel: (+49 203) 521    Fax: (+49 203) 522 42 67

### Key personnel
Managing Directors:
  Norbert Epler
  Dipl-Ing Manfred Redeker
Operating Manager: Dr Ing Jan Fischer

Gauge: 1,435 mm
Track length: 604 km
Electrification: 183 km at 1.5 kV DC

### Organisation
EH is the industrial railway system of the Thyssen steelworks. It serves several other industrial clients, but is not a common carrier. The company operates two private ports on the river Rhine at Schwelgern and Walsum.

### Freight operations
Originally operating in the Duisburg, Dinslaken and Oberhausen areas, EH is now also responsible for the operation of industrial lines at Mülheim, Krefeld and Witten. About one-third of traffic is exchanged with DB.

EH locomotives run freight trains over DB lines, while DB locomotives penetrate into the EH network.

Traffic statistics for 1999 were 63.6 million tonnes and 320.6 million tonne-km.

### Traction and rolling stock
EH operates 111 diesel locomotives (51 of these are dual-mode electric locomotives and have a diesel generator). All locomotives are equipped for remote control. Electric traction to be abandoned gradually by 2007. Also in the fleet are 2,169 freight wagons of different types.

Germany/**RAILWAY SYSTEMS** 157

## EKO Trans

EKO Transportgesellschaft mbH
Werkstrasse 1, D-15890 Eisenhüttenstadt
Tel: (+49 3364) 37 50 60   Fax: (+49 3364) 37 22 30

**Key personnel**
Managing Director: Dr Hans-Joachim Krüger
Operations Manager: Dipl-Ing (FH) Udo Thiede

Gauge: 1,435 mm
Track length: 155 km

**Organisation**
The industrial system of the EKO steelworks, the operator also runs freight trains over DB lines.

**Freight operations**
Traffic statistics for 1999 were 6.4 million tonnes and 50.6 million tonne-km.

**Traction and rolling stock**
EKO operates 17 diesel locomotives and 257 wagons.

## Elbe-Weser Railways (EVB)

Eisenbahnen und Verkehrsbetriebe Elbe-Weser GmbH
Bahnhofstrasse 67, D-27404 Zeven
Tel: (+49 4281) 94 40   Fax: (+49 4281) 944 30
e-mail: info@evb-elbe-weser.de
Web: http://www.evb-elbe-weser.de

**Key personnel**
Managing Director: Dipl-Vw Ulrich Koch
Operating Manager: Heinz Schulze

Gauge: 1,435 mm
Route length: 285 km

**Organisation**
EVB was formed in 1981 by the merger of the Bremervörde–Osterholz and the Wilstedt–Zeven–Tostedt railways, which only carried freight traffic. In 1991 the Bremerhaven–Bremervörde–Stade, Bremervörde–Rotenburg–Brockel and Hesedorf–Hollenstedt lines, totalling 156 km, were taken over from DB. In 1993 the Buxtehude–Harsefeld Railway was taken over.

**Passenger operations**
Passenger services are operated from Bremerhaven via Bremervörde-Harsefeld to Buxtehude and onwards over DB tracks to Hamburg-Neugraben, where a connection is available to the Hamburg S-Bahn. Traffic statistics for 1999 were 910,000 passengers and approximately 13.8 million passenger-km, compared with 878,000 passengers and some 13.0 million passenger-km in 1997.

**Freight operations**
EVB handles container traffic between the deep-sea ports of Hamburg, Bremen and Bremerhaven. EVB trains also run over DB lines, including container trains between Bremerhaven and Munich and Hamburg and Munich. Traffic statistics for 1998 were 195,000 tonnes and approximately 6 million tonne-km, compared with 193,000 tonnes in 1997.

**Traction and rolling stock**
Five dmus (similar to DB Class 628), five diesel railcars and 10 diesel locomotives.

## Erfurter Industriebahn (EIB)

Am Rasenrain 16, D-99086 Erfurt
Tel: (+49 361) 74 20 70   Fax: (+49 361) 742 07 27
e-mail: info@erfurter-bahn.de
Web: http://www.erfurter-bahn.de

**Key personnel**
Managing Director: Dipl-Betr wirt Heidemarie Mähler
Operating Manager: Erwin Nönig

Gauge: 1,435 mm
Route length: 15 km

**Organisation**
Originally an industrial freight line owned by the city of Erfurt. Since 1991 EIB has provided passenger services under contract to Thüringen state.

**Passenger operations**
Railcars are operated under contract to Thüringen state over the Erfurt–Döllstadt–Leinefelde line (84 km), alternating with DB RE (regional) trains. In May 1999, services were extended to Kassel Wilhelmshöhe and in May 2000 EIB commenced operations on the Gotha–Bad LangenSalza line.

**Freight operations**
The main commodity carried is coal for a power station. EIB also runs an industrial line in a chemical plant at Rudolstadt-Schwarza. Traffic statistics in 1997 were 399,000 tonnes and 2.3 million tonne-km, compared with 625,000 tonnes and 3.8 million tonne-km in 1996.

**Traction and rolling stock**
Five Adtranz RegioShuttle RS 1 diesel railcars and three diesel locomotives. An additional 26 RegioShuttles were ordered in 1999 for delivery in 2001.

*EIB Adtranz RegioShuttle lightweight diesel railcar (Quintus Vosman)*
0063197

## Rhenus Keolis

NL Bielefeld, Meisenstrasse 65, D-33607 Bielefeld
Tel: (+49 521) 927 37 12   Fax: (+49 521) 927 37 22
Web: http://www.eurobahn.de

**Key personnel**
Managing Director: Jörg Kiehn

**Background**
Formerly Eurobahn, Rhenus Keolis is a joint venture owned by Keolis and Rhenus to operate regional rail services in Germany. The company also operates the Freiberger Eisenbahngesellschaft (qv).

**Passenger operations**
In May 2000, the company took over passenger operations on the Bielefeld–Herford–Bünde–Rahden line (the 'Ravensberger Bahn') and the Bielefeld–Lemgo line, both in Nordrhein-Westfalen. During the previous year, the company took over operations on the Alzey–Kirchheimbolanden line in Rheinhessen.

In December 2000, the company commenced an open access service over DB tracks between Bielefeld and Cologne.

**Traction and rolling stock**
Services are provided with Adtranz RS1 RegioShuttle single-unit railcars: three are employed on Ravensberger Bahn services, two on the line in Rheinhessen.

*UPDATED*

## Farge—Vegesacker Eisenbahn (FVE)

Farger Strasse 128, D-28777 Bremen
Tel: (+49 421) 686 46   Fax: (+49 421) 68 35 60

**Key personnel**
Managing Directors
  Dipl-Ing Heinz Thomas Schare
  Heinz Wolfgramm
Operations Manager: Martin Mertens

Gauge: 1,435 mm
Route length; 10 km

**Organisation**
Associated with and operated by Connex Cargo Logistics GmbH.

**Freight operations**
FVE connects with DB at Bremen-Vegesack. Traffic is mainly coal for a power station. Traffic statistics for 1997 were 490,000 tonnes and 5 million tonne-km.

**Traction and rolling stock**
Four diesel locomotives.

## Frankfurt–Konigsteiner Eisenbahn AG (FKE)

Bahnstrasse 13, D-61462 Königstein
Tel: (+49 6174) 290 10   Fax: (+49 6174) 29 0 15
e-mail: mail@fke-online.de
Web: http://www.fke-online.de

### Key personnel
Chief Executive: Dipl-Ing Peter Berking
General Manager, Rail: Wolfgang Köhler

Gauge: 1,435 mm
Route length: 46 km (includes Taunusbahnen – see below)

### Organisation
Controlled by Hessische Landesbahn (qv), which has a 51 per cent stake, FKE's own line extends from Frankfurt-Höchst to Königstein (16 km). Since 1989 FKE has also operated the former DB Friedrichsdorf-Grävenwiesbach line (29 km) on behalf of Verkehrsverband Hochtaunus (Taunusbahnen). Since 1997 FKE has worked the Frankfurt-Höchst-Bad Soden line (7 km) under contract to DB.

### Passenger operations
A busy suburban carrier, FKE connects with the Frankfurt S-Bahn at Frankfurt-Höchst and Friedrichsdorf. Some peak-hour trains run through over DB tracks to Frankfurt (Main) Hbf. Traffic statistics for 1997 were 5.3 million passengers and 48.7 million passenger-km, compared with 5.1 million passengers in 1994. These figures include bus services using a fleet of 130 vehicles.

### Traction and rolling stock
FKE operates 25 dmus (20 VT 2E built by LHB in 1987-92, and five VT 628 units built by Duewag in 1994/95).

## Freiberger Eisenbahngesellschaft mbH (FE)

Am Bahnhof 17, D-09599 Freiberg
Tel: (+49 3731) 30 07 77   Fax: (+49 3731) 300 77 22
e-mail: info@freiberger-eisenbahn.de
Web: http://www.freiberger-eisenbahn.de

Gauge: 1,435 mm
Route length: 31 km

### Background
FE is a subsidiary of Eurobahn (qv), a joint venture formed by VIA GTI and Rhenus.

### Passenger operations
In November 2000 FE took over the operation of the Freiberg–Mulda–Holzhau line in Saxony.

### Traction and rolling stock
Three Adtranz RegioShuttle RS1 single-unit railcars.

## Georgsmarienhütte Eisenbahn (GET)

Georgsmarienhütte Eisenbahn und Transport GmbH
Neue Hüttenstrasse 1, D-49110 Georgsmarienhütte
Tel: (+49 5401) 39 43 60   Fax: (+49 5401) 39 43 73

### Key personnel
Managing Directors
 Wilfried Hülsmann
 Dipl-Ing Hubert Unland (also Operations Manager)

Gauge: 1,435 mm
Route length: 7.3 km

### Organisation
Industrial steelworks line.

### Freight operations
GET connects with DB at Hasbergen. Line haul traffic is now handled by DB with through trains from Osnabrück, while GET handles shunting movements and internal works traffic. Traffic statistics for 1997 were 721,000 tonnes and 5.3 million tonne-km, compared with 554,000 tonnes and 4.3 million tonne-km in 1996.

### Traction and rolling stock
One diesel locomotive.

## German Railways Group (DB)

Deutsche Bahn Gruppe
Potsdamer Platz 2, D-10785 Berlin
Tel: (+49 30) 29 70   Fax: (+49 30) 29 72 61 30
Stephensonstrasse 1, D-60326 Frankfurt am Main
Tel: (+49 69) 973 30   Fax: (+49 69) 97 33 75 00
Web: http://www.bahn.de

### Key personnel
Chairman of the Supervisory Board: Dr Michael Frenzel
Directors
 Chairman and Managing Director: Hartmut Mehdorn
 Finances and Controlling:
  Dipl-Betriebsw Diethelm Sack
 Marketing: Klaus Daubertshaüser
 Personnel and Social Affairs: Stefan Garber
 Property, Law and Passenger Stations: Dieter Ullsperger
 Research and Technology: Dr Karl-Friedrich Rausch
 Passenger Traffic:
  Dr Phil Christoph Franz
 Freight Traffic: Dr Bernd Malmström
 Infrastructure: Dipl-Ing Roland Heinisch
 Infrastructure Business and Network Planning:
  Dr Thilo Sarrazin
 Purchasing and Materials: Klaus-Bend Bapp
 Department of International Affairs: Klaus Ebeling
 Public Affairs: Dieter Hünerkoch

Gauge: 1,435 mm; narrow gauges
Route length: 38,384 km; 66 km
Electrification: 18,652 km (15 kV 16⅔ Hz AC except for Berlin and Hamburg S-Bahn systems)

### Political background
Under the Restructuring of the Railways Act 1993 (*Eisenbahnneuordungsgesetz (ENeuOG)*), which came into force on 1 January 1994, the former West German *Deutsche Bundesbahn*, East German *Deutsche Reichsbahn*, and the Railway Property in West Berlin were fused as the Federal Railway Assets. These were then divided into a public section and a commercial section. The public section is divided into the Federal Railway Office (*Eisenbahn-Bundesamt (EBA)*), and the Office for Federal Railway Assets (*Bundeseisenbahnvermögen (BEV)*), which deals with the non-operational railway estate, the civil service personnel of the former state railways (who could not because of their status pass under the control of a joint-stock company), and inherited debts. The commercial section of the railway became Deutsche Bahn AG, charged with managing the railway industry according to good business principles in line with German company law. To do this, business sectors, each with its own bottom-line responsibility, were established.

During the 1999 financial year DB AG was converted into a holding company, the *Deutsche Bahn Gruppe* (German Railways Group), under which come five subsidiaries, each with its own bottom-line responsibility. These are:
**DB Netz**, which operates, maintains, and markets the 64,821 km of track belonging to DB and provides infrastructure capacity and services in return for track access charges to some 100 railway traffic operators;
**DB Reise&Touristik**, which runs more than 1,400 long-distance passenger trains a day carrying some 400,000 passengers and, through 13 subsidiaries ranging from the AMEROPA travel agency to the MITROPA AG catering undertaking, provides tourism-related services at home and abroad;
**DB Regio**, which carries some 4 million passengers a day in 29,000 trains linking principal centres and in the regions;
**DB Cargo**, which runs some 6,200 goods trains a day to transport some 300 million tonnes of freight a year and owns some 131,000 goods wagons with a capacity of some 6 million tonnes, as well as more than 4,300 locomotives;
**DB Station&Service**, which operates 5,794 passenger stations and stopping-places throughout Germany.

The changes were envisaged from the start of the restructuring programme and are intended to pave the way for private-sector participation in the national railway.

Further changes were agreed early in 2000. Whilst not affecting the devolution of bottom-line responsibility brought in with the second stage of the railway reforms at the beginning of 1999, these are designed to match responsibilities to customer expectations and to remove divisions of answerability, experience having shown that the structure developed since the 1994 reforms is too complex and not sufficiently customer-focused. It has also become clear that the multitude of individual businesses adds unnecessary costs. The main changes involve the creation of a Marketing Division at Group Management level, bringing the whole of the passenger business together into a single Business Sector, concentration of purchasing into the Chairman's Division from 1 January 2001, creation of a special Property Sector, and rearrangement of groups and service areas like Communications or Legal Services whose activities cross Divisional boundaries. As far as possible, the Sectors will have largely parallel structures, with central functions for finance and audit, marketing and commerce, personnel, and either production and technology or operations.

As a result of these alterations there are now three organisational levels in DB. At the top of the pyramid comes the Group Management. The middle level is made up of five Business Sectors: Infrastructure, Passenger Traffic, Goods Traffic, Passenger Stations and Property. At the base level are the Business Units that have the task of delivering the products for the Business Sectors. These are essentially the existing companies and their structure is not changed – they continue to have full responsibility for production and bottom line. They are: Long Distance Passenger Traffic, Regional Passenger Traffic, Urban Passenger Traffic, European Freight, Regional Freight, Logistics, Stations and Construction & Repair.

In late 2000 the federal government announced an additional DM2,000 million a year of state support for the railway.

### Performance Indicators (€ million)

|  | 1999 | 2000 |
|---|---|---|
| Turnover | 15,630 | 15,465 |
| Pre-tax profit | 91 | 37 |
| Employees at 31 December | 241,638 | 222,656 |
| Fixed assets | 34,071 | 32,815 |
| Balance sheet total (equity & liabilities) | 37,198 | 39,467 |
| Equity capital | 8,701 | 8,788 |
| Gross investment | 8,372 | 6,892 |
| Net investment* | 3,229 | 3,250 |
| Depreciation | 1,966 | 2,052 |
| Pre-tax cash-flow** | 2,107 | 2,113 |

**Notes:** * Gross investment less grants towards construction costs from the federal, Land, and/or local authorities.

** Pre-tax profit plus depreciation of fixed assets and changes in pension reserves.

# Germany/RAILWAY SYSTEMS

*Class 605 ICE TD tilting diesel trainset for Dresden–Nuremberg services* (David Haydock) 2001/0114245

**DB's ICE Fleet**

| Type | No | Introduced | Seating capacity | Max speed km/h |
|---|---|---|---|---|
| ICE 1 | 59 | 1991 | 700 approx | 280 |
| ICE 2 | 44 | 1996 | 368 | 280 |
| ICE 3 | 50 | 2000 | 391 | 330 |
| ICE T | 43 | 1999 | 398 | 230 |
| ICE TD | 20 | 2000 | 196 | 200 |

**Traffic** (million)

| | 1998 | 1999 | 2000 |
|---|---|---|---|
| **DB Reise&Touristik** | | | |
| Passenger journeys | 149 | 146.5 | 144.8 |
| Passenger-km | 34,275 | 34,897 | 26,226 |
| **DB Regio** | | | |
| Passenger journeys | 1,450 | 1,534 | 1,568 |
| Passenger-km | 31,324 | 37,949 | 38,162 |
| **DB Cargo** | | | |
| Freight tonnes | 289 | 279 | 301 |
| Freight tonne-km | 73,273 | 71,494 | 80,634 |

## Traction and rolling stock

All the Deutsche Bahn Gruppe's traction units and rolling stock is assigned to the separate businesses. Overall, at the end of 2000, the total stock stood at 12 steam locomotives, 3,514 electric locomotives, 2,248 diesel locomotives, and 1,262 shunting locomotives. There were 2,076 electric multiple-units (excluding the DC stock of the Berlin and Hamburg S-Bahn systems), 2,001 diesel multiple-units, and 216 railbuses. At the end of 2000 the ICE fleet included 120 ICE 1 power cars and 46 ICE 2 power cars.

DB Regio had 1,637 bilevel passenger coaches. DB Reise&Touristik had 705 ICE 1 trailer cars and 309 ICE 2 trailer cars (45 of them being driving trailers). There were 264 ICE 3 vehicles and 42 ICE T trainsets. In addition to these, there were 1,847 IC/EC coaches and 1,518 IR/D coaches. The night stock comprised 631 vehicles.

DB Cargo had 131,178 freight wagons, and there were 60,611 privately owned wagons and 5,510 hired wagons on the system. Of the owned freight wagons, 33,169 were covered, 40,406 open, 55,895 flats, and 1,708 silo wagons.

*The InterCity Express (ICE) family*
The ICE 1 and ICE 2 fleets are complete.

One ICE 1 was destroyed in the Eschede accident in June 1998, the cause of which appears to have been a broken tyre. All except two of the fleet of 60 ICE 1s had been equipped with Class 064 resilient wheels, authorised for use in 1992, in order to try to eliminate vibration problems that had been encountered. At the instance of the EBA these have now been exchanged for monobloc wheels of the type used in the ICE 2s, at a total cost of some DM30 million. The change brought a recurrence of the vibration problems that led to the introduction of the tyred wheels in the first place, and as a provisional solution DB has specified turning the wheels every 240,000 km. In parallel, investigations are going on into the possibility of inserting a 10 mm damper layer between rail and sleeper on the high-speed lines to reduce the vertical stiffness of the track (which is a contributing factor to the problem). In the longer term DB hopes to be able to return to the use of tyred wheels with ultrasound monitoring. The railway is also examining a suggestion for the acoustic monitoring of bogies during the journey.

In August 1994 DB AG placed a 'run-on' order for 50 eight-car ICE 2-2s from Siemens/AEG. In fact, these trains, of which the first entered service in 2000, are very different from their predecessors and are now designated ICE 3. The design reduces weight still further, cuts fuel consumption and costs, and produces a train suitable for pan-European operation. The ICE 3 is a genuine unit-train: traction is distributed throughout the entire train, with roughly every second axle powered. Advantages include better transmission of tractive effort to rail, reduction of slipping, more seats for the same train length, and a more favourable weight distribution. Axleload is under 17 tonnes. Maximum speed is 330 km/h and the train can work on gradients of up to 40 pro mille. Four trains are to be three-voltage (15 kV 16⅔ Hz AC, 1.5 kV DC, and 25 kV 50 Hz AC) and nine are to be four-voltage (adding the Belgian 3 kV DC) for cross-border workings; the remaining 37 trains are to be equipped only for the German/Austrian/Swiss 15 kV 16⅔ Hz AC (though trains working into Switzerland, of course, require an additional pantograph). Four similar trainsets are being supplied to Netherlands Railways (qv) for services into Germany. Studies are being undertaken into the possibility of equipping a second series of DB AG ICE 3s with tilt.

In 2001 an additional 13 ICE 3s and 28 ICE Ts were ordered. In late 2001, DB withdrew from the planned joint procurement with its Austrian and Swiss counterparts ÖBB and SBB of a fleet of 116 tilting trainsets for TEE Alliance cross-border services. DB had intended to acquire 50 units.

DB has indicated that locomotive haulage of long-distance passenger services will end by 2010, by when trainsets of the ICE family will be used for all traffic of this type.

*Tilting trains*
DB AG's experience of tilting trains dates back to the highly successful introduction of the Fiat-system Class VT610 trains in North Bavaria in the early 1990s. The success of this operation led to a general reappraisal of future policy (also connected with tighter financial conditions), as a result of which three new types of tilting train were ordered.

For InterCity services on electrified lines 40 tilting unit-trains of Classes 411 and 415 are being delivered. The first units came into service in 1999 on Stuttgart–Zurich services. Externally, these trains resemble the ICE family, and they share internal design and equipment with the ICE 3 units. The ICE Ts use the latest, all-under-floor, Fiat tilt technology. With up to 8° body-tilt and a maximum uncompensated lateral acceleration of 2.0 m/s$^2$, the ICE Ts can run through curves up to 30 per cent faster than classic stock and can reduce journey times by 15 to 20 per cent. Top speed is 230 km/h and the trains are formed of five or seven vehicles, the majority being seven. Because the ICE T has a slightly smaller profile than the ICE, on account of the need to allow for the tilt, there is a marginal reduction in comfort. The motors are positioned lengthways under the floors and deliver a performance similar to that of the ICE 3 (though with a lower maximum speed). The seven-car sets include a restaurant, the shorter sets have a bistro.

For InterCity services on non-electrified lines, 20 diesel-powered four-car 200 km/h tilting trains (Class 605) are being built in a DM280 million contract with Siemens (with its Duewag AG subsidiary) and Deutsche Waggonbau AG. The first vehicles were in production at the start of 1998 and the trains came into use in April 2001 on Dresden–Nuremberg services. Each train offers 195 seats (41 first, 148 second, and six in a mother-and-child compartment) and there is an all-standing bar-area. Addition of a fifth car for strengthening is possible, and the sets can run in multiple. Motors and tilt-mechanism (the Siemens electromechanical system) are bogie-mounted.

The third new class of tilting train is designed for local passenger traffic and is the Class 611. Adtranz has supplied 50 diesel-powered two-car units with a top speed of 160 km/h which use a tilt technology with a military origin, developed from that in the Leopard tank, and a Voith hydraulic transmission. Each train offers 141 seats,

*ICE T set forming a Singen–Stuttgart service at Horb* (Colin Boocock) 2000/0089563

*Class 611 RegioSwinger tilting dmus forming a Cologne–Saarbrücken service at Saarburg* (John C Baker) 2001/0114246

and a closed toilet system is used. There have been many problems with these trains. A further 197 generally similar Class 612 two-car units were ordered by DB Regio from Adtranz (now Bombardier Transportation), while 21 were ordered by DB Reise&Touristik. Deliveries were in progress in 2001.

*New electric locomotives*
In 1994 DB AG ordered equipment to a value of DM4 billion. In addition to the ICE 3 and the three classes of tilting trains mentioned above, 420 locomotives (of the three types described below) and 339 S-Bahn units were ordered, with options for a further 500 locomotives and 200 S-Bahn units to a value of DM3.5 billion. Deliveries began before the end of 1996, and the arrival of the new stock is allowing a large part of the obsolete equipment from the 1960s and 1970s, now unreliable and expensive to maintain, to be scrapped. The urgent need for the replacement of locomotives is proved by the fact that 20 per cent of all daily perturbations in traffic are currently caused by locomotive faults and failures.

Class 103 has been replaced by the new Adtranz Class 101, of which 145 have been built. These three-phase, AC drive, 6,000 kW locomotives have a top speed of 220 km/h. They are being used initially on the InterCity network, but as more ICEs and ICTs come on stream they will gravitate towards freight traffic.

There will be 170 representatives of the new Class 152 from Krauss-Maffei/Siemens. This class, based on the EuroSprinter supplied to Spain, Portugal, and most recently Greece, is a heavy freight locomotive, also with a 6,000 kW rating and a 140 km/h maximum speed. Deliveries began in 1997. Along with the 101s, these machines will replace the 30-year-old Class 150s.

Over the next few years Classes 110, 139, 140, 141 and 143, some of them more than 30 years old, will begin to be replaced by a first delivery of 80 of Adtranz's new Hennigsdorf-built Class 145, of 4,200 kW continuous power and with a 140 km/h maximum speed. Delivery began in early 1998. Like the new Class 101, Class 145 belongs to the Adtranz modular family of locomotives, so major components have all already been fully tested in Class 101. In 2001 deliveries commenced from Bombardier of 31 Class 146 locomotives, a 160 km/h passenger version of the Class 145. An option for a further 400 similar machines was taken up in July 1998; these will be designated Class 185 and will be dual-frequency, to allow their use in cross-border freight traffic as well as in domestic traffic. Deliveries commenced in April 2001. They are being delivered at 50 a year from the beginning of 2001, flowing on from completion of the Class 145 order at the end of 2000. Three pre-serial production locomotives will be built. Other multisystem locomotives on order in 2001 were 25 Class 182 dual-voltage (25 kV AC/15 kV AC) Siemens 'Taurus' units and 100 Class 189 machines. The first of the former type was to be handed over to DB Cargo in August 2001.

*Diesel locomotives*
In 2001, orders were placed by DB Cargo for replacement engines to modernise 140 Class 232 Soviet-built diesel-electric locomotives. The existing Kolomna 5D49 engine is being replaced by a 2,235 kW 12D49 unit from the same manufacturer. The move followed the earlier trial installation of similar engines in two locomotives of the same class.

*Multiple-unit fleet renewal*
DB Regio is spending almost DM6 billion in the greatest ever investment programme in new trains for local traffic, designed to fit services for the new century. Included in the orders are 440 S-Bahn sets and electric units for regional traffic as well as the Class 605 diesel sets discussed in the 'Tilting trains' section above. Additionally, more lightweight and double-deck units are being bought. A further DM1 billion will go on the modernisation of existing stock.

The Munich, Stuttgart, and Frankfurt/Main S-Bahn systems are receiving 100 new Class 423 units, built by Adtranz with the participation of Alstom and having a floor height of 998 mm. These replace the Class 420/421 equipment dating from 1972. There is an option for a further 200 sets.

An order for 60 units of a new Class 424 was placed with a consortium of Adtranz, Siemens, and DWA (Bombardier Transportation). These were to have a 760 mm floor height, and the electronics were to be largely underfloor. Of the 60, 45 were for the new Hannover Expo 2000 S-Bahn, Dresden, and Leipzig; the remainder were to be deployed in the Mannheim area.

*Class 101 electric locomotive at Singen with an InterRegio service* (David Haydock)

**DB AG lightweight diesels unit on order/delivered**

| Class | Type |
|---|---|
| 640 001 to 640 030 | Alstom single-unit trains |
| 641 001 to 641 040 | De Dietrich DB/SNCF joint local units similar to Class 640 |
| 642 001 to 642 150 | Siemens-Duewag two-unit trains |
| 643 001 to 643 075 | Bombardier-Talbot diesel-hydraulic dmus |
| 644 001 to 644 058 | Bombardier-Talbot diesel-electric dmus |
| 646 001 to 646 030 | Adtranz GTW2/6 |
| 648 001 to 648 ??? | Alstom Coradia LINT two-car units |
| 650 101 to 650 127 | Adtranz single-unit RegioShuttle RS1 |
| 670 101 to 670 128 | Double-deck railbuses of the second series |

**Electric railcars or multiple-units (excluding Berlin and Hamburg S-Bahn stock)**

| Class | Cars per unit | Line voltage | Motor cars per unit | Motored axles/car | Power kW | Speed km/h | Weight tonnes | No in service | First built | Builders Mechanical | Electrical |
|---|---|---|---|---|---|---|---|---|---|---|---|
| 401 [1] | - | 15 kV | - | - | 4,800 | 280 | 80 | 120 | 1989 | KM, Krupp, Henschel | ABB, AEG, Siemens |
| 402 [2] | - | 15 kV | - | - | 5,000 | 280 | 80 | 44 | 1996 | - | - |
| 403 | 8 | 15 kV | - | - | 8,000 | 330 | - | 37* | 1999 | - | - |
| 406 | 8 | 15 kV | - | - | 8,000 | 330 | - | 13* | 1999 | - | - |
| 411 | 7 | 15 kV | - | - | 4,000 | 230 | - | 32* | 1999 | DWA/Duewag/Fiat | Siemens |
| 415 | 5 | 15 kV | - | - | 3,000 | 230 | - | 11* | 1999 | DWA/Duewag/Fiat | Siemens |
| 420/421 | 3 | 15 kV | - | - | 2,400 | 120 | 138 | 480 | 1971 | MBB/MAN | AEG/BBC/SSW |
| 423 | 4 | 15 kV | - | - | 2,350 | 140 | - | 190* | 1999 | Adtranz | Alstom |
| 424 | 4 | 15 kV | - | - | 2,350 | 140 | 108 | 40* | 1999 | Adtranz/DWA/Siemens | - |
| 425 | 4 | 15 kV | - | - | 2,350 | 160 | 108 | 156* | 1999 | Adtranz | Alstom |
| 426 | 2 | 15 kV | - | - | 1,175 | 160 | 60.9 | 43* | 1999 | Adtranz/DWA/Siemens | - |
| 445 | 3 | 15 kV | - | - | 3,600 | 140 | 179 | 1* | 1999 | Adtranz/DWA/Siemens | - |
| 450 | 3 | 15 kV/750-V | - | - | 560 | 100 | - | 4 | 1994 | Duewag/ABB/WV | - |
| 'Thalys' [3] | - | 4-cur | - | - | 8,800 | 300 | - | 4 | 1997 | Alstom | Alstom |

**Note:** [1] ICE 1 power car  [2] ICE 2 power car  [3] Thalys power car  *Number ordered

*Class 423 articulated emu built by Adtranz for Cologne services* (Colin Boocock)

The same consortium was given an order for a further 136 four-car units designated Class 425, a variant of the Class 424 design with more seats, fewer doors, and a 160 km/h maximum speed, for Express S-Bahn work on longer routes, together with 43 two-car units designated Class 426 and essentially shortened Class 425s. Classes 425 and 426 are provided with entry steps to allow them to work on lines without high station platforms. All three classes were to be articulated. It was then announced in early 1996 that the Class 424 design would not be built. Instead, an additional 60 Class 425s are being constructed, provided that automatic entry steps can be provided to deal with platform heights of 380, 560, and 760 mm. Examples of both Class 425 and 426 entered service with DB Regio in 2001.

The new Class 474 units for Hamburg's S-Bahn began to enter service in August 1997. All were in traffic by July 2001. Floor level in the new units is 100 mm lower than in their predecessors, to help all passengers but especially the disabled. Glass dividing walls allow a good view through the whole unit, and each vestibule has facilities for voice connection to the driver, thus contributing to greater passenger safety. DB's 2005 energy-saving programme is taken into account, and the braking systems return energy to the overhead line. The total DM800 million order was for 103 trains.

*Lightweight multiple-units*
To revitalise its regional services, DB AG has ordered large numbers of new lightweight diesel units mainly from the 'RegioSprinter' and 'Talent' families.

*Coaching stock*
Bilevel cars now feature significantly in local operations all over Germany. A series of such vehicles, and matching driving trailers, have been produced with a 160 km/h capability to work on RE services in the Berlin area. DB Regio has ordered a further 98 bilevel cars from Deutsche Waggonbau GmbH. These include 23 driving trailers and 75 trailers. This latest order is part of a contract dating from 1996 which provided for the delivery of 250 vehicles and an option for 350 more. The 98 are ordered under that option. The 160 km/h cars are being built in Görlitz at a total cost of DM185 million. There will be first-class-only vehicles in which the seats will have fold-down tables and in which the saloons will be closed off by glass doors to try and prevent the draughts that passengers have complained of, and six vehicles will have a Train Caf catering area, with wardrobe. There will be a satellite information system to show the next stop as well as the normal p/a installation. There will be provision for fitting ticket-machines at a future date.

In 2001 a major programme of withdrawal of old restaurant cars began.

All DB AG passenger vehicles are to be fitted with retention toilets by 2002 as another step in the railway's general environmental-awareness programme.

*Freight vehicles*
DB Cargo followed up its summer 1998 order for 1,570 new wagons and other transport-units with a further order for 1,600 goods wagons and swapbodies. Additionally, 1,550 wagons were to be converted in railway workshops, thus bringing its investment to more than DM500 million. The new order included 550 17.25 m slide-wall wagons for the transport of high-value industrial and commercial goods (like washing-machines, dishwashers, or coffee-makers) and palletised goods from the chemical industry, and there is an option on a further 300 of the same sort. Of this fleet, 300 wagons were to conform to European gauge, whilst the other 250 will be to the larger German gauge. The balance of the second order comprised a further 200 covered four-axle self-unloading wagons for potash and other fertiliser; 350 bilevel car-transporters (150 of them with modern gauge-change equipment); 100 bogie-wagons with rolling roof for water-sensitive clay transport from the Westerwald to Italy and France, some of them with the now automatic coupler; 100 covered bogie wagons with heavy-duty unloading equipment and radio local control for plaster (Rea-Gips); 200 heavy-duty swap-bodies for roll-paper transport; another 100 special wagons with sliding doors for car-part movement and the conversion of 1,850 carriers for combined transport, 50 of them with a 22.5-tonne axleload.

DB Cargo is currently investing a substantial amount in a large number of new and refurbished freight vehicles. On top of the summer 1998 order for 1,570 new wagons and a further order for 1,600 new vehicles and 1,550 conversions, the company announced a 1999-2000 shopping list including 2,450 units (new builds, rebuilds, and rentals).

Further large orders for new freight rolling stock have been placed as part of the ongoing modernisation of the fleet, including a DM21 million order in the spring of 2001, split as DM8 million for 50 new bulk lime wagons and DM13 million for rebuilding 200 more wagons for timber transport.

The CargoSprinter, a freight dmu which appeared in October 1996 and which was described in earlier editions, saw regular commercial service on trains between Frankfurt airport and the north but is no longer in regular use.

In conjunction with the railways of Austria and Italy, DB AG has been developing a 'quiet' freight train for the Brenner route. An experimental train of 30 wagons features disc brakes, bogie shrouds and special wheels to minimise transmissions of vibrations.

### Signalling and telecommunications

DB AG holds 50.2 per cent of the telecommunications company Mannesmann Arcor AG & Co, based in Frankfurt am Main. Arcor has at its disposal a national ISDN network of 40,000 km, with which it aims to be Germany's second national telecommunications operator as well as to provide for all the telecommunications requirements of a modern railway. In 2000, the company

### Electric locomotives

| Class | Origin | Line voltage | Wheel arrangement | Power kW | Speed km/h | Weight tonnes | No in service | First built | Builders Mechanical | Builders Electrical |
|---|---|---|---|---|---|---|---|---|---|---|
| 101 | - | 15 kV | Bo-Bo | 6,000 | 220 | - | 145 | 1997 | Adtranz | Adtranz |
| 103 | DB | 15 kV | Co-Co | 7,440/7,780 | 200 | 114 | 129 | 1970 | Henschel | Siemens |
| 109 | DR | 15 kV | Bo-Bo | 4,200 | 120 | 82 | 4 | 1962 | LEW | LEW |
| 110 | DB | 15 kV | Bo-Bo | - | 140 | 86.4 | 374 | 1956 | Krauss-Maffei | Siemens |
|  | DB | 15 kV | Bo-Bo | 3,620/3,700 | 140 | 86[1] |  | 1963 |  | Henschel/Krupp AEG/BBC |
| 111 | DB | 15 kV | Bo-Bo | 3,620/3,700 | 160 | 83 | 226 | 1974 | Krauss-Maffei | Siemens |
| 112 | DR | 15 kV | Bo-Bo | 4,200 | 160 | 83 | 128 | 1991 | LEW | LEW |
| 113 | DB | 15 kV | Bo-Bo | 3,620/3,700 | 120 | 86 | 11 | 1962 | Krauss-Maffei/Henschel | Siemens |
| 120 | DB | 15 kV | Bo-Bo | 4,400/5,600 | 160/200[2] | 84 | 62 | 1979 | Krauss-Maffei/Krupp/Henschel/Thyssen | BBC |
| 127 | - | 15 kV | Bo-Bo | 6,400 | 230 | - | 1 | 1993 | - | Siemens |
| 128 | - | 15 kV | Bo-Bo | 6,400 | 220/250 | - | 1 | 1994 | - | AEG |
| 139[3] | DB | 15 kV | Bo-Bo | 3,620/3,700 | 110 | 86 | 47 | 1957 | Krauss-Maffei/Krupp/Thyssen/Henschel | AEG, BBC |
| 140 | DB | 15 kV | Bo-Bo | 3,620/3,700 | 110 | 83 | 792 | 1957 |  | Siemens |
| 141 | DB | 15 kV | Bo-Bo | 2,310/2,400 | 120 | 67 | 379 | 1956 | Henschel | BBC |
| 142 | DR | 15 kV | Bo-Bo | 2,920 | 100 | 82 | 54 | 1962 | LEW | LEW |
| 143 | DR | 15 kV | Bo-Bo | 3,720 | 120 | 82.8 | 634 | 1984 | LEW | LEW |
| 145 | - | 15 kV | Bo-Bo | 4,200 | 140 | - | 80 | 1998 | Adtranz | Adtranz |
| 146 | - | 15 kV | Bo-Bo | 4,200 | 160 | - | 31 | 2001 | Bombardier | Bombardier |
| 150 | DB | 15 kV | Co-Co | 4,410/4,500 | 100 | 126/128 | 168 |  | Krupp/Henschel/Krauss-Maffei | AEG, BBC, Siemens |
| 151 | DB | 15 kV | Co-Co | 5,982/6,288 | 120 | 118 | 169 | 1973 | Krupp/Krauss-Maffei | AEG/BBC/Siemens |
| 152 | - | 15 kV | Bo-Bo | 6,000 | 140 | - | 170 | 1997 | Krauss-Maffei | Siemens |
| 155 | DR | 15 kV | Co-Co | 5,400 | 120 | 123 | 267 | 1974 | LEW | LEW |
| 156 | DR | 15 kV | Co-Co | 5,880 | 125 | - | 4 | 1991 | - | - |
| 171 | DR | 25 kV | Co-Co | 3,660 | 80 | - | 11 | 1965 | - | - |
| 180 | DR | 15/3 kV | Bo-Bo | 3,080 | 120 | 84 | 20 | 1988 | Skoda | Skoda |
| 181 | DB | 15/25 kV | Bo-Bo | 3,000/3,240 | 150 | 84 | 1 | 1968 | Krupp | AEG |
| 181.2 | DB | 15/25 kV | Bo-Bo | 3,200/3,300 | 160 | 83 | 25 | 1975 | Krupp | AEG |
| 182 | - | 15/25 kV | Bo-Bo | 6,400 | 140 | - | 25[4] | 2001 | Siemens | Siemens |
| 184 | DB | 1.5/3/15/25 kV | Bo-Bo | 3,240 | 150 | - | 1 | 1967 | - | - |
| 185 | - | 15/25 kV | Bo-Bo | 4,200 | 140 | - | 400[4] | 2001 | Bombardier | Bombardier |

**Notes:**
[1] Nos 110.288 onwards, which are Class 110.3; remainder are Class 110.1
[2] Nos 120.001-4 only
[3] The principal difference between Classes 139 and 140 is that the former has rheostatic braking for heavily graded routes
[4] Number of locomotives ordered

### Diesel locomotives

| Class | Origin | Wheel arrangement | Power kW | Speed km/h | Weight tonnes | No in service | First built | Builders Mechanical | Builders Engine | Transmission |
|---|---|---|---|---|---|---|---|---|---|---|
| 202 | DR | B-B | 900 | 100 | 65 | 380 | 1969 | LEW | 12 KVD 21 AL-3 | H Pirna |
| 204 | DR | B-B | 1,100 | 100 | 65 | 65 | 1969 | LEW | 12 KVD 21 AL-4 | H Pirna |
| 211 | DB | B-B | 760 | 90/100 | 62 | 34 | 1961 | - | MTU MD 12 V 538 TZ MTU MB 12 V 493 TZ | H |
| 212 | DB | B-B | 930 | 100 | 63 | 241 | 1962 | - | MTU MB 12 V 652 TA | H |
| 213 | DB | B-B | 930 | 100 | 63 | 10 | 1962 | - | MTU MB 12 V 652 TA | H |
| 215 | DB | B-B | 1,430/1,849 | 140 | 77.5 | 133 | 1968 | - | MTU MB 16 V 652 TB MTU 12 V 956 TB 10 | H |
| 216 | DB | B-B | 1,300 | 120 | 77.5-77 | 138 | 1964 | - | MTU MB 16 V 652 TB | H |
| 217 | DB | B-B | 1,430 | 140 | 77 | 13 | 1965 | - | MTU MD 16V 652 TB | H |
| 218 | DB | B-B | 1,840/2,060 | 140 | 80 |  | 1968 | - | MTU MA 12 V 956 TB MTU 12 V 956 TB 11 Pielstick 16 PA 4 V 200 | H |
| 218.2-4 | DR | C-C | 1,470 | 120 | 95 | 404 | 1966 | Babelsberg | 2 × 12 KVD 18/21 A II | H Pirna |
| 218.9 | DR | B-B | 1,840 | 90/140 |  |  | 1979 | - | - | H |
| 219 | DR | C-C | 1,980/2,200 | 120 | 99 | 167 | 1962 | Bucharest | 2 × M820 SR | H |
| 229 | DR | C-C | 2,760 | 140 | - | 20 | 1992 | - | - | H |
| 232 | DR | Co-Co | 2,200 | 120 | 112.4 | 482 | 1973 | Voroshilovgrad | 5 D 49 | E Voroshilovgrad |
| 234 | DR | Co-Co | 2,200 | 140 | - | 64 | 1992 | - | - | E |
| 259 |  | Co-Co | 2,460 | 96 | 121 | 1 | 1990 | General Motors | General Motors | E General Motors |
| 290 | DB | B-B | 810 | 70/80[1] | 77/77.8 | 216 | 1964 | - | MTU MU 12 V 652 TA | H |
| 291 | DB | B-B | 810 | 80 | 76-90 | 46 | 1965 | - | Mak 8 M 282 AK | H |
| 293 | DR | B-B | 735 | 65 | 64 | 2 | 1981 | LEW | 12 KVD 18/21 A3 | H Pirna |
| 294 | - | B-B | 1,995 | 40/80 | - | 193 | - | - | - | H |
| 295 | - | B-B | 1,995 | 40/80 | - | 57 | - | - | - | H |
| 298 | DR | B-B | 750 | 80 |  | 80 |  |  |  |  |

**Notes:**
[1] Nos 290.001-20 only

was replacing its existing analogue radio network with a digital GSM-R network.

In a rationalisation move at the beginning of 1998, DB AG took over from Arcor all non-telecommunications services, bringing them under its own Anlagen und Haus (AHS) service-organisation and taking on 1,379 Arcor staff. AHS handles railway-specific services like the installation and servicing of ticket machines, safety systems, office and communications technology, information systems like destination indicators, platform clocks, and p/a systems.

A Central Control Office for the whole of DB's network, located in Frankfurt am Main and replacing previous control offices in Berlin and Mainz, came into use in 1997. This is the Rechnerunterstützte Zentrale Betriebsleitung (RZBL), where 40 staff directly supervise all Long Distance Passenger Business services trains as well as principal goods trains and special workings. Some 1,800 trains a day are watched from seven workstations from start to finish of their journeys in real time – and connections, substitute trains, special stops, and diversions can all be decided. Some 4,000 connections a day are supervised and each month the staff deal with between 12,000 and 15,000 cases of conflict. Additionally, the 15 Regional Traffic Offices are co-ordinated from here and contact is maintained with foreign administrations. DB Netz aims eventually to have the 17,000 km network on which 90 per cent of rail traffic flows controlled from just seven Traffic Centres.

At the end of 2000 there were 122 electronic signalboxes (ESTw) in use, an increase of 18 during the year. Some are very large installations, covering cities like Dresden, Frankfurt am Main and Hannover.

A serious accident to the *Gläserner Zug* in late 1995 dramatically illustrated the risks when a train leaves a platform against a red signal. To prevent such accidents in future, the Indusi (PZB) driver vigilance system is to be modified, the new form being designated PZB 90. Additional monitoring beyond the signal and additional stop monitoring are provided, so that if any train does start against the signal it will be braked at a speed as low as 25 km/h.

*Computer-aided control*
Nuremberg was the first hub on the historic system to commission a computer-aided traffic control centre (RZu). Similar installations are being completed at Frankfurt and Karlsruhe by SEL, which supplied the Nuremberg apparatus, and at Cologne and Hannover by Deutsche Philips. Total cost of these projects is DM126 million.

In an RZu, train movements are monitored by train describer apparatus, and visual display units (VDUs) in the control centre depict graphically train performance against schedule. In the light of real-time progress the computer will propose individual train priorities for optimal adherence to the timetable.

The CIR-ELKE (Computer Integrated Railroading – Erhöhung der Leistungsfähigkeit im Kernnetz) was fully commissioned in June 2001 on the 197 km Karlsruhe–Basle route (chosen because it can be worked on a self-contained basis in terms of motive power). It is now believed that the capacity-enhancement benefits expected from this system can be more than matched by the benefits that will come from more recent signalling developments, and it is unlikely that CIR-ELKE will be extended further. Nevertheless, expenditure on the system is not regarded as wasted, as much has been learnt and some features can be transferred.

### Track
**Standard rail:** Type S49, weighing 49.5 kg/m; Type S54, 54.5 kg/m; Type S64, 64.9 kg/m. Lengths generally 30-120 m
**Type of rail joints:** 4- and 6-hole fishplates
**Sleepers (crossties):** Wood; steel; reinforced concrete. Wood sleepers impregnated beech, fir or oak, 2,600 × 260 × 160 mm
Steel, 2,600 × 9 mm weighing 86.3 kg
The latest type of RC sleeper (Spannbetonschwelle B58) weighs 235 kg, is 2,400 mm long, 190 mm thick under rails, 280 mm wide at bottom and 136 mm at top
**Spacing:** 650-800 mm
**Rail fastenings:** Baseplates and bolts, clips and spring washers with thin rubber or wood (poplar) pad between rail and plate; resilient rail spikes with wood and concrete sleepers and resilient rail clips with steel sleepers.
**Max gradient:** Main lines: 2.5%
Secondary lines: 6.6%
**Max curvature:**
Main lines: 9.7° = min radius 180 m
Secondary lines: 17.5° = min radius 100 m
**Maximum superelevation:** 150 mm on curves of 300 m radius and above
**Rate of slope of superelevation:** Generally 1:10 V (V = speed in mph). On occasion this may be increased to 1:8 V up to 1 in 400. On reverse curves the permissible limit is 1:4 V up to 1 in 400
**Max altitude:** Main line: 967 m between Klais and Mittenwald. Highest station Klais, 933 m
Secondary line: 969 m between Bärenthal and Aha on the Titisee-Seebrugg line
**Max axleloading:** 22.5 tonnes

*UPDATED*

### Diesel railcars or multiple-units

| Class | Cars per unit | Motor cars per unit | Motored axles/car | Power kW | Speed km/h | Weight tonnes | No in service | First built | Mechanical | Builders Engine | Transmission |
|---|---|---|---|---|---|---|---|---|---|---|---|
| 605 | 4 | - | - | 1,700 | 200 | - | 20 | - | - | - | E |
| 610 | 2 | - | - | 970 | 160 | - | 20 | 1992 | Duewag/MAN | MTU | E |
| 611 | 2 | - | - | 1,118 | 160 | 116 | 50 | 1997 | Adtranz | - | H |
| 612 | 2 | - | - | 1,118 | 160 | 116 | 200 | 1999 | Adtranz | - | H |
| 614 | 3 | 2 | 2 | 370 | 140 | 124.5 | 42 | 1972 | O & K/Uerdingen | MAN | H |
| 624/634 [1] | 3 | 2 | 2 | 330 | 120 | 115.5-118.1 | 44 | 1961 | MAN/Uerdingen | MAN | H |
| 627 | 1 | 1 | 2 | 285/287 | 120 | 36 | 8 | 1974 | - | - | H |
| 628 | 2 | 1 | 2 | 2 × 210/1 × 375 | 120 | 64 | - | 1974 | Duewag/KGB MBB | - | H |
| 628.2 | 2 | 1 | 2 | 410 | 120 | | 466 | 1987 | Duewag/KGB/MBB | - | H |
| 628.4 | 2 | 1 | 2 | 485 | 120 | | | 1992 | | | - |
| 640 | 1 | - | - | 315 | 120 | 38.9 | 30* | 1999 | LHB 'LINT' | - | M |
| 641 | 1 | - | - | 514 | 140 | 47 | 40* | 1999 | De Dietrich | - | H |
| 642 | 2 | - | - | 514 | 120 | 66.1 | 150* | 1999 | Siemens/Duewag 'Regio-Sprinter' | - | M |
| 643 | 2 | - | - | 5-630 | 120 | 67 | 75* | 1999 | Bombardier-Talbot 'Talent' | - | H |
| 644 | 3 | - | - | 1,000 | 120 | 84.3 | 59* | 1999 | Bombardier-Talbot 'Talent' | - | E |
| 646 | 2 | - | - | 550 | 120 | - | 42* | 1999 | GTW/2/6 | - | E |
| 650 | 1 | - | - | 514 | 120 | 37.7 | 27* | 1998 | Adtranz/DWA 'RegioShuttle' | - | H |
| 670 | 1 | - | - | 250 | 100 | - | 5 | 1997 | DWA | - | M |
| 771/172 | Max 2 | 2 | 1 | 132 | 90 | 22 | 65 | 1960 | Bautzen | 6 kVD 18 | M Bautzen |
| 772/172 | Max 2 | 2 | 1 | 132 | 90 | 22 | 89 | 1964 | Bautzen | 6 kVD 18 | M Bautzen |
| 796 [2] | 1 | 1 | 2 | 110 | 90 | 20.9 | 329 | 1953 | MAN/Uerdingen/WMD | - | M |

**Notes:**
[1] Type 624 rebuilt with air suspension bogies
[2] Two-axle railbus: works as required with non-powered trailers, but not in permanent set formations
* Number of units ordered

## DB Netz

DB Netz AG
Theodor-Heuss-Allee 7, D-60486 Frankfurt am Main
Tel: (+49 69) 26 53 20 02    Fax: (+49 69) 26 53 20 07

### Key personnel
Board Members
  Chairman: Dipl-Ing Roland Heinisch
  Infrastructure: Prof Dr rer pol Ulf Häsler
  Marketing and Commercial Affairs: Dagmar Haase
  Operations: Dipl-Ing Gerhard Schinner
  Personnel: Leuthold Lewin
  Technology and Development:
    Dipl-Ing Holger Schulze-Halberg

In 2000 DB Netz had a turnover of €3,525 million and spent €3,896 billion on its capital account. The business employed 53,554 people. The 1997 figures were DM156 million, DM8.7 billion, and 78,370 employees.

To conform to EU directive 91/440, DB AG issued a price-list for the use of the railway network by all customers, internal and external in mid-1994. This was modified from 1 January 1995 after protests from the states about the impact of certain of its provisions on the regular interval services they wished to purchase for local routes. There were further substantial modifications to the system in 1998 and a completely new tariff, conforming to all national and EU requirements, was introduced in April 2001. The aim remains to cover the full costs for the use of the infrastructure through the access charges.

The Order for the Use of the Railway Infrastructure came into effect in December 1997. The infrastructure operator must seek consensus agreement between the parties where there are competing claims for paths but, if this cannot be achieved, the path is given to the party willing to pay most for it. The fact that one of the parties may be a more valuable customer by reason of his interest in other lines must play no role – this being to prevent the incumbent businesses of DB AG from overwhelming smaller undertakings. Under normal circumstances the infrastructure operator must not treat different applicants for the same line differently. To achieve pricing transparency the framework permits rebates for bulk capacity purchase within certain limits.

The Deutsche Institut für Wirtschaftsforschung (DIW) calculated that in 1996 only 52 per cent of full track costs were actually being met through access charges, as required by the 1994 reforms, with a payment of DM7.1 billion and full costs of DM13.5 billion. Only the Local Passenger Traffic Business was paying sufficient to meet fully its share of track costs. The DIW asserted both that a full coverage of costs would not be possible and that under existing conditions the lower access charges demanded by the states could not be obtained. It therefore urged abandonment of this aim and its replacement by a requirement to cover all recurrent costs in full but only a clearly defined portion of the capital costs.

After significant cost rises in major projects, the DB AG supervisory board decided to introduce common standards throughout the country for such schemes and to establish an investment committee to keep a close central view on progress. All major projects now require the approval of the chairman of the board of management and the finance director. Significant changes are also being made in the way in which routine engineering works are planned, by 'bundling' tasks for 22 designated corridors, to reduce costs and improve the use of time and facilities.

### New lines (Neubaustrecken – NBS)
After the creation of DB AG at the start of 1994 all outstanding new-line projects were reappraised in the light of both possible cuts in federal funding and an intention to pursue a wide-scale deployment of tilting stock. Although the aim remains to maintain investment levels, a significant portion of the money now comes from the sale of surplus lands rather than from the state.

The Hannover–Würzburg and Mannheim–Stuttgart new lines came into use in 1991 (although the Nantenbach Curve, the final section of the Hannover–Würzburg project, was not opened until three years later), and the Spandau–Oebisfelde line was brought into service in 1998. These lines are engineered for mixed traffic working, and the first two pass through geographically difficult and quite densely populated countryside. Construction was very expensive, with a substantial proportion of the cost attributable to environmentally necessitated measures. At an average of DM50 million per kilometre the Hannover–Würzburg line is the most expensive railway ever built (the French LGV Sud-Est cost only a third as much).

*Cologne–Frankfurt NBS*
Fixed-price contracts to a value of DM4,000 million were let during 1996 for the construction of this 300 km/h line and work is now well advanced over the whole length. The section serving the new Frankfurt Airport InterCity station was brought into use in May 1999. Completion of the whole project is expected in 2002, two years later than originally planned. There are problems of cost over-runs.

From Cologne two additional tracks are being built beside the present Right Rhine main line as far as Siegburg, where the new line turns away and follows the direct course of the A3 motorway through the hills. A third of the length is in tunnel. Because this is to be a purely passenger railway and because the terrain traversed is very difficult, the design parameters have been relaxed to allow a ruling gradient of 40 pro mille and a minimum curve radius of 3,500 m (use of slab track throughout allowing cant of up to 180 mm).

Cologne-Bonn airport will be served by a loop, the cost of which is being shared between the federal treasury, the Nordrhein-Westfalen *Land* government, and the airport authority.

*Nuremberg–Ingolstadt NBS*
The only other new line on which substantial progress is at present being made is that between Nuremberg and Ingolstadt. This 80 km new line (31 km in tunnel) is also due for completion in 2002. This is so far the only major rail construction project to be privately financed, the federal government having taken the necessary powers in the 1996 Finance Act. Optimisation in planning and construction and exploitation of all possibilities in awarding contracts made it possible to reduce the originally envisaged investment costs so that the total burden on the state sinks to DM622 million a year over 15 years, or roughly DM9 billion – well beneath the permitted level of DM622 million a year for 25 years (DM15.6 billion).

*Leipzig–Dresden NBS/ABS*
Work began in late 1993 on a scheme to create 106 km of new high-speed infrastructure between Leipzig and Dresden, partly by rebuilding the existing line and partly by long sections of new construction such as a Riesa avoiding line. Shortage of money forced a simplification of the plans and the Riesa avoiding line no longer figures. A significant portion of the work was completed in early 1999 (although no progress has been made so far on the final approach to Dresden, where decisions remain to be taken on the upgrading of the Berlin–Dresden main line).

*Rastatt–Offenburg NBS*
The 193 km Karlsruhe–Offenburg–Basle main line is being upgraded, part NBS and part ABS. One of Europe's principal international arteries, the route unites the main lines from Mannheim and Heidelberg at Rastatt and channels traffic from the whole of northwest Europe into Switzerland.

An NBS section over the 49 km between Rastatt and Offenburg, generally parallel to the existing line, was nearing completion in 2000. Between Offenburg and Basle the original plans envisaged reconstruction of the existing railway for 200 km/h operation and the provision of a third track, but an extra pair of tracks is now to be provided throughout because it is expected that Swiss schemes to increase trans-Alpine rail freight capacity will generate considerable additional traffic.

*Other schemes*
There is little progress to report on the NBS schemes for lines between Erfurt and Ebensfeld, Halle/Leipzig and Erfurt, and Stuttgart and Günzburg. A short section of the Leipzig–Erfurt line, at the Leipzig end, is under construction.

## Improvements to existing lines
*(Ausbaustrecken – ABS)*
Ausbaustrecken are lines that have undergone major upgrading, including, where necessary, realignments and the provision of additional tracks, to maximise the scope for 200 km/h running. All German railway lines on which speeds of over 160 km/h are operated must be equipped with LZB continuous cab signalling, and no level crossings are permitted.

The 1990 reunification brought a shift in priorities: during the 1980s emphasis had been on a strengthening of north-south links, but more recently the focus has been on east-west routes. In 1991 a programme of 17 major transport works, nine of them rail, was agreed under the title of the *Deutsche Einheit* programme.

The period 1991-97 saw DM42,000 million spent in the 'Five New Federal States', but even so plans for most of the schemes were simplified to save money. In 2001 work was still in progress on the Lübeck–Stralsund route.

As a consequence of the abandonment of the Berlin Hamburg 'Transrapid' project the already-modernised main line between the two cities is now being further upgraded to allow speeds of up to 230 km/h. The work being done includes the long-delayed total modernisation of the railway through Wittenberge.

Infrastructure schemes in progress in the 'new federal states' that are not elements of the *Deutsche Einheit* programme include:

A DM 900 million investment-programme on the so-called *Sachsenmagistrale* between Dresden and Hof being carried out in agreement with the states of Saxony and Bavaria. This forms part of the ABS across South Germany from Karlsruhe through Stuttgart and Nuremberg to Leipzig and Dresden. New ICE TD trains will in due course reduce the Dresden–Hof timing from 3 hours 21 minutes to 2½ hours and Dresden–Nuremberg from 5 hours to about 4 hours. Bayreuth will acquire a much-improved link with Hof by the construction of the Schlomener Kurve, commissioned on 1 September 2000, which will cut at least 10 minutes off local train timings between the two cities and also allow Bayreuth to be linked into DB Reise&Touristik's long-distance network.

There is a DM177 million programme for the doubling, upgrading, and resignalling of the Weimar–Gera line.

Modernisation of the 84 km main line east from Berlin to Frankfurt an der Oder and Poland should be completed in 2002. The line is being upgraded for 160 km/h operation and resignalled to reduce times by quarter of an hour to 36 minutes.

Upgrading between Berlin and Dresden: DB AG and ČD have agreed to accelerate services between the two cities by short-term renovation and modernisation of the existing infrastructure coupled with the introduction of tilting trains. There is, however, a serious delay in the delivery of the new rolling stock. The Berlin–Prague–Vienna/Bratislava–Budapest corridor is to be integrated into the European high-speed network, and the German share involves upgrading the 160 km/h Dresden line for 200 km/h operation.

Berlin's railway system is being restored and modernised. Work began in late 1995 on a DM10 billion north-south tunnel through the heart of the city with a new central station at the Lehrter Stadtbahnhof, where the north-south route is crossed by the Stadtbahn west-east main line and S-Bahn route. The old direct lines from the south, from Halle/Leipzig and Dresden, are to be restored and re-routed at Papestrasse to the new alignment. At its northern end the new line will connect both ways with the (Inner) Ring, currently under restoration, enabling trains from the west and north to reach the new low-level Lehrter Bahnhof platforms. On the Ring and a little to the east, work on the *Nordkreuz* junctions for main line and S-Bahn trains is now well advanced. Although the plan to run a new S-Bahn line parallel to the north-south main lines has been partially put on hold to save money, the alignment is being protected. Eastwards from Zoologischer Garten the 114-year-old Berlin Stadtbahn has been rebuilt. The new Berlin-Spandau station was completed at the end of 1998. Reconstruction of Gesundbrunnen station is in progress. By 2000, major concerns had arisen about cost over-runs and plans for savings were being made.

*Cologne–Aachen ABS*
The line from Cologne to the Belgian frontier beyond Aachen is the link between the Cologne–Frankfurt NBS and the West European high-speed network. Between Cologne and Düren 250 km/h main lines are being provided, and from Düren to Aachen the existing line is to be upgraded for higher speeds. The full scheme will not be complete until 2005.

*Dortmund–Kassel ABS*
This ABS scheme covers the 215 km line from Dortmund via Hamm and Paderborn to a junction with the Hannover–Würzburg NBS at Kassel. Financial constraints have brought about a simplification of the plans, and after 10 years the work has still not been completed.

*Ebensfeld–Nuremberg ABS*
Instead of continuing the future NBS from Erfurt through to Nuremberg, an ABS is proposed from Ebensfeld southwards, involving the laying of two additional tracks alongside the well-aligned existing railway at a cost of DM3.3 billion.

*Günzburg–Augsburg(–Munich) ABS*
This is the continuation of the proposed new line between Stuttgart and Günzburg to form a high-speed line between Stuttgart and Munich. Two additional tracks, suitable for 230 km/h working, are being built over the 43 km between Olching (near Munich, where the separate S-Bahn tracks end) and Augsburg in a 5-year project costing DM1.1 billion.

*Ingolstadt–Munich ABS*
This is the ABS continuation from the outskirts of Ingolstadt to Munich of the NBS south from Nuremberg to Ingolstadt. Work should be complete in 2003, when timings between Nuremberg and Munich will be cut to an hour.

*Karlsruhe–Basle*
As stated above, much more of the work on this 197 km line will now be NBS rather than ABS.

*Driving trailers working with refurbished double-deck coaches on local services at Kaiserslautern* (Colin Boocok)
*2001*/0114207

## RAILWAY SYSTEMS/Germany

*Fulda—Frankfurt am Main—Mannheim ABS*
This is the connection between the Hannover—Würzburg NBS at Fulda and the Rhine Valley route. The line passes through difficult country to gain the Rhine-Main plain, and over the first 25 km or so speeds are limited to 110 km/h. The ABS works will make 200 km/h possible over 55 km of the remainder of the section through to Frankfurt. Work on the 79 km *Riedbahn* line thence to Mannheim is now essentially complete. It has included the laying of a third track to allow overtaking at eight locations, the elimination of 27 level crossings, and realignments at 11 points to permit 200 km/h over 62 km of its length.

*Munich—Markt Schwaben—Mühldorf—Freilassing ABS*
Prospective EU single-market growth of north-south freight traffic, Austria's accession to the EU, and that country's restrictions on lorry transit-traffic demand an increase in cross-border capacity. An ABS scheme, including electrification, has been developed for the 120 km route from Munich to Freilassing through Markt Schwaben, to create a high-quality relief route for the heavily taxed main line from Munich to Freilassing via Rosenheim, at a cost of some DM1 billion. Mühldorf's considerable commuter traffic to Munich will also benefit from the electrification.

*Strasbourg—Appenweier and Saarbrücken—Mannheim ABS*
To connect the German ICE network with France's TGV-Est Européen from Paris to Strasbourg, there are ABS schemes for the lines between Strasbourg and Appenweier and between Saarbrücken and Mannheim. There is no progress to date.

*Other improvements*
The single-track line between Gross Gleidingen and Hildesheim is to be doubled over most of its length at a cost of DM175 million.

Prior to reunification, the Hannover—Hildesheim—Goslar—Bad Harzburg line was due for singling. Instead, the Hildesheim—Goslar section is being upgraded for use by NeiTec trains and DM100 million is to be spent further east on the Halberstadt—Halle line to bring it up to 160 km/h standards where possible, with the aim of an RE service with Class 612 tilting trains between Hannover and Halle taking about 2½ hours.

Work began in March 1998 on a second 1,300 m double-track tunnel to sort out the bottleneck between Mainz Süd and Mainz Hbf.

*Level crossings*
DB Netz, working together with federal, state, and local authorities, is engaged in a major programme to improve safety at the 26,000 level crossings remaining on the system. New and upgraded lines are free of crossings, since it is a requirement of the *Eisenbahn Bau- und Betriebsordnung* that there should be none on lines where trains run at speeds above 160 km/h, and the current aim is to eliminate all existing crossings on heavily trafficked routes by the end of the decade. Others will be provided with up-to-date safety technology. These measures are expected to cost roughly DM630 million a year.

**UPDATED**

## DB Reise&Touristik

DB Reise&Touristik AG
Stephensonstrasse 1, D-60326 Frankfurt am Main
Tel: (+49 69) 265 71 30   Fax: (+49 69) 26 51 42 88

**Key personnel**
Board Members
  Chairman: Dr phil Christoph Franz
  Marketing and Commercial Affairs:
    Dr rer pol Ingo Bretthauer
  Production and Technology:
    Dipl-Ing Karl-D Reemtsema
  Finance and Audit: Dr rer pol Rolf Kranüchel
  Personnel: Jens-Uwe Bruysten

In 2000 the Long Distance Passenger Business had a turnover of €3,463 million (1999: €3,257 million) and capital expenditure of €499 million. The business employed 30,293 staff.

*InterCity Express*
ICE 1s first entered service in 1992 on a route from Hamburg to Munich using both the Hannover—Würzburg and Mannheim—Stuttgart high-speed lines (*Neubaustrecken* (NBS)). All 60 first-generation trains were in service for the start of the 1993-94 timetable, running on four routes including a new one between Berlin and Munich via Frankfurt am Main. In the first serious incident with an ICE, one train was lost in the Eschede accident in June 1998.

The first ICE 2s were introduced in June 1996, as long trains without either restaurant cars or driving trailers. By June 1997 the catering vehicles were available and the trains took over the two-hourly Berlin—Cologne service, still as long trains. With the delivery of the driving trailers, the fleet was available for use as designed for the May 1998 timetable.

The ICE 3 came into service on special trains to the Hannover EXPO 2000 in the 2000-2001 timetable, both with DB and with NS. The ICE T seven-car units first came into revenue-earning service on the Stuttgart—Zürich service in the 1999-2000 timetable; they were also used during that timetable-year on a number of other services.

*Berlin-bound ICE 2 trainset at Duisburg—Kaiserberg (Wolfram Veith)*    2000/0089562

The five-car units came in with the 2000-2001 timetable on the Dresden—Frankfurt am Main service. The ICE TD entered commercial service in 2001 on trains between Dresden and Hof and between Munich and Zurich.

Two foreign designs of high-speed train now work into Germany. In December 1997 'Thalys' services worked by multivoltage TGV units began to run between Paris and Cologne, with one pair of trains being extended in 1998 to run to and from Düsseldorf, and in March 1998 Cisalpino services using Fiat Pendolino trainsets began working into Stuttgart from Zurich.

*Other long-distance services*
In addition to its ICE services, DB Reise&Touristik operates locomotive-hauled domestic IC (InterCity) and international EC (EuroCity), IR (InterRegio) services, and, through a subsidiary, various overnight services.

Most IC locomotive-hauled trains now run as fixed train-sets with driving trailers and are maintained in fixed formation. In 2001 the 117 trainsets were being repainted into the ICE livery and were also being internally refurbished. The aim is to offer a single image and a common quality standard for long-distance services.

InterRegio trains were planned to connect regional centres. In practice, the role of the IR services was never entirely clear and the numbers of such services have been cut back, most significantly in the June 2001 timetable. Replacing them are more stops by IC trains, extra regional services and some trains of a new category, the InterRegioExpress (IRE).

*TEE Alliance*
DB AG has established with ÖBB and SBB in Austria and Switzerland respectively the TEE Alliance, with the aim of offering customers common levels of service across the borders of the three countries. In 2001 the three railways were seeking tenders for the supply of 116 tilting trainsets, to enter service in 2003.

*Sleeper services (DB Nachtzug)*
In 1999 responsibility for all sleeper services was passed to the DB Reise&Touristik subsidiary DB AutoZug GmbH and plans were announced for the development by 2001 of a network of more than 20 routes, 10 of them appearing in the May 1999 timetable. Other rolling stock is being modernised to offer a consistent standard of comfort and service (including conversion of the four-bed compartments in the new bilevel sleeping-cars to two-bed compartments) and a clearer and simpler pricing system is to be offered. The Talgo ICN (InterCityNight) services has been integrated into the new concept.

Since September 2000 the night train between Berlin and Malmö has been operated by the Georg Verkehrsorganisation of Frankfurt am Main, using leased rolling stock. This is the first regular long-distance service to be taken over by a private operator.

*Metropolitan GmbH*
A DB Reise&Touristik subsidiary, Metropolitan GmbH, was formed to offer direct, fast connections between major centres. The first such service began running between Cologne and Hamburg in August 1999. Trains call only at Düsseldorf and Essen and take about 3 hours 20 minutes for the journey (significantly slower than was aspired to at the planning stage). The rolling stock used offered at first three different types of accommodation in one class, 'Silence' for those who wished to rest, 'Club' for those wanting to talk, and 'Office' for those wanting to get

*Hamburg—Cologne 'Metropolitan' service passing the new airport station at Düsseldorf (Wolfram Veith)*    2000/0089557

on with their work whilst on the train. There is now an additional type of accommodation so that second class can be catered for. Two Class 101 locomotives are dedicated to the service (and liveried accordingly). The first year's operations were viewed as successful though load-levels remained relatively low.

*Customer services*

In an attempt to accelerate and simplify ticket purchase DB Reise&Touristik has introduced large numbers of vending machines to sell long-distance tickets.

DB Reise&Touristik launched its 'Surf+Rail' scheme in late 1999. Fixed-price second-class tickets, inclusive of reservations, are available at four price-levels for a limited number of through connections between major cities only by Internet credit card purchase. The tickets are valid only in the designated train and only for the named passenger. The tickets must be booked at least three days before travel, must include a Saturday night away, cannot be exchanged, and have no validity on DB Regio. The customer receives a confirmation of the booking by e-mail and prints his/her own ticket on a sheet of A4 paper. This shows the booked connection, with times and seat numbers and the passenger's name. On-train staff have a list of Surf+Rail tickets for their train, which allows proper checking. The scheme was an immediate success and its scope has been significantly extended.

Since early 1999 it has been possible to reserve 'Mobile-telephone Seats' in non-smoking accommodation in all ICEs. The vehicles are marked with pictograms and the word 'Handy' is printed on the reservation-ticket. Repeaters in the trains ensure good reception in these vehicles. 'Quiet Areas' have also been introduced in the ICE fleet.

On the motive power side, DB Reise&Touristik aims to concentrate all its motive power maintenance in just four places: Berlin, Hamburg, Munich, and Saarbrücken.

## DB Cargo

DB Cargo AG
Rheinstrasse 2, D-55116 Mainz
Tel: (+49 6131) 15-9   Fax: (+49 6131) 156 02 19
Web: http://www.db-cargo.de

**Key personnel**
Board Members
  Chairman and Commercial Director:
    Dr Bernd Malmström
  Operations and Technology:
    Dr-Ing Eh Karl-Heinz Jesberg
  Finance and Audit: Wilhelm Wegscheider
  Personnel and Legal Affairs: Birgit Gantz-Rathmann

DB Cargo's turnover of €3,831 million in 2000 showed a rise of €290 million on the 1999 figure, and capital expenditure was €405 million, down on the €501 million of the previous year. There were 38,555 employees, against 40,995 a year earlier.

DB Cargo operates through five profit centres: Coal & Steel, Building Materials & Waste Disposal, Oil & Chemical Products, Industrial Goods, and Commercial Goods, Agriculture & Forestry.

In late 2000 DB AG announced plans for DB Cargo to reposition itself in all three of its product areas: trainload and mass goods traffic is increasingly to be worked using modern rolling stock, with prices adjusted to meet competitive needs; the railway will aim to double its share of the container traffic market; and because the wagonload traffic service no longer meets the needs of the market, it will be improved by concentration on fewer collection points and increased speeds. The company believes that it has to offer a wider range of container services to try to render redundant the present time-consuming marshalling, collecting and transhipment arrangements, and it aims to draw lorries and inland shipping into the railway's chain so as to be able to offer transport from a single supplier with improved punctuality. The plan is known as MORA C (Marktorientiertes Angebot Cargo). At the end of 2000 the wagonload business made up 40 per cent of the total freight business of 75,000 million tonne-km. Of this, 85 per cent came from 320 major customers, where there was a growth potential of at least 5 per cent, and the other 15 per cent came from a spread of some 7,000 customers whose needs amounted to only a few wagons each per week or month, with growth potential assessed at only 1.9 per cent. This part of the business was making a loss of DM168 per wagon moved. DB Cargo was to assess all its 2,100 goods locations and to undertake discussions with customers about how best their needs might be met. The range of products on offer would include containers worked in Combined Traffic service, a diversion of the traffic to other goods locations, and co-operation with other railways or road hauliers.

Under MORA C, DB Cargo aims to improve its wagonload traffic out-turn by at least DM500 million a year. The reforms are to be introduced in stages for completion in 2004, by which time DM5,000 million will have been invested, not just in modern rolling stock and locomotives, but also in GPS systems, general growth, development of a sharper customer focus and the raising of quality, all in order to improve rail's competitiveness. The company's long-term aim is to increase rail freight by 42 per cent over a 15-year period, raising performance from 75,000 million tonne-km in 2000 to 120,000 million in 2020.

The premium level of service is provided by the InterCargo trains, which guarantee overnight siding-to-siding connection with departures between 15.00 and 17.00 and arrivals between 07.00 and 09.00.

The international counterpart of InterCargo-Express is the EurailCargo network; this targets second-morning delivery over distances up to 1,500 km.

In June 1998 DB Cargo and NS Cargo declared their intention to fuse their two undertakings and establish a new European rail transport company (open to further partners), with a working name of Rail Cargo Europe. The new company, now known as Railion, is established under German law with headquarters in Mainz and it started operations at the end of 1999. DB Cargo is also entering into close working relationships with other railways.

In collaboration with SNCB/NMBS (Belgium) and NS (the Netherlands), DB AG is involved in the revivification of the so-called 'Iron Rhine' route between the Belgian port of Antwerp and the German river port of Duisburg. On 28 March 2000, the three countries signed an agreement providing for a resumption of a trail service of 15 trains a day, to start by the end of 2000 and to continue till 2008. On the German side, DM50 million is already earmarked

*Class 152 electric freight locomotive on an intermodal service at Ulm (David Haydock)* 2001/0114248

*A RoLa piggyback service heads south through Königstein towards the Czech Republic (Wolfram Veith)* 2000/0089560

*Gauge-changing system being developed by DB Cargo and Knorr Bremse to allow the exchange of traffic with broad-gauge networks of former Soviet countries (David Haydock)* 2001/0114244

for the work from the government's *Anti-Stau-Programm* funds.

### Intermodal operations
DB AG's KLV (*Kombinierter Ladungsverkehr*) intermodal unit operates trains carrying containers, swapbodies, and piggyback unaccompanied road trailers. The KLV portfolio also includes both domestic and international (Austria, the Czech Republic and North Italy) *Rollende Landstrasse (RoLa)*, or 'Rolling Highway' – trains using ultra-low-floor well-wagons on small-wheeled bogies to form a continuous roadway for the drive-on/drive-off conveyance of accompanied truck and truck-and-trailer rigs.

The *RoLa* service between Germany and Lovosice in the Czech Republic, up the Elbe Valley from Dresden, introduced in 1994 in an area where the roads are far from suitable for heavy traffic, has been very successful and Saxon and Czech negotiators have agreed both on improvements and on the maintenance of the service through to the start of the next century.

## DB Regio

DB Regio AG
Stephensonstrasse 1, D-60326 Frankfurt am Main
Tel: (+49 69) 26 56 10 70   Fax: (+49 69) 26 51 42 88
Web: http://www.dbregio.de

### Key personnel
Board Members
   Chairman: Dr Phil Christoph Franz
   Production and Technology: Dr-Ing Joachim Trettin
   Finance and Audit: Dr rer pol Armin F Schwolgin
   Personnel and Legal Affairs: Heinrich Brüggemann

### Subsidiary companies
S-Bahn Berlin GmbH
Invalidenstrausse 19, D-10115 Berlin
Tel: (+49 30) 29 74 38 16
S-Bahn Hamburg GmbH
Steinstrasse 12, D-20095 Hamburg
Tel: (+49 40) 39 18 39 04

DB Regio, the local passenger traffic business, had a total turnover in 2000 of €7,517 million (1998: €7,328 million), of which orders from the federal states accounted for €4,330.9 million (1999: €4,283.4 million). Capital expenditure was €1,305 million for the year, against €1,311 million in the previous year. There were 52,769 employees at the end of 2000 (1999: 55,605). There are 14 regions and eight workshops. The company owns 17 regional bus companies, four DB ZugBus companies, the S-Bahn companies for Berlin and Hannover, and the Usedomer Bäderbahn.

From 1 January 1996 responsibility for the support of local rail transport passed from the federal government, which had been spending about DM6 billion a year, to the states. These received additional money to buy in from DB AG those loss-making services they or local authorities deemed to be socially necessary, the support being based on the 1993-94 timetable's service pattern. They decide which services are to be retained and how they are to be provided. They can contract with DB AG to run them; they can negotiate with an existing independent railway to provide a service, using the general right of access to the national infrastructure; they can even buy the infrastructure involved for themselves; or they can buy a replacement road service.

It is to be noted that a 1997 DB AG report suggested that more than 11,000 km of the 40,000 km network was either completely unprofitable or offered no possibility of commercial exploitation in the longer term. New and more effective ways of managing local networks are currently being explored.

Local services are branded as Regional Express (RE), RegionalBahn (RB), and S-Bahn. A new category, the InterRegioExpress (IRE) was introduced in 2001 to indicate especially fast RE services or RE trains running to replace IR services.

DB Regio, like DB Reise&Touristik, is investing heavily in new rolling stock and has a 10-year programme to eliminate hauled-stock working.

*S-Bahn systems*
As long as no increase in subsidised operating costs is involved, the federal government has an obligation to grant-aid the capital cost of S-Bahn work. Under the 1967 Municipal Transport Finance Act *(Gemeindeverkehrsfinanzierunggesetz (GVFG))* the state dedicates part – currently DM0.054 per litre – of its oil tax revenues to meeting 60 per cent of the cost of urban transport infrastructure improvements approved and financially supported locally.

Two of the S-Bahn systems are now operated by separate companies set up as subsidiaries of the Deutsche Bahn Gruppe. These are S-Bahn Berlin GmbH, established in January 1995, and S-Bahn Hamburg GmbH, established two years later. In all other areas with S-Bahn operations, services are provided by DB Regio directly.

In Berlin, restoration of the S-Bahn network to its 1930s extent continues under a specially financed programme. Rolling stock is being replaced. Significant numbers of the new Class 481 trains are now running, but it will still be some time before all pre-war units have been replaced.

*Class 644 Talent dmus forming a Gummersbach service at Cologne Hbf (Colin Boocock)*   2000/0089564

In Hamburg more than DM900 million is being invested in the system over the next few years. A link to join Fulsbüttel Airport to the S-Bahn at Hamburg-Ohlsdorf is being planned. New trains of Class 474 are coming into service. An Adtranz/Alstom consortium is supplying 45 of these three-car emus, in which the end-cars in each set are powered by Adtranz equipment, with four water-cooled 125 kW asynchronous AC motors under GTO inverter control. An option to buy a further 58 units at a cost of some DM350 million has been exercised, with delivery starting in 1999.

The expansion of other S-Bahn systems continues apace. In Cologne, work is well under way on the provision of segregated S-Bahn tracks between Cologne and Düren as part of the Cologne–Aachen ABS project, and an airport link, is being built. In Dresden a DM326 million project sees the restoration of four tracks between Dresden Hbf and Pirna to allow the segregation of S-Bahn services from main line traffic on the international route to the Czech Republic. Other work involves station renewals and an airport link which was opened in early 2001, and further measures planned include widening of the Arnsdorf and Meissen lines – work on the latter being dependent on progress on the upgrading of the Dresden–Leipzig/Berlin main lines. In the Halle/Leipzig area the DM450 million Halle–Leipzig S-Bahn line is now under construction. At 32 km it will be 6 km shorter than the existing route, mainly because of a different approach to Leipzig. It will require some 26 km of new construction and will have 10 intermediate stations.

A substantial S-Bahn network was developed in Hannover in time for EXPO 2000. Lines are:
S1   Stadthagen–Wunstorf–Hannover Hbf–Weetzen–Haste (that is, forming a loop)
S2   Nienburg–Wunstorf–Hannover Hbf–Weetzen–Haste
S3   Hannover Hbf–Lehrte–Celle
S4   Bennemühlen–Hannover Hbf–Hameln
S5   Flughafen Langenhagen–Hannover Hbf–Hameln.

S1 and S2 running hourly gives a 30-minute service between Wunstorf and Haste via Hannover Hbf, as do S4 and S5 between Langenhagen and Weetzen. Total cost of the north-south S-Bahn is put at DM690 million.

The Rhine-Main S-Bahn system, centred on Frankfurt am Main, continues to grow. A 'Messe' S-Bahn station has been built in Frankfurt. In the Rhine-Neckar area an agreement was signed in 1996 for the construction and financing of the new DM340 million S-Bahn. MVV (Mannheimer Versorgungs- und Verkehrgesellschaft) and DB were originally competitors as potential operators, but in late 1996 they came together and put forward a joint proposal for working both the proposed Neustadt–Speyer–Ludwigshafen–

*Class 650 Adtranz RegioShuttle railcars at Ulm (David Haydock)*   2001/0114243

*Class 474 Hamburg S-Bahn third-rail emu at Hamburg Hbf* (Marcel Vleugels)     2000/0089561

Mannheim–Heidelberg–Biberach–Bruchsal regional line and all local traffic between the Palatinate and Odenwald. The Neustadt–Speyer–Ludwigshafen–Mannheim–Heidelberg–Bruchsal/Eberbach route is being modernised throughout, quadrupled between Ludwigshafen and Mannheim (with a new Rhine bridge, on which work began in 1997), and electrified between Speyer and Schifferstadt. There will be a half-hourly service, with trains dividing in Schifferstadt for Neustadt and Speyer and in Heidelberg for Bruchsal and Eberbach. Extensions to Mosbach (Baden), Karlsruhe, and Kaiserslautern are envisaged later, and further lines are proposed to follow the initial east-west route. A cost-benefit analysis has given positive forecasts for a Worms–Frankenthal–Ludwigshafen–Mannheim route with a connection to the BASF works station.

In 2001, DB Regio won a 12-year contract to operate a new Rhein–Neckar S-Bahn network of some 240 route-km around Mannheim and Heidelberg. Due to commence in December 2003, services will be provided by 40 Class 425 emus. Also under discussion is a route from the South Hessen towns of Biblis, Bürstadt and Lampertheim through Mannheim and on over the Rheintalbahn via Schwetzingen/Hockenheim to Karlsruhe. To the north, the Rhine-Ruhr-Wupper S-Bahn is to be extended from Dortmund to Hagen, and other extensions in the Dortmund area are being planned, and a new S9 line, between Haltern, Essen, and Wuppertal-Vohwinkel, is due for completion by the turn of the century.

In Bavaria, the Munich S-Bahn received its second connection to the new Munich Airport with the opening in 1998 of the so-called Neufahrner Spange, 6.7 km in length, to complete a 19 km route from Ismanning coming in from the west. The total airport service is now six trains an hour. A second tunnel is to be built to solve the problems of congestion on the Munich city tunnel line. Separation of local traffic is required on the future ABS Munich–Ingolstadt route, and a DM200 million quadrupling between Obermenzing and Dachau is planned to allow an expansion of the Munich–Dachau S-Bahn service. During 2001-02, 144 new Class 423 emus are being brought into service to provide a DM900 million upgrade for Munich's S-Bahn. In Nuremberg construction work on the 26 km section from Nuremberg to Roth currently being modernised should be complete by the turn of the century and planning for the future is now focused on the Nuremberg–Fürth–Forchheim axis.

In June 2001, work commenced on infrastructure work for the creation of a cross-city S-Bahn network in Leipzig. The project includes a double-track tunnel under the city to link the Bayerischer Bahnhof terminus, in the south, with Leipzig main station, which lies north of the centre.

*Mixed running*

Heavy rail shares tracks with light rail (the trams of the Albtal Railway (qv)) in the Karlsruhe area. The aim was to establish a large regional network at low cost by connecting light rail routes and DB AG, allowing trams to travel out into the surrounding areas on DB AG tracks shared with ordinary trains. By the end of 1994 a fleet of 36 dual-system light rail cars was available, able to operate on both 750 V DC and 15 kV AC. The initial route was opened in 1992 and other routes have been added. The operation is proving enormously successful and further extensions are planned.

Services began in the autumn of 1997 on a similar mixed system in Saarbrücken, on a first section between Saarbrücken and Saargemünd (France). This now extends northwards via Riegelsberg and Heusweiler to Lebach, giving a total length of 44 km of which 19 km is new construction, the remainder existing DB AG or SNCF tracks. Future connections to the University of the Saarland and to Forbach are planned. Total cost will be some DM540 million, with the federal government providing DM214 million through the GVFG and the *Land* Saarland DM224 million. The first 15 trains were built by Bombardier and in July 1998 the same manufacturer received an order for a further eight vehicles of the same type.

There is a development that sees vehicles built to heavy rail standards running on to a tramway in Zwickau, where the Regental Bahnbetriebs GmbH ordered 10 'RegioSprinters' equipped to meet tramway requirements so that they can run over the 3 km of tramway (which will be converted from metre-gauge to mixed-gauge) between Zwickau Hbf and the city's Neumarkt (new market place).

**UPDATED**

## DB Station&Service

DB Station&Service AG, D-60326 Frankfurt am Main
Tel:(+49 69) 26 50    Fax: (+49 69) 26 52 45 69

### Key personnel
Board Members
- Chairman: Dieter Ullsperger
- Station Development: Martin Lepper
- Finance and Audit: Dipl-Ing Maximilian Kittner
- Personnel: Alfred Possin

In 2000 the passenger stations business spent €552 million (1999: €554 million) on the maintenance of its 5,794 stations (1999: 5,876). There were 5,015 employees, against 5,593 the previous year.

*Major new stations*

'Station 21' projects have been announced for Dortmund, Frankfurt am Main, Lindau, Magdeburg, Mannheim, Munich, Saarbrücken, Stuttgart, and Ulm. The first and most advanced is 'Stuttgart 21', for which four schemes (from 27 submitted) were awarded prizes in the architectural competition. These are now being worked over prior to a final decision and funding questions are being carefully examined.

Following on from the successful completion of the DM400 million modernisation of Leipzig station, work on a DM130 million project at Cologne has been completed, providing a new travel and service centre, a high-quality waiting area, about 65 shop units, and a new second frontage, as well as a total restoration of the historic parts of the building. DM110 million were spent on a thorough modernisation of Hannover Hbf before Expo 2000. There is also to be a DM850 million rebuilding of Dortmund station. Major works programmes have been completed at Rostock, Stralsund, Berlin Lichtenberg and Berlin Ostbahnhof.

Modernisation continues at Frankfurt am Main. The first stage of major improvements to Schwerin station has also been completed. Dresden Hbf is to be restored and modernised according to the plans of the British architect Sir Norman Foster (who was responsible for the rebuilding of Berlin's Reichstag building as the home of the German parliament).

Alongside the projects already mentioned, DB Station&Service is engaged in major modernisation of other stations. These include Aachen, Bielefeld, Bochum, Bremen, Gelsenkirchen, Hamburg-Dammtor, Koblenz, Mannheim, Mülheim, Münster, Oberstorf, Oranienburg, Siegburg, and Weimar. In many cases the structures are listed. The longer-term aim is to modernise all 6,000 stations to make them customer-friendly transport centres, retaining wherever possible the old structures whilst equipping them to meet the needs of today's travellers. Some 70 per cent of all stations have so far seen improvement works.

Bookholzberg (between Bremen and Oldenburg) was the first station to receive the new *Plus-Punkt* treatment for

*Station improvement work in progress at Rostock* (Marcel Vleugels)     2001/0114208

upgrading small stations where facilities at present are either non-existent or very much run down. A basic element of a square, red module with glazed sides provides waiting space and houses information and service elements: ticket-machine, ticket-canceller, timetable-display, fares, route-diagram, area map, card-telephone with emergency button, and waste-bins. Additional 'packages' can then be added to provide features like video surveillance, a telephone with service-buttons (taxi-call, bus services), and drinks and snack machines, or even more elaborate facilities like toilets, cycle-stand, kiosk, complaints box, money-changer, newspaper sales, and so on. More than 1,000 stations will be provided with *Plus-Punkt* furniture.

Furthermore, DB Station&Service recently spent DM5 million on construction of its first modular station, at Memmingen (on the line from Ulm to Kempten). The prototype uses elements which can be adapted to suit any ground plan. In this instance 1,000 m² are covered by a single-storey building. The company is planning 20 such stations nationwide.

DB Station&Service now offers a 'KonferenzService' of meeting rooms at more than 40 of Germany's largest stations, with the advertising slogan 'Meeting rooms with ICE connections'.

### Rail-air links

Lufthansa and 22 foreign airlines offer air tickets including a coupon for internal German journeys to or from their international departure or arrival airport which can be exchanged for a rail ticket without further charge at stations or on a train. Deutsche Bahn offers all comers a Rail-&-Fly ticket for travel to and from airports on two zonally based scales with substantial discounts for family or group travel. Furthermore, deals are now in place with two major holiday firms for rail travel between home and departure airport to be included in the price of the holiday.

Reserved accommodation serviced by Lufthansa staff is provided in selected IC trains between Düsseldorf and Frankfurt Airport. Stuttgart passengers using Frankfurt Airport can check in or reclaim their baggage at Stuttgart Hbf and travel in reserved accommodation between there and the airport.

A frequent fast service between the centre of Berlin and Schönefeld Airport is made available by the provision of dedicated accommodation in certain RE services. The trains run between 04.30 and 23.00 and the fare is the standard flat fare of the Berlin-area transport system.

DB Reise&Touristik hopes to develop an InterCity connection to the new Munich Airport. Now the second S-Bahn link has been completed, construction of a short spur between the main line west of Munich Hbf at Pasing and S-Bahn Line S1 at Moosach would enable IC trains from the Augsburg direction to reach the airport station and, if required, to serve Munich Hbf as well by completing the S-Bahn circle to arrive in the city from the east.

In May 1999 the new Frankfurt Airport station was opened. Situated on the first section of the Cologne–Rhine/Main NBS to be brought into service, this new station has long-distance services not only to and from Frankfurt am Main Hbf but also direct to Mannheim and the south.

Main line and S-Bahn connections are under construction to serve Cologne/Bonn Airport, the costs being shared by the railway, the federal government, the *Land*, and the airport company. Rail links have been enhanced at Düsseldorf Airport by the construction, at a cost of DM87 million, of a new station on the Düsseldorf–Duisburg main line, to be linked to the airport by a people mover and served by some 88 long-distance trains a day, as well as S-Bahn services.

The Hannover S-Bahn system, completed in time for the opening of Expo 2000, includes a double-track branch to the airport at Langenhagen from the northern line of the S-Bahn system.

A new station serves the airport at Dresden, and one is planned for Hamburg. These will be for S-Bahn services.

## Hafen und Güterverkehr Köln (HGK)

Hafen und Güterverkehr Köln AG
Bayenstrasse 2, D-50678 Cologne
Tel: (+49 221) 39 00    Fax: (+49 221) 390 13 43
Web: http://www.hgk.de

### Key personnel

Chairman and Operations Manager: Werner Böllinger
Chief Financial Officer: Dr Dipl-Kfm Rolf Bender
Marketing Director: Horst Leonhardt
Assistant Operations Manager: Manfred Eising

Gauge: 1,435 mm
Route length: 102 km

### Organisation

Controlled by the city of Cologne, HGK was formed in 1992 by merging the freight operations of the Köln–Bonner Eisenbahn (KBE), the Köln–Frechen–Benzelrather Eisenbahn (KFBE) and Cologne's public ports and port railways.

In 1998 HGK established a joint venture with Zanders (a paper producer), P&O and the community of Bergisch Gladbach, creating BGE Eisenbahn Güterverkehr GmbH. The company opened an intermodal terminal in Bergisch Gladbach in October 1999.

In April 2002, HGK became a member of the Swiss Rail Cargo Köln consortium, with a shareholding of 44 per cent. Other members of the venture are Swiss Federal Railways (51 per cent) and Swiss intermodal operator, Hupac.

### Passenger operations

Interurban light rail services of Cologne and Bonn city transport authorities use HGK lines.

### Freight operations

HGK co-operates closely with DB. Through container trains between Cologne and Rotterdam are run in association with Short Lines of the Netherlands. Diesel locomotives run throughout between these two points (although the entire line is electrified), but a change of driver occurs at the border crossing at Venlo.

A second international container flow commenced in 2000 when HGK provided haulage for intermodal operator Hupac on the Cologne–Basel leg of a new service to Rome Pomezia.

In 2000 HGK carried 5.8 million tonnes, an increase of 9 per cent on the previous year.

### Traction and rolling stock

HGK operates 33 diesel locomotives, some 500 freight cars and two business railcars. The locomotive fleet includes three Type DE 1024 MaK-built 2,650 kW Co-Co demonstrators dating from 1989 and 16 Type DE 1002

*General Motors Type JT42CWR diesel-electric locomotive* (Edward Barnes)    *2002*/0524928

1,320 kW Bo-Bos built in 1987 by the same manufacturer. During 1999, these were supplemented by two General Motors JT42CWR Co-Co locomotives similar to the Class 66 machines supplied by the same manufacturer to EWS in the United Kingdom. A third example of the same type was hired from Porterbrook in 2002.

The fleet was supplemented in 2000/01 by five Type 145 electric locomotives supplied by Bombardier Transportation and leased from Porterbrook Leasing and an additional two Vossloh G1206 diesel locomotives. The electric locomotives are used for container trains in the Rhine/Ruhr area and on intermodal and bulk flows between Cologne and Switzerland.

***UPDATED***

## Hamburg Port Railway

Hafenbahn Hamburg
Freie und Hansestadt Hamburg, Wirtschaftsbehörde, Strom- und Hafenbau, Abteilung Hafenbahn
Dalmannstrasse 1, D-20457 Hamburg
Tel: (+49 40) 28 47 25 41

### Key personnel

General Manager: Dipl-Ing Reinhard Höfer
Assistant Manager: Dipl-Ing H-Michael Röfer

Gauge: 1,435 mm
Route length: 403 km

### Organisation

Hamburg port railway is not a public carrier. It is operated by DB, but carries out its own track maintenance.

### Freight operations

Traffic statistics for 1997 were 23.7 million tonnes and 106.8 million tonne-km, compared with 21.9 million tonnes and 98.6 million tonne-km in 1996.

### Traction and rolling stock

Two diesel locomotives.

## Harz Narrow Gauge Railways

Harzer Schmalspurbahnen GmbH (HSB)
Friedrichstrasse 151, D-38855 Wernigerode
Tel: (+49 3943) 55 81 10    Fax: (+49 3943) 55 81 12
Web: http://www.hsb-wr.de

### Key personnel

Managing Director: Matthias Wagener
Operations Manager: Jörg Bauer

Gauge: 1,000 mm
Route length: 132 km

### Organisation

HSB is owned by local authorities in the region within which it operates. The lines of the former Nordhausen–Wernigeroder Eisenbahn and Gernrode–Harzgeroder Eisenbahn were taken over from the former German State Railways (DR) in 1993.

## Passenger operations

HSB serves the Brocken mountain, a popular tourist destination not accessible by road. Suburban services between Nordhausen and Ilfeld, operated by diesel railcars, have been improved by introducing a fixed interval timetable and opening additional halts. Traffic statistics for 1999 were 1.1 million passengers and 30.7 million passenger-km.

## Freight operations

Transporter bogies replaced transporter wagons in 1996. Traffic statistics for 1999 were 39,000 tonnes and 751,000 tonne-km.

## Traction and rolling stock

HSB traction and rolling stock comprises 24 steam locomotives (of which four stored), 47 diesel railcars, 10 line-haul diesel locomotives, several diesel shunting locomotives, 87 coaches, 55 freight wagons and 30 transporter bogies.

# HellertalBahn

HellertalBahn GmbH
Bahnhofstrasse 1, D-57518 Betzdorf/Sieg
Tel: (+49 2741) 97 35 75
e-mail: info@hellertalbahn.de
Web: http://www.hellertalbahn.de

## Background

Formed in 1999, HellertalBahn GmbH is a joint venture between the Hessische Landesbahn (HLB) (qv), the Siegener Kreisbahn and the Westerwaldbahn.

## Passenger operations

Since September 1999, the HellertalBahn has provided regional services on the Betzdorf—Neunkirchen—Haiger—Dillenburg line, which runs through the states of Rheinland-Pfalz, Nordrhein-Westfalen and Hessen.

## Traction and rolling stock

Three Stadler GTW 2/6 dmus procured by the HLB.

# Hessische Landesbahn (HLB)

Hessische Landesbahn GmbH
Mannheimer Strasse 15, D-60329 Frankfurt
Tel: (+49 69) 242 52 40   Fax: (+49 69) 24 25 24 60

e-mail: mail@hlb-online.de
Web: http://www.hessenbahn.de
http://www.hlb-online.de

## Key personnel

Managing Director: Dipl-Ing Peter Berking
Directors
    Harald Chrysam
    Wolfgang Fischer
    Norbert Sittinger

## Organisation

HLB was founded in 1955 as holding company for the state-owned local railways in Hesse. At present it owns and operates the following railways:
    Butzbach—Licher Eisenbahn AG (qv)
    Frankfurt—Königsteiner Eisenbahn AG (qv)
    Kassel—Naumburger Eisenbahn AG (qv).
In addition, HLB participates in two joint venture rail operations:
    HellertalBahn GmbH (qv), jointly with the Siegener Kreisbahn and the Westerwaldbahn
    SüdThüringenBahn GmbH (qv), jointly with the Erfurter Industriebahn.

## Traction and rolling stock

Including units on order in 2000, HLB has procured jointly with the Erfurter Industriebahn 30 GTW 2/6 and 21 RS1 diesel railcars from Stadler/Adtranz/DWA.

*Type GTW 2/6 articulated lightweight railcar built for HLB by Stadler/Adtranz/DWA*
0063199

# Hohenzollerische Landesbahn (HzL)

Hohenzollerische Landesbahn AG
Hofgartenstrasse 39, D-73279 Hechingen
Tel: (+49 7471) 180 60   Fax: (+49 7471) 18 06 12
Web: http://www.hzl-online.de

## Key personnel

Chief Executive: Dipl-Kfm Günter Zeiger
Rail Operations Manager: Dipl-Ing Bernhard Strobel

Gauge: 1,435 mm
Route length: 107 km (owned); 286 km (operated)

## Organisation

HzL is local government-owned. Freight and passenger trains also operate over DB lines.

## Passenger operations

HzL passenger services operate between Hechingen and Sigmaringen. The Sigmaringen—Tuttlingen line (42 km) is operated under contract to Baden-Württemberg state. Other services are operated for DB. Traffic statistics for 1999 were 5.9 million passengers and 112.9 million passenger-km, these figures include bus operations (55 buses).

In 2000 HzL won a contract from the Baden-Württemberg regional authorities to operate a group of services in the Black Forest area. The company was due to take over the so-called 'Ringzug' services in 2001.

HzL also manages services on the Bodensee—Oberschwaben Bahn (BOB) (qv).

## Freight operations

Traffic statistics for 1999 were 328,000 tonnes and 27.2 million tonne-km. Principal traffic is industrial salt bound for Burghausen, Bavaria, which is hauled by HzL between Stetten and Ulm.

## Traction and rolling stock

Twelve diesel locomotives, 33 diesel railcars (including 22 Adtranz RegioShuttle units), five driving trailers and three trailers.

The procurement of additional diesel railcars for the 'Ringzug' services (see Passenger operations) was anticipated.

*Two HzL Adtranz RegioShuttle railcars at Tübingen with an Albstadt—Ebingen service (David Haydock)*
2001/0109847

# RAILWAY SYSTEMS/Germany

## Hörseltalbahn (HTB)

Hörseltalbahn GmbH
Adam-Opel-Strasse 100, D-99817 Eisenach
Tel: (+49 3691) 66 31 60
Web: http://www.hoerseltalbahn.de

Gauge: 1,435 mm
Route length: 9 km

### Organisation
HTB is a subsidiary of Connex Cargo Logistics GmbH.

### Freight traffic
HTB primarily serves an Opel car manufacturing plant at Eisenach.

### Traction and rolling stock
Three diesel locomotives.

## Karsdorfer Eisenbahn (KEG)

Karsdorfer Eisenbahngesellschaft mbH
Strasse der Einheit 25, D-06638 Karsdorf
Tel: (+49 3461) 745 75   Fax: (+49 3461) 744 90
e-mail: info@privatbahn.de
Web: http://www.privatbahn.de

### Key personnel
Managing Director: Bernhard van Engelen
Operations Manager: Dipl-Ing Konrad Höft
General Manager, Burgenlandbahn: Uwe Rückreim

Gauge: 1,435 mm
Track length: 30 km

### Organisation
KEG was founded in 1993 to take over the industrial railway of a cement works and subsequently entered the market as an open access freight operator. Since 1995 it has run passenger services for DB. In 1996 the company took over management of the Rügensche Kleinbahn (qv). In a joint venture with DB in 1999, KEG founded Burgenlandbahn GmbH to operate the national operator's former routes in the Naumburg/Zeitz/Merseburg region.

KEG also operates the Citybahn Chemnitz system in Stollberg and holds a contract to run the Rügensche Kleinbahn tourist railway (qv).

In June 2001 KEG, in consortium with General Motors, announced it was to take over state-owned Romanian locomotive manufacturer Electroputere in an agreement reached with the country's privatisation agency APAPs.

*KEG Class 2100 diesel-electric locomotives at Rheine depot (David Haydock)* 2001/0109848

### Freight operations
In 1997 KEG carried 43,000 tonnes for its own operations. In 1999, the company inaugurated a service conveying aviation fuel from Lingen (Ems) to Munich airport, a distance of some 840 km over DB tracks.

The company also operates permanent way maintenance trains under contract to DB.

### Traction and rolling stock
KEG operates more than 40 diesel locomotives, nine diesel railcars and 20 freight wagons. Delivered by Bombardier DWA in 1999 were 18 LVT/S lightweight railcars which are leased to Burgenlandbahn.

In 1999, KEG acquired from Romanian State Railways four Class 60 Sulzer-engined diesel-electric locomotives for use on the aviation fuel traffic detailed above. The 1,546 kW machines were overhauled before delivery from Romania. By mid-2001 additional acquisitions had brought to 14 the number of this type (KEG Class 2100) in the fleet. In the same year KEG introduced to traffic its first Type 7000 5,100 kW electric locomotive, a refurbished Electroputere/ASEA-built machine also acquired from Romanian State Railways.

## Kassel—Naumburger Eisenbahn (KNE)

Kassel–Naumburger Eisenbahn AG
Wilhelmshöher Allee 252, D-34119 Kassel
Tel: (+49 561) 93 07 40   Fax: (+49 561) 930 74 21
e-mail: mail@kne-online.de
Web: http://www.kne-online.de

### Key personnel
Chief Executive: Dipl-Ing Peter Berking
General Manager: Dipl-Ing Veit Salzmann

Gauge: 1,435 mm
Route length: 10 km

### Organisation
Majority-owned (51 per cent) and operated by Hessische Landesbahn (qv).

### Passenger operations
An extension of the Kassel tramways operates over 2.9 km of the KNE line in Baunatal, which has been electrified for the purpose. Passenger services over the former DB Wabern—Bad Wildungen line (17 km) is operated by KNE under contract.

Regionalbahn Kassel, a joint venture between KNE and the Kassel tram operator KVG, took over the Kassel–Kaufungen—Hessisch Lichtenau line, the 24 km Lossetalbahn, from DB in 1998 for conversion into an electrified light rail line. It is also planned to operate dual-mode railcars over other DB lines.

In 1997 KNE carried 3 million passengers. This figure includes bus services (27 buses).

### Freight operations
Freight traffic is mainly for the Volkswagen car plant at Baunatal. Traffic statistics for 1999 were 1.2 million tonnes and 9.7 million tonne-km.

### Traction and rolling stock
Two diesel locomotives, three Stadler GTW 2/6 diesel railcars for Kassel—Wabern—Bad Wildungen services and two electric tramcars operated in a pool with Kassel tramways.

## Laubag

Lausitzer Braunkohle AG – Zentraler Eisenbahnbetrieb
Knappenstrasse 1, D-01968 Senftenberg
Tel: (+49 3573) 780   Fax: (+49 3573) 78 24 24

### Key personnel
Chief Executive: Prof Dr Ing Kurt Häge
Director, Railway: Dipl-Geol Jürgen Kobus

Gauge: 1,435 mm
Route length: 376 km
Electrification: 325 km at 2.4 kV DC overhead

### Organisation
Laubag is an industrial railway system operated by a lignite mining company in the Cottbus area, serving five opencast mines and three power stations. Connections with DB are made at Peitz and Spreewitz. The railway also serves other industrial enterprises.

### Freight operations
Traffic statistics for 1999 were 52.7 million tonnes and 698.8 million tonne-km. Through lignite trains for Berlin and elsewhere are transferred to DB.

### Traction and rolling stock
The Laubag fleet comprises 72 Bo+Bo 1,380 kW Type EL2 electric locomotives built by LEW Hennigsdorf, 25 diesel locomotives and 476 freight wagons.

### Signalling and telecommunications
A Siemens SICAS centralised traffic control system was completed in 2000.

## Leuna

Infra-Leuna Infrastruktur und Service GmbH
Am Haupttor, Bürocenter, D-06236 Leuna
Tel: (+49 3461) 43 30 01   Fax: (+49 3461) 43 33 44

### Key personnel
Managing Directors: Andreas Hiltermann; Walter Kraus

Gauge: 1,435 mm
Track length: 56 km

### Organisation
Industrial line.

### Freight operations
Traffic statistics for 1999 were 4.9 million tonnes and 34.3 million tonne-km.

### Traction and rolling stock
Ten locomotives and 22 freight wagons.

Germany/**RAILWAY SYSTEMS** 171

## Molli

Mecklenburgische Bäderbahn Molli GmbH & Co KG
Am Bahnhof, D-18209 Bad Doberan
Tel: (+49 38203) 41 50   Fax: (+49 38203) 415 12
e-mail: molli-bahn@t-online.de
Web: http://www.molli-bahn.de

**Key personnel**
Managing Director: Dr jur Horst Metz
Operating Manager: Dipl-Ing Jan Methling

Gauge: 900 mm
Route length: 15 km

**Organisation**
The Bad Doberan–Kühlungsborn line was taken over from DB in 1995. Freight traffic was discontinued.

**Passenger operations**
Molli connects Kühlungsborn, a popular resort on the Baltic coast, with DB at Bad Doberan. The steam-operated line is also a tourist attraction. Traffic statistics for 1999 were 446,000 passengers and 4.4 million passenger-km.

**Traction and rolling stock**
Four steam locomotives and 37 coaches.

## Neukölln—Mittenwalder Eisenbahn (NME)

Neukölln—Mittenwalder Eisenbahn AG
Gottlieb-Dunkel-Str 47/48, D-12099 Berlin
Tel: (+49 30) 70 09 03 50   Fax: (+49 30) 703 30 78

**Key personnel**
Directors: Eberhard Conrad; Sven Tombrink
Operations Manager: Dipl-Ing Dieter Radzuweit

Gauge: 1,435 mm
Route length: 9 km

**Organisation**
NME is a freight line in southern Berlin, connecting with DB at Hermannstrasse (Berlin–Neukölln).

**Freight operations**
Principal commodities carried are household waste, coal and fuel oil. Traffic statistics for 1999 were 1.1 million tonnes and 6.2 million tonne-km.

**Traction and rolling stock**
Six diesel locomotives, eight freight wagons.

## Neusser Eisenbahn

Städtische Hafenbetriebe Neuss-Neusser Eisenbahn
Hammer Landstrasse 3, D-41460 Neuss
Tel: (+49 2131) 90 82 00   Fax: (+49 2131) 90 82 82

**Key personnel**
Principal: Dipl-Ing Ludwig von Hartz
Railway Operations Manager: Frank Türger

Gauge: 1,435 mm
Track length: 54 km

**Organisation**
The railway is a division of the Neuss municipal port authority.

**Freight operations**
The Neusser Eisenbahn serves 75 private sidings. It also operates freight services over DB lines. Traffic statistics for 1999 were 2.3 million tonnes and 9.3 million tonne-km.

**Traction and rolling stock**
Seven diesel locomotives, 78 freight wagons.

## Niederrheinische Verkehrsbetriebe (NIAG)

Niederrheinische Verkehrsbetriebe AG (NIAG)
Homberger Str 113, D-47441 Moers
Tel: (+49 2841) 20 50   Fax: (+49 2841) 20 56 70
e-mail: info@niag-online.de
Web: http://www.niag-online.de

**Key personnel**
Chief Executives: Dipl-Ing Otfried Kinzel (chair)
    Dr rer pol Dipl-Kfm Gerhard Brückner
Rail Operations Manager: Dipl-Ing Manfred Diehl

Gauge: 1,435 mm
Route length: 36 km

**Organisation**
NIAG is a county council owned transport company which provides road passenger services and rail freight services.

**Passenger operations**
Seasonal passenger excursion traffic at weekends only.

**Freight operations**
Lines owned by NIAG extend from Moers to Rheinberg and Hoerstgen/Sevelen. Ore and coal are the main commodities carried. The railway also operates its own port on the river Rhine at Orsoy. Freight trains are also operated over DB lines from Moers to Trompet and Homberg. Traffic figures for 1999 were 3.5 million tonnes and 32.5 million tonne-km, compared with 3.7 million tonnes and 35.4 million tonne-km in 1998.

**Traction and rolling stock**
Eight diesel locomotives, 80 freight wagons and two diesel railcars.

## Nordfriesische Verkehrsbetriebe (NVAG)

Nordfriesische Verkehrsbetriebe AG
Bahnhofstrasse 6, D-25899 Niebüll
Tel: (+49 4661) 98 08 80   Fax: (+49 4661) 58 79

**Key personnel**
Chief Executive: Ulrich Schütz
Director and Operations Manager: Gerhard Neumann

Gauge: 1,435 mm
Route length: 30 km

**Organisation**
Links DB station at Niebüll with Dagebüll, railhead for the islands of Föhr and Amrum.

**Passenger operations**
Exchanges through coaches with DB Intercity trains. Carried 733,000 passengers in 1997, including bus services with a fleet of 16 buses.

**Freight operations**
Parcels traffic only, approximately 2,000 tonnes annually over own line. Runs freight trains over DB/Danish State Railways (DSB) line from Niebüll to Tønder (Denmark), where it connects with Privatbanan Sønderjylland.

**Traction and rolling stock**
Two diesel railcars, one diesel locomotive, three coaches, seven freight wagons.

## Nord-Ostsee-Bahn (NOB)

Nord-Ostsee-Bahn GmbH
Diedrichstrasse 7, D-24143 Kiel
Tel: (+49 431) 73 03 60   Fax: (+49 431) 730 36 50
e-mail: post@nord-ostsee-bahn.de
Web: http://www.nord-ostsee-bahn.de

Gauge: 1,435 mm
Route length: 177 km

**Key personnel**
Managing Director: Karl-Heinz Fischer
Sales and Marketing Manager: Bela Bergemann

**Background**
NOB is a member of Connex Regiobahn GmbH.

**Passenger operations**
In November 2000 NOB took over operations on three routes in Schleswig-Holstein: Kiel—Rendsburg—Schleswig—Husum (102 km); Husum—Bad St Peter-Ording (44 km); and Kiel—Neumünster (31 km).

**Traction and rolling stock**
Nine Alstom LINT 41/H dmus.

## NordWestBahn (NWB)

NordWestBahn GmbH
Alte Poststrasse 9, D-49074 Osnabrück
Web: http://www.nordwestbahn.de

Gauge: 1,435 mm
Route length: 310 km

### Key personnel
Managing Directors: Hansrüdiger Fritz; Martin Meyer

### Background
NWB is a joint venture between the Connex-Gruppe and Stadtwerke Osnabrück AG, operating services on behalf of the regional transport authority, Landesnahverkehrgesselschaft Niedersachsen (LNVG).

### Passenger operations
In November 2000 NWB took over from DB Regio operation of a 310 km network covering Bremen–Delmenhorst–Osnabrück and Osnabrück–Oldenburg–Esens/Wilhelmshaven lines in the Weser-Ems region.

### Freight operations
In 2001, Connex-Gruppe and Stadtwerke Osnabrück AG established NordWestCargo with the aim of expanding its operations into the freight market.

*NWB Alstom-built LINT 41 dmus (David Haydock)*  2001/0109851

### Improvements to existing lines
NWB commissioned a new rolling stock maintenance facility in Osnabrück in September 2000.

### Traction and rolling stock
Services are provided using a fleet of 23 Alstom Coradia LINT 41 two-car dmus and six Siemens Desiro two-car dmus. In January 2002, LNVG placed an order with Alstom for 16 additional two-car Coradia LINT 41 dmus for delivery in 2003. Alstom also provides maintenance for the fleet under a 15-year service contract.

**UPDATED**

---

## Oberrheinische Eisenbahn Gesellschaft (OEG)

Oberrheinische Eisenbahn Gesellschaft AG (OEG)
Käfertaler Str 9-11, D-68167 Mannheim
Tel: (+49 621) 339 40   Fax: (+49 621) 339 41 18

### Key personnel
Chief Executives: Dipl-Ing (FH) Eduard Stephan (also Operations Manager)
   Dr rer pol Dipl-Wirtsch-Ing Karl Wimmer

Gauge: 1,000 mm
Route length: 63 km
Electrification: 750 V DC overhead

### Passenger operations
OEG is an interurban electric line with through running with Mannheim and Heidelberg tramways. Traffic figures for 1999 were 15.3 million passengers and 168 million passenger-km. Figures include traffic gained using a small bus fleet.

### Traction and rolling stock
The fleet comprises 43 multisection electric light rail vehicles.

---

## Osthannoversche Eisenbahnen (OHE)

Osthannoversche Eisenbahnen AG
Biermannstrasse 33, D-29221 Celle
Tel: (+49 5141) 27 60   Fax: (+49 5141) 27 62 58

### Key personnel
Chief Executive: Dr rer pol Jens Jahnke
Directors: Dipl-Ing Wolfgang Joseph; Heinrich Lindhorst; Dipl-Verw Betr wirt Henning Weize

Gauge: 1,435 mm
Route length: 326 km

### Passenger operations
Formed in 1944 by the merger of seven local railways, OHE operates the following lines:
   Celle–Wittingen (51 km)
   Wittingen–Rühen (35 km)
   Beedenbostel–Mariaglück (6 km)
   Celle–Soltau (59 km)
   Beckedorf–Munster (24 km)
   Soltau–Lüneburg (57 km)
   Winsen–Hützel (41 km)
   Winsen–Niedermarschacht (16 km)
   Lüneburg–Bleckede (24 km)

In 2001, a consortium led by OHE and including Bremer Strassenbahn (BSAG), Elbe-Weser Railways (EVB) and Hamburger Hochbahn (HHA) secured a contract to operate regional express services on Hamburg–Bremen and Hamburg–Uelzen routes from 2003.

### Freight operations
Since 1990 OHE has operated freight trains over DB lines and also provides locomotives for DB permanent way maintenance trains. Traffic statistics for 1999 are 846,000 tonnes and 50.1 million tonne-km.

### Traction and rolling stock
The fleet comprises 20 diesel locomotives, two diesel railcars for excursion traffic and 19 freight wagons.
   To equip the regional express services detailed above, the OHE-led consortium plans to procure 18 Class 146 electric locomotives and a fleet of double-deck coaches.

**UPDATED**

---

## OME

Ostmecklenburgische Eisenbahngesellschaft mbH
Warliner Strasse 25, D-17034 Neubrandenburg
Tel: (+49 395) 456 75 24   Fax: (+49 395) 456 75 07

e-mail: service@omebahn.de
Web: http://www.omebahn.de

Gauge: 1,435 mm
Route length: 241 km

### Background
OME is a member of Connex Regiobahn GmbH.

### Passenger operations
Operated by Vivendi (Connex), OME provides services over DB lines in northeast Germany from Schwerin to Neubrandenburg via Güstrow, from where a branch runs to the north to the port of Rostock. From Neubrandenburg, branches run south to Neustrelitz and northeast to Pasewalk and Ueckermünde. In 1999, 1.12 million passenger journeys were recorded.

### Traction and rolling stock
Passenger services are operated by 10 three-section Talent dmus supplied by Bombardier Transportation.

*One of OME's Talent dmus was displayed at the InnoTrans trade fair in Berlin in October 2000 (Ken Harris)*
2001/0103632

Germany/**RAILWAY SYSTEMS** 173

## PCK Raffinerie

PCK Raffinerie GmbH
Passower Chaussee 111, D-16303 Schwedt
Tel: (+49 3332) 460   Fax: (+49 3332) 46 54 80

### Key personnel
Managing Directors: Dr Hans-Otto Gerlach
   Hans-Joachim Knust

Director, Logistics: Ralph Fenselau
Rail Operations Manager: Dipl-Ing Jochen Bismark

Gauge: 1,435 mm
Track length: 120 km

### Organisation
Industrial railway of a petrochemical plant at Schwedt on the river Oder.

### Freight operations
Traffic statistics for 1999 were 4.7 million tonnes.

### Traction and rolling stock
Seven locomotives.

## Prignitzer Eisenbahn GmbH (PEG)

Pritzwalker Strasse 2, D-16949 Putlitz
Tel: (+49 3981) 805 06
Web: http://www.prignitzer-eisenbahn.de

### Passenger operations
Since 1996 PEG has operated regional lines around the Pritzwalk area, northwest of Berlin. In 2001 the company won a six-year contract to operate Duisburg–Oberhausen (9 km) and Oberhausen–Dorsten (27 km) services in the Ruhr, taking these over from DB in December 2002. Also in 2001, in partnership with Hamburger Hochbahn AG, PEG secured a contract to operate a 175 km network covering Hagenow Land–Ludwigslust–Parchim–Karow–Waren–Neustrelitz and Neustrelitz–Mirow. The contract takes effect in December 2002.

### Freight operations
Traffic includes construction materials which are hauled from Sachsendorf to the Berlin area using open access rights.

### Traction and rolling stock
Passenger services employ ex-DB railbuses. PEG also operates an ex-DB Class 403 'Lufthansa Express' emu.

*PEG railbuses at Pritzwalk* (David Haydock)   2001/0109850

For the Ruhr contract, the company is to procure six Bombardier Talent dmus. Five M62 main line diesel-electric locomotives sourced from Czech Railways and Polish State Railways after refurbishment are used for freight traffic.

For services in the Ruhr to be taken over from DB in December 2002, PEG has ordered six Bombardier 'Talent' dmus.

**UPDATED**

## Regentalbahn (RBG)

Regental Bahnbetriebs GmbH
Bahnhofsplatz 1, D-94234 Viechtach
Tel: (+49 9942) 946 30   Fax: (+49 9942) 94 65 66

### Key personnel
Managing Director: Dipl-Ing Willi Höppner
Operating Manager: Dipl-Ing Lutz Kühn

Gauge: 1,435 mm
Route length; 43 km (freight), 18 km (passenger, owned), 133 km (passenger, operated)

### Organisation
RBG's original line, from Gotteszell to Viechtach, is now freight only. The Lam–Kötzting line, taken over in 1973, is passenger only, with through running over the DB line to Cham. The Plattling–Bayerisch Eisenstein (72 km), Zwiesel–Grafenau (32 km) and Zwiesel–Bodenmais (15 km) lines are operated for DB using the 'Waldbahn' brand name.

In May 1998 a subsidiary company, Vogtlandbahn GmbH, was established to operate services over 263 km of DB lines in the Zwickau/Plauen area of Saxony under a 15-year contract. Extensions to the network in May 2000 included a cross-border service between Marktredwitz in Bavaria and Cheb in the Czech Republic and in June 2001 Vogtlandbahn services were introduced on the Hof–Marktredwitz–Weiden line.

In June 2001, Oberpfalzbahn, a joint company established by RBG and DB Regio, took over the operation of the Cham–Schwandorf–Waldmünchen–Furthinwald–Kötzting line.

A subsidiary company, Regental Fahrzeugwerkstätten GmbH, carries out a considerable amount of work for third parties and also acts as a dealer for used rolling stock.

### Passenger operations
Traffic statistics for 1999 were 177,000 passengers and 3.3 million passenger-km.

### Freight operations
Approximately 12,000 tonnes carried annually.

### New lines
Vogtlandbahn trains have been extended into the centre of Zwickau via tramway tracks. A third rail was laid for this purpose.

### Traction and rolling stock
Regentalbahn: three diesel locomotives, five diesel railcars, two driving trailers, three coaches.
Waldbahn: 13 diesel railcars (11 Adtranz RegioShuttle units, and two former DB battery railcars rebuilt in own workshops for diesel operation).
Vogtlandbahn: 18 Siemens Duewag RegioSprinter 1 and nine RegioSprinter 2 diesel railcars, of which 10 are equipped for street running over tramway tracks.
Oberpfalzbahn: five Adtranz RegioShuttle railcars.

*Vogtlandbahn Siemens Duewag RegioSprinter street-running in Zwickau* (David Haydock)   2001/0109849

## Regio-Bahn

Regionale Bahngesellschaft Kaarst-Düsseldorf-Mettmann mbH
Bergstrasse 1B, D-40822 Mettmann
Tel: (+49 2104) 30 50
Web: http://www.regio-bahn.de

Gauge: 1,435 mm
Route length: 33 km

### Key personnel
Managing Director: Wolfgang Teubner

### Passenger operations
In 1999 Regio-Bahn took over operations on Route S28 of the Düsseldorf S-Bahn, covering the Kaarst–Neuss–Düsseldorf (17 km) and Mettmann–Düsseldorf (16 km) branches.

### New lines
Plans exist to extend the Mettmann branch to Wuppertal by 2003.

### Traction and rolling stock
The fleet comprises eight Bombardier Talent two-car dmus. In 2001 four additional units of the same type were ordered.

www.janes.com   Jane's World Railways 2002-2003

## Regiobahn Bitterfeld (RBB)

Regiobahn Bitterfeld GmbH (RBB)
Zörbiger Strasse, D-06749 Bitterfeld
Tel: (+49 3493) 770 58   Fax: (+49 3493) 77 61 27

**Key personnel**
Managing Directors: Dipl-Ing Dieter Kruse
   Dipl-Ing Thomas Schare
   Dipl-Ing Peter Stockhausen

Gauge: 1,435 mm
Route length: 25 km

**Organisation**
This railway was created by the merger of three industrial lines and was taken over by DEG in late 1995 and now forms part of Connex Cargo Logistics GmbH. Thirty-five private sidings are served. Passenger services are envisaged.

**Freight operations**
Traffic statistics for 1997 were 634,000 tonnes and 4.8 million tonne-km, compared with 765,000 tonnes and 4.3 million tonne-km in 1996.

**Traction and rolling stock**
The RBB fleet comprises nine locomotives and 80 freight wagons.

## Rheinbraun

Rheinbraun Aktiengesellschaft – Gruben- und Grubenanschlussbahnen
Stüttgenweg 2, D-50935 Cologne
Tel: (+49 221) 48 00   Fax: (+49 221) 480 13 51
Web: http://www.rheinbraun.de

**Key personnel**
Chief Executive: Dr Dieter Henning
Operations Manager: Dipl-Ing Werner Koenigs

Gauge: 1,435 mm
Route length: 318 km
Eectrification: 6.25 kV AC 50 Hz overhead

**Organisation**
Industrial line of lignite mining company.

**Freight operations**
The railway carries rubble and lignite, connecting with DB and HGK lines. Axleload of 35 tonnes and loading gauge exceed those of DB. Traffic statistics for 1999 were 112.4 million tonnes and 2.1 billion tonne-km.

**Traction and rolling stock**
The fleet comprises 51 electric locomotives, 21 diesel locomotives and 818 freight wagons. Most of the electric locomotives are due for replacement, dating from the 1950s: in 1999, delivery commenced of 10 type EL 2000 machines ordered from Adtranz. These have been developed from the design of DB Class 101 and 145 locomotives.

*UPDATED*

## Rhein-Haardtbahn (RHB)

Rhein-Haardtbahn GmbH
Industriestrasse 3-5, D-67063 Ludwigshafen
Tel: (+49 621) 50 51   Fax: (+49 621) 505 27 60

**Key personnel**
Managing Directors: Dipl-Vw Giso Rocker
   Dipl-Ing Manfred Vogt
Local Operations Manager: Dipl-Ing Peter Kitzbihler

Gauge; 1,000 mm
Route length: 16 km
Electrification: 750 V DC

**Organisation**
RHB is an electrified interurban railway, associated with Ludwigshafen municipal tramways.

**Passenger operations**
RHB runs from Mannheim via Ludwigshafen to Bad Dürkheim with through running over Mannheim and Ludwigshafen tramways. Traffic statistics for 1999 were 1.7 million passengers and 14.6 million passenger-km.

**Traction and rolling stock**
Six electric railcars and two trailers. Ludwigshafen trams are also used over the line.

## Rügensche Kleinbahn (RüKB)

Rügensche Kleinbahn GmbH & Co
Binzer Strasse 12, D-18581 Putbus
Tel: (+49 38301) 80 10   Fax: (+49 38301) 801 15
e-mail: info@rasender-roland.de
Web: http://www.rasender-roland.de

**Key personnel**
Managing Director: Bernhard van Engelen
Operations Manager: Dipl-Ing Konrad Höft
Local Operations Manager: Jochen Warsow

Gauge: 750 mm
Route length: 24 km

**Organisation**
The Putbus–Göhren line on the island of Rügen was taken over from DB in 1996, and is operated by Karsdorfer Eisenbahn (qv).

**Passenger operations**
In 1997 131,400 train-km were operated.

**New lines**
The railway is to be extended from Putbus to Lauterbach (2 km) over DB tracks. A third rail needs to be laid for this purpose.

**Improvements to existing lines**
The line is to be completely rehabilitated at a cost of DM24 million. Maximum speed is to be increased from 30 to 50 km/h.

**Traction and rolling stock**
Six steam locomotives, one diesel locomotive, 29 coaches, 6 baggage cars. Three diesel railcars are on order for delivery in 2001.

## Ruhrkohle

Ruhrkohle Bergbau AG – RAG-Bahn und Hafenbetriebe
Talstrasse 7, D-45986 Gladbeck
Tel: (+49 2043) 50 13 20   Fax: (+49 2043) 50 15 60

**Key personnel**
Managing Directors: Dr-Ing Gerhard Hartfeld
   Dipl-Ing Norbert Rüsel

Gauge: 1,435 mm
Track length; 479 km
Electrification: 242 km at 15 kV AC 16⅔Hz

**Organisation**
The industrial railway of the Ruhrkohle AG coal mining company operates an extensive network of lines in the Ruhr industrial area, although the system is shrinking with the decline of coal mining. The railway connects with DB at 29 locations. Freight trains are also operated over DB lines, and Ruhrkohle owns and operates 12 ports on inland waterways.

The Werne-Bockum-Hövel railway (12 km) is the only line operated as a public carrier.

**Freight operations**
Traffic statistics for 1997 were 63.7 million tonnes and 265.1 million tonne-km, compared with 67.4 million tonnes and 288.2 million tonne-km in 1996.

**Traction and rolling stock**
Ruhrkohle operates a fleet of 106 diesel locomotives, 28 electric locomotives and 3,464 freight wagons. In 1999 11 1,500 kW B-B diesel-hydraulic locomotives were supplied by Vossloh.

*Ruhrkohle diesel locomotive with empty coal hoppers for the Fürst Leopold mine at Dorsten (Wolfram Veith)*
0063200

In June 2001, the first of six Bombardier Class 145 electric locomotives was delivered. Initial duties included coal traffic from the Oberhausen area to a power station at Lahde.

*UPDATED*

Germany/**RAILWAY SYSTEMS** 175

## Ruhr-Lippe Eisenbahn

Regionalverkehr Ruhr-Lippe GmbH (RLG)
Krögerweg 11, D-48155 Münster
Tel: (+49 251) 627 00   Fax: (+49 251) 627 02 22

**Key personnel**
Managing Director: Dr Ing Eberhard Christ
Rail Operations Manager: Dipl-Ing Hansrüdiger Fritz

Gauge: 1,435 mm
Route length: 42 km

**Organisation**
The local bus company, owned by WVG (qv), has responsibility for three separate railway lines connected with DB at Hamm, Soest and Neheim-Hüsten respectively. Hamm—Vellinghausen is the busiest line, with heavy coal traffic for a power station. Rail services are operated by WLE (qv).

**Freight operations**
Traffic statistics for 1997 were 823,000 tonnes and 8.4 million tonne-km, compared with 643,000 tonnes and 5.7 million tonne-km in 1996.

**Traction and rolling stock**
Three diesel locomotives.

## SüdThüringenBahn (STB)

**Background**
STB is a joint venture established by Erfurter Industriebahn (EIB) (qv) and Hessische Landesbahn (HLB) (qv) to operate regional services in Thüringen.

**Passenger operations**
In January 2001 STB commenced services on the Wernshausen—Zella—Mehlis line and in March took over some services on the Eisfeld—Eisenach route. Local trains between Erfurt and Meiningen were added to the network in June 2001.

**Traction and rolling stock**
Services are provided using Adtranz RS1 RegioShuttle railcars, including seven units ordered in October 2001 to serve lines in northern Thüringen.

*UPDATED*

## SWEG

Südwestdeutsche Verkehrs AG (SWEG)
Friedrichstrasse 59, D-77933 Lahr
Tel: (+49 7821) 270 20   Fax: (+49 7821) 27 02 35
e-mail: info@sweg.de
Web: http://www.sweg.de

**Key personnel**
Chairman: Hans Joachim Disch
Directors: Johannes Müller; Hans-Peter Schiff;
   Bernd Strobel

Gauge: 1,435 mm
Route length: 110 km

**Organisation**
The present company was formed in 1962 to consolidate various regional railways in the Baden part of Baden-Württemberg state, some of which were abandoned by their previous owners. Currently the company owns and operates the following lines:
   Schwarzach—Achern—Ottenhöfen (10 km)
   Biberach—Oberharmersbach (11 km)
   Bad Krozigen—Münstertal (Münstertalbahn) (13 km)
   Riegel-Endingen—Breisach (Kaiserstuhlbahn) (40 km)
   Meckesheim—Waibstadt—Aglasterhausen—
   Hüffenhardt (36 km, of which 19 km leased from DB)
   Bühl—Schwarzach—Söllingen (15 km, freight only)
SWEG also runs extensive bus operations with a fleet of 280 vehicles.

**Subsidiary companies**
Ortenau S-Bahn GmbH
Hauptstrasse 26, D-77652 Offenburg
Tel: (+49 781) 239 30   Fax: (+49 781) 923 93 10

A wholly owned subsidiary of SWEG, the Ortenau S-Bahn is a 104 km network radiating from Offenburg to Achern, Appenweier and Bad Greisbach, Hausach, and Kehl. Services are provided by Adtranz RS1 RegioShuttle railcars.

Breisgau S-Bahn GmbH (BSB)
Besanconstrasse 99, D-79111 Freiburg (Breisgau)
Fax: (+49 7821) 27 02 45

BSB is a joint venture between SWEG and Freiburger Verkehrs AG (VAG) providing a high-frequency service between Freiburg and Breisach using Adtranz RS1 RegioShuttle railcars.

**Passenger operations**
Traffic statistics for 1997 were 2 million passengers and 17.6 million passenger-km, compared with 2.1 million passengers and 16.6 million passenger-km in 1996.

**Freight operations**
Traffic statistics for 1999 were 203,000 tonnes and 2.9 million tonne-km.

**Traction and rolling stock**
Six diesel locomotives, 55 diesel railcars, 24 coaches and two freight wagons. The fleet includes 26 Adtranz RS1 RegioShuttle railcars. Nine vehicles of the same type are used on Breisgau S-Bahn services.

## Teutoburger Wald Eisenbahn (TWE)

Teutoburger-Wald-Eisenbahn AG (TWE)
Am Grubenhof 2, D-33330 Gütersloh
Tel: (+49 5241) 160 67   Fax: (+49 5241) 252 45

**Key personnel**
Managing Directors: Dipl-Ing Thomas Schare
   Dipl-Ing Thomas Schulte
   Heinz Wolfgramm
Operations Manager: Karl Gottwald

Gauge; 1,435 mm
Route length: 104 km

**Organisation**
Associated with and operated by Connex Cargo Logistics GmbH. The TWE workshops at Lengerich are a central facility for all Connex Gruppe railways and also carry out work for third parties.
   In 2000 it was reported that local authority funding was to finance the reopening to passenger traffic of the Gütersloh—Harsewinkel and Gütersloh—Verl lines by 2005.

**Freight operations**
The line extends from Ibbenbüren via Lengerich and Gütersloh to Hövelhof and connects with DB at each of these four locations. TWE freight trains also run over DB lines.
   Traffic statistics for 1997 were 391,000 tonnes and 25.6 million tonne-km, compared with 296,000 tonnes and 16.7 million tonne-km in 1996.

**Traction and rolling stock**
Five diesel locomotives and nine freight wagons.

## Trans Regio

Trans Regio Deutsch Regionalbahn GmbH
Schönbornstrasse 7, D-54295 Trier
Tel: (+49 651) 991 26 76
e-mail: info@trans-regio.de
Web: http://www.trans-regio.de

Gauge: 1,435 mm
Route length: 101 km

**Background**
Trans Regio is a joint venture between Trier-based bus operator Moselbahn Gesellschaft mbH and Rheinische Bahngesellschaft AG, Düsseldorf's public transport operator.

**Passenger operations**
In May 2000 Trans Regio took over passenger operations on two lines in the Rheinland-Pfalz region: Andernach—Mayen (subsequently extended to Kaisersesch (43 km)); and Kaiserslautern—Kusel (45 km). In June 2001 the company took over services on the Bullay—Traben-Trarbach 'Moselwein-Bahn' line (13 km).

**Traction and rolling stock**
Nineteen Adtranz RS1 RegioShuttle railcars.

## Usedomer Bäderbahn (UBB)

Usedomer Bäderbahn GmbH (UBB)
Am Bahnhof 1, D-17424 Heringsdorf
Tel: (+49 38378) 27 10   Fax: (+49 38378) 271 14

**Key personnel**
Managing Directors: Dipl-Ing Jörgen Bosse
   Dipl-Kfm Corinna Hinkel
Marketing and Technical Director:
   Dipl-Ing Hans-Joachim Kohl
Operations Manager: Dipl-Ing Andreas Pinske

Gauge: 1,435 mm
Route length: 79 km

*UBB GTW 2/6 railcar at Peenemünde from Zinnowitz (David Haydock)*

*2001*/0109852

# RAILWAY SYSTEMS/Germany

### Organisation
UBB is a wholly owned subsidiary of DB Travel & Tourism, serving the island of Usedom, a popular seaside resort. Lines were taken over from the parent company in 1995.

### Passenger operations
Traffic statistics for 1999 were 1.5 million passengers, compared with 1.2 million in 1998.

### New lines
A fixed link with the German mainland at Wolgast across the river Peene was completed in 2000. At the other end of the line an extension across the Polish border to Swinoujscie is planned, with a further extension to the border town of Garz, but there will be no physical connection with Polish State Railways.

### Traction and rolling stock
A fleet of 14 diesel railbuses and 11 trailers was replaced in 2000 by 14 Type GTW 2/6 class 646. One diesel railcar from Stadler/Adtranz/Bombardier. Two diesel locomotives are also operated.

## Verkehrsbetriebe Kreis Plön (VKP)

Verkehrsbetriebe Kreis Plön GmbH
Diedrichstrasse 5, D-24143 Kiel
Tel: (+49 431) 70 58 11   Fax: (+49 431) 70 58 60

### Key personnel
Managing Director: Dipl-Betr wrt Günter Gloe
Rail Operations Manager: Harald Hansen

Gauge: 1,435 mm
Route length: 24 km

### Organisation
VKP is a county council-owned transport company providing passenger services by road and freight services by rail.

### Passenger operations
Jointly with DEG (qv) VKP was the successful bidder for the operation of passenger services over DB lines from Kiel to surrounding locations in Schleswig-Holstein. A new company, Nord-Ostsee-Bahn (NOB) (qv) manages these operations.

### Freight operations
VKP owns and operates the Kiel–Schönberger Eisenbahn and also operates a short line serving a power station in Kiel. The main commodity carried is coal. Traffic statistics for 1999 were 761,000 tonnes and 6.1 million tonne-km.

### Traction and rolling stock
One diesel locomotive.

## Verkehrsbetriebe Peine-Salzgitter (VPS)

Verkehrsbetriebe Peine-Salzgitter GmbH (VPS)
Am Hillenholz 28, D-38229 Salzgitter
Tel: (+49 5341) 21 35 41   Fax: (+49 5341) 21 45 76

### Key personnel
Managing Directors: Dipl-Ing Arndt Frielinghaus (also Operations Manager)
Dipl-Kfm Detlef Mehl

Gauge: 1,435 mm
Route length: 69 km

### Organisation
UPS is a steelworks industrial railway which also serves other clients. Operations are split into three divisions: Peine; Salzgitter (connecting with each other); and Ilsenburg. VPS also runs freight trains over DB lines. VPS locomotives are available for lease and its workshops also carry out work for third parties. The company owns and operates two ports on inland waterways.

### Freight operations
Traffic statistics for 1999 were 34.5 million tonnes and 208 million tonne-km. About one third of all traffic is exchanged with DB.

### Traction and rolling stock
The VPS fleet comprises 53 diesel locomotives and 775 freight wagons. The company also develops special freight wagons for the needs of the steel industry.

## Volkswagen

Volkswagen Transport GmbH & Co OHG (VAG)
Porschestr 102, Südkopf-Center, D-38436 Wolfsburg
Tel: (+49 5361) 26 30   Fax: (+49 5361) 26 34 10

### Key personnel
Managing Director: Dipl-Kfm Johannes M Fritzen
Operations Manager: Dipl-Ing Gerd Schönitz

Gauge: 1,435 mm
Track length: 174 km

### Organisation
Industrial railway of the Volkswagen automobile plant.

### Freight operations
In 1999 5.7 million tonnes were carried.

### Traction and rolling stock
The fleet comprises 12 diesel locomotives and 295 freight wagons.

## Wanne—Herner Eisenbahn und Hafen (WHE)

Wanne—Herner Eisenbahn und Hafen GmbH (WHE)
Am Westhafen 27, D-44653 Herne
Tel: (+49 2325) 78 80   Fax: (+49 2325) 78 84 30

### Key personnel
Managing Director: Betr wirt Karl-Heinz Wick
Manager: Friedhelm Unger
Operations Manager: Ludwig Funke

Gauge: 1,435 mm
Route length: 13.7 km

### Organisation
WHE connects with DB at Wanne Übergabebahnhof and also connects with Ruhrkohle AG. It owns and operates a canal port for coal traffic.

### Freight operations
The main commodity carried is coal. WHE serves several collieries and a power station. Traffic statistics for 2001 were 4.6 million tonnes and 18.7 million tonne-km.

### Traction and rolling stock
The WHE fleet comprises 9 diesel locomotives and 131 freight wagons.

*UPDATED*

## Westerwaldbahn (WEBA)

Westerwaldbahn GmbH
Bindweide, D-57520 Steinebach
Tel: (+49 2747) 922 10   Fax (+49 2747) 92 21 20
e-mail: info@westerwaldbahn.de
Web: http://www.westerwaldbahn.de

### Key personnel
Operations Manager: Dipl-Ing Horst Klein

Gauge: 1,435 mm
Route length: 31 km

### Organisation
WEBA is operated directly by the county council running freight services on the Scheuerfeld–Bindweide–Oberdreisbach (17 km) and Bindweide–Rosenheim (3 km) lines. Since May 1998 the Westerwaldbahn has also operated freight services on behalf of DB Cargo on the Altenkirchen–Raubach line and is expected to assume ownership of this line in the future. The Betzdorf–Daaden line (10 km) was taken over from DB in 1994 and is operated for passenger traffic.

### Passenger operations
Traffic statistics for 1999 were 1.5 million passengers and 15.1 million passenger-km. This includes bus operations with a fleet of 20 buses.

### Freight operations
82,000 tonnes were carried in 1997.

### Traction and rolling stock
The WEBA fleet comprises one VT 628 dmu and one VT23/24 railcar for schools traffic, five diesel locomotives, nine freight wagons and one driving trailer.

## Westfälische Landes-Eisenbahn (WLE)

Westfälische Landes-Eisenbahn GmbH
Krögerweg 11, D-48155 Münster
Tel: (+49 251) 627 00   Fax: (+49 251) 627 02 22

### Key personnel
Managing Director: Dr Ing Eberhard Christ
Rail Operations Manager: Dipl-Ing Hansüdiger Fritz
Local Operations Manager: Reiner Maier

Gauge: 1,435 mm
Route length: 120 km

### Organisation
WLE is a subsidiary of Westfälische Verkehrsgesellschaft mbH (WVG) (qv). Its main line runs from Münster via

Neubeckum and Lippstadt to Warstein (102 km, including 6 km leased from DB). Freight services over DB lines are also operated in the Lippstadt area. Main traffic is stone from quarries at Warstein to cement works in the Beckum area. WLE is also responsible for operating the railway divisions of Regionalverkehr Münsterland and Ruhr-Lippe Eisenbahn (qv).

**Freight operations**
Traffic statistics for 1997 were 1.3 million tonnes and 78.1 million tonne-km, compared with 78.4 million tonne-km in 1996.

**Traction and rolling stock**
The WLE fleet comprises 17 diesel locomotives and 83 freight wagons.

## Westfälische Verkehrsgesellschaft mbH (WVG)

Westfälische Verkehrsgesellschaft mbH
Krögerweg 11, D-46155 Münster
Tel: (+49 251) 627 00   Fax: (+49 251) 627 02 22

**Key personnel**
Managing Director: Dr Ing Eberhard Christ
Deputy Managing Director: Dipl-Kfm Dieter Eichner

**Organisation**
WVG is a holding company for several bus companies and local railways owned by the Westfalen provincial administration. At present it owns and operates the following railways:
Regionalverkehr Münsterland GmbH
Ruhr-Lippe Eisenbahn GmbH (qv)
Westfälische Landes-Eisenbahn GmbH (qv).

## Wismut

Wismut GmbH – Anschlussbahn
Jagdschänkenstr 29, D-09117 Chemnitz
Tel: (+49 371) 81 20

Gauge: 1,435 mm
Track length: 57 km

**Organisation**
Wismut is the industrial railway of the former Soviet-German uranium mining company. Mining operations have ceased. The railway is still used in connection with site restoration work.

**Freight operations**
Traffic statistics for 1997 were 625,000 tonnes and 14.6 million tonne-km.

**Traction and rolling stock**
The fleet comprises nine diesel locomotives and 70 freight wagons.

## Württembergische Eisenbahn-Gesellschaft (WEG)

Württembergische Eisenbahn-Gesellschaft mbH
Seewiesenstrasse 21-23, D-71334 Waiblingen
Tel: (+49 7151) 30 38 00   Fax: (+49 7151) 303 80 19

**Key personnel**
Managing Directors: Dipl-Ing Thomas Schare
 Dipl-Ing Thomas Schulte
 Heinz Wolfgramm

Gauge: 1,435 mm
Route length: 134 km (91.6 km in passenger operations)

**Organisation**
WEG is a subsidiary of Connex Regiobahn GmbH. It owns and operates the following local railways in Württemberg:

Nebenbahn Ebingen—Onstmettingen (Talgangbahn)
Nebenbahn Gaildorf—Untergröningen (Obere—Kochertalbahn)
Nebenbahn Korntal—Weissach (Strohgäubahn)
Nebenbahn Nürtingen—Neuffen (Tälesbahn)
Nebenbahn Vaihingen—Enzweihingen (Stadtbahn).
WEG also operates the Schönbuchbahn (Böblingen—Dettenhausen) and the Wieslauftalbahn (Schorndorf—Rudersberg) for the respective local authorities. Passenger and freight trains of WEG also operate over DB lines.

**Passenger operations**
Certain trains of the Strohgäubahn run through to Stuttgart-Feuerbach over DB tracks to provide better connections with the Stuttgart S-Bahn. Traffic statistics for 1999 were 1.3 million passengers and 9.5 million passenger-km.

**Freight operations**
Traffic statistics for 1997 were 190,000 tonnes and 4.3 million tonne-km.

**Traction and rolling stock**
The fleet comprises 24 diesel railcars, including eight Adtranz RegioShuttle units, 11 trailers and two diesel locomotives.

# GHANA

## Ministry of Transport & Communications

PO Box M38, Ministry Branch Post Office, Accra
Tel: (+233 21) 66 64 65   Fax: (+233 21) 66 71 14

**Key personnel**
Minister: E K Salia
Deputy Ministers: P M G Griffiths, A K Peasah
Chief Director: Dr W A Adote
Director, Planning: E A Kwakye
Director, Administrative: G P Ansah
Planning Officer, Railways: P Azumah

## Ghana Railway Corporation (GRC)

PO Box 251, Takoradi
Tel: (+233 31) 21 81; 25 05   Fax: (+233 31) 237 97

**Key personnel**
Managing Director: M K Arthur
Deputy Managing Directors
  Engineering: Raymond Afeke
  Administration and Operations: S K Agboletey
Financial Controller: T Cofie
Personnel and Administrative Manager:
  J Y Domson-Appiah
Chief Civil Engineer: S Barnes
Chief Mechanical and Electrical Engineer: A A Edoh
Chief Signalling and Telecommunications Engineer:
  J Obeng
Traffic Manager: E R O Quaye
Controller of Supplies: G Nuamah
Chief Internal Auditor: R K Johnson
Principal, Central Training Institute: K Owusu-Adjei
Public Relations Officer: J Abaka-Amuah

Gauge: 1,067 mm
Route length: 953 km

**Political background**
In recent years traffic on GRC has declined as heavy road transport has taken much of its traffic. A problem of overstaffing was addressed by a series of redundancies announced in 1993, the staff complement being reduced to around 4,500 by 1995.
 A major policy review, the Railway Policy Reform and Restructuring Study, was undertaken by foreign consultants in 1995. This study proposed a range of substantial changes in GRC's organisational structure, financial restructuring, staff reduction to 1,500 and privatisation of non-core business activities.

**Organisation**
The railway network is in the form of a letter 'A', the apex being at Kumasi and the two feet at the port of Takoradi and at Accra; the chord connects Huni Valley and Kotoku on the two legs. Branch lines run to Sekondi, Prestea, Kade, Awaso and Tema.

**Passenger operations**
GRC operates daily passenger trains between Accra and Kumasi, in the north, and three services daily from Kumasi to Takoradi, in the southwest. The Accra—Takoradi direct service was suspended in 1998 due to heavy road competition. With the exception of two Kumasi—Takoradi return trains, most services are overnight trains conveying both seating and sleeping accommodation. Local services are operated between Accra and Koforidua and on the Dunkwa—Awaso branch. The long-awaited reopening of the Accra—Tema suburban line had not occured by mid-1999.

**Freight operations**
Freight traffic is mainly export-oriented and its main commodities are cocoa, timber, bauxite and manganese; the last two commodities together account for more than 90 per cent of the total freight tonnage. GRC is also engaged in haulage of cement and other imports from the coast to the interior, as well as agricultural produce from sources to marketing centres.
 Some 715,000 tonnes were carried in 1994 for 125.7 million tonne-km. The German consultancy DE-Consult has identified considerable potential traffic which would be available with a more reliable operation.
 All operations are hampered by the malfunctioning signalling system, poor quality infrastructure and badly maintained rolling stock. The relatively high derailment frequency (one every five days on average) is a natural outcome of some of these problems.

**Intermodal operations**
A potential intermodal terminal site has been identified at Fumisua, near Kumasi, for movement of container traffic from and to Takoradi and Tema ports. At the present time, however, there are no container handling facilities on GRC and the rail connnection to Tema was severed in 1995 as a result of road construction.

**New lines**
In 1990 Japanese aid was secured for construction of a 96.5 km line from the port of Tema to Akosombo, on Lake Volta, a valuable link in an intermodal transport chain to the north of the country and to Burkina Faso. However, when the link between Accra and Tema was severed in 1995 as a result of road construction, the future of the project was put in doubt.

# RAILWAY SYSTEMS/Ghana—Greece

**Diesel locomotives**

| Class | Wheel arrangement | Power kW | Speed km/h | Weight tonnes | No in service | First built | Builders Mechanical | Engine | Transmission |
|---|---|---|---|---|---|---|---|---|---|
| 2601 | Co-Co | 1,700 | 80 | 96.5 | 8 | 1993 | GEC Alsthom | CAT 3606L | E GEC Alsthom |
| 1851 | Co-Co | 1,380 | 96 | 84 | 2 | 1969 | English Electric | EE 12CSVT | E English Electric |
| 1661 | Co-Co | 1,119 | 80 | 86 | 3 | 1995 | ABB Henschel | GM 12-645E | E ABB Henschel |
| 1651 | Co-Co | 1,119 | 96 | 85 | 10 | 1978 | Thyssen-Henschel | GM 645E | E Thyssen-Henschel |
| 1401 | Co-Co | 966 | 100 | 83 | 3 | 1959 | Henschel | GM 567C | E Henschel |
| 751 | Bo-Bo | 508 | 88 | 54 | 2 | 1954 | English Electric | EE 6 SRKT | E English Electric |
| 721 | Bo-Bo | 501 | 80 | 57 | 4 | 1986 | Daewoo | MTU 8V396TC12 | E Toshiba SE-223 |
| 701 | Bo-Bo | 441 | 64 | 60 | 6 | 1982 | Brush | Rolls-Royce DV8TCE | E Brush |
| 541 | C (0-6-0) | 447 | 45 | 43 | 10 | 1975 | Thyssen-Henschel | Henschel 12V 1516A | H Voith L4, 4V2 |

In the longer term GRC is hopeful of building two other lines. One would run from Awaso to Sunyani, and the other from Bosuso to Kibi. Both would have exploitation of bauxite deposits as their objective.

### Improvements to existing lines
In the late 1980s, the railway completed a rehabilitation project on the Kumasi–Takoradi Western line (including the Awaso branch), which is the main export trunk route. Foreign exchange inputs for the project, totalling US$45 million, came mainly from the World Bank and African Development Bank, but also from donor countries (France, Switzerland and the UK). The project covered track rehabilitation, replacement of signalling (using solar power) and telecommunication equipment, rehabilitation of locomotives and rolling stock, equipment of wagons with roller bearings, workshop modernisation, setting up of a Central Training Institute and staff training. Unfortunately, by 1995 much of the rehabilitated equipment had fallen into disrepair, particularly the solar-powered signalling, leading to serious operational problems on the route.

In 1988 the Italian government granted US$30 million towards similar rehabilitation of GRC's Central and Eastern lines, and also towards a microwave radio network. With further World Bank support of US$9 million, work on the 306 km Eastern line from Accra to Kumasi was started. The available funds also provided for attention to the 182 km Kotoku–Huni Valley section of the Central line from Accra to Takoradi.

Ghana's railway network has excessive curvature in several sections, and this tends to reduce line capacity. For example, between Kumasi and Takoradi 32 per cent of the 270 km Western line consists of curved track. Replacement of existing 39.7 kg/m rail by 44.7 kg/m rail has been carried out on the Manso–Huni Valley section; despite possessing suitable equipment, only a very small section of GRC track has been continuously welded. In 1995 German consultants DE-Consult carried out an in-depth technical and economic survey of the Western line, which identified considerable traffic potential and recommended a programme of investment in new air-braked freight wagons and in technical rehabilitation measures, though falling short of proposing extensive realignment.

### Traction and rolling stock
In 1995 GRC operated 38 diesel locomotives and 10 diesel-hydraulic shunters, 139 passenger coaches and 810 wagons.

All of the passenger coaches currently in service were built in 1986 by the Görlitz and Bautzen factories in East Germany. These include buffet, first and second class day and sleeping cars and five tourist saloons.

With the aid of finance from the French Central Bank for Economic Co-operation, GRC took delivery of nine Type AD26C 1,850 kW diesel locomotives of the 2601 class from GEC Alsthom in 1993. The units are mainly employed on the Western line for manganese and bauxite haulage. The contract provided for GEC Alsthom to maintain the locomotives for four years and also to re-equip the railway's locomotive depot at Takoradi. In early 1998 French funding agency CFD approved a FFr 12.4 million grant to extend this maintenance contract until 1999.

In 1991 Ghana secured a US$96 million credit to assist the second Transport Rehabilitation Project. Besides infrastructure work, purchase and repair of locomotives and rolling stock, and procurement of technical and consultancy assistance would be undertaken with the money. During 1995 three Henschel locomotives of the 1661 class were delivered, together with the first tranche of 100 covered freight wagons equipped with Scheffel self-steering bogies. A total of 14 new General Motors locomotives were delivered in 1996.

### Signalling and telecommunications
Under a World Bank project, GRC changed from the previous semaphore system to colourlight signals powered by solar panels in all 42 stations on the Western line. Regrettably, by 1995, lack of maintenance and suitable spare parts meant that the only functioning section was the short stretch between Takoradi and Harbour Junction and between Angu and Tarkwa. On other sections of the Western line, operation is by a ticket system based on the stationmaster obtaining telephonic permission to proceed into a section from the next station. This system is unreliable and leads to excessive delays.

The telecommunications network is similarly only partly functioning, with the Takoradi control office being regularly out of contact with up-country stations.

**Type of coupler in standard use:** No 2 Alliance/ABC type

**Type of brake in standard use:** Locomotives, air; carriages and wagons, vacuum

### Track
**Standard rail, type and weight**

*Western line*
Takoradi–Manso: RBS 39.7 kg/m
Manso–Huni Valley: BSA 44.7 kg/m
Huni Valley–Kumasi: RBS 39.7 kg/m

*Eastern line*
Kumasi–Konongo: BS 29.8 kg/m
Konongo–Juaso: BA 'A' 39.7 kg/m
Juaso–Osino: RBS 39.7 kg/m
Osino–Tafo: BS 29.8 kg/m
Tafo–Accra: RBS 29.8 kg/m

*Central line*
Huni Valley–Nyinase: RBS 39.7 kg/m
Nyinase–Twifu: BS 'A' 39.7 kg/m
Twifu–Akenkausu: BS 29.8 kg/m
Akenkausu–Achiasi Junction: BSA 39.7 kg/m
Achiasi Junction–Kotoku Junction: RBS 39.7 kg/m
Prestea branch line: RBS 29.8 kg/m

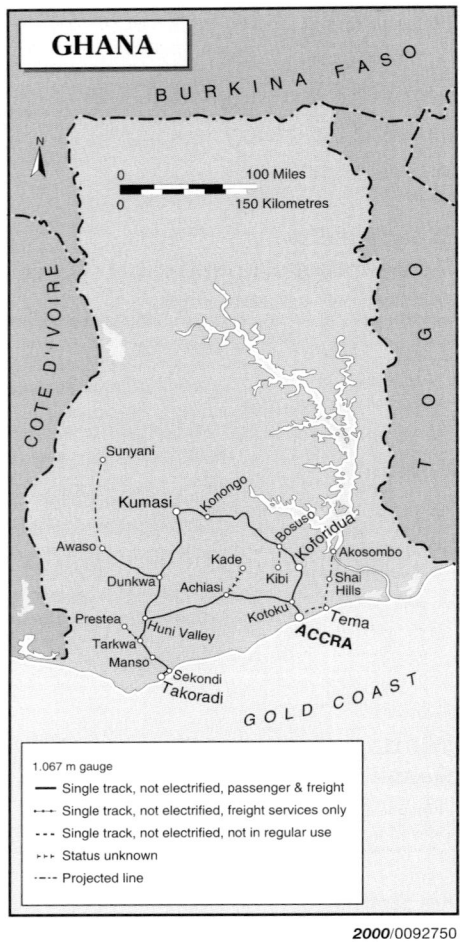

Awaso branch line: ASCE 37.2. kg/m
**Joints:** 4-hole fishplates
**Crossties (sleepers):** Standard steel; and wood 127 × 254 × 1,981 mm
**Spacing:** 1,365/km steel, 1,602/km wood
**Rail fastenings**
**Wood sleepers:** Dogspikes, Macbeth spike anchors, Type T3 (UK) elastic rail spikes. Elastic rail spikes Type ES18 and DS18 (Germany)
**Steel sleepers:** Keys, ABK clips
**Filling:** Mainly crushed granite and manganese ore, some gravel
**Max curvature**
Takoradi-Kumasi 8° 40' = radius of 202 m
Kumasi-Accra 8° 40' = radius of 202 m
Central line 8° 40' = radius of 202 m
Prestea branch 17° = radius of 103 m
Awaso branch 6° = radius of 291 m
**Max gradient:** 1.25% = 1 in 80; except Prestea branch 2.5% = 1 in 40
**Longest continuous gradient:** 10 km with ruling grade of 1.25% and max curves of 8° 40'
**Max altitude:** 286 m near Kumasi
**Max axleloading**
Takoradi-Kumasi-Accra 16 tonnes
Central line 16 tonnes
Prestea branch 12½ tonnes
Awaso branch 16 tonnes
**Gauge widening on sharpest curve:** 13 mm (theoretical)
**Superelevation on sharpest curve:** 89 mm (theoretical)
**Rate of slope of superelevation:** 13 mm per rail length

# GREECE

## Ministry of Transport & Communications

Xenofontos Street 13, GR-10191 Athens
Tel: (+30 1) 325 12 11-19  Fax: (+30 1) 323 90 39

**Key personnel**
Minister: Christos Verelis

UPDATED

## Hellenic Railways Organisation (OSE)

Organismos Sidirodromon Ellados
1-3 Karolou Street, GR-10437 Athens
Tel: (+30 1) 524 83 95  Fax: (+30 1) 524 32 90/524 62 39
Web: http://www.ose.gr

**Key personnel**
President: C Papageorgiou

Director General: A S Lazaris
Deputy Director General: I Rigas

Gauge: 1,435 mm; 1,000 mm; dual-gauge, 1,435 mm and 1,000 mm; 750 mm
Route length: 1,565 km; 961 km; 23 km; 22 km
Electrification: 764 km at 25 kV AC 50 Hz (in progress)
The railway from Athens to the Peloponnese, serving Patras and southern Greece, is metre-gauge.

# Greece/RAILWAY SYSTEMS

*Map caption:* 2002/0525465

## Organisation
A five-year modernisation and restructuring plan was started in 1998. The plan foresees investments of some Dr1,700 billion and the writing off by the government of accumulated debt.

| Traffic (million) | 2000 |
|---|---|
| Passenger journeys | 12.3 |
| Passenger-km | 1,583 |
| Freight-tonnes | 2.2 |
| Freight tonne-km | 350 |

## Passenger operations
OSE operates passenger services on two main lines from the capital, Athens. To the north, a standard-gauge line runs to Thessaloníki, with services beyond to Alexandroúpolis and the former Yugoslavia; to the south, a metre-gauge line runs to the Peloponnese, serving Patras and southern Greece.

## Freight operations
One of the most important lines for freight is that from Thessaloníki to Idomeni, on the border with Macedonia.

A new freight facilities complex and intermodal terminal for the Athens region is planned at Thriassio Pedio.

## New lines
Major developments to create an electrified standard gauge suburban network in Athens include a line from an interchange known as SKA, in the north of the city, to Spáta airport, scheduled for completion in late 2003, and a new double-track line from SKA to Corinth, including a new bridge over the Corinth Canal. Longer term plans foresee both lines being extended, from Koropi, junction for the Sáta airport spur, to Lávrion, and from Corinth to Patras respectively.

A new line to serve the port of Kavala is projected. This would link in with the Thesssaloníki–Alexandroúpolis line.

## Improvements to existing lines
The principal project, in hand since 1978, has been electrification, doubling and realignment of sections of the Athens–Thessaloníki–Idomeni main line, together with track renewal employing UIC54 continuously welded rail on two-block concrete sleepers, with minimum curve radius of 2,000 m. This axis carries more than half the railway's total traffic.

In December 1996, OSE appointed a 170-strong team to oversee a five-year Dr500 billion EU-backed infrastructure modernisation programme, including both its own personnel and engineering specialists from a consortium of consultants. The Hellas Rail Consult Joint Venture consortium comprises Halcrow Transmark of the UK (30 per cent); Metrotech of Greece (30 per cent); Obermeyer of Germany (25 per cent); and ILF Consulting Engineers of Austria (15 per cent). OSE has established a separate company, ERGOSE, to implement the improvements.

Among other work, the team has been supervising doubling of the track on the difficult mountain section between Evangelismos and Leptocarya (35 km). By 2008, travel time on the 510 km between Athens and Thessaloníki should be reduced from the 6 hours it takes today to 4 hours 20 minutes. Except between Larisa and Plati (134 km), electric signalling will be operative and a modern telecommunications system will cover the whole axis from Athens to Idomeni. There will be electrified double track over the whole route between Athens and Thessaloníki except for Lianokladi–Domokós (65 km) and the project includes driving two new tunnels through the foothills of Mount Olympus, in northern Greece.

The investment programme also includes upgrading the line from Thessaloníki to the Bulgarian border to provide an improved alternative link to Central Europe.

A subsidiary project has seen the 80 km metre-gauge Paleofarsalos–Kalambaka line converted to standard-gauge. The line connects with the Athens–Thessaloníki route.

## Traction and rolling stock
At the beginning of 2002 OSE operated 108 standard-gauge and 31 metre-gauge diesel locomotives, 130 standard-gauge and 83 metre-gauge dmu vehicles; 400 standard-gauge and 140 metre-gauge coaches.

For the Athens–Thessaloníki and Thessaloníki–Alexandroúpolis routes, German industry manufactured 12 four-car 160 km/h intercity dmus in 1989. In 1994, a further eight five-car trains were ordered from AEG Bahnsysteme (now Adtranz) for these lines. Assembly took place at the former AEG Hennigsdorf works. In 1995, eight extra trailer cars were ordered from DWA's Bautzen factory to make the second series into five-car sets.

Adtranz received a contract to build 26 Class A470 2,100 kW three-phase diesel-electrics for delivery by January 1998. The design of these locomotives allows for eventual conversion to electric traction. In late 1997 Siemens/Krauss-Maffei commenced delivery of six Class H560 EuroSprinter-based 5,000 kW electrics for hauling express passenger and freight trains over the newly electrified section from Thessaloníki to the Macedonian border. In March 1998 a further 24 of these locomotives were ordered from Siemens/Krauss-Maffei for delivery from 2000. These are intended for services on the Athens–Thessaloníki main line.

*Class A470 diesel-electric locomotive at Serre with a stopping service to Thessaloníki (Edward Barnes)* 2002/0524924

*Class H560 electric locomotives handle freight traffic on the line to Macedonia (Artemis Klonos)* 2002/0524927

# RAILWAY SYSTEMS/Greece

*Ganz-Mávag metre-gauge Class 6461 dmu at Corinth (Colin Boocock)* 2002/0524925

*LEW-built diesel trainsets, such as this example at Volos, are the mainstay of OSE intercity services (Edward Barnes)* 2002/0524923

For local services, OSE has ordered 29 GTW 2/6 low-floor diesel railcars from a consortium of Stadler and Hellenic Shipyards: 17 for the standard gauge system and 12 for the metre gauge network. Delivery of the standard gauge units was due to begin in 2002, while the metre gauge vehicles were to follow in 2003-04.

OSE's first emus were also ordered in March 1998, with a contract for 20 five-car units for Athens suburban services to be supplied by Siemens Transportation Systems in co-operation with Hellenic Shipyards. The 160 km/h aluminium-bodied articulated vehicles will be based on Siemens' Desiro design.

For the metre-gauge system, a total of 10 Class 6501 air conditioned three-car trainsets for intercity operation have been built by Hellenic Shipyards. Two of the cars in each unit have each bogie powered by a 398 kW 2,100 rpm engine. Ten two-car units were subsequently supplied from the same source and are designated Class 6521.

Recent coaching stock acquisitions include 185 intercity coaches ordered in 1998 from Siemens and constructed by local builders. Refurbishment of an additional 107 existing coaches and vehicles acquired secondhand from DB AG, Germany, was under way in 2002.

Freight wagon acquisitions include bogie tank wagons for kerosene transport and open wagons for sugar beet traffic.

In 2002, refurbishment was in progress of the eight MLW-built Class A500 diesel-electrics, with improvements to both engine and electronics.

## Electrification

Priority has been given to the 25 kV 50 Hz AC electrification of the 587 km Athens–Thessaloníki–Idomeni main line, which has the backing of the European Union. First section to be tackled the 76 km of single line from Thessaloníki to the former Yugoslav border at Idomeni, where track was renewed and curvature eased. This route carries three times the freight of the Athens–Thessaloníki line. Commissioning took place in 1997. In 1996 a consortium led by ABB and including Adtranz won a US$145 million contract to electrify the Athens–Thessaloníki route.

Also included in the project, and forming part of a plan to create an Athens electrified suburban network, is upgrading and electrification of the branch from Inoi, on the main Athens–Thessaloníki line, to Khalkis, due to be completed in 2006.

**Coupler in standard use:** 1,435 mm gauge, UIC 520-521
**Brake in standard use:** Air, mostly Knorr

## Track

**Rail:** 1,435 mm gauge, UIC 50, 54; narrow-gauge, 31.6 kg/m
**Sleepers:** 1,435 mm gauge, reinforced concrete twin-block (Vagneaux type) 680 × 290 mm; steel 2,550 × 260 mm; timber 2,600 × 250 mm. Narrow-gauge, steel and timber
**Fastenings:** 1,435 mm gauge, RN and Nabla for concrete sleepers; K direct fastenings for wood or steel
**Min curve radius:** 1,435 mm gauge, 300 m; narrow-gauge, 110 m
**Max gradient:** 1,435 mm gauge, 2.8%; narrow-gauge, 2.5%
**Max permissible axleload:** 1,435 mm gauge, 20 tonnes; narrow-gauge, 14 tonnes
**Max permissible speed:** 90-100 km/h; 120 km/h parts of Athens–Thessaloníki main line

### Diesel locomotives

| Class | Wheel arrangement | Power kW | Speed km/h | Weight tonnes | No in service | First built | Builders Mechanical | Engine | Transmission |
|---|---|---|---|---|---|---|---|---|---|
| **1,000 mm gauge** | | | | | | | | | |
| A9100 | Co-Co | 993 | 96 | 80.3 | 11 | 1965 | Alco | Alco 6-251D | E GE 761 A3 |
| A9200 | Co-Co | 1,200 | 90 | 80 | 13 | 1967 | Alsthom | P PA4-185/V12 | E GE Canada |
| A9400 | B-B | 2 × 240 | 90 | 48 | 17 | 1967 | Mitsubishi | G-M V8-71N | H Niigata |
| **1,435 mm gauge** | | | | | | | | | |
| A100 | C | 485 | 60 | 51 | 27 | 1962 | Krupp | M GT06A-V12 | H Voith L27 zub |
| A150 | B-B | 520 | 70 | 48 | 11 | 1973 | Faur | M-MB820Bb | H Voith |
| A170 | B-B | 560 | 70 | 48 | 6 | 1978 | Faur | M V12MB820Bb | H Voith |
| A200 | Bo-Bo | 785 | 105 | 64.6 | 7 | 1962 | Alco | Alco 251 B | E GE |
| A220 | Bo-Bo | 795 | 109 | 63.5 | 3 | 1973 | GE | C D398B-V12 | E GE |
| A450 | Co-Co | 2,015 | 149 | 120 | 20 | 1973 | MLW | Alco V12-251 F | E GE Canada |
| A470 | Bo-Bo | 2,100 | 160 | 90 | 25 | 1997 | Adtranz | MTU | Adtranz |
| A500 | Co-Co | 2,650 | 149 | 124 | 8 | 1974 | MLW | Alco V16-251 F | E GE Canada |

Abbreviations: C: Caterpillar; M: Maybach; Mek: Mekydro; P: Pielstick

### Diesel railcars or multiple-units

| Class (running numbers) | Car per unit | Motor cars per unit | Motored axles/car | Power/car kW | Speed km/h | No in service | First built | Builders Mechanical | Engine | Transmission |
|---|---|---|---|---|---|---|---|---|---|---|
| **1,435 mm gauge** | | | | | | | | | | |
| 601 | 4 | 2 | 4 | 1,180 | 160 | 12 | 1989 | LEW | MTU 396 TC13 | E S |
| 651 | 5 | 2 | 4 | 1,180 | 160 | 8 | 1995 | Adtranz | MTU 396 TC13 | E S |
| 91 | 3 | 2 | 2 | 895 | 140 | 6 | 1976 | G-M | G-M-SEMT | HD Voith L520-RO |
| 701 | 2 | 2 | 4 | 305 | 120 | 12 | 1990 | MAN | MAN D2842/ME | H Voith T320RZ |
| **1,000 mm gauge** | | | | | | | | | | |
| 6461 | 3 | 1 | 4 | 850 | 100 | 11 | 1983 | G-M | P 8PA4-185V | HD Voith KB380/1 |
| 6501 | 3 | 2 | 4 | 398 | - | 10 | 1991 | HS | - | - |
| 6521 | 2 | 1 | 2 | 305 | - | 10 | 1991 | HS | - | - |
| **750 mm gauge** | | | | | | | | | | |
| 3001-3003 | 2 | 1 | 2 | 260 | 40 | 3 | 1959 | Billard | Mer Y15-536 | E |
| 3004-3006 | 2 | 1 | 2 | 375 | | 3 | 1967 | Decauville | Mer MB836-B/L | E |

Abbreviations: G-M: Ganz-Mávag; HS: Hellenic Shipyards; Mek: Mekydro; Mer: Mercedes; P: Pielstick

### Electric locomotives

| Class | Wheel arrangement | Power kW continuous/ one-hour | Speed km/h | Weight tonnes | No in service | First built | Builders Mechanical | Electrical |
|---|---|---|---|---|---|---|---|---|
| H560 | Bo-Bo | 5,000 | 200 | 80 | 30* | 1997 | Krauss-Maffei | Siemens |

* Includes 24 on order in 2002

*Alco Class A9100 diesel-electric locomotive on the OSE metre-gauge system at Patras with a Piraeus–Kiparissia service (Colin Boocock)* 2002/0524926

**UPDATED**

# GUATEMALA

## Ministry of Communications and Public Works

Edificio Aeronautica Civil, Zona 13, Guatemala City
Tel: (+502 2) 51 27 69   Fax: (+502 2) 816 13

### Key personnel
Transport Minister: Fritz Garcia

## Bandegua Railway

Cia de Desarrollo Bananero de Guatemala Ltd
Edificio La Galeria 5° Nivel, 7 Avenue 1444, Zone 9, Guatemala City
Tel: (+502 2) 34 03 78   Fax: (+502 2) 32 21 52

### Key personnel
General Manager: G K Brunelle
Director of Engineering: E Casado
Railroad Superintendent: G Aguirre
Mechanical Superintendent: M Pérez

Gauge: 914 mm
Route length: 102 km

### Traction and rolling stock
The company operates 11 diesel locomotives, 17 diesel railcars, seven passenger coaches and 101 freight wagons.

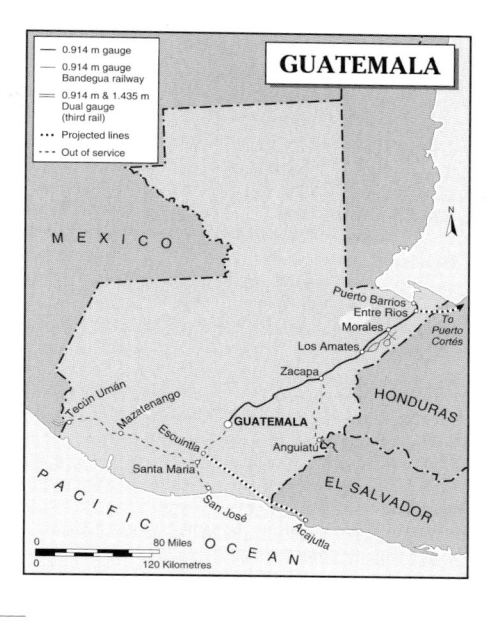

## Ferrovías Guatemala (FEGUA)

Compañia Desarrolladora Ferroviaria SA
24 Avenida 35-91, zona 12, Guatemala City
Tel: (+502 2) 485 01 30   Fax: (+502 2) 485 01 35

### Key personnel
General Manager: Renato Fernández Ravelo
Vice-President, Operations: William J Duggan

Gauge: 914 mm
Route length: 784 km

### Political background
Guatemala's railway was nationalised in 1968. At this time, the railway had significant flows of passengers, coffee and bananas, although a severe lack of investment in the ensuing 20 years effectively eroded this traffic base. From a 1980s yearly average in excess of 500,000 tonnes of freight carried, FEGUA was down to little more than 100,000 tonnes per year by the mid-1990s. All passenger traffic ceased in 1994, and the entire network closed in March 1996, just as the government had begun privatisation.

In 1997, US-based Railroad Development Corporation beat one other firm to win a 50-year concession to run the system, paying the government US$10 million, plus 5 per cent of revenues for the first two years of operation and 10 per cent annually thereafter. A further US$10 million will need to be spent on upgrading the main Guatemala City–Puerto Barrios line. RDC established a Guatemalan affiliate, Compañia Desarrolladora Ferroviaria SA (CODEFE) to prepare for a resumption of operations. The concession was signed in October 1997 and endorsed by Guatemala's congress in April 1998. Operations under new ownership commenced in 1999. The company trades as Ferrovías Guatemala.

The relocation of facilities in Guatemala City will involve RDC abandoning the present Central station in favour of a new container terminal in the industrial zone. The company also expects to generate extra income by selling right-of-way to pipeline, electricity, and fibre optic communications concerns.

### Passenger operations
No scheduled passenger services are operated and Ferrovías Guatemala has no plans to introduce such trains. However, charter trains for group travel are run and the first of these was operated in March 2000 as part of a five-day round-trip between Guatemala City and Puerto Barrios. Traction was provided by a Baldwin steam locomotive.

### Freight operations
Through freight operations resumed on the 318 km line between Guatemala City and Puerto Barrios in November 1999. Two or three trains daily run over the refurbished

*Prior to the granting of an operating concession to the Railroad Development Corporation, an MLW diesel locomotive heads an eastbound freight train near Agua Caliente*　0016434

line, journeys taking about 15 hours in each direction. Cement and other construction materials are the main commodities carried.

### New lines
The governments of Guatemala, Canada, El Salvador, Honduras, Mexico and the USA, together with the World Bank and the Interamerican Bank for Development have undertaken studies into a new international rail link to connect Guatemala, El Salvador and Honduras with the NAFTA states. In Guatemala, the scheme would necessitate rebuilding the existing line from Zacapa to Anguiatú and San Salvador, which is currently out of use, providing a link from El Salvador to Honduras.

### Improvements to existing lines
Despite difficulties such as stolen rail and washouts due to Hurricane Mitch, Ferrovías Guatemala has rehabilitated the Atlantic line between Puerto Barrios and Guatemala City. In a second phase, rehabilitation is planned of the Pacific route from Esquintla to Retalhuleu and Tecún on the Mexican border. This will serve as a feeder route into Mexico for containers. It is intended to establish a transhipment point for transferring this traffic from the 914 mm gauge of Guatemala to the Mexican standard-gauge network at the Mexican border station of Ciudad Hidalgo. Containers for Guatemala City will be unloaded at Esquintla. In a later phase, the Esquintla–Guatemala City line may be restored to service.

### Traction and rolling stock
Prior to the 1996 cessation of operations the FEGUA fleet totalled 28 General Electric diesel and two steam locomotives, 68 passenger coaches and 1,523 wagons. Recent additions are 10 Type MX620 1,492 kW locomotives from Bombardier; serviceable examples of this type and of 15 General Electric U10s locomotives will form the traction for RDC's revival of operations.

One of several Baldwin steam locomotives has been returned to traffic for passenger charter services and the restoration of two more was in hand for similar work in 2000.

### Track
**Rail:** 30 kg/m
**Sleepers:** Timber, spaced 1,800/km in plain track, 1,000/km in curves
**Max curvature:** 6°
**Max gradient:** 3.3%
**Max permissible axleload:** 20 tonnes

# GUINEA REPUBLIC

**Ministry of Trade, Transport & Tourism**

PO Box 715, Conakry

**Key personnel**
Minister: I Sylla
For map see entry for **Senegal**.

**Chemin de Fer de la Guinée (ONCFG)**

PO Box 581, Conakry

**Key personnel**
Director: M K Fofana

Gauge: 1,000 mm; 1,435 mm
Route length: 662 km; 175 km

**Organisation**
The railway links Kankan and the limit of navigability of the Upper Niger at Kouroussa with the port of Conakry. Crossing the Fouta Djalon mountains on gradients as steep as 2.9 per cent, and with curves of 100 to 150 m radius, it was lightly laid, without ballast, and has consequently deteriorated badly with rising axleloads. Some renovation of track and rolling stock has been carried out under foreign aid programmes.

The government's aim is to reconstruct the entire railway, regauging it to standard gauge. As part of this scheme, a 134 km standard-gauge line was built in 1974 with technical and financial aid from the USSR. Running from Conakry to Kindia, the line parallels the metre-gauge line for almost its entire length and is used exclusively for the transport of bauxite from mines at Kindia. The line is operated jointly by ONCFG and the Société de Bauxite de Kindia (SBK), its sole user. From Dabola, at Km 442 on the metre-gauge line, a branch line of some 140 km runs north to bauxite mines near Tougué. This line is jointly operated by ONCFG and the Société de Bauxite Dabola-Tougué (SBDT).

**Passenger operations**
Passenger operations using railcars between Conakry and Kankan ceased towards the end of the 1980s due to a lack of spare parts for rolling stock and poor track conditions. A limited passenger service has been run between Conakry and Kindia by attaching a passenger coach to a freight train twice-weekly but in many cases passengers are simply carried in a freight wagon. The total number of passengers carried in 1998 totalled around 50,000.

**Freight operations**
Freight operations are confined to the 442 km Conakry–Dabola section of the main line; east of Dabola there was in 2000 no traffic due to the poor state of the line's infrastructure. One daily train conveys bauxite from the mines at Tougué to Dabola, where the ore is transferred to metre-gauge wagons for movement to the port at Conakry. While bauxite accounts for around 80 per cent of traffic, iron ore, uranium, diamonds, graphite, chalk and gold are also transported. From Kindia to Conakry only bauxite is carried. Trains on this line are more frequent, and loading also takes place at Débélé, about midway on the route. Loadings from Tougué and Kindia total some 4 million tonnes annually.

**New lines**
With assistance from Slovakian Railways, the 140 km Dabola–Tougué line was completed in 1998, using second-hand rails from the Slovakian network. Additional projects include rebuilding the entire Kindia–Dabola–Kankan main line as a standard-gauge system. New lines from Kankan towards the border with Burkina Faso in the north and Ivory Coast in the south are also projected, although no steps have been taken towards their construction. Most of these projects date back to 1958 to 1984. During this period, in 1974, a new station was built at Simbaya, on the outskirts of Conakry, but never used for passengers. Adjacent USSR-built workshops are responsible for the maintenance of standard-gauge rolling stock.

**Traction and rolling stock**
The metre-gauge traction fleet consists of 30 main line diesel locomotives and several small shunters, although in 1999 only two Alsthom locomotives built in 1982 and two General Motors machines dating from 1986 were serviceable, together with a pair of two-axle French-built shunters. Two former Czech Railways Class 710 locomotives were acquired in 1998 and converted to metre gauge at Nymburk workshops in the Czech Republic. These are exclusively used on services to Dabola.

Standard-gauge locomotives for the line to Kindia consist of 13 USSR-built Type TEM 2T six-axle machines acquired in 1998. In July 1996, the Czech company Prime International obtained 18 former Czech Railways Class 770 and 771 diesel locomotives and 35 Falls-type freight wagons from Slovakian Railways originally purchased for a subsequently cancelled contract with Islamic Iranian Republic Railways. One of the locomotives and several of the wagons were lost in a storm during shipment: those vehicles which reached Guinea were in 2000 stored out of use at Simbaya. Three of the locomotives eventually entered service on the Dabola–Tougué line.

None of ONCFG's 16 metre-gauge railcars was serviceable at the end of 1999 and scrapping of most was reported to be imminent. Of 20 bogie passenger coaches, no more than five remained usable. Some 200 of the fleet of 500 freight wagons were serviceable, some of which were tank wagons that included eight-axle examples imported from Congo during the 1980s.

On the standard-gauge line to Kindia, most of the freight wagons are four-axle vehicles built in the USSR. Wagons regauged for metre-gauge operation are used on the Dabola–Tougué line.

**Industrial railways**
From Conakry, the metre-gauge Chemin de fer Conakry–Fria (CFCF) line runs parallel to the ONCFG main line for 30 km before diverging to the north to Fria, 142 km from Conakry. Owned by SBK and opened in 1960, the line serves Fria bauxite mines and its aluminium plant. It is single-track, with 46 kg/m rails on steel sleepers. Rolling stock comprises three Alsthom 820 kW diesel-electric locomotives and 61 50 tonne wagons. The line carries some 900,000 tonnes of bauxite annually.

Also operated by SBK is the Chemin de fer de Boké (CFB), located around 250 km northwest of Conakry. This standard-gauge line runs 136 km from the port of Kamsar via Boké to Sangaredi. Moving more than 12 million tonnes of bauxite annually from the mines at Sangaredi, at the foot of the Peul hills, it is the country's most important carrier of this commodity. Built by a consortium of European contractors and opened in 1973, the line has UIC 60 kg/m continuously welded rail laid on steel sleepers. As well as bauxite, around 50,000 tonnes of other merchandise and 150,000 passengers are carried annually in five trains a week in each direction. The railway owns 17 US-built diesel locomotives, 460 ore wagons, 39 other freight wagons and three passenger coaches.

# HONDURAS

**Ministry of Communications, Public Works and Transport**

Barrio La Bolsa, Comayaguela
Tel: (+504) 33 76 90   Fax: (+504) 33 92 27

**Key personnel**
Minister: G Aparicio

**Honduras National Railway (FNH)**

Ferrocarril Nacional de Honduras
PO Box 496, San Pedro Sula
Tel: (+504) 53 40 80; 53 18 79   Fax: (+504) 52 80 01

**Key personnel**
General Manager: Diego Zúniga Muñoz
Directors
   Administration and Finance: J O Garcia
   Commercial and Marketing Services:
      A Ramos Carrazco
   Mechanical: F Maury Martell
   Operations: J Manuel Benegas

Gauge: 1,067 mm; 914 mm
Length: 279 km; 420 km

**Organisation**
The existing FNH system includes 420 km of 914 mm gauge track which was formerly part of the Vaccaro and Standard Fruit system, which was nationalised in 1976. All lines are out of use but not dismantled. The former Tela Railroad lines, 164 km of 1,067 mm gauge, formerly leased to and operated by United Brands Company, were put under FNH control in 1983, but operated as a separate entity until the mid-1990s. About 90 km of this system remain serviceable. The remaining 115 km of 1,067 mm gauge track belongs to FNH and consists mainly of the Puerto Cortés–San Pedro Sula–Potrerillos main line and many smaller branches, of which that from Chamelecón to La Lima is the most important. Most of these lines are in operation or at least extant.

Damage to the railway by Hurricane Mitch principally affected the lines east of Tela and around La Ceiba, where all infrastructure was destroyed. Lines south of Puerto Cortés towards San Pedro Sula were affected to a lesser extent. After some minor repairs, freight services resumed during 1999 between Puerto Cortés and San Pedro Sula and other inland points.

**Passenger operations**
After a complete suspension of passenger services in mid-1998, no trains ran for almost 18 months. Early in 2000, FNH reinstated regular scheduled passenger services on the 76 km Puerto Cortés–Tela line with a round-trip every Friday and Sunday.

**Freight operations**
Most traffic runs between Puerto Cortés and San Pedro Sula and consists principally of fruit and other agricultural products. Some fertilisers and construction materials are also transported.

**New lines**
Nothing has resulted from a project unveiled in 1983 to construct up to 350 route-km of new lines. Work on the planned San Pedro Sula–Yoro line was initiated but halted, but this and other schemes, such as the Puerto Castillo–Sonaguera and Arenal–Rio Bonito lines, remain on the national agenda awaiting an improvement in economic conditions or private investment funds. Some of the projects form part of a scheme for a pan-Central American railway (see entry for Guatemala).

**Traction and rolling stock**
The 1,057 mm system is operated with two steam and 34 diesel locomotives, 37 passenger coaches, 22 diesel railcars and 1,960 wagons. The 914 mm fleet comprises eight diesel-electric and two diesel-mechanical locomotives, 17 diesel railcars, 16 passenger coaches and 530 wagons. Operations on the 1,067 mm Tela system are conducted with 28 diesel locomotives, 18 railcars, 70 passenger coaches and 1,324 freight wagons.

# HUNGARY

## Ministry of Transport, Communication & Water Management

PO Box 87, H-1400 Budapest (Dob utca 75-81)
Tel: (+36 1) 322 02 20   Fax: (+36 1) 322 86 95

**Key personnel**
Minister of Transport: János Fónagy
International Affairs: A Hardy
Railways: L Horváth

## Györ-Sopron-Ebenfurt Railway (GySEV/ROeEE)

Györ-Sopron-Ebenfurti-Vasút Rt
Raab-Oedenburg-Ebenfurter Eisenbahn AG
Szilágyi Dezsö-tër 1, H-1011 1 Budapest
Tel: (+36 1) 224 58 99   Fax: (+36 1) 224 58 08

**Key personnel**
General Manager: Dr János Berényi
Deputy General Managers:
   Dr László Fehérvári, Csaba Siklos
Director – Sopron: Dr Tibor Jozan
Director – Wulkaprodersdorf: Dr Csaba Székely
Personnel Director: György Tabori
Commercial Director: Dr Tibor Varga
Finance Director: Eszter Menich

Gauge: 1,435 mm
Route length: 101 km (Hungary), 65 km (Austria)
Electrification: 156 km at 25 kV 50 Hz AC

### Organisation
A majority shareholding in GySEV is owned by the Hungarian government (61 per cent), with the Austrian government holding 33.3 per cent. The Port of Hamburg owns 4.3 per cent of the equity.

### Passenger operations
In 2000, GySEV carried 1.35 million passengers. Fast services are operated between Sopron and Budapest. Sopron—Vienna services are operated by Austrian Federal Railways.

In 2001, GySEV took over services on the Sopron—Szombathely route. These were previously operated by MÁV.

### Freight operations
In 2000, GySEV handled 6.2 million tonnes of freight.

### Intermodal operations
In March 1996, Intercontainer-Interfrigo launched a new intermodal service between the Dutch port of Rotterdam and Sopron entitled 'Hansa-Hungaria-Container-Express'. This operates daily. At GySEV's Sopron terminal, which was expanded in 1999, containers are either transhipped to feeder trains for Hungary, the Balkan countries and Turkey or to road vehicles. Piggyback traffic is also significant, accounting for around one-fifth of freight tonnage.

*GySEV Class V43 electric locomotive* (Milan Šrámek)

### Traction and rolling stock
In 2000 the railway owned 15 Class V43 electric and 14 Class M44 diesel locomotives, two single-car and one two-car Austrian-built dmus, 42 passenger cars and 241 wagons.

In 2001, GySEV ordered five dual-voltage (15 kV AC/25 kV AC) Class 1116 'Taurus' electric locomotives from Siemens. Delivery was scheduled for 2002.

## Hungarian State Railways Co Ltd (MÁV)

Magyar Államvasutak Rt
Andrássy út 73-75, H-1940 Budapest
Tel: (+36 1) 322 06 60   Fax: (+36 1) 342 85 96
e-mail: mail@mav.hu
Web: http://www.mav.hu

**Key personnel**
Chairman: Dr István Endrédy
General Manager: Márton Kukely
Special Directors
   Passenger Services: Ferenc Vizsy
   Freight Services: István Bobál
Assistant General Managers
   Economics: Annamaria Benczédi
   Personnel: Dr Gábor Bajnai
   Infrastructure: József Pál
   Undertaking: Gyula Sárdi
Chief of International Affairs Department: József Lovas

Gauge: 1,524 mm; 1,435 mm; 760 mm
Route length: 36 km; 7,519 km; 219 km
Electrification: 2,628 km at 25 kV 50 Hz AC

### Political background
Like all railways of the former Communist East European countries, MÁV has steadily lost traffic since 1989 in the face of political and industrial change. Freight traffic more than halved in the 1989-94 period, from 104 to 44.2 million tonnes; in 1995, there was a modest rise, to 46.4 million tonnes. Passenger traffic, stagnant since the mid-1980s, dropped 30 per cent as unemployment rose and public and private road transport competition intensified. By 1994, MÁV was carrying 159 million passengers, compared to 225 million in 1989, but by 1995 the steep drop appeared to be over and carryings stabilised. In 2001, 43.8 million tonnes and 159.6 million passengers were carried.

State subsidies have been drastically falling since 1986. In response to the financial crisis, the payroll was cut to 57,000 in 1999 from 127,000 in 1990, and track and rolling stock maintenance has been delayed. At the end of 2001 the number of staff employed was 54,000. Ancillary businesses such as engineering departments were transferred to separate companies in the early 1990s.

From 1 January 1994 new legislation distinguished between the passenger and freight operations of MÁV and its infrastructure, each accounting separately within the organisation by 2004. Main lines will continue to be owned by the central government, while branch lines may

# RAILWAY SYSTEMS/Hungary

be handed over to local authorities. Private-sector firms will be able to apply to run railway services, subject to government licence.

In addition, under the Railways Act of 1993, since 1 February 1995 a contract has existed between the state and MÁV Ltd. It defines which infrastructure elements remain exclusively in state (treasury) ownership, the fee to be paid for their use and public service obligations whose deficits will be covered by the state. This contract contributes to the consolidation of MÁV's finances.

The government also repeatedly exempted MÁV from substantial historic debts, and increased its grant for passenger services, although this still lagged behind operating costs.

Keeping abreast of EU legislation the government decided in 2001 to establish a separate, independent body to manage the allocation of network capacity and to set fees for its utilisation.

| Traffic (million) | 1999 | 2000 | 2001 |
|---|---|---|---|
| Passenger journeys | 156.5 | 154.2 | 159.6 |
| Passenger-km | 9,418 | 9,595 | 9,902 |
| Freight tonnes | 43.6 | 43.6 | 43.8 |
| Freight tonne-km | 7,444 | 7,780 | 7,426 |

## Passenger operations

MÁV joined the western European EuroCity system with the 1988 conferring of EC status on the Vienna–Budapest 'Lehar'. EC links later added are the Cologne–Budapest 'Franz Liszt', the Munich–Budapest 'Béla Bartók', the Berlin–Budapest 'Hungaria' and the Prague–Budapest 'Comenius'. These use new MÁV Spanish-built (CCAF) cars. Other EC trains are the 'Polonia' from Budapest to Warsaw and the 'Traianus' from Budapest to Bucharest.

An international night train, the 'Kálmán Imre', links Munich with Budapest. A EuroNight service introduced in 1996, the 'Ister', gives a night connection to Bucharest. Altogether, 40 international passenger services operate over the MÁV network.

Domestically, MÁV runs 45 supplementary-fare intercity services radiating from Budapest covering eight routes ranging from 180 to 330 km.

From 1997, new InterPici services began, feeding into MÁV's intercity network in eastern Hungary. In 2002, these provided 31 train-pairs over 13 routes and employ refurbished dmus to provide connections with smaller communities at distances of up to 50 km from main centres and offer a standard of travel close to that of intercity services.

From June 2001 MÁV rebranded its premier intercity services 'InterCity Rapid'. Using 200 km/h CAF-built coaches and attracting higher-than-normal seat reservation fees, these limited stop services were initially introduced on Budapest–Debrecen–Nyíregyháza and Budapest–Pécs routes.

## Freight operations

Freight traffic has been badly affected by the political and economic changes in Hungary since 1989, with some plants which generated heavy traffic having closed and new private-sector road operators having taken other freight. Freight traffic more than halved in the 1989-94 period, from 104 to 44.2 million tonnes, but then stabilised, with 43.8 million tonnes in 2001. As Hungary is a landlocked country, international traffic is very important, with over half of MÁV's freight tonnage crossing the border. Delivery of stone and aggregates for motorway construction has provided a new domestic market.

MÁV's wagon fleet has been drastically reduced to reflect the reduced tonnage being carried, from a fleet of around 70,000 vehicles in the 1980s to 24,000 in 1998. Inadequacies of the wagon fleet in terms of obsolescence and unsuitability of vehicle types continue to hamper the development of freight traffic.

## Intermodal operations

To offset the drop in heavy industrial traffic such as coal and steel, MÁV is promoting container and piggyback transport.

The railway-owned international container company Intercontainer-Interfrigo (ICF), along with several business partners, established Pannoncont, a Budapest-based company, in mid-1992. An Intercontainer service, the 'Adria Express', runs daily between Budapest and Trieste in northern Italy, transiting Slovenia. Transit times are 24 hours. Other such services operate from Sopron to Hamburg (the 'Hansa Hungaria'), to Rotterdam (the 'Hungaria Express'), and also to the Balkans. A direct container block train between Budapest and Moscow, the 'Csardas', commenced experimental runs in 1999.

In conjunction with MÁV, Hungarokombi, the Hungarian member of UIRR (the international piggyback organisation), operates RoLa ('rolling motorway') services for trucks accompanied by their drivers. RoLa services were first introduced on a twice-daily basis between Wels (Austria) and Budapest in 1992. Since August 1993 services have operated three times daily between Wels and Kiskundorozsma, on the southeastern border of Hungary. Daily services started in 1994 between Sopron and Wels and in 1995 between Budapest and Ljubljana, Slovenia, replaced in 1997 by an alternative service into Slovenia, from Kiskundorozsma to Sežana. Hungarokombi doubled its shipments in 1995 and in 1996 Ganz-Hunslet built 50 RoLa wagons for MÁV. In 2001, 110,000 lorries were carried.

The Budapest Intermodal and Logistic Centre is to be developed with MÁV's participation on the southern perimeter of the city. With an annual capacity of 100,000 TEUs from 2001, the scheme's cost of some US$75 million will be funded in part by contributions from the Hungarian government and the European Union.

## New lines

A 44 km direct rail link between Hungary and Slovenia was officially opened in May 2001. The 19 km Hungarian section has been built for operations at up to 120 km/h and the alignment of the route has been designed to allow eventual upgrading for 160 km/h. The line includes a 1.4 km viaduct, claimed to be the longest in Central and Eastern Europe.

Plans to develop a 23 km rail link between Budapest Nyugati station and the city's Ferihegy airport have been developed. If adopted, the scheme would be implemented by a joint venture company in which MÁV would hold a majority shareholding. A study commissioned by MÁV and property developer TriGranit, which reported in early 2001, found that the link could be completed by 2003 at a cost of Ft15 to 20 billion. Some private sector funding would be required to complete the scheme. Around one-third of the line's route would entail new construction, including a 650 m tunnel to provide access to the airport terminal. A journey time of 19 minutes is foreseen, with a service frequency of three trains an hour.

## Improvements to existing lines

Major MÁV improvements planned with the help of European Union funding include: Zalalövö–Zalaegerszeg–Boba (83 km), which forms part of Crete Corridor 5, covering track upgrading and electrification; Budapest–Györ–Hegyeshalom (191 km, Crete Corridor 4), track and signalling improvements; and Budapest–Cegléd–Szolnok–Lökösháza (214 km, Crete Corridor 4), covering upgrading and track doubling.

EU funding is also helping to finance upgrading the Budapest–Ujszász–Szolnok route by the end of 2002 and the Cegléd–Kiskunfélegyháza line by 2005.

## Traction and rolling stock

At the end of 2001 MÁV was operating 463 electric locomotives, 550 diesel locomotives, 24 emus, 259 motor coaches and dmus, 3,067 hauled passenger cars (including 79 buffet/dining and 88 sleeper/couchette cars) and 19,600 wagons.

In 1998 a programme was launched to upgrade locomotive-hauled stock for suburban services. With the help of a loan from the European Bank for Reconstruction and Development, 200 vehicles have been refurbished and modernised. In addition, funding from the German *Kreditanstalt für Wiederaufbau* agency was to cover the purchase of 50 diesel railcars.

In 2000, work started on refurbishment and re-engineering with Caterpillar or MTU power units of some examples of Classes M40, M41, M47 and M62 diesel locomotives.

Examples of Class V43 electric locomotives have been refurbished and modified for operation with modernised Type Bhv push-pull coaching stock sets, forming the V43.2000 sub-series.

In October 2000 MÁV and GySEV (qv) jointly issued tenders for the supply respectively of 10 and five dual-voltage electric locomotives with an output of 5.6 MW and a maximum service speed of 200 km/h. This resulted in orders announced in May 2001 for locomotives of the 'Taurus' design, similar to the Austrian Federal Railways Class 1116.

In 2001 MÁV invited tenders for 13 articulated two-car dmus for regional services, with delivery required by the end of 2002. The company was also reported to be negotiating the acquisition of 40 Type RE-1 two-car dmus from Metrovagonmash in Russia under an arrangement intended to repay Russian debt to Hungary.

Repayment of debt was also a factor in the loan to MÁV by Croatian Railways of five Class 1142 electric locomotives, which entered service in March 2001.

In October 2001, MÁV awarded Bombardier Transportation a contract to refurbish 136 suburban coaches at its Dunakeszi facility. Deliveries are scheduled to take place between July 2002 and July 2003.

## Signalling and telecommunications

Nearly half of the system is equipped with automatic colourlight signalling and modern integral signalling centres have been installed at two-thirds of all stations: automatic block signalling is installed over 2,356 route-km, while a further 129 km are controlled by CTC; 749 km are controlled by centralised traffic supervision, including the 180 km route between Budapest and Hegyeshalom.

Track-to-train radio is operational on 1,400 km of the radial routes from Budapest.

In the southeast of the network three main line sections totalling some 300 km have been brought under the control of one centre at Szeged. Forward plans include development of this centre and resignalling at Budapest Ferencváros.

In consortium with Austria's Alcatel, MÁV has developed and installed a train control system on the Vienna–Budapest main line as a pilot project for Level 1 of the European Train Control System currently under development in other parts of Europe. A similar system was installed in 2002 on the new link to Slovenia.

Some World Bank aid has contributed to development of a computerised traffic management information system. This provides real-time data on traction and vehicle movements, marshalling yard operation and wagon distribution as well as fulfilling client information functions. Some 800 terminals throughout the railway will be linked to it; it was brought into operation in 1996, and the first clients went online during 1997.

The system is the first phase of a major development programme in MÁV informatics, valued at around US$150 million. Subsequent phases cover ticketing, seat reservations, and passenger information systems: these elements are being delivered by IBM, while information technology systems to manage MÁV finances were supplied by ICL in 2000. To serve these systems, and to create capacity for a competitive public telecommunications service, the programme included the construction by Siemens of a fully digital data transmission network of 2,600 km of fibre optic cables during the three-year period 1999 to 2001.

## Electrification

In 1997, Siemens was awarded a DM280 million contract to electrify the following routes: Székesfehérvár–Szombathely (170 km); Újpest–Vácrátót (30 km); and Balatonszentgyörgy–Murakeresztúr (45 km). Electric traction was introduced in 1998 on the last two routes, while the first-named was energised at the end of 2000.

Future electrification projects are likely to include: Csorna–Porpác (55 km); the new line from Boba to Hodos, Slovenia (100 km); Győr–Celldömölk (70 km); Szombathely–Nagykanizs (100 km); and Szombathely–Szentgotthárd (50 km).

## Track

**Rail:** 60, 54 or 48 kg/m, in some places lighter

*MÁV Class V43.2000 electric locomotive, refurbished and modified for push-pull operation, heading a Szolnok-bound suburban service at Budapest Keleti station (Milan Šrámek)* 2001/0109853

### Diesel locomotives

| Class | Builder's type | Wheel arrangement | Power kW | Speed km/h | Weight tonnes | No in service | First built | Builders Mechanical | Engine | Transmission |
|---|---|---|---|---|---|---|---|---|---|---|
| M28 | Rába M033 | B | 100 | 30 | 20 | 22 | 1955 | Rába | Ganz | M Rába |
| M31 | DHM2 | C | 330 | 60 | 45 | 5 | 1958 | Mávag | Ganz | H Voith |
| M32 | DHM6 | C | 260 | 60 | 36 | 15 | 1973 | Mávag | Ganz | H Ganz |
| M40 | DVM6 | Bo-Bo | 440 | 100 | 75.6 | 29 | 1966 | Mávag | Ganz | E Ganz Electric |
| M41 | DHM7 | B-B | 1,320 | 100 | 66 | 110 | 1973 | Mávag | Pielstick/Ganz | H Voith/Ganz |
| M43 | LDH45 | B-B | 330 | 60 | 48 | 104 | 1974 | Aug 23 | Aug 23 | H Brasso Hydrom |
| M44 | DVM2 | Bo-Bo | 440 | 80 | 62 | 117 | 1956 | Mávag | Ganz/Caterpillar | E Ganz Elec |
| M47 | LDH70 | B-B | 520 | 70 | 48 | 50 | 1974 | Aug 23 | Aug 23 | H Brasso Hydrom |
| M61 | M60 | Co-Co | 1,430 | 100 | 108 | 3 | 1963 | Nohab | GM | E GM |
| M62 | M62 | Co-Co | 1,470 | 100 | 120 | 94* | 1965 | Lugansk | Kolomna | E Charkov |
| M42 | DVM14 | Bo-Bo | 640 | 80 | 68 | 1 | 1994 | Ganz-Hunslet | MM/H | E Ganz Ansaldo |

*Includes 15 1,524 mm gauge

### Diesel railcars or multiple-units

| Class | Builder's type | Cars per unit | Motor cars per unit | Motored axles/car | Power/motor kW | Speed km/h | Units in service | First built | Builders Mechanical | Engine | Transmission |
|---|---|---|---|---|---|---|---|---|---|---|---|
| Bzmot 300 | Bzmot | 2 | 1 | 1 | 206 | 80 | 90 | 1995 | Studenka | Rába D10 | HM Voith |
| Bzmot 400 | Bzmot | 2 | 1 | 1 | 210 | 80 | 23 | 1997 | Studenka | Volvo | HM Voith |
| Bzmot 200 | Bzmot | 2 | 1 | 1 | 228 | 80 | 146 | 1998 | Studenka | MAN D2866 | HM Voith |

### Electric locomotives

| Class | Builder's type | Wheel arrangement | Speed km/h | Weight tonnes | No in service | First built | Builders Mechanical | Engine |
|---|---|---|---|---|---|---|---|---|
| V43 | VM14 | B-B | 130 | 80 | 350 | 1964 | Mávag | Ganz Electric |
| V46 | VM16 | Bo-Bo | 80 | 80 | 60 | 1983 | Mávag | Ganz Electric |
| V63 | VM15 | Co-Co | 120/160 | 116 | 53 | 1975 | Mávag | Ganz Electric |

### Electric railcars or multiple-units

| Class | Cars per unit | Motor cars per unit | Motored axles/car | Output kW | Speed km/h | No in service | First built | Builders Mechanical | Electrical |
|---|---|---|---|---|---|---|---|---|---|
| BDv | 4 | 1 | 4 | 1,444 | 120 | 19 | 1988 | Ganz-Hunslet | Ganz Electric |
| BV | 4 | 1 | 4 | 1,755 | 160 | 3 | 1995 | Ganz-Hunslet | ABB/Ganz Ansaldo |
| BVh | 4 | 1 | 4 | 1,755 | 120 | 2 | 1996 | Ganz-Hunslet | ABB/Ganz Ansaldo |

**Sleepers:** Concrete, steel and timber. Length, 2,420 mm; height, 190 mm; width, base, 280 mm; width, top, 200 mm

**Fastenings:** GEO 'K' type, SKL, Pandrol Fastclip, Nabla

**Min curve radius:** 150 m

**Max gradient:** 2%

**Max permissible axleload:** 22.5 tonnes

All new rail is 54.3 kg/m laid on prestressed concrete sleepers with a ballast depth of 500 mm. Minimum curve radius is 1,300 m and normal top speed is 140 km/h.

Under the Communist regime, five-year plans saw programmed upgrading of track for heavier axleloads and higher speeds. Due to lack of funding, this upgrading fell into abeyance for many years. The minimum aim is to eliminate most speed limitations related to the condition of track on the international main lines. In 1998 a rehabilitation programme was adopted to complete this task by 2010.

***UPDATED***

# INDIA

## Indian Railway Board (IR)

Rail Bhavan, Raisina Road, New Delhi 110 001
Tel: (+91 11) 338 89 31-41  Fax: (+91 11) 338 44 81
e-mail: secyrb@del3.vsnl.net.in

**Key personnel**
Minister for Railways: Nitish Kumar
Ministers of State for Railways: Dig Vijay Singh;
  O Rajagopalan

**Railway Board Members**
Chairman: Ashok Kumar
Financial Commissioner: P Rajagopalan
Electrical: N K Chidambavam

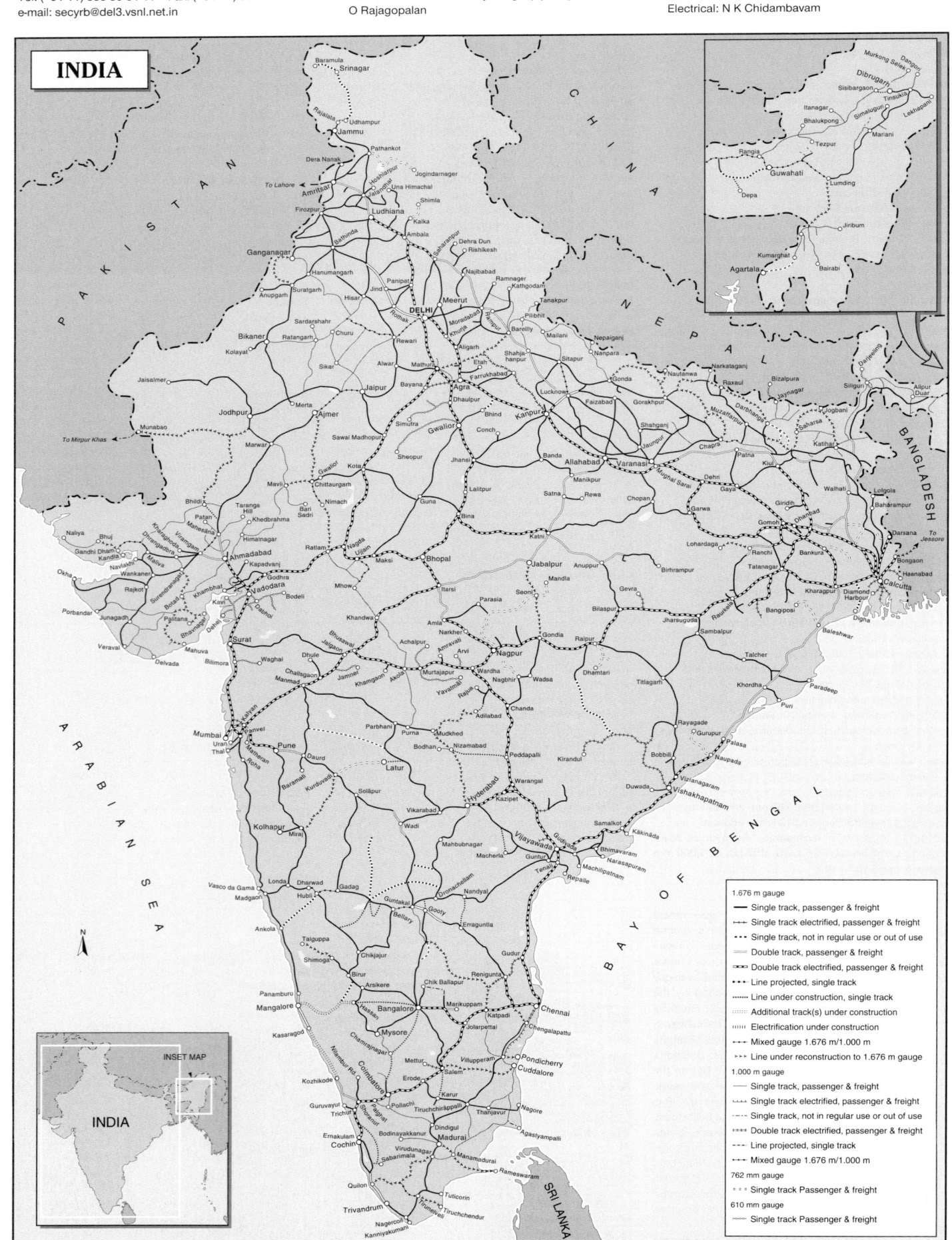

# India/RAILWAY SYSTEMS

Engineering: R N Malhotva
Mechanical: K B Sankavan
Staff: K Balakesari
Traffic: R K Thoopal
Secretary: R K Singh
Additional Members
  Staff: A S Gupta
  Budget: N Parthasarthy
  Civil Engineering: Arvind Kumar
  Commercial: A P Ramanam
  Computer and Information Systems: A K Saxena
  Electrical: A K Jain
  Finance: S Murli
  Mechanical: S Dhasarathy
  Mechanical, Production Units: Romesh Kumar
  Planning: Kanwarjit Singh
  Signalling Adviser: M L Gambhir
  Stores: N Sahu
  Telecommunications: R N Kumar
  Tourism and Catering: M C Srivastav
  Traffic: S S Bhandari
  Works: B S Sudhir Chandra
  Vigilance Adviser: R R Jauhar
Director General, Railway Protection Force: H D Rao
Director General, Health Services: Dr K Suresh
Officers on special duties:
  MS: J N Pant
  MIS and ER: V Ramkumar
  Safety: K K Chaudhury
  IRCTC: S K Malik
Executive Directors
  Coaching: M N Chopra
  Corporate Co-ordination: K Gupta
  Statistics and Economics: Balder Singh
  Accounts: R Sivadasan
  Efficiency and Research: R K Tandon
  Telecom Development: R C Sharma
  Signalling: K D Sharma
  Track: Shyam Kumar
General Managers, Manufacturing and other units
  Chittaranjan Locomotive Works: Arvind Sharma
  Varanasi Diesel Locomotive Works: O P Gupta
  Integral Coach Factory: A K Malhotra
  Wheel and Axle Plant: P Ramchandran
  Rail Coach Factory: K R Govindrajan
  Railway Electrification, CORE: A K Chopra
  Metro Railway, Calcutta: I I M S Rana
  NF Railway Construction: B M S Bisht
Research, Design and Standards Organisation:
  Hari Mohan
Principal, Railway Staff College: G C Bijlani
Director, IR Centre for Advanced Management and
  Technology: M L Gupta
Chief Administrative Officers
  Diesel Component Works: G K Wadhwa
  Central Organisation for Modernisation of Workshops:
    S A Singh
Chairman, Konkan Railway Corporation (ex officio):
  Ashok Kumar

Gauge: 1,676 mm; 1,000 mm; 762 mm and 610 mm
Route length: 44,382 km; 15,013 km; 3,363 km
Electrification: on 1,676 mm gauge 14,415 km at 25 kV 50 Hz AC, 429 km at 1.5 kV DC; 165 km of 1,000 mm gauge at 25 kV 50 Hz AC

## Organisation

Indian Railways, organised as a central government undertaking, is Asia's largest and the world's second largest state-owned railway system under unitary management. The Ministry of Railways functions under the guidance of the Minister of Railways. Day-to-day affairs and formulation of policy are managed by the Railway Board, comprising the Chairman, Financial Commissioner and functional members. The railway is made up of nine zonal systems: Central, Eastern, Northern, North Eastern, Northeast Frontier, Southern, South Central, South Eastern and Western. Due to the changing traffic patterns caused by large-scale gauge conversion and opening of the Konkan Railway (qv), IR is creating a further seven zones. These are the East Coast, East Central, North Central, North Western, South Western and West Central railways and the Bilaspur zone, with headquarters at Bhubaneswar, Hajipur, Allahabad, Jaipur, Bangalore, Jabalpur and Bilaspur. Work started in late 1996 on creation of the necessary administrative infrastructure, but this has not yet made much progress mainly due to lack of funds.

IR is a monopoly organisation and enjoys considerable economies of scale in its operations. Though the time is not yet ripe for its corporatisation, several changes in its conceptual framework are necessary in order to enable it to cope with the challenges of the twenty-first century.

For IR the major challenge in investment planning is to strike a proper balance between its dual role as a public utility on the one hand and a commercial enterprise to be run on sound business principles on the other. In a resource-strapped environment with dwindling budgetary support from the government, IR has objectively to assess the trade-off between targeting investment for capacity generation and investing in development projects which are unremunerative.

It has to be recognised that rail transport is likely to become a bottleneck in the growth of the economy unless adequate investments are planned in basic infrastructure in the ninth five-year plan (1997-2002). The revised estimated IR freight traffic projections in the terminal year (2001-02) of this plan are 500 million tonnes and 327 billion tonne-km, against 1996-97 (terminal year of the eighth five-year plan) figures of 423 million tonnes and 280 billion tonne-km. Revised estimated passenger traffic projections for 2001-02 are 4.927 billion passengers and 427.7 billion passenger-km, compared with 1996-97 figures of 4.153 billion passengers and 357 billion passenger-km, including suburban passengers.

A recent accident in which several vehicles of a mail train fell from a bridge in Kerala, killing over 50 people, has brought home the fact that arrears in the replacement of essential items due to shortage of funds has now started having a serious impact on railway safety. The government has therefore announced the establishment of a Rs170 billion non-lapsable railway safety fund for replacement of life-expired tracks, bridges, signalling systems, rolling stock and so on. The details of the fund were being worked out in 2001.

## Finance

In the railway budget for FY2001-02, IR's annual plan outlay had been kept at Rs110.90 billion, an increase of Rs10.88 billion over the revised estimate for FY2000-01. This outlay was to be financed by budgetary support from the government of Rs35.4 billion and balance resources were to be generated internally or through market borrowings by railways.

Budgetary support to IR from central government is being reduced over the years, mainly due to severe shortage of resources. On the other hand, there is a steady increase in working expenditure. For example, in FY1999-2000, working expenses inclusive of depreciation and miscellaneous expenses were higher by Rs30.27 billion than those in FY1998-99. It will therefore by necessary for IR to increase passenger fares, especially second class tariffs, gradually to achieve levels where services cover their operating costs.

As a populist measure, in the budget for 2001-02, there was no increase in the freight rates for essential commodities or in passenger fares. There was a marginal increase in the freight rates for other commodities.

IR's budget estimate for FY2001-02 is based on a target of 500 million tonnes of freight carried against a target of 475 million for FY2000-2001. For passenger traffic, a 9 per cent increase has been assumed. With these projections, freight earnings for FY2001-02 have been assessed at Rs247.35 billion and passenger receipts at Rs113.87 billion. With other income assessed at Rs25.67 billion, gross traffic receipts are estimated to be Rs394.39 billion. Working expenses are estimated at Rs386.84 billion compared with Rs349.3 billion for FY2000-01, an increase of 11 per cent.

The Railway Fare & Freight Committee set up to examine the whole structure of fares and freight rates has made several recommendations for attracting more traffic, raising additional revenue and reducing costs. Many of its recommendations have been accepted by IR, but implementation will be in stages. However, the government has yet to solve overmanning in the public sector, and the tradition that a public-sector post is effectively a job for life. IR's staff, for example, totalled 1.577 million in 1999-2000 for a wage bill of Rs162.88 billion, an increase of Rs6.69 billion over 1998-99.

As in the previous year, a major portion of the increase in the wages bill is a result of implementation of the Fifth Pay Commission.

IR has initiated several steps to augment earnings and curtail expenditure. The railway also plans to raise revenue from other non-traditional sources. These steps are expected to be pursued vigorously to ensure adequate funds are available to invest in the replacement of life-expired or obsolete assets and modernisation of the system.

| Revenue (Rs million) | 1997-98 | 1998-99 | 1999-2000 |
|---|---|---|---|
| Passengers | 81,401.4 | 91,757.0 | 104,060 |
| Freight | 198,663.8 | 199,603.8 | 220,610 |
| Other income | 5,400.0 | 6,646.2 | 6,573 |
| Total | 285,465.2 | 298,007.0 | 331,243 |

| Expenditure | 1997-98 | 1998-99 | 1999-2000 |
|---|---|---|---|
| Working expenditure | 206,050 | 232,546 | 256,449 |
| Reserve funds | 52,710 | 45,800 | 51,990 |
| Total | 258,760 | 278,346 | 308,439 |

| Traffic (million) | 1997-98 | 1998-99 | 1999-2000 |
|---|---|---|---|
| Passenger journeys | 4,340 | 4,411 | 4,585 |
| Passenger-km | 379,897 | 403,884 | 430,666 |
| Freight tonnes | 446 | 441.6 | 478.2 |
| Freight tonne-km | 286,771 | 284,270 | 308,039 |

## Gauge conversion

To boost the country's transport infrastructure and speed up development of the areas served by metre-gauge routes, IR had planned conversion of 6,000 km of busy metre-gauge routes to 1,676 mm gauge at a cost of Rs39 billion during the 1992-97 five-year plan. This was carried out successfully with conversion of 6,900 km during the period 1992-97, thus exceeding the 6,000 km target for the 1992-97 five-year plan by 900 km. Conversion of the 934 km Delhi–Ahmedabad route was completed in 1997 at a cost of Rs7.85 billion. An outlay of Rs5.11 billion has been provided in IR's budget for 2001-02 for gauge conversion work and a physical target of converting 165 km has been set.

## Passenger operations

Since 1950 IR's passenger traffic, measured in journeys, has risen by 243.5 per cent. Assessed in passenger-km of non-suburban rail travel, growth during the same period has been as much as 435 per cent. The rise in

*Passenger activity at New Delhi* (K K Gupta)

passenger-km has been due mainly to the increase in average journey length from 68.8 km in 1950 to 190.5 km in 1999-2000.

There is continuous demand for introduction of new trains and increased frequency of existing service, especially 'Rajdhani' and 'Shatabdi' expresses. During 1999-2000, 72 (single) trains were added to the timetable and 78 single extended. Additional main line emu and dmu services were introduced over several sections to segregate short- and long-distance traffic. Railbus service was introduced on some branch lines with low traffic densities. During FY1998-1999, 5,787 special trains were run and 18,723 extra coaches were provided to clear extra demand during summer, winter and Puja holiday periods.

Despite operational, resources and track capacity constraints, the introduction of 24 additional train services, increases in the frequency of nine pairs of trains and the extension or augmentation of several other services was proposed in the FY2001-02 budget to meet demand.

IR is now providing further improved facilities for passengers such as the installation of CCTV at important reservation offices to monitor the activities of touts and anti-social people; the provision of Rajdhani Express-type features on long-distance services; the installation of Interactive Voice Response System (IVRS), a computerised passenger enquiry system providing information on reservations, and train arrivals and departures – 157 stations had been equipped with IVRS by March 2000 and more were to follow; and the provision of instant confirmed reservations to passengers required to travel at short notice in over 100 long-distance trains on payment of a surcharge. Mumbai, Calcutta, Delhi, Chennai and Secunderabad passenger reservations systems (PRSs) have been linked so that it is possible to obtain a reservation for any train from any PRS terminal in the country. Computerised reservation facilities were available at 670 locations and are to be provided at an additional 71 sites.

### Freight operations

In FY1999-2000 revenue-earning freight grossed 456.4 million tonnes, some 35.5 million tonnes more than in the previous year. During the same period, indices for IR broad-gauge wagon utilisation were wagon turn-round – 7.7 days; wagon-km per day – 177.4 km; and net tonne-km per wagon day – 20.27.

The chief measures taken to enlarge freight operating capacity (and also to enhance productivity and efficiency) are recourse to more unit train working, block train segregation of high-capacity, roller bearing-equipped wagons, pursuit of as many 4,500 tonne trainloads as are feasible within existing passing loop parameters, and raising train speeds to a maximum of 80 km/h. Between 90 and 100 per cent of all coal, ore and petroleum product traffic moves in unit trains. Point-to-point fast freights known as 'Speed Link Express', introduced for movement of general goods between Delhi, Calcutta, Mumbai and Chennai, brought encouraging results and are to be extended to other corridors. IR also views upgrading of terminals as a means of improving freight traffic performance.

As a result of overall economic recovery, IR was set to achieve its freight budget loading target of 475 million tonnes during 2000-01, and a target of 500 million tonnes has been set for FY2000-01. However, IR is greatly concerned at slippage in its market share of freight traffic to 40 per cent. Its objective is to raise this share to 50 per cent during the first decade of the new millennium. IR is therefore making innovative marketing efforts to increase traffic in other sectors than core products like coal, iron and steel and raw materials for steel production. IR has reduced the classification of some commodities and is also giving 'volume discounts' to become more competitive. A two-point rake loading facility has been provided at some stations and wagon rakes are being made available in less than 48 hours. IR is planning to facilitate warehousing at existing railway terminals as well as at privately operated sites as a marketing tool to attract traffic.

IR is developing a computerised freight operations information and control system (FOIS) to provide real-time information to customers in regard to bookings, movements and delivery of freight consignments through customer service cells to be set up in all zonal railways. The system developed for specific application to unit train and rake operation has been commissioned on the Northern Railway and adjoining railways. It is being extended to the entire IR network.

*New-generation air conditioned passenger coach produced for IR by Alstom*

*Freight train hauled by a Class WDM2 diesel-electric locomotive (K K Gupta)*

*Class WAG7 25 kV AC electric freight locomotive built by CLW*

*Class WAG9 three-phase electric freight locomotive, built by CLW in collaboration with Adtranz (now Bombardier Transportation)*

## India/RAILWAY SYSTEMS

### Intermodal operations

The Container Corporation of India (Concor) was set up in 1988 under the administrative jurisdiction of the Ministry of Railways (see Indian Railway Board). Its remit is to market freight movement in containers and to develop the necessary infrastructure for multimodal operations. At present, Concor operates 40 domestic and international container-handling terminals. Traffic has risen from 66,187 TEU in FY90-91 to 1,044,728 in 2000-01. Package deals have been agreed with several major industries for through carriage of raw materials to production sites plus movement of finished products to destination.

Scheduled 'Contrac' trains with specified frequencies and guaranteed transit times run between key centres. New container-handling facilities were opened in 1998-99 at Moradabad, Madurai, Aurangabad, Ballabhgarh and Gwalior. During 1999-2000 and 2000-01, new terminals were added at Kanpur, Cossipur Road, Vadodra, Jodhpur and Guantur. Through the operations of Concor, IR is now firmly involved in multi-modal transport. Concor handles international traffic at the ports of Mumbai, Nhava Sheva, Chennai, Calcutta, Haldia, Kandla, Tuticorin, Cochin and Vizag. Concor plans to procure 3,800 high-speed wagons. Already 1,725 of these vehicles have entered service.

### Traction and rolling stock

During 1996-97, Adtranz completed delivery of 30 three-phase 4,475 kW locomotives under an order placed in 1993 for 20 six-axle freight locomotives with top speed of 100 km/h, and 10 for 160 km/h passenger service. The contract also involves transfer of technology to Chittaranjan Locomotive Works (CLW). After precommissioning tests, the freight units are being used on the Northern and Eastern railways, while the passenger locos are employed on Delhi—Howrah and Delhi—Kanpur 'Rajdhani' and 'Shatabdi' expresses. In 1998 CLW had started indigenous manufacture of the design, and in November 1998 it rolled out the first WAG 9 'Navyug' freight locomotive. By mid-2000, eight of this type had been completed. CLW is now taking up indigenous manufacture of WAP 5 passenger locomotives.

On the diesel side, in 1996 IR ordered 20 2,980 kW diesel-electrics with AC traction motors from General Motors USA, and undertook production of these locomotives, which are designated Class WDG4, from 1998-99 at its Diesel Locomotive Works (DLW) in collaboration with GM. The first of these was rolled out in August 1999.

With a view to developing export business in complete locomotives, a design and development centre has been created at CLW. During 1999-2000, IR production units manufactured 137 broad-gauge diesel and 120 electric locomotives, and 2,340 coaches including 152 suburban emu cars, 62 dmu cars and 5 main line emu cars.

The Railways Ministry 2001-02 budget provided for supply to IR of 90 diesel and 90 electric locomotives, 216 suburban emus, 48 main line emus and 60 dmus, 2,153 coaches and 23,000 wagons.

At 31 March 2000 IR's fleet comprised 35 MG and 21 NG steam, 4,651 diesel and 2,810 electric locomotives, 4,193 emu cars, 20 diesel railcars, 35,177 coaches, 1,963 service vehicles and 244,419 wagons.

**Type of coupler in standard use:** Passenger cars, screw and automatic buffer coupling; freight wagons, Alliance II and centre buffer.

**Type of brake in standard use:** Most broad-gauge freight stock built after 1982 is airbraked; others vacuum, as is all passenger stock except that for the 'Rajdhani' and 'Shatabdi' expresses which are airbraked. Phased programme under way for conversion of broad-gauge passenger stock to airbrakes.

### Signalling and telecommunications

Following an accident at Firozabad in 1995, IR is urgently pressing ahead with installation of track circuiting at block posts on all important main lines. Otherwise, the main emphasis is on replacement of mechanical interlockings at main line wayside stations by panel interlockings on an age/condition basis, and in busy yards by route-relay interlockings. At the end of FY1999-2000, IR had 1,970 panel and 210 route-relay systems and 14 solid state interlockings were in operation. New technologies are axle-counters, audio frequency track circuits, failsafe multiplexers and LED signal units.

Other areas of investment currently enjoying attention are increasing line capacity and improved safety, by provision of tokenless block, track circuiting, block-proving by axle counters, and interlocking of level crossings. During 1999-2000, 98 level crossings were

### Electric multiple-units

| Class | Cars per unit | Motor cars per unit | Motored axles/car | Output/motor kW | Speed km/h | First built | Builders Mechanical | Builders Electrical |
|---|---|---|---|---|---|---|---|---|
| **1.5 kV DC BG** | | | | | | | | |
| WCU14 | 3 | 1 | 4 | 139/187 | 105/80 | 1969 | Jessop/BEML | TDK/BHEL/Japan |
| WCU15 | 3 | 1 | 4 | 139/187 | 105/80 | 1970 | ICF/BEML/Jessop | BHEL |
| **25 kV AC BG** | | | | | | | | |
| WAU-4 | 3/4 | 1 | 4 | 167.3 | 80/90 | 1967 | ICF | BHEL/Hitachi |
| **25 kV AC MG** | | | | | | | | |
| YAU- | 4 | 1 | 4 | 126.5 | 65 | 1966 | ICF | Hitachi/Fuji |
| YAU- (Thyristor) | 4 | 1 | 4 | 90 | 65 | 1991 | ICF | GEC Alsthom/UK BHEL |
| MEMU | 4 | 1 | 4 | 163.3 | 100 | 1994 | ICF | BHEL |

### Electric locomotives

| Class | Wheel arrangement | Output kW continuous/one hour | Speed km/h | Weight tonnes | No in service | First built | Builders Mechanical | Builders Electrical |
|---|---|---|---|---|---|---|---|---|
| **Broad-gauge 1.5 kV DC** | | | | | | | | |
| WCM2 | Co-Co | 2,095/2,305 | 120 | 112.8 | 2 | 1957 | Vulcan Foundry | EEC |
| WCM6 | Co-Co | 3,430 | 105 | 120 | 2 | 1996 | CLW | CLW |
| WCG2 | Co-Co | 3,130/1,220 | 90 | 132 | 57 | 1971 | CLW | CLW |
| **Broad-gauge 25 kV AC** | | | | | | | | |
| WAM1 | Bo-Bo | 2,140/1,385 | 112 | 74.0 | 30 | 1960 | 50 c/s Group | 50 c/s Group |
| WAM2 | Bo-Bo | 2,080/2,170 | 112 | 76.0 | 4 | 1961 | Mitsubishi | Mitsubishi |
| WAM3 | Bo-Bo | 2,080/2,170 | 112 | 76.0 | 2 | 1964 | Mitsubishi | Mitsubishi |
| WAM4 | Co-Co | 2,715/2,870 | 120 | 112.8 | 474 | 1971 | CLW | CLW |
| WAP1/3 | Co-Co | 2,800/2,910 | 130/140 | 107 | 74 | 1980 | CLW | CLW |
| WAP4/6 | Co-Co | 3,730/3,990 | 140 | 107 | 150 | 1995 | CLW | CLW |
| WAP5 | Bo-Bo | 2,985/4,000 | 160 | 78 | 9 | 1996 | ABB | ABB (3 phase loco) |
| WAG1 | B-B | 2,160/2,185 | 80 | 85.2 | 10 | 1963 | 50 c/s Group/CLW | 50 c/s Group/CLW |
| WAG2 | B-B | 2,370/2,575 | 80 | 85.2 | 7 | 1964 | Hitachi | Hitachi |
| WAG3 | B-B | 2,350/2,680 | 80 | 87.32 | 9 | 1965 | 50 c/s Group | 50 c/s Group |
| WAG4 | B-B | 2,350/2,680 | 80 | 87.6 | 133 | 1971 | CLW | CLW |
| WAG5 | Co-Co | 2,870/3,250 | 80 | 118.8 | 1,176 | 1978 | CLW | CLW/BHEL |
| WAG7 | Co-Co | 3,730/3,990 | 100 | 123 | 537 | 1992 | CLW | CLW |
| WAG6A | Bo-Bo-Bo | 4,475/4,560 | 100 | 123 | 6 | 1988 | ASEA | ASEA |
| WAG6B | Bo-Bo-Bo | 4,475/4,560 | 100 | 123 | 6 | 1988 | Hitachi | Hitachi |
| WAG6C | Co-Co | 4,475/4,560 | 100 | 123 | 6 | 1988 | Hitachi | Hitachi |
| WAG9 | Co-Co | 4,565 | 100 | 123 | 25 | 1996 | Adtranz | Adtranz |
| **Broad-gauge dual-voltage 25 kV AC/1.5 kV DC** | | | | | | | | |
| WCAM1 | Co-Co | 2,715/2,870* 2,185 | 120/80 | 113 | 52 | 1975 | CLW | CLW |
| WCAM2 | Co-Co | 3,505* 2,160 | 120/80 | 113 | 20 | 1995 | BHEL | BHEL |
| WCAM3 | Co-Co | 3,730* 3,432 | 105 | 121 | 25 | 1996 | BHEL | BHEL |
| WCAG1 | Co-Co | 3,730* 3,432 | 100 | 128 | 12 | 1998 | BHEL | BHEL |
| **Metre-gauge 25 kV AC** | | | | | | | | |
| YAM1 | Co-Co | 1,215/1,300 | 80 | 52 | 20 | 1965 | Mitsubishi | Mitsubishi |

* First figures apply to AC operation, subsequent figures to DC

### Diesel locomotives

| Class | Wheel arrangement | Power kW | Speed km/h | Weight tonnes | First built | Builders Mechanical | Builders Engine | Builders Transmission |
|---|---|---|---|---|---|---|---|---|
| **Broad-gauge** | | | | | | | | |
| WDM1 | Co-Co | 1,340 | 104 | 112 | 1958 | Alco | Alco/V251B | E GE |
| WDM2 | Co-Co | 1,790 | 120 | 112.8 | 1962 | DLW | Alco/V251B | E BHEL |
| WDM2C | Co-Co | 2,310 | 120 | 112.8 | 1994 | DLW | Alco/V-251B/upgraded | E BHEL |
| WDG2 | Co-Co | 2,310 | | 123 | 1996 | DLW | Alco | E BHEL |
| WDP1 | Bo-Bo | 1,715 | 120 | 80 | 1995 | DLW | Alco | E BHEL |
| WDM4 | Co-Co | 1,965 | 120 | 113 | 1962 | GM | GM567D3 | E GM |
| WDM6 | Bo-Bo | 895 | 75 | 70 | 1981 | DLW | DLW/251D | E BHEL |
| WDM7 | Co-Co | 1,475 | 105 | 96 | 1987 | DLW | DLW-Alco/251-B 12 Eye | E BHEL |
| WDS2 | C | 330 | 54 | 51 | 1945 | Krauss-Maffei | MAN/W 8V-17-5/22A | H Voith |
| WDS3 | C | 460 | 65 | 57 | 1961 | MaK | Maybach/MD-435 | H MaK |
| WDS4 | C | 520 | 65/27 | 60 | 1969 | MaK/CLW | MaK/CLW/6M282A(k) | H/HM KPC Voith L4v2U2 |
| WDS4A | C | 490 | | | | | | H |
| WDS4B | | 520 | | | | | | H |
| WDS4D | | 450 | 65 | 60 | 1968 1969 1988 | CLW | MaK/6M282A(k) | H Voith L4r2u |
| WDS5 | Co-Co | 795 | 109 | 126 | 1967 | | Alco/251-B | E GE |
| WDS6 | Co-Co | 1,045 | 62.5 | 126 | 1977 | DLW | Alco/DLW/251D | E BHEL |
| **Metre-gauge** | | | | | | | | |
| YDM1 | B-B | 472 | 88 | 44 | 1955 | MaK/CLW | MaK/CLW/6M282A | H Voith |
| YDM-2 | B-B | 520 | 75 | 48 | 1986 | CLW | CLW/MaK/6M282A(k) | H Voith |
| YDM3 | 1B-B1 | 1,055 | 80 | 58.5 | 1961 | GM | GM 12 567c | E GM |
| YDM4 | Co-Co | 1,045 | 96 | 72 | 1961 | Alco/DLW | Alco 251-D | E BHEL |
| YDM4A | Co-Co | 1,045 | 96 | 67 | 1964 | MLW Canada | MLW/251-D | E GE Canada |
| YDM5 | C-C | 1,035 | 80 | 69 | 1964 | GM | GM 12 567c | E GM |
| **Narrow-gauge** | | | | | | | | |
| NDM1 | B'-B' | 110 | 33 | 29 | 1955 | Arn Jung | MWM TRHS/518 S | H Voith L33 U |
| NDM5 | B-B | 365 | 50 | 22 | 1987 | CLW | Cummins/KTA 1150L | H Voith L2r2zu2 |
| ZDM2 | B'-B' | 520 | 50 | 32 | 1964 | MaK | Maybach/MD 435 | HM MaK |
| ZDM3 | B'-B' | 520 | 32 | 35 | 1971 | CLW | CLW/MaK/6M282A(k) | HM Kirloskar |
| ZDM4A | 1B-B1 | 520 | 50 | 38.5 | 1984 | CLW | CLW/MaK/6M282A(k) | H Voith L4r 22 |

# RAILWAY SYSTEMS/India

interlocked. A selection of suitable pilfer-free Auxiliary Warning System (AWS)/Automatic Train Protection (ATP) systems for IR main lines is also now being given importance to prevent trains passing signals at danger. A radio-based pilot project in conjunction with the UIC is to be installed on the Delhi–Mathura section of line.

The Mumbai suburban network of the Central and Western railways is being equipped with train management systems.

On the telecommunications side, IR is replacing analogue microwave by digital systems, installing electronic telephone exchanges in place of electromechanical, and providing UHF radio links over busy sections. During 1999-2000, 333 route-km of long-haul digital microwave was installed. At the end of FY1999-2000 IR had fibre-optic communication on 2,737 route-km. It has been decided to provide such communications on all newly electrified sections of line, and for replacement of existing copper cables according to age and condition.

In 2000, IR decided to commercially exploit its right of way by laying and leasing optical fibre cables along over 62,000 km and to modernise the rail communications system to improve operation and safety. Rail Tel Corporation was set up to implement this plan.

During 1998-99 drivers and guards of trains running on A and B routes used walkie-talkie radios for emergency calls. This initiative has proved successful and is to be extended to all trains.

In IR's budget for FY2001-02, an outlay of Rs3,860 million has been provided for signalling and telecommunications work.

## Electrification

In 1925 1.5 kV DC traction was introduced on IR and at present this is confined to the 425 km suburban network on the Central and Western railways in the Mumbai area. The 25 kV 50 Hz system was adopted as standard in 1957 and has ben used for all subsequent electrification schemes. During recent years, the focus has been on electrifying the trunk routes linking Mumbai, Delhi, Calcutta and Chennai; and five of the seven major routes between these cities are energised. Electrification of the Chennai–Calcutta and Chennai–Mumbai routes is in progress, with energisation also planned for the high-density routes in and around the mineral-rich areas of Bihar, West Bengal and Orissa.

By March 2000, electrification extended to 14,984 route-km. This was 24 per cent of total route-km, but during 1999-2000 electric traction was handling 44 per cent of passenger train-km and 61 per cent of gross tonne-km on broad-gauge.

In 1991 the Asian Development Bank approved a loan worth US$225 million towards the US$617 million expansion of operating capacity between New Delhi and Calcutta. This focuses on creation of a second electrified route with modern signalling between the two cities. In 1992 IR consequently started electrification work on the 218 km from Patratu to Sonenagar, and began a third electrified track between Sonenagar and Mughalsarai, as well as various ancillary works including bidirectional signalling.

IR assigns high priority to electrification of the remaining high-density routes operated by diesel traction in a move to reduce dependence on imported petroleum products. During the eighth plan ending in March 1997, a total of 2,708 route-km were electrified. During the ninth plan, a target of electrifying 2,300 route-km has been set and the sections to be electrified during this period have been identified. During 1997-98 and 1998-99, the first two years of the ninth plan, 1,062 route-km were electrified. During 1999-2000, electrification of the Erode–Erknakulam, Adra–Midnapur and Kanpur–Lucknow lines (405 route-km) was completed. In the year 2001-02 an outlay of Rs2.25 billion has been assigned and a target of electrifying 350 route-km has been set. Now IR's aim is to complete electrification of the entire Kolkatta–Chennai route and provide an alternative electrified route on the Asansol–Mughalsarai section.

A 2 × 25 kV autotransformer system is now in operation on the heavy haul route Bina–Katni–Anuppur–Bishrampur/Chirimiri sections of Central and South Central Railways.

## Track

With the progressive introduction by IR of long-welded rail and concrete sleepers, the extension of mechanised track maintenance is a priority. The World Bank has financed substantial purchases of equipment. Besides using its own resources, IR is also resorting to funding from the Asian Development Bank and recourse to leasing and contracting of mechanised maintenance. During 1999-2000, 52,104 km of mechanised tamping was completed. High-output tampers are being used for straight track, and Unimat machines for turnouts. Dynamic track stabilisers and ballast regulators are also being used to improve retention of packing by tampers. Timber sleepers are being phased out and concrete sleepers are being installed extensively. At the end of FY1999-2000 IR had a total of 39,440 track-km and 10,146 turnouts laid on concrete sleepers.

In FY1999-2000 renewal was completed of 3,006 track-km. With rapid progress being made on gauge conversion, the aim is to liquidate all arrears of track renewal on the busiest broad-gauge sections. Ultrasonic rail testing has been introduced on all major routes. An outlay of Rs26.8 billion has been provided in IR's budget for FY2001-02 for track renewal (2,750 track-km of primary renewal and 650 track-km of secondary renewal).

## Research and development

Projects undertaken by IR's Research Standards & Development Organisation (RDSO) fall into four categories: improvements in traction and rolling stock; improving infrastructure; improving safety; and improving reliability. Some of the important projects undertaken by RDSO include: development of the 22.1 t higher axleload Box NHA wagon; development of dual-voltage three-phase emus for the Mumbai area to facilitate conversion of 1.5 kV DC traction to AC; design and development of high horsepower dmus. Other projects include: LED-based signal lamps; a train-actuated device for level crossings; integrated power supply for panel-interlocked stations; solid state interlocking (SSI) with two-out-of-three architecture; a point machine for thick-web and high-speed turnouts; a bogie-mounted brake system for freight cars; a derailment detection device; end-of-train telemetry; air springs for emu bogies; solid wheels for emus; emergency detrainment facilities for coaches; microcontroller-based speed recorder; and design of twin-beam headlight for locomotives.

It has been decided to set up a Railway Technology cell at the Indian Institute of Technology (IIT) at Kanpur and for this body to have close interaction with RDSO, academic and research institutions and industry.

*Manual track maintenance in progress on an electrified line* (K K Gupta)

*UPDATED*

---

# Central Railway

400001 Chatrapati Shivaji Terminus, Mumbai
Tel: (+91 22) 262 15 51   Fax: (+91 22) 262 45 55
Telex: 011 73819 crst in

### Key personnel

General Manager: Rajendra Nath
Additional General Manager: S K Aggarwal
Senior Deputy General Manager: B M Lal
Chief Administrative Officer: R S Varshney
Chief Electrical Engineer: P Punnuswami
Chief Commercial Manager: Ranbir Kashyab
Chief Operating Manager: S S Bhandari
Chief Engineer: A K Mahrotra
Chief Mechanical Engineer: S C SenGupta
Financial Adviser and Chief Accounts Officer:
  U V Acharya
Chief Signal and Telecommunication Engineer:
  R C Tripathi
Controller of Stores: G Siva Shankar
Chief Personnel Officer: P N Perti
Chief Security Officer: S P Srivastav
Chief Public Relations Officer: M Marwaha

Gauge: 1,676 mm; 762 mm; 610 mm
Route length: 6,149 km; 641 km; 220 km
Electrification: 2,719 km at 25 kV 50 Hz AC; 369 km at 1.5 kV DC

*Data logger at the route relay interlocking facility at Mumbai's central control cabin*

*Intercity emu of Central Railway*  0001709

## Organisation
CR serves six states: Maharashtra, Madhya Pradesh, Uttar Pradesh, parts of Rajasthan, Haryana and Karnataka, and has divisional headquarters at Mumbai, Bhusawal, Nagpur, Jabalpur, Solapur, Jhansi and Bhopal. Another division with headquarters at Agra is being established.

By virtue of its central location, CR is of pivotal importance to the IR network, connecting north and south India and east and west India. Besides carrying heavy transit traffic, it has a high loading potential of its own.

| Revenue (Rs million) | 1998-1999 | 1999-2000 |
|---|---|---|
| Passengers | 17,338 | 19,418 |
| Freight | 28,921 | 31,726 |
| Other income | 2,372 | 3,040 |
| Total | 48,631 | 54,184 |

| Expenditure (Rs million) | 1998-1999 | 1999-2000 |
|---|---|---|
| Staff/personnel | n/a | n/a |
| Materials and services | n/a | n/a |
| Depreciation | n/a | n/a |
| Financial charges* | n/a | n/a |
| Total | 43,397 | 48,357 |

* Pension fund and payment to general revenue

| Traffic (million) | 1998-1999 | 1999-2000 |
|---|---|---|
| Passenger journeys | 1,399 | 1,396 |
| Passenger-km | 101,902 | 104,839 |
| Freight tonnes* | 107.0 | 118.2 |
| Freight tonne-km | 44,085 | 48,870 |

* includes non-revenue traffic

## Passenger operations
CR transports over 3 million passengers on about 1,600 passenger trains every day. In 1999-2000, passenger-km constituted 24.3 per cent of the IR total and are the highest amongst the nine zonal railways.

The Mumbai area suburban services account for 83 per cent of the total originating passengers and 31.7 per cent of total passenger-km, with an average trip length in 1999-2000 of 28.3 km. Suburban traffic has grown from 452 million originating passengers to 971 million since 1970. CR runs 1,100 suburban trains a day. The network has also been extended by a double-track line across Thane Creek to a satellite city, New Mumbai on the mainland, to absorb population from the overcrowded Mumbai island.

In 1999-2000 originating passenger journeys totalled 1,184 million, compared to the previous year's total of 1,156 million, of which suburban traffic accounted for 971.4 million and non-suburban for 208.4 million on the broad-gauge system. The balance of 3.7 million passengers was carried on narrow-gauge lines. Total passenger-km was 104,839 million.

Future planning is based on an annual growth rate of 4 per cent for suburban and 3 per cent non-suburban traffic. To cater for the rise in suburban traffic, the network in the Mumbai area is being expanded. Track-doubling on the Belapur–Panvel line was completed in 2000. Construction of fifth and six lines between Kurla and Thane was also being undertaken on a priority basis. Additional emu rakes are being introduced and signalling works are under way. It is also planned to reduce progressively the headway of suburban services during peak hours initially from 5 to 4 minutes, and later 3 minutes. The pace of track renewal is being stepped up, and passenger information systems are being made more efficient.

In 1995, CR commissioned one of the two new terminal stations in Mumbai, at Kurla on the city's outskirts. Its five platforms can accommodate the 26-car trains which IR plans to introduce. This terminal is already being expanded to cater for three additional pairs of trains. A new station has also been built at Habibganj (Bhopal).

CR runs IR's fastest train, the air conditioned 'Shatabdi Express' which, with licence to run at up to 140 km/h on parts of the New Delhi–Bhopal route, averages 101 km/h over the 195 km from New Delhi to Agra and covers the 701 km to Bhopal in 8 hours.

## Freight operations
Freight consists chiefly of bulk commodities such as coal, cement, fertiliser, petroleum products, food grains and raw materials to steel plants. Total originating revenue traffic was 49.7 million tonnes in 1999-2000.

Until 1992-93, annual growth of originating and total traffic had been almost 4 per cent since the mid-1980s. To meet the increased demand, extensive electrification, doubling of tracks, track renewals and improved signalling are in various stages of completion. Higher capacity electric locomotives are also coming into service. Freight trains with trailing loads of 4,700 tonnes are already running and their number is being increased.

A rapid increase in ISO container traffic followed the 1989 opening of Jawaharlal Nehru Port at Nhava Sheva in New Mumbai. This is served by an offshoot of the new suburban line across Thane Creek.

## New lines
Several major new line construction projects are in progress: Panvel–Karjat; Guna–Etwah via Shiapur, Gwalior and Bhind (348 km); Amravati–Narkher (138 km); and Lalitpur–Satna and Rewa–Singrauli (541 km). Construction of the 250 km Ahmednagar–Parli Vaijnath line in the underdeveloped area of Marathwada is in progress. During 1998-1999, construction of an 82 km section of the Guna–Etawah line was completed. In the budget for 2001-2002 Rs730 million has been allocated for these projects.

## Improvements to existing lines
During 1999-2000 double-tracking of 49 km was completed. In the budget for FY2001-02, Rs461 million was provided for new double-tracking works and those in progress. Gauge conversion of 52 km of narrow-gauge between Pandhar and Kurduwadi was completed in 2000. Conversion of the Miraj–Latur narrow-gauge line (359 km) is in progress in 2001-02 and Rs50 million has been provided in the FY2001-02 budget for this work.

## Traction and rolling stock
At the start of 2000 the railway was operating on broad gauge 782 electric and 665 diesel locomotives, 374 emu motor cars and 751 trailers, 3,165 passenger coaches (including 1,360 sleeping and 49 dining cars), and 74,472 freight wagons (four-wheel equivalent). On narrow gauge the railway was operating three steam and 41 diesel locomotives, seven railcars, 287 passenger coaches and 1,008 freight wagons (four-wheel equivalent).

## Signalling and telecommunications
The present emphasis is on rehabilitation of ageing assets, along with enhancement of safety, reliability and application of modern technology. Safety aids are being installed like block-proving by axle counter, track circuiting of whole station areas, provision of two distant signals and introduction of route-relay and solid-state interlocking. Approval has been given for the provision of optical fibre cables on several new sections of the CR network, including: Delhi–Agracant; Bhusawal–Nagpur; Wardha–Ballarshah; and Pune–Wadi. During FY2001-02, Rs566 million have been allocated for these works.

## Electrification
A considerable electrification programme has been implemented. In 1992 the Delhi–Chennai route and the Mumbai–Delhi (via Bhusawal) routes were energised throughout. During 1994-95, 89 route-km were electrified and in 1995-96 electrification of the Bina–Katni east-west collieries route (263 km) was completed. IR's first 220/ 2 × 25 kV traction substation was commissioned on this section in 1993. A major project in progress is conversion of the Mumbai Division's traction power supply system from 1.5 kV DC to 25 kV AC.

**Coupler in standard use**
Passenger cars: Screw, Schaltbau (emus)
Wagons: CBC AAR-type screw; CBC Alliance II
**Braking in standard use**
Locomotive-hauled stock: Vacuum and air
Emus: Air

**Track (BG)**
**Rail:** 60, 52 and 44 kg/m FF
**Crossties (sleepers):** Monobloc concrete, 2,750 × 270 × 230 or 151 mm; wooden, 2,750 × 250 × 130 mm; steel, of various sizes
**Sleeper spacing:** 1,660/km on A routes; 1,540/km on B, C and D routes; 1,310/km on E routes
**Fastenings:** Keys, elastic fastenings such as Pandrol clip
**Max gradient:** 2.9% (1 in 34)
**Max permissible axleload:** 22.5 tonnes

*UPDATED*

---

## Container Corporation of India Ltd
2nd Floor, Le Meridian Commercial Tower, Raisina Road, New Delhi 110001
Tel: (+91 11) 375 31 64; 65; 67; 68; 69
Fax: (+91 11) 375 31 56
e-mail: concor.co@sprintrpg.ems.vsnl.net.in

### Key personnel
Managing Director: A K Kohl
Director, International Marketing and Operations: Karan Ahuja
Director, Domestic Division: R C Dubey
Director, Projects and Services: (vacant)
Director, Finance: B Ram

Group General Managers:
Finance: Runa Mukherjee
Planning and Development: S C Misra
Customs: R Pant
Technical: H Singh
Marketing and Commercial: A K Gupta
Operations: P S Nerwal

# RAILWAY SYSTEMS/India

## Organisation

Container Corporation (Concor) activities cover three distinct areas: carrier, terminal operator, and containerised freight service (CFS) operator. As a carrier, Concor conveys containerised international cargo by scheduled trains between ports and inland terminals. Terminal operations are carried out at 40 facilities throughout India. As a CFS operator, Concor provides value-added services by offering transport, warehousing and import/export cargo handling.

See also 'Intermodal operations' under the entry for 'Indian Railway Board'.

**UPDATED**

*Container train headed by two electric locomotives (K K Gupta)*

---

# Eastern Railway

17 Netaji Subhash Road, Calcutta 700 001
Tel: (+91 33) 222 71 20  Fax: (+91 33) 248 03 70

## Key personnel
General Manager: I I M S Rana
Additional General Manager: A Sen
Senior Deputy General Manager: S R Thakur
Financial Adviser and Chief Accounts Officer:
  G Thoopal
Chief Operating Manager: P K Chatterji
Chief Commercial Manager: A K Dutta
Chief Electrical Engineer: A Sen
Chief Personnel Officer: P K Chatterjee
Chief Engineer: S R Choudhury
Chief Mechanical Engineer: P N Garg
Chief Signal and Telecommunications Engineer:
  A K Varma
Controller of Stores: S Paul
Chief Public Relations Officer: K Mukhopadhejay

Gauge: 1,676 mm; 762 mm
Route length: 4,110 km; 132 km
Electrification: 2,004 km at 25 kV 50 Hz AC

## Organisation
ER is described as the 'Black Diamond' railway on account of its prime task of supplying coal to power stations. It runs mainly in the states of West Bengal and Bihar, and also in parts of Uttar Pradesh and Madhya Pradesh.

## Passenger operations
Originating passenger journeys amounted to 638 million in 1999-2000, for 44,121 million passenger-km. Of the total, some 1.3 million daily journeys were made on the Calcutta suburban network. Almost all main line passenger services are electrically operated, while Calcutta emu trains have been increased from eight to nine cars, with 10-car trains running on the Howrah and Sealdah divisions.

Each day ER runs 177 mail/express services, 869 emu services on the suburban sections of the Howrah and Sealdah lines, 96 non-suburban dmus and 59 main line emus (MEMUs). MEMU services were introduced on Barddhaman–Purulia and Asansol–Jhaja routes in August and September 1998 respectively.

As well as extending platorms to accommodate 24-coach trains, ER is taking additional steps to improve its services to passengers, including: provision of additional ticket counters; construction of platform shelters; the supply of drinking water; and the establishment of a system to communicate train running information. Computerised reservation is now available at 145 locations. Information regarding the availability of reservations on 21 important long-distance trains over Eastern and South Eastern networks is distributed via a cable TV service in Calcutta and surrounding areas.

## Freight operations
In 1999-2000 ER originated 69.15 million tonnes of revenue coal, which accounted for 86.4 per cent of freight traffic emanating from its territory. Revenue-earning freight as a whole aggregated 80.04 million tonnes and 33,245 million tonne-km.

## Improvements to existing lines
It is estimated that the freight and passenger traffic task will soon rise to 101 million tonnes and 731 million passenger journeys annually. Accordingly, several development works are in progress or planned to improve the infrastructure. These include: construction of new lines; restoration of dismantled routes; track-doubling of busy single-track lines; provision of a third bidirectional line between Dehri-on-Sone and Mughalsarai; and construction of new road overbridges.

During 1999-2000, double-tracking of 35 km was completed. ER's budget for FY2001-02 provides Rs1,010 million for construction of new lines, Rs60 million for the restoration of dismantled lines and Rs1,196 million for double- and triple-tracking of existing lines.

## Traction and rolling stock
At the start of 2000 the railway operated on broad gauge 412 electric and 516 diesel locomotives, 388 emu motor cars and 827 trailers, 4,104 passenger coaches, and 72,007 freight wagons (four-wheel equivalent). On narrow gauge the fleet comprised five diesel locomotives, four railcars and 45 passenger coaches.

*Eastern Railway main line emu at Asansol Junction (K K Gupta)*

*Coal train during loading on the Eastern Railway (K K Gupta)*

## Signalling and telecommunications

Apart from signalling works to improve line capacity on busy sections, ER is at present concentrating on replacement of old electromechanical installations by route-relay and panel interlockings. Some of these will be of the solid state (SSI) type. Track circuiting or provision of axle-counters has been sanctioned on all major ER routes and a number of level crossings are to be interlocked to improve operational safety. Optical fibre cable is being provided to replace copper cable in several sections, including the Howrah–Mughalsarai trunk route, on an 'age-cum-condition' basis. During FY2001-02 an outlay of Rs471 million has been provided for signalling and telecommunications work.

## Electrification

During 1995-96 and 1996-97, electrification of the 105 km Bandel–Katwa section was completed at a cost of Rs469 million. During 1998-99 and 1999-2000 electrification of 92 and 103 route-km respectively was completed. An outlay of Rs108 million is provided in the FY2001-02 budget.

## Coupler in standard use

Passenger cars: Drawbar with screw coupling
Freight cars: Centre buffer coupler; CBC with transition coupling; drawbar with screw coupling

## Braking in standard use

Locomotive-hauled stock: Air and vacuum brake

## Track (BG)

**Rail:** 52 and 60 kg/m in long welded rail panels
**Crossties (sleepers):** prestressed concrete – spacing 1,680-1,540 km CST-9 – spacing 1,562/km; wooden
**Fastenings:** Elastic rail clips and malleable or spheroidal graphite cast-iron inserts
**Min curvature:** 8°
**Max gradient:** 1.25%
**Max permissible axleload:** 22.5 tonnes

*UPDATED*

---

# Konkan Railway Corporation Ltd

Belapur Bhavan, Sector 11, CBD Belapur, Navi Mumbai (New Bombay) 400 614
Tel: (+91 22) 757 20 15; 20 16; 20 17; 20 18
Fax: (+91 22) 757 24 20
e-mail: general@konkanrailway.com

## Key personnel

Chairman (ex-officio): Ashok Kumar
Managing Director: B Rajaram
Director, Operations: Dr K K Gokhala
Director, Way and Works: D G Dirwate
Finance Director: R K Sinha
Financial Adviser and Chief Accounts Officer: R Ravikumar
Chief Engineer (HQ): Laxmi Narayan
Chief Mechanical Engineer: S C Agarwal
Chief Electrical Engineer: A K Bharadwaj
Chief Signal and Telecommunications Engineer: A A Bhatt
Chief Operating Manager: P B Murthly
Chief Manager, Information Technology: Sharad Saxena
Controller of Stores: R K Ahirwar

Gauge: 1,676 mm
Route length: 760 km

## Organisation

This major railway opened fully in January 1998. It extends from Roha, south of Mumbai, down the coast to Mangalore. It provides a much shorter route than the historic Mumbai–Mangalore line, which also entailed a break of gauge. The new line, in addition, opens up remote areas of Maharashtra, Goa and Karnataka states.

In 1990 the Konkan Railway Corporation was formed to take over construction of the 760 km route and operate it on completion. Initially the line is a single 1,676 mm gauge track with 58 intermediate stations, built through difficult country even by Indian standards. There are 171 major bridges, the longest of which is the Sharawati at 2,065 m, and the highest, Panvel Viaduct, 64 m, and a further 1,670 minor structures. The 92 tunnels total 83.6 km, with the longest, Karbute Tunnel, near Ratnagiri, extending to 6.5 km and using incrementally launched concrete box girder construction for the first time in India. Engineered for 160 km/h top speed, ruling gradient is 0.67 per cent and minimum curve radius 1,250 m. Track is 52 kg/m rail on prestressed concrete sleepers. The entire route is equipped with specially designed points and crossings with thick-web switches and laid on concrete sleepers. Stations have panel interlockings and colourlight signals; communication is by fibre optic link. All routine activities of the railway have been computerised, including ticketing, parcels booking and commercial coach and train operations.

*Konkan Railway passenger train crossing the 42-span Kalinadi River bridge (K K Gupta)*

KRC is at present operating nine pairs of Express and four pairs of passenger trains, including the Delhi–Trivandrum Rajdhani Express. However, freight traffic is at a level lower than expected. KRC has drawn up a prospective five-year plan to augment its earnings and is making strenuous efforts to develop its freight and tourism businesses. IR has also agreed where possible to divert goods traffic to the railway. Innovative initiatives, such as a ro-ro piggyback service, have been introduced, and it is expected that freight traffic overall will develop.

*UPDATED*

---

# North Eastern Railway

Gorakhpur 273012, Uttar Pradesh
Tel: (+91 551) 20 10 41   Fax: (+91 551) 20 18 42

## Key personnel

General Manager: V K Garg
Additional General Manager: M Sirajuddin
Senior Deputy General Manager: O P Agarwal
Chief Personnel Officer: Nepal Singh
Financial Adviser and Chief Accounts Officer: S Gupta
Chief Commercial Manager: Ashit Gupta
Chief Engineer: B R Sharma
Chief Administration Officer, Construction: Amar Singh
Chief Operations Manager: R N Agha
Chief Electrical Engineer: R K Sapre
Chief Signals and Telecommunications Engineer: P Swarup
Chief Mechanical Engineer: K R Govindrajan
Chief Medical Director: Dr M K Bhodale
Chief Public Relations Officer: R V Singh

Gauge: 1,676 mm; 1,000 mm
Route length: 2,255 km; 2,766 km

## Organisation

Increases of population and economic development now exert extreme pressure on the still predominantly metre-gauge network of the NER. It covers Bihar and Uttar Pradesh from Achnera in the west to Katihar in the east, and moves traffic for Nepal. It provides a vital link to the northeastern states of the country.

## Passenger and freight operations

In 1999-2000 originating passenger journeys totalled 187 million, of which 49.67 per cent were on broad gauge, for 35,867 million passenger-km. Originating freight amounted to 2.57 million tonnes, for 6,792 million tonne-km.

## Improvements to existing lines

Conversion to 1,676 mm gauge of NER's entire trunk route from Lucknow to Katihar was completed before the current programme. This had greatly improved rail access to Assam, while regauging of the Bhatni–Varanasi line simplified interchange of freight with the Central, Eastern and Northern railways.

Under the current programme, conversion of Burhwal-Sitapur (98 km), Varanasi–Allahabad (125 km) and Mankapur–Katra (90 km) has been completed. In addition, the Rampur–Kathgodam conversion/construction project enabled introduction of direct broad-gauge trains between Kathgodam and Delhi/Calcutta. Conversion of the Muzaffarpur–Raxaul section in 1994-95 has provided a direct broad-gauge route from several Indian ports to Nepal. During 1995-96, 208 km of metre-gauge route was converted, and conversion of the Mau–Shahganj and Sagauli–Narkatiaganj sections was completed in 1996-97. Conversion of the 72 km Bachwaya–Hajipur section was completed in 1997-98 and the 159 km Narkatiaganj–Gorakhpur and 55 km Indara–Phephna sections were completed in 1998-1999. Rs576 million has been allocated in the 2001-02 budget for further conversions. Due to the broad-gauge conversion of important rail sections, many metre-gauge sections have been isolated. Rail bus services have been provided in such sections.

Another major project is restoration of the line to Bagaha (29 km), completion of which is facilitating economic development in the area. The work involved construction of an 896 m road/rail bridge over the Gandak river. The railway's portion of the work on the bridge was completed in 1996.

## Traction and rolling stock

In March 2000 NER operated, on metre gauge, 129 diesel locomotives, 1,400 passenger coaches and 3,766 wagons (7,089 four-wheel equivalent); and on broad gauge, 143 diesel locomotives, 1,841 passenger cars and 2,657 wagons (5,600 four-wheel equivalent).

*UPDATED*

## RAILWAY SYSTEMS/India

## Northeast Frontier Railway (NFR)

Maligaon, Guwahati 781 011, Assam
Tel: (+91 361) 57 04 22   Fax: (+91 361) 57 11 24

### Key personnel
General Manager: B M S Bisht
General Manager, Construction: G R Madan
Additional General Manager: S P Chaudhury
Financial Adviser and Chief Accounts Officer:
  Mrs S Chonbey
Senior Deputy General Manager: M K Dev Varma
Chief Commercial Manager: A K Das
Chief Operating Manager: P Maluya
Chief Engineer: B K Agarwal
Chief Electrical Engineer: B S Dungriyal
Chief Mechanical Engineer: V D Sharma
Chief Signal and Telecommunications Engineer:
  C P Verma
Controller of Stores: S K Sen
Chief Personnel Officer: P K Sharma
Chief Public Relations Officer: Ms U Hazarika

Gauge: 1,676 mm; 1,000 mm; 610 mm
Route length: 1,575 km; 2,105 km; 87 km

### Organisation
NFR serves the whole of Assam and North Bengal, parts of North Bihar, the states of Arunachal, Manipur, Meghalaya, Mizoram, Nagaland, Sikkim and Tripura. Its 610 mm gauge component is the world-famous Darjeeling–Himalaya Railway. In December 1999, this mountain railway became the second line to be accorded 'World Heritage Site' status by UNESCO.

Besides playing a vital role in the transport of people and essential commodities, NFR is also of strategic importance, since the region is practically enveloped by international borders. NFR covers one of the most picturesque regions, overlooked by the Himalayas. Apart from serving well-known tourist centres like Darjeeling, Shillong and the wildlife sanctuaries of Kaziranga, Manas and Jaldapara, it also covers the vast tea-garden belts of North Bengal and Assam. From Darjeeling to Dibrugarh, several stretches of NFR are prone to damage by floods or landslides during monsoons. To maintain this vital communication link with the least interruption has always been a challenging task.

### Passenger and freight operations
Direct mail/express trains link Guwahati with Delhi, Mumbai, Bangalore, Calcutta, Chennai, Patna, Lucknow, Kanpur, Varanasi, Allahabad, Cochin and Trivandrum. In January 1998, the Delhi–Guwahati Rajdhani Express was extended once a week to Dibrugarh. In FY1999-2000 originating passenger traffic totalled 21.2 million journeys, for 6,654 million passenger-km.

Inward freight traffic consists mainly of essential commodities such as food grains, salt, sugar, cement and steel. Outward traffic, which is smaller in volume, comprises petroleum products, coal, bamboo, timber, jute, tea, and dolomite. In FY1999-2000 revenue-earning originating traffic totalled 6.25 million tonnes and 7,004 million tonne-km.

### New lines
Since 1979 NFR has had an independent construction organisation which has given a boost to the development of the railway network in the region. Present policy is to build rail links between the capitals of the region, and accordingly construction of a 119 km line from Kumarghat to Agartala was included in the 1996-97 budget and construction work on this project started in November 1998. During 1999-2000, construction of a new line between Goalpara and Kamakhya (124 km) was completed.

An important project was construction of the second rail/road bridge across the Brahmaputra river at Jogighopa, along with 142 km of broad-gauge line from Jogighopa and Goalpara and thence to Guwahati. The 2.3 km bridge and line from Jogighopa to Goalpara (20 km) was inaugurated in April 1998. A field survey and geotechnical investigation have been completed for a third rail/road bridge over the Brahmaputra at Bogibeel. The estimated cost is Rs10 billion.

### Improvements to existing lines
In 1998-99, conversion to broad gauge of the Mariani–Jorhat (18 km) and Sibsagar–Moranhat (39 km) sections was completed. Conversion of New Jalpaiguri–Siliguri–New Bongaigaon was approved in 1999 and work is in progress on several other sections. An outlay of Rs1,245 million has been provided in the FY2001-02 budget.

### Traction and rolling stock
At the start of 2000 NFR was operating, on 1,676 mm gauge, 116 diesel locomotives, 1,025 passenger cars and 11,917 wagons (four-wheel equivalent); on 1,000 mm gauge, 128 diesel locomotives, 548 passenger cars and 7,838 wagons (four-wheel equivalent); and on 610 mm gauge, 14 steam locomotives, 37 passenger cars and four wagons.

**Type of coupler in standard use:** Passenger cars, screw; freight cars, CBC/screw type
**Type of braking in standard use:** Vacuum

### Signalling and telecommunications
Signalling and telecommunications works are in progress throughout the region. The latest works programme includes laying of optical fibre cable on the Furkating–Tinsukia–Dibrugarh route at a cost of Rs187 million. Intra Voice Response System (IVRS) equipment has been installed at Guwahati and New Jalpaiguri stations, providing reservation status and availability information. IVRS was also being commissioned at other major stations. An outlay of Rs309 million for signalling and telecommunications works has been provided in the 2001-02 budget.

### Track
**Rail:** Flat-bottom 52, 44.61, 37.13, 29.76, 24.8 kg/m
**Crossties (sleepers):** Wood, steel trough, concrete
**Thickness:** Wood: BG, 127 mm; concrete, 210 mm
MG, 114 mm
NG, 114 mm
**Spacing**
Main lines: BG, 1,540/km
MG, 1,596/km
NG, 1,230/km
Branch lines: BG, 1,309/km
MG, 1,344/km
**Fastenings:** Wooden sleepers: CI/MS bearing plates and rail screws
Steel trough sleepers: loose jaws with keys
Cast-iron sleepers: keys
Concrete sleepers: elastic rail clips
**Max gradient:** BG 0.64%; MG 2.7%; NG 4.344%
**Max permissible axleload:** BG 22.9 tonnes; MG 12.7 tonnes; NG 7.6 tonnes

*Combined rail and road bridge over the Brahmaputra river at Jogighopa on the Northeast Frontier Railway*
2000/0089098

**UPDATED**

---

## Northern Railway

Baroda House, Kasturba Ghandi Marg, New Delhi 110 001
Tel: (+91 11) 338 72 27   Fax: (+91 11) 338 45 03
Telex: 3166329

*Northern Railway dmu (K K Gupta)*   2002/0114656

### Key personnel
General Manager: S Dhasarathy
Additional General Manager: K K Gupta
Senior Deputy General Manager: I P S Anand
Financial Adviser and Chief Accounts Officer:
  C S Saroy
Chief Commercial Manager: Jayanta Rai
Chief Engineer: S M Singla
Chief Mechanical Engineer: R N Aga
Chief Electrical Engineer: S C Nagpal
Chief Operations Manager: S B Bhatachariga
Chief Signal and Telecommunications Engineer:
  R L Arora
Chief Administrative Officer, Construction:
  S R Ujaiayan
Controller of Stores: Om Parkash
Chief Personnel Officer: Raj Kumar
Chief Public Relations Officer: Mrs C Mukherjee

Gauge: 1,676 mm; 1,000 mm; 762 mm
Route length: 9,104 km; 1,665 km; 261 km

Electrification: 1,239 km of 1,676 mm gauge at 25 kV 50 Hz AC

### Organisation
NR's territory extends from Delhi through Punjab, Haryana, Himachal Pradesh, parts of Jammu and Kashmir, Rajasthan and Uttar Pradesh states.

### Passenger and freight operations
In 1999-2000, the railway recorded 435 million originating passenger journeys, 72,778 million passenger-km, 34.56 million tonnes of originating revenue freight and 52,189 million tonne-km.

Eight out of 14 pairs of Shatabdi Express trains of the entire IR system run over NR and all 14 pairs of Rajdhani Express services originate or terminate in the Delhi area, which handles nearly 0.65 million passengers daily. NR operates over 450 special trains to different parts of the country during the summer season and over 80 special services during the Durga Puja holiday period. NR is now operating six pairs of 24-coach trains to increase passenger-carrying capacity. NR has introduced the facility of booking train tickets via the telephone. A Rail Credit Card system, launched in association with a multinational bank, has been introduced for this purpose.

NR carries food grains from the Punjab and Haryana to almost all parts of the country, and loads 1,400 to 1,500 wagons daily during harvest.

### New lines
Work on the new broad-gauge line from Jammu to Udhampur (53 km) is in progress. The project, which has high embankments, deep cuttings and a 2.5 km tunnel, is due to be completed by the end of 2001. It has been decided to extend this line from Udhampur to Srinagar and Baramula via Katra as a national project. An outlay of Rs1,901 million has been provided in the FY2001-02 budget for this and other new line projects. Work is also in progress on 83.74 km on the Nangal–Talwara broad-gauge project.

### Improvements to existing lines
Double-tracking works on the Muradnagar–Meerut city (29.5 km) and Gaziabad–Hapur sections was completed during FY2000-01 and work on several other sections is in progress. An outlay of Rs680 million for track-doubling projects has been provided in the FY2001-02 budget. During 1999-2000 electrification of 74 route-km, including that on Lucknow–Kanpur, was completed. Electrification of the Ambala–Kalka section was completed recently and work on the Ludhiana–Amritsar and Ambala–Moradabad sections was in progress in 2001.

Gauge conversion work was in progress on several sections, for which an outlay of Rs332 million has been provided in the 2001-02 budget, and Rs4,456 million has been provided for track renewals during this period.

### Traction and rolling stock
At the start of 2000 the railway operated on broad gauge 287 electric and 618 diesel locomotives, 67 emu motor cars, 136 emu trailers, five diesel railcars, 4,920 passenger cars and 25,334 freight wagons (48,667 four-wheel equivalent).

### Signalling and telecommunications
NR has installed the world's largest route relay interlocking (RRI) at Delhi main railway yard, for which it has been awarded a certificate by Guinness World Records Ltd.

Eleven stations on the Delhi–Ambala section have been equipped with networked dataloggers. These send data to a central computer where the data is processed and analysed to generate online reports which assist in monitoring the health of the signalling system.

*Passenger service hauled by a Class WAP3 electric locomotive (K K Gupta)*    2002/0114655

Besides fitting of track circuits to enhance operational safety, major works in progress on NR include: replacement of interlocking equipment at intermediate stations; replacement of route relay interlocking at Kanpur; provision of similar equipment at Tundla to replace existing signalling equipment; installation of train-to-control mobile communications on the Delhi–Ludhiana section; replacement of analogue by digital microwave; and provision of optical fibre cables.

In the 2001-02 budget, an outlay of Rs639 million has been provided for NR signalling and telecommunications works.

*UPDATED*

## South Central Railway

Rail Nilayam, Secunderabad 500 371, Andhra Pradesh
Tel: (+91 842) 735 83

### Key personnel
General Manager: N Krithivasan
Additional General Manager: C Ramakrishna
Senior Deputy General Manager: Ramesh Chandra
Financial Adviser and Chief Accounts Officer:
  N Krishnamurthi
Chief Administrative Officer (Construction): K Rangarajan
Chief Commercial Manager: B N C Segan
Chief Engineer: R K Sarkar
Chief Electrical Engineer: S C Goel
Chief Mechanical Engineer: Mahesh Chandra
Chief Signal and Telecommunications Engineer:
  R Sivaramakrishna
Chief Operating Manager: S B Ghoshdastidar
Controller of Stores: C M Pagar
Chief Personnel Officer: R K Rao
Chief Public Relations Officer: P Krishnaiya

Gauge: 1,676 mm, 1,000 mm
Route length: 5,623 km, 1,481 km
Electrification: 1,503 km of 1,676 mm gauge at 25 kV 50 Hz AC

### Organisation
SCR was set up in 1966 from portions of the Southern and Central railways. It covers the states of Andhra Pradesh and Goa, northwest Karnataka and southwest Maharashtra and Tamil Nadu.

### Passenger and freight operations
The principal raw material moved is coal, which in 1999-2000 accounted for 36.1 per cent of revenue freight. Other major bulk freight flow is iron ore from the Hospet-Bellary region to Chennai for export, which the railway moves in 4,500-tonne unit trains. Many new industries are arising in SCR territory, including steelworks, cement plants and a fertiliser plant at Kakinada, which promise considerable traffic growth. In the eight years from 1988, cement traffic increased by 51 per cent.

In FY1999-2000 originating revenue freight traffic grossed 51 million tonnes and 32,370 million tonne-km.

SCR has no considerable suburban traffic, relying mainly for passenger growth on improved intercity services. In FY1999-2000 originating traffic totalled 152.5 million journeys and 33,073 million passenger-km.

Prestigious Rajdhani Express services were introduced from Delhi to Secunderabad in January 1998. In 1999, the reservation system at Secunderabad was networked with those at New Delhi, Calcutta, Chennai and Mumbai, enabling reservations to be made to any station on the IR network.

### New lines
Construction of the new 35 km Karimnagar–Peddapali line has been completed. It opened to goods traffic in April 2000 and to passenger traffic in February 2001.

In the works programme for 1997-98, approval was given for construction of a 222 km line between Munirabad and Mehboudnager costing Rs4.39 billion. In the works programme for 2000-01, approval was given for the construction of a new line between Kotipalli and Narsapur (58 km) at a cost of Rs3.3 million. In 2001-02 an outlay of Rs651 million has been provided for work on new lines.

### Improvements to existing lines
Double-tracking of several sections is in progress. During 1998-99, track-doubling of 45 km was completed. Patch doubling of the Gooty–Renigunta section has been approved in the 2001-02 works programme at a cost of Rs3.04 billion. Gauge conversion work is in progress on several sections, with Muraj–Hubli (279 km) and Dinakonda–Giddalur (84 km) completed in 1994-95. In 1995-96, 1996-97, 1997-98 and 1998-99, gauge conversion of sections totalling 244 km, 223 km, 282 km and 15 km respectively was completed. When regauged throughout, the Goa–Hospet–Guntur line will provide a direct broad-gauge route between the east and west coasts. Gauge conversion of the Purna–Akola section (269 km) was approved in the 2000-01 works programme at an estimated cost of Rs2.28 billion.

In 2001-02 an outlay of Rs565 million has been provided for gauge conversion works.

### Traction and rolling stock
At the start of 2000 the railway operated on 1,676 mm gauge 277 electric and 446 diesel locomotives, 3,452 coaches and 47,728 wagons (four-wheel equivalent); and on metre-gauge 54 diesel locomotives, 351 coaches and 2,932 wagons (four-wheel equivalent).

### Electrification
In 1995-96, electrification of 166 route-km was completed, and in 1996-97 electrification of the entire 366 km Vijayawada–Vishakhapatnam portion of the Howrah–Chennai main line along the east coast was completed. Electrification of the Renigunta–Guntkal–Hospet section and the Toranagallu–Ranjitpura branch (448 km in total) has been frozen at present and funds diverted to other works. A new depot with capacity for 100 electric locomotives was opened in Lallaguda during 1995-96.

*UPDATED*

## South Eastern Railway

11 Garden Reach Road, Kidderpore, Calcutta 700 043
Tel: (+91 33) 439 12 81    Fax: (+91 33) 439 78 26
Telex: 021 2417 cosy

### Key personnel
General Manager: M C Srivastava
Additional General Manager: A K Roy
Senior Deputy General Manager:
  M R Ramkrishnan
Financial Adviser and Chief Accounts Officer:
  D Lakra
Chief Operating Manager: V K Sahay
Chief Commercial Manager: B Deb
Chief Mechanical Engineer: V Anand
Chief Engineer: S P S Jain
Chief Electrical Engineer: B M Lal
Chief Personnel Officer: G D Brahma
Chief Signals and Telecommunications Engineer:
  S C Gupta
Controller of Stores: A K Mukhopadhyay

Gauge: 1,676 mm; 762 mm
Route length: 6,278 km; 1,145 km
Electrification: 3,296 km at 25 kV 50 Hz AC

## Organisation
SER was created in 1955 and is the successor to the Bengal Nagpur Railway. It serves six states: West Bengal, Bihar, Orissa, Andhra Pradesh, Madhya Pradesh and Maharashtra.

## Passenger and freight operations
In 1999-2000, originating passenger traffic totalled 209.3 million journeys, of which 36 per cent was suburban, for 24,298 million passenger-km. SER is endeavouring steadily to improve and augment its passenger service levels, both by strengthening existing popular trains and by introducing additional services. During 2000-01, it has introduced six new express trains and two main line emus. It is also planning to increase the composition of popular trains to 24/26 coaches and emu rake size to 12 coaches from the existing 9/10 coaches.

SER originates over one-third of Indian Railways' total freight; 85 per cent of the railway's earnings come from freight traffic, which amounted to 166.58 million tonnes originating in 1999-2000. It is known as the 'blue chip' railway, serving all seven integrated steel plants and related mining belts, seven major coalfields, three major ports and a large number of aluminium, cement and fertiliser plants. In 1999-2000 its operating ratio was 76.5 per cent – the lowest of all Indian railways – and it achieved a surplus of Rs12.71 billion.

A new station in Calcutta for SER suburban trains is being built at Shalimar, and the city is also gaining a new freight terminal at Sankrail.

## New lines
Several major construction schemes have been in progress. To serve the new Vishakhapatnam steelworks, a 164 km line from Koraput to Rayagada was commissioned in 1995 at a cost of Rs4.85 billion. To improve access to Paradip port, provision of a bypass between Sambalpur and Talcher (174 km) was completed in 1998 at a cost of Rs4.64 billion. Construction work between Daitari and Banspani (155 km) is also making steady progress.

Development of Orissa is the objective of a major new route approved in the 1994-95 budget at a cost of Rs3.5 billion. This will link Khurda Road with Bolangar, 289 km distant. An 87 km line for Tamluk to the coast at Digha will benefit the tourist trade in West Bengal.

It was also proposed in the 1995-96 budget to start construction of a new line between Dallijahara and Jagdalpur (235 km) for transport of iron ore to Bhillai steelworks. It is being built on a shared-cost basis, with SER's portion being Rs1.28 billion.

An outlay of Rs1,490 million has been provided in the 2001-02 budget for these and other new line projects.

## Improvements to existing lines
Double-tracking of 29 km was completed in 1999-2000. Work is in progress on doubling or tripling several other busy sections for which an outlay of Rs1,338 million has been provided in the budget for 2001-02.

With completion of conversion of the 111 km Nagbir–Chandafort section, gauge conversion of the entire Gondia–Chandafort narrow-gauge line (242 km) was completed in 1997-98 at a cost of Rs2.42 billion. Conversion of Rupsa–Bangaposi (89 km) and the 285 km Gondia–Jabalpur (including Balaghat) narrow-gauge line at a cost of Rs4 billion is in progress. An outlay of Rs732 million has been provided in the 2001-02 budget for these and other gauge conversion projects.

## Traction and rolling stock
In March 2000 SER was operating on 1,676 mm gauge 507 electric and 557 diesel locomotives, 96 emu power cars and 208 trailers, 3,611 coaches and 117,888 wagons (four-wheel equivalent); and on its 762 mm gauge lines 70 diesel locomotives, 297 coaches and 1,368 wagons (four-wheel equivalent).

*Electrically hauled SER freight service* (K K Gupta)
*2002*/0114657

## Electrification
During 1999-2000 electrification of 126 route-km was completed.

## Track (BG)
**Rail:** 60, 52, 44.6 kg/m
**Crossties (sleepers):** Steel 106 mm thick; CST/9 122 mm thick; concrete 210 mm thick; timber 125 mm thick
**Spacing**
On straight track: 1,660/km, 1,540/km
On curves (438 m); 1,660/km, 1,540/km
**Fastening:** Elastic on cwr, conventional elsewhere
**Max gradient:** 2%
**Max axleload:** 22.86 tonnes

*UPDATED*

# Southern Railway

Park Town, Chennai 600 003
Tel: (+91 44) 535 41 41   Fax: (+91 44) 535 14 39

## Key personnel
General Manager: Ajit Kishore
Additional General Manager: S Gopalakrishnan
Senior Deputy General Manager:
  T Stanley
Financial Adviser and Chief Accounts Officer:
  V Vishwanathan
Chief Operating Manager: R Jayaram
Chief Engineer: P P Kunhikrishnan
Chief Mechanical Engineer: J K Kohli
Chief Commericial Manager: M Anauth
Chief Personnel Officer: P Murugan
Chief Electrical Engineer: D K Bansal
Chief Signals and Telecommunications Engineer:
  V Jayaraman
Controller of Stores: Hari Jeevan Alva
Chief Public Relations Officer: S Sridhar
Chief Administrative Officer, Construction: P S Iyer

Gauge: 1,676 mm; 1,000 mm
Length: 4,574 km; 2,570 km
Electrification: 1,188 km of 1,676 mm gauge at 25 kV 50 Hz AC; 166 km of 1,000 mm gauge at 25 kV 50 Hz AC

## Organisation
SR extends from Mangalore on the west coast and Kanya Kumari in the south to Renigunta in the northwest and Gudur in the northeast.

## Passenger and freight operations
Revenue freight traffic in FY1999-2000 amounted to 29.5 million originating tonnes for 15,787 million tonne-km.

Originating passenger traffic in FY1999-2000 grossed 423 million journeys and 40,458 million passenger-km. To meet increasing passenger demand, many important trains are now operated with 24 coaches. During summer 2001, SR ran over 454 special trains to handle holiday traffic.

As part of control office computerisation, SR has developed a Live Train Position Display System (LTPDS) and installed it at Chennai Central.

## New lines
The surface/elevated rapid transit between Chennai Beach and Luz was inaugurated in October 1997. The extension of the rapid transit line from Luz to Vellachery (10.3 km) was expected to be completed by 2002.

The new broad-gauge line between Penukanda and Puttaparthi was inaugurated on 22 November 2000. During 2001-02 a budget of Rs620 million has been provided for new line projects.

## Improvements to existing lines
As part of the gauge conversion project between Chennai Beach and Tiruchchirappalli, a parallel broad-gauge line has been opened between Beach and Tambaram (29 km). During 1998-99 conversion of Tambaram–Tiruchy (303 km), Tiruchy–Dindigul (93 km) and Mysore–Hassan (119 km) was completed and during 1999-2000

*Emu on the Southern Railway's recently completed Chennai Beach–Luz rapid transit line*   0019830

conversion of 80 km was completed. There are several other sections on which conversion work is in progress. In the 2000-01 works programme, conversion of two more sections, Tiruchy–Mana Madurai (150 km) and Villupuram–Kapadi (161 km), was approved, at an estimated cost of Rs1.75 billion each. In the 2001-02 budget an outlay of Rs456 million has been provided for conversion projects.

Track-doubling of several busy sections was in progress in 2001. An outlay of Rs1.56 billion has been provided for doubling projects in 2001-02.

SR is making rapid progress in track modernisation, with some 3,344 km already laid with concrete sleepers. A computerised track management system is being introduced on high-speed routes. During 1996-97 a total length of 6,344 km of track, including welds, was tested ultrasonically.

### Electrification
During 1999-2000 electrification of 35 route-km was completed. Electrification of the 324 km Erode–Palghat–Ernakulam section has since been completed.

### Traction and rolling stock
At March 2000 the railway operated on 1,676 mm gauge 201 electric and 389 diesel locomotives, 107 emu power cars and 259 trailers, 4,350 coaches and 30,045 wagons (four-wheel equivalent); and on metre-gauge 8 steam, 123 diesel and 20 electric locomotives, 69 emu power cars and 161 trailers, two diesel railcars, 956 coaches and 2,899 wagons (four-wheel equivalent).

In 1994-95, the railway introduced diesel push-pull trains to provide suburban-style services in non-electrified areas between Bangalore, Tumkar, Whitefield and Mysore, and on the Guruvayur–Ernakulam–Alleppey–Kottayam–Quilon route. During 2000-01 main line emu services between Arakkonam and Jolarpettai were introduced.

*UPDATED*

## Western Railway (WR)

Churchgate, Mumbai 400 020
Tel: (+91 22) 200 56 70   Fax: (+91 22) 201 76 31

### Key personnel
General Manager: V D Gupta
Additional General Manager: B S Kushwaha
Senior Deputy General Manager: S S Godbole
Chief Engineer: M S Ekbote
Chief Administrative Officer, Survey and Construction:
  Vinod Kumar
Chief Commercial Manager: S K Pande
Chief Electrical Engineer: V N Garg
Chief Mechanical Engineer: V Nanda
Chief Signal and Telecommunications Engineer:
  S Ramasubramanian
Chief Personnel Officer: S P Vatsa
Financial Adviser and Chief Accounts Officer:
  Sunita Awasthi
Controller of Stores: Arvind Kishore
Chief Operating Manager: V N Jaitley
Chief Public Relations Officer: Vinod Asthana

Gauge: 1,676 mm; 1,000 mm; 762 mm
Route length: 4,716 km; 4,427 km; 874 km
Electrification: 1,715 km at 25 kV 50 Hz AC; 63 km at 1.5 kV DC

### Organisation
Formed in 1951, WR is India's second-largest railway. It serves the whole of Gujarat state, most of Rajasthan and parts of Maharashtra, Madhya Pradesh, Haryana and Uttar Pradesh.

### Passenger operations
The railway is IR's busiest passenger carrier and its most profitable component, with an operating ratio of 81.51 per cent in FY1999-2000. WR covers the commuter network of Mumbai, running over 900 emu commuter trains daily and bringing a morning peak flow of almost 450,000 passengers into the city's Churchgate terminal, where trains arrive at 1.8 minute intervals.

Since 1960 greater Mumbai's population has trebled and WR's suburban passenger journeys soared from 236 million to 1,014 million in 1999-2000. But it has not been possible to raise the number of trains operated in proportion. Consequently, some peak-hour trains, with a seating capacity of only 900 or so, carry 3,000 to 3,500 commuters each. Some relief has been provided by raising the standard train formation from 9 to 12 cars, and more than 70 such sets are now in operation.

During 2000-01, WR introduced new long-distance trains between Okha and Dehradun and Ahmedabad and Nagpur, in addition to several other express trains, and increased the frequency of its two Rajdhani express trains to Delhi.

In 1999-2000, originating passenger journeys totalled 1,335 million, for 71,577 million passenger-km. Computerised reservation has now been extended to almost all major stations.

### Freight operations
WR was the first of the Indian railways to cater for container traffic in 1966, and current services include dedicated trains from Mumbai to the New Delhi dry port at Tughlakabad. WR also operates a guaranteed transit Mumbai–New Delhi wagonload service under the title 'Speed-Link Express'. Most of WR's bulk commodity unit trains, like three of the country's other major bulk-hauling railways, are now made up to 4,500-tonne formations of BOX-N wagons with double-headed locomotive power. In 1999-2000, originating freight traffic amounted to 35.9 million tonnes, for 41,600 million tonne-km.

### New lines
A major work in progress is a new 316 km line between Godhra and Indore, targeted for completion in December 2002. Total expenditure of Rs301 million has been provided for new line projects in the FY2001-02 budget.

### Improvements to existing lines
During 1994, a fifth track was completed between Mumbai Central and Santacruz to raise capacity for commuter trains. Extension of a fifth track from Santacruz to Andheri has been completed, and quadrupling between Borivali and Virar is in progress under the same scheme. During 1999-2000, renewal of 406 km of track was carried out. Provision of Rs2.85 billion has been made in the budget for FY2001-02 for track renewals.

Conversion of the important metre-gauge route between Delhi and Ahmedabad (934 km), the major portion of which is in WR's zone, was completed in April 1997. In addition, gauge conversion is in progress over several sections in Rajasthan and Gujerat, including Agra Fort–Bandikui (152 km) and Bhildi–Viramgram (157 km), which were approved in the 1997-98 works programme. An outlay of Rs1.15 billion has been provided in the 2001-02 budget for gauge conversion schemes.

### Traction and rolling stock
In March 2000 the railway was operating on 1,676 mm gauge, 324 electric and 361 diesel locomotives, 254 emu power cars and 491 trailers, 2,868 coaches and 41,995 wagons (four-wheel equivalent); on metre-gauge, 238 diesel and 23 steam locomotives, 1,169 coaches and 6,011 wagons (four-wheel equivalent); and on 762 mm gauge, 22 diesel and four steam locomotives, 124 coaches and 46 wagons (four-wheel equivalent).

### Signalling and telecommunications
Various signalling and telecommunications works in progress in 2001 include: provision of track circuits in station yards; block proving by axle-counters; replacement of existing electromechanical interlockings by panel interlocking, some of which will be SSI; provision of 4/6 quad cable and optical fibre cable; replacement of route relay interlockings at Bandra and Mahim; replacement of analogue microwave by digital microwave; provision of a train management system on the heavily used Churchgate–Virar section; and provision of a mobile train communications system. Some of the projects approved in the recent works programme include: interlocking of 85 level crossings; provision of automatic signalling on the Vadodra–Anand section; provision of axle-counters for block clearance proving at 24 stations; provision of optical fibre cable for the entire 1,250 km Mumbai–Mathura main line; and provision of data loggers at 34 stations for predictive maintenance. An outlay of Rs387 million has been provided for signalling and telecommunications in the FY2001-02 budget.

### Electrification
Work to convert the Mumbai suburban area 1.5 kV DC traction power supply system to 25 kV AC has been undertaken and the same is to be completed between Borivali and Virar in 2001. At that time special AC/DC emu rakes will be put into service.

### Coupler in standard use
Passenger cars: Screw
Freight cars: Centre buffer couplers and screw coupling

### Braking in standard use
Loco-hauled stock: Vacuum and air; emu: air

### Track

**Rail, types and weight**

| Broad-gauge | Type/specification |
|---|---|
| Flat bottom | |
| 65 kg steel rails | Gost 8160 & 8161.56 |
| Wear-resistant rails | |
| 60 kg/m | UIC 860/0 grade 'C' |
| Wear-resistant rails | |
| 52 kg/m | UIC 860/0 grade 'B' |
| Medium manganese | |
| flat bottom 60, 52 | IRS speen T12 |
| and 44.6 kg/m | |
| *Metre-gauge* | |
| Medium manganese | |
| 44.6, 37.1 and | IRS speen T12 |
| 29.7 kg/m | |

**Sleepers:** Wooden, cast-iron, concrete and steel sleepers. The standard now adopted for high-speed trunk routes is concrete

**Concrete:** Monobloc, thickness at centre 180 mm, thickness at rail level 210 mm, length 2,750 mm. With elastic rail clips

**Wooden**
1,676 mm gauge 2,750 × 250 × 130 mm
1,000 mm gauge 1,800 × 200 × 115 mm
762 mm gauge 1,500 × 180 × 115 mm

**Steel/cast-iron:** CST-9 for 1,676 and 1,000 mm gauge
**Spacing:** 1,660/km high-speed routes; 1,310 to 1,540/km other routes
**Max curvature:** 10° (175 m radius) on 1,676 mm gauge (BG)
**Max gradient:** 2.9% on BG
**Max axleload:** 22.9 tonnes on 1,676 mm gauge

*UPDATED*

---

# INDONESIA

## Department of Transport

8 Medan Merdeka Barat, 10110 Jakarta Pusat
Tel: (+62 21) 35 15 96; 36 13 08   Fax: (+62 21) 36 13 05

### Key personnel
Minister: Agum Gumelar

*UPDATED*

## Indonesian Railway Public Corporation (Perumka)

Perusahaan Umum Kereta Api
Jalan Perintis Kemerdekaan, 1, Bandung 40113, Java
Tel: (+62 22) 43 00 31; 430 39; 430 54
Fax: (+62 22) 43 00 62; 503 42

### Key personnel
Chief Director: Dr Anwar Suprijadi
Corporate Secretary: S Sonny
Director, Personnel: A S Harsono
Director of Finance: E Haryoto
Director of Marketing: T B Padmadiwirja
Director of Operations: Adi Witjaksono
Director, Technical: S E Saputro
Chief of Planning and Development: S Siregar
  Accounting: Hadijono
  Development: Soegeng G
  Way and Works: P J Sujatno
  Signalling and Telecommunications: M Iyad
  Workshops: Soeparman

# RAILWAY SYSTEMS/Indonesia

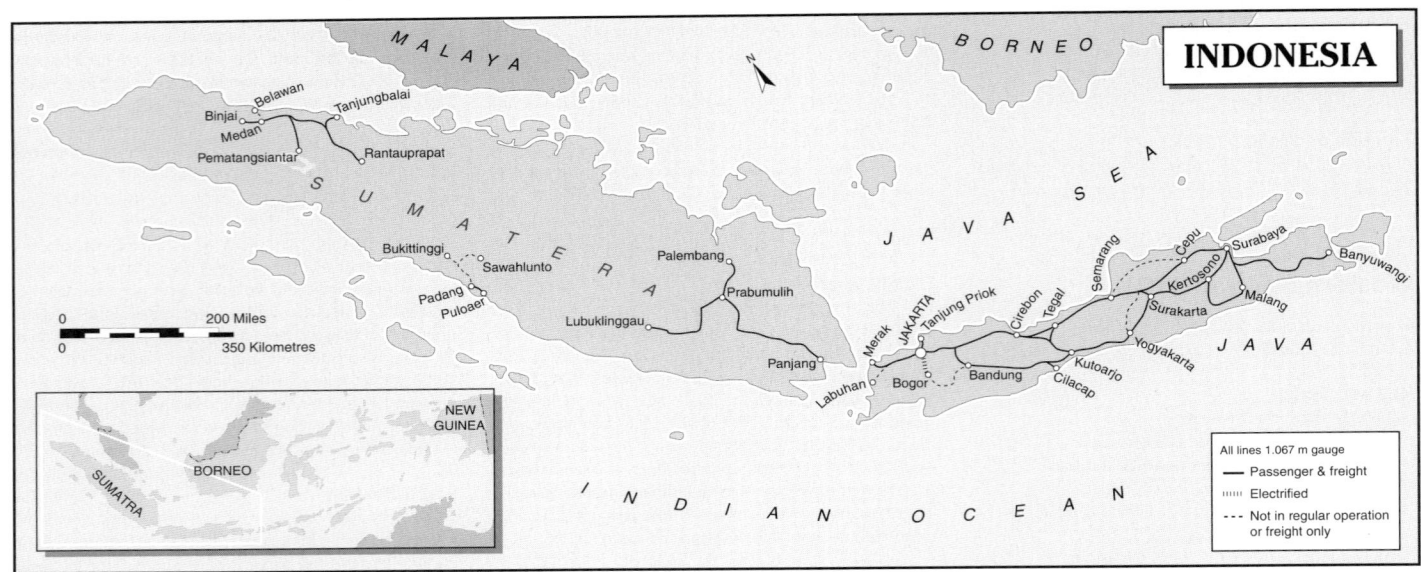

Traction: Soekamto
Rolling Stock: N Sumarna

Gauge: 1,067 mm; 750 mm
Route length: 5,961 km; 497 km (partly undergoing gauge conversion)
Electrification: 125 km at 1.5 kV DC

## Organisation

The railway network in Indonesia is confined to two islands: Java, where the main system of some 4,967 km is located, and Sumatra.

## Political background

Perumka's current concern is to overtake past shortfalls in investment so as to satisfy rising demand for its services. It has been helped by a government decision in 1992 to accept responsibility for maintenance of the railway infrastructure.

This followed liberalisation in 1991, when Perumka was released from full government control to become a public corporation, a move that was completed in 1992. It has commercial freedom in all but fixing third-class passenger fares; those remained under government control and at levels unvaried since 1984. Perumka also gained freedom to borrow in the domestic banking market.

Starting in 1992, Perumka planned to make some of its more intensively used lines in Java accessible to private passenger and freight service operators. The railway would continue to run its own services in competition with any private-sector entrepreneurs. The primary aim of the move was to satisfy rising demand for transport without straining Perumka's own resources. The first such private service started in late 1995.

## Passenger operations

Perumka draws almost two-thirds of its income from a passenger business that has steadily increased since the 1970s. In 1991 this sector recorded 66 million journeys and 10,417 million passenger-km, rising spectacularly to 95.4 million journeys and 12,224 million passenger-km in 1993. But with more than one-third of total volume represented by third-class travel at government-controlled fares in the Jakarta area, the growth has not been matched by a commensurate increase in revenue.

A through-ticketing deal agreed in 1992 with the Indonesian national airline Garuda is seen as one way of helping Perumka regain the business travellers lost to internal air services. Some upgrading of 'Eksekutif' class coaches has been undertaken and a few new vehicles ordered, but major purchases must await the fruits of Perumka's new flexibility to charge market fares for better quality accommodation.

A start was made during 1995 with introduction of a new faster service between Jakarta and Surabaya, christened JS950 in commemoration of the fiftieth anniversary of the national railway. Cutting four hours off current timings, the trains are formed of GE locomotives and a new fleet of coaches built locally by PT Inka.

## Freight operations

Annual freight carryings have soared even more strikingly, from 800 million tonne-km in 1982-83 to almost 4 billion in

### Diesel locomotives

| Class | Wheel arrangement | Power kW | Speed km/h | Weight tons | First built | Engine | Builders Transmission | Repowering |
|---|---|---|---|---|---|---|---|---|
| CC 200 | Co-Co | 1,200 | 90 | 96 | 1951 | GE 12V 244E | E | Alco 12V 250 (4 locos) |
| CC 201 | Co-Co | 1,450 | 100 | 82 | 1976 | GE 7 FDL 8 | E | |
| BB 200 | A1A-A1A | 650 | 120 | 74.8 | 1956 | GM 8567CR | E | |
| BB 201 | A1A-A1A | 1,000 | 120 | 78 | 1964 | GM G12 567C | E | |
| BB 202 | A1A-A1A | 745 | 100 | 65 | 1968 | GM GL8 645E | E | |
| BB 203 | A1A-A1A | 1,290 | 100 | 78 | 1978 | GE 7 FDL 8 | E | |
| BB 204 | B-2-B | 745 | 60 | 55 | 1982 | MTU 12V 396 TC 12 | H Voith hydrostatic | |
| BB 300 | B-B | 500 | 75 | 36 | 1956 | MB 820 B | H | |
| BB 301 | B-B | 1,120 | 120 | 52 | 1962 | MTU 12V 652 TR 11 | H L630 r U2 | MB 12V 652 TB11 (23 locos) |
| BB 302 | B-B | 820 | 80 | 44 | 1969 | MTU 12V 493 | H L520 r U2 | |
| BB 303 | B-B | 860 | 90 | 44 | 1971 | MTU MB12V 493 | H L52 r U2 | |
| BB 304 | B-B | 1,120 | 120 | 52 | 1974 | MTU 12V 652 | H L720 r U2 | |
| BB 306 | B-B | 640 | 75 | 40 | 1983 | MTU 8V 396TC 12 | H L4 r 42 U2 | |
| C 300 | C | 260 | 30 | 30 | 1964 | MB 836 B | H L203 U | |
| D 300 | D | 250 | 50 | 34 | 1956 | MB 836 B | H 2WIL1.15 | GM 8V92 (40 locos) |
| D 301 | D | 250 | 50 | 28 | 1960 | MB 836 B/2 | H 2WIL1.5 | GM 8V71 (6 locos) GM 12V 71 (6 locos) MWM TD 232V12 (13 locos) |

### Electric railcars or multiple-units

| Class | Cars per unit | Motor cars per unit | Motored axles/car | Output/motor kW | Speed km/h | First built |
|---|---|---|---|---|---|---|
| MCW 5 | 4 | 2 | 4 | 230 | 120 | 1976 |
| VCW 8 | | 2 | 4 | 230 | 120 | 1978 |
| BN-Holec | 4 | 2 | 4 | 180 | | 1993 |
| Hyundai-ABB | 4 | 2 | 4 | 180 | | 1993 |

*New station on the Jakarta—Merak line, on which upgrading was completed in 1996*

### Diesel railcars or multiple-units

| Class | Cars per unit | Motor cars per unit | Motored axles/car | Power/motor kW | Speed km/h | First built | Builders Engine | Transmission |
|---|---|---|---|---|---|---|---|---|
| MCDW 300/ MCW 300 | 1 | 1 | 4 | 160 | 90 | 1964 | 8V 71 | H Diwabus |
| MCW 301 | 2 | 2 | 2 | 135 | 90 | 1976 | DMH17H | H TC 2A |
| MCW 302 | 2 | 2 | 2 | 215 | 90 | 1978 | DMH17SA | H TCR 2-5 |

1993, when freight tonnage reached 15.7 million. This reflects the rapid advance of the country's liberalised economy, which has generated a 26 per cent rise of non-oil exports and a 12 per cent growth of non-oil manufacturing since 1983. Long-term estimates show an even more substantial rise than that envisaged for passenger traffic, with 35 million tonnes forecast by 2005.

### Intermodal operations

A recent feature in the freight sector has been intermodal development, which has increased ninefold since 1987 to over 24,000 TEU a year. The government plans creation of five rail-connected inland container terminals to serve maritime container traffic. To maximise potential, however, more track improvement is required and also some work on clearances, which in at least one area restrict the railway to movement of standard ISO container sizes.

Over its 180 km main line between Bandung and Jakarta Perumka runs a weekly unit train for maritime containers to American President Lines' charter. For domestic traffic Perumka's four 17-wagon container trains run daily each way between the port of Tangjungpriok, near Jakarta, and the Gedebage terminal near Bandung. Another container train plies between Cigading port and Bekasi, on the outskirts of Jakarta. A 17 km line has been built from Tangjungpriok to Cakung for the benefit of container traffic.

### Improvements to existing lines

The country has substantial coal reserves, which the government sees as a major source of exports, as well as fuel for much-needed additions to electricity-generating capacity and for cement manufacture.

The first major investment in Perumka's bulk freight capability was a US$1.3 billion project to upgrade the 410 km 1,067 mm gauge route in Sumatra for 40-wagon unit train movement of 2.5 to 3 million tonnes of coal a year from the Bukit Asam field to a new south coast port of Tarahan, for shipment thence to an electricity-generating station near Merak in West Java. Parts of the route are also used by other bulk freight flows. The works raised maximum permissible axleloadings from 13 to 18 tonnes and line speed to 60 km/h for freight and 90 km/h for passenger trains. Mechanical signalling was retained, but traffic control by single-line token has been superseded by radio control through a new UHF/VHF radio network.

The Bukit Asam-Tarahan port coal haul could eventually gross 12 million tonnes a year. The investment needed and the operational economics of quadrupling the scheme's present design capacity have been studied by a Canadian consultancy.

The Sumatran coal railway from Padang to Solok has been upgraded, as has the 120 km line from the port of Merak, west of Jakarta, to Serpong (needed for coal destined for a cement works at Cibinong in West Java).

In 1999 it was announced that the Asian Development Bank was to assist in financing a feasibility study into the reopening of the 486 km line from Langsa to Banda Aceh, on the northern tip of Sumatra. Total cost of rehabilitating the line, which runs through a region which has witnessed fighting between separatists and government security forces, is estimated at US$540 million.

*Jakarta–Merak upgrade*

In late 1996, Davy British Rail International Ltd (DBRI) completed the rehabilitation of the 120 km rail link between Jakarta and Merak, in a £45 million contract for Perumka.

The project involved the design of a new 30 km spur linking with the Jakarta–Merak line, and complete rerailing with 140 km of new R42 continuously welded rail, to give a traffic speed of 80 km/h. Other tasks included rehabilitating 14 existing stations and creating three new ones, with associated trackwork, and uprating 70 bridges – including masonry substructures and steel superstructures – to take increased axleloads.

In addition, the project team installed a new colourlight signalling system (based on centralised traffic control – CTC), a VHF utility radio system and a lineside telephone system; and provided a signalling and telecommunications training centre. Civil works comprised improvements to the track alignment, drainage and earthworks; and reballasting.

### Traction and rolling stock

In 1992 Perumka was operating 563 diesel locomotives, 30 four-car emus, 147 diesel railcars, 1,262 passenger cars and 12,683 freight wagons.

PT Inka, the BN Division of Bombardier Eurorail of Belgium and Holec of the Netherlands agreed joint production of seven four-car emus for the Jakarta suburban network, delivered in 1993. The first three trains were assembled by BN (now Bombardier Transportation) in Belgium, the remainder locally by PT Inka. A further 25 sets have been built by BN.

Meanwhile, Hyundai of Korea supplied two prototype four-car emus, of which the asychronous motors, GTO thyristors and Micas S power control system were provided by ABB.

Local builder Inka, in collaboration with Hitachi, in 1997 commenced delivery of 24 four-car emus for Jabotek services. The 1.6 kV DC stainless steel-bodied units feature AC traction motors and VVVF inverter control.

Passenger car needs, to cope with severe overcrowding in third class and satisfy government requests for more business travel capacity, comprised 420 economy class, 55 executive class and 245 business class coaches. Inka continues to meet this demand, in 1997 supplying 10 economy class and 18 executive class coaches. Bogies for 30 coaches for the Jakarta-Surabaya run were supplied by GEC Alsthom.

A further 24 diesel railcars were ordered from Mitsubishi/Hitachi.

In 1997 Inka was supplying Perumka with 118 coal hopper wagons.

### Signalling and telecommunications

Over 2,580 route-km is equipped with Siemens & Halske mechanical tokenless block, located at some 300 centres in Java and 45 in Sumatra. All-relay interlockings are operational at numerous traffic centres.

Under an A$115 million contract, Westinghouse Brake & Signal of Australia has installed new colourlight signalling controlled by the Westrace system on the 300 km route between Cirebon on the north coast and Yogyakarta in the southeast. Computerised signalling master control and communication centres are being established at Cirebon, Yogyakarta and Purwokerto; all 43 stations on the route have local control centres. One problem has been what to do about the many unofficial crossings on the line; under the old mechanical system, cans of stones suspended from the signal wires rattled when the signal changed, warning crossing keepers to drop bamboo barriers over crossings. This system will not be feasible with colourlights and how these crossings will be controlled, or if they will be allowed to continue in existence, has yet to be established.

Westrace signalling is also being installed on 130 km between Tasikmalaya and Kroya in central Java.

The railway's first solid-state interlocking has been installed by GEC Alsthom, along with Sigview ATC, to control a critical 20 km section of the Tanggerang line in suburban Jakarta.

### Electrification

The 1.5 kV DC electrified system in Java covers the line between Jakarta and Bogor (55 km) and some sections around the city of Jakarta. It is planned to expand electrification under the Jabotabek scheme into a regional network of nine lines and some 220 km embracing the satellite cities of Bekasi and Tanggerang.

So far work has chiefly concerned track renewal, double-tracking and installation of some new halts and signalling improvements. For example, GEC Alsthom Signalling was contracted in 1992 to modernise signalling on the 25 km Tanah Abang- Serpong line. Electrification proceeds – but slowly – on the Tanggerang line and also on the western line from Jakarta to Manggarai, where it is now operational over the new elevated alignment opened in 1992. Rolling stock shortages prevented immediate utilisation of this route for a 12 minute interval service between Jakarta and Gongondia.

Two further phases of the scheme were authorised in 1995, including rebuilding more track on elevated alignment.

In 1998, the Indonesian government announced proposals to electrify main lines on Java, with Japanese companies invited to finance and equip the scheme.

### Track

**Standard rail**
R54 54-43 kg/m; R50 50.4 kg/m; R14A 42.59 kg/m; R14 41.52 kg/m; R3 33.4 kg/m; R2 25.75 kg/m
750 mm gauge: R10 16.4 kg/m
600 mm gauge: ID 12.38 kg/m
**Crossties (sleepers):** Wood 130 mm thick; concrete 195 mm thick; steel 100 mm thick
**Spacings:** 1,666/km plain track, 1,700/km curves
**Rail fastening:** Rigid: dog or screw spike for R2 rail; Klem plate KI/KK for R42 rail; Klem plate KE/KF for R2 rail; Dorken spike; double elastic spring clip F type with rubber pad; double elastic Pandrol clip and rubber pad; single elastic Pandrol clip
**Max gradient:** 2.5%; 7% (rack sections)
**Min curvature radius**
Main line: 300 m
**Max altitude:** 1,246 m near Garut, Java
**Max axleload**
Main line: 14 tons

---

# IRAN

## Ministry of Roads & Transportation

PO Box 15185-1498, Shahid Kalantary Building, Tehran
Tel: (+98 21) 646 41 57   Fax: (+98 21) 564 70 86

### Key personnel
Minister: Dr Rahman Dadman
Vice Minister: Mohammad Saeidnejad

*UPDATED*

## Islamic Iranian Republic Railways (RAI)

Rahahane Djjomhouriye Eslami Iran
Shahid Kalantari Building, Rah Ahan Square, Tehran 13185-1498
Tel: (+98 21) 564 39 46   Fax: (+98 21) 565 05 32
e-mail: rail-rai@neda.net
Web: http://www.irirw.com

### Key personnel
Vice Minister, Roads and Transportation, Chairman and President, RAI: Mohammad Saeidnejad
Board Member and Acting President: Abbas Pourbasir
Board Member: Hormoz Ghotbi
Vice President, Planning and International Affairs: Seyed Hassan
Board Member, Vice President, Technical and Infrastructure: Abdolmajid Shahidi
Board Member, Managing Director, Raja Passenger Trains Co: Mohsen Pour Seyed
Vice President, Finance and Administration: Hassan Najafi
Vice President, Operations and Movement: Noureddin Aliabadi
Director General, International Affairs Bureau: Ali Jahandideh

# RAILWAY SYSTEMS/Iran

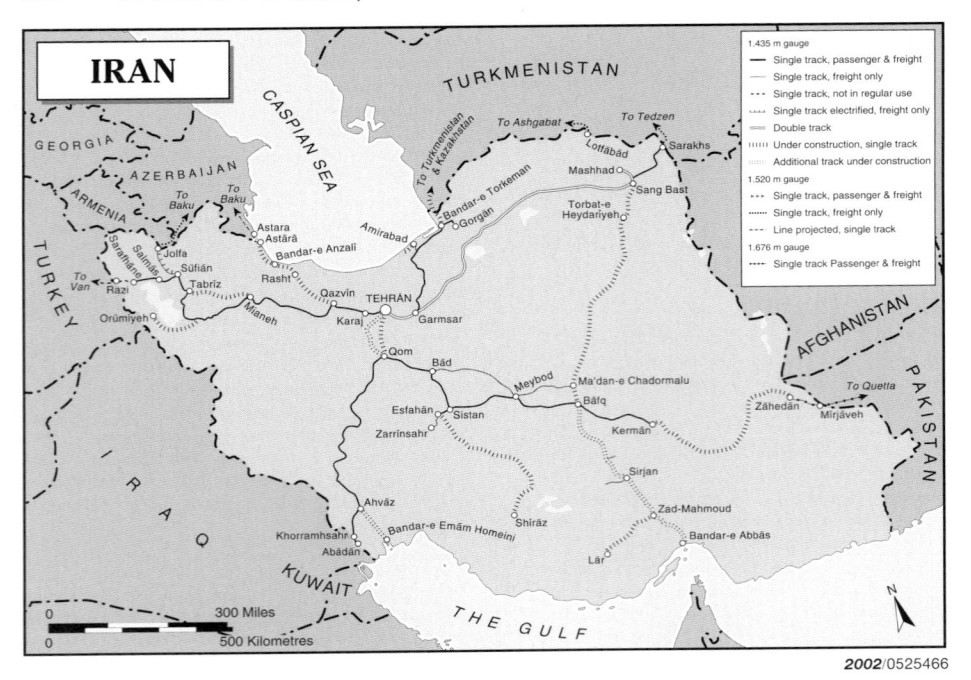

Director General, Statistics and IT Bureau:
Hassan Askarzadeh
Director General, Public Relations: Hamid Sediqpour

Gauge: 1,435 mm; 1,676 mm
Route length: 7,066 km; 94 km
Electrification: 146 km at 25 kV 50 Hz AC

## Political background
The structure of the railway was changed in 1990 from that of a state-owned entity to a limited company affiliated to the Ministry of Roads and Transport.

Restructuring has been based on decentralisation to 13 regional managements, with a split also effected between infrastructure and operations. Eventually, it is aimed to allow access to RAI tracks for private operators.

Market orientation was another key principle of the restructure. In the freight sector this has been marked by capacity increases to fit the railway for its role as a carrier of transit traffic, and development of door-to-door arrangements with improved intermodal transhipment.

Other priorities include improved facilities for staff training, including the establishment of a railway college, adoption of computer-based data transmission systems for strict vehicle control, and investment in mechanised track maintenance equipment.

## Organisation
RAI's key routes run from the ports of Bandar Khomayni and Khorramshar on the Persian Gulf to Tehran; from the capital northwest to Razi on the Turkish border and Djolfa on the Azerbaijan border. Tehran also radiates lines northeastward to Bandar Turkhman the Caspian sea port of Amirabad, Mashhad and Sarakhs on the Turkmenistan border, and southeast to Bafq, Kerman and the port of Bandar Abbas. Other key lines run southwest from Tehran to the Persian Gulf at Bandar-e-Khorramshahr and Bandar Emam Khomeini. Further to the southeast is a still isolated 94 km 1,676 mm gauge line from Zahedan to the Pakistan border at Mirjaveh, although RAI is constructing a link between this section and its main network.

The electrified part is the final 146 km of the route to Azerbaijan, from Tabriz to Djolfa. The electrification was undertaken by Technoexport and the traction is furnished by eight 3,600 kW locomotives based on Swedish Railways' Rc4. Built by SGP of Austria, the units have ABB electrical equipment.

In 1996 a government-owned affiliate company, Raja Passenger Trains (qv), was established to manage and operate passenger rail services on the RAI network. RAI-owned subsidiaries also include companies responsible for producing the railway's ballast and sleeper requirements.

| Traffic (million) | 1997 | 1998 | 1999 |
|---|---|---|---|
| Passenger journeys | 9.5 | 9.8 | 10.7 |
| Passenger-km | 6,103 | 5,631 | 6,451 |
| Freight tonnes | 24.4 | 21.6 | 23.0 |
| Freight tonne-km | 14,400 | 12,638.0 | 14,082.0 |

## Passenger operations
Passenger services on the RAI network are managed and operated by an affiliate company, Raja Passenger Trains (qv).

## Freight operations
In 2001-02, over 26 million tonnes were carried. Minerals generate 50 per cent of RAI's freight tonnage, oil products 16 per cent. Transit traffic to and from the Central Asian republics is of rapidly increasing importance, and completion of the line from Mashhad into Turkmenistan in 1996 places Iran astride major routes to Europe and the Persian Gulf. RAI anticipated that the opening of the Turkmenistan route and the commissioning of the Bafq–Bandar Abbas line would eventually raise freight tonnage to an annual 33 million tonnes.

## New lines
In 2002 RAI was constructing over 3,000 route-km of new lines, with a further 3,579 km under study.

### Bandar Abbas railway
Construction of a 700 km line from Bafq to Bandar Abbas, to connect the port of Shahid Rajai, iron ore mines of Golegohar, and copper reserves at Sarchesmeh to the existing railway network, was completed in 1995. This strategically important route also provides better access to the Persian Gulf than the line to Korramshahr.

A line running west from the Bafq–Bandar Abbas line at Zad Mahmoud to Lar was reported to be under construction in 1997.

### Silk Road railway
An important new international route opened in May 1996. This is the 180 km connection from Mashhad to Sarakhs on the Turkmen frontier, where it meets the 130 km line built simultaneously from the Central Asian main line at Tajan. Together with the new line to Bandar Abbas, this connection will give the Central Asian republics an important new outlet to the Persian Gulf and Europe. Bogie-changing facilities are provided at Sarakhs, where a free trade zone has been established. A 20 km branch from the line, 135 km from Mashhad, serves an oil refinery at Shahid Hashemi Nejad.

### Other projects
In 1997 RAI opened a 280 km new direct route between Bad and Maybod, reducing by some 100 km the distance between Tehran and Bafq.

Construction continued in 2002 on a 506 km line from Esfahän to Shiraz, Iran's only major city not served by rail. With very difficult terrain to surmount in its last 150 km through the Zagros Mountains and 19 significant tunnels, the line is not expected to be completed until 2004.

Provision of a still shorter route to the Persian Gulf is the aim of a direct Mashhad–Bafq line (800 km). This would reduce the distance from the Central Asian republics to Bandar Abbas by some 1,900 km. Work on the Sang Bast–Torbat-e-Heydariyeh section (148 km) was in progress in 2002.

A 219 km line from Ardakan to iron ore mines at Chadoor-Maloo, in Yazd province, was completed in March 1999 and connected to the network.

A start on another major new line, for which agreement was reached with Pakistan Railways in 1991, was also made in 1997. The two countries are undertaking joint construction of a 539 km line from Kerman to Zahedan, which is at present the terminal railhead of the 1,676 mm gauge cross-border line from Pakistan. While a change of gauge will be necessary at Zahedan, this line will complete a through rail connection between Europe and the Indian subcontinent. In 1999, it was reported that funding problems had slowed the rate of progress on this scheme.

A second link between Iranian and Turkmen networks would result from a Turkmenistan State Railways (qv) plan to construct a 225 km line south from Kizylgaia to Kizytaltrek, and then on to meet the RAI network at either Gorgan or Bandar Torkaman, on the Caspian Sea. Government approval for the Iranian element of the plan was given during 1997.

In northwest Iran a new more direct line is under construction between Mianeh and Tabriz, shortening the distance for traffic to and from Azerbaijan and Turkey. A branch of 180 km from the existing line between these two communities to Orumiyeh was under construction in 2002.

Work was in progress in 2002 on a second route from Iran into Azerbaijan, connecting with that country's line south from Baku to the Caspian Sea port of Astara. Leaving the Tehran–Mianeh line at Quazuin and running via Rasht, this will avoid the need to pass through Armenia using the present route into Azerbaijan via Djolfa.

## Improvements to existing lines
Doubling of track continues on lines where limits of capacity have been reached. Of late this has concerned the Tehran–Mashhad line (926 km), where continuous welded rail is also being provided. This project was completed in June 2002. Double-tracking of the Tehran–Ghom line (151 km) was completed in March 1999 and is to be extended to Esfahän. A second track is also planned for the Ahwaz–Bandar Khomayni (120 km) line.

Improvements to passenger facilities include provision of a new station at Bandar Abbas, construction of a third platform at Mashhad and the provision of additional stations on the Tehran–Qom and Bafq–Bandar Abbas routes.

With the increase of the length of trains and of their tonnage, the loops of all stations on the Tehran–Ghom, Tehran–Mashhad, Andimeshk–Ahwaz and Tehran–Tabriz lines have been lengthened.

## Traction and rolling stock
At the end of 2001 RAI's serviceable motive power fleet consisted of 284 diesel-electric and five electric locomotives, plus three diesel-hydraulic shunters, one dmu and the three Turbotrains bought from ANF-Frangeco in 1982. The wagon fleet totalled 15,158, and there were 898 passenger cars, including 62 restaurant and 345 sleeping and couchette cars. The passenger rolling stock fleet is assigned to RAI's affiliate, Raja Passenger Trains (qv).

At the end of 1997 a major contract was signed with GEC Alsthom for the supply of 100 Type AD43 C 2,880 kW diesel-electric locomotives. This largest-ever export order won by the company will see the first 20 locomotives and subassemblies for the next five manufactured in France. These latter machines and the remaining 75 units will be built by Wagon Pars at its plant at Arak, under a technology transfer arrangement which will also see some component manufacture in Iran. Thirty are to be supplied with modified suspension for passenger use; the remaining 70 will be ballasted to a 23-tonne axleload for freight traffic. First deliveries under this contract took place in July 2002.

RAI has modified and upgraded some General Motors GT26-CW locomotives for 160 km/h operation of passenger services.

In 2000 an order was placed with Siemens Transportation Systems to supply 20 four-car intercity dmus for use on the Tehran–Mashhad route. Five are to be built at Siemens' Vienna facility; the remainder will be supplied in kit form for assembly in Iran by Wagon Pars.

Two five-coach prototype Intercity diesel trains have been bought by Iran from DSB of Denmark; built in 1982, they were the forerunners of the successful Danish IC/3 Class. The two prototypes were refurbished at DSB's workshops in Århus before delivery to Iran in 1995; they have been put into service on the Tehran–Mashhad line.

In March 1998 the first batch of 135 refurbished ex-RENFE passenger coaches was shipped from Spain to Iran.

Many of RAI's freight wagon needs are met by Wagon Pars, but in 1999 the railway stated that it had reached agreement to purchase 1,000 vehicles from manufacturers in the Ukraine.

### Signalling and telecommunications

Recent major signalling projects include:

Shahr Rey (Tehran) –Sharud (Tehran–Mashhad line) (420 km). This is divided into two sections: Shahr Rey–Biabanak (200 km), covering 20 stations; and Semnan–Sharud, also 200 km and covering 12 stations. Both sections are being undertaken by Alcatel SEL AG as the foreign contractor and Maharan as the local supplier.

The 497 km Sharud–Mashhad signalling scheme covers 26 stations and is being undertaken by the Indian company, Ircon.

Siemens is the signalling contractor for the 176 km April–Mohammadieh scheme, which covers five stations. The same company has also been responsible for signalling on the 630 km Bafq–Bandar Abbas line and its 22 stations.

Telecommunication schemes include: the South Project, with NEC, Japan, providing telephone, fax and data transmission facilities over 800 route-km running south from Tehran to Qom, Dow Rud, Andimeshk, Khorramshahr and Bandar Emam Khomeyni; The Bafq–Bandar Abbas Project (630 km) with similar facilities provided by Siemens, Germany. In addition, radio communications systems are being provided by Tait, New Zealand in a phased project covering the following lines: Tehran–Mashhad–Sarakhs; Tehran–Bandar Abbas; Qom–Bandar Emam Khomeyni; Tehran–Jolfa–Razi; and Garmsar–Gorgan.

### Track

**Standard rail**
Type U33 46.3 kg/m (4,511 km installed)
Type IIA, 38.4 kg/m in 12.5 m lengths (149 km)
Type IIIA, 33.5 kg/m in 12 m lengths (109 km)
UIC 50 kg/m in 12.5 m lengths (31 km)
UIC 60 kg/m in 18 m lengths (Zahedan–Mirjaveh) and continuously welded (Mashhad–Sarakhs; Bafq–Bandar Abbas; and Tehran–Garmsar), (4,355 km)
**Rail joints:** 4- and 6-hole fishplates; and welding
**Crossties (sleepers):** Creosote-impregnated hard wood, steel and mono- or twin-block concrete. Wood 2,600 × 250 × 150 mm. Steel 2,550 × 260 × 60 mm. Concrete 2,500 × 290 × 24 mm. A mono-block concrete sleeper production plant at Shahroud was commissioned at the end of 1999.

### Diesel locomotives

| Builder's type | Wheel arrangement | Power kW | Speed km/h | Weight tonnes | No in service | First built | Mechanical | Builders Engine | Transmission |
|---|---|---|---|---|---|---|---|---|---|
| G8 | Bo-Bo | 715 | 84 | 68.4 | 6 | 1958 | GM-EMD | 567C | E |
| G12 | Bo-Bo | 980 | 105 | 72.7 | 49 | 1958 | GM-EMD | 567C | E |
| G18 | Bo-Bo | 746 | 105 | 64.8 | 2 | 1968 | GM-EMD | 567C | E |
| G22W | Bo-Bo | 1,118 | 105 | 77.2 | 24 | 1975 | GM-EMD | 645E | E |
| GT26-CW | Co-Co | 2,235 | 120 | 119.6 | 132 | 1971 | GM-EMD | 645E3 | E |
| GT26-CW2 | Co-Co | 2,235 | 120 | 119.6 | 132 | 1983 | GM Canada | 645E3B | E |
| HD10C | Bo-Bo | 798 | 100 | 69 | 21 | 1971 | Hitachi | 0398TA | E |
| LDE626 | Co-Co | | 100 | 120 | 1 | 1986 | Romania | Asea | E |
| U30C | Co-Co | 2,250 | 105 | 119.7 | 22 | 1992 | GE Canada | 7FDL | E |
| C307I | Co-Co | 2,250 | 110 | 132.1 | 21 | 1993 | GE Canada | 7FDL | E |
| 2M62 | 2 × Co-Co | 2,530 | 100 | 252 | 6 | - | Lugansk | 14D40 | E |
| Secmafer 16 | D | 550 | 60 | 45 | 1 | 1970 | Secmafer | Detroit | H |
| Secmafer 8 | B | 250 | 60 | 25 | 2 | 1970 | Secmafer | Poyaud | H |

### Electric locomotives

| Class | Wheel arrangement | Output kW | Speed km/h | Weight tonnes | No in service | First built | Mechanical | Builders Electrical |
|---|---|---|---|---|---|---|---|---|
| 40-700RCH | Bo-Bo | 3,480 | 135 | 78 | 5 | 1982 | Asea | Asea |

*Bridge on the border with Turkmenistan on the Silk Road route opened in 1996* 0003009

**Spacing:** 1,680/km (Steel 1,600/km)
**Rail fastenings**
Wood sleepers: sole plates, screws and bolts
Steel sleepers: clips and bolts
**Filling:** Part broken stone, and part river ballast; minimum 200 mm under sleepers
**Max curvature:** 7.9° = min radius 220 m
**Longest continuous gradient:** 16 km of 2.8% (1 in 36) grade between Firouzkouh and Gadouk

**Max altitude:** 2,177 m near Nourabad station
**Max axleloading:** 20 tonnes (25 tonnes Bafq–Bandar Abbas)
**Max permitted speed**
**Freight trains:** 55 km/h
**Passenger trains:** 80 km/h
170 km/h on parts of Tehran–Mashhad line, and 160 km/h on other new or upgraded lines

**UPDATED**

## Raja Passenger Trains

Raja Passenger Trains Company
159 Sanaee Street, Karimkhan Zand Avenue, Tehran
Tel: (+98 21) 883 55 75; 831 08 80
Fax: (+98 21) 883 43 40
e-mail: rajard@neda.net
Web: http://www.rajaco-ir.com

### Key personnel

Chairman and Managing Director:
Dr Mohsen Seyyed Aghaee
Directors: Eng Djavad Mosadeghi; Eng Mojtaba Shivapour; Eng Muhammad Moezziddin
Deputy Executive: Eng Abbas Ghorban Ali Beyg
Administration and Finance Deputy: Eng Seyyed Akhavan
Vice-President: Eng Seyyed Mustafa Kheradmand
Technical Deputy: Eng Mojtaba Shivapour

### Organisation

Established in October 1996, Raja Passenger Trains is a government organisation affiliated to Islamic Iranian Republic Railways (RAI) and charged with the operation, marketing and ticketing of all passenger services on the Iranian network. Its wide-ranging brief includes the development and upgrading of the passenger coaching fleet, including participating in the procurement of new locomotives and rolling stock, the development of domestic passenger services and facilities, managing the concessioning of train operations to private-sector companies, encouraging joint-venture projects to develop passenger rail transport in Iran and the development of new routes within Iran and passenger rail links with neighbouring countries. The company is also responsible for recruitment and training.

The company has three main departments, responsible for: operations; technical issues, mainly relating to rolling stock; and administration and finance. In 2001 2,983 staff were employed.

### Passenger operations

Services are operated on five main domestic routes linking major cities in Iran and on three international routes. Some domestic services are operated under concessions let by Raja Passenger Trains; the Simorgh Trains Company and the Sabz Train Company, two of the companies involved, providing train operations and high-quality onboard services.

In 2000-01 passenger numbers grew by 10 per cent to 11.7 million, totalling 7.13 billion passenger-km.

A cross-border service has been established from Tehran to Nakhichevan, Azerbaijan, and since March 2001, in co-operation with Syrian Railways and Turkish State Railways respectively, services have been introduced on Tehran–Damascus and Tehran–Istanbul routes. Future plans include the development of a service linking Tehran and Almaty, Kazakhstan.

### Traction and rolling stock

In 2001 Raja Passenger trains had at its disposal 976 passenger-carrying coaches, as well as 216 service vehicles, including catering cars, parcels/baggage vans and generator cars. Traction is provided by RAI.

Procurement intentions included in the company's structure plan, to be completed by March 2005, include 25 railcars and 20-30 trainsets, the purchase of locomotives and coaches, and the refurbishment of 500 coaches and 600 service vehicles.

## Tehran Urban & Suburban Railway Company

PO Box 4661, 37 Miramad Avenue, Tehran 15874
Tel: (+98 21) 874 01 10  Fax: (+98 21) 874 03 51

### Key personnel

Managing Director: A Ebrahimi

**Gauge:** 1,435 mm
**Route length:** 41 km
**Electrification:** 41 km at 25 kV 50 Hz AC

### Organisation

The Tehran Urban & Suburban Railway was established to develop and construct a 42 km electrified suburban heavy rail system serving the Iranian capital. Running west from the centre of Tehran at Ayatollah Kashani, where interchange is made with Line 2 of the Tehran metro system, the nine-station route provides connections to the satellite cities of Karaj and Mahr Shahr. The line has been constructed and equipped by the China International Trust, Investment and International Co-operation Corporation, the China National Technical Import and Export Corporation and the China North Industry

Corporation. Services began in 1999. An extension to Hashtgerd is planned.

The Chinese organisations are also responsible for the construction and operation of Tehran's four-line metro system.

### Traction and rolling stock
Services are provided by 12 3,200 kW SS5 Bo-Bo electric locomotives built by Zhuzhou Electric Locomotive Works and 48 double-deck coaches supplied by Changchun Railway Car Works, these operating as eight-car push-pull sets with a locomotive at each end.

### Signalling and telecommunications
The line is equipped with TVM300 automatic train control equipment supplied by Ansaldo subsidiary CS Transport under a subcontract placed by China North Industry Corporation.

*Type TM1 electric locomotive built by Zhuzhou Electric Locomotive Works for the Tehran Urban & Suburban Railway Company*
0063748

---

# IRAQ

## Ministry of Transport & Communications
Kanat Street, Baghdad

### Key personnel
Minister: A M Khalil

## Iraqi Republic Railways (IRR)
Damascus Square, Baghdad
Tel: (+964 1) 886 23 80   Fax: (+964 1) 537 22 26

### Key personnel
Director General: Eng Thabit Mahmud Ghareb
Assistant Director General: Eng Adnan Hassan Khalel
Directors
　Civil Engineering:
Eng Mohammed Abdul-Ghafor Al-Alawie
　Traffic and Operations: Eng Salam J Salum
　Mechanical and Electrical Engineering:
　　Eng Sabah R Arab
　Signalling and Telecommunications:
　　Eng Raad Moussa Geafar
　External Relations and Information:
　　Eng Sundus H Selman

Gauge: 1,435 mm
Route length: 2,603 km

### Organisation
Since closure of the metre-gauge network in 1988, IRR's network consists principally of a 1,435 mm gauge main line linking the Persian Gulf port of Um Qasr and Basra with Baghdad, there splitting to form routes to the Syrian border at Husaiba (opened in 1987) and El Yaroubieh. Branches to Kirkuk and Akashat to exploit mineral deposits are also of recent construction.

In 2000 IRR employed 7,385 staff.

| Traffic (million) | 1999 | 2000 |
|---|---|---|
| Passenger journeys | 1.27 | 1.0 |
| Passenger-km | 499.6 | 379.1 |
| Freight tonnes | 2.7 | 3.16 |
| Freight tonne-km | 830.2 | 872.2 |

### Passenger operations
Iraqi railways suffered serious disruption in the 1991 Gulf War and the subsequent international sanctions against the country.

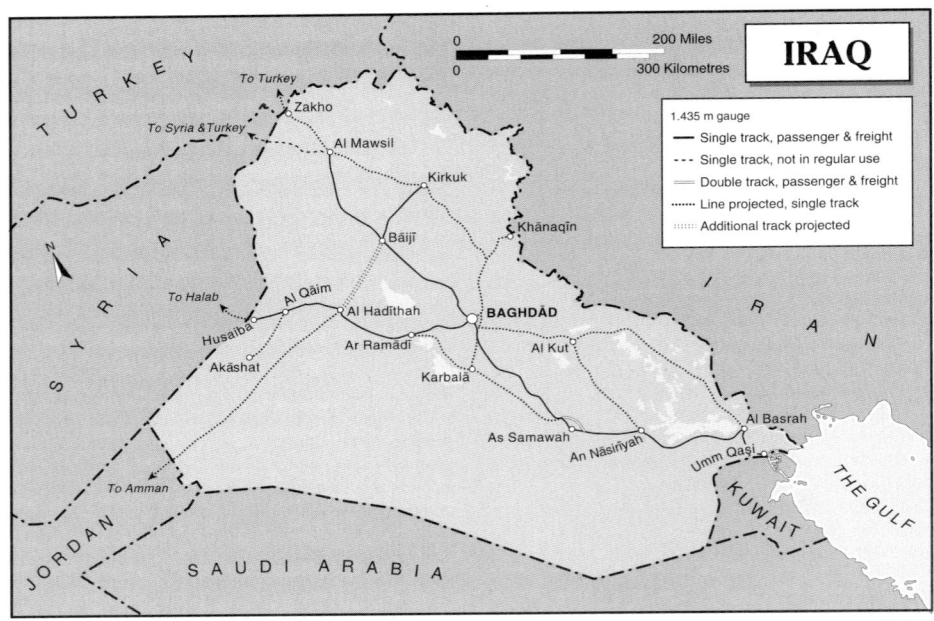

### Freight operations
In 1992 freight tonne-km amounted to no more than 115 million. In 2000 3.16 million tonnes were carried (872.2 million tonne-km).

### New lines
The first of several new line projects, completed in the 1980s, was a 404 km line from Baghdad via Radi and Haditha to the Syrian border at Husaiba, with a 115 km branch from Al Qaim to the phosphate mines at Akashat in the west, so as to link the latter with a fertiliser plant at Al Qaim, in the Euphrates valley. Like all new IRR lines, the Baghdad-Husaiba was engineered for 250 km/h, partly for ease of maintenance in the foreseeable future, when speeds would be limited to 140 km/h for passenger and 100 km/h for freight.

From Haditha on this route a 252 km transversal, built initially as single track with provision for later doubling, was completed via Baiji to Kirkuk in 1987. This project involved bridging the Euphrates, Tigris and Therthar rivers. The line is CTC-controlled with the complement of track-to-train radio and hot box detectors.

### Improvements to existing lines
The situation caused by the imposition of economic sanctions led IRR to seek assistance from India. Under an agreement signed in April 1996, India was to assist in rehabilitation of Iraq's railways and in execution of new projects. Among those cited was upgrading of the Baghdad-Basra route between Baghdad and Samawa.

### Traction and rolling stock
In 2000, the railway was reported to be operating 105 diesel-electric locomotives, 226 passenger cars and some 9,000 freight wagons.

During 2000-01, spare parts for IRR's fleet of 100 Class DES 3100 Co-Co diesel-electric locomotives were supplied by the Czech company Diesel International. The locomotives were originally delivered by ČKD Praha in 1979-82.

*UPDATED*

# IRELAND

## Department of Public Enterprise

44 Kildare Street, Dublin 2
Tel: (+353 1) 670 74 44   Fax: (+353 1) 670 96 33

**Key personnel**
Minister: Mary O'Rourke
Secretary: Brendan Tuohy

*UPDATED*

## Iarnród Éireann (IE)

Connolly Station, Amiens Street, Dublin 1
Tel: (+353 1) 836 33 33   Fax: (+353 1) 836 47 60
Web: http://www.irishrail.ie

**Key personnel**
Chairman: Dr John Lynch
Directors: Paul Cullen, Gerry Duggan, Plev Ellis, Tras Honan, Patrick Lynch, Anne Marie Mannix, Bill McCamley, Paul Prescott, Joe Meagher
Managing Director: Joe Meagher
General Manager, Infastructure Division: Joe Leahy
Manager, IE Freight: S Aherne
Manager, New Business (Freight): Donie Horan
Manager, InterCity: J P Walsh
Manager, Safety: Ted Corcoran
Manager, Human Resources: J Keenan
Manager, Finance and Administration and Company Secretary: Richard O'Farrell
Chief Engineer, Infrastructure: Brian Garvey
Chief Mechanical Engineer: J McCarthy
Manager, Strategic Planning: Tom Finn
Manager, Procurement and Materials Management: Pat Mullan
Manager, Resources and Central Traffic Control: O Doyle
Manager, Media and PR: Barry Kenny
Manager, Network Catering: Tom Mythen
Manager, Suburban Rail: Michael Murphy
Manager, Marketing: Ray Kelly
Manager, Passenger Services (South/West): Willie O'Connor
Manager, Passenger Services (North/East): Bertie Corbet
Manager, Navigator Freight Agency: Shay Hart
Manager, Bulk Freight: Patsy Mee
District Manager, Heuston: Noel McKenna
District Manager, Connolly: Tom Devoy
District Manager, Galway: Gerry Glynn
District Manager, Cork: Tim Sheehan
District Manager, Limerick: Brian Kelly
District Manager, Waterford: Paul Cheevers
District Manager, Suburban: Christy Stapleton
Port Manager, Rosslare Harbour: Walter Morrissey
Freight Manager, East (Dublin): Frank Spellman
Freight Manager, West (Galway): Gerry Mongan
District Freight Manager, Waterford: Peter Roche
District Freight Manager, Cork: Oliver O'Donovan
District Freight Manager, Limerick: Joe Whelan

Gauge: 1,602 mm on cwr track; 1,600 mm on jointed track
Route length (open to traffic): 1,947 km
Electrification: 45.5 km at 1.5 kV DC

### Political background
In late 2000 the government published proposals to restructure public transport in Ireland, with significant likely implications for IE. The proposed reforms foresee the division of IE into two independent companies responsible for infrastructure and operations, with the future possibility of either transferring the operations company to the private sector or of franchising all or some services. Also anticipated is the creation of an independent body to develop major projects in partnership with the private sector, establishing an independent public transport regulator and setting up a safety authority to cover all public rail operations. It was expected that legislation covering these reforms would be introduced in the Irish parliament during 2001. A second reform phase is expected to provide for the establishment as separate companies of the subsidiaries of Córas Iompair Éireann, the state transport holding company and parent of IE.

### Organisation
Iarnród Éireann is responsible for all rail services in the state including the Dublin Area Rapid Transit system. It is also responsible for rail freight and the company's own road freight services, for catering services, and for the operation of Rosslare Europort, which caters for sailings to the UK and the Continent.

At the end of 2001 IE employed 5,897 staff compared with 5,358 in 2000.

### Passenger operations
IE offers a nationwide service of diesel-hauled passenger trains, including a recently upgraded Enterprise service between Dublin and Belfast, while in the Dublin area it operates an electrified suburban system, known as Dublin Area Rapid Transit (DART). The DART system operates over 45.5 route-km electrified at 1.5 kV DC from Bray, south of Dublin Connolly Station, to Howth, in the north, with a fleet of 40 two-car emus. The DART is currently being extended southwards to Greystones and northwards to Malahide. Services over these extensions, which add 7.5 route-km to the network, commenced in April 2000 and June 2000 respectively.

| Traffic | 1999 | 2000 | 2001 |
|---|---|---|---|
| Passenger journeys (000) | 32,765 | 31,721 | 34,206 |
| Passenger-km (million) | 1,457.6 | 1,389.1 | 1,515.3 |
| Freight tonnes (000) | 2,901 | 2,707 | 2,612 |
| Freight tonne-km (million) | 526 | 490.8 | 515.7 |

### Freight operations
IE's major freight customers are the brewing, construction and fertiliser industries. The railway also hauls maritime containers and offers a parcels service known as 'Fastrack'.

Revenue from freight in 2001 increased by 3.0 per cent on the figure for 2000. Traffic increases were achieved in kegs, cement, mineral ores and ammonia distribution.

*Class 8200/8400 1.5 kV emu supplied by Alstom for DART suburban services undergoing commissioning at Dublin Fairview depot (Colin Boocock)*

*Class 201 diesel locomotive at Malahide with a Dublin Pearse—Drogheda service formed with a Mark 3 push-pull set (Colin Boocock)*

## Intermodal operations

Containers form an important part of IE's freight traffic, with around 130,000 TEU carried each year. IE provides daily (Monday to Friday) domestic common-user services between Dublin and Ballina, Dundalk, Galway, Limerick, Sligo, Waterford and Westport. Three common-user services run each day (Mondays to Fridays) between Dublin and Cork.

## Improvements to existing lines

As part of a €546 million safety investment programme, IE is upgrading almost 640 km of track, replacing jointed rail with cwr on concrete sleepers. This will result in improvements to all radial routes from Dublin on the Intercity network. Branch lines are also receiving investment.

The Safety Investment Programme, covering the period 1999-2003, was approved in 1999 by the Minister for Public Enterprise and also covers improvements to bridges and fencing, upgrading of signalling systems and improvements to level crossings.

## Traction and rolling stock

IE's motive power fleet at the start of 2002 consisted of 110 diesel locomotives, 64 dmu vehicles and DART emu. Freight wagons totalled some 1,830, and there were 181 passenger coaches.

In February 1998 IE placed an order with Alstom for five Class 8200/8400 two-car 1.5kV DC emus for DART suburban services. Assembly of the trains, which comprise a motor car plus trailer, was also undertaken in Spain, with delivery completed in 2000. The new vehicles are able to operate in multiple with existing DART stock.

In February 1999 IE placed an order with Mitsui, Japan, for 10 Class 2800 two-car diesel railcars and 16 Class 8500/8600 emu cars for DART services. Delivery of both types was completed in 2000. The Class 8500/8600 vehicles are formed as two two-car half-sets to create a four-car unit.

In 2000 IE ordered 15 Class 2900 four-car dmu vehicles from CAF in Spain. An additional five four-car units were added to the order in 2001.

IE expected to place contracts for the supply of new intercity coaches in 2002.

Talgo-Transtech in Finland received an order to supply 24 container flats by the end of 2001. These were due to enter service on the Dublin—Cork line in late 2002.

## Signalling and telecommunications

The Dublin suburban line is controlled from a computer-based VDU console at Connolly station. The system utilises automatic route-setting and optimisation of public road level crossing closures, the latter being supervised by closed-circuit television. The CTC building also houses a similar console for control of 458 route-km of main line railway. The system permits operation of cab signalling equipment fitted to all locomotives, as well as train radio, and is being extended to cover further lines. In 1997 coverage was extended on the Belfast route to reach the border with Northern Ireland.

DART electric trains in the Dublin suburban area are fitted with Automatic Train Protection (ATP) equipment, activated by coded currents passed through the running rails, detected by coils on the emus and processed on board. Lineside signalling has been retained for diesel-hauled trains on the route.

Locomotives are fitted with a Continuous Automatic Warning System (cab signalling). Both emus and locomotives are fitted with AEG-Telefunken train radio allowing two-way transmission of fixed-message telegrams and voice communication with the controlling signalman at the appropriate CTC centre (suburban or main line). Since 1996 this system has been extended beyond CTC-controlled areas, allowing drivers to maintain communications with local signal cabins at all times. The equipment also permits voice communication between train drivers and on-train staff using hand-held portable radios.

**Type of coupler in standard use:** Passenger cars, buckeye or screw; emus, Scharfenberg and Dellner automatic; freight cars, screw or Instanter

**Type of braking:** Locomotive-hauled stock, vacuum or air

## Track

**Standard rail:** Flat bottom 113, 95, 92 and 85 lb/yd, 54 kg/m, 50 kg/m; bullhead 95, 90, 87 and 85 lb/yd

**Crossties (sleepers):** Timber 2,590 × 255 × 125 mm; concrete 2,475 × 220 × 180 mm

**Spacing:** Concrete 1,144/km straight, 1,556/km curved track; timber, 1,313/km straight, 1,422/km curved track

**Rail fastenings:** Timber sleepers: CI chairs and sole plates; concrete sleepers: H-M (Vossloh) fastenings, Pandrol and H-M (Vossloh) on crossings

**Min curvature radius**
Running lines: 115 m
Sidings: 80 m

**Max gradient:** 1 in 40

**Longest continuous gradient:** 8.45 km, with 1% ruling gradient

**Max altitude:** 165 m at Stagmount, Co Kerry

**Max axleloads:** 18.8 tonnes for locomotives; 15.75 tonnes for wagons; 18.8 tonnes for specific traffic on bogie wagons

### Diesel locomotives

| Class | Wheel arrangement | Power KW | Speed km/h | Weight tonnes | No in Service | First built | Mechanical | Builders Engine | Transmission |
|---|---|---|---|---|---|---|---|---|---|
| 071 | Co-Co | 1,800 | 145 | 102 | 18 | 1976 | GM | GM12-645 E3C | E |
| 121 | Bo-Bo | 700 | 120 | 65 | 11 | 1961 | GM | GM 8-645CR | E |
| 141 | Bo-Bo | 700 | 120 | 68 | 35 | 1962 | GM | GM 8-645 CR | E |
| 181 | Bo-Bo | 820 | 120 | 68 | 11 | 1966 | GM | GM 8-645 E | E |
| 201 | Co-Co | 2,219 | 165 | 112 | 32 | 1994 | GM | GM 12-710G3 B | E |

### Electric multiple-units

| Class | Cars per unit | Motor cars per unit | Motored axles/car | Output/motor KW | Speed km/h | Cars in service | First built | Builders Mechanical | Electrical |
|---|---|---|---|---|---|---|---|---|---|
| 8100/8300 | 2 | 1 | 4 | 130 | 100 | 76 | 1983 | LHB | GEC Traction |
| 8200/8400 | 2 | 1 | - | - | 110 | 10 | 2000 | Alstom | Alstom |
| 8500/8600 | 2 | 1 | - | - | - | 16 | 2000 | Mitsui | - |

### Diesel multiple-units

| Class | Cars per unit | Motor cars per unit | Motored axles/car | Speed km/h | Cars in Service | First built | Mechanical | Builders Electrical | Transmission |
|---|---|---|---|---|---|---|---|---|---|
| 2600 | 2 | 2 | 2 | 110 | 17 | 1993 | Tokyu Car | Cummins NTA 855-R1 | H Niigata DW14G |
| 2700 | 2 | 2 | 2 | 120 | 25 | 1998 | Alstom | Cummins NTA-855 | H Niigata DW14G |
| 2800 | 2 | 2 | 2 | - | 20 | 2000 | Mitsui | Cummins | Niigata |
| 2900 | 4 | - | - | - | 80 | * | CAF | - | - |

*On order in 2001

*Mitsui-built Class 8500/8600 DART emu at Dublin Pearse forming a Howth—Bray service (Colin Boocock)*

*Mitsui-built Class 2800 dmus at Dublin Connolly (Colin Boocock)*

**UPDATED**

# ISRAEL

## Ministry of Transport

97 Jaffa Road, Jerusalem
Tel: (+972 2) 31 92 11   Fax: (+972 2) 31 92 03

### Key personnel
Minister: Efrayim Sne
Director General: Ing Ben-Zion Salman

**UPDATED**

## Israel Railways (IR)

Central Station, PO Box 18085, Tel Aviv 61180
Tel: (+972 3) 693 74 01   Fax: (+972 3) 693 74 80
Web: http://www.israrail.org.il

### Key personnel
Director General: Yossi Snir
Deputy General Directors
  Rolling Stock: Dudu Gabai
  Traffic: Harel Even
  Infrastructure: Yosi Mor
  Marketing: Avi Hefetz
  Finance & Economics: Dror Yaakobson
  Personnel & Human Resources: Isaac Seri
Directors
  Passenger Traffic: (vacant)
  Cargo Traffic: Yosi Carmeli
  Traction and Rolling Stock: Boby Solonikov
  Signalling and Telecommunications: Pinhas Katz
  Infrastructure and Civil Engineering: Illya Volkov

Purchase and Supply: Zur Ezyon
Economics, Budget & Trade: Eli Dalizky
Finance: Roni David
Public Relations and Spokesman: Benny Naor

Gauge: 1,435 mm
Route length: 640 km

### Political background

IR was long operated as a separate economic enterprise by the Ministry of Transport, but in 1988 the system became part of a new public enterprise, the Ports & Railways Authority. One objective was to reallocate some of the former Ports Authority's accumulated funds to railway investment; government policy for the past few years has been to renovate the railway, principally its passenger operations, as an attractive alternative to the rising volume of motor transport. Another aim of the change was to allow the railway more commercial freedom to react to changing market conditions.

In March 1997, IR was separated from the Ports & Railway Authority while remaining under its control. In March 1998 the Israeli government introduced to the Knesset legislation to establish IR as an independent fully state-owned company likely to be known as The Railways Company Ltd, with a nine-member board which would include appointees from National Infrastructure, Transport, and Finance ministries.

For the Rosh-Ha'Ayin—Kefar Saba suburban line in the Tel Aviv area, the government plans to invite tenders for an operating concession.

| Traffic (million) | 1998 | 2000 | 2001 |
|---|---|---|---|
| Passenger journeys | 6.4 | 13 | 15 |
| Passenger-km | 382.7 | - | - |
| Freight tonnes | 9.4 | 10 | - |
| Freight tonne-km | 1,059.8 | - | - |

### Passenger operations

In 1991 the Transport Minister approved investment in passenger services totalling NIS500 million. The railway's development plan, recently updated for the next decade, includes extension of passenger service to new routes and raising train frequency on existing lines. Under IR's 'Railway 2010' development plan, an annual target of 45 million passengers has been set for the end of the first decade of the new millennium. In the shorter term, IR forecasts that, subject to investment being sustained, it will be carrying some 20 million passengers annually by 2003.

Services from Tel Aviv to Be'er Sheva Central were introduced in 2000 following the opening of a new station there during September of that year. Infrastructure work to allow the introduction of suburban services in the Tel Aviv area, initially to the satellite towns of Kefar Sava and Petach Tikva, started in 1999. The new Hof Hacarmel station, opened in 1999, has become the southern terminus of Haifa suburban trains until the future extension to Tirat Hacarmel is completed. It is also to be an outer-suburban stop for main line trains.

In 1999, IR introduced collaboration with bus operators DAN and Egged, which provide bus services both in Haifa and nationally, to introduce a through rail/road ticketing scheme. Subsequently IR has worked with both companies to develop bus feeder services to stations.

### Freight operations

In 2000 the volume of freight rose to 10 million tonnes compared with 9.4 million tonnes in 1998. Rail's current market share is about 15 per cent of the total land transport task in terms of tonne-km, and this should rise as volume is expected to reach 15 million tonnes annually during the next decade.

Dominant traffic is potash from the Dead Sea and phosphates from Oron and Har Zin, which are conveyed

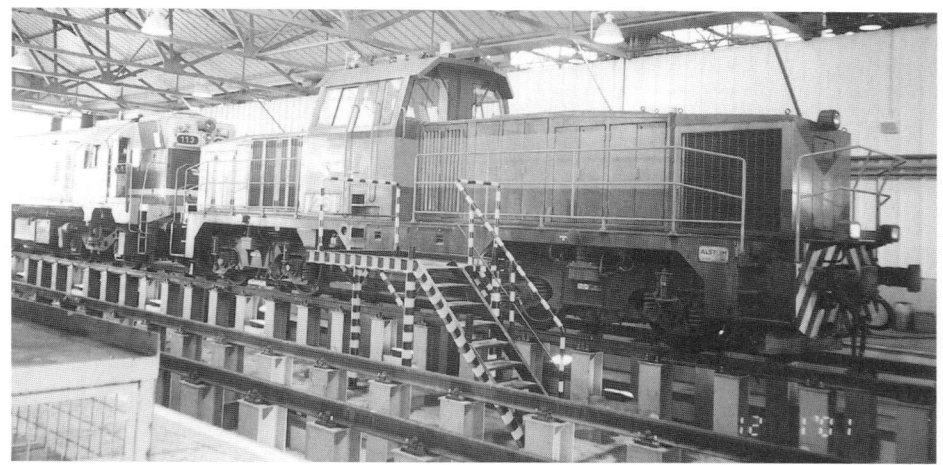

*Alstom GA 900 diesel-electric shunting locomotive in the newly constructed depot at Lod (Aharon Gazit)*

*IC3 diesel trainset leaving Bnei Brek for Tel Aviv (Aharon Gazit)*

# RAILWAY SYSTEMS/Israel

to the port of Ashdod in unit trains of up to 4,000 tonnes (west of Dimona) hauled by two GM Type G26CW 1,640 kW Co-Co diesel-electrics in multiple. Some goes to chemical plants on Haifa Bay, 310 km from Har Zin. For the rest, IR's freight is chiefly bulk movement of containers, grain and oil.

Potash from Sedom on the Dead Sea is carried by rail from Tzefa mainly to the port of Ashdod (155 km), but some for domestic purposes is taken to the industrial area north of Haifa (270 km). IR's coal traffic from the port of Ashdod to Ashqelon power station ceased with the commissioning of a maritime coal terminal at Ashqelon.

In early 1998 the Israeli government decided to switch from road to rail the haulage of domestic refuse from a concentration site at Hiriya, near Tel Aviv, some 150 km south to the Rotem Plain, southeast of Be'er Sheva.

## New lines

In the Tel Aviv area IR plans several lines as part of a developing suburban network, and electrification of some routes is proposed. Projects include: a new 19 km line from Tel Aviv South to Rishon Le-Zion West as part of the Rail 2000 project (see below); a 9 km branch from the Tel Aviv-Lod line to Ben Gurion International Airport, which has government approval. In the longer term, under IR's Master Plan, links are planned from Ramle to Modiin (14 km); Rishon Le-Zion to Ashdod (19 km); and Ben Gurion Airport to Modiin as part of a fast link to Jerusalem. Work on the Ben Gurion Airport link commenced in 2001 and was expected to be complete in 2002.

Master Plan projects also include construction of a new line from Rosh Ha'Ayin to Hadera to provide a north-south route bypassing Tel Aviv, and the creation of lines radiating from Haifa to serve Carmiel, Tamra, and Nazareth.

Design has been approved of a 21 km line in the south from Be'er Sheva to Ramat Hovav, and an extension of this line would complete a projected link to the Egyptian border at Nitsana.

The long-awaited project for a railway to Eilat has been postponed on financial grounds, but remains in IR's Master Plan. Preliminary design has been completed for a 161 km line from Har Tzin to the Red Sea port of Eilat, with a branch to the Jordanian port of Aqaba. A 32 km branch from this line would serve Israel's Sedom potash works at the southern end of the Dead Sea.

In early 1995 an accord was signed between the Israeli and Jordanian governments approving in principle construction of a line extending some 90 km from the port of Haifa to Irbid in northern Jordan, designed to provide access to the Mediterranean for Jordanian import/export traffic. The first section of the route would utilise the derelict alignment of the former Hedjaz Railway branch from Deraa to Haifa, which was closed when Israel was created in 1948.

In late 1996, Israel reached agreement with the autonomous Palestinian authority to restore the long-disused 18 km rail link between Ashkelon and Gaza, although no progress has been made due to the political situation in the country.

## Improvements to existing lines

Double-tracking of the Tel Aviv–Haifa line was completed in 1999 at a cost of NIS68 million. Together with other infrastructure improvements on this route, this has contributed to a cutting the journey time between the two cities to 45 minutes.

Plans to build two new stations on the cross-Tel Aviv 'Ayalon Railway', at Hahagana and University, were implemented in 2001. In November 2001, a third track was commissioned between University and Savidor (Tel Aviv Central) on the Ayalon Railway, increasing capacity by 50 per cent.

Extensive upgrading of existing lines has been under way under IR's Rail 2000 plan, a programme of network developments up to 2010 aimed at substantially increasing the capacity of both suburban and intercity links. Projects in the plan include: rehabilitating the existing Tel Aviv–Petah Tikva–Kefar Saba freight line (29 km) to create a high-density double-track electrified suburban line; either upgrading the existing Tel Aviv–Jerusalem line (87 km) to improve its alignment, or construction of a new 56.5 km double-track line extending eastwards from a 2 km branch off the Tel Aviv–Lod line to Ben Gurion International Airport; double-tracking of the Lod–Rehovot–Ashdod (30.3 km) line; and double-tracking and upgrading the Ramle–Naan (7 km) and Lod–Naan–Be'er Sheva (82 km) lines.

Work on this last scheme started in 1998, when NIS27 million was allocated to it. Resignalling and some realignment of the Lod–Naan section has been undertaken, and the project included reconstruction of Lod station. The project also included provision of a new signalling centre at Lod, commissioned in June 2000, which controls the Tel Aviv–Be'er Sheva line.

By mid-2001 a compromise solution was found for the long-running debate surrounding restoration of a Tel Aviv–Jerusalem rail link. This foresaw immediate reconstruction and upgrading of the existing alignment, which had remained out of use, while design work on a new fast line had been undertaken. However, the Israeli government has not totally abandoned the possibility of the eventual construction of a new Tel Aviv–Jerusalem line. Meanwhile, construction was under way in 2002 of the branch from the Tel Aviv–Lod line to Ben Gurion International Airport, with commissioning planned for July 2003, and initial planning was being carried out for 20 km extension of this line to Mod'in, with construction expected to start in 2003.

In 1999, first moves were made towards developing the Tel Aviv suburban line referred to above when a cornerstone for a new station was laid at the existing facility at Rosh-Ha'Ayin by former Prime Minister Binyamin Netanyahu. This marked the start of conversion of the Tel Aviv–Rosh Ha'Ayin section of the line to Kefar Saba. NIS160 million is being invested in infrastructure work related to this first stage of the scheme, which, when completed, is expected to carry two million passengers annually. Existing track is to be renewed with 54 kg/m rail on concrete sleepers laid on a new trackbed, two stations are to be rebuilt, and one new one, University, is to be constructed. The complete project will create a circular line serving 11 stations in greater Tel Aviv. It is forecast to convey 12 million passengers annually.

Tenders for the upgrading for the restoration of passenger services on the freight-only Be'er Sheva–Dimona line (36 km) were invited in 2001. Also being implemented in 2002 was the construction of a 3.5 km suburban line from Beer-Yaakov, on the Lod–Rehovot line, to Rishon-Le-Zion.

## Traction and rolling stock

Diesel locomotive stock at the end of 2000 comprised 61 main line units and three shunters. A fleet of 24 three-car

*Double-deck push-pull trainsets with Alstom 'Mega' locomotives stabled at Lod (Aharon Gazit)* 2002/0132087

### Diesel locomotives

| Class | Wheel Arrangement | Power kW | Speed km/h | Weight tonnes | No in service | First built | Mechanical | Builders Engine | Transmission |
|---|---|---|---|---|---|---|---|---|---|
| G12 | Bo-Bo | 1,230 | 105 | 76 | 13 | 1954-66 | GM | GM 12-645E | E GM |
| G16 | Co-Co | 1,450 | 107 | 124 | 3 | 1960-61 | GM 567C | GM 16-567C | |
| G26CW | Co-Co | 1,640 | 124 | 99 | 9 | 1971-79 | GM | GM 16-645E | E GM |
| G26CW-2 | Co-Co | 1,640 | 124 | 116 | 6 | 1982-86 | GM | GM 16-645E | E GM |
| GT26CW-2 | Co-Co | 2,200 | 124 | 119 | 1 | 1989 | GM | GM 16-645E3 | E GM |
| T44 | Bo-Bo | 1,230 | 105 | 76 | 1 | 1989 | Kalmar | GM 645E3 | E GM |
| Mega | Bo-Bo | 2,460 | 160 | 90 | 20 | 1998 | GEC Alsthom | GM 12-710G3B | E GM |
| Semi-Mega | Co-Co | 2,460 | 120 | 114 | 8 | 1998 | GEC Alsthom | GM 12-710G3B | E GM |
| GA900 | Bo-Bo | 900 | 80 | 14 | 3 | 1998 | GEC Alsthom | MTU 8V 396 | E GEC Alsthom |

### Diesel railcars or multiple-units

| Class | Cars per unit | Motor cars per unit | Motored axles/car | Rated power kW | Speed km/h | Units in service | First built | Mechanical | Builders Engine | Transmission |
|---|---|---|---|---|---|---|---|---|---|---|
| IC3 | 3 | 3 | 4 | 300 | 160 | 10 | 1992 | ABB-Scania | Deutz | H ZF |
| IC3-2/3 | 3 | 3 | 4 | 300 | 160 | 14 | 1995 | Adtranz Sweden | Deutz | H ZF |
| IC3-4 | 3 | 3 | 4 | 300 | 160 | 8 | 2001 | Adtranz | Deutz | H ZF |

*'Semi-Mega' Co-Co diesel-electric freight locomotive from Alstom in Spain (Aharon Gazit)* 0063308

IC3 dmus was also in operation. Coaching stock totalled 102, including buffet cars and generator cars. Railway-owned freight stock totalled 729 wagons; some 500 privately owned vehicles are also in use.

A significant upgrading of IR's traction fleet was initiated in 1998-99 when deliveries started of an order for 18 2,460 kW GM-powered diesel locomotives placed with GEC Alsthom Transporte of Spain (now Alstom Transport). The order was split into two versions of an essentially common design: 10 90 tonne 160 km/h Bo-Bo ('Mega') units; and eight 114 tonne 110 km/h Co-Co ('Semi-Mega') machines. Subsequently an additional 10 Mega locomotives were added in 2001. In 1998 GEC Alsthom Transporte also supplied three 900 kW Bo-Bo shunting locomotives. These are of the same design as locomotives supplied by the Spanish builder to Swiss Federal Railways. The majority of IR's elderly G12 locomotives were offered for sale in 2001.

In 2001 IR received the first of 14 double-deck three-car push-pull coaching stock sets from Bombardier Transportation's Görlitz plant in Germany. An option exists for 26 additional sets. The driving car of each set includes a generator to provide power for train services.

An additional eight three-car IC3 dmus were due to enter service from September 2001 and orders for seven more were expected. Under licence from GEC Alsthom Transporte, local builder Haargaz assembled 37 loco-hauled coaches, including five with driving cabs for push-pull operation and auxiliary diesel engines providing a train power supply. Older passenger coaches have been refurbished, and most of the fleet is now air conditioned.

### Signalling and telecommunications

In December 2001, IR invited tenders for the supply of a network management and traffic control system for the entire railway. This would take the form of a turnkey project including the supply of a centralised traffic control system and a network supervision centre system.

### Electrification

In November 2001, IR invited tenders for the electrification of its entire network. If approved, the project would be implemented in three phases: a feasibility and economic viability study; an electrification master plan; and the preparation by the selected bidder of a tender to design and implement the scheme as a turnkey project.

**Type of coupler in standard use:** Screw
**Type of brake in standard use:** Air

### Track

**Rail:** 60 kg/m (on order in 2001) 54 kg/m (351 km); 50 kg/m (226 km); 49 kg/m; 46 kg/m; 37 kg/m
**Crossties (sleepers):** Concrete monobloc 300 kg, timber, and steel
**Spacing:** 1,720/km, concrete; 1,666/km, timber and steel
**Fastenings:** Vossloh
**Min curvature radius:** 140 m; 600 m min, new projects
**Max gradient:** 2.68% (Bet Shemesh-Jerusalem)
**Max permissible axleload:** 22.5 tonnes

*UPDATED*

# ITALY

## Ministry of Transport and Infrastructure

Piazzale Porta Pia, I-00198 Rome
Tel: (+39 06) 064 41 21   Fax: (+39 06) 06 44 12 43 08
Web: http://www.infrastruttetrasporti.it

**Key personnel**
Minister: Pietro Lunardi

## Alifana Railway/Benevento–Naples Railway (FABN)

Managed by Government Commission, Rome
Gestione Governata Ferrovie Alifana e Benevento-Napoli
Via Don Bosco, I-80141 Naples
Tel: (+39 081) 599 32 54   Fax: (+39 081) 599 32 53
Web: http://www.alifana.it

**Key personnel**
Government Commissioner: F Giovanni
Director General: G Racioppi
Director, Alifana Railway: A Marescotti
Director, Benevento-Naples Railway: G de Iudicibus

Gauge: 1,435 mm
Route length: FA – 42 km, FBN – 49 km
Electrification: 49 km at 3 kV DC (FBN)

### Organisation

FABN comprises the former Alifana Railway (FA) Piedmonte Matese—Santa Maria Capua Vetere line (42 km) and the Benevento—Naples Railway (49 km), FA trains running through to Naples over FS metals. This line is now being electrified and FA has acquired one Firema Type E82b two-car emu so far. Progress is slow. FA also owns a 950 mm direct line to Naples via Trentola but this has not operated since damage in the Second World War. In 1996 the government agreed to fund 50 per cent (€50 million) of the cost of a new route from Piscinola to Capodichino airport, with the municipality providing an additional €155 million to extend tracks to Garibaldi/Centrale in central Naples. Work began in late 1997.

### Traction and rolling stock

FA operates 16 diesel railcars, three trailers, two diesel locomotives and nine freight wagons. FBN operates three electric locomotives, five electric railcars, one two-car emu, three three-car emus and eight wagons.

*UPDATED*

*FBN emu arriving at Caserta forming a Benevento–Naples service (David Haydock)*

## Appulo—Lucane Railways (FAL)

Corso Italia 6, I-70123 Bari, Italy
Tel: (+39 080) 572 25 11   Fax: (+39 080) 521 16 54
Web: http://www.fal-srl.it

**Key personnel**
Director General: Gaetano Morgese

Gauge: 950 mm
Route length: 183 km

**Organisation**
FAL was one of two railways formed in 1991 by splitting the former Ferrovie Calabro—Lucane into separate operations based on the Bari and Cosenza networks, the latter becoming Calabria Railways (qv). It became an independent company in January 2001. The FAL network connects Bari with Avigliano and Matera. In 1998, the railway achieved 70.2 million passenger-km, down from 78 million in the previous year.

**Traction and rolling stock**
Traction and rolling stock comprises 20 railcars and 22 trailers, six locomotives, 20 coaches and 95 wagons.

*UPDATED*

*FAL railcar at Altamura (Quintus Vosman)*
2000/0089565

## Arezzo Railways (LFI)

La Ferroviaria Italiana
Via Guido Monaco 37, I-52100 Arezzo
Tel: (+39 0575) 398 81   Fax: (+39 0575) 30 09 39
Web: http://www.lfi.it

**Key personnel**
General Manager: Marcello Grillo

Gauge: 1,435 mm
Route length: 85 km
Electrification: 85 km at 3 kV DC

LFI operates frequent passenger services from Arezzo to Sinalunga (40 km) and Pratovecchia Stia (45 km). The company is rebuilding a 5 km section of the Stia line with the intention of increasing speeds, avoiding risk of landslips and generating new freight traffic including block coal trains for a cement plant in Rassina. In 1999, LFI bought three Type AM56 two-car emus from Belgian National Railways and these entered service after refurbishment by Metalmeccanica Milanesio in Moretta.

In 2001 LFI was negotiating the takeover of both regional passenger and freight services over FS lines around Arezzo.

*LFI D341 Bo-Bo diesel-electric locomotive shunting stock at Arezzo (Colin Boocock)*   2000/0089566

The railway operates nine electric and five diesel locomotives, nine electric railcars, 18 trailers and 60 wagons.

*UPDATED*

## Bari-Nord Railway (FT)

Ferrotramviaria SpA-Ferrovia Bari-Nord
Piazza Moro 50B, I-70122 Bari
Tel: (+39 080) 521 35 77
Fax: (+39 080) 523 54 80; 524 36 41

**Key personnel**
President: Dr Oscar Pasquini
Managing Director: Dr Ing Nicola Nitti
Operations Manager: Dr Ing Cesare Soria
Administration Manager: Dr Giambattista Angiuli

Gauge: 1,435 mm
Route length: 70 km
Electrification: 70 km at 3 kV DC

**Organisation**
FT operates the Bari—Barletta line via Bitonto (70 km). The company is doubling much of this line and in 2002 was building a new 5 km line from Bari to San Paulo. This was to be followed by a new 7 km underground loop off the Bari—Bintorto line to serve Bari airport.

In early 2000, FT created a joint venture, known as Rail Traction Company (RTC), with three other partners, aimed at obtaining a licence to operate freight services from Verona to Munich, Germany.

**Traction and rolling stock**
The railway operates two electric and three diesel locomotives, one diesel shunter, 15 electric railcars and 11 control trailers, four coaches and 16 wagons. In 2002, four new three-car emus were on order from Alstom for the San Paulo service.

*UPDATED*

## Bologna—Portomaggiore Railway (FBP)

The FBP was one of four local railways which merged on 1 January 2001 to form the Emilia Rowagna Railway (FER) (qv).

*UPDATED*

## Calabria Railways (FC)

Via Crispi 117, I-88100 Catanzaro
Tel: (+39 0961) 89 61 11   Fax: (+39 0961) 74 70 07
Web: http://www.ferroviedellacalabria.it

**Key personnel**
Director General: Franco Natalizia

Gauge: 950 mm
Route length: 220 km

**Organisation**
FC was one of two railways formed in 1991 by splitting the former Ferrovie Calabro—Lucane into separate operations based on the Cosenza and Bari networks, the latter becoming Ferrovie Appulo—Lucane (qv). It became an independent company in January 2001. The FC network connects Cosenza with San Giovanni in Fiore and Catanzaro. In 1998, the railway achieved 23.9 million passenger-km, down from 25.3 million in the previous year.

**Traction and rolling stock**
Traction and rolling stock comprises 41 railcars and seven trailers, 12 locomotives, four coaches and 56 wagons.

*UPDATED*

Italy/**RAILWAY SYSTEMS** 209

## Casalecchio—Vignola Railway (ATC)

Azienda Trasporti Consorziali, Bologna
Via Saliceto 3, I-40128 Bologna
Tel: (+39 051) 35 01 11   Fax: (+39 051) 35 01 77
Web: http://www.atc.bo.it

**Key personnel**
General Manager: A Claroni
Railway Manager: F Monzali

Gauge: 1,435 mm
Route length: 24 km
Electrification: 3 kV DC

**Organisation**
ATC operates public transport in the city of Bologna as well as serving industrial sidings in and around the city. It became an limited company in 2000. In 1996, the 24 km Casalecchio—Vignola line and the 3 km branch Vignola—Confine were closed for rebuilding with the aim of introduction of a frequent Bologna—Vignola service. Opening of the first section from Casalecchio to Crespellano had been expected in September 2001 but was postponed due to the discovery of important archaeological remains during construction of a new station at Casalecchio.

**Traction and rolling stock**
The railway owns six electric and three diesel locomotives, and seven wagons. ATC has acquired two new Type E122 two-car emus from AnsaldoBreda and five two-car 1950s emus from Belgian National Railways for this service. ATC also has two diesel and five electric locomotives in working order.

*UPDATED*

## Central Umbria Railway (FCU)

Managed by Government Commission, Rome
Ferrovia Centrale Umbria
Largo Cacciatori delle Alpi 8, I-06100 Perugia
Tel: (+39 075) 57 54 01   Fax: (+39 075) 573 52 57
Web: http://www.fcu.it

**Key personnel**
General Manager: Luciano Tortorella

Gauge: 1,435 mm
Route length: 152 km
Electrification: 152 km at 3 kV DC

**Organisation**
In 1998, FCU achieved 41.8 million passenger-km, up from 39.8 km in the previous year.
In 2001 FCU let the contract to re-electrify its network to Alstom, ABB, Bonciane and Sirti. The Perugia Ponte San Giovanni—Perugia Santa Anna section was doubled in 2002.

**Traction and rolling stock**
The railway owns two electric and five diesel locomotives, 42 diesel railcars and 60 wagons. The diesel locomotives mainly haul coal trains from Perugia to Marsciano.

*UPDATED*

## Circumetnea Railway (FCE)

Managed by Government Commission, Rome
Ferrovia Circumetnea
Via Caronda 352A, I-95128 Catania
Tel: (+39 095) 43 10 02   Fax: (+39 095) 43 10 22
Web: http://www.circumetnea.it

**Key personnel**
Director General: Carlo Pino

Gauge: 950 mm; 1,435 mm
Route length: 110 km; 4 km
Electrification: 4 km at 3 kV DC

**Organisation**
This narrow-gauge railway forms an incomplete circle around Mount Etna in Sicily. In 1998, 31 million passenger-km were achieved, down from 36.7 million the previous year.
In June 1999, the on-street section of the railway in central Catania was replaced by a 3.8 km underground, standard-gauge electrified line from Porto to Borgo, where the narrow-gauge line now terminates. There are three intermediate stations. The 'metro' service is provided by three 1957-built OMS-TIBB electric railcars obtained from FCU. FCE received the first of four two-car emus on order from Firema in early 2001.

FCE intends to convert a further 20 km of line, to Paterno, with at least six new stations. There are also plans for a new branch from central Catania to Fontanarossa, 10 km to the north.

**Traction and rolling stock**
The railway operates 32 diesel railcars, 11 trailer coaches and three electric railcars.

*UPDATED*

## Circumvesuviana Railway (SFSM)

Managed by Government Commission, Rome
Gestione Governativa Della Circumvesuviana
Corso Garibaldi 387, I-80142 Naples
Tel: (+39 081) 772 26 72   Fax: (+39 081) 772 24 50
Web: http://www.vesuviana.it

**Key personnel**
Government Commissioner: Dr Ing Gaetano Danese
General Manager: Dr Fernando Rigo
General Secretary: Dr Domenico Sica
Rail Operations Director: Dr Ing Michele di Matteo

Gauge: 950 mm
Route length: 169 km
Electrification: 169 km at 1.5 kV DC

**Organisation**
The Circumvesuviana serves an extensive territory to the east of Naples stretching to Baiano, in the province of Avellino, and to Sarno in the province of Salerno, and also skirts the Bay of Naples to a terminus in Sorrento. The Sorrento branch is largely in tunnel, one of which under Monte Faito is 4.8 km long with a station inside the bore.
In 1998 passenger-km amounted to 349 million, down from 394 million the previous year.
The railway has a continuing programme of heavy engineering works to increase operating capacity and improve operation, see earlier editions of *Jane's World Railways* for details. Plans include: double-tracking of the Sorrento branch between Torre Annunziata and Castellamare di Stabia; double-tracking and realignment of the Sarno branch east of Scafati, a total of 14.5 km; and construction of a new 30 km double-track branch from the Baiano line at Nola to Avellino. Further extensions, double-tracking and realignments have been statutorily authorised, including a new line from Alfa Sud to Acerra.

*Two SFSM three-car articulated emus forming a Naples service at Sorrento (Colin Boocock)*   2000/0089567

**Traction and rolling stock**
The company operates 118 articulated three-car emus, three diesel shunting locomotives, four Bo-Bo electric locomotives, two coaches and 26 wagons.

*UPDATED*

## Cumana & Circumflegrea Railways (SEPSA)

Società per l'Esercizio di Pubblici Servizi Anonima
Via Cisternia dell'Olio 44, I-80134 Naples
Tel: (+39 081) 552 51 21   Fax: (+39 081) 552 02 61

**Key personnel**
General Manager: R Bianco

Gauge: 1,435 mm
Route length: 45 km
Electrification: 45 km at 3 kV DC

**Organisation**
The Cumana (19 km) and Circumflegrea (26 km) railways connect Naples with Torregaveta, serving a densely populated area with an all-day 20-minute service on each branch, doubling to 10 minutes all day within the boundaries of Naples.

## RAILWAY SYSTEMS/Italy

In 1996 the government allocated SEPSA Lit145 billion towards the Lit209 billion cost of the Mostra-Soccavo section of a new line to serve a university at Monte Angelo. Work started in 2001 on a 5.5 km connection with three new stations between Kennedy on the Cumana line and Soccavo on the Circumflegrea line.

### Traction and rolling stock
The railway operates 31 two-car emus, one diesel locomotive and 10 wagons.

*UPDATED*

*Firema-built Type ET 400 emu at Naples Montesanto (David Haydock)*
0063311

## Del Fungo Giera (DFG)

Del Fungo Giera Servizi Ferroviari SpA
Via Borra 35, Livorno
Tel: (+39 058) 682 96 05   Fax: (+39 058) 621 96 08
e-mail: domenico.libro@delfungogiera.com

### Organisation
This well-established transport company, which handles 2.5 million tonnes of freight per year, including 700,000 tonnes by rail, intends to expand into full operation of rail freight services.

### Traction and rolling stock
DFG has signed a contract with Alstom to purchase 50 tri-voltage electric locomotives similar to the SNCF Class BB 36000 and 30 Prima diesel-electric locomotives. Tests with an SNCF BB 36000 took place in May 2002.

*NEW ENTRY*

## Domodossola—Locarno Railway (SSIF)

Società Subalpina di Imprese Ferroviarie
PO Box 60, Via Mizzoccola 9, I-28845 Domodossola
Tel: (+39 0324) 24 20 55   Fax: (+39 0324) 452 42

### Key personnel
General Manager: Ing Daniele Corti

Gauge: 1,000 mm
Route length: 32 km (and 20 km in Switzerland)
Electrification: 32 km at 1.35 kV DC

### Organisation
SSIF operates through services to Locarno jointly with the Swiss railway FART.

### Traction and rolling stock
The railway operates 14 electric railcars, 11 coaches and 27 wagons.

In late 2001, SSIF invited tenders for two panoramic emus.

*UPDATED*

## Emilia Romagna Railway (FER)

Via Zandonai, I-44100 Ferrara
Tel: (+39 053) 297 93 06   Fax: (+39 053) 297 93 14

Gauge: 1,435 mm
Route length: 246 km
Electrification: 48 km at 3 kV DC

### Organisation
On 1 January 2001, four government-controlled independent operators in the province of Emilia Romagna merged to form FER. Participating railways were: the Bologna—Portomaggiore Railway (FBP) (48 km); Padane Railways (FP) (52 km); the Parma—Suzzara Railway (FPS) (82 km) (part of Venete Railways); and the Suzzara—Ferrara Railway (FSF) (82 km). The province also plans to reopen three lines to traffic by 2010: Modena—Vignola (20 km); Ferrara—Copparo (20 km); and Ostellato—Porto Garobaldi (30 km). In addition, there are plans to build a new line linking FBP and FP systems. It has also been reported that at a later date, Reggiane Railways (ATC), ATC Bologna and the Modena—Sassuola Railway (ATCM) could also become part of FER.

In April 2002, FER established a joint venture with ACT Reggio to develop freight in the Emilio Romagna region, especially in the Dinazzano area.

### Improvements to existing lines
In December 2001, the Portomaggiore—Bologna San Vitale line was extended underground to Bologna Centrale at a cost of €50 million.

All lines are to be electrified at 3 kV DC. The Ferrara—Semide—Poggio Rusco section (48 km) went live in March 2002.

FER is to build a line avoiding Ferrara station and eliminating reversals there at a cost of €29 million. The company has also developed a project to build a 25 km line from Adria to Codigaro, thus creating a new through route from Venice to Ravenna.

### Traction and rolling stock
FER owns 18 diesel locomotives and 48 diesel railcars. In April 2001, it took delivery of a rebuilt DB type V100 diesel locomotive.

The company plans to use the recently rebuilt FSF workshops at Sermide for traction and rolling stock maintenance.

In April 2002, FER invited tenders for the supply of three 3,000 kW 160 km/h electric locomotives.

*UPDATED*

*Fiat-built ex-FSF railcars on the Ferrara—Sermide line (Quintus Vosman)*
2000/0089569

## FS Holding SpA

Piazza della Croce Rossa 1, I-00100 Rome
Tel: (+39 06) 441 01   Fax: (+39 06) 44 10 51 86
e-mail: info@fs-on-line.it
Web: http://www.fs-on-line-it

### Key personnel
President: Giancarlo Cimoli

Directors
Finance and Administration: Gabriale Spazzadeschi
Human Resources: Francisco Forlenza
External Relations: Daniela Scurti

### Subsidiaries
Trenitalia SpA
Piazza della Croce Rossa, I-10061 Rome
Web: http://www.trenitalia.com

In 2000, FS split off its operating division as Trenitalia SpA. There are three train-operating divisions: Passegieri (long-distance passenger); Regionale (local passenger services including city suburban); and Cargo. Train fleets have been divided between the three (see 'Traction and rolling stock') and maintenance depots now specialise in work for one activity. Trenitalia's Rolling Stock Technology Unit (Unitá Tecnologie Materiale Rotabile), based in Florence, is responsible for the acquisition of new rolling stock and the technical specifications for modifications to or refurbishment of existing equipment.

*Grandistazioni SpA* (see separate entry)

*Italferr SpA* (see entry in *Consultancy services* section)
Italferr is the engineering consultancy division of FS.

*Medie Stazioni SpA*
In the mould of Grandistazioni, Mediestazioni was created by FS (60 per cent shareholding) and private companies to refurbish and restyle 103 medium-sized FS stations over a five-year period. The company allocated €175 million for this work.

*Metropolis SpA*
Via Arno 64, I-00198 Rome
Tel: (+39 06) 85 27 96 04   Fax: (+39 06) 85 27 95 77
Web: http://www.metropolis-spa.it

Metropolis SpA was established by FS in 1991 to manage and realise the value of the railway's real estate assets, including disused land.

### Political background
In 2000, FS reorganised according to EU rules, initially becoming the holding company for infrastructure authority RFI (qv) before it became an independent state-owned company in 2001, the train operating arm, Trenitalia, Grandi Stazioni (qv), formed to upgrade major stations, and TAV, responsible for building high-speed lines. The last-named is now a subsidiary of RFI. This followed approval by the Italian parliament in July 1998 of the adoption of European Union directives covering separate accounting of train operations and infrastructure functions.

As a result of this change, from 1 June 2000 Italian railways were liberalised on EU lines and any licensed operator can now operate over RFI tracks and use its passenger and freight facilities. FS licensed its own operating arm under the name Trenitalia. It operates long-distance passenger, regional passenger and freight services. Trenitalia has 63,000 staff and an annual turnover of some €2.8 billion. In 2001, the company moved into profit after a long period during which losses were incurred. This was mainly possible thanks to savings in labour costs. Due to the separation of infrastructure provision from operations, Trenitalia will have to pay track charges, as will other operators. FS retains exclusive rights to infrastructure management.

Initial requests from other operators wishing to be licensed included FNME, Rail Traction Company, and Rail Italy which intends to run tourist services. Italy has around 30 independent local railways, some of which are also keen to start open access services.

| **Traffic** (million) | 1997 | 1998 | 1999 |
|---|---|---|---|
| Passenger journeys | 461.0 | 425.9 | 432.2 |
| Passenger-km | 49,500 | 41,400 | 41,000 |
| Freight tonnes | 79.8 | 83.0 | 84.0 |
| Freight tonne-km | 25,280 | 24,700 | 23,780 |

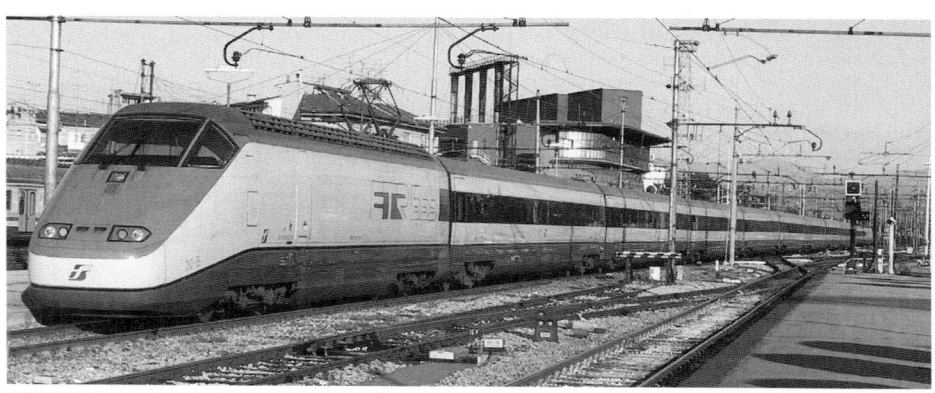

*ETR 500 high-speed trainset arriving at Florence Smista Mento on a Milan–Rome service* (David Haydock)

**Diesel locomotives**

| Class | Wheel arrangement | Power kW | Speed km/h | Weight tonnes | No in service | First built | Mechanical | Builders Engine | Transmission |
|---|---|---|---|---|---|---|---|---|---|
| D343 | B-B | 995/1,015 | 130 | 60 | 44 | 1967 | Fiat/OM/Sofer Omeca/Breda | Fiat 218 SSF/ Breda-Paxman 12YJCL | E TIBB/OCREN |
| D443 | B-B | 1,400 | 130 | 72 | 49 | 1966 | Fiat/OM/ Sofer/IMAM/ Reggiane | Fiat 2312 SSF/ Breda-Paxman 12YLCL | E ASG/OCREN |
| D345 | B-B | 995 | 130 | 61 | 145 | 1974 | Breda/Sofer/ Savigliano | Fiat 218SSF | E TIBB/Marelli/ Italtrofo |
| D445 | B-B | 1,560 | 130 | 72 | 149 | 1974 | Fiat/Omeca | Fiat 2112SSF | E Ansaldo |
| D141 | Bo-Bo | 515 | 80 | 64 | 29 | 1962 | TIBB/Reggiane | Fiat MB 820B | E TIBB |
| D143 | Bo-Bo | 420 | 70 | 65 | 49 | 1942 | TIBB/OM | OM | E TIBB |
| D145 | Bo-Bo | 850 | 100 | 72 | 100 | 1982 | Fiat/TIBB | BRIF ID 36 SS12V Fiat 8,297.22 × 2 | E TIBB/Parizzi |
| 235 | C | 160 | 50 | 34 | 17 | 1957 | Badoni | BRIF 1D36 N8V | H Voith |
| 225 | B | 129 | 50 | 32 | 125 | 1955 | Breda/Jenbach/ Greco/Sofer/ IMAM | Breda/Jenbach/ Deutz | H Breda/Voith |
| 245 | C | 258 | 65 | 48 | 407 | 1962 | Reggiane/OM/ Breda/IMAM/ Ferraro/Greco | MB820-Fiat D26N12V BRIF JW 600 CNTR OM-SEV | H BRIF-Voith Llt24 |
| 214 | B | 95 | 35 | 22 | 494 | 1964 | Badoni/Greco | Fiat 8217-02,001 | H BRIF-Voith Llt33 |
| 216 | B | 118 | 30 | 21 | 53 | 1965 | Badoni/Simm | OM DGL | H Von Roll |
| 255 | C | 500 | 53.5 | 53 | 30 | 1991 | Badoni/Greco | BRIF ID 3658V | H Voith |

### Finance
FS announced its first-ever surplus in 2001 of €20 million, compared with a loss of €689 million in 2000 and €1,487 million in 1999. Traffic receipts rose by 8.1 per cent to €3,002 million, while the cost of production fell from €4,668 million to €4,644 million.

To help FS towards financial self-sufficiency, the state took over its accumulated debt and met the costs of a programme begun in 1990 to reduce staff numbers through voluntary retirement. Between 1989 and 1997 the workforce was cut from 209,000 to 120,000 and productivity (measured in traffic units per employee) rose by 55 per cent. By 1999, staff numbers had been further reduced to 114,500.

*Loss-making routes to close*
In the 1993-95 period a core network of some 5,200 route-km was defined, where FS would have freedom of commercial judgement and operate without subsidy. Over the rest of the system it was initially anticipated that some 2,000 route-km of heavily loss-making regional lines would close in order to eliminate up to 80 per cent of historic government cash support of the railway's revenue. However, these heavy cuts did not take place, and decisions on the future of unremunerative regional lines was being transferred to the regions in 2001-02.

*Investment*
In 2001, total investment was €4,700 million, of which €1,860 was for high-speed lines.

*Independent railways*
There are 24 secondary railways in Italy running with a government concession. Since 1936, 13 of these (FABN, FAL, FAS, FC, FCE, FCU, FdS, FER, FGC, FSE, FV, SFSM, the other company no longer running trains) have been directly controlled by the Ministry of Transport through government commissioners and became Ferrovie in Concessione Commissariale Governativa. In 1998, these had a combined length of 2,462 km, traffic of 861 million passenger-km, 7,737 staff and revenue of €96 million against costs of €676 million. All lines are heavily loss-making, average coverage of direct costs being 24.6 per cent, the railways serving the poor south of Italy and Sardinia covering as little as 8.6 per cent of costs.

In 1997, commissionership of the first 16 was transferred to FS for restructuring and development. This arrangement ended in October 2000 (December 2001 for FCE and FdS). The remaining 11 railways are known as Ferrovie in Concessione Governita and have a government concession but are not directly controlled. It is the intention that between 2003 and 2005 control of all 24 railways will be passed to regional government.

### Passenger operations
*Long-distance*
These are operated by Trenitalia's Passeggieri division. In 1997 FS implemented its plans for a three-tier network of long-distance regular-interval services. Services operated between Italy's principal cities and to France and Switzerland with tilting and non-tilting high-speed rolling stock are marketed as Eurostar Italia, connecting with second-tier Intercity trains serving regional centres and provincial capitals. The third tier is formed by

*Class E464 single-cab electric locomotive powering a Rome Termini–Fiumicino Airport 'Leonardo Express' service* (Quintus Vosman)

# RAILWAY SYSTEMS/Italy

'Interregionali' regional trains radiating from principal nodes. By the end of 1997 Eurostar had captured a 12 per cent share of Italy's long-distance passenger market, with FS aiming at achieving a 35 per cent share by 2000.

FS is gradually converting IC services to ETR 500 operation where a high-speed line forms part of the journey.

*International*
FS and SNCF of France have formed joint ventures to market and develop high-speed and overnight services between Italy and France. Handling some 1 million passengers a year by the start of 1995, overnight services linking Paris with Milan, Florence, Venice and Rome were restructured in 1995 with improved timetables and new fares, and are now marketed under the Artesia brand-name. New or refurbished rolling stock was provided in 1996-97.

September 1996 saw introduction of two daily return services worked by SNCF TGV Réseau high-speed trainsets on the Paris–Turin–Milan route, with a journey time of 6 hours 35 minutes for Paris–Milan. At the same time, FS ETR 460 trainsets began working one return Milan–Lyon and two return Turin–Lyon services.

*Regional services*
Regional passenger services are operated by Trenitalia's Regionale division. These are divided into longer distance Inter Regionale, Trasporto Regionale and Metropolitano, the last for suburban services (see below). Trasporto Regionale carries about one million passengers daily.

The provinces are increasingly taking over responsibility for investment in local rail networks and rolling stock. Toscana is to finance a variety of local passenger and freight schemes worth €83 million. The Veneto region is investing in the creation of a local network known as Sistema Ferroviario Metropolitano Regionale. The estimated cost of the first phase is €350 million, while a €300 million second phase will include new rail links to Venice and Verona airports.

In early 2001, Trasporto Regionale announced that it would re-staff many of its 1,500 unstaffed stations, reopen waiting rooms, install ticket and vending machines and security video cameras. Voluntary organisations were to be invited to set up in some stations.

*Suburban*
Suburban operations are managed by 21 local business units which are structured to facilitate their eventual privatisation or separation from FS proper. Funding is now sourced locally, with FS receiving five-year contracts to operate services. However, initially optional competitive tendering will become mandatory when contracts fall due for renewal. In 1995 Rome suburban services came under a common fares scheme also adopted by the city's bus, tram and metro networks.

On 1 February 2001, Trenitalia, together with Naples city council and municipal transport operator ANM, founded Metronapoli, a common subsidiary to operate local transport. The company is licensed to run over RFI lines and includes city transport plus the 17 km RFI Napoli Gianturco–Pozzuoli Solfatara line, which is largely underground and known as the Passante. Metronapoli has taken over 20 FS Class ALe 724 four-car emus, which operate an all-stations service over the Passante, running every six minutes in the peaks.

## Freight operations
In the freight sector, FS was mandated to lift its market share from 12.5 per cent in 1997 to 14.5 per cent by 2000, when a rise to 28.9 billion train-km has been targeted as part of the company's latest strategic plan. Traffic for 2000 totalled 25.6 billion tonne-km, slightly below the record year of 1997. Revenue in 2000 was €700 million.

Investment totalling €2.05 billion is to take place during the period up to 2000. Strategy centres on moulding FS as a door-to-door carrier and priorities include provision of more specialised wagons and the ability to run top-rate merchandise and intermodal trains at 140 to 160 km/h. New private sidings are to be encouraged with incentives; joint ventures with foreign partners have been sought, to foster cross-border traffic; and EDI development will be energetic. The FS freight division is involved with the private sector in joint venture companies which specialise in the management, operation and retailing of intermodal operations and terminals, road collection and delivery, warehousing, information technology for freight services and the carriage of dangerous goods by rail.

Controllo Centralizzato Rotabili (CCR), a central real-time and computer-based data transmission system, now

*Four-car double-deck TAF emu forming Varese–Milan 'Passante' service seen at Rho (Quintus Vosman)*

*ETR 480 Pendolino tilting trainset at Bologna (Quintus Vosman)*

*Class E402B electric locomotive with a passenger service at Chiusi (Quintus Vosman)*

**Diesel railcars**

| Class | Motored Axles/car | Power/motor kW | Speed km/h | No in service | First built | Mechanical | Builders Engine | Transmission |
|---|---|---|---|---|---|---|---|---|
| ALn668 | 2 | 110-170 | 110-130 | 713 | 1956 | Omeca/Breda/ Fiat Savigliano | Fiat | M |
| ALn663 | 2 | 170 × 2 | 120/130 | 120 | 1983 | Fiat Savigliano | Fiat 8217.32 | M |

# Italy/RAILWAY SYSTEMS

monitors freight operation through input via 400 terminals of activity at all 2,800 freight-generating and reception points.

Approximately half of FS freight is international. There have been considerable gains in traffic with Germany as a result of the extra trains scheduled following new Austrian restrictions on transit road freight (for details see Austria entry). Despite fierce competition, rail holds 45 per cent of the Italo-German market, carrying 15.8 million tonnes in 1998. Traffic conveyed by block trains includes Italian cars for the German market, and fresh fruit and vegetables carried in temperature-controlled wagons to Cologne and Munich. In 1995 FS and DB AG agreed to set up a business unit to manage all Italo-German traffic, except cars and intermodal business. Rail carries 22 per cent of traffic through the country's ports – 54 per cent through Trieste, 34 per cent at La Spezia, 30 per cent at Livorno and 29 per cent through Genoa, Italy's busiest port.

Over 50 per cent of FS Cargo's traffic is concentrated in the northern part of the country and only 10 per cent in the far south.

A strategic alliance between FS and SBB in Switzerland was signed in March 1998 to improve the competitiveness of international rail freight between the two countries. The Cargo Suisse-Italie Sarl company became operational in the Summer of 1998. Initially the agreement was to cover marketing and sales, and provide Swiss access to Italian ports and Italian access to Swiss terminals serving northern Europe. Moves towards a full merger have faltered but FS Cargo and SBB have agreed to reorganise management of services between Italy and northern Europe via Switzerland. FS now manages all 'corridor' freight trains while SBB manages trains which link the Milan area via Switzerland. Eventually the company foresees joint procurement of dual-voltage locomotives, ownership of its wagon fleet and terminals, and its own operating staff.

FS has collaborated with Swiss (BLS and SBB), German, and Dutch rail networks to establish the North-South Freightway, which became operational in February 1998. Linking Italian ports to northern Europe, this allocates and manages train path through participating countries via a single control centre.

Trenitalia Cargo has a subsidiary, SerFer (Servizi Ferroviari srl) which manages private sidings and freight terminals including the port networks of Genoa and Naples. SerFer moves 600,000 wagons annually, has 400 staff and a fleet of over 170 locomotives. In early 2002, SerFer gained an open access freight licence.

## Intermodal operations

Intermodal freight is managed by Italcontainer, of which a 65 per cent share is held by the wholly owned FS subsidiary Nuova INT, 25 per cent by Intercontainer-Interfrigo, and 10 per cent by CEMAT, the Italian piggyback company. In intermodal business FS itself is essentially a wholesaler of track space and train operation.

Intermodal traffic now constitutes 37 per cent of FS freight. Trenitalia Cargo is Europe's leading intermodal carrier, with 33.8 million tonnes handled in 1999. Recent improvements have included a move from 100 to 120 km/h operation of intermodal trains on the north-south trunk route from Milan and a 3 per cent advance in the commercial speed of such services. In 2000, intermodal traffic grew by 10.2 per cent.

*Grants for equipment and terminals*
Legislation of 1990 provided financial inducements for companies to invest in rail-based intermodal transport. A 20 per cent contribution to capital cost is on offer for purchase of containers or swapbodies and other apparatus needed for intermodal operation, and a 10 per cent rebate of the cost of rail movement.

Legislation of 1990 put up almost €500 million towards the creation in key commercial areas of multifunction 'freight villages', or Interporti, equipped to deal in both conventional rail and intermodal freight, and where the rail installations are surrounded by warehousing and other value-adding activities that combine to offer a full logistics service. FS is supported in this programme by CEMAT, and further finance for most of the Interporti has come from local authorities, banks and other private-sector bodies. The nine 'first level' Interporti are members of Assointerporti, a European Economic Interest Group set up to associate similar enterprises throughout the EU.

At the end of 1997 logistics director Maurizio Bussolo announced that FS was to withdraw from logistics services provision, despite this business generating some 3 per cent of company turnover. The aim of the move was to release investment funds for core FS activities. FS is also gradually to withdraw from postal traffic.

*Adtranz-built Class E412 electric locomotives at Chiusa/Klausen, on the Brenner line (Quintus Vosman)*
2000/0089799

*Type Z intercity coach converted into a driving trailer for use on the Venice–Milan route (David Haydock)*
2002/0524931

*Refurbished Class E444 electric locomotive passing Rho with a Paris–Milan overnight train (Quintus Vosman)*
2000/0089801

## Traction and rolling stock

Total FS rolling stock resources at the beginning of 1999 comprised 1,826 electric locomotives, 405 diesel locomotives, 105 electric trainsets, 529 electric railcars, 832 diesel railcars, 1,376 shunting locomotives, 1,316 diesel, 60 electric, 10,951 hauled passenger coaches and 67,502 freight wagons.

During 1999, FS divided its locomotive fleet by activity: Passeggieri (long-distance passenger) has 301 electric and 35 diesel locomotives; Regionale (regional passenger) has 654 electric and 139 diesel locomotives; FS Cargo has 870 electric and 217 diesel locomotives. All high-speed trainsets have been allocated to Passegieri and all dmus, emus and railcars are assigned to Regionale.

*Pendolino trainsets*
FS ordered 30 ETR 460 tilt-body trainsets from Fiat, capable of 250 km/h. These are nine-car, like the earlier ETR 450, but with only six cars motored, due to the use of more powerful three-phase asynchronous motors with GTO inverter control. Body width is 2.8 m, and improved sound insulation and full pressure sealing have been applied to the aluminium alloy bodies. The first ETR 460s entered service in 1995. Three trainsets configured for operation at the Italian and French DC voltages (3 kV and

1.5 kV respectively) entered service between Milan and Lyon in 1996.

Production of a batch of 15 dual-voltage ETR 480 trainsets prepared for subsequent fitting of 25 kV 50 Hz AC equipment for eventual operation on Italian high-speed routes was completed in 1999. Trials of a prototype tilting two-car ATR 410 diesel-electric trainset, developed and funded by Fiat from the ETR 460, started in late 1997. The prototype is equipped with three-phase transmission and synchronous traction motors, and has a maximum speed of 160 km/h.

Nine dual-voltage ETR 470 electric trainsets with the Fiat active body-tilt system operate on the Geneva-Milan, Basle/Berne-Milan and Stuttgart-Zurich-Milan routes. A joint venture company, Cisalpino AG (qv in 'Operators of international rail services in Europe' section) has been established to manage these services.

*ETR 500*
Track parameters for Italy's planned high-speed (AV) network, dictated by need to make the new lines usable by fast freight as well as passenger trains, obviated need of body-tilt in the Type ETR 500 train for dedicated AV operation at 300 km/h. Design of a prototype was entrusted to a Breda-led consortium known as TREVI and background to its development is covered in past editions of *Jane's World Railways*.

The decision taken in 1993 to electrify the new AV routes at 25 kV 50 Hz AC has resulted in design changes to the ETR 500. The initial batch of 30 ETR 500 trainsets was ordered before this decision was taken, and thus has been delivered configured for DC only (although AC equipment is expected to be retrofitted at a later date). Deliveries of the second batch of 30 ETR 500 trainsets equipped with both AC and DC traction equipment was completed in 2001. Both batches will be able to operate from a 1.5 kV DC supply (the norm in southern France) at half power. Other modifications in comparison with the prototypes include reduction of maximum axleloading from 19 to 17 tonnes, which would permit operation over the French high-speed network.

*Electric locomotives*
FS has a long history of ordering Bo-Bo-Bo designs due to the number of mountainous routes on the Italian network. Of the present fleet of 1,826 electric locomotives, 1,490 are of Bo-Bo-Bo designs. Current deliveries are all of the Bo-Bo axle configuration.

Five Class E402 prototypes were built by a consortium including Ansaldo, Fiat and Breda. Equipped with a three-phase drive, the E402 is an 84-tonne, 5,600-kW, Bo-Bo locomotive designed for 250 km/h, with a tractive effort of 180 kN at 102 km/h and of 92 kN at 200 km/h.

Following delivery of 40 E402A (3 kV DC only), FS has received 80 E402B (3 kV DC/25 kV AC 50 Hz) electric locomotives, which operate both passenger and freight services. Twenty of the latter will also be equipped to operate freight traffic to and from Lyon, in France under the 1.5 kV DC system.

From mid-1997, FS took delivery of 20 Class E412 locomotives from Adtranz. Designed for international services to Austria and Germany, this 200 km/h design can run under both 3 kV DC and 15 kV AC 16⅔ Hz catenary, and at reduced performance under 1.5 kV DC. In 2002, Trenitalia Cargo agreed to buy from Bombardier 42 Class E405 electric locomotives originally destined for Poland. These are 3 kV DC only versions of the E412 three-voltage machines.

In 1996 FS placed an order valued at €88 million with Adtranz (now Bombardier) for 50 lightweight E464 electric locomotives. The 3,000 kW (continuous) locomotives, which feature a driving cab at one end only, are to be used on regional and suburban push-pull passenger services. Delivery of the first batch was completed in 2000 and examples from a subsequent order for 180 more were being delivered in 2002.

*TAF emus*
From 1997 to 2001 FS and FNME took delivery of 72 four-car aluminium-bodied double-deck electric multiple-units. Construction is being undertaken by a consortium of Ansaldo, Adtranz, Breda and Firema. Designated TAF (Treno ad Alta Frequentazione), each trainset comprises two motor and two trailer cars, with a maximum speed of 140 km/h and accommodation for 475 seated passengers. Duties for early FS deliveries included services linking Rome city centre with Fiumicino airport. In 2001 FS ordered an additional 27 units and FNME ordered five more.

### Electric trainsets

| Class | Cars per unit | Line voltage | Motor cars per unit | Motored axles/car | Output/motor kW | Speed km/h | No in service | First built | Builders Mechanical | Electrical |
|---|---|---|---|---|---|---|---|---|---|---|
| ETR 401 | 4 | 3 kV | 2 | 4 | 260 | 250 | 1 | 1976 | Fiat | Fiat |
| ETR 450 | 9 | 3 kV | 9 | 2 | 315 | 250 | 15 | 1987 | Fiat | Marelli |
| ETR 460 | 9 | 3 kV | 6 | 4 | 500 | 250 | (30) | 1988 | Fiat | Parizzi |
| ETR 480 | 9 | 3 kV* | 6 | 4 | 500 | 250 | (15) | 1996 | Fiat | Parizzi |
| ETR 500 | 13 | 3 kV** | 2 | 4 | 1,100 | 300 | (60)† | 1992 | Trevi | Trevi |

\* Prepared for 25 kV
\*\* Five also equipped for 1.5 kV DC and 25 kV AC
† 30 3 kV DC and 5 3 kV DC/25 kV AC in service 2000, 25 dual-voltage on order

### Electric locomotives

| Class | Wheel arrangement | Line Voltage | Output kW continuous/one hour | Speed km/h | Weight tonnes | No in service | First built | Builders Mechanical | Electrical |
|---|---|---|---|---|---|---|---|---|---|
| E412 | Bo-Bo | 3/15 kV | 6,000 | 200 | 87 | 20 | 1997 | Adtranz | Adtranz |
| E402A | Bo-Bo | 3 kV | 5,600 | 250 | 84 | 42 | 1988 | Reggiane/Fiat/Breda | Ansaldo |
| E402B | Bo-Bo | 3/15 kV | 5,600 | 250 | 84 | (80)* | 1996 | Ansaldo/Fiat/Breda | Ansaldo |
| E424 | Bo-Bo | 3 kV | 1,500/1,660 | 100/120 | 73 | 125 | 1943 | Breda/Savigliano/Ansaldo/Reggiane/Brown Boveri/OM | Breda/Savigliano/Ansaldo/Marelli/Brown Boveri/CGE |
| E444 | Bo-Bo | 3 kV | 4,000/4,440 | 200 | 83 | 113 | 1967 | Savigliano/Breda/Casaralta/Fiat | OCREN/Asgen/Savigliano |
| E464 | Bo-Bo | 3 kV | 3,000/3,500 | 160 | 72 | (140)* | 1999 | Adtranz | Adtranz |
| E636 | Bo-Bo-Bo | 3 kV | 1,890/2,100 | 110 | 101 | 345 | 1941 | Breda/Brown Boveri/Savigliano/OM/Reggiane/Pistoiesi | Breda/Brown Boveri/Savigliano/CGE/Ansaldo |
| E645 | Bo-Bo-Bo | 3 kV | 3,780/4,320 | 120 | 110 | 96 | 1958 | Breda/Brown Boveri/Savigliano/OM/Reggiane/Pistoiesi/IMAM | Breda/Brown Boveri/Savigliano/CGE/Marelli/Ansaldo/OCREN |
| E646 | Bo-Bo-Bo | 3 kV | 3,780/4,320 | 140 | 110 | 198 | 1961 | Breda/Brown Boveri/Savigliano/OM/Reggiane/Pistoiesi/IMAM | Breda/Brown Boveri/Savigliano/CGE/Marelli/Ansaldo/OCREN |
| E652 | B-B-B | 3 kV | 4,950 | 160 | 106 | 176 | 1989 | ABB/Sofer/Casertane | ABB/Ansaldo/Marelli |
| E656 | Bo-Bo-Bo | 3 kV | 4,200/4,800 | 150 | 120 | 453 | 1975 | TIBB/Sofer/Casaralta/Reggiane/Casertane | TIBB/Italfrafo/Asgen/Marelli/Ansaldo/Retam |
| E632 | B-B-B | 3 kV | 4,350/4,900 | 160 | 103 | 65 | 1982 | Fiat/TIBB/Sofer | Ansaldo/Marelli/TIBB |
| E633 | B-B-B | 3 kV | 4,350/4,900 | 130 | 103 | 143 | 1979 | Fiat/TIBB/Sofer | Ansaldo/Marelli/TIBB |
| E321 | C | 3 kV | 190 | 50 | 36 | 26 | 1960 | FS | |
| E322 | C | 3 kV | 190 | 50 | 36 | 16 | 1961 | FS | TIBB |
| E323 | C | 3 kV | 190 | 32/60 | 46 | 30 | 1966 | TIBB | TIBB |
| E324 | C | 3 kV | 190 | 32/60 | 45 | 10 | 1966 | TIBB | TIBB |

\* Includes examples on order

### Electric multiple-units: power cars

| Class | Cars per unit | Line Voltage | Motor cars per unit | Motored axles/car | Output/motor kW | Speed km/h | No in service | First built | Builders Mechanical | Electrical |
|---|---|---|---|---|---|---|---|---|---|---|
| ALe 5401 | | 3 kV | 1 | 4 | 180 | 150 | 8 | 1957 | OCREN/Stanga | OCREN/Stanga/Sacfem |
| ALe 5822/4 | | 3 kV | 1/2 | 4 | 280 | 140 | 90 | 1987 | Breda | Marelli/Ansaldo |
| ALe 6011 | | 3 kV | 1 | 4 | 218 | 200 | 50 | 1961 | Casaralta | Casaralta/OCREN |
| ALe 8033* | | 3 kV | 1 | 4 | 218 | 130 | 53 | 1961 | Stanga/Savigliano/IMAM | Savigliano/Sofer |
| ALe 8401 | | 3 kV | 1 | 4 | 180 | 130 | 8 | 1950 | OCREN/OM/OTO | OCREN/OM |
| ALe 8014** ALe 9404** | | 3 kV | 2 | 4 | 218 | 140 | 62 | 1976 | Stanga/Fiore/Aetal/Lucana Sofer | Marelli/Stanga/Fiore/Lucana Sofer |
| ALe 6444 | | 3 kV | 1 | 4 | 415 | 140 | 6 | 1980 | Breda | Breda |
| ALe 7244 | | 3 kV | 1 | 4 | 305 | 140 | 89 | 1982 | Breda | Marelli/Ansaldo |
| ALe 8414 | | 3 kV | 2 | 4 | 218 | 200 | 18 | 1994 | Converted from ALe 601 | |
| ALe 6422-3 | | 3 kV | 1/2 | 4 | 305 | 140 | 60 | 1991 | Breda/Fiore | Ansaldo/Lucana |
| ALe 4264† | | 3 kV | 2 | 2 | 318 | 140 | (82) | 1997 | Breda/Firema | Adtranz/Ansaldo |

\* Including two Type Le 803 trailers
\*\* Including two Type Le 108 trailers
† Including two Type Le 736 trailers + ALe 506 power car
†† Includes examples on order

*New emus and dmus*
In early 2001, Trenitalia ordered 200 three-car 'Minnetta' trainsets from Alstom, broken down as 110 160 km/h emus and 90 130 km/h dmus for regional services. The value of the contract was €650 million. The first firm order is for 14 emus for Trenitalia, four for Arezzo province and three for Salerno province, plus 10 dmus for Trenitalia and six for Trento province. Deliveries were scheduled to begin in 2004. All the trains will be articulated, with partial low floors and air conditioned. Dmus will be powered by Iveco engines with hydraulic transmission.

In addition, the Regionale division has embarked on a policy of adding air conditioning equipment to all rolling stock with a medium-term projected service life. This includes the majority of diesel railcars and, from 2001, Piano Ribassato low-floor locomotive-hauled stock.

As in France and Germany, regional authorities in Italy are beginning to finance and own rolling stock dedicated to services for which they are responsible.

*New shunting locomotives*
Trenitalia has ordered 33 Class D146 900 kW B-B diesel-hydraulic locomotives from Firema to replace Classes D141 and D143, the latter dating from 1942. The first of the new machines was delivered in May 2002.

Trenitalia is also re-engining 134 Class 245 diesel shunters with Fraschini engines.

*UPDATED*

## Genoa—Casella Railway (FGC)

Managed by Government Commission, Rome
Ferrovia Genova-Casella
Via alla Stazione per Casella 15, I-16122 Genoa
Tel: (+39 010) 83 73 21   Fax: (+39 010) 837 32 48
Web: http://www.ferroviagenovacasella.it

**Key personnel**
Manager: Paolo Gassani

Gauge: 1,000 mm
Route length: 25 km
Electrification: 24 km at 3 kV DC

**Organisation**
In 1998, FGC achieved 4.8 million passenger-km, down from 5.4 million the previous year.
Future plans include the construction of a new cut-off 4.5 km in length and of a new terminus in Genoa to connect with the upper station of the Granarolo funicular.

**Traction and rolling stock**
The railway operates 12 electric railcars, three electric and one diesel locomotives, 16 coaches and 24 wagons. Recent fleet acquisitions include two Adtranz-built Type E46A electric railcars.

*UPDATED*

## Grandistazioni

Via G Giolitti 34, I-10185 Rome
Tel: (+39 06) 47 84 11   Fax: (+39 06) 482 39 51
e-mail: info@grandistazioni.it
Web: http://www.grandistazioni.it

**Background**
With 60 per cent of its capital, FS founded the company Grandistazioni in 1998 with the aim of remodelling 12 of the biggest stations in Italy. Roma Termini served as a model and was completed in January 2000. Rebuilding of the remaining stations started in September 2001, the work expected to be completed over a period of two years. Cost will be some €350 million.

*NEW ENTRY*

## Metropolitana di Roma SpA (Met.ro)

Via Volturno 65, I-00185 Rome
Tel: (+39 06) 46 95 20 27   Fax: (+39 06) 46 95 22 84
e-mail: direzione@atac.roma.it
Web: http://www.atac.roma.it/metro

**Key personnel**
Chairman: C Vaciago
General Manager: D Mazzamurro
Deputy General Manager: E Sciarra
Manager, Commuter Railways Concession: A Curci

Gauge: 1,435 mm, 950 mm
Route length: 131 km, 18.5 km
Electrification: 102 km of 1,435 mm gauge at 3 kV DC, 29 km of 1,435 mm gauge at 1.5 kV DC, 18.5 km of 950 mm gauge at 1.5 kV DC

**Political background**
In 1995 Rome bus and tram operator ATAC merged with COTRAL, which operated three suburban rail routes, the Rome metro and regional bus services and in 2000 was brought under the same management as Rome's metro network as Metropolitana di Roma SpA (Met.ro). An integrated fares structure including FS suburban services was introduced following the merger.

**Passenger operations**
The Met.ro suburban passenger network comprises three electrified routes: Rome—Viterbo (102 km, 1,435 mm gauge); Rome—Lido di Ostia (29 km, 1,435 mm gauge); and Rome—Pantano Borghese (18.5 km, 950 mm gauge).

**Improvements to existing lines**
The Rome Piazzale Flaminio—Prima Porta section of the Viterbo route (Line F) has been upgraded and doubled. Doubling was in progress in 2002 on the line to Montebello. The rest of the Viterbo line is to be modernised at a cost of €97 million. The Pantano Borghese route has being rebuilt to light rail standards on its inner section to become semi-metro Line G, connecting with metro Lines A and B at Termini via a new city-centre tunnel. Further out, the Pantano Borghese line is to be rebuilt to metro standards with segregated tracks.

The inner section of the Lido di Ostia route (Line E) is being rebuilt between Piramide and Magliana, with a new station at San Paolo. In 1996 the government agreed to provide 50 per cent of the €125 million cost of building a new Mezzocamino—Spinaceto—Tor de Cenci section. A project to extend the Met.ro network to Osteria del Curato is also under development.

**Traction and rolling stock**
Met.ro's electric multiple-unit fleet comprises 41 cars for the Viterbo route, 34 vehicles for the Pantano Borghese route and 162 cars for the Lido di Ostia route.
Six double-articulated trainsets were ordered from the same manufacturer for the Pantano route. In 2002, delivery was in progress of 10 three-car emus from Alstom and Costaferroviaria for the Viterbo line. These are to operate on the Rome—Viterbo line. The order included an option on a further six units.

*UPDATED*

## Monfer

Via Angeli, I-12100 Cuneo
Tel: (+39 0171) 34 42 99   Fax: (+39 0171) 34 40 99
e-mail: info@monfer.net
Web: http://www.monfer.it

**Organisation**
Monfer was founded in 1970 to transport cereals. In 2002, the company gained an open access licence to use the Italian domestic network for freight services.

*NEW ENTRY*

## North Milan Railway (FNME)

Ferrovie Nord Milano Esercizio SpA
Piazza Cadorna 14, I-20123 Milan
Tel: (+39 02) 851 11   Fax: (+39 02) 851 17 08
e-mail: infocare@ferrovienord.it
Web: http://www.ferrovienord.it

**Key personnel**
President: Luigi Roth
General Manager: Ing Arnaldo Siena
Production and Operations Manager, North Milan:
  Ing Luigi Legnani
Operations Manager, Brescia-Edolo:
  Ing Federico Bonafini
Commercial Director: Gianni Scarfone

Gauge: 1,435 mm
Route length: 326.8 km, of which 308.6 km in use
Electrification: 200.3 km at 3 kV DC

**Political background**
In 1995 FS, FNME and the Lombardy region signed an agreement to create Servizio Ferroviario Regionale (SFR), which from November 1997 became responsible for regional and suburban railway services within Lombardy. As part of the formation of SFR, FS was eventually to acquire a 50 per cent shareholding in FNME, although in 2001 only 10 per cent was held, and staff from both operators were eventually to transfer to the new undertaking.

**Organisation**
FNME serves the north Milan suburbs with a main four-track route to Saronno, where it forks to Como and to Laveno on Lake Maggiore. The latter is single track beyond Malnate. Also from Saronno a single-track branch heads west to Novara, and a freight-only branch east to Seregno. A further double-track route runs from Bovisa to Seveso, beyond which single track extends to Canzo-Asso. In 1993 FNME took over operation of the 108 km non-electrified Brescia North Railway, linking Edolo with Rovato and Brescia.
In 2000 FNME registered itself as an open access operator and in summer 2001 launched freight services

*Class E620 electric locomotive with double-deck stock at Milan Nord Cadorna station (Colin Boocock)*
2000/0089568

# RAILWAY SYSTEMS/Italy

from Brescia to Great Britain and Belgium via the Lötschberg route in collaboration with Railitaly. The company uses its Class E630 electric locomotives to reach Domodossola.

## Traffic
In 2000, FNME carried 51 million passengers and 300,000 tonnes of freight.

## Improvements to existing lines
In 1984 the government approved execution of a €134.3 million modernisation plan. The main item was 17 km of further four-tracking on FNME's Como main line between Bovisa and Saronno, accompanied by level crossing elimination and station reconstruction, plus two new stations. This project was finished in 1999. Completion halved the Milan—Como journey time to 30 minutes. This development is germane to the integration of FNME and FS as SFR, operating a regional rail system based on the new Passante cross-city line (for details see under FS).

The 4 km from FNME's present Milan terminus to Bovisa, which is common to all FNME services, carries over 300 trains a day, two-thirds of which continue to Saronno. It is intended to widen this section from two to four tracks. Quadrupling beyond Bovisa to Cadorna will enable separation of fast and slow services. This is scheduled for completion in 2002.

The first phase of a €237.6 million scheme to serve Milan's Malpensa airport, by doubling 20.5 km of the Saronno—Novara branch and constructing from it an airport link, was begun in 1990 with double-tracking and realignment between Saronno, Busto Arsizio and Vanzaghello. In 1998 a €67.7 million contract was placed to construct the 13 km branch from Busto Arsizio to the airport. Work began in February 1998 and was completed during 1999. FNME launched a 'Malpensa Express' from its Cadorna terminus in Milan in May 1999, shortly after Malpensa airport began to handle scheduled international flights.

## Traction and rolling stock
Rolling stock in service at the start of 1996 comprised 24 electric locomotives, 19 diesel locomotives, 79 emu power cars, 17 diesel railcars, 252 trailer vehicles and passenger coaches and 96 freight wagons. The fleet includes many double-deck coaches, which often operate in with Class E750 single-deck railcars.

In 1994 FS and FNME ordered 50 four-car double-deck TAF (Treni ad Alta Frequentazione) electric multiple-units for Passante services (see FS entry); FNME's share of the order amounts to 19, four of which have been branded for Malpensa Express airport services. The type has received the FNME designations EA 760 for the driving motor cars and EB 990 for the intermediate trailers. An additional five units were ordered in 2001. FNME purchased nine 3,290 kW Bo-Bo electric locomotives built (but never delivered) by Škoda for Czechoslovakian State Railways and 19 coaches from SNCB, Belgium. In late 1997 FNME workshops completed its first Class EB 880 driving trailer converted from one of the ex-SNCB vehicles.

In 2001, FNME invited tenders to supply six 3,000 kW electric locomotives, six emus for Malpensa Express services (with an option for an additional six trains) and 18 three-car and nine five-car double-deck emus, with options for 12 and six more units respectively.

## Signalling and telecommunications
Automatic block controls 89.8 route-km, of which 63.8 km is double-track and 17 km quadruple-track. FS-type semi-automatic block controls 4 km. There are 287 signal-protected level crossings on the system. FNME has been testing an experimental track-to-train radio installation between Milan and Saronno.

## Track
**Rail (km installed):** RA 36 kg/m (42.4); FS 46 kg/m (4.9); UNI 50 kg/m (427.5); UNI 60 kg/m (2.1)
**Sleepers (km installed):** Timber (124.5), FS concrete monobloc (94.4) and bibloc (254.3)
**Size:** Timber 2,600 × 260 × 150 mm
Monobloc 2,300 × 300 × 190 mm
Bibloc 2,300 × 263 × 217 mm
**Spacing:** 1,500 per km
**Fastenings:** Direct for RA 36; Type K for FS 46; Direct UNI 50 for monobloc sleepers; Type RN and Nabla for bibloc sleepers
**Min curve radius:** 250 m
**Max gradient:** 3%
**Max permissible axleload:** 20 tonnes

*TAF double-deck emu for Malpensa Express airport service, seen from the cab of a sister unit* (M Tolini)

*TAF four-car double-deck emu for Passante line services* (M Tolini)

### Electric locomotives

| Class | Wheel arrangement | Line voltage | Output kW | Speed km/h | Weight tonnes | No in service | First built | Builders Mechanical | Electrical |
|---|---|---|---|---|---|---|---|---|---|
| 600 | Bo + Bo | 3 kV | 1,030 | 75 | 63 | 5 | 1928 | OM | CGE |
| 610 | Bo + Bo | 3 kV | 1,030 | 80 | 61 | 4 | 1949 | Breda | CGE |
| 620 | Bo + Bo | 3 kV | 2,250 | 130 | 72 | 6 | 1985 | TIBB | Ansaldo |
| 630 | Bo + Bo | 3 kV | 3,650 | 120 | 80 | 9 | 1991 | Škoda | Škoda |

### Electric railcars

| Class | Line voltage | Motored axles/car | Output/motor kW | Speed km/h | No in service | First built | Builders Mechanical | Electrical |
|---|---|---|---|---|---|---|---|---|
| 700 | 3 kV | 4 | 183 | 80 | 22 | 1929 | OM | TIBB |
| 730 | 3 kV | 4 | 272 | 80 | 3 | 1932 | Tallero | TIBB |
| 740 | 3 kV | 4 | 272 | 80 | 7 | 1929 | Tallero | CGE |
| 740 | 3 kV | 4 | 272 | 90 | 9 | 1953 | Breda | CGE |
| 740 | 3 kV | 4 | 272 | 90 | 8 | 1957 | Breda | CGE |
| 750 | 3 kV | 4 | 280 | 130 | 24 | 1982 | Breda | Ansaldo/Marelli |
| 760 | 3 kV | 4 | 910 | 140 | 24[1] | 1998 | Breda/Firema | Adtranz/Ansaldo |

[1] Includes five units ordered in 2001

### Diesel locomotives

| Class | Wheel arrangement | Power kW | Speed km/h | Weight tonnes | No in service | First built | Mechanical | Builders Engine | Transmission |
|---|---|---|---|---|---|---|---|---|---|
| 500 | Bo-Bo | 383 | 75 | 47 | 5 | 1971 | TIBB | Fiat | E |
| 510 | A-A | 103 | 30 | 18 | 2 | 1966 | TIBB | Fiat | E |

*UPDATED*

## Padane Railways (FP)

The FP was one of four local railways which merged on 1 January 2001 to form the Emilia Romagna Railway (FER) (qv).

**UPDATED**

## Rail Traction Company (RTC)

### Organisation
Rail Traction Company was formed by motorway operator Autobrennero (40 per cent), private operator FT (20 per cent), former FS director Guiseppe Sciaronne (20 per cent) and road transport companies Fercam and Sae (10 per cent each) as an open access freight operator.

### Freight operations
Operations commenced in October 2001 with two pairs of intermodal trains between Verona and Munich (Reim) on behalf of CEMAT and Kombiverkehr, initially providing haulage as far as Brennero.

In April 2002, RTC commenced handling the movement of new Volkswagen cars between Munich and Verona and in July 2002 was expected to add similar Verona–Brescia services.

### Traction and rolling stock
The company acquired from Bombardier Transportation eight Class EU43 electric locomotives originally built for Polish State Railways (PKP). These are dual-voltage (3 kV DC/15 kV AC) machines.

**UPDATED**

## Railitaly

### Organisation
Railitaly, which is 73 per cent owned by the Brescia metallurgical group Duferco, runs passenger charter trains using a former DB 'TEE' dmu. The company also launched two services in conjunction with the North Milan Railway (FNME) (qv) in June 2001 from northern Italy to Belgium and Great Britain via Switzerland.

### Traction and rolling stock
Railitaly ordered five 2,200 kW diesel locomotives from Vossloh in late 2000. In 2001/02, two former Czech Railways Class 753 locomotives were acquired after refurbishment and re-engining by ČMKS Holdings and Inekon Group.

**VERIFIED**

## Reggiane Railways (ACT)

Azienda Consorziale Trasporti
Viale Trento Trieste 11, I-42100 Reggio Emilia
Tel: (+39 0522) 92 76 11   Fax: (+39 0522) 92 76 74
Web: http://www.actre.it

### Key personnel
General Manager: S Cavaliere

Gauge: 1,435 mm
Route length: 77 km

### Organisation
ACT is owned by the city of Reggio di Emilia and other local towns, operating passenger services on lines from Reggio Emilia to Guastalla (28 km), Sassuolo (22 km) and Caino d'Enza (26 km). The Sassuolo line serves Europe's main ceramics industry and ACT hauled 1.7 million tonnes of incoming clay and outgoing tiles in 2000, connecting with FS at Reggio Emilia. The freight yard at Dinazzano is to be expanded in the next few years to cope with growing traffic. Plans have been developed by ACT to create a joint venture with FS to manage this facility, with the company taking a shareholding of 60 per cent. The station at Sassuolo is to be rebuilt as a common underground facility with ATCM (qv). ACT has also revealed a plan to reopen the 17 km Carpi–Bagnolo in Piano line for passenger and freight traffic. The project would cost €142 million. ACT also operates local buses.

### Traction and rolling stock
The railway operates six main line and six shunting locomotives plus 22 railcars. The railway hired two Vossloh G1206 diesel locomotives in April 2000 and is to purchase up to six new 2,200 kW diesel-hydraulic locomotives.

**UPDATED**

## Rete Ferroviaria Italiana (RFI)

Piazza della Croce Rossa 1, I-00100 Rome
Web: http://www.rfi.it

### Key personnel
Chief Executive: Mauro Moretti

Gauge: 1,435 mm
Route length: 16,030 km
Electrification: 10,358 km at 3 kV DC

### Subsidiary
TAV
Treno Alta Velocita SpA
Via Mantova, I-00198 Rome
Tel: (+39 06) 47 84 11   Fax: (+39 06) 482 39 15
Web: http://www.tav.it

### Political background
RFI was formed as an independent state-owned company in 2001, taking in Italian Railways' former infrastructure division (Divisione Infrastruttura). RFI owns and manages the Italian rail network, initially taking over those lines on which Trenitalia trains operate but later adding lines over which independent companies operate.

RFI has control over TAV, the subsidiary responsible for building new high-speed lines. TAV was initially owned by FS (45 per cent) and by a dozen banks, nine of them Italian, two French and one German, which together put up 60 per cent of the company's starting capital. In 1998 the company became 100 per cent FS-owned. TAV was granted a 50-year concession to design, construct and market the high-speed network in 1991. Train operation and rolling stock and infrastructure maintenance will be the responsibility of FS.

### New lines
*Rome–Florence Direttissima*
Italy's first high-speed line, the Rome–Florence Direttissima, became fully operational in 1992 with the opening of its final 44 km section from Arezzo South to Figline. It is electrified on the 3 kV DC system. The final stretch was made traversable at 300 km/h to allow for testing of new ETR 500 rolling stock. Currently, all trains are limited to 250 km/h in commercial service over the Direttissima.

A total of €238 billion is to be spent on upgrading the Direttissima for 300 km/h operation throughout, to be completed for the projected opening of the Rome–Naples high-speed route. At its northern end, the Direttissima is to be linked to the Florence–Bologna high-speed line by an orbital line around Florence running mostly on the surface.

*High-speed routes: network plan*
In 1991 a mixed holding company, Treno Alta Velocita (TAV), was formed to carry forward plans for a high-speed (Alta Velocita, or AV) network approved in 1986 by the FS board. The network was to be T-shaped, running south-north from Battipaglia (south of Salerno) to Milan via the Rome-Florence Direttissima, and west-east from Turin to Venice via Milan.

In 1993 the government made available the funds for a start of the high-speed project, having agreed to provide 40 per cent of the total cost of the infrastructure. The components authorised were Rome–Naples, Florence–Bologna, Bologna–Milan and Milan–Turin. Some 70 per cent of the state funding for these sections was provided in the 1993 and 1994 national budgets, with the remainder in the 1995 spending round. The total cost of building the approved high-speed infrastructure (964.7 km) has been put at €14.9 billion.

Delays to the high-speed programme have been caused by the vetting of construction contracts following allegations of corruption and by opposition on environmental grounds, although the new routes have been designed to follow existing motorway corridors where possible.

The new high-speed routes are to be electrified at 25 kV 50 Hz AC rather than 3 kV DC, and have a minimum curve radius of 5,450 m and a maximum gradient of 1.8 per cent. Maximum axleload is to be 18 tonnes. Signalling and train control will be derived from the French TVM 430 system, supplied by Ansaldo Trasporti and its French subsidiary CS Transport. Although the new lines are to be engineered for a maximum speed of 300 km/h, in 1995 it was announced that high-speed services would not operate above 250 km/h for an indeterminate period, in response to environmental concerns. Passenger services over the new routes will be provided by high-speed trainsets and locomotive-hauled trains operating at up to 220 km/h. The high-speed network will also be used by freight trains (principally intermodal services) operating at up to 160 km/h.

*High-speed routes: Rome–Naples*
Work began on the Rome–Naples high-speed line at 11 sites in 1994. Completion of the line is expected by 2003. The route follows the A1 motorway for most of its length and comprises 204.5 km of new construction and 15.5 km of upgraded infrastructure to gain access to Rome and Naples. Other connections with existing routes are to be provided at Frosinone, Caserta and Cassino. A train ran for the first time in February 2002 over a part completed section of the line.

*High-speed routes: Florence–Bologna*
The final alignment of the 78.3 km Florence–Bologna high-speed line was approved in 1995. Work started in 1996, after Italferr-SIS TAV signed a contract valued at €2.01 billion with a consortium led by Fiat and construction company Impregio to build the major part (71.5 km) of the route to the outskirts of Florence. It is expected that construction of most of the line will be completed by 2005. Crossing the Apennine range, 66.8 km of the principal 71.5 km section will be in tunnel. A new station, to be served only by high-speed services, is to be built in Florence.

*High-speed routes: Bologna–Milan*
The existing route between Bologna and Milan is one of the most congested on the FS network. The cost of the new route has risen to €5.68 billion. There are to be eight connections with existing lines and an intermediate station at Reggio Emilio. Work started in November 2000

for completion in 2006. The start of construction was delayed by a redesign to allow freight trains to use the line more easily.

The high-speed route comprises 182 km of new infrastructure starting at Melegnano, 21 km south of Milan Central. The subject of controversy during the early planning stages, much of it runs parallel to the A1 motorway as far as Bologna's outskirts. Some 38 km of the alignment is carried on viaducts and bridges. The new line is to pass below Bologna in tunnel, with a station below the existing FS facility. The line will cut the Milan–Bologna journey time from 1 hour 45 minutes to 1 hour.

With future high-speed services in mind, two extra tracks were commissioned in 1996 on the Milan–Melegnano route between Milan Rogoredo and San Giuliano Milanese (7 km).

*High-speed routes: Milan–Turin*
The alignment of this 125 km route has caused controversy, particularly in the Novara area, and is planned to follow the A2 motorway. New infrastructure is to begin at Certosa, 9 km from Milan Central, and run to Settimo Torinese, 8 km from Torino Porta Nuova. Connections with existing lines were to be provided at Novara. The cost of the project is estimated at €6.7 billion.

Construction started in February 2002 and completion is planned for 2006. When complete, the line will cut the Turin–Milan journey time from 1 hour 40 minutes to 50 minutes.

*High-speed routes: Milan–Venice*
Construction has been costed at €2.79 billion, excluding connections to existing lines. The route comprises 212 km of new line, starting 20 km from Milan Central at Melzo. It follows the SS1 motorway to Brescia (where connections with the existing network are to be provided), and then the A4 motorway to south of Verona where it rejoins the existing FS system. The remainder of the high-speed route links Verona and Padua, with a connection to the existing network at Vicenza. High-speed services will reach Venice over the existing Padua-Mestre route, upgraded and expanded. Construction is planned to start in 2004 for completion by 2008.

*High-speed routes: Lyon–Turin*
In September 2000, the French and Italian governments agreed to build a base tunnel of 52.7 km between St Jean-de-Maurienne and Susa, on the Lyon–Turin route. Work started in early 2002 and completion is scheduled for 2015 and the project will cost an estimated €10 billion. The main aim of the scheme is to divert freight traffic via the tunnel, which would be built to allow 'rolling highway' services (see entry for French Railways Infrastructure Authority). Both French and Italian authorities will link the tunnel to their respective high-speed networks. By 2006/07, the two railways will enlarge the existing loading gauge to UIC 'B' standards. In 1994 FS and SNCF of France formed the Alpetunnel joint venture to undertake technical and economic studies for the base tunnel (see entry for France).

*Cross-city routes: Milan*
In 1982 construction started of a new cross-Milan line, known as the Passante, as the first step toward creation of an integrated public transport system for the conurbation. The 18.4 km Passante will extend from Rogoredo, south of the city on the FS Bologna main line, to Certosa, on the line to Turin. The centrepiece is a 5.9 km double-track tunnel between Lancetti and Porta Vittoria, with six new stations below ground.

Besides connecting main lines to and from the south (Genoa and Bologna), east (Bergamo, Cremona and Treviglio, by a 3.1 km branch from Porta Vittoria) and northwest (Turin and Domodossola), the link will throw off a connection between Lancetti and Villa Pizzone to the North Milan Railway (FNME) system at Bovisa, enabling integration of FNME and FS services.

An initial 10 minute shuttle service operated by North Milan Railway (FNME) (qv) commenced in December 1997 between Bovisa and Porta Venezia although this section is not yet connected to the rest of the network. Through FS services running half-hourly to/from Gallarate were introduced in May 1999.

In November 2000, tenders were called for construction of the eastern section from Porta Venezia to Bivio Lambro on the line to Venice. The Passante was extended to Villa Pizzone on 4 July 2002. The rest of line is expected to open at the end of 2005.

Services will eventually operate every 20 minutes at peak periods and hourly at other times on five routes: Novara–Lodi, Gallarate–Codogno, Malpensa–Brescia, Saronno–Treviglio and Seveso–Pavia.

Further FS investment associated with the scheme has included four-tracking from Pioltello to Treviglio (22 km), approved in 1995 for completion around 2000 at an estimated cost of €362 million. Two extra tracks were commissioned in 1996 between Rogoredo and San Giuliano Milanese (7 km), on the route to Lodi and Codogno. The upgrading of the Milan orbital route connecting Certosa, Lambrate, Porta Vittoria, Rogoredo and Porta Romana has also been proposed; four-tracking between Pioltello and Lambrate has also been undertaken.

In 1995 FS, FNME and the Lombardy region signed an agreement to create Servizio Ferroviario Regionale (SFR), which from November 1997 became responsible for regional and suburban railway services within Lombardy. As part of the formation of SFR, FS is to acquire a 50 per cent shareholding in FNME and staff from both operators are eventually to transfer to the new undertaking.

*Cross-city routes: Turin*
In 1983 FS signed an agreement with the Turin city authorities aiming to establish a regional rail system similar to Milan's. A minimal through service started operation in September 1997 and a 3.3 km route from Lingotto to Porta Susa via Zappata opened in September 1999. The long-term aim is to increase capacity from Porta Susa to Dora to link FS and SATTI (qv) services. SATTI is building a new station on its Dora to Ceres line to serve Turin's Caselle airport.

*Bridge to Sicily*
A long-standing project to build a road/rail bridge over the Straits of Messina to Sicily was approved in 2001. The cost of the 3.3 km span is put at €5.7 billion and about 40 per cent this is sought from private sources. The bridge would allow up to 200 trains per day to cross between Reggio di Calabria and Messina. At present passenger and freight trains cross on ferries.

## Improvements to existing lines

*Brenner route*
In 1991 the Transport Ministers of Italy, Austria and Germany agreed on a long-term initiative to advance construction of a Brenner Pass base tunnel (for details see Austrian Railways entry). In the meantime, €645 million was to be invested in the Verona–Brennero portion of the existing route, with funding provided in part by loans from the European Investment Bank. Four new tunnels have been bored, partly to bypass speed-restricting curvature and partly to protect areas vulnerable to rock falls. Work was completed in November 1999 and the route now satisfies UIC 'C' loading gauge parameters. A 'rolling highway' service introduced in March 2000 from Wörgl to Trento was the first to benefit from this work.

*Pontebbana route*
The Pontebbana route between Villach, Austria, and Trieste/Venice via the Tarvisio Pass and Udine already carries 11 per cent of FS international traffic, almost the same as the Brenner, and is heading for major growth of its freight traffic. Its single line and outdated electrification have consequently become more of a burden year by year, prompting FS to launch a programme of double-tracking, track rebuilding for heavier axleloads, realignment and grade easement, re-electrification and resignalling with automatic block for reversible working. New tunnelling is involved in obtaining an alignment for the second track over 85 per cent of the route. Work was completed in 2001.

*Rome*
Major projects in the Rome area have included a new orbital link from St Peters via Vigna Clara to the Rome-Florence route north of Tiburtina. The link includes a 4.6 km tunnel under Rome's northern suburbs. Other upgrading projects include the double-tracking of the Tiburtina–Guidonia route and quadrupling between Casilina and Ciampino.

In 2000, work was completed on doubling the San Pietro–Cesaro line and on complete electrification of the route between San Pietro and Viterbo (82 km). Thirteen stations have been rebuilt.

These projects form the basis of a scheme to dramatically increase suburban rail provision in Rome by 2000. Cross-city services would be provided between Fiumicino and Fara Sabina and between La Storta and Ciampino, sharing the southern Trastevere–Ostiense–Tuscolana orbital route and operating in conjunction with St Peters–Vigna Clara–Tiburtina and Tiburtina–Guidonia services. Investment totalling €2.07 billion would be required for the scheme, which also includes refurbishment work at Rome's Termini, Tiburtina, St Peters, Ostiense and Trastevere stations.

*Other schemes*
FS is gradually upgrading the Verona–Bologna and Bologna–Ancona–Foggia–Bari Adriatic route. Work includes track-doubling and elimination of level crossings.

In 1999, FS and Swiss Federal Railways announced that they would reopen a 15 km line from Mendrisio to Varese via Stabio, which was closed in 1928, in order to improve passenger links to Milan Malpensa airport and freight traffic access to Novara. FS is also to reopen and electrify the Merano-Malles line by 2002.

A new 12.6 km double-track tunnel was opened in late 2001 between Messina and Villafranca Tirrena in Sicily, replacing a 5.5 km single-track structure with adverse gradients. The new tunnel cuts Messina–Palermo journey times by 20 minutes and the use of banking locomotives for freight trains has been eliminated.

Swiss Federal Railways and Italian Railways are studying a new 18 km line from Mendrisio, Switzerland, to Arcisate, Italy, to create a more direct route from the Gotthard line to Varese, Milan and Malpensa airports. The cost of the project, due to open in 2006, is estimated at €100 million.

Additional central government funding has been secured to fund upgrading of existing routes: Padua–Mestre (€176 million); Orte–Falconara (€206.6 million); Caserta–Foggia (€279 million); the Sardinian network (€103.3 million); and Palermo–Messina–Catania (€372 million).

## Signalling and telecommunications

For speeds above 150 km/h, automatic block with coded current cab repetition is being adopted. Cab repetition is integrated with automatic speed control. For speeds up to 250 km/h on the Rome–Florence Direttissima the following speeds are encoded (km/h): 250-230-200-150-100-60-30.

In 1996 Ansaldo completed the first phase of the €98 million Naples–Reggio di Calabria route modernisation project, comprising the 200 km between Battipaglia and Paola. This section, controlled by a new CTC installation with 22 interlockings at Sapri, received automatic block signalling with coded current cab repetition, a centralised hotbox detection system and improved public address and wayside telephone systems.

In 1997 Ansaldo Trasporti was awarded a €129 million contract to build operations control centres at Genoa, Naples and Venice covering traffic on Genoa-Rome, Bologna–Brennero, and Bologna–Bari routes. Implementation of the entire programme is scheduled for the end of 2000.

In 2002, Siemens received a €168 million contract from RFI to develop a GSM-R mobile radio communication system to be introduced in 2005, replacing existing equipment.

## Electrification

The historic network in Italy, and the Rome–Florence high-speed line, is electrified at 3 kV DC; however, future high-speed lines will be energised at 25 kV 50 Hz AC.

In 1997, 64.6 per cent of the network was electrified compared with 55.2 per cent in 1985. Lines being electrified in 2001 included: Merano–Malles (line reopening) and Pisa–Vada. Reopening and electrification of the Treviso–Portogruaro line was completed in 2000.

## Track

Monoblock prestressed concrete sleepers are being used almost exclusively in current track upgrading and doubling projects (though a test installation of slab track was recently completed). Length of sleeper is 2.3 m but for new track, where speeds may exceed 160 km/h, a new design with a length of 2.6 m is being adopted. For rail renewals, and all new lines, UIC 60 (60 kg/m) rails are being used, fastened with K-type clips. RFI replaces about 850 km of track each year.

*NEW ENTRY*

Italy/**RAILWAY SYSTEMS** 219

## San Severo—Peschici Railway (FdG)

Ferrovie del Gargano Srl
Strada Communale 82 S Ricciardi, I-71016 San Severo
Tel: (+39 0882) 22 14 14   Fax: (+39 0882) 24 76 45

**Key personnel**
Director General: V Scarcia
Operating Manager: A Oliva

Gauge: 1,435 mm
Route length: 56 km
Electrification: 56 km at 3 kV DC

**Organisation**
FdG operates the Peschici—San Severo line, with some services running over FS metals to Foggia.

In 2002, work should be completed on reopening the former FS Foggia—Lucera line (20 km), on which FdG is to take over operations.

The company gained an open access licence in 2002.

**Traction and rolling stock**
The railway operates four electric locomotives, 10 electric railcars, nine passenger cars and 28 freight wagons.

*UPDATED*

## Sangritana Railways (FAS)

Gestione Governativa Ferrovia Adriatico-Sangritana
Via Dalmazia 9, Piazzale della Stazione, I-66034 Lanciano
Tel: (+39 0872) 70 82 12   Fax: (+39 0872) 78 85 00
Web: http://www.sangritana.it

**Key personnel**
Managing Director: Dr Ing Antonio Bianco

Gauge: 1,435 mm
Route length: 126 km
Electrification: 103 km at 3 kV DC

**Organisation**
In January 2001 FAS became a limited liability company, wholly owned by the Abruzzo region. FAS operates the following lines: Marina San Vito (FS)—Lanciano—Crocetta—Archi—Castel di Sangro (104 km); Ortona Marina—Crocetta (38 km), of which only Ortona Marina—Caldari (10 km, freight only) is open at present; Torino di Sangro (FS)—Piazzano di Atessa (9 km, freight only). A new line, Lanciano—San Vito, is under construction to eliminate level crossings. Through Lanciano—Pescara journey times will be cut from 60 to 25 minutes. Another new line, from Torino di Sangro to Archi, is under construction.

The Caldari line may be reopened to Guardiagrele if freight traffic warrants. The Piazzano line was built in the 1980s to serve a car production plant and has been managed by FAS since 1991. The railway also has ambitions to take over the management of other local industrial branches and, possibly, local freight workings from FS, including services on the Teramo—Giulianova line.

In 1998, FAS recorded 14.1 million passenger-km, down from 16.8 million the previous year. Freight traffic amounted to 50,000 tonnes and 1 million tonne-km a year.

**Traction and rolling stock**
The railway operates four electric and six diesel locomotives, 11 electric railcars, six coaches and 28 wagons.

*FAS two-car refurbished emu at Lanciano (Quintus Vosman)*   2000/0089570

In February 2002, FAS received the first of four former Czech Railways Class 752 diesel locomotives for expanded services. An earlier locomotive acquisition, in June 2001, was an MaK G1100 diesel-hydraulic from the Vossloh hire fleet. In 1999, FAS bought 10 Type AM56 two-car emus from Belgian National Railways which were refurbished in 2000.

*UPDATED*

## Sardinian Railways (FdS)

Managed by Government Commission, Rome
Ferrovie della Sardegna
Via Cugia 1, I-09129 Cagliari

Tel: (+39 070) 34 23 41   Fax: (+39 070) 34 07 80
Web: http://www.ferroviesardegna.it

**Key personnel**
Director General: E Porceddu

Gauge: 950 mm
Route length: 614 km

**Organisation**
FdS was formed in 1989 with the merger of Strade Ferrate Sardegna and Ferrovie Complementari della Sardegna. Routes operated are Cagliari—Sorgono/Arbatax, Tresnuraghes—Macomer—Nuoro and Alghero—Sassari—Palau Marina. In 2000, regular passenger services were operating over 219 km of the network on the following routes: Sassari—Alghero (30 km); Sassari—Nulvi (35 km); Sassari—Sorso (11 km); Macomer—Nuoro (61 km); and Cagliari—Isili (82 km). The remainder of the system was used by freight and tourist services only.

In 2001 a 950 mm gauge tramway system was under construction in Sassari. The eventual aim is to take over FdS lines to Sorso and Alghero, with a 10 km extension to Fertilia airport in prospect from the latter location.

In 1998, FdS recorded 39 million passenger-km, down from 44.1 million the previous year.

**Traction and rolling stock**
The railway operates four steam locomotives, 16 diesel locomotives, 39 diesel railcars, 53 coaches and 19 wagons.

*UPDATED*

*FdS LDe500 Breda-built diesel-electric locomotive at Nulvi with a permanent way train (Edward Barnes)*
2002/0524936

## Sassuolo—Modena Railway (ATCM)

Azienda Trasporti Consorziale de Modena
Piazza Manzoni 21, I-41100 Modena
Tel: (+39 059) 30 80 11   Fax: (+39 059) 30 42 99
Web: http://www.atcm.mo.it

**Key personnel**
President: Liliana Albertini
General Manager: Dr Ing Giancarlo Della Casa

Gauge: 1,435 mm
Route length: 16 km
Electrification: 16 km at 3 kV DC

**Organisation**
A new, partially underground 3 km connection is being built from Modena ATCM station to the more central FS station. This will allow interchange with other passenger and freight services. Opening is expected in late 2002. The intention is that ATCM should operate a cross-city service to Carpi over the FS line to Suzzara.

## 220 RAILWAY SYSTEMS/Italy

ATCM gained an open access freight licence in mid-2002.

**Traction and rolling stock**
The railway operates two electric locomotives, five emus, six coaches and 10 wagons. The emu fleet includes three-car units acquired second-hand from Belgian National Railways.

*UPDATED*

*ATCM emu and ex-SNCB unit (left) at Modena (David Haydock)*
*2001/0114253*

## Società Trasporto Alto Adige (STA)

**Organisation**
STA is to operate the Merano–Málles line, which is to reopen in early 2004, on behalf of Bolzano province, which has financed its refurbishment.

**Traction and rolling stock**
Eight Stadler GTW 2/6 emus have been ordered for this service at a cost of €23.2 million.

*NEW ENTRY*

## South Eastern Railway (FSE)

Managed by Government Commission, Rome
Ferrovie del Sud-Est
Via G Amendola 106, I-70126 Bari
Tel: (+39 080) 546 21 11   Fax: (+39 080) 546 22 80

**Key personnel**
Director General: Dr Carlo Bombrini

Gauge: 1,435 mm
Route length: 473 km

**Organisation**
This is geographically the largest private railway in Italy, operating most lines in the Otranto peninsula: Bari–Mungivacca–Conversano–Putignano–Martina Franca–Taranto (113 km); Mungivacca–Casamissima–Putignano (43 km); Martina Franca–Francavilla Fontana–Lecce (103 km); Lecce–Zollino–Nardo–Gallipoli–Casarano (75 km); Zollino–Maglie–Gagliano Léuca (47 km); Novoli–Nardo–Casarano–Gagliano–Léuca (75 km); and Maglie–Otranto (18 km).

In 1998, FSE achieved 120.2 million passenger-km, down from 125.3 million the previous year.

In 1996 FSE was allocated government funding of €646 million for improvement projects.

**Traction and rolling stock**
The railway operates 28 diesel locomotives, 52 diesel railcars and 31 trailers, 50 coaches and 181 wagons. In late 1999, FSE received the first of four new two-car dmus from Fiat. Each car is powered by two diesel engines of 280 kW each with Voith hydraulic transmission.

FSE has acquired from FS 10 ALn 668.1400 Fiat single-unit railcars, which are being modernised and converted into two-car sets at Alitransport's Leon d'Oro works. The first unit was handed over to FSE in August 2001. Type designation is Class AD 120. The company also tendered for 13 new two-car dmus in late 2000.

*UPDATED*

*FSE diesel locomotive heading a passenger service at Lecce (David Haydock)*
*2001/0114254*

## Suzzara–Ferrara Railway (FSF)

The FSF was one of four local railways which merged on 1 January 2001 to form the Emilia Romagna Railway (FER) (qv).

*UPDATED*

## Trento–Malè Railway (FTM)

Ferrovia Trento–Malè SpA
Via Secondo da Trento 7, PO Box 93, I-38100 Trento
Tel: (+39 0461) 43 11 11   Fax: (+39 0461) 82 02 56
e-mail: agoale@fertm.it
Web: http://www.fertm.it

**Key personnel**
Chairman: Giorgio Giuliani
Operating Manager: Dr Ing Agostino Alessandrini

Gauge: 1,000 mm
Route length: 56 km
Electrification: 56 km at 3 kV DC

**Organisation**
Principally a passenger operator (1.808 million journeys in 1998), the railway also moves 1,435 mm gauge freight

*FTM emu at Malè (David Haydock)*
*2001/0114255*

Jane's World Railways 2002-2003

wagons using a fleet of 12 transporter bogies and four transporter wagons. There is a 2.3 km dual-gauge section connecting the FS network at Trento with a factory at Gardolo.

Construction of a 10 km, four-station extension from Malè to Marilleva was expected to be completed in 2002 and studies have been conducted into a further 7 km extension to Fucine. As part of a continuing upgrading programme, 40 km of track between Taio and Terzolas was renewed in 1998.

### Traction and rolling stock
The rolling stock fleet comprises one electric locomotive, five electric railcars and two trailers, and nine three-car articulated emus. Twelve two-car low-floor Coradia emus were ordered from Alstom in March 2002 to enable service frequencies to be increased on Trento–Mezzo Lombardo and Trento–Malè routes. Delivery is planned for 2004.

*UPDATED*

## Turin Local Railways (SATTI)

SpA Torinese Trasporti Intercomunali
Corso Turati 19/6, I-10128 Turin
Tel: (+39 011) 576 41    Fax: (+39 011) 576 43 40
e-mail: satti@satti.it
Web: http://www.satti.it

### Key personnel
President: G Guiati
General Manager: Ing R Notaro

Gauge: 1,435 mm
Route length: 82 km
Electrification: 55 km at 3 kV DC

### Organisation
SATTI operates local services over two routes, Turin–Ceres (electrified as far as Germagnano) and Turin–Pont Canavese. A total of 2.6 million passenger journeys and 63.2 million passenger-km were recorded in 1996.

The Turin–Germagnano line reopened in April 2001 after construction of a new deviation to serve Turin airport and an underground deviation serving Caselle on the Turin–Ciriè section. Service frequencies have since been more than doubled. Rebuilding after a landslip plus re-electrification on the Germagnano–Ceres section was continuing in 2001. Electrification of the 22 km Settimo Torinese–Rivarolo Canevese line was completed in March 2002 at a cost of €5.2 million.

In the long term, the Turin–Ceres route is to be upgraded to regional metro standards and connected to the cross-city route currently under construction for FS (see Italian Railways entry).

Co-ordination of FS and SATTI services started on 1 September 1997 with a dmu service linking FS at Chieri via the city centre to Rivarola Canavese, on SATTI's non-electrified line. A second through service is planned linking SATTI's Germagnano station on the Ceres line via the city centre to a new destination which remains to be finalised.

Operations for both SATTI lines are to be controlled from a single new centre at Ciriè.

SATTI has been awarded the contract to manage construction and operation of Turin's first metro line.

*Former Belgian National Railways two-car emus in service with SATTI, photographed at Borgaro* (Quintus Vosman)    2002/0524921

The company gained an open access licence in September 2001.

### Traction and rolling stock
At the beginning of 1997 SATTI operated four diesel and four electric locomotives, 20 diesel railcars and 12 trailers, eight ex-Belgian National Railways emus, 15 coaches and 15 wagons. Seven Type Y 0530 two-car low-floor emus have recently been supplied by Fiat.

In 2001, tenders were called for 12 three-car emus.

*UPDATED*

## Venete Railways (FV)

Managed by Government Commission, Rome
Gestione Commissariale Governativa Ferrovie Venete
Piazza Giacomo Zanellatos 5, I-35131 Padua
Tel: (+39 049) 74 49 99    Fax: (+39 049) 77 43 99

### Key personnel
Director: Sergio Bertonasco

Gauge: 1,435 mm
Route length: 73 km

### Organisation
Until 2000, the Venete Railways group comprised two geographically separate routes, the Ferrovia Adria–Mestre (FAM) (57 km) and the Ferrovia Udine–Cividale (FUC) (16 km).

FV holds an open access licence.

Traffic in 1998 totalled 40.5 million passenger-km, up from 38.8 million the previous year.

### Traction and rolling stock
In 1999, rolling stock totalled 28 diesel railcars, seven driving trailers, eight diesel locomotives and six coaches.

*UPDATED*

*Two FV diesel railcars cross at Piove de Sacco, on the Ferrovia Adria–Mestre (FAM) line* (David Haydock)    2001/0114256

# JAMAICA

## Ministry of Transport and Works

1C-1F Pawsey Road, Kingston 5
Tel: (+1 809) 75 41 90 01; 754 25 84 92
Fax: (+1 809) 754 25 95
Web: http://www.mtw.gov.im

### Key personnel
Minister: Robert Pickersgill
Permanent Secretary: Dr Alwin Hayes

*UPDATED*

## Alcoa Railroads

Alcoa Minerals of Jamaica Inc
May Pen PO
Tel: (+1 809) 986 25 61
Fax: (+1 809) 986 20 26; 27 52; 27 53

### Key personnel
Manager, Railroad Operations: J Shim You
Superintendent, Maintenance: J R Graham

Gauge: 1,435 mm
Length: 40 km

### Traction and rolling stock
The railway operates three diesel locomotives and 90 freight wagons.

## Jamaica Railway Corporation (JRC)

PO Box 489, 142 Barry Street, Kingston
Tel: (+1 809) 922 66 20/15 31    Fax: (+1 809) 922 45 39
Gauge: 1,435 mm
Route length: 207 km

### Political background
In 1994 potential buyers of the largely defunct state-owned JRC system were invited to submit expressions of interest to the National Investment Bank of Jamaica. Interested parties were reported to include a Jamaican consortium comprising J Wray and Nephew, Desnoes and Geddes, Grace Kennedy and the Caribbean Cement Company. This process did not result in a revival of the system, and in late 1997 the Bank commissioned RITES of India to study rehabilitiation of the network for both passenger and freight traffic. The study found the system to be potentially profitable provided the emphasis remained on freight traffic, and the Jamaican government was reported as intending to initiate preparations for a revival of services by the end of 1998.

In 1999 no trains were running and all rolling stock remained in storage.

## Kaiser Bauxite Railway

Kaiser Jamaica Bauxite Co
Discovery Bay PO, St Ann
Tel: (+1 809) 973 22 21

### Key personnel
General Manager: R D Honiball
Chief Engineer: A H Gordon

Gauge: 1,435 mm
Length: 25 km

### Traction and rolling stock
The railway operates four diesel locomotives and 88 freight wagons.

# JAPAN

## Ministry of Transport

1-3, 2-chome, Kasumigaseki, Chiyoda-ku, Tokyo
Tel: (+81 3) 35 80 31 11

### Key personnel
Minister: Hajime Morita
Parliamentary Vice-Minister: Sei-ichi Eto
Administrative Vice-Minister: Minoru Toyoda

## Japan Railway Construction Public Corporation (JRCC)

Sanno Grand Building, 2-14-2, Nagata-cho, Chiyoda-ku, Tokyo
Tel: (+81 3) 35 06 18 94    Fax: (+81 3) 35 06 18 90

### Key personnel
President: Sumio Shiota

### Organisation
The Corporation was set up in 1964 to construct railways on behalf of the government for subsequent leasing or transfer to railway operating companies. It is responsible for the construction of all new Shinkansen lines and has taken over much other new construction work from the JR Group and other railways.

## Japan Railways Group (JR)

### Political background
*Privatisation*
Japanese National Railways (JNR) was statutorily disbanded in 1987 and its assets, operations and liabilities were distributed among a number of new companies, known as the Japan Railways Group. The dismemberment legislation provided that JNR's passenger business, its infrastructure and its assets, on JNR's 1,067 mm gauge network be distributed geographically between six companies, three on Honshu island and one each on Hokkaido, Shikoku and Kyushu.

Initially, all remained in the public domain. Only the Hokkaido, Shikoku and Kyushu companies started free of any inherited debt liabilities, but all three required subsidy for their current operations, which was provided through government- established Management Stabilising Funds.

Privatisation of the new companies was the ultimate objective of JNR's dismemberment. At the start of 1991 the Transport Ministry announced that two million shares in each of the three biggest companies, JR East, JR Central and JR West, would be put on the market in 1992, but, with the subsequent serious downturn of the Tokyo stock market, the placing was postponed. The sale of half the JNR Settlement Corporation's holding of four million JR East shares eventually took place in October 1993 and was heavily oversubscribed. JR Central and JR West flotations were scheduled for 1994-95 but the adverse effects of the Kobe earthquake on revenue and profitability led to postponement; sales of JR West shares took place in 1996, and JR Central followed in October 1997. The proceeds from the sales are intended to be used to reduce the ¥26,200 billion debt inherited from JNR.

Since 1984 over 35 local companies have been established to take over loss-making JNR/JR rural lines. The new operators are known as third-sector companies, because they are a hybrid of private and local community finance.

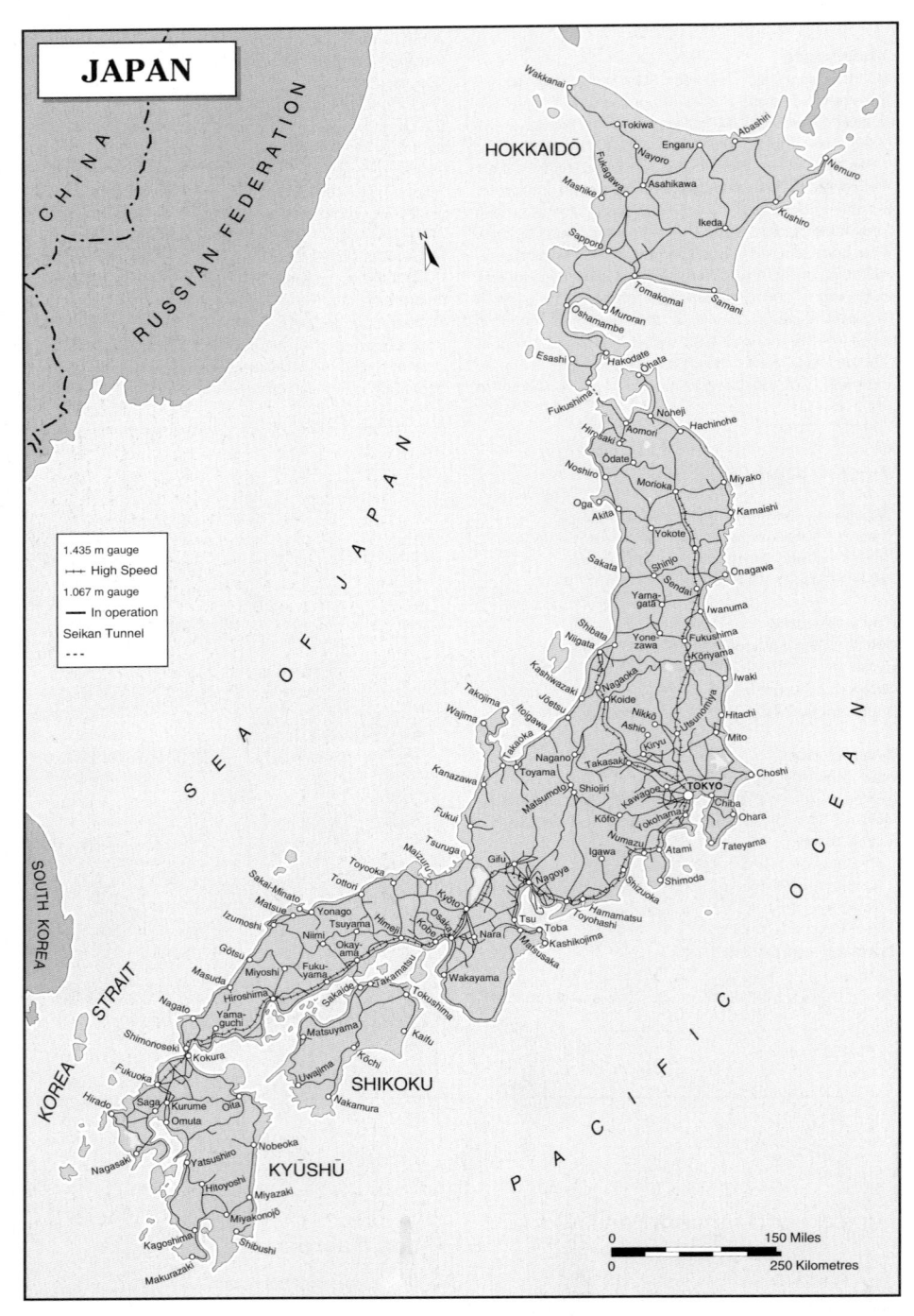

Previously, Japanese railway business was governed by two sets of statutes, one to regulate JNR and one covering other railways. This has been superseded by new legislation covering all railway business. It has reduced the degree of regulation, with provisos that railway safety and customer services are not impaired. A licence is required to run a railway business and railway facilities are subject to inspection. Furthermore, fares and charges must be approved in advance by the Minister of

Transport, although written notice is considered adequate for discounted fares and charges. Finally, train schedules must be submitted to the Ministry in advance of implementation.

*Shinkansen network*
The 1,435 mm gauge Shinkansen network was at first vested in a Shinkansen Property Corporation, which leased the infrastructure to the new companies for train operation. The companies were responsible for upkeep of the infrastructure. After protracted negotiations, terms were agreed in 1991 for sale of the network later in the year to the three companies operating it.

The proceeds were applied in part to the financing of Shinkansen network extensions begun in 1992, and also to clearing by the JNR Accounts Settlement Corporation of more of the accumulated debt left from the JNR regime.

## East Japan Railway Co (JR East)

2-2-2 Yoyogi, Shibya-ku, Tokyo 152-1578
Tel: (+81 3) 53 34 11 51  Fax: (+81 3) 53 34 11 10
Web: http://www.jreast.co.jp

**Key personnel**
Chairman: Masatake Matsuda
President and Chief Executive Officer: Mutsutake Otsuka
Executive Vice-Presidents
 Life-style Business Development Headquarters:
  Eiji Hosoya
 Railway Operations Headquarters: Yoshio Ishida
 Corporate Planning Headquarters: Satoshi Seino
Executive Directors
 Railway Operations Headquarters, Facilities and Construction Departments: Nobuyuki Hashiguchi
 Finance, Personnel and Health and Welfare Departments: Makoto Natsusme
 Railway Operations Headquarters, Marketing, Transport and Rolling Stock and Credit Card Development Departments and IT Business Project: Yasutomo Shirakawa
 Technology Planning Department, Corporate Planning Headquarters, JR East Research and Development Center, Transport Safety Department, Railway Operations Headquarters: Yukio Arimori
 Tokyo Branch Office: Hiroshi Okawa
 Administration, Inquiry and Audit, Public Relations and Legal Departments: Tetsujiro Tani
 Life-style Business Development Headquarters: Yoshiaki Arai

Gauge: 1,067 mm; 1,435 mm (Shinkansen)
Route length: 6,573.1 km; 956.3 km
Electrification: 2,671.6 km at 1.5 kV DC (1,067 mm); 1,887.4 km (1,067 mm) at 20 kV 50 Hz AC and 956.3 km (1,435 mm) at 20 kV 50 Hz AC

## Organisation

The railway runs rail passenger transport and related activities in the Tohoku region and the Tokyo metropolitan region, including the Tohoku and Joetsu Shinkansen. Some 304 Shinkansen and 12,192 conventional trains were operated daily from December 2001. In April 2002, 74,050 staff were employed.

**Finance** (million yen) Consolidated
| | 2000-01 | 2001-02 |
|---|---|---|
| Operating revenue | 2,546,041 | 2,543,378 |
| Operating expenditure | 2,222,289 | 2,227,038 |
| Transportation, other services and cost of sales | 1,722,744 | 1,712,324 |
| Sales, general and administrative expenses | 499,546 | 514,714 |
| Operating income | 323,751 | 316,339 |

*Series 215 bilevel 10-car suburban emu at Odawara (Wolfram Veith)*  0023015

*Series 209 'disposable' emu*  0001710

**Operating revenues and expenses**
In FY2001 (2001-02), operating revenue decreased by 0.1 per cent from ¥2,546 billion in FY2000 (2000-01) to ¥2,543.4 billion (US$19,123 million). This was due to a decrease in revenues from passenger transport, partially offset by an increase in revenues from the station space utilisation business.

Revenues from railway operations were ¥1,667.6 billion (US$12,538 million), a decrease of 0.8 per cent. Revenues from Shinkansen passes increased but revenues from non-pass travellers decreased on both Shinkansen and conventional lines.

Shinkansen network revenues decreased 1.0 per cent to ¥458.4 billion (US$3,447 billion) as the proportion of passengers using bargain-priced travel products increased despite an expansion of Shinkansen passenger-km. Revenue from Shinkansen passes was up 5.1 per cent to ¥21.3 billion (US$161 million) and revenue other than that from passes was down 1.3 per cent to ¥437.1 billion (US$3,286 million).

Tokyo metropolitan area network revenues decreased 0.3 per cent to ¥841.5 billion (US$6,327 million). Revenue from commuter passes was down 0.7 per cent to ¥346.1 billion (US$2,602 million). Non-commuter revenues remained at the same level as the previous year at ¥495.5 billion (US$3,725 million).

Intercity and regional network revenues declined 1.5 per cent to ¥367.6 billion (US$2,764 million). Commuter pass revenues decreased 0.2 per cent to ¥119.9 billion (US$901 million) and non-commuter revenues were down 2.0 per cent to ¥247.7 billion (US$1,863 million).

Revenues from businesses other than railway activities increased 1.1 per cent to ¥875.8 billion (US$6,585 million). This was mainly attributable to increases in revenues in retail businesses and restaurants within stations.

Operating expenses increases 0.2 per cent (¥4.7 billion) from ¥2,223.3 billion in FY2000-01 to ¥2,227.0 billion (US$16,745 million). Operating expenses accounted for 87.6 per cent of operating income in FY2001 and 87.3 per cent in FY2000.

| Traffic (million) | 1999-2000 | 2000-01 | 2001-02 |
|---|---|---|---|
| Passenger journeys | 5,893 | 5,862 | 5,846 |
| Passenger-km | 125,998 | 125,344 | 124,916 |

## Passenger operations
*Tokyo metropolitan area network*
The Tokyo metropolitan area network consists of 1,117.4 km of lines operating within a radius of approximately 100 km from Tokyo station, an area with a population of over 32 million. This network accounts for 61.01 per cent of JR East's total passenger-km and 44.3 per cent of its total operating revenues. Demand for commuter rail services is immense and the metropolitan area is the focus of considerable investment, aimed at reducing the serious overcrowding and lack of capacity. The company's Tokyo New Network 21 project involves lengthening trains, increasing train services and running faster trains on existing lines, together with infrastructure improvements – such as the electrification of the outer suburban Hachiko line which was completed in 1996.

On the Yamanote line orbiting central Tokyo, where the peak service operates at 2½ minute headways, standard train formations have been extended by one car to 11. The line's latest emu cars have six pairs of double doors in each bodyside to accelerate passenger loading and detraining, and foldaway seats to increase peak standing space to ease congestion. Similar cars were introduced on the Yokohama line in 1994, allowing an increase in train length from seven to eight cars, and on the Keihin–Tohoku line in May 1995 and subsequently on the Saikyo and Chuo–Sobu lines. Extra capacity is also provided by bilevel cars inserted in Series 211 electric trains operating south of Tokyo on the Tokaido line. In 1992 a new Series 215 design of 10-car emu formed exclusively of bilevel cars was introduced between Tokyo and Odawara. A further capacity increase has been provided by opening up freight tracks for new passenger services, notably the extension of the Saikyo Line to Ebisu and the Shonan–Shinjuku line, which commenced operations in 2001.

*Introduction of new cars in the Tokyo metropolitan area*
Series 209 10-car trainsets were introduced on the Keihin–Tohuku line in April 1993. Including the six-car sets operating on the Nambu line from Kawasaki from September 1996, the total in 2002 stood at 624 cars in service. These lightweight trains cost only two-thirds of that of a conventional emu. An extended maintenance cycle produces a further reduction in costs. JR East replaces some 400 cars each year to replace existing commuter stock, around 200 of which have been manufactured at the company's own Niitsu Rolling Stock Plant, supplemented by deliveries from traditional suppliers.

The low cost concept has also been employed in the development of the 15-car Series E217 outer suburban emus which now operate many services on the Sobu–Yokosuka lines. These units include two double-deck 'Green Class' cars and 13 standard class cars, 10 of which have only longitudinal seats to maximise capacity.

The Series E501 emus built for services on the Joban line incorporate converter-inverters made in Germany by Siemens. The Series E501 features 50 Hz AC/DC dual-mode and inverter control.

Series E231 cars were introduced in 2000. These are built to a wider profile as a congestion reducing measure, feature a Train Information System (TIMS) and are of a design that minimises maintenance requirements.

*Intercity and regional networks*
The intercity and regional networks operate on 5,464.4 km of rail lines serving areas throughout eastern Honshu, and include all non-Shinkansen lines outside the Tokyo metropolitan area, generating 24.8 per cent of the company's passenger-km and 19.3 per cent of total operating revenue.

Intercity services are being upgraded through the provision of improved connections with Shinkansen lines, increased frequencies, faster speeds, and through the introduction of newly designed trains tailored to the requirements of specific services. The Series 255 'Boso View Express' emus which were introduced in 1993 for limited express 'Super View Sazanami' and 'Super View Wakashio' services between Tokyo and the Boso Peninsula are designed for business and leisure travel, featuring both individual and group seating arrangements and compartments for stacking surfboards and golf bags.

Series E351 emus began running on 'Super Azusa' limited express services on the Chuo line between Tokyo (Shinjuku) and Nagano prefecture (Matsumoto) in December 1993. This series features an innovative suspension system for a smoother ride, longer trainsets giving 30 per cent more seating capacity and large windows for panoramic views.

New types of energy-saving Series E257 cars for express services were introduced on the Joban line 'Fresh Hitachi' train in 1997, on the Tohoku line 'Super Hatsukari' in 2000 and on the Chuo line 'Azusa' and Kaiji' in 2001. Series 701 AC emu cars have been introduced in the Tohoku region to reduce travel times and increase operational efficiency. These trains incorporate lightweight, stainless steel bodies that offer energy consumption and maintenance savings. The Series 701 has a maximum speed of 110 km/h and is operated as a two-car or three-car set. The latest variant is the two-car 701-5000, 10 sets of which have provided local services on the Tazawako Line (Akita Shinkansen) since March 1997. Series E127 emu cars have been introduced in DC electric sections in the Nagano district in Niigata prefecture.

In April 1999 JR East relaunched overnight services between Sapporo and Ueno using 12-car double-deck emus. The trains are operated under the 'Cassiopeia' brand-name.

*Shinkansen*
JR East's Shinkansen started operations in 1982 and currently covers a network extending in five directions: Tohoku; Yamagata; Akita; Joetsu; and Nagano. The number of trains currently operating each day is 304, three times the figure at the start of operations. Some 250,000 passengers use these services daily.

*Tohuku Shinkansen* (Tokyo–Morioka – 535.3 km)
The Tohoku Shinkansen commenced operations in June 1982 between Omiya and Morioka. Subsequently the section between Omiya and Ueno opened in March 1985

*Series E3 train for the Akita Mini-Shinkansen coupled to an older Series 200 unit at Omiya* (Wolfram Veith)
0023017

*Series 215 intercity emu forming 'Super View Odoriko No 1' service from Tokyo to Matsumoto* (Wolfram Veith)
0023016

*Series E2 Shinkansen trainset*

*JR East Series E1 double-deck Shinkansen trainset*

and that between Ueno and Tokyo in June 1991. From a figure of 94 daily services to and from Tokyo in 1987, JR East in December 2001 was running 153 trains each day. Initially trains ran at a top speed of 210 km/h but this was increased to 275 km/h in March 1997 with the introduction of new rolling stock. As a consequence, travel times between cities served has been reduced dramatically to 2 hours 21 minutes between Tokyo and Morioka (a reduction of 48 minutes compared with the 1987 journey time). In December 2002, the section between Morioka and Hachinohe (96.6 km) was scheduled to open, reducing the fastest journey between Tokyo and Hachinohe by 40 minutes to 2 hours 50 minutes. The number of passengers commuting to work or school by Shinkansen is also growing rapidly within 100 km of Tokyo as the commuting area expands and capacity during morning and evening peaks is being enhanced by increasing the number of trains, introducing double-deck trains that provide seating for 1,634 passengers and other measures.

*Joetsu Shinkansen* (Tokyo–Niigata – 333.9 km)
The Joetsu Shinkansen commenced operations in November 1982, six months after the commissioning of the Tohoku Shinkansen, and was completed between Tokyo and Niigata in June 1991. One feature of its operations is a large number of passengers during winter months travelling to and from a ski resort near Echigo-Yuzawa station, creating seasonal variations in demand. The number of daily trains has increased from 65 in 1987 to 95 in 2002. Maximum speed permitted in 275 km/h and the fastest trains connect Tokyo and Niigata in 1 hour 37 minutes. As with the Tohoku Shinkansen, the number of commuters using Joetsu Shinkansen services is increasing rapidly within 100 km of Tokyo and capacity is being increased by the deployment of double-deck eight- and 12-car trainsets, the latter providing seats for 1,229 passengers.

*Yamagata and Akita Shinkansen* (Tokyo–Yamagata – 359.9 km; Tokyo–Akita – 662.6 km)
Yamagata services between Tokyo and Yamagata were inaugurated in July 1992 and extended from Yamagata to Shinjo in December 1999. Thirty trains are operated daily between Tokyo and Yamagata, 16 of these extended to Shinjo. Akita Shinkansen services were inaugurated in March 1997. A total of 28 daily services operate between Tokyo and Akita, with two additional trains running between Sendai and Akita.

Yamagata Shinkansen trains between Tokyo and Fukushima and Akita Shinkansen services between Tokyo and Morioka run over the Tohoku Shinkansen line and are coupled to that route's trains. Through operation over Shinkansen and converted conventional lines eliminates the need for passengers to change trains at intermediate stations. The maximum speed on converted lines, which necessitated a large-scale gauge conversion programme, was raised to 130 km/h, greatly reducing travelling times: the fastest journey time between Tokyo and Yamagata is now 2 hours 29 minutes (a reduction of 53 minutes) and that between Tokyo and Akita 3 hours 49 minutes (a reduction of 77 minutes). This through operation does not add to train density between Tokyo and Omiya, where each Shinkansen competes for capacity, or to demand for the use of platforms at Tokyo station.

*Nagano Shinkansen* (Tokyo–Nagano – 222.4 km)
Nagano Shinkansen services were inaugurated in October 1997, just before the Nagano Olympics. This was the first new 'full standard' Shinkansen line in Japan for 15 years. Initially, 24 return services were provided between Tokyo and Nagano and four between Tokyo and Karuizawa. This has since been amended to provide 27 return services on the Tokyo–Nagano route and one between the capital and Karuizawa.

Features of the Nagano Shinkansen include a continuous gradient with a maximum of 3 per cent between Annaka-Haruna and Karuizawa and an alignment between Tokyo and Nagano for which 54 per cent is in tunnel. Maximum line speed is 260 km/h and the fastest Tokyo–Nagano journey time is 1 hour 19 minutes. Future plans foresee extension of the line to Kanazawa, in the Hokuriku area.

## Traction and rolling stock

As of April 2002, JR East owned two steam, 109 electric and 113 diesel locomotives, 11,699 Shinkansen and emu cars, 546 dmu cars, and 324 hauled passenger coaches.

In parallel with the increase in transport volume, the

### Principal JR East diesel locomotives

| Class | Wheel arrangement | Power kW | Speed km/h | Weight tonnes | No in service | First built | Mechanical | Builders Engine | Transmission |
|---|---|---|---|---|---|---|---|---|---|
| DD51 | B-2-B | 2,200 | 95 | 84 | 6 | 1966 | H/Me/K | 2 × 745 kW DML61Z | H 2 × DWZA |
| DD14 | B-B | 1,000 | 70 | 58 | 12 | 1966 | K | 2 × 373 kW DMF31SB-R | H 2 × DS1.2/1.35 |
| DD15 | B-B | 1,000 | 70 | 55 | 4 | 1961 | N | 2 × 373 kW DMF31SB | H 2 × DS1.2/1.35 |
| DE10 | AAA-B | 1,350 | 85 | 65 | 46 | 1969 | K/N/H | DML61ZB | H DW6 |
| DE11 | AAA-B | 1,350 | 85 | 70 | 9 | 1970 | K/N | DML61ZA, B | H DW6 |
| DE15 | AAA-B | 1,350 | 85 | 65 | 27 | 1970 | N | DML61ZB | H DW6 |

### Principal JR East diesel railcars

| Class | Cars per unit | Motor cars per unit | Motored axles/car | Power/motor kW | Speed km/h | Weight tonnes | Cars in service | First built | Mechanical | Builders Engine | Transmission |
|---|---|---|---|---|---|---|---|---|---|---|---|
| 28 | 1 | 1 | 1 | 135 | 95 | 34.1 | 11 | 1961 | F/NT | DMH17H D/S/NT | TC2A S/NC |
| 58 | 1 | 1 | 2 | 135 × 2 | 95 | 39.4 | 32 | 1961 | F/NT | DMH17H D/S/NT | TC2A S/NC |
| 30 | 1 | 1 | 1 | 135 | 95 | 32.4 | 3 | 1962 | F/NT/N | DMH17H D/S/NC | TC2A S/NC |
| 52 | 1 | 1 | 2 | 135 × 2 | 95 | 36.6 | 24 | 1962 | F/NT/N | DMH17H D/S/NC | TZ2A S/NC |
| 40 | 1 | 1 | 1 | 165 | 95 | 37.3 | 110 | 1977 | F/NT | DMF15HSA D/S/NT | DW10 S/NC |
| 47 | 1 | 1 | 1 | 165 | 95 | 35.9 | 28 | 1977 | F/NT | DMF15HSA D/S/NT | TC2A S/NC |
| 48 | 1 | 1 | 1 | 165 | 95 | 36.2 | 71 | 1979 | F/NT | DMF15HSA D/S/NT | TC2A S/NC |
| 100/101 | 1 | 1 | 1 | 245 | 100 | 24.9 | 64 | 1990 | F/NT | DMF11HZ DMF14HZT | DW14B NC |
| 110 | 1 | 1 | 1 | 313 | 100 | 29.4/29.9 | 89 | 1990 | F/NT | DMF13HZA DMF14HZA | DW14A Voith |
| 111 | 1 | 1 | 1 | 313 | 100 | 28.9/29.4 | 47 | 1991 | F/NT | DMF13HZA DMF14HZA | DW14A-B NC |
| 112 | 1 | 1 | 1 | 313 | 100 | 28.4/28.9 | 47 | 1991 | F/NT | DMF13HZA DMF14HZA | DW14A-B NC |

Abbreviations: D: Daihatsu Motor; F: Fuji Heavy Industries Ltd; Fe: Fuji Electric; H: Hitachi; K: Kawasaki Heavy Industries; Kn: Kinki Sharyo; Me: Mitsubishi Electric; Mh: Mitsubishi Heavy Industries; N: Nippon Sharyo Seizo; NC: Niigata Converter; NT: Niigata Engineering; S: Shinko Engineering; Se: Shinko Electric; T: Toshiba; To: Toyo Denki Seizo

### Principal JR East electric railcars or multiple-units

| Class | Cars per unit | Motor cars per unit | Motored axles/car | Output/motor kW | Speed km/h | Cars in service | First built | Mechanical | Builders Electrical |
|---|---|---|---|---|---|---|---|---|---|
| **1.5 kV DC** | | | | | | | | | |
| 103 | 10 | 6 | 4 | 110 | 100 | 935 | 1964 | N/T/H/K/Kn | H/T/Me/Fe/To |
| 107 | 2 | 1 | - | - | 100 | 54 | 1988 | | |
| 201 | 10 | 6 | 4 | 150 | 100 | 781 | 1979 | N/T/H/K/Kn | H/T/Me/Fe/To |
| 203 | 10 | 6 | 4 | 150 | 100 | 170 | 1982 | N/T/H/K/Kn | H/T/Me/Fe/To |
| 205 | 10 | 6 | 4 | 150 | 100 | 1,413 | 1984 | N/T/H/K/Kn | H/T/Me/Fe/To |
| 207 | 10 | 6 | 4 | 150 | 100 | 10 | 1986 | | |
| 209 | 10 | 4 | 4 | 95 | 110 | 1,028 | 1993 | R/T | M/T/To |
| 113 | 4 | 2 | 4 | 120 | 100 | 766 | 1963 | N/T/H/K/Kn | H/T/Me/Te/To |
| 115 | 4 | 2 | 4 | 120 | 100 | 718 | 1966 | N/T/H/K/Kn | H/T/Me/Fe/To |
| 211 | 10 | 4 | 4 | 120 | 110 | 575 | 1985 | N/T/H/K/Kn | H/T/Me/Fe/To |
| 215 | 10 | 4 | 4 | 120 | 120 | 40 | 1992 | N/N | To/Se |
| 165 | 3 | 2 | 4 | 120 | 110 | 55 | 1962 | N/T/H/K/N | H/T/Me/Fe/To |
| 167 | 4 | 2 | 4 | 120 | 110 | 35 | 1965 | | |
| 169 | 3 | 2 | 4 | 120 | 110 | 15 | 1968 | | |
| 251 | 10 | 6 | 4 | 120 | 120 | 40 | 1990 | R/S | To/Se/M |
| 253 | 3 | 2 | 4 | 120 | 130 | 99 | 1991 | T/S | H/M/Se/To |
| 301 | 10 | 8 | 4 | 110 | 100 | 50 | 1966 | | |
| E127 | 2 | 1 | 4 | 120 | 110 | 50 | 1994 | K | To/Me |
| E217 | 11 | 4 | 4 | 95 | 120 | 745 | 1994 | K/Tk | Me/To |
| 255 | 9 | 4 | 4 | 95 | 130 | 45 | 1993 | Kn/Tk | T/To |
| E351 | 8 | 4 | 4 | 150 | 130 | 60 | 1993 | H/N | H/To |
| E231 | 10 | 4 | 4 | 95 | 120 | 953 | 2000 | NI/K/Tk | Me/H/T/Fe |
| **Dual-voltage 1.5 kV/20 kV** | | | | | | | | | |
| 417 | 3 | 2 | 4 | 120 | 100 | 15 | 1978 | | |
| 403 | 4 | 2 | 4 | 120 | 100 | 40 | 1966 | | |
| 415 | 4 | 2 | 4 | 120 | 100 | 303 | 1971 | N/K/Kn | H/T/Me/Te/To |
| 455 | 3 | 2 | 4 | 120 | 110 | 105 | 1962 | N/T/H/K/Kn | H/T/Me/Fe/To |
| 183 | 4 | 2 | 4 | 120 | 120 | 195 | 1972 | N/T/K/Kn | H/T/Me/Fe/To |
| 185 | 4 | 2 | 4 | 120 | 110 | 227 | 1980 | N/T/K/H/K | H/T/Me/Fe/To |
| 189 | 9 | 3 | 4 | 120 | 120 | 118 | 1974 | | |
| 485 | 4 | 2 | 4 | 120 | 120 | 252 | 1968 | N/T/H/K | H/T/Me/Fe/To |
| 489 | 9 | 6 | 4 | 120 | 120 | 2 | 1971 | | |
| 583 | 4 | 2 | 4 | 120 | 120 | 24 | 1968 | N/T/H/K/Kn | |
| 651 | 17 | 4 | 4 | 120 | 130 | 99 | 1988 | K | |
| E501 | 10 | 4 | 4 | 120 | 120 | 60 | 1994 | Tk | Si/H/T |
| **20 kV AC** | | | | | | | | | |
| 717 | 3 | 2 | - | - | 110 | 30 | 1985 | | |
| 719 | 3 | 1 | - | - | 110 | 108 | 1990 | | |
| 200* | 12 | 12 | 4 | 230 | 240 | 384 | 1980 | N/T/H/K | H/T/Me/Fe/To/Se |
| 400* | 6 | 6 | 4 | 210 | 240 | 84 | 1990 | T/H/K | H/T/M/Fe To |
| 701 | 2 | 1 | 4 | 125 | 110 | 266 | 1992 | K | Me/T/Fe |
| **25 kV AC** | | | | | | | | | |
| E1* | 12 | 6 | 4 | 410 | 240 | 72 | 1993 | H/K | H/T/Me/To |
| E2* | 8 | 6 | 4 | 300 | 275 | 232 | 1995 | H/K/N | H/Me/T/To |
| E3* | 5 | 4 | 4 | 300 | 275 | 116 | 1995 | K/TK | H/T/Me/To |
| E4* | 8 | 4 | 4 | 420 | 240 | 192 | 1997 | H/K | Me/To/H/T |

* Shinkansen

Abbreviations: D: Daihatsu Motor; F: Fuji Heavy Industries Ltd; Fe: Fuji Electric; H: Hitachi; K: Kawasaki Heavy Industries; Kn: Kinki Sharyo; Me: Mitsubishi Electric; Mh: Mitsubishi Heavy Industries; N: Nippon Sharyo Seizo; NC: Niigata Converter; NI: JR East Niitsu Sharyo Seisakusho; NT: Niigata Engineering; S: Shinko Engineering; Se: Shinko Electric; T: Toshiba; To: Toyo Denki Seizo; TK: Tokyu Sharyo; Si: Siemens

Note: JR East leases Series 400 and Series E3 trains from Yamagata JR through Superexpress Holding Co and Akita Shinkansen Trains Holding Co respectively.

number of Shinkansen cars has also been increased. With the planned extension of the Tohoku Shinkansen to Hachinohe in December 2002, the E2 trainset fleet is being expanded. The existing 15 eight-car Series E2 trainsets are being increased to 10-car sets and 14 additional units will be progressively added to the fleet. By 2005, 120 Series 200 emu trainsets will be refurbished and 240 Series 200 emu cars will be renewed.

JR East has converted its maintenance works at Niitsu, Niigata prefecture, into a full-scale manufacturing plant for the production of a proportion of its own rolling stock. Production began in 1993, and the annual output between 1994 and 2001 was 1,319 cars. Vehicles produced comprise Series 209, E217 and E231 cars.

### Signalling and telecommunications

The principal signalling systems comprise:
ATS-P (Automatic Train Stop-Pattern): 1,422 km
ATC (Automatic Train Control): 1,022 km
CTC (Centralised Traffic Control): 6,206 km
ATOS (Autonomous Decentralized Transport Operation Control System): 570 km
Fibre optic cables: 2,906 km

ATS-P is an automatic brake control and signalling system which is being installed on busy sections in the Tokyo metropolitan area. Its computerised system checks intervals between trains and train speed using data sent from a signal to the train.

ATOS employs the latest computer and information technology and is also used on busy sections of the Tokyo metropolitan area. It provides the control centre with detailed information on train position and delay status and incorporates functions automatically to control train routes according to the schedule database and their routeing within stations. This enhances provision of passenger information in event of service disruption. In addition, safety during track maintenance is enhanced by the ability of staff to use a computer terminal to prevent trains entering a work site.

Fibreoptic cables have been laid in the Tokyo metropolitan area to provide a self-supporting communications network which will ensure the maintenance of safe and reliable train operations and also act as a network for various kinds of information.

### Track

**Rail type and weight:** 50 kg N rail; 60 kg N rail
**Sleepers**
PC (concrete) sleepers:
Shinkansen: 2,400 × 254.6 × 330 mm
Conventional lines: 2,000 × 174 × 240 mm
Wood sleepers:
Conventional lines: 2,100 × 140 × 200 mm
**Fastenings**
Shinkansen: direct fastening 8-type for slab track; 102-type and Pandrol-type for PC sleeper ballasted track
Conventional lines: 5-type; Pandrol-type
**Min curve radius:** Shinkansen: 4,000 m
**Min curvature radius on trunk lines:** 300-800 m, depending on train speed and tonnage carried, as well as on the number of sleepers used
**Max gradient:** Tohoku and Joetsu Shinkansen 3.5%, Yamagata and Akita Shinkansen 3.8%; conventional lines 3.5%
**Max permissible axleload:** 17 tonnes

**Sleeper spacing per km**
1st grade line, PC (prestressed concrete): 1,760; wood: 1,920
2nd grade line, PC: 1,560; wood: 1,640
3rd grade line, PC: 1,560; wood: 1,560
4th grade line, PC: 1,480; wood: 1,480
On sharp curves and sharp gradient sections, the number of wood sleepers shown is increased by 2/25 m.
Shinkansen lines: 1,720

***UPDATED***

### Principal JR East electric locomotives

| Class | Wheel arrangement | Line voltage | Output kW | Speed km/h | Weight tonnes | No in service | First built | Builders |
|---|---|---|---|---|---|---|---|---|
| ED75 | B-B | 20 kV | 1,900 | 100 | 67.2 | 12 | 1968 | Me/H/T |
| EF64 | B-B-B | 1.5 kV | 2,550 | 115 | 96 | 14 | 1964 | T/K/To |
| EF65 | B-B-B | 1.5 kV | 2,550 | 115 | 96 | 19 | 1965 | T/To/N |
| EF81 | B-B-B | 1.5 kV 20 kV | 2,550 2,370 | 115 | 100.8 | 61 | 1968 | H/Me |

## Central Japan Railway Co (JR Central)

Head office: JR Central Towers, 1-1-4 Meieki, Nakamura-ku, Nagoya, Aichi 450-0003
Tel: (+81 52) 564 23 17   Fax: (+81 52) 587 13 00
Tokyo office, International Department: Yaesu Center Building, 1-6-6 Yaesu, Chuo-ku, Tokyo 103-8288
Tel: (+81 3) 32 74 97 27   Fax: (+81 3) 52 55 67 80
Web: http://www.jr-central.co.jp

### Key personnel

Chairman: Hiroshi Suda
President: Yoshiyuki Kasai
Vice-Presidents: Masayuki Matsumoto; Takao Watanabe
Senior Executive Directors
  Personnel and Public Relations: Masataka Ishizuka
  Finance, Property Management and Audit:
    Takeshi Shida
Executive Directors
  Conventional Lines Operations: Okio Shozawa
  Shinkansen Operations: Sakio Masunaga
  Marketing and Chubu International Airport:
    Toshiaki Araya
  Corporate Planning: Yoshiomo Yamada
  Secretariat, Administration and Legal Affairs:
    Akihiro Amaya
  Linear Express Development: Akio Seki
  Affiliated Enterprises: Kazuaki Udagawa
  Shizuoka Branch Office: Kyohei Kimura
  Technical Research and Development: Hiraku Honda

Gauge: 1,067 mm; 1,435 mm (Tokaido Shinkansen)
Route length: 1,425 km; 553 km
Electrification: 944 km at 1.5 kV DC (1,067 mm); 553 km at 25 kV 60 Hz (1,435 mm)

### Organisation

Successful flotation of JR Central took place on the Tokyo Stock Exchange in October 1997. The core of JR Central's operations is the Tokaido Shinkansen, linking Tokyo, Nagoya and Osaka. The company also operates a network of conventional lines in central Japan. It has diversified into 40 subsidiary companies forming the Central Japan Railway Group. JR Central Towers, the core project of the group's affiliated business diversification plan, houses rental office units, a department store, hotel and other facilities.

On 31 March 2001 JR Central employed 21,727 staff.

### Finance

Improvement in the Japanese economy remained unclear in FY2000-01, which ended 31 March 2001, despite temporary signs of recovery in corporate capital investment and earnings. Persistent concern about a further slowdown in the domestic economy was an especially negative factor during the year.

In this economic environment, JR Central continued to place top priority on assuring transport safety and reliability, the fundamental strengths of the railway business. Specifically, the company focused on improving services in response to customer needs and worked to secure higher revenues through effective promotion and sales activities.

Various medium- and long-term projects were in progress. First, JR Central established autumn 2003 as the scheduled season for opening of the Tokaido Shinkansen's new Shinagawa station, together with a service improvement plan. A key element of the plan is the operation of seven Nozomi-type trains each hour. To put the plan into practice, the company made steady progress in constructing the new station and in introducing new Series 700 rolling stock. Geological, topographical and other tests covering the entire route of the Chuo Shinkansen also continued. In addition, the company made progress in the development of maglev railway technologies by conducting running tests aimed at verifying long-term durability and reducing costs.

Operations at all businesses located in JR Central Towers began in May 2000. Attracting numerous visitors, this complex located above Nagoya station made a healthy start, with occupancy surpassing initial business targets.

As a result, consolidated revenues in FY2000-01 amounted to ¥1,333 billion, up 9 per cent from the previous year. Factors contributing to this increase included a rise in transportation volume on the Tokaido Shinkansen service. Consolidated net income increased by 40.6 per cent to ¥53 billion and net income per share was ¥23,643. Consolidated total long-term debt at the fiscal year-end totalled ¥4,710 billion, down ¥232 billion from the previous year.

*A Series 700 Shinkansen trainset forming a JR Central Nozomi service crosses the Fujikawa river* (Wolfram Veith)
*2001/0099122*

| Finance (million yen) | 1998-99 | 1999-2000 | 2000-01 |
|---|---|---|---|
| **Operating revenues** (non-consolidated) | | | |
| Railway | 1,097,430 | 1,081,501 | 1,095,997 |
| Other | 9,434 | 8,898 | 8,894 |
| Total | 1,106,864 | 1,090,399 | 1,104,891 |
| **Operating expenses** (non-consolidated) | | | |
| Railway | 764,800 | 757,323 | 774,860 |
| Other | 6,581 | 6,285 | 5,298 |
| Total | 771,381 | 763,608 | 780,158 |

| Traffic (million) | 1998-99 | 1999-2000 | 2000-01 |
|---|---|---|---|
| Passenger journeys | 502 | 496.5 | 497.3 |
| Passenger-km | 48,538 | 47,892 | 48,674 |

### Passenger operations

*Tokaido Shinkansen*
The Tokaido Shinkansen operates at a maximum speed of 270 km/h to cover the 515.4 km between Tokyo and Shin-Osaka in a best time of 2 hours 30 minutes. Business volumes are considerable, with ridership of 357,000

passengers daily and 130 million annually. There are 285 departures per day (11 per hour from Tokyo during peak periods) and the average deviation from schedule is 0.6 minute per train. Safety is assured by an automatic train control system.

Currently, there are three types of Shinkansen service: Nozomi, the fastest service between Tokyo and Osaka, which stops at major stations; Hikari, which stops at selected stations; and Kodama, which stops at every station.

The company endeavoured to improve services. For example, in October 2000 a timetable revision was implemented that increased the number of Nozomi departures and doubled the number of Nozomi trains stopping at Shin-Yokohama station. As a result, annual transportation volume on the Tokaido Shinkansen rose by 2 per cent to 39,670 million passenger-km and revenues from operations climbed to ¥932 billion.

*Nozomi services*
In FY91-92, the company took a significant step in reducing travel time by bringing the Series 300 Nozomi train into service. In FY92-93, the frequency of Nozomi train departures from Tokyo station was increased to one per hour, and through operation to Hakata station, a terminal of the Sanyo Shinkansen, began. In November 1997, in response to greater demand for Nozomi services, departure frequency from Tokyo station was raised to two per hour in peak periods.

In late 2001, the frequency of Nozomi train departures was raised to one every 30 minutes, further improving the service.

JR Central has developed the Series 700 high-speed trainset jointly with JR West as the successor to the Series 300. It was introduced from the March 1999 timetable revision. As well as offering increased passenger comfort and performance, the Series 700 contributes to enhanced operational efficiency and flexibility by enabling common operation with Series 300 trainsets.

*Conventional lines network*
JR Central's network of conventional lines comprises the Tokaido line and 11 other lines, which cover a total route length of 1,430.9 km. Providing services principally in and around Nagoya and Shizuoka to meet commuter and intercity express demand, these lines play an important role in central Japan's transport network.

JR Central has introduced a number of types of train on its conventional lines designed to meet specific journey needs. The Series 383 Shinano Express emu employs a controlled tilting system, self-steering bogies and VVVF control to allow operation at higher speeds on twisting routes in mountainous areas while enhancing passenger comfort. Other types include the Series 85 Hida and Nanki dmus; the Series 371 Asagiri emu, which provides through services to the Odakyu Lines in the Tokyo metropolitan area; and the Series 313 emu, which has improved comfort for users of local services and reduced average operating and maintenance costs.

In July 1998, JR Central and JR West commenced operating the 'Sunrise Express' sleeping car service, the first new overnight service since the reform of Japanese National Railways. The service targets strong demand for transport between eastern and western Japan after airlines have stopped flying for the day.

JR Central has pursued a strategy of enhancing its local commuter services as well as developing intercity products, by introducing new rolling stock and by revising the timetables of individual lines better to accommodate customer needs. This process also involves increasing the number of departures and improving connections between express trains and the Tokaido Shinkansen to maximise utilisation of the company's total rail network. JR Central also intends to implement innovative measures to enhance the responsiveness of its services to diverse regional transport needs.

JR Central's conventional railway services in the Nagoya metropolitan area benefited from the power of the newly opened JR Central Towers in drawing customers. Due to reduced patronage of limited express trains and other factors, however, annual transportation volume on the conventional network fell by 0.1 per cent to 9,004 million passenger-km and revenues from operations decreased 0.9 per cent to ¥109 billion.

**New lines**
*The Chuo Shinkansen Maglev project*
The projected Chuo Shinkansen is a new high-speed railway linking Tokyo and Osaka. It is intended to support Japan's socio-economic development, help strengthen

*T4 Doctor Yellow test train for evaluating track condition and power supplies on Shinkansen lines* 2002/0113593

*JR Central continues development of its superconducting maglev technology at its test track in Yamanashi prefecture* 0063326

*Series 383 Shinano Express tilting trainset (Wolfram Veith)* 0063325

*Driving cab of a Series 700 trainset* 2002/0113581

the country's preparedness against natural disasters and contribute to energy conservation and global environmental conservation. In view of the important role of the Chuo Shinkansen, the implementation of the project is keenly anticipated.

As the future management entity of the Chuo Shinkansen, JR Central considers the Superconducting Maglev to be suitable for adoption on realisation of the Chuo Shinkansen because of its advanced characteristics and high-speed performance. The company has pursued the practical application of the Superconducting Maglev since April 1997 by conducting running tests on the Yamanashi Maglev Test Line in co-operation with the Railway Technical Research Institute.

On 14 April 1999 a manned trainset reached a world record speed of 552 km/h, enabling JR Central to confirm the operability of maglev technologies at the planned maximum service speed of 500 km/h. On 16 November 1999 passing tests were conducted using two trainsets which achieved a closing speed of 1,003 km/h. In March 2000 the practicability of a high-speed mass transit system using Superconducting Maglev technology was confirmed by a Ministry of Transport committee. JR Central is to continue running tests on the Yamanashi Maglev Test Line until 2005, to bring the system closer to practical perfection. These will include running tests aimed at further confirming durability and reducing costs.

### Improvements to existing lines

In September 2001 JR Central introduced a new multiple inspection train, claimed to be the first in the world to measure track, catenary, signalling and telecommunications facilities while travelling at speeds of up to 270 km/h. The train is intended for use on the Tokaido and Sanyo Shinkansen lines.

### Traction and rolling stock

As at 31 March 2001 Shinkansen rolling stock (1,435 mm gauge) comprised 122 16-car trainsets of three types (see table). In March 1999, timetables were revised and Series 700 trainsets commenced commercial Nozomi services. Developed jointly by JR Central and JR West as a next-generation Shinkansen design for both railways, the 16-car 270 km/h unit features an innovative aerodynamic nose shape, aluminium alloy bodyshells and VVVF control.

On 1,067 mm gauge JR Central operated 1,119 emu cars and 229 dmu cars. Also included in the fleet were eight electric and 10 diesel locomotives and 26 hauled passenger cars.

In 1991 JR Central began remotoring its diesel railcars with Cummins engines. The initial programme embraced 41 Kiha 11 and 80 Kiha 85 cars. Over 200 JR Central railcars are now powered by Cummins C-DMF14HZ engines including the Kiha 75 and Kiha 85 dmus.

The company introduced Series 313 emu trains in FY1999-2000, improving comfort levels in local trains while also reducing operating and maintenance costs.

### Signalling and telecommunications

The Tokaido Shinkansen's ATC (Automatic Train Control) system features innovative two-frequency equipment which permitted the introduction of 270 km/h operation in early 1992. The Tokaido Shinkansen facilities support one of the safest and most reliable high-speed railway services in the world. JR Central is currently developing a new Automatic Train Control (ATC) system to replace the existing equipment. The new system will control train operating speeds using a design that will allow for higher levels of safety, reliability and maintainability, as well as smoother train control.

JR Central has made steady investments in centralised traffic control for its conventional lines, and by the end of FY2000-01 the system was controlling 96 per cent of the 1,067 mm gauge network. A new automatic train stop system known as ATS-ST is now standardised throughout the network. A modification to the system activates an emergency brake application if a driver ignores a signal at danger.

### Track

(1,067 mm gauge lines)
**Rail:** 30.1 to 60.8 kg/m (on main routes 60.8 or 50.47 kg/m)
**Sleepers:** Prestressed concrete or timber 2,000 × 240 × 174 mm, spaced 1,480 to 1,920/km according to grade of route
**Fastenings:** elastic or rigid
**Min curve radius:** 300 to 800 m, according to maximum speed

### Diesel locomotives

| Class | Wheel arrangement | Power kW | Speed km/h | Weight tonnes | No in service | First built | Builders Engine | Transmission |
|---|---|---|---|---|---|---|---|---|
| DE10 | AAA-B | 1,350 | 85 | 65 | 6 | 1970 | DML61ZB | H DW6 |
| DE15 | AAA-B | 1,350 | 85 | 65 | 2 | 1978 | DML61ZB | H DW6 |
| DD51 | B-2-B | 2,200 | 95 | 76 | 2 | 1971 | 2 × DML61Z | H 2 × DW2A |

### Electric locomotives

| Class | Wheel arrangement | Output kW | Speed km/h | Weight tonnes | No in service | First built |
|---|---|---|---|---|---|---|
| 1.5 kV DC | | | | | | |
| EF58 | 2C + 2C | 1,900 | 120 | 113-115 | 2 | 1957 |
| EF64 | B-B-B | 2,550 | 115 | 96 | 3 | 1964 |
| EF65 | B-B-B | 2,550 | 115 | 96 | 2 | 1969 |
| ED18 | A1A-A1A | 915 | 70 | 66 | 1 | 1954 |

### Diesel railcars or multiple-units

| Class | Cars per unit | Motor cars per unit | Motored axles/car | Power/motor kW | Speed km/h | No in service | First built | Bodies | Builders Engine | Transmission |
|---|---|---|---|---|---|---|---|---|---|---|
| 28 | 2 | 2 | 1 | 180 | 95 | 2 | 1962 | | DMH17H | H TC2A or DF115A |
| 58 | 2 | 2 | 2 | 180 × 2 | 95 | 3 | 1962 | | DMH17H | H TC2A or DF115A |
| 58-5000 | 2 | 2 | 2 | 350 | 110 | 2 | 1965 | | DMF14HZB | H C-DW14A |
| 65-3000 | 2 | 2 | 2 | 500 | 95 | 1 | 1970 | | DML30HSD | H DW4F |
| 65-5000 | 2 | 2 | 2 | 500 | 110 | 1 | 1969 | | DML30HSD | H DW4F |
| 11-0, -100, -200 | 1 | 1 | 2 | 330 | 95 | 35 | 1988 | | C-DMF14HZA | H C-DW15 |
| 11-300 | 1 | 1 | 2 | 350 | 95 | 6 | 1999 | | C-DMF14HZB | H C-DW15 |
| 40 | 1 | 1 | 1 | 350 | 95 | 14 | 1979 | | DMF14HZ | H DW10 |
| 47 | 2 | 2 | 1 | 220 350 | 95 | 5 | 1976 | | DMF15HSA DMF14HZB | H DW10 H DW10 |
| 48 | 2 | 2 | 1 | 350 220 | 95 | 40 | 1979 | | DMF14HZ BMF15HSA | H DW10 H DW10 |
| 85 | 3/4/5 | 3/4/5 | 2 | 350 × 2 | 120 | 80 | 1988 | N/F/Nt | DMF14HZ | H DW14A |
| 75 | 2 | 2 | 2 | 350 × 2 | 120 | 40 | 1993 | N | DMF14HZB | H DW14A |

Abbreviations: N: Nippon Sharyo Seizo Ltd; F: Fuji Juko; Nt: Niigata Tekko

### Electric railcars or multiple-units

| Class | Cars per unit | Motor cars per unit | Motored axles/car | Output/motor kW | Speed km/h | Cars in service | First built |
|---|---|---|---|---|---|---|---|
| 1.5 kV DC | | | | | | | |
| 103 | 3, 7 | 2, 4 | 4 | 100 | 100 | 10 | 1965 |
| 113 | 3, 4, 6 | 2, 4 | 4 | 120 | 100 | 218 | 1963 |
| 115 | 3 | 2 | 4 | 120 | 100 | 63 | 1966 |
| 117 | 4 | 2 | 4 | 120 | 110 | 72 | 1982 |
| 119 | 1, 2 | 1 | 4 | 110 | 100 | 57 | 1982 |
| 123 | 1 | 1 | 4 | 120 | 100 | 7 | 1988 |
| 165 | 3 | 2, 4 | 4 | 120 | 110 | 12 | 1963 |
| 211-0 | 4 | 2 | 4 | 120 | 110 | 8 | 1986 |
| 211-5000 | 3, 4 | 2 | 4 | 120 | 110 | 242 | 1988 |
| 213 | 2 | 1 | 4 | 120 | 110 | 28 | 1989 |
| 285 | 7 | 2 | 4 | 220 | 130 | 14 | 1998 |
| 311 | 4 | 2 | 4 | 120 | 120 | 60 | 1989 |
| 311 | 2, 3, 4 | 1, 1.5, 2 | 2, 4 | 185 | 120 | 77 | 1999 |
| 313 | 2, 3, 4 | 1, 2, 2 | 4, 2 | 185 | 120 | 187 | 1999 |
| 371 | 7 | 5 | 4 | 120 | 120 | 7 | 1990 |
| 373 | 3 | 1 | 4 | 185 | 120 | 42 | 1995 |
| 381 | 4, 6 | 2, 4 | 4 | 120 | 120 | 16 | 1973 |
| 383 | 2, 4, 6 | 1, 2, 3 | 4 | 155 | 130 | 76 | 1994 |

### Shinkansen trainsets (1,435 mm gauge)

| Class | Cars per unit | Motor cars per unit | Motored axles/car | Output/motor kW | Speed km/h | Weight tonnes | Cars in service | First built |
|---|---|---|---|---|---|---|---|---|
| 25 kV 60 Hz | | | | | | | | |
| 100 | 16 | 12 | 4 | 230 | 220 | 57.8 | 592 | 1985 |
| 300 | 16 | 10 | 4 | 300 | 270 | 44.4 | 976 | 1989 |
| 700 | 16 | 12 | 4 | 275 | 285 | 44.3 | 384 | 1997 |

*JR Central Class 211 emu, used for local services (Wolfram Veith)*

Max gradient: 1 to 3.5%, according to maximum speed
Max axleloading: 16 tonnes

**Track**
(Tokaido Shinkansen)
Rail type: 60.8 kg/m
Sleepers: Prestressed concrete 2,400 × 330 × 255 mm, or 2,400 × 300 × 219 mm, spaced 1,720/km
Fastenings: Elastic
Min curve radius: 2,500 m
Max gradient: 2%
Max axleloading: 18 tonnes

*Series 313 suburban emu with VVVF control*
*2002*/0113592

# West Japan Railway Co (JR West)

4-24, Shibata 2-chome, Kita-ku, Osaka, 530-8341
Tel: (+81 6) 375 89 81   Fax: (+81 6) 375 89 19
e-mail: ir@westjr.co.jp
Web: http://www.westjr.co.jp

**Key personnel**
Chairman: Masatake Ide
President: Shojiro Nanya
Executive Vice-President: Takeshi Kakiuchi
Senior Managing Directors: Kazuyoshi Kudo, Sunao Moritake, Masayuki Sakata
Directors: Akio Nomura, Yoshio Tateishi

Gauge: 1,067 mm; 1,435 mm (Sanyo Shinkansen)
Route length: 4,435 km; 644 km
Electrification: 3,217 km at 1.5 kV DC (1,067 mm); 645 km (1,435 mm) and 320 km (1,067 mm) at 20 kV AC 60 Hz

**Organisation**
The railway runs passenger transport and related activities in the Hokuriku region and western Honshu, an area of 43 million inhabitants – 34 per cent of Japan's population. The network totals 50 lines, with 289 Shinkansen and 7,988 conventional trains operated daily in 2001. The company has steadily diversified into activities such as the travel trade and affiliated business, including restaurants and retail shops.

A total of 31.72 per cent of the shareholding in the company is owned by the state-owned Japan Railway Construction Public Corporation (qv), which was established in 1987 upon the reform of the former Japanese National Railways and partial privatisation of the network. Legislation introduced in 2001 created conditions which could lead to the eventual sell-off of this residual state shareholding.

**Finance**
During 2000-01, the company's financial performance continued to reflect the impact of the economic environment in Japan, with no sign of improvement in the labour market and consumer spending remaining depressed. Operating revenues from rail operations fell by 0.4 per cent but there was an improvement in net income of 1.6 per cent.

| Finance (million yen) | 1998-99 | 1999-2000 | 2000-01 |
|---|---|---|---|
| Operating revenue | 909,484 | 885,144 | 881,486 |
| Operating expenses | 796,781 | 786,089 | 784,428 |
| Operating income | 112,702 | 99,054 | 97,058 |
| Net income (loss) | (5,640) | 25,578 | 25,985 |

(Figures relate to JR West rail business only)

| Traffic (million) | 1998-99 | 1999-2000 | 2000-01 |
|---|---|---|---|
| Passenger journeys (rail only) | 1,843 | 1,823 | 1,812 |
| Passenger-km | 53,526 | 52,588 | 52,551 |

*Series 281 emu on 'Haruka' service at Nishioji connecting Kyoto and Osaka with Kansai International Airport* (Wolfram Veith)
*2001*/0099125

*Class 201 1.5 k V DC emu forming a local service at Kyoto* (Marcel Vleugels)
*2002*/0132664

*'Sunrise Express' bilevel 1,067 mm gauge emu for overnight service*
*2001*/0099128

*One of JR West's few locomotive-hauled services is the 'Twilight Express' sleeping car train linking Osaka and Sapporo. It is seen at Shin-Osaka behind a Class EF81 electric locomotive (Marcel Vleugels)*
*2002*/0132666

*JR West Series 700 'Rail Star' Shinkansen trainset forming a Tokyo—Hakata service at Hakata (Marcel Vleugels)*
*2002*/0132665

## Passenger operations
*Services on 1,067 mm gauge*

JR West's conventional lines comprise the Urban Network of 14 commuter lines serving the metropolitan areas of Kyoto, Osaka and Kobe; major intercity and regional lines; and local lines. On the urban network, ridership fell in 2000-01 by 0.2 per cent to 1,431 million passenger journeys but volume increased by 0.1 per cent to 28,331 passenger-km. Passenger numbers on other conventional lines fell by 2 per cent to 400 million for 10,414 passenger-km, a decrease of 2.3 per cent.

Recent improvements to the urban network include: the introduction in March 2000 of two new services, JR Kobe (Kobe—Osaka) and JR Kyoto (Osaka—Kyoto), on the Biwako line between Kyoto and Nagahama, both using Series 223 Special Rapid 130 km/h emus; double-tracking between Hanazono and Nijo on the Sagano line; increased use of Rapid trains on the Nara line following provision of double-track between JR Fujinomori and Kyoto stations; the opening in March 2001 of Universal-city station to serve the Universal Studios Japan theme park.

On other conventional lines, the introduction of Series 683 emus has enabled JR West to increase the frequency and shorten journey times of its Thunderbird interurban limited express services.

In 1998 JR West introduced a new luxury sleeping car train developed in collaboration with JR Central, the 'Sunrise Express'. This complements the existing Osaka—Sapporo 'Twilight Express' sleeping car service.

Local lines account for about 30 per cent of the total network but only 3 per cent of passenger-km. Some lines have been transferred to third-sector companies, and JR West has established 27 regional operating units aimed at upgrading service and enhancing the profitability of the remaining lines on an individual basis. Operating economies introduced include staff undertaking a wider range of duties.

*Shinkansen services*

In 2000-01, Sanyo Shinkansen services carried 58 million passengers, a decline of 0.2 per cent on the previous year, although volume increased by 1.3 per cent to 13,805 million passenger-km. Series 500 high-speed trainsets operate Nozomi services between Shin-Osaka and Hakata (Fukuoka) in 2 hours 17 minutes, while since March 2000 Series 700 trains have provided Hikari Rail Star services over this route. During the period 2000-01, these latter services achieved an average passenger load of 87 per cent of capacity.

Since October 2001, Nozomi services have additionally called at Shin-Kobe station to improve their competitiveness with airlines and three Hikari Rail Star services on the Shin-Osaka—Hiroshima route have been extended to Hakata.

## New lines

JR West is a partner with Osaka city and prefecture in a third-sector venture to rebuild and introduce passenger services on the 20.4 km orbital Joto freight line running from Shin-Osaka around the eastern suburbs of the city.

The proposed Naniwasuji line would form a north-south route through the centre of Osaka from Shin-Osaka via

### JR West diesel locomotives

| Class | Wheel arrangement | Output kW | Speed km/h | Weight tonnes | No in service | First built | Builders Mechanical | Engine | Transmission |
|---|---|---|---|---|---|---|---|---|---|
| DD14 | B-B | 745 | 70 | 58 | 3 | 1965 | K/D | DMF31SB-R/S | H DS1.2/1.35 |
| DD15 | B-B | 745 | 70 | 55 | 11 | 1961 | N/D | DMF31SB/S | H DS1.1/1.35 |
| DD16 | B-B | 600 | 75 | 48 | 1 | 1971 | K/S/D | DML61Z/H/K | H DW2A |
| DD51 | B-2-B | 1,640 | 95 | 84 | 23 | 1966 | H/Mh/K/S/D | DML61Z/H/K | H DW2A |
| DE10 | AAA-B | 1,000 | 85 | 65 | 31 | 1969 | K/N/H/S/D | DML61ZB/H/K | H DW6 |
| DE15 | AAA-B | 1,000 | 85 | 65 | 12 | 1970 | N/K/S/D | DML61DZB/H/K | H DW6 |

### JR West diesel railcars

| Class | Cars per unit | Motor cars per unit | Motored axles/car | Output/motor kW | Speed km/h | Weight tonnes | Cars in service | First built | Builders Mechanical | Engine | Transmission |
|---|---|---|---|---|---|---|---|---|---|---|---|
| 191 | 2 | 2 | 2 | 330 | 120 | 46.7 | 2 | 1968 | F/D/S/NC | DML30HSF | H DW4F/S/NC |
| 181 | 3 | 3 | 2 | 370 | 120 | 44.6 | 70 | 1968 | F/NT/N/D/S/NC | DML30HSE | H DW4E/S/NC |
| 28 | 2 | 2 | 1 | 135 | 95 | 34.3 | 115 | 1961 | F/NT/N/D/S/NC | DMH17H | H TC2A/DF115A/S/NC |
| 23 | 1 | 1 | 1 | 135 | 95 | 34.2 | 9 | 1966 | F/NT/N/D/S/NC | DMH17H | H TC2A/DF115A/S/NC |
| 33 | 1 | 1 | 1 | 185 | 95 | 34 | 2 | 1988 | GW/D/S/NC | DMF13HS | H DF115A/NT/S |
| 35 | 2 | 2 | 1 | 135 | 95 | 32 | 8 | 1961 | F/NT/N/D/S/NC | DMH17H | H TC2A/DF115A/S/NC |
| 37 | 2 | 2 | 1 | 155 | 95 | 31.6 | 2 | 1982 | NT/D/S/NC | DMF13S | H TC2A/DF115A/S/NC |
| 40 | 1 | 1 | 1 | 160 | 95 | 36.4 | 63 | 1979 | F/NT/D/S/NC | DMF15HSA | H DW10/S/NC |
| 47 | 2 | 2 | 1 | 160 | 95 | 35.5 | 184 | 1976 | F/NT/D/S/NC | DMF15HSA | H DW10/H S/NC |
| 48 | 2 | 2 | 1 | 160 | 95 | 35.9 | 5 | 1971 | F/NT/D/S/NC | DMF15HSA | H DW10/S/NC |
| 52 | 1 | 1 | 2 | 135 × 2 | 95 | 36 | 7 | 1962 | F/NT/N/D/S/NC | DMH17H | H TC2A/DF115A/S/NC |
| 53 | 1 | 1 | 2 | 135 × 2 | 95 | 39.7 | 6 | 1966 | F/NT/N/D/S/NC | DMH17H | H TC2A/DF115A/S/NC |
| 58 | 2 | 2 | 2 | 135 × 2 | 95 | 39.4 | 114 | 1961 | F/NT/N/D/S/NC | DMH17H | H TC2A/DF115/S/NC |
| 65 | 2 | 2 | 2 | 375 | 95 | 42.9 | 19 | 1969 | F/NT/N/D/S/NC | DML30HSD | H DW4F/S/NC |
| 120 | 1 | 1 | 1 | 225 | 95 | 26.7 | 89 | 1992 | NT/D/S/NC | SA6D125H-1 | H TACN-22-1605/S/NC |

### JR West electric locomotives

| Class | Wheel arrangement | Output kW | Speed km/h | Weight tonnes | No in service | First built | Builders Mechanical | Electrical |
|---|---|---|---|---|---|---|---|---|
| | **1.5 kV DC** | | | | | | | |
| EF15 | 1-C-C-1 | 1,900 | 75 | 102 | 1 | 1947 | H | H/T/Mh/F/To |
| EF58 | 2-C-C-2 | 1,900 | 100 | 115 | 1 | 1946 | T | H/T/Mh/F/To |
| EF59 | 2-C-C-2 | 1,350 | 90 | 106.6 | 1 | 1963 | H | H/T/Mh/F/To |
| EF60 | B-B-B | 2,550 | 100 | 96 | 1 | 1962 | To | H/T/Mh/F/To |
| EF64 | B-B-B | 2,550 | 100 | 96 | 2 | 1964 | T/K/To | H/T/Mh/F/To |
| EF65 | B-B-B | 2,550 | 110 | 96 | 23 | 1969 | K/To/T/N | H/T/Mh/F/To |
| EF66 | B-B-B | 3,900 | 110 | 100.8 | 13 | 1973 | K/To | H/T/Mh/F/To |
| EF81* | B-B-B | 2,550/2,370 | 110 | 100.8 | 16 | 1968 | H/Mh | H/T/Mh/F/To |

*Dual-voltage 1.5 kV/20 Kv
Abbreviations: D: Daihatsu; F: Fuji Heavy Industries; GW: Goto Workshop; H: Hitachi; K: Kawasaki Heavy Industries; Ki: Kinki Sharyo; Mh: Mitsubishi Heavy Industries; Me: Mitsubishi Electric; MW: Matto Workshop; N: Nippon Sharyo Seizo; NC: Niigata Converter; NT: Niigata Engineering; S: Shinko Engineering; T: Toshiba; Tk: Tokyu Haryo; To: Toyo Denki Seizo; Ty: Toyo Electric

Umeda to the JR Namba station, providing improved access to Kansai International Airport from northern Osaka and the Kyoto and Hyogo prefectures.

### Traction and rolling stock
In 2001 the company operated on 1,067 mm gauge five steam, 53 electric and 73 diesel locomotives, 4,638 emu cars, 630 dmu cars, 340 hauled passenger coaches and 258 wagons. Shinkansen rolling stock comprised 812 emu cars.

JR West was able to deploy nine Series 500 sets by 1999. The first new-generation Series 700 Shinkansen trainsets, developed jointly with JR Central, commenced service in March 1999. Branded 'Rail Star', each set comprises eight cars, of which six are motored. Total seating capacity is for 816 passengers.

### Signalling and telecommunications
ATS-P (Automatic Train Stop-Pattern) train protection equipment has been installed on the Hanwa line, including the Kansai Airport branch, the Osaka loop line, and the Tozai line. Future planned installations will cover the Osaka–Maibara section of the Kyoto line and Osaka–Aboshi on the Kobe line.

### Track
(1,067 mm gauge lines)
**Rail:** 30 to 60.8 kg/m

**Sleepers:** Wood 140 × 200 × 2,100 mm; and concrete 174 × 156-240 × 2,000 mm
**Sleeper spacing:** Wood 1,480-1,920/km depending on class of route; concrete 1,480-1,760/km. On Class 2, 3 and 4 track with wooden sleepers, increased by 80 through curves of 600 m radius or less
**Fastenings:** Wooden sleepers, spike or spring clip with plate and pad; concrete sleepers, spring clip with pad
**Min curve radius:** 800, 600, 400 and 300 m for maximum speeds respectively of 110 km/h or over, 90-110 km/h, 70-90 km/h and 70 km/h
**Max permissible axleload:** 19 tonnes

**Track** (Shinkansen lines)
**Rail:** 60.8 kg/m
**Sleepers:** Concrete 255 × 172-300 × 2,400 mm
**Sleeper spacing:** 1,720/km in plain track
**Fastenings:** Spring clip with pad
**Min curve radius (main line):** 4,000 m
**Max permissible axleload:** 17 tonnes

### Principal JR West electric railcars or multiple-units (1,067 mm gauge)

| Class | Cars per unit | Motor cars per unit | Motored axles/car | Output/motor kW | Speed km/h | Cars in service | First built | Builders Mechanical | Electrical |
|---|---|---|---|---|---|---|---|---|---|
| **1.5 kV DC** | | | | | | | | | |
| 103 | 7 | 4 | 4 | 110 | 100 | 777 | 1964 | K/Ki/H/N/Tk | H/T/Me/F/Ty |
| 105 | 2 | 1 | 4 | 110 | 100 | 121 | 1980 | Ki/H/Tk | H/T/Me/F/Ty |
| 113 | 4 | 2/4 | 4 | 120 | 110 | 531 | 1963 | K/Ki/H/N/Tk | H/T/Me/F/Ty |
| 115 | 4 | 2/4 | 4 | 120 | 110 | 476 | 1962 | K/Ki/H/N/Tk | H/T/Me/F/Ty |
| 117 | 6 | 2/4/6 | 4 | 120 | 115 | 122 | 1979 | K/Ki/N/Tk | H/T/Me/F/Ty |
| 165 | 3 | 2 | 4 | 120 | 110 | 35 | 1962 | K/Ki/N/Tk | H/T/Me/F/Ty |
| 167 | 4 | 2 | 4 | 120 | 110 | 4 | 1965 | | |
| 183 | 4 | 2 | 4 | 120 | 120 | 70 | 1990 | K/Ki/H/N | H/T/Me/F/Ty |
| 201 | 7 | 4 | 4 | 120 | 100 | 224 | 1981 | K/Ki/H/N/Tk | H/T/Me/F/Ty |
| 205 | 7 | 4 | 4 | 120 | 110 | 48 | 1986 | Ki/N | H/T/Me/F/Ty |
| 207 | 3/4/7 | 1/2/3 | 4 | 155 | 120 | 147 | 1991 | K/Ki/H | H/T/Me/F/Ty |
| 207-1000 | 2/6 | 1/3 | 4 | 200 | 120 | 257 | 1994 | K/Ki,H | H/T/Me/F/Ty |
| 211 | 2 | 1 | 4 | 120 | 120 | 2 | 1988 | Ki | H/T/Me/Ty |
| 213 | 3 | 1 | 4 | 120 | 110 | 37 | 1986 | K/Ki/H/N/Tk | H/T/Me/F/Ty |
| 221 | 2/4/6/8 | 1/2/3 | 4 | 120 | 120 | 474 | 1988 | K/Ki/H/N | H/Ts/Me/Ty |
| 223 | 2/6 | 1/3 | 4 | 180 | 120 | 68 | 1994 | K/Ki | H/Mh/Me/T/Ty |
| 223-1000 | 4/8 | 2/3 | 4 | 220 | 130 | 124 | 1995 | K/Ki/H | H/Mh/Me/T/Ty |
| 281 | 5 | 2 | 4 | 180 | 130 | 63 | 1994 | K/Ki | H/Mh/Me/T/Ty |
| 381 | 7 | 4 | 4 | 120 | 120 | 189 | 1978 | K/Ki/H/N | H/T/Me/F/Ty |
| 283 | 3/6 | 1/2 | 4 | 220 | 130 | 18 | 1996 | K/Ki/H | |
| **1.5 kV DC/20 kV AC** | | | | | | | | | |
| 413 | 3 | 2 | 4 | 120 | 110 | 31 | 1975 | MW | H/T/Me/F/Ty |
| 415 | 3 | 2 | 4 | 120 | 100 | 33 | 1990 | K/Ki/H/N/Tk | H/T/N/F/Ty |
| 419 | 3 | 2 | 4 | 120 | 100 | 45 | 1975 | MW | H/T/Me/F/Ty |
| 457 | 3 | 2 | 4 | 120 | 110 | 80 | 1969 | H | H/T/Me/F/Ty |
| 485 | 10 | 6 | 4 | 120 | 130 | 238 | 1968 | K/Ki/H/N/Tk | H/T/Me/F/Ty |
| 489 | 9 | 6 | 4 | 120 | 130 | 86 | 1971 | | H/T/Me/F/Ty |
| 583 | 10 | 6 | 4 | 120 | 120 | 60 | 1968 | K/Ki/H/N | H/T/Me/F/Ty |
| 681 | 9 | 3 | 4 | 190 | 160 | 84 | 1992 | K/Ki/H | T/M/Ty |

### Sanyo Shinkansen electric multiple-unit cars

| Class | Cars per unit | Motor cars per unit | Motored axles/car | Output/motor kW | Speed km/h | Cars in service | First built | Builders Mechanical | Electrical |
|---|---|---|---|---|---|---|---|---|---|
| **25 kV 60 Hz** | | | | | | | | | |
| 0 | 16 | 16 | 4 | 185 | 220 | 275 | 1969 | K/Ki/H/N/Tk | |
|   | 12 | 12 | 4 | | | | | | |
|   | 6 | 6 | 4 | | | | | | |
| 922 | 7 | 6 | 4 | 185 | 210 | 7 | 1979 | K/Ki/N/Tk | F/H/M/S/T/Ty |
| 100 | 16 | 12 | 4 | 230 | 230 | 256 | 1987 | K/Ki/H/N/Tk | F/T/M/H/Ty |
| 300 | 16 | 10 | 4 | 300 | 270 | 144 | 1992 | K/Ki/N/Tk | T/Ty/N |
| 500 | 16 | 16 | 4 | 300 | 300 | 144 | 1995 | K | |

Abbreviations: D: Daihatsu; F: Fuji Heavy Industries; GW: Goto Workshop; H: Hitachi; K: Kawasaki Heavy Industries; Ki: Kinki Sharyo; Mh: Mitsubishi Heavy Industries; Me: Mitsubishi Electric; MW: Matto Workshop; N: Nippon Sharyo Seizo; NC: Niigata Converter; NT: Niigata Engineering; S: Shinko Engineering; T: Toshiba; Tk: Tokyu Haryo; To: Toyo Denki Seizo; Ty: Toyo Electric

*UPDATED*

## Hokkaido Railway Co (JR Hokkaido)
1-1 Nishi 15-chome, Kita 11-jo, Chuo-ku, Sapporo 060
Tel: (+81 11) 700 57 17  Fax: (+81 11) 700 57 19

### Key personnel
Chairman: Yoshihiro Omori
President: Shin-ichi Sakamoto
Executive Director, Manager of Railway Operations: Koichi Fujita
Managing Director, Planning: Akio Koike
Managing Director: Takashi Nagano

Gauge: 1,067 mm
Route length: 2,628 km
Electrification: 431 km at 20 kV 50 Hz AC

### Organisation
The company is responsible for rail passenger transport and related activities in Hokkaido, the northernmost Japanese island which has a low population density. It operated 1,267 trains daily from March 1997. Approximately 1,450 route-km of loss-making rural lines were closed by JNR before the formation of JR Hokkaido but some very unremunerative lines are still operated; only one line has been transferred to third-sector operation, the 140 km Chihoku line. The most recent closure was the rural 120 km Shinmei line between Fukagawa and Nayoro which was replaced by a bus service in September 1995.

| Finance (million yen) | 1993-94 | 1994-95 | 1995-96 |
|---|---|---|---|
| Operating income | 106,000 | 102,000 | 101,864 |
| Operating expenses | 151,000 | 144,000 | 142,520 |
| Non-operating profit | 46,000 | 42,000 | 39,247 |
| Pre-tax profit | 700 | 400 | −2,247 |

### JR Hokkaido diesel locomotives

| Class | Wheel arrangement | Power kW | Speed km/h | Weight tonnes | No in service | First built | Builders Mechanical | Engine | Transmission |
|---|---|---|---|---|---|---|---|---|---|
| DD51 | B-2-B | 1,618 | 95 | 84 | 15 | 1967 | H/M/K | DML61Z S/NT/D | H DW2A H/K |
| DE10 | AAA-B | 993 | 85 | 65 | 12 | 1973 | K/N | DML61ZB S/NT/D | H DW6 H/K |
| DE15 | AAA-B | 993 | 85 | 65 | 24 | 1969 | N | DML61ZB S/NT/D | H DW6 H/K |

### Electric locomotives

| Class | Wheel arrangement | Output kW | Speed km/h | Weight tonnes | No in service | First built | Builders Mechanical | Electrical |
|---|---|---|---|---|---|---|---|---|
| ED76 | B-2-B | 1,900 | 100 | 90.5 | 1 | 1968 | M/T | H/M/T |
| ED79 | B-B | 1,900 | 100 | 68 | 34 | 1971 | H/M/T | H/M/T |

### JR Hokkaido electric railcars or multiple-units

| Class | Cars per unit | Motor cars per unit | Motored axles/car | Output/motor kW | Speed km/h | Cars in service | First built | Builders Mechanical | Electrical |
|---|---|---|---|---|---|---|---|---|---|
| 711 | 3 | 1 | 4 | 150 | 110 | Mo 38 Tr 76 | 1966 | H/T/K | H/T/M/Fe/To |
| 781 | 4 | 2 | 4 | 150 | 120 | Mo 24 Tr 24 | 1978 | H/K | H/T/M/Fe/To |
| 721 | 3/6 | 2/4 | | 150 | 130 | Mo 67 To 47 | 1988 | | |
| 785 | 2/4 | 1/2 | | 190 | 130 | Mo 15 Tr 15 | 1990 | H | |

Abbreviations: D: Daihatsu; F: Fuji Heavy Industries; H: Hitachi Ltd; K: Kawasaki Heavy Industries Ltd; M: Mitsubishi Heavy Industries; NC: Niigata Converter Co Ltd; NT: Niigata Engineering Co Ltd; S: Shinko Engineering Co Ltd; T: Toshiba Corp; To: Toyo Denki Seizo KK
Mo: motor car; Tr: trailer car

### Passenger operations
In 1995-96 JR Hokkaido recorded 129 million passenger journeys and 4,795 million passenger-km.

JR Hokkaido is responsible for operation through the Seikan Tunnel, where in 1991 the maximum permissible speed for 1,067 mm gauge trains was raised to 140 km/h.

# RAILWAY SYSTEMS/Japan

Since it took over the Hokkaido system from JNR, the company has been concerned to develop more attractive services within the island, both interurban for the island's own population and to its tourist areas for visitors. This has involved introduction of new types of diesel train that are more competitive against road transport, in terms both of passenger amenities and speed.

The company has introduced a small number of individually styled dmus for use on a network of tourist services to ski resorts including the four-car 'Crystal Express' set, which incorporates a double-deck car, and the 'North Rainbow Express' set, which features panoramic windows. Modern conventional stock has also been introduced on some local lines in the form of Kiha 130 railbuses and Series 150 dmus. Journey time reductions have been achieved on longer distance services with the introduction of Series 785 emus on the 'Super White Arrow' and 'Lilac' limited expresses between Sapporo and Asahikawa and with the use of rebuilt Series 183 'Super Tokachi' sets between Sapporo and Obihiro.

Production seven-car Series 281 tilting diesel trainsets, derived from the 'HEAT 281' experimental train completed in 1992, entered service in 1994, cutting the fastest journey time between Sapporo and Hakodate to 3 hours.

Following tests with a prototype Series 283, developed from the earlier Series 281, operational use has begun on the Sapporo-Kushiro route. The Series 283 'Furico' sets operating these 'Super Oozora' limited expresses have independent wheel bogies and a four-speed gear system. In spite of difficult operating conditions, including sharp curves and heavy winter snowfall, the three return services in each direction take 3 hours 45 minutes, about 50 minutes less than older stock.

In contrast to the rest of Hokkaido, suburban services in the Sapporo area have seen growth of 3 to 10 per cent a year. Four new three-car Series 731 emus able to carry 435 passengers (152 seated) entered service in December 1996. Additionally, four new three-car Series 201 dmus allow an increase in capacity on services operating into Sapporo from the unelectrified section of the Hakodate main line west of Otaru.

## Traction and rolling stock

In April 1996 the railway operated 35 electric and 51 diesel locomotives, 511 diesel railcars and 306 emu cars.

Loco-hauled passenger trains are no longer operated, apart from through trains from Honshu via the Seikan tunnel.

### Principal JR Hokkaido diesel railcars or multiple-units

| Class | Motored axles/car | Power/motor kW | Speed km/h | Weight tonnes | No in service | First built | Mechanical | Engine | Transmission |
|---|---|---|---|---|---|---|---|---|---|
| 27 | 1 | 132 | 95 | 35 | 8 | 1962 | T/NT/N | DMH17H S/NT/D/JNR | H TC2A/DF115A S/NC |
| 56 | 2 | 132 | 95 | 38.9 | 17 | 1986 | NT | DMH17H S/NT/D/JNR | H TC2A/DF115A S/NC |
| 29 | 1 | 132 | 95 | 33.8/38.3 | 3 | 1966 | T | DMH17H S/NT/D/JNR | H DF115A NC |
| 59 | 2 | 132 | 95 | 41.4 | 2 | 1983 | NT | DMH17H S/NT/D/JNR | H TC2A/DF115A S/NC |
| 40 | 1 | 162 | 95 | 36.4/37.6 | 141 | 1976 | F/NT | DMF15HSA S/NT/D | H DW10 S/NC |
| 48-300 | 1 | 162 | 95 | 36.6 | 3 | 1982 | NT | DMF15HSA S/NT/D | H DW10 S/NC |
| 480-1300 | 1 | 162 | 95 | 36.3 | 4 | 1982 | NT | DMF15HSA S/NT/D | H DW10 S/NC |
| 182 | 2 | 324 | 100 | 42.6/45.2 | 65 | 1978 | F/NT | DML30HSI D/S/NT | H DW9A S/NC |
| 182-500 | 2 | 405 | 110 | 38.8 | 38 | 1986 | F/NT | DML30HSJ | H DW12 |
| 183 | 1 | 162 | 100 | 47.4 | 24 | 1979 | F/NT | DMF15HSA D/S/NT | DW10 S/NC |
| 183-100 | 1 | 162 | 100 | 43.8 | 4 | 1981 | F/NT | DMF15HSA D/S/NT | H DW10 S/NC |
| 183-500 | 2 | 405 | 110 | 40.9 | 7 | 1986 | F/NT | DML30HSJ D/S | H DW12 S/NC |
| 183-1500 | 1 | 184 | 110 | 40.3 | 23 | 1986 | F/NT | DMF13HS NT | H DW12 NC |
| 184 | 1 | 162 | 100 | 44.2 | 8 | 1981 | F/NT | DMF15HSA D/S/NT | H DW10 S/NC |
|  | 1 | 162 | 100 | 46.6 | 1 | 1979 | F | DMF15HSA D/S/NT | H DW10 S/NC |
| 80 | 2 | 132 | 100 | 41.2/43 | 2 | 1964 | F/NT | DMH17H S/NT/D/JNR | H TC2A/DF115A S/NC |
| 83 | 1 | 132 | 100 | 41.2 | 3 | 1986 | NT | DMH17H S/NT/D/JNR | H DF1125A NC |
| 84 | 2 | 132 | 100 | 41.2 | 4 | 1986 | NT/F | DMH17H S/NT/D/JNR | H DF115A NC |
| 54 | 2 | 184 | 95 | 38.7/39.3 | 29 | 1986 | F/NT | DMF13HS NT | H TC2A/DF115A NC |
| 130 |  |  | 95 | 27.5 | 10 | 1988 |  | DMF13HS | H N-DW130 |
| 400 | 1 |  | 95 | 40.9 | 9 | 1988 |  | DMF13HZ-B | H DW14B |
| 480 |  |  | 95 | 37.6 | 4 | 1988 |  | DMF 13HZ-B | H DW14B |
| 141 |  |  | 95 | 34.5 | 14 | 1989 |  | DMF13HS | H DF115A |
| 142 |  |  | 95 | 40.1 | 15 | 1989 |  | DMF13HS | H DF115A |
| 281 | 3 |  | 130 | 41.0 | 27 | 1992 |  | DMF11HZ | H N-DW15 |
| 283 | 2 | 355 | 130 | 43.6 | 3 | 1995 | F | DMF11HZ | H N-DW18 |

Abbreviations: D: Daihatsu; F: Fuji Heavy Industries; H: Hitachi Ltd; K: Kawasaki Heavy Industries Ltd; M: Mitsubishi Heavy Industries; NC: Niigata Converter Co Ltd; NT: Niigata Engineering Co Ltd; S: Shinko Engineering Co Ltd; T: Toshiba Corp; To: Toyo Denki Seizo KK

## Kyushu Railway Co (JR Kyushu)

3-25-21 Hakataekimae, Hakata-ku, Fukuoka 812-8566
Tel: (+81 92) 474 25 01   Fax: (+81 92) 474 48 05
e-mail: service@jrkyushu.co.jp
Web: http://www.jrkyushu.co.jp

### Key personnel

Chairman: Koji Tanaka
President: Susumi Ishihara
Director General, Business Development/Urban Development: Akimasa Hayami
Managing Directors
  Director of Travel Services/Marketing and Sales /Railway Operations/Ferry Operations: Yasuharu Maruyama
  Director General of Corporate Planning/ Administration/Tokyo Branch Office/Okinawa Branch Office/JR Kyushu Hospital: Suichi Honda
Director General of Railway Operations: Toshiro Kameyama
Senior Executive Advisor: Yoshitaka Ishii
Directors
  Nashi-Kagoshima Station Development: Yoshihisa Kamino
  General Manager, Northern Kyushu Regional Head Office: Takao Nishimura
  Deputy Director, General Business Development/ General Manager, Administration: Hisaji Akizuki
  General Manager, Finance and Accounting/Auditing: Keisuke Saeki
  General Manager, Oita Regional Office: Keio Kawano

Gauge: 1,067 mm
Route length: 2,101.1 km
Electrification: 1,126 km at 20 kV 60 Hz AC; 51.1 km at 1.5 kV DC

### Organisation

The company runs rail passenger transport and related activities in the Kyushu region. It operated 2,791 trains daily from April 2001. Since formation of JR Kyushu in 1987, several local lines have been transferred to third-sector undertakings. The company also runs a hydrofoil service between Hakata and Pusan, South Korea. The company's bus services subsidiary was divested in April 2001.

Other parts of the JR Kyushu Group cover the development and exploitation of station buildings, leisure and retail activities, construction and food service businesses.

In 2000 JR Kyushu employed 11,660 staff.

| **Finance** (100 million yen) | 1998 | 1999 | 2000 |
|---|---|---|---|
| Passenger revenue | 1,222 | 1,189 | 1,175 |
| Other revenue | 368 | 422 | 430 |
| Total revenue | 1,590 | 1,611 | 1,605 |
| Operating expenses | 1,721 | 1,740 | 1,729 |
| Pre-tax profit/loss | −130 | −129 | −123 |

| **Traffic** (million) | 1998 | 1999 | 2000 |
|---|---|---|---|
| Passenger journeys | 3,911 | 3,865 | 3,831 |
| Passenger-km | 200 | 197 | 196 |

### Passenger operations

Operations cover 21 routes and serve 572 stations.

JR Kyushu has introduced several new types of rolling stock over recent years to upgrade its services. Refurbished Series 485 emus predominate on intercity services, but these are now supplemented by Series 783 'Hyper Saloon' emus introduced since 1990 and by nine-car Series 787 emus. The latter were introduced on 'Tsubame' services between Hakata and Kagoshima in

*Brunel Award-winning Series 883, which dominates JR Kyushu east coast line services between Hakata and Oita (Wolfram Veith)*
0023028

1992 to counter competition from parallel expressway bus services and short-distance air routes. Since March 1994, Series 787 units have also operated daily 'Kamome' return services between Hakata and Nagasaki.

March 1995 saw the introduction of a new 'Wonderland Express' service between Hakata and Oita operated by four seven-car Sonic 883 VVVF emus with active body-tilt. These units feature a distinctive exterior design and a colourful interior based on an amusement park theme; they have a variety of seating patterns and a panoramic section.

In March 2000, Series 885 'Kamome' six-car tilting emus were introduced on Hakata-Nagasaki limited-stop express services, providing 16 daily return trips in each direction. The introduction of these trains marked the completion of a programme of enhancements to JR Kyushu's network of limited express services, 308 of which were being operated daily by the company in 2000.

Series 811 commuter emus have been introduced on the Town Shuttle network of routes linking the main urban areas in northern Kyushu.

On non-electrified lines, new Kiha 200- and 220-type dmus have been introduced on local services. Since 1992, Kiha 185 express dmus have been running on the Trans-Kyushu Highland Express routes linking Hakata with the Mount Yofu area and Kumamoto with the Mount Aso region.

In the 14 years up to 2000, JR Kyushu had opened 45 new stations on its network.

### New lines

Construction began in 1991 of the 127 km Yatsushiro–Nishi-Kagoshima section of JR Kyushu's first Shinkansen line, the Kagoshima Route. The 257 km line will link Hakata, where connection will be made with the Sanyo Shinkansen, and Nishi-Kagoshima. A 120 km branch to Nagasaki will leave the main line at Shin-Tosu; the alignment for this line was announced in February 1998. The Kagoshima Route is being built with infrastructure suitable for 1,435 mm gauge but will initially be laid with 1,067 mm gauge track.

In March 1998, work started on the Yatsushiro–Funagoya section, mostly covering land acquisition and tunnel excavation, but in 2000 no work had been carried out on the 40 km northern section between Funagoya and Hakata.

Stations served by the new line will include four new facilities and four where extensions will be made at existing sites. The southern terminus station at Nishi-Kagoshima was completed in June 1996.

The Shinkansen will be worked by a new design of 1,067 mm gauge trainset designed for operation at a maximum speed of at least 200 km/h. The design may emerge from development work being carried out by the Japanese Railway Technical Research Institute on a design known as 250X, with the aim of attaining 250 km/h on 1,067 mm gauge. This envisages short and low-slung 14 m lightweight bodies equipped with automatic body-tilt and active suspension that are articulated over single-axle bogies with independent wheels.

### Improvements to existing lines

Recent developments include the opening of a short (1.4 km) branch linking Tayoshi on the Nichinan line with Miyazaki airport on 18 July 1996. Services are operated by refurbished two-car Series 713-900 emus as well as limited expresses. The 22.6 km section of the Hohi line between Kumamoto and Higo-Ozu is to be electrified, with funding by JR Kyushu and local government (Kumamoto Prefecture) as a third-sector project.

A recent electrification project covered the Sasaguri Line, betwen Yoshizuka and Keisen, the Chikuho Main Line, between Orio and Keisen, and part of the Kagoshima main line, between Kurosaki and Orio. Together, the scheme covered 64.8 route-km and was undertaken to stimulate economic and social regeneration following a rundown in coal mining in the Chikuho area. The cost of the ¥14 billion scheme was shared by JR Kyushu (¥5.6 billion), Fukuoka Prefecture and communities along the line (¥6.4 billion), and government funding under legislation introduced in 1961 to assist the regeneration of former coal mining areas (¥2 billion). The JR Kyushu funding also includes a ¥4 billion interest-free loan provided under similar regeneration legislation.

Included in the project were: trackside power supply systems; additional crossing places to increase line capacity; and a new depot for the Class 817 emus introduced to serve the line. Five stations were renovated and one, at Kotake, is to serve as a future 'park and ride' facility.

A major development of facilities at Kokura station was due for completion in early 1998, providing enhanced intermodal interchange.

### Traction and rolling stock

In 1997 the company operated 17 electric and 15 diesel locomotives, 1,145 emu cars and 426 dmu cars, 216 other passenger coaches, including 159 sleeping cars, and 61 freight wagons.

Between 1987 and 2000, JR Kyushu invested ¥123.3 billion in new passenger rolling stock, acquiring 773 new trains. Of these, 664 were emus, including 345 for commuter services, and 89 were dmus. Most recent deliveries have included Series 885 Kamome

*Hitachi-built Series 883 Kamome tilting emus entered service between Hakata and Nagasaki in March 2000*

**JR Kyushu electric locomotives**

| Class | Wheel arrangement | Output kW | Speed km/h | Weight tonnes | No in service | First built | Builders |
|---|---|---|---|---|---|---|---|
| EF81 | B-B-B | 2,550 | 100 | 100.8 | 4 | 1968 | H |
| ED76 | B-2-B | 1,990 | 100 | 90.5 | 13 | 1965 | T/M/H |

Abbreviations: H: Hitachi; M: Mitsubishi; T: Toshiba

**JR Kyushu diesel locomotives**

| Class | Wheel arrangement | Power kW | Speed km/h | Weight tonnes | No in service | First built | Builders Mechanical | Engine | Transmission |
|---|---|---|---|---|---|---|---|---|---|
| DD16 | B-B | 800 | 75 | 48 | 2 | 1971 | K | DML61Z | H DW2A |
| DE10 | AAA-B | 1,350 | 85 | 65 | 13 | 1969 | K/N | DML61ZB | H DW6 |

Abbreviations: K: Kawasaki; N: Nippon Sharyo

**JR Kyushu diesel railcars or multiple-units**

| Class | Cars per unit | Motor cars per unit | Motored axles/car | Power/motor kW | Speed km/h | No in service | First built | Builders Mechanical | Engine | Transmission |
|---|---|---|---|---|---|---|---|---|---|---|
| 65 | 1 | 1 | 1 | 500 | 95 | 24 | 1969 | N, F | DML30HSD | N DW4D |
| 58 | 1 | 1 | 2 | 360 | 95 | 71 | 1961 | Nt, F, N, TE | DMH17H N | N TC2A DF115A |
| 28 | 1 | 1 | 1 | 180 | 95 | 42 | 1961 | Nt, F | DMH17H N | N TC2A DF115A |
| 66 | 2 | 2 | 1 | 440 | 95 | 15 | 1975 | Nt, F | DML30HSH | N DW9 |
| 67 | 2 | 2 | 1 | 440 | 95 | 15 | 1975 | Nt, F | DML30HSH | N DW9 |
| 40 | 1 | 1 | 1 | 220 | 95 | 25 | 1978 | Nt, F | DMF15HSA | N DW10 |
| 47 | 1 | 1 | 1 | 220 | 95 | 76 | 1979 | Nt, F | DMF15HSA | N DW10 |
| 52 | 1 | 1 | 2 | 360 | 95 | 1 | 1961 | Nt | DMH17HSN | N TC2A DF115A |
| 31 | 1 | 1 | 1 | 250 | 95 | 23 | 1987 | F, N | DMF15HS | N, F TC2A DF115A |
| 185 | | | 1 | 250 | 110 | 20 | 1986 | Nt, F, N | DMF13HS | N TC2A DF115A |
| 200 | 2 | 2 | 1 | 420 | 110 | 40 | 1990 | | DMF13HZA | R-DW4 |

Abbreviations: F: Fuji; N: Nippon Sharyo; Nt: Niigata; TE: Teikoku; Tk: Tokyu

**JR Kyushu electric railcars or multiple-units**

| Class | Cars per unit | Motor cars per unit | Motored axles/car | Output/motor kW | Speed km/h | No in service | First built | Builders |
|---|---|---|---|---|---|---|---|---|
| **20 kV AC** | | | | | | | | |
| 423 | 4 | 2 | 4 | 120 | 100 | 87 | 1961 | H/Tk/Ki/TE/R |
| 415 | 4 | 2 | 4 | 120 | 100 | 184 | 1971 | H/N/S/Tk/R |
| 713 | 2 | 1 | 4 | 150 | 100 | 8 | 1982 | H/Tk |
| 715 | 4 | 2 | 4 | 120 | 100 | 28 | 1985 | H/N/S/R |
| 717 | 2 | 2 | 4 | 120 | 100 | 16 | 1985 | R/S/H |
| 475/457 | 2 | 2 | 4 | 120 | 100 | 111 | 1965 | R/S/Tk |
| 485 | 4 | 2 | 4 | 120 | 120 | 188 | 1969 | Ki/Tk/N/R/S |
| 811 | 4 | 2 | 4 | 150 | 120 | 112 | 1989 | H/S |
| 783 | 5/6 | 3/3 | 4 | 150 | 130 | 90 | 1987 | H/J/S |
| 787 | 9 | 6 | 4 | 150 | 130 | 137 | 1992 | H/J/S |
| 883 | 7 | 3 | 4 | 190 | 130 | 50 | 1994 | H |
| 885 | 6 | | | | 130 | 42 | 1999 | H |
| **1.5 kV DC** | | | | | | | | |
| 103 | 3 | 4 | 4 | 110 | 100 | 54 | 1964 | H/R |

Abbreviations: H: Hitachi; J: JR (Kokura); Ki: Kisha; N: Nippon Sharyo; R: Kawasaki; S: Kinki Sharyo; TE: Teikoku; Tk: Tokyu

six-car tilting emus from Hitachi for Hakata–Nagasaki services.

Refurbishment of over 300 vehicles has been undertaken, recent projects including Series 485 emus.

For the electrification of the Sasaguri and Chikuho lines (see 'Improvements to existing lines'), new Class 817 emus were introduced. Construction of these includes the use of materials considered friendly to the environment, such as aluminium, wood, glass and leather. Interior features include reversible seats made of wood and leather.

### Signalling and telecommunications
CTC (Centralised Traffic Control) controls 80 per cent of the system; programmable route control covers 81 per cent of the system. The first phase of JR Hakata traffic control centre scheme was completed in 1997 as part of a strategy to integrate dispersed control functions.

### Track
**Rail:** 50.4 and 60 kg/m
**Sleepers:** Prestressed concrete or timber 2,100 × 200 × 140 mm spaced 1,480, 1,560 or 1,760/km according to class of route
**Fastenings:** Elastic
**Max axleload:** 18 tonnes

*UPDATED*

## Shikoku Railway Co (JR Shikoku)

8-33, Hamano-cho, Takamatsu 760-8580
Tel: (+81 87) 825 16 22  Fax: (+81 87) 825 16 23
e-mail: knt20008@mail.kagawa-net.or.jp
Web: http://www.jr-shikoku.co.jp

### Key personnel
Chairman: Hiroatsu Ito
President: Toshiyuki Umehara
Senior Managing Director: Shozo Nakayama
Managing Director: Kiyohiro Matsuda

Gauge: 1,067 mm
Route length: 856 km
Electrification: 236 km at 1.5 kV DC

### Organisation
The company runs passenger transport and related activities in the Shikoku region. It operated 990 trains daily from March 2000.

### Passenger operations
Traffic has risen significantly since the introduction of through trains from Honshu island over the Seto bridges opened in 1988. In 1999-2000 the railway recorded 57.4 million passenger journeys and 1,764 million passenger-km, compared with 59.2 million and 1,815 million respectively the previous year.

The service of 35 rapid trains each way daily to Shikoku connects with the Sanyo Shinkansen at Okayama. There is also an overnight Tokyo–Shikoku sleeper service.

### Traction and rolling stock
At the beginning of 2000 the railway operated seven diesel locomotives, 215 dmus, 67 single diesel railcars, 104 emus and 36 single electric railcars.

Equipment includes three Type TSE-2000 diesel trainsets with a top speed of 120 km/h. Employed on cross-island services between Okayama/Takamatsu and Kochi, they are the world's first diesel-powered vehicles to be equipped with an active body-tilt system, which is designed to raise acceptable curving speed by 20 to 30 per cent depending on curve radius. An upgraded version, the N2000 Special Express (Series 2400/2450/2500), with a top speed of 130 km/h, was introduced in 1995. This two-car unit features 260 kW engines to improve acceleration, calliper disk brakes and automatic wheelslip prevention.

The Series 8000 emus used on the electrified Okayama/Takamatsu–Matsuyama routes also feature active body-tilting. These units have VVVF three-phase drive motors, a maximum speed of 160 km/h and carbodies carried on pendulum roller bolsters. An onboard memory checks the train location through the ATS system and issues tilting signals. The pantographs are mounted on an independent carriage on guiderails, with linkages to the bogies to ensure correct positioning of the pantographs when body-tilt is activated.

In 1996 JR Shikoku introduced the new three-car Series 6000 suburban emu with inverter control for use on the Seto–Ohashi line.

### Signalling and telecommunications
A centralised traffic control centre and headquarters in Takamatsu opened in 1997, controlling the entire network.

### Electrification
Electrification was begun to tie in with completion of the Seto bridge complex. Catenary between Takamatsu and Iyo on the Yosan line (206.3 km) was completed in early 1993, with Okayama-Matsuyama services in the hands of Series 8000 tilting emus from March of that year.

### Track
**Rail:** 60 kg/m (33 km), 50 kg/m (740 km) and 40 kg/m
**Sleepers:** Prestressed concrete or wood spaced

*N2000 130 km/h dmu with active tilting system*

*Class 2000 dmu forming a westbound service from Takamatsu (Wolfram Veith)*

**JR Shikoku diesel railcars or multiple-units**

| Class | Motored axles/car | Power/motor kW | Speed km/h | No in service | First built | Mechanical | Builders Engine | Transmission |
|---|---|---|---|---|---|---|---|---|
| 1000 | 1 | 300 | 110 | 56 | 1989 | NT | SA6D125-HD-1 | NT DW14 |
| TSE-2000 | 2 | 245 × 2 | 120 | 3 | 1989 | F | SA6D125-H | NT TACN 22-1600 |
| 2000 | 2 | 245 × 2 | 120 | 10 | 1989 | F | SA6D125-H | NT TACN 22-1600 |
| 2100 | 2 | 245 × 2 | 120 | 22 | 1989 | F | SA6D125-H | NT TACN 22-1600 |
| 2150 | 2 | 245 × 2 | 120 | 7 | 1989 | F | SA6D125-H | NT TACN 22-1600 |
| 2200 | 2 | 245 × 2 | 120 | 18 | 1989 | F | SA6D125-H | NT TACN 22-1600 |
| 2400 | 2 | 260 × 2 | 130 | 6 | 1995 | F | SA6D125-H | NT TACN 22-1600 |
| 2450 | 2 | 260 × 2 | 130 | 6 | 1995 | F | SA6D125-H | NT TACN 22-1600 |
| 2500 | 2 | 260 × 2 | 130 | 4 | 1997 | F | SA6D125-H | NT TACN 22-1600 |
| 185 | 1 | 185 × 2 | 110 | 32 | 1986 | NT/F/N | DMF13HS NT | S/NC TC2A DF115A |
| 65 | 2 | 375 | 95 | 7 | 1969 | NT/F/N | DML30HSD NT/S/D | S/NC DW4F |
| 58 | 1 | 135 × 2 | 95 | 16 | 1962 | NT/F/N | NT/S/D | S/NC TC2A DF115A |
| 54 | 1 | 185 × 2 | 95 | 12 | 1987 | NT/F | DMF13HS NT | S/NC TC2A DF115A |
| 47 | 1 | 165 | 95 | 42 | 1980 | NT/F | DMF15HSA NT/S/D | S/NC DW10 |
| 40 | 1 | 165 | 95 | 11 | 1981 | NT/F | DMF15HSA NT/S/D | S/NC DW10 |
| 32 | 1 | 165 | 95 | 22 | 1987 | NT/F | DMF13HS NT DMH17H | S/NC TC2A DF115A |
| 28 | 1 | 135 | 95 | 8 | 1961 | NT/F/N | NT/S/D | S/NC TC2A DF115A |

Abbreviations: D: Daihatsu; F: Fuji Juko; K: Komatsu Seisakusyo; N: Nippon Sharyo Seizo Ltd; NC: Niigata Converter; NT: Niigata Tekko; S: Shinko Zouki

Japan/**RAILWAY SYSTEMS**

1,560/km in plain track, 1,640/km in curves
**Fastenings:** Spike (wood sleeper) or double elastic
**Min curve radius:** 200 m
**Max gradient:** 3.3%
**Max axleload:** 17 tonnes

### JR Shikoku diesel locomotives

| Class | Wheel arrangement | Power kW | Speed km/h | Weight tonnes | No in service | First built | Mechanical | Builders Engine | Transmission |
|---|---|---|---|---|---|---|---|---|---|
| DE10 | AAA-A | 1,250 | 85 | 65 | 7 | 1966 | K/N/H | DML61ZB NT/S/D | H DW6 KH |

### JR Shikoku electric railcars or multiple-units

| Class | Cars per unit | Motor cars per unit | Motored axles/car | Output/motor kW | Speed km/h | No in service | First built | Builders Mechanical | Electrical |
|---|---|---|---|---|---|---|---|---|---|
| 111 | 4 | 2 | 1 | 100 | 100 | 3 | 1962 | N/K | H/T/M/To/Se |
| 113 | 4 | 2 | 4 | 120 | 100 | 4 | 1963 | NT/H/K/Kn | H/T/M/Se/To |
| 121 | 2 | 1 | 1 | 110 | 100 | 19 | 1986 | H/K/Kn/Tk | H/T/M/To |
| 6000 | 3 | 1* | 4 | 160 | 110 | 2 | 1996 | N | T |
| 7000 | 1 | 1* | 4 | 120 | 110 | 36 | 1990 | K | Fuji |
| 8000 | 3/4/5 | 2* | 4 | 185 | 140 | 12 | 1992 | N/H | To/T |

* VVVF Inverter control
Abbreviations: H: Hitachi Ltd; K: Kawasaki Heavy Industries; Kn: Kinki Sharyo; M: Mitsubishi; N: Nippon Sharyo; Se: Shinko Electric; T: Toshiba; To: Toyo Denki Seizo

## Japan Freight Railway Co

6-5, Marunouchi 1-chome, Chiyoda-ku, Tokyo 100
Tel: (+81 3) 32 85 00 71  Fax: (+81 3) 32 12 69 92

### Key personnel
Chairman: Masashi Hashimoto
President: Yasushi Tanahashi
Vice-President: Hisashi Ueda
Vice-Chairman: Yoshio Kaneda
General Managers: Naohiko Itoh, Shigeho Nimori, Hiroshi Hatanaka

### Organisation
Freight service is managed and marketed by JR Freight nationwide on the 1,067 mm gauge network. This concern owns its locomotives, wagons and terminals, but hires its track space from the six passenger railway companies. It has no marshalling yards and dedicates itself to bulk commodity and container traffic in trains using rolling stock modified to permit operation at up to 130 km/h. Some maintenance is subcontracted to the passenger railways.

### Finance
JR Freight is a drastically slimmed-down enterprise compared with the freight activity of JNR at its end, when wage costs alone exceeded freight revenue by 25 per cent. The company has withdrawn from a third of the route-km served by JNR and is running 40 per cent fewer daily trains. It has also discarded most individual wagonload traffic in favour of complete trainloads from one terminal to another and increased labour productivity.

As a result of these measures JR Freight was operating profitably, but the continuing Japanese recession, combined with the high value of the yen and a poor harvest, took its toll, with the company recording its first annual loss in 1993-94. Operating revenues fell slightly to ¥196.3 billion in 1995-96. However, a pre-tax profit of ¥1.7 billion was achieved, mainly through the sale of surplus land.

### JR Freight diesel locomotives

| Class | Wheel arrangement | Power kW | Speed km/h | Weight tonnes | No in service | First built | Builders Mechanical | Engine | Transmission |
|---|---|---|---|---|---|---|---|---|---|
| DE10 | AAA-B | 1,000 | 85 | 65 | 143 | 1967 | K/N/H | DML6ZB | H DW6 (2000 series) |
| DE11 | AAA-B | 1,000 | 85 | 70 | 4 | 1979 | K/N | DML61ZA/B | H DW6 |
| DD51 | B-2-B | 1,650 | 95 | 84 | 140 | 1966 | H/M/K | 2 × DML61Z | H 2 × DW2A |
| DF200 | B-B-B | 2,500 | 110 | 96 | 7 | 1992 | K/T | MTU 12V396TE14 | E |

To counter deteriorating performance the company adopted 'Freight 21', a 10-year management plan, in November 1994 with the aim of enhancing marketing, improving cost competitiveness, promoting planned capital investment and expanding non-railway business. Measures are in hand to restructure container services (into high-speed direct services between major terminal cities, express services between medium-size cities and local feeder services), to reduce terminal transfer times, to improve timetable efficiency by co-ordinating the speed of freight and passenger trains and to transfer more paper, tobacco and chemical products to containers. In the longer term, the company also intends to increase the number of wagons per train on the Tokaido line, to introduce new locomotives to speed up services and to reduce railway employee numbers from 11,000 to 7,000 by 2003 through expansion of its early retirement scheme.

| Finance (million yen) | 1993-94 | 1994-95 | 1995-96 |
|---|---|---|---|
| **Operating revenues** | | | |
| Railway | 180,684 | 171,700 | |
| Other | 25,160 | 25,200 | |
| Total | 205,844 | 196,900 | 196,293 |
| **Operating expenses** | | | |
| Total | 203,954 | 201,000 | 199,294 |
| Pretax profit/loss | –3,800 | –7,000 | 1,698 |
| Profit/loss after tax | –2,700 | –8,000 | 701 |

| Traffic (million) | 1993-94 | 1994-95 | 1995-96 |
|---|---|---|---|
| Freight tonnes | 54.0 | 53.5 | 52.5 |
| Freight tonne-km | 25,100 | 25,500 | 26,300 |

### Freight operations
A further decline in traffic levels occurred in 1995-96, with total freight tonnes down 1.8 per cent to 52.5 million, but tonne-km increased 0.3 per cent to 26.3 billion. Bulk commodities fell by 7.2 per cent to 31.52 million tonnes while container traffic rose 5.4 per cent to 20.58 million tonnes, the first rise in four years.

The most significant bulk commodities by weight are petroleum (34 per cent of total carryings), cement (19 per cent), limestone (14 per cent), paper and pulp (6 per cent), chemicals (4 per cent) and coal (2 per cent). However, containers are the biggest single traffic component, travelling 900 km on average compared to 200 km or so for other traffic, and yielding 60 per cent of JR Freight's total revenue.

The company's total number of daily scheduled trains stood at 844 in 1993 compared to 906 in 1992.

### Intermodal operations
In 1994, 329 container trains were running daily over trunk routes extending from Asahikawa and Kushiro in Hokkaido down to Fukuoka, Nagasaki and Kagoshima in Kyushu. One service runs throughout from Fukuoka to Sapporo, a distance of 2,130 km. 'Superliner' container trains connecting the main cities such as Tokyo, Osaka, Hiroshima and Fukuoka are permitted a top speed of 110 km/h. In all, 148 terminals are served by the container train system.

Most container traffic moves in JR Freight's own stock of 76,400 distinctively sized containers, but some 17,600 privately owned containers are also employed in rail transport. Width is the difficult dimension rather than height; since 1987 JR Freight has raised the latter from 8 ft (2.4 m) to 2.5 m in its own stock. Length was at first a standard 20 ft, but now JR Freight has available numerous 30 ft containers with 47 m³ capacity; that approximates to the cube available in the Japanese trucking industry's most widely used vehicles. JR Freight also deploys refrigerated and live fish containers, as well as boxes, tanks, hoppers and open tops.

JR Freight has now accumulated a stock of new low-floor flatcars that can carry 40 ft, 8 ft 6 in high ISO containers of 30 tonnes gross weight, or two 20 ft boxes with a total gross weight of 40 tonnes.

Because of its inherited scant terminal cranage, JR Freight partnered lorry manufacturer Izuku to develop a craneless transhipment technique for swapbody business. Known as 'Slide Vanbody', this uses a system of electrically powered winches and rollers with which the move from rail to road vehicle can be effected by one person.

*Class EF200 electric locomotive hauling an intermodal service through Nagoya (Anthony Robins)* 0001714

# RAILWAY SYSTEMS/Japan

From early 1995 JR Freight introduced a daily car transporter service between Nagoya and Niigata using new fully enclosed 'Car Rack' wagons. The sides and roof of the rail wagons lift upwards to accommodate a total of eight cars carried on two levels. These wagons can accommodate ordinary containers as return cargo.

*Piggyback services*
Recently perfected, too, is a low-floor flatcar with wheels of 610 mm diameter. That has enabled JR Freight to pursue ro-ro piggyback train service for the smaller size of road freight vans in common Japanese use. Over 300 truck movements a day are now made on 18 daily piggyback services. The wagon can also take 9 ft 6 in high containers.

Test running of a new concept known as 'Super Piggyback' began in 1993, with regular services introduced in 1994. Super Piggyback wagons accommodate three 6.5 m 'Freight Liner' road vans, each designed to carry 30 m$^3$ compared to conventional piggyback wagons which carry two 8.5 m vans with a capacity of 28.5 m$^3$ each.

## Traction and rolling stock
In September 1996, JR Freight operated 594 electric and 293 diesel locomotives and 11,647 wagons.

Recent deliveries include Hitachi-built Class EF200 1.5 kV DC Bo-Bo-Bos with inverter-controlled asynchronous motors and a dual-voltage EF500 prototype built by Mitsubishi/Kawasaki which is being evaluated for hauling container trains from Tokyo to Hokkaido via the Seikan tunnel. Following a one-year trial with a prototype DF200 diesel-electric 'Inverter Hi-Tech Loco' built by Kawasaki, JR Freight has taken delivery of a further six production versions for use on timber trains in Hokkaido. The DF200 has a maximum speed of 120 km/h, with power supplied by two MTU 12V396 engines (total output 2,500 kW at 1,800 rpm), each of which drives an alternator.

In 1996 trials commenced with a prototype Class EF210 1.5 kV DC 4,000 kW output electric locomotive designed for 110 km/h container services on the main Tokaido/Sanyo trunk route. Construction costs have been reduced by the use of inverters to control pairs of traction motors. From 1997 onwards, JR Freight plans to take delivery of 100 production Class EF210 locomotives to replace Class EF65 locomotives which have seen over 25 years service.

*Class EF66 electric locomotive near Atami with Tokyo-bound intermodal freight comprising piggyback and container traffic (Wolfram Veith)*

### JR Freight electric locomotives

| Class | Wheel arrangement | Output kW | Speed km/h | Weight tonnes | No in service | First built | Builders |
|---|---|---|---|---|---|---|---|
| **1.5 kV DC** | | | | | | | |
| ED62 | B-1-B | 1,560 | 90 | | 7 | | |
| EF64 | B-B-B | 2,550 | 100 | 96 | 113 | 1964 | T/K/To |
| EF65 | B-B-B | 2,550 | 100 | 96 | 184 | 1964 | K/To/T/N |
| EF66 | B-B-B | 3,900 | 110 | 100.8 | 73 | 1968 | K/To |
| EF67 | B-B-B | 2,850 | 100 | 99.6 | 8 | 1981 | To |
| EF200 | B-B-B | 6,000 | 120 | 100.8 | 21 | 1990 | H |
| **20 kV AC** | | | | | | | |
| ED75 | B-B | 1,900 | 100 | 67.2 | 89 | 1963 | M/H/T |
| ED76 | B-2-B | 1,900 | 100 | 87 | 24 | 1967 | H/M/T |
| ED79 | B-B | 1,900 | 110 | 68 | 10 | 1989 | T |
| **Dual-voltage 1.5 kV/20 kV** | | | | | | | |
| EF81 | B-B-B | 2,550/2,370 | 110 | 100.8 | 64 | 1968 | H/M |
| EF500 | B-B-B | 6,000 | 120 | 100.8 | 1 | 1990 | M/K |

Abbreviations: H: Hitachi; K: Kawasaki; M: Mitsubishi; N: Nippon Sharyo Seizo; T: Toshiba; To: Toyo Denki Seizo

## Shinkansen network development

The network in operation at the start of 1999 and its owning and operating railways comprised:

JR East:
- Tohoku Shinkansen — Tokyo to Morioka
- Joetsu Shinkansen — Omiya to Niigata
- Nagano Shinkansen — Takasaki to Nagano
- Yamagata Mini-Shinkansen — Fukushima to Yamagata
- Akita/Ou Mini-Shinkansen — Morioka to Omagari/Ou

JR Central:
- Tokaido Shinkansen — Tokyo to Shin-Osaka

JR West:
- Sanyo Shinkansen — Shin-Osaka to Hakata

The Shinkansen programme agreed in 1988 specified three types of extension:

**Type 1.** To full Shinkansen 1,435 mm gauge standard, engineered for 260 km/h by present equipment, 300 km/h by the next generation equipment in design.

**Type 2.** Addition of a third rail to existing 1,067 mm gauge, possibly with some realignment, with the use of small-profile trainsets restricted to 130 km/h on mixed-gauge.

**Type 3.** Infrastructure to full Shinkansen 1,435 mm gauge standard, but initially laid with 1,067 mm gauge track, engineered for 160 to 200 km/h.

Application of these concepts to the extensions approved in 1990 was as follows:

**Hokuriku (later Nagano) Shinkansen**
- Type 1: Takasaki-Karuizawa (41 km)
- Type 1: Karuizawa-Nagano (75 km)
- Type 3: Nagano-Kanazawa (89 km)

**Tohoku Shinkansen**
- Type 2: Morioka-Aomori (125 km)
- Type 1: Numakunai-Hachinohe (but dual-gauged for use also by freight trains)

**Kyushu Shinkansen**
- Type 3: Yatsushiro-Kagoshima (128 km)

Construction work began on the Karuizawa-Nagano section of the Hokuriku, the Morioka-Aomori extension of the Tohoku, and the Yatsushiro-Kagoshima section of JR Kyushu's first Shinkansen in September 1991. Construction commenced in October 1993 on the Itoigawa Uozu section of the Hokuriku Shinkansen. All were being built by the Japan Railway Construction Corporation (see above). Construction costs were to be shared between central government (40 per cent) and the JR companies, which will pay their share out of receipts from the Shinkansen lines they now own.

The outcome of a government review of the Shinkansen programme was announced at the beginning of 1994. The previously authorised sections of the Hokuriku, Tohoku and Kyushu lines retained priority. Environmental assessment studies of the Takefu-Osaka section of the Hokuriku line, the Nagasaki and Hokkaido branches of the Kyushu line and the Hokkaido line from Aomori to Sapporo commenced in 1994-95, although work on these sections was not to start before the next programme review in 1997.

A change in government policy saw a 25 per cent increase in funding for Shinkansen construction, which has enabled work to progress on some additional sections of the network. About 90 per cent of the ¥228 billion budget was allocated to the Takasaki-Nagano section of the Hokuriku Shinkansen, but work has also progressed on the Kumamoto section of the Kyushu line and the Morioka-Numakunai section of the Tohoku line, which will now be built to Type 1 rather than Type 2 standard.

The Takasaki-Nagano section was opened for public services in October 1997, but no date has been announced for completion of the section beyond Nagano to Toyama and Kanazawa.

## Shinkansen rolling stock

### Series 0
During the first 20 years after the opening of the Tokaido-Sanyo Shinkansen, rolling stock of essentially the same performance and accommodation was employed. The original cars of this Series 0 have now all been replaced.

### Series 100
Series 0 has been complemented on the Tokaido-Sanyo Shinkansen by the Series 100, which combines pursuit of better aerodynamics, more effective noise control and economy in energy consumption with improvement of passenger comfort and amenities. Earlier Shinkansen types had all cars powered, but in the Series 100 four of a set's 16 cars are trailers. The powered cars, which are paired, each have a 230 kW motor of lighter (828 kg) and more compact design on each axle. A Series 100 set is lighter than a Series 0 set, even though two (or in some sets all) of a Series 100's four trailers are bilevels (the other two are the end cars with driving cabs). The comparison is 922 tonnes as against 967 tonnes for 16

*JR Central Series 300, Series 100 and Series 0 trainsets at Osaka depot* (Wolfram Veith)

cars with a full complement of 1,277 passengers. Maximum axleloading, at 15 tonnes, is one tonne below that of a Series 0.

Aerodynamic improvements in the Series 100 include a longer and reshaped nose and closer attention to smooth exterior surfaces, in particular by avoiding recessed windows. The effect has been to reduce drag coefficient by 20 per cent, compared with Series 0, and also noise emission. Moreover, even though the total installed power of a Series 100 (11,040 kW) is less than that of a Series 0 16-car unit, the Series 100 has proved 17 per cent more economical in power consumption on a Tokyo-Sanyo 'Hikari' schedule. The 1.6 km/h/s acceleration rate of a Series 100 compares with the 1.0 km/h/s of a Series 0. Nose shaping is a factor in noise control as well as reduction of drag, since the noise emanating from an accelerating train's front end rises by a factor of between the fifth and sixth power of its speed.

With eddy current brakes on its non-motored trailers to complement the regenerative braking of the powered cars, the Series 100 has a braking performance superior to its predecessors.

### Series 200

Advances in Shinkansen speed resulted from an exhaustive programme of research and high-speed tests begun in the late 1970s. It proved possible to limit lineside noise at 240 km/h to 79 dB(A), the figure previously achieved at 210 km/h to respect the statutory limit of 80 dB(A), largely by increasing the frequency of rail grinding to eliminate surface defects, and by pantograph alterations.

As built for JR East's Joetsu and Tohoku lines, the Series 200 trainsets were formed of two-car units, each of which had to run with a pantograph operative. The normal 12-car formation now runs with only three pantographs raised and a 25 kV bus-line laid along the tops of the cars distributes the current. Noise has been further curbed by adoption of three-stage pantograph springing to sustain contact with the overhead wire and to minimise the intermittent arcing that has been a perennial cause for environmentalist complaints; and by surrounding the pantograph with shielding, which limits transmission of noise to the lineside.

A programme of replacement of Series 200 units was expected to commence after the opening of the Nagano and Akita Shinkansen projects in 1997. However, in 1998 JR East commenced a refurbishment programme covering at least 100 cars.

### Series 300

Test programmes demonstrated that speeds up to 300 km/h were feasible on the present track of all Shinkansen, but not with existing sets, which at that speed would break both the 80 dB(A) noise limit and also generate unacceptable vibration. Also, aerodynamic drag in tunnels would be too high. Consequently a new Series 300 train was designed and, as described above, was put into public service by JR Central on the Tokaido Shinkansen in 1992.

The Series 300 is distinguished externally by a dramatically reshaped nose-end and low-slung body. Floor level is 1.15 m and roof crown 3.6 m above rail, compared with 1.3 m and 4 m respectively for the Series 100. A considerable reduction of weight results from adoption of aluminium alloy body construction and more powerful traction motors. With six of a set's 16 cars non-motored, total weight is 691 tonnes, compared with the 922 tonnes of a Series 100. Maximum axleloading in the bolsterless bogies is 14 tonnes. Like the Series 100, the 300 adds eddy current to its braking systems; a change is that the 300 has regenerative instead of dynamic braking.

Traction is provided by three-phase AC 300 kW motors, four per motor car, supplied by a 3,000 kW pulse-width modulation converter with 4,500 V, 2,000 A GTO thyristors feeding 1,760 kVA VVVF inverters. Power-to-weight ratio is 17.37 kW/tonne. Designed top speed is 300 km/h.

### Series 300X

In 1994 JR Central took delivery of a six-car series 300X experimental trainset, designed for commercial speeds of 350 km/h, and is undertaking a two-year programme of high-speed trials on an upgraded section of track between Kyoto and Maibara. The 300X achieved a record speed for Japan of 443 km/h in July 1996. The train features two different nose configurations (cusp shape and rounded-wedge shape) to test air resistance and noise, reduced cross-section smooth-sided aluminium-bodied cars with coupling bellows and undercarriage skirts, pantograph covers, dampers between cars, tilting system and active control system. Individual cars have been constructed by four different manufacturers using different body fabrication techniques in order to assess the scope for further weight reductions.

The Series 300X forms the basis for trains that may be required for the Chuo Shinkansen between Tokyo and Osaka via Kofu if the proposed maglev line does not proceed.

### Series 400

For its Yamagata Mini-Shinkansen, as described above, JR East acquired 12 small-profile six-car Series 400 sets. All axles are powered by thyristor-controlled 220 kW motors. The cars are of the same height as those of the Series 200, to which the sets are coupled when running over the Tohoku Shinkansen and run at up to 240 km/h between Tokyo and the divergence of the Mini-Shinkansen at Fukushima. But the bodies are significantly narrower, so that each seating bay has one seat less per row than in a Series 200. A seventh car was subsequently added to each set.

In September 1991 a Series 400 was run at up to 345 km/h on the Tohoku Shinkansen.

### Series E1

To meet rising demand for commuter services on its Tohoku and Joetsu lines, JR East launched the all double-deck 12-car Series E1 'MAX' (Multi Amenity Express) in March 1994, and commercial services commenced in July 1994. Because the car height has been increased, the front cars have been given an ultra-streamlined shape to improve their appearance. Doors have been widened to prevent congestion around the entrances and wheelchair lifts are installed in two cars. Cars are equipped with electronic information displays and FM radio receivers. Vending machines are available in some cars in place of restaurant or buffet facilities. Half the cars are motored, with 24 traction motors providing a total continuous rating of 9,840 kW. Maximum speed is 240 km/h.

### Series E2

Services on the Nagano (formerly Hokuriku) Shinkansen are operated by eight-car Series E2 trainsets designed to achieve 260 km/h and climb 3.5 per cent gradients. Performance trials began following the delivery of a prototype set in May 1995, and revenue services began in October 1997. The train features a low-profile cross-section as on the Series 300 and a streamlined nose to reduce pressure when entering tunnels. To reduce aerodynamic noise, underfloor equipment is enclosed, plug doors are fitted flush with body sides and pantographs are surrounded by shields. VVVF-controlled 300 kW motors are fitted to six power cars and accept power supply at 50 or 60 Hz. The Series E2 and E3 units are designed so that noise and vibration levels at 275 km/h do not exceed those of existing 240 km/h trains.

An initial series of 19 trainsets was to be expanded by an additional nine units by March 2000.

### Series E3

A prototype five-car Series E3 unit was delivered in April 1995 for test running prior to commercial operation on the Akita Shinkansen from 1997. Series E2 and E3 share main electrical components and bogies to reduce construction and maintenance costs but the E3 has a smaller cross-section to meet clearances on the Akita line. The unit features asynchronous motors and a maximum speed of 270 km/h, though speed is limited to 130 km/h on the regauged line between Morioka and Akita. Power is supplied at 25 kV 50 Hz AC on the Shinkansen and 20 kV 50 Hz AC on the converted line. Due to limited underfloor space, some equipment is roof-mounted under an aerodynamically designed cover. Series E3 sets are coupled to Series 200 or E2 trains for the run between Tokyo and Morioka. Five five-car units were initially constructed. In 1998 it was announced that these would be increased to six-car sets and that a further train, also of six cars, would be built.

### Series E4

JR East introduced the new double-deck Series E4 from December 1997 on the Tohoku Shinkansen to alleviate rush-hour congestion, particularly on the Omiya to Oyama section. The newly designed 16-car trainset, consisting of two eight-car units, has total seating capacity of 1,634 and runs at 240 km/h. This will make it the highest capacity high-speed train in the world. Bodyshells are of aluminium alloy, contributing to an axleload of only 16 tonnes when fully laden. Four cars are motored and VVVF traction equipment is used. One-hour rating is 6,720 kW. Initially three sets were ordered by JR East and delivered in 1997. A further seven have been ordered for entry into service by March 2000.

### STAR 21

A prototype nine-car train was completed for JR East by Kawasaki in 1992. Tagged STAR 21 (Superior Train for the Advanced 21st Century Railway), it is designed to prove various components and technologies with a view to future operation at 300 to 400 km/h. Consequently, it features some alternative concepts, a peculiarity most apparent in the differing outlines of its two end cars. Of these, one is designated Series 952, the other Series 953.

The unit features three types of body in which aerospace techniques and materials have been employed for weight saving, which has been so effective that the maximum axleloading is 10.5 tonnes. For the first time in Shinkansen rolling stock development, five of the cars are articulated. Eight different designs of bolsterless bogie have been applied to the unit. Hollow axles and aluminium axleboxes are features.

Four of the cars are motored for a continuous rating of 2,640 kW to serve a total train weight of 256 tonnes. The motors are three-phase AC under VVVF control, and draw their current from pantographs on the third and seventh cars.

In November 1992 STAR 21 set a Japanese speed record of 358 km/h and in December 1993 reached 425 km/h, at that time second only to the French TGV-A's 515 km/h. Further work is now in progress to reduce noise levels associated with high-speed running.

### Series 500

In 1992 JR West unveiled a six-car prototype variously designated Series 500 and WIN 350, the latter to mark its objective of commercial operating speed. As with JR East's STAR 21, the unit featured differently styled end cars for investigation of aerodynamics and noise suppression at high speed. Test running of the WIN 350 train enabled the development of measures to respond to environmental concerns and to ensure passenger comfort at operational speeds of 300 km/h.

In January 1996 JR West took delivery of a 16-car Series 500 preproduction train, based on the results of the WIN 350 research. The 500 entered commercial service at a maximum speed of 300 km/h between Shin-Osaka and Hakata in March 1997 and was scheduled to operate through to Tokyo in late 1997. This new train features a reduced cross-section lightweight aluminium body, 'smooth' surfacing technology with plug doors and enclosed underfloor equipment modules, a distinctive 15 m long aerodynamic pointed nose, a wing-shaped pantograph to reduce aerodynamic and wire contact noise and active suspension to allow curves to be negotiated up to 20 km/h faster than other trains. All axles are motored and bolsterless bogies reduce vibration. The passenger capacity of 1,323 is the same as the 'Nozomi' trainsets. Series 500 trainsets entered service with JR West in March 1997.

### Series 700
Test running of a prototype Series 700 Shinkansen trainset developed by rolling stock engineers from JR Central and JR West began in October 1997. The 16-car train has been designed as a low-noise, low-maintenance replacement for the Tokaido and Sanyo Shinkansen routes. Hollow extruded aluminium sections filled with sound insulation has been used for the bodyshell, while computer-controlled secondary suspension and inter-car dampers are provided to improve ride quality and reduce vibration. Twelve cars are motored, giving a total power rating of 13,200 kW. Seating capacity is for 1,323 passengers. Top speed is 270 km/h, although 285 km/h was expected to be the maximum on the Sanyo Shinkansen.

### ATLAS
Japan's Railway Technical Research Institute is also working up designs for a 350 km/h Shinkansen train, in a project dubbed ATLAS (Advanced Technology for Low Noise and Attractive Shinkansen).

## The rump of JNR
What remains of JNR was reorganised as the Japanese National Railways Settlement Corporation, which retains all the assets and liabilities that are not transferred to successor companies (including the Japan Railway Construction Corporation). Its tasks are:
Reimbursement of long-term liabilities and payment of interest;
Disposal of real estate and other assets in order to raise the necessary money;
Execution of necessary business activities to utilise the rights and meet the obligations transferred to the company from JNR;
Action to achieve re-employment of personnel made surplus by the Reform. (Some 93,000 JNR personnel were surplus to the needs of the new companies at the latter's formation.)
JNR Settlement Corporation
6-5, Marunouchi 1-chome, Chiyoda-ku, Tokyo 100
Tel: (+81 3) 32 14 79 59   Fax: (+81 3) 32 40 55 86

### Key personnel
Chairman: Yasuo Nishimura
The corporation's function is disposal of the assets and long-term liabilities not transferred to new companies during the restructuring of 1987, and promotion of the re-employment of surplus employees. JNRSC took on most of the JNR debt in order to facilitate the privatisation of the ex-JNR companies, but 10 years after the JNR break-up the continued existence of ¥28,100 billion of debt (equivalent to nearly 6 per cent of gross domestic product) was a political embarrassment. Reduction of the inherited JNR debt is proving difficult because of lower than expected proceeds from railway privatisation and land sales due to the sluggish economy and collapse in property values. A proposal put forward in early 1997 was that the government should assume ¥13,800 billion of the outstanding debt; land sales might cover a further ¥8,000 billion. The balance of ¥6,300 billion required to enable the winding up of JNRSC might be financed by a surcharge on rail fares, an idea which is being strongly resisted by the ex-JNR companies. A subsequent government plan provided for outstanding long-term debt being paid off over a 50-year period and JNRSC being wound up. In October 1998 legislation was passed by the Japanese parliament to wind up the JNR Settlement Corporation. The government took over debt of ¥23,500 billion, to be written down over 60 years, while an outstanding sum of ¥4,300 billion was passed back to railway undertakings in Japan, which would be expected to recover a comparable figure from the disposal of property.
Japan Telecom Co
1-7-4 Kudan-kita, Chiyoda-ku, Tokyo 102
Tel: (+81 3) 32 22 66 51   Fax: (+81 3) 32 22 66 60

### Key personnel
Chairman: Kazumasa Mawatari
President: Koichi Sakata

*The two MLX-01 maglev vehicles at the Yamanashi test centre*

Maintenance of railway telecommunication equipment and provision of general telecommunication services.
Railway Information Systems Co Ltd
6-5, Marunouchi 1-chome, Chiyoda-ku, Tokyo 100
Tel: (+81 3) 32 14 46 95   Fax: (+81 3) 32 40 55 93

### Key personnel
Chairman: Yoshisuke Mutoh
President: Hiroyuki Hayashi
Information processing for railway companies, and related computerised information services.
Railway Technical Research Institute
2-8-38, Hikari-cho, Kokubunji-shi, Tokyo 185
Tel: (+81 425) 73 72 19   Fax: (+81 425) 73 72 55
Tokyo Office
Tel: (+81 3) 32 40 96 72
Miyazaki Maglev Centre
Tel: (+81 982) 58 13 03

### Key personnel
Chairman: Yoshinosuke Yasoshima
President: Hiromi Soejima
Executive Directors: Nobuhisa Izumi, Toshiaki Sasaki

### Organisation
Research and development activities to meet the requirements of the railway companies.

*High-speed 1,067 mm gauge design*
The Institute has developed a preliminary design for a 12-car lightweight train with active tilt-body apparatus for high-speed operation on the country's 1,067 mm gauge routes.

*ATLAS Shinkansen project*
As noted above, the Institute is developing a 350 km/h Shinkansen train design under the title of ATLAS.

*Maglev system*
Maglev is being considered as an option for the second Tokyo-Osaka high-speed route (see JR Central entry above). The objective is to operate at 500 km/h so as to cover the Tokyo-Osaka distance in 1 hour. To further this aim, the government authorised construction as a national project of a 43 km Yamanshi test track, roughly 100 km from Tokyo. The test track is being used to study vehicle behaviour in tunnels and when passing another car running in the opposite direction; operation and control of a full train service; permissible gradient and curvature parameters; and turnout performance. Progress with construction of the test track has been held up due to lack of government finance and land acquisition difficulties, but the Japan Railway Construction Corporation and JR Central have now completed an 18.4 km priority section (16 km in tunnel) between Sakaigawa and Akiyama.

A three-car test train known as MLX-01 was delivered in July 1995. This first MLX-01 comprises a 'double cusp' end car built by Mitsubishi, an 'aero wedge' end car by Kawasaki and a Nippon Sharyo middle car. The cars are linked by articulated levitation bogies which incorporate superconducting magnets and retractable take-off and landing wheels for use at low speeds. Aircraft technology has been used for the ultra-lightweight bodyshells which are constructed in a semi-monocoque style to a slightly smaller cross-section than Series 300 Shinkansen trains. A second five-car MLX-01 train was delivered in October 1997, permitting trials with two trains in operation at the same time.

Trials in superconducting mode, but without levitation, began in February 1997. Test running in levitation mode followed in May 1997. A manned record speed of 531 km/h was achieved in December 1997, and later the same month an unmanned speed of 550 km/h was reached. Tests continued in 1999, with the aim of proving the practicality of maglev in regular service by 2000.

## Major private and third sector railways
In addition to the JR Group Companies there are over 125 private and third-sector railways in Japan, excluding metros, tramways and new transit systems. These range from major private interurban networks to individual rural lines, many of which were former loss-making JNR/JR lines that have been taken over by third-sector companies.

## Chichibu Railway
Chichibu Tetsudo
1-1, Akebono-cho, Kumagaya-shi 360
Tel: (+81 485) 23 33 11   Fax: (+81 485) 26 05 51

### Key personnel
President: K Kakihara

Gauge: 1,067 mm
Route length: 79.3 km
Electrification: 79.3 km at 1.5 kV DC

### Organisation
The railway operates passenger services on two lines which connect at Kumagaya in Saitama prefecture; the 14.9 km Hanyu line and 56.8 km Chichibu line. The latter serves a mountainous area northwest of Tokyo which attracts sightseers and provides limestone for cement, an

important source of freight traffic for the railway. Interchange is available with JR, Tobu and Seibu lines and some Seibu services run through between Tokyo and Chichibu line destinations, mainly on Sundays and holidays; a steam-hauled tourist service also operates on the Chichibu line. A 7.6 km freight connection provides for the transfer of freight traffic to and from the JR network. Rolling stock comprises 22 electric locomotives, 67 emu cars and 168 wagons.

## Hankyu Corporation

Hankyu Dentetsu
16-1, Shibata 1-chome, Kita-ku, Osaka 530
Tel: (+81 6) 373 50 92    Fax: (+81 6) 373 56 70

### Key personnel
Chairman: Kohei Kobayashi
President: Motohiro Sugai
Senior Managing Directors: Yoshihito Utahashi, Norikazu Matsubara

Gauge: 1,435 mm
Route length: 146.8 km
Electrification: 146.8 km at 1.5 kV DC

### Organisation
The Corporation was set up in 1907 to construct an interurban railway to develop suburban Osaka, and is now a diversified enterprise. The railway remains the cornerstone of the group, but other activities range from bus and taxi companies to real estate development, department stores, recreation centres and audio-visual entertainment.

### Finance
Revenue from railway operations constitutes approximately 54 per cent of total operating revenue.

### Passenger operations
The railway serves nine lines with 84 stations and runs over 1,000 eight-car trains daily on its Kobe line and to Kyoto, and over 700 a day to Takarazuka. The terminal in Osaka, built in the 1970s, has 10 platforms and is located in a complex including a 17-storey office building and an underground shopping mall. The rail exit from the terminal is six-track. The company is currently implementing a programme to replace existing Automatic Train Stop (ATS), Total Train Control (TTC) and other safety equipment with more advanced systems. Elevated tracks are under construction at six locations to eliminate level crossings.

**Hankyu electric multiple-units**

| Class | Cars per unit | Motor cars per unit | Motored axles/car | Output/motor kW | Speed km/h | Cars in service | First built | Builders Mechanical | Electrical |
|---|---|---|---|---|---|---|---|---|---|
| 2000 | | | | | 110 | 38 | 1960 | Alna Koki | |
| 2300 | 4/7 | 2/4 | 4 | 150 | 110 | 78 | 1960 | Alna Koki | Toshiba/Toyo Denki |
| 2800 | 4/7 | 2/4 | 4 | 150 | 110 | 28 | 1964 | Alna Koki | Toyo Denki |
| 3000 | 3/4/6/8 | 2/4 | 4 | 170 | 110 | 114 | 1964 | Alna Koki | Toshiba |
| 3100 | 3/4/8 | 2/4 | 4 | 120 | 110 | 40 | 1964 | Alna Koki | Toshiba |
| 3300 | 6/8 | 4/6 | 4 | 130 | 110 | 126 | 1967 | Alna Koki | Toshiba/Toyo Denki |
| 5000 | 8 | 4 | 4 | 170 | 110 | 47 | 1968 | Alna Koki | Toshiba |
| 5100 | 8/10 | 4/6 | 4 | 140 | 110 | 90 | 1971 | Alna Koki | Toshiba |
| 5200 | 4/6 | 2/4 | 4 | 170 | 110 | 12 | 1970 | Alna Koki | Toshiba |
| 5300 | 6/7/8 | 4/6 | 4 | 140 | 110 | 105 | 1972 | Alna Koki | Toshiba/Toyo Denki |
| 2200 | 4 | 2 | 4 | 150* | 110 | 10 | 1975 | Alna Koki | Toshiba |
| 6000 | 6/8/10 | 4/6/8 | 4 | 140 | 110 | 130 | 1976 | Alna Koki | Toshiba |
| 6300 | 8 | 4 | 4 | 140/150 | 110 | 72 | 1975 | Alna Koki | Toshiba/Toyo Denki |
| 7000 | 6/8/10 | 4/5/6 | 4 | 150 | 110 | 210 | 1980 | Alna Koki | Toshiba |
| 7300 | 6/8/10 | 3/4/5/6 | 4 | 150/180* | 110 | 83 | 1982 | Alna Koki | Toshiba/Toyo Denki |
| 8000 | 6/8/10 | 3/4/5 | 4 | 170* | 110 | 90 | 1988 | Alna Koki | Toshiba |
| 8300 | 6/7/8 | 3/4 | 4 | 170* | 110 | 61 | 1989 | Alna Koki | Toshiba/Toyo Denki |
| 8200 | 2 | 1 | 4 | 200 | 110 | 4 | 1995 | Alna Koki | |

* VVVF inverter control

Passenger journeys declined from 789 million in 1993-94 to 758 million in 1994-95 due largely to Japan's economic downturn and the effects of the Hanshin earthquake of January 1995. The railway experienced severe damage in the earthquake with services suspended on the main line between Nishinomiya and Kobe and on the Itami and Koyoen branch lines. Reconstruction works costed at ¥85.2 billion were completed by June 1995.

### Rolling stock
The railway owns 1,343 emu cars, all air conditioned. The most recent motored cars have VVVF inverter control and the new Series 8200 units feature seats which fold away during the rush hour to increase passenger capacity.

### Track
**Rail:** 50.4 or 60.8 kg/m
**Sleepers:** Wood: 230 × 2,400 mm; prestressed concrete: 300 × 2,400 × 170 mm
**Fastenings:** Double elastic
**Spacing:** 1,760/km
**Min curvature radius:** 100 m
**Max gradient:** 3.5%
**Max permissible axleload:** 17.78 tonnes

## Hanshin Electric Railway

Hanshin Denki Tetsudo
1-24 Ebie 1-chome, Fukushima-ku, Osaka 533
Tel: (+81 6) 457 21 23

### Key personnel
Chairman: Shunjiro Kuma
President: Masatoshi Tezuka

Gauge: 1,435 mm
Route length: 40 km
Electrification: 40 km at 1.5 kV DC

### Organisation
The Hanshin Electric Railway is at the centre of the Hanshin Group of approximately 60 affiliated companies extending into transport, retailing, real estate, sports, leisure, construction and computer-related business. Rail operations account for 41 per cent of group turnover.

### Passenger operations
The railway operates a main line between Osaka and Kobe with two branches. In 1993-94 the railway recorded 240 million passenger journeys and 2,249 million passenger-km. The Hanshin earthquake of January 1995 affected performance in 1994-95 with passenger journeys down to 229 million and passenger-km down to 2,187 million.

Services extend via the underground Kobe Rapid Railway on to the Sanyo Electric Railway to the west of Kobe; reciprocal through running services are operated, providing a metro-style service across central Kobe.

All cars and underground stations are equipped with air conditioning. Programmed Traffic Control (PTC) and Automatic Train Stop (ATS) systems have been introduced. The proportion of main line in tunnel or elevated is due to rise to 87 per cent within 10 years through elimination of level crossings.

The railway was severely damaged in the January 1995 earthquake, with buses replacing trains between central Kobe and the eastern suburbs and all through-running services via the Kobe Rapid Railway suspended. Full service was restored, however, by June 1995. From the total fleet of 314 cars, 41 were written off as a result of earthquake damage. New replacement vehicles comprised two 4-car Series 5500 units, three Series 8000 cars and five 6-car Series 9000 units delivered during 1995-96.

## Iyo Railway

Iyo Tetsudo
4-1, Minatomachi 4-chome, Matsuyama-shi 790
Tel: (+81 899) 48 33 21

### Key personnel
President: H Nagano

Gauge: 1,067 mm
Route length: 33.9 km
Electrification: 24.5 km at 750 V DC and 9.4 km at 600 V DC

### Passenger operations
The railway operates 53 electric multiple-unit cars on two lines serving Matsuyama, on the island of Shikoku. Apart from its 33.9 km railway, it operates a 6.9 km urban tramway system in Matsuyama with 36 cars. There were 24 million passenger journeys in 1994-95.

## Izu Hakone Railway

Izu Hakone Tetsudo
300, Daiba, Mishima-shi 411
Tel: (+81 559) 77 12 00

### Key personnel
Chairman: Yoshiaki Tsutsumi
President: Kakuro Kato

Gauge: 1,067 mm
Route length: 29.4 km
Electrification: 29.4 km at 1.5 kV DC

### Passenger operations
The railway operates two electric locomotives and 60 emu cars on the 9.6 km Daiyousan line in Kanagawa prefecture and the 19.8 km Sunzu line in Shizuoka prefecture. JR East limited express 'Odori-Ko' trains run through from Tokyo to the Sunzu line. The company also operates two funiculars. Railway operations account for 15 per cent of the company's revenue.

## RAILWAY SYSTEMS/Japan

## Izukyu Corporation

Izu Kyuko (Izukyu)
1-21-6 Dogenzaka, Shibuya-ku, Tokyo 150-0043
Tel: (+81 3) 34 96 71 55

**Key personnel**
President: Shun-ichi Oki

Gauge: 1,067 mm
Route length: 45.7 km
Electrification: 45.7 km at 1.5 kV DC

**Passenger operations**
The railway, opened in 1961, serves the eastern coastline of the Izu peninsula from Ito to Izukyu-Shimoda. For the most part this is territory of the Fuji Hakone Izu national park, not far from Tokyo, and at Ito the railway connects with the JR East branch from Atami. Most local services operate through to Atami and JR 'Odori-Ko' limited expresses run through from Tokyo to Izukyu destinations. The railway operates 68 emu cars and its operations account for 37 per cent of the company's revenue.

## Keifuku Electric Railway

Keifuku Denki Tetsudo
3-20, Mibu-kayo-goshomachi, Nakagyo-ku, Kyoto 604
Tel: (+81 75) 841 93 81

**Key personnel**
Chairman: Minoru Miyashita
President: Seiya Yamakami

Gauge: 1,067 mm
Route length: 59.2 km
Electrification: 59.2 km at 600 V DC

**Passenger operations**
The railway operates 30 emu cars and two electric locomotives on three 1,067 mm gauge lines totalling 59.2 km at Fukui. It also operates a separate 11 km 1,435 mm gauge tramway system in Kyoto with a fleet of 28 cars. Railway operations account for 27 per cent of the company's revenue.

## Keihan Electric Railway Co Ltd

Keihan Denki Tetsudo
2-27, Shiromi 1-chome, Chuo-ku, Osaka 540
Tel: (+81 6) 944 25 21   Fax: (+81 6) 944 25 01

**Key personnel**
Chairman: Minoru Miyashita
President: Akio Kinba
Executive Vice-President, Accounts, Finance, Purchases, Subsidiaries: Yutaka Ogura
Senior Managing Director, Railway Operation, Electrical Engineering, Rolling Stock: Rikuro Kimura
Chief Manager, New Business Planning and Development: Hiroshi Yoshida
Managing Director, Personnel, Audit, Information Systems: Junzo Takai
Deputy Chief Manager, Business Planning and Developments: Toru Nakanishi
Otsu Branch: Kazuyuki Hasegawa
Director, New Line Construction: Kihachiro Nakaichi
Railway Operation: Kimio Nishimura
Accounting and Finance: Hiroichi Shimizu

Gauge: 1,435 mm
Route length: 91.5 km
Electrification: 66.3 km at 1.5 kV (Keihan line); 25.2 km at 600 V DC (Otsu line)

**Passenger operations**
The railway's main Keihan line runs 51.6 km from its Yodoyabashi station in Osaka to the underground Demachi Yanagi station in Kyoto City, with two branches, the Uji and Katano lines. The 11.5 km of continuously elevated quadruple-track between Temmabashi and Kayashima stations is the longest on any Japanese private railway. The Otsu line is light rail extending 25.2 km from Kyoto Sanjo to Hamaotsu, Ishiyama-dera and Sakamoto.

Serving 89 stations, the railway recorded 401 million passenger journeys and 5,319 million passenger-km in 1994-95.

The railway generates 58 per cent of the company's income. The rest is derived from 65 subsidiary and affiliated companies covering activities ranging from bus, taxi and leisure boat services to hotels, retail stores and construction.

Future developments include through operation from Otsu to Kyoto City's new Tozai underground line with new Series 8000 four-car emus delivered in readiness for this and construction of a Nakanoshima line westward through Osaka City to connect with a new line serving the Kansai International Airport.

### Keihan electric railcars or multiple-units

| Class | Cars per unit | Motor cars per unit | Motored axles/car | Output/motor kW | Speed km/h | Cars in service | First built | Builders Mechanical | Builders Electrical |
|---|---|---|---|---|---|---|---|---|---|
| **Keihan line 1.5 kV DC** | | | | | | | | | |
| 9000 | 8 | | | | | | 1995 | | |
| 8000 | 7 | 4 | 4 | 175 | 110 | 70 | 1989 | K/S/N | To/T/M |
| 7000 | 7 | 3 | 4 | 200 | 110 | 28 | 1989 | K/S/N | To/T/M |
| 6000 | 8 | 4 | 4 | 155 | 110 | 112 | 1983 | K/S/N | To/T/M |
| 5000 | 7 | 4 | 4 | 155 | 110 | 49 | 1970 | K/S/N | To/T/M |
| 3000 | 7 | 4 | 4 | 175 | 110 | 9 | 1971 | K/S/N | To/M |
| 2600 | 4/5/6 7 | 2/3 4 | 4 | 155 | 110 | 131 | 1978 | K/S/N | To/T/M |
| 2200 | 7/8 | 4 | 4 | 155 | 110 | 100 | 1964 | K/S/N | To/T/M |
| 2400 | 7 | 4 | 4 | 155 | 110 | 42 | 1969 | K/S/N | To/M |
| 1000 | 7 | 4 | 4 | 155 | 110 | 42 | 1977 | K/S/N | T/M |
| 1900 | 5 | 4 | 4 | 108 | 110 | 45 | 1956 | S/N | T/M |
| 7200 | 1/3/4 | 1/2 | 4 | 200 | 110 | 16 | 1995 | K/S | |
| **Otsu line 600 V DC** | | | | | | | | | |
| 700 | 2 | 2 | 2 | 70 | 70 | 10 | 1992 | Ke/S/N | To/T |
| 600 | 2 | 2 | 4 | 53 | 70 | 20 | 1984 | Ke/S/N | To/T |
| 80 | 2 | 2 | 4 | 45 | 65 | 16 | 1961 | Ki/N | To/T |
| 260 | 2 | 2 | 4 | 45 | 65 | 8 | 1957 | Ki/N | To |
| 350 | 2 | 2 | 2 | 85 | 65 | 7 | 1966 | Ki/N | To |

Abbreviations: K: Kawasaki; Ke: Keihan; Ki: Kinki; M: Mitsubishi; N: Nabco; S: Sumitomo; T: Toshiba; To: Toyo Denki Seizo

### Traction and rolling stock
Series 8000 stock is for limited express services and features onboard television and a telephone booth. Five double-deck cars were ordered for delivery in 1997 and another five in 1998. They are based on the double-deck car incorporated into an older Series 3000 unit in December 1995 and will eventually see all limited express units including a double-deck car. The latest emu type is the eight-car Series 9000.

### Signalling and telecommunications
Autonomous decentralised traffic control system (ADEC) is installed throughout the Keihan line. It links central control's mainframe computer and local processors by fibre optic cable, and allows overall traffic control to proceed simultaneously with independent control of an area's operation where that has become irregular.

**Coupler in standard use:** Tightlock automatic couplers; rotary key-block Tightlock automatic couplers; rod couplers

**Braking in standard use:** Electric command digital and electric pneumatic brake

### Track
**Rail:** Keihan line: 50 kg/m (144.2 km) and 60 kg/m; Otsu line 40 kg/m (47.8 km) and 50 kg/m
**Crossties (sleepers):** Keihan: concrete, thickness 170 mm; spacing 1,760/km; Otsu: wood, thickness 150-170 mm; spacing 1,520/km
**Fastenings:** Elastic (spring clip or F type)
**Min curvature radius:** Keihan line: 200 m; Otsu line:45 m
**Max gradient:** Keihan: 3.3%; Otsu: 6.7%
**Max permissible axleload:** Keihan: 15 tonnes; Otsu: 8-15 tonnes

*Double-deck car added to existing Series 3000 set* (Anthony Robins)

## Keihin Electric Express Railway

Keihin Kyuko Dentetsu
2-20-20, Takanawa, Minato-ku, Tokyo 108-8625
Tel: (+81 3) 32 80 91 23   Fax: (+81 3) 32 80 91 93
Web: http://www.keikyu.co.jp

### Key personnel
Chairman: Ichiro Hiramatsu
President and Representative Director: Masaru Kotani
Senior Managing Directors: Nobukuni Ishii,
    Masaru Okino, Yukimasa Saitoh
Managing Directors: Tsuneo Ishiwata, Takayuki Goseki

Gauge: 1,435 mm
Route length: 87 km
Electrification: 1.5 kV DC

### Background
Keihin Electric Express Railway is part of the Keikyu Group, which comprises 74 companies covering diverse sectors including property, tourism and leisure and distribution, as well as transport. The Transportation Group consists of 18 companies, including scheduled bus services near 576 routes totalling 5,100 km and trucking businesses.

### Finance
In FY2001-02, the company posted transport operating revenues of ¥116.1 billion, a rise of 1.1 per cent from the previous year. Operating income was ¥17.9 billion, a rise of 15.9 per cent compared with the previous year.

### Passenger operations
The railway extends from Shinagawa in Tokyo, southward to Yokohama and the Miura peninsula, and exercises through-running over the Asakusa line of the Tokyo metro. The railway recorded some 414 million passenger journeys in 2001-02.

In 1993 through services commenced between Keihin Kyuko's Haneda branch line, serving Haneda airport, and central Tokyo via the Asakusa line metro. Initially, passengers were required to transfer to the newly extended Tokyo Monorail for final access to the airport, but in November 1998 an underground extension of the Haneda line to the new airport terminal building was commissioned. Through services between Haneda and Narita airports, in collaboration with other operators, were implemented in November 1998, using Class 600 eight-car emus manufactured by Kawasaki and Tokyu Car Corporation with Mitsubishi and Toyo Denki Seizo GTO traction equipment.

The railway owns 760 emu cars. Its track is laid with 50 kg/m rail on 165 mm-thick prestressed concrete sleepers with elastic fastenings, with a minimum curvature of 60 m radius. Maximum axleloading is 13.7 tonnes.

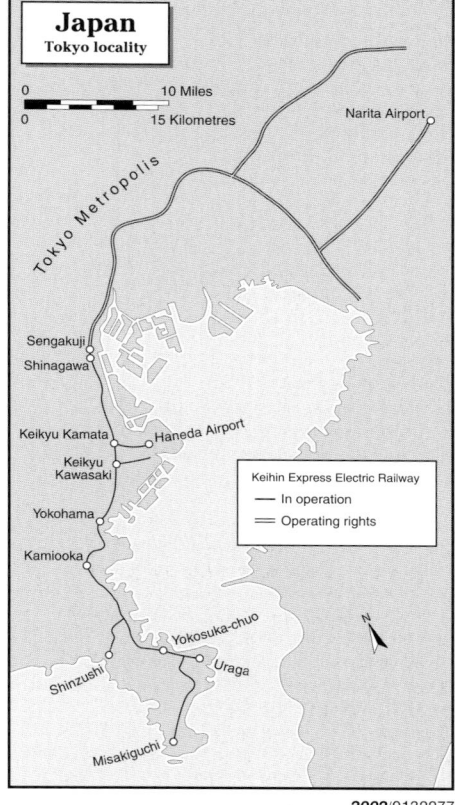

### Keihin electric railcars or multiple-units

| Class | Cars per unit | Motor cars per unit | Motored axles/car | Output/motor kW | Speed km/h | Cars in service | First built | Builders Mechanical | Electrical |
|---|---|---|---|---|---|---|---|---|---|
| 1000 | 2 | 2 | 4 | 75/90 | 110 | 170 | 1958 | K/Tk/S | M/To/Ko |
|  | 4 | 4 | 4 | 75/90 |  |  |  |  |  |
|  | 6 | 6 | 4 | 75/90 |  |  |  |  |  |
|  | 8 | 8 | 4 | 90 |  |  |  |  |  |
| 800 | 6 | 6 | 4 | 100 | 100 | 132 | 1978 | K/Tk/S | M/To/Ko |
| 2000 | 8 | 6 | 4 | 120 | 120 | 72 | 1982 | K/Tk/S | M/To/Ko |
|  | 4 | 3 | 4 | 120 |  |  |  |  |  |
| 700 | 4 | 2 | 4 | 150 | 110 | 44 | 1967 | K/Tk/S | M/To/Ko |
| 1500 | 6-8 | 6 | 4 | 100/120 | 120 | 166 | 1988 | K/Tk/S | M/To/Ko |
|  | 4 | 4 | 4 | 100 | 120 |  |  |  |  |
| 600 | 8 | 6 | 4 | 120 | 120 | 88 | 1993 | K/Tk/S | M/To/Ko |
|  | 8 | 4 | 4 | 180 |  |  |  |  |  |
|  | 4 | 2 | 4 | 180 |  |  |  |  |  |
| 2100 | 8 | 4 | 4 | 190 | 120 | 80 | 1998 | K/Tk/S | Siemens/M/To/Ko |
| N1000 | 8 | 4 | 4 | 190 | 120 | 8 | 2002 | K/Tk/S | Siemens/M/To/Ko |

Abbreviations: K: Kawasaki; Ko: Koito; M: Mitsubishi; S: Sumitomo; Tk: Tokyu; To: Toyo Denki Seizo

**UPDATED**

## Keio Teito Electric Railway

Keio Teito Dentetsu
9-1, Sekido 1-chome, Tama City, Tokyo 206
Tel: (+81 423) 37 31 41

### Key personnel
Chairman: K Kuwayama
President: H Nishiyama

Gauge: 1,372 mm; 1,067 mm
Route length: 72 km; 12.8 km
Electrification: 84.8 km at 1.5 kV DC

### Organisation
The railway runs northwest from Shibuya in Tokyo and southwest from Shinjuku, exercising through running over the Shinjuku line of the Tokyo metro. The railway, one of 46 companies in the group, generates 64 per cent of the group's income. It operates 848 emu cars, and in 1996-97 recorded some 587 million passenger journeys and 6,938.1 million passenger-km, compared with 588 million and 6,954.7 million respectively in 1995. New Series 1000 emus with 20 m long cars have been introduced to increase capacity on the narrow-gauge Inokashira line.

The company employs 4,303 staff.

*VVVF inverter-controlled Series 1000 narrow-gauge emu on Keio's Inokashira Line* (Takashi Kasai)

## Keisei Electric Railway

Keisei Dentetsu
1-10-3 Oshiage 1-chome, Sumida-ku, Tokyo 131
Tel: (+81 3) 36 21 22 31

### Key personnel
President: Hiroto Senoo

Gauge: 1,435 mm
Route length: 91.6 km
Electrification: 1.5 kV DC

### Organisation
The railway stretches eastward from Ueno in Tokyo to Chiba and to the station in the international airport of

### Keisei electric railcars

| Class | Cars per unit | Motored axles/car | Output/motor kW | Speed km/h | First built | Builders Mechanical | Electrical |
|---|---|---|---|---|---|---|---|
| AE 100 | 6 Mo 2 Tr |  |  |  | 1990 | Tk/N |  |
| AE | 6 Mo 2 Tr | 4 | 140 | 120 | 1972 | Tk/N | T/To/M |
| 3600 | 4 Mo 2 Tr | 4 | 140 | 120 | 1981 | Tk/N | T/To/M |
| 3500 | 4 Mo | 3 | 100 | 120 | 1972 | Tk/N/K | T/To/M |
| 3050 | 4 Mo | 4 | 75 | 120 | 1959 | N/Ki/Te | T/To/M |
| 3100 | 4 Mo | 4 | 75 | 120 | 1960 | N/Ki/Te | T/To/M |
| 3150 | 4 Mo | 4 | 75 | 120 | 1963 | N/Ki/Te | T/To/M |
| 3200 | 4 Mo/6 Mo | 3 | 100 | 120 | 1964 | N/Ki/Tk | T/To/M |
| 3300 | 4 Mo/6 Mo | 3 | 100 | 120 | 1968 | N/Ki/Te | T/To/M |
| 3700 | 6 Mo 2 Tr |  |  |  | 1991 | N |  |
| 3400 | 6 Mo 2 Tr |  |  |  | 1993 |  |  |

Abbreviations: Ki: Kisha; M: Mitsubishi; N: Nippon; T: Toshiba; Te: Teikoku; Tk: Tokyu; To: Toyo
Mo: motor; Tr: trailer

## 242 RAILWAY SYSTEMS/Japan

Narita, to which it operates its 'Skyliner' expresses at half-hour frequency. It has a reciprocal through service with the Asakusa line of the Tokyo metro and with the Chiba Express Electric Railway. Passenger journeys in 1994-95 totalled some 280.4 million, passenger-km 3.860 billion. Rail revenues form 62 per cent of the company's gross, the remainder coming from buses and real estate. The company has a half-share in Tokyo's Disneyland, but has no rail connection with the site. The railway operates 496 emu cars.

### Track
**Rail type and weight:** 50N 50 kg/m
**Crossties (sleepers):** Type K2
**Thickness:** 172 mm
**Spacing:** In plain track 1,560/km; in curves 1,680/km
**Fastenings:** Dogspike (double elastic fastening)
**Min curvature radius:** 160 m
**Max gradient:** 3.5%
**Max axleload:** 14.75 tonnes

## Kinki Nippon Railway

Kinki Nippon Tetsudo (Kintetsu)
6-1-55, Uehommachi, Tennoji-ku 6-chome, Osaka 543
Tel: (+81 6) 775 34 44   Fax: (+81 6) 775 34 68

### Key personnel
President: Wa Tashiro
Chairman: Shigeichiro Kanamori

Gauge: 1,435 mm; 1,067 mm; 762 mm
Route length: 404.4 km; 162.4 km; 27.4 km
Electrification: 1.5 kV DC: (394.2 km of 1,435 mm gauge; 159.1 km of 1,067 mm gauge)
750 V DC: (10.2 km of 1,435 mm gauge; 27.4 km of 762 mm gauge)

### Organisation
The Kinki Nippon Railway is part of the Kintetsu group of about 150 associated companies, ranging from hotels and construction concerns to bus and taxi companies, and including Japan's largest railway rolling stock manufacturer, Kinki Sharyo.

The Kinki Nippon has the most extensive route-km of any of Japan's private railways and lies third in the table of passenger movement, carrying two million daily. Extending eastward from Namba and Abenobashi termini in Osaka to Kyoto, Nara, Nagoya and Ise Bay, the railway runs limited expresses throughout the Kinki and Tokai areas. Its main line is intercity, running 186 km from Osaka to Nagoya, and it also serves Nara, Kyoto and the Ise-Shima National Park (136 km from Osaka). A 10.2 km extension, 4.7 km of it in tunnel, was opened from Ikoma to Nagata in 1986; at Nagata it makes a junction with the Osaka metro, over which through service is run to central Osaka.

The railway has its own research laboratory and generates 79 per cent of the income of its parent company.

*Series 30000 'Vista Ex' emu with two double-deck cars added to original four-car formation (Anthony Robins)*
0023035

### Passenger operations
In 1995-96 the Kinki Nippon recorded 825 million journeys and 15,251 million passenger-km. It introduced computer-based seat reservation as early as 1960 and has since computerised its timetabling.

### Traction and rolling stock
Rolling stock comprises two electric locomotives and 2,071 emu cars, including bilevel and vista-dome vehicles.

The company operates a fleet of luxury six- and eight-car emus known as 'Urban Liner' on its non-stop service between Nagoya and Osaka. These trains were built by Kinki Sharyo.

Recent deliveries include Series 16400 'ACE' two-car sets for the 1,067 mm gauge Minami-Osaka system introduced from June 1996 and the 'Vista Ex', a Series 30000 remodelled with two new intermediate double-deck cars and operated between Vehonmachi (Osaka) and Kashikojima.

## Kobe Electric Railway

Kobe Dentetsu
1-1, Daikai-dori 1-chome, Hyogo-ku, Kobe 652
Tel: (+81 78) 575 22 36   Fax: (+81 78) 577 24 67

### Key personnel
President: Yasuo Ipponmatsu

Gauge: 1,067 mm
Route length: 64.4 km
Electrification: 1.5 kV DC

### Organisation
This Hankyu subsidiary operates to Ao, Sanda and the hot-spring resort of Arima-Onsen via a steeply graded route through the Rokko mountain range north of Kobe. Within Kobe trains operate over 0.4 km of Kobe Rapid Railway tracks to an underground terminus at Shin-Kaichi where interchange is available with Hankyu, Hanshin and Sanyo services. A 5.5 km branch to serve a new town at Kobe-Sanda Garden City was completed in March 1996. Rolling stock comprises one electric locomotive and 167 emu cars. Railway operations represent 68 per cent of the company's revenue.

The Kobe earthquake of January 1995 caused damage estimated at ¥14.9 billion and resulted in the suspension of services between central Kobe and Suzurandai, a distance of 7.5 km, for approximately six months.

## Konan Railway

Konan Tetsudo
23-5, Kita-Yanagida, Hommachi, Hiraka-machi, Minami-Tsugaru-gun, Aomori 036-01
Tel: (+81 172) 44 31 36

### Key personnel
President: T Tarusawa

Gauge: 1,067 mm
Route length: 36.9 km
Electrification: 30.7 km at 1.5 kV DC

### Organisation
The railway operates two unconnected electrified lines and a non-electrified former JNR line in and around Hirosaki, Aomori prefecture. Rolling stock comprises three electric locomotives, three diesel railcars and 43 emu cars.

## Nagoya Railroad

Nagoya Tetsudo (Meitetsu)
1-2-4, Meikei, Nakamura-ku, Nagoya 450
Tel: (+81 52) 571 21 11   Fax: (+81 52) 581 60 60

### Key personnel
Chairman: Seitaro Taniguchi
President: Sokichi Minora

Gauge: 1,067 mm
Route length: 539 km
Electrification: 479 km at 1.5 kV DC; 59 km at 600 V DC

### Organisation
Between 1941 and 1944 the private urban railways of the Nagoya region were knitted into a coherent regional network by the conversion of city-centre tram tracks into an inter-system connection focused on a new underground Shin-Nagoya station alongside the Japan Rail station. Since then the system has been rationalised by some closures, but new lines have been laid to cater for fresh suburban development, such as the Chita line in 1980. The network includes 59.4 km of 600 V DC tramway and light rail in Gifu prefecture and a 1.2 km monorail line operating six cars. Besides the Nagoya Railroad, the diversified Meitetsu Corporation also runs bus, taxi, road freight, sea ferry and air-taxi services, hotels, restaurants and travel agencies, but the railway produces 59 per cent of total revenue.

### Passenger operations
Shin-Nagoya station handles over 800 trains a day, with 25 trains hourly each way on the main route between Shin Gifu/Inuyama and Toyohashi/Toko-name/Kowa. Reciprocal through-running services operate between the Toyota and Inuyama lines and the Tsurumai line of the Nagoya metro. Electrification was progressively standardised at 1.5 kV DC after the unification of the system, but 600 V DC survives on tramway and light rail

## Japan/RAILWAY SYSTEMS

**Principal Nagoya Railroad electric railcars or multiple-units**

| Class | Cars per unit | Motor cars per unit | Motored axles/car | Output/motor kW | Speed km/h | Cars in service | First built | Builders Mechanical | Electrical |
|---|---|---|---|---|---|---|---|---|---|
| 1000 | 4 | 2 | 4 | 150 | 120 | 92 | 1988 | N | T |
| 1200 | 6 | 4 | 4 | 150 | 120 | 64 | 1991 | N | T |
| 7000 | 4 | 4 | 4 | 75 | 110 | 106 | 1961 | N | T |
| 7500 | 6 | 6 | 4 | 75 | 110 | 42 | 1963 | N | To |
| 6500 | 4 | 2 | 4 | 150 | 110 | 96 | 1984 | N | T |
| 6800 | 2 | 1 | 4 | 150 | 110 | 78 | 1987 | N | M |
| 3500 | 4 | 2 | 4 | 170 | 120 | 136 | 1993 | N | To |

Abbreviations: M: Mitsubishi; N: Nippon; T: Toshiba; To: Toyo

**Principal Nagoya Railroad diesel railcars or multiple-units**

| Class | Cars per unit | Motor cars per unit | Motored axles/car | Power/motor kW | Speed km/h | Cars in service | First built | Builders Mechanical | Engine | Transmission |
|---|---|---|---|---|---|---|---|---|---|---|
| 20 | 1 | 1 | 2 | 187.5 | 80 | 5 | 1987 | Fuji | Nissan | Shinko |
| 30 | 1 | 1 | 2 | 187.5 | 80 | 4 | 1995 | Fuji | Nissan | Niigata |
| 8500 | 2/3 | 2/3 | 2 | 262.5 | 120 | 5 | 1991 | Nippon | NTA-855-R | Niigata |

lines in Gifu and to the north of that city. Passenger traffic amounted to 399 million journeys a year and over 7.313 billion passenger-km.

### Traction and rolling stock
Rolling stock comprises 1,023 emu cars, 42 tramcars, six monorail cars, 16 diesel railbuses, 13 electric locomotives and 28 wagons. The fleet includes three types of distinctively styled limited express units: 'Panorama Car' (introduced 1961); 'Panorama DX' (1984) and 'Panorama Super' (1988). New stock entering service for the April 1997 timetable revision comprised eight further 1000 Series 'Panorama Cars', 28 cars of the new 3100 Series (two-car emu) and 3700 Series (four-car emu) plus four new 780 Series cars for the 600 V DC system.

Coupler in standard use: Passenger cars: Tightlock automatic; freight cars: automatic
**Braking in standard use:** Electromagnetic

**Track**
**Rail:** 50 kg/m; 37 kg/m
**Crossties (sleepers):** Prestressed concrete: 200 × 160 × 2,000 mm; wood: 200 × 140 × 2,100 mm

*Series 3100 two-car emu introduced in 1997* (Anthony Robins) 0001716

**Spacing:** 1,640/km
**Fastenings:** Tie plate, dogspike
**Min curvature radius:** 160 m
**Max gradient:** 3.5%

## Nankai Electric Railway

Nankai Denki Tetsudo
1-60 Namba 5-chome, Minami-ku, Osaka 542
Tel: (+81 6) 644 71 20

### Key personnel
Chairman: Shigeo Yoshimura
President: Taiji Kawakatsu

Gauge: 1,067 mm
Route length: 171.7 km
Electrification: 157.4 km at 1.5 kV DC; 14.3 km at 600 V DC

### Passenger operations
The railway operates 724 emu cars, and in 1995-96 recorded 302.6 million passenger journeys. The main line runs from Namba in Osaka to Wakayama (64.2 km), with five branches, and the Koya line links Osaka with the pilgrimage and resort destination of Koya-San. Reciprocal through-running services operate over the Semboku Rapid Railway, built to serve new town development to the south of Osaka. The company also operates a 14.3 km 600 V DC line at Wakayama and a 0.8 km funicular. Railway operations represent 63 per cent of the company's revenue.

### New lines
A new 8.8 km spur connecting Nankai's main line with the new offshore Kansai International Airport opened in September 1994, with Nankai's 'Rapi:t' airport service operated by new Series 50000 stock. These distinctively styled five-car units have porthole-shaped side windows and an unusual external cab design. To compete with JR for airport traffic, Nankai proposes to lay mixed-gauge track along its 1,067 mm gauge main line to enable airport services to operate through central Osaka via the 1,435 mm gauge Sakaisuji line metro and on to Kyoto and Nara via the Hankyu, Keihan and Kintetsu systems.

*Series 31000 three-car emu* 0063750

## Nishi Nippon Railroad

Nishi Nippon Tetsudo
11-17 Tenjin 1-chome, Chuo-ku, Fukuoka 810
Tel: (+81 92) 761 66 31   Fax: (+81 92) 722 14 05

### Key personnel
Chairman: Reinosuke Ohya
President: Hisayuki Hashimoto

Gauge: 1,435 mm; 1,067 mm
Route length: 100 km; 21 km
Electrification: 1.5 kV DC; 600 V DC

### Organisation
The railway, which owns 355 emu cars, operates a 75 km main line from Fukuoka to Omuta, with branches, and a separate 21 km line from Kaizuka in the eastern suburbs of Fukuoka to Tsuyazaki. It also operates a 5 km 600 V DC line with 19 cars.

Track is laid with 37, 40 and 50 kg/m rail on timber and prestressed concrete sleepers spaced at 1,560/km and allowing 16 tonnes maximum axleloading; minimum curvature is 160 m. Traffic totalled some 154.3 million passenger journeys and 2.105 billion passenger-km in 1994-95. Railway operations represent 17 per cent of the company's revenue.

## Odakyu Electric Railway

Odakyu Dentetsu
1-8-3 Nishi Shinjuku, Shinjuku-ku, Tokyo 160-8309
Tel: (+81 3) 33 49 21 51   Fax: (+81 3) 33 46 18 99

### Key personnel
President: M Kitanaka
Managing Director, General Manager, Transportation: K Kurihara

Managing Director: Y Nojiri
Director, General Manager, Planning: S Suzuki
General Managers
Operations: T Harada

Track and Structures: M Yuhara
Electrical Engineering: T Isoya
Rolling Stock: Y Obuchi

Gauge: 1,067 mm
Route length: 120 km: also a 1.1 km monorail
Electrification: 1.5 kV DC

### Organisation

The railway runs southwest from Shinjuku, Tokyo, to Odawara, Hakone, the Mount Fuji region and the coast west of Yokohama. It has through service arrangements with the Chiyoda line of Tokyo's Eidan metro. The 1.1 km Mukogaoka-Yuen monorail, the 15 km Hakone Tozan Railway (a subsidiary company) and a 10 km light rail system, the Enoshima Electric Railway, are also operated by the group, which has more than 100 individual companies and obtains 67 per cent of its income from rail transport. Other group transport activities include long-distance and charter bus services, and taxi and hire businesses.

At the beginning of April 1997 the company employed 4,140 staff.

### Passenger operations

In 1995-96 the railway recorded 704 million passenger journeys and 11,263 million passenger-km. At peak periods the railway's core handles 29 trains each way per hour. It owns 1,055 emu cars and two monorail cars. In 1996 10-car Series 30000 'Romance Car EXE' emus were introduced for limited express service.

The railway has adopted ATP (Automatic Train Protection) based on coded frequency circuitry and a total traffic control system with both relay and electronic interlockings. Double-tracking between Kitami and Izumi-Tamagawa was completed in June 1997, and the installation of level crossing obstacle equipment has been adopted to improve service performance and safety. Track is formed of 50 or 60 kg/m rail on prestressed concrete sleepers spaced at 1,640/km in plain track, 1,760/km in curves; minimum curvature radius is 200 m, maximum gradient 2.7 per cent and maximum permissible axleload 17 tonnes. Recent construction projects have included the installation of extra tracks in suburban Tokyo and measures to allow 10-car express train operation.

**Odakyu Railway electric railcars or multiple-units**

| Class | Cars per unit | Motor cars per unit | Motored axles/car | Output/motor kW | Speed km/h | Cars in service | First built | Builders Mechanical | Electrical |
|---|---|---|---|---|---|---|---|---|---|
| 3100 | 11 | 11 | 2 | 100 | 130 | 77 | 1963 | N/K/S | T/M/Te |
| 7000 | 11 | 9 | 2 | 140 | 110 | 44 | 1980 | N/K/S | T/M/Te |
| 10000 | 11 | 9 | 2 | 140 | 110 | 44 | 1987 | N/K/S | T/M/Te |
| 2600 | 6 | 3 | 4 | 117 | 100 | 122 | 1964 | N/K/Tc/S | M/T/Te |
| 4000 | 6 | 4 | 4 | 135 | 110 | 60 | 1966 | N/K/Tc/S | M/T/Te |
|  | 4 | 2 | 4 | 135 | 110 | 32 | 1969 | N/K/Tc/S | M/T/Te |
| 5000 | 6 | 4 | 4 | 135 | 110 | 120 | 1978 | N/K/Tc/S | M/T/Te |
|  | 4 | 2 | 4 | 140 | 110 | 60 | 1984 | N/K/Tc/S | M/T/Te |
| 8000 | 6 | 4 | 4 | 140 | 110 | 96 | 1982 | N/K/Tc/S | M/T/Te |
|  | 4 | 4 | 4 | 110 | 120 | 64 | 1972 | N/K/Tc/S | M/T/Te |
| 9000 | 4/6 | 4 | 4 | 110 | 120 | 90 | 1973 | N/K/Tc/S | M/T/Te |
| 1000 | 4 | 2 | 4 | 175 | 120 | 100 | 1987 | N/K/Tc/S | M/T/Te |
|  | 6 | 3 | 4 | 175 | 120 | 48 | 1988 | N/K/Tc/S | M/T/Te |
|  | 8 | 4 | 4 | 175 | 120 | 8 | 1993 | K | M/T/Te |
|  | 10 | 5 | 4 | 175 | 120 | 40 | 1992 | N | M/T/Te |
| 20000 | 7 | 4 | 4 | 140 | 120 | 14 | 1990 | N/K | M/T/Te |
| 2000 | 8 | 4 | 4 | 175 | 120 | 16 | 1995 | N/K | M/T/Te |
| 30000 | 10 | 4 | 4 | 195 | 120 | 20 | 1996 | N | M/T/Te |

Abbreviations: K: Kawasaki; M: Mitsubishi; N: Nippon Sharyo Seizo; S: Sumitomo; T: Toshiba; Tc: Tokyu Car; Te: Toyo Electric

*Refurbished Series 3100 emu*  0023036

# Ohmi Railway

Ohmi Tetsudo
3-1 Daito-cho, Hikone-shi 522
Tel: (+81 749) 22 33 01

### Key personnel
President: T Kaida

Gauge: 1,067 mm
Route length: 59.5 km
Electrification: 59.5 km at 1.5 kV DC

### Organisation
This company is a Seibu Railway subsidiary. It operates 33 emu cars, 10 electric and one diesel locomotive, five diesel railbuses and 20 wagons. Emus operate between Maibara, an interchange with the Tokaido Shinkansen, and Ohmi-Hachiman, and also on the Toga branch line, but diesel railbuses have been introduced between Yokaichi and Kibukawa to reduce costs.

# Sagami Railway

Sagami Tetsudo
2-9-14 Kitasaiwai, Nishi-ku, Yokohama 220
Tel: (+81 45) 319 21 11

### Key personnel
Chairman: Masahiro Hoshino
President: Kojiro Tsushima

Gauge: 1,067 mm
Route length: 33 km
Electrification: 1.5 kV DC

### Passenger operations
This Yokohama suburban system comprises a 24.6 km main line from Yokohama to Ebina with a branch to Izumi-chuo. A 3.1 km extension from Izumi-chuo to connect with the Odakyu Enoshima line and extended Yokohama metro at Shonan-dai is planned.

In April 1995 the railway operated 460 emu cars of seven types built by Hitachi and Tokyu Sharyo, four electric locomotives and 15 freight wagons. Annual passenger journeys totalled 248.1 million and passenger-km 2,822.7 million in 1994-95. Railway operations represent 28 per cent of the company's revenue.

# Sanyo Electric Railway

Sanyo Denki Tetsudo
1-1, Oyashiki-dori 3-chome, Nagata-ku, Kobe 653
Tel: (+81 78) 611 22 11

### Key personnel
Chairman: Tadashi Suzuki
President: Masami Ohkuni

Gauge: 1,435 mm
Route length: 63.3 km
Electrification: 63.3 km at 1.5 kV DC

### Passenger operations
The railway operates between Himeji and Kobe with a fleet of 199 emu cars.

Within Kobe, trains run via the underground Kobe Rapid Railway and on to the Hankyu and Hanshin systems under a reciprocal through-service agreement. Through-running services were suspended, however, between January and June 1995 following the Hanshin earthquake which severely damaged the Kobe Rapid Railway. Railway operations represent 74 per cent of the company's revenue.

# Seibu Railway

Seibu Tetsudo
1-11-1 Kusunokidai, Tokorozawa-shi, Saitama 359
Tel: (+81 429) 26 20 35   Fax: (+81 429) 26 22 37

### Key personnel
Chairman: Yoshiaki Tsutsumi
President: Hiroyuki Toda

Gauge: 1,067 mm; 762 mm
Route length: 176 km; 3.6 km (rubber-tyred)
Electrification: 1.5 kV DC

### Organisation
Part of a multifaceted corporation that includes hotels, Japan's busiest department store, housing and road transport among its businesses, the railway serves the western suburbs of Tokyo with two main routes radiating from terminals on or near JR East's city-centre Yamanote loop, the 43.8 km Ikebukuro and 22.6 km Shinjuku lines.

These lines throw off and are in some cases interconnected in the suburbs by 10 branches. The Ikebukuro terminus deals with an average of 700 train workings daily, with departures at 1½ minute headways in the evening peak. There is a reciprocal through service with the Yurakucho line of the Tokyo metro. The Ohmi Railway is a Seibu subsidiary.

### Passenger operations
Traffic ran at some 661.8 million passenger journeys (9,489 million passenger-km) in 1994-95, 67 per cent of which was made on season tickets which generate 46 per cent of total receipts. The railway's operating ratio is approximately 87 per cent. Railway operations represent 46 per cent of the company's revenue.

### Traction and rolling stock
The fleet of 1,133 emu cars comprises 12 types. Further Series 10000 seven-car units built by Hitachi have been introduced to allow an increase in limited express services on the Ikebukuro and Shinjuku lines.

*Series 2000 emu formation* (Hiroshi Naito)  0023037

## Shimabara Railway

Shimabara Tetsudo
7385-1 Bentencho 2-chome, Shimabara-shi 855
Tel: (+81 95) 762 22 31

### Key personnel
President: D Shirakuta

Gauge: 1,067 mm
Route length: 78.5 km

### Passenger operations
The railway operates one diesel locomotive and 25 diesel railcars on its line serving the Shimabara peninsula in Nagasaki prefecture. Complete service over the line was restored in April 1997 following closure of part of the middle section of the line due to volcanic activity.

## Shin Keisei Electric Railway

Shin Keisei Dentetsu
16-16 Hatsutomi, Kamagaya-shi 273-01
Tel: (+81 473) 84 31 51

### Key personnel
Chairman: Haruo Hosokawa
President: Naoyuki Takeuchi

Gauge: 1,435 mm
Route length: 26.5 km
Electrification: 1.5 kV DC

### Passenger operations
The railway was constructed to serve suburban housing development in Chiba prefecture to the east of Tokyo, and connects with its parent Keisei Railway at Tsudanuma and with JR East's Joban line at Matsudo. Rolling stock comprises 194 emu cars operated as six- and eight-car trains. Railway operations represent 56 per cent of the company's revenue.

## Tobu Railway

Tobu Tetsudo
1-2, 1-chome, Oshiage, Sumida-ku, Tokyo 131
Tel: (+81 3) 36 21 50 57

### Key personnel
Chairman: Kaichiro Nezu
President: Takashige Uchida

Gauge: 1,067 mm
Route length: 464 km
Electrification: 464 km at 1.5 kV DC

### Organisation
The railway's main line runs 135 km northward from Asakusa in Tokyo to Shimoimaichi and Nikko, with branches to Utsunomiya and Isezaki and through-service arrangements with the Hibiya line of the Tokyo metro. The Tojo line runs 75 km from Ikebukuro in Tokyo to Yorii, with through running from the Yurakucho line of the Eidan metro. There are 88 companies in the group, which earns 66 per cent of its revenue from the railway.

### Passenger operations
Its daily average of almost 2.5 million passengers ranks second in the table of the busiest private railways in Japan; the total in 1994-95 was 945.3 million passenger journeys and 14,366 million passenger-km.

### Improvements to existing lines
The railway is currently undertaking ¥84 billion worth of infrastructure improvements, including work completed at the important interchange of Kita-Senju. A further ¥196.1 billion will be spent on works including connection of the Isezaki line to the new Number 11 underground line. These projects are scheduled to be completed in 2004.

*Series 100 'Spacia' limited express emu* (Anthony Robins)  0001717

### Traction and rolling stock
Rolling stock comprises 10 electric locomotives, 1,848 emu cars and 13 wagons.

## Tokyo Express Electric Railway

Tokyo Kyuko Dentetsu (Tokyu)
5-6 Nanpeidai-cho, Shibuya-ku, Tokyo 150
Tel: (+81 3) 34 77 61 11   Fax: (+81 3) 34 96 29 65

### Key personnel
President: Shinobu Shimizu
Executive Vice-President: Ototaro Horie
Senior Managing Directors: K Endoh, T Endoh, K Ihara, H Nagatoshi

Gauge: 1,372 mm; 1,067 mm
Route length: 5 km; 96 km
Electrification: 5 km (1,372 mm gauge) at 600 V DC; 96 km at 1.5 kV DC

## Organisation

The railway is part of the Tokyu Corporation, the flagship of the massive Tokyu Group, which embraces 390 companies and nine non-profit institutions covering real estate enterprises, bus and taxi companies, department stores, supermarkets, construction companies, road freight, railcar building, advertising agencies, construction companies, shipping, airline (Japan Air System, the country's third largest carrier) and air freight activity. Railway operations represent 40.2 per cent of the company's revenue, in 1996 generating turnover of ¥113.4 billion.

The rail network is located in the southwest of the Tokyo metropolitan area and runs from Shibuya, Meguro and Gotanda on JR's Yamanote line to Kanagawa prefecture and Yokohama. The 9.4 km Shin-Tamagawa line out of Shibuya is effectively a metro, and the railway also has through-service arrangements with the Tokyo metro's Hibiya and Hanzomon lines.

## Passenger operations

With a total of 950.8 million passenger journeys a year the Tokyo Express Electric Railway is the busiest railway in the capital's suburban area, and carries more than any other private railway in the country. Services are provided on eight lines. Although it claims to be the cheapest Japanese railway to ride, it also claims to generate the biggest revenue per track-km. Average length of passenger journey is only 9.1 km. Annual passenger-km totals 8,680 million.

## Improvements to existing lines

On its Toyoko line the railway is undertaking a track-quadrupling programme costing ¥210.8 billion which was due to be completed in 1997. It is also elevating more of its infrastructure to alleviate road congestion. In 1996-97 reconstruction started of the Mekama line, eliminating 16 level crossings. Construction started in 1995 on a 3.3 km underground section replacing part of the existing Mekama line and providing a connection with Tokyo's Namboku and Mita metro lines to allow for through services. Reconstruction and extension of the Oimachi line was also being undertaken to allow central Tokyo passengers to bypass the Den-en Toshi and Shin-Tmagawa lines.

## Traction and rolling stock

In 1996 Tokyu operated 1,054 emus, most on 1,067 mm gauge, but including 18 two-car units on 1,372 mm gauge. Most of the vehicles have been built in the Corporation's own workshops. Tokyu Car Corporation is one of the group's subsidiaries.

## Signalling and telecommunications

Automatic Train Control (ATC) is in use on 61.1 km of the system.

## Track

Tokyu employs 50 kg/m rail on prestressed concrete sleepers of 150 to 160 mm thickness, with double elastic fastenings. Minimum curve radius is 160 m, maximum gradient 4 per cent, and maximum permissible axleload 15.5 tonnes.

### Electric railcars or multiple-units

| Class | Cars per unit | Motor cars per unit | Motored axles/car | Output/motor kW | Speed km/h | No in service | First built | Builders Mechanical | Electrical |
|---|---|---|---|---|---|---|---|---|---|
| **1.5 kV DC** | | | | | | | | | |
| 7000 | 2 | 2 | 4 | 70 | 100 | 2 | 1962 | Tokyu | Hitachi |
| 7200 | 3 | 2 | 4 | 110 | 100 | 32 | 1967 | Tokyu | Hitachi/Toyo |
| 7600*† | 3 | 2 | 4 | 110 | 110 | 9 | 1986 | Tokyu | Toyo |
| 7700*† | 4 | 2 | 4 | 170 | 120 | 56 | 1987 | Tokyu | Toyo |
| 8000 | 5, 8 | 3, 6 | 4 | 130 | 120 | 187 | 1969 | Tokyu | Hitachi |
| 8090 | 5, 8 | 3, 6 | 4 | 130 | 120 | 90 | 1980 | Tokyu | Hitachi |
| 8500 | 10 | 8 | 4 | 130 | 120 | 400 | 1975 | Tokyu | Hitachi/Toyo |
| 9000 | 5, 8 | 3, 4 | 4 | 170 | 120 | 117 | 1986 | Tokyu | Hitachi/Toyo |
| 1000 | 4, 8 | 2 | 2 | 130 | 120 | 113 | 1988 | Tokyu | Hitachi/Toyo |
| 2000 | 10 | 6 |  | 170 | 120 | 30 | 1991 | Tokyu | Hitachi |
| **600 V DC** | | | | | | | | | |
| 70 | 2 | 2 | 2 | 48.5 | 40 | 8 | 1942 | Kawasaki | GE |
| 80 | 2 | 2 | 2 | 74.6 | 40 | 6 | 1950 | Hitachi/Toyo | Hitachi |
| 150 | 2 | 2 | 2 | 60 | 40 | 4 | 1964 | Tokyu | Toyo |

* VVVF inverter control
† 7600 rebuilt from 7200; 7700 rebuilt from 7000

# Toyama Chiho Railway

Toyama Chiho Tetsudo
1-36 Sakuramachi 1-chome, Toyama-shi 930
Tel: (+81 764) 32 51 11

### Key personnel
President: H Ogata

Gauge: 1,067 mm
Route length: 93.2 km

Electrification: 93.2 km at 1.5 kV DC; 6.4 km at 600 V DC

### Passenger operations

The Toyama Chiho Railway operates three routes from Toyama serving the coastal area and providing access to the northern Japan Alps. 'Alpen Express' trains connect the tourist destinations of Tateyama and Unazuki Onsen, with onward travel to Mount Tateyama and the Kurobe Dam being available via the Kurobe Gorge Railway. Rolling stock comprises 51 emu cars, two electric and six diesel locomotives, and three wagons. In 1995 the company acquired a three-car set of ex-Seibu 'Red Arrow' stock which has been modified for use on express services. The company also operates an urban tramway in Toyama with 19 cars.

# JORDAN

## Ministry of Transport

PO Box 4448, Amman
Tel: (+962 6) 489 54 14   Fax: (+962 6) 489 41 17

### Key personnel
Minister: Eng Nader Zahabi
Secretary General: Issa Ayyoub
Director, Rail: Yahya Jdaitawi

**UPDATED**

## Aqaba Railway Corporation (ARC)

PO Box 50, Ma'an
Tel: (+962 3) 213 21 14   Fax: (+962 3) 213 18 61

### Key personnel
Director General: Abdallah Kh Al Khattab
Assistant Director General: Eng Yasin Al-Tarawneh
Assistant Director General, Administrative:
  A Maitah
Directors
  Aqaba Branch: Eng Malek Abu-Rahmon
  Planning and Training (acting): Eng Osama Shalabi
  Operations and Mechanical (acting):
    Eng Naif Rawashdah
  Traffic and Communications: Eng Ibrahim Al-Chorbadji
  Train Control: Subhi Rasheed
  Permanent Way: Nabil Deknash
  Finance: A Abu Taha

Internal Control: Nabel M Al-Rawad
Material and Stocks: Mahdi Darweesh
Director General's Office Manager: Odeh Zayadnah

Gauge: 1,050 mm
Route length: 292 km

### Organisation

ARC is a public corporation, the sole function of which is haulage of phosphates from mines at El-Abyad and El-Hasa to the Red Sea port of Aqaba over a network of new and reconstructed lines, which are passed for 16 tonne axleloads. Part of the route, from El-Hasa to Hettiya, is the original Hedjaz Railway rehabilitated; the remainder is new. ARC also connects with HJR at Batn-el-Ghul. In 1997 the Jordanian government engaged Canadian consultants CPCS Transcom to assist in the privatisation of the railway. Late in 1998 a consortium led by Wisconsin Central Transportation Corporation (WCTC), with a shareholding of 33 per cent, and also including Raytheon Mitsubishi Corporation, Athens-based consolidated contractors and Jordanian investment organisations, was selected as preferred bidder for a 25-year operating concession to run ARC in return for a single payment to the Jordanian government of JD20 million. An agreement was signed in August 1999. The Jordanian government is to retain ownership of the infrastructure. The concession terms include provision to construct and operate branches to Shediya and Wadi II (see below). Increased business generated by these two branches is expected to raise freight traffic to 10 million tonnes annually by 2002.

| ARC traffic (million) | 1999 | 2000 |
|---|---|---|
| Freight tonnes | 2.68 | 2.55 |
| Freight tonne-km | 622 | 575 |

### Freight operations

In 2000, ARC carried 2.55 million tonnes of phosphates traffic and around 65 per cent of the total output of the country's major producer, the Jordan Phosphate Mining Corporation. Construction of a branch to a mine at Shediya is seen as a key to capturing a greater share of remaining traffic, which is currently handled by road transport. The competitiveness of rail has been increased by weight restrictions imposed on trucks.

The new operators of the line have stated their intention to study possible Aqaba–Amman general freight services, using the disused Hedjaz Jordan Railway north of Menzil.

### New lines

Under the WCTC-led concession, long-planned proposals for a 45 km route linking phosphate mines at Shediya with ARC at Batn-el-Ghul, and a 16 km link from Aqaba port to a new fertiliser plant in an industrial area known as Wadi II will be fulfilled. Work on the Shediya branch started in 2000.

### Improvements to existing lines

The originally designed capacity of the line was 1.5 million tonnes annually, but it has carried two-and-a-half times as much. A prime concern has therefore been the limitations of the existing infrastructure, with its curves of as little as

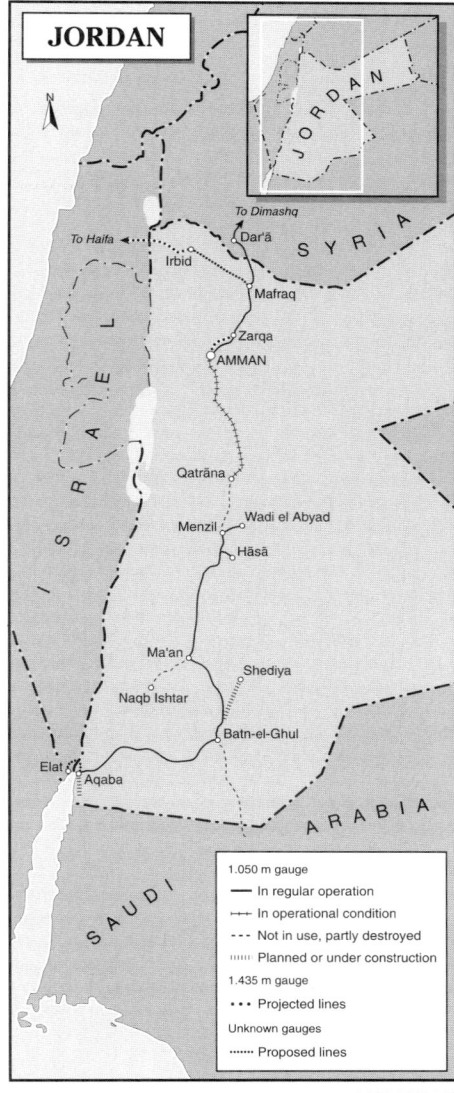

# Jordan/RAILWAY SYSTEMS

*ARC mechanised track maintenance (Stephanie Genkin)*

125 m radius and a 30 km gradient in places as steep as 1 in 37 near Aqaba. That incline restricts train length to 35 wagons of 42 tonnes payload and 64 tonnes gross each. The curvature has dictated adoption of Scheffel cross-braced bogies in recent wagon deliveries from Gregg of Belgium and Samsung of South Korea.

On the original Hedjaz Railway segment between El-Hasa and Ma'an, 49 kg/m rail, concrete-sleeper track is being laid in place of 30 kg/m, wooden-sleeper track on the existing route, under a three-phase programme, partly funded by a World Bank loan. Contracts covering a further 10.4 km, funded by the World Bank, were let to British companies in 1992, while renewal of a further 19.1 km between El-Hasa and Ma'an has been financed from ARC's own budget.

The block signalling between El-Hasa and Umran is controlled by UHF radio, employing fail-safe frequency-division multiplex apparatus. Westinghouse Westbloc coded block colourlight signalling controls operation at five stations. A VHF radio system, using mobile sets, connects train and station staff with the Ma'an control centre.

### Diesel locomotives

| Class | Wheel arrangement | Power kW | Speed km/h | Weight tonnes | No in service | First built | Builders Mechanical | Engine | Transmission |
|---|---|---|---|---|---|---|---|---|---|
| UL17C | Co-Co | 1,305 | 120 | 94.3 | 8 | 1975 | GE | 7FDL8 | E GE |
| U18C | Co-Co | 1,380 | 120 | 94.3 | 3 | 1978 | GE | 7FDL8 | E GE |
| U20C | Co-Co | 1,600 | 120 | 108 | 11 | 1981 | GE | 7FDL12 | E GE |

### Traction and rolling stock
ARC's traction fleet comprises 24 diesel-electric locomotives and the wagon fleet totals 313.

**Type of coupler in standard ARC use:** AAR Alliance 2
**Type of braking in standard ARC use:** Air 26 Lavi

### Track
**Rail:** S-49 (49 kg/m); BSS 70A (34.8 kg/m); and S-30 (30 kg/m)
**Sleepers:** Wood and monobloc concrete
**Spacing:** 1,666/km, 1,755/km in curves less than 300 m radius
**Fastenings:** DS 18 and Pandrol E2000
**Min curvature radius:** 125 m, 13.9°
**Max gradient:** 2.7%
**Max permissible axleload:** 16 tonnes

*UPDATED*

---

## Hedjaz Jordan Railway (HJR)

PO Box 4448, Amman
Tel: (+962 6) 489 54 13    Fax: (+962 6) 489 41 17

### Key personnel
Director General: Eng Abdel Razzak Abu Al Filat
Deputy Director General:
    Eng Oussama Suleyman Kreychee
Administration: Zuhair Momany
Infrastructure: Eng Maarouf Al-Soudi
Building: Eng Khalif Mehawesh
Mechanical: Eng Rayed El-Helo
Procurement: Issa Mahmud
Personnel: Ahmed Al Nueymat
Traffic: Eng Ali Hassan Djad Allah
Traction and Rolling Stock: Eng Hani Nesour
Finance (acting): Nada Al Saadi

Gauge: 1,050 mm
Route length: 212.5 km

### Political background
Even before the country's problems occasioned by the 1991 Gulf War, HJR was carrying little traffic. It is of marginal importance in the country's economy. However, in December 2001, the governments of Jordan, Saudi Arabia and Syria agreed to reconstruct the railway, including the cross-border section from Batn-el-Ghul to Al Madinah in Saudi Arabia.

### Passenger operations
There is a daily service from Amman across the border to Damascus in Syria. In 2000, 27,647 passengers were carried.

### Freight operations
In 1999 freight traffic amounted to 5,189 tonnes. There is service across the border to Damascus in Syria.

### New lines
The prospect of a new 1,435 mm gauge line in Jordan was raised in 1995 following an agreement with the Israeli government for joint construction of a 90 km line from Irbid in northern Jordan to Haifa in Israel. This would give prized access to the Mediterranean for Jordanian imports and exports. No timescale has been set for construction, nor indication made as to funding.

### Improvements to existing lines
In 1992 plans were announced to improve the railway between Amman and Zarqa. Some realignments as well as track renewals were envisaged. A strengthened passenger service was in mind, but its provision would involve procurement of additional rolling stock. The upgrading might also enable HJR to launch an oil feed service to the phosphate mines from Zarqa refinery. HJR would also like to break into grain haulage from Aqaba to Amman, but for that would need four additional locomotives and some 60 wagons, for which no funds are forthcoming.

### Traction and rolling stock
HJR owns five GE Type U10 670 kW Caterpillar-engined diesel-electric locomotives of which only three were operating in 1993, and six oil-fired steam locomotives. Passenger rolling stock comprises nine coaches and there are 113 wagons.

**Type of coupler in standard use:** Hook
**Type of braking in standard use:** Vacuum (locomotives air and vacuum)

### Track
**Rail:** 21.5 kg/m flat-bottom
**Sleepers:** Steel fish-type, 1,830 mm long × 20 mm thick
**Spacing:** 1,450/km plain line, 1,600/km curves
**Fastenings:** Angle-type four bolt
**Min curvature radius:** Main line 100 m, turnouts 91.5 m
**Max gradient:** 2%
**Max axleload:** 10.5 tonnes

*UPDATED*

# KAZAKHSTAN

## Ministry of Transport and Communications

Abay Prospekt 49, Astana
Tel: (+7 3172) 32 62 77; 32 42 47
Fax: (+7 3172) 32 10 58

**Key personnel**
Minister of Transport: Serik Burkitbaiev
Head of Railways Department: N Baydauletov

*UPDATED*

## Kazakhstan State Railways (KTZ)

Pobedy Prospekt 98, 473000 Astana
Tel: (+7 3172) 77 07 11    Fax: (+7 3172) 75 38 91
Web: http://www.railways.kz

**Key personnel**
Managing Director: B A Baimukhanov
Executive Director: Kanat Tulemetov
Head of Administrative Board: R T Kuzembaev

Gauge: 1,520 mm
Route length: 13,601 km
Electrification: 3,661 km at 3 kV DC and 25 kV AC

### Political background

Kazakhstan is large and sparsely populated. It is the ninth largest country in the world, extending from the Caspian Sea to northern China, and yet has a population which is the same size as Belgium's. With a history as the southern side of the Russian empire, its cities were built as fortresses on the frontier and communications links are chiefly long lines towards the heart of Russia, with few routes to the rest of Asia. Kazakhstan appeared as an independent entity upon the collapse of the USSR in 1991; the capital city has been moved from the frontier city of Almaty to Astana, in the centre of the country. Kazakhstan has maintained amicable and increasingly close relations with Russia.

Steady replacement of Russian by the local language, among other things, has stimulated a large-scale exodus of Russian technical staff, and the number of Kazakh replacements is not yet sufficient to fill the gap. In addition, many freight customers have failed to pay for the service provided, thus putting considerable financial pressure on the railway. To reduce losses the railways requested a 35 per cent freight rate increase in 1995, but the State Price Commission allowed only 8 per cent.

The current government programme for the railways emphasises a restructuring on commercial lines of freight and passenger tariffs, developing the transport market, and transferring to local authorities the railway health and educational institutions. In 1997 there were already signs that the railway was emerging from crisis. There was a small traffic recovery, operating income rose by 31 per cent over 1997, and wage backlogs were paid off.

In 1995, an American company, RailTex Distribution Services (see RailTex entry in the USA section) took on management responsibility for the 105 km route between Kulsary and Tengiz.

In early 2001 it was announced that the railways were to be restructured within the next two years. The intention was to create four businesses, of which two would be private, with rolling stock and infrastructure remaining in state ownership. However, later in the same year the government indicated that although restructuring would go ahead, ownership of all business would remain wholly in state hands.

### Organisation

The network comprises most of the former Almaty, Tselinnaya and West Kazakhstan railways of the former SZhD. In 1996-97 there was a series of reorganisations, with these three constituent railways shedding divisions in order to create three new railways, making six, with limited independence. One of them was subsequently re-absorbed, leaving five operating regions, that are no longer subdivided into divisions, and have the status of state enterprises under the close supervision of Kazakhstan State Railways.

There are several lengthy main lines traversing regions of low population. The principal route is the 1,507 km Trans-Kazakhstan Railway running from Petropavlovsk on the Trans-Siberian Railway through Kokchetav, Astana and Solonichki to the Karaganda coalfield. This was later extended to Chu, on the Turkestan–Siberian route, and Lugovoy where it connects with lines into Kyrgyzia and Uzbekistan. The Turkestan–Siberian route runs 1,445 km from Semipalatinsk via Aktogay and Zhangiz-Tobe to Almaty and Chu. From Aktogay the line to the Chinese border at Druzhba now forms part of a through route from the Chinese capital Beijing to Russia. This, the Trans-Asian route, provides a Japan–Western Europe link that is claimed to be 2,500 km shorter than the Trans-Siberian route.

A third main line in the west of the country links Tashkent, in Uzbekistan, with Orenburg in Russia, via Aralsk, Kandagach and Aktyubinsk, a distance of 1,854 km.

The Kazakhstan system has many long stretches of single track; over one third of the network is double track.

In 1999, the railway employed around 140,000 staff.

### Passenger operations

Following independence, passenger traffic was at first affected by rolling stock shortages, leading to a big reduction in through services to Russia, but business has recovered following delivery of new coaches and improved maintenance arrangements. In 1993, the railway recorded 20 billion passenger-km but by 1995 this had declined to 13.2 billion and continued to fall subsequently. In 1999, traffic was down to 8.89 billion passenger-km (14.3 million passenger journeys).

Since the collapse of the Soviet Union, fare evasion has been a serious problem, reaching levels of 50 per cent or more. One idea put forward by western consultants would be to turn all of the platforms on Kazakhstan's 82 stations into airport-style closed zones, accessible only to passengers with tickets.

A temporary ban on passenger trains originating in Uzbekistan, Tajikistan and Kyrgyzia was imposed in October 2000, because of problems caused by mass ticketless travelling, overcrowding, and contraband activities.

### Freight operations

In 1999 KTZ accounted for 78 per cent of Kazakhstan's freight transport. The railway's principal traffic is coal from the Karaganda and Ekibastuz fields. Most of this is moved over the busiest of the routes, the east-west Pavlodar–Tobol line, once part of a Soviet trunk route. Since independence, coal movements from Ekibastuz to various parts of the former Soviet Union have held up well, while other freight traffic has declined substantially. Freight statistics for 1993 were 218 million tonnes, 190 billion tonne-km. In 1996, 108 billion tonne-km were achieved. In 1999, 91.7 billion tonne-km were produced, tonnage carried being 124 million.

Preliminary figures indicated a 28 per cent rise in freight traffic in 2000. Freight traffic exchange with China through Druzhba increased by almost 50,000 tonnes in 2000, totalling about 4 million tonnes.

A boost to the freight business may come from the agreement signed in late 1994 with the six other countries promoting the so-called Eurasian Railway route to China via the Alatau Pass. To help revive industry, tariffs on coal and some other minerals were reduced by up to 50 per cent in 1998, the resultant losses being made up from the railway's reserves.

### New lines

With the aim of creating a more 'national' network, a number of new cut-off lines are under construction or planned. The 184 km Konechnaya–Aksu line was started in 1998 and opened in June 2001. This, and the Charskaya–Zaschita line connecting Zhangiz-Tobe and Ust Kamenogorsk, will avoid Russian territory, while the new Zhezqazghan–Kzyil Orda and Chelkar–Beyneu lines will provide a shorter and all-Kazakh route between the Caspian Sea and China.

An agreement was signed in 1997 between the governments of Kazakhstan and Turkmenistan to promote the building of a north-south corridor. This would link Yerelyevo on the Caspian Sea with Turkmenbashi in Turkmenistan, forming a direct rail route avoiding Uzbekistan. Major traffic flows between Russia and Iran are expected for this route.

Since 1999, discussions have been taking place between railway officials from Kazakhstan, Belarus, China, Poland and Russia to examine the possibility of creating an 11,000 km trans-Asia northern corridor to provide a freight land-bridge between the Chinese Yellow Sea port of Lianyungang and Rotterdam. Some 2,000 km of the route would be in Kazakhstan.

### Improvements to existing lines

Efforts are now concentrated on easing and smoothing the well-paying international transit traffic. Developing the approaches to Druzhba has priority, especially work on the Aktogay–Druzhba line. The north-south line linking Russia via Kandagach with Uzbekistan will also be improved.

In 2000, KTZ tendered for a wide range of track maintenance equipment to be funded by a load from the European Bank for Reconstruction and Development.

### Traction and rolling stock

In 1995, the railway was operating 738 electric (Class VL70C) and 2,327 diesel locomotives (each double or triple locomotive is counted as a single in this total). The principal locomotive classes in service are the TE10, TEP70, VL60K and VL80 families. The locomotive fleet is showing its age, with a continual need to top up engine oil due to heavy losses en route; as much as half the diesel fleet is out of use. In the absence of new locomotives, it is estimated that by 2000 all passenger electrics and about two-thirds of the main line diesel fleet will be life-expired.

In a tie-up with GE of the USA, 16 Ukrainian-built 2TE10M twin diesel locomotives are being rebuilt with 7FDL-12 engines. One unit from the West Kazakhstan Railway was shipped to the USA for rebuilding, and GE is supplying kits for the other 15 to be rebuilt locally. In 2001, bids were invited for the modernisation of 85 locomotives over a period of six to eight years, and for the supply of 130-150 locomotives or components for their assembly over a similar period.

In 2000 KTZ agreed to purchase two gauge-convertible Talgo trains (46 cars initially). These could be used for future services into China, or could cut the 21 hour schedule between the old and new capitals Almaty and Astana to 13 hours.

The locomotive depots at Atbasar and Chu now undertake capital repairs, making Kazakhstan State Railways independent in this respect. In 2001, tenders were called for the provision of cleaning and painting facilities at these installations.

Since independence, some 200 main line coaches have been imported from Germany and Russia, among them 99 air conditioned long-distance cars from Germany's DWA. In 1995 the coaching stock comprised 1,197 seating coaches, 658 sleeping cars, 102 restaurant cars and 206 other vehicles. In 1995 the wagon fleet stood at 17,820 covered wagons, 39,510 low-sided wagons, 14,130 flat wagons, 11,570 tank wagons, 2,240 refrigerated wagons, 15,760 other designs. By 1998 it was reported that due to write-offs, the wagon stock had been reduced to 90,000. However, 982 wagons were delivered in 1998 and 1,302 in 1999.

### Electrification
The Trans-Kazakhstan is electrified at 25 kV to Karaganda, along with several other routes converging on Astana. Further electrifications are proceeding slowly. The 62 km Chu–Chokpar section was electrified in 1995, and electrification of the line from Chu to Almaty continued in 2001.

### Track
There is a serious backlog of track maintenance; one third of the track is reported as overdue for replacement, with frequent temporary speed restrictions as a result.

*UPDATED*

# KENYA

## Ministry of Transport & Communications

PO Box 52692, Ngong Road, Nairobi
Tel: (+254 2) 72 92 00  Fax: (+254 2) 72 63 62

**Key personnel**
Minister: Titus Naikuni
Permanent Secretary: S N Arasa

## Kenya Railways Corporation (KR)

PO Box 30121, Nairobi
Tel: (+254 2) 22 12 11  Fax: (+254 2) 34 00 49; 22 41 56

**Key personnel**
Chairman: M Mohammed
Managing Director: Andrews Wayandeh
General Managers
  Commercial: J O A Nyerere
  Freight: N O Aloys
  Human Resources: R Shako
  Technical: J K Nyue
Chief Mechanical and Electrical Engineer: A O Okuku
Chief Civil Engineer: V On'gon'go
Chief Signal and Telecommunications Manager: V Hagono
Chief Traffic Manager: J Kinara
Chief Accountant: A K Musau
Chief Internal Auditor: S J N Maritim
Supplies and Procurement Manager: P E Okiring
Corporate Planning Manager: (vacant)
Human Resources Manager: F Muzungyo
Information Systems Manager: J K Njau
Business Development Manager: S K Kisoryo
Central Workshops Manager: G Onyango
Passenger Services Manager: T C Masha
Quality and Safety Manager: B M Kimau
Public Relations Manager: S M Chanzu
Director, Railway Training Institute: M O Mugasia
Corporation Secretary: I K Mbito
Estates Manager: P K Mutua
Security Services Manager: J S N Muli

Gauge: 1,000 mm
Route length: 2,778 km

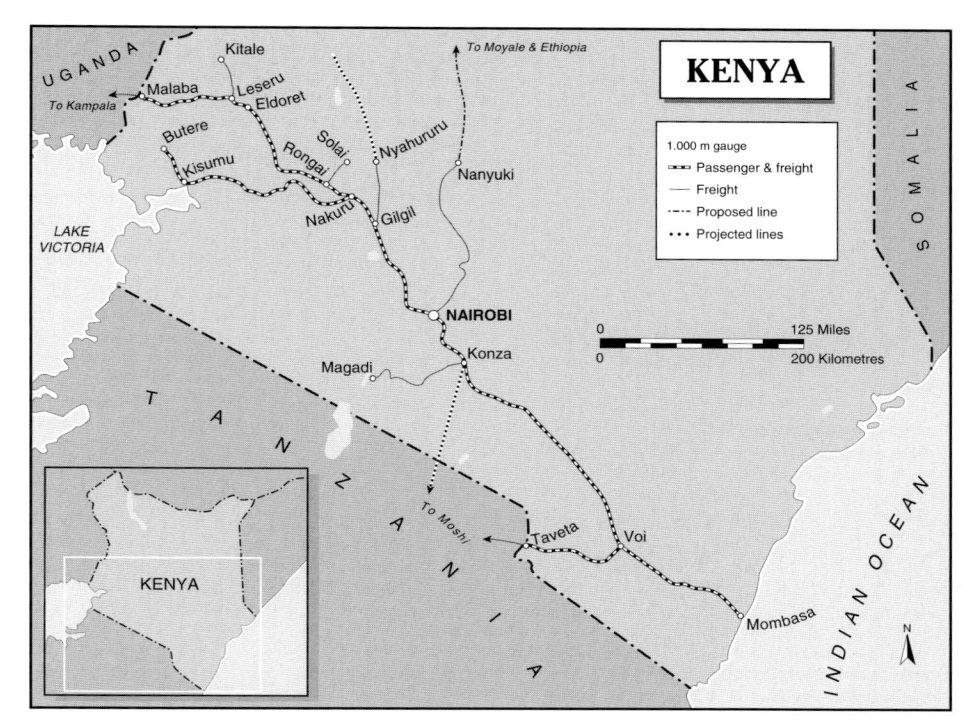

### Political background
The railway has been freed from tariff controls and a system of state compensation for provision of uneconomic services has been established. KR has been given managerial freedom by the government and is following a staff reduction programme. But economic liberalisation in Kenya has exposed the railway to increased competition from the roads, prompting KR to restructure its marketing strategy to address the needs of its customers.

### Passenger operations
KR handles substantial passenger traffic volumes on the Nairobi–Mombasa route. It also operates commuter services in Nairobi and its surrounding area. In 2000-01, 5.6 million passenger journeys were recorded.

### Freight traffic
In 2000-01, KR carried 2.4 million tonnes of freight. It expected to achieve 3 million tonnes in 2002-03, adopting a new marketing strategy to boost loadings. Key features of this strategy were: more flexible competitive tariffs; rationalisation of tariffs, especially on container movements, to increase the railway's competitiveness with road hauliers; an offer of rebates and discounts based on business volume and special seasonal rates; and an aggressive sales and marketing campaign by KR managers.

### Improvements to existing lines
The line connecting the capital, Nairobi, with the Indian Ocean port of Mombasa is the most important in the country and has been the subject of recent upgrading.

Transit traffic bound for Uganda over Lake Victoria has increased in importance. On the line from Nairobi to Lake Victoria, radio links were enhanced during 1997 in a US$517,000 project.

**Diesel locomotives**

| Class | Wheel arrangement | Power kW | Speed km/h | Weight Tonnes | No in service | First built | Mechanical | Engine | Transmission |
|---|---|---|---|---|---|---|---|---|---|
| 94XX | Co-Co | 2,172 | 72 | 101.8 | 10 | 1978 | GE (US) | GE 7F DL12 | *E* GE (US) |
| 93XX | Co-Co | 1,947 | 72 | 101.8 | 25 | 1978 | GE (US) | GE 7F DL12 | *E* GE (US) |
| 92XX | 1 Co-Co 1 | 1,901 | 72 | 118 | 12 | 1971 | MLW | Alco 251F | *E* GE (Canada) |
| 87XX | 1 Co-Co 1 | 1,372 | 72 | 104.7 | 22 | 1960 | EE | EE12CSVT | *E* EE |
| 72XX | 1 Bo-Bo 1 | 925 | 72 | 73 | 3 | 1972 | GEC | EE8CSVT | *E* GEC |
| 71XX | 1 Bo-Bo 1 | 925 | 72 | 71 | 1 | 1967 | EE | EE8CSVT | *E* EE |
| 62XX | B-B | 552 | 72 | 38 | 32 | 1977 | Henschel | MTU493TZ | *H* Voith L520rU2 |
| 47XX | D | 391 | 28 | 53 | 27 | 1977 | Hunslet | MTU396TC RRDV8TCE | *H* Voith L2r3ZU |
| 46XX | D | 2 × 257 | 32 | 49 | 16 | 1967 | Barclay | +BPC-Metro Cummins NT380 | *H* Twin Disc CF 11500 |

### Traction and rolling stock
Fleet numbers at the start of 2002 were 156 diesel locomotives, 588 passenger coaches, and 6,827 freight wagons.

In 2002, refurbishment of locomotives of Classes 93 and 94 by General Electric was in progress.

**Type of coupler in standard use:** PH/DA
**Brake system:** Graduated automatic air

### Track
**Rail:** 50, 60, 80 and 95 lb FB
**Crossties (sleepers):** Steel
**Spacing:** 1,485/km (1,568/km in curves)
**Fastenings:** 'K' type (Pandrol)
**Max gradient:** 3.5%
**Max axleload:** 18 tonnes

*UPDATED*

# KYRGYZIA

## Ministry of Transport and Telecommunications

ul Isanov 42, 720017 Bishkek
Fax: (+7 3312) 21 36 67

**Key personnel**
Minister of Transport and Telecommunications:
 Kubanyeh Bekzhumaliyev

*UPDATED*

## Kyrgyzia Railways

Kyrgyzia Zhelezni Darogy (KZD)
ul L'va Tolstogo 83, 720009 Bishkek
Tel: (+7 3312) 25 30 54

**Key personnel**
General Director: Isa Ormukulov

Gauge: 1,520 mm
Length: 470 km

### Political background
This state system emerged from the collapse of the USSR in 1991.

### Organisation
The main railway, formerly part of the USSR's Alma-Atinskaya Railway, is a 323 km branch from the Trans-Kazakhstan line to the capital, Bishkek (formerly Frunze), and its terminus at Issyk-Kul (Balykchi) on the shores of Lake Issyk-Kul. There are also several short branches in the south linking such cities and towns as Tashkumyr, Dzhalal-Abad, Osh and Kyzyl-Kia with the eastern Uzbekistan system.

### Passenger operations
In 1999, there were 31.3 million passenger-km travelled.

In 2001 it was reported that passenger services (all originating at Bishkek) consisted of a daily train to Moscow, a mixed train into Kazakhstan, and a seasonal service to Dzhalal-Abad over the railways of Kazakhstan, Uzbekistan and Tajikistan. Domestic services were limited to a daily train to Balykchi (Issyk-Kul) and four suburban services.

### Freight operations
In 1999, there were 2.9 million tonnes travelling for 350 million tonne-km; virtually all freight crosses the border. Major commodities are coal (932,000 tonnes) and petroleum products (862,000 tonnes).

Most of the coal is imported: several lines built to serve domestic collieries are now closed. Domestic freight traffic is very sparse except between Bishkek and Tokmak.

### New lines
The 60 km line from Balykchi (Issyk-Kul) to Kochkorka was opened in 2000. This is the first phase of a Trans-Kyrgyzia line across the seismic Pamir range to link the northern railways with the southern railways at Dzhalal-Abad. According to a law passed in late 2000, part of this line will be incorporated in an international project providing a new link between China and Europe; a line will be built south from the Trans-Kyrgyzia line, probably from Kazarman, to connect with Chinese Railways at Kashgar (Kashi). An accord agreeing to construction of the 256 km line was signed in June 2001 by the presidents of Kyrgyzia and China and tendering was in progress to select consultants to undertake design of the project. The line is expected to open in 2005-06.

### Traction and rolling stock
The railway is entirely diesel worked. There are 34 main line locomotives of classes 3TE10 and 2TE10, and 23 shunting locomotives of classes TEM2 and ChME3.

The rolling stock fleet comprises 520 coaches (of which 79 were out of use in 1996) and 2,616 wagons (727 not in use).

To satisfy complaints by other railways, a wagon repair workshop is to be established on the frontier at Belovskaya to ensure that freight vehicles requiring attention are rectified before leaving Kirghiz territory.

*UPDATED*

---

# KOREA, NORTH

## Korean State Railway (ZČi)

Zosun Tchul Zosun Mindzuzui Inminhoagug
Pyongyang
Fax: (+8502) 381 45 27

**Key personnel**
Minister of Railways: Kim En Sam

Gauge: Almost entirely 1,435 mm, but some narrow-gauge
Route length: 5,214 km
Electrification: approximately 3,500 km at 3 kV DC

### Organisation
ZČi is organised into five regional operating divisions, each responsible for the Ministry of Railways. The Ministry is also responsible for the country's railway manufacturing industry.

### Passenger operations
At last report, annual passenger journeys totalled some 35 million, passenger-km 3,400 million.

### Freight operations
At last report, freight carryings totalled some 38.5 million tonnes and 9,100 million tonne-km. Around 70 per cent of the country's freight is reported to be carried by rail.

### New lines
Recent completions include an 80 km railway from Jukchon to Onchon, for more direct access to the port of Nampo, and a 252 km line from Hyesan to Kanggye via Manpojin. In 1997 a 100 km electrified line between Wonsan and Mount Kumgang was inaugurated.

A new double-track route is planned for the Russian Federation border crossing, between Tumangang and Hassan near Najin.

### Improvements to existing lines
The year 1992 was marked by launching of a programme of modernisation of the country's rail infrastructure and industry. The first sign of action was production of a plan for reconstructing the strategic northern main line parallel to the Chinese border between Hyesan and Musan, on which capacity was to be raised to 50 million tonnes a year. Double-tracking of the 337 km route started in 1993 and was carried out in two stages.

Studies published in South Korea in 1998 indicate that major investments are required on many major routes, including Pyongyang-Kaesong and Pyongyang-Sinuiji. On both of these lines, demand is reported to exceed capacity.

*Domestically manufactured 'Red Flag' twin section 3 kV DC electric locomotive at Pyongyang (Thomas E Fischer)*

# Korea, North—Korea, South/RAILWAY SYSTEMS

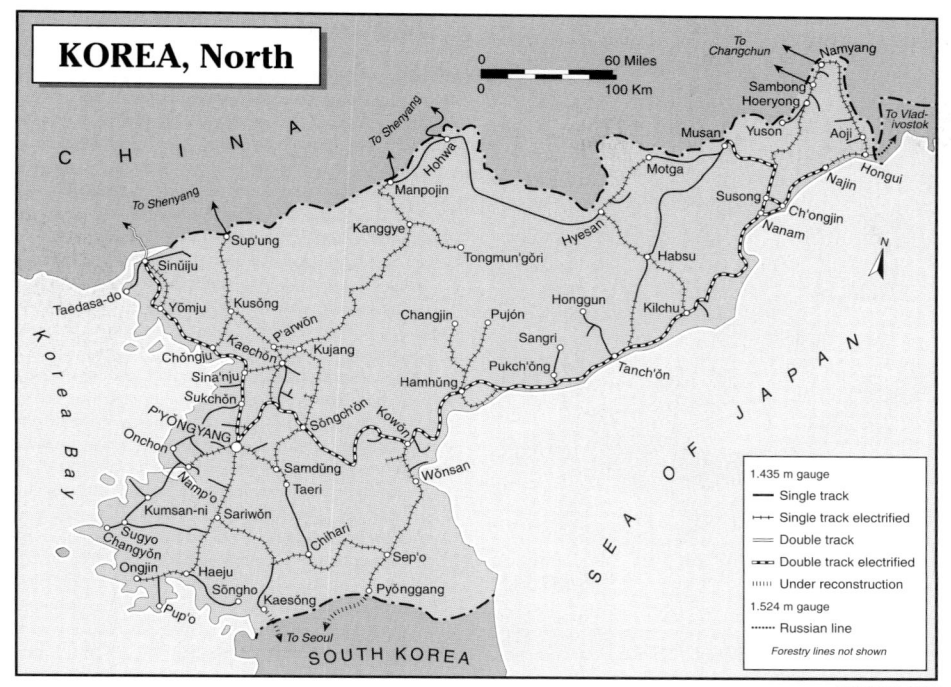

## KOREA, North

In 2000, reduced political tension between North and South Korea led to an agreement to reinstate the railway linking the two countries. This will necessitate reconstruction of a 20 km section of line from Pongdong-ni, in North Korea, across the border and the demilitarised zone to Munsan. Work on the South Korea portion of the link started late in 2000.

Improvements are also expected to be made to the rail link between North Korea and Russia following a meeting between the leaders of the two countries in 2000. Following an evaluation of the condition of the North Korean network, the Russian government indicated its willingness to assist in upgrading the line from Pyongyang to the border crossing at Hongui as part of a broader scheme to link the South Korean port of Pusan with the Trans-Siberian route at Khazan, Russia.

### Traction and rolling stock
No details are known of the numbers of locomotives, coaches and freight wagons, but a fleet of more than 300 electrics is believed to be available. With just over 80 per cent of the network now under wires, 90 per cent of all freight is reported as hauled by electric traction. The latter began with importation of 10 2,030 kW Škoda Bo-Bos similar to the Type E449.0 of CSD, and of some USSR-built locomotives. Since the early 1980s locomotives as well as rolling stock have been produced by the country's Kim Jong Tae factory at Pyongyang. Production has focused on 8-axle twin section 'Red Flag' locomotives, which form the core of the electric traction fleet. In 1992 this plant was reported to be building bilevel passenger cars. Chinese-built passenger coaches are also in service.

Local production of rolling stock has been supplemented by delivery of seven French-built 3,600 hp diesel-electric Co-Cos similar to those delivered to Iraq. A first batch of seven was supplemented in 1987 by five more, built by De Dietrich with Alsthom electrical equipment.

In December 1996, six ex-DR Class 220 Type M62 diesel locomotives built at the Voroshilovgrad locomotive works arrived in North Korea from Germany, supplementing large numbers of similar machines presumed to have been procured from the former Soviet Union. In May 2000, 10 similar machines were delivered: six from Poland (former PKP Class ST44); three from Slovakia (former ŽSR Class 781); and one from Germany (former DB Class 220).

### Electrification
In 1992 electrification was reported complete on the Singhung-Hamjiwan stretch of the Lake Pujon line in the northeast; this line is to be wired throughout. By the close of 1992 electrification was completed from Haeju to Ongjin, completing the wiring from Pyongyang to the southwest extremity of the country.

Electrification is continuous throughout the 780 km from Pyongyang northeast to Vladivostok, and through passenger service (involving a bogie change at Tumangang, near Najin in Korea) between Pyongyang and Moscow was launched in 1987.

Electrification of the link to China via Hoeryong was completed in 1995, and upgrading to carry heavier traffic is in progress. Another partially built cross-border route in the region is being completed to cope with the increasing traffic with China.

---

# KOREA, SOUTH

## Ministry of Construction and Transport

1 Joongang-Dong, Kwacheon-shi, Kyungki-Do, 100162 Seoul
Tel: (+82 2) 504 90 24   Fax: (+82 2) 504 91 99

**Key personnel**
Minister: Lim, In-taik

*UPDATED*

## Korea High Speed Rail Construction Authority

20th Floor, Kumhwa Building, 949-1 Togok-Dong, Kangnam-Gu, 135270 Seoul
Tel: (+82 2) 569 31 37   Fax: (+82 2) 554 82 24

**Key personnel**
Chairman: Chae, Young Suk

### Political background
KHRC is the government body set up to plan and build high-speed railways, first from Seoul to Pusan and later on other axes. The Seoul—Pusan scheme is funded jointly by government (45 per cent) and KHRC (55 per cent), the latter via foreign borrowings, bond issues and private capital.

### New lines
In 1989 the country's President announced his support for construction of both the Seoul—Pusan, or Kyongbu, high-speed line and of new electrified lines from Seoul to the east coast at Kangnung and Bukpyong, and from Taejon on the Seoul—Pusan line southwest to Mokpo.

The 412 km Seoul—Pusan line was selected to be built first. However, in late 1997 came government confirmation that completion of the Seoul—Pusan line would be delayed by two years after the target date, resulting in cost over-runs due to the extension of the construction period and for other reasons. This followed a review by a government commission into all major infrastructure projects in Korea in the light of worsening economic conditions. Subsequently, in 1998, it was decided that initially only the section from Seoul to Taegu would be constructed, with completion expected in 2003.

The existing Taegu—Pusan line is being electrified to allow high-speed trainsets to work throughout. This revised scheme reduces the distance between Seoul and Pusan to 409.8 km. Commercial services over the new line between Seoul and Taejon and over the newly electrified existing Taejon—Pusan line are scheduled to begin in 2004. Construction of an initial portion of this first

## RAILWAY SYSTEMS/Korea, South

*KTX high-speed trainset on the portion of the Chonan–Taejon test section of track inaugurated in December 1999* 0088213

phase of the project, a 57.2 km test section between Chonan and Taejon, began in June 1992 and an initial 34.4 km was inaugurated in December 1999.

In late 2001 the government authorised KHRC to build the second phase of the scheme between Taejon and Pusan via Kyongju, completing the high-speed alignment between Seoul and Pusan. The target date for completion of this 130.4 km section is 2008, two years earlier than originally envisaged.

The original performance objective was a 300 km/h top speed to achieve a two-hour Seoul–Pusan non-stop timing. There were to be four intermediate stations. Those at Chonan, Taejon (population 1.2 million) and Taegu (population 2.1 million) have been uncontroversial. The fourth, planned for the ancient city of Kyongju (population 1.1 million), ran into problems on environmental grounds; in 1997 a decision was taken to relocate it at nearby Hwachon-ri. The consequent replanning of the southern section of the line, from Hwachon-ri to Pusan, was a prime cause of delays to the high-speed project.

To mollify the city of Ulsan, whose residents will now have to travel further to reach the high-speed station, a promise has been made that the line from Kyongju to Ulsan will be electrified.

The mountainous character of the country requires about 38 per cent of the high-speed route to be in tunnel. Ruling gradient is generally 1.5 per cent, but is in places 2.5 per cent, and minimum curve radius is 7,000 m.

Tunnels are of 100 $m^2$ cross-sectional area, and within them distance between track centres is 5 m. Track capacity will be 240 movements a day, with trains running at four-minute intervals during peak periods.

After an intensely fought competition between French, German and Japanese industries, a US$2.1 billion contract covering rolling stock, catenary, signalling, maintenance, and other services was awarded in June 1994 to the Korea TGV Consortium (KTGVC). Led by Alstom and Eukorail, this grouping also includes Cegelec, CSEE Transport and Korean partners which include Daewoo, Hanjin, and Hyundai (now trading jointly as Koros) for rolling stock, and LG Cable, LG Industrial Systems, Goldstar, Iljin, and Samsung for fixed equipment.

Rolling stock is based on TGV/Eurostar technology, with 935-seat capacity trainsets comprising two power cars and 18 trailers, with the outer bogie of each end 'trailer' motored. Under the technology transfer element of the contract, two preseries and 10 production trainsets have been constructed by Alstom in France, while 34 are being built in Korea. The first French-built set was completed in May 1997 and subsequently tested on SNCF high-speed lines before shipment to Korea. KHRC subsequently adopted the branding 'KTX' for its trainsets.

Associated engineering from other French companies was included in the KTGVC bid. Cegelec is to supply the catenary and be responsible for its assembly and commissioning, while CSEE Transport is installing the TVM 430 track-to-train signalling system, and an automatic train speed control system. About 50 per cent of the equipment is being made in Korea.

Several other high-speed lines are envisaged in the long term, including the Honam (about 270 km from Chonan to Mokpo via Nonsan), the East-West (240 km from Seoul to Kangnung), the Kyongjeon (about 315 km from Kwangju to Pusan), and the East Coast (about 388 km from Kyongju to Kangnung).

*UPDATED*

## Korean National Railroad (KNR)

920, Tunsan-dong, So-ku, Taejon 302-701
Tel: (+82 42) 472 30 14   Fax: (+82 42) 472 30 10
e-mail: cph-icd@mail.korail.go.kr
Web: http://www.korail.go.kr

### Key personnel
Administrator: Son, Hak-lae
Deputy Administrator: Park, Chull-kyu
Directors General
  Corporate Planning: Shin, Kwang-soon
  Administration: Lee, Guen-Guk
  Supply: Kim, Jeong-Yeoul
  Safety and Environment: Kim, Hyung-park
  Transportation Business: Lee, Yong-kee
  Business Development: Park, Jong-kun
  Civil Engineering: Hong, Man-Yong
  Electrical Engineering: Chung, Yong-chull
  Rolling Stock: Lee, Yong-Il
  Construction: Im, Yong-Hyeon
  High-Speed Rail and Research: Yoo, Hee-Bok
Director, International Cooperation Division: Yoo Hee-Bok

Gauge: 1,435 mm
Route length: 3,125 km
Electrification: 642.1 km at 25 kV 60 Hz AC; 19.2 km at 1.5 kV DC

*Class 8100 electric locomotive* 0089056

### Political background
The Korean government's attempt in January 1996 to convert KNR into a public corporation was cancelled due to the threat of a strike by staff and the high cost of the process. Instead the government established 'The Special Law for National Railway Management Improvement', a five-year plan covering the period 1997-2001. As well as including measures to secure KNR's managerial independence, such as a separation of accounting for the operation of the railway and for new construction schemes, and the vesting of more authority in the company's administrator, the plan seeks to achieve an urgently needed reduction in expenditure. Over the five-year period of the plan, staff numbers will be cut from the 37,000 employed at the beginning of 1998 to 30,000. If this reduction is achieved by 2001, KNR's cost of wages will be reduced from 62 per cent of revenue in 1996 to 38 per cent. By the end of 1998 staff numbers had fallen to 34,600.

### Organisation
At the end of 2001, the KNR system encompassed 64 routes totalling 3,125 operational km.

The backbone of the railway system is the 444 km double-track Kyongbu line, running between the nation's two principal cities, Pusan on the southeast coast and the capital city of Seoul in the northwest. 'Saemaeul' express services link the two cities in around four hours. Principal intermediate cities reached by this route include Taegu and Taejon. While it constitutes less than 15 per cent of total route-km, the line accounts for nearly half of the system's operating revenues.

Diverging to the southwest from the Kyongbu line at Taejon, the Honam line reaches into the rich agricultural plain of North and South Cholla provinces and to the important southwestern port of Mokpo. Branching from the Honam line at Iri is the Cholla line, which extends southward to Yosu, an important southern port and the site of a major oil refinery.

The Yongdong line, which links the east coast with the Chungang line at Yongju, extends northward to the major east coast city of Kangnung.

| Revenue (billion Swon) | 2000 | 2001 |
|---|---|---|
| Operating revenue | 1,457 | 1,527 |
| Other revenue | 407 | 454 |
| Non-operating revenue | 86 | 99 |
| Non-current revenue | 27 | 36 |
| Total | 1,977 | 2,116 |

| Expenditure (billion Swon) | 2000 | 2001 |
|---|---|---|
| Operating expenditure | 2,105 | 2,235 |
| Non-operating expenditure | 3 | 5 |
| Other expenditure | 13 | 27 |
| **Total** | 2,121 | 2,267 |
| Profit/loss | −144 | −151 |

| Traffic (million) | 1999 | 2000 | 2001 |
|---|---|---|---|
| Passenger journeys | 823 | 816 | 911 |
| Passenger-km | 28,356 | 28,097 | 29,228 |
| Freight tonnes | 42.1 | 45.2 | 45.1 |
| Freight tonne-km | 10,071 | 10,803 | 10,492 |

## Passenger operations

Passenger traffic, which has risen steadily in recent years, is KNR's principal source of income. In 2001, an increase of 12 per cent was experienced in the number of passenger journeys compared with 2000 (see table).

Principal intercity services are formed of 150 km/h Saemaul Express diesel-hydraulic trainsets comprising six trailers and two power cars equipped with MTU engines and Voith transmission.

## Freight operations

Freight traffic has been in decline in recent years, falling from 60 million tonnes in 1993 to 45 million in 2001. Freight revenue is around a quarter of that derived by KNR from passengers.

## New lines

For information on the Seoul-Pusan high-speed line see Korea High Speed Rail Construction Authority entry. However, until the opening of the second phase of the project in 2010, high-speed services between Seoul and Pusan will make use of 174.4 km of the existing network.

In June 1998, KNR invited prequalification bids for a 30-year concession to build and operate a 61.5 km electrified line from central Seoul to Kimpo airport and on to the new Inchon International airport. A consortium led by Hyundai Engineering and Construction was selected to undertake the scheme, which is due to be completed in 2005.

## Improvements to existing lines

KNR is working on a 10-year upgrading of the 199 km Cholla line between Iri and Yosu. Realignment to eliminate the most severe curvature will cut journey time by 45 minutes, and with other works will raise capacity from 27 to 53 trains daily.

## Traction and rolling stock

As at June 2002, the fleet comprised 493 diesel and 96 electric locomotives, 1,672 emu cars, 610 dmu cars and three railcars. Other passenger stock in operation totalled 1,639 locomotive-hauled cars and there were 13,494 wagons. Some 5,000 privately owned freight wagons were also in use on the network.

In 2000, KNR took delivery of one of two prototype Class 8100 electric locomotives. Built by Daewoo Heavy Industries and Siemens and based on German Rail's Class 152 machines, these are the first three-phase asynchronous-drive electric locomotives to be used in Korea and are expected to form the basis of a future standard multipurpose design for the KNR network. The 88-tonne locomotives have a rated output of 5,200 kW and a top speed of 150 km/h. Completed in 1998, the two locomotives were undergoing acceptance tests before formal handover to KNR. Series production will take place in Korea, with mechanical design the subject of a technology transfer agreement between Korea Rolling Stock Corporation and Krauss-Maffei.

## Signalling and telecommunications

CTC (Centralised Traffic Control) is installed in the Seoul suburban area and on the Kyongbu, Changhang, Taebaek and Yongdong lines. In total, 1,117.4 route-km are so controlled. Automatic Train Stop (ATS) equipment is installed over 3,119.9 route-km, with Automatic Train Control (ATC) over 52.1 km.

At the end of 1999, two resignalling schemes were under way: centralised traffic control was being installed on 106.6 km between Chollam and Kangnung (Yongdong line) and on 60.7 km between Sodaejon and Kangkyung (Honam line).

## Electrification

Electrification in place in 2002 amounted to 642.1 km being electrified at 25 kV 60 Hz AC and 19.2 km at 1.5 kV DC. Sections being wired include: Cheongnyangui–Yeongju (218.8 km); Yeongju–Donghea (148.5 km); Jecheon–Baeksan (103.8 km); and 174.9 km in the Seoul suburban area.

In the longer term, KNR aspires to electrify all its main lines by 2020.

**Type of coupler in standard use:** Passenger cars — tight lock type; freight cars — Shibada (E-Type)
**Type of braking in standard use, locomotive-hauled stock:** Air brake

## Track

Main lines are mostly laid with 50 kg/m rail, but since 1981 KNR has laid continuously welded 60 kg/m rail to heavily trafficked sections and 344.3 track-km is now installed. Some secondary lines also have 50 kg/m rail, others 37 kg/m. Sleepers on main lines are now mostly of locally manufactured concrete, with Pandrol fastenings securing long-welded rail. On branch lines, timber sleepers prevail.

**Rail:** flat-bottom 37, 50 and 60 kg/m
**Crossties/sleepers**
**Material:** Wooden or prestressed concrete ties
**Dimensions**
Common tie: 15 × 24 × 250 cm
Switch tie: 15 × 25 × 280-460 cm or 23 × 23 × 250-300 cm
**Total number installed**
In plain track: 1,600 per km
In curves: 1,700 or a few more per km
**Fastenings type**
Wooden tie: elastic fastening type
PC tie: Pandrol fastening type
**Min curvature radius:** 200 m
**Max gradient:** 3.5% (3°)
**Max permissible axleload:** 25 tonnes

**UPDATED**

### Diesel locomotives

| Class | Wheel arrangement | Power kW | Speed km/h | Weight tonnes | No in service | First built | Mechanical | Builders Engine | Transmission |
|---|---|---|---|---|---|---|---|---|---|
| 2000 | Bo-Bo | 596 | 105 | 95.5 | 6 | 1955 | GMC | GMC | E GMC D27 |
| 2100 | Bo-Bo | 746 | 105 | 87 | 28 | 1961 | GMC | GMC | E GMC D75D |
| 3000 | Bo-Bo | 653 | 105 | 75 | 39 | 1956 | GMC | GMC | E GMC D47B |
| 3200 | Bo-Bo | 653 | 105 | 73 | 26 | 1966 | Alco | GMC | E GMC GE761 |
| 4000 | Bo-Bo | 977 | 105 | 78.5 | 5 | 1963 | GMC | GMC | E GMC D57B1 |
| 4100 | Bo-Bo | 977 | 105 | 88.5 | 7 | 1966 | GMC | GMC | E GMC D77B |
| 4200 | Bo-Bo | 977 | 105 | 88 | 20 | 1967 | GMC | GMC | E GMC D75B |
| 7000 | Co-Co | 2,238 | 150 | 113 | 15 | 1986 | Hyundai | GMC | E Hyundai D77B |
| 7100 | Co-Co | 2,238 | 150 | 132 | 86 | 1975 | GMC/Hyundai | GMC | E GMC/Hyundai D77B |
| 7200 | Co-Co | 2,238 | 150 | 132 | 39 | 1971 | GMC/Hyundai | GMC | E GMC/Hyundai D77B |
| 7300 | Co-Co | 2,238 | 150 | 124 | 83 | 1989 | Hyundai | GMC | E Hyundai D77B |
| 7400 | Co-Co | 2,238 | 150 | 126 | 59 | 1997 | Hyundai | GMC | E Hyundai D77B |
| 7500 | Co-Co | 2,238 | 105 | 132 | 54 | 1971 | GMC/Hyundai | GMC | E GMC/Hyundai D77B |
| 7500 | Co-Co | 2,238 | 150 | 124 | 20 | 1996 | Hyundai | GMC | E Hyundai D77B |

### Electric locomotives

| KNR series | Wheel arrangement | Output kW | Speed km/h | Weight tonnes | No in Service | First built | Builders Mechanical | Electrical |
|---|---|---|---|---|---|---|---|---|
| 8000 | Bo-Bo-Bo | 3,900 | 85 | 132 | 90 | 1972 | BN/Alsthom | Alsthom/ACEC AEG/ABB |
| 8000 | Bo-Bo-Bo | 3,900 | 85 | 132 | 4 | 1986 | Daewoo | Daewoo/Woojin |
| 8100 | Bo-Bo | 5,200 | 150 | 88 | 1 | 2000 | Korea Rolling Stock Corporation | Siemens |

### Diesel railcars or multiple-units

| Class | Cars per unit | Motor cars per unit | Motored axles/car | Power/car kW | Speed km/h | No in Service | First built | Mechanical | Builders Engine | Transmission |
|---|---|---|---|---|---|---|---|---|---|---|
| DHC | 6 | 2 | 4 | 1,469 | 150 | 4 | 1987 | Daewoo/Hyundai | MTU 12V396TC13 | H Voith L520RU |
|  | 8 | 2 | 4 | 1,469 | 150 | 51 | 1988 | Daewoo/Hyundai/Hanjin | MTU 16V396TC13 | H Voith L520 RZU2 |
| DEC | 5 | 2 | 4 | 723 | 110 | 2 | 1980 | Daewoo | Cummins KTA 2 300L |  |
| NDC | 4 | 2 | 4 | 231 | 120 | 9 | 1984 | Daewoo | Cummins NT855R1 | H NT855R4 T211R |
| CDC | 5 | 3-5 | 2 | 231 | 120 | 36 | 1996 | Daewoo | Cummins NT855R1 | H Voith T211YZ |

### Electric railcars or multiple-units

| Class | Cars per unit | Motor cars per unit | Motored axles/car | Power/motor KW | Speed km/h | Units in service | First built | Builders Mechanical | Electrical |
|---|---|---|---|---|---|---|---|---|---|
| **Dual-voltage 25 kV/1.5 kV** | | | | | | | | | |
| 1000 | 10 | 6 | 4 | 120 | 110 | 66 | 1974 | Hy/D/H | D/Hy/W/C/T/M |
| 2000 | 10 | 5 | 4 | 200 | 110 | 30 | 1994 | Hy/D/H | Hy/W/C/T/M |
| 5000 | 10 | 5 | 4 | 200 | 110 | 42 | 1997 | Hy | Hy/W/T/M |
| **25 kV** | | | | | | | | | |
| 2000 | 6 | 3 | 4 | 200 | 110 | 22 | 1994 | Hy/D/H | Hy/W/C/T/M |
| 9000 | 10 | 6 | 4 | 120 | 110 | 2 | 1980 | D | D/T |
| **1.5 kV** | | | | | | | | | |
| 3000 | 10 | 5 | 4 | 200 | 110 | 16 | 1995 | Hy | Hy/M |

Abbreviations: C: Chung Gye, D: Daewoo, H: Hanjin, Hy: Hyundai, M: Mitsubishi, T: Toshiba, W: Woojin

# KOSOVO

## Kosovo Railway Enterprise

Hekurudha e Kosoves/Kosovske Zeleznice
Gauge: 1,435 mm
Route length: 330 km

### Organisation
The Kosovo Railway Enterprise was set up by UNMIK to administer rail operations following the 1999 war. Initially, all trains were driven by KFOR soldiers, but these duties were due to be transferred to civilian hands by September 2000. Representatives of the railways of Croatia, France and Germany were training local drivers and fitters.

### Passenger operations
In 2000, there were two daily return trips between the good station at Pristina and Skopje Volkovo, Macedonia, and on the Kosovo Polje—Mitrovica—Zvecan line. Trains were formed of two or three coaches and were unheated. All were heavily guarded by KFOR troops.

### Freight operations
In 2000, freight trains carrying mainly KFOR and humanitarian supplies were operating on the two lines which were seeing passenger services and on the Prizren—Pec, Pristina—Prizren and Kosovo Polje—Leposavic lines.

### Improvements to existing lines
In 2000, parts of the system remained unusable due to war damage. Work was under way to repair the tunnel at Sinji, north of Pristina, which for some years has been used as a waste dump and parking area.

### Traction and rolling stock
In mid-2000, the Kosovo Railway Enterprise had at its disposal three Yugoslav Railways Class 661 diesel-electrics, two former SNCF Class 63000 diesel-electrics and six former German Rail Class 202 diesel-hydraulics. It was reported that 18 Norwegian State Railways Class Di3 diesel locomotives were to be transferred to Kosovo in September 2000.

The locomotive maintenance facilities at Kosovo Polje were reopened in January 2000.

# LAOS

## Ministry of Transport

Vientiane

### Key personnel
Spokesman: Songkane Luangmuninthorne

### New lines
Laos has been without railway lines until now, but a 1,000 mm gauge rail link has been planned across the recently completed Friendship Bridge across the Mekong river, which is the border with Thailand (see Thailand entry for details). However, work on the 20 km line linking Vientiane, the Laotian capital, with the bridge was suspended in 1998 as a result of regional economic difficulties. The line was being funded by a joint venture of the Shaviriya Group of Thailand (75 per cent), through its subsidiary Pacific Transportation, and the Laotian government (25 per cent). The company was to have a 60-year operating concession, property development and telecommunications rights along the route and tax breaks on the first 18 years of operating revenues.

Under discussion by the joint venture partners are construction of a west-east new line from Vientiane to the Vietnamese capital Hanoi, and a line striking northwards from Vientiane to the Chinese border, and a line south-east from Vientiane to Champasak.

No work had started on the initial phase of the project by the end of 1999, and the Laotian government was reported to be seeking possible new partners to take it forward.

# LATVIA

## Ministry of Transport

Gogola iela 3, Riga LV-1743
Tel: (+371 7) 22 69 22  Fax: (+371 7) 21 71 80

### Key personnel
Minister: Anatolij Gorbunovs
Director, Railway Department: Janis Veidemanis

## Latvian Railway (LDZ)

Valsts akciju sabiedrība Latvijas Dzelzceļš
Gogoļa iela 3, Riga LV-1547
Tel: (+371 5) 83 49 40  Fax: (+371 7) 82 02 31
e-mail: info@ldz.lv
Web: http://www.ldz.lv

### Key personnel
Director General: Andris Zorgevics
First Deputy Director General: Staņislav Baiko
Deputy Director General: Rihards Peders
Directors
 Passenger: Vasilijs Hristins
 Freight: Ériks Šmuksts
 Finance: Igors Nikolajevs
 Strategic Development: Jánis Vèvers
 Personnel: Edgars Elksnis
 Economic: Vladimirs Grjaznovs
 Infrastructure: Mihails Jagodkins
 Rolling Stock: Jánis Pètersons
 Real Estate: Andris Burtnieks
 Legal: Uldis Pètersons
 Computer Centre: Valentins Vèvers

Heads of key units
 Personnel: Edgars Elksnis
 Technical Inspection: Árijs Sinàts
 Stores: Nikolajs Vasiļjevs
 External Relations: Valérijs Turko

Gauge: 1,520 mm; 750 mm
Route length: 2,314 km; 33.2 km
Electrification: 270.4 km of 1,520 mm gauge at 3 kV DC

### Political background
The rail system of this Baltic state became legally established in August 1991 and started independent operations in January 1992 with a workforce of around 24,000; by December 2001, the number of employees was down to 15,200.

LDZ is the largest transport company in the Baltic states, its most significant function to provide services on the east-west and north-south transit corridors and to the Main Latvian ports of Ventspils, Riga and Liepája. In 2001, the railway handled 37.9 million tonnes of freight, 4 per cent up on the figure achieved in 2000 and 14.1 per cent more than in 1999. Transit traffic accounted for 82.6 per cent of freight carried and port traffic represented 75 per cent of total shipments. Increases in both overland transit and maritime traffic is attributed to successful co-operation with operators in Russia, Belarus, Estonia, Lithuania, Kazakhstan and Ukraine among others.

LDZ is in the process of restructuring. This was initiated to adjust the railway to the requirements of a market economy. As a result, the formerly centralised undertaking has been transformed into a vertically integrated railway company with functional business units operating in different market areas.

On 5 May 2000, an LDZ shareholders' meeting approved the Restructuring Action Programme for 2000-03, anticipating the establishment as a holding company. Within this, member companies would operate in their respective market segments as independent legal entities. The restructuring programme had the support of the Latvian Cabinet of Ministers.

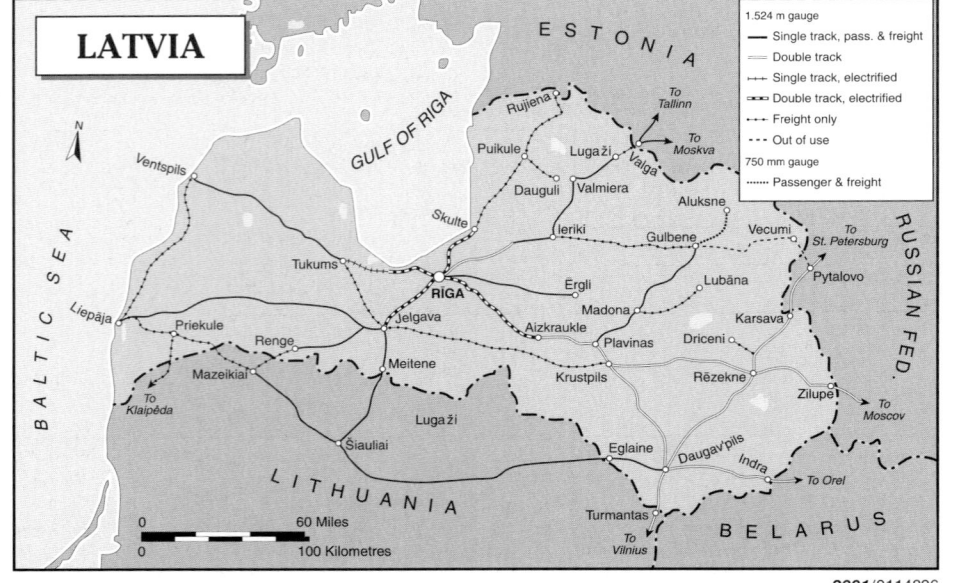

At the end of 2001, the first subsidiary company was established. Named Pasažieru Vilciens, it is responsible for domestic passenger services, this first subsidiary company combined the activities of the former Elektrovilciens ('Electric Train') and Dīzeļvilciens ('Diesel Train') divisions. During 2002, it was planned to establish three rolling stock overhaul and repair units and the international traffic business unit as subsidiary companies.

### Finance
In 2000, LDZ's audited profit was lat3.5 million. This successful result was attributed to market-oriented management, a flexible tariff policy and an efficient marketing strategy, providing for a responsive freight rates structure, reduced costs and improved use of financial resources.

Income from passenger traffic declined by 5 per cent compared with the previous year. The fall was attributed to competition from road transport operators, which receive government operating subsidies, whereas LDZ must cross-subsidise loss-making passenger activities from freight profits. This policy is in conflict with the requirements the country's restructuring legislation and with current European Union directives.

**Finance** (000 lats)

| Revenue | 1998 | 1999 | 2000 |
|---|---|---|---|
| Passengers | 13,511 | 10,746 | 10,122 |
| Freight | 78,222 | 66,759 | 76,227 |
| Parcels and mail | 3 | 7 | 3 |
| Other income | 5,717 | 3,936 | 11,293 |
| Total | 97,453 | 81,448 | 97,645 |

| Expenditure | 1998 | 1999 | 2000 |
|---|---|---|---|
| Staff/personnel/materials/Services | 86,158 | 83,507 | 83,835 |
| Depreciation | 14,742 | 5,137 | 9,631 |
| Total | 100,900 | 88,644 | 93,466 |

| Traffic | 1998 | 1999 | 2000 |
|---|---|---|---|
| Passenger journeys (000) | 30,100 | 24,862 | 20,259 |
| Passenger-km (million) | 1,059 | 984 | 708 |
| Freight tonnes (000) | 37,857 | 33,208 | 37,884 |
| Freight tonne-km (million) | 12,995 | 12,210 | 14,179 |

### Passenger operations
Passenger rail services in Latvia are provided by three companies: the state-owned Latvijas Dzelzceļš (LDZ), which runs international trains; Pasažieru Vilciens, which operates domestic services; and Gulbenes-Alūksnes Bānītis Ltd, which provides passenger services over the 750 mm gauge Gulbene–Alūksne line in the northeast of the country.

International services comprise the following: the 'Latvijas Ekspresis' (Moscow–Riga, daily); the 'Jūrmala' (Moscow–Riga, daily); and the 'Baltija' (St Petersburg–Riga, daily). There are also seasonal services to holiday destinations, such as Simferopol and Adler.

The main domestic lines link the capital Riga with Daugavpils, 218 km away in the southeast of the country, Rēzekne, in the east (224 km), Jelgava, in the south (43 km) and Lugaži, in the northeast (164 km).

Since 15 August 2001, services on the Riga–Ventspils and Riga–Liepāja routes have been suspended due to poor patronage and rolling stock shortages. Services were being maintained on the busiest sections of these routes, between Riga and Tukums and Riga and Jelgava respectively.

Most routes are operated with Class DR1A and DR1P dmus. Suburban lines around Riga are operated by ER2 and ER2T 3 kV emus.

### Freight operations
The decline of heavy industry since the break-up of the Soviet Union and the rise of road-based freight transport have seen freight tonnages on LDZ decline from around 50 million tonnes annually two decades ago to 28.8 million tonnes in 1995, although volumes recovered in 1997 to reach 41 million tonnes.

Following a further considerable decline in traffic in 1998 and 1999, volumes started to grow in 2000 and in 2001, almost 38 million tonnes were carried. As in previous years, international transit traffic accounts for the largest share – 82.6 per cent in 2001, including petroleum products, fertilisers, chemical products, ferrous metals, coal, foodstuffs, grain and timber.

Major investments are being made to develop container terminals at Latvian ports. At Ventspils the Nord Natie Ventspils Terminàls facility has been commissioned, while wagon handling capacity at the port has also been increased.

*Class 2TE10U twin-unit diesel-electric freight locomotive at Valga* (Eddie Barnes)

*LDZ Class TEP70 on a cross-border passenger service at Šiauliai, Lithuania* (Eddie Barnes)

*Class ER2 four-car emu at Jelgava* (Norman Griffiths)

### Diesel locomotives

| Class | Wheel arrangement | Power KW | Speed km/h | Weight Tonnes | No in service | First built | Builders Mechanical | Engine | Transmission |
|---|---|---|---|---|---|---|---|---|---|
| **1,520 mm gauge** | | | | | | | | | |
| TEP70 | Co-Co | 2,900 | 160 | 129 | 23 | 1981 | Kolomna | 2A-5D49 | E Kharkov |
| 2TE10M | 2 × Co-Co | 2 × 2,200 | 100 | 2 × 138 | 10 | 1981 | Lugansk | 10D100 | E Kharkov |
| 2TE10U | 2 × Co-Co | 2 × 2,200 | 100 | 2 × 138 | 14 | 1990 | Lugansk | 14D40 | E Kharkov |
| 2M62 | 2 × Co-Co | 2 × 1,270 | 100 | 2 × 120 | 42 | 1976 | Lugansk | 14D40 | E Kharkov |
| 2M62U | 2 × Co-Co | 2 × 1,270 | 100 | 2 × 126 | 30 | 1988 | Lugansk | 14D40 | E Kharkov |
| M62 | Co-Co | 1,270 | 100 | 119 | 33 | 1965 | Lugansk | 14D40 | E Kharkov |
| ChME3 | Co-Co | 993 | 95 | 121 | 58 | 1964 | ČKD | K6S310DR | E ČKD |
| TEM2 | Co-Co | 882 | 100 | 120 | 7 | 1960 | Bryansk | PD1M | E Kharkov |
| TGM3 | B-B | 550 | 30/60 | 68 | 2 | 1959 | Ludinovo | M753 | H Kaluga |
| **750 mm gauge** | | | | | | | | | |
| TU2 | Bo-Bo | 240 | 50 | 32 | 2 | 1958 | Kaluga | 1D12 | E Dinamo |
| TU7 | B-B | 294 | 50 | 24 | 2 | 1988 | Kambarka | 1D12 | H Kaluga |

### Improvements to existing lines
An Infrastructure Improvement Study was commissioned by the European Union towards the end of 1997, aimed at identifying bottlenecks in the existing rail network, and in particular those parts affecting the east-west transit corridor. Following this study, in late 1998 LDZ was lent US$41 million by the European Investment Bank to upgrade some 300 km of single track between the Russian border and Latvian ports to provide additional capacity. A second loan of US$20 million from the European Bank for Reconstruction and Development was to finance LDZ's new marshalling yard at Jūras Parks (Sea Park) and a northern rail bypass for the port of Ventspils.

In 2002, EU ISPA was to allocate funding to modernise signalling and hot box detection systems in the east-west corridor and for the construction of a new reception yard at Rèzekne II station, where east-west and north-south corridors cross.

A US$6 million project to refurbish Riga's main station was started in 1998 by a Latvian-Norwegian joint venture company, Linstow Varner. The first phase of this project was completed in June 2001.

### Traction and rolling stock
Outside the Riga suburban system, trains are diesel-hauled. The decline in traffic has prompted withdrawal of older locomotives, with all remaining steam locomotives scrapped or sent to museums and many diesel locomotives taken out of service.

At the start of 2002 the broad-gauge fleet comprised 219 diesel locomotives, 150 dmu cars and 245 emu cars (180 Type ER2 and 65 Type ER2T units). There were 265 passenger coaches (including 15 dining, 124 sleeper and 109 couchette cars) and 6,185 freight wagons.

### Signalling and telecommunications
Automatic block signalling systems cover 1,046 km of LDZ's network, including 698 km on lines equipped with centralised traffic control (CTC) systems; the 'Minsk' CTC system covers 81 km, the 'Neva' 431 km and the 'PChDC' 186 km. Semi-automatic block systems cover 942 km.

Various types of relay-based interlockings are installed at 161 of LDZ's 178 stations, operating 2,631 electrically locked sets of points. In June 2001, LDZ commissioned its first electronic interlocking, of the Ebilock-950 type. One of the largest of its type in Europe, this was supplied by Adtranz Signal (now Bombardier Transportation) and controls movements at Riga passenger station and at Tornakalns.

LDZ's telecommunications network consists of 555 km if fibre-optic cables with STM-1 and STM-4 SDH equipment, 500 km of microwave radio lines and 300 km of HDSL 2 Mb lines using copper cables. The telephone network has 114 exchanges supplied by Nortel.

### Diesel railcars or multiple-units

| Class | Cars per unit | Motor cars per unit | Motored axles/car | Power/motor kW | Speed km/h | Cars in service | First built | Builders Mechanical | Engine | Transmission |
|---|---|---|---|---|---|---|---|---|---|---|
| DR1A | 3/6 | 1 | 2 | 735 | 120 | 98 | 1973 | Riga | M756 | H Kaluga |
| DR1P | 3/6 | 1 | 2 | 735 | 120 | 21 | 1973 | Riga | M746 | H Kaluga |
| DR1Am | 3 | 1 | 2 | 745 | 120 | 30 | 1997* | Riga | MTU | H Voith |
| AR2 | 1 | 1 | 2 | 320 | 120 | 1 | 1997 | Riga | NTA855R4 | H Voith |

* Rebuilt from Class DR1A

### Electric railcars or multiple-units

| Class | Cars per unit | Motor cars per unit | Motored axles/car | Output/motor kW | Speed km/h | Cars in service | First built | Builders Mechanical | Electrical |
|---|---|---|---|---|---|---|---|---|---|
| ER2 | 4-8 | 2-4 | 4 | 200 | 130 | 180 | 1962 | Riga | Riga |
| ER2T | 4-8 | 2-4 | 4 | 235 | 130 | 65 | 1987 | Riga | Riga |

### Track
**Rails:** 75, 65, 50, 43 kg/m; 65 and kg/m is the most common, covering 1,572 km
**Sleepers:** Wood (2,750 × 180 × 250 mm), concrete (2,700 × 300 × 219 mm)
**Spacing:** 1,840/km in plain track, 2,000/km on curves
**Fastenings:** screw types: KB, W-14, SB-3, KD
**Min curve radius:** 200 m
**Max gradient:** 1.4%
**Max axleloading:** 23.5 tonnes

*UPDATED*

# LEBANON

## Office des Chemins de Fer et du Transport en Commun (CEL)

PO Box 11-0109, 1107-2010 Beirut
Tel: (+961 1) 44 21 98  Fax: (+961 1) 44 70 07

### Key personnel
President and Director General: Radwan Bou Nasreddine
Chief of Traffic and Operation: Faouzi Kharboutly
Chief of Traction and Rolling Stock:
  Ing Ahmad Abded Aziz
Chief of Track and Structures: Ing Sayed Aouad
Chief of Finance: Gabriel Menassa
Head of Accounts: Carlos Maamari
Head of Administration: Fahed Choueiri
Chief of Stores: Fadi Baini
Chief of Personnel: R Chedid

Gauge: 1,435 mm; 1,050 mm
Route length: 319 km; 82 km

### Organisation
The hostilities that ravaged the country during the 1980s affected the railway very severely and major parts of the system became unusable. The only services to have operated in recent years are short suburban service in Beirut operated with railbuses, and oil traffic south from Beirut to Saida. By 1999, these had been suspended.

Proposals developed during the early 1990s by French consultants Sofrerail to upgrade and electrify the Beirut–Tripoli line and to restore services on the line to Akkari in Syria have not been pursued.

In April 2001, the Czech consultancy firm Sudop Praha completed a study into rehabilitation of the section of line between Tripoli and Jôunié, north of Beirut.

In 2001 it was reported that tenders had been invited for the supply of rails for the reconstruction of the line from Beirut to the Syrian border.

*UPDATED*

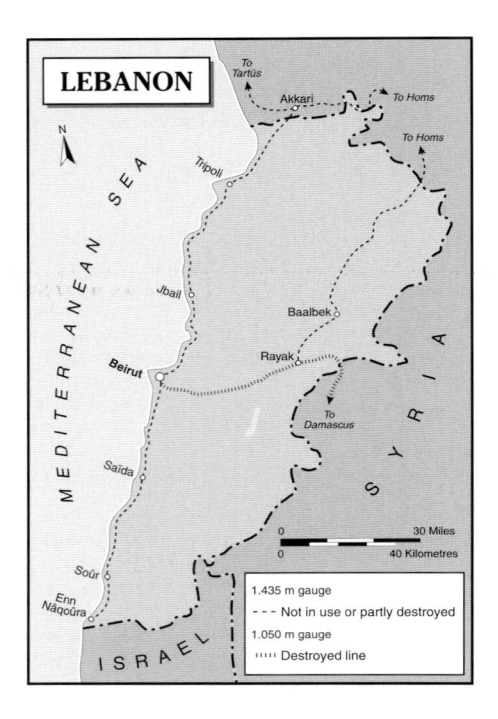

0058564

# LIBERIA

## Introduction
There are three railways in Liberia, all originally constructed for iron ore transport. After several years of civil war, there is no report that any of the three are in operation.

## Bong Mining Company

PO Box 538, Monrovia
Gauge: 1,435 mm
Length: 78 km
At the start of the 1990s, before the onset of civil war, annual freight traffic grossed 6.7 million tonnes and 860 million tonne-km.

## Lamco Railroad
Roberts International Airport
Gauge: 1,435 mm
Route length: 267 km

### Organisation
Lamco, the Liberian American-Swedish Minerals Company, is an iron ore mining company which mined at Nimba and Tokadeh. The railway served principally to move ore, latterly amounting to some 6.5 million tonnes annually, from these mines to the deep water port in Buchanan. There were 24 diesel-electric locomotives and 545 wagons. Operations ceased in 1989.

## National Iron Ore Company Ltd

PO Box 548, Monrovia
Gauge: 1,067 mm
Length: 145 km

### Organisation
The railway was opened in 1951. It operated 12 diesel locomotives, 253 ore and 28 other wagons. Annual traffic before the civil war totalled approximately 1 million tonnes.

## LIBYA

### Department of Communications

PO Box 14527, Bab Ben Ghashir, Tripoli
Tel: (+218 21) 499 32   Fax: (+218 21) 401 06

**Key personnel**
Director General: Izz Al-din Al-Hinshiri
Director, Railways: Eng Alaeddin Al Weyfati

### Railways Executive Board

PO Box 41748, Al Khames
Tel: (+218 21) 361 37 97; 360 94 85
Fax: (+218 21) 360 94 85
e-mail: genmana@libyanrailways.com
Web: http://www.libyanrailways.com

**Key personnel**
Chairman: Eng Mohammed Abdulssamed Ali
Director, General Affairs Office: Ali Mohammed Gholeh
General Managers
  Engineering Administration: Eng Abu Bakr Saeed
  General Administration of Materials:
    Eng Youssel Abdalla Al-Kabir
  Administrative and Financial Affairs:
    Mohammed Abdalla Al-Fitouri
  General Administration and Planning:
    Mohammed Bachir Al-Sayeh
  General Administration, Training and Operations:
    Eng Zayed Ali Al-Ghzeioui

**Political background**
With the dismantling of the British projection of 1,435 mm gauge from Egypt to Tobruk laid in the Second World War, no railways have run in Libya since 1965. Also discarded is the 950 mm system built around Tripoli and Benghazi on the eve of the First World War.

The present government, however, has revived plans to build a new 1,435 mm gauge system comprising a line along the Mediterranean coast from the Tunisian frontier via Tripoli to the Egyptian frontier and a line south from Surt to Sebha, in the heart of a mineral resource area.

In 1992 the General Projects Office was established to take forward plans to develop the system and in 2000 this organisation became the Railways Executive Board. In March 2000 the Board signed a contract with the China Civil Engineering Construction Corporation (CCECC) to build the first phase of the network, from Ras Ajdir to Tripoli. This followed the establishment in 1998 of a joint Libyan-Chinese committee to oversee initial stages of the project.

Arrangements for operating the new railway remain to be decided, with concessioning stated to be one possible option.

In late 2000 the Board employed some 750 staff.

**New lines**
Current plans foresee an eventual network of 3,170 km comprising: a 2,170 km line from Ras Ajdir, at the Tunisian frontier, eastwards via Tripoli, Benghazi and Tobruk to make a connection with the Egyptian system at Musa'id; and a line of some 1,000 km south from Surt via Waddan to Sebha, with a branch westwards to Tarot. A total of 96 stations will be provided.

The coast line is expected to carry both passenger and freight traffic, especially agricultural and petroleum products, while the line to the south will primarily carry iron ore from the Sebha area to a steelworks at Misratah, east of Tripoli.

The contract signed in 2000 with CCECC, valued at US$477 million, covers construction of the first section of the network, a 163 km line from Ras Ajdir to Tripoli and a 28 km link to the capital's port area. The contract also covers maintenance of the line for two years after its completion. The line is to be provided with 16 stations and will be laid with UIC 54 continuous welded rail on concrete sleepers. It will feature 45 bridges but no tunnels.

Construction of the network is being divided into four sectors, with the Ras Ajdir–Tripoli line forming part of the first sector, which covers the section from the Tunisian frontier to Surt. In 2001 site preparation work had been completed and construction of this sector was in progress, with completion expected by 2003 at an estimated cost of US$10 billion. The remaining sectors cover: Surt–Benghazi; Benghazi–Musa'id; and Surt–Sebha. On the Benghazi–Musa'id section preparatory work was in progress between Tobruk and Musa'id in 2000.

**Traction and rolling stock**
The Railways Executive Board has estimated that it will require 244 diesel locomotives and some 8,600 passenger and freight vehicles to equip the complete network.

**Signalling and communications**
Tenders for equipping the system call for CTC, colourlight signalling and automatic train control. Radio communication between train and control centre is also called for, together with a fibre optic telecommunications system.

*UPDATED*

---

## LITHUANIA

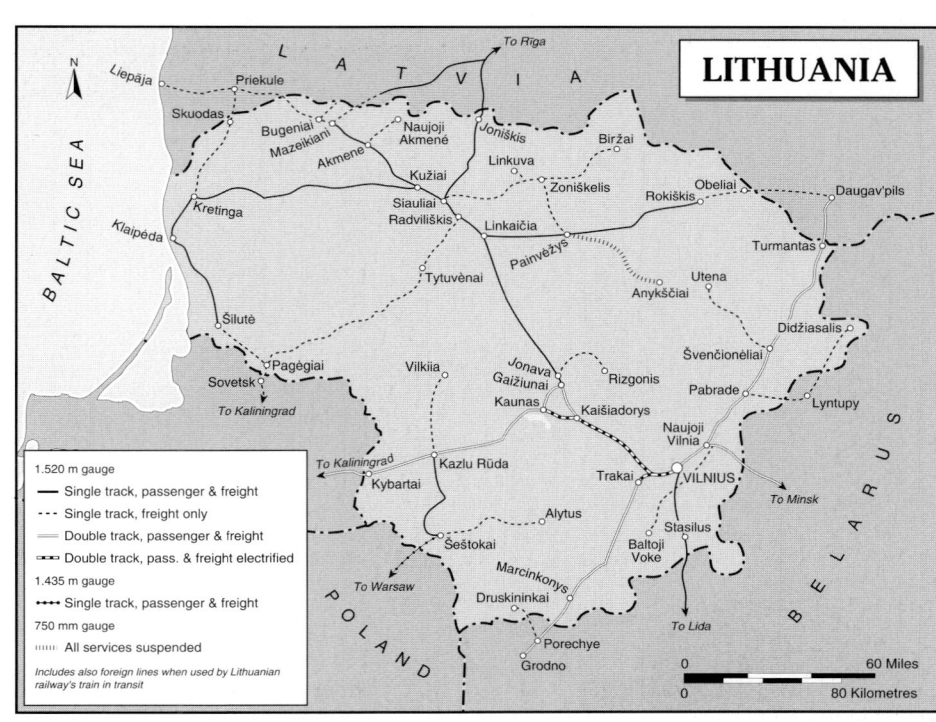

### Ministry of Transport

Gedlimino 17, Vilnius 2679
Tel: (+370 2) 62 14 45   Fax: (+370 2) 22 43 35

**Key personnel**
Minister: Gintaras Striaukas
Director of Rail Transport: A Zubkevicius

### Lithuanian Railways (LG)

Lietuvos Geležinkeliai
Mindaugo 12-14, Vilnius 2600
Tel: (+370 2) 69 20 38   Fax: (+370 2) 61 83 23
e-mail: lr-24@litrail.lt

**Key personnel**
Director General: K Dirgela
First Deputy Director General: V Kuzabavičius
Reforms and Estate Director: Vytautas Jaržemskis
Operations Director: V Vizbaras
Managers
  Reform and Development: Alfredas Zubkevičius
  Passenger: S Pieslikas
  Freight: Rimvydas Valys
  Rolling Stock: S Razgus
  Economics: A Špuraite
  Signalling and Power Supply: Romanas Račas
  Infrastructure: A Panavas
  Legal and Real Estate: Saulius Braziulis
  Personnel: L Apulskis
  Legal: L Sarkisianc
  International Relations: Helma Jankauskaite
  Chief Safety Inspector: V Ramonas
Tel: (+370 2) 69 26 18   Fax: (+370 2) 22 34 62

Gauge: 1,520 mm; 1,435 mm; 750 mm
Route length: 1,807 km; 22 km; 169 km
Electrification: 122 km at 25 kV 50 Hz AC

**Political background**
The independent transport system of Lithuania was re-established at the break-up of the USSR in 1991, when sea, air and railway transport were transferred to the Ministry of Transport of the Republic of Lithuania.

Early in 1994, the Lithuanian government approved the National Transport Development Programme up to 2010, and later the same year, it approved the schedule for the implementation of its main points for the period of 1995-1997. These included integrating the national transport system into the Western European transport network and market, and retaining the traditional transport relations with CIS countries; harmonising the fundamental transport law to comply with the transport legislation and standards of the European Union and other western countries; making available funding for investment from public funds; breaking up of state-owned monopolies and privatisation of the state transport sector providing commercial services; and promotion of private investment in the transport sector.

Relations with neighbouring countries, particularly Russia, are of paramount importance since domestic traffic accounts for less than 10 per cent of the total freight volume in tonne-km. Despite signing a regional traffic protocol in 1994, Russia is actively seeking alternative sea

# RAILWAY SYSTEMS/Lithuania

and land routes to the Kaliningrad enclave which would bypass Lithuania.

The principle of organisational separation of infrastructure and open access was incorporated in the 'Code on Railway Transport' issued in June 1996, which effectively incorporates the terms of the European Union Directive 91/440.

A European Union Phare-financed project to assist LG in the necessary restructuring process and preparation for implementation of 91/440 started in 1998.

## Finance

Losses on LG have continued from previous years, though at a reducing rate. The 1996 deficit of US$1.68 million led to some line closures and withdrawal of passenger traffic.

## Passenger operations

A generally efficient network of express buses, using an upgraded road infrastructure, has reduced rail passenger traffic significantly since independence. Other than the small electrified suburban network around the capital Vilnius and the link to Kaunas, all passenger services are diesel-worked, the majority in a fleet of ageing dmus built by Ganz of Budapest and RVR of Riga. Passenger numbers continue to decline, the 1996 total of 13.2 million being 13 per cent lower than the previous year, while the figure declined again in 1997 to 11.3 million although recovering to 11.5 million in 1999. A residual passenger service is also still operated over the 56 km 750 mm gauge line between Panevežys and Anyksciai.

International passenger traffic has also declined significantly, the former through daily Tallinn–Warsaw train now operating on alternate days only, with a change of train necessary at the gauge-change station Sestokai. Only one through train, operating overnight, remains to connect Vilnius with the Latvian capital Riga.

## Freight operations

In 1998 LG freight traffic improved, though still very low compared with the pre-independence levels. Some 30.9 million net tonnes were moved, with 8.27 billion tonne-km, showing an increase over the 1995 levels of 26.0 million and 7.69 billion respectively. There was a further decline in 1999 to 28.3 million tonnes and 7.8 billion tonne-km. There have been some increases in transit traffic, affecting particularly the throughput of the ice-free port of Klaipeda.

The operations at Klaipeda have seen significant changes since the rail ferry service to Mukran in the then German Democratic Republic were inaugurated in 1986. The dedicated rail ferry service to Mukran has been replaced by a combined ro-ro road/rail operation using one Lithuanian and one German ferry, and additional ro-ro road-only services also operate to other ports in Germany, Denmark and Sweden. In 1996, the total of 22,259 rail wagons moved can be compared with 54,638 unaccompanied road semi-trailers and 28,943 road lorries.

Most of the non-domestic rail traffic is interchanged with other former USSR railways, particularly operating in the east-west direction. North-south international traffic is much less important, the major interchange point being at Sestokai with the Polish (PKP) system, where a change of gauge takes place. There are plans to extend the standard gauge within Lithuania as described below.

*Vilnius station, with ER9M emu* (Norman Griffiths)

*Class M62 diesel locomotive in passenger service at Vilnius* (Norman Griffiths)

### New lines

A Government Decree issued in October 1997 plans the construction of a standard-gauge (1,435 mm) line from the Polish border, for a distance of 86.5 km via Mariajampole to Kaunas, Lithuania's second city. Here, it is planned to establish a common border station, a freight distribution centre and automatic gauge-changing facilities. The current plans do not envisage the line running to the centre of Kaunas, but rather to a road/rail interchange at Rokai on the southern outskirts. Construction is scheduled for the period 2001-2003 at an estimated cost of Ecu220 million. The scheme is expected to be funded by a combination of state, European Union and, in the case of the planned freight terminal, private-sector sources.

Further extension of the line towards Riga and possibly Tallinn is also seen as a long-term objective despite a marked lack of enthusiasm in Latvia and Estonia, both of which see their future traffic potential being firmly on the east-west axis rather than north-south.

### Improvements to existing lines

An extensive programme of track renewal is in progress, which is expected to be completed by 2000. In addition, European Investment Bank funding of US$44 million, to upgrade some 81 km of deteriorating rail infrastructure and signalling equipment, has been agreed for implementation in 1999-2000. The primary objective of the work is to restore the main lines to 100-120 km/h running speeds. By the end of 1998, 215 km of track had already been renewed and five heavy track maintenance machines had been procured.

A high priority is being given to modernising traffic management and telecommunications systems. Communications systems on the Kaišiadorys–Radviliškis line have been modernised with the help of a Danish government loan; a credit from the European Investment Bank is to fund modernisation of signalling on the same section. This scheme will be completed in 2001. During 1999, telecommunications are being renewed on the Vilnius–Kaišadorys and Šiauliai–Radviliškis lines. Work on laying fibre optic cable on the Kazlų–Ruda–Polish border line also started in 1999.

Improvements to border stations aimed at speeding up transit traffic have also been implemented: reconstruction and development of Kybartai station has been started for completion in 2000 and a similar scheme at Kena, funded by the European Union's Phare programme, was due to start in 1999.

Recent developments at Šeštokai (Mockava), terminal point for the standard-gauge line from Poland, include installation of a 40-tonne gantry crane and commissioning of a liquid gas transfer facility, both in 1997. In a bid to

*Class TU2 750 mm gauge diesel-hydraulic locomotive at Panevežys* (Eddie Barnes)

increase its capacity to handle international traffic, LG plans to install an automatic gauge-changing facility at Mockava in 1999.

In the longer term, LG foresees electrification of trunk lines, including Klaipeda–Siauliai–Vilnius and Kybartai–Kaunas–Vilnius and upgrading of the former route for 160 km/h operation. The target date for completion of these works is 2015.

### Traction and rolling stock
At the end of 1998, LG had on its books 199 main line diesel locomotives, 99 diesel shunters, 53 dmus and 16 emus. In addition, one prototype RVR (Riga) single-unit AR2-type railcar was being evaluated. However, a proportion of the book fleet is currently in storage. M62 (54 examples) and 2M62 (101) types formed the bulk of the locomotive fleet. The dmu fleet comprised 42 Class D1 and 14 Class DR1 types, while the emus were of the ER9M type.

At the end of 1998 the passenger coach fleet totalled 245 1,520 mm gauge and 13 750 mm gauge vehicles. DWA (now Bombardier Transportation) at Ammendorf in Germany has supplied a small fleet of long-distance passenger carriages in recent years, and a carriage refurbishment programme was implemented in 1998.

The freight wagon fleet totalled 10,118 freight wagons for 1,520 mm gauge, 50 for 1,435 mm and 267 for 750 mm.

### Diesel locomotives

| Class | Wheel arrangement | Power kW | Speed km/h | Weight tonnes | No in service | First built | Mechanical | Engine | Transmission |
|---|---|---|---|---|---|---|---|---|---|
| **1,520 mm gauge** | | | | | | | | | |
| M62 | Co-Co | 1,470 | 100 | 119 | 54 | 1970 | Lugansk | 14D40 | E Kharkov |
| 2M62 | 2 × Co-Co | 2,940 | 100 | 238 | 101 | 1980 | Lugansk | 14D40 | E Kharkov |
| TEP60 | Co-Co | 2,206 | 160 | 127 | 12 | 1970 | Kolomna | 11D45 | E Kharkov |
| TEP70 | Co-Co | 2,942 | 160 | 129 | 4 | 1993 | Kolomna | 2A-5D49 | E Kharkov |
| L | - | 1,520 | 80 | 124 | 16 | - | - | - | - |
| TEM2 | Co-Co | 883 | 100 | 120 | 56 | 1965 | Bryansk | PD1M | E ETM |
| ChME3 | Co-Co | 994 | 95 | 121 | 41 | 1980 | ČKD | K6S310DR | E ČKD |
| **750 mm gauge** | | | | | | | | | |
| TGK2 | B-B | 169 | 60 | 28 | 2 | - | - | - | H |
| TU2 | B-B | 221 | 50 | 32 | 12 | - | Kambarka | - | H Kaluga |

### Signalling and telecommunications
Centralised traffic control covers 169 km, automatic block 445 km, and semi-automatic block 1,323 km.

### Electrification
25 kV 50 Hz electric multiple-units operate between Vilnius and Kaunas, as well as providing commuter service for Vilnius.

### Track
In 1997, LG issued a tender notice for track renewal and maintenance equipment worth ECU39 billion. Also required were 52,000 concrete sleepers and 53 switches.

**Rails:** UIC 60
**Crossties (sleepers):** Concrete
**Sleeper spacing:** 1,640/km in plain track, 1,840/km in curves
**Fastenings:** Screws/bolts – DO type; in concrete sleepers – KB type
**Min curve radius:** 497 m
**Max gradient:** 1.5%
**Max axleload:** 25 tonnes

---

# LUXEMBOURG

### Ministry of Transport
Boulevard Royal 19-21, L-2918 Luxembourg
Tel: (+352) 478 44 01   Fax: (+352) 24 18 17

**Key personnel**
Minister: Henri Grethen
Director, Rail: Paul Schmit

*UPDATED*

### EuroLuxCargo SA
P O Box 1803, L-1018 Luxembourg
Tel: (+352) 49 90 47 00   Fax: (+352) 49 90 47 09

**Key personnel**
Director: Alex Kremer

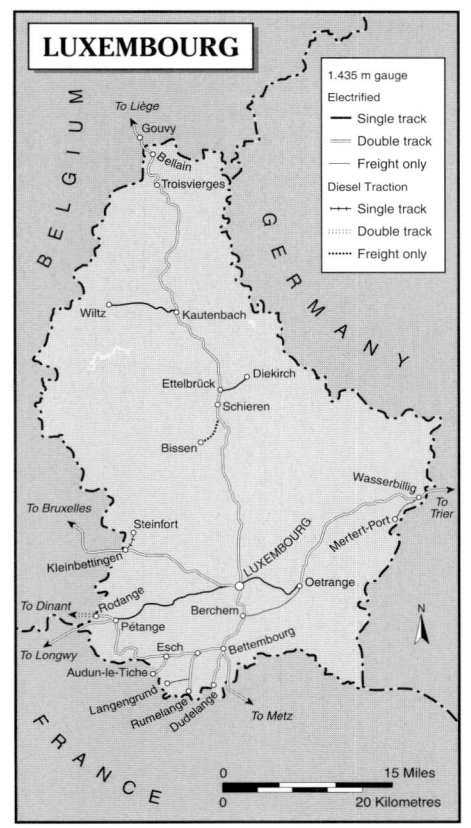

### Organisation
EuroLuxCargo is a subsidiary of Luxembourg Railways (CFL) which in 2001 acquired a minor German railway, the Norddeutsche Eisenbahn Gesellschaft (NEG) that held a licence to operate throughout the country's main line network. The company has taken over from DB Cargo some German freight services around Trier, feeding these into the CFL network at Wasserbillig.

*NEW ENTRY*

### Luxembourg Railways (CFL)
Société Nationale des Chemins de Fer Luxembourgeois
9 place de la Gare, L-1616 Luxembourg
Tel: (+352) 499 01   Fax: (+352) 49 90 44 70
e-mail: info@cfl.lu
Web: http://www.cfl.lu

**Key personnel**
President: Jeannot Waringo
Director General: Alex Kremer
Directors: François Jaeger, Nicolàs Welsch, Marc Wengler
Company Secretary: Edouard Schwinninger
Managers
  Network: Claude Mersch
  Finance: Gilber Schuck
  Operations: Paul Lorang

Traction and Rolling Stock: Marcel Barthel
Fixed Plant and Signalling: Jean-Marie Franziskus
Personnel: Nico Bollendorff
Data Systems: Michelle Hainaux
Passenger Business: Monique Buschmann
EuroLuxCargo: Alex Kremer

Gauge: 1,435 mm
Route length: 274 km
Electrification: 242 km at 25 kV 50 Hz AC; 19 km at 3 kV DC

### Political background
Since its creation, shares in CFL have been owned by the Luxembourg, Belgian and French governments. In 1996, the Luxembourg government increased its stake in CFL from 63.25 to 94 per cent and took over responsibility for the railway's debt as part of a reorganisation plan. The state became sole owner of CFL's infrastructure and the government became responsible for infrastructure maintenance and modernisation. Belgium's share of CFL has fallen from 24.5 to 4 per cent and France's from 12.25 to 2 per cent.

CFL operates bus services which complement the rail network

### Organisation
CFL is directed by a joint board which includes members from the Luxembourg government, CFL, and the French and Belgian governments.

*Class 2100 diesel railcar for local services (Eddie Barnes)*

# RAILWAY SYSTEMS/Luxembourg

CFL is managed in four 'activity units' covering operations, technical, commercial and central services. Apart from these, there are eight subsidiaries, including businesses responsible for tourism, freight, intermodal, wagons, Rhealys (see TGV Est), site development and insurance. In 2001, one of those subsidiaries, EuroLuxCargo, acquired a minor German private railway, Norddeutsche Eisenbahn Gesellschaft (NEG). NEG operates a 4.1 km line near Hamburg but holds operating rights over the entire German main line network.

In 2001, CFL employed 3,158 staff.

## Finance

CFL invested €117.5 million in 2001.

In 2001, CFL revealed details of performance by activity for the first time. While passenger activities were held to be 'in surplus', freight made a loss of €24.6 million.

| Finances (€ million) | 1999 | 2000 | 2001 |
|---|---|---|---|
| **Revenue** | | | |
| Passenger traffic | 25.29 | 27.44 | 29.06 |
| Freight traffic | 83.74 | 89.53 | 91.96 |
| Other* | 114.3 | 134.67 | 161.99 |
| Compensation for public service obligations | 67.97 | 72.23 | 76.17 |
| Other | 36.36 | 37.58 | 52.94 |
| Total | 327.67 | 368.47 | 412.12 |

* Remuneration for management of infrastructure ('Infragrant')

| Expenditure | | 2000 | 2001 |
|---|---|---|---|
| Linked to passenger services | | 10.21 | 10.87 |
| Linked to freight services | | 51.91 | 55.31 |
| Materials | | 21.75 | 20.50 |
| Personnel | | 171.44 | 188.64 |
| Other | | 113.16 | 136.80 |
| Total expenditure | | 368.47 | 412.12 |
| Profit | | 0 | 6.13 |

| Traffic (million) | 1999 | 2000 | 2001 |
|---|---|---|---|
| Freight tonnes | 19.3 | 20.0 | 18.6 |
| Freight tonne-km | 660 | 683 | 634 |

## Passenger operations

CFL no longer compiles annual totals for domestic passenger-km and passenger journeys as it offers only two types of ticket for travel within Luxembourg. These comprise a short-distance ticket and a day ticket valid over the entire CFL network. Passenger counts showed traffic of 300,611 in 2001, up 4.9 per cent on 2000. Of these, 78 per cent were to or from Luxembourg station.

In 2001 domestic passenger revenue rose by 2.9 per cent, while revenue from international traffic rose by 7.2 per cent.

A major promotional relaunch of the railway was initiated in 1992. With the benefit of new emus, passenger services were intensified by some 40 per cent. Passenger numbers rose by 30 per cent from 1991 to 1995. In May 1998, services were again completely recast in an operation known as TAKT 98, with a reinforcement of regular-interval operation on six routes. A new feature was north-south and east-west cross-Luxembourg services timed to interconnect with each other. In June 2001, this system was abandoned. To avoid unreliability on one line transferring to another, routes were split. This also helped match train size to demand. Commuter traffic from countries bordering Luxembourg has grown very strongly in recent years thanks to new season tickets and additional services. In 2001, for example, traffic from Metz grew by 21 per cent and from Longuwy by 346 per cent.

There are five main international services serving the country: Brussels–Luxembourg–Strasbourg–Basle–Italy; Luxembourg–Metz–Paris; Luxembourg–Metz–Nancy; Luxembourg–Trier; and Luxembourg–Liège.

*Cross-border improvements*
Electrification of the 'Athus–Meuse' line in December 2002 (see 'Electrification' below) will allow most freight services to be diverted away from the direct Namur–Luxembourg line via Libramont. Following this, CFL and SNCB wish to invest in upgrading the line to bring down the Luxembourg–Brussels journey time which is currently 2 hours 27 minutes at best for 234 km.

CFL is to acquire 12 double-deck emus in common with SNCF for services to Metz and Nancy.

In May 2000, SNCB Type AM96 air conditioned emus were introduced on the Brussels–Luxembourg service.

The Luxembourg–Paris service will be significantly accelerated in 2006 thanks to the new TGV Est Européen line (see section on France).

*Alstom-built Class 3000 electric locomotive with a Liège–Luxembourg intercity service at Schieren (John C Baker)*

*LRT proposals*
Proposals for a light rail scheme employing on-street operation in the city centre and CFL tracks beyond have been deferred following changes in government in Luxembourg.

## Freight operations

CFL freight traffic fell by 7.2 per cent in 2001, although revenue rose by 2.6 per cent. The Luxembourg steel industry generates 36 per cent of all CFL freight traffic. The nature of this traffic has changed due to conversion to electric furnaces. Transport of traditional, heavy raw materials including iron ore, coke, limestone and fuel oil in block trains has to some extent been replaced by the movement of the new raw material, scrap metal, in wagonload services and traffic in semi-finished products. Transit traffic is now the most important sector, generating 43 per cent of traffic. However, in 2001 this fell by 15 per cent, mainly due to a long strike by SNCF personnel.

On 14 January 1998, Luxembourg became the control centre for the newly created international 'freight corridor' from Muizen in Belgium via Namur, Luxembourg, Metz and Dijon to Milan and Gioia Tauro, Italy and via Marseille, France to Barcelona, Spain. The corridor was used by an average of 110 trains per month in 2000.

EuroLuxCargo (see Organisation) has used its licence to operate in Germany, feeding traffic into the CFL network at Wasserbillig.

## Intermodal operations

Transiting intermodal traffic has increased considerably in the last decade, Luxembourg being situated on the main Rotterdam/Antwerp–Switzerland–Italy route.

The Bettembourg terminal is being developed as an international intermodal traffic hub and offers connections to Germany, France, Switzerland, Italy and Spain. Most of the intermodal traffic is generated by the ports of Rotterdam and Antwerp, and Milan.

## New lines

In September 1992 the Transport Ministers of France and the Grand Duchy signed an agreement guaranteeing that Luxembourg would be served by TGV Est Européen trains when that French high-speed line becomes operational. Luxembourg will contribute €67 million to the cost of a spur from TGV Est Européen at Beaudrecourt. Luxembourg will get four daily TGV services from Paris and – when TGV Est Européen is extended that far – one from Strasbourg. From 2006, Luxembourg will be 2 hours from Paris compared with 3 hours 30 minutes in 2001.

The Transport Minister has suggested that over the 16 km between the French frontier and Luxembourg City, where the existing double track is already heavily occupied, a third track should be added for TGVs. It could be arranged for a higher speed than the 140 km/h maximum of the present double track without incurring insupportable civil engineering costs.

CFL is part of Rhealys, the joint venture which will operate international TGVs on the Est Européen high-speed line.

## Improvements to existing lines

In September 1994, a new single-line chord was opened at Aubange near the frontier between Belgium and

*2,650 kW diesel-electric locomotive, one of six on hire to CFL from Siemens Dispolok, photographed at Oetrange (David Haydock)*

Luxembourg which allows freight trains from the Namur–Bertrix–Virton line to run directly to Rodange instead of locomotives turning round at Athus. This streamlined operations in the south of the country and means that Belgian locomotives now operate regularly over the Pétange–Bettembourg line.

CFL and DB AG are studying access from Luxembourg to the future Frankfurt–Cologne high-speed line. Initial conclusions suggest that tilting rolling stock will be required, as well as significant improvements to infrastructure.

### Traction and rolling stock

In mid-2001 CFL operated 30 electric, 18 line-haul (plus six on hire) and 27 shunting diesel-electric locomotives, 11 diesel tractors, six diesel railcars, 32 emu sets (62 cars) plus two Belgian three-car emus used on the Brussels service and two two-car dmus maintained by DB, 76 passenger coaches (including 16 Corail coaches of the SNCF-CFL pool) and 2,821 freight wagons.

In December 1995, CFL and SNCB ordered 80 5,000 kW dual-voltage locomotives with three-phase asynchronous AC motor drives from Alstom. This pool of locomotives will be jointly operated, mainly on freight over the Antwerp–Luxembourg–Metz (France) route (see 'Electrification') via the to-be-electrified 'Athus–Meuse' line and passenger/freight on the Luxembourg–Liège line. CFL's share of the fleet is 19 Class 3000 locomotives. All CFL and SNCB locomotives were in service by early 2002.

CFL owns two SNCB Type AM80 three-car emus as its contribution to Brussels–Luxembourg services. The stock is maintained in Belgium. CFL also owns two DB Class 628.4 dmus, used in a pool with DB sets on the Luxembourg–Trier service, and maintained by DB.

At the end of 2000, CFL ordered from Alstom six Class 2100 single-unit diesel railcars based on the SNCF Class X73500. They are used on branch lines, releasing emus for busier routes.

In 2001, CFL ordered 12 three-car double-deck emus from a consortium led by Alstom and with significant participation by Bombardier. Based on the TER2N NG design ordered by SNCF, the units are intended primarily for cross-border services on the Luxembourg–Thionville–Metz route. Delivery is scheduled for 2004-2006.

To operate freight services into Germany, CFL has hired six 2,650 kW Type ME26 diesel-electric locomotives from Siemens and equipped five Class 1800 diesel locomotives with DB's standard Indusi driver vigilance equipment. In the longer term CFL is to order new diesel locomotives in common with SNCF. A new maintenance and servicing facility on the site of CFL's Luxembourg depot will eventually replace existing workshops.

**Diesel locomotives**

| Class | Wheel arrangement | Power kW | Speed km/h | Weight tonnes | No in Service | First built | Mechanical | Builders Engine | Transmission |
|---|---|---|---|---|---|---|---|---|---|
| 800 | Bo-Bo | 600 | 80 | 74 | 6 | 1954 | AFB | GM 8-567B | E GM |
| 850 | Bo-Bo | 615 | 105 | 72 | 8 | 1956 | B & L | SACM MGO V-12 SH | E B & L |
| 900 | Bo-Bo | 690 | 105 | 72 | 13 | 1958 | B & L | SACM MGO V-12 SHR | E B & L |
| 1800 | Co-Co | 1,435 | 120 | 110/114 | 18 | 1963 | BN | GM 16-567C | E ACEC/SEM |

**Electric locomotives**

| Class | Wheel arrangement | Output kW | Speed km/h | Weight Tonnes | No in service | First built | Builders Mechanical | Electrical |
|---|---|---|---|---|---|---|---|---|
| 3600 | Bo-Bo | 2,650 | 120 | 84 | 10 | 1958 | MTE | MTE |
| 3000 | Bo-Bo | 5,000 | 200 | 90 | 19 | 1998 | Alstom | Alstom |

**Electric railcars and multiple-units**

| Class | Cars per unit | Motor cars per unit | Motored axles/car | Output/motor KW | Speed km/h | Units in service | First built | Builders Mechanical | Transmission |
|---|---|---|---|---|---|---|---|---|---|
| 250 | 2 | 1 | 2 | 308 | 120 | 6 | 1975 | Carel et Fouché | MTE |
| 260 | 3 | 1 | 2 | 308 | 120 | 2 | 1970 | Carel et Fouché | CEM |
| 2000 | 2 | 1 | 4 | 308 | 160 | 22 | 1990 | De Dietrich | GEC Alsthom |

**Diesel railcars**

| Class | Cars per unit | Motor cars per unit | Motored axles/car | Power/motor kW | Speed km/h | Units in service | First built | Builders Mechanical | Engine | Transmission |
|---|---|---|---|---|---|---|---|---|---|---|
| 2100 | 1 | 1 | 2 | 258 | 140 | 6 | 2000 | Alstom/DDF | - | Voith |

During 2001, CFL increased its wagon fleet by 12 per cent to 330 vehicles.

### Signalling and telecommunications

CFL is pursuing a plan to concentrate signalling of each route on a single centre, supported by the new installation at Luxembourg. Most of the network is currently controlled from five signalling centres.

Following two head-on crashes in 1997, CFL has introduced a simple safety system known as MEMOR II+ to prevent a train passing a red signal. In the longer term, CFL is to be one of the first railways to introduce ERTMS/ETCS.

The SNCF KVB system is to be installed on the Luxembourg–Bettembourg frontier line.

### Electrification

Electrification of Luxembourg's main routes was completed in 1993. Ninety-five per cent of Luxembourg's rail lines are now electrified, all on the 25 kV 50 Hz AC system, except the cross-border line from Brussels and Namur in Belgium which is electrified at 3 kV DC. International expresses travelling between Belgium and France via Luxembourg change locomotives in Luxembourg station. Most transiting freight trains are now hauled by SNCB Class 13/CFL Class 3000 dual-voltage electric locomotives from Belgium to France via Luxembourg.

SNCB completed electrification of the Luxembourg–Liège route in 2000. SNCB is also wiring the 'Athus–Meuse' route from Rodange in Luxembourg via Virton and Bertrix to Dinant at 25 kV 50 Hz AC, to be completed in December 2002.

### Track

**Rails:** UIC 60, 54 and U33
**Crossties (sleepers):** Wood
**Thickness:** 150 mm
**Spacing:** 1,435/km
**Rail fastenings:** 'K' fastenings

---

# MACEDONIA

## Ministry of Transport & Communications

91000 Skopje

**Key personnel**
Minister: Ljupco Balkovski

## Macedonian Railways (MŽ)

Makedonski Železnici
PO Box 543, Železnička 50b, 91000 Skopje
Tel: (+389 91) 22 79 03   Fax: (+389 91) 41 10 21

**Key personnel**
Director General: Živko Gelevski
Assistant Directors General
  Marketing: Panče Kovačev
  Finance: Vera Panova
  Legal Affairs: Ilja Zdraveski
  Traffic: Branko Isijanovski
International Affairs: Kosta Markovski

Gauge: 1,435 mm
Route length: 699 km
Electrification: 233 km at 25 kV 50 Hz

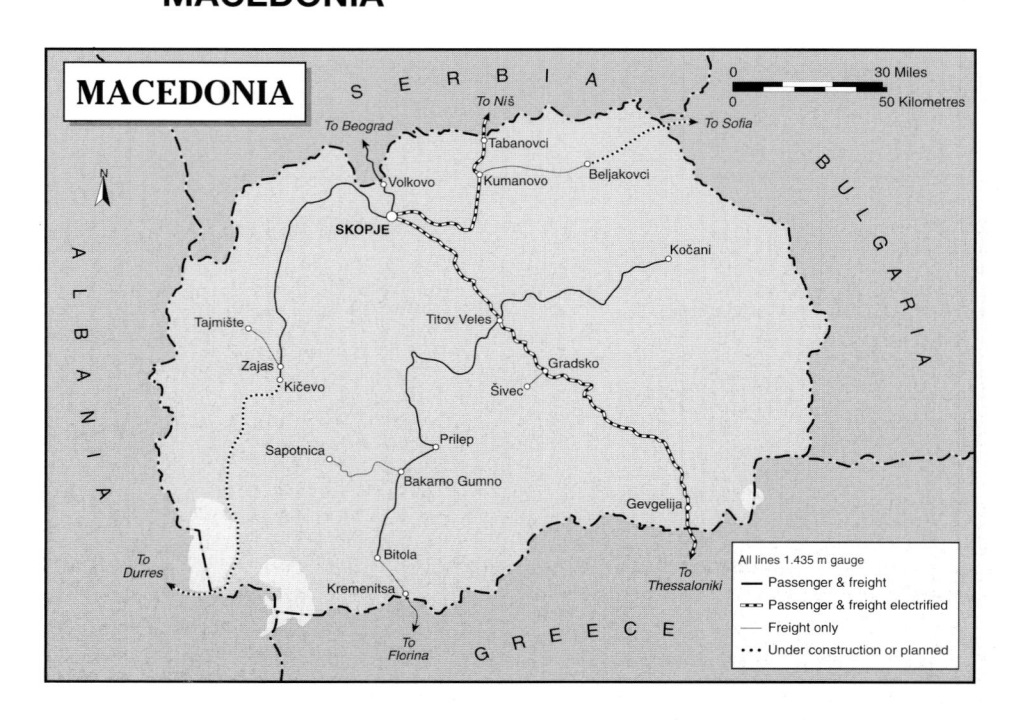

## RAILWAY SYSTEMS/Macedonia—Madagascar

### Political background
MŽ came into being as the result of Macedonia declaring its independence from the former Yugoslavia in 1991. It is a member of the UIC (International Union of Railways) and employed 4,297 staff at the end of 1998.

Part of a US$32 million loan in 1999 from the World Bank was to finance a replacement computer system, modern communications equipment and a radio despatching system for train operations. Also covered by the loan was funding for reorganisation and management training.

### Passenger operations
The most important routes run south from the capital Skopje to Gevgelija (206 km) on the Belgrade-Thessaloniki-Athens route (three pairs of trains a day) and Bitola (229 km, six trains a day).

| Traffic (million) | 1997 | 1998 |
|---|---|---|
| Passenger journeys | 1.712 | 1.715 |
| Passenger-km | 141 | 149 |
| Freight tonnes | 2.101 | 2.694 |
| Freight tonne-km | 280 | 408 |

### New lines
The main line through Macedonia runs from the Greek border in the south to the Yugoslav border in the north. A new east-west line is under construction in the north of the country to complement this north-south line. This route, 56 km in length, will run from Kumanovo to the Bulgarian border. It is eventually intended to form part of an Adriatic to Black Sea through link, from Durrës in Albania to Burgas in Bulgaria; in Macedonia, this will require construction of another new line from Kičevo to the Albanian border.

### Traction and rolling stock
At the end of 1998 MŽ was operating 13 electric and 54 diesel locomotives, four electric and 16 diesel multiple-units, and one diesel railcar. Coaching stock amounted to 169 vehicles, including 18 sleeping cars and 21 couchette cars; there were 2,431 freight wagons.

In 2001-02, the fleet was supplemented by the acquisition of three Class 442 electric locomotives, converted by Končar from former Croatian Railways (HŽ) Class 1141 machines.

### Signalling and telecommunications
Automatic block signalling is being installed on 39 km from Klisura to Gevgelija; it is already in place on a further 172 km between Tabanovci and Gevgelija.

**Type of coupler in standard use:** U-85t

### Track
**Rail:** 30-54 kg/m; 49 kg/m rail is the most common, being installed on 483 km
**Sleepers:** Wooden (1,030,900 installed), concrete (6,300), metal (16,500)
**Sleeper spacing:** 1,660 per km, in plain and curved track
**Fastening type:** K system
**Minimum curve radius:** 250 m
**Max gradient:** 2.6%
**Max permissible axleload:** 22.5 tonnes

*Former Croatian Railways Class 1141 electric locomotive modernised by Končar and now designated MŽ Class 442*　2002/0122618

#### Diesel locomotives

| Class | Wheel arrangement | Power kW | Speed km/h | Weight tonnes | No in service | First built | Builders Mechanical | Engine | Transmission |
|---|---|---|---|---|---|---|---|---|---|
| 661 | Co-Co | 1,434 | 124 | 108 | 29 | 1961 | GM | GM | E EMD |
| 643 | Bo-Bo | 680 | 80 | 65 | 3 | 1967 | B & L | MGO | E B & L |
| 642 | Bo-Bo | 606 | 80 | 63 | 8 | 1961 | Duro Daković | MGO | E Končar |
| 734 | C | 440 | 60 | 48 | 8 | 1960 | MAK | Maybach GT06 | H Voith |
| 732 | C | 397 | 60 | 43.5 | 4 | 1965 | Duro Daković | Jenbacher 600 | H Voith |
| 667 | Co-Co | 882 | 100 | 120 | 2 | 1981 | BMZ SSSR | BMZ | E BMZ SSSR |

#### Electric locomotives

| Class | Wheel arrangement | Output kW continuous/ one hour | Speed km/h | Weight tonnes | No in service | First built | Builders Mechanical | Electrical |
|---|---|---|---|---|---|---|---|---|
| 441 | Bo-Bo | 3,860/4,080 | 140 | 82 | 8 | 1973 | ASEA/Končar | ASEA/Končar |
| 442 | Bo-Bo | 3,860/4,080 | 120 | 82 | 3 | 2001* | Končar | Končar |
| 461 | Co-Co | 5,100/5,400 | 120 | 120 | 5 | 1978 | Electroputere | Electroputere |

* Modernised ex-Croatian Railways locomotives

#### Diesel railcars and multiple-units

| Class | Cars per unit | Motor cars per unit | Motored axles/car | Power/motor kW | Speed km/h | Units in service | First built | Builders Mechanical | Engine | Transmission |
|---|---|---|---|---|---|---|---|---|---|---|
| 712 | 3 | 2 | 4 | 206 | 120 | 16 | 1976 | MACOSA/ Duro Daković | MAN | H Voith |

#### Electric railcars and multiple-units

| Class | Cars per unit | Motor cars per unit | Motored axles/car | Output/motor kW | Speed km/h | Units in service | First built | Builders Mechanical | Electrical |
|---|---|---|---|---|---|---|---|---|---|
| 412 | 4 | 2 | 4 | 170 | 120 | 4 | 1985 | Riga | Riga |

**UPDATED**

# MADAGASCAR

## Ministry of Transport & Meteorology

PO Box 4139, Anosy, Antananarivo
Tel: (+261 2) 246 04　Fax: (+261 2) 240 01

### Key personnel
Minister: Aimé Rakotondrainibe

## Société d'État Réseau National des Chemins de Fer Malagasy (RNCFM)

PO Box 259, 1 Avenue de l'Indépendance, Antananarivo 101
Tel: (+261 2) 205 21　Fax: (+261 2) 222 88

### Key personnel
Director General: R Andriantsoavina
Director of Finance: J C Rajemialisoa
Director of Technical Services: J P Andriantsilavo
Heads of Department
　Human Resources: E Rakotomavo
　Transport: M Rakotomanga
　Studies: J C Rafanomezantsoa
　Engineering: J Rakotondrainibe
　Finance and Accounting: J C Randrianarivelo
　Manpower: S Rakotondravao
　Track and Infrastructure: A B Rabarijoely
　Toamasina Region: P Razafimahatratra
　Timber Impregnation: E Randriantsilany
　Quarry Production: M Rakotomalala
　Inspection: C E Ramaroson

Gauge: 1,000 mm
Route length: 732 km

### Political background
Since 1982, the railway has been established as a state-owned society operating under the country's laws governing limited companies, which allow some independence in commercial policy-making.

Neglect of the infrastructure has left the railway poorly equipped, and there is no foreign exchange available for essential spare parts. Election of a new government on a liberalisation ticket in 1993 led to moves to open railway operations to private contractors, and in 1998 Canadian consultant CPCS Transcom was assisting the government in awarding concessions to operate the northern network. An initial 20-year operation concession was proposed, with possible extension for a further five years under a 'sliding concession' arrangement. Covered by the concession would be operation of rail services, partial renewal and redeployment of existing rail infrastructure, and railway property management. The selection of a successful concessionaire was expected to be made during 1999.

## Principal diesel locomotives

| Class | Wheel arrangement | Power kW | Speed km/h | Weight tonnes | No in service | First built | Builders Mechanical | Engine | Transmission |
|---|---|---|---|---|---|---|---|---|---|
| BB 220 | Bo-Bo | 1,200 | 70 | 58 | 18 | 1973 | Alsthom/SACM | UD 30 V12R5 | E |
| BB 250 | Bo-Bo | 1,600 | 70 | 64 | 5 | 1986 | Alsthom/SACM | UD 30 V16R5 | E |

## Diesel railcars

| Class | Cars per unit | Motor cars per unit | Motored axles/car | Power/car kW | Speed km/h | No in service | First built | Builders Mechanical | Engine | Transmission |
|---|---|---|---|---|---|---|---|---|---|---|
| ZE 800 | 3 | 1 | 2 | 500 | 70 | 3 | 1958 | De Dietrich | MGO V8 | E Alsthom |
| ZE 700 | 4 | 1 | 2 | 900 | 70 | 1 | 1983 | Soulé | MGO V12 | E Alsthom |

## Organisation

The system lies mostly in the central-eastern region of the country. Its northern system comprises three main and two branch lines: the TCE (Antananarivo-Eastern Coast) 371 km, connecting Antananarivo inland with the port of Toamasina (formerly Tamatave); the MLA (Moramanga-Lac Alaotra), which is connected to the TCE at Moramanga and runs 167 km to Ambatosoratra on the shore of Lake Alaotra, the rice-producing region; and the TA (Antananarivo-Antsirabé) serving the high plateau south of Antananarivo (153 km). The branches are: the TWA, running from Antananarivo to the Alarobia industrial area (5 km); and the VMC, which diverges westwards from the MLA line at Vohidiala to Morarano-Chrome (19 km). Construction has started of two further branch lines, Antsirabé-Vinaninkarena and Ambatosoratra-Imerimandroso, but these have not been completed due to a lack of finance.

The southern system consists of one main line, the FCE (Fianarantsoa-Eastern Coast). This 163 km route serves the Fianarantsoa semi-industrial region from Manakara harbour. The FCE has been threatened with closure several times.

The railway suffered serious damage and disruption as a result of three cyclones, Grételle in 1998, and Eline and Gloria in February and March 2000 respectively. While the Toamasina–Antananarivo main line was rebuilt immediately by RNCFM, no government financial assistance was provided for rebuilding the southern line. Here, restoration of the Fianarantsoa–Manakara line was undertaken by volunteers with the help of Swiss Federal Railways and some Swiss regional railway companies, enabling RNCFM to provide at least a minimum level of service.

## Passenger operations

Passenger traffic has declined since 1989 from already insubstantial levels on account of the poor state of the national economy.

| Traffic | 1994-95 | 1995-96 |
|---|---|---|
| Passenger journeys | 536,624 | 338,942 |
| Passenger-km (million) | 21.272 | 18.048 |
| Freight tonnes | 473,249 | 254,264 |
| Freight tonne-km (million) | 78.340 | 43.431 |

## Freight operations

Freight tonnage, which had dipped below the half-million mark for the first time in 1992, reached 506,000 tonnes in 1993. A sharp drop to 254,200 tonnes was reported in 1995.

Rice production was being developed at the northern end of the MLA. In the rainy season road traffic is severely handicapped, so a 35 km rail extension was planned from Ambatosoratra around Lake Alaotra to Imerimandroso to facilitate shipment of rice from the territory. However, due to a lack of finance the project was not completed.

The busiest line is that from Antananarivo to Toamasina, which bears about 85 per cent of RNCFM's traffic but which is now in competition with a recently completed macadamised road and its encouragement of higher capacity road freight vehicles. Freight traffic includes a rising component of containers; a terminal at Toamasina has been complemented by one on the outskirts of Antananarivo at Soanierana.

## New lines

In the south of the country the mountainous territory has extraordinarily rich and very diverse mineral deposits. RNCFM has built a 27 km extension of the TA to a new cement works 1,800 m above sea level in the Ibity mountain massif. The previous government had ordered a feasibility study of an extension of almost 900 km from Antsirabé and Ibity south to Toliara through almost uninhabited terrain, to exploit the barely tapped mineral resources of the area. At last report, 10 km of new line was in place as far as Vinaninkarena. An 8 km stretch of the projected Imerimandroso route is in place to Ambohidava but no work is believed to have taken place on either project since 1987.

## Traction and rolling stock

In 1998 the railway's serviceable fleet comprised 16 diesel locomotives, 29 passenger coaches, three diesel railcars (including one rubber-tyred 'Micheline' dating from the French colonial era) and 610 freight wagons.

## Signalling and telecommunications

With World Bank aid under the Third Railway Project, the MLA line has been equipped with a radio telecommunications system that should greatly improve the efficiency of traffic control and train use in the chrome ore export flow to Toamasina, and in rice movement.

**Type of coupler in standard use:** Freight cars, Willison automatic, Madagascar type; passenger cars, De Dietrich, Soulé

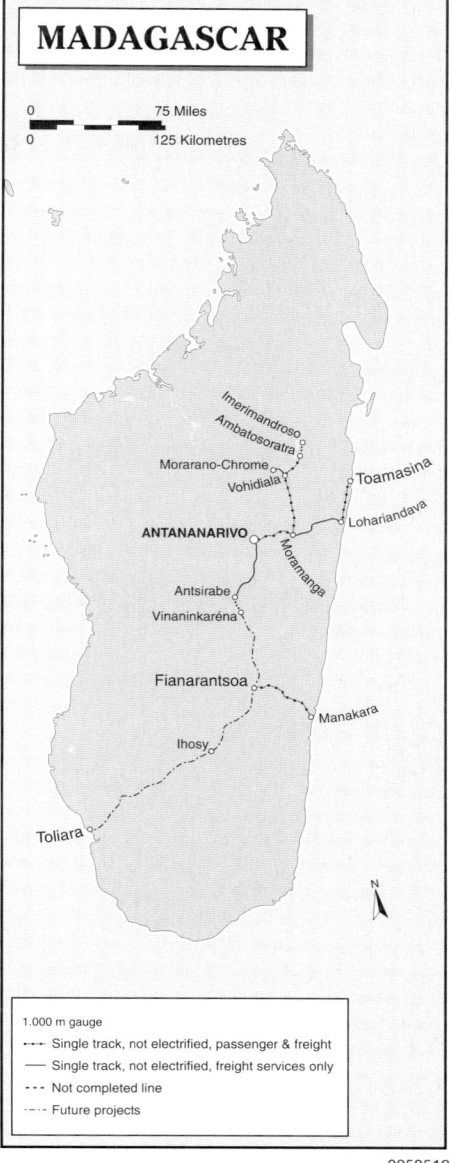

**Type of brake in standard use, locomotive-hauled stock:** Automatic air; direct air; and vacuum

## Track

**Rails:** S25, 26, 30, 36, 30 US, 30 East, 37 English
**Sleepers:** Wood 1,920 × 220 × 150 mm; steel 1,900 × 294 × 147 mm
**Spacing:** 1,666/km wood; 1,500/km steel
**Fastenings:** Screw (wood sleepers); frog (steel sleepers)
**Min curvature radius:** 80 m
**Max gradient:** 3.5%
**Max axleload:** 16 tonnes

---

# MALAWI

## Ministry of Transport and Civil Aviation

Private Bag 322, Capital City, Lilongwe 3
Tel: (+265) 73 01 22  Fax: (+265) 73 38 26

### Key personnel

Minister: Harry Thomson
Principal Secretary: J L Kalemera

For map see **Mozambique** entry.

## Malawi Railways (1994) Ltd

PO Box 5144, Limbe
Tel: (+265) 64 08 44  Fax: (+265) 64 06 83

### Key personnel

Chairman: Dean Lungu
General Manager: E R Limbe
Assistant General Managers
 H T Thindwa, K S J Chenjerani, J A Kazembe
Chief Accountant: M Ndenya
Company Secretary: Vacant
Chief Marketing Manager: T Nnensa
Chief Traffic Manager: M F Mlenga
Chief Mechanical Engineer: H Chimwaza
Chief Engineer (Telecoms and Electrical): M F Kuntiya
Supplies Manager: H P Nyasalu

Gauge: 1,067 mm
Route length: 797 km

### Political background

A major restructuring of the railway was carried out in 1995 under the auspices of the World Bank, and in 1996 the Malawi government invited consultants to advise on strategies for possible privatisation, with the aims of stimulating economic growth, increasing transport sector competition, and reducing government funding pressures.

During 1997, the Canadian-based Hickling Transcom (now CPCS Transcom) consultancy completed a study of the feasibility of privatisation; this led to a call for prequalification bids by early 1998 from organisations interested in taking over an operating concession and in 1999 Mozambique Ports & Railways (CFM) was selected to run the system. Under privatisation proposals,

# RAILWAY SYSTEMS/Malawi—Malaysia

infrastructure would remain government-owned but would be maintained by the concessionaire. Passenger services would be supported by a public service obligation subsidy. Other details of the concession structure remained to be finalised. The confidence of prospective bidders was being raised by indications that the government of neighbouring Mozambique, through whose rail network Malawi traffic must pass for the transport of external trade, was planning to offer concessions to operate its CFM(N) rail network (qv) and the port of Nacala. The Malawi government has also announced that the winning bidder for the Malawi concession would be free to bid for the Mozambique operations, raising the prospects for unified management of the so-called 'Nacala rail corridor'. However, in 1999 the Malawi government was reported to be dissatisfied with the 16 per cent minority shareholding being offered in such a concession by the Mozambique government.

## Organisation
A single-track line runs from Mchinji near the Zambian border through Lilongwe and Blantyre to the southern border with Mozambique. This line connects with the Mozambique port of Beira. A line from Nkaya to Nayuchi on the eastern border with Mozambique connects with the port of Nacala.

Following restructuring, passenger and cargo services on Lake Malawi are now run by a separate company, Malawi Lake Services. These connect with the rail system at Chipoka at the south end of the water.

| Traffic (000) | 1994-95 | 1995-96 |
|---|---|---|
| Passenger journeys | 537 | 339 |
| Passenger-km | 21,272 | 18,048 |
| Freight tonnes | 473 | 254 |
| Freight tonne-km | 78,340 | 43,431 |

| Finance (MK 000) | | |
|---|---|---|
| Revenue | 1994-95 | 1995-96 |
| Passengers | 4,209 | 4,424 |
| Freight | 50,362 | 43,851 |
| Miscellaneous | 78,283 | 10,856 |
| Total | 132,854 | 59,131 |

| Expenditure | 1994-95 | 1995-96 |
|---|---|---|
| Staff/personnel | 78,939 | 19,791 |
| Materials and services | 100,199 | 15,671 |
| Depreciation | 6,199 | 17,422 |
| Financial charges | 7,912 | 3,378 |
| Total | 193,249 | 56,262 |

## Passenger operations
In the early 1990s the railway was handling over 1 million passenger journeys annually. However, this has fallen sharply to around 30 per cent of this level. In the second half of the 1990s just a handful of passenger services remained, with no trains at weekends. Five times a week there is a mixed train between Balaka and Limbe, supplemented by an additional Blantyre-Limbe service on the north-south main line. On the eastern line a twice-weekly mixed train runs between Nkaya and Nayuchi, providing connections with international services to and from Cuamba in Mozambique.

The fall in traffic is attributed to slow journey times due to track conditions, leaving rail vulnerable to strong competition from fast and frequent bus services. Residual train services are mainly patronised by passengers travelling to markets with goods not permitted on buses.

## Freight operations
Traffic has declined since the 1980s, when around 1 million tonnes annually were transported, to a current level of some 300,000 tonnes. Approximately half of this is international traffic. Main commodities carried are cement, grain, fuel products, fertilisers, and tobacco. Consultancy studies suggest that international traffic offers the best growth potential, especially via the Nacala corridor.

## New lines
Proposals exist to develop a line from the Moatize coalfield in Mozambique through Malawi to connect with the existing line to Nacala. This would reach the Malawi system from the west at a point between Blantyre and Nkaya. The still unfinished line from Lilongwe to Mchinji would also be completed and a connecting line would be built westwards from Mchinji to Chipata (27 km) into eastern Zambia. Some earthworks for the Chipata extension were undertaken several years ago but no progress was made after a decision by the Zambian government to transfer track materials to Zambia Railways. However, in 1999 Malawi Railways announced that it intended to resume work on the project.

## Improvements to existing lines
Rehabilitation of the Nkaya-Nayuchi line to the border of Mozambique (44 km) has been undertaken following agreement in mid-1995 of World Bank and USAID credits totalling US$28.6 million. Of the total, US$9.53 million is being spent on track rehabilitation, which includes bridge and structure strengthening, points and crossing work, production of 17,000 sleepers, rental of a track tamper and purchase of gang and inspection trolleys.

*Examples of MR's two locomotive types are seen at Limbe: a recently refurbished MLW (Bombardier) Co-Co dating from 1980 and one of five CMI shunters built in 1993 (Eddie Barnes)* 0023147

### Diesel locomotives

| Wheel arrangement | Power kW | Speed km/h | Weight tonnes | No in service | First built | Mechanical | Builders Engine | Transmission |
|---|---|---|---|---|---|---|---|---|
| Co-Co | 1,120 | 116 | 86 | 12 | 1980 | Bombardier | Alco 8-251-E | E Canada GE |
| C | 380 | 56 | 43.5 | 5 | 1993 | CMI | Cummins KTA 19L | H Twin Disc |

## Traction and rolling stock
The locomotive fleet at the start of 1998 comprised 12 main line diesel-electrics (all now refurbished under a USAID programme), and five diesel-hydraulic shunters. The latter machines were supplied in 1993 by Cockerill Mechanical Industries of Belgium. The rolling stock fleet consisted of 389 freight wagons, 47 engineering service wagons, 29 passenger coaches and one special coach.

**Type of coupler in standard use:** AAR 10 Automatic profile
**Type of brake in standard use:** Vacuum

## Track
**Standard rail:** BSR 30 kg/m, length 12.2 m; BSA 30 kg/m, length 48.8 m; BSA 40 kg/m, length 48.8 m and cwr
**Sleepers:** Timber, steel and concrete

| | Spacing in plain track | Spacing in curved track |
|---|---|---|
| Timber | 1,310/km | 1,476/km |
| Steel (30 kg) | 1,310/km | 1,476/km |
| Concrete | 1,460/km | 1,640/km |

**Fastenings:** Pandrol clips on concrete sleepers, clip and steel key, elastic rail spikes
**Min curve radius:** 111 m
**Max gradient:** 2.27%
**Max axleload:** 15 tonnes (old track) 18 tonnes (new track)

---

# MALAYSIA

## Ministry of Transport

Wisma Perdana, Tingkat 3-9, Jalan Dungun, 50616 Kuala Lumpur
Tel: (+60 3) 254 81 22   Fax: (+60 3) 255 70 41

**Key personnel**
Minister: Dato'Seri Dr Ling Liong Sik
Secretary General: Othman Rijal

*UPDATED*

## Express Rail Link

Express Rail Link Sdn Bhd
25th Floor, Wisma UOAII, 21 Jalan Pinang, 50450 Kuala Lumpur
Tel: (+60 3) 21 64 22 77   Fax: (+60 3) 21 66 70 69
Web: http://www.myERL.com

**Key personnel**
Executive Chairman: Mohamed Nadzmi Mohamed Salleh
Chief Executive Officer: Dr Adnan Aminuddin
Vice-President, Marketing and Sales: Woo Yew Seong

Gauge: 1,435 mm
Route length: 57 km
Electrification: 57 km at 25 kV AC 50 Hz

### Political background
In August 1997 Express Rail Link (ERL) was granted a 30-year government concession, with a 30-year extension option, to design, finance, construct, manage, operate and maintain an express rail system linking Kuala Lumpur Sentral at Brickfields and the city's new international airport (KLIA) at Sepang, south of the capital. Land acquisition for the scheme was undertaken by the Malaysian government. After some delay as a result of regional economic conditions, in October 1998 a DM1.3 billion turnkey contract to build the system was placed with SYZ, a consortium led by the Transportation Systems Group of Siemens AG, which owns a shareholding of 59 per cent, after a financing package was secured from Germany. Construction work is being undertaken by local consortium partner Yeoh Tiong Lay Sdn Bhd (YTL). Operations commenced on 19 April 2002.

## Organisation

Shareholding in ERL, which was formally incorporated on 29 January 1996, is by Tabung Haji Technologies (60 per cent) and YTL Corporation (40 per cent).

Under a contract signed in November 1999, a subsidiary company, ERL Maintenance Support Sdn Bhd (E-MAS), has been established to operate and maintain the system for three years. Ownership of E-MAS is divided between Siemens (51 per cent) and ERL (49 per cent). It is intended that ERL will assume Siemens share of E-MAS after three years of operation of the system. At the start of operation in April 2002, E-MAS employed 327 staff.

## Passenger operations

ERL plans to operate two services: KLIA Express, a non-stop service linking KL Sentral and KLIA, with a journey time of 28 minutes; and KLIA Transit, a commuter service linking the same two points but with additional stops at the three stations listed in 'New lines'. KL CAT, which is located in the KL Sentral development, offers city centre check-in and baggage transfer for departing passengers and a baggage check-out facility for arriving passengers. A service frequency of 15 minutes is provided for 21 hours each day. Revenue operations began in April 2002.

For KLIA Transit, a half-hour frequency is planned, with a 36 minute journey time. Interchange will be made at Bandar Tasik Selatan with KTM Komuter main line services and with the STAR light rail system and with the Putrajaya Monorail at Putrajaya's Western Transport Terminal. At KL Sentral, interchange will be made with KTM Komuter and main line services, the Putra rapid transit system and KL Sentral Titiwangsa services. Commencement of KLIA Transit revenue operations is scheduled for June 2002.

## New lines

The project entailed construction of a 57 km double-track standard-gauge line, electrified at 25 kV AC 50 Hz. The alignment starts at a new Kuala Lumpur City Air Terminal (KL CAT), around 1 km south of the existing main KTM station, and parallels the existing line for some 17 km before diverging south to Sepang. Civil works started in June 1997, and include 39 bridges and three short cut-and-cover tunnels. Three intermediate stations are located at Bandar Tasik Selatan, Putrajaya, and Salak Tinggi. Depot and workshop facilities are located north of the last station. Track and signalling systems have been designed for train operations at speeds up to 160 km/h. Siemens has supplied system engineering services, including power supply, signalling, telecommunications and SCADA systems, as well as providing overall project management.

## Traction and rolling stock

As part of the turnkey contract, Siemens Transportation Systems has supplied 12 four-car articulated emus based on the design of the Class ET 425 vehicles supplied to Deutsche Bahn AG and designated Type Desiro ET. Eight of the units are for KLIA Express services, and feature higher levels of comfort and seating for 156 passengers, as well as a stowage area for baggage containers; the remaining four units are high-density vehicles with seating for 144 but standing capacity for 396 passengers. Body construction is of extruded aluminium sections and all vehicles are air conditioned.

Assembly of the ERL fleet has been undertaken at the Siemens SGP Verkehrstechnik facility in Vienna, with bodyshell components produced at Uerdingen, Germany and bogies coming from Siemens' Graz, Austria plant.

## Signalling and telecommunications

All train operations are controlled by a Traffic Management System (TMS), which has input/output devices in the Operations Control Centre (OCC), located at Salak Tinggi. Trains are driver-controlled under the guidance and control of an Automatic Train Protection (ATP) system.

An optical fibre bearer network centred on the OCC is employed to carry communications functions, including public address, clock and CCTV services. A SCADA system located at the OCC manages the traction power supply system and station infrastructure facilities for the entire network.

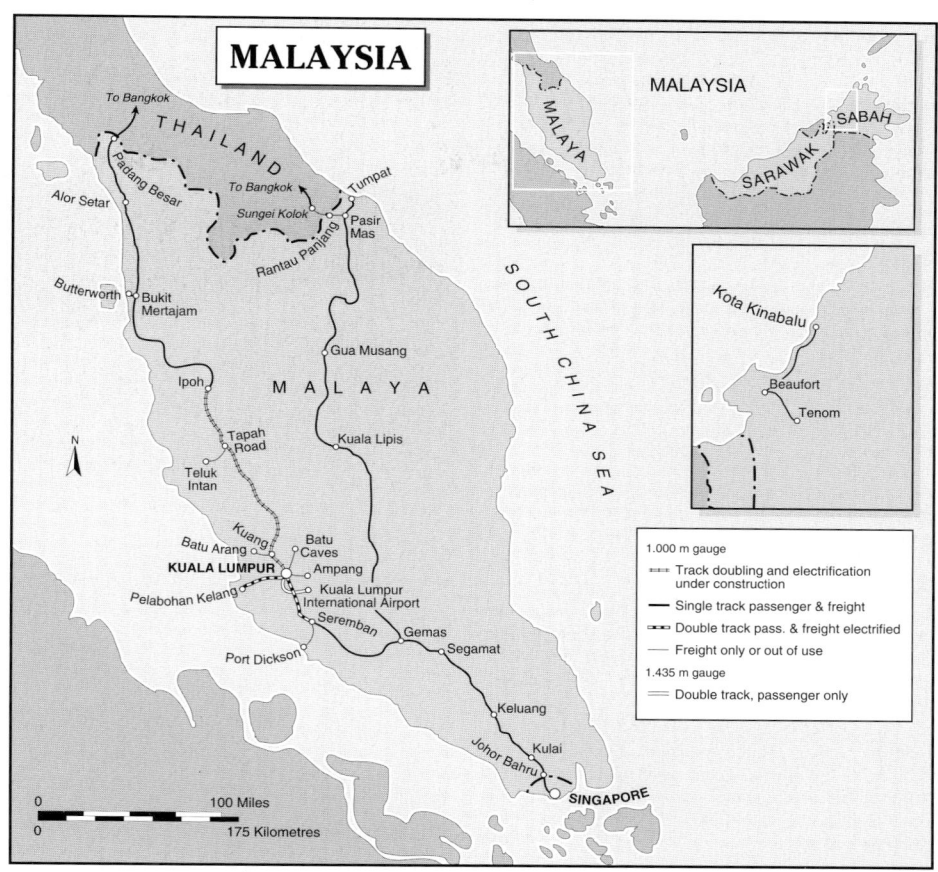

*Siemens-built four-car Desiro ET articulated emu for the KLIA Express airport link*

### ERL electric multiple-units

| Class | Cars per unit | Motor cars per unit | Motored axles/car | Output/motor kW | Speed km/h | Units in service | First built | Mechanical | Electrical |
|-------|---------------|---------------------|-------------------|-----------------|------------|------------------|-------------|------------|------------|
| ERL   | 4             | 2                   | 4(1)              | 225             | 160        | 8                | 2001        | Siemens    | Siemens    |
| CRS   | 4             | 2                   | 4(1)              | 225             | 160        | 4                | 2001        | Siemens    | Siemens    |

Notes
(1) Units are articulated

### Track
**Rail:** UIC 54, continuously welded
**Sleepers:** prestressed concrete monobloc; slab track used in KLIA ERL station

**UPDATED**

---

## Malayan Railway (KTM)

Keretapi Tanah Melayu Berhad
Jalan Sultan Hishamuddin, 50621 Kuala Lumpur
Tel: (+60 3) 274 94 22   Fax: (+60 3) 272 39 36

### Key personnel
Executive Chairman: Tan Sri C Selvarajah
Managing Director: Abdul Rahim Osman
Directors
 Operations and Customer Service: Mohd Zin Yusop
 Special Projects: P Satyamoorthy
 Finance: K Sinnappu
 Corporate Services: Dr Ismail Rejab
 Human Resources: Md Fauzi Hj Said
 Engineering: Haji Mazlan Waad

# RAILWAY SYSTEMS/Malaysia

**General Managers**
- Permanent Way: Z A Salleh
- Fleet Engineering: Madzin Majid
- Signalling and Communications: R Paranchothi
- Human Resources (Services): Abdul Mokti Zakaria
- Human Resources (Training): Khaeruddin Sudharmin
- Safety Operations: S Apputhurai
- Corporate Communications: Hamdan Ahammu
- Training and Development: K Sudharmin
- Traffic Operations: Sarbini Tijan
- Electrification: Dzulkifli Mohd Ali
- Freight Services: Abd Radzek Abd Malek
- Passenger Services: Zainab Hashim
- Commuter Services: Azhar Darus
- Property Management: Mahmud Hashim
- Corporate Planning: Hilmi Mohamad
- Information Technology: Shafiin Yunus
- Finance: Azman Ahmad Shaharbi

Company Secretary: Nor Aida Othman

Gauge: 1,000 mm
Route length: 2,227 km
Electrification: 150 km at 25 kV 50 Hz AC

## Political background

The government has long been seeking to privatise KTM. In early 1998 discussions regarding full privatisation continued between the government and the Marak Unggul consortium, comprising Renong, DRB-Hicom, and Bolton Properties, which had already taken over management control of the railway. Marak Unggul was reported to have commissioned consultants to review all aspects of KTM operations and development projects.

Rolling stock maintenance is now in the hands of a private-sector company, Rail Tech Industries, in which KTM has a 26 per cent holding.

## Organisation

The railway's prime route is the 787 km main line from Singapore north through the capital, Kuala Lumpur, to Butterworth, one of Malaysia's principal sea ports on the west coast of the peninsula. Short branches reach sea ports at Port Klang, Pasir Gudang and Port Dickson. The other major route is the 528 km East Coast line running northwards from a junction with the Singapore-Butterworth line at Gemas to Kota Bharu and Tumpat. Both lines link with the State Railway of Thailand.

At the beginning of 1997 KTM employed 6,300 staff.

## Passenger operations

KTM operates both electric commuter services (branded 'Komuter') around the capital, Kuala Lumpur, and long-distance trains.

Long-distance travel soared spectacularly in the 20 years to 1991, lifting the total of annual passenger-km from 620 million to 1,850 million; thereafter patronage began to fall. Following opening of the North-South Expressway (NSE) road in 1994, passenger-km declined to 1,348 million; in 1995, there was a further fall, to 1,270 million. An encouraging revival to 1,396 million passenger-km (5.9 million passenger journeys) was recorded in 1996.

The stiff competition focused attention on the long-term need to reduce journey times between Kuala Lumpur and Singapore. This will be achieved by the introduction of tilting trains, which were ordered in November 1996 from Fiat Ferroviaria of Italy (see 'Traction and rolling stock' section).

In addition to ordinary train services, KTM operates day and night Singapore-Kuala Lumpur and Kuala Lumpur-Butterworth express trains, and a single daily express between Gemas and Tumpat on the East Coast line. In conjunction with the State Railway of Thailand, KTM runs a daily International Express between Butterworth and Bangkok. All express and night trains on the north-south main line are air conditioned.

Orient-Express Hotels of the UK, operators of the Venice Simplon-Orient Express in Europe, runs a weekly luxury cruise train service, the Eastern & Oriental Express, between Singapore, Kuala Lumpur and Bangkok.

| Traffic | 1994 | 1995 | 1996 |
|---|---|---|---|
| Passenger journeys (000) | - | - | 5,900 |
| Passenger-km (million) | 1,348 | 1,270 | 1,396 |
| Freight tonnes (million) | 5.2 | 5.2 | 5.4 |
| Freight tonne-km (million) | 1,463 | 1,416 | 1,417 |

*Deliveries began in 1997 of 22 three-car emus built by Union Carriage with GEC Alsthom traction equipment* 0010319

### KTM diesel locomotives

| Class | Wheel arrangement | Power kW | Speed km/h | Weight tonnes | No in service | First built | Builders Mechanical | Engine | Transmission |
|---|---|---|---|---|---|---|---|---|---|
| 17 | C | 305 | 56 | 35.6 | 10 | 1964 | KSK | GM 12V-71 | H Niigata |
| 18 | 0-6-0 | 450 | 24 | 46.25 | 10 | 1979 | Brush | MTU 6V 396 TC 12 | E Brush |
| 19 | Bo-Bo | 480 | 78 | 58.4 | 10 | 1983 | Hitachi | MTU 6V 396 TC 12 | E Hitachi |
| 22 | Co-Co | 1,275 | 96.5 | 84 | 38 | 1979 | EE-AEI | EE8CSVT-MK 111 | E EE |
| 23 | Co-Co | 1,610 | 110 | 90 | 15 | 1983 | Hitachi | SEMT/ SP12 PA4V | E Hitachi |
| 24 | Co-Co | 1,790 | 120 | 90 | 26 | 1987 | Toshiba | SEMT/16V-PA4 | E Toshiba |
| 25 | C-C | 1,120 | 107 | 89.6 | 12 | 1990 | GM | EMD 8-645E 3C | E GM |

### Electric railcars or multiple-units

| Class | Cars per unit | Motor cars per unit | Motored axles/car | Output/motor kW | Speed km/h | Units in service | First built | Builders Mechanical | Electrical |
|---|---|---|---|---|---|---|---|---|---|
| EMU | 3 | 2 | 4 | 190 | 120 | 18 | 1994 | Jenbacher | Holec |

## Freight operations

Traffic has remained stable in recent years. Cement is one of the most important commodities carried.

In 1997, Bradford Kendal of Australia was building 500 wagons for KTM, with axles coming from SWASAP in South Africa.

KTM has developed in house and begun to implement a computerised rolling stock control known as SPOT.

## Intermodal operations

Container traffic is a fast-growing business. Begun in 1974, this has become KTM's second biggest freight earner, surpassed only by cement, traditionally KTM's major freight traffic. A significant component of the growth has been containers from southern Thailand, which have a quicker haul across the border at Padang Besar to a Malaysian port than to Bangkok. Around a quarter of southern Thailand's rubber exports are shipped through Butterworth. In April 1999, KTM launched a twice-weekly container landbridge service between Bangkok and Port Klang, providing a journey time of 60 hours.

The government has been promoting intermodal transport, and KTM has formed a wholly owned subsidiary, the Multimodal Freight Company, which has acquired 20 highway tractors and 100 trailers so as to offer door-to-door service. This operates from the inland container depots at Kuala Lumpur, Ipoh, Prai, Port Klang and Padang Besar.

Improvement and expansion of rolling stock has been a recent KTM priority. A further 1,000 TEU of flatcar capacity was added in 1995-96, bringing the total to 3,200 TEU. Structures have been modified to gain clearance for 9 ft 6 in cube containers.

## New lines

A line to the new Kuala Lumpur International Airport is planned (see entry for 'Express Rail Link').

Design and supervision contracts for the construction of a 3 km branch from Butterworth to the port's north terminal were awarded in late 1997.

In 1998, Canadian consultancy Canarail was commissioned by Malaysian oil company Petronas to design an 80 km industrial line from its facilities around Kerteh to the port of Kuantan. Canarail had earlier completed a feasibility study into the project.

In 1999, Ircon International of India was awarded a contract to construct a 34 km line linking Pelabauhan with the new port of Tanjung Pelebas. The project was expected to be completed by the end of 2001.

## Improvements to existing lines

The 787 km Butterworth-Kuala Lumpur-Singapore line is to be upgraded for the introduction of tilting trains. The aim is a 4 hour Singapore-Kuala Lumpur timing. Ircon International of India has completed double-tracking of the Rawang-Seremban line.

The KTM network forms an element of a regional project under discussion by seven ASEAN countries to create a Trans-Asia Rail Link, with an upgrade of existing infrastructure favoured to improve connections with neighbouring Thailand.

## Traction and rolling stock

At the beginning of 1997 KTM's traction fleet comprised 101 diesel locomotives. The passenger stock totalled 359, plus 18 three-car emu trains. Freight stock totalled 3,206 vehicles.

For the Butterworth-Kuala Lumpur-Singapore line improvement project (see 'Improvements to existing lines' section above) in November 1996 KTM ordered seven tilting trains of six cars each from Fiat Ferroviaria of Italy, with an option for a further 15 sets. The trains on option could have as many as 10 cars. The first trains are due to be in service in 1999.

To supplement the 18 emus supplied by Hunslet Transportation Projects/Jenbacher, two further batches of 22 three-car sets each were ordered in late 1995 from Mitsubishi/Hyundai and GEC Alsthom/Union Carriage. Deliveries of both series began in 1997.

Motive power shortages have been alleviated by delivery of 30 Indian Railways' Class YDM4 Co-Cos, hired on a power-by-the-hour basis from Ircon, which is also maintaining the locos with its own staff. There are also four MKA-2000 Co-Cos remanufactured and regauged by Morrison Knudsen Australia; they are English Electric units surplus to Australian National's requirements in Tasmania, which in 1995 were leased to the Malaysian firm Rail Tech Services for use by KTM as required. MKA retains another three such locomotives which are available to be sent to Malaysia if needed.

Ircon has also undertaken refurbishment of 12 Class 22 diesel-electric locomotives, and in 1997 was reported to be negotiating a contract to refurbish and maintain a further 15.

**Coupler in standard use:** Hook and knuckle. Hook couplers are being progressively replaced by the automatic knuckle-type on all wagons; this should permit increases of up to 50 per cent in gross freight train weights.
**Braking in standard use:** Air and vacuum

### Signalling and telecommunications
KTM is modernising signalling and communications on the south main line between Seremban and Johor Bahru. Route relay interlockings at stations and automatic block signalling, when completed, will have the entire distance from Singapore to Ipoh controlled by colourlight signals.

### Electrification
Operation of the country's first electric trains started in 1995 with commissioning of the Kuala Lumpur suburban network. With 25,000 passengers daily being recorded within six months, capacity of the 18 three-car emus very quickly became strained, and a further 44 sets were ordered (see 'Traction and rolling stock' section for details) to cover Kuala Lumpur and the new Johor Bahru services detailed below.

Completion of the scheme saw the launch of an air conditioned commuter emu service on the routes from Kuala Lumpur to Port Klang, Seremban and Rawang. The new emus have cut Kuala Lumpur-Port Klang journey time from 70 to 30 minutes and Kuala Lumpur-Seremban time from 90 to 45 minutes. Especially within the Klang Valley area, operating capacity for freight as well as passenger traffic is markedly improved.

The main line from Butterworth to Singapore via Kuala Lumpur is now being electrified. As a preliminary, the first 60 km of the route from Singapore to Kulai is being energised in a separate project to create an electrified network around the city of Johor Bahru in the far south of the country.

### Track
**Standard rail:** Flat bottom in 12.2 m (40 ft) lengths
**Main line:** 40 and 60 kg/m
**Rail fastening:** Elastic spikes
**Crossties (sleepers):** Malayan hardwoods 242 × 127 × 2,000 mm
**Spacing:** 1,666/km
**Filling:** 6 cm (2½ in) limestone ballast to a depth of 15 cm (6 in) under sleepers
**Max curvature:** 12.25° = radius of 142 m
**Ruling gradient:** 1%; except Taiping Pass 1.25%
**Longest continuous gradient:** 8.2 km on Prai-Singapore main line, with 1.25% grade, sharpest curve 142 m radius for a length of 320 m
**Max altitude:** 137 m near Taiping
**Max axleload:** 16 tons

## Sabah Ministry of Transport and Communications
88999 Kota Kinabalu, Sabah
Fax: (+60 88) 23 98 52

**Key personnel**
Minister: W M Bumburing
Assistant Secretary, Railways: H Gunggut

*Hitachi-built Bo-Bo diesel electric at Tanjong Aru (Eddie Barnes)*  0023148

## Sabah State Railways
Jabatan Keretapi Negeri Sabah
Karung Berkunci 2047, 88200 Kota Kinabalu, Sabah
Tel: (+60 88) 546 11   Fax: (+60 88) 23 63 95

**Key personnel**
General Manager: M T Jaafar

Gauge: 1,000 mm
Route length: 134 km

### Organisation
The railway links Tanjong Aru with Beaufort, running along the coastal strip before climbing inland along the Padas river to Tenom.

### Freight and passenger operations
In 1992 the railway carried 0.4 million passengers and some 2.2 million tonnes of freight, mainly rice, rubber and timber products.

There is a daily return mixed train and several short workings by ancient diesel railcars.

### Traction and rolling stock
In 1992 the fleet comprised 15 diesel locomotives, 21 coaches, 3 diesel railcars and 215 wagons.

# MALI

## Ministry of Public Works and Transport
PO Box 260, rue Baba Diarra, Bamako
Tel: (+223) 22 59 67; 8   Fax: (+223) 22 83 88

**Key personnel**
Minister: Mohammed Ag Erlaf
Director of Cabinet: M Sidibe
Technical Adviser, Railways: M Traore
For map see entry for **Senegal**.

## Chemins de Fer du Mali (RCFM)
PO Box 260, rue Baba Diarra, Bamako
Tel: (+223) 22 59 68   Fax: (+223) 22 59 67

**Key personnel**
Director General: Lassana Kone
Deputy Director General: Hamadoun Assouman Cisse
Directors
 Traffic: Daouda Diane
 Finance: Djibril Nama Keita
 Technical: Tounko Danioko
 Planning: Mady Konate
 Purchasing: Mohamed Traore
 Personnel: Fodé Traore

Gauge: 1,000 mm
Route length: 729 km

### Political background
The governments of Mali and Senegal have retained Canadian consultants CPCS Transcom to assist in the preparation and allocation of a concession to handle international traffic operations on the Bamako-Dakar line. Expressions of interest were being reviewed in early 1998.

### Organisation
The former Dakar-Niger Railway starts at Dakar in Senegal and runs inland via Kayes to the River Niger. The present CF du Mali is that portion of the line inside its territory, the remainder being the CF du Senégal. To give Mali an alternative outlet to the Atlantic, a new line linking Bamako, capital of Mali, with Conakry, capital of Guinea, is planned with a route length of 800 km, of which 600 km will be in Guinea.

At the beginning of 1997 RCFM employed 1,686 staff.

### Passenger operations
In 1996 RCFM recorded 189 million passenger-km and carried 763,000 passengers.

### Freight operations
In 1996 RCFM recorded 256 million tonne-km of freight and carried 574,000 tonnes.

Recovery of a major international traffic role is a prime management objective and this has been recognised in the railway's contract with the government. The latter has proclaimed RCFM to be its main means for spurring development in the west of the country.

### Traction and rolling stock
At the beginning of 1997 RCFM owned 25 line-haul diesel locomotives, 16 diesel-electric railcars and trailers, 41 passenger coaches and 382 freight wagons. The locomotive fleet includes Alsthom Type BB1100, GM Canada CC2200 and Alsthom CC2400 machines.

In common with RCFS of Senegal (qv), RCFM has recently acquired and adapted for metre-gauge 20 redundant French Railways Type B10t passenger cars of the 'Bruhat' type.

## MAURITANIA

### Ministry of Transport

Centre Administratif, Nouakchott

**Key personnel**
Minister: S M Deina
For map see entry for **Senegal**.

### Mauritanian National Railways (SNIM)

PO Box 42, Nouadhibou
Tel: (+222) 574 51 74
Fax: (+222) 574 53 96; 574 90 13; 574 90 27

*Paris office*
SNIM, 7 rue du 4 Septembre, F-75002 Paris, France
Tel: (+33 1) 42 96 80 90   Fax: (+33 1) 42 96 12 26

**Key personnel**
Director General: Mohamed Saleck Ould Heyine
Director of Railway and Port:
   Mohamed Khalifa Ould Beyah
Head of Rolling Stock: Mohamed El Moctar Ould Taleb
Head of Permanent Way: Sidi Ould Sid'Ahmed
Head of Railway Studies: Cheikhna Ould elemine

Gauge: 1,435 mm
Route length: 717 km

**Organisation**
The line, completed in 1963, runs from Nouadhibou to Tazadit for the transport of iron ore from the mines at F'Derik. Built and originally operated by Miferma, the line was nationalised in 1974 and is now operated by Société Nationale Industrielle et Minière (SNIM).

At the beginning of 2001, SNIM employed 1,533 staff.

**Freight operations**
Principal traffic is iron ore, carried in trainloads of 230 wagons grossing around 23,000 tonnes and hauled by three or four locomotives. Three return trips are made daily. Passenger traffic, carried on a daily service between Nouadhibou and Zouerate, is negligible.

| Traffic (million) | 1999 | 2000 | 2001 |
|---|---|---|---|
| Freight tonnes | 10.6 | 11.3 | 10.3 |
| Freight tonne-km | 7,136 | 7,766 | - |

**Traction and rolling stock**
Equipment at the beginning of 2000 consisted of 31 main line diesel-electric locomotives, eight shunting diesel-electrics of 630 kW, 1,177 freight wagons and six passenger coaches. General Motors delivered a batch of five SDL40-2 locomotives in 1997.

**Signalling and telecomunications**
Operations are controlled by manual dispatching with HF and VHF radio.

**Diesel line-haul locomotives**

| Wheel arrangement | Power kW | Speed km/h | Weight Tonnes | No built | First built | Mechanical | Builders Engine | Transmission |
|---|---|---|---|---|---|---|---|---|
| Co-Co | 1,865 | 60 | 138 | 10 | 1961 | Alsthom | SACM MGO V16 BSHR | E Alsthom |
| Co-Co | 2,460 | 60 | 145 | 21 | 1982 | EMD | EMD 645 E3 | E EMD |
| Bo-Bo | 630 | 70 | 73 | 8 | 1961 | B&L | SACM MGO V12 ASHR | E B&L |
| Co-Co | 2,240 | 60 | 145 | 6 | 1994 | EMD | EMD | E EMD |
| Co-Co | 2,240 | 60 | 145 | 5 | 1997 | EMD | EMD | E EMD |

**Track**
Standard rail: 54 kg/m UIC
Welded joints: Practically the whole line was laid with long-welded rails; 8 × 18 m railbars were flash-butt welded at the depot into 144 m lengths, which after laying were Thermit welded into continuous rail. Longest individual length of welded rail is 80 km
Crossties (sleepers): Type U28 steel and timber, weight 75 kg
Spacing: 600 mm
Rail fastening: Clips and bolts to metal sleepers, Nabla ties to timber sleepers
Max curvature: 1.75° = min radius of 1,000 m
Max gradient: 0.63% against loaded trains
   1.3% against empty trains
Max altitude: 400 m
Max axleload: 26 tonnes
Max speed: Loaded trains 50 km/h; empty 60 km/h
Type of signalling: Radio control

*UPDATED*

---

## MEXICO

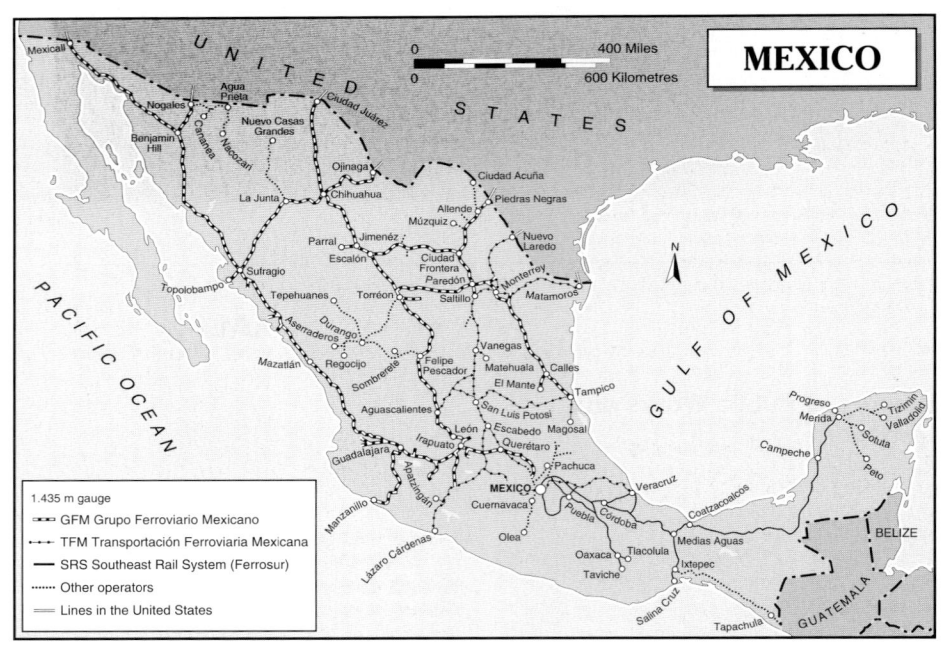

### Secretariat of Communications & Transport

Avenida Universidad y Xola, Col Narvarte, 03028 Mexico City 12, DF
Tel: (+52 5) 519 74 56; 92 03   Fax: (+52 5) 519 06 92

**Key personnel**
Secretary: Carlos Ruiz Sacristán
Under-Secretary: Aaron Dychter

**Organisation**
Overseeing the privatisation of the state railway industry is the Railway System Restructuring Committee, which is chaired by Carlos Ruiz Sacristán. The committee forms part of the overall Inter-Ministerial Divestiture Commission, tasked with disposing of state assets. Representatives from both Mexican railways and the government sit on the committee, with CS First Boston and Banca Serfin acting as financial advisors and Mercer Management Consulting co-opted as primary consultant. These private sector organisations have been valuing assets, overseeing the bidding process and facilitating due diligence financial investigations.

### National Railways of Mexico (FNM)

Ferrocarriles Nacionales de México
Avenida Jesús Garcia Corona 140, Col Buenavista,
Delegación Cuauhtémoc, 06358 Mexico City, DF
Tel: (+52 5) 547 94 58   Fax: (+52 5) 547 06 23

**Political background**
Legislation for FNM privatisation was passed in 1995 as part of a programme to inject some US$12 billion of foreign capital into the economy following the devaluation of the Mexican peso. The process gathered momentum in November 1995 when potential bidders for 50-year concessions to operate freight services were invited to register their interest. The Mexican government was to retain ownership of railway infrastructure, with concessionaires responsible for maintenance and future investment. FNM rolling stock was to be divided between the concessions, with the new operators free to set their own staff requirements and meet them from any source. The government was to continue to meet the costs of some 55,000 FNM pensions and the company's accumulated debt of US$400 million, as well as retaining responsibility for redundancy payments to FNM employees displaced by privatisation.

Given the presence of North American railway companies in the early bids and the lack of interest from potential operators from other parts of the world, political pressure to impose restrictions on foreign bidders resulted in changes to later concession documents.

For the purposes of privatisation, the FNM network was divided into three regional systems, a terminal company serving the Valley of Mexico (greater Mexico City) area and a series of short lines. The regional systems and the Mexico City terminal operation came into being as FNM divisions on 1 January 1996; a fifth division covered the largest short line, the 1,510 km Chihuahua-Pacific network connecting Topolobampo on the Gulf of California with the US border at Ciudad Juárez and Ojinaga.

FNM's principal routes, which carried over 90 per cent of its total freight traffic in 1994, formed the basis of the three regional systems radiating from Mexico City.

The North East network (3,960 km), serving the US border crossings at Nuevo Laredo and Matamoros and the ports of Veracruz, Tampico and Lázaro Cárdenas, generated some 14 billion tonne-km and peso 1.02 billion of

# Mexico/RAILWAY SYSTEMS

revenue in 1994. This network was sold and trades as Transportación Ferroviaria Mexicana (TFM) (qv).

The North-Pacific network (6,200 km) generated some 17.2 billion tonne-km and peso 1.23 billion of revenue in 1994, comprising routes from Mexico City to Nogales and Mexicali via Guadalajara, to Ciudad Juárez via Torreón, and from Torreón to Piedras Negras, Monterrey and Tampico. This network was sold and trades as Ferromex (qv).

Some 3.2 billion tonne-km and peso 0.27 billion of revenue were generated in 1994 by the South East network (2,200 km), linking Mexico City with Veracruz, Coatzacoalcos, Salina Cruz, Campeche and Mérida. The Sureste is Mexico's third most important railway, carrying 9 per cent of the country's rail freight, much of it to the port of Veracruz. Considerable potential exists for growth in container and bulk traffic. The concession was to include an option to acquire the Mayab Railway running from Coatzacoalcos to Mérida in Yucatan. This system was taken over in December 1998 by the Ferrosur (qv) consortium.

In late 1997 the government decided that the 300 km line linking Salina Cruz on the Pacific coast to the port of Coatzacoalcos on the Gulf of Mexico would not form part of the Sureste concession. Ownership would be retained by the state to ensure access by other private-sector rail operators, with the aim of setting up a landbridge alternative to the Panama Canal. This led to the establishment in 1999 of the Ferrocarril del Istmo de Tehuantepec (FIT) (qv), a state-administered infrastructure company owning the Salina Cruz—Media Aguas section of the coast-to-coast route, which is to be completed by the construction of a new 96 km line to the port of Coatzacoalcos.

After the awarding of the Sureste concession, the Valley of Mexico network was to be the next portion of FNM to be privatised, transferring to the private sector in April 1998 to become Terminal Ferroviaria del Valle de México. Each of the three major concessionaires took a 25 per cent stake in this company.

In addition to the Chihuahua—Pacific network, short line concessions were to be offered for six routes/clusters: Nogales—Nacozari; Escalón—Ciudad Frontera; Durango—Torreón/Felipe Pescador; Mexico City—Cuernavaca/Puebla; routes in Yucatan east of Mérida; and the line from Ixtepec to the Guatemalan border. In 1994 these routes and the Mexico City terminal operation generated 2.9 billion tonne-km on 8,000 km of track. In 1997, IXE Banco SA was appointed to oversee the sell-off of branches as short lines. Marginal routes excluded from the short line and regional concessions were thought likely to close. Two new operators to emerge from this process were Ferrocarril Coahuila a Durango (LCD) (qv) and Ferrocarriles Chiapas-Mayab (FCCM) ) (qv).

An FNM subsidiary company was set up to run the national railway's fibre optic communications network. This includes the SICOTRA computerised train control system. Concessionaires have bought into this system, although this is not obligatory. In 1999 options for privatising this network were being considered by the Mexican government.

On 1 September 1999, FNM ceased to operate any part of the Mexican rail network. By May 2000, the legislation necessary to terminate the existence of FNM had still not been presented to the country's parliament despite presidential authorisation for the process to be initiated. Around 9,000 of the railway's workforce remained on the payroll pending liquidation of the organisation.

### Passenger operations

In Mexico, rail is reckoned to command as little as 1 per cent of the national travel market, and passenger traffic has experienced steady decline since 1983, when 25.6 million passenger journeys and 5,997 million passenger-km were recorded. This trend became more pronounced as passenger and mixed train services were trimmed under an economy programme initiated in the early 1990s. FNM mixed trains accounted for 894 million tonne-km and 2,671 million train-km in 1993.

Between 1995 and 1997, services on lines where more than one daily train was running were reduced to just once daily, using first-class rolling stock and calling at all stations. However, after 1996 several branch lines lost all passenger services and the only mixed trains which survived were operating around Oaxaca and east of Mérida in Yucatán province. These, too, have either since been withdrawn or are under threat.

During 1997-98 many long-distance services were also suspended, such as Mexico City—Guadalajara—Benjamin Hill—Mexicali/Nogales, Mexico City—Ciudad Juárez and Mexico City—Lázaro Cárdenas. In early 1998 virtually all local trains were suspended except those where the absence of suitable roads precluded an alternative bus service.

In the privatised railway environment, some scheduled passenger services survive, mostly operated with a subsidy for social reasons. Some tourist services are also operated. Details are included in the entries for individual railway companies.

### Mexico City suburban network

The Secretariat for Communications and Transport (SCT) has developed plans for a 239.5 km three-line commuter rail system for Mexico city, which, with a population 20 million, endures severe traffic congestion and pollution. Each line would have one core route with several branches and in some cases the double-track electrified line north of the capital's Buenavista station could be used. Remaining lines would be diesel-operated initially, but future electrification is said to be a possibility.

The three routes which have been identified are: to the north, Buenavista—Cuautitlán, with branches from San Rafael to Tacuba, Cuautitlán to Huehuetoca and Lecheri to Jalcotan; to the northeast and east, Ecatepec—Teotihuacán and Teotihuacán—Tecamac; and to the southeast, Los Reyes—San Juan de Aragón with branches from San Juan de Aragón to San Rafael and Chalco to Texcoco.

Development of the network is estimated to cost around US$400 million. To operate the network, SCT plans to award a 30-year concession, with the concessionaire responsible for acquisition of rolling stock.

## Ferrocarril Coahuila a Durango (LCD)

Durango, Dgo

Gauge: 1,435 mm
Route length: 978 km, plus trackage rights over 285 km

### Organisation

Commonly known as the Línea Coahuila a Durango, Ferrocarril Coahuila a Durango SA operates several branch and secondary lines in the states of Chíhuahua, Coahuila, Durango and Zacatecas that were not taken over by the neighbouring Ferromex and TFM systems. Both of these larger railways provide trackage rights for LCD. The lines forming the system were transferred from FNM in April 1998.

LCD connects with Ferromex at Barroterán, Ciudad Frontera, Escalón, Felipe Pescador and Torreón and with TFM at Monclova, near Ciudad Frontera. The network comprises the Felipe Pescador—Durango—Torreón line, including parts of the former branches around Durango, and the Escalón—El Rey—Ciudad Frontera line, including the Sierra Mojada branch and several short branches around Barroterrán, in the northeast of Coahuila state. Several smaller branches and parts of secondary lines have been taken out of service due to a lack of traffic.

The company is owned and operated by Indústrias Peñoles, a Mexican mining and natural resources company, and Acerero del Norte, a steel producer. US short line operator Genesee & Wyoming acts as technical and operational advisor.

### Passenger operations

The central part of the Ciudad Frontera—Escalón line is served by a mixed passenger and freight train running three times a week in each direction between Cuatro Cienegas and Sierra Mojada. The service is operated for social reasons because the region has poor road access. There are plans to extend the service to Ciudad Frontera.

### Freight operations

Coal, iron ore, limestone and timber generate about 70 per cent of freight traffic, with the remainder consisting mainly of petroleum products and paper. Indústrias Peñoles and AHMSA (Altos Hornos de México SA) are by far the most significant customers. Almost all freight is exchanged with neighbouring railways.

### Traction and rolling stock

LCD owns 27 GE U23B diesel locomotives acquired second-hand from Norfolk Southern in the USA. There are also six passenger coaches and an unknown quantity of freight wagons, mostly ex-FNM.

## Ferrocarril del Istmo de Tehuantepec (FIT)

### Key personnel

Director General: Gustavo Baca

Gauge: 1,435 mm
Route length: 207 km

### Political background

Administered by the Secretariat of Communications and Transport (qv), FIT was established in 1999 as the infrastructure operator of a single-track line from Medias Aguas, 93 km inland from the Atlantic coast, to the port of Salina Cruz on the Pacific coast, connecting at Medias Aguas with Ferrosur and at Ixtepec with Ferrocarriles Chiapas-Mayab (FCCM). The line was retained by the government mainly for strategic reasons, providing the key element of a coast-to-coast route. FIT does not run its own trains: Ferrocarriles Chiapas-Mayab has trackage rights over the entire line.

FIT has received funding of peso123 million from the proceeds of the privatisation of FNM. Of this, peso53 million is to be spent on track upgrading and maintenance, civil engineering work and acquisitions, while an additional peso12 million will be invested in improvements at the port of Salina Cruz. Remaining funds will be spent on engineering facilities and planning for the new Medias Aguas—Coatzacoalcos line (see below).

### Passenger operations

See entry for Ferrocarriles Chiapas-Mayab (FCCM).

### Freight operations

All freight operations are run by FCCM, which pays for trackage rights. FIT expects eventual annual traffic volumes to and from Salina Cruz to total 2.4 million tonnes, mostly in containers.

### New lines

In April 1999, a 3 km line was opened at Salina Cruz to provide access to a new container handling terminal.

FIT plans a new 96 km line paralleling the existing Medias Aguas—Coatzacoalcos route owned by Ferrosur, thus completing a nationally owned coast-to-coast corridor.

## Ferrocarriles Chiapas-Mayab SA de CV (FCCM)

Calle 43, 429C, Entre 44 y 46, Colonia Industrial, Mérida, Yucatán 97000
Tel: (+52 99) 930 25 00   Fax: (+52 99) 930 25 39
Web: http://www.gwrr.com

### Key personnel

President and General Manager: Paul M Victor
Chief Financial Officer: Carlos Pereyra
Superintendent, Transportation: Sergio Tonioni Vega
Chief Mechanical Officer: Homero Walss
Chief Engineer: Fernando Osorio Rodriguez
Marketing Manager: Alejandro Garcia

Gauge: 1,435 mm
Route length: 1,805 km, plus trackage rights over 321 km

### Organisation

FCCM is a wholly owned subsidiary of US short line operator Genesee & Wyoming (qv in the United States of America section) which took over former FNM lines in the states of Campeche, Chiapas, Oaxaca, Tabasco, Veracruz and Yucatán in September 1999. Its lines run from Coatzacoalcos to Mérida, with some branches in the Yucatán peninsula and from Ixtepec south to Tapachula and the border with Guatemala, including a short stretch into Guatemala to Tecún Umán station. This last facility is laid with mixed − gauge track to allow the entry of standard-gauge trains. FCCM also has trackage rights over Ferrocarril del Istmo de Tehuantepec (FIT) and Ferrosur lines (qv). Connection is made with the Ferrosur network at Coatzacoalcos and Medias Aquas.

The unused branches to Peto and Sotuta, totalling 181 km south and east of Acanceh, were to be dismantled by FCCM.

### Passenger operations
FCCM runs a few government-subsidised socially desirable passenger services. These consist of trains three times a week in each direction between Coatzacoalcos and Campeche and between Coatzacoalcos and Tapachula. On behalf of the Yucatán state government, a weekend tourist train also runs between Mérida and Izamal.

### Freight operations
Principal commodities carried include cement, cereals, chemicals, fertilisers, petroleum products, propane and sugar. FCCM also carries containers over FIT and Ferrosur tracks between the ports of Coatzacoalcos and Salina Cruz. Container movements on behalf of FIT were expected to reach 2.4 million tonnes from 2000. Apart from coast-to-coast traffic, most freight is carried on the Coatzacoalcos−Mérida line, with Ixtepec−Tapachula and Tapachula−Técun Umán lines also seeing significant tonnages. The branches from Mérida to Acanceh, Valladolid and Tizimin see very little traffic and the Mérida−Progreso branch remained out of use in 2000, despite the presence of port facilities at the latter location.

The interchange of traffic with Guatemala consists of a train running most days conveying cement, chemicals and fertilisers from Mexico and agricultural products in the opposite direction. Road-rail trans-shipment is undertaken at Tecún Umán. Traffic may increase sharply when the Guatemalan line from Tecún Umán to Ciudad de Guatemala is restored to use, with the possible introduction of cross-border container services via a connection at Ciudad Hidalgo.

### New lines
In collaboration with the states of Yucatán and Quintana Roo, FCCM is planning a 100 km line from Valladolid to Cozumel, connecting Quintana Roo to the Mexican railway network for the first time.

*UPDATED*

## Ferromex

*US office*
10 Eddy Street, Alamogordo, New Mexico 8831
Tel: (+1 915) 534 37 32   Fax: (+1 915) 534 37 40

### Key personnel
Director: Xavier García de Quevedo

Gauge: 1,435 mm
Route length: 10,461 km

### Political background
In June 1997, Grupo Ferroviario Mexicano (Ferromex) was awarded the second 50-year concession to be offered by the government in its railway privatisation programme, for the Pacific North network. Formal transfer took place on 19 February 1998. GFM is made up of mining concern Grupo México, with a 74 per cent stake and Union Pacific of the USA, with 26 per cent. A 13 per cent shareholding held by Constructoras ICA, part of Mexico's biggest construction group, was sold to Union Pacific in 1999. GFM bid peso 4.2 billion (US$528 million) for the system, which exceeded the government's minimum price. The government has agreed to sell 100 per cent of the system despite its original intention to retain a 20 per cent stake.

GFM agreed to invest peso 3.4 billion in the network. Priorities would be upgrading of track and purchase of new locomotives and rolling stock. Of the original staff of around 14,000, only 6,200 have been taken on by the new operator.

GFM has also been awarded the Topolobampo−Ojinaga (944 km) short line concession, for which it paid US$421.3 million.

### Organisation
Ferrocarril Pacifico Norte comprises routes from Mexico City to Nogales and Mexicali via Guadalajara, to Ciudad Juárez via Torreón, and from Torreón to Piedras Negras, Monterrey and Tampico. In 1996 the network carried some 40 per cent of Mexico's total rail freight, generating 4.5 million tonne-km. GFM plans to double this within 10 years, although this will only be possible if line speeds are also doubled. It is hoped that with just modest upgrading, 35 per cent of freight handled by road transport will switch to rail within five years.

### Passenger operations
Ferromex operates the daily 'Chepe' (Chihuahua al Pacífico) tourist train and the daily 'Tarahumara' service, both on the Chihuahua−Los Mochis route. The Chepe is a fully air conditioned train conveying a restaurant car. The Tarahumara is formed of modernised non air conditioned economy class coaches and express freight cars. Another tourist train, the 'Tequila Express', runs on Saturdays between Guadalajara and Tequila and includes first class and buffet cars. Rolling stock for all three trains has been completely refurbished. Passenger facilities at Chihuahua have been transferred from the old FdeC station to the former FNM facility. During 2000, several chartered tourist trains were due to run over various Ferromex lines. These were to include around 30 trips by the 'Sierra Madre Express', operated with its own vehicles by Rail Passenger Services Inc of Tucson Arizona (qv in the 'Locomotives and powered/non-powered passenger vehicles' section).

In January 2000, Ferromex ceased to run state-subsidised passenger trains on the Torreón−Aguascalientes, Ciudad Victoria−Tampico and Piedras Negras−Saltillo−San Luís Potosí lines.

### Freight operations
Main commodities carried include cement, coal and grain, while Ferromex is pursuing opportunities to increase intermodal traffic using routes cleared for double-stack operation by FNM before concessioning.

In 1999, Ferromex was reported to be planning a joint venture with Canadian Pacific to develop rail freight links between Canada and Mexico.

### Traction and rolling stock
Ferromex inherited 435 locomotives from FNM and has leased additional traction to bring the fleet total to 496 in 1999. First deliveries of an order placed with General Electric for 50 AC4400 machines were expected during 1999. Locomotive maintenance and overhaul is subcontracted to two companies, GIMCO and MPI de México.

Some 10,700 freight wagons were inherited from the Ferrocarril Pacifico Norte and Chuihuahua-Pacific fleets and further procurements are planned.

Ferromex owns 55 passenger coaches, 31 of which have been refurbished for the regular and tourist services detailed in 'Passenger operations'. In 2000, the fleet for the Chihuahua−Los Mochis services consisted of: 11 air conditioned first class coaches; nine economy class; two smoking lounge cars and three restaurant cars. Tequila Express vehicles comprised five first class coaches and one buffet car. Three box cars have been converted for express freight ('Paquetería') services and operated as part of passenger train formations. All vehicles are ex-FNM.

## Ferrosur

### Key personnel
Director General: Frantz Guns
Chief Operating Officer: Luis García

Gauge: 1,435 mm
Route length: 1,479 km

### Political background
FNM's former Sureste (Southeastern) railway was the third and smallest division of the former national railway to be privatised when Ferrosur, a consortium of aggregates and construction company Tribasa (66.6 per cent) and the Inbursa financing group, took over operations on 18 December 1998. Ferrosur paid peso 2.9 billion for a 50-year concession. The Tribasa stake was subsequently sold to Frisco, a mining company which is part of the Grupo Carso conglomerate.

### Organisation
The Ferrosur network extends southeast from Mexico City to serve the port of Veracruz via Orizaba, to Coatzacoalos and to Puebla. Ferrosur is also responsible for operations on the 366 km Puebla−Oaxaca line, which carries very little freight traffic and was not privatised separately due to its poor business prospects. There is no connection with the US network.

### Passenger operations
Ferrosur operates two passenger services, one running from Mexico City to Apizaco (153 km) on the Veracruz line, the other from Tehuacán to Oaxaca (240 km). Both services are subsidised and maintained for social reasons. Until mid-1999, Ferrosur operated several other passenger services, including Mexico City−Veracruz and Veracruz−Coatzacoalcos, but these were discontinued due to a lack of political support.

### Freight operations
Cement, chemicals and minerals are the main commodities carried, while significant opportunities exist to develop container, automotive and grain traffic at Veracruz.

### Traction and rolling stock
Ferrosur took over 170 diesel locomotives, all of GE manufacture and mainly C30-7, B23-7 and U36C types. An additional 26 locomotives, mostly C30s and GM SD-40s have been hired from TFM and other railways. Around 3,400 wagons were taken over from FNM and additional more specialised vehicles may be acquired in due course. Ferrosur also received several passenger coaches from FNM but no more than eight of these were in active service in 2000. None is air conditioned and no sleeping or catering cars are in operation.

## Terminal Ferroviaria del Valle de México (TFVM)

Gauge: 1,435 mm
Route length: 297 km

### Political background
The Mexico City Terminal Railway (TFVM) was privatised on 30 April 1998, with the three main freight railway concessionaires, Ferromex, Ferrosur and TFM, each taking a 25 per cent stake.

### Organisation
TFVM operates marshalling yard and terminal facilities in the Mexico City area. These include the Valley of Mexico marshalling yard, which has recently undergone a modernisation programme to increase its capacity from 800 to 2,000 wagons a day. The capital's only intermodal facility, at Pantaco, is also run by TFVM.

### Traction and rolling stock
TFVM took over 46 diesel locomotives and 192 freight wagons from FNM.

## Transportación Ferroviaria Mexicana (TFM)

Transportación Ferroviaria Mexicana SA de CV
Av de La Cúspide No 4829, Col Parquest del Pedregal,
Mexico, DF, CP 14010
Tel: (+52 5) 447 58 79; 447 58 36
Fax: (+52 5) 447 58 30

### Key personnel
Chief Executive Officer: Chris Aadnesen
General Director: Mario Mohar

Gauge: 1,435 mm
Route length: 4,283 km

*For map see Kansas City Southern entry in US section.*

### Political background
On 29 November 1996, three consortia were shortlisted for the 50-year concession with a 50-year extension option on offer for the North East network of FNM (qv), with the award eventually going to a joint venture known as Transportación Ferroviaria Mexicana (TFM) on 5 December 1996. TFM, which assumed operational control of the railway on 24 June 1997, consists of the Mexican multimodal transport company, Transportaciónes Marítimas Mexicanas and Grupo Servin (38.5 per cent), and the US firm Kansas City Southern Industries (37 per cent). It won control of the North East network after having agreed to pay US$1.4 billion for 80 per cent of all common stock of the railway, with the remaining 24.5 per cent retained by the Mexican government, which was expected to sell its stake in 1999. The high level of the bid caused much surprise, being almost three times higher than that of two rival bidders. Financing of the deal almost fell apart, but the Mexican government agreed to help by injecting US$200 million in the form of a bridge equity stake, in addition to retaining a 20 per cent interest in the line. During 1999, this remaining government share was bought by Kansas City Southern and Transportaciónes Marítimas Mexicanas.

The North East network serves the US border crossings at Nuevo Laredo and Matamoros and the ports of Veracruz, Tampico and Lázaro Cárdenas. The port of Veracruz is an extremely important traffic generator in its own right, handling around a quarter of all maritime cargo. The network's new operators believe that the 1997 freight volume of some 8 million tonne-km can be doubled within three to four years.

In January 1998 a four-year US$553 million investment programme was announced. This was expected to generate a compounded annual business growth rate of 15 per cent over the succeeding three to five years from both increased NAFTA traffic and from improved market share.

### Passenger operations
Until January 2000, TFM operated a passenger service three times each week in collaboration with Ferromex, linking Saltillo and San Luis Potosí. Due to a lack of political backing, this and a few other passenger services, such as Mexico City–Querétaro–Veracruz via Jalapa, were discontinued.

In March 2000, US national passenger operator Amtrak made a trial run with a cross-border service and has developed plans to introduce a regular train from San Antonio, Texas via Laredo and Nuevo Laredo to Monterrey using TFM tracks in Mexico. The new service, the 'Aztec Eagle', was expected to include coach class and sleeping accommodation and to include dining facilities. The carriage of express freight and mail was also reported to be likely. The train, the first US-Mexico cross-border passenger service for some 50 years, was expected to be introduced late in 2000 or early in 2001, depending on negotiations with TFM and customs authorities.

### Freight operations
Principal markets served include the agriculture, metals, automotive and chemicals industries.

### Intermodal operations
In 1999, some 6 per cent of TFM's business was intermodal, with double-stack services operated on Nuevo Laredo–Mexico City and Veracruz–Mexico City routes. A new intermodal terminal opened in East Laredo, Texas in late 1998 and a similar facility in Monterrey was commissioned in 1999. Costing some US$7.5 million, the facility at East Laredo is intended to handle cross-border traffic and will triple existing capacity.

### Traction and rolling stock
TFM inherited 371 diesel locomotives from FNM in addition to the 22 examples of a fleet of 33 General Electric E60C electric locomotives used on the Mexico City–Querétaro line. TFM has not adopted electric traction for this section and trade-in of these machines formed part of an operating lease arrangement with General Electric for 75 AC4400 diesels.

TFM inherited 6,573 wagons from FNM. These have been progressively overhauled and supplemented by leased-in equipment from the USA, with a particular focus on container-carrying wagons.

A 17-year contract valued at US$419 million has been awarded to Motive Power Industries to overhaul and maintain 168 diesel locomotives at San Luis Potosi, replacing an earlier contract with FNM. Wagon maintenance is undertaken by Grup Fyl, a subsidiary of Progress Rail Services Corporation.

In 1999 TFM began taking delivery of an order for 75 SD70-MACs from General Motors, Electro-Motive Division. Assembly was being undertaken locally.

### Signalling and telecommunications
Train movements are controlled by centralised traffic control (CTC) over nearly one third of the network and by track warrants for the remainder. In 1999 TFM was working to extend CTC to the Monterrey–Nuevo Laredo line. The company has established a train operations centre at Monterrey. The SICOTRA traffic monitoring system (see 'Signalling and telecommunications' section in FNM entry) has been adopted by the company but is being upgraded.

### Electrification
The 25 kV AC 60 Hz electrified section of line between Mexico City and Querétaro remains energised for possible future use as part of a proposed suburban network for the capital but the use of electric traction was not adopted by TFM.

*Before privatisation and handover to TFM, two FNM General Electric C30-7 locomotives head freight for Mexico City past Querétaro (Michal Málek)* 0058802

# MOLDOVA

## Ministry of Transport and Communications

Boulevard Stefan cel Mare 134, MD-2012 Kishinev
Tel: (+373 2) 62 89 11  Fax: (+373 2) 24 15 53

### Key personnel
Minister: Anatol Kuptsov
Head of Railways Directorate: Gheorghe Turcanu

**UPDATED**

## Moldovan Railways (CFM)

Căile Ferate Moldova
Vlaiku Pirkelab Str 48, 277012 Kishinev
Tel: (+373 2) 23 35 83; 25 22 54
Fax: (+373 2) 22 13 80

### Key personnel
President: I Curkan
Assistant Director General: Georgui Efrim

Departmental Heads
International Relations: Grigori Ignakov
Freight: Victor Garkoucha
Passengers: Dionisi Semeniouk
Finance: Marina Kniazeva
Traffic: Alexi Kouz
Rolling Stock: Edouard Rastorgouev
Traction: Ivan Vasilaki

Gauge: 1,520 mm
Route length: 1,300 km

### Political background
Moldovan Railways was formed in 1992 in the break-up of SZhD (Soviet Railways), and comprises the latter's Moldovan section. Two lines traverse the rebellious Dnestr region in the east of the country. Civil war disrupted the fledgling independent railway, meaning that much of it has been out of action – but by 1995 most lines were back in traffic, including those in the Dnestr region.

With peace, the railway has an opportunity to build up transit traffic: the main line bisecting the country from east to west joins the Ukrainian port of Odessa with Romania. Traffic development therefore largely depends on a revival of the Ukrainian and Russian economies.

In 1997 the government relieved the railways of the hitherto heavy property taxes. Some lines are to be closed and others are losing their automatic block signalling. The labour force at the beginning of 1998 numbered about 20,000.

In 2000 the European Commission invited tenders to advise the Moldovan government on restructuring and/or privatising the railway system.

### Passenger operations
International passenger trains operate to the Ukraine and several cities in the Russian Federation. There are also international trains, mostly at night, to Romania, operating over the main east-west line via Ungheni. Restoration of passenger service to Romania across two freight-only links over the Prut river, at Prut and Reni, is under discussion.

Most internal day trains are operated by Riga-built diesel multiple-units, at speeds up to 100 km/h. There are plans to increase speeds on the main east-west line to 140 or 160 km/h.

Traffic statistics for 1996 were 10.3 million journeys, 0.88 billion passenger-km (in 1995 11.7 million and 1.02 billion respectively). In a bid to stem losses, domestic rail fares were sharply increased, which largely explains why passenger-km declined from 656 million in 1998 to 343 million (4.1 million passenger-km) in 1999.

### Freight operations
Most freight traffic is in transit between Romania and countries formerly in the Soviet Union. Agricultural goods make up much of the internally generated traffic. Maximum weight for freight trains is 2,800 tonnes.

As elsewhere in the former Soviet bloc, freight traffic has dropped off rapidly in recent years. Traffic statistics for 1996 were 12.5 million tonnes, 2.79 billion tonne-km. In 1999, 1.46 billion tonne-km were achieved, against 3.0 billion in 1995.

### New lines
The Romanian and Moldovan governments have discussed construction of a new line from Nicolina in Romania to the Moldovan capital Kishinev. The new line, to be built at 1,435 mm gauge, would run parallel to the CFM's existing east-west 1,520 mm gauge line, a few kilometres to the south.

### Traction and rolling stock
At the beginning of 1997 the CFM fleet totalled 218 diesel locomotives (mainly of the 2TE10M, 3TE10M, M62 and ChME3 Classes, with about half serviceable), 36 dmus, mostly of Class D1, and 130 various stored steam locomotives including standard-gauge ex-German Class TE 2-10-0s. There were also about 500 loco-hauled coaches and over 13,000 wagons – with less than 50 per cent of the latter serviceable. Financial problems make acquisition of spare parts difficult.

### Track
**Rail:** 65 kg/m on main lines, 45-55 kg/m on secondary lines
**Sleepers:** Mostly wooden, spaced at 1,840 per km
**Max axleload:** 24 tonnes

---

# MONGOLIA

## Ministry of Transport and Railways
PO Box 1104, Ulaanbaatar 11
Fax: (+976 1) 31 06 12

### Key personnel
Minister: Gavaagiyn Batchuu

## Mongolian Railway (MTZ)
Mongolin Tömör Zam
PO Box 376, Ulaanbaatar
Tel: (+976 1) 32 21 17   Fax: (+976 1) 32 83 60

### Key personnel
President: Radnaabazaryn Rash
Chief Engineer: J Nyamaa
Deputy Directors General: N Batmonkh, Y Batsaihan

Gauge: 1,520 mm
Route length: 1,815 km

### Organisation
MTZ's core main line, the Transmongolian Railway, extends 1,111 km from the Russian Federation frontier at Sühbaatar to the Chinese border at Dzamïn-Uüd, with a line to Erdenet (164 km) and six other branches. There is an isolated 349 km line, the Oriental Railway, in the east of the country which links the Mongolian-Russian Federation border station at Solovyevsk with Choybalsan, and throws off a branch to Erdes.

### Passenger operations
Passenger traffic declined less dramatically than freight through to 1993. An increase was recorded in 1994, and there was a slight fall again in 1995. The 2.8 million passengers carried in that year represented about 30 per cent of national passenger-km.

### Freight operations
From a peak of 17.8 million tonnes hauled in 1988, freight traffic has declined inexorably; by 1992 tonnage had halved to 8.5 million and fell further in 1993 and 1994. In that year, due to the continuing political and economic upheaval in neighbouring countries, transit traffic fell to a new low of 0.2 million tonnes – more than 1 million tonnes down on the 1988 figure. As a consequence of the fall-off in movements, many fewer trains are being run and more than 30 passing loops have been taken out of use until business improves.

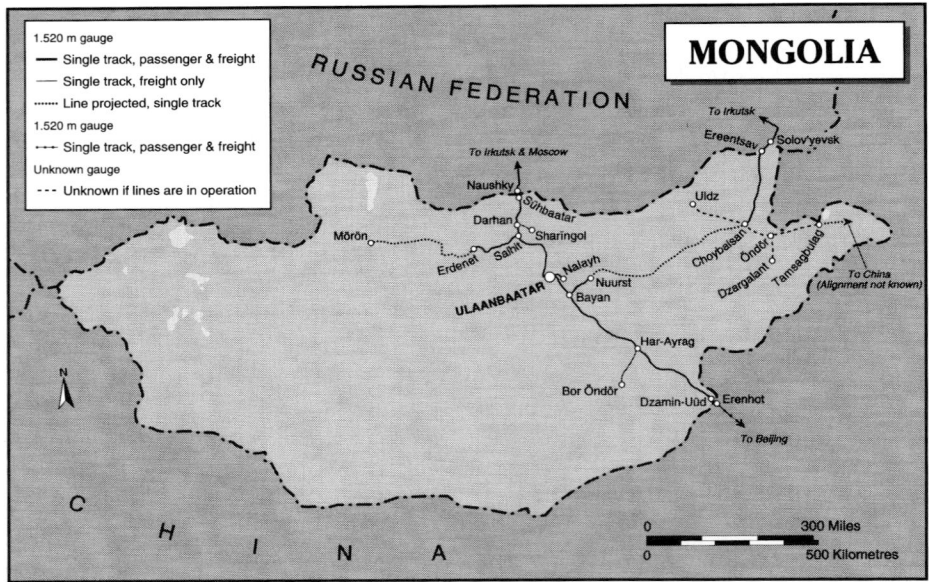

Internal traffic has fared better, with rail still handling some 80 per cent of total tonne-km. Movements comprise mainly bulk minerals and imported goods.

There was an improvement in this trend in 1995, when tonnage rose 3.5 per cent to 7.3 million tonnes.

| Traffic (million) | 1994 | 1995 |
|---|---|---|
| Passenger journeys | 2.884 | 2.827 |
| Passenger-km | 788.8 | 681.0 |
| Freight tonnes | 7.077 | 7.325 |
| Freight tonne-km | 2,150.3 | 2,284.0 |

| Revenue (tugrik million) | 1994 | 1995 |
|---|---|---|
| Passengers | 4,133.0 | 4,793.3 |
| Freight | 8,875.5 | 10,741.4 |
| Other income | 513.0 | 840.5 |
| Total | 13,521.5 | 16,375.2 |

| Expenditure | 1994 | 1995 |
|---|---|---|
| Staff/personnel | 1,401.4 | 2,698.7 |
| Materials and services | 507.1 | 1,068.8 |
| Depreciation | 3,895.5 | 3,973.6 |
| Fuel | 4,351.5 | 4,952.2 |
| Other | 1,872.7 | 2,956.5 |
| Total | 12,028.2 | 15,649.8 |

### New lines
Considerable benefits would accrue from linking the isolated Oriental Railway with the main network, feasibility studies for which were carried out in 1986. This remains a long-term goal, but a new shorter route to China from the Oriental Railway at Choybalsan is much favoured as a means of opening up eastern Mongolia and accessing the Tumen river economic zone. Also planned is a line from Erdenet to the Mörön region, principally for fertiliser movement.

There are better prospects for a line from Airag to tap the huge reserves of coking coal at Tavantolgoi. Prefeasibility studies were made in the late 1980s, but construction would depend on availability of foreign funding and technical assistance.

### Improvements to existing lines
Several capacity improvement projects are under way or planned to cope with transit traffic once the business revives. A major procurement programme agreed in 1994 and funded by OECF Japan loans was to see purchases of new passenger coaches and wagons, rail and track accessories, and computers, raising track maintenance standards and using rolling stock availability at pinch points.

Allied to this plan is establishment of a concrete sleeper manufacturing plant, capable of turning out 200,000 units a year, and raising output of ballast from 60,000 to 400,000 tonnes annually.

Rehabilitation of the existing fleet is addressed in a World Bank scheme which will finance procurement of spare parts and materials. Still awaiting a source of funding is the proposed central workshops at Ulaanbaatar, construction of which would eliminate the need to send locomotives and coaches to other countries for repair.

Japanese funding is also involved in a programme of works at the Chinese border station of Dzamïn-Üüd, where Mongolian 1,520 mm gauge tracks meet those of 1,435 mm gauge in the People's Republic. Additional and improved transhipment facilities have been provided for transit traffic to and from China, including a new container loading platform.

### Traction and rolling stock
The stock of 105 diesel-electric locomotives is formed chiefly of USSR-built Type 2M62 4,000 hp 2 × Co-Cos and TEM2 1,200 hp Co-Cos. There are also 13 M62 units of 2,000 hp. Passenger cars total 202 and freight wagons 1,981.

At the beginning of 1996 there were two Co-Co diesel-electrics on order, as well as 30 coaches (DWA Ammendorf) and 455 wagons (Roszheldorsnab, Russia). Funding for these purchases was made available by the World Bank and OECF Japan.

### Signalling and telecommunications
Semi-automatic block is in operation between Ulaanbaatar and Dzamïn-Üüd and on several branches, totalling 1,577 km, while the Choybalsan–Ereentsav line (237 km) is worked by electric token.

### Diesel locomotives

| Class | Wheel arrangement | Power kW | Speed km/h | Weight tonnes | No in service | First built | Builders Mechanical | Builders Engine | Transmission |
|---|---|---|---|---|---|---|---|---|---|
| 2M62 | 2 × (Co-Co) | 2 × 1,472 | 100 | 2 × 120 | 64 | 1981 | Lugansk | Lugansk | E Lugansk |
| M62 | Co-Co | 1,472 | 100 | 120 | 13 | 1987 | Lugansk | Lugansk | E Lugansk |
| TEM2 | Co-Co | 883 | 100 | 120 | 28 | 1972 | Briansk | Penza | E Briansk |

### Track
**Rail:** Type R-43, 44.65 kg/m; Type R-50, 51.5 kg/m; Type R-65, 64.64 kg/m
**Crossties (sleepers):** Wood, 200 × 250 × 2750 mm
**Fastenings:** Conventional, Russian Federation standard
**Min curvation radius:** 296 m
**Max gradient:** 1.8%
**Max axleload:** 23.5 tonnes

# MOROCCO

## Ministry of Transport and Merchant Marine
Rabat
Fax: (+21 27) 77 45 78

### Key personnel
Minister: Abdelsalam Znined
Secretary General: Mohamed Margaoui

*UPDATED*

## Moroccan Railways (ONCFM)
Office National des Chemins de Fer du Maroc
8 bis rue Abderrahmane Al Ghafiki, Rabat-Agdal
Tel: (+212 7) 77 47 47   Fax: (+212 7) 77 44 80
Web: http://www.oncf.org.ma

### Key personnel
Director General: Ing Karim Ghellab
Director, Finance and Management:
  Mohamed Lahbib El-Gueddari
Traffic Manager: Abdesselam El Ghissassi
Transport Manager: Mohamed Smouni
Commercial Manager: Mohamed Rabie Khlie
Traction and Rolling Stock Manager (Central):
  Mohamed Soufi
Traction and Rolling Stock Manager:
  El Hassane Leqsiouer
Track Manager: Moha Khaddour
Electrification, Signalling and Telecommunications Manager: Rachid Bouslama
Human Resources Manager: Ali El Karram
Management and Finance Manager:
  Mohamed El Gueddari
Inspector General: Mustapha Benmoussa
Supply Manager: Bouchaib Belhaj
Data Processing Manager: Rokia Belkebir
International Relations: Larbi Aidi

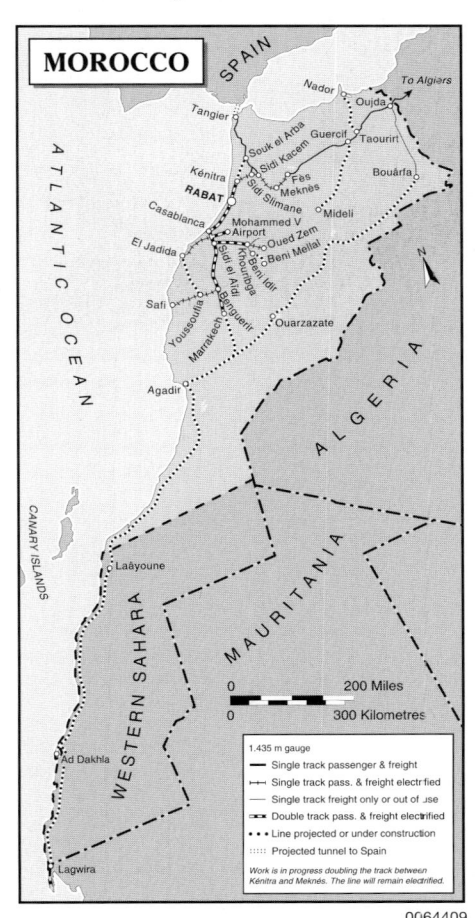

Gauge: 1,432 mm
Route length: 1,907 km
Electrification: 1,003 km at 3 kV DC

### Political background
ONCFM is a state-owned enterprise with its own legal entity and financial autonomy, working under the administrative umbrella of the Ministry of Transport. The Moroccan transport market was deregulated in 1993.

Relationships with government are currently managed by a Contract Plan signed in September 1996 and covering the five-year period up to 31 December 2000. This plan provides a budget of Dh2.2 billion for capital investment purposes. To coincide with the signature of this plan and to secure investment funding from international lending institutions, the government took over ONCFM's long-term debts at the end of 1996 and implemented a commercially based restructuring programme.

In early 1997, the World Bank and European Investment Bank approved loans of US$195 million towards the US$600 million cost of this restructuring and investment programme.

### Organisation
The railway runs about 220 km south from Tangier to the Sidi Kacem junction with the northwest coastal line to Rabat. The latter continues to Marrakech via Sidi el Aïdi and has a spur to Oued Zem and east to Oujda, via Fès, to link up with Algerian Railways at the frontier. A line running south from Oujda skirts the Moroccan-Algerian frontier as far as the southeast railhead at Bouârfa.

At the beginning of 2001 ONCFM employed 10,308 staff.

| Traffic (million) | 1999 | 2000 |
|---|---|---|
| Passenger journeys | 12.2 | 13.1 |
| Passenger-km | 1,880 | 1,956 |
| Freight tonnes | 28.13 | — |
| Freight tonne-km | 4,794 | — |

### Passenger operations
The 90 km main line between Rabat and Casablanca has been upgraded for 140 to 160 km/h over 76 km and is exploited by an hourly TNR (*Train Navette Rapide*) service provided by emus built in Belgium by BN (now Bombardier Transportation) and ACEC (now Alstom) to a design based on SNCB's Type AM80. But, whereas the SNCB AM80 has regenerative braking, the Moroccan units have rheostatic. The Moroccan three-car sets can operate in multipled pairs. Completion of upgrading of the Kénitra–Meknès corridor in 2002 will see TNR services extended to Sidi Kacem.

UIC Type X air conditioned cars (see below), designed for 160 km/h operation, equip named trains between Rabat and Marrakech; Casablanca, Tangier, Fès and Oujda; Tangier and Marrakech; and Oujda and Marrakech.

A 13 km electrified branch connects the main line out of Casablanca to the south with the King Mohamed V International Airport. Belgian-built emus are also used on this service.

*Class E 1300 electric locomotive with a mixed freight train at Rabat (Quintus Vosman)*

# RAILWAY SYSTEMS/Morocco

## Freight operations
Phosphates, which account for around one-third of freight tonnage, are moved for export shipment in 78 three-axle wagon trains of 3,900 tonnes payload, 4,680 tonnes gross, over the Beni Idir–Khouribga/Sidi Daoui–Casablanca and Sidi Azouz/Youssoufia–Safi electrified routes.

## New lines
A long-projected rail connection from Taourirt to the Mediterranean port of Nador appeared more likely in 1999 when a ministerial statement backed the scheme.

In 1999, government proposals were revealed to construct a new line eastwards from Tangier to Tetouan and the Spanish territory of Cueta.

## Improvements to existing lines
In March 1997, ONCFM commenced a US$233 million upgrading of the 140 km main line between Kénitra (40 km north of Rabat) to the city of Meknès. An initial phase covers the 85 km section between Kénitra and Sidi Kacem, and involves double-tracking with new 54 or 60 kg/m continuously welded rail, realignment for 160 km/h running, elimination of level crossings, and renewal of overhead power supply equipment. Tenders were invited in September 1997 for the Sidi Kacem–Meknès section. The complete scheme is due to be completed by the end of 2002.

The line between Fès and Oujda has been relaid with 60 kg/m rail.

In 1999, catenary renewal was carried out on the Sidi el Aïdi–Oued Zem line and in the Casablanca area.

## Traction and rolling stock
The fleet in 2000 included 131 diesel locomotives, 80 electric locomotives and 14 three-car emus. The passenger coach fleet totalled 414.

Under an agreement with De Dietrich, UIC Type X air conditioned cars of side-corridor layout have been built locally for ONCFM by Société Chérifienne du Matériel Industriel et Ferroviaire (SCIF), though some parts were supplied from France. In addition, 52 cars for local service have been acquired second-hand from Belgian Railways (SNCB).

Three Class DF French-built main line diesel locomotives have been refurbished.

In December 1996, seven 4,400 kW electric locomotives were ordered from GEC Alsthom, with an option on two more; ONCFM has now ordered 27 electric locomotives of this type. Alsthom-built Class E 900 electric locomotives were refurbished from 1999.

At the beginning of 2001, the ONCFM freight wagon fleet stood at 6,894.

## Signalling and telecommunications
In 1999, ONCFM placed a Euro53 million contract with Alstom to renew signalling between Sidi el Aïdi and Marrakech and Kenitra and Oujda. The scheme covers 700 route-km and involves modernisation of 55 stations, including Casablanca, where a new electronically controlled signalling centre will be provided. First phases of the project are due to be commissioned early in 2001.

Manual block has been installed under the 1994-98 plan on the principal non-electrified lines from the Algerian border at Oujda to Fès and Tangier to Sidi Kacem. Other recent works include equipping the main line between Fès and Sidi el Aïdi with automatic speed control.

## Electrification
The 584 km Fès–Marrakech line was electrified in the 1930s by the Paris-Orleans Railway. Renewal of catenary features in the upgrading and double-tracking of the Kénitra–Meknès line (see 'Improvements to existing lines').

ONCFM aspires to electrify its complete network, allowing it to make use of indigenously produced hydro-electric power rather than imported oil.

## Track
**Rail:** Less than 45 kg/m (657 km); 45-54 kg/m (1,154 km); 54 kg/m over (1,253 km)
**Crossties (sleepers) material:** Concrete, 1,464 km; steel, 1,541 km; timber, 59 km
**Number per km:** 1,666 km
**Fastenings type:** Nabla and rigid fastenings
**Min curvation radius:** 300 m
**Max gradient:** 2.5%
**Max permissible axleload:** 22 tonnes

*UPDATED*

*Class E 1250 electric locomotive at Sidi Bou Othmane with a Rabat—Marrakech train formed of Corail coaches built in Morocco under licence (Quintus Vosman)*  2001/0059398

*Class DF French-built diesel-electric locomotives at Sidi Kacem (Quintus Vosman)*  2001/0059399

### Electric locomotives

| Class | Wheel arrangement | Power kW continuous/one-hour | Speed km/h | Weight tonnes | No built | First built | Builders Mechanical | Electrical |
|---|---|---|---|---|---|---|---|---|
| E 700 | Bo-Bo | 1,220 | 110 | 88 | 14 | 1948 | Alsthom | Alsthom |
| E 800 | Co-Co | 2,295 | 80 | 132 | 7 | 1959 | Alsthom | Alsthom, CEM |
| E 900 | Co-Co | 2,425 | 125 | 114 | 7 | 1969 | Alsthom | Alsthom, MTE |
| E 1000 | Co-Co | 3,000 | 125 | 120 | 23 | 1975 | Pafawag | Dolmel |
| E 1100 | Co-Co | 2,850 | 100 | 120 | 22 | 1977 | Hitachi | Hitachi |
| E 1200 | Co-Co | 2,850 | 100 | 132 | 8 | 1982 | Hitachi | Hitachi |
| E 1250 | Co-Co | 3,900 | 160 | 120 | 12 | 1984 | Hitachi | Hitachi |
| E 1300 | B-B | 4,000 | 160 | 85.5 | 27 | 1989 | GEC Alsthom | GEC Alsthom |

### Diesel locomotives

| Class | Wheel arrangement | Power kW | Speed km/h | Weight tonnes | No built | First built | Mechanical | Builders Engine | Transmission |
|---|---|---|---|---|---|---|---|---|---|
| DF | C-C | 2,250 | 135 | 108 | 14 | 1968 | Alsthom | SACM-AGO V16 ESHR | E Alsthom |
| DG | Bo-Bo | 588 | 90 | 72 | 75 | 1973 | Fablok | HCP 8 VCD22T | E Dolmel |
| DH | Co-Co | 2,427 | 105 | 117 | 18 | 1974 | GM | EMD 16-645E3 | E GM |
| DK | Co-Co | 1,470 | 105 | 125 | 11 | 1983 | GM | EMD 12-645E3 | E GM |
| DI | Bo-Bo | 735 | 85 | 88 | 18 | 1983 | GM | EMD | E GM |
| DJ | Bo-Bo | 820 | | | 19 | 1992 | Brush | | E Brush |

# MOZAMBIQUE

## Ministry of Transport & Communications
PO Box 2158, Maputo
Tel: (+258 1) 42 71 73   Fax: (+258 1) 42 77 46

**Key personnel**
Minister: Paulo Muxanga

## Mozambique Ports & Railways (CFM)
PO Box 2158, Maputo
Tel: (+258 1) 42 71 73   Fax: (+258 1) 42 93 57

**Key personnel**
Chairman: Rui Fonseca
Director General: Mário A Dimande
Directors
    Engineering: Eng Anibal Laice
    Finance: B M Cherinda
    Commercial: D Gomes
    Computer Services: Avito Jequicene
    Purchases and Stores: Sancho Quipiço
    Personnel: I R Júnior
    Southern Railway: A Manave
    Central Railway: J A Felipe
    North Railway: F J Nhussi
    Zambésia Railway: O J Jaime

Gauge: 1,067 mm; 762 mm
Route length: 2,983 km; 140 km

### Political background
In 1990 the Mozambique Railways (CFM) were joined with the country's ports of Maputo, Beira and Nacala in a new state corporation, Mozambique Ports & Railways. This changed the status of both activities from government agency to a financially accountable corporation.

In the following year a new law was enacted to give impetus to plans for revitalisation of CFM, envisaging for the first time the possibility of private-sector participation.

Freight traffic performance has been at the mercy of low motive power availability and poor security, both at Maputo port and en route. In an attempt to address the endemic congestion at Maputo in particular, several of the port's facilities have been franchised to private operators. Another long-standing problem demanding attention is the need for dredging at Maputo and Beira to permit larger vessels to call at the ports.

Because of CFM's poor performance, donor governments have been pressing for outright privatisation of the railway as a means of strengthening operational control. World Bank assistance was obtained in 1993 for the Maputo Corridor Revitalisation Technical Assistance Project, designed to review the options for private-sector involvement and negotiate its implementation.

In the second half of 1997, five operating concessions in the Maputo Corridor were put up for sale. The five concessions cover the 93 km from Komatipoort (South Africa) to Moamba and Maputo, the 528 km Limpopo line from Chicualacuala to Maputo, the 69 km route from Goba in Swaziland, the harbour at Maputo and CFM's motive power workshops. In 1998, Spoornet (qv) was named preferred bidder to operate freight services between Maputo and South Africa, while the Consortia 2000 group was selected as the successful bidder for two other freight concessions into the port, providing links to Chicualauala (and on to Zimbabwe) and to Goba (and on to Swaziland). In mid-1999, negotiations continued on all three concessions amid reports of difficulties reaching contract terms.

In February 1999, the Sociedade de Desenvolvimento do Corredor de Nacala (SDCN) consortium was named preferred bidder for an operating concession for the CFM-North line between the port of Nacala and the Malawi border. SDCN members include Railroad Development Corporation and Edlow Resources, both based in the USA, and Mozambique and Portuguese investors. A stake of 16 per cent was also to be offered to interests in Malawi, although reports in 1999 suggested dissatisfaction in Malawi at the size of this proposed shareholding. Transfer to SDCN was expected to occur on 1 October 1999.

### Organisation
The railway is made up of five distinct systems linking the coastal ports to the hinterland, managed from four regional headquarters. These are:

*CFM-North*
Gauge: 1,067 mm
Route length: 919 km
This line runs from the port of Nacala, with a branch (at present closed) to Lumbo westward to Cuamba and Lichinga. A recently built line from Cuamba connects at Entre Lagos, on the border, with Malawi Railways and affords Malawi rail access to the port of Nacala.

*CFM-Centre*
Gauge: 1,067 mm
Route length: 994 km
From the port of Beira the line runs westwards to connect with Zimbabwe Railways at Machipanda. From Dondo Junction, 29 km from Beira, a line runs northward to connect with Malawi Railways with an extension from Dona Ana to Moatize. A branch line of 83 km links Inhamitanga with Marromeu.

*CFM-Zambésia*
Gauge: 1,067 mm
Route length: 145 km
An isolated line running from the coastal town of Quelimane to Mocuba.

*CFM-South*
Gauge: 1,067 mm; 762 mm
Route length: 930 km; 143 km
Three major international routes run from the port of Maputo to the Swaziland border at Goba (64 km); to the South African border at Ressano Garcia (88 km); and the Limpopo line to the Zimbabwe border at Chicualacuala (528 km).

The first joins up at the border of Swaziland with the Swaziland Railway, which connects the Umbovu Ridge iron ore complex at Kadake with the port of Maputo. The second continues into South Africa. The third line goes through Zimbabwe to Zambia, Botswana and the southeast of the Democratic Republic of Congo.

CFM-South also operates the two isolated lines linking Xai-Xai with Mauele and Chicomo (762 mm gauge), and Inhambane with Inharrime (1,067 mm gauge, 90 km).

At the beginning of 1997 CFM employed 10,558 staff.

### Passenger operations
Improved passenger services depend on rolling stock availability; currently there are insufficient coaches to run through trains to Swaziland and Zimbabwe, though the Johannesburg-Maputo train resumed thrice-weekly operation in 1994 using Spoornet stock. A local service introduced between Maputo and Manhica proved popular immediately. Some relief was provided by delivery of 25 coaches second-hand from South Africa in 1994, and a batch of new vehicles was ordered from Zimbabwe builders.

Traffic figures for 1996 were 5.7 million journeys (5.5 million in 1995), 358 million passenger-km (251 million in 1995).

### Freight operations
In the 1980s operation was severely disrupted by hostilities, with serious consequences for neighbouring railways for which Mozambique's ports provide a shipment outlet. Now that relations are improving, the prospects for rail are similarly reviving. In the short term, close attention is being given to retaining existing freight business, while new export traffic is being sought on the rehabilitated corridors. Closer co-operation with neighbouring railways should see more through running, joint cross-border operations, and streamlined customs and accounting practices.

Traffic figures for 1996 were 4.1 million tonnes (3.1 million in 1995), 983 million tonne-km (886 million in 1995).

### New lines
Under study in 1998 was a 180 km line to convey iron ore from central Zimbabwe to Manica, on CFM's Beira line. Here a smelting facility established in a special trade zone would produce iron briquettes for export via Beira.

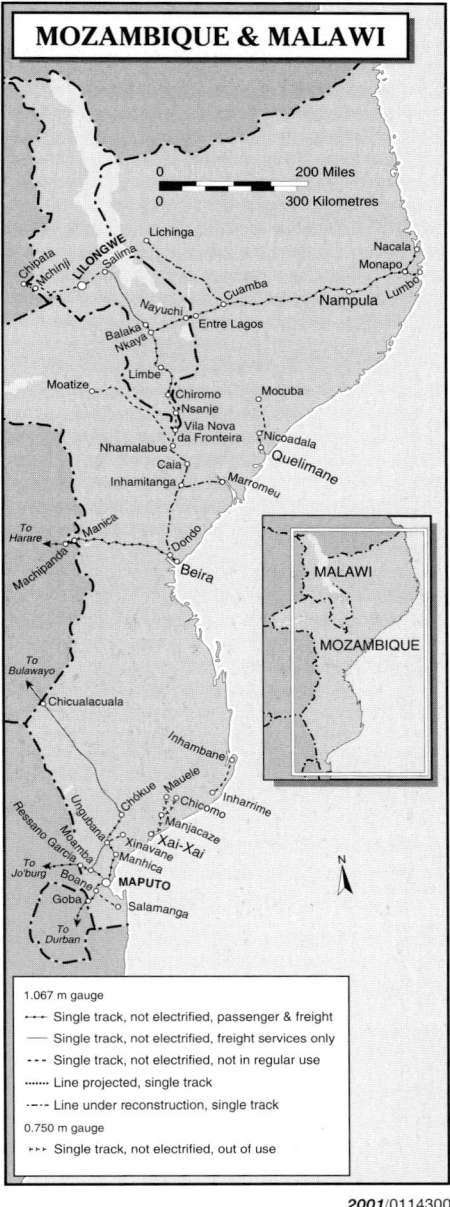

### Improvements to existing lines
Reconstruction of CFM's deteriorated trunk route tracks has been a top priority, first in view of the demands for access to the ports for traffic to and from the country's landlocked neighbours, and latterly in the light of the new political situation following normalisation of relations with South Africa.

Loans from Canadian, French and Portuguese sources helped to fund a US$195 million rebuilding of the 538 km Northern line from Nacala to Cuamba with 40 kg/m long-welded rail on concrete sleepers for 20 tonne axleloadings. Work on the remaining 77 km section from Cuamba to the Malawi border at Nayuchi was also being undertaken in 1999 with the help of a grant from the Portuguese government. There is also a plan to boost passenger service on the route with EU assistance. In early 1998 CFM was also working on a two-phase US$ 26 million renovation of the branch north from Cuamba to Lichinga.

Export/import traffic is moving again in the Limpopo corridor northwards from Maputo, over which a partial renovation was completed in 1993. Nevertheless, a further programme of works is necessary before the line can be considered fully operational, and British, Canadian, German, Portuguese and Kuwaiti donors have proffered a further US$65 million towards the US$200 million cost.

Rehabilitation of the Goba line is also being undertaken, with 45 kg/m rail on concrete sleepers and resignalling. Assistance provided by the Italian government funded work on the initial 20 km from Goba to Boane, while a start on the remaining 63 km awaits funding from other sources.

A grant from the UK of US$20 million supported rehabilitation of the Beira corridor line west of Dondo Junction, starting with the severely graded 100 km near the Zimbabwe border, where 30 kg/m rail was replaced by 40 kg/m, curves eased to a minimum radius of 500 m and ruling gradient from 1.2 to 2.4 per cent. The objective is to double-track and resignal the 27 km between Beira and Dondo. Further work planned for this route will benefit from technical assistance provided by the Australian government. All relaying is being carried out with 54 kg/m rail on concrete rather than timber sleepers. The upgrading has led to a rapid growth in transit traffic between Zimbabwe and the container terminal at Beira port.

Rehabilitation of the Beira line to Malawi remains to be funded, after international assistance provided under the Beira Corridor Authority programme ended in 1996. A combined project, involving dredging and other works at Beira with upgrading of the railway, is costed at US$381 million.

Funding for a R65 million rehabilitation of the Maputo-Ressano Garcia line is being provided jointly by Spoornet of South Africa, CFM, and the private sector. Early completion of the route's rehabilitation, along with dredging of the harbour at Maputo, will allow this port once again to fulfil its role as the nearest to Pretoria and Johannesburg. However, the scheme also includes construction with private finance of a toll road to Maputo from Witbank in South Africa.

**Traction and rolling stock**
At the beginning of 1997 CFM's fleet comprised 83 diesel and 18 steam locomotives, 17 diesel railcars, 152 passenger cars and 7,186 wagons.

The most recent traction acquisitions have been 15 GEC Alsthom Type AD26C 1,850 kW diesel locomotives

**Diesel locomotives**

| Class | Power kW | Speed km/h | Weight tonnes | No in service | First built | Builders Mechanical | Engine | Transmission |
|---|---|---|---|---|---|---|---|---|
| 1a | 2,150 | 103 | 96 | 1 | 1966 | GE | 7FDL-12B3 | E |
| 2a | 2,150 | 103 | 96 | 5 | 1968 | GE | 7FDL-12B7 | E |
| 3a | 2,150 | 103 | 120 | 17 | 1973 | GE | 7FDL-12D10 | E |
| 4a | 2,150 | 108 | 96 | 11 | 1979 | GE do Brasil | 7FDL-12D29 | E |
| 5a | 2,150 | 108 | 96 | 17 | 1980 | GE do Brasil | 7FDL-12D29 | E |
| 6a | 2,150 | 108 | 96 | 6 | 1984 | GE | 7FDL-12 | E |
| 7a | 2,150 | 103 | 96 | 5 | 1990 | GE | 7FDL-12 | E |
| 8a | 1,850 | 103 | 108 | 15 | 1991 | GEC Alsthom | 3606 | E |
| DH-125 | 1,250 | 80 | 68 | 28 | 1980 | Faur | 6LDA 28B | H Brason |
| 10a | 1,100 | 70 | 64 | 6 | 1991 | GE | 3512 | E |
| 200 | 1,200 | 80 | 82.5 | 1 | 1963 | AEI | Sulzer-6LDA-28B | E |

powered by Caterpillar Series 3606 engines, for use in the Limpopo corridor, and six World Bank-financed General Electric Caterpillar Series 3512-engined Type U10B 1,100 kW diesel locomotives delivered to the Beira Corridor Authority. Both series were supplied in 1991-2.

**Signalling and telecommunications**
Much of the existing signalling is deficient and the long-term aim is to resignal throughout the network. Rehabilitation of the Goba line includes installation of a new traffic control system, while resignalling and some doubling of the Ressano Garcia line is under study as part of the rehabilitation project mentioned above.

One of the most striking advances has been in the application of computers. A second phase of computerised traffic control was implemented in 1991, bringing on line a second computer to improve data capture. The system now encompasses wages, traffic and routeing statistics, and movement of ships at the port of Maputo. It will be extended to cover all financial, personnel and commercial matters and stores control.

In an associated project, US Aid has financed computerisation of all clerical activities at the port. The microwave link between Maputo and the South African border at Ressano Garcia is being supplemented by another between Maputo and the Zimbabwe border at Chicualacuala, bringing this route into the data capture system.

**Track**
**Standard rail:** 54 kg/m is replacing 30, 40 and 45 kg/m section when rehabilitation takes place
**Crossties (sleepers):** Timber, 2 × 0.24 × 0.13 m Concrete and twin-block concrete, 2 × 0.24 × 0.13 m
**Spacing:** In plain track, 1,500/km
**Min curve radius:** 100 m
**Max gradient:** 2.7%
**Max axleload:** 20 tonnes

# MYANMAR (BURMA)

## Ministry of Rail Transport

PO Box 118, Yangon

**Key personnel**
Minister: U Win Sein

## Myanmar Railways (MR)

PO Box 118, Bogyoke Aung San Street, Yangon
Tel: (+95 1) 28 44 55

**Key personnel**
Managing Director: U Thaung Lwin
General Manager: U Aye Mu
Departmental Heads
 Operating: U Tin Shwe
 Mechanical and Electrical: U Tun Aye
 Civil Engineering: U Kyaw San
 Finance: U Nyan Win
 Commercial: U Myint Wai

Gauge: 1,000 mm
Route length: 3,955 km

**Organisation**
The most important line connects the two principal cities, Yangon (Rangoon) the capital, and Mandalay 619 km to the north. MR has no connections with neighbouring railways. Extension of the Bago-Moatama line over the Salween river and into Thailand at Phisantouk has been studied, but is not seen as a priority.

**Passenger operations**
Just over five billion passenger-km were travelled in FY95-96.

Principal passenger services are operated on Yangon-Mandalay, Mandalay-Lashio, Mandalay-Myitkyina, Yangon-Ye, Thazi-Myingyan and Yangon-Pyay routes. Some overnight services on longer routes, such as Yangon-Mandalay, offer sleeping accommodation.

**Freight operations**
In FY95-96 traffic totalled 926 million tonne-km, almost double what it had been five years before. Principal freight commodities are timber, rice, sugar cane and aggregates.

**New lines**
A 102 km line south from Ye to Tavoy was opened in March 1999, having taken nearly five years to construct. The line was built by defence services personnel and members of the local population.

In 1999, defence personnel were working on the final stages of a new line from the regional capital of Pakokku to Gangaw and Kalay. New railway (and road) construction is carried out under the auspices of the State Peace and Development Council, which since 1988 has constructed nearly 1,400 km of new lines.

Rebuilding of the so-called 'Death Railway' link to Thailand was discussed by the two governments in 1996 but the project has not been taken forward.

**Improvements to existing lines**
Foreign aid has been sought to finance several major projects. One is conversion of Yangon's orbital commuter line to an electrified system operated by 19 locomotives and 105 passenger cars, the total cost of which is put at US$86.7 million. In 1992 bids were invited for resignalling of this line, but satisfactory tenders were not forthcoming. The work was readvertised at the start of 1996.

A second aspiration is the first stage of relaying the Yangon-Mandalay main line and equipping it with a VHF communications system.

**Traction and rolling stock**
At the beginning of 1996 MR's resources included 16 serviceable steam and 205 operational diesel locomotives. Additional locomotives were under repair or out of use. Some 600 passenger coaches and 3,800 freight wagons were also owned by the railway.

The greater part of MR's diesel fleet is French-built, with Alsthom Bo-Bo-Bos of 900 kW, 1,200 kW and 1,500 kW prominent. 1980s acquisitions included seven 375 kW diesel-hydraulic locomotives from Kawasaki and Sumitomo of Japan and 19 820 kW diesel-hydraulic locomotives from Krupp of Germany.

In 1993 MR took delivery of six Class DF 2016 1,500 kW diesel-electric locomotives from the Dalian rolling stock plant in northeast China's Liaoning province. A further six such locomotives were ordered later, along with four Class DF1264 900 kW units. In 1995 further orders valued at US$40 million were placed with Chinese builders for locomotives, rolling stock and spare parts, including nine MTU-powered diesel-electrics from Quingdao works.

Under a technology transfer arrangement in the 1980s, Daewoo of South Korea set up a factory at Mandalay capable of producing 60 passenger cars and 120 wagons a year.

In 1997, MR awarded a US$11 million order for 400 wagons to Fabrika Vagona Kraljevo of Yugoslavia.

**Signalling and telecommunications**
Most of the network remains under the control of semaphore signals and wire-based communications. Bids were sought in early 1996 for resignalling of the Yangon suburban network and three other locations.

**Track**
**Standard rail:** Flat bottom BS
**Main line:** 75 and 60 lb/yd (37.2 and 29.8 kg/m) in 39 ft lengths
**Main branches:** 60 lb/yd (29.8 kg/m)
**Other branches and sidings:** 50 lb/yd (24.9 kg/m)
**Joints:** Suspended; joint sleepers 14 in centres. Rails joined by fishplates and bolts
**Welded track:** 117 ft (35.7 m) lengths. Thermit welded *in situ*
**Crossties (sleepers):** Hardwood (Xylia Dolabriformis) and creosoted soft wood, 8 in × 4½ in × 6 ft (203 × 115 × 1,829 mm)
**Spacing**
Main line: N × 3
Branch line: N × 2 (N = length of rail in linear yards)
**Rail fastening:** Dog spikes, elastic rail spikes
**Filling (ballast):** Broken stone, 70 mm, shingle on branch lines
**Thickness under sleeper:** 150 mm
**Max curvature**
Main line: 6° = radius of 955 ft (291 m)
Branch line: 17° = radius of 338 ft (103 m)
**Max gradient**
Main line: 0.5% = 1 in 200 compensated
Branch line: 4.0% = 1 in 25 compensated
**Max permitted speed**
Main line: 48 km/h
Branch line: 32 km/h
**Max axleload:** 12 tons on 75 and 60 lb/yd rail
**Bridge loading:** Indian Railway Standard ML

# NAMIBIA

## Ministry of Works, Transport and Communication

Ministry of Works, Transport and Communication
PO Box 13341, 9000 Windhoek
Tel: (+264 61) 208 91 11    Fax: (+264 61) 22 85 60

**Key personnel**
Minister: Hon Moses Amweelo
Permanent Secretary: S T Hiveluah
Under Secretary for Transport: E H Lowe (acting)

*UPDATED*

## NamRail

Private Bag 13204, Windhoek 9000
Tel: (+264 61) 298 11 11    Fax: (+264 61) 22 79 84
e-mail: rail@transnamib.com.na

**Key personnel**
Managing Director: Stinus Brink

Gauge: 1,065 mm
Route length: 2,382 km

### Political background
In 1988 the Namibian rail, road and air services, previously worked by South African Transport Services under contract, were formally handed over to the Namibian body that was renamed TransNamib in 1989. This followed a *de facto* transfer in 1985. The government is the principal shareholder. The state owns the railway infrastructure, with the Ministry of Finance the shareholding ministry and the Ministry of Works, Transport and Communication the regulatory ministry. The rail, road and air services are run as separate business units. In 1996, the whole future of TransNamib was considered by the Independent Task Force to Review TransNamib Ltd, with German consultants DE-Consult looking specifically at the future of the rail operations. As a result, a complete restructuring of TransNamib Ltd was carried out. This saw the creation of a holding company, TransNamib Holdings Ltd, and four independently accountable subsidiary companies. TransNamib Transport (Pty) Ltd became the new subsidiary handling group rail and road transport services, with three other companies responsible for air transport, property and travel. Formerly TransNamib Rail, NamRail is the rail-operating subsidiary.

NamRail and TransNamib Rail have operated without outside funding or subsidy since its inception. At the start of 1997 it had 1,700 employees.

**Finance** (Namibia Dollars 000)

| Revenues | 1993-94 | 1994-95 | 1995-96 |
|---|---|---|---|
| Passengers | 2,233 | 2,113 | 2,888 |
| Freight | 151,641 | 152,316 | 161,274 |
| Other income | 1,745 | 2,511 | 1,575 |
| Total | 155,619 | 156,940 | 165,737 |

| Expenditure | 1993-94 | 1994-95 | 1995-96 |
|---|---|---|---|
| Staff/personnel | 48,223 | - | - |
| Materials and services | 89,416 | - | - |
| Depreciation | 2,130 | 2,174 | 2,965 |
| Total | 139,769 | 148,487 | 153,264 |

| Traffic | 1993-94 | 1994-95 | 1995-96 |
|---|---|---|---|
| Passenger journeys | 91,869 | 110,462 | 123,771 |
| Passenger-km (million) | 24.2 | 34.7 | 48.3 |
| Freight tonnes (million) | 1.684 | 1.733 | 1.760 |
| Freight tonne-km (million) | 1,075 | 1,077 | 1,082 |

### Passenger operations
In the early 1990s, business suffered from the expansion of minibus operations, some actually poaching passengers at stations. TransNamib responded by offering improved service at lower prices. In order to stem losses, the organisation revamped the whole passenger service by introducing coaches refurbished with airline-type seating and air conditioning attached to timetabled freight trains; these are known as 'StarLine' services and have proved very popular. They have replaced traditional overnight sleeper services, and resulted in a doubling of the number of passenger journeys between 1993 and 1998 to some 50 million. NamRail also operates an extensive network of connecting bus services. In 2000, StarLine buses were also providing services on the Keetmanshoop–Lüderitz route, on which rail services were suspended due to poor track conditions.

At the seaside resort of Swakopmund, NamRail has joined forces with a developer to build a hotel complex incorporating the town's imposing station building. TNR and Air Namibia introduced a luxury 'Desert Express' for tourists in April 1998, to operate three times weekly between Windhoek and Swakopmund/Walvis Bay. Sleeping car and restaurant facilities are included in the train formation.

A cross-border passenger service to Upington in South Africa has been restored, but through trains onwards to De Aar remain suspended since their withdrawal in late 1994.

NamRail has been studying a possible commuter service between Windhoek and Rehoboth (90 km).

### Freight operations
The main constituents of the freight business are mining products, bulk liquids, building materials and containers.

In 1995, tonnage of local traffic constituted 69.5 per cent of the total, while imports, at 24.7 per cent of total tonnage, decreased slightly. Exports, amounting to 5.8 per cent of total tonnage, also showed a decrease. This shift in the pattern of movements was due to the increased volumes entering the country through the port of Walvis Bay rather than over the southern border with South Africa. Improvements to port facilities in progress at Walvis Bay in 1999 offered the prospect of increased traffic for NamRail. The rail link with South Africa has declined significantly since independence as a result of severe road competition and shorter road distances from the Transvaal area. Traffic volumes of freight for South Africa have been boosted by the establishment of a NamRail depot at Upington, within South Africa, where cargo is transferred to road.

### New lines
Construction of a 248 km northern extension of the railway from Tsumeb to connect with Angola's Namibe

*General Electric U20C locomotive at Gobabis with a passenger train for Windhoek (Marcel Vleugels)*

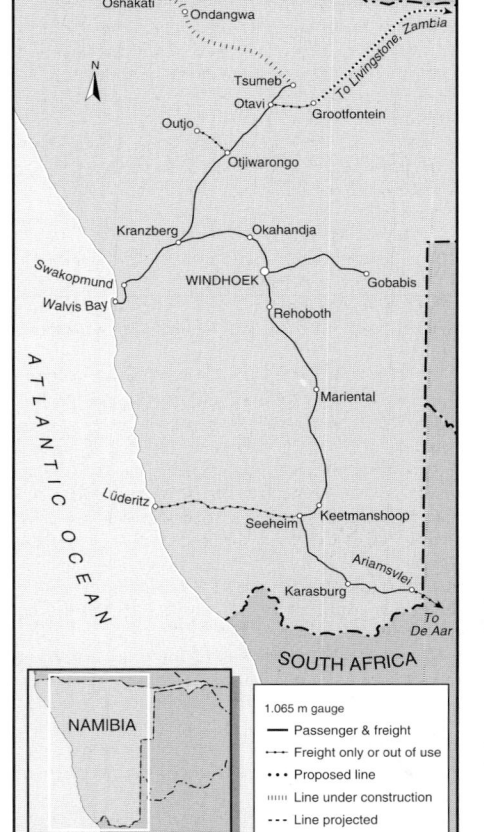

*Two General Electric U20C locomotives lead a Windhoek-bound freight at Dsona. The train includes tank wagons containing aviation spirit (Marcel Vleugels)*

Railway (qv) was in progress in 2001, with completion expected in early 2004. The so-called Northern Railway Extension project involves a new line northwest from Tsumeb to Oshikango, close to the border with Angola and the location of a tax-free export processing zone. On the Angolan side the line is to be extended to join the Namibe system at Cassinga.

A rail link between Namibia and Zambia moved closer to being realised in 1999, when the governments of the two countries agreed to construct a bridge over the Zambesi at Sheseke. This would be reached by extending the existing NamRail Walvis Bay–Grootfontein line to met a new Zambia Railways (qv) line diverging from its Livingstone–Mulobezi line. European Union funding for studies into this project was obtained in 2001.

**Improvements to existing lines**
In 2000, rehabilitation was under way of the 139 km Aus–Lüderitz section of the Seeheim–Lüderitz line (318 km), on which the rails had deteriorated to such an extent that passenger services were suspended. Rails salvaged from track upgrading in Botswana and reconditioned in South Africa were being used, enabling line speeds to be raised to 80-100 km/h and axleloads from 11.5 to 18.5 tonnes. The project is due to be completed in 2004.

**Traction and rolling stock**
The railway operates six GE U18C1 1,475/1,340 kW 1-Co-Co-1 and 65 GE Type U20C 1,605/1,490 kW Co-Co diesel-electric locomotives (some of the diesels are stored). It also has two steam locomotives for special trains. Other rolling stock comprises 113 passenger cars, including two catering, one lounge and 86 sleeping cars; and 1,626 freight wagons.

**Signalling and telecommunications**
Radio control now covers operation throughout the railway.

**Coupler in standard use:** SASKOP Type M on passenger cars, and Types M and S on wagons

**Braking in standard use:** Vacuum; two daily fast trains are air-braked

**Track**
**Rail type and weight:** HCOB 22 kg/m (185.4 km), 30 kg/m (1,405.8 km), 48 kg/m (916.5 km), 57 kg/m (78 km)
**Crossties (sleepers):** Concrete, steel, timber (on bridges and 1:12 pointwork)
Concrete, 2,057 × 230 × 250 mm
Steel, 1,917.7 × 305 × 106 mm
**Spacing:** In plain track 1,429/km, in curves 1,538/km
**Rail fastening:** Fist and Pandrol on concrete sleepers, bolt and nut in steel, screw on timber
**Min curve radius:** 200 m
**Max gradient:** 1.5%
**Max axleload:** 16.5 tonnes on 48 and 57 kg/m rail, 15 tonnes on 30 kg/m rail, 11.5 tonnes on 22 kg/m rail

*UPDATED*

# NEPAL

## Ministry of Works & Transport

Babar Mahal, Kathmandu
Tel: (+977 1) 22 65 37   Fax:(+977 1) 22 59 93

**Key personnel**
Minister: Bijaya Gachhedar

## Janakpur Railway (JR)

Jaynagar

**Key personnel**
Manager: P P K Poudyal
Traffic Officer: K G D Upadhya
Assistant Engineer: D B Khadka

## Nepal Government Railway (NR)

Birganj

**Key personnel**
Manager: Devendra Singh
Traffic Officer: Pratap Bahadur

Gauge: 762 mm
Route length: 6 km

**Organisation**
There are only two short railways within Nepal, operating in the Terai, a fertile and level strip adjacent to the border with India, the Janakpur Railway (qv) and the Nepal Government Railway (NR).

Gauge: 762 mm
Route length: 53 km

**Organisation**
The Janakpur Railway (JR) runs from Jaynagar in Bihar State, India, across the Nepal border north and west to Janakpur (32 km) and on to Bizulpura (21 km). JR is a subsidiary of the Nepal Transport Corporation.

The railway was originally built as a timber line designed to open the virgin jungle to the north of Janakpurdam. As the forest has long since been cut, the railway now operates primarily to provide access in an area with few roads. Passengers are the main source of revenue, with pilgrims to the temples of Janakpurdam forming the bulk of traffic. At latest report the railway recorded 1.6 million passenger journeys and 22,000 tonnes of freight.

NR runs a mere 6 km from Raxaul on the North Eastern Railway in India's Bihar State across the Nepal border to Birganj. The line was originally built as a key link in the railway-road-ropeway transport system that supplied the mountain-locked valley of Kathmandu, closed to the outside world until the early 1950s. The line formerly continued north to the base of the Siwalik Hills at Amlekhganj (48 km).

**New lines**
The government is now undertaking to develop Hetauda into a new industrial centre. As part of the scheme, preliminary feasibility studies have been made for construction of a new rail line from the limit of Indian metre-gauge at Raxaul to Hetauda.

**Improvements to existing lines**
In recent years JR has been upgrading track by laying new sleepers and second-hand 16 kg/m rail to replace existing 12.5 kg/m profile. Locomotives (including two Garratts) and wagons released from the Nepal Railway were rebuilt and pressed into service. Recent stock comprised 10 steam locomotives, 25 passenger cars and 52 freight wagons.

In 1991 India undertook to finance upgrading of the line from Bizulpura to Janakpur. In 1994 modernisation came in the form of two ZDM5 diesel locomotives and six coaches supplied by IR. These were operating two return Janakpur-Jaynagar trips daily, while the Bizulpura line was being operated separately by a single diesel. The steam fleet remained in reserve.

**Improvements to existing lines**
Plans emerged in 1993 for regauging the cross-border line to eliminate transhipment of freight from metre- to broad-gauge wagons once the NER line to Raxaul is converted to broad-gauge. Rites, the India Railways consultancy, was contracted to carry out a feasibility study, and will supply two diesel locomotives and 12 coaches, as well as technical support, for the project.

**Traction and rolling stock**
The Nepal Government Railway operates seven steam locomotives, 12 passenger cars and 82 freight wagons.

# NETHERLANDS

## Ministry of Transport & Water Management

Plesmanweg 1-6, PO Box 20901, NL-2500 EX Den Haag
Tel: (+31 70) 351 61 71   Fax: (+31 70) 351 78 95
Web: http://www.minvenw.nl

**Key personnel**
Minister: Mrs T Netelenbos
Secretary of State: Mrs M de Vries
Secretary-General: R Pans
Director-General, Passenger Transport: M van Eeghen
Director, Mobility and Market: P Boot
Director, Infrastructure and Policy: M Olman
Head, Rail Infrastructure Investment and Maintenance: P. de Booij
Directors General, Freight Transport:
 B Westerduin, F J P Heuer
Head, Freight Transport Sectors: K Van Hout

Head, Railfreight: Mrs T Zwartepoorte
Head, Repositioning Government Agencies: K van Hout

Within the framework of the railway reforms which are taking place in the Netherlands, the Minister of Transport has launched a policy document called '*De derde eeuw spoor*' (The Third Age of Rail). Its aim is to strengthen the position of rail transport. In three main areas it calls for action to be taken to improve the role played by rail.

The first is restructuring the managerial responsibilities for rail traffic. Progressively, responsibility for regional train services will be decentralised to regional authorities (provinces) and the services tendered. The first to be tendered will be the so-called 'contract sector services', which the national authorities pay NS Reizigers to run. This process will take into account the size of prospective operators' market shares: those with a share considered too large will be excluded.

In 1999, for some 30 services contracts have been made between the government and NS at a cost to the state of NS G155 million a year. The state will continue to be responsible for national train services. NS Reizigers will have the exclusive concession for running the national core network, which is currently served by most IC services and some fast trains. NS Reizigers will also have the exclusive right to operate domestic high-speed services on the HSL-Zuid line. For both exclusive concessions a performance contract will be made between NS Reizigers and the state in which obligations for NS are based on maintaining specified levels of service.

The second area addressed by the policy document concerns the balance between control by the authorities and the market. It is supposed that demands will be made on performance by the operators. Important here are growth of the numbers of peak-hour passengers and punctuality, but also some other points. It is probable that a bonus or penalty regime will be linked to performance.

The third area concerns the publicly owned, government-financed agencies within NS Holding: Railned, NS Railinfrabeheer BV and NS Verkeersleiding BV

(Traffic Control). These all undertake tasks for which the government is responsible and will remain so after the separation of infrastructure and operations, as well as the opening up of the network for other or new operators. The government's intention is to take these three agencies out of NS Holding from 1 January 2000. In 1999 it was likely that an independent public institution would be established to handle capacity management, operations control and access. Possibilities about the way to organise infrastructure maintenance and construction projects were still being studied.

A track access charge is to be introduced on 1 January 2000. In fact, track access fees already notionally exist but the charge is rated at G0 per km. European directives prescribe the existence of a rating system for track access charges and the present Dutch one is in accordance to this legislation. The proposed change planned in January 2000 is in fact a change in rating. In mid-1999 a final decision remained to be taken regarding the method by which operators would pay these charges. The Minister of Transport has proposed that a total charge must generate G400 million annually across the network. This amount does not cover the costs incurred by the government for track maintenance. NS Reizigers, which operates a majority of trains on the network, is to pay G250 million and decentralised, regional and tendered train service operators are to pay G100 million. Freight should pay between zero and G50 million. The charge is to be introduced in stages, eventually with different tariffs for freight and passenger transport. The proposal is not definitive and is still under discussion. All train operators oppose the track access charge.

To implement the policy described above, the Minister of Transport is planning new legislation for public transport, including public train operations, and this was expected to be in parliament during 1999. The new law will also define rules governing competition and tendering for regional train services. Another move by the Minister of Transport aims to renew existing railway legislation to meet contemporary requirements. The new legislation will be in accordance with European Union directives, and will define the tasks and competences of the various authorities involved with rail traffic. It will also define the position of the three publicly financed government agencies mentioned above. The Minister aims to make the new law effective by 2001.

Freight traffic and limited passenger services have been liberalised. In theory, if an operator fulfils the conditions to operate services, there are no legal or policy obstacles to entering the market. In practice, conflicts can occur scheduling freight between other trains. Much of the capacity of the Netherlands network is used by the high-density passenger services operated by NS Reizigers, which runs trains to a rigid pattern and with high frequencies, especially on the main corridors. This makes it difficult to run freight services during daytime. Rules for managing the line capacity were being developed in 1999.

*Open access*
Recently the Dutch railway network has been opened up to new operators, who must fulfil certain conditions. Open access and other rail reforms on the Dutch railway network are currently founded on a temporary, non-legislative basis, but are to be covered by the new legislation detailed above. Until then the procedure for setting up a train operating company focuses on three main points: access to the profession; access to the market; and access to the traffic. The Ministry of Transport and the three publicly financed government agencies, Railned, NS Railinfrabeheer and NS Verkeersleiding, all part of the NS Holding, are involved in this process. Railned, which is responsible for track capacity management, timetables and safety, and is considered to act independently, serves as the interface between the operator and the other two agencies.

First, prospective entrants to the market must be recognised by the Minister of Transport as being a train operating company. For access purposes, rail traffic is split up into three categories: freight, limited/charter train services and public services. For the last, public transport legislation approved by the Minister of Transport is needed. For freight or restricted passenger services, recognition by the Minister is sufficient. An access contract comes into force if it is clear that the new operator is capable of running his intended services, staff have been examined satisfactorily, rolling stock has been approved and if the new operator accepts specific legal responsibilities. The operator must also have a certificate of safety, issued by Railned.

In 1996 Lovers Rail was the first company to operate public services after withdrawal of the NS monopoly of passenger traffic, introducing trains between Amsterdam and the coastal town of IJmuiden. Unclear what kind of competition in public transport might emerge, the Minister of Transport decided that no new operators could enter this market of public transport, fearing the prospect of 'cherry-picking', companies bidding only to operate profitable routes, while NS Reizigers continued to run a nationwide network which included loss-making services. The minister will continue to refuse to grant licences for public services until the new legislation is in place.

In May 1998 another public passenger train service was started by a new train operator, Oostnet. In this case there was no cherry-picking; NS was unwilling to continue services on the Almelo-Mariënberg regional line for the subsidy offered by the government. In a pilot project for the decentralisation and tendering of regional train services, Oostnet, the regional bus operator in the eastern Netherlands, took over services, which are partially supported financially by regional and local authorities. It is thought that regional authorities will be responsible for tendering for local transport services under the provisions of the new legislation.

By 1 April 1999, 22 operators had been recognised by the ministry. Twelve of these had received safety certificates and 10 had not. The safety certificate allows an operator to run independently on the Dutch rail network. The operators listed are involved in the operation of public and limited passenger transport, freight and historic train services.

Operators with a safety certificate: ACTS; Bentheimer Eisenbahn; Lovers Rail; NBM Rail; NS Cargo; NS Materieel; NS Reizigers; Oostnet; Short Lines; Structon Railinfra Materieel; Volker Stevin Rail & Traffic; and Zuidlimburgse Stoomtrein mij.

Operators without a safety certificate: Chem Trans Logistic; Nederland ERS Railways BV; Holland Spoor; Hoogovens Staal; HST/VEM; NDX Intermodal; NS Ultrasoonbedrijf; Rasrail; Stichting Museum Buurtspoorweg; and Stichting Stadskanaal Rail.

## State Transport Inspectorate

Rijksverkeersinspectie
Johanna Westendijkplein 115, NL-2521 EN Den Haag
PO Box 10700, 2501 HS Den Haag
Tel: (+31 70) 333 70 00  Fax: (+31 70) 305 27 99

The rail division of the State Transport Inspectorate has been wound up. Its duties have been transferred to the rail safety division of Railned, leaving just one individual responsible for monitoring Railned's safety operations.

## Transport Safety Board

Raad voor de Transport veiligheid
Prins Clauslaan 18, P.O.Box 95404, NL-2509 CK Den Haag
Tel: (+31 70) 333 70 00

**Key personnel**
President: HRH Prince Pieter van Vollenhoven
President, Rail Bureau: Mrs Schmitz

The Transport Safety Board assumed its responsibilities from 30 June 1999. The Board investigates all major transport accidents, including those on the rail network. The Board can also make recommendations regarding transport safety and the environment. Administratively, it is formed of four bureaux, of which one is responsible for rail.

## Association of Rail Operators (BVS)

Branche Vereniging van Spoorvervoerders
PO Box 19040, NL-3501 DA Utrecht
Tel: (+31 30) 236 88 44  Fax: (+31 30) 236 83 38

**Key personnel**
President: J. Hoekwater

**Political background**
BVS was established to take care of the interests of the new rail operators in the Netherlands. These interests concern subjects such as procedures and difficulties in setting up train operating companies, relationships with government and government agencies such as Railned, RIB and other parts of NS Holding, and technical harmonisation issues. BVS is also concerned with the education and training of personnel.

## RAILWAY SYSTEMS/Netherlands

**Organisation**
The members of the association can be split up into three categories: professional train operating companies, both of passenger and freight services; track maintenance and infrastructure construction companies; and railway museum operators who want to run trains on the Dutch network. In early 1999 there were nine members: ACTS Nederland; Lovers Rail; NBM Rail NV-materieel; Oostnet Groep; Short Lines; Stichting Holland Spoor; Structon Railinfra Materieel; Vereniging Historisch Railvervoer Nederland; and Volker Stevin Rail and Traffic.

## ACTS Nederland BV

PO Box 19040, 3501 DA Utrecht, Kromme Nieuwegracht 58
Tel: (+31 30) 236 88 44   Fax: (+31 30) 236 83 38
Web: http://www.acts-nl.com

**Key personnel**
Director: Ir J Hoekwater
Director, Finance: P H A van der Schoot

**Freight operations**
ACTS specialises in the transport of household waste. Initially, ACTS did not operate its own trains, instead hiring its CATS container-carrying wagons to other operators, with haulage provided by NS Cargo. In early 1998 the company started to run its own trains, at first using Class 2200 diesel locomotives hired from infrastructure company Strukton and then a former German State Railways Class V100 locomotive owned by a preservation society. During that year around 85,000 tonnes were carried.

ACTS has since expanded its activities, in March 1999 taking over from NS Cargo the domestic container service between the port of Rotterdam (Maasvlakte) and Veendam, in the far northeast of the Netherlands, and Leeuwarden, to the north.

In June 2002, the company added two international services to Germany to the five already operated domestically.

**Traction and rolling stock**
Services are operated by five Class 6700 diesel locomotives, former Class 62/63 machines, bought by ACTS from Belgian National Railways. During 1998 ACTS also obtained from NS six Class 1200 electric locomotives, two of which were for spares. Four were overhauled by Nedtrain Services, Tilburg, and delivered at the end of March 1999. Subsequently, a fifth example of this type was added to the fleet. As well as operating on non-electrified lines, the Class 6700 units will also provide assistance to the Class 1200s on the heaviest trains and a form of remote control is being developed to allow the driver of the leading electric locomotive to operate the diesel. A V100 diesel locomotive is used for shunting at Leeuwarden and ACTS has also procured four former German Type V60 shunters.

*UPDATED*

*Former Netherlands Railways Class 1200 electric locomotive refurbished by NedTrain for ACTS, photographed at Amsterdam Westhaven yard alongside a Railion Class 6400 diesel locomotive (Quintus Vosman) 2002/0137108*

## Lovers Rail

Lovers Rail BV, PO Box 2109, 1000 CC Amsterdam
Tel: (+31 20) 421 22 02   Fax: (+31 20) 421 09 97
Web: http://www.lovers.nl/rail

**Key personnel**
Director: Y Lallemant

**Organisation**
Lover's Rail is 70 per cent owned by the French Vivendi (CGEA) group, having been originally formed as the rail subsidiary of a maritime company set up to take advantage of new opportunities for open access operators on the Dutch railway system.

In September 1999, the company discontinued its 'Optio' services between Amsterdam CS and Haarlem which it had been operating using hired Class 25.5 Belgian National Railways dual-voltage locomotives and 17 Class M2 coaches bought second-hand from the same source. In 1999 Lovers Rail also withdrew its diesel-operated Amsterdam–Ijmuiden 'Kennemer Strand Express' service.

Lovers Rail retains its licence to operate in the Netherlands and was considered a potential bidder for the provision of integrated regional transport services, possibly in co-operation with other Vivendi group bus operators.

## Netherlands Railways (NS)

NV Nederlandse Spoorwegen
PO Box 2025, NL-3500 HA Utrecht
Moreelsepark 1, NL – 3511 EP Utrecht
Tel: (+31 30) 235 91 11   Fax: (+31 30) 233 24 58
Web: http://www.ns.nl

**Key personnel**
President and Chief Executive, NS Holding:
    Rob den Besten
Corporate Staff
    Communications: Mrs J C B Straatman
NS Reizigers BV (passenger business unit)
    Managing Director: H Huizinga
    Director, Marketing & Sales: M M D van Eeghen
    Operations Director: W A G Doebken
    Director, Staff & Organisation: R Lantain
NS Cargo BV (freight business unit)
Web: http://www.nscargo.nl; cargoweb.nl/NScargo
    Managing Director: E Smulders
    Commercial Director: Z van Asch van Wijck
    Finance Director: R van Haaren
NS Materieel BV (rolling stock engineering)
    Managing Director: Tj Stelwagen
    Commercial Director: R Knipping
    Finance Director: A Valk
NS Stations BV (station management)
    Directors: P Stulp; A van Engelen
NS Vastgoed BV (Property)
    Director: H Portheine
NS Opleidingen (training)
    Director: D Kruijd
NS Verkeersleiding BV (traffic control)
    Director: Mrs J Arts
NS Railinfrabeheer (rail infrastructure)
    Director: R Oliemans
Railned (capacity management)
    Director: P Ranke
NS Railway Police
    Directors: M van Asch van Wijck, G van Beek

Gauge: 1,435 mm
Route length: 2,808 km
Electrification: 2,061 km at 1.5 kV DC

**Political background**
NS has been transformed into an independent, commercially oriented business following the 1992 report of the Wijffels select committee, appointed by the Dutch minister of transport. Changes centred on separation of rail operations and infrastructure management – completed in 1994 – and the progressive change of NS from a block-subsidised organisation to one of separately accountable business units. In June 1998, it was announced that NS Cargo was to merge with its German counterpart, DB Cargo, to form a new joint company, Rail Cargo Europe. The fusion of the two organisations was expected to be complete by late 1999, when operations would be managed from new headquarters in Mainz, Germany.

Further changes now being implemented see the advent of limited on-rail competition in a transitional period which will stretch up to 2000. Lovers Rail (qv), a private company, began passenger operations on the line between Amsterdam and IJmuiden in August 1996. Several other new operators plan to introduce freight services.

In early 1998, the competitive model for rail transport after 2000 had not been decided upon, but the transport ministry was moving to prevent any one operator, including NS, from having more than 50 per cent of the country's rail market. NS was pressing the government to grant it exclusive rights to the intercity network and to end uncertainty as its proposals for rolling stock acquisition and upgrading had to be put on hold.

In 1996, NS drew state financial support of G66 million for operations in respect of unremunerative services and fare reductions deemed socially necessary. An agreement has been reached with the government over the continuation in service until at least mid-1999 of 29 unprofitable lines and the operation of seven new stations. For the period mid-1998 to mid-1999, the government has agreed to pay G155 million for this. A list of around 30 loss-making lines was drawn up in the mid-1990s and the Dutch government has moved to open up their operation to international tender. From May 1998 the company Oostnet is to take over the Almelo–Mariënberg line, initially using NS rolling stock. There are now moves to open up complete local stopping train networks to tender rather than concentrating on individual lines.

Jane's World Railways 2002-2003                                                                                                                                                    www.janes.com

*Two NS Cargo Class 6400 diesel locomotives head grain hoppers near Gilze-Rijen* (Alex Dasi-Sutton) 0023254

## Organisation

In recent years NV Nederlandse Spoorwegen has been transformed into an independent commercially oriented business. The restructuring followed the method advised by the Wijffels select committee, appointed by the Dutch minister of transport. The first phase of this process has been completed and in mid-1999 the second stage was due to start soon. Its main feature will be the removal from railway control of the state-financed government-commissioned agencies, Railned, NS Railinfrabeheer and NS Verkeersleiding (see below). Although involved in performing functions in which neutrality and objectivity are required, these agencies currently remain part of NS Holding. This was a result of implementing European Union Directive 91/440, separating infrastructure and operations. The next phase will see a split between organisations with public functions and commercially oriented business units.

NS Holding is divided into two groups of companies: one comprises the three government-commissioned agencies mentioned above; the other is formed by NS Groep NV and includes the railway's commercial business units, each of which has independent company status. The business units are: NS Reizigers, NS Cargo, NS Stations, NS Vastgoed NS Materieel, NS Beveiliging Services, NS Facilitaire Bedrijven and NS Opleidingen. Some of these business units have shares or a participation in other companies, such as NS Reizigers, which is one of the three parties involved in the Syntus regional integrated transport company (qv). In mid-1998 it was announced that NS Cargo was to merge with DB Cargo, the freight business of German Rail. NS Holding will have a minority shareholding in the resulting new company, Rail Cargo Europe. NS Cargo was still recording losses during 1998, but the deficit had declined to G2 million. Break even was forecast to occur in 1999, just before the merger was due to take place.

State subsidies have been withdrawn in steps. NS received its last subsidy for train operations in 1997, marking the end of a five-year reduction process. On the contrary, NS chairman Rob den Besten proposed paying the shareholder, in the form the state, a dividend worth some G9 million from the positive results achieved during the year. Capital contributions from the state to help strengthen the commercial position of NS in its market were due to finish in 1999.

A new financial relationship was made between NS Reizigers and the state for running loss-making services. In addition, some services were 'bought' by the state to provide a public transport alternative to heavily congested roads. For 29 loss-making lines NS Reizigers receives G112 million annually, these payments continuing until the adoption of a tendering procedure for local or regional services. In the first years of the new millennium it is expected that tendering for providing service on regional networks – both rail and integrated rail and bus networks – will have become widespread. In future NS is expected to be given a 10-year concession to operate the national IC network, with a contract that incorporates service and performance obligations.

NS Reizigers is acting strategically so far as regional tendering is concerned, joining with other companies to form joint ventures. The government requires that no participant in such a joint company operating in the Dutch public transport market has a share larger than 50 per cent. For example, NS Reizgers has one third of the shares in the Syntus joint venture company.

### Business units

The passenger (NS Reizigers) and freight (NS Cargo) businesses are described under 'Passenger operations' and 'Freight operations'.

NS Materieel manages major rolling stock workshops at Tilburg, Amersfoort and Haarlem. Smaller workshops are located at Maastricht, Rotterdam Fijenoord, Amsterdam Zaanstraat, Zwolle and Onnen (Groningen). NS Materieel has suffered from overcapacity and the company has been restructured with a reduced workforce and modernised processes at its facilities. Work is sought from domestic and foreign clients as well as from NS companies.

NS Stations develops commercial activities at stations under exclusive rights granted to it by government. The total number of retail outlets rose from 1,231 in 1997 to 1,268 in 1998, when revenues of G1.05 billion and profits of G139 million were generated. At some stations where a ticket office is considered too expensive to operate, tickets are sold at a Wizzl, a small supermarket selling products to passengers. Provision of new retail space is regarded as an essential element of station improvement schemes.

NS Vastgoed handles the group's property portfolio, developing commercial property in and around stations, including the provision of accommodation at new or rebuilt stations.

### Service units

Other business units, which mostly sell services to other NS Holding companies, are: NS Beveiliging Services (Security); NS Facilitaire Bedrijven, responsible for administration, documentation and research; and NS Opleidingen (training). Some parts of NS Beveiliging Services have been sold. The railway police service, managed on a non-commercial basis by NS Beveiliging Services, is to be removed from NS from 1 January 2000 to become part of the national police force.

### Joint ventures

NS and British Telecom have established a joint telecommunications company, Telforty, which operates a mobile telephone network in the Netherlands. Over G1 billion is being invested annually in the company and losses resulting from these start-up costs have had a negative effect on the consolidated results of NS Groep.

NS also has a stake in a rail infrastructure construction company, Strukton Groep BV and in engineering consultancy Holland Railconsult. Both were formerly part of the old NS organisation.

### Government agencies

Outside the NS Groep but in 1999 still within NS Holding are three government-commissioned agencies: Traffic Control (NS Verkeersleiding) which regulates the allocation of train paths on a day-to-day basis between NS businesses and possible private-sector operators under the European Union's open access provisions; Railned, a capacity management agency which conducts forward planning of train paths; Rail Infrastructure (NS Railinfrabeheer) which is responsible for the management, upkeep, expansion and development of the system including the commissioning of contractors for the execution of work. These tasks are financed from the government infrastructure fund, Infrafonds. NS Railinfrabeheer contracts outside firms for maintenance, renewal and repair work; these include Strukton Railinfra bv (qv in Permanent Way Equipment and Services section), a joint venture which has taken over the assets of NS Infra Services Materieel.

## Finance

NS finished 1997 with a positive result of G164 million, up from G105 million in 1996. Overall, revenue rose by 5 per cent.

The average number of full-time employees in the company during 1997 was 25,938, against 28,191 in 1996.

| **Traffic** (million) | 1996 | 1997 | 1998 |
|---|---:|---:|---:|
| Passenger journeys | 306 | 316 | 321 |
| Passenger-km | 14,091 | 14,485 | 14,879 |
| Freight tonnes | 20.8 | 22.9 | 24.7 |
| Freight tonne-km | 3,123 | 3,406 | 3,778 |

## Passenger operations

The performance the NS Reizigers passenger business unit continues to improve. In 1998 profits rose to G362 million compared with G158 million the previous year. Revenue rose by 9 per cent and much progress was made on efficiency and cost reductions. Passenger volume rose by 2.9 per cent in 1998 to 14.9 billion passenger-km. Punctuality rose slightly during 1998, from 82.9 per cent in 1997 to 83.0 per cent. NS Reizigers' target is 87 per cent. Preventive measures against poor punctuality are to include avoiding vulnerable scheduling in timetable planning and a reduction in the coupling and splitting of portion trains, which will sometimes result in longer than necessary trains being run at certain times.

Between 1992 and 1998 state subsidies for passenger services have declined from almost G300 million to zero in 1998. In 1997 NS received G66 million for operations.

Passenger operations in the Netherlands are characterised by high-frequency, regular-interval services. For domestic services the lowest frequency is hourly. Most lines see two trains an hour, while on main lines the frequency is generally much higher, and routes like Amsterdam–Utrecht are served by four IC services an hour.

Although the three passenger service types introduced by NS in the early 1990s, Aglo/Regio, Interregio and Intercity, were perpetuated by NS Reizigers, these names

*Class DM 90 two-car dmus at Zwolle* (Quintus Vosman) 0058794

have been abandoned recently. Nevertheless, the split of services into the three categories is in effect taking place. NS is aiming to run faster IC services by omitting calls at some stations, while adding fast service stops at other stations where traffic levels justify this. Other stations are served by stopping services which NS Reizigers can withdraw if loss-making. If the government wishes to retain loss-making services, it can sign a contract with NS Reizigers to run them. In 1999 the two parties signed a G155 million contract covering the operation of such services. A government programme to combat road congestion, called 'Samen Werken Aan Bereikbaarheid' (Working Together on Sustainability) partly covers the addition of further train services to NS operations.

In the 1998-99 timetable NS added 5 per cent more passenger services – 250 trains – compared with the previous year. NS claims that the new services generated some 10,000 additional passengers daily.

NS Reizigers is making preparations to run domestic high-speed IC services on the HSL-Zuid line. New rolling stock is to be ordered, but in 1999 its design had not been determined, although double-deck equipment seemed most likely.

In 1998 NS withdrew from operating the Almelo-Mariënberg regional non-electrified line, considered the heaviest loss-making of all Dutch train services. Services were taken over by Oostnet, a regional bus operator and part of the VSN-1 group, after a tendering procedure. More regional services are to be abandoned by NS Reizigers, although it will take shareholdings in joint venture companies tendering to operate such services.

Transvision is a successful co-operative venture between taxi companies and NS Reizigers, carrying passengers to and from stations for a G6 ticket. Another alliance has been formed covering international passenger services: NS, KLM Royal Dutch Airlines, Schiphol airport, and Belgian and French National Railways have signed an agreement to develop a strategic co-operative alliance to operate trains using the HSL-Zuid to link the Netherlands, Brussels and Paris.

**Freight operations**
During 1998 NS Cargo freight traffic increased by 8 per cent up to 24.7 million tonnes. Much of this rise was attributable to a doubling of coal movements from the ports of Amsterdam and Rotterdam compared with 1997. The trailing load of such coal trains has been increased from 2,400 tonnes to 3,800 tonnes.

Container transport also rose by 10 per cent to a total of 490,000 units, although in a move to rationalise activities, NS Cargo withdrew most of its domestic container services. In 1999 NS Cargo lost its largest domestic container service, between Rotterdam Maasvlakte and Veendam container terminal, to ACTS (qv). In 1998 three new container services have been started: Rotterdam-Warsaw; Rotterdam-Mainz/Mannheim; and the Amsterdam-Frankfurt airfreight shuttle. Almelo-Poznan and Rotterdam-Barcelona, on behalf on Transfracht, were withdrawn. Traffic between Rotterdam and Eastern Europe, including Russian Federation countries, is growing rapidly. Nevertheless, rail's share in the market port's freight transport market was only 16 per cent in 1997.

Other freight sectors performed well in 1998: lime and cement traffic was up by 25 per cent to 300,000 tonnes and grain doubled up to 550,000 tonnes. Chemical transport was up by just 1 per cent.

An improving financial performance by NS Cargo saw losses decline from G6 million in 1997 to G2 million in 1998. NS Cargo was expected to break even in 1999, the year in which the merger with DB Cargo was due to take place. Revenue rose by 4 per cent to G371 million. The workforce was reduced from 1,837 in 1997 to 1,723. This includes approximately 300 drivers (240 in 1997) who were on loan from NS Reizigers. During 1999 drivers were assigned permanently either to NS Cargo or NS Reizigers.

International developments include fitting five Class 6400 diesel locomotives Class 6400 with Belgian automatic train protection and communications systems to enable them to operate intermodal services between the ports of Rotterdam and Antwerp, avoiding traction and crew changes at the border. Three more locomotives are to be similarly equipped. Four Belgian Class 25.5 dual-voltage electric locomotives, already equipped with the Dutch ATB train protection system, are being employed in through services between the two ports.

International through working of Dutch-German freight traffic was also to be introduced following the fitting of five Class 6400s with the German Indusi train protection system. These locomotives are to operate trains between the Ruhr and the port of Rotterdam, as well as regional freight services. DB Cargo is to equip five Soviet-built Class 232s with Dutch ATB equipment to haul heavy coal trains between Germany and Rotterdam and Amsterdam.

Freight services in the Arnhem area will be served from Oberhausen, Germany, instead of NS Cargo's principal yard at Kijfhoek, Rotterdam, from which freight is distributed throughout the Netherlands. Although the merger of NS Cargo and DB Cargo had not been completed when these changes were initiated, they can be seen as a consequence of the intention to combine.

**New lines**
There are two high-speed line projects in the Netherlands: the HSL-Zuid (high-speed south) line, linking Amsterdam with Belgium and France, and the HSL-Oost (high-speed east) line to Germany.

*HSL-Zuid*
Most of the legal procedures on the HSL-Zuid project have been completed and work was due to start in the second half of 1999, with completion planned for 2005. The 100 km project consists of two portions: from Hoofddorp (just south of Schiphol airport) to Rotterdam; and from the south of Rotterdam to the Dutch/Belgian border near Breda, mostly following the alignment of the E19 motorway. The line connects with the Belgian network at Antwerp. A link is to be provided to the existing Dutch network at Breda, enabling domestic services to use the high-speed line. The line will be engineered for 300 km/h and will employ a 25 kV AC 50 Hz power supply. For domestic services NS Reizigers is to order trains for speeds of 220 km/h or possibly higher. It is anticipated that running domestic services on the high-speed line will change the IC network dramatically, yielding significant time savings over the relative short-distance journeys which characterise the Dutch rail system. An Amsterdam-Rotterdam journey using the high-speed line will take 28 minutes instead of the present 1 hour 5 minutes and Amsterdam-Breda will take 48 minutes compared with 1 hour 40 minutes. International services will also benefit: the Amsterdam-Paris journey time will be reduced from present 4 hours 44 minutes to 3 hours 3 minutes.

To minimise the environment impact of the new line, its southern part will mostly run parallel to the E19 motorway or the existing Rotterdam-Breda line. On the section between Rotterdam and Hoofddorp a 7 km twin-bore tunnel is planned to avoid disturbing of the 'Green Heart of Holland'.

The government has planned the HSL-Zuid project as a partnership between public and private sectors. At 1998 prices, the project will cost an estimated G8.9 billion, of which an Investment contribution of G1-1.5 billion is expected from the private sector. The line will be operated under a 25-year infrastructure management concession to be awarded by the government.

*HSL-Oost*
The HSL-Oost project is to be achieved by a major upgrading and extension of the present line from Utrecht to Arnhem and on into Germany. Options for raising line speeds were still being studied in 1999. However, for the heavily used Arnhem-Utrecht line partial quadrupling is considered unavoidable. The HSL-Oost project focuses on the line from Utrecht to the German border, but the Utrecht-Amsterdam line can also be considered part of this project. Plans for improving this section are running ahead of the main HSL-Oost scheme and are expected to receive ministerial approval in 1999.

*Betuweroute*
In 1994 the Dutch parliament approved construction of an east-west freight-only rail corridor, the so-called Betuwe line. Total cost is estimated at G9 billion at 1997 price levels. To distinguish the new freight-only line from the existing Dordrecht-Geldermalsen-Tiel-Elst line, the new corridor is now known as the Betuweroute. Its length will be 112 km, from Kijfhoek yard, Rotterdam, to the Dutch/German border near Emmerich, Germany. Most of the line will run parallel to the A15 motorway. At Valburg, between Arnhem and Nijmegen, a container terminal is planned. At Zevenaar, the Betuweroute will connect with the existing line from Arnhem to Germany to reach Emmerich. Construction work has started and most legal procedures had been completed by 1999. The Betuweroute is to be completed in 2005 and by 2010 is expected to carry some 43 million tonnes of freight. This projected figure compares with 24 million tonnes carried by NS Cargo in 1998.

Also part of the Betuweroute is the 48 km Havenspoorlijn (harbour line) which will act as a feeder for the port of Rotterdam. This will run west from Kijfhoek yard to the Maasvlakte. Work on the project has started and is due to be completed by 2003. A bridge at the Dintelhaven was completed in 1998 and at the beginning of 1999 work started on boring the Botlek tunnel in the port of Rotterdam. The Havenspoorlijn is to be electrified using the 25 kV AC 50 Hz power supply system. This will form a pilot project for this system, which will also be used throughout on the new sections of the Betuweroute.

Extensive measures have been necessary to protect the environment from the impact of the new line. There are five major civil engineering works between Kijfhoek and the German border: four tunnels and one bridge. The bridge will cross the Amsterdam-Rhine Canal at Tiel. The tunnels will also serve as crossings of rivers and canals. Although the operation of double-stack container services has so far not been approved, tunnels and bridges are being constructed with clearances adequate to accommodate them at a later stage.

The German and Dutch governments have reached agreement on investments in German network infrastructure to handle traffic generated by the new line. About EUR1 billion is to be spent upgrading German routes to be used by freight services destined for the Netherlands. Improvements will focus on the Emmerich-Oberhausen line and bottlenecks in the Ruhr. Despite the agreement, there were reported to be concerns among Dutch politicians about the implementation of these improvements.

Studies are being carried out into extensions of the Betuweroute northeast to the German border crossing at Bentheim and to the south from Nijmegen towards Venlo.

*Line 11*
Proposals are being developed for another international freight-only line, between the Netherlands and Belgium. Called 'Line 11', this would give direct access from the port of Antwerp to the Dutch network, connecting with the Vlissingen-Roosendaal line just south of Bergen op Zoom. Several options are being studied. The new line is needed because, in spite of the construction of the high-speed line between Rotterdam and Antwerp, the classic Roosendaal-Antwerp line is still projected to reach maximum capacity. There are also concerns that capacity will be exhausted on the Rotterdam-Roosendaal-Breda triangle. A decision about Line 11, or at least a solution to capacity problems between Roosendaal and Antwerp, is envisaged by 2003.

*DDAR double-deck stock propelled by an mDDM power car (Quintus Vosman)*

*The 'Iron Rhine'*
Besides Line 11, the Belgian government has been pressing for a direct, fast freight-only line between the port of Antwerp and the Ruhr, in Germany. Talks have taken place between Dutch, Belgian and German authorities for the reopening of the so-called 'Iron Rhine' from Antwerp to Mönchengladbach via the Dutch towns of Weert and Roermond. The infrastructure for this route exists but the Dutch-German border link east of Roermond has been closed, though not officially. A high-frequency service will require significant upgrading of the Dutch portion of the route and some new infrastructure may be required.

*The Hanzelijn*
The 'Hanzelijn' or Hanseatic line, is planned between Zwolle and Lelystad, although a definitive route has not yet been set. If built for standards suitable for 200 km/h running, journey time savings for IC services on the Zwolle-Amsterdam route could be over 20 minutes. Upgrading the existing Zwolle-Amersfoort-Amsterdam route would be very expensive, due to the high number of level crossings to be eliminated. Currently the project is scheduled for completion by 2007 at a cost of G2 billion.

*Light rail*
In 1997 the Minister of Transport selected six light rail projects for development, considering these a valuable contribution to solving traffic and transport problems. Most of the plans remain the subject of studies. The six projects are:

- IGO+, which was to start in May 1999. This project aims to provide good-quality public transport based on integrating bus and rail services in a region in the east of the Netherlands. Rail routes involved are Doetinchem-Winterswijk and Winterswijk-Zutphen. Initially rail services are provided by hired NS conventional dmus but lightweight diesel railcars have been ordered. Decisions about infrastructure modifications are still to be made. (See entry for 'Syntus' later in the Netherlands section.)
- The introduction of light rail is being studied in south Limburg (Maastricht-Heerlen-Kerkrade). Tendering for the provision of regional services is envisaged. Infrastructure implications are not yet clear: some signalling and safety problems have occurred with the use of lightweight rail vehicles on the Dutch network and infrastructure modifications would be necessary. However, it is expected that the number of passengers could double as a result of the initiative.
- RandStadRail concentrates on the Rotterdam/Den Haag/Zoetermeer triangle and has been proposed by NS, regional bus operator ZWN and the city transport authorities of Rotterdam (RET) and Den Haag (HTM) to relieve road congestion by linking main line and urban rail systems and adapting the existing Den Haag-Zoetermeer and Den Haag-Rotterdam Hofplein lines for light rail vehicles. Studies continue into a pilot project which could be operational by 2003.
- Randstadspoor Utrecht is a proposal to develop a regional public transport network in the Utrecht area and is based on the existing rail network around the city. The scheme is closely linked to urban planning in the region. In anticipation of the Randstadspoor Utrecht project, the minister has approved the construction of a new station to serve a new housing development at Houten.
- The Rijn-Gouwe light rail project covers the Gouda-Alphen and Rijn-Leiden lines. Train services are considered to be loss-making while road traffic is congested in the area. Options differ from running regional services with light rail vehicles on existing lines to creating a new route, based on the Karlsruhe model, for light rail vehicles through the centre of Leiden to the coastal communities of Katwijk aan Zee and Noordwijk. Plans are being studied.
- RegioNet is a plan for an extending and integrating public transport around Amsterdam by making comparatively small investments. The proposal calls for more studies in possible connections between different kinds of rail systems.

### Diesel locomotives

| Class | Wheel arrangement | Power kW | Speed km/h | Weight tonnes | No in service | First built | Builders Mechanical | Engine | Transmission |
|---|---|---|---|---|---|---|---|---|---|
| 200/300 | Bo | 64 | 60 | 21 | 82 | 1934 | Schneider | Stork | E Heemaf/ETI |
| 600 | C | 300 | 30 | 41 | 45 | 1949 | EE | EEC 6KT | E EEC |
| 2200 | Bo-Bo | 650 | 100 | 74 | 8 | 1955 | Schneider | Stork/Schneider | E Westinghouse |
| 6400 | Bo-Bo | 1,180 | 120 | 80 | 120 | 1988 | MaK | MaK | E ABB |

### Diesel railcars or multiple-units

| Class | Cars per unit | Motor cars per unit | Motored axles/car | Power/motor kW | Speed km/h | No in service | First built | Builders Mechanical | Engine | Transmission |
|---|---|---|---|---|---|---|---|---|---|---|
| DE-II | 2 | 2 | 2 | 193 | 110 | 3 | 1953 | Allan | Cummins | E Smit |
| DE-III | 3 | 1 | 4 | 182 | 130 | 41 | 1960 | Werkspoor | SACM | E Smit |
| DH-I | 1 | 1 | 2 | 212 | 100 | 19 | 1983 | Uerdingen | Cummins | H Voith |
| DH-II | 2 | 2 | 2 | 212 | 110 | 30 | 1981 | Uerdingen | Cummins | H Voith |
| DM 90 | 2 | 2 | 2 | 320 | 140 | 53 | 1995 | Duewag | Cummins | H Holec |

### Electric locomotives

| Class | Wheel arrangement | Output kW | Speed km/h | Weight tonnes | No in service | First built | Builders Mechanical | Electrical |
|---|---|---|---|---|---|---|---|---|
| 1300 | Co-Co | 2,885 | 135 | 111 | 15 | 1952 | Alsthom | Alsthom |
| 1200 | Co-Co | 2,235 | 130 | 108 | 9 | 1951 | Werkspoor-Baldwin | Heemaf-Westinghouse |
| 1100 | Bo-Bo | 1,925 | 135 | 83 | 13 | 1950 | Alsthom | Alsthom |
| 1600 | B-B | 4,540 | 160 | 83 | 58 | 1981 | Alsthom | Jeumont-Schneider |
| 1700 | B-B | 4,540 | 160 | 86 | 81 | 1991 | GEC Alsthom | Schneider |

### Electric railcars or multiple-units

| Class | Cars per unit | Motor cars per unit | Motored axles/car | Output/motor kW | Speed km/h | No in service | First built | Builders Mechanical | Electrical |
|---|---|---|---|---|---|---|---|---|---|
| mP | 1 | 1 | 4 | 145 | 140 | 7 | 1965 | Werkspoor | Smit |
| 64-II | 2 | 2 | 2 | 246 | 140 | 242 | 1964 | Werkspoor | Heemaf/Smit |
| 64-IV | 4 | 2 | 4 | 246 | 140 | 31 | 1964 | Werkspoor | Heemaf/Smit |
| SGM-II | 2 | 2 | 4 | 330 | 125 | 30 | 1975 | Talbot/SIG | Oerlikon/Holec |
| SGM-III | 3 | 2 | 4 | 330 | 125 | 60 | 1980 | Talbot/SIG | Oerlikon/Holec |
| ICM-III | 3 | 1 | 4 | 312 | 160 | 94 | 1977 | Talbot/Wegmann | Heemaf/Smit |
| ICM-IV | 4 | 2 | 4 | 312 | 160 | 50 | 1991 | Talbot/Wegmann | TCO/Holec |
| SM 90 | 2 | 2 | 4 | 300 | 160 | 9 | 1993 | Talbot | Holec |
| DD-IRM-III | 3 | 2 | 2 | 200 | 160 | 34 | 1994 | Talbot | Holec |
| DD-IRM-IV | 4 | 2 | 2 | 200 | 160 | 47 | 1994 | Talbot/De Dietrich | Holec |

### Improvements to existing lines
As track capacity limits on much of the Dutch rail system were reached at the end of the 1980s, the government decided to execute a fast investment plan to solve the worst problems in the network. This investment programme was called Prorail. Major projects included: extending Utrecht CS station; quadrupling the Leiden-Den Haag-Rijswijkline; quadrupling the Schiphol line between Hoofddorp and Amsterdam; and providing better access to Amsterdam CS from the west by increasing the number of tracks from four to six. The Prorail projects have all been completed except the Schiphol quadrupling and station expansion from three to six platform tracks: this is scheduled for completion in 2001.

Much of the Prorail investment programme contained investments proposed by NS's own Rail 21 plan. However, one major difference between Rail 21 and Prorail was that NS proposed quality improvements while Prorail's aim was to raise rail traffic volumes.

A second wave of investments is now being implemented under the TTP (Second Tactical Package) programme, with a target completion date of 2005. Most TTP projects are in the Randstad and the main corridors to and from it. Most attention is paid to access to Amsterdam Schiphol airport and the port of Rotterdam.

Just one large investment was announced for a provincial line in the Netherlands: a partial doubling of the Groningen-Sauwerd line, where the line diverges to Delfzijl, Roodeschool and Eemshaven. This is the single-track line with the highest traffic density in the Netherlands.

There is one new line to be constructed under the TTP programme: the Hanzelijn, connecting Zwolle and Lelystad (see 'New Lines' section). Some of the projects have reached the construction phase, while for others plans are still being developed or have been delayed for financial reasons.

Many improvement schemes aimed at increasing track capacity have been planned or implemented, especially in the dense network in the west of the Netherlands. Capacity on the Amsterdam-Rotterdam-Dordrecht route has been raised by quadrupling the Leiden-Den Haag-Rijswijk section. Quadrupling of the Schiphol line, which serves the international airport, is in progress for completion by 2001. The underground Schiphol station is being enlarged from three to six tracks. South of Schiphol,

*DD-IRM emu on an Amsterdam-Utrecht service (Quintus Vosman)* 0058796

*Class 1600 electric locomotive on an IC service at Den Haag CS* (Quintus Vosman) 0058798

at Hoofddorp, the layout of the station has been expanded from two to four tracks and a flyover has been constructed to avoid conflicting movements. The line between Dordrecht and Rotterdam has been quadrupled, except one small section at Barendrecht. A flyover at Rotterdam Lombardijen has been built to ease freight movements, and preparations have been made to connect the HSL-Zuid high-speed line and the new Havenlijn (harbour line), which will be part of the freight-only Betuweroute.

Other major infrastructure projects recently completed include: station and the junction improvements at Amersfoort; extension of the western access to Amsterdam CS; quadrupling the Utrecht CS–Utrecht Overvecht line and construction of junction flyovers; doubling the single-track line between Heerhugowaard and Schagen and partially doubling the non-electrified Groningen–Leeuwarden line, where the maximum speed has been raised to 140 km/h.

Still in progress in 1999 were quadrupling of the Boxtel–Eindhoven section which is shared by Amsterdam–Maastricht and Rotterdam–Venlo services, with a flyover and extended station layout at Boxtel and a new layout at Arnhem station, including a flyover. The Woerden bottleneck has also been eased and recently ministerial approval was given for the quadrupling of the line between the Woerden station and the junction east of the station, where lines to Utrecht and Amsterdam diverge. Between Houten and Houten Castellum, on the Utrecht–Den Bosch line, a third track will be constructed. More capacity enhancements on this line are expected once plans for a suburban heavy rail operation in addition to existing main line traffic are approved.

Major improvements are also planned for the Amsterdam–Utrecht line: between Utrecht and Duivendrecht the line is to be quadrupled to separate fast and slow trains and to raise line speeds and a bilevel junction is to be constructed at Breukelen. This project was expected to be approved by the Minister of Transport during 1999.

Upgrading of the non-electrified Zwolle–Wierden line for 140 km/h running has been completed. In 1999 NS Reizigers introduced a DM 90-operated fast service on this route with an extension to Enschede.

While most investment has been focused on the western Netherlands, the Minister of Transport has approved the partial doubling of the non-electrified Groningen–Sauwerd line.

At some locations new links are to be provided, making new services possible. Government approval has been given for the Gooiboog, a link by which trains can run directly from Utrecht to Almere via Hilversum. A new link near Amsterdam Sloterdijk is being studied so that trains can run directly from Zaandam to Schiphol airport. There are also plans to extend track capacity at some stations. Other investments at stations concern improved parking provision for cycles.

An investment programme of G300-350 million is being implemented to raise freight train axleloads to 22.5 tonnes. The programme is split up into three parts, the first of which started in 1997. The second was due to start during 1999 and the third in 2001.

Investments have also been made necessary to ensure environmental protection, and programmes to reduce noise on running lines and in yards are being developed. Some yards have posed particular problems: for example, the Amsterdam Watergraafmeer yard suffers from a permanent legal threat of closure due to violations of noise control legislation.

In the longer term other improvements to the existing rail network are being studied. Two of these are aimed at raising capacity without adding to existing infrastructure or constructing new lines. One possibility explored is overhead power supply conversion from the present 1.5 kV DC to 25 kV AC 50 Hz. So far it has been decided only to introduce 25 kV on two new lines: the HSL-Zuid southern high-speed line and the Betuwe line. Also being studied is the introduction of new train control and capacity management system, BB 21. This would be a moving block system based on Level 3 of the ERTMS (European Rail Traffic Management System). No decision to introduce either system has yet been made.

### Traction and rolling stock

During the 1980s and 1990s NS replaced a major part of its first generation of post-war traction and rolling stock. The Class 1200 electric locomotives were withdrawn in 1998, apart from six bought by ACTS (qv), and remaining Class 1100 units were expected to be withdrawn during 1999. Older types of emus and dmus have also been withdrawn. The Mat' 54 two-car and four-car emus were withdrawn in 1997 and the Plan X two-car dmus were retired in 1998, finally replaced by DM 90 dmus on the international link between Heerlen and Aachen, Germany.

Replacement of ageing stock has been made possible by recent deliveries of new equipment, most significantly 290 Class DD-IRM inter-regional emu cars, 53 Class DM 90 two-car dmus and 50 mDDM power cars to operate three- and four-car DD-AR push-pull sets. With the arrival of the last of the mDDM vehicles at the end of 1998, there were no outstanding items of traction or rolling stock on order by any of the NS train operating businesses.

The rapid delivery of the mDDM motorcoaches freed about half of the Class 1700 electric locomotives, which had been used exclusively with double-deck push-pull sets. The displaced locomotives have had their automatic couplers removed and are now used with conventional hauled stock. Modifications to their braking system are required before they can haul freight trains.

In 1997 DM 90 'Buffalo' dmus entered service on the Arnhem–Winterswijk and Nijmegen–Venlo–Roermond routes. Due to the relatively light weight of these units, it has been necessary to install axle-counter equipment on the lines served by them, as well as the latest ATB-NG (new generation) automatic train protection system. DM 90s are also used on the Leeuwarden–Groningen, Zwolle–Enschede and Heerlen–Aachen (Germany) routes, each of which have been provided with axle-counting equipment. For the last-named service three sets have been equipped with the German Indusi train protection system. It took some two years for approval to operate the DM 90 on the German network.

Due to the rapid growth in its passenger numbers, NS Reizigers decided in 1998 to refurbish the four-car Plan T (Mat' 64) emus. Originally these 31 units were to be withdrawn from 1999. A new interior is being provided and the luggage compartment has been converted into a second class non-smoking saloon, adding 31 seats per set. In all, around 1,000 seats will have been added to the NS Reizigers fleet and the trains are to run for a further eight years.

In 1999 NS was waiting to assess political attitudes towards the future of rail transport. The Minister of Transport's 'Third Age of Rail' policy statement, published in 1998, indicated a key role for NS Reizigers, which promptly announced its intention to order 128 coaches to lengthen its DD-IRM emus. Four-car units are to be extended to six cars and three-car sets to four. For the domestic IC services on the HSL-Zuid line, NS Reizigers plans to order high-speed double-deck trains with capability at least of 220 km/h and possibly higher.

Due to continuing growth in passenger volumes, NS Reizigers has been forced to take short-term steps to avoid a lack of seating capacity. Several of the oldest double-deck coaches have been modified for normal locomotive-hauled services, in combination with ICR coaches. In 1998 NS decided to return several Plan W coaches to service; they had been withdrawn in 1996. A further 25 of these vehicles were to be recommissioned in 1999. In addition, NS and Belgian National Railways (SNCB) have reached agreement to hire 80 Type K4 coaches, which had been sold to SNCB by French National Railways. They were due to start running with existing locomotive-hauled stock on Den Haag–Heerlen and Den Haag–Venlo IC services in late 1999. This would add a further 6,000 seats each day. The hire contract was to last for two years with a option for a further two years. In addition, a mid-life overhaul of the ICR fleet – including those used on 'Benelux' services – has been started.

In January 1999 the NS rolling stock fleet was split up, mainly between NS Reizigers and NS Cargo. All emus, dmus and coaches have been assigned to NS Reizigers, together with 81 Class 1700 and 20 Class 1600 (1638-1658) locomotives. During 1999 the latter were to be renumbered into Class 1800. All remaining Class 1100 and Class 1300 locomotives are now owned by NS Cargo.

Most of the diesel locomotive fleet was assigned to NS Cargo in the form of 120 Class 6400s and six Class 2200s. NS Reizigers has become the owner of some Class 600 diesel shunters, while other shunting locomotives have been acquired by other NS Holding business units, such as NS Materieel and Railpro. Others considered to be a surplus were sold to third parties like ACTS.

*High-speed trainsets*

NS owns two TGV trainsets for Amsterdam–Paris services. At the end of 1999 delivery from Siemens of the first of four ICE-M six-car four-voltage high-speed trainsets for Amsterdam–Cologne–Frankfurt services was due to take place. During 1998 and 1999 the type has been tested in Germany and was expected for trials on the Dutch network during the second half of 1999. Services using the new trains are due to begin in 2000. NS also had an option on another two ICE-M sets for services between Amsterdam and Berlin but by mid-1999 this had been converted into a firm order. Until introduction of the ICE-M sets on the international services between the Netherlands and Germany, DB IC coaches will be used for Amsterdam–Cologne trains, while Swiss stock will be employed on direct services between Amsterdam and Switzerland until ICE-M sets take over these services in 2002.

### Signalling and telecommunications

NS is participating in European studies into the possibilities for capacity expansion by introducing new control and safety systems. Part of the research is concentrated on a system for the improved use of infrastructure capacity by means of automatic regulators and recommended speeds.

In September 1994, NS opened a new Siemens SIMIS type microcomputer interlocking signalling centre in Rotterdam, the largest of its type in Europe, to replace the existing relay-based centre. In 1995 a new traffic control centre was opened near Amsterdam Centraal station. Further centres are under construction in Amersfoort and Arnhem.

### Electrification

A total of 75 per cent of the NS system is electrified at 1.5 kV DC, including all main routes. The only extension to this in progress at present is the electrification of the Rotterdam dock line. After previously rejecting the idea, NS decided in 1994 to reconsider the gradual conversion of its existing electrification from 1.5 kV DC to 25 kV 50 Hz AC. This merits consideration in the context of connections with the emergent continental high-speed network and because intensification of passenger traffic will demand traction equipment with enhanced acceleration and braking characteristics. The first applications of 25 kV 50 Hz AC will be on the Amsterdam–Belgium and Amsterdam–Germany high-speed lines and the Betuwe freight route. Apart from new traction orders, it is possible that Class 1600 and 1700 locomotives will be converted to dual-voltage operation. The decision on conversion to 25 kV 50 Hz AC will be made by the Dutch government.

### Track
**Standard rail, weights**
**Main lines:** UIC 54 kg/m (3,025 m installed)
**Branch lines:** 46 kg/m (3,436 m installed)
**Crossties (sleepers):** Wood, 250 × 150 × 2,600 mm; twin-block concrete 230 × 300 × 2,250 mm; monobloc concrete 230 × 300 × 2,500 mm
**Spacing:** 1,667/km; 1,333/km

**Fastenings:** Wood, bolt or DE-clip; twin-block concrete, DE-clip; monobloc concrete, Vossloh clip
**Min curvature radius:** 300 m; 500 m on track with monobloc sleepers
**Max axleload:** 22.5 tonnes (20 tonnes on twin-block concrete-sleeper track)

## NoordNed Personenvervoer BV

PO Box 452, NL-8901 BG Leeuwarden, Netherlands
Tel: (+31 58) 233 56 38   Fax: (+31 58) 233 56 36
Web: http://www.noordned_ov.nl

### Key personnel
Director: H Donker

### Political background
In 1999, NoordNed took over regional train services on two lines in the province of Friesland, in the far north of the Netherlands, after a tendering procedure. The two lines, Leeuwarden–Stavoren (51 km) and Leeuwarden–Harlingen Haven (26 km), both of which are not electrified, were among 33 routes on which NS Reizigers had indicated no continuing interest. Subsequently NS Reizigers transferred to NoordNed services between Leeuwarden and Groningen (54 km).

In May 2000, NoordNed extended its operations to cover all non-electrified routes in the north of the Netherlands. This followed a second tendering procedure covering the non-electrified Groningen–Sauwerd–Roodeschool, Groningen–Sauwerd–Delfzijl and Groningen–Nieuweschans regional lines in the province of Groningen. The last of these is partly double-track, the others single-track. Arriva was already active in the province of Groningen, operating both regional and city bus services.

The Groningen Noord–Sauwerd section, which is shared by trains to Delfzijl and Nieuweschans as well as by freight traffic to Eemshaven, is being partially doubled with government funding to increase capacity, the work including provision of a double-track bridge across the Van Starkenborch Canal. Completion is for 2003.

Still unclear in late 2000 was the situation regarding international service between Groningen and Leer in Germany, which crosses the border at Nieuweschans. Initially, NoordNed was also to take over this service, but German local authorities pulled out of the negotiations and NS Reizigers insisted that it would no longer operate the service, terminating the hire of the German Rail (DB AG) Class 624 diesel trainsets used for it. NoordNed has no rolling stock approved for operation on the German network. Meanwhile, upgrading of the link between the two communities for freight traffic was under way for completion in 2000, funded by the Dutch and German governments and the European Union.

### Organisation
NoordNed shares are held by NS Reizigers, British bus operator Arriva and banking interests. None of the parties has a share of more than 49 per cent. As a condition of tendering procedures, the Netherlands Minister of Transport demands that no party is allowed to have over 50 per cent ownership of an operating company.

### Passenger operations
NoordNed is an integrated regional passenger transport operator, providing both train and bus services in Friesland. There is one train per hour between Leeuwarden and Stavoren, the frequency doubled to two trains per hour on the Leeuwarden–Sneek section. Three services per hour in each direction are provided between Leeuwarden and Groningen following infrastructure upgrading and a partial track-doubling completed in 1999.

### Traction and rolling stock
NoordNed has leased DM 90 and DH 'Wadloper' two-car and single-unit dmus from NS Financial Services, a newly created NS business unit based in Dublin, Ireland. The DM 90s, the newest type of dmu in the Netherlands, have undergone modifications to their control equipment to allow them to operate with the 100 km/h DH trainsets. The Leeuwarden–Groningen service is operated with DM 90s running at 140 km/h.

For the contract secured in May 2000, NoordNet was expected to continue to use the stock operated by NS Reizigers, the remaining Class DH single-unit railcars and Class 3100 and 3200 two-car dmus, again leased from NS Financial Services. It was also likely that some ageing Class Plan U diesel-electric three-car dmus from the early 1960s would be added to the fleet.

*NoordNet Class DH-2 dmu at Franeker, on the Leeuwarden–Harlingen line (Quintus Vosman)* 2001/0103633

## Short Lines BV

Zaltbommelstraat 10, NL-2089 JK, Rotterdam
Tel: (+31 10) 428 31 20   Fax: (+31 10) 429 49 84
Web: http://www.shortlines.nl

### Key personnel
Directors: R Spierings, J Herijgers

### Organisation
Short Lines was founded in 1997 to run open access freight services, the first operator to compete on the Dutch network with NS Cargo. The company has concluded an agreement with HGK, the Cologne port operator, for the provision of traction for intermodal services both between Rotterdam and Germany and within the Netherlands. HGK subsequently acquired a 25.1 per cent shareholding in Short Lines.

### Freight operations
In mid-1998 a daily intermodal service was launched between Rotterdam and Born, some 20 km north of Maastricht, on behalf of a terminal operator at the latter location. In March 1999 a Rotterdam–Cologne intermodal service for Transfracht was started jointly by Short Lines and HGK. This runs six days a week and also conveys wagons for Munich and Austria. Trains run through without a locomotive change, although HGK and Short Line crews change at the border.

In 2000, after competitive tendering, Short Lines took over from Railion the operation of a major daily flow for Dutch chemicals group DSM. This train runs between the port of Rotterdam and a major chemical plant at Geleen, some 15 km north of Maastricht. DSM ranks among Railion's five biggest customer. Also in 2000, Short Lines ordered two Cargo Sprinter freight dmus for just-in-time services between the Eindhoven and Rotterdam areas. The company was understood to be considering possible international services with such equipment.

### Traction and rolling stock
Short Lines has no fleet of its own at present. Trains are hauled by three heavy MaK DE-1024 diesel locomotives, prototype machines which have been proven by German Rail (DB) as Class 240. These are the most powerful diesels to run on the Dutch network and have been equipped with three automatic train protection systems: Indusi (DB), an ATP-system for running on the HGK docks network and ATB, the Dutch ATP system. MaK DE-1002 locomotives are also now approved for access on the Dutch network, subject to the provision of ATP equipment, and it was expected that some HGK machines of this type would be adapted for this system, possibly to work domestic services.

The Cargo Sprinters mentioned above were due to be delivered at the beginning of 2001.

In 2000 Short Lines was using some 140 container wagons.

*HGK-owned MaK Type DE-1002 diesel locomotive operating a Short Lines container service between Rotterdam and Born (Quintus Vosman)* 2001/0103634

## Syntus

PO Box 17, NL-7000 AA Doetinchem
Tel: (+31 314) 35 01 60   Fax: (+31 314) 33 26 51
Web: http://www.syntus.nl

### Key personnel
Director: F van Setten

### Organisation
Syntus is a new train operator, founded in December 1998. In May 1999 it took over regional passenger services on the Winterswijk–Doetinchem and Winterswijk–Zutphen lines from NS Reizigers. It also took over the Almelo-Mariënberg services from Oostnet, which has since been dissolved. The services on the last-named line are run on behalf of VSN-1, the holding company to which Oostnet belonged. Shares in Syntus are divided equally between three companies: NS Reizigers, VSN-1 and Cariane, a French regional bus operator. As well as the rail routes mentioned above, the company operates the regional bus network, which is closely integrated with its train services. The project is seen as a first step towards creating a light rail-based regional integrated transport system.

With the approval of the Netherlands Minister of Transport, Syntus and NS Reizigers reached agreement that Syntus would take over the operation services on the Arnhem—Doetinchem line from 10 June 2001. Through services between Arnhem and Winterswijk have also been restored. When Syntus commenced operations, this service was split into two portions, with NS operating between Arnhem and Doetinchem and Syntus between Doetinchem and Winterswijk.

### Passenger operations
The new operator has doubled all frequencies during the day, offering throughout its network a bus or train every 30 minutes rather than at best hourly, as before. Remarkably, subsidies have remained unchanged. Efficiencies achieved include flexible staff deployment, with personnel equally likely to drive a train or bus or handle revenue protection tasks.

### Traction and rolling stock
In April 1999 Syntus ordered 11 two-car Lint 41 lightweight diesel railcars from Alstom. These are to be delivered during the first half of 2001, replacing existing stock on both the Winterswijk–Zutphen and Winterswijk–Doetinchem lines as well as Almelo-Mariënberg. Currently rolling stock is hired from NS Reizigers in the form of four DM 90 two-car dmus and three three-car Plan U units, as well as the remaining two Plan X two-car dmus bought from the dissolved Oostnet.

For the restoration of through Arnhem—Winterswijk services, Syntus leased additional DM 90 dmus from NS. Lint 41 units were also thought likely to be used for this route. For additional Arnhem—Zevenaar services, Syntus was expected to hire Plan U three-car dmus from NS.

---

# NEW ZEALAND

## Ministry of Transport – Land Transport Safety Authority

PO Box 27459, Wellington, New Zealand
Tel: (+64 4) 382 83 00   Fax: (+64 4) 385 57 99
e-mail: info@ltsa.govt.nz
Web: http://www.ltsa.govt.nz

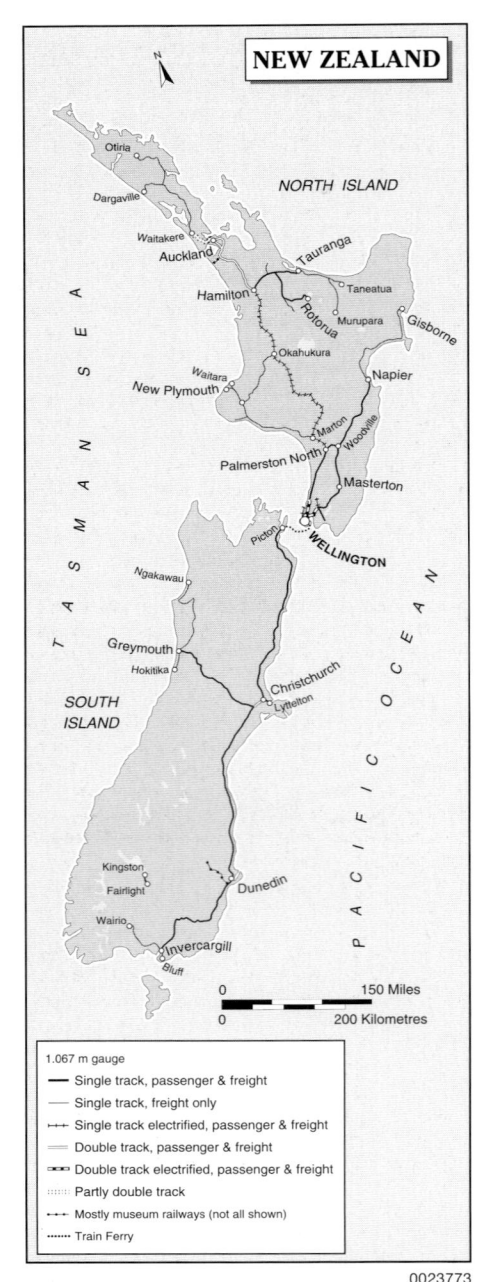

### Key personnel
Minister: M Gosche
Director, LTSA: David Wright

### Political background
The Land Transport Safety Authority is a regulatory authority responsible to the minister of transport; it has responsibility for licensing and audit of safety on the railway.

*UPDATED*

## Tranz Rail

Tranz Rail Limited
Wellington Railway Station, Private Bag, Wellington
Railway Station Building, Bunny Street, Wellington
Tel: (+64 4) 498 30 00   Fax: (+64 4) 498 32 59
e-mail: info@tranzrail.co.nz
Web: http://www.tranzrail.co.nz

### Key personnel
Chairman: Robert H Wheeler
Director and Managing Director: Michael Beard
Group General Managers:
    Human Resources and Change Management:
        Jeff Heisler
    Rail Services Operations: Lloyd Major
    Engineering Services: William Peet
    Rail Services: Noel Coom
    Process and Technology: Michael Thomas
    Interisland Line: Thomas Davis
National Manager, Motive Power: Bill Whall
Executive Manager and Chief Financial Officer:
    Mark Bloomer

Gauge: 1,067 mm
Route length: 3,898 km
Electrification: 95 km at 1.5 kV DC, 411 km at 25 kV 50 Hz AC

### Political background
For more than a century, railways in New Zealand were run as a government department. In 1982, New Zealand Railways Corporation was established as a statutory corporation with a commercial mandate. In 1986, it became a state-owned enterprise and in October 1990 the New Zealand government established New Zealand Rail Ltd as a limited liability company.

The deregulation of the transport industry and major restructuring were the hallmarks of these years. Staff numbers were reduced from more than 21,000 to around 5,000, productivity improved by nearly 300 per cent and the organisation was transformed from a loss maker into a profitable business, trends which have continued through to the present day.

The restructuring culminated in December 1992 when the New Zealand government announced its intention to sell New Zealand Rail. On 20 July 1993, it announced the sale to a consortium comprising local banking interests, with rail expertise coming from the US railroad Wisconsin Central Transportation Corporation. The sale was completed on 30 September 1993, with the company maintaining a lease from the Crown to occupy land for its railway operations until 2030. The company changed its name to Tranz Rail Ltd on 18 October 1995, and was floated on the New Zealand stock exchange and the Nasdaq national market in the United States on 14 June 1996. It now has almost 3,700 shareholders, the majority of the holding New Zealand-based.

Tranz Rail's purchase in 1993 included the tracks but not the land occupied by the railway, which remains in government ownership. This complicates the situation for anyone wanting to establish a competing operation or, as has been mooted, replace Tranz Rail as the operator of suburban passenger services, such as those in Auckland.

The company's two largest shareholders, Canadian National (formerly Wisconsin Central Transportation) and Fay, Richwhite, which together own 38 per cent of the shares, have announced their intention of selling their stakes. This process commenced in early 2002.

Tranz Rail has a 27 per cent holding in Australian Transport Network, the consortium that has taken over the railway system on the island of Tasmania and has a standard-gauge operation in Australia.

### Corporate development
The company has decided to dispose of non-core (other than freight haulage) business. In December 2001, the partial sale was finalised of the Tranz Scenic operation to the two founders of and shareholders in the Australian-based West Coast Railway, Don Gibson and Gary McDonald. The sale agreement provided for the establishment of a new company, Tranz Scenic 2001 Ltd (qv), in which Tranz Rail would retain a passive stake of 50 per cent. The agreement also foresaw existing staff being offered positions in the new company.

In December 2001, the Auckland rail corridor was sold by Tranz Rail to the New Zealand government under an agreement that would see the rail operator providing train control, track maintenance and other services for five years and passenger services under an existing contract until June 2003 at least. The agreement passes responsibility for suburban passenger rail services to Auckland Regional Council but preserves Trans Rail's freight traffic access rights to the lines concerned.

In early 2002, negotiations were in progress to conclude the sale of the Wellington Tranz Metro suburban electric operation.

### Organisation
Tranz Rail operates a nationwide rail network, interisland ferry services and an extensive owner/driver truck network; it is New Zealand's largest freight carrier. The company's vision is to move from being primarily a railway operator to a multimodal transport provider. The company has sold assets that are not essential to its core business.

With the December 2001 divestment of its Tranz Scenic long-distance passenger business, the sale of its Auckland commuter operations and the impending disposal of the Wellington Tranz Metro business, Tranz Rail created a new structure for its residual core activities. This consists of three distinct businesses: Rail Services, providing scheduled long-haul point-to-point services of fixed capacity; Distribution Services, providing mode-neutral supply chain management under the Tranz Link brand name; and The Interisland Line, offering passenger and freight transport services across the Cook Strait.

At March 2000, Tranz Rail had 4,158 employees, a further decrease on previous years. About 5 per cent of company shares are held by management and staff.

| Finance (NZ$ million) | 1999-2000 | 2000-01 |
|---|---|---|
| **Revenue** | | |
| Freight | 446.0 | 463.5 |
| Passenger | 127.1 | 143.9 |
| Miscellaneous | 21.4 | 21.0 |
| Total | 594.5 | 628.4 |
| **Expenditure** | | |
| Normal | 523.7 | 583.2 |
| Abnormal* | | 21.3 |
| Operating profit | | |
| After abnormals | 70.8 | 23.9 |
| Before abnormals | 70.8 | 45.2 |
| Interest and finance | 20.4 | 22.9 |
| Net profit | 50.4 | 1.0 |

* abnormal costs due to reorganisation, for example, redundancies and ferry reconfiguration

Tranz Rail is listed on the New Zealand stock market and the Nasdaq National Market in the USA.

## Passenger operations

*Long-distance services*
In December 2001, Tranz Rail sold its long-distance passenger operations to Tranz Scenic 2001 Ltd (qv) as part of its restructuring programme.

*Urban commuter services*
Tranz Metro, which operates urban commuter services in Wellington (electric multiple-units) and Auckland (diesel multiple-units), carried 12.1 million passengers in 1999-2000. Diesel services are also operated in Wellington: the 'Wairarapa Connection' services link Masterton (91 km) with the capital city and the 'Capital Connection' return service links Palmerston North (136 km) with Wellington. Passenger numbers continue to rise year by year.

In 2002, plans were being taken forward by Tranz Rail to sell the Wellington suburban operation as part of its restructuring programme.

In December 2001, the Auckland commuter rail corridor was sold to the New Zealand government. Tranz Rail was to continue operating services at least until the expiry of its current contract in June 2003, using railcars formerly operated in Perth, Western Australia. Responsibility for the development of commuter rail passenger services passed to Auckland Regional Council, while Tranz Rail retains track access rights for freight services.

## Freight operations

Since privatisation in 1993, Tranz Rail has continued to move record amounts of freight. Each week about 530 trains run on the North Island and 220 on the South Island. While tonnages continue to rise, much of this increase is carried over shorter distances. Major traffics are: agricultural and food products (35 per cent of total tonnage); forest products (17 per cent); manufactured goods (18 per cent); and coal (6 per cent). The Auckland–Wellington (North Island Main Trunk) section carries about 36 per cent of the total volume.

Tranz Rail is investing in a wide range of freight handling improvements. The most significant is a NZ$27 million upgrade of the Middleton yard and freight facility in Christchurch which opened in October 1998. This integrates on one site operations which were spread over a large area around Christchurch, bringing together for the first time train arrivals and departures, wagon sorting and marshalling, and freight handling.

Tranz Link has also expanded its freight services in Auckland with the purchase of a new warehouse and logistics centre. Included in this facility is a 2,000 m² chiller complex which will allow wagon and truck unloading within the complex to ensure the cold chain process is maintained. Coupled with new intermodal trailer units with integrated refrigeration units, this facility will significantly improve the cold chain process for New Zealand food processors.

Tranz Rail has also expanded into bulk milk transport with four consists running twice daily seven days each week at the peak of the season between Oringi, near Woodville, on the Napier branch, and Hawera, on the Taranaki branch. The customer is one of New Zealand's largest dairy companies. Finished dairy products from the same customer are also hauled by train to the port of New Plymouth.

Tranz Rail's Tranz Link division provides freight transport by rail, road (emphasised by the development of a network of more than 300 owner/drivers) or sea. It also offers warehousing, distribution and freight management services, including a freight forwarding division based in Australia.

Tranz Rail has pioneered the use of remotely controlled shunting locomotives. Forty locomotives of three classes have been equipped with the system, which enables safer and more precise shunting to take place. The system has been extensively tested and is fail-safe, as the locomotive stops if it does not receive a continuous signal from the shunter's equipment. In the future the equipment may be fitted to certain main line locomotives to enable a single-crewed locomotive to be used for wayside shunting.

Tranz Link has an Amicus 11 computer system connected to all freight terminals to monitor consignments. This has improved revenue collection and billing accuracy and has also allowed paperless documentation. The company has also introduced Ontrac, a state-of-the-art freight tracking system, using barcode technology applied to individual freight items rather than tracking the paper trail that goes with the freight, as with conventional systems.

An extension of Ontrac, Ontrac Direct, allows customers to track the progress of their freight in close to real time. Using the Internet, customers can follow their own consignments. A secure access procedure protects customers' commercially sensitive information.

The opening of the Tranz Rail Service Centre represents another step in the company's philosophy of providing the best possible customer service. The facility provides a single point of customer contact around the clock seven days a week.

Tranz Rail operates three roll-on/roll-off train ferries, and a seasonal fast ferry, across Cook Strait between Wellington and Picton. The ferries now operate 24-hour sailings, with over 5,000 sailings a year. They connect the 2,500 km of North Island track with the 1,500 km of South Island track. About 80,000 wagons are carried between the islands annually. A freight train from Auckland to Christchurch is run, providing a 24-hour transit time.

A programme to upgrade the ferry fleet has resulted in the building in Spain of the 'Aratere', the first new ferry bought by the company in 15 years. One of the most modern vessels in New Zealand and specifically designed for travel across Cook Strait, she has a crossing time of 3 hours and will help reduce overall transit times for freight operators.

Tranz Rail has won initial resource consent to build a new ferry terminal at Clifford Bay (38 km south of Blenheim) to replace Picton, which is reached through a sound. The cost of building the port would be offset by savings in the rail haul. The sea trip would be reduced by 30 minutes and the land trip to Christchurch by a similar time.

The coal producer, Solid Energy, has renewed a contract for the carriage of coal across the South Island. World over-supply of coal has resulted in reduced tonnages. Solid Energy has conducted trials in shipment

*Goninan-built dmu used for Tranz Metro Auckland area urban commuter services* (Brian Webber)

*Two Class DFT locomotives flanking a DQ on an empty milk train at Kai-iwi* (Brian Webber)

*Two Class Dx locomotives with loaded Type CB coal wagons at Stillwater* (Brian Webber)

by barge, reminding Tranz Rail it is not entirely dependent on the rail link.

**Freight traffic**

| | 1997-98 | 1998-99 | 1999-2000 |
|---|---|---|---|
| Freight tonnes (million) | 11.71 | 12.9 | 14.7 |
| Freight tonne-km (billion) | 3.5 | 3.6 | 3.5 |

### Intermodal operations

Tranz Rail has sought to increase carryings of containers and swapbodies, introducing 'Spaceliner' swapbodies in a bid to compete with road transport. Another new design of swapbody, the 'Iceliner', is a refrigerated swapbody that has been specially designed for Tranz Rail's temperature-controlled meat and fish transport market.

A new traffic being developed in conjunction with the road industry is the transport of domestic waste to country areas for disposal. Six wagons have been adapted to carry the containers and to enable them to be transferred to road vehicles without cranes or forklifts.

### Improvements to existing lines

Twelve bridges and about 150 km of track between Stillwater and Ngakawa (South Island west coast) have been upgraded to enable two DX locomotives to be used on export coal trains to Lyttelton, Christchurch's port. These trains work through the 8.6 km Otira tunnel, where, following the installation of a new ventilation system, the assistance of electric locomotives is no longer required. A new triangular connection near Westport, opened in July 1996, enables coal trains to run directly from Ngakawa to the east coast.

To cater for the increase in traffic on the Taranaki line caused by the highly successful milk trains, two crossing loops previously removed have been reinstated.

### Traction and rolling stock

At 30 June 2000, Tranz Rail operated 187 diesel main line, 129 diesel shunting, and 27 electric locomotives, 124 electric units, 38 diesel railcars, 159 main line passenger cars and 6,728 wagons. The wagon fleet comprised 2,964 container flat wagons, 746 hopper wagons, 1,586 box wagons, 493 log wagons and 160 special wagons.

The December 2001 sale by Tranz Rail of its main line passenger operations to Tranz Scenic 2001 Ltd included the transfer of 13 operational main line locomotives, nine other locomotives, 76 coaches, three dmus and 16 other passenger and generator vehicles. Also transferred were rolling stock maintenance facilities at Christchurch and Otahuhu.

Since 1995, Tranz Rail has purchased 25 second-hand Clyde-GM locomotives (now designated Class DQ) from Queensland Rail in Australia. These are being overhauled and progressively released to traffic. In 1998 Tranz Rail acquired further second-hand locomotives in the form of nine Class A and one Class AB machines from Westrail, Australia. These GM-powered locomotives, which are generally similar to the DQ units, await refurbishment and modifications at Tranz Rail's Hutt workshops.

Other locomotives are being equipped with a new wheel-slip control device, ditch lights and larger fuel tanks as they pass through workshops. A feature to improve employee safety is the provision of shunter's steps behind the locomotive headstock. The final eight DF class locomotives have been fitted with turbochargers. A DX Class locomotive has been rebuilt with an upgraded engine developing 2,460 kW compared with the 2,050 kW output of others of the class.

Tranz Rail has purchased a locomotive driving simulator to train drivers and encourage economical train running.

In December 2001, Alstom Transport won a seven-year contract, effective from April 2002, to take over the maintenance of all Tranz Rail's 180 diesel-electric, electric and shunting locomotives. The contract covers both preventative and corrective maintenance and overhaul and entails Alstom taking over the railway's Hutt workshops in Wellington.

Upgrading work continues on a fleet of insulated wagons for the meat and dairy sectors. A new class of CC coal wagon, with a tare of 20 tonnes and designed to carry 70 tonnes, has been introduced. Upgrading of track will be required before a 22.5 tonne axleload can be accommodated. Twenty used coal hoppers (class CW) were purchased from Australia's Westrail in 1996 for Midland line traffic.

Tranz Rail has introduced a new class of box wagons equipped with plug-type glass fibre doors. Some 75 of the class, ZH, are being built at Tranz Rail's Hillside workshops. The wagon has two doors on each side which move to open fully their half of the wagon side, making loading by forklift simple.

In 2002, Tranz Rail's Hillside workshops commenced delivery of 22 new coal hoppers for Solid Energy New Zealand Ltd for traffic between the west coast and Lyttelton. Export coal traffic totalled 1.7 million tonnes in 2001 and Tranz Rail expects to double that figure by 2006.

Overhaul of many of Wellington's Ganz-Mávag multiple-units has been completed. The 44 two-car units date from 1982 and work most services.

### Signalling and telecommunications

Most trains operate under either CTC (Centralised Traffic Control) or TWC (Track Warrant Control). Tranz Rail has centralised its train control operations in Wellington.

### Electrification

The North Island Main Trunk line between Palmerston North and Hamilton is electrified at 25 kV 50 Hz AC.

The 95 km Wellington suburban passenger system is electrified at 1.5 kV DC.

### Track

In a mountainous country like New Zealand, it is not surprising that the railway includes 149 tunnels (87 km) and 2,178 bridges (74 km). The three longest tunnels are Kaimai (8.9 km) between Tauranga and Morrinsville; Rimutaka (8.5 km) between Upper Hutt and Featherston; and Otira (8.6 km) between Otira and Arthur's Pass. Tunnel clearances are being increased to cater for continuing increases in the height of 'standard' containers. The longest bridge is over the Rakaia River (Christchurch–Picton) spanning 1,743 m, while the highest is over the Mohaka River (Hawkes Bay) standing 97 m over water height.

Tranz Rail owns an EM80 track evaluation car which regularly checks track standards.

### Rail

**Type of coupler in standard use:** Passenger cars and unit trains: AAR 'E'

Freight wagons: 'Norwegian' hook and pin; emus and railcars: Sumitomo tightlock

**Type of braking in standard use:** Air

**Main line:** 50 kg/m; 91 lb/yd; 85 lb/yd

**Provincial lines:** 91 lb/yd; 85 lb/yd; 75 lb/yd; 70 lb/yd

**Branch lines:** 70 lb/yd; 55 lb/yd

**Welding method:** Flash-butt in depot, Thermit in field. New rails flash-butt welded in depots into 76.8 m lengths and transported to site for laying. Short rail in track may be Thermit-welded into similar lengths. Continuous welded rail is formed by Thermit process with termination joints at extremities and epoxy glue joints, or Benkler encapsulated joints, and anchored. About half of the track (70 per cent of main and provincial lines) comprises continuous welded rail.

**Crossties (sleepers)**

NZ Pinus radiata (all lines) 67 per cent

Concrete (main lines only) 19 per cent

Hardwood remainder

**Spacing**

**Main line:** Timber 600 mm; concrete 700 mm

**Fastenings**

**Main lines:** Timber: Pandrol spring fastenings on bedplates; clips, crew spikes, spring washers on double-shoed bedplates. Spring clips and screw spikes without bedplates

Concrete: Pandrol spring fastenings with rubber or plastic pads and nylon insulators

**Branch lines:** Timber: screw spikes and bedplates and cascaded from higher ranking lines

**Laying method:** Concrete: by Tranz Rail designed and built sleeper-laying machine or by spot resleepering machinery

Timber: Laid manually either in face or by spot resleepering machinery

**Dimensions**

Concrete: 254 × 190 × 2,134 mm

Timber: 200 × 150 × 2,134 mm

**Max gradient:** 1 in 33

**Max altitude:** North Island – 814 m at Waioru, 290 km north of Wellington on the North Island Main Trunk; South Island – 737 m at Arthur's Pass on the Midland line.

**Max permitted speed:** 100 km/h – passenger trains; 80 km/h – freight trains

### Diesel locomotives

| Class | Wheel arrangement | Power kW | Weight tonnes | No in service | First built | Mechanical | Builders Engine | Transmission |
|---|---|---|---|---|---|---|---|---|
| Dbr | A1A-A1A | 709 | 68 | 10 | 1980 | GM | 8-645C | E |
| Dc | A1A-A1A | 1,230 | 82.75 | 82 | 1978 | GM | 12-645E | E |
| Dft | Co-Co | 1,830 | 87.6 | 30 | 1992 | GM | 12-645E3C | E |
| Dx | Co-Co | 2,050 | 99 | 47 | 1972 | GE | 7 FDL-12 | E |
| Dxr | Co-Co | 2,350 | 102.5 | 1 | 1993 | GE | 7 FDL-12 | E |
| Dh | Bo-Bo | 678 | 54 | 6 | 1978 | GE | CAT D398 B | E |
| Dsc | Bo-Bo | 2 × 175 | 41 | 45 | 1962 | AEI/NZR | 2 × Cummins NT855 | E |
| Dsj | Bo-Bo | 354 | 54 | 5 | 1987 | Toshiba KTA-1150-L | Cummins | E |
| Dsg | Bo-Bo | 2 × 354 | 56 | 24 | 1981 | Toshiba KTA-1150-L | 2 × Cummins | E |
| DQ | Co-Co | 977 | 90 | 6 | 1964 | Comeng | 12-567C | E |
| Tr | C (0-6-0) | 110-135 | 20 | 45 | 1936-77 | Price/Hitachi/Drewry/Bagnall | Cummins NH/Gardner GL | H |

### Electric locomotives

| Class | Wheel arrangement | Power kW | Weight tonnes | No in service | First built | Mechanical | Builders Electrical |
|---|---|---|---|---|---|---|---|
| Eo | Bo-Bo | - | 55 | 5† | 1968 | Toshiba | Toshiba |
| Ef | Bo-Bo-Bo | - | 106.5 | 20 | 1988 | Brush | Brush |

† stored

### Electric multiple-units

| Class | Power kW | Weight tonnes | No in service | First built | Mechanical | Builders Electrical |
|---|---|---|---|---|---|---|
| DM/D | 450 | 42.4 | 15/20 | 1936-47 | EE | EE |
| EM/ET | 400 | 72.1 | 44/44 | 1982 | Ganz-Mávag | - |

### Diesel railcars

| Class | Power kW | Weight tonnes | No in service | First built | Mechanical | Builders Engine | Transmission |
|---|---|---|---|---|---|---|---|
| Rm | 750 | 111 | 3 | 1973 | KHI Toshiba | CAT D398 | E |
| ADK/ADB | 276 | 33/16 | 9/10 | 1969 | Comeng/WAGR | Cummins | HM |
| ADL/ADC | 424 | 43/36 | 10/10 | 1981 | Goninan | Cummins | H |

*UPDATED*

## Tranz Scenic 2001 Ltd

### Organisation
Tranz Scenic 2001 Ltd was established to take over the long-distance passenger operations of Tranz Rail (qv) upon their sale in December 2001. The company is equally owned by Don Gibson and Gary McDonald, founders and shareholders of the West Coast Railway in Australia, and Tranz Rail, whose stake in the business is passive. However, its continued involvement was expected to ensure effective co-operation on issues such as track access. All former Tranz Scenic staff were offered positions in the new company. Selected stations were also transferred to Tranz Scenic 2001 Ltd.

### Passenger operations
Services taken over by the new company in mid-December 2001 included: the Auckland—Wellington 'Northerner' and 'Overlander'; the Picton—Christchurch 'TranzCoastal'; and the Christchurch—Greymouth 'TranzAlpine', which runs over the Southern Alps. Also included in the business are the 'Capital Connection' long-distance commuter service between Palmerston North and Wellington and the Tranz Scenic charter business. Not included was 'The Southerner', linking Invercargill and Christchurch, which Tranz Rail would continue to operate pending the outcome of a viability study into its future.

*Spectacular views are offered to passengers on the 'Overlander' as it crosses Rangitikei viaduct, near Taihape (Brian Webber)* 2002/0121177

### Traction and rolling stock
The sale of former Tranz Rail assets included 13 operational main line locomotives, nine other locomotives, 76 coaches, three dmus and 16 generator and observation cars. Vehicle maintenance facilities at Christchurch and Otahuhu were also transferred to Tranz Scenic 2001 Ltd.

**NEW ENTRY**

# NICARAGUA

## Ministry of Construction and Transport

PO Box 5, Managua

### Key personnel
Minister: P Virgil

### New lines
The former Ferrocarril de Nicaragua closed down in 1994, but in 1996 plans emerged for an ambitious new railway linking the Atlantic ocean with the Pacific. The idea was that the 370 km line would provide a landbridge alternative to the Panama Canal, shifting containers and other freight from a new port at Monkey Point on the Atlantic seaboard to one of three sites being investigated on the Pacific coast.

In 1998 the Nicaraguan government named the international CINN consortium as preferred bidder to prepare a feasibility study into the scheme, the cost of which has been estimated at US$1.5 billion. A less costly but longer alternative has been proposed by a rival consortium, SIT Global.

## Ferrocarril Ingenio San Antonio

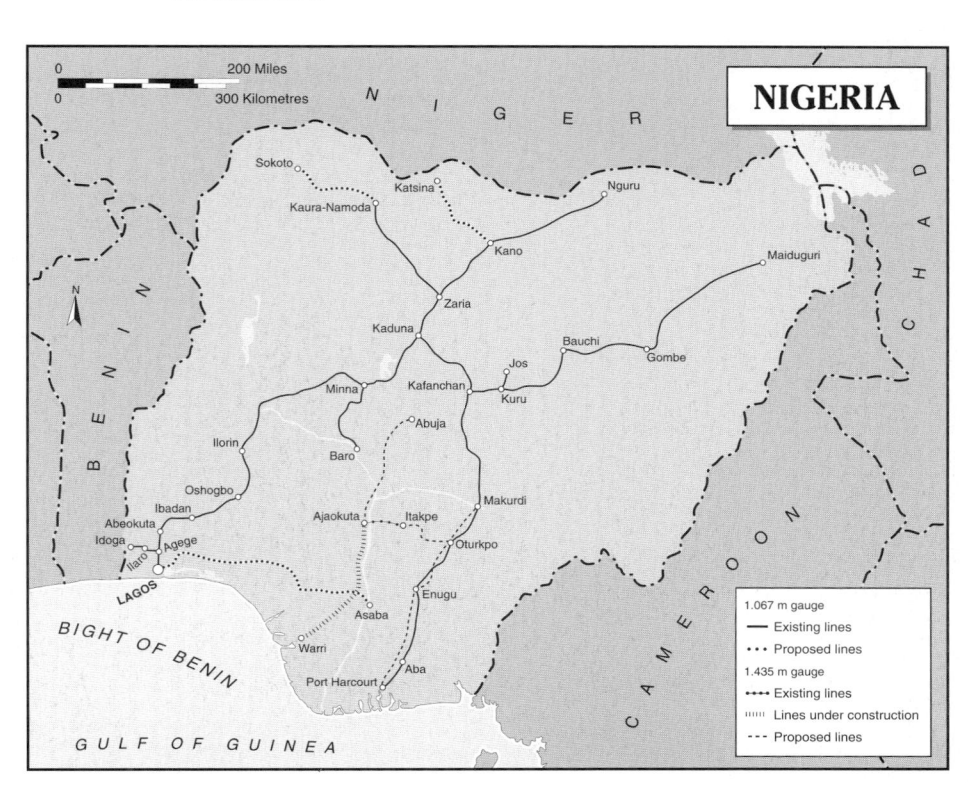

Gauge: 1,067 mm
Route length: 6 km

This line runs from Chichigalpa to Ingenio San Antonio. Initially built as a sugar cane railway, it has subsequently become a common-carrier, operated by Nicaragua Sugarestados. After an interruption of around a year caused by traction failures, operations resumed in 1999 following the repair of one of the fleet of three Davenport locomotives. Several converted freight wagons serve as passenger vehicles, carrying 150 to 250 passengers daily in three pairs of scheduled services. Travel is free of charge. Freight traffic is very limited, although molasses are carried occasionally.

# NIGERIA

## Ministry of Transport & Communications

1 Joseph Street, Marina, Lagos
Tel: (+234 1) 263 76 11    Fax: (+234 1) 263 50 10

### Key personnel
Minister: Alhaji Isah Yuguda

**UPDATED**

## Nigerian Railways Corporation (NRC)

PMB 1037, Ebute Metta, Lagos
Tel: (+234 1) 83 43 00

### Key personnel
Administrator: Gregory C Ilukwe
Secretary: Tijani Shehu
Directors
  Administration and Finance: A Abubakar
  Operations: L O Öshinubi
  Mechanical and Electrical Engineering: C E Okoye
  New Lines: D Olabinrin
  Internal Audit: S A Ekedebe
Managers
  Signalling and Telecommunications: O Olugbodi
  Legal: I Onyeabor
  Stores: P I Ricketts

Gauge: 1,067 mm; 1,435 mm
Route length: 3,505 km; 52 km

### Political background
Political debate raged around the structure of the railway in the early 1990s, but little progress was made with the vital task of rehabilitating the railway's rundown assets until mid-1996. At this time the Nigerian government approved funding for a substantial programme of track and signalling renewals (see 'Improvements to existing lines' section below), and further restructuring of management, costed at N16.8 billion. Two-thirds of that sum has already been made available, reportedly on account of improved government revenues from oil exports.

### Organisation
As part of a major rehabilitation of the Nigerian rail network, Chinese specialists in 1997 embarked on a programme to retrain NRC staff.

In 1994 NRC employed 11,346 staff.

### Passenger operations
The poor state of the infrastructure and rolling stock contributed to a dramatic decline in traffic after 1989, with a nadir reached in 1992 when 1.6 million passengers were carried (451 million passenger-km).

In an attempt to bring some relief to the appalling traffic conditions in Lagos, NRC has been running limited peak-hour passenger services between Ifo and Lagos. These were carrying nearly 6 million passengers annually in the 1980s. In 1992 the Lagos state government made available N5 million to fund new rolling stock to upgrade these services.

### Freight operations
The poor state of the infrastructure and rolling stock contributed to a dramatic decline in traffic after 1989; in 1992 less than 200,000 tonnes were hauled (50 million tonne-km). In 1992 a new marketing strategy was introduced aimed at raising the miserable freight tonnage.

### New lines
The 1,435 mm line linking ore deposits at Itakpe with a steelworks at Ajaokuta opened in 1992. Construction of a 270 km link from the steelworks to the sea at Warri is now proceeding.

In 1997, plans were announced for a new line to link Port Harcourt with the Federal Ocean Terminal oil and gas terminal at Onne.

### Improvements to existing lines
The greater part of the funds made available in mid-1996 (see 'Political background' section above), N13 billion, was to pay for renewal of 720 km of track and realignment at 40 locations where severe curvature imposes operating restraints. Rehabilitation of signalling and telecommunications equipment was to absorb a further N2.6 billion.

In 1997 China's Civil Engineering Construction Corporation embarked on a large-scale rehabilitation of the network. Due for completion in October 1998, the project was aimed at doubling line speeds to 80 km/h.

### Traction and rolling stock
At last report in 1994, NR owned 200 diesel locomotives, 287 passenger cars and some 4,000 freight wagons. The diesel locomotive fleet was reported to suffer from very low availability.

A grant from the Korean Export-Import Bank was agreed in 1993. This was to provide some N292 million to fund purchase of five diesel locomotives, along with technical assistance for rolling stock rehabilitation and track maintenance programmes.

In 1991 traction resources were supplemented by seven ex-Newfoundland GM-EMD Type G12 diesel locomotives bought from Canadian National's CANAC consultancy subsidiary and refurbished by Bombardier before shipment.

In 1993 15 diesels were ordered from South Korean builders, funded by Korean Eximbank, along with 36 coaches.

In 1997, Dalian Locomotive Works of China was building 50 1,800 kW Class 2101 CKD8A diesel locomotives for Nigeria for 1997-99 delivery.

In mid-1997, NR began taking delivery of new air conditioned passenger coaches from the Sifang plant in China.

### Track
As much as 80% of NR track is reported in need of overhaul
**Rail:** BS60R 29.8 kg/m; BS70A 34.7 kg/m; BS80R, 80A 39.7 kg/m
**Crossties (sleepers):** Steel, 130 × 7.5 mm
**Fastenings:** Pandrol: K Type

---

# NORWAY

## Ministry of Transport & Communications
Akersgata 59, PO Box 8010 Dep, N-0030 Oslo
Tel: (+47) 22 24 90 90   Fax: (+47) 22 24 95 70
e-mail: postmottak@sd.dep.telemax.no
Web: http://odin.dep.no/sd

### Key personnel
Minister: Torild Skogsholm
Under-Secretary of State: Arnfinn Ellingsen
Secretary General: Per Sanderud
Director General, Rail: Pål Tore Berg

*UPDATED*

## Norwegian National Rail Administration (JBV)
Jernbaneverket
PO Box 1162 Sentrum, 0107 Oslo
Tel: (+47) 22 45 51 00   Fax: (+47) 22 45 54 99
Web: http://www.jernbaneverket.no

### Key personnel
Director General: Steinar Killi
Executive Directors
  Infrastructure Management: Jon Frøisland
  Traffic and Public Relations: Svein Horrisland
  Rail Systems: Jens Melsom
  Resources and Strategy: Stein O Nes
  Safety: Ove Skordahl
  International and Administrative Affairs:
    Ole M Drangsholt

Gauge: 1,435 mm
Route length: 4,178 km
Electrification: 2,518 km at 15 kV 16⅔ Hz AC

### Organisation
Established on 1 December 1996 under legislation passed by the Norwegian parliament, Jernbaneverket is responsible for managing and maintaining Norway's rail infrastructure and for the regulation and planning of the rail system in general. The infrastructure function was previously a separate division within Norwegian State Railways (NSB).

The network is divided into four geographical regions for development, maintenance and operations purposes.

Jernbaneverket's head office in Oslo is responsible for regulatory functions, comprising planning, operational safety and allocation of track capacity, and for centralised administrative and support functions.

The traffic control function was transferred to Jernbaneverket on 1 January 1998, having remained with NSB initially for operational convenience.

At 31 December 2001, Jernbaneverket had a total of 3,577 staff.

### Finance
Parliament fixes annual appropriations for infrastructure maintenance and investment. The charges paid by train operators for use of the infrastructure are also set by parliament. Track charges reflect long-term marginal costs and may therefore differentiate between different types of rail traffic. They also take account of environmental factors and parity with other modes.

Jernbaneverket's expenditure is governed by a 10-year plan drawn up by the government and subject to annual review by parliament. The National Transport Plan for the period 2002-11 recommends capital expenditure on new infrastructure of NKr16.7 billion of which more than half will go towards improvements in the Greater Oslo area. Over the same period, the plan recommends allocating a total of NKr26.9 billion to operation and maintenance of the rail network.

### New lines
*Airport line*
Oslo's new international airport at Gardermoen, northeast of the city, opened in October 1998. It is served by a new 48 km double-track line, engineered for 200 km/h.

Construction of the line involved driving a 13.8 km tunnel between Bryn and Lillestrøm, to segregate airport and intercity trains from local services on the existing route, and a new railway from Lillestrøm to Eidsvoll via the airport. Problems with water seepage delayed the opening of the tunnel until August 1999. The tunnel's opening reduced the journey time from Oslo central station to the airport from 35 to 19 minutes.

### Improvements to existing lines
At the end of 2001 the Norwegian rail network had a total of 209 route-km with double track. In recent years priority has been given to extending double-tracking in the Greater Oslo area and on the Østfold (Oslo–Moss) and Vestfold (Drammen–Skien) lines, a policy which will be continued under the National Transport Plan 2002-11.

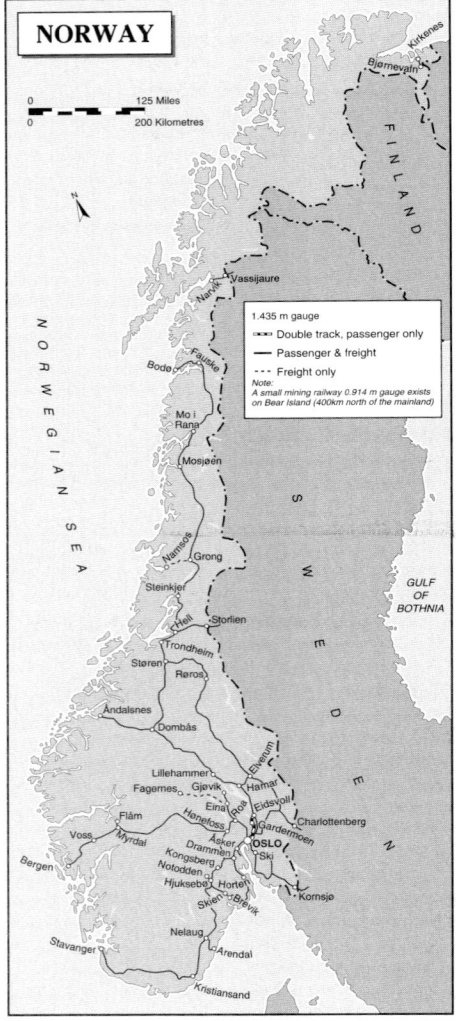

On the Østfold line, double-tracking of the 7 km Såstad–Haug section (between Moss and Halden) was completed in 2000, enhancing opportunities for trains to pass on this busy section of the Oslo—Gothenburg route.

On the Vestfold line, two new double-track sections of 6.9 km and 5.8 km near Åshaugen opened in 2001. A 500 m passing loop at Nykirke was scheduled to open in 2002.

Necessary infrastructure modifications to allow the introduction of tilt-body rolling stock on the Oslo–Kristiansand–Stavanger, Oslo–Bergen and Oslo–Trondheim lines were largely completed in 2001.

A similar programme of modifications is under way on the Kongsvinger (Oslo–Charlottenberg) and Østfold (Oslo–Kornsjø) lines, which will also benefit cross-border services from Oslo to Stockholm and Gothenburg respectively.

Meanwhile, work continues to improve track alignments, reduce the risk of snow blockage and provide additional passing loops on the mountain section of the Oslo–Bergen line. In 1999 work was completed on a new 5.2 km section at Gråskallen, east of Tunga.

Construction of an enlarged Nationaltheatret station in Oslo's east-west tunnel was completed in 2000. The station is the country's second busiest in terms of passenger numbers and had become a major traffic bottleneck. The scheme has created a second station chamber parallel to the existing one, doubling the number of tracks to four.

To increase capacity on the busy Oslo–Drammen line, construction work started in 2001 on a new section of line between Sandvika and Asker. The scheme comprises 11.6 km of new double or multiple track through a built-up area, with bridges over two rivers and a motorway. Much of the new line will run in tunnel or concrete culverts.

### Signalling and telecommunications
At 31 December 1997, a total of 2,617 route-km was equipped with centralised traffic control (CTC) and 2,342 route-km with automatic train control (ATC). Installation of CTC and ATC was under way on a further 70 route-km.

In 2001, Jernbanverket decided to install an emergency stop system on lines without CTC.

### Track
**Rail type:** S 49 (49.43 kg/m), S 54 (54.54 kg/m), UIC-54 (53.90 kg/m), UIC-60 (60.34 kg/m)
**Sleepers:** Concrete, length 2,400-2,600 mm
**Spacing:** 1,700/km
**Rail fastenings:** Pandrol (PR341A, e-clip, Fastclip)
**Max curvature:** 8°
**Max gradient:** 2.5% (5.5% on Myrdal-Flåm line)
**Max permissible axleload:** 22.5 tonnes (25 tonnes on Narvik-Riksgränsen ore line)

*UPDATED*

---

## Norwegian State Railways (NSB)

Norges Statsbaner AS
Prinsensgate 7-9, N-0048 Oslo
Tel: (+47) 23 15 00 00    Fax: (+47) 23 15 31 46
Web: http://www.nsb.no

### Key personnel
Chairman: Olav Fjell
President and Chief Executive: Einar Enger
Deputy Chief Executives: Arne Wam; Vidar Østreng
Directors
   Corporate Affairs: Rolv Roverud
   Passenger Services, Eastern Norway: Arne Fosen
   Passenger Services, Regions: Arne Vidar Hesjedal
   Traffic Safety: Tom Ingulstad
   Rolling Stock: Jan Runesson
   Operations: Øystein Risan
   Administration: Steinar Norli
   Strategy and Finance: Kjell Haukeli
   Communications: Audun Tjomsland
   Marketing: Marianne Ødegaard Ribe
   Sales: Karen K Hancke
   Central Services: Margareth Nordby
Managing Directors, subsidiaries
   Flytoget AS (airport line): Thomas Havnegjerde
   CargoNet AS (rail freight): Kjell Froyslid
   NSB Ekspressgods AS (parcels): Eivind Stangeby

### Political background
Under legislation that came into force on 1 December 1996, Norwegian State Railways was reconstituted as a special limited company (NSB BA) with all shares held by the state. On the same date, the operations of the former NSB infrastructure sector were transferred to the Norwegian National Rail Administration (Jernbaneverket) (qv). With effect from 1 July 2002, the Norwegian government changed the status of NSB to that of a normal limited company, and NSB BA became NSB AS.

Although NSB has greater commercial freedom than it previously enjoyed, the structure established by the legislation specifically provides for a degree of continuing political control, in the form of public purchasing of services and parliamentary approval for investment plans. The minister of transport acts as the sole shareholder, appointing the company's non-executive directors and approving major decisions.

### Organisation
A major restructuring of the group from 1 January 2002 saw NSB AS becoming primarily a passenger train operator. The freight business was hived off into a separate company, CargoNet AS, owned 55 per cent by NSB and 45 per cent by Green Cargo, the Swedish rail freight company. The parcels business likewise became a separate company, Ekspressgods AS, but wholly owned by NSB. Other non-core activities, such as maintenance, cleaning and IT, were also incorporated as separate subsidiary companies.

Flytoget AS runs trains on the high-speed line serving Oslo international airport (see Norwegian National Rail Administration entry). In June 2002, the Norwegian government announced that Flytoget AS was to be separated from NSB to become a free-standing publicly owned company.

*Class BM71 'Flytoget AS' Gardermoen Airport Express emu at Lillestrøm* (Edward Barnes)   2002/0524938

At 31 December 2001, the NSB Group had 9,358 employees (8,022 full-time equivalents).

### Finance
In 2001, the NSB Group recorded a loss of NKr33 million. The parent company, NSB BA, made a profit of NKr26 million. Passenger train operations returned a profit of NKr56 million, while rail freight operations showed a loss of NKr146 million.

As a limited company, NSB AS is responsible for raising its own investment capital on the private loan market and is no longer subject to government borrowing consents. In 1999 NSB established a European long-term borrowing programme with a ceiling of €750 million and at 31 December 2001 loans of NKr3,539 million had been taken up. NSB BA has established a financial reserve of NKr2 billion via a syndicated credit facility which expires in July 2004. A government loan of NKr2.1 billion was converted to equity in 2001.

| Finance (NKr million) | 1999 | 2000 | 2001 |
|---|---|---|---|
| Sales and other operating income | 5,633 | 5,622 | 5,595 |
| Public purchase of services | 1,279 | 1,303 | 1,530 |
| Operating profit/loss | 20 | −304 | 108 |
| Net loss after tax | −1,081 | −325 | −33 |
| | | | |
| Assets | 17,517 | 12,968 | 13,101 |
| Interest, bearing liabilities | 11,452 | 6,584 | 4,197 |
| Equity | 3,463 | 3,978 | 6,078 |

| Traffic (million) | 1999 | 2000 | 2001 |
|---|---|---|---|
| Passenger journeys | 54.1 | 54.9 | 53.5 |
| Passenger-km | 2,895 | 2,811 | 3,260 |
| Freight tonnes | 8.3 | 8.0 | 8.2 |
| Tonne-km | 2,456 | 2,328 | 2,412 |

*Class BM73 'Signatur' high-speed tilting trainset at Oslo after arrival from Trondheim* (Wolfram Veith)   2001/0114217

## Passenger operations

NSB runs commuter services in the Oslo, Trondheim, Bergen, Stavanger and Kristiansand areas and long-distance trains throughout the country.

As new rolling stock enters service, three new brands are being introduced for passenger services: Puls (commuter), Agenda (regional) and Signatur (long-distance).

NSB is introducing Signatur tilt-body electric trainsets on its main long-distance routes (see 'Traction and rolling stock' section). Once technical problems have been resolved and the new stock is able to operate at full speed, journey times from Oslo will be as follows (previous best times in brackets): Kristiansand 3 hours 55 minutes (4 hours 45 minutes); Stavanger 6 hours 25 minutes (7 hours 30 minutes); Bergen 5 hours 30 minutes (6 hours 30 minutes); Trondheim 5 hours 30 minutes (6 hours 40 minutes).

Other long-distance services from Oslo to Stavanger, Bergen and Trondheim are operated with modern locomotive-hauled stock, built in the 1980s and refurbished in 1994-96. As far as possible, day coaches and sleeping cars on these services now operate in fixed-formation rakes.

Class BM70 four-car emus, introduced in 1992, operate services from Oslo to Skien, Lillehammer and Halden. The Class BM70 is designed for 160 km/h operation and is receiving Agenda branding as sets are refurbished internally.

In May 2000, NSB and its Swedish counterpart, SJ, formed a joint venture company, Linx AB, to market and operate passenger services on the Oslo–Stockholm and Oslo–Gothenburg–Copenhagen routes. Operations began in June 2001.

## Freight operations

Since 1 January 2002, rail freight services in Norway have been operated by CargoNet AS, owned 55 per cent of NSB and 45 per cent by Green Cargo, the Swedish rail freight operator. As part of the deal, Green Cargo's intermodal subsidiary, RailCombi, became a wholly owned subsidiary of CargoNet.

CargoNet offers three products: intermodal solutions (CombiXpress), wagonload services and trainload services. The company is focusing on expansion in the intermodal sector, and to this end has signed co-operation agreements with Hupac in Switzerland and Kombiverkehr in Germany.

Iron ore traffic from Kiruna in Sweden to Narvik, a port in northern Norway, previously accounted for the bulk of NSB's freight tonnage. On 1 July 1996 this operation was transferred to a new Swedish company, Malmtrafik AB (MTAB), in which NSB holds a 24.5 per cent stake. Locomotives, depot facilities and staff connected with ore operations at Narvik were taken over by MTAB's Norwegian subsidiary, Malmtrafikk AS.

A mixed freight service from Oslo to Narvik via Sweden, known as Arctic Rail Express (ARE), was introduced by NSB and the then Swedish State Railways (SJ) in 1993. The service now runs seven days a week and has markedly increased rail's share of freight transport between Oslo and northern Norway. The 900-tonne train completes the 1,950 km transit in 27 hours. In 1996 a second ARE service was introduced, linking Narvik with Malmö in southern Sweden.

The ARE services paved the way for closer co-operation between NSB and SJ (now Green Cargo) in other areas, culminating in the formation of CargoNet AS. In January 1997 a twice-weekly service was introduced under the name Scandinavian Rail Express (SRE), linking Oslo with the Swedish port of Trelleborg, with onward connections to the Continent via the train ferry to Germany. SRE services were expanded in January 1998 to comprise five weekly shuttle trains for semitrailers, containers and swapbodies.

In November 1998 a service named Aladdin was introduced to transport aviation fuel from Oslo harbour to the new Gardermoen airport 50 km northeast of the city. The block train concept was developed by the German company Vereinigte Tanklager und Transportmittel GmbH (VTG) on the basis of its experience in the chemical industry. The 15 tank wagons transport around a million litres of fuel a day, equivalent to 38 road tanker loads.

A reduction in the number of freight wagons from 3,600 in 1996 to 2,200 by 2002 was achieved through better capacity utilisation, shorter turnround times and standardisation of wagon types.

## Traction and rolling stock

At 31 December 2001, NSB's motive power fleet consisted of 90 electric locomotives, 35 diesel locomotives, 135 electric multiple-units, 28 diesel

*Bombardier-built Class BM93 tilting 'Talent' dmu operating an Agenda service at Hamar (Edward Barnes)*

*CargoNet Class Skd 226 diesel-hydraulic shunter (in NSB Gods livery) acquired from Swedish State Railways (Edward Barnes)*

*Class BM70 emu at Lillehammer (William A Willard)*

multiple-units and 16 Airport Express emus. Other rolling stock comprised 393 passenger coaches and 2,182 freight wagons.

Following successful trials with a General Motors T66 locomotive on the Nordland line (Trondheim–Bodø) in 2000-01, CargoNet AS announced in early 2002 that it was to lease five of these locomotives. This will alleviate a shortage of modern diesel motive power following the rejection by NSB in 1998 of the 11 Class Di6 locomotives ordered from Siemens.

Siemens completed delivery in 1997 of 20 Class Di8 diesel-electric Bo-Bo locomotives for short-haul freight and shunting duties. The design is based on the Netherlands Railways Class 6400, but has a 1,570 kW Caterpillar engine.

Delivery was also completed in 1997 of 22 Class El18 electric locomotives built by Adtranz Norway to a Bo-Bo design based on the Swiss Federal Railways Class 460. The locomotives have an output of 5,880 kW and a top speed of 200 km/h, though initially they are limited to 140 km/h. Although a mixed-traffic design, Class El18 is at present confined to passenger duties.

Sixteen Class BM71 high-speed electric trainsets for the Gardermoen airport line were delivered by Adtranz Norway in 1998. The three-car units, fully air conditioned and pressure sealed, are designed for 210 km/h operation and seat 170 passengers. The design includes provision for the fitting of tilt equipment, and one set was delivered with this in place.

After successful trials with a Swedish X 2000 train on the Oslo-Kristiansand route in 1996, NSB placed a follow-on order with Adtranz in March 1997 for 16 tilt-body trainsets based on the airport train design. Designated Class BM73, the four-car units feature a revised interior for Signatur long-distance services with accommodation for 207 passengers. The trains will operate the Oslo–Kristiansand–Stavanger, Oslo–Bergen and Oslo–Trondheim routes. Although the first sets entered service on the Kristiansand route in November 1999 and the Trondheim route in January 2000, they had to be withdrawn temporarily at the end of June 2000 pending investigation of an axle problem which caused a set to derail on the Kristiansand line.

Until Bombardier Transportation completes the necessary re-engineering work is completed, the sets are limited to the same line speeds as conventional stock. Likewise, the Class BM71 Airport Express trains are restricted to 160 km/h.

A second follow-on order placed in early 2000 called for a further six sets, but with a revised interior layout (seating 243) for Agenda medium-distance services (Class BM73B). These were originally scheduled to enter service on the Østfold line (Oslo–Halden) from January 2002, but have been re-assigned to less onerous duties between Kristiansand and Stavanger until the axle re-engineering programme is completed.

In September 1997, NSB placed an order for 36 Class BM72 'Puls' new-generation commuter emus with Italian manufacturer Ansaldo Trasporti. The four-car low-floor units seat 300 passengers and were delivered at the rate of three sets a month from July 2000, operating from mid-2002 on local services in the Oslo and Stavanger areas. NSB has an option on two further batches, each of 20 sets.

For services on the unelectrified Dombås–Åndalsnes, Hamar–Røros and Trondheim–Bodø lines, NSB ordered 11 lightweight tilt-body dmus from Bombardier Transportation subsidiary Waggonfabrik Talbot in November 1997. The design of the two-car units is based on the German manufacturer's Talent prototype, which was tested by NSB in 1996, but has been adapted for longer routes and Norwegian winter conditions. The low-floor units, each seating 90 passengers and with a top speed of 140 km/h, entered service in 2000-01 as Class BM93.

The Class BM70 emus dating from 1992 are being refurbished to meet the standards adopted for NSB Agenda services.

*Class El18 electric locomotive with an intercity service at Ål (Edward Barnes)*  2002/0524941

### Electric locomotives

| Class | Wheel arrangement | Output kW | Speed km/h | No in Service | First Built | Builders Mechanical | Electrical |
|---|---|---|---|---|---|---|---|
| El11 | Bo-Bo | 1,676 | 100 | 7 | 1951 | Thunes | NEBB |
| El13 | Bo-Bo | 2,648 | 100 | 18 | 1957 | Thunes | NEBB |
| El14 | Co-Co | 5,076 | 120 | 31 | 1968 | Thunes | NEBB |
| El16 | Bo-Bo | 4,440 | 140 | 17 | 1977 | Strømmen/Nohab/Hamjern | ASEA |
| El17 | Bo-Bo | 3,400 | 150 | 12 | 1981 | Henschel | NEBB/BBC |
| El18 | Bo-Bo | 5,880 | 200 | 22 | 1997 | Adtranz | Adtranz |

### Diesel locomotives

| Class | Wheel arrangement | Power kW | Speed km/h | Weight tonnes | No in Service | First built | Mechanical | Builders Engine | Transmission |
|---|---|---|---|---|---|---|---|---|---|
| Di2 | C | 441 600 | 50/80 | 47 | 26 | 1961 | Thunes | BMV LT6 | H |
| Di4 | Co-Co | 2,430 | 140 | 112.8 | 5 | 1980 | Henschel | GM 16-645E 3B | E GM-BBC |
| Di5* | C | 485 | 60 | 47.4/53.0 | 13 | 1956 | MaK | MTU GTU 6 | H Voith |
| Di8 | Bo-Bo | 1,570 | - | - | 20 | 1997 | Siemens | Caterpillar | E |
| Skd226 | B | 218 | 70 | 34 | 15 | 1971 | Kalmar | KHD F12 M 716 | H Voith |

* Acquired from DB in 1985-87

### Electric railcars or multiple-units

| Class | Cars per unit | Motor cars per unit | Motored axles/car | Output/motor kW | Speed km/h | Units in service | First built | Builders Mechanical | Electrical |
|---|---|---|---|---|---|---|---|---|---|
| BM68A | 3 | 1 | 4 | 160 | 100 | 21 | 1956 | Skabo | NEBB |
| BM68B | 3 | 1 | 4 | 160 | 100 | 9 | 1960 | Skabo | NEBB |
| BM69A | 2 | 1 | 4 | 297 | 130 | 13 | 1970 | Strømmen | NEBB |
| BM69B | 2-3 | 1 | 4 | 297 | 130 | 19 | 1973 | Strømmen | NEBB |
| BM69C | 3 | 1 | 4 | 297 | 130 | 14 | 1975 | Strømmen | NEBB |
| BM69D | 3 | 1 | 4 | 297 | 130 | 35 | 1983 | Strømmen | NEBB |
| BM69E* | 3 | 1 | 4 | 297 | 130 | 2 | 1983 | Strømmen | NEBB |
| BM70 | 4 | 1 | 4 | 430 | 160 | 16 | 1992 | ABB | ABB |
| BM71 | 3 | 3 | 2 | 325 | 210 | 16 | 1997 | Adtranz | Adtranz |
| BM72 | 4 | 2 | 2 | 637 | 160 | 36 | 2000 | AnsaldoBreda | AnsaldoBreda |
| BM73 | 3 | 3 | 2 | 325 | 210 | 22 | 1999 | Adtranz | Adtranz |

* Rebuilt from BM69D in 1994   NEBB = Norsk Elektrisk-Brown Boveri

### Diesel railcars or multiple-units

| Class | Cars per unit | Motor cars per unit | Motored axles/car | Power/motor kW | Speed km/h | No in service | First built | Mechanical | Builders Engine | Transmission |
|---|---|---|---|---|---|---|---|---|---|---|
| BM92 | 2 | 1 | 2 | 2 × 360 | 140 | 15 | 1984 | Duewag | 2 × Daimler-Benz OM 424A | E BBC |
| BM93 | 2 | 2 | 2 | 2 × 360 | 140 | 11 | 2000 | Bombardier | Cummins N14E-R | M |

**UPDATED**

# PAKISTAN

## Ministry of Railways

Islamabad
Tel: (+92 51) 82 52 47   Fax: (+92 51) 82 88 46

**Key personnel**
Federal Railways Minister: Javed Ashraf

## Pakistan Railways (PR)

31 Sheikh Abdul Hameed Bin Badees, Lahore
Tel: (+92 42) 636 19 00   Fax: (+92 42) 30 61 93

**Key personnel**
Chairman, Executive Board: Muhammad Nasir
Managing Directors
  Freight: Muhammad Aslam
  Passenger: Abdul Quayyum
  Infrastructure: Nasir Amin
  Railway Resettlement Authority: Bashir Ahmad

Gauge: 1,676 mm; 1,000 mm
Route length: 7,718 km; 445 km
Electrification: 293 km of 1,676 mm gauge at 25 kV 50 Hz AC

**Political background**
Some faltering steps were made towards privatisation in the early 1990s. In 1992 it was announced that as a first step the government proposed to franchise out the lines from Lahore to Narowal and Faisalabad, and the Lodhran–Pakpattan route. Initial reports suggested that the franchisees, which took over at the beginning of 1993, had raised income on the routes, but this was due more to tighter security and control of ticketless travel than any immediate improvement to the train services. Both original franchises were later terminated and readvertised, but government approval for new leases was not immediately forthcoming.

In July 1997, disappointed by the lack of progress and the chaotic state of the railways, the government instituted a radical shake-up. World Bank-inspired reforms would see the railways and communications ministries merged into a single transport ministry, a rail regulatory authority set up, and PR divided into three bodies responsible for freight, passengers and infrastructure. A fourth business would manage railway-owned facilities such as schools and hospitals and would be responsible for the disposal of non-core businesses. Within three years they would be privatised. A task force, headed by economic affairs secretary Javed Burki, has been created to implement the restructuring plan, which was to include replacement of the existing board of management. The plan also foresaw massive cuts in PR's 110,000-strong workforce and the transfer of schools and hospitals for railway staff and their families to local authorities.

The division of PR into four businesses took place in September 1998, when rolling stock assets were divided between freight and passenger businesses. Management of the network, including signalling and train control functions, is being handled by the infrastructure unit. Coinciding with this restructuring was the creation of a new senior management board. Through the Privatisation Commission, the government plans to offer for sale or by concession its three core businesses, freight, passenger and infrastructure, as well as non-core activities such as rolling stock plants and sleeper manufacturing facilities and railway land and other property.

## Organisation

PR comprises the whole of the North-Western system of the former British India rail network with the exception of lines in the southwestern Punjab. The main routes connect Karachi with Hyderabad, Multan, Lahore, Rawalpindi, Peshawar, Quetta and Zahedan. It was known as Pakistan Western Railway from 1961 to 1974. The 445 km metre-gauge network is in the southeast of the country.

Following a railways ministry order that railway operation be divorced from non-railway activity, PR is now structured in several management units. These are: Railway Operations; Production Unit I, which includes the Islamabad coach works and the Moghalpura steel works; Production Unit 2, which includes the new Risalpur locomotive works; Production Unit 3, covering concrete sleeper manufacture and rail welding; Property Management & Development; and PR's Consultancy Service (PRACS).

## Finance

PR's financial situation deteriorated rapidly during 1993-94 and, in mid-1994, the outgoing General Manager, Syed Zahoor Ahmad, warned of impending crisis if the bias in favour of road transport was not reversed and rehabilitation of the rail network begun. Matters declined further during 1995, and it was forecast that PR's deficit would rise from Rs1.3 billion in 1994-95 to Rs2.3 billion in 1995-96. In fact, the deficit for FY95-96 was Rs8 billion, an outcome which brought the railway close to bankruptcy.

Government's response in the eighth five-year plan (1993-98) was to allocate PR a share of some 30 per cent of investment planned for the transport sector, whilst road projects were to receive 57 per cent. But, due to poor economic conditions nationally, little of this money was forthcoming; by mid-1996 only Rs7.7 billion had been made available for the entire plan period, and this figure subsequently fell victim to the restructuring process detailed above.

*Investment*
Concerned that almost a third of its diesel locomotives are life-expired, PR developed plans to remanufacture 101 Alco units, but foreign exchange shortages meant that only six units had been re-engined by the start of 1996. The project was revived after agreement of a further loan of Rs5 billion from Japan in late 1995, but was subsequently cancelled under 1997 restructuring plans. However, procurement of 30 Blue Tiger diesel locomotives from Adtranz/General Electric went ahead.

## Passenger operations

Passenger journeys reached a record 85 million in 1988-89. By 1994-95, this had fallen to 73.7 million journeys, for 18,904 million passenger-km. PR has since maintained this level of traffic.

Prospects were not improved by the poor condition of many coaches, with some services being withdrawn on account of rolling stock shortage. Multan works started a

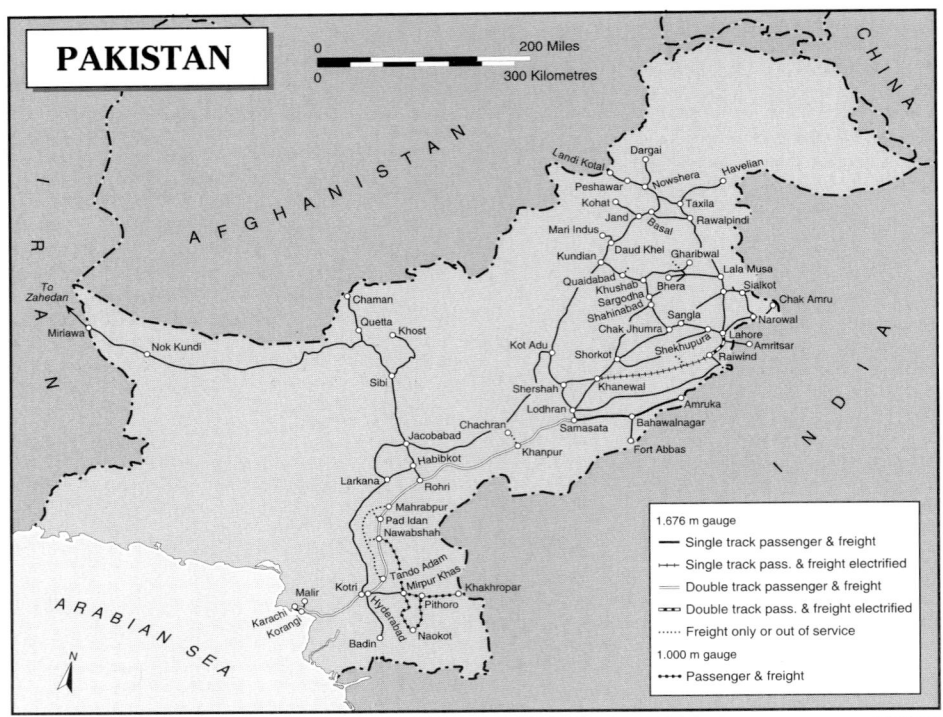

*PR Adtranz-built 'Blue Tiger' 2,500 kW diesel-electric locomotive*

*General view at Rawalpindi station, with improvements in progress (John Bamforth)*

crash programme of light refurbishment to raise comfort standards. More coaches have been air conditioned, and upholstery has replaced hard seating in many second- and third-class cars. Some trains now have video entertainment.

In 1995 there was a move to reduce operating costs by substituting railcars for locomotive-hauled trains, but suitable cars were not available and the cost of construction or conversion was thought too high for the plan to succeed.

At various times during the 1990s plans were canvassed for introduction of high-speed trains, including construction of a new alignment between Karachi and Hyderabad. While the high cost militated against such schemes, PR nevertheless aims to equip all expresses with air conditioned coaches in an attempt to improve business prospects. By 1998, Islamabad works had built 250 air conditioned cars, including 150 economy-class saloons, 50 sleeping cars and 50 generator vans. Of these, 175 have been financed under an agreement with German donors which also covered technology transfer. The first 15 coaches were built in Germany.

## Freight operations

In 1991-92 freight tonnage reached a low point of 7.6 million tonnes, for 5,962 million tonne-km. In the period 1993-98 tonnage was on average 5 to 6 million tonnes annually, with 5.1 billion tonne-km generated in 1995-96. PR has faced strong competition from road hauliers.

The first private-sector freight operators to run trains over PR tracks are likely to be involved in a scheme to raise three-fold, to 1.8 million tonnes, the amount of oil moved by rail to up-country power stations. Private operators would be permitted to run their own rolling stock over designated routes, and investment of some US$200 million will be required for 48 locomotives and 1,300 tank wagons. Several Canadian, US and South African parties expressed interest in running freight trains, but later complained of government lassitude in progressing the scheme. The franchise was readvertised by the government in June 1996, and by mid-1998 expressions of interest were reported to have been submitted by 14 prospective bidders.

In 1999, the private operation of container trains between Port Qasim, Lahore and Faisalabad was the subject of tender invitations from PR.

## New lines

Surveying has started on the first new railway to be built with private-sector funding. This is a 150 km line into the Thar desert from the Badin terminus of PR's branch from Hyderabad. Designed to tap reserves of coal and other minerals, the line will also facilitate construction of a 1,300 MW power station in the midst of the vast coalfield at Islamkot. The concession to build both railway and power station has been granted to a consortium of Hong-Pak United Power Generation, Tanson Development and American United Corporation.

In 1991 PR and Islamic Iranian Republic Railways signed an agreement to co-operate in development of the two systems. It provided for construction of the long-discussed 375 km connection between PR at Zahedan and IIRR at Kerman, although funding constraints have led to little progress with the scheme. A 40 km branch is to be built from the Zahedan line at Taftan to a copper mining development at Saindak.

Construction of several other lines has been canvassed in recent years, most recently a 650 km direct line from Quetta to Karachi, but the pressure on the investment budget makes it unlikely that a start will be made on any of them.

## Traction and rolling stock

Under the 1998 restructuring, the passenger unit took over 268 locomotives and 2,239 coaches; the freight unit inherited 267 locomotives and 26,755 wagons.

Electric traction is used between Lahore and Khanewal using a fleet of 29 British-built Bo-Bo locomotives.

In 1996, PR ordered 30 'Blue Tiger' diesel locomotives from a consortium of Adtranz, Germany, and General Electric, USA. The new machines were delivered in 1998. With a rated output of 2,500 kW, and weighing 132.6 tonnes in service, these will comprise 20 110 km/h freight units and 10 150 km/h machines for passenger service.

In accord with a policy of self-sufficiency in rolling stock manufacture, a diesel-electric locomotive manufacturing works has been constructed near Risalpur at a total cost of Rs1,993 million. The foreign exchange component of that sum was Rs1,237 million. The project has the support of the Japanese government and a technology transfer agreement has been concluded with Hitachi. The first locomotive, a 150 kW shunter, was rolled out at the end of 1993, but the target of 18 locomotives set for 1995 had still not been achieved in 1998. Projected output is 25 locomotives per annum.

In 1998/1999 the Pakistan Railways Carriage Factory in Islamabad was undertaking mid-life refurbishment of PR passenger coaches, and in 1999 PR was given authority to refurbish 102 diesel locomotives.

## Signalling and telecommunications

A major signalling project has been implemented comprising both conventional and modern signalling works, such as provision of colourlight signals on the double-track main line between Lahore and Raiwind and of tokenless block on other important lines, starting with Lodhran-Khanewal-Faisalabad and Sangla Hill-Wazirabad. Following a call for international tenders, orders for design, supply and installation of the equipment were placed with Siemens.

Signalling over some 2,000 route-km of main lines is to be upgraded in a programme agreed in 1993. Japan's Marubeni Corp will carry out the work, with much equipment to be supplied by Siemens' local subsidiary.

A modern train and traffic control system has been installed on the Rawalpindi–Peshawar Cantt section of main line over a length of 174 km. The equipment was supplied by Aydin Monitor System of the USA.

Further projects, which had been scheduled for 1994-95 completion, provided for UHF communication over 598 km covering the Rawalpindi–Peshawar Cantt and Kot Adu-Attock City sections; and track circuiting of storage sidings at 94 stations on the Hyderabad–Peshawar line.

### Diesel locomotives

| Class | Builder's type | Wheel arrangement | Power kW | Speed km/h | Weight tonnes | No in service | First built | Mechanical | Builders Engine | Transmission |
|---|---|---|---|---|---|---|---|---|---|---|
| HGMU-30 | TV6125A2 | Co-Co | 2,462 | 120 | 120 | 30 | 1985 | Henschel | GM USA 16-645E3C | E GM USA |
| GMU-30 | GTCW-2 | Co-Co | 2,238 | 122 | 114.95 | 36 | 1975 | GM | GM USA 16-645E3 | E GM USA |
| GMU-15 | GL-220 | Co-Co | 1,119 | 122 | 85.44 | 32 | 1975 | GM | GM USA 12-645E | E GM USA |
| GMCU-15 | G22CU | Co-Co | 1,119 | 122 | 86.90 | 30 | 1979 | GM Canada | GM USA 12-645E | E GM Canada |
| GEU-61 | - | Bo-Bo | 455 | 80 | 67.84 | 1 | 1954 | GE | Cooper Bessemer USA-FWL-67 | E GE USA |
| GEU-15 | U-15-C | Co-Co | 1,492 | 122 | 83.00 | 23 | 1970 | GE | GE USA E 7FDL-B4 | E GE USA |
| GEU-20 | U-20-C | Co-Co | 1,119 | 122 | 96.00 | 40 | 1971 | GE | GE USA 7FDL-B11 | E GE USA |
| HAU-10 | HFA-10A | Co-Co | 746 | 72 | 120 | 4 | 1980 | Hitachi | Alco USA 6-251E | E Hitachi |
| HAU-20 | HFA-22A | Co-Co | 1,492 | 120 | 102.6 | 28 | 1982 | Hitachi | Alco USA 12-251GE | E Hitachi |
| HBU 20 | HFA-22B | Co-Co | 1,492 | 125 | 105 | 60 | 1986 1987 | Hitachi/ Bombardier | Bombardier 12-251C4 | E Hitachi |
| HPU-20 | HFA-24P | Co-Co | 1,492 | 120 | 101.3 | 10 | 1982 | Hitachi | Pielstick 12PA4200VG | E Hitachi |
| ALU-95 | DL-531 | Co-Co | 709 | 104 | 73.98 | 25 | 1958 | Alco | Alco USA 6-251B | E GE |
| ALU-12 | DL-535 | Co-Co | 895 | 96 | 75.00 | 49 | 1962 | Alco | Alco USA 6-251B | E GE |
| ALU-18 | DL-541 | Co-Co | 1,343 | 120 | 96.00 | 24 | 1961 | Alco | Alco USA 12-251B | E GE |
| ALU-20 | DL-543 | Co-Co | 1,492 | 120 | 102 | 52 | 1962 | Alco | Alco USA 12-251C | E GE |
| ALU-24 | DL-560 | Co-Co | 1,790 | 120 | 112.44 | 21 | 1967 | Alco | Alco USA 16-251B | E GE |
| ALU-20R | DL-543 | Co-Co | 1,492 | 120 | 102 | 6 | 1986* | Alco | Bombardier 12-251G4 | E GE |
| ARP-20 | DL-212 | AIA-AIA | 1,492 | 120 | 109.06 | 23 | 1977* | Alco | Bombardier 12-251C4 | E GE |
| ARU-20 | E-1662 | AIA-AIA | 1,492 | 120 | 111.9 | 26 | 1976* | Alco | Bombardier 12-251C4 | E GE |
| ARPW-20 | DL-500C | Co-Co | 1,492 | 120 | 102 | 42 | 1982* | Alco | Bombardier 12-251C4 | E GE USA/ Canada |
| FRAU-75 | - | Bo-Bo | 560 | 69 | 68 | 2 | 1980* | Alsthom | Pielstick SEMT PA-4 | E Alsthom |

* Date of rebuilding

### Electric locomotives

| Class | Wheel arrangement | Output kW | Speed km/h | Weight tonnes | No in service | First built | Builders Mechanical | Electrical |
|---|---|---|---|---|---|---|---|---|
| BCU-3DE | Bo-Bo | 2,230 | 120 | 81.3 | 29 | 1966 | AEI/Met Cam | English Electric |

**Type of coupler in standard use:** Screw
**Type of braking in standard use:** Passenger cars (at 2/92): air, 872 cars; vacuum, 1,467 cars.
**Freight cars:** vacuum all

## Electrification

In order to get the full benefits of electric traction and to remove operational bottlenecks, extension of electrification from Khanewal to Sama Satta is considered essential. Though planned for more than 20 years, and included in the eighth plan, the project has never been accorded any funds. Estimated cost is Rs1,174 million. Tenders to execute the electrification were called in 1989, but no contracts were let.

## Track

**Rail:** 50 kg RE, 45 kg R BSS, 37.5 kg R BSS

**Crossties (sleepers)**

| Type | Thickness | Spacing |
|---|---|---|
| PSC Monobloc | 234 mm | 1,640/km |
| RCC twin-block | 231.77 mm | 1,562/km |
| Wooden | 125.152 mm | 1,562/km |
| Steel trough | 106.36 mm | 1,562/km |
| CST 9 (cast-iron plates joined with tie bar) | 133.35 mm | 1,562/km |

**Fastenings**
PSC/RCC sleepers: RM Type
Wooden sleepers: WI bearing plates with dog spikes; CI bearing plates with round spikes and keys
Steel trough sleepers: Mills spring loose jaws with keys
CST/9 CI plate sleepers: Keys
**Min curvature radius:** 10°
**Max gradient:** 4%
**Max permissible axleload:** 22.86 tonne

# PANAMA

## Ministry of Public Works

PO Box 1632, Panama 1
Tel: (+507) 32 55 05; 32 55 72   Fax: (+507) 32 57 58

**Key personnel**
Minister: J A Dominguez
Secretary: E Perez Y

## Chiriquí Land Company Railways

Chiriquí Land Company, Puerto Armuelles, Chiriquí, Apartado 6-2637 or 6-2638, Estafeta El Dorado, Panama City
Tel: (+507) 70 76 41   Fax: (+507) 70 80 64

**Key personnel**
General Manager: Cameron Forsyth
Assistant General Manager: Ricardo Flores
Technical Services Manager: Victor Mirones

Gauge: 914 mm
Route length: 152.5 km

**Organisation**
The railway, which was formerly divided into the Armuelles (133 km) and Bocas (243 km) Divisions, is dedicated to the transport of bananas. In 1992, the network was reduced to 152 km in length. Track is formed of 30 kg/m rails spiked to wooden sleepers spaced 1,600/km in plain track, 1,700/km in curves. Maximum permissible axleload is 20 tonnes and the maximum gradient 2 per cent.

**Freight operations**
Freight traffic in 1993 amounted to 410,670 tonnes.

**Traction and rolling stock**
The railway operates 17 diesel locomotives, seven diesel railcars and 380 freight wagons. Most powerful traction units are five 700 hp Caterpillar-engined locomotives, one a Whitcomb unit of 1948, the remainder GE of 1959 and 1970. Standard coupler is knuckle-type and braking of vehicles mechanical.

## Chiriquí National Railroad

Ferrocarril Nacional de Chiriquí
PO Box 12B, David City, Chiriquí

**Key personnel**
General Manager: M Alvarenga

Gauge: 914 mm
Route length: 126 km

**Organisation**
The railway, operated by the government of Panama, consists of a single line linking David City with Puerto Armuelles, in the region of the Costa Rican border.

**Traction and rolling stock**
The fleet comprises five diesel locomotives, five diesel railcars, five passenger coaches and 24 freight wagons.

## Panama Canal Railroad (PCRC)

Panama Canal Railway Company
PO Box 2023, Estafeta de Balboa, Panama
Tel: (+507) 32 60 81; 32 60 86   Fax: (+507) 32 53 43

**Key personnel**
Director: Darío Benedetti

Gauge: 1,524 mm
Length: 76 km

**Political background**
National austerity kept the former Ferrocarril de Panamá (FCP) short of investment funds, with the result that both infrastructure and rolling stock became badly rundown, and traffic declined sharply. In 1996, a 50-year concession to operate the line was granted to a joint venture consisting of the US firms Kansas City Southern Industries, which owns Kansas City Southern Railway, and Mi-Jack Products (equipment supplier and terminal operator). A final contract was approved by the Panama government in March 1998 and signed in June of that year. The concession, which called for no initial purchase cost, requires PCRC to rehabilitate, operate and develop the 76 km line, together with its intermodal terminals, infrastructure and equipment, and to pay the government 5 per cent of gross revenue until its initial investment has been recovered and 10 per cent thereafter.

PCRC plans to offer an alternative to the parallel Panama canal between the coastal ports of Manzanillo (Cristobál) and Balboa. The company eventually expects to run 32 trains a day, giving a capacity of 500,000 containers annually, although initially 75,000 are expected to be handled as a complementary service to the parallel canal.

**Passenger operations**
Passenger operations between Cristobál and Balboa resumed in July 2001.

**Freight operations**
Freight operations resumed in October 2001, with up to 10 container trains per day provided. The completion in December 2002 of a planned expansion in port capacity at Manzanillo was expected to boost traffic.

**Improvements to existing lines**
Reconstruction and the construction and equipping of terminals took place over a two-year period at a cost of US$75 million. The entire trackbed was renewed by Kansas City Southern, and standard-gauge track laid with continuous welded rail. Some realignment was undertaken to raise speeds to 65-95 km/h. Work was completed in 2001.

**Traction and rolling stock**
The new operators were reported as intending to acquire eight diesel locomotives and 48 container-carrying wagons. Passenger services are operated using locomotives and coaches acquired second-hand from Amtrak in the USA.

*UPDATED*

# PARAGUAY

## Ministry of Public Works & Communications

2° Piso-Gral, Diaz y Alberdi, Asunción

**Key personnel**
Minister: Gen Víctor Segovia Ríos
Under-Secretary: A Gomez Optiz

## Ferrocarril Presidente Carlos Antonio López (FCPCAL)

PO Box 453, Calle Mexico 145, Asunción
Tel: (+595 21) 44 32 73; 44 57 17
Fax: (+595 21) 44 78 48

**Key personnel**
President: J J Servían
Secretary General: J D Galeano
Directors
  Technical: W C Vallejos
  Administrative: M Franco
  Financial: H Guth
Managers
  Traffic: R Aguirre
  Tariff and Commercial: R V Bareiro
  Materials: C Insfran
  Way and Works: J Adorno
  Traction and Workshops: G Leon Samaniego

Gauge: 1,435 mm
Route length: 441 km

**Political background**
At the end of 1991, the Paraguayan government passed a law effectively making it possible to privatise all state enterprises. Modernisation work was to be undertaken with a view to privatising the system. In 1997, the government pledged US$150 million to prepare the

railway for privatisation. In February 1999 talks took place between representatives of the Paraguay government, FCPCAL and Spanish National Railways aimed at restoring services on the system and modernising it.

### Organisation
Paraguay's only common carrier railway, the state-owned Ferrocarril Presidente Carlos Antonio López (FCPCAL), extends from Asunción southeast via Villarrica to Encarnación and Pacú-Cuá (375 km) with a branch from San Salvador to Abaí 65 km long. The railway employed some 800 staff as of mid-1995.

### Passenger operations
In 1994 FCPCAL recorded 24,000 passenger journeys. In mid-1995, it was reported that passenger services comprised occasional Asunción–Aregua running at weekends. A study delivered to the government in late 1997 stated that reinstatement of passenger services between Asunción and Ypacarai would necessitate the repair of 25 bridges and investment in locomotives and rolling stock.

### Freight operations
Freight traffic amounted to 182,000 tonnes in 1994. As of mid-1995, weekly freight services were reported in operation between Asunción and General Artigas, continuing to Encarnación whenever possible. International traffic between Encarnación and Posadas in Argentina comprised exports of Paraguayan soya beans and imported goods moving in containers.

### New lines
In 1997, plans emerged to build a new line serving Ciudad del Este, which is on the eastern border with Brazil and Argentina.

### Improvements to existing lines
Improvements to the decrepit FCPCAL main line are sorely needed. The opening of the fixed link between the Paraguayan and Argentine railway systems was expected to boost traffic, but the poor condition of the Asunción–Encarnación route stands in the way of any sustained system wide growth. Previous strategies for modernisation have focused on the renewal of track throughout the Villarrica–Encarnación corridor (and the 140 km section between Villarrica and General Artigas in particular) and replacement of the railway's antique rolling stock.

As of mid-1995, FCPCAL operations were hampered by seasonal flooding of the River Paraná severing the main line between Encarnación and General Artigas. The level of the Paraná has risen due to the construction of a dam at Yacyreta and the possibility of relocating the FCPCAL main line appears remote.

### Traction and rolling stock
The FCPCAL fleet comprises 24 mainly British-built wood-burning steam locomotives, eight passenger coaches and 195 freight wagons. As of mid-1995, some nine locomotives were reported as serviceable.

Many of the freight and passenger vehicles latterly in use were on loan from Argentine Railways. It was reported in mid-1995 that its successor as FCPCAL's international connection, the private Ferrocarril Mesapotámico General Urquiza SA, was allowing its wagons to proceed no further into Paraguay than Encarnación due to the risk of damage and delay.

# PERU

## Ministry of Transport & Communications

Avenida 28 de Julio 800, Lima
Tel: (+51 1) 433 12 12   Fax: (+51 1) 433 04 27

### Key personnel
Minister: Juan Castilla Meza
Secretary General: Dr J J Quelopana Rázuri

## ENAFER-Peru

Empresa Nacional de Ferrocarriles del Perú
PO Box 1379, Jr Ancash 207, Lima 01
Tel: (+51 1) 428 94 40   Fax: (+51 1) 428 09 05
e-mail: comercial@mail.enafer.com
Web: http://www.enafer.com/

### Key personnel
Chairman: Davis San Roman Benvante
Managers
  General: Raúl Rosales Trelles
  Operations: Alberto Mori Ito
  Financial and Administration: Carlos Reyes Huerta
  Commercial: Raúl Salas Cornejo
  Privatisation: Terry Medina Llerena
  Public Relations: José Luis Sánchez León Mantilla

Gauge: 1,435 mm; 914 mm
Route length: 1,296 km; 314 km

### Political background
In 1990 the Peruvian government announced its intention to privatise ENAFER. At the same time it issued a decree permitting the construction of new railways competitive with the state system by private enterprise. In November 1991 President Fujimori confirmed that he intended to end the state regulation of the transport market and abolish the state railway's monopoly. It was proposed that management of infrastructure would be split from day-to-day operation of trains, with private companies invited to run services and paying rent for the use of the track.

In 1997, the Commission for the Promotion of Private Industry was preparing proposals for privatisation; Mercer Consulting of the USA was assisting in the process.

In July 1999 a group of investors led by Sea Containers Limited, which owns the UK's Great North Eastern Railway franchise, was announced as the winning bidder for a 30-year concession, to operate ENAFER, extendable by an additional 30 years. The bidding vehicle was a divisible consortium, with Peruvian investors led by Oleacha & Co taking over the Central Line from the port of Callao to Puno and Cusco and Sea Containers and Peruval Corporation managing the Southern and Machu Picchu lines through the PeruRail SA consortium. The two companies each have a share of 50 per cent in PeruRail, but Sea Containers retain the right to make decisions on capital investments. A subsidiary of PeruRail will be the principal operator of the Southern and Machu Picchu lines which will have to pay access charges to its parent.

In turn, PeruRail will also charge other operators for using its networks and for provision of rolling stock. PeruRail is required to pay the Peruvian government 33.375 per cent of such access charges, although during the first 5 years of the concession these payments may be offset by the cost of infrastructure improvements.

The concession includes all track, signalling, stations, workshops, ships and rolling stock. There is no purchase price for the concession other than US$5 million for spare parts and office equipment. All three networks are to be taken over by the respective operator from 21 September 1999. Sea Containers will manage the Southern and Machu Picchu lines for a fee and lease new rolling stock to both railways.

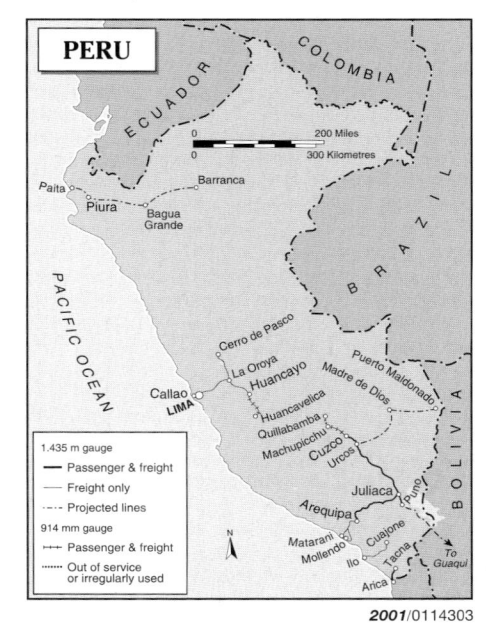

### Diesel locomotives

| Class | Wheel arrangement | Power kW | Speed km/h | Weight tonnes | First built | Mechanical | Builders Engine | Transmission |
|---|---|---|---|---|---|---|---|---|
|  | 0-6-0 | 256 | 30 | 42 | 1964 | Yorkshire Engine | Rolls-Royce C8TEL | H Rolls-Royce |
|  | 0-6-0 | 140 | 20 | 32.6 | 1950 | Hunslet | Gardner 863 | M Hunslet |
| DL-531 | Co-Co | 671 | 80 | 71.6 | 1958 | Alco | Alco 6251B | E GE |
| DL-532-B | Bo-Bo | 708 | 80 | 69.4 | 1974 | MLW | Alco 6251B | E GE |
| DL-535-A | Co-Co | 895 | 80 | 69.7 | 1967 | Alco | Alco 6251C | E GE |
| DL-535-B | Co-Co | 895 | 80 | 81.4 | 1963 | Alco | Alco 6251B | E GE |
| DL-535B | Co-Co | 895 | 80 | 80.7 | 1976 | MLW | Alco 6251B | E GE |
| DL-535D | Co-Co | 895 | 80 | 80.7 | 1964 | MLW | Alco 6251B | E GE |
| DL-500-C | Co-Co | 1,342 | 110 | 104 | 1956 | Alco | Alco 12251C | E GE |
| DL-543 | Co-Co | 1,491 | 110 | 110 | 1962-63 | Alco | Alco 12551B | E GE |
| DL-560-D | Co-Co | 1,789 | 105 | 110 | 1964-66 | Alco | Alco 16251B | E GE |
| DL-560-D | Co-Co | 1,789 | 105 | 110 | 1974 | MLW | Alco 16251E | E GE |
| GT-26CW-2 | Co-Co | 2,237 | 105 | 116 | 1982 | GM | GM 16-645E3B | E GM |
| GT-26C2-2 | Co-Co | 2,237 | 105 | 116 | 1983 | GM | GM 16-645E3B | E GM |

### Organisation
ENAFER was formed in 1972 with the nationalisation of The Peruvian Corporation railways, a private company which ran most of Peru's railways and the Lake Titicaca ferry services. The system now comprises the Central, Southern and South Eastern Railways (the Machu Picchu line) with headquarters in Lima, Arequipa and Cusco respectively.

### Passenger operations
Systemwide, ENAFER achieved 1.8 million passenger journeys (216 million passenger-km) in 1995. By mid-1995, passenger services had been suspended on the Central Railway (except for some weekend excursion services to San Bartolomé) but were in operation on the South Eastern Railway between Cusco and Quillabamba, and on the Cusco–Puno and Puno–Arequipa sections of the Southern Railway.

### Freight operations
ENAFER carried 1.7 million tonnes of freight and generated 484 million tonne-km in 1994. In 1995, these figures declined to 1.5 million tonnes, 407 million tonne-km.

### New lines
A US$1 billion, 1,800 km railway between the port of Bayover and Acre in Brazil has been proposed.

In 1997 the Peruvian government commissioned consultants to undertake a technical and economic feasibility study for a 150 km mixed-gauge line between Puno and Desaguadco. This would replace the existing Lake Titicaca ferry service, which imposes limitations on international services to Bolivia, with disruptions and reliability problems caused by low water levels in the lake. In recent years Bolivian transit traffic has been lost to the line serving the Chilean port of Arica, where road and rail connections are better.

In 1998 the Peruvian government announced it was to study three new non-connected lines: from the port of Paita, in the north of the country, to Barranca (650 km);

# RAILWAY SYSTEMS/Peru

from Tambo del Sol, on the existing Cerro de Pasco line, to Pucallpa (350 km); and Urcos, on the Southern Railway, to Puerto Maldonado, near the border with Bolivia (300 km).

**Track**
**Standard rail:** 34.7 and 39.7 kg/m
**Crossties (sleepers):** Peruvian hardwood
Made-up sleepers consisting of two blocks of reinforced concrete joined by a piece of used rail have been used in sidings and on straight stretches of main line

**Spacing**
Main line: 1,600-1,720/km
Branch line: 1,365-1,700/km
**Rail fastenings**
Soleplates and ⅞ in coachscrews
Soleplates and ⅝ in dog spikes
Pandrol fastenings are being fitted where new 35 kg/m rail is being laid
**Max curvature:** 17.5° = min radius 100 m
**Max gradient:** 4.7% (Central Railway), 4% (Southern Railway)

**Max altitude:** 4,839 m on Central Railway at La Cima siding on the Ticlio-Morococha branch, 173 km from Callao. On main line 4,782 m inside Galera Tunnel, 172 km from Callao
**Max axleloading**
Central Railway: 1,435 mm, 18 t; 914 mm, 14 t
Southern Railway: 1,435 mm, 17 t; 914 mm, 14 t
Tacna-Arica: 19.5 t
**Bridge loading:** Cooper E-40

## Central Railway

ENAFER-Ferrocarril del Centro (FCC)
PO Box 1379, Ancash 207, Lima
Tel: (+51 1) 427 66 20   Fax: (+51 1) 428 10 75

**Key personnel**
Manager: Ing Terry Medina Llerena
Chief of Operations: Raul Liao Rengifo
 Infrastructure: Jorge Vigil Rojas
 Mechanical: Manuel Pinto Podesta
 Commercial: Fernando Tovar Madueño

Gauge: 1,435 mm
Route length: 380 km

**Political background**
The 332 km Lima-Huancayo line, plus the Cerro de Pasco line of the Empresa Minera del Centro del Perú (132 km) and the 127 km 914 mm Huancayo-Huancavelica line have been bundled together as a single concession for privatisation purposes.

**Organisation**
The standard-gauge main line runs from Callao to Huancayo where it connects with the 914 mm gauge line to Huancavelica, which was privatised in 1996. There are 66 tunnels with aggregate length of 8.9 km, 59 bridges and nine zig-zags (reversing stations).

The main line climbs from sea level to its highest point of 4,782 m in the Galera Tunnel in 171 km from Callao on an average gradient of 4 per cent. The highest point on the system is 4,818 m at a siding at La Cima on the Ticlio-Morococha branch. This makes it the highest standard-gauge line in the world. The steepest gradients occur in the first 222 km from Callao, at sea level, to La Oroya at 3,726 m above sea level.

**Passenger operations**
In 1999 an occasional tourist passenger service was being operated between Lima and Huancayo.

**Traction and rolling stock**
The Central Railway operates 25 diesel locomotives, 41 passenger coaches and 972 freight wagons.

## Empresa Minera del Centro del Perú (Centromin Perú) SA

Railway Division
PO Box 2412, Lima 100
Tel: (+51 1) 476 10 10   Fax: (+51 1) 476 97 56

**Key personnel**
Chairman: J C Barcellos
General Manager: J Merino
Central Manager of Operations: J C Huyhua
Services Manager: L Pérez
Superintendent of Railways: J Chávez
Chief Operations Officer: V Zúñiga
Chief Mechanical Officer: C A Hoyos
Supervising Engineer, Way and Structures: A Chang Way
Accountant, Railways: J Gutiérrez

Gauge: 1,435 mm
Route length: 212.2 km

**Political background**
In 1997, the government announced that the company would be merged with ENAFER (qv) prior to letting concessions for the operation of that railway. The Cerro de Pasco line has been bundled with the Central Railway for privatisation purposes. The transfer will be overseen by the Commission for the Promotion of Private Industry.

**Organisation**
The railway division of the Centromin mining company comprises two lines lying east of Lima branching from ENAFER's Central Railway. These are La Oroya-Cerro de Pasco (132.2 km) and Pachacayo-Chaucha (80 km), operated for the transport of concentrates, ores, raw materials and spare parts. Centromin's railway operations employed a staff of 282 at the end of 1996.

**Finance** (US$ million)

| Revenue | 1994 | 1995 | 1996 |
|---|---|---|---|
| Freight | 3.176 | 3.069 | 5.812 |
| Other income | 1.684 | 1.242 | 0.077 |
| Total | 4.860 | 4.311 | 5.889 |

| Expenditure | 1994 | 1995 | 1996 |
|---|---|---|---|
| Staff/personnel | 2.801 | 3.272 | 3.197 |
| Materials and services | 0.655 | 0.493 | 0.552 |
| Depreciation | 1.059 | 0.540 | 0.482 |
| Total | 4.515 | 4.305 | 4.231 |

| Traffic (million) | 1994 | 1995 | 1996 |
|---|---|---|---|
| Freight tonnes | 0.884 | 0.885 | 0.888 |
| Freight tonne-km | 103.497 | 101.347 | 105.866 |

**Traction and rolling stock**
The fleet in 1996 consisted of 10 diesel locomotives and 627 freight wagons.

**Diesel locomotives**

| Class | Wheel arrangement | Power kW | Speed km/h | Weight tonnes | No in service | First built | Mechanical | Builders Engine | Transmission |
|---|---|---|---|---|---|---|---|---|---|
| GR-12 | Co-Co | 980 | 105 | 174 | 5 | 1964 | GM | GM 12/567C | E GM |
| GA-8 | Bo-Bo | 635 | 70 | 173 | 3 | 1964 | GM | GM 8/567C | E GM |
| G22CW | Co-Co | 1,120 | 105 | 107 | 2 | 1976 | GM | GM 12/645E | E GM |
| G18W | Bo-Bo | 745 | 115 | 66 | 1 | 1976 | GM | GM 8/645E | E GM |

**Coupler in standard use:** Sharon 10A
**Braking in standard use:** Air (valves K, AB, ABD Wabco Westinghouse)

**Signalling and telecommunications**
The railway uses a combination of mechanical, hand, telegraph, telephone and radio signalling.

**Track**
**Rail type and weight:** 9,020 45 kg/m (158 km); 7,040 35 kg/m (112 km)
**Crossties (sleepers):** Wood; 500,000 installed, spacing 1,850/km
**Fastenings:** Cut track spikes
**Min curvature radius:** 15° (La Oroya-Cerro de Pasco); 16° (Pachacayo—Chaucha)
**Max gradient:** 2.44% (La Oroya-Cerro de Pasco); 4.15% (Pachacayo-Chaucha)
**Max permissible axleload:** 19.8 tonnes

## Ilo-Toquepala Railway

Ferrocarril Ilo-Toquepala
PO Box 2640, Lima
Tel: (+51 1) 436 15 65   Fax: (+51 5) 472 63 44

**Key personnel**
Manager: R D Alley
Resident Engineer: G Pasut
General Foreman: T L Chapman
Operations: D M Krinovich
Maintenance of Way Foreman: R Lungstrom

Gauge: 1,435 mm
Route length: 219 km

**Organisation**
The railway connects the port of Ilo with copper mines at Toquepala, with a branch serving deposits at Cuajone.

**Traction and rolling stock**
The railway operates 41 diesel locomotives and 629 freight wagons.

## South Eastern Railway

ENAFER-Ferrocarril Sur-Oriente (FCSO)
Estación Marko Jara Schenone, Cuzco
Tel: (+51 84) 22 19 31   Fax: (+51 84) 23 35 51

**Key personnel**
Manager: Alberto Cruzado

Gauge: 914 mm
Route length: 186 km

**Political background**
Plans did exist to convert this to a standard-gauge line but not privatise it. However, both decisions have since been reversed, and the line is now to be sold off as a separate concession.

**Organisation**
Formerly managed as part of the Southern Railway, the 914 mm gauge route from Cuzco to Quillabamba via Machu Picchu emerged as a separate division in 1993.

**Passenger and freight operations**
The primary traffic is tourism, from Cuzco to Puente Ruinas, the station nearest to the Inca remains of Machu Picchu, for which there is no road access from Cuzco. This lack of a parallel road also dictates that most of the available freight traffic travels by rail, with transhipment at Cuzco. In 1997 there were two daily trains from Cuzco to Puente Ruinas and one mixed train from Cuzco to Quillabamba. Trailing load is severely restricted by the zigzags and gradients from Cuzco San Pedro terminus up

to El Arco. In addition to drinks and snack, onboard services on passenger trains include first aid.

### Traction and rolling stock
The South Eastern Railway operates seven 900 kW diesel locomotives, one MLW Type DL535 and six MLW Type DL535A/B, eight diesel railcars (2 Ferrostaal, 6 Macosa), 36 passenger coaches and 88 freight wagons.

*MLW Type DL535A diesel locomotive on passenger service at Cuzco San Pedro (Norman Griffiths)*
0023264

## Southern Railway

ENAFER-Ferrocarril del Sur (FCS)
PO Box 194, Avenida Tacna y Arica 201, Arequipa
Tel: (+51 54) 24 90 03   Fax: (+51 54) 23 16 03

### Key personnel
Manager: Ing Terry Medina Llerena
Chief of Operations: Nicólas Rodríguez Nieto
  Mechanical: Víctor Franco Velarde
  Infrastructure: Ernesto Medina Barzola
  Commercial: Alejandro Torres Delgado

Gauge: 1,435 mm
Route length: 855 km

### Organisation
The 1,435 mm gauge main line of the Southern Railway runs from the ports of Matarani and Mollendo on the Pacific coast to Juliaca, 462 km, where the line divides to Puno, 47 km, on Lake Titicaca; and to Cuzco, 338 km, where it connects with the 914 mm gauge South Oriental Railway to Quillabamba. The main line climbs from sea level to its highest point at Crucero Alto, 4,477 m, in 359 km from Matarani on an average gradient of 3 per cent.

ENAFER's Southern Railway operates shipping services on Lake Titicaca at an altitude of 3,818 m. The highest ferry service in the world runs on a 204 km route from Puno in Peru to Guaqui in Bolivia. The fleet includes one train ferry, one mixed passenger/freight vessel and one dredger.

### Finance
Investment totalling US$22.15 million was planned for the Southern Railway in 1996, with US$12.6 million to be spent on major track improvements. Other major investment items included US$5.43 million to be spent on refurbishing diesel-electric locomotives, US$1.63 million on freight wagons and US$1.22 million on track maintenance machinery.

### Passenger operations
In 1996 the Southern Railway recorded 267,943 passenger-km, down from the previous year's 302,447.

| Traffic (million) | 1995 | 1996 |
|---|---|---|
| Freight tonnes | 0.5 | 0.5 |
| Freight tonne-km | 216 | 259 |

### Traction and rolling stock
The Southern Railway's serviceable fleet at the beginning of 1998 comprised 26 diesel locomotives, 33 diesel railcars, 81 passenger coaches and 917 freight wagons. Diesel locomotives types operated are Alco-built DL-535 and DL-543 models, Bombardier DL-560s, and General Motors GT26CW-2s.

### Track
**Standard rail:** 39.7 kg/m (517 km) and 36.7 kg/m (315 km)
**Crossties (sleepers):** Hardwood (576 km) and concrete twin-block (217 km)
**Spacing**
Plain track: 1,700/km
Curves: 1,760/km
**Rail fastenings:** Tirafondos and Pandrol
**Min curve radius:** 102 m
**Max gradient:** 4.2%

# PHILIPPINES

## Department of Transport & Communications

Philcomcen Building, Ortigas Avenue, Pasig, Metro Manila
Tel: (+63 2) 631 87 61   Fax: (+63 2) 639 99 85

### Key personnel
Secretary: Vincente Riveira

## Philippine National Railways (PNR)

Torres Bugallon Street, Kalookan City, Metro Manila
Tel: (+63 2) 362 24 06   Fax: (+63 2) 362 08 24

### Key personnel
General Manager: Jose Dado
  Assistant General Management: Rafael Mosura, Jnr
Acting Assistant General Managers
  Maintenance: Erasto Laiz
  Operations: Ramon Jimenez
  Finance and Administration: Francisco Aure
Managers
  Legal Department: Antonio Holgado
  Public Affairs Department: Hilario Rojo
  Performance and Efficiency Board: Lynna Goyma
  OIC, Security and Investigation Services:
    Alexander Josol
  Training Operations Department: Ramon Jimenez
  Station Operations Department: Bonaparte Roque
  Rolling Stock Maintenance Department: Erasto Laiz
  Permanent Way Maintenance Department:
    Antonio Garcia Jnr
  Materials Management Department: Francisco Aure
  Controllership Department: Edilberto Manalo
  Treasury Department: Stalin Landas
  Personnel Services Department: Salvacion Bundoc
  Hospital Services: Armando Fuentes
  Real Estate Development: Edna Ramos

Gauge: 1,067 mm
Route length: 897 km, of which 492 km in operation

### Political background
Plans to privatise PNR had been expected to be put before Congress in 1998 as a way of arresting the deterioration of the network. Ownership of infrastructure was expected to remain with the state, with private-sector concessionaires taking over operation, maintenance and upgrading of the system. No progress with these plans had been reported by early 1999.

### Organisation
Much of the northern part of the network remains closed due to the poor condition of the infrastructure. Operations are currently concentrated on the 478 km Southern line from Manila to Legaspi City, on which major rehabilitation work was completed in 1995. Only the final 41 km from Polangui to Legaspi remain closed. Suburban trains run south from Manila on this line as far as Carmona.

### Passenger operations
Passenger traffic has suffered from the poor state of the system; the number of journeys declined by more than half between 1990 and 1993. Long-distance passenger figures have continued to languish, but Manila suburban services bounced back sharply in 1993 following commissioning of 10 new diesel locomotives. Passenger journeys doubled to 4.6 million, holding steady for the following two years. Reopening throughout of Main Line South (see 'Improvements to existing lines' section below) is expected to improve carryings.

### Freight operations
With nearly half the system closed, traffic has been in decline for several years. Tonnage amounted to only 5,000 in 1992 for 0.9 million tonne-km. By 1995 there had been a mild recovery, with 14,000 tonnes moving 3.9 million tonne-km, although the transport of construction materials for the Main Line South reconstruction artificially improved the figures.

Since 1997 container services operated by the Manila port authority have been run to a terminal near Santa Rosa (45 km).

### New lines
There are long-term plans for construction of two new lines, once rehabilitation of the existing network is complete. A 153 km line to Sorsogon from Main Line South is planned, along with a 281 km route to open up the Cagayan Valley in the north of the country.

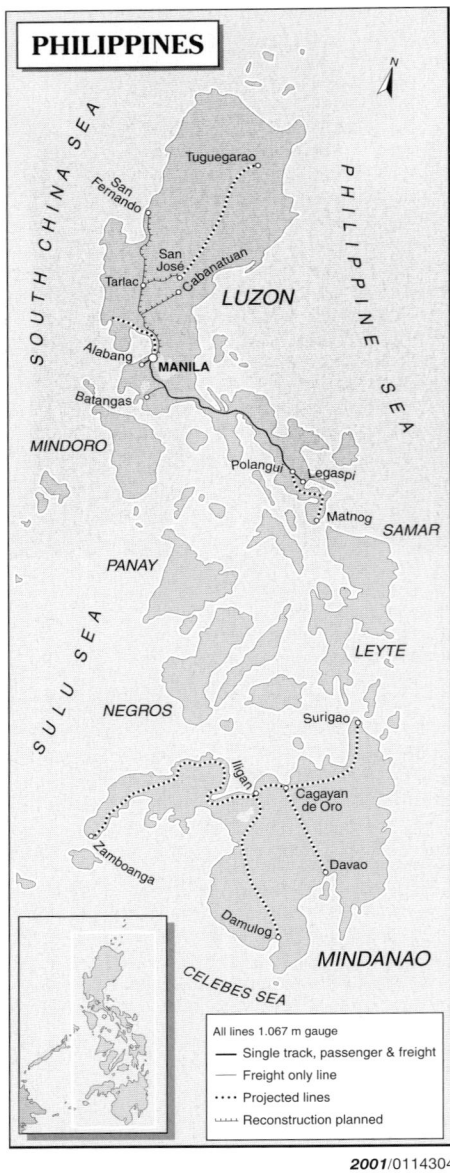

## RAILWAY SYSTEMS/Philippines—Poland

# PHILIPPINES

22 locomotives and 112 coaches. The consortium will own the trains and operate services, but the government has insisted that the track be handed to it upon completion so that other operators can use it.

*Manila-Clark Rapid Railway System*
In August 1997 government go-ahead was given to build a 130 km/h 102 km link, the Manila-Clark Rapid Railway System (MCRRS), from Manila to the development area on the former US Clark airbase. This involves reconstruction and electrification of the 25 kV Main Line North from Manila to 1,435 mm gauge, with construction of a short branch from Dan to Clark. Construction had been expected to get under way in 1998 following granting of a concession to North Luzon Railways (Northrail), a consortium in which the government-owned Bases Conversion Development Authority is the principal shareholder and in which PNR and RENFE of Spain also feature. However, Asian regional economic problems delayed the start of work, although the scheme's prospects looked brighter in 1999 with the acquisition of a 25 per cent stake in construction of the first phase by a Filipino-Japanese consortium, Fil-Estate Management, which is backed by Mitsui and Nishimatsu Construction, both of Japan. The government also took the opportunity to restructure the scheme, with construction entrusted to state-owned firms and private-sector companies required to invest in rolling stock.

The first 40.6 km phase, estimated to cost US$650 million, will run from Monumento, in Caloocan City, to Calumpit, in Bulacan province, ending at Clark airport. Under the second phase, the line will be extended to Subic, then to San Fernando La Union and San Jose.

*Mindanao*
In 1995 a plan to build a 2,000 km railway system on the Philippines' second largest island, Mindanao, was put forward by a consortium led by Malaysian engineering company Promet. Members include Spanish companies CAF and Cobra. A joint public/private-sector task force has been formed to take forward the proposed scheme, which would be constructed under a 12-year build-operate-transfer (BOT) scheme. In mid-1999 the government was close to inviting tenders for the project, which is expected to cost US$541 million. A high priority was being given to construction of the network, half of which the government expected to be operational by 2002.

One other important rail-related project is for construction of toll roads above PNR rights-of-way, allied to development of housing for up to 12,000 families. This is designed to remove the large number of squatters who currently live in shacks alongside the tracks.

**Improvements to existing lines**
A major project for the total rehabilitation of PNR's 437 km Main Line South, from Manila to Polangui (the remaining 42 km to Legaspi have been closed since landslip damage in 1976) was largely completed in 1995. In 1996, rehabilitation of the sections from Naga to Legaspi (96 km) was carried out by the Australian contractor John Holland, with consultants TMG International undertaking supervision. PNR's goal was to have 10 trains a day running at speeds of up to 75km/h; the route is expected to carry 2.5 million passengers annually.

Except for a commuter train service from Manila to Malolos (37 km from Manila), the whole of the 266 km

*Reconstruction of the line to Legaspi has seen the previous formation rebuilt with concrete sleepers, fresh ballast and part-worn rail* 0003028

Main Line North from Manila to San Fernando La Union and the 55 km branch line from Tarlac to San Jose Nueva Ecija are closed to train operations due to heavy damage caused by storms. Local interests are co-operating with international investors in proposing a US$100 million package of improvements to the Main Line North, to serve K-Line's new container port at Subic.

Rehabilitation of the 56 km Calamba-Batangas branch is planned.

**Traction and rolling stock**
Chronic availability problems have plagued every PNR effort to improve services. In 1995 PNR operated 25 diesel locomotives, including 16 Japanese-built 1,120 kW machines supplied in 1992, 21 diesel railcars, 30 passenger cars and 266 wagons.

Acquisition of six more diesel-electric locomotives, repair of five others and refurbishment of 20 passenger coaches was going ahead under the Main Line South improvement project.

**Signalling and telecommunications**
In the Manila terminal area 13.6 km of double-track line with semaphore signals is controlled from interlocked cabins. On single-track lines elsewhere trains operate on the English 'staff' system or by telegraph or telephone communication and VHF radio from station to station.

**Track**
Standard rail
  Main line: 32.2 kg/m in 30 and 33 ft lengths
  37.2 kg/m in 60 and 25 ft lengths
  Branch lines: 32.2 kg/m in 30 and 33 ft lengths
**Rail joints:** Angle bars with slots for spikes
**Crossties (sleepers)**
  Main line: 'Molave' wood, 127 × 203 × 2,133 mm, spaced at 610 mm
  Branch line: 'Molave' wood, 127 × 203 × 2,133 mm, spaced at 610 mm
  Bridge ties: 'Yacal' wood, 203 × 203 × 2,438 mm, spaced at 406 mm
  A limited number of steel ties are also used
**Rail fastenings:** Track spikes; bolts with square nuts; 'Hipower' nutlock washer, elastic rail spikes
**Max curvature**
  Main line: 9.2° = min radius 190 m
  Branch line: 11½° = min radius 150 m
**Max gradient:** 1.2%
**Max axleload:** 16 tonnes
**Max permitted speed:** 60 km/h

Reinstatement of the 92 km Balagtas-Cabanatuan branch is also planned.

In 1997 it was reported that international funding was being sought for construction of a 134 km line from PNR's Main Line South at Comun to Matnog, the capital of Albay Province.

*MCX*
In March 1997, a 25-year concession to build a commuter line south from Manila was let by the government to a consortium led by property developer Ayala Land Inc. The US$600 million plan is to reconstruct and electrify the line from Manila to Calamba along the shore of Laguna de Bay. This would form part of a more ambitious scheme, the so-called MCX project, to link the capital with the port of Batangas, 100 km to the south. Rolling stock planned is

---

# POLAND

## Ministry of Transport & Shipping

ul Chalubińskiego 4, PL-00-928 Warsaw
Tel: (+48 22) 624 43 00  Fax: (+48 22) 30 02 61

**Key personnel**
Minister: Jerzy Widzyk
Head of Railways Department: Krzysztof Celinski

## Polish State Railways (PKP)

Polskie Koleje Państwowe
ul Chalubińskiego 4-6, PL-00-928 Warsaw
Tel: (+48 22) 624 43 38  Fax: (+48 22) 624 44 10

**Key personnel**
President & Director General: Jan Janik
Deputy Director General: Jerzy Zalewski
Board Members
  Motive Power: Jerzy Smialkowski
  Personnel: Henryk Pawłowski
  Operations and Commercial: Jerzy Zabecki
Directors
  Strategic Planning: Marian Łukasiak
  Passenger, Commercial: Grzegorz Uklejewski
  Freight, Commercial: Jan Tymoszuk
  Economic Office: Zbigniew Cieślik
  Director General's Office: Jerzy Wiśniewski
  Operations: Czesław Dudziak
  Traction and Rolling Stock: Romuald Keller

  Track Maintenance: Bogdan Grzegorzewski
  Data Systems: Aleksander Słupczyński
  Signalling and Telecommunications: Kazimierz Frak
  Research and Development: Radosław Żołnierzak
  Personnel: Andrzej Krawczyk
  Training Office: Bogdan Ciszewski
  Procurement Office: Artur Dudziak
  Legal Affairs: Anna Žmuda-Bednarczyk
  Investment: Ryszard Sikora

Gauge: 1,524 mm; 1,435 mm; 1,000, 785, 750 and 600 mm
Route length: 646 km; 21,639 km; 1,135 km
Electrification: 11,591 km at 3 kV DC; 35 km at 600 V DC

## Political background

Poland's railways have suffered the same difficulties as those of the other former eastern bloc countries in adapting to the closure of heavy industry and other structural changes in the economy following the political changes of 1989. However, Poland has been one of the more successful ex-Comecon countries in acclimatising to change: it is one of the three countries (the Czech Republic and Hungary being the other two) which accounted for over 90 per cent of inward capital flows to the region in 1995. Inflation was around 30 per cent in 1995, in the middle of the range for the region.

An austerity programme in the early 1990s saw the withdrawal of around a thousand little-used passenger trains, and marginal freight terminals have been closed. Nevertheless, losses continued to mount: in 1998 the railway recorded a deficit equivalent to US$333 million and the figure for 1999 was expected to exceed this considerably. The government has subsequently pushed through other reforms of the railway system, privatising ancillary operations of PKP and introducing legislation allowing open access operation in November 1997. Operating licences were automatically to pass to PKP and to four existing freight operators in Poland. New open access operators must be registered in Poland before applying to use the network.

In July 1998 a new structure for PKP was implemented, creating separate business units covering infrastructure, passenger and freight operations, thus complying with European Union Directive 91/440. A Directorate of Traction & Workshop Support had already been established in 1997. In mid-1999 the government was expecting that PKP would become a state-owned joint stock company by 1 January 2000 and was considering the precise form of eventual privatisation. At least six foreign investors were reported to have expressed an interest in participating in the privatisation, including US-based Wisconsin Central and German Rail.

Of the 412,000 railway staff at the beginning of 1993, some 80,000 were already separated from PKP, as they were employed in maintenance and construction activities that had been or were about to be privatised. By mid-1999 PKP's labour force was down to 208,000; at the beginning of 1996 the railway employed a staff of 233,000.

## Passenger operations

Passenger traffic has fallen steadily since the collapse of communism. In 1988 there were 984 million passenger journeys; by 1993 this was down to 540 million, and the total for 1996 was 335 million (19.8 billion passenger-km).

An intercity passenger network embraces 20 major centres and thereby 50 per cent of the country's urban population. The domestic network has been steadily expanded and regular-interval service has been established on several routes. Trains now consist uniformly of PKP's latest 160 km/h rolling stock and all convey a restaurant car. PKP acquired its first EuroCity (EC) service, the Berlin–Warsaw 'Berolina', with the May 1992 timetable change. The train's schedule was improved to 6 hours 24 minutes for the 569 km end-to-end distance, an improvement of 1 hour 26 minutes over the previous best. Further significant improvement occurred in May 1998, when completion of upgrading of the Warsaw-Poznan-Kumowice E20 corridor cut the journey time to 4 hours 45 minutes. Other EC services have since been added. PKP's first EuroNight overnight service, the Warsaw–Cologne 'Jan Kiepura', commenced operation in May 1998.

Both domestic intercity and EC services operate profitably, but many other PKP passenger services incur heavy losses. In 1998, as part of the restructuring process detailed above, PKP was reviewing its future policy towards unremunerative services. Options were reported to include service cuts, a system of subsidies, operation with lower-cost equipment, and the transfer of responsibility for local services to regional authorities.

PKP has adopted DB AG's KURS 90 computer-based system of ticket issue, seat reservation and timetable database for dealing with passenger enquiries.

## Freight operations

The steep decline of freight traffic that took place after the collapse of communism levelled out in the mid-1990s but there was a substantial reduction in 1998, a decline attributed to reduced demand for movements of coal. Some 202.3 million tonnes (60.9 billion tonne-km) were recorded in 1998. By comparison, 419 million tonnes of freight were carried in 1985.

In spite of the decline experienced in 1998, coal remains PKP's principal traffic, accounting for around half

*Class ED72 3 kV DC emu at Czestochowa* (Marcel Vleugels)

*Class EU07 electric locomotive on passenger service at Wrocław Slowny station* (Marcel Vleugels)

# RAILWAY SYSTEMS/Poland

*Class SM42 diesel-electric locomotive at Krakow (Marcel Vleugels)* 0058820

the tonnage carried. PKP hauls unit trains of coal from Silesia to power stations, industrial plants and ports, employing rotary tipper or Talbot-system self-discharge hopper wagons. It signed agreements with other operators allowing them to use its tracks, with these operators handling about 40 million tonnes per year. Under the Polish government's open access policy, these companies have inherited operating licences to use the rail network.

### Intermodal operations
Intermodal development is a priority; traffic levels in 1995 were about the same as in 1994, due to delays in establishing new services.

A national piggyback company has been formed in partnership with haulage operator Pekaes, forwarding agents C Hartwig and several shipping firms including Polish Ocean Lines. The new organisation operates under the name Polkombi. A joint venture container company, Polcont, has also been created by PKP, Hartwig and Intercontainer. In addition to domestic services linking a total of 15 terminals, regular container/swapbody services are operated to Germany and Italy (Udine).

A new intermodal terminal at Plonsk, northwest of Warsaw, was opened in 1997.

### New lines
At present Warsaw's airport south of the city at Okecie has only a bus link with Warsaw Central station. PKP has proposed a rail link. As a first step, a dedicated shuttle train service could be run between Warsaw East, Warsaw Central and the existing suburban station of Okecie, on the line to Krakow, whence a bus shuttle would run to the international airport terminal. In a subsequent phase, PKP suggests, a loop serving an airport station could be created by double-tracking and electrifying an existing freight branch to the airport, and extending it to rejoin the Krakow main line.

### Improvements to existing lines
Since 1993 funding totalling EUR487 million from the European Investment Bank, the European Union's Phare assistance plan for central Europe and the European Bank for Reconstruction and Development have been obtained by PKP to complement domestic funding for an upgrade of its 473 km western sector of the Warsaw–Berlin main line, the so-called E20 corridor. The line extends from the Polish capital via Poznań to the frontier at Kunowice. Work was continuing in 1999 and includes track and bridge renewal, resignalling and reinforcement of the traction current supply, making the route suitable for 160 km/h passenger train operation and 120 km/h freight train running with 22.5 tonne axleloads. Work started in 1999 on the 211 km eastern sector of the E20 corridor, from Warsaw to Terespol, the principal point of interchange with the railway system of Belarus. The estimated cost of this project is EUR480 million, with completion scheduled for 2005. This will coincide with completion of upgrading of the entire Berlin–Moscow east-west corridor.

In May 1997, agreement was reached in principle with neighbouring governments on upgrading of the Gdansk–Warsaw–Krakow–Katowice–Vienna/Bratislava north-south corridor. UK consultancy Gibb Rail was commissioned to study the needs of the corridor under the EU's Phare programme. It is planned to operate tilting trainsets over this route (see 'Traction and rolling stock' section).

### Traction and rolling stock
At the end of 1998 PKP's traction fleet comprised 62 steam, 1,940 electric and 2,472 diesel locomotives, 1,222 emus and 14 diesel railcars. Also in service were some 7,000 passenger coaches and 108,000 freight wagons. A further 35,810 privately owned vehicles were present on the network.

In 1997, two major vehicle manufacturing industry developments set the foundations for replacement of worn-out locomotives in PKP's fleet and modernisation of the Polish locomotive manufacturing industry. The multinational group Adtranz bought from the Polish state a 75 per cent stake in Pafawag of Wroclaw. Adtranz undertook to invest US$28 million over the succeeding six years in the Wroclaw plant. Pafawag subsequently received an order from PKP to build eight Class EU43 mixed traffic 200 km/h 7,000 kW electric locomotives similar to the Italian Type E412, with financing arranged with a 10-year US$209 million loan to PKP from a group of five Polish banks. They are to be dual voltage to allow through operations under Austrian and German 15 kV systems. The first locomotives were delivered in early 1998. Adtranz is also building 42 Class E11 electric locomotives for domestic services. These are based on the builder's Class 101 design for German Rail.

Also in 1997 GEC Alsthom acquired a 60 per cent stake in vehicle manufacturer Konstal, and announced plans to invest in the company's plant at Chorzów to provide an effective response to PKP passenger vehicle requirements.

A refurbishment programme for emus of Classes EN57 and EN71 has been initiated.

Future new vehicle investments could include up to 200 lightweight diesel railcars for regional lines.

### Tilt-body trainset interest
After tests in 1994 with a Fiat ETR 460 Pendolino tilting trainset, PKP invited bids for nine 250 km/h units with an option for a further six. Fiat Ferroviaria was subsequently named as preferred supplier for 16 Pendolino trainsets for which funding was being arranged during 1999. The two routes particularly of interest for this technology are Warsaw–Gdansk–Gdynia and Warsaw–Krakow–Katowice, with possible subsequent extension to Vienna.

PKP also concluded an agreement for collaboration with Spanish industry with a view to acquiring Talgo tilt-body rolling stock. PKP studied the use of variable-gauge Talgo trainsets for its services into Belarus, Ukraine and the Baltic states, and also in possible rerouteing of

### Diesel locomotives

| Class | Wheel arrangement | Power kW | Speed km/h | Weight tonnes | First built | Builders Mechanical | Engine | Transmission |
|---|---|---|---|---|---|---|---|---|
| SM 40/41 | Bo-Bo | 441 | 80 | 61.7 | 1958 | Ganz-Mávag | Ganz XVI IV 170/240 | E Ganz |
| SM 03 | B | 111 | 45 | 24 | 1959 | Fablok | Nowotko | M Zastal |
| SM 30 | Bo-Bo | 257 | 58 | 36 | 1959 | Fablok | Nowotko DVSa-350 | E Dolmel |
| SM 42 | Bo-Bo | 588 | 90 | 72 | 1963 | Fablok | HCP 8 VCD22T | E Dolmel |
| SP 42 | Bo-Bo | 588 | 90 | 70 | 1966 | Fablok | HCP 8 VCD22T | E Dolmel |
| ST 43 | Co-Co | 1,544 | 100 | 116 | 1965 | Craiova | Sulzer 12 LDA 28 | E BBC |
| ST 44 | Co-Co | 1,471 | 100 | 116 | 1966 | Voroshilov-grad | Kolomna 14D20 | E Charkow |
| SP 45 | Co-Co | 1,287 | 100 | 96 | 1967 | HCP | HCP Fiat 2112SFF | E Dolmel |
| SU 46 | Co-Co | 1,650 | 120 | 102 | 1974 | HCP | HCP Fiat 2112SSF | E Dolmel |
| SM 31 | Co-Co | 882 | 80 | 120 | 1976 | Fablok | HCP | E Dolmel |
| SM 48 | Bo-Bo | 882 | 100 | 116 | 1976 | PZM-Lugansk | PDG-YM | E Charkow |
| SP 32 | Bo-Bo | 1,300 | 100 | 74 | 1985 | 23 August | 23 August M820SR | E Craiova |
| SP 47 | Co-Co | 2,200 | 140 | 114 | 1978 | HCP | HCP Fiat 2116SSF | E Dolmel |

### Electric multiple-units

| Class | Cars per unit | Motor cars per unit | Motored axles/car | Output/motor kW | Speed km/h | First built | Builders Mechanical | Electrical |
|---|---|---|---|---|---|---|---|---|
| **3 kV DC** | | | | | | | | |
| EW 55 | 3 | 1 | 4 | 145 | 110 | 1959 | Pafawag | Dolmel |
| EN 57 | 3 | 1 | 4 | 145 | 110 | 1961 | Pafawag | Dolmel |
| EN 71 | 4 | 2 | 4 | 145 | 110 | 1974 | Pafawag | Dolmel |
| ED 72 | 4 | 2 | 4 | 175 | 110 | 1994 | Pafawag | Dolmel |
| EW 58 | 3 | 2 | 4 | 206 | 120 | 1975 | Pafawag | Dolmel |
| **600 V DC** | | | | | | | | |
| EN 94 | 2 | 2 | 2 | 56.5 | 80 | 1969 | Pafawag | Dolmel |

### Electric locomotives

| Class | Wheel arrangement | Output kW continuous/one hour | Speed km/h | Weight tonnes | First built | Builders Mechanical | Electrical |
|---|---|---|---|---|---|---|---|
| ET 21 | Co-Co | 1,860/2,400 | 100 | 112 | 1957 | Pafawag | Dolmel |
| EU 06/07 | Bo-Bo | 2,000/2,080 | 125 | 80 | 1963 | Pafawag | Dolmel |
| ET 22 | Co-Co | 3,000/3,120 | 125 | 120 | 1971 | Pafawag | Dolmel |
| EP 05 | Bo-Bo | 2,032/2,344 | 140/160 | 80 | 1973 | Skoda | Skoda |
| EP 08 | Bo-Bo | 2,080/3,000 | 140 | 80 | 1973 | Pafawag | Dolmel |
| ET 40 | Bo-Bo + Bo-Bo | 4,080/4,680 | 100 | 164 | 1976 | Skoda | Skoda |
| ET 41 | Bo-Bo + Bo-Bo | 4,000/4,160 | 125 | 167 | 1978 | Cegielski | Dolmel |
| ET 42 | Bo-Bo + Bo-Bo | 4,480/4,840 | 100 | 164 | 1978 | Novocherkassk | Novocherkassk |
| EP 09 | Bo-Bo | 2,920/3,230 | 100 | 84 | 1986 | Pafawag | Dolmel |
| EM 10 | Bo-Bo | 960 | 80 | 72 | 1990 | Ciegelski | Dolmel/Elta/IEL |

Warsaw–Bucharest services via a shorter route through ex-USSR territory instead of through the Czech Republic. However, no investment case could be proved and the scheme has not been taken forward.

### Signalling and telecommunications
PKP has used part of a World Bank loan worth US$145 million to develop its Katowice signalling works for the production of solid-state interlocking equipment. A contract was let to NKT of Denmark for a pilot scheme embracing installation of optic fibre cabling, fail-safe transmission for signalling and associated equipment over a 40 km section between Gdansk and Tczew.

Bidirectional four-aspect signalling of exclusively Polish manufacture is operative throughout the 224 km Central Trunk Route. PKP had been trying to install this type of equipment at the rate of 300 route-km per annum, but the rate of progress has had to be severely reduced.

### Electrification
PKP uses a 3 kV DC system of electrification, except on the 35 km Warsaw–Grodzisk Mazowiecki suburban line electrified at 600 V DC.

### Track
On main trunk routes UIC 60 rail is being laid and on other primary lines UIC 60 or S49 rail. With wooden sleepers up to 250 mm ballast depth is prescribed, with concrete sleepers, up to 300 mm.
**Rail, type and weight:** UIC 60 60.34 kg/m; S49 49.43 kg/m; S42 42.48 kg/m

**Crossties (sleepers)**
**Wooden:** Types: IB, IIB, IIO thickness 150 mm; IIB, IIIO, IVO thickness 140 mm
**Concrete:** Types: BL-3 thickness 210 mm; INBK-3 thickness 202 mm; INBK-4 thickness 180 mm; INBK-7 thickness 190 mm; INBK-8 thickness 183 mm; PBS-1 thickness 180 mm
**Spacing**
Traditional track: 1,566, 1,600, 1,720, 1,733/km
cwr: 1,680 and 1,700/km
**Max gradient**
Main trunk and primary: 0.6%
Secondary: 1%
Local: 2%
**Min curve radius:** 200 m
**Max axleload:** 20 tonnes, 22.5 tonnes on some sections

---

# PORTUGAL

## Ministry of Planning, Transport and Territorial Administration
Praca do Comércio, Ala Oriental, P-1100 Lisbon Codex
Tel: (+351 1) 87 95 41   Fax: (+351 1) 86 76 22

**Key personnel**
Minister: Ferro Rodrigues

## Portuguese Railways (CP)
Caminhos de Ferro Portugueses
Calçada do Duque 20, P-1294 Lisbon Codex
Tel: (+351 1) 346 31 81   Fax: (+351 1) 347 65 24

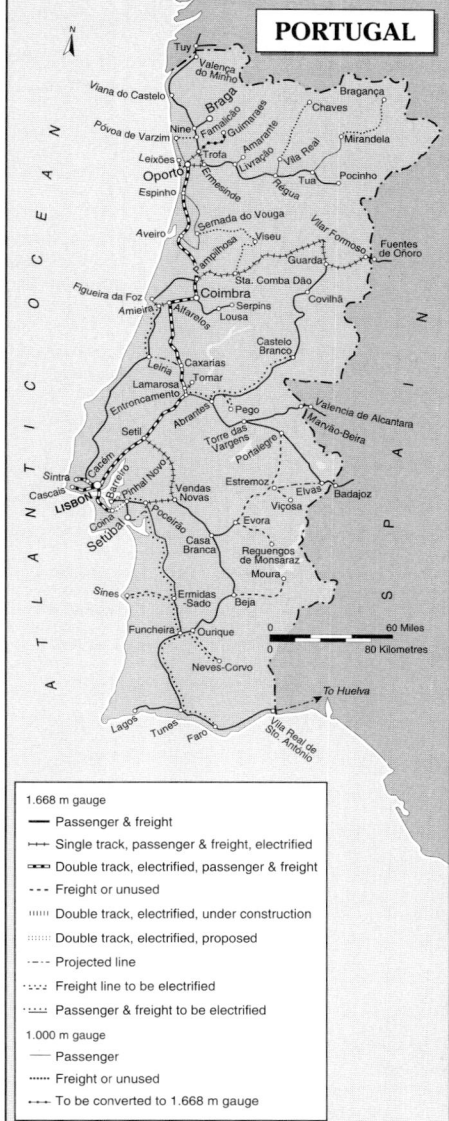

**Key personnel**
Board of Directors
Chairman: Crisóstoma Teixeira
Members: Eng Vilaça e Moura, Dr Elsa Roncon Santos, Dr Silva Rodrigues, Dr Moura Calhão, Eng José Espinha, Dr Braancamp Sobral
Directors General
  Infrastructure: Eng Francisco Carapinha
  Engineering and Investment: Eng Nuno Leandro
  Operations: Dr Oliveira Monteiro
  Sintra Line Business Unit: Eng Martins de Brito
Directors
  Planning: Vacant
  Innovation and Development: Eng Tiago Ferreira
  Data Processing: Eng Guimares da Silva
  Legal Affairs: Dr Almeida Coragem
  Finance: Dr Viegas de Barros
  Audit: Eng Vitor Biscaia
  Human Resources: Dr Maria João Tender Arroja
  Investment Management: Dr Tavares Fernandes
Administration Secretariat: Dr Luis Beato
Public Relations: Dr Américo Ramalho
Regional Managers
  Northern Region: A Villaverde
  Southern Region: Eng Alberto Grossinho
  Cascais Line: Eng João Cunha
  Sintra and Circle Lines: Eng Conceição e Silva

### Political background
The government announced a radical restructuring of the Portuguese railway sector in 1996, apparently prompted by CP's worsening financial performance. In 1995 CP recorded a deficit of Esc59.961 billion, following deficits of Esc48.37 billion in 1994 and Esc54.275 billion in 1993. As part of the restructuring, the government agreed to assume Esc450 billion of debt owed by the railways.

A new body, REFER (Rede Ferroviária – qv), began taking over responsibility for infrastructure on 1 July 1997, while the remainder of CP was to continue to operate the railway. The bill creating REFER was passed by the parliament in February 1997. Signalling centres were to be the final responsibility assumed by REFER, in January 1999.

Open access rights will encourage new operators to come into the industry, and a regulatory body is to be set up to ensure fair treatment of all companies using the network. Through restructuring, the government hoped to determine which socially necessary services would continue to be subsidised. It was suggested that regional services might be provided under contract by private companies and more public/private partnerships set up, such as the Mirandela Metro venture between CP and local government on the Tua-Mirandela route (see 'Passenger operations' section below). Operation of commuter services over the 25 de Abril bridge (see 'New lines' section in REFER entry) is to go out to tender.

In 1998 CP was reorganised into five business units: Greater Lisbon Suburban (USGL); Greater Porto Suburban (USGP); Traction & Rolling Stock (UMAT); Interurban & Regional (UVIR); and Freight & Logistics (UTML). The first to come into operation, in February 1998, was UTML, where traffic rose by 27 per cent in 1997. This unit, which operates from 12 to 18 terminals across Portugal, may be privatised within three years.

USGL came into existence in March 1998, managing Sintra, Cascais and Azambuja services, as well as the Lisbon circle (Cintura) line and Barreiro-Setúbal services on the south bank of the Tagus. USGP manage four lines, and became operational in 1998 following completion of certain infrastructure projects.

Outright privatisation of CP is not on the agenda at present.

### Organisation
CP has created over 10 subsidiary companies to manage more peripheral activities. Private companies have a stake in some of these subsidiaries, such as those involved in the movement of containers and cars by rail and the sale of advertising space on railway sites. Recently created subsidiaries include SOFLUSA, managing CP's Lisbon-Barreiro ferry service, door-to-door (using passenger trains) parcel carrier TEX and EMEF. The latter undertakes work for CP and other operators at four ex-CP heavy-repair sites with a workforce of 1,930.

CP staff numbers have fallen from 21,037 at the end of 1991 to 13,024 at the end of 1997. This reduction has

*Class 1800 diesel locomotive heading Vila Real de Santo António–Barrreiro passenger service at Tunes (Chris Wilson)*

# RAILWAY SYSTEMS/Portugal

*Class 5600 electric locomotive on Alfa Porto–Lisbon passenger service at Oporto Campanha (Colin Boocock)*
0023365

*Class 2200 Sintra line emu at Campolida (Colin Boocock)*
0023366

been achieved in part through early retirement and voluntary redundancy schemes.

### Finance
In early 1998 the government partially offset CP's accumulated debt of Esc450 billion by allocating to the railway shares in Electricidade de Portugal worth Esc151.5 billion, making it the latter company's largest shareholder, although without voting rights. This has effectively boosted CP's capital from Esc128.5 billion to Esc280 billion.

| Traffic (million) | 1996 | 1997 |
|---|---|---|
| Passenger journeys | 177.15 | 178.1 |
| Passenger-km | 4,503 | 4,563 |
| Freight tonnes | 7.9 | 9.3 |
| Freight tonne-km | 1,857 | 2,247 |

### Passenger operations
CP's passenger traffic, in steady decline since the early 1990s, saw a modest increase in 1997. Whilst express and interregional services have grown in popularity, this has not been able to compensate for the decline in regional, suburban and international traffic, largely put down to increased car ownership, an improving road network and a higher standard of living for many sectors of the population.

In 1997 suburban services accounted for 59.9 per cent of total CP passenger-km. Total passenger traffic in terms of passenger-km rose marginally by 1.3 per cent between 1996 and 1997; suburban services achieved an increase of 1.8 per cent in passenger-km, while the figure for long- and medium-distance and regional services was 0.6 per cent.

The first of a fleet of 10 six-car Pendoluso tilting trainsets (see 'Traction and rolling stock' section) began operating between Lisbon and Porto in May 1998, although CP's aim of cutting journey times using this equipment were frustrated by major delays to infrastructure upgrading.

Exclusive rights to operate from Cachão to Mirandela (14 km) on CP's 1,000 mm gauge Tua–Mirandela route have been granted to Mirandela Metro Co. Owned mostly by the municipality of Mirandela, with CP holding the remaining 10 per cent, the company began operating over an initial 4.1 km section from Mirandela in July 1995. Operations with four LRV 2000 railbuses are eventually to be extended to Cachão.

*Cross-Tagus link*

In December 1997 three groups entered bids to manage cross-Tagus suburban services using the new link described below (see entry for REFER). In mid-1998 the Fertagus consortium, which includes CGEA Transport of France, was selected for a 30-year operating concession. Services commenced in June 1999.

For the first three years, Fertagus is to operate under financial safeguards, but thereafter will be compensated with lower track charges if passenger numbers are lower than expected and with higher fees if traffic exceeds expectations.

### Freight operations
In 1998 CP's freight activities were consolidated to become one of the railway's five business units, UTML (Unidade de Transportes de Mercadorias e Logística).

Significant increases in freight traffic were recorded in 1997. Turnover rose 23.5 per cent to Esc14.1 billion, while tonnage grew 17.7 per cent from 7.9 to 9.3 million. Receipts from intermodal traffic increased by 37.1 per cent and tonnage was up 31.5 per cent, while conventional international freight tonnage rose by 58.9 per cent. Tonnage increases for specific commodities included: timber products 71.6 per cent; aggregates 59.7 per cent; iron and steel 46.8 per cent; coal 26.3 per cent; and automotive components 16.7 per cent.

An express service known as CEMI (Comboio Expresso de Mercadorias Internacional) is operated on the Lisbon–Barcelona route in conjunction with RENFE of Spain. Specialising in the movement of palletised consumer goods, CEMI offers door-to-door service with collection and onward distribution by road.

### Intermodal operations
Three new regular intermodal services to and from Spain were launched in 1995: an Intercontainer service from Lisbon and Leixões (Oporto) to Santurce (Bilbao); an Intercontainer service from Lisbon and Leixões to Algeciras/Cádiz; and a service for Liscont moving refrigerated containers between Lisbon and Vigo. Lisbon's Beirolas container terminal was replaced by a new facility at Bobadela which opened on 24 July 1995. CP eventually hoped to restructure its freight operations around Bobadela and three other principal terminals at Oporto, Aveiro and Setúbal.

Pecobasa, which owns 10 bimodal Transtrailer bogies, has asked CP to purchase 30 similar bogies to allow the establishment of a Lisbon–Barcelona service.

### Traction and rolling stock
In 1998 a separate business unit, UMAT (Unidade de Material e Tração), was established to manage CP's rolling stock fleet. Its remit includes the sale of traction services to external clients.

In 1996, CP's 1,668 mm gauge rolling stock fleet comprised 220 diesel locomotives (including shunters), 82 electric locomotives, 195 emus, 80 dmus, 487 passenger coaches and 3,976 freight wagons. For its 1,000 mm gauge network, CP had at its disposal 10 diesel locomotives, 50 diesel railcars, 15 passenger coaches and 5 freight wagons.

### Diesel locomotives

| Class | Wheel arrangement | Power kW | Speed km/h | Weight tonnes | No in service | First built | Builders Mechanical | Engine | Transmission |
|---|---|---|---|---|---|---|---|---|---|
| 9001/003 | Bo-Bo | 425 | 70 | 46 | 3 | 1959 | Alsthom | SACM/MGO | E Alsthom |
| 9004/006 | Bo-Bo | 440 | 70 | 46 | 3 | 1959 | Alsthom | SACM | E Alsthom |
| 9021/031 | Bo-Bo | 530 | 70 | 46.65 | 11 | 1976 | Alsthom | SACM | E Alsthom |
| 1001/1006 | C | 120 | 41.5 | 30.4 | 6 | 1948 | Drewry | Gardner | M Sinclair |
| 1021/1025 | B | 320 | 65 | 36 | 5 | 1968 | Moyse | Deutz | E Moyse |
| 1051/1068 | B | 90 | 38 | 28.3 | 13 | 1955 | Moyse | Moyse | E Moyse |
| 1101/1112 | Bo-Bo | 190 | 56 | 41.2 | 11 | 1946 | GE | Caterpillar | E GE |
| 1151/1186 | C | 190 | 58 | 42 | 36 | 1966 | Sorefame | Rolls-Royce | H Rolls-Royce |
| 1201/1225 | Bo-Bo | 480 | 80 | 64.7 | 25 | 1961 | Sorefame | SACM | E B&L |
| 1321/1337 | Co-Co | 750 | 120 | 87 | 17 | 1968 | Alco | Alco | E GE |
| 1401/1467 | Bo-Bo | 765 | 105 | 64.4 | 65 | 1967 | Sorefame | EE | E EE |
| 1501/1521 | A1A-A1A | 1,290 | 120 | 111 | 17 | 1948 | Alco | Alco | E GE |
| 1551/1570 | Co-Co | 1,290 | 120 | 89.7 | 20 | 1973 | MLW | MLW/Alco | E GE Canada |
| 1801/1810 | Co-Co | 1,530 | 140 | 110.3 | 10 | 1968 | EE | EE | E EE |
| 1961/1973 | Co-Co | 1,680 | 120 | 121 | 13 | 1979 | MLW | MLW | E GE Canada |
| 1901/13 | Co-Co | 2,240 | 100 | 120 | 13 | 1981 | Sorefame | SACM | E Alsthom |
| 1931/47 | Co-Co | - | 120 | 116 | 17 | 1981 | Sorefame | SACM | E Alsthom |

### Electric locomotives

| Class | Wheel arrangement | Power kW | Weight tonnes | No in service | Builders Mechanical | Electrical |
|---|---|---|---|---|---|---|
| 2501-2515 | Bo-Bo | 2,116 | 72 | 15 | 50 c/s Group | 50 c/s Group |
| 2551-2570 | Bo-Bo | 2,116 | 70.5 | 20 | Sorefame | 50 c/s Group |
| 2601-2629 | B-B | 2,940 | 78 | 21 | Alsthom | 50 c/s Group |
| 5600 | Bo-Bo | 5,600 | 88 | 30 | Sorefame | Siemens |

**Diesel railcars**

| Series | Power kW | Speed km/h | Weight tonnes | No in service | First built | Builders Mechanical | Engine | Transmission |
|---|---|---|---|---|---|---|---|---|
| 9101/103 (NG) | 240 | 70 | 22 | 3 | 1949 | Nohab | Scania Vabis | H Lisholm-Smith |
| 9301/310 (NG) | 320 | 70 | 37 | 8 | 1954 | Allan | AEC | E Smith |
| 9601/622 (NG) | 383 | 90 | 64.36 | 22 | 1976 | Alsthom | SFAC | E Alsthom |
| 0101/115 (BG) | 252 | 100 | 33.3 | 12 | 1948 | Nohab | Saab-Scania | H Voith |
| 0301/325 (BG) | 360 | 100 | 5.5 | 24 | 1954 | Allan | SSCM | E Smith |
| 0401/419 (BG) | 560 | 110 | 94.1 | 19 | 1965 | Sorefame | Rolls-Royce | H Rolls-Royce |
| 0601/0640 (BG) | 775 | 120 | 110 | 20 | 1979 | Sorefame | SFAC | H Voith |
| 9701-40 (NG) | 720 | 60 | 92 | 10 | - | Fiat* | | M |
| 9501/502 | 245 | 84 | 30 | 2 | 1995 | Fiat/Volvo | Volvo | H Voith |
| 9401/406 | 222 | 51 | 30 | 6 | 1993 | Fiat | Volvo | H Voith |

* (acquired from Yugoslav Railways)

**Electric railcars**

| Class | Output kW | Speed km/h | Weight tonnes | No in service | First built | Builders Mechanical | Electrical |
|---|---|---|---|---|---|---|---|
| 2001/2025 | 1,095 | 90 | 117 | 24 | 1956 | Sorefame | Siemen/AEG/Oerlikon |
| 2051/2074-2082/2090 | 1,095 | 90 | 123.6 | 33 | 1956 | Sorefame | Siemens/AEG/Oerlikon |
| 2101/2124 | 1,280 | 120 | 132.8 | 24 | 1970 | Sorefame | Siemens/AEG/Oerlikon |
| 2151/2168 | 1,280 | 120 | 132.8 | 18 | 1977 | Sorefame | Siemens/AEG/Oerlikon |
| 2201/2215 | 1,280 | 120 | 132.8 | 15 | 1984 | Sorefame | EFACEC |
| 2301/2342 | 3,100 | 120 | - | 42 | 1992 | Sorefame | Siemens |

In early 1998 CP was reported to be dissatisfied with levels of traction availability, and was to negotiate new maintenance contracts with EMEF (see 'Organisation' above). Competitive tendering for these services was foreseen if availability did not improve.

*Intercity trains*
CP's target end-to-end timing of 2 hours 15 minutes for its upgraded Lisbon-Oporto route is based on the use of automatic body-tilting vehicles. In March 1996 an order for 10 six-car Pendoluso trainsets, valued at approximately Esc25 billion, was placed with Fiat (bodyshells and tilting equipment) and Siemens (electrical equipment), with Adtranz Portugal (formerly Sorefame) undertaking final assembly of the fleet; the first five units were to be delivered by mid-1998, in time for Expo '98, with the remainder in service by the end of 1999. However, subsequent manufacturing delays led to the first five trainsets being delivered at a rate of one per month from July 1998. CP negotiated compensation from Fiat Ferroviaria in the form of services and spares valued at Esc1.4 billion.

Meanwhile, upgrading has been undertaken on the existing intercity fleet: 44 passenger coaches have been refurbished by CP's EMEF subsidiary at a cost of Esc5 billion. The upgrading features remounting on Y32 bogies, fitting of retention toilets, double-glazing, high-capacity air conditioning and power doors. CP has also installed telephones on the premium 'Alfa' trainsets of the Lisbon-Oporto service and introduced a business car on this route.

Many types in the dmu and emu fleets have also been the subject of refurbishment programmes, including 19 two-car dmus and 34 Cascais line emus. In addition, CP has been studying the acquisition of lightweight diesel railcars to improve the performance and economics of regional and local services.

*Cross-Tagus trains*
A contract for the supply of 18 double-deck four-car electric multiple-units for operation on the cross-Tagus link (see 'New lines' section in REFER entry) went to a GEC Alsthom-led consortium that also included CAF. The first trains were delivered in 1998.

A follow-on order for 12 similar sets was placed in December 1997 for Lisbon-Azambuja suburban services.

*Suburban trains*
Refurbishment of 34 Cascais line trains in Lisbon is being undertaken by EMEF as part of a Esc13.8 billion upgrade programme for the line.

In 1998 Adtranz Portugal and Siemens were awarded a contract to supply a further four four-car emus for the Lisbon-Sintra line for delivery in 1999.

Tenders have also been invited for 22 new emus, 12 of which will be for Cascais services and 10 for suburban services around Oporto. These could be double-deck units, and the eventual contract will include options for a further 22 trains.

## Portuguese National Rail Administration (REFER)

Rede Farroviária Nacional

### Key personnel
President: Dr Manuel Frasquilho

Gauge: 1,668 mm; 1,000 mm
Route length: 2,576 km; 274 km
Electrification: 1,668 mm gauge, 598 km at 25 kV 50 Hz AC; 25 km at 1.5 kV DC

### Political background
REFER began trading as Portugal's new rail infrastructure authority on 1 July 1997. Transfer of track was to be gradual, to be completed by 1 January 1999. Initially, 500 former CP employees were employed by the new company, with 2,000 more due to be taken on in 1998 and a further 3,000 in 1999.

REFER generates income from a combination of track access charges, property rental from operators and other businesses, and government subsidy.

REFER anticipated making a trading loss of Esc2-3 billion for the half-year ending 31 December 1997, with the Finance Ministry due to transfer Esc1.5-3 billion to balance the accounts. As part of its first half-year's trading, REFER invested Esc100 billion, much of which was sourced from the state or from the European Union. Esc120 billion of infrastructure investment has been budgeted for 1998.

The organisation's plan for the period up to 2000 is to spend some Esc600 billion on modernising its network. Half of this figure has already been allocated, with the cross-Tagus project in Lisbon absorbing Esc130 billion and the modernisation of the Lisbon-Oporto main line accounting for a further Esc200 billion. Overall priority is to be given to this latter line, where contracts for upgrading work on the Braça de Prata-Pampilhosa Da Serra section were awarded in 1997, and for Quitães-Ouar in 1998. Around Esc300 billion is allocated for the suburban networks of Lisbon and Oporto.

REFER has absorbed the two public-sector organisations set up to manage major rail infrastructure schemes in Lisbon - GECAF, which has been responsible for the addition of a rail deck to the cross-Tagus 25 de Abril bridge, and GNFL, the Lisbon Railway Network Office. Also absorbed is GNFP, which was charged with managing rail investment in the greater Oporto area.

### Organisation
Functional divisions within REFER's organisational structure cover operations, maintenance, infrastructure engineering, and construction projects, and will report to a board of directors. They are supported by finance and personnel departments. The maintenance division was established in January 1998, while an operations division started functioning in January 1999.

### New lines
*Cross-Tagus link*
Construction of the Esc140 billion 22 km cross-Tagus link for Lisbon suburban traffic between Chelas on the north bank and Fogueteiro on the south bank has been completed, enabling services to commence in June 1998. The project involved the installation of a rail deck to carry 700 tonne trains on the 25 de Abril suspension bridge, opened in 1967 for road traffic. Between Chelas and Campolide the link makes use of CP's existing Lisbon orbital (Cintura) route, widened to four tracks, but the remainder of the project has involved new construction.

Existing stations at Chelas, Areeiro, Entrecampos, Sete Rios and Campolide are served, and new stations have been built at Alvito, Pragal, Corroios, Foros de Amora and Fogueteiro. It is hoped eventually to extend the link from Fogueteiro via Coina and Penalva to the CP system at Pinhal Novo, thereby providing an alternative to the ferry connection between Lisbon city centre and Barreiro on the south bank of the Tagus, the terminus for passenger trains to and from the south of Portugal. The necessary link to complete this scheme, between Coina and Penalva, will be financed by the state.

*International links*
In May 1996 representatives of the Portuguese government met with European Commission officials to discuss the possibility of European Union funding for a new international passenger service. Using existing or planned infrastructure and a new connection between the Portuguese and Spanish networks over the River Guadiana, presumably at Vila Real de Santo António, the new service would run between the Spanish cities of La Coruña and Seville via Oporto, Lisbon and Faro.

Various other options have been examined for connecting Lisbon to Europe's developing high-speed network. An upgrade of the Beira Baixa (Entroncamento-Castelo Branco-Guarda) route was proposed in May 1996, whilst CP is known to have considered a direct Lisbon-Irún link. RENFE of Spain has expressed a preference for a route feeding into its emerging Madrid-Barcelona high-speed line.

### Improvements to existing lines
*Lisbon-Oporto upgrading*
The electrified Lisbon-Oporto line (Linha do Norte) generates half CP's income, and its redevelopment became an urgent need with the 1991 completion of a motorway between the two cities. Following a study by the UK consultancy Transmark, in April 1991 the government authorised investment in infrastructure and new rolling stock to allow 220 km/h passenger operation between Lisbon and Oporto, with tilt-body trains covering the 340 km in two hours. A lift of maximum freight wagon axleload to 25 tonnes was also an objective.

On 26 July 1994 CP signed a Esc5.5 billion five-year project and construction management contract for the Linha do Norte upgrading programme with a consortium of ICF Kaiser International, W S Atkins and Fernando Braz Oliveira. A total of Esc190 billion is being spent on infrastructure, which includes renewal of 600 track-km, realignment of 60 track-km for 220 km/h operation and provision of an additional 75 track-km. UIC 60 rail on monobloc sleepers is being installed and the project involves the construction of 160 new bridges and a 1 km viaduct.

Catenary on the Linha do Norte is being renewed and the route resignalled. Level crossings are being eliminated or given automatic protection in conjunction with installation of CTC and the Ericsson ATP system, which will permit a lifting of maximum passenger train speed. Layouts at 42 stations are being remodelled to reduce path conflicts of trunk and local trains, and to avoid speed restriction of non-stopping trains.

REFER has inherited the Linha do Norte upgrading programme and intended to complete it by 2001. However, by 1999 serious delays and unforeseen work were threatening to put back completion until 2010. Costs had also risen substantially. These factors were prompting a renewed assessment of the case for a new high-speed line between the two cities.

*Lisbon network redevelopment*
Before the establishment of REFER CP allocated Esc3.2 billion for raising capacity on the 27 km Lisbon–Sintra line. The money was to be spent on resignalling the route as far as Cacém with ESTWL90 equipment, eliminating level crossings, renovating stations and remodelling track layouts. It is planned to introduce centralised traffic control, permitting 25 trains an hour in each direction. Four tracks in place of the present two will eventually be in service between Lisbon and Cacém (17.3 km). The route between Campolide and Benfica (3.1 km) has been expanded to four tracks, with trains operating at 4 minute headways at peak hours and serving a new station at Queluz-Massamá.

In addition to minor works to improve interchanges with the Lisbon metro, a modernisation programme costed at Esc60 billion has been proposed for the Lisbon–Cascais route. Level crossing elimination, better bus interchanges and new car parks for rail commuters form the major objectives of the programme, which could be completed by 2002.

*Oporto improvements*
Recent investment programmes have made provision for a new train maintenance facility at Oporto and the conversion of the 1,000 mm gauge Lousado-Guimarães branch to 1,668 mm gauge. The 1,000 mm gauge Oporto-Póvoa de Varzim and Senhora da Hora-Trofa routes (49.4 km in total) are to form part of a new Esc100 billion light rail system planned for Oporto. A contract to build and initially operate the 68 km network was awarded in early 1997 to Siemens, following competition with GEC Alsthom, a consortium led by Adtranz and a consortium of Spie Batignolles, Bombardier and Ansaldo.

Elsewhere on the CP Oporto network, doubling from two to four tracks between Oporto and Ermesinde is planned. Electrification from Ermesinde eastwards to Marco de Canaveses and double-tracking between Ermesinde and Caíde (completed as far as Valongo in 1995) has been undertaken.

*Beira Alta route*
Modernisation of REFER's prime international route to Spain, the Beira Alta, was a priority identified by CP. The line runs 201.6 km from Pampilhosa, south of Oporto on the Lisbon main line, to the Spanish border at Vilar Formoso; from here there is a direct Spanish route to the French border via Salamanca and Burgos. The 202 km of single track within Portugal has been electrified, resignalled and has undergone substantial realignment to ease its most severe curves and permit 160 km/h operation. This will entail complete reconstruction of two segments, in addition to level crossing elimination. Completion has cut as much as two hours from Lisbon–Paris passenger train timings, and the Esc38 billion cost of the project has been supported in part by the European Union.

### Signalling and telecommunications
In recent years CP has concentrated signalling of its main line network on five electronic control centres, at Oporto, Coimbra, Entroncamento, Lisbon and Setúbal.

Two technologies have been adopted. One is the British SSI (Solid-State Interlocking), which has been supplied by Dimetronic SA of Spain and Westinghouse Brake & Signal. The other is ESTWL90, a German system similar to one adopted by that country's DB AG, which has been furnished by Alcatel's Portuguese subsidiaries, Alcatel SEL and Alcatel Portugal. The local company Efacec assisted in various aspects, including track circuiting, cabling, level crossing automation and installation.

EB Corporation of Norway (now Adtranz) received a CP contract for the delivery of Ericsson-type ATP speed-control equipment for installation on the Lisbon–Oporto line. The contract covers equipment for 300 vehicles. The local partner in this project is Efacec.

### Track
**Standard rail**
1,668 mm gauge: 30-55 kg/m in 8 and 18 m lengths
1,000 mm gauge: 20-36 kg/m in 8 and 12 m lengths
**Welded rail**
Thermit process is used. Rail used weighs 54, 50, 45, 40 kg/m in 18 and 24 m lengths. The length of continuous welded rail is usually 840 m but occasionally 950 m
**Crossties (sleepers)**
1,668 mm gauge: 260 × 130 × 2,600 mm, spacing 605 mm
1,000 mm gauge: 230 × 120 × 1,800 mm, spacing 820 to 850 mm
**Rail fastening:** Screw spikes or bolts. RN flexible fastenings used with welded rail
**Filling:** Broken stone, gravel or earth
**Max curvature**
1,668 mm gauge: 5.9° = min radius 300 m
1,000 mm gauge: 29° = min radius 60 m
**Longest continuous gradient**
1,668 mm gauge: 8.3 km of 1.4% gradient with curves varying from 590 to 1,501 m in radius
1,000 mm gauge: 7.2 km of 2.5% gradient with curves varying from 75 to 500 m in radius
**Max gradient**
1,668 mm gauge: 1.8% = 1 in 55½
1,000 mm gauge: 2.5% = 1 in 40
**Max altitude**
1,668 mm gauge: 812.7 m
1,000 mm gauge: 849.7 m
**Max axleload**
1,668 mm gauge: 19.5 tonnes
1,000 mm gauge: 11 tonnes
**Max permitted speed**
1,668 mm gauge: 160 km/h
1,000 mm gauge: 80 km/h

# PUERTO RICO

## Ponce & Guayama Railway

Corporación Azucarera de Puerto Rico
Aguirre, Puerto Rico 00608
Tel: (+1 809) 853 38 10

**Key personnel**
Executive Director: A Martinez

General Superintendent: J Rodriguez
Roadmaster: R Rodriguez
Traffic Manager: J Lopez
Purchasing Manager: R Rivera
Accountant: T Cartagena

Gauge: 1,000 mm
Route length: 96 km

### Traction and rolling stock
The railway operates 22 diesel locomotives and 1,280 freight wagons.

# ROMANIA

## Ministry of Transport

Bd Dinicu Golescu 38, Bucharest 78123
Tel: (+40 1) 617 20 60   Fax: (+40 1) 312 32 05

**Key personnel**
Minister: Miron Mitrea

### Political background
Within the Ministry of Transport, the Railways Directorate has responsibility for overall regulation and strategy. The directorate is also responsible for implementing the changes needed to meet European Union directives as Romania prepares for membership of the community. It is also the body which agrees annual contracts with CFR SA and CFR-Calatori.

*UPDATED*

## Romanian Railway Authority (AFR)

Autoritatea Feroviara Romana
Bucharest

**Key personnel**
General Manager: Ispas Eugen
Chief State Inspector: Dobrescu Lucian

### Political background
AFR was established on 1 November 1998 to oversee the licensing of operators, railway safety and issues such as conflicts in track access demands.

*VERIFIED*

## CFR Calatori SA

Bd Dinicu Golescu 38, 77113 Bucharest 1
Tel: (+40 1) 222 25 18   Fax: (+40 1) 411 20 54

**Key personnel**
Chairman and Chief Executive Officer: Valentin Bota

### Organisation
CFR Calatori is the passenger business created on the October 1998 restructuring of Romanian National Railways. After the unsuccessful introduction of a devolved structure in 2000, CFR Calatori is now centrally managed, with a separate unit responsible for intercity business. However, the establishment of a four-region structure is foreseen. In 2001, approximately 22,500 staff were employed.

Subsidy for unremunerative services is provided via passenger service contracts negotiated with government via the Railways Directorate. A current four-year contract runs from 2001 to 2004.

| Traffic (million) | 2000 |
|---|---|
| Passenger journeys | 117 |
| Passenger-km | 18,000 |

### Passenger operations
Intercity services linking Romania's major centres of population form a key part of CFR Calatori's business, accounting for some 50 per cent of passenger journeys.

In May 2000, an hourly 'Litoral 2000' premium service was introduced on the Bucharest–Constanza–Mangalia route.

### Traction and rolling stock
In 2001, CFR Calatori operated 361 electric and 456 diesel locomotives. There were also some 4,200 coaches in use.

In July 2001, the Transportation Systems Group of Siemens AG announced that it had signed a contract to supply 120 Desiro dmu cars to CFR Calatori. To be supplied as two- and four-car units, the trains were to be delivered between 2001 and 2005. They are to be deployed on regional non-electrified lines around Bucharest and other major Romanian cities. The first five units are to be constructed by Siemens, leaving the remainder to be built locally, although in mid-2001 the partner supplier was still to be named. CFR Calatori also foresees the purchase of 90 emu cars for delivery in 2003-05.

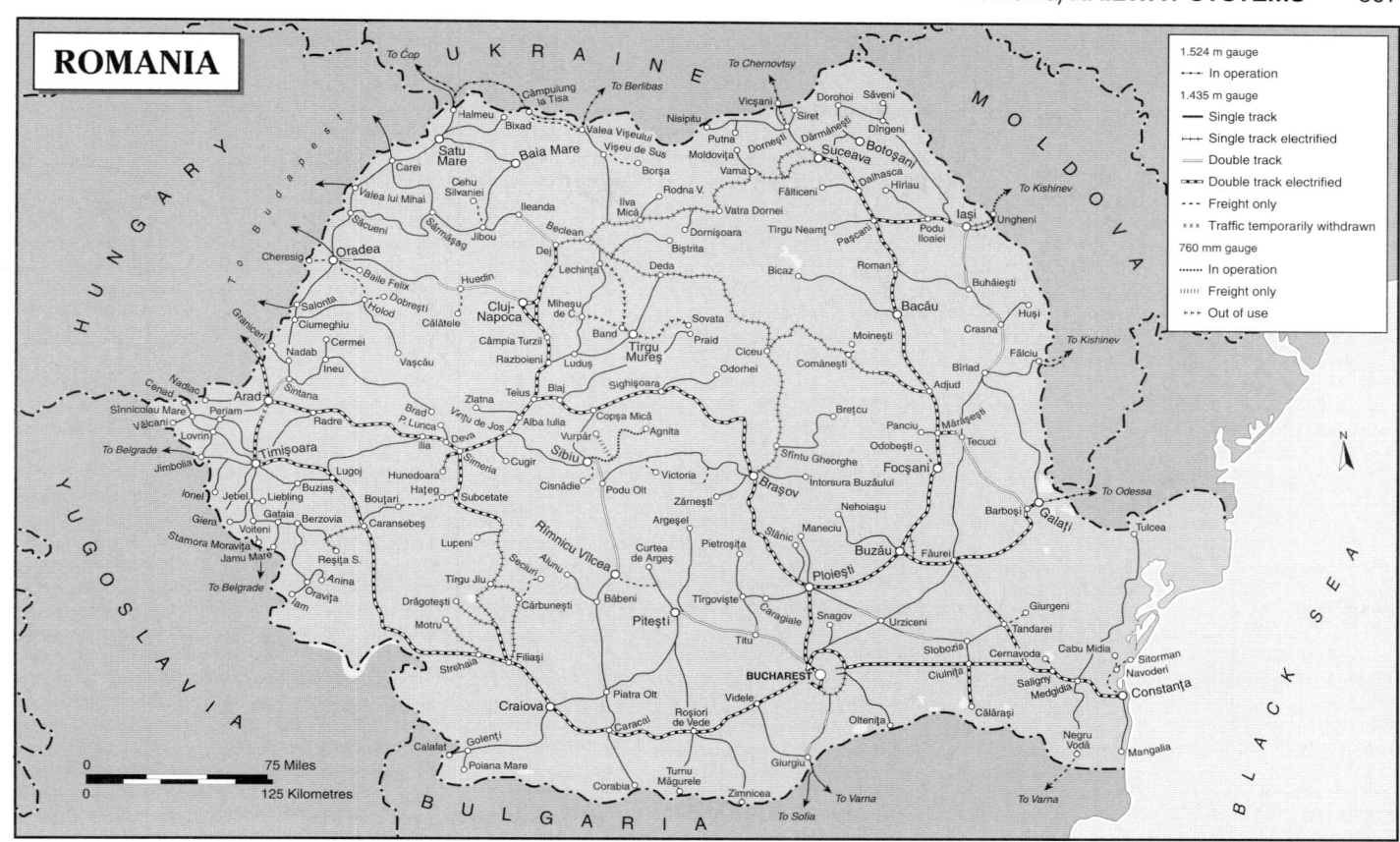

# Romania/RAILWAY SYSTEMS

*Class 60 Co-Co diesel-electric locomotive at Tulcea with a service to Bucharest Nord (Colin Boocock)*

Siemens has also refurbished 24 Class 40 and 41 5,100 kW electric locomotives in collaboration with Electroputere. The modernised locomotives have become Class 45. The modernisation of up to 70 Class 60 and 62 Sulzer-engined diesel-electric locomotives has also been started. This follows the successful refurbishment in 2000 of two prototypes, installing a General Motors eight-cylinder 710 series engine in place of the original unit. Modified locomotives have become Class 63. A third locomotive refurbishment programme covers Class 80 and 81 B-B diesel-hydraulic machines, four of which were modernised by ALSTOM and Faur in 1999, with their original Sulzer engines replaced by Caterpillar or MTU engines to become Classes 82 and 83.

In addition, CFR Calatori has awarded contracts for the refurbishment of some of its coaching stock fleet.

**NEW ENTRY**

*Class 45 electric locomotive, refurbished by Electroputere in collaboration with Siemens, at Medgidia with a Mangalia—Bucharest Nord service (Colin Boocock)*

## CFR Marfa

Bd Dinicu Golescu 38, 77113 Bucharest 1
Tel: (+40 1) 638 55 88   Fax: (+40 1) 312 47 00

**Key personnel**
Director General: Vasile Tulbure

**Organisation**
CFR Marfa is the freight business created upon the October 1998 restructuring of Romanian National Railways. Tariffs are deregulated and the company receives no state subsidy. CFR Marfa faces competition from independent operators which have taken advantage of open access rights included in the legislative reforms of 1998.

In 2001, studies into possible privatisation of CFR Marfa were undertaken with the aim of determining the extent and nature of private sector involvement. Subsequently, the government announced its intention to privatise the business based on guidelines to be recommended by the World Bank.

The company is structured as eight regional divisions, with headquarters offices in Bucharest. In 2001, it employed 29,000 staff.

| Traffic (million) | 2000 |
|---|---|
| Freight tonnes | 71.5 |
| Freight tonne-km | 18,000 |

**Freight operations**
Overall freight traffic grew by 13.6 per cent in 2000, accounting for some 41 per cent of total freight tonne-km in Romania. Rail links exist with Bulgaria, Hungary, Moldova (1,524 mm gauge), Serbia and Ukraine (1,524 mm gauge), while CFR Marfa operates Black Sea train ferry services linking Constanţa and ports in Georgia and Turkey. In 2000, international traffic accounted for one quarter of tonne-km and is viewed by the company as an area for potential growth. Both piggyback and container services are operated.

**Traction and rolling stock**
In 2001, CFR Marfa operated 376 electric, 289 main line diesel locomotives and 289 shunters. Plans exist to refurbish some 100 electric locomotives and part of the diesel shunter fleet. The main line diesel fleet is to be renewed from 2005. In 2001, there were also some 63,800 wagons in the fleet, many of which were regarded as surplus to the operator's needs.

*NEW ENTRY*

## CFR SA

Bd Dinicu Golescu 38, 77113 Bucharest 1
Tel: (+40 1) 638 55 88   Fax: (+40 1) 312 47 00

**Key personnel**
President: Mihai Necolaiciuc

Gauge: 1,435 mm; 1,524 mm; 760 mm
Route length: 10,898 km; 60 km; 427 km
Electrification: 3,888 km at 25 kV AC 50 Hz

**Political background**
CFR SA is the infrastructure business created on the October 1998 restructuring of Romanian National Railways. As a legally independent, state-owned company, it manages and maintains Romania's national rail network under an indefinite concession. Operations are mainly funded by access charges from CFR Calatori and CFR Marfa (both qv), together with some direct state subsidy and access charges from a small number of independent operators. International loans to fund major investment projects are underwritten by the government. Licensing and regulation of all rail operators is the responsibility of a separate state agency, AFER (qv).

**Organisation**
The business is managed via a devolved regional structure, supported by headquarters departments overseeing strategic and technical issues.

**Improvements to existing lines**
In 2001, work was in hand to upgrade a key section of European Corridor IV, between Braşov and Bucharest (160 km). The section from Braşov to Ploieşti also forms part of Corridor IX. The upgrading project includes infrastructure improvements, track renewal and some realignment and upgrading of the catenary. The European Investment Bank is providing a loan covering 75 per cent of the cost of the work; the remaining funding is being provided by the Romanian government.

International loans have also been negotiated to cover much of the cost of modernising the Bucharest–Constanţa line (225 km).

**Signalling and telecommunications**
Improvements to Corridor IV include the provision by SEL Alcatel of new electronic interlockings at Arad, Braşov, Bucharest and Timişoara. Siemens TS has provided an electronic interlocking at Ploieşti, the first such installation commissioned by the railway.

CFR SA plans to modernise its telecommunications system with an optical fibre network.

**Electrification**
Most key routes are electrified using the 25 kV AV 50 Hz system. Lines identified by CFR SA for possible future electrification include: Cluj-Napoca–Oradea and beyond to the border with Hungary; Iaşi–Tecuci; and Constanţa–Mangalia.

*NEW ENTRY*

# RUSSIAN FEDERATION

## Ministry of Railways

Novo-Basmannaya 2, Moscow 107174
Tel: (+7 095) 262 16 28   Fax: (+7 095) 262 90 95

**Key personnel**
Minister of Railways, Russian Federation:
  N E Aksyonenko
First Deputy Ministers: V I Ilyin; M V Ivankov
Deputy Ministers
  A V Annenkov, E N Vinogradov, S N Gapaev,
  Y M Gerasimov, S A Grishin, A N Kondratenko,
  V M Mironov, A S Misharin, V N Morozov, V N Pustovoi,
  V T Semenov, P A Shevopukov, A Tselko
Heads of Departments
  Economics: B M Lapidus
  Finance: P G Korotkevich
  Freight Operations: (vacant)
  Passenger: V N Shataev
  Traction: A D Rusak
  Freightcar: S S Barbarich
  Track and Structures: S A Rabchuk
  Safety and Ecology: P S Shanaitsa
  Freight and Commercial: Yu M Kosov
  Signalling and Train Control: V A Milyukov
  Electrification and Power Supply: G B Yakimov
  Information Technology: V S Voronin
  Personnel and Training: N M Burnosov
  Health: O N Sorokin
  Technical Policy: V S Nagovitsyn
  Railway Restructuring: P K Chichagov
  Capital Construction: (vacant)
  Clerical: V G Dolzhenko

External Relations: N V Antipov
Wages and Working Conditions: S M Danilov
Statistics: G V Bugrov
Real Estate: A M Vaigel
Legal: A A Melnikov
Internal Organisation: E P Chernyavskii

## Russian Railways

Rossiiskie Zheleznie Dorogi (RZhD)
Novo-Basmannaya 2, Moscow 107174
Tel: (+7 095) 262 16 28   Fax: (+7 095) 262 24 11

**Key personnel**
Regional Managers
Moskovskaya (Moscow): G M Fadeev
  Krasnoprudnaya ul 20, 107040 Moscow
  Tel: (+7 095) 262 51 65
Oktyabr'skaya (October): G P Komarov
  Ostrovskogo Pl 2, 191011 St Petersburg
  Tel: (+7 812) 168 60 40
Severnaya (Northern): V Ya Petrov
  Volzhskaya nab 59, 150028 Yaroslavl'
  Tel: (+7 0852) 29 44 00
Gor'kovskaya (Gorkii): Kh Sh Zabirov
  Oktyabr'skoy Revolyutsii ul 61, 603011 Nizhnii Novgorod
  Tel: (+7 831) 48 44 00   Fax: (+7 831) 48 44 77
Severo-Kavkazskaya (North Caucasus):
  A S Bogatyrev
  Teatral'naya Pl 4, 344719 Rostov-on-Don
  Tel: (+7 8632) 59 44 00

Yugo-Vostochnaya (South East): M P Akulov
  Revolyutsii Pr 18, 394621 Voronezh
  Tel: (+7 0732) 50 44 60/50 44 50
  Fax: (+7 0732) 50 48 93
Privolzhskaya (Volga): M P Likhachev
  Moskovskaya ul 8, 410013 Saratov
  Tel: (+7 8452) 90 40 13
Kuibyshevskaya (Kuibyshev): E M Plokhov
  Komsomolskaya Pl 2-3, 443030 Samara
  Tel: (+7 8462) 39 44 00
Sverdlovskaya (Sverdlovsk): B I Kolesnikov
  Cheluskintsev ul 11, 620013 Ekaterinburg
  Tel: (+7 3432) 53 92 16
Yuzhno-Ural'skaya (Southern Urals): U M Dyakonov
  Revolyutsii Pl 3, 454000 Chelyabinsk
  Tel: (+7 3512) 33 84 82
Zapadno-Sibirskaya (Western Siberia): V Starostenko
  Vokzalnaya Magistral ul 12, 630004 Novosibirsk
  Tel: (+7 3832) 22 88 22
Krasnoyarskaya (Krasnoyarsk): P G Kucherenko
  Gorkogo ul 6, 660049 Krasnoyarsk
  Tel: (+7 000) 221 17 64
Vostochno-Sibirskaya (Eastern Siberia): A I Kasyanov
  Karla Marska ul 7, 644638 Irkutsk
  Tel: (+7 3952) 29 44 00
Zabaikal'skaya (Trans Baikal): V Sekhin
  Leningradskaya ul 34, 672092 Chita
  Tel: (+7 30222) 613 57
Dal'nevostochnaya (Far East): A A Strel'nik
  Muraveva-Amurskogo ul 20, 680000 Khabarovsk
  Tel: (+7 421) 27 22 63

Kaliningradskaya (Kaliningrad): V G Budovskii
Kievskaya ul 1, 263039
Tel: (+7 011) 233 00

Sakhalinskaya (Sakhalin): V A Chernichkin
Kommunisticheskii Prospekt, 693000 Yuzhno-Sakhalinsk
Tel: (+7 42422) 71 48 48

Gauge: 1,520 mm; Sakhalin: 1,067 mm
Route length: 86,200 km; Sakhalin: 957 km
Electrification: 18,800 km at 3 kV DC; 21,500 km at 25 kV 50 Hz AC

### Political background

In the days of the Soviet command economy, SZhD (Soviet Railways) carried over two and a half times the total freight carried by all 16 Class 1 carriers in the US (SZhD's 1990 freight volume was 3,857 million tonnes, 3,717 billion tonne-km). In passenger traffic, SZhD carried about twice as many passenger-km as the railways of France, Germany, Italy and the UK combined (in 1990 SZhD carried 4,273 million passenger journeys, 417 billion passenger-km).

The railways are still by far the most important mode of transport in Russia. RZhD (Russian Railways) accounts for almost half of all passenger-km travelled, and over three-quarters of all non-pipeline tonne-km carried in the country. But with the break-up of the Soviet Union in late 1991 and the transition to a market economy, the former enormous traffic volumes are no longer assured, and in the short term the railway is having to adapt to compete with other modes. Nevertheless, by length of line Russia claims second place in the world, after the USA, and in terms of electrified route it occupies first place. It is the world's third biggest carrier of freight (after China and the USA) and of passengers (after Japan and India).

Both the Railways Ministry and consultants commissioned in 1992 by the European Bank for Reconstruction and Development were opposed to railway privatisation, but both accepted that adaptation to the market economy was urgent. The railways were already introducing flexibility to rate fixing, and were establishing premium freight centres, where clients could negotiate the whole transportation process, including pick-up and delivery, storage and documentation, with a single service point. Exploitation of modern information technology has progressively enabled these centres to monitor freight transits for the benefit of clients. Privately owned wagons were encouraged with special rates, although some clients subsequently found those rates too high.

In July 1995 the Federal Railway Law was ratified. This specified that, while non-transport-related facilities might be privatised, the operating railway was not liable to denationalisation. (However, in early 1996 the Railways Minister found it necessary to promise strong opposition to the suggestion that the railways might nevertheless be privatised in response to pressure from Western banks.) The Railway Law also forbade strikes of operating workers and allowed the railways to sell off shipments whose transportation had not been paid for. The general strengthening of the railways' hand meant that stronger measures were taken against recalcitrant debtors. For a few days in 1995 the railways refused to provide mail cars, and relented only when the Federal Postal Service agreed to pay its enormous debts. However, in subsequent years some railways were again refusing to handle mail until the postal service paid its debts.

Some ancillary enterprises like equipment supply works have been privatised. In the case of train and station catering services, privatisation brought a decline in an already unappetising performance and the railways in some cases have been allowed to take them back.

After a change of minister in April 1997 (the second such change within a year), the government stated that the immediate task of the railways was to reduce freight tariffs and at the same time pay the specified taxes and contributions to the pension fund. By 2001 pension fund arrears had been almost paid off. Wages were paid promptly, and most overdue taxes settled. The federal taxation service had dropped its practice of despatching squads with sub-machine guns to sequester railway cash at stations and depots, but was still pursuing some railways in the courts. On the Moscow Railway, big cost reductions were obtained by eliminating the night shift wherever possible.

Several detailed proposals for reforming the railways, a so-called 'natural monopoly', were put forward, including one by the Transport Ministry, responsible for non-railway transport, which proposed taking over the railways as well. The Railway Ministry described other competing proposals as simply versions of the derided 'English approach', and it was the Ministry's own proposal that, in early 1998, was favoured by the government. Somewhat clarified, it was finally accepted by the government in 2001, although since 1998 much exploratory work had been done by the Ministry's new Department for Railway Reform. In the first stage (2001-02) the already existing railway-founded passenger operating companies are to settle down, while independent freight operating companies for specialised traffic continue to develop. In the second stage (2003-05) the passenger operating companies will be partially sold off, and subsidiary companies will be formed to handle general freight. In stage 3 (2006-10) it is expected that genuine competition will appear. Meanwhile, the Ministry of Railways' two roles, as state supervisor of railways and railway operator, will be split; a restructured Russian Federal Railways is expected to be established in 2002. At arm's length from the Ministry, this will be responsible for operation and steadily develop into a holding company responsible for affiliate companies for passenger and freight services, infrastructure, and maintenance services. Initially, the Ministry of Railways valued reform as a means of ending cross-subsidy of passenger by freight traffic, but now appreciates it as a means of raising long-needed capital.

There were 15 independent freight operating companies in early 2001. These were tied to a particular industry: several, notably Linkoil-SPb, BaltTransServis, and Russkii Mir, were oil carriers and the last two seemed likely to acquire their own motive power in 2001. Another big operator was Severstal'trans, established by the Northern Steel company. In addition, there were two early Ministry of Railways companies, GUP-Konteiner for container and Refservis for refrigerator services; the latter was going through difficult times.

*Less money from government*

In 1994 central government severely restricted its grants for major projects and agreed to maintain finance only for the final tunnel, the Severo—Muiskii, on the Baikul—Amur Magistral (BAM), the Amur bridge reconstruction at Khabarovsk and 130 new passenger vehicles. Overall, by 1995 government investment was about 96 per cent less than it had been three years earlier and this was further diminished. By 1999 the government was paying only about one-tenth of the Severo—Muiskii tunnel costs. Most capital projects are now financed by RZhD itself, but local authorities sometimes assist, especially with station construction/rebuilding projects and occasionally with the purchase of new rolling stock for commuter services. Some local authorities, providing funds to offset commuter service losses in the expectation that this money would buy new trains, have been disappointed. Meanwhile in 1999 the RZhD introduced new depreciation indices to permit investment to rise from the 16 billion roubles of 1998 to 21 billion in 1999.

No major line closures have occurred yet, but they have become a possibility: up to 3,000 km of routes were provisionally listed for closure in 1995-96. Some 9,000 km are regarded as warranting closure, and to lessen local opposition it is hoped that some of these will become industrial railways. In 2000 the Krasnoyarsk regional government expressed willingness to take responsibility for the loss-making 259 km Reshoty—Karabuda branch, and it was hoped that other governments would make similar offers.

### Organisation

The Russian system had 19 principal railways or regions, including the Kaliningrad and Sakhalin systems. These railways were further subdivided into over 100 divisions. However, a start was made in reducing the number of divisions, with a view to their complete elimination as a management level. By 1999, when the process was temporarily abandoned, about 40 divisions had been eliminated. Merging of the railways was recommended, leading to the formation of five or six big organisations. The BAM Railway was divided between the Far Eastern and East Siberian railways, and the Kemerovo Railway was merged with the West Siberian. However, there was opposition to such amalgamations, largely from local political administrators reluctant to lose their 'own' railway and the tax-base it represents.

In 1999 agreement of local authorities to the elimination of the Krasnoyarsk Railway became unlikely to be forthcoming after the election of the powerful General Lebedev as Governor of Krasnoyarsk. The merging of the Sakhalin Railway into the Far Eastern never took place, although it remains a distant intention. The total number of railways is now 17. These are not financially independent: their incomes are channelled to the Ministry of Railways (which is in effect RZhD) and it decides how much money to allocate back to each railway.

In 1999 there were about 1,600,000 workers on the railway payroll, of whom 1,236,100 were operating workers (compared to 1,521,000 in late 1996). Further reductions are expected.

### Finance

The former SZhD ran at a profit. Interest on capital was not charged as an expense, but even so it is thought that the railway made sufficient profit to cover this.

Traditionally, profits from freight operations have been used to cover losses generated by passenger operations. During the early 1990s, with freight traffic declining faster than passenger traffic, this arrangement seemed threatened. But all RZhD regions (except Sakhalin) returned a profit in 1994 with an overall profitability, after subsidies, of 21.9 per cent of income. This fell to 10.2 per cent in 1997 but recovered to 24.5 per cent in 1999. In that year freight operating profit was 48,511 million roubles, while there was a 17,629 million rouble loss registered by passenger services. The balancing of passenger with

*Prototype of Kolomna-built Class EP200 eight-axle AC electric passenger locomotive (Zheleznodorozhnoe Delo/Ivan Khil'ko)*

# RAILWAY SYSTEMS/Russian Federation

*Class ChS7 3 kV DC electric locomotive with a Nizhniy Novgorod—Tyumen express at Yekaterinburg (Milan Šrámek)*
2001/0059400

*New Demikhovo-built Class ED4MK emu providing the three-class supplementary-fare Moscow—Ryazan service (Zheleznodorozhnoe Delo/N Ermolaev)*
2000/0085815

freight profits has aroused complaints from Siberia, where passenger traffic is low and freight traffic is high.

Freight tariffs and long-distance passenger fares are now inflation-indexed. Problems and losses occur, however, when the government orders a price-freeze, as happened for the duration of the fourth quarter of 1995. Local authorities are involved in the setting of fares for commuter services, and many of them make a financial contribution. Highway competition, as well as a desire to stimulate traffic, has led to flexible (negotiated) freight tariffs for some commodities, while political pressures have dictated reduced rates for freight moving over 3,000 km in Siberia and the east. Further differentiation of tariffs can be expected. Rates for low-value freight were reduced from one third to one half in 1995, with slight increases for high-value traffic. The railways have made agreements with certain regional governments whereby rates on a region's prime produce are reduced (thereby widening the market) in return for prompt payment, price reductions for products and services bought by the railway, and other concessions. However, there have been disappointments. Traffic has not significantly responded to tariff cuts and the Magnitogorsk metallurgical complex, after gaining a substantial rate cut, increased its steel prices to the railways by one third. In 2000 and 2001 there were significant rate increases, but the much-criticised discrimination between international and internal rates was being eliminated.

About 25 per cent of railway income is paid as taxes, compared to 6 per cent in 1991. The railways duly but unenthusiastically make their contribution to the Road Tax.

## Passenger operations

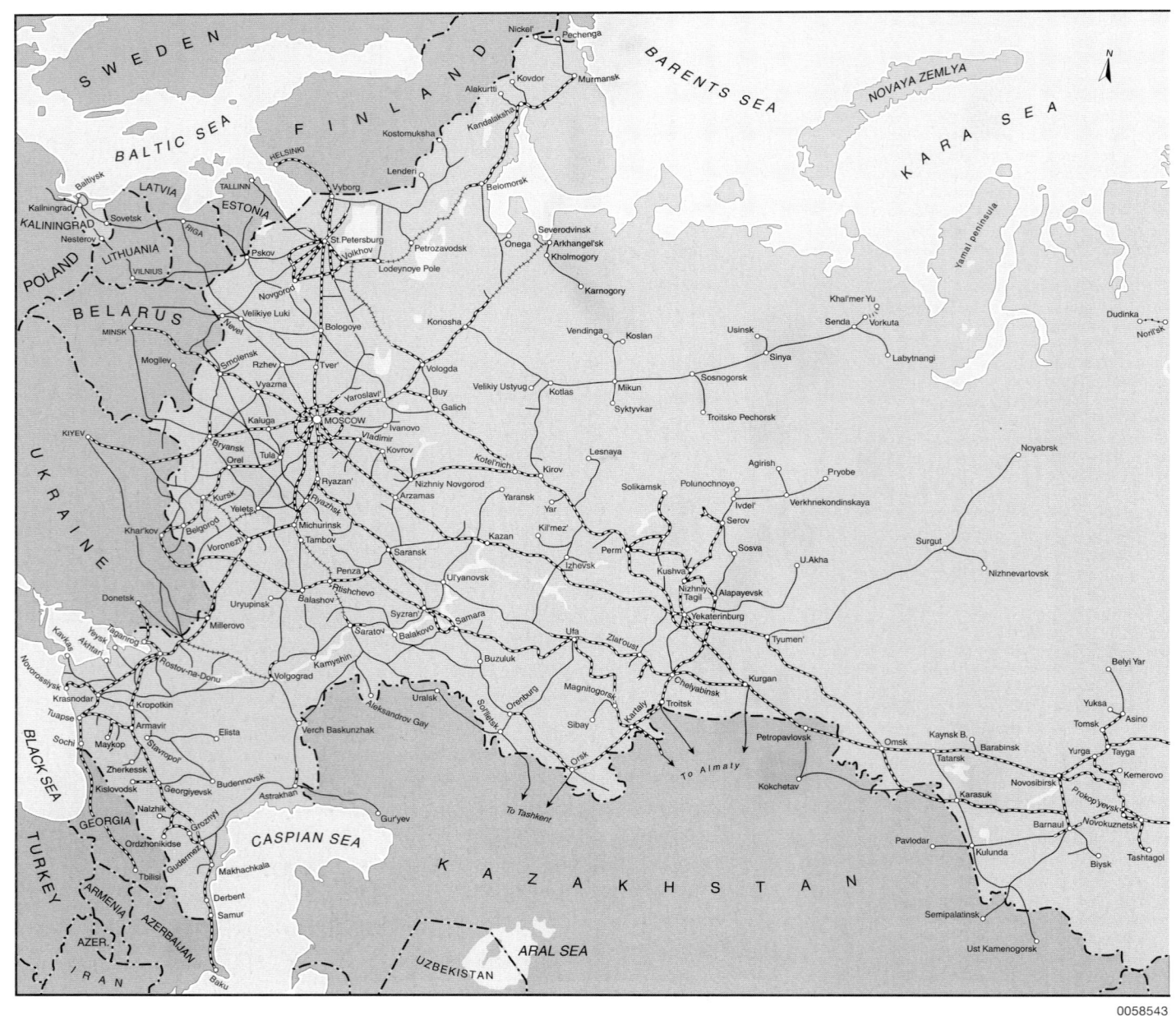

Passenger statistics are compromised by the high proportion of commuter passengers who do not purchase a ticket. To solve this problem, turnstile access is being introduced at main stations. At Moscow stations, commuter revenues were said to have increased by twice and even three times after these changes were made. In general, passenger traffic held up better than freight over the 1990s, and in 1999 there was an unexpected recovery in long-distance summer traffic.

Services operating between the republics of the former Soviet Union now undergo lengthy customs inspections at the new state frontiers. For this reason, services from the centre to the Caucasus and the Black Sea are now routed via Voronezh rather than through Ukraine.

Obtaining reservations has become less time-consuming for passengers due to the spread of RZhD's electronic reservation system. The St Petersburg Railway Agency now offers international reservations through the European START-AMADEUS system.

1999 was a good year for safety, with no passenger fatalities in train accidents. Nevertheless passengers perceive rail travel as not entirely safe, largely because of the incidence of on-train crime. Railway police now cover some late-night commuter trains and also selected long-distance services. It is the policy to direct foreign tourists to long-distance trains that are thus protected.

Overall the quality of customer service remains patchy, albeit improving. There have been some fare reductions even though the previous fare level ensured that passenger trains could never make a profit (although long-distance services might become profitable if fare reduction and free travel concessions were less widespread; currently there are over 60 categories of passenger entitled to them). Creation of separate passenger companies has been accepted as a policy and a number of city commuter companies are being developed. On the October Railway, *Transservis* operates longer-distance passenger trains and *Transkom* operates commuter services. There is a similar commuter company at Samara (*Samaratransprigorod*) and a variation is being introduced at Moscow, while at Novosibirsk the *Ekspress-prigorod* is a joint-stock company. The West Siberian Railway has established a long-distance passenger subsidiary. Premium service (supplementary fare) trains are becoming more widespread and in early 1999 *Transkom* was demonstrating its first premium-service commuter train. Other railways have since instituted extra-fare local trains, offering the rare (for Russia) division into first, second and third classes. Some do not accept discounted tickets, but are nevertheless well patronised. The prototype ER200 trainset was withdrawn for complete refurbishment and replaced by an identical trainset which performed the Moscow–St Petersburg route twice-weekly.

In December 2000 twice-daily high-speed services were introduced between Moscow and St Petersburg, but this schedule soon relapsed into the previous once-weekly high-speed train. However, in 2001 it was expected that an enhanced service would be restored. Final choice of equipment had not yet been made; a high-speed stainless-steel trainset built by the Tver Works was to undergo trials, the Sokol train was already on trial, and Talgo trains were also a possibility.

| **Traffic** (million) | 1997 | 1998 | 1999 |
|---|---|---|---|
| Passenger journeys | 1,595 | 1,471 | 1,300 |
| Passenger-km | 170,000 | 152,200 | 141,062 |
| Freight tonnes | 855.8 | 834.1 | 947.3 |
| Freight tonne-km | 1,096,000 | 1,006,00 | 1,204,600 |

Freight traffic in 2000 grew to 1,373,000 tonne-km. Passenger traffic was reported to have increased by a fifth, but part of this was probably a statistical manifestation of reduced fare evasion.

**Main commodities carried by rail** (000 tonnes)

|  | 1998 | 1999 |
|---|---|---|
| Coal | 208,600 | 227,000 |
| Coke | n/a | n/a |
| Oil and oil products | n/a | n/a |
| Manganese and iron ore | 72,000 | 84,700 |
| Ferrous metals | 43,700 | 52,700 |
| Chemical and mineral fertilisers | 28,300 | 33,700 |
| Cement | 16,700 | 19,100 |
| Timber | 31,900 | 42,700 |
| Grain and flour | 15,400 | 15,500 |
| Construction materials | 134,000 | 145,600 |

### Freight operations

The economic changes in Russia, featuring the decline of heavy industry and the emergence of private enterprise road hauliers, have led to a decline in carryings on RZhD. All the main commodity groups saw a decrease in carryings in 1996 compared to 1992.

The 1999 figures may, at last, mark the end of decline. Meanwhile, the railways' share of total common-carrier shipments rose from 75 per cent in 1995 to 86 per cent in 1999, thanks to the decline of water-borne traffic.

The division of the SZhD freight wagon fleet amongst the republics of the former Soviet Union took place amicably, but the new states often suspect their neighbours of sending them wagons in doubtful order that require repair before being returned to the owning system. An automated wagon registration system at frontiers, with charges levied for the use of foreign wagons, was instituted.

*Industrial railways*
Non-common-carrier lines belonging to particular industries, varying from short factory sidings to large local

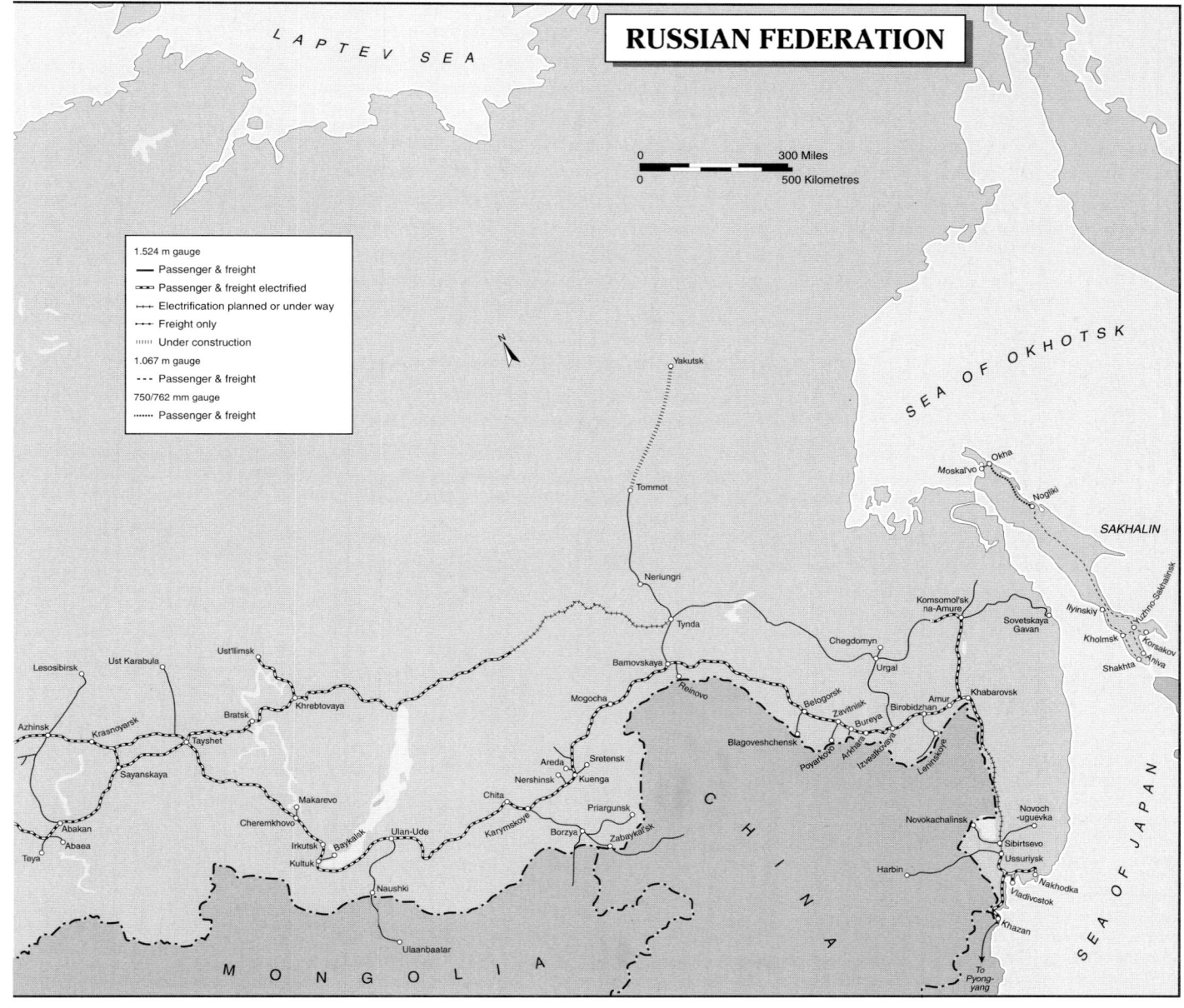

*Class 2TE116 two-section diesel-electric locomotive on a transfer freight at Narva, Estonia* (Eddie Barnes)

networks, are said to originate three-quarters of Russian railway freight. Total extent of these lines is probably around 30,000 km. In industrial areas they tend to be amalgamated into industrial railway transport enterprises which have steadily become privatised. One of the largest is the Moscow City Industrial Railway Company which serves 120 sites and owns 50 diesel shunters.

### Intermodal operations

As yet, most container services operate 'by train path' rather than 'by timetable'. That is, they run to fixed schedules but only when traffic seems to require them. This irregularity is probably one reason why shippers have shown a certain indifference to container services. But since 1996 there has been a nightly St Petersburg–Moscow container train, and the Moscow–Tallinn (Estonia) service is also regular. Helsinki–Moscow container trains are also showing promise. The Berlin–Moscow container train ran about 500 times in 1995-98. In 1998 the Budapest–Moscow train ran 41 times, but most of its containers were transhipped to and from the highways at the Brest break-of-gauge. On the Trans-Siberian route, which showed great promise in the 1980s, traffic fell with deteriorating service and increasing pilferage. Efforts are being made to improve its attractions and it now provides a secure and swift service (12 days from Pacific port to the Polish frontier), but shippers are slow to return. In 1998, there were 129 container trains operated over this route (47 westward and 82 eastward).

A regular service, carrying motor trucks and their drivers, now links Novorossiysk on the Black Sea with Moscow. Those who criticised it as an inherently uneconomic procedure failed to take into account its main appeal: freedom from the compulsory bribes levied by highway police. In 1998, less than one per cent of traffic was handled in containers, although it was planned to increase this to 16 million tonnes by 2005. The lack of a railway organisation solely interested in container traffic was one brake on development, but in 2000 a new state subsidiary company (*GUP-Konteiner*) was set up, with affiliate companies on each railway.

A new multimodal freight terminal is being built at St Petersburg. Advice on the location, design, specifications, marketing and management of this terminal was provided by Sir Alexander Gibb and Partners of the UK, thanks to European Union funding.

### New lines

*Moscow–St Petersburg high-speed line*

In September 1991 President Yeltsin decreed that a new high-speed route be created between Moscow and St Petersburg (formerly Leningrad).

A special company, RAO VSM, was formed to study, build and operate the high-speed route. Initially, a strong argument for the line was the need to relieve the existing St Petersburg–Moscow railway, but this lost its validity with the drastic fall of freight traffic after 1990.

The present proposal, which only received final ecological approval in 1999, is for new line from the outskirts of Moscow to the outskirts of St Petersburg, with existing routes being used for the terminal sections. Initially, trains would run at up to 300 km/h, and later at 350 km/h. The line would be passenger-only and would close for maintenance at night.

RAO VSM is a company independent of Russian Federal Railways even though the October Railway, part of Russian Federal Railways, is a joint founder (the others were the Moscow and St Petersburg governments and the Leningrad regional government). On its formation, the government transferred to the new company controlling shares in state industries about to be privatised. These included rolling stock building plants at Torzhok and Tikhvin. With the successful exploitation of these industries, and its land holdings, RAO VSM might well prosper even if the railway were not built.

Successive railway ministers have been lukewarm in their attitude towards the line (the only minister who was enthusiastic had an unexpectedly short tenure), and there are legitimate doubts about the traffic projections. Meanwhile the Railways Ministry has almost completed the reconstruction of the existing railway with a view to running trains at up to 200 km/h.

Almost all the needed land has been acquired, but work so far done has been limited to clearing the proposed route of wartime land mines and the beginning of the construction of a station/hotel complex as the terminal in St Petersburg. The latter is the responsibility of a British contractor and has been financed by British banks. Meanwhile the Torzhok Works has been building electric commuter trains while Tikhvin, with associate companies, has produced the *Sokol* prototype high-speed train.

In 1999 and 2000, RAO VSM was unable to redeem some of its due bonds. These were guaranteed by the government, which has taken an appropriate proportion of the company's assets in recompense. The prevailing opinion is that the line will not be built until about 2020, and probably not by the existing company. The Railways Ministry is hoping that high-speed lines will also be built in the 2020s between Moscow and the South and Moscow–Brest, in joint private/public ventures. In the meantime, 200 km/h services are anticipated between Moscow, Omsk and Novosibirsk over existing lines, the upgrading of which is in course.

*Finnish connections*

A new 126 km route between Kochkoma and Ledmozero in Karelia, near the Finnish border, was nearing completion in 2001. Constructed by a private company, Gelleflint, the line has been designed to tap the mineral and forestry resources of the region. Gelleflint will interchange with RZhD at Kochkoma and with Finnish State Railways (VR) at the border.

Gelleflint proposes the development of a second line, a 180 km line from Karnogory to Vendinga, which, in combination with the first new line and existing RZhD routes, would establish the so-called No-We (North-West) rail link from northeast Russia to ice-free Finnish ports on the Baltic. A start on construction was proposed for 1997.

In another development, agreement has been reached between VR and RZhD on a 68 km new line from Ruchei Karelski to the border with northern Finland at Alakurtti, with reinstatement of a 6.5 km line on an abandoned trackbed on the Finnish side of the border. This would allow mineral deposits in the Murmansk area to be tapped. Construction was due to begin in 1995.

*New link with China*

Several Japanese firms have entered joint ventures associated with development of the port of Zarubino, at the southeastern extremity of Russia, below Vladivostok.

On the initiative of the Far Eastern Railway, the 'Golden Link' company was formed to build a line from Kraskino, south of Vladivostok, to link with Chinese Railways. This was finished in 1999 but traffic has failed to develop because it is a private railway, and therefore, as yet, has no legal status.

Another attempt to develop traffic for the Trans Siberian Railway is a link between that railway and South Korea. Russian Railways has offered to help upgrade the North Korean sector of this route.

*Dagestan*

A new 80 km line avoiding Chechnya has been built in Dagestan. This also reduces the length of the trunk route linking Russia with Azerbaijan.

*Yamal peninsula line*

Construction of a 400 km line from Vorkuta to gas and oilfields on the Yamal peninsula, which was put on hold in the early 1990s, has restarted; the line was 250 km long by late 1995. This will be the world's northernmost railway.

*Amur–Yakutsk Railway*

Construction of this 850 km line from Neryungri to Yakutsk has proved difficult, but 380 km have been laid, and completion is expected in 2005.

### Improvements to existing lines

Apart from the Moscow–St Petersburg reconstruction, the lines from Moscow to Nizhnii Novgorod and Voronezh are also to be reconstructed. The EBRD is assisting in all three of these projects.

Track renewal and regauging to 1,435 mm gauge on the 47 km main line from Kaliningrad to Mamonova on the Polish frontier was completed in 1992/93 with German financial assistance. Elsewhere on the RZhD system, the condition of bridges requiring renewal or replacement has imposed a large number of speed restrictions.

An important new idea is to develop the Moscow ring railway as an outer circle line of the city metro system.

*Container traffic on the Nakhodka–Brest route* (Cniitei Mps)

Freight traffic on the ring railway is down by half, while the existing Circle line of the metro is heavily congested. Metro services will be introduced gradually section by section alongside, but separated from, continuing freight traffic. There will be about 30 new stations and interchange points with the existing metro system. If authorised, the first trains could be running by late 2000.

A Russian-Finnish railway accord was signed on 16 April 1996. Projects include upgrading of the St Petersburg–Helsinki line for high-speed operation by 1999 with Pendolino tilting trains. International travel on this line grew by 32 per cent in 1994 and is forecast to reach 1 million passengers per year by 2000. The Finnish Railways invested a European Union credit of US$335 million and undertook to find a further US$358 million by 1999. Some US$185-200 million is needed for the Russian section. Through high-speed trains to Turku are planned for 2005.

On the BAM line in Siberia, work on building the Severo–Muiskii tunnel has continued despite lack of cash and was finished in 2001. The BAM has excess capacity, and is in need of greatly increased economic activity in the area. For this reason, two branches to mineral deposits are being constructed. Work has already started on a 65 km line to Udokan which will tap substantial deposits of several minerals. A 320 km branch to the Elginskii coal deposits was begun in 2001 and when finished (some time after 2006) should also bring more traffic to the BAM.

A new 150 km industrial railway is being built in the Urals, linking the mainline railway with the Srednii Timan bauxite mine.

An improvement project has been proposed for railways on the island of Sakhalin in the Pacific, which were built to the 1,067 mm gauge. Freight from the mainland at present is shipped across the Gulf of Tartary on 1,520 mm gauge wagons on eight train ferries, and transhipped on the island into 1,067 mm gauge wagons for onward transit. To allow uninterrupted rail transit, there is a proposal to introduce a bogie changing facility at the port of Kholmsk on the island; clearances would also be enlarged in nine tunnels on the island's main line. For the longer term, regauging of Sakhalin's railways at 1,520 mm and construction of a tunnel to the mainland are under study.

A rather more exotic proposal is a two-tunnel rail link between Japan, Sakhalin and the Siberian mainland.

### Traction and rolling stock

In 1993 the rolling stock fleet available for use comprised some 2,653 diesel and 5,043 electric locomotives, 37,940 passenger cars and 548,000 wagons plus over 16,000 multiple-unit coaches.

In 1998, the total (including reserve) freight wagon stock was about 660,000, of which 254,000 were open cars, 95,000 box cars, 74,000 flat cars, and 91,000 tank cars (8-axle tank cars totalled 8,600). The working stock was 385,000 in 1998 and 426,700 in 1999. The working stock of passenger cars was 19,959 in 1999. In 2000, 23 per cent of the operational freight wagons were in private ownership, and this percentage was expected to increase when more favourable tariffs for private-owner wagons were introduced. About 100,000 of the private-owner vehicles are tank wagons.

RZhD's strained finances have continued to restrict deliveries of new rolling stock. Only 29 electric and 35 diesel locomotives were delivered in 1994, and the 1995 programme for new passenger coaches was cut from 980 to 320. Deliveries of electric locomotives were six in 1998 and 20 in 1999, and of diesel locomotives (expressed in sections) 10 and 17. In total 607 passenger cars were delivered in 1999, up from 423 in 1998. In 1997, an order worth ECU48 million was placed with Adtranz for 21 electric locomotives, designated as Class EP10. This Co-Co design has dual power supply and asynchronous motors, and nearly 80 per cent of components will be supplied by Russian factories.

Under an accord between the German and Russian governments reached in 1994, RZhD is taking delivery of 10 electric locomotives from Adtranz (worth DM40 million) and, at a concessionary price of DM500 million, 500 passenger coaches from former East German builder DWA; 191 new coaches were supplied in 1994.

Also approved by the Railways Ministry was the import of 26 electric locomotives from Škoda, 16 to be bought with hard currency and the remainder to be bartered for supply of electricity to the Czech Republic. In 1998 Škoda was also undertaking refurbishment and upgrading of nine ChS200 3 kV DC electric locomotives. Dating from the late 1970s, the 8,000 kW locomotives was returned to service in 1999 on the Moscow–St Petersburg line, where

*Class ChS200 8,000 kW DC electric locomotive recently refurbished and modernised by Škoda (Milan Šrámek)*

*Prototype asynchronous-motored dual-voltage Class EP10 electric locomotive built by a consortium of Adtranz and Novocherkassk (Zheleznodorozhnoe Delo/Ivan Khil'ko)*

*One of a trial batch of Class EP1 six-axle AC electric passenger locomotives built by Novocherkassk (Zheleznodorozhnoe Delo/Ivan Khil'ko)*

RhZD plans 200 km/h running. Meanwhile Škoda is co-operating in establishing a repair works at Yaroslavl for the several Škoda-built electric locomotive types.

A shortage of passenger locomotives is forcing widespread use of freight traction for passenger services: an average of 800 to 1,200 electric and 605 diesel locomotives were in use in this way in 1995. Loco-hauled stock is being used to cover a shortfall of multiple-units; almost every diesel class appears on such work. A modernisation programme has been agreed for Hungarian-built class D1 dmus using a Zvezda engine and Kaluga electrical equipment.

Recently, numbers of new freight wagons delivered to the railway have fallen well below the number of withdrawals. RZhD acquired 10,400 wagons in 1993 and 7,600 in 1994, falling further to 2,102 in 1998 and 1,557 in 1999. While some new designs are currently being prepared for series production, the cheaper alternative of thoroughly reconstructing older vehicles is also being pursued, with 20,000 such rebuildings scheduled for 1999.

Two Russian sleeping cars have been refurbished in Spain at RENFE's Malaga works as a pilot project for a possible 1,500 carriages.

*New locomotive plans*
Many of the traction suppliers to the former SZhD were located outside the Russian Federation. Procurement for the RZhD has been reorganised to minimise hard currency expenditure on imports and protect domestic employment.

Škoda in Czechoslovakia was SZhD's principal supplier of passenger electric locomotives in the days of the Comecon trading bloc. The Russian freight electric locomotive production facilities at Novocherkassk have been expanded to produce diversified passenger locomotives as well. The EP1 is a passenger locomotive derived from Novocherkassk's VL65 AC electric. VL65 production has now ended, only 48 units having been built, but 28 of the replacement EP1 were built by the end of 2000. To replace the bigger Czech locomotives the 8-axle 7,200 kW EP200 has been built, to be followed by its DC version, the EP100. The EP201 and EP101 will be similar but designed for 160 km/h instead of 200 km/h. The EP10 is a dual-voltage machine of which 21 are being built by a consortium of Adtranz and Novocherkassk. These are the first Russian locomotives to be equipped with GTO asynchronous technology. The first EP10 was built in 1998 and is still on trial. This type will be followed by the somewhat similar Russian-built EP2 (DC) and EP3 (AC). It is forecast that over 1,000 units each of the EP2 and EP3 will be built.

With the 'loss' of diesel loco-building capacity in Ukraine, steps are being taken to raise output from Russia's own plants. At Lyudinovo a new generation of standard diesel-electrics is to be developed in co-operation with GE Transportation Systems of the US, under a technology transfer agreement signed in July 1995. A prototype 3,000 kW TEP400 mixed-traffic diesel locomotive is scheduled from Lyudinovo. Kolomna plans to construct TEP80 and TEP71 passenger diesel locos. Limited imports may continue in the form of 2TE116UP mixed-traffic locomotives from Lugansk. Later additions to the programme include the 3,600 hp TEP100 diesel passenger and the TEM18G gas-fuelled diesel yard locomotive. The prototype of the latter has already been built at Bryansk.

Further co-operation is wanted with foreign firms concerning the latest semiconductor transformers, three-phase traction motors, microprocessor control and frame-hung traction motors. Foreign investment in more joint ventures is also being sought.

A Talgo tilting train was on test on the October Railway in early 1996, including high-speed trials on the Moscow–St Petersburg line.

In 2000 an agreement was signed establishing a joint Russo-Spanish company for the production of Talgo convertible-gauge freight and passenger wagons and coaches. The first gauge-convertible passenger trains were expected to be used for international services to Berlin and Warsaw.

*New emu and dmu plans*
Short-haul commuter travel is booming at weekends, despite draconian fare increases, because the government has provided suburban land for city inhabitants in a bid to encourage food production and cure urban shortages. More than half of the commuter vehicles are life-expired, or approaching that age, and cannot cope with the still dense suburban traffic.

*Class TEM18G gas-fuelled diesel shunting locomotive built by Bryansk (Cniitei Mps)*

### Electric locomotives

| Class | Wheel arrangement | Output kW continuous/one hour | Speed km/h | Weight tonnes | First built | Builders Mechanical | Builders Electrical |
|---|---|---|---|---|---|---|---|
| **3 kV DC** | | | | | | | |
| VL8 | 2 × Bo+Bo | 3,760/4,200 | 80/100 | 184 | 1953 | N/T | N |
| VL10 | 2 × Bo-Bo | 4,600/5,360 | 100 | 184 | 1976 | N/T | T |
| VL10u | 2 × Bo-Bo | 4,600/5,360 | 100 | 200 | 1974 | N/T | T |
| VL11 | 2 × Bo-Bo | 4,600/5,360 | 100 | 184 | 1975 | T | T |
| VL11m | 2 × Bo-Bo | NA/6,680 | 100 | 184 | 1987 | T | T |
| VL15 | 2 × Bo-Bo-Bo | 8,400/9,000 | 100 | 300 | 1984 | T | T |
| VL22m | 2 × Co+Co | 1,860/2,400 | 80 | 132 | 1941 | N | N/D |
| VL23* | Co+Co | 2,740/3,150 | 100 | 138 | 1956 | N | N |
| ChS2 | Co-Co | 3,708/4,200 | 160 | 125 | 1958 | Škoda | Škoda |
| ChS2t | Co-Co | 4,080/4,620 | 160 | 126 | 1972 | Škoda | Škoda |
| ChS200 | 2 × Bo-Bo | 8,000/8,400 | 220 | 156 | 1975 | Škoda | Škoda |
| ChS6 | 2 × Bo-Bo | 8,000/8,400 | 190 | 164 | 1979 | Škoda | Škoda |
| ChS7 | 2 × Bo-Bo | 6,160/7,200 | 180 | 172 | 1983 | Škoda | Škoda |
| EP100 | Bo-Bo-Bo-Bo | 9,600/NA | 200 | 180 | 1999 | Kolomna | Škoda |
| **25 kV AC** | | | | | | | |
| VL60K* | Co-Co | 4,050/4,650 | 100 | 138 | 1962 | N | N |
| VL60pk | Co-Co | 4,050/4,650 | 110 | 138 | 1965 | N | N |
| VL65 | Bo-Bo-Bo | 4,680/5,000 | 120 | NA | 1992 | N | N |
| VL80K | 2 × Bo-Bo | 5,920/6,320 | 110 | 184 | 1963 | N | N |
| VL80T | 2 × Bo-Bo | 5,920/6,320 | 110 | 184 | 1967 | N | N |
| VL80R | 2 × Bo-Bo | 5,920/6,320 | 110 | 192 | 1967 | N | N |
| VL80S | 2 × Bo-Bo | 5,920/6,320 | 110 | 184/192 | 1979 | N | N |
| VL85 | 2 × Bo-Bo-Bo | 9,360/10,000 | 110 | 288 | 1983 | N | N |
| VL86F | 2 × Bo-Bo-Bo-Bo | NA/10,800 | 120 | 288 | 1985 | N | N |
| ChS4 | Co-Co | 4,920/5,100 | 180 | 123 | 1965 | Škoda | Škoda |
| ChS4t | Co-Co | 4,920/5,100 | 180 | 126 | 1971 | Škoda | Škoda |
| ChS8 | 2 × Bo-Bo | 7,200/NA | 180 | 175 | 1983 | Škoda | Škoda |
| EP200 | Bo-Bo-Bo | 8,000/NA | 200 | 180 | 1996 | Kolomna | N |
| **Dual voltage 3 kV DC/25 kV AC** | | | | | | | |
| VL82m | 2 × Bo-Bo | 5,760/6,040 | 110 | 200 | 1972 | N | N |
| EP10 | Bo-Bo-Bo | 7,200/NA | 160 | 132 | 1998 | N | Adtranz |

*Also operated in twin- and triple-unit versions
Abbreviations: D: Dinamo; N: Novocherkassk; T: Tbilisi

### Diesel locomotives

| Class | Wheel arrangement | Power kW | Speed km/h | Weight tonnes | First built | Builders Mechanical | Builders Engine | Builders Transmission |
|---|---|---|---|---|---|---|---|---|
| TE3 | 2 × Co-Co | 2,944 | 100 | 254 | 1953 | V/K/Ko | 2 × 2D 100 | E ETM |
| TE7 | 2 × Co-Co | 2,944 | 140 | 254 | 1956 | V/K | 2 × 2D 100 | E ETM |
| 2TE10M* | 2 × Co-Co | 4,416 | 100 | 276 | 1981 | V/K | 2 × 10 D100 or M1 | E ETM |
| 2TE10L | 2 × Co-Co | 4,416 | 100 | 260 | 1962 | V/K | 2 × 10 D100 | E ETM |
| 2TE10u | 2 × Co-Co | 4,412 | 100 | 276 | 1989 | V/K | 2 × 10 D100M1 or M2 | E ETM |
| 2TE10ut | 2 × Co-Co | 4,412 | 120 | 276 | 1989 | V/K | 2 × 10 D100M1 or M2 | E ETM |
| 2TE10V | 2 × Co-Co | 4,416 | 100 | 276 | 1974 | V/K | 2 × 10 D100 | E ETM |
| 4TE10S | 4 × Co-Co | 8,824 | 100 | 552 | 1983 | V/K | 4 × 10 D100 | E ETM |
| TEM1 | Co-Co | 736 | 90 | 126 | 1958 | B | 2D50 | E ETM |
| TEP10 | Co-Co | 2,208 | 140 | 129 | 1960 | V/K | 10 D500 | E ETM |
| TEP60 | Co-Co | 2,208 | 160 | 129 | 1960 | Ko | 11D45 | E ETM |
| TEP70 | Co-Co | 2,944 | 160 | 135 | 1973 | Ko | 2A5D49 | E ETM |
| TEP80 | Bo+Bo+Bo+Bo | 4,412 | 160 | 180 | 1988 | Ko | 2-20DG | E ETM |
| M62† | Co-Co | 1,470 | 100 | 116.5 | 1964 | V/Ko | 14D40 | E ETM |
| 2TE116 | 2 × Co-Co | 4,500 | 100 | 276 | 1971 | V/Ko | 2 × 1A5D49 | E ETM |
| 2TE136 | 2 × Bo-Bo+Bo-Bo | 8,832 | 120 | 400 | 1984 | V/Ko | 120DG(D49) | E ETM |
| 2M62u | 2 × Co-Co | 2,942 | 100 | 252 | 1987 | V/Ko | 2 × 14D40 | E ETM |
| TEM2 | Co-Co | 883 | 100 | 120 | 1960 | V/B/P | PDIM or PDI | E ETM |
| TEM2um | Co-Co | 994 | 100 | 126 | 1988 | B/P | 1PD-4A | E ETM |
| TEM7 | Bo+Bo-Bo+Bo | 1,472 | 100 | 180 | 1975 | L/Ko | 2-2D49 | E ETM |
| ChME2 | Bo-Bo | 552 | 80 | 64 | 1958 | ČKD | 65310DR | E ČKD |
| ChME3‡ | Co-Co | 993 | 95 | 123 | 1964 | ČKD | K65310DR | E ČKD |
| ChME5 | Bo+Bo-Bo+Bo | 1,470 | 95 | 168 | 1985 | ČKD | K85310DR | E ČKD |

* Also operated in triple-unit version (3TE10M)
† Also operated in twin- and triple-unit versions (2M62, 3M62)
‡ A variant is classified ChME3T
Abbreviations: B: Bryansk; K: Kharkov; Ko: Kolomna; L: Lyudinovsk; P: Penza; V: Voroshilovgrad

The former source of emu car supply was the Riga works in Latvia, which Russia now finds expensive. In 1992, 100 emu vehicles were ordered from the Riga works, but the Russians are now developing their own domestic sources of supply.

Emu vehicles have been produced by the Torzhok missile wagon works, while the Tikhvin converted military plant has manufactured motor bogies. Current plans envisage an annual capacity of 750 carriages by 2001.

Novocherkassk produced its first 10-car emu in early 1996 (Class EN1) and the ENZ asynchronous emu was expected to appear in 1999. A lack of funds means that this works' capacity for emu construction remains badly utilised.

The Demikhovo works, formerly a builder of narrow-gauge wagons for the mining industry, completed the first of 50 four-car emus in December 1992; Czech builder Škoda has a US$20 million stake in the new concern. Classes ED4 and ED6 were to enter series production in 1996 and 1999 respectively, with Novocherkassk electrical equipment. By 2000 the factory is intended to produce over 1,000 cars per year; 24 10-car trains were produced in 1998 and the Railways Ministry was to acquire about 50 new emu sets in 1999, about half the number urgently required.

The prototype *Sokol* high-speed train has been on trial since 1999. This is a 12-car formation with four dual-current motored vehicles. It is designed to run at up to 250 km/h. It may be purchased for use on the reconstructed St Petersburg—Moscow line.

To replace the Hungarian, Latvian and Czech suppliers of dmus and railcars, the Lyudinovo locomotive plant has begun production of Class DL2 dmu motor cars which, in combination with trailer cars supplied by Tver, results in the DL2B12 12-car dmu. Meanwhile, the Mytischii works has produced Russia's first railbus, the RA1, which has been on trial since early 1998; this is based on that works' metro vehicles.

The DP2 diesel train of completely new design began trials in 2000. It is a joint product of the Lyudinovo diesel locomotive works and the Tver passenger coach works.

*Other passenger coach developments*
Double-deck vehicles are slow to appear, despite earlier agreements with ANF-Industrie (now Bombardier) of France and GEC Alsthom Transporte (now Alstom) of Spain. With the end of German imports, the Tver passenger coach works is now the supplier of long-distance coaches and it was hoped production there would increase to 500 annually in 2000. It is concentrating on high-comfort designs. Meanwhile the Voitovich Works is reconstructing time-expired vehicles and also designing a new range of coaches. In 2000, it was due to deliver the first of 16 new coaches for the *Avrora* Moscow—St Petersburg service. These were to be air conditioned and provided with ecological toilets. The latter are also a feature of vehicles now in the Helsinki—St Petersburg services, which also include Russia's first coaches with wheelchair access.

### Signalling and telecommunications
About 63,000 km of the RZhD network is equipped with the automatic block system. Microprocessor-based control centres cover about 25,000 km, and this system is being extended, although much signalling equipment dating from the 1950s and 1960s will need to be replaced at the same time. Several systems of automatic locomotive signalling are in use, but only one is regarded as satisfactory.

Large-scale electronic systems include the *Ekspress* passenger train reservation facility, the *DISPARK* freight car control system and the *DISLOK* network which monitors locomotives and their crews. The laying of fibre optic cables between St Petersburg and the Black Sea,

### Electric railcars or multiple-units

| Class | Cars per unit | Motor cars per unit | Motored axles/car | Output/motor kW | Speed Km/h | First built | Builders Mechanical | Electrical |
|---|---|---|---|---|---|---|---|---|
| **3 kV DC** | | | | | | | | |
| ER1 | 10 | 5 | 4 | 200 | 130 | 1957 | Riga/Kalinin | REZ, Dinamo |
| ER2 | 10-12 | 5-6 | 4 | 200 | 130 | 1962 | Riga/Kalinin | REZ |
| ER22 | 8 | 4 | 4 | 220 | 130 | 1964 | Riga | REZ |
| ER200 | 10 | 8 | 4 | 240 | 200 | 1974 | Riga | REZ |
| ER2R | 10-12 | 5-6 | 4 | 240 | 130 | 1979 | Riga | REZ |
| ER2T | 10-12 | 5-6 | 4 | 235 | 130 | 1987 | Riga | REZ |
| ET2 | 10 | 6 | 4 | NA | 130 | 1993 | Torzhok/Tikhvin | Tikhvin |
| ED2T | 10 | 5 | 4 | NA | NA | 1992 | Demikhovo/Tikhvin | Tikhvin |
| **25 kV AC** | | | | | | | | |
| ER-9 | 10 | 5 | 4 | 180 | 130 | 1961 | Riga/Kalinin | REZ |
| ER9P | 10-12 | 5-6 | 4 | 200 | 130 | 1964 | Riga | REZ |
| ER9M | 10-12 | 5-6 | 4 | 200 | 130 | 1976 | Riga | REZ |
| ER9E | 10-12 | 5-6 | 4 | 200 | 130 | 1981 | Riga | REZ |
| ER 9T | 10-12 | 5-6 | 4 | 200 | 130 | 1988 | Riga | REZ |

### Diesel railcars or multiple-units

| Class | Cars per unit | Motor cars per unit | Motored axles/car | Power/motor kW | Speed km/h | First built | Builders Mechanical | Engine | Transmission |
|---|---|---|---|---|---|---|---|---|---|
| D1 | 4 | 2 | 2 | 540 | 120 | 1963 | Avad/Ganz-Mavag | Ganz-Jendrassik 12VFE17/24 | HM |
| DR1 | 6 | 2 | 2 | 736 | 120 | 1963 | Riga | Zvezda M756B | H |
| DR1P | 6 | 2 | 2 | 736 | 120 | 1969 | Riga | Zvezda M756B | HM |
| DR1A | 6 | 2 | 2 | 736 | 120 | 1973 | Riga | Zvezda M756B | H |
| ACh2 | 1/2 | 1 | 2 | 736 | 120 | 1984 | Studenka | Zvezda M756B | H |

and between Moscow and Vladivostok, is well advanced. The first ground station for satellite communication is being built in the Urals, although earlier experiments were carried out at Krasnoyarsk. The Railways Ministry will have enough capacity to enable its *Transtelekom* subsidiary, already a substantial telephone service provider, to offer a competitive direct-dialling long-distance service to the public.

### Electrification
RZhD operates the world's most extensive electrified railway network and about two-thirds of all freight traffic is electrically hauled. Lines around Moscow and in the Urals are electrified on the 3 kV DC system. Most lines electrified since 1956 have been equipped with the 25 kV 50 Hz AC system.

The astonishing pace of electrification between the 1960s and the 1980s has slowed in recent years for economic reasons. In 1990 the 25 kV electrification of the Baikal—Amur Railway from Ust-Kut reached Chara. Two other routes electrified at 25 kV in the Far East were Khrebtovaya—Ust Ilimsk and Khabarovsk—Kruglikovo.

The Trans-Siberian has been electrified as far as Khabarovsk (8,531 km) for many years, and work is proceeding steadily on converting the Khabarovsk—Vladivostok section.

Electrification at 25 kV is proceeding on the North Caucasus Railway. In 1993 wiring was completed of a 50 km section from Krymskaya to Novorossiysy, while 1994 saw the start of work on a further two section, Krasnodar—Tikhoretskaya and Krymskaya—Afimskaya, totalling 180 km. Work on the Tikhoretskaya—Salsk and Likhaya—Morozovskaya sections (290 km) began one year later. After completion it will be possible to employ electric traction to the Volga Railway via Morozovskaya and Kotelnikovo.

In 1997 electrification began on a 158 km section between Sviyazhsk and Tsima, connecting the Gorki and Kuibyshev Railways. The changing geopolitical situation following the break-up of the Soviet Union calls for a further upgrading and electrification of an additional 470 km of north-south lines to avoid passing through Ukraine.

On the South East Railway the Voronezh—Kastornaya route was electrified at 25 kV early in 1998 and work has since switched to the 187 km Elec—Kastornaya—Stariy Oskol section.

In 1996 the 130 km Vologda—Buy line was electrified and work on a westward extension to Cherepovets (124 km) has since been started. Further north, electrification of the Konosha—Milenga—Arkangelsk line (423 km) is in progress and a 126 km section from Nyandoma, north of Konosha, and Plesetskaya was completed in 1998. Both projects employ the 25 kV system.

Electrification at 3 kV DC of the Volkhovstroy—Belomorsk section of the busy Northern Railway's St Petersburg—Petrozavodsk—Belomorsk—Murmansk line is close to completion. In mid-1996 the 121 km Volkhovstroy—Lodeynoye Pole section was completed; an extension northwards to Svir followed in mid-1998. A section from Belomorsk to Idel was energised in August 1997 and a further 165 km south to Medvezhya Gora was completed by the end of 1998. Electrifying the gap between Svir and Medvezhya Gora will eliminate remaining diesel operation over the 1,455 km St Petersburg—Murmansk line, significantly reducing journey times.

Conversion from 3 kV DC to 25 kV AC 50 Hz of the Mineralnye Vody—Kislovodsk (65 km) and Zima—Slyudyanka (453 km) lines was completed in 1996. The latter forms part of the Trans-Siberian route.

### Track
A severe backlog in track maintenance work has developed on RZhD in recent years. Ballast is in poor condition in many places. The EBRD report recommended that lighter, more mobile track maintenance equipment and advanced tampers should be used, and advocated a revision of maintenance methods. Western track machines have been purchased and a start made on producing Russian versions of them which initially will be devoted to the Moscow—St Petersburg, Moscow—Smolensk and Moscow—Samara main lines. A trial order was placed for Swedish sleepers with Pandrol clips.

**Rails:** 75, 65, 50 kg/m
**Continuous welded rail:** 40,400 km (1999)
**Sleepers:** Ferro-concrete on 56,800 km (1999)
**Sleeper spacing:** 1,840/km on plain track, 2,000/km on curves of less than 1,200 m radius
**Sleeper dimensions:** 2,750 × 250 × 180 (wood); 2,700 × 250 × 193 (concrete)
**Max axleload:** 23.5 tonnes

# SAUDI ARABIA

## Saudi Railways Organisation

PO Box 36, Dammam 31241
Tel: (+966 3) 871 30 01; 871 51 51
Fax: (+966 3) 827 11 30; 827 10 71

### Key personnel
President: Khalid H Alyahya
Vice-President: Fahad S Al-Balawi
Vice-President, Operations: Abdul Aziz S Al-Tammami
Directors General
   Administration and Finance: Abdulla Ghanim Al-Oraini
   General Superintendent of Maintenance:
    Nasser Refaei
   Riyadh Branch: Abdulaziz S Al-Tobayyeb
   Projects: Hamad Abdulqadir
   Transportation & Marketing: Saud Al-Tobbeyab
Operations: Adbulaziz H Al-Harbi
Development & Training: Adbulamir A Al Sunni
Directors
   Personnel: Ibrahim H Al-Khashan
   Finance: Saad A A Al-Abbad
   Motive Power and Equipment: Shahab Abdulla
   Telecommunications: Fahad A Al-Aqeel
   Planning and Budget: Kazim M Al-Mirza

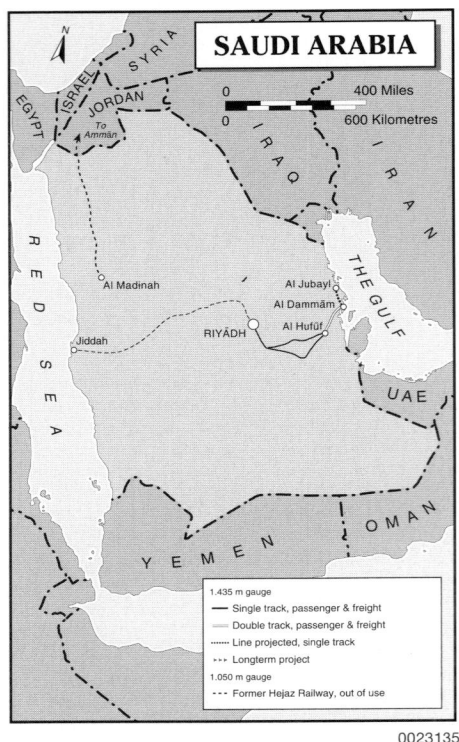

# RAILWAY SYSTEMS/Saudi Arabia

*SRO passenger service headed by GM-built SD50 locomotive* 0058803

*Dry port at Riyadh* 2000/0087935

Maintenance of Way: Abdulla Bin Al-Haddad
Purchasing: Yousuf A Al-Farhan
Stores: Khalid A Al-Turaki
Legal: Yousuf A Al-Owais
Representative for UIC Affairs: Nasser Refaei

Gauge: 1,435 mm
Route length: 1,392 km (with branch lines & sidings)

## Organisation
At the end of 2000 SRO employed 1,826 staff.

**Finances** (SR million)

| Revenue | 1997 | 1999 |
|---|---|---|
| Passengers | 17.866 | 23.269 |
| Freight | 69.528 | 84.810 |
| Other income | 17.689 | 15.964 |
| Total | 105.083 | 124.043 |

| Expenditure | 1997 | 1999 |
|---|---|---|
| Staff/personnel | 118.275 | 109.704 |
| Materials and services | 48.985 | 49.752 |
| Depreciation | 101.369 | 101.538 |
| Total | 268.629 | 260.994 |

| Traffic | 1997 | 1999 | 2000 |
|---|---|---|---|
| Passenger journeys | 634,000 | 804,000 | 854,000 |
| Passenger-km (million) | 213 | 267 | 288 |
| Freight tonnes (million) | 1.78 | 1.87 | 1.66 |
| Freight tonne-km (million) | 838 | 900 | 832 |

## Passenger operations
Passenger services are operated between Dammam and Riyadh.

## New lines
Studies were completed in 2000 for two new lines: an east-west line between Riyadh and Jeddah; and a direct line from Riyadh to the port of Jubail and on to phosphates deposits in the northeast. In 2001 funding options were being studied. Construction of the two lines is expected to take around five years.

## Improvements to existing lines
Principal infrastructure project of the 1980s was transformation of the Dammam–Riyadh main line. The 140 km of the existing route from Dammam to Hofuf were double-tracked and realigned for 120 km/h maximum speed, with continuously welded UIC 60 rail on concrete sleepers on the new line, manufactured in a plant established locally at Hofuf. Beyond Hofuf a new and direct double-track route of 308 km was built for 150 km/h running. This line is used by passenger trains only. There is a second double-track line from Hofuf to Riyadh (416 km), passing through Haradh and Al-Kharj. The old line from Dammam to Hofuf and from Hofuf to Riyadh via Haradh and Al-Kharj is used for freight only. At present 449 km of the network carries passenger traffic.

New stations were built at Riyadh, Dammam and Hofuf. Traffic is controlled by voice orders through the telecommunications system via radio terminals and repeater stations. Some level-crossing automatic barriers are worked by soft-lead batteries recharged by solar power.

## Traction and rolling stock
In 2000 the railway was operating 59 diesel locomotives, 58 passenger cars (including nine restaurant cars) and 2,262 freight wagons.

### Diesel locomotives

| Class | Wheel arrangement | Power kW | Speed km/h | Weight tonnes | No in service | First built | Engine | Builders Transmission |
|---|---|---|---|---|---|---|---|---|
| 1100 (G18W) | Bo-Bo | 746 | 110 | 67 | 16 | 1968 | EMD | E EMD |
| 1100 (SW1001) | Bo-Bo | 746 | 110 | 84 | 5 | 1981 | EMD | E EMD |
| 2250 (GP38-2) | Bo-Bo | 1,678 | 110 | 107 | 1 | 1973 | EMD | E EMD |
| 2000 (GT22CW) | Co-Co | 1,492 | 110 | 109 | 3 | 1976 | EMD | E EMD |
| 3500 (SD50) | Co-Co | 2,611 | 160 | 124 | 6 | 1981 | EMD | E EMD |
|  |  |  |  | 125 | 10* | 1985* | EMD | E EMD |
|  |  |  |  | 120 | 7 | 1998 | EMD | E EMD |
| 3600 (CSE 26-21) | Co-Co | 2,450 | 160 | 126 | 6 | 1981 | Alco/Francorail | E Jeumont Schneider |

* With dynamic braking

**Type of coupler, passenger and freight:** AAR Type E
**Type of brake:** Westinghouse air

### Track
All main line track renewals are undertaken with continuously welded UIC 54 kg/m rail on prestressed concrete sleepers with elastic fastenings.

**Rail types and weights:** 110 lb RE, 115 lb RE, UIC 54, UIC 60
**Crossties (sleepers):** Prestressed concrete, 215 mm thickness, 2,600 mm long; some wooden
**Spacing:** 1,667/km
**Rail fastenings:** Elastic, ballast cushion of 300 mm
**Min curve radius:** 565 m
**Max gradient:** 1%
**Max permissible axleload:** 22 tonnes

**UPDATED**

---

## General Railway Corporation

### Key personnel
Chairman: Dr Nasser M Al-Salloum, Minister of Communications

### Political background
The purpose of this body, which was established in the late 1990s, is to stimulate the transfer of freight from road to rail. The government has commissioned studies into two possible projects to promote this goal: a 1,200 km east-west line from Jeddah to Jubail, on the Arabian Gulf; and a rail link between Jubail and Ras al-Jalameed, an area rich in phosphates and bauxite. The new lines would be built by the private sector as build, operate, transfer (BOT) projects, with a likely concession length of 20 years. Total cost of the two lines is estimated at US$4 billion. Both Saudi and foreign investors will be encouraged to participate and a number of European and Malaysian organisations are reported to have expressed an interest.

# SENEGAL

## Ministry of Equipment and Land Transport
Administrative Building, Dakar

**Key personnel**
Minister: Landing Sone

## Société Nationale des Chemins de Fer du Sénégal (SNCS)
PO Box 175, Cité Ballabey, Thiès
Tel: (+221 39) 53 50   Fax: (+221 951) 13 93

**Key personnel**
Director General: Ibrahima Niang
Directors
    Infrastructure and Co-ordination: Badara Talla
    Personnel: Ndaraw Fall
    Financial: Serigne Ndiaye
    Equipment: Abdoulaye Lo
    Operations: Mamadou Gueye
    Studies, International Relations, Computerisation and Property: Baba Diankha

Gauge: 1,000 mm
Route length: 906 km

### Organisation
As one of West Africa's most industrialised countries, Senegal has a railway system comprising two main lines running from Dakar to St Louis and Linguère in the northeast and the border with Mali in the east. The system was originally part of the Federal West African Railway Authority (AOF) before transfer to the Mali Federation in 1960. The disintegration of the Mali Federation caused the division of the former Dakar-Niger system into two networks. The principal line extends 1,286 km from Dakar in Senegal to Koulikoro, the terminus of the railway in the landlocked neighbouring country of Mali.

SNCS was established in November 1989 as successor to the former RCFS; it is an independent semi-public corporation and as such agrees a performance contract each year with the government.

In recent years, the growth of road transport has been a significant challenge for SNCS.

In 1997 the governments of Senegal and Mali retained Canadian consultancy CPCS Transcom to prepare a concession and assist in the selection of a concessionaire to operate international services on the Dakar-Bamako (Mali) line. Expressions of interest were submitted by February 1998 but no further progress was evident until February 2001, when the Senegal and Mali governments revived efforts to select a concessionaire with access to finance to upgrade the infrastructure and commercial expertise to develop traffic.

### Passenger operations
There are four international expresses a week from Dakar to Bamako, the capital of Mali, which are overseen by a joint management board. Typically, these trains carry between 4,000 and 5,000 passengers a month.

A frequent push-pull service operates on the 29 km suburban route from Dakar to Thiaroye and Rufisque. Patronage on this route has boomed, with the service handling some 6 million passengers in a year.

### Freight operations
In terms of weight, the principal freight traffic is phosphates, transported by rail to the port of Dakar for export. In 2000, one daily train was serving Taiba, a single weekly train was serving Lam-Lam, and a single daily train was serving Allou Kagne.

In 2000, SNCS was operating two trains of chemical products a day for the chemicals company Sefics between Taiba and Dakar, using wagons owned by Sefics.

In 2000, international traffic on the Dakar—Bamako line totalled 345,704 tonnes, 4.3 per cent down on the 1999 figure of 361,293 tonnes. Freight traffic revenue in 2000 was CFAFr7 billion.

### Improvements to existing lines
Two projects are being assigned priority. First is the CFAFr19.6 billion renewal of track on the international main line between Tambacounda and Kidira.

The other project is installation of a third track between Hann and Thiaroye on the Dakar suburban route; this would be for the exclusive use of passenger trains, freeing up the other two tracks for freight. This would ease the flow of traffic on the Dakar—Thiès line and improve access for freight trains to terminals at Bel Air and Mbao.

### Traction and rolling stock
The stock of 29 diesel locomotives is mostly French built; French aid is financing Alstom maintenance of the railway's Alsthom AD16B locomotives. In 1996, a protocol was signed between the governments of Senegal and Canada that provided a grant of C$12.5 million to pay for five new locomotives from General Motors Canada; a further C$1 million from Senegalese sources funded acquisition of a pool of spare parts. The locomotive fleet is more than adequate for current SNCS traffic requirements, to such an extent that in 2001 three 1,790 kW machines were leased to RCFM in Mali, in addition to an additional three that were outbased there.

At the end of 2000, the number of passenger cars totalled 102. SNCS has acquired from France 24 stainless steel SNCF 'Mistral' cars of the 1950s and their four generator cars; these are now being used on the international trains to Mali. In 2001, SNCS also had 20 passenger coaches refurbished by Pakistan Railway Carriage Factory. This was in part to provide capacity for traffic generated by the African Cup football competition.

The 'Little Blue Train' suburban service in Dakar was launched in 1987. There are seven five-car trains, with 10 dedicated Type AD16 locomotives as motive power. SNCS has refurbished 41 SNCF Type B10t 'Bruhat' passenger cars, and fitted them with ex-freight wagon metre-gauge bogies with their suspension refined.

In 2000, the freight wagon fleet totalled 1,015. SNCS and Mali have recently added 140 new wagons to the international pool.

### Signalling and telecommunications
Automatic block colourlight signalling is operative on the 70 km of double track between Dakar and Thiès. Further improvements to signalling and telecommunications systems have been identified as a priority, especially for routes carrying suburban traffic.

*SNCS diesel railcar at Dakar forming a train to Saint Louis (Eddie Barnes)*

**UPDATED**

# SLOVAKIA

## Ministry of Transport, Post and Telecommunications

Stefánovičova 6/I.2902, SK-801 00 Bratislava
Tel: (+421 2) 59 49 41 11   Fax: (+421 2) 25 48 00

**Key personnel**
Minister: Jozef Macejko
Director, Railways: Dusan Turanovič

**UPDATED**

## Slovakian Republic Railways (ZSR)

Seleznice Slovenskej republiky
Klemensova 8, SK-813 61 Bratislava
Tel: (+421 2) 32 52 42; 548 70 05
Fax: (+421 2) 548 70 44
Web: http://www.zsr.sk

**Key personnel**
Chairman of Executive Committee: Michal Balog
General Manager: Ladislav Saxa
General Inspector: Vojtech Štefan Kobetič
General Manager's Office – Under-Secretaries
  Economy: Dušan Zelinka
  Management and Personnel Resources: Ján Žačko
  Technical Development: Ladislav Dimun
  Operations: Milan Solárik
Management Board
  Legal Affairs: Alojz Ceizel
  Control and Investigation: Mária Surovcová
  Strategy: Július Daubner
  Technical Development and Ecology: Ján Hanúsek
  Investment: Jozef Bošanský
  Information: Peter Banič
  Finances: Jaroslav Mikla
  Controlling: Anton Kukučka
  Property Management: Ján Prosuch
  Signalling: Ivan Bartoš
  Power and Electrical Engineering: Dušan Mitošinka
  Economy: Rastislav Sirkovský
  Human Resources: Eva Schwarczová
  Operations: Miloslav Barčiak
  Marketing: Milan Nevidanský
  Protection and Security: Ivan Bernát
  International Relations: Peter Havrila
  Public Relations: Ján Keresteš

Gauge: 1,435 mm; 1,520 mm; 1,000 mm; 750 mm
Route length: 3,511 km; 106 km; 46 km; 5 km
Electrification: 786 km at 25 kV 50 Hz AC; 737 km at 3 kV DC; 42 km at 1.5 kV DC; 2 km at 15 kV AC 16⅔ Hz

### Political background

Mirroring the severance of Slovakia from the Czech Republic, the Czechoslovak railway system (ČSD) was divided in 1993 into Slovakian Railways (ŽSR) and Czech Railways (ČD). The railways now operate independently of each other. On all EuroCity and InterCity trains as well as most other services, the same electric locomotive will work across both countries.

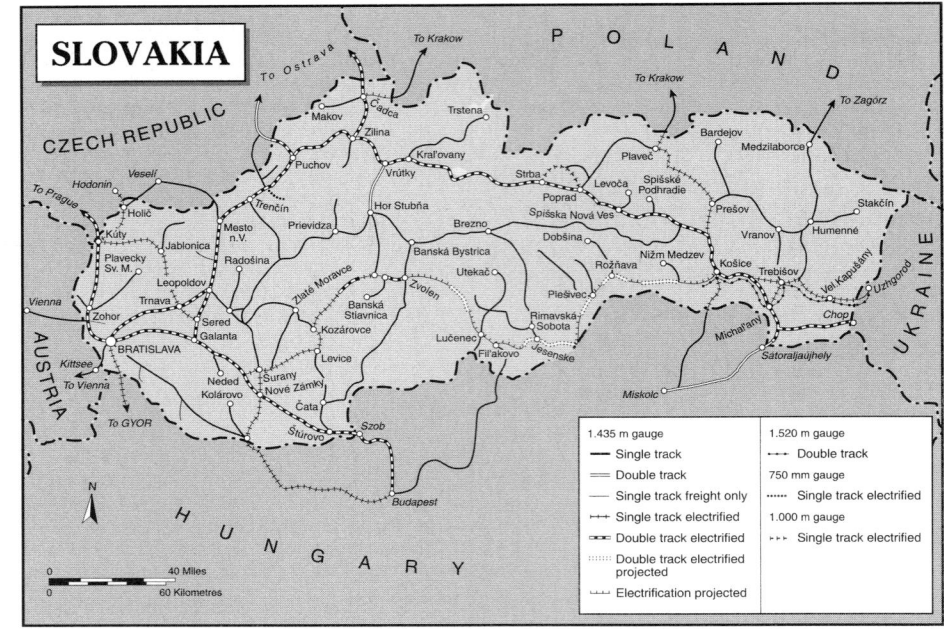

A new Railway Act was approved by the Slovak National Council in May 1996. This provided for the separation of ŽSR on the western European model into three functions: infrastructure ownership, infrastructure management and train operation.

On 18 October 2000, the Slovak government endorsed a project to restructure ŽSR into two separate businesses. The Slovak National Council ratified the final division on 14 June 2001 and the Ministry of Transport followed on 8 August of the same year. The split formally took place on 1 January 2002. The state-owned company, Železnice Slovenskej republiky (ŽSR as), retains responsibility for railway infrastructure. It will also assume responsibility for managing residual assets and disposing of surplus railway property. Ancillary businesses will be converted in three stages into 17 service companies which will be offered for sale at a later date. ŽSR will employ around 10,000 staff.

Železničná spoločnost (ŽS), legally incorporated on 6 December 2001, became a joint-stock commercial and operating enterprise, initially with some 35,000 staff. The debt-free company has been divided into three divisions responsible for: passenger operations (DOP); freight operations (DNP); and rolling stock (DŽKV). They are overseen by the company's general management, based in Bratislava. Splitting off the freight operation by 2010 into a dedicated subsidiary, ŽS Cargo, is foreseen.

The aim of the restructuring project is the creation of an economically healthy customer-oriented commercial company with a share of 50-60 per cent of Slovakia's transport market, able to survive without state subsidy in a strongly competitive environment and ready after 2005 for full privatisation with the participation of a strong foreign shareholder.

*Privatisation*

A programme to transform the economics of ŽSR's rural lines was drawn up in 1996. This was to see 32 loss-making regional routes totalling 623 km either transferred to local authorities, privatised or closed. In 1998, operations on regional lines made losses of Kcs858.2 million, of which 583.2 million were recorded by freight traffic and the remainder by passenger services. In a way that mirrors the model adopted in the neighbouring Czech Republic, a process is under way of allowing private operators to run their own trains on ŽSR tracks. The first company to take advantage of this is a Košice-based steel-producing firm, US Steel Košice, which signed an agreement with ŽSR in December 1999 for the operation of its own block trains over the national network under a licence granted by the Slovak Railway Authority (Štátny dráhový úrad). The monopoly of ŽS for operating rail services on the Slovakian network will come to an end in 2003, when the system will be fully liberalised and open to any operator holding a licence granted by the Ministry of Transport.

On 1 February 2000, US Steel Košice began operation of three pairs of its own freight trains on a 23 km section of ŽSR's Zvolen–Košice route. Formed of Class 770.5 diesel-electric locomotives and Type Facc and Faccs hopper wagons, the trains convey limestone from a quarry at Turňa nad Bodvou to a steelworks at Velká Ida in eastern Slovakia, close to the Hungarian border. Other private operators planning to run services include TSS Bratislava and ŽS Košice.

### Organisation

ŽSR is controlled by the Ministry of Transport, Post and Telecommunications through an executive committee.

ŽS is based on a similar model and is overseen by a supervisory board.

Ancillary activities such as civil engineering, mechanical engineering, design, catering, and the three major traction and rolling stock workshops at Trnava, Zvolen and Vrútky, were all sold off by the end of 1993 under the privatisation programme. In January 1996 Wagon Slovakia took over from ŽSR as private operator of dining and sleeping cars on international services to 14 European countries.

At the end of 2001, ŽSR employed 42,742 staff, compared with 45,251 at the end of 2000.

On 23 July 1999, ŽSR was granted a state-guaranteed credit totalling €200 million from the European Investment Bank. This was to be spent on the acquisition of 35 new passenger coaches, the purchase or modernisation of 180 freight wagons, modernisation of the telecommunications network, refurbishment of the Čadca-Skalité route and upgrading the Bratislava-Trnava line for 160 km/h running (see 'Improvements to existing lines'). The government plans to cut overall state support from Kcs5.8 billion in 1999 to Kcs1.7 billion by 2007.

*Class 773 diesel-electric locomotive rebuilt from a Class 771 machine (Michal Málek)*

## Slovakia/RAILWAY SYSTEMS

*Class 350 dual-voltage 25 kV AC/3 kV DC electric locomotive at Bratislava Hlavná Stanica (Colin Boocock)*
*2002/0132668*

During this period, the number of employees will be reduced to around 30,000.

| **Finances** (Kcs million) | 1999 | 2000 | 2001 |
|---|---|---|---|
| Expenditure | 29,197 | 32,910 | 30,500 |
| Revenue | 23,994 | 28,876 | 26,627 |
| Profit/loss | −5,203 | −4,034 | −3,873 |
| Government subsidy to cover passenger losses | 2,521 | 3,950 | 3,610 |

| **Traffic** (million) | 1998 | 1999 | 2000 |
|---|---|---|---|
| Passenger journeys | 70.0 | 69.4 | 66,81 |
| Freight tonnes | 56.5 | 49.1 | 54,12 |

### Passenger operations

The political and economic changes that took place in the wake of the 'Velvet Revolution' have resulted in declining passenger numbers. Passenger-km dropped from 6.2 billion in 1989 to 2.9 billion in 1999; road coaches are proving formidable competitors. Reflecting the fall in rail patronage, services in Slovakia were cut by some 10 to 15 per cent in 1993, and further cuts took place in December 1995. ŽSR now accounts for 25 per cent of the country's total passenger journeys.

Slovakia is served by three year-round EuroCity services, the 'Hungaria', the 'Comenius' and the 'Csárdás', running on the Prague—Budapest axis. Another EuroCity service, the 'Polonia', crosses Slovak territory en route from Warsaw to Budapest and two pairs of InterCity trains, the 'Košičan' and the 'Odra', run between Košice and Prague via Žilina.

There are two pairs of InterCity trains on the main transversal line from Bratislava to Košice via Žilina, the 'Tatran' and the 'Kriváň. The fastest of these accomplishes the 445 km trip serving Slovakia's largest cities in 4 hours 55 minutes; 10 years ago the trip took over 7 hours. Route upgrading to 160 km/h speeds should eventually bring the time down to 3 hours 30 minutes. Another InterCity train connects Bratislava with Zvolen via Levice.

In 2001, revenues covered just 16 per cent of total expenditure in passenger traffic. During that year the government budgeted support of Kcs3.61 billion to cover loss-making passenger operations up by 30 per cent compared with 1999. The cost of operating passenger services during 1999 reached Kcs8.7 billion, but revenues of only Kcs1.69 billion were received despite a 35 per cent increase in fares in February 1999. In 2000, passenger revenues were slightly up, reaching Kcs2.018 billion.

### Freight operations

The political and economic changes in central and eastern Europe have resulted in a major reduction in freight traffic, with the decline of heavy industry, a reduction in north-south transit traffic between the former Eastern Bloc countries and a decline in trade with the former USSR heavily influencing tonnage figures. Tonne-km more than halved between 1989 and 1995, dropping from 25 to 12 billion. By 1995, the situation had stabilised, with freight revenue rising by 5 per cent in that year to reach Kcs12.8 billion, and rising again in 1998 to Kcs14.172 billion against operating costs of Kcs13.3 billion. ŽSR still remains Slovakia's principal mode of heavy freight transport, although its market share fell between 1994 and 2001 from 66.3 to 60.3 per cent. Transit traffic accounts for some 26 per cent of this figure.

Freight traffic accounted for 86.95 per cent of ŽSR's revenues in 1999, earning the railway a total of Kcs14.69 billion. The same year, ŽSR traffic reached a total of 9.856 billion tonne-km. Of this, 36 per cent was formed by import cargo, 26 per cent by export, 21 per cent internal freight and 17 per cent transit business. In 2001, ŽSR was operating 899 regular freight trains each day. The main commodities transported are iron ore, coal, construction materials, chemicals, metal products and timber.

On 1 March 1996, ŽSR joined with Czech Railways (ČD) and Czech forwarding company ISD Děčín to initiate a door-to-door parcels service. Named 'Interkurýr', the service is provided at 17 stations on the ŽSR network.

### Intermodal transport

Intermodal traffic is still at an early stage of development, accounting for just under 1 per cent of the railway's freight volume at 505,000 tonnes in 2000. Much of the trade with the former USSR was transported in containers; the break-up of the Eastern Bloc resulted in a dramatic fall in intermodal traffic. Of late, ŽSR has been making efforts to rebuild this traffic. In October 1996, a new Kcs100 million terminal was opened at Čierna nad Tisou-Dobrá on the Ukrainian border, where the gauge changes. Two months later a weekly container service was launched between the new terminal and Moscow, Russia. A letter of intent has been signed with the port authorities in Padua, Italy, providing for transport through the terminal of 300,000 tonnes annually of containerised freight bound for eastern markets.

In November 1996 the Slovak government adopted a plan to develop intermodal traffic, with Combi Slovakia Eurotrans Žilina selected as the national operator. ČSKD-Intrans and Metrans Danubia also operate in this market.

The 'Tatranexpress' unit container train between Bratislava-Pálenisko and Rotterdam and the 'Tatranexpress II' between Čierna nad Tisou and Rotterdam, both launched in 1997, were discontinued due to poor loadings. Subsequently, in July 1999, a Netherlands-based company, European Rail Shuttles (ERS), in co-operation with local partners ČSKD-Intrans in Prague and SPAP of Bratislava, launched a new container shuttle between Prague Žižkov and Bratislava ÚNS/Pálenisko. Running three times-weekly, this provides a direct connection with ERS's daily 'Bohemia Express' service between Prague Žižkov and Rotterdam Maasvlakte/Walhaven. In 2001, Slovakia was also served by the following container shuttles: Praha Žižkov—Budapest Jozsefváros and Praha Žižkov—Bucuresti Sud (operated by ERS Rotterdam); Budapest Jozsefváros—Hamburg/Bremerhaven (Kombiverkehr, Frankfurt); and by a north-south piggyback service between Budapest Jozsefváros and Gliwice (Flott Trans Kft Eger, Polkombi and Klevytrans Sturovo).

In 1998 the government undertook to provide funding of Kcs30 million to support combined transport, with a further Kcs60 million allocated for 1999. In 1998 attention was focused on the development of piggyback services using wagons produced domestically by Tatravagónka Poprad since 1997. Studies were being carried out on the introduction of piggyback services on two routes to the Czech Republic: Čierna nad Tisou—Otrokovice and Bratislava—Lovosice.

ŽSR now has at its disposal five international intermodal terminals: Bratislava-ÚNS, Čierna nad Tisou; Košice; Ružomberok-Lisková; and Žilina. It plans to open an additional facility at Zvolen. A regional terminal opened at Ružomberok in May 1998 and a further five are to be built in Lučenec, Nitra, Poprad, Strážske and Trenčianska. There are also privately owned terminals at Dunajská Streda and Nové Zámky (Metrans Danubia/Ozon). Multipurpose combined transport centres are located at Bratislava-Pálenisko and Čierna nad Tisou-Dobrá.

In May 1998 a new swapbody service, the 'Assi Domän Express', was introduced between Štúrovo and Bologna, Italy. Operated by Klevyttrans Štúrovo, the fortnightly service was suspended temporarily in June 1999.

In December 1998, ŽSR and Polish State Railways signed an agreement for the operation of intermodal trains over the Čadca—Slakité—Zwardoń—Bielsko-Biala cross-border route.

Using funds from the state budget, ŽSR had acquired 152 Type Sgnss container flats by the end of 2000 in a programme to eliminate the 1970s-built Type Pasy vehicles which were barred from international services from the start of 2000. Also meeting RIV international standards are 97 Hungarian-built Type Sgjs container flats and 60 new Type Sdgnss wagons for piggyback operations by Tatra-vagónka.

### New lines

In 1994 construction began of a new cross-border alignment from Petržalka, a suburb of the Slovak capital, to Kittsee, in Austria, partly using the trackbed of the Bratislava-Berg-Vienna line, built in 1914 and closed in April 1945. The new single-track line was built by the 'Rýchla trať' (Fast Line) consortium of construction companies, with the Slovak portion just 1.76 km in length. Construction has also involved electrification at 15 kV AC

*ČKD-built Class 770.5 diesel-electric locomotive and limestone train operated by VSŽ Košice over ŽSR tracks under open access rights, photographed at Veľka Ida (Michal Málek)*
*2001/0062505*

# RAILWAY SYSTEMS/Slovakia

16⅔ Hz as far as Petržalka, the installation of new signaling and safety equipment and the erection of new station buildings at Petržalka and Kittsee.

The official opening of the line took place on 15 December 1998 and revenue operations began on 7 January 1999, with one pair of fast passenger trains operating between Bratislava-Petržalka and Vienna Südbahnhof. An additional three non-stop return workings each day were introduced from the 1999/2000 timetable change in May 1999, when full electric operation also commenced. These trains are hauled by ÖBB Class 1046 and ŽSR Class 240 electric locomotives. Initially, problems with customs authorities prevented the introduction of new local passenger services between Petrzalka and Parndorf; eight pairs of local stopping services using ÖBB Class 4010 and 4020 emus were finally introduced from 1 August 1999. All but one are coupled to Neusiedl-Vienna trains at Bruck/Leitha to provide through services to and from the Austrian capital. Commissioning the new line has reduced journey times betwen the two capitals to 45 minutes compared with the previous best of 1 hour 7 minutes via Devínská Nová Mes and Marchegg. ŽSR intends to reroute some 50 per cent of all north-south freight transit traffic via the new line, which forms part of the Warsaw–Vienna north-south international corridor (see 'Improvements to existing lines' section).

Following an agreement between ŽSR and ÖBB, direct freight trains between Vienna and Bratislava-východ from 7 January 2002, followed by direct express passenger services between the Austrian capital and Bratislava hlavná stanica from 27 January. These operate without the need for a customs stop at Petržalka. All these services are hauled by ÖBB Class 1116 dual-voltage electric locomotives.

In 1996, Austria and the Slovak Republic agreed to set up a joint venture to establish a link between Vienna's Schwechat airport and the Ivanka pri Dunaji airport in Slovakia. The so-called Neu Pressburger Bahn would run through Wolfsthal, Kittsee and Bratislava, partly on existing lines and partly new construction.

A 14.5 km cross-border connection into Poland was reopened to freight traffic in June 1996. Up to six pairs of freight trains daily use this line. The Kcs150 million project links Medzilaborce and Lupków. ŽSR introduced cross-border passenger services from Humenné to Zagórz in June 1999.

## Improvements to existing lines

In the period 1997-2010 ŽSR plans to invest a total of Kcs33.7 billion, of which Kcs21.5 billion will go towards the upgrading of three trunk corridors which are responsible for three-quarters of ŽSR's traffic volume. In mid-1997 ŽSR obtained a loan of Kcs5.8 billion, of which Kcs0.5 billion was intended for modernisation of the 113 km Kúty–Zohor–Bratislava–Galanta section and Kcs2.8 billion for the 46 km Bratislava–Rača–Trnava section.

Modernisation was under way in 1998 on the 20.2 km line between Čadca and Skalité-Serafínov on the Polish border, which was opened for freight operation in May 1994. The Kcs1.62 billion project involving electrification at 3 kV DC, upgrading 15 bridges and rebuilding the border station at Čadca, under way since 1993, will allow maximum loads for freight trains to be increased from 400 to 800 tonnes and the line speed to be raised from 60 to 100 km/h. ŽSR predicts completion during 2002.

Modernisation of the 265 km north-south transversal route is seen as a priority. This route runs from Skalité-Serafínov near the Polish border to the Austrian border at Kittsee (via a new cross-border connection – see 'New lines' section above), via Žilina, Trenčín and Bratislava (European Corridor VI), and forms part of the Warsaw-Vienna international route.

In April 2000, ŽSR began upgrading the first section of Corridor VI between Bratislava-Rača and Trnava. The 39.1 km section is being upgraded to raise the maximum line speed from 120 km/h to 160 km/h, the project including new overhead catenary and modernisation of signalling equipment. The cost of the project, which is divided into 11 sections, is Kcs7.1 billion.

The first 8.4 km section between Trnava and Cífer, completely rebuilt at a cost of Kcs383 million, was officially opened on 30 September 2000 by Slovakia's prime minister Mikuláš Dzurinda. The Bratislava—Rača-Svätý Jur and Pezinok—Šenkvice sections (13.5 km) were completed at the end of 2001 and the whole route between Bratislava and Trnava scheduled for completion in 2004. A second phase of the Corridor VI project covers modernisation of the 52 km Trnava—Nové Město nad Váhom line at a cost of Kcs8.7 billion and a third phase will add the 58 km Nové Město nad Váhom—Púchov section at a cost of Kcs7.6 billion. By 2010, route modernisation is due to reach Žilina, 203 km north of Bratislava.

*Class 812 two-axle diesel railcar rebuilt from a Class 011 non-powered trailer (Milan Šrámek)* 2002/0132669

The double-track 25 kV AC route linking Prague and Budapest which runs from Kúty through Bratislava and Nové Zámky to the Hungarian border at Štúrovo (European Corridor IV) is also to be upgraded for 160 km/h operation. Of the 218 km in Slovak territory, 167 km will have track renewed, with level crossings eliminated and tunnels through Bratislava refurbished. Work on the Kcs19.8 billion project is expected to continue until 2010. In 2001, work on the first two sections, Devínske Jazero—Zohor (8.3 km) and Malacky—Vel'ke Leváre (7.6 km), was to be undertaken.

Another project concerns the east-west trunk route from Žilina to Čierna nad Tisou via Košice (European Corridor V), which is a transit route to the Ukraine. It is already double-track and electrified at 3 kV, but upgrading to 120 to 140 km/h on the 242 km Žilina-Košice section is scheduled for 2006-2010 at a cost of Kcs21.2 billion; the 95 km from Košice to the Ukrainian border at Čierna would follow, with upgrading for 140 to 160 km/h running at a cost of Kcs12.1 billion.

Work started in the 1970s on the 442 km Bratislava–Levice–Zvolen–Košice southern transversal with the aim of double-tracking and electrifying it throughout, but only slow progress has been made. By the start of 1995, less than half of the route had been doubled, and a similar proportion electrified mainly at 25 kV 50 Hz AC. Track upgrading was complete on the 84 km section west from Košice. ŽSR has divided the line into five sections with the aim of accelerating the programme, but lack of funds means that completion is unlikely before 2000.

In December 2001, ŽSR commenced modernisation of the Slovak-Ukrainian border station at Cierna nad Tisou. Undertaken by ŽS Košice, ŽS Bratislava and ELTRA Košice, the Kcs1.5 billion project is being carried out in three stages and covers: track and overhead catenary renewal at marshalling yards; installation of new telecommunications systems; and environmental protection measures. The first phase covers the 1,520 mm gauge part of the station and is estimated to cost Kcs547 million.

The 5.4 km 760 mm gauge Trenčianska Teplá–Trenčianske Teplice line in northwest Slovakia underwent heavy maintenance during 2000, involving renewal of the trackbed and catenary masts.

In 1999 just 8.4 per cent of ŽSR's network was fit for 120 km/h operation and 18 per cent for 100 km/h services.

## Traction and rolling stock

In mid-2000, ŽSR operated 527 electric locomotives, 694 diesel locomotives, 23 electric multiple-units, 268 diesel railcars, 1,529 hauled passenger coaches and 22,907 freight wagons (excluding narrow-gauge).

By 2005, ŽSR's SK21 billion modernisation programme envisages: complete refurbishment of Class 350 dual-voltage and Class 131 3 kV DC twin-unit electric locomotives; conversion of Class 770 and 771 diesel locomotives into Class 773; complete modernisation of Class 460 3 kV DC emus; refurbishment of 26 Hungarian-built coaches; partial modernisation of Type A, AB and B

*Type Sdgnss wagon for piggyback services, built in the late 1990s by Tatravagónka Poprad (Michal Málek)* 2002/0132670

*Class 425.95 low-floor articulated metre-gauge 1.5 kV DC emu for service in the High Tatras (Milan Šrámek)*
2001/0062507

passenger coaches; the purchase of Teams freight wagons; and the purchase of lightweight dmus for regional routes.

ŽSR has started to fit its fleets of Class 350 and 363 Škoda-built dual-voltage electric locomotives with MIREL microprocessor control to equip them to run at 160 km/h. The first Class 350 upgraded for 160 km/h running on the Bratislava–Prague route was handed over in March 2000, followed by two more later in the same year.

Since early 1999, a requirement for additional high-speed dual-voltage electric locomotives has led to bogie exchanges between classes. Fifteen Class 363 120 km/h dual-voltage electric locomotives have been fitted with 140 km/h bogies from Class 162 3 kV DC machines and redesignated Class 362. The Class 162 machines which receive 120 km/h bogies have become Class 163.1. A lack of funds prevents ŽS from purchasing new electric locomotive designs, although the company has been considering buying three 25 kV/15 kV AC dual-system machines based on the Austrian Federal Railways Siemens-built Class 1116 for operation over the Bratislava Petržlka–Kittsee border crossing (see *New lines*).

In September 1997 the first example of a Class 755 diesel-electric locomotive appeared, rebuilt from Class 753 by the private-sector Martinská mechatronická and ŽOS Zvolen companies. The 76 tonne 100 km/h Bo-Bc is powered by a Pielstick Type 12PA-185 engine rated at 1,500 kW, becoming ŽSR's most powerful diesel type, and features a new-style body. The locomotive is equipped with electro-dynamic braking and electronic control. A contract was signed to rebuild an additional two locomotives during 1999.

A programme to modernise ŽSR's diesel locomotive fleet made good progress in 1998, when three new rebuilds emerged. The Class 772 six-axle 111-tonne diesel-electric was reconstructed from a Class 771 by Martinská mechatronická and Vagónka Trenišov. It is powered by a 960 kW Pielstick 8PA4-185M4 engine licence-built by ZTS TEES Martin and is intended for heavy shunting duties.

The most successful conversion from Class 771 is a Class 773 prototype, featuring a 1,300 kW Caterpillar engine. Weighing 112 tonnes and intended for heavy shunting and main line freight services, the locomotive has a central cab with lowered hoods and incorporates Theimeg remote-control equipment supplied by Krauss-Maffei. Construction was undertaken by ZTS-KV Dubnica nad Váhom. Series modernisation began in 1999 and by mid-2001, eight locomotives had been completed. ŽSR plans to have 35 of the type operational by 2005.

The 64-tonne Class 736, which features AC/DC transmission, has been rebuilt y ŽOS Zvolen from a Class 735 locomotive and is equipped with a Caterpillar engine. It is designed for shunting and light main line operations. The prototype was placed in service on the Zvolen–Košice main line in mid-2001. Conversion of a second example was completed in late 2001.

Vrútky workshop has undertaken a programme to rebuild Type Baafx railcar trailers into new Class 811 diesel-electric railcars. The Class 811 is used to provide faster and more comfortable services on ŽSR branch lines. Two prototypes powered by a Liaz M1.2C 640F engine emerged late in 1995 and underwent trials on the 56 km route between Kralovany and Trstená. Class 811 is equipped with microprocessor control by NES Nová Dubnica. ŽSR ordered a first series-built batch of 10 railcars fitted with a modified Type M1.2c 640s engine of 237 kW, of which six were manufactured by ŽOS Vrútky and four by ŽOS Zvolen. These were completed in 1997-98. In April 1997, a second batch of 17 railcars was ordered from ŽOS Zvolen at a cost of Kcs173.5 million. Delivery was made during 1999 and an additional seven vehicles were delivered in 2000. The type has entered service on six regional routes. Prototypes of Type 011 trailers and 912 driving trailers for use with these railcars emerged in late 1996, built in collaboration with ŽOS Zvolen and Správkárna vozů Stúrovo The first example of a similar modernisation emerged in September 2001 from ŽOS Zvolen. The new Class 812 lightweight two-axle diesel railcar prototype is a rebuild from a Class 011 trailer. It is powered by a MAN engine rated at 257 kW and has Voith Type DIWA 863.3 hydro-mechanical transmission. The vehicle has a top speed of 88 km/h and seats 53 passengers. It is also equipped with a MIREL microprocessor control system. A total of 10 such conversions has been ordered, all destined for the difficult 93 km Margecany–Červená Skala regional line. ŽS intends to undertake a similar modernisation project covering the entire fleet of 129 Class 810 railcars built 1975-84 by Vagónka Studénka over a 10-year period.

In August 2000, the EMU GTW-Vysoké Tatry consortium, incorporating Stadler Fahrzeuge AG, Adtranz and ŽOS Vrútky, rolled out a prototype of a series of Class 425.95 low-floor articulated emus for ŽSR's 1.5 kV DC metre gauge network in the High Tatras mountains. A fleet of 14 of these aluminium-bodied vehicles, which are based on Stadler's GTW 2/6 design, replacing obsolete Class 420.95 units built by Tatra Smíchov in 1963-70. Revenue operations began in June 2001, and by the end of that year seven of the emus were in service. Built under licence in Slovakia, each unit consists of two non-powered driving cars and an intermediate powered section. Rated output is 600 kW with a top speed of 80 km/h. Total cost of the contract, which was signed in September 1998, is Kcs1.5 billion.

A prototype of a diesel-electric version of this type was due to emerge from the Vrútky plant during 2001. This standard-gauge vehicle is destined to operate on the Poprad–Starý Potok–Tatranská Lomnica and Poprad–Plaveč–Orlov non-electrified lines. Six examples are due to be in service by the end of 2002. In early 2002, a similar consortium, named DMU GTW Slovensko, won a contract to supply 35 lightweight diesel vehicles for regional lines. Rated at 650 kW, they will replace 13 Class 830, 10 Class 850 and seven Class 851 dating from 1950-60. Construction will be undertaken at the Vrútky workshops under Swiss supervision.

In 1997 ŽSR purchased from DWA (Bombardier Transportation) 10 Class WLABmee couchette cars originally built for Russian Railways. They have operated international services from the May 1998 timetable change.

The private maintenance company, ŽOS Vrútky, has been undertaking coach refurbishment. In conjunction with Hungarian company DVJ Dunakeszi of Budapest, by the end of 1996 the firm had refurbished 23 160 km/h coaches for use on Bratislava-Košice InterCity trains. Improvements include disc brakes, upgraded interiors with air conditioning, and plug doors. After a three-year break due to a lack of funds, modernisation of a second batch of 26 Hungarian-built coaches was finally ordered in August 1999. Of these, 10 are first-class Type Aheer, 10 second-class Type Bheer, three first-class/restaurant Type Arpeer and three second-class/service cars of Type Bdseer. Work commenced at the ŽOS Vrútky workshops in September 1999 and involved close collaboration with DVJ Dunakeszi of Budapest. Improvements since the refurbishment of the first batch of these vehicles include new anti-skid protection and

**Electric locomotives (1,520 and 1,435 mm gauge)**

| Class | Wheel arrangement | Output kW continuous/one hour | Speed km/h | Weight tonnes | No in service | First built | Builders Mechanical | Electrical |
|---|---|---|---|---|---|---|---|---|
| **3 kV DC** | | | | | | | | |
| 110 | Bo-Bo | 800/960 | 80 | 72 | 22 | 1971 | Škoda | Škoda |
| 121 | Bo-Bo | 2,032/2,344 | 90 | 88 | 12 | 1960 | Škoda | Škoda |
| 125.8* | 2 × Bo-Bo | 4,080/4,680 | 90 | 170 | 21 | 1976 | Škoda | Škoda |
| 131† | 2 × Bo-Bo | 2 × 2,240/2,500 | 100 | 2 × 85 | 2 × 50 | 1980 | Škoda | Škoda |
| 140 | Bo-Bo | 2,032/2,344 | 120 | 82 | 17 | 1953 | Škoda | Škoda |
| 163/163.1 | Bo-Bo | 3,060/3,400 | 120 | 85 | 12/26 | 1986/92 | Škoda | Škoda/ČKD |
| 162 | Bo-Bo | 3,060/3,400 | 140 | 85 | 7 | 1992 | Škoda | Škoda/ČKD |
| 182 | Co-Co | 2,790/2,890 | 90 | 120 | 60 | 1963 | Škoda | Škoda |
| 183 | Co-Co | 2,790/3,000 | 90 | 120 | 37 | 1971 | Škoda | Škoda |
| **25 kV AC** | | | | | | | | |
| 210 | Bo-Bo | 880/984 | 80 | 72 | 36 | 1973 | Škoda | Škoda |
| 240 | Bo-Bo | 3,080/3,200 | 120 | 85 | 95 | 1968 | Škoda | Škoda |
| 263 | Bo-Bo | 3,060/3,400 | 120 | 85 | 10 | 1988 | Škoda | Škoda/ČKD |
| **Dual-voltage** | | | | | | | | |
| 350 | Bo-Bo | 4,000/4,200 | 160 | 87.6 | 18 | 1974 | Škoda | Škoda |
| 363 | Bo-Bo | 3,060/3,400 | 120 | 87 | 35 | 1980 | Škoda | Škoda/ČKD |
| 362 | Bo-Bo | 3,060/3,400 | 160 | 88 | 16 | 1990 | Škoda | Škoda/ČKD |

Note: * Designed for the Haniska–Matovce 1,520 mm gauge line
† These locomotives can be operated as single Bo-Bo units when uncoupled

**Electric multiple-units (1,435 mm gauge)**

| Class | Cars per unit | Motor cars per unit | Motored axles/car | Output kW Continuous/one hour | Speed km/h | No in service | First built | Builders Mechanical | Electrical |
|---|---|---|---|---|---|---|---|---|---|
| **3 kV DC** | | | | | | | | | |
| 460 | 5 | 2 | 4 | 2,000/2,160 | 110 | 16 | 1974 | MSV | MEZ |
| **25 kV AC** | | | | | | | | | |
| 560 | 5 | 2 | 4 | 1,680/1,860 | 110 | 8 | 1970 | MSV | MEZ |

hydraulic shock-absorbers. The coaches will be used for international express services. There are aspirations to reconstruct a further 150 vehicles and give light refurbishment to another 345 vehicles. Reconstruction of Class A, B and AB Hungarian-built coaches of both classes is being carried out by ŽOS Trnava and ŽOS Zvolen.

ŽSR plans to invest Sk11.25 billion in around 800 wagons from domestic builder Tatravagónka Poprad and from Czech builders during the four to five years from 1998. These are to meet the needs of a radically changed market, and will mainly comprise sliding-roof, sliding-wall, container flats and piggyback types. In June 1997 the first Type Sdgnss piggyback wagon was manufactured by Tatravagónka Poprad. By the end of 1997 28 such wagons were delivered with a further 32 following in the first half of 1998 at a total cost of some Kcs300 million.

A prototype of a new Type Rils wagon with fixed ends and sliding roof was purchased in 1998 from ŽOS Trnava. Rebuilt from a Type Res flat wagon, it is intended for carrying bulk and palletised goods. In October 1998 200 new four-axle Type Shimmns steel coil transporters were handed over by Tatravagónka Poprad.

In August 2000, ŽOS Trnava rolled out the first Type Hirrs four-axle twin-unit freight wagon, rebuilt in collaboration with Greenbrier in Germany from two Type Gbkks two-axle wagons. It was also agreed that 204 Type Rils and Rilns wagons with removable tarpaulin roofs and 450 Type Eas high-sided wagons for the transport of substrates would be rebuilt in collaboration with Ahaus-Altstätter Eisenbahn Cargo AG (AAE). The wagons will first be sold to AAE, then leased back and eventually purchased again by ŽSR.

By April 2001, 200 Type Eas 52 and Eas 53 wagons had been upgraded, followed by the modernisation of 250 Type Eas 11 by December of the same year. All three types now have an axleload capacity of 22.5 tonnes and a maximum speed of 100 km/h.

### Signalling and telecommunications

Automatic block signalling is in operation on 764 route-km, 20 per cent of the ŽSR system.

Following introduction of automatic block equipment on the 31 km section between Žilina and Považská Bystrica in October 1995, work switched to the 35 route-km from Považská Bystrica through Púchov to the Czech border. This scheme was completed by AŽD Bratislava and formally opened in February 2000 at a cost of Kcs505.9 million.

In mid-1997 ŽSR signed an agreement with Bell Canada, Noram Ltd and EDC to modernise its communications system. The US$10 million contract was due to be fulfilled within one year. Optical cable laying started between Košice and Žilina.

On 5 November 2001, Alcatel Slovakia won a contract to upgrade the ŽSR telecommunications network. Modernisation began in December 2001 and is scheduled for completion by the end of 2004. Work is being carried out in three stages: the first covers Bratislava–Zvolen–Košice–Čierna nad Tisou, the second Bratislava–Žilina–Košice and the last Vrútky–Banská Bystrica–Zvolen and Turčianske Teplice–Prievidza–Nitra–Nové Zámky–Štúrovo/Komárno.

The European Investment Bank is providing Kcs1.5 billion towards the cost of upgrading ŽSR's telecommunications subsidiary, ŽSR Telekomunikácie.

### Electrification

Over 40 per cent of the ŽSR network is electrified, with electric traction in 2000 handling 84.1 per cent of the railway's traffic. The Púchov–Žilina–Košice–Čierna nad Tisou main line with branches, the Plaveč–Prešov–Košice–Čaňa north-south axis and the 1,520 mm gauge Haniska–Trebišov–Kapušány (ŠRT) route are electrified at 3 kV DC, with the 25 kV 50 Hz AC system having been chosen for the remainder of the 1,435 mm gauge electrification. The only junction of the electrification systems is located at Púchov, 45 km southwest of Žilina.

The 1,000 mm gauge High Tatras system and the 750 mm gauge Trenčianska Teplá–Trenčianske Teplice route are electrified at 1.5 kV DC.

Work has been under way on the 25 kV 50 Hz AC electrification of the 120 km Šurany–Levice–Zvolen route: the first electrically powered train to Zvolen ran in August 1995. Two new substations were built in Kozárovce and Zvolen. Electrification of the 21 km Zvolen–Banská Bystrica route at 25 kV 50 Hz AC, postponed several times, is now scheduled for completion by 2005 at a cost of approximately Kcs1 billion.

Electric operation on the sinuous 56 km line between Plaveč and Prešov in the country's far east began on 1 June 1997. Started in May 1995, electrification work at 3 kV DC has been carried out by ELTRA Košice at a cost of Sk594 million. Also on 1 June 1997 electrically powered services commenced over the formerly non-electrified 11 km gap from Čaňa, south of Košice, to the Hungarian border, completely energising this important north-south corridor.

In 1998, work started on the 3 kV DC system of the 20.2 km single-track line between Čadca and the Polish border, which forms part of ŽSR's north-south transit corridor. The project will cost Sk620 million, including a new substation at Skalité. Infrastructure will be completely renewed and equipped with new signalling to allow through international passenger operation and intermodal traffic.

### Track

**Rail:** 65 kg/m Type R (1,611 km installed); 60kg/m Type UIC (27.2 km installed); 49 kg/m Type T and S (2,727 km installed); 44 kg/m Type A (300 km installed)
**Max axleload:** 22.5 tonnes (1,435 mm gauge); 24.5 tonnes (1,520 mm gauge)
**Min curve radius:** 350 m (main lines); 200 m (secondary routes)
**Sleepers:** Wood and concrete spaced 1,640-1,720 per km
**Fastenings:** Vossloh Sk1 12, 14
**Max gradient:** 2.7%

*UPDATED*

### Diesel locomotives (1,520 and 1,435 mm gauge)

| Class | Wheel arrangement | Power kW | Speed km/h | Weight tonnes | No in Service | First built | Builders Mechanical | Engine | Transmission |
|---|---|---|---|---|---|---|---|---|---|
| 701 | B | 147 | 40 | 22 | 10 | 1957 | ČKD | Tatra 930-51 | M ČKD |
| 702 | B | 147 | 40 | 24 | 2 | 1968 | ZTS Martin | Tatra 930-51 | M ČKD |
| 710 | C | 302 | 60 (30) | 42 | 26 | 1961 | ČKD | 12V 170DR | H ČKD |
| 720 | Bo-Bo | 551 | 60 | 61 | 3 | 1958 | ČKD | 6S 310DR | E ČKD |
| 725 | B-B | 515 | 70 (35) | 56.6 | 2 | 1962 | ČKD/ZTS | K12 170DR | H ČKD |
| 726 | B-B | 515 | 70 (35) | 56.6 | 5 | 1963 | ZTS Martin | K12 170DR | H ČKD |
| 721 | Bo-Bo | 551 | 80 | 74 | 121 | 1963 | ČKD | K6S 310DR | E ČKD |
| 731 | Bo-Bo | 880 | 70 | 72 | 11 | 1988 | ČKD | K6S 230DR | E ČKD |
| 735 | Bo-Bo | 926 | 90 | 64 | 41 | 1973 | ZTS Martin | 12PA 4 186 | E ČKD |
| 742 | Bo-Bo | 883 | 90 | 64 | 82 | 1977 | ČKD | K6S 230DR | E ČKD |
| 751 | Bo-Bo | 1,102 | 100 | 75 | 78 | 1964 | ČKD | K6S 310DR | E ČKD |
| 752 | Bo-Bo | 1,103 | 100 | 74 | 26 | 1969 | ČKD | K6S 310DR | E ČKD |
| 753 | Bo-Bo | 1,325 | 100 | 73.2 | 24 | 1968 | ČKD | K12V 230DR | E ČKD |
| 750 [1] | Bo-Bo | 1,325 | 100 | 71.7 | 47 | 1991 | ČKD | K12V 230DR | E ČKD |
| 754 | Bo-Bo | 1,460 | 100 | 74.4 | 26 | 1975 | ČKD | K12V 230DR | E ČKD |
| 770 | Co-Co | 993 | 90 | 114.6 | 30 | 1963 | ČKD/Dubnica | K6S 310DR | E ČKD |
| 771 | Co-Co | 993 | 90 | 115.8 | 50 | 1968 | SMZ/Dubnica | K6S 310DR | E ČKD |
| 770.8 [2] | Co-Co | 993 | 90 | 114.6 | 10 | 1983 | SMZ/Dubnica | K6S 310DR | E ČKD |
| 771.8 [2] | Co-Co | 993 | 90 | 114.6 | 9 | 1970 | Dubnica | K6S 310DR | E ČKD |
| 781 | Co-Co | 1,472 | 100 | 116 | 35 | 1966 | Lugansk | VSZ 14D 40 | E Kharkov |
| 781.8 [2] | Co-Co | 1,472 | 100 | 116 | 4 | 1966 | Lugansk | VSZ 14D 40 | E Kharkov |
| 755 [3] | Bo-Bo | 1,500 | 100 | 76 | 1 | 1997 | ČKD/Martinskă/Žos | 12PA4-185 | E ČKD |
| 772 [4] | Co-Co | 960 | 90 | 110 | 1 | 1998 | Martinská/Vagónka Trebišov | 8PA4-185M4 | E Martinská |
| 773 [4] | Co-Co | 1,300 | 100 | 112 | 9 | 1998 | ZTS-KV Dubnica | Cat 3512 DI-TA/2 | E Siemens |
| 736 [5] | Bo-Bo | 990 | 90 | 64 | 2 | 1998 | ŽOS Zvolen | Cat 3512 DI-TA | E Siemens |

*Note:* [1] A reconstructed Class 753 locomotive with electric 3,000 V heating
[2] Designed for the Haniska–Matovce 1,520 mm gauge line
[3] Rebuilt from Class 753, equipped with electronic control
[4] Rebuilt from Class 771, equipped with electronic and remote control
[5] Rebuilt from Class 735, equipped with electronic control

### Diesel railcars (1,520 and 1,435 mm gauge)

| Class | Cars per unit | Motor cars per unit | Motored axles/car | Power/car KW | No in service | First built | Builders Mechanical | Engine | Transmission |
|---|---|---|---|---|---|---|---|---|---|
| 811 | 1 | 1 | 2 | 180/237** | 29 | 1995 | VS | Liaz M1.2C640S | E ČKD† |
| 810 | 1 | 1 | 1 | 156 | 125 | 1975 | VS | Liaz ML634 | HM Praga |
| 810.8* | 1 | 1 | 1 | 156 | 2 | 1982 | VS | Liaz ML634 | HM ČKD |
| 812† | 1 | 1 | 1 | 257 | 1 | 2001 | VS | MAN D2866 LUH21 | HM Voith |
| 820 | 1 | 1 | 2 | 206 | 31 | 1963 | VS | Tatra T930-4 | H ČKD |
| 830 | 1 | 1 | 2 | 301 | 28 | 1949 | VS | ČKD 12V170DR | E ČKD |
| 850 | 1 | 1 | 2 | 515 | 25 | 1962 | VS | ČKD 12V170DR | H ČKD |
| 851 | 1 | 1 | 2 | 588 | 22 | 1967 | VS | ČKD 12V170DR | H ČKD |

*Note:* VS – Vagénka Studénka
* Designed for the Haniska–Matovce 1,520 mm gauge line
** First two prototypes equipped with Liaz M1.2C 640F 180 kW engine
† Rebuilt from Type Baafx trailer at ŽOS Vrútky and ŽOS Zvolen maintenance shops

---

## Železničná spoločnost as (ŽS)

Žabotova 12, SK-811 04 Bratislava

### Key personnel

Chairman of Supervisory Board: Dušan Pajdlhauser
Chairman: Andrej Egyed
First Under-Secretary: Pavol Kužma
Management Board
  Freight Traffic: Jozef Šimlovič
  Passenger Traffic: Jiří Jančík
  Rolling Stock: Miroslav Dzurinda
  Commercial Controlling: Pavol Gábor
  Finances: Anton Jaborek
  Marketing: Ján Dančej
  Strategy and Technical Development: Peter Červenka
  Control and Inspection: Peter Krcho
  Internal Relations: Ladislav Martinkovič
  Human Resources Management: Jozef Luha
  Communication: Miloš Čikovský

### Political background

ŽS is the joint-stock company established on 1 January 2002 to conduct the train operations of Slovakian Republic Railways (ŽSR). See the ŽSR entry for more details.

*NEW ENTRY*

# SLOVENIA

## Ministry of Transport and Communications

Presernova 23, SL-61000 Ljubljana
Tel: (+386 61) 125 22 85   Fax: (+386 61) 21 87 07

**Key personnel**
Minister: Anton Bergauer
State Secretary, Railways: S Hanžel

## Slovenian Railways (SŽ)

Slovenske Železnice
Kolodvorska ul 11, 1506 Ljubljana
Tel: (+386 61) 131 31 44   Fax: (+386 61) 133 41 84

**Key personnel**
Director General: Marjan Rekar
Assistant Director General, Infrastructure Development:
  Bogdan Zgonc
Directors
  Operations: Peter Rutar
  Freight and Passenger Marketing: Mario Škrinjar
  Infrastructure: Boris Zrimc
  Finance and Planning: Franc Hočevar
  Personnel, Administration and Legal Affairs:
    Igor Hauptman
  Rolling Stock: Vojko Kraševec
International Affairs Manager: Mirjam Kastelic
Press Officer: Olga Zvanut

Gauge: 1,435 mm
Route length: 1,201 km
Electrification: 489 km at 3 kV DC; 9.4 km at 25 kV 50 Hz AC; 0.7 km at 15 kV 16⅔Hz AC

### Political background

Slovenian Railways is part of the former Yugoslav network. Slovenia is a natural junction of transport routes which connect central and western Europe with the Near East or southern Europe. When part of the Yugoslav system, Slovenia's railways transported more than 22 million tonnes of freight and about 21 million passengers in inland and international traffic. However, in the early 1990s, the break-up of Yugoslavia and the ensuing war cut Slovenia's railway links with the former southern republics. This resulted in a drastic fall of Slovenian transport volume. This was reflected also in the reduction of the number of employees, which dropped from 15,206 in 1990 to 11,900 in 1993. By the end of 1996 the number had declined further to 9,737.

By the mid-1990s, the Slovenian economy was one of the best performers in the former Eastern Bloc, with growth of 4.8 per cent in 1995. This, combined with the restoration of normal political conditions in the region, boosted carryings, with SŽ freight traffic up to 13.8 million tonnes (2.9 billion tonne-km) in 1995, and passenger traffic at 13.3 million journeys and 595 million passenger-km. In 1996, passenger traffic continued to grow, rising to 13.7 million passenger journeys (613 million passenger-km), but freight traffic slipped back to 13.2 million tonnes (2.6 billion tonne-km).

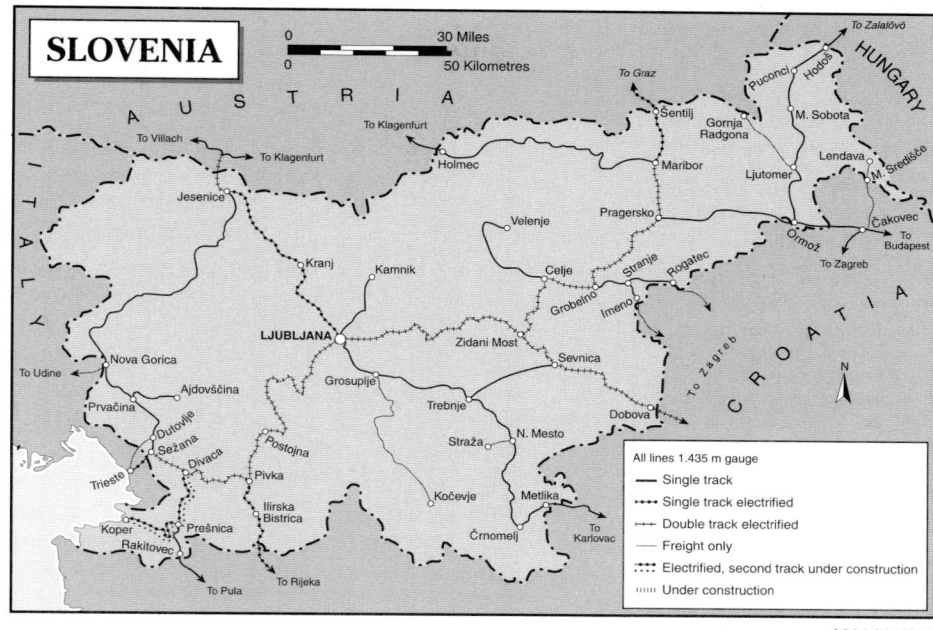

| Traffic (million) | 1995 | 1996 |
|---|---|---|
| Passenger journeys | 13.3 | 13.7 |
| Passenger-km | 595 | 613 |
| Freight tonnes | 13.8 | 13.2 |
| Freight tonne-km | 2,881 | 2,560 |

### Passenger operations

SŽ operates international passenger trains from the capital Ljubljana to Trieste in northern Italy (165 km) and Graz in Austria (246 km). Slovenia is also served by international trains linking neighbouring countries, such as the 'Simplon Express' (Zagreb–Ljubljana–Trieste–Venice–Geneva) and the Munich–Zagreb overnight service.

Domestically, the most important line is from Ljubljana to Maribor (278 km, two-hourly service), on which Fiat-built Class 310 Pendolino trainsets were introduced during 2000. Branded Inter City Solvenia (ICS), the new service replaced the former Želeni vak (green train) operation provided by German-built Class 711 dmus.

A cross-country diesel-worked route runs from Jesenice to Sežana (149 km). For its summer 2000 timetable, SŽ introduced a car-carrying service on this route, eliminating the need for motorists to use the difficult road over the Bohinjsko Pass.

### Freight operations

Freight carryings are rebounding following the restoration of peace in the Balkan region (see 'Political background'). SŽ's largest marshalling yard at Zalog outside Ljubljana has been modernised; GEC Alsthom and local supplier Iskra re-equipped the yard to raise sorting capacity from 1,500 to 2,500 wagons daily, using 39 classification tracks. Work was completed in mid-1997.

### Intermodal operations

SŽ operates container terminals in Ljubljana, Celje and Maribor and, together with the Port of Koper, the container terminal in Koper. Traffic figures for SŽ in 1996 were a total of 46,000 TEU, consisting of 16,000 TEU imports, 13,000 TEU exports and 17,000 TEU transit traffic.

There are hopes that Koper will become a major entry port for Austria and other parts of central Europe, served by feeder ships from a Mediterranean hub port; this route could save boxes from Asia between five and seven days in transit time, compared to landing at Rotterdam. Koper is only 20 km from the established port of Trieste in Italy, but operating costs are lower. Volumes passing through Koper grew rapidly in 1996, reaching 70,000 TEU, and were expected to reach 85,000 TEU in 1997; much of this traffic is moved by rail.

### New lines

SŽ awarded construction contracts in 1999 for a 25 km link from Murska Sobota to the Hungarian border near Hodoš; Hungarian Railways (MÁV) has built a 19 km line on its side of the frontier. Opened in May 2001, the combined link shortens the route for freight running between eastern Europe and the West and the port of Koper in the Adriatic. This substantially increases the importance of SŽ, for this link enables an important part of potential eastern European freight to go by sea (see 'Intermodal operations' above). Some of the funding for the €80 million project has been provided by the European Union under its PHARE programme.

In February 2001, the Slovenian and Italian governments agreed on the route through their countries of the European Union's Corridor 5 high-speed line linking Milan–Venice–Trieste–Ljubljana–Budapest–Kiev. Work is expected to start in 2005 with a target completion date of 2015.

### Improvements to existing lines

Projects include an upgrade of the Divaca–Koper route, including provision of a second track using a new alignment. However, use of part of the planned Trieste–Ljubljana high-speed line (see New lines) is being considered as an alternative. EU funding is also being provided to upgrade the line from the Austrian border at Jesenice to Ljubljana and on to Croatia via Dobova, which forms the SŽ portion of the 'Crete Corridor X'. The single-track section from Jesenice to Ljubljana is to be doubled.

In 1995, SŽ invited tenders for the renewal of overhead line equipment on sections of the Ljubljana–Sežana and Ljubljana–Zidani Most lines. A contract covering the supply of solid state interlocking equipment for the former line was placed with Siemens in 1999.

### Traction and rolling stock

In 1999 SŽ operated 95 electric and 101 diesel locomotives, 30 emu and 92 dmu sets, 225 hauled passenger cars (including six dining, 27 sleeping and four

*Newly built Class 312-0 'Desiro' two-car emu during trials at Siemens' test facility at Wildenrath, Germany (Ken Harris)*

couchette cars) and 7,273 freight wagons. Electric locomotives are of French and Italian origin while the bulk of the main line diesel fleet is formed by General Motors designs. Procurement of new electric locomotives is planned, with a 6,000 kW asynchronous motor type favoured.

During 2000 SŽ received three three-car Class 310 Pendolino tilting trainsets ordered from Fiat Ferroviaria in 1998. They are intended for intercity services between Ljubljana and Maribor. Purchase of a further eight sets for international services is likely. These will be dual-voltage units capable of operating on the 25 kV systems of neighbouring Croatia and Hungary.

In September 2000 SŽ received from Siemens the first of 10 two-section and 20 three-section 'Desiro' articulated emus for use on its Koper–Postojna and Ljubljana–Zidani Most routes. Designated Classes 312-0 and 312-1 respectively, the vehicles are due to replace Pafawag-built Class 311 and 315 emus.

The first five units were built at Siemens plants in Germany, while the remainder are being assembled at the Siemens-owned TVT Nova plant in Maribor.

### Electrification

Principal rail routes in Slovenia (Ljubljana–Maribor, Ljubljana–Jesenice, Ljubljana–Koper/Trieste) are electrified on the 3 kV DC system.

Electrification is planned of the Jesenice–Nova Gorica–Sezana line.

### Track

**Rail type and weight (kg/m):** UIC 60, 54, 49, 45
**Crossties (sleepers)**
Wood: 26 × 16 × 260 cm
Concrete: 31-24 × 21-18 × 260 cm
**Number per km**
 in plain track: 1,660
 in curves: 1,660
**Fastenings:** K, Pandrol, SKL 2
**Min curvature radius:** 250 m
**Max gradient:** 0.26%
**Max permissible axleload:** 22.5 tonnes

*Class 310 Pendolino tilting trainset, seen at Ljubljana shortly after delivery* (Quintus Vosman) 2001/0110186

#### Diesel locomotives

| Class | Wheel arrangement | Power kW | Speed km/h | Weight tonnes | No in service | First built | Builders Mechanical | Engine | Transmission |
|---|---|---|---|---|---|---|---|---|---|
| 661 | Co-Co | 1,440 | 112 | 114 | 7 | 1961 | GM | GM 567 | E GM |
| 642 | Bo-Bo | 452 | 80 | 64 | 21 | 1960 | DD | MGO | E B&L |
| 643 | Bo-Bo | 507 | 80 | 67.2 | 28 | 1967 | B&L/DD | MGO | E B&L |
| 644 | A1A-A1A | 1,357 | 120 | – | 25 | 1973 | Macosa | GM | E GM |
| 664 | Co-Co | 1,496 | 124 | – | 20 | 1984 | DD | GM | E GM |

B&L: Brissoneau & Lotz; DD: Djuro Djakovic; GM: General Motors

#### Electric locomotives

| Class | Wheel arrangement | Power kW continuous | Speed km/h | Weight tonnes | No in service | First built | Builders Mechanical | Electrical |
|---|---|---|---|---|---|---|---|---|
| 342 | Bo-Bo | 2,280 | 120 | 76 | 40 | 1968 | Ansaldo | Ansaldo |
| 362 | Bo-Bo-Bo | 3,400 | 120 | 112 | 17 | 1960 | Ansaldo | ASGEN |
| 363 | C-C | 2,830 | 125 | 114 | 38 | 1976 | Alsthom | Alsthom |

**UPDATED**

# SOUTH AFRICA

## Department of Public Enterprises

Private Bag X842, Pretoria 0001
Tel: (+27 12) 342 71 11   Fax: (+27 12) 342 72 24

**Key personnel**
Minister: Jeff Radebe

## Department of Transport

Strubenstreet, Forum Building, Pretoria
Tel: (+27 12) 45 72 60   Fax: (+27 12) 461 68 45

**Key personnel**
Minister: Dullah Omar
Director General of Transport: Khetso Ghordan

**UPDATED**

## Alfred County Railway

**Key personnel**
Directors: Allen Jorgensen, Charlie Lewis

**Freight operations**
Alfred County Railway is a privately owned common carrier operating in Alfred County.

## South African Rail Commuter Corporation Ltd (SARCC)

Private Bag X2, Sunninghill 2157
Tel: (+27 11) 804 29 00   Fax: (+27 11) 804 38 52

**Key personnel**
Chairman: J T M Edwards
Managing Director: Wynand P Burger
Chief Executive Officers
 Metro Rail: Zandile Jakavule
 Intersite Property Management: J Prentice
Senior Group General Managers
 Finance: Jakkie van Niekerk
 Communications: Mrs Connie Nkosi
 Management Services: Saag Jonker

Gauge: 1,065 mm
Length: operates over 2,228 km
Electrification: 3 kV DC

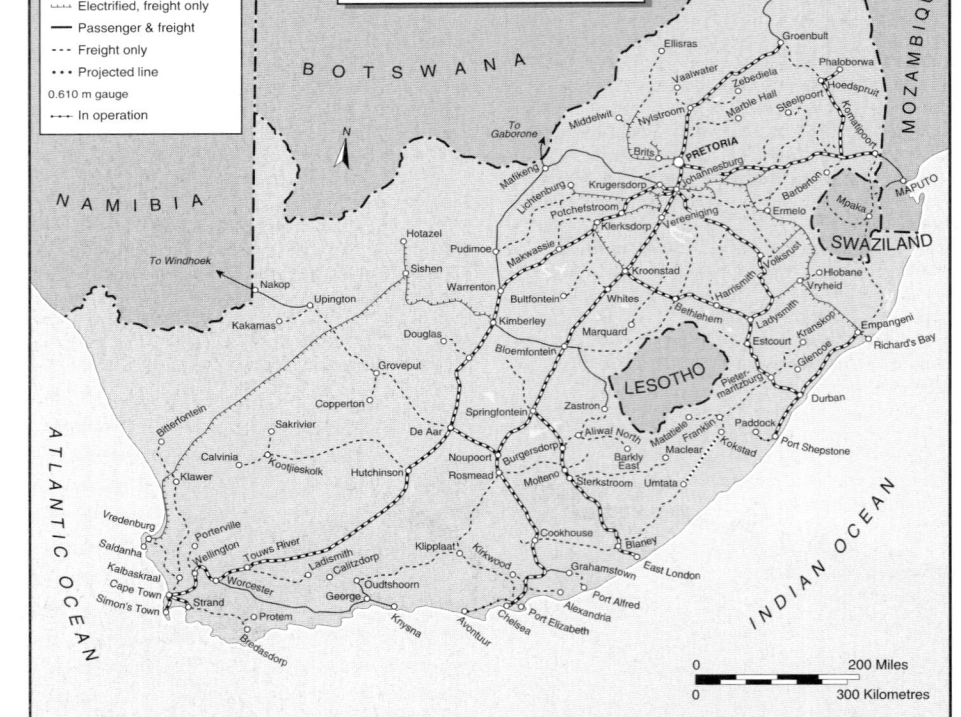

2001/0114308

### Political background

In 1990 SARCC took over the infrastructure and rolling stock of the country's suburban services, with Spoornet running them under contract for the first few years but SARCC taking over from 1995 onwards. The company is a wholly owned subsidiary of the Transnet holding

# South Africa/RAILWAY SYSTEMS

*Metro Rail emus leave Dal Josafat on the Cape Town network (Colin Boocock)* 0058829

company (see 'Political background' section in Spoornet entry).

Some stations have been transferred to SARCC ownership to encourage their commercialisation as a source of subsidiary revenue.

In 1996, discussions were under way with a view to making city authorities responsible for commuter services in their areas. Concessioning on the Argentinian model is anticipated, with between five and eight concessions likely.

## Organisation

SARCC's rail operations are branded 'Metro Rail'. This division of the company employed 10,357 people at the close of 1996. Services are operated in four metropolitan regions: Cape Town, Durban, Johannesburg and Pretoria.

Intersite is the division responsible for management and development of the company's property holdings. Its employee total at the close of 1996 was 80.

Overseeing the two divisions is SARCC's head office, employing about 40 people.

## Passenger operations

Metro Rail services operate around the larger coastal cities – Cape Town, Durban, Port Elizabeth and East London – and in the Johannesburg/Vereeniging/Pretoria metropolitan area.

In the newly stable political situation, patronage has started to grow again after declining substantially since the mid-1980s. This was largely due to strong competition from kombi-taxis and latterly the high level of violence prevalent on some commuter routes. From a peak of 638 million passenger journeys in 1985-86, traffic reached a low point of 373 million journeys in 1992-93, but has progressively grown again to reach 458 million in 1996-97 following successful efforts to counter politically motivated violence, which is now at an end.

## New lines

A dozen new lines or extensions are proposed to extend rail service to developing suburban areas and seven, totalling 61 km, have been accorded priority for detailed studies. Varying in length from 3 to 18 km, the seven are costed out in total at R2.4 billion.

A 7 km extension from Kathlehong to Kweisini, in the Gauteng district of Johannesburg, was due to open in March 2000.

## Improvements to existing lines

The government's programme of National Reconstruction and Development has identified good-quality and inexpensive rail service as an essential part of the process of improving conditions in the township areas surrounding major cities. Accordingly, SARCC is embarking on a 10-year R600 million investment programme to improve and extend its services. The rolling stock fleet will be rehabilitated, and new stations are planned at several locations where substantial residential or educational developments are under way.

The entire 2,228 km of electrified track has been surveyed to ascertain its condition, and a start made on rehabilitation of 69 km of overhead on the Natal South Coast. Uniquely, heavily corroded steel is being replaced by glass fibre structures.

## Traction and rolling stock

In 1998 the rolling stock fleet totalled 1,331 powered emu cars and 3,233 trailers. Apart from a few trains built in the 1980s, all stock is based on a design of 1957 vintage. Some R2.8 billion is to be spent on refurbishment of 4,000 cars in a 15-year programme. The aim is to raise comfort standards and reduce opportunities for vandalism.

Service improvements and the proposed extensions will require purchase of a further 300 cars, but the need to import technology and the devaluation of the rand has made such purchases problematic. In 1996, a R260 million loan from the Japanese government was being finalised for the purchase of new trains. In 1998 UK-based Interfleet Technology was retained to develop a specification for an initial five Class 9M 12-car trains to be procured under this arrangement. It was expected that an order for these would be placed in 1999.

## Signalling and telecommunications

In 1997, automatic block was being installed on 70 km from Pretoria to Gauteng.

### Rail Commuter Corporation electric multiple-units

| Class | Cars per unit | Motor cars per unit | Motored axles/car | Output/motor kW | Speed km/h | No of sets | First built | Builders Mechanical | Electrical |
|---|---|---|---|---|---|---|---|---|---|
| 5M | 11-14 | 3-4 | 16 | 220 | 100 | 350 (all series) | 1957 | UCW | GEC |
| 6M | 14 | 8 | 32 | 245 | 110 | 1 (prototype) | 1983 | Hitachi | Hitachi |
| 7M | 6 | 6 | 24 | 290 | 110 | 1 (prototype) | 1984 | MAN | Siemens/AEG/BBC |
| 8M | 6 | 6 | 24 | 245 | 110 | 8 | 1987 | Dorbyl | Hitachi |

# Spoornet

South African Railways
Umjanshi House, 30 Wolmarans Street, Johannesburg 2000 (Private Bag X47, Johannesburg 2000)
Tel: (+27 11) 773 87 57   Fax: (+27 11) 773 82 50
e-mail: Johanh@transnet.co.za
Web: http://www.spoornet.co.za

## Key personnel

Deputy Managing Director (Transnet): M Mkwanazi
Chief Executive: Z Jakavula
General Managers
   Marketing and Sales: (Vacant)
   Information Systems: Dr C R Jardine
   Specialist Businesses: H Evert
   Rail and Terminal Services: S Lushaba
   Engineering: B J van der Merwe
   Finance: H L van der Westhuizen
   Human Resources: A Mofokeng
   Restructuring and Joint Ventures: R Nair
   Planning and Technology: L Petkoon
Executive Business Managers: H M Mashele; L Miller
Executive Managers
   COALlink: Peet Cronjé
   Orex: H Green
   Corporate Affairs: Dr V V Mkhize

Gauge: 1,065 mm; 610 mm
Route length: 19,756 km; 314 km
Electrification: 5,040 km at 3 kV DC; 861 km at 50 kV AC; 2,298 km at 25 kV AC; 9 km dual-current (3 kV DC/25 kV AC)

## Political background

Spoornet is the largest division of Transnet, a state-owned company established in 1990 as a result of government policy to commercialise its transport business interests and deregulate the industry in South Africa. As well as its rail business, Transnet has port management, pipeline, road haulage and air carrier divisions.

*Spoornet 610 mm gauge Class 91 diesel locomotives on a freight service at Port Elizabeth (Marcel Vleugels)*
2001/0099134

*Four General Electric Class 34 locomotives form a heavy freight at Oudtshoorn (Colin Boocock)* 0058827

# RAILWAY SYSTEMS/South Africa

Since the mid-1980s the South African road transport industry has grown considerably to become a major competitor for rail. Initially road was an attractive mode for light manufacturing industries but more recently has made inroads into heavy manufacturing and certain sectors of the mining industry. In response Spoornet has restructured itself to provide integrated freight logistics solutions with the aim of maintaining its leadership in the heavy haul sector and repositioning its other freight and passenger transport businesses.

## Organisation

Recent restructuring has seen the centralisation of service planning and control in place of the previous geographical organisation, a move aimed at improving customer service. In 1996 the Two Streams Spoornet programme was introduced, separating the processes of marketing the company's logistics capabilities and its production but retaining customer orientation as the primary goal. Dedicated business units, COALlink and Orex, manage Spoornet's coal and iron ore traffic over the Richards Bay and Sishen–Saldanha lines respectively. The General Freight Services division is grouped into 15 industry-based segments.

Separate units manage Spoornet's Main Line Passenger Services and Blue Train business.

In a bid to help reduce the debt of Spoornet parent Transnet, reported to be R27 billion in 2000, a restructuring plan was announced. This would see the establishment of the company's main operational divisions as separate entities. A further restructuring was expected to follow a re-examination of core and non-core activities.

Since 1991, the Spoornet workforce has dropped from nearly 120,000 to 43,736 in March 1999. The South African Rail Commuter Corporation (Metrorail) business was divested in 1998.

## Finances (R million)

| Revenue | 1997-98 | 1998-99 |
|---|---|---|
| Passengers (including commuter) | 263.498 | 284.136 |
| Freight | 8,710.006 | 8,817.751 |
| Other income | 573.082 | 555.369 |
| Total income | 9,546.586 | 9,657.256 |
| **Expenditure** | | |
| Labour | 3,739.359 | 4,140.710 |
| Materials and services | 3,878.781 | 4,406.972 |
| Depreciation | 864.903 | 772.786 |
| Total operating costs | 8,483.043 | 9,320.468 |
| Operating surplus/(shortfall) | 1,063.543 | 336.788 |

| Traffic (million) | 1997-98 | 1998-99 |
|---|---|---|
| Freight tonnes | 186.8 | 182.7 |
| Freight tonne-km | 103,866 | 102,777 |
| Passenger journeys | 5.0 | NA |
| Passenger-km | 1,775 | 1,794 |

## Passenger operations

Spoornet is principally a freight operator, but its Main Line Passenger Services division runs some long-distance passenger trains, including several semi-luxury services. The company also operates the prestigious Blue Train on four routes: Pretoria–Cape Town; Pretoria–Victoria Falls (Zimbabwe); Cape Town–Port Elizabeth (The Garden Route); and Pretoria–Hoedspruit (Valley of the Olifants), Northern Province. Blue Train coaching stock has undergone a refurbishment and relaunch programme costing some R70 million. Reports in 1999 suggested the possible sell-off or concessioning of the Blue Train operation.

## Freight operations

In 1997-98 Spoornet carried 182.7 million tonnes of freight. This represented a fall of 2.2 per cent on the previous year's figure of 186.8 million tonnes.

In 2000, Spoornet was reported to be seeking strategic equity partners for its COALlink and Orex (iron ore) transport activities.

During FY97-98 a five-year contract worth R400 million was signed by Spoornet and Chrome Resources to convey up to 500,000 tonnes annually of ferrochrome to Richards Bay for export. The Intermodal Wholesale business segment reached agreement with Maersk Lines to convey containers between Gauteng and principal ports.

*Electrically hauled heavy coal train at Three Rivers* (Marcel Vleugels)

### Spoornet diesel-electric locomotives

| Class | Wheel arrangement | Power kW | Speed km/h | Weight tonnes | No in service | First built | Mechanical | Builders Engine | Transmission |
|---|---|---|---|---|---|---|---|---|---|
| 33-000 | Co-Co | 1,605/1,490 | 100 | 91 | | 1965 | GE | GE 7 FDL-12 | GE 761 A6 |
| 33-200 | Co-Co | 1,640/1,490 | 100 | 91 | 43* | 1966 | EMD | EMD 16-645-E | EMD D 29CC-7 |
| 33-400 | Co-Co | 1,605/1,490 | 100 | 91 | | 1968 | GE | GE 7 FDL-12 | 5 GE 761 A6 |
| 34-000 | Co-Co | 2,050/1,940 | 100 | 111 | | 1971 | GE | GE 7 FDL-12 | GE 5 GE 761 A13 |
| 34-200 | Co-Co | 2,145/1,940 | 100 | 111 | | 1971 | EMD | EMD 16-645-E3 | EMD 29B |
| 34-400 | Co-Co | 2,050/1,940 | 100 | 111 | | 1973 | GE | GE 7 FDL-12 | GE 5 GE 761 A13 |
| 34-500 | Co-Co | 2,050/1,940 | 100 | 111 | 388** | 1977 | GE | GE 7 FDL-12 | GE 5 GE 761 A13 |
| 34-600 | Co-Co | 2,245/1,940 | 100 | 111 | | 1974 | GM SA | EMD 16-645-E3 | EMD D 29B |
| 34-800 | Co-Co | 2,140/1,940 | 100 | 111 | | 1978 | GM SA | EMD 16-645-E3 | EMD 29B |
| 34-900 | Co-Co | 2,050/1,940 | 100 | 111 | | 1979 | GE | GE 7 FDL-12 | GE 5GE 761 A13 |
| 35-000 | Co-Co | 1,230/1,160 | 100 | 82 | | 1972 | GE | GE 7 FDL-8 | GE 5GE 764-C |
| 35-200 | Co-Co | 1,195/1,065 | 100 | 82 | 324† | 1974 | EMD/GM SA | EMD 8-645-E3 | EMD D 29CCBT |
| 35-400 | Co-Co | 1,230/1,160 | | 82 | | 1976 | GE | GE 7 FDL-8 | GE 5GE 764-C1 |
| 35-600 | Co-Co | 1,195/1,065 | 100 | 82 | | 1976 | GM SA | EMD 8-645-E3 | EMD D29 CCBT |
| 36-000 | Bo-Bo | 875/800 | 100 | 72 | 217†† | 1975 | GE | GE 7 FDL-8 | GE 5GE 764-C1 |
| 36-200 | Bo-Bo | 875/800 | 90 | 72 | | 1980 | GM SA | EMD 8-645-E | D29B |
| 37-000 | Co-Co | 2,340/2,170 | 100 | 125 | 85 | 1981 | GM SA | EMD 16-645E-3B | EMD D31 |
| 38-000 | Bo-Bo | 1,500/780 | 100 | 74 | 49 | 1993 | UCW | CAT 3508 | Siemens ABB/6 FRA 5252 |
| 91-000 | Bo-Bo | 52/480 | 50 | 44 | 16 | 1973 | GE | CAT D 379 | GE 5GE 778 |

\* Total for 33 Class
\*\* Total for 34 Class
† Total for 35 Class
†† Total for 36 Class

*Two Class 6E electric locomotives at the head of Spoornet's prestigious 'Blue Train'* (Wolfram Veith)

## Signalling and telecommunications

At the beginning of 1999 6,365 route-km was CTC-controlled, 3,530 km mechanically signalled and 609 km under local control.

In 1999 Webb Industries was awarded a contract to install GSM radio equipment on the Richards Bay–Ermelo line.

## Electrification

Electrification of the De Aar–Kimberley route is planned.

## Traction and rolling stock

At the start of 2000 the railway was operating 2,146 electric and 1,403 diesel locomotives, 1,851 passenger cars (including 72 catering vehicles and 525 miscellaneous including luggage vans, steam-heat coaches), and 123,750 wagons.

In 1999 Class 6E electric locomotives were the subject of a refurbishment programme using Agate traction control electronics supplied by Alstom.

**Type of braking**: Vacuum and air
**Type of coupler in standard use**: SAR M-type and S-type (AAR-compatible), AAR E-type and AAR F-type (rotary and non-rotary)

## Track

**Rail**: 60 kg (1,950 km), 57 kg (4,370 km), 48 kg (9,290 km), 40 kg (1,580 km), 30 kg (2,803.3 km) and 22 kg (99.7 km)
**Crossties (sleepers)**
PY/FY concrete 2,200 × 250 × 200 mm
P2/F4 concrete 2,057 × 203 × 200 mm
Steel 40 and 30 kg 2,060 × 260 × 115 mm
Wood  2,100 × 250 × 125 mm;  2,100 × 250 × 175/185 mm
**Fastenings**: Pandrol, Fist, E3131 chairs

### Spoornet electric locomotives

| Class | Wheel arrangement | Output kW continuous/ one hour | Speed km/h | Weight tonnes | No in service | First built | Builders Mechanical | Electrical |
|---|---|---|---|---|---|---|---|---|
| **3 kV DC** | | | | | | | | |
| 5E1 | Bo-Bo | 1,458 | 97 | 86 | 229 | 1963 | UCW | GEC |
| 6E | Bo-Bo | 2,252 | 105 | 89 | 42 | 1970 | UCW | GEC |
| 6E1 | Bo-Bo | 2,252 | 105 | 89 | 702 | 1969 | UCW | GEC |
| 8E | Bo-Bo | 704 | 75 | 81 | 82 | 1983 | UCW | 50 c/s Group |
| 10E | Co-Co | 3,090 | 90 | 125 | 50 | 1985 | UCW | Toshiba |
| 10E1 | Co-Co | 3,090 | 90 | 126 | 100 | 1987 | UCW | GEC |
| 10E2 | Co-Co | 3,330 | 100 | 126 | 25 | 1989 | UCW | Toshiba |
| 12E | Bo-Bo | 2,252 | 150 | 84 | 5 | 1963 | UCW | GEC |
| 17E | Bo-Bo | 2,252 | 105 | 90 | 140 | 1979 | UCW | GEC |
| 18E | Bo-Bo | 2,252 | 105 | 90 | 4 | 1979 | UCW | GEC |
| **25 kV AC** | | | | | | | | |
| 7E | Co-Co | 3,000 | 100 | 123 | 67 | 1978 | UCW | 50 c/s Group |
| 7EI | Co-Co | 3,000 | 100 | 125 | 50 | 1980 | Dorman Long | Hitachi |
| 7E2 (Series 1 and 2) | Co-Co | 3,000 | 88 | 126 | 64 | 1982 | UCW | 50 c/s Group |
| 7E3 (Series 1 and 2) | Co-Co | 3,000 | 100 | 124 | 85 | 1983 | Dorbyl | Hitachi |
| 11E | Co-Co | 3,900 | 90 | 168-172 | 45 | 1985 | GMSA | GM/ASEA |
| **50 kV AC** | | | | | | | | |
| 9E | Co-Co | 3,840 | 90 | 166 | 31 | 1978 | UCW | GEC |
| **Dual-voltage 3 kV DC/25 kV AC** | | | | | | | | |
| 14E | Bo-Bo | 4,080 | 140 | 92 | 3 | 1990 | SLM | 50 c/s Group |
| 14E1 | Bo-Bo | 4,000 | 140 | 97 | 10 | 1998 | UCW | 50 c/s Group |

Abbreviations: UCW: Union Carriage & Wagon

**Spacing**: 700 mm: 1,440/km; and 650 mm: 1,538/km
**Minimum curvature radius**: 90 m
**Max gradient**: 1.67%
**Max axleload**: 29 tonnes (locomotives); 26 tonnes (wagons)

# SPAIN

## Ministry of Development

Plaza de la Castellana 67, Nuevos Ministerios, E-28071 Madrid
Tel: (+34 91) 597 70 00   Fax: (+34 91) 597 85 02

### Key personnel
Minister: Francisco Alvarez Fernandez
Director General of Rail Transport: Manuel Niño

## Catalan Railways (FGC)

Ferrocarrils de la Generalitat de Catalunya
Av Pau Casals 24, 8è, E-08021 Barcelona
Tel: (+34 93) 366 30 00   Fax: (+34 93) 366 33 50
e-mail: mllevat@fgc.catalunya.net
Web: http://www.fgc.es

### Key personnel
Chairman: Antoni Herce Herce
Director: Miquel Llevat Vallespinosa
Operating Director: Albert Tortajada Flores
Technical Director: Josep Lluís Arques Patón
Administration Director: Lluís Huguet Viñallonga
Personnel Director: Josep Lluís Portabales Iglesias

Gauge: 1,435 mm (Catalunya i Sarrià line); 1,000 mm (Catalans and Ribes–Núria (Abt rack) lines)
Route length: 45 km; 139 km (Catalans) and 13 km (Ribes–Núria)
Electrification: 1,435 mm gauge: 45 km at 1.5 kV DC
1,000 mm gauge: 63, 12 and 35 km at 1.5 kV DC

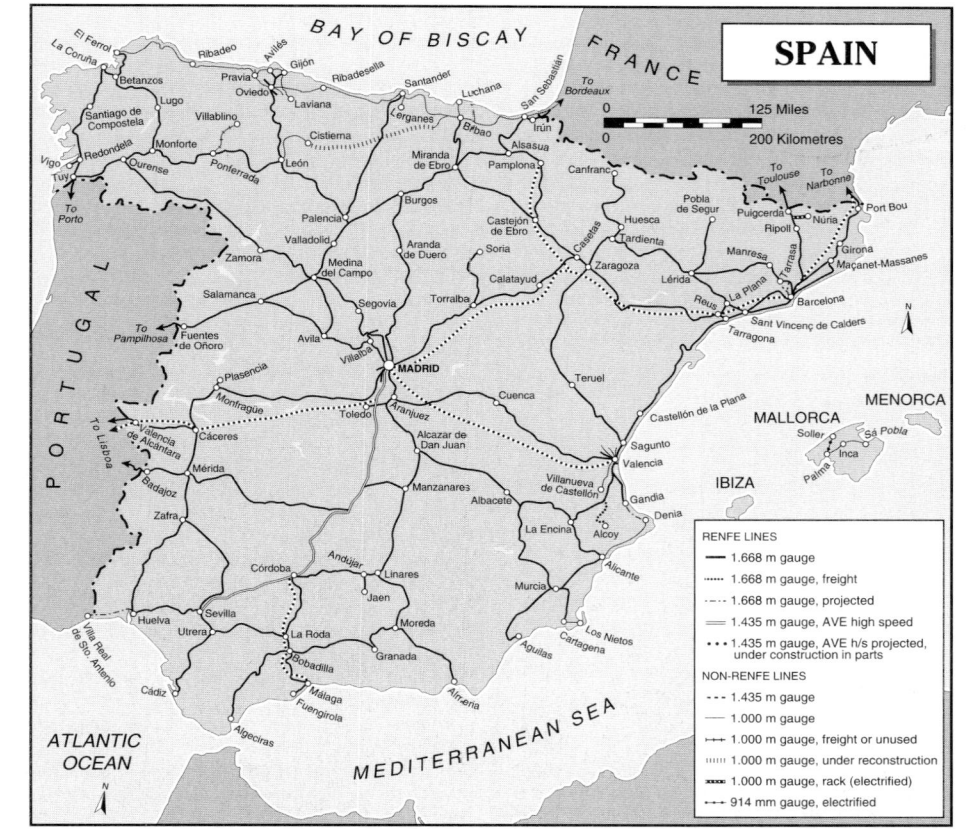

### Organisation

FGC was created in 1979 and operates local railways in the Barcelona area. Its 1,435 mm gauge Catalunya i Sarrià line runs from the Plaça Catalunya terminus in Barcelona to Sant Cugat where it forks to serve Tarrasa and Sabadell. A short branch (2 km) leaves the route at Gràcia within Barcelona itself to serve Avinguda Tibidabo.

FGC's 1,000 mm gauge Catalans line links Igualada and Manresa with Barcelona Plaça Espanya via Martorell. The 1,000 mm gauge Abt rack line between Ribes and Núria is isolated from the Catalans and Catalunya i Sarrià lines, connecting at Ribes with RENFE's 1,668 mm gauge Barcelona–La Tour de Carol route. FGC also operates one cable car system and four funicular railways.

At the end of 1999, FGC employed 1,396 staff.

| Traffic (million) | 1997 | 1998 | 1999 |
|---|---|---|---|
| Passenger journeys | 46.84 | 52.71 | 57.0 |
| Passenger-km | 551.86 | 594.73 | 627.2 |
| Freight tonnes | 0.782 | 0.543 | 0.651 |
| Freight tonne-km | 47.04 | 30.05 | 38.8 |

### Passenger operations

In 2000 the main FGC network carried 60.7 million passengers, an increase of 6.5 per cent on the previous year. Since 1996 passenger demand has grown by over 35 per cent.

### Freight operations

FGC is basically an intensive passenger service operator, but there are significant flows of common and potassium salts along the Catalans line. This traffic originates at mines served by the Súria and Sallent freight-only branches at the northwestern extremity of line and gains access to the port of Barcelona via another freight-only branch leaving the Catalans line at Sant Boi. Trains load up to 1,200 tonnes gross.

### Improvements to existing lines

Work in progress in 2000-01 included double-tracking to improve capacity on the Metro del Baix Llobregat line and remodelling and capacity improvements on the Metro del Vallès line.

In June 1999, FGC unveiled a plan to reinstate the 5 km rack railway between Monistrol, on the Manresa–Barcelona line, and the mountain tourist destination,

Montserrat. The line is expected to be reopened in 2002.

### Traction and rolling stock
At the start of 2000 FGC was operating two electric and 12 diesel locomotives, 70 emus, eight other passenger cars and 182 freight wagons.

In 1995 FGC ordered 20 Type 213 three-car emus from CAF, GEC Alsthom Transporte and ABB for the Catalans line. Derived from the Type 112 and similarly equipped with three-phase traction motors, the Type 213 entered service in February 1999 following electrification of the Martorell–Igualada section. The central trailer vehicle of the Type 213 has a low-floor section to facilitate boarding from low platforms.

The Ribes–Núria Abt rack line is operated with two 265 kW units of 1929 vintage for haulage of a fleet of eight passenger cars, and four two-car trainsets with two 181 kW motors per car, delivered in 1985 and 1995. A diesel locomotive for the Ribes–Núria line was delivered by Stadler/SLM/ABB in 1994, as were two railcar trailers from GEC Alsthom Transporte for the Catalans line. Authorisation to procure two new trainsets for the Ribes–Núria rack line was given in May 2001.

In 2000 an order was placed with Stadler Rail for five Type Beh 2/6 rack versions of the company's GTW lightweight vehicle for use on the reinstated Monserrat line.

Eight Class 400/500 emus have been sold to Cuban Railways.

Two three-car Class 3000 dmus rendered surplus by electrification of the Martorell–Igualada line in 1999 were sold to Ferrocarriles de la Generalitat Valenciana.

In May 2001 the purchase was authorised of six new trains for Metro del Vallès services.

### Signalling and telecommunications
The Catalunya i Sarrià line has ATP and CTC in operation along its entire length. Installation of ATO is planned for the Barcelona urban area (between Plaça Catalunya, Sarrià and Avinguda Tibidabo), to enable an appreciable increase in train service frequency, especially in the peak hours. The aim was to have 36 trains an hour departing Plaça Catalunya by 1997, a 20 per cent increase.

The Catalans line is equipped with the DIMFAP trainstop system between Barcelona and Manresa and between Martorell and Igualada (98 km).

Satellite tracking using the GPS system is now operational on all freight-only lines, and also on the Martorell–Igualada line.

### Electrification
Electrification of the Martorell–Igualada branch (35 km) of the Catalans line was commissioned in February 1999. Budgeted at Pta1.2 billion, this project was the major new scheme for the main FGC network covered by the funding agreement signed in 1995.

### Track
**Rail:** 1,000 mm gauge: UNE 45 kg/m; UIC 54 kg/m. Abt rack line only: 20 kg/m
1,435 mm gauge: UIC 54 kg/m
**Sleepers:** Wood 2,400 × 240 × 140 mm*; and 2,000 × 230 × 140 mm
Concrete 2,400 × 300 × 200 mm*; and 1,900 × 260 × 209 mm
**Fastenings:** Direct or indirect elastic and direct rigid with ribbed plate on wooden sleepers
**Min curvature radius:** 150 m*; 100 m
**Max gradient:** 4.4%*; 2.5%
**Max axleload:** 20 tonne*; 15 tonne
* Catalunya i Sarrià line. Other dimensions refer to Catalans line

*Class 213 emu for the metre-gauge Catalans line* 0045998

*Two- and three-car class M211/T281/T291 Catalans line emus at Manresa Alta (D Trevor Rowe)* 0016436

#### Diesel locomotives

| Class | Wheel arrangement | Power kW | Speed km/h | Weight tonnes | No in service | First built | Builders Mechanical | Engine | Transmission |
|---|---|---|---|---|---|---|---|---|---|
| **Catalans line** | | | | | | | | | |
| 700/1,000 | Bo-Bo | 570 | 70 | 44 | 5 | 1955 | Alsthom | Alsthom | E Alsthom |
| 700/1,000 | Bo-Bo | 590 | 70 | 48 | 3 | 1965 | Alsthom | Alsthom | E Alsthom |
| 254 | Co-Co | 1,200 | 90 | 79 | 3 | 1990 | Meinfesa | GM 645 E3C | E GM/Cenemesa |
| **Ribes–Núria line** | | | | | | | | | |
| D9 | B | 300 | 37 | 23 | 1 | 1994 | Stadler | Daimler-Benz 12 V 183 TA12 | E ABB |

#### Electric locomotives

| Class | Wheel arrangement | Line voltage | Output kW | Speed km/h | Weight tonnes | No in service | First built | Builders Mechanical | Electrical |
|---|---|---|---|---|---|---|---|---|---|
| **Ribes–Núria abt rack line** | | | | | | | | | |
| E | C | 1,500 DC | 135 | 30 | 23 | 3 | 1929 | SLM | BBC |

#### Electric multiple-units

| Class | Cars per unit | Motor cars per unit | Motored axles/car | Output/motor kW | Speed km/h | No in service | First built | Builders Mechanical | Electrical |
|---|---|---|---|---|---|---|---|---|---|
| **Llobregat–Anoia line** | | | | | | | | | |
| M211/T281/T291 | 3 | 1 | 4 | 276 | 90 | 7 | 1987 | Macosa | Alsthom |
| M211/T291 | 2 | 1 | 4 | 276 | 90 | 3 | 1987 | Macosa | Alsthom |
| M213/T283 | 3 | 2 | 4 | 180 | 90 | 20 | 1999 | CAF/Alstom | Adtranz |
| **Barcelona–Vallés line** | | | | | | | | | |
| M111/T181 | 3 | 2 | 4 | 276 | 90 | 20 | 1983 | MTM/Alsthom | Alsthom |
| M112/TM122/T182 | 4 | 3 | 4 | 180 | 90 | 16 | 1995 | CAF | ABB |
| **Ribes–Núria abt rack line** | | | | | | | | | |
| A | 2 | 2 | 2 | 181 | 37 | 4 | 1985 | GEC Alsthom/SLM | ABB |

## Euskotren

Eusko Trenbideak/Ferrocarriles Vascos SA (ET/FV)
Calle Atxuri 6, E-48006 Bilbao
Tel: (+34 94) 433 95 00   Fax: (+34 94) 433 60 09
Web: http://www.jet.es/euskotren/

### Key personnel
President: C Garcia
Secretary-General: L F Escudero
Controller: J A Crucelegui
Technical Secretary: C Sarachu
Directors
   Vizcaya Region: V Ayarza
   Guipuzcoa Region: A Gagarain
Commercial: O Gomez
Works and Maintenance: J A Gorostiza
Organisation and Human Resources: J Ortega

Gauge: 1,000 mm
Route length: 202 km
Electrification: 202 km at 1.5 kV DC

### Political background
The Bilbao-San Sebastián (Donostia) line, the Bilbao suburban railways and branches formerly operated by FEVE were transferred in 1979 to a local railway administration controlled by the Basque government.

### Passenger operations
In 1996 ET/FV adopted the name Euskotren for marketing purposes and unveiled a 1996-2000 strategic plan aiming to boost its share of the Basque passenger transport market from 29 per cent to 46 per cent. This was to be achieved largely through a Pta27.284 million investment plan concentrating on infrastructure improvements.

In mid-1998 Euskotren introduced two new long-distance services: the EuskoPullman, linking Bilbao, San Sebastián and Hendaye with three other intermediate stops; and the InterCity, which also operates between Bilbao and San Sebastián, with seven intermediate stops.

### New lines
A 1.2 km single-track extension of the Bilbao-Lezama route was completed in 1994, taking the railway into the centre of Lezama from its previous terminus in the La Cruz district of the town. The extension has been built to allow for a further 3.4 km of new construction to Larrabetzu, and the two former stations at Derio have been replaced by a single new facility. A new station at Elotxelerri-Loiu is planned.

*Bilbao metro*
A major portion of ET/FV's former Bilbao San Nicolás-Plentzia suburban line is now part of Line 1 of the Bilbao metro, connected to a new underground route from San Inazio to Casco Viejo opened in 1995. Line 1 was scheduled to be extended to Bolueta (and an interchange with ET/FV's Bilbao-San Sebastián route) during 1997, and eventually reach Basuari.

At Casco Viejo, Line 1 of the Bilbao metro was to eventually have an interchange with an ET/FV Bidarte-Lezama line formed of the existing Bilbao-Lezama route (which is to be upgraded) and a new line to Bidarte connected by a tunnel between Bilbao Calzadas and Bilbao San Nicolás. At present the respective termini of the Lezama and Plentzia routes, these two stations are to be replaced by the ET/FV facility at Casco Viejo, which will house the control centre for the Bidarte-Lezama route.

### Improvements to existing lines
The Basque government produced a railway investment plan for 1994-99 which, from a total of Pta51.782 billion, has allocated Pta19.387 billion for infrastructure, Pta2.585 billion for electrification and Pta3.686 billion for signalling. The plan makes provision for strengthening power supplies and double-tracking the following sections: Herrera-Molinao; Rentería-Oiartzun; Oiartzun-Gaintzurizketa; Landetxe-Belaskoenea; Amorebieta-Euba; Lasarte-Amara; and Axpe-Sukarrieta. The railway is to be covered over at Anoeta, Amara and Durango, and on certain portions of the route between Anoeta and Amara. Station works are to take place at Molinao, Irún Colón, Galdakao and Bermeo.

Many of these schemes and the projects associated with construction of the Bilbao metro also feature in ET/FV's 1996-2000 strategic plan and the Basque government's 1996-98 'Euskadi XXI' development plan. The latter was published in 1996, costed at Pta295 billion.

*Bilbao-San Sebastián route*
In recent years, traffic has increased significantly on this route. In 1992, 5.1 million passengers were conveyed, prompting ET/FV to announce a Pta4 billion upgrading and modernisation plan which began in 1993. The plan included double-tracking from Bilbao Atxuri to the junction with the Bermeo branch at Amorebieta, plus the 4.5 km Lemoa-Amorebieta portion.

Widening the Lemoa-Amorebieta section to two tracks has cost Pta1.3 billion and involved 2.1 km of new alignment, a new station at Amorebieta-Etxano, two new road overbridges, a new bridge over the River Arratia for the extra track and a new deck for the existing bridge over the River Ibaizábal.

### Traction and rolling stock
The railway operates seven electric and three diesel locomotives, 62 electric multiple-units, 10 diesel multiple-units, 98 coaches and 23 wagons.

The 1994-99 investment plan allocates Pta6.268 billion for rolling stock and ET/FV may order up to 11 UT400 sets within a budget of Pta3.2 billion. The purchase of 10 trailer cars for the UT200 fleet is anticipated.

Rolling stock workshops and stabling facilities are allocated Pta4.78 billion in the 1994-99 investment plan, which anticipates renovation of existing facilities at Luchana and construction of new facilities in the San Sebastián area.

*Type UT300 electric multiple-unit at San Sebastián forming a service from Hendaye (Bryan Philpott)*
0023699

### Signalling and telecommunications
To raise capacity, the 1994-98 investment plan recommended installation of bidirectional signalling on all ET/FV routes, provision of electric interlocking at all stations and crossings, and installation of CTC throughout the network. All points would be motored, ground-to-train radio installed and an ATC/ATS system introduced.

## Spanish Narrow-Gauge Railways (FEVE)

Ferrocarriles Españoles de Vía Estrecha
General Rodrigo 6, Parque de las Naciones, E-28003 Madrid
Tel: (+34 91) 453 38 00    Fax: (+34 91) 453 38 25
e-mail: info@feve.es
Web: http://www.feve.es

### Key personnel
President: Eugenio Damboriena
Director General: Juan de la Cruz Pacheco
Deputy Director General: Juan Carlos Albizuri Higuera
Secretary General: Ignacio González Arrate
Directors
  Rolling Stock: Juan Carlos Menoyo
  Economy, Finance and Personnel: Miguel Pérez Pérez
  Infrastructure: Juan de la Cruz
  Operations: José Luis Pello
  Communications: Aurora Moya Rodríguez

Gauge: 1,000 mm
Route length: 1,267 km
Electrification: 337.4 km at 1.5 kV DC

### Political background
FEVE is a state-owned company established in 1965 to operate Spain's extensive network of narrow-gauge railways. Operation of several of these systems has since been transferred to local public operators, namely those established by the regional governments of Catalonia, Valencia, Majorca and the Basque country.

Having lived a hand-to-mouth existence throughout most of its history, FEVE eventually signed a contract programme with the government in 1997 covering the period 1997-2001. Investments are financed under the government's Infrastructure Plan, the current plan in force covering 2000-07.

The León—Guardo line is independently financed by the regional government of Castilla y León.

### Organisation
The FEVE system comprises two main routes: Ferrol–Bilbao; and Bilbao–León (the La Robla line). In addition, FEVE operates the 19 km Cartagena—Los Nietos passenger line on the Mediterranean coast.

Structurally FEVE is organised as eight divisions covering: general secretariat; economics/finance; human resources; infrastructure; operations; traffic management; rolling stock; and communications and presidential functions. The presidency, general secretariat and some of the divisions are located in Madrid. The company employs around 2,000 staff.

**Traffic** (million) | 2000
--- | ---
Passenger journeys | 12
Passenger-km | 218.0
Freight tonnes | 3.2
Freight tonne-km | 451.4

### Passenger operations
FEVE provides passenger services in the provinces of Asturias and Cantabria as well as in Vizcaya, where the Bilbao—Balmaseda line alone carries more than 1.8 million passengers annually. Passenger services are also provided on León—Guardo and Ferrol—Ortiguiera routes. The Bilbao—León line has been partially closed to passenger traffic since 1991 due to track conditions but was to be reopened throughout on completion of rehabilitation work, expected in 2002.

FEVE also operates the 10-car 'Transcantábrico' land-cruise train on week-long trips from Santander to the west coast for connections to Santiago de Compostela and back. The trainset is available for private hire out of season, and has been used in conjunction with university seminars and other congresses in the area. In 2000 FEVE introduced a second set of Transcantábrico vehicles in the form of 11 coaches refurbished in its own workshops.

### Diesel locomotives

| Class | Wheel arrangement | Power kW | Speed km/h | Weight tonnes | No in service | First built | Builders Mechanical | Engine | Transmission |
|---|---|---|---|---|---|---|---|---|---|
| 1000 | Bo-Bo | 625 | 70 | 48 | 9 | 1954 | Alsthom | SACM-MGO V12 | *E* Alsthom |
| 1050 | Bo-Bo | 680 | 70 | 48 | 14 | 1954 | Alsthom | SACM-MGO V12 | *E* Alsthom |
| 1600 | Bo-Bo | 1,177 | 90 | 58 | 14 | 1982 | MTM | SACM-MGO V16 | *E* Alsthom |
| 1650 | Bo-Bo | 1,177 | 90 | 60 | 10 | 1985 | MTM | SACM-MGO V16 | *E* Alsthom |
| 1400 | B-B | 883 | 60 | 56 | 4 | 1964 | Henschel | SACM-MGO V12 | *H* Voith |
| 1500 | B-B | 772 | 80 | 56 | 10 | 1965 | GECO | Caterpillar | *E* GECO |
| 1300 | C | 207 | 28 | 33.5 | 4 | 1964 | SECN | Rolls-Royce | *M* Yorkshire |
| 1300 | C | 161 | 28 | 33.5 | 9 | 1964 | Westinghouse | Rolls-Royce | *M* Yorkshire |

### Diesel railcars or multiple-units

| Class | Cars per unit | Motor cars per unit | Motored axles/car | Power/motor kW | Speed km/h | No in service | First built | Builders Mechanical | Engine | Transmission |
|---|---|---|---|---|---|---|---|---|---|---|
| 2500 | 2 | 2 | 2 | 250 | 80 | 1* | 1987 | MTM | Pegaso | *E* ABB-MTM |
| 2400 | 3 | 2 | 2 | 228 | 80 | 10 | 1983 | MTM | MAN | *E* BBC |
| 2400 | 2 | 2 | 2 | 228 | 80 | 15 | 1985 | MTM | MAN | *E* BBC |
| 2300 | 2 | 2 | 2 | 154.5 | 80 | 24 | | CAF/Macosa | Pegaso | *H* Voith |
| 2300 | 1 | 1 | 2 | 154.5 | 80 | 7 | | Babcock | | *H* |
| 2200 | 1 | 1 | 4 | 220 | 75 | 6 | 1959 | Esslingen | Bussing | *H* ZF |

* Prototype

### Electric railcars or multiple-units

| Class | Cars per unit | Motor cars per unit | Motored axles/car | Output/motor kW | Speed km/h | No in service | First built | Builders Mechanical | Electrical |
|---|---|---|---|---|---|---|---|---|---|
| 3500 | 2 | 1 | 4 | 4 × 121 | 80 | 2 | 1981 | CAF | AEG/GEE |
| 3500 | 3 | 1 | 4 | 4 × 121 | 80 | 6 | 1984 | CAF | AEG/GEE |
| 3500 | 3 | 1 | 4 | 4 × 121 | 80 | 13 | 1981 | CAF | AEG/GEE |
| 3800 | 2 | 1 | 4 | 4 × 119 | 80 | 16 | 1992 | CAF | AEG/GEE |

## Freight operations

Between 1995 and 2000 FEVE freight traffic increased by 114 per cent. Principal commodities carried are steel products and coal. In recent years FEVE has invested in improving access to ports such as those at Avilés, Gijón and Santander.

## Improvements to existing lines

Investment to improve infrastructure for Asturias region suburban services has included Pta272 million for the Gijón-Pola de Laviana route and Pta900 million allocated to upgrading the Oviedo–Pravia–San Esteban and Gijón–Pravia–Cudillero routes in 1996.

On the Oviedo–Santander route, the station layout at El Berrón has been remodelled at a cost of Pta80 million. In 1996 the Cartagena–Los Nietos route was assigned investment of Pta150 million, and FEVE routes into Ferrol and León Pta150 million and Pta100 million respectively.

Thanks to the new long-term financing agreement with the state, FEVE will be able to reopen the Gijón–El Ferrol line, from which services were withdrawn because of poor track. Pta1.5 bilion has been made available, with Cudillero–Ribadeo already reopened in 1998.

The León–Balmesada route is being upgraded by 2001 at a cost of Pta6.9 billion. The Guardo–Bedcedo section will be reopened as part of the project.

## Traction and rolling stock

At the end of 1999 FEVE operated 65 diesel locomotives, 21 electric and 50 diesel trainsets, 13 diesel railcars, 21 hauled passenger cars and 1,008 freight wagons.

FEVE has been refurbishing its dmu and emu fleet. Class 2300 dmus have been rebuilt to become Class 2600 dmus and Class 3600 emus under an extensive modernisation programme that covers 21 two-car and five single-car units; 27 Class 2400 demus have been refurbished, including provision of new engines; 22 Class 3500 three-car emus used on Bilbao suburban services have been refurbished by Temoinsa; and 16 Class 3800 emus based in the Gijón area have been subjected to interior modernisation.

In 2000 FEVE embarked on a programme to repower Class 1600 and 1650 diesel locomotives with Caterpillar 3512-B engines in place of the original SACM-MGO units. Also proposed is the reconstruction of 10 Class 1000 and 1500 diesel locomotives into electric locomotives to meet haulage demands on FEVE's growing electrified network.

**Type of coupler in standard use:** Alliance
**Type of braking:** Air and vacuum

## Signalling and telecommunications

In 2000 FEVE announced that it was to extend automatic block signalling, automatic train protection and CTC to all routes under a Pta1.5 billion investment programme in safety improvements.

## Electrification

Electrification of the 74.4 km Langreo line from Gijón to Pola de Laviana was completed in 1994 at a total cost of Pta1.2 billion. Electrification of the Oviedo—Pola de Siero section of the Santander–Oviedo route has also been undertaken.

In conjunction with the Bilbao authorities, FEVE has electrified its Bilbao—Balmaseda line (33 km) and installed double track on the 3.6 km between Zaramillo and Aranguren.

## Track

**Rail:** 35 kg/m, 45 kg/m and 54 kg/m
**Sleepers:** Concrete monobloc; and timber 2,000 × 240 × 130 mm
**Sleeper spacing:** 1,500/km plain track, 1,600/km in curves
**Min curvature radius:** Main line 100 m
**Average curvature radius:** 250 m
**Max gradient:** 3.6% between Cartegena and Los Nietos
**Max permissible axleload:** 15 tonne
**Longest tunnel:** 4 km, La Florida, between Gijón and Pola de Laviana

---

# Railway Infrastructure Authority (GIF)

Gestor de Infraestructuras Ferroviarias (GIF)
Madrid

## Political background

GIF was established as Spain's rail infrastructure authority to take responsibility for the construction of new lines, with the possibility that all state-owned lines might eventually be transferred to its control. At the start of 1998 GIF's capital was Pta91 billion; this was expected to rise to Pta250 billion by 2000. For the present, the government remains sole shareholder.

GIF's principal current responsibility is the Madrid-Barcelona-French border high-speed line. Once completed, this will be managed by GIF, which will allocate track paths and recover costs by levying access charges. The national development ministry will select and plan all future high-speed projects, which GIF will implement and manage.

## New lines

*Madrid–Barcelona high-speed line*
The original cost of the country's first high-speed line between Madrid and Seville, opened in 1992, had been calculated at Pta75 billion, although the final cost turned out to be Pta262.5 billion, excluding rolling stock. This drastic cost overrun has considerably influenced plans for the Madrid–Barcelona high-speed link, which is to be constructed in stages. The new route is likely to reach the Barcelona area from the northwest via Martorell and serve a new station at La Sagrera within the city before continuing onwards to the French border and Narbonne. The Madrid terminus of the new line would be Atocha, the present and future hub of all 1,435 mm gauge routes serving the city.

By the end of 1998 work was under way over half of the 760 route-km line. Madrid–Lleida is expected to be completed by 2002, allowing Talgo Pendular trainsets to cut the Madrid-Barcelona journey time initially to 4 hours 40 minutes and to 2 hours 30 minutes when the Lleida-Barcelona section is completed in 2004.

The first two sections of the Madrid-Barcelona high-speed line were initially conceived to relieve serious operating bottlenecks on the existing network and are to be built with sleepers allowing for conversion from 1,668 mm gauge to the 1,435 mm gauge of the Spanish high-speed system. Until the opening of the remainder of the Madrid-Barcelona high-speed route, the Calatayud-Ricla and Zaragoza-Lleida sections are to be used by 1,668 mm gauge trains travelling at up to 220 km/h.

The new Madrid–Barcelona route is to be engineered for a maximum speed of 350 km/h throughout, with a minimum curve radius of 6,000 m, 4.5 m between track centres and a maximum gradient of 2.5 per cent. Electrification and signalling will follow Madrid–Seville practice and RENFE is aiming for a Madrid-Barcelona journey time of 2 hours 30 minutes (less than half that of the fastest train to date) with an average speed of 242 km/h over the 605 km distance.

The government has undertaken to fund Pta250 billion of the estimated Pta1,000 billion cost (1997 figures) of the project using revenues from the sale of state-owned industries. A further Pta150 billion will come from the EU's Cohesion Fund, with track access charges paying for the remainder of the scheme's cost.

*Barcelona–Narbonne high-speed line*
The Madrid-Barcelona-Narbonne-Montpellier high-speed axis featured amongst the 11 infrastructure projects selected to receive a total of ECU68.5 billion by 2010 at the 1994 Corfu summit of European ministers. In 1995 RENFE and SNCF formed a *Groupement Européen d'Intérêt Economique* known as SEM (*Sud Europa Mediterraneo/Sud Europe Méditerranée*) to carry forward the project for a high-speed line linking Barcelona with Narbonne. The joint venture will be responsible for development of the project and will oversee construction of the 280 km line, scheduled to open in 2004. Connecting with SNCF's TGV Méditerranée high-speed line at Montpellier, the new route will permit Barcelona-Paris journey times of around 4 hours 30 minutes, and will be used by freight trains between Barcelona and Perpignan operating at up to 160 km/h.

The total cost of the Spanish portion has been estimated at Pta170 billion and SEM's financial and economic studies for the project were to include the feasibility of placing the construction and operation of the route in the hands of a private-sector concessionaire. It was anticipated that provision would be made for the concessionaire to receive financial support from the Spanish and French governments and the European Union.

In 1995 the Spanish and French governments signed an agreement covering the international Figueras-Perpignan section, including an 8 km tunnel under the Pyrenean chain at the Col du Perthus, as SEM arrived at an outline design for the route. By early 1996, SEM was updating earlier technical studies undertaken by Catalan Railways (FGC) from 1986 at the behest of the Catalan government, and it was hoped to revise earlier environmental impact studies by the end of 1996 with a view to defining a Barcelona-Narbonne alignment in 1997. FGC's studies had considered a route engineered for a maximum speed of 250 km/h. It was expected that trains would run at 300 km/h between Barcelona and Girona, at 250 km/h through Girona and at 350 km/h to the French border. Work is expected to start on the Barcelona-French border section in 2000.

*Madrid–Valencia high-speed line*
In 1998 it was announced that feasibility studies and final route selection would be completed during 1999 on a new high-speed line linking Madrid and Barcelona at an estimated cost of Pta400 billion. This option would involve 360 km of new construction routed via Albacete and following existing routes between Albacete and Valencia. For the first 119 km, trains would make use of the existing AVE line between Madrid and Seville. A Madrid-Valencia journey time of 2 hours 33 minutes is anticipated. Significantly, this line would attract 5.6 million passengers per year, compared with 2.09 million on the Madrid-Seville line. Capital costs would be recovered from revenues within 20 years, leaving a 30-year concession-holder with 10 years of potentially profitable operation. Spurs giving access to Alicante, Cartagena and Murcia would generate similar benefits.

*Other high-speed projects*
In addition to the the Basque Y between Irún, Vitoria and Bilbao and the Zaragoza-Basque Y link, the revised PDI infrastructure plan makes provision for 1,435 mm gauge high-speed lines between Madrid and Valencia (with a branch to Albacete) and Madrid and Valladolid. The latter, along with the V-shaped Vitoria-Bilbao portion of the Basque Y, is intended to be built to 1,668 mm gauge for later conversion to 1,435 mm gauge. Existing infrastructure between Valladolid and Vitoria is to be upgraded. RENFE has asked for work on this line, known as the Guadarrana Deviation, to start as soon as possible. The cost of the scheme, which will be engineered for 220 km/h, is Pta200 billion. Construction will take four years, and completion of the project will enable RENFE to compete with parallel roads.

With a view to starting construction of the Madrid–Valladolid and Vitoria-Bilbao routes in 1997, initial environmental appraisals were carried out in 1994. A 1996-98 infrastructure investment programme published by the Basque government in 1996 allocated Pta2.370 billion to the Basque Y project, but did not anticipate construction work starting before 2000. The Basque Y would take some 10 years to complete at an estimated cost of Pta400 billion; the project was allocated Pta150 million of central government funding in 1995 and Pta100 million in 1996.

The revised PDI infrastructure plan makes mention of the following branches from the Madrid-Seville high-speed route: Seville-Cádiz, Seville-Huelva and Córdoba-Málaga via Bobadilla. European Union funding for studies into the last-named scheme was made available during 1999. The new 157 km line will reduce journey times between the capital and Málaga from the present best of 4 hours 10 minutes to 2 hours 20 minutes.

*Fixed link with Morocco*
In 1996 the governments of Spain and Morocco announced plans to build a 38.7 km rail tunnel under the Strait of Gibraltar from near Tarifa in Spain to a point near Tangier in Morocco. Similar in design to the Channel Tunnel, the fixed link would comprise two single-track rail tunnels (7.5 m in diameter) either side of a smaller service tunnel (4.8 m in diameter). Shuttle trains carrying cars, road coaches and trucks would share the tunnel with through passenger and freight services.

The rail link between Spain and Morocco would be 1,435 mm gauge and would probably be connected to the proposed extension of Spanish high-speed network from Seville to Cádiz. It was hoped to open the tunnel (possibly with a single rail bore at first) by 2010, with forecasts suggesting that it might carry 10.7 million passengers and 7.6 million tonnes of freight a year by 2025. Although it was hoped to offer a concession to the private sector to build and operate the tunnel for up to 30 years, it was anticipated that public funding would be required to meet part of the estimated Pta500 billion cost of the project.

## Majorca Railways (SFM)

Serveis Ferroviaris de Mallorca
Calle Aragon s/n Son Rullán, E-07009 Palma de Mallorca
Tel: (+34 97) 170 60 91  Fax: (+34 97) 170 60 49

Gauge: 1,000 mm
Route length: 47 km

### Political background
Responsibility for the 29 km Palma–Inca line on the island of Majorca was transferred by FEVE to SFM in 1994. In turn, SFM reports to the regional development ministry.

### Passenger operations
In 2001, 44 trains were operated daily on weekdays between Palma and Inca and 30 between Palma and Sa Pobla.

### Improvements to existing lines
In 1997 Pta900 million was invested by SFM, with an additional Pta400 million spent on station refurbishment. The Palma terminus has been completely redeveloped. Contracts were awarded in early 1999 to reinstate the 18 km extension of the existing line from Inca to Sa Pobla and revenue-earning services on this section commenced in January 2001.

In 2001 construction work was in progress on the Inca–Manacar line, which is due to open in 2003. Further network developments include: a line linking Sa Pobla–Alcudia–Pollensa, which was at the development stage in 2001; reopening the line to Palma airport and Santanyí; and a new line to Palma University.

### Traction and rolling stock
The SFM fleet comprises six dmus, four three-car and two two-car, supplied by CAF in 1995. Each is powered by two Cummins NTA855R4 engines with Voith hydraulic transmission. Servicing is undertaken at a new maintenance facility established at Son Rullán. A Batignolles/CAF diesel shunter is also retained for works trains.

## Sóller Railway

Ferrocarril de Sóller SA
Castañer 7, E-07100 Sóller, Majorca
Tel: (+34 971) 63 01 30  Fax: (+34 971) 63 12 22

### Key personnel
Chairman: J M Puig Morell
Vice-President: J Puig Rullan
Director: R A Sierra

Gauge: 914 mm
Route length: 28 km
Electrification: 28 km at 1.2 kV DC

### Passenger operations
Operating between Palma and Sóller, this privately owned railway carries around 1 million passengers annually, 90 per cent of which are tourists.

### Traction and rolling stock
The railway operates one diesel locomotive, four 350 kW electric railcars, 15 trailers and 3 baggage cars.

## Spanish National Railways (RENFE)

Red Nacional de los Ferrocarriles Españoles
Avenida Pío XII n° 110, E-28036 Madrid
Tel: (+34 91) 733 60 37  Fax: (+34 91) 315 03 84
Web: http://www.renfe.es

### Key personnel
President: Miguel Corsini Freese
Deputy President: Ramón Escribano Méndez
Secretary to the Board of Management:
  José Luis Marroquín Mochales
Directors General
  Operations: José Luis Villa de la Torre
  Infrastructure: Juan Antonio Villaronte Martínez
  Corporate Affairs: José María Lasala
Directors
  Organisation and Human Resources: Juan Fernández
  President's Office: Ramón Escribano
Secretary to the Board and Legal Affairs:
  Joaquín de Fuentes Bardaji
Managing Directors
  Long-Distance Passenger: A Gómez Templado
  High-Speed Passenger: J L Martín Cuesta
  Regional Passenger: Francisco Javier Villón
  Suburban Passenger: Abelardo Carrillo
  Freight: Carlos Sánchez
  Intermodal: Sagrario López Bravo
  Traction: Juan Carlos Carril
  Rolling Stock Maintenance: Arturo Delgado
  Traffic: José Eladio Seco
  Infrastructure Maintenance: Manuel Benegas
  High-Speed Infrastructure Maintenance:
    Antonio Fernández Gil
  Commercial Stations: Francisco Bonache
  Property: Gerardo García Merino
  Information Systems: Eduardo Fernández

Gauge: 1,668 mm; 1,435 mm; 1,000 mm
Route length: 11,804 km; 410 km; 18 km
Electrification: 1,668 mm gauge: 6,409 km at 3 kV DC
1,435 mm gauge: 481 km at 25 kV 50 Hz AC
1,000 mm gauge: 18 km at 1.5 kV DC

### Political background
RENFE was conferred new legal status in 1994, bringing it in line with EU Directive 91/440 on the separation of accounting for infrastructure and operations and allowing for the possibility of access to the system for other operators. Legislation to facilitate such access was drawn up in late 1995 and a general election in March 1996 brought in a new administration keen to see more private freight operators.

The new government appointed a new RENFE president and indicated that less public funding would be made available to the Ministry of Development (formerly the Ministry of Public Works, Transport & Environment) for investment in railway infrastucture projects. Schemes attracting private investment were likely to be given priority by the government. Wholescale privatisation of RENFE had not been an election issue, but the new administration appeared well-disposed towards selling off certain subsidiary companies.

### Organisation
President Miguel Corsini consolidated the company's top tier of management into three divisions each headed by a director general in 1996. Central functions such as finance and administration, human resources and planning fall within the remit of the Corporate Affairs division, also responsible for the information technology business unit. RENFE's production activities are divided into 14 such business units, each with their own budgets and managers responsible for their financial performance.

The Operations division comprises four business units responsible for passenger traffic (high-speed, long-distance, regional and suburban); freight and intermodal business units; and business units responsible for traction and rolling stock maintenance. The business units responsible for property and urban planning, stations, infrastructure maintenance, high-speed infrastructure maintenance and traffic (network operation) form the Infrastructure division.

Rolling stock and infrastructure maintenance is undertaken both by RENFE business units and external contractors. RENFE has examined the possibility of creating subsidiary companies from its rolling stock maintenance, infrastructure maintenance and information technology business units; the rolling stock maintenance business unit has already performed work for external customers such as component overhaul and the painting of road vehicles. The first RENFE internal contract was signed in late 1995 by the infrastructure maintenance and suburban passenger business units, initially covering the commuter networks of Madrid and Barcelona.

Staff levels have continued to fall: at the end of 1997 RENFE employed 36,023 staff compared with 36,821 at the end of the previous year.

### Finance
Under the provisions of the 1994-98 Contract Programme, RENFE received a total of Pta308.1 billion in state support, including Pta46.9 billion for suburban and regional passenger services, Pta137.3 billion for infrastructure management, Pta52.5 billion for debt servicing and Pta71.1 billion for other loss-making activities.

RENFE's 1996 profit of Pta2.1 billion was achieved even though government subsidy was cut by Pta18 billion to just Pta231 billion. During this period the state 'invested' a further Pta58 billion in RENFE.

*Targets for 1998*
The 1994-98 Contract Programme involves an overall reduction in state spending in the order of Pta160 billion. RENFE is expected to provide some Pta332.665 billion for investment in service quality (targeted at its suburban operations) from internally generated savings and improved financial performance. Infrastructure investment between 1994 and 1998 will largely be determined by the PDI plan (see below) and undertaken by the government.

Between 1994 and 1998 RENFE received a total of Pta683.104 billion for infrastructure management. This grant was fixed for the five-year period, and RENFE was to make efficiency savings to offset its decline in real terms. Under the Contract Programme, suburban services received a total of Pta197.2 billion in subsidy, and regional services Pta35.885 billion. The suburban business unit was set the objective of meeting 56.9 per cent of its costs in 1998 (46.6 per cent of costs were met in 1994), and the regional business unit the target of 69.3 per cent (58.2 per cent were met in 1994).

It was originally intended that RENFE's other business units, now operating without state support, would all be in profit or breaking even by 1998. RENFE expected that high-speed services would be in profit by then, but has revised its forecasts for the long-distance passenger, freight and intermodal business units. A combined deficit of some Pta43 billion is now anticipated, due to the allocation of costs between business units and the government's refusal to allow RENFE to trim its workforce to below 35,141. RENFE's original forecasts had been based on reducing its workforce from some 41,000 in 1994 to 31,430 by 1998. At the end of 1997, RENFE employed 36,023 staff.

To meet the objectives of the Contract Programme, the combined income of the freight business units has to grow by 10 per cent annuallly, and that of the combined passenger businesses by 5.1 per cent. In 1994 passenger income was provided mainly by the long-distance business unit (46.2 per cent), followed by the suburban (27.3 per cent), high-speed (16.5 per cent) and regional (10 per cent) business units. In 1998 it was forecast that

# RAILWAY SYSTEMS/Spain

*Irún—Alicante train formed of older Talgo stock at Vitoria behind Class 352 B-B diesel-hydraulic locomotive (Bryan Philpott)* 0023704

long-distance will provide 38.1 per cent of passenger income, suburban 34.4 per cent, high-speed 18.5 per cent and regional 9 per cent.

### PDI Infrastructure Plan
This national infrastructure plan, drawn up by the Ministry of Public Works, Transport & Environment (now the Ministry of Development) and covering the period 1993 to 2007, allocated Pta2,915 billion towards improving RENFE's interurban links. By April 1994 this had been increased to Pta3,222 billion, to be administered according to five-year spending programmes. The new administration elected in 1996 indicated that PDI schemes would have to rely more on private finance in the future, possibly leading to a change in established priorities.

New lines to be financed as part of the plan are the Madrid–Barcelona–French border high-speed line, the so-called Basque Y linking Bilbao with Vitoria and Irún, as well as a high-speed connection between this system and the new Madrid–Barcelona route. The high-speed network would grow from 471 km in 1993 to 1,590 km by 2007. Investment in the classic broad-gauge network would increase to 3,200 km lines capable of 200 to 220 km/h running.

| **Traffic** (million) | 1996 | 1997 | 1998 |
|---|---|---|---|
| Passenger journeys | 377,892 | 395,220 | 402,169 |
| Passenger-km | 15,605 | 16,579 | 17,478 |
| Freight tonnes | 24.512 | 25,399 | 25,652 |
| Freight tonne-km | 9,794 | 11,027 | 11,316 |

### Passenger operations
Aiming to break even by 1998 under the provisions of the 1994-98 Contract Programme, RENFE's long-distance passenger business unit has embarked upon a recovery programme to reverse the continuous decline in ridership and income recorded since 1986. Traditional overnight services were to be withdrawn in favour of hotel trains and more emphasis placed on day trains. A simpler market-based fares structure was to be adopted, with higher fares applying to those routes where rail journey times are better than or close to those of the road competition. Such routes were to receive the newest rolling stock, with improved standards of information and service for passengers and airline-style catering. In 1997 RENFE also achieved a marked increase in its load factor following a narrowing of differentials compared with second-class tariffs.

The business unit's rolling stock strategy includes the replacement of conventional locomotive-hauled services with multiple-units and Talgo formations. The Murcia–Barcelona Mediterranean Corridor has received six 1,668 mm gauge AVE high-speed trainsets (see 'Traction and rolling stock' section) branded 'Euromed' and, between late 1996 and June 1997, fixed-formation rakes of 27 Series 10200 coaches refurbished by RENFE's Málaga workshops for 200 km/h operation behind Class 252 locomotives. A fleet of 10 Intercity 2000 electric trainsets with active body-tilt was ordered in January 1996 for the Madrid–Valencia route. These were introduced in February 1999 under the 'Alaris' branding. From September 2000, 10 daily return workings running at 200 km/h will complete the 490 km journey in 3 hours 30 minutes. On the same route RENFE has introduced a new locomotive-hauled service. Operating under the 'Arco' branding, the trains operate at up to 200 km/h and are formed of Class 252 electric locomotives and refurbished Type B11 coaches.

*Class 592 Regionales dmu at El Repilado (Eddie Barnes)* 2001/0099135

### International joint ventures
From September 1996, the 'Trenes de Talgo Transpirenaicos' joint venture (a *Groupement Européen d'Intérêt Economique*) was formed by RENFE and SNCF of France to manage Madrid–Paris, Barcelona–Paris, Barcelona–Milan and Barcelona–Zurich service for a period of five years. As only Talgo rolling stock (with gauge-changing axles) was to be used by the new venture, SNCF purchased 44 Talgo coaches for Pta2 billion.

### High-speed services
Inauguration of AVE (*Alta Velocidad Española*) services over the new Madrid–Seville high-speed route coincided with opening of the Seville Expo in April 1992. The high-speed services were reckoned to have increased their market share by 29 per cent at the expense of air, 24 per cent from private cars and by 3 per cent from coaches. The percentage of high-speed traffic generated by rail itself, rather than abstracted from other modes, was in the region of 34 per cent. In its first five years of operation more than 17 million passengers were carried, paying revenues of Pta80 billion. In 1997 punctuality stood at 99.3 per cent – down from the figure of 99.9 per cent achieved in 1995.

In 1997 patronage rose by 304,000 to reach 4.4 million. In June of that year, AVE operations made a Pta217 million profit, the first time such a result had been achieved and 18 months ahead of target. Operational profitability had been achieved in 1994, but financial costs had converted this into a loss.

### Regional services
Regional Express services with air conditioned rolling stock run between La Coruña and Vigo in Galicia; on routes radiating from Madrid to León, Valladolid, Burgos, Irún and Jaén; from Ciudad Real to Albacete and Alicante; and in Andalucía, using Class 592 diesel multiple-units refurbished by RENFE's Valladolid workshops.

*Broad-gauge 'Euromed' AVE at Tarragona on a Valencia–Barcelona service (Bryan Philpott)* 0006169

This policy was taken a step further with creation in 1992 of the 'Catalunya Exprés' network for services focused on Barcelona. Major cities within the region now have a regular interval timetable, with trains every 1 or 2 hours; regular travellers can buy multiple-journey tickets at discounted prices. By 1995, the network had expanded from 18 weekday services to 32, operated with a fleet of four Class 432 and 14 refurbished Class 444 emus. The regional passenger business unit's aim of maintaining annual growth of between 6 and 10 per cent by operating 45 to 50 services each weekday, would require additional rolling stock.

The Regional Express concept was subsequently introduced to Andalucía. Under an 'Andalucía Express' branding, five Class 470 (refurbished Class 440) emus began operation on a Seville–Cádiz, Seville–Córdoba–Jaén and Seville–Huelva services in 1994. A Córdoba–Málaga service was introduced in January 1995 and by June of that year over 700,000 passengers had been carried on the Andalucía Express network, then comprising 18 daily services operated with six Class 470 emus.

Regional Diesel Trains (TRDs) were introduced on La Coruña–Vigo services in September 1997.

Regional services carried an extra 1.6 million passengers in 1997 to reach 23.9 million for the year, a rise of 7.3 per cent. In 1994-96 subsidy fell by Pta3.2 billion.

*Suburban services*
A combination of high inner-city house prices and spiralling interest rates has driven many young householders into the suburbs to find new accommodation. As a result, RENFE's suburban business unit has experienced considerable traffic growth. Suburban services are provided in 11 metropolitan areas: Asturias, Barcelona, Bilbao, Cádiz, Madrid, Málaga, Murcia, San Sebastián, Santander, Seville and Valencia, of which Madrid and Barcelona are by far the most heavily used, followed by Bilbao and Valencia. Fares on all RENFE local passenger services in the metropolitan Madrid area form part of the scheme administered by an authority also comprising the city's bus and metro operators. A similar authority was to be created for the greater Barcelona area in 1996, with a unified fares structure to follow, and for the greater Bilbao area.

In 1997 passenger journeys rose by 4.3 per cent to 354.36 million.

By 1995, Pta198.995 billion had been invested in new or refurbished rolling stock for suburban services and Pta25 billion in stations. With the business unit's target for 1998 of increasing ridership by 8 per cent in mind, rolling stock remained a priority, with a further Pta47.5 billion invested by 1998. Total station investment projected for 1994-98 totalled Pta20.105 billion, with passenger information and AFC systems both priorities.

**Freight operations**
A three-year investment plan costed at Pta7.2 billion was announced in 1996, aiming to restructure freight operations around seven different types of service and offer complete door-to-door logistics packages incorporating warehousing and onward distribution. Bulk traffic was to be conveyed by 'Indutren' services for different customers and products from the same sector, such as the petrochemicals industry; 'Maxitren' for single commodities, such as coal; 'Autotren' for car parts for different customers; and 'Jumbotren' for large volumes of general traffic. Non-bulk products were to be carried by general 'Almac' services, 'Logal' trains for consumer goods and 'Serliauto' trains for finished cars.

Elimination of wagonload business has been a major influence on the improved financial performance of the freight business sector. It has been estimated that wagonload traffic was carrying 20 per cent of freight traffic but responsible for 80 per cent of the sector's losses. By 1995 the network of freight depots served had been cut from 1,330 to 430 and the wagon fleet slashed from 36,000 to 1,500.

As part of its trainload strategy, the freight business unit complemented its established single-client regular 'Tren-Cliente' and seasonal 'Tren-Campaña' operations with a network of regular door-to-door services offering warehousing and distribution facilities. The first spokes in the TEM (Express Freight Train) network were daily Madrid–Barcelona and Madrid–Seville services introduced in 1994, carrying mainly consumer products such as drinks. The TEM network was eventually to comprise further radial services linking Madrid with Bilbao, La Coruña, Vigo and Valencia and Barcelona–Valencia–Seville and Barcelona–Vigo–La Coruña flows avoiding the capital.

All new RENFE freight wagons are designed for 100 km/h running with 22.5 tonne axleloads or 120 km/h with 20 tonne axleloads. The freight business is supported by SACIM, a systemwide, real-time data transmission system for traffic monitoring and control. It derives its data from a total of 257 terminals located throughout the rail system. Development of a real-time information system for freight customers known as 'Loginfo', to report the status of shipments, formed part of investment plans announced in 1996.

*International traffic*
International traffic has recently been growing at double the rate of domestic traffic and by 1995 represented some 25 per cent of non-intermodal freight business. A network of regular international freight services (TEMI), centred on Barcelona, is being established to complement the internal TEM services. A Barcelona–Cologne service was

*Class 269 electric locomotive with Talgo Pendular stock at Barcelona* (Marcel Vleugels)

*AVE trainset at Puertollano forming a Madrid–Seville high-speed service* (Colin Boocock)

*Class 448 emu at Madrid Chamartín* (Colin Boocock)

introduced in 1994, and by mid-1995 was operating three days each week with a journey time under 30 hours. In 1995 a thrice-weekly Setúbal–Lisbon–Oporto–Barcelona service was introduced; Italy, France, UK, Denmark, Belgium, Holland, Switzerland, Austria and Eastern Europe were under consideration as future additions to the TEMI network. A weekly service to Sweden began in 1996, using wagons owned by Nordwaggon and serving a new Combitrans terminal at Vicálvaro, near Madrid.

Rolling stock operating beyond the French border passes through the wheelset-changing facilities at Irún/Hendaye and Port Bou/Cerbère. RENFE has owned a 20 per cent shareholding in Transfesa, the operator of these facilities, since 1995; SNCF has a shareholding of the same size. Wheelset-changing is preferred where less robust commodities such as new cars, car parts, citrus fruit and finished consumer goods are being carried. Cargoes such as wood, cereals and iron and steel products are usually transhipped, as are containers and swapbodies. Some 4,600 wagons belonging to other European railways are permitted to operate in Spain, and private wagon owners inside Spain (such as Transfesa) have 7,600 vehicles suitable for cross-border operation.

In 1998 RENFE, SNCF, logistics company Decoexsa and TMF founded the Cadaler joint venture to manage flows of iron and steel traffic from the south to the north of Europe. The company is based at Port Bou, where it operates handling equipment and 6,000 m$^2$ of warehousing. Logistics, reception and sorting of products takes place here, while additional intermodal distribution centres are located at Valencia and Barcelona. A forecast 25,000 tonnes are expected to be dealt with annually at Port Bou.

## Intermodal operations

In 1997 RENFE's intermodal business continued to grow, recording a 15.5 per cent increase in tonnage (16.9 per cent in tonne-km) to follow the 12.8 per cent in 1996 and a 5.4 per cent increase in tonne-km. At the start of 1996, over 60 container trains were in operation daily, serving some 34 terminals. In addition to port services and trains for single clients, some 55 timetabled TECO multiclient container trains were in operation daily, including services between Madrid and 14 centres, Barcelona and six centres, and Valencia and four centres.

Madrid Abroñigal forms the hub of the TECO network, but a larger replacement has been approved in the shape of the government-sponsored Madrid Dry Port at Coslada, inside the triangle formed by the Madrid Chamartín–Hortaleza–Guadalajara, Guadalajara–Vicálvaro–Madrid Atocha and Vicálvaro–Hortaleza routes. The terminal, costed at Pta2 billion, is being largely financed by a consortium including the ports of Algeciras, Barcelona, Bilbao and Valencia, which will benefit from daily services of intermodal block trains. RENFE also expected to participate in funding the facility, which will have capacity for an annual throughput of 100,000 TEU. Transfesa and Urbaser have been selected as operators.

### Azuqueca de Henares dry port

In 1997 services ceased to the dry port at Azuqueca de Henares, located between Alcalá de Henares and Guadalajara on the Madrid–Zaragoza main line. Services to the facility were the first established in Spain under EU open access legislation and were operated and marketed by TCC Sea Train. Freight companies Transfesa and Cedes Logística Integral joined the Port of Barcelona and Barcelona Free Port to form TCC Sea Train, which itself is part of the TCC Puerto Seco consortium responsible for the development and management of the Azuqueca de Henares dry port. Unsuccessful attempts were made to persuade RENFE to take a financial stake in TCC Sea Train, and in early 1998 it looked likely that the company would be wound up. The Coslada scheme detailed above is being developed as an alternative.

### Bimodal operations

RENFE, in partnership with intermodal operator Transportes Olloquiegui and rolling stock manufacturer TAFESA, has founded Bi-Modal Trailer to promote wider use of the Transtrailer bimodal vehicle. Transportes Olloquiegui is running Spain's first domestic bimodal service, consisting of Volkswagen car components between plants in Pamplona and Barcelona. These trains are formed of up to 16 bimodals and semi-trailers. Transportes Olloquiegui was also seeking to establish a daily international service between Zaragoza and Cologne via Hendaye. This follows successful trials with Renault car components between Zaragoza and Douai, in France.

### Electric locomotives

| Class | Wheel arrangement | Output kW | Speed km/h | Weight tonnes | No in service | First built | Mechanical Builders | Electrical Builders |
|---|---|---|---|---|---|---|---|---|
| **3 kV DC** | | | | | | | | |
| 250 | C-C | 4,600 | 140/100 | 124 | 40 | 1982 | Krauss-Maffei/CAF/MTM | BBC |
| 251 | B-B-B | 4,650 | 140/100 | 138 | 30 | 1980 | Mitsubishi/CAF | Westinghouse |
| 269 | B-B | 3,100 | 140/80 | 88 | 105 | 1973 | Mitsubishi/CAF | Cenemesa |
| 269.200/400/500/600 | B-B | 3,100 | 160/90 | 88 | 157 | 1973 | CAF | Westinghouse |
| 276.200 | Co-Co | 2,208 | 110 | 120 | 3 | 1956 | Alsthom/Macosa/CAF/MTM/Euskalduna/Babcock & Wilcox | Alsthom/Sice/GEE/Oerlikon/Westinghouse |
| **3 kV DC/25 kV AC** | | | | | | | | |
| 252 | Bo-Bo | 5,600 | 220/100 | 90 | 74 | 1991 | Krauss-Maffei/ABB/Henschel/Meinfesa/CAF | Siemens ABB |
| **1.5 kV DC/3 kV DC** | | | | | | | | |
| 279 | B-B | 2,700 | 130/80 | 80 | 15 | 1967 | Mitsubishi/CAF | Mitsubishi/Cenemesa |
| 289 | B-B | 3,100 | 130/80 | 84 | 28 | 1967 | Mitsubishi/CAF | Mitsubishi/Cenemesa |

### Diesel locomotives

| Class | Wheel arrangement | Power kW | Speed km/h | Weight tonnes | No in service | First built | Mechanical | Builders Engine | Transmission |
|---|---|---|---|---|---|---|---|---|---|
| 319-200* | Co-Co | 1,190 | 120 | 110 | 57 | 1984 | Macosa | GM 567 C | E WESA |
| 319-300 | Co-Co | 1,372 | 140 | 119 | 40 | 1991 | Meinfesa | GM 645 E | E GM |
| 319-400 | Co-Co | 1,372 | 120 | 116 | 10 | 1992 | Meinfesa | GM 645 E | E GM |
| 321 | Co-Co | 1,250 | 120 | 111 | 54 | 1967 | Alco/CAF/Naval/Euskalduna | Alco | E GE, GEE |
| 333 | Co-Co | 1,875 | 146 | 120 | 93 | 1974 | Macosa | GM 645 E 3 | E GM |
| 352 | B-B | 1,470 | 140 | 76.3 | 10 | 1964 | Krauss-Maffei/Babcock & Wilcox | 2 × Maybach-Mercedes MD 650/18 | H Maybach-Mercedes |
| 353 | B-B | 1,668 | 180 | 88 | 3 | 1969 | Krauss-Maffei | 2 × Maybach-Mercedes MD6652 | H Maybach-Mercedes |
| 354 | B-B | 2,340 | 180 | 80 | 8 | 1982 | Krauss-Maffei | 2 × Maybach-Mercedes MD 6652 | H Maybach-Mercedes |
| 316 | Co-Co | 1,457 | 120 | 109 | 2 | 1955 | Alco | Alco 251 | E GE |
| 318 | Co-Co | 1,457 | 120 | 110 | 16 | 1958 | Alco | Alco 251 | E GE |
| 308 | Bo-Bo | 520 | 120 | 64 | 39 | 1966 | GE/Babcock & Wilcox | Caterpillar D-398 | E GE |
| 309 | C | 515 | 50 | 54 | 20 | 1986 | MTM | MTU-Bazan 6V396TC13 | H Voith |
| 310 | Bo-Bo | 930 | 114 | 78 | 60 | 1990 | Macosa | GM 645 E3 | E GM/Indar |
| 311 | Bo-Bo | 504 | 90 | 80 | 61 | 1990 | MTM | MTU 8V396TC13 | E MTM |
| 313 | Co-Co | 743 | 120 | 84 | 1 | 1965 | Euskalduna/Alco | Alco 251 | E GE, GEE |

Note: Classes 352, 353 and 354 are Talgo locomotives
* Seven are 1,435 mm gauge

### Electric multiple-units

| Class | Cars per unit | Motor cars per unit | Motored axles/car | Output/motor kW | Speed km/h | No in service | First built | Mechanical Builders | Electrical Builders |
|---|---|---|---|---|---|---|---|---|---|
| **1.5 kV DC** | | | | | | | | | |
| 442 | 2 | 1 | 4 | 524 | 60 | 5 | 1976 | MTM | BBC |
| **3 kV DC** | | | | | | | | | |
| 432 | 3 | 1 | 4 | 290 | 140 | 17 | 1971 | CAF/Macosa | Mitsubishi/Westinghouse |
| 440 | 2/3 | 1 | 4 | 290 | 140 | 72 | 1974 | CAF/Macosa | Mitsubishi/CENEMESA |
| 440R* | 3 | 1 | 4 | 290 | 140 | 95 | 1981 | CAF/Macosa | Mitsubishi/CENEMESA |
| 440R† | 3 | 1 | 4 | 290 | 140 | 8 | 1981 | GEC Alsthom/CAF | GEC Alsthom |
| 444 | 3 | 1 | 4 | 290 | 140 | 14 | 1980 | CAF/Macosa | Melco/GEC |
| 446 | 3 | 2 | 4 | 300 | 100 | 170 | 1989 | CAF/MTM/Macosa | Mitsubishi/ABB |
| 447 | 3 | 2 | 4 | 300 | 120 | 117 | 1993 | CAF/GEC Alsthom | Siemens/ABB |
| 448 | 3 | 1 | 4 | 290 | 160 | 31 | 1987 | CAF/Macosa | Melco/GEC |
| 450 | 6 | 2 | 4 | 370 | 140 | 24 | 1994 | GEC Alsthom/CAF | GEC Alsthom |
| 451 | 3 | 1 | 4 | 370 | 140 | 12 | 1994 | GEC Alsthom/CAF | GEC Alsthom |
| 470 | 3 | 1 | 4 | 290 | 140 | 37 | 1981 | CAF/Macosa | Mitsubishi/Cenemesa |
| Euromed | 10 | 2 | 4 | 675 | 220 | 6 | 1996 | GEC Alsthom | GEC Alsthom |
| **3 kV DC/25 kV AC** | | | | | | | | | |
| AVE | 10 | 2 | 4 | 1,100 | 300 | 18 | 1991 | GEC Alsthom | GEC Alsthom |

* Rebuilt for suburban services
† Rebuilt for regional services

### Diesel multiple-units

| Class | Cars per unit | Motor cars per unit | Motored axles/car | Power/motor kW | Speed km/h | No in service | First built | Mechanical | Builders Engine | Transmission |
|---|---|---|---|---|---|---|---|---|---|---|
| 592 | 2/3 | 2 | 2 | 213 | 120 | 69 | 1981 | Macosa/Ateinsa | MAN | H Voith |
| 593 | 3 | 2 | 2 | 206 | 120 | 50 | 1981 | CAF/BWE | Fiat | M Fiat |
| 594 | 2 | 2 | 2 | 300 | 160 | 16 | 1997 | CAF | MAN | H Voith |
| 596 | 1 | 1 | 2 | 206 | 120 | 12 | 1997 | CAF/BWE | Fiat | M Fiat |

### International services

By mid-1996, RENFE's intermodal business unit was handling 270 services each week between Spain and other European countries, a substantial increase from the six international services operated in 1992. Regular multiclient 'Euroteco' services link Spain with France, Germany, Italy, the Netherlands and Portugal.

In September 1997 NDX implemented its fourth European international freight service, linking the ports of Barcelona and Rotterdam twice-weekly using axle-changeable wagons.

ICF intermodal services to and from Spain carried 120,000 TEU in 1995, with the bulk of this traffic (70,000 TEU) moving between Spain and Germany and mostly comprising chemicals and car components. The remainder of ICF Spanish traffic was carried to and from France, Italy, Switzerland, the UK, Scandinavia, the Netherlands, Belgium and Portugal. In January 1996 ICF introduced additional services to Italy and Portugal, a Barcelona-Milan train operating four days a week in each direction and a weekly Bilbao-Lisbon/Leixões train.

Combiberia and Kombiverkehr retail space for containers and swapbodies on Tarragona/Granollers–Mannheim/Cologne and Zaragoza/Pamplona–Mannheim/Cologne services that mainly carry Opel car parts.

## Improvements to existing lines

*PDI projects*

The revised PDI plan makes provision for upgrading the following existing lines for speeds of 200-220 km/h: Valladolid–Venta de Baños–Burgos–Vitoria, Venta de Baños–León–Monforte de Lemos, Madrid–Manzanares–Ciudad Real/Santa Cruz de Mudela, and Valencia–Alicante–Murcia. Complementary investment is earmarked for the modernisation of other routes, namely Monforte de Lemos–Orense–Vigo, Orense–Santiago–La Coruña, Fuentes de Oñoro–Valladolid, León–Pola de Lena, Palencia–Santander, Miranda–Castejón de Ebro, Madrid–Cáceres–Valencia de Alcántara, Cáceres–Mérida–Badajoz, Algeciras–Bobadilla, Santa Cruz de Mudela–Linares–Moreda–Almería, Linares–Córdoba, Moreda–Granada and Albacete–Murcia–Cartagena. In 1997 it also emerged that the Development Ministry was seeking to establish a dedicated high-speed freight line linking Vigo with the Portuguese city of Oporto.

*Mediterranean Corridor*

As part of an ongoing programme scheduled for completion around 1999, the Murcia/Alicante–Valencia–Barcelona Mediterranean Corridor received Pta20.75 billion of investment in 1996. The programme aims to raise line speeds to 200-220 km/h over the 69 km of double track between Valencia and Castellón; curves are being eased, track and catenary renewed, and improved signalling installed.

Between Castellón and Tarragona the single track is being doubled and realignments undertaken that will shorten the distance from 206 km to 185 km. A new alignment is under construction between Alcanar and Camarles which includes bridging with a deck height of 29 m above the River Ebro at Amposta y L'Aldea. Development Ministry contracts valued at Pta5.5 billion were placed in 1998 covering Valencia–Tarragona and Castellón–Las Palmas track-doubling and improvements on the Alcanar–Camarles section. New routes through the towns of Benicàssim and Castellón are to be constructed at a cost of Pta23.5 billion, with funding provided by central government, the region of Valencia and local and municipal authorities.

Upgrading work between Font de la Figuera and Xátiva includes track-doubling and installation of CR220 catenary for 220 km/h operation. A proposed cross-city tunnel under Valencia, connecting the route to Barcelona with those to Madrid and Alicante, has been costed at Pta51 billion. Forming part of the Valencia Intermodal strategy, the project includes a station beneath the city's existing RENFE terminus and would improve connections with metro and bus services.

*Andalucian investment plan*

The Andalucian regional government made public for consultation its own PDIA infrastructure plan early in 1994. Of a total budget of Pta4.9 billion, Pta319.2 million was earmarked to be spent on improvements to the rail network in the region up to 2007. Andalucia's strategy, which would involve greater spending than anticipated by central government for the area, has four principal objectives forming successive stages of the plan.

The first objective is the creation of a regional network from RENFE's existing Huelva–Bobadilla–Almería, Córdoba–Málaga, Cádiz–Jaén–Linares and Linares–Almería routes. This would involve upgrading the existing infrastructure and electrifying those sections of the putative network still operated with diesel traction, namely Utrera–La Roda, Bobadilla–Granada–Moreda and Linares–Moreda–Almería.

The second objective is upgrading principal routes for services operating at 200-220 km/h to and from the high-speed line to Madrid at Seville and Córdoba. The routes concerned are Seville–Huelva, Seville–Cádiz, Córdoba–Málaga, Bobadilla–Granada, Córdoba–Linares and Espeluy–Jaén. The first three on this list feature on the national PDI plan as candidates for new broad-gauge high-speed feeders for the Madrid–Seville high-speed route.

Studies are being undertaken for building a Córdoba–Málaga high-speed line for use by standard-gauge AVE trainsets. See entry for 'Railway Infrastructure Authority (GIF)' for more details.

Better links between Andalucia in the far south of Spain and the European rail network form the ambitious third stage of this far-reaching plan. In order to achieve this, new railway lines between Cádiz and Algeciras (the existing Bobadilla–Algeciras route is conspicuous by its absence from PDIA investment proposals) and Almería and Aguilas in Murcia are proposed. A further new line along the coast has been suggested to link Algeciras with Almería; the region's PDIA plan makes provision for a feasibility study.

Suburban services for the Seville, Málaga and Cádiz areas are the focus of the fourth stage, which foresees construction of new links and the reopening of the Huelva–Ayamonte line. In contrast, under the PDIA proposals, marginal routes, such as Zafra–Huelva, Los Rosales–Zafra, Cordoba–Almorchon and Ronda–Bobadilla, might be turned over to non-railway uses with potential for tourism such as long-distance footpaths.

*Suburban networks*

As part of a 1990-98 investment strategy totalling Pta73.9 billion, the Ministry of Transport allocated Pta10.9 billion to suburban routes and railway access to cities in 1995. Madrid's suburban system was to receive the largest share (Pta5.75 billion), followed by Barcelona (Pta3.45 billion), Asturias (Pta900 million), Valencia and Seville (Pta400 million each). Part of a European Investment Bank long-term loan of ECU412.3 million secured in 1994 was to be spent on infrastructure upgrading work in Madrid, Barcelona and Valencia.

In 1996 the government produced an investment plan for the Bay of Cádiz area, which proposed to spend Pta30.916 billion between 1996 and 2001 on infrastructure improvements for suburban services in Cádiz, San Fernando, Puerto Real, Puerto de Santa Maria and Jerez de la Frontera.

The 1996-2001 Madrid investment plan makes provision of Pta20 billion for a new 7.2 km line from Cantoblanco Universidad north of the city to stations at Valdelasfuentes and Avenida de España, serving the communities of Alcobendas and San Sebastián de los Reyes. Civil engineering contracts for the project were let in 1996. Southwest of the capital, the Madrid regional government hoped to complete a new 29 km route from Vicálvaro to Rivas Vaciamadrid and Arganda del Rey in late 1998. Running for part of its length alongside an existing 1,000 mm gauge industrial railway, the new single-track 1,668 mm gauge electrified route was to be built with the help of private capital.

## Traction and rolling stock

At the end of 1998, RENFE's motive power comprised 452 electric locomotives (including 13 AVE Class 252s), 293 line-haul diesel locomotives (including 21 Talgo locomotives), 181 diesel shunting locomotives, 18 AVE trainsets, six Euromed trainsets, 602 emus and electric railcars and 147 dmus. The hauled passenger rolling stock fleet comprised 4,293 vehicles. In total, 24,737 freight wagons were in service, excluding vehicles used for internal purposes.

Since the beginning of 1999, the locomotive fleet has been allocated to RENFE's individual business sectors.

Recent electric traction developments include a programme to convert Class 279 and 289 locomotives into permanently coupled tandem units. Undertaken by RENFE's Villaverde, Madrid workshops, the first conversion appeared in June 1999. RENFE planned to create a fleet of 20 similar machines.

*Intercity 2000 trainsets*

RENFE's long-distance passenger business unit invited tenders in 1994 for the supply of 10 Intercity 2000 electric trainsets for around Pta10 billion, capable of seating up to 200 passengers at speeds up to 220 km/h. On 30 January 1996 10 three-car tilting trainsets based on the ETR 460 design for FS of Italy were ordered from a consortium of GEC Alsthom (now Alstom) and Fiat for Pta9.058 billion. These trains entered service in February 1999 under the 'Alaris' brand-name on the Madrid–Valencia route.

*TRD dmus*

Adtranz-designed CAF-built Class 594 TRD two-car dmus entered regional service with RENFE in 1997. These are based on the Flexliner design but are not articulated. The original 16 vehicles were to be supplemented by an additional seven ordered in 1999 for delivery by the end of 2000.

*The Talgo fleet*

The latest model of Talgo coaching stock, the Talgo Pendular, has a passive body-tilting system designed to permit curve negotiation at a 20 per cent higher speed than the normal limit without discomfort to passengers. The range includes sleeping-car sets with wheelsets adjustable to gauge-change for international services. For details of these cars, see *JWR 1996-97*.

Talgo cars are owned by RENFE but maintained by the builder under contract. The present five-year contract, which also covers Class 352, 353 and 354 diesel-hydraulic locomotives built for Talgo haulage, specifies high-season coach availability of 97 per cent, dropping to 88 per cent in periods of low demand. In service, each trainset carries a Talgo engineer who can deal with any malfunction that may occur.

*Class 447 suburban electric multiple-unit (Alex Dasi-Sutton)* 0023703

## RAILWAY SYSTEMS/Spain

### Signalling and telecommunications
At the end of 1998, RENFE had 1,665 km of its network equipped with automatic block signals and 3,985 km under the control of Centralised Traffic Control (CTC). Manual block equipment was in use on 6,177 km. Cab signalling (LZB system) was in use on 478 km of the network. Track-to-train radio is in operation on 3,850 route-km, with equipment installed in 1,065 traction units.

In 1996 a contract to equip the La Encina–Valencia and Valencia–Barcelona routes with 32 Class 252 electric locomotives and six 1,668 mm gauge AVE trainsets with Automatic Train Protection equipment over a period of four years was awarded to a consortium of ABB (now Adtranz) and Dimetronic. Fully compatible with the emerging European Train Control System, the ATP system for the Mediterranean Corridor incorporates ABB Ebicab 900 and Dimetronic TBS technology.

At the end 1996, automatic block signalling was being installed between Vara de Quart and Ribarroja (18 km) in the Valencia area. In Barcelona CTC was being installed between Moncada and Tarrasa (23 km), and between Sagrera and Arenys. The LZB cab-signalling system was being installed on the Móstoles–Fuenlabrada route (42 km), which carries half of Madrid's total suburban traffic, to allow trains to run at 2 minute intervals.

### Track
**1,435 mm gauge routes**
**Rail:** UIC 60 kg/m
**Sleepers:** Type DW monobloc concrete, spaced 1,667/km
**Fastenings:** Vossloh Type HM
**Spacing between tracks:** 4.3 m
**Max gradient:** ; 1.25%
**Min curve radius:** In general 0.5°, except stations and 30 km at 0.8°
**Max axleload:** 22.5 tonnes (up to 200 km/h); 17.2 tonnes (up to 270 km/h)

**1,668 mm gauge network**
**Standard rail**
**Main lines:** 60 kg/m, 54.5 kg/m, 45 kg/m and UIC 54.1 kg/m in 12 and 18 m lengths
**Sleepers**
**Wooden:** Mainly creosoted oak, pine, and sometimes beech, 2,600 × 240 × 140 mm for ordinary track. For points, crossings 3, 3.5, 4 and 4.5 m of same width and thickness (centre crossing sleeper being 4,500 × 300 × 14 mm), and for expansion joints 2,600 × 350 × 140 mm. Special sleepers of up to 6.2 m used for diagonals on double track
**Reinforced concrete:** Type RS or monobloc, thickness 250 mm
**Spacing:** 1,667/km
**Rail fastenings:** Screw spikes on wood sleepers and elastic clamps on reinforced concrete sleepers. Elastic fastenings for wood sleepers are also being tested.

*Class 252 locomotive and Talgo Pendular set on a Barcelona–Madrid working at Lleida (Bryan Philpott) 0023700*

**Min curve radius:** In general 250 m
**Max gradient:** 4.2% on Ripoll–Puigcerdá line
**Longest continuous gradient:** 8.27 km of 2%, with 5.85° curves (300 m radius) on 4.84 km
**Max altitude:** 1,494 m on Ripoll-Puigcerdá line
**Max axleload:** 22.5 tonnes

---

## Valencia Railways (FGV)

Ferrocarrils de la Generalitat Valenciana
Partida de Xirivelleta s/n, B de S Isidro, E-46014 Valencia
Tel: (+34 96) 357 81 03   Fax: (+34 96) 357 82 58

### Key personnel
Managing Director: V Contreras
Managers
  Operations: F Garcia
  Finance: Jesus Cerverón Esteban
  Marketing: Jorge Beltrán Oliver
  Industrial Relations: Antonio Ruiz
  Rolling Stock: Manuel Sansano
  Workshops: Gonzalo Romero
  Communications: J Canales

Gauge: 1,000 mm
Route length: 123.6 km in Valencia; 92.6 km in Alicante
Electrification: 113.5 km at 1.5 kV DC

### Political background
FGV was created in 1986 to take over from FEVE the local railways in the Valencia area, and also operates the non-electrified Alicante-Denia line.

### Passenger operations
A rise in patronage of 5.23 per cent was reported in 1997, when 21 million passengers were carried. Light rail Line 4 carried 3.5 million pasengers, a gain of 27.8 per cent on the year.

### Improvements to existing lines
*Valencia*
FGV has completed the integration of the city's 1,000 mm gauge Llíria, Bétera and Villanueva de Castellón lines (Lines 1 and 2) as a regional metro via a 6.8 km city centre tunnel with eight underground stations.

Under an expansion programme for 1991-99 costed at Pta86 billion, an existing suburban line between Ademuz and El Grao was rebuilt as a 9.7 km double-track LRT route. Known as Line 4, the route opened in 1994.

Line 3 has been renovated between Rafaelbunyol and Palmaret (11 km) and the overground Palmaret–Pont de Fusta section was abandoned in 1995 in favour of a new underground route to Alameda (3 km). From 1998 Line 3 will connect at Alameda with Line 5 to Avinguda, currently under construction. Line 5 will eventually link Nuevo Cauce in the west of the city with Cabanyal in the east.

*Alicante*
A total of Pta1 billion has been spent on upgrading work on the Alicante–Denia line, although no progress has been made on improving this isolated line's connection with the city centre at Alicante.

### Electric railcars or multiple-units

| Class | Cars per unit | Motor cars per unit | Motored axles/car | Output/motor kW | Speed km/h | No in service | Builders Mechanical | Electrical |
|---|---|---|---|---|---|---|---|---|
| UTA | 2 | 2 | 1 | 220 | 80 | 40 | CAF | ABB |
| 3900 | 3 | 2 | | | | 18 | GEC Alsthom | GEC Alsthom |

### Diesel railcars or multiple-units

| Class | Cars per unit | Motor cars per unit | Motored axles/car | Power/motor kW | Speed km/h | No in service | First built | Builders Mechanical | Engine | Transmission |
|---|---|---|---|---|---|---|---|---|---|---|
| MAN | 2 | 1 | 2 | 210 | 80 | 8 | 1965 | MAN | MAN | M Voith DIWA |

### Traction and rolling stock
At the start of 1994 FGV operated two 845 hp diesel-electric and two 465 hp diesel-mechanical locomotives, 61 electric and eight diesel trainsets.

### Track
**Rail:** 45 and 54 kg/m
**Sleepers:** Stedef bibloc concrete 1,800 × 260 × 220 mm with Nabla fastenings; monobloc concrete 1,900 × 240 × 130 mm with HM-Vossloh fastenings; timber 1,900 × 240 × 130 mm
**Sleeper spacing:** 1,000-1,500/km in plain track; 1,250-1,500/km in curves
**Max gradient:** 2.4%
**Max permissible axleload:** 15 tonnes

# SRI LANKA

## Ministry of Transport, Highways and Aviation

PO Box 588, D R Wijewardana Mawatha, Colombo 10
Tel: (+94 1) 68 73 11; 68 72 12
Fax: (+94 1) 69 45 47

### Key personnel
Minister: Dinesh Gunawardane
Advisor: P Rajagopal

**UPDATED**

## Sri Lanka Railway (SLR)

PO Box No 355, Colombo 10
Tel: (+94 1) 43 11 77   Fax: (+94 1) 44 64 90
e-mail: rly@visual.lk

### Key personnel
General Manager: Priyal de Silva
Additional General Manager (Administration): H M Rupasinghe
Additional General Manager (Operations): K A Premasiri
Commercial Superintendent: P H Silva
Chief Engineer (Way and Works): C R Vithanage
Chief Signal and Telecommunications Engineer: V S Balasubranamiam
Chief Mechanical Engineer: P P Wijesekera
Chief Engineer (Motive Power): B A P Ariyaratne
Operating Superintendent: GRP Chandratillake
Transportation Superintendent (planning): S W Munasinghe
Stores Superintendent: S P Samaranayake
Chief Accountant: A K Theiventhren

Gauge: 1,676 mm
Route length: 1,449 km

### Poltical background
SLR is a government department functioning under the Ministry of Transport, Highways and Aviation. The government intends to reconstitute the management structure of SLR, giving it more authority and flexibility in carrying outits maintenance and development programmes. Considerable disruption has been caused to SLR operations by the so-called liberation tigers of Tamil Eelam, which has been outlawed by the government as a terrorist organisation.

In 1998 a business unit was established to open up the network to private-sector freight operators, who would pay access charges and be responsible for maintenance of infrastructure.

The Railway Management Council was established in 2001 to pursue the objectives of a restructuring programme. Amendments to existing legislation were being considered to facilitate public/private partnerships in the operation of the railway.

### Organisation
The SLR network is centred on Colombo, from where nine lines radiate north along the coast to Periyanagavilu, south to Matara and east to the Central Highlands. The 339 km Northern Line branches off the Colombo–Badulla Main Line (290 km) at Polgahawela and crosses north-central and northern provinces to the city of Kankesanturai, although train services beyond Vavuniya have been suspended because of the civil war in the north.

In June 1997 SLR employed 18,070 staff.

The installation of a management information system and a computerised ticketing system feature in SLR's 2001-05 investment programme.

### Diesel locomotives

| Class | Wheel arrangement | Power kW | Speed km/h | Weight tonnes | No in service | First built | Mechanical | Engine | Transmission (Builders) |
|---|---|---|---|---|---|---|---|---|---|
| M2 | A1A-A1A | 1,063 | 80 | 79 | 12 | 1954 | GM | GM 12-567C | E GM |
| M2C | Bo-Bo | 1,063 | 80 | 79 | 2 | 1961 | GM | GM 12-567C | E GM |
| M2D | A1A-A1A | 977 | 80 | 79 | 2 | 1966 | GM | GM 12-567E | E GM |
| M4 | Co-Co | 1,305 | 80 | 97.68 | 14 | 1975 | MLW | Alco 12-25 103 | E Generator GT 581PJ1 |
| M5 | Bo-Bo | 1,175 | 80 | 66 | 6 | 1975 | Hitachi | MTC-Ikegai 12V652TD11 | E Alternator H1-503-Bb |
| M5A | Bo-Bo | 1,175 | 82 | 66 | 1 | 1993* | Hitachi | MTU 396 | E Alternator |
| M5B | Bo-Bo | 1,175 | 82 | 66 | 4 | 1997* | Hitachi | Caterpillar 3516 | E Alternator |
| M6 | A1A-A1A | 1,230 | 80 | 85.5 | 14 | 1980 | Henschel | GM 12-645E | E Generator D 25L |
| M7 | Bo-Bo | 746 | 80 | 67 | 15 | 1981 | Brush | GM 08-645E | E BA 1004A/BAE/507A |
| M8 | Co-Co | 2,400 | 120 | 109.8 | 6 | 1996 | DLW | 251-B16-DLW | E Alco |
| M9 | Co-Co | 1,340 | 80 | 100 | 10 | 2000 | Alstom | Ruston 12 BK | E Alstom |
| W1 | B-B | 857 | 80 | 60.55 | 10 | 1969 | Henschel | Caterpillar 3312 | H MTU-Mekydro K 102-1016 PS |
| W2 | B-B | 1,173 | 80 | 65.3 | 3 | 1969 | Lokomotivbau | Paxman 16YJXL | H MTU-Mekydro K 182 BU |
| W3† | B-B | 857 | 80 | 65.3 | 6 | 1979 | Henschel | Caterpillar | H Voith |
| Y | 0-6-0 | 410 | 45 | 28 | 20 | 1969 | Hunslet | Rolls-Royce DV 8T | H Rolls-Royce CF 13800 |
| P1 |  | 98 | 32 | 20.12 | 2 | 1950 | Hunslet | Ruston Hornsby 6 VPH | H Hunslet axle drive |
| N1 | 1-C-1 | 367 | 32 | 41.17 | 2 | 1953 | Fried Krupp | Deutz 33 | H Krupp LIB |
| N2 | B-B | 447 | 32 | - | 2 | 1973 | Kawasaki | Detroit Diesel 16V71K | H Niigata DBG-138 |

Note: * Date of re-engining   † Class W1 re-engined

### Diesel railcars or multiple-units

| Class | Cars per unit | Motor cars per unit | Motored axles/car | Power/motor kW | Speed km/h | No in service | First built | Mechanical | Engine | Transmission (Builders) |
|---|---|---|---|---|---|---|---|---|---|---|
| S3 | 4 | 1 | 4 | 656 | 80 | 6 | 1959 | MAN | MAN L 12V18/21 | H Maybach K 104 U |
| S5 | 4 | 2 | 4 | 577 | 80 | 3 | 1970 | Hitachi | Paxman 8Y JXL | H MTU-Mekydro K 102 UB/55 |
| S6 | 4 | 1 | 4 | 869 | 80 | 8 | 1975 | Hitachi | Paxman 12Y JXL | H MTU-Mekydro K 102 UB |
| S7 | 4 | 1 | 4 | 760 | 80 | 8 | 1977 | Hitachi | Cummins KTA-2300L | H Hitachi DW 2A |
| S8 | 5 | 1 | 4 | 1,005 | 100 | 20 | 1990 | Hitachi/Hyundai | MTU 12V 396 TC13 | H |
| S9 | 5 | 1 | 4 | 1,015 | 100 | 15 | 1999 | Sifang | MTU 12V 396 TC14 | E |

*Hitachi-built dmu at Fort (Ralph Oakes-Garnett)*

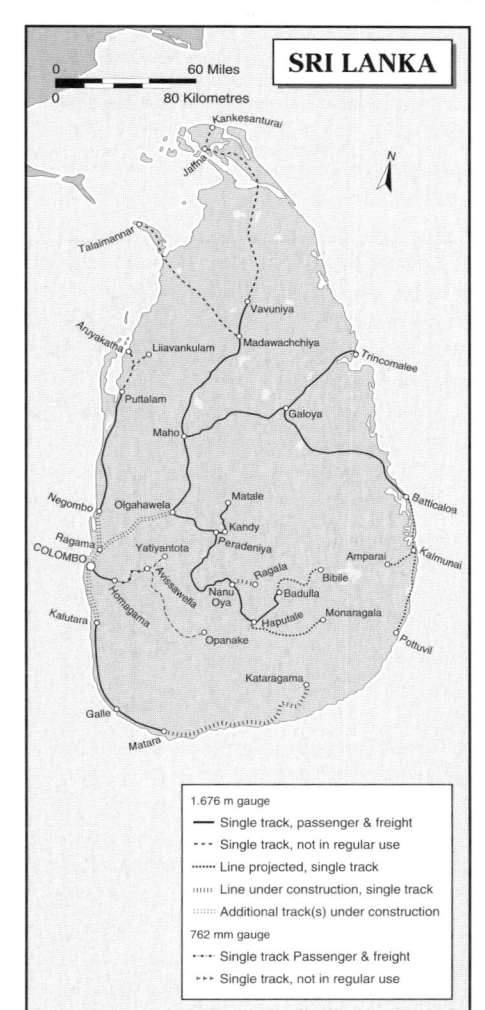

**SRI LANKA** map showing 1.676 m gauge and 762 mm gauge lines:
- Single track, passenger & freight
- Single track, not in regular use
- Line projected, single track
- Line under construction, single track
- Additional track(s) under construction

762 mm gauge:
- Single track Passenger & freight
- Single track, not in regular use

*Sifang-built dmu, one of is supplied from 1999*

# RAILWAY SYSTEMS/Sri Lanka—Sudan

**Finances** (SLRs million)

| Revenues | 1999 | 2000 |
|---|---|---|
| Passengers | 678.5 | 740.9 |
| Freight | 209.6 | 133.3 |
| Parcels | 39.4 | 32.1 |
| Other | 110.9 | 108.1 |
| Total | 1,038.4 | 1,014.5 |

| Expenditure | 1999 | 2000 |
|---|---|---|
| Staff/personnel | 1,186.6 | 1,777.0 |
| Materials and stores | 78.6 | 86.5 |
| Fuel/lubricants | 742.9 | 538.9 |
| Pensions/other | 182.5 | 283.4 |
| Total | 2,885.6 | 2,685.8 |

| Traffic (million) | 1999 | 2000 |
|---|---|---|
| Passenger journeys | 83.2 | 85.9 |
| Passenger-km | 3,176 | 3,430 |
| Freight tonnes | 1.160 | 1.194 |
| Freight tonne-km | 94.5 | 88.2 |

## Passenger operations
Besides commuter services around Colombo and long-distance services on the Main Line and the Coast Line to Matara, intercity trains also operate between other major cities, such as Colombo–Kandy and Colombo–Galle. In all, 170 stations and 155 stops are served.

SLR passenger-km have increased every year since 1991, but in recent years service development has been hampered by inadequate investment. Daily passenger services operated include: 260 Colombo suburban; 35 long-distance; and 21 local.

## Freight operations
Freight traffic has suffered from lack of motive power, as the few locomotives which are available are often taken to power passenger trains. In 2001, SLR operated 20 daily freight services, with petroleum products, cement and foodstuff the principal commodities carried.

In early 2001, the Freight Business Unit (FBU) was established to lead a revival in rail freight traffic. An open access policy was also being purchased to facilitate private sector participation with the aim of increasing rail's marketshare from 10 to 50 per cent.

## Intermodal operations
Having performed poorly in recent years, container traffic was to be revived during the period 2001-06. A new facility, the Internal Container Depot, was to be established near Ragama station, 13 km north of Colombo and the line linking the SLR network with Colombo port was to be rehabilitated in 2002. Plans were being pursued to establish container handling yards closer to main export processing zones.

## Improvements to existing lines
A continuing track rehabilitation programme underway in 2001 aimed to allow 100 km/h running by 2005. In 2001, negotiations were underway for financial assistance for this programme from Japanese banking institutions. To some extent track maintenance has been mechanised in recent years.

Provision of a third track on the Main Line between Colombo and Ragama has reduced congestion at peak times. Track-doubling between Wadduwa and Aluthgama (17 km) on the Coast Line and between Ragama and Negombo (14 km) on the Puttalam Line was in progress in 2001. Construction of five bridges in connection with further track-doubling was scheduled to commence in 2002, and an additional eight minor bridges were due to be rehabilitated during the period 2002-04.

Construction of a Mass Rapid Transit for the outer Colombo area, upgrading the Colombo–Katunyaka Airport service, extension of the network to link industrial and agricultural zones and the electrification of Colombo suburban services were all the subject of continuing feasibility studies in 2001.

## Traction and rolling stock
At the beginning of 2001 SLR operated 129 diesel locomotives, 53 diesel railcars, 1,128 passenger cars and 2,000 freight wagons on 1,676 mm gauge.

During the period 1994-2001, SLR strengthened its fleet by 30 diesel locomotives and 15 dmus for suburban services.

## Signalling and telecommunications
Rehabilitation or replacement of the CTC system installed in 1960 has been identified as a major project. In addition, in 2001 SLR planned to install level crossing protection systems at 244 locations.

Phase 2 of the installation by NMA Signalling of colour light signalling on the Coast Line was scheduled for completion by 2003.

**Type of coupler in standard use:** Auto and screw, ARR standard
**Type of braking:** Vacuum

## Track
**Rail:** 43 and 39 kg/m (382 km and 866 km)
**Crossties (sleepers):** Wood (1,248 km) and concrete, spaced 1,550/km; installation of concrete started in 1996
**Fastenings:** Dog and elastic spikes, Pandrol clips
**Min curvature radius:** 100.6 m
**Max gradient:** 2.7%
**Max axleload:** 16.5 tonnes

*UPDATED*

---

# SUDAN

## Ministry of Transport

PO Box 300, Khartoum

### Key personnel
Minister: Lam Okol

## Sudan Railways (SRC)

PO Box 1812, Khartoum
Tel: (+249 11) 77 40 09   Fax: (+249 11) 77 06 52

### Key personnel
General Manager: Eng Omer Mohamed Mohamed Noor
Deputy General Manager, Infrastructure:
  Eng Abdel Rahim M Abdel Rahim
Deputy General Manager, Research and Development:
  Eng Aarad El Kareem Ali Abdel Wahab
Deputy General Manager, Operations:
  Abdel Haleem Ahmeidi Taha
Deputy General Manager, Technical:
  Eng Samel Ahmed Samel
Deputy General Manager, Finance:
  Gaafar Hub Alla Saeed
Regional Managers
  Northern: Musa Mohammed Musa
  Eastern: Eng El Hassan Abbas
  Central: Eng Bushara Gantoor
  Southern: Eng Mohammed Hamid
  Western: Eng Ali El Tayeb
Managers:
  Traction and Rolling Stock:
    Eng Magdi Mohammed Bilal
  Tracks and Construction:
    Eng Abdel Rahman Aldaw
  Operation and Traffic:
    Abdel Wahab Suliman
  Signalling and Telecommunication:
    Adam Ibrahim Shurbaike
  Finance: Mohammed Abdel Rahman Ibrahim
  Personnel: Mustafa Ibrahim Hassan
  Training: Mahgoub Hassan M Haiba
  Planning and Statistics: Elsheikh Abdel Mutalab Omer
  Projects: Eng Abdel Rahman Mohamed Ahmed
  Safety: Eng Hassan Bakry Hamad
  Police: Brig Abdel Adil Ali Haroon
Internal Auditing: Mohammed Ali Tamimi
Stores: Abdalla Jubartalla
Legal Administration: Joseph Sabit Ija
Purchasing: Ibrahim Bashari Ali
Public Relations: Omer Mahmoud Mohammed
Co-operative Corporation for Commerce and Services:
  Mohammed Omer Awad El Kareem

Gauge: 1,067 mm
Route length: 4,595 km

## Political background
The single-track railway used to be the main transport mode in Sudan, but from the late 1970s onwards the mode has been in serious decline. Some rehabilitation was undertaken with foreign aid during the 1980s famine, but lack of spares and consequent poor availability of motive power severely hampered operations in the early 1990s; the situation eased when 10 new diesel locomotives arrived in January 1995.

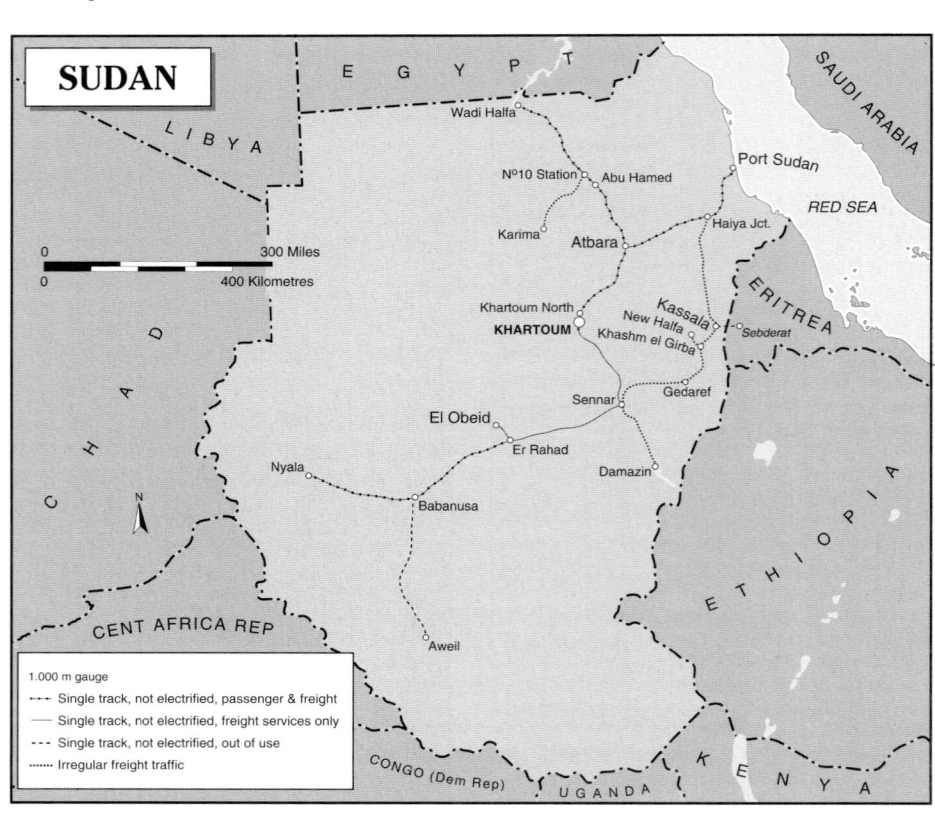

The main line linking the capital Khartoum to Port Sudan carries over two-thirds of SRC's traffic.

In 1999 the government announced its intention to privatise freight and passenger operations by the end of 2001, leaving SRC responsible for infrastructure, which was to be upgraded.

## Organisation
At the end of 2001 SRC employed 13,698 staff.

| Traffic | 1999 | 2001 |
|---|---|---|
| Passenger journeys | 257,690 | 157,957 |
| Passenger-km (million) | 129 | 78 |
| Freight tonnes (million) | 1.64 | 1.25 |

## Passenger operations
There is a weekly train from the capital Khartoum to Wadi Halfa in the north of the country, Port Sudan on the Red Sea and Nyâlâ in the southwest. Political and operating difficulties have disrupted the network for much of the 1990s, with many trains cancelled for lack of motive power and substantial portions of the network closed, including the line to Wau.

There have been some improvements. Super-Express service introduced on the Port Sudan-Khartoum route cut the best timing from 36 to 19 hours. Improvements have also resulted from private sector participation in the running of services.

## Freight operations
In 1996, crude oil from a new find near El Mujlad in western Sudan began flowing by rail to a refinery at El Obeid; the distance travelled is 466 km and quantities range from 2,000 to 5,000 tonnes a day. Around 1,750 tonnes a day of fuel oil is being transported from the refinery to Khartoum and other towns. More than US$30 million had to be invested in the network for this traffic, which amongst other things covered rehabilitation of 10 locomotives, track repairs and provision of workshop facilities.

## New lines
In 2000 the Sudan government commissioned studies into new lines to provide links with Chad, the Central African Republic and Ethiopia to provide rail access for these countries to Sudan's parts.

### Diesel locomotives

| Class | Wheel arrangement | Power kW | Weight tonnes | No in service | First built | Builder |
|---|---|---|---|---|---|---|
| 600 | C | 335 | 48 | 22 | 1968 | H Kawasaki |
| 700 | C | 375 | - | 19 | 1975 | H Henschel |
| 1000 | Co-Co | 1,380 | 99 | 8 | 1960 | E EE/Vulcan |
| 1500 | A1A-A1A | 1,120 | 78 | 5 | 1990 | E Hitachi |
| 1601 | Co-Co | 1,230 | 53 | 10 | 1981 | H Henschel |
| 1700 | Co-Co | 1,230 | 79.2 | 9 | 1975 | E GE |
| 1750 | A1A-A1A | 1,360 | 79.2 | 6 | 1991 | E GE |
| 1800 | Co-Co | 1,715 | na | 18 | 1975 | E GE |
| 1850 | Co-Co | 2,000 | na | 10 | 1985 | E GE |
| 1860 | Co-Co | 2,000 | na | 6 | 1995 | E GE |
| 1900 | Co-Co | 1,865 | 76 | 20 | 1975 | E Henschel/GM |
| 1950 | Co-Co | 1,790 | 94.1 | 10 | 1981 | E GM |

## Improvements to existing lines
A specialist team of engineers has carried out a detailed inspection of structures between Port Sudan and Khartoum, prior to preparation of a rehabilitation plan. On the line to Wau and Babanousa, reconstruction of the Guti bridge permitted trains to resume running after disruption by terrorist action.

## Traction and rolling stock
At the beginning of 2001 SRC owned 111 diesel locomotives, although over half of these were out of service or under repair. Also on the stock list were three diesel railcars, 196 passenger coaches and 4,309 freight wagons. Many of the latter were out of use.

In 1996, SRC put into service 200 tank wagons leased from Spoornet of South Africa on the new oil flow from El Mujlad to El Obeid; more than half SRC's 600 tank wagons are employed on this flow.

In 1998 SRC ordered 500 freight wagons and 600 bogies from Wagon Pars of Iran.

## Signalling and telecommunications
Mechanical lower quadrant signalling is used throughout the system with absolute block working between stations. In some cases both points and signals are operated from signalboxes, but in others points are hand-operated individually or from ground frames. The primary communication link is a lineside open pole route, over which SRC serves block instruments and block telephone, selective ringing telephones and a station-to-station telephone and telegraph system. This open route has been vulnerable to theft and destruction, but rehabilitation has been carried out between Atbara and Khartoum using old rail as termite-proof replacement poles. In addition a manual Morse telegraph operates.

SRC has an HF radio link for voice communication between major centres throughout the rail network. Now it is considering introduction of radio signalling and solar power.

A central control point at Atbara is responsible for a dispatching system for the Khartoum-Port Sudan main line.

## Track
**Standard rail:** Flat bottom, 24.7 kg/m in lengths of 9.14 m and 37.2 kg/m in lengths of 10.97 m; joined by fishplates and bolts
**Crossties (sleepers):** Steel; and wood impregnated under pressure in mixture of creosote and oil (1:1). Concrete used in a few cases as an experiment
**Max curvature:** Main line 4.5°
**Max gradient:** 0.66%, except on section in Red Sea Hills between Summit and Port Sudan 1%. Gradient compensation for curves 0.04% per 1° curvature
**Max axleload**
75 lb track: 16½ tonnes; 50 lb track: 12½ tonnes
**Max speed**
50 lb track: 50 km/h; 75 lb track: 60 km/h
**Max altitude:** 918.5 m at Summit station on Port Sudan line

*UPDATED*

# SWAZILAND

## Ministry of Works & Communications

PO Box 58, Mbabane
Tel: (+268) 423 21    Fax: (+268) 423 64

### Key personnel
Minister: E Magagula

## Swaziland Railway (SR)

PO Box 475, Johnstone Street, Mbabane
Tel: (+268) 424 86    Fax: (+268) 450 09

### Key personnel
Chairman: L Sithebe
Chief Executive Officer: G J Mahlalela
Directors
    Financial: U Makhubu
    Operating: S Z Ngubane
    Human Resources and Development: M B Mabuza
    Engineering: T Ndlovu

Gauge: 1,067 mm
Route length: 301 km

## Political background
In October 2001, the Swaziland government approved the concessioning of SR as a single entity as a public-private partnership with strong local participation.

## Organisation
Swaziland's railway was completed in 1964. The main route is from Ka Dake to the Mozambique border at Goba, with lines from Phuzumoya to Lavumisa/Golela and Mpaka to Komatipoort.

A 120 km link from Mpaka to Komatipoort in the eastern Transvaal was opened in 1986; 58 km is in Swaziland and 62 km in South Africa. The line provides a through north-south line to South Africa via the Mpaka–Phuzumoya section of the Ka Dake–Mlawula line and the 95 km Phuzumoya–Golela southern link.

## Passenger operations
The twice-weekly 'Trans-Lubombo' service, operated by Spoornet between Durban, Mpaka and Maputo, was discontinued in January 2001. This left tourist trains from South Africa and private charters as the only passenger services using the Swaziland network.

## Freight operations
Annual traffic totals around 4 million tonnes, 700 million tonne-km, and includes sugar industry products, minerals and ores from eastern Transvaal, phosphoric acid, fruit, timber and containers.

A major traffic source is Matsapha Dry Port, an inland clearance terminal where export containers are loaded. The success of this facility has led SR to develop plans for a second terminal at Mpaka.

## New lines
In 1997 SR unveiled plans to construct a western link with the South African system, from Matsapha via Siphoco to Lothair, terminus of a Spoornet branch from Ermelo. The line, which SR is developing with South African partners, would provide a direct link to Johannesburg and cut the distance from Matsapha by 200 km.

## Improvements to existing lines
In 1998 rehabilitation was in progress on SR's west-east corridor, from Matsapha to Siweni and the border with Mozambique.

## Traction and rolling stock
Traction is provided by diesel locomotives leased from South Africa's Spoornet; there are three passenger cars and 420 wagons.

## Track

| | Kadake–Goba | Phuzumoya–Golela |
|---|---|---|
| Rail | 40 kg/m | 48 kg/m (sidings 30 kg/m) |
| Sleepers | hardwood | concrete |
| Thickness | 127 mm | 200 mm |
| Spacing | 814 mm | 700 mm |
| Fastenings | sole plates and coachscrews | Fist BBR |
| Welded rail | 126 km | 92 km |

*UPDATED*

# SWEDEN

## Ministry for Industry, Employment & Communications

Jakobsgatan 26, SE-103 33 Stockholm
Tel: (+46 8) 405 10 00  Fax: (+46 8) 411 36 16
e-mail: registrator@industry.ministry.se
Web: http://naring.regeringen.se/index.htm

**Key personnel**
Minister: Björn Rosengren
Under-Secretary of State, Transport: Birgitta Heijer

**Political background**
*Separation of infrastructure and operations*
In 1988 the state assumed responsibility for upkeep and development of the railway's infrastructure. For the first time in Europe, management of infrastructure and operations was separated, infrastructure becoming the responsibility of Banverket (BV), the National Rail Administration.

Under legislation passed by the Swedish parliament in 1998, track access charges were reduced substantially to improve rail's ability to compete with road transport. The charges paid by train operators in 1996 totalled SKr1,045 million, but the new system has reduced the annual total to SKr275 million. The previous charging method has been replaced with a system of variable access fees based on socioeconomic marginal costs.

The 1,053 km Inland Railway from Mora to Gøllivare is a special case. Under a 20-year agreement concluded in 1993, it and three connecting branches were transferred to the control of Inlandsbanan AB (IBAB, qv), a consortium of local authorities along the route.

With effect from 1 January 2001, the business of the former Swedish State Railways (SJ) was split up into six independent companies: SJ AB (passenger services), Green Cargo AB (freight services), Jernhusen AB (real estate), TraffiCare AB (train cleaning and station services), EuroMaint AB (mechanical engineering and maintenance) and Unigrid AB (information technology services). TraffiCare and Unigrid were privatised in 2001.

*Phased deregulation*
Access to the rail network was liberalised with effect from 1 July 1996. Although SJ AB retains its monopoly on unsubsidised long-distance passenger services, regional transport administrations and the state can now contract other operators for subsidised services on any line.

For freight traffic, any licensed operator has the right to run services over any part of the network, though established traffic has priority in track allocation. Responsibility for track allocation and traffic control rests with Banverket.

Further legislation passed in 1998 aims to secure non-discriminatory access to all parts of the rail network by transferring responsibility for industrial sidings, platform structures and passenger information systems to Banverket.

Responsibility for procuring commercially unviable long-distance passenger services was transferred to a new agency, Rikstrafiken (qv), from 1 January 2000.

New legislation that came into force on 1 April 2002 abolished the previous distinction between trunk and regional lines. As a consequence, SJ AB now has operating rights for passenger traffic on all lines belonging to the state railway infrastructure, but no obligation to run services.

SJ AB does not run services that are not commercially viable. These are procured by the state, via Rikstrafiken, and by the 24 regional transport administrations (länstrafikhuvudmän).

**UPDATED**

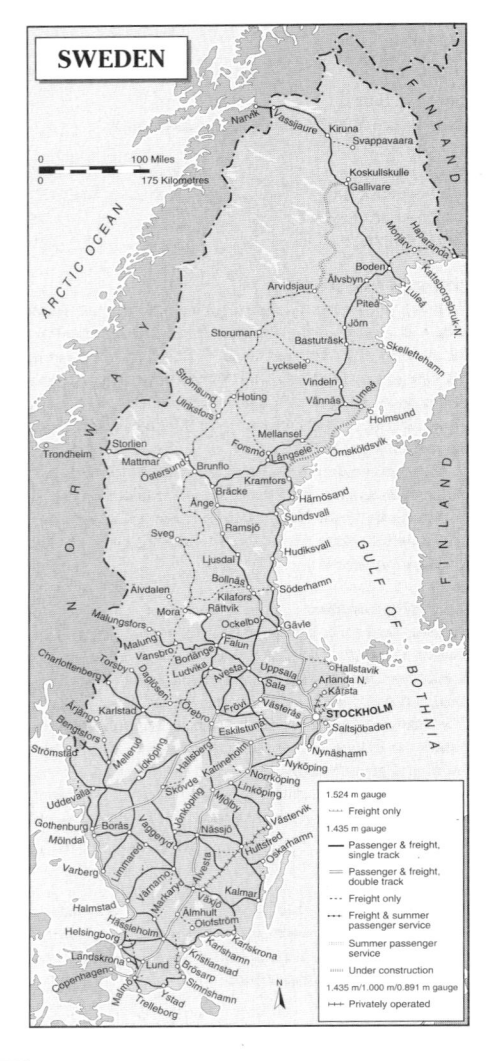

## Arlanda Express

A-Train AB
PO Box 130, SE-101 22 Stockholm
Tel: (+46 8) 58 88 90 00  Fax: (+46 8) 58 88 90 01
e-mail: arlandaexpress@atrain.se
Web: http://www.arlandaexpress.com

**Key personnel**
Chief Executive: Göran Lundgren
Finance Director: Göran Karlsson
Project Director: Torsten Bjuggren
Operations Director: Roman Willenfelt
Marketing Director: Tomas Kreij
Public Relations Manager: Inger Fjordgren
Sales Manager: Maria Bohman

**Passenger operations**
The direct line between Stockholm Central station and three underground stations at Arlanda airport, 40 km to the north, opened in November 1999. The link provides travellers with a dedicated airport shuttle (Arlanda Express), as well as allowing regional and long-distance passenger trains to serve the airport terminal.

Under its contract with the government, in return for building and financing the line, A-Train AB has the right to operate the shuttle service and retain ticket revenues until 2040.

The Arlanda Express service has a maximum speed of 200 km/h. The journey takes 20 minutes and trains depart every 15 minutes, increasing to every 10 minutes at peak times. Check-in facilities for air passengers are provided at Stockholm Central station, where luggage can be tagged for collection from designated drop-off points on arrival at the airport.

Platform 1 at Stockholm Central has been converted into a terminal for the Arlanda Express with its own entrances. Taxis and cars can stop outside these entrances, and the nearest metro station is 50 metres away.

Three separate rock tunnels have been blasted beneath the airport area. Two of these are single-track tunnels for the Arlanda Express, with two stations serving the airport's four terminals. The third tunnel is double-track and is used by regional and long-distance trains, with a single station beneath the airport's central service area, Sky City. Lifts and escalators provide direct access from the stations to the various terminals.

*Arlanda Express trainset at Stockholm Central (Norman Griffiths)*

**Traction and rolling stock**
The seven airport shuttle trains, built in the UK by Alstom, are four-car emus seating 190 passengers. Car floors are entirely at platform level, and there is special accommodation for wheelchairs and accompanying passengers.

**VERIFIED**

Sweden/**RAILWAY SYSTEMS** 341

## Banverket

See Swedish National Rail Administration, below

## BK Tåg AB

PO Box 28, SE-571 21 Nässjö
Tel: (+46 380) 55 44 00   Fax: (+46 380) 55 44 44
e-mail: info@bktag.se
Web: http://www.bktag.se

### Key personnel
Managing Director: Rolf Torwald
Deputy Managing Director: Tommy Nilsson

### Passenger operations
BK Tåg has been operating in this market since 1990 and currently holds contracts with regional transport administrations to run services on the following lines: Hallsberg–Lidköping–Herrljunga in western Sweden, Ystad–Simrishamn in the far south of the country and a group of routes radiating from Nässjö in the southern province of Småland.

In December 1998 a consortium, in which BK Tåg has a 10 per cent stake, won a five-year contract to operate the suburban network in Stockholm from 1 January 2000. The other partner in the consortium is the French company Keolis. A new company, Citypendeln (qv), has been set up to operate this network, which covers 185 route-km and carries over 60 million passengers annually.

In 2001, BK Tåg won a renewed contract to operate a number of routes in the counties of Halland, Jönköping and Småland in southeast Sweden. These include the Jönköping–Värnamo–Alvesta–Växjö line. The five-year contract commenced in August 2002.

*Class Y1 diesel railcar operated by BK Tåg AB for Jönköpings Länstrafik AB (JLT), photographed at Jönköping* (Edward Barnes)
2001/0114221

### Freight operations
In March 1998, BK Tåg began operating container traffic between Karlstad and Gothenburg, in conjunction with the Port of Gothenburg. In addition, the company now transports containers from the Absolut Vodka plant at Åhus to Gothenburg, for onward export to the USA.

Since 1996 the subsidiary company has operated timber traffic over the southern section of the Inlandsbanan between Östersund and Mora.

In March 2000, BK Tåg acquired the business of BSM Järnväg AB, and with it the running of daily block trains carrying liquefied petroleum gas between the Neste Gas terminal at Timrå (near Sundsvall) and the SSAB steelworks at Borlänge.

### Traction and rolling stock
BK Tåg AB has a fleet of 11 diesel locomotives. Two Class Da electric locomotives are hired from Shortline Väst AB (qv) for the Karlstad–Gothenburg traffic. Haulage for Inlandsbanan timber trains is hired from Inlandsbanan AB (qv). The company owns six Class Y1/YF1 diesel railcars for passenger services to supplement the rolling stock provided by the regional transport administrations. The company has 65 freight wagons.

Jönköpings Lönstrafik has ordered four two-car and six three-car Itino dmus from Bombardier Transportation, for delivery by mid-2003. These will be operated by BK Tåg on the Jönköping–Võrnamo and Nässjö–Halmstad lines.

*BK Tåg Class TMX diesel-electric locomotive, acquired from Danish State Railways, with a freight service at Mellerud* (Edward Barnes)
2002/0524943

**UPDATED**

## Botniabanan AB

Strandgatan 7, SE-891 33 Örnsköldsvik
Tel: (+46 660) 29 49 00   Fax: (+46 660) 29 49 10
e-mail: info@botnianbanan.se
Web: http://www.botniabanan.se

### Key personnel
Chief Executive Officer: Lennart Westberg
Project Manager, Railway Systems: Håkan Hellqvist
Communications Manager: Jan Bergman

### Political background
Botniabanan AB was founded by the Swedish government (91 per cent) and local authorities (9 per cent) to finance, design and construct a new railway serving the Norrland coast, linking Nyland and Umeå. This followed parliamentary approval in 1997 to build the line, which is intended to provide better communications and improve the economy of a region currently poorly served by rail. The Swedish National Rail Administration (Banverket) is responsible for preliminary evaluation, planning, design planning and permits. On completion of construction of the line, it will be leased to Banverket, which will undertake operations and maintenance for a 40-year period. The cost of construction is estimated at SKr10.9 billion at January 2001 prices, making the Botniabanan Sweden's largest rail project in modern times. Financing will be provided by loans through the National Debt Office and by possible contributions from the European Union.

### New lines
The 190 km Botniabanan (Bothnia Line) will run from a junction with the Sundsvall–Sollefteå Ådalsbanan north of Nyland via Örnsköldsvik, Husum and Nordmaling to Umeå. Designed for possible eventual 250 km/h running, the standard gauge line will be single-track with passing loops and will be electrified at the Swedish standard 15 kV 16 ⅔ Hz AC system. Initial maximum operating speed will be 200 km/h. Maximum permitted axleload will be 25 tonnes, with a maximum gross train weight of 1,600 tonnes.

The line will feature around 20 tunnels totalling 25 km, two of these over 5 km, and some 140 bridges, including three of 1 km or more. The heaviest engineering works will be on the southernmost section between Nyland and Örnsköldsvik. Seven stations are to be constructed at: Örnsköldsvik North; Örnsköldsvik Central; Husum; Nordmaling; Hörnefors; Umeå East; and Umeå Central. These will be closely integrated with other transport modes.

Block signalling will be provided, together with automatic train control. All road-rail crossings will feature grade separation. GSM-R radio communications equipment will be provided together with pulse code modulation (PCM) transmission technology and a fibreoptic telecommunications network.

Work on the Örnsköldsvik–Husum section started in 1999. Construction of the central Örnsköldsvik section was due to begin in 2002 and of the Nyland–Örnsköldsvik section in 2003. Work on the Husum–Umeå section, for which planning approvals were still awaited at the end of 2001, was also due to begin in 2003. The entire line is due to be commissioned in 2008.

**NEW ENTRY**

## Citypendeln Sverige AB

Varuvägen 34, SE-125 30 Älvsjö
Tel: (+46 8) 762 27 00   Fax: (+46 8) 762 27 75
e-mail: info@citypendeln.se
Web: http://www.citypendeln.se

### Key personnel
Chairman: Tord Hult

### Passenger operations
Under a five-year contract with the regional transport administration, Storstockholms Lokaltrafik (SL), Citypendeln took over the running of trains and stations on the Greater Stockholm suburban network from 6 January 2000. These services were previously provided by Swedish State Railways (SJ).

The majority shareholder in Citypendeln, with a 90 per cent stake, is the French transport group Keolis. The remaining 10 per cent of shares are held by Swedish rail operator BK Tåg AB (qv).

The business has a turnover of €93 million, a workforce of 900, and transported 61 million passengers in its first year of trading. As well as train operations and maintenance, Citypendeln is responsible for managing 50 suburban stations.

Services operate on two lines, totalling 185 route-km: a northwest-southeast line from Bålsta via the city to Västerhaninge and Nynäshamn; and a northeast-southwest line from Märsta via the city to Södertälje and Gnesta. Both lines run in parallel through the city centre.

### Traction and rolling stock
Services are operated with a fleet of around 150 Class X1 and X10 emus owned by SL.

*UPDATED*

## Citytunneln

Citytunnelkonsortiet i Malmö
Lilla Nygatan 7, Box 4012, SE-203 11 Malmö, Sweden
Tel: (+46 40) 32 14 00   Fax: (+46 40) 32 15 00
e-mail: info@citytunneln.com
Web: http://www.citytunneln.com

### Key personnel
Managing Director and Chief Executive Officer:
  Kjeld Boye-Møller
Technical Director: Örjan Larsson
Project Director, Railway: Patrik Magnusson
Project Director, Malmö C: Lennart Stenman
Project Director, Tunnels: Laust Ladefoged
Manager, Public Relations: Anders Mellberg

### Political background
The Citytunnelkonsortiet is a joint venture partnership established by the Swedish National Rail Administration (Banverket), Swedish State Railways (SJ), the City of Malmö and the Skåne (Scania) regional authority to plan, construct and commission improved rail links to and through Malmö and to the Öresund Fixed Link with Denmark. The aim of the scheme is to provide additional capacity to handle traffic generated by the Öresund Fixed Link and to facilitate an expansion of regional rail services.

Government approval of the scheme was given in 2002, while environmental endorsement was expected in 2003, enabling construction to begin that year. Commissioning is scheduled for 2008. The cost of construction is estimated at SKr7.7 billion at 1996 prices.

### New lines
The Citytunneln project foresees construction of 18 km of electrified main line railway, comprising a 12 km double-track line from Malmö Central station to the Öresund Fixed Link and 6 km of single line to provide new links to the ports of Trelleborg in the south and Ystad in the east. The project also includes major expansion of Malmö Central station and new stations at Hyllie and Triangeln.

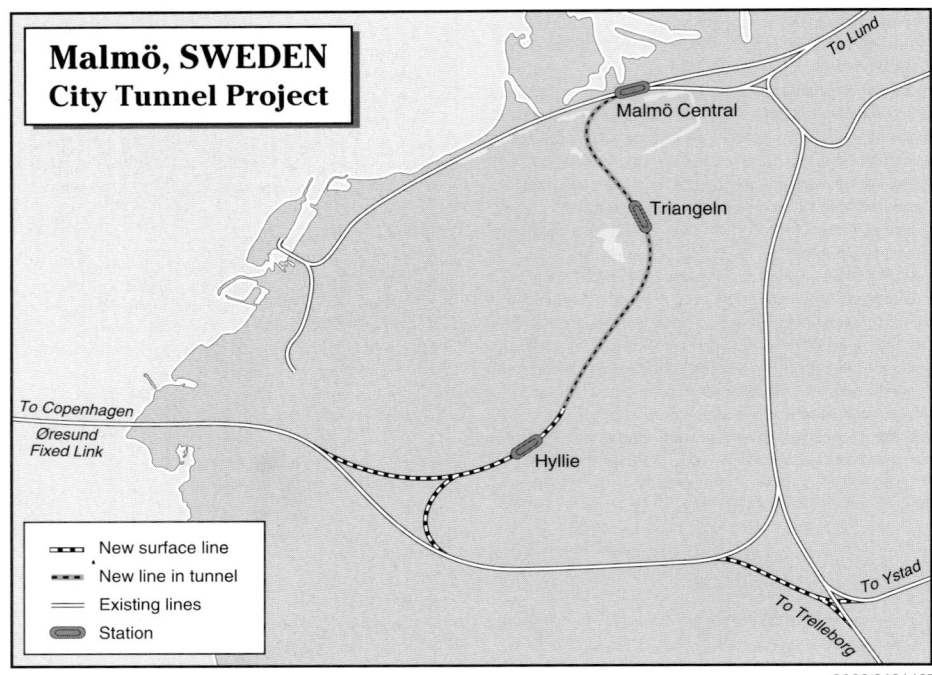

The principal feature of the project is the proposed construction of twin 6 km tunnels under central Malmö. Some 4.5 km of these will be bored, the remainder constructed using the cut-and-cover method. Triangeln station, which will serve the city's commercial and cultural centre, will be located in the tunnelled section; Hyllie will be at surface level. Proposals for expanding facilities at Malmö Central station include provision of two underground island platforms served by four tracks.

*NEW ENTRY*

*Malmö, SWEDEN City Tunnel Project*
2002/0131467

## Green Cargo AB

PO Box 39, SE-17111 Solna
Tel: (+46 8) 762 40 00   Fax: (+46 8) 791 72 21
e-mail: info@greencargo.com
Web: http://www.greencargo.com

### Key personnel
Managing Director: Jan Sundling
Directors
  Operations: Kjell Färnström
  Road and Logistics: Roland Hoijar
  Marketing and Sales: Mats Hanson
Corporate Communications: Anna Bergqvist
Human Resources: Rune Karlsson
Finance: Gunnar Andersson
Information and Communications Technology:
  Kerstin Stenberg
Market Support: Ingela Roos af Hjelmsäter

### Organisation
Green Cargo AB, formed from the freight division of the former Swedish State Railways, began trading on 1 January 2001. The company is wholly owned by the Swedish state and has a workforce of around 3,900.

The company had a turnover of SKr6.3 billion in 2001 and traffic equivalent to 17 billion net tonne-km in 2000.

Green Cargo's business is organised into four main divisions: Operations (rail transport), Road and Logistics, Marketing and Sales, and Market Support.

| Traffic (million) | 1997 | 1998 | 1999 |
|---|---|---|---|
| Freight tonnes | 30.5 | 30.2 | 30.4 |
| Freight tonne-km | 15,169 | 15,171 | 15,381 |

(Data applies to former SJ Cargo Group)

### Freight operations
Green Cargo AB offers rail-based logistics solutions with the highest safety, quality and environmental standards. The Swedish freight market has grown considerably in recent years as a result of economic growth. Customers are becoming increasingly environmentally aware in their transport and logistics requirements, to the benefit of rail.

Rail currently has a market share of just over a fifth of the total Swedish freight market. Green Cargo is responsible for around 80 per cent of freight traffic on the

*Green Cargo is the name adopted for the former SJ Cargo Group, one of whose Rc4 electric locomotives is seen at Borlänge (Norman Griffiths)*   2001/0114222

Swedish rail network, operating from 29 terminals and logistics centres.

The company's customers are predominantly in the manufacturing sector. Over two-thirds of turnover derives from long-distance freight movements for a number of core customers, including AssiDomän, Stora-Enso, SCA, SSAB and AvestaSheffield.

Green Cargo has adopted a strategy of increasingly offering planning and management of entire material supply chains in partnership with its customers. This involves the company taking overall and continuing responsibility for all aspects of its customers' transport and logistics requirements. Rail transport may be only one of the services provided.

The Green Cargo business includes the following subsidiaries and associated companies:
- Green Cargo Road & Logistics AB, which provides domestic and international road distribution and third-party logistics services.
- Nordisk Transport Rail AB (NTR), one of Scandinavia's leading freight forwarding companies, with offices in 11 countries and an annual throughput equivalent to around 72,000 freight wagons, or one in three wagons travelling between Sweden and continental Europe.
- TGOJ Trafik AB (qv), one of Sweden's largest short line freight operators, specialising in trainload traffic for heavy industry. The company also hires out locomotives, wagons and traincrew to third parties.
- Sve Rail Italia AB, owned equally by Green Cargo AB and Via Trenitalia SpA to provide rail freight services between the Nordic countries and Italy.
- CargoNet AS, formerly the freight division of Norwegian State Railways (NSB). Green Cargo took over a 45 per cent stake in the business from 1 January 2002, the remaining 55 per cent remaining with NSB.
- Rail Combi AB, which specialises in intermodal transport (trailers, swapbodies and containers) through a network of 14 rail-connected terminals across Sweden, with links to Norway and Denmark. Since 1 January 2002, Rail Combi has been a subsidiary of CargoNet AS.

**Traction and rolling stock**

Green Cargo AB has a fleet of 450 locomotives, 10,000 wagons and 290 road vehicles.

*UPDATED*

*T44 diesel locomotive shunting the train ferry to Sassnitz at Trelleborg (David Haydock)* 2001/0114258

**Diesel locomotives**

| Class | Wheel arrangement | Power kW | Speed km/h | Weight tonnes | No in service | First built | Builders Mechanical | Engine | Transmission |
|---|---|---|---|---|---|---|---|---|---|
| T44/ | Bo-Bo | 1,235 | 90 | 76 | 109 | 1968 | Nohab | GM 12-645E | E GM |
| T44R | | | | | | 1983 | Kalmar | | |
| V4 | C | 460 | 70 | 48 | 10 | 1972 | Henschel | Deutz BF12M716 | H Voith/Gmeinder |
| V5 | C | 460 | 70 | 48 | 40 | 1975 | Henschel | Deutz BF12M716 | H Voith/Gmeinder |
| Z66 | B | 218 | 70 | 32/34 | 7 | 1971 | Kalmar | KHD F12 M 716 | H Voith/Gmeinder |
| Z70* | B | 333 | 70 | 34 | 48 | 1990 | ABB-Rac | Saab-Scania DSI 14 | H Voith L3r 4U2 |

\* Rebuilt from former Class Z65

**Electric locomotives**

| Class | Wheel arrangement | Output kW | Speed km/h | Weight Tonnes | No in service | First built | Builders Mechanical | Electrical |
|---|---|---|---|---|---|---|---|---|
| Rc1 | Bo-Bo | 3,600 | 135 | 80 | 19 | 1967 | Nohab/ASJ/Motala | ASEA |
| Rc2 | Bo-Bo | 3,600 | 135 | 77 | 72 | 1969 | Nohab/ASJ/Motala | ASEA |
| Rc4 | Bo-Bo | 3,600 | 135 | 78 | 128 | 1975 | Nohab/Kalmar | ASEA |
| Rm | Bo-Bo | 3,600 | 100 | 92 | 6 | 1977 | Nohab | ASEA |

Notes: Class Rc and Rm, thyristor control

# IKEA Rail AB

Box 228, SE-260 35 Odäkra
Tel: (+46 42) 25 73 80   Fax: (+46 42) 25 73 80)
Web: http://www.ikea.com

**Key personnel**
Managing Director: Christer Beijbom

**Background**
This subsidiary of IKEA, the international home furnishings retail chain, was established in April 2001 to develop its own rail services to distribute the company's products in Europe. Its first train ran on 27 June 2002.

IKEA Rail claims to be the first private company to operate its own freight trains across international borders in Europe.

**Freight operations**
At its launch, IKEA Rail was operating five return trains each week between Älmhult, Sweden, and Duisburg, Germany. Additional routes were at the planning stage in mid-2002.

**Traction and rolling stock**
IKEA Rail uses hired-in traction for its services: between Älmhult and Copenhagen, a TGOJ Trafik General Motors-built Class T66 diesel-electric locomotive is used; between Copenhagen and Padborg, Denmark, trains are hauled by a pair of TraXion Class MY diesels; and from Padborg to Duisburg, a pair of RAG Bahn und Hafen Class 145 electric locomotives take over. IKEA expected the diesel traction employed on the Swedish and Danish legs to be replaced by dual-voltage electric locomotives operating throughout by late 2003 or early 2004.

*NEW ENTRY*

# Inlandsbanan AB (IBAB)

Köpmangatan 22B, PO Box 561, SE-831 27 Östersund
Tel: (+46 63) 19 44 00   Fax: (+46 63) 19 44 06
e-mail: info@inlandsbanan.se
Web: http://www.inlandsbanan.se

**Key personnel**
Chairman: Leonard Persson
Managing Director: Ulf Johanisson
Marketing Manager: Dan Humble
Finance Manager: Lars E Grenholm

Gauge: 1,435 mm
Route length: 1,056 km

**Political background**
The Inlandsbanan (Inland Railway) extends for 1,053 km from Mora to Gällivare, through some of the most sparsely populated territory in Sweden. After years of declining services and uncertainty over the line's future, parliament agreed in 1992 to lease the line for 20 years to the 15 district councils along the route.

Inlandsbanan AB (IBAB), a company owned by the 15 councils, assumed responsibility for managing the line in 1993. The addition of three connecting branch lines has brought the total route-km managed by IBAB to 1,096, some 10 per cent of the Swedish rail network.

Following expiry of the initial five-year government funding agreement in 1997, IBAB can now apply for subsidy on an annual basis.

**Organisation**
IBAB is responsible for passenger services, infrastructure and stations, as well as traffic control and safety. Freight services are run by Green Cargo AB (qv), BK Tåg (qv), TGOJ Trafik AB (qv), and Inlandsgods AB (qv). Infrastructure maintenance services are procured by competitive tendering. The train operators pay fees to IBAB for access to infrastructure, locomotives and rolling stock.

The board of IBAB has stipulated that the company must operate within the bounds of the finance provided in the transfer agreement and the revenue generated by operations; apart from equity capital, no funding will be required from shareholders. Together with the train operators, IBAB works to develop traffic and to secure the Inlandsbanan as an essential part of the transport system in northern Sweden.

**Passenger operations**
IBAB has concentrated on developing tourist services, which attracted 23,000 passengers in 1999. In 1997, IBAB took over the operation and marketing of these services itself, rather than contracting them out as in previous years.

From late June until mid-August, railcars provide daily workings in each direction over both the southern section from Östersund to Mora (322 km) and the northern section from Östersund to Gällivare (746 km). The 'Wilderness Express', a locomotive-hauled train conveying ordinary second-class accommodation, vintage first-class cars and a restaurant car, returned to the route in 1998.

Since 1996, local railway preservation societies have operated a series of steam-hauled specials on different sections of the Inlandsbanan during the summer season.

### Freight operations

Timber transport has always been the mainstay of the Inlandsbanan. Freight traffic has grown by 50 per cent in wagonload terms since IBAB took over the line; Green Cargo AB now operates a daily return journey all the way from Östersund to Storuman, whereas previously the policy was for freight trains to travel the shortest possible distance on the Inlandsbanan.

Inlandsgods AB operates timber trains on the southern section between Östersund and Mora plus peat trains between Sveg and Mora and onward via Banverket lines to Uppsala.

In total 37,000 wagonloads were carried on the line in 1999, corresponding to about 1,100 trainloads.

### Improvements to existing lines

Under the 1992 transfer agreement, IBAB is committed to completing upgrading work planned by the former SJ and Banverket covering the 494 route-km to which the former SJ's freight operations were previously confined. In view of the increase in freight traffic, IBAB aims to extend the upgrading to other sections, while remaining within budget. The aim is that the entire line should permit the same maximum axleload (22.5 tonnes) as Banverket's network.

In 1998/99, IBAB upgraded Vilhelmina–Dorotea (56 route-km) and Hoting–Ulriksfors (52 route-km). A five-year programme of work on the line between Bruntlo and Sveg (170 route-km) commenced in 2000.

Some of the upgrading work has taken the form of employment training projects, operated in conjunction with regional government. It has also been necessary for IBAB, at its own expense, to upgrade several sections where maintenance had been deferred.

### Traction and rolling stock

IBAB's diesel motive power comprises three Class Z65 shunters and four Class TMX A1A-A1A locomotives acquired from Danish State Railways in 1994.

Nine preserved steam locomotives have been acquired for use by railway societies along the line.

*UPDATED*

## Inlandsgods AB

Heffnersvägen 1, SE-856 33 Sundsvall
Tel: (+46 60) 10 17 70   Fax: (+46 60) 10 08 16
e-mail: info@inlandsgods.se
Web: http://www.inlandsgods.se

### Key personnel
Managing Director: Tomas Säterberg

### Freight operations

Inlandsgods AB was set up in 1993, initially to provide haulage for works trains operated on behalf of Inlandsbanan AB (qv).

In 1997 the company began operating freight services in its own right and signed a five-year contract to carry peat from Sveg (on the Inlandsbanan) to Uppsala, north of Stockholm.

By 2002 traffic was in excess of 500,000 tonnes per year, making Inlandsgods Sweden's largest private rail freight operator. The principal commodities carried are timber, woodpulp and biofuels.

*UPDATED*

## Jernhusen AB

Box 520, SE-101 30 Stockholm
Tel: (+46 8) 762 45 00   Fax: (+46 8) 762 33 50
Web: http://www.jernhusen.se

### Key personnel
Managing Director: Lasse Jerbéus

### Organisation

Formerly SJ Properties, the land and property company created by Swedish State Railways as part of the restructuring resulting from its break-up, Jerhusen AB owns or manages 900 stations, workshops, freight terminals, warehouses and development assets in Sweden. The present company was established in 2001 and remains state owned.

The company acts as station manager for train and bus traffic operators at some 190 locations in Sweden; it manages tenancies at railway properties; it is responsible for optimising the value of property and land no longer needed for railway use; and it has a remit to draw up development plans for stations in major towns and cities.

*NEW ENTRY*

## Malmtrafik i Kiruna AB (MTAB)

SE-981 86 Kiruna
Tel: (+46 980) 710 00   Fax: (+46 980) 109 02
e-mail: info@mtab.com
Web: http://www.mtab.com

### Key personnel
Managing Director: Åke Boström

Gauge: 1,435 mm
Route length: 447 km in Sweden (BV), 42 km in Norway (JBV)

### Organisation

The Iron Ore Line (Malmbanan) links the mines at Kiruna, Malmberget and Svappavaara with the harbours at Narvik (Norway) and Luleå. Since 1988 operating rights for the Swedish part of the line have rested with the mining company LKAB, which initially contracted Swedish State Railways (SJ) to run the trains on its behalf, together with Norwegian State Railways (NSB).

In 1995 it was decided to establish the ore transport operations as a separate company, Malmtrafik AB (MTAB), originally owned 51 per cent by LKAB, 24.5 per cent by SJ and 24.5 per cent by NSB. MTAB established a Norwegian subsidiary, Malmtrafikk AS (MTAS), to acquire the former NSB assets and staff.

On 1 July 1996, MTAB and MTAS took over all locomotives, wagons and depot facilities connected with the ore operations. Infrastructure maintenance remains the responsibility of Banverket (Sweden) and Jernbaneverket (Norway).

Since 1 January 2000, MTAB has been a wholly owned subsidiary of LKAB.

The infrastructure authorities are upgrading the line for 30-tonne axleloads, which will allow the operation of 8,160-tonne trains compared with the previous maximum of 5,200 tonnes. Upgrading of the southern section, between Malmberget and Luleå, was completed in 2001. Work on the northern section, between Kiruna and Narvik, is in progress.

### Traction and rolling stock

At January 2002, MTAB and MTAS operated 24 electric line-haul locomotives: 15 Class Dm3 (7,200 kW, ex-SJ), six Class El15 (5,406 kW, ex-NSB) and three of the new class IORE (see below). In addition, the companies owned 985 ore wagons, together with seven diesel locomotives for shunting and terminal operations and one back-up electric locomotive.

In 1998 the company placed an order with Adtranz (now Bombardier Transportation) for nine electric locomotives to replace classes Dm3 and El15. Each Class IORE locomotive will comprise two close-coupled six-axle units (Co-Co + Co-Co) with a total power output of 10.8 MW and a maximum tractive effort of 1,200 kN. The first example was delivered in 2000 and underwent extensive testing prior to series delivery in 2002-04.

In 1999 tests commenced with five prototype Series Uno ore wagons from Transwerk of South Africa. A preliminary batch of 68 additional wagons was delivered in December 2000, and MTAB has an option to purchase a total of 209 such wagons.

Upgrading of the line for 30-tonne axleloads will permit a reduction in the fleet to nine locomotives (Class IORE) and around 700 wagons.

*UPDATED*

*Bombardier Transportation Class IORE two-section 10.8 MW electric locomotive*   2001/0103974

## Öresund Consortium

Öresundskonsortiet
Kalkbrottsgatan 141, PO Box 4278, SE-203 14 Malmö
Tel: (+46 40) 676 60 00   Fax: (+46 40) 676 65 80
e-mail: info@oeresundsbron.com
Web: http://www.oeresundsbron.com

### Key personnel
Managing Director: Sven Landelius
Directors
   Finance: Teddy Jacobsen
   Technical: Peter Lundhus
   Public Affairs (Sweden): Leif-Göran Persson

### New lines

In 1991 the Swedish and Danish governments signed an agreement to complete a fixed Öresund link between Malmö and Copenhagen. The link opened on 1 July 2000.

The 15.5 km rail and road link comprises a 7.8 km bridge from Lernacken on the Swedish shore to an artificial island close to Saltholm, where it passes into a 3.5 km tunnel, emerging via an artificial headland on Amager, close to Copenhagen's Kastrup airport.

The link's managing authority, Öresundskonsortiet, split the project into three construction contracts: the central high bridge section with the approach bridges on either side; the artificial island and headland; and the tunnel entry into Denmark.

The bridge is a twin-deck design, with motorway on the upper and railway on the lower deck. The central cable-stayed section is 1,092 m in length, with a shipping clearance of 57 m and a pylon height of 203.5 m.

*VERIFIED*

## Rikstrafiken

National Public Transport Agency
PO Box 473, SE-856 06 Sundsvall
Tel: (+46 60) 67 82 50   Fax: (+46 60) 67 82 51
e-mail: registrator@rikstrafiken.se
Web: http://www.rikstrafiken.se

**Key personnel**
Director General: Kjell Dahlström
Administrative Director: Kerstin Söderland
Chief Procurement Officer: Elisabeth Forslin
Public Relations Officer: Håkan Jacobsson

**Political background**
Legislation passed by the Swedish parliament in 1998 set up a new agency to promote the development of a nationwide integrated public transport system. Rikstrafiken came into being on 1 July 1999, and on 1 January 2000 it assumed responsibility for procuring long-distance passenger services which SJ AB has declared commercially unviable. It has similar responsibilities in respect of air and ferry services.

Subsidies totalling SKr800 million are allocated to public transport in the state budget, which includes central government support to the regional transport administrations. These funds have now been transferred to Rikstrafiken, but in future will no longer be earmarked for a particular mode. Instead, Rikstrafiken will allocate subsidies to the most appropriate mode on the basis of an overall socioeconomic assessment of public transport requirements.

Commercially unviable long-distance rail services have been subject to competitive tendering since 1993, but it was not until 1999 that private operators succeeded in breaking SJ's long-distance monopoly. Since January 2000, overnight services linking Stockholm and Gothenburg with the far north have been run by Svenska Tågkompaniet AB (qv). Following retendering in 2002, the contract to operate these services for five years from June 2003 was awarded to a new operator, Connex Transport AB. In May 2001 a contract to operate services between Sundsvall and Östersund from June 2002 was awarded to Svenska Tågkompaniet. The remaining state-subsidised services remain in the hands of SJ.

*UPDATED*

## Shortline Väst AB

Per Anders gata 24, SE-521 32 Falköping
Tel: (+46 515) 834 23

**Key personnel**
Managing Director: Jan-Erik Astonius

**Freight operations**
Shortline Väst AB was set up in 1994 and has operated feeder freight traffic on the Borås—Herrljunga line (43 km) since January 1995. The company's original service between Herrljunga and Lidköping (55 km) ceased in early 1998.

The company has three electric locomotives, three diesel locomotives and two locotractors. It also provides workshop facilities and has responsibility for shunting duties at Falköping and Borås.

*VERIFIED*

## SJ AB

Centralstationen, SE-105 50 Stockholm
Tel: (+46 8) 762 20 00   Fax: (+46 8) 411 12 16
e-mail: sjinfo@sj.se
Web: http://www.sj.se

**Key personnel**
Chairman: Daniel Johanesson
Managing Director: Jan Forsberg
Directors
　Personnel: Peter Blomqvist
　Production: Jan G Forslund
　Rolling Stock: Jan Kyrk
　Political and International Affairs: Magnus Persson
　Marketing and Communications: Gunilla Asker
　Subsidiary Businesses: Christer Jernberg
　Sales: Björn Nilsson
　Long-distance Services: Mikael Wikström
　Götland Region: Gunnar Wulff
　Svealand Region: Mats Wilhelmsson

**Organisation**
SJ AB, formerly the passenger division of Swedish State Railways, began trading as a limited company on 1 January 2001. The company is wholly owned by the Swedish state and employs around 3,500 people.

The company had a turnover of SKr5.5 billion in 2001. Traffic for the year (excluding contract traffic) totalled 30.6 million passenger journeys and 5.5 billion passenger-km.

SJ AB is structured into seven head office departments, a long-distance division, two regional divisions, and divisions for sales, rolling stock, production and subsidiary businesses. Operational and profit responsibility is devolved to the business units.

| Traffic (million) | 1997 | 1998 | 1999 |
|---|---|---|---|
| Passenger journeys | 106.8 | 110.9 | 114.9 |
| Passenger-km | 6,814 | 6,997 | 7,434 |

(Data applies to former SJ Passenger Traffic subsidiary)

**Passenger operations**
SJ AB's product portfolio includes long-distance, regional and local services. Around 20 per cent of business consists of contracted traffic purchased by the public sector through Rikstrafiken (qv) and the 24 regional transport administrations. The remaining 80 per cent of business is made up of commercial traffic on the trunk network.

In recent years SJ has significantly increased its share of the business travel market. On the major business travel routes (Stockholm to Gothenburg, Malmö and Sundsvall) served by X2000 services, SJ has strengthened its position. X2000 services are operated with Adtranz-built Class X2 tilt-body trainsets, designed for 200 km/h operation. X2000 services also operate from Stockholm to Karlstad, Arvika, Falun, Mora, Härnösand, Jönköping, Karlskrona and Helsingborg. The Mälar and Svealand lines serving the populous area west of Stockholm are also operated with Class X2 trainsets. A shortened version of the X2, known as the X2-1, operates on interregional services in the south of Sweden.

*New services*
The link enabling SJ to provide services to Stockholm's Arlanda airport was opened at the beginning of 2000 and the Öresund Link was opened in July 2000, offering a direct connection to Copenhagen and its airport at Kastrup. The provision of new services to the large airports in Copenhagen and Stockholm are strategically important for SJ, which realises that such effective rail links offer substantial benefits for both train and airline

*Y2K 'Kustpilen' dmu at Lund forming a Malmö—Copenhagen service (David Haydock)*   2001/0114259

*SJ AB Class Rc6 electric locomotive waiting at Oslo Central with a return cross-border service to Gothenburg (Wolfram Veith)*   2001/0114223

**Electric locomotives**

| Class | Wheel arrangement | Output kW | Speed km/h | Weight Tonnes | No in service | First built | Builders Mechanical | Electrical |
|---|---|---|---|---|---|---|---|---|
| Rc3 | Bo-Bo | 3,600 | 160 | 77 | 32 | 1970 | Nohab/ASJ/Motala | ASEA |
| Rc6 | Bo-Bo | 3,600 | 160 | 78 | 100 | 1982 | Hägglunds | ASEA |

passengers. SJ and the Scandinavian airline SAS are already co-operating with through ticketing, enabling passengers to use one ticket for travel on both modes.

Together with Norwegian State Railways (NSB), SJ is working on a project to develop high-speed services linking Stockholm and Oslo in 4 hours 30 minutes. A new company, Linx AB (qv in *Operators of International rail services in Europe* section) owned jointly by SJ and NSB and based in Gothenburg, has been set up to take over the running of Oslo–Karlstad–Stockholm and Oslo–Gothenburg–Copenhagen services from 2001/2002.

### Traction and rolling stock

SJ AB on its formation took over 121 Class Rc3 and Rc6 electric locomotives from Swedish State Railways, as well as most of the dmu and emu fleet.

Of the initial batch of 27 three-car dual-voltage emus supplied by Adtranz to the Swedish and Danish railways for operating services via the Öresund fixed link, 10 units are owned by SJ AB, which has a further eight units on order (Class X31).

In January 2001, six Adtranz Regina two-car emus (Class X50) were introduced on local services from Västerås, operated by SJ AB on behalf of the Västmanland regional transport administration. SJ AB also won the contract to run local services in the Bergslagen region from June 2001, for which 12 Regina and two Itino units are being leased.

In its own right, SJ AB has agreed to lease 11 two-car and five three-car Regina units for operation on Stockholm–Västerås services and a pair of two-car units for Coast-to-Coast services (Gothenburg–Kalmar/Karlskrona).

When current orders are completed, SJ AB will have a total of 36 Regina emus in service on contracted and commercial services.

The first order placed by the new SJ AB, in early 2001, calls for 43 bilevel emus for services in the Mälardalen region such as Stockholm–Västerås. The units, to be supplied by Alstom, will have a top speed of 200 km/h. Of the trains, 27 will be three-car units, seating 319 passengers, while the remaining 16 will be two-car units with 202 seats. Delivery is scheduled to begin in late 2003 and be completed by the end of 2004.

A fleet of 27 hauled coaches built in the 1980s was refurbished in 2001-02 to provide back-up and relief capacity for X2000 services. The refurbished stock, known as BlueX trains, is to operate in six-car sets, offering comparable levels of comfort to Class X2 trainsets. Although maximum speed was initially limited to 160 km/h, five Class Rc electric locomotives are being modified and reclassified Rc7 to provide haulage at up to 180 km/h.

*Class X50 emu operated by SJ AB for Tåg i Bergslagen at Borlange (Edward Barnes)* 2002/0524944

#### Diesel railcars or multiple-units

| Class | Cars per unit | Motor cars per unit | Motored axles/car | Power/motor kW | Speed km/h | No in service | First built | Builders Mechanical | Engine | Transmission |
|---|---|---|---|---|---|---|---|---|---|---|
| Y1 | 1 | 1 | 2 | 147 | 130 | 19 | 1979 | Fiat/Kalmar | Fiat 8217.12.150 | H Fiat SRM |
| Y1 | 1 | 1 | 2 | 210 | 130 | 17 | 1979 | Fiat/Kalmar | Volvo THD 102 KB | H Allison |
| YF1 | 1 | 1 | 2 | 147 | 130 | 4 | 1981 | Fiat | Fiat 8217.12.150 | H Fiat SRM |
| Y2 | 3 | 2 | 2 | 294 | 180 | 14 | 1990 | ABB-Scandia | KHD BF8LV 513CP | M ZFS HP 600 |
| Y2* | 3 | 2 | 2 | 310 | 180 | 6 | 1996 | Adtranz | Cummins NTAA 855 R7 | M ZFS HP 600 |

* Fitted with catalytic converters and particle filters

#### Electric railcars or multiple-units

| Class | Cars per unit | Motor cars per unit | Motored axles/car | Output/motor kW | Speed km/h | No in service | First built | Builders Mechanical | Electrical |
|---|---|---|---|---|---|---|---|---|---|
| X1 | 2 | 1 | 4 | 280 | 120 | 94 | 1967 | ASJ/Kalmar | ASEA |
| X2 | 7 | 1 | 4 | 815 | 210 | 23 | 1990 | ABB | ABB |
| X2 | 6 | 1 | 4 | 815 | 210 | 3 | 1994 | ABB | ABB |
| X2-1 | 5 | 1 | 4 | 815 | 210 | 17 | 1994 | ABB | ABB |
| X9 | 3 | 2 | 2 | 170 | 115 | 5 | 1960 | Carlsson | ASEA |
| X10 | 2 | 1 | 4 | 320 | 140 | 54 | 1982 | Hägglunds | ASEA |
| X11 | 2 | 1 | 4 | 320 | 140 | 47 | 1982 | Hägglunds | ASEA |
| X12 | 2 | 1 | 4 | 320 | 160 | 18 | 1991 | ABB | ABB |
| X14 | 2 | 1 | 4 | 320 | 160 | 18 | 1994 | ABB | ABB |
| X31† | 3 | 2 | 4 | 480 | 180 | 18 | 1999 | Adtranz | Adtranz |
| X50 | 2 | - | - | - | - | 31 | 2001 | Bombardier | Bombardier |
| X50 | 3 | - | - | - | - | 5 | 2001 | Bombardier | Bombardier |

† Dual-voltage (15 kV AC/25 kV AC)

*UPDATED*

## Svedab

Svensk-Danska Broförbindelsen AB
Djäknegatan 23, PO Box 4044, SE-203 11 Malmö
Tel: (+46 40) 30 65 65    Fax: (+46 40) 30 00 21

### Key personnel
Managing Director: Karl-Otto Sicking
Public Affairs Director: Leif-Göran Persson

### New lines
Svedab is the public enterprise responsible for landworks on the Swedish side of the Öresund link (see Öresund Consortium entry above). A double-track railway and four-lane motorway run in parallel for 10 km from the bridge abutment at Lernacken to Fosieby, south of Malmö. The railway then swings north to join the existing Continental Line linking Malmö, Trelleborg and Ystad, which has been double-tracked throughout.

A proposal for a 4 km rail tunnel beneath central Malmö, to allow through running to the Öresund crossing without reversal at Malmö Central, was finally approved by the government in late 1996. The project will involve construction of a subsurface through station at Malmö Central, a tunnel station at Triangeln in the city centre, and a new surface station at Hyllie, south of the city. The estimated SKr7 billion cost of the scheme will be shared by central and regional government. Construction work will start around 2002 and should be completed in 2006.

*VERIFIED*

## Svenska Tågkompaniet AB

PO Box 45, SE-971 02 Luleå
Tel: (+46 920) 23 33 33    Fax: (+46 920) 23 33 39
Web: http://www.tagkompaniet.se

### Key personnel
Managing Director: Jan Johansson
Operations Director: Sven Malmberg
Marketing Director: Björn Nyström

### Passenger operations
Tågkompaniet was set up by a group of senior managers previously employed by Swedish State Railways (SJ) and is jointly owned by its three founder directors and the venture capital company Fylkinvest AB. Operations commenced on 10 January 2000, following the award of a two-year contract to run the state-subsidised overnight

*Tågkompaniet Rc2 electric locomotive with a passenger service at Gällivare (Edward Barnes)* 2002/0524945

services linking Stockholm and Gothenburg with the northern cities of Umeå and Luleå and the Norwegian port of Narvik.

Under a new five-year contract awarded in June 2002, these services are to be taken over by a new operator, Connex Transport AB, from June 2003. Tågkompaniet has lodged an appeal against this decision.

Tågkompaniet's contract also covers passenger services on the Iron Ore line (Luleå–Kiruna–Narvik). In a separate initiative, the company is running a daily return service from Luleå to the Finnish border at Haparanda during the summer months, which has entailed the reopening to passengers of eight stations.

Further expansion came in June 2000, when Tågkompaniet took over the operation of commuter services between Uppsala and Tierp (on the Stockholm–Gävle main line) under a five-year contract with the regional transport administration, Upplands Lokaltrafik.

Tågkompaniet has also won the contract to operate local services for X-Trafik, the regional transport administration in the neighbouring country of Gävleborg. The five-year agreement, which took effect in June 2001, covers services on the main lines north from Gävle to Ljusdal and Sundsvall.

In May 2001 Tågkompaniet was awarded a contract to run services between Sundsvall and Östersund from June 2002, initially for three years but with an option for a further two.

### Traction and rolling stock

Motive power for the services to the far north is provided by 12 Class Rc6 and two Class Rc2 electric locomotives hired from SJ. Initially, a fleet of 93 carriages (including 26 sleeping cars, 30 couchette cars and six cinema cars) was also hired from SJ.

To reduce its dependence on hired stock, the company has since purchased 10 carriages from the Swiss tour operator Reisebüro Mittelthurgau: five ex-DB 'Rheingold' panoramic observation cars, and five recently refurbished sleeping cars which latterly operated the Nostalgie Istanbul Orient Express land cruise. Tågkompaniet and Mittelthurgau have joined forces to market services using this stock to foreign tourists under the Polar Express name.

Tågkompaniet's motive power and rolling stock is maintained under contract by TGOJ (formerly a subsidiary of SJ) at its Notviken works near Luleå.

The Uppsala–Tierp service is operated with Class X12 emus hired from SJ by Upplands Lokaltrafik. Tågkompaniet has established a small depot at Tierp for cleaning and day-to-day maintenance.

The X-Trafik services are operated with five Regina two-car emus delivered in 2001 by Adtranz Sweden (now Bombardier Transportation). Additional Regina units will be deployed on the Sundsvall–Östersund service from mid-2003.

*UPDATED*

## Swedish National Rail Administration (BV)

Banverket
Jussi Björlings väg 2, SE-781 85 Borlänge
Tel: (+46 243) 44 50 00   Fax: (+46 243) 44 50 09
e-mail: banverket@banverket.se
Web: http://www.banverket.se

### Key personnel
Chairman: Mats Hulth
Director General: Bo Bylund
Deputy Director General: Per-Olof Granbom
Directors
 Technical: Rune Lindberg
 Infrastructure Management: Hans Öhman
 Strategy: Lena Ericsson
 Marketing: Lars-Åke Josefsson
 Administration: Per-Olof Granbom
 Finance: Bo Wikström
 Communications: Karin Rosander
 Banverket Production: Claes Sandgren
 Industrial Division: Tommy Forslund
 Banverket Consulting: Björn Östlund
 Information Technology: Rune Lidman
 Banverket Telecom: Lars-Göran Bernland
 Railway Training Centre: Jan Hammarqvist
Directors, Independent Administrative Units
 Rail Traffic Administration: Sven Bårström
 Railway Inspectorate: Dick Ivarsson

Gauge: 1,435 mm
Route length: 9,978 km
Electrification: 7,527 km at 15 kV 16⅔ Hz AC

### Organisation
Banverket is a state authority responsible for the railway network in Sweden. At the end of 1996 its role was expanded from that of infrastructure provider to one of overall responsibility for the development and co-ordination of the rail system.

Day-to-day scheduling, train control and passenger information functions were fully integrated into Banverket during 2001. An independent unit, the Rail Traffic Administration, decides on operating rights and track allocations, and acts as an arbitrator in the event of disputes.

The state takes full responsibility for the maintenance and upgrading of rail infrastructure, while train operators pay fees to Banverket for using the tracks. Track access charges are based on socioeconomic marginal costs and total around SKr275 million per annum.

Banverket maintains embankments and tracks, marshalling yards and electrical, signalling and telecommunications installations. It is responsible for the upgrading of existing lines and the construction of new lines.

Banverket's main lines generally allow speeds up to 130 km/h, but a gradual programme is under way to upgrade the most important routes for 160 to 200 km/h. Double or multiple track exists on the following lines:
- Stockholm–Gothenburg
- Stockholm–Malmö
- Stockholm–Gävle and some additional sections onwards to Östersund
- Most of Stockholm–Västerås–Kolbäck
- About 110 km between Gothenburg and Lund
- Frövi–Örebro–Hallsberg

Axleload is normally 22.5 tonnes, but a design standard of 25 tonnes is now applied when upgrading track (for example, by use of UIC-60 rail) and replacing bridges on major lines. The Iron Ore line (Luleå–Kiruna–Narvik) is being upgraded to 30 tonnes axleload.

### Finance
Banverket is funded by annual government appropriations. In 2001, Banverket's total volume of operations was SKr10.2 billion. SKr2 billion was spent on maintenance and operations and SKr858 million on reinvestment. Investment in new lines totalled SKr3.3 billion, and Banverket received SKr1 billion for regulatory duties. External contracts generated SKr1.2 billion.

### Improvements to existing lines
*Ten-year investment plan*
A 10-year rolling investment programme for Sweden's railway infrastructure is produced every four years. The current plan, approved by the government in June 1998, allocates a total of SKr38 billion to new investment in the national rail network between 1998 and 2007. The principal projects are:
- West Main Line, Stockholm–Gothenburg: Upgrading for operation with 200 km/h tilting trains has been completed and has reduced the journey time to under 3 hours. The line has also been upgraded between Hallsberg and Gothenburg to accommodate 25 tonnes axleload and containers 50 per cent wider than normal.
- South Main Line: Upgrading for 200 km/h was completed from Stockholm to Malmö in 1997. Proposed additional works are aimed mainly at improving travelling comfort and increasing station capacities.
- West Coast Main Line: Double-tracking throughout of the Gothenburg–Malmö line is intended to bring journey time down from 3 hours 15 minutes to about 2 hours, and to remove the route's present restrictions on freight train length and operating capacity. Construction of two parallel 8.5 km tunnels under the Hallandsås hills was originally scheduled for completion in 1996, but the difficult nature of the rock encountered has put the project seriously behind schedule. Banverket has suspended work as a result of environmental problems and greatly increased costs, and the solution is currently in the hands of the Swedish government.
- North Link: As part of plans to develop the Gothenburg–Oslo route for 200 km/h operation, several stretches of new alignment will be needed, along with double-tracking in the Göta valley.
- Coast to Coast Line: The Karlskrona/Kalmar–Alvesta–Gothenburg route is to be upgraded for 160 km/h over much of its length.
- East Coast Line: This route has already been fettled up for 200 km/h from Stockholm through Uppsala to Gävle and will now be substantially upgraded to Sundsvall, cutting Stockholm–Sundsvall journey time from 3 hours 15 minutes to 3 hours. A new single-track section north of Söderhamn is nearing completion. Double-tracking between Uppsala and Gävle will be undertaken on an incremental basis over the 10-year period. The route north of Gävle will remain largely single-track, as demand is lower on this section.
- Bothnia Line: This will run from Nyland, north of Sundsvall, to the northern university city of Umeå, a major growth area. A special-purpose company, Botniabanan AB (qv) has been formed by the government and local authorities to finance, design and construct the 190 km line. Commissioning is scheduled for 2008.
- North Main Line: The line from Gävle that forks to Östersund and to Luleå is a vital freight corridor in need of more operating capacity, which is to be progressively created.
- Mälar Line and Svealand Line: These are new lines on the northern and southern shores respectively of Lake Mälar, west of Stockholm. Work began in 1992 and funds have been provided (85 per cent from the state and 15 per cent from other sources) to finance completion by 2003. North of the lake the result will be new 200 km/h double track from Stockholm to Västerås and Kolbäck, then single track upgraded for 160 km/h on to Arboga. A cut-off between Arboga and Örebro, suitable for 200 km/h operation, has helped cut Stockholm–Örebro journey time by 15 minutes. South of the lake a new 200 km/h single track, with a

*Banverket snowplough-fitted Class DLL-Tb diesel locomotives with a ballast train at Abisko Östra (Edward Barnes)*

short double-track section, has reduced Stockholm–Eskilstuna journey time by 40 minutes. The Svealand Line was completed in 1997 and most of the Mälar Line in 1999, apart from a remaining bottleneck near Stockholm.

- Malmö City Tunnel: The project to build a tunnel beneath Malmö city centre, costed at SKr5 billion, is now under way. Construction will start around 2002 and should be completed in 2006. The tunnel will accommodate all passenger traffic to and from the Öresund fixed link, as well as regional services.
- Storvik–Frövi–Hallsberg–Mjölby route: On this important north-south freight corridor, a short double-track section opened at the beginning of 1998 and a further 15 km of double track opened in 2000 between Hallsberg and Mjölby (see entry for Malmtrafik).
- Iron Ore Line: Upgrading to 30 tonnes maximum axleload has started between Gällivare and Luleå. Another project under discussion, but not figuring in the current 10-year plan is:
- Götaland Line: Promoted by the three regional governments whose territory it would traverse and by the construction company NCC, this would be a longer but faster route from Stockholm to Gothenburg than the present West Main Line. The Götaland concept envisages upgrading the line from Stockholm to Mjölby and Tranås, then building 140 km of new infrastructure through Jönköping to Borås, and finally upgrading from Borås to Gothenburg.

*Systemwide projects*
Banverket is spending SKr500 million across the network to reduce noise pollution from railway operations by installing soundproof triple glazing in homes near railway lines and constructing sound barriers. A total of SKr500 million is also being spent on fitting some level crossings with automatic barriers and eliminating others.

### Signalling and telecommunications
The project to find replacements for 40-year-old relay-based interlockings at small stations, and for traditional line blocking equipment, has reached the design phase. The system is being developed by a Swedish company, Novosignal, and a prototype installation is expected to be made at Gemla station on the Alvesta–Växjö line in 2002.

Since 1997, a new generation of control system for marshalling yards has been successfully in use at Borlänge. The same kind of system, based on an open system concept with PLC and PC hardware and Windows NT software, has now also been introduced at Sävenäs marshalling yard.

A generic specification of functional safety requirements has been drawn up and used for formal verification of some of Banverket's interlocking systems. Further research in this field is in progress.

A human factors research project concerning safety-related issues and the working environment of train drivers was completed in mid-2000. The first stage of a research project concerning man/machine interaction in CTC systems was completed in 1998.

*Telecommunications*
The Banverket Telecom system comprises about 20,000 km of metal cable, 10,000 km of fibre optic cable, 90 digital telephone exchanges and 800 radio base stations. There are 26,000 subscriptions, of which 16,000 are used by Banverket or SJ and 10,000 are trackside telephones.

The fibre optic cable is a 12-fibre single-mode cable. Capacity is 2.5 Gb/s or 622 Mb/s long-distance and 34 Mb/s short-distance. In addition, wavelength multiplexing (WDM) is used on major long-distance routes.

Capacity in the fibre optic cable is sold on commercial terms to external customers, of which SJ is one. Other major clients include Tele 2, Comviq, Telenordia and Worldcom, reflecting the deregulated telecommunications market in Sweden.

In July 1998, Banverket placed a contract with Siemens to supply a digital mobile radio communications network. It will employ GSM-R technology, developed to meet the specific requirements of railway operations. Banverket is a member of ERIG (EIRENE Radio Implementation Group), which brings together the railway administrations introducing the EIRENE GSM-R system. The new system, MobiSIR, was inaugurated at the end of May 2001.

In June 2002, AerotechTelub (part of the Saab Group) signed a two-year contract to supply Banverket with radio link systems from Nokia, which will be used for communication between radio base stations and from radio base stations to an exchange in MobiSIR.

### Electrification
The existing extension programme for the 132 kV 16⅔ Hz power transmission line was completed in 2000 with the Ockelbo–Ryggen–Borlänge–Ludvika–Bäckhaga–Hallsberg and Borlänge–Rättvik sections, bringing its total length to around 1,900 km extending from Boden in the north to Stockholm and Hallsberg in the south. Total installed power in the system is 300 MVA, 250 MVA with static frequency converters and 50 MVA with rotary converters. Extension of the line further south is being considered.

The total electrified railway system in Sweden comprises 7,527 km of track with catenary, 660 MVA of static frequency converters and 500 MVA of rotary converters.

For some lines, the 132 kV transmission line is not the most viable option. A 2 × 15 kV 16⅔ Hz autotransformer (AT) system has been investigated, and a thorough study comparing the AT system with the existing booster transformer system concluded in 1998. The study focused particularly on power capacity, rail potentials and disturbance. A 50 km single-end fed section of the Iron Ore Line, Råtsi (Kiruna)–Svappavaara, was converted from booster transformer to AT system in 1998. The results have been encouraging, so the AT system may be used on other lines in future.

### Track
**Standard rail:** Type UIC-60 (60 kg/m) or BV 50 (50 kg/m)
On secondary lines: BV 43 (43 kg/m)
**Crossties (sleepers)**
Concrete
Type B10: 320 × 222 × 2,500 mm
Type S3: 320 × 250 × 2,500 mm
Wooden
Type 1: 240 × 165 × 2,600 mm
**Rail fastenings**
Wooden sleepers
On main lines: Hey-Back
On secondary lines: spikes, normally with baseplate
Concrete sleepers: Pandrol
**Sleeper spacing**
On main lines: 1,538/km on plain track; 1,538 or 1,667/km in curves of less than 500 m radius
On secondary lines: 1,333/km
Number of sleepers is increased to 2,000/km on the Kiruna-Riksgränsen ore line
**Min curve radius:** 300 m
**Max gradient:** 2.5%
**Max permissible axleload:** 22.5 tonnes (25 tonnes on the Kiruna–Riksgränsen ore line)

*UPDATED*

---

## Tågåkeriet i Bergslagen AB (Tågab)
Bangårdsgatan 2, SE-681 30 Kristinehamn
Tel: (+46 550) 875 00   Fax: (+46 550) 875 03

### Key personnel
Managing Director: Lars Yngström

### Freight operations
With over 15,000 wagonloads a year, Tågab is one of Sweden's largest short line operators. Since 1994, the company has run feeder services on two lines in west central Sweden: Hällefors–Filipstad–Kristinehamn (105 km) and Bofors–Degerfors (18 km).

Tågab supplies locomotives and drivers for some Green Cargo trains from Kristinehamn to Hallsberg and Karlstad. Haulage is also provided on occasion for Banverket works trains, and in early 1999 the company signed a five-year contract with Jernbaneverket, the Norwegian infrastructure authority, to provide two locomotives and crews for works trains in Norway.

The company's main shareholders are its principal customers: Ovako Steel and crispbread manufacturer Wasabröd. Kristinehamn council holds a minority stake. Other traffic includes processed timber and liquefied petroleum gas.

### Traction and rolling stock
Tågab operates three main line diesel locomotives (ex-Danish State Railways Class MY) and four diesel shunters. In 2001, the fleet was supplemented by the acquisition of nine Class 1043 electric locomotives from Austrian Federal Railways. Their design is similar to that of Green Cargo's Rc2 machines.

The company has its own workshop for heavy maintenance, which also undertakes work for other operators.

*UPDATED*

*Former Danish State Railways Tågab Class TMY diesel locomotives at Namsskogen, Norway (Edward Barnes)*
2002/0524942

---

## TGOJ
TGOJ Trafik AB
Järnvägsplan, SE-631 92 Eskilstuna
Tel: (+46 16) 17 26 00   Fax: (+46 16) 17 26 01

### Background
TGOJ Trafik AB is a subsidiary of Green Cargo, the freight business created by the break-up of the former Swedish State Railways (SJ). SJ took over the company in 1989.

### Passenger operations
TGOJ operates passenger services under contract to Västmanlands Länstrafik using a fleet of five emus.

## Freight operations

TGOJ is an open access operator mostly specialising in trainload freight movements for heavy industry. Operations are mainly concentrated on two routes: Börlange–Kolbäck–Eskilstuna–Oxelösund; and Hallsberg–Frövi–Västerås–Kolbäck–Eskilstuna.

Locomotives, wagons and train crew are also hired to other operators, including IKEA Rail AB (qv), which in 2002 commenced services as a train operator.

## Traction and rolling stock

At the beginning of 2001 the TGOJ fleet comprised 20 Class Ma 3,960 kW electric locomotives, 19 diesel main line and 14 diesel shunting locomotives. The diesel fleet includes two General Motors Class T66 machines delivered in late 2000 and of the same design as the Class 66 locomotives supplied to EWS in the UK. TGOJ also operates five emus and has a fleet of some 800 freight wagons.

**UPDATED**

*TGOJ Class Ma electric locomotive at Börlange (Norman Griffiths)*

# SWITZERLAND

## Ministry of Transport, Communications & Power

Bundeshaus Nord, CH-3003 Bern
Tel: (+41 31) 322 57 11   Fax: (+41 31) 322 58 11

### Key personnel
Minister: Moritz Leuenberger
Director General, International Railway Office:
  Hans-Rudolf Isliker

### Political background

The federal government assumes financial responsibility for Swiss Federal Railways' (SBB) fixed installations, except where directly connected with SBB operations, workshops and traction current supply installations. The state's responsibility is purely financial. In its commercial sector, comprising InterCity passenger, wagonload, container and less-than-wagonload traffic, SBB, as a joint stock company, has managerial freedom and is required to make an annually predetermined contribution to infrastructure costs. The company returned to profitability in 1999.

The 57 so-called private railways (their private shareholders are in fact minimal) are supported by their Cantons. The federal government is statutorily obliged to top up their subsidy in two ways. It stabilises the railways' finances, including capital investment, at levels of contribution that reflect each railway's assessed value to the national or a regional transport system. Thus, support for the Bern–Lötschberg–Simplon (BLS), a trunk system of national importance, or the metre-gauge Rhaetian, socioeconomically vital to the Grisons Canton, is much more generous than the backing for short local lines in less hostile terrain. Secondly, in the case of Alpine territory, railways like the Rhaetian or Bernese Oberland, federal subsidy finances local passenger and freight tariffs based on SBB prices; because of their abnormal upkeep costs such railways charge non-residents much higher rates.

In 1994, the federal council approved revision of the country's Railway Law to put the SBB's Regional services on the same footing as those of the private railways. The Cantons are required to share the costs of all Regional services, whoever provides them, sharing with the federal administration the annual determination of the total amount of subsidy to be provided, and the detail of services to be operated. This may in some instances be in conflict with the 'Bahn 2000' regular-interval service concept (see 'Political background' section in Swiss Federal Railways entry).

Major change is now in progress. New rail legislation has been passed to adapt Swiss railways to the principles of open access for third-party operators, with track charge for infrastructure use, such as are being introduced into surrounding European Union countries. This involves far-reaching changes to the concession principle of ownership and operations which has previously guided Swiss public and private rail competences. The new law came into effect on 1 January 1998.

In 1999, the Bundesrat brought the regulations for the funding of major railway projects into force, backdating them to 1 January 1998. The fund receives the revenues from the flat-rate HGV charge and part of the excise duties on mineral oils (the total amount being SFr200 million in 1998). The flat-rate HGV charge was to be doubled at the start of 2000, and then to be phased out in 2001 in favour of a levy based on actual journeys. There was also to be an increase in VAT. The fund will allow the construction of the new Alpine tunnels, Rail 2000, noise abatement measures, and connections with the European high-speed network.

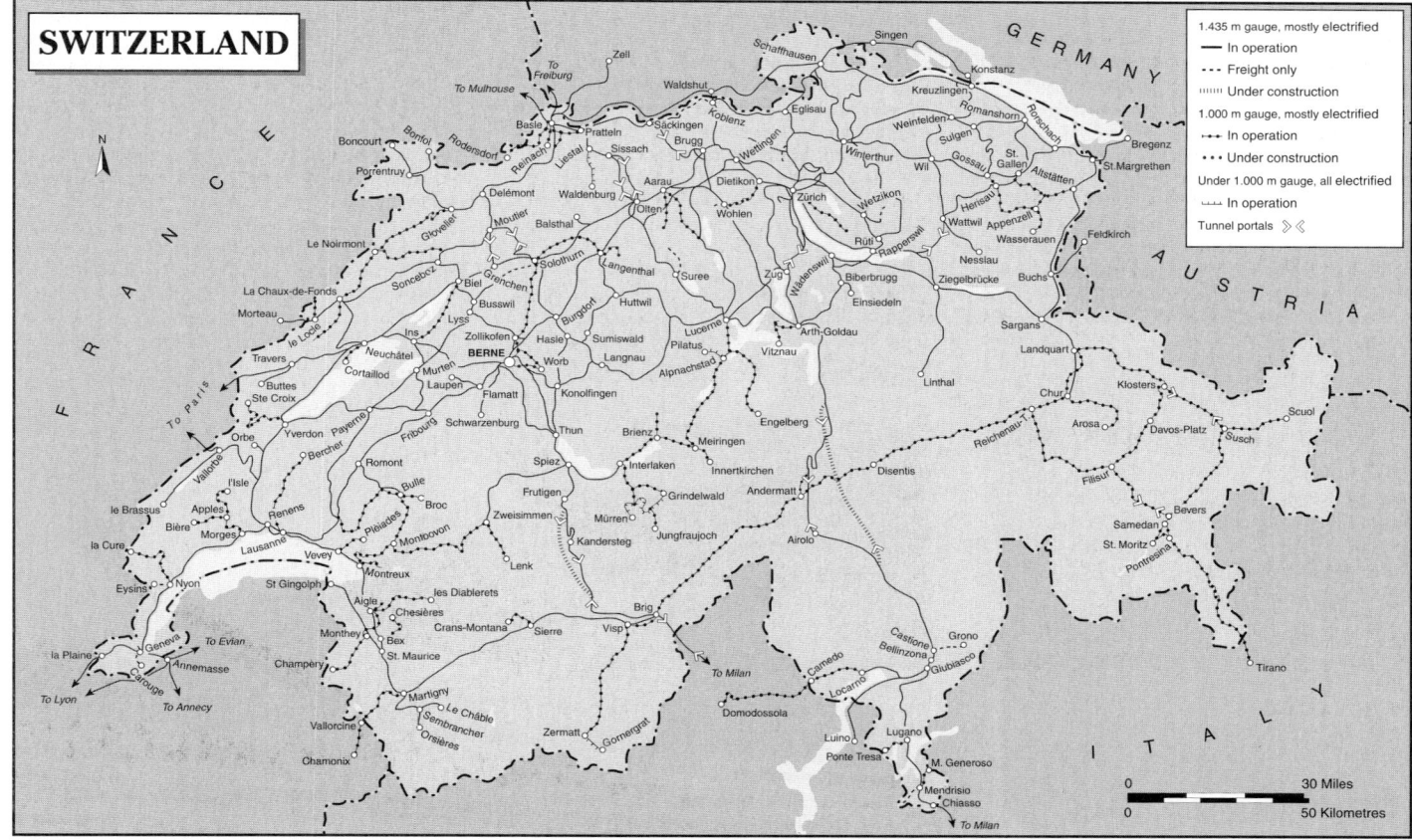

## Appenzell Railway (AB)

Appenzeller Bahnen
Bahnhofplatz 10, CH-9101 Herisau
Tel: (+41 71) 354 50 60   Fax: (+41 71) 354 50 65
e-mail: info@appenzellerbahnen.ch
Web: http://www.appenzellerbahnen.ch

### Key personnel
Director: Martin Vogt
Marketing Manager: Hanspeter Müller

*AB Type BDeh 4/4 emu at Herisau (David Haydock)*   2001/0109858

Gauge: 1,000 mm
Route length: 59.76 km (4.15 km of rack rail)
Electrification: 59 km at 1.5 kV DC

### Organisation
The system results from the 1988 merger of the Appenzell with the neighbouring St Gallen–Gais–Appenzell Railway. A 32 km line runs from Gossau, on the SBB St Gallen–Zurich main line, to Herisau, Appenzell and Wasserauen, in the Säntis mountain area, and attains a summit of 903 m above sea level at Gonten. A 20 km line extends from St Gallen to Teufen, Gais and Appenzell and is worked by seven rack-equipped electric trainsets. The third, 7 km line connects Gais and Altstätten Stadt and features a ruling gradient of 16 per cent.

Appenzeller Bahnen revenue from passengers in 1999 was SFr5,688,263 with a further SFr201,415 from freight. Total income was SFr24,717,212, of which SFr16,919,931 came in the form of support. Expenditure was SFr11,538,994 on staff costs, SFr7,373,412 on materials and services, and SFr5,561,796 on depreciation.

### Passenger and freight operations
AB's passenger performance in 1998 was 2,940,312 journeys for 29.7 million passenger-km. In 1999 these figures rose to 3,004,135 and 30.6 million respectively. On the freight side, 9,114 tonnes were carried for 214,150 tonne-km in 1998, falling to 8,020 tonnes and 199,810 tonne-km in 1999.

### Traction and rolling stock
In total the railway owned in 1998 one steam, two electric and one diesel locomotives; 14 electric trainsets; eight electric and one diesel railcars; and 76 other passenger cars (of which two incorporated a buffet). AB also operated 24 freight wagons for transporting standard-gauge wagons.

### Signalling and telecommunications
Centralised traffic control (CTC) manages 52 route-km. In 1998 automatic block equipment was being installed between St Gallen and Appenzell (20 km) and Gossau and Wasseraven (32 km)

## Bern–Solothurn Railway (RBS)

Regionalverkehr Bern–Solothurn
Bahnhofhochhaus, PO Box 119, CH-3048 Worblaufen
Tel: (+41 31) 925 55 55   Fax: (+41 31) 925 55 66
e-mail: info@rbs.ch
Web: http://www.rbs.ch

### Key personnel
Director: P Scheidegger
Deputy Director: Hans-Jakob Stricker
Vice-Director: Hans Amacker

Gauge: 1,000 mm; mixed 1,435 and 1,000 mm
Route length: 56 km
Electrification: 52 km at 1.25 kV DC; 11 km at 600 V DC overhead

### Organisation
RBS was formed by merger of the Solothurn–Zollikofen–Bern Railway (SZB) and Bern–Worb Railways (VBW). The Bern Zytlogge–Worb Dorf line is electrified at 600 V DC, the voltage of the Bern city tramway network with which both SZB and VBW were connected before the 1960s. At that time SZB's original surface route into Bern was superseded by a new segregated double-track route from Worblaufen which finally tunnelled 1.2 km to a new four-platform terminus beneath the reconstructed Bern main station. The SZB system was then mostly re-electrified at 1.25 kV DC and its route modified to funnel its trains into the new Bern subterranean terminus.

RBS also operates feeder bus services over 12 routes totalling 53 km.

*RBS Type ABe 4/12 low-floor emu leaving Zollikofen for Bern (David Haydock)*   2001/0062442

### Passenger and freight operations
In 2000 RBS carried a total of 18.9 million rail passengers. Limited amounts of freight are carried including some in standard-gauge wagons carried on RBS transporter wagons.

### Traction and rolling stock
In 2001 RBS operated six electric and two diesel locomotives; 59 emu/light rail cars; nine control trailers; five passenger cars; 12 freight wagons; and 45 transporters for 1,435 mm gauge wagons. Some historic passenger vehicles are retained for special traffic.

During 2001 intermediate low-floor trailers were added to 11 of the fleet of 16 Type Be 4/8 light rail vehicles. The lengthened vehicles are designated Type ABe 4/12.

*UPDATED*

## Bière–Apples–Morges Railway (BAM)

Chemin de Fer Bière–Apples–Morges
En Riond Bosson 3, CH-1110 Morges
Tel: (+41 21) 811 43 43   Fax: (+41 21) 801 90 17
e-mail: bam@swisscraft.ch
Web: http://www.swisscraft.ch/bam

### Key personnel
Director: P Gaillard

Gauge: 1,000 mm
Route length: 30 km
Electrification: 30 km at 15 kV 16⅔ Hz AC

*BAM Type Ge 4/4 III locomotive together with railcar at Apples (D Trevor Rowe)*
0021784

## Organisation

The BAM line is located between Lake Geneva and the Jura foothills. Investment up to the year 2000 will amount to SFr11 million, of which SFr5.6 million is approved by the Vaud Canton, and SFr2 million from local communities.

## Passenger and freight operations

In 1997, the BAM carried 1.2 million passengers (5.813 million passenger-km) and 67,000 tonnes of freight (999,700 tonne-km).

## Traction and rolling stock

BAM's rolling stock fleet comprises two electric locomotives, one diesel locomotive, six railcars, 11 trailers and 48 freight wagons.

# BLS Lötschbergbahn (BLS)

BLS Lötschbergbahn AG
Genfergasse 11, CH-3001 Bern
Tel: (+41 31) 327 27 27   Fax: (+41 31) 327 29 10
e-mail: media@bls.ch
Web: http://www.bls.ch

### Key personnel

Management
 Director: Mathias Tromp
 Infrastructure: Kees van Hoek
 Transit Traffic: Bruno Schaller
 Regional Traffic: Beat Luginbühl
 Alp Transit Traffic: Franz Kilchenmann
 Finance: Hans Flury
 Secretary General: Thomas Müller
Divisions
 Personnel: Erwin Látsch
 Safety: Eduard Wymann
 Installations: Urs Graber
 Operations: Walter Flühmann
 Development: Hans Faust
 Property: Hans Peter Lehmann
 Long-Distance Passenger Traffic: Franz Máder
 Freight Traffic: Urs Wyttenbach
 Rolling Road: Carlo Degalo
 Car-shuttle Traffic: Bernhard Schmidt
 Regional Rail and Bus Passenger Traffic:
  Peter Jaggi
 Passenger Traffic Distribution: Hansueli Kunz
 Traction: Peter Gerber
 Workshops Josef Stöckli
 Ships: Peter Ochsenbein
Public Affairs
 Publicity: Peter Senn
 Media Relations: Hans Martin Schaer

Route length: 245 km
Electrification: 245 km at 15 kV 16⅔Hz AC

## Organisation

The BLS main line from Frutigen through the Lötschberg Tunnel to Brig was opened in 1913. Certain regional railways with special guarantees from the Canton of Bern were then incorporated in the Lötschberg system, though each retained separate financial and operating identity. The BLS embraces the Spiez–Erlenbach–Zweisimmen line, the Gürbetal–Bern–Schwarzenburg line and the Bern–Neuchâtel line. Much interoperation of rolling stock takes place. In 1997, the company's shareholders approved the merger of all group railway operations into one new company, BLS Lötschbergbahn AG. The group also owns 18 Lake Thun and Lake Brienz ships and the Interlaken bus company, Auto AG. The BLS company also owns BLS Alp Transit AG, a subsidiary set up to manage the planning and building of the Lötschberg Base Tunnel.

*Class 465 6,400 kW electric locomotive at Spiez (Colin Boocock)* 2000/0088200

The BLS system covers the main lines from Thun to Spiez and Interlaken, and from Spiez via the Lötschberg Tunnel to a junction with SBB at Brig. The Lötschberg route is one of Europe's vital international rail links. BLS also owns the Grenchenberg tunnel line between Lengnau and Moutier (MLB), which forms part of the shortest route between Geneva and Basel.

At the end of 2000 BLS employed 1,567 staff.

BLS revenue from passengers in 1998 was SFr84 million, with a further SFr37 million from freight, SFr4 million from parcels and mail traffic. Total earnings from traffic were SFr167.1 million and total income was SFr36,517 million. Total expenditure was SFr361.4 million with SFr154.8 million spent on staff and SFr66.3 million for depreciation.

Under an agreement announced in August 2000, there is to be enhanced collaboration between BLS and SBB. BLS is to take over the Bern S-Bahn lines currently worked by SBB and SBB will be responsible for all long-distance traffic and the network management of both railways. SBB will hold a minority stake of up to 34 per cent in BLS.

## Passenger operations

In 1998, the BLS group carried 19.2 million passengers.

Bern Canton supports integration and development of an RER (Regional Express) network (see Swiss Federal Railways entry). For BLS this will principally entail part double-tracking of the Bern–Neuchâtel line, double-tracking throughout of the Bern–Belp line, and provision of additional rolling stock. These requirements are only in part covered by investments planned with credits from federal and cantonal supports for the private railways covering the period up to 1997.

BLS provides the route for the Cisalpino (qv in International Operators section) tilting trains running between Basel and Milano from October 1996, bringing substantially reduced journey times.

*Car shuttle*

BLS runs a push-pull shuttle service for accompanied cars and coaches through the Lötschberg Tunnel between terminals at Kandersteg and Goppenstein. The trains are formed of 28 Talbot-built car-carriers, giving an hourly capacity of 550 vehicles.

## Freight operations

In 1998, BLS carried 7.4 million tonnes, slightly down on the 7.556 million tonnes handled in 1997. BLS carries significant numbers of Intercontainer intermodal trains between Northern Europe and Italy, formerly routed through France, and in 2000 a piggyback corridor with enlarged profile will be opened between Freiburg im Breisgau and Novara via the BLS route.

## New lines

The federal council's transalpine tunnel decision of 1989 (see 'New lines' section in the Swiss Federal Railways (SBB) entry) provided for construction of both Gotthard and Lötschberg base tunnels.

The Lötschberg base tunnel will form part of a new 34.5 km route from Frutigen to a junction with the SBB's Rhône Valley main line, with ruling gradient 1 per cent. Like the Gotthard Base Tunnel, the Lötschberg will have clearance for piggybacked 4.2 m high lorries, as also the Simplon Tunnel, following the latter's track-lowering and equipment with a rigid traction current contact system (see 'Improvements to existing lines' section in SBB entry). The federal government will meet the cost, recovering roughly a quarter from road transport fuel taxation.

The twin-bore base tunnel begins at Frutigen. Planned to fork at Km 27, the western arm will emerge, 34.5 km from Frutigen, on the SBB's Rhône Valley main line at Steg, giving a politically important automobile-carrying train service to the Canton Valais, replacing an Alpine motorway connection struck from the programme; it also completes a through route from the Lötschberg line to Lausanne and Geneva. The eastern arm will lead into the Rhône Valley main line at Raron, west of Visp. Tunnel length to Raron Ost will be 34.5 km underground; this will feed traffic for Italy into the approach to the Simplon tunnel. Preliminary work began in 1994 and construction proper began in 1998 after two referenda. Completion of the base tunnel should be in 2006.

## Improvements to existing lines

Frutigen station has been rebuilt and Spiez station has been reconstructed and enlarged. Spiez is also to have a new signalling centre. In parallel to the SBB, the BLS is installing ZUB 121 automatic train-control equipment.

The Bern–Thun section is one of the best-aligned high-speed stretches in Switzerland. In a SFr86.7 million programme its 20.8 km from Gümligen to Thun has been

*Class RABe 'NINA' three-car low-floor emu at Neuchâtel (David Haydock)* 2001/0109859

# RAILWAY SYSTEMS/Switzerland

### Electric locomotives

| Class | Wheel arrangement | Output KW | Speed km/h | Weight tonnes | No in service | First built | Builders Mechanical | Electrical |
|---|---|---|---|---|---|---|---|---|
| Re 465 | Bo-Bo | 6,400 | 230 | 84 | 18 | 1994 | SLM | ABB |
| Re 4/4 | Bo-Bo | 4,980 | 140 | 80 | 36 | 1964 | SLM | ABB |
| Ae 4/4 | Bo-Bo | 2,940 | 120 | 80 | 4 | 1944 | SLM | ABB |
| Ae 8/8 | Bo-Bo + Bo-Bo | 6,470 | 120 | 160 | 2 | 1959 | SLM | ABB |
| Eea 3/3 | C (shunter) | 600 | 75 | 50 | 1 | 1991 | SLM | ABB |

### Electric railcars

| Class | Cars per unit | Motor cars per unit | Motored axles/car | Output kW | Speed km/h | No in service | First built | Builders Mechanical | Electrical |
|---|---|---|---|---|---|---|---|---|---|
| ABDe 4/8 | 3* | 2 | 2 | 1,180 | 125 | 6 | 1964 | SIG/BBC | ABB/SAAS |
| RBDe 4/4 | 3* | 1 | 4 | 1,620 | 125 | 22 | 1982 | SIG/SWS/SWP | ABB |
| RABe 4/8 | 3 | 2 | 4 | 1,000 | 140 | 14** | 1998 | Bombardier | Alstom |

\* Most of these railcars are operated with additional trailers (some driving) as three- or four-car emus
\*\* Additional 18 on order in 2002

cleared for 160 km/h, with complete track renewal, easing of four curves, strengthening of 52 bridges, station improvements and resignalling for two-way working on each track.

While unaccompanied trailers up to 4 m high can be accepted on the Lötschberg route, tractor and trailer rigs of these dimensions are currently unable to use the line. Pending completion of the base tunnel, an interim SFr125 million has been drafted to enable Lötschberg RoLa ('rolling motorway') movement of trucks up to 4 m high at their roof corners.

The interim plan, proposing at first a gauntleted third track aligned near the bore's crown, was dropped in favour of lowering one of the tunnel's lines, rebuilding it with concrete slab track, and modifying the spacing of the two tracks, to secure the required clearance for bidirectional RoLa working on the one lowered line. This clearance cannot be obtained exclusively on one line through the approach tunnels, so RoLa trains will have to make more than one crossover between the two running lines, protected by special signalling, between Spiez and Brig.

### Traction and rolling stock

In 1998, BLS operated 52 electric locomotives, six electric shunting locomotives, 36 electric railcars, nine electrodiesel shunters, 27 diesel shunters, 34 control trailers, 172 other passenger coaches (including two restaurant cars), 31 baggage cars and some 200 freight wagons (including Lötschberg Tunnel car-carrying shuttle cars). There is also one steam locomotive.

In 1996, BLS ordered eight part-low-floor NINA (Niederflur-Nahverkehr) commuter trains from a consortium led by Vevey (since acquired by Bombardier Transportation). Bombardier Talbot supplied bodies and bogies and Holec (subsequently Alstom Transport) the electrical equipment. Used for Bern area regional services, the first of the articulated three-section 47.4 m long trains was delivered in late 1998. An order for six similar units for Bern S-Bahn services was placed in 2000, followed by a subsequent contract in December 2001 for 18 more.

It was announced at the end of 1999 that BLS was to buy six air conditioned driving trailers (IC-Bt) from SBB. With these, the present 32 EW IV vehicles, six Corail baggage cars and six Re 465 locomotives, the railway formed six push-pull trainsets. Three more EW IV cars were acquired from SBB (which SBB had exchanged with the South Eastern Railway). The 35 passenger coaches and the six baggage cars were then fitted out for push-pull working and equipped with closed toilet systems. The works were completed in time for the move to all push-pull working for IC trains in Switzerland from the 2001 timetable.

### Track
(BLS only)
**Rail**
SBB IV (UIC 54E), 54 kg/m
**Crossties (sleepers):** Timber and concrete
Thickness: 150 mm timber, 235 mm concrete
Spacing: 1,666/km
**Fastenings**
Timber: Ke (bolted spring clips SKL 3)
**Min curvature radius**
Lötschberg line: 300 m
Other lines: 280 m
**Max gradient**
Lötschberg line: 2.7%
Other lines: 3.5% (Bern—Schwenenburg)
**Max axleload**
Lötschberg line: 22.5 tonnes
Other lines: 20 tonnes

*UPDATED*

---

## Bodensee—Toggenburg Railway (BT)

In December 2001, BT amalgamated with the South Eastern Railway (SOB) (qv).

*UPDATED*

---

## BVZ Zermatt-Bahn (BVZ)

BVZ Zermatt-Bahn
Nordstrasse 20, CH-3900 Brig-Glis
Tel: (+41 27) 921 41 11   Fax: (+41 27) 921 41 19
e-mail: zermatt-bahn@bvz.ch
Web: http://www.bvz.ch

### Key personnel
Managing Director: Hans-Rudolf Mooser
Group Managment: Marcel Mooser
Permanent Way: W In-Albon
Rolling Stock and Traction: H Tribolet
Finance and Control: Beat Britsch
Marketing Centre: Marcel Mooser

Gauge: 1,000 mm
Route length: 44 km, of which 8.9 km Abt rack system
Electrification: 44 km at 11 kV 16⅔Hz AC

### Organisation
BVZ is part adhesion, part Abt rack (four sections Visp—Zermatt, ruling gradient 12.5 per cent). Between Visp and Zermatt the railway climbs 955 m. Single-line throughout, with passing loops, the busiest section of the BVZ is the final 5.6 km from Täsch to Zermatt; the former is the limit of other transport to Zermatt, which is kept inaccessible to most road vehicles. Over this section the basic service of 15 Brig—Zermatt trains each way daily is supplemented by a push-pull shuttle between Zermatt and Täsch car parks. The BVZ car park at Visp is toll-free. To enable 2,000 passengers an hour to be moved each way between Täsch and Zermatt in peak seasons, this section is provided with an automatically controlled passing loop at Kalter Boden.

In 2002 it was announced that, subject to shareholder approval, BVZ was to merge with Furka-Oberalp Railway (FO) in January 2003.

*Gornergrat Railway*
BVZ also controls the 1,000 m gauge Abt rack Gornergrat—Monte Rosa—Bahnen (GGB) from Zermatt to Gornergrat. This 10 km line, electrified at 725 V DC 50 Hz three-phase, operates three electric locomotives and 22 electric railcar sets.

### Passenger and freight operations
In 1998, BVZ recorded 2.598 million passenger journeys and 45.197 million passenger-km; 40,902 tonnes of freight were carried, for 1.4 million tonne-km.

To facilitate the bulk transport of domestic refuse from Zermatt, BVZ employs the Tuchschmid ACTS container transfer system.

### Traction and rolling stock
On its main system BVZ operates nine electric, two diesel-electric and one historic steam locomotive; four diesel tractors; nine electric motor coaches; nine driving trailers; 57 hauled passenger cars; four baggage and mail cars; and 90 freight and service wagons. The electric locomotive fleet is headed by five HGe 4/4 II 1,750 kW electric locomotives similar to those of the Furka—Oberalp Railway and Brünig line of SBB.

In 2000, BVZ ordered two three-car articulated emus from Stadler Bussnang, with traction equipment to be supplied by Bombardier Transportation. To be designated Class BDSeh 4/8, the trains were due to enter service in August 2002.

### Signalling and telecommunications
The BVZ network is controlled by automatic block signalling.

*UPDATED*

---

## Furka Oberalp Railway (FO)

Furka Oberalp Bahn
PO Box 256, CH-3900 Brig, Valais
Tel: (+41 27) 922 81 11   Fax: (+41 27) 922 81 01
e-mail: info@fo-bahn.ch
Web: http://www.fo-bahn.ch

### Key personnel
Director: Rolf Escher
Deputy Director: Peter Maurer

Managers
Operations: Peter Rüttimann
Finance: Anton Zeiter
Marketing: Arnadé Perrig
Construction: Bernhard Glor
Workshops: Franz Karlen

Gauge: 1,000 mm
Route length: 120 km, of which 22.9 km Abt rack-equipped
Electrification: 120 km at 11 kV 16⅔Hz AC

### Organisation
FO is the central link in a 1,000 mm gauge route from Zermatt to St Moritz and Chur, the itinerary of the famous 'Glacier Express'. The FO section extends from Brig, junction with the BVZ, to Disentis, junction with the Rhaetian. The FO employs the Abt rack system to negotiate maximum gradients of 11 per cent. Minimum curvature radius is 70 m.

Centrepiece of the FO route is the 15.44 km Furka Base Tunnel, single track with two crossing loops, completed in 1982. It bypasses the former rack-worked section from

Oberwald to Realp which used to close to traffic between October and April each year, lying mostly between 2,000 and 3,000 m above sea level. A private organisation, the Dampfbahn Furka-Bergstrecke AG, has restored the historic route of the 'Glacier Express' between Realp and Gletsch over the Furka Pass and the Rhône glacier, which was closed in 1982, and runs special trains on it.

In 2001 FO employed 331 staff.

### Developments
In 2002, the FO and the BVZ Zermatt-Bahn (qv) announced their intention to merge their operations from 1 January 2003.

### Passenger operations
In 2001, FO recorded 1.7 million passenger journeys.

The international success of the year-round 'Glacier Express' requires three trains bearing this name to be operated each way daily between Zermatt and St Moritz via FO. In summer each 'Glacier Express' is frequently operated as two distinct trains, one reserved for package tour parties and the other for general travellers.

### Freight operations
FO operates a shuttle service for road vehicles and their occupants through the adhesion-worked Furka Base Tunnel, between terminals at Oberwald and Realp. Around 15,000 shuttle trains use the tunnel annually.

From 2003, FO was to move large volumes of material generated by construction of the Gotthard Base Tunnel, which forms part of the AlpTransit project. This traffic will use the FO line between Disentis and Sedrun, which has been upgraded.

### Improvements to existing lines
FO has undertaken a comprehensive reorganisation of its installations at Brig, including the platforms it shares with BVZ in the SBB station and the adjoining workshops. The programme was made possible by construction of a bypass to relieve the main road through Brig on which the station stands.

### Traction and rolling stock
In 2001 FO was operating two diesel-electric, one diesel-hydraulic and 16 electric locomotives; five Type BDeh 2/4 and 11 Type Deh 4/4 electric power cars; 79 passenger coaches; four baggage cars; 30 car-carriers; 67 freight wagons; and maintenance vehicles including nine powered units and 11 powered snow-ploughs. Passenger stock included four panoramic saloons with deep side and roof windows, built by Ramseyer and Jenzer of Biel.

In 2001, 19 new coaches for 'Glacier Express' services were acquired jointly by FO, BVZ and RhB.

### Signalling and telecommunications
A control centre at Brig enables train, signal and point control throughout the system to be integrated with passenger information, operations planning and management functions.

### Track
FO was the first railway to employ 'Y' form steel sleepers developed by Peine Salzgitter in Germany for rack-equipped track. They have been installed in the new 374 m Grind Tunnel bored between Andermatt and Nätschen to replace an existing tunnel which had deteriorated.

**UPDATED**

*FO Class HGe4/4 II rack-equipped electric locomotive entering the rack section at Grengiols viaduct with the Zermatt–Chur 'Glacier Express' (Andrew Marshall)*
2001/0109862

## Jungfraubahnen

Berner Oberland-Bahnen (BOB), Wengernalp-Bahn (WAB) and Jungfraubahn (JB)
Hardstrasse 14, CH-3800 Interlaken
Tel: (+41 33) 828 71 11   Fax: (+41 33) 828 72 64
e-mail: jb@jungfrau.ch
Web: http://www.jungfraubahnen.ch

### Key personnel
Chief Executive Officer: Walter Steuri
Head of Operations: Christian Balmer
Vice-President, Technical Director: Hans Schlunegger
Vice-President, Marketing and Operations Director: Urs Kessler
Vice-President, Director of Finance: Christoph Seiler

### Organisation
The Jungfraubahnen Group comprises the Berner Oberland-Bahnen (BOB), Wengernalp-Bahn (WAB) and Jungfraubahn (JB) systems, plus two rope-worked funiculars, and the Harderbahn at Interlaken.

*Berner Oberland-Bahnen*
BOB operates 38.367 route-km of 1,000 mm gauge from Interlaken Öst to Lauterbrunnen and Grindelwald, electrified at 1.5 kV DC. Sections of route employ Riggenbach rack to cope with maximum gradients of 1 in 11.

Double track has been installed over a 2.5 km section between Wilderswil and Zweilütschinen at a cost of SFr30 million, and curve radius eased from 120 to 200 m over a further 5 km, enabling line speed to be raised from 40 to 70 km/h.

In 2000 the BOB acquired five Type ABt driving trailers from Regionalverkehr Bern-Solothurn (RBS).

The BOB's latest rolling stock is three ABeh 4/4 II 43-tonne motor coaches and matching BDt control trailers. Each motor coach is powered by four ABB 314 kW series-wound DC motors. The braking system for direct-coupled DC motors is a combined regenerative and resistance brake with automatic changeover according to conditions in the supply system. The added control functions are performed by ABB's MICAS programmable system. Maximum speed is 70 km/h.

The railway also operates the 7.3 km 800 mm gauge Riggenbach rack Schynige Platte mountain railway (SPB) from Wilderswil, electrified at 1.5 kV DC, and the Bergbahn Lauterbrunnen–Mürren (BLM). The BLM comprises a cable funicular from Lauterbrunnen to Grütschalp and a metre-gauge line on the Lauterbrunnen valley's western wall from Grütschalp to Mürren.

### Jungfraubahnen lines

| Railway | BOB | SPB | WAB | JB | BLM |
|---|---|---|---|---|---|
| Route length | 38.367 km | 7.26 km | 29.366 km | 11.827 km | 5.7 km |
| Max gradient | 12% | 25% | 25% | 25% | 5% |
| Minimum curve radius | 90 m | 60 m | 60 m | 100 m | 40 m |
| Maximum axleload | 20 t | - | - | 11.5 t | 16 t | - |
| Steam locomotives | - | 1 | - | - | - |
| Electric locomotives | 2 | 10 | 10 | 5 | - |
| Electric railcars | 10 | - | 28 | 14 | 4 |
| Passenger cars | 41 | 22 | 44 | 18 | - |
| Baggage cars | 10 | - | - | - | - |
| Freight wagons | 31 | 7 | 63 | 20 | 4 |

### Diesel locomotives

| Class | Wheel Arrangement | Power kW | Speed km/h | Weight tonnes | No in service | First built | Mechanical | Builders Engine | Transmission |
|---|---|---|---|---|---|---|---|---|---|
| **BOB** | | | | | | | | | |
| Tm 2/2 | B (shunter) | 110 | 30 | 15 | 1 | 1946 | Stadler | Saurer E | BBC |
| HGm 2/2 | B (shunter) | 296 | 30 | 19.5 | 1 | 1986 | Steck | Deutz H | Steck |

### Electric locomotives

| Class | Wheel Arrangement | Output kW | Speed km/h | Weight tonnes | No in service | First built | Builders Mechanical | Electrical |
|---|---|---|---|---|---|---|---|---|
| **BOB** | | | | | | | | |
| **1.5 kV DC** | | | | | | | | |
| HGe 3/3 | Co | 295 | 45 | 36 | 2 | 1914 | SLM | BBC |
| **SPB** | | | | | | | | |
| **1.5 kV DC** | | | | | | | | |
| He 2/2 | B | 220 | 12 | 16 | 10 | 1914 | SLM | BBC/Alioth |
| **WAB** | | | | | | | | |
| **1.5 kV DC** | | | | | | | | |
| He 2/2 | B | 220 | 12 | 16 | 7 | 1909 | SLM | BBC/Alioth |
| He 2/2 | B | 460 | 22 | 16 | 2 | 1995 | Stadler/SLM | ABB |
| **JB** | | | | | | | | |
| **1.125 kV AC 3 phase** | | | | | | | | |
| Hc 2/2 | B | 283 | 18 | 15 | 5 | 1904 | SLM | BBC |

*Double-tracking on the Wilderswil–Zweilütschinen section of the BOB*
2000/0088197

## Wengernalp-Bahn

Recording over 3.5 million passenger journeys annually, WAB operates a 29.366 km 800 mm gauge line running from Grindelwald and Lauterbrunnen to Kleine Scheidegg, 2,060 m above sea level and immediately below the Jungfrau mountain chain. It is electrified at 1.5 kV DC, and employs Riggenbach rack throughout. In 1996, an interlocking system with Alcatel-SEL axlecounter track release, specially designed for multitrain operation, was introduced between Lauterbrunnen and Allmend. A control centre is located in Wengen.

The WAB fleet includes two locomotives for the operation of freight services to the village of Wengen, which is prohibited to road traffic. In 1998, Stadler was due to deliver four low-floor articulated driving trailers.

## Jungfraubahn

JB records annually some 940,000 passenger journeys. It operates an 11,827 km 1,000 mm gauge line starting from Kleine Scheidegg, which tunnels through the Jungfrau range to attain the highest altitude of any European railway at Jungfraujoch, 3,454 m above sea level, on the ridge between the Jungfrau and Mönch mountains. It employs the Strub rack system and is electrified at 1,125 V 50 Hz three-phase AC.

### Electric railcars or multiple-units

| Class | Cars per unit | Motor cars per unit | Motored axles/car | Output/motor kW | Speed km/h | Units in service | First built | Builders Mechanical | Electrical |
|---|---|---|---|---|---|---|---|---|---|
| **BOB** | | | | | | | | | |
| **1.5 kV DC** | | | | | | | | | |
| ABeh 4/4 | 1 | 5 | 4 | 261 | 70 | 5 | 1965 | SLM/SIG | BBC |
| ABeh 4/4 | 1 | 1 | 4 | 261 | 70 | 1 | 1979 | SLM/SIG | BBC |
| ABeh 4/4 II | 1 | 3 | 4 | 314 | 70 | 3 | 1987 | SLM | ABB |
| **WAB** | | | | | | | | | |
| **1.5 kV DC** | | | | | | | | | |
| BDeh 4/4 | 11 | 11 | 4 | 110 | 25 | 11 | 1947 | SLM | BBC |
| BDeh 4/4 | 7 | 7 | 4 | 110 | 25 | 7 | 1963 | SLM | BBC |
| BDeh 4/8 | 6 | 4 | 4 | 110 | 25 | 6 | 1988 | SLM | BBC/Sécheron |
| BDeh 4/8 | 4 | 4 | 4 | 201 | 28 | 4 | 1988 | SLM | BBC |
| **JB** | | | | | | | | | |
| **1.125 kV AC 3 phase** | | | | | | | | | |
| BDeh 2/4 | 6 | 6 | 2 | 440 | 24 | 6 | 1955 | SLM | BBC |
| BDeh 2/4 | 4 | 4 | 2 | 440 | 24 | 4 | 1966 | SLM | BBC |
| BDeh 4/8 | 2 | 4 | 4 | 201 | 27 | 8 | 1992 | SLM/Stadler | ABB/Bombardier |
| **BLM** | | | | | | | | | |
| **560 V DC** | | | | | | | | | |
| BDe 2/4 | 1 | 3 | 2 | 49 | 25 | 1 | 1913 | SIG | Alioth |
| Be 4/4 | 3 | 3 | 4 | 51 | 30 | 3 | 1963 | SIG | BBC |

In 2002, Stadler was due to deliver an additional four Type BDeh 4/8 units similar to those supplied in 1992.

**UPDATED**

# Lausanne—Echallens—Bercher Railway (LEB)

Compagnie du Chemin de Fer Lausanne—Echallens—Bercher
Place de la Gare 9, CH-1040 Echallens
Tel: (+41 21) 886 20 00    Fax: (+41 21) 886 20 19
Gauge: 1,000 mm
Route length: 24 km
Electrification: 24 km at 1.5 kV DC

## Passenger operations

The LEB provides a commuter service between Lausanne and communities to the north of the city, serving some 20 stations. Around 2.1 million passengers are carried annually, 80 per cent of these season ticket holders. Unusually, the railway is not directly linked to the Swiss Federal Railways national network; connections with it in Lausanne are made via light rail and rack metro services. Dining services are also operated and steam specials are run in high season.

## Freight operations

LEB freight traffic, mostly agricultural produce, is handled by a fleet of road vehicles.

## Improvements to existing lines

In May 2000, a 1.1 km tunnelled extension was completed from the LEB's Lausanne terminus of Chauderon to a more conveniently located site at Flon. This has resulted in improved connections with Métro Lausanne—Ouchy (LO), Lausanne—Gare (LG) and Métro Ouest (TSOL) urban rail services and will also provide a link with the proposed Métro Nord-Est line.

## Traction and rolling stock

At the beginning of 2000, LEB operated two single-unit electric railcars and six two-car Class Be 4/8 emus, the latter dating from 1985-1991, as well as two driving trailers and seven trailer cars. One steam locomotive is also retained for special traffic. The maintenance fleet comprises two shunting tractors and seven operational wagons.

*LEB emus cross at Cheseaux (David Haydock)*

**UPDATED**

# Lucerne—Stans—Engelberg Railway (LSE)

Luzern—Stans—Engelberg Bahn
Stanserstrasse 2, CH-6362 Stansstad
Tel: (+41 41) 618 85 85    Fax: (+41 41) 618 85 89
e-mail: info@lse-bahn.ch
Web: http://www.lse-bahn.ch

## Key personnel

Managing Director: Christoph Tanner
Managers
 Operations: Werner Peterhans
 Finance: Hansruedi Odermatt
 Sales: Hugo Birchmeier
 Construction: Gerhard Kurmann
 Rolling Stock and Workshops: Peter Berger
 Electrical Installations: Karl Amstutz

Gauge: 1,000 mm
Route length: 25 km, of which 1.5 km on Riggenbach rack
Electrification: 25 km at 15 kV 16⅔Hz AC

## Passenger operations

The railway combines a commuter service for the outskirts of Lucerne with access to the resorts of the Engelberg and Titlis areas. In 1998, a total of 1.99 million passenger journeys and 21.64 million passenger-km were recorded.

## Freight operations

In 1998, LSE carried 7,560 tonnes and recorded 77,670 tonne-km.

## Improvements to existing lines

For 'Bahn 2000', LSE is to carry out realignment of its final rack section from Obermatt into the Engelberg basin, requiring a new 4 km tunnel and easing the gradient from 25 to 10.5 per cent. This will triple existing line capacity by allowing longer trains and the through working of locomotive-hauled LSE or combined SBB Brünig rolling stock. Work on the project started in March 2001 and commissioning is planned for the 2005/06 winter season.

*LSE Class BDeh 4/4 electric railcar and trailers forming an Engelberg—Lucerne service at Hergiswil (John C Baker)*

## Traction and rolling stock

The railway operates eight BDeh 4/4 electric railcars (736 kW, Schindler/SLM/BBC, 1964) and 28 trailers in three-car trainsets; two De 4/4 electric locomotives (894 kW, SLM/BBC, 1942) for Stans—Lucerne—Sachseln commuter services; and five diesel shunters.

## Mittel-Thurgau Railway (MThB)

Mittel-Thurgau Bahn
Schützenstrasse 15, CH-8570 Weinfelden
Tel: (+41 71) 622 33 22   Fax: (+41 71) 622 34 23

### Key personnel
Director: Peter Joss
Deputy Director: Ursula Widmer
Managers
  Commercial: Rolf Knecht
  Operations: Alfred Hartmann
  Technical: Robert Gamper
  Finance: Rino Cavallet

Gauge: 1,435 mm
Route length: 43 km
Electrification: 43 km at 15 kV 16⅔Hz AC

### Organisation
The original MThB system runs from Wil, on the SBB Zurich–St Gallen main line, northwards to the SBB station at Weinfelden, and thence to Kreuzlingen; from here SBB tracks are used to Konstanz. MThB also operates all local trains on DB AG's Konstanz–Singen–Engen route in Germany and Schaffhausen–Kreuzlingen–Romanshorn cross-border services.

In Switzerland, MThB also operates the 1,000 mm gauge, 18 km Frauenfeld–Wil Railway, electrified at 1.2 kV DC. It was the first Swiss private railway company to compete with SBB and in Germany for operating concessions under new legislation, and operates local services on SBB's Lake Constance shore route.

In November 2000 MThB formed an alliance with Swiss Federal Railways, Regionalbahn Ostschweiz (RBO), to bid for concessions to operate regional services both in Switzerland and elsewhere.

A consequence of this initiative was an announcement in September 2002 that MThB and SBB were to form a joint-venture company, Thurbo AG, to operate regional services over a 550 km network in eastern Switzerland from December 2002. These operations are to cover the cantons of Thurgau, St Gallen and Zurich.

### Passenger operations
In May 1994, MThB introduced a cross-border fixed-interval service. With financial support from the German Baden-Württemburg provincial and local administrations, the service runs from Weinfelden to Konstanz and over DB AG tracks to Singen and Engen. It is furnished with four new SBB-type 'Colibri' three-car electric multiple-units which were taken from a current SBB order for these units. In addition, the entire existing MThB rolling stock fleet has been adapted to meet DB AG standards, including the fitting of INDUSI automatic train control equipment.

*Type Be 4/4 motor car and driving trailer at Wil on the Frauenfeld–Wil Railway, which is operated by MThB (David Haydock)*

### Freight operations
In 1994 MThB and the South Eastern Railway (SOB) jointly formed Lokoop, initially to acquire and manage a traction fleet at first formed by surplus Class 142 electric locomotives from the former East German system. Subsequently Lokoop entered the freight haulage business as an open access operator, taking advantage of railway reforms introduced by the Swiss parliament in 1999. The company has signed partnership agreements with DB Cargo in Germany and NS Cargo in the Netherlands and has been especially successful in capturing oil products traffic, including cross-border services to Germany. Other recent contracts cover the movement of construction materials.

In 1999 MThB and SOB secured a contract to run postal services between Frauenfeld, St Gallen, Landquart and Chur and in 2000 MThB ordered new rolling stock for such traffic.

### Traction and rolling stock
MThB operates one electric and three diesel locomotives, 10 electric power cars, 10 trailers and 14 other passenger cars. In 1998 MThB acquired 10 GTW 2/6 lightweight emus from Stadler for services in the Bodensee area. Five ex-DB 'Rheingold' vista-dome observation cars and historic 'Orient Express' cars are maintained for land-cruise train operations organised by the associated travel agency company Reisebüro Mittelthurgau.

The 1,000 mm gauge Frauenfeld–Wil Railway operates nine Be 4/4 motor cars, four driving trailers and 32 carriers for transport of 1,435 mm gauge wagons.

In 2000 MThB ordered three electrically powered versions of the CargoSprinter freight dmu developed in Germany, with an option for 10 more, for use on postal contracts.

In 2000 the Lokoop fleet comprised 19 ex-DR Class 142 (Class 477) electric locomotives, one Re 4/4 II, four ex-SBB Class Re 4/4 I (Class 416) electric locomotives and six new Class 486 electric locomotives supplied during the year by Adtranz and based on the DB Class 145 design. The Class 486 locomotives are equipped to operate on the Austrian and German networks, as well as the domestic system.

The GTW 2/6 emus are to become part of the Thurbo AG fleet when the company commences operations in December 2002. They will be supplemented by an additional 80 vehicles of an improved but generally similar design to be supplied by Stadler/Bombardier by 2007.

**UPDATED**

---

## Mittelland Regional Railways (RM)

Regionalverkehr Mittelland
Bucherstrasse 1-3, CH-3401 Burgdorf

Tel: (+41 34) 424 50 00   Fax: (+41 34) 424 50 80
e-mail: info@rm-rail.ch
Web: http://www.regionalverkehr.ch

### Key personnel
Director: Martin Selz
Central Services: G Schoch
Technical Manager: P Dübi
Operations Manager: J Zeder
Commercial Manager: J-P Hubmann

Gauge: 1,435 mm
Route length: 167 km
Electrification: 155.8 km at 15 kV 16⅔ Hz AC

### Organisation
RM was created in 1997 by merger of the Emmentahl-Burgdorf-Thun Railway with railways which had been under its management: the Solothurn-Moutier (SMB); Solothurn-Burgdorf-Hasle-Rüegsau-Konolfingen-Thun and Hasle-Rüegsau-Langnau (EBT); and Ramsei-Sumiswald and Langenthal-Huttwil-Wolhusen (VHB). The RM group of railways connects the north and south of the Canton of Bern, and also reaches out to the hinterland of Lucerne.

### Passenger and freight operations
There are eight interchange stations with SBB, and RM connects with the Bern RER system. Passenger services on minor branches have been replaced by bus (Sumiswald-Wasen in 1994), but the intensification of services on through routes and a growing freight business have required conversion to double track of several critical sections.

*RM Type RBDe emu arriving at Oberburg (David Haydock)*

# RAILWAY SYSTEMS/Switzerland

In 1996, the RM constituents carried 5.9 mill on passengers for 63.1 million passenger-km and 2.8 mill on tonnes of freight for 39 million tonne-km.

### Traction and rolling stock
At the beginning of 1997, the RM fleet comprised two Class Re 456 electric locomotives dating from 1993; 10 Class Be 4/4 locomotives of 1932-53 (withdrawn in 2000); five Class Re 436/Re 4/4 locomotives of 1969-83; four Class De 4/4 and one BDe 2/4 motor luggage vans; eight RBDe 566 (1973-74), three BDe 576 (1966) and 13 Class RBDe 566 (1984-85) electric railcars; 27 control trailers; 50 other passenger and baggage cars; 19 electric and 13 diesel shunting tractors.

In 2000 RM ordered eight Type GTW 2/6 lightweight emus from Stadler, as well as three driving trailer cars.

## Montreux—Oberland Bernois Railway (MOB)

Chemin de Fer Montreux—Oberland Bernois
PO Box 1426, Rue du Lac 36, CH-1820 Montreux 1
Tel: (+41 21) 989 81 81   Fax: (+41 21) 963 89 96
e-mail: mob@mob.ch
Web: http://www.mob.ch
  http://www.goldenpass.ch

### Key personnel
President, Managing Board: W von Siebental
Group Director General: Richard Kummrow
Managing Director: M Sandoz
Marketing Manager: H-J Spirgi
Traffic Manager: J C Gétaz
Way and Works Manager: G Bridevaux
Traction and Workshops Manager: J M Forclaz

Gauge: 1,000 mm; 800 mm
Route length: 85.7 km; 10 km
Electrification: 95.7 km at 860 V DC

### Organisation
The MOB Group comprises three electrified railways, funiculars (including the automatic 1.6 km Vevey–Chardonne–Mont Pèlerin Railway), ski lifts, coach operations, travel agencies and hotels and restaurants. The principal railway is the 75.3 km 1,000 mm gauge Montreux—Oberland Bernois (MOB); the Montreux–Territet–Glion–Naye (800 mm gauge, 10 km) and Vevey Electric (CEV) (1,000 mm gauge, 10.4 km) railways have an essentially local role.

MOB's main line runs from Montreux via Gstaad to Zweisimmen. Its climb from Lake Geneva to Les Avants and the 2.4 km Col de Jaman Tunnel, at 7.3 per cent ruling grade, is the steepest adhesion line in Switzerland. The summit is 1,269 m above sea level. From Zweisimmen a branch runs to Lenk.

### Passenger operations
Starting life as a local cross-country line, MOB began to court the tourist market in 1979 with introduction of the 'Panoramic Express'. The 'Super Panoramic Express' followed in 1985, and the 'Crystal Panoramic Express' in 1993. Completely new stock was provided in May 2000, running between Montreux and Lenk as the 'Golden Pass Panoramic', while 1999 saw the introduction of a new trainset on the CEV, operating under the name of 'Train des Etoiles'.

In June 2001, it launched a marketing alliance with BLS Lötschbergbahn and Swiss Federal Railways' metre-gauge Brünig line to promote integrated panoramic rail travel from Montreux to Lucerne via the Bernese Oberland. A development of the MOB's 'Golden Pass Panoramic' service concept, the 'GoldenPass Line' brand name has been adopted and locomotives and rolling stock used by each operator on the group of services carry a gold and white livery. Routes served are: Montreux–Zweisimmen (MOB); Zweisimmen–Interlaken (BLS, standard gauge); and Interlaken–Lucerne (SBB Brünig line). Together these total 250 km.

In 2000, MOB carried 1.74 million passengers (40.9 million passenger-km) and 38,900 tonnes of freight (0.89 million tonne-km).

*MOB Class Ge 4/4 electric locomotive with a tank train at Montreux (Andrew Marshall)*   2001/0109866

*Montreux-Zweisimmen 'Golden Pass Panoramic' trainset near Allières (Andrew Marshall)*   2001/0109867

### Diesel locomotives

| Class | Wheel arrangement | Power kW | Speed km/h | Weight tonnes | No in Service | First built | Mechanical | Builders Engine | Transmission |
|---|---|---|---|---|---|---|---|---|---|
| Gm 4/4 | Bo-Bo | 575 | 80 | 44 | 2 | 1976 | Moyse | Poyaud | E Moyse-Leroy-Sommer |
| Tm 2/2 | B-B | 115 | 33 | 15 | 2 | 1953* | KHD | Deutz | H Voith-Turbo |

* Rebuilt 1983-84

### Electric locomotives

| Class | Wheel arrangement | Output kW | Speed km/h | Weight tonnes | No in service | First built | Builders Mechanical | Electrical |
|---|---|---|---|---|---|---|---|---|
| De 6/6 | Bo-Bo-Bo | 1,230 | 55 | 63 | 2 | 1931 | SIG | ABB |
| GDe 4/4 | Bo-Bo | 1,432 | 100 | 50 | 4 | 1983 | SLM | ABB |
| Ge 4/4 | Bo-Bo | 2,400 | 120 | 62 | 4 | 1995 | SLM | ABB |

### Traction and rolling stock
MOB operates eight electric and two diesel locomotives, two diesel shunting tractors, 20 motored passenger units, 52 passenger cars and 112 freight wagons, plus numerous service vehicles. Four new Stadler/Adtranz/SLM Class Be 2/6 low-floor electric railcars entered service in 1998.

**UPDATED**

## Rhaetian Railway (RhB)

Rhätische Bahn
Bahnhofstrasse 25, CH-7002 Chur
Tel: (+41 81) 254 91 00   Fax: (+41 81) 254 91 01
Web: http://www.rhb.ch

### Key personnel
Director: Silvio Fasciati
Chief Engineer: W Altermatt
Chief Mechanical Engineer: E Mannes
Chief of Finance and Services: H Bauschatz
Chief of Marketing and Operations: E Bachmann

Gauge: 1,000 mm
Route length: 375 km
Electrification: 304.4 km at 11 kV 16⅔ Hz AC; 60.7 km at 1 kV DC; 3 km at 1.5 kV DC

### Organisation
The Rhaetian Railway is a vital means of communication in the mountainous southeast of Switzerland. Serving the Engadine, the valley of Poschiavo, the Davos area, Arosa and the Grisons Oberland, the railway connects the canton with the SBB network at Chur and Landquart, with the Furka-Oberalp Railway in Disentis/Muster, and with FS of Italy in Tirano. The territory is the most sparsely populated in Switzerland, with a population of some 170,000 averaging 23 per km².

The core of the RhB network is electrified at 11 kV 16⅔ Hz, but the Bernina Railway from St Moritz to Tirano was electrified at its construction in 1908-10 at 1 kV DC and retains that system. The Bernina is the only Swiss

Switzerland/**RAILWAY SYSTEMS** 357

*Class Ge 4/4 III electric locomotive with a Chur–St Moritz passenger service at Filisur* (Andrew Marshall)
*2001*/0109868

transalpine line that avoids tunnelling, attaining a summit of 2,253 m above sea level at Ospitio Beining; for 27 km, or 44 per cent of its total distance, it is graded at 7 per cent but is worked entirely by adhesion. The Chur–Arosa Railway of 26.4 route-km, which RhB absorbed in 1943, was converted from a 2.4 kV DC power supply system to the standard 11 kV AC on 1 December 1997; on this line the ruling gradient is 6 per cent.

In 1999 RhB employed 1,364 staff and 118 trainees.

**Finance** (SFr million)

| Revenue | 1997 | 1998 | 1999 |
|---|---|---|---|
| Passengers | 65.7 | 64.4 | 69.3 |
| Freight | 16.1 | 17.0 | 15.9 |
| Subsidy | 97.6 | 100.2 | 103.0 |
| Financial income | 2.1 | 2.1 | 1.8 |
| Other | 30.4 | 29.4 | 30.7 |
| Total | 211.9 | 213.1 | 220.7 |

| Expenditure | 1997 | 1998 | 1999 |
|---|---|---|---|
| Staff/personnel | 124.9 | 121.5 | 124.6 |
| Materials/services | 46.1 | 49.2 | 56.7 |
| Depreciation | 34.5 | 36.3 | 37.4 |
| Finance costs | 6.4 | 6.1 | 2.0 |
| Total | 211.9 | 213.1 | 220.7 |

| Traffic (million) | 1997 | 1998 | 1999 |
|---|---|---|---|
| Passenger journeys | 7.862 | 8.041 | 8.252 |
| Passenger-km | 290.1 | 286.8 | 288.6 |
| Freight tonnes | 0.818 | 0.814 | 0.711 |
| Freight tonne-km | 41.3 | 42.6 | 39.2 |

### Passenger operations
RhB marked the conversion of the Chur–Arosa line to an 11 kV AC power supply in December 1997 with the introduction of the blue-liveried 'Arosa Express' service between the two communities.

### Freight operations
Main constituents of RhB's considerable freight traffic are construction materials, accounting for nearly half of 1997 tonnage carried, cement, drinks, chemicals, petroleum products, fuel oil and timber. The wagon fleet includes sliding wall, insulated vans with electric heating and cooling to provide for winter haulage of fresh produce; power is provided by a busline from the train's locomotive.

RhB has a developing container and swap-body traffic between Landquart and St Moritz. It is developing a Bernina line terminal on the Italian frontier at Campocologno, believing that this route has all-weather advantages for traffic from northern Italy.

During 2000 RhB took delivery of 21 wagons designed to carry ACTS roll-on/roll-off containers. These are used for domestic waste traffic.

### New lines
In 1981, RhB initiated plans for a 22.3 km cut-off from Klosters to Lavin, between Samedan and Scuol-Tarasp, which halves journey times between Landquart and the Lower Engadine. Journey times to Scuol-Tarasp from Zurich and Chur have been cut by 135 and 100 minutes to 2 hours 40 minutes and 1½ hours respectively.

The cut-off includes the 19.05 km single-track Vereina Tunnel under the Silvretta mountain range. The tunnel has one passing loop and a ruling gradient of 1.5 per cent, and is large enough to accommodate wagons conveying road vehicles up to 3.5 m in height. Maximum speed through the tunnel is 100 km/h, allowing passage in 17 minutes.

From the Selfranga vehicle-loading terminal at Klosters, a semicircular single-line tunnel on a gradient of 2.5 per cent leads to the Vereina Tunnel portal via a short section of track in the open. The south terminal is at Sagliains, between Susch and Lavin. Each terminal has two loading tracks.

Total cost of the project, including SFr36 million for rolling stock, was estimated at SFr571 million in 1985; the federal government agreed to provide 85 per cent of the funding and gave its approval in 1986. Construction began in 1991 and commercial services started in November 1999. The standard hourly service in each direction is one conventional passenger train and one or two vehicle shuttles; the latter increases to three in peak periods. There are one or two daily freight services.

### Improvements to existing lines
Plans exist to relieve congestion at Chur by creating new underground station facilities to handle Arosa, Landquart and Thusis services. This will necessitate a new 2 km alignment to provide access for Arosa line services, obviating street-running through Chur.

Construction of the standard-gauge Gotthard base tunnel, part of Switzerland's AlpTransit project, will necessitate upgrading the line from Disentis, on the Furka Oberalp railway, to Chur, to handle heavy construction traffic.

### Traction and rolling stock
In 1997, RhB operated 61 electric, 6 diesel and three electro-diesel locomotives; 41 electric railcars; 25 diesel and six electric shunting tractors; three steam locomotives (used for special trains); 335 passenger coaches (including eight restaurant cars); 50 baggage and mail cars; and 850 revenue freight wagons.

During 1999, RhB took delivery from Adtranz of three Class Ge 4/4 III electric locomotives, supplementing the fleet to handle services through the Vereina Tunnel. These latest machines are equipped with IGBT technology, whereas the nine earlier locomotives of this type have GTO converters.

In 2001, RhB rebuilt its two Class Gem 4/4 electro-diesel locomotives, equipping each with two Cummins 709 kW engines, new electrical equipment and improved cabs. Their 1 kV DC capability enables them to operate on RhB's Berninabahn, linking St Moritz and Tirano.

In 2000 Stadler supplied 10 Panorama coaches and eight driving trailers for RhB 'Bernina Express' services.

### Signalling and telecommunications
The RhB system, mostly single track, is colourlight signalled with automatic block under the oversight of seven control centres. The majority of passing loops can be switched for automatic operation by trains when their stations are unmanned. The entire system and all power units are equipped with the Integra 79 ATC system. Ground-to-train radio has been installed throughout the railway's network. The RhB has always relied upon Hardy vacuum brakes for its passenger and freight trains, enhanced by electric braking on all locomotives.

*UPDATED*

*Road vehicle boarding a Vereina Tunnel shuttle service at Sagliains* (David Haydock) *2001*/0109869

## Sihltal–Zurich–Uetliberg Railway (SZU)

Sihltal–Zurich–Uetliberg Bahn
Manessestrasse 152, CH-8045 Zurich
Tel: (+41 1) 206 45 11   Fax: (+41 1) 206 45 10
Web: http://www.szu.ch

### Key personnel
Chairman: Dr Thomas Wagner
Chief Executive Officer: Christiane V Weibel

Gauge: 1,435 mm
Route length: 29 km
Electrification: 19 km (Sihltal line) at 15 kV 16⅔ Hz; 10 km (Uetliberg line) at 1.2 kV DC

### Organisation
SZU operates an intensive passenger service from Zurich over two routes, one to Sihlbrugg (the Sihltal line) and the other to Uetliberg.

### Improvements to existing lines
Following the opening of SZU's tunnel extension from the outskirts of Zurich to the city's main SBB station in 1990,

passenger traffic on the Sihltal line grew by 75 per cent. On the Uetliberg line, traffic grew by more than 130 per cent. As a result, the federal and canton governments financially supported a SFr137 million investment, which included some double-tracking and new rolling stock.

### Traction and rolling stock
SZU operates the Sihltal line with eight electric and four diesel locomotives, five electric railcars and 29 trailers, and 32 other passenger coaches. The Uetliberg line is operated with 14 electric railcars, four trailers and two other passenger coaches.

*SZU railcar at Zurich Giesshübel with a train from Uetliberg (David Haydock)*
2001/0109870

## South Eastern Railway (SOB)

Schweizerische Südostbahn AG
Bahnhofplatz 1a, Postfach, St Gallen
Tel: (+41 71) 228 23 23  Fax: (+41 71) 228 23 33
e-mail: info@suedostbahn.ch
Web: http://www.suedostbahn.ch

### Key personnel
Director: Dr Guido Schoch
Managers
  Marketing and Services: Ernst Wittmer
  Production (Operations): Heinrich Güttinger
  Finance: Paul Furrer
  Technical: Frédy Vogler
  Infrastructure: Marcel Latscha

### Subsidiary company
Voralpen-Express (jointly with SBB)
Merkurstrasse 3, CH-8820 Wädenswil
Tel: (+41 1) 780 31 57  Fax: (+41 1) 780 37 56
e-mail: vae-info@suedostbahn.ch
Web: http://www.voralpen-express.ch

Gauge: 1,435 mm
Route length: 112.6 km
Electrification: 112.6 km at 15 kV 16⅔ Hz AC

### Organisation
In December 2001, the SOB and the Bodensee–Toggenburg Railway (BT) merged, more than doubling the route length of this important cross-country system. The original SOB segment runs from Rapperswil to the SBB station at Pfäffikon, and from there to connect with the SBB at Arth-Goldau. Branches serve Wädenswil and Einsiedeln. The former BT line starts at the SBB station at Romanshorn on Bodensee (Lake Constance), joins SBB tracks to St Gallen and then runs on SOB's own line to Wattwil, where it branches to its terminus at Nesslau-Neu St Johann. From Wattwil, however, SOB operates over SBB tracks to Rapperswil. Together, these two portions of the network form a through Romanshorn–St Gallen–Lucerne route.

### Passenger operations
The principal service is the hourly 'Voralpen-Express' operated jointly with SBB and, until December 2001, BT. This connects Romanshorn, St Gallen, Wattwil, Pfäffikon, Arth-Goldau and Lucerne. The operation and marketing of this branded service is managed by Voralpen-Express, the management organisation established jointly by SOB and SBB.

### Traction and rolling stock
At the end of 1996 the SOB comprised four electric locomotives and one diesel, 11 emus and six electric railcars, as well as 44 passenger cars, including three with buffets. Ten of the coaches, delivered from 1997, are Revvivo refurbished vehicles supplied by Schindler Technik, and incorporate prefabricated interior modules formed of composite materials. No revenue freight wagons are owned.

In 1994, SOB purchased a surplus DR Class 142 electric locomotive for its exclusive use and subsequently agreed with Mittel-Thurgau Railway (MThB) to acquire a further 20 locomotives jointly. Two were sold to Fribourg Railways and four (equipped with rheostatic braking) entered service with SOB through a leasing arrangement agreed with Lokoop AG (see MThB entry).

*SOB Colibri-type four-car emu forming an Einsiedeln service at Biberbrugg (David Haydock)*
2001/0109872

**Electric locomotives**

| Class | Wheel arrangement | Output kW | Speed km/h | Weight tonnes | No in service | First built | Builders Mechanical | Electrical |
|---|---|---|---|---|---|---|---|---|
| Re 4/4 IV | Bo-Bo | 4,960 | 160 | 80 | 4 | 1982 | SLM | ABB |
| Re 4/4 | Bo-Bo | 3,200 | 130 | 68 | 6 | 1987 | SLM | ABB |
| Be 4/4 | Bo-Bo | 1,180 | 80 | 66 | 1 | 1931 | SLM | SAAS |

**Electric railcars**

| Class | Cars per unit | Motor cars per unit | Motored axles/car | Output/motor kW | Speed km/h | Weight tonnes | No in service | First built | Builders Mechanical | Electrical |
|---|---|---|---|---|---|---|---|---|---|---|
| ABe 4/4 | 1 | 1 | 4 | 186 | 80 | 46.5 | 3 | 1939 | SIG/SLM/SWS | ABB/MFO/SAAS |
| BDe 4/4 | 1 | 1 | 4 | 515 | 110 | 72 | 10 | 1959 | SIG | ABB/MFO/SAAS |
| RBDe 4/4 | 2 | 1 | 4 | 428 | 140 | 70.5 | 4 | 1995 | SWG/SIG | ABB |
| RBDe 4/4 | 4 | 1 | 4 | 425 | 125 | | 6 | 1982 | FZA/SIG | BBC |
| BDe 4/4 | 4 | 1 | 4 | 526 | 110 | | 4 | 1960 | SIG | BBC |
| Be 3/4 | 1 | 1 | 3 | 295 | 80 | | 1 | 1938* | SIG | SAAS |

* Modernised 1981

*Former BT Type Re 4/4 electric locomotive at Lucerne (L T Peacock)*
2002/0109860

Four two-car emus of SBB's 'Colibri' type were delivered to SOB by Schindler Waggon in 1995.

SOB's portion of the fleet of coaching stock used on Voralpen-Express services includes 29 'revvivo' vehicles created by installing new glass-fibre modular interiors into existing vehicle bodyshells. The original SOB fleet was supplemented in December 2001 by former BT locomotives and rolling stock. This included seven electric locomotives, 11 emus/railcars, some 60 passenger coaches and nine shunting locomotives.

**Track**
**Rail**: SBB-profile type I, 46 kg/m
**Crossties (sleepers)**: Steel, concrete, wood, 150 × 260 mm
**Spacing**: 1,667/km
**Fastenings**: K and W on wood and steel sleepers. A on steel sleepers, B on concrete sleepers
**Min curvature radius**: 143 m
**Max gradient**: 5%
**Max axleload**: 22.5 tonnes

*UPDATED*

## Swiss Federal Railways

Schweizerische Bundesbahnen (SBB AG)
Chemins de Fer Fédéraux Suisses (CFF)
Ferrovie Federali Svizzere (FFS)
Hochschulstrasse 6, CH-3000 Bern 65
Tel: (+41 51) 220 11 11   Fax: (+41 51) 220 42 65
e-mail: railinfo@rail.ch
Web: http://www.rail.ch

### Key personnel
Board of Directors
  President: Thierry Lalive d'Epinay
  Chief Executive Officer: Benedikt Weibel
  Finance: Claude-Alain Dulex
  Personnel: Daniel Nordmann
  Passenger Traffic: Paul Blumenthal
  Freight Traffic: Daniel Nordmann
  Infrastructure: Pierre-Alain Urech
  Secretary General: Peter Fülistaler
  Deputy Secretary General: Walter Moser
  Corporate Risk Management: Annette Zimmerli
  Head of Communications: Werner Nuber
Passenger Traffic Business
  Director: Paul Blumenthal
  Long-Distance Traffic: Vincent Ducrot
  Finances: Guy Luginbühl
  Business Development: Peter Grossenbacher
  Project Expo 01: Markus Dössegger
  Project ICN: Theo Weiss
  Regional Traffic: Philippe Gauderon
  Customer Services: Peter Lehmann
  Production: Hannes Wittwer; Serge Anet
  Logistics, Personal Security: Buchs Daniel
  Rolling Stock and Maintenance: Ferdinando Gianella
  Personnel: Annick Kalantzopoulos
Freight Business (SBB Cargo)
  Director: Daniel Nordmann
  Marketing: Jürg Scheidegger
  Business Development: Hanspeter Vogel
  Information Technology: Burkhard Schulz
  Home Sales: Raphael Waeber
  Foreign Sales: Dirk Broek
  Production: Nicolas Perrin
  Human Resources: Thomas Aebischer
  Customer Services Centre: Samuel Ruggli;
    Dominique Boucrot
Infrastructure Business
  Director: Pierre-Alain Urech
  Rail 2000 and Major Projects: Paul Moser
  Logistics of Works and Purchases: Max Lehmann
  Telecommunications Management: Eduard Stiefel
  Development and Technology: Peter Winter
  Network and Path Management, Finances:
    Hans-Jürg Spillmann
  Management of Installation: Erwin Rutishauser
  Management of Maintenance: Reto Burkhardt
  Operational Management: Felix Loeffel
  Property Management: Urs Schlegel
  Personnel: Eric Pétremand

Gauge: 1,435 mm; 1,000 mm
Route length: 2,836 km; 74 km
Electrification: 1,435 mm gauge, 2,836 km at 15 kV 16⅔ Hz AC; 1,000 mm gauge, 74 km at 15 kV 16⅔ Hz AC

### Political background
Heavy losses during the 1990s prompted the Swiss government to put pressure on SBB to improve productivity and financial results. The railway has had considerable success in this, and returned to profitability in 1999.

Under a reform package approved by the Swiss Council of States in October 1997 and subsequently ratified by the National Council, SBB became a limited company on 1 January 1999, with all shares owned by the state.

At the end of March 1999, the Bundesrat set out the strategic and operational objectives for SBB for the years 1999 to 2000 as required under the new arrangements for the railway. These objectives require the railway to win a greater share of the passenger market and at least to hold its current position *vis-à-vis* road in the goods market. Productivity must improve by 5 per cent a year in both sectors, and infrastructure costs must be reduced by at least 5 per cent.

The workforce will have been cut from 39,000 in 1990 to 28,000 in 2000.

In March 2000, SBB and the rail unions signed a new General Employment Agreement (Gesamtarbeitsvertrag (GAV)) which came into force on 1 January 2001. For the first time in the railway's history, all conditions of work are dealt with in a single agreement between employers and representatives of the employees. Among the main provisions of the new agreement are formalisation of the flexible working agreements established when the 39-hour week was introduced on 1 June 2000, a major expansion of working-together arrangements between management and unions, a pay structure with a performance element, and guaranteed employment.

*Bahn 2000*
In the 'Bahn 2000', or 'Bahn + Bus 2000' programme, the federal government is financing development of an expanded and closely integrated public passenger transport service nationwide by the next century. For railways, parliament in 1986 approved expenditure of SFr5.4 billion on SBB projects embodied in the plan. At the end of 1991 the federal government budgeted SFr1.3 billion to support the country's 57 private railways' 'Bahn 2000' investments.

SBB's expanded passenger train service plan for 'Bahn 2000' centred on hourly cycling throughout the timetable at critical interchange points. On key routes, however, the 'Bahn 2000' plan doubles InterCity or direct train service from hourly to half-hourly. Realisation of this increase of service frequency began in 1999.

The 'Bahn 2000' scheme called for about 130 km of new 200 km/h route, to secure competitive transit times and to cut running time between neighbouring hubs to the 1 hour required. (For details, see under 'New lines' section.)

SBB's major 'Bahn 2000' projects have not proceeded to plan. The initial cost estimate of SFr5.4 billion had, by 1993, swollen to SFr14-16 billion with increased construction industry costs, and through the addition of environmental safeguards enforced by objectors to several schemes.

In 1993, the Bundesrat required SBB to recast the 'Bahn 2000' plan to keep total cost within the 1987 budget, SFr8.1 billion, with subsequent cost inflation. This was exclusive of investment associated with the AlpTransit scheme for new transalpine base tunnels (see 'New lines' section). The revised plan is now expected to cost SFr 6.4 billion. This curtailed programme will achieve most objectives of 'Bahn 2000' by 2005. It will not, however, accommodate the increased traffic expected from completion of the AlpTransit base tunnel plan. With tilt-body technology and double-deck coaches for InterCity services, some costly civil engineering to increase speed and capacity has been saved.

### Organisation
In 1997, SBB completed the implementation of a major restructuring intended to bring management decision-making closer to the market and to comply with the provisions of European Union Directive 91/440, even though Switzerland is not an EU member. The new structure provided for a complete separation of infrastructure and operations, and allowed the Swiss network to be opened up to operators other than SBB.

A further step was taken at the start of 1999. The state railway was transformed into a limited liability company wholly owned by the state, headed by a President and with a Chief Executive Officer. Within 'Schweizerische Bundesbahnen SBB' (SBB AG) three divisions have bottom-line responsibility (Passenger Traffic, Freight Traffic and Infrastructure). There is also a Finance Department and a Personnel Department. An Executive Board is made up of the Chief Executive Officer, the heads of passenger, freight and infrastructure divisions and the heads of the finance and personnel departments. Simplification (to achieve a more effective structure) and decentralisation (to bring the railway closer to its customers) continues; an entire layer has been removed by the elimination of the regional directions in Lausanne, Lucerne and Zurich. Regionalverkehr, the regional traffic business, has established a much firmer presence 'on the ground', able to deal directly and easily with the cantons. It produces more than half the total train-km of SBB's passenger traffic operation, amounting to some 2,600 million passenger-km on more than 120 routes in 1998. Over the last five years costs have been reduced by SFr100 million even though the number of train-km produced has gone up by 2.3 per cent. The new regions, with their headquarters, are: Léman (Lausanne), Wallis (Sion), Arc jurassien (Neuenburg), Mittelland (Bern), Zentralschweiz (Lucerne, Tessin (Bellinzona), Nordwestschweiz (Basel), Solothurn-Aargau (Olten), Zürich (Zürich), Nordostschweiz (Winterthur), Säntis-Bodensee (St Gallen), Graubünden-Walensee (Chur). The head of each region is the formal point of contact between SBB and the regional authorities. Grants towards regional traffic are falling – in 2000 at SFr545.7 million they were down SFr82.7 million on the figure for the previous two years – but the service is being expanded, and in the next few years some 50 new stations are to open for regional trains. In order to prepare for the joint-venture freight business with FS (see below), the SBB freight business was converted into a wholly owned limited liability subsidiary, SBB Cargo AG, at the beginning of 2000, as

*Class 460 electric locomotive with a Basel Chur IC service passing the Rhätische Bahn Station at Zizers (Andrew Marshall)*
*2000*/0088192

this was a prerequisite for entering into international agreements.

Open access for goods traffic and for the local traffic 'bought' by the cantons also came into force at the beginning of 1999 and SBB has established a one-stop shop to sell the paths. A new timetable gives priority to InterCity and international services, after which paths for sale can be established. SBB's own timetable is already projected forward to 2010.

### Finance

SBB had a deficit of SFr496 million in 1995. Energetic measures turned this round to a net profit of SFr120 million in 1999, the first year as a joint-stock company.

Productivity measures being introduced include one-person crews for regional trains and further substitution of buses for trains on poorly used regional services. Stations are being closed or destaffed as their operational facilities are brought under remote control. And a 'lean infrastructure' programme has rigorously embarked upon the removal of all track, points, crossings, and so on, surplus to normal requirements.

SBB's current aim is to improve the results of its freight division annually by SFr290 million up to 2002. To achieve this, productivity must be increased by SFr150 million, which requires a further reduction in personnel.

A federal law of 1987 requires rail and road to satisfy stringent noise emission standards by 2002. Meeting these standards will cost SBB approximately SFr2 billion.

**Finances** (SFr million)

| Income | 1998 | 1999 | 2000 |
|---|---|---|---|
| Passenger traffic | 1,533.7 | 1,603.6 | 1,630.3 |
| Goods traffic | 979.7 | 1,012.5 | 1,081.2 |
| Traffic earnings for services | 105.1 | 113.8 | 113.8 |
| Traffic earnings/Infrastructure | 14.7 | 9.6 | 11.9 |
| Grants for regional services | 628.4 | 557.9 | 545.7 |
| Grants for piggy-back traffic | 110.0 | 125.0 | 75.1 |
| Property rentals | 233.9 | 242.7 | 247.4 |
| Subsidiary earnings | 515.4 | 487.9 | 530.7 |
| Other income | 26.4 | 7.4 | 14.7 |
| Internal services | 383.0 | 382.4 | 456.6 |
| Federal contributions | 1,249.0 | 1,273.0 | 1,316.0 |
| Reductions in income | (−39.7) | (−64.7) | (−72.5) |
| Total | 5,738.6 | 5,751.1 | 5,950.9 |

| Expenditure | 1998 | 1999 | 2000 |
|---|---|---|---|
| Materials | (−324.9) | (−304.0) | (−340.5) |
| Staff costs | (−3,142.8) | (−2,990.3) | (−2,863.8) |
| Other costs | (−900.9) | (−959.8) | (−1,231.1) |
| Depreciation | (−938.3) | (−830.7) | (−879.1) |
| Inactive investments | (−257.3) | (−304.2) | (−326.4) |
| Taxation | (−58.9) | (−86.9) | - |
| Total expenditure | (−5,623.1) | (−5,475.9) | (−5,641.9) |
| Operational result | 115.5 | 275.2 | |
| Financial earnings | 143.9 | 108.3 | 132.8 |
| Financial costs | (−202.8) | (−178.5) | (−343.5) |
| Sale of real estate | 27.6 | 41.1 | 34.1 |
| Extraordinary earnings | 58.0 | 83.1 | 102.4 |
| Extraordinary expenditure | (−163.5) | (−208.9) | (−104.9) |
| Profit | (−21.3) | 120.3 | 139.9 |

| Traffic (million) | 1998 | 1999 | 2000 |
|---|---|---|---|
| Passenger journeys | 266.1 | 276.0 | 286.8 |
| Passenger-km | 12,484.8 | 12,615.0 | 12,835.0 |
| Freight tonnes | 52.3 | 57.3 | 60.5 |
| Freight tonne-km | 9,540.0 | 9,797.0 | 10,800.0 |

### Passenger operations

Four out of five of SBB's customers use local services; just one passenger in every five makes a journey exclusively on long-distance trains. A customer survey showed that in 2000 84.7 per cent of its customers were 'very satisfied' with SBB, a railway on which 94 per cent of trains reach their destination on time or no more than four minutes late.

The cutbacks in 'Bahn 2000' civil engineering investment (see 'Political background' section above) mean that, outside the key Basel—Bern—Zurich triangle, within-the-hour scheduling of InterCity (IC) services between all adjoining pairs of hub stations will not be feasible. Half-hourly service frequency on some routes, such as Basel—Lucerne, may be limited to business peak hours. The objective of connectional interlacing of regional and long-haul trains to offer once-every-daytime-hour service between any pair of SBB stations is affected by cuts in lightly used off-peak trains on many regional services.

The first three 'avec' shops at stations opened in 1999, at Schüpfen, Brügg, and Mettmenstetten. These are a joint venture between SBB, Migros and Kiosk AG, and they sell rail tickets, groceries, and kiosk goods. Open 365 days a year between 06.00 and 20.00 (or longer), they have been very well received by customers. It is planned to develop 50 more over the next few years at middle-sized stations. From the railway's point of view the great advantage is that the most important of the railway's products can be available in these stations without a need for SBB sales staff.

On 1 December 1999 SBB introduced a new national enquiry number, 0900 300 300, available 24 hours a day, to replace the old 157 22 22 number (which closed down at nights). Night service is provided from Zürich, while the other offices in Lausanne, Biel, Bern, Lucerne, Basel, Glaris, St Gallen and Lugano keep to their existing working hours. Four languages are available (English being the fourth), and the cost of the service is SFr1.19 per minute.

SBB is involved with the Swiss Post and the Public Transport Association (VöV) in the so-called 'EasyRide' project. In stages up to 2005 it will become possible to use the entire Swiss public transport system without the need for advance purchase of a ticket. Sensors on each of the 11,000 vehicles of the national public transport system will register each passenger's entry and exit and send the information for calculation of the tariff valid at that time, taking into account any applicable rebates and if the passenger will be invoiced at regular intervals. The system will cost some SFr600 million and it will cut the annual cost of ticketing by some SFr450 million. It will also provide data for timetable compilation and deployment of vehicles. Extension of the system to other modes (for example taxis, ski subscriptions, car-sharing) are provided for at a future stage. The aim is eventually to cover 80 per cent of all mobility. A preliminary study was completed in autumn 1999.

### Impuls 97

The June 1997 timetable change saw the introduction of the major train service innovations connected with 'Bahn 2000' and launched under the 'Impuls 97' branding. The first of an initial batch of 58 'InterCity 2000' double-deck coaches entered service on St Gallen—Interlaken services; train service frequency on Zurich—Bern, Zurich—St Gallen and Bern—Fribourg routes was doubled to half-hourly. Experience has shown that the half-hourly interval timetables are a commercial success.

The 1999 timetable offered an additional 8,000 train-km a day (6,000 in long-distance traffic and 2,000 in local traffic). The routes between Zürich and Lucerne, and Fribourg and Lausanne both received a half-hourly service throughout the day. The main beneficiary of the year's changes was Romandie, as a result of progress on the 'Bahn 2000' construction works: trains can run directly between Lausanne and the Broye again on completion of work on the three tunnels between Palézieux and Lausanne. Delivery of more bilevel coaches means that these can replace older stock on the Basel—Zürich—Chur, Interlaken—Bern—Zürich—St Gallen, and Zürich—Lucerne lines, with the stock displaced being made available for new IC and IR trains on the Lucerne—Basel and Basel—Biel—Geneva lines. The first ICN trains entered service in 2000. The 1999 timetable also saw complete Fly-Baggage-Check-In for almost all airlines in offer at 23 stations, with more due to be added to the list.

SBB entered into partnership with its Austrian and German counterparts ÖBB and DB in the Trans Europe Excellence (TEE) Alliance, which aims by 2005 to offer a common profile, cross-border service. The three railways were initially seeking bids to supply 116 tilting trains for the new through services; 34 of these will be owned by SBB. However, in late 2001 DB withdrew its intention to procure a share of a common fleet of trains, confining its participation in the TEE Alliance to marketing.

### Zurich RER

The Zurich RER (Regional Express) service, some 300 route-km, was inaugurated in 1990 (see *Jane's World Railways 1996-97* for details). In 2001, work started on a further expansion phase of the network. This covers track-doubling between Bubikon and Rüti to boost frequencies to Rapperswil, work to enhance capacity on the line to Winterthur, extension of route S3 to Dietikon, and completion of the Zimmerberg tunnel, raising capacity on lines serving Pfäffikon and Zug. The extension of line S3 is

*Interlaken Ost—St Gallen service formed of IC2000 bilevel stock and propelled by a Class 460 locomotive at Faulensee* (Andrew Marshall)

*Zurich S-Bahn Class 450 emu at Zürich Altstetten with an Uster service* (David Haydock)

due to be completed by 2004; the remaining projects are to be commissioned by 2006.

In a referendum held in September 2001, residents in the Zurich region approved plans for a fourth expansion of the S-Bahn network, at an estimated cost of SFr1.45 billion. To be completed by 2012, the scheme includes construction of a second underground through station beneath Zurich Hbf. A new 4.8 km tunnel from Zurich Hbf to Oerlikon will release capacity on the existing line for long-distance traffic.

*Bern RER*
May 1998 saw a major expansion of the Bern S-Bahn (first established in 1995). The two existing lines running through the city (S1 Thun–Bern–Fribourg/Laupen and S2 Langnau–Bern–Schwarzenburg) were joined by two new through lines, S3 (Biel–Lyss–Zollikofen–Bern–Ausserholligen–Weissenbühl–Belp–Seftigen–Thun and S4 (Langnau–Ramsei–Hasle–Rüesgau–Burgdorf–Zollikofen–Bern–Bern Bümpliz Nord). And the regional trains on the line from Bern to Neuchâtel via Kerzers now run under the S5 designation. The 138 stations on the network are served by more than 400 trains a day carrying some 40,000 passengers. As well as SBB, BLS Regionaiverkehr Mittelland, the Sensetalbahn, and the RBS network are involved, all operating as equal partners under the S-Bahn brand name (using the symbol of a blue 'S' on a yellow ground) to serve the cantons of Bern, Fribourg, Solothun, Waadt and Neuenburg. Under the close working agreement between SBB and BLS, the latter will take over SBB's share of Bern S-Bahn operations.

*Other S-Bahn operations*
Following on from the development of cross-border local services in the Basel area with SNCF, SBB is now to introduce an S-Bahn service across the border into Germany in collaboration with DB. Trains will run between Basel SBB and Offenbach via Basel Bad and Freiburg (Brsg). On the German side this new service will take over the existing Upper Rhine regional traffic. At present the only rail connection between Basel Bad and Basel SBB is provided by long-distance trains.

SBB has been entrusted with the planning of the proposed S-Bahn system for Central Switzerland, on which a decision was expected by the middle of 2001.

*Regional operations*
In September 2001, SBB announced that it was to form a jointly owned subsidiary with the Mittel-Thurgau Railway (MThB) (qv) to operate regional passenger services over a 550 km network in the Thurgau, St Gallen and Zurich areas of eastern Switzerland. Named Thurbo AG, the new company was due to commence operations in December 2002. Thurbo was to take over ownership of 10 existing MThB Type GTW 2/6 lightweight emus and order additional similar vehicles (see 'Traction and rolling stock').

## Freight operations
Major changes in SBB's freight business were foreshadowed on 30 March 1998 with the signature of an agreement between SBB and Italian State Railways (FS) to establish a joint rail freight business. With headquarters offices in Milan, the new company, Cargo Schweiz Italien GmbH, is to create a 'quality centre' to manage commercial and operational aspects of the two companies' international freight traffic. A second joint venture between SBB and FS undertakes the integration of the two railways' freight operations, creating a separate organisation with dedicated rolling stock, terminals and staff. Josef Egger, previously head of SBB's Central Department for Informatics, moved to the management of the new combined goods operation as Head of Informatics with the task of bringing the different systems of the two railways together. He was heavily involved in the negotiations that led to the establishment of the joint venture.

The two railways hoped to bring the joint operation into life at the start of 2001, but they have since agreed that a step-by-step approach to full union of their freight activities is required because of the much greater complexity of the project than was at first anticipated.

In 2000, SBB freight tonnage increased to a record 60.5 million.

SBB wants to raise the maximum speed of freight trains from 80 to 100 km/h to help obtain greater capacity on the mixed traffic network without new investment by harmonisation of speeds.

*Classes Re 6/6 and Re 4/4 II locomotives with a train of new light commercial vehicles at Wassen, on the southbound ascent of the Gotthard line (Andrew Marshall)*

*Northbound Gotthard line RoLa piggyback service at Göschenen (David Haydock)*

**Diesel locomotives**

| Class | Wheel arrangement | Power KW | Speed km/h | Weight tonnes | No in service | First built | Builders Mechanical | Engine | Transmission |
|---|---|---|---|---|---|---|---|---|---|
| 842 | Bo-Bo | 611 | 75 | 66 | 1 | 1939 | SLM | Sulzer | E ABB |
| 840 | Bo-Bo | 620 | 75 | 72 | 26 | 1960 | SLM | SLM | E Sécheron |
|  | Bo-Bo | 620 | 75 | 72 | 20 | 1968 | SLM | SLM | E Sécheron |
|  | Co-Co | 956 | 75 | 106 | 4 | 1954 | SLM | Sulzer | E ABB/Sécheron |
|  |  |  |  |  | 10 | 1960 |  |  |  |
| 930 | C | 326 | 65 | 49 | 5 | 1959 | SLM | SLM | E ABB/Sécheron |
|  |  | 326 | 65 | 49 | 35 | 1962 | SLM | SLM | E ABB/Sécheron |
| 863 | Co-Co | 1,440 | 85 | 111 | 6 | 1976 | Thyssen-Henschel | Chantiers de l'Atlantique | E ABB |
| Em 6/6 | Co-Co | 393 | 65 | 104 | 6 | 1971 | SLM | SLM | E SAAS/ SSB/ABB |
| 831 | C | 900 | 60 | 54 | 3 | 1992 | RACO | Cummins | H |
| 842 | Bo-Bo | 1,120 | 90 | 80 | 2 | 1992 | Krupp | MTU | H |

A new freight strategy was announced in 2001 under which SBB will aim to improve standards of both service and productivity. This replaces the strategy based on rapid fusion with FS Cargo and on the aim of offering a complete logistics service.

On the broader European front, SBB will seek direct relationships with customers in key geographic markets, will develop its own production in Germany and will seek to further its partnerships with FS (leading to fusion), with Hupac for combined traffic and with HGK as an additional partner in the north. Basel will be developed as a modern, high-performance 'Eurohub' and SBB Cargo will move its headquarters there.

On the domestic front the most important change is the redefinition of SBB Cargo's activities to just those areas where rail can be strong. Four products are envisaged: *CargoRail*, for overnight wagonload traffic; *CargoExpress*, for accelerated transits for single wagons overnight between 55 centres; *CargoClientNet* (working title) for trainload services for major customers between specific centres; and *CargoTrain* (working title), for single-product trainload services. *CargoExpress* was launched in June 2001.

## Intermodal operations
SBB is purely a wholesaler of train capacity to intermodal marketing concerns, notably the Swiss company Hupac (for contact details, see UIRR entry in 'Operators of International Rail Services in Europe' section), and the Swiss-based international company Intercontainer (qv),

both of which own fleets of intermodal wagons. Hupac deploys a fleet of 345 RoLa ('Rolling Highway') low-floor well wagons for ro-ro movement of complete (tractor and trailer) road trucks. Hupac also operates 25 couchette cars for RoLa trains' trucker crews and 1,750 pocket wagons for carriage of unaccompanied trailers and swapbodies.

Hupac's RoLa trains for accompanied lorries run between Basel and Lugano, between Freiburg-im-Breisgau (just inside Germany) and Lugano or Milan Greco Pirelli, and from Rielasingen to Milan Rogoredo. The RoLa operation, however, cannot be marketed at a cost-covering price and is federally supported out of road-users' petrol/diesel tax.

In April 2001 SBB and Hupac formed a joint venture subsidiary, S-Rail Europe (SRE), which has been registered in Germany as an open access operator. A Class 1116 electric locomotive, acquired by Hupac in 2000, was transferred to SRE and two similar machines were ordered from Siemens. The locomotives are similar to the Austrian Federal's Class 1016/1116 Taurus machines.

A further development in 2001 was the establishment by SBB, BLS and Hupac of the RAlpin joint company to operate RoLa services between Freiburg im Breisgau, Germany and Novara, Italy. Each company holds a 30 per cent shareholding in the venture, with FS Cargo in Italy holding the remaining 10 per cent. Using the Lötschberg route, RAlpin services commenced in June 2001 with an initial four train pairs per day.

Since late 2000 lorry drivers on the Germany–Italy run have been able to put their vehicles on trains and take their rest periods during the rail trip through Switzerland. A 1992 agreement between the EU and Switzerland included the creation of a rolling motorway, set the capacity (105,000 lorry-spaces), and named the terminals (Freiburg im Breisgau, and Novara). A spur was given to the plans by the 1994 Alpine Initiative. In 1998 the federal government sought tenders for operating the Lötschberg–Simplon route, and early in 1999 it was announced that a consortium of SBB, BLS, and Hupac SA had been successful. Revenue of SFr22.4 million in 2001, rising to SFr65 million in 2005, is envisaged. Subsidy will remain constant at about SFr30 million a year. On the infrastructure front, the Lötschberg tunnel is cleared for trains carrying lorries up to 4 m high and 2.4 m wide. In the Simplon area, works have been completed on the Varzo–Preglia section. Works on the Iselle–Domodossola and Domodossola–Novara sections were completed by September 2000. And on the Varzo–Iselle section one line became available in September 2000, the other in March 2001.

*New intermodal systems*
The first bimodal operation was launched by the Swiss food distribution company Migros, which annually sends 1.2 million tonnes of freight by rail. Ten Kombitrailers and 20 rail bogies operate from Migros' main Neuendorf centre to St Margrethen.

SBB and the private railways are partners in ACTS SA, a company formed to promote local container traffic. This achieves road-rail transfer without cranage; the Type Rs-x rail wagons, 800 of which are supplied by Tuchschmid AG of Frauenfeld, each have three 20 ft long platforms that can be swung outwards to back up to the rear of a road vehicle chassis equipped with a mechanism to slide a container from one vehicle to the other.

*Gotthard route upgrade*
The federal government allocated SFr1.46 billion for works, chiefly on the Gotthard route, and on approach routes Basel–Brugg–Arth–Goldau, to expand capacity for transit intermodal traffic pending completion of the new transalpine base tunnels (see 'New lines' section). The aim was to treble the Gotthard route's intermodal piggyback capacity from 160,000 to 470,000 units a year. This embraced unaccompanied semi-trailers, and RoLa movement of highway trucks. There would also be scope for annual throughput of some 330,000 containers and swapbodies.

The works were completed at the end of 1993. As a result, the maximum permissible format of Gotthard piggyback trains rose from 17 to 36 flat wagons with a gross laden weight of 2,000 tonnes. Southbound, single-headed 16-wagon trains run to Dottikon, where they are coupled, so that the locomotive of the rear train becomes the radio-controlled mid-train power. A third locomotive is added to double-head the combined train. Northbound, combined trains are formed during the essential change-of-voltage repowering at the FS-SBB yard in Chiasso. The aim is to power these trains exclusively with the tranche of 75 Class 460 locomotives which SBB expressly ordered for the service. In 1994, the Gotthard route carried 44 piggyback intermodal trains daily.

The clearances of the Gotthard route allow unaccompanied trailers, 3.9 m high at their roof corners, on so-called 'pocket' wagons. If they have deflatable air suspension, 4 m high box trailers can be safely accommodated on the latest type of pocket wagon. But RoLa piggybacked trucks must not be higher than 3.8 m, whereas virtually unrestricted admissibility to RoLa trains of European trucks requires clearance for 4.2 m road vehicle height. That will be built into the new transalpine base tunnels.

### New lines
*'Bahn 2000' works*
The longest stretches of new 200 km/h infrastructure proposed in the original 'Bahn 2000' plan were to be on the Basel–Bern route: one of 34 km between Muttenz, on Basel's outskirts, and Olten (which entailed tunnels of 4.7 and 12.8 km length, the Adler and Wisenberg respectively); and another of 54 km between the Olten area at Rothrist and Mattstetten, near Bern, with a branch to the Olten–Zofingen–Lucerne line. These give the 22 minute cut in Bern–Basel timings needed to secure under-the-hour timing of direct trains, as between Bern and Lucerne or Zurich. But four-tracking between Basel and Bern would also handle the doubled direct passenger train frequency and anticipated extra international freight traffic via the Bern area following completion of the BLS Lötschberg route double-tracking.

The Rothrist–Mattstetten high-speed route survived the reappraisal of the 'Bahn 2000' project, and work started in 1996. It runs parallel to the N1 motorway and close to the existing railway as far as the region of Herzogenbuchsee, with a branch to an existing secondary line to Solothurn, to be upgraded to a fast route for trunk trains from Biel to Basel or Zurich. At Mattstetten the new line will make an end-on junction with the new Grauholz bypass. The line is expected to open on 19 December 2004.

The 9.5 km Grauholz bypass opened in 1995; it includes a 6.3 km tunnel. Its purpose is to keep Bern–Olten traffic clear of Zollikofen, where the old Olten–Bern and Biel–Bern lines saw some 300 trains a day. With full implementation of 'Bahn 2000' the total would rise to 500, including eight pairs of IC trains in each hour. The bypass starts 4 km out of Bern at Bern-Löchligut. The Grauholz bypass permits half-hourly Bern–Zurich IC service. Further east, the Rupperswil–Aarau segment, including Aarau station and a new tunnel under the town, will become a four-track high-speed section.

Of the planned Muttenz–Olten high-speed segment, the Muttenz–Liestal section (including the Adler Tunnel) opened in December 2000. This section segregates the Hauenstein and Bözberg routes out of Basel. The advantages offered by a continuation through a new Wisenberg Tunnel were held not to be worth the cost, but SBB is now engaged in new studies for an additional tunnel through the Jura chain. A decision is expected in time for the second stage of Rail 2000.

A third stretch of 200 km/h track, 9 km in length, was to be between Zurich Airport and Winterthur. This stretch required boring of the 8.4 km Brüttener Tunnel between Kloten and Winterthur. The entire scheme is now deferred.

Finally, 31 km of 200 km/h line were planned between Vauderens and Villars-sur-Glâne, on the main line from Lausanne to Bern. This, the only 200 km/h project with the sole aim of shortening transit time, was cut back to construction of a new tunnel at Vauderens that is essential to provide adequate clearance for the new double-deck IC trainsets. Construction began in 1998 on the 2.9 km of double track between Vauderens and Prezvers-Siviriez, which includes the 1,975 m tunnel. The section will cost SFr90 million and its completion will allow the existing 1862 tunnel to be abandoned.

Among the SBB's other major 'Bahn 2000' schemes, the short section of the Simplon route still single – the 4.6 km between Salgesch and Leuk in the canton of Wallis – is now being bypassed. The 6.6 km double-track new, 4.2 km in tunnel, will be completed in 2005 and will allow 160 km/h instead of today's 100 km/h. The job is a big one: the railway will be realigned through the Pfynwald, the A9 autobahn will take the alignment of the present T9 cantonal main road and the T9 will take the present railway alignment. The total final cost will be SFr239 million, of which 60 per cent will be borne by the canton and the Federal Roads Department.

In April 2001 the new 10.5 km double-track line from Onnens to St-Aubin via Gorgier was opened and this allows tilting trains to run into Romandie. After this, the next opening expected is of the double-track 10 km new line between Zürich and Thalwil, in 2003, which will relieve the lakeside line of traffic and allow improvements to local services.

*New base tunnels*
The federal government's AlpTransit plan for new Gotthard and Lötschberg base tunnels, to enable the

### Electric locomotives

| Class | Wheel arrangement | Speed km/h | Weight tonnes | No in service | First built | Builders Mechanical | Electrical |
|---|---|---|---|---|---|---|---|
| 610 | Co-Co | 125 | 120/124 | 120 | 1952 | SLM | ABB/Oerlikon |
| 410 | Bo-Bo | 125 | 57 | 10 | 1946 | SLM | ABB/Oerlikon |
| 411 | | 125 | 57 | 17 | 1950 | SLM | Sécheron |
| 420 | Bo-Bo | 140 | 80 | 273 | 1964 | SLM | ABB/Oerlikon/Sécheron |
| 430 | Bo-Bo | 125 | 80 | 21 | 1971 | SLM | ABB/Oerlikon/Sécheron |
| 450 | Bo-Bo | 130 | 71 | 115 | 1989 | SLM | ABB |
| 460 | Bo-Bo | 100 | 81 | 119 | 1993 | SLM | ABB |
| 620 | Bo-Bo-Bo | 140 | 120 | 88 | 1972 | SLM | ABB/Sécheron |
| 930 | C | 40/50 | 39/45 | 118 | 1928 | | ABB/Oerlikon/Sécheron |
| Ee 6/6 | C + C | 45 | 90 | 2 | 1952 | SLM | ABB/Sécheron |
| 962 | Co-Co | 85 | 107 | 10 | 1980 | SLM | ABB |
| Eem 6/6 | Co-Co | 65 | 104 | 1 | 1970 | SLM | SAAS |
| **15 kV/25 kV** | | | | | | | |
| Ee 3/3 II | C | 45 | 46 | 14 | 1957 | SLM | ABB |
| **1.5 kV/3 kV/15 kV/25 kV** | | | | | | | |
| 934 | C | 60 | 48 | 10 | 1962 | SLM | Sécheron |

New classifications have been reserved for forthcoming locomotives as follows:
453 Possible three-voltage unit for Geneva and Basel S-Bahn projects
462 Planned dual-voltage version of Re 4/4 VI

### Electric railcars or multiple-units

| Class | Cars per Unit | Motor cars Per unit | Motored axles/car | Output/motor kW | Speed km/h | No in service | First built | Builders Mechanical | Electrical |
|---|---|---|---|---|---|---|---|---|---|
| **15 kV AC** | | | | | | | | | |
| RAe 2/4 | 1 | 1 | 2 | 197 | 125 | 1 | 1935 | SLM | ABB/MFO/SAAS/SBB |
| 511 | 3 | 3 | 4 | 204 | 125 | 18 | 1965 | SWP/FFA | SAAS/ABB |
| 512 | 4 | 2 | 4 | 281 | 125 | 4 | 1976 | SWS/SWP/SIG | SAAS |
| 560 | 2 | 1 | 4 | 412 | 140 | 84 | 1984 | FFA/SIG/SWP/SWA | ABB |
| 540 | 1 | 1 | 4 | 497 | 125 | 80 | 1959 | SIG/SWS | ABB/MFO |
| 536 | 1 | 1 | 4 | 294 | 110 | 2 | 1952 | SLM/SWP | ABB/MFO/SAAS |
| 546 | 1 | 1 | 4 | 201 | 75 | 1 | 1927 | SIG/SWS | SAAS |
| **1.5 kV DC** | | | | | | | | | |
| Bem 550 | 2 | - | - | 600 | 100 | 5 | 1994 | SWG-A/SWG-P/SIG | ABB |
| **1.5 kV/3 kV/15 kV/25 kV** | | | | | | | | | |
| 506 | 6 | 1 | 6 | 577.5 | 160 | 3 | 1961 | SIG | MFO |

near-trebling of transalpine capacity for rail-based intermodal traffic, was approved by national referendum in 1992. The federal council adopted the AlpTransit plan, to resist European Union (EU) demands for a transalpine road corridor for 40 tonne trucks, in face of Switzerland's 28 tonne gross loaded weight truck limit, prohibition of night driving, a levy on heavy goods road transit, and noise and emissions controls. Railways claim 68 per cent of the Swiss transit freight market, although substantial diversion of road traffic via France or Austria occurs.

Using rights under the Swiss constitution, a private environmentalist initiative led to a national referendum on transit highway freight in 1994. Against federal government advice, in view of the likely strain on relations with the EU, the country voted to bar Swiss roads to all transit highway freight by 2004. Since neither transalpine base tunnel would be finished by then, rail congestion is inevitable.

Exploratory boring for the Gotthard base tunnel route began in 1995 (the Lötschberg project is dealt with in the BLS Lötschbergbahn entry). It will extend approximately 125 km from Arth-Goldau to the outskirts of Lugano, with the 57 km base tunnel as its centrepiece. The base tunnel, starting at Erstfeld on the northern side, will be the world's longest rail bore; its summit, 550 m above sea level, will be some 600 m below that of the present Gotthard tunnel. The route is described in *JWR 1996-97*.

Clearances will be contoured for piggybacking of road lorries 4.2 m high. The base tunnel itself will be aligned and built so as to simplify its possible elaboration at some future date into the 'Y' form sought by eastern Switzerland. Other schemes exist, subject to financing, to improve access to the Gotthard base tunnel from eastern Switzerland, south Germany and Austria. Use of the Bodensee—Toggenburg line (qv) from St Gallen southwestwards would bring Gotthard traffic from the east and northeast to Pfaffikon, up the SBB's Zurich line to Au and through a new Hirzel Tunnel, to a 'Y' near Zug with a new north-south double-track Zimmerberg Tunnel, to be bored from Thalwil to benefit traffic from Zurich (and the Stuttgart area of Germany) to Arth-Goldau.

The Lötschberg tunnel will be completed in 2006, the Gotthard in 2012. Internal differences in the Swiss Cabinet in 1994 led in 1995 to an independent reappraisal of the cost (about SFr15 billion) and returns, and it was shown that the SBB and BLS could not, as originally planned, pay back the cost from traffic income. Since this was a condition on which the 1992 popular approval was given, a further vote was due to be held on a revised finance package, including increased use of fuel revenues. An agreement reached in January 1998 between Switzerland and the European Union provides for a gradual relaxation of the 28 tonne gross laden weight limit for trucks up to 2005, when a 40 tonne ceiling would be permitted. A transit tax on each lorry and a quota system were considered by the Swiss government sufficient both to provide funding for the two base tunnels and their related works – as well as for other rail infrastructure investments in Switzerland – and to appease public opinion and the concerns of environmentalists.

In May 1998, a new SBB subsidiary, 'AlpTransit Gotthard AG' was founded in Bern with a capital of SFr5 million to be responsible for the planning and construction of the AlpTransit Gotthard Axis.

In mid-1998, final test results showed that all the strata through which the Gotthard Base Tunnel passes are firm throughout, so that no special problems are to be expected in tunnelling, either by boring machine or by explosive. On 29 November 1998, in two referenda, the Swiss people accepted the so-called FinöV proposals and thus approved the funds to allow a solid financing of major rail projects, allowing work on the two Alpine Base Tunnels to move from the planning phase into the building phase.

Tunnelling began in November 1999 and the Base Tunnel is expected to open by 2012.

## Improvements to existing lines

The Rhône Valley main line to the Simplon Tunnel has been upgraded. Complete renewal of track with heavier rail and higher-speed pointwork, realignments at Riddes and Ardon, renewal of overhead equipment, and resignalling accompanied by computer-based control, track-to-train radio and automatic speed control, equip the Martigny—Sion section for 200 km/h. There is provision for solid-state interlockings at Martigny and Sion. A new double-track tunnel will replace the last single-track section, the 5 km in difficult terrain between Salgesch and Leuk. Here, from Leuk to Visp, and (later) through the Simplon Tunnel the speed limit will be 160 km/h.

To achieve clearance for piggybacked trucks of 4.2 m corner height, and to provide for higher passenger train speeds, the Simplon Tunnel's track is being renewed and its bed lowered. At the same time, a rigid traction current conductor replaces traditional catenary. The rigid conductor is closer to the tunnel crown, giving 300 to 400 mm of extra clearance for intermodal piggyback trains. To avoid unacceptable interference with traffic, the works are executed in the least busy periods of the year, covering 3 to 5 km at a time, and the project is expected to take six to eight years in total.

A seven-year reconstruction and upgrading programme for Zürich's main station was announced in April 1998.

In March 1999, work began on the construction of the third line over the 13.5 km between Coppet and Geneva. Completion will be between 2003 and 2005. Provision of this third track will allow the demands of the 'Bahn 2000' timetable to be met by separating out regional services from long-distance traffic.

In the period up to 2005 the approaches to Zürich station are being totally renewed within the scope of the 'Bahn 2000' project. Trains will be sorted at Killwangen-Spreitenbach, Altstetten, Thalwil and Oerlikon, thus allowing crossing movements in the *Hauptbahnhof* throat to be avoided and raising reliability and efficiency. The chosen solution, coupled with the quadrupling of the Wipkingen line, will allow up to 15 parallel movements – necessary if the number of trains is to be raised by 22 per cent in four stages over the next seven years, from 1,350 in 1996 to 1,650. A new four-platform S-Bahn station between Line 3 and the Sihlpost will eliminate problems in the station itself. From 2005 Zürich will have half-hourly services in all directions. At Altstetten Süd SFr176.4 million are to be spent on the improvements, including provision of a single-track S-Bahn underpass.

SBB is currently concerned to establish a more robust power supply and as part of this work it is spending SFr22 million on the 25 km Burgdorf—Wanzwill section of the second Central Switzerland electrical link between its transformer stations in Kerzers and Rupperswil. This is to relieve a 1927 link which is no longer adequate by providing an additional link between the power stations group in Wallis and that in the Gotthard region. The 132 kV connection will also feed the planned substation in Wanzwil which is to feed the 'Bahn 2000' new line between Mattstetten and Rothrist. The link will be built as a 90 per cent joint exercise with other electricity companies. And in mid-September 1998 the Amsteg hydro-electric power station, completely renovated over a five-year period at a cost of SFr460 million, began to supply power. The old Amsteg station produced current for SBB for more than 70 years. For the new one, SBB and the canton of Uri founded in 1992 a Kraftwerk Amsteg KG company with a capital of SFr80 million (90 per cent SBB) to build and operate the new installations. The new equipment generates up to 120 MW.

## Traction and rolling stock

By January 2000 SBB's locomotive fleet had been divided between the Passenger and Freight business sectors, with 234 going to the former and 397 to the latter. Depots and personnel are also now similarly assigned to the one business or the other. A decision on main workshops was due to be taken at the end of November 2000.

In 1999, SBB operated 803 standard-gauge electric locomotives; 255 electric power cars; 121 diesel locomotives; 163 electric shunters; and 916 tractors. The rolling stock fleet of 4,392 passenger cars included 53 restaurant, 12 sleeping and 60 couchette cars. Freight wagons totalled 16,111, Swiss Post Office-owned postal cars 561 and baggage cars 333. Over 6,460 privately owned wagons were in use.

*Tilting train order*

In 1996, SBB ordered 24 nine-car ICN tilting trains from a consortium of Swiss industry in a contract worth some SFr500 million. The consortium is led by Bombardier and also involves Alstom. The trains are capable of travelling at 200 km/h and are for use on curvaceous routes; SBB decided to opt for tilting trains to cut down the work required on building new lines for 'Bahn 2000'.

Delivery began in December 1999 and will be completed in 2001. The first route on which the trains ran is the Jura corridor between Lausanne and St Gallen; Geneva to Basel will follow. The tilt trains are marketed under the 'ICN 2000' tag (the bilevel cars run as 'IC 2000').

The tilting trains have a multiple-unit format, with power distributed along the train. Two units can work in multiple at peak times.

In June 2001, SBB ordered an additional 10 seven-car ICN trainsets, with an option on 10 more. Delivery is scheduled in 2004.

*Rack-equipped Class 101 (HGe 4/4) Brünig line metre-gauge electric locomotive at Lucerne* (L T Peacock)

*Full seven-car production ICN tilting trainset near Ligerz*

SBB also plans to procure an additional 34 tilting trainsets as its contribution to the TEE Alliance project (see 'Passenger operations').

*Other developments*
In October 2001, SBB Cargo ordered 10 dual-voltage (15 kV AC/25 kV AC) 4,200 kW electric locomotives from Bombardier. These are to be of a design similar to that of DB Cargo's Class 185. Construction will take place in Germany, with delivery commencing in February 2002.

SBB Cargo has equipped 10 locomotives of classes Re 460 and Re 4/4 II for working into Germany. This requires the provision of a German-size pantograph, Indusi (and probably LZB), and German train-radio. Up to now only the Re 4/4 II machines 11195 to 11200 have been equipped with pantographs that allow them to work into Lindau. Target station is Ludwigshafen, a centre for chemical traffic.

In 2000 SBB ordered from Stadler 17 GTW 2/8 three-section lightweight emus for services on the Lucerne–Lenzburg line in the Seetal region. Designated Type ABe 520 by SBB, they are to be delivered in 2002 and will be the first three-section examples of the Stadler GTW family. In collaboration with Adtranz, Stadler also supplied 50 Tm 234 service tractors during 2000.

The Thurbo AG subsidiary (see 'Passenger operations') established jointly by SBB and the Mittel-Thurgau Railway (MThB) (qv) plans to acquire an additional 80 GTW-type articulated lightweight emus from Stadler/Bombardier by 2007, supplementing the existing fleet of 10 similar vehicles.

*Coach fleet*
SBB is investing between SFr260 million and SFr290 million a year up to 2002 in the modernisation of the passenger fleet. Following on from the initial order for 58 air conditioned InterCity 'Bahn 2000' bilevel cars placed in 1993 and the follow-up order for 144 vehicles placed in late 1997, a third series of 48 bilevel InterCity carriages has been ordered at a cost of SFr143 million, to bring this fleet up to 250 units within three years – including, from 2000, vehicles with a bistro section. This order included 19 first class cars, three driving trailers and 26 second class/bistro cars. In place of compartments on the lower level, these last have a bistro-bar with kitchen and office. There are 14 seats and standing room at the bar, and on the upper level there are eight groups of four seats for take-away service. These cars were ordered in place of classic restaurant cars because of the poor economics of the latter and ever-shortening journey times. Also, research has shown that a bistro will appeal to a broader cross-section of the public than a traditional restaurant car.

An order for a fourth series of 70 vehicles, valued at SFr217 million, was placed with an Adtranz/Alstom consortium in February 2001. Deliveries will be made between 2002 and 2004 and will bring the total fleet to 320 cars. No further orders for IC2000 bilevel stock are envisaged.

The standard formation of a push-pull bilevel IC set consists of a Class 460 locomotive, seven intermediate vehicles and a driving trailer, offering a total of 712 seats. Trains can be worked in multiple, allowing division en route to serve two destinations.

The modernisation programme includes SFr248 million to update by 2005 the InterCity fleet of 449 Type IV (EW IV) coaches and the EuroCity fleet. In addition, five baggage cars are to be bought from French National Railways (SNCF), 15 restaurant cars are to be converted for international service, 36 EC coaches are to be rebuilt as driving trailers and baggage compartments are to be built into the first class InterCity cars. The EW IV vehicles are still in good shape after 10 or more years of service and do not yet require major overhaul, so a facelift is to be applied: new furnishings and carpets, a sealed toilet system, electric hand-driers, cycle platforms and a better passenger information system, as well as replacement of the air conditioning and electronic systems. They will be equipped for push-pull operation and 200 km/h running. The EC cars will acquire a closed toilet system. After this work the refurbished vehicles and the new bilevel vehicles will all be fit for use on the new line between Mattstetten and Rothrist.

With push-pull 'InterCity 2000' services in mind, 60 driving trailers were ordered in 1994 and were in widespread service in 1997. Some 300 cars of earlier build, at present limited to 140 km/h, are being modified for 160 km/h operation.

### Signalling and telecommunications
Some 99.7 per cent of SBB lines are colourlight signalled with the Swiss standard system. The remaining 0.3 per cent of lines still have mechanical signalling. Some 45 per cent of the system (1,267.2 km) is equipped with automatic block with axle-counters; 26.5 per cent (742.3 km) has automatic block with track circuits; manual block with continuous current serves 28 per cent (788.8 km), and manual block indicators the remaining 0.5 per cent (11.9 km).

SBB has so far not required cab signalling, though this would be useful in the Lakeland areas of the country where mists and fog can make lineside equipment hard to see. However, some of the new lines due to be opened in the next few years will allow speeds at which cab signalling is required. Accordingly a 32 km test section is to be equipped, between Zofingen and Sempach. This is a Gotthard feeder line which suffers from a good many foggy days. Some stations will need alteration, as on safety grounds island platforms will need to be replaced by lineside platforms. 53 vehicles will be equipped with the necessary cab signalling: nine local units, 37 locomotives for goods and passenger traffic, and eight shunting locomotives. The system used will be the world's first ERTMS Level 2 installation in commercial service and is being supplied by Adtranz. The contract covers the radio block centre, the GSM-R radio transmission system, onboard equipment for 66 locomotives and some 200 track beacons (balises). Testing began in May 2000. Signalling on the whole Olten–Lucerne line is being modernised, involving SFr55.4 million replacement of mechanical installations dating from 1908 to 1932 in Brittnau-Wikon, Reiden, Dagnersellen, Nebikon, Wauwil, Sursee and Nottwill – which are not suitable for the 200 km/h speeds required for the future – by two new ESTW installations, at Dagmersellen and Sursee.

Since April 1998, it has been possible to use train-to-shore radio throughout the 19.803 km length of the Simplon No 1 tunnel. Broadband coverage (160-900 MHz) is available. The total installation project for both tunnels involves the drilling of some 40,000 holes into the tunnel walls. The radio system replaces the telephone system previously in place.

SBB and SNCF have decided to link up their traffic management systems, *Brehat* and *Surf*, thus providing controllers with a picture of operations on both networks and allowing the possibility of more effective intervention in case of problems.

Almost as needy of renewal is the third of SBB's interlockings that are electromechanically controlled, and thus difficult to adapt for remote control from new route-setting panels. SBB is also one of Europe's leading railways in use of Automatic Vehicle Identification, using trackside radio-wave readers and transponder tags, designed by Alcatel-Amtech to UIC standard. The first installations at Erstfeld, on the Gotthard route, and at Italian and French border stations in 1993, were followed by implementation throughout Switzerland, giving much-improved rolling stock control and better customer information.

In common with the Lucerne-Stans-Engelberg Railway (qv), with which it shares tracks between Hergiswil and Lucerne, the Brünig route has been equipped with a ZSL90 system of ATP specially developed for narrow-gauge railways.

A thorough modernisation of the railway telephone service was being undertaken in 2001, affecting all exchanges and all 18,000 handsets. New equipment was being supplied by Ascom. Total cost of the project is SFr15 million. A project for the modernisation of public information services is running in parallel. This work was expected to cost SFr98 million.

### Track
**Rail:** SBB 1, 46 kg/m (538 km); SBB IV UIC 54E, 54 kg/m (2,382 km); SBB VI UIC 60, 60 kg/m (1,553 km)
**Crossties (sleepers):** wood (1,765 km); steel (1,096 km); concrete (1,612 km)
**Spacing:**
In plain track: 1,667/km
**Min curvature:** 176 m
**Max gradient:** 4%
**Max axleload:** 22.5 tonnes

*UPDATED*

---

## Thurbo AG

Postfach, CH-8280 Kreuzlingen
e-mail: info@thurbo.ch
Web: http://www.thurbo.ch

### Key personnel
Chairman: Paul Blumenthal
Vice-President: Peter Joss
Managing Director: Dr Ernst Boos
Product Director: Ruedi Signer
Managers
    Marketing and Sales: Gallus Heuberger
    Transport: Martin Hochreutener
    Production: Alfred Hartmann
    Customer Service: Christian Saxer

### Organisation
Thurbo AG was founded in September 2001 jointly by SBB AG and Mittelthurgaubahn AG (qv) to operate and develop regional services in northeast Switzerland. Full operations were expected to commence in December 2002, by which date the company would employ some 150 staff.

### Passenger operations
From December 2002 Thurbo AG is to operate regional services over a 543 km network in an area defined by the Bodensee (Lake Constance) in the east, Koblenz and Winterthur in the west and Uznach in the south. Also covered are cross-border services to Stockach, Singen and Engen, in Germany. At the commencement of operations it was expected that the company's services would carry some 22.5 million passengers for 335 million passenger-km annually.

### Traction and rolling stock
Existing MThB and SBB equipment is to be supplemented or replaced progressively from the end of 2003 by a fleet of 80 Type GTW 2/6 lightweight articulated emus supplied by Stadler. All 80 units are to be in service by the end of 2007.

*NEW ENTRY*

---

## Transports Public Fribourgeois (TPF)

Rue des Pilettes 3, CH-1700 Fribourg
Tel: (+41 26) 351 02 00    Fax: (+44 26) 351 02 90

### Key personnel
General Manager: Claude Barraz

Gauge: 1,435 mm; 1,000 mm
Route length: 50 km; 50 km
Electrification: 50 km of 1,435 mm gauge at 15 kV 16⅔ Hz AC; 50 km of 1,000 mm gauge at 900 V DC

### Organisation
Formed in 1942, the former GFM group (Chemins de Fer Fribourgeois Gruyère-Fribourg-Morat) comprised: a 49 km 1,000 mm gauge route from Montbovon MOB via Gruyères to Palézieux (SBB), and from Bulle to Broc; an 18 km 1,435 mm gauge route from Bulle to Romont (SBB); and an isolated 32 km 1,435 mm gauge line from Fribourg via Morat to Anet (BLS-BN).

In July 2000 GFM merged with Fribourg's public transport operator, Transports Publics de Fribourg (TPF), creating the present company.

## Passenger and freight operations

In 1995, 2,124,000 passengers were carried (26.5 million passenger-km), and 302,000 tonnes of freight (5.6 million tonne-km). In 1996, traffic declined to 2.0 million passengers (24.9 million passenger-km) and 243,000 tonnes of freight (4.1 million tonne-km).

## Traction and rolling stock

In 1995, GFM's 1,435 mm gauge fleet comprised: 13 electric power cars; two Ae 417 electric locomotives, former DR Class 142 obtained through leasing company Lokoop AG; 13 passenger trailer cars; two electric and five diesel tractors; and four freight wagons.

GFM's 1,000 mm gauge fleet comprised in 1994: two Type GDe 4/4 1,000 kW electric locomotives; 11 electric power cars; 20 other passenger coaches; four electric and two diesel tractors; 45 freight wagons; and 52 transporter bogies for conveyance of 1,435 mm gauge wagons.

*TPF (former GFM) Type RABDe standard-gauge railcar leaving Fribourg with a freight service (David Haydock)*
*2001*/0109861

# SYRIA

## Ministry of Transport

PO Box 134, Damascus
Tel: (+963 11) 33 68 01    Fax: (+963 11) 332 33 17

**Key personnel**
Minister: Murfid Abdul Karim

## Chemin de Fer du Hedjaz

PO Box 134, Place Hidjaz, Damascus
Tel: (+963 11) 221 29 50    Fax: (+963 11) 222 71 06

**Key personnel**
Director General: Ing Salah Ahmad
Head of Director General's Office: Youssef Dakhlallah
Directors
　Operations and Marketing: Ing Hussein Nasser
　Traction and Rolling Stock: Ing Faysal Alnen
　Information Technology, Signalling and
　　Communications: Ing Ousama Al-Abiad
　Finance: Mohamed Osman
　Planning: Younes Al-Nasser
　Infrastructure: Ing Wafik Al-Homsy
　Training: Ing Faez Breshe
　Compliance: Rifaat Suleyman

Gauge: 1,050 mm
Route length: 251 km

### Political background

In December 2001, the governments of Jordan, Saudi Arabia and Syria agreed to reconstruct the railway.

### Organisation

In addition to its own route length, the CF du Hedjaz also operates the 67 km narrow-gauge Damascus–Zerghaya line on behalf of the Syrian government. Traffic has been at a very low level for several years. Work on a standard-gauge line to supersede this line was started but has been suspended (see CFS entry).

### Traffic

In 1999 the railway carried 94,000 passengers and some 2,000 tonnes of freight.

### Traction and rolling stock

The railway owns five (of 29) serviceable steam and three (of nine) diesel locomotives, six railcars, 35 passenger cars and 311 freight wagons.

*UPDATED*

## Chemins de Fer Syriens (CFS)

PO Box 182, Aleppo
Tel: (+963 21) 221 39 00; 221 39 01
Fax: (+963 21) 222 84 80; 222 56 97
e-mail: cfs-syria@net.sy

**Key personnel**
President and Director General:
　Ing Mohamad Iyad Ghazal
Deputy Directors General:
　Ing I A M El-Bonn
　Adnan Al-Hussein
Directors
　Rolling Stock and Traction: Ing A M Battikh
　Movement and Traffic: Ing Ismail Badenkhan
　Fixed Installations: Ing Mahmoud Ismail
　Administrative: Messab Al-Nokkary
　Financial Affairs: Hassan Mamlouk
　Accounts: Abdul-Karim Taleb
　Planning and Statistics: Fariza Moulayes
　Marketing: Ing M Kattash
　Signalling and Telecommunications:
　　Dr Ing Anas Fattouh
　Technical: Ing Shaden Wafai
　Central Region Operations: Ing M Yassin Ghreir
　Eastern Region Operations: Ing Saoud Al-Kassem
　Northern Region Operations: Ing M Al-Adna
　Institute of Railways: Ing Khaled Jneid
　Professional Training Centre: S Barakat
　International Relations: H Hamam
　Medical: Dr Ihsan Assy
　Auto-Control: Monzer Alemdar
　Studies: Dr Ing Ammar Kaadan
　Legal: J Masri
　Informatic: Mahmoud Al-Hamid
　Public Relations: Marwan Zarka

Gauge: 1,435 mm
Route length: 2,425 km

### Organisation

All standard-gauge lines in Syria are operated by CFS, and comprise the lines from the Lebanese border via Homs and Aleppo to the Turkish border and, in the northeast, the connecting line between the Turkish and Iraqi borders. A line runs from the oilfields of Kamechli in the north to the port of Latakia (750 km). The Homs–Palmyra line was opened to phosphates traffic (destined for the port of Tartus) in 1980.

The extension of the railway from Homs southwards to Damascus (194 km) was opened in 1983 and the 80 km Tartus-Latakia line in 1992.

For operational purposes CFS is divided into three regions: Central, Eastern and Northern.

At the end of 2001 CFS employed 11,151 staff.

### Passenger operations

In 2001, CFS recorded 1.2 million journeys for 304 million passenger-km compared with 0.9 million (216 million passenger-km) in 2000. Traffic has suffered from competition from faster, cheaper coaches using Syria's developing road network.

Sixteen daily services are operated (20 in summer), and some overnight trains are run, for example between Damascus and Latakia.

### Freight operations

In 2001, traffic amounted to 5.29 million tonnes, for 1,491 million tonne-km.

Freight traffic is strong in bulk freight commodities such as petroleum products, phosphates, cereals and cement. Traffic is exchanged with the Turkish network at Maydan Ikbis. A train ferry link with Greece, possibly from Latakia to Vólos, has been proposed.

### New lines
In 1981, a Soviet loan was secured to build a line from Deir Ezzor to Abou–Kemal on the Iraqi frontier (150 km). This was to link up with Iraq's new Baghdad–Husaiba line. Some 40 km of trackbed was under construction in 2002.

A study has also been undertaken of a new 203 km line from Palmyra to Deir Ezzor, but no work on the project had been undertaken by late 1997.

In 1996, work started on a 1,435 mm gauge line of 101 km from the outskirts of Damascus to Deraa, near the Jordanian frontier, to supersede the Syrian section of the 1,050 mm gauge Hedjaz Railway. The new line, which was to have a branch from Sheikh Miskin to Suweida, would be engineered for 160 km/h operation. However, construction was suspended pending commencement by Jordan of its part of the scheme.

In 1997, planning had been authorised for a project to realign access to the capital from the southern section of the Homs–Damascus line. A new Damascus central station is projected.

### Improvements to existing lines
In September 1997, tenders were invited to upgrade CFS's busiest line, from Tartus to Homs, relaying the most steeply graded sections on new alignments. Earlier proposals to electrify this line have been abandoned.

A two-year track renewal programme on the Aleppo-Maydan Ikbis line was started in September 1997.

### Traction and rolling stock
In 1999, the railway was operating 184 diesel locomotives, 479 passenger cars, 33 baggage vans and 5,226 freight wagons.

In June 1997, CFS signed a FFr350 million contract with GEC Alsthom, now Alstom, to purchase 30 diesel locomotives, with funding from a letter of credit from the French government. The 1,715 kW Type AD33C Co-Co machines are powered by Alstom Ruston 12RK215 engines with IGBT control equipment and asynchronous traction motors. The first example was completed at Alstom's Belfort, France facility in late 1999.

Poor reliability of the Soviet-built Class LDE 2800 locomotives has led CFS to embark on a repowering programme for 32 of the type using General Electric engines and traction equipment, with new cooling and air filter systems.

*Type AD33C diesel-electric locomotive supplied to CFS by Alstom*    2000/0088111

### Diesel locomotives

| Class | Wheel arrangement | Power kW | Speed km/h | Weight tonnes | No built | First built | Mechanical | Builders Engine | Transmission |
|---|---|---|---|---|---|---|---|---|---|
| LDE 650 | Bo-Bo | 485 | 60 | 60 | 9 | 1968 | B&L | SACM | E B&L |
| LDE 1200 | Co-Co | 895 | 100 | 120 | 11 | 1972 | (Soviet-built) | | E |
| LDE 2800 | Co-Co | 2,090 | 100 | 120 | 80 | 1974 | Voroshilovgrad | 5D49 | E Jaricov |
| LDE 2800 | Co-Co | 2,090 | 120 | 120 | 30 | 1984 | Voroshilovgrad | 5D49 | E Jaricov |
| LDE 1800 | Co-Co | 1,342 | 110 | 90 | 15 | 1976 | General Electric | 7 FDL-8 | E General Electric |
| LDE 1800 | Co-Co | 1,342 | 135 | 90 | 15 | 1976 | General Electric | 7 FDL-8 | E General Electric |
| LDE 1500 | Co-Co | 1,120 | 90 | 120 | 25 | 1985 | ČKD | K6S 310 DR | E ČKD |
| AD33C | Co-Co | 1,715 | – | – | 30 | 1999 | Alstom | 12RK215 | E Alstom |

Most passenger coaches were supplied by manufacturers in the former German Democratic Republic, although 77 are of Romanian origin.

CFS placed orders with Wagon Pars of Iran for 559 tank wagons for petroleum products, 360 cereal wagons and 45 cement wagons.

### Signalling and telecommunications
On the Latakia–Aleppo–Kamechli line, signalling and telecommunications are of Soviet origin, dating from 1967. Mechanical interlockings control movements at stations, while a relay semi-automatic block system is used between stations. The Aleppo–Homs, Homs–Tartus and Homs–Mahin–Damascus lines are equipped with full relay interlockings at stations and relay semi-automatic block signalling between stations. This was supplied by German Democratic Republic companies in the 1980s.

### Track
**Rail:** 30, 37, 43 and 50 kg/m
**Crossties (sleepers):** concrete, metal
**Spacing:**
In plain track: 1,600/km
In curves: 1,840/km
**Fastenings:** Russe KB, K2 and RN
**Min curvature radius:** 300 m
**Max gradient:** 2.5%
**Max axleload:** 20 tonnes

*UPDATED*

---

# TAIWAN

## Ministry of Transportation & Communications

2 Chang-Sha Street, Taipei
Tel: (+886 2) 349 29 00   Fax: (+886 2) 381 22 60

**Key personnel**
Minister: Lin Fong-cheng

## Taiwan High Speed Rail Corporation (THSRC)

3rd Floor, 100 Hsin Yi Road Section 5,
Taipei, Taiwan 110
Tel: (+886 2) 87 89 20 00
Web: http://www.thsrc.com.tw

**Key personnel**
Chairman: Nita Ing
President: George Liu

### Political background
In 1991, revised plans were approved for a US$17 billion, 350 km high-speed line from Taipei to Kao-hsiung. A budget was approved in mid-1995 to cover the initial phases of land acquisition, planning and administration, and it was decided later that a minimum of 40 per cent of the projected cost would be sought from the private sector. Land acquisition started in late 1995 and in September 1997 the Taiwan High Speed Rail Consortium (THSRC) was named preferred bidder to construct and equip the line under a 35-year 'build-operate-transfer' (BOT) contract. THSRC comprises five Taiwanese companies: Continental Engineering Corporation; Evergreen Marine Corporation (Taiwan) Ltd; Fubon Insurance Co Ltd; Pacific Electric Wire & Cable Co Ltd; and TECO Electric & Machinery Co Ltd. Completion of the project had been planned for July 2003 but this was subsequently revised to October 2005.

### New lines
Taiwan's 350 km high-speed railway will be a double-track standard-gauge line extending from the capital city Taipei in the north to the second largest city Kaohsiung in the south. The line is being designed for 350 km/h but initially maximum speeds will be limited to 300 km/h.

The line is to extend for most of the length of the island, linking several of the larger cities located along the densely populated west coast, where about 75 per cent of Taiwan's population lives. The existing transportation facilities in this corridor, consisting of highways, the 1,067 mm gauge existing railway and air services, are heavily utilised, and high-speed rail was seen as an obvious way to ensure that growing demand for rapid and convenient travel along the corridor would be met.

*Civil engineering works*
The project is one of the largest railway construction projects under way in the world. The nature of the topography and difficulties associated with land acquisition have resulted in the railway generally being located on viaduct or in tunnel, with only short sections at grade. The guideway consists of the following:
Viaducts and bridges – 255 km

Mined tunnels (36, including 4 long tunnels) – 39 km
Cut and cover tunnels – 11 km
Embankments and cuttings – 32 km.

On the southern section of the line, where the topography is generally flat, there will be a section of viaduct extending continuously for almost 160 km.

For the major civil construction work 11 contracts were signed with international joint ventures between March and May 2000. The twelfth and last civil contract covering a short section at the southern end of the line was let in early 2001. All of these contracts are of the design-and-build type so that initial efforts were focused on investigative and design activities. Construction began in earnest in early 2001, with most attention being given to the longer tunnels which will be critical in terms of the time required for completion.

Taiwan is located in an area of high seismic activity so particular attention is being paid to this factor in the design of the civil structures. Other engineering challenges include poor geotechnical conditions at some tunnel sites and the presence of three active earthquake faults that will need to be traversed.

The most northern section of the line, of approximately 20 km through Taipei, is not included in the 12 civil contracts. Here the high-speed line is to be located in an already constructed tunnel that passes through the city centre and presently accommodates the existing 1,067 mm gauge main line. The intention is for the two railways to share this infrastructure.

*Stations and depots*
The high-speed line will initially have seven stations located at Taipei, Taoyuan, Hsinchu, Taichung, Chiayi, Tainan and Tsoying, on the northern outskirts of Kaohsiung. Provision will be made in the design for five additional stations to be added at appropriate times in the future.

In central Taipei the existing main railway station is to be used. The other six initial stations are being designed under four consultancy contracts and tenders for construction of these were due to be called in mid-2001. Most of these stations will be elevated structures constructed around the guideways being built under the civil contracts.

Five depots and maintenance facilities for various activities are to be constructed along the route of the line with several more planned in the Taipei area. Detailed design of most of these was under way in 2001.

*Trackwork*
Four trackwork contracts are to be let covering the new guideway sections, while a fifth will cover the track to be installed in the existing tunnel through central Taipei. At present both slab and ballasted track are specified for different sections but there is a possibility that this will be changed to all slab track to minimise maintenance requirements. The trackwork contracts are to be of the design and install type.

The high-speed line is to be double-track standard-gauge, using 60 kg/m rail. The two tracks will be 4.5 m apart.

*Core System (Rolling stock and mechanical and electrical equipment)*
After intense competition between European and Japanese consortiums, the Core System contract was awarded in late December 1999 to the Japanese TSC group, which includes Mitsui, Mitsubishi Corporation, Mitsubishi Heavy Industries, Kawasaki and Toshiba. This provides for the supply, installation, commissioning and testing of all rolling stock, traction power supply, signalling and telecommunications equipment.

The line will be electrified at 25 kV 60 Hz AC.

Thirty trainsets are being obtained initially, with options for another 25 sets. They will be derived from the Series 700 Shinkansen train and will each consist initially of 12 cars. The first train is due for delivery to Taiwan in early 2004. Testing and initial training is to take place over a section of the main guideway that has been programmed for early completion at the southern end of the line.

All trains will have ATO and ATP as well as onboard fault diagnosis and monitoring systems.

*Train operations*
To meet the anticipated passenger demand at acceptable levels of service, several different types of service will be operated with minimum intervals of four minutes between trains.

The fastest services between Taipei and Kaohsiung will include a stop at Taichung and will take 90 minutes for the full journey. The slowest trains, that will stop at all the stations to be built, will take approximately 2 hours 15 minutes for the journey from Taipei to Kaohsiung. A number of services that operate only over the Taipei–Taichung section will also be provided.

## Taiwan Railway Administration (TRA)

3 Peiping West Road, Taipei
Tel: (+886 2) 23 81 52 26   Fax: (+886 2) 23 81 13 67
e-mail: railway@railway.gov.tw
Web: http://www.railway.gov.tw

### Key personnel
Managing Director: T P Chen
Deputy Managing Directors: H J Sy; Y N Sheu; C T Lin
Chief Secretary: C N Ma
Chief Engineer: M Z Huang
Directors
  Operations: C L Shu
  Civil Engineering: S C Chen
  Mechanical Engineering: K N Liu
  Electrical Engineering: C C Chang
  Purchase and Stores: Y I Chen
  Planning: C W Wang
  Freight: K I Chao
  Accounting: C D Chung
  Personnel: C S Chi
  Data Processing: L T Lai
  Anti-Corruption Office: J L Lin
  Administration: C N Ma

Gauge: 1,067 mm
Route length: 1,108 km
Electrification: 519 km at 25 kV 60 Hz AC

### Finance
TRA benefits from state funding for its major projects financed by the country's massive accumulation of foreign exchange reserves, which in 1991, standing at over US$82.4 billion, were the biggest of any country in the world. But TRA itself is in deficit, largely because of a burden of excessive staff and pensioners, and of government control of its charges.

| Finances (NT$ million) | | | |
|---|---|---|---|
| **Revenue** | *1996* | *1997* | *1998* |
| Passenger | 13,547 | 14,429 | 15,713 |
| Freight | 1,886 | 1,797 | 1,661 |
| Parcels and mail | 80 | 71 | 63 |
| Other | 4,471 | 4,845 | 4,711 |
| Total | 19,984 | 21,143 | 22,148 |
| **Expenditure** | | | |
| Staff | 17,378 | 18,076 | 18,725 |
| Materials/services | 5,687 | 5,357 | 5,760 |
| Depreciation | 2,791 | 2,910 | 3,066 |
| Financial charges | 3,290 | 5,024 | 4,941 |
| Total | 29,146 | 31,368 | 32,492 |
| **Traffic** (million) | *1996* | *1997* | *1998* |
| Passenger journeys | 159.4 | 165.2 | 172.0 |
| Passenger-km | 8,969 | 9,254 | 9,784 |
| Freight tonnes | 16.5 | 16.9 | 17.1 |
| Freight tonne-km | 1,540 | 1,467 | 1,366 |

### Passenger operations
In the passenger sector TRA pursues principally the development of quality long-distance services with air conditioned rolling stock. These are the most remunerative because, although there is government control of fares, the ceiling imposed on long-distance fares is well above that set for local and commuter travel.

The cross-city tunnel in Taipei, opened in 1990, has eliminated traffic congestion caused by level crossings on Chunghua Road. It has also established a transport centre in the Taipei station area as a foundation for the emerging mass transit system. The project involved a new line starting from west of Sungchiang Road to the east of Wanhua station. It threads a new subterranean Taipei Main station. This multilevel through station, replacing the former terminal, hosts a cross-city emu service between Chi-lung and Hsin-chu.

### Freight operations
In the freight sector, bulk commodities account for 60 per cent of the tonnage, with cement, limestone, grain and coal topping the list. Through its Railway Freight Service (RFS), TRA offers a total service, from door-to-door rail-and-truck transits between a dozen main centres to warehousing, responsibility for customs clearance and insurance. RFS has headquarters in Taipei, branch offices in eight other cities and service offices at 69 locations of the rail network.

### Intermodal operations
TRA has two container terminals of its own at Chi-lung, one at Chi-Tu and the other at Wu-Tu. In addition, the railway serves the United Container Terminal's installation at Pu-Hsui. TRA is also one of the financial backers of the China Container Terminal Corp and its Wu-Tu Inland Terminal in the Chi-lung suburbs. The railway has further port container terminals at Tai-chung and Su-ao, and a Taipei area terminal at Cheng-kung.

The Chi-lung and Kao-hsiung port terminals and the Taipei inland terminal are interconnected by eight dedicated container trains each way daily. TRA has some 600 four-axle flat wagons capable of carrying 40 ft ISO containers.

### New lines
*Chiang Kai-Shek airport line*
In May 1998, the Ministry of Transport & Communications selected Chang Sheng International Development Co to construct a 35 km rail link from Taipei to Chiang Kai-Shek International airport. The ministry expects the four-track line, which will also incorporate 15 stations to serve commuter traffic, to be open in 2003.

*TR Class DR 1000 single-unit railcar built by Nippon Sharyo*     0063615

## Improvements to existing lines

Following completion of double-tracking of the main line down the western side of the island of Taiwan, the government is funding double-tracking of the route on the eastern side, southward from Su-ao to Hua-lien; and also electrification of this line and its adjoining double-track line to the north, so as to have wiring throughout from Pa Tu, in the far north, to Hua-lien. South of Hua-lien, the North Link is to be upgraded with 50 kg/m rail to Tai-tung and the junction with the new South Coast Link. CTC is to be installed on this section. Target date for completion was 1998.

Continuation of the Taipei cross-city tunnel for 5.3 km from the main station eastward to Huashan and Sungshuan is proceeding. Over 2.7 km of the distance the rail alignment is integrated with a government expressway road project. The latter will be elevated above surface highways; and between the surface highway and the rail tunnel underground parking lots will be inserted. Plans have been laid for a western extension from Wanhua under the Tamshui river to an interchange at Panchaio with the metro and the prospective high-speed line.

### Diesel locomotives

| Class | Wheel arrangement | Power kW | Speed km/h | Weight tonnes | No in service | First built | Builders Mechanical | Engine | Transmission |
|---|---|---|---|---|---|---|---|---|---|
| R20/R50 | A1A-A1A | 1,060 | 100 | 78 | 52 | 1960 | EMD | EMD | E EMD |
| R100 | Co-Co | 1,237 | 100 | 78 | 39 | 1970 | EMD | EMD | E EMD |
| R150 | Co-Co | 1,237 | 110 | 89 | 25 | 1970 | EMD | EMD | E EMD |
| R180 | Co-Co | 1,237 | 110 | 89 | 4 | 1992 | EMD | EMD | E EMD |
| R190 | Co-Co | 1,237 | 110 | 89 | 4 | 1992 | EMD | EMD | E EMD |
| S200 | A1A-A1A | 712 | 100 | 65 | 12 | 1960 | EMD | EMD | E EMD |
| S300 | Bo-Bo | 667 | 75 | 54 | 11 | 1966 | EMD | EMD | E EMD |
| S400 | Bo-Bo | 825 | 75 | 54 | 4 | 1970 | EMD | EMD | E EMD |
| R0 | Co-Co | 1,154 | 100 | 85 | 1 | 1960 | Hitachi | MAN | E Hitachi |

### Diesel railcars or multiple-units

| Class | Cars per unit | Motor cars per unit | Motored axles/car | Output/motor kW | Speed km/h | Units in service | First built | Builders Mechanical | Engine | Transmission |
|---|---|---|---|---|---|---|---|---|---|---|
| 2100 | 1 | - | - | - | 105 | 4 | 1931 | TRA | Cummins | H |
| 2200 | 1 | - | - | - | 105 | 2 | 1933 | TRA | Cummins | H |
| 2300 | 1 | - | - | - | 105 | 7 | 1935 | TRA | Cummins | H |
| 2400 | 1 | - | - | - | 105 | 5 | 1935 | TRA | Cummins | H |
| 2500 | 1 | - | - | - | 110 | 2 | 1966 | Tokyu Car | Cummins | H |
| 2700 | 1 | - | - | - | 110 | 25 | 1966 | Tokyu Car | Cummins | H |
| 2800 | 3 | - | - | - | 110 | 15 | 1982 | Tokyu Car | Cummins | H |
| 2900 | 3 | - | - | - | 110 | 5 | 1987 | Hitachi | Cummins | H |
| 3000 | 3 | - | - | - | 110 | 27 | 1990 | Hitachi | Cummins | H |
| 3100 | 3 | - | - | - | 110 | 8 | 1998 | Nippon Sharyo | Cummins | H Nico |
| 1000 | 1 | - | - | - | 110 | 8 | 1998 | Nippon Sharyo | Cummins | H Nico |

### Electric railcars

| Class | Cars per unit | Motor cars per unit | Motored axles/car | Output/motor kW | Speed km/h | Units in service | First built | Builders Mechanical | Electrical |
|---|---|---|---|---|---|---|---|---|---|
| 100 | 5 | 1 | 4 | 310 | 120 | 11 | 1979 | BREL | GEC |
| 200 | 3 | 2 | 4 | 116 | 120 | 10 | 1988 | Socimi | Brush |
| 300 | 2 | 3 | 4 | 125 | 120 | 8 | 1986 | UCW | GEC |
| 400 | 2 | 4 | 4 | 125 | 110 | 12 | 1991 | UCW | GEC |
| 500 | 2 | 3 | 4 | 250 | 110 | 86 | 1995 | Daewoo | Siemens |

## Traction and rolling stock

At the start of 1999 the fleet comprised 180 electric and 152 diesel locomotives, 165 dmus, five diesel railcars, 508 emus power cars, 1,742 passenger coaches and 2,956 freight wagons.

In the mid-1990s, delivery was taken of 344 electric multiple-unit cars for Taipei suburban services being built by Daewoo Heavy Industries in South Korea. The cars have Siemens electrical equipment, comprising VVVF propulsion and control systems, and bogies by Adtranz.

Recent acquisitions include first examples of an order for 36 Class DR 1000 single-unit diesel railcars from Nippon Sharyo for suburban and branch line services and 10 Class DR 3100 three-car dmus from the same builder. Two of the DRC units and one dmu were manufactured in Japan, while the remaining vehicles were assembled in Taiwan from knocked-down components.

## Signalling

Computer-aided CTC has been installed between Chang-hua, Tai-nan and Ping-tung, and covers a total of 510 route-km. ABS is in service over 311 km.

## Electrification

Under way is wiring of the East Trunk line from Pa Tu, near Chi-lung in the north, as far as Hua-lien, a distance of 171 km. Altogether, wiring of 519 km was in progress at the end of 1996.

## Type of coupler

Passenger cars: Tight lock automatic AAR-H
Freight cars: AAR E Type automatic
**Type of braking:** AAR Westinghouse air

## Track

**Rail:** 37 and 50 kg/m; 100 lb/yd
**Crossties (sleepers):** In tangent track and curves over 600 m radius: 174 × 240 × 2,000 mm
In curves of 300 to 600 m radius: 201 × 240 × 2,000 mm
**Spacing**
In plain track: 1,760/km (wood), 1,640/km (concrete)
In curves: 1,800/km for radii less than 400 m
**Rail fastenings:** Pandrol clip
**Min curvature radius:** 5.82°
**Max gradient:** 2.5%
**Max axleload:** 18 tonnes

---

# TAJIKISTAN

## Ministry of Transport

Nazarshojev 35, 734012 Dushanbe
Fax: (+737 72) 21 44 48

### Key personnel
Minister: F Mukhiddinov
Deputy Minister: Abdurahmon Rasulov

*UPDATED*

## Tajik Railways

Tajikskaya Zheleznaya Doroga (TZD)
Nazarshojev 35, 734012 Dushanbe
Fax: (+737 72) 21 44 48

### Key personnel
President: M Nuralyev
Chief Engineer: B Shodiyev
Traffic Manager: A Bulugin
Finance Director: M F Narzyev

Gauge: 1,520 mm
Route length: 482 km

## Political background

The railway was founded as an independent organisation in October 1994.

Traffic has declined precipitously since independence. The disturbed political situation has resulted in a mass exodus of Russians, and 90 per cent of railway specialist staff have been lost as a result. Further decline will occur if Uzbekistan completes its proposed Angren bypass of the Tajik Railways' northern section. This section was closed by military activities for a week in November 1998.

In 1996, an agreement was made with the Uzbekistan railway covering standardisation, cross-border workings of personnel, and access of Tajik students to Uzbek railway training institutions. Unfortunately this has not led to any noticeable improvement in cross-border operations.

In 1997, the accounts of all 38 enterprises making up the railway were frozen because of overdue tax. They were later unfrozen, and the railway also made inroads into its wages backlog. The average railwayman's wage is five times higher than the national average, which is exceptional for a former Soviet state.

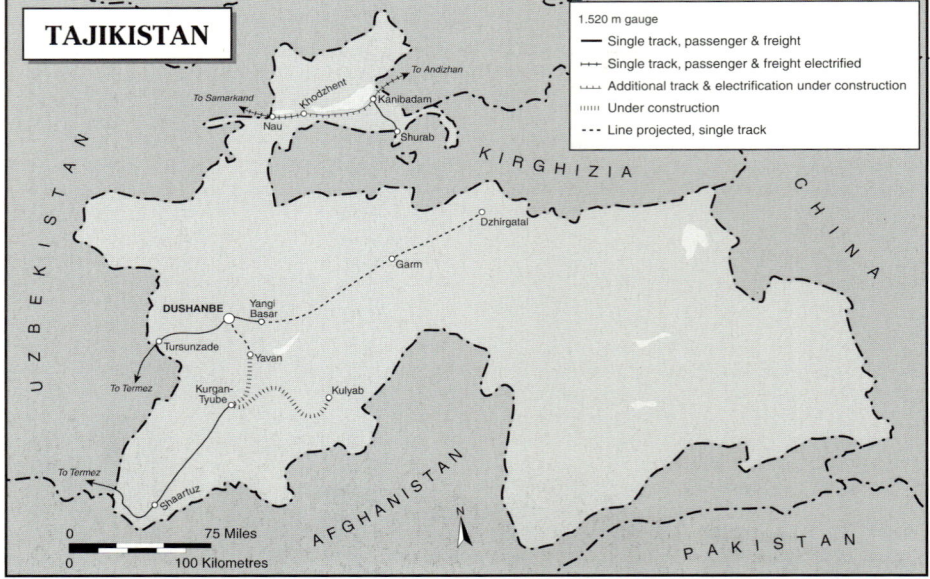

In December 1998, the Asian Development Bank announced a US$21.5 million loan and technical assistance package to assist in the reform of Tajikistan's transport and energy sectors. Among the programme's aims were the separation of regulatory and operational functions of the railway network and providing state enterprises increased autonomy and incentives to run on commercial lines.

In July 2001, the government announced increased funding for the network to pay for a programme of improvements and to meet debts owed to the Uzbekistan Railway.

### Organisation
Formerly part of the USSR's Central Asian Railway, Tajik Railways consists of three lines, each isolated from the others by neighbouring states. In the south there are two branch lines from Termez in Uzbekistan, one to the Tajik capital Dushanbe and Yangi Basar (93 km) and one to Kurgan-Tyube and Vakhsh (220 km). In the north, some 110 km of the east-west Andizhan–Samarkand line runs through Tajikistan. This portion is electrified eastwards as far as Khodzhent (formerly Leninabad), but electrification work on the 59 km section towards Kanibadam has been suspended. A branch from Kanibadam stretches 53 km to Shurab.

The number of operating workers in 1999 was 4,235.

| Traffic (million) | 1997 | 1999 |
|---|---|---|
| Passenger journeys | 0.64 | 0.65 |
| Passenger-km | 150.2 | 61.2 |
| Freight tonnes | 0.62 | 0.90 |
| Freight tonne-km | - | 1,300 |

### Passenger operations
In December 1995, Russian Railways refused to handle the Dushanbe–Moscow through service, citing poor quality rolling stock and mass ticketless travel. The through train was reintroduced on a thrice-weekly basis from October 1996, taking 87 hours for the journey.

A weekly Dushanbe–Volgograd train, reputed to carry mainly ticketless travellers in unhygienic conditions, was established during 1997.

### New lines
In August 2001, the government authorised planning for a new line from Dushanbe to Dzhirgatal via Garm, with the eventual intention of extending it to the border with Kyrgyzia. Also planned is a line from Dushanbe to Yavan.

In 2001, work was well advanced on the lines from Kurgan-Tyube to Yaran and to Kulyab.

### Improvements to existing lines
Despite a shortage of track components, remedied partly by the lifting of redundant sidings, electrification and double-tracking of the northern line is taking place over busy sections. The first 53 km of this 128 km line were opened in 1998 and the remainder in September 1999. Upgrading continued into 2000, and the bi-weekly passenger train now covers the 128 km in five hours.

### Traction and rolling stock
Having initially only 29 locomotives, stationed at the country's only depot at Dushanbe, and finding itself with no track maintenance equipment upon independence, the railway has depended, to some extent, on equipment loaned by Uzbekistan's railway.

In 1997, the locomotive fleet comprised two double-unit locomotives of Type 2TE10, purchased in 1996; 24 double-unit locomotives of Type 2TE10V/L, of which 16 were serviceable; 10 shunting locomotives of Type TEM2 (all serviceable) and five shunting locomotives of Type ChME3 (of which only one was serviceable). The rolling stock fleet comprised 355 passenger coaches and 2,112 freight wagons.

*UPDATED*

---

# TANZANIA

## Ministry of Communications & Transport

PO Box 9423, Dar es Salaam
Tel: (+255 51) 376 41   Fax: (+255 51) 364 62

### Key personnel
Minister: William Kusila

## Tanzanian Railways Corporation (TRC)

PO Box 468, Dar es Salaam
Tel: (+255 51) 11 05 99   Fax: (+255 51) 11 06 00
e-mail: trc-plan@ud.co.tz

### Key personnel
Director General: L Mboma
Chief Commercial Manager: Rukia D Shamte
Chief Mechanical Engineer: M Kabipe
Chief Civil Engineer: J Mabeyo (acting)
Chief of Manpower Development: N N Msoffe
Chief Supplies Manager: L R S Baseka
Chief of Finance: S A Riwa
Chief of Corporate Development and Management Services: J J Mungereza
Chief Signals and Communications Engineer: R J Kisanga

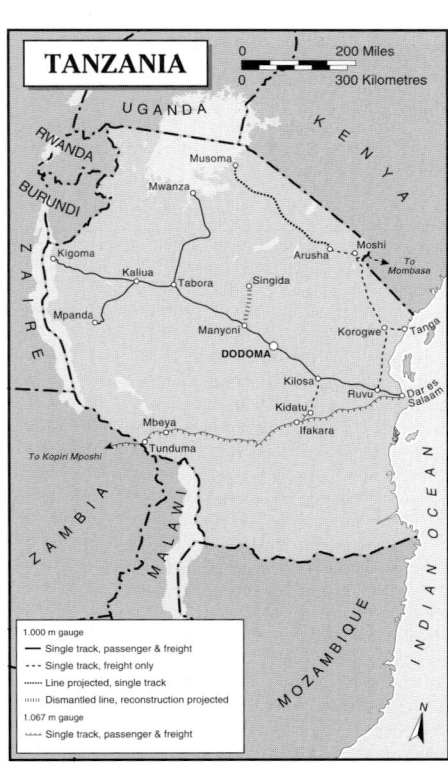

Gauge: 1,000 mm
Length: 2,721 km

### Political background
Following the formal break-up of the East African Railways Corporation in 1977, Tanzania set up the independent Tanzanian Railways Corporation to operate the former EAR lines wholly within Tanzania.

By the end of the 1980s, TRC was rundown and in urgent need of investment capital. In a series of World Bank-inspired reforms, the railway's extensive lake-shipping operation was hived off into a separate profit centre, staff numbers have been reduced (down to 9,500 by the end of 1998) and tariffs increased. Some rehabilitation of the system has been possible with funds made available from Canadian, European and Chinese sources. In 1999, it was reported that the Tanzanian government intended to privatise TRC by concessioning.

| Traffic (million) | 1997 | 1998 |
|---|---|---|
| Passenger journeys | 0.557 | 0.570 |
| Passenger-km | 362.2 | 262.8 |
| Freight tonnes | 1.073 | 0.955 |
| Freight tonne-km | 1,108 | 708 |

### Passenger operations
Passenger traffic levels continue to run at less than half the level achieved in the mid-1990s. Bus competition accounts for some of the decline in traffic, and has led to a discontinuation of shuttle services on the Dar es Salaam–Moshi and Dar es Salaam–Tanga lines.

Delivery of new Indian-built coaches in 1998-99 (see 'Traction and rolling stock') has eased a severe shortage of seating capacity.

### Diesel locomotives

| Class | Wheel arrangement | Power kW | Speed km/h | Weight tonnes | First built | Mechanical | Builders Engine | Transmission |
|---|---|---|---|---|---|---|---|---|
| 35 | C | 205 | 25 | 36.6 | 1973 | Barclay | Paxman 8RPHL Mk 7 | H Voith L320V |
| 36 | C | 244 | 25 | 36.2 | 1979 | Brush | Ruston-Paxman | E Brush |
| 37 | C | 295 | 25 | 36.2 | 1985 | Henschel | MTU Type 6Y 396 | H Voith TC12 |
| 64 | B-B | 559 | 72 | 38.3 | 1979 | Henschel | MTU Type EB | H Voith L520-UZ 12V 396 TCII |
| 72 | 1Bo-Bo1 | 925 | 72 | 68.86 | 1972 | GEC Traction | Ruston-Paxman 8CVST | E GEC |
| 73 | Co-Co | 1,003 | 96 | 72 | 1975 | Varanasi | YDMA4 | E Varanasi |
| 87 | 1Co-Co1 | 1,370 | 72 | 101.4 | 1966 | Eng Elec | Ruston-Paxman 12CVST | E Eng Elec |
| 88 | 1Co-Co1 | 1,490 | 72 | 110.9 | 1972 | MLW | Alco 251C | E GE Canada |

### Freight operations
Freight traffic has continued its gradual decline since 1996, when 1.2 million tonnes were lifted, generating 1,236 million tonne-km. In 1998, less than 1 million tonnes were lifted, for 708 million tonne-km.

Since 1993, TRC has provided dedicated trains for Burundi traffic between Dar es Salaam and its western terminus at Kigoma, where goods are transhipped to road vehicles for the cross-border journey to Burundi. New freight-handling depots at Dar es Salaam and Kigoma provide rapid customs clearance facilities, and a special fleet of 80 wagons for the service has been donated by European Union sources (see below).

The Burundi service is seen as the prototype for similar operations serving other neighbouring countries, as TRC strives to regain the transit traffic lost at the start of the 1990s. A through service to and from Kenya via the Moshi–Taveta–Voi link was restored in 1996 after a 20-year interruption.

### New lines
In 1991, Uganda and Tanzania reached agreement in principle for extension into Uganda of TRC's line from the port of Tanga to Arusha. The proposal is to project this line to Musoma on Lake Victoria and install a train ferry to connect Musoma with Uganda's capital, Kampala. A feasibility study, funded partly by Uganda, was carried out during 1994, but no further progress has been reported.

### Traction and rolling stock
In 1998, TRC owned 73 main line diesel locomotives, 129 passenger coaches and 1,802 freight wagons.

Adtranz has carried out heavy overhaul on 11 Class 36 diesel shunters, and refurbished 79 passenger coaches at TRC's Dar es Salaam works. A batch of 27 third-class coaches was supplied by India's ICF in 1998-99. During the same period 80 covered bogie wagons were added to the freight fleet.

**Type of coupler in standard use:** MCA-DA
**Type of brake in standard use:** Automatic air, Type EST4d

**Track**
**Rail:** 55, 60 and 80 lb/yd
**Crossties (sleepers):** Steel plain track, wood turn-outs
**Fastenings:** Fish bolts and nuts, fishplates, screw spikes, coach screws, Pandrol

**Spacing:**
55 lb/yd: 1,430/km plain, 1,540/km curved track
60 lb/yd: 1,405/km plain, 1,485/km curved track
80 lb/yd: 1,402/km plain, 1,482/km curved track
**Min curve radius:** 8°

**Max gradient:** 2.5%
**Max axleload:** 14 tonnes

## Tanzania-Zambia Railway Authority (TAZARA)

PO Box 2834, Dar es Salaam
Tel: (+255 51) 86 03 40; 76 41 91; 9
Fax: (+255 51) 86 51 87; 86 51 92

**Key personnel**
Chairman: S Musoma
Co-Chairman: Ronald Makuma
Directors
  Finance: Method A Kashonda
  Corporate Planning: Michael J Ngonyani
  Traffic: J Y Minsula
  Technical Services: L M Nsofwa
Regional Manager, Zambia: Morrison S Banda
Regional Manager, Tanzania: Hamis M Teggisa

Gauge: 1,067 mm
Route length: 1,860 km (891 km in Zambia, 969 km in Tanzania)

### Diesel locomotives

| Class | Wheel arrangement | Power kW | Speed km/h | Weight tonnes | No in service | First built | Mechanical | Builders Engine | Transmission |
|---|---|---|---|---|---|---|---|---|---|
| 1A (DFH1) | Bo-Bo | 1,000 | 50 | 60 | 14 | 1971 | Chintao | 12V 189ZL* | SF 2010 |
| 1B (DFH-2) | Bo-Bo | 2,000 | 100 | 80 | 57 | 1971 | Chintao | 12V 180ZL (28 locos)*/ MTU 12V 396TC12 (29 locos) | SE 2010 / SE2010 |
| DE (U30C) | Co-Co | 3,200 | 100 | 120 | 29 | 1983 | Krupp | GE 17 FDL 12HT | E GE |
| CKD8B | - | 2,200 | - | - | 6 | 1997 | Loric | - | - |

* Class is being re-engined with MTU units

### Political background

The Tanzania-Zambia Railway (TAZARA) was constructed following an agreement signed in 1967 between the governments of Tanzania, Zambia and the People's Republic of China. Under the agreement, China provided finance and technical services for construction of a railway from Dar es Salaam in Tanzania to Kapiri Mposhi in Zambia, together with equipment, two workshops and other auxiliary facilities. Operation began in 1975.

The loan repayment was to commence in 1983 and to be spread over 30 years, with each country responsible for 50 per cent. Due to their economic problems, however, both countries agreed in 1983 to reschedule the repayment terms; the start of repayment of the main loan was put back 10 years. In 1997, a further loan agreement was signed, with China extending the 30-year contract to provide additional development funding of Y100 million. This was intended to cover staff training and the provision of microwave communications technology on the section of the railway in Zambia.

The Council of Ministers, consisting of three Ministers each from Zambia and Tanzania, is the body established by the two governments to exercise overall control on the railway. All the railway assets are vested in TAZARA, a corporate body whose principal organ is the Board of Directors; this consists of 10 members, five appointed by each government. For operational purposes, the railway is divided into two regions for Tanzania and Zambia, with headquarters at Dar es Salaam and Mpika.

TAZARA's gauge permits through traffic with contiguous railways in Central Africa, in particular Zambia Railways. Its performance, however, has been handicapped by serious problems of traction, rolling stock and track maintenance, of inadequate funds, and the international political strains of the continent. Whereas the railway's designed capacity was 5 million tonnes of freight a year, it has yet to register more than 1.5 million tonnes.

In the 1980s, TAZARA benefited from export/import traffic from Botswana, Malawi, Zaire, Zambia and Zimbabwe seeking to use Dar es Salaam instead of South African ports, but in the 1990s political change in South Africa enabled the landlocked states to resume use of ports in that country. By 1997, TAZARA was in deep trouble, with carryings down to 600,000 tonnes per year. An estimated US$7 million was owed by customers and there were few prospects of being able to collect the money.

In an effort to reverse the decline, the railway adopted a commercialisation policy with an aggressive approach to marketing. Armed police ride with freight trains to deter pilferers. Transit times have been cut, with the fastest freight trains taking four days (as opposed to 10 in the past) to traverse the line. Gantry cranes were being installed at four freight terminals. By 1999, the workforce had been reduced to 5,000 and it was planned to cut this to 3,000 by 2003.

In 1999, it looked increasingly likely that some degree of privatisation would be introduced to TAZARA.

### Passenger operations

A long-established passenger service runs the length of the TAZARA line, from Dar es Salaam to Kapiri Mposhi, twice a week. In 1997, a twice-weekly express service, named 'Mukaba' eastbound and 'Kilimanjaro' westbound, was introduced.

There are also three-a-week services running on the Tanzanian and Zambian sections respectively.

Around 1.6 million passenger journeys were recorded in 1998-1999.

### Freight operations

Zambian exports, principally copper, have been the mainstay of TAZARA freight tonnage, but much of this is now routed through South Africa. Some traffic diversification has been achieved.

### Improvements to existing lines

In a project funded by the Austrian government, long-welding of rail is being installed between Dar es Salaam and Makambako (657 km); this project was more than two-thirds complete in 1999. Completion throughout the route will remove a source of frequent delays due to misaligned or broken rail joints.

### Traction and rolling stock

At the start of 1993 TAZARA operated 100 diesel locomotives (many of GE design), 97 passenger coaches (including nine restaurant cars) and 2,230 freight wagons.

In 1997, six CKD8B 2,200 kW diesel locomotives were delivered from Chinese manufacturers, funded by a Chinese government loan of Y200 million. The same loan was to allow the purchase of 80 tank wagons for petroleum products, a breakdown crane, and spares for locomotives and rolling stock.

### Signalling and telecommunications

A digital microwave radio system was to be installed over the entire TAZARA system by 2000-01 at a cost of US$500,000.

**Type of coupler in standard use:** Top action
**Type of braking in standard use:**
Passenger: Air
Freight cars: Air, vacuum

**Track**
**Rail:** 45 kg/m, 12.5 m length
**Crossties (sleepers):** Prestressed concrete 195 × 208 × 272 mm
**Spacing:** 1,520/km
**Fastening:** Electric (spring clip and bolt)
**Min curvature:** 200 m
**Max gradient:** 1 in 50
**Max altitude:** 1,789.43 m, Uyole near Mbeya
**Max axleload:** 20 tonne

---

# THAILAND

## Ministry of Transport & Communications

5 Rajdammern Avenue, Bangkok 10100
Tel: (+66 2) 281 34 22   Fax: (+66 2) 280 17 14

**Key personnel**
Minister: Wan Muhammad Nor Matha
Permanent Secretary: Srisuk Chandrangsu

*UPDATED*

## State Railway of Thailand (SRT)

Rong Muang Road, Pathumwan, Bangkok 10330
Tel: (+66 2) 220 42 60; 22 04 26 67
Fax: (+66 2) 225 38 01

**Key personnel**
Governor: (vacant)
Deputy Governors
  Operations 1: Niyom Diovilai
  Operations 2: Dr Chitsanti Dhanasobhon
  Administration: Bancha Kongnakorn
  Development and Planning: Sriyoudh Sirivedhin
  Special Affairs: Thira Ratanavit
Assistant Governors: Nakorn Chantasorn;
  Pijarn Rattanaratree; Youdtana Tupcharoen
Inspector General: Clong Clongpayaban;
  Thavat Katesorn
Personnel Manager: Wacharin Teevakul
Director, Finance and Accounting Department:
  Narapan Chimroylap
Traffic Manager: Somnug Ruecha
Marketing Manager: Viroj Treamphongpun
Chief Mechanical Engineer: Narong Pisitbannakorn
Chief Civil Engineer: Chalermchai Cholpaisal
Chief Signalling and Telecommunications Engineer:
  Suchai Roywirutn
Chief Construction Engineer: Narong Changlum
Directors
  Information Systems: Yolchai Kemungkorn
  Stores: Charoeng Chomsurintr
  Property Management and Development:
    Anuwong Sooksiwong
  Internal Auditing: Wayupol Chaisiri
  Special Programme Development:
    Charnchai Anantasate
  Chief, Legal Bureau: Ithipon Paphavasit
  Chief, Medical Bureau: Dr Montree Changtor
  Chief, Training and Development Bureau:
    Anop Prachasaisoradej
  Chief, Governor Bureau: Charupha Pongtrachoo

Gauge: 1,000 mm
Route length: 4,071 km

### Political background

The restructuring and privatisation of SRT has been government policy since November 1998. According to a

*Hitachi-built Class HID diesel-electric locomotive arrives at Bangkok with a passenger service (David Haydock)*
2002/0137110

*Class ASR British-built dmu at Bangkok (David Haydock)*
2002/0137109

*Double-tracking in progress between Hua Mak and Chachoengsao, on the Eastern line, with a container service passing on the existing single line*
2002/0122753

cabinet resolution, the railway will initially be separated into three business units: infrastructure; operations; and the non-rail businesses. In order quickly to ease SRT's serious cashflow problems, the government is to bear the cost of the infrastructure account through an allocation of its annual budget for the maintenance of track, signalling and telecommunications systems and other needs, such as track renewals. In addition, the government will temporarily allocate a budget covering the repayment of SRT's historic debt.

In 1999, the government employed consultants to review its proposals, with a view to implementing them by October 1999, in time for the 2000 budget. In the longer term, consultants were to be employed to create a strategic plan for restructuring and privatisation, which would then be considered by the government before implementation.

In 2000, the government decided to split SRT into four entities: the rail network, remaining as SRT; a train operating company; a rolling stock preparation and maintenance company; and an asset management company. This separation was to be undertaken using the Corporatization Act 2542 BE (1999). In February 2001, a new government took office and initiated workshops in July and September of that year to consider the future of SRT. This resulted in agreement that a separation of SRT into several companies or entities would result in a lack of overall vision for the system. The workshops further concluded that the objectives of each company or entity would be in conflict and that for SRYT to become an efficient and sustainable organisation, its restructuring would need to be undertaken step-by-step, beginning with internal reorganisation according to business needs. It was expected that in 2002, SRT would apply to government to revoke the cabinet resolution of 2000 to split up the organisation in favour of establishing an integrated, commercially-based railway company.

| Traffic (million) | 1998 | 1999 | 2000 |
|---|---|---|---|
| Passenger journeys | 60.8 | 55.2 | 55.5 |
| Passenger-km | 10,947 | 9,894 | 10,040 |
| Freight tonnes | 8.6 | 9.2 | 9.8 |
| Freight tonne-km | 2,874 | 2,981 | 3,384 |

### Passenger operations
In FY2000, SRT carried 55.5 million passengers and achieved 10,040 million passenger-km, increases compared with the previous year of 0.48 and 1.48 per cent respectively. This limited increase in passenger numbers was attributed by SRT to the adverse impact of various improvement projects. These included termination of the Hopewell Project in Bangkok and double-tracking schemes, which caused delays to services. In addition, track rehabilitation on lines in both the north and the south of the country aggravated delays.

### Freight operations
In FY2000, SRT transported 9.8 million tonnes of freight for 3,384 million tonne-km, increases of 5.88 and 13.52 per cent respectively. Much of this extra traffic was generated by container movements on the eastern line, from Lat Krabang Inland Container Depot to Laem Chabang deep-sea port, as well as by special services from Sungai-Way, Malaysia, to Bang Sue and Lat Krabang.

### New lines
Opened in late 1996, the Khlong Sip Kao–Kaeng Khoi line, an 82 km link between existing Eastern and Northeastern lines, completed SRT's long-term plan to remove most freight traffic from the congested route through the centre of Bangkok. The new line provides direct access to the Sattahip port branch from the north.

To extend the network to provide a connection with a proposed new railway in Laos, SRT started construction of a new station south of the city of Nong Khai in 1994 and later completed a 1.8 km rail connection to the centre of the Friendship Bridge, which forms a frontier link between the two countries. Work on a line from there to the Laotian capital, Vientiane, for which a Thai consortium had obtained a concession, was delayed by economic conditions prevailing in southeast Asia in the late 1990s. Work was revived in 2000 and SRT engaged a consultant to undertake detailed design of a 3.5 km line from the Friendship Bridge to Ban Ta Na Laeng, Laos. Completed in 2001, the design proposal was submitted to the Laotian government by its Thai counterpart. It estimated the construction cost to be US$6.827 million. However, despite the expected economic benefits of the projects, work on the Laotian side was reported in 2002 to have been suspended, again for funding reasons.

SRT plans four new lines: Den Chai–Chiang Rai (245 km), in the north of the country; Surat Thani–Phangnga (163 km) in the south; Mab Ta Phut–Rayong (24 km) in the east; and Bua Yai–Nakhon Phanom (368 km) in the northeast. The design of the first three of these had been completed by 2002, while the last still awaited detailed design. The Royal Decree of Land Acquisition Marking for the Den Chai–Chiang Rai and Surat Thani–Phang Nga lines was implemented in 2001 but no budget had been allocated to build these lines in view of domestic economic conditions. Land acquisition was expected to take two years, with construction of the two lines taking five and four years respectively.

In preparation for the commissioning in 2005 of the Second Bangkok International Airport (SBIA), also known as the 'Suwannabhumi' airport, SRT was assigned to construct a rail link to it from its eastern line at Lat Krabang, 30 km from Bangkok. A feasibility study was completed in February 2002 and design work was to be carried out in 2003. Construction was expected to be undertaken in 2004-05.

## Improvements to existing lines

With line capacity reaching its limits on various parts of the SRT network, additional tracks are required to handle an increasing number of trains. Apart from provision of a third track between Rangsit and Ban Phachi (61 km), completed in 1999, double-tracking on four routes was in progress in 2002: Bang Sue–Nakhon Pathom on the Southern line (56 km); Ban Phachi–Lop Buri on the Northern line (43 km); Ban Phachi–Map Kabao on the Northeastern line (44 km); and Hua Mak–Chachoengsao on the Eastern line (2 × 45 km). The first three of these was scheduled for completion in July 2002, while the last were due to be commissioned in April 2003, apart from signalling and telecommunications work.

In addition, double-tracking of the eastern seaboard line (the Sattahip line), 177 km from Si Racha to the Kaeng Khoi junction of the Nong Khai line via Chachoengsao Junction, is also planned to support the Thai government's Eastern Seaboard Area Development Programme. Design of the project has been completed and the construction cost has been estimated at Bt11,889 million. According to traffic demand and studies relating to train operations, the Si Racha–Chachoengsao section (69 km), estimated to cost Bt5,822 million, should be constructed first in response to forecasts of increasing passenger traffic and freight growth. In 2002, the project was under review by the agencies concerned prior to submission to the government.

Track rehabilitation projects are also being carried out. These cover: Lop Buri–Chumsaeng (141 km) and Hua Hin–Ban Krut (148 km), completed in October 2000; Chumsaeng–Phitsanulok (108 km) and Chai Ya–Thung Song (150 km), to be completed in July 2002; and Ban Krut–Chai Ya (244 km), to be completed in July 2002. Because of safety issues and the need for increased line capacity, track rehabilitation schemes are given very high priority by SRT and are being continuously implemented. Feasibility studies identifying a further 813 km of track to be treated as a priority have been completed and in 2002 awaited implementation approval.

For its commuter services, SRT has engaged a consultant to produce a master plan and feasibility study into improvement on its network, investigating and confirming the need for investment to improve operations in this sector. It was expected to be completed by August 2002.

## Traction and rolling stock

In 2001, SRT was operating five steam, 241 diesel-electric and 40 diesel-hydraulic locomotives, 51 shunters, 285 diesel railcars, 1,238 passenger cars (including 103 sleeping, 49 restaurant, and 92 baggage cars) and 7,901 freight wagons.

### Type of coupler in standard use:

Passenger cars: Type E, AAR-10A automatic, controlled-slack type
Freight wagons: Type E, AAR-10E automatic, controlled-slack type
Diesel railcars: Type E, AAR-10A, automatic tight-lock type

### Type of braking in standard use:

Locomotive-hauled stock: vacuum, air and dual-system

*SRT has a continuing programme of track rehabilitation*

### Sleepers

| Type | Untreated hardwood | Creosote-treated softwood | 2-block concrete (RS-type) | Monobloc pre-stressed concrete |
|---|---|---|---|---|
| Dimensions | 150 × 200 × 1,900-2,000 mm | 150 × 200 × 1,900 mm | 1,710 mm long, block 209 × 274 × 600 mm | 200 × 260 × 2,000 mm |
| Spacing | 1,430-1,666/km | 1,430-1,666/km | 1,666/km | 1,666/km |
| Fastenings | Dogspike, Dorken spike or Woodings clip | Dogspike, Dorken spike or Woodings clip | RN clip | Hambo, Fist, Pandrol, Vossloh, Stedef |

### Diesel locomotives

| Class | Wheel arrangement | Power kW | Speed km/h | Weight tonnes | No in service | First built | Mechanical | Engine | Transmission |
|---|---|---|---|---|---|---|---|---|---|
| Davenport | Bo-Bo | 375 | 82 | 48.12 | 16 | 1952 | Davenport | Caterpillar D397 | E Westinghouse |
| Davenport | Co-Co | 745 | 92 | 80 | 5 | 1955 | Davenport | Caterpillar D397 | E Westinghouse |
| HID | Co-Co | 2,135 | 100 | 90 | 22 | 1993 | Hitachi | Cummins KT7A 50-L | E Hitachi |
| GE | Co-Co | 985 | 103 | 75 | 49 | 1964 | GE | Cummins KT 38-L, KT 2300-L | E GE |
| Alsthom | Co-Co | 1,790 | 95 | 82.5 | 49 | 1975 | Alsthom | SEMT 16PA 4V.183 | E Alsthom |
| AHK | Co-Co | 1,790 | 100 | 82.5 | 30 | 1980 | Henschel/Alsthom/Krupp | SEMT 16PA4 185VG | E Alsthom |
| ALD | Co-Co | 1,790 | 100 | 82.5 | 9 | 1983 | Alsthom | SEMT 16PA4 185VG | E Alsthom |
| ADD | Co-Co | 1,790 | 100 | 82.5 | 20 | 1985 | Alsthom | SEMT 16PA4 185VG | E Alsthom |
| Hunslet | C | 180 | 19.5 | 30 | 3 | 1965 | Hunslet | Gardner 8L 3B | H Voith |
| Krupp | B-B | 1,120 | 90 | 55 | 20 | 1969 | Krupp | MTU 12V6 52 TB 11 | H Voith |
| HAS | C | 535 | 58 | 41.25 | 10 | 1986 | Henschel | MTU 6V3 96 TC12 | H Voith |
| GEA | Co-Co | 1,865 | 100 | 86.5 | 38 | 1995 | GE | Cummins KTA 50-L | E GE |

### Diesel railcars or multiple-units

| Class* | Cars per unit | Motor cars per unit | Motored axles/car | Power/motor kW | Speed km/h | No in service | First built | Mechanical | Builders Engine | Transmission |
|---|---|---|---|---|---|---|---|---|---|---|
| BPD/BTD | 2 | 1 | 2 | 175 × 2 | 85 | 14 | 1967 | Hitachi | Cummins N855-R2 | H Voith |
| BPD/BIN | 3 | 2 | 1 | 165 | 70 | 12 | 1971 | Tokyu | Cummins NHH-220-B-1 | H Nico |
| BPD | 2 | 2 | 1 | 175 | 100 | 40 | 1983 | Tokyu Hitachi Nippon | Cummins N855-R2 | H Nico |
| ASR | 2 | 2 | 1 | 210 | 120 | 18 | 1991 | BREL, UK | Cummins NTA 855 RL | H Voith |
| APD | 2 | 2 | 1 | 175 | 100 | 63 | 1985 | Nippon/Kinki/Kawasaki/Hitachi/Fuji/Niigata | Cummins N855-R2 | H Nico |
| APN | Intermediate motor car | | 1 | 175 | 100 | 10 | 1985 | Tokyu | Cummins N855-R2 | H Nico |
| APD | 2 | 2 | 1 | 261 | 120 | 12 | 1995 | Daewoo | Cummins NTA 855-R1 | H Voith |
| APN | Intermediate motor car | | 1 | 261 | 120 | 8 | 1995 | Daewoo | Cummins N855-R1 | H Voith |
| APD | 2 | 2 | 1 | 261 | 120 | 20 | 1995 | Daewoo | Cummins NTA 855-R1 | H Voith |
| APD | 2 | 2 | 1 | 134 × 2 | 95 | 23 | 1998 | (JRWest) | DMH 17H | H Nico |
| APN | Intermediate motor car | | 1 | 134 | 95 | 3 | 1998 | (JR West) | DMH 17H | H Nico |

* BPD = Bogie Power car for Diesel railcar with driving cab
BIN = Bogie trailer diesel railcar non-driving cab
APD = Air conditioned power diesel railcar with driving cab
BTD = Bogie Trailer for Diesel railcar with driving cab
ASR = Air conditioned Sprinter Railcar
APN = Air conditioned power diesel railcar non-driving cab

### Signalling and telecommunications

SRT's standard signalling systems are colour light signals, DC track circuit blocks and electric point machines. However, in addition to double-tracking of single-track sections, SRT has also introduced new signalling system, replacing all-relay interlockings with Computer-Based Interlockings (CBIs). The new signalling system must also support immunisation against possible future electrification and provision of Automatic Train Protection (ATP). Sections to be equipped with CBI-based systems are:

- Scheme ST1 (Northern line, third track Rangsit–Ban Phachi Junction, 61 km, 11 stations; and Southern line, double-track Bang Sue Junction–Taling Chan Junction, 14.66 km, three stations) - contract signed with Jasmine/LG Consortium on 7 September 2001. Work commenced 24 October 2001, with completion scheduled by 23 December 2003.
- Scheme ST2 (ST2/N Northern line, double track, Ban Phachi Junction Lop–Buri, 43 km, seven stations; ST2/NE Northeastern line, double track, Ban Phachi Junction–Kaeng Khoi–Map Kabao, 44 km, eight stations; ST2/S, Southern line, double track, Taling Chan Junction–Nakhon Pathom, 42 km, 10 stations) - tender documents issued May 2001. Signature of contracts scheduled for April 2002.
- Scheme ST3 (Eastern line, double track, Hua Mak–Chachoengsao, 45 km, 10 stations) - tender documents issued June 2001. Signature of contracts scheduled for May 2002.

### Track

**Rail**

| Type | Weight (kg/m) |
|---|---|
| BS 50 R | 24.8 |
| BS 60 R & 60 ASCE | 29.77 |
| BS 70 R | 34.76 |
| BS 70 A & 70 ASCE | 34.84 |
| BS 80 A | 39.8 |
| Others | 37, 37.5, 42.5 |

**Min curvature radius:** 180 m (turnouts 156 m)
**Max gradient:** 2.6%
**Max altitude:** 574.9 m
**Max axleload:** 15 tonnes

*UPDATED*

---

# TOGO

## Ministry of Commerce and Transport

Lomé

### Key personnel
Minister: Dedevi Michele Ekue
For map see entry for **Benin**.

## Compagnie Togolaise des Mines de Benin (CTMB)

Gauge: 1,000 mm
Track length: approximately 36 km

CTMB runs phosphate trains over a distance of 30 km from mines at Hahotoé to the port of Kpémé and on a 6 km branch serving mines at Kpogamé. Loaded trains to Kpémé are run approximately hourly around the clock, transporting around 120,000 tonnes of phosphates per month. Operations are suspended one day per week to enable track maintenance to be carried out. CTMB owns six Alsthom Bo-Bo diesel locomotives, 150 self-discharging phosphate hoppers and a few service vehicles. Traction and rolling stock maintenance is undertaken at a depot near Kpémé.

Main running lines are laid with heavy rail on steel sleepers on crushed stone ballast and are well maintained.

## Société Nationale des Chemins de Fer Togolais (SNCT)

PO Box 340, vis-à-vis de la Gare de Lomé, Lomé
Tel: (+228 21) 43 01

### Key personnel
President: David de Fanti
General Manager: Yawo Kalepe

Superintendents
  Administration and Finance: V K Dogbe-Tomi
  Rolling Stock and Motive Power: K Alfa
  Traffic: Polo Noelaki
  Infrastructure: Y Akakpo

Gauge: 1,000 mm
Route length: 525 km

### Political background

During 1997-98 the former Réseau des Chemins de Fer du Togo was restructured and its name changed to Société Nationale des chemins de Fer Togolais (SNCT) to facilitate eventual privatisation of both passenger and freight services. Branch lines in the phosphate mining area north of Kpémpé are operated by the Compagnie Togolaise des Mines du Benin (CTMB) (qv).

### Organisation

One main route extends from the port of Lomé to Blitta (276 km). There are several branches but many of them are out of service, including the Frontalière Lomé-Togblékové, Côtière Lomé-Aného lines and the short section from Agbonou to Atakamé. A 58 km branch linking Togblékové and Tabligbo, which was opened in 1979 but closed between 1984 and 1990, is used for clinker transport. Of the branches leading to the port of Lomé only the line to Dique Est remains in operation.

### Passenger and freight operations

Poor maintenance, due to lack of investment, led to a steady decline in traffic and as a result it was decided to let out railway operations in Togo to a private sector company under a management contract. This resulted in an upturn in traffic with 19 million tonne-km and 9 million passenger-km carried in 1994.

In mid-1998, remaining passenger services between Lomé and Blitta were withdrawn and then reinstated in November of that year, running on Saturdays to Blitta and returning on Sundays. This followed pressure from traders who felt isolated from markets at Lomé. The train is mixed, conveying passengers and commodities such as charcoal and agricultural products.

Freight traffic includes about 0.5 million tonnes of clinker annually on the Tabligbo–Lomé–Digue Est route, conveyed normally in two 20-wagon trains per day each carrying about 1,000 tonnes. Cement trains run regularly on the Lomé–Blitta route.

### Traction and rolling stock

SNCT's stock consists of one Soulé railcar, currently unserviceable, three Canadian-built GM Co-Co diesel electrics, three Alsthom diesels (two B-B and one Bo-Bo), two Henschel B-Bs and two small French-built shunters. One of the two Henschels, both of which had been out of service for some time, has been returned to traffic by robbing its sister of spares. There are 12 coaches, several of which are railcar trailers which are unusable in locomotive hauled formations due to coupler differences. Some vehicles were built locally by Sotometo in 1990. Of some 120 freight wagons, 80 are clinker hoppers.

### Signalling and telecommunications

All traffic is radio-controlled, the telephone communications system having been suspended completely.

### Track

**Rails:** Up to 40 kg/m on main lines, lighter on disused branches. Welded rail is in place on some parts of main routes
**Sleepers:** Mostly steel, on older line sections also wooden, rails are fixed with plates and screws
**Ballast:** Crushed stone on all lines built after 1960 and on some parts of older lines
**Max speed:** 35 km/h for railcars, lower for locomotive-hauled trains

---

# TUNISIA

## Ministry of Transport

Tunis

### Key personnel
Minister: Houcine Chouk

## Tunisian National Railways (SNCFT)

Société Nationale des Chemins de Fer Tunisiens
PO Box 693, 67 Avenue Farhat Hached, Tunis
Tel: (+216 1) 33 44 44   Fax: (+216 1) 34 40 45; 34 85 40

### Key personnel
President/Director General: Ing Abdel Aziz Chaaban
Deputy Director General: Med Nejib Fitouri
Headquarters Directors
  Management and Finance: Lofti Ben Fadhl
  Rail Business: Sami Khanfir
Bureau Heads
  Environment and Energy: Faouzia Gardallou
  Development and Strategy: Faika Dali
  Organisation and Information: Hédi Belguith
Directors
  Tunisian Rail Network Unit: Abdulsalam Ben Dhiab
  Railway Sector: Sami Khanfir
  International Affairs: Mohamed Chabbi
  Administration and Finance: Mohamed Touj
  Administrative Division: Ahmed Ezzine
  Finance Division: Faouzia El Ghardallou
  Planning and Control: Chazli Al-Kaizani
  Purchasing: Mokhtar Baati
  Main Line Passenger Services: Fayçal Klibi
  Tunis Suburban Services: Abderrahmene Gamha
  Sahel Suburban Services: Hemadi Ben Osman
  Freight Services: Mouldi Zouaoui
  Phosphates Traffic: Djamal Al-Dine Hamza
  Infrastructure Operations and Maintenance:
    Salha Zaidi
  Operations: Jalel Ben Dana
  Property: Khaled Jeddi
  Strategic Development: Abdelhamid Jemmali
  Infrastructure Development: Mokhtar Fennira
  Planning and Operations Control: Chadly Guizani
  External Relations Division: Mahmoud Souayah
  Information Technology: M Yangui

Gauge: 1,435 mm; 1,000 mm; mixed 1,435/1,000 mm
Route length: 468 km; 1,674 km; 10 km
Electrification: 65 km of 1,000 mm gauge at 25 kV 50 Hz AC

### Political background

For the first time, a contract plan was agreed between the government and SNCFT for the period of the Ninth Economic and Social Development Plan (1996-2001). This sets specific targets for the railway to achieve by the end of the period. These include: managing the railway under strictly commercial terms, pursuing only markets where rail offers economic and financial advantages compared with other modes, to achieve a balanced financial result after state subsidies are taken into account; improving service quality, comfort, punctuality, information provision and the safe handling of freight traffic, with standards monitored by performance indicators.

# RAILWAY SYSTEMS/Tunisia

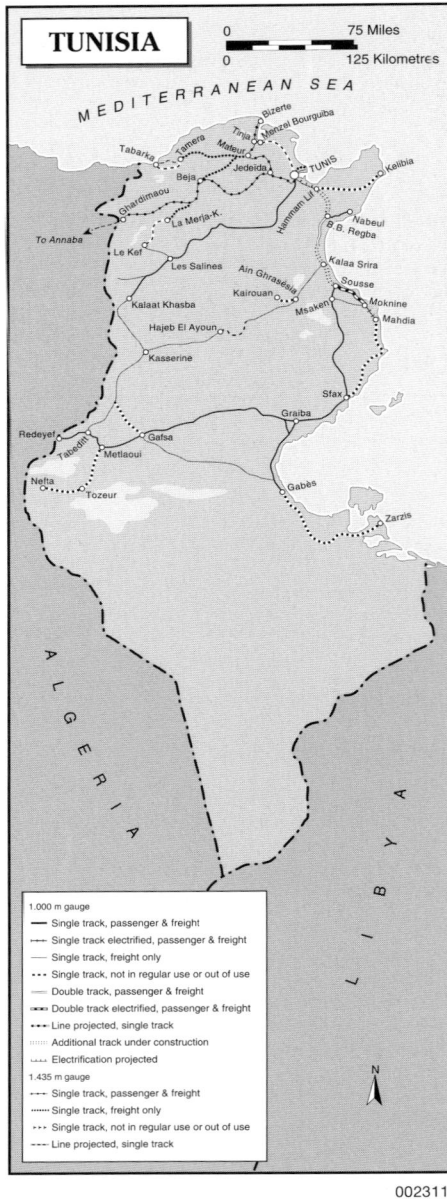

### Diesel locomotives

| Class | Wheel arrangement | Power kW | Speed km/h | Weight tonnes | No in service | First built | Builders |
|---|---|---|---|---|---|---|---|
| 060 GR12 | Co-Co | 1,047 | 100 | 92 | 5 | 1964 | E GM |
| 040 DF | Bo-Bo | 698 | 90 | 59 | 9 | 1965 | E GM |
| 040 DG | Bo-Bo | 698 | 80 | 48 | 6 | 1967 | E Traction |
| 060 DH | Co-Co | 1,640 | 100 | 93 | 5 | 1973 | E GM |
| 060 DI | Co-Co | 1,604 | 114 | 90 | 22 | 1973 | E MLW |
| 040 DK | Bo-Bo | 895 | 116 | 64 | 20 | 1978 | E MLW |
| 040 DL | B-B | 1,323 | 110 | 62 | 10 | 1981 | H Ganz Mávag |
| 060 DN | Co-Co | 1,862 | 114 | 89 | 19 | 1983 | H GE |
| 060 DP | Co-Co | 1,764 | 130 | 91 | 20 | 1984 | H Bombardier |
| 040 DO | B-B | 1,764 | 130 | 64 | 20 | 1985 | H Ganz Mávag |
| 040 DD | Bo-Bo | 294 | 70 | 39 | 8 | 1958 | E Alsthom |
| 040 GE | Bo-Bo | 446 | 96 | 49 | 4 | 1962 | E GE |
| 040 GE | Bo-Bo | 515 | 96 | 49 | 4 | 1965 | E GE |
| 060 DS | Bo-Bo | 466 | 103 | 64 | 9 | 1977 | E GE |
| 040 DM | Bo-Bo | 522 | 114 | 64 | 28 | 1983 | E GE |

Under the contract plan the government would provide US$346 million of financial aid to SNCFT over the plan period, with US$300 million to be devoted to infrastructure. The remainder would take the form of subsidy for unremunerative services. All rolling stock investments are to financed by SNCFT.

To achieve the objectives set out in the contract plan, SNCFT is required to implement a diversified and flexible tariff policy, with a special focus on developing door-to-door multimodal transport business. Private sector operators will be allowed to operate selected suburban and tourist passenger and freight services. Concessioning of railway property is also to be adopted.

## Organisation

The reorganisation of SNCFT in compliance with its contract plan with the government has led to the adoption of a more commercially-oriented structure. This comprises seven business units: two suburban passenger units; main line passenger; phosphates traffic; freight; maintenance; and railway infrastructure. At the end of 2000 SNCFT employed 6,634 staff.

Operationally SNCFT is divided into three sectors: the Northern standard-gauge sector, covering lines north and northeast of Tunis; the Northern narrow-gauge sector, covering the route south of Tunis to Sfax; and the Southern narrow-gauge sector, responsible for lines south of Sfax. Important equipment differences restrict the cohesion of the two narrow-gauge sectors as a network: rolling stock of the Northern sector (the former Compagnie des Phosphates de Gafsa) employs single buffers with a coupler located underneath, while the Southern sector uses vehicles with two buffers and a coupler between. SNCFT does not employ bogie-changing between narrow and standard gauges.

Connection between Tunisian and Algerian standard gauge networks is made in the northwest at Ghardimaou while in the future SNCFT will be connected to the system under construction in Libya via a 185 km standard gauge line linking Gabès and Ras Jedir, effectively completing a trans-Maghreb rail link.

| Traffic (million) | 1999 | 2000 |
|---|---|---|
| Passenger journeys | 11.6 | - |
| Freight tonnes | 12.2 | 13 |

## Passenger operations

In 2000 SNCFT introduced two pairs of fast trains linking Tunis and Sfax (278 km) using refurbished first class and grand comfort coaches only.

Other routes to benefit from improved services include Tunis–Sousse, which in 2000 had 10 pairs of trains each weekday. Most long-distance services are formed of refurbished Ganz-Mávag coaches.

## New lines

Several new lines have been proposed, including rebuilding the former Cap Bon line from Fondouk Djedid to Henchir Lebna and extending it to Kelibia. Other schemes include two new north-south lines, one from Borj Mcherga to Kairouan and connections with the prospective Sousse-Kasserine route; and another further west from Gafour to Sidi Bouzid, whence there would be a fork southwest to Gafsa and southeast to Mazouna. A new route around the coast from Monastir to Sfax via Mahdia has also been projected.

## Improvements to existing lines

Under its Ninth Plan period (1999-2001), SNCFT aims to complete double-tracking the key metre-gauge main line from Tunis southward to Sousse, Sfax and Gabès; in October 1997, SNCFT received a loan of €25 million from the European Investment Bank for track renewals, bridge strengthening and repair work on this route, and for the purchase of track maintenance equipment; a further loan of €50 million was made by the EIB for this scheme in 2001. Extension of this line beyond Gabès to Medenine has begun, with ultimate projection to Tripoli in view. Other projects covered by the plan include bridge improvements in Tunis, and procurement of train communications equipment.

During the Tenth Plan period (2002-2006) SNCFT will implement electrification of the 23 km Tunis Ville–Borj Cedria suburban line. To be funded by a loan from the Japan Bank for International Co-operation, work was due to start during 2001.

It has been reported that the Tunis–Tebourba surburban line may also be a candidate for future electrification.

Reopening of several routes has been proposed, including: the line from Mateur to Tabarka, closed since 1984; the Mateur–Jedeida connection; the Mastouta–Merja link further south; and of line southwest from Sousse to revive a through route from the coast to Kasserine.

## Traction and rolling stock

At the end of 1999, SNCFT operated 127 main line and 45 shunting diesel locomotives, 11 diesel railcars and 60 trailers, six emus and 12 trailers, 305 passenger cars and 3,326 freight wagons.

All railcars, locomotives and passenger cars are capable of bogie change and of operation on either gauge, although in practice this facility is rarely used. Most passenger services have hitherto been provided by diesel railcars, but, except for sets delivered by Alsthom in 1975, those used in secondary services are now elderly and inadequate to meet today's requirements. However, many Tunis area commuter services are operated using diesel locomotives with push-pull coaching stock formations.

Sousse—Mahdia electrified services are operated by six three-car emus supplied by Ganz-Mavág. Some 50 additional emu cars are to be purchased for the Tunis Ville–Borj Cedria electrification.

In 1999, General Motors of Canada commenced deliveries of 21 GT18B diesel-electric locomotives for passenger services.

## Signalling and telecommunications

In 1996, SNCFT commissioned its first CTC system. Supplied by Ansaldo Trasporti and located at Tunis Ville station, the equipment controls the 24 km Tunis–Bordj Cedria section, which handles around 200 trains daily.

Automatic block installation, operative throughout the Tunis-Sousse-Sfax-Gabès single line, with relay interlockings at crossing stations, is being extended to the sections from Tunis to Djedeeda and Beja, Bir Kassa to Gafour, Sfax to Gabès and Gabès to Gafsa. The section

*Three-car metre-gauge emu built by Ganz-Mavag for suburban services south of Tunis* (Marcel Vleugels)

from Sfax to Gafsa and Métlaoui has been experimentally equipped with track-to-train radio. All telephone lines are being progressively placed in ground-level ducts.

### Electrification
Electrification of suburban lines south of Tunis in 2000, following feasibility studies by Systra and Tunisian consultants Scet. Lines covered by the scheme are Tunis—Bordj and Tunis—Tebourka.

### Track
**Standard rail**
Standard-gauge: Flat bottom, 36-46 kg/m in lengths of 12-18 m
Metre-gauge: Flat bottom, 25-36 kg/m in lengths of 7, 8, 12 m
**Welded joints:** Thermit welding of rail joints
**Crossties (sleepers):** Oak impregnated with creosote; metal; concrete RS type
Standard-gauge: 120 × 220 × 2,600 mm
Metre-gauge: 120 × 220 × 2,200 mm
**Spacing:** 1,500/km
**Rail fastenings:** Wood sleepers: spikes
Metal sleepers: clips and bolts
Concrete sleepers: special resilient fittings
**Filling:** Broken stone
**Max curvature**
Standard-gauge: 7° = min radius 250 m
Metre-gauge: 11.6° = min radius 150 m
**Max gradient:** 1 in 50
**Max altitude:** 952 m on Haidra to Kasserine line
**Max speed, standard-gauge**
Railcars: 100 km/h
Diesel trains: 70 km/h
**Max axleload**
Standard-gauge: 21 tonnes
Metre-gauge: 18 tonnes

**UPDATED**

*Class 040 DO diesel-hydraulic locomotive on passenger service at Bir Ben Regba (Marcel Vleugels) 2001/0059403*

# TURKEY

### Ministry of Transport and Communications
Ulâstirma Bakanligi, Ankara
Tel: (+90 312) 212 67 30   Fax: (+90 312) 212 49 00

**Key personnel**
Minister: Enis Öksüz
Director General, Land Transport: M Mendilcioglu

### Turkish State Railways (TCDD)
Türkiye Cumhuriyeti Devlet Demiryollari
Genel Müdürlüğü Talatpaşa Bulvari, 06330 Ankara
Tel: (+90 312) 309 05 15   Fax: (+90 312) 312 32 15

**Key personnel**
Director General and Chairman of the Board:
    (Acting): Turgay Doludeniz
Chairman and Deputy Director General: Cahit Söyler
Deputy Directors General: Tayyar Hindistan,
    Aydiner Sarikaya, Cevat Oktay
Head of Board of Inspection: Cemil Tatli
Legal Consultant: Necdet Alkan
Head of Security Secretariat: Kemal Çiftçi
Public Relations Counsellor: Erhan Demirkol
Directors
    Permanent Way: Nurullah Tatarağasigil
    Traction: Nail Adali
    Commercial: Bedri Palamut
    Financial: Ercan Cici
    Operations: Süleyman Yavuz
    Health: Kadriye Çetinkaya
    Personnel (Acting): Hüseyin Öztürk
    Purchasing: Nizamettin Gülşener
    Ports: Nizamettin Arslan
    Construction: Erol Inal
    Research, Planning and Co-ordination: Feridun Akyüz
    Training: Yalçin Cevahir Tolu
    Data Processing: Ümran Özbozduman
    Installations: Mehmet Uras
    Real Estate: (Acting) Oktay Fidaner
Affiliated companies
Tülomsaş (Locomotive and Motor Corporation of Turkey):
    Zeki Daloğlu
Tüvasaş (Wagon Industry Corporation of Turkey):
    Mehmet Göktürk
Tüdemsaş (Railway Machinery Industry Corporation of Turkey): Halil Torun

Gauge: 1,435 mm
Route length: 8,607 km
Electrification: 2,131 km at 25 kV 50 Hz AC

### Political background
In late 1997, the Turkish government announced its intention to restructure TCDD in readiness for privatisation. At present the railway still has to balance its books with the aid of a considerable state subsidy. This covers track maintenance and the losses of uneconomic lines and services, but does not currently meet in full the shortfall between TCDD's revenue and expenditure.

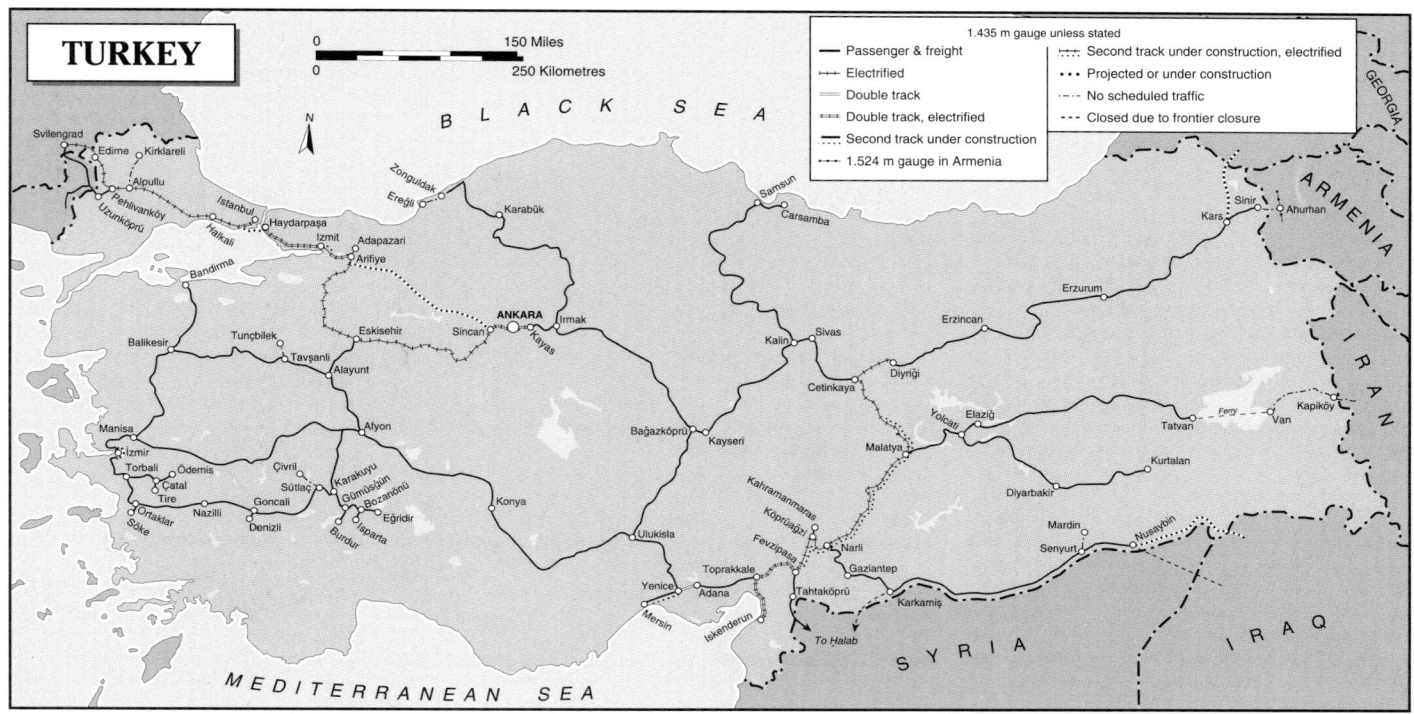

Financially, TCDD has benefited from the rapid growth of traffic through the seven ports it manages: these now provide about a third of the corporation's revenues (about the same proportion as rail traffic, while government subsidy and non-operating revenues such as those from real estate make up the rest). Sale of the ports is likely to figure in the government's privatisation plans, which have already seen TCDD divest itself of a number of peripheral activities. The disposal of railway workshops, after modernisation, has also been identified as a likely early feature of privatisation policy.

Mainspring of the railways' turnaround has been an attack on the inefficiencies which previously prevented TCDD from grasping all commercial opportunities. The unacceptably high ratio of unserviceable locomotives, for instance, has been much reduced. TCDD has also invested substantial sums to modernise and rationalise the activity of its vehicle workshops. Manufacture of new high-capacity bogie freight wagons is being concentrated on the Tüdemsasş plant at Sivas. A drive has also been mounted to improve wagon productivity, in part by imposing demurrage charges on customers who are lethargic in unloading their cargoes. This has secured an improvement of about 10 per cent in turnaround times.

TCDD's fundamental handicap persists, however, in that it cannot add competitive transit speeds to the considerable price advantage it offers over road transport, and to its availability when road movement is hobbled by winter conditions. Far too much of the rail system is still single-track and beset by sharp curves and severe gradients.

## Organisation

Currently, TCDD has no sound costing and financial management system that can be considered a meaningful indicator for performance measurement. Such a system is considered vital for the development of successful marketing and commercial programmes. Under recent restructuring, new business profit centres were established, making effective financial control essential. TCDD has therefore made the implementation of its Financial Management Information System (FMIS) a top priority. The cost of the project has been estimated at US$4 million.

TCDD in 2000 was also evaluating tenders to supply an Operational Management Information Systems (OMIS), aimed at improving the effectiveness if its passenger and freight operations. OMIS will comprise three subsystems: an operational control system; a train planning system; and a rolling stock information system. The estimated costs of the project, covering hardware and software, is US$20 million, 85 per cent of which was expected to be provided by foreign credit and the remainder from equity.

At the end of 1998, TCDD employed 41,819 staff.

| Revenue (TL million) | | | 1998 |
|---|---|---|---|
| Passenger | | | 13,266,318 |
| Freight | | | 89,710,940 |
| Other income | | | 12,033,232 |
| Subsidies | | | 27,148,412 |
| Total | | | 142,158,902 |

| Expenditure (TL million) | | | 1998 |
|---|---|---|---|
| Railway personnel | | | 103,304,903 |
| Other expenditure | | | 175,949,469 |
| Total | | | 279,254,372 |

| Traffic (million) | 1995 | 1996 | 1998 |
|---|---|---|---|
| Passenger journeys | 104 | 98 | 110 |
| Passenger-km | 5,797 | 5,229 | 6,160 |
| Freight tonnes | 15.1 | 16.2 | 16.0 |
| Freight tonne-km | 8,409 | 9,018 | 8,466 |

## Passenger operations

Passenger business divides roughly half and half (in terms of passenger-km) between suburban and main line. Sirkeci has the most commuter traffic (955 million passenger-km in 1998), followed by Haydarpaşa (721 million), Ankara (463 million), Basmane (27 million) and Alsancak (22 million).

A feature in the long-haul sector is the development of good quality, first-class-only services. Recent additions to the long-haul rolling stock include business cars with telephone, telex and data modem equipment, new day cars and sleeping cars with individual shower/WC facilities for each compartment.

In 1991, a private company, Nesa of Istanbul, began operating its own premium-fare luxury car on Ankara-Istanbul trains; the company linked this rail operation with hire car facilities from each terminal. TCDD's service on the route was relaunched in 1994 following completion of electrification throughout. Now the 'Baskent Express' covers the 567 km from Ankara to Haydarpaşsa (over the straits from Istanbul) in under five hours, with air conditioned cars providing a high standard of comfort.

For short-haul service TCDD has begun local manufacture of diesel railcars, while new Fiat dmus have been introduced on suburban lines round Izmir pending electrification. It also operates 20 two-car railbus sets bought second-hand from Germany.

## Freight operations

The most important commodity is iron ore, at over 4 million tonnes, while coal (over 2 million tonnes) and construction materials (1.7 million tonnes) are also significant. International traffic is around one million tonnes annually.

## Intermodal operations

In 2000, TCDD planned to commission a feasibility study aimed at developing a strategy for combined transport in Turkey, defining steps to be taken by the three modes (sea, rail and road), and defining organisational, regulatory and investment requirements. The study would also consider equipment requirements.

In the longer term, TCDD envisages the construction of inland intermodal terminals at Ankara, Balikesir, Denizili, Gaziantep, Kayseri, Konya and Kahramanmaraş. By making these investments, TCDD aims to relieve the pressure on ports which has resulted from the growth in containerisation and move the emphasis on handling freight closer to centres of production and demand.

As part of a major ports modernisation programme, partly funded by the European Investment Bank, the facilities at Haydarpaşa, Izmir and Mersin are being provided with container-handling equipment.

## New lines

Feasibility studies into a proposed high-speed passenger link between Ankara and Istanbul continued during 1999, although government statements indicated that this is a long-term project. Nevertheless, in 1999 it was announced that the Ministry of Transport had been given the go-ahead to invite bids for the line's construction. Government support has been forthcoming for the planned Bosphorus rail tunnel, which has been broadened into a major electrified suburban rail scheme and is now known as the Marmaray project. An initial 13.3 km tunnel section, including 1.8 km of 'immersed tube' construction, is to form the centrepiece of a 63 km cross-Bosphorus line linking Halkali and Gebze. In early 1998, the construction cost of the tunnel was estimated at US$650 million, while the associated suburban lines, which will serve 41 stations, were costed at US$600 million.

Still at the study stage in 2000 was a long-projected 124 km single-line electrified railway between Kars and Tbilisi, Georgia, intended to provide improved links between Turkey, the central Asian republics and Russia. Most of the route, 92 km, would be in Turkish territory. Construction would take four years.

Several routes have been proposed to reduce the distance between Ankara and the Armenian and Iranian borders, but high cost rules out early construction of any. Better founded is a proposed line round the north shore of Lake Van, where elimination of the difficult train ferry crossing would allow TCDD to raise capacity closer to the substantial demand on this international axis.

## Improvements to existing lines

Several large-scale projects feature in TCDD's medium- and long-term network improvement programmes.

International tenders were received in 2000 for a major rehabilitation and upgrade of the 567 km Istanbul–Ankara main line. The four-year project aims to reduce the journey time between the two cities from 7 hours 30 minutes to 5 hours after completion of its first phase and to 4 hours after the second phase. The estimated cost of the scheme is US$237 million.

*Class E 52 electric locomotive at Istanbul Sirkeci* (D Trevor Rowe)

### Diesel locomotives

| Class | Wheel arrangement | Power kW | Speed km/h | Weight tonnes | No in service | First built | Mechanical | Builders Engine | Transmission |
|---|---|---|---|---|---|---|---|---|---|
| DH 33100 | C | 450 | 50 | 41.2 | 30 | 1953 | MAK | KTA-1150 | H Voith |
| DH 44100 | D | 800 | 80 | 58.9 | 2 | 1955 | MAK | MTU 8V 396TL | H Voith |
| DH 6500 | C | 650 | 60 | 49.6 | 13 | 1960 | Krupp | Maybach | H Voith |
| DH 3600 | C | 360 | 50 | 40.5 | 7 | 1968 | MAK ELMS | MTU 12V 183 | H Voith |
| DH 3600 | C | 450 | 50 | 40.5 | 11 | 1968 | MAK ELMS | Cummins | H Voith |
| DH 7000 | C | 522 | 50 | 51 | 18 | 1995 | Tülomsasş | Cummins KTA19L | H Voith |
| DH 9500 | B-B | 710 | 40/80 | 68 | 5 | 1999 | Tülomsasş | MTU 8V 396 | H Voith |
| DH 11500 | B-B | 810 | 100 | 62 | 2 | 1960 | MAK | Mercedes mB 820 B6 | H Voith |
| DE 21500 | Co-Co | 1,600 | 114 | 111.6 | 11 | 1965 | GE | GEFDL 12 | E GE |
| DE 24000 | Co-Co | 1,580 | 120 | 112.8 | 291 | 1970 | Tülomsasş | Pielstick 16PA4-185 | E Alsthom |
| DE 18000 | Bo-Bo | 1,325 | 120 | 80 | 1 | 1970 | MTE | Pielstick 12PA4-185 | E Alsthom |
| DE 18100 | A1A-A1A | 1,325 | 120 | 87 | 16 | 1978 | Tülomsasş-MTE | Pielstick 12PA4-185 | E Alsthom |
| DE 22000 | Co-Co | 1,470 | 120 | 117 | 86 | 1985 | GM | GM 645 E | E GM |
| DE 11000 | Bo-Bo | 735 | 80 | 68 | 80 | 1985 | Tülomsasş | MTU 8V 396 | E GEC |

### Electric locomotives

| Class | Wheel arrangement | Output kW | Speed km/h | Weight tonnes | No in service | First built | Builders Mechanical | Electrical |
|---|---|---|---|---|---|---|---|---|
| E4000 | Bo-Bo | 1,620 | 90 | 77.5 | 3 | 1955 | Alsthom | Alsthom |
| E40000 | B-B | 2,945 | 90/130 | 77 | 12 | 1969 | 50 C/S Group | 50 C/S Group |
| E43000 | Bo-Bo-Bo | 3,180 | 90/120 | 120 | 45 | 1987 | Tülomsasş/ Toshiba | Toshiba |

In 2000, a feasibility study was under way into electrification, resignalling and provision of a new telecommunications system for the Ulukişla–Yenice–Mersin–Adana–Toprakkale–Iskenderun line. The cost of the two year scheme is estimated at US$229.5 million.

At the prefeasibility stage in 2000 was the procurement of 290,000 tonnes of rail at an estimated cost of US$140 million. Under its Permanent Way Mechanisation Project (IV) TCDD plans to acquire permanent way construction and maintenance equipment by international tender. The estimated cost is US$15.3 million.

Short-term and small-scale improvement projects to be completed by 2000 include: renewal of 400 km of track at a cost of US$44 million; achieving 15,400 rail welds (US$1.1 million); renewal of 250 switches (US$3 million); rehabilitation of tunnels (US$3.5 million); curve alignments and deviations (US$524,000); and the construction and renewal of tunnels, bridges and culverts.

### Traction and rolling stock

At the end of 1998 the fleet comprised 508 main line and 78 shunting diesel, 68 electric and 50 steam locomotives, 93 emu cars and 57 diesel railcars. In addition, the railway operated 1,081 passenger coaches, among them 110 sleeping, 101 couchette, and 73 restaurant cars; and 16,989 freight wagons.

**Type of coupling:** Screw
**Type of brake:** Knorr and Westinghouse air

### Signalling and telecommunications

In 2000, nearly 1,900 km of the TCDD network was supervised by CTC.

### Electrification

The ore line wiring between Iskenderun and Diyrigi (577 km), was completed in mid-1995. The next line being tackled is the 701 km Kayasş–Çetinkaya artery, to link the ore line electrification with Ankara, due for completion in 2000.

In 1999, contracts were placed with a Turkish consortium to upgrade and electrify 79 km of suburban lines serving Izmir. Routes covered by the scheme are Basmane–Menemen–Aliaga and Alsança–Cumaovasi.

*Class E 43 Bo-Bo-Bo electric locomotive with an Istanbul–Ankara express at Izmit, with new station work in evidence* (D Trevor Rowe)  0063619

#### Diesel multiple-units

| Class | Cars per unit | Motor cars per unit | Motored axles/car | Power/motor LP | Speed km/h | No in service | First built | Builders Mechanical | Engine | Transmission |
|---|---|---|---|---|---|---|---|---|---|---|
| MT 5600 | 1 | 1 | 2 | 2 × 550 | 140 | 11 | 1992 | Tüvasaş | Cummins KTA 19 R | H Voith T 320 RZ |
| MT 5700 | 1 | 1 | 2 | 2 × 280 | 120 | 30 | 1993 | Fiat | Iveco | H Voith T211R |
| MT 3000 | 3 | 1 | 2 | 2 × 150 | 90 | 4 | 1960 | Uerdingen | Bussing U10 | EM |
| MT 5500 | 3 | 2 | 4 | 4 × 145 | 90 | 9 | 1961 | Fiat | Fiat | H |

#### Electric multiple-units

| Class | Cars per unit | Motor cars per unit | Motored axles/car | Output/motor kW | Speed km/h | No in service | First built | Builders Mechanical | Electrical |
|---|---|---|---|---|---|---|---|---|---|
| E 8000 | 4 | 2 | 2 | 255 | 90 | 28 | 1995 | Alsthom | Alsthom |
| E 14000 | 3 | 1 | 2 | 520 | 119 | 72 | 1979 | Tüvasaş/50 C/S Group | 50 C/S Group |

### Track

**Rails:** 49 kg/m (4,868 km); 46 kg/m (1,733 km); 39 kg/m (1,634 km)
**Sleepers:** concrete (B55-B58); wooden (2,600 × 160 × 260 mm); steel (2,600 × 240 × 100 mm)
**Spacing:** 1,612/km
**Fastenings:** K, HM, N
**Min curvature radius:** 250 m
**Max gradient:** 2.7%
**Max axleload:** 20 tonnes

# TURKMENISTAN

## Ministry of Transport

Turkmenbashi Shaely 7, 744007 Ashkhabad
Fax: (+993 12) 47 39 58

### Key personnel
Minister: Sedar Djepbarov

## Turkmenistan State Railway

Türkmenistanyn Döwlet Demir Yoly (TDDY)
Turkmenbashi Shaely 7, 744007 Ashkhabad
Fax: (+993 12) 47 39 58

### Key personnel
President: Atdabek Agodzhanov
Chief Engineer: G G Neroubaiski
Directors
   Commercial and Operations: Z T Bakhalov
   Traction: A B Khommadov
   Rolling Stock: D I Nourberdyev
   Passenger Services: S A Dourdyev
   Purchasing: T Y Yazlakov
   Personnel and Infrastructure: G A Veguentchova
   Signalling and Telecommunications:
     A Gueldymouradov
   Finance: S O Perliev
   Technical: G A Sakhatdourdyeva
   Legal: E M Kouziat
Chief Economist: O Khoudaiberdyev
External Relations Manager: M K Biachimova

Gauge: 1,520 mm
Route length: 2,440 km all single track; no electrification

### Political background

Turkmenistan is investing in its rail network to develop the country's role as a transport hub in Central Asia. Bilateral agreements covering rail freight links have been signed with the governments of Azerbaijan, Georgia and Uzbekistan, and connections with Iran improved in 1996 with the opening of the Sarakhs–Mashhad line. The Turkmenistan rail system also features in a project supported by the EU to develop a transport corridor between Europe, the Caucasus region and Asia.

### Organisation

The network comprises the western portion of the former Soviet Railways Central Asian Railway. Its main route is the 1,141 km trans-Caspian line linking the port of Turkmenbashy (formerly Krasnovodsk), the capital Ashkhabad and Chardzhou, near the border with Uzbekistan. A branch from Mary to Kushka (Gushgi) on the Afghan frontier is rarely used because of the unrest in Afghanistan.

In 1997, Japan's Overseas Economic Co-operation Fund granted a US$40 million credit to modernise the Ashkhabad locomotive depot, assimilate new repair technologies, and establish a computerised traffic control system.

# RAILWAY SYSTEMS/Turkmenistan—Uganda

Additional funding valued at €35.6 million for modernisation of the network was committed in early 2000 by the Japanese Overseas Economic Co-operation Fund.

Workers engaged in the 'main activity' (railway work) totalled 18,535 in 1998, of which 14,283 were operating workers.

### Passenger operations
Passenger traffic in 1995 amounted to 1.9 billion passenger-km. In 1999, 2.3 million passengers were carried (0.7 billion passenger-km). A new fast service was introduced in 1993 from Turkmenbashy to the regional capital of Tashauz, covering the 1,600 km in 36 hours.

### Freight operations
Traffic is mainly cotton and other crops, and oil. In 1993, 18.5 million tonnes of freight were carried, falling to 8.7 million in 1997 and then recovering to 9.8 million in 1999. In that year 7 billion tonne-km were recorded.

### New lines
Construction of the 122 km Tedzhen—Sarakhs—Mashhad line, linking Turkmenistan with Iran, has been completed; the line was opened in May 1996.

The branch to Kushka is to be the spring-off point for the proposed trans-Afghan railway, which was the subject of an accord signed between the Pakistan, Afghan and Turkmenistan governments in March 1994. The 800 km route, which has the strong support of the Pakistan government, would link Kushka with Chaman in Pakistan, via Herat, Farah and Kandahar in Afghanistan.

A new link from Chardzhou in a southeasterly direction was opened in early 2000. This line runs along the south side of the Amu Darya river to Kerki where a new bridge has been constructed with a link to the present isolated line at Kerkichi (on the Karshi—Termez (both in Uzbekistan) route). This new river crossing relieves pressure on the life-expired bridge at Chardzhou, for which a replacement is also being planned.

In 1997, a Japanese-led consortium agreed to build a 450 km line from Yeraliyev, in Kazakhstan, to Turkmenbashy (formerly Krasnovodsk). This will provide improved access from western Russia to the Persian Gulf via Sarakhs and through Iran to the port of Banda' Abbās.

Construction of the 530 km Ashkhabad—Tashauz line began in 2000, with completion expected in 2005.

### Traction and rolling stock
The current fleet of locomotives comprises some 233 double-unit locomotives of the 2TE10 derivatives, of which about 120 are available for service. Additionally, there are 98 shunters of types TEM2 and ChME3 of which about 60 are serviceable. Interest has been expressed in a potential re-engining exercise for the 2TE10M locomotives using General Electric (USA) technology.

Hard currency earned from exports of cotton have enabled the railway to purchase spare parts for the rehabilitation at Chardzhou workshops of unserviceable locomotives. The same source has provided funding for new locomotives: in 1995 the railway bought 33 Type 2TE10U two-section diesel-electrics from Lugansk of Ukraine.

Fifteen passenger cars were bought in 1998, but none in 1999. No freight cars were delivered in those years.

# UGANDA

## Ministry of Transport and Communications
PO Box 7087, Amber House, Kampala
Tel: (+256 41) 25 50 28; 23 57 30

**Key personnel**
Minister: AK Kivejinja
Permanent Secretary: W O Wanyama

## Uganda Railways Corporation (URC)
PO Box 7150, Nasser Road, Kampala
Tel: (+256 41) 25 49 61; 25 80 51
Fax: (+256 41) 24 44 50

**Key personnel**
Managing Director: E K Tumusiime
Chief Mechanical Engineer: S Kwesiga
Chief Civil Engineer: H Akora
Chief Rail Operations Manager: C Ntegakarija
Chief Administration Manager: G Kahangi
Chief Construction Unit Manager: C Musuuza
Financial Controller: S Sebunjo (Acting)
Assistant Chief Marketing Manager: E Hashaka
Assistant Chief Planning and Development Officer: F Mugenyi
Assistant Chief Signal and Telecommunications Officer: Ruth Kyohairwe
Public Relations Manager: E K Kabatangale

Gauge: 1,000 mm
Route length: 1,241 km

*Class 73 locomotives*

### Political background
Uganda Railways Corporation (URC) was created after the 1977 dissolution of East African Railways (EAR). Since then it has suffered seriously from political dissension between its former partner countries in EAR, from the civil war in its own country and resultant damage, and from a decline in the performance of Ugandan industry and agriculture.

During 1995 and 1996 an easing of political tensions between the former EAR partner countries led to serious consideration of the practicality of reviving both the East African Community and much closer co-operation between URC and the neighbouring railways in Kenya and Tanzania, particularly in the areas of marketing, tariffs and accounting.

Privatisation of URC is still intended and, in anticipation of this, efforts have been made to reduce staff numbers.

### Passenger operations
In 1990, traffic amounted to 1.5 million passenger journeys but fell off subsequently, with URC recording a mere 200,000 journeys (30 million passenger-km) in 1995. By 1997, all passenger services had been suspended, save for the weekly through international passenger train between Nairobi and Kampala (which was reintroduced in 1994 following reduction of political tension in the region). This uses URC locomotives and Kenya Railways coaches.

In late 2000 URC announced that it was to undertake studies into the restoration of passenger services on the Kampala—Tororo, Kampala—Kasese and Tororo—Gulu lines. This will entail complete reconstruction of the Kampala—Kasese line, where freight services have been withdrawn due to poor track conditions. The Tororo—Gulu line also needs partial rehabilitation.

## Freight operations

In 2001 the Tororo (Kenya) to Kampala corridor was the only operational railway in Uganda. This includes access to Kampala port, where freight arriving by boat across Lake Victoria is transferred to rail. In 1999, URC carried 753,488 tonnes of freight compared with 600,182 tonnes in 1998. This increase in rail freight volume has been attributed to a reduction in maximum permissible loads for road transport, a unique step taken by the Ugandan government and one not attempted by any other African country. The theft of goods in transit continues to prove a problem for URC, with raids on freight trains en route from the Kenyan border to Kampala a frequent occurrence.

In 2001 discussions continued with Spoornet in South Africa via its Comazar joint venture regarding a proposed inland port at Namanve, near Kampala.

### Train ferry service

As a member of the African Central Corridor transport system, Uganda benefited from the provision of European funds for improvement of wagon ferry terminals and port facilities on Lake Victoria at Jinja, Port Bell, Mwanza, Musoma and Bukoba. Two URC train ferries ply between Port Bell in Uganda, Kisumu in Kenya and Mwanza in Tanzania, with occasional use of the Jinja terminal for traffic from the east of the country.

### Improvements to existing lines

URC started rehabilitation under a National Recovery Programme in 1980, commencing with signalling modernisation, financed by French aid, with station interlocking and tokenless block (which has since fallen into disuse); the construction of a workshop at Nalukolongo using German bilateral aid; new locomotive and rolling stock orders; and construction of new Lake Victoria wagon ferries.

A seven-year modernisation of the Tororo–Pakwach line was completed in mid-1993.

### Traction and rolling stock

At the start of 1997 URC was operating 57 diesel locomotives, 85 passenger coaches and 1,384 freight wagons. In 1991, the railway received 300 freight wagons from More Wear Industries of Zimbabwe, followed by a further 300 from the same source in 1992; 51 hoppers were delivered by Spain's CAF, also in 1992.

# UKRAINE

## Ministry of Transport

Gorki ul 51, 252150 Kiev
Tel: (+380 44) 227 73 51   Fax: (+380 44) 227 03 23

### Key personnel

Minister: Leonid Kostiuchenko
First Deputy Director, Railways: G Kirpa

## Transcarpathian Railroads

294017 Uzhgorod, Universitetskaja Str 1
Tel: (+380 31) 224 26 62   Fax: (+380 31) 223 78 01

### Key personnel

Managing Director: Ivan Ustich

### Organisation

Transcarpathian Railroads is a private-sector company set up to develop narrow-gauge railways in southwest Ukraine and neighbouring countries. Its first ambition was to take over the 80 km Beregova–Kusnitsa line run by the Ukrainian Ministry of Transport.

## Ukrainian National Rail Transport Administration (UZ)

Derzhavna Administratsiya Zaliznichnogo Transportu Ukraïni (Ukrzaliznitsya, UZ)
Vulitsa Lysenko 6, 252601 Kiev-34
Tel: (+380 44) 223 63 05
Fax: (+380 44) 227 65 93; 03 23
Web: http://www.uz.kiev.ua

### Key personnel

General Director: G Kirpa

Gauge: 1,520 mm
Route length: 22,473 km
Electrification: 4,320 km at 25 kV 50 Hz AC, 4,930 km at 3 kV DC

### Political background

UZ resulted from the 1992 break-up of Soviet Railways (SZD), and consisted of the six railway administrations that served Ukraine: the Donetsk, Lviv (Lvov), Odessa, Dnipro (Dnepr), South West and Southern railways. Its headquarters was established in Kiev and is subordinated to the Railway Department of the Transport Ministry. Of Ukraine's seven neighbours, the Russian Federation, Belarus and Moldova share the same 1,520 mm gauge. Although there are a few short cross-border 1,520 mm gauge lines, most freight is transhipped to standard gauge when it passes to and from the Polish, Slovakian, Hungarian and Romanian railways.

Due partly to the unsettled political situation, and partly to the economic downturn that followed the break-up of the USSR, the UZ administration was faced with a critical situation. It endeavoured to cut costs, but could not always achieve its goals; in 1996 it planned to close 89 low-traffic subdivisions, but local resistance halved that number. An attempt to merge railway divisions aroused wide opposition and may have been one of the factors in the summary dismissal of the General Director in 1997, which came at a time when the apparently excessively reorganised Dnipro Railway was facing possible bankruptcy and there were calls for the establishment of an independent Crimean Railway.

More serious, perhaps, was the growth of crime and corruption and apparently the 1997 upheaval did little to stop this. Early in 2000, following a critical report commissioned by the national security council, there was

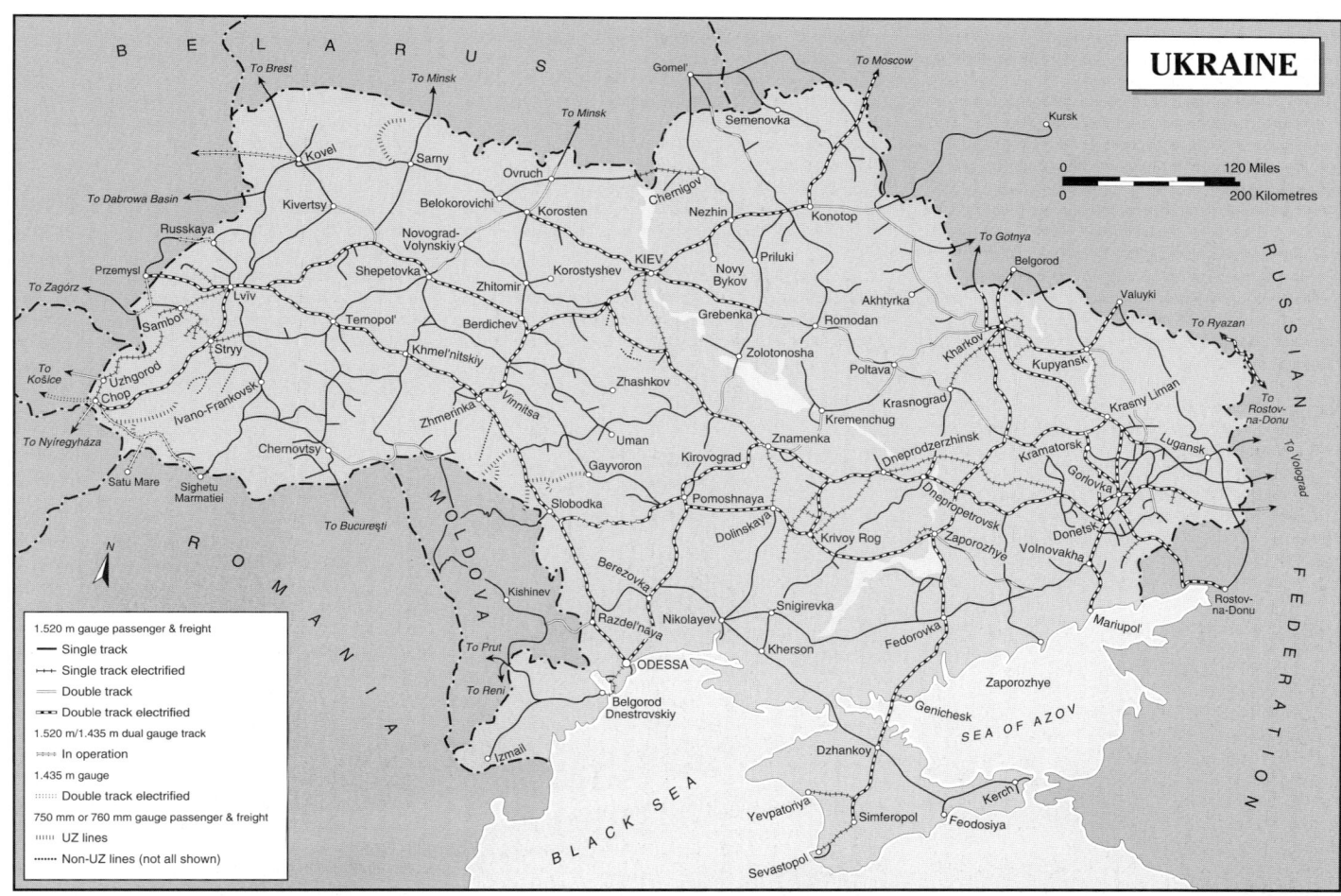

*Class ER9M 10-car emu at Fastov, forming a Kiev-bound service (Colin Boocock)* 2001/0059406

*Class 2M62U diesel-electric locomotive at Zhitomir with a Chop–Kharkov service (Colin Boocock)* 2001/0059404

another hasty change of General Director. The new man, G Kirpa, formerly head of the Lviv Railway, declared his intention to 'disinfect' UZ from railway heads down to cleaners. Five out of the six railway heads, accused of incompetence and financial unreliability and of 'hiding behind the skirts of local administrators,' were dismissed, together with half of the General Director's deputies. It was announced that real money would be required from clients (hitherto only 22 per cent of internal freight charges were paid in ready cash, the rest was payment in kind or credit notes). The host of middlemen and self-proclaimed freight forwarders was to be eliminated, and railway organisations were to be strictly audited and required to use UZ's EkspressBank for all their transactions. In June 2000, apparently as a first fruit of this cleansing, freight traffic increased by six per cent but freight revenue by 47 per cent. Wages began to be paid on time and in full.

UZ had earlier accepted the restructuring principles of EU Directive 91/440 and additionally has been advised by the European Bank for Reconstruction and Development. However, the present intention is to proceed slowly, probably towards transforming UZ into a holding company.

### Finance

High inflation (2,500 per cent in 1994 but much less subsequently) has to be taken into account when comparing different years. In 1997, income from freight was 4,026 million karbovanets, 11 per cent more than in 1996. Corresponding figures for passenger income were 652 million and 6.6 per cent more. The share of passenger income had grown considerably from the barely 5 per cent of 1992.

Reluctance or inability of customers to pay their bills has caused problems. In 1997, on the eve of a conscription call-up period, the railway refused to issue military concession tickets until the Defence Ministry agreed to pay its debts.

Since separation from Russia, heavy increases in the costs of energy in the Ukraine – both diesel oil and electricity – have meant that these now form a much higher proportion of the railway's costs than formerly.

The number of workers (excluding those in non-railway activity) was 367,879 in 1999, of which 276,729 were operating workers. A high proportion of staff works less than full time.

### Passenger operations

In 1995, passenger traffic stood at 577 million journeys (1994 = 631 million); passenger-km stood at 63.759 billion (1994 = 70.881 billion). By 1999 these figures had fallen respectively to 487 million and 47.6 billion and passenger operations were continuing to return an operating loss.

The railways have no financial support from the state. In the five years 1992-96 only 17 passenger cars were purchased. For long-distance passenger services in 1997, 11,300 vehicles were needed but only 9,000 were serviceable, of which one third were obsolete. Although the Crimean government relieved the railways of land tax, most local governments paid little heed to the government's exhortation to help the railways with passenger subsidies. In 1996, the railways therefore cut some services and put other pressures on local authorities, but with little result. From mid-2000 children under 16 have been carried free. Passenger trains are increasingly accompanied by transport militia. On the Dnipro Railway, 35 daily passenger trains were so escorted by late 2000.

There is little road competition for passenger traffic; this reflects the high cost of fuel oil and the railway fares structure. In contrast to other former Communist countries, private interurban bus operation has not developed to any great extent, though there is already competition on the Moscow–Kiev–Kishinev (Moldova)–Bucharest–Turkey corridor from Turkish coach operators. Most mail now moves by road.

### Freight operations

The major source of freight traffic is the heavily industrialised Donetsk region in the southeast.

Since the break-up of the USSR and SZD, freight traffic has declined by about 50 per cent. In 1995, the railway carried 360 million tonnes (1994 = 408 million); tonne-km stood at 195.762 billion (1994 = 200.423 billion). In 1996, 342.5 million tonnes were carried, of which iron ore amounted to 50 million, and ferrous metals 28.5 million. In 1999, 156.3 billion tonne-km were produced. Tonnes originated totalled 284.2 million, of which coal contributed 82 million.

As with many neighbouring countries, the principal reasons for the decline in traffic are the reduction in industrial output following the loss of traditional markets combined with an upsurge of competition, particularly from road hauliers for international traffic flows.

Thanks to ill-judged tariff increases, much transit traffic was lost in the late 1990s. About a quarter of transit traffic is originated by Intertrans, the forwarder established by the Transport Ministry in 1992.

UZ's Ukrpromzheldortrans (Ukrainian Industrial Railway Transport Combine) operates much, though not all, of the industrial feeder mileage, charging industries directly for work done (but rarely being paid in full). In 2000 it was said to possess 224 diesel locomotives, of which 80 were serviceable. It is being restructured, the first moves being the combination of its 14 industrial railways in Kiev, and a smaller merger at Odessa.

### Traction and rolling stock

At the end of 1997, the effective (although not neccesarily operating) rolling stock fleet comprised: 515 passenger electric locomotives, 139 passenger diesel locomotives, 1,349 freight electric locomotives, 1,211 main line diesel freight locomotives, 1,869 diesel shunting locomotives, 1,032 dmu cars and 2,982 emu cars.

The main electric Classes are: VL8, VL10, VL11/11m, VL80 and VL82 families, ChS2, ChS4, ChS7 and ChS8, with emus mainly from the Riga-built ER2 and ER9 groups. The main diesel fleets are: TE3, TE7, TEP60, TEP70, 2TE10 family, M62 family, 2TE116 and 2TE121; dmus are of Classes D1 (Ganz-Mávag), DR1, DR1A and DR1P (Riga).

During 1994, the financial situation had deteriorated to such an extent that freight traffic, wherever feasible, was being routed solely over electrified lines in order to reduce the consumption of diesel oil. More than 20 steam locomotives were returned to service on shunting and trip work, mainly in the Lviv area.

New construction approved by the government for 1998 was 40 dmu cars, eight emu cars and six mixed-traffic DC electric locomotives. It was decided soon after independence that electric locomotives would be built at an engineering works in Dnepropetrovsk, while the existing main line diesel locomotive works at Lugansk would add emu and dmu designs to its product range. The Dnepropetrovsk Electric Locomotive Works (NPO DEVZ) is to build twin-section Bo-Bo freight and passenger designs for both AC and DC operation. The first, the DC freight Type DE1, appeared in 1996 but was seven tonnes overweight. The six mixed-traffic units scheduled for construction in 1998 were to be based on this design and were to be followed in 1999 by an AC version. DC and AC passenger electric prototypes were to appear in 1999 and 2000. Siemens Transportation Systems is supplying three-phase traction equipment based on that used in its Class 152 and 189 locomotives supplied to DB for 21 Class DS3 25 kV AC electric locomotives to be constructed by NPO DEVZ. Construction of a prototype commenced in 2000. The series batch of 20 is to be completed by 2006. The 4,800 kW machines will have a maximum speed of 160 km/h.

*Class VL80T 25 kV AC electric locomotive at Fastov (Colin Boocock)* 2001/0059405

To extend the life of ChS4 passenger locomotives for 15 years beyond 2000, the Zaporozhe repair works, with assistance from Škoda, is refurbishing these units. Kharkov Works has produced diesel engines with which to re-engine the Soviet 2TE116 freight design, while Lugansk has produced a passenger version of the latter.

In early 1998 it was announced that Uzbekistan was to participate in a joint venture to manufacture diesel locomotives at Lugansk.

In 1992, 330,000 freight wagons of the Soviet stock were allocated to Ukraine, of which 225,000 were in the operational stock. In January 1996 there were 280,000, of which 100,000 were in the working stock. New acquisitions have been few (only 2,200 wagons were acquired in 1994, for example).

Five coaches were rebuilt with Spanish help in 1996, following which it was decided to obtain assistance from the same source to refurbish coaches older than 20 years to bring them up to European standards. The Dnepropetrovsk repair works commenced refurbishment of 100 coaches in 1999. With some technical assistance from De Dietrich in France, it was expected that the Kryukov wagon works would build new passenger vehicles.

In 1999, 22 passenger coaches were bought, as against 10 in 1998 and nil in 1997. Delivery of freight wagons, however, decreased from 1,416 to 772.

### Signalling and telecommunications
The following types of signalling are in use on UZ (with km controlled in brackets): automatic block (13,605 km); interlocking control (3,355); semi-automatic block (7,466); automatic cab signalling (15,113); dispatcher control (8,495).

### Electrification
Some 41 per cent of the system is electrified, divided almost equally between 25 kV AC and 3 kV DC. Encouraged by the high price of diesel fuel, the administration adopted a 10-year electrification plan in 1994 which is now in arrears. It envisaged 2,148 km of new electrification. The east-west Russian frontier–Poltava–Kiev line has been the most important objective, as well as the Ternopol–Zhmerinka line. In 1998 the final section of the Moscow–Hungary route was electrified. 187 km were electrified in 1999.

### Track
To overcome a shortage of rail, in 1995, each of the six railways in UZ was required to close 200 km of poorly utilised track in order to provide materials for maintaining the main lines.

The Lvov–Kiev main line, part of one of the nominated European transport corridors, is being upgraded to accept 140 km/h running, with the European Bank for Reconstruction and Development providing financial help.

Considerable investment is to be made in increasing line capacity in and around the ports of Odessa and Ilichevsk.

**Rail:** 65 kg/m (34,620 km); 50 kg/m (11,330 km)
**Sleepers:** Concrete, wood
**Spacing:** 1,840/km in plain track, 2,000/km in curves
**Min curve radius:** 200 m
**Max gradient:** 1.4%
**Max axleload:** 22.5 tonnes

---

# UNITED KINGDOM

## Department for Transport

Eland House, Bressenden Place, London SW1E 5DU
Tel: (+44 20) 79 44 30 00   Fax: (+44 20) 79 44 46 69
Web: http://www.detr.gov.uk

**Key personnel**
Secretary of State for Transport: Alistair Darling
Minister for Transport: John Spellar

### Organisation
The privatised railway in the UK is regulated by three autonomous bodies: the Strategic Rail Authority (qv), the Office of the Rail Regulator (qv) and Railway Inspectorate HM (qv). However, the Department for Transport retains direct responsibility for the administration of subsidies for environmentally beneficial transfer of freight from road to rail. Since April 1994, grants have been payable not only for rail loading and unloading facilities that remove freight from roads, as they had been since 1974, but also to offset track access charges.

In April 2001 the government published its 10-year transport plan, Transport 2010. This foresees investments in rail transport of £60 billion over the period of the plan, with £15 billion provided by the state, £34 billion by the private sector and £11 billion of public resource expenditure. The plan envisages growth of 50 per cent in passenger traffic and 80 per cent in rail freight.

*UPDATED*

## HM Railway Inspectorate Health and Safety Executive

Rose Court, 2 Southwark Bridge, London SE1 9HS
Tel: (+44 20) 77 17 65 01   Fax: (+44 20) 77 17 65 47

**Key personnel**
Chief Inspector of Railways: V Coleman
Deputy Chief Inspector, Technical Division (RI 1): A Cooksey
Head of HMRI Strategy, Planning and Safety Cases Division (RI 2): M Power
Deputy Chief Inspector, Field Operations Division (RI 3): R J Smallwood

### Organisation
HM Railway Inspectorate monitors the safety of railway operations in Great Britain and advises government ministers on railway safety matters. Established in 1840, it is the oldest such body in the world. The Chief Inspector publishes an annual report on railway safety in Great Britian.

Organised into the three branches mentioned above, the Inspectorate at 1 February 1998 had 54 inspector grades supported by 36 administrative staff.

## Office of the Rail Regulator

1 Waterhouse Square, 138-142 Holborn, London EC1N 2TQ
Tel: (+44 20) 72 82 20 00   Fax: (+44 20) 72 82 20 40

**Key personnel**
Rail Regulator: Tim Winsor
Directors
  Railway Network: Michael Beswick
  Operator Regulation: Melanie Leech
  Economics and Finance: Paul Plummer
  Strategy, Planning and Communications: Keith Webb
Chief Legal Adviser: M R Brocklehurst
Head of Communications: C I Cooke

### Political background
The role of the Rail Regulator in the privatised British railway network is to protect the consumer, both passenger and freight, from abuses of monopoly power. This he does by licensing operators, approving agreements for track, station and light maintenance depot access and investigating closure proposals. Through the network of rail users' consultative committees, he also protects the interests of passengers.

In performing those functions he has a duty to promote: the use of the rail network; competition in the provision of rail services; and efficiency and economy by those providing services.

The Rail Regulator also has a role in facilitating through ticketing and other benefits associated with a national network.

*Competition Act 1998*
The Regulator has concurrent powers with the Director of Fair Trading with the introduction on 1 March 2000 of powers under this Act.

The Regulator has published draft guidelines for the benefit of rail industry partners and their customers.

## Strategic Rail Authority (SRA)

55 Victoria Street, London SW1H 0EU, UK
Tel: (+44 20) 76 54 60 00   Fax: (+44 20) 76 54 60 10
Web: http://www.sra.gov.uk

**Key personnel**
Chairman and Chief Executive Officer: Richard Bowker
Deputy Chairman: David Quarmby
The Secretary: Peter Trewin
Executive Directors
  Franchise Replacement/Management: Nick Newton
  Strategic Routes: Chris Kinchin-Smith
  Regional Networks: Gary Backler
  London and South East: Richard Morris
  Freight: Julia Clarke
  Infrastructure: Peter Hansford
  Finance: Martin McGann
  Human Resources: Sandra Jenner
  Corporate Services: Terence Jenner
  External Relations: Chris Austin

### Political background
The SRA has been established by the UK government to provide focus and strategic direction for Britain's railways and to promote their development. It is a non-departmental public body charged with advising government and with implementing government policy for the railway network. Its main roles are: to promote the use of the railway network for the carriage of passengers and freight; to secure the development of the railway network; and to contribute to the development of an integrated system of transport of passengers and freight.

Pending the legislation which enabled its formal establishment, the SRA was set up in mid-1999 as the Shadow Strategic Rail Authority (sSRA), using the powers of the Office of Passenger Rail Franchising (OPRAF) and the British Railways Board (BRB). The functions of both organisations were absorbed by the SRA on 1 February 2001, following Royal Assent of the 2000 Transport Act. In Scotland, the SRA is subject to Directions from the Scottish Minister for Transport. At the same time, the SRA assumed responsibility for the consumer support responsibilities of the Office of the Rail Regulator and the freight and international operations responsibilities of the Department for Transport.

A long-delayed first Strategic Plan was published by the SRA in January 2002. This placed emphasis on achieving the government's target of increases of 50 per cent on passenger-k and 80 per cent in freight tonne-km by 2010. It also indicated a policy change in confirming a greater role for the SRA in taking forward major infrastructure schemes on a project basis in partnership with the successor to Railtrack, contractors and other bodies. These would be undertaken by 'special purpose vehicles', organisations established specifically for each scheme.

## Organisation
Following the appointment of a new SRA chairman and chief executive in late 2001, plans were revealed to create a new structure for the organisation. This would comprise three groups, responsible for: operations, dealing with day-to-day relationships with train operating companies, Railtrack's successor and rolling stock leasing companies; strategic planning, covering projects and investment plans; and transactions, embracing financing and private sector partnerships for major projects.

*Passenger services*
The SRA assumed responsibility for the management and development of the system of franchises which form the basis of most passenger rail services in Great Britain. Between 1995 and 1997, 25 franchises were established based on the lowest bid for subsidy against predictions of little growth. It was subsequently recognised that this arrangement did little to encourage investment, especially as many of the franchises were short: 18 were due to expire by mid-2004. In the five years to March 2000, passenger-km increased by 33 per cent.

In response, the sSRA initiated several changes to the franchise replacement process. Most significant among these were proposals, unveiled in June 2000, to amend geographically the structure: of the existing 25 franchises, changes are planned for six, three would be incorporated into other franchises, seven new franchises would be created and nine would remain unchanged. In addition, the sSRA in September 1999 began the process of replacement of existing franchises for which the geographical structure would not significantly change, giving priority to those with less than five years to run. The Strategic Plan included refinements to this process, including combining franchises serving London termini in a move aimed at increasing station capacity and operational flexibility.

The SRA also administers the Rail Passenger Partnership project (RPP) scheme, a government initiative to provide support for innovative proposals aimed at encouraging new rail passengers or at promoting modal shift and integration. Typically, these provide financial support for additional rolling stock and services. By mid-2001, 25 RPP projects were approved at a cost of £33 million over three years.

*Freight services*
Freight operations on the railway network in Great Britain are in the hands of private sector companies, including some third party or own-account operators running services under the provisions of the 1993 Railways Act. Under the 2000 Transport Act, the SRA has a responsibility to promote rail freight. The SRA's freight strategy is designed to support growth through network and access investment and targeted revenue support. It pursues a policy of the retention of existing freight capacity and of the enhancement of both capacity and capability of the network.

Since full vesting of the SRA on 1 February 2001, the organisation has taken over responsibility for administering rail freight grants in England. This function was previously undertaken by Department of Transport, local government and the Regions. Similar grants in Scotland and Wales are administered by the Scottish Executive and the National Assembly for Wales respectively, in both cases in consultation with the SRA.

In December 1999, the sSRA announced a scheme to award financial incentives totalling up to £6 million for innovative solutions for rail-based logistics. Three awards were announced in June 2000 covering: a two-year trial using a piggyback concept for cement distribution; the development of a freight dmu; and the development of a high-speed flat wagon to convey mini-containers for express parcels traffic on Anglo-Scottish routes.

*Infrastructure*
In its role of securing the development of the railway network, the SRA plays a key part in reviewing network utilisation and capacity, assessing how this is expected to change and identifying priorities for network enhancement as part of the longer term process of investment planning. The sSRA/SRA has led or participated in several major studies, including: the Review of Rail Capacity in the West Midlands; London North-South Integration and London East-West Study schemes; the South London Metro feasibility study; studies into a new high-speed line linking London and Scotland; and Manchester area study. The SRA also participates in the evaluation of route reinstatement and upgrading schemes proposed by train operators and/or local authorities.

The Strategic Plan published in January 2002 detailed major infrastructure projects that the SRA was backing. These include Crossrail, two cross-city lines in London, for which the SRA has established an eponymous organisation jointly with Transport for London (see 'Crossrail' entry). Also listed in the plan for development are: Great Western Main Line upgrade and a new north-south high-speed line.

*Rolling stock*
While provision of passenger rolling stock is primarily the responsibility of train operating companies, working with leasing companies and manufacturers, it is a key to the SRA's objectives of securing progressive improvements in service quality. The introduction of new rolling stock is also a requirement of many franchise agreements.

In February 2000, the sSRA announced that it was to invite expressions of interest from manufacturers and financing organisations for the supply of up to 1,500 new vehicles to replace Mark 1 slam-door stock. This equipment is due to be replaced on safety grounds by 1 January 2003, or, by 1 January 2005, if modified with coupler improvements to prevent over-riding in the event of a collision. The move was intended both to guarantee manufacturing capacity during a period of franchise uncertainty and to prevent franchise bidders using Mark 1 replacement as a bargaining level during negotiations. No orders had resulted from this process by the end of 2001.

*UPDATED*

---

## Association of Train Operating Companies

3rd Floor 40 Bernard Street, London WC1N 1BY
Tel: (+44 20) 79 04 30 00   Fax: (+44 20) 79 04 30 20
Web: http://www.rail.co.uk/atoc/public

### Key personnel
Chairman: Christopher Garnett
Director: George Muir

Director, Distribution and Marketing Services: David Mapp
Engineering Director: Rebeka Sellick

### Political background
The Association of Train Operating Companies (TOCs) was set up to administer schemes that required the joint participation of the 25 passenger TOCs formed out of the old British Rail. ATOC's most important role is to administer the division of monies derived from tickets for journeys which cross TOC boundaries, but it also performs a role as a trade association, acting for the TOCs where there is benefit to them in acting collectively.

*UPDATED*

---

## Anglia Railways

Anglia Railways Train Services Ltd
St Clare House, Princes Street, Ipswich IP1 1LY
Tel: (+44 1473) 69 39 00   Fax: (+44 1473) 69 39 15
Web: http://www.angliarailways.co.uk

### Key personnel
Chairman: Jeremy Long
Managing Director: Tim Clarke
Finance Director: Richard Drake
Human Resources Director: Stephen Taylor
Corporate Affairs Director: Jonathan Denby
Operations Director: Mark Pickersgill
Sales and Marketing Director: Liz Mullen

### Political background
Under the arrangements put in place by the 1993 Railways Act, the franchise to run operations on Anglia Railways was let in December 1996 to GB Railways Group plc, a company set up to run rail franchises by Michael Schabas, formerly transport adviser to property developers Olympia & York. Shares in GB Railways are traded on the London Alternative Investment Market.

The franchise was let for a term of seven years and three months. Anglia Railways was to receive from the Franchising Director support, in 1996 prices, of £35.9 million in the first full financial year of the franchise, declining to £6.3 million in the last year of the franchise.

In March 2001, the company employed 762 staff.

*Anglia Railways Class 170/2 Turbostar dmu forming a London Crosslink service from Chelmsford near its destination at Basingstoke (Ken Harris)*

## Passenger operations

Anglia Railways operates main line passenger services over 661 route-km between London's Liverpool Street terminus and Ipswich and Norwich. It also operates local trains on branches in East Anglia.

Under the franchise agreement, GB committed to running a half-hourly weekday service on the London–Norwich route by September 2000, an innovation actually implemented in May 1999.

In May 2000, Anglia commenced the first stage of its new London Crosslink service between Chelmsford and Basingstoke. The service has received funding of £2.8 million from the Rail Passenger Partnership Fund. Further RPP funding of £9.2 million was made to Anglia for a new direct Norwich–Cambridge service, commencing October 2002.

| Traffic (million) | 1998-99 | 1999-2000 | 2000-01 |
|---|---|---|---|
| Passenger journeys | 6.8 | 7.9 | 8.3 |
| Passenger-km | 635 | 701 | 755 |
| Train-km | 6.8 | 7.9 | 9.0 |

### Diesel railcars or multiple-units

| Class | Cars per unit | Motor cars per unit | Motored axles/car | Power/motor kW | Speed km/h | Cars in service | First built | Builders Mechanical | Builders Engine | Transmission |
|---|---|---|---|---|---|---|---|---|---|---|
| 150/2 | 2 | 2 | 2 | 210 | 120 | 20 | 1986 | BREL | Cummins NT855R5 | HM Voith T211r |
| 153 | 1 | 1 | 2 | 213 | 120 | 7 | 1987 | Leyland Bus | Cummins NT855R5 | HM Voith T211r |
| 170/2 | 3 | 3 | 2 | 315 | 160 | 24 | 1999 | Adtranz | MTU 6R183TD | HM Voith T211r |
| 170/3 | 2 | 2 | 2 | 315 | 160 | 2 | | Adtranz | MTU 6R183TD | HM Voith T211r |

### Traction and rolling stock

On the London–Norwich route Anglia uses 11 trains of Mk 2 stock, powered in push-pull mode by Class 86/2 locomotives mostly leased from HSBC Rail (UK) Ltd. Refurbishment of the coaching stock commenced in 1998. For local services 10 Class 150/2 two-car dmus and seven Class 153 railcars are leased from Porterbrook.

In 1999, Anglia purchased eight three-car Class 170/2 'Turbostar' air conditioned dmus from Adtranz (now Bombardier Transportation) under a £26 million contract financed by Porterbrook Leasing Company. Bombardier is also maintaining the trains, which are deployed on services between East Anglia and London Liverpool Street, as well as through services to Anglia destinations with no previous direct London trains. The company has also leased from Porterbrook a two-car Class 170/3 'Turbostar' demonstrator and in 2002 was to procure four additional two-car Class 170 dmus for its new Norwich–Cambridge services.

*UPDATED*

---

# Arriva plc

Admiral Way, Doxford International Business Park, Sunderland SR3 3XP
Tel: (+44 191) 520 40 00   Fax: (+44 191) 520 41 15
Web: http://www.arriva.co.uk

### Key personnel
Chief Executive: Bob Davies
Managing Director, Arriva Trains: Euan Cameron
Finance Director, Arriva Trains: Peter Telford
Rail Development Director, Arriva Trains: Roger Cobbe
Human Resources Director, Arriva Trains: Julie Allan

A major UK-based bus operator, Arriva entered the domestic passenger rail market in February 2000 when it acquired MTL (qv), which held the Merseyrail Electrics and Northern Spirit franchises. Arriva was to operate these franchises for one year (until February 2001) before changes were made to their structures.

In February 2001 both franchises were extended by the Strategic Rail Authority for a further two years.

Arriva is also a joint venture partner with Netherlands Railways in Noordned (qv), which operates integrated rail and bus services in Friesland, and also operates some train services in Groningen.

*UPDATED*

---

# Arriva Trains Merseyside

Rail House, Lord Nelson Street, Liverpool L1 1JF
Tel: (+44 700) 427 74 82   Fax: (+44 151) 702 30 74
Web: http://arriva.co.uk

### Key personnel
Managing Director: Bob Hind
Deputy Managing Director: John Skinner
Directors
  Personnel: Alan Haynes
  Commercial: Ian Bullock
  Customer Services: Dean Nicholson
  Safety and Quality: Lesley Cusick

### Political background

Under the arrangements put in place by the 1993 Railways Act, the franchise to run operations on the then Merseyrail Electrics system was let in January 1997 to MTL Services plc, formerly MTL Trust Holdings Ltd, a group with roots in bus operations in Liverpool. In January 2000, the Arriva bus-operating group made a takeover bid for MTL Services and this subsequently received approval from the Shadow Strategic Rail Authority. Arriva was initially to operate the franchise for a maximum of 12 months under existing terms and conditions, during which period it would be re-let. In 2001 Arriva was granted a two-year extension of the franchise until February 2003. Arriva also runs the Arriva Trains Northern (formerly Northern Spirit and Regional Railways North East) franchise (qv). From March 2001 Merseyrail Electrics was renamed Arriva Trains Merseyside.

The franchise was originally let for a term of seven years and two months. Unlike other franchises, the Arriva Trains Merseyside one is essentially a management contract, with Merseytravel (the local authority) retaining the revenue risk, setting the fares, marketing train services and controlling timetables. Merseytravel is responsible for approximately 89 per cent of the funding of the network.

Passenger revenue in FY98-99 was £17.9 million, including estimated concessionary and multimodal revenue; in March 2000, the company employed 930 staff.

### Passenger operations

Arriva Trains Merseyside runs services on two lines comprising 120 route-km serving the Liverpool suburban area. The Wirral line, extending under the river Mersey, links Liverpool with West Kirby, Ellesmere Port, New Brighton and Chester. The Northern line links Liverpool with Ormskirk, Kirkby, Southport and Hunts Cross.

*Arriva Trains Merseyside Class 507 emu forming a Kirkdale–Liverpool Central Northern Line service at Kirkdale (Colin Boocock)*

### Arriva Trains Merseyside electric multiple-units

| Class | Cars per unit | Motor cars per unit | Motored axles/car | Power/motor kW | Speed km/h | Cars in service | First built | Builders Mechanical | Builders Electrical |
|---|---|---|---|---|---|---|---|---|---|
| 507 | 3 | 2 | 4 | 82 | 120 | 96 | 1978 | BREL | GEC |
| 508 | 3 | 2 | 4 | 82 | 120 | 63 | 1979 | BREL | GEC/Brush |

| Traffic (million) | 1998-99 | 1999-2000 | 2000-01 |
|---|---|---|---|
| Passenger journeys | 23 | 24 | 23.8 |
| Passenger-km | 256.2 | 263.8 | 254.3 |
| Train-km | 5.9 | 5.9 | 5.8 |

### Traction and rolling stock

The Arriva Trains Merseyside system is electrified on the 750 V DC third rail system. The company runs 32 Class 507 and 21 Class 508 emus leased from Angel Train Contracts. An additional six Class 508s leased from Angel Trains Ltd are stored out of use.

Four Class 73 electric-diesel locomotives are retained but in 2002 were offered for sale.

Early in 2001 Merseyrail Electrics indicated its intention to procure a new fleet of rolling stock to replace existing equipment.

*UPDATED*

# RAILWAY SYSTEMS/UK

## Arriva Trains Northern

Station Rise, York YO1 1HT
Tel: (+44 1904) 65 30 22   Fax: (+44 1904) 52 30 75
Web: http://www.arrivatrainsnorthern.co.uk

### Key personnel
Directors
  Managing: Ray Price
  Safety and Standards: Gary Stewart
  Human Resources: Dave Welham
  Finance: (acting) Frank McQuade
  Fleet: Ion Papworth

### Political background
Under the arrangements put in place by the 1993 Railways Act, the franchise to run operations on Regional Railways North East was let in March 1997 to MTL Rail Ltd, a subsidiary of MTL Services plc (formerly MTL Trust Holdings Ltd) qv), a group with roots in bus operations in Liverpool. MTL also ran the Merseyrail Electrics (now Arriva Trains Merseyside) franchise (qv). In June 1998, the company adopted the new name Northern Spirit Ltd, and started rebranding its services to reflect this new identity.

The franchise was let for a seven year and one month term. MTL was to receive from the Franchising Director and local authorities support, in 1997 prices, of £224.5 million in the first full financial year of the franchise, declining to £145.6 million in 2003-04.

### Corporate developments
In February 2000, the Northern Spirit franchise was taken over by Arriva plc when it acquired MTL Rail Ltd. Initially Arriva was to operate the franchise for one year only, but in early 2001 this was extended to February 2003. In May 2001 Arriva Trains Northern rebranding was adopted, demonstrating the company's long-term commitment to the business.

### Passenger operations
Arriva Trains Northern runs services on a 2,055 km network in northern England, including express services across the Pennines and local services around big cities such as Leeds and Newcastle. Some services are supported by and operate to the specifications of Passenger Transport Executives in Greater Manchester, Tyne and Wear (Nexus), South Yorkshire and West Yorkshire.

| Traffic (million) | 1998-99 | 1999-2000 | 2000-01 |
|---|---|---|---|
| Passenger journeys | 43.7 | 46.6 | 45.9 |
| Passenger-km | 1,384.5 | 1,450.1 | 1,424.1 |
| Train-km | 33.5 | 35.8 | 35.8 |

### Traction and rolling stock
The majority of Arriva Trains Northern services are run with second-generation diesel multiple-unit vehicles.

Class 158 dmus (25 two-car and 16 three-car) leased from Porterbrook operate the company's Trans-Pennine services, while Class 142, 144, 153, 155 and 156 dmus are used on local services. The Class 156 units have been refurbished. On electric services from Leeds to Doncaster, three Class 321/9 emus leased from Porterbrook are employed, while on the Leeds–Skipton line 16 Class 333 three-car emus ordered by MTL under the terms of its franchise agreement and supplied by Siemens entered service in early 2001, replacing life-expired Class 308 emus.

In 2000 and 2001 orders were placed for additional intermediate trailers to strengthen all 16 Class 333s to four-car units. Conversion was due to be completed by the end of 2003.

*Arriva Trains Northern Class 156 dmu forming a Sheffield-bound service at Scunthorpe (Colin Boocock)*
2002/0137112

### Arriva Trains Northern diesel multiple-units

| Class | Cars per unit | Motor cars per unit | Motored axles/car | Power/motor kW | Speed km/h | Cars in service | First built | Mechanical | Builders Engine | Transmission |
|---|---|---|---|---|---|---|---|---|---|---|
| 142 | 2 | 2 | 1 | 170 | 120 | 56 | 1985 | BREL | Cummins LTA10R | H Voith T211r |
| 144 | 2/3 | 2/3 | 1 | 170 | 120 | 46 | 1986 | Alexander | Cummins LTA10R | H Voith T211r |
| 150 | 2 | 2 | 2 | 213 | 120 | 24 | 1986 | BREL | Cummins NT855R5 | HM Voith T211r |
| 153 | 1 | 1 | 2 | 213 | 120 | 12 | 1987* | Leyland Bus | Cummins NT855R5 | HM Voith T211r |
| 155 | 2 | 2 | 2 | 213 | 120 | 14 | 1988 | Leyland Bus | Cummins NT855R5 | HM Voith T211r |
| 156 | 2 | 2 | 2 | 210 | 120 | 54 | 1987 | Met-Cam | Cummins NT855R5 | HM Voith T211r |
| 158/0 | 2/3 | 2/3 | 2 | 275/300 | 145 | 92 | 1989 | BREL | Cummins NTA855R/ Perkins 2006-TWH | HM Voith T211r |
| 158/9 | 2 | 2 | 2 | 275 | 145 | 20 | 1989 | BREL | Cummins NT855R1 | HM Voith T211r |

* Rebuilt 1991

### Arriva Trains Northern electric multiple-units

| Class | Cars per unit | Motor cars per unit | Motored axles/car | Power/motor kW | Speed km/h | Cars in service | First built | Builders Mechanical | Electrical |
|---|---|---|---|---|---|---|---|---|---|
| 321/9 | 4 | 1 | 4 | 268 | 160 | 12 | 1991 | BREL | Brush |
| 333 | 3/4* | 2 | 4 | 175 | 160 | 56 | 2000 | CAF | Siemens |

* All units to become four-car by 2003

***UPDATED***

## c2c

c2c Rail Ltd
Central House, Clifftown Road, Southend-on-Sea, Essex SS1 1AB
Tel: (+44 1702) 35 78 89   Fax: (+44 1702) 35 78 23
Web: http://www.c2c-online.co.uk

### Key personnel
Director and General Manager: Andrew Chivers
Finance Director: Ken Bird
Production Director: Richard McClean
Head of Sales and Marketing: Ali Naqvi
Brand Manager: Andrew Ayers

### Political background
Under the arrangements put in place by the 1993 Railways Act, the LTS Rail franchise was won by Prism Rail (qv) in May 1996. Prism also ran the Cardiff Railway (now Valley Lines), Wales & West and West Anglia Great Northern franchises. The franchise was let for 15 years on the understanding that Prism would acquire new rolling stock. The franchisee also gave undertakings to invest at least £14 million on station improvements, and to build a new interchange station at West Ham in east London.

LTS Rail was to receive financial support from the Franchising Director, in 1996 prices, of £29.5 million in the first year, declining to £11.2 million in 2010-11. Total income for LTS Rail was £84.6 million in 1997-98.

In 2000, LTS Rail adopted the branding 'c2c'.

### Corporate developments
In July 2000, Prism sold its rail operating businesses to National Express Group.

### Passenger operations
LTS Rail operates commuter services on the lines out of London Fenchurch Street to Tilbury, Southend and Shoeburyness, with the route network extending to 129 km in all.

### LTS Rail electric multiple-units

| Class | Cars per unit | Motor cars per unit | Motored axles/car | Power/motor kW | Speed km/h | Cars in service | First built | Builders Mechanical | Electrical |
|---|---|---|---|---|---|---|---|---|---|
| 312 | 4 | 1 | 4 | 201 | 145 | 68 | 1976 | BREL | EE |
| 317 | 4 | 1 | 4 | 247 | 160 | 16 | 1983 | BREL | GEC |
| 357 | 4 | 3 | 2 | 250 | 160 | 296* | 1999 | Adtranz | Adtranz |

* Includes vehicles on order

| Traffic (million) | 1998-99 | 1999-2000 | 2000-01 |
|---|---|---|---|
| Passenger journeys | 24.7 | 25.8 | 26.6 |
| Passenger-km | 733 | 762 | 783 |
| Train-km | 5.95 | 6.12 | 6.12 |

### Traction and rolling stock
LTS Rail inherited 78 ageing 25 kV electric multiple-units leased from HSBC Rail (UK) (40) and Angel Trains (38). The five oldest units, Class 302, were withdrawn in July 1998, replaced by sliding-door-equipped Class 317 units released by West Anglia Great Northern by the introduction into service there of new Class 365 Networker Express trains.

To meet the requirements of the 15-year franchise term, LTS Rail had to acquire stock to replace slam-door units by the turn of the century. In March 1997, Adtranz was selected to fulfil a £17 million order for 44 'Electrostar' four-car emus to be acquired by Porterbrook and leased to LTS Rail. The first of these Class 357 units was delivered in 1999, although it was not until 2001 that the vehicles became widely used in public service. Two additional units were supplied by the former Adtranz as compensation for late entry into service of the type and order for 28 additional Class 357 units was placed with Adtranz in December 1999.

**UPDATED**

*c2c Class 357 emu at Pitsea forming a London Fenchurch Street—Tilbury service* 2002/0524947

## Central Trains

Central Trains Ltd
102 New Street, Birmingham B2 4JB
Tel: (+44 121) 64 44 44   Fax: (+44 121) 654 12 34
Web: http://www.centraltrains.co.uk

### Key personnel
Managing Director: Andy Cooper
Commercial Director: Mike Haigh
Service Delivery Director: Tony Wright

### Political background
Under the arrangements put in place by the 1993 Railways Act, the franchise to run operations on Central Trains was let in March 1997 to National Express Group plc (qv), a bus and airport operator which has also won the Midland Mainline, Gatwick Express, ScotRail and North London Railways (now Silverlink) franchises.

The franchise was let for a term of seven years and one month. NEG will receive from the Franchising Director and the local authority Centro support, in 1997 prices, of £187.5 million in the first full financial year of the franchise, declining to £132.6 million in 2003-04.

In October 2001, all Central Trains operations in northeast and mid-Wales were handed over to the new Wales & Borders Trains train operating company (qv).

Under a deal negotiated in March 2002, the Strategic Rail Authority will pay £115 million additional subsidy to Central Trains and its sister company ScotRail over the remaining two years of their franchises to enable them to break even. The parent company, National Express Group, will contribute £57 million. In mid-2002, work was in progress on proposals for a two-year extension of the Central Trains franchise until March 2006.

### Passenger operations
Central Trains operates services over a 2,400-km route network covering large part of central England, with many lines extending into South Wales and East Anglia. It also operates an extensive network of local services in the Birmingham/Wolverhampton conurbation for Centro, the local Passenger Transport Executive.

| Traffic (million) | 1999-2000 | 2000-01 | 2001-02 |
|---|---|---|---|
| Passenger journeys | 36 | 36.7 | 36.4 |
| Passenger-km | 1,292.1 | 1,320.3 | 1,332 |
| Train-km | 30.9 | 34.3 | 30.2 |

### Traction and rolling stock
For electric services around Birmingham, Central uses 22 three-car Class 323 emus (13 from Porterbrook, nine from Centro). For its premier diesel-worked long-distance routes, the business leases Class 158 dmus from Angel Trains. Other trains in use include Class 150, 153 and 156 dmus.

*Central Trains Class 158 dmu approaching Cardiff with a service from Birmingham* (Ken Harris)   2002/0137113

**Central Trains diesel multiple-units**

| Class | Cars per unit | Motor cars per unit | Motored axles/car | Power/motor kW | Speed km/h | Cars in service | First built | Mechanical | Builders Engine | Transmission |
|---|---|---|---|---|---|---|---|---|---|---|
| 150/0 | 3 | 3 | 2 | 210 | 120 | 6 | 1985 | BREL | Cummins NT855R5 | HM Voith T211r |
| 150/1 | 2 | 2 | 2 | 210 | 120 | 62 | 1985 | BREL | Cummins NT855R5 | HM Voith T211r |
| 150/2 | 2 | 2 | 2 | 210 | 120 | 10 | 1986 | BREL | Cummins NT855R5 | HM Voith T211r |
| 153 | 1 | 1 | 2 | 213 | 120 | 20 | 1987* | Leyland Bus | Cummins NT855R5 | HM Voith T211r |
| 156 | 2 | 2 | 2 | 210 | 120 | 40 | 1987 | Met-Cam | Cummins NT855R5 | HM Voith T211r |
| 158/0 | 2 | 2 | 2 | 275/300 | 145 | 50 | 1989 | BREL | Cummins NTA855R | HM Voith T211r |
| 170/5 | 2/3 | 2/3 | 2 | 315 | 160 | 76 | 1999 | Adtranz | MTU 6R183TD | HM Voith T211r |

* Rebuilt 1991

**Central Trains electric multiple-units**

| Class | Cars per unit | Motor cars per unit | Motored axles/car | Power/motor kW | Speed km/h | Cars in service | First built | Builders Mechanical | Electrical |
|---|---|---|---|---|---|---|---|---|---|
| 323 | 3 | 1 | 4 | 146 | 144 | 66 | 1993 | Hunslet TPL | Holec |

To handle predicted growth in demand and to provide new services, in March 1998 Central ordered 13 Class 170/5 'Turbostar' dmus from Adtranz. Delivery began during 1999. Subsequently the company ordered a further 30 units of the same type for delivery by May 2000. The orders provided 23 two-car and 10 3-car units.

**UPDATED**

## Chiltern Railways

Western House, 14 Rickfords Hill, Aylesbury, Buckinghamshire HP20 2RX
Tel: (+44 1296) 33 21 00   Fax: (+44 1296) 33 21 26
Web: http://www.chilternrailways.co.uk

### Key personnel
Managing Director: Adrian Shooter
Finance Director: Tony Allen
Deputy Managing Director (Franchise Replacement): Mark Beckett

### Directors
Engineering: Andy Hamilton
Production: Stuart Griffin
Marketing: Cath Proctor
Finance: Ian Walters
Head of Procurement and Property: Guy Franklin

### Political background
Under the arrangements put in place by the 1993 Railways Act, the Chiltern Railways franchise passed in July 1996 to M40 Trains, a joint venture of the Chiltern's management, the John Laing construction group and venture capitalists 3i. The new owners undertook to cut subsidy levels over a seven-year franchise from £16.5 million in the first year to £3.3 million in the final year, acquire new trains and increase the level of services prevailing when it took over. Subsequently, the 3i shareholding in M40 Trains was acquired by John Laing, giving it a stake of 84 per cent.

In April 2001 Chiltern Railways announced that it had reached agreement with the Strategic Rail Authority to amend its franchise. Chiltern was to receive a one-off subsidy payment in 2000-01 of £2.4 million, bringing the total for that year to £5.1 million, enabling the company to

# RAILWAY SYSTEMS/UK

*Two Class 168/1 dmus forming a London Marylebone—Birmingham Snow Hill service near Banbury (David Cobbe)* 2001/0114226

make investments of £11 million in a range of safety and customer service improvements.

In 2000 M40 Trains was named preferred bidder for a new 20-year franchise to take effect from July 2003. The bid is based on a major programme of capacity enhancement schemes to be completed by October 2002 under Phase 1 of 'Project Evergreen'. These include reinstating double track between Bicester and Aynho Junction, quadruple track at Beaconsfield and between West and South Ruislip, raising the line speed to 160 km/h between Banbury and South Ruislip, and signalling improvements. Also foreseen by October 2002 are capacity improvements in the Birmingham area, including the reopening of terminal platforms at Moor Street station. Phase 2 of Project Evergreen will provide two additional platforms at London Marylebone station, as well as other capacity enhancements.

## Passenger operations
Chiltern runs services over 272 km on two routes out of London's Marylebone station: to Aylesbury via Amersham and to Birmingham Snow Hill via High Wycombe. The franchisee's ambitious revenue growth plans assumed changing the character of the company's operation from one where commuter traffic to London predominates to one where medium-distance traffic, from such places as Leamington Spa to London, is of significance as well. Supporting these growth plans, Railtrack has restored double track on the 29 km Bicester—Princes Risborough section.

During 1998 Chiltern introduced five Class 168 dmus (see 'Traction and rolling stock'), which were used to launch its Birmingham—London Marylebone 'London Clubman' service. The trains' 160 km/h capability, coupled with the infrastructure improvements detailed above, were to reduce the company's best journey time between the two cities by 25 minutes.

An additional three three-car dmus were ordered to provide extra capacity to coincide with the opening of Warwick Parkway station in October 2000.

In May 2001 Chiltern extended some services beyond Birmingham Snow Hill to Stourbridge and in 2002 it plans to extend these further to Kidderminster.

On completion in 2002 of its Project Evergreen programme of capacity enhancements and line improvements, Chiltern plans to double the frequency of its London Marylebone—Birmingham Snow Hill service to half-hourly, with reduced journey times.

| Traffic (million) | 1998-1999 | 1999-2000 | 2000-01 |
|---|---|---|---|
| Passenger journeys | 9.6 | 10.4 | 11.4 |
| Passenger-km | 427 | 484 | 546 |
| Train-km | 7.1 | 7.1 | 7.7 |

## Traction and rolling stock
Chiltern initially operated a fleet of modern 'Turbo' Class 165 diesel multiple-units owned by the Angel Trains leasing company with 23 two-car and 11 three-car units. Maintenance of the fleet was subcontracted out to the trains' manufacturer, Adtranz. Refurbishment of this fleet commenced in mid-2001, when a prototype upgraded set was returned to traffic. In July 2002, Bombardier Transportation received a contract to refurbish the remainder of the fleet.

With finance being provided by Porterbrook, the company subsequently ordered from Adtranz five new four-car 160 km/h units to improve services on its Birmingham route; designated Class 168/0, these entered service in 1998. In 2000, Chiltern procured a further five two-car dmus of similar design to become Class 168/1. These units took one of the intermediate cars from the four-car Class 168/0 units to become three-car sets.

In February 2000, Chiltern Railways ordered from Adtranz an additional three three-car Class 168/1 units. Delivered in late 2000, they brought to 13 the total of Class 168/0 and 168/1 units procured.

As part of the agreement announced in 2001 covering the amendment of its existing franchise, Chiltern undertook to procure an additional seven dmu cars during 2002.

Over the period of its new 20-year franchise, during which passenger volumes are predicted to double, Chiltern expects to procure more than 200 additional dmu cars.

### Chiltern Railways diesel multiple-units

| Class | Cars per unit | Motor cars per unit | Motored axles/car | Power/motor kW | Speed km/h | Cars in service | First built | Builders Mechanical | Engine | Transmission |
|---|---|---|---|---|---|---|---|---|---|---|
| 165/0 | 2/3 | 2/3 | 2 | 260 | 120 | 79 | 1990 | BREL | Perkins 2006-TWH | Voith T211r |
| 168/0 | 3 | 3 | 2 | 315 | 160 | 15 | 1998 | Adtranz | MTU | Voith |
| 168/1 | 3 | 3 | 2 | 315 | 160 | 24 | 2000 | Adtranz | MTU | Voith |

***UPDATED***

## Connex South Eastern

A subsidiary of the Vivendi (formerly Compagnie Générale d'Enterprises Automobiles) group of France
Connex Rail Ltd
Friars Bridge Court, 41-45 Blackfriars Road, London SE1 8PG, UK
Tel: (+44 20) 76 20 55 05  Fax: (+44 20) 76 20 55 22
Web: http://www.connex.co.uk

### Key personnel
Chairman: Antoine Hurel
Managing Director: Olivier Brousse
Directors
  Finance: Chantal Estragnat
  Engineering: Gary Cooper
  Human Resources: Gary Smith
  Operations Performance: Stewart Palmer
  Operations: Charles Horton
  Commercial: Glen Charles
  Legal: Dominique Ryder
  Planning and Development: Stephen Grant
  Corporate: Tony Robinson

### Political background
Under the arrangements put in place by the 1993 Railways Act, the franchise to run operations on the former South Eastern Division of British Rail was let to Connex, a wholly owned subsidiary of the French CGEA group, in August 1996. In 1998 CGEA adopted the new

*Two Class 375/6 emus forming a Connex South Eastern Service from Victoria to Ramsgate at Gillingham (Alex Dasi-Sutton)* 2002/0114658

# UK/RAILWAY SYSTEMS

name Vivendi. Connex also ran the neighbouring South Central franchise (qv) until August 2001.

The franchise was let for a 15-year term; it is expected to become profitable in that time. Connex will receive from the Franchising Director support, in 1996 prices, of £124.5 million in the first year of the franchise, turning to a premium payment of £2.8 million in 2011.

In January 2001, Connex South Eastern employed some 3,500 staff.

### Passenger operations
Connex South Eastern runs services on a 772 km network out of London's Charing Cross and Victoria stations to south London, Kent and East Sussex. South Eastern is the biggest of the 25 train operating companies in terms of passenger-km; it moves around 115,000 commuters into London every weekday morning.

| Traffic (million) | 1998-99 | 1999-2000 | 2000-01 |
|---|---|---|---|
| Passenger journeys | 123.16 | 128 | 132.2 |
| Passenger-km | 2,976 | 3,114 | 3,215 |
| Train-km | 27.2 | 27.52 | 28.32 |

### Traction and rolling stock
All Connex South Eastern's territory is electrified on the 750 V DC third rail system.

The company's inner-suburban services are run with modern Class 465 Networker emu trains (674 vehicles) leased from the Angel Trains and HSBC companies.

**Connex South Eastern electric multiple-units**

| Class | Cars per unit | Motor cars per unit | Motored axles/car | Power/motor kW | Speed km/h | Cars in service | First built | Builders Mechanical | Electrical |
|---|---|---|---|---|---|---|---|---|---|
| 411/9 | 3 | 2 | 2 | 185 | 145 | 54 | 1956 | BR | EE |
| 411/5 | 4 | 2 | 2 | 185 | 145 | 116 | 1956 | BR | EE |
| 421/4 | 4 | 1 | 4 | 185 | 145 | 84 | 1970 | BREL | EE |
| 423 | 4 | 1 | 4 | 185 | 145 | 296 | 1967 | BR | EE |
| 465/0 | 4 | 2 | 4 | 140 | 120 | 388 | 1992 | ABB/Brush | GEC |
| 465/2 | 4 | 2 | 4 | 140 | 120 | 200 | 1992 | GEC | GEC |
| 466 | 2 | 1 | 4 | 140 | 120 | 86 | 1993 | GEC | GEC |
| 365/5* | 4 | 2 | 4 | 140 | 160 | 64 | 1994 | ABB | GEC |
| 375/3 | 3 | 2 | 2 | 250 | 160 | 30† | - | Bombardier | Bombardier |
| 375/6 | 4 | 3 | 2 | 250 | 160 | 30† | 1999 | Bombardier | Bombardier |
| 375/7 | 4 | 3 | 2 | 250 | 160 | 60† | - | Bombardier | Bombardier |
| 375/8 | 4 | 3 | 2 | 250 | 160 | 228 | - | Bombardier | Bombardier |
| 508 | 3 | 1 | 4 | 82 | 120 | 33 | 1980 | BR | GEC |

* Dual-voltage 750 V DC/25 kV AC, operates only on DC lines
† Includes cars on order

In mid-1998, many longer-distance services were still being operated with a fleet of over 500 Mk 1 slam-door emus of Classes 411, 421 and 423 dating from the 1950s and 1960s. Plans were formulated for retiring these vehicles. South Eastern's share of the Class 365 Networker Express fleet owned by HSBC (formerly Forward Trust) was introduced into service on routes from London Victoria in July 1997. However, with only 16 trains (64 vehicles), this made only a limited impact on the fleet of Mk 1 stock.

In June 1997, Connex announced plans for replacing the Class 411s: 30 Class 375 four-car 'Electrostar' trains were ordered from Adtranz (now Bombardier Transportation), with the first new trains delivered in 1999. Revenue-earning services with the type commenced in 2001.

Subsequent orders for the same type have added an additional 72 four-car and 10 three-car units to the fleet.

In July 2002, Connex placed a further contract for Electrostar emus with Bombardier to replace its remaining slam-door trains. This order was for 36 five-car units for South London suburban services. Delivery was due from July to December 2004.

*UPDATED*

## Crossrail

Telstar House, Eastbourne Terrace, London W2 6LG
Tel: (+44 20) 73 08 44 00    Fax: (+44 20) 73 08 46 80
e-mail: rupert@crossrail.co.uk
Web: http://www.crossrail.co.uk

### Key personnel
Chairman: Sir Christopher Benson
Acting Chief Executive: Keith Berryman

### Background
Cross London Rail Links (Crossrail) is a joint venture, formed in 2001, of the Strategic Rail Authority (SRA) (qv) and Transport for London (TfL) equally, the authority responsible for the capital's public transport. It was established to undertake feasibility studies and to acquire parliamentary powers to construct two heavy rail, high-capacity urban passenger rail routes across central London.

Crossrail Line 1 is a projected east-west line, the core of which would be a new tunnelled alignment linking the City of London commercial district with Paddington station. Services in the east would possibly extend to Romford and Shenfield. A branch would serve the Docklands commercial development. In the west, services would extend to Reading, with an option to serve Heathrow Airport.

Crossrail Line 2 is a proposal for a southwest-northeast route which also requires substantial tunnelling under central London. This would be linked to the southwest London suburban network at Clapham Junction, running via Victoria, the West End of London and King's Cross to Hackney and London's northeast suburbs.

Crossrail's 'best case scenario' foresees construction of Line 1 starting in 2006 and Line 2 in 2009, with services commencing in the periods 2010-12 and 2013-16 respectively.

*NEW ENTRY*

## Direct Rail Services

A subsidiary of British Nuclear Fuels plc
Kingmoor Depot, Etterby Road, Carlisle CA3 9NZ
Tel: (+44 1228) 40 66 00
Web: http://www.directrailservices.com

### Key personnel
Managing Director: Neil McNicholas
Head of Engineering: Ted Cassady

### Political background
Under the 1993 Railways Act, the government made provision for third party and own-account operators to begin rail freight operations on the Railtrack network.

Two traditional customers of the railways initially took advantage of the legislation by setting up their own rail freight operations: National Power, which in 1998 transferred its operations to EWS (qv), and British Nuclear Fuels Ltd. BNFL established a new subsidiary for the purpose: Direct Rail Services.

### Freight operations
DRS began freight operations in December 1995. Its initial operations centred on BNFL's own requirements, carrying flasks of imported spent nuclear fuel from the port at Barrow about 60 km along the Cumbrian coastline to the BNFL reprocessing plant at Sellafield, and also chemicals from further afield required by the plant. In 1999, DRS took over from EWS the movement of spent nuclear fuel rods travelling between power stations around Great Britain and Sellafield. The growing DRS traction fleet has also found useful employment covering locomotive shortages being experienced by other operators and as emergency traction during service disruptions on northwest England and southern Scotland.

In February 2001, DRS commenced a 10-year contract with road haulier and logistics company WH Malcolm to provide rail services between Grangemouth, Scotland and Daventry International Freight Terminal in the Midlands region of England.

### Traction and rolling stock
At the end of 2001, the operational DRS locomotive fleet comprised 15 Class 20/3, six Class 20/9, one Class 33 and six Class 37/6 machines. In addition, the company had acquired an additional 25 Class 20s, eight Class 33s and 16 Class 37s, all of which were non-operational. While some of these were to be refurbished and returned to traffic, others were to serve as sources of spare parts.

The wagon fleet included some 60 special-purpose vehicles for the transport of nuclear materials.

*Two DRS Class 20/9 locomotives with a nuclear flask train north of Cheltenham (Ken Harris)    2002/0126830*

*UPDATED*

## English Welsh & Scottish Railway

English Welsh & Scottish Railway Ltd
310 Goswell Road, Islington, London EC1V 7LW
Tel: (+44 20) 77 13 23 00    Fax: (+44 20) 77 13 23 11
Web: http://www.ews-railway.co.uk

### Key personnel
Chairman: Carl Ferenbach
Chief Executive: Philip Mengel
Chief Operating Officer: Allen Johnson
Directors
    Finance: Steve Bodger
Engineering: Stuart Boner
Planning: Graham Smith
Human Resources: Rachel Bennett
Head of Corporate Communications: Sue Evans
Head of Safety: Barry Evans
Safety Development Manager: Gordon Hunt

# RAILWAY SYSTEMS/UK

*Class 66 diesel locomotive with an Avonmouth(Bristol)—Didcot coal train formed of recently delivered Type HTA wagons* (Ken Harris)
*2002*/0132672

## Political background
English, Welsh & Scottish Railway (EWS) is the UK's largest rail freight company. Formed in 1996, the company was initially owned by a consortium led by US regional railroad Wisconsin Central Transportation Corporation (WCTC), with financial partners Fay Richwhite & Co from New Zealand, Berkshire Partners from the USA and Goldman Sachs from the UK.

In November 1997, EWS purchased Railfreight Distribution, British Rail's international freight carrier.

EWS operates freight, mail and passenger charter trains throughout Great Britain, as well as freight services to and from mainland Europe via the Channel Tunnel.

In 2002 the company employed some 6,100 staff.

In October 2001, the purchase of WCTC by Canadian National (CN) was completed. As a result, CN acquired WCTC's 42 per cent shareholding in EWS and nominated three representatives to join the company's board.

While a private company, EWS operates in a regulated industry for which the UK government has broad objectives, including growth of 80 per cent in rail freight traffic between 2000 and 2010. The company therefore has dealings with the Office of the Rail Regulator and the Strategic Rail Authority (both qv), as well as with the Scottish Executive and the Welsh Assembly.

## Organisation
EWS operations are managed from a purpose-built Customer Service Delivery Centre (CSDC) in Doncaster. This facility was commissioned in October 1998, replacing a separate, geographically distributed operations structure. Staffed by approximately 400 personnel, the CSDC is organised as six commodity teams, together with units responsible for train planning, locomotive control, wagon management and performance analysis and improvement.

In September 2001, EWS launched its Rail Industry Services sector. This brought together the previously separate Rail Services and Infrastructure Services units and is responsible for operating trains and providing resources for other railway industry companies and for providing works trains and hauling infrastructure materials for railway infrastructure and engineering companies.

EWS also provides contract maintenance services and facilities for other train operators (see *Manufacturers – Vehicle maintenance equipment and services*).

## Passenger operations
Although principally a freight carrier, EWS holds a nationwide operating licence for passenger trains. This allows the company to run more than 1,000 charter trains annually, including steam-hauled trains for tour operators.

| **Traffic** (million) | 1996/97 |
|---|---|
| Freight tonnes | 83.533 |
| Freight tonne-km | 14,547 |

## Freight operations
Bulk freight carried by EWS chiefly comprised coal for electricity generation and industrial use, finished and semi-finished steel products, aggregates for the construction industry and petroleum products.

While there has been a significant switch from coal to gas for electricity generation in the UK in the last few years, the volume of coal moved by rail has held up well following aggressive marketing. New contracts for the supply of coal to the power generators came into force in early 1998, effecting changes to the delivery patterns to power stations. In addition, growth in the use of imported coal has created an increase in long-distance movements by rail. In March 1998, EWS acquired the rail business of National Power, which had taken advantage of open access legislation to establish an own-account operation conveying coal from source to power stations. Recent developments affecting coal traffic include the provision of a rail link to the Portbury Docks complex in Bristol. From January 2002, up to seven daily trains of imported coal have been operated both to a recently commissioned power station at Fifoots Point, Newport, and to power stations in the Midlands.

Despite an almost complete cessation of the road-building programme, EWS's aggregates business continues to develop.

The British steel industry has performed well in recent years and this was reflected in the steady growth in tonnages moved by rail. Further expansion is now complete at EWS's steel terminal at Wolverhampton, where a new extension to the covered warehouse has more than doubled the covered accommodation available for steel coil. To create more space at Wolverhampton, a new facility for billet has opened at nearby Walsall.

Changes in UK steel production have had both positive and negative impacts on EWS steel traffic. The termination in 2001 of steel production at the Corus steelworks at Llanwern, Newport, brought to an end the transport of iron ore to the plant from Port Talbot. In contrast, the continuation of rolling at the plant has led to the commencement of long-distance flows of steel slabs to Llanwern from Lackenby, in northeast England. In December 2001, EWS announced that it had secured from Corus a contract to move over 200,000 tonnes annually of steel billet between Scunthorpe and Aldwarke, Rotherham.

EWS now handles only one surviving flow of iron ore, that between Immingham and Scunthorpe.

Other metals sector traffic includes flows of both domestic and imported scrap for steel-making and raw materials and finished products for the aluminium manufacturing industry.

In the petroleum market, rail is still extensively used for a whole range of products, including niche products such as LPG and bitumen. In 2001, the movement by rail of petroleum products from Grangemouth to Fort William, Scotland, resumes after a gap of eight years. This was the first of a number of new flows from Grangemouth to destinations in Scotland.

In addition to moving freight for industrial customers, EWS moves ballast, rail and other construction materials for railway infrastructure engineering work. Railtrack is currently tackling a backlog of renewal work with an expanded works programme that sees intensive use of EWS resources. In 1999, a major new contract was signed between Railtrack and EWS for the provision of infrastructure train services. EWS has also been involved in all the recent major rail infrastructure projects, including the Channel Tunnel Rail Link. EWS also provides engineering maintenance services and hires locomotives and drivers to other parts of the railway industry.

As well as looking for growth in the traditional bulk haul markets, EWS is actively developing its Enterprise wagonload business that has already proved popular with the general merchandise market. Seven trains a day in each direction now run over the core route between Warrington and Glasgow, with some services available for 120 km/h running and one London-Glasgow train running non-stop. A hub at Doncaster to serve the network on the east side of Great Britain came into use at the end of 1998.

Enterprise has been particularly aimed at bringing new markets to rail. Forest products continues to be a major growth area, with key companies in this sector now moving significant quantities by rail. Food and drink is another area where Enterprise is starting to make significant breakthroughs, with some of the best known names in retailing now using rail for specific distribution services.

Enterprise caters not only for movements within the UK, but also into Europe via the Channel Tunnel.

The movement of cars and car components makes use of both block trains and the Enterprise network, as shippers react to the exacting requirements of this market. Recent successes in this market include contracts to move export versions of Jaguar's X-type model from Halewood (Liverpool) to Southampton and BMW Minis from Oxford to Purfleet, east London. Other automotive customers include Ford, Land Rover, Nissan, Rover and Vauxhall.

### Royal Mail traffic
EWS has a 10-year contract for the movement of mail by rail. While many European countries are abandoning rail for this traffic, the Royal Mail division of the Post Office

*Class 67 diesel locomotives heading a postal train northwards from Bristol* (Ken Harris)
*2002*/0132673

made a strategic decision in the early 1990s that it would continue to use this method of transport. A new way of working known as 'Railnet' was devised and took effect in September 1996. The Post Office invested £150 million to establish Railnet, with additional EWS investment in rolling stock. The key to the Railnet operation is a purpose-built hub at Willesden in northwest London. Other depots are located in Doncaster, Glasgow, Newcastle, Stafford, Tonbridge and Warrington. Railnet services use 16 purpose-built Class 325 four-car dual-voltage emus, together with a fleet of specially converted vans, in addition to the traditional travelling post office vehicles.

The company also provides a daily Glasgow–London piggyback service for Parcel Force, the parcels subsidiary of the Post Office.

In August 2001 and October 2001 respectively, EWS launched daily high-speed parcels and packages services between Motherwell (Glasgow) and Inverness and the West Midlands and Aberdeen, in both cases offering transit times much better than those available by road.

*Intermodal operations*
EWS is now a major force in the operation of intermodal services in the UK. Channel Tunnel trains continue to be run under the EWS International banner, but there are increasing intermodal movements from key ports to inland terminals. These take place as part of the Enterprise network, and are attracting new business sectors to rail, principally white goods and food and drink. Three of the UK's leading supermarket chains are now regular users of rail.

In September 2001, EWS commenced services to an intermodal facility at Grangemouth, Scotland, operated by TDG, which provides supply chain logistics.

Plans for gauge enhancements across key parts of the network, specifically between the Channel Tunnel and Scotland, continue to be refined. These plans form part of Railtrack's strategy for West Coast Main Line improvements (see Railtrack entry), and EWS is providing input, although there are increasing concerns that there will be insufficient capacity for freight.

*International traffic*
International traffic handled by EWS via the Channel Tunnel includes cars and automotive products, newsprint, china clay and general wagonload freight, serving destinations in Belgium, France, Germany, Italy and Spain. Dedicated intermodal services are operated between the several terminals in the UK and Belgium (Muizen), France (Metz, Paris and Perpignan) and Italy (Bari, Milan, Novara and Turin). In 2001-02, international traffic was facing serious disruption as a result of the activities of asylum-seekers attempting to breach security measures at Calais and the French entrance to the Channel Tunnel.

**Traction and rolling stock**
In 2001, EWS owned a fleet of 566 main line diesel, 136 diesel shunting and 65 electric locomotives and

### Diesel locomotives

| Class | Wheel arrangement | Power kW | Speed km/h | Weight tonnes | No in service | First built | Mechanical | Builders Engine | Transmission |
|---|---|---|---|---|---|---|---|---|---|
| 08 | C | 261 | 24 | 49 | 133 | 1958 | BR | EE 6KT | E EE |
| 09 | C | 261 | 43 | 49 | 33 | 1958 | BR | EE 6KT | E EE |
| 37/0 | Co-Co | 1,305 | 129 | 105 | 8 | 1960 | EE | EE 12CSVT | E EE |
| 37/3 | Co-Co | 1,305 | 129 | 107 | 2 | 1960 | EE | EE 12CSVT | E EE |
| 37/4 | Co-Co | 1,305 | 129 | 107 | 14 | 1960 | EE | EE 12CSVT | E EE |
| 37/5 | Co-Co | 1,305 | 129 | 107 | 15 | 1960 | EE | EE 12CSVT | E EE |
| 37/7 | Co-Co | 1,305 | 129 | 119 | 13 | 1960 | EE | EE 12CSVT | E EE |
| 47/4 | Co-Co | 1,925 | 120 | 123 | 3 | 1963 | Brush or BR | Sulzer 12LDA28C | E Brush |
| 47/7 | Co-Co | 1,925 | 120 | 119 | 48 | 1963 | Brush or BR | Sulzer 12LDA28C | E Brush |
| 56 | Co-Co | 2,425 | 130 | 128 | 55 | 1976 | Electroputere or BR | Ruston Paxman 16RK3CT | E Brush |
| 58 | Co-Co | 2,460 | 130 | 130 | 17 | 1983 | BREL | Ruston Paxman RK3ACT | E Brush |
| 59/2 | Co-Co | 2,460 | 96 | 121 | 6 | 1994 | General Motors | GM 645E3C | E GM |
| 60 | Co-Co | 2,310 | 96 | 129 | 100 | 1989 | Brush | Mirlees MB275T | E Brush |
| 66 | Co-Co | 2,385 | 120 | 127 | 250 | 1998 | General Motors | GM 710 | E GM |
| 67 | Bo-Bo | 2,385 | 200 | 90 | 30 | 1999 | Alstom | GM 710 | E GM |
| 73* | Bo-Bo | 1,190/450 | 145 | 75 | 5 | 1965 | EE | EE 4SRKT | E EE |

* Class 73 is electro-diesel; 1,190 kW is output under electric power

### Electric locomotives

| Class | Wheel arrangement | Power kW continuous | Speed km/h | Weight tonnes | No in service | First built | Builders Mechanical | Electrical |
|---|---|---|---|---|---|---|---|---|
| 86/2 | Bo-Bo | 2,985 | 160 | 80 | 3 | 1966 | BR or EE | AEI |
| 86/4 | Bo-Bo | 2,685 | 160 | 80 | 7 | 1966 | BR or EE | AEI |
| 90/0 | Bo-Bo | 3,360 | 177 | 84 | 25 | 1988 | BREL | GEC |
| 92 | Co-Co | 5,000 | 145 | 126 | 30 | 1996 | Brush | ABB |

approximately 18,500 wagons. There are also around 500 vans used exclusively for Royal Mail trains. Also operated by EWS are 15 Class 325 emus owned by Royal Mail. In addition, EWS operates Mendip Rail's fleet of eight privately owned Class 59/0 and 59/1 diesel locomotives used on aggregates trains, plus many privately owned wagons.

To meet business growth and to enable life-expired locomotives to be replaced, EWS took delivery of 250 Class 66 (Model JT42CWR) diesel-electric locomotives from General Motors between 1998 and 2000. Rated at 2,385 kW, these feature radial steering bogies, microprocessor control and slow speed control. In 1999-2000, EWS also received 30 Class 67 high-speed diesel-electric locomotives for its mail and parcels businesses. Also rated at 2,385 kW, these were supplied by General Motors and built by Alstom in Valencia, Spain. Their design speed is 200 km/h but in service they are currently restricted to 176 km/h.

EWS has also developed a business supplying for export purposes locomotives surplus to its current requirements. In April 2001, the company shipped the first of 14 Class 37/7 diesel locomotives to Spain, where they are used on construction trains in connection with the new high-speed line between Barcelona and Madrid. They have been supplied under a four-year contract, which includes maintenance and driver training, with Continental Rail, a joint venture between Vias y Construcciones and Continental Auto. This followed an earlier contract to supply 42 Class 37 locomotives for use during construction of the TGV Méditerranée high-speed line in France.

The first of 2,500 new wagons was delivered in August 1998 from US wagon builder Thrall Car. Thrall has taken over part of the former Adtranz plant at York and converted it to a wagon-building facility. An option exists to increase the order by a further 2,500 wagons over the next five years. The first wagons to be delivered were 310 steel carriers. These were being followed by 100 container wagons, 300 open box wagons and further container wagons to differing specifications. In December 2000, Thrall commenced deliveries of an order for 845 Type HTA 102 tonne high-capacity coal hoppers intended to replace existing two-axle vehicles. The new wagons have a payload capacity of 75 tonnes and are able to operate at 120 km/h.

***UPDATED***

## Eurostar (UK) Ltd

Eurostar House, Waterloo Station, London SE1 8SE
Tel: (+44 20) 79 22 61 80  Fax: (+44 20) 79 22 44 24
Web: http://www.eurostar.com

**Key personnel**
Chairman: Rob Holden
Chief Executive: Richard Brown
Chief Operating Officer: Jacques Damas
Executive Director of Finance: Ian Nunn
Directors
 Corporate Affairs: Debra Aspin
 Corporate and Legal Affairs: Victoria Wilson
 Customer Services and Human Resources:
  Lynne Graham
 Production: Steve White
 UK Sales and Distribution: Adrian Watts

**Background**
Eurostar (UK) Ltd is responsible, in conjunction with the Belgian and French national railways, for the operation of international high-speed passenger services between London, Paris and Brussels via the Channel Tunnel. The company has a shareholding of 32.5 per cent in the Eurostar Group. It was previously known as European Passenger Services Ltd (EPSL).

*A Waterloo-bound Eurostar Class 373/0 trainset on Railtrack 750 V DC lines near Otford Junction, on the Ashford–Maidstone–Swanley diversionary route* (Ken Harris)   2001/0110187

In May 1994, EPSL was transferred out of British Rail ownership and became a company owned directly by the government. This was in preparation for the transfer of EPSL to the private sector consortium chosen to build the Channel Tunnel Rail Link, a new £3 billion, 108 km high-speed line from London to the tunnel. Assets worth some £800 million would be transferred, comprising the British share of the fleet of Eurostar trains, Waterloo International station in central London and the North Pole Eurostar maintenance depot in west London.

In June 1994, four private-sector consortia were invited to bid to build the line on a build-and-operate basis: the winning consortium was London & Continental Railways (LCR). LCR (qv) was awarded the assets of Eurostar and there was also to have been a cash injection of about £1.4 billion from the government. The government also wrote off £1.3 billion of debt in Eurostar.

LCR took control of EPSL in May 1996 and in October changed the company's name to Eurostar (UK) Ltd. However, in January 1998, LCR's bid to construct the CTRL failed after the government refused additional state funding for the scheme to make good a shortfall in forecast revenues from Eurostar operations. As a result, the operation of Eurostar services passed from LCR, which remains an umbrella company for the construction of the CTRL, to Inter Capital and Regional Rail Ltc, a consortium formed by National Express Group (40 per cent), SNCF (35 per cent), SNCB (15 per cent) and British Airways (10 per cent). The consortium is to operate Eurostar under a management contract valid until 2010. Continuing government subsidy will be required for the immediate future to cover a revenue shortfall against costs.

### Passenger operations

Eurostar's principal routes are between London and Paris (17 trains a day in 2002) and London and Brussels (eight trains a day in 2002). Services on these routes were first introduced in November 1994, using Waterloo International as the London terminal. Some services stop at the intermediate stations at Ashford, Calais Fréthun and Lille. The London–Paris train takes 3 hours, the London–Brussels trip 2 hours 40 minutes since the opening of the Belgian high-speed line in December 1997 (for details see Belgian entry).

A direct daily train from Waterloo serves Marne-la-Vallée on the LGV Jonction (Paris bypass line), for the nearby Disney complex. Seasonal skiing trains to the French Alps were introduced in 1997, with three Eurostar trains adapted to take 1.5 kV DC supplies from the overhead in the French regions.

In July 2002, Eurostar launched a summer Saturday direct London–Avignon service.

In 2000, plans to introduce services between the Continent and destinations north of London were abandoned as no case could be put forward for operating these on a commercially viable basis. As a consequence, some examples of the Eurostar (UK) Class 373/3 fleet were leased during 2000 to Great North Eastern Railway (qv) for domestic traffic.

In the longer term, the high-speed Channel Tunnel Rail Link promises to cut journey times from London to the tunnel by 35 minutes, as well as improving prospects for effective links to Railtrack's East and West Coast Main Lines to serve destinations north of London (see entry for London & Continental Railways) thanks to the planned use of St Pancras as the London terminal for Eurostar services. Eurostar (UK) ticket sales and seat reservations are handled by the company's ELGAR distribution system, which is accessible to some 4,000 UK travel agents and has links with Galileo (UK), Sabre, Amadeus and Worldspan global distribution systems. The system also has a link to the Association of Train Operating Companies (ATOC) ticket sales system, providing travel industry access to the UK's 25 train operating companies.

### Traction and rolling stock

For the London–Paris/Brussels 'Three Capitals' service via the Channel Tunnel, 31 300 km/h Eurostar trainsets were built by GEC Alsthom.

Each Three Capitals train consists of 18 trailers, articulated in two separable rakes and with a 68 tonne power car at each end of the train. The power car has to accommodate three voltages (25 kV on SNCF, 3 kV on SNCB and 750 V in the UK) but within a 17 tonne axleload maximum. Three sets have been modified to operate from SNCF's 1.5 kV DC system to allow the trains to work through France to Alpine ski resorts.

Each air conditioned trainset includes first- and standard-class accommodation, two bar-buffet cars, two family compartments and facilities for nursing mothers. Each set is arranged as two self-contained power cars and nine trailer halves, easily separable from each other in case of emergency in the Channel Tunnel.

Plans were announced in 2001 to undertake interior refurbishment of the fleet by 2003.

For the once-intended through services between Paris and the British provinces, a 14-trailer format is used. The failure to implement these services has enabled Eurostar (UK) to lease three sets daily (from a pool of four) to Great North Eastern Railway for use on its London Kings Cross–Leeds domestic route. Two of the four units have been repainted in GNER livery.

Eurostar (UK) Ltd's share of the Eurostar trainset fleet is 11 18-trailer and all seven 14-trailer units. Of the remaining 18-trailer sets the SNCF's share is 16 and the SNCB's four. (Details in the table refer to the half trains into which the Eurostar units are separable.)

Eurostar (UK) has sold to Direct Rail Services (qv) three of its six Class 37/6 locomotives converted for the UK legs of overnight services to the Continent, which were never introduced. These are used for stock movements, emergency standby purposes and general hire. Previously, six members of the sub-class were sold to Direct Rail Services. In 2000, Eurostar (UK) also put up for sale the seven Class 92 dual-voltage electric locomotives which it notionally owns. These were also procured for overnight trains and have been operated as part of a common Class 92 pool which also includes EWS and SNCF machines.

The Eurostar (UK) traction fleet also includes two Class 73/1 locomotives, adapted with special drawgear for trainset stock movements, and one Class 08 shunter.

***UPDATED***

#### Eurostar electric trainsets

| Class | Cars per half-set | Line voltage | Motor cars per unit | Motored axles/car | Output/motor kW | Speed km/h | No in service | First built | Builders Mechanical | Electrical |
|---|---|---|---|---|---|---|---|---|---|---|
| 373/0 | 10 | 25 kV AC 750 V DC 3 kV DC | 2 | 4/2 | 100 | 300 | 22* | 1994 | GEC | GEC/Brush |
| 373/3 | 8 | 25 kV AC 750 V DC 3 kV DC | 2 | 4/2 | 100 | 300 | 14** | 1995 | GEC | GEC/Brush |

* Eurostar (UK) allocation of half-trains for London–Paris/Brussels services. A further 32 half-trains are allocated to France and 8 to Belgium
** Four units for a hire pool for GNER; remainder stored

---

## Eurotunnel

Operating headquarters: *France*
Siège d'exploitation, BP69, Coquelles, Cedex, F-62904
Tel: (+33 3) 21 00 60 00   Fax: (+33 3) 21 00 60 01
Web: http://www.eurotunnel.com

*United Kingdom*
Cheriton Parc, Cheriton High Street, Folkestone CT19 4QS
Tel: (+44 1303) 28 22 22   Fax: (+44 1303) 85 03 60

**London office**
Golden Cross House, 8 Duncannon Street, London WC2N 4JF
Tel: (+44 20) 74 84 50 16   Fax: (+44 20) 74 84 51 55

**Paris office**
19 Blvd Malesherbes, F-75008 Paris
Tel: (+33 1) 55 27 39 59   Fax: (+33 1) 55 27 37 75

### Key personnel
Chairman (Non-executive): Charles Mackay
Group Chief Executive: Richard Shirrefs
Managing Director, Eurotunnel Shuttle Services:
   Bill Dix
Directors
   Railway Relations: Jerome Requillart
   Technical: Dave Pointon
   Railway Services, Plan and Development:
      Alain Bertrand
   Communications: Alison Bourgeois
   Business Services: Pascal Sainson
   Public Affairs: John Noulton
   Commercial Director (B to B): Lawrence Strover
   Commercial Director (B to C): Rob Lamond
Chief Financial Officer: Roger Burge

Gauge: 1,435 mm
Route length: 60 km
Electrification: 60 km at 25 kV, 50 Hz

*Cars leaving a Eurotunnel shuttle service*

### Political background

Anglo-French government agreement to construction of a rail-only tunnel under the English Channel was announced on 20 January 1986. The scheme chosen by the British and French governments was that proposed by the consortium of the Channel Tunnel Group and their French partners, France Manche (CTG-FM), which is now known as Eurotunnel.

Agreement on payments to be made by British and French Railways for use of the Channel Tunnel was reached in May 1987 after protracted negotiation. Minimum usage charges will be paid each month, even if the traffic in any one month does not reach the forecast level. The railways agreed to pay these usage charges for the first 12 years of the Tunnel operation. In return, the railways won entitlement to use 50 per cent of the capacity of the Tunnel, as varied from time to time through the concession period. Protection clauses allowing for reduction in minimum usage payments if the Tunnel is not available for use were also written into the agreement.

The Tunnel was handed over by the builders, Trans Manche Link, to the operators, Eurotunnel, in December 1993. The Tunnel complex comprises a service tunnel 4.8 m in diameter, connected every 375 m by cross-passages on either side to two railway tunnels 7.5 m in diameter. These tunnels run for 50 km, with 38 km under the sea, connecting terminals at Cheriton near Folkestone, Kent, and Coquelles, near Calais in northern France.

Eurotunnel spent the first half of 1994 on final commissioning work, and the Tunnel was formally opened by Her Majesty Queen Elizabeth II and President François Mitterrand on 6 May 1994. However, as tests were still incomplete, revenue-earning services were unable to start straightaway. The first shuttle trains carrying lorries ran on 19 May, while the first conventional freight train (carrying new Rover cars bound for Italy) ran on 1 June. Through London—Paris/Brussels Eurostar passenger trains and car-carrying shuttles began in late 1994.

### Finance
Construction of the Tunnel system cost some £10 billion. This was well in excess of preconstruction estimates, and the cost over-run put some strain on the funding of this wholly privately financed project. Over 60 per cent of the revenue was expected to be derived through tourist traffic in the summer months: Eurotunnel was hoping that its first summer of full operations, in 1995, would be sufficiently fruitful to see the company through to a steady income stream. However, fierce competition from ferries constrained revenues and in September 1995 Eurotunnel suspended interest payments on its £8 billion debts in order to force its creditor banks into a financial restructuring of the company's debt load.

An £8.5 billion restructuring of the company's finances, which involved the banks swapping debt for equity and the two governments agreeing an extension of the company's concession beyond 2052 until 2086, was approved by the company's shareholders in July 1997. The concession extension also received the approval of the two governments in return for payment of 59 per cent of Eurotunnel's pre-tax profits between 2052 and 2086.

### Passenger operations
Passenger operations through the Channel Tunnel are of two types. Cars and road coaches are transported through the Tunnel on Eurotunnel's shuttle trains, while London—Paris/Brussels foot passengers are conveyed on Eurostar trains (for description of the latter, see Eurostar (UK) Ltd entry).

The 'Eurotunnel' car-carrying trains began operations in July 1994, initially for shareholders and other invitees. Full commercial services began in December 1994. Eurotunnel trains operate between elaborate terminals just beyond the tunnel portals, at Cheriton in England and Coquelles in France. The main running lines at each are in a loop, with a flyover to avoid conflict between incoming and outgoing trains, so that Eurotunnel trains are in continuous Anglo-French circuit without reversal. Terminal-to-terminal journey time is 35 minutes.

To use Eurotunnel shuttle trains, car and coach drivers simply drive off the motorway into the Eurotunnel terminal, negotiate customs and immigration posts and then drive on to the train. Unlike the 'Eurotunnel Freight' services for lorries, the car and coach users of the service stay with their vehicles for the transit of the Tunnel, and no railway coaches with seating are provided for them.

### Freight operations
Freight operations through the Channel Tunnel are of two types. Lorries are transported through the Tunnel on Eurotunnel's 'Eurotunnel Freight' trains, while intermodal and conventional rail freight is conveyed in trains operated by the national rail operators, EWS and SNCF.

To use the Eurotunnel Freight service, lorry drivers simply drive off the motorway into the Eurotunnel terminal, negotiate customs and immigration posts and then drive on to the train. A minibus driving along the platform picks the drivers up and delivers them to a club car for transit of the Tunnel. Another minibus on the other side of the Channel takes the drivers back to their vehicles. Journey time is 35 minutes start to stop.

### Traction and rolling stock
*Locomotives*
Eurotunnel initially bought 38 5.6 MW Bo-Bo-Bo electric locomotives with GTO converter three-phase AC drive for shuttle operations. They were built by Brush of Loughborough, with electrical equipment from ABB (now Adtranz) of Switzerland. There is a locomotive at each end of each shuttle train, with either machine capable of powering the shuttle should the other one fail.

In May 1996, an additional four locomotives to the same design were ordered from the same builders, this order subsequently increased to six. The first was handed over in April 1998. In 1999 Eurotunnel ordered an additional seven locomotives to handle increased freight vehicle traffic. Delivery was due to begin in March 2001.

Eurotunnel has also purchased five Krupp/MaK diesel-electric locomotives for yard and maintenance work.

*Passenger shuttles*
The Euroshuttle Consortium Wagon Group, comprising chiefly the Canadian-owned multinational Bombardier, was contracted to build 108 covered single-deck transporters for coaches; 108 double-deck covered passenger transporters for private cars; and 18 single-deck and 18 double-deck loading cars.

The passenger shuttle cars are formed into nine single-deck and nine double-deck sets, each of 12 transporters. Each set is flanked by loader vehicles. The normal passenger train shuttle format combines a bilevel and single-level set, each with its two loader cars, and has a locomotive at each end. It thus totals 30 vehicles and is 792 m long.

The 26 m long passenger transporters were built to a height of 5.6 m and a width of 4.1 m, with floor level 1,050 mm above rail. The single-level cars can thus accommodate vehicles up to 4.2 m high. Each rake is a continuous roll-on/off roadway – on both floors in the bilevel rakes. There are 6 m wide side-loading/exit doors on each side of the bilevel rakes' 26 m long loading vehicles (DDL), with separate entrances/exits for each deck: internal ramps lead from the relevant entrance/exit doors to the upper deck. The unprecedented 4.1 m width of the cars achieves an internal width of 3.75 m on each deck, leaving room for auto passengers to dismount and use toilet facilities in the transporters during the journey. The bilevel cars (DDC) are semi-permanently coupled in threes, with the centre car housing stairs and WCs.

To avoid the structural problems of doorways big enough to pass road coaches, the single-deck rakes' 26 m long loading vehicles (SDL) have telescopic hoods of steel coil-carrying wagon character, so that 18 m of their floor length can be laid open during loading/unloading.

*Freight shuttles*
The shuttles for road freight vehicles were built by an Italian consortium comprising Breda and Fiat Ferroviaria. There are 228 single-deck transporters for heavy road freight vehicles, 33 loading wagons for same, and nine club cars in which the lorry drivers ride through the Tunnel. A standard 'Eurotunnel Freight' consist is: Bo-Bo-Bo locomotive, club car, loading/unloading wagon, 14 lorry transporter wagons loading/unloading wagon, Bo-Bo-Bo locomotive.

In March 1996, Eurotunnel ordered sufficient extra wagons to make up a further two freight shuttles (with an option on four more). The order was placed with Arbel Fauvet Rail of Douai, France and all 72 shuttle wagons were delivered in 1998. An option on 144 additional wagons was taken up and delivered in 1999. Costamasnaga of Italy was contracted to build three new club cars, with an option on another two.

### Signalling and telecommunications
The initial operating plan provides for a 3 minute headway in each direction. Half the 20 hourly paths in each direction can be occupied by Eurotunnel's shuttle trains. The Tunnel is equipped with the TVM430 signalling and Automatic Train Protection (ATP) system adopted for French Railways' TGV Nord. The maximum speed possible is 200 km/h, but in practice the Eurotunnel shuttle trains are limited to 140 km/h, Eurostar trains to 160 km/h and freight trains to 100 km/h.

### Track
**Rail:** UIC 60 kg/m
**Sleepers:** Twin block concrete encased in rubber boot and cast into floor slab with no tie bars
**Spacing:** 600 mm
**Fastenings:** Sonneville S75
**Max gradient:** 1.1%

*UPDATED*

---

## FirstGroup plc

3rd Floor, Macmillan House, Eastbourne Terrace Entrance, Paddington Station, London W2 1FG
Tel: (+44 20) 72 91 05 05  Fax: (+44 20) 76 36 13 38
Web: http://www.firstgroup.com

*Operational headquarters*
395 King Street, Aberdeen AB24 5RP
Tel: (+44 1224) 65 01 00  Fax: (+44 1224) 65 01 40

### Key personnel
Chief Executive: Moir Lockhead
Chief Operating Officer: Dr Mike Mitchell
Managing Director, Railways: Dean Finch
Managing Director, Buses: David Leeder

### Political background
Bus operator FirstBus took advantage of the 1993 Railways Act, winning the Great Eastern Railway franchise and securing a stake in Great Western Holdings, which won the Great Western Trains and North Western Trains franchises. In March 1998, having changed its name to FirstGroup plc, the company acquired the remaining 74.7 per cent shareholding in GWH. Subsequently the company's three franchises have been renamed First Great Eastern, First Great Western and First North Western.

FirstGroup also operates the Tramlink light rail system in Croydon.

*UPDATED*

---

## First Great Eastern

First Great Eastern Ltd
35 Artillery Lane, London E1 7LP
Tel: (+44 20) 79 04 33 20  Fax: (+44 20) 79 04 33 01
e-mail: customer-service.ger@ems.rail.co.uk
Web: http://www.ger.co.uk

### Key personnel
Managing Director: Dave Kaye
Sales and Marketing Director: Theo Steel
Finance Director: Dave Gansby
Engineering Director: Steve Rees
Operations Director: Danny Fox

### Political background
Under the arrangements put in place by the 1993 Railways Act, the franchise to run operations on Great Eastern Railway was let in January 1997 to FirstBus plc, a bus operator which also has a stake in Great Western

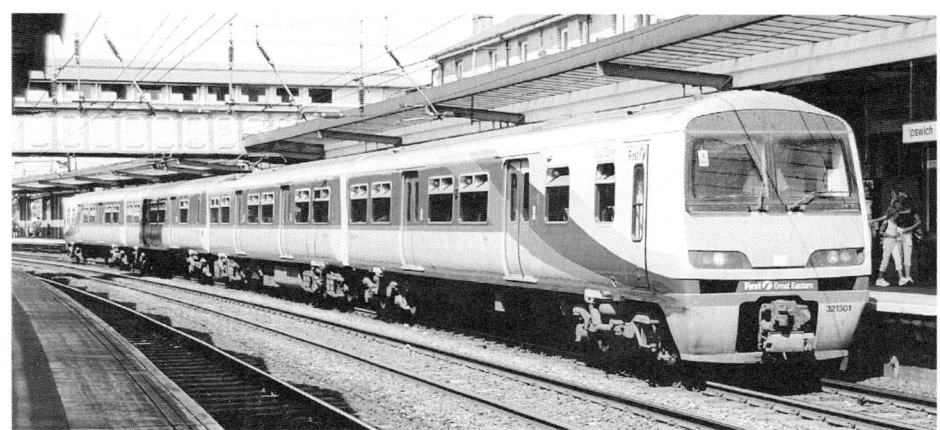

*First Great Eastern Class 321 emu at Ipswich forming a service to London Liverpool Street (Colin Boocock)*

Trains (qv). In early 1998, FirstBus adopted the new name FirstGroup and Great Eastern Railway was subsequently renamed First Great Eastern (FGE).

The franchise was let for a seven year and three months term. FirstGroup will receive from the Franchising Director support, in 1997 prices, of £29.0 million in the first full financial year of the franchise, reversing to a premium payment to the Franchise Director of £9.5 million in 2004.

FGE revenue in FY98-99 was £170 million and in December 1999 the company employed 1,126 staff.

### Passenger operations

FGE runs suburban services on a 264 km route network out of London's Liverpool Street terminus, serving Clacton, Colchester, Harwich, Ipswich and Southend.

| Traffic (million) | 1998-99 | 1999-2000 | 2000-01 |
|---|---|---|---|
| Passenger journeys | 54.4 | 57.8 | 57.5 |
| Passenger-km | 1,625 | 1,771 | 1,802 |
| Train-km | 11.8 | 12.6 | 12.6 |

#### First Great Eastern electric multiple-units

| Class | Cars per unit | Motor cars per unit | Motored axles/car | Power/motor kW | Speed km/h | Cars in service | First built | Builders Mechanical | Electrical |
|---|---|---|---|---|---|---|---|---|---|
| 312 | 4 | 1 | 4 | 201 | 145 | 96 | 1976 | BREL | EE |
| 315 | 4 | 2 | 2 | 82 | 120 | 172 | 1980 | BREL | GEC |
| 321/3 | 4 | 1 | 4 | 268 | 160 | 308 | 1988 | BREL | Brush |
| 360 | 4 | 2 | 4 | 194 | 160 | - | * | Siemens | Siemens |

* On order for service entry in 2002

### Traction and rolling stock

Almost all of FGE's territory is electrified on the 25 kV AC system. The company's rolling stock fleet comprises 24 Class 312 emus leased from Angel and 43 Class 315 and 77 Class 321 emus leased from Forward Trust. The first results of a Class 312 refurbishment programme were revealed in January 1998. In 2000, Class 321 units were undergoing full refurbishment as part of a C6X overhaul programme.

In July 2000, Siemens Transportation Systems concluded a contract to supply to FGE 21 four-car 'Desiro UK' aluminium-bodied emus. To be financed by Angel Trains, the new Class 360 vehicles are due to enter service in 2002, replacing the Class 312 slam-door units.

For its non-electrified Sudbury service FGE hires an Anglia Railways Class 153 diesel unit.

*UPDATED*

## First Great Western

First Great Western Trains Ltd
Milford House, 1 Milford Street, Swindon SN1 1HL
Tel: (+44 1793) 49 94 00  Fax: (+44 1793) 49 94 51
Web: http://www.greatwesterntrains.co.uk

### Key personnel

Managing Director: Chris Kinchin-Smith
Operations and Safety Director: Alison Forster
Finance Director: Wilma Allan
Engineering Production Director: Richard Noble

### Political background

Under the arrangements put in place by the 1993 Railways Act, Great Western Holdings took over the operation of intercity services out of London Paddington terminus in February 1996; GWH also acquired the North Western Trains (now First North Western) franchise (qv). GWH was formed as a joint venture between the former British Rail management on the line, the FirstBus company and the 3i investment company. In March 1998 FirstGroup (renamed from FirstBus) acquired the stakes owned by GWH management and investment companies to become sole shareholder. Subsequently the company was renamed First Great Western (FGW). FirstGroup also holds the franchise for First Great Eastern (formerly Great Eastern Railway) (qv).

Following a commitment by GWH (now FGW) to invest £36 million in new rolling stock, the length of the franchise was extended to 10 years. FGW will receive less than its original 10-year support payments in years five to 10 of the franchise. In 2000/01 the company received £42.9 million, falling to £8.8 million in year 2004/05, and in 2005/06 will repay £2.8 million.

### Passenger operations

FGW operates high-speed services on a 1,367 km route network out of London Paddington to South Wales and the West of England. It also operates a sleeper service out of London Paddington to Devon and Cornwall.

FGW increased the frequency on the London—Bristol route to half-hourly in the summer 1999 timetable and on the London—Cardiff route at the introduction of the summer 2001 timetable.

FGW has fulfilled a franchise commitment to relaunch Motorail accompanied car services between London and Cornwall, in southwest England, launching these in May 2000.

In 1999, jointly with Thames Trains, FGW launched a Bristol—Oxford service, employing Thames Class 166 dmus and using traincrew from both companies.

In 2001 FGW employed some 2,500 staff.

| Traffic (million) | 1998-99 | 1999-2000 | 2000-01 |
|---|---|---|---|
| Passenger journeys | 16.9 | 18.0 | 18.6 |
| Passenger-km | 2,326.6 | 2,400.3 | 2,401.01 |
| Train-km | 14.3 | 15.1 | 16.8 |

### Traction and rolling stock

FGW leases 39 InterCity 125 sets from Angel Trains Contracts. It also leases seven Class 47/8 locomotives and some 11 sleeping cars. In addition, FGW owns 11 Class 08 shunting locomotives. In 2001, FGW leased from Porterbrook a prototype Class 57/6 locomotive, created by refurbishing a Class 47/8 machine and equipping it with a General Motors engine. To provide the additional demand for seating capacity created by an increase in its services, FGW in 1999 arranged to lease 24 Mk 2d and 2e locomotive-hauled coaches from HSBC Rail (UK). The vehicles were refurbished by Adtranz. Additional coaches were refurbished and leased in 2001 pending introduction of Class 180 trainsets (see below).

FGW's high-speed train trailer coaches have been refurbished in a £50 million four-year mid-life programme at Railcare, Wolverton. Also refurbished were the coaches used on FGW's London—West of England sleeper services.

In 1997, the former GWH ordered eight Class 180 'Adelante' five-car 200 km/h dmus from Alstom at a cost of £36 million, with service entry planned for 2001. Subsequent orders were placed for six additional five-car sets. After some commissioning delays, the type entered regular service in 2002.

*UPDATED*

*Two Class 180 'Adelante' dmus forming a London Paddington—Bristol service near Didcot* (Ken Harris)
2002/0524951

## First North Western

First North Western
First Floor, Bridgewater House, 58 Whitworth Street, Manchester M1 6LT
Tel: (+44 161) 228 21 41  Fax: (+44 161) 228 50 03
e-mail: fnwcustomer.relations@gwt.firstgroup.com
Web: http://firstnorthwestern.co.uk

### Key personnel

Director and General Manager: Vernon Barker
Engineering Director: Steve Rees
Commercial Director: Paul Bunting

### Political background

Under the arrangements put in place by the 1993 Railways Act, the franchise to run operations on North Western Trains (NWT) was let in March 1997 to Great Western Holdings, the GW management/FirstBus/3i joint

*Alstom-built Class 175 'Coradia' dmu* (Colin Boocock)
2002/0524948

venture which acquired the franchise for Great Western Trains, now First Great Western (qv). In March 1998, FirstGroup (renamed from FirstBus) acquired the stakes owned by GWH management and investment companies to become sole shareholder. Subsequently the company's name was changed to First North Western. FirstGroup also operates the Great Eastern Railway franchise.

The franchise was let for a seven years and one month term. GWH received from the Franchising Director and local authorities support, in 1997 prices, of £184.3 million in the first full financial year of the franchise, declining to £125.5 million in the final year.

### Passenger operations

FNW operates local services on a 2,102 km route network in northwest England, including all the suburban services around Manchester, and in north Wales. The company collaborates with three metropolitan Passenger Transport Executives: Greater Manchester, Merseytravel and West Yorkshire.

| Traffic (million) | 1998-99 | 1999-2000 | 2000-01 |
|---|---|---|---|
| Passenger journeys | 27.6 | 29.9 | 30.0 |
| Passenger-km | 813 | 833 | 839 |
| Train-km | 28.0 | 27.4 | 26.6 |

### Traction and rolling stock

FNW has a large stud of second-generation dmus. From Angel Trains, the business leases 46 two-car Class 142s and 29 two-car Class 150s. From Porterbrook, 12 single-car Class 153, 18 two-car Class 156 and eight two-car Class 158 dmus are leased, along with 17 three-car Class 323 emus. On the North Wales coast line and interurban services, FNW has introduced Class 175 two- and three-car dmus. This has resulted in the cascading of other modern rolling stock and the elimination of most first-generation dmus and emus.

**First North Western diesel multiple-units**

| Class | Cars per unit | Motor cars per unit | Motored axles/car | Power/motor kW | Speed km/h | Cars in service | First built | Mechanical | Builders Engine | Transmission |
|---|---|---|---|---|---|---|---|---|---|---|
| 142 | 2 | 2 | 1 | 165 | 120 | 92 | 1985 | Leyland/BREL | Cummins | HM Voith T211 |
| 150/1 | 2 | 2 | 2 | 210 | 120 | 36 | 1985 | BREL | Cummins NT855R5 | HM Voith T211r |
| 150/2 | 2 | 2 | 2 | 210 | 120 | 22 | 1986 | BREL | Cummins NT855R5 | HM Voith T211r |
| 153 | 1 | 1 | 2 | 213 | 120 | 12 | 1987* | Leyland Bus | Cummins NT855R5 | HM Voith T211r |
| 156 | 2 | 2 | 2 | 210 | 120 | 36 | 1987 | Met-Cam | Cummins NT855R5 | HM Voith T211r |
| 158/0 | 2 | 2 | 2 | 260 | 145 | 16 | 1989 | BREL | Cummins NTA855R | HM Voith T211r |
| 175 | 2/3 | 2/3 | 2 | 335 | 160 | 70 | 1999 | Alstom | Cummins N14RE | HM Voith T211 |

* Rebuilt 1991

**First North Western electric multiple-units**

| Class | Cars per unit | Motor cars per unit | Motored axles/car | Power/motor kW | Speed km/h | Cars in service | First built | Builders Mechanical | Electrical |
|---|---|---|---|---|---|---|---|---|---|
| 323 | 3 | 1 | 4 | 146 | 144 | 51 | 1993 | Hunslet TPL | Holec |

Supplied by Alstom, the Class 175 order comprised 16 three-car sets (Class 175/1) and 11 two-car sets (Class 175/0). Some £1.5 million has been allocated to the refurbishment of existing Class 142 and Class 150 trains, including vehicles used for Greater Manchester and Merseytravel PTE services.

*UPDATED*

## Freightliner

Freightliner Ltd
3rd Floor, The Podium, 1 Eversholt Street, London NW1 2FL
Tel: (+44 20) 72 14 93 57   Fax: (+44 20) 72 14 92 79
Web: http://www.freightliner.co.uk

### Key personnel

Chairman: Norman Broadhurst
Directors
   Managing: Alan Galley
   Finance: Douglas Downie
   Strategy: Bob Goundry
   Joint Managing Director, Freightliner Ltd:
      Peter Maybury
   Joint Managing Director, Freightliner Ltd: Neil McLean
   Managing Director, Freightliner Heavy Haul Ltd:
      Eddie Fitzsimons
   Personnel and Safety: Ian McDicken

### Organisation

Formerly the division of British Rail running deep-sea container services from ports to inland terminals, Freightliner was privatised in 1996. Since then, the company has moved into profitability and has improved its service delivery in the container and heavy-haul sectors of the market.

### Freight operations

Freightliner container services link the UK's five major deep-sea ports with eight main inland terminals. Services are also provided at the ports of Belfast and Dublin, Ireland and at six other terminals.

In February 2001, the company opened the European Rail Freight Terminal for Wales at Wentloog, Cardiff. Its inland service network includes Daventry and Widnes. In Scotland, additional facilities have been provided at Grangemouth and Deanside to give better coverage of the central belt.

In November 2001, Freightliner inaugurated a ten-year contract to provide a dedicated container service between the ports of Southampton and Manchester for Orient Overseas Container Line.

Freightliner's road services arm, Inland Logistics, has also benefited from investment in 75 new Volvo tractor units and new trailers which allow loading and unloading at locations without specialised handling equipment.

In 2000, Freightliner moved into the UK's conventional freight market and by early 2002 was operating more than 300 trains each week. Freightliner Heavy Haul now serves the coal, cement, car, household waste, petroleum and gas markets and undertakes rail infrastructure work for Railtrack. Usually it dedicates staff and equipment to its customers to ensure the reliability and security of its innovative, bespoke transport solutions.

In December 2001, Freightliner Heavy Haul secured a contract to deliver 720,000 tonnes of ballast from north Kent to the site of the Channel Tunnel Rail Link.

*Freightliner Class 66/5 locomotive and Greenbrier-built hopper wagons with coal imported via Hull for power station use (Ken Harris)*
2001/0059929

*Freightliner Class 57 locomotive rebuilt from a Class 47 on a Southampton—Glasgow service near Reading (Ken Harris)*
2001/0059928

## Traction and rolling stock

Recent additions to Freightliner's traction fleet include 12 Class 57 locomotives, converted from Class 47 locomotives by re-engining with a General Motors 645-12E3 power plant to provide increased haulage capabilities and reliability, and 65 General Motors Class 66 locomotives. An additional 12 of these machines were ordered in 2002. Financing has been provided by both HSBC and Porterbrook.

Freightliner also operates: 29 Class 47 diesels, 10 Class 90 and 28 Class 86 25 kV AC electric locomotives.

For its recently won coal haulage contracts, Freightliner has acquired 250 bogie hopper wagons from Greenbrier. These are leased to the company by Porterbrook Leasing.

In January 2002, Freightliner Heavy Haul launched a new type of car-carrying wagon, the Autoflat, for its Autoliner business. The new wagon is intended to provide a means of transporting larger cars within the restrictive British loading gauge.

### Diesel locomotives

| Class | Wheel arrangement | Power kW | Speed km/h | Weight tonnes | No in service | First built | Builders Mechanical | Engine | Transmission |
|---|---|---|---|---|---|---|---|---|---|
| 08 | C | 298 | 24 | 50 | 15 | 1955 | BR | EE 6KT | E EE |
| 47 | Co-Co | 1,550 | 120 | 120 | 14 | 1963 | BR, Brush | Sulzer 12LDA28C | E Brush |
| 57 | Co-Co | 1,507 | 120 | 121 | 12 | 1997* | BR, Brush | GM 645-12E3 | E Brush |
| 66/5 | Co-Co | 1,850 | 120 | 64 | 65** | 2000 | GM | GM 12N-710G3B | E GM |
| 66/6 | Co-Co | 1,850 | 105 | 121 | 12** | 2000 | GM | GM 12N-710G3B | E GM |

\* Rebuilt and re-engined by Brush
\*\* Including examples on order

### Electric locomotives

| Class | Wheel arrangement | Power kW continuous | Speed km/h | Weight tonnes | No in service | First built | Builders Mechanical | Electrical |
|---|---|---|---|---|---|---|---|---|
| 86 | Bo-Bo | 2,680 | 120 | 83 | 30 | 1965 | BR | AEI |
| 90 | Bo-Bo | 3,730 | 120 | 84.5 | 10 | 1987 | BREL | GEC |

**UPDATED**

---

# Gatwick Express Ltd

A subsidiary of National Express Group
Gatwick Express Ltd
52 Grosvenor Gardens, London SW1W 0AU
Tel: (+44 20) 79 73 50 00   Fax: (+44 20) 79 73 50 48
Web: http://www.gatwickexpress.co.uk

## Key personnel
Managing Director (acting): Nick Brown
Deputy Managing and Finance Director: David Stretch

## Political background
The Gatwick Express franchise was won by the National Express Group in 1996 and was the only one let by the Franchising Director that did not require a subsidy from the outset. The franchisee paid a premium (in 1996 prices) of £4.6 million in the first year, increasing to £22.6 million in 2010-11.

## Passenger operations
Gatwick Express operates a shuttle service over the 43 km route between Gatwick Airport (London's second largest – Heathrow is the biggest) and the terminus at Victoria in central London. The service works on a quarter-hourly frequency throughout the day, and hourly throughout the night. The trip takes 30 minutes.

In April 2000 Gatwick Express and Heathrow Express (qv) formed a marketing alliance, Airport Express, to promote the two companies' services to the travel industry. In December 2000 Stansted Express, part of the West Anglia Great Northern franchise (qv) joined the alliance.

| Traffic (million) | 1998-99 | 1999-2000 | 2000-01 |
|---|---|---|---|
| Passenger journeys | 4.5 | 4.4 | 4.7 |
| Passenger-km | 197.1 | 189.7 | 201.2 |
| Train-km | 2.4 | 2.57 | 2.57 |

*Gatwick Express Class 460 electric trainset en route from London Victoria to Gatwick Airport at Coulsdon*
2002/0524922

### Gatwick Express electric multiple-units

| Class | Cars per unit | Motor cars per unit | Motored axles /car | Power /motor kW | Speed km/h | Units in service | First built | Builders Mechanical | Electrical |
|---|---|---|---|---|---|---|---|---|---|
| 460 | 8 | 4 | 2 | 270 | 160 | 8 | 2000 | Alstom | Alstom |

## Traction and rolling stock
Gatwick Express operations are mainly undertaken with a fleet of eight eight-car Class 460 750 V DC third rail electric trainsets supplied by Alstom to their Juniper design and leased from Porterbrook. The first was handed over on July 2000, although final commissioning of the fleet was still in progress in mid-2002. This left some services still in the hands of the Class 73/2 electro-diesel locomotives and push-pull formations of Mk 2 coaches which were employed before the Class 460s were delivered.

**UPDATED**

---

# GB Railfreight

15-25 Artillery Lane, London E1 7HA
Tel: (+44 20) 79 04 33 94   Fax: (+44 20) 73 75 25 94
Web: http://www.gbrailfreight.com

## Key personnel
Chief Executive: Jeremy Long
Managing Director: John Smith
Executive Director: Max D Steinkopf

## Organisation
GB Railfreight was established as an open access freight-operating subsidiary of GB Railways Group plc, which holds the Anglia Railways (qv) passenger train contract. The company obtained its train-operating licence in mid-2000, shortly before securing an eight-year contract to haul infrastructure materials and maintenance trains for Railtrack to and from work sites in the east of England. The Railtrack contract commenced on 31 March 2001. In 2002, the company also secured contracts for general freight and container flows from Felixstowe to Selby and the West Midlands respectively.

## Traction and rolling stock
GB Railways initially ordered seven Class 66/7 locomotives from General Motors in Canada. Financed by HSBC Rail, they were delivered in February 2001. An additional five similar locomotives were delivered by General Motors in June 2002.

**UPDATED**

*GB Railfreight Class 66/7 locomotives seen at their handover at General Motors' London, Ontario plant in January 2001 (Philip Sutton/Rail Express)*
2001/0103975

## GB Railways

GB Railways Group plc
15-25 Artillery Lane, London E1 7HA
Tel: (+44 20) 74 65 90 13   Fax: (+44 20) 73 75 35 94
e-mail: info@gbrailways.com
Web: http://www.gbrailways.com

### Key personnel
Chairman: Lord Sheppard of Didgemere
Deputy Chairman and Chief Executive: Jeremy Long
Directors: Michael Schabas; Max D Steinkopf

### Corporate development
GB Railways was established to bid for rail franchises let under the 1993 Railways Act, successfully winning a seven-year three-month contract to run the Anglia Railways (qv) franchise from January 1997. In September 2000 GB Railways, in a joint venture with Renaissance Railways, launched Hull Trains (qv) to provide a service between London King's Cross and Hull. In April 2001 the company's freight subsidiary, GB Railfreight (qv) commenced operations, making GB Railways the only company to undertake both passenger and freight operations on the Railtrack network.

Together with the East West Rail Consortium (EWRC), a grouping of 30 local authorities and other stakeholders, GB Railways has produced proposals to develop and upgrade the route from the important east coast port of Felixstowe, the UK's largest container port, to Oxford, including the restoration of an abandoned 24 km section between Cambridge and Bedford. The line would carry both passenger and freight traffic. In March 2001 GB Railways announced that it and EWRC had selected Skanska Construction Group as the preferred bidder to develop a joint special purpose company to seek parliamentary approval to develop the scheme, at an estimated cost of £250 million. Completion of the project is anticipated in 2006, from when the upgraded line would be operated as part of the Railtrack network.

In December 2000 GB Railways, through its subsidiary GB Railways Eesti AS, signed an agreement to purchase the assets of Estonian rail operator Edelaraudtee AS (qv), which operates passenger and freight services in the southwest of the country.

## The Go-Ahead Group

The Go-Ahead Group plc, Level 16, Cale Cross House, Pilgrim Street, Newcastle upon Tyne NE1 6SU
Tel: (+44 191) 232 31 23   (+44 191) 221 03 15
Web: http://www.go-ahead.com

### Key personnel
Group Chief Executive: Martin Ballinger
Group Deputy Chief Executive: Chris Moyes
Chief Executive, Rail: Keith Ludeman

### Political background
The Go-Ahead Group plc originated from the management buyout in 1987 of the Northern bus company. The company remains a major bus operator, especially in London and northeast England, and subsequently acquired stakes in two rail franchises created by the break-up of British Rail: initially a shareholding of 65 per cent is held in Victory Holdings, which held the Thames Trains franchise (qv), full control being taken in March 1998; and Go-Ahead is a joint venture partner with the French transport group, VIA-GTI, in GOVIA Ltd, which holds the franchise for Thameslink Rail (qv). In 2000 GOVIA Ltd was named preferred bidder to take over the Connex South Central franchise, which it planned to rename New Southern Railway.

## Great North Eastern Railway

A subsidiary of Sea Containers Ltd
Main Headquarters Building, Station Rise, York YO1 6HT
Tel: (+44 1904) 65 30 22   Fax: (+44 1904) 65 33 92
Web: http://www.gner.co.uk

### Key personnel
Chief Executive: Christopher Garnett
Chief Operating Officer: Jonathan Metcalfe
Directors
  Marketing and Sales: Lysanne McCallion
  Production: Richard McClean
  Human Resources: Mike Gooddie
  Finance: Philip Pacey

### Political background
Under the arrangements put in place by the 1993 Railways Act, Great Northern Railway, a subsidiary of the shipping and hotels group Sea Containers, was awarded the franchise for the InterCity East Coast route in March 1996; the trading name of the line was changed later that year to Great North Eastern Railway. The franchise runs for seven years, with subsidy declining from £67.3 million in the first year to zero in the seventh year.

### Passenger operations
GNER operates intercity services on a 1,518 km network out of King's Cross terminus in London to West Yorkshire, the North East of England and Scotland.

| Traffic (million) | 1998-99 | 1999-00 | 2000-01 |
|---|---|---|---|
| Passenger journeys | 13.9 | 15.9 | 13.6 |
| Passenger-km | 3,490 | 3,953 | 3,933 |
| Train-km | 17.4 | 17.9 | 19.0 |

*GNER HST diesel high-speed trainset forming an Aberdeen–London King's Cross service, photographed after crossing the Forth Bridge, north of Edinburgh (Colin Boocock)* 2002/0524950

### Traction and rolling stock
GNER operates 31 InterCity 225 electric trains owned by HSBC Rail and nine diesel InterCity 125s (HSTs) owned by Angel Train Contracts. Mid-life refurbishing of the diesel trains has been completed. Class 91 InterCity 225 locomotives have been undergoing refurbishment by a consortium of Bombardier and Alstom aimed at improving their reliability. The first example to be treated was handed over in February 2001; the programme was due to be completed by the end of 2002. In July 1997, Sea Containers bought 12 Mk 3 sleeping cars which had been in use on charter trains; these have been refurbished and fitted with seats, to provide an extra vehicle in GNER's InterCity 125 trains.

From the May 2000 timetable change, GNER introduced Class 373/2 Eurostar sets on domestic services between London Kings Cross and York in a move intended to increase capacity. Built for international services from UK regional centres to Brussels and Paris, which were not implemented, the trains had been stored out of use. The three trains required for daily service are drawn from a pool of four under a three-year 'wet' lease contract with Eurostar (UK) Ltd. Two of the sets in use by GNER carry the company's blue livery, while the other two retain Eurostar colours but without branding.

*UPDATED*

## Heathrow Express

4th Floor, Macmillan House, Paddington Station, London W2 1FT
Tel: (+44 20) 73 13 43 52   Fax: (+44 20) 79 22 43 25
Web: http://www.heathrowexpress.co.uk

### Key personnel
Chairman, Heathrow Express and BAA Rail:
  Vernon Murphy
Managing Director: Brian Raven
Commercial Director: Jeremy Job
Customer Services Director: Malcolm MacKenzie

### Passenger operations
Heathrow Express provides a dedicated airport express service between London's principal airport, Heathrow, and the rail terminus at Paddington. The company is wholly owned by airport operator BAA.

The exit from Paddington is electrified at 25 kV AC. At Heathrow Junction, 19 km out of Paddington, a 7 km line owned by Heathrow Express runs to the airport. The line is double track to a station under the Central Terminal Area, and then single track to a station under Terminal Four; if a fifth terminal is built at the airport, another line will be built to T5 from the CTA, with trains splitting for Terminals 4 and 5 from the CTA.

The service comprises four trains an hour in each direction travelling at a maximum of 160 km/h, with the Paddington-Heathrow journey taking 15 minutes. Full baggage check-in services are provided at Paddington.

### Traction and rolling stock
Rolling stock consists of 14 Class 332 four-car emu trains supplied by Siemens Transportation Systems, with CAF of Spain undertaking mechanical construction. Siemens also undertakes maintenance on a contract basis at a purpose-built depot at Old Oak Common.

In July 2001 Heathrow Express ordered an additional five intermediate trailer cars from CAF to strengthen members of the existing fleet. Due to enter service in late 2002, the new cars will allow five- and nine-car trains to be operated.

A rolling refurbishment programme commenced in 2001, introducing safety improvements and enhanced passenger amenities.

*UPDATED*

# RAILWAY SYSTEMS/UK

## Hull Trains

Premier House, Ferensway, Hull HU1 3UF
Tel: (+44 1482) 21 57 45  Fax: (+44 1482) 21 57 45

### Key personnel
Managing Director: Jim Morgan

### Corporate development
Hull Trains is a joint venture established between GB Railways (qv) (80 per cent) and Renaissance Railways (20 per cent) to run passenger services between London and Hull under a four-year open access agreement with Railtrack. Services between the two cities commenced in November 2000 and are operated without subsidy.

### Passenger operations
Hull Trains' timetable provides four weekday and one Sunday return services between London King's Cross and Hull, serving Grantham, Doncaster, Selby and Brough.

### Traction and rolling stock
Services are provided using examples of Anglia Railways' fleet of eight Class 170/2 Turbostar dmus.

**UPDATED**

## Island Line

Island Line Ltd
St John's Road Station, Ryde, Isle of Wight PO33 2BA
Tel: (+44 1983) 81 25 91  Fax: (+44 1983) 81 78 79
e-mail: comments@island-line.co.uk
Web: http://www.island-line.co.uk

### Key personnel
Managing Director: Andrew Haines
General Manager: Steve Wade

### Political background
Under the arrangements put in place by the 1993 Railways Act, the franchise to run operations on the 13.6 km railway on the Isle of Wight was let in October 1996 to Stagecoach Holdings plc (qv), a bus operator.

The franchise was let for a term of five years. Stagecoach will receive from the Franchising Director support, in 1996 prices, of £2.012 million in the first full financial year of the franchise, declining to £1.751 million in the last year.

In 2001, a two-year extension to Stagecoach's franchise was concluded with the Strategic Rail Authority, extending the contract to September 2003.

### Passenger operations
Island Line operates passenger services on a 13.6 km line between Ryde and Shanklin on the eastern coast of the Isle of Wight.

### Island Line electric multiple-units

| Class | Cars per unit | Motor cars per unit | Motored axles/car | Power/motor kW | Speed km/h | Cars in service | First built | Builders Mechanical | Electrical |
|---|---|---|---|---|---|---|---|---|---|
| 483* | 2 | 2 | 2 | 130 | 75 | 12 | 1938 | Met-Cam | GEC |

* Built for London Transport, converted for Isle of Wight 1989-90

| Traffic (million) | 1998-99 | 1999-2000 | 2000-01 |
|---|---|---|---|
| Passenger journeys | 0.7 | 0.7 | 0.8 |
| Passenger-km | 5.3 | 5.8 | 5.9 |
| Train-km | 0.29 | 0.29 | 0.30 |

### Traction and rolling stock
Island Line is operated with former London Underground electric trains leased from HSBC Rail.

**UPDATED**

## London & Continental Railways

3rd Floor, 183 Eversholt Street, London NW1 1AY
Tel: (+44 20) 73 91 43 00  Fax: (+44 20) 73 91 44 01
e-mail: helpline@ctrl.co.uk
Web: http://www.ctrl.co.uk

### Key personnel
Chairman: John Neerhout Jr
Head of Public Affairs: Bernard Gambrill

### Subsidiary companies
Union Railways (South) Ltd
Union Railways (North) Ltd
London & Continental Stations & Property Ltd
Eurostar (UK) Ltd

### Political background
London & Continental Railways is the consortium which in 1996 won the build-and-operate concession for the Channel Tunnel Rail Link (CTRL), the high-speed line from the Channel Tunnel to London, with operation of the UK's share of Eurostar services intended to provide a revenue stream during the project's construction. Revised plans for the scheme were announced by the government in June 1998 following the collapse of LCR's financing proposals. These provided for the line to be built in two phases by LCR, with Railtrack taking over the first phase upon completion and having first option to take over the second phase. Railtrack subsequently gave up this second phase option. The operation of Eurostar services passed to a management consortium which includes British Airways and National Express (see entry for Eurostar (UK) Ltd).

### New lines
In December 1996, parliamentary approval was granted for the building of a new high-speed route between London and the Channel Tunnel. The new route, then planned to open in 2003, would reduce the journey time between London and Paris via the tunnel by some 35 minutes to around 2 hours 15 minutes and that to Brussels to 2 hours.

Construction of the first section of the new route formally began in October 1998 and is being project-managed by Rail Link Engineering (RLE), a joint venture of LCR's four engineering shareholders (Bechtel, Ove Arup, Sir William Halcrow and Systra). Financing for this first section is being assisted by a £200 million loan from the European Investment Bank, which also advanced £100 million for the design phase of the line.

Of the new route's 108 km, 26 km will be in tunnel, the main structure being a 20 km tunnel on the approaches to St Pancras. The line includes junctions on to the 750 V DC existing route near Ashford so that international trains from the high-speed line can serve Ashford International station on the existing route; non-stop trains will be able to bypass Ashford. Another link to the existing network near Gravesend will allow trains to access the Waterloo terminal on the south side of London. The government has selected Ebbsfleet, in north Kent, as a site for an intermediate station, and LCR also plans to develop a new international station at Stratford in east London. LCR plans a link from the high-speed line to the West Coast main line, which would permit services from British provincial cities on the West Coast main line to the Continent.

Under the terms of the government's agreement with LCR, the Franchise Director would have access to a number of paths on the high-speed line for express commuter services to St Pancras. Between Ashford and Ebbsfleet two paths have been set aside in the off-peak, four in the peak; from Ebbsfleet to St Pancras, four paths in the off-peak and eight in the peak have been reserved for the Franchising Director's use. Connex South Eastern

*This bridge will carry the Channel Tunnel Rail Link across the River Medway, which is also traversed at this location by the M2 motorway*  
2002/0122559

(qv) will be offered first refusal on operation of these services.

The first phase (67 km) will run from the Channel Tunnel to Fawkham Junction, near Dartford, connecting with the existing network to Waterloo International terminal. Work started in October 1998 for completion by 2003. Railtrack has agreed to purchase this phase for its construction cost of £1.9 billion ('out-turn' cost). Eurostar journey times will be reduced by 15 minutes.

While, at 42 km, phase two of the project is shorter, it is more complex, with extensive tunnelling and major works at St Pancras to create a new London terminal. This is reflected in the out-turn cost of £3.3 billion. Construction of this section began in 2001 for completion by the end of 2006. The public sector contribution for both phases is a total of £3.1 billion. This second phase will cut a further 20 minutes from Eurostar journey times from London to the Channel Tunnel.

Waterloo International currently provides the London terminal for Eurostar services. At the second London station for international services at St Pancras, LCR intends to make full use of the magnificent St Pancras train shed, designed by the nineteenth century engineer William Barlow, and St Pancras Chambers, designed by Sir Gilbert Scott. Six platforms in the train shed will be given over to international services. Platforms will be built outside the trainshed for Midland Mainline and CTRL domestic services. Two low-level platforms will be provided on the west side of the station for Thameslink services, to replace the present cramped station at King's Cross Thameslink.

The CTRL station at Stratford, east London, also part of phase two of the line due to open in 2007, will provide an intermediate stop for international and domestic services using the Channel Tunnel Rail Link. Two island platforms, largely underground, are planned. The new station will have a wide range of connectional opportunities with domestic main line, London Underground and Docklands Light Railway services.

*UPDATED*

## Mendip Rail

Mendip Rail Limited, The Pavilion, Torr Works, East Cranmore, Shepton Mallet, Somerset BA4 4SQ
Tel: (+44 1373) 45 67 22   Fax: (+44 1749) 88 01 41
e-mail: alan.taylor@mendip-rail.co.uk

### Key personnel
Managing Director: Alan Taylor
Commercial Manager: Alan Freemantle

### Freight operations
Mendip Rail provides transportation services in conjunction with English, Welsh and Scottish Railway for two aggregates companies, Foster Yeoman and Hanson Aggregates, to manage the rail movement of stone from the company's quarries in the west of England. Mendip Rail owns nine 2,460 kW General Motors-built Class 59 diesel locomotives, plus a fleet of 413 wagons. In 1998, Mendip Rail conveyed 6.13 million tonnes, compared with 5.7 million in 1997. In 1999, the company employed 25 staff.

In 1997, one of Mendip's Class 59s was dispatched to Germany, where it works in a joint venture with DB AG (German Railways) on the haulage of stone delivered by ship from Scotland to northwest German ports and then transported by rail for the reconstruction of Berlin.

*Mendip Rail Class 59 locomotive in the latest Foster Yeoman livery near Westbury with aggregates for west London* (Phil Marshall)   0063646

Recent contracts cover the movement of 2 million tonnes of construction material to Sevington, Kent for the Channel Tunnel Rail Link, on behalf of Foster Yeoman (October 1999 – October 2001) and 500,000 tonnes of material to Allington, Kent for Hanson Aggregates (March 2000 – March 2001).

In mid-2000, Mendip Rail became a licensed non-passenger train operating company.

## Midland Mainline

Midland Mainline Ltd
Midland House, Nelson Street, Derby DE1 2SA
Tel: (+44 1332) 26 20 40   Fax: (+44 1332) 26 25 61
e-mail: feedback@midlandmainline.com
Web: http://www.midlandmainline.com

### Key personnel
Directors
  Managing: Alan Wilson
  Train Services: Heidi Mottram
  Sales and Marketing: Malcolm Brown
  Projects: Peter Garrood
  Finance: Sharon Stone
  Station Services and Human Resources:
    Barry Brown

### Political background
Under the arrangements put in place by the 1993 Railways Act, the Midland Mainline franchise was let to the National Express Group (qv) in April 1996 for a 10-year term.

A subsidy of £16.5 million was to be paid by the Franchising Director in the first year, with decreasing amounts thereafter until Year 5, when the franchise was forecast to turn profitable. In the second half of the franchise there were to be payments to the Franchising Director by the franchisee, with the premium being around £10 million in Year 10.

In August 2000, NEG was awarded a two-year extension of the franchise, until April 2008. As part of the negotiations which resulted in this extension, premium payments due to be made under the original franchise agreement would be retained by Midland Mainline for investment in its network.

### Passenger operations
Midland Mainline operates intercity passenger services on a 708 km route network running out of London St Pancras station to Leicester, Derby, Nottingham, Sheffield, Leeds, Burton-on-Trent, Matlock and Scarborough.

| Traffic (million) | 1998-99 | 1999-2000 | 2000-01 |
| --- | --- | --- | --- |
| Passenger journeys | 6.8 | 8.2 | 8.6 |
| Passenger-km | 934.3 | 1,075.8 | 1,096.7 |
| Train-km | 5.6 | 9.5 | 11.4 |

### Improvements to existing lines
In January 2001, Midland Mainline received planning approval to develop a new East Midlands Parkway station close to the M1 motorway and East Midlands Airport.

### Traction and rolling stock
Midland Mainline leases 13 HST diesel trainsets from the Porterbrook Leasing Company. Refurbishment of these by Adtranz was completed in early 1998.

In June 1997, the company ordered 13 two-car Class 170/1 Adtranz 'Turbostar' diesel multiple-units with finance from Porterbrook; the deal included maintenance of the new trains by the manufacturer. In October 1997, a further four two-car units of the same type were ordered. In April 2000, 10 intermediate cars were ordered to strengthen some existing Class 170/1 units to three-car sets. Since May 1999, the new dmus have been used to

*Midland Mainline Class 170/1 dmu at Derby forming the inaugural Barnsley–London St Pancras service in May 1999* (Colin Boocock)   2001/0099140

provide frequent services to smaller intermediate stations on the route, allowing an increase in frequency to principal stations using HSTs. A hub at Leicester provides an interchange between dmus and HSTs. Deployment of the additional trains amounts to a 97 per cent increase in services.

In February 2001, Midland Mainline placed an order with Bombardier Transportation for 127 diesel-electric multiple-unit cars based on the design of the Class 220 and 221 Voyager and Super Voyager trains supplied to Virgin CrossCountry. To be designated Class 222 and branded 'Meridian' units, the trains are to be configured as seven nine-car and 16 four-car sets. Finance is being provided by HSBC Rail (UK) Ltd and delivery is due to take place between the second quarter of 2004 and January 2005. The contract with Bombardier Transportation also includes maintenance provision initially for four years, with an option to extend this to 15 years. Maintenance is to be undertaken at a new depot at Beighton, Sheffield, at a recommissioned facility at Cricklewood, north London, and at Bombardier's Central Rivers depot near Burton-on-Trent. Delivery of the Class 222 units will enable the Class 170/1 dmus to be transferred to other National Express franchises.

Also in 2001, Midland Mainline indicated that it was to overhaul and refurbish its 13 HST diesel trainsets, with some re-engining likely. A backlog in the maintenance of this fleet led to the introduction of a daily locomotive-hauled diagram in February 2001, using hired traction and rolling stock.

## MTL

MTL Services plc
Edge Lane, Liverpool L7 9LL

### Political background
As MTL Trust Holdings Ltd, MTL Services plc was a bus operator which took advantage of the 1993 Railways Act to enter the rail industry, winning the Regional Railways North East and Merseyrail Electrics franchises. In February 2000, the company was acquired by Arriva plc (qv).

## National Express Group

National Express Group plc
75 Davies Street, London W1K 5HT
Tel: (+44 20) 75 29 20 00    Fax: (+44 20) 75 29 21 00
e-mail: info@natex.co.uk
Web: http://www.nationalexpressgroup.com

### Key personnel
Chief Operating Officer: Ray O'Toole

### Trains Division
Midland House, Nelson Street, Derby DE1 2SA

Chief Executive: Ian Buchan
Train Retailing Director: Mark Powles

### Political background
National Express Group was a coach, bus and airport operation which took advantage of the 1993 Railways Act, winning five out of the 25 passenger franchises on offer, making it the largest single operator. The franchises won were Gatwick Express, Midland Mainline, Central Trains, North London Railways (now Silverlink) and ScotRail; the group is also a member of the consortium contracted to manage Eurostar international services following the failure of the London & Continental Railways (of which National Express was a shareholder) concession to build and operate the Channel Tunnel Rail Link.

In July 2000, National Express announced a takeover bid for Prism Rail, which was operating four franchises: c2c (formerly LTS Rail); Valley Lines (formerly Cardiff Railway); Wales & West; and West Anglia Great Northern. The offer, which was subject to approval by the Rail Regulator and shareholders, valued Prism Rail at £166 million. From October 2001, the Wales & West franchise and certain adjoining franchises were restructured to form two 'managerial units': Wales & Borders Trains, and Wessex Trains. As part of this process, the Valley Lines franchise was integrated with the new Wales & Borders Trains managerial unit.

The company has established a national call centre for its Trains Division. Located in Sheffield, the centre handles internet ticket sales and oversees development of commercial retailing strategy.

*UPDATED*

## Northern Ireland Railways (NIR)

Northern Ireland Railways Co Limited
Central Station, East Bridge Street, Belfast BT1 3PB
Tel: (+44 1232) 89 94 00    Fax: (+44 1232) 89 94 01
Web: http://www.translink.co.uk

### Key personnel
Managing Director: Edward Hesketh
Directors
  Finance: S Armstrong
  Human Resources: Alan Mercer
  Operations: Andy Watt
  Technical: Mal McGreevy
  Marketing: Ciaran Rugan
Manager, Railway Services: Seamus Scallon

Gauge: 1,600 mm
Route length: 357 km

### Political background
In 2000 consultants Arthur D Little presented a strategic safety review commissioned by Translink that suggested that investments of £183 million were required to restore the NIR system to full effectiveness. Key areas of expenditure recommended by the report included: £72.3 million on rolling stock; £67.2 million on track and structures; and £26.6 million on signalling and telecommunications. The study prompted the UK government to establish a Task Force to consider the findings. The interim report of the Task Force found that there were three main options for the network and presented these to the Northern Ireland Assembly in September 2000. The options were: mothballing the network apart from the Belfast–Dublin route; consolidating the existing system with priority given to commuter lines; and enhancing and expanding the network. No clear route forward had been chosen by the Assembly by early 2002, although steps to upgrade the rolling stock fleet (see 'Traction and rolling stock') suggested that abandonment of most of the network was unlikely.

### Organisation
Northern Ireland Railways is part of Translink, a state-owned corporation which manages public transport in the province.

| Traffic (million) | 1998-99 | 1999-2000 | 2000-01 |
|---|---|---|---|
| Passenger journeys | 5.8 | 6.0 | 6.0 |

*Class 8450 demu at Belfast Great Victoria Street with a Bangor–Londonderry service (Colin Boocock)*
2001/0109876

### Diesel locomotives

| Class | Wheel arrangement | Power kW | Speed Km/h | Weight tonnes | No in service | First built | Mechanical | Builders Engine | Transmission |
|---|---|---|---|---|---|---|---|---|---|
| 201 | Co-Co | 2,390 | 143 | 112 | 2 | 1995 | GM | EMD 12-710 G3B | E GM |
| 111 | Co-Co | 1,678 | 129 | 102 | 3 | 1980 | GM | EMD 12-645E3B | E GM |

### Diesel railcars or multiple-units

| Class | Cars per unit | Motor cars per unit | Motored axles/car | Output/motor kW | Speed km/h | Units in service | First built | Builders Mechanical | Engine | Transmission |
|---|---|---|---|---|---|---|---|---|---|---|
| 80 | 3 | 1 | 2 | 175 | 112 | 21 | 1974 | BREL | EE 4SRKT | E EE |
| 8450 | 3 | 1 | 2 | 175 | 112 | 9 | 1985 | BREL | EE 4SRKT | E EE |

### Passenger operations
NIR operates the cross-border intercity 'Enterprise' service jointly with Irish Rail between Belfast and Dublin. This was relaunched in October 1997. It also operates services within the province from Belfast on routes to Bangor, Larne and Londonderry.

### Freight operations
A limited freight service operates in Northern Ireland, in the form of cross-border traffic worked to and from Adelaide yard in Belfast by Irish Rail. A flow of timber traffic from Londonderry to Dublin also commenced in 1999.

## New lines

A £29 million Belfast cross-harbour rail link incorporating the longest bridge in Ireland was opened in 1994. The route comprises a 2 km single-track line, 1,424 m of it on viaduct, between Yorkgate and Belfast Central stations.

The project represented a significant advance for NIR, as it allowed the railway to consolidate all its passenger activities on Belfast Central station; before construction of the bridge, Larne services terminated at Belfast Yorkgate, on the other side of the river Lagan.

Upgrading to passenger standards of the line from Bleach Green to Antrim to capitalise on the cross-harbour link was completed in June 2001, cutting Belfast–Londonderry journey times by some 20 minutes and permitting operation of through Dublin–Londonderry services without reversal. This led to the abandonment of regular passenger services over the Lisburn–Antrim line.

## Improvements to existing lines

The 9.7 km Coleraine–Portrush branch was closed for a three-month period during 2000 for complete renewal of track.

Track on the Belfast–Bangor line was renewed in 2001-02.

An integrated rail and bus station was opened in Bangor in April 2001.

Major refurbishment of Belfast Central station was due to be completed in 2002.

## Traction and rolling stock

NIR has five diesel-electric locomotives, 30 dmus and 36 passenger cars. Two of the locomotives are Class 201 2,390 kW JT42HCW Co-Co General Motors diesel-electric locomotives, NIR's contribution to a pool of four such locomotives jointly maintained with Irish Rail for Enterprise cross-border services. A pool of coaches was also ordered from De Dietrich by the two organisations for this service (see Irish Rail entry for details).

In 2001 Porterbrook Leasing concluded an agreement to make available to NIR eight former Gatwick Express vehicles. These were refurbished and regauged in Great Britain prior to transfer to NIR, where they are to be powered by Class 111 locomotives on Newry–Belfast services.

In 2002, NIR's York Road, Belfast workshops were refurbishing the railway's 14 De Dietrich coaches used on the Belfast–Dublin Enterprise service.

In 2002 NIR placed an order with CAF in Spain for 23 three-car dmus to replace the Class 80 vehicles. They are due to enter service in 2004.

## Signalling and telecommunications

NIR uses two signalling systems. Centralised traffic control (CTC), with entry-exit colourlight route setting panels, controls 215 km.

## Track

**Rail:** 113 A FB (135 km); 95 lb BH (72 km); 50 kg FB (171 km)

**Crossties (sleepers):** Prestressed concrete and timber, spaced 1,150/km in plain and 1,300/km in curved track.

**Fastenings:** Pandrol PR401
**Min curvature radius:** 180 m
**Max gradient:** 1.25%
**Max axleload:** 18 tonnes

## Railtrack

Railtrack plc
Railtrack House, Euston Square, London NW1 2EE
Tel: (+44 20) 75 57 80 00   Fax: (+44 20) 75 57 90 00
Web: http://www.railtrack.co.uk

### Key personnel

Chairman: John Robinson
Chief Executive: Steve Marshall
Chief Engineer: Andrew McNaughton
Directors
    Operations Service: Derek Holmes
    Safety and Environment: Chris Leah
    Technical: Richard Middleton
    Business Development: Sebastian Bull
    Corporate Affairs: Sue Clark
    Human Resources: Deborah Page
    Information Systems: Thiaga Kathirasoo
    Investment Delivery: Robbie Burns
    Network Development: Nicholas Pollard
    Property: John O'Brien
    Regulation and Government: John Smith
Head of Freight: Barbara Barnes
Head of Major Stations: Deborah Richards
Head of Passenger Business: Richard Wightman
Company Secretary and Solicitor: Simon Osborne
Zone Directors
    Scotland: Janette Anderson
        Tel: (+44 141) 332 98 11
    North West: Mike Cowman
        Tel: (+44 161) 228 88 88
    London North Eastern: Robin Gisby
        Tel: (+44 1904) 65 30 22
    Midlands: Richard Fearn
        Tel: (+44 121) 345 35 59
    Great Western: John Curley
        Tel: (+44 1793) 51 52 08
    East Anglia: Ray Price
        Tel: (+44 20) 79 04 40 00
    Southern: Michael Holden
        Tel: (+44 20) 79 28 51 51

Gauge: 1,435 mm
Route length: 16,536 km
Electrification: 2,970 km at 25 kV, 50 Hz AC overhead; 1,958 km at 750 V DC third rail

### Political background

Railtrack was set up in the reforms engendered by the 1993 Railways Act. It is the rail infrastructure authority on the UK mainland, owning the track, stations and signals and controlling the timetabling of trains. Its income comes from the train paths it sells to train operating companies; charging policy is subject to scrutiny by the Rail Regulator. The charging regime for the period 2001-06 was agreed between Railtrack and the Rail Regulator in August 2000.

Railtrack was floated on the London Stock Exchange in May 1996, in an exercise which raised some £1.9 billion for the UK government.

A condition of Railtrack's licence to operate the national rail infrastructure is that it is required to publish an annual Network Management Statement in which it records its achievements and sets out its plans and aims

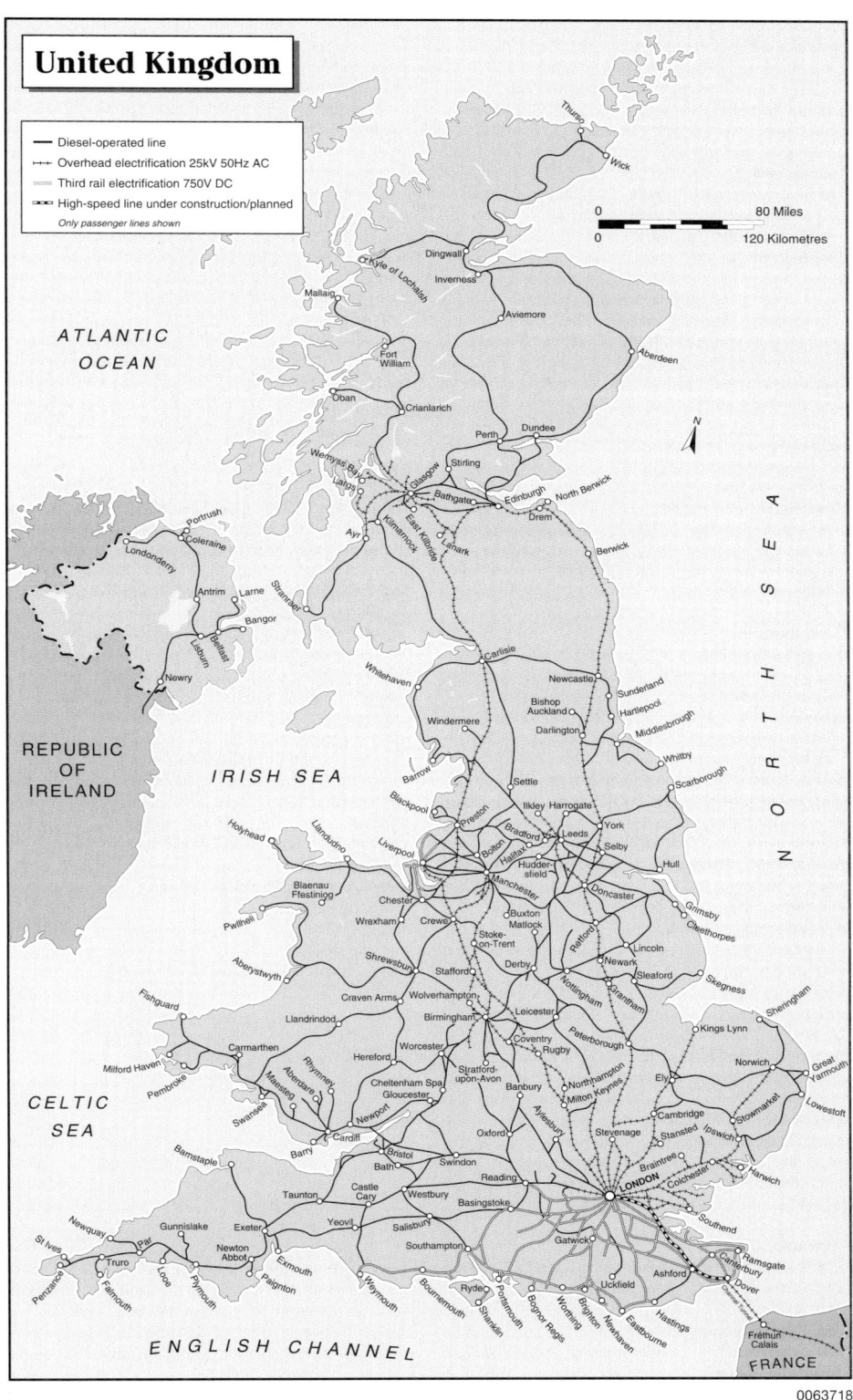

# RAILWAY SYSTEMS/UK

to develop the system.

In a major development in October 2001, Railtrack ceased trading as a public limited company when the government refused to meet requests from the company for further state funding and placed the company in administration. The government stated that it intended to replace Railtrack with a not-for-profit company limited by guarantee. Bids to take over Railtrack were expected both from the government and from private sector groups.

### Safety
Railtrack's relationships with government and its customers, and public perception of it, has in recent years been dominated by safety-related issues. In particular, three accidents resulting in passenger fatalities, Southall (September 1997, seven deaths), Ladbrooke Grove/ Paddington (October 1999, 31 deaths) and Hatfield (October 2000, four deaths), have resulted in the introduction of major safety programmes aimed at reducing the risk of such catastrophic accidents.

In the case of the first two events, the primary cause of each was determined to have been a signal or signals being passed at danger (SPAD). In response, Railtrack launched a nationwide programme to install a train protection warning system (TPWS), with some 11,000 signals to be equipped by December 2002. Effective at lower speeds, TPWS initiates train braking if a SPAD occurs. In addition, extra controls have been implemented at signals with a history of SPADs. In the longer term, the UK rail industry is to continue the examination and development of European Rail Traffic Management System (ERTMS) technology on lines on which trains operate at speeds of 160 km/h or above.

The Hatfield accident was caused by a broken rail, precipitated by gauge corner cracking. The consequences for the UK rail network were severe, with speed restrictions imposed at many locations while the extent of gauge corner cracking was assessed. Railtrack subsequently implemented a national recovery programme involving extensive rail replacement covering some 800 km of track and 1,100 switches and crossings. The network was returned to full normal timetable operation in May 2001.

The extensive examination of the network that followed the Hatfield accident revealed that the system was in poorer condition than previously thought, leading to an extensive review of the company's approach to infrastructure engineering.

In January 2000, a wholly owned not-for-profit subsidiary company, Railway Safety (qv), was set up to take over most of the activities of Railtrack's former Safety and Standards directorate.

### Organisation
Operationally, Railtrack is organised as seven territorial regions, or zones, each with its own director and management team. Each zone is responsible for placing contracts for the maintenance and renewal of infrastructure within its territory.

At a central level, the business is managed in three distinct areas: core network operations, covering the safe operation of the system and the quality and effectiveness of its assets; enhancements and major programmes, managing new network developments; and property and new business, concerned with optimising Railtrack's property portfolio, including using this to increase rail usage, and the development of new activities such as joint ventures in ticket retailing.

Railtrack's assets include around 2,500 station. Most are leased to train operating companies but 14 major facilities are owned and managed by the company. They are: Birmingham New Street; Edinburgh Waverley; Gatwick Airport; Glasgow Central; Leeds City; London Bridge (London); London Charing Cross; London Euston; London King's Cross; London Liverpool Street; London Paddington; London Victoria; London Waterloo; and Manchester Piccadilly. Connections are provided to more than 1,000 freight terminals and 90 maintenance depots are leased to train operators and contractors.

In 2001, Railtrack employed over 11,000 staff, some 50 per cent of which were signalling staff.

### Finance
In 2000-01, Railtrack recorded turnover of £2,476 million (£2,547 the previous year) and operating profits of £261 million (£363 million). Revenue from franchised passenger train operators totalled £2,089 million, while revenue from freight operators stood at £162 million. Rental income from property generated an additional £146 million. Operating costs for 2000-01 were £2,215 million. Production and management expenses accounted for £568 million, joint industry costs were £221 million, infrastructure maintenance costs were £706 million and depreciation stood at £720 million. In addition to these costs, Railtrack reported exceptional items for the year totalling £733 million. Of this, £644 million was for performance and other payments to train operating companies, additional operating costs and additional depreciation arising from the Hatfield accident. In May 2001, after conclusion of Railtrack's 2000-01 financial year, the company agreed to make compensation payments totalling over £100 million to Virgin Group in respect of service disruption following the Hatfield accident.

In April 2001, in return for accelerated funding of £1.5 billion, Railtrack agreed with the Strategic Rail Authority and government not to exercise its option to purchase phase two of the Channel Tunnel Rail Link on its completion (see New lines).

### New lines
#### Channel Tunnel Rail Link
Under June 1996 government proposals for the restructuring of London & Continental Railways, the company was awarded the build-and-operate concession for the 109 km high-speed Channel Tunnel Rail Link. Responsibility for construction is to remain with L&CR, but Railtrack will acquire at construction cost the first phase of the line from Folkestone to Fawkham Junction upon completion, planned for 2003. The company initially had first option on purchasing the second phase of the project, from Gravesend to St Pancras, due for completion in 2007. However, in April 2001 this option was relinquished in favour of accelerated funding following agreement between the company, the SRA and government. To defray its investment costs, Railtrack will earn income from access charges paid by Eurostar, domestic commuter service operators, and other operators, including rail freight companies.

### Improvements to existing lines
#### Thameslink 2000
An £830 million plan to upgrade an existing north-south line through London to RER (Regional Express) standards was agreed by the government and Railtrack in the run-up to flotation of the company in early 1996. Railtrack agreed to undertake the project, known as Thameslink 2000, in exchange for being floated with lower debt levels than would otherwise have been the case. In 2001, the scheme was in the final stages of obtaining parliamentary approval under the Transport and Works Act.

The historic Thameslink route beneath the City of London, which has been used by through trains since 1988, suffers from serious capacity constraints. Thameslink 2000 involves major infrastructure work to eliminate some flat junctions south of the river Thames, and at St Pancras a new low-level station and new connections to adjacent main lines will be built as part of the rebuilding of the station for the Channel Tunnel Rail Link (see Eurostar (UK) entry). Power supplies in the central tunnelled section will be enhanced.

On completion of the project, probably in 2006, the present Thameslink service between Bedford and Brighton will be supplemented by services between King's Lynn and Peterborough north of the Thames, and Ashford, Dartford, Horsham and Guildford, south of London. The number of stations served will increase from 50 to 169.

#### West Coast modernisation
The West Coast main line, which connects London with Birmingham, Manchester, Liverpool and Glasgow, has had only limited investment since its electrification in the mid-1960s. Plans by British Rail to modernise it in the early 1990s came to nothing and a decision on investment in the route had to await privatisation of the railways.

With the reorganisation of the railway industry, Railtrack took on responsibility for the infrastructure side of the West Coast project. In October 1996, the then Franchise Director and Railtrack reached agreement on an infrastructure upgrading programme on the route, while the franchise agreement for West Coast Trains signed by Virgin (qv) in early 1997 ensured that new trains would be built for the line: orders for 53 advanced tilting trains were announced in early 1998. Before that, in October 1997, Railtrack and the Virgin Rail Group announced a collaborative deal under which a two-stage upgrade – costed at £2.1 billion – would go ahead, funded partly by track access charges and partly by a revenue-sharing arrangement agreed by the two companies. This received approval from the Franchise Director and the Rail Regulator in early 1998.

The infrastructure upgrading programme includes signalling system upgrading, catenary renewal, upgrading of the traction current supply system and some minor work to improve alignments. A first phase, known as 'PUG 1' (Passenger Upgrade One), will see the most heavily used London Euston–Crewe section upgraded for a maximum speed of 200 km/h by May 2002, with relief lines improved for 160 km/h operation. A second phase, PUG 2, will be completed by 2005 and will provide for line speeds up to 225 km/h. PUG 2 is underwritten by Virgin's agreement to double service levels to use 11 train paths per hour into and out of Euston station. Total cost of the scheme is £6.3 billion.

A central plank of the upgrade project is renewal of the signalling on the line. For this, Railtrack plans a radio Transmission Based Train Control System (TBTCS), with cab displays of the speed permitted and elimination of traditional wayside signals (except at busy junctions where signals would be retained for non-TBTCS-equipped rolling stock). In early 1996, Railtrack awarded two parallel development contracts for the TBTCS to Transig (a consortium of Adtranz and Westinghouse Signals) and a consortium of Alstom and Siemens. In May 1998 Alstom was named as the successful bidder to develop and implement the system, with Siemens and Alcatel as subcontractors. The system will conform to Level 3 of the European Train Control System.

#### East Coast Main Line
Phase one of a £1.6 billion upgrade of the East Coast Main Line has commenced, with a major remodelling of Leeds station completed in early 2001 at a cost of £165 million.

#### Cross Country
A £168 million scheme to modernise routes used by Virgin CrossCountry services is in progress for completion in late 2003. Timed to coincide with the

*For duties such as vegetation management, Sandite application during the leaf-fall season and other infrastructure functions, Railtrack has recently acquired from Windhoff a fleet of Multi-Purpose Vehicles (MPVs) (Ken Harris)*

introduction by Virgin of new Class 220 and 221 Voyager and Super Voyager demus on the services, the infrastructure works include track capacity and line speed enhancements.

*Tyne & Wear Metro Extension*
A £90 million scheme to be completed by January 2002 will enable Tyne & Wear Metro services to share Railtrack tracks with heavy rail local passenger and freight services south from the Newcastle metropolitan area to Sunderland.

*Network enhancements*
In its annual Network Management Statements Railtrack identifies key network locations where congestion is currently experienced or is predicted with traffic growth. The company has evaluated and developed possible solutions to capacity constraints at each location.

In 2001, Railtrack was exploring new methods of funding enhancements which might otherwise fall victim to its investment constraints. One device under study was the special purpose vehicle, an organisation established specifically to develop, finance and deliver an individual scheme.

### Signalling and telecommunications
Solid-State Interlocking (SSI) has been a standard feature of recent resignalling projects. The interlocking is performed centrally by microcomputers which communicate through serial datalinks with lineside terminals directly controlling signalling equipment. To achieve the required levels of safety and availability, cross-checking duplicate or triplicate systems are used (hardware redundancy). Built-in diagnostic facilities enable faults to be detected and rectified speedily.

Major resignalling schemes lately completed or under way adopt the Integrated Electronic Control Centre (IECC) concept.

In an IECC, solid-state interlocking is used to prevent conflicting routes being set and, in place of a conventional panel, high-resolution colour VDUs are employed. Automatic route-setting is provided for the entire control area; manual route-setting is necessary only in exceptional cases. The signalling system provides data for comprehensive passenger and management information systems within an integrated communications network.

IECCs installed include one at Ashford, Kent, which controls international trains from close to the Channel Tunnel mouth to within a few kilometres of the terminus at Waterloo.

Taking a further technological step forward, Railtrack now envisages the use of transmission-based signalling (see 'West Coast modernisation' in 'Improvements to existing lines'). In a policy document issued in early 1997, Railtrack envisaged three levels of signalling in future: transmission-based signalling on the main intercity routes; conventional colourlight signals in suburban areas where conversion of large numbers of trains to TBTCS would be uneconomic; and axle counter or radio electronic token system for rural lines.

In the shorter term, Railtrack has invested some £310 million on the widespread implementation of signalling safety schemes, most notably TPWS (see Political background/Safety).

### Electrification
Of the Railtrack network 38 per cent is electrified, using the 25 kV AC 50 Hz overhead or 750 V DC systems. Most of the latter is concentrated on the former Southern Region network in southeast England.

*UPDATED*

## Railway Safety

Evergreen House, 160 Euston Road, London NW1 2DX
Tel: (−44 20) 79 04 75 18   Fax: (+44 20) 75 57 90 72
e-mail: enquiries@railwaysafety.org.uk
Web: http://www.railwaysafety.org.uk

### Key personnel
Chairman: Sir David Davies
Director: Rod Muttram
Director, Policy and Standards: Aidan Nelson
Director, Safety Management Systems: Matt Walter

### Background
Railway Safety was established in January 2000 in the wake of the Southall and Ladbrooke Grove fatal accidents as a wholly owned not-for-profit subsidiary of Railtrack plc.

The organisation's role is to provide a centre of excellence for all matters relating to UK railway safety and to help the industry focus on improved safety management. It took over most of the functions of Railtrack's former Safety and Standards directorate.

*NEW ENTRY*

## ScotRail

ScotRail Railways Ltd
Caledonian Chambers, 87 Union Street, Glasgow G1 3TA
Tel: (+44 141) 332 98 11   Fax: (+44 141) 335 47 91
e-mail: enquiries@scotrail.co.uk
Web: http://scotrail.co.uk

### Key personnel
Managing Director (acting): Peter Cotton
Finance Director: Kenny McPhail
Operations Director: Steve Banaghan
Commercial Director: Mike Price
Fleet Director: Ian Mylroi
Head of Personnel: Donald Macpherson
Head of Safety and Standards: Jerry Farquharson
Head of Marketing: Don Roberts
Strathclyde Services Manager: Steve Montgomery
Fleet Engineer: John McCarron
Sleeper Services Manager: Jacqueline Dey
Franchise Partnership Manager: Alan Scott
Customer Relations Manager: Pamela Ballantyne
External Relations Manager: John Yellowlees
Media Relations Manager: Eddie Toal
Press and Information Officer: Carol Harris

### Political background
National Express Group commenced a seven-year franchise to operate ScotRail on 1 April 1997. At 1997 prices, support from the Franchising Director (now the Strategic Rail Authority) and Strathclyde Passenger Transport Authority (SPT) diminishes from £280.1 million in the first full financial year of the franchise to £202.5 million in 2003-04.

Under new terms agreed by the SRA and National Express in March 2002 to put the ScotRail and Central Trains franchises on a stable financial footing, the SRA is providing £115 million of additional subsidy to achieve a breakeven position between January 2002 and the end of the franchise period. In return NEG made a cash payment of £59 million and undertook to continue to operate additional services above the minimum level required in the franchise agreements.

Responsibility for funding the franchise was transferred to the Scottish Executive from 1 April 2001. In June 2002, the Executive issued Directions and Guidance to the SRA for the re-letting of the ScotRail franchise.

ScotRail revenue for 2001 was £142.6 million and the company employed 3,100 staff.

### Passenger operations
ScotRail operates services on a 3,035 km network. These include: interurban services linking the five Scottish cities;

*Alstom-built Class 334 'Juniper' emus at Glasgow central forming an SPT-supported service to Ayr (Colin Boocock)*

*Class 170/4 dmu at Glasgow Queen Street station forming a service to Edinburgh (Alex Dasi-Sutton)*

# RAILWAY SYSTEMS/UK

suburban services around Edinburgh and Glasgow, where the services supported by Strathclyde Passenger Transport comprise the largest suburban network in Great Britain outside London; rural services in Dumfries and Galloway and the West and North Highlands; and sleeper services linking Scotland with London. The company operates 335 stations and serves 354.

The franchise commitment to increase the frequency of services between Edinburgh and Glasgow from half-hourly to 15-minute was implemented six months early, in September 1999. Daytime services have also been doubled between Edinburgh and Fife, with an increase in peak-hour capacity funded by Fife Council. An additional 130,000 annual off-peak train-km have been provided on the Glasgow North Electrics network for SPT. New services over and above franchise requirements include: a Tain–Inverness commuter service; a new direct link between Cumbernauld and Falkirk; a new commuter service between Carstairs and Edinburgh; and a new Edinburgh Crossrail route, which opened in June 2002.

| Traffic (million) | 1999/2000 | 2000/01 | 2001-02 |
|---|---|---|---|
| Passenger journeys | 62 | 63.2 | 60.7 |
| Passenger-km | 1,902.7 | 1,928 | 1,953 |
| Train-km | 35 | 37 | 35 |

## Traction and rolling stock
ScotRail operates only multiple-unit trains, save for on its sleeper services, where Class 90 AC electric locomotives and Class 67 and 37 diesels are hired in from EWS to haul the Mk 3 sleeper vehicles on Anglo-Scottish and internal Scottish legs respectively.

NEG has invested some £200 million in new and refurbished rolling stock for ScotRail. The new trains are of two types: 40 Class 334 'Juniper' three-car emus from

### ScotRail diesel multiple-units

| Class | Cars per unit | Motor cars per unit | Motored axles/car | Power/motor kW | Speed km/h | Cars in service | First built | Mechanical | Builders Engine | Transmission |
|---|---|---|---|---|---|---|---|---|---|---|
| 150/2 | 2 | 2 | 2 | 210 | 120 | 24 | 1986 | BREL | Cummins NT855R5 | HM Voith T211r |
| 156 | 2 | 2 | 2 | 210 | 120 | 96 | 1987 | Met-Cam | Cummins NT855R5 | HM Voith T211r |
| 158/0 | 2 | 2 | 2 | 275/300 | 145 | 80 | 1989 | BREL | Perkins 2006-TWH | HM Voith T211r |
| 170/4 | 3 | 3 | 2 | 315 | 160 | 78 | 1999 | Adtranz | MTU 6R183 TD13H | H Voith T211rzze |

### ScotRail electric multiple-units

| Class | Cars per unit | Motor cars per unit | Motored axles/car | Power/motor kW | Speed km/h | Cars in service | First built | Builders Mechanical | Electrical |
|---|---|---|---|---|---|---|---|---|---|
| 303 | 3 | 1 | 4 | 155 | 120 | 36 | 1959 | Pressed Steel | Metro-Vick |
| 314 | 3 | 2 | 2 | 82 | 120 | 48 | 1976 | BREL | GEC/Brush |
| 318 | 3 | 1 | 4 | 268 | 145 | 63 | 1985 | BREL | Brush |
| 320 | 3 | 1 | 4 | 268 | 120 | 66 | 1990 | BREL | Brush |
| 322** | 4 | 1 | 4 | 268 | 160 | 20 | 1990 | BREL | Brush |
| 334 | 3 | 2 | 2 | 270 | 160 | 136* | 1999 | Alstom | Alstom |

* Total order is for 120 cars
** Sub-leased from West Anglia Great Northern

Alstom, all of which were due to be in service in early 2000, but many difficulties were experienced with reliability, leading to a wide-ranging programme of modifications by the manufacturer which succeeded in getting over three-quarters of the fleet operational by mid-2002; and 26 Class 170/4 'Turbostar' three-car dmus from Adtranz (now Bombardier), 24 of these for the interurban network and two for SPT as compensation for late delivery of Class 334 emus. Again, these new trains achieved poor reliability until in November 2001, their manufacturer, Bombardier Transportation, agreed to fund a re-engining programme which has shown promising results and is due for completion in late 2002.

The sleeper fleet, which comprises 53 sleeping cars, 10 lounge cars and 11 club/brake cars, have been the subject of a refurbishment programme which included provision of wheelchair-accessible cabins and the reinstatement of seated accommodation, a facility withdrawn by the former British Rail.

**UPDATED**

# Sea Containers

Sea Containers Services Ltd
20 Upper Ground, London SE1 9PF
Tel: (+44 20) 88 05 50 00   Fax: (+44 20) 88 05 59 03
Web: http://www.seacontainers.com

## Key personnel
President: James Sherwood
Vice-President, Rail: Christopher W M Garnett

## Political background
Sea Containers has its roots in the container leasing industry and has of late diversified into railways. It operates the luxury Venice–Simplon Orient Express tour train and in 1996 took over intercity operations on the London–Edinburgh/Aberdeen/Inverness, and London–Leeds routes, which it is marketing as the Great North Eastern Railway (qv).

**UPDATED**

# Silverlink

Silverlink Train Services Ltd
PO Box 689, Melton House, 65-67 Clarendon Road, Watford WD1 1XY
Tel: (+44 1923) 20 77 70   Fax: (+44 1923) 20 70 69
Web: http://www.silverlink-trains.com

## Key personnel
Managing Director: Charles Belcher
Finance Director: Phil Beanlands
Production and Planning Director: John Ratcliffe
Marketing Director: Steve Thompson
Director, County Services: John Brooks
Director, Metro Services: Charlie Beaumont
Franchise Extension Director: Richard Eccles
Group Financial Controller: Liz Pike
Communications Manager: Graham Bashford

## Political background
Under the arrangements put in place by the 1993 Railways Act, the franchise to run Silverlink (then North London Railways) operations was let in March 1997 to National Express Group plc, a bus and airport operator which also won the Midland Mainline, Gatwick Express, ScotRail and Central Trains franchises.

The franchise was let for a term of seven years and six months. NEG received from the Franchising Director support, in 1997 prices, of £48.6 million in the first full financial year of the franchise, declining to £16.9 million in 2003-04.

Silverlink revenue in FY99-2000 was £77.5 million and in December 2000 the company employed 998 staff.

## Passenger operations
Silverlink Train Services is the name adopted in September 1997 for the former North London Railways. The company operates suburban and regional services out of London's Euston station to Birmingham and on the North London orbital line; the route network extends to 321 km.

### Silverlink electric multiple-units

| Class | Cars per unit | Motor cars per unit | Motored axles/car | Power/motor kW | Speed km/h | Cars in service | First built | Builders Mechanical | Electrical |
|---|---|---|---|---|---|---|---|---|---|
| 313* | 3 | 2 | 2 | 82 | 120 | 69 | 1976 | BREL | GEC |
| 321/4 | 4 | 1 | 4 | 268 | 160 | 148 | 1990 | BREL | Brush |

* Dual-voltage 750 V DC/25 kV AC

*Silverlink Metro Class 313 dual-voltage emu on a Richmond–North Woolwich service near Caledonian Road, north London (Alex Dasi-Sutton)* 2000/0089574

| Traffic (million) | 1998-99 | 1999-2000 |
|---|---|---|
| Passenger journeys | 34.3 | 36.3 |
| Passenger-km | 899 | 974 |
| Train-km | 9.8 | 10.2 |

## Traction and rolling stock
Silverlink's principal route, from Euston to Northampton, is electrified at 25 kV AC overhead; for this line, the company leases 37 Class 321 emus from Forward Trust (formerly Eversholt). Local routes around London are electrified with a mixture of 25 kV AC overhead and 750 V DC third rail, and for these the business leases 23 Class 313 dual-voltage emus from Forward Trust.

On the Bletchley–Bedford and Gospel Oak–Barking diesel-worked branch lines, Silverlink leases seven Class 150/1 dmus.

# South Central

South Central Ltd
First Floor, Friars Bridge Court, 41-45 Blackfriars Bridge Road, London SE1 8NZ
Tel: (+44 20) 76 20 58 20   Fax: (+44 20) 76 20 56 80
Web: http://www.southcentraltrains.co.uk

## Key personnel
Directors
  Managing: David Franks
  Finance: Alan McKnespiey
  Commercial (acting): Paresh Patel
  Operations: Elwyn Roberts
  Human Resources: Nick Mitchell
  Engineering: David Sawyer

## Political background
Under the arrangements put in place by the 1993 Railways Act, the Network SouthCentral franchise was transferred to London & South Coast Ltd (later renamed Connex), a subsidiary of the French CGEA group, in April 1996. Services were operated under Connex South Central branding, while in 1998 CGEA adopted the new name Vivendi. The franchise was to have run for seven years.

Support payments from the Franchise Director to Connex South Central were to decline from £85.3 million in the first year to £34.6 million in 2003.

Connex's bid for a replacement franchise to take effect from 2003 was rejected by the Strategic Rail Authority in 2001. Instead, GoVia Ltd, which operates the Thameslink franchise (qv), was named as preferred bidder for a 20-year franchise for the service. Pending final signature of the franchise contract, expected in late 2002, GoVia took over the existing business on 26 August 2001, compensating Connex for the unfulfilled portion of its contract. The franchise was to be operated under the South Central brand name until signature of the new contract, when the business was to be renamed the New Southern Railway.

## Passenger operations
South Central runs services on a 724 km network mostly of 750 V DC electrified lines out of London's Victoria and London Bridge termini to Gatwick Airport, Brighton and other towns on the south coast of England.

Service innovations by the former franchise holder included the deployment of Class 319/2 refurbished emus on an upgraded London Victoria–Brighton 'Brighton Express' service, which was stepped up from hourly to half-hourly frequency in May 1998, and the launch of a Gatwick Airport–Rugby cross-London service in May 1997 using dual-voltage Class 319s. Subsequently, the Gatwick Airport–Rugby service was cut back on the West Coast Main Line leg to Watford Junction.

| Traffic (million) | 1998-99 | 1999-2000 | 2000-01 |
|---|---|---|---|
| Passenger journeys | 98.345 | 109 | 110.4 |
| Passenger-km | 2,309 | 2,525 | 2,591 |
| Train-km | 26.23 | 27.03 | 27.84 |

## Traction and rolling stock
South Central runs about 233 four-car and two-car electric multiple-units and 14 diesel-electric multiple-units (for the non-electrified Uckfield and Hastings—Ashford lines), on lease from the three ex-British Rail rolling stock leasing companies. Inner-suburban services are run by sliding-door units, while most of the longer-distance services are still run by slam-door stock built in the 1960s. There were no requirements in the franchise for the new owner of the company to make arrangements to renew any of the rolling stock, although there was a clause in the agreement which allowed for the franchise to be extended beyond seven years in the event of new trains being ordered. This bid was declined by OPRAF, predecessor of the SRA. Nevertheless, in July 1999 Connex Rail ordered 37 'Electrostar' emus from Adtranz (now Bombardier Transportation) for delivery from 2001. The order is split as 28 three-car (Class 375) and nine four-car units (Class 377). Subsequently, an additional 30 four-car units were ordered.

Although initially the subject of doubt due to transfer of the franchise to a new operator, GoVia confirmed this order in September 2001, with a revised date for commencement of deliveries of 2002.

In March 2002, GoVia placed a second order with Bombardier for an additional 115 four-car Class 377 emus, bringing the total of the type ordered to 28 three-car and 154 four-car sets (700 cars). Financing for both orders is being provided by Porterbrook Leasing Company.

*UPDATED*

### South Central diesel-electric multiple-units

| Class | Cars per unit | Motor cars per unit | Motored axles/car | Power/motor kW | Speed km/h | Cars in service | First built | Builders Mechanical | Engine | Transmission |
|---|---|---|---|---|---|---|---|---|---|---|
| 205/0-2 | 3 | 1 | 2 | 450* | 120 | 26 | 1957 | BR | EE 4SRKT | *E* EE507 |
| 207/0/1 | 2/3 | 1 | 2 | 450* | 120 | 11 | 1962 | BR | EE 4SRKT | *E* EE507 |

* Diesel engine rated at 450 kW

### South Central electric multiple-units

| Class | Cars per unit | Motor cars per unit | Motored axles/car | Power/motor kW | Speed km/h | Cars in service | First built | Builders Mechanical | Electrical |
|---|---|---|---|---|---|---|---|---|---|
| 319/0* | 4 | 1 | 4 | 247 | 160 | 52 | 1987 | BREL | GEC |
| 319/2* | 4 | 1 | 4 | 247 | 160 | 28 | 1987 | BREL | GEC |
| 375* | 3 | 2 | 2 | 250 | 160 | 84** | 2002 | Bombardier | Bombardier |
| 377* | 4 | 3 | 2 | 250 | 160 | 616** | 2002 | Bombardier | Bombardier |
| 421/7 | 3 | 1 | 4 | 185 | 145 | 33 | 1964 | BR | EE |
| 421 | 4 | 1 | 4 | 185 | 145 | 348 | 1970 | BREL | EE |
| 422/2 | 4 | 1 | 4 | 185 | 145 |  | 1965 | BR | EE |
| 422/3 | 4 | 1 | 4 | 185 | 145 |  | 1970 | BREL | EE |
| 423 | 4 | 1 | 4 | 185 | 145 | 200 | 1967 | BR | EE |
| 455 | 4 | 1 | 4 | 185 | 120 | 184 | 1982 | BREL | GEC |
| 456 | 2 | 1 | 2 | 268 | 120 | 48 | 1990 | BREL | Brush |

* Dual-voltage 750 V DC/25 kV AC
** Total on order

*Class 319/2 emu forming a London Victoria–Brighton 'Brighton Express' service at Croydon (Ken Harris)*
2001/0099137

---

# South West Trains

A subsidiary of Stagecoach Holdings
South West Trains Ltd
Friars Bridge Court, 41-45 Blackfriars Road, London SE1 8NZ
Tel: (+44 20) 76 20 52 29   Fax: (+44 20) 76 20 50 15
e-mail: via website
Web: http://www.southwesttrains.co.uk

## Key personnel
Managing Director: Andrew Haines
Operations Director: Stewart Palmer
Commercial Director: Rufus Boyd
Engineering Director: David Hornby
Finance Director: Andy West
Human Resources Director: Beverley Shears
Retail Director: James Burt

## Political background
Under the arrangements put in place by the 1993 Railways Act, a franchise to run South West Trains for seven years passed to the bus company Stagecoach (qv) in February 1996; Stagecoach also operates the Island Line franchise. Subsidy from the Franchise Director is set to fall from £54.7 million in the first year of operation to £40.3 million in the final year. In April 2001 Stagecoach was named preferred bidder by the Strategic Rail Authority to continue to operate the South West Trains franchise under a proposed 20-year contract, with an option to reduce this to 15 years if capacity enhancement plans are not implemented.

### South West Trains diesel multiple-units

| Class | Cars per unit | Motor cars per unit | Motored axles/car | Power/motor kW | Speed km/h | Units in service | First built | Builders Mechanical | Engine | Transmission |
|---|---|---|---|---|---|---|---|---|---|---|
| 159* | 3 | 3 | 3 | 300 | 145 | 22 | 1992 | ABB/Babcock | Cummins NT855R1 | *HM* Voith T211r |
| 170 | 2 | 2 | 2 | 315 | 160 | 8 | 2000 | Adtranz | MTU | *HM* Voith |

* Built as Class 158 and converted before entering service

*Alstom-built Coradia Juniper Class 458 emu at Guildford (Ken Harris)*
2002/0126829

## RAILWAY SYSTEMS/UK

At the end of 2001 the company employed approximately 4,700 staff.

### Passenger operations
SWT operates commuter trains in southwest London and long-distance services from London Waterloo to a triangular area of southern England stretching from Portsmouth in the east to Exeter in the west. Total route-km operated: 940.

| Traffic (million) | 1998-99 | 1999-2000 | 2000-01 |
|---|---|---|---|
| Passenger journeys | 122.9 | 132 | 142.4 |
| Passenger-km | 3,687.9 | 3,925.2 | 4,167 1 |
| Train-km | 33.5 | 34.7 | 37.8 |

### Traction and rolling stock
Most of the area covered by SWT is electrified on the 750 V DC system. SWT operates 270 four- and five-car electric multiple-units owned by all three of the ex-British Rail rolling stock leasing companies, plus 22 three-car Class 159 diesel units owned by Porterbrook which are used on the line from Waterloo to Salisbury and Exeter. In 1997, SWT placed a £90 million order with Alstom, with financing from sister company Porterbrook Leasing, for 30 new four-car emus to replace slam-door stock. Designated Class 458, 12 of these were in service at the end of 2001.

In the closing weeks of 2000, SWT took delivery of eight Class 170/3 two-car Turbostar dmus from Adtranz.

Following its selection in April as preferred bidder for a new 20-year contract to operate South West Trains, Stagecoach placed a £1 billion order with Siemens Transportation Systems for 785 Desiro UK emu cars to replace all existing slam-door stock by 2004. Built at Siemens plants in Uerdingen, Germany and Vienna, the new trains are being supplied as: 45 Class 444 five-car units for express services; 100 four-car Class 450 suburban units; and 32 Class 450 five-car suburban units. An option exists for an additional 321 cars to be delivered by 2009. Financing for the new trains is being provided by Angel Trains. An additional contract covers the provision by Siemens of maintenance services, for which a new depot is being built in the Southampton area.

*The first SWT Class 450 Desiro UK emu at Siemens' Wildenrath Test Centre (Ken Harris)* 2002/0137116

#### South West Trains electric multiple-units

| Class | Cars per unit | Motor cars per unit | Motored axles/car | Power/motor kW | Speed km/h | Units in service | First built | Builders Mechanical | Builders Electrical |
|---|---|---|---|---|---|---|---|---|---|
| 411 | 4 | 2 | 4 | 185 | 145 | 28 | 1957 | BR | EE |
| 412 | 4 | 2 | 4 | 185 | 145 | 7 | 1957 | BR | EE |
| 421/4 | 4 | 1 | 4 | 185 | 145 | 12 | 1970 | BREL | EE |
| 421/5 | 4 | 1 | 4 | 185 | 145 | 22 | 1970 | BREL | EE |
| 422 | 4 | 1 | 4 | 185 | 145 | 6 | 1970 | BREL | EE |
| 423 | 4 | 1 | 4 | 185 | 145 | 66 | 1967 | BR | EE |
| 442 | 5 | 1 | 4 | 300 | 160 | 24 | 1988 | BREL | EE |
| 444 | 5 | 2 | 4 | 187 | 160 | 45** | 2002 | Siemens | Siemens |
| 450 | 4 | 2 | 4 | 187 | 160 | 100** | 2002 | Siemens | Siemens |
| 450 | 5 | 2 | 4 | 187 | 160 | 32** | 2002 | Siemens | Siemens |
| 455 | 4 | 1 | 4 | 185 | 120 | 91 | 1982 | BREL | GEC |
| 458 | 4 | 3 | 2 | 270 | 160 | 30* | 1998 | Alstom | Alstom |

\* Under delivery in 2001  \*\* Under delivery in 2002

SWT also operates a solitary Class 73/1 electro-diesel locomotive for rolling stock movements.

**UPDATED**

## Stagecoach

Stagecoach Group plc
10 Dunkeld Street, Perth PH1 STW
Tel: (+44 1738) 44 21 11   Fax: (+44 1738) 64 36 48
e-mail: info@stagecoachgroup.com
Web: http://www.stagecoachgroup.com

### Key personnel
Acting Non-Executive Chairman: Robert Spiers
Acting Chief Executive: Brian Souter
Executive Director, Rail Operations: Graham Eccles
Business Development Director, Rail: Andy Pitt
Major Projects Director: Allison Ingram
Group Finance Director: Martin Griffiths

### Political background
Stagecoach has its roots in the bus industry, having grown fast following bus deregulation in the UK in the 1980s. With that market approaching maturity, it turned its attentions to overseas bus acquisitions and to the opportunities offered by the 1993 Railways Act in the UK. It won the first franchise to be let, South West Trains (qv), and subsequently acquired the Island Line franchise. It also purchased Porterbrook (qv), one of the three rolling stock leasing companies formed with the British Rail rolling stock fleet. Porterbrook was initially sold to a management buyout team and then acquired by Stagecoach in late 1996. In April 2000, Porterbrook was sold to Abbey National for a consideration valued at £1.4 billion. In 1997, Stagecoach acquired a 26-year operating franchise for the Sheffield-based Supertram light rail system.

In June 1998, Stagecoach announced that it had taken a 49 per cent stake in the Virgin Rail Group for a purchase price of £158 million. The move followed the purchase by Stagecoach of the 59 per cent shareholding by Virgin's venture capital backers and the subsequent transfer of 10 per cent of the equity back to Virgin, giving it a controlling stake.

In April 2001 Stagecoach was named preferred bidder for a new 20-year franchise to operate South West Trains.

**UPDATED**

## Thames Trains Ltd

Venture House, 37-43 Blagrave Street, Reading RG1 1PZ
Tel: (+44 118) 908 36 78   Fax: (+44 118) 957 96 48
Web: http://www.thamestrains.co.uk

### Key personnel
Director and General Manager: Terry Worrall
Finance Director: Ken Watson
Human Resources Director: Hugh Dunglinson
Group Communications Director: Martin Walter

### Political background
Under the arrangements put in place by the 1993 Railways Act, the franchise to run operations on Thames Trains was let in October 1996 to Victory Railways Holdings Ltd, a joint venture between bus operator The Go-Ahead Group plc and the management of Thames Trains. The Go-Ahead Group is also part of a joint venture running Thameslink (qv). In early 1998, The Go-Ahead Group acquired the 34.8 per cent shareholding in Victory Railways by management and staff to take full control of the company.

The franchise was let for a term of seven years and six months. Victory Railways was to receive from the Franchising Director support, in 1996 prices, of £33.2 million in the first full financial year of the franchise, declining to zero in the last year of the franchise.

In 2000 the company employed approximately 960 staff.

*Thames Trains refurbished Class 166 dmu forming a Reading—Gatwick Airport service approaches its destination (Ken Harris)* 2002/0126828

#### Thames Trains diesel multiple-units

| Class | Cars per unit | Motor cars per unit | Motored axles/car | Power/motor kW | Speed km/h | Units in service | First built | Mechanical | Builders Engine | Transmission |
|---|---|---|---|---|---|---|---|---|---|---|
| 165/0 | 2 | 2 | 2 | 260 | 120 | 5 | 1990 | BREL | Perkins 2006-TWH | H Voith T211r |
| 165/1 | 2/3 | 2/3 | 2 | 260 | 145 | 36 | 1992 | ABB | Perkins 2006-TWH | H Voith T211r |
| 166 | 3 | 3 | 2 | 260 | 145 | 21 | 1993 | ABB | Perkins 2006-TWH | H Voith T211r |

## Passenger operations

Thames Trains operates suburban services out of London's Paddington station along the Thames valley to Reading and Oxford. The company also runs services between Oxford and Hereford, Oxford and Stratford-upon-Avon, Reading and Basingstoke and Reading and Gatwick Airport. Total route-km operated is 581.

As part of the franchise agreement, Victory increased the Oxford-Paddington weekday frequency to half-hourly in 1998. The Franchise Director's approval of Go-Ahead taking full control of Thames Trains was conditional on service improvements and innovations which included a new route, Oxford-Swindon-Bath-Bristol, which was inaugurated in June 1998. This service is operated in partnership with First Great Western.

| Traffic (million) | 1998-99 | 1999-2000 | 2000-01 |
|---|---|---|---|
| Passenger journeys | 31 | 33.3 | 36.4 |
| Passenger-km | 888 | 939 | 1,012 |
| Train-km | 12.9 | 13.5 | 13.8 |

### Traction and rolling stock

Thames Trains uses only modern 'Turbo' diesel units built by Adtranz. The fleet consists of Class 165 and 166 dmus leased from Angel Train Contracts. In 2000, a fleet refurbishment programme was initiated, the Class 166 units being treated first.

*UPDATED*

# Thameslink

Thameslink Rail Ltd
Friars Bridge Court, 41-45 Blackfriars Bridge Road, London SE1 8NZ
Tel: (+44 20) 76 20 52 22   Fax: (+44 20) 76 20 50 99
Web: http://www.thameslink.co.uk

### Key personnel

Managing Director: Keith Ludeman
Director and General Manager: Mark Causebrook
Finance Director: Ken Watson
Group Marketing Director: Martin Walker

### Political background

Under the arrangements put in place by the 1993 Railways Act, the franchise to run operations on Thameslink was let in March 1997 to GOVIA, a joint venture combining the British bus operator Go-Ahead Group plc and Via GTI, the French transport group.

The franchise was let for a seven year and one month term. GOVIA was to receive from the Franchising Director support, in 1997 prices, of £2.5 million in the first full financial year of the franchise, reversing to a premium payment to the Franchise Director of £28.4 million in 2004.

Thameslink revenue in FY98-99 was £104 million and in March 2000 the company employed 700 staff.

### Passenger operations

Thameslink runs cross-London suburban operations through a tunnel linking King's Cross to Blackfriars. Long-distance services run between Bedford and Brighton via Gatwick Airport, and inner-suburban services between Luton and Wimbledon. Total route-km operated over: 224.

| Traffic (million) | 1998-99 |
|---|---|
| Passenger journeys | 34.4 |
| Passenger-km | 1,142.3 |
| Train-km | 10.9 |

### Improvements to existing lines

Railtrack is committed to a £560 million upgrade of the Thameslink lines in a project known as Thameslink 2000. This will see upgrading of the power supply and signalling through the central London tunnels, improvements in track layouts to increase capacity in south London, and a new station adjacent to St Pancras to replace the cramped King's Cross Thameslink station. Target completion date is 2006, at which point Peterborough, King's Lynn and Letchworth to the north of London, along with Littlehampton, Eastbourne, Horsham, Dartford and Ashford to the south of London, will be brought into the service net.

The Franchising Director wishes to be in a position to refranchise the services currently operated by Thameslink at the time of the introduction of Thameslink 2000 services. Accordingly, under the terms of the franchise agreement, while the franchise can continue until 1 April 2004, the Franchising Director will have the right to terminate the franchise agreement at any time from five and a half years after the commencement date.

### Traction and rolling stock

Thameslink operates over 25 kV AC overhead electrified lines to the north of London and 750 V DC third rail in the south. The changeover point is at Farringdon in central London.

The company's rolling stock comprises Class 319 dual-voltage emus leased from Porterbrook; there are 66 four-car units in the fleet. From the end of 1997, these have been refurbished and divided into two sub-classes: 26 have become Class 319/3 for inner suburban work, while the remaining 40 units are designated Class 319/4 and incorporate two-class accommodation for long-distance work. During refurbishment the vehicles have been reliveried.

In 1999, Thameslink signed an innovative contract with Porterbrook under which the entire 264-vehicle fleet is operated under a contract hire agreement which includes all maintenance. This was claimed to be the first time such an arrangement was used in the UK rail industry.

*Thameslink Class 319/4 emu forming a Bedford–Brighton service at Gatwick Airport* (Ken Harris) 2000/0084686

### Thameslink Rail electric multiple-units

| Class | Cars per unit | Motor cars per unit | Motored axles/car | Power/motor KW | Speed km/h | Cars in service | First built | Builders Mechanical | Electrical |
|---|---|---|---|---|---|---|---|---|---|
| 319/3 | 4 | 1 | 4 | 247 | 160 | 104 | 1987 | BREL | GEC |
| 319/4 | 4 | 1 | 4 | 247 | 160 | 160 | 1990 | BREL | GEC |

# Virgin Trains

Virgin Rail Group Ltd
West Wing Offices, Euston Station, London NW1 2HS
Tel: (+44 20) 79 04 32 11   Fax: (+44 20) 79 04 32 34
Web: http://www.virgintrains.co.uk

### Key personnel

Chairman: Sir Richard Branson
Co-Chairman: Keith Cochrane
Chief Executive: Chris Green
Executive Directors
  Operations and Human Resources: Chris Tibbits
  Commercial: Paul Griffiths
  Customer Service: Brenda Klug
  Finance: Sue Murphy
  Corporate Affairs: Denize Quest
  Major Contracts: Tony Collins
Director, Safety and Quality: Andy Holl
Director, Service Development and Implementation:
  Philippa Creswell

### Political background

Under the arrangements put in place by the 1993 Railways Act, the franchise to run operations on British Rail's InterCity CrossCountry network was awarded to the Virgin Rail Group in January 1997. The franchise for InterCity West Coast services followed in March 1997. Both were awarded for 15 years.

In October 1998, Stagecoach Holdings (qv) acquired a 49 per cent shareholding in the Virgin Rail Group. The remaining 51 per cent is owned by Richard Branson Trusts.

### Organisation

The two franchises held by the Virgin Rail Group are overseen by an integrated management team and trade collectively as Virgin Trains, although to meet the rules of the Strategic Rail Authority they are legally separate entities.

*UPDATED*

# Virgin CrossCountry

CrossCountry Trains Ltd
See entry for Virgin Trains for address details and key personnel

### Political background

Under the arrangements put in place by the 1993 Railways Act, the franchise to run operations on British Rail's InterCity CrossCountry division was let in January 1997 to the Virgin Rail Group Ltd (qv), a subsidiary of the Virgin airline company. Virgin also runs the West Coast franchise (qv).

The franchise was let for a 15-year term. Virgin will receive from the Franchising Director support, in 1997 prices, of £112.9 million in the first full financial year of the

# RAILWAY SYSTEMS/UK

franchise, reversing to a premium payment from Virgin to the Franchising Director of £10 million in 2011-12.

### Passenger operations
Virgin CrossCountry runs long-distance passenger services throughout Britain, although few of its services reach London. Its route map has the form of a cross intersecting in Birmingham, with northern axes serving Scotland, northeast and northwest England and southern axes serving the west of England, the south coast and South Wales. On summer Saturdays holiday trains operate to the resorts of Newquay, Ramsgate and Weymouth. CrossCountry revenue in FY98-99 was £140 million and in 1999 the company employed 867 staff.

| Traffic (million) | 1998-99 |
|---|---|
| Passenger journeys | 13.8 |
| Passenger-km | 2,112 |

### Traction and rolling stock
Virgin CrossCountry operates InterCity 125 HST diesel trains leased from Angel and Porterbrook and seven-coach conventional trains hauled by Class 86 electric and Class 47 diesel locomotives. In addition Virgin CrossCountry operates five two-car Class 158 dmus leased from Porterbrook.

In March 1998, the Virgin Rail Group announced that it had selected Bombardier Transportation to supply a new fleet of trains for the franchise. Originally this was to comprise a mixture of tilting dmus and non-tilting trainsets formed of a power car plus trailers. This was subsequently revised to an all dmu fleet formed of 40 five-car and four four-car Class 221 Virgin Super Voyager tilting dmus and 34 four-car non-tilting Class 220 Virgin Voyager units. The contract includes maintenance of both existing and new traction and rolling stock fleets for the remainder of the 15-year franchise. The first trains of both types are due to be delivered in 2000.

Most existing traction and rolling stock will be returned to their leasing companies on delivery of the new trains, although some HST sets will remain on lease until 2004.

*Class 220 Voyager diesel-electric trainset supplied by Bombardier for Virgin CrossCountry services, photographed during test running in Belgium*
2001/0103635

### CrossCountry diesel locomotives

| Class | Wheel arrangement | Power kW | Speed km/h | Weight tonnes | No in service | First built | Builders Mechanical | Engine | Transmission |
|---|---|---|---|---|---|---|---|---|---|
| 43 | Bo-Bo | 1,680 | 200 | 70 | 52 | 1976 | BREL | Paxman Valenta 12 RP2000L | E Brush MB190 |
| 47/4 | Co-Co | 1,920 | 153 | 125 | 27 | 1963 | BR/Brush | Sulzer 12LDA28C | E Brush TM64-68 |
| 47/7* | Co-Co | 1,920 | 153 | 125 | 2 | 1963 | BR/Brush | Sulzer 12LDA28C | E Brush TM64-68 |

*Hired from English, Welsh & Scottish Railway

### CrossCountry electric locomotives

| Class | Wheel arrangement | Output kW | Speed km/h | Weight tonnes | No in service | First built | Builders Mechanical | Electrical |
|---|---|---|---|---|---|---|---|---|
| 86/2 | Bo-Bo | 3,010 | 160 | 86.2 | 18 | 1965 | BR/EE | EE |

## Virgin West Coast

West Coast Trains Ltd
See entry for 'Virgin Trains' (above) for address details and key personnel

### Political background
Under the arrangements put in place by the 1993 Railways Act, the franchise to run long-distance passenger services on the West Coast main line was let to Virgin Rail Group (qv), a subsidiary of the airline operator Virgin, in March 1997. Virgin also runs the CrossCountry franchise (qv).

The franchise was let for a 15-year term; it is expected to move into profit in 2002-03. Virgin will receive from the Franchising Director support, in 1997 prices, of £76.8 million in the first full year of the franchise, turning to a premium payment of £220.3 million in 2011-12.

### Passenger operations
Virgin West Coast runs services on a 1,164 km network out of London's Euston terminus to the West Midlands, the northwest of England and central Scotland.

| Traffic (million) | 1998-99 | 1999-2000 |
|---|---|---|
| Passenger journeys | 15.9 | 16.6 |
| Passenger-km | 3,128 | 3,418 |

### Improvements to existing lines
In October 1997, Virgin Rail Group and Railtrack (qv) jointly announced their agreement of a two-stage scheme to upgrade and re-equip the West Coast main line, with the £5.8 billion cost funded by a combination of track access charges and a revenue-sharing arrangement. A first phase, to be completed by June 2002, would allow Virgin trains to operate between London Euston and Crewe at speeds up to 200 km/h, while a second phase, scheduled for commissioning by 2005, would further increase speeds to 225 km/h. The investment would allow Virgin to double the number of paths it uses into and out of Euston station.

### Traction and rolling stock
The West Coast main line is electrified at 25 kV AC and long-distance services are currently in the hands of Class 86 (leased from Forward Trust (formerly Eversholt)), 87 and 90 locomotives (both leased from Porterbrook) powering push-pull trains of Mk 2 and Mk 3 stock. HST diesel high-speed trainsets are also operated, serving the non-electrified North Wales coast route.

The centrepiece of Virgin's plan for the line is a new fleet of high-speed tilting trains for delivery from 2001 onwards, allowing services to be operated initially at 200 km/h starting in 2002 (the current maximum is 175 km/h), and at 225 km/h from 2007. In March 1998, a joint venture of Fiat Ferroviaria and Alstom was named as the chosen supplier for these trains under a £1.2 billion contract which also includes maintenance of this fleet and of existing equipment. Designated Class 390, the new fleet was originally ordered as 44 eight-car and nine nine-car trains. In November 2000 an order was placed for an additional 44 cars to make all trains nine-car sets.

The new trains will bring the current 2 hour 40 minute journey time between London and Manchester down to 2 hours in 2003 and to 1 hour 50 minutes by 2005, while 25 minutes will be lopped off the current 1 hour 35 minute Birmingham timings.

On delivery of the Class 390 trainsets, all existing traction and rolling stock will be returned to the leasing companies.

### West Coast electric locomotives

| Class | Wheel arrangement | Output kW | Speed km/h | Weight tonnes | No in service | First built | Builders Mechanical | Electrical |
|---|---|---|---|---|---|---|---|---|
| 86/2 | Bo-Bo | 3,010 | 160 | 86.2 | 7 | 1965 | BR/EE | EE |
| 87/0 | Bo-Bo | 3,730 | 176 | 83.3 | 35 | 1973 | BR/EE | AEI |
| 90/0 | Bo-Bo | 3,730 | 176 | 82.5 | 15 | 1987 | BREL | GEC Alsthom |

*The first Class 390 Pendolino tilting trainset for Virgin West Coast Services at Alstom's Old Dalby test facility in February 2001 (Alstom/Virgin Trains/Milepost 92½)*
2001/0062510

# Wales & Borders Trains

Brunel House, 2 Fitzalan Road Cardiff CF24 0SU
Tel: (+44 29) 20 43 04 00  Fax: (+44 29) 20 43 02 14
Web: http://www.walesandborderstrains.co.uk

### Key personnel
Managing Director: Chris Gibb

### Political background
Under the arrangements put in place by the 1993 Railways Act, the franchise to run operations on South Wales & West Railway was let in October 1997 to Prism Rail plc, a company set up by a consortium of bus companies. Prism also ran the Cardiff Railway (subsequently Valley Lines), LTS Rail (c2c) and West Anglia Great Northern franchises. The company subsequently changed the name of the franchise to Wales & West Passenger Trains Ltd.

The franchise was let for a term of seven years and six months. Prism was to receive from the Franchising Director support, in 1996 prices, of £70.9 million in the first full financial year of the franchise, declining to £38.1 million in the last year of the franchise.

Similarly, a franchise to run operations on the Cardiff Railway was let in October 1997 to Prism Rail plc, the franchise becoming Valley Lines. The franchise was also let for a term of seven years and six months with support payments declining from £19.9 million in the first year of the franchise to £13.3 million in the final year.

In July 2000, Prism sold its rail operating business to National Express Group.

In 2001, agreement was reached with the Strategic Rail Authority to extend both franchises to no later than April 2004, when Wales & West services were to form part of new Wales & Borders and Wessex franchises.

In October 2001, Valley Lines services and former Wales & West services within Wales and to some English destinations were combined to form the Wales & Borders Trains managerial unit pending the eventual awarding of a new franchise contract, which was expected to be awarded in 2003. Services formerly operated by Central Trains to northeast and mid-Wales were also transferred to the Wales & Borders franchise. Services in southwest England formerly part of the Wales & West franchise are now operated by a managerial unit trading as Wessex Trains (qv). Both managerial units are part of National Express Group.

### Passenger operations
The former Valley Lines network covers 138 route-km centred on the Welsh capital, Cardiff. Trains run up the valleys to the north of Cardiff and Barry and Penarth in the south. Former Wales & West routes now forming part of the Wales & Borders managerial unit include interurban routes from Cardiff to west Wales, Holyhead, Liverpool, Manchester, Birmingham, Bristol, London Waterloo, Plymouth and Penzance. Former Central Trains routes extend to Aberystwyth and Pwllheli.

### Traction and rolling stock
Wales & Borders is an all-diesel-operated business worked with second-generation dmus. For its interurban routes, the company employs Class 158 dmus leased from Angel Trains. For local services, it leases Class 142 dmus and Class 153 single cars from Angel and Class 143 and 150/2 dmus from Porterbrook. Wales & Borders Trains also leases in Class 37/4 locomotives from EWS, providing Rhymney line peak-hour services with Mk 2 coaches.

### Wales & Borders Trains diesel multiple-units

| Class | Cars per unit | Motor cars per unit | Motored axles/car | Power/motor kW | Speed km/h | Cars in service | First built | Builders Mechanical | Builders Engine | Transmission |
|---|---|---|---|---|---|---|---|---|---|---|
| 142 | 2 | 2 | 1 | 170 | 120 | 28 | 1985 | BREL | Cummins LTA10R | H Voith T211r |
| 143 | 2 | 2 | 1 | 152 | 120 | 28 | 1985 | Alexander/Barclay | Cummins LTA10R | H Voith T211r |
| 150/2 | 2 | 2 | 2 | 210 | 120 | 12 | 1986 | BREL | Cummins NT855R5 | HM Voith T211r |
| 153 | 1 | 1 | 2 | 213 | 120 | 8 | 1987* | Leyland | Cummins NT855R5 | HM Voith T211r |
| 158/0 | 2 | 2 | 2 | 275/300 | 145 | 80 | 1989 | BREL | Cummins NTA855R | HM Voith T211r |

* Rebuilt 1991

*Former Valley Lines Class 142 dmu at Caerphilly* (Ken Harris)

**UPDATED**

# Wessex Trains

2nd Floor, Broadwalk House, Southernhay West, Exeter EX1 1TS
Tel: (+44 1392) 47 31 00
Web: http://www.wessextrains.co.uk

### Key personnel
Managing Director: Charles Belcher

### Political background
Under the arrangements put in place by the 1993 Railways Act, the franchise to run operations on South Wales & West Railway was let in October 1997 to Prism Rail plc, a company set up by a consortium of bus companies. Prism also ran the Cardiff Railway (subsequently Valley Lines), LTS Rail (c2c) and West Anglia Great Northern franchises. The company subsequently changed its name to Wales & West Passenger Trains Ltd.

The franchise was let for a term of seven years and six months. Prism was to receive from the Franchising Director support, in 1996 prices, of £70.9 million for the first full financial year of the franchise, declining to £38.1 million in the last year of the franchise.

In July 2000, Prism sold its rail operating business to National Express Group.

In 2001, agreement was reached with the Strategic Rail Authority to extend the franchise to no later than April 2004, when Wales & West services would be split to form new franchises.

In October 2001, former Wales & West services from Wales to some English destinations and within England were combined to form the Wessex Trains managerial unit, pending the eventual awarding of a new franchise contract. It is expected that services on the Waterloo–Salisbury–Exeter and Reading–Portsmouth/Brighton routes, currently operated by South West Trains, will eventually fall within the Wessex franchise. Services in Wales formerly part of the Wales & West franchise and the former Valley Lines franchise are now operated by a managerial unit trading as Wales & Borders Trains (qv). Both managerial units are part of National Express Group.

### Passenger operations
Wessex Trains runs interurban Alphaline-branded services from Bristol to Cardiff, Portsmouth, Brighton, Exeter, Plymouth and Penzance and local services to Birmingham, Swindon, Weymouth and throughout southwest England.

*Former Wales & West Class 158 dmu, now part of the Wessex Trains fleet, near Southampton forming a Portsmouth—Cardiff service* (Ken Harris)

### Wessex Trains diesel multiple-units

| Class | Cars per unit | Motor cars per unit | Motored axles/car | Power/motor kW | Speed km/h | Cars in service | First built | Builders Mechanical | Builders Engine | Transmission |
|---|---|---|---|---|---|---|---|---|---|---|
| 143 | 2 | 2 | 1 | 152 | 120 | 22 | 1985 | Alexander/Barclay | Cummins LTA10R | H Voith T211r |
| 150/2 | 2 | 2 | 2 | 210 | 120 | 48 | 1986 | BREL | Cummins NT855R5 | HM Voith T211r |
| 153 | 1 | 1 | 2 | 213 | 120 | 13 | 1987* | Leyland | Cummins NT855R5 | HM Voith T211r |
| 158/0 | 2 | 2 | 2 | 275/300 | 145 | 24 | 1989 | BREL | Cummins NTA855R | HM Voith T211r |

* Rebuilt 1991

### Traction and rolling stock
Wessex trains is an all-diesel-operated business worked with second-generation dmus. For its interurban routes, the company employs Class 158 dmus leased from Angel Trains. For local services, it leases Class 153 single cars from Angel and Class 143 and 150/2 dmus from Porterbrook.

**NEW ENTRY**

## West Anglia Great Northern

West Anglia Great Northern Railway Ltd
Hertford House, 1 Cranwood Street, London EC1V 9QS
Tel: (+44 20) 79 28 51 51   Fax: (+44 20) 77 13 21 02

### Key personnel
Managing Director: Dominic Booth
Finance Director: Robert Smyth
Production Director: Richard Lockett
Commercial Director: Mark Powles
General Manager, Stansted Express: Debbie Ellis

### Political background
Under the arrangements put in place by the 1993 Railways Act, the franchise to run operations on West Anglia Great Northern was let in December 1996 to Prism Rail plc (qv), a company set up to run rail franchises by a consortium of bus companies. Prism also ran the Cardiff Railway (now Valley Lines), Wales & West and LTS Rail (c2c) franchises. In November 2000, Prism sold its rail operating businesses to National Express Group.

The franchise was let for a term of seven years and three months. Prism was to receive from the Franchising Director support, in 1996 prices, of £52.9 million in the first full financial year of the franchise, reversing to a premium payment of £24.8 million in 2004.

### WAGN Railway electric multiple-units

| Class | Cars per unit | Motor cars per unit | Motored axles/car | Power/motor kW | Speed km/h | Cars in service | First built | Builders Mechanical | Electrical |
|---|---|---|---|---|---|---|---|---|---|
| 313* | 3 | 2 | 2 | 82 | 120 | 123 | 1976 | BREL | GEC |
| 315 | 4 | 2 | 2 | 82 | 120 | 72 | 1980 | BREL | Brush/GEC |
| 317 | 4 | 1 | 4 | 247 | 160 | 224 | 1981 | BREL | GEC |
| 365 | 4 | 2 | 2 | 140 | 160 | 100 | 1994 | ABB | GEC |

* Dual-voltage, 25 kV AC, 750 V DC

### Passenger operations
WAGN operates suburban services on a 413 km route network out of London's King's Cross, Moorgate and Liverpool Street stations, with services reaching as far north as King's Lynn and Peterborough. The company also provides a high-frequency 'Stansted Express' fast service between Liverpool Street and Stansted Airport.

| Traffic (million) | 1997-98 | 1998-99 | 1999-2000 |
|---|---|---|---|
| Passenger journeys | 52.8 | 55.7 | 61.2 |
| Passenger-km | 1,612 | 1,774 | 1,950.8 |
| Train-km | 16.5 | 18.0 | 18.3 |

### Traction and rolling stock
WAGN is exclusively operated by electric multiple-unit trains operating on the 25 kV AC overhead system, apart from a short 750 V DC section to Moorgate. The company leases 41 Class 313s, 18 Class 315s, 56 Class 317s, five Class 322s and 25 Class 365s. All are leased from Forward Trust, except the Class 317s which are owned by Angel Trains.

Prism has committed to refurbishing all the units used on outer-suburban services to a standard comparable to the new Class 365s, and to install more comfortable seats on the Class 315s.

The first of nine refurbished Class 317/7 emus dedicated to Stansted Express services entered service in August 2000. Each contains two galley areas to support an on-board trolley catering service.

*WAGN Class 317/6 emus forming a King's Lynn service at London Liverpool Street (Colin Boocock)*
2001/0099143

---

# UNITED STATES OF AMERICA

## Department of Transportation

400 7th Street SW, Washington DC 20590
Tel: (+1 202) 366 40 00

### Key personnel
Secretary: Rodney Slater
Deputy Secretary: Mortimer L Downey
Associate Deputy Secretary and Director, Office of Intermodalism: Michael P Huerta
General Counsel: Stephen H Kaplan
Assistant Secretaries
  Government Affairs: Steven O Palmer
  Public Affairs: Steven J Akey
  Policy: Frank E Kruesi
  Budget and Programmes: Louise F Stoll
Director, Executive Secretariat: Margarita Rogue

### Surface Transportation Board
1925 K Street NW, Washington DC 20423-0001
Tel: (+1 202) 565 16 74   Fax: (+1 202) 927 61 07

### Key personnel
Chairman: Linda J Morgan
Vice-Chairman: Gus A Owen
General Counsel: Henri F Rush
Secretary: Vernon A Williams

### Organisation
A proposal to reorganise the US Department of Transportation (USDOT), first made in January 1995, has not been acted upon. Under the proposal as formulated by the Secretary's office, 10 agencies would be consolidated into three, one of which would be an Intermodal Transportation Administration, including both the current Federal Transit Administration and Federal Railroad Administration, with the intent of streamlining operations and procedures for greater efficiency. A companion proposal called for some 30 capital grant programmes to be consolidated into one US$24 billion annual Unified Transportation Infrastructure Investment Program (UTIIP).

In place of the suggested reforms, the Secretary's office announced in January 1996 the Operation Timesaver initiative, with an emphasis on an Intelligent Transportation Infrastructure (ITI) to be built in the next decade, especially in the 75 most populous urban centres. The rail industry does not appear to play a major part in this initiative, except as an element of Intelligent Transportation Systems (ITS) projects in the areas of traveller information systems and improved rail-highway crossing devices.

USDOT field offices are expected to show greater responsiveness to state and local agencies, which are generally taking on more decision-making responsibilities. In 1997, the Administration introduced its NEXTEA (for National Economic Crossroads Transportation Efficiency Act) to succeed the ISTEA (Intermodal Surface Transportation Efficiency Act) which was in its last year of six. The Administration proposal was pegged at $175 billion for six years, compared to $157 billion for ISTEA. The levels are about the same if the effect of inflation over six years is taken into account. Several technical studies undertaken by USDOT during 1996, to ascertain the extent to which ISTEA funds have reached the intermodal industry, are being published.

Also receiving much attention recently is the ITS (Intelligent Transportation Systems) initiative, which consultants forecast will be a $400 billion market by 2015, although that figure is 87 per cent consumer-related product development and placement. Again, as a public policy issue, it is uncertain how much, if any, investment will be targeted towards either freight transportation, rail industry activity, or urban goods movement.

*Surface Transportation Board*
USDOT now includes the three-member Surface Transportation Board (STB), which replaced the Interstate Commerce Commission (ICC) and assumed its responsibilities in matters such as rail mergers. In July 1996, the STB unanimously approved the $3.9 billion acquisition of Southern Pacific by Union Pacific (UP). STB was to monitor the acquisition for five years, watching for any adverse competitive developments that would require additional conditions, and to ascertain that the substantial trackage rights granted by UP to Burlington Northern Santa Fe were being utilised effectively.

In the matter of Conrail (qv), the STB essentially told CSX and Norfolk Southern to agree to a disposition of the assets or the STB would rule on such a disposition. By the second quarter of 1997, all three companies had entered a joint petition with the STB for an expedited proceeding. STB approval of the two railroads' agreed formula for the division of Conrail assets was given in June 1998.

A 1996 ruling by the STB makes mergers and acquisitions between short lines, where neither party has revenue in excess of $20 million, not subject to Board approval.

Under the terms of the ICC Termination Act the STB is authorised to exist until September 1998. It may then be disbanded or change status.

The annual budget of the 'Surfboard' is $12.3 million, with about a quarter of that coming from fees.

## Federal Railroad Administration

1120 Vermont Street NW, Washington DC 20005
Tel: (+1 202) 493 60 14   Fax: (+1 202) 493 64 01
Web: http://www.dot.gov

### Regional Administrators of Railroad Safety

Region 1: 55 Broadway, 10th Floor, Room 107, Cambridge, Massachusetts 02142
Tel: (+1 617) 494 23 21

Region 2: Scott Plaza 2, Suite 550, Philadelphia, Pennsylvania 19113
Tel: (+1 610) 521 82 00

Region 3: 1720 Peachtree Road NW, Suite 440 North Tower, Atlanta, Georgia 30309
Tel: (+1 404) 347 27 51

Region 4: 111 N Canal Street, Suite 655, Chicago, Illinois 60606
Tel: (+1 312) 353 62 03

*Region 5:* 8701 Bedford Euless Road, Suite 425, Hurst, Texas 76053
Tel: (+1 817) 334 36 01

*Region 6:* 1807 Federal Building, 911 Walnut Street, Kansas City, Missouri 64106-2095
Tel: (+1 816) 426 24 97

*Region 7:* 650 Capital Mall, Room 7007, Sacramento, California 95814
Tel: (+1 916) 551 12 60

*Region 8:* Murdock Building, 703 Broadway Street, Suite 650, Vancouver, Washington 98660
Tel: (+1 206) 696 75 36

**Key personnel**
Administrator: Allan Rutter
Deputy Administrator: Betty Monro
Chief Counsel: S Mark Lindsey
Directors
    Budget: D J Stadtler
    Civil Rights: Carl Ruiz
    International Policy: Ted Krohn
Research and Development: Steve Ditmeyer
Associate Administrators
    Railroad Development: Mark Yachmetz
    Safety: George Gavalla
    Policy (Acting): Jane Bachner
    Public Affairs: Rob Gould
    Administration (Acting): Peggy Reid

**Organisation**
The Federal Railroad Administration develops rules and regulations to implement national transportation law affecting railroads. FRA rules apply to some 40 major areas, including driver qualifications; maximum permissible hours of service for railroad personnel; conduct of railroad police; rolling stock safety standards; alcohol and drug testing; and level crossing and signalling system safety.

FRA also manages research and development projects and contracts to operate FRA's Transportation Technology Center in Pueblo, Colorado with the Association of American Railroads.

***UPDATED***

## Federal Transit Administration (FTA)

Department of Transportation, 400 7th Street SW, Washington DC 77820-590
Tel: (+1 202) 366 40 40   Fax: (+1 202) 366 98 54

**Key personnel**
Administrator: Gordon J Linton
Deputy Administrator: Nuria Fernandez
Director, Public Affairs: Bruce Frame
Director, Policy Development: Richard Steinman

**Organisation**
The Federal Transit Administration (FTA) was formerly the Urban Mass Transportation Administration and is the agency responsible for providing federal financial assistance to US cities to improve mass transit. Grants for capital projects, including the acquisition of rolling stock, involve 80 per cent federal and 20 per cent local funding; FTA also provides funds for public transport planning, research and operations.

FTA has 10 field offices.

## CLASS I FREIGHT RAILROADS

The following section lists Class I railroads. In June 1992, the Interstate Commerce Commission revised its definition of railroad classifications. The annual qualifying revenue threshold for Class I status was raised from a gross of $92 million to $250 million. One Class I carrier reclassified in consequence was Florida East Coast; it was replaced by Wisconsin Central (qv) which exceeds $250 million since the acquisition and integration of the Algoma Central and the ex-UP Duck Creek subdivision.

The second section lists the more important companies in the Class II (gross revenue $20 million to $249.9 million) and Class III categories. The Class II category includes 15 Regional railroads.

Following this is a section on passenger operators. This includes Amtrak, which is a Class I railroad.

## Boston & Maine Corporation

A subsidiary of Guilford Rail System
Iron Horse Park, North Billerica, Massachusetts 01862
Tel: (+1 508) 663 11 30   Fax: (+1 508) 663 11 99
Web: http://www.guilfordrail.com

**Key personnel**
See entry for 'Guilford Rail System'

Gauge: 1,435 mm
Length: 2,532 km

**Organisation**
The principal lines of the Boston & Maine run north and west from Boston through the states of Maine, New Hampshire, Vermont, Massachusetts and in eastern New York state, where it makes connections at Albany and Schenectady with other lines.

In 1983, Guilford Transportation Industries (GTI) took over the B&M. GTI also owns the Maine Central. The railroads preserve their separate identities in some areas (for example equipment), but are being operated as an integral system with common management. As a result of past disputes with the labour force over working practices, management is exercised by another GTI subsidiary, the Springfield Terminal Railway Co.

Since the second quarter of 1995 all shipping documents have carried the Guilford name in order to simplify relations with customers. Guilford is privately held and revenue and performance data are not a matter of public record.

**Passenger operations**
The Northern New England Passenger Rail Authority (NNEPRA) has endorsed the upgrading of the main line from Plaistow, New Hampshire to Portland, Maine, for passenger operations at speeds of up to 126 km/h. Work began in January 1999 and was expected to take two years.

**Freight operations**
About 85 per cent of B&M's freight tonnage is received from connecting lines and two-thirds of it terminates on the system. Forest products from northern New England and Canada predominate.

**Intermodal operations**
B&M has built a major new intermodal facility called the Devens Inland Port and Distribution Center which opened in late 1993. This facility handles domestic and international containers, piggyback traffic and bulk transfer services; it serves as an extension of the port of Boston. Both the Devens Port and the Ayer automobile facility (see below) are targets of Norfolk Southern in a run-through arrangement which will see NS negotiating reciprocal rights with CP (St Lawrence & Hudson) in order to reach Albany, then a similar arrangement with B&M to serve Massachusetts, since CSX is acquiring Conrail's assets in New England.

**Improvements to existing lines**
The state of Massachusetts has announced a plan to spend $158 million to raise clearances across the state to accommodate double-stack trains. Phase I has consisted of clearing the section from Devens to Mechanicville, New York, to make connection to CP (St Lawrence & Hudson division).

In 1993, B&M upgraded the Ayer automobile unloading facility and installed 112 lb continuous welded rail on the Worcester main line.

**Traction and rolling stock**
The railroad operates with a fleet of 45 diesel locomotives of which the largest tranche is 32 GP40/GP40-2 models.

Recent rolling stock acquisitions include 384 boxcars for the transport of paper and paper products and 98 covered hoppers for cement traffic.

*Maine Central-lettered GP40 at the Boston & Maine yard in East Somerville, Maryland (F Gerald Rawling) 0021587*

## Burlington Northern Santa Fe (BNSF)

2650 Lou Menk Drive, PO Box 96105, Fort Worth, Texas 76161-0057
Tel: (+1 817) 333 20 00   Fax: (+1 817) 352 79 25
Web: http://www.bnsf.com

**Key personnel**
Chairman and Chief Executive Officer: Robert D Krebs
President and Chief Operating Officer: Matthew K Rose
Senior Vice-Presidents
    Chief Financial Officer: Tom Hind
    Operations: Carl Ice
    Growth Initiatives: Gregory T Sweinton
    Law, and General Counsel: Jeffrey R Moreland
    Employee Relations: James D Dagnon
Executive Vice-President and Chief Marketing Officer:
    Charles L Schultz
Group Vice-Presidents
    Agricultural Products: Steve Bobb
    Coal: Tom Kraemer
    Consumer Products: Steve Branscum
    Industrial Products: Dave Garin
Vice-Presidents
    General Counsel: Shelley Venick
    General Tax Counsel: Daniel J Westerbeck
    Litigation: Gary L Crosby
    Government Relations: A R (Skip) Endres
    Finance, and Treasurer: Patrick J Ottensmeyer
    Controller: Dennis Johnson
    Investor Relations and Corporate Secretary:
        Marsha K Morgan
    Corporate Relations: Richard A Russack
    Business Unit Operation and Customer Service:
        Fritz Draper
    Service Design and Performance: Rollin Bredenburg
Transportation: Dave Dealy
    Safety, Training and Operations Support:
        Greg Stengem

Gauge: 1,435 mm
Length: approximately 54,400 route-km

*For map, see Union Pacific section.*

### Organisation

BNSF was created in 1995 with the merger of two major railroads, namely the Burlington Northern and the Santa Fe. BNSF's territory lies principally to the west of the Mississippi river, serving 27 US states and two Canadian provinces; a major rival is the Union Pacific/Southern Pacific system.

BN itself was the product of a 1970 merger involving the Chicago, Burlington & Quincy; Great Northern; Northern Pacific; and Spokane, Portland & Seattle railways. In 1980, BN bought out the St Louis-San Francisco Railway (the Frisco). The core of the Santa Fe Railway was a high-speed Chicago-Los Angeles route, with feeder lines in the western and mid-western states.

The integrated system is now operated as 22 geographical divisions.

At the beginning of 1999, BNSF employed some 44,500 staff.

*Union Pacific/Southern Pacific merger*

In response to some significant opposition to the UP/SP merger, the UP sold the BNSF some 560 km of track and additionally arranged up to 6,100 km in trackage rights in order to provide competition in areas that would otherwise have had only single-carrier service. The three principal elements of the deal were (a) allowing BNSF into New Orleans directly, (b) connecting BNSF's extensive Pacific northwest trackage with California's Central Valley and Bay area, via Oregon (Klamath Falls) and northern California to offer a single line haul much shorter than the alternative through Idaho, Wyoming and over the Rockies again, and (c) giving BNSF access to the Denver-Stockton corridor which would otherwise have been a UP monopoly.

Typical of the new service options under trackage rights available is a Houston-Memphis service with interline connection via the former Illinois Central route to Illinois. Systemwide, nearly 1,000 major manufacturing and distribution services can now call on BNSF for service. The Surface Transportation Board has stated that it will require periodic reports from BNSF in order to determine that the trackage rights concessions have achieved their purpose in satisfying shippers' concerns about competition.

### Finance

The BNSF concluded 1997 with $8,413 million in total freight revenues. For 1996, BNSF reported $8,141 million. Performance during the year was hampered by severe winter weather during the first quarter, and the consequences of Union Pacific's difficulties later in the year. Despite the latter problem and a nationwide shortage of intermodal wagons, BNSF achieved a revenue improvement of 5 per cent compared with the same period in 1996.

In 1997, revenue ton-km totalled 683.29 billion, up 3.3 per cent on 1996.

**Finances**

| (US$ millions) | *1996* | *1997* |
|---|---|---|
| Revenues | 8,141 | 8,413 |
| Operating income | 1,748 | 1,767 |
| Income after taxes and other items | 889 | 885 |

### Line sales

BNSF's line/track rationalisation programme has been relatively conservative compared to those of other Class I railroads. Sales in 1998 included the 438 km Camas Prairie Railroad in southeast Washington and western Idaho, which was jointly owned with Union Pacific, to North American RailNet, Inc.

### Freight operations

Part of the rationale for the merger of BN and the Santa Fe was that the two companies were major players in different traffic areas: the BN's top commodities were coal, lumber and forest products out of the northwest, and agricultural commodities, while Santa Fe was pre-eminent in intermodal business and the distribution of automobiles. By merging two largely complementary territories, the BNSF offers single-line service from the Gulf of Mexico to Canada and from the southwest to the upper midwest. As a product of the trackage agreement with UP/SP, the BNSF will increase its presence in transborder traffic to and from Mexico.

*During 1998 Dash 9-44CW locomotives built by GE for BNSF were entering service partially painted to keep traffic moving* (F Gerald Rawling) 0021586

Transport of coal is BNSF's largest source of rail freight tonnage, contributing 23 per cent of revenue in 1997, although the combined automotive and intermodal sectors accounted for $2,691 million (32 per cent) of turnover – an increase on 1996 of $269 million.

Over 200 million tonnes of coal was again originated by the combined properties in 1997. Low sulphur coal from the Powder River Basin of Montana and Wyoming accounts for most of BNSF's originations. This is hauled to close to 60 coal-burning electricity generating stations chiefly in the north central, south central, mountain and Pacific regions. Hauls to power plants in the east are rising (some coal is transferred onto navigable rivers at the limit of BNSF trackage).

Nearly all the coal tonnage originated by BNSF is carried in unit trains and 99 per cent of the business is run under contract. The trains typically consist of 108 wagons and, depending on the difficulty of the grades encountered, from three to six locomotives. On a typical working day BNSF has about 190 unit coal trains on the move; about three-quarters of them will be formed of customer-owned wagons.

BNSF serves a significant area of the major grain-producing regions located in the midwest and Great Plains and transports large quantities of whole grains to domestic feed lots, major milling centres, and to the Pacific northwest, Gulf and western Great Lakes ports for export. In 1997, agricultural commodities produced 13 per cent of revenues.

BNSF serves the timber-producing regions of the Pacific northwest and the southeast, hauling significant volumes of lumber, plywood and structural panels, wood chips, wood pulp, paper and paper products. For 1996 this group produced 6.8 per cent of revenues. Fluctuations in the level of forest products traffic result from general economic conditions as reflected in new housing starts and levels of industrial production, from competition with other modes, and export demand.

In other commodity groups, in the first half of 1996 chemicals accounted for 9.3 per cent of 1996 revenues; consumer products, 5.7 per cent; minerals, 3.9 per cent; metals, 4.9 per cent; vehicles and machinery, 4.8 per cent.

*New international links*

With the introduction of the North American Free Trade Agreement (NAFTA), BNSF spread its net to encompass service to both Canada and Mexico (via El Paso), as well as its US heartland.

Premerger partnerships had been struck with CP Rail, where BNSF operates intermodal trains between Texas and Toronto and Montreal, and with CN North America for movement of freight between western Canada and Chicago.

An agreement with the South Orient Railroad Co signed in 1992 gives BNSF alternative access to the Mexican rail network. Trains from Ojinaga in north Mexico travel via Presidio, Texas, to join the BNSF system at Dallas/Fort Worth. The UP-SP merger conditions also gave BNSF access to Eagle Pass, Texas, from San Antonio.

### Intermodal operations

Increasing containerisation of internal US freight has benefited both the former BN (which had been moving for several years into domestic container business) and the former Santa Fe. Intermodal freight is now the number one revenue producer for BNSF, generating $2.09 billion in 1996.

Since 1991 both the Santa Fe and BN components of the railroad have been teamed up with road haulier J B Hunt to provide intermodal service between the midwest and Pacific northwest; this partnership continues. Other partnerships are in effect with UPS and its refrigerated MarTrac subsidiary, as well as several LTL (Less than TruckLoad) carriers.

In 1996, BNSF, Norfolk Southern and Conrail formed a domestic intermodal equipment project called NACS (North American Container System), which will encourage shippers to use containers in most major markets where there is double-stack service available and taking advantage of the restriction-free interchange of NACS 48 ft containers. By 1999 some 6,000 of these units were available for use by participating operators. The network has subsequently expanded to include Canadian National, CSX Intermodal, Kansas City Southern and, from May 1999, Norfolk Southern.

BNSF now offers double-stack service for refrigerated containers in international traffic. Power for the refrigeration plant in up to nine containers conveyed on a five-platform double-stack wagon is supplied from a container, carried in the centre platform, which holds two diesel-generator sets (one for back-up) and a large fuel tank.

Recent additions to BNSF's stack-train resources include 106 stand-alone heavy-lift 'Husky-Stack' well wagons from Gunderson. The builder claims that the car, designed primarily for domestic market weighty container traffic, can accept 60 per cent more load than conventional articulated double-stack wells. It is therefore adaptable to such freight as lumber, plywood, paper and solid waste. The 48 ft well can take a 48 ft container below and stack a 53 ft container above.

Since the UP/SP merger, BNSF has introduced dedicated intermodal services on the following new lanes: New Orleans-Arizona and New Orleans-California; St Paul, Minnesota-California; and Texas-Pacific northwest/Vancouver. As recently as April 1994, BN had withdrawn from the Texas market.

Intermodal handling capacity was increased at several locations during 1997, including the Cicero and Corwith hubs in the Chicago area, Kansas City and Los Angeles.

### Improvements to existing lines

BNSF's 1997 capital expenditures were over $2 billion, and the 1998 forecast anticipates a similar level of investment. The 1998 figure includes a projected $90 million on terminal expansion, line improvements and information technology. Planned projects include: a $44 million investment in increased track capacity to serve the Powder River Basin, allowing the operation of more than 50 daily coal trains; removal of a single-track 588 m tunnel at Guernsey, Wyoming, on a key coal route, and replacing it with 5.6 km of double track; and double-tracking some 120 km of the Chicago-Los Angeles trunk route in New Mexico at a cost of $150 million.

Some $800 million has already been directed at capacity expansion projects, including negotiations with the Washington Central (qv) for track to reach the Pacific northwest.

Finding itself acutely short of capacity to the northwest ports and major markets, BNSF purchased and re-opened the Stampede Pass line to create a third route. The company has budgeted $125 million in the 1997-99 period for upgrades, including raising clearance in the 2.9 km Stampede Pass tunnel to accommodate double-stack container trains.

The Argentine Yard in Kansas City was re-commissioned in 1997 after a complete $90 million rehabilitation, and is now BNSF's largest sorting facility. Improvements here, together with those at Galesburg, completed in 1996, allow the company to avoid the overcrowded Chicago network as an interchange facility. Intermodal lifting facilities at several locations also benefited during 1997 from investments totalling $10 million.

### Traction and rolling stock

At the beginning of 1998 the BNSF locomotive fleet totalled some 4,400 units, including machines on hire.

BNSF became the first North American freight railroad to opt in volume for AC three-phase traction motors, ordering 350 SD70M-AC 4,000 hp (3,000 kW) locomotives from Electro Motive Division of General Motors in March 1993, subsequently adding 54 to the order. The locomotives have Siemens electrics, EMD's EM 2000 microprocessor control package and a new radial bogie. They are being promoted for their all-weather traction, improved fuel efficiency, lower emissions and lower maintenance requirements. BNSF estimates that three of the new machines do the work of five SD40s. Most of the new locomotives have been used on coal service.

In May 1997, BNSF announced an order for an additional 405 locomotives to be delivered in the period 1997-2000. From EMD 26 SD75I units came in 1997 and 105 SD70MAC units in 1997-98, with a further 104 (unspecified) to come in 1999 and 2000. From GE came 170 Dash 9-44CW units in 1997-98. As part of the agreement with EMD a contract maintenance facility will be built at BNSF's intermodal property in City of Commerce, California. EMD already operates four such facilities in Chicago; Barstow, California; Alliance, Nebraska; and Glendive, Montana.

*'Power by the Hour'*
BNSF continues with its 'Power by the Hour' contractual arrangements with locomotive manufacturers. The contracts involve 100 General Electric Dash 8 units through a leasing intermediary, LMX Inc, and 100 SD60 units from GM-EMD via another intermediary, Oakway Inc; actual fleets in 1995 had been reduced to 197 by attrition and accidents and these units also were beginning to show up more off-line during 1996.

The suppliers (LMX and Oakway) guarantee availability in the form of a number of kilowatt hours from the fleet. The manufacturer, supplier and the purchaser (BNSF) negotiate support functions – basically the manufacturers oversee BNSF workshop employees in the performance of a maintenance regimen.

*AllRailer*
BNSF is collaborating with Wabash National, the builder, to develop the AllRailer, a fully enclosed car transporter and the first such vehicle for Wabash. It will be changeable between a two-tier and a three-tier configuration and use the same slack-free couplers from RoadRailer. Performance tests have been conducted at Pueblo and in-service (revenue) trials started in 1997.

### Signalling and telecommunications
BN opened its $120 million Network Operations Centre (NOC), called the James J Hill Center and designed in co-operation with Union Switch & Signal, in Fort Worth, Texas, in April 1995. The centre provides tactical control of four functions, namely:
- Business Processes and Functions (that is trains, crews and power) through TSS (Transportation Support Systems);
- Information Technology (that is asset management, strategic and tactical planning systemwide);
- Human Resources;
- Facility Design.

BNSF is adopting the DigiCon dispatching system, and dispatchers from offices in St Paul, Minnesota; Alliance, Nebraska; Springfield, Missouri; and Seattle, Washington, were moved to Fort Worth during 1997.

The 125 workstations at Fort Worth are individually climate and lighting controlled and include personal storage spaces. The building is built to withstand tornadoes; its walls are of half a metre thick, steel-reinforced concrete.

There is design capacity to include Santa Fe properties; SF opened its own similar facility within the last two years using a different systems architecture and different software, though the management objectives were the same. Combining and/or reconciling the two systems is a continuing systems engineering challenge.

BNSF and the UP have been co-operating with the Federal Railroad Administration to test Positive Train Separation (PTS) on 1,350 km of track in the Pacific northwest, comprising some track owned separately by each participant and some jointly operated, with the UP on the BNSF under trackage rights. Amtrak is a participant. GE Harris Railway Electronics is the systems integrator, involving both Forth Worth (BNSF) and Omaha (UP) dispatch centres. PTS displays safe train operating instructions in the cab, alerts train crew to potential conflicts and overrides, that is stops the train, if there is no crew response. The results will be shared nationally with

# Conrail
Consolidated Rail Corporation

### Political background
Conrail was created as a private profit-making corporation by an Act of Congress and began operations in April 1976. It comprised most of the rail properties of a group of bankrupt companies: the Central of New Jersey, Erie Lackawanna, Lehigh & Hudson River, Lehigh Valley, Penn Central and Reading lines. Following an unsuccessful attempt by the government to sell off Conrail to Norfolk Southern, the federal 85 per cent stake in Conrail was floated on the open market in 1987. The flotation was successful and realised $1.9 billion. Conrail thus remained an intact system until broken up in 1999.

*Break-up of Conrail*
On 15 October 1996, CSX Corporation agreed to buy Conrail for $8.1 billion in a friendly deal that would have required the approval of the Surface Transportation Board (qv). Norfolk Southern countered with a $9.1 billion offer. The issue was fought out in the pages of the nation's business press as well as in the courts. Conrail stockholders opposed the 'friendly low bid' by CSX. Also in consideration was a legal issue of whether the virtual monopoly in the New York market, given to Conrail to improve its start-up position in 1976, could be transferred to CSX if there was a challenger (NS). The Surface Transportation Board effectively told the parties to agree between themselves on a settlement, tacitly recognising the break-up of Conrail. By the second quarter of 1997 the deal was in two parts:
(a) CSX would acquire Conrail for $10.5 billion (the price after having been bid up by NS)

(b) NS would immediately acquire about 58 per cent of Conrail for $5.9 billion, approximately.

The three parties then each withdrew their separate positions before the STB and jointly filed for an expedited proceeding. In June 1997, the STB said it would rule on the deal within a year. Approval was given by the STB in June 1998, and CSX and NS took over control of their respective portions of the Conrail network in June 1999.

Under the deal, CSX took control of the St Louis-Indianapolis-Cleveland-Buffalo-Syracuse-Albany-New York route (the once New York Central 'water level' route).

NS took over the ex-Pennsylvania line Chicago-Pittsburgh-East Coast (some of which, at the west end, it had been buying up already) and the 'southern tier' line across New York State.

Areas around Detroit, Philadelphia, in New Jersey and in the Monongahela coalfield are jointly owned, but NS also received the old Reading route between Hagerstown and New York.

*Line disposals*
Before asset disposition being put on hold pending break-up of Conrail, a significant component of Conrail's disposal programme was the 'Conrail Express' partnership project in which lines were spun off in 'clusters' around a hub, analagous to the way in which feeder services in the airline industry work. The extent of imitation even allowed for Conrail to paint the short line motive power in a 'Conrail Express' paint scheme. During 1996 Conrail disposed of a 125 km cluster in Connecticut (to RailTex); 157 km of track in Pennsylvania to the Reading and Northern; parts of the Pekin Secondary, the former Peoria and Eastern Railroad in

Illinois, to Norfolk Southern; 61 km of the Williamsburg cluster and about 50 km of the Carnegie cluster, both in Pennsylvania.

In the first quarter of 1997 the project was suspended while CSXT and Norfolk Southern examined all of Conrail's remaining properties.

### Traction and rolling stock
At the beginning of 1998 the Conrail locomotive fleet totalled nearly 2,000 units. Its most recent order, announced in December 1997, was for 39 General Motors SD-70 locomotives, of which 15 were to be AC-powered and the remainder DC. Assembly was being undertaken from kits at the railroad's Juniata workshops at Altoona, Pennsylvania, with all locomotives scheduled to be in service by November 1998. Under the planned break-up of Conrail, the AC units passed to CSX, while the DC machines became the property of NS.

## CSX Intermodal Inc (CSXI)

301 West Bay Street, Jacksonville, Florida 32202
Tel: (+1 904) 633 10 00
Web: http://www.csxi.com

### Key personnel
President and Chief Executive Officer: M McNeil Porter
Senior Vice-Presidents
   Operations: Michael G Peterson
   Sales and Marketing: J Ganson Evans
   Ronald T Sorrow
Vice-Presidents
   Operations: Frank K Turner
   Marketing and Pricing: Alan Peck
   Finance: Asok Chaudhuri
   Sales: Jim Williams
   International Sales and Marketing: Steven E Rand
   Business Planning: Peter Rutski
   Human Resources: William Schultz
Vice-President and General Counsel: Mark Hoffman

### Organisation
CSXI, formed in 1988, is an integrated door-to-door intermodal carrier, operating both a nationwide container distribution service (with the backbone of the traffic being the inland haulage of containers landed by sister CSX company Sea-Land) and piggyback trains in the east of the country on the CSX system. CSXI's double-stack container trains use the CSX system to reach destinations in the east of the country but also serve other areas on other railroads.

CSXI operates independently of parent CSX Corporation but during 1995 was brought closer to the parent in several ways, including a relocation. Employment was reduced by 16 per cent in 1995, partly in response to flat demand for trailer business which was adversely affected by aggressive truck competition. CSXI has its own autonomous senior management group and, since 1993, has reported separate financial results.

Assets owned and leased at the end of December 1997 were 5,322 domestic containers, 5,119 rail trailers, 33 intermodal terminals, 23 motor carrier operations terminals and 18 servicing facilities. CSXI's 33 fully mechanised intermodal terminals, staffed by its own employees, serve every major port. CSXI manages and monitors over 300 dedicated weekly intermodal trains, including 13 transcontinental double-stack trains. Trucking operations are fully integrated, and CSXI's drayage operations, if considered alone, would constitute the largest such service in North America. A subsidiary, CSX Services, handles chassis leasing and equipment maintenance at 17 facilities, manages the container pick-up and delivery process and schedules availability.

In a restructuring and asset management move in June 1996, CSXI grouped its terminals into six geographic regions, each with a general manager. The average number of staff employed in 1997 fell to 800, compared with 1,090 in 1996.

### Finance
CSXI recorded operating revenue of $669 million in 1997, compared with $660 million in 1996. Expenses were $623 million, producing net operating income of $46 million, a 31 per cent increase over 1996.

International traffic volume rose by 7 per cent in 1997, while domestic volume increased by 4 per cent.

### Intermodal operations
Service extends to all continental US states, three adjoining Canadian provinces and Mexico. CSXI's sister company Sea-Land connects to Alaska. The company's fastest growing service is its 48 ft domestic container network dubbed 'Frequent Flyer', which offers nationwide door-to-door service. Recently, especially buoyant flows have been the Pacific Northwest to Southeast (the Carolinas, Georgia, Florida) and California to New England, the Northeast and middle Atlantic states.

In the area of customer service CSXI has the USA's first advance ordering system for domestic containers, which was expanded to include trailers in 1993, and operates CSXI Customer Service, 24 hour, seven-day shipment tracing using EDI.

During 1997, CSXI began expansion of its terminal facilities in Atlanta and New York/New Jersey, and expanded its domestic container fleet by over 30 per cent. Further capital investments in 1998 were to be aimed at expansion of facilities in preparation for the integration of Conrail. These included the new $39 million 59th Street terminal in Chicago, which was opened in September 1998. During the same year approval was obtained to construct a new intermodal terminal at Fairburn, some 32 km south of Atlanta. The first phase was due to open in 1999.

In May 1998, CSX and Norfolk Southern were awarded rights jointly to operate the 11 km Staten Island Railroad, providing access to New York's Howland Hook Marine Terminal. Reports suggested that resulting traffic could rise to 400,000 containers annually.

*Transferring containers between drayage truck and double-stack train*

## CSX Transportation Inc (CSXT)

A business unit of CSX Corporation
500 Water Street, Jacksonville, Florida 32202
Tel: (+1 904) 359 31 00   Fax: (+1 904) 359 18 99
Web: http://www.csxt.com

### Key personnel
President and Chief Executive Officer:
   Ronald J Conway
Executive Vice-Presidents
   Law and Corporate Affairs: Mark G Aron
   Operations: Carl N Taylor
   Finance: Paul R Goodwin
   Sales and Marketing: John Q Anderson
   Employee Relations: Donald D Davis
Senior Vice-Presidents
   Corporate Services: Andrew B Fogarty
   Employee Relations: Frank H Nichols
   Technology: John F Andrews
   Sales and Marketing: Aden C Adams
   General Counsel: P Michael Giftos
   Charles J O Wodehouse
Vice-Presidents
   Corporate Secretary: Patricia J Aftoora
   Employee Relations: R H Cockerham
   Merchandise Marketing: John E Giles
   Engineering: J N Reese
   Mechanical: W Michael Cantrell
   Field Operations: C W Gooden
   Financial Planning and Analysis: Frederick J Favorite
   Service Design: Renee D Rysdahl
   Corridor Development: A B Aftoora
   Operations Support: F E Pursley
   Human Resources: Sally B Basso
   Supply and Services: John W Basso
   Chemicals: C P Jenkins
   Coal Sales and Marketing: R L Sharp
   Automotive: D R Hawk
   State Relations: M J Ruehling
   Risk Management: J Edward Codd
   Northeast Commercial Operations: James A Howarth
   Real Estate and Industrial Development:
      J Randall Evans
   Corporate Communications and Public Affairs:
      T M Fiorentino
   Controller: Frank E Herczeg Jr
Chief Engineers
   Maintenance of Way: R A Cross
   System Reliability: R Kenneth Beckham
   Train Control: R M Kadlick
Chief Mechanical Officers
   Locomotive Operations: David L Petway
   Cars: M L Wall
   Engineering and Quality Control: G C Martin
Vice-President and General Manager, Chesapeake & Ohio Business Unit: T G Forst
General Manager, Cumberland Coal Business Unit:
   D S Green
General Manager, Florida Business Unit: P D Sandler

Gauge: 1,435 mm
Route length: approximately 36,500 km

### Organisation
CSXT is a rail transportation and distribution company operating in 20 US states, the District of Columbia and Ontario, Canada. It is one of five related transportation companies that make up CSX Corporation. The other component CSX companies are:
- Sea-Land Service Inc, a container shipper operating 98 ships and 220,000 containers of various kinds serving 120 ports;
- CSX Intermodal Inc (CSXI – qv) which operates over 300 dedicated trains each week serving a network of 33 intermodal terminals in North America and offers

# USA/RAILWAY SYSTEMS

*A GE DAH8-40CW locomotive leads two GM-EMD SD40-2s at Sand Patch Summit on CSXT's Baltimore-Pittsburgh main line (Phil Marshall)* 0063696

truck drayage, chassis management and leasing services;
- American Commercial Lines (ACL), the largest barge operator in the US with 135 towboats and 3,800 barges together with supporting marine facilities;
- Customised Transportation Inc (CTI), which is a contract logistics services company.

Non-transportation holdings of CSX include Mobil Five-Star and AAA Five-Diamond hotels, the Greenbrier resort in White Sulphur Springs, West Virginia and Grand Teton lodge in Moran, Wyoming. A majority interest is held in Yukon Pacific Corporation in Anchorage, Alaska, which is promoting the Trans-Alaska Gas System. CSX Real Property Inc disposes of CSX assets surplus to operating requirements.

The holding company, CSX Corporation, is publicly traded on the New York Stock Exchange.

*Formation of CSXT*
In 1980, Chessie System Inc merged with Seaboard Coast Line Industries to form the CSX Corporation. At first the rail constituents, Chessie System Railroads and Seaboard System Railroad (a revised title), maintained their separate identities, managements and operations, but in 1986 they were co-ordinated into a single system, CSX Transportation Inc (CSXT). A multimodal structure was developed to maximise deregulation's opportunities, stress the importance of the train as a link in a total distribution chain, and structure a competitively credible door-to-door transport system. Thus CSXT and its trucking operation, Chessie Motor Express, were welded into a new total transport system.

In early 1986, CSXT bid successfully for control of Sea-Land, the major container shipping line. This gave CSXT control of Sea-Land terminals throughout the world. To optimise the scope for synergies of its marine and land intermodal activity a new company, CSX Intermodal (CSXI), was formed to handle all CSXT and Sea-Land intermodal operations. It became operational at the start of 1988.

*Conrail acquisition*
In October 1996, CSX made an agreed bid for Conrail (qv), valuing the Philadelphia-based company at $8.1 billion. As expected, Norfolk Southern (qv) vigorously contested the merger and initiated a hostile bid valued at $9.1 billion. By January 1997, CSX had acquired about 20 per cent of Conrail stock and NS about 10 per cent. Conrail stockholders ceased to tender to CSX. The Surface Transportation Board expressed a desire to see the parties reach a 'negotiated and balanced' settlement. NS then sent CSX and Conrail a proposal to divide Conrail. CSX agreed to amend its merger proposal, rebid for Conrail at $115 share (a gross valuation of $10.5 billion) and resell about 58 per cent of Conrail to NS. CSX has acquired much of what was once the New York Central plus a shared interest in desirable trackage around Detroit, New York/New Jersey and in the Pennsylvania/West Virginia coalfields. Approval of the joint acquisition by the STB was given on 8 June 1998 and CSX began operating its share of the former Conrail system on 1 June 1999.

With the additions of the trackage acquired from Conrail, the CSX system has expanded to some 36,500 route-km, and annual revenues are projected to be $6.4 billion. Network benefits include the ability to bypass congestion in Chicago, allowing CSX to reduce transit times to Burlington Northern Santa Fe and Union Pacific destinations by one day, and the use of modern classification facilities at Indianapolis to free capacity at Cincinnati to speed up shipments to southeastern states.

CSX planned to invest nearly $500 million in capital improvements to its share of the former Conrail network, and is to deploy 190 additional locomotives to the 820 it inherits from Conrail.

*Lines and territories*
The Chessie System principally comprised the former Chesapeake & Ohio and Baltimore & Ohio Railroads and their subsidiaries, such as the B&OCT (Baltimore & Ohio Chicago Terminal). The ex-Chesapeake & Ohio Railway's principal lines extend from the coalfields of southern West Virginia and eastern Kentucky eastward to the port of Newport News; westward to Louisville, Cincinnati and Chicago; and northward through Colombus and Toledo to Detroit.

The former Baltimore & Ohio system operates in 11 states and the District of Columbia. Principal lines extend from Philadelphia, through the port of Baltimore and Washington to Cumberland, Pennsylvania, and thence by separate routes to Chicago and St Louis.

Seaboard System was formed in 1983 through the merger of Seaboard Coast Line Railroad and the Louisville & Nashville Railroad. Former Seaboard main lines extend from Chicago to the Gulf of Mexico along the Atlantic coastal plain, serving all major Atlantic ports from Virginia to Florida; the system also serves several ports on the Gulf of Mexico, including Tampa, Mobile, Pascagoula and New Orleans.

In the south and southeast, ex-Seaboard lines serve the rich coal-producing fields of eastern Kentucky.

*Business units*
In early 1994 CSXT established the C&O Coal Business Unit. This unit manages all aspects of the railroad's business operations on the principal coal-hauling lines of the former Chesapeake & Ohio Railway. Strategic business units established previously are CSX Intermodal; Cumberland Coal Business Unit, covering coal operations on the lines of the former Baltimore & Ohio Railroad; and Florida Business Unit for phosphate and fertiliser in south-central Florida.

*Service lanes*
CSXT has established four service lanes (out of a projected seven); in each lane a large geographic area is supervised by a general manager responsible for all transportation functions. In many respects the lanes are a recreation of pre-CSXT rails, for example the Chicago lane is essentially the one-time Louisville & Nashville and Monon. Service lane management, the business units, and system support from sales and marketing are meshed in each territory to improve customer response, service reliability and asset deployment.

| Finance, rail only (US$ million) | 1995 | 1996 | 1997 |
|---|---|---|---|
| Operating revenue | 4,819 | 4,909 | 4,989 |
| Total operating expenditure | 3,951 | 3,782 | 3,760 |
| Operating income (loss) | 868 | 1,127 | 1,229 |
| Net income after other charges | 727 | 855 | - |
| Operating ratio | 77.9 | 77.0 | 75.4 |

### Finance
CSX reported consolidated transportation operating revenue of $10.6 billion in 1997, the third consecutive year over the $10 billion mark and a sixth year of increase. Gross expenses were $9.038 billion. Of those figures, rail contributed $4.989 billion to group revenue, up $80 million from the previous year. Rail operating expenses were $3.760 billion compared to $3.782 billion in 1996. The operating ratio (operating expenses as a percentage of income) declined to 75.4 per cent from 77.0 per cent a year earlier.

As a result of agreements negotiated in 1993 and similar ones reached previously, CSXT now operates through freight trains with only a conductor and driver on virtually its entire system. Efforts are now under way to extend these agreements to local and yard crews; the declared target is a systemwide crew size of 2.25 compared to the 2.4 in 1995 (and 2.7 in 1993).

The average CSXT rail workforce in 1996 was 28,500 employees. CSXT announced early in 1997 that it was going to set up several locomotive driver training courses in colleges and universities to train drivers as many existing drivers were expected to retire in the near future.

Including locomotive purchases, the annual capital investment programme for CSXT in 1996 was $764 million, a level unchanged from the previous year. Similar annual programmes were expected to be in the range of $600 million to $650 million in the years up until 1998.

### Passenger operations
CSX is principally a freight railway, but it operates commuter services for Maryland's Rail Commission on lines to/from Washington Union station (see MARC entry). In 1996, CSX and MARC signed a five-year contract extension.

### Freight operations
In 1997, total rail merchandise wagon loads (at 4.69 million) represented a modest increase on the previous year's 4.57 million, but revenues in most commodity sectors showed improvement. Year to year comparisons for wagon loads and revenues are shown in the accompanying table.

**Rail commodities by wagon loads**

|  | Wagon loads in thousands | | | Revenue in $ millions | | |
|---|---|---|---|---|---|---|
|  | 1996 | 1997 | Change % 1996-1997 | 1996 | 1997 | Change % 1996-1997 |
| Automotive | 367 | 387 | +5.4 | 520 | 543 | +4.4 |
| Chemicals | 408 | 435 | +6.6 | 721 | 747 | +3.6 |
| Minerals | 430 | 445 | +3.4 | 381 | 394 | +3.4 |
| Food and consumer | 134 | 149 | +1.1 | 148 | 163 | +10.1 |
| Agricultural products | 261 | 269 | +3.1 | 343 | 347 | +1.2 |
| Metals | 277 | 316 | +14.1 | 290 | 314 | +8.3 |
| Forest products | 466 | 471 | +1.1 | 499 | 499 | N/C |
| Phosphates and fertiliser | 511 | 506 | -0.1 | 279 | 292 | +4.7 |
| Coal | 1,711 | 1,714 | +0.2 | 1,584 | 1,560 | -1.5 |
| **Total** | 4,566 | 4,692 | +2.8 | 4,765 | 4,859 | +2.0 |
| Other revenues |  |  |  | 144 | 130 |  |
| **Total rail revenue** |  |  |  | 4,909 | 4,989 | +1.9 |

## Improvements to existing lines

A 20 ft (6 m) vertical clearance, suitable for double-stack operations, has been achieved on the Atlanta-New Orleans-Jacksonville triangle. CSXT will construct similar clearances in the Chicago-Nashville-Augusta (Georgia), traffic lane and the Nashville-Birmingham (Alabama)-Macon (Georgia) corridor.

In 1998, CSXT completed a $220 million project to upgrade and double-track the Greenwich, Ohio-East Gary, Indiana corridor, improving links between New England and the Atlantic coast ports and Chicago and the Midwest. Around 400 km of track has been reconstructed or upgraded and some 160 km of new rail laid. The scheme has involved the creation of several new links with ex-Conrail lines as well as the provision of bi-directional signalling.

In 1999, CSXT planned to invest $462 million in infrastructure renewals and upgrades.

## Traction and rolling stock

At the close of 1997 and before the acquisition of part of Conrail, CSXT listed 2,781 diesel locomotives, including leased machines; the higher horsepower units arriving on the railway will displace several of the older, smaller classes which will be made available to short lines and third parties. At the same date, the wagon fleet totalled 97,478.

In June 1999, CSXT placed a contract with GE Harris Electronics to equip its locomotive fleet with a Pinpoint GPS tracking system. Some 2,800 locomotives are to be adapted in a bid to improve utilisation and fuel efficiency.

Investment plans for 1999 included: 89 GE AC6000 locomotives; 50 GE AC4400s; 30 GM-EMD SD70MACs; and modifications and upgrades valued at $4.7 million to the existing locomotive fleet. In addition the company planned to invest $142 million in freight wagons, including 1,331 new vehicles and 9,563 modified or refurbished.

## Signalling and telecommunications

CSXT has been developing a pilot Advanced Train Control System (ATCS) on its Bone Valley line east of Tampa, Florida, which was also CSXT's testing ground for AEI (Automatic Equipment Identification). Predominantly involved in phosphates haulage from mines to ports, this line is well suited to the trial because its traffic is hauled by a dedicated stud of locomotives.

## Track

**Rail type & weight:** T-rail, 17.6 kg/m to 69.6 kg/m
**Sleepers:** Hardwood (101.5 million) 2,600 × 180 × 230 mm; concrete (250,000) 2,600 × 210 (railseat)/180 (centre) × 270 mm. Spaced 1,950/km (wood) and 1,640/km (concrete)
**Fastenings:** Cut spike, wood; Pandrol clips, wood in more than 6° curves and for concrete sleepers
**Max curvature:** 14°, main line; some branches up to 30°
**Max gradients:** approx 2.5%, main line; approx 2.9% branch lines
**Max permissible axleload:** 34.8 tonnes

---

# Illinois Central Railroad

Gauge: 1,435 mm
Length: 4,320 km (excluding Chicago, Central & Pacific)

## Organisation

In February 1998, Illinois Central Corporation and Canadian National Railway Company announced plans to merge their railway interests. ICC's principal subsidiary, the Illinois Central Railroad (IC), had become the sixth largest Class I railroad in the US at 4,320 km: a merger with the Canadian company was intended to create a network spanning Canada from coast to coast, and crossing the USA from Chicago to the Gulf of Mexico at New Orleans. The CN takeover valued the equity of IC at $2.4 billion. CN also took over IC's debt of $560 million. Integration of the two systems commenced on 1 July 1999, following approval in May of the takeover by the Surface Transportation Board.

IC was incorporated in 1851 as the United States' first land grant railroad. The railway worked through a 20-year cycle of acquisitions, mergers and divestments from 1972 to 1992, to attain a core operation in six states in the heartland of America, running on a north-south axis from the Great Lakes to the Gulf of Mexico and providing freight rail connection between some 2,000 communities, including Chicago, St Louis, Memphis, New Orleans and Mobile. IC interchanged little of its traffic with other railroads; it still originated 74 per cent of its traffic on its own territory (the highest figure in the industry) and 46 per cent never left the IC.

Its last major divestiture was the sale of the electrified commuter network in Chicago and south suburbs to Metra (qv). A merger with Kansas City Southern was discussed in 1994 but was not consummated. In 1996, it took a step toward turning back the clock when it agreed to acquire one of its earlier spin-offs, the Chicago, Central & Pacific. The company was formerly the Iowa Division of the Illinois Central Gulf Railroad, which sold it off for $75 million in 1985. Together with the small Cedar Valley Railroad, it made up CC&P Holdings Inc, which the present Illinois Central bought back in June 1996 for $139 million plus taking over $18 million of capital leases.

The principal CC&P routes run 817 km from Chicago to Council Bluffs, Iowa, and 206 km from Tara to Sioux City, Iowa.

## Finance

In 1997, IC reported revenues of $699.8 million (up 6.4 per cent on 1996); operating income of $263.9 million (an increase of 9.4 per cent) and net income of $150.2 million (10 per cent up on 1996).

## Freight operations

IC's prime commodity in terms of tonnage is coal, which in 1997 accounted for 16 per cent of the year's 1,031,000 carloadings and for 12.1 per cent of total revenues. Coal business in 1997 suffered from a major fire at one of the company's shippers and from network congestion in western states.

Grain, milled grain and food products together represented 17 per cent of carloads, and revenues were up by 17 per cent, mainly reflecting the inclusion of CCP traffic for the first year. However, demand for export grain was low. The railroad had established itself as an integral part of the nation's grain distribution system by providing year-round service to the agricultural sector. IC maintained a strong advantage over other rail carriers as it provided a direct access to the Gulf of Mexico. IC was also well positioned to supply feed to the burgeoning poultry industry in southeast states. Grain, at 39 per cent, was the prime *raison d'être* for the CCP.

At the southern end of the railroad, chemical complexes produced a significant contribution to IC's traffic base in the form of 16 per cent of carloads and, significantly, 25 per cent of revenues. The 145 km stretch between Baton Rouge and New Orleans is particularly rich in such natural resources as lime, salt, sulphur, crude oil and natural gas.

One of the nation's heaviest paper mill concentrations is to be found in the IC-served states of Alabama, Tennessee and Louisiana. Since IC was the major railroad in Mississippi, a major timber-producing state, the wood, pulp, and paper products industries combined to generate 14 per cent of total carloadings and 15.6 per cent of revenues in 1997. Metals, bulk commodities and consumer products made up the balance of loads.

## Intermodal operations

Intermodal activity continued strongly from 1996 into 1997, with a 9 per cent increase in revenues. However, IC lost some of its business from UPSP, a major client.

Transit time for dedicated intermodal trains between Chicago and New Orleans was under 27 hours.

IC's former classification yard at Harvey, Illinois, has been transformed into an intermodal facility called the Moyers Intermodal Terminal. After a $6 million partial re-engineering, Wisconsin Central became a tenant and by the end of 1996 Canadian National moved its 95,000 loads a year passing through Chicago into a 67 acre (27 ha) site within the IC yard but with exclusive access/egress separate from the Moyers gate. Inclusive cost for four parallel simultaneous 2.7 km tracks and supporting infrastructure was $16.8 million.

## Traction and rolling stock

In 1997, IC rostered an all-GM fleet of 405 locomotives, of which 358 were active at the year-end. IC's recent locomotive acquisitions included 20 SD70s rated at 4,000 hp (3,000 kW) and costing $26 million; these were delivered in 1995. The railroad had not bought new for 20 years previously. Owned or leased freight wagon stock totalled 16,7128. IC also owned 900 pieces of highway equipment (tractors and trailers).

## Signalling and telecommunications

All 4,320 km of the core railroad is controlled by a DigiCon CTC (Centralised Traffic Control) system. IC adopted Union Pacific Technologies' Transportation Control System for monitoring of traction and freight car status, car distribution, and generation of shipping documents and switching orders.

---

# Kansas City Southern Railway Company

114 West 11th Street, Kansas City, Missouri 64105-1804
Tel: (+1 816) 983 13 03  Fax: (+1 816) 983 11 92
Web: http://www.kcsi.com

## Key personnel

President and Chief Executive Officer:
  Michael R Haverty
Senior Vice-President, Chief Financial Officer:
  Robert H Berry
Senior Vice-President, General Counsel and Secretary:
  Richard P Bruening
Senior Vice-President, Chief Operating Officer:
  Albert W Rees
Senior Vice-President, Transportation:
  Donald H Gill
Senior Vice-President, Marketing and Sales:
  William W Graham
Vice-Presidents
  Transportation: John Fenton
  Sales: Robert D Wood
  Marketing: David C Bastress
  Business Unit Operations: Steve Hefley
  Intermodal Business Unit: Vaughan Short
  Engineering: David W Brookings
Vice-President and Chief Mechanical Officer: Eric R Post
Director, Purchasing: Sammie L McCain
Superintendent of Locomotives: Fred Haywood III
Superintendent, Car Department: John E Foster
Signal Engineer: Stanley R Taylor

Gauge: 1,435 mm
Length: 5,259 route-km (including Texas-Mexican Railway and GWWR)

## Organisation

Kansas City Southern Industries (KCSI) is a diversified holding company. Transportation Services is one of three principal operations and the railway (KCSR) is the largest component of that group. In 1996, KCSI entered into a joint venture with GATX to create Southern Capital Corporation to continue the leasing operations of rolling stock and maintenance equipment, with KCSI as its major client. In 1997, Transportation Services contributed 54.2 per cent of KCSI consolidated revenues.

In June 1993, KCSI acquired for $213 million the 78 per cent shareholding of MidSouth Corporation which it had not previously purchased, and the two railroads were officially merged from 1 January 1994. KCSI is a partial owner of the Kansas City Terminal Railway Co.

The KCSR network serves a nine-state region and connects northern and eastern US railroads to south-western US states and Mexico. It also offers the shortest rail route between Kansas City and major ports along the Gulf of Mexico. The railway's east-west corridor, the 'Meridian Speedway', provides an effective link between Meridian, Mississippi and Dallas, Texas.

At the end of 1997, KCSR employed 2,570 staff.

*NAFTA railroad*

KCSI has become a major player in the Mexican market. The roots of this expansion date back to 1995, when the company formed an alliance with Transportación Maritima Mexicana (TMM) to explore joint venture prospects in connection with the North American Free Trade Agreement (NAFTA) cross-Gulf intermodal movements, and privatisation of the Mexican railways. Through the partnership, Mexrail Inc, KCSI acquired a 49 per cent stake in the Texas-Mexican Railway (qv), which operates the primary US-Mexico rail gateway from Corpus Christi to Laredo.

Of greater significance, though, was the allegiance KCS formed with TMM to bid successfully on the 50-year concession to run the Ferrocarril del Noreste, 3,850 km of track which is reported to carry 60 per cent of Mexico's rail freight. The core line is Mexico City-San Luis Potosi-Monterrey-Nuevo Laredo, with branches to Veracruz, Tampico, Aguascalientes, Metamoros. The operating company is named Transportacion Ferroviaria Mexicana (Grupo TFM), and one-quarter of the stock remains with the Mexican government for two years: at the end of December 1997, KCSI owned 37 per cent of the shares in Grupo TFM. The purchase price, US$1.4 billion was almost triple that bid by the UP and a partner and is almost five times revenues. Industry observers and market analysts were surprised, but for TMM it represents a step toward vertical integration across modes. For KCS it represents a link in the NAFTA railroad and a potential single carrier through route, Mexico City-Chicago, as well as access to an estimated 80 per cent of the Mexican population.

KCS will connect with the new I&M Rail Link property (qv) at Kansas City which will extend its reach to the upper Midwest and Canada.

To put another piece in the jigsaw, KCSR has created a new subsidiary, KCS Transportation Co, which in 1997 acquired the Gateway Western (qv). By linking up the GWWR, the KCS and the Tex-Mex, KCSR has created 'the NAFTA railroad' from Chicago to the Mexico border. At the same time KCSR will connect to CSXT at East St Louis. Also in 1997, KCSR entered a marketing agreement with I&M Rail Link, providing access to the key Chicago and Minneapolis markets.

Further expanding its interests in Latin America, KCSI formed a partnership with Mi-Jack Products and a consortium of Panamanian business interests to win an exclusive 25-year concession to rehabilitate and operate the 76 km Panama Railroad Company (qv) to provide an intermodal alternative to the Panama Canal. Reconstruction was due to start during 1999 for completion by mid-2000.

*Divisions restructured*

In December 1995 the railroad was formally restructured into two divisions. One is centred upon KCSR's spine line which runs south from Kansas City to Beaumont and Port Arthur, Texas, with trackage rights to Omaha, Topeka, Houston and Galveston. The second route division basically is east-west from Alabama to Texas and includes the line to New Orleans. The main freight yard, Deramus, is at Shreveport, Louisiana; KCSR also has its principal car and locomotive shop at Shreveport.

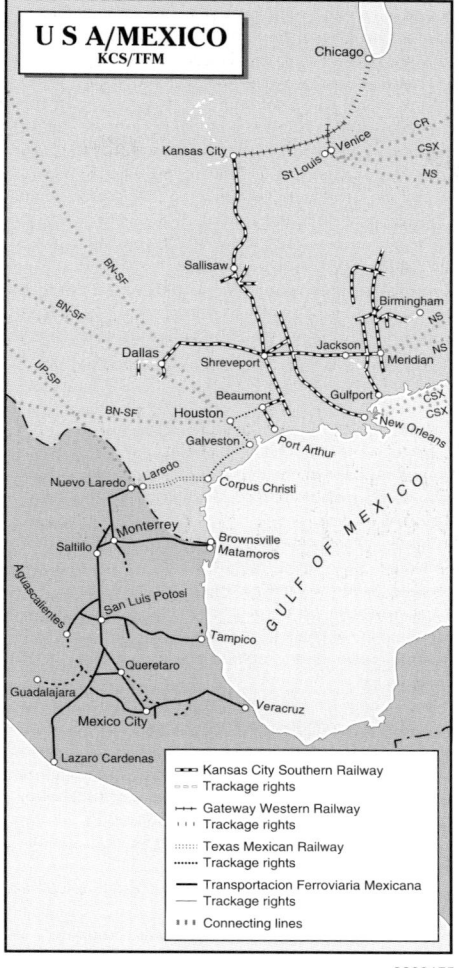

### Finance

KCSR produced revenues in 1997 of $517.8 million (5.1 per cent up on 1996); expenses rose from $415.3 million to $502.6 million. Net income after taxes and interest expenses was $27.4 million, compared with $17.1 million in 1996. The operating ratio (operating expenses as a percentage of income) stood at 83.4 per cent, excluding non-recurring costs and expenses. However, in the last six months of 1997, a figure of 79.3 per cent was achieved.

### Freight operations

Carloadings in 1997 totalled 821,400, a rise of 1.7 per cent on the previous year. Coal loads continued to lead the commodity sectors at 177,083 (21.6 per cent of total), followed by intermodal (19.7 per cent); chemicals (12.0 per cent); pulp and paper (11.2 per cent) and lumber/wood (8.9 per cent).

### Intermodal operations

Intermodal business, chiefly between New Orleans and Dallas, increased modestly for several years but took off in 1994. Growth continued in 1995 and again in 1996; revenue in 1997 totalled $43.2 million, an increase of 7.2 per cent on the previous year.

KCSR signed a new agreement with trucking company Schneider National in January 1994 to handle traffic through Kansas City. Later in the year KCSR created a service partnership with Norfolk Southern to operate each way daily in the Dallas-Atlanta market, offering a 'Hotshot 20' train to compete with trucks on parallel Interstate 20. KCSR handles the train west of Meridian, Mississippi, and installed seven new sidings to facilitate crossing trains travelling in the other direction on the single-track line. KCSR calls its section west from Meridian 'the Meridian Speedway'. United Parcel Service and J B Hunt are now also major intermodal partners.

KCSR owns and operates six intermodal facilities: Dallas, Texas; Kansas City, Missouri; Sallisaw, Oklahoma; Shreveport and New Orleans, Louisiana; Jackson, Mississippi.

### Improvements to existing lines

Around 63 per cent of KCSR's main line track-km is continuously welded rail (cwr). During 1997, 79 km of track was relaid with cwr, new sleepers installed totalled 332,000, and ballast poured stood at 305,000 tonnes.

As a result of the track programme, systemwide speeds on the core system have been raised to 85.90 km/hour and future investment can be at a more conservative rate.

On the Texas-Mexican Railway new yard and intermodal facilities at Laredo, on the border with Mexico, were completed in late 1998.

### Traction and rolling stock

Traction and rolling stock at the end of 1997 comprised 412 diesel locomotives (113 owned and 299 leased), of which 351 were main line units, and 16,520 freight cars (75.6 per cent leased). The locomotive fleet is composed entirely of GM-EMD models and has an average age of 22.8 years. The newest units are 10 MK-remanufactured 3,600 hp (2,685 kW) SD45-3s leased from Helm in 1995; 22 ex-CN GP40-2LW units also from Helm and also rebuilt by MK, retaining the original Canadian comfort cabs; and 20 rebuilt SD40-2s via VMV. In addition to the Deramus shop at Shreveport, Louisiana, KCSR has a locomotive repair facility in Pittsburg, Kansas and a car repair shop in Dallas, Texas.

The MidSouth locomotive roster was made up entirely of units transferred from Illinois Central when MidSouth was spun off from IC a decade ago; fleet rationalisation has already led to the retirement of the CF7 Class. Many of the surviving lower power GP model locomotives have been drafted into service with The Texas-Mexican Railway to augment power on trackage rights newly acquired from UP between Corpus Christi and Beaumont, Texas.

### Signalling and telecommunications

KCSR has Centralised Traffic Control (CTC) over 1,505 track-km with a centralised computer-aided dispatching system. It has 96 track-km of Automatic Block System (ABS). The entire system is cable-controlled by microwave and/or fibre optic cables.

**KCS diesel locomotives**

| Model | Number | Builder/Rebuilder | Date of delivery (or of last rebuild) |
| --- | --- | --- | --- |
| GP7 | 1 | EMD | 1955-58 |
| GP9 | 5 | EMD | 1953 |
| GP10 | 76 | EMD/ICG | (1968-74) |
| GP18 | 2 | EMD | 1960-63 |
| SW1001 | 3 | EMD | 1974-81 |
| SW900 | 1 | EMD | 1988 |
| SW1500 | 44 | EMD | 1966-72 |
| MP15 | 5 | EMD | 1975 |
| GP38-2 | 34 | EMD | 1973-78 |
| GP40-2LP | 86 | EMD | 1979-81 |
| SD40 | 7 | EMD | 1966-71 |
| SD40-2 | 89 | EMD | 1972-80 (1995) |
| SD40X | 4 | EMD | 1979 |
| SD45-3 | 10 | EMD/Helm | (1996) |
| SD50 | 9 | EMD | 1981 |
| SD60 | 46 | EMD | 1989-91 |
| Total* | 435 | | |

*Does not include 10 slugs or 4 F9s (in business train use)

## Norfolk Southern Corporation

Three Commercial Place, Norfolk, Virginia 23510-2191
Tel: (+1 757) 629 26 00   Fax: (+1 757) 629 23 45
Web: http://www.nscorp.com

**Key personnel**

Chairman, President and Chief Executive Officer:
  David R Goode
Vice-Chairmen
Chief Marketing Officer: L I Prillaman
Chief Financial Officer: Henry C Wolf
Chief Operating Officer: Stephen C Tobias
Executive Vice-Presidents
  Law: James C Bishop Jr
  Corporate: R Alan Brogan
Senior Vice-Presidents
  Public Affairs: John F Corcoran
  Operations: Jon L Manetta
  Planning: James W McClellan
  Engineering: Phillip R Ogden
Vice-Presidents
  Human Resources: Paul N Austin
  Properties: David A Cox
  Marketing Services: Timothy P Dwyer
  Intermodal: Thomas L Finkbiner
  Vice-President: Nancy S Flieschman
  Public Relations: Robert C Fort

# RAILWAY SYSTEMS/USA

*Coal accounted for over 30 per cent of NS operating revenue in 1997, with 134 million short tons carried*
0021588

Coal Marketing: John W Fox Jr
Public Affairs: James L Granum
Transportation: Lewis D Hale
Taxation: James A Hixon
Internal Audit: Thomas C Hostutler
Corporate Affairs: H Craig Lewis
Mechanical: Mark D Manion
Public Affairs: Harold C Mauney Jr
Research and Tests: Donald W Mayberry
Financial Planning: Kathryn B McQuade
Information Technology: Charles W Moorman
Controller: John P Rathbone
Treasurer: William J Romig
Operations Planning and Budget: John M Samuels
Merchandise Marketing: Donald W Seale
Labour Relations: Robert S Spenski
Quality Management: Rashe W Stephens Jr
Safety and Environmental: Charles J Wehrmeister
Law: William C Wooldridge
Corporate Secretary: Dezora M Martin

Gauge: 1,435 mm
Length: 34,560 km

## Organisation
Norfolk Southern Corporation (NS) is a Virginia-based holding company that owns all the common stock of and controls the Norfolk Southern Railway Company and a natural resources company, Pocahontas Land Corporation. The railroad system's lines extend over some 23,200 km in 20 states, primarily in the southeast and midwest, and in the province of Ontario, Canada. Pocahontas Land manages approximately 1.2 million acres of coal, natural gas and timber resources in Alabama, Illinois, Kentucky, Tennessee, Virginia and West Virginia.

*Route structure*
The Norfolk & Western and Southern Railway merger, which created NS, was an end-to-end consolidation. The N&W stretched from Norfolk, Virginia, west to Kansas City, Missouri, and north into the key markets of Chicago, Detroit and Cleveland. The Southern blanketed the southeast, from New Orleans, Louisiana; Mobile, Alabama; and Jacksonville, Florida, north to Cincinnati, Ohio; and Washington DC; from the St Louis 'gateway' and Memphis, Tennessee, eastwards to the Atlantic ports of Norfolk, Virginia; Charleston, South Carolina; Savannah and Brunswick, Georgia. The railroads connected at 17 common points, with major connections at East St Louis, Cincinnati and throughout Virginia and North Carolina.

*Conrail break-up*
NS and CSX Corporation filed a joint application with the Surface Transportation Board (STB) on 23 June 1997 for authority to acquire control of Conrail's 11,000 km system in the northeastern United States. The application resulted from an agreement the previous April between NS and CSX to acquire Conrail for approximately $10 billion, a solution which ended efforts by both NS and CSX to obtain sole control of the carrier. Support from shippers, public officials and other railroads for the transaction, which is intended to reshape the rail system in the eastern states and restore competition, is thought to be the strongest ever offered for a rail control application, and contributed to STB approval for the application in June 1998. NS and CSX took over control of Conrail operations on 1 June 1999.

Under the agreement, NS obtained the right to operate routes and other assets accounting for 58 per cent of Conrail's 1995 revenues. Services are provided over a combined 34,560 km system in 22 states, the District of Columbia and Ontario, Canada.

## Finance
During the 1997 accounting period, the investment in Conrail has been accounted for under the equity method, with the NS portion of Conrail earnings included in non-operating income.

Shortly after the year-end, NS disposed of its North American Van Lines motor carrier subsidiary, with completion of the sale achieved in March 1998. As a result, American Van Lines is presented as a discontinued operation in NS financial statements, and all prior-period amounts have been reclassified to conform to this presentation.

Net income for 1998 was $734 million, up 2 per cent from 1997. Included in 1998 results were Conrail-related items that reduced net income by $156 million: excluding these items, net income for 1997 was $890 million, an increase of 7.5 per cent on the previous year. Income from railway operations was $1.05 billion, down 13 per cent over 1997. At $4.2 billion, railway operating revenues were unchanged from 1997.

The operating ratio rose to 75.1 per cent, compared with 71.3 per cent in 1997.

Capital expenditure in 1998 was budgeted at $903 million, including $149 million related to Conrail. The figure for 1999 as $1.07 billion, including some $300 million of Conrail-related expenditure. Of the total, $651 million was to be spent on infrastructure and $387 on traction and rolling stock, including 138 six-axle locomotives.

## Freight operations
*Coal*
Coal is NS's most important commodity. Reserves of some seven billion tonnes of coal, much of it of low-sulphur, exist in Central Appalachia, where NS originates most of its traffic in this sector. The principal sources are mines in West Virginia, Kentucky, Virginia and Tennessee. Export coal is shipped through the NS pier at Lambert's Point in Norfolk, Virginia. In 1997, the volume of export coal handled at this facility increased by 6 per cent to 27.9 m llion short tons, the highest level since 1992.

NS and several coal-producing customers opened four new Thoroughload batch-weigh loading installations during 1997. The Thoroughload system reads individual wagon capacity information from electronic tags located on vehicle sides to optimise loading and equipment utilisation. The system also facilitates billing by transmitting load information via EDI. NS expects to load 13 million tonnes annually through the four facilities equipped with the system.

In 1997, NS and South Carolina Electric and Gas (SCE&G) opened a rail-truck coal transfer operation at Branchville, South Carolina, to provide daily deliveries of coal to local generating stations. Using this facility and a similar operation opened in Augusta, Georgia in 1996, NS expects to increase coal deliveries to SCE&G by almost 25 per cent in 1998 compared with 1997.

NS continues to participate in movement of low-sulphur coal out of Wyoming to southern states and midwest utilities. Many power generators are considering using coal from Wyoming's Powder River Basin as a means of complying with the strict $SO^2$ emission reductions called for in Phase II of the Clean Air Act Amendments of 1990.

*Agricultural products*
Agricultural traffic declined 3 per cent and revenue fell by 1 per cent in 1997. This performance is attributed to a poor soya bean crop and a lack of good corn supplies to serve midwest processors. The forecast for 1998 was for growth of 2 per cent. Inbound feed grain to the poultry industry will especially benefit from the completion of a new feed mill in 1998, while inbound wheat shipments were expected to increase after the completion of three new flour mills.

*Automotive*
Automotive traffic was flat in 1997, with a 2 per cent increase in carloads and a 1 per cent rise in revenues. Future prospects looked brighter: 1997 was the first full year of production for a recently opened General Motors assembly plant at Wentzville, Missouri, and for the same company's retooled assembly plant at Doraville, Georgia. Mercedes-Benz and Toyota also began production at assembly plants in Alabama and Kentucky, and the latter company expects to begin production at its expanded truck manufacturing facility at Princeton, Indiana in the first quarter of 1999. BMW is also to expand its Greer, South Carolina factory to produce sport utility vehicles from 1999. NS currently transports over 20 per cent of all new vehicle production in the USA and Canada.

During 1997, NS designed and commissioned a comprehensive network to handle the distribution of over 3 million Ford vehicles annually through four 'mixing centres' located at Chicago, Fostoria (Ohio), Shelbyville (Kentucky) and Kansas City. To support the network, NS has developed an information system that monitors the movement of every Ford-manufactured vehicle from assembly plant to its release to dealer delivery. An all-new train service network has been created involving NS and six other rail carriers to handle vehicles via the mixing centre network. When fully operational, NS expects the network will increase its handling of Ford vehicles by 60 per cent. Shipments of vehicles on a staggered roll-out plan for the network began on 5 January 1998.

NS has also completed construction of two new vehicle distribution facilities at Jacksonville and Titusville, Florida.

*NS double-stack container train headed by a General Electric Dash 9-40CW locomotive*
0021589

These will be used by several manufacturers to distribute vehicles in Florida, southern Georgia and South Carolina.

NS has expanded its 'Lead Rail Logistics Provider' programme to include on-site managers of rail services at the two General Motors assembly plants mentioned earlier, Doraville and Wentzville, and at four Ford assembly plants at Norfolk, Atlanta, Kansas City and Chicago. A Ford assembly facility in St Louis was expected to be incorporated into the programme in early 1998. Under the programme, the flow of parts into each plant is monitored against production requirements to ensure a smooth inward flow and effective management of rail resources.

NS JIT (just-in-time) Rail Centers in Detroit and Buffalo are operated to supply assembly plants in the USA and in Mexico with vehicle parts as needed for production. Trucks are operated on daily 'milk runs' to collect parts from local suppliers for consolidation into boxcar loads for each assembly plant. During 1997 the Detroit and Buffalo centres handled 13,113 carloads, an increase of 27 per cent over 1996. A third JIT Rail Center, to be constructed in Dayton, Ohio, was expected to add an annual 4,800 carloads to the network in 1999.

NS continues to test 20 AutoRailers (a bimodal car-carrying wagon produced by RoadRailer) in connection with Triple Crown Services.

### Intermodal operations

In 1997, intermodal traffic volume increased by 11 per cent and revenue increased by 12 per cent, both figures exceeding the records set in 1996. Capacity expansion at major terminals, combined with a healthy domestic and international economy, enabled NS to achieve a third year of double-digit growth in a four-year period. Container traffic increased by 12 per cent, trailer volume rose by 8 per cent, and Triple Crown Services Company traffic was up 11 per cent.

NS is continuing to work with partner railroads to improve the speed and reliability of interline rail services: in March 1997 the company introduced an improved service between Louisville, Kentucky and Burlington Northern Santa Fe destinations. This faster service uses the less congested gateway of Kansas City and allows BNSF destinations such as Fresno, Phoenix and San Diego to be served for the first time. The development has also allowed BNSF to close its Louisville facilities.

In November 1997, NS launched a premium intermodal service between Greensboro, North Carolina and Chicago, offering a transit time of a day and a half. The service competes with trucking times at a lower price.

The installation of SIMS, the Strategic Intermodal Management System, has been completed at all NS intermodal facilities. SIMS is an internally produced comprehensive information system applied to the identification and movement of containers and trailers, allowing the company to improve terminal productivity and increase profitability. As a marketing tool, SIMS provides NS with an opportunity to explore peak-season pricing as well as other premium service options.

Trans Atlantic Rail Express (TARES) is an intercontinental joint venture of inland operators, in which NS has allied itself with one US and three European partners to offer a complete door-to-port and port-to-door service covering both continents. TARES offers a single price and one point of contact, and covers all transport, storage, customs clearance and EDI shipment tracking services. It covers all European ports and those in the eastern USA, but excludes ocean freight movements, leaving customers free to negotiate separate alliances with shipping lines and forwarding agents.

*Triple Crown Services Company*

In April 1993, NS and Conrail entered into an equal partnership named Triple Crown Services Company (TCSC) to offer domestic intermodal services based on a Chicago-New York-Atlanta triangle, using RoadRailer bimodal equipment. Through the partnership, NS and Conrail developed highway-competitive intermodal services in geographic and commodity market segments that were under-served by conventional intermodal operations. Since the Conrail transaction, Triple Crown have been operated solely by NS.

Triple Crown markets its products primarily through an internal retail sales force. The door-to-door service includes drayage provided by a contracted fleet run mainly by dedicated owner-operators. TCSC handles all services in a modern RoadRailer fleet with an average age of less than four years. Trailer acquisitions during 1998 boosted the number of 53 ft trailers to 90 per cent of the fleet, leaving just a small number of the 48 ft Mark IV units.

Since its formation, TCSC has expanded its system to include Dallas, the New York metropolitan region and southeastern Pennsylvania. In 1998, the company expected to commence services to southern Texas.

*Distribution Services Group*

Responsibility for NS's rail-to-truck transfer operations, known as Thoroughbred Bulk Transfer (TBT) terminals, has been transferred to the recently created Distribution Services Group. Existing terminals are located at: Jacksonville, Florida; Atlanta and Dalton, Georgia; Detroit; Winston-Salem, North Carolina; Cincinnati, Cleveland (Euclid) and Columbus, Ohio; Chattanooga, Tennessee; and Petersburg, Virginia. During 1998, four new TBT terminals were due to open at: Miami; Charlotte, Buffalo; and Spartanburg, South Carolina. These 14 terminals will handle a range of dry and liquid chemicals and food products.

Western Intermodal has opened an ISO 9002-certified heat- and humidity-controlled metals warehouse in Charlotte. This is the latest of 27 privately operated metals distribution facilities intended to serve non-rail NS customers.

Distribution of off-rail and forest products is handled through a network of 17 paper distribution centres and 38 timber handling facilities strategically located to serve consumers.

### Traction and rolling stock

In June 1999, when NS took over operations on the former Conrail portion of its expanded network, the diesel locomotive fleet totalled some 3,500 Recent additions included 120 Dash 9-40CW units built by General Electric during 1997. These are rated at 4,000 hp (3,000 kW) but are provided with electronics for 4,400 hp (3,280 kW), and feature the wide-body air conditioned cabs. They were followed by a further 116 Dash 9-40CWs in 1998.

The combined freight wagon fleet on 1 June 1999 stood at approximately 126,000.

In 1999, acquisitions were due to include multilevel automobile racks, 60 ft cars for automotive parts and covered steel coil carriers.

A programme continues to increase the capacity and extend the life of the existing coal wagon fleet. In February 1998, NS completed its 25,000th vehicle to be rebodied, increasing capacity by some 10 per cent and extending its life for a further 20 years.

### Signalling and telecommunications

A contract has been negotiated to provide a Unified Train Control System (UTCS) for all nine NS divisions and the divisions of Conrail that have been added to the existing system. All division headquarters are to remain at existing locations with train despatch responsibilities. UTCS will link all headquarters via a communications Wide Area Network (WAN), allowing any division to be operated from any other division headquarters in event of failure or emergency. Two UTCS control centres will be located in Roanoke (Virginia) and Atlanta. The system incorporates computer-aided despatching. Software design was in progress in early 1998, and the Georgia Division was due to be commissioned in July 2000. The last division to go live, apart from any Conrail divisions which may be added, was due to be Piedmont in June 2002.

### Track

In 1997, NS installed 726 km of track and installed 2.2 million new sleepers.

**Rail type and weight:** Chiefly 132 lb/yd, 65.6 kg/m; 115 lb/yd, 57 kg/m; 100 lb/yd, 49.6 kg/m; and 85 lb/yd, 42.2 kg/m.
**Crossties (sleepers):** Wood
**Spacing:** 1,970/km
**Fastenings:** 6 in cut spikes
**Max curvature:** 22°
**Max gradient:** 4.4%
**Max permissible axleload (lb):** 71,500±, 36 in diameter wheels; 78,750±, 38 in diameter wheels

---

## Union Pacific Railroad Company

1416 Dodge Street, Omaha, Nebraska 68179-0605
Tel: (+1 402) 271 50 00   Fax: (+1 402) 271 55 72
Web: http://www.uprr.com

### Key personnel

Chairman and Chief Executive Officer:
  Richard K Davidson
Vice-Chairman: James A Shattuck
President and Chief Operating Officer: Ike Evans
Executive Vice-Presidents
  Network Design and Integration: R Bradley King
  Marketing and Sales: John J Koraleski
  Operations: Dennis J Duffy
Senior Vice-Presidents
  Information Technologies: L Merrill Bryan Jr
  Marketing and Sales: Arthur W Peters
  Human Resources: Barbara W Schaefer
Vice-Presidents
  Energy: Henry L Arms
  Regional, South: Stephen R Barkley
  General Manager, Intermodal: Randall S Blackburn
  Planning and Analysis: Eric L Butler
  Manifest Products: Drew R Collier
  Premium Products: John W Holm Jr
  Supply: Michael J Cronin
  Harriman Dispatching Center: Dennis H Jacobson
  Law: James V Dolan
  Risk Management: Gayla L Fletcher
  General Manager (Business Development):
    John T Gray II
  Regional, North: Michael F Kelly
  General Manager, Energy: Robert M Knight Jr
  General Manager (Agricultural Products):
    Diane D Knudsen
  Field Operations: Jeff H Koch
  General Manager (Industrial Products): Alex Kummant
  General Manager (Automotive): Joseph W Leppert III
  Labour Relations: John J Marchant
  Quality and Process Improvement:
    Stanley J McLaughlin
  Bulk Products: Joseph E O'Connor
  Network and Service Planning: John H Rebensdorf
  General Manager (Chemicals): J Edward Sims
  National Customer Service Center: William R Turner
  Regional, West: Jeffrey L Verhaal
  Engineering: William E Wimmer
Senior Assistant Vice-President, Communications:
  Jim Hildreth
Director, Public Affairs: John Bromley

Gauge: 1,435 mm
Route length: 54,241 km

### Organisation

Union Pacific Railroad Company (UPRR) is one of three business units of the holding company, Union Pacific Corporation. The other units are Overnite Transportation, a trucking company; and UP Technologies, a developer and retailer of computer systems and software. Three subsidiaries were sold in recent years: USPCI in 1994; UP Resources, a gas, coal and soda ash company, in 1996; and Skyway Freight Systems, a logistics and transportation company, in 1998. Board approval to dispose of Overnite Transportation was given in May 1998 but the sale was abandoned due to market conditions.

Union Pacific is a publicly traded company listed on the New York Stock Exchange.

Union Pacific's aggressive acquisitions policy has made it the second mega-system in the US West after the merged Burlington Northern/Santa Fe entity (qv). It operates nearly 55,000 km in 23 states and in mid-2000 employed 52,523 people.

During 1997, UP and a consortium of partners were granted a 50-year concession to operate the Ferrocarril Pacifico Norte and Chihuahua—Pacific lines in Mexico, together with a 25 per cent stake in the Mexico City Terminal Company for a price of $525 million. UP initially held a 13 per cent share in the consortium. An additional 13 per cent ownership was acquired in 1999. The consortium took over operational control of both lines in early 1998.

*Operating Plan*
Union Pacific's Operating Plan has a strong echo of the structure of the former Southern Pacific, acquired in

# RAILWAY SYSTEMS/USA

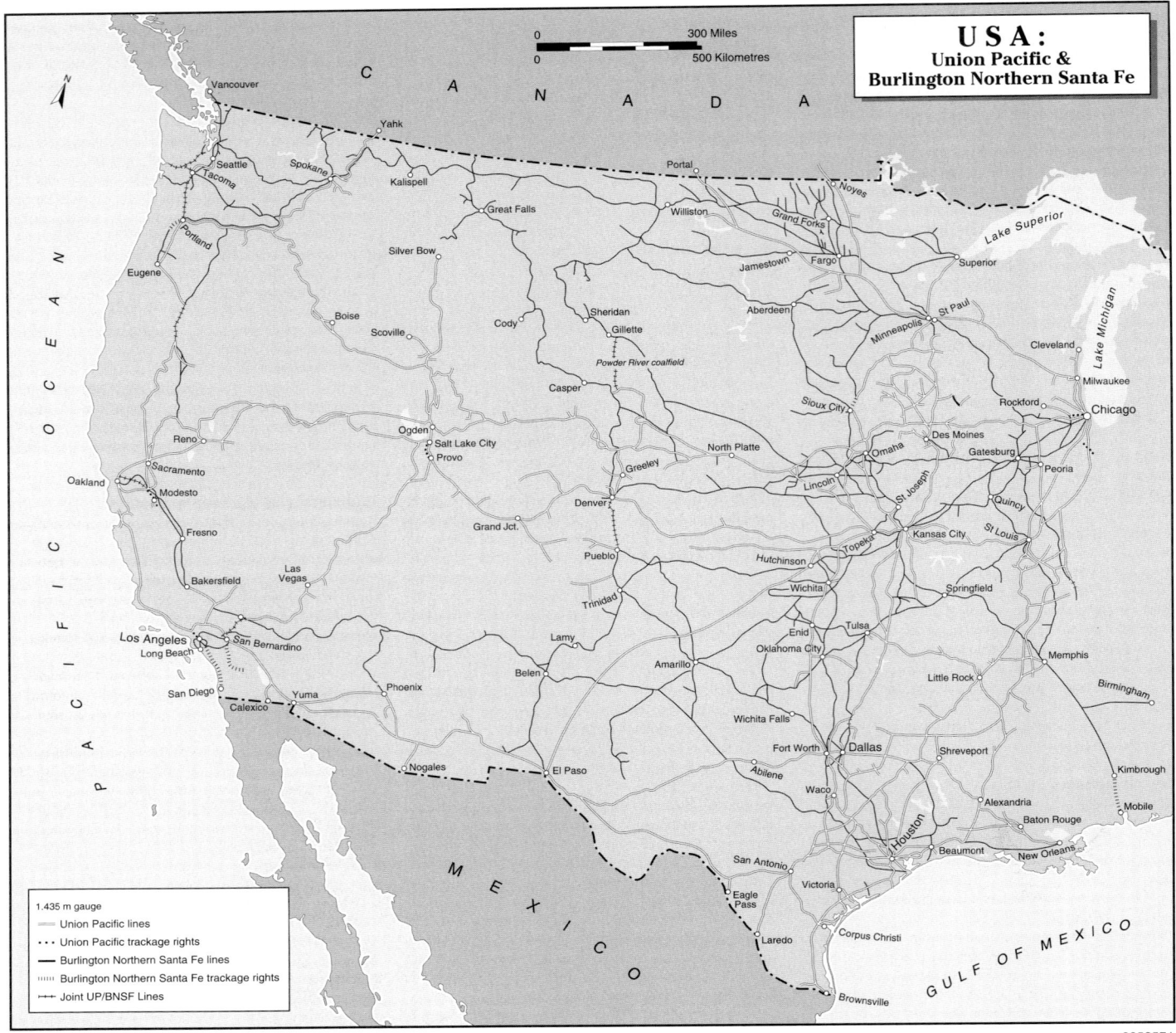

**USA: Union Pacific & Burlington Northern Santa Fe**

*1.435 m gauge*
— Union Pacific lines
··· Union Pacific trackage rights
— Burlington Northern Santa Fe lines
⸽⸽⸽ Burlington Northern Santa Fe trackage rights
⊢⊣ Joint UP/BNSF Lines

September 1996, in that it features discrete routes, namely:
- the I-5, or West Coast, Corridor: California to Seattle;
- the Sunset Route: Los Angeles–Houston–New Orleans;
- the Overland Route: Midwest to Northern California;
- the Golden State Route: Midwest to Southern California;
- the Kansas–Pacific Route: Kansas City to Denver;
- Memphis–Texas–California route;
- Midwest–Arkansas–Texas route.

Some of these routes are to be the subject of major investment, for example, more than 160 km of additional double track is to be installed in the Sunset corridor and CTC will control the Golden State corridor.

The Kansas–Pacific Route will be used to return empty coal trains to the Powder River basin via Topeka and Denver.

## Finance

Union Pacific Corporation recorded a net profit of $810 million in 1999, turning round a loss of $633 million in 1998 as the railway recovered from its service delivery problems in 1997-98. Rail operating revenue was $10.176 billion (up from $9.37 billion in 1998); operating income was $1,804 million, up from a deficit of $171 million. In 1999, the operating ratio (operating expenses as a percentage of income) fell to 84.0 from 101.6 the previous year. Overall carloadings were up 5.7 per cent over 1999, to 8,556,000.

For 2000, UP planned capital investments of between $1.9 and $2.1 billion, including continuing expenditure upgrading infrastructure in the Texas area.

## Passenger operations

In 1993, UP started commuter services, providing four daily trains each way on a 96 km line between Riverside and Los Angeles under contract to the Southern California Regional Rail Authority (qv); the contract permits up to 10 trains each way. Amtrak is the designated operator on the rest of the SCRRA Metrolink system.

As a consequence of the takeover of Chicago & Northwestern, UP is now contract operator to Metra for three Chicago area lines. UP has set up a commuter rail development team to identify new opportunities by emphasising rail's 'green' credentials.

## Freight operations

UP has a wide traffic mix, with coal from the Powder River Basin, intermodal traffic from the Californian ports, and grain from the prairie states being important commodities. In 1999 it was operating some 2,000 trains daily.

By business unit and measured in carloadings the year-to-year changes from 1998 to 1999 were: *intermodal* – up 8 per cent; *energy* – up 6 per cent; *automotive* – up 10 per cent; *chemicals* - up 3 per cent; *agricultural products* – up 8 per cent; *industrial products* – up 6 per cent.

### Reorganisation

With the acquisition of CNW and SP, UP almost doubled the size of its system. This, coupled with the severe network congestion which occurred in 1997-98, led the company in the third quarter of 1998 to undertake organisational changes based on two initiatives. First, field operations were decentralised from the Omaha headquarters to three operating regions covering the north, south and west. They are now responsible for all local and through freight services, yard operations and mechanical, traction and rolling stock issues. Second, UP established a Network Design and Integration team to integrate market and resources planning based on three product categories: premium, bulk and manifest (mixed freight). The aim is to achieve a better match between customer requirements and UP's operational capabilities.

### Significance of coal

Coal is the prime commodity on the Union Pacific, accounting for 22 per cent of revenue in 1999. Output from the Powder River Basin is now in excess of 100 million tonnes and train lengths have risen to 135 cars. This coalfield generated an average of 24.7 loaded trains a day in 1998, compared with 23.9 trains per day in 1997. In September 1998, UP loaded its 75,000th Powder River Basin coal train. In 1999, UP handled a record 1.9 million carloads of coal.

### SIT yards

UP has continued to develop storage-in-transit (SIT) yards to serve the Gulf Coast chemical industries. Effectively 'rolling warehouses', these are small yards where hopper cars loaded with commodities such as plastic pellets can be stabled to be called in by customers at short notice. In 1998, work commenced on an expansion programme for the Spring, Texas SIT yard and a seven-track facility was opened at Longview, Texas.

### Customer service

The national Customer Service Center in St Louis interacts with UP's computerised Transportation Control

*A UP coal train loading at the Rochelle mine in Wyoming's Powder River Basin*

System (TCS), which provides service representation with billing information and a profile of customer requirements, as well as online information on the status of shipments and the availability of wagons. Shippers have the ability to interact directly with Union Pacific's TCS system. By using personal computers they can order wagons, trace shipments and enter billing information directly.

## Intermodal operations

UP serves all major West Coast and all Gulf Coast ports. Most container traffic runs between West Coast ports and midwestern cities or New York, but regular double-stack trains also run between Houston and New Orleans. The fastest Chicago-Los Angeles double-stack train schedule is now 50 hours, following the introduction of a new premium service.

In addition to these double-stack container trains, UP runs numerous dedicated container/piggyback trains daily between its major city and port hubs. Besides through services, competitive intercity connections are augmented by scheduled interchange between a number of trains at North Platte, Nebraska.

Intermodal traffic in terms of carloads rose by 8 per cent in 1999, driven by strong demand for imports from Asia.

For the past decade these trains have been handled through the Intermodal Container Transfer Facility at Long Beach. SP signed a long-term lease until 2036 on the ICTF, which now covers 96 ha. An average of 75 trains a week serve the terminal, moving containers mostly for Pacific Rim shippers. The $100 million facility, a joint venture between UP and the ports of Los Angeles and Long Beach, is 6.5 km from the ports. It has 11 km of track and can load and unload five double-stack trains simultaneously.

In years to come the ICTF will be complemented by the $1.8 billion Alameda Corridor project. Designed jointly by the ports and the city authorities, the aim is to create a new high-capacity rail freight corridor linking the former Southern Pacific, Santa Fe and Union Pacific networks with container yards at the dockside. The ex-SP San Pedro branch forms the basis of the project, but it will be much improved and expanded. The corridor is designed to remove trucks hauling containers from the streets, and further to relieve traffic congestion by eliminating grade crossings on rail lines near the ports; to this end, part of the 32 km corridor will be sunk below street level, with streets crossing over the top of the trench. There will be rail access from the Corridor to the ICTF and Dolores yard. The project is being touted by the Administration as a paradigm in the area of innovative financing: USDOT has advanced a $400 million loan. Target project completion date is 2000.

Improvements introduced in 1997 included a restructured Midwest—California service connecting Chicago, St Louis and Kansas City with California, and the inauguration of dedicated Interstate 5 Corridor intermodal trains between Los Angeles and Seattle, providing third morning deliveries in both cities. In June 1998, Southern Pacific's Sunset Route intermodal services were entirely recast: these connect Memphis, New Orleans, Houston and San Antonio with El Paso, Tucson, Phoenix and southern California.

*Into Mexico*

Since 1991, UP has operated run-through service into Mexico from the US, via Laredo, with American President Companies as the major customer. Expedited customs clearance and a dedicated intermodal terminal at Huehuetoca have strengthened the business.

SP also had important links with Mexico in its own right. Ex-SP double-stack container operations include a twice-weekly service from the Long Beach ICTF to Mexico City, interchanging with FNM (National Railways of Mexico) at El Paso/Ciudad Juarez.

Privatisation of Mexico's railways (see Mexico entry) has focused US attention on this market. Having lost out in a bid for the Ferrocarril del Noreste (Mexico's busiest line) to rival KCSI, UP gained a foothold with an initial 26 per cent stake, later increased to 39 per cent, in the Ferromex consortium which was successful in bidding for the 6,000 km Pacific-North route, which runs along Mexico's western coast.

**Consolidated financial performance (in US$ millions)**

|  | 1997 | 1998 | 1999 |
|---|---|---|---|
| Rail revenues | 9,712 | 9,368 | 10,176 |
| Trucking revenues | 946 | 1,034 | 1,062 |
| Other revenues | 421 | 151 | 35 |
| All | 11,079 | 10,553 | 11,273 |
| Operating expenses | 9,935 | 10,724 | 9,469 |
| Operating income | 1,144 | (171) | 1,804 |
| Income, net of taxes, Interest, charges | 432 | (633) | 810 |

## Improvements to existing lines

Recent investments aimed at increasing network capacity included:

- completion in 2000 of triple-tracking 173 km between North Platte and Gibbon, Nebraska, part of a four-year project to raise capacity for coal movements from the Powder River Basin;
- capacity expansion projects in Texas and Louisiana aimed at speeding traffic to and from Mexico;
- upgrading the Tucumcari line between El Paso and Chicago, speeding the movement of intermodal services from the Midwest to the ports of southern California.

Recent yard improvements include a $145 million complete reconstruction of the facility at Roseville, northern California, completed in 2000, and the creation of a $70 million intermodal terminal at Marion, Arkansas, to serve the greater Memphis area. This project was completed in July 1998.

*Oregon double-tracking project*

UP plans to spend more than $100 million in the years up to 2002 in double-tracking much of its main line through the Blue Mountains of eastern Oregon. Once completed, the more than 80 km of new double track will increase line capacity by at least 50 per cent. Most of the construction will be in 4 to 8 km segments. In many instances, it will link sidings to complete long stretches of double-track main line.

UP's main line over the Blue Mountains carries an average of 26 freight trains per day as well as two Amtrak passenger trains. During some periods, volumes reach up to 40 trains daily. While the number of trains has grown, so has the average length of trains. As a result, bottlenecks have developed on the line where long bulk commodity trains, forced to travel at low speeds due to track grade and curvature, occupy the main line track for long periods. This prevents high-speed, time-sensitive trains from passing. The track-doubling will overcome these difficulties.

## Traction and rolling stock

At the beginning of 2000, the UP fleet totalled 6,328 freight locomotives, 512 switching units and seven passenger locomotives. During 1999, 187 new locomotives were purchased or leased. General Motors

*UP double-stack container train led by a GE Dash 8-41CW locomotive*

*UP freight between Tucson and Benson, Arizona, hauled by GM SD60 and SD50 locomotives (Phil Marshall)*

designs accounted for 66.26 per cent of the fleet, with most of the remainder supplied by General Electric. The average age of the freight fleet was 15.4 years compared with 14.6 in 1999.

In 1999, UP announced a major deal with General Motors to lease 1,000 SD70 4,300 hp (3,285 kW) diesel locomotives. To be delivered by 2003, the new locomotives are intended to enable some 1,500 older machines to be withdrawn and to reduce the number of types operated from 33 to 18.

*Distributed power*

UP continues to set the pace for the development of 'distributed power', in which radio-controlled unmanned helper sets are put in mid-train or at the end of long consists, with the result that undesirable 'slack action' will be reduced by 50 per cent or better and track capacity can be increased.

Whereas UP used to split its unit coal, grain and soda ash trains to cross the Blue Mountains of Oregon in two sections, both crewed and requiring manned helper sets, the move can now be made with one crew and a total of six or seven distributed locomotives. Distributed power s also being applied to very long (180 to 190 wagons) soda ash trains between Green River, Wyoming, and North Platte, Nebraska, and to many of the longer (135-car) coal trains.

Carrying the development a step further, UP has equipped three pairs of GE units with a 20,000 gallon (75,700 litre) fuel tender (one per pair) as a means to increase the range of its power without a refuelling stop, and stabilise the onboard fuel weight, and therefore the all-in locomotive weight, contributing to more consistency in applied tractive effort.

*Freight wagons*

UP's assets at the start of 2000 included over 114,500 revenue-earning freight wagons, either owned or leased and including service vehicles. During 1999, UP added 453 new freight cars.

In 1999, UP designated Thrall Car as its preferred partner for future freight wagon development.

The wagon fleet had a 94.6 per cent availability in 1999.

### Signalling and telecommunications

*Harriman Dispatching Center*

Union Switch & Signal has consolidated control of all UP trackage into the Harriman Dispatching Center in Omaha. The most striking feature of the office is its panoramic, video-projected display of the UP system. While this wall display provides summary information, a visual display unit at each dispatcher's console offers a detailed view of operations at any of the 1,800 or so signal control points throughout the system.

The Harriman Center employs Computer-Aided Dispatching System (CADS). Using auto-routeing, dispatchers assign an identity and priority to each train. The computer then takes over and routes trains according to priority, while also automatically determining the meeting and passing of trains on single-track sections.

*Transportation Control System*

UP's marketing strategy rests on one of the most advanced technical bases in the industry. The heart of UP's service operations, the National Customer Service Center, would be impossible without the Transportation Control System (TCS) and the Automatic Call Directing (ACD) system. TCS schedules and monitors rail operations and performs the accounting function on every item shipped on the railroad.

A new work order reporting system connects TCS computers directly with UP locomotives, enabling customers to have their data communicated to trains en route. This new system is being developed in conjunction with ATCS (Advanced Train Control System) and is expected to improve customer service and cut expenses by more than $20 million a year.

Completion of the process of incorporating the former SP network into the TCS system was achieved in July 1998.

### Track

**Rail:** 133 AREA, 60.3 kg/m
**Crossties (sleepers):** Wooden, 7 × 9 in × 9 ft
**Spacing:** 2,019/km
**Fastenings:** ⅝ × 6¼ in cut track spikes; Portec curve blocks for curvative in excess of 6°
**Max curvature:** 20°; exceptionally 12°
**Max gradient:** Main line 2.33%, 4.0% branch lines
**Max axleload:** 65,750 lb (unrestricted operation), 78,750 lb (restricted)

## Wisconsin Central Transportation Corporation

The acquisition of Wisconsin Central Transportation Corporation by Canadian National Railroad Company (qv) was approved by the US Surface Transportation Board in September 2001.

## Other selected US railroads

**Note:** There are more than 500 regional and short line railroads in the US of which about twelve are Class II. A Class II is designated as a railroad with annual operating revenues of more than $20 million, but less than $250 million. Railroads of less than that range of operating revenues are Class III. These 500 properties operate approximately one quarter of US freight trackage, employ 12 per cent of railroad workers and generate 10 per cent of industry freight revenue. Around 80 per cent are members of the American Short Line Railroad Association (see 'Associations and Agencies' section for contact details).

## Aberdeen, Carolina & Western Railway Co

102 Depot Street, North Carolina 27356
Tel: (+1 910) 428 90 30   Fax: (+1 910) 428 29 66

**Key personnel**
President: Robert M Menzies II
General Manager: Bill Bartosh

**Organisation**
The company owns: 18 GM-EMD locomotives (eight GP16, three GP38, two GP9, three GP7, one GP18 and one SW7) and leases four GP40s. It operates over 224 track-km. It has 25 employees. Connection is made to CSXT at Aberdeen and with NS at Charlotte and Gulf. The present ACWR was created in 1987 and in 1989 became the contract operator of Norfolk Southern's Charlotte-Gulf line under the terms of the NS 'Thoroughbred Short Line Program'. The Charlotte-Gulf line has benefited from a US$2 million improvement programme. Total tonnage carried in 2001 was 1,420,440.

*UPDATED*

## Aberdeen & Rockfish Railroad Co

PO Box 917, 101 East Main Street, Aberdeen, North Carolina 28315
Tel: (+1 910) 944 23 41   Fax: (+1 910) 944 97 38
e-mail: aberdeen.rockfish.rr@worldnet.att.net
Web: http://www.aberdeen-rockfish.com/

**Key personnel**
President: E A Lewis
Vice-President, Traffic: Paul McArdle

A&RR has 75 route-km, making connections with CSXT in Aberdeen and both CSXT and NS in Fayetteville, North Carolina. The company operates 10 locomotives (four GP16s; one each of Classes CF7, GP7, GP18, GP38, plus two switchers) and 75 freight wagons. The company also owns the Pee Dee River railway in South Carolina. Annual average carloadings for both lines are 12,000.

## Alabama & Florida Railway Co

1510 East Three Notch Street, Andalusia, Alabama 36420

A subsidiary of Pioneer Railcorp
1318 S Johansen Road, Peoria, Illinois 61607
Tel: (+1 309) 697 14 00   Fax: (+1 309) 697 53 87
Web: http://www.pioneer-railcorp.com

**Key personnel**
See entry for Pioneer Railcorp

Gauge: 1,435 mm
Route length: 123 km

**Organisation**
Acquired from A&F Inc in November 1992, the AF runs from Georgiana, Alabama, where it interchanges with CSXT, to Geneva. Main commodities carried are chemicals, forest products and agricultural products.

*NEW ENTRY*

## Alabama & Gulf Coast Railway

224 North Mount Pleasant Avenue, PO Box 339, Monroeville, Alabama 36461
Tel: (+1 251) 575 50 08   Fax: (+1 251) 575 19 41
Web: http://www.railamerica.com

**Key personnel**
General Manager: Mike Brigham

Gauge: 1,435 mm
Route length: 225 km

**Organisation**
Acquired by RailAmerica as a result of its takeover in January 2002 of the interests of StatesRail, the AGR runs from Kimborough, Alabama, to Pensacola, Florida. The railway handles approximately 40,000 carloads annually, mainly of forest products, chemicals, clay and food products. Interchange is made with BNSF at Magnolia, Alabama, via trackage rights from Kimborough, with CSXT at Hybart via trackage rights from Atmore and with CSXT at Cantonment, Florida.

*NEW ENTRY*

## Alabama Railroad Co

RR2, Box 209, Monroeville, Alabama 36460

A subsidiary of Pioneer Railcorp
1318 S Johansen Road, Peoria, Illinois 61607
Tel: (+1 309) 697 14 00   Fax: (+1 309) 697 53 87
Web: http://www.pioneer-railcorp.com

**Key personnel**
See entry for Pioneer Railcorp.

Gauge: 1,435 mm
Route length: 89 km

**Organisation**
Acquired from CSX Transportation in October 1991, the ALAB runs from Flomaton, Alabama, where it interchanges with CSXT, to Corduroy. Main commodities carried are forest products and cement.

*NEW ENTRY*

## The Alaska Railroad

The Alaska Railroad Corporation
PO Box 107500, Anchorage, Alaska 99510-7500
Tel: (+1 907) 265 23 00   Fax: (+1 907) 265 23 12

**Key personnel**
President and Chief Executive Officer:
  William Sheffield
Vice-Presidents
  Transportation Services: George Erickson
  Maintenance and Engineering: Robert Stout
  Corporate Affairs: James B Blasingame

USA/**RAILWAY SYSTEMS** 421

*Alaska Railroad General Motors GP38-2 locomotive at Portage with a car shuttle train for Whittier (Wolfram Veith)*
0063699

**Alaska Railroad diesel locomotives**

| Class | Wheel arrangement | Transmission | Rated power kW | Max speed km/h | Total weight tonnes | No in service | First built (rebuilt) | Mechanical | Builders Engine | Transmission |
|---|---|---|---|---|---|---|---|---|---|---|
| 1550 (MP15) | B-B | DC Elec | 1,120 | 115 | 115 | 4 | 1978 | EMD | EMD 12-645 | EMD |
| 2000 (GP38-2/38U) | B-B | AC/DC Elec | 1,492 | 113 | 116 | 8 | 1985 | EMD | EMD 16-567 | EMD |
| 2500 (GP35/35U) | B-B | DC Elec | 1,865 | 115 | 118 | 4 | 1981 | EMD | EMD 16-567 | EMD |
| 2800 (GP49) | B-B | AC/DC Elec | 2,087 | 115 | 113 | 9 | 1983 | EMD | EMD 12-645 | EMD |
| 3000 (GP40-2/40U) | B-B | AC/DC Elec | 2,238 | 115 | 121 | 19 | 1975 | EMD | EMD 16-645 | EMD |

Real Estate and Project Planning: James Kubitz
Finance and Administration: Jerry Anderson
Vice-President and General Counsel: Phyllis C Johnson
Superintendent of Transportation: Patrick C Shake
Chief Engineer: Tom E Brooks
Chief Mechanical Officer: John Kincaid
Chief Mechanical Engineer: Joshua D Coran
Directors
  Communications: Ernie Piper
  Freight Services: Steve Silverstein
  Passenger Services: Laurie Herman
  Transportation Services Administration: Bruce Carr
  Transportation Services: Jim Seeberger
  Customer Services: Adrie Setton

Gauge: 1,435 mm
Length: 846 km

**Organisation**
The Alaska Railroad (ARR) runs a single-track main line of 756 km from the ports of Seward on the Gulf of Alaska, and Whittier on Prince William Sound, northward through Anchorage and Denali (formerly McKinley) National Park to Fairbanks, and eastward to Eielson Air Force Base, with a branch to Palmer.

The ARR was built in 1923 by the federal government to open up the state and was transferred to state ownership in 1985. It is a quasi-public corporation with a seven-member board of directors appointed by the Governor of Alaska. Unique as the only full-service US railroad still offering both passenger and freight services, ARR operates flag-stop passenger service along a large section of the system. In season (May-September) there are two scheduled passenger trains with company-owned passenger and dome cars, and dome car services provided by Princess Tours and Holland America (Westours). Also in season there is a car and driver/passenger shuttle between Whittier and Portage on the main line. Year-round local passenger service operates on Saturdays/Sundays to link the state's two major cities.

Freight connections are made with the US and Canadian rail systems to the south via Crowley Marine Service (rail wagons and loose-stowed freight on barges) from Seattle and CN Rail's Aquatrain (rail wagons on barges) from Prince Rupert.

Recognising the essential nature of the service to the state's inhabitants, the Federal Railroad Administration has in recent years awarded grants to the railroad for trackwork to improve the performance of the passenger operations, which operate at 50 km/h overall.

**Traction and rolling stock**
In service in 1998 were 44 diesel-electric locomotives, 20 passenger cars, four RDCs and 1,115 wagons. Six locomotives were leased for the summer of 1998 to power infrastructure trains. Between late 1999 and 2000 ARR will add six new General Motors SD70MAC locomotives to its fleet.

**Type of coupler in standard use:** AAR Automatic Knuckle
**Type of braking in standard use:** AAR Standard Air

**Track**
Rail: 115 lb/yd RE-Standard Carbon (57.16 kg/m)
Crossties (sleepers): Treated fir and hardwood 2,045 × 203 × 178 mm
Spacing: 2,019/km
Fastenings: 4- or 6-hole angle bars, steel spikes
Max curvature: 14.5°
Max gradient: 3%
Max axleload: 30.726 tonnes (67,750 lb)

## Allegheny & Eastern Railroad Inc

See Genesee & Wyoming Inc entry.

## Anacostia & Pacific Company Inc

Suite 335, 53 West Jackson Boulevard, Chicago, Illinois 60604
Tel: (+1 312) 362 18 88  Fax: (+1 312) 362 14 02
e-mail: info@anacostia.com
Web: http://www.anacostia.com

*New York office*
535 Fifth Avenue, 33rd Floor, New York, New York 10174
Tel: (+1 212) 687 95 00  Fax: (+1 212) 687 95 01

**Key personnel**
President: Peter A Gilbertson
Vice-President and Chief Financial Officer:
  Bruce A Lieberman

The company is a railroad investment and management firm, with US and foreign interests. It deals in acquisitions, start-ups and restructuring as well as management and management support. Equity interest varies; it is up to 100 per cent in some cases. The company has formed a subsidiary, Rail Logistics Services Inc, to expand into switching equipment, yard services, and track maintenance. In February 2002 principal affiliates consisted of: Anacostia Rail Holdings; Chicago SouthShore & South Bend RR (qv); Louisville & Indiana RR (qv); New York & Atlantic RR (qv); Pacific Harbor Line (qv). All these lines are in the USA. Outside the USA, A&P's interests are the Nuevo Central of Argentina (qv) and the Ferrocarril del Pacifico in Chile (qv).

## Apalachicola Northern Railroad Co

A subsidiary of St Joe Company
PO Box 250, Port St Joe, Florida 32457
Tel: (+1 850) 229 74 11  Fax: (+1 850) 229 27 55

**Key personnel**
Vice-President: R Wayne Parrish

ANR has 154.9 route-km, six locomotives (three SW1500 and three GP15T, all GM-EMD) and 149 freight wagons.

**Track**
Rail: 66, 55 and 45 kg/m
Crossties (sleepers): Concrete, 305 × 203 × 2,590 mm
Fastenings: Tru-Temper rail clips
Max curvature: 6°
Max gradient: 1.2%
Max axleload: 29.5 tonnes
Spacing: In plain track, 1,415/km; in curves, 1,650/km

## Arizona & California Railroad

1301 California Avenue, Parker, Arizona 85344
Tel: (+1 928) 669 66 62  Fax: (+1 928) 669 66 66
Web: http://www.railamerica.com

**Key personnel**
General Manager: John Scott
Regional Vice-President and General Manager:
  Gene Shepherd

Gauge: 1,435 mm
Route length: 557 km

**Organisation**
Operated by RailAmerica, the ARZC is a former Santa Fe line linking Cadiz, California, with Matthie, Arizona, via Rice, California, and Parker, Arizona. From Rice, a branch runs south to Ripley. The railway handles approximately 18,000 carloads annually, commodities carried including cement, asphalt, forest products and steel. Interchange is made with BNSF at Cadiz and at Phoenix, Arizona.

## Arizona Eastern Railway Company

PO Box 2200, Claypool, Arizona 85532
Tel: (+1 520) 473 24 47  Fax: (+1 520) 473 24 49
Web: http//www.railamerica.com

Gauge: 1,435 mm
Route length: 217 km

**Organisation**
Formerly a Statesrail company and now owned by RailAmerica, the AZER runs southeast through eastern Arizona from Miami to Bowie. The railway handles approximately 16,000 carloads of copper cathode and related materials annually. Interchange is made with UP at Bowie.

## Arkansas & Missouri Railroad Co

306 East Emma Street, Springdale, Arkansas 72764
Tel: (+1 501) 751 86 00  Fax: (+1 501) 751 22 25
e-mail: arkmo@ipa.net
Web: arkansasmissouri-rr.com

**Key personnel**
President: J Anthony Hannold
Senior Vice-President and General Manager:
  G Brent McCready
Executive Vice-President: Larry Bouchet
A&M has 222 route-km and 19 Alco locomotives. The railroad operates 800 freight cars and four passenger cars.

# 422  RAILWAY SYSTEMS/USA

Connections are made to BNSF at Monnett, Missouri, and to UP at Van Buren, Arizona. Annual carloads totalled 22,900 in 1998; tonnage amounted to 2.3 million. From April to mid-November the railway runs a tourist special from Springdale to Van Buren and return, which carried 16,000 passengers in 1998.

## Ashley, Drew and Northern Railway Company

PO Box 757, Crossett, Arkansas 71635
Tel: (+1 501) 364 90 04   Fax: (+1 501) 364 45 21

### Key personnel
President: S Russell Tedder
Vice-President and General Manager: Philip H Schueth
Administration: David W Smith
Customer Services: James D Harrison
Chief Engineer: Robert G McManus
Transportation Manager: L B Coffey

The ADN was one of four railroads administered from the same address by the Georgia Pacific Company. Surviving traffic and a short 8 km track section were transferred to the Fordyce & Princeton which connects to the UP (ex-SP) at Fordyce. The other two roads are the Gloster Southern and the Arkansas, Louisiana & Mississippi (which connects to UP and KCS) and the three together now total 240 route-km and operate a combined fleet of 14 road and switch engines of various GM-EMD models plus 2,222 freight cars. Georgia Pacific also owns and operates the Amador Central in California and has sent some ex-ADN GM units there to replace Alcos.

## Atlantic & Gulf Railroad Co

1019 Coast Line Avenue, Albany, Georgia 31705
Tel: (+1 912) 435 66 29   Fax: (+1 912) 436 45 71

### Key personnel
President: H P Claussen
Executive Vice-President: W T Hart
Vice-Presidents
  General Manager: K V Douglas Jr
  Engineering: D O Cochran
  Mechanical: Larry S Daniel

The company took over from CSX in February 1991 its 125 route-km line that runs from a CSX connection at Thomasville, Georgia, to Albany and Sylvester. Its locomotive fleet comprises seven GP10s. Employees: 16; annual carloadings: 10,000.

## Bangor & Aroostook Railroad Company

RR2, Box 45, Northern Maine Junction Park, Bangor, Maine 04401
Tel: (+1 207) 848 42 00   Fax: (+1 207) 848 43 43

### Key personnel
President and Chief Executive Officer, Iron Road Railways: Robert T Schmidt
Senior Operating Officer: Ted Michon

Gauge: 1,435 mm
Route length: 701.5 km

### Organisation
The BAR was sold in 1993 by the then owner Amoskeag Corporation to Fieldcrest-Cannon Inc, which resold it in March 1995 to Bangor & Aroostook Acquisition Corporation acting for Iron Road Railways Inc (qv). Major commodities transported include lumber, logs, paper and potatoes. Originating much traffic, the BAR has been profitable in recent years. Interchange is made with Canadian National at St Leonard, the Canadian American Railroad and the Eastern Maine, both at Brownville Junction. Connections to the south are via the Guilford system.

Recent developments focused on the development of intermodal facilities, with the establishment of a terminal at Bangor.

In December 2001, BAR was declared insolvent, although operations were continuing pending the appointment of a trustee.

### Traction and rolling stock
At the time of the sale, the BAR equipment fleet consisted of 38 locomotives, comprising GM-EMD F3, BL2, GP7, GP9 and GP38 types; and 2,805 freight wagons, 61 per cent of which are boxcars. The fleet is being standardised, and remanufactured GP38s were being delivered in 1996.

### Track
**Rail:** 115 RE 57.05 kg/m; 112 RE 55.56 kg/m, 100 ARA 49.61 kg/m, 80 ARA 39.74 kg/m
**Crossties (sleepers):** Treated hardwood, thickness 152.4 mm
**Spacing:** 1,772/km
**Fastenings:** 178 × 304.8 mm Dbl sh 1:40 cant
**Max curvature:** 10°
**Max gradient:** 1.25%
**Max axleload:** 28.5 tonnes unrestricted, 29.5 tonnes with restrictions

*UPDATED*

*A Bangor & Aroostook GP38 locomotive heads a GP40 and two SD40s in the Chicago area, while on loan to Canadian Pacific (F Gerald Rawling)*  0006191

## Bay Colony Railroad Corporation

420 Washington Street, Braintree, Massachusetts 02184
Tel: (+1 781) 380 35 56   Fax: (+1 781) 380 48 20
Web: http://www.baycol.com

### Key personnel
Chairman and Chief Executive Officer:
  Gordon H Fay
Senior Vice-President, Marketing: Bernard M Reagan
Vice-President, Administration: Susan J Fay
Superintendent, Operations and Maintenance:
  John F Pimentel Sr

### Organisation
BARC operates 204 route-km formed of six unconnected lines in southeastern Massachusetts (four are presently active); it has 10 locomotives and 26 freight wagons. The operating centre is Wareham on the Cape Cod line. All connections are to CSXT.

*UPDATED*

## Belt Railway Company of Chicago

6900 South Central Avenue, Chicago, Illinois 60638
Tel: (+1 708) 496 40 00   Fax: (+1 708) 496 40 05

### Key personnel
President: Ronald Batory
Vice-President, General Counsel:
  Woodrow M Cunningham

Superintendents
  Transportation: Joseph R Spano
  Motive Power: Kenneth H Smith
  Car Dept: James D Mowery
Engineer, Maintenance of Way: Kenneth Diemer
Supervisor, Communications and Signals: Tyree F Bell
Secretary/Treasurer: Ruth A Taylor

Gauge: 1,435 mm
Route length: 43.5 km

The BRC is the innermost of three Chicago-area connecting railroads (see also Indiana Harbor Belt; Elgin, Joliet & Eastern). Its 13 shares are owned by eight of the North American Class I railroads. It makes connections with other railroads, including all Chicago trunk lines, at 21 locations. BRC's massive Clearing Yard measures 9 km from east to west and carries out classification and blocking for UP (ex-SP), Grand Trunk, Wisconsin Central and CSX, and services locomotives for several railroads. Total yard trackage is 480 km. The BRC also serves around 100 online industries. It serves the new I&M Rail Link (qv).

Since 1990, the BRC has undertaken a rationalisation and modernisation programme including bidirectional signalling, installation of remote signals and switches and the introduction of computerised train dispatching. Since 1990 employment has risen from 200 to 500, revenues have reached $50 million (from $16.5 million) and the operating ratio has improved to 75. BRC hosts several unit coal train run-throughs, and since mid-1996 it has been cleared throughout for double-stack container trains. Since picking up some extra traffic diverted from Proviso yard as a result of the UP/CNW merger, the BRC Clearing Yard is virtually at capacity; the company is embarking upon an analysis mapping out a plan for the future, with the participation of the Chicago Operating Rules Association.

In 1996, BRC handled 1,077,128 wagons in intermediate service and 918,159 additional cars were dispatched subject to trackage rights agreements.

### Traction and rolling stock
BRC owns 48 GM-EMD and Alco diesel-electric locomotives, of which seven are twin cow and calf (cabless) units for switching and hump duties. Early in 1997 GE scheduled its back-up lease fleet – a dozen of the first Dash 7 units – through the BRC for a full-service overhaul.

*SW1500 locomotive on Belt Railway of Chicago (F Gerald Rawling)*  0006192

*Jane's World Railways 2002-2003*                                                                        www.janes.com

# Bessemer & Lake Erie Railroad Company

PO Box 68, Monroeville, Pennsylvania 15146
Tel: (+1 412) 829 66 00

**Key personnel**
President and Chief Executive Officer:
  Robert S Rosati
Vice-Presidents
  Law: Robert N Gentile
  Finance: Joseph W Schulte
  Operations: Frank J Habic
  Marketing: Rade Vignovic
General Manager, Operating: George E Steins
Superintendent, Mechanical: E W Richardson
Chief Engineer: F Houston Morris
General Supervisor, Signals and Communications:
  David K Vogou

The B&LE has 341 route-km; 39 locomotives (all EMD six-axle) and 4,830 freight wagons. It is a US Steel/Transtar (qv) property.

# Bethlehem Steel Corporation

Rail Operations Division, Martin Tower, 1170 8th Avenue, Bethlehem, Pennsylvania 18016
Tel: (+1 610) 694 59 37    Fax: (+1 610) 694 33 16
Web: http://www.bethintermodal.com

**Key personnel**
President: J Michael Zaia
Vice-President, Operations: Patrick R Loughlin
Vice-President, Finance: August N Fix Jr
Vice-President, Business Development:
  Patrick A Sabatino

The BSC operates nine railroads, each of which serves a company mill (the Steelton, Pennsylvania, works, for example, produces rail) and any receivers/shippers located on line. Each railroad's resident superintendent is responsible for its own business plan and asset management.
The railroads are:
- Brandywine Valley Railroad, Coatesville, Pennsylvania
  Tel: (+1 610) 383 26 69
- Conemaugh & Black Lick, Johnston, Pennsylvania
  Tel: (+1 814) 533 71 50
- Cumberland Valley Business Park, Chambersburg, Pennsylvania
  Tel: (+1 610) 694 59 74
- Lake Michigan and Indiana, Burns Harbor, Indiana
  Tel: (+1 219) 787 79 88
- Patapsco & Black Rivers, Baltimore, Maryland
  Tel: (+1 410) 388 79 37
- Philadelphia, Bethlehem & New England, Bethlehem, Pennsylvania
  Tel: (+1 610) 694 33 92
- Steelton & Highspire, Steelton, Pennsylvania
  Tel: (+1 717) 986 24 55
- South Buffalo Railway, Lackawanna, New York
  Tel: (+1 716) 821 36 30
- Upper Merion and Plymouth, Conshohocken, Pennsylvania
  Tel: (+1 610) 383 26 69

Total route length of the nine railroads is 528 km. Rolling stock comprises 103 locomotives and 638 freight wagons. Interchange traffic totals around 160,000 carloads annually, while internal traffic amounts to over 170,000 carloads.

# Birmingham Southern Railroad Co

PO Box 579, 6200 E J Oliver Boulevard, Fairfield, Alabama 35064
Tel: (+1 205) 783 41 18    Fax: (+1 205) 783 45 07

**Key personnel**
President and Chief Executive Officer: Robert S Rosati
Vice-Presidents
  Operations: Peter Stephenson
  Law: Robert N Gentile
  Marketing: J C Pranaitis
  Finance: Joseph W Schulte
General Superintendent: J L Neis

BSRC has 135 route-km; it operates 37 GM-EMD locomotives (three MP1500, four GP38-2, three SW1000, 12 SW1001, one SW7, three SW9C, 10 SD9R and one slug unit) and 1,118 freight wagons. It is a US Steel/Transtar (qv) subsidiary.

# Buffalo & Pittsburgh Railroad

Genesee & Wyoming Inc
New York/Pennsylvania Region
1200-C Scottsville Road, Suite 200, Rochester, New York 14624
Tel: (+1 585) 463 33 08    Fax: (+1 585) 463 33 57
Web: http://www.gwrr.com

**Key personnel**
Senior Vice-President: Dave Collins
Vice-President, Marketing and Sales: Ron Klein
Vice President, Transportation: Dave Malay
Vice-President Mechanical: Gene Evans
Chief Engineer: David Baer
Director of Customer Service: Dan Wahle

**Organisation**
Together with the Rochester & Southern Railroad, the Buffalo & Pittsburgh Railroad forms the New York/Pennsylvania Region of Genesee & Wyoming Inc (qv), and totals some 1,050 route-km. The Buffalo & Pittsburgh runs south from Buffalo, New York, and Erie to a network of lines serving Driftwood in the east, Freeport in the south and, via trackage rights over the CSX Transportation system, to New Castle in the west. The Rochester & Southern Railroad runs south from Rochester, New York, to Dansville and Silver Springs, and is connected to its sister railway via trackage rights over NS metals from Silver Springs to Buffalo. Traffic for the combined system totals some 80,000 carloads annually, with coal, petroleum products, metals and forest products as the main commodities carried.

*UPDATED*

# California Northern Railroad

129 Klamath Court, American Canyon, California 94503
Tel: (+1 707) 557 28 68    Fax: (+1 707) 557 29 41
Web: http://www.railamerica.com

**Key personnel**
General Manager: Vernon Colbert
Regional Vice-President and General Manager:
  Gene Shepherd

Gauge: 1,435 mm
Route length: 410 km

**Organisation**
Operated by RailAmerica, the CFNR comprises a line from American Canyon, California, north to Tehama, with branches, and an unconnected line from Tracy, southwest of Oakland, to Los Banos. The railway handles approximately 30,000 carloads annually of industrial and agricultural products. Interchange is made with UP at Davis, Suisan, Tehama and Tracy, with the Northwestern Pacific at Schelville and with the Napa Valley line.

# Camas Prairie Railroad Co

325 Mill Road, PO Box 1166, Lewiston, Idaho 83501
Tel: (+1 208) 743 29 40

**Key personnel**
Manager: Verne J Hoes

Gauge: 1,435 mm
Route length: 437 km

Formerly an operating company for the Union Pacific and BNSF railroads, the Camas Prairie Railroad was sold in April 1998 to Camas Prairie RailNet, Inc, a wholly owned subsidiary of North American RailNet, Inc. Previously, the company owned no equipment except for a rotary snow-plough.
The line leaves the UP at Riparia, Washington, and breaks into three branches to Kooskia, Washington; Reveling, Idaho; and Grangeville, Idaho. Principal commodities carried are logs and lumber products, while intermodal traffic generated by the port of Lewiston has also grown.

Employees: 70; annual carloadings: 18,000.

# Carolina Piedmont Railroad

268 East Main Street, Laurens, South Carolina 29360
Tel: (+1 864) 984 00 40    Fax: (+1 864) 984 00 43
Web: http://www.railamerica.com

**Key personnel**
General Manager: Lamont Jones
Business Development Manager: Kim Greer

Gauge: 1,435 mm
Route length: 79 km

**Organisation**
Operated by RailAmerica, the CPDR links East Greenville and Laurens, South Carolina. The railway handles approximately 5,000 carloads annually, carrying commodities which include forest and paper products, food and farm products, chemicals, petroleum and coal. Interchange is made with NS at Greenville and with CSXT at Laurens.

*NEW ENTRY*

# Cascade & Columbia River Railroad

901 Omak Avenue, Omak, Washington 98841
Tel: (+1 800) 992 72 65    Fax: (+1 509) 826 38 66
Web: http://www.railamerica.com

**Key personnel**
General Manager: Buck Workman
Business Development Manager: Tom Hawksworth

Gauge: 1,435 mm
Route length: 209 km

**Organisation**
Operated by RailAmerica, the CSCD is a shortline which runs north through central Washington from Wenatchee, east of Seattle, to Oroville. The railway handles approximately 8,000 carloads annually, mostly of forest and agricultural products. Interchange is made with BNSF at Wenatchee.

*NEW ENTRY*

# Cedar Rapids and Iowa City Railway Co

See IES Transportation Inc entry.

# Central Kansas Railway

1825 West Harry, Wichita, Kansas 67213
Tel: (+1 316) 263 31 13    Fax: (+1 316) 263 83 46
Kansas Southwestern Railway affiliate
Tel: (+1 316) 263 32 40    Fax: (+1 316) 263 32 54

Two OmniTrax (qv) properties, CKRY and the adjacent Kansas Southwestern Railway (KSWR), serve a total of 480 km of ex-Missouri Pacific and 1,440 km of ex-Santa Fe trackage, principally for the transport of outbound agricultural produce.

# Central Michigan Railway Co

1410 S Valley Center Drive, Bay City, Michigan 48706-9998
Tel: (+1 517) 684 50 88    Fax: (+1 517) 684 52 60

**Key personnel**
President and General Manager:
  Charles A Pinkerton III
Operations Manager: Rick Ziermer
CMRC is one of a dozen subsidiaries of a diversified holding company, the Straits Corporation, but the only railway.

# Central Montana Rail Inc

PO Box 868, Denton, Montana 59430
Tel: (+1 406) 567 22 23    Fax: (+1 406) 567 22 23
e-mail: cmrail@ttc-cmc.net

**Key personnel**
Chairman: Larry Barber
Vice-Chairman: Henry Nomec

Secretary/Treasurer: Jim Woodburn
General Manager: Carla R Allen

Gauge: 1,435 mm
Route length: 137 km

**Organisation**
CMRI operates under lease a former BNSF branch which is owned by the state of Montana. Connection is with BNSF at Mocassin, Montana. In 2001, CMRI had eight employees.

Track is 75 ASCE, 90RA, 90RB and 100RE rail. Maximum curvature is 8°, maximum gradient 1.5 per cent and maximum permissible axleload 28.5 tonnes.

**Traction and rolling stock**
CMRI has five EMD GP9 locomotives. Wagons are supplied by BNSF.

*UPDATED*

## Central Oregon & Pacific Railroad

PO Box 1083, Roseburg, Oregon 97470
Tel: (+1 541) 957 59 66    Fax: (+1 541) 957 06 86
Web: http://www.railamerica.com

**Key personnel**
General Manager: Dan Loveday
Business Development Manager: Tom Hawksworth

Gauge: 1,435 mm
Route length: 723 km

**Organisation**
Formerly owned by RailTex and operated by RailAmerica since February 2000, the CORP comprises two adjoining lines: from Eugene, Oregon, southwest to Coquille; and from Springfield Junction, Oregon, south to Black Butte, in northern California. The railway handles approximately 44,000 carloads annually, with a diversified traffic base. Interchange is made with UP at Black Butte and with other shortline operators at Eugene, Springfield Junction, White City and Gardiner Junction, Oregon, and at Montague, California.

## Central Railroad of Indiana

497 Circle Freeway Drive, Suite 230, Cincinnati, Ohio 45246
Tel: (+1 513) 860 10 00    Fax: (+1 513) 682 46 45
Web: http://www.railamerica.com

**Key personnel**
General Manager: Terry Wilson
Marketing and Sales Managers: Dour Ernstes,
   Doug Loughead

Gauge: 1,435 mm
Route length: 137 km

**Organisation**
Operated by RailAmerica, the CIND links Cincinnati, Ohio, with Shelbyville, Indiana. From Cincinnati, the railway has trackage rights to Springfield, Ohio, and from Shelbyville rights exist to Indianapolis and Frankfort. Approximately 7,000 carloads are handled annually, commodities carried including cereals, minerals and aggregates, food products, fertilisers and iron and steel.

*NEW ENTRY*

## Central Railroad of Indianapolis

c/o Indiana & Ohio Railway
497 Circle Freeway Drive, Suite 230, Cincinnati, Ohio 45246
Tel: (+1 765) 454 79 03    Fax: (+1 765) 454 79 08
Web: http://www.railamerica.com

**Key personnel**
General Manager: Terry Wilson
Business Development Manager: Warner Clark

Gauge: 1,435 mm
Route length: 137 km

**Organisation**
Operated by RailAmerica, the CERA comprises lines in northern Indiana northwest from Marion to Amboy and west from Marion to Kokomo. Haulage rights exist beyond Kokomo to Frankfort. The railway handles around 3,600 carloads annually.

*NEW ENTRY*

## Chesapeake & Albemarle Railroad

1500 Lexington Drive, Elizabeth City, North Carolina 27909
Tel: (+1 252) 338 37 77    Fax: (+1 252) 338 56 34
Web: http://www.railamerica.com

**Key personnel**
General Manager: Carl Hollowell
Business Development Manager: Kim Greer

Gauge: 1,435 mm
Route length: 338 km

**Organisation**
Operated by RailAmerica, the CA links Chesapeake, Virginia, with Elizabeth City and Edenton, North Carolina. The railway handles approximately 8,600 carloads annually, consisting mainly of limestone, forest products, grain and scrap metal.

*NEW ENTRY*

## Chicago Central & Pacific Railroad Co

See Illinois Central entry.

## Chicago Rail Link

2728 E 104th Street, Chicago, Illinois 60617-5766
Tel: (+1 312) 978 86 37    Fax: (+1 312) 374 66 05

**Key personnel**
President: David Lyons
Director, Marketing and Sales: Mike McGee

The CRL has 57 route-km. It provides switching and industry service in and around Chicago. Its accounts include the Illinois International Port (for export grain), the UP (former Missouri Pacific) intermodal yard on 26th Street and Metra, to which it delivers cars produced by Amerail (formerly MK Transit) at its Pullman plant. Connections are made with seven Class I railroads and seven regional or short lines. CRL is an OmniTRAX company (qv) and draws from its locomotive fleet, principally GP7s and GP9s.

## Chicago SouthShore & South Bend Railroad

505 North Carroll Avenue, Michigan City, Indiana 46360-5082
Tel: (+1 219) 874 42 21    Fax: (+1 219) 879 37 54
Web: http://www.anacostia.com/css

**Key personnel**
Chairman: Peter A Gilbertson
President: H Terry Hearst
Controller: Lance Werner

Gauge: 1,435 mm
Length: 293 km

The railroad operates 10 GM-EMD GP38-2 diesel locomotives and 600 freight wagons, some 350 of which are gondolas. Its workforce totals 65.

In 1989, the railroad was acquired by Anacostia & Pacific Co Inc (qv), which began operations in January 1990. In early 1991, the new owners completed sale to the Northern Indiana Commuter Transportation District (NICTD) (qv) of the 146 km of 1.5 kV DC electrified line used by commuter services between South Bend, Indiana, and the Indiana-Illinois state line. NICTD assumed exclusive responsibility for the passenger service, but the CSS&SB retained trackage rights for its freight operations, which total approximately 50,000 wagonloads in a year, with coal accounting for over 50 per cent of freight revenue. The system also serves major steel and utilities facilities and connects with all transcontinental, regional and local railroads in the Chicago area.

The line is entirely signalled by automatic block. Track is mostly 50 kg RE continuously welded rail on oak sleepers. Maximum curvature is 8°, maximum gradient 2.5 per cent.

## Cimarron Valley Railroad

PO Box 249, Satanta, Kansas 67870
Tel: (+1 316) 649 32 80    Fax: (+1 316) 649 32 81

**Key personnel**
Manager of Operations: Henry Hale
A 1997 start-up on 384 km of former BNSF trackage in the Kansas grain belt.

## Colorado & Wyoming Railway Co

PO Box 316, Pueblo, Colorado 81002
Tel: (+1 719) 561 63 59    Fax: (+ 1 719) 561 68 37

**Key personnel**
General Manager: Robert E Porter
General Superintendent: Robert Cesario

This property is now essentially a switching operation serving the CF&I steel mill in Pueblo (rail is one product) and connecting to both BNSF and UP.

It has 25 km of track, eight locomotives and 200 wagons.

## The Columbia Basin Railroad

6 East Arlington, Yakima, Washington 98901
Tel: (+1 509) 453 91 66    Fax: (+1 509) 452 93 49
Web: http://www.cbrr.com

**Key personnel**
President: Brig Temple
Senior Locomotive Mechanic: Bob Sluys

Gauge: 1,435 mm
Route length: 135 km

**Organisation**
Formerly part of the Washington Central Railroad Company (WCRC), which was acquired in 1986 from the former Burlington Northern (BN), the Columbia Basin Railroad (CBRW) was established in 1996 following the merger of BN and Santa Fe to form BNSF. BNSF re-acquired the former WCRC lines except the 135 km that now form CBRW. The locally owned line runs from a junction with BNSF's Spokane–Portland route at Connell to Moses Lake, both in Washington. It carries mainly agricultural products, including grain, potatoes and fertilisers, as well as chemicals and paper products.

**Traction and rolling stock**
In 2002, CBRW operated 12 locomotives: two GP-38s, two SD-9s, four GP-9s and four SW-1200s.

*UPDATED*

## Connecticut Southern Railroad

190 Park Avenue, East Hartford, Connecticut 06108
Tel: (+1 860) 291 17 00    Fax: (+1 860) 291 17 03
Web: http://www.railamerica.com

**Key personnel**
Assistant General Manager: Charles Fooks
Business Development Manager: Sally Larner

Gauge: 1,435 mm
Route length: 126 km

**Organisation**
Operated by RailAmerica, the CSO runs south from East Alburg, Vermont, through New Hampshire and Massachusetts to New London, Connecticut. The railway handles approximately 16,000 carloads annually, including forest products, metal products, minerals, food and chemicals. Interchange is made with CSXT at West Springfield, Massachusetts, and New Haven, Connecticut.

*NEW ENTRY*

## Copper Basin Railway Inc

PO Drawer 1, Highway 177, Hayden, Arizona 85235
Tel: (+1 520) 356 77 30    Fax: (+1 520) 356 63 04

**Key personnel**
President: K Earl Durden

Vice-President and General Manager: L S Jacobson
Chief Mechanical Officer: Michael J McGinley
CBRI has 112.6 route-km. It operates 14 GM-EMD locomotives (three GP18, five GP9, four SD39 and two GP39) and 115 wagons. Annual carloadings are in the order of 125,000.

## D & I Railroad Co

PO Box 5829, 300 South Phillips Avenue, Suite 200, Sioux Falls, South Dakota 57117-5829
Tel: (+1 605) 334 50 00   Fax: (+1 605) 334 3656

**Key personnel**
President: Dan Kuper
Vice-President: Matt Ellefson
Master Mechanic: Gerald Fox

The D&IRR operates 222 route-km of former Milwaukee Road track between Dell Rapids, South Dakota, and Sioux City, Iowa, owned by the state of South Dakota. Its main activities are hauling aggregates, gravel and railroad ballast from its principal online shipper and owner of the working assets, the L G Everist Company. A former CNW line from Hawarden to Beresford is now a branch of the D&I and generates as many as 100 grain trains in a season. BNSF is the local service provider on two segments, Sioux Falls to Canton and Elk Point to Sioux City. Interchange is available via BNSF at Sioux Falls, South Dakota, and with BNSF, UP and IC (formerly CC&P) at Sioux City, Iowa.

D&IRR operates 12 GM-EMD GP9, two GP20, two GP7, two SD45 and two SD39 locomotives. Rolling stock comprises 250 open-top hoppers and 75 gondolas.

## Dakota, Minnesota & Eastern Railroad Corporation

PO Box 178, 337 22nd Avenue South, Brookings, South Dakota 57006
Tel: (+1 605) 697 24 00   Fax: (+1 605) 697 24 99
e-mail: dmemain@dmerail.com
Web: http://www.dmerail.com

**Key personnel**
President and Chief Executive Officer: Kevin V Schieffer
Vice-President, Marketing, Strategic Planning and Public Affairs: Lynn A Anderson
Vice-President, Finance: Kurt V Feaster
Chief Transportation Officer: Vernon L Colbert
Chief Mechanical Officer: Daniel L Goodwin
Chief Engineer: Steve O Scharnweber

Gauge: 1,435 mm
Route length: 1,825 km

**Organisation**
DM&E, formed in 1986, was the first railroad to be created by a major sale of Chicago & North Western trackage. It is the second longest US regional railroad, with Winona–Rapid City and Waseca–Mason City main lines as its core.

In May 1996, DM&E acquired from UP the 325 km 'Colony line' from Chadron, Nebraska, to Colony, Wyoming, which was also an ex-Chicago & North Western property. The DM&E meets this line at Rapid City, South Dakota.

In February 2002, the DM&E announced that it had reached agreement to acquire the assets of I&M Rail Link (IMRL) (qv), a 2,763 km network to the east linking Chicago with Kansas City and Minneapolis. The IMRL was to be acquired by a wholly owned DM&E subsidiary, Iowa, Chicago & Eastern Railroad Corporation (IC&E). Both DM&E and IC&E would eventually come under the common management of Cedar American Rail Holdings Inc. The transaction was expected to be completed in late 2002, subject to regulatory approval and financing arrangements.

**Passenger operations**
DM&E owns three restored historic passenger coaches which it uses for tourist excursions, community meetings and corporate purposes.

**Freight operations**
The DM&E handles approximately 60,000 carloads annually. Grain is the main commodity, comprising approximately 45 per cent of wagonloads in 1999. Other important commodities are bentonite, kaolin, cement, metal products, paper, foodstuffs, scrap metal, grain products and woodchips.

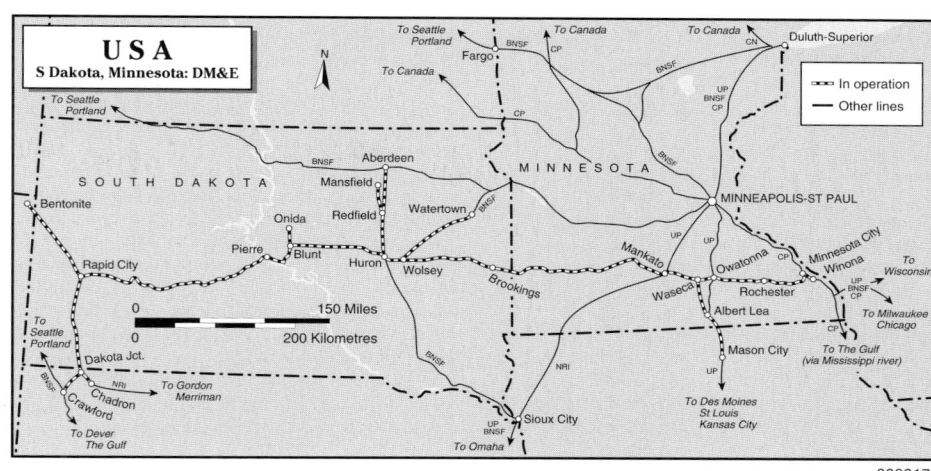

**New lines**
In June 1997, DM&E unveiled a plan for a $1.4 billion new project to extend into the Powder River Basin coalfield in Wyoming. The 965 km line from Winona, Minnesota, to Wasta, South Dakota, would be rebuilt, and a new 450 km link would be built into the coalfields. The plan received the approval of the Surface Transportation Board in January 2002. Completion is expected to take five years.

**Traction and rolling stock**
DM&E operates 70 locomotives, all of GM-EMD origin. The railway also owns or leases around 3,200 wagons, of which 1,225 are of recent manufacture.

## Dakota, Missouri Valley & Western Railroad Inc

1131 22nd Street South, Bismarck, North Dakota 58504
Tel: (+1 701) 223 92 82

**Key personnel**
President: Larry C Wood
Executive Vice-President: Jeff Wood
Vice-President: Diane J Wood
Vice-President, Marketing: Dennis Ming
General Manager: Roger C Wood
Transportation Manager: J P Ankenbauer
Manager, Mechanical: Randy Adin

DMV&WR has 505.7 route-km and operates three GP9 and 10 GM-EMD GP35 locomotives.

The company was created in 1990 to operate trackage leased from Soo Line (now Canadian Pacific) in North Dakota, principally from Oakes westward through Bismarck and north to Max. Freight wagons are supplied by CP Rail.

## Dakota Southern Railway Company

PO Box 436, Chamberlain, South Dakota 57325
Tel: (+1 605) 734 65 95   Fax: (+1 605) 734 65 95

**Key personnel**
Chairman: Richard H Huff
President and General Manager: George A Huff IV

DSR operates over 299 route-km of track owned by the state of South Dakota; it has eight locomotives, including one Alco C420, one Alco S3, two GM-EMD SD7 and two SD9 and one GE 70-ton unit.

The line, from Mitchell to Kadoka, generates 1,600 carloads a year, almost entirely grain, and connects at Mitchell to BNSF. DSR has 220 covered hopper wagons on lease.

## Dallas, Garland & Northeastern Railroad

403 International Parkway, Suite 500, Richardson, Texas 75081
Tel: (+1 972) 808 98 00   Fax: (+1 972) 808 99 00
Web: http://www.railamerica.com

**Key personnel**
General Manager: Dave Eyermann
Business Development Manager: Robin Bergeron

Gauge: 1,435 mm
Route length: 301 km

**Organisation**
Operated by RailAmerica, the DGNO comprises lines running north from Dallas to Sherman and to Trenton using trackage rights between Dallas and Garland. The railway handles approximately 46,000 carloads annually. Interchange is made with KCS and UP at Dallas, with BNSF at Irving and with a sister company, the Texas Northeastern Railroad, at Trenton.

*NEW ENTRY*

## Decatur Junction Railway Co

308 South Chestnut Street, Assumption, Illinois 62510
A subsidiary of Pioneer Railcorp
1318 S Johansen Road, Peoria, Illinois 61607
Tel: (+1 309) 697 14 00   Fax: (+1 309) 697 53 87
Web: http://www.pioneer-railcorp.com

**Key personnel**
See entry for Pioneer Railcorp
Gauge: 1,435 mm
Route length: 61 km

**Organisation**
Operated under lease until 31 December 2006 from a consortium of grain dealers, the DT comprises two segments of track in east central Illinois, including 13 km of trackage rights over the Canadian National system through Decatur, Illinois. Main commodities carried are grain, fertilisers and plastics.

*NEW ENTRY*

## Detroit, Toledo & Ironton Railroad

The DT&I was an independent railroad until 1982 when it was bought by Canadian National. In 1996, CN put it up for sale and the preferred bidder was RailTex (qv), at a reported $27 million, which would secure 233.5 km of track, 175 km of rights, and 110,000 annual carloads. It serves as a bridge line between Detroit and Cincinnati. Two major commodities are car parts northbound and finished autos southbound.

## Delaware Otsego Corporation

1 Railroad Avenue, Cooperstown, New York 13326
Tel: (+1 607) 547 25 55   Fax: (+1 607) 547 98 34

The Delaware Otsego Corporation is a privately held non-rail holding company whose principal asset is the New York, Susquehanna and Western Railway, a wholly owned subsidiary. The holding company also engages in real estate development to augment the railroad's traffic base. In January 1996, the company acquired a 40 per cent interest in the Toledo, Peoria & Western Railway (qv) for cash and stock valued at $2.25 million.

## Duluth, Missabe and Iron Range Railway Company

500 Missabe Building, Duluth, Minnesota 55802
Tel: (+1 218) 723 21 15   Fax: (+1 218) 723 21 27

**Key personnel**
President: Robert S Rosati

# RAILWAY SYSTEMS/USA

Vice-Presidents
  Law: Robert N Gentile
  Finance: Joseph W Schulte
  Operations: F J Habic
  Marketing: R Vignovic
General Manager: J C Pranaitis
Superintendent, Locomotive: T C Sample
Superintendent, Car: M J Urie
Superintendent, Transportation: J D Paschke
Chief Engineer: D B Moore
Signals and Communications Engineer:
  Timothy R Luhm

DMIRR is a US Steel/Transtar (qv) property and has 736 km in track. It operates 69 locomotives, predominantly SD9s and SD38s, and 4,242 freight wagons. In 1995, the DMIRR acquired five reconditioned SD45T-3s from VMV and three more in 1996. Several SD9s were cascaded to other Transtar properties. The railway connects the Missabe Range iron ore deposits with the ports of Duluth and Two Harbors on Lake Superior, from where the ore is shipped to steel mills in the Great Lakes region. In 1994, DMIRR began to ship ore to Geneva Steel in Utah via Wisconsin Central and Southern Pacific.

## Eastern Alabama Railway

2413 Hill Road, PO Box 658, Sylacauga, Alabama 35151
Tel: (+1 256) 249 11 96   Fax: (+1 256) 249 11 98
Web: http://www.railamerica.com

### Key personnel
General Manager: Larry Nordquist
Gauge: 1,435 mm
Route length: 40 km

### Organisation
Operated by RailAmerica, the EARY is formed of branches from the CSXT Birmingham–Phenix City line in eastern Alabama. Interchange is also made with NS. The railway handles approximately 12,000 carloads annually.

*NEW ENTRY*

## Eastern Shore Railroad

PO Box 312, Cape Charles, Virginia 23310-0312
Tel: (+1 757) 331 10 94   Fax: (+1 757) 331 27 72

### Key personnel
President and General Manager: Larry Le Mond
Transportation Superintendent: Ira T Higbee

ESHR has 113 route-km and operates one GM-EMD GP38 and four GM-EMD GP10 locomotives, and 27 freight wagons. It provides a rail link from the Hampton Roads area to the eastern shore of Virginia by floating wagons across Chesapeake Bay.

*UPDATED*

## Elgin, Joliet and Eastern Railway Company

1141 Maple Road, Joliet, Illinois 60432
Tel: (+1 815) 740 69 03   Fax: (+1 815) 740 67 29

### Key personnel
President (of Transtar): Robert S Rosati
Vice-Presidents
  Law: Robert N Gentile
  Operations: Frank J Habic III
  Finance: Joseph W Schulte
  Marketing: Rade Vignovic

General Manager: Mel S Turner
Director, Asset Management: J M Hayes

EJ&E is a US Steel/Transtar (qv) property. Its route length is 320.2 km, and it has 58 locomotives and 4,355 freight wagons.
The EJ&E is the outermost of the three belt railroads encircling the Chicago area. Via 14 interchanges it connects with every Class I operator in the region. During 1996, several large railroads expressed interest in purchasing the EJ&E; UP has declared its intention to make a connection into the EJ&E in the vicinity of West Chicago and the EJ&E has granted overhead trackage rights. There is substantial civic opposition to this move in West Chicago. Metra (qv) has undertaken a feasibility study into the possibility of running circumferential commuter operations in the future on the EJ&E, to connect several routes radiating from Chicago.

## Elkhart & Western Railroad Co

PO Box 1468, Elkhart, Indiana 46515
A subsidiary of Pioneer Railcorp
1318 S Johansen Road, Peoria, Illinois 61607
Tel: (+1 309) 697 14 00   Fax: (+1 309) 697 53 87
Web: http://www.pioneer-railcorp.com

### Key personnel
See entry for Pioneer Railcorp
Gauge: 1,435 mm
Route length: 13 km

### Organisation
Acquired from Conrail in 1996 to become the Elkhart & Western Division of the Michigan Southern Railroad (qv), the EWR runs from Elkhart to Mishawaka, Indiana. Interchange is made with Norfolk Southern at Elkhart and the EWR has a haulage agreement to CSXT at Fort Wayne, Indiana. Commodities carried include building materials and cement.

*NEW ENTRY*

## Emons Transportation Group Inc

See entry for Genesee & Wyoming Inc.

*UPDATED*

## Escanaba and Lake Superior Railroad

One Larkin Plaza, Wells, Michigan 49894
Tel: (+1 906) 786 06 93   Fax: (+1 906) 786 80 12

### Key personnel
President: John C Larkin
Secretary and Treasurer: A K Larkin
Director, Marketing & Customer Services:
  Thomas J Klimek

ELSR operates 555 route-km with 21 locomotives, including several Baldwins. It owns 357 wagons and leases a further 550.
ELSR has connections through Green Bay to the Wisconsin Central system. There are several connections in other locations with the WC and its Sault Ste Marie subsidiary.
Principal traffic is paper waferboard and pulpwood outbound; chemicals and fertilisers inbound. Volume in 1997 was 14,000 carloads.

## Farmrail System Inc

PO Box 1750, 136 E Frisco Street, Clinton, Oklahoma 73601-1750
Tel: (+1 405) 323 12 34   Fax: (+1 405) 323 45 68

### Key personnel
Chairman, President and Chief Executive Officer:
  George C Betke Jr
Chief Operating Officer: Richard S Shaw

Farmrail System Inc comprises 566.4 km of line in western Oklahoma. It owns 286.4 km (ex-Burlington Northern) as Grainbelt Corp. It operates 284.8 km (ex-Rock Island and ex-Santa Fe) owned by the state of Oklahoma as Farmrail Corp. Employees: 32; locomotives: 15. Connections are made to Burlington Northern Santa Fe, Union Pacific and two short lines.
In mid-1995, the company assigned three GP9s to start up a subsidiary, Finger Lakes Railway, operating 176 km of lines centred on Geneva in upstate New York.

## Florida East Coast Railway Company

Florida East Coast Industries Inc
1 Malaga Street, St Augustine, Florida 32084
Tel: (+1 904) 829 34 21

### Key personnel
Chairman, President and Chief Executive Officer:
  Carl F Zellers Jr
Vice-President, Secretary and Treasurer:
  T Neal Smith
Comptroller: J Richard Yastrzemski

### Organisation
FECRC is a Class II carrier. Its common stock is 54.5 per cent held by the St Joe Corp, Florida's largest private landowner. FECRC is one of two wholly owned subsidiaries of Florida East Coast Industries Inc, which also owns Gran Central Corporation, a property company which redevelops surplus rail property and other sites. Also wholly owned is International Transit Inc (ITI), a trucking subsidiary which provides transportation services between the company's railheads and customers' facilities.
In May 1997, St Joe made a $428 million bid for the 46 per cent of FEC it did not already own. However, negotiations ended in November 1997 with no transaction having taken place.
In March 1997, the company signed a trackage agreement with the South Central Florida Express Railroad (qv).
The railway's physical plant is 561.6 km of main track between Jacksonville and Miami; there is a 145.6 km branch line to Belle Glade on Lake Okeechobee. In addition, there are 251.2 km of yard and switching tracks and 294.4 km of second main and passing track. Main track is 132 lb rail on concrete sleepers; branch/yard track is 112/115 lb rail on timber sleepers. With an average number of employees of 1,178 in transportation in 1997, the company has pared its workforce by 20 per cent since the start of 1993.

### Finance
Revenues from transportation in 1997 were $185 million compared with $172.9 million in 1996, and $65.5 million from property compared with $35.1 million. Income before taxes in net of taxes was $40.1 million ($30.4 million in 1996). The increase in transportation revenue was mainly due to increases in traffic, especially in aggregates, intermodal and automotive sectors.

### Passenger operations
As part of an attempt to increase its transportation business, in 1997, FEC undertook to study the reintroduction of passenger services.

### Freight operations
In addition to intermodal traffic, principal commodities are automobiles, crushed stone, cement, consumer products and foodstuffs. Traffic was basically flat or in slight decline in FY95-96, except for automotives which rose by 9.3 per cent. Gross tonne-km for 1996 were 6.5 billion.

### Intermodal operations
Historically known for its interline intermodal business, especially through the ports of Jacksonville and Miami, FEC now originates or terminates 46 per cent of revenues online.

*EJ&E SD40 (left) and SD9 locomotives at the company's Joliet roundhouse (F Gerald Rawling)* 0021593

FEC opened a leased intermodal facility at Macon, Georgia, in March 1995, to extend its reach, but closed it in February 1996. The explanation for this was that growth was forecast to outgrow the facility but not by such a margin as to justify the expense of building, and owning, a larger site.

**Traction and rolling stock**
The all-GM-EMD locomotive fleet comprises 41 GP40 and GP40-2 units; 22 rebuilt GP9s; 11 GP38-2s; two SW9s; and two SW1200s. In 1994, FEC ordered its first six-axle units, four of which entered service on unit mineral trains and intermodal expresses.

At the close of 1996, the railway operated 2,635 freight wagons.

## Forth Smith Railroad Co

22 North B Street, Fort Smith, Arkansas
A subsidiary of Pioneer Railcorp
1318 S Johansen Road, Peoria, Illinois 61607
Tel: (+1 309) 697 14 00   Fax: (+1 309) 697 53 87
Web: http://www.pioneer-railcorp.com

**Key personnel**
See entry for Pioneer Railcorp
Gauge: 1,435 mm
Route length: 13 km

**Organisation**
Originally a 79 km system for which a 20-year operating lease was acquired by Pioneer Railcorp from Missouri Pacfic in 1991, the line was cut back to its present length in 1995. Connection is made at Fort Smith with Kansas City Southern and Union Pacific. Commodities carried include iron and steel, forest products and food and beverages.
*NEW ENTRY*

## Garden City Western Railway

708 North View Road, Garden City, Kansas 67846
A subsidiary of Pioneer Railcorp
1318 S Johansen Road, Peoria, Illinois 61607
Tel: (+1 309) 697 14 00   Fax: (+1 309) 697 53 87
Web: http://www.pioneer-railcorp.com

**Key personnel**
See entry for Pioneer Railcorp
Gauge: 1,435 mm
Route length: 72 km

**Organisation**
Acquired by Pioneer Railcorp in May 1999, the GCW comprises two branches running from Garden City, Kansas, where interchange is made with Burlington Northern Santa Fe. Main commodities carried are grain and other agricultural products, fertilisers and foodstuffs.
*NEW ENTRY*

## Gateway Western Railway

15 Executive Drive, Fairview Heights, Illinois 62208
Tel: (+1 618) 624 47 00   Fax: (+1 618) 624 47 31

**Key personnel**
President: Don Gill
Vice-President Engineering and Mechanical:
    Paul Fetterman

**Organisation**
In May 1997, the Surface Transportation Board gave approval for the acquisition of the GWWR by the Kansas City Southern Railway Company (qv).

GWWR's route length is 656 km, of which 602 km was solely owned; the remainder was owned jointly or operated under rights. Annual carloadings: 60,000; employees: 250.

The railway was formed in 1990 to take over lines linking Kansas City, St Louis and Springfield, Illinois, and associated branches, formerly owned by the bankrupt Chicago, Missouri & Western. It has a long-term contract with BNSF (ex-Santa Fe) for haulage of that railroad's freight between Kansas City and East St Louis.

In 1995, it took over the Mill Street yard and six locomotives to service customers of the Kansas City Terminal railroad. Also in 1995, the GWWR reached agreement with Conrail to haul the latter's intermodal traffic from St Louis to Kansas City where previously it went by highway. GWWR also owned trackage rights from Springfield to Chicago.

GWWR operated a fleet of GM-EMD locomotives, comprising 10 GP38 and four GP40 line-haul units and 13 SW1500 switchers.

## Genesee & Wyoming Inc

66 Field Point Road, Greenwich, Connecticut 06830
Tel: (+1 203) 629 37 22   Fax: (+1 203) 661 41 06
Web: http://www.gwrr.com

**Key personnel**
Chairman and Chief Executive Officer:
    Mortimer B Fuller III
President and Chief Operating Officer: Charles N Marshall
President, Marketing and Development:
    Charles W Chabot
Executive Vice-President, Corporate Development:
    Mark W Hastings
Chief Financial Officer: John C Hellmann
Senior Vice-President, GWI Rail Switching Services:
    James W Benz
Senior Vice-President and Chief Accounting Officer:
    Alan R Harris
Senior Vice-Presidents
    Louisiana: Forrest L Becht
    Canada: Carl P Belke
    Illinois: Spencer D White
    New York & Pennsylvania: David J Collins
    Oregon: Robert I Melbo
    GWI Rail Switching Services: James W Benz
    Australia: Martin D Lacombe
    Mexico: Paul M Victor
Finance and Treasurer: Thomas P Loftus
Administration and Human Resources: Shayne L Magdoff

**Organisation**
GWI is an operator of shortlines and regional railroads. Its properties in the USA are:
- Buffalo & Pittsburgh RR
- Carolina Coastal Railway
- Commonwealth Railway
- Illinois & Midland RR
- Louisiana & Delta RR
- Pittsburgh & Shawmut RR
- Portland & Western RR
- Rochester & Southern RR
- Utah Railway Company
- Willamette & Pacific RR.

Through its joint-venture affiliate in Canada, Genesee-Rail-One (qv in Canada section), the company operates:
- Québec Gatineau Railway
- Huron Central Railway.

In Australia, through its joint venture subsidiary with Wesfarmers Ltd, Australian Railroad Group Pty Ltd (ARG) (qv in Australia section), GWI owns or operates:
- Australia Southern Railroad
- Australia Northern Railroad
- Australia Western Railroad
- Westnet Rail

In Bolivia GWI is a strategic investor in:
- Empresa Ferroviaria Oriental SA (qv in Bolivia section)

In Mexico GWI operates:
- Ferrocarriles Chiapas—Mayab SA de CV (FCCM) (qv in Mexico section)

In 1996, GWI acquired an industrial switching subsidiary, Rail Link Inc, which it has subsequently developed. By 2002, Rail Link was handling rail operations at some 25 locations in 10 states, including port authorities, coal mines and power utilities companies, and was operating seven short line railroads.

In December 2001, GWI announced that it was to acquire Emons Transportation Group, which operated short line railroads in Maine, New Hampshire, Pennsylvania and Vermont, and in Quebec, Canada. The acquisition was completed in February 2002. US railroads added to the GWI portfolio as a result of this acquisition were:
- Penn Eastern Rail Lines
- York Railway Company

Canadian lines acquired were:
- St Lawrence & Atlantic Railroad (Quebec) Inc
- St Lawrence & Atlantic Railroad Company

In August 2002, GWI acquired the Utah Railway Company (qv) from Mueller Industries Inc.

In mid-2002, GWI owned or leased approximately 9,600 km of track and operated over an additional 3,780 km under access arrangements.

**Traction and rolling stock**
At the beginning of 2000, the company operated 252 locomotives in its North American businesses.
*UPDATED*

## Georgia Southwestern Railroad

PO Box 69, 216 Long Drive, Smithville, Georgia 31787
Tel: (+1 229) 846 40 21   Fax: (+1 229) 846 40 25
Web: http://www.railamerica.com

**Key personnel**
General Manager: Terry Small
Business Development Manager: Anita Horton
Gauge: 1,435 mm
Route length: 164 km

**Organisation**
Formerly owned by RailTex, the GSWR was operated by RailAmerica between February 2000 and March 2002. In March 2002, RailAmerica sold the track to the state of Georgia and the capital stock of the GSWR, together with eight locomotives, to a local private operator, which runs the railway on behalf of the state. The railway comprises a network of lines from Columbus in the northwest of the state to Vidalia in the east, Bainbridge in the south and via trackage rights to Albany and to White Oak, Alabama, in the west. Approximately 12,000 carloads are handled annually. Interchange is made with CSXT at Bainbridge and Cordele, with NS at Albany, Americus, Arlington and Helena and with the Georgia Central Railway at Vidalia.
*UPDATED*

## Gettysburg & Northern Railroad Co

750 Mummasburg Road, Gettysburg, Pennsylvania 17325
A subsidiary of Pioneer Railcorp
1318 S Johansen Road, Peoria, Illinois 61607
Tel: (+1 309) 697 14 00   Fax: (+1 309) 697 53 87
Web: http://www.pioneer-railcorp.com

**Key personnel**
See entry for Pioneer Railcorp
Gauge: 1,435 mm
Route length: 40 km

**Organisation**
Acquired by Pioneer Railcorp from private interests in February 2001, the Gettysburg & Northern runs north from a connection with CSXT at Gettysburg, Pennsylvania, to Mount Holly Springs, where a connection is made with Norfolk Southern. Main commodities carried are paper products, foodstuffs and grain.
*NEW ENTRY*

## Grand Rapids Eastern

10 Enterprise Drive, Vassar, Michigan 48768
Tel: (+1 800) 968 19 75   Fax: (+1 989) 823 37 94
Web: http://www.railamerica.com

**Key personnel**
General Manager: Larry Ross
Business Development Manager: Mike Bobic
Gauge: 1,435 mm
Route length: 70 km

**Organisation**
Operated by RailAmerica, the GR links Grand Rapids with Ionia in the east and Marne in the west. The railway handles approximately 3,200 carloads annually, comprising mainly chemicals, paper, farm products and automotive components. Interchange is made with CSXT and NS at Grand Rapids and with a sister company, the Mid-Michigan Railroad (qv), at Lowell.
*NEW ENTRY*

## Great Western Railway Company of Colorado

Taylor Avenue Shops, PO Box 537, Loveland, Colorado 80539
Tel: (+1 303) 667 68 83   Fax: (+1 303) 667 14 44

**Key personnel**
President: David L Lafferty

GWR serves customers on 88 route-km of track. Interchanges are made with BNSF and UP; the latter brings corn in unit trains to GWR. The railway is an OmniTRAX company (qv) and undertakes major locomotive repair and rebuilding at Loveland for member companies as well as on contract. In 1996, GWR added two reconditioned SD9s to its locomotive fleet, in order to have sufficient power for the unit trains.

## Green Mountain Railroad Corp

PO Box 498, Bellows Falls, Vermont 05101-0498
Tel: (+1 802) 463 95 31    Fax: (+1 802) 463 40 84

**Key personnel**
President and General Manager: Jerome M Hebda
Vice-President and Chief Engineering Officer:
  D M Lamoureux
Chief Mechanical Officer: S J Whitney
Operations Officer: K L Smith

GMRC has 83.9 route-km and operates five locomotives (one Alco RS1, four EMD GP9 ), 100 freight wagons, and eight passenger cars, including a dining car.
In 1996, the railroad recorded 4,000 carloads, 400,000 tonnes of freight, over 20 million freight tonne-km, 30,000 passenger journeys and 1.25 million passenger-km. The corporation is the operator of a mid-June to mid-October 'Green Mountain Flyer' tourist train.
GMRC is a partner in a marketing initiative that links up with the St Lawrence & Atlantic, the New England Central and the Providence & Worcester railroads.

## Guilford Rail System

Iron Horse Park, North Billerica, Massachusetts 01862
Tel: (+1 508) 663 11 30
Web: http://www.guilfordrail.com

**Key personnel**
President: Thomas F Steinger
Executive Vice-President: David A Fink
Vice-Presidents
  Transportation: Sid Culliford
  Engineering: Steve Nevero
  Mechanical: James Coffin
  Finance: Sonya Clay
  Marketing: Richard Willey

Guilford is the holding company for several rail assets, namely:
- Boston & Maine Corporation (qv)
- Maine Central Railroad (qv)
- Springfield Terminal Railway.

At the end of April 1998, Guilford Transportation Industries acquired Pan Am Corporation for $28.5 million.

## Harbor Belt Line

See Pacific Harbor Line entry.
See also Anacostia & Pacific Co Inc entry.

## Housatonic Railroad Co Inc

67 Main Street, PO Box 298, Centerbrook, Connecticut 06409
Tel: (+1 860) 767 74 76    Fax: (+1 860) 767 74 19

**Key personnel**
President: John R Hanlon Jr
Vice-Presidents
  Operations: Peter E Lynch
  Finance: Thomas E Curtin
  General Counsel: Edward J Rodriguez

The Housatonic RR, together with its subsidiary Danbury Terminal RR, operates freight service for 45 accounts on 259 km of tracks in the states of Connecticut, New York and Massachusetts; the lines are ex-New Haven, New York Central, Conrail, and Boston & Maine. HRRC also has freight rights to 141 km of Metro-North owned trackage. Connections are made to Conrail at Pittsfield, Massachusetts and Beacon, New York; and to the Boston and Maine at Derby, Connecticut. Paper products, limestone, chemicals and lumber are the principal commodities; total carloadings for the entire railroad are 4,500-5,000 per year. It operates a lumber reload centre at Hawleyville, Connecticut.

## Houston Belt & Terminal Railway Co

501 Crawford Street, Houston, Texas 77002
Tel: (+1 713) 222 11 33

**Key personnel**
President and General Manager: Harlan W Ritter
Vice-President, Finance: Michael A Schensted
Chief Engineer: Satish C Malhotra
Superintendent, Signals and Communications:
  Richard M Sanders

Length: 435 km

The railway purchased eight model MK1500D switchers featuring Caterpillar engines and MK-LOC microprocessors from MK Rail which displaced its previous fleet of 12. The contract for acquisition and long-term support is valued at $30 million. (See also the Port Terminal Railroad Association entry.)

## Huron & Eastern Railway

101 Enterprise Drive, Vassar, Michigan 48768
Tel: (+1 800) 968 19 75    Fax: (+1 517) 823 37 94
Web: http://www.railamerica.com

**Key personnel**
General Manager: Larry Ross
Business Development Manager: Mike Bobic
Gauge: 1,435 mm
Route length: 275 km

**Organisation**
A RailAmerica subsidiary since March 1986, the HESR comprises a network of shortlines east of Saginaw, Michigan. The railway handles approximately 9,500 carloads annually, traffic including agricultural commodities, automotive components, chemicals, sugar beet and sugar products, fertiliser and aggregates. Interchange is made with CSXT at Saginaw and with the Central Michigan Railway (qv) at Buena Vista, Michigan.

## IES Transportation Inc

2330 12th Street SW, Cedar Rapids, Iowa 52404
Tel: (+1 319) 398 45 97    Fax: (+1 319) 398 41 71

**Key personnel**
Vice-President and General Manager:
  Paul H Treangen
Chief Mechanical Officer: Angie Perez

The railway has 85 route-km; it operates 13 GM-EMD locomotives (five SW8; one SW900; one SW9; two SW1200; and four GP9 which were remodelled by National Railway Engineering in 1996) and 307 freight wagons.
IES is a holding company for the Cedar Rapids & Iowa City Railway, plus a barge terminal in Dubuque and a rail-to-track transfer facility in Cedar Rapids.
In 1996, a feasibility study was conducted (with Wilbur Smith, consultants, as prime contractor) to assess the potential for commuter rail on this system. The conclusion was that passenger services were unlikely to be justifiable.

## I&M Rail Link

1910 East Kimberley Road, Davenport, Iowa 52807-2033
Tel: (+1 319) 344 76 00    Fax: (+1 319) 344 77 00
Web: http://www.imrail.com

Gauge: 1,435 mm
Length: 2,763 km

**Organisation**
Created in 1997, I&M Rail Link LLC serving Illinois, Iowa, Missouri and Minnesota, includes a main line linking Minneapolis/St Paul, Chicago and Kansas City. Originally a Milwaukee Road route, it was merged into the Soo Line in 1986 and later came under the control of Canadian Pacific in 1990 before becoming a Washington Company. The company employs around 700 people.
In February 2002, the acquisition of I&M by Dakota, Minnesota & Eastern Railroad Corporation was announced. The merger was expected to be completed by the end of 2002.
The I&M connects with all railroads in Chicago, offering a direct intermodal service between Chicago, Davenport, Kansas City and the Twin Cities. Major branch lines serve the rich agricultural areas of northern Iowa and southern Wisconsin. The line also serves a variety of industrial customers, including cereals processors and manufacturers of machinery and agricultural and industrial heavy equipment. Bulk products such as cement and coal are also carried, and a branch to Rockford, Illinois transports automobile parts to assembly plants and warehouses.

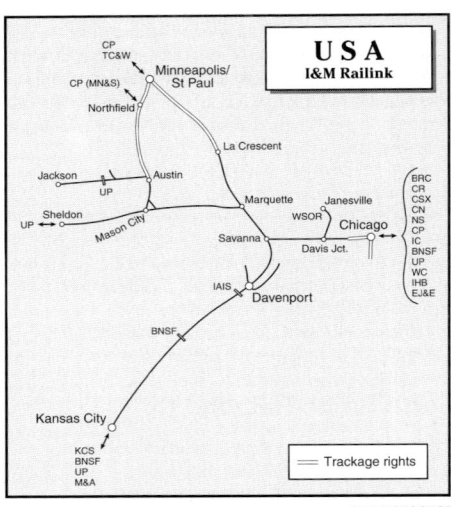

**Traction and rolling stock**
The locomotive fleet totals 115, including General Motors SD-40 and SD-45 models, and the railway owns some 2,300 freight wagons.

## Illinois & Midland Railway Co

1500 North Grand Avenue East, Springfield, Illinois 62702
Tel: (+1 217) 788 86 01    Fax: (+1 217) 788 86 60
Web: http://www.gwrr.com

**Key personnel**
President and General Manager:
  Spencer White
Executive Vice-President: Raquel Swan
Chief Transportation Officer: Terry Holderread
Superintendent: Jim Rodden
Chief Mechanical Officer: Hal Bast
Chief Engineer: Allan Johnson
Manager, Marketing and Customer Services:
  Mike Vetter
Manager, Purchasing, Stores, Lumber Transfer:
  Kay Hutchcraft

Gauge: 1,435 mm
Length: 194.7 km

**Organisation**
Formerly the Chicago & Illinois Midland Railway Company, the I&M acquired its current name following acquisition in 1996 by Genesee & Wyoming (qv). The railway runs south from Peoria, Illinois, via Havana to Springfield and Taylorville. Interchange is made with BNSF, CN, NS and UP, and via the Gateway Western with CSX Transportation. Coal features prominently in the I&M's traffic, with some 3 million tonnes delivered annually from the Powder River Basin to the Kincaid generating plant. Other commodities carried include agricultural products, building materials and domestic and industrial waste.

**Traction and rolling stock**
The I&M fleet numbers 17 (four SW1500s; two SD18s; four SD9s; five SD20s; two RS1325s).    *UPDATED*

## Indiana & Ohio Rail System

497 Circle Freeway Drive, Suite 230, Cincinnati, Ohio 45246
Tel: (+1 513) 860 10 00    Fax: (+1 513) 682 46 45
Web: http://www.railamerica.com

**Key personnel**
General Manager: Terry Wilson
Marketing and Sales Managers: Doug Ernstes,
  Doug Loughead
Gauge: 1,435 mm
Route length: 792 km

## Organisation

Formerly operated by RailTex and owned by RailAmerica since February 2000, the Indiana & Ohio Rail System comprises two geographically separate railways: the Indiana & Ohio Railway (IORY) is a network of lines centred on Springfield, Ohio, and running north to Diann, Michigan, southeast to Washington Court House and via trackage rights southwest to Cincinnati. From here, using the tracks of a sister company, the Central Railroad of Indiana, and trackage rights, the IORY extends its services northwest to Frankfort, Indiana, and beyond. The Indiana & Ohio Central Railroad (IOCR) runs from Columbus, Ohio, southwest to Logan.

Together the two railways handle approximately 110,000 carloads annually. Commodities carried include soda ash, limestone, cars, trucks and automotive components, railway equipment, fertiliser, and forest products.

## Indiana Harbor Belt Railroad

2721 161st Street, Hammond, Indiana 46323-1099
Tel: (+1 219) 989 47 03    Fax: (+1 219) 989 47 07
Web: http://www.ihbrr.com

### Key personnel
President: T Ingram
General Manager: Gary L Gibson
Comptroller: D J R Smith
Senior Manager, Business Development:
    J R Szamatowicz

### Organisation

Comprising 252 route-km, Indiana Harbor Belt (IHB) provides industrial switching and transfer services in northwest Indiana and northeast Illinois, especially to several steel plants in Indiana and corn milling plants in Illinois. It operates yards at Hammond, Indiana and Riverdale, Illinois. IHB is 51 per cent owned by NS/CSX and 49 per cent by CP. In 2001, traffic totalled 612,952 wagon loads, up 3,503 on the previous year. Revenues in 2001 were US$75.6 million.

In 2001, IHB employed 779 staff.

### Traction and rolling stock

IHB operates 83 locomotives: two GP38-2s; two SD38-2s; six SD20s; 33 NW2s; 10 SW-7s; and 23 SW-1500 units. In recent years the railroad has acquired more main line locomotives and begun to reduce its fleet of switchers. The railroad also operates five power boosters, three diesel hump trailers and 1,536 freight wagons, of which 48 per cent are gondolas and 34 per cent coil cars.

*UPDATED*

## Indiana Hi-Rail Corporation

4301 SR1 North, Connersville, Indiana 47331
Tel: (+1 317) 825 03 49    Fax: (+1 317) 825 04 53

### Key personnel
Trustee: R Franklin Unger
Vice-Presidents
    Operations: Pete Bell
    Marketing: Tim Yaeger
    Finance: James Owens

In 1997, the company was in Chapter 11 receivership and its assets were being sold off. The Evansville area trackage had been sold and the Connersville-Evansville line was not operated. Trackage north from Connersville was on offer to a venture capital firm, Transmark.

## Indiana Rail Road Co

101 West Ohio Street, Suite 1600, Indianapolis, Indiana 46204
Tel: (+1 317) 262 51 40    Fax: (+1 317) 262 33 14
Web: http://www.inrd.com

### Key personnel
President and Chief Executive Officer: Thomas G Hoback
Executive Vice-President and Chief Operating Officer:
    John A Rickoff

### Organisation

Indiana Rail Road Co (IRRC) provides freight service over 249 route-km. In 1985, the company bought 188 route-km serving coalfields in southern Indiana from Illinois Central and has since expanded. Its main line extends southwest from Indianapolis via Bloomington, Indiana, to Newton and Lis, Illinois. North of Indianapolis, trackage rights exist to Noblesville.

*UPDATED*

## Indiana Southern Railroad

PO Box 158, Petersburg, Indiana 47567
Tel: (+1 812) 354 80 80    Fax: (+1 812) 354 80 85
Web: http://www.railamerica.com

### Key personnel
General Manager: Charles Fooks
Business Development Managers: Doug Ernstes;
    Doug Loughead

Gauge: 1,435 mm
Route length: 283 km

### Organisation

Operated by RailAmerica, the ISRR runs southwest from Indianapolis to Evansville, Indiana. The railway handles approximately 65,000 carloads annually, commodities carried including coal, metal products, petroleum products, grain and grain products, foodstuffs, fertilisers, forest products and alcohol.

*NEW ENTRY*

## Indiana Southwestern Railroad Co

603 Allen Lane, Evansville, Indiana 47710
A subsidiary of Pioneer Railcorp
1318 S Johansen Road, Peoria, Illinois 61607
Tel: (+1 309) 697 14 00    Fax: (+1 309) 697 53 87
Web: http://www.pioneer-railcorp.com

### Key personnel
See entry for Pioneer Railcorp

Gauge: 1,435 mm
Route length: 40 km

### Organisation

Acquired by Pioneer Railcorp from the Evansville Terminal Railway Company in April 2000, the ISW runs from Evansville via Poseyville to Cynthiana, Indiana. Interchange is made with CSXT and Norfolk Southern at Evansville. Main commodities carried are grain, plastic and rail equipment.

*NEW ENTRY*

## Iowa Interstate Railroad Ltd

800 Webster Street, Iowa City, Iowa 52240-4806
Tel: (+1 319) 339 95 01    Fax: (+1 319) 339 95 33

### Key personnel
Chairman: Henry Posner III
President and Chief Executive Officer:
    Frederic W Yocum Jr
Executive Vice-President and Chief Financial Officer:
    Robert C Finley
Vice-Presidents
    Marketing: William A Haggerty
    Operations: William J Duggan
Superintendent, Operations: Gilbert P Peters
Chief Mechanical Officer: Frederick D Cheney Jr
Chief Engineer: Mark G Peterburg
General Manager, Intermodal: David Howland

The Iowa Interstate Railroad (IAIS) operates the former Rock Island main line from Council Bluffs, Iowa, to Bureau, Illinois, (724 route-km). Within Illinois, IAIS operates between Bureau and Blue Island over CSXT and Metra, connecting with all major railroads in the Chicago gateway. It also operates south from Bureau into Peoria, by exercising trackage rights over CSXT and the 59 km of the Lincoln & Southern. At Peoria it can offer an outlet for Iowa grain on the Illinois river and to Gulf ports.

The railroad's 1996 capital investment programme included a $5 million combined state, local and company investment in a new yard at Newton, Iowa, with intermodal capability. Newton is the location of the railroad's largest customer, Maytag Corporation.

In 1996, the IAIS turned over its entire intermodal operations to the C H Robinson Company. This contract is a new venture for both parties.

The IAIS locomotive fleet consists of 37 road diesels, chiefly GM-EMD GP38 (including four rebuilds from VMV added in 1994), GP7, GP8, GP9 and GP10. The railroad also operates five Alco diesels, including three ex-Providence & Worcester M420s rebuilt by Conrail in 1994 as M420Rs, and has leased two GP16s and four SD20s from National Railway Equipment to ease a continuing locomotive shortage. IAIS owns 469 freight wagons.

## Iowa Northern Railway Co

PO Box 640, 113 North Second Street, Greene, Iowa 50636
Tel: (+1 515) 823 58 70    Fax: (+1 515) 823 48 16

### Key personnel
General Manager: Mark A Sabin

Iowa Northern (224 route-km) connects with Illinois Central (previously CC&P) and Iowa Interstate at Cedar Rapids, with Canadian Pacific (Soo) at Plymouth and with Union Pacific at Manly. Much of its annual 15,000 to 20,000 carloads of traffic is interchanged with the latter two railroads.

In December 1995, the company was bought by Iron Road Railways (qv) which is restructuring the business as a switching carrier. At the end of 1995, Iowa Northern operated seven GM-EMD GP9 locomotives and 40 freight wagons and employed 26 staff.

## Iron Road Railways Inc

44 Canal Center Plaza, Suite 303, Alexandria, Virginia 22314
Tel: (+1 703) 299 99 44    Fax: (+1 703) 299 99 45

### Key personnel
President and Chief Executive Officer: Robert T Schmidt
Chairman: John F DePodesta
Vice-Presidents: Daniel R Sabin, B F Collins, K R Ziebarth

Iron Road Railways was incorporated in 1993 to acquire, manage and invest in short line and regional railways. Aggregated annual revenues are approximately $55 million.

At the beginning of 2000 the eight operating units in the IRR stable were:
Bangor & Aroostook Railway
Canadian American Railway
Windsor & Hantsport Railway
Iowa Northern Railway
Québec Southern Railway (Chemins de Fer du Québec Sud)
Northern Vermont Railway
Van Bureu Bridge Company
Logistics Management Systems Inc.

The Québec Southern is the St Jean to Lennoxville section of the erstwhile Canadian Atlantic plus two branches; the Northern Vermont is all former CP trackage off the Canadian Atlantic extending south to Wells River, Vermont. The QSR also has trackage rights to reach the St Luc yard of the St Lawrence & Hudson (qv in Canada section). In June 2000, the Northern Vermont was awarded an operating contract over an additional 67 km of track owned by the State of Vermont from Wells River Junction to White River Junction, where connections are made with several other carriers.

The IRR combination of properties in upper New England and Québec is targeting traffic lost to truck haulage in the last decade and, in co-operation with several New England states, has begun to research the passenger market for east-west movement over the several contiguous properties. Its Logistics Management Systems unit offers a full range of warehouse and transloading services at Bangor, Maine, York, Pennsylvania and other online points.

## Kankakee Beaverville & Southern Railroad Co

Po Box 136, Beaverville, Illinois 60912
Tel: (+1 815) 486 72 60

### Key personnel
President: Kevin D Stroo
Secretary and Treasurer: C F Hall

The railroad operates 408 route-km and has eight interchanges with other systems. The rolling stock fleet comprises seven locomotives and 290 freight wagons.

## Kansas South Western Railway

See Central Kansas Railway entry.

## Keokuk Junction Railway Co

17 Water Street, Keokuk, Iowa 56232
A subsidiary of Pioneer Railcorp
1318 S Johansen Road, Peoria, Illinois 61607
Tel: (+1 309) 697 14 00  Fax: (+1 309) 697 53 87
Web: http://www.pioneer-railcorp.com

### Key personnel
See entry for Pioneer Railcorp
Gauge: 1,435 mm
Route length: 83 km

### Organisation
Acquired by Pioneer Railcorp from the KNRECO in March 1996, the KJRY runs from Keokuk, Iowa, where interchange is made with Burlington Northern Santa Fe, to LaHarpe, Illinois, where interchange is made with the Toledo, Peoria and Western Railroad. In February 2002, the KJRY was extended by the acquisition of an additional 19.5 km of line from LaHarpe to Lomax, Illionois, together with 25 km of trackage rights over BNSF's main line from Lomax to Fort Madison, Iowa. Here interchange is made with Union Pacific. Main commodities carried are foodstuffs.
*NEW ENTRY*

## Kiamichi Railroad

PO Box 786, Hugo, Oklahoma 74743
Tel: (+1 580) 326 83 57  Fax: (+1 580) 326 66 06
Web: http://www.railamerica.com

### Key personnel
General Manager: Mitch Becker

### Organisation
Operated by RailAmerica since 1987, the KRR is an east-west line linking Anthony, Arkansas, and Madill, Oklahoma. At Hugo, branches run north to Antiers and south to Paris. The railway handles approximately 35,000 carloads annually. Traffic includes aggregates, cement, foodstuffs, forest products and paper, grain and grain products, metals, fertiliser and coal. Interchange is made with BNSF at Madill, with KCS at Ashdown, Arkansas, with DQE at Valiant, Oklahoma, and with UP at Durant, Oklahoma, and Hope, Arkansas.

## Kyle Railroad Co

PO Box 566, Third & Railroad Avenue, Philipsburg, Kansas 67661
Tel: (+1 785) 543 65 27  Fax: (+1 785) 543 96 46
Web: http://www.railamerica.com

Gauge: 1,435 mm
Route length: 1,114 km

### Organisation
Operated by RailAmerica, KYLE comprises a group of lines linking Limon, Colorado, in the west and Salina and Bellville, Kansas, in the east, together with a geographically separate line between Lincoln and Arbor, Nebraska. The railway handles approximately 42,000 carloads annually including grain and other agricultural products, coal, asphalt and aggregates. Interchange with BNSF is made at Courtland, Kansas, with UP at Salina and Colby, Kansas, and at Limon.

## Lake Superior & Ishpeming Railroad Co

105 East Washington Street, Marquette, Michigan 49855-4385
Tel: (+1 906) 228 79 79  Fax: (+1 906) 228 79 83

### Key personnel
President and General Manager: John F Marshall
Vice-President, Controller: Dewayne D Nygard
Superintendent, Transportation: William J Cooke
Chief Engineer: Theodor O Stokke

Lake Superior & Ishpeming (LS&I) is a self-contained private railroad which also shares tracks with Wisconsin Central. First built in 1896, LS&I is currently owned by the Cleveland-Cliffs Iron Co which has an interest in Empire and Tilden, the last two active iron ore mines in the Marquette range.

In 1996, the railroad handled 115,000 carloads, totalling 9.5 million tonnes. Of the 9.5 million, 8 million tonnes is outbound ore pellets and the balance is inbound materials, notably bentonite. Ore is moved in 11,000 tonne trains and loaded into lake shipping at LS&I dock, Marquette. The dock closes when Lake Superior freezes over, which usually occurs between January and April every year.

LS&I employed 175 people at the start of 1997. The railway amounts to 80 route-km, of which the 31 km main line is laid with 132 lb rail; the rest of the trackage consists of yards or spurs serving mines.

The rolling stock fleet at the start of 1994 consisted of 1,371 including 1,250 ore hoppers and 13 U30C and three U23C locomotives built by GE.

## Laurinburg and Southern Railroad Co

PO Box 1929, Laurinburg, North Carolina 28353
Tel: (+1 910) 276 07 86  Fax: (+1 910) 276 28 53

### Key personnel
President: Pete Claussen
General Manager: Rick Pearson

The railway owns 45.1 route-km and also operates the 19 km Red Springs & Northern. Connection is directly to CSX or via the Aberdeen & Rockfish (qv) to NS. On 31 July 1998, the railway was purchased by Gulf & Ohio Railways System. Traction includes two locomotives purchased from the line's previous owner, Murphy Evans, with others operated by Murphy Evans' L&S holding company.

## Louisiana & Delta Railroad

402 W Washington Street, New Iberia, Louisiana 70560
Tel: (+1 337) 364 96 25  Fax: (+1 337) 369 14 87
Web: http://www.gwrr.com

### Key personnel
President: James W Benz
Vice-President, Operating Services: William A Jasper
Vice-President, Sales and Marketing: C Murray Cook
General Manager: Billy C Eason
Director of Sales and Marketing: Carl T Broussard

### Organisation
The railroad is a Genesee & Wyoming (qv) property and operates 14 branches totalling 183 route-km owned and an additional 148 km of trackage rights.

It connects to the BNSF which bought the line into New Orleans as a condition of the UP-SP merger. The railway is managed as a unit of the Genesee & Wyoming subsidiary, Rail Link Inc. Annual traffic totals some 12,000 carloads. Principal commodities carried are carbon black, sugar and molasses, pipes, rice and paper products.

*UPDATED*

## Louisville & Indiana Railroad Company

500 Willinger Lane, Jeffersonville, Indiana 47130
Tel: (+1 812) 288 09 40  Fax: (+1 812) 288 49 77
Web: http://www.anacostia.com/lir

### Key personnel
Chairman and Chief Executive Officer:
  Peter A Gilbertson
President and Chief Operating Officer:
  John K Secor
General Superintendent: John H Sharp

Gauge: 1,435 mm
Route length: 171 km (owned); 182 km (operated)

### Organisation
Louisville & Indiana (LIRC) is a wholly owned subsidiary of Anacostia & Pacific Co Inc (qv). Formed in 1994, the LIRC operates 171.2 km of main line and some secondary track between Indianapolis and Louisville, Kentucky, formerly worked by Conrail. Annual carloadings amount to 23,000 and the railroad employed 40 people in 2002. LIRC connects with CP, CSXT, NS and PAL.

The LIRC main line between Indianapolis and Louisville has been designated as a high-speed rail corridor by the US Department of Transportation.

### Traction and rolling stock
The locomotive fleet consists of 13 locomotives, mostly GP7/GP9 units.

## Maine Central Railroad Company

Subsidiary of Guilford Transportation Industries Rail Division
20 Rigby Road, South Portland, Maine 04106
Tel: (+1 207) 828 64 03  Fax: (+1 207) 828 64 03

### Key personnel
Chairman, President and Chief Executive: David A Fink
Vice-Presidents
  Transportation: Sydney P Culliford
  Marketing and Sales: Thomas F Steiniger
  Mechanical: James P Coffin
  Finance: Michael A Holmes

Gauge: 1,435 mm
Length: 1,187 km

Maine Central lies within the state of Maine, but another Guilford company, Springfield Terminal Railway, actually operates the system on account of the labour agreements advantageous to Guilford which are in force on the Springfield Terminal Railway.

Guilford has contributed $1.5 million to a $7 million new intermodal facility in Waterville, aimed at capturing truck traffic. Waterville is also the originating/terminating point for the 'DownEast Express' operation started jointly with Conrail (qv).

Maine Central is also being positioned to combine with Boston & Maine (qv) and the New Brunswick Southern (qv in Canada section) to create an import-export business to and from New England via the port of Halifax, Nova Scotia.

At the start of 1994, 36 locomotives were in service: five GP7, two GP9R, eight GP38, one SD39, 10 U18B, four U23B and six Alco C424M.

## Manufacturers Railway Co

2850 South Broadway, St Louis, Missouri 63118-1895
Tel: (+1 314) 577 17 49  Fax: (+1 314) 577 31 36

### Key personnel
President and Chief Executive Officer:
  Edward R Goedeke
Treasurer and Controller: Barbara J Houseworth
Senior Operations Director: Randy J Weitzel
Mechanical Superintendent: Amund L Whittley
Director of Engineering: Kem E Conrad

### Organisation
The railway operates over 68.2 route-km and connects with all major carriers in the St Louis gateway, via Alton & Southern (qv) in particular. It is a wholly owned subsidiary of the brewing company Anheuser-Busch. In addition to switching the flagship brewery in St Louis, distributing certain beer brands nationally for which the railway maintains a fleet of 200 boxcars and grain hopper cars and hauling grain, the subsidiary secures income from contract wagon and locomotive repair and modification.

There is also a subsidiary trucking operation that furnishes cartage (130 purpose-designed trailers) and warehousing services at two locations to serve the parent brewing company and others.

### Traction and rolling stock
Manufacturers Railway operates seven GM-EMD SW1500 and SW1001 locomotives. In late 1996, the company overhauled a trainset (two 'F' units plus six passenger cars) owned by the St Louis Car Company, which is now available for charter service.

*UPDATED*

## Maryland & Delaware Railroad Co

106 Railroad Avenue, Federalsburg, Maryland 21632
Tel: (+1 410) 754 57 35  Fax: (+1 410) 754 95 28

### Key personnel
President: John C Paredes
General Manager: Eric Callaway

The company owns 191.5 route-km, four diesel locomotives.

## Maryland Midland Railway Inc

PO Box 1000, 40 North Main Street, Union Bridge, Maryland 21791-0568
Tel: (+1 410) 775 77 18  Fax: (+1 410) 775 25 20
e-mail: mmid@erols.com

**Key personnel**
Chairman and: Henry F LeBrun
President, Chief Executive Officer and Chief Operating Officer: Paul D Denton
Senior Vice-President and Chief Financial Officer: David W Bordner
Director, Marketing: Barbara Denton
Manager, Transportation: David B Hart
Manager, Track and Structures: Gary W Smith

Maryland Midland operates 108 route-km and connects with CSXT at Highfield and Emory Grove. In 1998, the railroad employed 30 staff and handled 8,062 carloads of freight, an increase of 0.16 per cent on the previous year. Cement, stone, coal and timber accounted for 92 per cent of traffic. Gross operating revenues of $5.779 million were recorded in 1998, compared with $3.803 million in 1997. Net income after tax in 1997 was $513,628.

The railway has proposed a strategic alliance with CSX to develop traffic resulting from the latter company's acquisition of part of the Conrail system.

Maryland Midland operates six diesel locomotives (three GP9s and three GP38s) and 240 wagons.

## Maryland and Pennsylvania Railroad Co

See Emons Transportation Group Inc.

## Michigan Shore Railroad

101 Enterprise Drive, Vassar, Michigan 48768
Tel: (+1 800) 968 19 75   Fax: (+1 989) 823 37 94
Web: http://www.railamerica.com

**Key personnel**
General Manager: Larry Ross
Business Development Manager: Mike Bobic

Gauge: 1,435 mm
Route length: 11km

**Organisation**
Operated by RailAmerica, the MS is a shortline in the Muskegon, Michigan area handling approximately 3,200 carloads annually of sand and chemicals. Interchange with CSXT is made at Muskegon.

*NEW ENTRY*

## Michigan Southern Railroad Co

PO Box 239, White Pigeon, Michigan 49099
A subsidiary of Pioneer Railcorp
1318 S Johansen Road, Peoria, Illinois 61607
Tel: (+1 309) 697 14 00   Fax: (+1 309) 697 53 87
Web: http://www.pioneer-railcorp.com

**Key personnel**
See entry for Pioneer Railcorp
Gauge: 1,435 mm
Route length: 78 km

**Organisation**
Located in southern Michigan and owned by Pioneer Railcorp, the MSO connects with Norfolk Southern at White Pigeon, Michigan, and via haulage rights with CSXT at Fort Wayne, Indiana. Main commodities carried include scrap metal, paper, fertiliser, aggregates and food products.

*NEW ENTRY*

## Mid-Michigan Railroad

101 Enterprise Drive, Vassar, Michigan 48768
Tel: (+1 800) 968 19 75   Fax: (+1 989) 823 37 94
Web: http://www.railamerica.com

**Key personnel**
General Manager: Larry Ross
Business Development Manager: Mike Bobic

Gauge: 1,435 mm
Route length: 176 km

**Organisation**
Formerly owned by RailTex and since February 2000 operated by RailAmerica, the MMRR comprises two lines in Michigan: Paines–Elwell and Lowell–Greenville. Approximately 8,200 carloads are handled annually. Interchange is made with CSXT at Paines and Elmdale, with a sister company, Grand Rapids Eastern, at Lowell, and with TSBY at Alma.

## Minnesota Commercial Railway

14047 Petronella Drive, Suite 201, Libertyville, Illinois 60048
Tel: (+1 651) 632 90 00   Fax: (+1 651) 632 90 37

**Key personnel**
Chairman and President: John W Gohmann
Chief Maintenance of Way Officer: Joe Krajcrewski
Chief Mechanical Officer, Cars: John Walsh
Chief Mechanical Officer, Locomotives: Scott Wardrope
Chief Accounting Officer: Galen Miller
Director of Operations: Wayne Hall Jr

**Organisation**
The company operates over some 190 route-km in the Metro Twin Cities, Minnesota area. In 2000, 63,800 revenue units were handled and the company employed 85 people. The company also operates a warehousing and trucking subsidiary through Commercial Transload of Minnesota. It also owns a heated warehouse in Fridley, Minnesota and specialises in steel transloading, storage and transportation, as well as large bulkier items.

**Traction and rolling stock**
The fleet consists of 35 locomotives and includes five six-axle units: three C-30-7 and two Alcos, one of which has been repowered with a Caterpillar engine. The stock also includes 10 B-23-7 and B-30-7 and 10 Alco units, three EMD switching engines and 21 freight wagons.

*UPDATED*

## Mississippi Central Railroad Co

642 East Van Dorn Avenue, Holly Springs, Mississippi 38635
A subsidiary of Pioneer Railcorp
1318 S Johansen Road, Peoria, Illinois 61607
Tel: (+1 309) 697 14 00   Fax: (+1 309) 697 53 87
Web: http://www.pioneer-railcorp.com

**Key personnel**
See entry for Pioneer Railcorp
Gauge: 1,435 mm
Route length: 91 km

**Organisation**
Acquired by Pioneer Railcorp as the Natchez Trace Railroad from Kyle Railways Inc in April 1992, the MSCI runs from Oxford, Mississippi, to Grand Junction, Tennessee. Interchange is made with Norfolk Southern at Grand Junction and with Burlington Northern Santa Fe at Holly Springs, Mississippi. Main commodities carried include cotton products, steel, forest products, fertiliser and chemicals.

*NEW ENTRY*

## Mississippi Export Railroad Co

PO Box 8743, Moss Point, Mississippi 39562-8743
Tel: (+1 601) 475 33 22

**Key personnel**
President: D Gregory Luce Jr
Vice-President and General Manager: Michael W Bagswell

The company owns 167.3 route-km; four GM-EMD locomotives (two GP38-2, one GP9, one SW1500); 526 wagons.

## Missouri & Northern Arkansas Railroad

PO Box 776, Carthage, Missouri 64836
Tel: (+1 417) 358 88 00   Fax: (+1 417) 358 60 05
Web: http://www.railamerica.com

**Key personnel**
General Manager: Al Satunas
Business Development Manager: Anita Horton

Gauge: 1,435 mm
Route length: 848 km

**Organisation**
Formerly owned by RailTex and since February 2000 operated by RailAmerica, the MNA runs northwest from Diaz, Arkansas, to Pleasant Hill, Missouri, continuing via trackage rights to Kansas City. The railway handles approximately 110,000 carloads annually, commodities carried including coal, foodstuffs and farm products, forest products and paper, fertiliser, minerals, chemicals and steel. Interchange is made with UP at Kansas City, Missouri, and Newport, Arkansas, with BNSF at Aurora, Lamar and Springfield, Missouri and with KCS at Joplin, Missouri.

## Mohawk Adirondack & Northern Railroad Corporation

8364 Lewiston Road, Batavia, New York 14020-1245
Tel: (+1 716) 343 53 98   Fax: (+1 716) 343 43 69

**Key personnel**
President: David J Monte Verde
Vice-President and General Manager: Jeffrey P Baxter
Marketing and Chief Financial Officer: Charles J Riedmuller

Totalling 244.8 route-km, Mohawk Adirondack & Northern (MA&N) is the largest of five railroads in the states of New York and Pennsylvania that together make up the Genesee Valley Transportation Company (GVTC). The others are Depew, Lancaster & Western; Lowville & Beaver River; and Falls Road Railroad, all in New York; and Delaware-Lackawanna in Pennsylvania.

During 1996 GVTC purchased 73.6 km of track from Conrail with a connection at Lockport, New York. GVTC also purchased an out-of-use yard in Niagra Falls, New York, which it will develop as a business park for customers.

MA&N operates several Alco models, RS11s, RS18s, displaced from the ex-Central Vermont.

## Montana Rail Link Inc

PO Box 16390, Missoula, Montana 59809-6390
Tel: (+1 406) 523 15 00   Fax: (+1 406) 523 16 19
Web: http://www.montanarail.com

**Key personnel**
President: Daniel K Watts
Vice-President, Operations: John L Grewell
Operating Superintendent: Michael R Lemm
Chief Engineer: Richard L Keller
Chief Mechanical Officer: Joseph R Richardson
Executive Director, Marketing/Customer Service: Howard E Nash
Controller: R Dirk Cloninger

Gauge: 1,435 mm
Length: 1,534 route-km (including 110 km BNSF trackage rights)

Montana Rail Link (MRL) is a subsidiary of Washington Companies, a diversified natural resources conglomerate. Equity held by Anacostia & Pacific Co Inc (qv) was acquired by Washington Companies in August 1997. Also owned by Washington Companies are: I&M Rail Link and the Southern Railway of British Columbia.

Formed in 1987 to run Burlington Northern's ex-Northern Pacific main line through Montana as a regional railroad, MRL provides a major corridor for rail traffic between central and southern US states and the Pacific northwest and Canada. Its western end is Spokane, its eastern end is Huntley near Billings; it traverses the Belt Mountains via Bozeman Pass, west of Livingston, at an altitude of 5,561 ft above sea level; it crosses the Continental Divide via Mullan Pass, west of Helena, at 5,546 ft above sea level. It also provides local service to more than 100 listed stations. Connection is made with: BNSF at Helena and Laurel, Montana and at Spokane, Washington; with Montana Western at Garrison, Montana; and with Union Pacific at Sandpoint, Idaho.

MRL is among the larger Class II railroads formed in the US in the last 25 years. Employees numbered 1,000 in 2001. Two-thirds of its route-km are cleared for 96 km/h operation, equipped with CTC and automatic block signalling.

Revenue units for 2000 were 227,863, 18 per cent up on the previous year.

**Traction and rolling stock**
In 2001, MRL rolling stock comprised 120 locomotives and 2,100 freight wagons (half of them boxcars) and cabooses. The largest locomotive class is around 50 SD45/SD45-2s.

*UPDATED*

## Nashville & Eastern Railroad Corporation

514 Knoxville Avenue, Lebanon, Tennessee 37087
Tel: (+1 615) 444 14 34   Fax: (+1 615) 444 46 82

**Key personnel**
President: William J Drunsic
General Manager: Craig Wade

The N&ERR is the contracted operator for a four-county rail authority which owns the property. The company serves 210 route-km with eight ex-CSX U30Bs and one U36B locomotive; it connects with CSX at Nashville. Of the 10,000 annual carloads, 80 per cent are inbound and the primary commodities are lumber, plastics and beer.

For three summers, the state of Tennessee has funded an experimental commuter service into Nashville to relieve parallel Interstate 40. N&ERR provides passenger counts. The practice has not gone year round; outside of the summer season the parking facilities at the stations revert to bus park-and-ride lots.

## Nebraska Central Railroad Company

400 Braasch, Suite B, Norfolk, Nebraska 68701
Tel: (+1 402) 371 90 15   Fax: (+1 402) 371 45 88

NCRC operates two former UP grain branches, the Stromsberg and Ord lines. The first branch connects to UP at Grand Island, the second at Central City. NCRC uses its own GP38s and borrows locomotives from UP when grain volumes reach unit train levels.

## Nebraska, Kansas & Colorado RailNet Inc

See North American RailNet Inc entry.

## New England Central Railroad

2 Federal Street, St Albans, Vermont 05478
Tel: (+1 802) 527 34 11   Fax: (+1 802) 527 34 82
Web: http://www.railamerica.com

**Key personnel**
General Manager: Mike Olmstead
Business Development Manager: Sally Larner

Gauge: 1,435 mm
Route length: 528 km

**Organisation**
Formerly owned by RailTex and since February 2000 operated by RailAmerica, the NECR runs south from East Alburg, Vermont, on the border with Canada, through New Hampshire and Massachusetts to New London, Connecticut. The railway handles approximately 34,000 carloads annually, commodities carried including forest and paper products, plastics, copper, coal and flyash. Interchange is made with CN at East Alburg, with CSXT at Palmer, Massachusetts, and with the Providence & Worcester Railroad (qv) at New London.

## New England Southern Railroad

8 Water Street, Concord, New Hampshire 03301
Tel: (+1 603) 228 85 80/(+1 617) 472 24 25
Fax: (+1 603) 228 95 71

**Key personnel**
President and General Manager: Peter M Dearness

The company owns and operates two properties, the NESR in New Hampshire and the Quincy Bay Railroad in Massachusetts. The NESR averages 2,200 carloads annually and the QBR moves 900. The NESR connects to the Boston & Maine (Guilford) at Manchester, New Hampshire; the QBRR connects to Conrail at Braintree, Massachusetts.

During 1996 and 1997, the company has a contract with the MBTA (qv in Passenger operators section) to perform two services:
(a) it brings in track materials for the contractor rebuilding the Old Colony lines (via the QBR);
(b) it will conduct running-in trials for the rolling stock that will be used in the Old Colony lines, namely 23 rebuilt locomotives from the former AMF Technotransport and 47 ex-Pullman cars being refurbished by Amerail (trials on the NESR).

## New Orleans Public Belt Railroad

PO Box 51658, New Orleans, Louisiana 70151
Tel: (+1 504) 896 74 10   Fax: (+1 504) 896 74 52

**Key personnel**
President: Marc H Morial
General Manager: Ray Duplechain

The company owns 198 route-km; six GM-EMD locomotives (three SW1001 and three SW1500); and connects with UP, KCS and IC. It serves the Port of New Orleans and online industries.

## New York & Atlantic Railway

68-01 Otto Road, Glendale, New York 11385
Tel: (+1 718) 497 30 23   Fax: (+1 718) 497 33 64
Web: http://www.anacostia.com/nya

**Key personnel**
Chairman and Chief Executive Officer:
  Bruce A Liebermann
President: Fred Krebs
Superintendent of Transportation: Joel Torres

Gauge: 1,435 mm
Route length: 433 km

**Organisation**
The company has contracted to operate freight services that were previously provided by the Long Island Rail Road (qv); operations began in May 1997 and involve 30 employees. NYA is a subsidiary of the Anacostia & Pacific Company Inc (qv). Annual carloadings amount to 15,000, including forest products and paper, aggregates and construction materials and food products. Interchange is made with CP, CSXT, NS and two shortlines.

**Traction and rolling stock**
NYA operates 11 diesel locomotives and 60 gondola cars.

## New York, Susquehanna and Western Railway Corporation

1 Railroad Avenue, Cooperstown, New York 13326
Tel: (+1 607) 547 25 55   Fax: (+1 607) 547 98 34

**Key personnel**
President and Chief Executive Officer: W G Rich
Executive Vice-President and Chief Operating Officer:
  C David Soule
Executive Vice-President, TP&W: Gordon R Fuller
Vice-President, NYS&W: Robert A Kurdock
Senior Vice-President and Chief Financial Officer:
  William B Blatter
Vice-Presidents
  Administration: William H Matteson
  Engineering: Richard J Hensel
  Operations: Joseph G Senchyshyn
  Controller: Robert E Pierce
  Treasurer: Frank Quattrocchi
  Marketing and Sales: Paul Garber
General Counsel and Corporate Secretary:
  Nathan R Fenno
Mechanical: David Boyd
Revenue Accounting: Jane McArdle

New York, Susquehanna and Western (NYS&W) is wholly owned by the Delaware Otsego Corporation (qv) and operates over 800 route-km, of which 320 km is trackage rights. NYS&W covers territory from Syracuse and Utica, New York, through Pennsylvania to northern New Jersey. Between Binghamton and Buffalo, NYS&W has a haulage agreement with CP, using NYS&W supplied power and fuel.

From its junction with Conrail at Syracuse, NYS&W is now the regular route of Sea-Land double-stack container trains from the west coast to the New York/New Jersey area. This was made possible by a renegotiated interchange agreement with Conrail and a $7 million investment in the line between Syracuse and Binghamton. The alternative route via Buffalo and the Norfolk Southern system is still used for CSXI domestic container trains from Chicago. Trains are handled at the CSXI-owned Little Ferry terminal in New Jersey. NYS&W has secured Hanjin's Pacific Rim-Northeast Coast container service, which is handled at a North Bergen terminal, and partners Union Pacific and Norfolk Southern in a weekly coast-to-coast stack train service from Long Beach, California.

NYS&W serves food-grade transfer facilities for liquid sweeteners at Oakland and Riverdale, New Jersey. The railroad also has an automobile loading facility in North Bergen, operated by CT Services, and brings lumber to the New York/New Jersey metropolitan market via a distribution centre operated by National Distribution in conjunction with Georgia Pacific. These facilities complement an already-strong sugar and plastics bulk transfer business.

Total revenue for 1997 declined to $32.1 million.

Rolling stock comprises 24 diesel locomotives (including three GM-EMD SD70M, four GM-EMD SD45, one GM-EMD F45, four GE B40-8, two Alco C430, one GM-EMD GP38, one GM-EMD GP40, three GM-EMD GP18 and one GM-EMD NW2); 45 freight wagons; and 15 passenger coaches.

The 1997 capital programme anticipated spending of $15 million: $8 million for track and structures; $7 million for yards, terminals and related real estate; $1 million for motive power and equipment.

## North American RailNet Inc

2300 Airport Freeway, Suite 230, Bedford, Texas 76022
Tel: (+1 817) 571 23 56   Fax: (+1 817) 571 23 35

**Key personnel**
Chairman and Chief Executive Officer:
  Robert F McKenney
President and Chief Operating Officer: Roger H Nelson
Executive Vice-President: William E Glavin

The company began operations in 1996. Its first property is the Nebraska, Kansas & Colorado RailNet Inc, 669 km in its namesake states and operated with six locomotives initially. Its second property, the 92 km Illinois RailNet, commenced operations in 1997.

## North Carolina & Virginia Railroad

214 North Railroad Street, Ahoskie, North Carolina 27910
Tel: (+1 252) 332 27 78   Fax: (+1 252) 332 33 25
Web: http://www.railamerica.com

**Key personnel**
General Manager: Carl Hollowell
Business Development Manager: Kim Greer

Gauge: 1,435 mm
Route length: 87 km

**Organisation**
Formerly owned by RailTex and since February 2000 operated by RailAmerica, the NCVA comprises two lines running north from Kelford to Tunis, North Carolina, and to Boykins, Virginia. The railway handles approximately 2,900 carloads annually, carrying grain, forest products and peanut products. Interchange with CSXT is made at Boykins. **NEW ENTRY**

## Northern Plains Railroad

Fordville, North Dakota 58321
Tel: (+1 701) 229 33 30

**Key personnel**
President: Gregg Haug
Manager, Accounting/Administration: Cheryl Sanderson

**Organisation**
Established in January 1997, NPR was set up to operate 615 km of leased Canadian Pacific track, mostly in the state of North Dakota, commonly referred to in the industry as 'the Wheat Lines'. Connections to Canadian Pacific are available at Thief River Falls, Minnesota, or Kenmare, North Dakota. CP provides the grain cars, sets the rates and markets the services. **UPDATED**

## Northwestern Pacific Railroad

4 West 2nd Street, Eureka, California 95501
Tel: (+1 707) 441 16 25   Fax: (+1 707) 441 13 24

**Key personnel**
Executive Director and Chief Executive Officer:
  Dan Hauser
Manager, Passenger Operations: Arthur Lloyd

NPRR uses 16 locomotives (4 SD9s, 12 GP7/9s) to operate between Eureka and Schellville. Trains meet at Willets and take four days to traverse the 560 km length. The NPRR started up in 1996 after the public agency, the North Coast Railroad Authority, purchased the Willets to Schellville section (it has previously acquired the Eureka to Willets section). The contract operator, California Northern, was displaced by NPRR but still provides a vital bridge 29 km from Schellville to Suisun City to connect to UP (ex-SP). Carloads for NPRR average 600 per month. In an inauspicious start, the line was badly impacted by the west coast floods in 1997, incurring an estimated $5 million in damage.

Long-term, the public authority is reviewing property south into the area of San Rafael and Tiburon (in Marin County) as a commuter railway opportunity. Right-of-way is there and some out-of-service track. The commuter operator would be the Golden Gate Transit District.

## Ohio Central Railroad Inc

136 South 5th, Coshocton, Ohio 43812
Tel: (+1 614) 622 8118   Fax: (+1 614) 622 3941

### Key personnel
President: William A Strawn
Chief Executive Officer: Jerry J Jacobson
Executive Vice-President: Michael J Connor
Director of Marketing: Marty Pohlod
Chief Engineering Officer: John Dulac
Manager of Motive Power: T K Young
Chief Mechanical Officer: T J Sposato
Manager of Car Repair: J A DeGallo
Chief Accounting Officer: B A Fogle

### Organisation
The Ohio Central System is the collective name for the Ohio Central, Columbus & Ohio River, Ohio Southern, Pittsburgh & Ohio Central, Mahoning Valley, Youngstown & Austinstown Youngstown Belt, Warren & Trumbull and Ohio & Pennsylvania railroads, totalling 560 km. Together, the six railroads operate 35 diesel (five GP40s; one GP38; two GP35s; two GP30s; eight GP10s; two SW1500s; four SW1200s; one SW10; plus several Alcos and four slugs) and three steam locomotives for excursion trains (150,000 passengers/year), 13 passenger coaches and 38 freight wagons.

The company offers repair and rebuild service to other short lines in Ohio and Indiana and to independents such as grain elevator operators. It also has bought a number of ex-Conrail slugs and cannibalised them to make four serviceable units.

Track is 90 to 155 lb/yd rail on timber sleepers with plate and spike fastening. Maximum permissible axleloading is 35 short tons.

### Traction and rolling stock
At the end of 2001, the fleet comprised three EMD SD40-2 and three Alco M-420 locomotives, five steam locomotives and four passenger coaches. **UPDATED**

## OmniTRAX Inc

252 Clayton Street, 4th Floor, Denver, Colorado 80206
Tel: (+1 303) 393 00 33   Fax: (+1 303) 393 00 41

### Key personnel
Chairman and Chief Executive Officer: Robert E Smith
President: Dwight N Johnson
Vice-President, Research & Analysis: Dennis N Lindberg
Vice-President, Business Development: Stephen Gregory
Vice-President, Operations: Dennis McDougal
Vice-President, Real Estate: Clark Robertson
Managing Director: Mike Ogborn
Manager, Marketing and Sales: John P Reilly

OmniTRAX Equipment Inc
3310 Woodcrest Drive, Bettendorf, Iowa 52722-55378
Tel: (+1 319) 332 79 59   Fax: (+1 319) 332 85 05

### Key personnel
President: John Gallagher
Vice-President: Jim H Griffiths
Quality Terminal Services Inc
2400 Westpost Parkway West, Haslet, Texas 76052
Tel: (+1 817) 224 71 56   Fax: (+1 817) 224 71 72

OmniTRAX Inc is the management company for properties owned or operated by the Broe Companies Inc. It is also involved in locomotive and wagon leasing through OmniTRAX Equipment Inc.

OmniTRAX also has property and other non-railroad subsidiaries. OmniTRAX Logistics provides distribution and inventory management services. OmniTRAX Switching Services Inc offers company or plant-specific switching. Quality Terminal Services Inc, a shared-ownership subsidiary, operates the 125 acre (50.6 ha) Alliance, Texas, intermodal terminal for BNSF, including switching and repair of trailers, containers, chassis. At the end of 1996, the operating companies in the OmniTRAX portfolio were:
   Central Kansas Railway Inc
   Chicago Rail Link
   Chicago West Pullman & Southern RR Co
   Georgia Woodlands RR Co
   Great Western Railway of Colorado Inc
   Great Western Railway of Iowa
   Great Western Railway of Oregon Inc
   Kansas Southwestern Railway Co
   Manufacturers Junction Railway Co (Chicago)
   Newburgh & South Shore RR Co
   Northern Ohio & Western
   Panhandle Northern RR Co.

In November 1996, OmniTRAX was designated the successful bidder on 1,295 km of lines in northern Manitoba which are operated by Canadian National (qv).

## Otter Tail Valley Railroad

200 North Mill Street, Fergus Falls, Minnesota 56357
Tel: (+1 800) 726 79 21   Fax: (+1 218) 736 76 36
Web: http://www.railamerica.com

### Key personnel
General Manager: Pam Slifka
Business Development Manager: Robin Bergeron

Gauge: 1,435 mm
Route length: 116 km

### Organisation
Operated by RailAmerica, the OTVR runs from South Moorhead (Fargo) to southeast Fergus Falls, in western Minnesota. From Fergus Falls, branches extend east to Hoot Lake and West to Foxhome. The railway handles approximately 9,000 carloads annually, mostly carrying coal, grain and fertiliser. Interchange with BNSF is made at Dilworth Yard, Fargo. **NEW ENTRY**

## Pacific Harbor Line Inc

340 Water Street, Wilmington, California 90744
Tel: (+1 310) 834 45 94   Fax: (+1 310) 513 67 89
Web: http://www.anacostia.com/phl/phl.htm

### Key personnel
Chairman and Chief Executive Officer:
   Peter A Gilbertson
President: Andrew Fox
Vice-President: Bill Roufs
Superintendent: Russell R Tomren
Chief Engineer: Robert Giannoble
Controller: R Scott Morgan

Pacific Harbor Line Inc is an affiliate of Anacostia & Pacific (qv). The ports of Long Beach and Los Angeles selected Anacostia & Pacific to manage and operate the 128 km of ports-owned trackage, beginning in November 1997. Connections are made to Union Pacific and BNSF. The company employs 90 staff, operates 15 locomotives and handles some 30,000 carloads annually, excluding intermodal traffic. **UPDATED**

## Paducah & Louisville Railway

1500 Kentucky Avenue, Paducah, Kentucky 42003
Tel: (+1 270) 444 43 00   Fax: (+1 270) 444 43 88
e-mail: r/rushin@palrr.com

### Key personnel
President and Chief Executive Officer: Anthony V Reck
Vice-President, Marketing: R L Rushing
Vice-President and Chief Financial Officer: T A Green
Associate Vice-President, Mechanical and
   Environmental: William O Albritton
Chief Engineer: Robbie A Buchanan
Director, Communications: D E Pflueger

The company was formed in 1986 and operates 448 route-km of ex-Illinois Central trackage. The principal commodity carried is coal, some 64 per cent of total traffic volume. At 90,000 carloads annually, the railroad leads all Class II, Class III and regional systems for originated coal, loaded into barges at four rail-served facilities, while traffic received from the East & West Chemicals company accounts for 17 per cent of carloads and 44 per cent of revenues.

Track is largely 67.6 kg/m cwr on 7 × 9 in × 8 ft 6 in wood sleepers with cut spike fastenings. Maximum curvature is 6°, maximum gradient 1.3 per cent and maximum permissible axleload 29.89 tonnes.

Motive power varies, but includes 30 GP10, 22 GP8, three GP7, four GP30, one GP35, one GP39 and 11 switchers. Total freight wagons owned and leased in 1997 totalled 1,300.

## Patapsco & Black Rivers Railroad

See Bethlehem Steel Corporation entry.

## Peoria & Pekin Union Railway

301 Wesley Road, Creve Coeur, Illinois 61610
Tel: (+1 309) 694 86 00   Fax: (+1 309) 694 86 08

### Key personnel
President: P D Feltenstein
Chief Engineer: J H Rada

P&PU operates 194 km of track (128 km owned and 66 km contracted), of which 77 per cent is yard, siding or industrial trackage. It owns eight locomotives and 53 freight cars. Net operating income in 1997 was $2,319,000 on gross income of $13 million. Net after taxes and other provisions was $1,264,000.

The P&PU's 10,000 shares are held by the IC – 47 per cent; Conrail – 26 per cent; Norfolk Southern – 15 per cent; UP – 12 per cent.

## Philadelphia, Bethlehem and New England Railroad Co

See Bethlehem Steel Corporation entry.

## Pinsly Railroad Company

53 Southampton Road, Westfield, Massachusetts 01085
Tel: (+1 413) 568 64 26   Fax: (+1 413) 562 84 60

### Key personnel
President: Marjorie P Silver
Executive Vice-President: John Levine
Director of Operations: David M Kruschwitz

Pinsly is a holding company for five short line railroads, totalling 480 km in four states with 125 employees, $14 million in annual revenues, and a logistics company, Rail Road Distribution Services. It owns a fleet of 20 locomotives. Rolling stock is leased. In the Pinsly portfolio at the end of 1996 were:
   Pioneer Valley Railroad, Massachusetts
   Florida Central Railroad
   Florida Midland Railroad
   Florida Northern Railroad
   Arkansas Midland Railroad.

In April 1997, the Greenville & Northern was sold to RailTex, which had been operating it under lease through its Carolina Piedmont subsidiary.

## Pioneer Railcorp

1318 S Johansen Road, Peoria, Illinois 61607
Tel: (+1 309) 697 14 00   Fax: (+1 309) 697 53 87
Web: http://www.pioneer-railcorp.com

### Key personnel
President and Chief Executive Officer:
   Guy L Brenkman
Chief Operating Officer: B Allen Brown
Chief Financial Officer: J Michael Carr
Superintendent, Roadway and Structures:
   Gregory L Gilmer
Director, Customer Service: Kelly J Vansaghi
Director of Marketing: Catherine Busch
General Counsel: Jonathan L Kazense
Right of Way Agent: Frank C May

Pioneer is a holding company which owns and/or operates some 694 km of track in 15 locations as follows:
   Alabama Railroad Co
   Alabama & Florida Railway Co

Decatur Junction Railway Co, Illinois
Fort Smith Railroad Co, Arkansas
Garden City Western Railroad, Kansas
Gettysburg & Northern Railroad Co, Pennsylvania
Indiana Southwestern Railway Co
Kendallville Terminal Railway Co, Indiana
Keokuk Junction Railroad, Illinois
Michigan Southern Railroad
Minnesota Central Railroad Co
Mississippi Central Railroad Co
Shawnee Terminal Railway Co, Illinois
Vandalia Railroad Co, Illinois
West Michigan Railroad Co, Michigan.

Pioneer Railcorp also operates the Gettysburg Scenic Railway tourist line.

The company owns 95 locomotives in the 1,000 to 1,800 hp (746 to 1,340 kW) range and over 1,400 wagons, plus materials for reuse or sale. Pioneer Railroad Equipment Company hires out and repairs the assets. Pioneer Railroad Services Inc provides administrative and management support functions. **UPDATED**

## Port Terminal Railroad Association

501, Crawford Street, Houston, Texas 77002
Tel: (+1 713) 546 33 04 Fax: (+1 713) 546 33 40

### Key personnel
General Manager: Jack Jenkins

The 51.6 km property, of which 14.5 km are CTC-equipped, is owned 50 per cent by the UP and 50 per cent by the BNSF. Fees are assessed on the basis of use. In a transaction valued at $90 million, the railroad replaced all its switchers with 24 units of type MK1500D from MK Rail during 1996. The contract includes a 30-year maintenance provision.

In 1996 the company handled 494,920 carloads.

## Portland & Western Railroad Inc

Genesee & Wyoming Inc
Oregon Region
650 Hawthorn Avenue SE, Suite 220, Salem, Oregon 97301
Tel: (+1 503) 365 77 17 Fax: (+1 503) 365 77 87
Web: http://www.gwrr.com

### Key personnel
President: Larry Phipps
Director of Customer Service: Ron D Vincent
Chief Mechanical Officer: Jack G Russell
Manager of Asset Utilization: Tom G Cresswell
Assistant Vice-President, Transportation: David A Farrell
Assistant Vice-President, Engineering:
  Charles S Kettenring
Director of Marketing: Susan C Walsh-Enloe

### Organisation
Together with the Willamette & Pacific Railroad, the Portland & Western Railroad forms the Oregon Region of Genesee & Wyoming (qv), and totals some 715 route-km. The network runs northwest from Portland to Astoria, west to Stimson-Forestex and south to Salem, Albany and Toledo, with a connection via trackage rights over UP to Eugene. Connections are made with both BNSF and Santa Fe. Traffic amounts to some 60,000 carloads annually, comprising mainly paper and forest products, steel, grain, fertilisers, chemicals and aggregates.
**UPDATED**

## Providence & Worcester Railroad Co

PO Box 16551, 75 Hammond Street, Worcester, Massachusetts 01610
Tel: (+1 508) 755 40 00 Fax: (+1 508) 795 07 48

### Key personnel
Chairman: Robert H Eder
President: Orville R Harrold
Treasurer and Controller: Robert J Easton
Secretary and General Counsel: Heidi J Eddins

Providence and Worcester came into being in 1973 to operate a 69 km line between its namesake towns whose stockholders had declined to form part of the then emerging Conrail. Since 1973, Providence & Worcester has expanded to a 756 km system, partly by buying up sections of the Boston & Maine and many of Conrail's low-density lines in Connecticut and Rhode Island. Rights to provide local freight service on the Amtrak route from Providence to New Haven have been acquired; P&W also has rights on Metro-North (MN) from New Haven to South Norwalk and over two MN branches to reach Danbury. Its principal interchange points are Worcester and New Haven with Conrail; Gardner, Massachusetts, with Springfield Terminal; New London, Connecticut, with the RailTex subsidiary New England Central.

Conrail has offered for sale all its remaining track in Connecticut and most of its assets and interests in Massachusetts. Both P&W and Railtex (qv) were in negotiations with Conrail until the events leading up to Conrail's imminent break-up. Since October 1996, P&W has reached Fresh Pond Junction, in Queens, New York to interchange with the New York and Atlantic (qv) where previously it (P&W) had to interchange to Conrail at New Haven. Access to Boston is an issue which has yet to be resolved.

In October 1997, P&W signed an agreement to purchase the Connecticut Central Railroad Company (Conn Central), which operates 27 km based on Middletown, Connecticut, and has trackage rights over a further 18 km, on which P&W intends to restore services.

P&W is a public company traded on the American Exchange (as of 1997). In 1997 the company had retained income of $1.927 million on $22.083 million of operating revenues, which was a 13.5 per cent increase over a year earlier and mainly attributable to increased freight volumes. The railroad handled over 31,000 carloads of freight, compared with 27,241 carloads in 1996, of an eclectic commodity mix that included chemicals, plastics and minerals. Two container terminals in Worcester handled more than 43,000 containers compared with 39,701 in 1996.

P&W owns 24 locomotives, a mix of GE and GM types, 66 freight cars and five passenger cars. In 1998 the company planned to acquire 40 100-ton gondolas for scrap metal, wire rod and bulk products traffic.

Track is primarily 50 kg/m, spiked to wood (oak) ties spaced 1,969 per km. Maximum permissible axleload is 32.5 tonnes and substantially all of P&W property is FRA Class 3, that is 40 mph for freights. The capital expenditure programme in 1997 was $2.5 million for track and structures, and $2 million was expected to be spent in 1998.

The company continues to develop a deep water port facility, Wilkesbarre Pier, in East Providence, Rhode Island, the so-called 'South Quay' project, which it aims to develop as an intermodal terminal. It also continues to be closely involved in developments in the New Haven-Boston electrification project in terms of freight access, siding/passing tracks to segregate freights, and clearance for future double-stack services. The company is sharing costs with the state of Rhode Island for a major track and bridges project, which was due to be completed in 1997. Similarly, the commonwealth of Massachusetts will contribute $5.5 million to improvements on P&W as part of a statewide programme to increase double-stack clearances on certain lines.

## Puget Sound & Pacific Railroad

PO Box L-2, Elma, Washington 98541
Tel: (+1 360) 482 49 94 Fax: (+1 360) 482 39 66
Web: http://www.railamerica.com

### Key personnel
General Manager: Brad Chapman
Regional Vice-President and General Manager:
  Gene Shepherd

Gauge: 1,435 mm
Route length: 241 km

### Organisation
Operated by RailAmerica, the PSAP comprises a network of lines radiating from Elma, Washington. The railway handles approximately 14,000 carloads annually. Traffic includes forest and paper products, fertiliser and metal products. In addition, freight is carried for the US Navy, which has an interchange with PSAP at Shelton. Interchange is also made with BNSF at Centralia and with UP at Blakeslee Junction. **NEW ENTRY**

## RailAmerica, Inc

5300 Broken Sound Boulevard NW, Boca Raton, Florida 33487
Tel: (+1 561) 994 60 15 Fax: (+1 561) 994 46 29
Web: http://www.railamerica.com

### Key personnel
Chairman, President and Chief Executive Officer:
  Gary O Marino
Executive Vice-President, Chief Administration Officer and Secretary: Donald D Redfearn
Executive Vice-President and Chief Operating Officer:
  Gary M Spiegel
Senior Vice-President, International Rail Group:
  W Graham Claytor III
Senior Vice-President and Chief Financial Officer:
  Bennett Marks
Chief Executive Officer, Freight Australia:
  Marinus van Onselen
Senior Vice-President, Strategic Planning: Walter Zorkers
Senior Vice-President, North American Rail Group:
  Robert C Parker
Senior Vice-President-North, North American Rail Group:
  Jack F Conser
Senior Vice-President-South, North American Rail Group:
  Joe Conklin
Vice-President, Real Estate: Todd N Cecil
Vice-President, Information Systems: Michael E Emmons
Vice-President, Human Resources: Terry K Forsman
Vice-President and Treasurer: Michael J Howe
Vice-President and General Counsel: John T 'Jack' White
Vice-President, Engineering: M Scott Linn
Vice-President, Mechanical: James H Wagner

### Corporate background
RailAmerica Inc is the world's largest operator of shortline and regional railways, owning 50 companies operating more than 21,500 route-km in the USA, Canada, Australia and Chile.

In North America, the company's railroads operate in 28 states and five Canadian provinces. Outside North America, the company also operates an additional 6,920 route-km under track access arrangements in Argentina and Australia. In October 2001, RailAmerica was ranked eighty-fifth in Forbes magazine's list of the 200 Best Small Companies in America; in July 2001, the company was named in the Russell 2000 (R) Index. RailAmerica is a public company, traded on the New York Stock Exchange under the symbol 'RRA'.

The company was formed in 1986 with the purchase of the Huron & Eastern Railway Co (133 km) in the state of Michigan. In November 1992, RailAmerica held its initial public offering, setting the foundation for greater expansion. Its third railroad, the South Central Tennessee Railroad (80 km), was acquired in February 1994.

During 1994-95, RailAmerica added significantly to its management team at both officer and director levels. It acquired two additional shortline railroads, Dakota Rail in Minnesota and the West Texas & Lubbock Railroad in Texas. This growth continued in 1996 with the acquisition of three additional US shortlines.

In early 1997, RailAmerica acquired its first railroad outside the USA with the purchase of the 3,621 km Chilean railway, Ferronor. Ferronor is the only north-south railway in northern Chile, extending from Iquque, 194 km south of the border with Peru, to LaCalera, near Santiago. In October 1997, a RailAmerica subsidiary, RailAmerica Australia Pty Ltd, through its membership in the Great Southern Railway Ltd consortium, expanded into Australia with the acquisition of the 6,500 km transcontinental Australian passenger rail service concession.

RailAmerica acquired its eleventh US railroad and twelfth overall in August 1998, with the purchase of the 21 km Ventura County Railroad, located at Oxnard, California. In early 1999, it acquired its first railway in Canada with the purchase/lease of the 294 km Esquimault and Nanaimo Railway Company (E&N) on Vancouver Island from Canadian Pacific.

In April 1999, RailAmerica completed its largest acquisition to date with the purchase of Australia's V/Line Freight railway from the Victorian government for US$103 million. The transaction included the purchase of 107 locomotives and 2,800 wagons. The railway provides freight services over approximately 5,120 km. Now known as Freight Australia, operations under RailAmerica ownership commenced on 1 May 1999.

RailAmerica completed another large North American acquisition in July 1999 with the purchase of the outstanding stock of Canada's third largest rail system, RaiLink Ltd, for US$70 million, including the assumption of debt. On 26 July 1999, the company commenced running this 4,060 km system, with operations or interests in 11 regional or shortline railways in Alberta, New Brunswick, Northwest Territories, Ontario and Quebec.

# USA/RAILWAY SYSTEMS

On 3 September 1999, RailAmerica took over the operation of one of its largest US rail acquisitions, the 966 km Toledo, Peoria & Western Railroad (TPW), based in Peoria, Illinois. The US$18 million acquisition included 22 locomotives, numerous wagons and vehicles, track maintenance equipment and two fully equipped intermodal facilities.

In October 1999, RailAmerica announced that it was to acquire RailTex, North America's largest shortline freight railroad company. Completed in February 2000, the US$325 million acquisition enabled RailAmerica to claim to be the world's largest operator of shortline and regional freight railroads.

In October 2001, RailAmerica announced that it would acquire StatesRail, a leading US shortline operator, for US$90 million. Completed in January 2002, the acquisition added seven freight railroads and a tourist railway in Hawaii to RailAmerica's portfolio. This included approximately 2,680 km of track in 11 states, approximately 100 locomotives and 2,600 wagons.

In November 2001, RailAmerica announced plans to acquire ParkSierra, an operator of three shortline railroads covering 1,220 km in four western US states. Completed in January 2002 for US$48 million, the acquisition added three more railroads and 31 locomotives to the company's West Coast Region and brought to 50 the number of railways operated by RailAmerica.

## Freight operations

RailAmerica undertakes freight operations on the following railways. See also individual entries for each railway.

*Australia*
Freight Australia
Great Southern Railway (consortium member, passenger service)

*Canada*
Cape Breton & Central Nova Scotia Railway
Central Western Railway
E&N Railway Company (1998)
Goderich-Exeter Railway
Lakeland & Waterways Railway
Mackenzie Northern Railway
Ottawa Valley Railway
Southern Ontario Railway

*Chile*
Ferronor

*USA*
Alabama & Gulf Coast Railway
Arizona & California Railroad
Arizona Eastern Railway
California Northern Railroad
Carolina Piedmont Railroad
Cascade & Columbia River Railroad
Central Oregon & Pacific Railroad
Central Railroad of Indiana
Central Railroad of Indianapolis
Chesapeake & Albemarle Railroad
Connecticut & Southern Railroad
Dallas, Garland & Northeastern Railroad
Eastern Alabama Railway
Georgia Southwestern Railroad
Grand Rapids Eastern
Huron & Eastern Railway
Indiana & Ohio Rail System
Indiana Southern Railroad
Kiamichi Railroad
Kyle Railroad Company
Lahaina, Kaanapali & Pacific Railroad (tourist passenger railway)
Michigan Shore Railroad
Mid-Michigan Railroad
Missouri & Northern Arkansas Railroad
New England Central Railroad
North Carolina & Virginia Railroad
Otter Tail Valley Railroad
Puget Sound & Pacific Railroad
Saginaw Valley Railway
San Diego & Imperial Valley Railroad
San Joaquin Valley Railroad
San Pedro & Southwestern Railway
South Carolina Central Railroad
Texas Northeastern Railroad
Toledo Peoria & Western Railroad
Ventura County Railroad
Virginia Southern Railroad
West Texas & Lubbock Railroad *

* Assets leased to Permian Basin Railways Inc

**UPDATED**

## Rarus Railway Co

(Formerly the Butte, Anaconda & Pacific Railway)
PO Box 1070, Anaconda, Montana 59711
Tel: (+1 406) 563 28 51

### Key personnel
President: William T McCarthy

Rarus Railway Co has 40 route-km. Rolling stock comprises eight locomotives (three 1,500 hp (1,120 kW) GP7 and five 1,750 hp (1,305 kW) GP9) and 32 freight wagons. Rarus Railway employed 13 people at the start of 1999. Gross revenues for 1999 were $1.32 million against $0.83 million in expenses.

## Reading & Northern Railroad Co

PO Box 218, Port Clinton, Pennsylvania 19549
Tel: (+1 215) 562 21 00

### Key personnel
President: Andrew Muller Jr

The R&N is a holding company which began operation in 1990. It took over from Conrail a total of 199.5 km, chiefly serving anthracite mines, radiating from Port Clinton, Pennsylvania; connection is via Conrail at Reading. There are two operating subsidiaries: the Blue Mountain Reading & Northern is the freight hauler, the Blue Mountain & Reading is a stand-alone tourist property. Locomotives: one GE U33B, three U23B, four GM-EMD SW8 and one SW7, two CF7.

In 1996, the Reading & Northern joined Conrail's 'Conrail Express' programme (qv in Conrail entry), bought an additional 157 km of track and several additional U23B locomotives.

## Red River Valley & Western Railroad Co

PO Box 608, 116 S 4th Street, Wahpeton, North Dakota 58074
Tel: (+1 701) 642 82 57   Fax: (+1 701) 642 35 34
Web: http://www.rrvw.net

### Key personnel
Chairman: Kent P Shoemaker
President and Chief Executive Officer: William F Drusch

### Organisation
RRVW owns approximately 800 route-km and connects with BNSF and CP. BNSF supplies most of the empty rolling stock to RRVW. The traffic base is approximately 40,000 cars annually and includes outbound grain, sugar, corn syrup and feeds; inbound traffic includes steel, coal and fertilisers.

### Traction and rolling stock
RRVW operates five GP20C and six GP15C diesel locomotives. **UPDATED**

## Rochester & Southern Railroad Inc

See Buffalo & Pittsburg Railroad entry. **UPDATED**

## St Lawrence & Atlantic Railroad Co

See Emons Transportation Group Inc entry.

## Saginaw Valley Railway

101 Enterprise Drive, Vassar, Michigan 48768
Tel: (+1 800) 968 19 75   Fax: (+1 517) 823 37 94
Web: http://www.railamerica.com

### Key personnel
General Manager: Larry Ross
Business Development Manager: Mike Bobic

Gauge: 1,435 mm
Route length: 89 km

### Organisation
Operated by RailAmerica, the SGVY run eastwards from Saginaw, Michigan, to Marietta and Brown City. The railway handles approximately 2,000 carloads annually, mainly of agricultural commodities, fertiliser, chemicals and aggregates. Interchange is made with CSXT at Saginaw, with a sister company, the Huron and Eastern Railway (HESR), at Denmark Junction, Michigan, and with the Central Michigan Railway via the HESR at Buena Vista, Michigan. **NEW ENTRY**

## San Diego & Imperial Valley Railroad

1501 National Avenue, Suite 200, San Diego, California 92113-1029
Tel:(+1 619) 239 73 48   Fax: (+1 619) 239 71 28
Web: http://www.railamerica.com

### Key personnel
General Manager: Doug Verity
Business Development Manager: Mike Ortega

Gauge: 1,435 mm
Route length: 262 km

### Organisation
Formerly owned by RailTex and since February 2000 operated by RailAmerica, the SDIY runs south from San Diego, California, enters Mexico, before re-entering California to reach Campo, from where trackage rights extend to Plaster City. A second connected line runs northeast from San Diego to El Cajon. The railway handles approximately 4,400 carloads annually, traffic including liquefied petroleum gas, forest products, grain and foodstuffs.

## San Joaquin Valley Railroad

221 North 'F' Street, PO Box 937, Exeter, California 93221
Tel: (+1 559) 592 18 57   Fax: (+1 559) 592 18 59
Web: http://www.railamerica.com

### Key personnel
General Manager: Rex Bergholm

Gauge: 1,435 mm
Route length: 549 km

### Organisation
A former SatesRail system now operated by RailAmerica, the SJVR comprises a network of lines centred on Bakersfield, Exeter and Fresno, California. The railway handles approximately 32,000 carloads annually, traffic including consumer products, agricultural and food products, paper, metals and petrochemicals. Interchange is made with BNSF at Fresno and with UP at Bakersfield.
**NEW ENTRY**

## San Pedro & Southwestern Railway

796 East Country Club Drive, PO Box 1420, Benson, Arizona 85602
Tel: (+1 520) 586 22 66   Fax: (+1 520) 586 29 99
Web: http://www.railamerica.com

### Key personnel
General Manager: Tanya Cecil

Gauge: 1,435 mm
Route length: 126 km

### Organisation
A former SatesRail system now operated by RailAmerica, the SWKR runs southeast from Benson, Arizona, to Bisbee Junction and Paul's Spur. The railway handles approximately 3,200 carloads annually. Interchange is made with UP at Benson and Paul's Spur.
**NEW ENTRY**

## Seminole Gulf Railway

4110 Centerpoint Drive, Fort Myers, Florida 33916
Tel: (+1 813) 275 60 60   Fax: (+1 813) 275 05 81

### Key personnel
President and Treasurer: Gordon H Fay
Executive Vice-President: George E Bartholomew
Vice-Presidents
  Administration: Susan J Fay
  Marketing and Sales: Bernard M Reagan

SGR has 190 route-km; it operates with eight GM-EMD GP9 locomotives and 26 freight wagons.

## South Buffalo Railway Co

See Bethlehem Steel Corporation entry.

## South Carolina Central Railroad Inc

PO Box 1083, 101 South 4th Street, Hartsville, South Carolina 29550
Tel: (+1 843) 332 75 84   Fax: (+1 843) 332 12 22

**Key personnel**
General Manager: Lamont Jones
Business Development Manager: Kim Greer

Gauge: 1,435 mm
Route length: 93 km

**Organisation**
Formerly owned by RailTex and since February 2000 operated by RailAmerica, the SCRF comprises two unconnected shortlines in South Carolina: Cheraw–Society Hill and Bishopville–Florence. The railway handles approximately 25,000 carloads annually. Interchange is made with CSXT at Cheraw and Florence.

## South Central Florida Express Inc

Division of United States Sugar Corporation
900 South W C Owen Avenue, Clewiston, Florida 33440
Tel: (+1 941) 983 31 63   Fax: (+1 941) 983 67 73
e-mail: scferr@gate.net

**Key personnel**
President: L D Sugar
General Manager: Richard H Conley

Formerly the South Central Florida Railroad, this property now employs 38 people, operates 12 locomotives (four GP7s, three GP8s, one GP9 and two GP16s and two GP18s), 48 wagons and 167.3 route-km. The principal commodities are raw and refined sugar, raw sugar cane and fertilisers. In 1998 the railroad handled 2.05 million tonnes in total volume.

## South Kansas & Oklahoma Railroad Inc

1230 South Walnut, Coffeyville, Kansas 67337
Tel: (+1 316) 251 36 00

**Key personnel**
General Superintendent: James P Herman

SK&O has 490 route-km and seven GM-EMD GP7 locomotives. The company, a subsidiary of WATCO of Coffeyville, purchased its three lines from Santa Fe in 1990. Its annual traffic is about 12,000 wagonloads.

## Southwestern Railroad Co

**New Mexico Division**
PO Box 126, Hurley, New Mexico 88043
Tel: (+1 505) 537 20 04   Fax: (+1 505) 537 26 24

**Key personnel**
Operations Manager: Ron Lindsey
Southwestern Railroad Co
**Texas Division**
2 North Main Street, Perrytown, Texas 79070
Tel: (+1 806) 435 23 22

SR has 194.6 route-km and eight GM-EMD locomotives (three GP7Us, one GP30R, two GP35Rs and two SD45Rs).

## Tennessee Southern Railroad Co Inc

100 Railroad Street, Mt Pleasant, Tennessee 38474
Tel: (+1 615) 379 58 24   Fax: (+1 615) 379 58 26

**Key personnel**
President: Dennis T Prince

TSR operates over 174.4 route-km; it has 10 GM-EMD locomotives (two SD18s, three GP30s and five GP9s) and 51 freight wagons. The company bought one of its lines and leased the other from CSX in 1989. It is controlled by Shortlines Inc.
Employees in 1996: 26.

## Terminal Railroad Association of St Louis

700 North Second Street, St Louis, Missouri 63102
Tel: (+1 314) 231 51 96   Fax: (+1 314) 539 47 05

**Key personnel**
President: W Dennis Spencer
Vice-President, Traffic: Richard G Weidner
General Manager and Superintendent: A F Williams Jr

TRRA has 330 track-km, 27 diesel locomotives (10 GM-EMD SW1200 and 17 GM-EMD SW1500) and five slugs. During 1996 it had on trial two MK1500D units loaned by Houston's Port Terminal Railroad. The TRRA is seeking to interest its owners (the largest is Union Pacific with 43 per cent of shares) in investing in a common-user intermodal terminal capable of 250,000 annual lifts.

## Texas Mexican Railway Co

PO Box 419, 1200 Washington Street, Laredo, Texas 78042-0419
Tel: (+1 956) 728 67 00   Fax: (+1 956) 723 74 06
Web: http://www.txmx.com

**Key personnel**
President and Chief Executive Officer: Larry D Fields
Vice-Presidents
 Finance and Comptroller: Zaragoza Solis III
 Transportation: Pat Watts
Secretary and Treasurer: Walter Winters, III
Manager, Sales: B B Lacey

TMR operates over 252.6 route-km, from Corpus Christi, Texas, to Nuevo Laredo, Mexico, connecting with Transportacion Ferroviaria Mexicana (TFM) (qv in entry for Mexico). In 1996 it acquired 589 km of trackage rights from Corpus Christi to Beaumont, Texas. The rolling stock fleet comprises 19 GM-EMD locomotives (two GP60, seven GP38-2, four GP38, three GP18, one each GP35, GP9 and GP7) augmented by about 20 machines on lease. Its wagon fleet numbers 1,400. Statistics for 1996 were 3.8 million tonnes of freight carried; net income of $3 million on gross revenues of $27 million.

**Track**
Rail: 90 lb RA (43.74 kg/m); 100 lb RE (49.6 kg/m); 110 lb RE (54.56 kg/m); 115 lb RE (57.05 kg/m); 136 lb RE (67.46 kg/m)
Crossties (sleepers): Wooden, thickness 7 in
Spacing: 1,988/km
Fastenings: ⅝ × 6 in track spikes, 7 E 11 in tie plates, anchors and so on
Max curvature: 6°
Max gradient: 0.75%

## Texas-New Mexico Railroad

82 West Broadway Street, Brownfield Texas 79316
Tel: (+1 806) 637 83 23   Fax: (+1 806) 637 80 74
Web: http://www.railamerica.com

**Key personnel**
General Manager: Dave Eyermann
Business Development Manager: Robin Bergeron

Gauge: 1,435 mm
Route length: 172 km

**Organisation**
Formerly owned by RailTex and from February 2000 until May 2002 operated by RailAmerica, the TNMR was then sold to Permian Basin Railways Inc, a wholly owned subsidiary of Iowa Pacific Holdings. The line runs north from Monahans, Texas, to Levington, New Mexico, and handles approximately 2,700 carloads annually. Commodities carried include hazardous waste, liquefied petroleum gas, chemicals, scrap metal and minerals. Interchange is made with UP at Monahans.   **UPDATED**

## Texas Northeastern Railroad

425 North 5th Street, Garland, Texas 75040
Tel: (+1 972) 487 81 80   Fax: (+1 972) 487 79 80
Web: http://www.railamerica.com

**Key personnel**
General Manager: Dave Eyermann
Business Development Manager: Robin Bergeron

Gauge: 1,435 mm
Route length: 172 km

**Organisation**
Formerly owned by RailTex and since February 2000 operated by RailAmerica, the TNER comprises two unconnected lines in northeast Texas: from Sherman eastwards to Paris; and from Texarkana westwards to New Boston. The railway handles approximately 13,800 carloads annually, mainly carrying consumer products, railroad cars, metals and agricultural products. Interchange is made with UP at Dennison, Texas, with BNSF at Sherman, Texas, and with a sister company, the Dallas, Garland and Northeastern Railroad, at Trenton, Texas.   **NEW ENTRY**

## Toledo, Peoria & Western Railroad

1990 East Washington Street, East Peoria, Illinois 61611-2961
Tel: (+1 309) 698 26 00   Fax: (+1 309) 698 26 79
Web: http://www.railamerica.com

**Key personnel**
General Manager: Alan Satunas, Jr
Carloads Business Development Manager: Warner Clark
Intermodal Business Development Manager: Ron Benson

Gauge: 1,435 mm
Route length: 594 km

**Organisation**
Operated by RailAmerica since September 1999, the TPW mainly consists of an east-west line from Loganport, Indiana, to Dallas City, Illinois. The railway handles approximately 65,600 carloads annually, commodities carried including automotive components, chemicals, coal, fertiliser, food products and steel. Interchange is made with BNSF, CN, CSXT, UP and other railways at various locations.

## Transkentucky Transportation Railroad Inc

205 Winchester Street, Paris, Kentucky 40361
Tel: (+1 606) 987 15 89

**Key personnel**
President: C Randall Clark
Manager, Operations: Russell S Rogers

The TTI moves trainloads of coal out of the eastern Kentucky and Cumberland Valley coalfields to a rail-to-barge transloading facility at Maysville, Kentucky. It is effectively a short cut for CSXT, which delivers 90-120 wagon trains to TTI at Paris; the latter are moved in two blocks of 60. Capacity is capped at the 6 million tonnes per annum that the transloader can handle. The once exclusive fleet of 20 GE U28B units has been reduced to nine through attrition; as an addition to the fleet nine U36Bs have been acquired.
 The 80 km line was sold off to TTI in 1979 by the (then) Louisville & Nashville RR. Successor company, CSXT bought it back in 1992.

## Tuscola & Saginaw Bay Railway

PO Box 550, 308 West Main Street, Suite 303, Owosso, Michigan 48867-0550
Tel: (+1 517) 725 66 44   Fax: (+1 517) 723 82 26

**Key personnel**
Chairman and Chief Executive Officer:
 James E Shepherd
President and General Manager: Larry M McCloud
Vice-President, Operations: Raymond J Robinson

TSBR has 690 route-km, 10 diesel locomotives (two Alco, eight EMD GP35) and five freight wagons.
 Traffic is primarily outbound grains, lumber, sand and aggregates.
 Connections are made to CSX and CN/IC.

## Twin Cities & Western Railroad Co

2925 12th Street East, Glencoe, Minnesota 55336
Tel: (+1 320) 864 72 00   Fax: (+1 320) 864 72 20
Web: http://www.tcwr.net

## USA/RAILWAY SYSTEMS

**Key personnel**
Chairman and Chief Executive Officer:
 Kent P Shoemaker
President: William F Drusch
Senior Vice-President, Marketing:
 David E Thompson
Vice-President, Marketing: Lloyd T Host
General Manager, Operations: Daniel C Rickel
Manager, Transportation Services: Diane M McCall
Director, Mechanical and Maintenance: Tim K Jeske

TCW has 331 km (226 km owned, 105 km of trackage rights); nine leased GP20Cs (Caterpillar power plants installed by Generation II locomotives) and 350 wagons, mostly hoppers. In 1991 the newly formed company purchased the Soo Line route from Hopkins, on the outskirts of Minneapolis-St Paul, to Appleton, Minnesota, and trackage rights for connection with all railroads serving the Minneapolis-St Paul conurbation (the Twin Cities). Annual carloadings: 20,750; total tonnes handled in 1998: 2.7 million; employees: 45.

Track is 50 kg, spiked to wood ties spaced 2,046/km. Maximum permissible axleload is 33.75 tonnes.

## Union Railroad Co

PO Box 68, Monroeville, Pennsylvania 15146
Tel: (+1 412) 829 66 00   Fax: (+1 412) 829 66 07

**Key personnel**
President: Thomas W Sterling
Vice-Presidents
 Administration: James P Bobich
 Law: Robert N Gentile
 Finance: John A Yokim
General Manager: James L Neis
Chief Engineer and Superintendent, Mechanical:
 Joseph P Coessens
Superviser, Signals and Communications:
 Eugene L Polliard

**Organisation**
URR operates over 338.7 route-km; it has 33 diesel locomotives and 603 wagons.

It is a Transtar (qv) property and became the first railroad in the US to be certified under ISO 9002 quality standards. ***UPDATED***

## US Steel Company/Blackstone Partners/Transtar Inc

The one-time US Steel Company rail properties are now jointly owned by US Steel and Blackstone Partners, a venture capital firm. Each road is operated by an on-site team with separately registered rolling stock and managed by Transtar Inc, which is located on the Union Railroad (qv). The properties (1997) are:
 Bessemer & Lake Erie RR (qv)
 Birmingham Southern RR (qv)
 Duluth, Missabe & Iron Range RR (qv)
 Elgin, Joliet & Eastern RR (qv)
 Lake Terminal, Ohio, RR
 Union Railroad.

## Upper Merion and Plymouth Railroad Co

Member of Lukens Inc Rail Division
PO Box 404, Conshohocken, Pennsylvania 19428
Tel: (+1 610) 828 75 36/(+1 610) 383 22 37
Fax: (+1 610) 828 67 90/(+1 610) 383 24 40

**Key personnel**
President: Gary R Shields
Controller: John W Jankowski

UM&PR has 17.7 route-km; it operates three GM-EMD locomotives (one SW9, SW1 and NW2) and has 3,246 freight wagons. It handles between 6,000 and 9,000 loads a year, connecting to Conrail at Coatsville.

Another Lukens subsidiary, the Brandywine Valley Railroad, handles 100,000 loads and empties annually, plus provides 30,000 revenue switches to online customers, connecting with both Conrail and CSXT.

## Utah Railway Company

340 Hardscrabble Road, Helper, Utah 84526
Tel: (+1 435) 472 34 07   Fax: (+1 435) 472 37 44
Web: http://www.gwrr.com

**Key personnel**
General Manager: James N Davis

Gauge: 1,435 mm
Route length: (owned) 72 km; (trackage rights) 608 km

**Organisation**
Acquired in August 2002 from Mueller Industries Inc by Genesee & Wyoming Inc (qv), the Utah Railway Company (UTAH) operates a 680 km network that includes trackage agreements with UP between Provo, Utah, and Grand Junction, Colorado, and with BNSF between Provo and Ogden, Utah. The company also serves industrial customers in the Salt Lake City area through trackage rights with the Utah Transit Authority. The principal commodity carried is coal, especially low-sulphur material to power stations in Utah and Nevada. Switching services are also provided by UTAH for BNSF and the Salt Lake City Southern Railroad.

**Traction and rolling stock**
UTAH operates a fleet of 23 diesel locomotives, mostly General Motors SD40s. ***UPDATED***

## Ventura County Railroad

333 Ponoma, Port Hueneme, California 93041
Tel: (+1 877) 855 72 45   Fax: (+1 805) 488 65 17
Web: http://www.railamerica.com

**Key personnel**
General Manager: Doug Verity
Business Development Manager: Mike Ortega

Gauge: 1,435 mm
Route length: 21 km

**Organisation**
Operated by RailAmerica, the VCRR is a network of freight-carrying shortlines in and around Port Hueneme, California. The railway handles approximately 3,100 carloads annually. Interchange is made with UP at Oxnard. ***NEW ENTRY***

## Vermont Railway Inc

One Railway Lane, Burlington, Vermont 05401
Tel: (+1 802) 658 25 50   Fax: (+1 802) 658 25 53

**Key personnel**
President: David W Wulfson
Executive Vice-President and Treasurer: Lisa W Cota
Vice-Presidents
 Jerome M Hebda
 Marketing: David M Ploof
 Operations: Charles H Bischoff

The Vermont Rail system comprises four short line railroads totalling 320 km:
 Vermont Railway Inc
 Green Mountain Railroad Corporation
 Clarendon & Pittsford Railroad Company
 Washington County Railroad Company.
Connections are made with other carriers at: Whitehall, New York (Canadian Pacific); Burlington and Bellows Falls, Vermont (New England Central); Bellows Falls (Springfield Terminal Railroad); and Palmer, Maine (CSX Transportation, via NECR).

In 2000, the railroad operated 14 locomotives and annually carried around 23,000 carloads.

## Virginia Southern Railroad

Keysville Depot, Keysville, Virginia 23947
Tel: (+1 804) 736 88 62   Fax: (+1 804) 736 99 68
Web: http://www.railamerica.com

**Key personnel**
General Manager: Carl Hollowell
Business Development Manager: Kim Greer

Gauge: 1,435 mm
Route length: 121 km

**Organisation**
Formerly owned by RailTex and since February 2000 operated by RailAmerica, the VSRR runs south from Burkville, Virginia, to Oxford, North Carolina. The railway handles approximately 6,800 carloads annually, commodities carried including coal, food products and forest products. Interchange is made with NS at Burkville and at Oxford. ***NEW ENTRY***

## West Michigan Railroad Co

15 Industrial Drive, Paw Paw, Michigan 47079
A subsidiary of Pioneer Railcorp
1318 S Johansen Road, Peoria, Illinois 61607
Tel: (+1 309) 697 14 00   Fax: (+1 309) 697 53 87
Web: http://www.pioneer-railcorp.com

**Key personnel**
See entry for Pioneer Railcorp

Gauge: 1,435 mm
Route length: 24 km

**Organisation**
Acquired by Pioneer Railcorp as the Kalamazoo, Lakeshore & Chicago Railroad in October 1995, the WMI runs from Harford to Paw Paw, Michigan. Interchange is made with CSXT at Paw Paw. Main commodities carried are food products and beverages. ***NEW ENTRY***

## West Texas & Lubbock Railroad

821 West Broadway Street, Brownfield, Texas 79315
Tel: (+1 806) 637 83 23   Fax: (+1 806) 637 80 74
Web: http://www.railamerica.com

**Key personnel**
General Manager: Dave Eyermann
Business Development Manager: Robin Bergeron

Gauge: 1,435 mm
Route length: 167 km

**Organisation**
Operated by RailAmerica from November 1995 until May 2002, the WTLR runs from Lubbock, Texas, southwest to Seagraves and west to Whiteface. In May 2002, Permian Basin Railways Inc, a wholly owned subsidiary of Iowa Pacific Holdings, signed a long-term operating lease for the line. The railway handles approximately 4,000 carloads annually, commodities carried including cotton and cotton products, sodium sulphate, chemicals, fertiliser, scrap metal and steel. Interchange is made with BNSF at Lubbock and with UP at Amarillo, Texas. ***UPDATED***

## Wheeling & Lake Erie Railway

100 E First Street, Brewster, Ohio 44613
Tel: (+1 330) 767 34 01/(+1 330) 767 43 27

**Key personnel**
Chief Executive Officer: Larry R Parsons
President and Chief Operations Officer: Steve Wait
Vice-Presidents
 Law: William A Callison
 Transportation: James I Northcraft
 Marketing, Sales, Real Estate: Reginald M Thompson
Chief Engineer: Jim J Ganzales

The Wheeling & Lake Erie operates over 933 km; it has 44 locomotives (seven SD45, 14 SD40 and 23 GP35) and 1,216 freight wagons. This regional railroad was formed in 1990 from sale by Norfolk Southern of lines that once formed the original Wheeling & Lake Erie and the Akron Canton & Youngstown and Pittsburgh & West Virginia Railroads. The transaction also covered lease from NS of 44 locomotives still numbered in the NS roster, and 1,297 freight wagons. W&LE is a wholly owned subsidiary of the Wheeler Corporation.

During 1995, the railway restructured financially, and received a $2.4 million investment from the state of Ohio; in 1996 the Stark County Development Board used a $10 million state loan to build NEOMODAL, a North East Ohio intermodal facility at Masillon, which is targeted at a large market within a 180 km radius focusing on consumer perishables inbound and manufactured goods outbound. One feature of NEOMODAL is that all three MiJack cranes in the terminal are remote controlled, with units supplied by MaxTec International of Chicago. W&LE interchanges with Conrail, CSX and NS. In 1995, after an interval of 10 years, the railway reactivated the former Norfolk & Western ore dock at Huron, Ohio, for the purpose of moving taconite to a Wheeling-Pittsburgh Steel Company mill at Steubenville, Ohio.

In 1997, WLE received its first new car deliveries in several years, 23 covered coil cars.

## Wichita, Tillman & Jackson Railway Co, Inc

4420 West Vickery Boulevard, Suite 110, Fort Worth, Texas 76107
Tel: (+1 817) 737 72 88   Fax: (+1 817) 732 26 10

**Key personnel**
Chairman, President and Chief Executive Officer of Rio Grande Pacific Corporation: Richard D Bertel
Vice-President, RGPC: J Scott Traylor

**Organisation**
The WT&J operates over 163.5 route-km; it has six GM-EMD GP7 locomotives. The railroad consists of two segments, one from the UP at Wichita Falls, Texas (with connections to BNSF) running northwest to Altus, Oklahoma, and the other connecting Waurika, Oklahoma, on the Union Pacific with Walters, Oklahoma. Track in Texas is leased from the UP; in Oklahoma it is leased from the state. Annual carloadings are 7,700; wheat and sand are the main commodities.

WT&J is part of a holding company, Rio Grande Pacific Corporation, that also has the Nebraska Central (qv) and the Idaho, Northern and Pacific, each of which is locally managed. **UPDATED**

## Willamette & Pacific Railroad Inc

See Portland & Western Railroad entry. **UPDATED**

## Winchester & Western Railroad Co

**Virginia Division**
PO Box 264, 126 East Piccadilly Street, Winchester, Virginia 22601
Tel: (+1 540) 662 26 00   Fax: (+1 540) 667 36 92
e-mail: wwrail@visuallink.com (Virginia Division only)

**Key personnel**
President: W P Light
Agent: S D Vessella

**New Jersey Division**
PO Box 1024, Burlington Road, Bridgeton, New Jersey 08302
Tel: (+1 609) 451 64 00   Fax: (+1 609) 451 70 16

**Key personnel**
Trainmaster: M T Luczkiewicz
General Agent: F A Winkler

**Organisation**
W&WR has 164 route-km of unsignalled trackage. The New Jersey Division operates with seven GM-EMD GP9 locomotives and one road slug. The Virginia Division operates with six GP9s and one road slug. Winchester & Western has 624 freight wagons. Tonnage moved in 2001 was 1.0 million, compared with 1.12 million in the previous year.

## Wisconsin & Southern Railroad Co

PO Box 9229, 5300 N 33rd Street, Milwaukee, Wisconsin 53209-0229
Tel: (+1 414) 438 88 20   Fax: (+1 414) 438 88 26

**Key personnel**
President and Chief Executive Officer: William E Gardner
Secretary and Treasurer: Lucy Stone-Gardner
Controller: T J Karp
Director, Sales and Marketing: J V Lombard
Superintendent of Transportation: H M McConville
Superintendent, Maintenance of Way: B M Meighan

The company has 912 route-km, in three line clusters, including 418 km acquired with the purchase of the Wisconsin & Calumet Railroad from Chicago West Pullman Transportation Corporation in August 1992. Wisconsin & Southern (WSOR) connects with Wisconsin Central, Union Pacific (formerly CNW) and Canadian Pacific at several locations. In addition, the railroad enjoys trackage rights over Metra between Fox Lake and Cragin and thence over Belt Railway of Chicago to reach BRC's Clearing Yard to connect with eastern and southern railroads. In 1998, 46,000 carloads were recorded. The railway carries a varied range of commodities, including grain and grain products, coal, timber, paper and paper products, fertiliser, chemicals and aggregates.

WSOR has an all-GM fleet of 40 locomotives of several models, and 786 freight wagons. Additionally, six passenger cars are retained for excursion traffic. The company also operates the Northern Railcar workshop in Cudahy, Wisconsin, that specialises in rebuilding and maintaining privately owned passenger and freight vehicles and in custom-painting.

## Wyoming Colorado Railroad Inc

452 Snowy Range Road, Laramie, Wyoming 82070
Tel: (+1 307) 721 29 07

**Key personnel**
President: David L Durbano
Vice-President, Operations: Gregory L Kissel
General Manager: W Q Penno

WCRI operates over 186.6 route-km; it has five GM-EMD locomotives (two F7A, one F7B and two GP7).

## Yadkin Valley Railroad Co

401 Henley Street, Knoxville, Tennessee 37902
Tel: (+1 615) 525 94 00   Fax: (+1 615) 546 37 17

**Key personnel**
President: H Peter Claussen
Executive Vice-President: W Terry Hart
General Manager: Andy Anderson

This property was first sold by Norfolk Southern in 1989 as an element of NS's 'Thoroughbred' short line leasing initiative, then acquired in 1994 by Gulf & Ohio Railways. The YVRR totals 160 route-km based on Rural Hall, South Carolina. Annual carloadings are 11,000; corn, coal and soyabean meal are the three primary commodities. Interchange is with NS. The railway is operated with five GM-EMD GP9 and four GM-EMD GP10 rebuilds.

# PASSENGER OPERATORS

In certain conurbations regional authorities operate 'heavy rail' commuter services with their own equipment over track belonging to or acquired from railroad companies; elsewhere services are operated by railroads under contract. Details on these are included in this section.

Also included in this section is Amtrak, the federally owned Class I intercity passenger operator.

Proposals for high-speed passenger services in the USA and emerging commuter operations follow in separate sections.

## Altamont Commuter Express Authority (ACE)

PO Box 1810, Stockton, California 95201
Tel: (+1 209) 468 56 00   Fax: (+1 209) 468 56 10
e-mail: Stacey@acerail.com
Web: http://www.acerail.com

**Key personnel**
Chairman: Phillip Pennino
Executive Director: Stacey Mortensen
Rail Operations Manager: Brian Schmidt

Altamont Commuter Express (ACE) provides weekday commuter rail services over a 138 km corridor from Stockton, in the richly agricultural San Joaquin Valley, to San Jose, at the heart of the US computer manufacturing industry. Services operate over Union Pacific (UP) tracks via intermediate station stops at Stockton, Manteca/Lathrop, Tracy, Livermore (2), Pleasanton, Fremont, Santa Clara and San Jose.

The ACE train currently undertakes three daily runs at peak commuter times, with a fourth run in the planning stage. Following a strong start-up in October 1998, nearly 3,200 commuters use the ACE service each day, helping to relieve three of the most notorious highway bottlenecks in the greater San Francisco area. Farebox recovery ratio after three years of operation has been targeted at between 5 and 60 per cent. The contracted operator is Herzog Transit Services.

Additional shuttle services connect ACE with San Francisco's BART metro system at Pleasanton, with Santa Clara Valley Transportation Authorities light rail system at Santa Clara, and with Amtrak's San Jose-Oakland corridor.

Services are operated with five 3,200 hp (2,385 kW) F40PHM-3Cs from Boise Locomotive and 20 Bombardier gallery cars, including nine cab cars.

At the end of 2001, ACE employed 35 staff.

**UPDATED**

## Amtrak

National Railroad Passenger Corporation
Washington Union Station, 60 Massachusetts Avenue, New England, Washington DC 20002-4285
Tel: (+1 202) 906 38 57   Fax: (+1 202) 906 38 65
Web: http://www.amtrak.com

**Key personnel**
President and Chief Executive Officer: George D Warrington
Executive Vice-President: Barbara J Richardson
Chief Financial Officer: Arlene Friner
Vice-Presidents
  High-Speed Rail Development: David J Carol
  Procurement and Administration: (vacant)
  Government Affairs: Sandra J Brown
President, Northeast Corridor Strategic Business Unit: E S Bagley Jr

Gauge: 1,435 mm
Route length owned: 1,256 km; network operated: 35,200 km
Electrification: 735 km (554.6 km at 12 kV AC 25 Hz; remainder at 25 kV AC 60 Hz)

**Political background**
Amtrak was created when the Rail Passenger Service Act was enacted in 1970. Services began in May 1971, establishing the first nationwide rail passenger service under one management in the USA.

Amtrak's rail passenger service is totally dependent upon the condition of track and related facilities that are owned, designed, maintained and operated by the private freight-hauling railroads. The only exceptions to this are where Amtrak owns its own track: in the Boston-New York-Washington North East Corridor (NEC), on short sections of track elsewhere, and in several major cities where the corporation has acquired passenger terminals.

Amtrak has been supported by federal capital and operating grants, the amount of which is annually budgeted by Congress as part of the overall transportation authorisation. The process generally consists of a joint House and Senate committee reconciling a House figure and a Senate figure with the requests submitted by Amtrak and by the Administration.

Amtrak's has stated the avowed aim of doing without any operating subsidy by 2002. An unwritten aspect of this intention was that Amtrak should be provided with adequate capital assistance.

Amtrak's fortunes improved significantly in December 1997, when President Clinton signed into law the operator's reauthorisation bill, which, contrary to

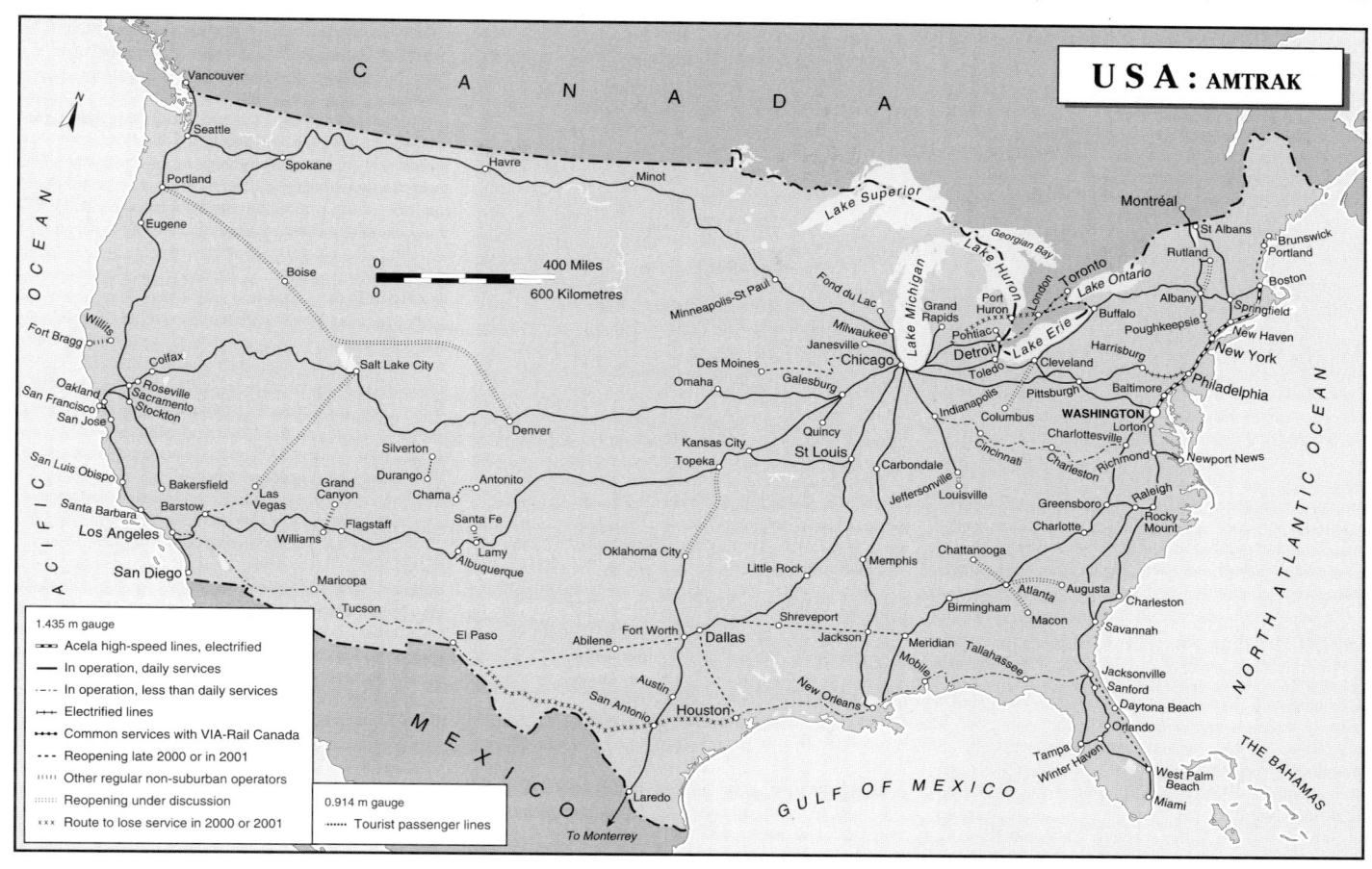

## USA: AMTRAK

**Map legend:**
- 1.435 m gauge
- Acela high-speed lines, electrified
- In operation, daily services
- In operation, less than daily services
- Electrified lines
- Common services with VIA-Rail Canada
- Reopening late 2000 or in 2001
- Other regular non-suburban operators
- Reopening under discussion
- Route to lose service in 2000 or 2001
- 0.914 m gauge
- Tourist passenger lines

expectations, had been passed by the US Congress during the previous month. The Amtrak Reform and Accountability Act made available until 2000 a further $2.3 billion in capital improvements, as well as providing operating and capital investment funds of up to $4 billion. The law also relaxes labour agreements to allow Amtrak to contract out certain functions: this practice is currently confined by federal law to the area of food service, now seen as a potential source of profit for Amtrak. Amtrak will also be allowed more freedom to determine the routes on which services are provided on the basis of demand.

### Finance

In FY97, Amtrak lost $761.9 million on total revenues of $1,673.7 million compared with figures of $763.6 million and $1,554.8 million in FY96. After federal grants the overall loss in FY97 was $70.4 million ($82.2 million in FY96).

A General Accounting Office (GAO) report published in May 1998 on Amtrak's financial performance concluded that the operator remained in a 'very precarious financial position' and would continue to be dependent on federal funding to meet operating and capital expenses. The report found that Amtrak spends $2 for every dollar of revenue and that only Washington DC-New York Metroliner services were profitable. Services on 39 other routes were loss-making to some degree. The GAO report also concluded that in spite of Amtrak's goal of eliminating the need for operating subsidies by 2002, the company would continue to need federal capital and operating support until that year and beyond. However, the report also observed that the financial performance of some routes had improved, thanks to Amtrak having negotiated support payments from the states served, and quoted California as an example. It would therefore appear that prospects for retention of the existing network and its subsequent development will depend on the willingness of state and local governments to provide support as well as on continued federal funding. However, in spite of these positive signals, the break-up of Amtrak remains a possibility if financial viability is not achieved by 2002.

In its four-year business plan for the period 1999-2002 Amtrak aims to improve its annual operating performance by $426 million. Much of this is to be achieved by increasing ridership by 21 per cent over the four years: in 1998 21 million passengers journeys were made. Full implementation of high-speed 'Acela Express' services on the Northeast Corridor (see below), planned for late 2000, is expected to generate annual revenues of $180 million by 2002, and the Mail and Express business is also expected to show significant growth.

Amtrak's federally funded capital investment plan for FY99 includes: $165 million for infrastructure; $142 million for equipment overhaul and replacement; and $313 million for new business development. In addition, the plan foresaw investments of $144 million in new corridors. A further $303 million is to be generated in funding from outside partners in the public and private sectors in areas such as revenue support and property.

### Passenger operations

Amtrak's operations cover most of mainland USA, but services vary in frequency. The most frequent services are on the Northeast Corridor (NEC) from Washington DC to New York City, where two or more trains operate each hour at speeds up to 200 km/h; services are also frequent between New York City and Boston and on certain routes in California. Additional trains introduced to key routes in 1996 left only two national routes with less-than-daily service.

As part of a 1996 restructuring exercise, Amtrak's activities were reorganised into three strategic business units, namely Northeast Corridor, West Coast and Intercity. The company also created a 'sub' business unit in the Northeast Corridor. Trains other than Metroliners are marketed as 'Northeast Direct', with a modified colour scheme which may provide a source of ideas for similar sub-units with geographic identities.

Metroliner stock is being refurbished and a first 'Concept 2000' trainset was introduced during 1996. As a stand-alone product package, Metroliner operated in the black in 1996.

*Track access*

In the Northeast Corridor Amtrak owns its own tracks, but on other routes it has to buy track access from the freight railroads. The original track access contracts between freight railroads and Amtrak expired in April 1996 after a period of 25 years. By September 1996, negotiations had been concluded with several of the host companies and contract extensions agreed with Illinois Central (for 15 years) and Conrail (10). An impasse with Burlington Northern Santa Fe was referred to the Surface Transportation Board, then an agreement signed in October 1996 for a 15-year renewal. CSXT and Norfolk Southern have both commented publicly on the 'incompatibility' of freight and passenger services.

Under the track access agreements, Amtrak makes performance incentive payments to host railroads for dispatching its trains over their lines on time. An exponential formula has been adopted, so that at 90 per cent on-time performance, the host railroad has lost 50 per cent of its incentive opportunity; Amtrak's payouts are running in the order of one-third of potential maximum. In 1996, on-time performance across the Amtrak network was 71 per cent; by 1997, this figure had risen to 90 per cent.

*AEM7 electric locomotive on a Northeast Corridor service at Newark, New Jersey* (Marcel Vleugels)

*The success of trials with Talgo tilting stock on Amtrak's Pacific Northwest services has led to orders for three trainsets jointly funded by the operator and Washington State* 0021597

*Northeast Corridor*
Amtrak continues to enjoy a dominant presence in the Northeast Corridor, having raised its market share between Washington DC and New York City to 43 per cent; it now carries more passengers than either of the competing air shuttles and NEC is the only Amtrak business unit to produce a positive budget result. In the intermediate market its share is over 70 per cent. Improvements in onboard amenities and services (telephone, fax and conference facilities and complimentary meal service in extra-fare Club class) continue to encourage demand.

In 1999, the NEC was to see the first fruits of an investment programme which will have extended electrification to Boston (see 'Electrification') and seen the introduction of the first of a fleet of 20 new high-speed tilting trainsets (see 'Traction and rolling stock). Running at up to 240 km/h and branded 'Acela Express', these will cut 30 minutes off the current 3 hour Washington-New York journey time and reduce the New York-Boston timing from 4 hours 30 minutes to 3 hours. Amtrak expects to generate 2.5 million new passengers during the first full year of service using the new trains.

*Pacific Northwest Rail Corridor*
New rolling stock was introduced in January 1999 on the Pacific Northwest Rail Corridor, which extends 746 km between Vancouver, British Columbia and Eugene, Oregon. In 1998, Amtrak services on this route carried 550,000 passengers, an increase of 137 per cent over 1993, when the operator began a partnership with the states of Washington and Oregon to develop rail to provide an alternative mode to road. To replace existing leased equipment, two dedicated sets of Talgo tilting coaches have been acquired by the state of Washington for Seattle-Portland-Eugene services and a third set has been placed in service by Amtrak for Seattle-Vancouver services. Services are operated under the 'Amtrak Cascades' branding. The corridor is also served by Amtrak's daily Los Angeles-Seattle 'Coast Starlight'.

*'403(b)' services*
Under the Rail Passenger Service Act of 1970, Amtrak can add new services to its existing network provided it has the equipment available and the additions will cover their operating costs requiring no additional federal support. Since this is rarely the case, Section 403(b) of the Act authorised Amtrak to initiate new routes with financial support from a non-Amtrak source. The latter could be a state, a group of states, a regional or local agency, or even an individual with the requisite financial backing.

Amtrak's conditions for considering new so-called 403(b) services are: that a state or states will shoulder 70 per cent of long-term losses, and that Amtrak's absorption of the remaining 30 per cent is subject to a maximum of $1 million annually; and that capital expenditure for station construction and other infrastructure improvements needed to initiate service are negotiated so that Amtrak's share does not exceed 30 per cent. Amtrak's ability to undertake a 403(b) service also depends on availability of spare rolling stock and Amtrak's ability to accept its share of any losses incurred in operation. The cost of using Amtrak's rolling stock must be shared by the applicant state(s), or the latter can provide their own. An applicant is free to shoulder all costs to get a service started if Amtrak is financially unable to take on any of the expenses involved, and in recent years the trend in new starts and service expansions has been towards 100 per cent state/local funding.

While several states made use of the legislation beforehand, Section 403(b) assumed greater importance when Amtrak introduced service cuts in 1995; a few states, such at Illinois, agreed to take a financial responsibility for specified intra-state services.

California has been a major player in the 403(b) arena, using the proceeds of a $1 billion bond issue in 1990 to purchase rolling stock for these services. In 1996, the California legislature passed a 'permissive' bill that allows local authorities to assume 403(b) responsiblity if they can offer current levels of service more cheaply or add service for the current expenditure. Several counties in the Bay Area have formed a Joint Powers Authority with a view to BART (Bay Area Rapid Transit) acting as manager of rail services with Amtrak still the provider.

A consortium of eight midwest states (Illinois, Indiana, Iowa, Michigan, Minnesota, Nebraska, Ohio, Wisconsin) joined under the leadership of Wisconsin to fund a $688,500 study for what amounted to a 'Midwest business unit'. Missouri became the ninth state to join the consortium, which subsequently adopted the name Midwest Regional Rail Initiative (MWRRI) and also included participation by the Federal Railroad Administration. The focus of the initiative is to develop a series of high-speed corridors emanating from Chicago and serving Carbondale, Cincinnati, Cleveland, Detroit, Milwaukee, Omaha, St Louis and St Paul, with journey times cut by between 30 and 50 per cent.

In January 1999, Amtrak announced plans to invest an initial $25 million to introduce high-speed services to the midwest, including: $5 million to stage a demonstration in 2000 with high-speed rolling stock; $5 million to improve rail access from the south side of Chicago, eliminating a time-consuming reversing movement into the city's Union station; $2 million towards the redevelopment of Kansas City Union station; and $3 million for station improvements in St Louis and Milwaukee. In addition, Amtrak was to spend $6 million on further preparatory research for high-speed services at Chicago Union station, the Chicago-Detroit corridor and other related projects.

Other corridors being studied in 1999 with a view to pursuing growth opportunities included:

The California Corridor, developing two existing routes: Los Angeles and San Diego; San Joaquin Valley from Bakersfield to Oakland, which in 1997 saw ridership increase by 21 per cent compared with the previous year;

The Southeast Corridor, for which Amtrak and the state of North Carolina are developing a 715 km high-speed corridor using existing tracks between Washington DC and Charlotte;

The Gulf Coast Corridor, where Amtrak is targeting the Atlanta-New Orleans route for ridership growth;

The Empire Corridor between New York, Albany and Buffalo, where Amtrak has reached agreement with the state of New York to share the cost of $140 million worth of infrastructure improvements and $45 million in rolling stock upgrades;

The Keystone Corridor between Philadelphia and Harrisburg, which in 1999 was the subject of negotiations between Amtrak and the Commonwealth of Pennsylvania concerning a multi-year investment programme.

*Commuter contracts*
Amtrak revenue from operating commuter services under contract to local agencies has continued to grow. In 1999, commuter rail services were operated by or for the following agencies:

Connecticut Department of Transportation (Shoreline East);

Peninsula Corridor Joint Powers Board (Caltrain);

Maryland Department of Transportation (MARC);

Massachusetts Bay Transit Authority (MBTA);

North San Diego County Transit Development Board (Coaster);

Southern California Regional Rail Authority (Metrolink);

Virginia Railway Express (VRE);

In addition, in 1999 Amtrak secured a 10-year contract from Central Puget Sound Regional Transit Authority (Sound Transit) to provide maintenance services for the equipment to be used on 'Sounder' commuter services to be introduced between Seattle and Tacoma late in 1999.

### Intermodal operations
Joint trials with the US Postal Service concluded with sufficient promise for Amtrak to order 13 RoadRailer bimodal van trailers, two intermediate rail bogies and 18 'Couplermate' adaptors from Wabash National. In late 1996, a pilot project was launched between Chicago and Philadalphia, plus Philadelphia and Jacksonville. From Jacksonville, trailers are hauled over the road to Orlando, Tampa and Miami postal stations.

In February 1998, Amtrak deployed eight 'ReeferRailer' temperature-controlled bimodal units on its Philadelphia-Chicago-St Paul and Philadelphia-Jacksonville services.

Amtrak's plans to lease up to 600 freight cars to pursue express freight opportunities and capture such business from trucks were scaled down in mid-1998. The company had suggested that up to $400 million of annual revenue could result from providing capacity for premium freight on its trains, but the company's increasing losses, coupled with strong opposition from freight railroads, led to this expectation being halved. Federal approval for the plan was given in June 1998, in spite of opposition from Union Pacific.

### Improvements to existing lines
Excluding sections totalling 151 km that are owned by six regional commuter authorities, Amtrak has owned the 735 km Boston-New York-Washington Northeast Corridor route since 1976, including five of its stations: Baltimore, Wilmington, Philadelphia (30th Street), New York (Pennsylvania Station) and Providence. An improvement project (NECIP) on this route was completed in 1999. The last stage to be inaugurated included electrification to Boston (see 'Electrification' section), and upgrading the New York-Washington section to prepare for the introduction of high-speed trainsets.

### Traction and rolling stock
In 1999, Amtrak's locomotive fleet totalled 343, of which 65 were electrics.

Amtrak and New York state (see 'High-speed rail projects' section) have co-operated to repower two existing Turboliner sets. The two partners have secured finance to convert all seven RTL sets at an inclusive cost of approximately $20 million (50 per cent local, 50 per cent federal money).

Amtrak received the first of its new 4,000 hp (2,985 kW) AMD-103 locomotives (known as the 'Genesis' fleet and also designated P40B) from General Electric Transportation Systems in mid-1993, and the order for 44 units was completed in the first half of 1994. A follow-on order for 98 additional 4,250 hp (3,170 kW) diesel-electric locomotives from General Electric was announced by Amtrak in May 1995, and subsequent orders had increased the fleet size of this P42B version to 121 examples by the end of 1997.

The first 1991-era series of GE units, the B-32 model, have been moved from California to Chicago for midwest short-haul routes, with a mid-life overhaul in the GE shops. By the end of 1998, 16 GE 3,200 hp (2,385 kW) dual-mode (diesel and third-rail electric) P32AC units had entered service, ordered to replace ageing FL9 locomotives.

In 1996 Amtrak ordered 15 high-powered electric locomotives for use on Northeast Corridor long-distance services. They are being supplied by Alstom and Bombardier to a design based on that of the power cars of the Acela Express high-speed trainsets ordered for the upgrade of NEC services.

At the start of the second quarter of 1997 Amtrak announced an order for 21 F59PHI units from GM, to be assigned to the West Coast Business Unit, for use on California 403(b) services and on Pacific northwest services.

*High-performance trainsets*
In March 1996 Amtrak placed a contract with the Bombardier/GEC Alsthom consortium for 18 trainsets with active body-tilt, capable of 240 km/h operation, and

# USA/RAILWAY SYSTEMS

the 15 electric locomotives (see above) for use throughout the Northeast Corridor in conjunction with infrastructure improvements currently under way. In July 1998, a follow-up order for a further two trainsets was announced. Each 'Acela Express' trainset will consist of two power cars each developing 4,600 kW, flanking six coaches (one first, four standard and one bistro car) with a seating capacity of 301 per set; the trains will be equipped with the latest in electronic office suites and telecommunications to appeal to the business market. Total value of the contract for the rolling stock and up to three maintenance facilities is $754 million ($611 million for rolling stock only) and US/Canadian content will be 51 per cent or better. The operating contract contains significant performance specifications and penalties for failure to meet targets.

The first trainset was completed in March 1999 and transferred to the test track at the Association of American Railroads' Transportation Technology Center in Pueblo, Colorado. Revenue services with the new equipment were due to commence late in 1999.

*Passenger coaches*
Total coaching stock at the start of 1999 was 2,272.

In February 1998, Amtrak awarded GEC Alsthom Transportation Inc (now Alstom) a $100 million order for eight five-car bilevel trainsets for 'San Diegan' services in the southern and central coast regions of California. Manufacturing will take place at Alstom's Hornell facility in New York state, with the new fleet scheduled to enter service in 2000.

For its successful Northwest Corridor 'Cascades' services, Amtrak and the Washington State Department of Transportation have funded the construction of three 12-car passive-tilt trainsets designed by Patentes Talgo and assembled locally by Pacifica Inc. The order followed the leasing by WSDOT for evaluation and demonstration purposes of two Talgo sets. The two agencies have funded one and two sets respectively, while Patentes Talgo is financing the construction of two more sets in a bid to generate a market for its design. The end-cars of the 'Cascades' vehicles incorporate glass fibre streamlined fins intended to harmonise their low-slung appearance with that of the F59PHI locomotives which power the trains. Delivery of the three sets was completed early in 1999.

Deliveries of 195 new Superliner II coaches from Bombardier, begun in early 1994, were completed in 1997. The first series of Amfleet cars, the first new coaching stock ordered by the company, is now some 20 years old and several are being reconfigured for continuation in the Northeast Corridor business service. Amtrak had intended that the Viewliner coach, in several configurations, would become the standard single-deck car.

## Signalling and telecommunications
*Advanced signalling tests*
Amtrak is participating in tests of three different advanced positive train control systems, to be carried out in conjunction with the Federal Railroad Administration. The new systems aim to allow higher operating speeds, provide increased track capacity and improve safety.

On Burlington Northern Santa Fe and Union Pacific routes in the northwest US, Amtrak is participating in trials of GE-Harris Positive Train Separation equipment in a mixed high-speed passenger/freight environment. In Illinois, the Advanced Train Control System developed in-house by the Association of American Railroads is being tested on the Chicago-St Louis route between Dwight and Springfield. In Michigan, the Incremental Train Control System developed by Amtrak and Harmon Industries is being tested on the 100 km between New Buffalo and Kalamazoo belonging to Amtrak.

## Electrification
*Extension to Boston*
In total, 482.7 route-km of the Northeast Corridor is electrified at 12 kV 25 Hz AC. From New York to Boston, only the first 120.7 km as far as New Haven was electrified, and is mostly operable at 200 km/h.

With the financial backing of Congress, the US Department of Transportation, and the Coalition of Northeastern State Governors (CONEG) electrification has been extended from New Haven to Boston on the 25 kV 60 Hz AC system. The overall cost of the project has been estimated at $1.06 billion, with one-third of that for the electrical infrastructure and two-thirds for trackwork.

*Three General Electric P42 'Genesis' units bring the Chicago-bound 'California Zephyr' into Sacramento* (Ken Harris)

*F59PHI locomotive and 'California Cars' at Jack London Square, Oakland station with a train from Sacramento* (Ken Harris)

In May 1992, a contract worth approximately $300 million for the electrification component was awarded to a consortium of Morrison Knudsen, L K Comstock & Co Inc and Spie Group Inc. In light of Morrison Knudsen's then precarious financial condition, a new contract worth $321 million was signed in 1995 with a consortium of Balfour Beatty Group and Massachusetts Electrical Construction Corporation; Siemens was the subcontractor responsible for substations. Work began in July 1996 and the project was completed in 1999, when the best New York-Boston journey time was to be cut by almost 1 hour to 3 hours.

| Class | Wheel arrangement | Power kW | Speed km/h | Weight short tons | No in service | First built | Builders Mechanical | Engine |
|---|---|---|---|---|---|---|---|---|
| **Diesel locomotives** | | | | | | | | |
| F40PH | Bo-Bo | 2,240 | 165 | 130/131 | 85 | 1976 | GM | 16-645 E3B |
| F59PHI | Bo-Bo | 2,240 | 175 | - | 21 | 1997 | EMD | 12-710 G3B |
| FL9* | Bo-A1A | 1,300 | 165 | 145 | 6 | 1957 | GM | 16-645 E |
| GP40H | Bo-Bo | 2,240 | 165 | 132 | 8 | 1966 | GM | 16-645 E3B |
| P-32BH | Bo-Bo | 2,390 | 165 | 129 | 18 | 1991 | GE | FDL12 |
| AMD-103 | Bo-Bo | 2,990 | 165 | 127 | 43 | 1993 | GE | FDL16 |
| AMD-103 | Bo-Bo | 3,135 | 165 | 127 | 98 | 1996 | GE | FDL16 |
| AMD-110DM* | Bo-Bo | 2,390 | 175 | 127 | 10 | 1996 | GE | FDL12 |
| **12 kV AC electric locomotives** | | | | | | | | |
| E60CP | Co-Co | 3,580 | 145 | 183 | 2 | 1975 | GE | |
| E60MA | Co-Co | 3,580/3,800 | 145 | 183 | 11 | 1975 | GE | |
| AEM-7 | Bo-Bo | 5,200 | 200 | 91 | 52 | 1980 | GM/ASEA | |

*Dual-mode: diesel and electric DC

**Turboliners**

| Class | Cars per unit | Motor cars per unit | Motored axles/car | Power/motor kW | Speed km/h | Weight short tons | No in service | First built | Builders Mechanical | Engine | Transmission |
|---|---|---|---|---|---|---|---|---|---|---|---|
| RTL | 5 | 2 | 2 | 1 × 820<br>1 × 1,195 | 175 | 309 | 14 | 1976 | ANF/Rohr | Turmo III<br>Turmo XII | Voith |

**Track**
**Rail:** 70 kg RE
**Crossties (sleepers)**
Concrete: Thickness 241 mm, spacing 1,584/km
Wood: Thickness 178 mm, spacing 1,950/km
**Fastenings:** Concrete ties: Pandrol E2055
Wood ties: Cut spikes
**Min curvature radius:** 175 m (10.5°)
**Max gradient:** 1.9%
**Max axleload:** 32.88 tonnes

# RAILWAY SYSTEMS/USA

## Connecticut Department of Transportation

2800 Berlin Turnpike, PO Box 317546, Newington, Connecticut 06131-7546
Tel: (+1 860) 594 29 00   Fax: (+1 860) 594 29 13

### Key personnel
Commissioner: J William Burns
Deputy Commissioner and Rail Bureau Chief:
   Harry P Harris
Rail Administrator: Lawrence J Forbes

### Passenger operations
Amtrak is contracted to run an 81.4 km service between New London and New Haven, called 'Shoreline East', serving six intermediate stations. Coaching stock consists of the 10 Pullman-Standard cars that were bought from Pittsburgh in 1990, plus 10 Bombardier Comet cars and 11 depowered Budd SPV2000 railcars that were remodelled by Amtrak's Wilmington workshops.

At the beginning of 1996 service was still basically weekday peak-only with two counter (stock positioning) movements; ridership increased during the year by 6.5 per cent to 1,185. Farebox recovery is in the range of 12 per cent. Six 3,000 hp (2,238 kW) diesel locomotives have been delivered from AMF Technotransport to improve service speeds in anticipation of overall corridor speed improvements as the result of electrification (see Amtrak entry).

The Connecticut DoT also oversees and subsidises jointly with the New York Metropolitan Transportation Authority the New Haven line commuter service into New York operated by Metro-North (qv). Connecticut funds approximately 60 per cent of the New Haven line's operating shortfall and 63 per cent of capital costs.

ConnDot has been promoting bus shuttles to its stations to encourage 'reverse' commuting, which are now operating in Greenwich, Stamford, New Haven and Norwalk.

Overall, since 1989, the ConnDoT supported lines have seen a 121 per cent increase in intra-state commuting and an 89 per cent increase in trips 'imported' to Connecticut. ConnDoT has a $500 million capital projects 'wish list' for stations, parking, bridgework and so on – but there is no funding in place for these items at yet.

## Long Island Rail Road

93-02 Sutphin Boulevard, Jamaica Station, Jamaica, New York 11435
Tel: (+1 718) 558 74 00   Fax: (+1 718) 558 82 12
Web: http://www.mta.nyc.ny.us

### Key personnel
President: Kenneth J Bauer
Executive Vice-President: Albert M Cosenza
Vice-Presidents
   Senior Vice-President, Operations: James Dermody
   Market Development and Public Affairs: Brian P Dolan
   Planning, Technology Development and Capital
      Program Management: John W Coulter Jr
   Chief Financial Officer: Nicholas DiNola
   General Counsel and Secretary: Tricia Troy Alden
Chief Engineer, Capital Program Management:
   Joseph Ferrara
Chief Transportation Officer: Raymond P Kenny
Chief Engineer: Dennis George
Chief Mechanical Officer: Charles Kalkhof
Chief Program Executive, East Side Access:
   Anthony F Japha
Chief Procurement and Logistics Officer:
   Gary Dasaro
Assistant Chief Engineers
   Signals, Communications and Power: Kenneth Lettow
   Maintenance of Way: Joseph Sais

Gauge: 1,435 mm
Length: 1,120 km
Electrification: 237 km at 750 V DC third rail

### Political background
Long Island Rail Road (LIRR) is a wholly owned subsidiary of the Metropolitan Transportation Authority (MTA), an agency of the State of New York, whose members constitute the railroad's board of directors.

### Finance
LIRR's 2000-04 five-year plan, an element of the New York MTA's budget, calls for a US$2.5 billion capital investment programme which is focusing on rolling stock renewal (US$1 billion), infrastructure maintenance (US$743 million) and stations (US$314 million).

### Passenger operations
Passenger journeys in 2000 amounted to 85.3 million, up 3.1 per cent on 1999 and the ninth consecutive year of growth and a 12-year high. Off-peak ridership rose by more than 835,000 and sales of weekly and monthly tickets also rose, stimulated by gains in the New York City employment market.

The railroad serves the Long Island suburban counties of Nassau and Suffolk as well as certain communities in eastern Queens. It has nine branches which feed into three western terminals in New York City: Penn Station, Flatbush Avenue (Brooklyn) and Hunters Point Avenue (open only in peak hours and served only by diesel-powered trains). Penn Station handles 240,000 passengers daily; another 40,000 travel via Brooklyn and Hunters Point Avenue.

The focal point of the system is the eight-platform Jamaica station, where eight of the nine branches and the three approaches to the New York City terminals converge. During the rush hour, a train movement takes place on average every 30 seconds at Jamaica.

### Freight operations
LIRR's freight division was sold to Anacostia & Pacific Company Inc (qv), which formed the New York and Atlantic Railway subsidiary to operate the 430 km acquired, beginning in April 1997.

### Improvements to existing lines
LIRR's US$190 million Penn Station Improvement Project improved access to, mobility through, and comfort and information in the Manhattan terminal. As a result of this project, LIRR's 240,000 daily patrons have experienced a 20 per cent increase in pedestrian space and a 40 per cent increase in access points throughout the station; five stairways, three escalators, five lifts to LIRR platforms and a new entrance on 34th Street have been provided. Other improvements include upgraded signage and a master destination board, a new public address system, improved lighting, a customer waiting area with toilets and a climate-control system incorporating air conditioning for LIRR patrons on the concourse level.

LIRR has conducted studies into access to Grand Central terminus. This has resulted in the adoption of the East Side Access (ESA) Project, a 10-year $3.2 billion scheme which will provide LIRR with its own 10-track five-platform terminal at Grand Central's lower level. As well as involving new and reconstructed tunnels between Long Island City and Manhattan, the ESA Project also includes improved LIRR passenger access at Grand Central, a new station at Sunnyside Yard, new carriage stabling facilities in Queens and improved traction power supply, signalling and communications systems.

### Traction and rolling stock
In March 1995, LIRR awarded $412 million in contracts for the supply of locomotives and coaches. General Motors supplied 23 DE30AC diesel-electric locomotives with Siemens AC transmission and 23 DM30AC dual-mode locomotives of similar design, but equipped to operate from LIRR's 750 V DC third-rail supply. Mitsui supplied 134 air conditioned double-deck coaches for push-pull operation, in an order valued at $234 million. The order

*Type DE30AC diesel-electric locomotive built for LIRR by General Motors, Electro-Motive Division, with Siemens AC traction equipment*   0023716

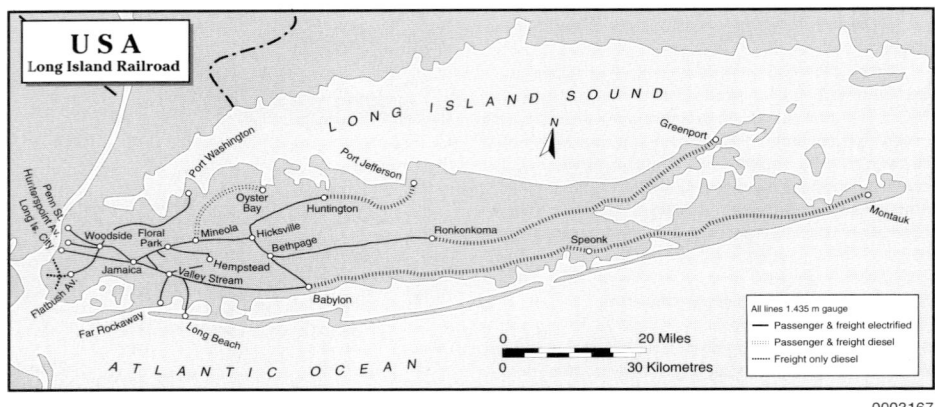

USA Long Island Railroad   0003167

### Electric railcars or multiple-units

| Class | Cars per unit | Motor cars per unit | Motored axles/car | Output/motor kW | Speed km/h | No in service | First built | Builders Mechanical |
|-------|---------------|---------------------|-------------------|-----------------|------------|---------------|-------------|---------------------|
| M-1   | 2             | 2                   | 4                 | 640             | 129        | 744           | 1968        | Budd                |
| M-3   | 2             | 2                   | 4                 | 704             | 129        | 172           | 1984        | Budd                |

includes 23 driving trailers, 67 intermediate trailers and 44 trailers with ADA-compliant (Americans with Disabilities Act) toilet facilities.

Responding to local content requirements in contracts involving New York state funds, GM assembled the locomotives in the Schenectady area. Mitsui subcontracted final assembly to Kawasaki Heavy Industries in Yonkers, with Siemens of Germany collaborating on carbody design.

For yard, transfer and maintenance work, LIRR operates eight SW1001 switchers of 1,000 hp (745 kW). LIRR leased seven switcher units to NY&A at the freight company's start-up.

The fleet of 1,050 passenger vehicles includes 760 Class M-1 multiple-unit cars, operated on inner suburban electrified lines in New York City, Nassau and Suffolk counties, and 172 Class M-3 cars acquired in 1984-86.

### Track
**Rail:** 100 PS, 112, 115, 119 RE, 130
**Sleepers:** Wood 7 × 9 in by 8 ft 6 in, spaced 2,983/mile
**Fastenings:** Cut spike and Pandrol
**Max curvative:** 9° main line
**Max gradient:** 2.0%
**Max permissible axleload:** 33 short tons

*UPDATED*

## Maryland Mass Transit Administration: Maryland Rail Commuter Service (MARC)

5 Amtrak Way, PO Box 8718, BWI Airport, Maryland 21240-8718
Tel: (+1 410) 859 74 01   Fax: (+1 410) 859 57 13
Web: http://www.mtamaryland.com

### Key personnel
MTA Administrator: Ronald L Freeland
Manager and Chief Operating Officer: Kathryn D Waters
Chief Mechanical Officer: John Kopke
Chief Transportation Officer: Ira Silverman

### Passenger operations
MARC provides Perryville–Baltimore–Washington DC services over 121.6 km of Amtrak's Northeast Corridor route (electrified at 12 kV 25 Hz AC) and Baltimore–Washington DC services over 61 km of CSXT. A Martinsburg-Washington DC service is provided over 116.8 km of CSXT track.

Amtrak operates the Washington–Baltimore–Perryville service with four electric and two diesel locomotives and MARC's newer Japanese-built coaches. Two diesel-powered services are operated for MARC by CSXT. One is over former Baltimore & Ohio tracks between Washington's Union station and Baltimore Camden station. The other is from Washington to Brunswick, Maryland, and Martinsburg, West Virginia. On weekdays, 78 trains are operated; there is no weekend service.

In 2000, MARC was negotiating new operating contracts with CSXT and Amtrak to replace agreements, which expired on 31 December 1999.

| Traffic (000s) | 1997 | 1998 |
|---|---|---|
| Passenger journeys | 4,656 | 4,739 |
| Passenger-km | 225,149 | 229,454 |

### Improvements to existing lines
Federal funding has been appropriated in an amount of US$13.5 million toward the total cost of extending the MARC network by 21.6 km to Frederick. The total cost of the project, including land acquisition, infrastructure improvements, stations and rolling stock has been estimated at US$91.3 million. Construction work started early in 2000 and services to Frederick are scheduled to start in late 2001. MARC is also constructing additional stabling facilities at Washington's Union Terminal. MARC is also contributing capital funding for a new station and platforms at BWI, in conjunction with Amtrak.

### Traction and rolling stock
MARC's locomotive fleet consists of four AEM7 electric locomotives; 19 GP40WH-2 (3,000 hp/2,238 kW) and six GP39-2 (2,300 hp/1,716 kW) diesel locomotives rebuilt by Morrison Knudsen.

In July 1997, MARC placed a US$37.6 million order with a consortium of Bombardier and GEC Alsthom for six 200 km/h electric locomotives of the 'American Flyer' design being built for Amtrak.

The fleet of 103 coaches comprises 43 refurbished ex-New Jersey Transit vehicles and 60 coaches, including cab cars, built by Sumitomo.

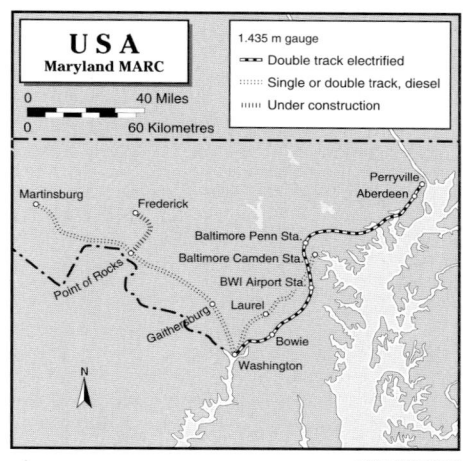

*2001/0088736*

In March 1995, MARC placed an order for 50 double-deck coaches, valued at US$82 million, with Kawasaki Heavy Industries. The coaches are being assembled at Kawasaki's Yonkers, New York, facility, with first deliveries made in February 2000. Their introduction will allow 39 50-year-old coaches to be sold or leased.

### Signalling and telecommunications
CTC covers all but 29.5 km of track, which is controlled by automatic block signals. All signalling is owned by Amtrak or CSXT.

*MARC Type GP40WH-2 diesel locomotive at Brunswick, Maryland (Eddie Barnes)*   *2000/0087654*

## Massachusetts Bay Transportation Authority (MBTA)

10 Park Plaza, Room 5720, Boston, Massachusetts 02116
Tel: (+1 617) 222 33 02   Fax: (+1 617) 222 45 39

### Key personnel
General Manager: Patrick J Moynihan
Director, Railroad Operations: John Brennan III
Chief Transportation Officer: Robert H Prince
Chief Finance and Administrative Officer:
 Ann O D Hartman
Chief Engineering and Maintenance Officer:
 William A MacDonald
Chief Mechanical Officer: David Diaz
Chief of Planning and Construction: Charles B Steward

### Passenger operations
MBTA provides commuter service over 11 routes into Boston covering 435.9 route-km of ex-Penn Central and

*One of 23 GP-40MC rebuilds acquired by MBTA from AMF Technotransport in Canada, photographed at the operator's newly completed maintenance facility at Somerville; bilevel cars are by Kawasaki, single-deck vehicles are from Pullman-Standard (F Gerald Rawling)*   *0021598*

Boston & Maine trackage purchased in the 1970s. In 1988, the range of its services was extended along Amtrak's Northeast Corridor route to Providence, Rhode Island. All MBTA's services are operated by Amtrak (qv) under contract.

MBTA is also the operator of a co-ordinated network of four metro lines, five light rail lines, four trolleybus and 155 bus routes. An integrated fare system is in place allowing use of all modes, including heavy rail, with an inclusive, zone-based monthly ticket. The state of Massachusetts, directed by the governor's office, is looking into prospects for MBTA privatisation, beginning with functional areas such as revenue accounting, payroll and property management.

As of 1995, MBTA heavy rail operations were recording some 23 million passenger journeys and 675 million passenger-km a year, with revenues grossing between $40 million and $45 million. The heavy rail services recover about 33 per cent of their costs from farebox revenues.

### Improvements to existing lines
MBTA began operations over a 36.8 km extension of its network from Framingham to Worcester in late 1996. The project has been costed at US$80 million, with the contract for infrastructure and signalling improvements awarded to Conrail.

Old Colony Railroad services over three routes to Middleboro and Kingston in southeastern Massachusetts started in late 1997, while trains on the restored link from Ipswich to Newburyport commenced in October 1998.

MBTA is receiving 23 rebuilt locomotives from the former AMF Technotransport (now owned by Alstom) and 47 remodelled ex-Pullman cars. Before entering service on Old Colony trains these were to be run in on the New England Southern (qv). The Old Colony services will use the extensively remodelled South Station which is now a major bus, taxi and metro interchange.

Several other network extensions, to both the north and south of Boston, are either under way, as in the case of lines to Fall River and New Bedford, or the subject of studies.

### Traction and rolling stock
MBTA operates 81 diesel locomotives, including the rebuilds arriving from AMF Technotransport for the Worcester and Old Colony services, and 403 passenger cars. Rolling stock includes 25 F40PH-2C locomotives from GM-EMD, 18 F40PH and 12 F40PHM2 locomotives remanufactured by Morrison Knudsen and two GP9s for shunting and maintenance duties.

The passenger coach roster includes 67 from MBB of Germany, 147 from Bombardier, 75 double-deck vehicles by Kawasaki and 58 coaches by Pullman-Standard. A further 17 Kawasaki vehicles have been ordered for 1997-98 delivery at a cost of $32 million and Amerail is performing mid-life overhaul on 51 Pullman-Standard vehicles for $30 million at the former MK Transit facility in Hornell, New York. A tranche of the MBB units has been reconfigured to serve as cab cars on the Old Colony lines.

In 1998 MBTA completed a $166 million contract for the reconstruction of its Commuter Rail Maintenance Facility in Somerville.

### Track
**Rail:** 65.5 kg/m
**Crossties (sleepers):** Wood 177.8 × 228.6 × 2,590.8 mm, spaced 2,017/km; and concrete 254 × 266.7 × 2,090.8 mm, spaced 1,641/km
**Fastenings:** Cut spikes with double shoulder tie plates or resilient fasteners with appropriate tie plates or adaptors
**Max curvature:** 13°
**Max gradient:** 3%
**Max permissible axleload:** 29.85 tonnes

---

## Metra

Chicago Commuter Rail Service Board
(Northeast Illinois Regional Commuter Railroad Corporation)
547 W Jackson Blvd, Chicago, Illinois 60661-6840
Tel: (+1 312) 322 69 00
Web: http://www.metrarail.com

### Key personnel
Chairman: Jeffrey R Ladd
Executive Director: Philip A Pagano
Deputy Executive Director: G Richard Tidwell
Chief Operations Officer: Vaughn L Stoner
Heads of Department
  Corporate Administration: Michael J Nielsen
  General Development: Jack Groner
  Real Estate and Planning: Patrick McAtee
  Human Resources: Gail Washington
  Treasury and Finance: Frank M Racibozynski
  Materials Management: Paul Kisielius
  Transportation: George Hardwidge
  Mechanical: Richard Soukup
  Engineering: William K Tupper

Gauge: 1,435 mm
Route length: 335.6 km
Electrification: 98.95 km at 1.5 kV DC

### Passenger operations
Metra is the commuter railroad operating arm of the Chicago Regional Transportation Authority (RTA). Its commuter rail system takes in the six counties of northeast Illinois. Including the operations conducted for Metra by Burlington Northern Santa Fe (BNSF – formerly Burlington Northern) and Union Pacific (UP – formerly Chicago & North Western) on their own infrastructure, the system embraces over 800 route-km and 1,930 track-km, and covers most of the northeast Illinois region. Trains operate seven days a week over 11 main routes and four branches, serving 228 stations.

BNSF (one route) and UP (three routes) operate commuter services in the Chicago RTA area with Metra-owned equipment and under Metra direction through purchase-of-service contracts. Metra itself owns and runs the former Illinois Central (electric), Milwaukee Road and Rock Island services with its own train crews and equipment; since June 1993 it has operated the Norfolk Southern line to Orland Park, now called SouthWest Service, under long-term lease.

Metra also operates its North Central service via trackage rights on Canadian National right-of-way. There are also three Heritage Corridor trains each way daily between Chicago and Joliet on the Canadian National route.

Total ridership in 2000 was 81.9 million, up 2.5 per cent on 1999. On-time performance was reported at 97.1 per cent overall.

### Improvements to existing lines
Metra's 2001 capital programme was set at US$372 million, considerably higher than in 2000. The programme includes: US$66 million for engineering projects; US$53 million for stations and parking; US$110 million for rolling stock; US$18 million for support facilities and equipment; US$33 million for signalling and telecommunications; US$81 million for acquisitions, extensions and service expansion; and US$10 million for other investments.

Metra is a partner in evaluating the potential for commuter service on three routes: (a) the Waukegan–Lynwood segment of the Elgin, Joliet & Eastern (qv) belt line; (b) an orbital route linking O'Hare and Midway airports using Indiana Harbor Belt trackage; and (c) on the CSX line south to Beecher.

### Metra diesel locomotives

| Class | Builder's type | Wheel arrangement | Power kW | Speed km/h | Weight tonnes | No in service | First built | Builders Mechanical | Engine | Transmission |
|---|---|---|---|---|---|---|---|---|---|---|
| B32A | F40PH | Bo-Bo | 2,390 | 142 | 118 | 28 | 1977 | EMD | 16-645E3B | E EMD |
| B32A | F40PH-2 | Bo-Bo | 2,390 | 142 | 118 | 57 | 1979 | EMD | 16-645E | E EMD |
| B32A | F40PHM-2 | Bo-Bo | 2,390 | 142 | 120 | 30 | 1991 | EMD | 16-645E3B | E EMD |
| C32A | F40C | Co-Co | 2,390 | 142 | 165 | 15 | 1974 | EMD | 16-645E | E EMD |

### Metra electric railcars

| Class | Cars per unit | Motor cars per unit | Motored axles/car | Output/motor kW | Speed km/h | No in service | First built | Builders Mechanical | Electrical |
|---|---|---|---|---|---|---|---|---|---|
| SA2A | 1 | 1 | 4 | 120 | 130 | 8 | 1982 | Nippon Sharyo | GE |
| MA3A | 1 | 1 | 4 | 120 | 121 | 129 | 1971 | St Louis Car | GE |
| MA3B | 1 | 1 | 4 | 120 | 121 | 36 | 1978 | Bombardier | GE |

USA/**RAILWAY SYSTEMS** 445

**Traction and rolling stock**
At the end of 2001, Metra owned 130 diesel locomotives for revenue service, plus 173 electric railcars and 791 push-pull passenger coaches.

**Track**
**Rail:** 115, 119, 131, 132, 136 lb/yd
**Crossties (sleepers):** Wood and concrete
**Thickness:** 7 × 9 in
**Spacing:** 1,988/km

**Fastenings:** Rail anchors
**Max curvature:** 7° 26′
**Max gradient:** 1.75%
**Max axleload:** 65,000 lb

*UPDATED*

## Metro-North Railroad Co

347 Madison Avenue, 4th Floor, New York, New York 10017
Tel: (+1 212) 340 30 00   Fax: (+1 212) 340 40 37
Web: http://www.mta.nyc.ny.us

### Key personnel
MTA Chairman: E Virgil Conway
MTA Executive Director: Marc V Shaw
President and General Manager, Metro-North:
  Donald N Nelson
Executive Vice-President: Genevieve T Firnhaber
Vice-Presidents
  Operations: George F Walker
  Planning and Development: Howard Permut
Assistant Vice-President, Operations: George F Walker
Chief Mechanical Officer: G Robert Bott
Director, Infrastructure Maintenance: Robert Lieblong
Staff: 5,393

Gauge: 1,435 mm
Route length: 428 km
Electrification: Hudson and Harlem lines (139 km), 600 V DC third rail; New Haven line (116 km), 11 kV 60 Hz AC overhead

### Organisation
Metro-North is one of five operating divisions of New York's Metropolitan Transportation Authority (MTA).

### Finance
Revenue from passengers and other income totalled $300.4 million in 1996 (compared to $287.1 million in 1995) which was 58.7 per cent of expenses. On the New Haven line this figure reaches 66 per cent. Targets for Metro-North were set at 62.3 per cent in 1997 and 64.6 per cent by 1998. The MTA's internal cost control programme requires $3 billion in reduced expenses and $1.5 billion in increased revenue in the span of the 1995-99 five-year plan. Among other contributions, Metro-North has pared its employee total by 10 per cent.

Metro-North's capital investment programme is included in the overall MTA budget. Since 1983, Metro-North has expended $3 billion out of MTA's $22 billion. The 1995-97 Metro-North capital programme amounted to $12 billion.

### Passenger operations
Metro-North's three main lines that run north out of New York City and east of the Hudson river are the Hudson, Harlem and New Haven lines. These three routes operate out of New York's Grand Central Terminal.

Service on the 158.4 km, 29-station New Haven line, and its New Canaan, Danbury and Waterbury branches totalling 95.6 km and 17 stations, is provided by Metro-North pursuant to a contract between the Connecticut Department of Transportation (ConnDoT) and MTA/Metro-North. Stamford is the busiest station, boarding almost 5,000 passengers per weekday and receiving 2,100 arrivals. At New Haven connection is made with ConnDoT's Shoreline service which runs to New London. Capital improvements in Connecticut are funded by ConnDoT, which owns the infrastructure.

Metro-North also provides services west of the Hudson in the New York state counties of Orange and Rockland on the Port Jervis and Pascack Valley lines; trains on these lines run out of the Hoboken terminal on the New Jersey shore of the Hudson. These services are operated by New Jersey Transit (qv) under contract to Metro-North, which assigns part of its rolling stock fleet to NJT.

On the three main lines (Hudson, Harlem and New Haven), total passenger journeys in 1996 were 61.6 million. This was the highest figure recorded since 1945 and the sixth consecutive increase. Growth is occurring in weekend travel and reverse commuting, up 3.6 per cent and 6 per cent respectively, while the more traditional commuter market into New York City is essentially flat.

### Improvements to existing lines
In 1996, Metro-North built its first new station since 1983, at Cortland, on the Hudson line, at a cost of $11 million, including parking. A further $9.6 million was spent on four major station upgrades on the Dover Plains line.

In 1998, construction started on an 8 km extension of the Harlem line beyond its current terminus at Dover Plains to Wassaic for opening in 2000. Metro-North also plans to extend the Hudson line northwards by 26 km from Poughkeepsie to Rhinecliff

### Traction and rolling stock
At the end of 1995, resources comprised three electric and 48 diesel locomotives (10 of which are owned by ConnDoT), 683 emus and 88 conventional coaches (of which 30 are owned by ConnDoT). An additional eight locomotives are assigned to west of Hudson services and numbered in with NJ Transit rosters.

The majority of Metro-North's passenger cars serving the third-rail electrified Hudson and Harlem lines are emus of Types M-1, M-2 and the most recent tranche of 54 M-6 three-car emus, which were delivered by Tokyu Car in

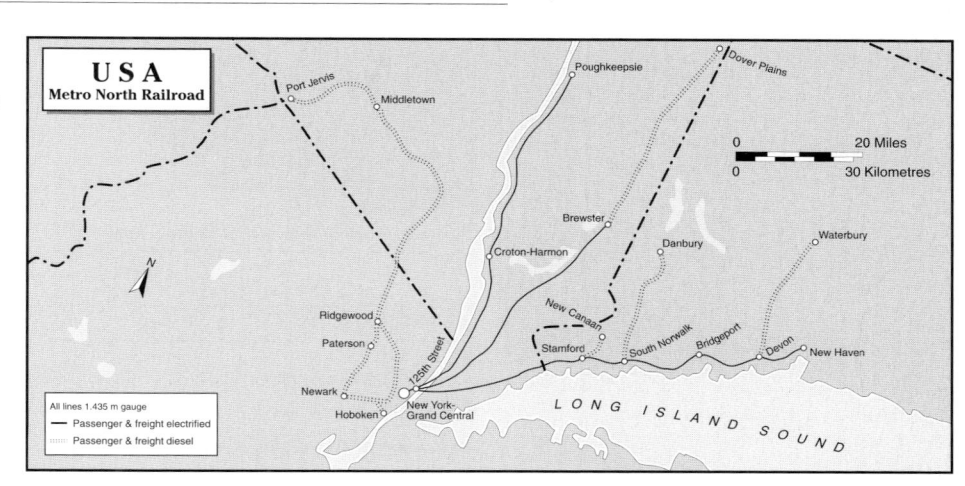

*Metro-North General Electric Type P32AC-DM dual-mode locomotive at Poughkeepsie* (Eddie Barnes) 0063703

**Diesel and electrodiesel locomotives (with third-rail pick-up shoes)**

| Class | Wheel arrangement | Power kW | Speed km/h | Weight short tonnes | No in service | First built | Mechanical | Builders Engine | Transmission |
|---|---|---|---|---|---|---|---|---|---|
| FL9 | Bo-A1A | 1,340 | 143 | 141 | 27 | 1957 | EMD | GM 567 C | *E* EMD |
| FL9AC | Bo-A1A | 2,310 | 160 | 137.5 | 7 | 1993 | ABB | GM 710G3 | *E* EMD |
| P32AC-DM | Bo-Bo | 2,390 | 160 | na | 5 | 1995 | GE | GE | *E* GE |
| F10A | Bo-Bo | 1,300 | 130 | 125 | 4 | 1979 R | EMD | GM 567 | *E* EMD |
| GP35R | Bo-Bo | 1,490 | 110 | 131 | 6 | 1994 R | EMD | GM 567 | *E* EMD |
| GP7u | Bo-Bo | 1,120 | 105 | 124.5 | 1 | 1953 | EMD | GM 567 C | *E* EMD |
| GP9 | Bo-Bo | 1,300 | 105 | 125.5 | 1 | 1955 | EMD | GM 567 C | *E* EMD |
| GP40 FH2* | Bo-Bo | 2,240 | 169 | 128.1 | 7 | 1988 92R | EMD/MK; EMD/CR | GM 16 645 | *E* EMD |

R year of rebuilding
* in New Jersey service

**Electric locomotives**

| Class | Wheel arrangement | Line voltage | Output kW | Speed km/h | Weight tonnes | No in service | First built | Builders Mechanical | Electrical |
|---|---|---|---|---|---|---|---|---|---|
| E10B | Bo-Bo | 600 DC | 745 | 50 | 126 | 3 | 1952 | GE | GE |

www.janes.com

Jane's World Railways 2002-2003

# RAILWAY SYSTEMS/USA

1987. As part of a major overhaul programme, 22 M-2 emus received attention in 1995, and a similar number were overhauled in 1996; the programme continues under outside contract while some M-1s, some M-3s and some Bombardier coaches were overhauled in-house.

Non-electrified lines are worked by locomotive-hauled trains, using a variety of diesel traction including FL9 electro-diesels equipped with third-rail pick-up shoes for operating into Grand Central Terminal. Seven FL9s have been modernised: they have been rebuilt by ABB (now Adtranz) as FL9AC units with three-phase AC traction motors and a 3,200 hp (2,387 kW) EMD engine.

Five 3,200 hp (2,387 kW) P32AC-DM Genesis electro-diesel locomotives from General Electric entered service in the third quarter of 1995 and a further seven, costing $30 million, were ordered for 1998 delivery. In 1996, Bombardier completed an order for 34 passenger coaches valued at $41.5 million. Final assembly was undertaken at Plattsburgh, New York, and an option for a further 15 vehicles for 1997 delivery was exercised. Some of the new coaches were allocated to services west of the Hudson. Metro-North has contracted for design specifications for a coach body which can be built as either a conventional coach or an emu.

*Maintenance*
Heavy rolling stock repairs are undertaken at Croton-Harmon, while running repairs can also be carried out at Brewster and North White Plains. Some component repair is performed by outside contractors. There is a running repair facility at New Haven, Connecticut, for M-2, M-4 and M-6 emus. ConnDoT has funded the construction of an overhaul workshop in New Haven and a new maintenance and repair facility at Stamford.

For track, signalling, and electrification maintenance work, Metro-North operates a fleet of over 150 wagons and six GP35R locomotives rebuilt by Conrail's Altoona workshops.

### Electric railcars or multiple-units

| Class | Cars per unit | Line voltage | Motor cars per unit | Motored axles/car | Output/motor kW | Speed km/h | No in service | First built | Builders Mechanical | Electrical |
|---|---|---|---|---|---|---|---|---|---|---|
| M-1 | 2 | 600 DC | 2 | 4 | 110 | 160 | 178 | 1971 | Budd | GE |
| M-2 | 2 | 600 DC and 12.5 kV AC | 2 | 4 | 120 | 160 | 242 | 1973 | GE | GE |
| M-3 | 2 | 600 DC | 2 | 4 | 120 | 160 | 142 | 1982 | Budd | GE |
| M-4 | 3 | 600 DC and 12.5 kV AC | 2 | 4 | 120 | 160 | 54 | 1987 | Tokyu Car | GE |
| M-6 | 3 | 700 DC and 13.2 kV AC | 3 | 4 | 120 | 160 | 48 | 1993 | Morrison Knudsen | GE |
| ACMU | 1 | 600 DC | 1 | 4 | 75 | 120 | 61 | 1962 | Pullman-Standard | GE |

### Push-pull locomotive-powered single coaches

| Class | Speed km/h | Weight short tons | No in service | First built | Builder |
|---|---|---|---|---|---|
| Shoreliner Coach | 160 | 45.5 | 136 | 1985 | Bombardier |

### Signalling and telecommunications

In 1991, Metro-North completed installation of CTC (centralised traffic control), cab signalling and ATC (automatic train control) throughout its main line system; this had been phased in over nine years for an outlay of $82.7 million. A new command centre, designed and built by GRS, has been completed on the sixth floor of Grand Central Terminal.

The only remaining segments without cab signalling are the single-track Danbury and Waterbury branches, and the Brewster North-Dover Plains section of the Harlem line. Metro-North dispatches for Amtrak and freight activity as far as New Haven.

### Track

**Rail:** 119 RE and 132 RE predominantly, some 140 and 127
**Crossties (sleepers):** 7 × 9 in × 8 ft 6 in
**Spacing:** 1,968/km for wood ties; 1,640/km for concrete
**Fastenings:** Tie plates and cut spike for wood; Pandrol clips for concrete and some wood
**Min curvature radius:** 109 m
**Max gradient:** 3%
**Max axleload:** E72 loading for track design

---

## New Jersey Transit Rail Operations Inc

One Penn Plaza East, Newark, New Jersey 07105 22461
Tel: (+1 201) 491 70 00    Fax: (+1 201) 491 82 18

### Key personnel
Executive Director: Jeffrey A Warsh
Vice-President and General Manager of Rail Operations: Robert A Randall
Deputy General Manager, Hoboken Division Operations: William R Knapp
Deputy General Manager, Infrastructure Engineering: Alison Conway-Smith
Deputy General Manager, Support Operations: Michael J Rienzi
Director, System Operations: James V Samuelson
Acting Assistant General Manager, Administration: Edward C McGittigan
Assistant General Manager, Contracts and Capital Programs: D C Agrawal
Chief Financial Officer: Charles Wedel
Gauge: 1,435 mm
Route length, owned: 513.4 km; Trackage rights: 231.5 km

Electrification, owned: 107.6 km at 25 kV 60 Hz AC; 26.4 km at 12 kV 25 Hz AC; 25.4 km at 12 kV 60 Hz AC; trackage rights: 93.5 km at 12 kV 25 Hz AC

### Passenger operations

New Jersey Transit (NJT) Rail in 1997-98 carried 52.1 million passengers over nine routes into Newark, Hoboken and New York City. NJT Rail employs train crews, owns rolling stock and much of its network infrastructure (except Conrail and Amtrak routes), together with 145 stations.

On the Jersey Coast line from New York Penn Station to Bay Head Junction, NJT operates its 'Jersey Arrow' electric multiple-units (as far as Long Branch) and trains hauled by GP40PH-2, GP40PH-2B, F40PH-2, and GP40FH-2 diesels. At weekends, diesel-powered trains from Bay Head terminate at Long Branch where passengers transfer to emu services.

The North East Corridor service from Penn Station to Trenton and the branch to Princeton is provided by 'Arrow' emus. Services on the Raritan Valley line from Newark are powered by a range of new and rebuilt GM locomotive types (qv) and in 1994 was extended 13 km to a new terminus at Hackettstown.

The Morris and Essex lines, rewired to 25 kV AC in 1984, are operated principally with emus; some diesel-powered trains also run. As part of the major restructuring of services in association with the opening of the Kearny connection, push-pull trainsets powered by new ALP44 locomotives were introduced.

The Boonton, Port Jervis and Pascack Valley lines are served by diesel push-pull trains. Because the Port Jervis and Pascack Valley routes both extend into New York state, compatible equipment supplied by Metro-North (qv) is deployed alongside NJT stock.

*Atlantic City service*
Introduced in 1989, this service was extended into Philadelphia in 1993; it had previously terminated at Lindenwold for a metro connection to the city centre. In 1994, Amtrak pulled out of the Atlantic City market altogether and NJT rescheduled its service to provide all-day coverage. The service is run with a small fleet of five diesel locomotives and 18 coaches which are kept at Amtrak's yard north of 30th Street station. This service to Atlantic City continues to lose money out of proportion to other NJT rail services.

### Improvements to existing lines

NJ Transit has continued to make significant progress in advancing major rail projects that will enable the state of New Jersey to meet forecast increases in demand through the 1990s and beyond 2000. Among these is the $69 million Kearny Connection project that in June 1996 was completed to link the Morris and Essex lines with the Northeast Corridor. This service is now marketed under the brand name MidTOWN DIRECT. The connection enables through services to reach Penn Station in Manhattan, instead of terminating at Hoboken on the New Jersey shore of the Hudson, where a transfer to ferries or the PATH metro is necessary to reach Manhattan. In September 1996, the MidTOWN DIRECT service was extended to weekends also.

Construction started in 1998 on the Bay Street Connection, a link between the end of the Montclair branch (on the Morris and Essex line) to the Boonton line; this will allow Boonton services to gain access to the Kearny Connection and will permit closure of the southern end of the Boonton line into Hoboken. Completion is scheduled for mid-2001. A major new station serving Newark International Airport is being developed.

*New Jersey Transit Type ALP44 electric locomotive with a commuter service at Dover, New Jersey (Eddie Barnes)* 0063704

# USA/RAILWAY SYSTEMS

*Single-unit electric railcar forming Princeton—Princeton Junction shuttle service (Quintus Vosman) 2001/0099144*

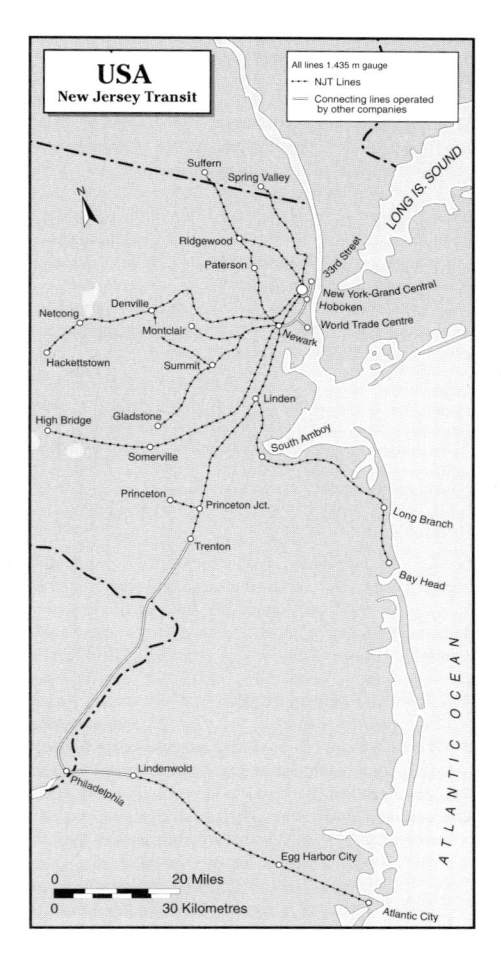

In 1999, studies were being conducted in to a restoration of services between West Treton and Bound Brook, and on three routes in Bergen County.

A consortium of rail projects together is called the Urban Core Programme, which has been substantially supported by the US Congress and the FTA (qv).

### Capacity at Penn Station
In conjunction with Amtrak and Long Island Rail Road, NJT has implemented a project to increase train frequency into New York City's Penn Station and raise total station capacity at peak periods from 20 to 30 trains. Work has included the design and construction of a new high-speed signalling system as well as improvements in and around Penn Station to accommodate increased passenger movements. Completion is scheduled for late 2001.

STV Consultants have been engaged in a large-scale simulation study of track occupancy between Newark and Jamaica on Long Island, involving the timetables of NJT, Long Island Rail Road and Amtrak. The study includes the routes to Spuyten Duyvil in the Empire Corridor and to New Rochelle in the Northeast Corridor. The instrument of analysis has been a family of software programs from Comreco and built around their RailPlan module.

### Secaucus Transfer
Ground was broken in 1995 on this station (also part of the Urban Core Project) that will create a major New Jersey public transport interchange embracing all of NJT's north New Jersey lines. The multilevel facility, to be located in the Jersey Meadowlands (and estimated to cost $448 million by completion in 2002), will facilitate connections to Manhattan's Penn Station from all three lines in New Jersey that presently terminate in Hoboken. An interchange is preferred to a direct rail connection as the north New Jersey lines are diesel-worked and only electric rolling stock is permitted in Penn Station. Services to Newark, the Jersey Coast, Trenton and Amtrak destinations will also be available via Secaucus.

### Southern New Jersey Light Rail Transit System
In 1999, the Southern New Jersey Light Rail Group, led by Adtranz and Bechtel, was awarded a design-and-build contract to design, construct and operate for 10 years a 55 km line between Camden and Trenton. The system, which was due to open in late 2002, will include 20 stations and will be operated with European-designed lightweight diesel railcars. A feasibility study was commissioned in 1999 into extending the line beyond Trenton station to the state capitol (1.6 km).

### New York, Susquehanna & Western
A proposed passenger service on the New York Susquehanna & Western railroad continues to be the subject of a consultant's planning and environmental impact study. The new service would call at Secaucus Transfer and diverge from the NJT Bergen line at Hawthorne to run into northern New Jersey or southern New York. Strategies for implementation have become increasingly complex as levels of freight traffic over the relatively basic infrastructure in question have increased significantly since the concept was first developed and have been further complicated by the jockeying for access to the New York—Northern New Jersey freight market as a by-product of the Conrail break-up.

### Traction and rolling stock
At the end of 1999, NJT operated 32 electric and 79 diesel locomotives, 300 emu cars and 514 other passenger coaches.

In 1999, NJT placed an order with Adtranz for 24 multi-current electric locomotives based on the design of the German Rail Class 101 machines. Delivery of the first two of these was scheduled for the end of 2001. Also ordered from Adtranz were 20 GTW lightweight diesel railcars as part of the design-and-build contract with Bechtel for the 55 km Camden—Trenton light rail project.

Also ordered in 1999 were 48 driving trailers and 22 intermediate trailers from Alstom in a joint procurement project with Metro-North. These are part of a fleet modernisation and expansion programme covering 200 single-deck and 200 double-deck coaches, as well as 33 diesel locomotives and the Adtranz electric locomotives mentioned above.

### Track
**Rail:** New rail standard 132 lb/yd (65.5 kg/m)
**Crossties (sleepers):** Hardwood
**Thickness:** Main lines 178 × 229 mm, yards 152 × 203 mm
**Spacing:** Running lines 1,989/km; yards 1,802/km
**Fastenings:** 152 mm cut spike, drive-on rail anchors
**Min curvature radius:** Running lines 194 m, yards 122 m
**Max axleload:** 20 tonnes at unrestricted speed; locomotives to 32.7 tonnes at restricted speed

### Diesel locomotives

| Class | Wheel arrangement | Power kW | Speed km/h | Weight tonnes | No in service | First built | Builders Mechanical | Engine | Transmission |
|---|---|---|---|---|---|---|---|---|---|
| GP40PH-2 | Bo-Bo | 2,238 | 169 | 133.8 | 13 | 1968 | EMD | 16-645 E3B | E EMD D77 |
| F40PH-2 | Bo-Bo | 2,238 | 169 | 118.6 | 17 | 1996R | EMD/CR | 16-645 E3B | E EMD D77 |
| GP40FH-2 | Bo-Bo | 2,238 | 169 | 128.1 | 21 | 1987-1990* | EMD/MK | 16-645 E3 | E EMD D77 |
| GP40FH-2 | Bo-Bo | 2,238 | 169 | 128.1 | 19 | 1994R | EMD/CR | 16-645 E3 | E EMD D77 |

* year of rebuild

### Electric locomotives

| Class | Wheel arrangement | Output kW | Speed km/h | Weight tonnes | No in service | First built | Builders Mechanical | Electrical |
|---|---|---|---|---|---|---|---|---|
| ALP44 | Bo-Bo | 4,320 | 201 | 92.5 | 32 | 1990 | ABB | ABB |

### Electric railcars or multiple-units

| Class | Cars per unit | Motored axles/car | Output/motor kW | Speed km/h | No in service | First built | Builders Mechanical | Electrical |
|---|---|---|---|---|---|---|---|---|
| Arrow II | 2 | 4 | 120 | 160 | 34* | 1974 | GE-AVCO | GE |
| Arrow III | 2 | | | | 91 | 1976 | GE-AVCO | GE |
| Arrow III | 1 | | | | 29 | 1976 | GE-AVCO | GE |

* Arrow II withdrawals started in 1997

## Northern Indiana Commuter Transportation District

33 E US Highway 12, Chesterton, Indiana 46304-3514
Tel: (+1 219) 926 57 44   Fax: (+1 219) 929 44 38

### Key personnel
Chairman: David L Niezgodski
General Manager: Gerald R Hanas
Chief Operating Officer: Kenneth R Peterson
Chief Counsel: Bjarne R Henderson
Chief Financial Officer: Dario M Brezene
Director, Marketing and Planning: John N Parsons

### Passenger operations
Following sale of the Chicago SouthShore & South Bend Railroad, Northern Indiana Commuter Transportation District (NICTD) took over full responsibility for its passenger services between Chicago and South Bend. From Chicago to Kensington operation is over Metra's electrified Illinois Central route. In 1992, a 1 km extension was opened to South Bend Airport.

NICTD owns 109.3 route-km, leases 20.2 route-km and has trackage rights over 22.9 km. Electrification at 1.5 kV DC overhead covers 141.4 km. Annual ridership is 3.6 million; the line continues to attract latent demand such that peak-hour trains average 110 per cent of seat capacity. Income from all sources including fares was US$27 million in 2000.

A major investment study was completed in 2000 and recommended a new service between Chicago, Illinois, and Valparaiso, Indiana, with a second phase to Lowell, Indiana. Power would be supplied by dual-mode locomotives with overhead power from Munster to Chicago and diesel power to a proposed terminal at either Lowell or Valparaiso.

### Improvements to existing lines
NICTD's capital investment programme for the near term involves continued improvements to infrastructure, especially parking facilities, bridges and passenger facilities.

### Traction and rolling stock
NICTD operates a fleet of 58 Nippon Sharyo electric railcars and 10 trailers ordered through Sumitomo in three batches delivered in 1982-83, 1992 and 2000. Each power car in the two earlier series has four GE 104 kW traction motors and maximum speed is 120 km/h. NICTD has built an extension to its Michigan City workshops for mid-life overhauls of the first batch.

The overhaul includes new Toshiba AC propulsion drives. The 2000 order from Sumitomo is also equipped with a similar propulsion system.

*UPDATED*

## North San Diego County Transit Development Board

810 Mission Avenue, Oceanside, California 92054
Tel: (+1 760) 967 28 27   Fax: (+1 760) 967 09 41
e-mail: ekasparik@uctd.org

### Key personnel
Executive Director: Martin C Minkoff
Director of Transportation Services: Thomas Lichterman
Manager of Rail Services: Edward Kasparik
Manager of Maintenance-of-Way: James Merritt
Rail Contract Compliance Officer: Wayne Penn

### Passenger operations
In February 1995, North San Diego County Transit Development Board (NCTD) began operating its Coast Rail Express or 'Coaster' service over a 67.2 km San Diego—Oceanside route in California.

The Coaster runs over the former Santa Fe 'Surf Line', which, together with the Oceanside—Escondido branch, provides a total network of 134 km. The main line has eight stations, each of which has extensive free parking facilities and connecting bus services. The line is maintained for 145 km/h operation and is equipped with ATS and CTC. Approximately two-thirds of the line remains single-track, although several projects were under way in 2002 to convert sections to double-track. The service is also operated under the name of San Diego Northern Railway.

Amtrak is the current designated operator under a five-year contract. It is also contracted to undertake track maintenance and, under a subcontract with Motive Power Inc, to maintain rolling stock.

In 2002, 22 Coaster services were run each weekday and eight on Saturdays. There was no service on Sundays. Coaster services share tracks with 22 daily Amtrak 'Surfliner' intercity services and four BNSF freight trains each day. Ridership averages 4,300 each weekday. Trains are push-pull operated, the usual formation comprising one locomotive, four trailers and a cab control coach.

### Traction and rolling stock
Motive power consists of five remanufactured F40PHM-2C diesel locomotives supplied by Morrison-Knudsen, supplemented by one leased Amtrak F40PH. Two EMD F59PHI locomotives were delivered in 2001. Bombardier has supplied 22 bilevel coaches and cab control coaches. In 2001, five additional coaches and one cab car were ordered for delivery in 2003. All motive power and rolling stock is maintained at a maintenance and stabling facility at Stuart Mesa, 8 km north of Oceanside.

*UPDATED*

## Peninsula Corridor Joint Powers Board

PO Box 3006, 1250 San Carlos Avenue, San Carlos, California 94070-1306
Tel: (+1 650) 508 62 00   Fax: (+1 650) 508 63 65
Web: http://www.caltrain.com

### Key personnel
Executive Director: Michael J Scanlon
Director, Rail Services: Jerome Kirzner
Manager of Operations: Walt Stringer
Manager of Equipment: Steve Coleman

### Organisation
In 1992, the Peninsula Corridor Joint Powers Board, a three-county agency, purchased the 75.6 km Southern Pacific main line from San Francisco to San Jose for $242.3 million. This is a long-standing commuter route previously operated under the sponsorship of the California Department of Transportation (Caltrans). There were options to purchase additional trackage on three branches (including the Tracy branch and its Dumbarton Bridge over San Francisco Bay) and an additional 40.9 km of line south to Gilroy. Amtrak was awarded the contract to operate the line; management is provided for the board by the San Mateo County Transit District. Amtrak's contract has been extended through to June 2000, with a fixed price formula designed to contain cost overruns.

### Passenger operations
The Peninsula commuter service, marketed as Caltrain, comprises a weekday service of 33 San Francisco—San Jose return trains. Four of these trains in each direction serve Gilroy beyond San Jose. Under a 10-year plan, service levels are to rise to over 100 trains a day. Weekday ridership averages 27,000, of which 800 presently comes from the San Jose—Gilroy section. Annual journeys totalled 8.6 million in 1998, which was 3.2 per cent up on the previous year.

There are 34 stations, including an interchange facility at Tamien, 2 miles south of central San Jose, served by Santa Clara County's light rail system. Since January 1998, the San Francisco terminal has been served by the city's Muni Metro light rail system, which now provides a direct link via the N-Judah line (see 'Improvements to existing lines').

*Bicycle accommodation*
Caltrain market research has established that 9 per cent of passengers cycle to the station, and about 1,700 then use their bikes from station to work. Caltrain continues to install racks and lockers (now 700) at stations. Bikes are also conveyed on trains: each bike car provides space for 24 machines, and on some services two bike cars are included in the train formation.

### Improvements to existing lines
The Joint Powers Board has deferred a long-term plan to relocate its San Francisco terminus to Beale and Market Streets to connect with the city's light rail, metro, ferry, cable car and bus services. A conservative estimate for a project of this scope is in the order of $600 million to $650 million.

*Improvements to San Francisco station include the provision of an enlarged concourse, which is enclosed in glass and steel*    0063705

The Muni light rail underground system was opened to the current terminal at 4th Street & King Street on 10 January 1998, providing improved service integration until such time as an extension of the commuter line can be engineered.

A new station at Millbrae will provide connections with the extension of the BART metro system to San Francisco International Airport, replacing the existing shuttle bus.

Work started in December 1997 on a $5 million scheme to improve and modernise passenger facilities at the Caltrain San Francisco terminal. Much of the work on the interior of the station was completed in December 1998, notably including a new concourse, which is enclosed in glass and steel. Further work on the exterior of the station was completed in April 1999.

In December 1998, a $1 million station restoration project at the Renaissance-style Gilroy station was completed.

# USA/RAILWAY SYSTEMS

An $8.6 million programme to replace jointed track with continuously welded rail was initiated in August 1997 between San Jose Diridon and Lawrence stations.

In August 1998, Caltrain awarded a $1.5 million contract for the construction of a new station at Mountain View, San Antonio. Services to this facility started in April 1999.

In January 1999, a $41 million contract was awarded to Kiewit Pacific Co for a series of 30 construction schemes known collectively as the Ponderosa Project. Work to be completed in the third quarter of 2000 includes replacement of some 43,000 sleepers, reconstruction of 11 bridges and 15 km of track and major work at four stations.

In October 1998, the Caltrain board received a series of recommendations for improving commuter services in a report known as the Rapid Rail Study. The study outlines some $900 million in improvements that would lead to an electrified system early in the next century, with track and signalling upgraded for 144 km/h operation. The report also details rehabilitation projects costing some $220 million, which would increase operating speeds to 126 km/h and improve reliability.

### Traction and rolling stock
Three F40 locomotives from Boise Locomotive entered service in 1998. They joined the existing fleet of 20 3,200 hp (2,385 kW) F40PH locomotives from GM-EMD and 73 double-deck gallery coaches from Nippon Sharyo. The coaches include 21 push-pull cab control trailers. A $15 million mid-life overhaul programme on the existing locomotives has been carried out by Alstom in Montreal, including the addition of head-end power to 15 machines. The project was completed by December 1999. In November 1999, Alstom was also awarded a $34.7 million contract covering routine overhaul of the passenger coach fleet.

In 1997, an order was placed with Sumitomo for 19 double-deck coaches. This has since been increased to 20, with first deliveries scheduled for the third quarter of 1999.

Caltrain is proceeding with planning for a new full-service maintenance facility in the San Jose area.

## Sound Transit Board

Central Puget Sound Transit Authority

### Key personnel
Director, Sounder Commuter Trains: Paul Price

### Passenger operations
'Sounder' peak-hour commuter services operated by the Sound Transit Board between Tacoma and Seattle (130 km) in the state of Washington were expected to begin by the end of 1999. Extensions are planned north from Seattle to Everett and south from Tacoma to Lakewood by 2001. The implementation of services forms part of the 10-year 'Sound Move' regional transport plan developed by the Central Puget Sound Transit Authority.

### Traction and rolling stock
An initial fleet of six General Motors locomotives and 38 bilevel Bombardier coaches has been ordered and it is expected eventually to add an additional five locomotives and 20 coaches to the fleet. In 1999, Amtrak was awarded a 10-year programme to provide fleet maintenance services. These will be undertaken at the national operator's King Street facility in Seattle.

## Southeastern Pennsylvania Transportation Authority (SEPTA)

1234 Market Street, Philadelphia, Pennsylvania 19107-3780
Tel: (+1 215) 580 84 00
Web: http://www.septa.org

### Key personnel
Chairman: Pasquale Deon
Chief Operating Officer and General Manager:
  John K Leary
Chief Operations Officer, Railroad: W Benjamin Dwinnel

Gauge: 1,435 mm
Route length: 902 km
Electrification: 902 km at 12 kV 25 Hz AC

### Passenger operations
SEPTA operates a multimodal network of public transport services throughout the five-county region of southeastern Pennsylvania. The commuter rail portion consists of 13 electrified lines radiating from Philadelphia. These are operated as eight cross-city routes.

The present Regional Rail system was formed in 1984 when the commuter lines formerly operated by the Pennsylvania and Reading railroads were linked by a four-track connection beneath central Philadelphia.

SEPTA has extended service over Amtrak's Northeast Corridor to Newark, Delaware, under contract to the Delaware Transportation Authority.

### New lines
With the neighbouring Berks Area Reading Transportation Authority (BARTA), SEPTA has conducted studies into public transport alternatives for the 100 km Schuylkill River Valley corridor between Philadelphia and Reading. In July 2000, a commuter rail solution was selected as the 'locally preferred alternative' by SEPTA and BARTA. This foresees an electrified railcar service, provisionally branded MetroRail, operating over existing route R6 lines from Philadelphia to Norristown and then via a Norfolk Southern alignment to Wyomissing, west of Reading. The new line would replace route R6. In 2002, public consultation continued. Subject to funding, construction could begin in 2003, resulting in commissioning in 2007-08.

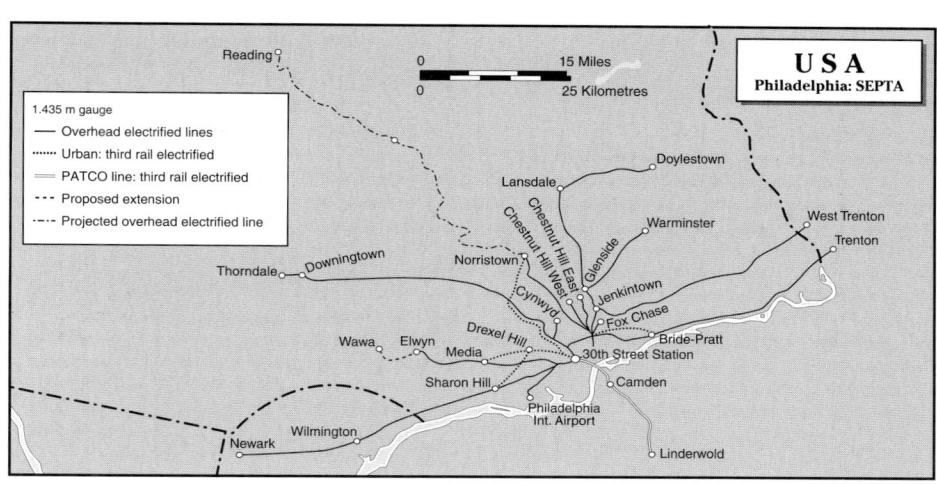

### Traction and rolling stock
The Regional Rail service is operated chiefly by a fleet of 304 Silverliner electric multiple-unit cars.

SEPTA also operates a fleet of 45 Bombardier-built passenger coaches operated as push-pull trainsets with AEM7 electric locomotives. A refurbishment programme for the Silverliner 4 fleet was completed in 2001.

**Type of coupler in standard use:** N2A (emus) Tightlock Knuckle (push-pull cars)

**Type of braking in standard use:** 26C, PS68
Brake air and blended rheostatic (Silverliner 4 cars)

### Track
**Rail:** 140 PS and RE, 132 RE, 131 RE, 130 REHF, 115 RE, 112 RE, 107 NH, 100 PS
**Crossties (sleepers):** Wood, thickness 175 × 200 mm
**Spacing:** 530 mm
**Fastenings:** Pandrol and spike
**Min curvature radius:** 125 m
**Max gradient:** 1 in 25

### Electric railcars or multiple-units

| Class | Cars per unit | Motor cars per unit | Motored axles/car | Output/motor kW | Speed km/h | No in service | First built | Builders Mechanical | Electrical |
|---|---|---|---|---|---|---|---|---|---|
| Silverliner 2 | 1 | 1 | 4 | 110 | 135 | 36 | 1963 | Budd | GE |
| Silverliner 2 | 1 | 1 | 4 | 110 | 135 | 17 | 1964 | Budd | GE |
| Silverliner 3 | 1 | 1 | 4 | 110 | 135 | 20 | 1967 | St Louis Car Co | GE |
| Silverliner 4 | 1 | 1 | 4 | 140 | 150 | 47 | 1974-75 | GE | GE |
| Silverliner 4 | 2 | 2 | 4 | 140 | 150 | 184 | 1975-76 | GE | GE |

*UPDATED*

## Metrolink

Southern California Regional Rail Authority
700 South Flower Street, Suite 2600, Los Angeles, California 90017
Tel: (+1 213) 452 02 00  Fax: (+1 213) 454 04 29
Web: http://www.metrolinktrains.com

### Key personnel
Chief Executive Officer: David R Solow
Assistant Executive Officer: Tracy Daly

Directors
  Strategic Development and Communications:
    Stephen H Lantz
  Operations: John Kerins
  Equipment: William Lydon
  Construction and Engineering: Mike McGinley
  Finance: Mark Dubeau

Gauge: 1,435 mm
Route length operated: 669 km

### Political background
The Southern California Regional Rail Authority (SCRRA) is a joint powers authority formed in August 1991 by five member agencies to develop a commuter rail system for the Los Angeles region. Its member agencies are: Los Angeles County Metropolitan Transportation Authority; Orange County Transportation Authority; Riverside County Transportation Commission; San Bernardino Associated Governments; and Ventura County Transportation Commission. Its activities are governed by

# RAILWAY SYSTEMS/USA

*Metrolink F59PH locomotive with Bombardier bilevel stock at Los Angeles Union station (Colin Boocock)*
0021600

a board of 11 directors drawn from these agencies. In 1992 SCRRA purchased 544 km of right-of-way from Santa Fe, whose successor, Burlington Northern Santa Fe, retains trackage rights for freight traffic over the remaining mileage. Services on the first three of the present network of six lines commenced in October 1992.

In mid-2001, SCRRA employed 743 staff.

### Passenger operations
SCRRA services operate under the Metrolink branding. In mid-2001, 128 trains were operated daily over a six-line, 49-station network. The six lines are: Antelope Valley Line (Lancaster–Los Angeles, 123.3 km); Inland Empire-Orange County Line (San Bernardino–San Juan Capistrano, 114.1 km); Orange County Line (Oceanside–Los Angeles, 140.3 km); Riverside Line (Riverside–Los Angeles, 94.5 km); San Bernardino Line (San Bernardino–Los Angeles, 90.4 km); and the Ventura County Line (Oxnard–Los Angeles, 106.4 km).

In July 2001, daily ridership stood at 32,682, an increase of 3.8 per cent on the figure for July 2000.

### Traction and rolling stock
Metrolink services are operated by Amtrak under contract, using 23 low-emission GM-EMD F59PH locomotives, 10 F59PHI units ordered by California Department of Transportation (CalTrans) and 119 double-deck coaches bought from Bombardier or on lease from GO Transit of Canada. In mid-2001, four additional locomotives and 28 coaches were on order.

In April 1998, Bombardier Transportation was awarded a three-year contract valued at US$36 million covering maintenance of SCRRA's locomotive and rolling stock fleet at Metrolink's Taylor Yard facility in Los Angeles. The contract includes two one-year extension options.

### Track
**Rail:** 136, 119, 115
**Crossties (sleepers):** 83% wood; 17% concrete
**Spacing:** Wood: 2,006/ km; concrete: 1,630/km
**Fastenings:** (concrete) Pandrol clip, McKay Safelok
**Min curvature radius:** 10°
**Max gradient:** 3%

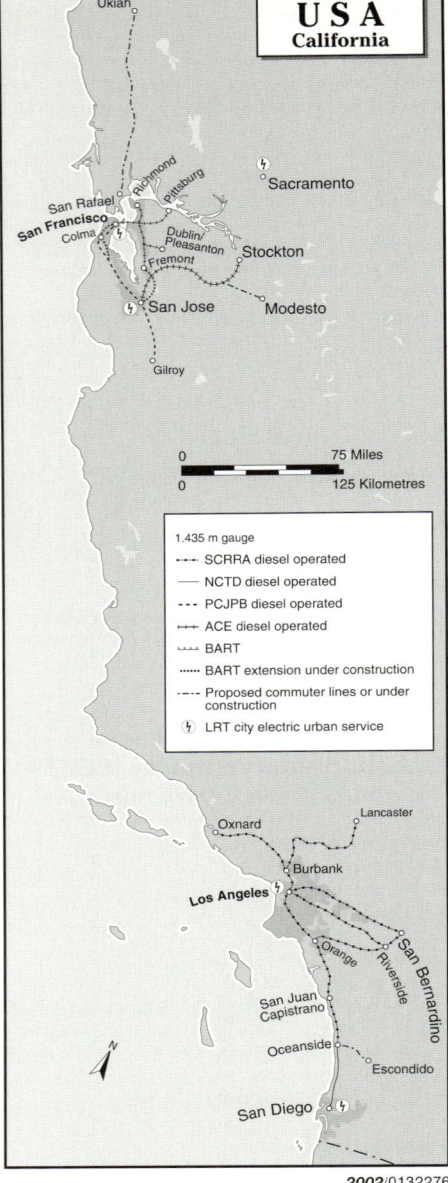

*UPDATED*

2002/0132276

## Tri-County Commuter Rail Authority: Tri-Rail

800 NW 33rd Street, Suite 100, Pompano Beach, Florida 33064
Tel: (+1 954) 942 72 45   Fax: (+1 954) 788 78 78
Web: http://www.tri-rail.com

### Key personnel
Executive Director: Joe Giulietti

### Passenger operations
The Tri-Rail commuter service, funded by the Florida Department of Transport, was introduced over 107 route-km of former CSXT tracks between Miami and West Palm Beach in January 1989. An extension north from West Palm Beach to Mangonia Park has made the service 114.3 km overall. There are now 18 stations on the line. The state of Florida financed the purchase of the Miami-West Palm Beach line for US$264 million. Amtrak and CSXT continue to share the line; CSXT is responsible for maintenance.

Contract management of Tri-Rail operations is being provided until 2002 by Herzog Transit Services Inc for US$10 million a year. Tri-Rail serves all three of the area's international airports which are at Miami, Fort Lauderdale/Hollywood and Palm Beach. Operating at weekends as well as on weekdays, Tri-Rail carries some 2.5 million passengers annually. Transfers to local buses and the Miami metro system have remained free. Connection with the metro is made at Tri-Rail/Metro Transfer station.

### Improvements to existing lines
In 2002, the final stage of Tri-Rail's Double Track Corridor Improvement Program was in progress. Covering 71.3 km, the Segment 5 Project is due to be completed in March 2005. This is intended to enable Tri-Rail services to run at 20 minute headways during peak periods, and will

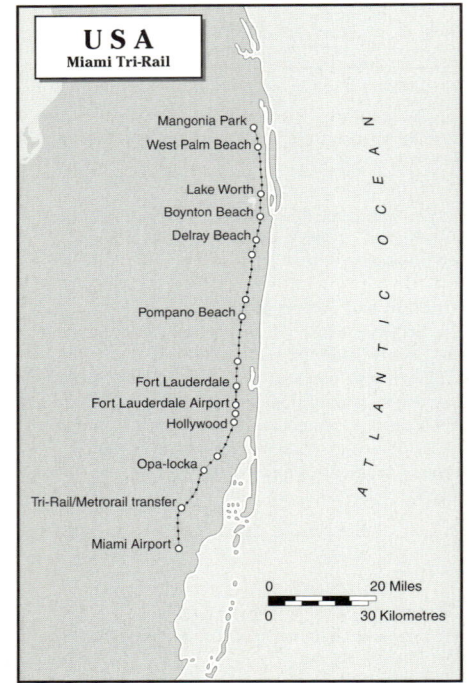

2002/0132275

*Tri-Rail F40PHL-2 locomotive with bilevel stock (Van Wilkins)*
2002/0069419

also reduce congestion and scheduling conflicts with Amtrak and CSXT traffic.

**Traction and rolling stock**
In 2002, Tri-Rail's road fleet consisted of 26 double-deck coaches (11 are cab cars), five F40PHL-2 locomotives, three F40PHC-2C rebuilt locomotives from Morrison Knudsen, and two ex-Amtrak reconditioned F40s.

**Signalling and telecommunications**
A 900 MHz radio control system has been recently installed and in 1997 electronically coded rail signalling replaced a system dating from the Second World War.

*UPDATED*

## Trinity Railway Express

PO Box 660163, Dallas, Texas 75266-7210
Tel: (+1 214) 749 30 88   Fax: (+1 214) 749 36 09
Web: http://www.trinityrailwayexpress.org

**Key personnel**
Director, Trinity Railway Express: Bonnie J Duhr

Gauge: 1,435 mm
Route length: 54.7 km

**Passenger operations**
Dallas Area Rapid Transit (DART), in conjunction with Fort Worth Transportation Authority (theT), introduced commuter services on a Union Pacific route to Fort Worth which is now owned by the two cities. The first stage, a 16 km three-stop service between Dallas and the South Irving Transit Center and branded Trinity Railway Express, opened on the last day of 1996; the line was subsequently extended to Richland Hills and then, in late 2001, to Fort Worth. Here, the city's Intermodal Transportation Center was opened in January 2002, providing interchange with Amtrak's long-distance services and local light rail and bus services. CentrePort/DFW Airport station provides access to Dallas/Fort Worth International Airport via a free shuttle bus. There are 10 stations. Services are managed under contract by Herzog Transit Services.

In 2000-01, Trinity Railway Express carried 1.3 million passengers.

**Traction and rolling stock**
Services are provided by 13 ex-VIA RDC diesel railcars, which were refurbished by GEC Alsthom/AMF Technotransport (now Alstom), four General Motors F59PH-2 locomotives and 14 bilevel coaches obtained from GO Transit in Toronto and refurbished.

*UPDATED*

## Virginia Railway Express (VRE)

1500 King Street, Suite 202, Alexandria, Virginia 22314
Tel: (+1 703) 684 10 01   Fax: (+1 703) 684 13 13
e-mail: gotrains@vre.org
Web: http://www.vre.org

**Key personnel**
Chief Operating Officer: Pete Sklannik Jr
Director of Capital Programs and Facilities: Ed Barber
Superintendent, Railroad Services: David A Snyder
Superintendent of Equipment: (Vacant)
Director, Planning, Customer Service and Public Affairs: Dale Zehner
Chief Financial Officer: Barbara Dripps

**Organisation**
Virginia Railway Express (VRE), a partnership of the Northern Virginia Transportation Commission (NVTC) and the Potomac and Rappahannock Transportation Commission (PRTC), began commuter operations in June 1992 over two lines into Washington Union station, from Fredericksburg (87 km) and Manassas (53 km), serving 18 stations. Operating aspects of VRE are overseen by the VRE Operations Board, consisting of seven commissioners, three each from NVTC and PRTC and the Director of the Virginia Department of Rail and Public Transportation.

**Passenger operations**
From a daily ridership of 3,700 at start-up, patronage had climbed to over 10,300 by January 2001.

Ticketing is a proof-of-purchase system with extensive use of ticket vending machines. VRE pursues a vigorous marketing programme, including free parking, free bus transfers; guaranteed ride home outside train times; and use of Amtrak trains in the same service corridors. Some services also now include catering provision. VRE has combined with Washington Metropolitan Area Transit Authority to develop a joint fare structure. Free transfer is also permitted to some MARC (qv) services.

Connections with Amtrak services are provided at Washington Union Station and at Alexandria, Fredericksburg, Manassas, Quantico and Woodbridge. Connections with Metrorail services are provided at Alexandria (King Street), Crystal City, L'Enfant, Franconia-Springfield and Union Station.

**Traction and rolling stock**
VRE motive power consists of 10 GP39-2C locomotives rebuilt by Morrison Knudsen, five GP40P-2C units rebuilt by Morrison Knudsen and AMF Technotransport and two F40s leased from Amtrak.

The latest additions to the passenger coach fleet are 13 Kawasaki-built double-deck coaches (four driving trailers and nine intermediate trailers) purchased as part of an option on a MARC contract for similar vehicles. These were introduced in January 2000. At the beginning of 2001, they were supplemented by 38 vehicles built new by Mafersa (10 driving trailers and 28 intermediate trailers) and nine 'heritage' vehicles leased from MARC.

## HIGH-SPEED RAIL PROJECTS

At the federal level, the Intermodal Surface Transportation Efficiency Act (ISTEA) required the US Department of Transportation to identify corridors where there is presently, or there can reasonably be expected to develop in the near future, 145 km/h or better operations. USDOT identified six corridors as follows:
(1) Washington-Charlotte: 815 km
(2) Detroit-Chicago-St Louis/Milwaukee: 1,002 km
(3) Miami-Orlando-Tampa: 573 km
(4) San Diego-Los Angeles-Sacramento: 1,048 km
(5) Vancouver BC-Eugene OR: 742 km
(6) The Texas triangle (which was the subject of the Texas High-Speed Rail Authority) was added in 1996.

These corridors were added to two previously recognised corridors, namely the Washington-New York-Boston Northeast Corridor and the New York City-Albany Empire Corridor.

Dependent upon actual appropriations, each of these corridors was eligible to receive up to $1 million per year for the six years (1992-97) of ISTEA for level crossing hazard elimination. The FY97 appropriations bill for the Department of Transportation made the following provisions through the Federal Railroad Administration:

$20.1 million for general railroad research and development;
$195 million for the Northeast Corridor project, including $80 million towards the high-speed train sets;
$24.7 million for Next Generation High-Speed Rail studies, corridor planning, demonstration and implementation.

No provision was made for the National Magnetic Levitation Prototype Development programme.

In July 1998, the ISTEA was succeeded by the Transportation Equity Act for the 21st century (TEA 21), which is intended to balance the funding requirements of road and public transport over a six-year period. A minimum of $36 billion is guaranteed for public transport projects. The number of high-speed corridors qualifying for TEA 21 funding rose to 10 and $1.01 billion was authorised for maglev development.
Federal Railroad Administration – High Speed Rail division
(For address, see main FRA entry)
Tel: (+1 202) 366 65 93   Fax: (+1 202) 366 03 46

**Key personnel**
Director, High Speed Rail Staff: Mark Yachmetz

At the state level, several intercity corridors have been the subject of high-speed passenger rail attention. These are detailed in the following entries (except for the Northeast Corridor Improvement Programme, for details of which see Amtrak entry).

## Alabama/Louisiana/Mississippi

**Houston-New Orleans-Birmingham**
Under TEA-21, Houston-New Orleans-Birmingham (1,150 km), the so-called Gulf Coast Corridor, has been designated as a high-speed rail route, to be achieved by making incremental improvements to existing lines. Ridership and feasibility studies were being conducted in 1999 and the three states were working together to obtain funding for the scheme.

## California Department of Transportation (CalTrans)

Division of Rail
PO Box 942874 Sacramento, California 94274-0001
Tel: (+1 916) 327 62 19

**Key personnel**
Chief, Special Projects: Steve Zimrick
Division of Rail Transportation, Manager: Warren Weber

California Intercity High-Speed Rail Authority
PO Box 942874, MS-74 Sacramento, California 94274-0001
Tel: (+1 916) 324 15 41

**Key personnel**
Executive Director: Dan Leavitt

The California High-Speed Rail Commission released its *Final Summary Report and 20-Year Action Plan* in December 1996, after which it was disbanded. The Authority replaces the Commission, with the task of raising both public support and funding, most probably with a bond issue referendum. The California ballot in 2000 has been set as a target for placing funding proposals before the electorate.

In the Commission Report HSR was determined feasible, at a cost of $21 billion for an inclusive very-high-speed rail technology or $29 billion for maglev, with average speeds of 350 and 495 km/h respectively, though very-high-speed rail would be slowed to 200 km/h or so in city limits. Annual ridership forecasts are 20 million for very-high-speed rail, 26 million of maglev. Both would have a positive farebox recovery ratio but both would require almost 100 per cent capital financing – which implies a statewide or regional tax of some kind to retire any bonds.

The core segment, San Francisco-Los Angeles via Bakersfield, would be covered in 2 hours 49 minutes by very-high-speed rail; 2 hours 3 minutes by maglev. The Commission opted for an inland, as opposed to coast route for the Los Angeles-San Diego section. Ridership estimates for the high-sped rail option were for 19.8 million passengers annually by 2015 and for the maglev option were 26.4 million by the same date.
California Maglev Transportation Corporation

**Key personnel**
President: Joseph Vranich

This corporation has been formed in Nevada with the intention of developing a Transrapid maglev route between southern California and Las Vegas, Nevada. It has begun attempts to obtain venture capital, secure the use of highway rights-of-way and construct a test track from Las Vegas to the California state line. A franchise from the California Public Utilities Commission would be required for operations within that state.

## Florida Department of Transportation: Rail Office

605 Suwannee Street, Tallahassee, Florida 32399-0450
Tel: (+1 904) 414 45 00   Fax: (+1 904) 922 49 42
Web: http://www.dot.state.fl.us/rail

**Key personnel**
Secretary of Transportation: Tom Barry
State Public Transportation Administrator: Marion Hart Jr
Managers
    Rail Office: J Fred Wise
    Rail Operations: Anne Brewer
    Seaports and Intermodal: Rob Hebert
    Rail Planning and Safety: Jack Heiss

**Statewide Intercity Rail Passenger System**
In February 1996, Florida's Department of Transportation (DOT) announced the award of a 40-year franchise to the Florida Overland Express (FOX) consortium to develop a public/private partnership to construct and operate a 523 km high-speed system connecting Miami, Orlando and Tampa. The consortium comprised Fluor Daniel, GEC Alsthom (now Alstom) and Bombardier, and proposed the adoption of French TGV technology. Florida pledged annual support of $70 million for 14 years and it was also proposed to use federal funding when available and where appropriate.

Early in 1999, the Governor of Florida, Jeb Bush announced a decision to withhold funding for the scheme in the FY1999-2000 budget, effectively terminating it.

## Illinois Department of Transportation

**Chicago-St Louis**
Illinois Department of Transportation (IDOT) has studied this corridor and work to date has emphasised the Chicago-Joliet-Bloomington-Springfield-St Louis alignment, a distance of 451 km. A consultant's report suggested that investment in the order of $420 million is required to attain 200 km/h speeds and 3.5 hour journey times with tilting diesel or turbine equipment. However, more likely is a series of incremental improvements which would allow line speeds to be raised from the current limit of 126 to 176 km/h.

In 1999, the IDOT was working on a draft environmental impact statement for the corridor and collaborating with the Association of American Railroads and the Federal Railroad Administration to develop a level crossing arrestor net to restrain road vehicles when a train approaches and an automatic train protection system suitable for higher speeds.

The cost of upgrading is estimated at $350 million. Once that is complete, IDOT is expected to select a private-sector partner to operate services, which could begin in 2003.

## Illinois/Wisconsin

**Chicago-Milwaukee**
In 1994, the states of Illinois and Wisconsin completed a feasibility study covering a Chicago-Milwaukee high-speed rail corridor. This identified the existing Amtrak route (136 km) between the two cities as the preferred option, with improvements to permit 176 km/h running. Most of the upgrading work falls within the area covered by the Wisconsin Department of Transportation, which has not yet started construction work or set a date for a commencement of accelerated services, although some high-speed running is anticipated by 2006.

## Michigan Department of Transportation

425 W Ottawa, Lansing, Michigan 48909
Tel: (+1 517) 335 29 26   Fax: (+1 517) 373 92 55

**Key personnel**
Intermodal Policy Division: Robert L Kuehne

**Detroit-Chicago**
Michigan continues to work with Amtrak and the US Federal Railroad Administration (FRA) in the incremental development of higher speeds and more frequent service over a 450 km system in the Detroit-Chicago Corridor, also linking these two cities with Ann Arbor and Kalamazoo. Improvements are proposed to train control systems, track work, stations, and rolling stock, allowing speeds to be increased to 176 km/h. In 2002, intercity passenger services were operating at up to 144 km/h. The cost of upgrading the corridor is estimated at $535 million. The Michigan Department of Transportation estimates that by 2010, some 2.6 million passengers annually will use the corridor.

*UPDATED*

## New York State Department of Transportation (NYSDOT)

Office of Passenger and Freight Transportation
Building 7A, Room 302, Albany, New York 12232
Tel: (+1 518) 457 10 46   Fax: (+1 518) 457 31 83
Web: http://www.dot.state.ny.us

**Background**
The state of New York contains the entire New York City-Albany-Buffalo-Niagara Falls Empire Corridor and sections of Amtrak's Northeast Corridor. Consequently, the state, through NYSDOT, has acted in partnership with Amtrak to implement programmes to support the introduction of high-speed rail services on both routes.

*Empire Corridor (New York-Albany-Buffalo)*
Under TEA-21 legislation, the Empire Corridor was officially designated a high-speed rail route in September 1998. The line is mainly owned by CSX, but some sections are owned by Amtrak or the Metropolitan Transportation Authority's Metro North Commuter Railroad. The state and Amtrak are sharing equally the cost of the US$200 million Empire Corridor Improvement Program to upgrade the route, with US$140 million of this figure being invested in infrastructure improvements and the remainder in rolling stock upgrades.

Infrastructure investments include: double-tracking the Albany-Schenectady section (29 km); rehabilitating the Livingstone Avenue swing bridge over the Hudson River in Albany; expanding and improving Amtrak's Rensselaer rolling stock maintenance facility in Albany; improvements to track condition and alignment south of Albany and west of Schenectady; and grade crossing improvements.

Rolling stock expenditure covers the refurbishment of seven RTL III Turboliner gas turbine-powered high-speed trainsets originally built under licence to French designs by Rohr Corporation. The first rebuilt trainset was successfully tested at 200 km/h in February 2001. Refurbishment of the remaining units was in progress in early 2002 at Super Steel Industry's plants near Schenectady. Each trainset comprises two power cars and three trailers, one of which is a café car. While primarily turbine-powered, they are also equipped with third rail collector shoes for operation in New York City tunnels.

Using the refurbished trains on upgraded infrastructure will enable Amtrak to cut 20 minutes from the New York City-Albany (229 km) journey time and 1 hour 30 minutes from existing timings between New York City and Buffalo (690 km). Empire Corridor ridership is expected to rise from 1.2 million passenger journeys annually to 3 million.

*Northeast Corridor*
As a contribution to the Northeast Corridor upgrade, NYSDOT has acted in partnership with Amtrak on several projects, including the provision of a connection between the NEC and the Empire Corridor at Pennsylvania Station in New York City and the redevelopment of the James A Farley Post Office Building as the intercity rail component of the restructured terminal.

*UPDATED*

## North Carolina/Virginia

**Washington DC-Charlotte**
The states of North Carolina and Virginia have been working together to develop a passenger rail corridor between Washington DC and Charlotte, which was identified as a high-speed route under ISTEA legislation. A preliminary engineering study has been undertaken by the North Carolina Department of Transportation and the Virginia Department of Rail and Public Transportation, and in early 1999 an environmental impact study was in progress. The proposed 624 km link would connect the two cities via Richmond, Raleigh and Greensboro, using existing rail alignments with improvements to allow operating speeds of up to 176 km/h. As an interim measure, the state of Virginia has approved a six-stage programme of improvements covering the Washington-Richmond section, which should allow 144 km/h running by 2002.

## Pennsylvania

The Harrisburg-Philadelphia route (166 km) has been identified as a high-speed route under TEA-21 legislation. The existing infrastructure is already electrified, although few electric trains use it, and some sections are suitable for 144 km/h running. Since receiving a request in 1995 from Amtrak for financial assistance to save the deteriorating right-of-way, the Pennsylvania Department of Transportation (PennDOT) has been contributing $2.6 million annually to its upkeep. Future plans foresee track and station improvements and renewal of overhead power supply equipment, as well as the procurement of new trains for 176 km/h operation. No date has been set for the commencement of accelerated services.

A study prepared by the former Pennsylvania High Speed Rail Commission suggested a maglev system to provide a link between Philadelphia and Pittsburgh. Estimated cost of the system is $7.5 billion. An initial $1.3 billion section from Greater Pittsburgh International Airport to Greensburg has been proposed.

## Railroad Commission of Texas

Rail Division, PO Box 12967, Austin, Texas 78711-2967
Tel: (+1 512) 463 70 01   Fax: (+1 512) 463 71 53
Web: http://www.rrc.state.tx.us

**Key personnel**
Director: Jerry L Martin
Special Projects Director: Michael N Jones

A Texas High Speed Rail Authority was created by the Texas legislature's High Speed Rail Act to investigate the possibilities of high-speed rail in Texas, and to grant franchises for the construction, operation, maintenance and financing of high-speed rail routes in Texas, if such routes were determined to be in the public convenience and necessity.

An attempt by the Authority to initiate construction of a TGV route in the early 1990s failed to come to fruition and under Texas law the Authority's independent existence ended in August 1995, when the enabling legislation was repealed. As a matter of law, any party wishing to build a high-speed rail system in Texas can secure a railroad company charter under Texas railroad statutes and can then utilise the right of eminent domain to acquire right-of-way. The main reason for granting a franchise under the now repealed High Speed Rail Act was to confer exclusive rights to a high-speed developer so that it would be easier to finance a capital-intensive project.

*UPDATED*

## Washington Department of Transportation

Transportation Building, PO Box 47383, Olympia, Washington 98504-7383
Tel: (+1 360) 705 79 01   Fax: (+1 360) 705 68 21

**Key personnel**
Rail Program Manager: Ken Uznanski

Strong interest continues in the 540 km Portland (Oregon)-Tacoma/Seattle (Washington)-Vancouver (British Columbia) 'Pacific Northwest' corridor, using Burlington Northern Santa Fe trackage for both high-speed services and commuter trains. The former are operated by Amtrak in partnership with the states of Washington and Oregon, while the latter have been approved as a congestion mitigation strategy competitive with the cost of new highway construction.

Washington DOT secured contract engineering analyses to define track and other improvements necessary for 125 km/h services throughout and a 3 hours 55 minutes journey time. The eventual target is 200 km/h, with related upgrading costs estimated at $1.865 billion.

Phase I investment, committed by the state DOT, was directed at CTC installation, track superelevation, work on crossings, bridges and passing loops and some station modernisation for a total of $24 million (plus an additional $4 million from BNSF), out of a projected all-inclusive corridor cost of $315 million. In March 1994, Washington DOT leased a tilting 12-car Talgo Pendular 200 set from Patentes Talgo of America for what became a popular six-month trial on Amtrak's Portland-Seattle (298 km) 'Mount Adams' service.

In July 1996, Washington DOT announced it had contracted to lease two Talgo sets, one each for the 'Mount Adams' and the 'Mount Baker International', introduced in May 1995 between Seattle and Vancouver.

In March 1997, Patentes Talgo awarded a $50 million contract to a new company, Pacifica, of Seattle, which was formed by the International Association of Machinist & Aerospace Workers for the purpose of building five trainsets. Branded 'Amtrak Cascades', three trainsets entered service in January 1999, powered by examples of Amtrak's order for F59PHI locomotives (see Amtrak entry) with de-engined F40 locomotives forming driving trailers. While the last two of the five-train order were to have been built speculatively for sale to buyers outside the Pacific Northwest, one of these was expected to be used on a second daily Seattle-Vancouver service.

## Emerging Commuter Operations

The following section contains details of commuter projects that appeared well advanced in 1999.

## Denver Regional Transportation District

1600 Blake, Denver, Colorado 80202
Tel: (+1 303) 628 90 00

Denver Regional Transportation District has been considering several new services, with the active participation of Union Pacific (UP) and Burlington Northern Santa Fe (BNSF). On UP, possible destinations from Denver include Golden, Boulder, Fort Collins and Cheyenne, Wyoming, and a service to Denver International Airport has also been proposed. UP ran a test train over 40 km of its tracks; some $140 million of capital acquisition and construction will be required to make a viable airport connection and commence service. Services would operate out of Denver Union station, as would those using BNSF routes.

## Georgia Department of Transportation

The Georgia State Transportation Board commissioned a study by LS Transit Systems Inc which concluded that there were 12 operable lines radiating from Atlanta. The most promising six could be in service by 2010 at a cost of $480 million for capital requirements and would then need $18 million a year in operating assistance. A multimodal transportation centre has been designed to anchor the system in Atlanta but no construction funding has yet been committed by either the public or the private sector.

## Other US Metropolitan Areas

The New York, Susquehanna & Western (qv) started a service called OnTrack in September 1994 in **Syracuse**, New York, using four RDC diesel railcars, of which two had been reconditioned by the operator. There is a midweek 'City Express' shuttle service connecting the Carousel Center shopping complex to a newly constructed Armory Square station and Syracuse University. On days when there is a major Syracuse University sporting event a shuttle runs from Armory Square to the Carrier Dome all-weather arena.

The Michigan Department of Transportation has signed a $400,000 study contract with DeLeuw Cather & Company to develop a plan and programme for the reintroduction of passenger services for **Detroit** and southeastern Michigan. The city of Detroit, General Motors, and the United Auto Workers have all endorsed the project.

The regional plan for **Cleveland**, Ohio, proposes service to Akron and Canton over Conrail trackage. The intended 1996 start-up was not attained but the proposal has received $7.7 million in development funding from the Federal government and has been endorsed by the Ohio Rail Development Commission.

The 20-year plan for metropolitan **St Louis** includes restoration of commuter service over 51 km to Pacific, Missouri, and intermediate suburbs, including Kirkwood which already has Amtrak service. A Union Pacific line south to DeSoto is under review. Consultancy Booz, Allen & Hamilton has been retained to carry out a feasibility study and preliminary design.

In North Carolina, plans have been developed for a 56 km commuter rail system linking **North Raleigh**, **Raleigh** and **Durham** with possible future extensions.

In Utah, Union Pacific has offered 37 km of track, between **Salt Lake City** and Draper, to the regional transit authority in anticipation of major reconstruction on a parallel highway in the near future. Service could eventually be provided from Ogden through Salt Lake City to Provo, a total distance of around 150 km.

Three counties in the **Tampa Bay** area of Florida are studying commuter rail options; the first service is likely to be between Tampa and Lakeland, half the distance to Orlando on CSXT. Federal funds of $2 million were made available in the FY97-98 appropriation bill.

The North Coast Transportation Authority has bought over 195 km of Northwestern Pacific (a subdivision of Southern Pacific's Western Division) trackage between **Willitts** and **Schellville**. The authority opted to be the freight operator while retaining ownership of the property as a potential commuter route for Marin County and San Francisco.

# URUGUAY

## Ministry of Transport & Public Works

Rincón 561, 8to piso, Montevideo
Tel: (+ 598 2) 96 05 09; 95 70 13   Fax: (+598 2) 96 28 83

**Key personnel**
Minister: L Cáceres Behrens

## State Railways Administration (AFE)

Administración de Ferrocarriles del Estado
PO Box 419, Calle La Paz 1095, Montevideo
Tel: (+598 2) 94 08 05   Fax: (+598 2) 94 08 47

**Key personnel**
President: V Vaillant
Vice-President: Dr F Caride B
Directors: O Lopez Balestra, J C Hernandez, E Silveira
Secretary General: V Varela
General Manager: M Anastasia
Deputy General Manager: H Chapuis
Directors
 Legal Affairs: Dr R Jimenez
 Audit: E Garcia
 Special Projects: A Santos
Managers
 Finance and Accounting: G Leva
 Human Resources: J Ceriani
 Operations: H Riccardi
 Rolling Stock: J Lopez Baggi
 Infrastructure: G Tettamanti
 Communications: A Lujambio

Gauge: 1,435 mm
Route length: 2,073 km

### Political background

In October 1991, legislation was passed which effectively reduced the role of AFE to that of track authority with responsibility for maintaining track and co-ordinating operations. It was to be financed via taxation and by charging fees to operators. The rump of AFE has been permitted to compete with private operators in providing services, although the future of the country's railways will depend on private companies owning and running their own motive power and rolling stock.

Of the current network, some 461 km are closed and a further 460 km only in partial operation. Track quality has been seriously prejudiced by the financial cuts of 1988 when substantial numbers of permanent way staff were shed. Total AFE staff numbers fell from 10,000 in 1987 to 2,100 at the start of 1994.

### Finance

By 1997 annual revenue stood at around US$3 million. Recent policy has emphasised tighter cost control, resulting in a reduction of US$1 million in overall operating costs. This will enable subsidy to be cut by US$45 million.

AFE's projected investment strategy for 1994-97 had US$30 million earmarked for track repairs and US$11.8 million to be spent on rolling stock. The remainder was reserved for the purchase of intermodal equipment. During 1996, out of a total investment budget of US$6.53 million, US$4.16 million was to be spent on major track improvements, US$1.55 million on freight wagon refurbishment and US$0.35 million on communications.

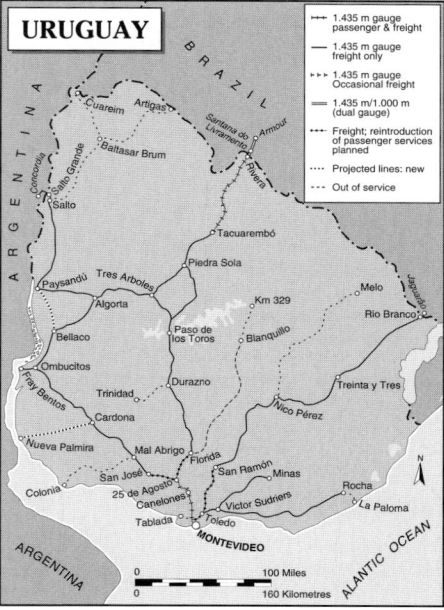

### Passenger operations

In 1988 passenger services were withdrawn as an economy measure. In March 1990 a new political administration set out to restore passenger services by encouraging AFE to undertake joint ventures with the private sector. Between 1990 and 1992 several 'charter' trains were run and in January 1993 regular passenger services were restored on the 118 km Tacuarembó–Rivera line in the north of the country.

Suburban services resumed between Montevideo and 25 de Agosto on 25 August 1993. By November of that year, the four trains running in each direction were carrying over 1,200 passengers a day on the 64 km route. In 1997 476,900 passengers were carried. These two restored passenger services were managed by the private company Luxtol SA, which was responsible for ticket sales, onboard service and the cleaning of trains and stations. AFE received a fixed amount per train-km which covered the hire of train crews and rolling stock.

Expansion and extension of the existing 25 de Agosto services to San José de Mayo and Florida was proposed. However, the return of the anti-rail political party in 1996 had a dramatic effect. The Ferrotransporte company managed by Luxtol had its August 1993 concession withdrawn. AFE itself took over the running of all trains in January 1997 and suspended indefinitely the deep rural Tacuarembó–Rivera train due to its lack of profitability. Although upgrading work on the 118 km route had resulted in a 2 hours 40 minutes end-to-end timing in 1993, by 1996 this had lengthened to 3 hours 45 minutes, despite faster railcars having replaced diesel locomotives and coaches. Intense political lobbying resulted in the Tacuarembó–Rivera train being reinstated on 3 March 1997. Furthermore, the timetabled four trains a day on the Montevideo–25 de Agosto commuter service were increased to five following the reinstatement of the Peñarol–Sayago feeder service.

A further suspension of the Tacuarembó–Rivera service occurred on 31 December 1998 but trains resumed running in April 1999.

### Freight operations

Around 1.5 million tonnes of freight were carried in 1997, compared with an average of 1 million tonnes in the preceding 10 years.

In early 1998, the Compañía Uruguya de Cemento Portland acquired 28 Czech-built second-hand hopper wagons to convey clinker over the 118 km Verdum–Montevideo route using AFE traction.

AFE and the Ministry of Transport and Public Works have invited expressions of interest for a concession to operate timber trains between Montevideo and both Rivera and Blanquillo. The railway expects its timber traffic to increase and is investing in track improvements accordingly: its 10 new GE locomotives were purchased with this timber traffic in mind, and were expected to enable AFE to increase train lengths by 50 per cent and modify the pattern of its freight operations. New sidings to serve industrial customers, silos, containers and handling equipment for containers and pallets are also the subject of investment.

### Intermodal operations

AFE's investment strategy for 1994-97 made provision for the purchase of two container cranes (US$0.56 million) and 150 bulk containers (US$0.9 million). By August 1994, 44 containers had been purchased for US$350,000.

### New lines

Recent planning objectives have included development of the Littoral line and extension of the Central line northwards to a point known as Km 441 from its present terminus at Km 329. In conjunction with the latter project, US$3 million was spent on a new rail bridge across the Río Negro, but the scheme was later abandoned and the bridge converted for use by road traffic.

AFE has been reported as studying the possibility of constructing a new branch from the Montevideo–Fray Bentos line at Cardona to the recently expanded port of Nueva Palmira. The branch would be 70 km long.

### Improvements to existing lines

In 1997 AFE embarked on a two-and-a-half year track renewal programme. The use of 50 kg/m rail and new sleepers has cut derailments by 40 per cent. However, line speeds of 20-60 km/h are still prevalent. Funding for the project is achieved through productivity improvements and cost savings. By mid-1997, repairs were under way on 1,339 km of the 1,926 km operational network. A further 422 km were due for upgrading. The Uruguay army undertook repairs on the 250 km San José–Mercedes route, which had been closed since 1994, and work was reported to have switched to the 98 km Reboledo–Nico Pérez line. The World Bank has provided US$20 million to renovate 587 km to meet the needs of forestry products traffic; this has been matched by US$20 million from the government.

Electrification of the Montevideo–Progreso (26.4 km) section of AFE's route to 25 de Agosto was proposed as part of an LRT scheme under development in 1996. The upgraded infrastructure would be used by dual-mode LRVs similar to those adopted by the German cities of Karlsruhe and Saarbrücken.

In 1998 AFE called for tenders for a light rail line, to be known as 'Tren de la Costa', linking Montevideo and El Pinar. Ten consortia had already expressed an interest in developing the scheme.

### Traction and rolling stock

At the start of 1993 the locomotive fleet comprised 24 Alco/GE and 18 Alsthom 825 hp (615 kW) diesel-electrics, seven diesel-hydraulics for shunting duties and four steam locomotives. In November of that year, AFE took delivery of 10 1,800 hp (1,340 kW) Type C18-7i diesel-electric locomotives built by GE Canada. The investment programme for 1994-97 made provision for the rebuilding of three shunting locomotives.

Passenger services are operated with refurbished equipment, namely six 200 hp (150 kW) Brill 60 railcars of 1936 vintage and 10 Fiat-Materfer coaches. The latter are hauled by Alsthom or newer GE locomotives. AFE has begun refurbishing four Ganz-Mavag diesel trainsets; the first was returned to service in September 1994. Its fleet of passenger equipment also comprises five ex-DB Uerdingen railbuses and 97 other passenger coaches (including 21 wooden-bodied vehicles and 10 Allan trailers used for charter trains), of which half have latterly been unserviceable. In early 1998, AFE was reported to be considering leasing five Class 593 dmus from RENFE in Spain in a package which would include maintenance.

At the start of 1993, AFE operated 2,413 freight wagons. In 1998 delivery was expected from Czech builders of 150 wagons for timber or container traffic and 150 low-sided wagons.

### Track

**Rail:** 20 kg/m (529 km); 30-40 kg/m (1,361 km); 40-50 kg/m (969 km); 50 kg/m or heavier (132 km)
**Sleepers:** Steel and timber
**Min curve radius:** Generally 500 m; less than 500 m over 97 km

---

## Líneas Férreas Uruguayas (LFU)

Guaviyú 2941, 11800 Montevideo
Tel: (+598 2) 203 67 42   Fax: (+598 2) 203 67 42
Swiss project office:
Fahrplancenter, Tellstrasse 45, CH-8400 Winterthur, Switzerland
Tel: (+41 52) 213 12 20   Fax: (+41 52) 213 12 20

### Key personnel

Uruguay:
  Marcelo Benoit; Esteban Martínez; Alvaro Saavedra
Switzerland:
  Peter Lais; Samuel Rachdi

### Political background

In 1988 the State Railways Administration (AFE) withdrew all rail passenger services throughout Uruguay. In 1993 services were reinstated on two short sections of line, Montevideo–25 de Agosto and Tacuarembó–Rivera, leaving all remaining towns and cities without access to passenger rail transport. Many of these towns are not served by the main national roads network and some are inaccessible during adverse weather. Líneas Férreas Uruguayas (LFU), a Uruguayan-Swiss consortium, plans to reintroduce passenger services over as many lines as possible. In 1999 LFU had received network access approval from AFE for modest charges and was to operate without government subsidy. The consortium was seeking low-cost second-hand lightweight rolling stock. In Uruguay the consortium was finalising the most appropriate form that the operating company should take.

### Passenger operations

In a first phase, the proposed fleet of railbuses would operate services on three types of route: lines with no parallel road; lines between major communities; and suburban lines around Montevideo and in the Salto/Paysandú area. Three daily long-distance services are planned: one from Rivera, in the north of the country, to Salto in the west and connecting at Tres Arboles with a service to Montevideo; one serving the densely populated Montevideo-Paso de los Toros corridor, complementing the service from Tres Arboles, which takes the same route; and a third possible weekly service between Montevideo and Treinta y Tres. Proposed short-haul services include Salto—Paysandú, Rio Branco—Treinta y Tres, Treinta y Tres—José Pedro Varela, Florida—Sarandí del Yí and Montevideo—La Floresta. The consortium has also expressed an interest in taking over the Tacuarembó—Rivera service should AFE wish to withdraw from it.

LFU was aiming at a commencement of services by the end of 1999.

A second planned phase of service development by LFU foresees the possible procurement of 20 to 25 X4500 'Caravelle' railcars from France for deployment on long-distance services and to equip a reintroduction of services from Montevideo to Fray Bentos, Colonia, Melo, Rocha and Rivera and between Sarandí del Yí and Islas de la Paloma. In this phase LFU would also take over responsibility for track maintenance over lines no longer used by AFE.

---

# UZBEKISTAN

## Ministry of Transport

ul T Shewchenko 7, 700061 Tashkent
Fax: (+7 3712) 59 52 51

### Key personnel

Head of Rail Transport: Normat Ermetov

**UPDATED**

## Uzbekistan Railway (UTY)

Uzbekistan Temir Yullari
T Shevchenko 7, 700061 Tashkent
Tel: (+7 3712) 32 44 00   Fax: (+7 3712) 59 52 51

### Key personnel

President: Ravshan Zakhidov

Gauge: 1,520 mm
Route length: 3,950 km
Electrification: 620 km at 25 kV AC

### Organisation

This network comprises the greater part of the former Soviet Railways Central Asian Railway, centred on the artery from Chardzhou in Turkmenistan to Bukhara, Samarkand, Dzhizak and Tashkent. It became an independent entity from January 1992. The northwest and far-eastern sections could only be accessed through the neighbouring states of Turkmenistan and Tajikistan respectively which, given the political tensions in the whole region, complicated the railway's operations considerably.

Due mainly to clients' continued failure to pay their debts, the railways were in severe financial difficulties in 1999. The labour force remained excessive, and electric locomotives were reported, on average, to spend only seven per cent of their day actually hauling trains.

However, in March 2001 a presidential order converted UTY into an open share company, with the aim of introducing competition and encouraging investment.

The railway is divided into five regional administrations: Tashkent, Ferganar, Bukhara, Aral and Karshi.

The labour force (excluding workers in non-rail activity) was 45,223 in 1999, compared to 53,842 in 1997. Operating workers in 1999 totalled 29,406.

### Passenger operations
The passenger business stood at 20.4 million journeys in 1993, for 5.9 billion passenger-km. By 1999, passenger journeys had declined to 13.3 million and passenger-km to 1.9 billion. A number of passenger trains were withdrawn in 1999. To cut costs further, remaining passenger services in the capital were concentrated on the Central station.

The extra costs associated with catering for this growth led to an increased financial loss for the railway, as a result of which fares were raised substantially in early 1995. Local authorities contributed towards the cost of running new high-quality trains between major cities. Some trains were leased to their staffs, and were said to be very presentable.

No new coaches had been purchased for the Central Asian Railway in the two years before the break-up of the USSR, and subsequently the lack of repair facilities has exacerbated the shortage of passenger stock. Steps were taken in 1998 to alleviate this situation (see 'Traction and rolling stock').

### Freight operations
Freight traffic has slumped following the break-up of the Soviet Union, with freight tonnage down from 90.8 million in 1991 to 57 million in 1993. An expected recovery in 1994 failed to materialise, with tonnage falling to 40 million. However, in 1995 volume increased to 46 million tonnes following improved international transits. But by 1997 it was down to 41 million. In 1999, 41 million tonnes were again carried, but tonne-km were 13.9 billion, down from 16.5 billion in 1997. The railway carries nine-tenths of the total common-carrier freight of the republic. The dominant traffics are cotton and construction materials.

### New lines
From early 2001 freight services to the northwest began to use the new 341 km cut-off route Uchkuduk–Misken–Nukus, thereby avoiding transit across Turkmenistan. The 115 km Misken–Sultanuizdag line was completed in 1999, linking the Aral region with central Uzbekistan. There is also a project to link the Karshi–Kitab and Termez–Denau lines in the south, again bypassing Turkmenistan.

Work on this 124 km Guzar–Kumkurgan line began in 1996.

In the east, a bypass is proposed from Angren to the Kokand–Namangan line, hitherto accessed from Khavast through Tajikistan. However, the very difficult terrain makes any early start on this project unlikely.

In 1997, construction began of the 50 km Shavat–Dzhurmurtau line.

A works for track products has been opened, producing some 400 categories of material formerly imported.

### Improvements to existing lines
The modernisation, including electrification, of the main trunk route between Bukhara, Samarkand and Tashkent is continuing. In 1998 a loan worth US$100 million was made available by the Asian Development Bank to upgrade 320 km of this route from Chengel'dy (Kazakhstan) to Tashkent and Samarkand. Then, in late 2000, the Bank approved a loan to help modernise the 341 km Samarkand–Bukhara–Khodzha Davlet main line, with additional investment from UTY.

### Traction and rolling stock
The current traction is as follows:
Diesel (main line) locomotives 2TE10/3TE10 variants: 1,082 units (480 ½ double and triple locomotives);
Diesel (shunting) locomotives TEM2/chME3: 313 locomotives (all single units);
Electric (main line) locomotives 3VL80/VL80, 2VL60/VL60: 173 units (84 double and triple locomotives); electric multiple-units ER2, ER9: 90 units (45 sets).

The ER2 units (24 two-car units) are stored out of use.

In early 1998, the government of Uzbekistan announced that it was to participate in a joint venture with Ukraine to manufacture diesel locomotives at the latter country's Lugansk plant and in 2001 negotiations were proceeding for the acquisition of 30 Skoda-built electric locomotives.

Five new coaches were acquired in 1998 and a Russian-built Demikhovo emu has been on trial. In the same year an additional 25 vehicles were ordered from Bombardier Transportation's DWA subsidiary in German, using Japanese finance. A Japanese-financed passenger car depot at Tashkent should also ease the situation and this facility may also build new passenger stock.

No new passenger cars were received in 1999, but there were 100 new freight cars (50 in 1998, nil in 1997). Passenger coaches total 1,450 (many are no longer serviceable). Freight wagons total 32,500 (many are no longer serviceable).

In 2001, the European Bank for Reconstruction and Development granted a loan to assist with the refurbishment and rehabilitation of diesel locomotives. Also planned was the construction of a new locomotive repair shop in Tashkent, with some funding provided by the Overseas Economic Co-operation Fund of Japan.

### Signalling and communications
Provision of fibre optic communications technology for the 630 km section from Bukhara to Keles, on the border with Kazakhstan, forms a key feature of a five-year modernisation programme commenced in 2000.

### Electrification
Apart from the 354 km between Tashkent and Samarkand, a few short industrial lines have been electrified. Some routes in the Fergana basin were electrified in 1993, including Khavast–Bekabad. In 1999 the Samarkand–Marakand and Misken–Sultannuisdag lines were energised, which brought electrified mileage to 620 km. Another 1,340 km are to be electrified over the longer term.

This includes the 275 km section between Samarkand and Bukhara, electrification of which was in progress in 2002.

*UPDATED*

---

# VENEZUELA

## Ministry of Transport & Communications

Caracas

**Key personnel**
Minister: C Zaa

## Venezuelan State Railways (Ferrocar)

Instituto Autónomo Ferrocarriles del Estado
PO Box 146, Avenida Lecuna, Parque Central, Torre Este, Piso 45, Caracas 1010
Tel: (+58 2) 509 35 00;1    Fax: (+58 2) 574 70 21

**Key personnel**
President: Ing Juan Carlos Hiedra Cobo
Vice-President: O Ramirez Osio
Vice-President, Legal Affairs: C Salazar
Vice-President, Marketing: Antonio Zapata

Vice-President, Internal Accounting: L Morales
Managers
    Construction: Olegario Braga
    Operations: C Alberto Buenaño
    Administration and Finance: I Antunez
    Planning and Budgets: G Vanorio
    Personnel: Mercedes Polo Mimo
    Property: R Gosselain

Gauge: 1,435 mm
Route length: 434 km

### Political background
Recent legislation pertaining to Venezuela's ambitious railway construction programme has made provision for private funding to be used alongside public money.

### Organisation
The Ferrocar system consists of the 176 km Puerto Cabello–Barquisimeto route with branches from Yaritagua to Acarigua and Morón to Tucucas.

Freight traffic, amounting to 422,541 tonnes (54.5 million tonne-km) in 1997, consists of grain, fertiliser, sand and sugar cane waste (bagasse), often moving via private sidings serving industry.

Ferrocar has in the past operated passenger services on the 173 km Puerto Cabello–Barquisimeto line, but at last report no passenger services were operating.

At the end of 1997, Ferrocar employed nearly 500 people.

### Finance
Ferrocar's provisional investment budget for 1996 amounted to Br14.963 billion, including Br1.341 billion for major track improvements, Br567 million for workshops and repair facilities and Br13.055 billion for new lines, of which Br12.493 billion was to pay for civil works on the Cua–Puerto Cabello project.

### New lines
*National Railways Plan*
Venezuela's revised National Railways Plan aims to create a 3,447 km system of lines of local, regional and national

# RAILWAY SYSTEMS/Venezuela

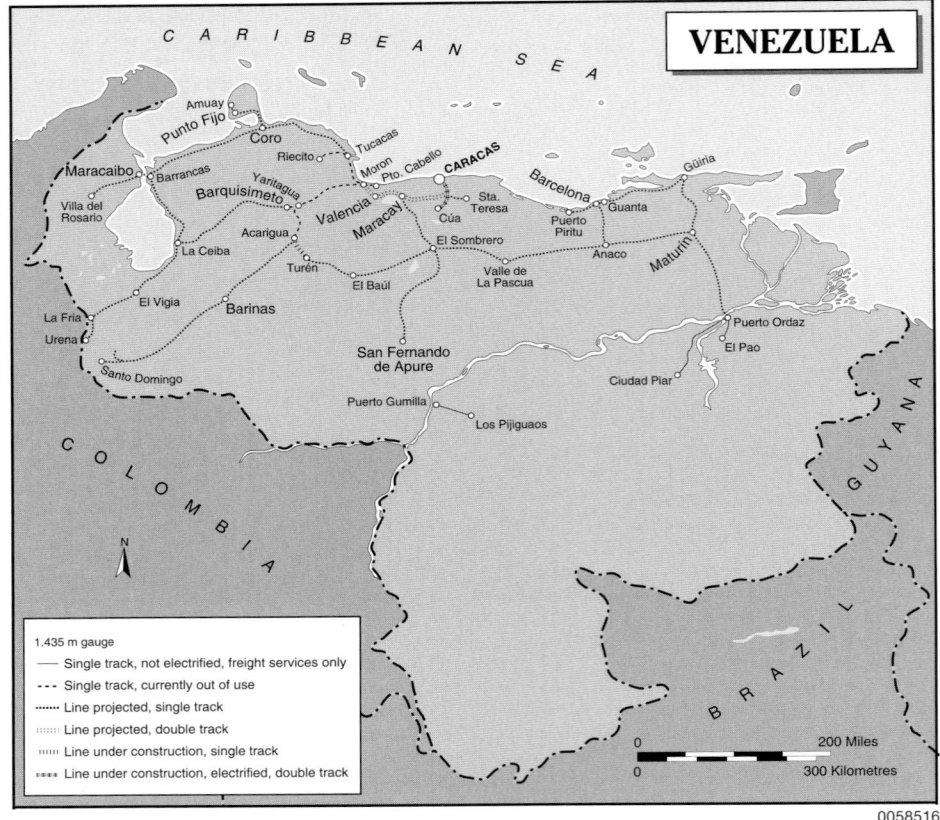

**Map legend:**
1.435 m gauge
— Single track, not electrified, freight services only
--- Single track, currently out of use
······ Line projected, single track
∷∷∷ Line projected, double track
∥∥∥ Line under construction, single track
▬▬▬ Line under construction, electrified, double track

importance by 2020. The programme involves the eventual creation of four interconnecting systems that are known as the Central Western, Central Region, Eastern Plains and Western railways.

### Central Western Railway

Ferrocar's existing routes form the core of this system. Extension of the branch leaving the main line at Morón beyond its present terminus at Tucacas to Riecito, to a total length of 109 km, had been completed in early 1998 but not inaugurated. Construction, costed at a total of Br2.3 billion, has been funded by Ferrocar and the national oil company PDVSA, as the line will carry phosphates from deposits at Riecito to a petrochemical works at Morón. This traffic is eventually expected to amount to some 1.2 million tonnes a year, and Ferrocar sees potential for tourist services in the Tucacas and Chichiriviche areas.

A proposed 285 km extension would take the Riecito branch to Coro, Puerto Cardón and Amuay for oil industry traffic. This has been costed at Br15.5 billion for infrastructure and Br8.5 million for rolling stock. A total of Br10 million was allocated in 1996 to studies for a 185 km Yaracal–Coro route.

In 1991, work began on a 45 km extension from Acarigua to Turén, for which financing had been approved. The majority of the civil engineering work had been completed by early 1994, but further funding was required before tracklaying and terminal construction could begin. Costed at Br0.7 billion, the Acarigua–Turén extension is expected to carry some 500,000 to 800,000 tonnes of freight (mostly agricultural produce) a year with potential for traffic to grow by 20 per cent a year.

From Turén, a 115 km extension is planned to El Baúl. From El Baúl, a further eastward extension would connect the Central Western system with the proposed Eastern Plains network at El Sombrero.

### Central Region Railway

The major Ferrocar enterprise now under way is the long-planned new east-west Central Region system, also known as the Central Trunk. This will extend from Caracas to Puerto Cabello via Cúa, Maracay and Valencia, and will link the capital and the central region of the country with the Central Western trunk at Puerto Cabello. It has been designated a project of national importance. At Puerto Cabello the Central Trunk would also connect with the Central Western, enabling the latter to rail coal and minerals to the Caracas conurbation.

After a call for tenders in 1989, an Italian-Japanese-Venezuelan consortium, Contuy Medio, led by Cogefar-Impresit SpA of Milan, won in 1991 the competition to build the first 43 km from Caracas to Cúa, serving the expanding new town of Tuy Medio. A contract valued at US$800 million was eventually signed with the Venezuelan government on 29 May 1996, whereby the consortium agreed to meet 50 per cent of the construction cost. Ferrocar's 1996 investment budget made provision for a Br12.493 billion advance payment for civil works on the Caracas–Cúa route, expected to open in 2001 and initially to carry some 64,000 passengers per day, rising to 110,000 per day by 2007.

This first stage traverses difficult terrain, with a difference of 623 m in level between its extremities, and will involve a ruling gradient of 2.3 per cent and 10.6 km of tunnelling, including one bore of 6.8 km. The line will be electrified at 25 kV 60 Hz AC, and laid with a single track later to be doubled.

Maximum speeds of 120 km/h will be exploited by 13 Japanese-built four-car emus consisting of two motor cars enclosing two trailers, with a capacity for 448 passengers. CTC will be located in Caracas and there will be two intermediate stations. The Caracas terminus will be at Mercado for interchange with Line 3 of the city's metro system, currently under construction.

The second stage of the Central Region system is the 176 km Cúa–Puerto Cabello section. Private finance was expected to fund the project, costed at Br52.7 billion for civil works and Br12.6 billion for rolling stock; Ferrocar allocated Br213 million to further studies in 1996. The Cúa–Puerto Cabello route is to be engineered for 180 km/h passenger operation, but is also expected to carry heavy freight traffic once Venezuela's national network emerges. Ferrocar expects to eventually handle 96,000 passengers and 139,000 tonnes of freight between Caracas and Puerto Cabello every day. A construction contract, possibly as part of an operating concession, was due to be awarded in early 1998. Groups from Canada, France and Mexico were reported to have expressed an interest.

### Eastern Plains Railway

A proposed Eastern Plains system will be formed of south-north and east-west axes together totalling 938 km. The 394 km south-north route would start at Puerto Ordaz on the River Orinoco, connecting with the existing 141 km route to Ciudad Piar operated by Ferrominera for the transport of iron ore. From Puerto Ordaz, the new line heads north through Maturín for a deep sea port at Puerto Guiria on the Gulf of Cariaco, in the state of Sucre. Costed at Br32.5 billion for civil works and Br4.3 billion for rolling stock, the south-north axis is expected by Ferrocar to carry 12 to 21 million tonnes of iron ore a year.

In 1995, Br45 million was spent on surveying work for the Puerto Ordaz–Maturín–Guacarapo component (342 km) of the project, allocated Br75 million for further studies in 1996. In 1995, Ferrocar concluded agreements with the states of Anzoategui, Bolívar and Monagas to proceed with the south-north axis of the Eastern Plains system (with branches to Barcelona and Guanta on the Caribbean) to be built either as a mixed private/state venture or by offering concessions. Expressions of interest were sought in 1996 by mining company CVG Bauxilum (see Los Pijiguaos Railway) to construct a route from Ciudad Guayana (east of Puerto Ordaz) to Puerto Guiria or another Caribbean port.

The 544 km east-west line would run from Maturín via Zaraza and El Sombrero to a junction with the Central Trunk at Cagua. Traffic would consist mainly of agricultural produce moving westwards from the eastern plains, estimated to be in the region of 8 million tonnes a year. The Maturín–Cagua route has been costed at Br45.3 billion for civil works and Br6.5 billion for rolling stock.

### Western Railway

This system's principal traffic would be coal and phosphates from deposits in the southwest of Venezuela, moving to tidewater for export. International links have also been considered and, in May 1996, Ferrovias of Colombia announced proposals for a new 126 km route from Cúcuta across the border to La Concha and La Ceiba on Lake Maracaibo in Venezuela. The proposed Western Railway's initial 116 km section from La Fría to La Concha would carry some 3 million tonnes a year, and has been costed at Br10.6 billion for civil works and Br0.9 billion for rolling stock. Construction of this route has been deemed a priority and was to be publicly funded to the tune of 50 to 80 per cent. In 1995, Br31.3 million was spent on initial studies for the Urena–La Fría–La

*Ferrocar GM-EMD GP15-1 diesel-electric locomotive at Barquisimeto* (Eddie Barnes)

Concha–La Ceiba route, including geotechnical and hydrological work, and further La Frí–La Ceiba (243 km) studies received Br198 million in 1996.

The Western Railway would also include three other routes. The first is El Vigía–La Ceiba–Barquisimeto (417 km), connecting the La Fría–La Concha–La Ceiba route with the Central Western system and costing Br33.2 billion for civil works and Br6.9 billion for rolling stock. This line would carry 7.9 milion tonnes a year according to Ferrocar's forecasts. Much of this traffic would be coal and agricultural products.

A second line, 472 km long, would head north from La Fría to a new port on the Gulf of Venezuela, known as Puerto Nuevo, via Maracaibo and the coal mining area of Guasare. Civil works are costed at Br41.9 billion. The third route runs for 446 km from Santo Domingo via Barinas to the southern branch of the Central Western at Turén. This route would carry 10 million tonnes of traffic a year, principally coal and phosphates. Civil works have been costed at Br38 billion.

### Improvements to existing lines

In anticipation of heavier traffic expected to be generated by the extension of its branches (roughly twice the present amount) and the construction of other connecting trunk routes, upgrading work was undertaken on the track of the Puerto Cabello–Barquisimeto main line of the Central Western Railway in the early 1990s. However, in late 1997 Ferrocar admitted that track had badly deteriorated, and that US$67 million had been assigned to fund an 18 month upgrading programme.

### Traction and rolling stock

At the start of 1998, Ferrocar operated 17 diesel locomotives, namely six GM-EMD 1,300 kW GP9s, four GM-EMD 1,100 kW GP15-1s and two 110 kW shunting locomotives. Other rolling stock comprised 14 passenger coaches and 264 freight wagons.

**Type of coupler in standard use:** US Type E
**Type of braking in standard use:** Air

### Track
**Rail:** ASCE 49 kg/m and UIC 60 kg/m
**Sleepers:** Dywidag concrete, 2,500 × 227 × 300 mm
**Spacing:** 1,670/km, 1,336/km in curves
**Min curve radius:** 800 m
**Max gradient:** 1.4%
**Max permitted axleload:** 31.75 tonnes
**Max speed:** 70 km/h

## Ferrominera

CVG Ferrominera Orinoco CA
PO Box 399, Puerto Orduz, Bolívar State
Tel: (+58 86) 30 31 11   Fax: (+58 86) 30 36 56

### Key personnel
General Superintendent, Piar Division: E Carabello
Superintendents
 Pao Division: H Brazon
 General Shops: M Aro G

Track and Structures: D Massiah R
General Supervisor: J Diaz

Gauge: 1,435 mm
Route length: 196 km

### Freight operations
Ferrominera, a state-owned company, operates two railways in eastern Venezuela principally for the transport of iron ore to the River Orinoco. The line linking Ciudad Piar in the Cerro Bolívar range with Puerto Ordaz on the river is 141 km long, and that connecting El Pao with Palua on the Orinoco 55 km long. Annual carryings amount to some 30 million tonnes of freight.

### Traction and rolling stock
Ferrominera operated a fleet of 36 diesel locomotives and 1,587 freight wagons in 1990. In 1996, Freios Knorr of Brazil was contracted to supply the company with 100 braking systems to be fitted to new wagons ordered from Transimpex of Bulgaria.

## Los Pijiguaos Railway

CVG Bauxilum
Carretera Nacional Caicara-Puerto Ayacucho, Los Pijiguaos, Bolívar State
Tel: (+58 2) 572 16 20   Fax: (+58 2) 993 76 85

### Key personnel
President: Pedro Mantellini
Executive Vice-President: José L Garcia G
General Manager: Gustavo Quintero
Mineral Handling Manager: Oscar Portes
Traffic and Railway Maintenance Superintendent:
 Juan Carlos Fermin

Gauge: 1,435 mm
Route length: 52 km

### Freight operations
CVG Bauxilum operates a 52 km railway linking bauxite deposits at Los Pijiguaos with the Orinoco river port of Gumilla. Opened in 1989, the line carried 5 million tonnes in 1995.

### Improvements to existing lines
A new mineral handling system has been installed which will allow the railway to carry 5.3 million tonnes of bauxite a year. The system incorporates an automatic loading station and an automatic car dumper, both with a capacity of 3,600 tonnes an hour, and allows six trains carrying 2,500 tonnes each at 60 km/h to be operated in a period of 8 hours.

### Traction and rolling stock
At the end of 1995, the railway operated five diesel-electric locomotives, including GM-EMD SD38-2 and SW900 types, and 119 freight wagons, mostly 90 tonne gondolas.

**Type of coupler in standard use:** F150
**Type of braking in standard use:** 26L, 24RL, 6BL

### Track
**Rail:** AREA 132 RE, 54.75 kg/m
**Sleepers:** Dywidag concrete, 2,500 × 227 × 300 mm
**Spacing:** 1,667/km
**Fastenings:** RN 300
**Min curve radius:** 36°
**Max gradient:** 1%
**Max permissible axleload:** 30 tonnes

# VIETNAM

## Ministry of Communications and Transport

80 Tran Hung Dao, Hanoi
Tel: (+84 4) 25 20 79

### Key personnel
Minister: Buy Danh Luu
Railways Director: Nguyen Hieu Liem

## Vietnam Railways (DSVN)

Duong Sat Viet Nam
118 Duong le Duan, Hanoi
Tel: (+84 4) 822 14 68   Fax: (+84 4) 825 49 98
e-mail: vr.hn.irstd@fpt.vn

### Key personnel
Director General: Dr Dao Dinh Binh
Deputy Directors General:
 Nguyen Trong Bach, Vuong Dinh Khanh,
 Nguyen Huu Bang, Phan Van Gian,
 Dang Duc
Directors
 Hanoi Division: Nguyen Phat
 Da Nang Division: Bui Tan Phuong
 Ho Chi Minh City Division: Dang Ngoc Thanh
 Planning and Investment: Nguyen Ngockhoi
 International Relations – Science and Technology:
  Nguyen Dat Tuong

Deputy Director, International Relations – Science and Technology: Phan Quoc Hung

Gauge: 1,435 mm; 1,000 mm; mixed gauge
Route length: 209 km; 2,625 km; 308 km

### Political background
After a long period of stagnation, DSVN underwent reorganisation in 1994-95, following the government's agreement to separate infrastructure and operating costs from the beginning of 1995. The railway, freed from responsibility for upkeep and renewal of its infrastructure, nevertheless continues to manage day-to-day execution of these tasks and retains control over rolling stock maintenance and procurement. It is required to cover its operating costs as well as remitting 10 per cent of revenues to the government as a track access charge. In return, the government shoulders all costs associated with track, signalling, telecommunications and structures.

DSVN is not entirely free from government control, however, as it cannot set domestic fares at an economic level. In its first year of operation without subsidy, DSVN turned in a loss of D134 billion, but in 1995 it achieved the balance of revenue and expenditure that was intended to be the norm under the restructuring programme, largely by means of big increases in freight rates. This trend continued through 1996-98.

Despite the restructuring, funding remains problematical. Clearing the huge backlog of infrastructure and rolling stock maintenance could absorb as much as D400 billion annually, a sum which can only be delivered by new funding sources such as joint ventures with the private sector. DSVN controls all the country's railway manufacturing and service companies, many of which would benefit from foreign participation.

### Organisation
The most important route is the main line linking Hanoi with Ho Chi Minh (Saigon) (1,726 km); other routes radiate from Hanoi to the port of Haiphong (96 km) and Quan Trieu (mixed-gauge, 54 km), while two lines run to the border with China – northwest to Lao Cai and northeast to Dong Dang (mixed-gauge). A 1,435 mm gauge line runs from Quan Trieu to Kep and Halong.

Hanoi has a western orbital route, built in the 1980s, which diverges from the main line to the north at Dong Anh, crosses the Red River on the Thang Long bridge, and joins the southern main line to Ho Chi Minh (Saigon) at Van Dien.

Operationally, the railway is divided into three divisions based on Hanoi, Da Nang and Ho Chi Minh.

At the end of 1998 DSVN employed 42,330 staff, compared with 65,000 ten years earlier.

| Traffic (million) | 1997 | 1998 | 1999 |
|---|---|---|---|
| Passenger journeys | 9.3 | 9.7 | 9.3 |
| Passenger-km | 2,476 | 2,535 | 2,727 |
| Freight tonnes | 4.8 | 4.8 | 5.0 |
| Freight tonne-km | 1,533 | 1,327 | 1,398 |

### Passenger operations
By 1994, passenger traffic had fallen below 8 million journeys annually, with some 80 per cent of the

## Diesel locomotives

| Class | Wheel arrangement | Power kW | Speed km/h | Weight tonnes | No in service | First built | Builders Mechanical | Engine | Transmission |
|---|---|---|---|---|---|---|---|---|---|
| D4H | Bo-Bo | 290 | 50 | 24 | 190[1] | 1968 | Kambarka | 1D12-400 | H |
| D4H | Bo-Bo | 325 | 50 | 24 | 1 | 1997 | Dong Co | 368 MTU 12V 183 | H |
| D5H[2] | Bo-Bo | 347 | 50 | 40 | 13 | 1968 | Walkers | CAT D-355 | H |
| D9E | Bo-Bo | 670 | 100 | 52 | 28 | 1963 | GE | D 379 | E |
| D11H[3] | Bo-Bo | - | - | - | (58) | 1979 | 23 August | - | H |
| D12E | Bo-Bo | 736 | 80 | 56 | 40 | 1985 | ČKD | K6S 230DR | E |
| D13E | Co-Co | 895 | 100 | 72 | 12 | 1984 | DLW | 251-D | E |
| D18E | Co-Co | 1,472 | 100 | 84 | 16 | 1982 | CMI | LTR 240-C | E |

[1] 11 locomotives operational on 1,435 mm gauge
[2] Purchased second-hand from Queensland Railways 1993-96
[3] Whole fleet of 58 out of service

passenger-km logged by the Hanoi–Ho Chi Minh (Saigon) route. Traffic on this artery is expected to grow to more than 14 million journeys a year, a renaissance which started in 1994 with the commissioning of a new premium service, the Reunification Express, which cut the transit time by half to 36 hours.

Further growth is expected on the two routes to the Chinese border. At Dong Dang, a metre-gauge DSVN train connects twice-weekly with a 1,435 mm Chinese Railways service to Pinxiang. On the 530 km all-metre-gauge route from Hanoi via Lao Cai to Kunming in China, an inaugural direct service ran in April 1997. Four services a week were planned.

Radical improvement must await delivery of new rolling stock. Introduction of high-quality air conditioned coaches is seen as vital to help DSVN retain its share of the middle-distance traffic which has not yet yielded to bus competition. DSVN's Gia Lam works at Hanoi can now turn out coaches to a higher standard than the basic accommodation deemed satisfactory for local trains. These are based on the most recent cars supplied from India, but air conditioning equipment requires costly foreign exchange and it will be some time before sufficient cars are available to make a real impact.

### Freight operations

Recent years have seen considerable growth in freight traffic. Tonne-km in 1994 were 1.37 billion; this figure rose to 1.75 billion in 1995. Severe weather in 1996 pegged traffic at 1.68 billion tonne-km and a modest decline occurred in 1997 and 1998, attributed to the Asian economic environment. However, a modest revival to 1.4 billion tonne-km was achieved in 1999.

There is considerable potential for increased traffic with China, both over the 1,435 mm gauge route via Dong Dang and the metre-gauge line that provides a through connection from the port of Haiphong to Kunming. On the Dong Dang route (on which trans-shipment is required at the gauge change at the border) international services resumed in 1996, after having been broken off during a border dispute in 1979; there are now four freight services daily, aggregating 6,400 tonnes.

### Intermodal operations

A joint venture between VSDN and New Zealand interests known as Rail Express has opened up the route between the port of Haiphong and Hanoi with a US$5 million investment package. Just over US$3 million was contributed to this by the venture's New Zealand partner, Minzr Containers Ltd, a company established by engineering conglomerate McConnell International which is drawing in rail expertise from Tranz Rail.

VSDN has improved the track between the two cities and an on-dock rail terminal has been built in Haiphong. Rail Express obtained its operating licence in August 1996 and expected to start running three container trains a day (total capacity 60 TEU) between Haiphong and the capital during 1997. More powerful locomotives and new wagons are needed if the venture is to expand.

Once it is better established, Rail Express intends to expand by beginning services on the Ho Chi Minh-Hanoi route. The port of Ho Chi Minh has a throughput of 300,000 TEU, but currently none of these boxes goes by rail.

### New lines

DSVN has long sought a link with Thailand, but this would require a line across intervening Laos (qv) which is only now building its first railway line. A line from Ho Chi Minh to Phnom Penh in Cambodia (Kampuchea) also figures in ASEAN proposals for improved links between member countries.

In 1995, ITF Intertraffic, a subsidiary of Germany's Daimler-Benz, studied proposals for a 15 km cross-city elevated railway to be built through the congested centre of Hanoi. Funding for feasibility and preliminary engineering studies was being sought in 1996, and the current five-year plan includes a proposal to buy diesel railcars for suburban services. More recently, a 120 km line from Ho Chi Minh to the seaside resort of Vung Tau has been canvassed.

New links to ports are being studied. A 90 km line from the port of Vung Tau to Ho Chi Minh via Dong Nai could be built using the build-operate-transfer form of contract. In 2000, a feasibility study was completed for this project, which could carry 3 million tonnes of cargo and 9.5 million passengers annually. Good access to a new deep sea port being built at Cai Lan, which will open in 2000, would be assured by construction of a 42 km cut-off between Yen Vien near Hanoi and Pha Lai.

Other proposed links are from Ho Chi Minh to the tourist region of Dalat, and a railway from Lok Ninh to Da Nang.

### Improvements to existing lines

The mammoth rehabilitation task continues to be hampered by funding shortages. Trackwork is largely ancient and in poor condition, with worn-out 30 kg/m rail. A particularly critical problem is the state of the system's numerous bridges and viaducts – 1,658 of them, with a total length of some 39 km. Over many metal bridges a speed limit of 5 km/h is imposed because of corrosion or other weaknesses.

Rehabilitation of the Hanoi–Ho Chi Minh main line, aimed at increasing passenger train speeds to 120 km/h, remains the priority in the investment plan for the years through to the end of the century. Re-laying of 400 km of track with 40 kg/m rail, replacement of nine bridges and strengthening of 70 other structures is costed at D2.5 billion. Japanese loans totalling US$55 million were to fund the reconstruction of eight bridges on this line.

A reduction in journey times will also result from work on the important route linking Hanoi with the port of Haiphong. Since 1995, passenger services have covered this 102 km route in 2 hours, an average speed of 51 km/h. DSVN commissioned UK-based Balfour Beatty and Adtranz to undertake a modernisation study which would include complete track renewal and the installation of new signalling equipment with the aim of increasing passenger trains speeds to 80-100 km/h and freight to 60-80 km/h.

The two routes to China, via Lao Cai and Dong Dang, are also earmarked for early attention.

Swiss assistance was sought for rehabilitation of the 89 km rack-and-adhesion line between the coastal town of Thap Cham and the central highlands city of Da Lat. Steam-worked before its closure in 1976, the restored line will be worked by new diesel locomotives.

Japanese loans agreed in 1995 have been used in part to fund rehabilitation work, in particular reconstruction of the many damaged or substandard bridges. Queensland Rail has also supplied technical assistance with rehabilitation, while India's Rites has been working with DSVN since the 1970s.

### Signalling and telecommunications

1,096 route-km are controlled by toneless semi-automatic block signalling, and token block working applies to 638 km. Semaphore signals and token-block working on the Hanoi–Ho Chi Minh–Dong Dang and Haiphong–Lao Cai lines are to be replaced by colourlights and semi-automatic block. Vulnerable lineside telecommunications cabling would be replaced by a digital telephone and information system that would eventually cover the entire network.

### Traction and rolling stock

At the beginning of 1999, the railway owned 67 steam and 325 diesel locomotives, but of the latter only 300 were serviceable and only 180 or so in daily operation. Steam traction remains in use on account of the plentiful local supply of coal. The rolling stock fleet totalled 760 passenger cars and 4,066 freight wagons, although some of these were unserviceable.

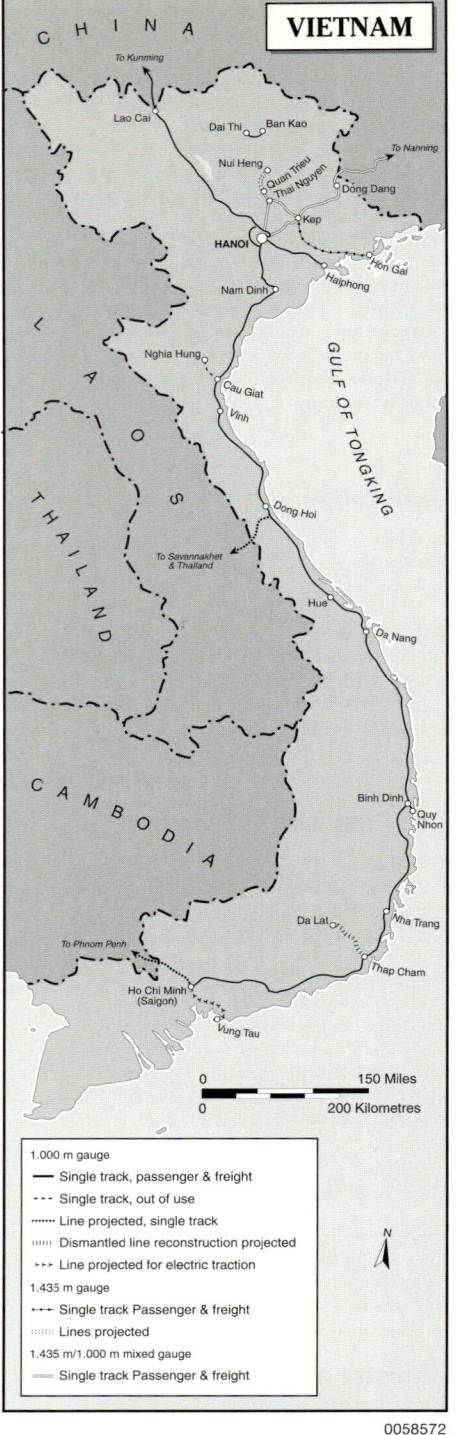

Recent deliveries include 15 1,000 kW, 251 D-engined diesel-electric Co-Co locomotives, similar to Indian Railways' Type YDM4, from India's Projects & Equipment Corp (PEC); and from Belgian industry came 16 1,300 kW, 84 tonne diesel-electric Co-Cos with Cockerill engines. ČKD Praha has delivered 10 750 kW, 56-tonne Type DEV-736 diesel-electric locomotives for metre-gauge. Other diesel traction includes GE and Russian-built Type TY 300 kW units, and 13 locos bought second-hand from Queensland Rail in 1994.

In 1997, the domestic Dong Co works completed its first refurbishment of a Russian-built Class D4H diesel-electric locomotive, equipping it with a 325 kW MTU engine. DSVN plans to re-engine a further 50 D4H locomotives as well as the entire fleet of 58 Romanain-built Class D11H machines, which in 1999 were all out of service.

In April 1999, the Vietnamese government finally agreed to the purchase of a further batch of 10 Class D12E 736 kW 56 tonne Bo-Bo diesel-electrics from ČKD Praha of the Czech Republic. The order was valued at

US$300 million, with financing guaranteed by the Vietnamese government. Deliveries started in the first half of 1999.

The railway's urgent requirement is for locomotives of higher power, and hopes are pinned on the possibility of a technology transfer agreement with an overseas manufacturer that would equip Gia Lam works for diesel loco construction. A similar deal would probably be the only way of meeting the need for some 500 new coaches by 1999.

### Track
**Rail:** 43 kg/m rail is installed over 2,274 track-km; 37 kg/m rail is installed over 378 track-km

**Sleepers:** concrete (1,157 km); steel (1,103 km); wood (482 km)
**Min curve radius:** 90 m
**Max gradient:** 1.7%
**Max permissible axleload:** standard gauge – 16 tonnes; metre gauge – 14 tonnes

---

# YUGOSLAVIA, FEDERAL REPUBLIC

## Ministry of Transport & Communications

Boulevard Avnoj 104, Belgrade

### Key personnel
Minister: Z Vuković
Head of Rail Transport Division: B Djikanović

## Yugoslav Railways (JŽ) 2002

Zajednica jugoslovenskih železnice
Community of Yugoslav Railways
Nemanjina 6, Belgrade 11000
Tel: (+381 11) 361 67 22; 48 11    Fax: (+381 11) 361 67 97

### Key personnel
Director: Predrag Nikolić
Deputy Director: Zoran Radivojević
Assistant Director, Traffic and Commercial Affairs:
  Dr Savo Vasiljević
Assistant Director General, Finance, Credit, Settlement and Analysis: Nadežda Milićević
Directors
  Traffic: Dragan Miladinović
  Technical: Miroljub Stojanović
  Commercial: Vasilije Krstić
  Finance, Credit and Settlement: (vacant)
  Planning, Analysis and Accounting: Tomislav Živković
  Legal and Personnel Affairs: Mila Djordjević
  Revenue Control: Slobodan Mandić
  Rolling Stock: Vladimir Vainhal
  International Loans: Zadik Danon
  Security: Branislav Stanković
  International Affairs: Željko Valentić
Head of Communications: Rade Vojvodić

### Subsidiaries
ŽTP Beograd
Železničko transportno preduzeće 'Beograd'
(Belgrade Railway Transport Enterprise)
Nemanjina 6, 11000 Belgrade
Tel: (+381 11) 361 67 22; 48 11
Director General: Slobodan Rosić

Željeznica Crne Gore a d
(Montenegro Railways Joint Stock Co)
Trg Golootočkih žrtava 13, 81000 Podgorica
Tel: (+381 81) 63 34 98   Fax: (+381 81) 63 39 57
Director General: Ranko Medenica

*Passenger traffic activity at Belgrade's main station*    0063706

Gauge: 1,435 mm
Route length: 4,059 km
Electrification: 1,364 km at 25 kV 50 Hz AC

### Organisation
In 2002, JŽ continued a process of reconstruction and rehabilitation following heavy damage inflicted on the system by the NATO bombing campaign during the Kosovo crisis in 1999 and the adverse effects of trade sanctions imposed by the UN. A major problem has been a shortage of motive power due to deferred maintenance and a lack of spares. The position has progressively improved as overhauls have been undertaken and some traction has been hired in, including main line diesels from Bulgaria. Sources of funding for network rehabilitation and development have included the European Bank for Reconstruction and Development (EBRD), which in October 2001 agreed a €57 million loan covering locomotive refurbishment and maintenance, track maintenance equipment and funding for a reduction in personnel numbers.

Organisational reform of ŽTP Beograd, which is responsible for the Serbian portions of JŽ, was expected to be implemented in 2002. This would see the business divided into two independent companies, one managing the railway's infrastructure and the other responsible for train operations and rolling stock maintenance.

| Traffic (million) | 1996 | 1997 | 1998* |
|---|---|---|---|
| Passenger journeys | 23.1 | 20.5 | 12.6 |
| Passenger-km | 1,830 | 1,737 | 1,614 |
| Freight tonnes | 8.88 | 10.9 | 10.8 |
| Freight tonne-km | 2,062 | 2,443 | 2,570 |

Note: * 1998 figures estimated

### Passenger operations
Passenger traffic declined from 29.8 million passenger journeys in 1995 to an estimated 12.6 million in 1998. By 1998, international express services had been restored to nine countries, and the introduction of new rolling stock and improvements to infrastructure had been expected to rebuild ridership. Further setbacks to recovery resulted from the Kosovo crisis in 1999, but by 2002 many services had been restored despite severe shortages of traction.

### Freight operations
Freight traffic suffered heavily as a result of the NATO bombing and UN sanctions. This was exacerbated by the damage inflicted on the country's industrial infrastructure. However, by 2002 some international transit traffic between western Europe and Greece had resumed.

### New lines
Completion of the 68 km Valjevo–Loznica line, on which work started in 1992, remains an aim of JŽ, and further funds were committed to the scheme in 1997. The single-track line will incorporate 20 tunnels totalling around 10 km and 69 bridges. The most difficult tunnel, at Trifković (1,719 m), was completed in 1998.

### Improvements to existing lines
In the wake of the 1999 Kosovo crisis, rehabilitation of the system has been top priority for JŽ, with the EBRD and the European Investment Bank (EIB) among institutions to

provide funding. Reconstruction and modernisation of the 874 km Yugoslav section of European Corridor X has also been identified as a key development priority. Corridor X (Salzburg—Ljubljana—Zagreb—Belgrade—Niš—Skopje—Thessaloniki, with its Belgrade—Budapest and Niš—Sofia branches) forms the shortest and fastest route between central and western Europe and southeastern Europe and the Middle East. Part of an EIB loan of €85 million finalised in March 2002 was intended to assist with the rehabilitation of sections of Corridor X in Yugoslavia.

Corridor X also features in a joint international project to reduce delays to trains crossing the border into and out of the JŽ system. Based on the UIC's 'Action Border Crossing' (ABC) methodology, steps to reduce stopping times and simplify border formalities were to be implemented at four crossing points: Subotica—Kelebia (MÁV/Hungary); Šid—Tovarnik (HŽ/Croatia); Preševo—Tabanovci (MŽ/Macedonia); and Dimitrovgrad—Dragoman (BDŽ/Bulgaria).

### Traction and rolling stock

At the start of 1999, JŽ owned 189 electric and 293 diesel locomotives, 45 emu and 106 dmu sets, 722 hauled passenger cars and 17,169 freight wagons. While only one locomotive (a Class 441 electric) is reported lost during the conflict with NATO over Kosovo, just one third of the traction fleet was estimated to be serviceable in 2000.

Steps taken by JŽ to overcome its motive power shortage have included sending Class 441 and 461 electric locomotives for overhaul to Electroputere in Romania and hiring in Class 06 diesel-electric locomotives from Bulgaria. An EIB loan agreed in March 2002 was to fund the refurbishment of 60 electric locomotives.

In 1998, JŽ received the first 23 of an order for 100 200 km/h long-distance passenger coaches from local manufacturer Goša. The new vehicles were to be deployed on international services with the introduction of the 1998-99 timetable.

### Signalling and telecommunications

About 50 per cent of railway stations are equipped with station relay signalling; automatic block system or interlocking are installed on about 40 per cent of lines, and Automatic Train Control (ATC) on 34 per cent of lines. CTC was commissioned on the Belgrade—Bijelo Polje line (311 km) and between Belgrade and Bar (481 km) during 1996, while automatic block is being installed over the Subotica—Belgrade—Niš—Preševo main line, totalling 840 route-km.

Lineside telecommunication cables and dispatching telephone systems with selective dialling and identification are installed on 37 per cent of lines.

### Electrification

The only project in progress in 1997 was the energisation of the 152 km Lapovo—Kraljevo—Požega route, which would provide alternative access to the Bar line for electric trains, and is estimated to save 10,000 tonnes of fuel oil annually.

Further electrification plans include routes from Pančevo to Vršac and the Romanian border, and from Niš to Dimitrovgrad and the Bulgarian border.

### Track

**Rail:** UIC 45A is installed over 2,121.7 km; UIC 49 over 1,790 km; and UIC 60 over 146 km

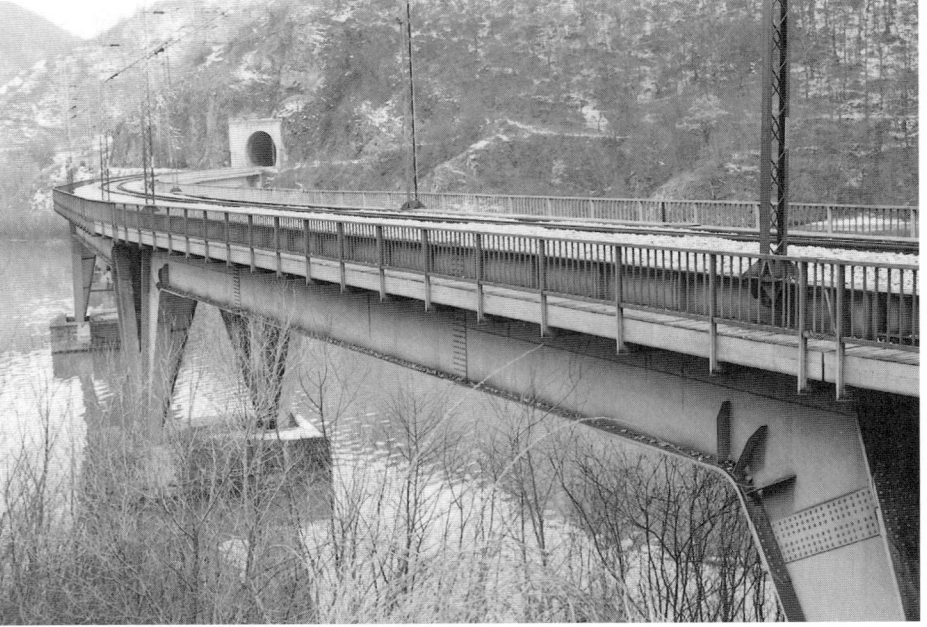

*Bridge on the electrified Belgrade—Bar line*   0063707

### Diesel locomotives

| Class | Wheel arrangement | Power kW | Speed km/h | Weight tonnes | No in service | First built | Mechanical | Builders Engine | Transmission |
|---|---|---|---|---|---|---|---|---|---|
| 641-100 | Bo-Bo | 441 | 80 | 62 | 65 | 1960 | Mávag | Ganz | E Ganz-Mávag |
| 641-300 | Bo-Bo | 685 | 80 | 64 | 40 | 1985 | Ganz-Mávag | Pielstick | E Ganz-Mávag |
| 642 | Bo-Bo | 606 | 80 | 64 | 28 | 1960 | DD | MGO | E B&L |
| 643 | Bo-Bo | 680 | 80 | 67.2 | 14 | 1967 | B&L/DD | MGO | E B&L |
| 645 | A1A-A1A | 1,820 | 120 | 100.2 | 3 | 1981 | GMF/DD | GM | E GM |
| 661 | Co-Co | 1,933 | 112 | 108/114 | 99 | 1961 | GM | GM | E GM |
| 662 | Co-Co | 1,212 | 120 | 99 | 2 | 1965 | DD | MGO/DD | E R Končar/Sever |
| 664 | Co-Co | 1,617 | 124 | 99/103 | 11 | 1972 | GM | GM | E GM |
| 734* | B-B | 478 | 60 | 48/54 | 12 | 1960 | MAK | Maybach GT06 | H Voith |
| 666 | Co-Co | 1,845 | 122 | 100 | 4 | 1978 | GM-USA | GM | E GM |

* Ex-German Federal Class 260/261
B&L: Brissonneau & Lotz; DD: Duro Dakovic; RK: Rade Končar Zagreb

### Electric locomotives

| Class | Wheel arrangement | Power kW | Speed km/h | Weight tonnes | No in service | First built | Mechanical | Builders Electrical |
|---|---|---|---|---|---|---|---|---|
| 441 | Bo-Bo | 3,400/4,080 | 140 | 78 | 96 | 1970 | ASEA/R Končar | ASEA/R Končar |
| 461 | Co-Co | 5,100/5,400 | 120 | 126 | 97 | 1972 | Electroputere | Electroputere |

### Diesel railcars or multiple-units

| Class | Cars per unit | Motor cars per unit | Motored axles/car | Power/motor kW | Speed km/h | Cars in service | First built | Mechanical | Builders Engine | Transmission |
|---|---|---|---|---|---|---|---|---|---|---|
| 712 | 2 | 1 | 4 | 2 × 213 | 120 | 15 | 1980 | Duro Dakovic | MAN | H Voith |
| 811 | 4 | 2 | 2 | 367 | 118 | 11 | 1974 | Ganz-Mávag | Ganz-Mávag | M Ganz-Mávag |
| 812 | 1 | 1 | 1 | 110 | 90 | 80 | 1958 | Goša | MAN | M MAN |

### Electric railcars or multiple-units

| Class | Cars per unit | Motor cars per unit | Motored axles/car | Output/motor kW | Speed km/h | Cars in service | First built | Builders Mechanical | Electrical |
|---|---|---|---|---|---|---|---|---|---|
| 412 | 4 | 2 | 4 | 170 | 120 | 45 | 1980 | RVR | RVR |

**Crossties (sleepers):** Wooden, 2,600 × 260 × 160 mm; concrete, 2,400 × 300 × 192 mm
**Spacing:** 1,670/km
**Fastenings:** K, SKL-2 and Pandrol

**Min curvature radius:** 250 m
**Max gradient:** 2.5%
**Max axleload:** 22.5 tonnes

*UPDATED*

# ZAMBIA

## Ministry of Communications & Transport

PO Box 50065, Block 33, Fairley Road, Ridgeway, Lusaka
Tel: (+260 1) 25 14 44
Fax: (+260 1) 25 32 60; 26 24 41

### Key personnel
Minister: David Saviye
Deputy Minister: Gilbert Mululu
Permanent Secretary with responsibility for railways: R C Mukuma

## Zambia Railways Ltd (ZRL)

PO Box 80935, Corner of Buntungwa Street and Ghana Avenue, Kabwe
Tel: (+260 5) 22 22 01; 9   Fax: (+260 5) 22 44 11

### Key personnel
Chairman: P S Chamunda
Managing Director: Robert Crawford
Directors
   Technical Services: Igwa U Sichula
   Traffic and Marketing: Chris C Musonda
   Finance: Goodson M Moonga
   Personnel: Angela Malawo
General Managers
   Workshops: Bedford Lungu
   Central: H C K Nyimbili
   South: Baxton Siwila
   North: Kingston Mkandawire
Chief Civil Engineer: Yubya Mwanawina
Chief Mechanical and Electrical Engineer:
   Webster Mutambo

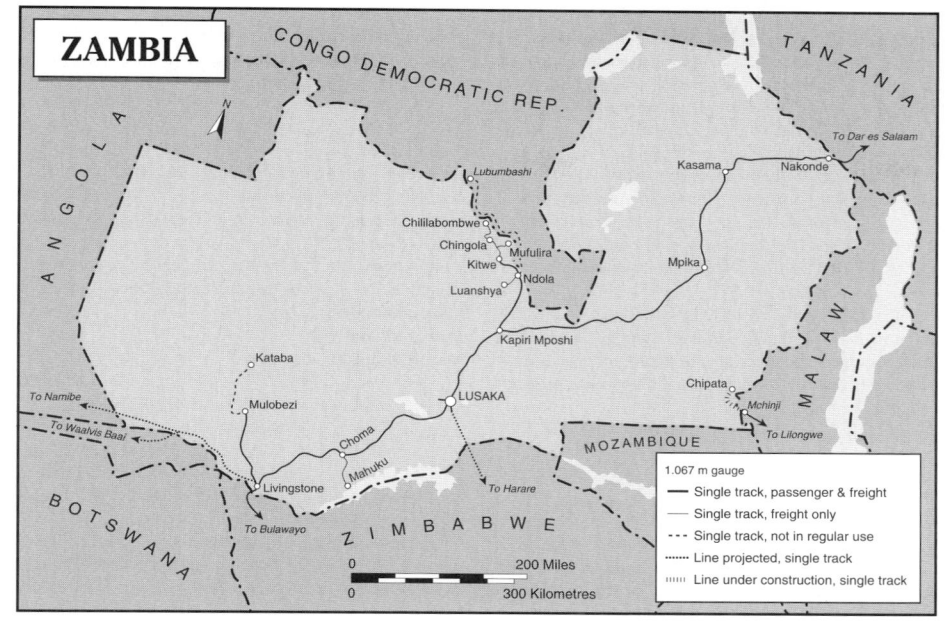

# Zambia/RAILWAY SYSTEMS

*[Map of Zambia showing railway network, 1.067 m gauge. 2001/0114313]*

Chief Signal and Telecommunications Engineer:
 P C Lumumbe
Managers
 Traffic: David Mwaliteta
 Finance: A L Fernando
 Marketing: Frank Kangwa
 Purchasing and Stores: Francis Zulu
 Passenger Services: Luke Mwanza
 Freight Services: Hilary Mphuka
Gauge: 1,067 mm
Route length: 1,266 km

## Political background

Formerly part of Rhodesia Railways (RR), Zambia Railways was segregated as an autonomous system in 1976. It comprises the old RR system north of the Victoria Falls Bridge, to which was added in 1970 the 164 km Zambesi Sawmills Railway from Livingstone to Mulobezi. RR remained a legal entity until 1996, when its assets were eventually divided between ZRL and National Railways of Zimbabwe.

Since its independence, ZRL has been handicapped by the political crises in the region and the problems of some neighbouring railways, which have clouded definition of the land-locked country's rail routes to the sea ports with uncertainty. Rail outlets are of critical importance to Zambia's copper industry, which generates 90 per cent of its exports. The TAZARA system's operating difficulties (see Tanzania entry) have restricted the potential of its route to Dar-es-Salaam, originally envisaged as Zambia's primary export rail route, and the Benguela Railway to Lobito in Angola has been affected by the unrest to the west. Assignment of copper traffic to the TAZARA or Victoria Falls routes is decided by the government.

Since 1984, ZRL has been a limited company, with freedom to set its own tariffs, though it is still subject to a fuel oil tax, the revenues from which support road infrastructure.

ZRL is one of the poorest performers in the country's transport sector, and this has led to the government of Zambia seeking foreign aid in order to implement a comprehensive restructuring plan. Funding was agreed with the Swedish International Development Agency (SIDA) in 1997, the terms of which required the board of directors of ZRL to recruit and select a new management company to take over the railway for a period of up to 2.5 years. A consortium consisting of the Swedish company Hifab and German rail consultants DE-Consult was selected for this role and staff of the company duly took over the leading management positions in March 1998.

Before the new company commenced its work, staffing levels had been reduced from 8,500 in 1993 to 5,190 in 1997. Major problems experienced related almost exclusively to the very poor cashflow situation and constant lack of funds for investment, particularly in staff severance payments, infrastructure rehabilitation and traction and rolling stock repair and refurbishment.

In March 2000, the Zambian government approved in principle plans to privatise ZRL. In August 2001, the Zambia Privatisation Agency invited bids for a long-term concession to operate the ZRL system and manage its assets. This followed agreement with the World Bank to provide a loan to fund selective rehabilitation of track, locomotives and freight wagons. The closing date for bids was 7 December 2001.

## Passenger operations

In 1997, ZRL was running a daily service over the 851 km between Livingstone and Kitwe (augmented by a thrice-weekly service on the Livingstone–Lusaka section of the route), two daily return trips between Livingstone and Victoria Falls (13 km) and a twice-weekly service between Livingstone and Mulobezi (163 km). For service details on the TAZARA line see Tanzania entry.

Passengers benefited from introduction of refurbished coaching stock in 1991, but this did little to attract extra patronage. Traffic figures for 1997 were 1.26 million passenger journeys, 267 million passenger-km – little more than half what they had been a decade before.

## Freight operations

Around two-thirds of all freight carried is copper, but this has been vulnerable to road competition. In addition to the constraints on performance due to fallible equipment, traffic growth has been restricted by several factors: slow turn-round of wagons at customers' sidings and on neighbouring railways; inflation and the depreciation of the Kwacha; and unsettled politics and strife in neighbouring countries. Traffic figures for the year to 31 March 1998 were 1.4 million tonnes – less than half what they had been only five years previously. However, a modest recovery was achieved in 1999, when the railway was expected to carry 1.8 million tonnes.

## Traction and rolling stock

In 1997, ZRL owned 66 diesel locomotives (44 operational, 35 in use), mostly comprising General Electric U20C 1,330 kW units, plus 12 General Electric U15C 1,016 kW shunters. ZRL's most recently acquired traction is a batch of 15 Type GT36CU-MP locomotives from GM Canada, delivered from 1993.

The wagon fleet in 1997 totalled 6,345, of which 3,345 were in use. There were 77 passenger cars, including six sleepers, 19 standard class, 36 economy class, three buffet/dining and six snack cars. Other recent deliveries were 100 bogie covered wagons from BN and 25

*ZRL General Motors GT36CU-MP diesel-electric locomotive at Kapiri Mposhi with a freight service (Oubeck.com)* 2002/0114660

*General Electric Co-Co diesel-electric locomotive at Livingstone with a ZRL passenger service (Oubeck.com)* 2002/0114661

container flats from BREC, Belgium, while Braithwaite of India was supplying 20 sulphuric acid tank wagons in 1996-97.

**Type of coupler in standard use:** Alliance automatic, bottom-operated, Contour 10A
**Type of brake in standard use:** Vacuum

### Signalling and telecommunications

The 851 km in total from Livingstone to Ndola and the Copperbelt branch section between Ndola and Kitwe are controlled by CTC (centralised traffic control) with multiple-aspect colourlight signals. Sections outside CTC territory are worked on the token block system or, in the Copperbelt, on the train staff system. The CTC system was installed during 1961-64 and utilised open-wire carrier circuits along the line or rail. Operating from a centre at Kabwe, the CTC has now been renewed with all-electronic apparatus by Siemens AG at a cost of US$15.8 million. A total of 61 relay interlockings are remote-controlled from Kabwe, while a further six stations have locally controlled relay interlockings.

The overhead line carrier system has been replaced by radio transmission because of theft and vandalism of wires, generators and batteries, with resultant interruption of the new CTC. The African Development Bank funded the US$9.14 million conversion which was finished in 1990.

Other recent projects include installation of a Mitsui digital multiplex microwave radio system between Ndola and Livingstone and upgrading of a computer mainframe. A start was made with purchase of hand-held radios for communication between yard staff and signalboxes. Installation of mains electricity was completed at a further 15 stations, replacing diesel generators.

### Track
**Rail:** 45.13 kg/m
**Crossties (sleepers):** Wood, 127 mm thickness; concrete, 200 mm thickness; spaced 1,340/km in plain track, 1,400/km in curves, for concrete, 1,400/km in both cases for wood
**Fastenings:** Coach screw, clip and spring washer (triple coil) for wood, Pandrol for concrete sleepers
**Min curve radius:** 8.7°
**Max gradient:** 1.75%
**Max axleload:** 15.25 tonnes

*UPDATED*

## Njanji Railways
PO Box, Lusaka

**Key personnel**
Managing Director: C Mayatwa

Gauge: 1,067 mm
Route length: 16 km

### Organisation

This operation, started-up by the state copper mining company and now run independently, established a cross-city commuter service from Chilenje to George in Lusaka in 1990, largely over existing tracks. The two diesel railbuses originally employed proved inadequate for the demand, and now the service is provided by two locomotives and 10 coaches hired from ZR.

The success of the limited service offered has stimulated plans for extension over ZR's main line to serve Ngwerere in the north and Chilanga to the south.

It is possible that ZR will take over the management of the line, which would then be run as a self-contained business unit.

# ZIMBABWE

## Ministry of Transport and Communications

PO Box Cy 595, Kaguvi Building, Causeway, Harare
Tel: (+263 4) 70 06 93   Fax: (+263 4) 70 82 25

**Key personnel**
Minister: Dr Swithun Mombeshora
Deputy Minister: Paul Mangwana
Permanent Secretary: Paul Kodzwa

## National Railways of Zimbabwe (NRZ)

PO Box 596, Bulawayo
Tel: (+263 9) 36 35 21   Fax: (+263 9) 36 35 43

**Key personnel**
General Manager: Samson Zumbika
Assistant General Managers
  Finance: Alfred Nyalila
  Marketing: Welcome P Lugube
  Technical Services: E S Marowa
  Operations: G T W Tyamzashe
Chief Internal Auditor: D Sithole
Chief Accountant: L D Mkandla
Chief Traffic Manager: A Munzara
Chief Planning Manager: Lewis Mukwada
Chief Mechanical Engineer: N Marange
Chief Manpower Manager: Eliot Mashingaidze
Chief Civil Engineer: J Nyawura
Chief Electrical Engineer: E C Dube
Chief Signal Engineer: D J Scott
Manager, Supplies and Stores: K P Magunda
Manager, Legal Affairs: N Marechera
Manager, Safety: P Mukoki
Manager, Security: P M Mbondiah
Manager, Computer Services: Lovemore Ndlovu
Public Relations Manager: G T Rungani
Manager, Marketing Development:
  Chenjerai Nziramasanga
Manager, Eastern Area: V Sithole
Manager, Southern Area: O Shiriyapenga

Gauge: 1,067 mm
Route length: 3,077 mm (includes 318 km BBR line)
Electrification: 313 km at 25 kV 50 Hz AC

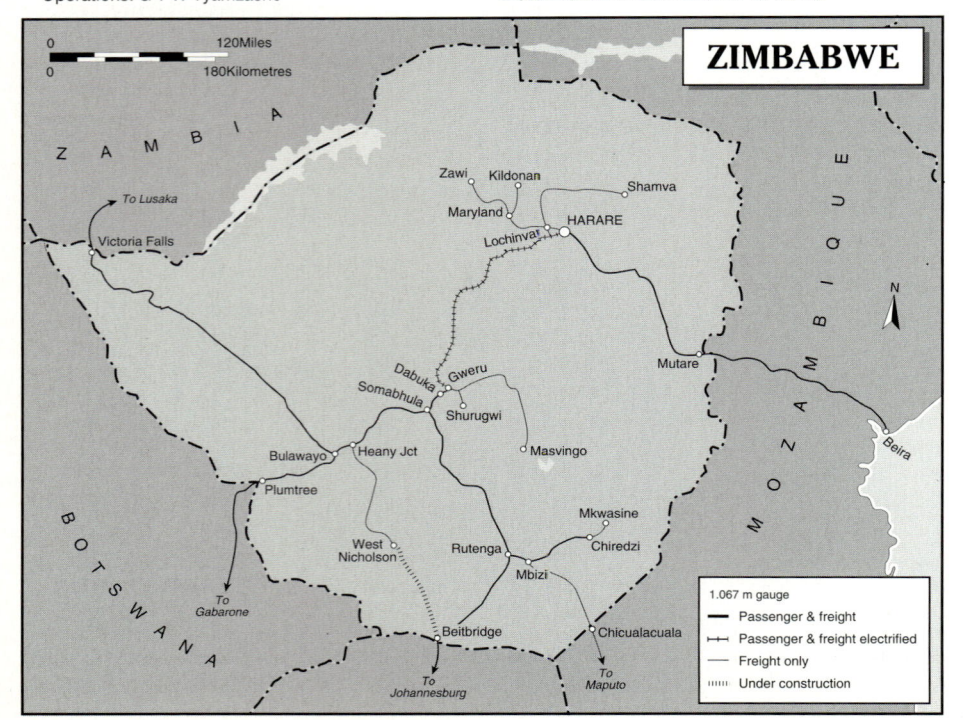

### Political background

NRZ was created in 1967 out of Rhodesia Railways (RR), the northern portion of which became Zambia Railways. The old RR remained a legal entity until 1996, when division of its assets between the two countries was finally agreed.

An important condition attached to the Railway II Project agreed in 1991 was that the country's Railways Act be amended to give NRZ more commercial and financial freedom of decision making. NRZ would be required to act on normal business principles, with government involvement limited to appointment of the railway's management board.

The revised Act made provision for government assumption of financial responsibility for upkeep of rail infrastructure, for use of which NRZ would pay tolls. In 1995, the government decided that NRZ would be split into separate operating and infrastructure divisions, with the aim of improving the railway's ability to compete with road transport.

No progress was made with this restructuring. In 2000/01, the Privatisation Agency of Zimbabwe was considering how best NRZ might be restructured, and from January 2001 a new board of directors took office. Its remit included the commercialisation of NRZ and freeing the railway from government control.

In 2001, NRZ was adversely affected by fuel shortages and in the early months of the year was operating at about 50 per cent below its capacity. The situation was eased by supplies of oil from customers and neighbouring railways. A lack of foreign exchange was also having an impact on the procurement of spares for traction and rolling stock.

| Traffic | 1997 | 1998 |
|---|---|---|
| Passenger journeys (000) | - | - |
| Passenger-km (million) | 583,379 | 408,223 |
| Freight tonnes (000) | 12,428 | 18,338 |
| Freight tonne-km (million) | 4,871 | 7,049 |

### Passenger operations

There is a daily train between the two largest cities, the capital Harare and Bulawayo, and tourist services between Bulawayo and Victoria Falls. The daily service between Harare and Mutare on the Beira Corridor route was relaunched with new rolling stock in 1999. There are also services between Somabhula and Chiredzi in the southeast of the country.

A 1986 proposal for a Harare suburban electric system has been revived in part, and the project is being handled by the Ministry of Local Government, with NRZ's participation limited to technical advice. Sofretu undertook a feasibility study of a 28 km link between the city and its satellite town of Chitungwiza, and work on this scheme started in 1999.

In July 2001, NRZ launched a daily commuter service between Marimba and Harare. This is operated jointly with Zimbabwe United Passenger Services Company (Zupco), which provides feeder bus services. This was followed later in the same year on the Ruwa and Tafara routes in Harare and the Luveve/Mabvuku route in Bulawayo. It was expected that additional routes would be added.

### Freight operations
The downward trend in freight movement apparent over five years was reversed in 1995, when tonnage rose by 14 per cent to 12.3 million for 4,754 million tonne-km. This was some 10 per cent over budget, with increases in maize, chrome ore, cement, coke and sugar cane more than offsetting decreases in iron ore and tobacco. In 1997, 12.4 million tonnes (4,871 million tonne-km) were carried, falling slightly in 1998 to 11.8 million and 4,603 million respectively.

NRZ operates a merry-go-round operation supplying ore from Ngezi (on the Somabhula–Rutenga section) and coal from the Wankie Colliery Co at Hwange to the state-owned ZISCO iron and steel manufacturing complex at Redcliff. The trains employ purpose-built rotary tippler wagons by ZECO of Zimbabwe, the coal wagons having aluminium body sides; ore wagon payload capacity is 58.5 tonnes, that of a coal wagon 60.5 tonnes. Both iron ore and coal are loaded with trains on the move beneath overhead bunkers. Hauled by GM Class DE 10A 1,678 kW locomotives, the trains are formed of 60 wagons grossing over 4,500 tonnes, each powered by four DE 10A units. From loading to destination tippler takes 8 hours, while from Hwange source to Redcliff takes a coal train 16 hours. Coal for other destinations generally moves in unit trains of about 34 wagons.

In 1999, NRZ reached agreement with Zambia Railways and Congo National Railways (SNCC) in Congo, Democratic Republic to rehabilitate and develop the existing railway links between the three countries as a commercial freight corridor. The first train to result from these agreements arrived in Harare in September 1999, conveying copper concentrates from Congo for Mhangura copper mines. A weekly general freight service also runs between Harare and Congo, taking seven days for the journey. To promote further traffic growth between the two countries, NRZ was to provide assistance with the rehabilitation of lines in Congo.

In 2001, NRZ commenced a contract to convey sulphuric acid from a plant in Masasa, Harare, to Zambia on behalf of Chemplex Corporation.

### Intermodal operations
Almost 90 per cent of the country's tobacco crop is exported in containers, along with tea, coffee, graphite, hides and skins, nickel and tin. Containerised imports for the Harare area's extensive industrial development include machinery, lubricants, bricks, iron and steel. NRZ's two container terminals are Dabcon, at Dabuka near Gweru, and Locon, at Lochinvar near Harare.

### New lines
Freight services over the new 350 km Beitbridge–Bulawayo line commenced in July 1999. Developed as a private-sector 'Build, Operate and Transfer' (BOT) scheme, the BBR provides a direct link from South Africa to Bulawayo and on to Zambia and to Mutare, close to the border with Mozambique. As a result of the opening of the line, journey times between Bulawayo and Durban have been cut from 25 to four days. A 30-year concession to operate and maintain the line has been acquired by the Bulawaya–Beitbridge Railway Company, in which a 15 per cent stake is held by NRZ, 40 per cent by the New Limpopo Bridge Company, and the remainder by Gensec, Nedcor, Old Mutual and Sanlam. Spoornet of South Africa is contracted to run train services.

In 1999, government approval was given to develop plans to extend the Harare–Lion's Den (Zawi) line northwest to Kafue, in Zambia, via the border crossing at Chirundu. This would provide landlocked Zambia with an effective link through Zimbabwe to the port of Beira in Mozambique.

In 1999, work started on a 28 km commuter line from Harare to Chitungwiza, south of the capital.

### Improvements to existing lines
In 1998, upgrading of the Zimbabwean section of the Beira Corridor at Mufeseri, between Timber Mills and Eagle's Nest, was completed, eliminating sharp reverse curves and steep gradients in this area. The centrepiece of the scheme is a 62 m girder bridge designed by NRZ engineers.

In 1998, NRZ installed its first hydraulically operated level crossing barriers in the Harare area. The units have been designed and manufactured by NRZ's Signals Branch.

### Traction and rolling stock
At the beginning of 2000, NRZ owned 30 electric, 42 steam and 152 diesel locomotives; 325 passenger cars (including 17 buffet/dining, and 117 sleeping cars) and 11,387 freight wagons.

NRZ is continuing a major rationalisation and updating of its diesel locomotive fleet. For historic reasons, the fleet was a mix of 11 classes, embodying nine types of engine, and featuring both electric and hydraulic transmissions. A programme inaugurated in 1992 saw scrapping of 110 locomotives, mainly of Classes DH2, DE7 and DE8/8A. The principal Classes retained are DE10A (GM-EMD GT22LC-2), DE9A (refurbished GE U10B and U11B), and DE6 (refurbished GE U20C). A few steam locomotives are retained, mostly for tourist specials.

A re-engining programme for DE6 diesel shunting locomotives has been undertaken. General Electric 7FDL-12 engines have been fitted with funding from the European Bank for Reconstruction and Development.

For the future, NRZ is studying the possibility of using engines able to burn lower-grade fuels, microprocessor control systems, three-phase AC drives and electro-diesel designs. The last-mentioned is of interest because at present tonnages are not great enough to justify the capital costs of major electrification extensions, so that the ability of a locomotive to work unchanged from non-electrified into electrified territory would be valuable.

In 1997, NRZ ordered 56 coaches from a consortium formed by Union Carriage & Wagon and locally based More Wear Industries. These comprise 24 economy class, 20 standard class and eight sleeping cars. Refurbishment of 265 existing coaches is also being undertaken. In 1999, NRZ signed an agreement to lease 20 of these vehicles to Congo National Railways (SNCC) for two years, with a renewal option.

In 1998, NRZ commenced a programme at its Mutare workshops to convert 27 petroleum tank wagons to tallow wagons in response to a growing demand to handle this commodity.

**Type of coupler in standard use:** Automatic centre buffer coupler, Alliance No 1 and 2 heads
Passenger cars: 5 × 5 in, 5½ × 5 in shanks
Freight wagons: 8 × 6 in, 7 × 5 in shanks
**Type of braking in standard use:** Vacuum on passenger and freight stock except for liner train wagons, which are on direct release airbrakes

### Signalling and telecommunications
A new CTC (centralised traffic control) supervisory and remote-control system supplied by Siemens Zus was commissioned on the Victoria Falls–Bulawayo section in 1993. However, its usefulness was reduced by continuing dependence on a vulnerable copper-wire pole route for communications. CTC now extends to around 1,250 route-km.

Radio control is employed between Harare and Mutare (the 300 km Zimbabwean section of the Beira Corridor export route to the Indian Ocean), replacing the signalling system dating from 1960. Following a funding agreement with the African Development Bank, a Z$83 million contract for this was let to Siemens in January 1997.

Reliability problems have also plagued the railway trunk dialling system in the coalfields and other areas. Use of Post Office facilities as a back-up continues to cost a substantial sum every year. Hot box detectors on the North Line have been removed due to poor telecommunications. As a result, accidents caused by broken axles are rife, causing losses running into millions of dollars.

*Class DE 10 diesel-electric locomotive hauling Rovos Rail's 'Pride of Africa' train at Victoria Falls* (Colin Boocock)
0063695

**Diesel locomotives**

| Class | Wheel arrangement | Power kW | Speed km/h | Weight tonnes | No in service | First Built | Builders Mechanical | Engine | Transmission |
|---|---|---|---|---|---|---|---|---|---|
| DE 6 | Co-Co | 1,559 | 116 | 90.84 | 9 | 1966 | GE-USA | GE 7-FDL-12 (re-engined 1998) | E GE-USA |
| DE 9 | Bo-Bo | 732 | 103 | 61.3 | 64 | 1975 | GE (U11B) | D 3512 D11 JWAG Caterpillar (re-engined 1992-94) | E GE |
| DE 10 | Co-Co | 1,678 | 107 | 94.35 | 61 | 1982 | GM USA/Canada | 12-645E3 B (GM) | E GM |
| DE 11 | Co-Co | 2,508 | 102 | 113.998 | 13 | 1992 | | 16-645E3B | E |

**Electric locomotives**

| Class | Wheel arrangement | Output kW | Speed km/h | Weight tonnes | No in service | First built | Builders Mechanical | Electrical |
|---|---|---|---|---|---|---|---|---|
| EL1 | Co-Co | 2,400 | 100 | 114 | 30 | 1983 | ZECO/SGP | 50 c/s Group |

# RAILWAY SYSTEMS/Zimbabwe

Following the success of a temporary freight traffic control centre set up to cope with the additional grain traffic handled in 1992-93 under the drought relief programme, NRZ has established a permanent control centre to monitor freight operations countrywide.

## Electrification
The 313 km route between Harare and Gweru is electrified on the 25 kV 50 Hz AC system. Rewiring was carried out in 1995 of 22 km of catenary over the original electrification test section between Gado and Samwari, where contact-wire breakages had been giving trouble for years.

NRZ has more Class EL1 electric locomotives than current traffic levels demand, so locomotive availability is maintained by cannibalising mothballed machines.

## Track
**Rail:** UICE Class B standard 54 kg/m (313 km of main line only); remainder of main line BS45 kg/m; branch lines BS45, 40 and 30 kg/m. A new standard rail, BS90A, has been adopted for all future use

**Crossties (sleepers)**

| Type: | Thickness (under seat) |
|---|---|
| Concrete | 226 mm |
| Hardwood | 115 mm |
| Steel | 10 mm; 13 mm |

**Spacing:** 1,429/km

**Min curvature radius:** Main line 600 m, branch lines 400 m
**Max gradient:** 1 in 80 (main line)
**Max axleload:** 18.6 tonnes

# OPERATORS OF INTERNATIONAL RAIL SERVICES IN EUROPE

# OPERATORS OF INTERNATIONAL RAIL SERVICES IN EUROPE

## PASSENGER

### Cisalpino AG

Postfach 5757, Parkterrasse 10, CH-3001 Bern, Switzerland
Tel: (+41 31) 329 09 09   Fax: (+41 31) 329 09 19
e-mail: info@cisalpino.com
Web: http://www.cisalpino.com

**Key personnel**
President: Dr Luca Barbera
Managing Director: Ing Lucio Gastaldi

**Organisation**
Cisalpino AG was set up jointly in November 1993 by the Swiss and Italian railways to operate an international train service using ETR470 tilting trainsets. FS Spa (Italian Railways) has a 50 per cent holding; SBB (Swiss Federal Railways) 40 per cent, and BLS Lötschbergbahn 6 per cent; the remaining 4 per cent is held jointly by certain Swiss cantons.

The catering service on the Cisalpino trains is the responsibility of a separate Rome-based company, Cremonini.

**Services**
In 2002, services were operated on the following routes:
Zurich–Milan
Stuttgart–Zurich–Milan
Zurich–Milan–Florence
Geneva–Milan–Venice
Basle–Milan

Four train pairs operate via the Gotthard route, two pairs use the Simplon route and one pair runs via the Lötschberg line. For the route between Zurich and Stuttgart Cisalpino AG acts as a leasing company.

**Traction and rolling stock**
Cisalpino's rolling stock fleet comprises nine tilting ETR470 trains built by Fiat Ferroviaria. The nine-car trains each comprise a restaurant/bar car, three first- and five second-class cars.

The ETR470s have dual-voltage capability, allowing them to cope with the Italian (3 kV DC) and Swiss and German (15 kV 16⅔ Hz AC) electrical systems. Apart from this, they are much the same technically as the ETR460 Pendolino trains operating Italian domestic services. Traction is provided by asynchronous three-phase AC traction motors with GTO thyristor control, with a motor to each bogie's own axle on the six powered cars in each set. For Alpine conditions, the ETR470s are differently geared from an ETR460 so as to obtain higher tractive effort but with a reduced maximum speed of 200 km/h.

**UPDATED**

*Cisalpino ETR470 tilting trainset at Domodossola forming a Milan–Geneva service* (Andrew Marshall)

### CityNightLine

CityNightLine CNL AG
Postfach 7377, Bahnhofplatz 15, CH-8023 Zurich, Switzerland
Tel: (+41 1) 225 75 75   Fax: (+41 1) 225 75 76

**Key personnel**
Director: Christian Zogg

**Organisation**
CityNightLine CNL AG was set up by the national railways of Germany, Austria and Switzerland to operate luxury 'CityNightLine' sleeper services on international routes between the three countries. In the face of poor financial results, OBB pulled out of the consortiium in 1996, leaving just DB AG of Germany (60 per cent) and SBB of Switzerland (40 per cent) as shareholders.

**Services**
CityNightLine services operate nightly on three routes: Hamburg-Zurich (the 'Komet'), Berlin-Zurich (the 'Berliner') and Vienna-Dortmund (the 'Donau Kurier'). A fourth route, Vienna-Zurich (the 'Wiener Walzer'), was taken over by ÖBB when it left the consortium and is now run as a conventional EuroNight service.

CityNightLine services comprise three levels of accommodation. At the top end are 'A' class deluxe sleeping compartments, with toilet and shower in the compartment. 'B' class is similar to conventional sleepers, with beds and wash basins in the compartments. 'C' class features reclining seats. Continental breakfast is served to A and B class passengers.

**Traction and rolling stock**
The double-deck sleeping cars accommodating A and B class passengers were built new for CityNightLine services. Schindler of Switzerland, SGP of Austria and Bombardier Talbot of Germany built 18 cars each.

### Eurostar Group

Eurostar House, Waterloo Station, London SE1 8SE, UK
Tel: (+44 20) 79 22 61 80   Fax: (+44 20) 79 22 44 24
Web: http://www.eurostar.com

**Key personnel**
Chairman and Chief Executive: David Azéma
Executive Directors
   Sales and Marketing: Pascal Tomasso
   Operations: Jacques Damas
   Budget and Human Resources: Daniel Piana
Director of Customer Services: Maurits Kalff

**Organisation**
Formed in March 1999, the Eurostar Group determines the commercial direction and service development of the overall Eurostar business. Its board includes representatives of the three companies which jointly operate the service, Belgian National Railways, Eurostar (UK) Ltd and French National Railways (all qv).

**Passenger operations**
Responsibility for the day-to-day operation of Eurostar services rests with the three companies detailed above; details are provided in entries in each respective country in the *Railway systems* section.

In 2000, 7.666 million tickets were sold for Eurostar services, compared with 7.046 million in 1999. This represented an increase of 8.8 per cent. In the first eight months of 2000, Eurostar achieved market shares of 46 per cent and 63.4 per cent respectively in the total London–Brussels and London–Paris air and rail markets. Total Eurostar revenues in 2000 were £439 million, an increase of 12 per cent over the 1999 figure of £393 million.

From June 2000 Eurostar's catering contract was taken over by the Momentum consortium, a joint venture between Granada Food Services of the UK and Italian caterer Cremonini SpA.

*A London–Paris Eurostar set photographed soon after leaving the Channel Tunnel, with Calais Fréthun station in the background* (David Haydock)

# OPERATORS OF INTERNATIONAL RAIL SERVICES IN EUROPE/Passenger

As well as providing passenger travel, Eurostar offers a range of services for the carriage of urgent packages. Esprit Europe provides a fast door-to-door delivery service from London and Ashford to Brussels and Paris, while Esprit Global and Esprit UK respectively offer similar worldwide and domestic UK services.

### Traction and rolling stock
The Eurostar fleet of high-speed trainsets is shared among the three railways which form the Eurostar Group. Details are provided within their individual entries.

Under Eurostar Group auspices, interior refurbishment of the fleet is scheduled to take place in 2002/03.

## Linx AB

Box 249, SE-401 24 Gothenburg
Tel: (+46 31) 10 49 51   Fax: (+46 31) 10 49 93
e-mail: webmaster@linx.se
Web: http://www.linx.se

### Key personnel
Managing Director: Reidar Jignéus
Directors
   Rolling Stock: Arne Jonsson
   Operations: Jarl Samuelsson
   Marketing: Øyvind Rørslett
   Human Resources: Bjørn Bjørnsson
   Finance: Ulla Grath

### Organisation
Linx AB is a joint venture, equally owned by Norwegian State Railways (NSB) and Swedish State Railways (SJ), established in May 2000 to develop, operate and market intercity services on the Oslo–Karlstad–Stockholm and Oslo–Gothenburg–Malmo–Copenhagen corridors.

### Passenger operations
Linx took over services on the Copenhagen–Gothenburg–Oslo and Oslo–Karlstad–Stockholm routes in June 2001.

### Traction and rolling stock
Linx is initially leasing seven X2000 high-speed tilting trainsets from SJ, equipped for dual-voltage operation to enable them to use the Øresund Link to Denmark. The trains will be refurbished internally and branded in Linx livery by TGOJ at its Tillberga works. The first refurbished trainset was scheduled for completion in early 2002.

**UPDATED**

## Lyria

56 rue de Londres, F-75008 Paris, France
Tel: (+33 1) 42 93 38 74   Fax: (+33 1) 42 93 39 02

### Organisation
Under its original name, Rail France Suisse SAS, Lyria was formed in January 2000 by French National Railways (SNCF) and Swiss Federal Railways (CFF/SBB) as a Société par Actions Simplifiée (SAS), a company with a simplified corporate structure, to develop high-speed train services on the Paris–Lausanne and Paris–Neuchâtel–Bern–Zurich routes. It succeeded the TGV France-Suisse joint venture formed by the two railways in 1993. The name Lyria was adopted in March 2002. The company is responsible for service quality, development and delivery; pricing policy; marketing; promotion; and contracts for provision of on-board services. Since March 2002, the last has been undertaken by Chef-Express, part of the Italian Agape group.

### Services
Services are operated under the branding 'Ligne de Coeur', using TGV trainsets. Paris–Lausanne is served by up to five trains daily in each direction, while two daily return trains (one on Saturdays) link Paris with Zurich. During the ski season, some Lausanne services are extended to Brig at weekends.

### Traction and rolling stock
TGV France-Suisse services are provided by nine three-current TGV-PSE trainsets, one of which was formally acquired by SBB in 1993. A two-year fleet refurbishment programme was completed in 1999.

**UPDATED**

## Thalys International SC

20 Place Stéphanie, B-1050 Brussels, Belgium
Tel: (+32 2) 548 06 00   Fax: (+32 2) 511 29 44
Web: http://www.thalys.com

### Key personnel
Director-General: Jean-Philippe Dupont
Deputy Director-General: Michel Jadot

### Organisation
Originally named Westrail International, Thalys International was established as a joint-venture company by Belgian National Railways (SNCB) and French National Railways (SNCF) to develop and manage high-speed rail services on the Paris–Brussels–Antwerp–Amsterdam and Paris–Brussels–Liège–Cologne routes. German Rail (DB AG) and Netherlands Railways (NS) participate in the operation by commercial agreement and retain the option to become full joint-venture partners as services develop to and from their domestic networks. The company is responsible for service quality, development and delivery; communications; marketing; and contracts for provision of onboard services.

### Services
Services are operated with high-speed trainsets under the 'Thalys' branding. Routes operated are: Paris–Brussels; Paris–Brussels–Cologne–Düsseldorf; Paris–Brussels–Antwerp–Rotterdam–Amsterdam; Brussels-Roissy-Charles de Gaulle–Marne la Vallée–Bourg en Bresse-Geneva; Amsterdam–Brussels–Roissy-Charles de Gaulle–Marne las Vallée–Lyons–Valence. Two levels of service, Confort 1 and Confort 2, are available, the former offering access to a personal steward and increased onboard and off-train facilities.

From March 2001, five daily Thalys services in each direction between Brussels Midi and Roissy-Charles de Gaulle replaced all Air France flights between the Belgian capital and Paris's principal airport following a partnership agreement between the two carriers.

### Traction and rolling stock
Thalys services are provided by 17 four-voltage PBKA (Paris–Brussels–Köln–Amsterdam) high-speed trainsets and 10 three-voltage PBA sets bearing Thalys livery. Nine of the PBKA sets are owned by SNCB, of which two are leased to DB AG, six belong to SNCF, and two to NS. The PBA units are owned by SNCF. The trains are used in a common pool. Technical details can be found in the entry for France in the Railway systems section.

## VSOE

Venice Simplon-Orient-Express Ltd
A division of Orient-Express Hotels Inc
Sea Containers House, 20 Upper Ground, London SE1 9PF, UK
Tel: (+44 20) 78 05 50 60   Fax: (+44 20) 78 05 59 08

### Key personnel
President: Simon M C Sherwood
Chief Executive: Nicholas R Varian
Vice-President and Treasurer: Peter Parrott
Director of Public Relations: Pippa Isbell

### Services
VSOE operates the following services:
A luxury train between London, Paris, Düsseldorf and Venice, Florence, Rome and Prague.
A vintage Pullman train on day and weekend excursions within the UK.
A luxury train in Asia between Singapore, Kuala Lumpur, Bangkok and Chiang Mai.
A deluxe river cruiser on the Ayerarwady river in Myanmar.

In December 1998, VSOE, in partnership with Queensland Rail, was to launch the luxury 'Great South Pacific Express' service from Brisbane to Cairns and Sydney.

*Thalys PBKA trainsets pass on the LGV Nord high-speed line in northern France (David Haydock)*

*RTV service from Paris arriving at Zurich Hbf (John C Baker)*

# FREIGHT

## BTZ

Bayerische Trailerzuggesellschaft mbH
Poccistrasse 7, D-83306 München, Germany
Tel: (+49 89) 609 70 25  Fax: (+49 89) 609 50 00

**Key personnel**
Managing Director: Dipl Volksw Heiner Rogge
Rail Operations: Dipl Ing Hartmut Thiele

**Services**
In June 1995, BTZ began operating RoadRailer bimodal vehicles on a trans-Alpine route from Munich, Germany, to Verona, Italy.

In October 1996, the service between Munich and Hamburg was added and in November 1996, a service between Munich and Cologne was begun.

BTZ operates 60 curtain-sided trailers, 210 reefer trailers, 20 dry van (box) trailers, 166 tilt trailers and 20 container/swapbody chassis.

## European Rail Shuttle BV

PO Box 59018, NL-3008 PA Rotterdam, Netherlands
Boompjes 40, NL-3011 XB Rotterdam, Netherlands
Tel: (+31 10) 425 52 22  Fax: (+31 10) 428 52 12
Web: http://www.ersrail.com

**Key personnel**
Managing Director: Frans Zoetmulder

**Services**
Operates intermodal shuttle services between Rotterdam, Italy, Germany, the Czech Republic and Poland.

*UPDATED*

## Hupac SA

Viale R Manzoni 6, CH-6830 Chiasso, Switzerland
Tel: (+41 91) 695 28 00  Fax: (+41 91) 695 28 01
Web: http://www.hupac-intermodal.ch

**Key personnel**
Chairman: Hans-Jörg Bertschi
Deputy Chairman: Daniel Nordmann
Secretary: Peter Hafner

**Background**
Founded in 1967 and owned by road hauliers (72 per cent) and railway companies (28 per cent), Hupac SA is a holding company for a group of firms providing intermodal transport and logistics services.

In 1998, Hupac SA acquired a majority shareholding in the Netherlands-based intermodal transport company, Trailstar NV.

In April 2001, Hupac SA, BLS Lötschbergbahn (BLS) and Swiss Federal Railways (SBB) established a joint venture company RAlpin AG, to run a 'rolling highway' piggyback service between Freiburg in Breisgau, southwest Germany, to Novara, Italy. This followed a tender invitation issued by the Swiss Federal Office of Transport to provide piggyback services via the upgraded Simplon route through the Alps. Each company has a shareholding of 30 per cent in the company; the remaining 10 per cent was reserved for Italian State Railways.

**Subsidiaries**
Fidia SpA
Viale Rimembranza 10/12, I-28047 Oleggio, Italy
Tel: (+39 0321) 99 81 55  Fax: (+39 0321) 913 42
Manager: Paolo Paracchini

Hupac Intermodal SA
Viale R Manzoni 6, CH-6830 Chiasso, Switzerland
Tel: (+41 91) 695 28 00  Fax: (+41 91) 695 28 01
Web: http://www.hupac-intermodal.ch
Chief Executive: Bernhard Kunz

Hupac GmbH
Zum Umschlagbahnhof 2, D-78224 Singen, Germany
Tel: (+49 7731) 87 90 60  Fax: (+49 7731) 87 90 65
Manager: Rudi Mager

Hupac SpA
Via Dogana 8/10, I-21052 Busto Arsizio, Italy
Tel: (+39 0331) 60 85 11  Fax: (+39 0331) 38 28 80
Manager: Francesco Crivelli

Termi SA
Viale R Manzoni 6, CH-6830 Chiasso, Switzerland
Tel: (+41 91) 695 29 55  Fax: (+41 91) 695 28 05

Terminal Singen TSG GmbH
Zum Umschlagbahnhof 2, D-78224 Singen, Germany
Tel: (+49 7731) 879 00  Fax: (+49 7731) 87 90 16
Directors: Hans-Joachim Güntner, Rudi Mager

Trailstar NV
A Plesmanweg 151, NL-3088 GC Rotterdam, The Netherlands
Tel: (+31 10) 495 25 22  Fax: (+31 10) 428 05 98
President: Theo Alleman
Director of Operations: Jan Groeneveld

**Services**
Hupac Intermodal SA provides intermodal container, swapbody, unaccompanied semi-trailer and accompanied piggyback services linking Italy and northern Europe, with some connecting services also running west to Perpignan, France, to destinations in Austria and to the Nordic countries. In Germany and Switzerland, Hupac has a train operating licence and provides traction for some of its services.

Hupac SpA operates the company's Busto Arsizio terminal near Milan; Hupac GmbH holds the company's operating licence in Germany; and Terminal Singen TSG GmbH operates the Singen terminal in southern Germany. Termi SA is responsible for the planning and development of intermodal terminals and transhipment facilities.

**Traction and rolling stock**
The Hupac fleet includes three Siemens ES 64 US EuroSprinter leased from Dispolok. The company also owns more than 2,400 wagons for its intermodal traffic.

*NEW ENTRY*

## Intercontainer-Interfrigo

Intercontainer-Interfrigo (ICF) sc
Margarethenstrasse 38, CH-4008 Basel, Switzerland
Tel: (+41 61) 278 25 25  Fax: (+41 61) 278 24 45
e-mail: icf@icfonline.com
Web: http://www.icfonline.com

**Key personnel**
Chairman and Managing Director: René Hellinghausen
Managers
  Sales and Operations: René Hellinghausen
  Operational Services, Combined Transport:
    Patrice Pinoli
  Central Services: Mark W Smith

**Organisation**
Intercontainer-Interfrigo is owned by 27 European railway companies. Its customers include freight forwarders, transport companies, shipping agents and shipping lines.
Joint-venture companies with ICF participation include:
  Allied Continental Intermodal Services, Reading, UK
  Bahnhof-Kühlhaus AG, Basel, Switzerland
  CLB, Bettembourg, Luxembourg
  Intercontainer Austria GesmbH, Vienna, Austria
  Intercontainer Scandinavia AB, Gothenburg, Sweden
  Intercontainer Ibérica, Madrid, Spain
  NV Interfery, Antwerp, Belgium
  Italcontainer SpA, Milan, Italy
  Optimodal Nederland BV, Rotterdam, Netherlands
  Pannoncont Kft, Budapest, Hungary
  Polcont, Spólka zoo, Warsaw, Poland
  Transthermos GmbH, Munich, Germany.

**Services**
One of Europe's leading international combined transport operators, Intercontainer-Interfrigo runs a network of customised intermodal services, including shuttles, block trains and hubs with connections to other terminals. These span western Europe and provide links with the Russian Federation and associated states. The company also provides temperature-controlled transport services using a fleet of specialised rail wagons.

## STVA

Société de Transport de Véhicules Automobiles
Immeuble Le Cardinet, PO Box 826, F-75828 Paris Cedex 17, France
Tel: (+33 1) 44 85 56 78  Fax: (+33 1) 44 85 57 00
e-mail: stva@stva.com
Web: http://www.stva.com

**Key personnel**
President of the Executive Board: J P Bernadet
Managing Director: Y Fargues
Deputy Managing Director, Commercial and Operations:
  J Henry
Deputy Managing Director, Finance and Administration:
  J J Pronzac

**Services**
Operates a fleet of automobile transporters and offers full service (predelivery operations) throughout Europe.

## Transfesa

Transportes Ferroviarios Especiales SA
Musgo 1, Urbanizacion La Florida, Aravaca, E-28023 Madrid, Spain
Tel: (+34 91) 307 65 85  Fax: (+34 91) 372 90 59

**Key personnel**
President and Executive Director:
  Emilio Fernández Fernández
Managing Director: Luis Del Campo Villaplana

**Services**
Operates cross-border rail services from Spain, including perishables traffic to northern Europe and car parts for Ford between Valencia, Spain, and Dagenham, UK, via the Channel Tunnel.

## UIRR SC

International Union of Combined Road-Rail Transport Companies
31 rue Montoyer, Bte 11 B-1000 Brussels, Belgium
Tel: (+32 2) 548 78 90  Fax: (+32 2) 512 63 93
e-mail: headoffice.brussels@uirr.com
Web: http://www.uirr.com

**Key personnel**
Chairman: Werner Külper
Director General: Rudy Colle

**Full members**
UIRR SC

**Austria**
Ökombi
Taborstrasse 95, A-1200 Vienna
Tel: (+43 1) 331 56 0  Fax: (+43 1) 331 56 300

**Belgium**
TRW
100 Avenue du Port, Bte 1, B-1000 Brussels
Tel: (+32 2) 421 12 11  Fax: (+32 2) 425 59 59

**Czech Republic**
Bohemiakombi
Opletalova 6, CZ-113 76 Prague 1
Tel: (+420 2) 24 24 15 76
Fax: (+420 2) 24 24 15 80

**Denmark**
Kombi-Dan
Thorsvej 8, DK-6330 Padborg
Tel: (+45 74) 67 41 81  Fax: (+45 74) 67 08 98

**France**
Novatrans
21 rue du Rocher, F-75008 Paris Cédex 08
Tel: (+33 1) 53 42 54 54  Fax: (+33 1) 43 87 27 98

**Germany**
Kombiverkehr
PO Box 940153, D-60459 Frankfurt/Main
Tel: (+49 69) 79 50 50  Fax: (+49 69) 79 50 51 19

# OPERATORS OF INTERNATIONAL RAIL SERVICES IN EUROPE/Freight

**Hungary**
Hungarokombi
Szilagyi Dezso tér 1, H-1011, Budapest
Tel: (+36 1) 224 05 50   Fax: (+36 1) 224 05 55

**Italy**
Cemat
Via Valtellina 5-7, I-20159 Milan
Tel: (+39 02) 66 89 51   Fax: (+39 02) 66 80 07 55

**Netherlands**
Trailstar
Albert Plesmanweg 151, NL-3088 GC Rotterdam
Tel: (+31 10) 495 25 22   Fax: (+31 10) 428 05 98

**Norway**
Kombi-Nor
c/o Kombi-Dan, Thorsvej 8, DK-6330 Padborg, Denmark
Tel: (+45 74) 67 41 81   Fax: (+45 74) 67 08 98

**Poland**
Polkombi
ul Targowa 74, PL-03-734 Warsaw
Tel: (+48 22) 619 79 14   Fax: (+48 22) 619 00 00

**Portugal**
Portif
Avenue Sidono Pais, 4-4-P.3, P-1000 Lisbon
Tel: (+351 1) 52 35 77   Fax: (+351 1) 315 36 13

**Slovakia**
Eurotrans
Kuzmanyho 22, PO Box B-2, SK-01092 Zilina
Tel: (+421 41) 62 24 47   Fax: (+421 41) 62 56 28

**Slovenia**
Adria Kombi
Tivolska 50, SLO-1000 Ljubljana
Tel: (+386 61) 131 01 57   Fax: (+386 61) 131 01 54

**Spain**
Combiberia
Rafael Herrera 11, 3° Pta 308, E-28036 Madrid
Tel: (+34 91) 314 98 99   Fax: (+34 91) 314 93 47

**Sweden**
Swe-Kombi
Hamntorget 3, S-252 21 Helsingborg
Tel: (+46 42) 12 65 65   Fax: (+46 42) 13 88 46

**Switzerland**
Hupac
Viale R Manzoni 6, CH-6830 Chiasso
Tel: (+41 91) 695 29 00   Fax: (+41 91) 683 26 61

**UK**
CTL
179/180 Piccadilly, London W1V 9DB
Tel: (+44 20) 73 55 46 56   Fax: (+44 20) 76 29 57 14

**Associate member**
CNC
8, avenue des Minimes, F-94302 Vincennes
Tel: (33 1) 43 98 70 00   Fax: (+33 1) 73 74 18 12

### Services

The UIRR was founded in 1970 and its central objective is to ensure a more sustained development of rail transport of swapbodies and containers as well as of semi-trailers and lorries by private transport hauliers.

UIRR members operate cross-border intermodal services throughout western Europe and control over 55 per cent of all European combined transport. Local road hauliers are major shareholders in the individual national member companies.

**UPDATED**

# Unilog

Unilog NV
Leuvensesteenweg 443, B-2812 Muizen, Belgium
Tel: (+32 15) 42 20 11   Fax: (+32 15) 42 38 29

### Key personnel

Commercial Manager: Tony Davis

### Services

Operates intermodal services between Belgium, Germany and the UK via the Channel Tunnel. In 2002 the company served three terminals in the UK at Daventry, Glasgow and Manchester.

Unilog has taken delivery of 50 60 ft wagons for joint use with its Multifret wagons from Arbel-Fauvet Rail, Douai, France. Unilog carries 70 to 80 per cent of its traffic in ISO or 20 ft, 30 ft and 40 ft units, with the rest being a mix of metric 13.6 and 7.15 swapbodies.

The headquarters for Unilog is at the new inland terminal of Muizen near Malines, halfway between Antwerp and Brussels. Called Dry Port Muizen, it started operation in 1994 and is operated by Inter Ferry Boats (majority owned by Belgian National Railways).

**UPDATED**

# MANUFACTURERS

Locomotives and powered/non-powered passenger vehicles
Diesel engines, transmission and fuelling systems
Electric traction equipment
Passenger coach equipment
Freight vehicles and equipment
Brakes and drawgear
Bogies and suspension, wheels and axles, bearings
Simulation and training systems
Signalling and communications systems
Passenger information systems
Revenue collection systems and station equipment
Electrification contractors and equipment suppliers
Cables and cable equipment
Permanent way components, equipment and services
Freight yard and terminal equipment
Vehicle maintenance equipment and services
Turnkey systems contractors
Information technology systems

# LOCOMOTIVES AND POWERED/NON-POWERED PASSENGER VEHICLES

## Alphabetical listing

Alcan Mass Transportation Systems
Alna Koki
ALSTOM Transport SA
ANSALDOBREDA
Astarsa
Astra
Babcock & Wilcox Española
Babcock Rail
Beijing
BEML
BHEL
BMZ
Bombardier Transportation
Breda
Brookville
Brush
Bumar-Fablok
CAF
CFC
CFD
Changchun Car Company
Changzhou Diesel and Mining Locomotive Plant
China National Railway Locomotive and Rolling Stock Industry Corporation (LORIC)
ČKD
ČKD VAGONKA as
CLW
Cockerill Mechanical Industries SA (CMI)
Costaferroviaria SpA
Dalian Locomotive and Rolling Stock Works
Datong Locomotive Works
De Dietrich Ferroviaire
DEVZ – Dnepropetrovsk State Electric Locomotive Factory
Diesel Locomotive Works (DLW)

Diesel Supply Co
Duro Daković
E G Steele
Electroputere
Energomachexport
Evans Deakin
Ferrostaal AG
FIREMA Trasporti SpA
Fuji Car Manufacturing Co
Fuji Heavy Industries
Ganz-Hunslet
Ganz Vagon Kft
Gemco
General Motors Corporation
GE Transportation Systems
Gevisa SA
Gmeinder
Hanjin
Hitachi Ltd
Hoogovens VAW
Hunslet-Barclay
ICF
Impco
INKA
Jessop
Kalugaputjmach
Kawasaki Heavy Industries Ltd
Alan Keef Limited
Keller Elettromeccanica SpA
Kinki Sharyo
Kockums
Kolmex
Kolomna
Končar – Električne Lokomotive dd
Luganskteplovozstroj

Lyudinovo Locomotive Works JSC
Mecanoexportimport
Metrowagonmash Joint Stock Company
Michurinsk Locomotive Works
Mitsubishi Electric Corporation
Moës
MotivePower Industries
Muromteplovoz
National Railway Equipment Company
NEVZ
Newag GmbH & Co KG
Niigata Engineering Co Ltd
Nippon Sharyo
OFV
Pakistan Railways Carriage
PEC Ltd
Peoria Locomotive Works
PFA
Price
Qishuyan
Qualter Hall
Rail Services International SA (RSI)
Reggiane
Relco
Republic Locomotive
Rocafort Ingenieros
Rotem Company
RSD
Ruhrthaler
RVR
Saalasti Oy
SAN Engineering and Locomotive Co Ltd
Santa Matilde
Schöma
Schalke

---

# VSFT
## Vossloh Schienenfahrzeugtechnik GmbH

### G 1700 BB
**Four axle diesel-hydraulic locomotive for heavy shunting and main line service**

| | |
|---|---|
| Axle arrangement | B'B' |
| Track gauge | 1.435 mm |
| Weight | 80 t |
| Length | 15.200 mm |
| Height | approx. 4.220 mm |
| Width | 3.080 mm |
| Wheel diameter new/worn | 1000/920 mm |
| Max. speed | 100 km/h |
| Diesel engine | CAT 3512 B - HB |
| Diesel engine performance | 1.700 kW |
| Diesel engine speed | 1.800 rpm |
| Turbo hydraulic gear | Voith L620 re U2 |
| Starting tractive power (μ=0,33) | 259 kN |
| Min. radius of curve | 60 m |
| Diesel tank capacity | 4.400 l |

**MaK Lokomotiven**

**Vossloh Schienenfahrzeugtechnik GmbH**
Falckensteiner Str. 2
D-24159 Kiel
Phone: +49 (0)431 3999-3089
Telefax: +49 (0)431 3999-2274
E-Mail: vertrieb.kiel@vsft.vossloh.com
Internet: www.vsft.de

**Servicezentrum Moers**
Klever Str. 48
D-47441 Moers
Phone: +49 (0)2841 1404-0
Telefax: +49 (0)2841 1404-50

# 474 MANUFACTURERS/Locomotives and powered/non-powered passenger vehicles

SCIF
SEMAF
Siemens Transportation Systems
Škoda Transportation Systems
Stadler Rail Group
Tafesa
Talgo
Talgo-Transtech
Tokyu Car Corporation

Toshiba
Transrapid International
Transwerk
Tülomsas
Unilok
Union Carriage
United Gonian
Ventra
Villares

Vossloh Schienenfahrzeugtechnik GmbH (VSFT)
Wabtec Rail Ltd
Wagon Pars
Yorkshire Engine Co Ltd (YEC)
Zeco
Zephir SpA
Zhuzhou Electric Locomotive Works
Zwiehoff GmbH

## Classified listing

**BODYSHELLS AND COMPONENTS**
ALSTOM
De Dietrich Ferroviaire
Ferrostaal
FIREMA Trasporti
Hoogovens
Impco

**DIESEL LOCOMOTIVES AND POWERED/NON-POWERED PASSENGER VEHICLES**
ALSTOM Transport
Astarsa
Babcock & Wilcox Española
Babcock Rail
Beijing
BHEL
BMZ
Bombardier Transportation
Brush Traction
Bumar-Fablok
CFC
CFD
Changchun Car Co
Changzhou Diesel and Mining
ČKD Vagonka as
CLW
CMI
Dalian Locomotive & Rolling Stock Works
Datong Locomotive Works
De Dietrich Ferroviaire
DEVZ
Diesel Supply Co
DLW
Electroputere
Evans Deakin
Faur
Ganz Vagon
General Motors Corporation
Gevisa
Hitachi
Jessop
Kalugaputjmach
Kawasaki
Keller Elettromeccanica SpA
Kinki Sharyo
Kockums
Kolomna
Koncar
Krauss-Maffei
Lugansktleplovozstroj
Lyudinovo Locomotive Works
Mecanoexportimport
Michurinsk Locomotive Works
Mitsubishi Electric
MotivePower Industries
Muromteplovoz
Newag
Niigata
Nippon Sharyo
NWRZ
OFV
Pakistan Railways Carriage
PEC
Peoria Locomotive Works
PFA
Price
Qishuyan
Railcare
Rautaruukki
Reggiane
Republic Locomotive
Rocofort Ingenieros
Rotem
RPS
RSD

RSI
SCIF
SEMAF
Siemens
Siemens SGP
Siemens Schienenfahrzeugtechnik
Siemens Transportation Systems
Stadler
Tafesa
Talgo-Transtech
Tokyu
Toshiba
Tülomsas
Union Carriage
Villares
Wagon Pars
Zeco

**DIESEL MULTIPLE-UNITS AND RAILCARS**
BWS
CFD
De Dietrich Ferroviaire
Faur
Fuji
Ganz Vagon
Hitachi
Hunslet-Barclay
Kinki Sharyo
Koncar
LHB
Mecanoexportimport
MSV
Niigata
Nippon Sharyo
Reggiane
RVR
Siemens SGP
Siemens Transportation
Stadler
Tokyu
Toshiba
Union Carriage
Wabtec

**ELECTRIC LOCOMOTIVES AND POWERED PASSENGER VEHICLES**
ANSALDOBREDA
Brush Traction
ČKD Vagonka as
CLW
Datong Locomotive Works
DEVZ
Electroputere
Evans Deakin
FIREMA Trasporti
Ganz Vagon
GE
Gevisa
Hitachi
Kawasaki
Krauss-Maffei
Mecanoexportimport
Mitsubishi Electric
NEVZ
PEC
Peoria Locomotive Works
Reggiane
Rotem
RSD
Siemens SGP
Siemens Schienenfahrzeugtechnik
Siemens Transportation Systems
Škoda
Talgo-Transtech
Toshiba

Tülomsas
Union Carriage
Villares
Zeco

**ELECTRIC MULTIPLE-UNITS AND RAILCARS**
ALSTOM
ANSALDOBREDA
Babcock & Wilcox Española
BWS
ČKD Vagonka as
De Dietrich Ferroviaire
Electroputere
Evans Deakin
Ferrostaal
FIREMA Trasporti
Fuji Car Manufacturing
Ganz Vagon
Hitachi
Hyundai
Kinki Sharyo
LHB
Mecanoexportimport
Niigata
Nippon Sharyo
PEC
Reggiane
Rotem
RSD
RVR
Santa Matilde
Schlegel Swiss Standard
SEMAF
Siemens SGP
Siemens Transportation
Škoda
Stadler
Tokyu
Toshiba
Union Carriage
Villares

**HIGH-SPEED TRAINSETS**
ANSALDOBREDA
De Dietrich Ferroviaire
Hitachi
Kinki Sharyo
Mitsubishi
Nippon Sharyo
Siemens Transportation

**INDUSTRIAL, MINING AND SHUNTING LOCOMOTIVES AND POWERED/NON-POWERED PASSENGER VEHICLES**
Brookville
CFD
Changzhou Diesel and Mining Locomotive Plant
CMI
Dalian Locomotive & Rolling Stock Works
Diema
Faur
Ferrostaal
Ganz Vagon
Gemco
Hunslet-Barclay
Kaelble-Gmeinder
Keef
Moës
Newag
PEC
Peoria Locomotive Works
Plymouth
Qualter Hall
Republic Locomotive
RFS(E)

# Locomotives and powered/non-powered passenger vehicles/MANUFACTURERS

RSD
Saalasti
SAN
Schöma
Steele
Ventra
Villares
YEC

**LIGHT RAIL VEHICLES AND TRAMS**
ANSALDOBREDA
BWS
De Dietrich Ferroviaire
FIREMA Trasporti
Fuji Car Manufacturing
Ganz-Hunslet
Kinki Sharyo
Nippon Sharyo
Rotem
Schlegel Swiss Standard
SEMAF
Siemens SGP
Siemens Transportation
Stadler
Talgo-Transtech

**LOCOMOTIVE COMPONENTS**
Diesel Supply Co
Electroputere
Lyudinovo Locomotive Works

Qualter Hall
Ruhrthaler

**LOCOMOTIVE REMANUFACTURE**
Brush Traction
Hunslet-Barclay
National Railway Equipment Company
Newag
Relco
Republic Locomotive
Transwerk
YEC

**METRO CARS, MONORAILS AND PEOPLE MOVERS**
ANSALDOBREDA
Astra
Babcock & Wilcox Española
CAF
Changchun Car Company
Evans Deakin
Fuji Car Manufacturing
Ganz-Hunslet
Hitachi
Kinki Sharyo
Matra Transport
Metrowagonmash
Mitsubishi Electric
Nippon Sharyo
Rautaruukki
Rotem

SEMAF
Siemens Transportation
Toshiba
Transrapid International
Union Carriage

**PASSENGER VEHICLE REFURBISHMENT AND REPAIR**
Electroputere
Faur
Hunslet-Barclay
Newag
Railcare
Škoda

**ROAD/RAIL LOCOMOTIVES AND POWERED PASSENGER VEHICLES**
CFD
Newag
Saalasti
Unilok
YEC
Zephir

**TILTING TRAINSETS**
Nippon Sharyo
Siemens Transportation
Talgo-Transtech

## Company listing by country

**ARGENTINA**
Astarsa

**AUSTRALIA**
Evans Deakin
Gemco
Goninan

**AUSTRIA**
Siemens SGP

**BELGIUM**
Cockerill Mechanical Industries SA (CMI)
Moës

**BRAZIL**
Gevisa SA
Santa Matilde
Villares

**CANADA**
Bombardier Transportation

**CHINA, PEOPLE'S REPUBLIC**
Beijing
Changchun Car Company
Changzhou Diesel and Mining Locomotive Plant
China National Railway Locomotive and Rolling Stock Industry Corporation (LORIC)
Dalian Locomotive and Rolling Stock Works
Datong Locomotive Works
Qishuyan
Zhuzhou Electric Locomotive Works

**CROATIA**
Duro Daković
Koncar

**CZECH REPUBLIC**
ČKD Vagonka as
Škoda Transportation Systems

**EGYPT**
SEMAF

**FINLAND**
Rautaruukki
Saalasti Oy
Talgo-Transtech

**FRANCE**
ALSTOM
CFD

De Dietrich Ferroviaire
Matra Transport
RSI

**GERMANY**
Adtranz
Ferrostaal
Gmeinder
Hoogovens VAW
Newag
PFA
Ruhrthaler
Schöma
Schalke
Siemens Transportation Systems
Transrapid International
VSFT
Zwichoff Gmbh

**HUNGARY**
Ganz-Hunslet
Ganz Vagon Kft

**INDIA**
BEML
BHEL
CLW
Diesel Locomotive Works (DLW)
ICF
Jessop
PEC Ltd
SAN Engineering and Locomotive Co Ltd
Ventra

**INDONESIA**
INKA

**IRAN**
Wagon Pars

**IRELAND**
Unilok

**ITALY**
ANSALDOBREDA
Breda
CFC
Costaferroviaria SpA
FIREMA Trasporti SpA
Keller Elettromeccanica SpA
OFV
Reggiane
Zephir SpA

**JAPAN**
Alna Koki
Fuji Car Manufacturing Co
Fuji Heavy Industries
Hitachi
Kawasaki
Kinki Sharyo
Mitsubishi Electric Corporation
Niigata
Nippon Sharyo
Tokyu Car Corporation
Toshiba

**KOREA, SOUTH**
Hanjin
Rotem

**LATVIA**
RVR

**MOROCCO**
SCIF

**NEW ZEALAND**
Price

**PAKISTAN**
Pakistan Railways Carriage

**POLAND**
Bumar-Fablok
Kolmex

**ROMANIA**
Astra
Electroputere
Mecanoexportimport

**RUSSIAN FEDERATION**
BMZ
Energomachexport
Kalugaputjmach
Kolomna
Lyudinovo Locomotive Works JSC
Metrowagonmash Joint Stock Company
Michurinsk Locomotive Works
Muromteplovoz
NEVZ

**SOUTH AFRICA**
RSD
Transwerk
Union Carriage

## MANUFACTURERS/Locomotives and powered/non-powered passenger vehicles

**SPAIN**
Babcock & Wilcox Española
CAF
Rocafort Ingenieros
Tafesa
Talgo

**SWEDEN**
Kockums

**SWITZERLAND**
Alcan Mass Transportation Systems
Stadler Rail Group

**TURKEY**
Tülomsas

**UKRAINE**
DEVZ – Dnepropetrovsk State Electric Locomotive Factory
Luganskteplovozstroj

**UNITED KINGDOM**
Babcock Rail
Brush
E G Steele
Hunslet-Barclay
Keef
Qualter Hall
Railcare
Wabtec Rail Ltd
Yorkshire Engine Co Ltd (YEC)

**UNITED STATES OF AMERICA**
Brookville
Diesel Supply Co
General Motors Corporation
GE Transportation Systems
Impco
MotivePower Industries
National Railway Equipment Company
Peoria Locomotive Works
Relco
Republic Locomotive
Siemens

**ZIMBABWE**
Zeco

The most important thing in trains are the people...

# rsi
RAIL SERVICES INTERNATIONAL

DESIGN • ENGINEERING • MAINTENANCE • REFURBISHMENT

DIRECTION INTERNATIONALE / 38, rue de la Convention • F-94270 Le Kremlin-Bicêtre
Tél. : +33 (0) 1 53 14 17 30 • Fax : +33 (0) 1 53 14 17 49 • E-mail : info@railsi.com • Site : www.railsi.com

# MANUFACTURERS/Locomotives and powered/non-powered passenger vehicles

## Alcan Mass Transportation Systems

(Alcan Alesa Engineering Ltd)
PO Box 1250, Max Högger-Strasse 6, CH-8048 Zurich, Switzerland
Tel: (+41 43) 497 44 22   Fax: (+41 43) 497 45 85
e-mail: roadrail@access.ch

### Key personnel
Managing Director: Hans-R Käser
Commercial Director: Giorgio Destefani

### Background
Alcan Mass Transportation Systems, formerly Alusuisse Road & Rail Ltd, is a member of the Fabrication Europe Division of Alcan Inc which operates plants in 37 countries. The Mass Transportation Systems Business Unit is the marketing, sales, engineering and project management organisation representing the Alcan group of companies in the transport market worldwide.

### Products
Development and design, stress, crash and vibration analysis as well as energy management calculation of aluminium and hybrid bodyshells which are built using extrusions and composite elements; development and design of complete vehicle interiors including systems integration, insulation, sound-dampening and decoration; manufacture of prototypes; static strain gauge and fatigue testing of bodyshells for all types of passenger rolling stock and components; supply of aluminium semis (large extrusions up to 800 mm width, sheets); structural subassemblies (such as complete cab fronts for locomotives and railcars) as well as interior components of composite materials and others.

### Contracts
Alcan Mass Transportation Systems has entered into co-operation agreements with more than 30 rolling stock manufacturers.

Recent contracts include low-floor regional trainsets for Austrian, Danish, French, Greek, Italian, Slovakian, Spanish, Swiss and USA railways; suburban trainsets for Barcelona, Helsinki and Melbourne; double-deck coaches for Czech, Finnish, French, Italian and Swiss railways; tilting trains for Czech, German, Italian, Portuguese, Slovenian, Spanish, Swiss and UK railways; high-speed trains for French, German, Italian, Spanish and USA railways; Transrapid Maglev train for Shanghai airport line.

**UPDATED**

## Alna Koki

Alna Koki Company Ltd
4-5 Higashi Naniwa-cho 1-chome, Amagasaki 660-8572, Japan
Tel: (+81 6) 401 72 83   Fax: (+81 6) 401 61 68

*Pendolino UK built by Alstom Transport*

### Key personnel
President: Juni.chi Konishiike
Managing Director, Sales and Production: Makato Hosoi
Managing Director, Engineering: Yutaka Kurita

### Products
Aluminium, mild steel and stainless-steel electric railcars, passenger coaches and light rail vehicles.

## ALSTOM Transport SA

Worldwide Headquarters of Transport Sector:
48, rue Albert Dhalenne, F-93482 Saint-Ouen Cedex France
Tel: (+33 1) 41 66 90 00   Fax: (+33 1) 41 66 96 66
Web: http://www.transport.alstom.com

### Key personnel
President, Transport Sector: Michel Moreau
Deputy President, Transport Sector: Gérard Blanc
Senior Vice President: Charles Carlier
Vice President: Jeffrey Done

### Background
ALSTOM, floated on the Paris, London and New York stock exchanges in June 1998, has a presence in over 60 countries and employs 113,700 people. For each of its main markets, ALSTOM offers a complete range of systems, components and services covering design and manufacture as well as commissioning and long-term maintenance. The company also has experience in large-scale systems integration and the management of turnkey projects.

In March 1999, ALSTOM and ABB announced their decision to merge their power generation activities in a 50-50 joint company to be known as ABB ALSTOM Power.

The company is organised into six sectors: Energy, Transmission and Distribution, Transport, Industry, Marine, and Local Contracting. All of these are supported by the ALSTOM Country Network.

The Transport Sector of ALSTOM employs nearly 25,000 people. It has production facilities in more than 20 countries. ALSTOM reports that one in every four metro trains in the world, in over 40 major cities, is an ALSTOM product: nearly 550 of ALSTOM-built TGV trainsets are in operation in seven countries.

ALSTOM has acquired or formed the following companies:

In July 2002, ALSTOM announced the signing of a joint venture agreement with German Rail (DB AG) to undertake locomotive renovation and leasing at a DB site at Stendal, Germany. Subject to approval by national and European regulatory authorities, operations by the venture, in which ALSTOM will hold a 51 per cent stake, was expected to start in September 2002. In the UK, ALSTOM acquired Railcare in 2001; it specialises in heavy overhaul and refurbishment of locomotives, dmus and emus and main line coaches. With facilities at Coventry, Springburn (Glasgow) and Wolverton, Railcare has become part of ALSTOM's Transport Services business as ALSTOM Railcare Ltd.

In November 2000, ALSTOM and General Motors Electro-Motive Division (EMD) announced the formation of a joint venture, ALSTOM EMD Services, to provide locomotive maintenance services worldwide.

In Italy, ALSTOM acquired a 51 per cent shareholding in Fiat Ferroviaria in October 2000. As well as the high-speed tilting trainsets for which it has become best known, Fiat Ferroviaria's product capabilities include dmus and emus, metro cars, LRVs, diesel and electric locomotives, passenger coaches, bogies and components.

In Canada, ALSTOM acquired Telecite Inc in 1999. Founded in 1986, Telecite specialises in developing, manufacturing and marketing real-time information and communication systems for public transport and other applications.

In France, ALSTOM increased its shareholding in De Dietrich Ferroviaire from 17.5 per cent acquired in 1995 to 68.75 per cent in 1998 and 98.75 per cent in January 1999.

In the UK, ALSTOM acquired Wessex Traincare in 1998; it specialises in heavy overhaul and refurbishment of main line coaches, and electrical multiple-units.

The SASIB railway signalling business was acquired in 1998. It is based in Italy and has a presence in Europe along with GRS in the USA.

Mafersa's stainless steel technology was bought by ALSTOM in 1997. Mafersa, Brazil, was founded in 1944 and its products include cars for suburban, metro and long-distance services, LRVs, car bodyshells, wheels and axles. It also undertakes the refurbishing and replacement of the main components of passenger cars.

Konstal, Poland, was bought in 1997. Its product range includes tramcars, LRVs and metros.

Also in 1997, an agreement was signed with the Fidelity and Deposit Company of Maryland to take possession of the Hornell facilities, New York, which were previously owned by the American Passenger Rail Car Company, LCC (Amerail).

*Series 10-000 emu for Tokyo Transportation Bureau*

The Canadian company AMF (now ALSTOM Canada Inc) was acquired in 1996 from Canadian National railway undertaking. It specialises in the maintenance and refurbishment of rolling stock, locomotives and coaches.

Linke-Hofmann-Busch (LHB) in Germany, became a subsidiary company in 1995. Its products include metro cars, low-floor LRVs and conventional tramway rolling stock. It also delivers emus, dmus and ICE cars.

ALSTOM Transport SA was set up in 1995 following the acquisition of the Romanian company, Faur. It builds rail vehicles in Romania and refurbishes rolling stock.

CMW, based in Brazil, was bought in 1995. It produces a range of signalling equipment for urban, suburban and national railway network management and security.

## Products

ALSTOM designs, manufactures, tests and commissions rolling stock for commuter, metro and light rail applications; as well as single- or double-deck, electric or diesel-electric trainsets for suburban, regional high-speed and very-high-speed use. ALSTOM also produces locomotives and freight wagons and markets traction and electromechanical subsystems to third-party wagon and carriage builders.

The company also designs, configures, integrates, tests and commissions rail transport network signalling systems for urban and main line rail infrastructure authorities. These include traffic management, traffic control, maintenance diagnostics and planning solutions, passenger information facilities and automatic driving systems.

These products and systems are also marketed by ALSTOM within a range of rail transport system solution packages, which may include: project management, project financing, civil works, life-time maintenance, and initial or long-term transport service operation. All this offering is backed up by a worldwide service organisation offering customers a range of service packages from basic warranty and parts to 'lifetime support'.

## Locomotives

ALSTOM has developed a new family of locomotives, named Prima, particularly for the European freight transport market. Prima locomotives can be equipped with each of the relevant train control systems to enable them to run on all electrified lines in Europe and are available in both diesel and multivoltage electric versions. The design is claimed to cut traction costs by up to 30 per cent, through its ONIX technology. It is offered as the world's first locomotive to use an IGBT traction system. A 4,200 kW 140 km/h multivoltage demonstrator has been produced.

## Passenger vehicles

ALSTOM has developed six comprehensive families of rolling stock to address the rail transport market, from LRVs and metros through commuter, regional and intercity trains, to high-speed and very-high-speed trains. Optionic Design© is the name given to ALSTOM's product design process, which integrates from the very beginning a wide range of configurations, based on international customers' evolving needs around the world.

The five families are: Citadis™ (light rail vehicles for city operation), Metropolis™ (metro cars for city operation), X'trapolis™ (commuter trainsets), Coradia™ (regional and intercity trainsets), Pendolino™ (high-speed trainsets) and TGV (very-high-speed trainsets).

All these families use what ALSTOM calls service-proven equipment, bogies and subassemblies such as ONIX™ Drive and Agate train control, produced by the many ALSTOM units around the world. These factors contribute to lower LCC and higher reliability and availability.

*TER double-deck emu for SNCF regional services* 2002/0525426

Citadis features include:
- modularity, with a choice of car dimensions, high or low floor
- improved vision and comfort, with 35 per cent more glass surfaces compared to a traditional tramway
- high safety levels for drivers and passengers, with reinforced cab structure and bodyshell structure easy maintenance thanks to centralised spare parts supply, with plug-in, pull-out layout of equipment interfaces
- quick repairability with easy-to-exchange windows and panelling.

Metropolis is the mass transit solution and addresses the different needs of customers worldwide, from the most traditional metro to the most sophisticated driverless version. Choices of train dimensions, train configurations, multiple-unit operation, train-monitoring architecture and manned or unmanned operation mean that customers are able to select design parameters to create the right metro for their network.

X'trapolis is a high-capacity commuter train. Like the Citadis and Metropolis families, it offers flexibility in train dimensions and configurations. Other features include: electrical multiple-units and passenger coaches, single- and double-decks, easy maintenance and upgrading to deal with different passenger flow requirements.

X'trapolis is designed to meet all track gauge, vehicle gauge and voltage requirements.

Coradia addresses the increasing trends of urban and outer-city development. Coradia regional and intercity trains are modular flexible products, designed to provide high standards of comfort, safety and performance. The Coradia family holds the record for the fastest dmu and double-deck emu (200 and 220 km/h respectively).

The Coradia Duplex double-deck train concept with distributed power has a new bodyshell based on a system of laser-cut interlocking pieces. In this way, the structure is flexible and can adapt to any specific gauge dimensions or body shapes for technical or aesthetic purposes. It can operate at up to 220 km/h in dmu, emu or locomotive-operated push-pull version.

The Pendolino family operates at maximum speeds in the 200-270 km/h range. Most of this family are tilting trains but in certain cases, such as the recent RENFE order, the tilting capability was not specified as the trains will only operate on high-speed lines.

The TGV family of very-high-speed trains includes single-deck, double-deck and the new AGV (Automotrice à Grande Vitesse). They are all based on the articulated trainset concept, which provides high security for passengers and drivers alike. The TGV Duplex features an aluminium bodyshell, high capacity and speeds of up to 320 km/h. The AGV can travel up to 350 km/h and has the advantage of distributed power throughout the trainset. A tilting TGV is also possible.

The Coradia, Pendolino and TGV product families can all be built as tilting trains, using ALSTOM's field-proven, third-generation Tiltronix technology. In future, up to 20 per cent of Coradia orders are expected to be tilting trains. For the TGV, Tiltronix would be applied to optimise performance if the train were required to leave dedicated high-speed routes and operate on traditional lines. ALSTOM's industrial unit in Savigliano, Italy, is the company's centre for Tiltronix technology.

## Contact points

**Brazil**
ALSTOM Transporte Ltda
Al Campinas 463-4 Floor, 01404-902 São Paulo
Tel: (+55 11) 30 69 07 22

**France**
ALSTOM Transport – La Rochelle Plant
avenue du Commandant Lysiak, 17440 Aytre BP 359,
F-17001 La Rochelle Cedex
Tel: (+33 5) 46 51 30 00

ALSTOM Transport – Valenciennes Plant
rue Jacquart – BP 45, F-59494 Petite Foret
Tel: (+33 3) 27 14 18 00

ALSTOM DDF
6 route de Strasbourg, F-67110 Reichshoffen
Tel: (+33 3) 88 80 25 00

**Germany**
ALSTOM LHB GmbH
Linke-Hofmann-Busch-Strasse 1, D-38239 Salzgitter
Tel: (+49 53) 41 21 05

**Italy**
ALSTOM Ferroviaria SpA
Via O Moreno 23, I-12038 Savigliano (CN), Italy
Tel: (+39 0172) 71 83 08   Fax: (+39 0172) 71 83 06

ALSTOM Transport SpA
Via Nazario Suro 38, Sesto San Giovanni, Milan, Italy
Tel: (+39 02) 248 82 62 02   Fax: (+39 02) 240 25 52

**Poland**
ALSTOM Konstal SA
Ul Katowicka 104/41 500 Chorzow
Tel: (+48 32) 349 10 00

**Spain**
ALSTOM Transporte – Barcelona Plant
Crta – B140 de Sta Perpetua a Mollet del Valles kM 7.5,
E-08120 Sta Perpetua de Mogoda, Barcelona
Tel: (+34 93) 575 50 00

**UK**
ALSTOM Transport UK
PO Box 248, Leigh Road, Washwood Heath, Birmingham
B8 2YJ
Tel: (+44 121) 695 36 00

*Coradia LINT 41 lightweight regional dmu for NordWest Bahn, Germany* 2002/0525429

# 480 MANUFACTURERS/Locomotives and powered/non-powered passenger vehicles

**USA**
ALSTOM Transportation Inc
353, Lexington Avenue Suite 800, New York, New York 10016
Tel: (+1 212) 557 72 62

ALSTOM Transport (ex-Amerail)
1 Transit Drive, Hornell, New York 14843
Tel: (+1 607) 324 45 95

### Systems solutions, systems integration and project financing
Project management, systems integration and supply packages. These packages are custom-designed from a set of modules which start with the rolling stock and signalling system and extend to embrace the remaining electrical and mechanical systems, the civil works, project finance, lifetime maintenance and even initial or long-term transport service operation.

ALSTOM Transport Systems
48 rue Albert Dhalenne, F-93482 Saint-Ouen Cedex
Tel: (+33 1) 41 66 90 00   Fax: (+33 1) 41 66 96 66
Vice-President and Executive Director: Charles Carlier

ALSTOM Transport Systems
PO Box 223, Block G, Booths Hall, Knutsford WA16 8GL, UK
Tel: (+44 1565) 75 86 05   Fax: (+44 1565) 75 83 70
Director: Julian Garrat

ALSTOM Transport Systems Infrastructure Business Unit
3 rue Eugene & Armand Peuguot, F-92508 Rueil-Malmaison Cedex
Tel: (+33 1) 47 52 80 00   Fax: (+33 1) 47 52 82 46
Director: Alain Goga

### Traction equipment and subsystems
ALSTOM supplies fully integrated propulsion system packages, traction equipment and support services for modern railway and urban transportation vehicles. It offers a range of products, services and expertise in transport electronics, and in electrical and mechanical engineering and establishes partnerships with its customers to support them throughout the life cycle of their equipment.

### Contact points
Traction equipment and auxiliary converters:
ALSTOM Ltd
Channel Way, Preston PR1 8XL, UK
Tel: (+44 1772) 25 47 77

Traction equipment, power modules and switchgear:
ALSTOM Transport SA
50 rue du Dr Guimier, PO Box 4, F-65600 Semeac
Tel: (+33 5) 62 53 41 21

Onboard electronic equipment:
ALSTOM Transport SA
11-13 Avenue de Bel Air, F-69627 Villeurbanne Cedex
Tel: (+33 4) 72 81 52 00

Motors:
ALSTOM Transport SA
7 Av De Lattre de Tassigny, BP 49, F-25290 Ornans Cedex
Tel: (+33 3) 81 62 44 00

Bogies and dampers:
ALSTOM Transport SA
1 rue Baptiste Marcet, PO Box 42, F-71202 Le Creusot Cedex
Tel: (+33 3) 85 77 60 00

Transport services:
ALSTOM Train Services
PO Box 248, Leigh Road, Washwood Heath, Birmingham B8 2YF
Tel: (+44 121) 695 36 00   Fax (+44 121) 327 56 31

### Maintenance, equipment and services section
Signalling systems:
ALSTOM Signaling
Head Office: 33 rue des Bateliers, PO Box 165, F-93404 Saint-Ouen, Cedex, France
Tel: (+33 1) 40 10 63 35   Fax: (+33 1) 40 10 61 00
Senior Vice-President: Gerard Blanc
See main entry in Signalling, communications and traffic control equipment

*Dublin DART emu*     2001/0104620

### Contracts
**Argentina:** ALSTOM received an order from Métrovias SA for the supply of 16 trainsets for Line A of the Buenos Aires metro system. The order calls for the manufacture of 80 stainless steel metro cars, to be equipped with ONIX traction systems and built in ALSTOM's Brazil unit.

**Australia:** ALSTOM signed contracts in 2000 with Metrolink for the supply and maintenance of new trams for the Yarra Trams network of Melbourne. Under the terms of the contracts, ALSTOM was to provide 36 Citadis 300 low-floor tramsets. ALSTOM is also responsible for maintaining the new fleet over 15 years. Deliveries commenced in 2001.

In 1999, ALSTOM Transport won an order to supply and maintain 58 three-car X'trapolis 100 suburban trains for the Connex Trains Melbourne network. Deliveries commenced in 2002. ALSTOM was also to maintain the existing fleet of 74 trains and assume responsibility for managing the whole network.

**Belgium:** SNCB (Société Nationale des Chemins de Fer Belges) placed an order in 1999 for 35 sets of six double-deck passenger coaches with a consortium composed of ALSTOM and Bombardier Transportation. The order is shared equally between the two consortium members. The six-car sets are configured in pairs to form 220 km/h locomotive-hauled formations to boost intercity services to and from Brussels.

**Brazil:** ALSTOM won a turnkey order from Metrofor for a metro system in Fortaleza, northeastern Brazil. The 24 km line, which will have 17 stations, of which three will be underground, will link Joao Felipe in the city centre to Villa Das Flores in the suburbs. It was due to be commissioned in 2001. The order covers 10 four-car trainsets, which incorporate the ONIX 3000 drive system, and the signalling system. In addition, ALSTOM is responsible for the management of the project and the integration and installation of the complete electrical and mechanical system. The overall system will be manufactured by ALSTOM's factories in São Paulo, with traction equipment supplied by ALSTOM's plant in Tarbes, France.

Companhia Paulista de Trens Metropolitanos (CPTM), the public sector organisation responsible for suburban railway transport in São Paulo State, selected the Sistrem Consortium, led by ALSTOM, to build its new 9 km line from Capão Redondo to Largo Treze. The Sistrem Consortium was formed to undertake the project on a turnkey basis. Within it, ALSTOM is responsible for the overall technical management of the project, systems integration, provision from its factories in Brazil and France of eight six-car Metropolis trainsets, the signalling system, operations control centre and various items of electrical and mechanical equipment for the stations. Other members of the consortium are:
- Siemens (Brazil and Germany), which will provide the high- and medium-voltage power supply equipment and auxiliary inverters for the rolling stock;
- Adtranz (Brazil) (now Bombardier), was to provide rectifiers and auxiliary substations, the overhead line and elements of the signalling system;
- CAF (Spain), which will provide bogies and couplers for the rolling stock.

The new line is the first phase of a project which it is planned to extend as far as Chacara Klabin station (Vila Mariana region) in the future.

**Canada:** ALSTOM was awarded an order by VIA Rail, Canada for the supply of 139 former Nightstock coaches. VIA Rail uses these coaches for overnight services, operating on its flagship routes between Halifax, Montreal and Toronto. The vehicles entered service in 2002.

**Chile:** In 2002, ALSTOM won a turnkey contract to equip the new 32 km Line 4 of the Santiago metro system. This includes the supply of 60 three-car Metropolis stainless steel-bodied metro trains. Commissioning of the system is scheduled for the end of 2005.

Also in 2002, Metro Regional de Valparaiso (Merval) selected ALSTOM to supply 28 two-car emus to provide main line suburban services between Valparaiso, Viña del Mar and Limache. Deliveries are scheduled for 2005. The contract also covers maintenance of the trains.

ALSTOM has signed a contract with Metro SA, operator of the Santiago metro, for the supply of rolling stock intended to strengthen the existing fleet. ALSTOM is to

*Pendolino S220 tilting trainset for Finnish Railways*     2002/0525425

*Juniper trainset for South West Trains, UK*
2001/0104614

supply 92 cars (10 eight-car trains, a seven-car trainset, and five trailer cars to be added to existing trainsets). The order includes the maintenance of the new trainsets for two years. The new trains will use the latest technology, including Agate Media, ALSTOM's passenger information system. The vehicles are designed with walkthrough gangways, which allow passengers to circulate freely throughout the train. The new vehicles will allow Metro SA to cope with rising traffic and to meet the needs linked to the extension of Lines 5 and 2 of its network. First deliveries were scheduled for early 2002 at a rate of one train per month. This contract is a follow-on to the order placed by Metro SA in 1997, which was for six seven-car trainsets.

**China:** In 2002, ALSTOM in partnership with Nanjing Puzhen Rolling Stock Works was selected by Nanjing Metro Company Ltd to supply 20 six-car Metropolis metro trains for Phase the city's North-South Line scheme. The first train is to be built at ALSTOM's plant in Valenciennes, France, with the remainder of the contract fulfilled by the Nanjing Puzhen Rolling Stock Works. Deliveries are due to take place between May 2002 and June 2006.

ALSTOM has been awarded a contract by the Shanghai Mass Transit Pearl Line Development Co Ltd for the supply of 28 six-car Metropolis trainsets, worth some Euro203 million, for Line 3 of the city's metro. The new line links the southeast to the north of the city. The trains' lightweight aluminium cars will be equipped with ALSTOM's ONIX 1500 drive propulsion system based on IGBT technology. A significant portion of work relating to the contract will be carried out in China by several factories, including the Shanghai ALSTOM Transport Electrical Equipment Company Ltd and Nanjing Puzhen Rolling Stock Works.

A contract for the new Shanghai tramway, the Xinmin line, covers the supply of 152 Metropolis cars, with an option for a further 148. This contract was between JIUSHI, a company representing the Municipality of Shanghai, and SATCO, a joint venture between ALSTOM (with a 40 per cent stake) and Shanghai Electric Corporation (SEC) (60 per cent).

**Czech Republic:** ALSTOM is a member of a consortium supplying to ČD seven three-voltage seven-car tilting trainsets (Series 680) based on the design of Italian Railways Class ETR 460 Pendolino trainsets. First deliveries are due in 2003.

**Denmark:** In 2002, Arriva Tog AS ordered 30 two-car Coradia LINT regional dmus for its Jutland franchise. The order includes an option for five additional vehicles. Delivery is scheduled for 2004.

**Egypt:** In September 2000, an order was received from Egyptian National Railways to supply 30 diesel shunting locomotives.

**Finland:** Options were exercised in 2002 to supply to VR-Group an additional eight of a possible 15 six-car Pendolino electric tilting trainsets to supplement the 10 Class Sm3 trains already in service or in production. Delivery of the first trainset is scheduled for early 2004.

At the same time, options were taken up by VR-Group to order 20 of an additional 40 Class Sm4 two-car aluminium-bodied suburban Coradia emus similar to 10 examples delivered by the former Fiat Ferroviaria in 1999. Deliveries are due to begin in May 2004.

**France:** The Communauté Urbaine de Bordeaux (CUB) has placed firm orders for 70 trams placed in batches of 38 and 32 vehicles. Delivery of the first tram took place in 2002. When commercial service begins in Bordeaux in 2003, the Citadis will become the first tramway to operate catenary-free in certain areas on its route. From the inception of this project, one of the customer's primary concerns was that its historic old city and city centre not be marred by unsightly overhead wires. ALSTOM was selected for a solution relying on new technology for powering the trams by ground, which is being supplied by Innorail under project management by ALSTOM.

An order placed in March 2002 for 40 vehicles brought to 299 the number of ATER regional railcars ordered by SNCF. The vehicles, part of ALSTOM's Coradia product family, are built in Reichshoffen, France.

In 2002, SNCF placed a contract with ALSTOM to supply 10 Type Z2N four-car double-deck emus for services in the Ile-de-France region. Delivery is scheduled for 2003.

In 2002, SNCF placed with ALSTOM an order to supply 29 Class Z 21500 TER three-car regional emus, bringing to 51 the number of vehicles of this type odered by the operator.

The Paris Transport Authority (RATP) is to order 161 metro trains (805 metro cars) from the consortium comprising ALSTOM, Bombardier Transportation and Technicatome. The trains are destined to replace some 40 per cent of the RATP's current metro fleet, beginning in 2005. Designated MF 2000, the new trains will be composed of five cars, three of which will be powered by ONIX traction systems. Similar equipment has also been supplied by ALSTOM to the Washington, DC metro. Construction is to be undertaken at Valenciennes. A pre-series train is to be delivered for testing on Line 2 of the Paris Métro in December 2003. Full production is scheduled to begin by mid-2004 and the first series train for Line 2 will be delivered by December 2005. Deliveries for Line 5 will begin in mid-2008, and for Line 9 in mid-2011. Final deliveries are scheduled for December 2015.

In July 1998 SNCF ordered 120 Prima locomotives with options on 180 more. Each has a power rating of 4,200 kW and a maximum speed of 140 km/h. Ninety of these locomotives are to be two-voltage (25 kV AC/1.5 kV DC); the remaining 30 will be three-current machines additionally equipped to operate from the German and Swiss 15 kV AC systems. Another order has been placed by SNCF for 30 passenger and freight Astride electric locomotives, rated at 6,000 kW and with a maximum speed of 220 km/h.

By 2000, ALSTOM had completed deliveries of an order to supply 80 TER2N two-car double-deck emus for the Nord-Pas-de-Calais, Provence-Côte d'Azur and Rhône-Alpes regions. SNCF subsequently notified ALSTOM of its decision to order 205 new-generation TER2N double-deck regional emu cars. This first firm order comes within the framework of an investment programme for 629 new cars, to be carried out over several years and financed by regional authorities. The new distributed power vehicle, part of the Coradia Duplex product family, will be able to operate at up to 160 km/h.

The order calls for 72 trainsets, composed of two to five cars, according to service requirements. The number of seated places will be 220 in two-car and 576 in five-car versions. First deliveries will begin in December 2003.

City operators which have ordered Citadis LRVs include Montpellier, which specified a partial low-floor, air conditioned vehicle (with low-floor access also at the front door), and a width of 2.65 m. The system was inaugurated in July 2000. Orleans specified a partial low-floor, air conditioned vehicle too (with low-floor access also at the front door), and a width of 2.32 m. Lyon selected a full low-floor vehicle with air conditioning and a width of 2.40 m. The system was inaugurated in December 2000. Valenciennes is taking 17 Citadis trams with ONIX traction systems. Each LRV is 30 m long, 2.4 m wide and has a partial low floor.

The Paris Transport Authority (RATP) notified ALSTOM in 2000 of its decision to order 13 Citadis trams, destined for existing or projected tramway lines in the Ile-de-France region. This firm order is part of a programme involving a total of 60 vehicles needed to strengthen services on tramway lines T1 (Saint Denis—Bobigny) and T2 (La Défense—Issy Val de Seine). Delivery of the new vehicles will begin in March 2002. For this order, ALSTOM will supply RATP with its new Citadis 300 tram.

In 1999, EOLE, the fifth line of the Paris region's Regional Express Network (RER), was officially inaugurated. It is served by MI2N trainsets designed and manufactured by ALSTOM. The MI2N's double-deck design provides a capacity for 3,000 people. For the MI2N project, ALSTOM acted as prime contractor in an industrial consortium with Bombardier Transportation (ANF Industrie). A major prerequisite was that the new trainset be equipped with three extra-wide doors per car to minimise station dwell times. These provide an entry and exit flow capacity of 1,100 passengers in less than 50 seconds. The MI2N is compatible with the signalling systems of both RER operators, SNCF and RATP. Initially 53 MI2N trainsets were ordered by SNCF, with options on 50 more, and 17 by RATP, with options on 23.

ALSTOM won a €230 million order for an additional 12 double-deck TGV Duplex high-speed trainsets for use on the new TGV Méditerranée line. The new line, linking Paris and Lyon with Marseille, opened in July 2001. Bombardier Transportation (ANF Industrie) has partnered ALSTOM in the manufacture of the trains, deliveries of which were due to run from September 2001 to the end of 2002. The new trains will be formed of eight passenger cars and two power cars. They will be added to SNCF's existing fleet of 30 TGV Duplex trainsets.

SNCF notified ALSTOM in 2001 of its intent to order 18 TGV Duplex double-deck high-speed trainsets to complement its firm order of 22 trainsets (placed in October 2000). The optional order for 18 trainsets and the initial order for 22 trainsets are part of an investment programme being carried out by the SNCF over several years. In all, the SNCF will have a fleet of 82 TGV Duplex trains by 2006. This total includes 30 TGV Duplex trains already in service in France as well as 12 TGV Duplex trains currently being built for an earlier order awarded to ALSTOM in July 1999. The new trains are to be used to strengthen the SNCF's high-speed service in France; they will be used on the Paris—Lyons line, to complement the 30 TGV Duplex trains currently in intense service on this line.

**Germany:** In 2002, Landesnahverkehrsgesellschaft Niedersachsen (LNVG) placed an order for 16 Coradia LINT two-car regional dmus for NordWestBahn services in northwest Germany. Delivery is scheduled for 2003. This

*Arlanda Express emu for service linking Arlanda Airport and Stockholm, Sweden*
2000/0092253

contract includes an option for 30 additional vehicles and follows an earlier order for 23 trains of this type. A 15-year service agreement covers fleet maintenance.

In 2001, Regionalbahn Kassel GmbH in co-operation with Kasseler Verkehrsgesellscahft placed a contract with ALSTOM to supply 28 Regio Citadis dual-voltage and diesel-hybrid tram-trains for suburban services around Kassel. Intended to operate over both heavy rail main lines and the city's tram system, the order comprises two vehicle types: 18 dual-voltage (600/750 V DC/15 kV AC 16 2/3 Hz); and 10 diesel-hybrid (600/750 V DC/diesel-electric). Delivery of the all-electric vehicles is scheduled to start in 2003, with the diesel-hybrid variant following in 2005.

**Iran:** ALSTOM is supplying RAI with 100 3,200 kW Prima DE 43C AC diesel-electric locomotives for passenger and freight traffic. To be delivered from March 2002, the locomotives are equipped with MAN B&W Ruston diesel engines and ONIX asynchronous drive systems. The first 20 locomotives are being manufactured at ALSTOM's factory in Belfort, eastern France. The remaining 80 units are being assembled in Iran by Wagon Pars, ALSTOM's local partner for the contract.

**Ireland:** ALSTOM has won orders to supply 26 Citadis tram sets, with an option for an additional 14, for Dublin's new LUAS LRT line. The low-floor vehicles, which use the ONIX 800 propulsion system with asynchronous traction motors, are approximately 30 m long, 2.4 m wide, and can carry up to 170 passengers. Delivery of the order began in October 2001 and was due for completion in May 2002. A further order was placed in August 2000 for 14 40 m partial low-floor vehicles for Dublin's Line B.

ALSTOM won an order to supply five dmus to Irish Rail (IE) for Dublin area suburban services.

**Israel:** In 1998 Israel Railways (IR) commissioned three new Bo-Bo diesel-electric shunters as part of its traction fleet modernisation programme. The 920 kW centre-cab machines were supplied by ALSTOM Spain, and are similar to locomotives delivered to Spanish National Railways and Swiss Federal Railways. IR has also taken delivery of 10 Bo-Bo and eight Co-Co Prima 2,460 kW main line diesel-electric locomotives from the same builder against a June 1996 contract and in July 2000 placed an order for an additional 10 Bo-Bo locomotives. They are powered by General Motors engines.

**Italy:** In 2002, Ferrovia Trento-Malè SpA ordered 12 two-car Coradia regional emus for services in the Trento province of northern Italy. Delivery is scheduled for 2004.

In January 2001, ALSTOM was awarded a contract by FS (Trenitalia) for 37 three-car articulated Coradia trains (20 emus and 16 dmus) for regional services. The trains will be assigned to Trenitalia (14 emus, 10 dmus) and the provinces of Arezzo (four emus), Salerno (three emus) and Trento (six dmus). Deliveries are due to begin in 2004. Options cover the supply of an additional 90 emus and 74 dmus.

ALSTOM won an order, in consortium with Costaferroviaria, to supply 10 emus, including an option for six, for the Rome—Viterbe line.

Other contracts include 28 partial low-floor vehicles delivered by 1999 for ATAC Rome, complemented by an earlier order in 1998 for 50 low-floor Citiway trams. Also,

*Nine-car Pendolino tilting electric trainset for Virgin Trains services on the UK's West Coast Main Line (Milepost 92.5)* 2001/0114314

for the same operator, 50 low-floor tramcars delivered by 2000. Turin Municipal Transport Authority is taking 55 tramcars with an option of up to 100, for delivery by December 2002 and Messina is taking 15 low-floor LRVs for delivery by July 2002.

**Luxembourg:** Luxembourg National Railways (CFL) authorised SNCF in 2001 to notify ALSTOM on its behalf that it will place an order for new-generation double-deck electrical multiple units. This order comes within the framework of a sales agreement schedule for 629 Coradia Duplex vehicles, signed by SNCF in 2000. The first firm order of this agreement, financed by the Regions of France, was for 205 vehicles. The new order for 36 vehicles (12 three-car trainsets), destined for CFL, was confirmed to ALSTOM in 2001. ANF Industries (Bombardier Transport) will participate in the manufacture of these trains.

**Mexico:** ALSTOM won a contract to refurbish NM 73B and MP 68 II rolling stock. ALSTOM also received an order from Bombardier Concarril and CAF for 13 six-car trainsets for Line A of the Mexico City metro. This was ALSTOM's first complete order for its new-generation ONIX traction system with Agate electronic power control.

**Netherlands:** ALSTOM secured a contract to supply 11 two-car Coradia Lint lightweight dmus to Syntus, a consortium formed by Netherlands Railways (NS Reizigers), the Dutch bus company VSN, and French-based public transport operator Cariane Multimodal International. The trains are used in the eastern Netherlands province of Gelderland, where a five-year concession to operate services was won by Syntus.

Rotterdam city transport authority RET selected ALSTOM to supply 60 new trams for its three Tram-Plus lines, which serve suburban areas not covered by the city's metro. ALSTOM will supply its full low-floor, unidirectional Citadis tram, featuring four double doors on one side of each vehicle. The new fleet of trams is due to go into service in 2003.

**Poland:** ALSTOM has supplied Metropolis trains for Line 1 of the Warsaw metro. The trains will run on the northern extension of the Kabaty Mlociny line, which will link Politechnika to Mlociny in 2004. The 108 metro cars will be operated in six-car train configurations, each able to carry up to 1,470 passengers. The first trains were commissioned in October 2000.

ALSTOM has also won an order to upgrade the Bytom to Katowice tramway for the Tramway Communication Company of Katowice in Silesia. As well as provision of new vehicles, the turnkey order includes the refurbishment of the rail infrastructure and stations on the existing 20 km Line 6/41. The trams, which will be supplied by the company's Polish subsidiary ALSTOM Konstal, will be fitted with ONIX traction drives.

**Singapore:** ALSTOM won an order to supply the Singapore Land Transport Authority (LTA) with 25 six-car Metropolis trainsets for its new North East Line. This was the largest electromechanical contract awarded within the current LTA development programme. It covers the design, implementation, production, and on-site testing of the trainsets. The driverless signalling and control system will also be supplied by ALSTOM.

In 2002, ALSTOM was confirmed as supplier of the third phase of the city's 34 km Circle Line system, which when completed will employ 26 three-car Metropolis trainsets. Deliveries of these are due to commence in 2004.

In 2000 LTA ordered a further 42 driverless Metropolis cars for the Marina Line (MCL).

**Slovenia:** The former Fiat Ferroviaria in 2000 completed deliveries to SZ of three three-car Class 310 Pendolino electric tilting trainsets.

**South Korea:** Hanjin Heavy Industries placed an order with ALSTOM for 168 electric traction systems for the Pusan metro. The order includes auxiliary converters and onboard information systems.

ALSTOM also won a contract for the development of a new 400 km high-speed rail link between Seoul and Pusan. This project involves a substantial amount of local input and ALSTOM is managing the technology transfer and co-production needed to meet these objectives. In 1994, 46 TGV trainsets were ordered to serve this line, with production split between ALSTOM and its Korean partners. Commercial service is expected to begin in 2004.

**Spain:** Spanish National Railways (RENFE) awarded a consortium of ALSTOM and CAF a contract for the supply and complete maintenance of 20 Pendolino Alaris high-speed regional trains. The trains, which will operate at

*Coradia 1000 200 km/h dmu for First Great Western, UK* 2001/0114485

250-270 km/h, are intended to run on Spanish high-speed lines. ALSTOM's share of the contract is approximately 61.5 per cent. As the consortium leader, the company is responsible for providing the traction system and 50 per cent of the mechanical equipment. The Alaris trains, a non-tilting product from ALSTOM's Pendolino range, will cover distances of up to 250 km on routes which include Madrid—Guadalajara, Zaragoza—Guadalajara, Zaragoza—Lleida and Barcelona—Lleida. Bodyshell production, general assembly and testing will be done in the ALSTOM unit in Santa Perpetua de Mogoda, Barcelona. Some electrical equipment will be produced in ALSTOM's Italian plants. CAF will carry out its portion of the mechanical work at its plants in Beasain (Guipúzcoa) and Zaragoza. Delivery of the first trains will begin in 2003.

Catalan Railways (FGC) introduced the first eight of 20 three-car metre-gauge Class 213 emus on its Barcelona—Igualada and Barcelona—Manresa 'Metro del Baix Llobregat' routes. Supplied by CAF and ALSTOM, the 1.5 kV DC units provide an hourly off-peak service in each direction, stepping up to 30 minutes at peak periods, and replace diesel operation of the Igualada branch.

Autoritat del Transport Metropolita Spa (ATM), the local transport authority acting on behalf of the Regional Government of Catalunya, the Municipality of Barcelona and other local municipalities and authorities, selected the Group TramMet consortium for its 16.8 km light rail project. Group TramMet is a consortium formed to undertake the project on a finance, design, build, operate and maintain (FDBOM) basis. Within it, ALSTOM is responsible for the overall technical management of the project and the supply of the electromechanical system, including the provision of 19 Citadis light rail vehicles, the signalling and communication systems, and the traction power supply system. ALSTOM is also to invest equity in the concession company which will be responsible for the system throughout the design and construction period and for the subsequent 25 years of operation. In 2002, again as part of the TramMet consortium, ALSTOM received a further contract from ATM to equip the second line of the city's light rail network, including the supply of 18 Citadis tramsets.

**Sri Lanka:** In 1998 ALSTOM received an order from Sri Lanka Railways for 10 Prima DE32CAC 1,870 kW diesel-electric locomotives. Deliveries began in August 2000.

**Sweden:** In 2002, AB Transitio/Storstockholms Lokaltrafik (SL) placed an order with ALSTOM to supply 55 six-car Coradia Lirex regional emus for operation in the greater Stockholm area. The contract includes an option for 50 additional trains. Deliveries are due to begin in 2005.

In 2000, ALSTOM was awarded a contract by SJ AB to supply 113 Coradia Duplex double-deck emu cars to be formed into two- and three-car sets. To be delivered between 2003 and 2004, the trains are destined for inter-regional services in the Lake Mälaren region.

**Switzerland:** The Administration of Switzerland's Vaud canton declared ALSTOM preferred bidder for the supply of rolling stock for the 'North-East' Lausanne metro project. This project calls for the delivery of 15 two-car trainsets, of which 10 are to be supplied in an initial phase. The tender called for the bidders to quote for the supply of rubber-tyred metro cars in view of the line's gradients (12 per cent). Rubber-tyred systems have also been supplied by ALSTOM for metros in Paris – most recently on the new Météor line – and also in Santiago, Chile.

As part of the Intercity Neigezüge SBB consortium, in 2001 ALSTOM received a contract to supply Tiltronix tilting technology and equipment for 10 additional ICN seven-car tilting trainsets for Swiss Federal Railways (SBB). This latest order will bering to 44 the number of ICN trainsets orderedby SBB.

**Thailand:** In September 2000, as part of the Nippon-Euro Subway Consortium, ALSTOM was selected by Bangkok Metro Company Ltd to become a partner in a 25-year concession to design, build, operate and maintain the 20 km Blue Line of the Bangkok metro. ALSTOM is to supply 21 three-car Metropolis trainsets, with an option on an additional four sets. The company is also responsible for overall management of E&M supply, systems integration, signalling, communications systems and provision of depot/workshop equipment.

**Turkey:** The first metro line for Istanbul was inaugurated in 2000. The 8 km Taksim—4.Levent metro will eventually provide transport for up to 1.5 million people per day. ALSTOM was largely responsible for this project, which it undertook on a turnkey basis in 1997. The company's participation encompassed the design, supply, and installation of all electromechanical systems including the operating control centre, communication and signalling systems. ALSTOM also supplied eight four-car aluminium-bodied trainsets.

**United Kingdom:** ALSTOM delivered the first completed tilting Pendolino train for the West Coast route in 2001. Virgin Trains have ordered 53 Pendolinos. The Pendolino is set to become the centrepiece of the West Coast upgrade when it starts full passenger service in 2002. The first trains were introduced on the West Coast route in summer 2002. They are built and tested for 225 km/h, but will run at a lower speed until the deferred infrastructure enhancement envisaged in Phase II of the West Coast upgrade is implemented.

To meet the train test and delivery programme, ALSTOM has created a testing facility in the UK, dedicated to improving train reliability and safety. The ALSTOM Midlands Test Centre, the first major off-line test facility in the UK, encompasses a 21 km fully electrified test track, the Asfordby Test Centre building, the TCS signalling and control centre and a dedicated TCS test track.

The first of eight eight-car Class 460 750 V DC third-rail electric trainsets for UK operator Gatwick Express entered service in 2001. Based on the company's Optionic modular Coradia Juniper emu concept, they were built at its Washwood Heath, Birmingham plant.

Fourteen five-car 200 km/h Coradia 1000 dmus have been built for First Great Western. Designated Class 180 by the operator and branded Adelante, first examples entered service in 2002. In addition, 11 two-car and 16 three-car Class 175 Coradia dmus have been supplied to First North Western.

ALSTOM has built a fleet of 40 Class 334 Coradia Juniper three-car 25 kV AC emus for ScotRail. First examples entered service in 2001. In addition, 30 Class 458 Coradia Juniper four-car 750 V DC emus have been built for South West Trains.

Thirty Class 67 Prima Bo-Bo diesel-electric locomotives have been built at ALSTOM's Valencia plant for freight operator EWS for express mail traffic. Each has a maximum speed of 200 km/h and is rated at 2,200 kW.

**USA:** In 2002, a consortium of ALSTOM and Kawasaki received an order from the Metropolitan Transportation Authority of New York City Transit (MTA-NYC) to supply 660 heavy rail subway cars. To be delivered in 2006-07, the new cars will replace existing Type R32, R38, R40 and R42 vehicles.

Also in 2002, ALSTOM was awarded a contract by the Washington Metropolitan Transportation Authority (WMATA) to supply 62 heavy rail subway cars for its Blue Line extension to Largo Town Centre. The contract includes an option to supply 120 cars for WMATA's Orange Line extension and for general traffic growth.

Six MARC Bo-Bo electric locomotives were delivered during 2000 to MTA Maryland by a consortium of ALSTOM and Bombardier Transportation. The locomotives are identical to 15 others delivered to Amtrak.

During 1999-2000 Amtrak was supplied with AME125 electric locomotives. Each is rated at 6,000 kW and has a top speed of 200 km/h.

In 2000, ALSTOM supplied Amtrak with eight five-car double-deck trainsets for services in the Southern and Central Coast regions of California.

In 2001 New Jersey Transit Corporation (NJT) voted to award ALSTOM a contract for the design and manufacture of a fleet of 33 new diesel-electric passenger locomotives, spare parts and an option for an additional five locomotives. NJT also has the option to award an additional 42 locomotives in the future.

The Chicago Transit Authority notified ALSTOM in 2001 of its decision to award the company a third optional contract for the refurbishment of 108 subway cars. This follow-on order comes within the framework of a base CTA contract awarded to ALSTOM in December 1997 for the overhaul of 284 subway cars.

The cars are being upgraded with ALSTOM's ONIX propulsion system and an advanced cab signal system. The interior refurbishment work includes the installation of air conditioning, a public address system and improved lighting. Further improvements for later optional contracts include vandal-proof shields for windows and silicone cleats to reduce long-term wear on the high-voltage cabling under the car. All work for the CTA contracts has been carried out at ALSTOM's industrial facilities in Hornell, New York. Deliveries will be made at a rate of 14 cars per month, with no disruption to CTA's revenue service, and finish in September 2003.

**Uzbekistan:** 15 Prima 25 kV 1,520 mm gauge 4,200 kW electric locomotives are being delivered.

**Venezuela:** ALSTOM, as part of the FRAMECA consortium, has been awarded a turnkey order from the Caracas metro authority, CAMC, for the 5.5 km Line 4 of the city's metro system, which is scheduled to enter service in 2002. In addition to supplying 44 metro cars and the signalling system, ALSTOM will carry out electrification of the line and provide a complete fire protection system.

*UPDATED*

# ANSALDOBREDA

Ansaldo Trasporti SpA
425 Via Argine, I-80147 Naples, Italy
Tel: (+39 081) 243 11 11   Fax: (+39 081) 243 26 98

**Key personnel**
Chief Executive Officer: Luigi Roth
Group Vice-President, Vehicle Business Unit:
  Claudio Artusi
Group Vice-President, Turnkey Systems Business Unit:
  Fausto Cutuli
Ansaldo Signal NV (Signalling and Automation):
  James Sanders

**Subsidiaries**
Transystem SpA, Italy
Ansaldo Signal NV
Breda Transportation Inc
261 Madison Avenue, New York 10016-2303, USA
Tel: (+1 212) 286 80 00   Fax: (+1 212) 286 07 00

*Ansaldo Class E402 dual-voltage locomotive*

**484  MANUFACTURERS**/Locomotives and powered/non-powered passenger vehicles

**Products**

Electric propulsion equipment, either rheostatic or electronic, for locomotives with AC and DC motors; electronic converters and controls; auxiliary apparatus; planning, designing and management methodologies for public transport: sale, assembly, start-up and servicing.

Stainless steel, carbon steel and aluminium alloy passenger coaches.

Contracts include Z1-type coaches for Italian Railways (FS); amenity coaches for Eurotunnel; panoramic coaches for BVZ, FO and MOB, Switzerland; trailer vehicles for ETR 500 high-speed trainsets for FS; and double-deck emu trailer cars for FS and North Milan Railway.

Traction equipment for 73 E652 chopper-controlled locomotives for Italian Railways (FS) has been supplied, also 60 ETR 500 high-speed trainsets for FS (supplied by the Trevi Consortium, of which Ansaldo Trasporti is a member); and 120 E402 electric locomotives with inverter drives and asynchronous traction motors for FS, with 80 equipped for operation at 3 kV DC and 25 kV 50 Hz AC.

Norwegian State Railways (NSB) Norway has awarded Ansaldo Trasporti a contract for the delivery of 36 emus for local traffic.

A contract has been won to build the Copenhagen metro and covers, on a turnkey basis, the design, construction, supply and installation of an automatic urban metro system with 15 km of track and 15 stations. It also covers the supply of 19 driverless vehicles with ATC.

## Astarsa

Astilleros Argentinos Rio de la Plata SA
Tucumán 1438, 1050 Buenos Aires, Argentina
Tel: (+54 1) 40 70 14   Fax: (+54 1) 372 86 47

**Works**
Calle Solis Rio Lujan, 1648 Tigre, Prov Buenos Aires
Tel: (+54 749) 10 71 78

**Key personnel**
Executive Vice-President: E G Nottage
General Manager, Rail: G Molinari

**Associated company**
General Motors Corporation

**Licences**
MTE and ALSTOM (France and UK)

**Products**
Diesel-electric locomotives.

## Astra Vagoane Călători SA Arad

1-3 Petru Rareş, R-2900 Arad, Romania
Tel: (+40 257) 23 36 51   Fax: (+40 257) 25 81 68
e-mail: astra@calatori.rdsar.ro

**Key personnel**
Administrator: Valer Blidar
General Manager: Romulus Nosner
Technical Manager: Gheorghe Vărşăndan

Commercial Manager: Raj Epuran
Head of Marketing Department: Ovidiu-Lucian Bologea

**Corporate development**
The company was formed in 1998 by splitting it from freight wagon and passenger coaches manufacturer Astra Vagaone Arad SA (qv).

**Products**
Certified ISO 9001 for the design, manufacture and refurbishment of passenger coaches and rail urban passenger vehicles. Passenger coaches for international and domestic traffic, metro cars, dmus, emus, light rail vehicles. Refurbishment is also undertaken and the company has renovated coaches for Romanian Railways, alone and in co-operation with Alstom.

Astra is licensed to build 200 km/h Corail coaches.

*UPDATED*

*Z1 UIC 200 km/h passenger coach AVA 200 – Corail licence*
*2002/0142356*

## Babcock & Wilcox Española

Babcock & Wilcox Española SA
PO Box 294, Alameda Recalde 27, E-48009 Bilbao, Spain
Tel: (+34 94) 424 17 61   Fax: (+34 94) 423 70 92

**Key personnel**
President: R Gonzalez-Orus
Railway Division Manager: L Zubia

**Products**
Main line diesel-electric and diesel-hydraulic units, shunting locomotives.

Exports have featured diesel-electric locomotives for Colombia, Guatemala and numerous African railways.

## Babcock Rail

Keith Road, Rosyth Royal Dockyard, Rosyth, Fife
KY11 2YD, UK
Tel: (+44 1383) 42 37 94   Fax: (+44 1383) 42 31 82
Web: http://www.babcockbes.co.uk

**Key personnel**
Managing Director: Douglas Lindsay
General Manager: Andy Somerville

**Products**
Manufacture of freight wagons and passenger rolling stock refurbishment.

Recent contracts include: intermodal freight wagon manufacture; relivery of MkIV coaching stock for the GNER fleet (continuing); relivery of Class 158 dmu for Scotrail, UK (continuing).

## Beijing

Beijing 'February 7th' Locomotive Works
Changxindian, Fengtai District, Beijing 100072, People's Republic of China
Tel: (+86 1) 269; 408   Fax: (+86 1) 325 76 54

**Key personnel**
Factory Director: Xu Xiaozeng
Deputy Director: Li Guoan

**Corporate structure**
Member of China National Locomotive Rolling Stock Industry Corporation.

**Products**
Diesel locomotives; diesel engines; hydraulic transmissions; fuel injectors; fuel injection pumps; cardan shafts; and bogies.

The BJ series of diesel-hydraulic locomotives is produced in 1,990 kW B-B and 3,980 kW B-B versions. The B-B has been in series production since 1975. Both models employ the Type 12V240ZJ-1 12-cylinder 1,000 rpm engine, which is also manufactured in the works. The B-B weighs 92 tonnes, has a starting tractive effort of 23.1 t, a continuous tractive effort of 16.27 t at 24.3 km/h and a maximum speed of 120 km/h.

The works also manufactures the Model DF7 Co-Co diesel-electric locomotive, for heavy shunting. It is fitted with a four-stroke 12-cylinder Vee engine of Type 12V240ZJ-1, exhaust turbocharged with intercooling, which has a rating of 1,470 kW at 1,000 rpm. The transmission is AC/DC alternator, employing silicon rectifiers.

The Model DF7B Co-Co diesel-electric locomotive produced for freight traffic has a rating of 1,840 kW at 1,000 rpm and is equipped with rheostatic braking.

To meet the needs of industrial and mining industries the works produces the Model GK1E diesel locomotive with a hydrostatic transmission system. The locomotive is powered by a six-cylinder Vee diesel engine, which has a 240 mm bore and a stroke of 260 mm, producing a maximum rating of 1,000 kW at 1,100 rpm.

# BEML

Bharat Earth Movers Ltd
BEML Soudha, 23/1 4th Main, SR Nagar,
Bangalore 560 027, India
Tel: (+91 80) 222 44 58    Fax: (+91 80) 229 19 80
e-mail: techrnd@vsnl.com
Web: http://www.bemlindia.com

### Works
Bangalore Complex, New Thippasandra,
Bangalore 560 075, India
Tel: (+91 80) 524 24 14    Fax: (+91 80) 524 55 45

### Key personnel
Chairman and Managing Director: Dr K Aprameyan
Director, R&D: V S Venkatanathan
Executive Director: M P Sriram
Deputy General Manager (R&D): V S Bharadwaj

### Products
Electric multiple-units, diesel railbuses, railcoaches.

### Contracts
Recent contracts for Indian Railways include the supply of a lightweight, two-axle, 1,676 mm gauge diesel railbus and electric multiple-units with 25 kV AC traction equipment.

Lightweight passenger coaches of integral welded steel construction of all types including sleeper coaches, day travel coaches, treasury vans, postal vans, parcel vans, brake and luggage vans and motor-cum-parcel vans.

The division has supplied over 12,000 coaches of different types for Indian Railways. Coaches have also been exported to Bangladesh and Sri Lanka.

**UPDATED**

*BEML electric multiple-unit*

*25 kV AC emu for Indian Railways*

*Two-axle 1,676 mm-gauge diesel railbus for India's Eastern Railway*

# MANUFACTURERS/Locomotives and powered/non-powered passenger vehicles

## BHEL

Bharat Heavy Electricals Ltd
Bhopal 462 022, India
Tel: (+91 755) 58 61 00   Fax: (+91 755) 54 04 25
Head Office
BHEL House, Siri Fort, New Delhi 110049

**Key personnel**
Executive Director: R C Aggarwal
General Manager, Switchgear and Control Gear: D P Joshi
General Manager, Transportation: S P Bindra

**Group Companies**
Bharat Heavy Electricals Ltd
Jhansi 284 129, India
Tel: (+91 517) 44 02 40; 44 06 15; 44 09 44
Fax: (+91 517) 44 31 08; 44 43 60
General Manager: Ashok Gupta
Product Manager, Locomotives: P S Kulshreghtha

**Products**
Electric locomotives, diesel-electric shunting locomotives, traction transformers and fabricated bogies.
Bharat Heavy Electricals Ltd
Transportation Business Department, Lodhi Road, New Delhi 110003, India
Tel: (+91 11) 461 65 44 (Marketing)
Fax: (+91 11) 462 94 23
General Manager: S C Chopra
Electric locomotives for 25 kV AC, 1.5 kV DC and dual-voltage operation. Diesel-electric locomotives for shunting and main line duties from 261 kW (350 hp) to 1,940 kW (2,600 hp).

AC electric production includes 75 Class WAG-5 locomotives, 20 Class WCAM2 locomotives, 53 Class WCAM3 locomotives, all for Indian Railways, with delivery between 1996 and 1998. A 5,000 hp prototype with thyristor control has been manufactured.

## BMZ

JSC Bryansk Engineering Works
ulica Ulyanova 26, 241 015 Bryansk, Russian Federation
Tel: (+7 832) 55 86 73; 00 30   Fax: (+7 95) 203 33 95

**Key personnel**
Senior Marketing Manager: Natali Skrobova
Marketing Manager: Dmitri Melnichuk

**Products**
Diesel shunting locomotives, generator vans.

## Bombardier Transportation

Management Offices
1101 Parent Street, Saint-Bruno, Québec J3V 6E6, Canada
Tel: (+1 450) 441 20 20   Fax: (+1 450) 441 15 15
Web: http://www.transportation.bombardier.com

Saatwinkler Damm 43, D-13627 Berlin, Germany
Tel: (+49 30) 383 20   Fax: (+49 30) 38 32 20 00
Web: http://www.transportation.bombardier.com

**Key personnel**
President and Chief Operating Officer: Pierre Lortie
Vice-President Communications: Linda Coates
Vice-President Marketing and Product Planning: Trung Ngo
Executive Vice-President and Chief Procurement Officer: Jacques Lamotte

Bombardier Transportation
North America
1101 Parent Street, Saint-Bruno, Québec J3V 6E6, Canada
Tel: (+1 450) 441 20 20   Fax: (+1 450) 441 15 15
President, North America: William Spurr

Bombardier Transportation Regional and Commuter Trains
Am Rathenaupark, D-16761 Hennigsdorf, Germany
Tel: (+49 33) 330 28 90   Fax: (+49 33) 33 02 89 20 88
President, Regional and Commuter Train: Jürgen Fleischer

Bombardier Transportation Intercity Trains
Place des Ateliers, BP 1, F-59154 Crespin, France
Tel: (+33) 327 23 53 00   Fax: (+33) 327 35 16 24
President, Intercity Trains: Rik Dobbelaere

Bombardier Transportation Metros
Litchurch Lane, Derby, Derbyshire DE24 8AD, UK
Tel: (+44 1332) 34 46 66   Fax: (+44 1332) 26 62 71
President, Metros: Olof Persson

Bombardier Transportation Light Rail Vehicles
Donaufelder Strasse 73-79, A-1211 Vienna, Austria
Tel: (+43 1) 251 10   Fax: (+43 1) 25 11 08
President, Light Rail Vehicles: Walter Grawenhoff

Bombardier Transportation Locomotives & Freight
Brown-Boveri Strasse 5, PO Box 8384, CH-8050 Zürich, Switzerland
Tel: (+41 1) 318 22 13   Fax: (+41 1) 318 27 27
President, Locomotives & Freight: Wolfgang Toelsner

Bombardier Transportation Total Transit Systems
PO Box 220, Station A, Kingston, Ontario K7M 6R2, Canada
Tel: (+1 613) 384 31 00   Fax: (+1 613) 384 52 44
President, Total Transit Systems: Patrice Pelletier

Bombardier Transportation Propulsion and Controls
Brown-Boveri Strasse 5, CH-8050 Zürich, Switzerland
Telephone: (+41 1) 318 33 33   Fax: (+41 1) 318 15 43
President, Propulsion and Controls: Åke Wennberg

Bombardier Transportation Rail Control Solutions
Letcombe Street, Reading, Berkshire RG1 2HW, UK
Tel: (+44 118) 953 83 94   Fax: (+44 118) 953 84 83
President: Javier Rión

Bombardier Transportation Services
West Street, Crewe, Cheshire CW1 3JB, UK
Tel: (+44 1270) 50 03 33   Fax: (+44 1270) 53 88 33
President, Services: Andrew Lezala

**Australia**
Lars Persson
Tel: (+61 73) 858 24 81   Fax: (+61 73) 367 24 22

**Austria**
Bernhard Rieder
Tel: (+43 1) 25 11 01 78   Fax: (+43 1) 25 11 05 31

**Belgium**
André Detollenaere
Tel: (+32 50) 40 11 11   Fax: (+32 50) 40 18 40

**Brazil**
Serge van Themsche
Tel: (+55 11) 37 48 97 00   Fax: (+55 11) 37 48 99 31

**Canada**
Carol Sharpe
Tel: (+1 450) 441 81 56   Fax: (+1 450) 441 30 90

**China**
Jian Wei Zhang
Tel: (+86 10) 85 29 91 00   Fax: (+86 10) 85 29 91 09

**Czech Republic**
Josef Schorm
Tel: (+42 02) 22 83 22 50   Fax: (+42 02) 22 83 22 51

**Denmark**
Kirstin Petersen
Tel: (+45 86) 42 53 00   Fax: (+45 86) 41 45 64

**Finland**
Christoffer Enckell
Tel: (+35 81) 02 22 62 10   Fax: (+35 81) 022 20 67

**France**
Florence Macarez
Tel: (+33 3) 27 23 58 04   Fax: (+33 3) 27 23 72 86

**Germany**
Ulrich Bieger
Tel: (+49 30) 38 32 11 78   Fax: (+49 30) 38 32 20 20

**Greece**
Tonia Petrovits
Tel: (+30 12) 89 15 40   Fax: (+30 12) 89 15 39

**Hungary**
Janos Ujhelyi
Tel: (+36 27) 54 21 47   Fax: (+36 27) 39 01 43

**India**
Mahesh Kumar Ahuja
Tel: (+91 11) 618 67 94   Fax: (+91 11) 618 66 51

*Bombardier Talent dmu for Regiobahn, Germany*   2000/0116586

*ICE-tilting train for Deutsche Bahn*   2000/0116578

## Locomotives and powered/non-powered passenger vehicles/MANUFACTURERS

*Bombardier NINA emu for BLS, Switzerland*    2000/0116583

*Bombardier bilevel commuter car for Seattle*    2000/0116575

**Indonesia**
Darryl Sailor
Tel: (+65 65) 49 71 50    Fax: (+65 65) 49 72 92

**Italy**
Cristiana Solinas
Tel: (+39 01) 92 89 05 80    Fax: (+39 01) 92 89 05 92

**Korea**
Kathryn Nickerson
Tel: (+1 613) 384 31 00    Fax: (+1 613) 384 52 40

**Latin America (except Brazil and Mexico)**
Francisco Garcia
Tel: (+613 3) 84 31 00    Fax: (+613 3) 84 52 40

**Malaysia**
Regis Beauchesne
Tel: (+603 20) 31 08 39    Fax: (+603 20) 31 08 42

**Mexico**
Alejandro Gutierrez Marcos
Tel: (+52 55) 50 93 77 00    Fax: (+52 55) 50 93 77 51

**Norway**
Tom Korstad
Tel: (+47 63) 80 96 58    Fax: (+47 63) 80 97 76

**Philippines**
Don Lavoie
Tel: (+66 266) 192 18    Fax: (+66 226) 409 19

**Poland**
Janusz Kucmin
Tel: (+48 71) 356 25 96    Fax: (+48 71) 355 57 31

**Portugal**
Luis Ramos
Tel: (+35 12) 14 96 95 54    Fax: (+35 12) 14 96 93 94

**Russia**
Dorothea Hafner
Tel: (+49 30) 67 93 12 57    Fax: (+49 30) 67 93 12 07

**Singapore**
Darryl Sailor
Tel: (+65 65) 49 71 50    Fax: (+65 65) 49 72 92

**Spain**
Salvador Luelmo
Tel: (+34 91) 383 62 08    Fax: (+34 91) 383 61 99

**Sweden**
Bengt Lindwall
Tel: (+46 21) 31 70 04    Fax: (+46 21) 32 38 47

**Switzerland**
Alfred Ruckstuhl
Tel: (+41 1) 318 27 33    Fax: (+41 1) 318 30 80

**Taiwan**
Kathryn Nickerson
Tel: (+1 613) 384 31 00    Fax: (+1 613) 384 52 40

**Thailand**
Don Lavoie
Tel: (+66 266) 192 18    Fax: (+66 226) 409 19

**Turkey**
Ali Savci
Tel: (+90 21) 22 16 80 54    Fax: (+90 21) 22 17 09 66

**United Arab Emirates**
Kathryn Nickerson
Tel: (+1 613) 384 31 00    Fax: (+1 613) 384 52 40

**United Kingdom**
Neil Harvey
Tel: (+44 1332) 26 64 70    Fax: (+44 1332) 26 64 72

**United States**
Carol Sharpe
Tel: (+1 450) 441 81 56    Fax: (+1 450) 441 30 90

**Vietnam**
Darryl Sailor
Tel: (+65 65) 49 71 50    Fax: (+65 65) 49 72 92

### Background
Serving a diversified customer base around the world, Bombardier Transportation is the global leader in the rail equipment, manufacturing and servicing industry. Its range of products includes passenger rail cars and complete rail transportation systems. It also manufactures locomotives, freight wagons, propulsion and controls and provides rail control solutions.

Bombardier Transportation entered the mass transit market in 1974 with a first contract involving the supply of 423 rapid transit cars for the Montréal metro. It subsequently embarked on a dynamic growth strategy, which combines internally generated expansion with a focus on acquisitions of other companies that have proven designs, know-how and technologies.

On 1 May 2001, Bombardier Transportation acquired Adtranz, one of the largest players in the international railway industry, with a history dating back to the mid-19th century. Bombardier Transportation's revenues for the fiscal year ended January 31, 2002 were in excess of Cdn$7 billion (€5 billion). Headquartered in Montreal, Canada with European headquarters in Berlin, Germany, Bombardier Transportation employs 36,000 people and has an international manufacturing presence with production facilities in 23 countries.

Bombardier Transportation is a unit of Bombardier Inc, a Canadian-based diversified manufacturing and service company, world-leading manufacturer of business jets, regional aircraft and motorised recreational products. The Corporation also provides financial services and asset management in business areas aligned with its core expertise. Bombardier Inc's revenues for its fiscal year ended 31 January 2002 totalled Cdn$21.6 billion (€15.6 billion). The Corporation has a workforce of some 80,000 people in 24 countries throughout the Americas, Europe and Asia-Pacific.

### Products
Bombardier Transportation offers a full range of rail vehicles for urban, commuter/regional and intercity/high-speed operation as well as modernisation of rolling stock and operations and maintenance services. Products include metro cars, light rail vehicles/trams, single and

*Bombardier Class 146 electric locomotive for DB regional services*    2001/0116281

*Bombardier three-car express emu for Öresund Link services*    2001/0116283

*Bombardier Class E464 single-cab electric locomotive for Italian Railways passenger services* (Ken Harris)

*Bombardier Voyager demu for Virgin Trains*

double-deck electric multiple units (emus), diesel multiple units (dmus) and coaches; tilting trains and high-speed trains. Complete transportation systems encompass fully automated transit systems, people movers and monorails, as well as light rail and metro systems. Bombardier Transportation also offers electric and diesel locomotives; propulsion and controls; rail control solutions, and freight cars.

## Contracts

**Australia:** In 2002, in a joint venture with EDI-Rail, Bombardier Transportation received an order from the Western Australian government to supply 31 three-car stainless steel-bodied emus, with an option for 10 additional units, for commuter services on the southern leg of the Perth Urban Rail Development project. Bombardier was to undertake vehicle design and supply of propulsion and electrical equipment, while EDI-Rail was to be responsible for bodyshells and bogies. Assembly was to be carried out at a Bombardier Transportation/EDI-Rail joint venture plant in Queensland. Deliveries are scheduled to take place from mid-2004 to 2006. A contract was signed in 2001 with National Express and the Victorian State Government to build 29 two-car diesel multiple-units for Victoria's country and regional services. The agreement also covers the maintenance of these trains for the next 15 years. Deliveries are scheduled to take place between October 2004 and July 2006. The stainless steel trains will be manufactured at Bombardier's Dandenong facility in Victoria with some components and technical input being supplied by local Australian engineering firms. Bombardier Transportation's facility in Derby, UK will be providing the bogies.

**Austria:** In 2001, Austrian Federal Railways ordered 40 four-car and 11 three-car Talent emus from Bombardier Transportation and ELIN EBG Traction. 18 low-floor Street-Trams type Cityrunner for the city of Graz were delivered in 2001.

In 1999, Bombardier Transportation was awarded a contract for the supply of 21 low-floor trams for Linz; delivery began in late 2001.

**Belgium:** In 2001, De Lijn ordered 10 low-floor intermediate cars to equip existing vehicles, with subsequent contracts to be placed for 22 similar cars. In 1999, SNCB (Belgium National Railways) ordered 210 double-deck coaches from Bombardier Transportation.

STIB Brussels took delivery of 25 metro cars.

**Canada:** In 2000, GO Transit placed a contract for 16 wheelchair-accessible bi-level commuter cars for Greater Toronto Area services. Bombardier Transportation had already delivered more than 300 bi-level suburban vehicles to this operator.

In 1999, Ottawa-Carleton Regional Transit Commission ordered three Talent diesel multiple-units for its O-Train service launched in 2001.

**China:** In 2001 Bombardier Transportation and the Changchun Car Company (CCC) announced that their joint venture CARC had received an order from Shenzhen Metro Co Ltd for the supply of 114 metro cars (19 six-car trains). The vehicles will be used for Phase 1 of the new metro system under construction in Shenzhen City. Shenzhen is located in the South of China, neighboring both Hong Kong and Guangzhou. The first train will be manufactured in Hennigsdorf, Germany with the remaining 18 trains to be built at the CARC plant in Changchun, Jilin Province in northeast China. Bombardier's facility in Västeras, Sweden will provide the propulsion. The metro trainsets are planned to be delivered between early 2004 and the second half of 2005. Revenue service is scheduled to commence in December 2004.

In 1999, Bombardier Transportation received an order to build 300 intercity coaches at its joint venture manufacturing facility in China.

In 1998 an X2000 high-speed trainset supplied by the former Adtranz commenced services between Guangzhou and Hong Kong. The company was also consortium leader in the supply of 11 seven-car Airport Express and 12 seven-car Tung Chun Line emus operating on Hong Kong's Airport Railway.

**Denmark:** In 2001, an order was received from UK-based Porterbrook Leasing Company Ltd for 42 double-deck passenger coaches to be leased to Danish State Railways (DSB) for services between Copenhagen and Kalundborg. The order comprised 33 intermediate trailers and nine driving cars. In 2002, a further order was received from Porterbrook for 25 additional double-deck coaches. These vehicles were also to be leased by DSB for use on Copenhagen Lolland/Falster and Copenhagen Seeland routes. Assembly was to take place at Bombardier's Görlitz plant for delivery at the end of 2002.

Other contracts fulfilled in Denmark include 48 IR4 Flexliner emus for DSB and 13 Flexliner L2D dmus for several independent Danish railways.

**Egypt:** In 1998, Egyptian National Railways took delivery of 23 DE 2550 Abu Tartour diesel-electric locomotives.

**Finland:** In 2000, Finnish Railways (VR-Group Ltd) took up an option for an additional six Class Sr2 electric locomotives, bringing to 46 the number of this type ordered. Deliveries of a second batch of 20 locomotives commenced in January 2001.

In 2000, Helskinki City Transport (HKL) exercised an option for 20 additional low-floor Variotrams. Deliveries commenced of the first batch of 20 trams. Deliveries started of 12 two-car metro trainsets to Helsinki City Transport.

**France:** In 2001, Bombardier Transportation signed a contract with SNCF covering the supply of 500 high-capacity Type AGC (Autorail Grande Capacité) for regional services. The initial form part of the contract was for 192 trains. The AGC design provides for diesel, electric or dual-powered versions of the train. Deliveries were due to commence during the first quarter of 2004.

In 2001, a consortium of Bombardier Transportation and Alstom received an order from French National Railways (SNCF) for 18 TGV Duplex double-deck high-speed trainsets. These represent part-confirmation of an option on 60 vehicles included in the contract placed in 2000 (see below). Bombardier's share of the contract, which was to be fulfilled between March 2004 and March 2005, covers the manufacture of two first class and one second class vehicle and six carrying bogies for each 10-car trainset.

In 2001, Bombardier received an order from RATP, the Paris transport authority, for 161 five-car Type MF-2000 metro trains in consortium with ALSTOM Transport and Technicatome.

In 2000, in a consortium comprising Bombardier Transportation and ALSTOM Transport received an order from the French National Railways (SNCF) for 72 TER 2N NG (New Generation) emus consisting of 30 two-car, 25 three-car and 17 four-car units. The city of Nantes took delivery of the first of 23 low-floor light rail vehicles. Bombardier Transportation signed a contract in 1998 with the transport company of Nancy for the supply of 25 trams on tyres.

**Germany:** In 2002, Bombardier Transportation received an order to manufacture 60 LF2000 low-floor trams for the city of Frankfurt/Main, Germany. Also in 2002, a consortium comprising Bombardier Transportation, Siemens and Alstom received an order from Deutsche Bahn for the delivery of 28 seven-car ICE T high-speed trains.

An order was received from the Local Transport Authority of Lower Saxony (LNVG) for 10 Class 146 15 kV AC electric locomotives and 66 double-deck passenger coaches. To be delivered between July and October 2003, the trains will provide regional express services on

*Bombardier ICN tilting high-speed trainset for Swiss Federal Railways* (David Haydock)

Hamburg–Bremen and Hamburg–Uelzen routes. The locomotives were to be manufactured at the company's Kassel plant, while the coaches would be produced at Görlitz.

In 2001, a consortium of Bombardier Transportation Systems and Siemens Transportation Systems received an order from German Rail (DB AG) to supply 40 Class 425 four-car emus for delivery between April and November 2003. The trains are intended for Rhein-Neckar regional and commuter services. In 2001, Bombardier Transportation received an order from the Dresden transport authority, DVB, for 20 low-floor trams, with an option for an additional 50 vehicles.

In 2001 a Deutsche Bahn subsidiary, DB Regionalbahn Rheinland GmbH, ordered 26 two-car Talent dmus, converting an option on an earlier order for 75 units. Deutsche Bahn also ordered an additional 117 double-deck suburban vehicles. So far, Deutsche Bahn has ordered over 1,000 vehicles of this type.

In 2001 a contract was awarded by the transport authority of Halle (Hallesche Verkehrs AG, Germany) for the supply of 30 low-floor street-trams type LF2000. The delivery of the vehicles is scheduled between the end of 2003 and the end of 2005.

Bombardier Transportation in Bautzen will be responsible for the development and production of the vehicles as well as for the system integration. Bombardier Transportation in Mannheim will supply the electrical equipment.

Also in 2001, Bombardier Transportation was awarded a contract by the Bonn transport authority (SWB) for 15 high-floor trams, in partnership with Kiepe Elekrik. Bombardier Transportation delivered the last of 28 three-car S1000 Tram-Train LRVs to Saarbrücken.

In 2000, an order was received from the Dessau transport authority, DVG, for 10 trams. In the same year a contract was signed for 55 high-floor trams for Cologne. This order included an option for an additional 91 trams.

Deliveries commenced in 2000 of a DB Cargo order for 400 Class 185 dual-voltage electric locomotives, derived from the Class 145 4,000 kW single-voltage design which was rolled out in 1999. Eighty Class 145 locomotives have been delivered to DB and two have been procured by chemicals company BASF for open access operations. In 2001, deliveries commenced to DB of 31 Class 146 locomotives, a derivative of Class 145 for regional passenger services. Earlier DB had received 145 Class 101 electric locomotives for intercity services.

In 2000, Deutsche Bahn took up an option for an additional 46 Class 612 two-car 'Regio-Swinger' tilting dmus, bringing to 250 the number of the type and its Class 611 predecessor ordered by this operator.

Also in 2000, DB received the last examples of an order for 110 Class 423 four-car emus for suburban services and was taking delivery of an order for 160 Class 424 low-floor four-car S-Bahn emus being supplied by a consortium of Bombardier and Siemens.

**Greece:** National operator OSE has received 25 DE2000 diesel-electric locomotives which are capable of later conversion to electric traction. Bombardier is also a member of a consortium which received a contract placed by the Athens-Piraeus Electric Railways Company for 40 three-car metro trainsets.

**Israel:** In 2001, the delivery commenced to Israel Railways (IR) of 57 double-deck passenger coaches comprising 15 power cars and 42 coaches.

In 2001, 20 three-car dmus based on the Danish IC3 design were ordered by IR.

**Italy:** In 2002, Italian Railways (Trenitalia) placed a contract with Bombardier Transportation for 42 Class EU11 6 MW 3 kV DC Bo-Bo electric locomotives.

In 2000, Trenitalia received the last of 50 Class E464 single-cab 3,000 kW electric locomotives and placed a follow-up order for an additional 90 locomotives of the same type. In 2001, Trenitalia placed an order for an additional 100 locomotives of this type, bringing to 240 the number of Class E464 locomotives ordered by this customer since 1996. Assembly takes place at Vado Ligure, Italy, with electrical equipment supplied by Bombardier's plant in Mannheim, Germany, and propulsion equipment from Zurich, Switzerland.

Between 1998 and 2001 Milan urban operator ATM received 20 Eurotram low-floor LRVs.

**Malaysia:** In 1998, revenue service started for the PUTRA rail system (70 advanced rapid transit cars) and in 1996 for the STAR light rail system (90 light rail vehicles).

**Mexico:** In 2000, Mexico City took delivery of the last cars of an order of 78 FM-95A rapid transit cars for Line A.

**Netherlands:** In 2002, Bombardier delivered the last of 81 vehicles on order by RET (Rotterdamse Elektrische Tram) in the Netherlands. In 1996, RET awarded to Bombardier Transportation an order for 42 metro vehicles, followed in 1998 by an additional order for 21 metro vehicles and 18 high-speed trams (sneltrams).

In 2001, an order was received from Netherlands Railways for 21 six-car Type IRM double deck emus. This followed a contract placed in 2000 for 252 vehicles, consisting of 13 four-car and 12 six-car double-deck units and 128 Type VIRM double-deck intermediate coaches.

**Norway:** In 2000, Bombardier Transportation started deliveries of 15 lightweight tilting Talent two-car dmus to Norwegian State Railways (NSB).

In 1999, NSB ordered an additional six Class BM73 four-car tilting emus, which are based on the design of the non-tilting Class BM71. In 1997, NSB received the last of 22 Class E118 5,880 kW electric locomotives based on the design of the Swiss Federal Railways Class 460.

**Pakistan:** Deliveries were completed in 2000 of a Pakistan Railways order for 30 DE-AC33CA Blue Tiger diesel-electric locomotives.

**Poland:** In 2000, the city of Lodz ordered 15 low-floor trams and in 1998, Krakow ordered 14 low-floor trams.

**Portugal:** In 2000, the company, in consortium with Siemens, received an order to supply 22 four-car emus to Portuguese Railways, for Oporto commuter service and 12 five-car emus to Cascais line.

**Romania:** In 2002, deliveries of 108 Movia started. The vehicle have been ordered for Line 2 of the Bucharest metro by Metrorex RA.

**Spain:** In 2001, a contract was awarded by Spanish National Railways (RENFE) for the construction of 16 high-speed trains for services on the standard-gauge line linking Madrid, Barcelona and the French border. Train configuration will comprise 12 trailer cars and power cars. The order followed the development by a consortium with Talgo of a prototype trainset, which completed trials at speeds up to 350 km/h.

RENFE has received 26 articulated two-car Flexliner TRD dmus for regional services in northern Spain.

**Sweden:** In 2001, the Stockholm Public Transportation Authority (SL) placed a contract with Bombardier Transportation to supply an additional 70 three-car Vagn 2000 metro units between September 2002 and early 2004. This brought to 270 the number of Vagn 2000 units ordered by SL. Production is undertaken at Bombardier sites at Kalmar and Västerås, Sweden, with bogies manufactured at its Derby, UK, plant.

In 2001, additional orders were received from Skånetrafiken for seven three-car Contessa intercity trainsets for Öresund Link services between Sweden and Denmark, bringing to 56 the number of trains of this type ordered by operators in the two countries.

In 2000 the first of nine two-section 10,800 kW 360 tonne three-phase electric locomotives for the LKAB iron ore mining company was handed over. Designed for use on the 540 km Luleå Kiruna Narvik line, the locomotives are based on the Octeon platform developed by the former Adtranz.

Fifty Regina regional emus (109 cars) have been ordered by VL X-Trafik and TiB, Västtrafol. SK and Västmanslands Lokaltrafik.

In 1999, SL Stockholm awarded took delivery of 12 trams based on the Cologne vehicles. In December 2000 an additional 10 vehicles were ordered.

**Switzerland:** In 2002, Bombardier Transportation has been awarded a contract by BLS Cargo AG in Switzerland to deliver 10 dual-voltage freight locomotives. The order is valued at approximately €30 million. Delivery of the locomotives, which BLS Cargo AG will put in service for the cross-border traffic between Germany and Switzerland, is scheduled to take place between December 2002 and July 2003. In Switzerland, 10 freight locomotives of the same type are already in service with SBB Cargo (the Swiss Federal Railways). Various private railway operators also operate freight locomotives of the same successful type, among which Deutsche Bahn, with more than 70.

In 2001, a consortium of Bombardier Transportation and Alstom Transport was awarded a contract by BLS Lötschbergbahn to supply 18 three-car NINA 15 kV AC emus for service in the regional network on the Bern area. Deliveries were to be made between June 2003 and December 2004. This followed an earlier order for eight similar units which had been in service since 1999.

*Bombardier emu for Long Island Railroad, USA*

*Bombardier Turbostar dmus for UK operators*

## 490  MANUFACTURERS/Locomotives and powered/non-powered passenger vehicles

*Bombardier high-capacity regional express train, France*  2002/0524861

*Bombardier Electrostar for c2c, UK*  2002/0524863

In 2001, an order was placed by Swiss Federal Railways with a consortium led by Bombardier Transportation and including Alstom Transport for 10 seven-car Class ICN tilting trainsets, with an option for an additional 10 trains. This followed earlier orders for 24 trainsets of this type, the first of which commenced commercial service in 2000. In 2001, the option on 10 additional trains was taken up for delivery in 2004.

The Mittelthurgau Railway (MThB) ordered six Class 145 electric locomotives for its Lokoop subsidiary.

In 2000 orders were received from three Swiss regional operators, BLS Lötschbergbahn, Transports de Martigny et Région and Transports Régionaux Neuchftelois for 11 NINA low-floor emu trainsets. Earlier the company had supplied eight three-car NINA trainsets to BLS Lötschbergbahn for Bern area services.

In March 2000, the VBZ (Verkehrsbetriebe Zürich) exercised an option for additional 58 Cobras increasing the total to 75 new trams for Zürich.

In the same year Swiss Federal Railways awarded a contract for 70 IC2000 double-deck intercity passenger coaches, the fourth order for vehicles of this type, which increases the total to 320 emus.

**Turkey:** In 2002, A consortium of Bombardier Transportation and engineering group Yapi Merkezi of Turkey was awarded a contract by the Eskisehir Greater City Municipality to supply a 14.2 km light rail transit system, including one year of operations and maintenance support.

In 2001, the Istanbul Transportation Company ordered 55 low-floor trams. Delivery will begin in 2002. In 2000, the Izmir Light Rail Transit system started operation. Bombardier is also involved in the current construction of a light rail system for the city of Adana which includes the delivery of 36 light rail vehicles.

**United Kingdom:** In 2002, Bombardier Transportation won a contract from Connex South Eastern for the manufacture of 228 additional Class 375 Electrostar emu cars complementing the previous Connex order for 210 cars (55 trains). The order also includes a 30-year maintenance agreement.

Bombardier Transportation also received an order for the provision of 45 Turbostar diesel-multiple-unit cars for Porterbrook Leasing Company Ltd in the UK, part of Abbey National Treasury Services plc.

*Regioswinger tilting dmu for Deutsche Bahn*  2002/0524870

In 2002, HSBC Rail UK Ltd on behalf of the UK train operator, Midland Mainline, placed an order with Bombardier Transportation for 127 high-speed diesel-electric cars. Technically similar to the Voyager units supplied for the Virgin Rail Group, the Meridian units will operate express services between London and Derby, Nottingham and Sheffield. Delivery was due to take place from mid-2004.

Also in 2002, UK operator Govia confirmed an additional order for 460 Class 375/377 Electrostar 750 V DC emus cars for services on its South Central network. Financed by Porterbrook Leasing Company Ltd, the contract brought to 700 the number of cars of this type ordered for this operator. Assembly takes place at Bombardier's Derby plant in the UK.

In May 2001, Virgin Rail Group took delivery of the first Voyager diesel-electric multiple unit. Bombardier Transportation is responsible for the design, supply and maintenance of 78 trainsets, comprising 352 diesel-electric cars, of which 216 are equipped with Bombardier's tilting technology.

Also in 2000, Bombardier Transportation received an order from Docklands Light Railway in London, for the delivery of 12 automated metro cars. This represented the conversion of an option on a 1999 contract, also for 12 vehicles.

Bombardier will supply 15 Incentro trams to the city of Nottingham and has already delivered 24 trams for Croydon Tramlink in London.

Turbostar dmus have been supplied to various UK rail operators, including: Anglia Railways (eight three-car and four two-car units); Central Trains (10 three-car, 23 two-car); Chiltern Railways (seven four-car and six three-car); Midland Mainline (10 three-car, seven two-car); ScotRail (26 three-car); and South West Trains (eight two-car).

Electrostar emus have been ordered by or supplied to three UK rail operators: c2c Rail Ltd (74 four-car 25 kV AC units); Connex South Eastern (45 four-car and 10 three-car, all 750 V DC); and South Central (154 four-car, 28 three-car all 750 V DC).

**USA:** In 2002, Bombardier Transportation received orders for its new generation of bilevel commuter cars from four North American Transportation Authorities: the North San Diego County Transit District; the Central Puget Sound Regional Transit Authority; the San Jaoquin regional Rail Commission; and the Fort Worth Transportation Authority. Together, these contracts were for 12 cab cars and 18 trailer coaches to be manufactured at the company's plants at Thunder Bay, Ontario, and Barre, Vermont, during 2003. Bombardier had earlier supplied 17 bilevel cars to the Peninsula Corridor Joint Powers Board for use from 2002 on Caltrain commuter services between San Francisco and San Jose.

In 2001, the Metropolitan Transportation Authority/Long Island Rail Road placed an order for 100 Type M-7 emu cars. The exercise of this option brought the total ordered to 326 cars. A further order for 352 emu cars placed in 2002 brought to 678 the number of cars of this type ordered by MTA/LIRR from Bombardier Transportation. Bodyshells are manufactured at the company's plant at La Pocatière, Quebec, while final manufacturing and assembly takes place at its Plattsburgh, New York, facility.

Also in 2001 an order was received from the Metropolitan Transport Authority/New York City Transit for 350 Type R142 metro cars. The contract represented the conversion of an existing option for 200 cars under a 1997 order and a new order for 150 cars required by NYCT to meet increased levels of ridership.

In 2001 Minneapolis Metropolitan Council placed an order for 18 low-floor light rail vehicles, with options for an additional 24.

New Jersey Transit has ordered 24 electric dual system locomotives derived from the DB Class 101 electric locomotive design.

In 2000, Amtrak started operation of its high-speed Acela Express Service. Bombardier, in a consortium with ALSTOM supplies 20 tilting trainsets, each consisting of two power cars and six coaches. In addition to being

*Bombardier electric locomotive for SBB Cargo, Switzerland*  2002/0524867

*Bombardier 'Xinshisu' tilting train, China*  2002/0524868

responsible for the complete design of the coaches, Bombardier manufactured the power cars, the coaches and 15 locomotives, and undertakes the integration of the trainsets.

The Port Authority of New York and New Jersey awarded Bombardier Transportation a contract for the design, construction, operation and maintenance of the New York JFK International Airport Automated Light Rail System. The contract called for the turnkey design and construction of the driverless light rail system and the supply of 32 vehicles.

**Uzbekistan:** In 1998, Bombardier Transportation signed a contract with the Japanese trade firm Marubeni Corporation for the supply of 25 passenger coaches to Uzbekistan.

### Developments

The SNCF regional train order marked the first time Bombardier Transportation was chosen as prime contractor in France. This is the first major example of the benefits of combining the complementary expertise of the new Bombardier Transportation, particularly in the propulsion field. Another breakthrough for Bombardier Transportation was for the supply of locomotives in the North American market, which was highlighted during the year with the introduction of the first of 29 electric locomotives ordered by New Jersey Transit.

Bombardier Transportation is also recognised for its ability to successfully develop advanced products that meet emerging needs. A concrete example is the development of a high-speed intercity train propelled by a turbine locomotive. This unique technology will allow for high-speed operation without the considerable cost of electrification required with alternative solutions. The Jet Train locomotive, developed in partnership with the United States Federal Railroad Administration, successfully underwent six months of testing in Colorado during 2002, travelling over 8,000 km and reaching speeds of 250 km/h. Bombardier Transportation is now promoting this product in North America.

*UPDATED*

## Breda

Breda Costruzioni Ferroviarie SpA
Via Ciliegiole 110b, I-51100 Pistoia, Italy
Tel: (+39 0573) 37 01   Fax: (+39 0573) 37 02 92
e-mail: mcmanzocco@bredacf.it

### Products

Stainless steel, carbon steel and aluminium alloy passenger coaches.

Contracts include Z1-type coaches for Italian Railways (FS); amenity coaches for Eurotunnel; panoramic coaches for BVZ, FO and MOB, Switzerland; trailer vehicles for ETR 500 high-speed trainsets for FS; and double-deck emu trailer cars for FS and North Milan Railway.

## Brookville

Brookville Mining Equipment Corporation
PO Box 130, 175 Evans Street, Brookville, Pennsylvania 15825, USA
Tel: (+1 814) 849 20 00   Fax: (+1 814) 849 20 10
e-mail: BMEC@bmec.com
Web: http://www.bmec.com

### Key personnel

President: Dalph S McNeil
Vice-President, Production: Larry J Conrad
Director of Marketing: Christine E Clinger
Sales: Chris Rhoades

### Products

Haulage equipment for mines, tunnelling and industrial applications.

The company produces 4 to 20 ton battery-powered locomotives, 4 to 45 ton diesel-powered locomotives and 45 to 150 ton diesel-electric locomotives for marshalling yard operations.

Support equipment includes diesel- or battery-powered haulage tractors, maintenance vehicles and personnel carriers for rail or road use.

Brookville also rebuilds/remanufactures existing locomotives to original OEM specifications.

## Brush

Brush Traction
PO Box 17, Loughborough LE11 1HS, UK
Tel: (+44 1509) 61 70 00   Fax: (+44 1509) 61 70 01
e-mail: sales@brushtraction.demon.co.uk
Web: http://www.brushtraction.com

### Key personnel

General Manager: A L Williams
Sales Manager: PL Needham

### Products

Diesel-electric and electric locomotives, also propulsion equipment including main and auxiliary alternators, traction motors and control equipment for both diesel and electric locomotives.

Contracts include Channel Tunnel shuttle locomotives for Eurotunnel, Class 92 electric locomotives for Railfreight Distribution and dual-mode battery-electric locomotives for Hong Kong MTRC. Of late, Brush has diversified into mid-life remanufacture of diesel locomotives and associated components. Contracts in this sector include 12 Class 57 locomotives for Freightliner, produced by remanufacturing a Class 47 locomotive with a General Motors engine. A Class 57/6 prototype with a power supply for the passenger train auxiliaries has also been produced.

## Bumar-Fablok

Fabryka Maszyn Budowlanych i Lokomotyw 'Bumar-Fablok' SA
ul Fabryczna 3, PL-32-500 Chrzanów, Poland
Tel: (+48 35) 623 22 31   Fax: (+48 35) 623 29 25
e-mail: info@fablok.com.pl

### Key personnel

General Manager: Piotr Majcherczyk
Manager, Marketing and Development: Andrej Smolana
Marketing Specialist: Grzegorz Kosobudzki
Assembly Department Chief: Antoni Jemielniak

### Products

Modernisation, repair and general overhaul of diesel locomotives; production driving axle-sets for electrical and diesel locomotives, motor bogies for power cars, mechanical gears, cylindrical gears, braking system components for rail vehicles, and brake adjusters.

*Bumar-Fablok diesel-electric shunter*  0021419

## CAF

Construcciones y Auxiliar de Ferrocarriles SA
Padilla 17, E-28006 Madrid, Spain
Tel: (+34 91) 435 25 00   Fax: (+34 91) 576 62 63
e-mail: export.caf@nexo.es
Web: http://www.caf.es

### Key personnel

Chairman: J I Cangas Herrero
Executive Deputy Chairman: J M Baztarrica Garijo
Commercial Manager: J M de la Rubia Burgos
Export Manager: L G de la Cuesta

### Works

Beasain, Zaragoza, Irún

### US Office

CAF USA
1401 K Street, N W Suite 803, Washington DC 20005, 3418, USA
Tel: (+1 202) 898 48 48   Fax: (+1 202) 216 89 29

### Products

Electric, diesel-electric and diesel-hydraulic locomotives; multiple-units and hauled coaches.

### Contracts

*Brazil:* In 2002, CAF was awarded a turnkey contract to construct and operate for 20 years a metro system in Salvador de Bahía. The project includes the supply of rolling stock.

A consortium led by CAF, and including Alstom and the former Adtranz, supplied 30 four-car emus to CPTM, São Paulo.

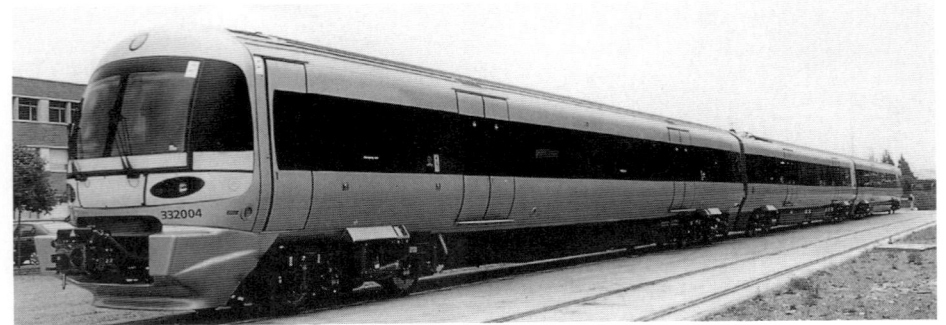

## 492 MANUFACTURERS/Locomotives and powered/non-powered passenger vehicles

*IGBT-powered Series S-600 two-car emu for Metro de Madrid*    2002/0114008

**China:** In collaboration with the former Adtranz, CAF supplied 184 aluminium-bodied emu cars to MTRC Hong Kong for its Airport Express (11 eight-car trains) and Lantau line commuter services (12 eight-car trains).

**Ireland:** In 2000, Irish Rail placed a contract with CAF to supply 15 Class 2900 four-car dmus.

**Italy:** In 2001, CAF signed a contract increasing from 33 to 45 the number of air conditioned six-car trains ordered by Comune di Roma for the capital's metro network.

**Portugal:** In collaboration with Alstom, CAF undertook construction of 36 cars of an order for 18 four-car double-deck emus for Lisbon cross-Tagus services.

**Spain:** In 2001, Spanish National Railways (RENFE) awarded a consortium of CAF and Alstom a contract to supply 12 AVE high-speed trainsets for the Madrid–Barcelona line. The trains are to be equipped with CAF's Brava gauge-changing system to enable them to operate on both the standard gauge high-speed lines and the broad gauge (1,668 mm) of the classic Spanish network.

In 2001, RENFE awarded CAF a contract to supply 21 three-car tilting dmus for regional services. Delivery was due to commence in 2003. These follow earlier deliveries of 16 Flexliner-type dmus supplied to RENFE for regional services.

In 2001, CAF, in consortium with Alstom, was awarded a contract by RENFE to supply 20 Alaris non-tilting four-car 270 km/h regional emus for use on the Madrid–Barcelona high-speed line.

Recent emu contracts for RENFE include batches of 29 and 46 Class 447 air conditioned emus.

Recent locomotive contracts for RENFE include the manufacture of 15 Class 252 high-speed electric locomotives and the reconstruction of four Class 269.600 electric locomotives for 200 km/h operation.

The most recent deliveries for the Madrid metro system have been of Type S-8000 three-car trainsets with IGBT technology. Earlier deliveries to Metro de Madrid included 44 S-600 and 72 Series 2000 trainsets.

The latest type to be supplied to the Barcelona metro system is the four-car Type S-550, which employs IGBT technology. Earlier deliveries were of the Series 2100 type.

CAF has also supplied 20 Class 213 three-car metre-gauge emus to FGC, Barcelona.

**UK:** In 2002, CAF received an order from the Northen Ireland government for 23 three-car dmus for service on the Northen Ireland Railways network from 2004.

In 2000, CAF commenced delivery of 16 Class 333 three-car 25 kV AC emus for Northern Spirit (now Arriva Trains Northern). Subsequently, orders were placed for 16 additional trailer cars to strengthen all sets to four-car units.

Acting as a general contractor, CAF, together with Siemens Transportation Systems, built 14 25 kV AC Class 332 four-car emus for Heathrow Express. In 2001, orders were placed for an additional five trailers to strengthen five of these trains.

**USA:** Recent contracts include: the supply of 192 metro cars for WMATA, Washington; supply of 40 LRVs to Sacramento Regional Transit District; and the supply of 28 new trams and the refurbishment of 55 existing vehicles for PATCO, Pittsburgh.

*UPDATED*

## CFC

Costruzioni Ferroviarie Colleferro SpA
A member of the Fiat Group
Via Sabotino, I-00034 Colleferro, Rome, Italy
Tel: (+39 06) 978 12 80   Fax: (+39 06) 978 27 46

**Key personnel**
President: Dr C Giancarlo
Delegate Administrator: Ing L Basta
Technical Director: Ing V Travaglini
Project Officer: Ing G Clementi
Production Officer: PI F Cherubini

Production Officer: Ing A Rigon
Import/Export Officer: Rag V Nobilio

**Products**
Passenger cars, freight cars, refrigerated wagons and containers.

## CFD

CFD Industrie
9-11 rue Benoît Malon, F-92156 Suresnes, France
Tel: (+33 1) 45 06 44 00   Fax: (+33 1) 47 28 48 84
e-mail: cfd@cfd.fr
Web: http://www.cdf.fr

**Key personnel**
President: F de Coincy
General Manager: P Esnault
Sales Manager: M Hallet

**Principal subsidiaries**
CFD Industrie, CFD Locorem, Belgium Desbrugeres, Batiruhr and CFD Bagnères, France

**Products**
Diesel locomotives from 150 to 2,000 kW, road-rail vehicles.

A new-generation diesel-electric industrial locomotive of 44 tonnes and 240 kW was supplied to the Evian mineral water company in late 1999. Three similar locomotives for metre gauge are currently under construction for the Tunisian chemical group GCT, as is a 1,790 kW bogie locomotive for the Swiss rail grinding company Scheuchzer SA. CFD Bagnères is executing a series of lightweight, articulated metre gauge dmus for the French State Railways (SNCF) to be used on the Blanc-Argent metre gauge line. Five units have been ordered with an option for a further nine vehicles.

*A new-generation diesel-electric industrial locomotive of 44 tonnes and 240 kW was supplied to the Evian mineral water company in late 1999*   2000/0092236

*CFD diesel locomotive for Holderbank cement works, Switzerland*   0002143

## Changchun Car Company

5 Qingyin Road, Changchun 130062, Jilin, People's Republic of China
Tel: (+86 431) 790 14 45   Fax: (+86 431) 293 07 92
e-mail: hhw@cccar.com.cn
Web: http://www.cccar.com.cn

**Key personnel**
Director of Factory: Ma Shu Kun
Manager of Sales and Marketing: Chen Wei

**Corporate developments**
In 1998 Adtranz (qv) and Changchun Car Company inaugurated the Changchun Adtranz Railway Vehicle Company for the production of metro trains, LRVs, people movers and dmus. The company has an initial capacity of 160 vehicles per year.

**Products**
Development, design, production, sales, installation, refurbishment, maintenance and aftersales service for

metro cars; electric multiple-units for main line applications; sleeping cars, dining cars, mail vans, generator vans and passenger coaches.

Metro cars include DK20 and the DK9 with chopper voltage control. All cars are motored (4 × 86 kW) and designed to operate in multiples of two, four or six.

Contracts include an order announced in 1996 for the supply of 29 six-car emus for Beijing Mass Transit Railway Co with AC traction and VVVF control.

Changchun has also supplied 217 DK21-DK27 metro cars to Iran, 48 double-deck coaches to Iran in May 1998 and 174 metro cars to Beijing at the end of 2000.

*Harbin diesel multiple-unit by Changchun*     2000/0089808

*High-speed electric multiple-unit by Changchun*     2000/0089809

## Changzhou Diesel & Mining Locomotive Plant

74 Xinshi Road, Changzhou, 213002 Jiangsu, People's Republic of China
Tel: (+86 519) 60 06 56  Fax: (+86 519) 60 04 43

**Key personnel**
Managing Director: Xie Yintang
Chief Engineer: Xu Di'an
Marketing Director: Wang Chenxian
Production Director: Wang Jianxun
Export Sales Director: Wu Leping

**Products**
Diesel locomotives from 60 to 750 kW. Electric locomotives for mining applications from 3 to 55 tonnes.

## China National Railway Locomotive and Rolling Stock Industry Corporation (LORIC)

10 Fuxing Road, 100844 Beijing, People's Republic of China
Tel: (+86 10) 63 51 16 20
Fax: (+86 10) 63 51 16 14; 63 24 78 35
e-mail: loric@public.bta.net.cn
Web: http://www.loric.com.cn

**Key personnel**
Chairman and Managing Director: Wang Tai-Wen
President of LORIC Import & Export Corporation Ltd: Cao Guo-Bing
Vice-President of LORIC Import & Export Corporation Ltd: Chen Da-Yong
Vice-President of LORIC Import & Export Corporation Ltd: Wang Xian
Senior Engineer of LORIC Import & Export Corporation Ltd: Yang Xiang-Jing

**Works addresses**
(the company comprises 34 production facilities and four research divisions)
Changchun Car Company (qv)
Dalian Locomotive & Rolling Stock Works (qv)
Datong Locomotive Works (qv)
Beijing February 7th Locomotive Works
Changxindian, Beijing 100072, China
Tel: (+86 10) 63 88 61 47  Fax: (+86 10) 63 25 76 54
Sifang Locomotive and Rolling Stock Works
16 Hangzhou Road, Quingdao 266031, Shandong, China
Tel: (+86 532) 371 81 68  Fax: (+86 532) 371 66 56
Qishuyan Locomotive and Rolling Stock Works
Qishuyan, Changzhou 213011, Jiangsu, China
Tel: (+86 519) 877 17 11  Fax: (+86 519) 877 03 58
Ziyang Diesel Locomotive Works
Ziyang 641301, Sichuan, China
Tel: (+86 832) 622 42 61  Fax: (+86 832) 622 71 76
Zhuzhou Electric Locomotive Works
Zuzhou 412001, Hunan, China
Tel: (+86 733) 844 13 31  Fax: (+86 733) 844 23 99
Taiyuan Locomotive & Rolling Stock Works
84 Jiefang North Road, Taiyuan 030009, Shanxi, China
Tel: (+86 351) 304 54 11  Fax: (+86 351) 304 95 63
Jinan Locomotive & Rolling Stock Works
73 Huaichun Street, Huaiyin District, Jinan 250022, Shandong, China
Tel: (+86 531) 795 59 30  Fax: (+86 531) 795 75 48
Yongji Electric Machine Factory

*CKD7 diesel-electric locomotive for Myanmar Railways*     0002145

*SS8 electric locomotive by LORIC*     0002146

# MANUFACTURERS/Locomotives and powered/non-powered passenger vehicles

24 Tiaoshan West Street, Yongjii 044502, Shanxi, China
Tel: (+86 359) 802 38 25   Fax: (+86 359) 802 20 90
Lanzhou Locomotive Works
210 Wuwei Road, Lanzhou 730050, Gansu, China
Tel: (+86 931) 286 69 01   Fax: (+86 931) 233 72 79
Tangshan Locomotive & Rolling Stock Works
3, Chanqian Road, Tangshan New District, Tangshan 063035, Hebei, China
Tel: (+86 315) 324 19 12   Fax: (+86 315) 324 29 39
Qiqihr Rolling Stock Group Company
10 Chanqian Street, Zhonghus East Road, Qiqihr 161002, Heilongjiang, China
Tel: (+86 452) 293 84 72   Fax: (+86 452) 251 44 64

## Products

Development, design, engineering, production, sales, installation, refurbishment, maintenance and after-sales service for electric, diesel-electric and diesel-hydraulic locomotives with various power ratings from 280 to 6,400 kW for passenger, freight and shunting services; passenger coaches; metro cars; freight wagons; rail-mounted cranes; diesel generator sets and components.

From 1990 to 1999, the corporation has built 6,310 diesel locomotives, 1,821 electric locomotives, 18,362 passenger coaches and 232,926 freight wagons.

The annual output is over 750 diesel locomotives, 300 electric locomotives, 2,500 passenger coaches and 38,000 freight wagons. Most are 1,435 mm gauge for China Railways.

The DF range of diesel-electric locomotives, with four-stroke turbocharged diesel engines, and with AC/DC transmission, are the main types of locomotive for both passenger and freight traffic. The locomotives run on three-axle bogies with roller bearings. The traction motors are full suspension with hollow shaft quill drive. The DF4C and DF8B are for heavy-duty freight trains, the DF4D, DF10F and DF11 are for high-speed passenger work and the DF5 and DF7 are for shunting work.

The GK range of diesel locomotives is intended for shunting and industrial applications. Most have hydraulic transmission and have B-B configuration to suit tight curves.

The SS range of electric locomotives features microprocessor control, anti-slip braking and AC/DC transmission. The SS4 eight-axle double units are suitable for heavy haul freight work and the SS8 is for high-speed passenger work.

The CK range of diesel locomotives is designed for markets other than China and features a lower axle load. These locomotives are in operation on the narrow-gauge railways of Thailand, Myanmar, Tanzania, Zambia and Nigeria.

LORIC is developing high-speed passenger trains with an operating speed of up to 300 km/h. An SS8 locomotive reached 212 km/h in 1997.

Recent deliveries have included 23 SS4B electric locomotives for the Shen-Suo mine, 15 1,800 kW diesel-electric locomotives for Nigeria, 143 metro cars for Iran and 54 metro cars (VVVF) for Beijing.

Other recent export contracts include the supply of 10 1,492 kW diesel-electric locomotives for Myanmar, 24 SS4B electric locomotives for the Shen-Suo mine, 15 diesel-electric locomotives for Nigeria, and 143 54 metro-cars for Beijing.

## New developments

Canadian companies, Bombardier Inc and Power Corporation of Canada have announced the creation of a joint venture with Chinese partner Sifang Locomotive and LORIC subsidiary Rolling Stock Works, Qingdao. It is for the manufacture of railcars and Bombardier and Power will own 50 per cent of the joint venture and Sifang will own 50 per cent. It is expected that bodyshells emus, double-deck cars, passenger coaches and other urban transport vehicles will be offered. In support of the joint-venture start-up Chinese Railways has agreed to purchase 300 inter city coaches with an option for 200 more. Newly developed is the Class S9 demu.

### LORIC electric locomotives

| Type | Wheel arrangement | Line voltage | Output (kW) continuous | Speed (km/h) | Weight tonnes | Length (mm) | First built | Builders |
|---|---|---|---|---|---|---|---|---|
| SS3B | Co-Co | 25 kV/50 Hz | 4,350 | 100 | 138 | 21,416 | 1992 | Zhuzhou, Dafong, Taiyuan |
| SS4B | 2(Bo-Bo) | 25 kV/50 Hz | 6,400 | 100 | 184 | 2 × 16,416 | 1995 | Zhuzhou |
| SS6B | Co-Co | 25 kV/50 Hz | 4,800 | 100 | 138 | 21,416 | 1992 | Zhuzhou |
| SS7 | Bo-Co-Bo | 25 kV/50 Hz | 4,800 | 100 | 138 | 22,016 | 1992 | Datong |
| SS7B | Bo-Co-Bo | 25 kV/50 Hz | 4,800 | 100 | 150 | 22,016 | 1997 | Datong |
| SS8 | Bo-Bo | 25 kV/50 Hz | 3,600 | 177 | 88 | 17,516 | 1994 | Zhuzhou |
| TM1 | Bo-Bo | 25 kV/50 Hz | 3,200 | 140 | 88 | 17,516 | 1998 | Zhuzhou |

### LORIC electric railcars and multiple-units

| Class | Cars per unit | Line voltage | Motor cars per unit | Wheel arrangement | Output (kW) per motor | Speed (km/h) | Weight (tonnes) per car | Total seating capacity | Length per car (mm) | No in service | First built |
|---|---|---|---|---|---|---|---|---|---|---|---|
| DK16 | 6 | 750 V DC | 6 | Bo-Bo | 76 | 80 | 35 | 188 | 19 | 116 | 1985 |
| DK20 | 6 | 750 V DC | 6 | Bo-Bo | 80 | 86 | 35 | Mc180/M190 | 19 | 42 | 1994 |
| DK21-27 | 3 | 750 V DC | 2 | Bo-Bo | 180 | 80 | 38 | 180 | 19 | 3 | 1998 |
| DK28 | 6 | 750 V DC | 6 | Bo-Bo | 180 | 80 | 38 | 230 | 25.5 | 4 | 1988 |
| Chun chen | 6 | 25 kV/50 Hz | 3 | Bo-Bo | 180 | 120 | 72 | Mc128 T64 | M25 T25.8 | 6 | 1999 |
| DDJ1 | 7 | 25 kV/50 Hz | 1 | Bo-Bo | 1,000 | 200 | M86 Tc52 T48/52 | Tc48 T64/76 T96 | M18.5 | 7 | 1999 |

### LORIC diesel locomotives

| Type | Wheel arrangement | Transmission | Power (kW) | Speed (km/h) | Weight tonnes | First built | Builders |
|---|---|---|---|---|---|---|---|
| 4E3DF4C | Co-Co | AC/DC | 2,650 | 100 | 138 | 1985 | Dalian |
| DF4D | Co-Co | AC/DC | 2,940 | 160 | 138 | 1996 | Dalian |
| DF5 | Co-Co | AC/DC | 1,213 | 80 | 135 | 1984 | Sifang, Dalian |
| DF6 | Co-Co | AC/DC | 2,940 | 118 | 138 | 1989 | Dalian |
| DF7C | Co-Co | AC/DC | 1,470 | 100 | 135 | 1991 | Feb 7th |
| DF7D | 2 (Co-Co) | AD/DC | 2 × 1,840 | 100 | 2 × 138 | 1995 | Feb 7th |
| DF8B | Co-Co | AC/DC | 3,680 | 100 | 150 | 1997 | Qishuyan |
| DF10F | 2 (Co-Co) | AC/DC | 2 × 2,200 | 160 | 2 × 123 | 1996 | Dalian |
| DF11 | Co-Co | AC/DC | 3,680 | 170 | 138 | 1992 | Qishuyan |
| GK1E | B-B | hydraulic | 790 | 40/80 | 92 | 1991 | Ziyang |
| GK1F | B-B | hydraulic | 1,200 | 50/80 | 92 | 1997 | Sifang |
| GK1H | B-B | hydraulic | 1,000 | 35/70 | 92 | 1996 | Sifang |
| GK1G-B | B-B | hydraulic | 1,000 | 35/70 | 100 | 1995 | Jinan |
| GK2 | C-C | hydraulic | 1,375 | 65/100 | 120 | 1994 | Ziyang |
| GKD1 | Bo-Bo | AC/DC | 990 | 80 | 84 | 1990 | Dalian |
| CK5 | B-B | hydraulic | 515 | 76 | 60 | 1992 | Ziyang |
| CKD6 | Bo-Bo-Bo | AC/DC | 880 | 90 | 66 | 1995 | Sifang |
| CKD7 | Bo-Bo-Bo | AC/DC | 1,250 | 90 | 76 | 1993 | Dalian |
| CKD8A | Co-Co | AC/DC | 1,800 | 100 | 96 | 1997 | Dalian |
| CKD8B | Co-Co | AC/DC | 2,200 | 100 | 120 | 1997 | Dalian |

### LORIC diesel railcars and multiple-units

| Class | Cars per unit | Motor cars per unit | Motored axles per motor car | Transmission | Rated power (kW) per motor | Speed (km/h) | Weight (t) per car | Seating capacity | Length per car (m) | First built | Builders |
|---|---|---|---|---|---|---|---|---|---|---|---|
| YZDD | 4 | 2 | 4 | AC/DC | 91 | 120 | Mc72, T68 | Mc95, T168 | Mc24.6 T25.5 | 1998 | Tangshan |
| ZXGW | 1 | 1 | 4 | AC/DC | 70 | 120 | 64 | 18 | 25.5 | 1996 | Tangshan |
| Tian'an | 1 | 1 |  | hydraulic |  | 120 | 72 | 13 | 25.5 | 1994 | Sifang |
| Nanchang | 6 | 2 |  | hydraulic |  | 140 | 76 | M33, T96 T128 | M25.5 T25.5 | 1998 | Sifang |
| NZJ1 | 11 | 2 | 4 | AC/DC | 600 | 180 | M122.4 T50 | T148 T108 | M20.6 T25.5 | 1999 | Qishuyan Puzhen |
| S9 | 6 | 1 | 4 | AC/DC | 230 | 100 | M66 T42 | M20, M54 T60, T180 DT46, DT144 | 21.5 | 2000 | Sifang |

*China National Class S9 demu*
2000/0089426

## ČKD

ČKD Dopravn Systémi AS
Ringhofferova 115/1, CZ-15500 Praha 5, Czech Republic
Tel: (+420 2) 20 32 28 30   Fax: (+420 2) 20 32 28 33
e-mail: ckddos1@mbox.vol.cz

### Key personnel
Managing Director: Bohumír Kráčmar
Commercial Director: Petr Bílek
Technical Director: Milan Šlitr

### Products
Diesel-electric shunting and main line locomotives, battery shunting locomotives, high-speed trains, tramcars, LRVs, metro cars, refurbishment, consultancy.

Class 680 high-speed three-voltage (3 kV DC, 15 kV AC and 25 kV AC) active tilt-body trainset.

T239.2: This is a newly introduced two-axle diesel locomotive with AC transmission and has been developed for shunting work and for hauling trains on 1,435 mm gauge railways. The range includes two-, four- and six-axle diesel-electric versions with outputs from 200 to 1,760 kW and 1,000, 1,435 and 1,520 mm track gauges.

Current production includes Class D12 and Bde 410 on metre gauge in Asia, Class 714 and 708 for main line railways and Class T239.1, T239.2 and T448.1 for industrial operators.

*New Class T239.2 two-axle diesel-electric locomotive with AC transmission*   0063349

*Class T448.1 locomotive for industrial operators*   0063350

## ČKD VAGONKA as

1 máje 3176/102, CZ-0931 Ostrava, Czech Republic
Tel: (+420 59) 747 71 11   Fax: (+420 59) 747 71 90
e-mail: info@vagonka.cz
Web: http://www.vagonka.cz

### Key personnel
Chairman of the Board of Directors: Luděk Votava
Vice-Chairman: Radimír Surák
Commercial Manager: Oldřich Strakoš

### Background
ČKD VAGONKA was founded by a Joint Stock Company ČKD PRAHA HOLDING in January 2000. The limited company was transformed into a Joint Stock Company in January 2001 and moved from Studénka to Ostrava in March the same year.

### Products
Development, design and manufacture of double-deck electric multiple-units using aluminium bodyshells; diesel-electric and diesel-hydraulic railcars and multiple-units; light regional vehicles; railcars; trailers and coaches.

### Contracts
Recent contracts include the supply of double-deck Class 471 emus for Czech Railways, Class Bzmot Interpici motor cars developed together with Hungarian industry, MVJ Szombathely, for MÁV and Class 843 motor units for Czech Railways. A contract has been granted to build a new type of regional diesel railcar for Finnish Railways, and also to build a new type of double systems inter-regional emu, Class 675.

*ČKD VAGONKA double-deck Class 471 emus for Czech Railways*   2002/0525452

**UPDATED**

## CLW

Chittaranjan Locomotive Works
Chittaranjan, 713331, Burdwan District, West Bengal, India
Tel: (+91 341) 52 56 42   Fax: (+91 341) 52 56 41
e-mail: secy@vsnl.net.in

### Key personnel
General Manager: N K Chidambaram
Chief Electrical Engineer: P C Seghal
Chief Mechanical Engineer: S Sah
Controller of Stores: K Mishra
Financial Adviser/Chief Accounts Officer: L C Majumdar
Chief Personnel Officer: S Gupta

### Background
CLW was the first production unit to be set up within Indian Railways. Established in 1950, CLW has turned out 2,351 steam locomotives of five different classes and seven classes of diesel locomotives. CLW currently manufactures only main line passenger and freight locomotives and, up to the end of March 1998, had manufactured 2,519 diesel locomotives.

A special feature of the plant is its in-house manufacturing facility for traction motors, control equipment and heavy steel castings. CLW has been awarded an ISO 9001 certificate for the locomotive works and an ISO 9002 certificate for the steel foundry in 1996-97.

# MANUFACTURERS/Locomotives and powered/non-powered passenger vehicles

*CLW WAG-7 25 kV AC high-adhesion Co-Co locomotive for Indian Railways freight service* 0063351

*CLW WAP-5 three-phase locomotive for passenger service* 0063353

### Products
Electric locomotives; traction motors, castings. The present product mix consists of the following types of locomotives:

*WAG7:* This is rated at 3,730 kW and can haul 4,500 t of freight up a 1 in 200 incline. It is for 25 kV operation and has a starting tractive effort of 42 t and a continuous tractive effort of 24 t. It has 630 kW type HS15250A traction motors and is designed for a speed of 100 km/h. It has a dual brake system with rheostatic braking and can be operated in multiple units.

*WAP4:* This is rated at 3,730 kW and can haul a maximum of 26 coaches at a maximum speed of 140 km/h. It operates on 25 kV and has a starting tractive effort of 30.8 t and a continuous tractive effort of 19 t. It has HS1525OA 630 kW traction motors and flexi-coil Co-Co steel bogies. It is suitable for hauling air-braked stock and is designed for multiple-unit operation.

*WAG9:* CLW has started manufacture of a three-phase 4,500 kW locomotive with GTO drive and microprocessor control through a technology transfer agreement from Adtranz. CLW has assembled 15 with SKD/CKD components from Adtranz. The first locomotive was handed over in 1998. It operates on 25 kV and has a starting tractive effort of 47 tonnes. It is designed for a maximum speed of 100 km/h. The locomotives are intended for heavy haulage work, due to their higher adhesion, and have regenerative braking and a microprocessor-based fault diagnostic system. Maintenance is reduced through the use of electronic controls and three-phase AC traction motors.

*WAP5:* CLW is starting manufacture of these three-phase 4,500 kW electric passenger locomotives with technology acquired from Adtranz Switzerland. The locomotive is designed to haul 26-coach trains at a maximum speed of 160 km/h.

## Cockerill Mechanical Industries SA (CMI)

Avenue Greiner 1, B-4100 Seraing, Belgium
Tel: (+32 4) 330 24 46; 330 21 11
Fax: (+32 4) 330 25 45; 330 25 82
e-mail: locos.diesel@cmi.be
Web: http://www.cmi.be

### Key personnel
President: L Levaux
Sales Director: J F Levaux
Contact: A Bruls (Manager, Locomotives & Diesel Engines)

### Products
Shunting locomotives 185 to 1,000 kW, on two, three or four axles, for all gauges and types of track. Amongst its latest products is a shunting/branch line locomotive featuring hydrostatic transmission.

Maintenance, rehabilitation and retro-fitting of shunting locomotives; radio remote-control.

**UPDATED**

*Cockerill Mechanical Industries shunting locomotive* 0063352

## Costaferroviaria SpA

Viale IV Novembre, I-23845 Costa Masnaga (LC), Italy
Tel: (+39 31) 86 94 11   Fax: (+39 31) 85 53 30
e-mail: info@costaferroviaria.it

### Key personnel
Managing Director: F Magni
General Manager: S Maluta
Sales Manager: Giuliano Felten

### Background
Costaferroviaria (formerly Costamasnaga) started building rolling stock in 1916. The company traditionally concentrated on wagons but, since 1980, has been constructing passenger cars. Since 1989, its technical department has been designing new vehicles for urban transport.

### Products
Electric multiple-units, passenger coaches, freight wagons and bogies.

Costaferroviaria manufactured 10 electric multiple-units for Consorzio Trasporti Pubblici Lazio (COTRAL), Rome. These are for regional and suburban service and include a motor, passenger and driving coach, with 236 seats. Total length is 64,420 mm, maximum speed is 90 km/h and the power is 1,200 kW.

**UPDATED**

*Costaferroviaria MRP236 for COTRAL, Rome*
2000/0089810

*Jane's World Railways 2002-2003*   www.janes.com

## Dalian Locomotive and Rolling Stock Works

51 Zhong Chang Street, 116022 Dalian, People's Republic of China
Tel: (+86 411) 419 88 29
Fax: (+86 411) 460 30 64
e-mail: DLW@pub.dl.lnpta.net.cn

### Key personnel
General Manager, Export Sales & International Marketing: Tan Fuqiang

### Products
Diesel locomotives of various power ratings for passenger, freight and shunting applications.

The DF4D passenger diesel locomotive is newly introduced and has a 16V240ZJD diesel engine, maximum power output of 2,940 kW. The locomotive is for main line passenger work and has a maximum speed of 145 km/h, and can haul 20 coaches.

The DF4D freight diesel locomotive has been developed on the basis of the DF4D passenger locomotive. It has an improved gear ratio (63:14) and a maximum starting tractive effort (480.5 kN) for heavy haul work in China.

The DF5 diesel electric shunting locomotive has a maximum power rating of 1,210 kW and an 8240ZJ diesel engine with three-phase AC/DC transmission and an axle loading of 22.5 tonnes. It is for shunting and industrial work.

The DF5B locomotive, based on the DF5 locomotive, is powered by the 12V240ZJF diesel engine with a maximum power rating of 1,840 kW. The locomotive is narrow, making it suitable for mining operations.

The DF6 locomotive is a new generation of high-power and high-performance units, built in co-operation with other firms. Its power unit, the 16V240ZJD has been improved in association with Ricardo Consulting Engineers, UK, while the electric transmission has been developed in co-operation with General Electric Co, USA. It features advanced technology including microprocessor control, diagnostic display system, dynamic brakes with three-stage expansion and anti-slip/slide devices. It has a maximum power rating of 2,940 kW.

The DFl0F passenger diesel locomotive is a new model for mainline passenger operation with a maximum speed of 160 km/h. It is in Co-Co axle configuration and has an axle loading of 20 t. The engine is predominantly used on main line work.

The CKD7 locomotive has been specially designed and built for main line work on Myanmar Railways. It has a CAT 3516 diesel engine as its power unit with a maximum power rating of 1,250 kW, and features two cabs and Bo-Bo-Bo arrangement. It has a dual vacuum-air brake system and rheostatic brake system.

The CKD8A locomotive, designed for Nigerian Railways, is equipped with the advanced 12V240ZJG diesel engine and has a maximum power rating of 1,800 kW. The turbocharger and fuel injection system can be specified from manufacturers other than Dalian. Passenger and freight work on narrow gauge (1,067 mm).

The CKD6 locomotive is also for Nigerian Railways. It is powered by the 6240ZJ diesel engine and has a maximum power rating of 1,200 kW. The wheel arrangement A 1 A-A 1 A, and the axle load is 12.5 t, with a tare weight of 75 t.

The CKD8B locomotive, with a 2,200 kW power rating, which is powered by the 12V240ZJD diesel engine, has been designed specially for the Tanzania-Zambia Railway.

The GK diesel-hydraulic shunting locomotive is for both shunting and light haulage. This locomotive, powered by the 6240ZJ diesel engine with a power rating of 990 kW, has a hydraulic transmission and hydraulic reversing instead of the original electric transmission mode which is cited as being lower in cost.

*Dong Feng 4D diesel passenger locomotive* 0063354

## Datong Locomotive Works

1 Daqing Road, Datong 03708, Shanxi, People's Republic of China
Tel: (+86 352) 509 01 24   Fax: (+86 352) 509 09 84
e-mail: dtjjc@public.dt.sx.cn

### Key personnel
Director: Zheng Xian Dao
Chief Engineer: Xie Bumin
Chief Chartered Accountant: Dai Baocheng

### Corporate developments
Datong ABC Castings Company Ltd (a Sino-American joint venture, Datong Works, owns 60 per cent of the shares) Datong Locomotive Works is part of LORIC (China National Railway Locomotive and Rolling Stock Industry Corporation) (qv).

### Products
SS3 passenger and freight electric locomotives; SS4/SS7 electric locomotives; DF4 diesel-electric freight locomotive; DT20 diesel-electric shunting locomotive; DF4, DF8 combined piston of steel crown and aluminium skirt; ND5 combined piston of steel crown and aluminium skirt for 7FDL diesel engines; forged aluminium piston and piston pins for diesel engines; bogies and parts for locomotives and rolling stock.

Contracts include supply of 20 DF4 diesel-electric locomotives, 44 SS3 electric locomotives and five SS7 electric locomotives for the Ministry of Railways, June 1999.

*Datong Works SS7 main line electric locomotive*
0063355

## De Dietrich Ferroviaire

PO Box 35, F-67891 Niederbronn Cedex, France
Tel: (+33 3) 88 80 25 00   Fax: (+33 3) 88 80 25 12

See ALSTOM entry in *Locomotives and powered/non-powered passenger vehicles* section.

## DEVZ – Dnepropetrovsk State Electric Locomotive Factory

13 Orbitalnaya Street, Dnepropetrovsk 49868, Ukraine
Tel: (+380 56) 258 51 33; 42 35; (56) 773 26 78
Fax: (+380 56) 773 29 17; 773 26 77

### Key personnel
General Director: Chumask Valery Victorovych

### Background
The firm was established in 1937 as Ukraine's major locomotive and repair works. In 1958 it switched to the manufacture of industrial electric locomotives.

## Products

Main line electric locomotives, mining electric locomotives, industrial narrow-gauge electric locomotives, repair, emergency renovation, electric traction components, starters for diesel locomotives, wheelsets.

The DS freight locomotive is for operation on 3 kV overhead lines and 1,520 mm gauge. It has a maximum power rating of 6,250 kW at a speed of 100 km/h.

## Contracts

Locomotives have been supplied for operation on rail lines and open-cast mines in Russia, Kazakhstan, Mongolia and other countries.

## Developments

In 1993-1995, under the programme of Ukraine's own enterprise encouraging diesel locomotive production, DEVZ produced a prototype model. Designs have been produced for advanced four- and eight-axle locomotives.

*DEVZ DS Class eight-axle freight locomotive*    2000/0092266

*DEVZ prototype advanced four-axle locomotive* 2000/0092267

# Diesel Locomotive Works (DLW)

Varanasi 221 004, (UP), India
Tel: (+91 542) 27 05 51; 55   Fax: (+91 542) 27 06 03
e-mail: gmdlw@nde.vsnl.net.in
Web: http://www.dlwindia.com

## Key personnel

General Manager: O P Gupta
Chief Mechanical Engineer: H S Pannu
Controller of Stores: N K Mehndiratta
Chief Design Engineer: H C Gupta
Chief Project Manager: Pramod Kumar
Chief Marketing Manager: Vishwa Bandhu
Chief Mechanical Engineer/Production: R B Srivastva

## Corporate background

DLW was set up in collaboration with Alco, USA, in 1962 and has so far supplied 4,094 locomotives, mainly to Indian Railways. DLW has been awarded ISO 9002 certification.

*DLW WDP2 high-speed aerodynamically styled twin-cab Co-Co diesel-electric locomotive for passenger work at speeds of up to 160 km/h*    0063358

## Products

Diesel-electric locomotives for 1,676 mm (broad gauge) and metre gauge; diesel engines of 1,000 to 2,300 kW and components for diesel locomotives.

Export orders include 15 metre-gauge 1,000 kW (1,350 hp) six-axle locomotives to Vietnam National Railways and six to Tanzanian Railways. Two 1,676 mm 1,940 kW (2,600 hp) six-axle WDM2 locomotives were supplied to Sri Lankan Railways in 1995. A repeat order for another six WDM2 locomotives was supplied to Sri Lankan railways in 1997. A 1,676 mm gauge 1,000 kW four-axle WDM6 shunting locomotive was supplied to a private cement company in Sri Lanka in 1997. Bangladesh Railways took delivery of 10 metre-gauge 1,000 kW six-axle twin-cab locomotives in 1996.

DLW has supplied 501 1,000 kW WDS6 class shunting locomotives, some with slow-speed creep control, to meet heavy-duty shunting requirements including those of steel plants and power stations.

*WDP1:* 1,676 mm gauge Bo-Bo loco for passenger work. It has a 251-C 12-cylinder diesel engine, upgraded to 1,715 kW. DLW reports that performance of this locomotive is comparable to the 1,940 kW WDM2

*WDG4 locomotive by Diesel Locomotive Works, India*    2000/0089811

passenger locomotive due to lower rolling resistance and lower total weight. So far, 63 have been built.

*WDG2*: 1,676 m gauge Co-Co high-adhesion locomotive for freight work with 16-cylinder 251-C engine, uprated to 2,300 kW. Starting tractive effort is 37.9 tonnes, compared to 30.4 tonnes with the WDM2 loco. So far 221 have been built.

Earlier, DLW had manufactured the *WDM2C* class locomotive with upgraded 16-cylinder 251-C engines, uprated to 3,100 kW. DLW has built 57 of these locomotives.

For high-speed operation (160 km/h) on broad-gauge, DLW has evolved the full-width twin-cab *WDP2* Co-Co locomotive with flexi-coil two-stage suspension and rated at 2,300 kW. Fourteen have been built so far.

In 1995, IR signed a contract with General Motors (EMD), USA, for 3,100 kW AC drive GT46MAC class freight locomotives, as well as 12- 16- and 20-cylinder diesel engines, produced at DLW. Thirteen assembled locomotives out of the 21 ordered from General Motors (EMD) are working on South Central Railway, six partially knocked down locomotives have also been assembled and commissioned, the remaining two CKD locomotives are being assembled, with full production continuing during 2000-2001.

A contract has recently been signed with Sri Lankan Railway for two 1,693 kW broad-gauge locomotives and Bangladesh Railways is considering procurement of 10 broad-gauge 1,940 kW WDM2 locomotives.

An agreement has been signed with General Motors (EMD) for 10 3,100 kW (4,075 hp) state-of-the-art AC-AC microprocessor-controlled WDP4 class passenger locomotives with production at DLW.

With the acquisition of AC technology from GM/EMD, DLW is offering Alco and GM technology worldwide.

DLW is manufacturing spares for diesel locomotives including 6-, 12- and 16-cylinder diesel power packs, cylinder blocks and engine components. An automated cylinder liner chrome plating facility was commissioned in 1996.

DLW is also manufacturing spares for diesel locomotives including the six-, 12- and 16-cylinder Alco power pack. DLW has also built diesel generator sets.

## Diesel Supply Co

Diesel Supply Co Inc
1601 Industrial Street, Hudson, Wisconsin 54016, USA
Tel: (+1 715) 386 39 01   Fax: (+1 715) 386 74 20

**Key personnel**
President: Paul J Kramer

**Products**
Supply of diesel-electric locomotives and locomotive components, including bearings, power assemblies, light bulbs and brake equipment.

## Duro Daković

Railway Vehicles Factory Ltd
PO Box 94, 55102 Slavonski Brod, Croatia
Tel: (+385 35) 24 19 26; 23 21 89
Fax: (+385 35) 23 24 54

**Key personnel**
General Manager: A Milović
Marketing Manager: Antun Kaurić

**Products**
Diesel locomotives – diesel-hydraulic 220 to 730 kW; diesel-electric 730 to 3,000 kW.

## E G Steele

E G Steele & Co Ltd
25 Dalziel Street, Hamilton ML3 9AU, UK
Tel: (+44 1698) 28 37 65   Fax: (+44 1698) 89 15 50
e-mail: egsteelecoltd@btinternet.com

**Key personnel**
Managing Director: David Steele

Logistics Manager/Director, Export Sales: Ian Hood
Quality Manager: Cameron Gibson

**Products**
Locopulsor shunting machine, a single-wheel vehicle capable of moving freight wagons weighing 160 to 200 tonnes on straight level track. It can also move wagons in curves, split a line of wagons and handle a wagon on a turntable.

UK agents for Trackmobile road/rail shunters.

**Contracts**
A Trackmobile 4500TM was supplied to Thrall Europa, York, in 1998.

**VERIFIED**

## Electroputere

SC Electroputere SA
Calea București 144, R-1100 Craiova, Romania
Tel: (+40 451) 14 77 53   Fax: (+40 451) 19 98 97

**Key personnel**
Managing Director: Ion Lupulescu

**Products**
Diesel-electric Co-Co locomotives from 1,570 to 3,000 kW; electric Co-Co locomotives of 5,100 kW; electric shunting locomotives of 1,250 kW.

Electroputere co-operates with a large number of other factories in Romania supplying auxiliary machines and apparatus, the braking system control and supply equipment, metering equipment lamps and so on. Diesel engines are manufactured by UCM Reșița and bogies by CAROMET Caransebeș.

## Energomachexport

Energomachexport
25A Protopopovsky per, 129010 Moscow, Russia
Tel: (+7 095) 288 84 56   Fax: (+7 095) 288 79 90
e-mail: in@eme.tsr.ru

(See also entry in *Bogies and suspension, wheels and axles, bearings* section)

**Key personnel**
General Director: M Nosanov

Director, Transmash Department: G Stepnov
Advertising Manager: Natalia Kuznetsova

**Products**
Metro cars.

## Evans Deakin

Evans Deakin Industries Ltd
PO Box 866, 12 Boundary Street, South Brisbane, Queensland 4101
Tel: (+61 7) 3840 22 22   Fax: (+61 7) 3840 23 70
Chief Executive Officer: Ross Dunning
e-mail: corp@evansdeakin.com.au
Web: http://www.evansdeakin.com.au
Clyde Engineering
PO Box 73, Factory Street, Granville, NSW 2142, Australia
Tel: (+61 2) 96 37 82 88   Fax: (+61 2) 96 37 67 83
e-mail: sales@clydeng.com.au

**Key personnel**
Group General Manager: John Hancox
Executive Sales Manager: Kevin Thomson

**Design and manufacturing facilities**
Bathurst, New South Wales; Kooragang Island, New South Wales; Cardiff, New South Wales (under construction); Campbellfield, Victoria; Forrestfield, Western Australia; Dry Creek, South Australia; Port Augusta, South Australia; Port Lincoln, South Australia; Sydney, New South Wales.
Walkers Pty Ltd
Walkers Pty Ltd
23 Bowen Street, Maryborough, Queensland 4650, Australia
Tel: (+61 71) 20 81 00   Fax: (+61 71) 22 44 00
e-mail: paulbennet@walkers.net.au

**Key personnel**
Group General Manager: Danny Broad
General Manager, Rolling Stock: Paul Bennett

**Products**
Diesel-electric and diesel-hydraulic locomotives; electric locomotives; electric and diesel tilting trainsets; emus; diesel railcars; diesel-electric and diesel-hydraulic rail cars; LRVs; traction motors; freight wagons; fabricated and cast steel bogies; maintenance of passenger trains, locomotives, and freight wagons.

*Artist's impression of Clyde Engineering 4GT double-deck passenger rail cars for the State Rail Authority (SRA) of New South Wales*   0063357

## MANUFACTURERS/Locomotives and powered/non-powered passenger vehicles

### Recent contracts executed and obtained

Clyde Engineering is designing and building 80 4GT double-deck passenger rail cars for the State Rail Authority (SRA) of New South Wales and will maintain them over 15 years. SRA may increase the order to 120 additional railcars and extend the maintenance period to 35 years.

Clyde is maintaining the former Australian National fleet of locomotives and wagons for 10 years to 2007 for Australia Southern Railroad.

Clyde also maintains the NSW State Rail Authority's 'Ready Power' fleet of 89 diesel-electric locomotives under a 15 year contract to 2011

Clyde Engineering is designing, and EDI companies Clyde Engineering, Walkers and Evans Deakin Engineering, are manufacturing 38 AC-powered narrow-gauge heavy-haul, diesel-electric locomotives for Queensland Rail. A separate contract will provide for 10 years supply of replacement parts (February 1998). Walkers recently supplied Queensland Rail with two narrow-gauge, six-car electric tilting trains, which entered service late in 1998. These vehicles have been built in collaboration with Hitachi Ltd of Japan and the Itochu Corporation.

Walkers is maintaining the tilt trains in Brisbane and Rockhampton for Queensland Rail.

Walkers has entered a design and development agreement with Queensland Rail for two, ten-unit diesel tilt trains for operation from Brisbane to Cairns (September 1998)

Walkers is building 90 suburban multiple units for Queensland Rail with final delivery expected in 2001.

*Six-car electric tilting train, built in collaboration with Hitachi Ltd of Japan and the Itochu Corporation*
0063356

## Ferrostaal AG

PO Box, Hohenzollernstrasse 24, D-45116 Essen, Germany
Tel: (+49 201) 818 01    Fax: (+49 201) 818 28 22
Telex: 897100fsd

### Key personnel
Head of Transport Systems Division: Georg Schwinning

### Products
Main line, shunting and mining locomotives with diesel-hydraulic, diesel-electric and electric traction. Electric or diesel-electric railcars, railbuses, light rail vehicles and other multiple-units for urban public transport; motor and trailer bogies; rolling stock components including wheels, axles, wheelsets, bearings, suspension parts and couplers.

Passenger coaches including special designs; inspection and service trolleys for track and overhead maintenance and track installation; motor and trailer bogies for freight wagons, passenger coaches, locomotives, railcars; rolling stock components such as wheels, axles, assembled wheelsets, bearings, suspensions, couplers and electrical equipment.

**UPDATED**

## FIREMA Trasporti SpA

c/o I D P Milano Fiorenza, Via Triboniano, 220 I-20156, Milan, Italy
Tel: (+39 02) 23 02 02 23    Fax: (+39 02) 23 02 02 34
e-mail: firema.com@firema.it
Web: http//www.firema.it

### Key personnel
Chairman: A de Benerdictis

Managing Director: L Rigno
Commercial Manager: S d'Arminio
Marketing Manager: M Fantini

### Head office
Via Provinciale Appia-Località Pontesélice, I-81110 Caserta, Italy
Tel: (+39 0823) 258 11    Fax: (+39 0823) 46 68 12

### Works
Officine Meccanica della Stanga
Corso Stati Uniti 3, I-35127 Padova, Italy
Tel: (+39 049) 899 62 11    Fax: (+39 049) 899 62 12

Officine Fiore Casertane
Via Provinciale Appia, I-81110 Caserta, Italy
Tel: (+39 0823) 25 81 11    Fax: (+39 0823) 46 76 91

Metalmeccanica Lucana
I-85050 Tito Scalo, PZ, Italy
Tel: (+39 0971) 42 41 11    Fax: (+39 0971) 48 50 72

Retam Service
Viale Edison 110, I-20099 Sesto S Giovanni, Milan, Italy
Tel: (+39 02) 249 41    Fax: (+39 02) 248 35 08

### Products
Electric locomotives, high-speed trainsets, electric multiple-units, railcars, advanced guided transit systems, metro rolling stock and light rail vehicles.

### Contracts
Contracts include mechanical parts for 20 single-voltage (3 kV DC) and 23 dual-voltage (3 kV DC and 25 kV 50 Hz AC) E402 electric locomotives for Italian Railways (FS); electrical equipment for 26 E652 electric locomotives for FS; and mechanical parts for 12 E652 locomotives for FS.

Other contracts include the supply of 20 power car bodyshells, 56 first-class and 38 second-class light-alloy trailers, 40 trailer bogies, 12 sets of AC traction motors and 60 auxiliary static converters for 30 ETR 500 high-speed trainsets for Italian Railways (FS); 20 power cars, 77 trailers, 30 motor bogies, 154 trailer bogies and electronic equipment for 30 dual-voltage (3 kV DC and 25 kV 50 Hz AC) ETR 500 trainsets for FS; six Type E82 two-car 3 kV DC emus for SEPSA, Naples (Cumana and

*Firema D146 diesel-hydraulic locomotive*    2000/0089812

Circumflegrea Railways); five Type E84A 3 kV DC emus for COTRAL (Rome—Viterbo); 104 power cars and 64 trailers for 72 four-car double-deck emus for FS and North Milan Railway (FNME); and four two-car emus for Circumetnea Railway. Firema has supplied 16 articulated low-floor LRVs for the Midland Metro in Birmingham and 30 double-articulated low-floor LRVs for Oslo Sporveier. Electrical equipment for both types supplied by ANSALDOBREDA (qv).

Recent orders include 25 diesel-hydraulic Bo-Bo locomotives Class D146 for Italian State Railways; 1 diesel-hydraulic locomotive Type D146 for Autorità portuale di Marina di Carrara, deliveries from the end of 2001; 100 bogie hopper wagons Type Talns for DB Cargo, deliveries from April 2000.

**UPDATED**

*TAF double-deck emu in service with FS*

## Fuji Car Manufacturing Co

Fuji Car Manufacturing Co Ltd
3 Shoho Building, 2-2-3 Nishishinsaibashi, Chuo-ku, Osaka 542, Japan
Tel: (+81 6) 213 27 11    Fax: (+81 6) 213 40 71

**Key personnel**
Export Sales: M Miyama

**Products**
People mover systems (FAST) and passenger coaches.

## Fuji Heavy Industries

Fuji Heavy Industries Ltd
Transportation & Ecology Systems Division
Subaru Building 7-2, Nishishinjuku 1-chome,
Shinjyuku-ku, Tokyo 160, Japan
Tel: (+81 3) 33 47 24 92   Fax: (+81 3) 33 47 24 75

**Main works**
Utsunomiya Manufacturing Division
1-11, Yonan 1-chome, Utsunomiya, Tochigi 320, Japan

**Key personnel**
General Manager, Overseas Group: Hideo Ueno

**Products**
Diesel trainsets, tilting dmus, passenger coaches and railcars.

## Ganz-Hunslet

Ganz-Hunslet Részvénytársaság
PO Box 29, H-1430 Budapest, Hungary
Tel: (+36 1) 210 11 77; 313 08 87
Fax: (+36 1) 210 11 75; 210 11 80
Sales office: (+36 1) 210 11 73

**Products**
Passenger coaches, trailer vehicles for electric multiple-units.

Recent contracts include the supply of a total of 40 commuter coaches to Hungarian State Railways (MÁV), for operation as locomotive-hauled stock or as part of an electric trainset.

Ganz-Hunslet has been awarded a contract by ALSTOM (qv) to supply 120 completed painted bodyshells for Juniper Class 334 modular emus for UK operator ScotRail. Ganz-Hunslet is delivering the bodyshells between December 1998 and December 1999 to ALSTOM's Birmingham factory for final assembly. Included in the contract is an option for a further 120 vehicles.

## Ganz Vagon Kft

Ganz-Mozdony, Vagon-és Jamugyárto Kft Vajda Péter utca 12, H-1430 Budapest, Hungary
Tel: (+36 1) 210 11 77; 303 90 46
Fax: (+36 1) 210 11 80; 303 94 11
e-mail: vagon.board@ganz-holding.hu

**Key personnel**
Managing Director: Tamás Fodor
Sales Director: István Szécsey
Technical Director: László Süveges

**Corporate developments**
Ganz Vagon was set up in 1999 as a joint venture of Ganz Gépgyár Holding Rt and the state liquidation company Reorg Rt to carry on railway engineering activity with the assets and personnel of the bankrupt Ganz-Hunslet Rt, which itself had evolved from Ganz & Co, established in 1844.

It is a member of Ganz Gépgyár Holding together with two other companies of Ganz Gépgyár Holding Rt, Ganz Motor Kft and Ganz David Brown Transmissions Kft, integrated in the vehicle construction division.

**Products**
Electric and diesel multiple-units, trams and LRVs, metro cars, passenger coaches, diesel-electric and diesel-mechanical locomotives; passenger coaches, trailer vehicles for electric multiple-units.

Deliveries: Three four-car intercity emus and two commuter emus have been supplied to MÁV Hungary and 18 Series 8100 three-car commuter emus have gone to KTMB Malaysia, all with three-phase motors.

*Ganz-Hunslet intercity emu for MÁV Hungary*

Ganz-Hunslet was awarded a contract by ALSTOM (qv) to supply 120 completed painted bodyshells for Juniper modular emus. The units have been constructed by the Anglo-French group for UK operator ScotRail. Ganz-Hunslet delivered the bodyshells between December 1998 and December 1999 to ALSTOM's Birmingham factory for final assembly. Included in the contract is an option for a further 120 vehicles.

Other contracts include the supply of a total of 40 commuter coaches to Hungarian State Railways (MÁV), for operation as locomotive-hauled stock or as part of an electric trainset.

## GE Transportation Systems

2901 East Lake Road, Erie, Pennsylvania 16531 USA
Tel: (+1 814) 875 22 40   Fax: (+1 814) 875 59 11
Web: http://www.getransportation.com

### Key personnel
President and Chief Executive Officer: John G Rice
General Managers
    Locomotive Commercial Operation: Michael Abrams
    Global Services Operation: David Tucker
    Global Supply Chain Management: Jack Fish
    Engineering Operation: Daniel Sheflin

### Affiliates
A Goninan & Co Ltd, Australia (licensee)
Dorbyl Transport Products, South Africa (licensee)
GE Harris Railway Electronics LLC, USA (joint venture)
GE Lubrizol, LLC USA (joint venture)
GEVISA SA, Brasil (joint venture)
PT GE Locomotif, Indonesia (joint venture)

### Products and services
Diesel-electric AC/DC and AC/AC freight and passenger locomotives (new, remanufactured, and modernised); electric locomotives; locomotive control systems; railway transportation management and electronics systems; global locomotive maintenance services (technical advisers, turnkey locomotive maintenance operations, and remote monitoring and diagnostic services); financing, and training programmes.

*Locomotive overview*
GE locomotives include the high-performance GE AC6000 CW™ and GE AC4400 CW™ locomotives, which use AC technology for higher horsepower, lower operating costs and fewer maintenance needs. The GE line also includes reliable DC propulsion DASH 7™, DASH 8™ and DASH 9™ locomotives. With performance-enhancing upgrades, customers can further improve tractive effort, reduce maintenance costs, lower fuel consumption and emissions, and achieve other efficiencies in these models. The GENESIS® Series locomotives are lightweight aerodynamic units designed for passenger service.

*Global Services*
Through global services, GE Transportation Systems is working to maximise locomotive performance and productivity for transportation customers around the world. GE supplies OEM new and remanufactured components for more than 20,000 locomotives in more than 75 countries, directly and through a network of distributors and sales representatives worldwide. The company also now performs EMD traction motor and component repair to OEM standards. (EMD is the Electro-Motive Division of General Motors Corporation and a trade designation of GM.)

Through component replacement services, the company offers performance-enhancing upgrades to increase adhesion of tractive/braking effort and to reduce maintenance costs, fuel consumption and emissions for older U-Series, ALCO™, DASH 7, DASH 8, DASH 9 and AC4400 models. Maintenance support ranges from routine visits by a technical adviser to full service contracts. Today, the company performs full-service maintenance on several thousand locomotives, ranging from U-Series to AC4400s, in the United States, Canada, Mexico, Kenya and Australia. In addition, GE Transportation Systems provides services such as technical support, materials management and logistics throughout the Americas, Africa, Asia and Australia. These programmes include reliability-centered maintenance, continuous training, supply chain integration and dedicated engineering support.

Through Customer Web Centers (CWCs) developed by GE, customers have greater access to information and solutions than ever before. Railways can check order status, view performance data, access technical information and more online. On the Internet, GE has also created TranShopNet.com™, an online global marketplace that links buyers and sellers of equipment, parts and supplies. TranShopNet.com gives users access to global markets and the opportunity to expand their customer base, drive efficient, negotiated pricing, and expedite the buying and selling process.

GE Transportation Systems' Expert On-Board™ is a remote monitoring and diagnostics service that links GE-

*GE AC4400 CW™ Locomotive for Ferrocarril del Sureste, SA de CV*

*GE service experts based in Erie, Pennsylvania, USA, use advanced communications and diagnostics tools to monitor locomotive fleets around the globe*

*PB32 AC-DM locomotive built for Metro-North Railroad*

*GE GENESIS® Series passenger locomotive for Amtrak's Empire Corridor*

## Locomotives and powered/non-powered passenger vehicles/MANUFACTURERS

*GE AC4400 locomotive for CSX*

based service experts with locomotives operating in the field. An intelligent monitoring system continuously assesses locomotive condition and delivers reliable, up-to-the-minute operating information. Automated diagnostics tools identify potential problems and offer probable causes. GE's remote capabilities, combined with the expertise of locomotive specialists, make it possible to identify service needs, spot potential problems and recommend repair solutions, all before actual need arises. GE's remote monitoring and diagnostics capabilities integrate with fluids condition and filtration systems developed by GE Lubrizol to lengthen maintenance intervals and predict equipment failures. The GE Lubrizol onboard product incorporates a common GE communication platform, providing the rail industry with a comprehensive solution in the search for extended maintenance and servicing.

GE Transportation Systems' training programmes focus on operator familiarisation, diagnostics, troubleshooting and continuing maintenance education. Courses can be scheduled individually or as part of a complete training programme, selected from existing programmes or custom-designed, and held at customers' sites or at the GE Learning Center in Erie, Pennsylvania. Educational methods include class instruction, videos, multimedia training modules, video conferencing, simulations and hands-on instruction.

*Locomotive Products*
GE AC6000 CW™ (6,000 hp, 4,474 kW), GE AC4400 CW™ (4,400 hp, 3,281 kW) and the Blue Tiger™ family (1,119-2,984 kW) diesel locomotives feature AC traction motors regulated by separate, computer-controlled inverters. The AC traction control system utilises the latest Insulated Gate Bipolar Transistor (IGBT) technology for improved reliability and packaging.

DASH 9™ and DASH 8™ diesel-electric locomotive propulsion systems use DC traction motors in full-time parallel configuration supplied by rectified, three-phase traction alternators (computer-regulated adhesion process). All models are microprocessor-controlled. Operator interface is made through computer displays that allow access to diagnostics and integrated ancillary systems information.

DASH 7™ diesel models include the Constant Horsepower Excitation Control (CHEC) and the speed-based adhesion control (Sentry) system with automatic wheel diameter calibration.

GENESIS® Series passenger locomotives are available either as straight diesel models with DC propulsion or as dual-mode with AC propulsion, able to operate from a third-rail electric supply or by using diesel power in non-electrified zones.

Electric locomotives utilise DC traction motors in full-time parallel configuration supplied by phased thyristor control and fast, analogue-regulated adhesion control.

*Locomotive Engines & Components*
GE offers two diesel engine families: the GE 7HDL™ 16-cylinder, 4,474 kW and the GE 7FDL™ 16-cylinder, 3,281 kW. The GE 7FDL 16-, 12-, and 8-cylinder can also be set at various power ratings.

All AC, DASH 9, DASH 8 and DASH 7 models feature a three-phase traction alternator feeding a full-wave bridge traction rectifier. The GMG-type alternator is used on 4,474 traction kW (AC) and 3,281 traction kW (AC, DASH 9 and DASH 8) models.

Most AC, DASH 9, DASH 8, and DASH 7 models include a single stator traction alternator output with sufficient capacity to accommodate all volt-amp requirements through the entire speed range.

All AC, DASH 9, DASH 8, and DASH 7 models feature traction motors connected in a full-time parallel configuration in the propulsion mode to provide consistent propulsion behaviour, to enhance speed-

*TranShopNet.com™, developed by GE Transportation Systems, is an online marketplace that links buyers and sellers of equipment, parts and supplies*

*GE Dash 9 locomotive built for Quebec North Shore & Labrador Railway*

*GE AC4400 locomotive for TFM Mexico*

tractive effort characteristics, and to eliminate motor transition contactor maintenance. The DC traction motor family consists of GE 752, GE 793, GE 794, GE 761 and GE 764 models. The AC traction motor family consists of GEB 13 and GEB 15 models.

*Locomotive Technologies*
GE's AC locomotives feature direct, air-cooled, easily replaceable phase module inverter systems (single inverter per axle). The GE AC traction motor includes a low-slip capability. IGBT technology delivers more reliability with the added benefits of less weight and volume. The units are air-cooled, as with the former GTO technology, yet have significantly reduced component count and complexity.

Electronic fuel injection (EFI) promotes fuel savings, reduces emissions, and lowers maintenance costs. Split cooling improves fuel efficiency and reduces engine temperatures.

HiAd™ (high adhesion) bogies feature a low-weight transfer design with 10-year overhaul intervals. The GE steerable bogie is a three-axle, three-motor, high-adhesion class bogie designed to reduce rail forces in curves. The steerable bogies allow locomotives to negotiate previously prohibited curved track.

GE Harris Railway Electronics, LLC designs advanced electronic train and railway products and systems such as LOCOTROL® distributed power, EP$^{X™}$ Direct Braking and Universal Control Valve™, TrainTalk™ intra-train communications, Precision Dispatch™, Navigator Dispatch™, Precision Train Control™, PINPOINT™ locomotive tracking and asset management system, and train defect detection systems. These and other GE Harris technologies are integrated into GE microprocessor-based locomotives through an open-architecture control system.

GE Lubrizol, LLC designs, develops, and produces real-time fluids condition and filtration systems that enable extended maintenance intervals and predict critical equipment failures. GE Lubrizol combines on-board hardware and software algorithms with off-board communication integration to prolong locomotive maintenance intervals to 180 days and beyond. GE Lubrizol products and services are also applicable to other diesel engine equipment used in the railroad, mining, marine and stationary markets. Future platforms include fuel level, fuel consumption, fuel delivery, and fuel optimisation services.

*Locomotive Leasing*
Locomotive Management Services (LMS) manages a variety of locomotive lease fleets including DASH 8 locomotives. The mission of LMS is to provide highly reliable and productive locomotives for lease to its customers on terms that are tailored to support the rail lines. Lease periods range from short-term operating leases to long-term commitments. Full-time (for a specified time period) leases over a multiyear commitment can be ordered.

## Gemco

George Moss Ltd
PO Box 136, Mount Hawthorn 6016, 461 Scarborough Beach Road, Osborne Park 6017, Western Australia, Australia
Tel: (+61 9) 446 88 44  Fax: (+61 9) 446 34 04

**Key personnel**
General Manager: R Jackson
Commercial Manager, Sales and Marketing: R Davison
Engineering Manager: R Leslie

**Products**
Industrial locomotives.

## General Motors Corporation

Electro-Motive Division
9301 West 55th Street, La Grange, Illinois 60525, USA
Tel: (+1 708) 387 60 00; 61 07
Web: http://www.gmemd.com

**Key personnel**
General Manager: R William Happel

**Canadian Manufacturing Facility**
PO Box 5160, London, Ontario N6A 4N5, Canada
Tel: (+1 519) 452 50 00

**Licensees**
General Motors has locomotive manufacturing licence agreements with the following companies:
Clyde Engineering Company Pty Ltd, Granville, New South Wales, Australia
Hyundai Rolling Stock Company, Seoul, South Korea
ALSTOM Transporte SA, Valencia, Spain
Turkish State Railways, Ankara, Turkey

**Products**
Diesel-electric freight and passenger locomotives from 746 to 4,476 kW (1,000 to 6,000 hp); remanufacturing and rebuilding services; locomotive leasing and contract maintenance.

*SD90MAC:* 4,476 kW (6,000 hp) AC-driven freight locomotive. It is offered as a 1:2 replacement for the SD40-2 locomotive. The H-engine has a 16 per cent improvement in fuel efficiency over that of the SD40-2 16-645E3B engined locomotive and it has a starting tractive and braking capability of 170,000 lbs continuous, 200,000 lbs starting tractive effort and 115,000 lbs braking. The SD90MAC has integrated cab electronics, EM2000 advanced computer, electronic air brakes, automatic parking brakes, WhisperCab and a patented radial bogie.

*GT46MAC:* 2984 kW (4,000 hp) heavy haul/high-speed AC traction locomotive, in production since 1993, fitted with 16-710G3B engine. Starting tractive effort 549 kN and braking 270 kN. A 12 per cent fuel efficiency improvement is cited over the 645E series. It has the EM2000 advanced computer system and HTSC bogie. Maintenance intervals are 90 days.

*JT42CWR:* 2,238 kW (3,000 hp) DC traction freight locomotive with 12N-710G3B-EC turbocharged engine, geared for a top speed of 124 km/h. A 12 per cent fuel efficiency improvement is cited over the 645E series. It has the EM2000 advanced computer system and HTSC bogie. Maintenance intervals are 90 days.

*GP15D/GP20D:* 1,119/1,679 kW (1,500/2,250 hp) shunting locomotives with EMD170 electronic fuel injection twin-turbocharged engines built by Caterpillar. Fitted with EM2000 control technology.

*F59PHI:* 2,238 kW (3,000 hp) DC traction, streamlined passenger locomotive with 12-710G3B-EC turbocharged diesel engine and top speed of 176 km/h (110 mph).

*SD90MAC locomotive for Union Pacific*  0003462

WhisperCab which isolates crew from noise and vibration, GP-SS bogies. Fitted with EM2000 control technology.

*DE30AC/DM30AC:* 2,238 kW (3,000 hp) AC traction passenger locomotive with 12-710 turbocharged engine with electronic fuel injection geared to top speed of 160 kph (100 mph), bolsterless bogie, integrated cab

*SD80MAC locomotive for Conrail*  0003463

electronics, EM2000 advanced computer and aerodynamic body. Dual-mode version can operate off third rail.

**New developments**
The company's newest development, Functionally Integrated Railroad Electronics (FIRE®) is an advanced locomotive management system.

## Gevisa SA

Gevisa SA
Praca Papa João XXIII, 28 Cidade Industrial, I-322210-100
Contagem MG, Brazil
Tel: (+55 31) 369 33 33   Fax: (+55 31) 369 33 34
e-mail: faleconosco.getrans@trans.ge.com
Web: http://www.getransportation.com.br

### Key personnel
Director, South American Operations, GE Transportation Systems: Marcelo Mosci

### Corporate developments
Established in 1992, Gevisa is owned by GE Brasil (44.5 per cent), Villares (44.5 per cent) and the Safra Group (Albatroz) (11.1 per cent).

### Products
Rolling stock: diesel-powered locomotives; refurbishment and repair; remanufacture/reconstruction; maintenance; painting/livery and spare parts. Traction/control: (diesel) complete traction package, engines, components, traction motors, generators, mechanical equipment, gears/shafts/couplings and turbochargers.

## Gmeinder

Gmeinder Lokomotiven- und Maschinenfabrik GmbH
PO Box 1355, D-74803 Mosbach, Baden, Germany
Tel: (+49 6261) 80 60   Fax: (+49 6261) 80 61 90
e-mail: info@gmeinder.de
Web: http://www.gmeinder.de

### Key personnel
Managing Director: Heinz Chr Mutz
Head of Rail Traction Division: Rudolf Mickel

### Products
Diesel locomotives with electric, hydrodynamic or hydrostatic power transmission systems and engine output up to 1,100 kW, suitable for narrow-, standard- or broad-gauge locomotives with dual-power systems, (diesel-electric/electric, battery/electric) for operations in tunnels; flameproof diesel locomotives for chemical industries and flameproof battery locomotives for underground mining operations; propulsion bogie systems for application to any kind of special railway vehicles, such as snow-ploughs, rail grinding and track maintenance vehicles.

Examples are the Type D60C diesel-hydraulic locomotive and the dual-mode service locomotive. The Type D60C is powered by an MWM water-cooled diesel engine producing 463 kW, which provides a maximum speed of between 30 and 50 km/h in forward and reverse. Total weight with ballast is 66 t. The locomotive is equipped with cardan shaft drive and hydraulic power transmission. The dual-mode service locomotive, which has been supplied to Berliner Verkehrsbetriebe (BVB), is fitted with a three-phase drive system and has a Bo-Bo axle arrangement. It is powered by a 1,100 kW diesel engine giving a maximum speed of 80 km/h. Radio-controlled push-pull running, operated from the control car, is available.

## Hanjin

Hanjin Heavy Industries Co Ltd
118, 2 Ka, Namdaemunro, Chung-ku, Seoul, South Korea
Tel: (+82 2) 728 54 41; 54 20
Fax: (+82 2) 755 09 28; 756 54 55
Web: http://www.hhic.co.kr

### Key personnel
President: Young Soo Song
Executive Vice-President: Soo Bu Lee
General Manager: Byung Chun Choi
General Manager: Moo Yeong Jeong

### Products
Electric and diesel multiple-units.

Recent contracts include 24 emu cars for the Bundang line in 1997; 402 emu cars for Seoul, Lines 7 and 8, in 1997; 336 emu cars for Pusan Line 2; 216 emu cars for Taegu Subway Agency No 1 Line which opened in 1997; 24 cars for the Kwacheon line; 20 emu cars for Seoul Metropolitan Subway Corporation; 36 cars for KNR Korea; 146 cars for the Seoul-Pusan high-speed line project (1994-2001).

A manufacturing facility is now in operation at Sang-Ju in Kyoung Sang North Province for construction of high-speed trains.

*Hanjin emu for Pusan Urban Transit Authority*

## Hitachi Ltd

Overseas Marketing Department
Transportation Systems Sales Division
6 Kanda Surugadai 4-chome, Chiyoda-ku, Tokyo 101-8010, Japan
Tel: (+81 3) 52 95 55 40   Fax: (+81 3) 32 58 52 30

### Key personnel
Managing Officer, Transportation Systems: Takazumi Ishizu
General Manager, Rolling Stock Systems Division, Transportation Systems: Chiaki Ueda
General Manager, Transportation Systems Sales Division: Gaku Suzuki
Chief Marketing Manager, Transportation Systems Sales Division: Hideo Inoue
Department Manager, Overseas Marketing Department: Jun Kataoka

### Main works
**Transportation Equipment**
Kasado Transportation Systems Product Division: 794 Higashitoyoi, Kudamatsu City, Yamaguchi Pref 744-8601
Mito Transportation Systems Products Division: 1070 Ichige, Hitachinaka-shi, Ibaraki Pref 312-8506
Hitachi works: 1-1, 3-chome, Saiwai-cho, Hitachi City, Ibaraki Pref 317-0073
Kokubu works: 1-1, 1-chome, Kokubu-cho, Hitachi City, Ibaraki Pref 316-8501

*Series 257 for JR East*

## MANUFACTURERS/Locomotives and powered/non-powered passenger vehicles

### Background
Hitachi is one of the world's leading global electrical engineering companies generating 1 per cent of Japan's GDP. It has 1,069 subsidiaries, including 335 overseas corporations and its share of the Japanese rolling stock market is approximately 40 per cent.

Hitachi has delivered vehicles into all market sectors, including Shinkansen, 'Limited Express', commuter emu and metro trains.

### Products
Hitachi manufactures and markets a wide range of products, including computers, semiconductors, consumer products, rolling stock and power and industrial equipment. It is a main supplier for Shinkansen, Monorail System, Linear Metro System, maglev system, Tilting Train, signalling and substation system, including: emus and dmus for city, urban and regional networks; monorail cars; linear induction motor-powered metro trains for small-bore tunnel; lightweight aluminium and stainless steel and steel bodyshells; AC propulsion system using IGBT inverter; auxiliary power supply; air conditioning; ATC, ATO and automatic train diagnostics systems.

Hitachi has developed an aluminium car body train with friction stir welding and module construction.

### Contracts
IGBT propulsion systems: IGBT inverters for Beijing Urban Railway Construction project, China.
High-speed train system: rolling stock, control system for Taiwan High Speed Rail Corporation, Taiwan.
Limited Express: Series 257 Limited Express for East Japan Railway Company, Japan; Series 683 Limited Express for West Japan Railway Company, Japan; Series 885 Limited Express for Kyushu Railway Company, Japan.
Commuter emu: KL3-97 stainless steel emu for Jabotabek suburban network in Jakarta, Indonesia; transit vehicle for Metropolitan Atlanta Rapid Transit Authority (MARTA) in USA; Series 20000 for Seibu Railway Company, Japan; Series 815 for JR Kyushu, Japan.
Metro emu: Series 12000 linear motor propulsion emu for Transportation Bureau of Monorail System; Series 2000 for Tokyo Monorail, Tokyo Metropolitan Government; Series 1000 for Tokyo Tama InterCity Monorail, Japan.

Current customers include: Beijing Urban Railway Construction Project; Taiwan Railway Administration; Russia; Hokkaido Railway Company, East Japan Railway Company, Central Japan Railway Company, West Japan Railway Company, Kyushu Railway Company, Teito Rapid Transit Authority, Transportation Bureau of Tokyo Metropolitan Government, Seibu Railway, Tokyo Corporation, Tobu Railway, and Kinki Nippon Railway, Japan.

*Series 683 for JR West Railway Company*

**UPDATED**

## Hoogovens VAW

Hoogovens VAW AG
Large Extrusion Technology Unit
Friedrich-Wöhler-Strasse 25, D-53117 Bonn 1, Germany
Tel: (+49 228) 552 02    Fax: (+49 228) 552 22 68

### Key personnel
Managing Directors: Wolfgang Beck, Rudolf Drach

### Products
Design and production of large aluminium extrusions up to 650 mm in width; fully automatic welding of extrusions up to 30 m in length and 2.8 m in width. Supply of machined/shaped extrusions and components. Manufacture of roof, wall and floor sections; and calculation of construction groups by means of the finite element method.

Projects in which VAW has been involved include:
Second generation of Fiat's tilting trainsets known as ETR460 (Nuovo Pendolino) for Italian State Railway (FS). VAW has been contracted for the design of the bodyshells and their static and dynamic calculations by means of the finite element method as well as the delivery of all extrusions for a first batch of 10 trainsets (90 vehicles in total). Main contractor Fiat (Italy).

A derivation of this tilting trainset has been built by Fiat and Oy Transtech Ltd (Finland) for Finnish State Railways (VR). VAW was responsible for design and finite element calculations of the bodyshells as well as the delivery of all extrusions for two prototype six-car trainsets known as Sm200. The contract included an option of 23 trainsets.

## Hunslet-Barclay

Hunslet-Barclay Ltd
Caledonia Works, West Langlands Street, Kilmarnock
KA1 2QD, UK
Tel: (+44 1563) 52 35 73    Fax: (+44 1563) 54 10 76

### Key personnel
Managing Director: A Barclay
Director: P E Kewney
Director: I McInnes
Sales Manager: M Douglas

### Corporate structure
Hunslet-Barclay is a member of the Auricon Group of Austria.

### Products
All Hunslet products within the Auricon Group are designed and built by Hunslet-Barclay Ltd in Kilmarnock.

The range includes design and manufacture of railbuses; conversion and repair of powered and non-powered passenger vehicles; diesel-hydraulic, diesel-electric and trolley/battery and electric surface and underground/metro locomotives; fully flame-proofed locomotives. Locomotives supplied range from 3 to 120 t and 50 to 1,000 kW to suit any rail gauge. Included are radio remote-controlled and robot locomotives incorporating programmable logic controller systems and wheel traction control.

*Hunslet-Barclay 600 kW radio-controlled diesel-hydraulic locomotive for Baoshan, China*

Specialist products include metro locomotives and rack-and-pinion locomotives.

A second batch of four 80 t 600 kW radio-controlled diesel-hydraulic locomotives has been supplied to Baoshan, China.

Three 544 kW 15 t diesel rack and pinion locomotives with Waagner-Biró driving trailer and non-driving trailer cars have been supplied for the Schneeberg Mountain Railway, Austria.

*One of three 544 kW 15 t diesel rack and pinion train sets supplied for the Schneeberg Mountain Railway*
0063361

## ICF

The Integral Coach Factory
Ministry of Railways, Chennai 600 038, India
Tel: (+91 44) 626 01 52; 00 54
Fax: (+91 44) 626 01 52; 00 54
e-mail: icfsecgm@md4.vsnl.net.in
Web: http://www.icf.gov.in

**Key personnel**
General Manager: A K Malhotra

**Corporate background**
ICF is a production unit of Indian Railways.

**Products**
Electric multiple-units for AC and DC traction; diesel railcars and multiple-units; relief medical vans; metro cars.

Air conditioned sleeper and chair cars; pantry cars; metro cars; tourist cars; coaches for intercity express trains; track recording cars; power cars; and double-deckers.

A recent product is the D-2000 diesel-electric multiple-unit. Powered by a 1,045 kW Cummins engine, the D-2000 is a four-car unit with seating for 384 passengers. Up to four sets can be operated in multiple. Top speed is 100 km/h.
**UPDATED**

*ICF D-2000 four-car diesel-electric multiple-unit*
2002/0126211

## Impco

Impco Products Inc
6047 Adams Lane, Allentown, Pennsylvania 18103, USA
Tel: (+1 215) 266 90 60   Fax: (+1 215) 266 02 11

**Key personnel**
President: Philip von Funk

**Products**
Sanding equipment, storage and dispensing of traction sand into the locomotive sand box.

## INKA

PT (Persero) Industri Kereta Api (PT INKA)
Jalan Yos Sudarso No 71, Madiun 63122, Indonesia

Tel: (+62 351) 522 71; 522 74   Fax: (+62 351) 522 75
e-mail: sekretariat@inka.go.id
Web: http://www.inka.go.id

**Key personnel**
President: Ir Istantoro
Marketing Director: Ir Haryono Subyantoro

**Products**
Assembly and renovation of freight wagons, passenger coaches, diesel and electric railcars, bogies.

Assembly and manufacture of emus are undertaken in collaboration with Bombardier Transportation and Hitachi.

Contracts include 10 economy class and 18 executive class cars for Indonesian Railway Public Corporation.

*INKA executive-class car for Indonesian Railway Public Corporation*
0023837

*Interior of executive-class car for Indonesian Railway Public Corporation*
0023838

## Jessop

Jessop & Company Ltd, Calcutta
63 Netaji Subhas Road, Calcutta 700001, India
Tel: (+91 33) 243 20 41; 243 34 20
Fax: (+91 33) 243 16 10

**Works**
Dum Dum Works, 21 & 22 Jessore Road, Calcutta 700 028, India
Tel: (+91 33) 551 99 22; 59 92   Fax: (+91 33) 551 28 68

**Key personnel**
Managing Director: A K Sur
Director (Engineering and Commercial):
  P C Bhattacharya
Director (Production): P K Mukherjee
Secretary: R D G Raghavan
Senior Manager (Exports): Amit Ghosh

**Products**
Rolling stock including electric multiple-unit coaches, LRVs, passenger coaches and freight wagons.

Contracts include 175 electric multiple-unit coaches for Indian Railways. A total of 51 such coaches was delivered to Indian Railways in 1993-94.

508  **MANUFACTURERS**/Locomotives and powered/non-powered passenger vehicles

## Kalugaputjmach

Kaluga Locomotive Works
PO Box 4, 248 612 Kaluga, Russian Federation

**Products**
Locomotives.

## Kawasaki Heavy Industries Ltd

World Trade Center Building, 4-1 Hamamatsu-cho 2-chome, Minato-ku, Tokyo 105, Japan
Tel: (+81 3) 34 35 25 88
Fax: (+81 3) 34 35 21 57; 34 36 30 37

**Works**
1-18 Wadayama-dori 2-chome, Hyogo-ku, Kobe 652, Japan
Tel: (+81 78) 682 31 33
Fax: (+81 78) 682 31 34; 671 57 84

**Key personnel**
President: Masamoto Tazaki
Managing Director and President, Rolling Stock, Construction Machinery and Crushing Plant:
    Takehiko Saeki

**Subsidiary**
Kawasaki Rail Car Inc, 1 Larkin Plaza, Yonkers, New York 10701, USA
Tel: (+1 914) 376 47 00   Fax: (+1 914) 376 47 79

**Products**
Electric, diesel-electric, diesel-hydraulic locomotives; high-speed trainsets; electric and diesel railcars; metro trainsets; automated guideway transit systems; passenger coaches.

**Contracts**
Contracts include the supply of a DC inverter locomotive with an output of 3,390 kW to the Japan Freight Railway.

*Kawasaki's R110A metro train for New York*

Tokyo-based private rail operator Keihin Electric Express Railway is taking five eight-car trains built by Tokyu Car Corporation and Kawasaki Heavy Industries. Siemens Transportation Systems will supply SIBAS 32 traction equipment with dynamic wheelspin/wheelslide control. Only four cars will be motored, compared with six in the earlier batch of trains, the reduction attributable to increased acceleration and braking rates achieved by the equipment's designers. The units also feature GTO power converters mounted in underfloor containers, the first time these have been installed in this way in Japan.

KCR West Rail, Hong Kong, is taking 250 emus built by a consortium of Kawasaki, Kinki Sharyo and Itochu. They are for the Kowloon—Canton railway and delivery is expected to be completed by 2003. Kawasaki has supplied 114 bilevel coaches for Long Island Rail Road Co, 50 for Maryland Mass Transit Administration, 13 for Northern Virginia Transit Corporation and 17 bilevel coaches for Massachusetts Bay Transportation Authority, USA.

*UPDATED*

## Alan Keef Limited

Lea Line, Ross-on-Wye HR9 7LQ, UK
Tel: (+44 1989) 75 07 57   Fax: (+44 1989) 75 07 80

**Key personnel**
Chairman: Alan Keef

**Products**
Design, construction and refurbishment of light railway equipment including diesel-hydraulic, diesel-mechanical, mining and surface locomotives, steam locomotives, rolling stock and trackwork. Sole suppliers of Simplex locomotives and related spares.

**Contracts**
Contracts include two K100 diesel locomotives for TPC Ltd, Tanzania for sugar cane haulage.

*UPDATED*

## Keller Elettromeccanica SpA

Zona Industriale I-09039, Villacidro, Cagliari, Italy
Tel: (+39 070) 933 62 02   Fax: (+39 070) 933 62 44
e-mail: info@keller.it
Web: http://www.keller.it

**Key personnel**
Chairman: Piero Mancini
Board members: Sergio Zanarini; Paolo Piombini; Giovanni Cappietti

**Other office**
Sales department
via Volturno, 10/12, I-50019 Sesto Fiorentino, Firenze, Italy
Tel: (+39 055) 34 08 80   Fax: (+39 055) 34 08 81
e-mail: commerciale@keller.it

**Background**
Established in March 2000, Keller Elettromeccanica is a private limited company owned by the Busi Impianti SpA group, Bologna, and the Ciet SpA group, Arezzo.

**Products**
Design and manufacture of passenger coaches and special purpose vehicles, including: UIC Z1 passenger coaches; measure coaches for diagnostic train substructures and superstructures; railway maintenance vehicles; luggage coaches manufacture for UIC Z1 diagnostic train.

*NEW ENTRY*

## Kinki Sharyo

The Kinki Sharyo Co Ltd
3-9-60 Inada-Shinmachi, Higashi-Osaka City, Osaka 577-8511, Japan
Tel: (+81 6) 67 46 52 40   Fax: (+81 6) 67 45 51 35
e-mail: KSRTAN@Kinsha.dp.u-netsurf.ne.jp
Web: http://www.kinkisharyo.co.jp

**Key personnel**
President and Chairman of the Board: Junro Ono
Executive Vice-President: Shunji Matsumoto
Senior Managing Director: Hirokazu Iyota
Managing Director Design and Manufacture Office: Masahiro Hotta
Managing Director, Sales: Yosuke Saida
Associate Director, Rolling Stock Management: Atsushi Tokatake
Export General Manager: Hitoshi Tomoda

*Kinki Sharyo commuter emu for KCRC, Kong Kong, supplied in 12-, seven- and four-car version*
2002/0134173

Locomotives and powered/non-powered passenger vehicles/**MANUFACTURERS** 509

**Subsidiary company**
Kinki Sharyo (USA) Inc
45 Shawmut Road, Canton, Massachusetts 02021, USA
Tel: (+1 617) 949 24 40   Fax: (+1 781) 828 80 25

**Background**
Kinki Sharyo Co Ltd is a subsidiary of the Kinki Nippon Railway.

**Products**
Electric multiple-units for main line, commuter, rapid transit, metro and light rail vehicles, double-deck passenger coaches.

**Contracts**
Recent orders include: commuter emus for KCRC, Hong Kong (East Rail and West Rails); Series E257 Limited Express emus for JR East; Series 700 Shinkansen for JR West; commuter emus for Kinki Nippon Railway; metro cars for NAT Cairo; LRVs for Denver; and 43 low-floor LRVs for Santa Clara Valley Transportation Authority, USA.

*UPDATED*

*Kinki Sharyo LRV for Santa Clara Valley Transportation Authority*
*2002*/0134178

## Kockums

Kockums Industrier AB
SE-205 55 Malmö, Sweden
Tel: (+46 40) 34 80 80   Fax: (+46 40) 34 87 75
e-mail: info@kiab@celsius.se

**Key personnel**
President: Thomas Abrahamsson
Senior Vice-President, Rolling Stock: Björn Widell

Senior Vice-President, Technical Department:
  Lars-Olof Nilsson
Senior Vice-President, Production: Lennart Ek

**Corporate background**
Kockums Industrier is owned by the Celsius Group.

**Products**
Between 1986 and 1997 Kockums carried out modernisation of 180 passenger coaches for SJ. It has also carried out design and development and has built 50 sleeping cars for SJ, including rebuilding of 20 sleeping coaches. Other work includes design and rebuilding of three passenger coaches for NSB Netherlands.

Kockums also designed and modernised 10 trams for Norrkoping and rebuilt a prototype X10 emu for Stockholm.

## Kolmex

Kolmex SA
Grzybowska 80/82, PL-00-844 Warsaw, Poland
Tel: (+48 22) 661 50 00   Fax: (+48 22) 620 93 81
e-mail: komexsa@kolmex.com.pl
Web: http://www.kolmex.com.pl

**Key personnel**
Chairman: Andrzej Nâlęcz
Commercial Director: Krystyna Stepaniuk

**Products**
Diesel and electric railcars, lightweight regional rail vehicles, low-floor tramcars, main line locomotives, battery locomotives.

First, second and first/second class coaches, Type Z1, for operation up to 200 km/h, with bogies equipped with disc brakes (track brake as an option), with or without air conditioning. Restaurant/bar and sleeping/couchette coaches for 200 km/h, with or without air conditioning, with bogies equipped with disc brakes (track brake as an option).

## Kolomna

Kolomna Plant Joint Stock Company
Partizan Street, 140408 Kolomna, Moscow Region, Russia
Tel: (+7 095) 381 52   Fax: (+7 095) 203 47 00

**Key personnel**
General Director: V N Vlasov
Chief Engineer: V A Shelemet'yev
Marketing Director: E N Gunchenko

**Products**
Passenger diesel electric locomotives TEP 70 rated at 4,000 hp and TEP 80 rated at 6,000 hp; rated speed is 160 km/h; locomotives use AC and DC electric transmission.

Diesel-electric locomotives rated at 2,940 kW and 4,410 kW, alternating current electric locomotives rated at 8,000 kW.

Recent production includes the Co-Co TEP70 and Bo+Bo-Bo+Bo TEP80 types. Powered by a four-cycle, 16-cylinder D49 engine, the 2,942 kW TEP70 has a maximum speed of 160 km/h. The TEP80 is rated at 4,413 kW and is powered by a four-cycle, 20-cylinder 2-20DG engine. Maximum speed is 160 km/h. Alternating current electric locomotives EP 200 and EP 201, line voltage – 25 kV power output – 8,000 kW, maximum operating speed 200 and 160 km/h.

| Engine type | Output | | | Dimensions mm | | Type of locomotive |
|---|---|---|---|---|---|---|
| | kW | hp | Length | Width | Height | |
| 4 LD49 | 300-750 | 408-1,020 | 3,090 | 1,580 | 2,300 | – |
| 6 LD49 | 470-1,100 | 637-1,500 | 3,930 | 1,580 | 2,310 | Shunting |
| 8 VD49 | 500-1,760 | 680-2,390 | 3,720 | 1,665 | 2,330 | TGM 6V, TGM 8 |
| 12 VD49 | 1,100-2,650 | 1,500-3,600 | 3,920 | 1,665 | 3,030 | 2TE 116, TEM 7A |
| 16 VD49 | 1,470-3,700 | 2,000-5,030 | 4,900 | 1,655 | 3,070 | 2TE 116, 2TE 121, TEP 70 |
| 20 VD49 | 3,700-5,000 | 5,300-6,800 | 6,270 | 1,665 | 3,190 | TE 136, TEP 80 |

Output is for ISO standard reference conditions.

*UPDATED*

*Kolomna EP 201 AC electric locomotive*
*2000*/0089815

www.janes.com

Jane's World Railways 2002-2003

# 510 MANUFACTURERS/Locomotives and powered/non-powered passenger vehicles

## Končar – Električne Lokomotive dd

Končar-Electric Locomotives Inc
Velimira Škorpika 7, HR-10090 Zagreb, Croatia
Tel: (+385 1) 349 69 59   Fax: (+385 1) 349 69 60
e-mail: uprava.ellok@koncar.tel.hr
Web: http://www.koncar.tel.hr/ellok

**Key personnel**
Managing Director: Želimir Bobinac
Deputy Managing Director: Vesna Boinović-Grubić
Marketing and Sales Manager: Zvonimir Cvijin
Technical Director: Jusuf Crnalić

**Products**
Electric locomotives for AC and DC traction; electric multiple-units; trams; shunting locomotives; light rail vehicles; parts, components and systems for electric traction.

*UPDATED*

Class E52 Bo-Bo 25 kV AC 50 Hz electric locomotive refurbished for Bulgarian State Railways
*2002*/0122615

Class 46 Co-Co 25 kV AC 50 Hz electric locomotive refurbished for Bulgarian State Railways
*2002*/0122617

---

## Luganskteplovozstroj

Lugansk Diesel Locomotive Works
ulica Frunze 107, 348 002 Lugansk, Ukraine

**Products**
Diesel locomotives.

---

## Lyudinovo Locomotive Works JSC

1 K Liebknecht Street, Lyudinovo, Kaluga region 249400, Russia
Tel: (+7 08444) 201 20; 252 59   Fax: (+7 08444) 252 59

**Key personnel**
General Director: Peter F Baum

Executive Director: Sergey M Fomin
Chief Engineer: Anatoly I Gerasimov
Import and Export, Sales: Nicolai N Denisov

**Products**
Diesel-hydraulic and diesel-electric locomotives 597 to 2,984 kW (800 to 4,000 hp) for industrial, shunting and main line applications. Spare parts for locomotives.

Lyudinovo LW also makes rail lubricating machines, rotary snow ploughs, track maintenance cars, dmus, narrow-gauge trains and tank wagons.

---

## Mecanoexportimport

Mecanoexportimport SA
30 Dacia Boulevard, Bucharest, Romania
Tel: (+40 1) 211 98 55   Fax: (+40 1) 210 78 94

**Key personnel**
Managing Director: Cornel Anghel

Technical Manager: Mahitar Dolmanian
Financial Manager: Ion Capatina
Head of Marketing Department: Ioana Rogoveanu

**Products**
Electric, diesel-electric and diesel-hydraulic locomotives, diesel railcars, emus, passenger coaches, multifunction road/rail vehicles, rotary snow-ploughs, axles, wheelsets and bogies.

Mecanoexportimport is the export sales company for the Romanian railway supply industry. For the majority of the locomotive designs available see the entries for Electroputere and Faur.

---

## Metrowagonmash Joint Stock Company

4 Kolontsov str, Mytishchi, 141009 Moscow, Russia
Tel: (+7 095) 581 12 56   Fax: (+7 095) 581 12 56
e-mail: metrowagonmash@mtu-net.ru
Web: http://www.mtu.net.ru

**Key personnel**
General Manager: J A Gulko
Technical Director: J P Soldatov
Deputy General Manager: A A Andreyev

**Subsidiaries**
Spola Spare Parts Production Co (Ukraine)
Vyshnevolotski Machine Building Plant

**Products**
Metro cars, railbuses, bogies, spare parts for metro cars.

---

## Michurinsk Locomotive Works

ulica Privokzalnaya 1, 393 740 Michurinsk, Tambov region, Russian Federation

**Products**
Locomotives.

---

## Mitsubishi Electric Corporation

Mitsubishi Denki Building, 2-3 Marunouchi 2-chome, Chiyoda-ku, Tokyo 100, Japan
Tel: (+81 3) 32 18 34 30   Fax: (+81 3) 32 18 28 95
Web: http://www.melco.co.jp/society/traffic/

**Key personnel**
President: Tamotsu Nomakuchi

Executive General Manager (Public Utility Systems Group): Takaaki Kijima
Division Manager (Transportation Systems Division): Mitsuo Muneyuki
Deputy Division Manager (Transportation Systems Division): Harami Shiumura
Manager (Transportation Overseas Marketing Dept): Takayuki Ogawa

**Subsidiaries**

*Australia*
Mitsubishi Electric Australia Pty Ltd
348 Victoria Road, Rydalmere, New South Wales 2116, Australia
Tel: (+61 2) 96 84

---

Jane's World Railways 2002-2003   www.janes.com

Locomotives and powered/non-powered passenger vehicles/**MANUFACTURERS**

**Electric locomotives equipped by Mitsubishi Electric since 1990**

| Class | Railway | Wheel arrangement | Line voltage | Rated output (kW) continuous | Max speed (km/h) | Weight (t) | No in service | Year first built | Builders Mechanical parts | Electrical equipment |
|---|---|---|---|---|---|---|---|---|---|---|
| EF 500 | JR Freight | Bo-Bo-Bo | 20 kV AC/ 1.5 kV DC | 6,000 | 120 | 100.8 | 1 | 1990 | Kawasaki Heavy Industry | Mitsubishi Electric |
| EF 210 | JR Freight | Bo-Bo-Bo | 1.5 kV DC | 3,390 | 110 | 100.8 | 30 | 1995 | Kawasaki Heavy Industry | Mitsubishi Electric |
| EF 510 | JR Freight | Bo-Bo-Bo | 20 kV AC/ 1.5 kV DC | 3,390 | 110 | 100.8 | 1 | 2002 | Kawasaki Heavy Industry | Mitsubishi Electric |

*Mexico*
Melco de Mexico SA de CV
Mariano Escobedo No 69, Tlanepantla 54030, Edo de Mexico
Tel: (+5 390) 73 44

*Singapore*
Mitsubishi Electric Asia Pte Ltd
307 Alexandra Road #05-01/02, Mitsubishi Electric Bldg, Singapore 159943
Tel: (+65) 473 23 08

*UK*
Mitsubishi Electric Europe BV
15th floor, Leon House, 223 High Street, Croydon, Surrey CR0 9XT, UK
Tel: (+44 20) 86 86 95 51

*USA*
Mitsubishi Electric Power Products Inc
1211 Avenue of the Americas, 43rd floor, New York, New York 10036, USA
Tel: (+1 212) 704 66 73

**Products**
Complete electric locomotives, diesel-electric locomotives, traction motors, VVVF inverters, main transformers, rectifiers, drive gears, flexible couplings, brake systems, static inverters.

**Contracts**
Recent contracts include: electrical equipment for 192 emus, New York MTA, Long Island Rail Road (USA), May 1999; electrical equipment for 250 emus, KCRC West/ East rail, Hong Kong, August 1999; electrical equipment for 104 emus, MTRC C651 Tsuen-Kwan-O extension, Hong Kong; electrical equipment for 328 emus, Seoul Metro Line 6, Korea; electrical equipment for 240 emus, Delhi Metro Railway Corporation, (India), May 2001.

*UPDATED*

# Moës

Moteurs Moës SA
62 Rue de Huy, B-4300 Waremme, Belgium
Tel: (+32 19) 32 23 52   Fax: (+32 19) 32 34 48

**Key personnel**
Chairman: C Froidbise
Managing Director: R Thirion
Sales Director: J Antoine

**Products**
Narrow-gauge diesel-hydraulic and diesel-mechanical locomotives (3 to 30 tonnes, 10 to 190 kW) for mine railways.

# MotivePower Industries

MotivePower Industries
1200 Reedsdale Street, Pittsburgh, Pennsylvania 15233, USA
Tel: (+1 412) 237 22 50   Fax: (+1 412) 321 77 56
Web: http://www.motivepower.com

**Works**
USA: Boise, Idaho; Braddock, Pennsylvania; Latham, New York; Jackson, Tennessee; Gilman, Illinois; Elk Grove Village, Illinois.
Mexico: San Luis Potosi, Acambaro.

**Key personnel**
Chairman: John C (Jack) Pope
President and Chief Executive Officer: Michael Wolf
Senior Vice-President and Chief Financial Officer:
    William F Fabrizio
Vice-Presidents
General Counsel and Secretary:
    Jeanette Fisher-Garber
Controller and Principal Accounting Officer:
    William D Grab
Treasurer: Thomas P Lyons
Human Resources and Administration:
    Scott E Wahlstrom
Investor and Public Relations: Timothy R Wesley

**Operating group management**
*Components Group*
Engine Systems Company Inc
President: James E Lindsay
Motor Coils Manufacturing Company
President: J Lynn Young
Power Parts Company
Executive Vice-President: David M Cullen
Touchstone Company
President: Theodore E Nelson

*Locomotive Group*
Boise Locomotive Company
President: Joseph S Crawford
Vice-President and General Manager: Francis X Larkin
MPI de Mexico SA de CV
Director-General: Carlos Vidaurreta

**Products**
Through its subsidiaries, MPI specialises in the manufacturing and distribution of engineered locomotive components and parts; provides locomotive fleet maintenance, remanufacturing and overhauls and manufactures environmentally friendly switcher, commuter and mid-range locomotives up to 4,000 hp (2,985 kW).

The company's main customers are freight and passenger railways including every Class 1 railroad in North America.

# Muromteplovoz

Murom Diesel Locomotive Works
ulica Filatova 10, 602 200 Murom, Vladimir region, Russian Federation
Tel: (+7 095) 291 31 68   Fax: (+7 09234) 443 03
e-mail: mteplo@cl.murom.ru
Web: http://www.cl.murom.ru

**Key personnel**
Director General: V Kharitinov
Director, Export Sales and Marketing: E Tretyakov

**Products**
Diesel shunting locomotives.

*Muromteplovoz Type TGM23D diesel shunting locomotive*
2001/0103977

## National Railway Equipment Company

14400 South Robey Street, PO Box 2270, Dixmoor, Ilinois 60426, USA
Tel: (+1 708) 388 60 02   Fax: (+1 708) 388 24 87

*International Division*
908 Shawnee Street, Mt Vernon, Illinois 62864, USA
Tel: (+1 618) 241 92 70   Fax: (+1 618) 241 92 75

**Key personnel**
President: Lawrence J Beal
Vice-Presidents: Wilfred A Burrows, Patrick C Frangella
Vice President International Sales: John Tooke

**Products**
National Railway Equipment Company has been engaged in the remanufacture of diesel-electric locomotives for nearly 20 years. Locomotives ranging from 447 to 2,686 kW in four- or six-axle configurations can be supplied.

In addition to complete locomotives, NREC supplies components including diesel engines, electrical rotating equipment and air compressors. Each is rebuilt to Original Equipment Manufacturer (OEM) specifications before dispatch.

NREC's inventory includes over 200 diesel locomotives which can be rebuilt to customer specifications.

Contracts include the design and remanufacture of 14 EMD SD39-2M locomotives for Ferrocarril Del Pacifico SA, Santiago, Chile; the rebuilding of U10B locomotives for Ferrovias, Colombia; the rebuilding and supply of EMD locomotives for Boke Trading, Guinea.

Recent USA contracts include 33 EMD SD40-2 locomotives for the Union Pacific Railroad and work for the Canadian National Illinois Central Railroad, Burlington Northern Santa Fe Railroad, the Kansas City Southern Railway company and the Gateway Western Railroad.

## NEVZ

Novocherkasskk Electric Locomotive Works
346 413 Novocherkassk, Rostov region, Russian Federation
Tel: (+7 86352) 344 46   Fax: (+7 86352) 338 38

**Key personnel**
General Director: Noskov Alexander Leonidovich
Deputy Director of Marketing:
   Podust Sergey Fyodorovich
Chief, Foreign Department: Budkov Alexander Markovich

**Products**
Main line passenger and freight electric locomotives.

*UPDATED*

## Newag GmbH & Co KG

Ripshorster Strasse 321, D-46117 Oberhausen, Germany
Tel: (+49 208) 86 50 30   Fax: (+49 208) 865 03 20
e-mail: info@newag.de

**Key personnel**
Managing Director: C Kohl
Technical Director: M Hanke
Sales Director: R Franz

**Products**
Diesel-hydraulic locomotives from 150 to 900 kW for gauges 750 to 1,676 mm. The remanufacture of diesel-electric and diesel-hydraulic locomotives of 20 to 2,240 kW.

**Developments**
Newag is offering the Jumbo 2000, a heavy-duty high-speed road/rail vehicle. (See *Permanent way components, equipment and services* section.)

*UPDATED*

## Niigata Engineering Co Ltd

10-1, Kamatahonchou, 1-chome, Ota-ku, Tokyo 144-8639, Japan
Tel: (+81 3) 57 10 77 00   Fax: (+81 3) 57 10 47 50

**Works**
9-3, Kamatahoncho 1-chome, Ohtaku, Tokyo 144-8640, Japan
Tel: (+81 3) 37 37 19 89   Fax: (+81 3) 37 37 19 51

**Key personnel**
President: Yoshihiro Muramatsu
Executive Managing Directors: Tsuneo Yanagida; Tomoya Okumura

**Subsidiary**
Niigata Converter Co Ltd
5-27-9 Sendagaya, Shibuya-ku, Tokyo 151, Japan
Tel: (+81 3) 33 54 71 11   Fax: (+81 3) 33 41 53 65

**Products**
Diesel and electric railcars; passenger coaches; rotary snow-ploughs; work cars. Diesel locomotives.

*Niigata type HK100 electric railcar for Hokuetsu Railway*

**Niigata diesel railcars (typical examples)**

| Class | Cars per unit | Motor cars per unit | Motored axles per motor car | Transmission | Rated power (kW) per motor | Max speed (km/h) | Weight (tonnes) Per car | Total seating capacity | Length per car (m) | No in service | Year first built | Mechanical parts | Builders Engine and type | Transmission |
|---|---|---|---|---|---|---|---|---|---|---|---|---|---|---|
| NDC | 1 | 1 | 2 | Hydraulic torque converter | 188 | 95 | 26.2 | 52 | 16.3 | 64 | 1988 | Niigata | Niigata DMF13HS | Niigata Converter TACN-22-1100 |
| KIHA 1,000 | 1 | 1 | 2 | hydraulic torque converter | 340 | 110 | 31.5 | 70 | 21.3 | 48 | 1990 | Niigata | Komatsu DMF11HZ | Niigata Converter DW14C |
| KIHA 200 | 2 | 2 | 2 | hydraulic torque converter | 340 | 110 | 34.5 | 52 | 21.3 | 28 | 1991 | Niigata | Niigata DMF13HZA | Niigata Converter R-DW4 |
| KIHA 111 | 2 | 2 | 2 | hydraulic torque converter | 320 | 100 | 39.8 | 60 | 20.0 | 81 | 1991 | Niigata | Niigata DMF13HZA | Niigata Converter DW14A-B |
| KIHA 125 | 1 | 1 | 2 | hydraulic torque converter | 250 | 95 | 29.5 | 59 | 18.5 | 27 | 1993 | Niigata | Niigata DMF13HZ | Niigata Converter TACN22-1600 |
| MRT300 | 2 | 2 | 2 | hydraulic torque converter | 250 | 95 | 33.2 | 66 | 21.3 | 4 | 1994 | Niigata | Niigata DMF13HZ | Niigata converter TACN22-1600 |

**Niigata electric railcars**

| Class | Cars per unit | Line voltage | Motor cars per unit | Motored axles per motor car | Rated output (kW) per motor | Max speed (km/h) | Weight (tonnes) per car | Total seating capacity | Length per car (m) | No ordered | Year first built | Mechanical parts | Builders Electrical equipment |
|---|---|---|---|---|---|---|---|---|---|---|---|---|---|
| HK 100 | 1 | 1.5 kV DC | 1 | 1 | 95 | 110 | 36.5 | 61 | 20.5 | 9 | 1996 | Niigata | Mitsubishi |

*UPDATED*

## Nippon Sharyo

Nippon Sharyo Ltd
Riverside Yomiuri Building, 11th Floor, 36-2 Nihombashi-Hakozaki-cho, Chuo-ku, Tokyo 103-0015, Japan
Tel: (+81 3) 36 68 33 30   Fax: (+81 3) 36 69 02 38

**Works**
Toyokawa Plant, 2-20 Honohara, Toyokawa, Aichi 442-8502, Japan

**Key personnel**
President: Kazuhisa Matsuda
Managing Director & General Manager, Rolling Stock Division: Akio Honda
Business Contact General Manager International Sales Department: Masataka Nakajima

**Subsidiary company**
Nippon Sharyo USA Inc
600 Third Avenue, 28th Floor, New York, New York 10016, USA
Tel: (+1 212) 949 22 28   Fax: (+1 212) 949 22 29

**Products**
High-speed trains, electric and diesel railcars, light rail vehicles, automated guideway transit vehicles. Diesel-electric, diesel-hydraulic locomotives. Bogies for transit vehicles.

Recent major deliveries include emus to the Kawasaki-Nippon Sharyo joint venture. Nippon Sharyo has also received an order for gallery cars (PC) from Metra, Chicago, USA.

*Series 700 Shinkansen emu*

*Series 9000 emu for Teito Rapid Transportation Authority*

### Recent Nippon Sharyo electric railcars or multiple-units

| Railway | Cars per unit | Line voltage | Motor cars per unit | Motored axles per motor car | Rated output (kW) per motor | Max speed (km/h) | Weight (t) per car (M-motor T-trailer) | Total seating capacity per car | Length per car (mm) | Rate of acceleration (m/s$^2$) | Year first built | Builders Mechanical parts | Electrical equipment |
|---|---|---|---|---|---|---|---|---|---|---|---|---|---|
| Central Japan Railway (JR Tokai) 700 series for Shinkansen | 16 | 25 kV AC | 12 | 4 | 275 | 285 | M 42.5 T 40.1 | 1,323/unit | 25,000 27,350 | 0.56 | 1998 | Nippon Sharyo | Toshiba/ Mitsubishi/ Hitachi/Fuji/Toyo |
| West Japan Railway (JR West) 500 series for Shinkansen | 16 | 25 kV AC | 16 | 4 | 285 | 300 | M 42.1 | 1,324/unit | 25,000 27,000 | 0.44 | 1997 | Nippon Sharyo | Toshiba/ Mitsubishi/ Hitachi |
| East Japan Railway (JR East) E2 series for Shinkansen | 8 | 25 kV AC | 6 | 4 | 300 | 275 | M 46.7 T 44.0 | 630/unit | 25,000 25,700 | 0.44 | 1995 | Nippon Sharyo | Hitachi/ Mitsubishi/ Toshiba |
| Central Japan Railway (JR Tokai) 285 series sleeping emu | 7 | 1.5 kV DC | 2 | 4 | 220 | 130 | M 50.3 T 40.3 | 150/unit | 21,670 21,300 | 0.50 | 1998 | Nippon Sharyo | |
| West Japan Railway (JR Nisinihon) 700-E series for Shinkansen | 8 | 25 kV AC | 6 | 4 | 275 | 285 | Tc 38.8 M 38.9 | 571/unit | 25,000 27,350 | 0.44 or 0.56 | 1999 | Nippon Sharyo | Toshiba/ Mitsubishi/ Hitachi |
| Central Japan Railway (JR Tokai) 313 series for commuter | 2, 3, 4 | 1.5 kV DC | 1, 1.5, 2 | 4 or 2 | 185 | 120 | Mc 36.6 M 32.7 T 27.5 Tc 31.6 | 203/unit (4 car set) | 20,000 20,100 | 0.72 | 1999 | Nippon Sharyo | Toshiba/ Mitsubishi |
| Teito Rapid Transportation Authority | 6 | 1.5 kV DC | 4 | 4 or 2 | 190 | 110 | Tc 26.6/ 26.8 M 28/8/32.5 | 306 unit | 20,660 20,000 | 0.92 | 1999 | Nippon Sharyo | Hitachi/ Mitsubishi |
| Nagoya Railroad co 800 series LRV | 1 | 1.5 kV/ 600 V DC | 1 | 2 | 60 | 40 | 18.9 | 30/car | 14,780 | 0.78 | 2000 | Nippon Sharyo | Mitsubishi |

### Recent Nippon Sharyo diesel railcars or multiple-units

| Railway | Cars per unit | Motor cars per unit | Motored axles per motor car | Transmission | Rated output (hp) per motor | Max speed (km/h) | Weight (t) per car (M-motor T-trailer) | Total seating capacity per car | Length per car (mm) | Year first built | Builders Mechanical parts | Engine and type | Transmission |
|---|---|---|---|---|---|---|---|---|---|---|---|---|---|
| Taiwan Railway Administration series 3100 for express | 3 | 2 | 1 | Torque converter | 350 | 110 | M 40.0 T 37.5 | 142/unit | 19,500 | 1998 | Nippon Sharyo | Cummins NTA855R1 | Niigata DBSF-100 |
| Taiwan Railway Administration | 1 | 1 | 1 | Torque converter | 350 | 110 | M 42.1 | 46/car | 19,000 | 1998 | Nippon Sharyo | Cummins NTA855R1 | Niigata DBSF-100 |
| Central Japan Railway (JR Tokai) 95 series for track inspection | 3 | 4 | 2 | Torque converter | 350 | 120 | M 41.3 T 31.2 | n/a | 21,400 | 1996 | Nippon Sharyo | Cummins C-DMF14HZB | Niigata C-DW14 |

**UPDATED**

## OFV

Officine Ferroviarie Veronesi SpA
Lungadige A Galtarossa 21, I-37133 Verona, Italy
Tel: (+39 045) 806 41 11   Fax: (+39 045) 803 28 76

**Key personnel**
President: Paolo Biasi
Technical Manager: Massimo Toniato
Sales Manager: Paolo Galbier

**Products**
Passenger coaches.

## Pakistan Railways Carriage

Head Office, Pakistan Railways, Headquarters Office, Lahore
Tel: (+92 42) 920 17 69; 630 80 97
Fax: (+92 42) 920 17 69; 630 80 97

**Main works address**
Sector I-11, Islamabad, Pakistan

Tel: (+92 51) 44 13 45; 44 27 76; 44 41 62
Fax: (+92 51) 44 27 76

**Key personnel**
Chairman, Pakistan Railways: Masood A Dhar
Managing Director, Mechanical Works:
   Abdul Wahid Khan
Deputy Chief Mechanical Engineer: Asad Ahsan
Works Manager: Jalal-ud-Din

**Products**
Passenger coaches.

The factory has so far produced over 1,698 passenger coaches, including 223 exported to Bangladesh. It is currently carrying out mid-term refurbishment of passenger coaches for Pakistan Railways.

## PEC Ltd

A Government of India Enterprise
Hansalaya, 15 Barakhamba Road, New Delhi 110 001, India
Tel: (+91 11) 331 63 72; 36 19; 47 23
Fax: (+91 11) 331 52 79; 47 97; 36 64
Telex: 031-65199 PEC-IN
Cable: PECOIND
e-mail: burman@peclimited.com

**Key personnel**
Chairman: A K Srivastava
Director: Manjit Yinayak
General Manager: S S Roy Burman

**Products**
Diesel-electric, diesel-hydraulic, electric, industrial and mining locomotives; spares for locomotives passenger coaches.

Diesel-electric locomotives and spares have been exported to Tanzania and to Vietnam.

*UPDATED*

## Peoria Locomotive Works

Peoria Locomotive Works
301 Wesley Road, Creve Coeur, Illinois 61610, USA
Tel: (+1 309) 694 86 62   Fax: (+1 309) 694 86 27

**Key personnel**
Manager – Engineer/Sales: Thomas L Derry

**Products**
Switching locomotives powered by Caterpillar diesel engines.

PLW also makes dual-mode (electro-diesel) locomotives for maintenance trains on transit railroads. It has built one such locomotive for the PATH metro system in New York which is used for ballast trains, snow-ploughing duties and for hauling passenger trains in the event of power cuts.

## PFA

Partner für Fahrzeug-Ausstattung GmbH
Zur Centralwerkstätte 11, D-92637 Weiden, Germany
Tel: (+49 961) 388 81 48   Fax: (+49 961) 388 89 99
e-mail: ma@pfa.de
Web: http://www.pfa.de

**Key personnel**
Commercial Manager: Dr Rainer Wagner
Technical Manager: Gero Rossbach
Sales Manager: Hans Kudlacek

**Corporate background**
The company was founded by the former Deutsche Bundesbahn together with Flachglas in 1985. Production started in 1988. The present partners are Schaltbau AG (50.2 per cent) and Berliner Elektro Holding AG (49.8 per cent).

**Products**
Rail vehicle manufacture and refurbishment, especially of passenger coaches.

Contracts include refurbishment of approximately 1,000 old express coaches to InterRegio vehicles for DB AG; refurbishment of 370 suburban coaches into CityBahn and Regional Express for DB AG, among them approximately 100 driving trailers. Other refurbishment work includes couchette UrlaubsExpress coaches for DB AG; airport express coaches for Lufthansa; modernisation of diesel power cars for DSB, Denmark; redesign of first generation of InterCity coaches for DB AG; refurbishment of InterCity driving trailers and PUMA (FA refurbishing concept with aluminium construction) coaches.

## Price

A & G Price
Division of CPD Engineering Ltd
Private Bag, Thames, New Zealand
Tel: (+64 7) 868 60 60   Fax: (+64 9) 309 28 19
e-mail: contracts@agprice.co.nz

**Works**
Beach Road, Thames, New Zealand

**Key personnel**
General Manager: John A Hillery
Commercial Manager: Neil Howe
Sales: Bill Lovell

**Products**
Passenger coach manufacture, modification and repair.

## Qishuyan

Qishuyan Locomotive and Rolling Stock Works
Qishuyan, Changzhou City, Jiangsu Province, People's Republic of China
Tel: (+86 519) 877 17 11   Fax: (+86 519) 877 03 58

**Key personnel**
President: Yang Weishu
Export Director: Xu Jun
Export Manager: Wang Jiazhen

**Products**
Diesel-electric locomotive manufacture, overhaul and repair; component manufacture for locomotives and rolling stock; rolling stock manufacture and repair.

In addition to meeting domestic needs, Qishuyan products have been exported to more than 30 countries in Europe, America, Asia and Africa. A major product is the 3,310 kW Dong Feng 8 freight diesel locomotive with AC/DC electric transmission, first built in 1984. It is powered by a single Vee-type, four-stroke diesel engine (Type 16V280ZJ) of 16 cylinders, each of 280 mm bore diameter and 285 mm piston stroke. The separately excited AC traction generator has a rated capacity of 3,330 kVA at 1,000 rpm. The 480 kW traction motors are series-excited DC. The cooling system comprises a plate-fin water radiator and static hydraulic-driven cooling fan. The two three-axle bogies, which are interchangeable, are pedestal-less, with no centre plate or balance beam.

The first Dong Feng 9 diesel locomotive with AC/DC transmission was manufactured in 1990. It is equipped with a 16V280ZJA diesel engine, similar to the Dong Feng 8, producing a maximum power of 3,610 kW.

Contracts include the supply of 27 Dong Feng 11 locomotives to Ministry of Railways, People's Republic of China.

**Dong Feng 11**
Track gauge: 1,435 mm
Wheel arrangement: Co-Co
Max speed: 170 km/h
Axle load: 23 t
Max starting tractive effort: 245 kN
Continuous tractive effort: 160 kN
Min curvature radius: 145 m
Max height (rail surface to top end): 4,736 mm
Max width: 3,304 mm
Length over couplers: 21,250 mm

## Qualter Hall

Qualter Hall & Co Ltd
PO Box 8, Johnson Street, Barnsley S75 2BY, UK
Tel: (+44 1226) 20 57 61    Fax: (+44 1226) 28 62 69

**Key personnel**
Managing Director: George Orton
Manufacturing Director: Keith Richardson

**Corporate structure**
Qualter Hall is a part of Waagner-Biro group of companies, Austria.

**Products**
Fabricated structures for rolling stock including locomotive superstructures; passenger and freight vehicles; narrow-gauge underground transportation systems including cabs, bolsters, underframes, and the company has shotblast and painting facilities.

Contracts include: the company is working on shuttle locomotives for the Channel Tunnel and has built and painted all the locomotive superstructures, weighing about 33 tons each, for the Channel Tunnel Shuttle operations; various steel components for main line multiple-units.

*UPDATED*

## Rail Services International SA (RSI)

Rue de la Presse, 4, B-1000 Brussels, Belgium
Tel: (+32 2) 227 11 52    Fax: (+32 2) 218 31 41
e-mail: info@railsi.com
Web: http://www.railsi.com

**Key personnel**
President: Sébastien Bazin
Vice-President: Serge Platonow
Managing Director: Philippe Aloyol

**Subsidiaries**
RSI Austria
Domaniggasse, 2, A-1100 Vienna, Austria
Tel: (+43 1) 617 77 71 12    Fax: (+43 1) 617 77 71 28
e-mail: info@railsi.at
Managing Director: Reinhard Rössler

RSI Belgium
Vaartblekersstraat, 29, B-8400 Oostende, Belgium
Tel: (+32 59) 70 09 08    Fax: (+32 59) 70 23 75
e-mail: info@railsi.be
Managing Director: Jan Baert

RSI France
38, rue de la Convention, F-94270 Le Kremlin-Bicêtre, France
Tel: (+33 1) 53 14 17 30    Fax: (+33 1) 53 14 17 49
e-mail: info@railsi.com
Managing Director: Philippe Aloyol

RSI Italia SpA
Via Sesto San Giovanni, 9, I-20126 Milan, Italy
Tel: (+39 02) 66 14 02 01    Fax: (+39 02) 66 10 09 61
e-mail: info@railsi.it
Managing Director: Renato Mantegazza
Unit Manager Milan: Guido Sarzilla
Unit Manager Rome: Pasquale Grieco

RSI Netherlands
Onderhoudpost Watergraafsmeer, Kruislaan, 254, NL-1098 Amsterdam SM
Tel: (+31 6) 15 03 67 70    Fax: (+31 6) 205 57 88 18
e-mail: info@railsi.nl

Managing Director: Jan Baert
Unit Manager: Bart Janssen

**Products**
Development, design, engineering and technical assistance for fitting out passenger car interiors. RSI's Study and Design Department works on new projects such as interiors and technical specifications for passenger cars. RSI carries out maintenance, overhaul and major refurbishment of all kinds of rolling stock at its four workshops (Milan, Oostende, Rome and Vienna) or at units in 20 European locations.

Customer support for railway operators, day-to-day operations, wheelset maintenance, repair, warranty, mobile operations at customer's plant and supply of spare parts.

*UPDATED*

## Reggiane

Officine Meccaniche Italiano SpA
PO Box 431, 27 Via Agosti, I-42100 Reggio Emilia, Italy
Tel: (+39 0522) 58 81    Fax: (+39 0522) 58 82 43

**Key personnel**
Managing Director: F Squadrelli Saraceno
Sales Director: O Chierci

**Products**
Electric, diesel-electric, diesel-hydraulic and diesel-mechanical locomotives; railcars; passenger coaches and rolling stock components.

The company also manufactures mechanical subassemblies for other companies, such as bogies for locomotives complete with quill drive or toothed gearing.

## Relco

Relco Locomotives Inc
113 Industrial Avenue, Minooka, Illinois 60447-0058, USA
Tel: (+1 815) 467 30 30    Fax: (+1 815) 467 30 39

**Key personnel**
Vice-President of Marketing: Eric C Bachman

**Products**
Diesel-electric shunting and main line locomotives for sale or lease. The company can also perform full service maintenance and heavy repairs throughout the USA and leases most of its units with full maintenance contracts. Relco offers remanufacture of motive power to factory-new specifications. Also performs aftermarket repowering with new, high-technology, low-emission engines and alternator/generator sets. Other products and services include new and remanufactured parts and components, supply/install/service locomotive radio remote-control systems and export capabilities. Relco is fully certified under the American Association of Railroads M-1003 quality assurance programme.

Contracts include the supply of locomotives and/or contract services to over 150 industrial companies, railways and government agencies.

*Diesel-electric locomotive remanufactured by Relco*

## Republic Locomotive

Republic Transportation Systems Incorporated
Suite 101, 131 Falls Street, Greenville, South Carolina 29601-2825, USA
Tel: (+1 864) 271 40 00    Fax: (+1 864) 233 21 03

**Works**
1861 West Washington Road, Greenville, South Carolina 29601, USA

**Key personnel**
President and Chief Executive Officer:
    Hugh B Hamilton Jr
Manufacturing Manager: Mike Dixon
Director of Engineering: Tim Armstrong

**Principal affiliates**
Republic Locomotive Works Inc
Republic Group Inc
Republic Raileasing Inc

**Products**
New or remanufactured locomotives for railway, industrial and passenger applications.

Republic has successfully tested the RD20 model diesel-electric locomotive, developed by Republic and Detroit Diesel. Available is a switching locomotive with AC traction motors.

# MANUFACTURERS/Locomotives and powered/non-powered passenger vehicles

## Rocafort Ingenieros

Rocafort Ingenieros SL
Pl El Regás, C/Ciencia 25, E-08850 Gavá (Barcelona), Spain
Tel: (+34 93) 633 39 10   Fax: (+34 93) 662 94 50
e-mail: rocafort@rocafort.net

**Key personnel**
President, General Manager: Gerardo Rocafort
Deputy General Manager: Gerardo Gállego
Technical Manager: Daniel Dedieu
Export Manager: José Cañelles

**Affiliated company**
PMS SA, Avenida Esplugas 77, E-08034 Barcelona, Spain
Tel: (+34 93) 205 10 11   Fax: (+34 93) 203 41 00
e-mail: pms@pms.es

**Products**
Systems for general interiors and refurbishment of railway vehicles, technology transfer, toilet modules and closed WC systems, touristic trains.

*UPDATED*

## Rotem Company

231 Yangjae-Dong, Soecho-ku, Seoul, Korea 137-938
Tel: (+82 2) 34 64 46 45   Fax: (+82 2) 34 64 47 92
Web: http://www.rotem.co.kr

**Key personnel**
President and Chief Executive Officer: Hak-Jin Chung

**Works**
Changwon plant
85 Daewon-dong, Changwon, Kyungsangnam-do, Korea
Tel: (+82 55) 273 15 41   Fax: (+82 55) 273 17 41

Uiwang plant/central research and development centre
462-18 Sam-dong, Uiwang, Kyunggi-do, Korea
Tel: (+82 31) 460 11 14   Fax: (+82 31) 461 19 13

Technical research institute
80-10 Mabook-ri, Guseong-eup, Yongin, Gyunggi-do, Korea
Tel: (+82 31) 288 11 14   Fax: (+82 31) 284 21 29

**Background**
Established as the Korea Rolling Stock Corporation (KOROS) in July 1999, Rotem adopted its present name on 1 January 2002. Earlier, in October 2001, Rotem became a member of the Hyundai Motor Group.

**Products**
High-speed trainsets, emus, dmus, diesel and electric locomotives, light rail vehicles, metro cars, maglev vehicles and passenger coaches.

**Contracts**
Rotem is the Korean local partner in the construction of TGV-derived high-speed trainsets for the Seoul–Pusan, or Kyongbu, line. The company is responsible for the construction of 34 of these trains, which are locally designated Type KTX13.

In July 2002, Rotem rolled out the first two of 92 aluminium-bodied metro cars for a new metro system in Kyongju. These were claimed to be the first Korean-built vehicles to employ aluminium construction.

In June 2001, the company secured a contract to supply 240 metro cars to the Delhi Metro Rail Corporation to equip the Indian capital's new system.

Other recent contracts include 92 metro cars for Istanbul, 44 for Seoul, 72 for Manila and 160 emu cars for Korean National Railroad (KNR). Rotem won a contract in August 2000 to supply 34 diesel locomotives to KNR.

*UPDATED*

*Rotem diesel electric locomotive*   2000/0092237

*Rotem KNR Type 8100 (DEL 01) locomotive*   2000/0092238

## RSD

Rolling Stock Division
PO Box 229, Boksburg East 1460, Transvaal, South Africa
Tel: (+27 11) 914 14 00   Fax: (+27 11) 914 38 85
e-mail: rsddor@africa.com
Web: http://www.de.dorbyl.com/rsd

**Key personnel**
Managing Director: Dr Thinus Gouws
Executive Director: Carl Render
Business Manager, Traction: Chris Sparcy
Business Manager, Rolling Stock: Norman Taylor

**Background**
RSD is the rolling stock manufacturer of the Dorbyl group of companies.

**Products**
Funkey mining and industrial locomotives, GE diesel electric mainline and industrial locomotives, freight wagons, couplers and drawgear, locomotive refurbishing, specialised vehicles, renewal parts and servicing for all products.

*UPDATED*

## Ruhrthaler

Ruhrthaler Maschinenfabrik GmbH & Co KG
PO Box 10 16 54, D-45416 Mülheim Ruhr, Germany
Tel: (+49 208) 44 51 31   Fax: (+49 208) 47 90 41

**Key personnel**
General Managers: Manfred Opp,
   Hilmar Rudolph Kuppe
Export Manager: Jutta Dudda

**Products**
Diesel-hydraulic narrow-gauge mining locomotives; suspended monorail diesel locomotives for underground transport of personnel and materials.

## RVR

Riga Carriage Building Works
201 Brivibas Gatve, Riga LV-1039, Latvia
Tel: (+371 2) 37 25 21   Fax: (+371 7) 55 52 19; 82 83 96

### Key personnel
President: Janis Anderson
Vice-President, Financial Director: Velerij Novarro
Vice-President, Technical Director: Robert Reingardt
Commercial Director: Sergey Chigorin
Sales and Marketing Manager: Vadim Maximov

### Corporate development
In May 1988, RVR was awaiting a rescue package from its creditors. RVR's majority shareholder is Latek, a joint venture of Latvian and Ukrainian companies.

### Products
1,435 and 1,529 mm gauge diesel and electric (AC and DC) multiple-units for local services.

Production includes the 1,520 mm gauge Type DR1B dmu, comprising two power cars (modified Type M62 Co-Co diesel-electric locomotives) and 10 trailers and the Type DR8. A development of the Type DR1A, the DR8 comprises two power cars with cabs and four trailers. Each power car has two 736 kW M787BR diesel engines driving GDP1000M hydraulic transmissions, with a maximum speed of 120 km/h. Driving trailer cars for DR1A and DR1B dmus are also available.

An experimental lightweight railcar, the AR2-01 has been placed in service with LDZ, Latvia, on the Krustpils-Jelgava service.

*RVR AR2-01 experimental lightweight railcar at Jelgava* (Norman Griffiths)

## Saalasti Oy

Juvan teollisuukatu 28, FIN-02920 Espoo, Finland
Tel: (+358 9) 251 15 50   Fax: (+358 9) 25 11 55 10
e-mail: info@salaasti.fi
Web: http://www.saalasti.fi

### Key personnel
Managing Director: Timo Saalasti
Director of Transport Machinery Department:
  Teijo Saalasti

### Products
Saalasti specialises in building vehicles and systems to customer requirements. Typical products include: diesel shunting locomotives and shunting robots; automatic shunting yard systems; road/rail vehicles for shunting; rail maintenance vehicles; ganger's trolleys; shunting couplings; snow ploughs.

The OTSO shunting locomotives range from 30 tonne, two-axle through to 100 tonne, four-axle bogies. Locomotives are equipped with Caterpillar engine and VoithTurbo fully hydraulic power transmission. Airbrake components including anti-slip and anti-skid devices are supplied from Knorr-Bremse. Locomotives can be equipped with radio-control, automatic Vapiti couplers and snow ploughs. The OTSO shunting robots range from 30 tonne, two-axle through to 100 tonne four-axle robots. Shunting robots are equipped with a Deutz water-cooled engine and hydrostatic power transmission. Hydraulic components are from Bosch Rexroth and Poclain. Shunting robots are radio controlled but can be equipped with automatic driving systems if required by the customer. Other possible accessories include a train brake controlling system with hydraulic compressor, snowplough and snowbrush. Saalasti Ganger's Trolley is a multipurpose vehicle which can be equipped for many kind of rail maintenance work. It is equipped with a Volvo horizontal diesel-engine and Clark-Hurth power shift transmission. An underfloor engine enables effective use of space and a variable design. The trolley can also be equipped with a crane, personal lifting device, snowplough and various hydraulic accessories.

### Contracts
Two OTSO-robot 100 automatic shunting locomotives to Stora-Enso's mill in Finland for wood unloading. Two ganger's trolleys to Electric Rail Oy for catenary construction work in northern Finland. All vehicles can be made to fulfil UIC regulations and for rail gauges 1,435 and 1,524 mm.

**Examples of Saalasti diesel shunting locomotives and Ganger's Trolley**

|  | OTSO-robot 50 | OTSO-robot 100 | OTSO 4 | OTSO 8 & 10 | Ganger's Trolley |
|---|---|---|---|---|---|
| Weight (t) | 50 | 100 | 40-44 | 80-90 | 1,500 |
| Power (kW) | 126 | 220 | 350 | 700-1,400 | 265 |
| Drawbar pull (kN) | 50 | 180 | 130 | 210-270 | 20 |
| Speed (km/h) | 4 or 8 | 4-8 | 25 | Up to 80 | Up to 100 |
| Axle arrangement | B | B+B | B | B'B' | B |
| Rail gauge (mm) | 1,435/1,524 | 1,435/1,524 | 1,435/1,524 | 1,435/1,524 | 1,435/1,524 |

*Saalasti OTSO 8 shunting locomotive*

**UPDATED**

## SAN Engineering & Locomotive Co Ltd

PO Box 4802, Whitefield Road, Bangalore 560048, India
Tel: (+91 80) 845 22 71-76
Fax: (+91 80) 845 22 60; 845 31 95
e-mail: rvm@san-engineering.com

### Key personnel
Managing Director: Milind S Thakker
Chief Executive Officer: Inder Mahadevan

### Principal subsidiary
Engineering Products Division
Plots 1 & 10, Hebbal Industrial Area, Belwadi Post, Mysore 571 106, India
Tel: (+91 821) 40 24 30; 40 23 21
Fax: (+92 821) 40 23 21
e-mail: mysore@san-engineering.com

### Products
Diesel-hydraulic and diesel-electric locomotives, transmissions for locomotives and industrial applications, gears and gearboxes, (spur, helical, spiral bevel).

# 518 MANUFACTURERS/Locomotives and powered/non-powered passenger vehicles

Diesel-hydraulic and electric rail cranes, self-propelled rail vehicles, including eight-wheeler OHE inspection cars, four-wheeler tower wagons, dmus, railbus, Granby cars/quenching cars, axle drives, power pack for dmus, traction gears and pinions for locomotives, heavy duty cardan shafts, custom-designed gearboxes, planetary gear boxes. Locomotives manufactured are used by industries such as cement plants, oil refineries, petrochemical complexes, steel plants, fertiliser plants, thermal plants and construction sites. Locomotives are tailored to customer needs.

The company also manufactures flameproof locomotives for refineries, fertiliser plants and underground mining applications.

Recent contracts include: diesel-electric 1,045 kW, six-axle, 126 tonne locomotive for Mormugao Port Trust; diesel-hydraulic 1,120 kW, Twin Power Pack, six-axle, 135 tonne locomotive for Jharkhand State Electricity Board.

**UPDATED**

*Eight-wheeler overhead inspection car for Indian Railways* 2000/0089817

## Santa Matilde

Cia Industrial Santa Matilde
Rua Frei Caneca 784, São Paulo, Cep 01307-000, Brazil
Tel: (+55 11) 852 24 76   Fax: (+55 11) 30 61 99 15

**Works**
Rua Isaltino Silveira 768, Cep 25804-020, Três Rios, Rio de Janeiro, Brazil

**Key personnel**
Marketing and Export Director:
  Eduardo Hubert K Monteiro

**Products**
Emus; passenger coaches.
Contracts include refurbishment of Series 160 and Series 401/431 stainless steel emus for CPTM, and refurbishment of two Series 500 and five Series 800 stainless steel emus for Flumitrens.

## Schalke

Schalke Eisenhütte Maschinenfabrik GmbH
Magdeburger Strasse 37, D-45881 Gelsenkirchen, Germany
Tel: (+49 2) 99 80 50   Fax: (+49 2) 99 80 51 55
e-mail: schalke-@t-online.de

**Products**
Design and construction of rail vehicles for local traffic, tunnelling and mining; hybrid battery and overhead electric vehicles; rail grinding vehicles; diesel/electric hybrid rail maintenance vehicle.

## Schöma

Christoph Schöttler Maschinenfabrik GmbH
PO Box 1509, D-49345 Diepholz, Germany
Tel: (+49 5441) 99 70   Fax: (+49 5441) 997 44

**Key personnel**
Chairman: Ing C Schlöttler
Sales Manager: Ing R P Bogs

**Products**
Standard- and narrow-gauge diesel-hydraulic locomotives for shunting duties and mining, works and tunnel construction systems in operation worldwide. The company has extended its product range to locomotives of 80 t weight and 600 kW output. Sales have included 14 CFL-500 VR works locomotives for London Underground Ltd's Jubilee Line Extension; 12 CEL-500R battery-electric locomotives for the North-East Line MRT in Singapore; various two-, three- and four-axled (Bo-Bo type) works locomotives of 22 t axle-load.

**UPDATED**

*Schöma locomotive for Jubilee Line Extension project in London*

## SCIF

Société Cherifienne du Matériel Industriel et Ferroviaire
PO Box 2604, Allée des Cactus, Aïn-es-Sebaa, Casablanca, Morocco
Tel: (+212 2) 35 39 11   Fax: (+212 2) 35 09 60

**Key personnel**
Deputy Director General: M Lahkim

**Products**
Passenger cars.

## SEMAF

Société Générale Egyptienne de Matériel des Chemins de Fer
Ein Helwan, Cairo, Egypt
Tel: (+20 2) 78 23 58; 78 21 77; 78 27 16
Fax: (+20 2) 78 84 13

**Key personnel**
Chairman: Eng T El-Maghraby
Technical Manager: Eng A Rahik
Commercial/Financial Manager: A Farid
Works Manager, Coach and Metro: Dr Eng L Melek
Works Manager, Wagon and Bogie: Eng El-Sherbini

**Products**
Power cars, passenger cars, railcar/trailers, trams and metro cars.

# Siemens Transportation Systems

PO Box 3240, D-91050 Erlangen, Germany
Tel: (+49 9131) 72 02 38   Fax: (++49 9131) 72 45 98
e-mail: internet@ts.siemens.de
Web: http://www.siemens.com/ts

### Corporate headquarters
Siemens AG
Transportation Systems
PO Box 910220, D-12414 Berlin, Germany
Tel: (+49 30) 385 50

### Key personnel
President, Transportation Systems Group:
  Herbert J Steffen
Group Vice Presidents: Hans-Dieter Bott;
  Thomas Ganswindt; Hans M Schabert

### Works

*Austria*
Siemens SGP Verkehrstechnik Ges mbH
Brehmstrasse 16, A-1110 Vienna
Tel: (+43 1) 74 06 90   Fax: (+43 1) 749 51 48
Siemens SGP Verkehrstechnik Ges mbH
Eggenberger Strasse 31, A-8021 Graz
Tel: (+43 2151) 45 00   Fax: (+43 2151) 45 02 14

*Germany*
Siemens AG
Transportation Systems
Duisburger Strasse 145, D-47829 Krefeld
Tel: (+49 2151) 45 00   Fax: (+49 2151) 45 02 14
Siemens AG
Transportation Systems
Krauss-Maffei-Strasse 2, D-80997 Munich
Tel: (+49 89) 889 90   Fax: (+49 211) 88 99 33 36

*Test centre*
Siemens AG
Transportation Systems
Friedrich-List-Allee 1, D-41844 Wegberg-Wildenrath
Tel: (+49 2432) 97 00   Fax: (+49 2432) 97 02 00

### Organisation
Siemens Transportation Systems (TS) is organised as eight business divisions based on the products or services supplied:
Locomotives (TS LM): electric locomotives; diesel-electric locomotives; special purpose locomotives; operating leases (Dispolok); and refurbishment
Trains (TS TR)): high-speed and intercity trains; commuter and regional trains; and passenger coaches
Heavy Rail (TS HR): metro vehicles; suburban trains; and running gear
Light Rail (TS LR): light rail vehicles
Rail Automation (TS RA) (see entry in *Signalling and communications systems* section): signalling and control systems; interlockings; automatic train control systems; signalling systems and components; and telecommunications systems
Electrification (TS EL) (see entry in *Electrification contractors and equipment suppliers* section): products and systems for main line and mass transit contact lines; and products and systems for main line and mass transit traction power supplies
Turnkey Systems (TS TK) (see entry in *Turnkey systems contractors* section): turnkey systems for mass transit and main line systems
Integrated Services (TS IS) (see entry in *Vehicle maintenance equipment and services* section): maintenance; refurbishment; spare parts; training; documentation; and consultancy

In March 2002, Siemens TS employed 15,690 staff.

### Subsidiary companies
Siemens Transportation Systems Ltd (UK) (100 per cent holding)
Siemens Transportation Systems Inc (USA) (100 per cent)
Locomotives, Heavy Rail, Trains, Light Rail
Siemens Dispolok GmbH (Germany) (100 per cent)
Siemens Duewag Schienfahrzeuge GmbH (Germany) (100 per cent)
Siemens Krauss-Maffei Lokomotiven GmbH (75 per cent)
Siemens SGP Verkehrstechnik GmbH (Austria) (74 per cent*)
Siemens Traction Equipment Ltd, Zhuzhou (People's Republic of China) (51 per cent)
Siemens kolejov vozidla sro (Czech Republic) (100 per cent)
TGB Technisches Gemeinschaftsbüro GmbH (Germany) (75 per cent)

*Rail Automation*
messMa GmbH (Germany) (100 per cent)
Siemens Integra Transportation Systems Sdn Bhd (Malaysia) (70 per cent*)
Siemens Signalling Ltd (China) (70 per cent*)
Siemens Tehnica Feroviara SRL (Romania) (100 per cent)
Siemens Transit Telematic Systems AG (Switzerland) (100 per cent*)
Siemens Transportation Systems SAS (France) (100 per cent*)

*Electrification/Turnkey Systems*
SPL Siemens Powerlines GmbH Co KG (Austria) (100 per cent)
Transrapid International GmbH & Co KG (Germany) (50 per cent)

*Integrated Services*
Dienstleistungensgesellschaft für Kommunikation des Stadt- und Regionalverkehrs mbH (Germany) (51 per cent)
ERL Maintenance Support Sdn Bhd (Malaysia) (51 per cent)
Leipziger Fahrzeug-Service Betriebe GmbH (Germany (50 per cent)
Leipziger Infrastruktur Betriebe GmbH (Germany) (50 per cent)
Nertus Mantienimiento Feroviario SA (Spain) (51 per cent)
Siemens Bahnelektrifizierung Services GmbH & Co KG (Germany) (100 per cent)
Siemens Rail Services Pty Ltd (Australia) (100 per cent)
* shareholding held by Siemens AG parent company in each country

### Corporate developments
In October 2001, Siemens acquired the passenger vehicle manufacturing interests of Czech rolling stock manufacturer ČKD Dopravní Systémi, forming these into a wholly owned subsidiary, Siemens kolejov vozidla sro. Its main products are vehicles for urban transport applications, including trams and metro cars.

In January 2001, Siemens 'Dispolok' leasing and rental business was established as a wholly owned subsidiary, Siemens Dispolok GmbH (see entry in *Rolling stock leasing companies* section).

### Products
Design, development and manufacture of: main line electric locomotives; diesel-electric locomotives; high-speed trainsets; diesel and electric tilting and non-tilting trainsets; emus; dmus with electric, hydraulic or mechanical transmission; passenger coaches; lightweight diesel or electric railcars; suburban and metro cars; and light rail vehicles and trams.
The current product portfolio includes:

*Eurosprinter*
Designed as a universal high-performance three-phase electric locomotive primarily for European networks, the Eurosprinter has a continuous rating of 6,400 kW and a top speed of 230 km/h. Siemens has received orders for the type both from national railway companies and from open access operators.

*Eurorunner*
The Eurorunner is a medium-powered multi-purpose main line diesel-electric locomotive aimed primarily at European markets. The first order for the type was for a 2,000 kW 140 km/h version from Austrian Federal Railways (see below).

*Class 189 electric locomotive for German Rail*

*Class 2016 Eurorunner diesel-electric locomotive for Austrian Federal Railways*

*Type SD70 MAC diesel-electric locomotive for Burlington Northern Santa Fe, built by General Motors with Siemens AC traction equipment*     2002/0525401

### ICE 3
This latest development in the ICE family of high-speed trains initially designed for the German Rail network features distributed power rather than the power car and trailers concept of earlier ICE units. As well as supplying examples of the type to DB AG, Siemens has won ICE 3 orders from NS, Netherlands, and RENFE, Spain.

### ICE T and ICE TD
Electric and diesel-electric tilting versions respectively of the ICE high-speed train, examples of both types have been supplied to DB AG.

### Venturio
The Venturio family has been developed for intercity and inter-regional applications where operations in the 160 to 250 km/h speed range are required. A modular platform enables trains to be supplied in tilting or non-tilting, electric or diesel-electric versions in formations from three to nine cars.

### Desiro
This modular family of articulated dmu and emu vehicles is intended for suburban, commuter and regional traffic. Diesel versions can be supplied in diesel-electric, -hydraulic or -mechanical versions. Customers include: DB AG (dmu Class VT 642 and emu Classes 424-426); SŽ, Slovenia (see below); and Express Rail Link, Malaysia (see below). A non-articulated version, Desiro UK, has been developed for the UK market.

### RegioSprinter
The RegioSprinter is a lightweight diesel railcar design for local and regional traffic. Examples have been supplied to operators in Germany and Denmark.

### MoMo
MoMo is an extended family of metro vehicle designs for applications worldwide and is based on the use of service-proven modular components. At the same time, a wide range of platforms is offered to meet the diverse needs of individual metro systems. Applications of the MoMo concept include vehicles for the Vienna U-Bahn and trainsets ordered for Bayside Trains, Melbourne.

### Avanto
The Avanto is a hybrid design of low-floor light rail vehicle intended to operate both on city centre tram routes and over outlying main line suburban networks. The vehicle concept is configured to allow multi-voltage operation and provision is made to incorporate a diesel engine to permit operations on non-electrified routes. The first order for the type was received from SNCF, France, in July 2002.

### Combino
The Combino is Siemens' modular design of low-floor tram, which can be configured in a range of lengths and widths, for single- or bidirectional operation and for various gauges. It can be adapted to suit the requirements of individual customers.

A key element of Siemens' product strategy is the company's Wildenrath Test Center in northwest Germany. Commissioned in January 1997, this facility includes five test tracks, the longest 6.083 km and four of them dual-gauge (standard/metre), together with a capability to energise the overhead power supply systems at various voltages. These features enable the company to undertake exhaustive test running and mileage accumulation of all types of vehicle.

### Contracts
Recent contracts include:

*Australia:* In 2002, Siemens delivered the first of 59 Combino trams to M>Tram, Melbourne. The order comprises 38 three-section and 21 five-section vehicles. Siemens also received a contract to supply 62 three-car MoMo metro vehicles for Bayside Trains, Melbourne.

*Austria:* Deliveries continued in 2002 of orders for 400 Class 1016 and 1116 (dual voltage) 6.4 MW Eurosprinter electric locomotives for Austrian Federal Railways (ÖBB).

In January 2002, Siemens handed over the first of 70 Class 2016 'Hercules' 1,600 kW diesel-electric locomotives to ÖBB. Placed in November 1998, the contract included an option on 80 similar locomotives, which are members of the Siemens Eurorunner family of locomotives.

*Belgium:* In December 2001, Siemens announced that it had won a contract from the Flemish transport operator De Lijn to supply 47 Hermelijn-type part-low-floor trams for services in Antwerp (30 single-ended vehicles) and Ghent (17 double-ended). The order followed earlier deliveries to De Lijn of 45 similar vehicles.

*Brazil:* In August 2000, a Siemens-led consortium handed over the first of 10 four-car 3 kV DC emus for CPTM, São Paulo, for use on express commuter services on the operator's South Line.

*China:* In January 2002, Siemens announced an order for five Eurorunner diesel-electric locomotives for the Kowloon Canton Railway Corporation, Hong Kong.

In 2001, through its joint-venture company Siemens Traction Equipment Ltd, Zhuzhou (STEZ), Siemens completed the first of 20 Class DJ1 three-phase 6,400 kW eight-axle 25 kV AC electric freight locomotives for Chinese Railways. The first three machines were built at the company's Graz, Austria, plant; the remaining 17 were to be constructed in Zhuzhou.

In June 2000, the Dalian Locomotive and Rolling Stock Works (DLRW) rolled out the first of two prototype Class DF4DAC diesel-electric locomotives equipped with Siemens IGBT converters and three-phase AC traction equipment. This was the result of a co-operation agreement signed by Siemens and DLRW in April 1999.

*Denmark:* In May 2000, Siemens handed over the first of 13 6.5 MW Class EG dual-voltage (25 kV AC/15 kV AC) electric freight locomotives for Danish State Railways (the freight division of which subsequently became Railion).

*France:* In July 2002, Siemens received an order from French National Railways) (SNCF) for 15 dual-voltage Avanto light rail 'tram-train' vehicles for use on an 8 km line between Aulnay-sous-Bois and Bondy, in the eastern suburbs of Paris. Delivery was due in 2004-05. The contract includes an option on 20 similar vehicles.

In May 2001, Siemens subsidiary Matra Transport International (now Siemens Transportation Systems SAS) was awarded a turnkey contract by SMTC, Toulouse, to supply and equip the city's second fully automated metro line, the 16 km Line B. The contract included the supply of 35 VAL 208 driverless metro vehicles. The line was scheduled to open in 2007.

*Germany:* In June 2002, Siemens as a member of a consortium led by Bombardier Transportation secured a follow-on order for 12 Type GT 8-100 D/2S-M dual-voltage (750 V DC/15 kV AC) light rail vehicles for VBK, Karlsruhe, with an option for eight more vehicles. Siemens is responsible for the mechanical portions of the contract, as well as the high-voltage equipment and dual-voltage technology. To be delivered in 2004, the new vehicles will bring to 111 the number of dual-voltage LRVs used on Karlsruhe's 'tram-train' network.

By May 2002, orders from Germany for the Eurosprinter 6.4 MW electric locomotive had been received from German Rail (DB AG) for 25 machines designated Class 182 and Siemens Dispolok for 38 locomotives for hire or lease.

In May 2002, as leader of the ICT2 consortium, which also includes Alstom Transport and Bombardier Transportation, Siemens signed a contract to supply to DB AG 28 seven-car Class 411 tilting ICE high-speed trainsets. Siemens was to be responsible for the supply of electrical equipment and the production of 91 vehicles, with delivery scheduled for June 2004-February 2006.

In December 2001, Siemens announced that in consortium with Bombardier Transportation it had won a contract to supply to DB AG 40 Class 425 four-car emus for service on the Verkehrsverbund Rhein-Neckar regional network from the end of 2003.

In November 2001, Siemens announced an order from Verkehrs AG (VAG), Nuremburg, to equip the new U3 automated metro line in the city and to retrofit the existing

*ICE T high-speed electric tilting trainset for German Rail*     2002/0525402

VAG U2 metro lines for automatic operation. The contract includes the supply of 30 Type DT 3 driverless trainsets, 16 for service on Line U3 and 14 for Line U2. Line U3 was to be commissioned in 2006 and Line U2 converted to automatic operation by the end of 2007.

In August 2001, SWU, the municipal operator in Ulm, ordered eight additional five-section single-ended metre-gauge Combino light rail vehicles for delivery in 2003. The order included an option on two more vehicles. At the same time, Rheinbahn, Düsseldorf, exercised its option to procure 15 Type NF 8 five-section Combinos, adding these to 36 seven section NF 10 vehicles previously ordered from Siemens.

In May 2001, Stadtwerke Augsburg GmbH ordered 13 seven-section single-ended metre-gauge Combino trams for delivery from September 2002. They were to join 16 similar vehicles already in service with this operator.

Other German operators to order Combino low-floor trams include: EVAG, Erfurt (36 five-section bidirectional, 12 three-section bi-directional); FVAG, Freiburg (18 seven section bidirectional metre- gauge); SNVS, Nordhausen (seven three-section one-directional metre-gauge); ViP, and Potsdam (48 five-section one-directional).

*Greece:* As a member of a consortium with Adtranz (now Bombardier Transportation), in August 2000 Siemens delivered the first of 40 three-car metro trains for Athens-Piraeus Electric Railways (ISAP). Siemens was responsible for the vehicles' traction, train control and safety systems.

*Hungary:* In September 2001, Siemens announced orders for 15 Type ES 64 U2 Eurosprinter dual-voltage (25 kV AC/15 kV AC) electric locomotives from operators in Hungary. Ten are to be supplied to Hungarian State Railways and five to the private operator, Györ-Sopron-Ebenfurt-Vasút (GySEV). Delivery was scheduled for June-December 2002.

*Italy:* In November 2001, as part of the VAL 208 Torino GEIE consortium, Siemens received an order for 46 automated four-car VAL 208 trainsets for the planned driverless metro in Turin. Assembly was to be carried out at Siemens two plants in Austria, with delivery scheduled for 2004-05.

Also in November 2001, Siemens won a turnkey contract to build and equip the first two tram lines in Verona, including the supply of 22 double-articulated bidirectional Combino trams. The system was due to be commissioned in 2004.

*Japan:* In 2002, Siemens was delivering 12 five section bidirectional Combino trams to Hiroden, Hiroshima.

*Malaysia:* In April 2002, the Express Rail Link system connecting Kuala Lumpur with its new international airport was commissioned. The line was built by a Siemens-led consortium and is served by 12 four-car Desiro ET articulated 25 kV AC emus. Eight of these are used for KLIA Express airport services, while the remaining four are assigned to high-density suburban services on the new line.

*Netherlands:* In March 2001, Siemens TS and Siemens Netherlands received follow-on order from GVBA Amsterdam for 60 five-section single-ended Combino trams. They were to join 95 similar vehicles ordered in March 2000; four of these were to be supplied as double-ended bi-directional vehicles. Delivery of the combined orders was due to run from November 2001 to the end of 2003.

*Portugal:* In February 2000, a Siemens-led consortium that included Adtranz (now Bombardier Transportation) secured a contract to supply 22 four-car and 12 five-car emus for commuter services in the Oporto and Lisbon suburban areas respectively. Siemens was to supply electrical and electronic equipment. Deliveries were due to be made between May 2002 and April 2004. The contract includes an option on 20 additional units.

*Slovenia:* In 2001, Siemens delivered the first of 30 Desiro 3 kV DC articulated emus to Slovenian Railways (SŽ). The order, placed in September 2000, was for 10 two-section (Class 312-0) and 20 three-section (Class 312-1) units.

*Spain:* In March 2001, Siemens announced that it had won a contract to supply Spanish National Railways (RENFE) with 16 ICE 3 trainsets for service on the Madrid Barcelona high-speed line.

*Class 450 Desiro UK emu for South West Trains*

*Desiro emu for Slovenian Railways*

*Emu for Keihin Express Railway*

*Switzerland:* Orders for Combino trams have been received from BVB, Basel (28 seven-section single-ended metre-gauge), and SVB, Berne (15 five-section single-ended metre-gauge).

*Taiwan:* In August 2001, Siemens announced that it had secured a contract from Kaohsiung Rapid Transit Corporation to equip two metro lines in the city, including the supply of 42 three-car trainsets. The system was due to be commissioned in 2007.

*Thailand:* As part of a turnkey contact awarded to Siemens in January 2002 to construct, equip and maintain the first metro line (20 km) in Bangkok, the company is to supply 19 three-car trainsets.

*Turkey:* As part of a Siemens-led turnkey contract to provide a two-line light rail system for Bursa, the company supplied 48 Type B 80 six-axle bidirectional high-floor LRVs. The first vehicle was handed over in November 2000.

# 522 MANUFACTURERS/Locomotives and powered/non-powered passenger vehicles

*Ukraine:* In February 2000, Siemens announced a contract to supply three-phase AC traction and control equipment for a prototype Class DS 3 4.8 MW electric locomotive to be built by NPO DEWZ, Dnepropetrovsk, for the Ukrainian National Rail Transport Administration (UZ), and for 20 similar machines to be constructed subsequently.

*UK:* In 2002, deliveries commenced of an order for 785 Desiro UK emu cars for South West Trains, with finance provided by Angel Trains. The trains were to be configured as 45 five-car sets for express services (Class 444), and 100 four-car and 32 five-car sets for suburban services (both Class 450). Deliveries were due to be completed by 2004. The contract includes an option on 321 additional cars to be delivered by 2009.

In July 2000, Angel Trains, a UK-based rolling stock leasing company, ordered 21 Desiro UK Class 360 four-car 25 kV AC emus for use on First Great Eastern services in eastern England. Delivery was scheduled for 2002.

In 2001 and 2000, orders were placed with Siemens and CAF to supply 16 intermediate trailer vehicles to strengthen Arriva Trains Northern Class 333 25 kV AC emus from three- to four-car units.

*USA:* In May 2002, Siemens received orders for LRV from operators in three US cities: three additional S 70 vehicles were ordered to complement an earlier order for 15 to equip a 12 km transit system being built by the company in Houston under a turnkey contract (see below); 11 S 70 LRVs were ordered for service in San Diego, with delivery due in 2004; and 22 SD 460 units were ordered for delivery by 2004 to the St Louis transit network.

In November 2001, Massachusetts Bay Transportation Authority (MBTA) placed an order with Siemens for the supply of 94 metro vehicles for its Blue Line, with delivery scheduled from the beginning of 2004. A locally based associate company, Transportation and Transit Associates Inc, was to take over final assembly of the vehicles under Siemens supervision. The contract also covers the refurbishment of existing vehicles.

In March 2001, Siemens announced that it had secured a turnkey contract to build and equip the first light rail line in Houston, Texas, for the Metropolitan Transit Authority of Harris County. Scheduled for completion by December 2003, the 12 km line is to be served by 15 Type S 70 low-floor LRVs.

*Venezuela:* In July 2000, Siemens secured a turnkey contract to construct and equip the first 6.9 km phase of Line 1 of a light rail system for Maracaibo, including the supply of 12 LRVs.

**UPDATED**

*Aerial view of Siemens' Wildenrath Test Centre*     2002/0525406

## Škoda Transportation Systems

Škoda Dopravni Technika sro
Tylova 57, CZ-31600 Plzeň, Czech Republic
Tel: (+420 19) 773 50 02   Fax: (+420 19) 773 90 59
e-mail: market@dop.skoda.cz
Web: http://www.skoda.cz

### Key personnel
Managing Director: Petr Karásek
Finance Director: Roman Lesny
Sales Director, Railway Vehicles Business Unit:
  Viktor König
Purchasing Manager: Tomaś Hajśman

### Products
Electric locomotives and power cars, electric and mechanical parts for rail vehicles. Locomotive refurbishment. Double-deck commuter emus; refurbishment of metro trainsets and low-floor tramcars.

The Škoda works in Plzeň has built more than 5,700 locomotives, many of them for the railways of the former Soviet Union, Bulgaria and Poland as well as those of the Czech Republic and Slovakia.

*Škoda-Inekon low-floor LRV*     0063369

### Škoda electric locomotives

| (Railway's own designation) | Manufacturer's type | Wheel arrangement | Line voltage | Rated output (kW) continuous | Max speed (km/h) | Weight (t) | Overall length (mm) | No in service 1995 | Year first built | Electrical equipment |
|---|---|---|---|---|---|---|---|---|---|---|
| SZD CS-200 | 66E | Bo-Bo+Bo-Bo | 3 kV DC | 8,000 | 200 | 156 | 33,080 | 12 | 1975 | Škoda |
| SHD | 27E | Bo+Bo+Bo | 1.5 kV DC | 2,190 | 65 | 155/165 | 21,560 | 40 | 1984 | Škoda |
| ČSD 210 | 51E | Bo-Bo | 25 kV 50 Hz | 880 | 80 | 72 | 14,400 | 74 | 1973 | Škoda + ČKD |
| ČSD 111 | 78E | Bo-Bo | 3 kV DC | 760 | 80 | 72 | 14,478 | 36 | 1977 | Škoda + ČKD |
| SZD CS-8 | 81E | Bo-Bo+Bo-Bo | 25 kV 50 Hz | 7,200 | 160 | 170 | 32,780 | 82 | 1983 | Škoda + ČKD |
| SZD CS-7, RŽD UZ | 82E | Bo-Bo+Bo-Bo | 3 kV DC | 6,160 | 160 | 172 | 34,040 | 321 | 1983 | Škoda |
| ČSD 363 | 69E | Bo-Bo | 3 kV DC/25 kV 50 Hz | 3,060 | 120 | 87 | 16,740 | 182 | 1981 | Škoda + ČKD |
| ČSD 263 | 70E | Bo-Bo | 25 kV 50 Hz | 3,060 | 120 | 85 | 16,800 | 12 | 1984 | Škoda |
| ČSD 163 | 71E | Bo-Bo | 3 kV DC | 3,060 | 120 | 84 | 16,740 | 60 | 1984 | Škoda + ČKD |
| ČSD 169 | 85E | Bo-Bo | 3 kV DC | 3,200 | 120 | 75 | 18,000 | 1 | 1987 | Škoda |
| BDŽ 61 | 56E | Bo-Bo | 25 kV 50 Hz | 960 | 80 | 74 | 14,460 | 20 | 1992 | Škoda |
| ČSD 372 | 76E | Bo-Bo | 3 kV DC | 3,080 | 120 | 84 | 16,800 | 15 | 1988 | Škoda |
| DR 230 | 80E | Bo-Bo | 3 kV DC/15 kV | 3,080 | 120/160 | 84 | 16,800 | 20 | 1988 | Škoda |
| ČSD 162 | 98E | Bo-Bo | 3 kV DC | 3,480 | 140 | 85 | 16,800 | 60 | 1991 | Škoda + ČKD |
| ČD 163 | 99E | Bo-Bo | 3 kV DC | 3,480 | 120 | 83 | 16,800 | 40 | 1992 | Škoda + ČKD |
| ŽSR 163 | 99E | Bo-Bo | 3 kV DC | 3,480 | 120 | 83 | 16,800 | 11 | 1992 | Škoda + ČKD |
| DNT | 93E | Bo-Bo-Bo | 3 kV DC | 5,220 | 90 | 120 | 20,270 | 4 | 1994 | Škoda + ČKD |
| FNME 630 | 99E2 | Bo-Bo | 3 kV DC | 3,480 | 120 | 80 | 16,800 | 9 | 1995 | Škoda + ČKD |
| DNT | 90E | Bo-Bo | 3 kV DC | 1,600 | 100 | 72 | 14,460 | (4) | 1996 | Škoda |

ČD: Czech Railways
ČSD: Czechoslovakian Railways
SZD: Former Soviet Railways
BDZ: Bulgarian State Railways
SHD: North Bohemian Coal District
DR: Former German State Railway
ŽSR: Slovakian Republic Railways
FNME: North Milan Railway, Italy
DNT: Tušimice Coal Mines, Czech Republic
RŽD: Russian Railways
UZ: Ukraine Railway

Locomotives for Czech Railways (ČD) and Slovak Railways (ŽSR) are the dual-voltage Class 363 (Škoda Type 69E), the 25 kV AC Class 263 (Škoda Type 70E) and the 3 kV DC Class 163 (Škoda Type 71E, 99E). All are in series production. Types embodying the same concepts and principles have been built for the Bulgarian and former Soviet railways.

Development of a third-generation range of locomotives is in progress. The locomotives feature induction motors in high- and low-speed variants, and with a vector control system. A Class 85E Bo-Bo prototype with Škoda asynchronous motors for 3 kV DC has been produced. Both variants of axle drive have been successfully tested, with the high-speed drive continuing in service.

Production has also included a series of dual-system (3 kV DC and 15 kV 16⅔ Hz AC) Type 80E locomotives for ČD and DB AG; a Class 61 thyristor-control shunting locomotive with regenerative braking for Bulgarian State Railways; four Type 93E locomotives featuring a new axle design and improved electrical systems (part-chopper with GTO thyristors and microprocessor control); four Type 90E locomotives for regional and shunting service equipped with voltage source inverters and three-phase drives; 30 Bo-Bo+Bo-Bo locomotives for UZ, Ukraine; 10 Bo-Bo+Bo-Bo locomotives for RZhD, Russia; and nine Bo-Bo locomotives for FNME, Italy. Refurbishment of Type 66E (CS 200) electric locomotives for RZhD, Type 52E (CS4) locomotives, 25 kV/50 Hz, 160 km/h for UZ and refurbishment of Type 65E and 76E locomotives for ČD to increase speed to up to 160 km/h.

Contracts for powered passenger vehicles include the supply of electrical equipment and bogies for double-deck commuter emus for Czech Railways (ČD). Delivery of emus is expected during 2000-2002 to ČD and for export. These suburban train units have been produced in association with ČKD Studénka, which supplied the electrical components.

Prague metro cars are being reconstructed and refurbished. The work included installation of IGBT drive and a communications system. Škoda has also fitted new cabs and modified bogies.

RZhD, Russia, is taking 20 sets of electrical equipment for Class EP100 (3 kV DC) and EP300 (3 kV DC/25 kV AC) 10,000 locomotives. The locomotives are being built at the Kolomna plant (qv).

A modular low-floor LRV with asynchronous drive has been introduced by Škoda-Inekon and it was awarded a gold medal at the 39th International Engineering Trade Fair, Brno, Czech Republic in 1997. Series production started in 1998 with orders from Czech cities and the United States.

### Developments

A high-performance traction motor with IGBT inverter control has been developed.

Škoda has won a competition to supply 20 sets of electrical equipment for Class EP 100 (3 kV DC) and EP 300 (3 kV DC/25 kV 50 Hz AC) 10,000 kW electric locomotives for Russian Railways (RZhD) passenger services. The eight-axle single-unit locomotives will be built at the Kolomna plant, near Moscow. Škoda will supply high-voltage IGBTs to feed eight 1,250 kW asynchronous traction motors. Kolomna has already developed prototypes of a Class EP 200 25 kV 50 Hz 8,000 kW design of similar configuration with asynchronous propulsion equipment of local origin. The EP 100 and EP 300 locomotives are being designed for express passenger services at speeds up to 200 km/h in harsh climatic conditions which include temperatures as low as −40°C.

*UPDATED*

## Stadler Rail Group

Stadler Bussnang AG
Bahnhofplatz, CH-9565 Bussnang, Switzerland
Tel: (+41 71) 626 21 20   Fax: (+41 71) 626 21 28
e-mail: stadler.bussnang@stadlerrail.ch

Stadler Bussnang AG
CH-9423 Bussnang, Switzerland
Tel: (+41 71) 626 20 21
e-mail: stadler.bussnang@stadlerrail.ch

Stadler Altenrhein AG
CH-9423 Altenrhein, Switzerland
Tel: (+41 71) 858 41 41   Fax: (+41 71) 858 41 42
e-mail: stadler.altenrhein@stadlerrail.ch

*Stadler Type GTW 2/6 articulated electric railcar built for Chemins de fer du Jura*   2002/0122867

Stadler Pankow GmbH
Lessingstrasse 102, D-13158 Berlin, Germany
Tel: (+49 30) 91 91 15 00   Fax: (+49 30) 91 91 21 50
e-mail: stadler.pankow@stadlerrail.de

### Key personnel

President and Chief Executive Officer, Stadler Rail Group:
  Peter Spuhler
Chief Operating Officer, Stadler Rail Group:
  Michael Daum
Director Marketing and Sales, Stadler Rail Group:
  Peter A Jenelten
Managing Director, Stadler Bussnang: Peter Spuhler
Managing Director, Stadler Altenrhein: Hans Kubat
Managing Director, Stadler Pankow: Michael Daum

### Corporate background

The major expansion of Stadler in the late 1990s was achieved by taking over the Altenrhein facility of Schindler Waggon in Switzerland and the Berlin-Pankow plant of Adtranz/Bombardier.

### Products

Dmus, emus, diesel-electric shunters and trams/light rail vehicles.

### Contracts

Stadler Bussnang AG has won an order to manufacture and supply 80 articulated trains GTW 2/6 (15 kV AC) for Thurbo AG Switzerland. The vehicles will operate in the eastern part of Switzerland. The total number of GTWs sold amounted to 323 units by the end of 2001 including orders for New Jersey Transit, Hellenic Railways Organisation (OSE) and Slovakian Railways.

The Stadler Rail Group has taken over the licence for the RegioShuttle RS1 (dmu) from Adtranz/Bombardier. 45 units were sold in 2001 for several private operators in Germany, increasing the overall number of RS1 trains to 265 units.

*Stadler Type GTW 2/6 articulated electric railcar built for Chemins de fer Electriques Veveysans*   2001/0103976

*UPDATED*

## Tafesa

Tafesa SA, Construcción y Reparación de Material Ferroviario
Carretera de Andalucía Km 9, E-28021 Madrid, Spain
Tel: (+34 91) 798 05 50   Fax: (+34 91) 798 09 61
e-mail: tafesa@lander.es

### Key personnel

Group Chairman: Paloma Fernández-Souza Faro
General Manager: Eileen Esteban González
Technical Director: Luis Peromarta Calvo
Marketing and Commercial Manager:
  Jesús Montes Chinchón

### Products

Manufacture and maintenance of passenger coaches.

## Talgo

Patentes Talgo SA
C/Gabriel Garcia Marquez 4, E-28230 Las Rozas, Madrid, Spain
Tel: (+34 91) 631 38 00; 27 00
Fax: (+34 91) 631 38 99
e-mail: comercial@talgo.com

### Key personnel

Chairman: J L Oriol
Chief Executive Officer: Francisco Lorenzo
Commercial Manager: F Lorenzo
Financial Manager: J L Rhodes
Technical Manager: J L López Gómez
Production Manager: S Vallejo

### Subsidiary companies

Talgo America
100 South King Street, Suite 320, Seattle, Washington 98104, USA
Tel: (+1 206) 748 61 40   Fax: (+1 206) 748 61 47
e-mail: info@talgoamerica.com

Talgo Deutschland GmbH
Revaler Strasse 99, D-10245 Berlin, Germany
Tel: (+49 30) 29 72 27 51   Fax: (+49 30) 29 72 11 43
e-mail: talgodeutschland@talgo.com

Talgo-Transtech Oy (qv)

### Corporate development

Patentes Talgo acquired Transtech in 1999 to form Talgo-Transtech (qv). Transtech was the railway division of Finnish steel manufacturer Rautaruukki.

### Products

Lightweight low-centre-of-gravity passenger coaches employing the Talgo system of suspension and wheel guidance, designed to permit higher curving speed without passenger discomfort or undue track wear (powered and non-powered). Also passenger coaches, electric locomotives, diesel-hydraulic and diesel-electric locomotives and LRVs.

Each Talgo low-floor vehicle (except trainset end vehicles) is carried on a single pair of half-axles with independent wheels. The design includes coaches with automatic variable-gauge axles and bogies for through running between Spain and France and coaches with pendular (passive tilt) suspension.

Automatic variable-gauge axles and bogies for freight wagons; modular pit lathes for wheels and disc brakes; automatic equipment for dynamic measurement of wheel characteristics.

Contracts include Talgo trains for RENFE; Washington State Department of Transportation, USA; Amtrak, USA; and German Railways (DB AG).

In March 2001 a consortium of Talgo and Adtranz was awarded a contract by RENFE, Spain, to supply 16 Talgo 350 high-speed electric trainsets (see 'Developments' section) for the line linking Madrid, Barcelona and the French border. The standard-gauge 25 kV AC 50 Hz trains are to be formed of two power cars and 12 trailers. Talgo

**524  MANUFACTURERS**/Locomotives and powered/non-powered passenger vehicles

is to undertake supply of the trailers and participate in developing the train's general concept.

### Developments
Talgo has produced a prototype of its Talgo XXI diesel-powered tilting trainset. Designed for operation at speeds of up to 220 km/h, the train comprises two power cars and three trailers. Production versions will be formed of two power cars and up to 12 trailers. These will be produced in two versions – club class, with seating for 29 passengers, and coach, accommodating 40. A bistro car also features in the configuration options.

Power cars are produced by Krauss-Maffei, and incorporate a 1,500 kW MTU diesel engine and Voith hydraulic transmission. The train concept includes optional provision of the Talgo RD automatic gauge-changing system. This allows through operations using the standard-gauge domestic high-speed line and cross-border running into France. A 'BT' type designation for the power car is a reference to a unique wheel arrangement, which provides one two-axle traction bogie at the leading end and a single Talgo Pendular tilting axle at the rear, this shared with the first trailer car.

Newly developed is an improved sealed bodyshell design to reduce noise levels and pressure peaks when trains pass, and a repositioning of the air conditioning units from within the bodyshell to the underfloor area, reducing the centre of gravity and providing extra seating space. Axleloading is 17.5 tonnes. Other features include reclining and rotating seats, allowing their reversal so as to face direction of travel, a GPS-driven system for passenger announcements and power points for laptop computers.

The Talgo 350 high-speed electric trainset has been developed jointly by Talgo and Adtranz. This comprises two 25 kV AC 50 Hz power cars and up to twelve 13 metre trailers of Talgo's Series 7 'new generation' design, employing the company's established articulated, single-axle concept. Each 20 metre power car has a continuous rating of 4,000 kW, with all axles powered by asynchronous traction motors. The power cars are supplied by Adtranz, which is responsible for the train's traction system, control equipment and onboard electronics. Maximum design speed is 350 km/h, with a 17 t axle-load.

## Talgo-Transtech

PO Box 209, FIN-90101 Oulu, Finland
Tel: (+358 8) 870 69 00   Fax: (+358 8) 870 69 70
e-mail: salesoulu@talgo-transtech.fi
Web: http://www.talgo-transtech.fi

### Key personnel
Managing Director: Tapani Tapaninaho
Sales Director: Matti Haapakangas
Sales Manager: Matti Asikainen

### Corporate development
Formerly Transtech, the railway division of Finnish steel manufacturer Rautaruukki, the company was acquired by Patentes Talgo (qv) in 1999.

### Products
Electric trainsets; passenger coaches and freight wagons.

### Contracts
VR Ltd (Finnish Railways): supply of 92 double-deck aluminium-bodied intercity passenger coaches; delivery began in 1998, with completion scheduled for 2002. Manufacture of 46 Class Sr2 electric locomotives, completion is scheduled for 2003.

**UPDATED**

*Talgo-Transtech double-deck intercity coach for VR Finland*   2000/0089427

## Tokyu Car Corporation

Head Office & Yokohama Plant
3-1 Ohkawa, Kanazawa-ku, Yokohama 236-0043, Japan
Tel: (+81 45) 785 30 09   Fax: (+81 45) 785 65 50

### Sales Department
4-1-1 Taishido, Setagaya-ku, Tokyo 154-0004, Japan
Tel: (+81 3) 54 31 10 91   Fax: (+81 3) 54 31 10 59
Web: http://www.tokyu-car.co.jp

### Works
Gunma Plant: 4120 Akahori, Oura-machi, Oura-gun, Gunma Prefecture 370-0614, Japan
Hanyuu plant: 2-705-23 Komatsudai 2-chome, Hanyu City, Saitama Prefecture 348-0038, Japan
Osaka plant: 3-200 Otoriminami-machi, Sakai City, Osaka 593-8325, Japan

### Key personnel
President: Takeo Momose
Executive Vice President: Yasuo Ajima

### Products
Electric and diesel railcars.

Production includes the East Japan Railway Series 209-950, which has a lightweight stainless steel bodyshell. One trainset consists of 10 cars including four motored cars. The main power source is a VVVF inverter, and a static inverter supplies auxiliary power supply. The brake system consists of an air brake with regenerative braking. The bogie is lightweight and bolsterless.

The Tokyo Express uses the Tokyu Electric Railway Series 3000 which is designed with LED information display, door chimes and IGBT inverter control to reduce the noise pollution of this stainless steel car body with single arm pantograph.

Series E3-1000 Mini-Shankansen is in use on the Yamagata Shinkansen line. It operates at a maximum of 240 km/h on high-speed lines (AC 25 kV) and at 130 km/h on gauge-converted conventional routes (AC 20 kV). It uses an automatic coupler for the Shinkansen Series 200,

*Series E257 trainset for JR East*   2002/0122823

*Series E3-1000 mini-Shinkansen in service on the Yamagata line for East Japan Railways*   2002/0079819

## Recent Tokyu electric multiple-unit

| Class (Railway's Own Designation) | Cars Per Unit | Line voltage | Motor cars Per unit | Motored axles per motor car | Rated output per motor (kW) | Max speed (km/h) | Weight (t) per car | Total seating capacity | Length per car (mm) | No in service | Rate of acceleration (km/h/s) | Year first built | Mechanical parts | Builders Electrical parts |
|---|---|---|---|---|---|---|---|---|---|---|---|---|---|---|
| Irish Rail 8510 | 4 | DC 1,500V | 2 | 4 | 135 | 110 | From 33.75 to a max of 39.25 | 40 | 20,130 or 20,000 | 12 | 3.3 | 2001 | Tokyu | |
| JR East | 9 | DC 1,500 V | 5 | 4 | 145 | 130 | from 30.1 to a max of 36.8 | 52, 54, 64, 68 or 72 | 20,000 or 20,500 | 69 | 2.0 | 2001 | Tokyu | |

and the Mini-Shinkansen uses an automatic folding step at each passenger door.

The Series E751 express train is an AC 20 kV 50 Hz vehicle with a car body shell made of double-skin aluminium. Because the unit is used in an area with heavy snowfalls the underfloor equipment has extra protection from snow and ice.

The Irish Rail Class 8510 emu is an upgraded version of the Class 8500 series manufactured in 2000. Main differences in the Class 8510 are increased fire performance (complying with BS6853 cat. Ib), installation of CCTV and its recording system. In addition, increased impact absorption is built into the carbody ends to provide improved safety for passengers and crew in the event of a collision. The traction equipment and bogies of the Class 8510 series are similar to those of Class 8500.

The E257 series has been designed and manufactured for express services between Tokyo and Nagano. The lightweight carbody employs a double-skin structure of aluminum alloy. Furthermore, the carbody structure is conceived for operation in areas subject to heavy snow falls and in tunnels with restricted clearances in mountain areas. Interior accommodation including the vestibule and toilet have been designed for passengers with impaired mobility. The air conditioning system was newly developed for the E257 series. The Train Information Management System (TIMS) is equipped as whole train formation control systems. TIMS not only controls the main and auxiliary circuits, but also undertakes train condition monitoring.

### Contracts
JR East has taken delivery of Series E653 emus for Tokyo—Tohoku district commuter services. Each aluminium-bodied seven-car unit features four powered cars employing VVVF inverters for traction purposes and static inverters for auxiliaries. Lightweight bolsterless bogies are employed, with blended air and regenerative braking. Passenger facilities include onboard telephone, vending machines and information displays and provision for travellers in wheelchairs.

The company has also supplied Type 10 'heritage-style' tramcars to the Enoshima Electric Railway for commuter and tourist services in Kamakura. Stainless and corrosion-resistant steel is used for the bodies of the two-car articulated vehicles.

KCR West Rail, Hong Hong, is taking 250 emus built by a consortium of Kawasaki, Kinki Sharyo and Itochu. They are for the Kowloon-Canton railway and delivery is expected to be completed by 2003.

**UPDATED**

## Toshiba

Toshiba Corporation, Railway Projects Department
Toshiba Building, 1-1 Shibaura 1-chome, Minato-ku, Tokyo 105, Japan
Tel: (+81 3) 34 57 49 24   Fax: (+81 3) 54 44 94 22

### European office
Toshiba International (Europe) Ltd
1 Roundwood Avenue, Stockley Park, Uxbridge UB11 1AR, UK
Tel: (+44 20) 87 56 60 00   Fax: (+44 20) 88 48 49 69

### Key personnel
President: Taizo Nishimuro
General Manager: Shigenori Yamakawa
Senior Manager, Railway Projects Dept: Shunji Uchino

### Products
Electric, diesel-electric and diesel-hydraulic locomotives; electric traction equipment; auxiliary power supply units. Electric and diesel railcars; trolleybuses; monorails; electric traction equipment; auxiliary power supply units; coach air conditioner; industrial rolling stock.

An order for Series 500 VVVF inverter-controlled traction equipment for nine Shinkansen trainsets (144 cars) has been received from JR West, Japan.

## Transrapid International

Transrapid International GmbH & Co KG
Pascalstrasse 10f, D-10587 Berlin, Germany
Tel: (+49 30) 39 84 30   Fax: (+49 30) 39 84 35 99
e-mail: transrapid.international@tri.de

### Other offices
Transrapid International-USA, Inc
400 Seventh Street, NW, Fourty Floor, Washington, Washington DC 20004, USA
Tel: (+1 202) 969 11 00   Fax: (+1 202) 969 11 03

### Key personnel
Managing Directors: Dr Karin Vomhof,
  Hans Georg Raschbichler

### Corporate structure
Transrapid International GmbH & Co KG (TRI) was founded as a joint company located in Berlin. Each of the founders, Adranz, Siemens and ThyssenKrupp had a one-third share in the company. In the beginning of 2001, Adtranz departed TRI and their share was divided equally between Siemens and ThyssenKrupp.

The activities of TRI include marketing the Transrapid System worldwide, the system engineering for projects, and the preparation of offers in cooperation with the parent companies, Siemens and ThyssenKrupp. At the realisation phase, TRI takes over the project management and during later operation, the maintenance management.

The TRI markets the Transrapid System worldwide, specifically in Mainland China, Germany, Netherlands and the USA.

### Products
The Superspeed Maglev System Transrapid is suitable for long-distance service, regional networks, and high-speed airport to city centre shuttle operation at speeds of 100 to 500 km/h.

The Transrapid system comprises aircraft-style trains running on a dedicated track composed of welded steel or reinforced concrete beams, which can be installed at grade or elevated.

Transrapid vehicles are levitated and guided without contact using magnetic force and a synchronous longstator linear motor provides non-contact propulsion and braking. Transrapid vehicles consist of two to 10 vehicle sections and are able to carry over 1,100 passengers or 175 tons of light freight. The Transrapid systems can cope with up to 10 per cent gradients and 16° superelevated curves.

Transrapid vehicles can reach 300 km/h in less than two minutes (4.5 km) and a two-minute station stop only adds four minutes to the total travel time.

A 31.5 km test track and facility has been in operation in Emsland, northern Germany since 1984. Certified as a public transportation system in Germany, Transrapid trains have accumulated in test and demonstration operation over 750,000 km and carried over 350,000 paying passengers (DM25 per person).

The current three-section pre-series vehicle TR08 was commissioned in late 1999 and has carried visitors at speeds up to 420 km/h in daily demonstration operation at the test site during the EXPO 2000 fair.

The first application route was abandoned after several years of planning in February 2000. The project partners,

*Transrapid's TR08 carrying out demonstrations at speeds up to 400 km/h*   2002/0132086

*Transrapid's TR08 carrying out demonstrations at speeds up to 400 km/h*   2000/0089818

# 526  MANUFACTURERS/Locomotives and powered/non-powered passenger vehicles

consisting of the Federal Government, Deutsche Bahn AG, and the parent companies of Transrapid International, are currently deciding on alternative routes in Germany.

The contract for the first application of Transrapid technology worldwide was signed on 23 January 2001 in Shanghai, People's Republic of China. The new Pudong International Airport is located 30 km outside the centre of Shanghai and is not yet connected by any public transport means. The trip time will be less than eight minutes, the maximum travel speed 430 km/h and the headway 10 minutes. The first demonstration run is scheduled for the beginning of 2003 and the commercial operations is scheduled for 2004.

**UPDATED**

## Transwerk

Transwerk, Business Development Section
Transwerk Park, Lynette Street, Kilner Park, Pretoria 0186, South Africa
Tel: (+27 12) 842 50 30   Fax: (+27 12) 842 59 78

### Products
Specialist in refurbishment and other services for developing countries including CKD kits for locomotive refurbishment.

Contracts include the continuing refurbishment of 3,700 locomotives, 3,000 coaches and 4,600 commuter cars and 150,000 freight wagons in South Africa.

## Tülomsas

The Locomotive and Motor Corporation of Turkey
Ahmet Kanatli Caddesi, TR-26490 Eskisehir, Turkey
Tel: (+90 222) 224 00 00
Fax: (+90 222) 225 72 72; 57 57
e-mail: tulomsas@tulomsas.com.tr
Web: http://www.tulomsas.com.tr

### Key personnel
Managing Director: D Zeki Daloglu
Assistant General Managers: Galip Pala, Cengiz Özan, Fatih Turan, Haluk Akova
Head of Marketing: Erol Çetin

### Products
Diesel-hydraulic and diesel-electric shunting and main line locomotives (545 to 1,790 kW); electric locomotives (3,200 kW); special purpose freight wagons including tank wagons, refrigerated hopper wagons and wagons for ore transport, tracked tanks and containers; diesel engines with outputs of 1,865, 2,200 and 2,400 hp; traction motors, motor generator sets, control equipment for electric locomotives, maintenance and repair work; bogies for locomotives and freight wagons; self-propelled rail vehicles for infrastructure maintenance including car equipped with hydraulic crane, catenary maintenance and inspection car.

**VERIFIED**

## Unilok

Unilokomotive Ireland Ltd
Oranmore, Galway, Ireland
Tel: (+353 91) 79 08 90   Fax (+353 91) 79 08 46
e-mail: sales@unilok.ie

### Key personnel
Managing Director: Michael Lalor

### Products
The Unilok range of road/rail shunting locomotives and special-purpose shunting and inspection vehicles. Uniloks are in service worldwide and are available in most rail gauges and coupler types. A wide range of diesel engines may be fitted according to customer preference. Engines may be air- or water-cooled from 60 to 110 kW. Uniloks are designed and built to the customer's specifications and can be supplied to haul loads up to 1,500 tonnes. Maximum speed on road and rail is 30 km/h. A wide range of optional equipment can be fitted, including snow-plough, road sweeper, hydraulic crane, front-end loader and radio remote control.

### Contracts
The supply of shunting vehicles to Mozambique, Syria and China.

**UPDATED**

## Union Carriage

Union Carriage & Wagon Co (Pty) Ltd
PO Box 335, Marievale Road, Vorsterkoon, Nigel 1490, Transvaal, South Africa
Tel: (+27 11) 814 44 11   Fax: (+27 11) 814 20 64
e-mail: union@ucw.co.za
Web: http://www.ucw.co.za

### Key personnel
Managing Director: L Talijaard
Financial Manager: G Blewitt
Project Manager: D Ward
Engineering/Product Development Manager: P R Watts
Manufacturing Manager: J McIlwraith
Publications and Media: E Wills

### Products
Electric, diesel-electric, diesel-hydraulic and diesel-mechanical locomotives from 50 to 180 t; railcars; electric and diesel-electric multiple-units; main line passenger coaching stock; specialised freight vehicles.

Recent contracts include the supply of 22 three-car emus to Malaysia (1998) and 64 push-pull Bo-Bo 25 kV electric locomotives for the Taiwan Railway Administration.

*Union Carriage main line economy-class coach for NRZ*   2000/0063694

Current contracts include 58 passenger coaches for NRZ, Zimbabwe; upgrades, refurbishments and crash repairs of metro and main line rolling stock; refurbishment and crash repairs of diesel-electric locomotives.

*Union Carriage three-car emu for Malaysia*   0063372

*Union Carriage push-pull Bo-Bo 25 kV electric locomotive for the Taiwan Railway Administration*   0063373

## United Goninan

Broadmeadow Road, Broadmeadow,
New South Wales 2060, Australia
Tel: (+61 2) 49 23 50 00   Fax: (+61 2) 49 23 20 60; 50 01
Web: http://www.unitedgroup.com.au

**Key personnel**
Managing Director: Allan Smith

**Corporate background**
A member of the United Group, the company changed its name from A Goninan & Co Ltd in February 2001.

**Products**
Diesel-electric locomotives. United Goninan is a licensee of GE Transportation Systems, USA. Diesel locomotive refurbishment.
  Powered single- and double-deck vehicles, light rail vehicles.
  Passenger coaches and passenger coach refurbishment.

**Contracts**
Contracts include: two two-car and one three-car 200 km/h Prospector dmus for the Western Australian Government Railways Commission; three GE Dash 9 diesel-electric locomotives to Hamersley Iron Ore Railway, in conjunction with GE Transportation Systems; 20 LRVs for KCRC's Tuen Mun System, Hong Kong, China.

*UPDATED*

*LRV designed by United Goninan for KCRC Hong Kong*

## Ventra

Ventra Locomotives Ltd
(A Division of the Dukes Retreat Ltd)
Works and Administration Office
Plot No 23-B, IDA, Patancheru, 502319, Medak District AP
Tel: (+91 40) 339 20 81   Fax: (+91 40) 339 42 13

**Key personnel**
Managing Director: Arvind N Vakil
General Manager, Operations: T O Verghese
Manager, Sales and Service: S Henry Samuel

**Products**
Diesel locomotives of up to 900 kW with hydraulic and electric transmissions; battery locomotives up to 75 kW; flameproof locomotives; self-propelled trolleys; electrically operated traversers; mine cars and OHE cars.

*UPDATED*

## Villares

Equipamentos Villares SA
Rua Alexander Levi 202, 01520 São Paulo, Brazil
Tel: (+55 11) 279 33 09   Fax: (+55 11) 270 05 11

**Key personnel**
Managing Director: M Silveira
Manufacturing Director: J Cassio Daltrini

**Products**
Multiple-unit trainsets; diesel locomotives under EMD licence; electric locomotives under ALSTOM licence; diesel shunting locomotives.

## Vossloh Schienenfahrzeugtechnik GmbH (VSFT)

PO Box 9293, D-24152 Kiel
Falckensteiner Strasse 2, D-24159 Kiel, Germany
Tel: (+49 431) 39 99 30 89   Fax: (+49 1) 39 99 22 74
e-mail: vertrieb.kiel@vsft.vossloh.com
Web: http://www.vsft.de

**Works**
Service-Zentrum Moers, Klever Strasse 48, D-47441 Moers, Germany
Tel: (+49 2841) 140 40   Fax: (+49 2841) 14 04 50

**Key personnel**
Board of Directors: Dipl Kfm Andreas Hopmann,
  Dipl Ing Hirich Krey

**Subsidiary companies**
VSFT has a 90 per cent shareholding in Locomotion Service GmbH which was established with UK-based Angel Trains (owners of the remaining 10 per cent) to maintain locomotives owned by Locomotion Capital Ltd (qv in the *Rolling stock leasing companies* section).

**Corporate developments**
In 1998 Vossloh AG wholly acquired Siemens Schienenfahrzeugtechnik GmbH, former Krupp MaK Maschinenbau, and renamed the company Vossloh Schienenfahrzeugtechnik GmbH (VSFT). Since then it has become a member company of the Vossloh Group.

**Products**
Diesel-hydraulic and diesel-electric locomotives ranging from 275 to 2,750 kW for all duties, gauges, speeds for both main line and industrial service. Rail vehicle components including bogies and cooling systems. Maintenance, rehabilitation and repowering of locomotives (in Moers).
  Under the brandname of 'Mak Locomotives' VSFT has delivered its vehicles in recent years to state railways as well as to private railways within Europe: G1206 (1,570 kW) to BV (Sweden), MK (390 kW) to DSB (Denmark), HLD77 (1,150 kW) to SNCB (Belgium), Rh2070 (738 kW) to ÖBB (Austria), G1206 B-B (1,500 kW) to SNCF (France). G400 B' (390 kW) G1206 B-B, G2000 B-B (2,240 kW) are already on duty at private railways in Germany, Switzerland, Italy, Luxembourg and Austria. Full certification is in preparation for Belgium, Austria, Netherlands and Italy.
  In 2002, VSFT is going to complete its range of diesel-hydraulic locomotives with the G1000 B-B (1,100 kW) and the G1700 B-B (1,700 kW) models.

*VSFT G2000 B-B diesel-hydraulic locomotives*

*UPDATED*

## Wabtec Rail Ltd

PO Box 400, Doncaster Works, Hexthorpe Road, Doncaster DN1 1SL, UK
Tel: (+44 1302) 79 00 27; 34 07 00
Fax: (+44 1302) 79 00 58; 34 06 93
e-mail: probinson@wabtec.com
Web: http://www.wabtec.com

### Key personnel
Managing Director: John Meehan
Engineering Director: Mike Roe
Finance Director: Robert Johnson
Operations Director: Chris Weatherall
Commercial Manager: Paul Robinson

### Corporate development
Wabtec Corporation of Pennsylvania, USA. WABCO is a leading North American manufacturer of equipment for locomotives, freight wagons and passenger coaches.

Wabtec Rail formerly traded as RFS(E), changing its name in March 2000.

### Products
Overhaul of dmu and emu bogies, with a 48 hour turnaround from collection to delivery, including the complete overhaul of wheelsets, gearboxes, air brake equipment and hydraulic dampers.

Recent contracts include the overhaul of over 1,000 bogies for Central Trains, including Class 150, 153, 156 and 158 dmu bogies and Class 323 emu bogies; classified repairs to Class 158 dmus for Porterbrook; repainting of Class 158s for Northern Spirit.

Wabtec overhauls shunting and industrial locomotives including the Sentinel range of modular construction locomotives complete with radio control and designed to suit arduous conditions including tunnel-working.

In addition, Wabtec has a range of industrial and shunting locomotives available for hire, supported by 'Fleetcare' operational maintenance support.

Ten Class 20 diesel electric locomotives have been refurbished for DRS and supplied with a 'Fleetcare' operational maintenance support package.

Wabtec has also manufactured the UK's heaviest shunting locomotive (150 t) for Tilcon. In addition, Wabtec supplies spare parts and maintenance support for all types of shunting and industrial locomotives.

*Wabtec refurbished Class 20 locomotive* 0063365

*Wabtec overhauled Class 08 locomotive for EWS* 0063366

*Wabtec repainted Class 158 for Northern Spirit* 0063367

## Wagon Pars

Wagon Pars Company
10 Azarshar Street, South Kheradmand Avenue, Tehran, 15846, Iran
Tel: (+98 21) 884 83 30; 83 39  Fax: (+98 21) 884 83 38

### Works
Km 4, Tehran Rd Arak
Tel: (+98 861) 330 46 50  Fax: (+98 861) 339 99

### Key personnel
Marketing Executive: Reza Esfahlani

### Products
Diesel locomotives, including the ME10 diesel-electric locomotive for shunting and other work for speeds up to 100 km/h. Eighty locomotives are being built under a technology transfer deal with the former GEC Alsthom (now ALSTOM).

Also builder of coaches and wagons (see *Freight vehicles and equipment*).

## Yorkshire Engine Co Ltd (YEC)

PO Box 66, Rotherham S60 1DD, UK
Tel: (+44 1709) 82 02 02   Fax: (+44 1709) 82 02 06
e-mail: yec@FSBDial.co.uk

**Works**
Unit A7, Meadowbank Industrial Estate, Rotherham, UK

**Key personnel**
Director: Peter Briddon
Sales Manager: Albert Shaw
Sales Administration: Karen Black

**Products**
YEC is a specialist industrial locomotive supplier, manufacturing shunting locomotives and railcars. Specialising in two and three-axle rigid frame locomotives up to 75 tonnes/750 bhp in diesel-hydraulic or diesel-electric. The company has experience in remote control of locomotives following the European standard, and currently offers 'call home' technology whereby YEC's DEMS2 control system automatically reports to YEC or client's base via the GSM network. YEC also produces specialised rail vehicles and is the UK agent for the *minilok* rail/road locomotive range. Hiring of locomotives, both in the UK and overseas, is a major part of the company's activities.

Recent contracts include: remanufactured/remote control locomotives for Sheerness steel and AES Fifoots power station, Newport; radio control conversions and hires to Corus (BSC); and repower to Caterpillar for Lindsey Oil Refinery; plus a wide range of repairs and conversions for organisations such as the UK MoD and Ford Motor Company.

## Zeco

ZECO (1996)
PO Box 1874, Bulawayo, Zimbabwe
Tel: (+263 9) 789 31   Fax: (+263 9) 722 59; 789 31
e-mail: ZECO@acacia.samara.co.zw

**Works**
38 Josiah Chinamano Road, Belmont, Bulawayo, Zimbabwe

**Key personnel**
Managing Director: M A Da Silva
Technical Director: K A Meth
Project Engineer: R McGann
Division Managers
　Rolling Stock: P Birnie
　Structural: M Sciscio
　Erection: S C Braddock

**Products**
Construction of diesel-electric, diesel-hydraulic and electric locomotives and rolling stock; overhaul and rebuilding of steam, diesel-electric, diesel-hydraulic and electric locomotives and rolling stock.

## Zephir SpA

85 Via Salvador Allende, I-41100 Modena, Italy
Tel: (+39 059) 25 25 54   Fax: (+39 059) 25 37 59
e-mail: zephir@zephirspa.com
Web: http://www.zephirspa.com

**Key personnel**
Managing and Sales Director: Vittorio Cereghini
Purchasing Manager: Fabrizio Della Rovere
Production Manager: Daniele Bergamini

**Products**
Rail/road shunting tractors. The Zephir range includes the IL Locotrattore for wagon handling which is able to travel on roads as well as on rails by means of four pneumatic tyres combined with four 400 mm railway-type flanged steel wheels. The latter are fitted to two hydraulic axles that are lowered by the operator once the machine has been driven on and aligned to the rails.

The tractor has a strong steel chassis and body structure, and is equipped with buffers at either end to allow the machine to operate in both directions.

The Lok series comprises 12 models with drawbar pulls from 2,500 to 23,000 kg and towing capacities up to 4,600 t. Optional equipment offered includes automatic coupling/uncoupling controlled from the driving position; airbraking system for wagons; remote control for rail operations; anti-explosion systems; and one or two cabs.

*UPDATED*

## Zhuzhou Electric Locomotive Works

Tianxin, Zhuzhou, Hunan, PR China 412001
Tel: (+86 733) 844 48 48; 13 51
Fax: (+86 733) 843 10 03; 23 99
e-mail: zelwwdy@public.zz.hn.cn

**Key personnel**
Director: Zhao Xiaogang
Executive President: Li Zhixuan

**Corporate background**
Zhuzhou Electric Locomotzve Works (ZELW) was founded in 1936.

**Products**
Four, six and eight-axle electric locomotives for passenger and freight operation, with an 80 per cent share of the Chinese electric locomotive market.

In recent years, ZELW has become a major supplier to the Chinese high-speed rail and heavy haulage field. It has supplied 158 Type SS8 locomotives which has increased the average passenger transportation speed on Chinese Railways by 50 per cent.

The locomotive reached a record speed of 240 km/h during a test run. The latest generation of DDJ emus is designed for high-speed operation with a top speed of 200 km/h. The 954B locomotive is playing an increasingly important role in rail freight transportation.

## Zwiehoff GmbH

Tegernseestrasse 15, D-83022 Rosenheim, Germany
Tel: (+49 8031) 21 96 01   Fax: (+49 8031) 21 96 03
e-mail: info@zwiehoff.com
Web: http://www.zwiehoff.com

**Key personnel**
Managing Director: Gerd Zwiehoff

**Products**
Road/rail vehicles for shunting loads of up to 3,000 tonnes or equipped as multipurpose vehicles; self-propelled Mini Shunter for loads of up to 150 tonnes; self-propelled Maxi Shunter for loads of up to 200 tonnes; forklift truck-propelled wagon shunter for loads of up to 300 tonnes; motorised one-seat track inspection car.

*UPDATED*

Visit us at **Railtex** from 26th – 28th November 2002 in Birmingham (Hall 2, Stand No. 770)

When the day comes and **the first train** heads for the **North Pole station** one thing's for certain—Voith Turbo technology will be on board

Industry | **Rail** | Road

Voith Turbo is a specialist in driveline and control solutions, cooling systems, and Scharfenberg couplers. Almost every freight or passenger train in the world has Voith Turbo equipment installed—for higher speed, higher comfort and lower noise levels. Our competence in the design of systems is based on decades of experience. This enables us to find individual solutions to every possible task, however complex and challenging it may be. We accept responsibility for our solutions, anywhere in the world, so that our customers can be confident even with their most ground-breaking projects. www.voithturbo.com

# VOITH
*Engineered reliability.*

# DIESEL ENGINES, TRANSMISSION AND FUELLING SYSTEMS

## Alphabetical listing

ALSTOM Engines
ALSTOM Engines, Mirrlees Blackstone
Behr Industrietechnik
Caterpillar Inc
CFD
China National Railway Locomotive & Rolling Stock Industry Corporation (LORIC)
Cockerill Mechanical
CTE
Cummins
Dalian
David Brown
Detroit Diesel
EMG
Eminox Ltd
Faur
Fiat
Freudenberg Schwab GmbH
Ganz-David Brown
GE
General Motors Corporation
Giro
GMD
Gmeinder
Grandi Motori Trieste
Haynes
Hidromecanica
Hitachi
Honeywell Serck
Hygate Transmissions Ltd
Jenbacher
JMA Railroad Supply Company
Kim Hotstart
Kolomna
Komatsu
L & M Radiator
MAN
M & J Diesel Locomotive Filter
MTU
MWM
NICO
Niigata
OMT
Paulstra
Prime
PSI
Scania
SEMT Pielstick
SILSAN
SM
TSM
Tülomsas
Turbomeca
Twiflex
Twin Disc
UCM Reşița
Unipar Inc
Voith Safeset
Voith Turbo
Volvo Penta
ZF Friedrichshafen AG
ZF Padova

## Classified listing

**COOLING AND FUELLING SYSTEMS**
Behr Industrietechnik
Giro
Haynes
Honeywell Serck
Kim Hotstart
L & M Radiator
M & J Diesel Locomotive Filter
OMT
Prime
SILSAN

**DIESEL ENGINES**
ALSTOM Engines
ALSTOM Engines, Mirlees Blackstone
Caterpillar
China National Railway Locomotive & Rolling Stock Industry Corporation (LORIC)
Cummins
Dalian
Detroit Diesel
Faur
Fiat
GE
General Motors
GMD
Grandi Motori Trieste
Jenbacher
Kolomna
Komatsu
MAN
MTU
MWM
Niigata
Perkins Engines
Scania
SEMT Pielstick
Tülomsas
UCM Reşița
Unipar
Volvo Penta

**ENGINE REMANUFACTURE**
Haynes
PSI

**EXHAUST SYSTEMS AND TURBOCHARGERS**
Eminox
Hidromecanica

**GAS TURBINES**
Turbomeca

**TRANSMISSIONS AND GEARBOXES**
CFD
CTE
David Brown
EMG
Fiat
Freudenberg Schwab
Ganz-David Brown
GE
Gmeinder
Hidromecanica
Hitachi
Hygate Transmissions
JMA Railroad Supply Company
Komatsu
NICO
Paulstra
Prime
SM
TSM
Twiflex
Twin Disc
Voith Safeset
Voith Turbo
Volvo Penta
ZF Friedrichshafen
ZF Padova

## MANUFACTURERS/Diesel engines, transmission and fuelling systems

## Company listing by country

**ARGENTINA**
GMD

**AUSTRIA**
Jenbacher

**BELGIUM**
Cockerill Mechanical

**CHINA, PEOPLE'S REPUBLIC**
China National Railway Locomotive & Rolling Stock Industry Corporation (LORIC)
Dalian

**FRANCE**
CFD
Paulstra
SEMT Pielstick
Turbomeca

**GERMANY**
Behr Industrietechnik
EMG
Freudenberg Schwab GmbH
Gmeinder
MAN
MTU
MWM
SM
Voith Turbo

Volvo Penta
ZF Friedrichshafen AG

**HUNGARY**
Ganz-David Brown

**ITALY**
CTE
Fiat
Grandi Motori Trieste
OMT
ZF Padova

**JAPAN**
Hitachi
Komatsu
NICO
Niigata

**ROMANIA**
Faur
Hidromecanica
UCM Reşiţa

**RUSSIAN FEDERATION**
Kolomna

**SWEDEN**
Scania
Voith Safeset

**TURKEY**
SILSAN
Tülomsas

**UNITED KINGDOM**
ALSTOM Engines
ALSTOM Engines, Mirrlees Blackstone
Cummins
David Brown
Eminox Ltd
Giro
Honeywell Serck
Hygate Transmissions Ltd
Twiflex

**UNITED STATES OF AMERICA**
Caterpillar Inc
Detroit Diesel
GE
General Motors Corporation
Haynes
JMA Railroad Supply Company
Kim Hotstart
L & M Radiator
M & J Diesel Locomotive Filter
Prime
PSI
TSM
Twin Disc
Unipar Inc

Diesel engines, transmission and fuelling systems/**MANUFACTURERS**

## ALSTOM Engines

Paxman Division
A division of ALSTOM Engines Group
Hythe Hill, Colchester CO1 2HW, UK
Tel: (+44 1206) 79 51 51   Fax: (+44 1206) 79 78 69

**Key personnel**
Managing Director: John Branscombe
Sales Director: Ashley Hammer

**Products**
Lightweight compact high-speed diesel engines, the VP185 and the Valenta, in the 840 to 2,520 kW power range, for rail traction applications.

The Valenta engine has now amassed over 20 million running hours in High-Speed Train (HST) power cars in the UK. These engines have successfully powered the XPT fleet for the State Railway Authority of New South Wales and are to be replaced by 12VP185s now on order.

The Paxman 12VP185 is now in service with a number of UK rail authorities, including First Great Western, GNER and Midland Mainline, demonstrating its capability for this demanding duty where low weight and high power are critical requirements. Many of the 12VP185 engines are equipped with Viking 22 electronic governors and controls supplied by sister company ALSTOM Regulateurs Europa.

*Paxman 12VP185 engines have been ordered to repower Countrylink XPT trainsets in New South Wales*
2000/0084682

| Engine type | Turbo-charged or turbo-charged/ inter-cooled | No of cylinders | Cont traction rating kW (bhp) | Engine speed rpm | BMEP bar (lbf/in²) | Piston speed m/s (ft/min) | Full load fuel con-sumption g/bhp/h (lb/bhp/h) | Bore mm (in) | Stroke mm (in) | Displace-ment litres (ins²) | Com-pression ratio | Length | Width | Height | Crank-case centre line height | Approx dry weight kg (lb) |
|---|---|---|---|---|---|---|---|---|---|---|---|---|---|---|---|---|
| Valenta 6CL | TC/I | 6 | 840 (1,126) | 1,500 | 17 (247) | 10.8 (2,125) | 167 (0.368) | 197 (7.75) | 216 (8.5) | 39.4 (2,405) | 12.8:1 | 2,673 (105.2) | 1,073 (42.2) | 1,803 (71.0) | 635 (25.0) | 4,400 (9,700) |
| Valenta 8CL | TC/I | 8 | 1,120 (1,500) | 1,500 | 17 (247) | 10.8 (2,125) | 167 (0.368) | 197 (7.75) | 216 (8.5) | 52.6 (3,207) | 12.8:1 | 1,937 (76.3) | 1,460 (57.5) | 2,337 (92.0) | 737 (29.0) | 5,300 (11,684) |
| Valenta 12CL | TC/I | 12 | 1,790 (2,399) | 1,500 | 18.1 (263) | 10.8 (2,125) | 165 (0.365) | 197 (7.75) | 216 (8.5) | 78.9 (4,811) | 12.8:1 | 2,457 (96.7) | 1,460 (57.5) | 2,318 (91.3) | 737 (29.0) | 7,500 (16,535) |
| Valenta 16CL | TC/I | 16 | 2,240 (3,003) | 1,500 | 17 (247) | 10.8 (2,125) | 167 (0.368) | 197 (7.75) | 216 (8.5) | 105.1 (6,415) | 12.8:1 | 2,978 (117.2) | 1,460 (57.5) | 2,426 (95.5) | 737 (29.0) | 9,600 (21,165) |
| Valenta 18CL | TC/I | 18 | 2,520 (3,380) | 1,500 | 17 (247) | 10.8 (2,125) | 166 (0.367) | 197 (7.75) | 216 (8.5) | 118.3 (7,217) | 12.8:1 | 3,207 (126.3) | 1,460 (57.5) | 2,337 (92.0) | 737 (29.0) | 10,800 (23,810) |
| 12VP185 | TC/I | 12 | 1,860/2,060 (2,761)/ (2,761) | 1,500/1,800 | 23.5/21.7 (341)/ (315) | 9.80/11.76 (1,926/ 2,314) | 151/158 (0.334/0.349) | 185 (7.28) | 196 (7.71) | 63.22 (3,856) | 13.1:1 | 2,971 (123.7) | 1,660 (56.7) | 2,175 (78.9) | 656 (25.8) | 7,406 (16,280) |
| 18VP185 | TC/I | 18 | 2,800/3,100 (3,753/ 4,955) | 1,500/1,800 | 23.5/21.7 (341/315) | 9.80/11.76 (1,926/ 2,314) | 151/158 (0.334/0.349) | 185 (7.28) | 196 (7.71) | 94.8 (5,784) | 13.1:1 | 3,798 (148.8) | 1,450 (58.2) | 2,178 (82.7) | 720 (28.3) | 10,100 (23,150) |

**Engine ratings:** Continuous traction rating are for a barometric pressure of 1,000 mbar, an air temperature of 30°C (85°F) and a water temperature to intercooler 45°C (113°F).
**Dimensions:** These are for engines with standard equipment.
**Engine weights:** These are for complete engines ready for installation and may vary slightly, depending on customer requirements.

## ALSTOM Engines, Mirrlees Blackstone

ALSTOM Engines Ltd, Mirrlees Blackstone
Hazel Grove, Stockport SK7 5AH, UK
Tel: (+44 161) 483 10 00   Fax: (+44 161) 487 14 65

**Key personnel**
Managing Director: Ralph Bennett

**Products**
Diesel engines.

## Behr Industrietechnik

Behr Industrietechnik GmbH & Co
Heilbronner Strasse 380, D-70469 Stuttgart, Germany
Tel: (+49 711) 896 20 11   Fax: (+49 711) 896 30 75

**Key personnel**
General Managers: Edgar Roeben
Sales Manager: Ruediger Wanner

**Products**
Radiators and cooling units for transformers, converters, traction motors and diesel engines.

Heating and air conditioning units for cabs and passenger coaches. Cooling plates (air and water cooled) for electronic devices, GTOs and IGBTs.

**UPDATED**

## Caterpillar Inc

100 NE Adams Street, Peoria, Illinois 61629, USA
Tel: (+1 309) 578 44 19   Fax: (+1 309) 578 72 76
e-mail: CAT-Power@CAT.com
Web: http://www.cat-engines.com

**Works**
Engine Products Division
PO Box 610, Mossville, Illinois 61552-6107, USA

**Key personnel**
Vice-President, Engine Products Division:
  Douglas R Oberhelman
Manager, Worldwide Locomotive Engine Sales:
  Kim S Neible

**Principal subsidiary companies**
Perkins Engines Company Ltd
MaK Motoren GmbH
F G Wilson (Engineering) Ltd
Solar Turbines Inc

**Products**
Diesel engines 3.7 to 15,000 kW (5 to 20,100 hp), for traction, electric power generation and maintenance-of-way equipment.

Caterpillar is one of the world's leading manufacturers of diesel and spark-ignited engines for a wide range of applications. With the acquisition of Perkins Engines in 1998 and the 1997 acquisition of MaK, Caterpillar manufactures a range of engines from 3.7 to 15,000 kW at plants in USA, Europe, India and Japan. Currently, parts are distributed through 26 Caterpillar distribution centres

# MANUFACTURERS/Diesel engines, transmission and fuelling systems

| Model | | 3612 | 3608 | 3606 | 3516B HD | 3516B | 3512B | 3508B | 3412E | 3456 | 3406E | 3176C | 3306 |
|---|---|---|---|---|---|---|---|---|---|---|---|---|---|
| Bore & stroke | mm | 280 × 300 | 280 × 300 | 280 × 300 | 170 × 215 | 170 × 190 | 170 × 190 | 170 × 190 | 137 × 152 | 140 × 171 | 137 × 165 | 125 × 140 | 121 × 152 |
| | (in) | (11 × 11.8) | (11 × 11.8) | (11 × 11.8) | (6.7 × 8.5) | (6.6 × 7.5) | (6.7 × 7.5) | (6.7 × 7.5) | (5.4 × 6) | (5.5 × 6.75) | (5.4 × 6) | (4.9 × 5.5) | (4.75 × 6) |
| No of cylinders | | V12 | 18 | 16 | V16 | V16 | V12 | V8 | V12 | 16 | 16 | 16 | 16 |
| Turbocharged | | Yes | Yes | Yes | Yes | Yes | Yes | Yes | Yes | Yes | Yes | Yes | Yes |
| Aftercooled | | Yes | Yes | Yes | Yes | Yes | Yes | Yes | Yes | Yes | Yes | Yes | Yes |
| Locomotive rating | bhp | 5,300 | 3,300 | 2,650 | 3,000 | 2,600 | 1,950 | 1,300 | 1,050 | 660 | 575 | 425 | 270 |
| | kW | 3,950 | 2,460 | 1,980 | 2,240 | 1,940 | 1,455 | 970 | 783 | 492 | 429 | 317 | 201 |
| | rpm | 1,000 | 1,000 | 1,000 | 1,800 | 1,800 | 1,800 | 1,800 | 2,100 | 2,100 | 2,100 | 2,100 | 2,200 |
| UIC rated power | kW | 4,330 | 2,710 | 2,300 | 2,460 | 2,130 | 1,600 | 1,065 | 860 | 540 | 470 | 350 | 220 |
| | rpm | 1,000 | 1,000 | 1,000 | 1,800 | 1,800 | 1,800 | 1,800 | 2,100 | 2,100 | 2,100 | 2,100 | 2,200 |
| Weight (dry) | kg | 25,100 | 20,400 | 16,700 | 7,500 | 7,500 | 6,080 | 4,310 | 2,435 | 1,353 | 1,300 | 932 | 970 |
| | (lb) | (55,220) | (44,880) | (36,740) | (16,500) | (16,500) | (13,400) | (9,500) | (5,365) | (2,979) | (2,867) | (2,050) | (2,140) |
| Length | mm | 4,120 | 4,540 | 3,720 | 3,366 | 3,366 | 2,675 | 2,135 | 1,723 | 1,532 | 1,532 | 1,287 | 1,270 |
| | (in) | (162) | (179) | (147) | (133) | (133) | (105) | (84) | (68) | (60) | (60) | (51) | (50) |
| Width | mm | 1,720 | 1,780 | 1,780 | 1,443 | 1,443 | 1,443 | 1,443 | 1,143 | 968 | 968 | 832 | 812 |
| | (in) | (68) | (70) | (70) | (57) | (57) | (57) | (57) | (45) | (38) | (38) | (33) | (32) |
| Height | mm | 2,741 | 2,741 | 2,631 | 1,980 | 1,980 | 1,839 | 1,839 | 1,319 | 1,375 | 1,375 | 1,287 | 1,160 |
| | (in) | (108) | (108) | (104) | (78) | (78) | (72) | (72) | (52) | (54) | (54) | (51) | (46) |

in 10 countries and a worldwide network of 207 independent dealers in 1,800 locations.

Caterpillar has been a supplier of diesel engine power to the rail industry since the mid-1930s. The company's 3400, 3500 and 3600 Families of engines are well-suited in size, power and performance for locomotive traction. The 3400 Family powered generator sets provide head end power in passenger locomotives and the full range of Caterpillar's small and medium sized engines can be found in permanent way maintenance equipment. Caterpillar also offers several engine models for use in underground, mining, tunnelling and other environmentally sensitive applications.

Advanced engineering features are offered by Caterpillar to meet emission standards worldwide. These include electronic controls, hydraulic unit injectors and other technologies that dramatically reduce engine emissions. Caterpillar reports that exhaust emission levels are well within the emission regulations set by the United States Environmental Protection Agency for non-road and locomotive applications. All Caterpillar diesel locomotive engines meet UIC 623 and ERRI 1997 emission limits.

The 3600 Family of engines is available in speeds of up to 1,000 rpm for main line locomotives. Model 3606 and 3608 engines are being used to repower Class 232-type locomotives operated by several railways including German Rail. These repowering projects utilise existing traction generators.

The 3500 Family of engines is used to power diesel-electric and diesel-hydraulic shunting and main line locomotives. The largest users are in Zimbabwe, Austria, Germany, Canada and the USA. In 2000, the range of power ratings for the fully electronic 3500B was further expanded. These engines continue to offer reduced fuel consumption, reduced emissions and system diagnostics. Operators of locomotives with 3500B engines include German Rail, FEVE (Spain), Romanian National Railways, and Chinese Railways. In 2000, additional units were on order for several European customers.

High-speed versions of the 3500 engine, packaged with a two-bearing traction alternator on an integral welded base, are being offered as an alternative to completely replace old and inefficient equipment. These employ a unique four-point rubber isolated mounting system, enabling them to be installed in many existing locomotive bodyshells. Caterpillar has started shipping packages using the 3500B unit to EMD (General Motors) for a new range of shunting locomotives. VSFT has started assembly of 20 locomotives with a Caterpillar 3516B engine rated at 2,240 kW (3,000 hp).

Low-speed 3500 Series engines offer a practical way to repower old locomotives that were previously powered by Caterpillar 6.25 in bore engines. These engines continue to be installed in locomotives in South America and South Africa.

The 3400 Family engines are used to power diesel-electric and diesel-hydraulic shunting locomotives. They are available with mechanical or electronic fuel systems and ratings up to 783 kW at 2,100 rpm. Currently, these engines are being sold into traction, power generation and maintenance-of-way applications. Recent contracts include 60 3412E engines rated at 746 kW (1,000 hp) for new locomotives for Austrian Federal Railways. 3400 generator set engines provide 50 and 60 Hz head-end power (HEP) in passenger locomotives and generator cars. The 3412 engine is a standard offering from EMD (GM) in their passenger locomotives for North America.

### General specifications

Cylinders: Removable wet-type cylinder liners of hardened cast iron. Alloy cast-iron cylinder heads with water directors and removable injectors. The 3500 and 3600 Family utilises individual cylinder heads for serviceability.
Fuel injection: Caterpillar-designed unit injectors and pump-and-line systems on all direct injection models. Standard arrangements utilise replaceable full-flow fuel filters.
Aspiration: All models utilise turbocharging and aftercooling (intercoolers).
Fuel: No 2 diesel fuel oil (ASTM specification D396).
Lubrication: Full pressure systems including gear-type pumps, replaceable full-flow filters and water-cooled oil coolers.
Cooling systems: Centrifugal-type circulating pumps with thermostatically controlled bypass. All systems are capable of pressurisation and designed to use antifreeze.
Starting: Air or electric.

## CFD

CFD Industrie
9-11 rue Benoît Malon, F-92150 Suresnes, France
Tel: (+33 1) 45 06 44 00   Fax: (+33 1) 47 28 48 84

### Key personnel
See entry in *Locomotives and powered/non-powered passenger vehicles* section.

### Products
Mechanical transmissions for mainline and shunting locomotives; power shift gearboxes (up to 900 hp input power); eight-speed hydromechanical 'Asynchro' transmissions; and locomotive final drives.

## China National Railway Locomotive & Rolling Stock Industry Corporation (LORIC)

10 Fu Xing Road, Beijing 100844, People's Republic of China
Tel: (+86 10) 63 51 16 20
Fax: (+86 10) 63 51 16 14; 63 51 16 00

### Works addresses and key personnel
See entry in *Locomotives and powered/non-powered passenger vehicles* section.

### Products
LORIC currently builds diesel engines, main alternators, traction motors, hydrodynamic transmissions, cardan shafts, turbochargers, intercoolers, injection pumps, fuel injectors, water pumps and oil pumps. The annual output of diesel engines rated at over 1,000 kW is 1,000, while for engines between 410 and 1,000 kW, the figure is 6,000.

The locomotive engine range includes Series 180, 240 and 280 from 660 to 3,860 kW rating. These units have direct injection, are four-stroke and have turbocharging and intercooling.

*LORIC 12V240ZJE diesel engine*
*2001/0099145*

**LORIC diesel engines**

| Type | No of Cylinder | Bore mm | Stroke mm | Swept volume litres | UIC rated power kW | Full-rated speed rpm | BMEP bar | Dimensions mm length | Dimensions mm width | Dimensions mm height | Dry weight kg | Builder |
|---|---|---|---|---|---|---|---|---|---|---|---|---|
| 6L180ZJC | L6 | 180 | 205 | 31.3 | 660 | 1,500 | 16.88 | 2,575 | 1,052.5 | 1,699 | 4,300 | Sifang |
| 12V180ZJC | V12 | 180 | 205 | 62.6 | 1,324 | 1,500 | 16.88 | 2,518 | 1,368 | 2,287 | 6,800 | Sifang |
| 6L240ZJ | L6 | 240 | 275 | 74.64 | 1,100 | 1,000 | 17.70 | 3,885 | 1,747 | 2,568 | 12,700 | Dalian, Ziyang |
| 6L240ZJA | L6 | 240 | 260 | 70.57 | 1,000 | 1,100 | 15.47 | 3,631 | 1,650 | 2,501 | 9,450 | Feb 7th |
| 8L240ZJ | L8 | 240 | 275 | 99.52 | 1,500 | 1,000 | 18.09 | 4,833 | 1,783 | 2,611.8 | 17,039 | Sifang |
| 12V240ZJ6 | V12 | 240 | 275 | 149.29 | 1,620 | 1,000 | 13.03 | 3,718 | 1,780 | 2,857 | 16,800 | Feb 7th |
| 12V240ZJ6A | V12 | 240 | 275 | 149.29 | 2,000 | 1,000 | 16.09 | 3,716 | 1,780 | 2,942 | 16,400 | Feb 7th |
| 12V240ZJ7 | V12 | 240 | 260/273.51 | 144.81 | 2,000 | 1,000 | 16.58 | 4,460 | 1,870 | 2,975 | 15,000 | Feb 7th |
| 12V240ZJD | V12 | 240 | 275 | 149.29 | 2,400 | 1,000 | 19.29 | 4,298 | 1,790 | 2,642 | 16,300 | Dalian |
| 12V240ZJG | V12 | 240 | 275 | 149.29 | 2,206 | 1,000 | 17.73 | 4,298 | 1,790 | 2,642 | 16,300 | Dalian |
| 16V240ZJC | V16 | 240 | 275 | 199.05 | 2,942 | 1,000 | 17.75 | 5,339 | 1,790 | 3,085 | 23,230 | Dalian |
| 16V240ZJD | V16 | 240 | 275 | 199.05 | 3,240 | 1,000 | 19.53 | 5,339 | 1,790 | 3,085 | 22,600 | Dalian |
| 16V240ZJE | V16 | 240 | 275 | 199.05 | 3,680 | 1,000 | 22.20 | 5,339 | 1,790 | 3,085 | 23,600 | Dalian |
| 16V280ZJ | V16 | 280 | 285 | 280.78 | 3,676 | 1,000 | 15.72 | 4,970.5 | 1,725 | 2,895 | 24,500 | Qishuyan |
| 16V280ZJA | V16 | 280 | 285 | 280.78 | 3,860 | 1,000 | 16.51 | 4,970.5 | 1,725 | 2,895 | 24,120 | Qishuyan |

*Cylinder block:* Cast iron for Series 180 and 280; cast welded steel for Series 240. Removable wet-type cylinder liners of hardened cast iron.

*Cylinder heads:* Unit alloy of cast iron cylinder with double bottom decks; water directors.

*Pistons:* Thin-walled nodular iron, steel-crowned combined aluminium-skirted or steel-crowned combined iron-skirted.

*Fuel system:* Unit multi-hole type injector and plunger pumps on all models of the direct injection type. Camshaft-actuated fuel injectors provide metering and timing.

*Aspiration:* All models utilise turbochargers and intercoolers.

*Lubrication:* Large-capacity gear pump provides pressure lubrication to all bearings and oil supply for piston cooling, replaceable full-flow filters and water-cooled oil coolers.

*Cooling system:* Gear-driven centrifugal water pump. Large-volume water passages provide even flow of coolant around cylinder liners, valves and injectors.

1,000 kW diesel generator sets are in service in Indonesia. Locomotives with 12V240ZJ engines are operating in Nigeria and Tanzania.

*Turbocharger by LORIC*
0063621

## Cockerill Mechanical Industries SA (CMI)

Avenue Greiner 1, B-4100 Seraing, Belgium
Tel: (+32 4) 330 24 46  Fax: (+32 4) 330 25 02
e-mail: locos.diesel@cmi.be
Web: http://www.cmi.be

**Products**
Launched in 1965, the present 240CO Series of diesel engines is now in its third generation. Developing 1,170 to 3,120 kW (1,590 to 4,240 hp) at 1,000 rpm, it is in use worldwide for rail traction, marine propulsion and power generation duties.

**UPDATED**

## CTE

CTE Srl Engineering
Corso Concordia 16, I-20129 Milan, Italy
Tel: (+39 02) 79 90 08  Fax: (+39 02) 79 43 18

**Products**
Reduction gears and drives for heavy and light rail vehicles. Wheelsets, electromagnetic track brakes and other electromechanical devices.

## Cummins

Cummins Engine Co, Rail Marketing
Royal Oak Way South, Daventry NN11 5NU, UK
Tel: (+44 1327) 88 63 29  Fax: (+44 1327) 88 61 15
e-mail: david.j.moore@notesbridge.cummins.com
Web: http://www.cummins.com

**Key personnel**
International Rail Director: David Peters
General Manager, Defence and Rail: David Moore

**Head Office**
PO Box 3005, Columbus, Indiana 47202-3005, USA
Tel: (+1 812) 377 33 55  Fax: (+1 812) 377 30 82

**Subsidiary companies**
Fleetguard (filtration systems)
Holset (turbochargers)
Nelson Industries (filtration systems)
Diesel ReCon (remanufactured engines and components)

**Products**
Diesel engines and power packs for locomotives, track equipment, passenger units and auxiliary power.

The engine range includes the QSK19-R, N14-R and M11-R with capacities of 19, 14 and 10.8 litres respectively. All three are horizontal for underfloor installation on railcars and dmus.

The QSK19 is an underfloor diesel engine rated at 410 to 560 kW and is intended for high-speed dmus.

*Aftercooler:* Large-capacity aftercooler results in cooler, denser intake air for more efficient combustion and reduced internal stresses for longer life. Aftercooler is located in the engine coolant system eliminating the need for special plumbing.

*Cooling system:* Gear-driven centrifugal water pump. Large-volume water passages provide even flow of coolant around cylinder liners, valves and injectors. A total of four modulating bypass thermostats regulate coolant temperature. Spin-on corrosion resistors

# MANUFACTURERS/Diesel engines, transmission and fuelling systems

| Engine | | Maximum rating hp | rpm | Continuous traction rating hp | rpm | Displacement litres (in³) | Bore and stroke mm (in) | Number of cylinders | Aspiration | Net weight kg (lb) |
|---|---|---|---|---|---|---|---|---|---|---|
| **Industrial engines** | | | | | | | | | | |
| 4B | 3.9L | 76 | 2,500 | 64 | 2,200 | 3.9 (239) | 102 × 120 (4.02 × 4.72) | 4 | N | 324 (715) |
| 4BT | 3.9L | 100 | 2,500 | | | 3.9 (239) | 102 × 120 (4.02 × 4.72) | 4 | T | 336 (740) |
| 4BTA | 3.9L | 116 | 2,500 | 91 | 2,200 | 3.9 (239) | 102 × 120 (4.02 × 4.72) | 4 | T/A | 348 (767) |
| 6B | 5.9L | 115 | 2,500 | | | 5.8 (359) | 102 × 120 (4.02 × 4.72) | 6 | N | 412 (908) |
| 6BT | 5.9L | 152 | 2,500 | 122 | 2,200 | 5.8 (359) | 102 × 120 (4.02 × 4.72) | 6 | T | 423 (933) |
| 6BTA | 5.9L | 177 | 2,500 | 141 | 2,200 | 5.8 (359) | 102 × 120 (4.02 × 4.72) | 6 | T/A | 439 (967) |
| 6C | 8.3L | 150 | 2,200 | 134 | 2,200 | 8.3 (505) | 114 × 135 (4.49 × 5.32) | 6 | N | 599 (1,320) |
| 6CT | 8.3L | 210 | 2,200 | 173 | 2,200 | 8.3 (505) | 114 × 135 (4.99 × 5.32) | 6 | T | 616 (1,359) |
| 6CTA | 8.3L | 234 | 2,200 | 199 | 2,200 | 8.3 (505) | 114 × 135 (4.49 × 5.32) | 6 | T/A | 636 (1,402) |
| **Locomotive engines** | | | | | | | | | | |
| N-855-L3 | | 235 | 2,100 | 210 | 2,100 | 14 (855) | 140 × 152 (5.5 × 6) | 6 | N | 1,175 (2,590) |
| NTA-855-L4 | | 335 | 2,100 | 285 | 2,100 | 14 (855) | 140 × 152 (5.5 × 6) | 6 | T/A | 1,191 (2,625) |
| NTA-855-L3 | | 400 | 2,100 | 340 | 2,100 | 14 (855) | 140 × 152 (5.5 × 6) | 6 | T/A | 1,247 (2,750) |
| NTA-855-L6 | | 450 | 2,100 | 380 | 2,100 | 14 (855) | 140 × 152 (5.5 × 6) | 6 | T/A | 1,270 (2,800) |
| KTA-19-L | | 600 | 2,100 | 510 | 2,100 | 19 (1,150) | 159 × 159 (6.25 × 6.25) | 6 | T/A | 1,588 (3,500) |
| KTTA-19-L | | 650 | 2,100 | 550 | 2,100 | 19 (1,150) | 159 × 159 (6.25 × 6.25) | 6 | T/A | 1,633 (3,600) |
| VTA-28-L3 | | 725 | 2,100 | 615 | 2,100 | 28 (1,710) | 140 × 152 (5.5 × 6) | 12 | T/A | 2,621 (5,780) |
| VTA-28-L2 | | 800 | 2,100 | 680 | 2,100 | 28 (1,710) | 140 × 152 (5.5 × 6) | 12 | T/A | 2,621 (5,780) |
| KT-38-L | | 900 | 2,100 | 765 | 2,100 | 38 (2,300) | 159 × 159 (6.25 × 6.25) | 12 | T | 3,315 (7,300) |
| KTA-38-L | | 1,200 | 2,100 | 1,020 | 2,100 | 38 (2,300) | 159 × 159 (6.25 × 6.25) | 12 | T/A | 4,200 (9,250) |
| KTA-50-L | | 1,600 | 2,100 | 1,360 | 2,100 | 50 (3,067) | 159 × 159 (6.25 × 6.25) | 16 | T/A | 5,455 (12,000) |
| KTTA-50-L | | 1,800 | 2,100 | 1,530 | 2,100 | 50 (3,067) | 159 × 159 (6.25 × 6.25) | 16 | T/A | 5,500 (12,100) |
| **Railcar engines** | | | | | | | | | | |
| N-855-R2 | | 235 | 2,100 | 210 | 2,100 | 14 (855) | 140 × 152 (5.5 × 6) | 6 | N | 1,185 (2,600) |
| NT-855-R5 | | 335 | 2,100 | 285 | 2,100 | 14 (855) | 140 × 152 (5.5 × 6) | 6 | T | 1,200 (2,700) |
| NTA-855-R1 | | 400 | 2,100 | 340 | 2,100 | 14 (855) | 140 × 152 (5.5 × 6) | 6 | T/A | 1,255 (2,800) |
| NTA-855-R3 | | 430 | 2,100 | 365 | 2,100 | 14 (855) | 140 × 152 (5.5 × 6) | 6 | T/A | 1,335 (2,944) |
| KTA-19-R | | 600 | 2,100 | 510 | 2,100 | 19 (1,150) | 159 × 159 (6.25 × 6.25) | 6 | T/A | 1,770 (3,900) |
| KTA-19-R2 | | 650 | 2,100 | 550 | 2,100 | 19 (1,150) | 159 × 159 (6.25 × 6.25) | 6 | T/A | 1,850 (4,080) |

check rust and corrosion, control acidity and remove impurities.

*Cylinder block:* Alloy cast-iron with removable wet liners. Cross-bolt support to main bearing cap provides extra strength and stability.

*Cylinder heads:* Alloy cast-iron. Each head serves one cylinder. Valve seats are replaceable corrosion-resistant inserts. Valve guides and crosshead guides are replaceable inserts.

*Cylinder liners:* Replaceable wet liners dissipate heat faster than dry liners and are easily replaced without reboring the block.

*Fuel system:* Cummins exclusive low-pressure PT system with wear compensating pump and integral dual-flyball governor. Camshaft-actuated fuel injectors give accurate metering and timing. Spin-on fuel filters.

*Lubrication:* Large-capacity gear pump provides pressure lubrication to all bearings and oil supply for piston cooling. All pressure lines are internal drilled passages in block and heads. Oil cooler, full flow filters and bypass filters maintain oil condition and maximise oil and engine life.

*Turbocharger:* Two AiResearch exhaust gas-driven turbochargers mounted at top of engine. Turbocharging provides more power, improved fuel economy, altitude compensation and lower smoke and noise levels.

### Developments
Electronic controllers have been introduced to meet emissions legislation and to improve performance.

## Dalian

Dalian Locomotive & Rolling Stock Works
51 Zhong Chang Street, Dalian, Liaoning, People's Republic of China
Tel: (+86 411) 460 20 43   Fax: (+86 411) 460 64 47

### Key personnel
See entry in *Locomotives and powered/non-powered passenger vehicles* section.

### Products
Diesel engines and diesel generating sets. The 240ZJ series of diesel engines features a cast welded engine block, an alloy modular cast-iron crankshaft, parallel connecting rods, wet cylinder liners, steel-crowned and aluminium-ringed pistons (or steel crowned, iron-ringed pistons), individual injection pumps, closed-type injection equipment, gas turbochargers and a constant speed and constant power hydraulic governor.

This range of engines can be equipped with various kinds of governors, fuel injectors, turbochargers and generators according to the number of cylinders and cylinder arrangement to provide a range of power outputs to meet various applications.

The 16V240ZJC model is a development of the 16V240ZJB which has been in production for many years. The power rating of the new engine has been increased by improvements in the design and construction of the crankshaft, connecting rods and cylinder liners.

The 16V240ZJD diesel engine has been developed by co-operation in technology with Ricardo Consulting Engineers, UK. Many of the main components, such as the crankshaft and cylinder head, have been improved. New parts including ABB VTC 254-13 turbochargers, Bryce FCVAB fuel injection pumps, NTDLB injectors and NOVA Swiss high pressure pipes, Glacier main journal and connecting rod bearing shells and a Woodward PGEV governor have been introduced.

The 16V240ZJE diesel engine, being improved, is a new generation based on 240ZJD in co-operation with Ricardo Consulting Engineers. It has maximum power rating of 3,300 kW and is designed for heavy haulage work.

### Developments
The new high power 280ZJ series diesel engines are under the course of development in co-operation with another company.

## David Brown Engineering

David Brown Engineering Ltd
Park Road, Huddersfield HD4 5DD, UK
Tel: (+44 1484) 46 55 00   Fax: (+44 1484) 46 55 86
e-mail: sales@davidbrown.com

**Key personnel**
Managing Director: C Reed
Sales and Marketing Director and Project Manager:
   N Crossley

**Subsidiaries**
Ganz-David Brown Transmissions Kft, Hungary
Hygate Transmissions, UK

**Background**
Part of Textron Power Transmission.

**Products**
Complete design, consultancy and manufacture of all types of gears and gearbox assemblies for railway applications.
  Spiral and hypoid bevel, spur and helical gears for spares to complete systems for light rail, mainline locomotives and multiple-units. The company also overhauls, designs new, or redesigns and upgrades existing gearboxes to meet customer requirements.

**Contracts**
Main line gearbox and coupling assemblies for China; LRV Eurotram gearboxes for Strasbourg phase 2 and for Milan; gearbox assemblies for Seoul Metro and spare gear sets for UK, Sweden, Pakistan, Holland and Korea.

*UPDATED*

---

## Detroit Diesel

Detroit Diesel Corporation
13400 Outer Drive West, Detroit, Michigan 48239-4001, USA
Tel: (+1 313) 592 50 00   Fax: (+1 313) 592 75 80
Web: http://www.detroitdiesel.com

**Key personnel**
Chief Executive Officer and Chairman:
   Roger S Penske
President and Chief Operating Officer: Ludvik F Koci
Vice-President, International: Paul A Moreton
Vice-President, Construction and Industrial Sales:
   Jeffrey Sylvester

**Products**
Diesel and alternative fuel engines from 5 to 10,000 hp. Generator sets.

*UPDATED*

---

## EMG

Elektro-Mechanik GmbH
Industriestrasse 1, D-57482 Wenden, Germany
Tel: (+49 276) 261 20   Fax: (+49 276) 261 23 31

**Key personnel**
Sales Director: E Greiner

**Products**
Cardan shaft axledrives for diesel railcars.

---

## Eminox Ltd

North Warren Road, Gainsborough DN21 2TU, UK
Tel: (+44 1427) 81 00 88   Fax: (+44 1427) 81 00 61
e-mail: jnperry@eminox.com
Web: http://www.eminox.com

**Key personnel**
Sales Manager, Rail: John Perry
Commercial Manager: Gerald Richards

**Products**
Stainless steel exhaust systems for use on diesel multiple-units and railcars, including exhaust after-treatment; catalyst and particulate filters.

*VERIFIED*

---

**Behr Industry – the right partner for demanding Jobs**

*It's working*

Behr Industry is the number one manufacturer of cooling units for locomotives and trainsets in Europe with more than 50 years of accumulated experience. Complete air conditioning systems for trains and compact air conditioning units for drivers cabs are also part of Behr Industry's product range.

As a part of the Behr company, whose specific core competences are cooling and air conditioning systems, Behr Industry develops specific solutions for cooling and air conditioning of railway vehicles, buses, construction vehicles, aircrafts, military vehicles and high range diesel engines.

Manufacturers and Operators of trains and locomotives are looking for complete system solutions, Behr Industry is the right partner for this demanding job.

Behr Industrietechnik GmbH & Co.
Heilbronner Straße 380, D-70469 Stuttgart
Tel.: +49 (0) 7 11/8 96-0, Fax +49 (0) 7 11/81 81 95
http://www.behrgroup.com

**BEHR INDUSTRY**

# MANUFACTURERS/Diesel engines, transmission and fuelling systems

## Faur

Basarabia Boulevard 256, Bucharest 3, R-73249, Romania
Tel: (+40 1) 255 15 13  Fax: (+40 1) 255 00 71

**Key personnel**
See entry in *Locomotives and powered/non-powered passenger vehicles* section.

**Products**
Cardan shafts for diesel-hydraulic locomotives and railcars. The basic range is for a torque range of 1,400 to 12,000 daNm with external flange diameters of 225 to 435 mm. Also manufactured under licence are Maybach-Benz and MTU diesel engines in the 130 to 930 kW range with ratings of 1,000 to 2,300 rpm and in 6-, 8- and 12-cylinder configurations. Models produced include: Faur 331 (6V331, 8V331 and 12V331); Faur 396 (6V396, 8V396 and 12V396); MB 836; MB 820; and MBM 836.

Other products include generator sets (130 to 800 kVA, 50 Hz, 3 × 400/231 V) and spare parts for diesel engines, including: crankshafts, pistons, cylinder jackets, connecting rods, cylinder heads and crankcases) either to Faur specifications or to customer requirements.

**VERIFIED**

## Fiat

Fiat Ferroviaria SpA
Piazza Galateri 4, I-12038 Savigliano (CN), Italy
Tel: (+39 0172) 71 81 11  Fax: (+39 0172) 71 83 06
e-mail: public.relation@fiatferroviaria.it

**Key personnel**
See entry in *Locomotives and powered/non-powered passenger vehicles* section.

**Principal subsidiary companies**
Elettromeccanica Parizzi
FiatSig Schienenfahrzeuge AG

**Corporate development**
In June 2000, Alstom Transport (qv) acquired a 51 per cent shareholding in Fiat Ferroviaria.

**Products**
Diesel engines for rail applications derived directly from Iveco large-volume power plants for road trucks.

Design and manufacture of components and transmission for rail vehicles, in particular diesel railcar transmissions, output ratings 147 to 205 kW (200 to 280 hp), both hydromechanical (hydraulic coupling and five-speed gearbox) and hydraulic (torque converter); recently, the mechanical version has been improved by introducing a microprocessor device for automatic control of transmission. Also drives for locomotives, metro car tractive units and tramcars in monomotor and twin-motor versions with traction motors mounted longitudinally or transversally. Drives for high-speed (up to 300 km/h) motor bogies are now in service after five years of development and trials.

## Freudenberg Schwab GmbH

Freudenberg Simrit KG
Höhnerweg 2-4, D-69465 Weinheim, Germany
Tel: (+49 1805) 74 67 48
e-mail: simrit.service@freudenberg.de
Web: http://www.simrit.de

**Key personnel**
See *Bogies and suspension, wheels and axles, bearings* section.

**Products**
Vibration control: rubber/metal elastic elements, standard as well as specially designed. Range includes elastic mountings for traction equipment and components for primary and secondary suspension, resilient couplings linking motor, gearbox and axle.

**UPDATED**

## Ganz-David Brown

Ganz-David Brown Transmissions Kft
Orczy út 46-48, H-1089 Budapest, Hungary
Tel: (+36 1) 210 11 50  Fax: (+36 1) 334 03 64
e-mail: gdb@mail.datanet.hu
Web: http://www.gdb.hu

**Key personnel**
General Manager: József Fáy
Marketing and Technical Manager: István Lörincz
Chief Engineer: Károly Fóti

Production Manager: Sándor Szluk
Engineering Manager: Laszló Meszaros

**Products**
Hydrodynamic and hydromechanical power transmissions for diesel railcars and locomotives. Axledrive units with helical and spiral bevel gears for railcars, locomotives and light rail vehicles. Wholly suspended axledrive units for monomotor bogies for metro trainsets. Helical gear pairs for high-speed locomotives and railcars, spiral bevel gear pairs for locomotives, railcars and light rail vehicles; drives for low-floor LRVs.

**Contracts**
Recent contracts include: 160 complete powered wheelsets for railbuses, 20 hydrodynamical power transmissions for dmus and 800 sets of traction gears for 'Trainitalia'; 113 hydrodynamic gearboxes have been delivered to CIS railways for modernisation of dmus.

**UPDATED**

## GE

General Electric Transportation Systems
2910 East Lake Road, Erie, Pennsylvania 16531, USA
Tel: (+1 814) 875 59 11  Fax: (+1 814) 875 64 87

**Key personnel**
See entry in *Locomotives and powered/non-powered passenger vehicles* section.

**Products**
Diesel engines and complete electric transmissions.

*Series HDL (16-cylinder, Vee) engine*
Type: four-stroke cycle, turbocharged and after-cooled (intercooled).
Cylinders: Bore 250 mm (9.84 in), Stroke 320 mm (12.60 in).
Fuel Injection: Individual injection and fuel pumps with EFI control.
Turbocharger: Two, single stage.
Lubrication and cooling: Forced full flow filtered oil to all bearings and pistons, gear-type engine-driven pump.

*Series FDL (8-, 12- and 16-cylinder Vee) engines*
Type: four-stroke cycle, turbocharged and after-cooled (intercooled).

**Current engine specifications**

| Model | 7FDL8 | 7FDL12 | 7FDL16 | 7HDL16 |
|---|---|---|---|---|
| No of cylinders | 8 | 12 | 16 | 16 |
| Output (UIC) standard | 2,000 | 3,300 | 4,100 | 6,250 |
| Stroke cycle | 4 | 4 | 4 | 4 |
| Cylinder arrangement | 45° Vee | 45° Vee | 45° Vee | 45° Vee |
| Bore | 228.6 mm (9 in) | 228.6 mm (9 in) | 228.6 mm (9 in) | 250 mm (9.84 in) |
| Stroke | 266.7 mm (10½ in) | 266.7 mm (10½ in) | 266.7 mm (10½ in) | 320 mm (12.60 in) |
| Compression ratio | 12.7:1 | 12.7:1 | 12.7:1 | 15.2:1 |
| Idle speed | 385 rpm | 385 rpm | 385 rpm | 350 rpm |
| Full-rated speed | 1,050 rpm | 1,050 rpm | 1,050 rpm | 1,050 rpm |
| Firing order | 1R-1L-2R-2L-4R-4L-3R-3L | 1R-1L-5R-5L-3R-3L-6R-6L-2R-2L-4R-4L | 1R-1L-3R-3L-7R-7L-4R-4L-8R-8L-6R-6L-2R-2L-5R-5L | 1R-1L-3R-3L-7R-7L-5R-5L-8R-8L-6R-6L-2R-2L-4R-4L |
| Turbocharger | One | One | One | Two |
| Engine dimensions | | | | |
| Height (excluding stack) | 2,191 mm (86¼ in) | 2,289 mm (90⅛ in)* | 2,289 mm (90⅛ in) | 2,611 mm (102.80 in) |
| Length (overall) | 3,264 mm (128½ in) | 4,051 mm (159½ in) | 4,902 mm (193 in) | 4,984 mm (196.24) |
| Width (overall) | 1,734 mm (68¼ in) | 1,740 mm (68⅜ in) | 1,740 mm (68⅜ in) | 1,700 mm (66.93 in) |
| Weight (dry) | 12,200 kg (27,000 lb) | 15,900 kg (35,000 lb) | 19,700 kg (43,500 lb) | 23,800 kg (52,500 lb) |

Cylinders: Bore 229 mm (9 in), Stroke 267 mm (10-1/2 in)
Swept volume, 668 cu in per cylinder. Individual unitised cast cylinder with renewable liner and head.
Fuel injection: Individual injectors and fuel pumps. Electronic fuel injection (EFI) available.
Turbocharger: One, single stage, exhaust-driven (no gear drive to crankshaft).

Lubrication: Forced, full-flow, filtered oil to all bearings and pistons, gear-type engine-driven pump.
Cooling system: Forced circulation water cooling of cylinders, turbocharger and intercoolers. The water passages are external of the crankcase and mainframe.

## General Motors Corporation

Electro-Motive Division
9301 West 55th Street, LaGrange, Illinois 60525, USA
Tel: (+1 708) 387 60 00

**Key personnel**
See entry in *Locomotives and powered passenger/non-powered vehicles* section.

**Products**
Electro-Motive Division first developed the Model 567 diesel engine in 1938 when it began locomotive manufacture at LaGrange, Illinois, USA.

To provide increased hp and greater efficiency, the Model 645 engine was introduced in mid-1965. The major change in the Model 645 over the 567 was the increase in cylinder liner bore from 216 mm (8½ in) to 230 mm (9⅛ in), the stroke remaining at 254 mm (10 in).

The turbocharged 645E3B engine introduced in 1979 and the turbocharged 645F3 engine introduced in 1981 were a result of the search for increased product reliability, performance and fuel economy. With increased hp and fuel economy these engines could haul more tonnage at the same speed or the same tonnage at a higher speed than their predecessors.

The 710G series of engines is an evolutionary development of GM/EMD's turbocharged, uniflow-scavenged, two-stroke cycle engine. The 16-cylinder 710G3B is rated at 4,250 hp at 900 rpm for locomotive applications and has a displacement of 710 in$^3$ per cylinder. This series is the result of a succession of improvements to the engine. From 1989 to 1991, for example, the fuel efficiency of the 710G was increased by 1.5 per cent. Greater displacement and an advanced turbocharger give the 710G the capacity for significant increases in hp.

Full load fuel consumption of the model 710G3B engine is down 11.5 per cent from the 1980 model and 4.9 per cent from the 1983 model in the 645 range. Among the ways fuel efficiency has been increased is improved turbocharger aftercoolers and fuel injectors, and low-restriction liner intake ports.

As compared to the 645 series engines, the 710 features a longer stroke and added displacement which led to these structural improvements in the engine: Model G crankcase; larger diameter plunger injectors; larger diameter crankshaft; new camshaft; longer cylinder liner; and longer piston and rod assembly. The 710G design also increased the overall dimensions: the new engine is 1⅝ in higher and 4⅝ in longer.

### Developments

The company's newest innovation, Functionally Integrated Railroad Electronics (FIRE ®) is an advanced locomotive management system.

| Model | | 16-645FB | 16-710G |
|---|---|---|---|
| Bore | in | 9.06 | 9.06 |
| Stroke | in | 10 | 11 |
| Displacement | in$^3$ | 645 | 710 |
| Cylinder spacing | in | 16⅝ | 16⅝ |
| Bank angle | | 45 | 45 |
| Compression ratio | | 16.0:1 | 16.0:1 |
| Engine speed | rpm | 950 | 900 |
| bhp | | 3,800 | 4,250 |

## Giro

Giro Engineering Ltd
Talisman, Duncan Road, Park Gate, Southampton SO31 7GA, UK
Tel: (+44 1489) 88 52 88   Fax: (+44 1489) 88 51 99
e-mail: giro@giroeng.com

### Key personnel
Managing Director: J P Williams
Commercial Director: C R Galley

### Products
Design and manufacture of diesel engine sheathed and unsheathed fuel injection pipes.

Unsheathed fuel injection pipes were supplied to Dalian Locomotive Works in 1997; unsheathed Alco fuel injection pipes were supplied to Indian Railways in 1997 and sheathed Mirrlees fuel injection pipes were sent to Mirrlees for railway applications in May 1997.

**UPDATED**

## GMD

Grandes Motores Diesel SA
Av Juan Bautista Alberdi 1001, 1678 Caseros, Buenos Aires, Argentina
Tel: (+54 1) 750 42 09; 90 19; 22 51
Fax: (+54 1) 750 14 76

### Works
Ruta 9, Km 694, 5123 Ferreyra, Córdoba, Argentina
Tel: (+54 51) 97 22 12; 21 06   Fax: (+54 51) 97 23 09

### Key personnel
President: Guillermo Scarsoglio
Vice-President and General Manager: Ing Enzo N Filipelli
Commercial Manager: Ing Antonio Maltana

### Group companies
Materfer SA
Centro de Actividades Termomécanicas (CAT) SA

### Products
GMD manufactures the Alco 251 engine under General Electric licence.

Together with CAT, the company manufactures spares for Fiat GMT engines.

## Gmeinder

Gmeinder Lokomotiven- und Maschinenfabrik GmbH
PO Box 1355, D-74803 Mosbach, Baden, Germany
Tel: (+49 6261) 80 60   Fax: (+49 6261) 80 61 90
e-mail: info@gmeinder.de
Web: http://www.gmeinder.de

### Key personnel
See entry in *Locomotives and powered/non-powered passenger vehicles* section.

### Products
Axle drives for lightweight rail vehicles, dmus and emus, tilting trainsets; axle drives for locomotives with cardan shaft drive; special vehicles such as cranes. Vehicles equipped include the RegioShuttle lighweight dmu, DB Class VT 628 dmu and VT 611/612 tilting dmus.

## Grandi Motori Trieste

Cantieri Navali Italiani SpA
Diesel Engines Division, Bagnoli della Rosandra 334, I-34018 Trieste, Italy
Tel: (+39 040) 319 31 11   Fax: (+39 040) 382 73 71

### Key personnel
Managing Director: G R Lami
Technical Director: F Bartoli

### Products
Diesel engines for railway traction, marine and industrial applications. Hydraulic and mechanical transmissions for locomotives and railcars. Axledrives for electric and diesel-powered vehicles. For rail traction, the Fincantieri locomotive engine range includes Series A210 and BL230 from 620 to 4,400 kW, and the 1700 Series from 225 to 2,000 kW.

In addition, Sulzer slow-speed engines are produced for the Italian market and a cross-licensing agreement exists with Sulzer for medium-speed engines of the A 32 and ZA 40 S types.

## Haynes

Haynes Corporation
3581 Mercantile Avenue, Naples, Florida 34104, USA
Tel: (+1 941) 436 15 78   Fax: (+1 941 ) 643 53 11
Web: http://www.haynesco.com

### Key personnel
Vice-President Sales: Greg L Schultz
Technical Sales Manager: Kirk D Leutz

### Corporate development
Haynes Corporation has acquired the EMD injector remanufacturing product line from DTC (Diesel Technologies Corporation).

### Products
Fuel injection systems and component systems for Alco, EMD and GE locomotives; factory rebuild unit exchange programme; just-in-time delivery programmes.

## Hidromecanica

Hidromecanica SA
78, 15 Noiembrie Boulevard, R-2200 Brasov, Romania
Tel: (+40 68) 33 32 34   Fax: (+40 68) 31 04 61; 33 14 12
e-mail: hidro@rdsbv.ro
Web: http//www.deltanet.rdsbv.ro

### Key personnel
General Director: Petre Sereteanu
Production Manager: Lucian Florea
Technical Manager: Liviu Nicoara
Commercial Manager: Romulus Verzea
Head of Marketing and Foreign Relations: Viorel Pavel
Chief of Sales Department: Constantin Belu

### Products
Turbochargers: VTR series turbochargers (257 to 1,193 kW) and TS series (883 to 2,942 kW) for railway applications.

Torque converters and power shift transmissions (37 to 736 kW) for shunting locomotives and other applications.

Hydraulic transmissions and reducers for rail traction (100 to 1,103 kW).

Customers include railway operators in Belgium, Canada, Cuba, Egypt, Hungary, Pakistan and Poland.

**UPDATED**

# 540 MANUFACTURERS/Diesel engines, transmission and fuelling systems

## Hitachi Ltd

Overseas Marketing Department
Transportation Systems Sales Division
6 Kanda Surugadai 4-chome, Chiyoda-ku, Tokyo 101-8010, Japan
Tel: (+81 3) 52 95 55 40  Fax: (+81 3) 32 58 52 30

**Key personnel**
See entry in *Locomotives and powered/non-powered passenger vehicles* section.

**Products**
Complete control equipment, electric transmissions and hydraulic transmissions.

*UPDATED*

## Honeywell Serck

Warwick Road, Birmingham B11 2QY, UK
Tel: (+44 121) 766 66 66  Fax: (+44 121) 766 60 14
e-mail: sind@serckht.co.uk

**Key personnel**
Chief Executive: Ian Dugan
Marketing and Sales Manager: John Brookes
Technical Sales Manager: Paul Egerton

**Corporate background**
Honeywell Serck is part of Honeywell Thermal Systems and a subsidiary of the Honeywell Corporation.

**Products**
Integrated cooling modules for cooling oil, water and air systems for diesel locomotives.
Recent contracts include: redesign of the engine cooling group for South West Trains' Class 159 dmus (UK); charge air cooling equipment for Countrylink (Australia) XPT power cars re-engined with MAN B&W Paxman 12VP185 engines; radiator elements for Sri Lanka Railway Class M7 locomotives and transmission oil coolers for the same operator's Hunslet shunting locomotives.

## Hygate Transmissions Ltd

Part of the David Brown Group (a Textron company)
Lower Bristol Road, Bath BA2 3EB, UK
Tel: (+44 1225) 33 40 00  Fax: (+44 1225) 31 85 82
e-mail: sales.hygate@davidbrown.com
Web: http://www.davidbrown.com/products/rail

**Key personnel**
Managing Director: C Reed
Sales and Marketing Director: N Crossley
Technical Sales Manager: N Antrobus

**Products**
Design and manufacture of gearbox assemblies and loose gears for main line, urban railway, mass transit systems and LRVs. Single and double reduction parallel shaft gearboxes and spiral bevel gearboxes. Double engagement gear couplings for rail applications. Redesign and upgrading of existing transmissions. Consultancy, maintenance, overhaul and repair services.

**Contracts**
Recent contracts include: locomotive gear sets for Belgium and Syria; gearboxes for Øresund Link and regional emus in Sweden and emus for Gatwick Express, ScotRail and SouthWest Trains in the UK; metro car gearboxes for Seoul Lines 6 and 7 and Pusan Line 2 in Korea; and gearboxes for trains in Milan and Rome.

*VERIFIED*

*Hygate double-reduction gearbox for Eurotram LRV stub axle mounted and carrying rail wheel and disc brake assembly as fitted for Strasbourg Phase 2*

## Jenbacher

Jenbacher Energiesysteme AG
Achenseestrasse 1-3, A-6200 Jenbach, Austria
Tel: (+43 5244) 60 00  Fax: (+43 5244) 632 55
Web: http://www.jenbacher.com

**Key personnel**
See entry in *Locomotives and powered/non-powered passenger vehicles* section.

**Products**
Diesel engines for rail vehicles.

*VERIFIED*

## JMA Railroad Supply Company

361 South Main Place, Carol Stream Illinois 60188, USA
Tel: (+1 630) 653 92 24  Fax: (+1 630) 653 90 40
e-mail: mkauck@jmarail.com (Marketing Enquiries)
e-mail: info@jmarail.com (Sales/General Info)
Web: http://www.jmarail.com

**Key personnel**
President: Jack Matthews
Vice-President, Sales: Kevin Masterson
Director of Short Line Sales: Kevin Bahnline
Chief Financial Officer: Bob Herigodti
Marketing Co-ordinator: Melissa Kauck

**Background**
Joint owners of JMA Railroad Supply Company are: JMA Rail Products; JMA Transit; New Vision Manufacturing and EngineAir Inc.

**Products**
Supply of locomotive air compressors and component parts, compressors, drain valves, cast-iron brake shoes, fuel injectors, heat exchangers, filters, air brake equipment, wheelset overhaul and a wide range of other components and refurbishing services for EMD and GE locomotives.

**Contracts**
Contracts with rail companies in the USA include starter motors for CSX transportation, governors for Illinois Central, electropneumatic operating valves, drain valves, lights and blowers for Union Pacific Railroad, air compressors for Metra and air dryers for Wisconsin Central. Blowers, fuel injectors and governors for CP Rail, Canada, Burlington Northern and Santa Fe, USA; fuel injectors for Norfolk Southern, USA.

*UPDATED*

## Kim Hotstart

Kim Hotstart Mfg Co
East 5723 Alki, Spokane, Washington 99212, USA
Tel: (+1 509) 534 61 71  Fax: (+1 509) 534 42 16

e-mail: sales@kimhotstart.com
Web: http://www.kimhotstart.com

**Key personnel**
Vice-President and General Manager: Rick Robinson
Director, Sales and Marketing: Terry Judge
Manager, Industrial Sales, Locomotive Division: Jason Barnes
International Sales Manager: Trond Liaboe

Diesel engines, transmission and fuelling systems/**MANUFACTURERS**   541

## Products

Winter layover heating systems for diesel and petrol engines. Available in 240 and 480 V AC three phase; special voltages on request. Heating systems designed to heat coolant only or combination of coolant and oil. Models range from 11 to 36 kW plus the patented Diesel Driven Heating System (DDHS) which includes a two-cylinder Lister-Petter water-cooled diesel engine with a water-circulation pump, plus a belt-driven 72 V DC alternator, the system operates independently of other locomotive systems.

Heavy-duty trickle chargers for locomotive applications. Available from 12 to 96 V DC.

## Contracts

Contracts include supply of systems to GE Transportation Systems in 2001, NJT (New Jersey Transit) 2001, Montana Rail Link 2001, Motive Power Inc and Turner Rail Services 2001.

***UPDATED***

## Kolomna

Kolomna Plant Joint Stock Company
Partizan Street, 140408 Kolomna, Moscow Region, Russian Federation
Tel: (+7 095) 381 52   Fax: (+7 095) 203 47 00

### Key personnel

General Director: V N Vlasov
Chief Engineer: V A Shelemet'yev
Marketing Director: E N Gunchenko

### Products

D49 series of diesel locomotive engines. The D49 series comprises four-stroke, turbocharged engines with four or six cylinders arranged in-line or eight, 12, 16 and 20 cylinders in Vee-versions.

D49 diesel engines and generating sets are in service in Europe and countries in Southeast Asia, Africa, South America as well as northern regions of Russia. Recent contracts include the supply of diesel engines to Germany, Latvia, Lithuania and Estonia.

*D49 diesel locomotive four-stroke turbocharged engines*
Bore: 260 mm
Stroke: 260 mm
Speed: min 750-1,000 rpm
Mean effective pressure: MPa 1.1-1.96
Mean piston speed: 6.8-8.6 m/s
Specific fuel consumption: g/kW/h 190 +5%
Four- and six-cylinder versions arranged in line and the 8, 12, 16 and 20 cylinder versions in V-configuration.

| Engine type | Output | | | Dimensions mm | | | Weight kg | Type of locomotive |
|---|---|---|---|---|---|---|---|---|
| | KW | hp | Length | | Width | Height | | Diesel engine |
| 4 LD49 | 300-750 | 408-1,020 | 3,090 | | 1,580 | 2,300 | 8,000 | - |
| 6 LD49 | 470-1,100 | 637-1,500 | 3,930 | | 1,580 | 2,310 | 11,000 | Shunting |
| 8 VD49 | 500-1,760 | 680-2,390 | 3,720 | | 1,665 | 2,330 | 10,070 | TGM 6V, TGM 8 |
| 12 VD49 | 1,100-2,650 | 1,500-3,600 | 3,920 | | 1,665 | 3,030 | 14,000 | 2TE 116, TEM 7A |
| 16 VD49 | 1,470-3,700 | 2,000-5,030 | 4,900 | | 1,655 | 3,070 | 17,460 | 2TE 116, 2TE 121, TEP 70 |
| 20 VD49 | 3,700-5,000 | 5,030-6,800 | 6,270 | | 1,665 | 3,190 | 20,900 | TE 136, TEP 80 |

Output, specific fuel consumption and weight values are for ISO standard reference conditions.

***UPDATED***

## Komatsu

Komatsu Diesel Co Ltd
Shuwa Tameike Bldg, 2-4-2 Nagatacho, Chiyoda-ku, Tokyo 100-0014, Japan
Tel: (+81 3) 35 03 19 01   Fax: (+81 3) 35 03 18 97
e-mail: yasuo_okamoto@kdl.komatsu.co.jp
Web: http://www.komatsu.com/kdl

### Works

400 Yokokura Shinden, Oyama-shi, Togichi 323-8558

### Key personnel

Director, Sales Development & Application Department: Y Okamoto

### Products

Diesel engines, torque converters, transmissions, hydraulic pumps, hydraulic motors, hydraulic control valves.

The engine range features light weight and compactness, making it suitable for use in tilting rolling stock, good cold-start capability, easy maintenance, low fuel consumption (through measures including improved

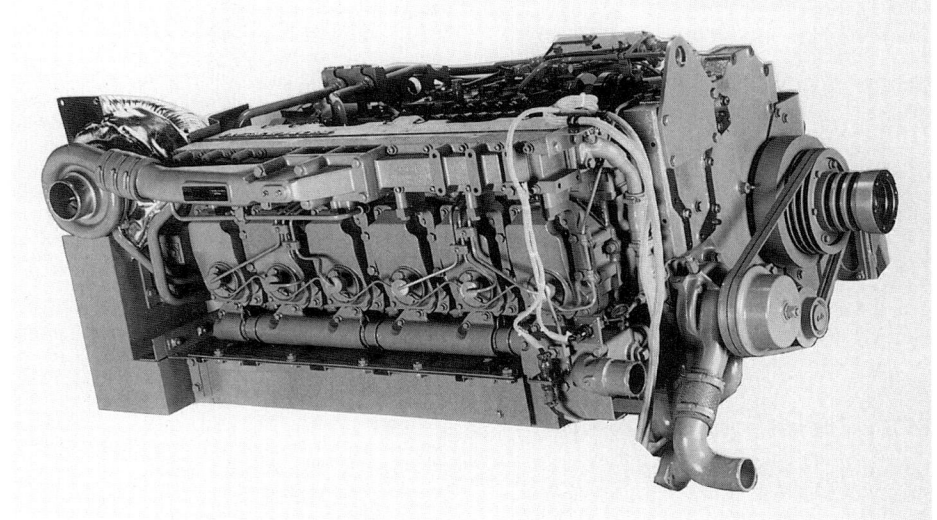

*Komatsu SA6D125-HD engine*   0063623

### Komatsu railcar engines

| Type | Cyl. No | Aspiration | Bore mm | Stroke mm | Displacement cc | Maximum rating kW (hp) | rpm | Continuous rating kW (hp) | per/min | Length mm | Width mm | Height mm | Weight kg |
|---|---|---|---|---|---|---|---|---|---|---|---|---|---|
| S6D125-H | Horizontal | 6 | T | 125 | 150 | 11,040 | 221 (296) | 2,200 | 199 (266) | 2,200 | 1,376 | 1,179 | 770 | 990 |
| SA6D125-H | Horizontal | 6 | T/A | 125 | 150 | 11,040 | 294 (395) | 2,200 | 265 (355) | 2,200 | 1,376 | 1,179 | 770 | 1,150 |
| SA6D125-HD | Horizontal | 6 | T/A* | 125 | 150 | 11,040 | 342 (459) | 2,100 | 309 (414) | 2,100 | 1,680 | 1,215 | 792 | 1,250 |
| SA6D140-H | Horizontal | 6 | T/A | 140 | 165 | 15,240 | 431 (577) | 2,000 | 386 (518) | 2,000 | 1,624 | 1,257 | 757 | 1,700 |
| SA6D140-HD | Horizontal | 6 | T/A* | 140 | 165 | 15,240 | 475 (636) | 2,000 | 427 (572) | 2,000 | 1,484 | 1,329 | 757 | 1,670 |

Note: * Dual Circuit Aftercooler

### Torque converter specifications

| Model | Max Input Power kW (hp) | rpm | Element | Torque Converter Stage | Phase | Weight kg | Overall Dimension Length mm | Width mm | Height mm | Type | Retarder (Option) Absorbed Power kW (hp) | per/min |
|---|---|---|---|---|---|---|---|---|---|---|---|---|
| KTF3335A | 257 (345) | 2,200 | 3 | 1 | 2 | 800 | 1,008 | 777 | 710 | Hydraulic | 147 (203) | 2,000 |
| KTF3345A | 331 (444) | 2,000 | 3 | 1 | 2 | 980 | 1,120 | 883 | 757 | Hydraulic | 147 (203) | 2,000 |

### Komatsu locomotive engines

| Type | Cyl. No | Aspiration | Bore mm | Stroke mm | Displacement cc | Maximum rating kW (hp) | rpm | Continuous rating kW (hp) | per/min | Length mm | Width mm | Height mm | Weight kg |
|---|---|---|---|---|---|---|---|---|---|---|---|---|---|
| S6D125 | Vertical | 6 | T | 125 | 150 | 11,040 | 221 (296) | 2,200 | 188 (252) | 2,200 | 1,350 | 699 | 1,134 | 880 |
| SA6D125 | Vertical | 6 | T/A | 125 | 150 | 11,040 | 276 (370) | 2,200 | 236 (316) | 2,200 | 1,350 | 699 | 1,135 | 900 |
| SA6D140 | Vertical | 6 | T/A | 140 | 165 | 15,240 | 405 (542) | 2,100 | 346 (464) | 2,100 | 1,515 | 780 | 1,210 | 1,230 |
| SA6D170 | Vertical | 6 | T/A | 170 | 170 | 23,150 | 552 (740) | 2,000 | 471 (632) | 2,000 | 1,938 | 998 | 1,685 | 2,440 |
| SA12V170 | Vee | 12 | T/A | 170 | 170 | 46,340 | 1,104 (1,480) | 2,100 | 942 (1,262) | 2,100 | 2,220 | 1,203 | 1,752 | 4,800 |
| SDA12V170 | Vee | 12 | T/A* | 170 | 170 | 46,340 | 1,545 (2,071) | 1,800 | 1,324 (1,775) | 1,800 | 2,220 | 1,203 | 1,752 | 4,900 |
| SA16V170 | Vee | 16 | T/A | 170 | 170 | 61,740 | 1,472 (1,972) | 2,100 | 1,251 (1,677) | 2,100 | 2,783 | 1,410 | 1,698 | 6,336 |

Note: * Dual Circuit Aftercooler

***VERIFIED***

542  MANUFACTURERS/Diesel engines, transmission and fuelling systems

intake port configuration and high pressure injection system) and multifunction electronic governor.

The K-ATOMiCS (Komatsu Advanced Transmission with Optimum Modulation Control System) automatic transmission system eliminates shift shock and prevents torque cut-off. A hydraulic retarder and a wheel spin control device can be installed. Maintenance costs are reduced by changing the durable rubber couplings by the engine flywheel.

Komatsu stared manufacturing diesel engines for railcar applications about 10 years ago and has gained a major share of the Japanese market. Recently the company has developed a new high-performance engine for locomotive use, the SDA12V170. Three units were produced in late 1999 for a new locomotive design developed for JR Freight, the DF200, or 'Eco-Power Red Bear', as it is popularly known.

The SDA12V170 develops 1,325 kW at 1,800 rpm. It is equipped with a dual-circuit aftercooler system which enhances combustion efficiency and power output while offering reduced fuel consumption and increased endurance through the use of Komatsu original cast pistons. Other features of the engine in the DF200 application include a starter system that controls current for both vehicle and engine control and engine condition-monitoring.

*Komatsu SA12V170 engine*    2001/0099146

*Komatsu KTF3335A torque converter*    0023832

## L & M Radiator

L & M Radiator, Inc
1414 East 37th Street, Hibbing, Minnesota 55746, USA
Tel: (+1 218) 263 89 93

**Key personnel**
President: Alex Chisholm
Vice-President: Richard Braun

**Products**
Radiators and radiator cores.

## MAN Nutzfahrzeuge Aktiengesellschaft

Dachauer Strasse 667, D-80995 Munich, Germany
Tel: (+49 89) 15 80 70 41  Fax: (+49 89) 15 80 31 70
Web: http://www.man-nutzfahrzeuge.de

**Works**
Engines Business Unit, Vogelweiherstrasse 33, D-90441 Nuremberg
Tel: (+49 911) 420 20 01  Fax: (+49 911) 420 19 32
e-mail: horst_lutter@mn.man.de

**Key personnel**
General Management: Dirk Wülfing
General Sales Manager: Kurt Heuser
Sales Manager Industrial Engines: Wolfgang Kuntze
Service Manager Industrial Engines: Werner Sontheimer

**Products**
Four-stroke direct-injection water-cooled diesel engines. These are six-cylinder in-line engines, rated at 160 to 300 kW at 2,100 rpm. The 300 kW D2866LUE602 engine meets the UIC and Euro-2 regulations. For railway applications MAN has released a new 12-cylinder engine available in two versions. The underfloor version for railcars is 870 mm in height. This was achieved by a special design of turbocharger attachment and a flat oil sump. The other version is for shunting engine applications. Both versions have a dry weight of 1,400 kg. The engines are rated at 500 and 588 kW at 2,100 rpm. Both engines meet Euro-2 emission standards.

MAN has also adapted its D2876 as a horizontal unit for rail vehicles. This six-cylinder engine has a swept volume of 12.81 litres and is available with three ratings – 294, 316 and 338 kW. All three engines meet Euro-2 emission regulations.

For auxiliary drives MAN produces six-cylinder in-line engines for generator sets, rated at 47-313 kW, V-8, V-10 and V-12 cylinder engines from 325 to 587 kW at 1,500 to 1,800 rpm.

Both engine applications are based on MAN's truck engine range.

Recent contracts include: 28 Type D2866 LUE602 engines for the CAF TRD592; 100 Type 2842 LE604 for re-engineering SNCF X2100/X2200 railcars; and 60 Type D2866 LUE602 for SNCF X-TER dmus in addition to 400 already delivered.

*UPDATED*

## M & J Diesel Locomotive Filter

805 Golf Lane, Bensenville, Illinois 60106, USA
Tel: (+1 630) 595 45 60  Fax: (+1 630) 595 06 46

**Key personnel**
President and Chairman of the Board: Harold O'Connor
Vice-President, Sales: Robert S Grandy
Executive Vice-President, Financial: Robert Holden

**Products**
Lube oil, fuel and air filters for diesel locomotives.

## MTU

MTU Friedrichshafen GmbH
D-88040 Friedrichshafen, Germany
Tel: (+49 7541) 90 28 40  Fax: (+49 7541) 90 39 49
e-mail: christos.ramnialis@mtu-online.de
Web: http://www.mtu-online.com

**Key personnel**
Senior Vice-President Sales:
  Peter Grosch
Director Rail Applications: Christos Ramnialis

**Background**
MTU Friedrichshafen in Germany and Detroit Diesel in the USA, have combined their off-highway activities in the new established DaimlerChrysler business unit, 'Powersystems'. With the joint range of their products a worldwide leading supplier of engines and systems has been set up covering marine, rail, mining, construction and industrial, defence and agriculture applications as well as power generation. The joint product programme includes compact diesel engines with a power output ranging from 40 to 9,000 kW, gas engines with ratings between 130 and 1,320 kW and gas turbines of 3 to 30 MW. It is complemented by electronic governing, monitoring and control systems.

With the rail industry, which is served by the brand MTU, the company has a long and close partnership. Since 1950, MTU and its predecessor companies have delivered more than 13,000 units for rail vehicles. The

### Engines for rail traction

| Engine | Speed rpm | Output (UIC) kW | Output (UIC) mhp | Length mm | Width mm | Height mm | Weight Kg (dry) | Exhaust emission |
|---|---|---|---|---|---|---|---|---|
| **Underfloor installation** | | | | | | | | |
| 6R 183 TD13H | 1,900 | 275 | 375 | 1,475 | 1,320 | 655 | 980 | EURO II |
| 6R 183 TD13H | 1,900 | 315 | 430 | 1,475 | 1,320 | 655 | 980 | EURO II |
| 12V 183 TD13 | 2,100 | 550 | 750 | 1,630 | 1,290 | 870 | 1,360 | EURO II |
| **Engine room installation** | | | | | | | | |
| 8V 183 TD13 | 2,100 | 390 | 530 | 1,330 | 1,300 | 1,040 | 1,035 | EURO II |
| 12V 183 TD13 | 2,100 | 550 | 750 | 1,630 | 1,290 | 870 | 1,360 | EURO II |
| 8V 4000 R41 | 1,800 | 1,000 | 1,360 | 1,895 | 1,555 | 1,800 | 4,590 | ERRI 2003 |
| 8V 4000 R41L | 1,860 | 1,100 | 1,495 | 1,895 | 1,555 | 1,800 | 4,590 | ERRI 2003 |
| 12V 4000 R41 | 1,800 | 1,500 | 2,040 | 2,500 | 1,430 | 1,800 | 6,300 | ERRI 2003 |
| 12V 4000 R41L | 1,860 | 1,650 | 2,245 | 2,500 | 1,430 | 1,800 | 6,300 | ERRI 2003 |
| 16V 4000 R41 | 1,800 | 2,000 | 2,720 | 2,955 | 1,635 | 1,800 | 7,280 | ERRI 2003 |
| 16V 4000 R41L | 1,860 | 2,200 | 2,990 | 2,955 | 1,635 | 1,800 | 7,280 | ERRI 2003 |
| 20V 4000 R42 | 1,800 | 2,700 | 3,670 | 3,370 | 1,480 | 2,065 | 8,430 | ERRI 2003 |

### Train electricity generation

| Engine | Output frequency | Speed rpm | Output (UIC) kW | Length mm | Width mm | Height mm | Weight Kg (dry) |
|---|---|---|---|---|---|---|---|
| 6R 183 TA12G | 50 Hz | 1,500 | 180 | 1,325 | 820 | 1,165 | 835 |
|  | 60 Hz | 1,800 | 195 | 1,325 | 820 | 1,165 | 835 |
| 8V 183 TA12G | 50 Hz | 1,500 | 240 | 1,295 | 1,060 | 1,060 | 930 |
|  | 60 Hz | 1,800 | 255 | 1,295 | 1,060 | 1,060 | 930 |
| 8V 183 TE12G | 50 Hz | 1,500 | 255 | 1,340 | 1,075 | 1,135 | 950 |
|  | 60 Hz | 1,800 | 295 | 1,340 | 1,075 | 1,135 | 950 |
| 12V 183 TA12G | 50 Hz | 1,500 | 360 | 1,415 | 1,215 | 1,095 | 1,220 |
|  | 60 Hz | 1,800 | 382 | 1,415 | 1,215 | 1,095 | 1,220 |
| 12V 183 TE12G | 50 Hz | 1,500 | 407 | 1,415 | 1,215 | 1,170 | 1,300 |
|  | 60 Hz | 1,800 | 459 | 1,415 | 1,215 | 1,170 | 1,300 |
| 12V 183 TB12G | 50 Hz | 1,500 | 441 | 1,415 | 1,215 | 1,170 | 1,300 |
|  | 60 Hz | 1,800 | 529 | 1,415 | 1,215 | 1,170 | 1,300 |

engines are installed in a large variety of applications and services with some of them operating under the most severe environmental conditions.

### Products
Engines for shunting/switching locomotives with frequent load changes, for multi-purpose and main-line services or a prime mover for train electricity supply. For diesel railcars and high-speed trains, the company has gained a capability to design and supply complete drive systems (powerpacks).

*UPDATED*

*MTU Series 16V 4000 R40 locomotive engine*
*2002*/0122656

## MWM (Motoren-Werke Mannheim AG)

(A Klöckner-Humboldt-Deutz company)
PO Box 102263, D-68140 Mannheim, Germany
Tel: (+49 621) 38 40   Fax: (+49 621) 38 43 28

### Products
Diesel engines for rail vehicles up to 2,000 kW.
Sales of diesel engines in the 380 to 7,400 kW range in the first half of 1997 were 80 per cent higher in a year-on-year basis.

*VERIFIED*

## NICO

Niigata Converter Company Ltd
405-3, Yoshinocho 1-chome, Omiya, Saitama 330-8646, Japan
Tel: (+81 48) 652 80 69   Fax: (+81 48) 652 87 19
e-mail: h-gocho@niigata-converta.co.jp
Web: http://www.niigata-converta.co.jp

### Key personnel
President: S Takeuchi
Managing Director: T Hayashi
General Manager, International Operation: A Ochiai

### Main works
Kamo plant: Gejyo Bo 405, Kamo-City, Niigata 959-1391, Japan
Omiya plant: 405-3 Yoshinocho 1-chome, Omiya, Saitama 330-8646, Japan
Muikamachi plant: Kawakubo 1095-1, Muikamachi, Minami-Uonuma, Niigata 949-6603, Japan

### Principal subsidiaries
Niigata Converter Co Ltd, Europe Office, Beursplein 37, NL-3011 AA Rotterdam, Netherlands
Tel: (+31 10) 405 30 89   Fax: (+31 10) 405 50 67

### Products
Single-stage torque converters, three-stage torque converters, power shift transmissions, hydraulic couplings for engines rated from 37 to 895 kW (50 to 1,200 hp).

Model TACN-22-1600 two-speed forward, two-speed reverse power shift transmission with Type 8 single-stage torque converter for 261 kW (350 hp) diesel railcars.
Model TACN-22-2000 two-speed forward, two-speed reverse power shift transmission with three-stage torque converter for 331 kW (444 hp) express diesel railcars.
Model TACN-33-3000 three-speed forward, three-speed reverse power shift transmission with Type 8 single-stage torque converter for 485 kW (650 hp) express diesel railcars.

*UPDATED*

## Niigata

Niigata Engineering Company Ltd
1-10-1 Kamata-Honchou, Ota-ku, Tokyo 144, Japan
Tel: (+81 3) 57 10 77 31   Fax: (+81 3) 57 10 47 52

### Key personnel
See entry in *Locomotives and powered/non-powered passenger vehicles* section.

### Products
Diesel engines for rail traction use up to 2,000 hp.

*12V16FX*
Type: 12-cylinder Vee, water-cooled, four-stroke turbocharged and charge air-cooled.
Cylinders: Bore 165 mm. Stroke 185 mm. Swept volume 3.96 litres per cylinder.

*DMF18HZ*
Type: 6-cylinder horizontal in-line, water-cooled, four-stroke turbocharged and charge air-cooled.
Cylinders: Bore 150 mm. Stroke 165 mm. Swept volume 2.92 litres per cylinder.

*General specifications for both models*
Cylinders: Monobloc cast-iron cylinder block and crankcase, removable cast-iron liners with integral water jacket. Cast-iron cylinder heads secured by studs.
Fuel injection: Bosch-type injectors and Bosch pump.
Lubrication: Forced feed.
Starting: Electric starter.

## OMT SpA

Via Ferrero 67/A, I-10090 Casine Vica, Rivoli (TO), Italy
Tel: (+39 011) 957 53 54   Fax: (+39 011) 957 54 74
Web: http://www.omt-torino.com

### Products
Diesel fuel injection equipment.

*UPDATED*

## Paulstra

61 rue Marius Aufan, F-92305 Levallois-Perret, France
Tel: (+33 1) 40 89 53 31   Fax: (+33 1) 47 58 75 16
e-mail: auto.levallois@hutchinson.fr
Web: http://www.hutchinson.fr

### Key personnel
See *Brakes and drawgear* section.

### Products
Tetraflex coupling of 4,000 Nm torque capacity, part of a family of power transmission couplings developed by Paulstra. Used between electric motors and gearboxes, they are characterised by a reduced axial thickness and a radial misalignment capacity of several millimetres. The torque range available is between 2,000 and 8,000 Nm with a maximum speed of 3,000 to 3,500 rpm.

*UPDATED*

# MANUFACTURERS/Diesel engines, transmission and fuelling systems

## Prime

Prime Manufacturing Corporation
PO Box 63, Oak Creek, Wisconsin 51354, USA
Tel: (+1 414) 764 14 00   Fax: (+1 414) 764 09 45

**Key personnel**
General Manager: Dan Croal
Sales Manager: Jeff Mueller

**Products**
Engineered locomotive products, including heating and cooling equipment, cooling water drain valves, mirrors, visors, sanding valves, check valves, refrigerators toilets and other cab equipment.
Nationwide service network for repair and remanufacture of HVAC equipment, drain valves, cab heaters and air conditioning units.

Products sold to North American original equipment manufacturers and to locomotive operators worldwide.

---

## PSI (Peaker Services Inc)

8080 Kensington Court, Brighton, Michigan 48116-8591, USA
Tel: (+1 810) 437 41 74   Fax: (+1 810) 437 82 80
Web: http://www.peaker.com

**Key personnel**
President: Richard R Steele
Marketing and Sales: Vance Shoger, Frank Boatwright
Sales Engineers: Kim Stone, Terry Warrick

**Products**
Diesel engine rebuilding and maintenance; exchange service for diesel engine components and personnel training.
PSI is an independently owned company specialising in medium-speed, large diesel engines manufactured by the Electro-Motive Division of General Motors Corporation. Services include engine conversions and upgrading, unit exchange components, engine overhaul (including repair of case and pan sections, power assemblies, pumps and governors), field repairs, service contracts, application studies, crankcase line boring and repairs, locomotive inspections and evaluations and personnel training in locomotive maintenance and repair.

*UPDATED*

---

## Scania – Industrial & Marine Engines

SE-151 87 Södertälje, Sweden
Tel: (+46 8) 55 38 10 00   Fax: (+46 8) 55 38 10 37
e-mail: info@scania.com
Web: http://www.scania.com

**Key personnel**
Head of Industrial and Marine Engines: L Hjelfe
Sales Manager: L Eriksson

**Products**
The company, which produced its first internal combustion engine in 1897 and its first diesel engine in 1936, specialises in high-speed engines.
Scania's industrial engine programme now comprises engines with outputs ranging from 146 to 460 kW. The programme is in part a preparedness for future demands for reduced emission levels in industrial engines. Here charge air-cooling is a distinct advantage in optimising the engines to meet more stringent regulations without loss of fuel economy.
The engines are specially adapted for operation with high average output. To reduce the danger of piston ringstick in extremely heavy operation, a keystone-ring is fitted as upper compression ring on the piston. A feature of Scania engines is a cylinder ring preventing coke build-up on the piston.
Generating set engines have been specially adapted for generator speeds of 1,500 and 1,800 rpm. The injection pump and single-speed Bosch RQ governor provides faster and more precise governing of engine speed. With this governor the requirements for Class A1 (high requirements of governing accuracy) in ISO 3046 are fulfilled. The new governor is also particularly well suited in parallel operation of multi-engine installations.

*UPDATED*

### Generator drive engines for power generation

| Model | Engine output gross | Prime duty* | | Limited time power** | | Emergency standby power*** | |
|---|---|---|---|---|---|---|---|
| | | 50 Hz | 60 Hz | 50 Hz | 60 Hz | 50 Hz | 60 Hz |
| D9   | kW | 146 | 156 | 146 | 156 | 161 | 182 |
| D9   | kW | 154 | 178 | 154 | 178 | 176 | 201 |
| D9   | kW | -   | 201 | 176 | 212 | 198 | 222 |
| DC9  | kW | 208 | 228 | 229 | 249 | 264 | 291 |
| DC9  | kW | 229 | 249 | 247 | 272 | -   | -   |
| DC12 | kW | 249 | 276 | 273 | 302 | 318 | 341 |
| DC12 | kW | 273 | 302 | 294 | 318 | 335 | 358 |
| DC12 | kW | 294 | 314 | 314 | 336 | 354 | 383 |
| DC12 | kW | 314 | 336 | 332 | 358 | 383 | 405 |
| DC12 | kW | -   | -   | 354 | 383 | 405 | -   |
| DI14 | kW | 285 | 341 | 314 | 361 | 366 | 419 |
| DI14 | kW | 316 | -   | 342 | -   | 398 | -   |
| DC14 | kW | 317 | 362 | 341 | 362 | 408 | 420 |
| DC14 | kW | 333 | 398 | 351 | 380 | 441 | 439 |
| DC14 | kW | 351 | -   | 376 | 398 | -   | 460 |
| DC14 | kW | -   | -   | 399 | 418 | -   | -   |

\* Prime duty: Rated power overloadable by 10% 1h/12h.
\*\* Limited time power: Continuous operation according to ISO 8528.
\*\*\* Emergency standby power: 300 h/year service.
Standards: ISO 3046, ISO 8528 and DIN 6280.

### Industrial engines

| Model | D9 | DI9 | DC9 | DI12 | D14 | DI14 | DC14 |
|---|---|---|---|---|---|---|---|
| Output* kW (hp) | 157 (213)-216 (294) | 169 (230)-244 (332) | 241 (328) | 269 (366)-316 (430) | 320 (435) | 353 (480) | 376 (511) |
| No of cylinders | 6 in-line | 6 in-line | 6 in-line | 6 in-line | V8 | V8 | V8 |
| Cylinder volume, dm³ | 9 | 9 | 9 | 11.7 | 14.2 | 14.2 | 14.2 |
| Max torque Nm | 826-1,098 | 888-1,339 | 1,306 | 1,544-1,801 | 1,662 | 1,890 | 2,032 |
| Specific fuel consumption at 1,500 rpm g/kWh | 202 | 196-202 | 194 | 197 | 207 | 200 | 199 |
| Weight (dry) kg | 825 | 835 | 890 | 995 | 1,160 | 1,180 | 1,256** |

\* Full power 1h/6h. No limitation on running hours. Standards: ISO 3046.
\*\* Weight including radiator and expansion tank.

---

## SEMT Pielstick

Paris Nord II – Bât Le Ronsard, 22 avenue des Nations, BP 50049 Villepinte, F-95946 Roissy CDG Cedex, France
Tel: (+33 1) 48 17 63 29   Fax: (+33 1) 48 17 63 49
e-mail: sales_traction@pielstick.com
Web: http://www.pielstick.com

**Key personnel**
Chairman of the Board of Management: Pierre Bousseau
Sales Director: Jean-Luc Cavellat

**Products**
High- and medium-speed diesel engines for mainline passenger and freight locomotives, including the PA4 (8 to 16 cylinders, 1,350 to 3,600 hp) and PA6 (6 to 16 cylinders, 2,820 to 7,520 hp) series.

*PA4-185 Series*
Type: 8, 12 and 16 Vee (90°), 4-cycle, water-cooled.
Cylinders: Bore 185 mm. Stroke 210 mm. Swept volume 5.65 litres per cylinder. Wet liners, individual cast-iron cylinder heads. Central precombustion chamber fitted with pintle-type injectors.
Fuel injection: Pintle-type injectors fitted to precombustion chambers. Monobloc injection pump located inside Vee, controlled by electronic governor.
Superchargers: Exhaust gas turbochargers, one for 6- and 8-cylinder engines, one for 12 cylinders and two for 16 and 18 cylinders, between cylinder banks. Air coolers arranged on timing gear side.
Cooling: Water pumps fitted on timing gear end of frame.
Starting: Either electrically or by compressed air.

*PA4-200 Series*
Type: 12 and 16 Vee (90°), 4-cycle, water-cooled, with variable geometry precombustion chamber (VG).
Cylinders: Bore 200 mm. Stroke 210 mm. Swept volume 6.6 litres per cylinder. Wet liners, individual cast-iron cylinder heads.
Pistons: Cast-iron pistons cooled by pressure lubricating oil fed through connecting rod and piston pin into an annular chamber level with top compression ring.
Fuel injection: Monobloc injection pump inside the Vee, controlled by electronic governor.
Superchargers: Exhaust gas turbochargers, one for 8-cylinder engine, two for 12 and 16 cylinders, between cylinder banks. Air coolers arranged on timing gear side.
Cooling: Water pumps fitted on timing gear end of frame.
Starting: Either electrically or by compressed air.

*PA5-255 Series*
Type: 6 and 8 cylinders in-line, 12 and 16 cylinders Vee, supercharged, water-cooled.
Cylinders: Bore 255 mm. Stroke 270 mm. Swept volume 13.79 litres per cylinder. Wet liners directly mounted in the crankcase, without cooling jackets. Individual cast-iron cylinder heads. Single combustion chamber. Direct injection.
Fuel injection: Direct injection by means of injectors of the multihole type. Individual injecting pump housed in the crankcase, directly controlled by the camshafts. Injection controlled by hydraulic speed governor.
Turbochargers: Two per engine, driven by a turbine on the exhaust gas, and housed in the centreline of the engine above each end of the crankcase. Air cooler at supercharger outlets, housed above the middle of the crankcase, and fed by the low temperature water circuit.
The PA5 engine has successfully run 100 hours UIC tests (12 PA5 V).

## Diesel engines, transmission and fuelling systems/MANUFACTURERS

### PA4-200 VGA

| | | |
|---|---|---|
| No of cylinders | 12(V) | 16(V) |
| Turbocharged | Yes | Yes |
| Charge air-cooled | Yes | Yes |
| Power rating (hp) | 2,400 | 3,600 |
| Engine speed (rpm) | 1,500 | 1,500 |
| Piston speed (m/s) | 10.5 | 10.5 |
| Bmep (bar) | 20.5 | 20.5 |
| Weight (dry) (kg) | 8,000 | 10,000 |
| Length (mm) | 2,630 | 3,630 |
| Width (mm) | 1,600 | 1,680 |
| Height (mm) | 1,975 | 1,875 |

### PA4-185 VG

| | | | | |
|---|---|---|---|---|
| No of cylinders | 8(V) | 12(V) | | 16(V) |
| Turbocharged | Yes | Yes | | Yes |
| Charge air-cooled | Yes | Yes | | Yes |
| Power rating (hp) | 1,340 | 2,000 | | 2,680 |
| Engine speed (rpm) | 1,500 | 1,500 | | 1,500 |
| Piston speed (m/s) | 10.5 | 10.5 | | 10.5 |
| Bmep (bar) | 17.3 | 17.3 | | 17.3 |
| Weight (dry) (kg) | 3,900 | 5,600 | | 7,100 |
| Length (mm) | 1,940 | 2,540 | | 3,140 |
| Width (mm) | 1,450 | 1,450 | | 1,450 |
| Height (mm) | 1,865 | 1,865 | | 1,865 |

### PA5-255

| | | | | |
|---|---|---|---|---|
| No of cylinders | 6(L) | 8(L) | 12(V) | 16(V) |
| Turbocharged | Yes | Yes | Yes | Yes |
| Charge air-cooled | Yes | Yes | Yes | Yes |
| Power rating (UIC) (hp) | 1,955 | 2,610 | 3,915 | 5,220 |
| Engine speed (rpm) | 1,000 | 1,000 | 1,000 | 1,000 |
| Piston speed (m/s) | 9 | 9 | 9 | 9 |
| Bmep (bar) | 19 | 19 | 19 | 19 |
| Weight (dry) (kg) | 10,500 | 13,500 | 17,000 | 22,200 |
| Length (mm) | 3,590 | 4,400 | 4,060 | 5,140 |
| Width (mm) | 1,300 | 1,310 | 1,980 | 2,070 |
| Height (mm) | 2,255 | 2,440 | 2,620 | 2,870 |

### PA6B-280

| | | | |
|---|---|---|---|
| No of cylinders | 8(L) | 12(V) | 16(V) |
| Supercharged | Yes | Yes | Yes |
| Charge air-cooled | Yes | Yes | Yes |
| Power rating (UIC) (hp) | 3,760 | 5,640 | 7,500 |
| Engine speed (rpm) | 1,000 | 1,000 | 1,000 |
| Piston speed (m/s) | 11 | 11 | 11 |
| Weight (dry) (kg) | 18,000 | 27,000 | 34,000 |
| Length (mm) | 4,820 | 4,480 | 5,270 |
| Width (mm) | 1,450 | 1,700 | 1,700 |
| Height (mm) | 2,755 | 2,890 | 2,890 |

*PA6B-280 Series*

Type: 6 and 8 cylinders in-line, 12 and 16 cylinders Vee, supercharged, water-cooled.
Cylinders: Bore 280 mm. Stroke 330 mm. Swept volume 20.3 litres per cylinder. Wet liners directly mounted in the crankcase, with cooling jackets. Individual cast-iron cylinder heads. Single combustion chamber. Direct injection.
Fuel injection: Direct injection by means of injectors of the multihole type. Individual injecting pump housed in the crankcase, directly controlled by the camshafts. Injection controlled by hydraulic speed governor.
Turbochargers: Driven by a turbine on the exhaust gas, and housed above the end of the crankcase.
 Air cooler at supercharger outlets, housed above the middle of the crankcase and crossed by a special waterline.
Cooling: Two water pumps of the centrifugal type, driven by the timing train, one for jacket and cylinder head line, the other for air cooler and lube oil line.

*360 hour UIC test*
The 12-cylinder 12PA6V-280 engine has officially run its 360 hour UIC locomotive test in accordance with ORE

**UPDATED**

## SILSAN

SILSAN AŞ
Mersin Yolu 10 km, TR-01210 Adana, Turkey
Tel: (+90 322) 441 00 12   Fax: (+90 322) 441 00 86

**Key personnel**
Sales: Çağhan Bacaksizlar

**Products**
Diesel engine components including cylinder liners for engines from Europe, USA and other countries.

**VERIFIED**

## SM

Strömungsmaschinen GmbH
Power Transmission Division
Königsbrücker Strasse 96, PO Box 100508, D-01075 Dresden, Germany
Tel: (+49 351) 599 34 13   Fax: (+49 351) 599 32 07

**Key personnel**
Managing Director: Dr Ing Carl Woebeken
Managing Director, Power Transmission Division:
 Jürgen Theimer

Manager, Rail Systems Division:
 Dr Ing Reinhard Kernchen

**Products**
Hydrodynamic power transmissions for diesel locomotives and diesel railcars. Over 8,800 units are installed in 16 countries. Features of the transmissions are: fully automatic working; infinitely variable torque and speed adjustment; vibration damping and shock reduction; and hydrodynamic braking for hydrodynamic reversing transmissions.

SM offers a wide range of transmissions with a nominal output of between 100 and 1,050 kW. The company has recently specialised in the repair and overhaul of hydrodynamic locomotive transmissions produced by other manufacturers.

SM offers an international servicing and technical consultancy service for retrofit programmes for diesel locomotive and railcar drive systems.

## TSM

TSM Inc
10765 Ambassador Drive, Kansas City, Missouri 64153, USA
Tel: (+1 816) 891 65 44   Fax: (+1 816) 891 93 29

**Key personnel**
See main entry in *Brakes and drawgear* section.

**Corporate developments**
In 1996, TSM was acquired by Rockwell. TSM is a subsidiary of the Railroad Electronics business of Rockwell.

**Products**
Microprocessor-based control and monitoring systems for diesel locomotives including temperature sensing and cooling control systems, electronic fuel gauges and fuel-management monitors. Wireline distributed power locomotive control systems.

## Tülomsas

The Locomotive and Motor Corporation of Turkey
Ahmet Kanatli Cad, TR-26490 Eskisehir, Turkey
Tel: (+90 222) 224 00 00   Fax: (+90 224) 225 72 72
e-mail: tulomsas@tulomsas.com.tr
Web: http://www.tulomsas.com.tr

**Key personnel**
See entry in *Locomotives and powered/non-powered passenger vehicles* section.

**Products**
Diesel engines with outputs of 1,865, 2,200 and 2,400 hp.

**VERIFIED**

## Turbomeca

F-64511 Bordes, France
Tel: (+33 5) 59 12 50 00   Fax: (+33 5) 59 53 15 12

**Key personnel**
President: Jean-Bernard Cocheteux
Executive Vice-President: Jean-Louis Chenard
Marketing Manager: Bernard Watier
Turbomeca Engine Corporation

**Subsidiary**
Turbomeca Engine Corporation
2709 Forum Drive, Grand Prairie, Texas 75052, USA
Tel: (+1 214) 641 66 45

## MANUFACTURERS/Diesel engines, transmission and fuelling systems

### Products
There are two turbines currently being marketed for railway use. The first is the Makila TM-1600. This engine is used for both traction motor drive as well as direct propulsion. The TM-1600 has a speed of 6,500 rpm and a power output of 1,050 kW (1,600 hp). It is a two-shaft engine and weighs 410 kg with a length of 1,850 mm.

The Astazou is a single-shaft 1,500 rpm engine with an output of 450 hp and 330 kW. It measures 1,500 mm and weighs 300 kg. It is used for running hotel power.

A third engine developed with Volvo and Ulstein is available. Called Eurodyn, it has a power of 2.5/3 mW and a efficiency of 34 per cent. Its lightness makes it suitable for high-powered locomotives.

## Twiflex Ltd

104 The Green, Twickenham TW2 5AQ, UK
Tel: (+44 20) 88 94 11 61   Fax: (+44 20) 88 94 60 56

### Key personnel
Sales and Marketing Director: Jonathan P Cooksley
Technical Director: Peter Wood

### Products
Advanced braking technology, industrial disc brakes, Layrub and Laylink flexible shafts and couplings; industrial and marine disc brakes and Flexi-clutch couplings.

Both Layrub and Laylink couplings incorporate compressed cylindrical rubber blocks. The Laylink coupling carries these blocks in links, while the Layrub coupling carries them in a carrying plate. The use of these couplings and flexible shafts allows large amounts of angular and axial misalignment to be accommodated; it also absorbs shock, controls vibrations and simplifies close coupling in confined spaces. The units need no servicing or lubrication and can cater for very high operating speeds and transmission of high power without loss.

**UPDATED**

## Twin Disc

Twin Disc Incorporated
1328 Racine Street, Racine, Wisconsin 53403-1758, USA
Tel: (+1 262) 638 40 00   Fax: (+1 262) 638 44 82
Web: http://www.twindisc.com

### Key personnel
Chairman, Chief Executive Officer: M E Batten
President, Chief Operating Officer: M H Joyce
Vice-President, Marine Marketing and Distribution: H C Fabry
Commercial Manager, Production Systems and Operations: J H Batten

### Principal subsidiaries
Twin Disc International SA, Chaussée de Namur 54, B-1400 Nivelles, Belgium
Tel: (+32 67) 88 72 11   Fax: (+32 67) 88 73 33
Twin Disc (Pacific) Pty Ltd, PO Box 442, Virginia, Queensland 4014, Australia
Tel: (+61 7) 265 12 00   Fax: (+61 7) 865 13 71
Twin Disc (South Africa) Pty Ltd, PO Box 40542, Cleveland 2022, South Africa
Tel: (+27 11) 626 27 14   Fax: (+27 11) 626 27 17
Twin Disc (Far East) Ltd, PO Box 155, Jurong Town Post Office, Singapore 9161
Tel: (+65) 261 89 09   Fax: (+65) 264 20 80

### Products
Universal joints; hydraulic torque converters, power shift transmissions and controls suitable for locomotives and railcars.

**VERIFIED**

## UCM Reşiţa

Uzina de Construct de Maşini Reşiţa SA
1 Golului Street, R-1700 Resita, Romania
Tel: (+40 55) 21 15 77; 21 71 11
Fax: (+40 55) 22 30 82; 22 01 13
e-mail: ucmr@tms.iiruc.ro
Web: http://www.ucmr.ro

### Key personnel
General Manager: Enache Barbu
Sales Manager: Sorin Gârz
Product Marketing Department: Dumitru Onea

### Products
High-speed diesel engines from 373 kW to 3,357 kW (500 to 4,500 hp) per unit; spare parts for R251, LDS/LDSR and Alco 251 engines; refurbishment of R251 and Alco 251 engines.

### R 251 series engines

| | | | | | | |
|---|---|---|---|---|---|---|
| No of cylinders | 4 | 6 | 8 | 12 | 16 | 18 |
| rpm range | 400-1,100 | 400-1,100 | 400-1,000 | 400-1,100 | 400-1,100 | 400-1,100 |
| Max, full load (HP) | 500-750 | 700-1,520 | 1,000-1,720 | 1,500-3,040 | 1,900-3,960 | 2,600-4,560 |
| Compression ratio | (12.5) 11.5 to 1 | | | | | |
| Bore & stroke (mm) | 228 × 267 | | | | | |
| Displacement (dm³) | 43.8 | 65.7 | 87.6 | 131.4 | 175.2 | 197.1 |
| Turbocharged | Yes | Yes | Yes | Yes | Yes | Yes |
| Aftercooled | Yes | Yes | Yes | Yes | Yes | Yes |
| Fuel system type | Mech | Mech | Mech | Mech | Mech | Mech |
| Heat dissipation rate | | | | | | |
| Oil (kcal/Hp.min) | 1.2 | 1.2 | 1.2 | 1.2 | 1.2 | 1.2 |
| Water (kcal/Hp.min) | 5.5 | 5.5 | 5.5 | 5.5 | 5.5 | 5.5 |
| Starting system | | air motor | - | | air motor | |
| Cum/start, average | 7 | 7 | 7 | 7 | 7 | 7 |
| Pressure range (bar) | 6-10 | | | | | |
| Weight - dry (tons) | 8.6 | 11.2 | 12.0 | 14.7 | 19.3 | 22.2 |
| - wet (tons) | 9.4 | 12.0 | 12.7 | 15.5 | 21.0 | 24.5 |

Note: Based on Alco licence. MDO operation also available.

### LDS/LDSR series engines

| | | | |
|---|---|---|---|
| No of cylinders | 6 | 12 | 12 |
| Compression ratio | 11.25 to 1 | | |
| rpm range | 350 – 750 | | |
| Max, full load (HP) | 1,250 | 2,100 | 2,500 |
| Bore & stroke (mm) | 280 × 360 | | |
| Displacement (dm³) | 133 | 266 | 266 |
| Turbocharged | Yes | Yes | Yes |
| Aftercooled | Yes | No | Yes |
| Fuel system type | Mech. | Mech. | Mech. |
| Heat dissipation rate | | | |
| Oil (kcal/Hp.min) | 1.3 | 1.8 | 1.3 |
| Water (kcal/Hp.min) | 5.6 | 4.4 | 5.6 |
| Starting system | * | ** | ** |
| Cum/start, average | 7 | 7 | 7 |
| Pressure range (bar) | 6-10 | | |
| Weight - dry (tons) | 10.5 | 28.0 | 29.3 |
| - wet (tons) | 11.3 | 29.5 | 30.8 |

Notes: * Based on Sulzer licence. External, traction generator or dyna-starter. Air motor on special request.  ** DC generator included. Engine start by DC generator. Air motor on special request.

**UPDATED**

## Unipar Inc

7210 Polson Lane, Hazelwood, Missouri 63042, USA
Tel: (+1 314) 521 81 00   Fax: (+1 314) 521 80 52

### Key personnel
Executive Vice-President: Dennis McClure
Sales Manager: Mark Cleveland

### Products
New and remanufactured replacement power assemblies for GM/EMD locomotives. Component parts for Alco, GE and GM locomotives.

**VERIFIED**

## Voith Safeset AB

Rönningevägen 8, SE-824 34 Hudiksvall, Sweden
Tel: (+46 650) 54 01 50   Fax: (+46 650) 54 01 65
e-mail: info@voithsafeset.se

### Corporate background
Since 1992, the company has been wholly owned by J M Voith.

### Products
Torque limiting couplings, including the Safeset® coupling for drivelines in high-speed trains, which in event of cardan shaft failure protects the driveline from overtorque.

The system has been supplied to Fiat Ferroviaria for ETR-series Pendolino tilting trainsets, to ALSTOM for Virgin Rail Group's West Coast Main Line Pendolinos in the UK and to AEA Technology for retrofitting on Class 91 electric locomotives operated by GNER in the UK.

**VERIFIED**

## Voith Turbo

Voith Turbo GmbH
PO Box 1930, D-89509 Heidenheim, Germany
Tel: (+49 7321) 370   Fax: (+49 7321) 37 76 03
e-mail: hydrodynamic-drives@voith.de
Web: http://www.voithturbo.de

### Key personnel
Managing Director: Günter Armbruster
General Manager, Turbo Transmissions: Manfred Lerch
General Manager, Axle Drives: Martin Wawra
General Manager, Service Centre: K Sing

Diesel engines, transmission and fuelling systems/**MANUFACTURERS** 547

**UK subsidiary**
Voith Engineering Ltd
6 Beddington Farm Road, Croydon CR0 4XB, UK
Tel: (+44 20) 86 67 03 33   Fax: (+44 20) 86 67 04 03
e-mail: alan.morris@voith.co.uk
Manager, Rail Products: A L Morris

**Products**
Hydrodynamic transmissions and retarders, torque converters and automatic hydromechanical transmissions. Final drive reduction gearboxes for mechanical or electrical drives in locomotives, metro cars and light rail vehicles. DIWA hydromechanical transmissions for light rail vehicles. Limited-slip differential device for metro cars and light rail vehicles.

Voith automatic hydrodynamic transmissions are designed specifically for installation in rail vehicles. The basic components are drainable hydraulic torque converters and fluid couplings, which in combination provide tractive effort over a wide speed range in an efficient and cost-effective manner. The filling characteristics ensure wear-free, smooth shifting without interruption of tractive effort. Turbo-reversing transmissions used in shunting locomotives extend the principle to allow direction shifting in a similar manner. All non-reversing turbo transmissions can be fitted with a wear-free retarder.

Voith final drives are available in bevel and spur gear configurations, from axle-hung drives to bogie or body-suspended quill-shaft drives, with single or double reduction.

Recent contracts include T211re.3 turbo transmissions for the Adtranz Turbostar vehicles as well as T211re.3 with KB190 retarders for the new TRD railcars of RENFE Spain. Major contracts have also been received from SNCB Belgium for L4r4 turbo reversing transmissions and from Eisenbahn und Häfen, Duisburg for L3r4 turbo reversing transmissions.

Orders have also been received for Voith's range of final drive reduction units which include the ET425 and 426 S-Bahn emus, ICE and ICT trainsets for DB AG, Germany, ICN tilting trainsets of SBB Switzerland as well as 560 units for Shanghai metro.

*Voith Turbo has developed the L620 re V2 turbo transmission with an input power of 2,300 kW for main line diesel locomotive*
2001/0105887

## Volvo Penta

Volvo Penta Central Europe GmbH
Redderkoppel 5, D-24159 Kiel, Germany
Tel: (+49 431) 399 42 07   Fax: (+49 431) 399 41 55
e-mail: vp.90040hm@memo.volvo.se
Web: http://www.volvo.com

**Key personnel**
Business Manager, Rail: Helmut Möller

**Products**
RailPac unit with Volvo DH10A horizontal diesel engine and Volvo Powertronic VT1605PT five-speed automatic transmission.

Volvo Penta engines are the power units in the 'Cargosprinter' Windhoff freight dmu, now in operation with DB Germany. Each power car has two Rail Pac engines, the front one driving the rear axle of the front powered bogie and the engine at the rear driving the front axle of the rear bogie. Each Rail Pac comprises a Volvo DH10-A360 engine rated at 265 kW, at 2,050 rpm, and meeting Euro-2 regulations. The drive is through a Volvo Powertronic Pt 1650 five-speed automatic gearbox which includes converter and retarder as well as electronic torque limiter.

The Volvo Penta DH10A-360 horizontal diesel engine is used to power the DWA LVT/S 64-seat railcar.

MAV Hungary is took delivery of Rail Pac engines for re-powering of Railcargo units in 1998/99.
**VERIFIED**

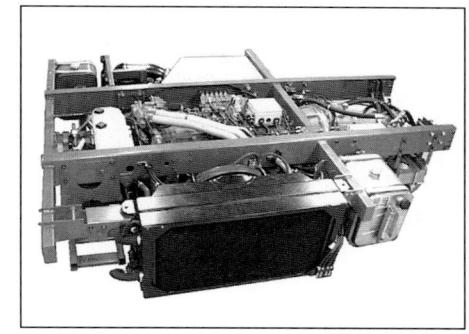

*Volvo Penta RailPac unit with DH10A diesel engine*
0063655

## ZF Friedrichshafen AG

D-88038 Friedrichshafen, Germany
Tel: (+49 7541) 77 17 70   Fax: (+49 7541) 77 90 80 00
Web: http://www.zf.com

**Key personnel**
Chief Executive Officer: Dr Siegfried Goll
Head of Marketing and Public Relations: M Lenz
Sales Manager: Dr D M Störk

**Subsidiaries**
ZF Passau GmbH
D-94030 Passau, Germany

Tel: (+49 851) 494 22 04   Fax: (+49 851) 494 21 91
Marketing Manager: J Weidemann

ZF Bahntechnik GmbH
D-88046 Friedrichshafen, Germany
Tel: (+49 7541) 306 01   Fax: (+49 7541) 30 64 00
Web: http://www.zf.com
Sales Manager: M C Cleobury

ZF Great Britain Ltd
Abbeyfield Road, Lenton, Nottingham NG7 2SX, UK
Tel: (+44 115) 986 92 11   Fax: (+44 115) 986 92 61
Marketing Manager: G A Buck

**Products**
Transmissions and driveline systems for locomotives, intercity, regional, city and metro applications, both electric and rail driven.

**UPDATED**

## ZF Padova

ZF Padova SpA
Via Penghe N 48, I-35030 Caselle di Selvazzano, Padua, Italy
Tel: (+39 049) 829 93 11
Fax: (+39 049) 829 95 50; 95 60; 95 70
e-mail: adriano.giuriati@zf.com

**Key personnel**
President: H G Harter
Managing Director: Roland Heil
Product Manager: Adriano Giuriati

**Background**
ZF Padova is owned by ZF Friedrichshafen AG based in Germany.

**Products**
Traction gears, special gearboxes. ZF Padova designs and manufactures case-hardened ground gears for rail transmissions with profile correction for long life and smooth running.

The company has developed computer programs for calculation and projecting custom-engineered gears. ZF Padova is currently supplying traction gears for Class E444, E633, E652 and E656 locomotives for Italian Railways; ground bevel gears for ETR 460 (Italian Railways) and IC Neil Tec (DB AG) tilting trainsets; traction gears for DB (BR423), SNCF and SNCB.

**VERIFIED**

# ELECTRIC TRACTION EQUIPMENT

## Alphabetical listing

3M Specialty Materials Markets
A K Fans
ALSTOM
ANSALDOBREDA
APS
BHEL
Bombardier Transportation
Brecknell, Willis
Brush
China National Railway Locomotive & Rolling Stock Industry Corporation (LORIC)
ČKD
Clyde
Continental Components Pvt Ltd
Daewoo
Dynex Semiconductor
EFACEC
EG & G
ELIN EBG Traction
Entrelec
Faiveley Transport
Ferraz
FIREMA
Freudenberg
Fuji Electric
Hamworthy
Hitachi
Hyundai
InfoSystems GmbH
Kiepe Elektrik
KMT-teknikka Oy
Končar – Električne Lokomotive dd
Lechmotoren
Lekov
Mitsubishi Electric
Morio Denki
National
Parizzi
Permali
RDS Technology Ltd
Riga Electric Machine Building Works
Rotem
SAFT
Sécheron SA
Siemens Rolling Stock Electronics
Siemens Westinghouse
SPII
Stemmann
Toshiba
Toyo Denki
Transportation Products
Tülomsas

**UPDATED**

## Classified listing

**BATTERY SYSTEMS**
SAFT

**CONTROL EQUIPMENT, CONVERTERS AND TRANSFORMERS**
ALSTOM
ANSALDOBREDA
APS
BHEL
Bombardier Transportation
Brush
ČKD
EFACEC
ELIN EBG Traction
Entrelec
FIREMA
Fuji Electric
Hitachi
Kiepe Elektrik
KMT-teknikka Oy
Lechmotoren
Lekov
Mitsubishi Electric
Morio Denki
Parizzi
RDS Technology
Riga Electric Machine Building Works
Rotem
Sécheron
Siemens
Siemens Electric
Siemens Rolling Stock Electronics
Siemens Transportation
Siemens Westinghouse
SPII
Toshiba
Toyo Denki
Transportation Products
Tülomsas

**COOLING SYSTEMS AND ACOUSTIC INSULATION**
3M Specialty Materials Markets
A K Fans
EG & G

**CURRENT COLLECTION EQUIPMENT**
Brecknell, Willis
Faiveley Transport
Ferraz
Fuji Electric
Hamworthy
InfoSystems GmbH
Lekov
Permali
Siemens
SMC
Stemmann
Toyo Denki

**TRACTION MOTORS AND TRANSMISSIONS**
ALSTOM
ANSALDOBREDA
BHEL
Bombardier Transportation
Brush
ČKD
China National Railway Locomotive & Rolling Stock Industry Corporation (LORIC)
Clyde
EFACEC
EG & G
Elin EBG Traction
Ematech
FIREMA Trasporti
Freudenberg
Fuji Electric
Mitsubishi Electric
National
Riga Electric Machine Building Works
Rotem
Siemens Westinghouse
Toshiba
Toyo Denki
Tülomsas

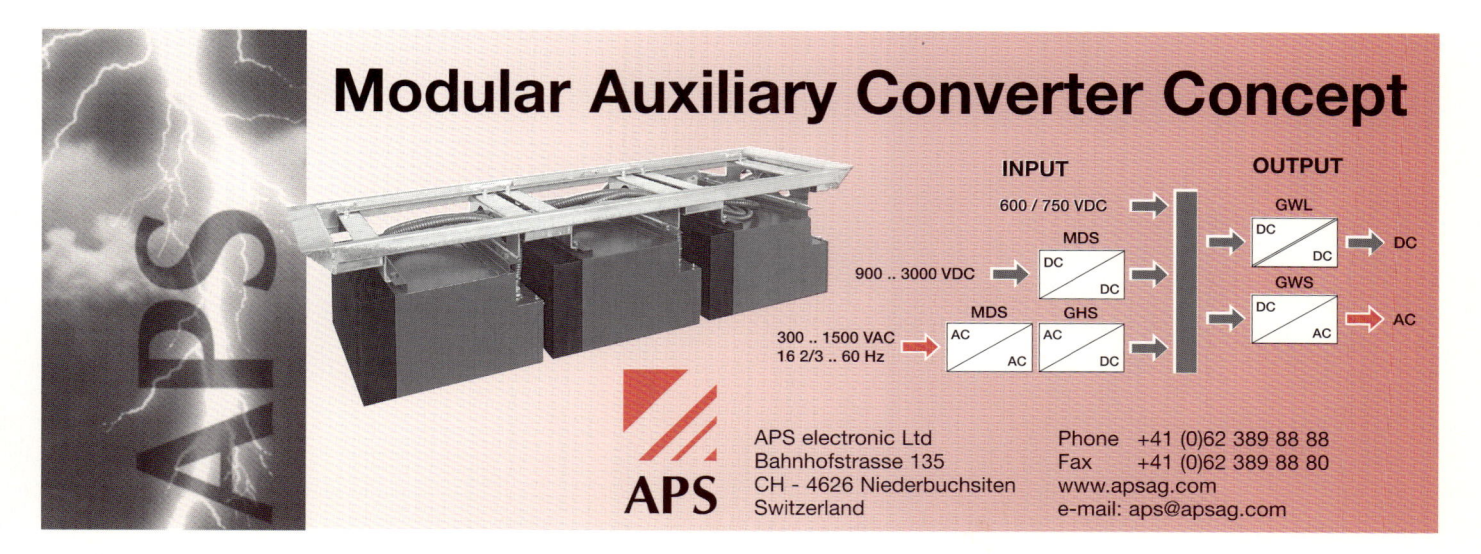

---

# Modular Auxiliary Converter Concept

INPUT
600 / 750 VDC
900 .. 3000 VDC
300 .. 1500 VAC
16 2/3 .. 60 Hz

MDS
MDS
GHS

OUTPUT
GWL
GWS
DC
AC

APS electronic Ltd
Bahnhofstrasse 135
CH - 4626 Niederbuchsiten
Switzerland

Phone +41 (0)62 389 88 88
Fax +41 (0)62 389 88 80
www.apsag.com
e-mail: aps@apsag.com

## MANUFACTURERS/Electric traction equipment

### Company listing by country

**AUSTRALIA**
Clyde
Siemens Westinghouse

**AUSTRIA**
ELIN EBG Traction

**CANADA**
Bombardier Transportation
Siemens Electric

**CHINA, PEOPLE'S REPUBLIC**
China National Railway Locomotive & Rolling Stock Industry Corporation (LORIC)

**CZECH REPUBLIC**
ČKD
Lekov

**FINLAND**
KMT-teknikka oy

**FRANCE**
ALSTOM
Faiveley Transport
Ferraz
SAFT

**GERMANY**
3M Specialty Materials Markets
Freudenberg
InfoSystems GmbH
Kiepe Elektrik
Lechmotoren
Siemens
Siemens Rolling Stock Electronics
Stemmann

**INDIA**
BHEL
Continental Components Pvt Ltd

**ITALY**
ANSALDOBREDA
FIREMA
Parizzi
SPII

**JAPAN**
Fuji Electric
Hitachi
Mitsubishi Electric
Morio Denki
Toshiba
Toyo Denki

**KOREA, SOUTH**
Daewoo
Hyundai
Rotem

**LATVIA**
Riga Electric Machine Building Works

**PORTUGAL**
EFACEC

**SWITZERLAND**
APS
Sécheron Ltd

**TURKEY**
Tülomsas

**UNITED KINGDOM**
A K Fans
Brecknell, Willis
Brush
Dynex Semiconductor
Entrelec
Hamworthy
Permali
RDS Technology Ltd

**UNITED STATES OF AMERICA**
EG & G
National
Siemens Transportation
Transportation Products

## Electric traction equipment/MANUFACTURERS

## 3M Specialty Materials Markets

c/o 3M Germany
Carl Schurz Strasse 1, D-41453 Neuss, Germany
Tel: (+49 2131) 14 24 17  Fax: (+49 2131) 14 27 49
e-mail: pbreloer@mmm.com

**Key personnel**
Market Development Manager: P Breloer

**Head office**
3M Center
St Paul, Minnesota 55144, USA
Tel: (+1 651) 736 38 95  Fax: (+1 651) 736 60 41
Web: http://www.mmm.com/

Vice President, Performance Materials: Dr Jay Ihlenfeld
Global Business Director, Specialty Fluids: Craig Schwalz

**Products**
Fluorinert dielectric liquids for converter system direct contact cooling; coolants for converters, systems (GTO and IGBT).

## A K Fans

A K Fans Ltd
32-34 Park Royal Road, London NW10 7LN, UK
Tel: (+44 20) 89 61 68 88  Fax: (+44 20) 89 65 06 01
e-mail: sales@akfansltd.btinternet.com

**Key personnel**
Managing Director: D C Moore
Financial Controller: R Brazell
Operations Manager: J M Brinkworth
Chief Engineer: A McArthur
General Sales Manager: G A Anderson
Rail Sales Manager: P Heapy

**Products**
Fan for rail traction applications; types include axial, centrifugal, mixed flow and crossflow, with AC or brushless DC motors. Applications include cooling of traction motors converters, auxiliary inverters, brake resistors, compressors and transformers. Cooling systems comprising matched fan and heat exchanger assemblies.

**Contracts**
Contracts include cooling underbody equipment on trains for Arlanda, Incheon, Manila, Adana and Gardermoen.

*UPDATED*

## ALSTOM

ALSTOM Transport SA
48 rue Albert Dhalenne, F-93482 Saint-Ouen Cedex, France
Tel: (+33 1) 41 66 90 00  Fax: (+33 1) 41 66 96 66
Web: http://www.transport.alstom.com

See also main entry in *Locomotives and powered/non-powered passenger vehicles* section.

**Contact points**
**Traction drives, power modules, switchgear**
ALSTOM Transport SA
50 rue du Dr Guimier, BP 4, F-65600 Semeac, Tarbes, France
Tel: (+33 5) 62 53 41 21  Fax: (+33 5) 62 53 40 01
Managing Director: J P Allavena

**On-board electronic systems**
ALSTOM Transport
11-13 Avenue du Bel Air, F-69627 Villeurbanne cedex, France
Tel: (+33 4) 72 81 52 00  Fax: (+33 4) 72 81 52 87
Managing Director: Antoine Doutriaux

**Motors**
ALSTOM Transport SA
7 Av De Lattre de Tassigny, BP 49, F-25290 Ornans Cedex
Tel: (+33 3) 81 62 44 00  Fax: (+33 3) 81 62 44 01
Managing Director: Christian Tonna

*ONIX 800 propulsion set for Virgin Trains Pendolino tilting trainset*  2001/0114492

**Traction drives, auxiliary converters**
ALSTOM Transport
50/52 rue Cambier Dupret 6001, Charleroi, Belgium
Tel: (+32 71) 44 54 11  Fax: (+32 71) 44 57 82
Managing Director: Chander S Bansal

**ALSTOM Transport Netherlands BV**
PO Box 3021, NL-2980 DA, Ridderkerk, Netherlands
Tel: (+31 180) 45 28 57  Fax: (+31 180) 45 28 60

ALSTOM Ltd
Channel Way, Preston PR1 8XL, UK
Tel: (+44 1772) 25 47 77  Fax: (+44 1772) 84 33 66
Managing Director: Brian Jones

ALSTOM Transportation Inc
1 Transit Drive, Hornell, New York 14843
Tel: (+1 607) 324 45 95  Fax: (+1 607) 324 23 68
Managing Director: Art Siegel
also: 4 Skyline Drive, Hawthorne, New York 10532-2160, USA
Tel: (+1 914) 345 51 11  Fax: (+1 914) 345 52 01

**Traction drives, auxiliary converters, switchgear, motors, transformers**
ALSTOM Transport Ltd
F - 4, East of Kailash, New Delhi 110 065, India
Tel: (+91 11) 628 77 16; 77 47; 77 48
Fax: (+91 11) 628 77 15
Managing Director: Pierre Jaquinandi

**Traction drives, auxiliary converters, switchgear**
Shanghai ALSTOM Transport Electrical Equipment Co Ltd
Room 915, Electric Power Building, 430 Xu Jia Hui Road, 200025 Shanghai, PR China
Tel: (+86) 21 64 72 51 57  Fax: (+86) 21 64 72 96 62

**Products**
The company's strategy for traction equipment centres on its IGBT propulsion system known as ONIX (Onduleur à Integration exceptionnelle). The know-how in advanced IGBT power modules, Agate control electronic systems and ONIX asynchronous traction motors provides a compact, lightweight, integrated traction system which is in reliable service around the world. ONIX is suitable for all line voltages (including the latest 3,000 V). In the ONIX range is the 350, for electric and trolleybuses (up to a line voltage of 400 V), 800 for metros and LRVs (up to a line voltage of 900 V), 1,500 for metros, emus, locomotives and high-speed trains (up to a line voltage of 2,000 V) and 3,000 V for emus, locomotives and high-speed trains (up to a line voltage of 3,000 V).

ONIX's modularity enables quick and easy maintenance and its flexibility allows a choice of cooling system to suit the local operating environment.

More than 5,500 units have been sold worldwide, representing 60 per cent of the world IGBT market.

ALSTOM's electric and electronic sub-systems include: electronic systems featuring the AGATE integrated family of traction control (AGATE Control), auxiliary control (AGATE Aux), Train Control Management Systems (AGATE Link), passenger information systems (AGATE Media, see Passenger Information Systems section), as well as depot monitoring systems.

A modular range of asynchronous, synchronous and DC motors, which are lightweight, compact and can be readily adapted to specific needs.

Auxiliary converters based on the modular CARA auxiliary power conversion and distribution packages.

A range of AC and DC switchgear, circuit breakers and cab equipment.

**Contracts**
Details of ALSTOM-built rolling stock contracts for which traction equipment has been ordered or supplied appear in the *'Locomotives and powered/non-powered passenger vehicles'* section.

**Australia:** ALSTOM won an order from Clyde Engineering to supply the traction equipment (80 ONIX 1500 IGBT inverters drives plus the new generation of Agate train management and passenger information systems), auxiliary power supplies and train operating system, as well as a comprehensive maintenance package, for a fleet of 20-four car double-deck train sets. The trains are operated by CityRail on Sydney's suburban rail network.

**Belgium:** ALSTOM has supplied ONIX 3000 traction drive systems for 24 AM96 emus for Belgian National Railways

**Brazil:** ALSTOM has won a turnkey order from Metrofor for a metro system in Fortaleza, north eastern Brazil. The order covers 10 four-car trainsets, which incorporate the new ONIX 3000 drive system supplied by ALSTOM's plant in Tarbes, France.

**France:** ALSTOM received an order from Bombardier Transportation in 1998 for 25 traction units for a fleet of rubber-tyred trams for Nancy. The contract includes the supply of the asynchronous ONIX 800 traction system and 56 kVA auxiliary converters.

A contract with RATP, the Paris public transport authority, for the refurbishment of MP89, MP73, MF67 and MS61 metro vehicles includes the supply of 2,500 ATM electromagnetic contactors.

**Germany:** In September 2000 ALSTOM received an order from Siemens to supply Type 22CB vacuum circuit breakers with silicon insulators and earthing switches to equip 100 Class 189 locomotives for DB AG.

**India:** Mitsubishi Electric (MELCO) awarded a contract to ALSTOM for the design, supply and testing of traction equipment for new rolling stock destined for the Delhi metro, now under construction. ALSTOM will manufacture, assemble and test MELCO-designed traction equipment: traction motors, AC control cases, inverter cases, converter/inverter cases, and auxiliary converter cases. ALSTOM's facility in Coimbatore, in

## 552 MANUFACTURERS/Electric traction equipment

southern India, will carry out case assembling, wiring and testing. Other ALSTOM units in India will be responsible for the remainder of the equipment. Delivery of the equipment was due to begin in early 2002 and will run through to November 2004. Testing of completed trains will be carried out in India. This order comes within the framework of a contract placed with the Mitsubishi/MELCO/KOROS consortium in May 2001 for 240 new metro cars destined for Delhi's first two metro lines, scheduled to begin commercial service in late 2002.

**Mexico:** ALSTOM received an order from Bombardier Concarril and CAF for 13 six-car trainsets for Line A of the Mexico City metro. This was ALSTOM's first complete order for its new-generation ONIX traction system with Agate electronic power control.

**Netherlands:** Recent contracts include: 10 trolleybuses for Arnhem; 15 trolleybuses for Solingen; 13 hybrid vehicles for Eindhoven; 36 articulated metro and rapid transit vehicles for Rotterdam; refurbishment of 71 articulated metro and rapid transit vehicles for Rotterdam and 2 electric motor car units for Netherlands Railways; 316 auxiliary power supply units for the Netherlands Railways.

In 2001 ALSTOM signed a contract for the supply and commissioning of electrical equipment for Netherlands Railways. The contract was awarded by Bombardier Transportation, which signed a major refurbishment contract with Dutch Railways (NS Reizigers) in July covering a major modernisation of 60 three-car suburban units. Each renovated train with two 1,500 V DC chopper installations and two static converters. The chopper installation replaces the resistor-controlled drive. Two prototypes, delivered in 1996, have already proved successful. The first delivery of a refurbished trainset to Dutch Railways is scheduled for April 2003.

**Russia:** Moscow Metro has placed an order with ALSTOM for 40 ONIX propulsion systems. The cars are a new design of light metro developed together by Moscow Metro, Metrowagonmash (the leading Russian metro car builder) and ALSTOM. They will operate initially on the new line under construction for the CITY Business centre in Moscow, and later on further lines planned in Moscow's districts. The ONIX IGBT propulsion which will power these new cars has already been tested on Moscow's heavy Yauza-type metro cars with three prototype drives.

**South Africa:** ALSTOM was selected by Spoornet to supply and install its Agate control electronics in 99 locomotives as part of its locomotive refurbishment programme.

**Spain:** Four new trainsets for the Barcelona metro have been fitted with ONIX 1500 traction control systems.

**Switzerland:** In consortium with Bombardier Transportation, ALSTOM in December 2001 received a contract to provide the complete electrical installation for 18 three-car Nina emus for BLS Lötschbergbahn. Equipment to be supplied includes: high-voltage current collection and distribution equipment; auxiliary power supply converters and equipment; and ONIX propulsion equipment. The contract follows earlier orders for 14 similar emus.

**UK:** ALSTOM Transport is supplying Bombardier Transportation with ONIX traction drive systems (352 ONIX IGBT inverter drives including ALSTOM's standard AGATE microprocessor system) and auxiliary equipment for the new fleet of 352 Class 220/221 demu cars which will be operated by Virgin CrossCountry on the UK network. First examples entered service in 2001. Under the terms of the contract ALSTOM is responsible for providing all spares for the trains until the end of the franchise in 2012.

**USA:** Work continued in 2002 on the refurbishment of 490 subway cars for Chicago Transit Authority, including the provision of an upgraded propulsion system and IGBT-based auxiliary inverters.

ALSTOM is also supplying Bombardier Transportation with 952 ONIX propulsion sets for the 680 new cars for the New York Subway. ALSTOM will supply 30 ONIX to NJT (New Jersey Transit Authority) as well as auxiliary converters.

ALSTOM is completely refurbishing 364 of the 764-car rapid transit fleet Washington Metropolitan Area Transit Authority (WMATA), which were built between 1983 and 1988. The contract includes replacing the existing propulsion systems with ONIX traction drives, and installing an advanced cab signalling system.

ONIX traction is being supplied for 30 Kinki Sharyo LRVs for Santa Clara.

60 ARC circuit breakers have been supplied to SPD Technology for the refurbishment of the Pittsburg tramway.

156 AGATE CCR propulsion control electronics have been supplied for Kawasaki LRVs operated by SEPTA, Philadelphia.

ALSTOM is supplying ONIX traction systems and CARA auxiliary converters for 70 railcar sets to train builder Kinki Sharyo for a follow-on order by Santa Clara Valley Transit Authority (SCVTA). Some 30 railcar sets from an initial order are already in production in ALSTOM's facility in Hornell, New York, making the total number of railcar sets ordered 100. First delivery was scheduled for August 2001, final delivery for October 2003.

*UPDATED*

## ANSALDOBREDA

Ansaldo Trasporti
425 Via Argine, I-80147 Naples, Italy
Tel: (+39 081) 243 11 11   Fax: (+39 081) 243 26 98

**Key personnel**
See entry in *Locomotives and powered/non-powered passenger vehicles* section.

**Products**
Electric propulsion equipment for mainline, urban and suburban railway vehicles with AC and DC traction motors; electronic converters and controls; auxiliary equipment; planning, design and management methodologies for public transport; sales, assembly, start-up servicing.

## APS

APS Electronic AG
Bahnhofstrasse 135, CH-4626 Niederbuchsiten Switzerland
Tel: (+41 62) 389 88 88   Fax: (+41 62) 389 88 80
e-mail: aps@apsag.com
Web: http://www.apsag.com
Formerly EAO Electro-Apparatebau Olten AG

**Key personnel**
Managing Directors: Urs Christen, Heinrich Naegelin

**Products**
Static converters; battery chargers; cooling equipment.
Over the past 10 years many contracts have been carried out for railway, metro, tramway and trolleybus operators in Europe.

*UPDATED*

## BHEL

Bharat Heavy Electricals Ltd
Bhopal, 462 022 India
Tel: (+91 11) 461 65 44   Fax: (+91 11) 462 94 23

**Key personnel**
See entry in *Locomotives and powered/non-powered passenger vehicles* section.
BHEL
Bangalore, 560 026, India
Tel: (+91 80) 852 01 92   Fax: (+91 80) 806 61 01 37

**Key personnel**
General Manager: V K Bhatnagar

**Products**
Electrical propulsion equipment for electric (AC and DC), diesel-electric and battery rail vehicles, including choppers, AC inverters and traction motors; equipment for traction substations. BHEL is the major supplier of electrical equipment to the locomotive and coach building works of Indian Railways and has supplied equipment to private rolling stock builders.

Power converter and controls for three-phase locomotives, AC-powered emus and AD/DC dual-voltage emus.

## Bombardier Transportation

1101 Parent Street, Saint-Bruno, Québec, Canada J3V 6E6
Tel: (+1 450) 441 20 20   Fax: (+1 450) 441 15 15
Web: http://www.transportation.bombardier.com

Saatwinkler Damm 43, D-13627 Berlin, Germany
Tel: (+49 30) 383 20   Fax: (+49 30) 38 32 20 00

**Key personnel**
See entry in *Locomotives and powered/non-powered passenger vehicles* section.

**Products**
Development, design, engineering, sales, production, installation, maintenance and after-sales service of propulsion equipment, Mitrac® CC onboard computer and diagnostic systems for all rolling stock applications. This includes products such as the Mitrac® TC traction converter family, the Mitrac® AU auxiliary converter and battery charger family, Mitrac® DR drives system with traction motors and transmission gears and various onboard computer system units (for example processor units, driver's display units).

Bombardier Transportation's experience in the development of propulsion and control systems encompasses innovative solutions such as the Integrated Total Drive, the IGBT power converter technology and the modular train control and communication system MITRAC. These systems are today an integral part of many rail vehicles around the world.

New developments in propulsion and controls technology help guarantee higher levels of performance,

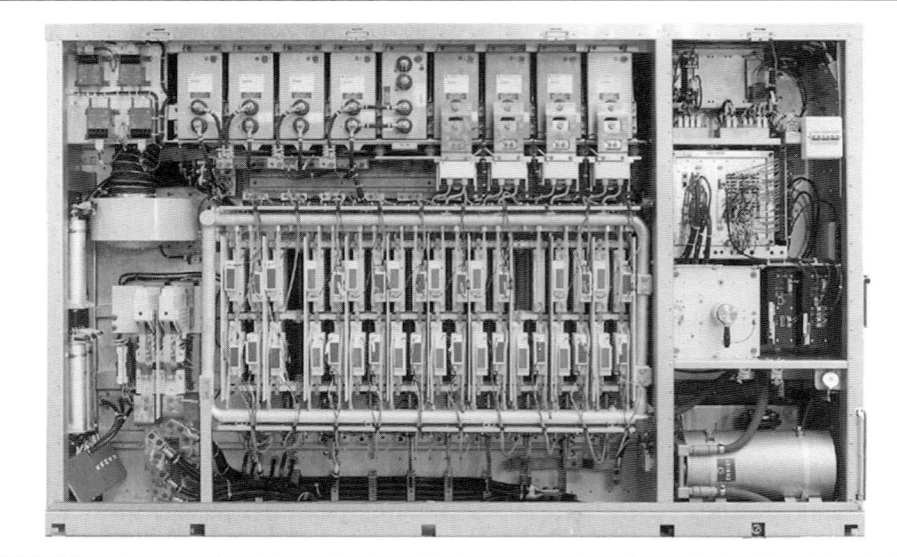

*Bombardier propulsion system for high power application*

0524873

Electric traction equipment/**MANUFACTURERS** 553

*Bombardier train control and communication, driver's desk* 2002/0524875

increased safety, improved Life Cycle Cost and reduced energy consumption.

### Contracts
Propulsion and control equipment for 250 Class 185 two system electric locomotives for the DB AG, Germany; Propulsion equipment for 76 4,475 kW diesel-electric locomotives developed in partnership with Zhuzhou Electric Locomotive Research Institute (ZELRI) for the Qishuyan Locomotive and Rolling Stock Works, China; Propulsion and control equipment for 10 Class DJ electric locomotive for the GSRC, China; Propulsion and control equipment for 26 trains to Guangzhou Metro Line 2, China; Propulsion and control equipment for 47 Class 8000 trains for Metro Madrid, Spain; propulsion and control equipment for the R142A metro cars to NYCT, USA; propulsion and control equipment for the Electrostar EMU to Connex and c2c, UK; Propulsion and control equipment for emu's Class OTU for SJ and DSB, Sweden and Denmark; Propulsion and control equipment for 64 People Movers for Dallas Forth Worth, USA; Traction equipment for various tram cars supplied to operators in Austria, Germany, Greece, Slovakia, Sweden and Switzerland.

*UPDATED*

---

## Brecknell Willis & Co Ltd

Member of the Fandstan Electric Group
PO Box 10, Tapstone Road, Chard TA20 2DE, UK
Tel: (+44 1460) 649 41   Fax: (+44 1460) 661 22
e-mail: brecknell.willis@ukonline.co.uk
Web: http://www.brecknell-willis.co.uk

### Key personnel
Chief Executive: Michael Bostelmann
Chairman: Lord Tanlaw
Managing Director: Tony White
Sales Manager, Trainborne Equipment: Andrew Hales
Chief Engineer: David Hartland

### Overseas office
Brecknell Willis Taiwan

*Brecknell Willis high-speed pantograph on Class 91 locomotive, UK* 0003094

### Products
Current collection and power distribution equipment for the transport sector. This includes the design, manufacture, supply and installation of complete systems.

The product groups are pantographs and third rail current collectors; conductor rail systems; light rail overhead systems and automatic gas tensioning equipment for overhead systems.

### Contracts
Current collector systems for all new UK emu vehicles, West Coast Main Line Pendolino and current collection equipment for Shanghai Maglev; current collectors for the new vehicles for Hong Kong, Delhi Metro, KL-Monorail.

BW has also delivered conductor rail systems and catenary to Dublin, Copenhagen, Vancouver and Manchester and conductor rails and collectors to Copenhagen.

*UPDATED*

---

## Brush

Brush Traction
PO Box 17, Loughborough LE11 1HS, UK
Tel: (+44 1509) 61 70 00   Fax: (+44 1509) 61 70 01
e-mail: sales@brushtraction.demon.co.uk
Web: http://www.brushtraction.com

### Key personnel
See entry in *Locomotives and powered/non-powered passenger vehicles* section.

### Products
Electrical propulsion equipment including control equipment, traction motors, transformers and electrical auxiliary equipment for electric multiple-units, metro cars and light rail vehicles utilising both DC and AC traction motors.

Recent contracts include the supply of GTO-controlled propulsion equipment for Class 465 emu trainsets in the UK. Further propulsion equipment was also supplied for the Central Line cars for London Underground Ltd, and also for the Docklands Light Railway, London.

---

## China National Railway Locomotive & Rolling Stock Industry Corporation (LORIC)

10 Fu Xing Road, Beijing 100844, People's Republic of China
Tel: (+86 10) 63 51 16 20
Fax: (+86 10) 63 51 16 14; 63 51 16 00

---

### Jane's Transport Finance

With need-to-know finance intelligence, including debt pricing, structure, arrangers and lenders for debt deals in the aircraft, shipping and rail rolling stock sectors, *Jane's Transport Finance* is the most complete source of transport financial information for both the debt and equity markets. This unique resource also features research from investment banks and rating agencies on finance trends, as well as recent orders and privatisation information – keeping you informed of the latest business developments.
Visit **http://jtf.janes.com** for further details and sample articles.

*For further information, please visit our online catalogue at www.janes.com*

## MANUFACTURERS/Electric traction equipment

*ZD109B traction motor by LORIC*

**Key personnel**
See entry in *Locomotives and powered/non-powered passenger vehicles* section.

**Products**
LORIC currently builds diesel engines, alternators, traction motors, hydrodynamic transmissions, cardan shafts, turbochargers, intercoolers, injection pumps, fuel injectors, water pumps and oil pumps.

## ČKD

ČKD Dopravni Systémi AS
Ringhofferova 115/1, CZ-155 00 Prague 5, Czech Republic
Tel: (+420 2) 20 32 28 30   Fax: (+420 2) 20 32 28 33
e-mail: ckddos1@mbox.vol.cz

**Key personnel**
See entry in *Locomotives and powered/non-powered passenger vehicles* section.

**Products**
Electric traction and auxiliary systems for diesel-electric locomotives, trams and LRVs; control and diagnostic systems; AC and DC traction motors; dynamos and alternators; rectifiers; choppers, converters, refurbishment; assembly of electrical equipment.

## Clyde

Clyde Engineering
Factory Street, Granville, PO Box 73, New South Wales 2142, Australia
Tel: (+61 2) 96 37 82 88   Fax: (+61 2) 98 97 21 74
A member of the Evans Deakin Industries Group

**Key personnel**
See entry in *Locomotives and powered/non-powered passenger vehicles* section.

**Products**
Traction motors.

## Continental Components Pvt Ltd

16 Hare Street, Calcutta 700 001, India
Tel: (+91 33) 248 23 91   Fax: (+91 33) 248 93 82
e-mail: ccpltd.cc@gems.vsnl.net.in

**Key personnel**
Managing Director: Y K Daga
Chief Executive: S Neogi

**Products**
Pantographs and trolley poles for LRVs and suburban transit systems, and modified versions for other requirements; heavy-duty pantographs for railways for various catenary voltages up to 25 kV, custom-designed and produced for any catenary arrangement; air-brake compressor with integral motor suitable for light rail systems.

*VERIFIED*

## Crompton Greaves Ltd

6th floor, CG House, Dr Annie Besant Road, Prabhadevi, Mumbai 400 025, India
Tel: (+91 22) 423 77 77   Fax: (+91 22) 423 77 88

Rail Transportation Systems Division
Vandhna 11, Tolstoy Marg, New Delhi 110 001, India
Tel: (+91 11) 331 21 47; 373 04 45
Fax: (+91 11) 331 43 60; 335 21 34
e-mail: rtsdm7@mantraonline.com
  harsh@mail.cgl.co.in

**Key personnel**
Managing Director: S M Trehan
General Manager, Rail Transportation Systems Division: A K Raina
All India Marketing Manager, Rail Transportation Systems Division: Harsh Dhingra

**Products**
AC and DC traction motors; traction alternators; AC and DC auxiliary motors; brushless alternators; locomotive transformers; power converters and auxiliary converters; control electronics for locomotives; surge arrestors; rotary converters; static inverters. Complete electrics for demus and Diesel-Electric Tower Cars (DETC).

**Developments**
Three-phase electric equipment for locomotives is under development.

*NEW ENTRY*

## Daewoo

Daewoo Heavy Industries Ltd
PO Box 7955, Daewoo Centre Building 23nd Fl, 541, 5-Ga, Namdaemun-Ro, Jung-Gu, Seoul, South Korea
Tel: (+82 2) 726 31 79; 31 82
Fax: (+82 2) 726 31 86; 756 26 79

**Key personnel**
See entry in *Locomotives and powered/non-powered passenger vehicles* section.

**Products**
Traction motors (AC, DC), static inverters (IGBT, GTO, PTR), propulsion equipment (VVVF, chopper, rheostatic control) and TCMS (Train Control & Monitoring System).
Recent contracts include technical licences wtih Magatherm Electronics Ltd, India, for the supply of four types of static inverters for Indian Railways.

## Dynex Semiconductor

Doddington Road, Lincoln LN6 3LF
Tel: (+44 1522) 50 05 00   Fax: (+44 1522) 50 00 20
e-mail: power_solutions@dynexsemi.com
Web: http://www.dynexsemi.com

**Key personnel**
President and Chief Executive Officer: Mike Legoff
Vice-President, Technology: Dr Paul Taylor
Vice-President, World-Wide Sales: Brian Boomer

**Products**
Power semiconductor devices: thyristors, diodes, transistors, IGBTs, gate turn-off thyristors, power modules, and air, oil, water and phase change cooling assemblies. These products may be used for onboard or track side applications.

**Contracts**
Contracts include Eurostar, TGV Nord, Sybic, Metro Interconnexion (RER), France; Hong Kong MTRC; London Underground Ltd's Jubilee Line, Class 325 emus for Royal Mail, Networker Class 465 in the UK; Seoul Metro, South Korea; and locomotives for Taiwan.

*UPDATED*

## EFACEC

EFACEC Sistemas de Electrónica SA
PO Box 31, P-4470 Maia, Portugal
Tel: (+351 2) 941 36 66   Fax: (+351 2) 948 54 28

**Products**
DC and AC traction motors, transformers.

*VERIFIED*

## EG & G Rotron

55 Hasbrouck Lane, Woodstock, New York 12498, USA
Tel: (+1 845) 679 24 01   Fax: (+1 845) 679 18 78

**Key personnel**
President and General Manager: Peter Stewart
Business Element Manager, Transportation: Norm Smith
Marketing Manager, Transportation: Keith Hallenbeck

**Products**
Maintenance-free brushless DC motors, blowers, pumps, fans and blowers for bus, LRV and locomotive applications. Also HVAC products, including boost pumps, ventilators and fuel pumps.

*UPDATED*

## ELIN EBG Traction GmbH

Cumberlandstrasse, 32-34 A-1141 Vienna, Austria
Tel: (+43 1) 899 90 22 87   Fax: (+43 1) 899 90 38 62
e-mail: contact@elinebgtraction.at

**Key personnel**
Chair: Peter Rauter
Head of Sales and Marketing: Christian Serjannis

**Products**
Development, design, manufacture, marketing, sales and installation of electric traction for main line locomotives,

*Continental Components Type IR-03H pantograph*

Electric traction equipment/**MANUFACTURERS** 555

railcars, light rail vehicles, trams, metro trainsets, mining and industrial locomotives.

ELIN EBG Traction produces traction transformers, force-ventilated and water-cooled three-phase asynchronous traction motors, water-cooled and air-cooled IGBT transistor traction inverters, microprocessor-based traction and vehicle control systems, IGBT transistor traction inverters for mining locomotives and auxiliary power supply inverters for locomotives, railcars and passenger coaches.

**Contracts**

Contracts include supply of high-voltage equipment, transformers and IGBT inverters for 15+13 dual-voltage LRVs for Saarbrücken, Germany. Traction inverters with IGBT technology are being supplied to Škoda for a new design of tram, to Konstal and to the Transport Authority of Lodz (Poland) for refurbishment of trams. As leader of a consortium with Siemens and Adtranz, the Vienna metro trains are being upgraded whereby DC traction equipment is being replaced by three-phase technology. In the same consortium, 60 new trains will be produced for the Vienna metro. The prototype was delivered in 2000. Delivery of IGBT traction inverters and motors for the 150 ultra-low-floor trams that were developed with Siemens.

Other contracts include drive units for a follow-up order for Vienna metro type T vehicles and locomotives for Austrian salt mining companies.

*UPDATED*

## Entrelec

Entrelec (UK) Ltd
Unit B6, Dolphin Way, Shoreham-by-Sea BN43 6NZ, UK
Tel: (+44 1273) 44 01 40   Fax: (+44 1273) 44 00 34

**Key personnel**
General Sales Manager: D Evans
Specification Manager: N Babb
Marketing Manager: M Wickens

**Products**
Rolling stock and side of track terminal blocks; terminal block assemblies; relay modules; contactors and control gear; circuit breakers.

## Faiveley Transport

Faiveley Transport SA
143 boulevard Anatole France, Carrefour Pleyel, F-93285 Saint-Denis Cedex, France
Tel: (+33 1) 48 13 65 00   Fax: (+33 1) 48 13 66 47
e-mail: info@faiveley.com

**Key personnel**
See entry in *Passenger coach equipment* section.

**Products**
Pantographs, collector shoes and trolley poles. Recent developments include the CX family of pneumatically cushioned pantographs, comprising the AX and CX designs. The AX can operate where other pantographs are extended at speeds up to 220 km/h; it has been fitted to SNCF Class BB22200 locomotives. The AX is fitted with a regulator that ensures that a constant pressure is maintained against the contact wire at all speeds, using aerodynamic devices.

The CX operates at speeds up to 320 km/h. The CX is controlled by a microprocessor which varies the contact force (via a servo-valve in the pantograph's pneumatic system) in line with the train's speed and direction of travel, the position of the pantograph and the type of catenary overhead. The CX also features an automatic drop device, a low-friction spring box suspension and a collection head with independent wear strips.

## Ferraz

Ferraz SA
PO Box 3025, F-69391 Lyon Cedex 03, France
Tel: (+33 4) 72 22 66 11   Fax: (+33 4) 72 22 67 13

**Works**
28 rue Saint Philippe, F-69003 Lyon, France
70 avenue de la Gare, PO Box 18, F-38290 La Verpilliere, France
rue Vaucanson, F-69720 St Bonnet de Mure, France

**Key personnel**
Marketing Manager: M Renart
Export Sales Manager: H Behr

**Principal subsidiaries**
Fouilleret, Ferraz Corporation (USA)
Nihon Ferraz (Japan)

**Products**
Earth return current units; brush-holders for electric traction motors; current-collecting device on live rail; fuses with very high breaking capacity for protection of power semiconductors; shoe fuses; automatic earthing device with large short-circuit capability; resistors, disconnectors and switches.

## FIREMA Trasporti SpA

c/o I D P Milano Fiorenza, Via Triboniano, 220 I-20156, Milan, Italy
Tel: (+39 02) 23 02 02 23   Fax: (+39 02) 23 02 02 34
e-mail: firema.com@firema.it
Web: http://www.firema.it

**Key personnel**
See entry in *Locomotives and powered/non-powered passenger vehicles* section.

**Products**
Electromechanical and electronic (chopper and inverter) traction equipment for mainline and suburban, metro and light rail applications. Traction motors for AC and DC equipment, main generators for diesel-electric locomotives.

**Contracts**
Contracts include electrical equipment for E652 and E402 locomotives for Italian Railways (FS); electrical equipment, including traction motors, for double-deck emus for FS/North Milan Railway; auxiliary static converters for ETR 500 high-speed trainsets for FS; and traction equipment for emus for Circumetnea Railway and remote control for Type Z1 coaches.

*UPDATED*

## Freudenberg

Freudenberg Simrit KG
Höhnerweg 2-4, D-69465 Weinheim, Germany
Tel: (+49 1805) 74 67 48   Fax: (+49 1805) 74 67 48
e-mail: simrit.service@freudenberg.de
Web: http://www.simrit.de

**Key personnel**
See entry in *Bogies and suspension, wheels and axles, bearings* section.

**Products**
Precision seals: radial shaft seals, complete sealing kits for electric motors, O-rings, seals and elastic materials.

(See also *Bogies and suspension, wheels and axles, bearings*, *Passenger coach equipment*, *Freight vehicles and equipment*, *Brakes and drawgear* and *Diesel engines, transmission and fuelling systems* sections).

*UPDATED*

## Fuji Electric Co Ltd

Gate City Ohsaki, East Tower 11-2, Osaki 1-chome, Shinagawa-ku, Tokyo 141-0032, Japan
Tel: (+81 3) 54 35 70 46   Fax: (+81 3) 54 35 74 23
e-mail: info@fujielectric.co.jp
Web: http://www.fujielectric.co.jp

**Key personnel**
Managing Director, Electrical Systems Company Group: H Itou
General Manager, Transportation Systems Sales Department: K Kimura

**Background**
The Transportation Systems Sales Department of Fuji Electric falls within the company's Electrical Systems Company Group.

**Products**
Traction motors with VVVF control, static auxiliary power supply (SIV) systems, power supply equipment; computer-based supervisory remote-control equipment; fluorocarbon-cooled silicon rectifiers. SF6 gas circuit breakers and mini high-speed circuit breakers; moulded transformers; control systems incorporating electric power management, station office apparatus control, data management and disaster prevention management.

*UPDATED*

## Hamworthy

Hamworthy Compressor Systems Ltd
Chequers Bridge, Gloucester GL1 4LL, UK
Tel: (+44 1452) 52 84 31   Fax: (+44 1452) 50 73 94
e-mail: indsales@hamworthy-compressors.co.uk

**Key personnel**
Managing Director: J Cahill
Product Manager: K J Tingle

**Products**
Pantograph air compressor: a compact air-cooled compressor direct-coupled to DC motor (0.7 kW). Constructed in heavy-duty cast iron, this compressor offers maximum scope for choice of mounting position on a locomotive. Charging rate: 126 litres/min over pressure range 0 to 75 psi (0 to 5 bar). Maximum operating pressure: 100 psi (7 bar). Dimensions: 46 × 26 × 27 cm; weight with motor, 43 kg.

*Singapore MRT train using Fuji Electric inverter control systems*

## 556 MANUFACTURERS/Electric traction equipment

## Hitachi Ltd

Overseas Marketing Department
Transportation Systems Sales Division
6 Kanda Surugadai 4-chome, Chiyoda-ku,
Tokyo 101-8010, Japan
Tel: (+81 3) 52 95 55 40   Fax: (+81 3) 32 58 52 30

**Key personnel**
See entry in *Locomotives and powered/non-powered passenger vehicles* section.

**Products**
Propulsion systems, auxiliary power supply, ATP/ATO equipment, computerised total systems for urban transportation, bogie and air conditioning equipment.

In view of the increasing use of asynchronous motor propulsion systems, Hitachi has been developing VVVF inverters for trainsets of 1,500 V DC railways.

The small size of Hitachi VVVF inverters has been achieved by use of 4,500 V high-voltage GTO thyristors. Direct digital control provides accuracy in constant speed control, slip-skid correction control and start control on up-gradients. The signalling system is protected from noise and electromagnetic interference by extensive shielding and optimised wiring layout.

Hitachi Cable has developed fibre optic cables for use in monitoring and control systems in electric trains. They are being used in the latest versions of the Tokaido and Sanyo Shinkansen cars.

*UPDATED*

## Hyundai

Hyundai Heavy Industries Ltd
Electro-Electric Systems
Hyundai Building, 140-2, Kye-dong, Chongro-ku,
Seoul 110-793, South Korea
Tel: (+82 2) 746 75 30   Fax: (+82 2) 746 74 79
e-mail: rolling.hhi.co.kr
Web: http://www.hhi.co.kr

**Products**
Traction motors, traction inverters; traction generators; auxiliary power systems; train information management systems.

## InfoSystems GmbH

Lorsenstrasse 124-135, D-22869 Schenefeld, Germany
Tel: (+49 40) 83 03 90   Fax: (+49 40) 83 03 91 15
e-mail: info@hamb.infosystem.de

Ullendahler Strasse 437, D-42109 Wuppertal, Germany
Tel: (+49 202) 709 50   Fax: (+49 202) 709 51 37
e-mail: info@wtal.infosystem.de
Web: http://www.infosystem.de

**Key personnel**
Managing Director: Dr Rolf-Dieter Krächter

**Corporate background**
InfoSystems GmbH is a member of the Schaltbau Group (qv in the *Passenger coach equipment* section).

**Products**
Krueger System third rail current collection equipment for urban mass transit and underground rail vehicles. Products include top-, side- and bottom-contact systems. Metro systems equipped include those in Berlin, Hamburg, Helsinki, London and Milan.

*NEW ENTRY*

## Kiepe Elektrik

Kiepe Elektrik GmbH & Co KG
Bublitzer Strasse 28, D-40599 Düsseldorf-Reisholz,
Germany
Tel: (+49 211) 749 70   Fax: (+49 211) 749 73 00
e-mail: info@kiepe-elektrik.com
Web: http://www.kiepe-elektrik.com

**Subsidiary company**
Kiepe Electric GmbH, Vienna, Austria

**Background**
Kiepe Elektrik is a member of the Schaltbau Group (qv).

**Key personnel**
Presidents: Thomas Weber, Jürgen Textor

**Products**
Propulsion control equipment for 600 and 750 V DC supply, including three-phase AC and DC chopper power electronics for LRVs with regenerative braking; dual-voltage (15 kV AC, 750 V DC) propulsion equipment.

Rotating camshaft controllers or contactor bank controllers (switched resistor) for metro vehicles or LRVs with microprocessor-based control electronics; DC contactors, reversers, switches; master controllers; braking resistors; power electronics; door and step controls; weight, speed and displacement transducers; time delay, light and blinker-relays; and static converters.

**Contracts**
Major contracts include three-phase AC traction equipment (direct pulse inverter) for LRVs for Vienna (Austria) and Bremen, Düsseldorf, Cologne, Kassel (Germany), Croydon (UK). Traction equipment for LRVs for Saarbrücken, Germany to operate on 750 V DC and 15 kV 16⅔ Hz AC; and for battery/line locomotives for various metro and LRV operators. Kiepe supplies components and subassemblies for most LRV and metro projects in Germany. The company also specialises in installing and wiring electrical equipment at the car builder's factory – for example, for the ICE train, Germany.

*UPDATED*

## KMT-teknikka Oy

PO Box 116, FIN-38701 Kankaanpää, Finland
Tel: (+358 2) 573 12 39   Fax: (+358 2) 573 22 80
e-mail: esa.pyoria@kmt.fi
Web: http://www.kmt.fi

**Key personnel**
Managing Director: Esa Pyöriä
Key Account Manager: Aki Tuononen

**Products**
Assembly of electric traction equipment, switchgear, pre-assembled electrical centres and control consoles; fabrication and manufacture of cabinets and enclosures in steel, stainless steel and aluminium for rail applications.

**Contracts**
Pre-assembly of main converter units for VR Class Sr2 electric locomotives built by Bombardier Transportation; assembly of control consoles for Class Sr2 locomotives; electrical distribution boxes, electrical control centres, heating elements and catering service lifts for VR Type ICS double-deck coaches built by Talgo; electrical control centres and neutral section sensor boxes for VR Pendolino trainsets built by Alstom.

*NEW ENTRY*

## Končar – Elecktrične Lokomotive dd

Končar-Electric Locomotives Inc
Velimira Škorpika 7, HR-10090 Zagreb, Croatia
Tel: (+385 1) 349 69 59   Fax: (+385 1) 349 69 60
e-mail: uprava.ellok@koncar.tel.hr
Web: http://www.koncar.hr/koncar/ellok/

**Key personnel**
See entry in *Locomotives and powered/non-powered passenger vehicles* section.

**Products**
Light rail vehicles; parts, components and systems for electric traction.

*UPDATED*

## Lechmotoren

Lechmotoren GmbH
Suedliche Roemerstrasse 12-16, D-86972 Altenstadt,
Germany

Tel: (+49 8861) 71 00   Fax: (+49 8861) 71 01 80
e-mail: lechmotoren@compuserve.com
Web: http://www.lechmotoren.de

**Products**
Converters, generators up to 1.5 kV, internal combustion generator sets, AC motors, asynchronous/synchronous motors, electronic components for urban transport applications.

## Lekov AS

Jirotova 375, CZ-336 01 Blovice, Czech Republic
Tel: (+420 185) 52 21 79
Fax: (+420 185) 52 21 81; 52 21 89
e-mail: lekov@lekov.cz
Web: http://www.lekov.cz

**Key personnel**
Managing Director: Michal Ovsjannikov
Finance Director: Alena Zoubková
Sales Director: Michal Kučera

**Products**
Components for trolleybuses, trams, metros and railways. These include high-speed circuit breakers, electromagnetic and electropneumatic contactors, master controllers, protection relays, reversers, disconnecting switches, earthing switches, pantographs, resistors and magnetic valves.

**Contracts**
Contracts include delivery of electrical equipment to Škoda for the refurbishment of Russian Railways Type CS200 and 82 E9 CS locomotives. Delivery of electrical devices to Škoda for 14 Tr trolleybuses to the city of Dayton, Ohio, USA. Currently supplying locomotive pantographs to Končar, Zagreb, Croatia. Supply of electrical units and pantographs to the city of Pilsen for the low-floor Astra tram through Škoda/Inekon. Supply of electrical units and pantographs to Pilsen for modernisation of T3 trams (through ČKD). Supply of electrical units and pantographs for the modernisation of Type T3 trams for the city of Liberec. Supply of pantographs for the RT6 low-floor tram for Liberec. Supply of electrical units to Czech Railways for LRV Type 47I. Supply of electrical devices and controllers to Škoda for the modernisation of the Prague metro.

*UPDATED*

## Mitsubishi Electric

Mitsubishi Electric Corporation
Mitsubishi Denki Bldg, 2-3 Marunouchi 2-chome,
Chiyoda-ku, Tokyo 100, Japan
Tel: (+81 3) 32 18 34 30   Fax: (+81 3) 32 18 90 48

**Key personnel**
See entry in *Locomotives and powered/non-powered passenger vehicles* section.

**Products**
Electric propulsion equipment (traction motors, VVVF inverters, chopper controllers, main transformers, rectifiers, drive gears, flexible couplings), brake systems, auxiliary electrical equipment (static inverters). Air conditioning systems, train control equipment (ATC, ATO, ATS). Integral control systems, communication systems, substation systems (DC and AC) and equipment, station depot and inspection equipment, magnetic and super conduction magnets.

## Morio Denki

Morio Denki Co Ltd
34-1 Tateishi 4-chome, Katsushika-ku, Tokyo 124-0012,
Japan
Tel: (+81 3) 36 91 31 81   Fax: (+81 3) 36 92 13 33
Web: http://www.morio.co.jp

**Main works**
2 Natooka, Ryugasaki City, Ibaragi Pref 301, Japan

## Key personnel
President: S Yamagata
Managing Director and General Manager, Marketing Division: K Miura

## Subsidiaries
Morio Engineering Service
Morio Robotek Co Ltd
Couterie Morio Ltd

## Products
Control equipment, including master controllers, switch boxes, distribution boards, junction boxes and conductor switches. Digital speedometers.

*UPDATED*

---

## National

National Electrical Carbon Corporation
PO Box 1056, Greenville, South Carolina 29602, USA
Tel: (+1 864) 458 77 77    Fax: (+1 864) 281 01 80

### Key personnel
General Manager: M Cox
Sales Director: D Klas
Director, International Sales: J T Tidswell
Director, International Marketing: K Osman

### Principal subsidiaries
Fulmer Company Inc Export, Pennsylvania, USA
National Electrical Carbon BV, Hoorn, Netherlands
National Electrical Carbon Canada, Mississauga, Ontario, Canada
National Electrical Carbon Limited, Sheffield, UK

### Products
Carbon brushes for all traction, commutator, motor generator and auxiliary equipment, carbon brush holders and wheel flange lubricators.

---

## Parizzi

Parizzi (a Fiat Ferroviaria company)
Elettromeccanica Parizzi SpA
Via C Romani 10, I-20091 Bresso, Milan, Italy
Tel: (+39 02) 66 52 31    Fax: (+39 02) 614 04 08

### Products
Energy converters: mono- and poly-current static converters fed by the primary power line to supply power for onboard auxiliary systems in three-phase 50 Hz AC (input voltages: 3,000 V DC, 1,500 V DC, 1,500 V AC, 50 Hz, 1,000 V AC 16⅔ Hz. Power: 40 to 85 kVA); mono- and poly-current static battery chargers fed by the primary power line (input voltages: as for auxiliary systems above, plus 600, 750 and 1,500 V DC. Power: 1, 5 to 14 kW); inverters and converters; UPS.

Traction equipment: variable frequency and voltage inverters for the supply and control of asynchronous traction motors for diesel-electric locomotives and electric trainsets; AC traction motors.

Components: electrical and electropneumatic components for railcars and locomotives; automatic starters; controllers and reverse switches; electrical connectors for multiple traction; various transducers.

Electromechanical devices: battery chargers operated from the axle of the bogie of railway vehicles.

Electronic systems: microprocessor-based control and diagnostic systems; centralised tachometric/tachographic and event-recording systems; electronic anti-slide devices to adapt the braking force to the instantaneous adhesion condition of railway vehicles; electronic anti-slip devices for locomotives; bivalent anti-slide/slip devices.

---

## Permali Gloucester Ltd

Bristol Road, Gloucester GL1 5TT, UK
Tel: (+44 1452) 52 82 82    Fax: (+44 1452) 50 74 09
e-mail: sales@permali-gloucester.co.uk
Web: http://www.permali.co.uk

### Key personnel
See entry in *Passenger coach equipment* section.

### Products
Halogen-free laminates for shoe beams, shoe arms and arc barriers for third rail current collection systems.

### Contracts
Contracts include the supply of shoe beams, shoe arms and arc barriers to London Underground Ltd and shoe beam and shoe arm assemblies for EWS Class 92 locomotives.

*UPDATED*

---

## RDS Technology Ltd

Cirencester Road, Minchinhampton, Stroud GL6 9BH, UK
Tel: (+44 1453) 73 33 00    Fax: (+44 1453) 73 33 22
e-mail: info@rdstec.com
Web: http://www.rdstec.com

### Key personnel
Managing Director: R Danby
Engineering Director: P Nelson
REM Business Director: J A Hawer

### Products
True Ground Speed Sensor (TGSS) for slip and traction control.

---

## Riga Electric Machine Building Works

31 Ganibu dambis, LV-1005 Riga, Latvia
Tel: (+371 7) 38 13 50    Fax: (+371 7) 733 41 33

### Products
Electric control sets for 3 kV DC and 25 kV AC trainsets; electrical control sets for passenger vehicle lighting and power supply; 100 to 280 kW DC traction motors for 3 kV DC emus; repair and refurbishment of DC motors; low voltage DC motors up to 20 kW for forklifts.

*UPDATED*

---

## Rotem Company

231 Yangjae-Dong, Soecho-ku, Seoul, Korea 137-938
Tel: (+82 2) 34 64 46 45    Fax: (+82 2) 34 64 47 92
Web: http://www.rotem.co.kr

### Key personnel
See entry in *Locomotives and powered/non-powered passenger vehicles* section.

### Background
See entry in *Locomotives and powered/non-powered passenger vehicles* section.

### Products
Rotem has developed and supplies fully integrated propulsion system packages, traction equipment and support services for modern railway and urban transportation vehicles.

Electrical equipment for emus; electric locomotive and light rail vehicles, including VVVF inverter control, chopper control equipment using IGBT or GTO technology, AC and DC traction motor, main transformer and auxiliary power supply.

### Contracts
GTO VVVF inverter AC drive systems have been supplied for Seoul metro line 7 and 8 and also more than 200 sets of chopper control system for Seoul metro line 3 and 4.

Rotem supplied more than 3,000 sets of AC/DC traction motors and more than 500 sets of static inverters using IGBT, GTO and power transistors for Seoul metro and Korean National Railroad (KNR).

Recent orders have included the 240 kW AC traction motor and 150 kVA IGBT static inverter for Taiwan Railway Administration (TRA) 600 series emu.

Rotem is fully equipped with test facilities and equipment. All products are performed with wide range of performance test and quality inspection.

*UPDATED*

---

## SAFT

156 avenue de Metz, F-93230 Romainville, France
Tel: (+33 1) 49 15 36 00    Fax: (+33 1) 49 15 34 00
Web: http://www.saftbatteries.com

### Key personnel
Managing Director Industrial Battery Group: Bertrant Olivesi
Marketing and Sales Director, Industrial Battery Group: Fred-Erik Hopiak
Railway Product Manager: Anne-Marie Billard
Railway Project Manager: Michael Lippert

### Subsidiaries
Argentina, Australia, Brazil, Cyprus, Germany, Hong Kong, Italy, Korea, Malaysia, Mexico, Netherlands, Norway, Singapore, Spain, Sweden, UK and USA.

### Products
Saft Nife Ni/Cd batteries, pocket plates or sintered/plastic bonded electrode types are for emergency supply, and security purposes. All items are lightweight and compact and are available in containers made of stainless steel, flame retardant or standard plastic containers. The SRX/SRM batteries need topping-up every two years with distilled water.

Saft offers an integrated battery assembly concept for onboard power for railways OEMs and railway networks by combining advanced Ni/Cd batteries with custom made containers, the weight and volume is reduced thus improving energy efficiency.

Saft has received contracts to supply SRX/SRM batteries for the West Coast Mainline, UK, Washington metro USA; Oeresund line, Sweden; Taipei metro and the metro and railways of Hong Kong.

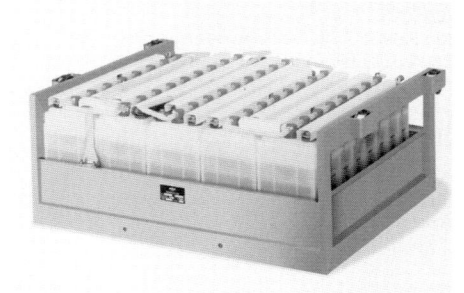

*Saft SRM battery pack*    0063628

---

## Sécheron SA

14 Avenue de Sécheron, CH-1211 Geneva 21, Switzerland
Tel: (+41 22) 739 41 11    Fax: (+41 22) 738 73 05
e-mail: info@secheron.com
Web: http://www.secheron.com

### Key personnel
Chief Executive Officer: C Durand
Chief Financial Officer: O Kunkel
PBU Components Director: J Murer
PBU Electronics Director: P Stanffer
PBU Systems Director: P Taurian

### Subsidiary companies
Secheron Tchequie sro, Czech Republic
Secheron Italia Srl, Milan
Secheron Inc, Washington, USA
Pixy AG, Baden, Switzerland

### Products
DC high-speed circuit breakers (HSCB); auxiliary converters; AC and DC power and auxiliary contactors, AC vacuum circuit breakers, disconnection and changeover switches, single-arm pantographs, master controllers, electronic speed measuring and data recording systems, pulse generators, multifunctional display systems, wheel flange lubricators, automatic centre-couplings.

Complete system engineering, installation and setting up of modular control electronics and associated traction/auxiliary components.

Recent projects include: various components for Class 223 and Class 209 emu of JR West and JR East; components for the Type DESIRO vehicles for SZ

## MANUFACTURERS/Electric traction equipment

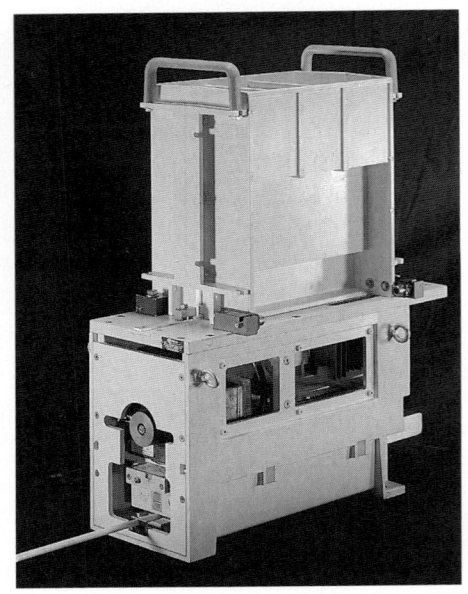

*Sécheron high-speed DC circuit breaker, Type HBP 45-81S (4,500 A-1,000 V)* 0002184

Slovenia; supply of auxiliary converters for type OCTEON electric locomotives for MTAB Sweden, FS Italy and other railways.

**UPDATED**

---

## Siemens Rolling Stock Electronics

Krauss-Maffei-Strasse 2, PO Box 500340, D-80973 Munich, Germany
Tel: (+49 89) 88 99 20 24   Fax: (+49 89) 88 99 28 50
e-mail: internet@ts.siemens.de
Web: http://www.siemens.com

### Key personnel
Managing Board: Dr Volker Kefer, Bruno Flad
Rolling Stock Electronics: Ralf Ruck
  Thomas Seger

### Corporate development
A majority shareholding of Siemens Rolling Stock Electric is owned by Siemens AG.

### Products
Modular, rail-proven microprocessor-based locomotive control, command and monitoring systems (KM-DIREKT) with integrated online diagnostics (K-MEMO) suited to safe (SIL 3) radio remote control; integrated and stand-alone wheelslip and -skid control and protection systems (K-MICRO and K-MICRO compact) for all kinds of rail vehicle; rugged contact- and wear-less active speed sensors (KMG-2H) and LCD displays (K-MONITOR); speed control/regulation and automation systems (KM-PROFA); sanding gear (KM-1sp and ED) and crash elements.

**UPDATED**

---

## Siemens Westinghouse

Siemens Westinghouse Technical Services
544 Church Street, Melbourne, Victoria 3121, Australia
Tel: (+61 29) 724 73 22   Fax: (+61 29) 726 97 57
e-mail: david.morris@siemens.com.au
Formerly Westinghouse Electric Australasia

### Works
49 Miowera Road, Villawood, New South Wales 2163, Australia

### Key personnel
Manager, Technical Services: Ken Cunningham
Business Field Manager: John Louth
NSW Regional Manager: Graham Barlow
National Marketing Manager, Australia: David Morris

### Products
Electric traction equipment; DC and AC traction motors; onboard transformers and reactors; compressor motors; replacement equipment; remanufacture of all rotating traction motors and generators; repairs and upgrades of transformers and switchgear.

---

## SPII

SPII SpA
Via Volpi 37, I-21047, Saronno VA, Italy
Tel: (+39 02) 962 29 21   Fax: (+39 02) 960 96 11

### Key personnel
Principal: Dr Ing Roberto Foiadelli

### Products
Electromechanical components for rail, tram and metro vehicles, including driver's control panels, master controllers, switch panels, circuit breakers, rotary switches, relays and isolators. Newly introduced are driver consoles, master controllers and switch panels for locomotives.

Other equipment by SP11 includes pneumatic selection switches, rotary switches for connecting batteries, controllers and multipole switches.

Contracts include complete driving control units for E412, E402, ETR500, ETR460, ETR470, ETR480, E652 and E633 locomotives.

---

## Stemmann

Stemmann-Technik GmbH
PO Box 1460, D-48459 Schüttorf, Germany
Tel: (+49 5923) 810   Fax: (+49 5923) 811 00
e-mail: info@stemman.de
Web: http://www.stemmann.de

### Corporate development
Stemmann-Technik is a member of the Fandstand Electric Group.

### Products
Standard pantographs for light rail vehicles, underground tramways and suburban transit systems per German DIN specification 43,187, and modified versions to suit customer requirements; heavy-duty pantographs for trunk railroads for all catenary voltages (up to 25 kV) in conventional (diamond) and contemporary single-arm style; pantographs for industrial locomotives, custom-designed to suit any catenary arrangement. Frost earthing contacts for railway vehicles.

---

## Toshiba

Toshiba Corporation
Railway Projects Department
Toshiba Building, 1-1, Shibaura 1-chome, Minato-ku, Tokyo 105, Japan
Tel: (+81 3) 34 57 49 24   Fax: (+81 3) 34 57 83 85

### Key personnel
See entry in *Locomotives and powered/non-powered passenger vehicles* section.

### Products
Electric traction equipment; auxiliary power supply units; coach air conditioner; industrial rolling stock.

One of the systems of advanced technology that has been under development, in this case in conjunction with Japanese National Railways, is the propulsion system for the next generation of Shinkansen Super-Hikari trainsets, which consists of a 3,000 kW pulsewidth modulation converter with 4,500 V-2,000 A GTO, 1,760 kVA VVVF inverter also with 4,500 V-2,000 A GTO, and eight 320 kW induction motors.

---

## Toyo Denki

Toyo Denki Seizo KK
Toyo Electric Manufacturing Co Ltd
No.1 Nurihiko Building, 9-2 Kyobashi 2-chome, Chuo-ku, Tokyo 104, Japan
Tel: (+81 3) 35 35 06 41   Fax: (+81 3) 35 35 06 50

### Works
Yokohama: 3-8 Fukuura 3-chome, Kanazawa-ku, Yokohama 236, Japan
Sagami: 6-32 Higashi-Kashiwagaya 4-chome, Ebina 243-04, Japan

### Key personnel
President: Mitsuru Ando
Vice-President: Jiro Tsukahara
Managing Director: Yoshitsugu Miura
Director: H Takei
General Manager of Transportation Division: T Hagiwara
General Manager, System Sales Department: H Kiyama
General Manager of Engineering Department: T Ohsawa

### Products
Electrical equipment for electric multiple-units, electric and diesel-electric locomotives, light rail vehicles, rubber-tyred vehicles and maglev systems. Propulsion equipment, including induction motors, DC traction motors, drive gear units, VVVF inverter control systems, master controllers, high-speed circuit breakers, unit switches and microprocessor-controlled electronic devices. Auxiliary power supply equipment, including static inverters and converters and brushless motor-alternators. Current collection devices, door actuators, train information control systems and speedometers.

---

## Transportation Products

Transportation Products Sales Co Inc
61 Cepi Drive, Suite B, Chesterfied, Missouri 63005, USA
Tel: (+1 314) 532 11 44   Fax: (+1 314) 532 14 82
e-mail: tpscerms@tpsc-arms.com

### Key personnel
President: Walter J Winzen
Vice-President: Hugo Schmitz

### Products
Batteries by GNB Technologies for starting diesel-electric locomotives. DC power systems for rail application electronics.

---

## Tülomsas

The Locomotive & Motor Corporation of Turkey
Ahmet Kanatli Cad, TR-26490 Eskisehir, Turkey
Tel: (+90 222) 224 00 00
Fax: (+90 225) 72 72; 57 57
e-mail: tulomsas@tulomsas.com.tr
Web: http://www.tulomsas.com.tr

### Key personnel
Managing Director: D Zeki Daloglu
Assistant General Managers: Galip Pala, Cengiz Özan, Fatih Turan, Haluk Akova
Head of Marketing: Erol Çetin

### Products
Traction motors, motor generator sets, control equipment for electric locomotives, bogies.

# PASSENGER COACH EQUIPMENT

## Alphabetical listing

3M Europe SA
A K Fans
Adams & Westlake
Advanced Structures Corporation
Aim Aviation (Henshalls)
Air International
Airscrew Ltd
Albatros
Albright International
Alna Koki
ALSTOM
Angst+Pfister
ApATeCh Electro
Astra
Atlas International
Autoroche Industrie
AVE Rail Products
Avery Dennison
Baier + Koppel GmbH & Co
Bayham
Behr Industry
Bekaert Composite
Bircher
Bode
Bosch Telecom
C&H Chemical
Carrier Sütrak GmbH
Carrier Transicold
CASAS-M
Channel Electric Equipment
Chapman Seating Ltd
Cleff
Clerprem SpA
CMC Interiors
Cole
Compin
Conbrako
Concargo
Connei
ContiTech Profile GmbH
Craig and Derricott
Cressall Resistors Transit Division
Cromweld Steels Ltd
Cytec Fiberite
Dansk Dekor-Laminat A/S
Deans Powered Doors
Deco Seating BV
Desso
Deuta-Werke AG
Deutsch Relays
Dewhurst
Dialight
Driessen Railway Interior Systems
Eagle Ottawa Callow & Maddox
EAO AG
Ebac
Ebo Systems
EC-Engineering Oy
Ederena Concept
EFACEC
EKE-Electronics Ltd
Elettromeccanica Parizza spa
Ellcon National
ELNO
ESW-EXTEL
EVAC
EVAC GmbH
Excil
FAGA
FAINSA
Faiveley Transport
FASI Seating Systems
Ferranti Technologies Ltd
Ferraz
Ferro
Ferro International A/S
Fersystem
Fiberline
Fine Products SA
Finnyards Materials Technology
Fischer Industries Pty Ltd
Flachglas Wernberg GmbH
Freudenberg Schwab GmbH
Fuji Electric
FY – Industries
GAI-Tronics
The Gates Rubber Co Ltd
Georg Eknes Industrier A/S
Georges Halais SA
GEZ
Geze
Giumma SpA
GMT
Grammer
Heinrich Helms Metallwarenfabrik GmbH
Hexcel Composites
HFG
Hitachi
Hodgson and Hodgson
Honeywell Serck
Howden Buffalo
HP
Hübner
Huck
IFE
IMI Norgren GmbH
International Metals Reclamation Co dbac (INMETCO)
International Nameplate Supplies Ltd
Irausa Loire
Jarmuszerelvenyt Guarto RT
John Holdsworth
Joyce-Loebl Ltd
Jupiter Plast
Kaba Gilgen AG
Kidde
Kiel
Kleeneze Sealtech Ltd
Klein Transport
KV Ltd
Lakeuden Kykmakeskus Oy (Lumikko)
Lazzerini
Lenord + Bauer
Liebherr-Verkehrstechnik Frankfurt
LM Glasfiber
Mafelec
Mechan
Merak
Microelettrica Scientifica SpA
Microphor
Mobile Climate Control Corporation
Monogram Sanitation
Morio Denki
MTB Equipment Ltd
NABCO LTD
Narita
Neu Systems Ferroviaires
Nieaf-Smitt
Northern Rubber Co Ltd
Nortrade
Orvec International
Parker Pneumatic
Pascal International AB
People Seating
Percy Lane Products
Permali
Phoenix
Pickersgill-Kaye Ltd
Pilkington Aerospace
Pintsch Bamag GmbH
Pixy AG
Polarteknik PMC Oy AB
Portaramp
Power-One AG
Powernetics Ltd
Powertron
Protec
RailTronic AG
Reidler Decal
Rex
RICA
Safenet
SAFT
Saint-Gobain Sully
Saint-Gobain Sully NA, Inc
SBF
Schaltbau GmbH
Schaltbau Holding AG
Schlegel Swiss Standard AG
Schunk
Selectron Systems AG
Semco Vacuumteknik
SEPSA
SERINOX
Siemens Rolling Stock Electronics
SMA
SMTC
Southco
Specialty Bulb
SPS Isoclima SpA
Stone India Ltd
Stone International
Stratiforme Industries
Supersine Duramark Limited
TBA
Techni Industrie SA
Technical Resin Bonders
Teknoware
Telephonics
Temoinsa
th-contact
The Network Connection
Thermo King
Thorn Transport Lighting
Tiflex Ltd
TODCO Inc
Toshiba
Toyo Denki
Transit Control Systems
Transmatic Inc
Transtechnik GmbH
Trevira
TriCon
Unicel
UniControls
USSC Group
Vapor Corporation
VBK
WABCO
Wabtec Rail Ltd
Walter Mäder Lacke
Westcode
Widney Transport Components
Winstanley
Woodville Polymer Engineering
XP

**UPDATED**

## Classified listing

**AIR CONDITIONING, HEATING AND VENTILATION SYSTEMS**

Airscrew Ltd
Air International
A K Fans
Albatros
ALSTOM
Behr Industry
Carrier Khéops Bac
Carrier Transicold
Channel Electric Equipment
CompAir
Compair Hydrovane
Cressall Resistors Transit Division
Ebac
Faiveley Transport
HFG
Hitachi
Hodgson and Hodgson
Honeywell Serck
Howden Buffalo
Kuckuck
Lakeuden Kykmakeskus Oy (Lummico)
Liebherr-Verkehrstechnik Frankfurt

## MANUFACTURERS / Passenger coach equipment

Morio Denki
Neu Systems Ferroviaires
Nortrade
Parker Pneumatic
Pintsch Bamag
Stone Iberica
Stone India
Stone International
Stone UK
Sütrak
Temoinsa
Thermo King
Toshiba
Transit Control Systems
Vapor
Westcode

### AUDIO SYSTEMS AND INFORMATION DISPLAYS
ALSTOM
Carrier Khéops Bac
ELNO
FY Industries
GAI-Tronics
IVS
Joyce-Loebl Ltd
Morio Denki
The Network Connection
Pixy AG
SEPSA

### CONVERTERS AND ELECTRICAL EQUIPMENT
Albright International
ALSTOM
Bombardier Transportation
Carrier Khéops Bac
Connei
Craig & Derricott
Deutsch Relays
Dewhurst
EAO Highland
Ebo Systems
EFACEC
Elettromeccanica
ESW-EXTEL
Excil
FAGA
Faiveley Transport
Ferranti Technologies
Ferraz
GEZ
Harting
IMI Norgren GmbH
Liebherr-Verkehrstechnik Frankfurt
Litton
Microelettrica Scientifica
Nieaf-Smitt
Pintsch Bamag
Power-One AG
Powernetics
Powertron
SAFT
Schaltbau GmbH
SEPSA
Siemens Rolling Stock Electronics
SMA
Stone India
Stone International
Toshiba
Transtechnik GmbH
UniControls
Vapor

### DATA RECORDERS, FIRE PROTECTION AND TRAIN MANAGEMENT SYSTEMS
ALSTOM
EKE-Electronics
GEZ
Kidde
Lenord + Bauer
Liebherr-Verkehrstechnik Frankfurt
SEPSA
Siemens
TBA
UniControls
Wood Group Fire Systems
XP

### DOOR SYSTEMS AND COMPONENTS
Berendsen Pimatic
Bircher
Bode
Conbrako
ContiTech
Deans Powered Doors
Dewhurst
EAO Highland
Faiveley Transport
Ferro International
FY Industries
Fuji Electric
Geze
HP
IFE
IMI Norgren GmbH
Kaba Gilgen
Kiekert
Kleeneze Sealtech
KV
LM Glasfiber
Morio Denki
NABCO
Narita
Nippon Signal
Parker Pneumatic
Phoenix
Pickersgill-Kaye Ltd
Pintsch Bamag
Portaramp
Schlegel Swiss Standard
Southco
Techni-Industrie
th-contact
TODCO Inc
Toyo Denki
USSC Group
Vapor
Westcode
Widney Transport Components

### GANGWAYS
Adams & Westlake
Faiveley Transport
Hübner
Narita
Northern Rubber
Woodville Polymer Engineering

### INTERIOR FITTINGS AND SEATING
Aim Aviation (Henshalls)
Alna Koki
ApATeCh Electro
Astra
Bekaert Composite
Bosch Telecom
CASAS-M
Chapman Seating Ltd
Clerprem SpA
Cole
Compin
Concargo
ContiTech
Cromweld Steels Ltd
Cytec Fiberite
Dansk Dekor-Laminet A/S
Deans Powered Doors
Decostone Europe BV
Desso
Driessen
Eagle Ottawa Callow & Maddox
EC-Engineering Oy
FAINSA
Ferro
Fiberline
FY Industries
Gates Rubber Co Ltd, The
George Eknes Industrier A/S
Georges Halais
Grammer
Hexcel
Hübner
Huck
IMI Norgren GmbH
IRAUSA LOIRE
John Holdsworth
Jupiter Plast
Kiel
MTB Equipment Ltd
Pascal International AB
Percy Lane
Lazzerini
LM Glasfiber
Narita
Orvec International
Parker Pneumatic
People Seating
Permali Gloucester Ltd
Phoenix
Protec
Railcare
RG Manufacturing
RICA
Sanivac
Schlegel Swiss Standard
SMTC
Sütrak
Technical Resin Bonder
Temoinsa
Tiflex
Trevira
TriCon
Unicel
USSC Group
VBK
Winstanley

### LIGHTING SYSTEMS AND COMPONENTS
Angst+Pfister
Atlas International
Autoroche Industrie
Dialight
Excil
GEZ
Morio Denki
RailTronic AG
SBF
Specialty Bulb
Teknoware
Thorn Transport Lighting
Toshiba

### PAINTING AND REPAIRS
3M Europe SA
Avery Dennison
C&H Chemical
RFS(E)
Supersine Duramark
Walter Mäder Lacke

### TOILET SYSTEMS AND COMPONENTS
Aim Aviation (Henshalls)
Bayham
Driessen
EVAC
Microphor
Monogram Sanitation
Parker Pneumatic
Protec
Sanivac
Schlegel Swiss Standard
Semco Vacuumteknik
SERINOX
Temoinsa

### UNDERFLOOR EQUIPMENT
Angst+Pfister
Baier + Koppel GmbH
Bayham
Carrier Khéops Bac
CompAir
Compair Hydrovane
Ellcon National
Freudenberg
GMT
Mechan
Narita
Phoenix
Wabtec

### WINDOWS AND WINDSCREENS
Alna Koki
Cleff
Conbrako
ContiTech
Deans Powered Doors
Flachglas Wernberg
Geze
Klein
Morio Denki
Percy Lane
Phoenix
Pilkington Aerospace
Sully North America
Sully Produits Spéciaux
USSC Group
Widney Transport Components

## Company listing by country

**AUSTRALIA**
Air International
Fischer Industries Pty Ltd

**AUSTRIA**
IFE
Schunk

**BELGIUM**
3M Europe SA
Bekaert Composite
FASI Seating Systems

**CANADA**
International Nameplate Supplies Ltd
Stone International

**CZECH REPUBLIC**
Thermo King
UniControls

**DENMARK**
Dansk Dekor-Laminat A/S
Ferro International A/S
Fiberline
Jupiter Plast
LM Glasfiber
Semco Vacuumteknik

**FINLAND**
EC-Engineering Oy
EKE-Electronics Ltd
EVAC
Finnyards Materials Technology
FY – Industries
Lakeuden Kykmakeskus Oy (Lumikko)
Polarteknik PMC Oy AB
Teknoware

**FRANCE**
ALSTOM
Autoroche Industrie
Compin
Ebo Systems
Ederena Concept
ELNO
Faiveley Transport
Ferraz
Fersystem
Georges Halais SA
Irausa Loire
Klein Transport
Mafelec
Neu Systems Ferroviaires
SAFT
Saint-Gobain Sully
SERINOX
SMTC
Stratiforme Industries
Techni Industrie SA

**GERMANY**
Baier + Koppel GmbH & Co
Behr Industry
Bode
Bosch Telecom
Carrier Sütrak GmbH
Cleff
ContiTech Profile GmbH
Deuta-Werke
ESW-EXTEL
EVAC GmbH
FAGA
Flachglas Wernberg GmbH
Freudenberg Schwab GmbH
GEZ
Geze
GMT
Grammer
Heinrich Helms Metallwarenfabrik GmbH
HFG
Hübner
IMI Norgren GmbH
Kiel
Lenord + Bauer
Liebherr-Verkehrstechnik Frankfurt
Phoenix
Pintsch Bamag GmbH
Protec
Sanivac
SBF
Schaltbau
Siemens
SMA
Transtechnik GmbH
Trevira
TriCon

**HUNGARY**
Jarmuszerelvenyt Guarto RT

**INDIA**
Stone India Ltd

**ITALY**
Clerprem SpA
Connei
Elettromeccanica Parizza spa
Giumma SpA
HP
Lazzerini
Microelettrica Scientifica SpA
Nortrade
RICA
SPS Isoclima SpA

**JAPAN**
Alna Koki
Fuji Electric
Hitachi
Morio Denki
NABCO LTD
Narita
Toshiba
Toyo Denki

**NETHERLANDS**
Avery Dennison
Deco Seating BV
Desso
Driessen Railway Interior Systems
Nieaf-Smitt

**NORWAY**
Georg Eknes Industrier A/S
VBK

**PORTUGAL**
EFACEC

**ROMANIA**
Astra

**RUSSIAN FEDERATION**
ApATeCh Electro

**SOUTH AFRICA**
Conbrako
Widney Transport Components

**SPAIN**
Albatros
CASAS-M
CMC Interiors
FAINSA
Fine Products SA
Merak
SEPSA
Temoinsa

**SWEDEN**
Pascal International AB
Safenet

**SWITZERLAND**
Angst+Pfister
Bircher
Kaba Gilgen AG
Pixy AG
Power-One AG
RailTronic AG
Rex
Schlegel Swiss Standard AG
Selectron Systems AG

**UNITED KINGDOM**
Aim Aviation (Henshalls)
Airscrew Ltd
A K Fans
Albright International
Atlas International
AVE Rail Products
Bayham
Channel Electric Equipment
Chapman
Cole
Concargo
Craig and Derricott
Cressall Resistors Transit Division
Cromweld Steels Ltd
Deans Powered Doors
Dewhurst
Dialight
Eagle Ottawa Callow & Maddox
EAO Limited
Ebac
Excil
Ferranti Technologies Ltd
Ferro
GAI-Tronics
Gates Rubber Co Ltd, The
Harting Ltd
Hexcel Composites
Hodgson and Hodgson
Honeywell Serck
Howden Buffalo
Huck
John Holdsworth
Joyce-Loebl Ltd
Kidde
Kleeneze Sealtech Ltd
KV Ltd
Mechan
MTB Equipment Ltd
Network Connection, The
Northern Rubber Co Ltd
Orvec International
Parker Pneumatic
People Seating
Percy Lane Products
Permali
Pickersgill-Kaye Ltd
Pilkington Aerospace
Portaramp
Powernetics Ltd
Powertron
Southco
Supersine Duramark Limited
TBA
Technical Resin Bonders
Thorn Transport Lighting
Tiflex Ltd
Wabtec Rail Ltd
Winstanley
Woodville Polymer Engineering
XP

**UNITED STATES OF AMERICA**
Adams & Westlake
Advanced Structures Corporation
C&H Chemical
Carrier Transicold
Cytec Fiberite
Deutsch Relays
Ellcon National
International Metals Reclamation Co dbac (INMETCO)
Microphor
Mobile Climate Control Corporation
Monogram Sanitation
Reidler Decal
Saint-Gobain Sully NA, Inc
Specialty Bulb
Telephonics
TODCO Inc
Transit Control Systems
Transmatic Inc
Unicel
USSC Group
Vapor Corporation
WABCO
Westcode

# MANUFACTURERS/Passenger coach equipment

## 3M Europe SA

Hermeslaan 7, B-1831 Diegem, Belgium
Tel: (+32 2) 722 45 00   Fax: (+32 2) 722 45 11

**Key personnel**
Marketing Communication Europe: Nicole N Roy
Commercial Graphics Marketing: Severine Soufflet

**Products**
Bonding systems and adhesive to replace traditional rivets, bolts, and screws in train interiors; anti-graffiti and anti-scratching films; graphics for rail vehicle liveries, interiors and advertising.

---

## Adams & Westlake

Adams & Westlake Ltd
PO Box 4254, 940 North Michigan Street, Elkhart, Indiana 46514, USA
Tel: (+1 219) 264 11 41   Fax: (+1 219) 264 11 46
e-mail: adlake@aol.com

**Key personnel**
General Manager and President: Don Chupp
Sales Manager: Rex Barton

**Products**
Lanterns, thrust blocks, locks, lathes, lamps, hooks, handles, curtains and third rail pickup equipment.

---

## Advanced Structures Corporation

235 West Industry Court, Deer Park, New York 11729, USA
Tel: (+1 631) 667 50 00   Fax: (+1 631) 667 50 15

**Products**
Lightweight stainless-steel metro car doors. These doors are stronger and lighter than aluminium doors and are designed to last 20 years compared to the average three years in other train door type construction. The key to the stronger lightweight construction is the use of very thin walled stainless-steel honeycomb bonded to lightweight stainless-steel skins and a high-strength stainless-steel welded channel structural frame.

New York City Transit Authority helped develop these lightweight metro car side, end and cab doors and, according to Advanced Structures Corporation, has found them to be longer lasting and more fire and corrosion resistant than other steel or aluminium doors. The Transit Authority has not experienced any failures with the lightweight all stainless-steel honeycomb doors.

---

## Aim Aviation (Henshalls)

Aim Aviation (Henshalls) Ltd
Abbot Close, Oyster Lane, Byfleet KT14 7JT, UK
Tel: (+44 1932) 35 10 11   Fax: (+44 1932) 35 27 92

**Key personnel**
Chairman and Chief Executive: J C Smith
Managing Director: K Robinson
Financial Director: M J Davis
Marketing Director: M Eyre

**Products**
Catering equipment for rolling stock, products for carriage interiors.

Recent contracts include the supply of wall-mounted grilles for the Channel Tunnel trains, and the supply of toilet cubicles for the Channel Tunnel nightstock.

*UPDATED*

---

## Air International Transit Pty Ltd

3 Distillers Place, Huntingwood, New South Wales, Australia 2141
Tel: (+61 2) 98 30 71 00   Fax: (+61 2) 96 72 10 18
e-mail: jschembri@airinter.com.au

**Key personnel**
Executive General Manager: Robert (Bob) C Grant
General Manager, Business Development:
   Joseph R Schembri

**Principal subsidiaries**
Air International Transit US Inc
Air International Transit UK Ltd

**Products**
Air conditioning and ventilation systems for rolling stock including saloon and locomotive cabs. Unit configurations include integrated roof mounts, split systems, wall/side mounts. Auxiliary power supplies. System controls using programmable logic control or relay logic with diagnostic facilities.

**Contracts**
Contracts include supply of equipment for LRVs in Hong Kong, USA, Philippines and Turkey, emus in Australia, Hong Kong, India and UK, double-deck trains in Australia, USA and locomotive cabs for Indonesia, Australia and Eurotunnel.

*UPDATED*

---

## Airscrew Ltd

111 Windmill Road, Sunbury-on-Thames TW16 7EF, UK
Tel: (+44 1932) 76 58 22   Fax: (+44 1932) 76 10 98
e-mail: mail@airscrew.co.uk
Web: http://www.airscrew.co.uk

**Key personnel**
Sales Manager, Rail Products: Peter Heapy
Marketing Director: Bryan Hiscock

**Associate company**
Aircontrol Technologies Limited

**Products**
Cooling fans and systems for locomotives, dmus and emus. Applications include transformer cooling units, converter cooling modules, traction motor blowers and brake compressor cooling fans.

Heating and ventilation units for rail vehicle cabs and saloons.

**Contracts**
Contracts include supply of traction motor blowers for UK Class 92 locomotives, Eurostar common block cooling, networker brake resistor cooling and equipment cask cooling for West Coast Main Line, UK.

*UPDATED*

---

## A K Fans

A K Fans Ltd
32-34 Park Royal Road, London NW10 7LN, UK
Tel: (+44 20) 89 61 68 88   Fax: (+44 20) 89 65 06 01
e-mail: sales@akfansltd.btinternet.com

**Key personnel**
See entry in *Electric traction equipment* section.

**Products**
Fans for rail traction applications; axial, centrifugal, mixed flow and crossflow with AC or brushless DC motors. Fan systems and allied equipment including cab heaters and cab ventilation units.

Contracts include fans for saloon heaters on London Underground Jubilee and Northern Line and cab air re-circulation systems for Victoria Line.

---

## Albatros Corporation

c/o Ruiz de Alarcón, 13, E-28014 Madrid, Spain
Tel: (+34 91) 532 41 81   Fax: (+34 91) 522 76 97
e-mail: albatros@albatros-sl.es

**Works**
Pol Ind 'La Estación', C/Gavilanes 16, E-28320 Pinto, Madrid, Spain
Tel: (+34 91) 495 90 00   Fax: (+34 91) 691 09 97

Albatros also has factories located in Barcelona (Spain), Alcázar de San Juan (Spain), Albany (USA) and Shanghai (China).

**Background**
Albatros is formed by the following companies:
Merak (qv) (formerly known as Stone Ibérica SA) which specialises in the design and manufacture of air-conditioning, ventilation and heating systems for trains, tramways and metros worldwide.
SEPSA (qv), dedicated to the design and subsequent manufacture of electronic equipment for railway vehicles, specialising in two products: static converters and information and control systems.
CMC Interiors (qv), which designs and manufactures modular components for railway vehicles, both externally and internally.

**Products**
Cab and saloon air conditioning and heating and ventilation systems and equipment for new-build and vehicle refurbishment projects; electronic and microelectronic control equipment; static converters; on-board passenger information and data communications systems; vehicle interior systems and components; inverter ballasts for train lighting applications; static speed regulators for asynchronous motors; pressure wave protection systems; battery charger protection relays.

Vehicles for which air conditioning equipment has been supplied include: Heathrow Express (UK); New York JFK International Airport automated light metro (USA); Boston Green Line light rail (USA); Chicago Transit Authority metro refurbishment (USA); Airport Express (Hong Kong, China).

*UPDATED*

---

## Albright International

125 Red Lion Road, Surbiton KT6 7QS, UK
Tel: (+44 20) 83 90 53 57   Fax: (+44 20) 83 90 19 27
Web: http://www.albright.co.uk

**Key personnel**
Joint Managing Directors: N Bedggood, A Catt
Sales, Home and Export: P Pickworth
Quality Assurance & Technical Manager: Peter Gigance

**Products**
DC solenoid switches, contactors and battery disconnecting switches. Albright contactors are used to switch the following equipment: cab and corridor lighting, windscreen demister, auxiliary compressor, pantograph heater, saloon half lighting, toilet trace heating, battery isolation.

The contactors are manufactured in five basic ranges, extending from 80 A to 600 A continuous rating and are available in normally open, normally closed and changeover configurations.

Magnetic blowouts can be fitted to most of the range to allow safe operation at voltages in excess of 48 V.

Operating coils can be wound to suit voltages from 6 to 240 for continuous or intermittent operation.

Emergency battery disconnect switches are made in single-pole and double-pole variants with current ratings of 100 A to 250 A. These switches are capable of rupturing full-load battery currents in an emergency.

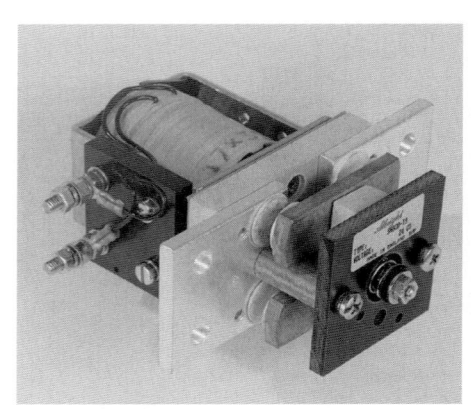

*Contactor by Albright International*   0023842

## Alna Koki

Alna Koki Ltd
4-5 Higashi Naniwa-cho 1-chome, Amagasaki 660-8572, Japan
Tel: (+81 6) 401 72 83   Fax: (+81 6) 401 61 68

**Key personnel**
See entry in *Locomotives and powered/non-powered passenger vehicles* section.

**Products**
Aluminium window sashes for rolling stock; honeycomb sandwich doors and panels for railcars and passenger coaches.

## ALSTOM Transport SA

48 rue Albert Dhalenne, F-93482 Saint-Ouen Cedex, France
Tel: (+33 1) 41 66 90 00   Fax: (+33 1) 41 66 96 66
Web: http://www.transport.alstom.com

**Key personnel**
See ALSTOM entry in *Locomotives and powered/non-powered passenger vehicles* section.

**Contact points**
ALSTOM Transport
Rue Cambier Dupret 50-52, B-6001 Charleroi, Belgium
Tel: (+32 71) 44 54 11   Fax: (+32 71) 44 57 82

**Products**
DC, AC and multivoltage static converters designed for the supply of rolling stock auxiliaries (AC and DC), such as air conditioning, heating and ventilation units, battery chargers and power equipment cooling.

ALSTOM Ltd
Channel Way, Preston PR1 8XL, UK
Tel: (+44 1772) 25 47 77

**Products**
Auxiliary converters for rolling stock and trolleybuses.
ALSTOM Transport SA
11-13, avenue de Bel Air, F-69627 Villeurbanne Cedex, France
Tel: (+33 4) 72 81 52 00   Fax (+33 4) 72 81 52 87

**Products**
Onboard railway electronic systems for train management, propulsion and auxiliary control and passenger information.

ALSTOM Transport Inc
1 Transit Drive, New York 14843, USA
Tel: (+1 607) 324 45 95   Fax: (+1 607) 324 45 68

**Products**
Auxiliary converters for rolling stock.

ALSTOM India
A-20 Kailash Colony, New Delhi 110048 India
Tel: (+ 91 11) 628 77 16

**Products**
Auxiliary converters for rolling stock.

*VERIFIED*

## Angst+Pfister

Angst+Pfister AG
Thurgauerstrasse 66, CH-8052 Zürich, Switzerland
Tel: (+41 1) 306 61 11   Fax: (+41 1) 302 18 71

**UK subsidiary**
Angst+Pfister Ltd
20 Rufford Court, Hardwick Grange, Woolston, Warrington WA1 4RF
Tel: (+44 1925) 85 26 88   Fax: (+44 1925) 85 26 87

**Key personnel**
Marketing Director: Andreas Ferrari

**Products**
Components for rail vehicles including plastics mouldings, washers, seals, valves and ducting.

## ApATeCh Electro

Zhukovsky Street 2, Building 131, Dubna, 141980 Moscow Region, Russian Federation
Tel: (+7 09621) 257 92   Fax: (+7 09621) 234 92
e-mail: electro@dubna.ru

**Products**
Glass-fibre plastic seating shells, and plastic interior panels and window frame casings for new and refurbished passenger rail vehicles.

## Atlas International

Atlas International Ltd
Merrington Lane, Spennymoor DL16 7UR, UK
Tel: (+44 191) 301 31 15   Fax: (+44 191) 301 31 10

**Key personnel**
Logistics Manager: T Burton

**Associate company**
Thorn Transport Lighting

**Products**
Lighting components for rail vehicles; inverter ballasts for fluorescent lighting 24, 36, 52, 70/72 and 110 V DC, AC; ballasts for various voltages; lampholders and other lighting accessories including luminaires and subassemblies of standard or special types; AC and DC converters for low-voltage tungsten halogen lamps for 12 V reading lights and locomotive headlights; inverter ballasts for fluorescent lamps to the European standard, and luminaires using compact fluorescent lamps.

An extended range of Atlas brand electronic lighting inverter ballasts has been introduced to operate at 15 to 40 W 26 to 38 mm tubes. Advances in production technology have enabled them to offer these compact electronic inverters in voltages covering 24 to 110 V DC. They meet RIA, European (EN), French (NF), International (UIC) and associated standards for rolling stock.

## Astra Vagoane Călători Arad SA/Arad

1-3 Petru Rareș, R-2900 Arad, Romania
Tel: (+40 257) 23 36 51   Fax: (+40 257) 25 81 68
e-mail: astra@calatori.rdsar.ro

**Key personnel**
See entry in *Locomotive and powered/non-powered passenger vehicles* section.

**Products**
Doors, windows, seats, luggage racks, toilet cubicles, sidewalls.

*UPDATED*

## Autoroche Industrie

3 rue de la Cotonnière, F-14000 Caen, France
Tel: (+33 2) 31 74 73 13   Fax: (+33 2) 31 74 75 98
e-mail: info@autoroche.com

**Subsidiary**
ABL Lights
50 Golf Club Boulevard, Mosinee, Wisconsin 54455, USA
Tel: (+1 715) 693 15 30   Fax: (+1 715) 693 15 34
Web: http://www.abllights.com

**Products**
Exterior lighting systems and indicators for rail vehicles.

## AVE Rail Products

Derby Carriage Works, Litchurch Lane, Derby DE24 8AP, UK
Tel: (+44 1332) 25 75 00   Fax: (+44 1332) 37 19 50
e-mail: admin@averail.co.uk
Web: http://www.averail.co.uk

**Key personnel**
Managing Director: M P Thompson
Sales Manager: G V Simpson

**Products**
Complete interior packages for rail vehicles. The company's expertise includes turnkey interior packages, cab and cabin modules, doors, exterior panels and structures, electrical services, powder coating, driver vigilance systems, train data recorders and onboard CCTV systems and the use of advanced manufacturing materials.

## Avery Dennison

Graphics Division
Rijndijk 86, PO Box 118, NL-2394 ZG Hazerswoude, The Netherlands
Tel: (+31 71) 342 15 00   Fax: (+31 71) 342 15 38
Web: http://www.averygraphics.com

**Products**
Anti-graffiti film for rail vehicles; glass protection film; adhesive colour vinyl film for livery applications and vandal and graffiti resistant.

## Bayham

Bayham Ltd
Rutherford Road, Daneshill West Industrial Estate, Basingstoke RG24 8PG, UK
Tel: (+44 1256) 46 49 11   Fax: (+44 1256) 46 43 66
e-mail: sales@bayham.demon.uk
Web: http://www.bayham.demon.co.uk

**Key personnel**
Chairman: J J Boulcott
Managing Director: E A Salter
Export Sales: C J Balment

**Subsidiary**
The Ranger Instrument Company Ltd

**Products**
R & G direct and remote reading fuel and coolant tank gauges, together with those for drinking water and lavatory flush tanks on passenger carriages; combination level indicators and switches on a single mounting flange give continuous level indication plus warning of low/high liquid level with optional automatic shutdown in the event of catastrophic coolant losses.

## Behr Industry

Heilbronner Strasse 380, D-70469 Stuttgart, Germany
Tel: (+49 711) 89 60   Fax: (+49 711) 896 30 75
Web: http://www.behrgroup.com

**Subsidiary**
Flinschstrasse 20, D-60388 Frankfurt/Main, Germany
Tel: (+49 69) 264 89 90   Fax: (+49 69) 26 48 99 11
Sales Manager: Wilfried Sonnenfeld

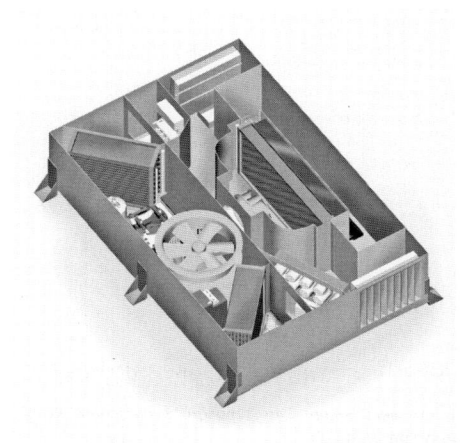

*HVAC module of a railway car air conditioning system*
2002/0114662

# MANUFACTURERS/Passenger coach equipment

### Background
Behr Industry is a subsidiary of Behr GmbH & Co, both of which have their head offices in Stuttgart. It has expanded its rail vehicle air conditioning division to all types of rail vehicles and has opened a subsidiary in Frankfurt/Main.

### Products
Air conditioning systems for trains, trams and commuter and subway trains; air conditioning systems for locomotive cabs and driving units. Capabilities include design of air ducting and air circulation in the vehicle, power supply for climate control and associated power electronics.

### Contracts
Air conditioning systems for vehicles used by: Deutsche Bahn AG, Austrian Federal Railways, Maintrain (UK), First Great Western, UK and RATP, France. Produced by Bombardier, Siemens, Kraus Maffei.

*UPDATED*

## Baier + Köppel GmbH + Co

Präzisionsapparatefabrik, Beethovenstrasse 14, D-91257 Pegnitz/Bayern, Germany
Tel: (+49 9241) 72 90   Fax: (+49 9241) 729 50
e-mail: beka@beka-lube.de;
 beka@beka-max.de
Web: http://www.beka-lube.de

### Products
FluiLub vehicle-mounted wheel flange lubrication systems.

*NEW ENTRY*

*FluiLub lubrication nozzle positioned to deliver lubricant to the wheel flange of a light rail vehicle*
2002/0126646

## Bekaert Composites

Industriepark De Bruwaan 2, B-9700 Oudenaarde, Belgium
Tel: (+32 55) 33 30 11   Fax: (+32 55) 33 30 50
e-mail: info@composites.bekaert.com
Web: http://www.bekaertcomposites.com

### Subsidiary company
Bekaert Composites Spain
Aritzbidea 67, E-48100 Munguia (Vizcaya), Spain
Tel: (+34 94) 674 03 16   Fax: (+34 94) 615 61 14

### Products
Components and modules in fibre-reinforced composites for rail vehicle applications. Both pultrusion and filament winding production processes are used.

*NEW ENTRY*

## Bircher

Bircher AG
CH-8222 Beringen, Switzerland
Tel: (+41 52) 687 11 11   Fax: (+41 52) 687 12 10

### Key personnel
President and Chief Executive Officer: Giorgio Behr
Executive Directors: Max Bircher, Otto Stehle
Managing Directors: Rémy Höhener, Ernst Bührer, Roland Kaufmann
Sales and Marketing Manager: Stefan Kellenberger

### Principal subsidiaries
Bircher America Inc
1865 Hicks Road, 909 East Oakton Street, Elk Grove Village, Illinois 60007, USA
President: Rémy Höhener
Bircher Asia Pacific Sdn Bhd
278 Jalan Simbang, Taman Perling, 812000 Johore Bahru, Malaysia
General Manager: Hanspeter Ritzmann
Bircher Deutschland GmbH
Leonberger Strasse 28, D-71063 Sindelfingen, Germany
General Manager: Erich Maier

### Products
Safety edges for train doors; safety mats for train entrances; switch mats for gangway doors between coaches; time delay relays for general control purposes; safety equipment for station platforms.

## Bode

Gebrüder Bode & Co GmbH
Ochshäuserstrasse 14, D-34123 Kassel, Germany
Tel: (+49 561) 500 90   Fax: (+49 561) 559 56
e-mail: bode@bode-kassel.com

### Key personnel
Managing Directors: Klaus-Peter Schwarz
 Rainer Wicke
Sales Manager: Jürgen Holz

### Background
Bode is a member of the Schaltbau Group.

### Products
Electric and pneumatic door systems for LRVs, metro and high-speed vehicles, outswing plug doors and inswing plug doors; pressure-sealed doors for high-speed trains; ramp systems; step systems; door controls.
 Contracts include supply of door systems to Hong Kong MTRC airport link; Amtrak Northeast Corridor; ICE and ICT, Germany; Transrapid, Germany; ICN, Switzerland; and Kuala Lumpur metro.

## Bosch Telecom

Bosch Telecom Öffentliche Vermittlungstechnik GmbH
Kölnerstrasse 5, D-65760 Eschborn am Taunus, Germany
Tel: (+49 6196) 97 96 40   Fax: (+49 6196) 97 96 13

### Head office
Robert Bosch GmbH
PO Box 106050, D-70049 Stuttgart
Tel: (+49 711) 81 10   Fax: (+49 711) 811 66 30

### Key personnel
Marketing: Norbert Kayser
Product Management: Heinz-Peter Schönberg

*Bosch radio terminal for Thalys*   0003467

### Products
The Ökart-Zug system is a card-operated telephone for trains. The machine, which is resistant to vandalism, scratching and graffiti, accepts a telephone card instead of money. The card can be either the equivalent of a prepaid number of charge units, or it can be used to debit the user's bank account protected by a PIN code.

## C&H Chemical

222 Starkey Street, St Paul, Minnesota 55107, USA
Tel: (+1 561) 227 4343   Fax: (+1 651) 227 2485
e-mail: 6112@softshare.com

### Key personnel
President: William Cammack
Vice-President: Tom Boemher
Technical Specialist: Terry McMahon

### Products
Exterior cleaners and degreasers, leak tracer dyes, radiator water treatments, parts cleaning detergents, spray cabinet detergents.
 Contracts include supply to BNSF, UP, CP and many other Class I, Class II and short line railways.

## Carrier Sütrak GmbH

Heinkelstrasse 5, D-71272 Renningen, Germany
Tel: (+49 7159) 92 30   Fax: (+49 7159) 92 31 08
Web: http://www.carriers.transicold.com

### Products
Air conditioning equipment for rail vehicles, people movers and buses; roof-mounted, integrated modular and compact configurations. All systems are available with R134a environmentally friendly refrigerant.

## Carrier Transicold

Carrier Transicold
Carrier Refrigeration Operations (Division of Carrier Corporation)
PO Box 4805, Carrier Parkway, Building TR20, Syracuse, New York 13221, USA
Tel: (+1 315) 432 64 34   Fax: (+1 315) 432 72 18

### Key personnel
President: Nick Pinchuk
Vice-President, Transport Air Conditioning:
 Lex van der Weerd

### Regional Sales Offices

*North America:*
Carrier Transicold-Transport A/C
715 Willow Springs Lane, York, Pennsylvania 17402, USA
Tel: (+1 717) 767 65 31   Fax: (+1 717) 764 04 01

*Latin America:*
Carrier Transicold-Mexico
Tezoquipa No 142 Col. La Joya, Deleg. Tlalpan 14090 Mexico DF
Tel: (+52 5) 573 55 55; 655 05 07
Fax: (+52 5) 655 21 02

*Europe/Middle East/Africa:*
Carrier-Sütrak, Heinkelstrasse 5, D-71272 Renningen, Germany
Tel: (+49 7159) 92 31 00   Fax: (+49 7159) 92 31 08

*Asia Pacific:*
Carrier Transicold-APO
12 Gul Road, Singapore 629343
Tel: (+65) 862 00 98   Fax (+65) 862 32 86

### Business units
Transport Air Conditioning Group
Transport Refrigeration and Air Conditioning

### Products
Air conditioning and heating systems for rail and bus applications, roof-mounted, rear-mounted or in-vehicle; air conditioners for small vehicles; components including compressors, evaporators and heater coils, open drive and semi-hermetic compressors; and replacement components.

## CASAS-M

CASAS-M SL
Poligono Santa Rita, PO Box 1333 E-08755 Castellbisbal, Barcelona, Spain
Tel: (+34 93) 772 08 59   Fax: (+34 93) 772 21 30

**Key personnel**
Export Manager: Umberto Ferrari Cassina
Marketing: Rosa Maria Casas

**Products**
Compas range of modular seating in aluminium, with or without backs, up to six seats in length. Impact and scratch-resistant material is used.
The Suma range is for seating up to six in length which can be joined together. The seats are fire, impact and scratch resistant.

**Contracts**
Provision of seating at Barajas and Antalya airports in 1997, Rio de Janeiro Airport and Belem International Airport in Brazil.

*UPDATED*

## Channel Electric Equipment

Bath Road, Thatcham RG18 3ST, UK
Tel: (+1635) 86 48 66   Fax: (+1635) 86 91 78

**Key personnel**
Managing Director: Neil Fraser

**Corporate background**
Channel Electric Equipment is a member of LPA Group plc.

**Product**
Beaufort blower for air conditioning units.
This fan system incorporates a single maintenance-free brushless DC motor. The Beaufort unit delivers airflow rates up to 36,000 litres/min and has a design life of eight years.

*Channel Electric Beaufort blower for upgrading air conditioning units*   0063682

## Chapman Seating Ltd

79 Mile Road, Mitcham CR4 3YL, UK
Tel: (+44 1932) 22 05 51   Fax: (+44 1932) 24 62 57

**Key personnel**
Sales Manager: G Elliott

**Products**
Passenger and crew seating.

*UPDATED*

## Cleff

Carl Wilhelm Cleff GmbH & Co KG
Postfach 260180, D-42243 Wuppertal, Germany
Tel: (+49 202) 64 79 90   Fax: (+49 202) 647 99 88
e-mail: marketing@cleff-wpt.de

**Products**
Windows for passenger vehicles and driving cabs; interior doors; luggage racks; interior lighting systems.

## Clerprem SpA

Via Bianche 10, I-36010 Carre (VI), Italy
Tel: (+39 0445) 86 97 00   Fax: (+39 0445) 86 97 77
e-mail: info@clerprem.com

**Products**
Seating systems for urban, suburban, regional and high-speed trains.

## CMC Interiors

Pol Ind Can Roca, C/Mar del Japon, Parcela 13, E-08130 Sta Perpetua de Mogoda, Barcelona, Spain
Tel: (+34 93) 544 66 66   Fax: (+34 93) 544 82 19
e-mail: cmc@cmc.albatross-sl.es

**Corporate background**
CMC Interiors is a member of the Albatros Group (qv).

**Products**
Concept, design and fabrication of complete interiors for new and refurbished passenger rolling stock.

*VERIFIED*

## Cole

Malcolm Cole Ltd
10 Chantry Park, Cowley Road, Nuffield Industrial Estate, Poole BH17 7UJ, UK
Tel: (+44 1202) 68 28 30   Fax: (+44 1202) 66 55 72
e-mail: cole@malcolm-cole.co.uk

**Key personnel**
Engineer: Max Dales

**Products**
Oval 316 stainless steel tube as used for grab handles and commode handles.
Contracts include the supply of tube for metro trainsets for London Underground Ltd and for rolling stock for Channel Tunnel overnight services.

## Compin

ZI de Netreville, 1, rue due Guesclin, F-27000 Evreux, France
Tel: (+33 2) 32 33 92 00   Fax: (+33 2) 32 33 92 80
e-mail: compin.commercial@wanadoo.fr

**Products**
Seating systems and accessories for urban, suburban, regional and high-speed trains.

## Conbrako

Conbrako (Pty) Ltd
PO Box 4018, Luipaardsviei 1743, Transvaal, South Africa
Tel: (+27 11) 762 24 21   Fax: (+27 11) 762 65 35

**Products**
Sliding doors; electropneumatic door mechanisms; coach windows.

## Concargo

Concargo Ltd
Old Mixon Crescent, Weston Super Mare BS24 9AH, UK
Tel: (+44 1934) 62 82 21   Fax: (+44 1934) 41 76 23
e-mail: sales@concargo.fsnet.co.uk
Web: http://www.concargo.co.uk

**Key personnel**
Managing Director: N Brown
Sales Manager: Andrew Morris

**Products**
Glass reinforced plastics components including side panels, window surrounds, skirts, ceiling panels, third-rail covers, seats, consoles, cab fronts. Materials include phenolic, epoxy and Class 1 polyester resin systems using the hand lay and resin transfer moulding process.

**Contracts**
Moulded components for London Underground Jubilee, Piccadilly and Northern lines; Turbostar and Electrostar interior and exterior mouldings.

*UPDATED*

## Connei

Connei SpA
Via Pillea 14-16, I-16153 Genoa, Italy
Tel: (+39 010) 60 08 21   Fax: (+39 010) 650 85 73/12 56

**Key personnel**
General Manager: Giuseppe Lancella
Export Sales Manager: Mauro Gramaccioni

**Products**
Electrical connectors (rectangular, rack and panel).

## ContiTech Profile GmbH

Vahrenwalder Strasse 9, D-30165 Hannover, Germany
Tel: (+49 511) 938 02   Fax: (+49 511) 938 27 66
e-mail: mailservice@contitech.de
Web: http://www.contitech.de

**Key personnel**
Customer Management, Rolling Stock: Manfred Hunze

**Corporate background**
ContiTech Profile GmbH is a member of the Contitech Group, part of Continental AG.

**Products**
Door and window sealing profiles.

*UPDATED*

## Craig and Derricott

Hall Lane, Walsall Wood, Walsall WS9 9DP, UK
Tel: (+44 1543) 37 55 41   Fax: (+44 1543) 45 26 10
e-mail: sales@cragder.com
Web: http://www.computaphile.com/craigder

**Key personnel**
Managing Director: Kevin Jones
General Manager and Head of Marketing:
  Bernadette Hanley
Financial Director: John Mills
Sales and Export: Gary Smith
Engineering: Robert Corbett
Operations: Paul Cranshaw
Distribution: Eric Neal

**Subsidiaries**
Teepee Electrical
Selector Switch Services

**Products**
Design, manufacture and supply of a range of switchgear and custom-designed control panels adapted to meet the control and safety requirements of the rail industry, control desks, uncouplers, control panels, equipment cases, switches, communication panels, safety related equipment and wiring harnesses. Specifically including: shunting control panels; customised rotary switches and isolators; rotary switches featuring high-security key locks; and mushroom-headed push-buttons used as both emergency stops and passenger alarm switches. Also supplied is a range of limit and reed switches suitable for mounting in or around all rail equipment.
Newly launched for 1999/2000 were low-profile push-button and LED indicator units, master drivers key switches, passenger alarm handles, drum switches and underframe starting switches.

# MANUFACTURERS/Passenger coach equipment

*Craig & Derricott's display model of a driver's desk with integrated switchgear, panels, wiring and connectors*
2000/0087705

Recent contracts include: supply of uncouplers, communication panels and kitchen harnesses for Virgin West Coast Main Line; supply of switch panels, servery and galley harnesses for Virgin Cross Country; supply of uncouplers and emergency stop boxes for Connex, and the supply of switches and passenger communication handles for MTRC.

## Cressall Resistors Transit Division

Transit Division, Peacock Way, Melton Constable NR24 2BZ, UK
Tel: (+44 1263) 86 05 81   Fax: (+44 1263) 86 14 17
e-mail: transit@cressall.com
Web: http://www.cressall.com

**Key personnel**
General Manager: Eric Williams
Finance Director: Dennis Cummins
Sales and Marketing Manager: Roger Mason
Principal Engineer: Russell Everett
Manufacturing Manager: Mark Dent
Purchasing Manager: John Crick

**Background**
Parent company is Cressall Resistors, Evington Valley Road, Leicester, LE5 5LZ.

**Products**
Power resistors for transport applications, including naturally cooled and forced cooled roof or under-car-mounted resistors, designed to meet the load requirements of each vehicle. Infra-red temperature monitoring and protection system offering remote indication and status.

*UPDATED*

## Cromweld Steels Ltd

The Old Vicarage, Tittensor, Stoke-on-Trent, Staffordshire ST12 9HY, UK
Tel: (+44 1782) 37 41 39   Fax: (+44 1782) 37 33 88

See entry in *Freight vehicles and equipment* section.

**Subsidiary**
Cromweld Steels
PO Box 1500, Cornelius, North Carolina 28031, USA
Tel: (+1 704) 896 81 14   Fax: (+1 704) 896 81 15

**Products**
3CR12 ferritic stainless steel. This material is claimed to offer a low stable cost stainless-steel option for passenger coach and light rail vehicles.

*VERIFIED*

## Cytec Fiberite

Cytec Fiberite Inc
2055 East Technology Circle, Tempe, Arizona 85284, USA
Tel: (+1 602) 730 20 00   Fax: (+1 602) 730 21 90

**Key personnel**
President: Michael Molyneaux
Vice-President, Sales: Steve Speak

**Products**
Composite materials, including resin systems, mainly epoxies and phenolics, prepegged on to a variety of fabrics such as graphite, glass, aramid and hybrids of these fabrics. These composites are used for the interiors of coaches for sidewall panels, ceilings, overhead storage bins and bulkheads, and conform to specific requirements for low smoke, flame and toxicity.

## Dansk Dekor-Laminat A/S

Grønlandsveg 197, DK-7100 Vejle, Denmark
Tel: (+45 7642) 82 82   Fax: (+45 7582) 71 21
e-mail: dd@dandekor.dk
Web: http://www.dandekor.dk

**Products**
Etronit-M high-pressure and compact laminates, DanDekor real veneer laminates and Alunit lightweight construction material for rail vehicle interiors. Applications include wall and ceiling panels, tables, partitions and door panels.

## Deans Powered Doors

(A trading division of Manganese Bronz Components Ltd)
PO Box 8, Borwick Drive, Grovehill Road, Beverley HU17 0JQ, UK
Tel: (+44 1482) 86 81 11   Fax: (+44 1482) 88 18 90

**Key personnel**
Managing Director: D Skidmore
Sales and Marketing Director: M Phillips
Technical Director: P Spencer

**Products**
Powered doors (electric and pneumatic) and door-operating mechanisms; handrail and handrail fittings. Power-operated access ramps for wheelchair users.

## Deco Seating

Deco Seating BV
Oude Baan 75, NL-4825 BL Breda, Netherlands
Tel: (+31 76) 571 60 06   Fax: (+31 76) 587 59 51

**Key personnel**
General Director: S Yntema
Commercial Director: Y De Corte

**Products**
Passenger seats for rail vehicles including frames and upholstery. Vandal-resistant upholstery for new or refurbished seating.
Contracts include supply of seating for NS Netherlands.

## Desso

Desso Hotel Aero-Marine Carpets International
Molenweg 81, NL-5349 AC Oss, Netherlands
Tel: (+31 4126) 679 11   Fax: (+31 4126) 351 65

**Products**
Carpets.

## Deuta-Werke

Vorm Deutsche Tachometerwerke GmbH
PO Box 200260, D-51432 Bergisch Gladbach, Germany
Tel: (+49 2202) 95 80   Fax: (+49 2202) 95 81 45

**Key personnel**
Manager Marketing and Sales: Wolfgang Fobek
Export Manager: Joachim Beamann

**Principal subsidiaries**
Shanghai Deuta Electronic & Electrical Equipment Co Ltd

**Products**
Sensors: pickups, AC generators, electronic/electric pulse generators, opto-electronic generators, microwave sensors.
Indicators: electric indicators, electric meters, eddy current tachometers, panel-mounted clocks, electric and mechanical counters, modular driver's cab indicators, multi-function displays, digital indicators.
Incident recorders: electric incident recorders, short-distance incident recorders, digital storage cassettes, evaluation software for data recorders.
System components: central distance and speed measuring units, electronic control units, multi-function modules.
IT solutions: speed, distance and position systems for train navigation and protection, tracing and tracking information systems for passenger and freight, train information systems, network databank systems for fleet management and diagnostics.

*UPDATED*

## Deutsch Relays

Deutsch Relays Inc
55 Engineers Road, Hauppauge, New York 11788, USA
Tel: (+1 631) 342 17 00   Fax: (+1 631) 342 94 55
e-mail: info@deutschrelays.com
Web: http://www.deutschrelays.com

**Key personnel**
President: Tom Sadusky
Marketing Manager, Railway: Rodolphe Leroy
Engineering and Quality Manager: Edward Cheswick
Purchasing Manager: Jack Dickinson

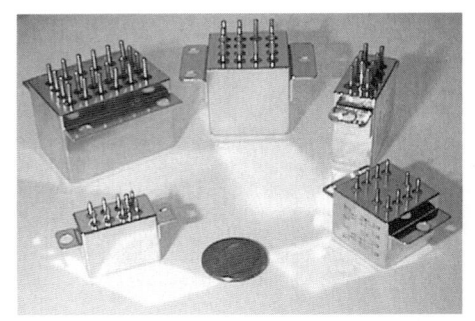

*Deutsch Relays hermetically sealed relays in standard metal enclosure*
2000/0087707

## Passenger coach equipment/**MANUFACTURERS**

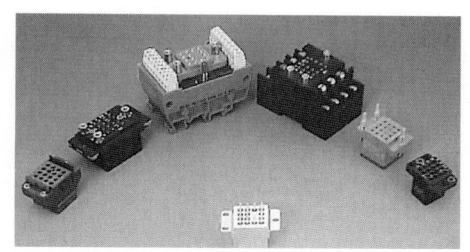

*Deutsch Relays railway sockets* 2002/0120204

**Overseas offices**
Relais Electroniques Deutsch
22 rue des Chaises, BP 96, F-45142 St. Jean de la Ruelle Cedex, France
Web: http://www.compagnie-deutsche.com
Division Manager: Jérome Avelange
Marketing Manager: Christophe Charpentier
Engineering Manager: Patrick Gautier

Deutsch GmbH
Postfach 17 19, D-82145 Martinsried, Munich, Germany
Tel: (+49 89) 899 15 70    Fax: (+49 89) 857 46 84
e-mail: info@compagnie-deutsch.de
Web: http://www.compagnie-deutsch.de
Division/Marketing Manager: Sebastian Bendak

**Products**
Hermetically sealed relays and mating sockets designed for reliable operation under severe environmental conditions. Relays, timers and sockets are available in a variety of terminations and mounting styles for track, PC board, panel, and wiring harness installations. Relays are designed for long life switching of low to medium current levels in 1, 2, 3, 4 and 6 pole configurations. Deutsch's design also features a single pivoting armature switching whereby all movable pole contacts switch together and 'non-overlapping', 'back-check', or 'force-guided' principles can be capitalised on. Applications include logic interface in automatic and manual train control systems, sensor and actuator interface, lighting, braking and other control and sensing systems. Operating temperature range: –40°C to +125°C, shock (any axis): 200 g.
 Contracts include relays, sockets and timers, designed for DART and VTA Kinki Sharyo LRVs, MTA New York R cars, NJT Hudsen-Bergen cars, Adtranz cars operated by SEPTA, Philadelphia, and Acela on the Northeast Corridor for the Bombardier/Alstom consortium. Developments include miniature ETX single break series.

*UPDATED*

## Dewhurst

Dewhurst plc
Inverness Road, Hounslow TW3 3LT, UK
Tel: (+44 20) 86 07 73 00    Fax: (+44 20) 85 72 59 86
e-mail: railsales@dewhurst.co.uk
Web: http://www.dewhurst.co.uk

**Key personnel**
Rail Product Manager: John Harris

**Principal subsidiary companies**
Dupar Controls, Canada
The Fixture Company, USA
Thames Valley Controls, UK
Australian Lift Company, Australia

**Products**
Push-button controls and indicators to meet the requirements of retrofit and new rolling stock vehicles. Standard ranges of vandal-resistant push-buttons, keypads and push-button control panels for internal and external passenger doors, vestibule doors, emergency call panels, drivers' cab controls, guard stations and crew access.
 Platform TR and RA signal boxes and signalling control panels.
 Contracts include LED bodyside status indicators on the new generation of Adtranz passenger vehicles.
 Other contracts include passenger door push-buttons for Heathrow Express and Stockholm LRVs. Driver's cab controls for MTRC Lantau Airport extension, Hong Kong. Upgrade to LED illumination of passenger controls on the Mk IV intercity fleet and status indicators on the Hammersmith and Bakerloo lines.

## Dialight

Exning Road, Newmarket CB8 0AX, UK
Tel: (+44 1638) 66 23 17    Fax: (+44 1638) 56 04 55

**Key personnel**
Vice-President, Sales and Marketing: Gary Durgin
European Business Manager: Gareth Eaton

**Products**
External LED indicator lights.

## Driessen Railway Interior Systems

De Stek 3, PO Box 28, NL-1770 AA Wieringerwerf, Netherlands
Tel: (+31 227) 606 55 71    Fax: (+31 227) 60 65 80
e-mail: railway@driessen.com

**Works**
Main works: address as above
Other works: 10781 Forbes Avenue, Garden Grove, California 92643, USA
Laan van Ypenburg 66, NL-2289 DV Rijswijk, Netherlands
Tel: (+31 70) 307 46 04

**Key personnel**
Marketing and Sales Director: D G W Dyxhoorn
President, Galley Inserts Division: G Driessen
President, Galley Division (USA): H Sprangers
General Manager, Galley Division (NL): M Dingerdis

**Principal subsidiary companies**
Van Riems Dyk Rotterdam BV (Cargo container manufacturing)
Driessen Interior Systems BV (Airplane and train interiors)

**Products**
Railcar interiors including lavatories and galley systems; passenger service equipment: meal/beverage trolleys, onboard sales carts; beverage containers.

**Contracts**
Contracts executed and obtained include supply of galleys and equipment to Amtrak (Bombardier); Queensland Rail (Walkers); CP Portuguese Rail (Adtranz); FS/SBB (Fiat Pendolino); Cisalpino/FS/SSG; Caltrans, USA; Acela/Amtrak, USA; AVE/RENFE; Virgin Rail; Thalys International; Rail Gourmet; Eurostar-Cross Channel Catering Company; Wagon Lits, Servair France.

*UPDATED*

## Eagle Ottawa Callow & Maddox

Sibree Road, Baginton, Coventry CV3 4FD, UK
Tel: (+44 1203) 63 93 93    Fax: (+44 1203) 30 87 21

**Key personnel**
Business Manager: T J Rogers
Sales Executive: P Deacon

**Products**
Seating for passenger vehicles.
 Contracts include supply of seating for London Underground Circle Line stock and Piccadilly Line stock.

## EAO AG

Tannwaldstrasse 88, CH-4601, Olten, Switzerland
Tel: (+41 62) 286 92 33
e-mail: info@eao.com
Web: http://www.eao.com

**Key personnel**
Contact: Stefan Zimmeroi

**Subsidiaries**
*Belgium*
Koning Albert 1 Laan 48, B-1780 Wemmel
Tel (+32 2) 456 00 10    Fax: (+32 2) 456 00 19
e-mail info.ebl@eao.com

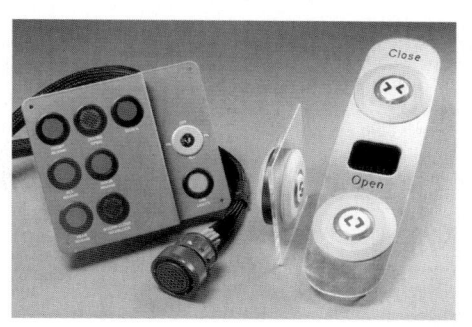

*EAO's panel combination* 2000/0087708

*France*
5 rue Henri François, BP 3, F-77831, Ozoir-La-Ferrière
Tel: (+33 1) 64 43 37 37    Fax: (+ 33 1) 64 43 37 48
e-mail: sales.ese@eao.com

*Germany*
Langenberger Straße 570, D-45277 Essen
Tel: (+49 0201) 858 71 99    Fax: (+49 0201) 858 72 57
e-mail: sales.ede@eao.com

*Hong Kong*
Unit A1, 1/F, Block A, Tin On Industrial Building, 777 Cheung Sha Wan Road, Lai Chi Kok, Kln
Tel: (+852 27) 86 91 41    Fax: (+852 27) 86 95 61
e-mail: sales.ehk@eao.com.hk

*Japan*
Daiichi Tomo BLDG. 4F, Minato-ku, Tokyo
Tel: (+81 3) 54 01 09 53    Fax (+81 3) 54 01 09 68
e-mail: sales.esj@eao.com

*Netherlands*
Kamerlingh Onnesweg 46, NL-3316 GL Dordrecht
Tel: (+31 78) 653 17 00    Fax: (+31 78) 653 17 99
e-mail: sales.enl@eao.com

*Sweden*
Gråhundsvägen 80, SE-128 22 Skarpnäck
Tel: (+46 8) 683 86 60    Fax: (+46 8) 724 29 12
e-mail: sales.esw@eao.com

*Switzerland*
Altgraben 441, CH-4624 Härkingen
Tel: (+41 62) 388 95 00    Fax: (+41 62) 388 95 55
e-mail: sales.ech@eao.com

*UK*
Highland House, Albert Drive, Burgess Hill RH15 9TN
Tel: (+44 1444) 23 60 00    Fax: (+44 1444) 23 66 41
e-mail: uksales@eao.com
Managing Director: Susan Fisher
Sales and Marketing Manager: Robert Davies

*USA*
198 Pepe's Farm Road, Milford, Connecticut 06460
Tel: (+1 203) 877 45 77    Fax: (+1 203) 877 36 94
e-mail: eus-digioia.d@eao.com

**Products**
Drivers cab and guards control components: push-buttons, rotary switches, emergency stop switches, indicators and Sonarlert sounders; toilet controls: halo illuminated push buttons for flush; door controls: halo illuminated push buttons and gated key switches.

**Contracts**
2001-2002 include: Class 458 emu, Class 170 dmu; Class 460 emu; Class 170/1 dmu, Class 170/2 dmu, Class 333 emu, Class 334 emu and, Class 375 emu.
1999-2000 include: Class 168 dmu; Class 170 dmu; Class 460 emu; Class 375 emu; Class 170/1 dmu; Class 458 emu; Class 170/2 dmu; Class 333 emu; Class 334 emu and, Class 375 emu.

*UPDATED*

## Ebac Ltd

MIRA Division, St Helen Trading Estate, Bishop Auckland, County Durham DL14 9AD, UK
Tel: (+44 1388) 60 60 74    Fax: (+44 1388) 60 61 82

**Key personnel**
Managing Directors: Farage Tarbah, Graham Higgs

## MANUFACTURERS/Passenger coach equipment

### Principal subsidiaries
Ebac Systems Inc
106 John Jefferson Road, Suite 102, Williamsburg, Virginia 23185, USA
(Enquiries to Ebac Ltd, UK)

Ebac Deutschland GmbH
Romerring 7, D-74821, Mosbach-Diedesheim, Germany
Tel: (+49 6261) 982 60   Fax: (+49 6261) 98 26 10

### Products
Design, manufacture, supply and overhaul of air conditioning, heating and ventilation systems for all types of rail vehicles. Heat pump technology; microprocessor-based controls and diagnostics; chilled water systems; low refrigerant content, R134a systems; roof-mounted, underframe-mounted and split systems.

*UPDATED*

---

## Ebo Systems

boulevard d'Europe, PO Box 10 F-67211, Obernai Cedex, France
Tel: (+33 3) 88 49 50 51   Fax: (+33 3) 88 49 50 14
e-mail: ebosystemsint@yahoo.com
Web: http://www.ebo-systems.com

### Key personnel
Managing Director: Peter Caldwell

### Products
Frp/grp (fibreglass reinforced polyester) cable management systems, cable trays, ground ducts, cable ladders, fixing and supporting material.

*Ebo Systems grp profiles*   0063685

---

## EC-Engineering Oy

Santaniitynkatu 12A, FIN-04250 Kerava, Finland
Tel: (+358 9) 294 03 27   Fax: (+358 9) 294 03 28
e-mail: ec-engineering@ec-engineering.fi
Web: http://www.ec-engineering.fi

### Key personnel
Managing Director: Tapio Ollanketo

### German office
EC-Engineering Oy
Büro Deutschland
Postfach 2029, D-32779 Lage, Germany
Tel: (+49 5232) 784 33   Fax: (+49 5232) 781 33
e-mail: ec-vs@t-online.de
Contact: Frhr Horst v Schleinitz

### Background
EC-Engineering Oy is a member of the Finnish Transportation Expertise Network (Finten) association.

### Products
Custom-designed sandwich panels and vacuum-formed GRP components for passenger rail vehicles, including complex shapes and products for heavy wear conditions. Applications include: window and wall elements; interior stairs for double-deck coaches; elements for vestibules.

### Contracts
Roof fairings for Pendolino trainsets (Talgo); exterior roof and wall panels for RegioShuttle dmu (Bombardier); floor panels for Class ET 423 emu (Alstom); and wall and window panels, interior dividing walls and roof panels for ICS double-deck coaches (Talgo).

*UPDATED*

---

## Ederena Concept

avenue du Parc, F-40230 St Vincent de Tyrosse, France
Tel: (+33 5) 58 77 46 46   Fax: (+33 5) 58 77 46 45
e-mail: sales@ederena.com
Web: http://www.ederena.com

### Products
Composite bonded materials, bonded structures, and sandwich panels.

*VERIFIED*

---

## EFACEC

EFACEC Sistemas de Electrónica, SA
PO Box 31, P-4470 Maia, Portugal
Tel: (+351 2) 941 36 66   Fax: (+351 2) 948 54 28

### Products
Static converters.

### Contracts
Recent contracts include supply of static converters for Corail-type coaches for CP.

*VERIFIED*

---

## EKE-Electronics Ltd

Piispanportti 7, FIN-02240 Espoo, Finland
Tel: (+358 9) 61 30 33 08   Fax: (+358 9) 61 30 33 00
e-mail: electronics@eke.fi
Web: http://www.eke.com

### Key personnel
Managing Director: Anssi Laakkonen
Development: Jyrki Keurulainen
Sales: Joni Juuth
Customer Projects: Samuel Krüger
Service and Technical Support: Mika Linden

### Products
EKE-Trainnet® TCN standard-based integrated train management systems. Products include a comprehensive set of modules, components and tools for complete train monitoring, diagnostics and control systems. System solutions include EKE-TMS train management systems and TCN gateways, EKE-TDR event recorders with protected memory, EKE-IVE in-vehicle passenger entertainment systems for on-demand audio and video, EKE-MMI user interface with display and keypad, and EKE-NMI ATC speedometers.

### Contracts
Recent contracts include: TMS, TCN gateway and remote control and user interface for Bombardier Transportation (FAGA, Israel double-deck project), 2000-01; TMS, TCN gateway and remote control, TMS, TDR and driver's interface for Walkers Pty Ltd (Cairns Tilt Train, Australia), 1999-2002; WTB Trainbus for Bombardier Transportation (Virgin CrossCountry demus, UK), 1999-2001.

*UPDATED*

*EKE-Trainnet® Gateway*   2002/0134728

---

## Elettromeccanica Parizza spa

Sesto San Giovanni, via Fosse Ardeatine 120, I-20099, Milan, Italy
Tel: (+39 02) 24 42 32 11   Fax: (+39 02) 24 42 33 99
e-mail: info@parizzi.it

### Key personnel
Managing Director: Giovanni Sciolla
Sales Manager: Massimo Maggioni

### Corporate developments
Parissa is a Fiat Ferroviaria company.

### Products
Energy converters: mono- and poly-current static converters fed by the primary power line to supply power for onboard auxiliary systems in three-phase 50 Hz AC (input voltages; 3,000 V DC, 1,500 V DC, 1,500 V AC, 50 Hz, 1,000 V AC 16 ⅔ Hz. Power: 35/220 k VA); mono- and poly-current static battery chargers fed by the primary power line (input voltages: as for auxiliary systems above, plus 600, 750 and 1,500 V DC. Power: 1.5 to 22 kW); inverters and converters; UPS.

Traction equipment: variable frequency and voltage inverters to supply and control asynchronous traction motor for diesel-electric locomotives and electric trainsets; synchronous and asynchronous traction motors.

Urban transport technology and applications: IGBT converters (chopper or inverter) for traction and electrical braking; digital traction controllers; asynchronous tractions motors; permanent magnet synchronous tractions motors. Water, heat pipes, natural or forced ventilated cooling systems.

Vehicle control system and diagnostic, integral low-floor tramways, low-floor trolleybus, bus and minibus, innovative guided rail vehicles.

Electronic systems: microprocessor-based control and diagnostic systems; centralised/tachometric/tachographic and event-recording systems; electronic anti-skid devices to adapt the braking force to the instantaneous adhesion condition of railway vehicles.

Recent contracts include: systems for Pendolino trains, VAL 208, for Virgin, ATM Milan and Tram Torino.

---

## Ellcon National Inc

50 Beechtree Boulevard, PO Box 9377, Greenville, South Carolina 29604-9377, USA
Tel: (+1 864) 277 50 00   Fax: (+1 864) 277 52 07
Web: http://www.ellcon.com

### Key personnel
Chairman: E P Kondra
President: Douglas E Kondra
Executive Vice-President: R A Nitsch
Treasurer: L F D'Alessio

### Licensee
Gregg Company Ltd
15 Dyatt Place, PO Box 430, Hackensack, New Jersey 07602-0430, USA

### Sales representatives
*Canada*
Pandrol Canada Ltd
8310 Cote de Liesse Road, Suite 100, Montreal, Quebec H4T 1G7

*Mexico*
Piedras Negras 35, Club de Golf 'La Hacienda', Atizapan de Zaragoza, Edo De, Mexico

### Products
Ball-style straight cocks, ball-style angle cocks, retaining valve, stainless-steel ball valves, electronic air brake system, 'Norson' pneumatic discharge gates, handbrakes, bogie-mounted brakes, empty load brakes, slack adjusters, branch pipe tees.

Body-mounted brake cylinders, dirt collector cut out chock.

*UPDATED*

## ELNO

BP 46-17 rue Jean Pierre Timbaud, F-95100 Argenteuil, France
Tel: (+33 1) 39 98 44 44   Fax: (+33 1) 39 98 44 46
e-mail: sales@elno
Web: http://www.elno.fr/

**Key personnel**
Chairman: Philippe Bertin
General Manager: Jacques Fedon
Export Manager: Gabriel Grosjean

**Subsidiary company**
Deutsche Elno, Germany

**Products**
Audio and video systems for passenger vehicles. Audio components including driver/guard handsets and microphones, loudspeakers, power amplifiers, passenger alarm units and remote/central communications and alarm management units. Active noise reduction system.

**Contracts**
Contracts include supply of equipment to Eurostar, TGV Atlantique (ALSTOM and Bombardier), SNCF/RATP, SNCFB and rail operators in UK.

*UPDATED*

---

## EWS-EXTEL Systems Wedel

Industriestrasse 33, D-22876 Wedel, Germany
Tel: (+49 4103) 60 36 71   Fax: (+49 4103) 60 45 03
e-mail: sales@esw-wedel.de
Web: http://www.esw-wedel.de

**Key personnel**
Marketing Manager: Rolf Forstmann

**Products**
Electric body tilting equipment.

*VERIFIED*

---

## EVAC

EVAC International Ltd
Purotie 1, FIN-00380 Helsinki, Finland
Tel: (+358 9) 50 67 61   Fax: (+358 9) 50 67 63 33

**Key personnel**
Managing Director: Matti Tanska

**EVAC companies**
EVAC Oy
(address above)
Managing Director: Olli Björkqvist

EVAC AB
SE-295 39 Bromölla, Sweden
Tel: (+46 456) 485 00   Fax: (+46 456) 279 72
Managing Director: Arne Ask

EVAC GmbH
Hafenstrasse 32A, D-22880 Wedel, Germany
Tel: (+49 41) 03 91 68 0   Fax: (+49 41) 03 91 68 90
Managing Director: Hans Wörmcke

Envirovac Inc
1260 Turret Drive, Rockford, Illinois 61115-1486, USA
Tel: (+1 815) 654 83 00   Fax: (+1 815) 654 83 06
Managing Director: Robert Schafer

EVAC Vacuum Systems (Shanghai) Co Ltd (EVSS)
Unit E, 13F, Jiu Shi Fu Xing Mansion, 918 Huai Hai Road (M), Shanghai, 200020, PR China
Tel: (+86 21) 64 15 95 80   Fax: (+86 21) 64 15 75 50
Managing Director: Nils Andersson

**Products**
Vacuum toilet and sewage handling systems.

*VERIFIED*

---

## EVAC GmbH

Hafenstrasse 32a, D-22880, Wedel, Germany
Tel: (+49 4103) 916 80   Fax: (+49 4103) 91 68 90
e-mail: sanivac@evac.de
Web: http://www.evacgroup.com

**Key personnel**
Sales and Marketing Director: Robert Gigengack

**Other offices**
EVAC International Ltd
Purotie 1, FIN-00380 Helsinki, Finland
Tel: (+358 9) 50 67 61   Fax: (+358 9) 50 67 62 33
e-mail: evac@evacgroup.com

EVAC Oy
e-mail: evac.marine@evac.fi
e-mail: evac.building@evac.fi

EVAC Sarl
Parc d'Activities des Bellevue, 35/37 Avenue du Gros Chêne, Herblay,
BP 98 F-95613 Cergy Pontoise Cedex, France
Tel: (+33 1) 34 21 99 88   Fax: (+33 1) 34 64 39 00
e-mail: evac@wanadoo.fr

Evac Aquamar GmbH
Zöllner Strasse 7, D-51491 Overath, Germany
Tel: (+49 2204) 972 40   Fax: (+49 2204) 97 24 29

EVAC GmbH
Hafenstrasse 32a, D-22880 Wedel, Germany
Tel: (+49 4103) 916 80   Fax: (+49 4103) 91 68 90
e-mail: info@evac.de

EVAC Representative Office
206, Tagore Lane, 787593 Singapore
Tel: (+65) 453 73 55   Fax: (+65) 453 52 07
e-mail: richard.moreira@evac.fi

EVAC AB
Rattens Gränd 1, S-295 39 Bromölla, Sweden
Tel: (+46 456) 485 00   Fax: (+46 456) 279 72
e-mail: evac.train@evac.se

Evac (UK) Limited
Unit A1, Darenth Works, Ray Lamb Way, Erith DA8 2LA, UK
Tel: (+44 1322) 35 17 00   Fax: (+44 1322) 35 18 00
e-mail: evac-uk.building@evac.fi

Envirovac Inc
1260 Turret Drive, Rockford Ilinois 61115-1486, USA
Tel: (+1 815) 654 83 00   Fax: (+1 815) 654 83 06
e-mail: aviation@evac.com
Web: http://www.envirovacinc.com

Evac Ltda
Rua Luiz Otávio, 2955 Taquaral, Brazil
Tel: (+55 19) 32 56 34 90   Fax: (+55 19) 32 56 46 61
e-mail: evac@evac.com.br

Evac Vacuum Systems
(Shanghai) Co Ltd (EVSS)
Unit E, 13F, Jiu Shi Fu Xing Mansion, 918 Huai Hai Road (M), Shanghai, 200020, PR China
Tel: (+86 21) 64 15 95 80   Fax: (+86 21) 64 15 75 50

**Background**
EVAC GmbH is a member of the Sanivac Corporation.

**Products**
Vacuum toilet; tanks and accessories.

*UPDATED*

---

## Excil Electronics Ltd

Ripley Drive, Normanton WF6 1QT, UK
Tel: (+44 1924) 22 41 00   Fax: (+44 1924) 22 41 11
Web: http://www.excil.co.uk

**Key personnel**
Managing Director: Phil Burns
Sales Manager: David Burley
Technical Manager: John Hesketh

**Background**
Excil Electronics is a member of LPA Group plc.

*Actuator by ESW-EXTEL Systems*

*Excil luminaire in UK rolling stock*

## MANUFACTURERS/Passenger coach equipment

**Products**
Passenger vehicle interior lighting systems; electronic lighting inverters; control and monitoring equipment.

**Contracts**
Interior lighting for London Underground Ltd Piccadilly line metro cars and luminaires for Northern and Jubilee line stock.

*UPDATED*

---

### Fahrzeugausrüstung Berlin GmbH (FAGA)

A subsidiary of Deutsche Waggonbau AG
Wolfener Strasse 23, D-12681 Berlin, Germany
Tel: (+49 30) 93 64 20   Fax: (+49 30) 93 64 23 02

**Key personnel**
Managing Director: Reinhard Schwarzenau

**Products**
Power supply systems, DC and AC generators, rectifiers, inverters, high-voltage equipment boxes in single and multitension design, switch cabinets, transistorised fluorescent ballasts, train/vehicle control systems, controlling and regulating and diagnostic devices.

*VERIFIED*

---

### FAINSA

Fabricación Asientos Vehículos Industriales SA
Calle Horta s/n, E-08107 Martorelles (Barcelona), Spain
Tel: (+34 93) 579 69 70   Fax: (+34 93) 570 18 38
e-mail: fainsa@fainsa.com

**Key personnel**
President: Juan Singla
Managing Director: Rafaél Roldán
Commercial Manager: Francesc Puig
Export Manager: Marc Vidal

**Subsidiary companies**
MTP Equipment (UK Sales)
FAINSA Corporation, USA

**Products**
Passenger seating for railway vehicles, LRVs and metro cars, including berths for sleeping cars.

Recent developments include: design of a rotatable seat for high speed train applications. Establishing new anti-vandalism systems; new production facilities in Plattsburg, New York; signature of several technology transfer agreements.

Recent contracts for RENFE in Spain include: D-200 vehicle refurbishment programme; seats for TRD dmus; Class 440 refurbishment; seats for Class 447 emus; second class seats for TALGO vehicles. FAINSA has also equipped refurbishment projects for FEVE, Spain.

Other contracts: dmu refurbishment for Chile; refurbishment of regional trains for TGOJ, Sweden; first and second class seats for ŽSR, Slovakia; seats for Sacramento and Washington metro cars; seats for passenger coaches for New Jersey; dmu seats for SNCB, Belgium; seats for Bombardier's Itino projects; second class seats for ENR, Egypt; seats for regional emus for the UK; tram seats for vehicles for Kassel, Milan, Prague and Turin; sleeping car berths for Greece.

*UPDATED*

---

### Faiveley Transport

Faiveley Transport SA
143 boulevard Anatole France, F-93285 Saint Denis Cedex, France
Tel: (+33 1) 48 13 65 00   Fax: (+33 1) 48 13 66 47
e-mail: info@faiveley.com

**Main works**
Electromechanical Division
Les Yvaudières, avenue Yves Farge, F-37705 Saint-Pierre-des-Corps, France
Tel: (+33 2) 47 32 55 55   Fax: (+33 2) 47 44 80 24
Production Centre, Electromechanics and Air Conditioning Division
ZI, 1 rue des Grands Mortiers, F-37705 Saint-Pierre-des-Corps, France
Tel: (+33 2) 47 32 55 55   Fax: (+33 2) 47 63 19 31
Electronics Division
rue Amélia Earhart, ZI du Bois de Plante, PO Box 43, F-37700 La-Ville-Aux-Dames, France
Tel: (+33 2) 47 32 55 55   Fax: (+33 2) 47 32 56 61

**Key personnel**
Chairman and Chief Executive Officer: Alain Bodel
Financial Director: Francois Couffy
Director, Electromechanical Products Division: Bernard Guillaume
Director, Electronics Division: Marc Chocat
Director, Air Conditioning Division: Jean-Jacques Maillard
Marketing and Communications Manager: Régine Lombard

**Subsidiaries**
Faiveley Española SA
Autovia Reus Km 5, Apartado 525, E-43080 Tarragona, Spain
Tel: (+34 977) 54 85 06   Fax: (+34 977) 85 79
e-mail: info-esp@faiveley.net
Faiveley Italia SpA
Via della Meccanica 21, Zona Industriale de Bassone, I-37139 Verona, Italy
Tel: (+39 045) 851 00 11   Fax: (+39 045) 851 00 20
e-mail: info-it@faiveley.com
Equipfer Faiveley do Brazil Ltda
Rua Major Paladino No241, Via Leopoldina, São Paulo SP, 05307.000 Brazil
Tel: (+55 11) 36 49 040   Fax: (+55 11) 36 49 041
e-mail: info-brasil@faiveley.com
NFL-Nabco Faiveley Ltd
45-2 Oi, 1-chome, Shinagawa-ku, Tokyo 104, Japan
Tel: (+81 3) 57 09 87 51   Fax: (+81 3) 57 09 87 58
e-mail: info-japan@faiveley.jp
Faiveley UK Ltd
Unit 10, Ninian Industrial Park, Ninian Way, Tamworth B77 5DE, UK
Tel: (+44 1827) 26 28 30   Fax: (+44 1827) 26 28 31
e-mail: info-uk@faiveley.com
HFG Hagenuk Faiveley GmbH
Industriestrasse 60, D-04435 Schkeuditz, Germany
Tel: (+49 34204) 853 00   Fax: (+49 34204) 853 02
e-mail: info@faiveley.de
HFG Hagenuk Faiveley GmbH
Philipp Reiss Weg 5, D-24148 Kiel, Germany
Tel: (+49 431) 600 70   Fax: (+49 431) 600 73 02
HFG Shanghai Hagenuk Refrigerating Machine Co Ltd
1481 Gong He Xin Road, Shanghai 200072, China
Tel: (+86 21) 56 62 58 04   Fax: (+86 21) 56 62 55 00
e-mail: info-china@faiveley.com
Faiveley Rail Inc
213 Welsh Pool Road, Pickering Creek Industrial Park, Exton, Pennsylvania 19341, USA
Tel: (+1 610) 524 9110   Fax: (+49 610) 524 91 90
e-mail: info-usa@faiveley.com
Faiveley Far East Ltd
Unit A, 26/F, Hang Shan Centre, 141-145 Queens Road East, Wanchai, Hong Kong, China
Tel: (+852) 28 61 17 88   Fax: (+852) 28 61 17 44
e-mail: info-asia@faiveley.com

**Products**
Onboard equipment and systems comprising door systems (electric and pneumatic operators, automatic external doors and steps, interior doors, automatic platform screen doors); air conditioning equipment (passenger coach and driver's cab units, duct systems, pressure protection systems, programmable controllers; electronics (data processing, speed control and monitoring equipment, event recorders, anti-slip and anti-skid protection, multiplexing, power converters); passenger counting systems and video surveillance systems, gangways and pantographs (see *Electric traction equipment* section).

---

### FASI Seating Systems

Clerprem Benelux, Rue des Ateliers no 10, B-7850 Petit Enghien, Belgium
Tel: (+32 2) 395 58 30   Fax: (+32 2) 395 64 96

**Products**
Seating systems.

---

### Ferranti Technologies Ltd

Cairo House, Waterhead, Oldham OL4 3JA, UK
Tel: (+44 161) 624 02 81   Fax: (+44 161) 624 52 44
e-mail: sales@ferranti-technologies.co.uk
Web: http://www.ferranti-technologies.co.uk

**Key personnel**
Managing Director: T C Scuoler
Finance Director: F Brinksman
Commercial Director: K R Mills
Operations Director: G J Lowe
Business Development Director: S R Warren

**Products**
Distance/Velocity Measurement Device (DVMD) utilising non-contact Doppler radar sensing and featuring integral processing electronics. Train-mounted applications include traction control, slip/slide protection, odometry and speed measurement; track-located applications for sensing speed and length of passing rolling stock.

Design, development and production of control electronics to customer specifications; manufacture and repair of third-party electronic and electromechanical assemblies.

Range of power conversion equipment, including transformer rectifier units, inverters, power supplies and other equipment for low-power auxiliary functions.

UV laser cable marking and manufacture of cable looms; environmental testing (UKAS-approved).

**Contracts**
Contracts include a DVMD device selected by ALSTOM Transport Service UK for integration into the traction control package of an overseas refurbishment programme.

Production for ALSTOM Traction Ltd, following previous design and development contracts, of a family of key electronic subsystems for use on the Juniper generic train.

*UPDATED*

*Ferranti Technologies distance/velocity measurement device*   0023846

---

### Ferraz

Ferraz SA
PO Box 3025, F-69391 Lyon Cedex 03, France
Tel: (+33 4) 72 22 66 11   Fax: (+33 4) 72 22 67 13

**Key personnel**
See entry in *Electric traction equipment* section.

**Products**
Earth return current units and associated resistors to prevent current flowing through bearing of axleboxes and associated resistors; fuses with very high breaking capacity for DC/AC converter protection and for heating circuits protection.

---

### Ferro

Ferro (Great Britain) Ltd, Powder Coatings Division
Westgate, Aldridge WS9 8YH, UK
Tel: (+44 1922) 74 13 00   Fax: (+44 1922) 74 13 27

**Key personnel**
General Manager: A J Pitchford
UK Sales Manager: M F Haines
Export Director: M Davies
Transportation Market Manager: A Phillips

## Products

Powder coatings for the rail industry for passenger vehicle interiors, station fittings and signage, cladding, trunking and switchgear assemblies.

Range includes: Bonalux AG 2000 anti-graffiti, 491 series polyesters, 4620 series epoxies, all fire resistant to BS 476 Pys 6 and 7 (Class 1) and smoke emission to BS 6853.

Ferro coatings have been supplied to London Underground Ltd's Central, Piccadilly, Northern and Jubilee lines and Hong Kong MTRC, Virgin Trains, First Great Western, Midland Mainline and specified by major rolling stock manufacturers.

*UPDATED*

## Ferro International A/S

Tirsbækvej 15, DK-7120 Vejle Ø, Denmark
Tel: (+45 75) 89 56 11   Fax: (+45 75) 89 59 37
e-mail: info@ferro-int.dk
Web: http://www.ferro-int.dk

### Key personnel
Managing Director: Erik Sørensen
Export Manager: Finn Bach Laursen

### Products
Sliding interior doors for passenger vehicles, including electric and pneumatic doors operated by push-buttons or automatically by sensors; curved electric sliding doors for toilet modules and compartments.

Recent contracts include: interior doors and gangway doors for Adtranz, VR, Talgo-Transtech, Bombardier and EVAC AB, Sweden; the supply of interior sliding doors to Adtranz, and curved automatic doors for EVAC.

## Fersystem

Parc d'activitiés de Conneuil, 1 avenue Léonard de Vinci, PO Box 30, F-37270 Montlouis-sur-Loire, France
Tel: (+32 2) 47 45 19 45   Fax: (+32 2) 47 45 11 34
e-mail: fersystem@wanadoo.fr

### Key personnel
President: Jean Chapouthier

### Products
Doors for rail vehicles and fire barriers.

Contracts include supply of door systems and fire barriers for Eurostar in partnership with Westinghouse Brakes & Signals.

## Fiberline

Fiberline Composites A/S
Nr Bjertvej 88, DK-6000 Kolding, Denmark
Tel: (+45) 75 56 53 33   Fax: (+45) 75 56 52 81
e-mail: fiberline@fiberline.com
Web: http://www.fiberline.com

### Key personnel
Sales Manager: Stig Krogh Pedersen

### Products
Lightweight corrosion-resistant grp profiles for rail vehicles.

Contracts include the supply of exterior panels for Talent dmus built by Bombardier Transportation for German Rail (DB AG).

## Fine Products SA

Polígono El Sequero, Parc 21, Aptdo 1617, E-26080 Logroño, Spain
Tel: (+34 941) 43 70 32   Fax: (+34 941) 43 71 85
e-mail: fine.p@fer.es

### Products
Emergency evacuation ramps for passenger rail vehicles; access ramps for mobility-impaired passengers; control desks; equipment cabinets; coupler fairings; luggage stacks; vehicle side skirts.

## Finnyards Materials Technology

Finnyards Ltd Materials Technology
Nosturikatu 7, FIN-37150, Nokia, Finland
Tel: (+358 3) 342 99 29   Fax: (+358 3) 342 99 14

### Key personnel
Director: Ari Vihersaari
Technology Director: Pekka Tammi
R & D Director: Pekka Lammassaari
Quality Manager: Asko Kylkilahti

### Products
Design, development and manufacture of composite structures for rail vehicles, ships, ballistic protection and buildings.

Advanced reinforced plastic composites are produced at the Nosturikatu works.

Contracts include design and development of aerodynamic driver's cab for the Pendolino train, supply of composite structures to Fiat Ferroviario, for 42 double-deck coaches for Rautaruukki.

## Fischer Industries Pty Ltd

13 Whiting Street, Atarmon, New South Wales 2064, Australia
Tel: (+61 2) 94 36 06 11   Fax: (+61 2) 94 38 24 35

### Key personnel
Technical Director: Peter Fischer
Marketing Manager: Warren Hocking

### Products
Events recorders/data loggers, vigilance systems, Train Management Systems (TMS), analogue and digital meters, door controllers, inverters/converters.

*UPDATED*

## Flachglas Wernberg GmbH

Nuernberger Strasse 140, D-92533 Wernberg-Koeblitz, Germany
Tel: (+49 9604) 480   Fax: (+49 9604) 483 98

### Key personnel
Sales Director: Martin Rädel

### Products
Module supplier of glass for special applications: low-E insulating glass; solar control glass; noise-reducing insulating glass; toughened glass; laminated glass; bullet-resistant glass; screen-printed glass with and without glazing system.

*UPDATED*

## Freudenberg Schwab GmbH

Postplate 3, D-16761 Hennigsdorf, Germany
Tel: (+49 3302) 206 20   Fax: (+49 3302) 20 62 77
e-mail: info@freudenberg-schwab.de
Web: http://www.freudenberg-schwab.de

### Key personnel
See *Bogies and suspension, wheels and axles, bearings* section.

### Organisation
See *Bogies and suspension, wheels and axles, bearings* section.

### Product
Noise reduction and vibration control systems and components especially multi-layer springs, cone springs, axle type bushes, ultra bushes, spherical bearings, buffers, spring seats, elastic coupling elements, hydrobushings, active vibration absorbers.

The company has worked with: ALSTOM, Bombardier Transportation, Deutsche Bahn AG, A Friedr Flender AG, Phoenix AG, Scharfenbergkupplung, SAB WABCO BSI Verkehrstechnik Products, Siemens, Voith Turbo, Vossloh Schienenfahrzeugtechnik, WATTEEUW Power Transmission Co and ZF Bahntechnik.

*UPDATED*

## Fuji Electric Co Ltd

Gate City Ohsaki, East Tower 11-2, Osaki 1-chome, Shinagawa-ku, Tokyo 141-0032, Japan
Tel: (+81 3) 54 35 70 46   Fax: (+81 3) 54 35 74 23
e-mail: info@fujielectric.co.jp
Web: http://www.fujielectric.co.jp

### Key personnel
See entry in *Electric traction equipment* section.

### Background
The Transportation Systems Sales Department of Fuji Electric falls within the company's Electrical Systems Company Group.

### Products
Static auxiliary power supply systems; linear motor-drive door systems for rail vehicles.

*UPDATED*

## FY – Industries

FY – Industries Ltd, Composites
Nosturikatu 7, FIN-37150 Nokia, Finland
Tel: (+358 3) 342 99 00   Fax: (+358 3) 342 99 14
e-mail: ari.vihersaari@FY.sci.Fi
Web: http://www.FY.composites.com

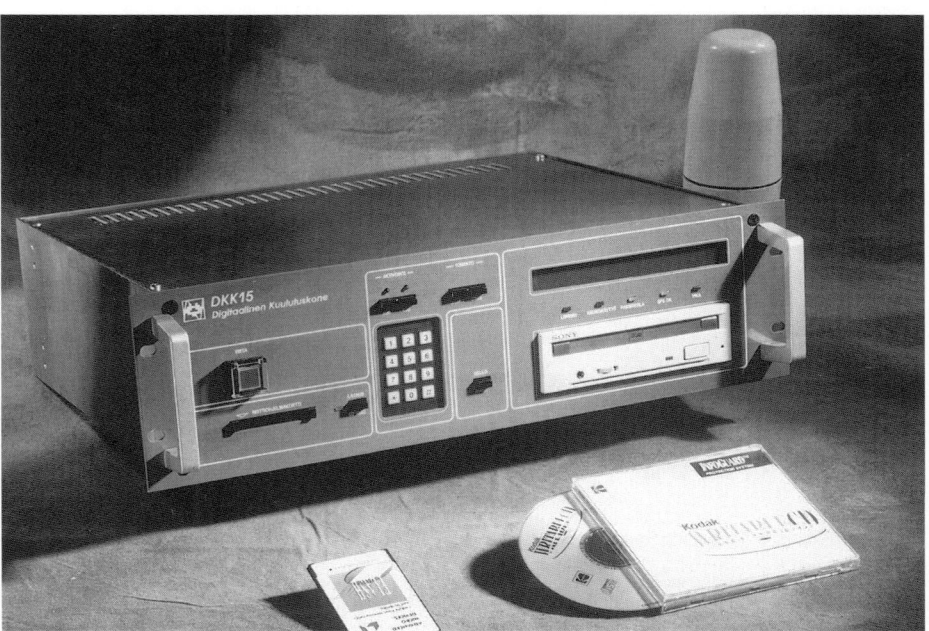

*The FY – Industries automatic on-train public address system uses a CD-ROM for the announcements*

## MANUFACTURERS/Passenger coach equipment

**Key personnel**
Director: Ari Vihersaari
Manager, Research & Development: Mika Mustakawgas
Manager, Production: Il Poahlstedt
Quality Manager: Asko Kylkigahti

**Products**
On-train automatic public address system which uses a Global Positioning System receiver to make announcements at predetermined locations. The system uses a CD-ROM for extra capacity in the recorded multilingual announcements. Finnish State Railways has been operating the system since 1995 and has over 225 modules in service.

## GAI-Tronics Ltd

Brunel Drive, Stretton Business Park, Burton on Trent DE13 0BZ, UK
Tel: (+44 1283) 50 05 00   Fax: (+44 1283) 50 04 00
e-mail: sales@gai-tronics.co.uk
Web: http://www.gai-tronics.co.uk

**Key personnel**
Business Unit Manager: Graham Lines
Financial Director: Toby Balmer
Engineering Manager, Applications: Steve Smith
Manufacturing Director: Mark Bradford
Sales Director: Steve Dade
Sales Manager, Transport: Anthony Rooryck
Commercial Manager: Roger Goodall
Marketing Consultant: Nicole Ireland

**Other offices**
GAI-Tronics Corporation, USA
Tel: (+1 610) 777 13 74   Fax: (+1 610) 775 65 40
Web: http://www.gai-tronics.com

GAI-Tronics Srl, Italy
Tel: (+39 02) 48 60 14 60   Fax: (+39 02) 458 56 25

GAI-Tronics Corporation, Malaysia
Tel: (+60 3) 637 60 91   Fax: (+60 3) 638 60 93

**Background**
GAI-Tronics Limited was established in 1964 to provide communications equipment to the mining industry. It has now expanded into the provision of specialised communications equipment for road and rail transportation industries.

**Products**
Onboard communications and information systems including passenger announcement system; crew communications; driver/control centre radio communications; emergency driver/passenger communications; disabled persons communications; on-train entertainment; audible warning and prerecorded digitised special messages.
The products and systems are developed for use in hazardous or hostile areas and are vandal- and weather-resistant.

*UPDATED*

## The Gates Rubber Co Ltd

Edinburgh Road, Heathhall, Dumfries DG1 1QA, UK
Tel: (+44 1387) 26 95 51   Fax: (+44 1387) 25 01 87
e-mail: info@floormaster-plus.com
Web: http://www.floormaster-plus.com

**Products**
Fire-safe, low-smoke, low-toxicity floor coverings for rail vehicle applications, including Floormaster 9200 M2F1 for surface stock and Floormaster Plus 9300 for use in metro vehicles.

## Georg Eknes Industrier A/S

N-5913 Elkangervåg, Norway
Tel: (+47 56) 35 75 00   Fax: (+47 56) 35 75 01
e-mail: transit@eknes.no
Web: http://www.eknes.no

**Products**
Hispek range of seating systems for rail vehicles.

*UPDATED*

## Georges Halais SA

5 rue Ambroise Croizat, BP 203, F-95190 Goussainville, France
Tel: (+33 1) 30 18 00 10   Fax: (+33 1) 30 18 00 11

**Key personnel**
Chief Executive Officer: M Cyril Josset

**Products**
Components for passenger car interiors including: stainless steel fittings, ceilings, interior doors and walls, table lamps, water heaters, lighting fixtures, handles and handrails, hinges, luggage racks, blinds, locks, slots for seat reservation cards, litter bins, ashtrays, picture frames, tables, folding tables and skirts.
Contracts include TGV (SNCF), MP89 (RATP), MI2N (SNCF/RATP) and TER2N (SNCF/RATP), Virgin.

## GEZ

GEZ Gesellschaft für Elektrische Zugausrüstung mbH
Flinschstrasse 20, D-60388 Frankfurt/Main, Germany
A member of the Schaltbau group
Tel: (+49 69) 420 90 60   Fax: (+49 69) 42 09 06 13

**Key personnel**
Export Manager: F Vasel

**Products**
Low-voltage equipment and electrical components for coaches, especially train lighting equipment, control panels, alternators, inverters.

## Geze

Geze GmbH
PO Box 1363, D-71226 Leonberg, Germany
Tel: (+49 7152) 20 30   Fax: (+49 7152) 20 33 10
e-mail: vertrieb.services.de@geze.com
Web: http://www.geze.com

**UK subsidiary**
Geze UK Ltd
Chelmsford Business Park, Colchester Road, Chelmsford, Essex CM2 5LA
Tel: (+44 1245) 45 10 93   Fax: (+44 1245) 45 11 08
e-mail: geze.uk@geze.com
Web: http://www.geze-uk.com

**Products**
Window and door systems (single, double and telescopic); closing mechanisms, electromechanical or electropneumatic drives for single- and double-leaf doors; actuators; boarding and alighting equipment for buses trams and trains. RWA and safety technology glass systems.

*UPDATED*

## Giumma SpA

Via Pian Masino 12A, I-16011 Arenzano, Genova, Italy
Tel: (+39 010) 91 32 51   Fax: (+39 010) 911 10 65
e-mail: giumma@giumma.com
Web: http://www.giumma.com

**Products**
Prefabricated interior packages in self-extinguishing resin with reinforced glass fibre for rail vehicles, including toilet modules, wall panels and gangways.

**Contracts**
Recent contracts include the supply of toilet modules to Fiat Ferroviaria for Pendolino trainsets for Finnish Railways, Italian State Railways, Portuguese Railways, Slovenian Railways and Virgin Trains in the UK.

*UPDATED*

## Grammer

Grammer AG
PO Box 1454, D-92204 Amberg, Germany
Tel: (+49 9621) 88 04 31   Fax: (+49 9621) 88 03 81
Web: http://www.grammer.de

*Subsidiary company*
Lazzerini & Co Srl
Via Toscana 1, I-60030 Monsano (AN), Italy
Tel: (+39 0731) 602 61   Fax: (+39 0731) 604 49
e-mail: cml.lazzerini@fastnet.it

**Works**
Amberg; Kümmersbruck

**Products**
Suspension driver seats, passenger seats and other passenger coach equipment. Three-point seat belts, tables and interior fittings and the passenger seat range includes the Comfort reclining seat with arm rest and leather trim.

*VERIFIED*

## Gummi Metall Technik GmbH (GMT)

5 Liechtersmatten, D-77815 Bühl, Germany
Tel: (+49 7223) 80 40   Fax: (+49 7223) 210 75
e-mail: sengstler@gmt-gmbh.de
Web: http://www.gmt-gmbh.de

**Key personnel**
Manager: S Engstler

**Sales offices**
*Austria*
GMT Gummi Metall Technik Ges mbH
Gewerbestrasse A-65082 Grödig
Tel: (+43 6246) 74 00 60   Fax: (+43 6246) 740 06 22

*Belgium*
GMT Belgium SA/NV
165 Chaussée de Louvain, B-5310 Eghezée
Tel: (+32 81) 81 14 40   Fax: (+32 81) 24 40
e-mail: gmt.be@skynet.be

*France*
GMT Filiale France
ZI Sainte-Agathe, rue Paul Langevin, F-57192 Florange
Tel: (+33 3) 82 59 33 90   Fax: (+33 3) 82 59 33 99
e-mail: gmt.france@wanadoo.fr

*Ireland*
GMT Ireland Ltd
Clifden Co Galway
Tel: (+353 95) 213 82   Fax: (+353 95) 217 04
e-mail: gmtirl@iol.ie

*Malaysia*
GMT Gummi Metall Technik (M) SDN BHD
Industrial Estate, PO Box 82, 33000 Kuala Kangsar/Perak
Tel: (+60 5) 776 17 42   Fax: (+60 5) 776 57 00
e-mail: rmtsb@jaring.my

*Switzerland*
GMT Gumeta AG
Kautschuk-Werk, Buchrainstrasse 2, CH-6030 Ebikon
Tel: (+41 440) 17 17   Fax: (+41 440) 50 60

*UK*
GMT Rubber Metal Tecnic Ltd
The Sidings, Station Road, Guiseley, Leeds LS20 8BX
Tel: (+44 1943) 87 06 70   Fax: (+44 1943) 87 06 31
e-mail: andrew@gmt.gb.com

*USA*
GMT International Corp
PO Box 117 Villa Industrial, USA-30180 Villa Rica, USA
Tel: (+1 770) 459 57 57   Fax: (+1 770) 459 09 57
e-mail: gmt@gmt-international.com

**Products**
Resilient wheel systems, rubber and metal elements for noise and vibration insulation, such as axle springs, ball joints, primary suspension and rubber springs.

**Contracts**
ICE and ICE II high-speed trains, Germany; DWA (Bombardier) railbus project. Clients include Alstom, Bombardier, SNCF, SNCB, DB, Siemens and Adtranz.

*UPDATED*

## Heinrich Helms Metallwarenfabrik GmbH

Department Kuckuck Lufter
Postfach 75 06 54, D-28726 Bremen, Germany
Tel: (+49 421) 66 96 40; 669 64 15
Fax: (+49 421) 669 64 29

**Key personnel**
Contact Partner: W Boehm

**Subsidiary company**
Kuckuck GmbH

**Products**
Electric-powered fans and ventilators for rail vehicles, including roof-mounted fan with low air resistance, suitable for high-speed rail applications.

## Hexcel Composites

Duxford, Cambridge CB6 2JR, UK
Tel: (+44 1223) 83 83 70   Fax: (+44 1223) 83 85 64
e-mail: communications@hexcel-eu.com
Web: http://www.hexcelcomposites.com

**Key personnel**
Head of Sales, Europe: Thierry Merlot
Head of Marketing (Global): Jon Stowell
Communications Manager: Rachel Atkinson

**Products**
Hexlite® sandwich panels for interiors and structures; honeycomb cores (metallic and non-metallic); honeycomb energy absorbers; epoxy and phenolic prepregs; reinforcement fabrics, Redux® film adhesives.

**Contracts**
Structural flooring for Bombardier IC2000 carriages, sandwich panels for Alstom Pendolino interiors, energy absorbers for TGV trainsets and prepregs for SNCF.

*UPDATED*

## Hagenuk Faiveley GmbH (HFG)

Industriestrasse 60, D-04435 Schkeuditz, Germany
Tel: (+49 34204) 850   Fax: (+49 34204) 853 02
e-mail: info@faiveley.de
Web: http://www.faiveley.de

**Works**
Philipp-Reis-Weg 5, D-24148 Kiel, Germany
Tel: (+49 431) 600 70   Fax: (+49 431) 600 73 02

**Key personnel**
General Managers: W D Karneboge, M Köhler
Engineering Manager: H Schmerler
Sales Manager, Northern Europe:
  B Lehmann-Matthaei
Sales Managers, Southern Europe and Overseas:
  S Net, J Kreutzmann

**Subsidiary company**
HFG Shanghai Hagenuk, Refrigerating Machine Co Ltd, 1481 Gong He Xin Rd, Shanghai, China, PC 200072

**Products**
Heating and ventilation, air conditioning, heaters for hot water supply and refrigeration systems including the Air-Cycle air conditioning system for rail vehicles; microcomputer-controlled temperature control systems; pressure protection systems.

Air-Cycle and air conditioning equipment has been supplied to DB for ICE3 and ICT trainsets; air conditioning equipment has been supplied to Metro Bangkok and Norway for the Gardemoen line (Oslo airport-city centre shuttle). Other contracts include refurbishment of trainsets for Belgrade and supply of air conditioning units to BVG Berlin for tram cabs.

*UPDATED*

## Hodgson and Hodgson

Hodgson and Hodgson Group Ltd
Winnington Hall Mews, Northwich CW8 4DU, UK
Tel: (+44 1606) 765 93   Fax: (+44 1606) 743 15
e-mail: hodgsons@easynet.co.uk

**Key personnel**
Chairman: G Balshaw-Jones
Managing Director: J Roberts
Technical Director: N Grundy
Commercial Director: P Rollinson
Export Sales Manager: E Fitzpatrick
Acoustic Consultant: P Eade

**Products**
Thermal and acoustic components for services for bus and railway traction units and rolling stock. Thermal and acoustic products for associated buildings. Design, manufacture and supply of finished products or components direct to site or the production line.

**Contracts**
Recent projects include: Waterloo Eurostar Terminal (buildings), St Petersburg Rail Terminal (buildings), Barratt Housing Project (trackside development), Eurotram (complete vehicle), Europa Transrapid (complete vehicle), MTRC Hong Kong (complete vehicle), Arlanda, Stockholm (complete vehicle), Gatwick Express (complete vehicle), Juniper, Turbostar and Electrostar (complete vehicles), West Coast Main Line (complete vehicle), First Bus, Mellor Vancraft, Optare and Marshalls (exhaust jacketing, moulded engine compartment and interior panelling).

*UPDATED*

## John Holdsworth

John Holdsworth & Co Ltd
Shaw Lodge Mills, Halifax HX3 9ET, United Kingdom
Tel: (+44 1422) 43 30 00   Fax: (+44 1422) 43 33 00
e-mail: info@holdsworth.co.uk
Web: http://www.holdsworth.co.uk

**Key personnel**
Managing Director: Michael Holdsworth
Sales:
  (Rail) Richard Field
  (Coach) Martin Gosnay
  (Bus/Ferry) Peter Hobson

**Subsidiary company**
Holdsworth North America

**Products**
Manufacturers of transport seating fabrics for the rail, bus, coach, airport and ferry markets worldwide, incorporating a bespoke design and styling service.

*UPDATED*

## Honeywell Serck

Warwick Road, Birmingham B11 2QY, UK
Tel: (+44 121) 766 66 66   Fax: (+44 121) 766 60 14
e-mail: sind@serckht.co.uk

**Key personnel**
See entry in *Diesel engines, transmission and fuelling systems* section.

**Corporate background**
Honeywell Serck is part of Honeywell Thermal Systems and a subsidiary of the Honeywell Corporation.

**Products**
Integrated cooling modules air conditioning systems for dmus, emus and passenger coaches.

Recent contracts include redesign of the air conditioning system in South West Trains (UK) Class 159 dmus.

## Howden Buffalo

Old Govan Road, Renfrew, Glasgow PA4 8XJ, UK
Tel: (+44 141) 885 75 00   Fax: (+44 141) 886 19 61

**Key personnel**
General Manager: Kevin M Bristow

**Products**
Cooling fans for locomotive engines, transformers, inverters and dynamic braking systems.

## HP

HP Srl
A Westinghouse Air Brake Company
Viale Regina Pacis 296, I-41049 Sassuolo, Modena, Italy
Tel: (+39 0536) 80 64 41   Fax: (+39 0536) 80 17 89
e-mail: hpdoors@sirnet.it

**Key personnel**
Managing Director: Luigi Camellini
Export Manager: Vinicio Mathis

**Products**
Sliding, slide-glide and plug doors for bus and rail vehicles, featuring infra-red sensitive edge and other passenger protection devices, body-end fire-proof doors, both pneumatic and electric drive units with control electronics, mobile steps, bridgeplates and bus ramps.

Recent orders include electric sliding plug doors for the Copenhagen automated metro, entrance doors, body-end fire doors and bridgeplates for bilevel commuter trains (TAF) for FS, all-electric slide-glide doors for citybuses, bus ramps, powered covers for couplers.

## Hübner Gummi- und Kunststoff GmbH

Heinrich Hertz Strasse 2, 15, D-34123 Kassel, Germany
Tel: (+49 561) 959 55 00   Fax: (+49 561) 959 55 55
e-mail: info@hubner-germany.com
Web: http://www.hubner-germany.com

**Key personnel**
Executive Chairman: Reinhard Hübner
Managing Director: Günter Schwind
Director: Ingo Brtizke

**Subsidiary companies**
Hübner Manufacturing Corporation, 355 Wando Place Drive, 29464 Mount Pleasant, South Carolina, USA
Tel: (+1 843) 849 94 00   Fax: (+1 843) 849 94 04
Hübner Sanfonas Industriais Ltda, Adhemar Pinto Siqueira 412, 12280 Caçapava Est de São Paulo, Brazil
Tel: (+55 122) 53 36 22   Fax: (+1 122) 52 47 04

**Products**
Folding bellows for buses and rail vehicles; vehicle articulation systems; rail vehicle gangways; moulded rubber parts; rubber profiles.

Hübner has supplied gangways for Class 158, 165, 168, Turbostar, Electrostar DB class 643 emus, Juniper and Pendolino emus, ICE cars, Berlin metro, Strasbourg metro and metros in Cologne, Amsterdam and Rotterdam.

**Developments**
Hübner has announced a new product range of front end gangways for the UK market, which includes a gangway connection that can be folded back inside the vehicle front end to give an aerodynamic front end.

*VERIFIED*

## Huck

Huck International Ltd
A Thiokol company
Unit c, Stafford Park 7, Telford TF3 3BQ, UK
Tel: (+44 1952) 20 46 52   Fax: (+44 1952) 29 04 59

## 574 MANUFACTURERS/Passenger coach equipment

**Key personnel**
Vice-President: John Coles

**Products**
Huckbolt fastener system.
Contracts include supply of Huck fasteners to Adtranz, Bombardier, ALSTOM and Siemens.

## IFE

IFE Industrie-Einrichtungen Fertigungs-AG
Patertal 20, A-3340 Waidhofen/Ybbs, Austria
Tel: (+43 7442) 51 50   Fax: (+43 7442) 515 13
e-mail: doors–vk@ife-ag.com

**Subsidiary companies**
IFE CR as, Czech Republic
IFE North America, USA
IFE-Tebel Australia Pty Ltd, Australia
IFE-Tebel Technologies BV, Netherlands
IFE UK Services Ltd
Kiekert-Automatiktüren, GmbH, Germany

**Key personnel**
General Manager: Ing Ferdinand Reich
Head of Automatic Door Division (Sales Director, Export and Marketing): Ing Manfred Teufl

**Corporate development**
Knorr-Bremse Systems for Rail Vehicles GmbH took a 49 per cent shareholding in IFE (Industrie-Einrichtungen Fertigungs-Atkiengesellschaft) Austria, in 1997.

**Products**
Plug, pocket and sliding door systems for rail vehicles and buses; external sliding doors, pocket doors, inside swing doors; movable steps; door control equipment.

## IMI Norgren GmbH

Actuator Division
Bruckstrasse 93, D-46519 Alpen, Germany
Tel: (+49 2802) 490   Fax: (+49 2802) 68 04
Web: http://www.norgren.com

**Corporate background**
IMI Norgren GmbH is part of the IMI Group.

**Products**
Pneumatic actuators for rail vehicle applications, including: internal and external door operation; door step control; seat adjustment; toilet operation; water preparation; pantograph retraction; brakes; de-coupling equipment; retractable mirrors; and body tilting systems.
Clients include Alstom Transport, Bode, Bombardier Transportation, DB AG, IFE, PFA and Stadler-Pankow.

*NEW ENTRY*

## International Metals Reclamation Co dbac (INMETCO)

245 Portersville Road, Ellwood City Pennsylvania 161117, USA
Tel: (+1 724) 758 55 15
e-mail: sthompson@inco.com
Web: http://www.inmetco.com

**Key personnel**
President: Kenneth L Money
Sales Representative: Shane M Thompson

**Products**
Recycling of batteries used in locomotives and rolling stock, radios, phones and computers.

*UPDATED*

## International Nameplate Supplies Ltd

1420 Crumlin Road, London, Ontario N5V 1S1, Canada
Tel: (+1 800) 565 35 09   Fax: (+1 519) 455 44 09
e-mail: sales@inps.on.ca
Web: http://www.inps.on.ca

**Key personnel**
Director: David Gibson

**Products**
Dead-front graphics (panels which have a dull finish, and hidden lights. They are commonly found on cars for the indicating lights). The company has the technology to form small runs of plastic without incurring the enormous tooling required for injection moulding. It also engraves serial plates, wire and hydraulic markers, warning and informational signs. Hot stamping of customer cards, wire markers, parking and expiration decals. Cutting of stencils and legends, corporate logos, painting patterns, vehicle identification, and numbering vehicles. Silk screen printing of warning and information nameplates, rate decals and corporate logos.
Stainless steel etching, aluminium anodising, screen printing and four colour process and reverse screened polycarbonate.
The latest development is a vacuum formed product for bus and passenger rail. It mounts inside the vehicle and acts as a permanent frame for advertising media.
Currently INPS is the sole supplier of locomotive graphics services to General Motors EMD division, CSX Transportation, and Amtrak including the development of the Braille specification for the DoT. INPS also engineers, manufactures and supplies National Steel Car, Bombardier Transportation, ALSTOM, New Flyer, NovaBus, Orion Bus, Thomas Built Bus and other companies. Advanced Thermo Dynamics Ltd is affiliated to IRR & INPS through joint ownership, and is involved in both transit, transportation and military projects and products that involve heating and cooling (HVAC) and generator set manufacture and design.

*VERIFIED*

## Irausa Loire

Irausa Loire SA
boulevard Blaise-Pascal, F-42230 Roche-la-Molière, France
Tel: (+33 4) 77 50 53 00   Fax: (+33 4) 77 50 53 01

**Parent company**
Group Antolin IRAUSA (Spain)

**Key personnel**
Managing Director: René Picout
Sales Director: André Bocchi

**Products**
Passenger and driver seats for railway equipment and other public transportation. The latest railway seat to be introduced is the Linea, which is designed to allow travel in the conventional sitting position (with a 17° reclined backrest) or in a semi-horizontal position (with a reclining backrest from 17 to 25°). The seat consists of an integrated head restraint, central/left and right armrests and a reversible and adjustable foot made of cast aluminium.

## Jarmuszerelvenyt Guarto RT

XV kerulet, Bacska utca 14, H-1153 Budapest, Hungary
Tel: (+36 1) 307 68 77   Fax: (+36 1) 307 04 52

**Background**
The company has manufactured passenger railway carriage and bus mountings for over 40 years and has experience in producing aluminium structures by using raw materials, mechanical cutting, cold deformation (bending, cutting, deep-drawing), welding (fusion welding and shield arc welding) grinding, oxide coating and mounting.

**Products**
Windows, luggage racks for Deutsche Bahn AG, entrance and bypass doors, cabin doors and other items for Hungarian Railways and Deutsche Bahn.

## Joyce-Loebl Ltd

390 Princesway, Team Valley Trading Estate, Gateshead NE11 0TU, UK
Tel: (+44 191) 420 30 00   Fax: (+44 191) 420 30 30
e-mail: mike@mwjl.freeserve.co.uk

**Products**
Integrated electronic onboard passenger information systems including: seat reservation displays; front of train displays; audio systems; video seat-back entertainment systems; side of train displays; and digital CCTV security systems.

## Jupiter Plast

Bakkedraget 1 DK-4793 Bogø, Denmark
Tel: (+45) 55 89 33 33   Fax: (+45) 55 89 33 66

**Products**
Passenger vehicle components in composite materials including toilet modules, door leaves and seat frames.

## Kaba Gilgen AG

Freiburgstrasse 34, CH-3150 Schwarzenburg, Switzerland
Tel: (+41 31) 734 41 11   Fax: (+41 31) 734 44 75

**Key personnel**
Sales Director: Konrad Zweifel
Project Director, Platform Screen Doors: Hans Kráhenbühl

**Products**
Automatic train door systems synchronised with platform screen doors.

## Kidde

Kidde Fire Protection Ltd
Bellvue Road, Northolt UB5 5QW, UK
Tel: (+44 20) 88 39 07 00   Fax: (+44 20) 88 45 43 04
e-mail: marketing@kfp.co.uk
Web: http://www.kfp.co.uk

**Key personnel**
Sales and Marketing Director: Philip Robertson
Marketing Co-ordinator: Brian Keeble
Sales Manager, Rail Systems: Ronnie Drugan
Project Manager: Richard Starczewski

**Products**
Fire protection systems for locomotives, dmus and rolling stock, including halon replacement gaseous fire suppression systems using FM-200, FE-13 & $CO_2$; AFFF (Aqueous Film-Forming Foam), Powder and Water.
Systems have been supplied for Class 169, 170, 175/1, 180 and 200 dmus, high-speed locomotives (Eurostar, Amtrak Flyer and ETR500); freight locomotives (Class 66 and 92); new product developments include passenger coach fire detection and control systems, along with Halon replacement with Argonite for Class 91s.
New systems developed for passenger vehicles also include emergency braking control and discharging, utilising the latest sanding technology.

*UPDATED*

## Franz Kiel GmbH & Co KG

Nürnberger Strasse 62, D-86720 Nördlingen, Germany
Tel: (+49 9081) 210 30   Fax: (+49 9081) 210 31 51
e-mail: info@kiel-sitz.de
Web: http://www.kiel-sitz.de

Passenger coach equipment/**MANUFACTURERS** 575

*Kiel Trend 2 range of seating* 0023850

*Kiel mother-child-seat* 0023849

**Products**
Seating for buses, coaches, main line and light rail vehicles, including mother-and-child seat.

*UPDATED*

### Kleeneze Sealtech Ltd

Ansteys Road, Hanham, Bristol BS15 3SS, UK
Tel: (+44 117) 947 51 49   Fax: (+44 117) 960 01 41
e-mail: enq@ksl.uk.com
Web: http://www.ksltd.com

**Key personnel**
Commercial Director: David Love
Export Manager: David Eggleden
Marketing Manager: Mrs Fitton

**Subsidiaries**
Record Industrial Brushes (sister company)
Kullen GmbH (parent company)

**Products**
Carriage door seals, industrial wire wheels for any rust, paint, corrosion removal and surface finishing, rodent brush, internal panel seals, pillar seals, cab door seals.

*VERIFIED*

### Klein Transport

221 avenue du Président Wilson, F-93218 La Plaine, Saint Denis Cedex, France
Tel: (+33 1) 49 17 87 41   Fax: (+33 1) 42 43 99 93
e-mail: g.klein@wanadoo.fr
Web: http://www.g_klein.fr

**Key personnel**
President: Remi Ulmann

Chief Executive Officer: Dominique LeMarchand
Marketing: Gilles Vacher

**Subsidiary companies**
Cantin, St Ouen l'Aumone, France
Sessna Klein Italia, Castronno, Italy
Quingdao Klein Railway Equipment Co Ltd, Quingdao, China
Systems G Klein Inc, Saint Bruno, Quebec, Canada
Klein Korea Co Ltd, Seoul, South Korea

**Products**
Windows for rail vehicles; window blinds and pans; specially made interior doors for rail vehicles; locks for doors; interior panels and bulkheads, and automatic gates for public transport authorities. In collaboration with Sofanor, Klein Transport supplies full interior sub-assemblies for new vehicles and refurbishment projects.

Recent contracts include: TGV, Korea 1999; Metro Cairo 1999; Juniper programme 1998-1999; Citadis programme 1999-2000; Metropolis Warsaw 2000; R142 Metro, New York 1997; ICT 1999 and Duplex/TGV 2000.

### KV Ltd

Presley Way, Crownhill, Milton Keynes MK8 0HB, UK
Tel: (+44 1908) 56 15 15   Fax: (+44 1908) 56 12 27
e-mail: sales@kvautomation.co.uk
Web: http://www.devicelink.com

**Key personnel**
Managing Director: A R Cersell
Export Sales Director: A C Hough
European Sales Director: I R Davies
Technical Director: H M Stoneman
Financial Director: B Kentish

**Subsidiary**
Instruments and Movements Ltd

**Products**
Pneumatic control components and modular systems for control of passenger, driver cab and internal coach doors, pneumatic components and systems for use on rail vehicles.

*UPDATED*

### Lakeuden Kylmäkeskus Oy (Lumikko)

PO Box 304, FIN-60101 Seinäjoki, Finland
Tel: (+358 6) 420 40 00   Fax: (+358 6) 414 19 21
e-mail: lumikko@lumikko.com
Web: http://www.lumikko.com

**Key personnel**
Production Manager: Kari Saikkonen

**Products**
Lumikko HVAC devices for locomotives, passenger coaches and other rail vehicles; systems are capable of operation in temperatures ranging from –40 to +40°C.

**Contracts**
Contracts include: the supply of over 500 cab air conditioning units for locomotives, dmus and emus operated by Finnish Railways (VR-Group Ltd); air conditioners for 12 VR-Group restaurant cars; refrigeration and freezing equipment for restaurant cars manufactured by Talgo Oy.

*NEW ENTRY*

### Lazzerini

Lazzerini & Co Srl
Via Toscana 1, I-60030 Monsano (AN), Italy
Tel: (+39 0731) 602 61   Fax: (+39 0731) 604 49
e-mail: cml.lazzerini

**Background**
Lazzerini is a subsidiary of Grammer AG (qv).

**Products**
Seating for passenger vehicles.

### Lenord, Bauer & Co GmbH

Dohlenstrasse 32, D-46145 Oberhausen, Germany
Tel: (+49 208) 996 30   Fax: (+49 208) 67 62 92
e-mail: info@lenord.de
Web: http://www.lenord.de

**Agents in UK**
Motor Technology Ltd
Motec House, Chadkirk Industrial Estate, Romiley, Stockport, Cheshire SK6 3LE, UK
Tel: (+44 161) 427 36 41   Fax: (+44 161) 427 13 06
e-mail: andrew@motec.co.uk

**Products**
Speed sensors and encoders for rail vehicles, applicable to motor speed monitoring systems; wheel slip protection systems; traction control systems; and door movement control systems.

*UPDATED*

*GEL 247 MiniCoder in a typical application scanning a toothed wheel to detect traction motor speed*
2002/0126826

### Liebherr-Verkehrstechnik Frankfurt

Liebherr-Verkehrstechnik Frankfurt GmbH
Hanauer Landstrasse 200, PO Box 101437,
D-60314 Frankfurt, Germany
Tel: (+49 69) 40 35 12 00   Fax: (+49 69) 40 35 13 85

**Key personnel**
Managing Director: Erich Seyer
Technical Manager: Gerd Höschler
Sales Manager: Wilfried Sonnenfeld

**Products**
Air conditioning, heating and ventilating equipment for locomotives and passenger, multiple-unit and rapid transit stock; split systems; unitary equipment; underfloor-mounted, ceiling integrated or rooftop installation. Microprocessor-based electronic controls for HVAC equipment with integrated diagnostic and control features for all pneumatic and electrical components of a coach. Storage and data transmission systems using PC104 system hardware.

The company Luwa pioneered the induction system in air conditioned passenger cars and invented the single-duct reheat principle.

The company has developed an air conditioning system for the ICE, German Railways' (DB AG) high-speed trainset, including special air valves and pressure protection systems to protect passengers and crew from any hazardous air pressure variation.

Contracts include development of an air conditioning system for ICE3 (DB AG); construction and starting-up of air handling equipment and regulation/controlling for the Transrapid maglev train (Adtranz, Germany); data transmission system for DB AG; air cycle air conditioning system for HST Mark III refurbishment (Angel Train Contracts, UK).

### LM Glasfiber

Industrial Division, Ole Rømersvej 25, Taulov DK-7000 Fredericia, Denmark
Tel: (+45) 75 51 44 08   Fax: (+45) 75 51 40 70

e-mail: info@lm.dk
Web: http://www.lm.dk

**Key personnel**
Divisional Manager: Michael Stahl

**Products**
Lightweight composite materials for rolling stock, for interior and exterior applications, supplied to the European rail industry.
Interior applications include wall covering, interior linings cupboards, control panels, luggage racks and partition walls.
Exterior applications include fronts, roofs, skirts and bodywork for rolling stock.
Also lightweight sandwich floor systems.

*UPDATED*

## Mafelec

F-38480 Chimilin, France
Tel: (+33 4) 76 32 07 33   Fax: (+33 4) 76 32 54 11
Web: http://www.mafelec.fr

**Products**
Automatic railway control components including man-machine interface, visualisation and display, connection, safety, engineering and electronics.

*UPDATED*

## Mechan Ltd

Thorncliffe Park, Chapeltown, Sheffield S35 2PH, UK
Tel: (+44 114) 257 05 63   Fax: (+44 114) 245 11 24
e-mail: admin@mechan.co.uk
Web: http://www.mechan.co.uk

**Key personnel**
Managing Director: A G Hague
Engineering Director: G L Cofield

**Subsidiary**
Mechan Technology: design and manufacture of advanced control systems.

**Products**
Battery boxes, obstacle deflectors, undercar boxes, undercar tanks.

*VERIFIED*

## Merak

Merak Sistemas Integrados de Climatización
A member of the Albatros group
Ruiz de Alarcón no. 13-3° E-28014 Madrid, Spain
Tel: (+34 91) 532 41 81   Fax: (+34 91) 522 76 97
e-mail: albatros@albatros-es.es

**Key personnel**
President: Nicolás Fúster
Managing Director: Julio Rey
Commercial Director: Carlos Rico

**Works**
C/Gavilanes 16, Polígono Industrial La Estación, E-28320 Pinto, Madrid
Tel: (+34 91) 495 90 00   Fax: (+34 91) 691 09 97
e-mail: merak@merak-sa.com

**Corporate development**
Merak (qv) formerly traded as Stone Ibérica SA and is a member of the Albatros Group (qv).

**Products**
Design, manufacture and maintenance of air conditioning equipment, heating and ventilation equipment, electronic and microprocessor controls, inverter ballasts for fluorescent tubes, and static speed regulator for asynchronous motors.

**Contracts**
Recent contracts include supply of air conditioning equipment for Vancouver Train (1999) Canada, Talgo Trains S-7 (1999) Spain, JFK Train (1999) USA, Flumitrens (1999) Brazil, DMU Belgica (1999), Northern Spirit (1999), USA, Oporto Metro (2000), Shanghai Metro (2000), Oporto Suburban Train, M-7 Train, USA.

*UPDATED*

## Microelettrica Scientifica SpA

Via Alberelle 56/58, I-20089 Rozzano (MI), Italy
Tel: (+39 02) 57 57 31   Fax: (+39 02) 57 51 09 40
e-mail: sales.contactors@microelettrica.com
sales.relays@microelettrica.com
sales.resistors@microelettrica.com
Web: http://www.microelettrica.com

**Key personnel**
Chief Executive: Dr Marco Boldrini

**Products**
Standard and custom-designed contactors for rail vehicles; analogue and digital electronic protection relays; power resistors for braking and other rail applications.

*VERIFIED*

## Microphor

452 East Hill Road, Willits, California 95490, USA
Tel: (+1 707) 459 55 63   Fax: (+1 707) 459 66 17
e-mail: info@microphor.com
Web: http://www.microphor.com

**Key personnel**
Vice-President, Operations: Ted Mayfield
Customer Service: Brian Banzhaf
Marketing and Sales Manager: Walter Hess

**Products**
Macerator and air-assisted flush toilets/waste retention and treatment systems (one quart and two quart per flush) for passenger vehicles and locomotives; vacuum toilets; thermoelectric refrigerators, low-temperature protection systems, rotary screw air compressors, ditch lights and accessories for locomotives; custom-manufactured components in plastic and sheet metal for locomotives, passenger vehicles and freight wagons.

**Contracts**
Contracts include the supply of toilets and waste retention/treatment systems to Metro-North, Amtrak, MARC, New Jersey Transit, Amerail, GE Transportation Systems and Electro-Motive Division, General Motors Corporation.
Products are supplied to customers in Australia, Canada, China, Mexico, South Africa, Vietnam and UK.

*UPDATED*

## Mobile Climate Control Corporation

80 Kincort Street, Toronto, Ontario M6M 5G1, Canada
Tel: (+1 416) 242 64 06   Fax: (+1 416) 242 64 06
Web: http://www.MCCII.com

**Subsidiaries**
Industrial Division
2050 Drew Road, Mississauga, Ontario L5S 1N3, Canada
Tel: (+1 905) 405 00 04   Fax: (+1 905) 405 99 94

USA East
2200 Dywer Avenue, Utica, New York 13501, USA
Tel: (+1 315) 738 15 00   Fax: (+1 315) 738 19 19

USA West
426 Winnebago Avenue, Fairmont, Minnesota 56031, USA
Tel: (+ 1 507) 238 27 83   Fax: (+1 507) 238 41 51

MCC Europe
AB Baldersgatan 24, Box 96, S-761 21 Norrtälje, Sweden
Tel: (+46 176) 20 78 00   Fax: (+46 176) 20 78 10

Soprano
Parc Technologique de l'Isle d'Abeau, 40 rue Condorcet, Vaulx Milieu F-38090, France

**Products**
Air conditioning in passenger coaches. The company has research and development facilities and laboratories in Ontario, Canada.

*UPDATED*

## Monogram Systems

A Zodiac company
800 West Artesia Boulevard, Compton, California 90224-9057, USA
Tel: (+1 310) 638 84 45   Fax: (+1 310) 638 84 58
e-mail: BMercer@monsan.com

**Key personnel**
President: Mike Rozenblatt
Vice-President, Sales and Marketing: James R Durso
Sales Manager: W I Mercer

**Products**
Waste collection systems for passenger vehicles. Water flush, vacuum waste collection systems capable of 72-hour full retention. Self-contained, single-position modular vacuum toilets. Waste compactors for café cars and buffet cars.

**Contracts**
Contracts include vacuum waste collection systems for 280 vehicles of Amtrak's Superliner I fleet, and the supply of vacuum waste collection systems to Bombardier of Canada for 38 Amtrak Superliner II coach cars. Other orders include 80 sets of full-retention vacuum waste systems for Amtrak's Horizon coach fleet and 300 sets of toilets for its Amfleet I refurbishment programme. Monogram is supplying systems for 35 RTLIII Turboliners for Super Steel, New York.

*UPDATED*

## Morio Denki

Morio Denki Co Ltd
34-1 Tateishi 4-chome, Katsushika-ku, Tokyo 124-0012, Japan
Tel: (+81 3) 36 91 31 81   Fax: (+81 3) 36 92 13 33
Web: http://www.morio.co.jp

**Key personnel**
See entry in *Electric traction equipment* section.

**Products**
Fluorescent ceiling lights, headlights and tail-lights, destination display systems, heating systems, door-operating switches.

*UPDATED*

## MTB Equipment Ltd

7-9 Barton Road, Water Eaton, Bletchley MK2 3HX, UK
Tel: (+44 1908) 37 95 21   Fax: (+44 1908) 27 06 04
e-mail: info@mtb-equipment.com
Web: http://www.mtb-equipment.com

**Key personnel**
Managing Director: J W Mainwaring
Sales Director: A D Berrington

**Products**
Seating, roller blinds, vehicle interior equipment.

*NEW ENTRY*

## NABCO LTD

Railroad Products Division, 9-18 Kaigan 1-chome, Minato-ku, Tokyo 105-0022, Japan
Tel: (+81 3) 54 70 24 01   Fax: (+81 3) 54 70 24 24
e-mail: takashi_koyama@nabco.co.jp

**Key personnel**
See entry in *Brakes and drawgear* section.

**Products**
Plug and sliding door systems; platform doors (manufactured and supplied by NABCO Building Products division); pressure-sealing systems for passenger coaches; windscreen wiper motors.

**Contracts**
Recent contracts include the supply of automatic sliding door systems to JR East for E231 commuter trainsets, to Ireland (Iarnród Éireann) for emu/dmu cars. NABCO supplied over 24,500 sets of automatic electric sliding door systems (licensed by Faiveley) for various Japanese operators including JR East commuter trainsets.

*UPDATED*

## Narita

Narita Manufacturing Ltd
20-12 Hanaomote-cho, Atsuta-ku, Nagoya 456, Japan
Tel: (+81 52) 881 61 91   Fax: (+81 52) 881 67 48
e-mail: sinarita@narita.co.jp
Web: http://www.narita.co.jp

**Key personnel**
President: Masatoshi Narita
Executive Director: Terutoshi Narita
Executive Director, General Affairs and Quality Assurance: Haruo Narita
Director (Sales and Purchasing): Yasushi Fujii
Director (Export Sales and Marketing): Shuichi Narita

**Products**
Gangway systems (including automatic type); vestibule diaphragms; rubber bellows; inter-car barriers; door leaves; interior panels of carbody; car body ducts for air conditioning systems; driving consoles; fuel and water tanks; parts and accessories.

**Contracts**
Recent contracts include: gangways for Singapore LTA C751 and C751B emu, August 1999; balancers of cab door window for NYCTA, New York, USA R142A emu, January 2000; automatic gangways, series 1600 emu for Nagoya Railroad, May 1999; series 783 emu for JR-Kyushu, March 2000 and series 261 dmu for JR-Hokkido, September 1999; emu for Melbourne Bay, February 2001; two cars for Guangzhou Metro Line, November 2001; Series 700 emu for JR Shinkansen, September 2001; Series 817 suburban emu (including semi-automatic gangways) for JR Kyushu, February 2001; Series 3000 commuter emu for Odakyu Electric Railway, February 2001; sliding side doors for Nagoya Railroad Series 300 commuter emu, August 2001; Series 700 emu for JR-Central Shinkansen, June 2001; Series 300 commuter emu for Nagoya Railroad, August 2001; inside panels for passenger interiors for JR Shinkansen Series 700 emu, September 2001.

*UPDATED*

*Narita lifting side door (sky door) for JR Maglev MLX01 car*  0063687

## The Network Connection

The Mill, Lodge Lane, Derby DE1 3HB, UK
Tel: (+44 1332) 20 21 72
e-mail: uk@tncx.com
Web: http://www.projectrainbow.com

**Key personnel**
Managing Director: Stephen J Ollier
Commercial Director: Philip Campbell
Sales and Marketing Director: Julian Burrell
Engineering Director: Dominic Newton

**Parent company**
Global Technologies Ltd
1911 Chestnut Street, Suite 120 Philadelphia, Pennsylvania 19103, USA
Tel: (+1 215) 972 81 91   Fax: (+1 215) 972 81 83

**Products**
Services include hardware provision and integration into the rail vehicle, service support for the agreed life of product, automated content loading via integrated telecommunications systems, content provision, revenue generation management.

## Neu Systems Ferroviaires

PO Box 2026, 70 rue du Collège, F-59700 Marcq en Baroeul, France
Tel: (+33 3) 20 45 65 46   Fax: (+33 3) 20 45 64 98
e-mail: mail@neu-nsf.com
Web: http://www.neu-nsf.com

**Key personnel**
Chief Executive Officer: Guy Leblon
Commercial Manager: Franck Vinchon
Export Assistant: Caroline Dufour

**Subsidiaries**
Atelier Neu Systems Ferroviaires
ZI Neuville en Ferrain, Voie Nouvelle, rue de Reckem, F-599960 Neuville en Ferrain

Conestra
Trupbacher Strasse 26a, D-57072 Siegen, Germany
Tel: (+49 271) 372 05 03; 372 05 05

Contact: Karl Heinz Brull

Neu SF Polska
ul Krucza 28, PL-00522 Warsaw, Poland
Tel: (+48 22) 622 84 71; 622 84 72

**Products**
Air conditioning, heating and ventilation equipment, control systems for HVAC, exhaust fans, cooling fans, high-pressure fans for adjustment of pressure inside coach.

Contracts include heating and ventilation equipment for Rotterdam metro (168 units), Z2N driving cabs for SNCF (800 units), NINA cars for BLS Switzerland (Bombardier Transportation Vevey, 24 units).

Recent contracts: Rotterdam metro for Bombardier; Z2N driving cabs for SNCF; NINA/BLS; Metro VAL 208, Lille for MATRA; TVR Nancy for Alstom de Dietrich; Warsaw metro for Alstom Konstal; metro VAL 208 Rennes for Siemens and Citadis for Alstom.

## Nieaf-Smitt BV

PO Box 7023, NL-3502 KA, Utrecht, Netherlands
Tel: (+31 30) 288 13 11   Fax: (+31 30) 289 88 16
e-mail: sales@nieaf-smitt.nl
Web: http://www.nieaf-smitt.nl

**Key personnel**
Managing Director: A J Wijnmaalen
Sales Manager: A B Mann
International Sales Manager: C S Hu

**Products**
Plug-in instantaneous relays; plug-in measuring, timing and monitoring relays; signal treatment systems; system solutions (complete panels) for refurbished and new projects and panel indicators (speedometers); differential high voltage/current relays.

*UPDATED*

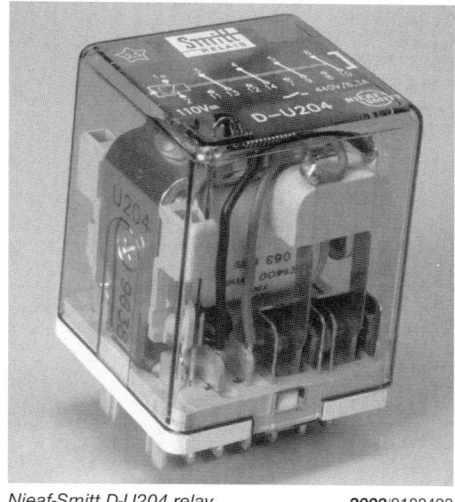

*Nieaf-Smitt D-U204 relay*  2002/0122493

## Northern Rubber Co Ltd

Northern Rubber Co Ltd
Retford DN22 6HH, UK
Tel: (+44 1777) 70 67 31   Fax: (+44 1777) 70 97 39
e-mail: nroboffice@aol.com

**Key personnel**
Managing Director: M Thompson
Sales and Marketing Director: A Gibson
Sales Manager, Export: D Simpson

**Products**
Gangway diaphragms, inter-car gap protection systems and other fabric-reinforced rubber products. Fire-resistant kick straps on ticket gates, inter-car protection mouldings.

Contracts include inter-car gap protection mouldings for ALSTOM rolling stock for London Underground Northern and Jubilee Lines; fire-resistant kick strips on WCL ticket gates for London Underground.

*Northern Rubber inter-car protection mouldings for London Underground rolling stock*  0002379

## Nortrade

Nortrade srl, Railway Division
Cacciagrande, I-58040 Tirli (GR), Italy
Tel: (+39 0564) 94 42 03   Fax: (+39 0564) 94 41 13

## MANUFACTURERS/Passenger coach equipment

e-mail: railway@nortrade.it
Web: http://www.nortrade.it

**Key personnel**
Commercial Director: Marco Galleri

**Products**
Heating, ventilation and air conditioning systems and equipment for drivers' cabs and passenger vehicle interiors.

---

## Orvec International

Orvec International Ltd
Malmo Road, Hull HU7 0YF, UK
Tel: (+44 1482) 87 91 46   Fax: (+44 1482) 62 53 25
e-mail: info@orvec.co.uk

**Key personnel**
Managing Director: Graham Stonehouse
Financial Director: Gary Layus
Sales Manager: Philip Underwood

**Products**
Bespoke and customised antimacassars, headrest covers, disposable headrest covers, tray mats (including non-slip), blankets, amenity packs, pillows and pillow covers.

*UPDATED*

---

## Parker Pneumatic

Parker Hannifin plc
Pneumatic Division, Walkmill Lane, Bridgtown, Cannock, Staffordshire WS11 3LR, UK
Tel: (+44 1543) 45 60 00   Fax: (+44 1543) 45 60 01

**Key personnel**
Application Manager: Brian Umney

**Products**
Parker manufactures pneumatic systems with a range of applications in rolling stock, including seat adjustment cylinders (Italian ETR 500 high-speed train), pneumatic circuit blocks for onboard toilet flush (French TGV), door opening control panel (ETR 500), valves and cylinders for heating and ventilating.

---

## Pascal International AB

Box 33, SE-280 10 Sösdala, Sweden
Tel: (+46 451) 660 80   Fax: (+46 451) 603 70
e-mail: contact@pascal-system.com
Web: http://www.pascal-system.se

**Products**
DUX spring technology for passenger rail vehicle seating. The system comprises a self-contained spring unit consisting of multiple rows of springs mounted into channels of non-woven fabric.

---

## People Seating

People Seating Ltd
Unit 9, Washington Street Industrial Estate, Netherton, Dudley DY2 9RE, UK
Tel: (+44 1384) 25 71 24   Fax: (+44 1384) 24 21 06

**Key personnel**
Managing Director: David J Poston

**Products**
Passenger and driver seating, interior trim components.

*VERIFIED*

---

## Percy Lane Products

Lichfield Road, Tamworth B79 7TL, UK
Tel: (+44 1827) 638 21   Fax: (+44 1827) 31 01 59
e-mail: main@percy-lane.co.uk
Web: http://www.percy-lane.co.uk

**Key personnel**
Executive Chairman: G H Fowler
Managing Director: P S Wright
Sales Director: J W Whetton
Business Development Director: N Greenhalgh
Purchasing Manager: L Clarkson

**Sales offices**
*Denmark*
Gertsen & Olufsen AF 1993 AS
Savsvinget 4, DK-2970 Horsholm

*France*
CCD
31 sentier des Fours à Chaux, F-77700 Coupvray

*Spain*
World Class
Heros, 15 Bajo Centro, E-48009 Bilbao

**Products**
Windows, sashes, impact-resistant windscreens, luggage racks, detrainment devices, Beclawat range of products; aluminium fabrications, including gangway frames, doors.

Contracts include bodyside glazing for MP89 stock for Paris metro (for ALSTOM); detrainment device for London Underground Northern line (for ALSTOM); bodyside glazing for Connex vehicles (for Adtranz); emergency exit doors and detrainment ramp for Singapore SMRT (for ALSTOM); bodyside windows for Virgin CrossCountry (for Bombardier) and for Docklands Light Railway vehicles.

*UPDATED*

---

## Permali Gloucester Limited

Bristol Road, Gloucester GL1 5TT, UK
Tel: (+44 1452) 52 82 82   Fax: (+44 1452) 50 74 09
e-mail: sales@permali-gloucester.co.uk
Web: http://www.permali.co.uk

**Key personnel**
See entry in *Permanent way components, equipment and services* section.

**Products**
Decorative laminate, Permaglass MFM, used in rail vehicles for interior lining where a high degree of scratch and graffiti resistance is required, a halogen-free, fire retardant electrical insulation. Sandwich panels for flooring and thermal barriers.

*UPDATED*

---

## Phoenix

Phoenix AG
PO Box 900854, D-21048 Hamburg, Germany
Tel: (+49 40) 76 67 20 01   Fax: (+49 40) 76 67 24 10
Web: http://www.phoenix-ag.com

**Key personnel**
See entry in *Bogies and suspension, wheels and axles, bearings* section.

**Products**
Doorseals and windowseals.

---

## Pickersgill-Kaye Ltd

Pepper Road, Hunslet, Leeds LS10 2PP, UK
Tel: (+44 113) 277 55 31   Fax: (+44 113) 276 02 21
e-mail: sales@pkaye.co.uk
Web: http://www.pkaye.co.uk

**Key personnel**
Managing Director: Peter Murphy
Sales Manager: Harry Griffiths

**Products**
Lock assemblies for internal and external applications; passenger emergency alarm handles and emergency talkback units; K-Tex emergency window breaker device; LED indicators for door status, driver's desk.

*UPDATED*

---

## Pilkington Aerospace Ltd

Eckersall Road, Kings Norton, Birmingham B38 8SR, UK
Tel: (+44 121) 606 41 00   Fax: (+44 121) 606 41 91
e-mail: pilkaero@aol.com

**Key personnel**
General Manager: R A Harper

**Products**
Design and manufacture of heated/unheated, curved/flat, framed/unframed impact-resistant transparencies for railway and transit industries.

*UPDATED*

---

## Pintsch Bamag Antriebs-und Verkehrstechnik GmbH

PO Box 10 04 20, D-46524 Dinslaken, Germany
Tel: (+49 2064) 60 20   Fax: (+49 2064) 60 22 66
e-mail: info@pintschbamag.de
Web: http://www.pintschbamag.de

**Key personnel**
See entry in *Signalling and communications* section.

**Corporate background**
Pintsch Bamag is a member of the Schaltbau Group (qv).

**Products**
Power supply equipment, inverters for train lighting, electronic door controls and air conditioning equipment, tail lights. System for the control and supervision of folding, hinged and sliding coach doors which features fault diagnosis.

*UPDATED*

---

## Pixy AG

Bruggerstrasse 37, CH-4500 Baden, Switzerland
Tel: (41 56) 221 71 10   Fax: (+41 56) 21 72 59
e-mail: sales@pixy.ch
Web: http://www.pixy.ch

**Corporate background**
Pixy AG is a member of the Sécheron Group.

**Products**
Rail vehicle and locomotive diagnostic supervision and control systems and in-cab displays.

*NEW ENTRY*

---

## Polarteknik PMC Oy AB

Klaavolantie 1, FIN-3270 Huittinen, Finland
Tel: (+358 2) 560 15 00   Fax: (+358 2) 56 85 01
e-mail: jouni.saarnia.polarteknik.com
Web: http://www.polarteknik.com

**Key personnel**
Project Manager, Door Systems: Jouni Saarnia

**Background**
Previously Berendsen PMC Oy Ab, Pimatic. The company is a member of the Hexagon Group.

### Products
Pimatic automatic interior door systems; pressure-sealed gangway doors; interior doors; fire barrier doors; electro-pneumatic and electric-powered door gear for rail vehicles; pneumatic bus actuators.

### Contracts
Contracts include the supply of interior door systems for Bombardier Transportation projects, including Electrostar emus for the UK, and for double-deck intercity coaches supply to VR, Finland, by Talgo.

*UPDATED*

## Portaramp

Roman House, Roman Way, Fison Way Industrial Estate, Thetford IP24 1QT, UK
Tel: (+44 1842) 75 01 86   Fax: (+44 1842) 75 02 29

### Key personnel
General Manager: Keith Jones

### Products
Portable wheelchair ramp, to provide access to rail vehicles for wheelchair users. Available in four standard lengths and fully DIPTAC (Disabled Persons Transport Advisory Committee) compliant; manufactured from lightweight strong aluminium alloy; folds in half for compact easy storage.

## Powernetics Ltd

Jason Works, Clarence Street, Loughborough LE11 1DX, UK
Tel: (+44 1509) 21 41 53   Fax: (+44 1509) 26 24 60
e-mail: sales@powernetics.co.uk
Web: http://www.powernetics.co.uk

### Key personnel
See entry in *Electrification contractors and equipment suppliers* section.

### Products
Static inverters/converters; static frequency changers; switch mode power supplies; DC-DC converters.

### Contracts
Contracts include DC-DC converters for the Stoneblower project for Railtrack, UK; static converters for Bombardier (for London Underground); static inverters for lighting, air conditioning and fans for Hong Kong Tramways.

*UPDATED*

## Power-One AG

Ackerstrasse 56, CH-8610 Uster, Switzerland
Tel: (+41 1) 944 82 16
e-mail: info@power-one.com
Web: http://www.power-one.com

### Key personnel
President: Hans Grüter
Product Manager: Claude Abächerli

### Background
Power-One products were formerly marketed under the Melcher name.

### Products
DC-DC converters, inverters, battery chargers – 80 product families with output power in a range of 1 to 1,000 W. All Power-One power products are ISO 9001 certified. Miniature-size switching regulator.

*NEW ENTRY*

## Powertron Ltd

Glebe Farm Technical Campus, Knapwell, Cambridge CB3 8GG, UK
Tel: (+44 1223) 72 20 00   Fax: (+44 1223) 72 20 50
e-mail: sales@powertron.co.uk

### Key personnel
Managing Director: Miles Rackowe
Technical Director: Andy Dickeson
Director of Sales: Mike Carter

### Products
High-reliability switch mode power supplies and DC-DC converters in the power range 10 W to 2 kW. A principal area of activity is DC-DC converters for use on railway rolling stock. Applications include lighting, communications, brake monitoring equipment, fire protection equipment and train management systems.

*UPDATED*

## Protec

Partner für Umweittechnick GmbH
A member of the Schaltbau Group
Parksteiner Strasse 51, D-92637 Weiden, Germany
Tel: (+49 961) 67 00 60   Fax: (+49 961) 670 06 20

### Products
Bio toilet system.

## RailTronic AG

Postfach, Fabrikstrasse 10, CH-8370 Sirnach, Switzerland
Tel: (+41 71) 969 37 73   Fax: (+41 71) 969 37 74
e-mail: info@railtronic.com
Web: http://www.railtronic.com

### Products
Electronic ballasts, timetable illuminators, high-voltage charging and power supply systems and complete interior systems for urban and main line rail vehicles.

*NEW ENTRY*

## Reidler Decal

The Reidler Decal Corporation
1 Reidler Road, Industrial Park, St Clair, Pennsylvania 17970, USA
Tel: (+1 717) 429 18 12   Fax: (+1 717) 429 15 28

### Key personnel
President: Richard Reidler
Vice-President, Operations: Barry Frey

### Products
Rail-Cal™ decals for rail vehicles, featuring heavy adhesive for pitted surfaces and a double-baking process for chemical and solvent protection; prismatic delineators to make rail vehicles more visible in poor light conditions and full graphics wrap programs.

*UPDATED*

## Rex

Rex Articoli Tecnici SA
Via Catenazzi 1, CH-6850 Mendrisio, Switzerland
Tel: (+41 91) 640 50 50   Fax: (+41 91) 640 50 55
e-mail: rex.sa@tinet.ch
Web: http://www.rex.ch

### Key personnel
General Manager: M Favini

### Products
Design and manufacture of rubber and elastic thermoplastic products for the rail industry.

## RICA

Via Podgora 26, I-31029 Vittorio Veneto (TV), Italy
Tel: (+39 0438) 91 01
Fax: (+39 0438) 91 22 36; 91 22 72; 91 03 26
e-mail: rica@zoppas-industries.it
Web: http://www.rica.zoppas-industries.it

### Corporate development
RICA is a member of the Zoppas Industries group.

### Products
Heating systems for rail vehicles, including: finned element duct heaters; air conditioning duct heaters; insulator mounted heaters; horizontal upflow heater units; wall and floor heating elements; cab heater units; vertical convection heaters; toilet heater units and boilers; waste tank heaters; windscreen defrosting systems; flexible heater systems; coach entrance floor heating systems; locomotive anti-slip system heating systems; and pipe and exhaust tank heating systems.

## Safenet

Safenet AB
Beragarden, SE-24010 Dalby, Sweden
Tel: (+46 46) 20 33 43   Fax: (+46 46) 20 33 47
e-mail: lars.linden@safenet.se
Web: http://www.safenet.se

### Products
Manufacture of pneumatic and electric door opening systems for trains, buses, ships and buildings.

## SAFT

156 avenue de Metz, F-93230 Romainville, France
Tel: (+33 1) 49 15 36 00   Fax: (+33 1) 49 15 34 00
Web: http://www.saftbatteries.com

### Key personnel
See *Electric traction equipment* section.

### Products
Saft Nife Ni/Cd batteries, pocket plates or sintered/plastic bonded electrode types are for emergency supply and security purposes. All items are lightweight and compact and are available in containers made of stainless steel, flame retardant or standard plastic containers.

The company has supplied railway companies in 56 countries and recent contracts include supply to the pendolino tilting trainsets, passenger coaches for SNCB, RENFE, Taipei and Pakistan.

## Saint-Gobain Sully

16 route d'Isdes, F-45600 Sully-sur-Loire, France
Tel: (+33 2) 38 37 30 00   Fax: (+33 2) 38 37 30 40

### Key personnel
Marketing Manager: Guy Pajot

### Products
Locomotive windscreens. Traction fitted with Sully windscreens includes the Thalys TGV, the ETR 500 high-speed train, Series 700 Shinkansen (Japan) and Acela trainsets for Amtrack (USA).

*UPDATED*

## Saint-Gobain Sully NA, Inc

2175 Kumry Road, PO Box 70, Trumbauersville, Pennsylvania 18970-0070, USA
Tel: (+1 215) 536 03 33   Fax: (+1 215) 536 68 72
e-mail: douglasjones@msn.com

### Key personnel
General Manager: Scott Switzer
Sales Manager, Railroad: Douglas Jones

### Corporate background
Saint-Gobain Sully NA is part of the Saint-Gobain Corporation.

### Products
Windscreens and other glass for rolling stock including frames and safety glazing with high-impact resistance and

# MANUFACTURERS/Passenger coach equipment

good optical quality, wire grid heating elements for glazing, solar protection.

Contracts include supply of glazing to Bombardier Transportation for Northeast Corridor; for New York CTA R142 and R142A cars; Los Angeles metro; St Louis metro.

*UPDATED*

## SBF

SBF Spezialleuchten Wurzen GmbH
Badergraben 16, D-04808 Wurzen, Germany
Tel: (+49 3425) 92 01 81   Fax: (+49 3425) 92 01 78

**Key personnel**
Managing Director: Hans D Sehn
Sales Manager: Fritz Strobelt

**Products**
Light fittings for passenger car interiors and exteriors.
Recent contracts include the supply of light fittings to DB AG, Bombardier Transportation DWA and Adtranz.

## Schaltbau GmbH

Klausenburger Strasse 6, D-81677 Munich, Germany
Tel: (+49 89) 93 00 50   Fax: (+49 89) 93 00 53 50
e-mail: schaltbau@schaltbau.de

**Key personnel**
Managing Director: Hans-Rainer Quaas
Sales Director: Hans Kudlacek

**Corporate background**
Schaltbau GmbH is a member of the Schaltbau Group (qv).

**Products**
High-voltage equipment for passenger coaches; electrical equipment for diesel-hydraulic railcars; electrical components for locomotives, LRVs and passenger coaches.

*NEW ENTRY*

## Schaltbau Holding AG

PO Box 801540, D-81615 Munich, Germany
Tel: (+49 89) 93 00 50   Fax: (+49 89) 93 00 53 50
e-mail: schaltbau.schaltbau.de
Web: http://www.schaltbau.de

**Key personnel**
Board Members: Dr Jürgen Cammann, Klaus A Feix, Thomas Weber

**Works**
Industrie Strasse 12, D-84149 Velden/Vils, Germany
Dietmar-von-Ayst Strasse 10, D-94501 Aldersbach, Germany

**Corporate background**
Schaltbau Holding AG is a holding company for several companies in the railway equipment market.

**Subsidiary companies**
Schaltbau GmbH (qv)
Gebrüder Bode & Co GmbH (qv)
InfoSystems GmbH (qv)
Kiepe Elektrik GmbH & Co KG (qv)
Pinstch Bamag Antriebs- und Verkehrstechnik GmbH (qv)

Schaltbau Electric America Inc
705 Interchange Boulevard, Newark, Delaware 19711, USA
Tel: (+1 302) 266 05 00 Fax: (+1 302) 266 77 47
e-mail: info@schaltbau.com
Managing Director: Jim Brown

TA Technologies
10 rue Désiré Granet, F-95104 Argenteuil, France
Tel: (+33 1) 39 98 49 49 Fax: (+33 1) 39 81 92 64
e-mail: cna@easynet.fr
Managing Director: Jacques Meunier

Xi'an Schaltbau Electric Corporation Ltd
43 Golden Flower South Road, Xi'an, Shaanxi, People's Republic of China
Managing Director: Siegfried Hohm

*UPDATED*

## Schlegel Swiss Standard AG

CH-9423 Altenrhein, Switzerland
Tel: (+41 71) 858 45 45   Fax: (+41 71) 858 45 90
e-mail: info@schlegel.ch
Web: http://www.schlegel.ch

**Key personnel**
Managing Director: Roland Kressbach
Business Development and Marketing: Pieter de Ruijter

**Corporate development**
Schlegel Swiss Standard took over the passenger coach interiors business of Schindler Technik AG.

**Products**
Seats; interior fittings including luggage racks and wall-mounted tables; interior doors and door systems; self-contained submodules for all kinds of passenger coaches, walls, ceilings and other interior components and complete subsystems.

Schlegel Swiss Standard offers complete interiors.

Recent contracts include the supply of lighweight seats for Swiss Federal Railways (SBB), featuring wooden frames and other biodegradable/recyclable components.

*UPDATED*

*First-class seat by Schlegel Swiss Standard*   0063688

## Schunk Bahntechnik GmbH

Aupoint 23, A-5101 Bergheim bei Salzburg, Austria
Tel: (+66 2) 45 92 00   Fax: (+66 2) 459 20 01
e-mail: office@schunk-group.at
Web: http://www.schunk-group.com

**Subsidiary companies**
Schunk Kohlenstoff technik GmbH
Schunk Metall und Kunststoff GmbH

**Key personnel**
Director: F Rabacher

**Products**
Electric traction equipment, pantographs for locomotives, high-speed trains, LRVs and trams, earthing contacts and ground switches.

*UPDATED*

## Selectron Systems AG

Transport Division
Bernstrasse 70 CH-3250 Lyss, Switzerland
Tel: (+41 32) 387 61 51   Fax: (+41 32) 387 62 84
e-mail: transport@selectron.ch

**Subsidiary company**
Selectron Systems GmbH
Schupfer Strasse 1 (90482), Postfach 310262, D-90202 Nürnberg, Germany
Tel: (+49 911) 95 08 90   Fax: (+49 911) 950 89 30
e-mail: info.nbg@selectron.de

**Corporate background**
Selectron Systems is a member of the Schneider Electric Group.

**Products**
Complete control systems for rail vehicles, including MAS-Traffic open control and communication system, including train bus and vehicle bus. This integrates traction and propulsion monitoring, braking, vehicle speed control, power supply, lighting, heating, ventilation, air conditioning, toilets, doors and other functions.

Selectron Systems also supplies control components and undertakes hardware manufacturing and engineering for vehicle subsystems and for stationary applications.

Selection Systems control technology is in service with operators in Austria, Czech Republic, Germany, Netherlands and Switzerland.

*NEW ENTRY*

## Semco Vacuumteknik

CWO Semco Vacuumteknik A/S
PO Box 157, Svendborgvej 226, DK-5260 Odense S, Denmark
Tel: (+45) 65 68 33 00   Fax: (+45) 65 95 73 74
Web: http://www.semcovakuumteknik.dk

**Key personnel**
Department Manager: Horst Kirchner
Sales Engineer: Sten Frydensbjerg

**Products**
Vacuum toilet systems; complete toilet compartments; toilet system components, effluent tanks, water tanks and sensors.

Contracts include 210 toilet systems for Bombardier Transportation for M6 coaches for SNCB, 239 vacuum toilets for Bombardier Transportation for TER'2N'NG, 294 vacuum toilets for ALSTOM for A-TER and Z-TER, 249 toilet modules for ANSALDOBREDA for IC4, 505 toilet modules for Siemens AG, VT642 – DESIRO and vacuum toilets for Australia, Korea, Russia, USA and many other countries.

*UPDATED*

## SEPSA

Sistemas Electrónicos de Potencia SA
Albatros 7 and 9, (Pol Ind) La Estación, E-28320 Pinto, Madrid, Spain
Tel: (+34 91) 495 70 00   Fax: (+34 91) 495 70 60
Web: http://www.sepsa.es

**Key personnel**
President: Nicolas Fuster
General Manager: Felix Ramos
Commercial Director: Antonio Sosa
Technical Director: Carlos de la Viesca

**Background**
SEPSA is a member of the Albatros Group (qv).

**Products**
Static converters with large power range up to 400 kVA. DC and AC inputs and multivoltage outputs to feed auxiliary rail equipment such as air conditioning, heating,

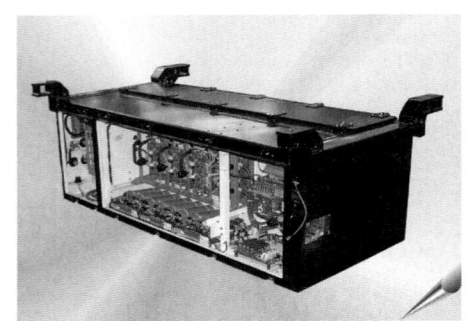

*SEPSA 65.5 kVA static converter for Washington Metro*   2002/0125399

compressors and lighting. Power electronic equipment for railway applications includes converters, inverters, choppers, rectifiers and battery chargers. Microprocessor control, high-switching frequency and IGBT technology.

Passenger information systems, public address, station announcers and displays (IRIS). Monitoring and Controlling System (PLC) to drive both auxiliary equipment and traction. CESIS crash event recording equipment.

### Contracts
Recent contracts include equipment for R-142 in New York, M-7 for LIRR, WMATA 5000 and WMATA 2000/3000 RATP, vehicles for Washington, Paris, London Underground, Madrid Metro S7000/8000 and Talgo Series 7 vehicles.

**UPDATED**

---

## SERINOX
route de Sainte Marguerite, PO Box 70, F-63307 Thiers Cedex, France
Tel: (+33 4) 73 80 22 01   Fax: (+33 4) 73 80 72 85

### Key personnel
General Manager: Philippe Furodet

### Products
Steel components for toilet systems and toilet compartments, including retention tanks, toilet bowls, litter bins, door handles and wash basins.

---

## Siemens Rolling Stock Electronics
Krauss-Maffei-Strasse 2, PO Box 500340, D-80973 Munich, Germany
Tel: (+49 89) 88 99 20 24   Fax: (+49 89) 88 99 28 50
e-mail: internet@ts.siemens.de
Web: http://www.siemens.com

### Key personnel
See entry in *Electric traction equipment* section.

### Background
A majority shareholding of Siemens Rolling Stock Electronics is owned by Siemens AG.

### Products
Modular, rail-proven microprocessor-based locomotive control, command and monitoring systems (KM-DIREKT) with integrated online diagnostics (K-MEMO) suited to safe (SIL 3) radio remote control; integrated and stand-alone wheelslip and skid control and protection systems (K-MICRO and K-MICRO compact) for all kinds of rail vehicle; rugged contact- and wear-less active speed sensors (KMG-2H) and LCD displays (KMONITOR); speed control/regulation and automation systems (KM-PROFA); sanding gear (KM-1sp and ED) and crash elements.

**NEW ENTRY**

---

## SMA
SMA Regelsysteme GmbH
Hannoversche Strasse 1-5, D-34266 Niestetal, Germany
Tel: (+49 561) 952 20   Fax: (+49 561) 952 21 00
e-mail: bahn@sma.de
Web: http://www.sma.de

### Key personnel
Managing Director Power Engineering: Günther Cramer
Sales Managers: Birgit Wilde-Velasco, Uwe Kleinkauf

### Products
Single- and multi-voltage power supply systems for passenger coaches; power electronics and microprocessor systems for railway applications; battery chargers; battery converters; diagnostic systems.

---

## SMTC
F-85600 St Georges de Montaigu
BP 115-85601 Montaigu Cedex, France
Tel: (+33 2) 51 09 25 25   Fax: (+33 2) 51 06 39 54
e-mail: info@smtc.fr

### Key personnel
General Manager: Alain Saracchi
Commercial Manager: Christian Dartayre
Technical Manager: Gilles le Masson

### Subsidiaries
*Germany*
SMTC GmbH
Merzigerstrasse 8, D-66763 Dillingen
Tel: (+49 68) 31 76 84 40   Fax: (+49 68) 31 76 84 15
e-mail: SMTC@IPN-GmbH.de

*UK*
NVM
Tel: (+44 1993) 83 13 47   Fax: (+44 1993) 83 00 67
e-mail: bill@gsf-limited.demon.co.uk

### Products
Rail interior products including tables, flooring systems, ceilings, fittings, partitions, bar car tables, interior doors, platforms, floors, light roofings, electrical cubicle partitions.

---

## Southco
Southco Europe Ltd
Midway House, Staverton Technology Park, Cheltenham GL51 6TQ, UK
Tel: (+44 1452) 71 54 00   Fax: (+44 1452) 71 54 92
e-mail: preichle@southco.com

### Key personnel
Marketing Manager: Petra Reichle

### Products
Latches and access fasteners including the new Vise Action™ compression latch line with flush design that can be mounted from the back of the door with minimal intrusion.

---

## Specialty Bulb
The Specialty Bulb Co Inc
80 Orville Drive, Bohemia, New York 11716-0231, USA
Tel: (+1 631) 589 33 93   Fax: (+1 631) 563 30 89
e-mail: info@bulbspecialists.com
Web: http://www.bulbspecialists.com

### Key personnel
President: Judith Beja
Vice-President, Technical: Caden Zollo
Vice-President, Sales and Marketing: Edie Muldoon

### Products
Major supplier to rail and mass transit industry of USA and European lamps for car, signal, headlights and other applications.

---

## SPS Isoclima SpA
Via Degli Scipiono 268a, I-00192 Rome, Italy
Tel: (+39 06) 081 11   Fax: (+39 06) 00 01 70
e-mail: isoroma@attglobal.net

### Key personnel
Director, Transport Products Division: Filippo Ugolini

### Works
Via Enico Mattei I, I-35046 Aletto (PD), Italy
Tel: (+39 0429) 895 44   Fax: (+39 0429) 89 92 94

### Products
Windscreens: flat, curved, heated, framed with antispall, high-impact-resistant for high-speed trains, locomotives, emus, dmus, LRVs, trams and buses; glass for light covers, interior glazing and partitions.

---

## BODE DOOR SYSTEMS

**PROVEN**

Trust in our know-how, our constructive abilities and the high reliability of our systems.

**SAFE**

Talk to us about your special tasks for vehicle door systems – we fulfil them.

**RELIABLE**

Gebr. Bode & Co. GmbH
Ochshäuser Str. 14
D-34123 Kassel
Postfach 31 03 27
D-34059 Kassel
Phone +49 561 50090
Fax +49 561 55956

Bode

# MANUFACTURERS/Passenger coach equipment

Recent contracts include: all windows for Fiat Pendolino trains (from 1992 to date); high-speed train and Eurotram windscreens and side windows for Adtranz NSB and Adtranz Strasbourg; windscreens for ALSTOM Scottish Rail; ETR500 HST for Breda Italian Rail; windows for Talgo Pendular.

## Stone India Ltd

16 Taratalla Road, Calcutta 700 088, India
Tel: (+91 33) 401 46 61   Fax: (+91 33) 401 48 86
e-mail: stonein@cal.vsnl.net.in

**Key personnel**
See entry in *Brakes and drawgear* section

**Products**
Train lighting alternators, air conditioning equipment, pantographs and rubber components.   **VERIFIED**

## Stone International

A member of Vapor Group
10655 Henri Bourassa West, Montreal, Quebec H4S 1A1, Canada

Stone UK Limited (Stone International)
Unit 9, Crossways Business Park, Stone Marshes, Dartford, DA2 6QG, UK
Tel: (+44 1322) 28 93 23   Fax: (+44 1322) 28 92 82
Managing Director: Anthony J Walsh

Stone Safety Service
240 South Main Street, South Hackensack, New Jersey 07606, USA
Tel: (+1 201) 489 02 00   Fax: (+1 201) 489 93 62
Vice-President: Vincent Mirandi

**Products**
Air conditioning, heating, pressure ventilation and temperature control equipment, static inverters, battery chargers, alternators, DC motors.

## Stratiforme Industries

26 route Nationale, F-59235 Bersee, France
Tel: (+33 3) 20 84 90 10   Fax: (+33 3) 20 59 28 00
Web: http://www.stratiforme.com

**Production facility**
Technoforme
26 route Nationale, F-59235 Bersee, France
Tel: (+33 20) 849 00   Fax: (+33 20) 84 90 22

**Testing laboratory**
Compreforme
BP 8, F-21402 Chatillon sur Seine, France
Tel: (+33 80) 91 09 85   Fax: (+33 80) 91 40 61

**Products**
Polyester thermohardening plastics to manufacture phenolic resin moulded pieces with in-mould gelcoat coating. Stratiforme has two production units, at Bersee and Chatillon sur Seine, with a testing laboratory at Chatillon.
Moulded pieces for driver cabins, front ends, driver consoles, toilet cubicles, stairways, side panels, seats and interior liner panels.
Front ends for the French, Spanish, Italian, Korean and Eurostar TGV high-speed trains; urban and suburban rolling stock.
Underground passenger cars for Paris, Caracas, New York, Taipei, Jacksonville, Chicago, Atlanta, San Francisco; tramways and streetcars for Lille, Brussels, Grenoble, Cologne and Saarbrücken; and interior fittings for Intercity trains.

*Stratiforme moulded structural units are used in Talent dmus*   2000/0085461

## Supersine Duramark Limited

Freemantle Road, Lowestoft, Suffolk NR33 0EA, UK
Tel: (+44 1502) 50 12 34   Fax: (+44 1502) 58 35 44
e-mail: sales@ssdm.co.uk
Web: http://www.ssdm.co.uk

**Products**
System Deco self-adhesive laminates for use on trains as an alternative to paint, with anti-graffiti options. Glass protection film applied to windows to protect them from vandalism. SSDM On-line, developed by SSDM's electronic media company, Clear Interactive Ltd. The Internet-based system allows for artwork approvals and instant ordering around-the-clock.

## TBA

TBA Textiles Ltd
PO Box 40, Rochdale OL12 7EQ, UK
Tel: (+44 1706) 474 22   Fax: (+44 1706) 35 42 95

**Key personnel**
Managing Director: Dr A V Ruddy

**Products**
Fireblocking and anti-vandal fabrics for passenger transport seating. Fire resisting/insulating liners for use within the bodywork. Moulded fire-resistant seat pans.

## Technical Resin Bonders

12 Clifton Road, Huntingdon, Cambridgeshire PE29 7EN, UK
Tel: (+44 1480) 523 81   Fax: (+44 1480) 41 49 92
e-mail: sales@trbonders.co.uk
Web: http://www.trbonders.co.uk

**Key personnel**
Sales Manager: Robert Hodgson

**Corporate development**
Formerly part of Ciba Geigy, Technical Resin Bonders is part of the Bondsword Group.

**Products**
Lightweight structural and decorative honeycomb panels for vehicle new build and refurbishment programmes, including: aluminium honeycomb floors; external doors; internal doors; partitions; draught screens; table tops; ceiling panels; lower body sides; tables for passengers with disabilities; toilet modules; catering modules; overhead lockers; train skirts; energy absorbers; driver protection panels and cladding panels.

## Techni Industrie SA

ZI de la Chambrouillère, F-53960 Bonchamp-les-Laval, France
Tel: (+33 2) 43 59 23 80   Fax: (+33 2) 43 59 23 89
e-mail: contact@techni-industrie.fr

**Key personnel**
Chairman: Gérard Lelasseux
Commercial and Technical Manager: Dan Diaconu

**Products**
Components for powered passenger vehicles including front ends and chassis for LRVs and bodyshell parts for TGV high-speed trainsets. Locomotive cabs and chassis.

## Teknoware

Teknoware Oy
Ilmarisentie 8, FIN-15200 Lahti, Finland
Tel: (+358 3) 88 30 20   Fax: (+358 3) 883 02 40
e-mail: sales@teknoware.fi
Web: http://www.teknoware.fi

**Key personnel**
Sales Director (Austria, Czech Republic, Croatia, Germany, Hungary, Romania, Slovakia, Slovenia, Switzerland, Yugoslavia): Olli-Pekka Porkka
Sales Director (rest of world): Esa Melkko

**Products**
Interior lighting electronics and lighting systems; inverters/ballasts and fluorescent lighting systems for LRVs and passenger coaches.
Recent developments include an increased range of halogen converters and dimmable lighting inverters/ballasts.

## Telephonics

Telephonics Corporation
815 Broad Hollow Road, Farmingdale, New York 11735, USA
Tel: (+1 631) 549 60 62   Fax: (+1 631) 549 60 18

**Key personnel**
Vice-President, Business Development, Commercial Operations: Phil Greco
Manager, Business Development: Norbert Trokki

**Products**
Integrated digital communications systems for rail vehicles, including public address/crew intercom, automated announcements, radio communications; vehicle CCTV systems; vehicle condition monitoring systems; train line multiplexers; car network controllers.

**Contracts**
Vehicle communication/passenger entertainment for Caltrans, (USA); vehicle communication, train line multiplexer, network controller for New York City Transit R143 212 subway cars; vehicle communication, train line multiplexer, network controller for New York City Transit R142 1550 subway cars; vehicle communication, radio network door observation CCTV for South Eastern Pennsylvania Transit Authority; vehicle communication for Massachusetts Bay Transit Authority LRV; vehicle communication, health monitoring, vehicle CCTV for Hudson Bergen Light Rail System LRV; integrated wayside communication for Newark APM.
Recent developments include: train line multiplexer for transport of vehicle controls and digital audio using E1 standards; car network controller used to convert LON to propulsion/brake commands; onboard CCTV for door observation; public address and customer information systems based on industry standard, internet technologies.

**UPDATED**

## Técnicas Modulares e Industriales SA (Temoinsa)

Polígono Industrial Congost, Avenida San Juliá 100, E-08400 Granollers, Barcelona, Spain
Tel: (+34 93) 860 92 00   Fax: (+34 93) 860 92 13
e-mail: temoinsa@redestb.es
Web: http://www.temoinsa.com

**Key personnel**
Chairman: Alvaro Colomer
Chief Executive Officer: Miguel de Sagarra
General Manager: Jose M Pedret
Commercial Manager: Antonio Fábregas

**Products**
Design, manufacture, engineering and technical assistance of components for fitting out passenger coach interiors with fully developed modular systems, including air conditioning, heating and ventilation, vacuum toilet systems; high-technology composites, control systems, passenger information systems and electric panels.
Turnkey projects for complete interiors of new vehicles and refurbishment.
Developments include a passenger information modular system (Telink) and high-technology composite materials.

## Contracts

Contracts include fitting out coaches for ENR and SEMAF (Egypt); s/440 units for RENFE (Spain); double-deck coaches for ALSTOM (Spain); saloon, sleeper and buffet coaches for KTMB (Malaysia), coach interiors for MOVO (Czech Republic); club cars for AMF Canada; double deck coaches for CP Tagus Crossing (Portugal); Heathrow Express toilet modules for CAF (Spain); MUN coaches for Wagons-Lits, (France); metro coaches destined for Copenhagen and Atlanta for Breda (Italy); emus to Brazil for Siemens (Austria); saloon coaches for FEVE (Spain); metro coaches destined for Madrid for Breda (Italy); different types of coaches for OSE (Greece); bistro coaches for Amtrak (USA); toilet modules for Virgin Cross Country for Bombardier (France); toilet modules destined for Long Island for Bombardier (Canada); coaches for WCML for ALSTOM (UK); toilet modules for Adtranz (UK).

**VERIFIED**

## th-contact AG

Schönmattstrasse 6, CH-4153 Reinach, Switzerland
Tel: (+41 61) 716 75 75   Fax: (+41 61) 711 77 67
e-mail: info@th-contact.ch
Web: http://www.th-contact.ch

### Subsidiary companies

*France*
550 av du Général De Gaulle, BP 203, F-88106 Saint-Dié, Cédex
Tel: (+33) 329 56 23 82   Fax: (+33) 329 56 10 42
e-mail: the-contact@wanadoo.fr
Web: http://www.th-contact.fr

*UK*
Unit 9, Lion Industrial Park, Northgate Way, Aldridge, Walsall WS9 9RL
Tel: (+44 1922) 45 22 12   Fax: (+44 1922) 45 54 17
e-mail: sales@th-contact.co.uk
Web: http://www.th-contact.co.uk

*USA*
th-contact inc
2121 South Oneida, Suite 515, Denver, Colorado 80224
Tel: (+1 303) 757 62 00   Fax: (+1 303) 757 68 00
e-mail: info@th-contact.com
Web: http://www.th-contact.com

### Corporate development

In December 2001, a co-operation agreement was announced between th-contact AG and German-based Escha Bauelemente GmbH.

### Products

Switching devices and indicator lamps for public transport.

**NEW ENTRY**

## Thermo King

Thermo King Corporation
Rail Climate Control Head Office
Ostrovskeho 34, 15128 Prague 5, Czech Republic
Tel: (+420 2) 57 10 91 11   Fax: (+420 2) 51 56 21 87

### Headquarters office

314 West 90th Street, Minneapolis, Minnesota 55420-3693, USA
Tel: (+1 612) 887 22 00

### Key personnel

Chief Executive Officer: Sean Kinsela
Vice-President, Bus and Rail, HVAC Sales and Marketing: Philip Veenboer
Director, Business Development, Rail Climate Control: Don King
Director, Engineering, Bus and Rail HVAC: John Gough

### Products

Since 1984 Thermo King has been a system supplier of climate control (heating, ventilation and air conditioning) for new rail vehicles and for the retrofit of existing cars. This includes the design, manufacture, supply, installation, service and maintenance of complete climate control systems.

System components include passenger climate control, driver's cab climate control, electronic controllers and software. Thermo King's family of units is designed specifically for the rail industry to achieve high reliability and low life-cycle costs. For passenger climate control a low-profile styled design is totally self-contained, hermetically sealed and able to deliver a wide range of capabilities (25 to 42 kW) within the same structure. For the driver's cab, Thermo King supplies a unit with a range of capacities from 3 to 6 kW.

The units feature the latest scroll compressor technology, environmentally friendly refrigerant, advanced corrosion protection on all heat transfer surfaces and a microprocessor controller to ensure ease of use and precise temperature control.

Retrofit contracts for Thermo King have included the ALN project in Italy, vehicles for Vietnam Railways and Giubileo del 2000 in Rome. Contracts for climate control systems for new rail vehicles include ALSTOM's X'Trapolis project in Melbourne, Siemens-built LRVs for Salt Lake City and Metro Line 3 in Manila.

## Thorn Transport Lighting

3 King George Close, Eastern Avenue West, Romford, Essex RM7 7PP, UK
Tel: (+44 1708) 77 63 75   Fax: (+44 1708) 77 63 37
e-mail: jim.hayes@thornlight.com
Web: http://www.thornlight.com

### Key personnel

Manager, Transport Lighting Division: Jim Hayes

### Products and Services

A major designer and manufacturer of interior saloon luminaries. Design, manufacture and supply of Luminaires for all types of rail vehicles, comprising fluorescent, tungsten halogen downlighters and fibre optic emergency egress lighting.

### Contracts

Contracts include the design, manufacture, test and supply of saloon luminaries for the Kowloon-Canton railway project, Hong Kong airport rolling stock, GNER HST vehicles, Swedish 2000 tilting train and Class 321 project.

### Developments

Fibre optic emergency egress lighting for use on rolling stock.

**UPDATED**

## Tiflex Ltd

Tiflex House, Liskeard, PL14 4NB, UK
Tel: (+44 1579) 32 08 08   Fax: (+44 1579) 32 08 02
e-mail: treadmaster@tiflex.co.uk
Web: http://www.tiflex.co.uk

### Key personnel

Managing Director: N A Spearman
Sales and Marketing Director: P V Stiles
Product Manager: Barry Curtis

### Products

Treadmaster smoke and fire-resistant floor coverings, slip-resistant floor coverings, for rail and road vehicles and for buildings; specialist stair nosings.

Contracts include the supply of floorings for the Heathrow Express trainsets, Midland Metro LRVs and MoD Naval vessels.

**UPDATED**

## TODCO Inc

7167 Route 353, Cattaraugus, New York 14719-9537, USA
Tel: (+1 716) 257 34 75   Fax: (+1 716) 257 91 14

### Products

Door panels for rail vehicles. Panels are produced without seals, glazing or furniture and in primed-only condition. Recent products include the Partner door, which is capable of being operated in sliding-plug configuration.

## MANUFACTURERS/Passenger coach equipment

### Toshiba

Toshiba Corporation
Railway Projects Department, Toshiba Building, 1-1 Shibaura 1-chome, Minato-ku, Tokyo 105, Japan
Tel: (+81 3) 34 57 49 24   Fax: (+81 3) 34 57 83 85

**Key personnel**
See entry in *Locomotives and powered/non-powered passenger vehicles* section.

**Products**
Air conditioning equipment; exhaust fans; orbit fans; heaters; refrigerators; water coolers; beer coolers; lighting equipment; alternators; static GTO inverters.

### Toyo Denki

Toyo Denki Seizo KK
Toyo Electric Manufacturing Co Ltd, Yaesu Mitsui Building, 7-2 Yaesu 2-chome, Chuo-ku,
Tokyo 104, Japan
Tel: (+81 3) 32 71 63 74   Fax: (+81 3) 32 71 46 93

**Key personnel**
See entry in *Electric traction equipment* section.

**Products**
Door operating systems and equipment, including door actuators, opening/closing switches and control systems.

### Transit Control Systems

11451 North Ocean Circle, Anaheim, California 92806, USA
Tel: (+1 714) 234 30 30

**Key personnel**
President: Peter J Anello
Vice-President, Marketing and Contracts:
 Jimmie C Collins
Chief Engineer: J Kiel

**Products**
Drivers' consoles, manual controllers, fault monitoring, controls, communications, heating and air conditioning subsystem equipment. TCS also supplies locomotive heating and air conditioning systems.

**Contracts**
Contracts include: Heating, Ventilation and Air Conditioning (HVAC) equipment for MBTA Red Line cars; drivers' consoles and control equipment for Los Angeles; HVAC and communication equipment for Septa Norristown cars; drivers' consoles for NYCTA; knife switch assembly for St Louis LRVs; drivers' consoles control and communication equipment for BART's C2 cars; trainsets and the HVAC overhaul of WMATA's 298 Rohr cars; and manual controllers for Atlanta's MARTA CQ312 cars.

*UPDATED*

### Transmatic Inc

6145 Delfield Industrial Drive, Waterford, Michigan 48329, USA
Tel: (+1 248) 623 25 00   Fax: (+1 248) 623 28 39

**Key personnel**
President: O K Dealey Jr
Vice-President, Sales and Marketing: M T Hoffman
Vice-President, Environmental Systems:
 D Scott McConnell

**UK subsidiary**
Transmatic Europe Ltd
Unit 2, City Park Industrial Estate, Gelderd Road, Leeds LS12 6DR, UK
Tel: (+44 1131) 279 99 89   Fax: (+44 1131) 279 41 27
e-mail: sales@transmatic.co.uk
Managing Director: Terry Calnon

**Products**
Interior lighting and advertising coving for buses and urban transit vehicles, multipurpose lighting/air conditioning duct modules, surface-mounted fluorescent lighting, destination sign lighting, interior cleaning systems for buses and rail vehicles.

### Transtechnik GmbH

Ohmstrasse 1-3, D-83607 Holzkirchen, Germany
Tel: (+49 80 24) 99 00   Fax: (+49 80 24) 99 03 00
e-mail: info@transtechnik.com
Web: http://www.transtechnik.com

**Key personnel**
Managing Directors: Robert Sterff, Wolf-Dieter Deggau
Manager, Marketing Communications: Rosi Marx
Sales: Dr Ralf Cremer

**Other offices**
*UK Marketing Office*
Transtechnik PSI
Chiltern House, High Street, Chalfont St Giles HP8 4QH
Tel: (+44 1494) 87 15 44   Fax: (+44 1494) 87 31 18
Sales: Robin Cochrane

*Italy Sales and Marketing Office*
ITP (International Technical Products di Maurizio Favini & Co) SA
Via Cilea 78, I-20151 Milan
Tel: (+39 02) 353 45 61   Fax: (+39 02) 353 45 61
Marketing Manager: Bruno Favini

*Australia Marketing Office*
Transtechnik Asia Pacific Pty Ltd
Unit 2, 42-44 Whyalla Place, Prestons,
New South Wales 2170
Tel: (+61 2) 95 19 23 11   Fax: (+61 2) 95 19 23 77
e-mail: wwachs@ozemail.com.au
Sales: William Wachsmann

*France Sales and Marketing Office*
11 rue des Vosges, F-57444 Reding
Tel: (+33 3) 87 03 59 19   Fax: (+33 3) 87 03 59 26
Sales Manager: Serge Colle

*USA Sales and Marketing Office*
Transtechnik Corporation USA
27 McKee Drive, Mahwah, Bergen County, New Jersey 07430
Tel: (+1 201) 828 98 04   Fax: (+1 201) 828 98 13

**Products**
Auxiliary power converters for all rail vehicle and trolleybus onboard services and special power electronic applications.

**Developments**
Diagnostics software 'ttProDiag' with Windows interface and tt2000 hardware.

**Contracts**
Power converters for 59 Combino low-floor streetcars for Swanston Trams, Melbourne, Australia, worth €1.2 million; nine auxiliary power supply systems for the Prospector/Avonlink replacement high-speed diesel railcars for Western Australian Government Railway Commission.

*UPDATED*

### Trevira

Trevira GmbH & Co KG
Lyoner Strasse 38a, D-60528 Frankfurt am Main, Germany
Tel: (+49 69) 305 68 75   Fax: (+49 69) 305 81822
e-mail: treviracs@fra.trevira.com
Web: http://www.treviracs.com

**Key personnel**
Marketing Manager: Dr Zimmermann

**Products**
Flame-retardant textiles for rail vehicle seating, carpet and interior trim applications.

*VERIFIED*

---

## Efficient KINEMATICS

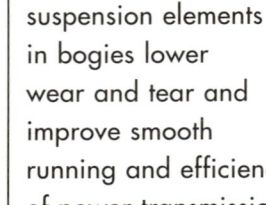

Kinematic and suspension elements in bogies lower wear and tear and improve smooth running and efficiency of power transmission

- **Kinematics**
- **Acoustics**
- **Suspension**

**Freudenberg Schwab GmbH**

Freudenberg Schwab GmbH
Postplatz 3
16761 Hennigsdorf, Germany
Tel. +49-3302-20620
Fax. +49-3302-206277
www.freudenberg-schwab.de
e-mail: info@freuddenberg-schwab.de

Schwab Schwingungstechnik AG
Soodstrasse 57, CH-8134 Adliswil
Tel. +41 (0)1-711 17 17
Fax +41 (0)1-710 05 42
www.schwab-ag.ch
schwingungstechnik@schwab-ag.ch

## TriCon

TriCon Design GmbH
Liebigstrasse 5-7, D-92637 Weiden, Germany
Tel: (+49 961) 39 06 60   Fax: (+49 961) 39 06 66 20
e-mail: TriCon-Design@t-online.de

**Key personnel**
Managers: Thomas König, Frank Schuster

**Products**
Components for the railway industry; interior and exterior design of passenger coaches.

Recent contracts include the development of the airport shuttle at Kuala Lumpur, design of sleeper coaches and Puma coaches for DB AG.

## Unicel

Unicel Corporation
Transportation Composites Division
1520 Industrial Avenue, Escondido, California 92029, USA
Tel: (+1 619) 741 39 12   Fax: (+1 619) 741 88 32

**Key personnel**
Sales Manager: Michael Henderson

**Products**
*Cres Floor* lightweight stainless steel honeycomb floor panels. Lightweight composites and honeycomb panels for passenger vehicle interiors including floors, partitions, windscreens, ceilings, external and internal doors, luggage racks and luggage bins.

## UniControls

UniControls AS
Kreniká 2257, CZ100 00 Prague 10, Czech Republic
Tel: (+420 2) 781 78 85   Fax: (+420 2) 781 44 75
e-mail: unic@unicontrols.cz
Web: http://www.unicontrols.cz

**Products**
Communications and control systems for trains and rail vehicles, including: train communication network, wire-train-bus equipment; multivehicle communications equipment; vehicle communication devices; and driver's cab equipment and displays.

Contracts include train communications and control systems for refurbished Russian-built Prague metro stock; train communications system for St Petersburg metro stock; train and vehicle communications system and driver's cab equipment for Czech Railways Class 471 emus; automatic train control system for Czech Railways Class 680 tilting trainsets; driver's cab equipment for refurbished Class 772 locomotive.

## USSC Group

USSC Group Inc
20 Union Hill Road, West Conshohocken, Pennsylvania 19428, USA
Tel: (+1 610) 83 47 28   Fax: (+1 610) 834 05 23
e-mail: info@usscgroup.com

**Key personnel**
President: Christian Hammarskjold

**Products**
Cab seats, windows, solar screens/blinds, mirrors, upholstery fabrics, automatic lubrication systems and other interior components; ergonomic design contracts.

## Vapor Corporation

A Westinghouse Air Brake Company
6420 West Howard Street, Niles, Illinois 60714, USA
Tel: (+1 847) 967 83 00   Fax: (+1 847) 965 98 64; 33 95
Web: http://www.vapordoors.com

**Key personnel**
Executive Vice-President and General Manager: K N Nippes
Vice-President, Sales and Marketing: W J Kleppinger
Vice-President, Engineering: J M Jackson

**Associated companies**
Vapor Canada Inc
10655 Henri Bourassa West, Ville St-Laurent, Quebec H4S 1A1, Canada
Tel: (+1 514) 335 42 00   Fax: (+1 514) 335 42 31

Vapor UK
2nd Avenue, Centrum 100, Burton on Trent DE14 2WF, UK
Tel: (+44 1283) 74 33 00   Fax: (+44 1283) 74 33 33

HP srl
Viale Regina Pacis, 296, I-41049 Sassuolo, Modena, Italy
Tel: (+39 0536) 80 64 41   Fax: (+39 0536) 80 17 89

Stone Air
10655 Henri Bourassa West, Ville St-Laurent, Quebec H4S 1A1, Canada
Tel: (+1 514) 335 42 00   Fax: (+1 514) 335 42 31

Stone UK
2nd Avenue, Centrum 100, Burton-on-Trent DE14 2WF, UK
Tel: (+44 1283) 74 33 00   Fax: (+44 1283) 74 33 33

**Products**
Automatic door systems; passenger car heating, ventilation and air conditioning systems, relays and contactors.

## VBK

VBK Transport Interior AS
Godthaab, Strandveien 50, N-1324 Lysaker, Norway
Tel: (+47 33) 02 07 20   Fax: (+47 33) 02 07 45
e-mail: sales@vbkti.no
Web: http://www.vbkti.com

---

**Resilient components for rail vehicles**

ISO 9001 certified

**GMT® GUMMI · METALL · TECHNIK · GMBH**
Liechtersmatten 5 · 77815 Bühl · Germany
email: info@gmt-gmbh.de · www.gmt-gmbh.de
Telephone +49/7223/804-0 · Fax +49/7223/21075

# MANUFACTURERS/Passenger coach equipment

**Key personnel**
Managing Director: Jo Laaveg
Sales and Marketing Manager: Kristin Helgesen

**Subsidiaries**
VBK Transport Interior Scandinavia AS
PO Box 780, N-3196 Horten, Norway
Tel: (+47 33) 02 07 20    Fax: (+47 33) 02 07 45

VBK TI France Sarl
c/o Norwegian Trade Consul, 2 rue de Marignan, F-75008 Paris, France
Tel: (+33 1) 56 59 20 40    Fax: (+33 1) 56 59 20 41

VBK Transport Interior Ltd
'O' Shop, Derby Carriage Works, Litchurch Lane, Derby DE24 8AD, UK
Tel: (+44 1332) 22 39 00    Fax: (+44 1332) 22 39 19
e-mail: vbkuk@btconnect.com

**Products**
Turnkey solutions for complete vehicle interiors. Seats for passenger vehicles. Interior fittings for passenger vehicles, including luggage racks and grab rails; supply of interior fittings on a turnkey basis.

Contracts include the supply of interiors for 13 Class 71 three-car emus for the Gardermobanen plus interiors and seats for 16 Class 72 four-car tilting emus, both built by Adtranz Sweden for NSB; seats for 17 trams built by Ansaldo/Firema for Oslo Sporveier; seats for regional trains for DSB Denmark and interior modules for vehicles built by Adtranz Derby for UK operators.

## WABCO

Westinghouse Air Brake Company
1001 Air Brake Avenue, Wilmerding, Pennsylvania 15148, USA
Tel: (+1 412) 825 10 00    Fax: (+1 412) 825 10 19

**Key personnel**
See entry in *Brakes and drawgear* section.

**Principal subsidiaries**
Cardwell Westinghouse Company
Pulse Electronics Inc
Motive Power
Railroad Friction Products Corp
Universal Railway Devices Inc
Vapor Corporation
Young Touchstone

**Products**
Electronic data recorders, end-of-train units, speed indicators, alertness devices, onboard computers, fault monitors/annunciators, fuel level indicators; electromechanical and electropneumatic door actuators for passenger vehicles; air conditioning equipment for passenger vehicles.
*NEW ENTRY*

## Wabtec Rail Ltd

PO Box 400, Doncaster Works, Hexthorpe Road, Doncaster DN1 1SL, UK
Tel: (+44 1302) 79 00 27; 34 07 00
Fax: (+44 1302) 79 00 58; 34 06 93
e-mail: probinson@wabtec.com
Web: http://www.wabtec.com

**Key personnel**
See entry in *Locomotive and powered/non-powered passenger vehicles* section.

**Corporate developments**
Wabtec Rail formerly traded as RFS(E), changing its name in March 2000.

**Products**
Passenger coach classified repairs, crash damage and repainting; bogie overhaul including wheelsets, air brake equipment and hydraulic dampers.

## Walter Mäder Aqualack GmbH

Gewerbepark 40, D-59069 Hamm, Germany
Tel: (+49 2385) 935 60    Fax: (+49 2385) 93 56 49
e-mail: info@maeder-aqualack.de

**Products**
Water-borne and solvent-borne paints and coatings for rail vehicles of all types.
*NEW ENTRY*

## Westcode Inc

1372 West Chester, Pennsylvania 19380, USA
Tel: (+1 610) 738 12 00    Fax: (+1 610) 696 74 20
Web: http://www.westcodeus.com

**Key personnel**
Chairman and Chief Executive Officer: Edward J Widdowson

**Subsidiary company**
Westcode (UK) Ltd
PO Box 1582, Chippenham SN15 3ZR, UK
Tel: (+44 1249) 78 34 56    Fax: (+44 1249) 78 36 66
Managing Director: David A Thompson

**Products and services**
Manufacture and refurbishment of rail vehicle heating, ventilation and air conditioning (HVAC) systems; design, manufacture and overhaul of train door systems; design and manufacture of pneumatic systems, including brake control and air supply equipment and test rigs.

**Contracts**
HVAC equipment for urban operators in Puerto Rico, Taipei and Toronto; refurbishment of HVAC equipment for 439 cars for BART, San Francisco; HVAC equipment for ScotRail, UK and IE, Ireland; over 40,000 door systems for operators in North America; test equipment for NYCTA, New York and TRTC, Taipei.
*NEW ENTRY*

## Widney Transport Components

Widney Transport Components (Pty) Ltd
PO Box 124167, Alrode 1450, South Africa
Tel: (+27 11) 864 48 04    Fax: (+27 11) 908 18 56

**Key personnel**
Managing Director: S R Jennings
Export Marketing Director: P Pretorius
Technical Director: G Szabo
General Manager: P N Van den Biggelaar

**Products**
Windows for passenger vehicles, including sliding, hopper and double-glazed types; doors for locomotives and passenger vehicles; locks and general carriage fittings.

Contracts include the supply of hopper windows for suburban rolling stock.

## Winstanley

Winstanley & Co (Kings Norton) Ltd
Racehorse Road, Pinvin Industrial Estate, Pershore WR10 2DG, UK
Tel: (+44 1386) 55 22 78    Fax: (+44 1386) 55 65 31

**Key personnel**
Chairman: John Foley
Managing Director: Jerry King
Commercial Director: Trevor Clews

**Subsidiary companies**
Portable Balers Ltd
Adcon Modular MRF Systems

**Products**
Design, manufacture and finishing of aluminium, steel and stainless steel fabrications, primarily for the railway industry. Factoring of products made in composites or wood and the supply of complete railway vehicle interiors and ancillary equipment to the major rolling stock passenger coach equipment.

Contracts include components for Eurostar, European Nightstock Services, Jubilee and Northen line metro cars, Arlanda (Sweden) airport link, KCRC Hong Kong refurbishment and upgrade of 317 to 365 stock.

Latest contracts include components for Electrostar and Turbostar new stock and First Great Western/North Western new build.

## Woodville Polymer Engineering

Hearthcote Road, Swadlincote DE11 9DX, UK
Tel: (+44 1283) 22 11 22    Fax: (+44 1283) 22 29 11
e-mail: gmiller@woodvillepolymer.co.uk
Web: http://www.woodvillepolymer.co.uk

**Key personnel**
Managing Director: Roger Kent
General Manager, Rail: Martin Clarke
General Sales Manager, Rail: Gary Miller
Contracts Manager, Rail: Bruce Cresswell

**Background**
Woodville Polymer Engineering is part of The Smiths Group.

**Products**
Design, development and manufacture of gangways, flexible treadplates and rail accessories fabrication and industrial engineering services.

**Contracts**
Recent contracts include: Bombardier/Virgin CrossCountry, UK; Koros/MTRC TKE line, Hong Kong; MTRC LAL and AEL, Hong Kong; Bombardier Canada/Vancouver Sky Train 1998-99; Arlanda Airport Express; Alstom Juniper emus, UK; Øresund Link emus; Delhi Metro; Manila Metro.
*UPDATED*

## XP

XP plc
Horseshoe Park, Pangbourne RG8 7JW, UK
Tel: (+44 118) 984 55 15    Fax: (+44 118) 984 34 23
e-mail: sales@xpplc.co.uk
Web: http://www.xpplc.co.uk

**Key personnel**
Managing Director: James Peters
Technical Director: Gary Bocock
Divisional Director (Railways): Jamie Henderson

**Products**
Electronic power supplies and DC/DC converters that meet UK and European standards RIA13 and 13 for rail applications.

*XP modular DC/DC converters that meet UK and European standards*    0003469

# FREIGHT VEHICLES AND EQUIPMENT

## Alphabetical listing

ABRF Industries
ACF
Alna Koki
ALSTOM
Amherst
Arbel
Astra
Babcock Rail
Bharat Wagon & Engineering
BMZ
Bombardier Transportation
Bradken Rail
Braithwaite
Bratsvo
BREC
Breda
Burn Standard
CAF
Callegari
Cattaneo
CCC
CFC
China National Railway Locomotive and Rolling Stock Industry Corporation (LORIC)
Cimmco International
Cometal
Cometarsa
Costaferroviaria
Cromweld Steels
Daewoo
Dalian Locomotive and Rolling Stock Works
Davis
Dorsey
Duro Daković
EKA
Energomachexport
Evans Deakin
Ferrostaal AG
Fiat
Finsam
FIREMA Trasporti SpA
FM Industries
Freudenberg Schwab GmbH
Fuji Car
Ganz Vagon Kft
Goša
Graaff
Greenbrier Companies, The
Gregg Company, The
Gunderson
Gunderson-Concarril
Haacon
Hanjin
HEI
Holland Company LP
Hoogovens
Hunslet-Barclay
Hyundai
INKA
Intamodal-Eimar
Jenbacher
Jessop
Johnstown America Corporation
Kawasaki
K & M
Kawasaki
Keller Elettromeccanica
Kinki Sharyo
Kockums
Kolmex
Kryukovsky
K T Steel
Lyudinovo Locomotive Works JSC
Manoir Industries
Marcroft Engineering Ltd
Marrel
MÁV
Mecanoexportimport
Meva
More Wear Industries
MSV
National Steel Car Ltd
Nippon Sharyo
OFV
Oleo
Orval
Pakistan Railways Carriage Factory
PEC
Portec
Price
Procor Ltd
Progress Rail Services
Qiqihar
Qishuyan
Ray Smith
Reggiane
Rolanfer
Rotem
RSD
SABB
Santa Matilde
SCIF
SEEC
SEMAF
Soma
Stag AG
Strick
Tafesa
TATRAVAGÓNKA
Texmaco Ltd
Thrall
TrentonWorks Ltd
Trinity Difco
Tuchschmid
Tülomsas
Union Tank
United Goninan
Unity
Uralvagonzavod
Wabash National
Wabtec Rail Ltd
Wagon Pars
WagonySwidnica SA
Wakamatsu Sharyo
Zastal
Zeco
Zhuzhou

# MANUFACTURERS / Freight vehicles and equipment

## Classified listing

**CONTAINERS AND SWAPBODIES**
BMZ
Bratsvo
CFC
Davis
Finsam
Graaff
Intamodal-Eimar
Kolmex
Nippon Sharyo
Ray Smith
SEEC
Strick
Tafesa

**FREIGHT HANDLING EQUIPMENT**
Braithwaite
Cometal
EKA
Haacon
Marrel
Portec
Ray Smith
Strick
Tuchschmid

**FREIGHT WAGONS AND COMPONENTS**
ABRF Industries
ACF
Alna Koki
ALSTOM
Amherst
Arbel
Astra
Babcock Rail
Bharat Wagon & Engineering
BMZ
Bombardier Transportation
Braithwaite
Bratsvo
BREC
Breda
Burn Standard
CAF
Callegari
Cattaneo
CCC
CFC
China National Railway Locomotive and Rolling Stock Industry Corporation (LORIC)
Cimmco International
Cometal
Cometarsa
Costaferroviaria
Cromweld Steels
Daewoo
Dalian Locomotive
Davis
Dorsey
Duro Daković
Energomachexport
Evans Deakin
Ferrostaal
Fiat
FIREMA
FM Industries
Freudenberg Schwab
Fuji Car
Ganz-Hunslet
Goša
Graaff
Greenbrier Companies, The
Gregg Company, The
Gunderson
Gunderson-Concarril
Hanjin
HDC
Hoogovens
Hunslet-Barclay
Hyundai
INKA
Jenbacher
Jessop
Johnstown America
Kawasaki
Keller
Kinki Sharyo
Kockums
Kolmex
Kryukovsky
K T Steel
Lyudinovo Locomotive Works
Marcroft Engineering
MÁV
Mecanoexportimport
Meva
More Wear Industries
MSV
National Steel Car
Nippon Sharyo
OFV
Oleo
Orval
Pakistan Railways Carriage Factory
PEC
Portec
Price
Procor
Progress Rail Services
Qiqihar
Qishuyan
Rautaruukki
Reggiane
Rolanfer
RSD
SABB
Santa Matilde
SCIF
SEMAF
Siemens SGP
Soma
Stag
Tafesa
TATRAVAGÓNKA
Texmaco
Thrall
TrentonWorks
Trinity Difco
Tülomsas
Union Tank
United Goninan
Unity
Uralvagonzavod
Wabtec Rail
Wagon Pars
WagonySwidnica
Wakamatsu Sharyo
Zastal
Zeco
Zhuzhou

**INTERMODAL SYSTEMS**
Breda
Dorsey
Kolmex
Manoir Industries – Sambre et Meuse
MÁV
Wabash National

**WAGON CONVERSION, MAINTENANCE AND REPAIR**
ALSTOM
Bombardier Transportation
CCC
Hunslet-Barclay
Marcroft Engineering
MÁV
Progress Rail Services
Rolanfer
Soma
Trinity Difco
Wabtec Rail
Zastal

## Company listing by country

**ARGENTINA**
Callegari
Cometarsa
SABB

**AUSTRALIA**
Evans Deakin
Perry
Rotem
United Goninan

**AUSTRIA**
Jenbacher
Siemens SGP

**BELGIUM**
BREC

**BRAZIL**
CCC
Santa Matilde
Soma

**CANADA**
Bombardier Transportation
National Steel Car Ltd
Procor Ltd
TrentonWorks Ltd

**CHINA, PEOPLE'S REPUBLIC**
China National Railway Locomotive and Rolling Stock Industry Corporation (LORIC)
Dalian Locomotive and Rolling Stock Works
Qiqihar
Qishuyan
Zhuzhou

**CROATIA**
Duro Daković

**CZECH REPUBLIC**
MSV

**EGYPT**
SEMAF

**FRANCE**
ABRF Industries
Arbel
Manoir Industries
Marrel
Orval
Rolanfer

**GERMANY**
Ferrostaal AG
Freudenberg Schwab GmbH
Graaff
Haacon
Hoogovens

**HUNGARY**
Ganz Vagon Kft
MÁV

**INDIA**
Bharat Wagon & Engineering
Braithwaite
Burn Standard
Cimmco International
HEI
Jessop
K T Steel
PEC
Texmaco Ltd

**INDONESIA**
INKA

**IRAN**
Wagon Pars

**ITALY**
Breda
CFC

## MANUFACTURERS/Freight vehicles and equipment

Costaferroviaria
Fiat
FIREMA Trasporti SpA
K & M
OFV
Reggiane

**JAPAN**
Alna Koki
Fuji Car
Kawasaki
Kinki Sharyo
Nippon Sharyo
Wakamatsu Sharyo

**KOREA, SOUTH**
Daewoo
Hanjin
Hyundai

**MEXICO**
Gunderson-Concarril

**MOROCCO**
SCIF

**MOZAMBIQUE**
Cometal

**NEW ZEALAND**
Price

**NORWAY**
Finsam

**PAKISTAN**
Pakistan Railways Carriage Factory

**POLAND**
ALSTOM
Kolmex
WagonySwidnica SA
Zastal

**ROMANIA**
Astra
Mecanoexportimport
Meva

**RUSSIAN FEDERATION**
BMZ
Energomachexport
Lyudinovo Locomotive Works JSC
Uralvagonzavod

**SLOVAKIA**
TATRAVAGÓNKA

**SOUTH AFRICA**
RSD

**SPAIN**
CAF
Intamodal-Eimar
Tafesa

**SWEDEN**
Kockums

**SWITZERLAND**
Cattaneo
Stag AG
Tuchschmid

**TURKEY**
Tülomsas

**UKRAINE**
Kryukovsky

**UNITED KINGDOM**
Babcock Rail
Cromweld Steels
Davis
EKA
Hunslet-Barclay
Marcroft Engineering Ltd
Oleo
Railcare
Ray Smith
Wabtec Rail Ltd

**UNITED STATES OF AMERICA**
ACF
Amherst
Dorsey
FM Industries
Greenbrier Companies, The
Gregg Company, The
Gunderson
Holland Company LP
Johnstown America Corporation
Portec
Progress Rail Services
SEEC
Strick
Thrall
Trinity Difco
Union Tank
Unity
Wabash National

**YUGOSLAVIA, FEDERAL REPUBLIC**
Bratsvo
Goša

**ZIMBABWE**
More Wear Industries
Zeco

# 590 MANUFACTURERS/Freight vehicles and equipment

## ABRF Industries

Ateliers Bretons de Réalisations Ferroviaires Industries
PO Box 19, ZI rue Lafayette, F-44141 Châteaubriant Cedex, France
Tel: (+33 2) 40 81 19 20   Fax: (+33 2) 40 28 02 02

**Key personnel**
General Manager: Jean-Luc Remondeau
Commercial and Technical Director: Gérard Gueguin
Commercial Engineer: Jean-Pierre Cadiou

**Products**
Freight wagons, including 'Easiloader' curtain hood wagon for general merchandise, tank, container and hopper wagons.

## ACF

ACF Industries Inc
620 North Second Street, St Charles, Missouri 63301, USA
Tel: (+1 636) 940 50 00   Fax: (+1 636) 940 50 20

**Key personnel**
President: Roger Wynkoop
Vice-President, Sales and Marketing: Brian Evdo

**Products**
Specialised covered hopper and tank wagons, including the Pressureaide® pressure differential covered hopper capable of operating with internal pressure up to 14.5 lb/in$^2$, for fast and efficient unloading of dry bulk products to remote silos. Freight wagon components, outlets, valves and trailer hitches.

## Alna Koki

Alna Koki Company Ltd
4-5 Higashi Naniwa-cho 1-chome, Amagasaki 660-8572, Japan
Tel: (+81 6) 401 72 83   Fax: (+81 6) 401 61 68

**Key personnel**
See entry in *Locomotives and powered/non-powered passenger vehicles* section.

**Products**
General-purpose freight wagons; low-floor wagons; tank wagons; dump wagons.

## ALSTOM

ALSTOM Konstal SA (ex Konstal SA)
Ul Katowicka 104, PL-415-00 Chorzow, Poland
Tel: (+48 32) 241 10 51   Fax: (+48 32) 241 33 97
e-mail: Konstal@konstal.com.pl

**Key personnel**
See main entry in *Locomotives and powered/non-powered passenger vehicles* section.

**Products**
Freight wagons, including self-discharging hopper wagons; four-axle, six-axle and eight-axle pocket wagons; tank wagons; and specialised wagons for the transport of extra-heavy and extra-long loads, including hollow-platform wagons for transport of extra-long loads.

Contracts include delivery of 3,100 freight wagons to First Union Rail Corporation, the leasing division of First Union National Bank. The contract calls for the production of four types of vehicle over a five-year period. The first type to be produced will be a steel coil carrier, 500 of which are being manufactured at ALSTOM's Montreal plant.

*ALSTOM Konstal Type 213Z container flat wagon* 0023861

## Amherst

Amherst Industries Inc
Port Amherst, Charleston, West Virginia 25306, USA
Tel: (+1 304) 926 11 22   Fax: (+1 304) 926 11 36

**Key personnel**
President: Charles T Jones

**Products**
Freight wagons; interior linings for tank and hopper wagons.

## Arbel

Arbel Fauvet Rail
68 rue de Villiers, F-92532 Levallois-Perret, Cedex France
Tel: (+33 1) 40 89 69 00   Fax: (+33 1) 40 89 69 57

**Works**
140 rue du Paradis, F-59500 Douai, France

**Key personnel**
President: Michel Frambourg
Managing Director: Jacques Sellier
Sales Manager: Luc le Formal

**Subsidiaries**
Lormafer – maintenance, repair and refurbishment of goods wagons
AFBS – maintenance and repair

**Products**
Design, manufacture and refurbishment of a wide range of freight wagons and tank containers. Wagon range includes container, open high-sided, covered, tank, hopper, car-carrying (double-deck), shuttle (for Eurotunnel), coil-carrying, chemical tank containers and shunting locomotives.

Contracts include supply of 108 lorry-carrying wagons, 130 tank wagons for chemical and LPG, 180 coupled Multifret-type wagons, 580 coupled container wagons, and a co-operation contract for bogie design between Arbel and the Ministry of Railways of the People's Republic of China.

## Astra

Astra Vagoane Arad SA
Calea Aurel Vlaicu 41-43, R-2900 Arad, Romania
Tel: (+40 57) 23 12 55; 23 53 79   Fax: (+40 57) 20 22 60
e-mail: mihai.danciu@trinityraileurope.com

**Key personnel**
General Director: Eng Mihai Danciu
Sales Director: Eng Sandu Albulescu

**Corporate background**
Astra Vagoane Arad SA is a member of the Trinity Rail Group.

**Products**
Freight wagons, including: flat wagons of type RBS, Sgnss, Lgns, Sgmmns; underframes for tank wagons; 70, 86, 90, 93 and 95 m$^3$ tank wagons; Tadgs and Tagps grain wagons, Eaos open wagons; Fals wagons; and pocket wagons for transporting lorries and containers; Rijmmns wagons; Shimmns wagons.

**Contracts**
Recent contracts include: 200 Lgnss flat wagons for container transport for a Belgian customer; 500 Sgnss flat wagons for Belgium; 65 78 m$^3$ tank wagons for KVG, Austria; and 125 86 m$^3$ tank wagons for EVA, Germany.

*UPDATED*

## Babcock Rail

Keith Road, Rosyth Dockyard, Rosyth, Fife KY11 2YD, UK
Tel: (+44 1383) 42 37 94   Fax: (+44 1383) 42 31 82

**Key personnel**
See entry in *Locomotives and powered/non-powered passenger vehicles* section.

**Products**
Freight wagons.

## Bharat Wagon & Engineering

Bharat Wagon & Engineering Company Ltd
(A Government of India undertaking)
C Block, 5th Floor, Maurya Lok, Dak Bungalow Road, Patna 800 001, India
Tel: (+91 612) 22 66 99   Fax: (+91 612) 22 21 47

**Key personnel**
General Manager: S P Singh

**Products**
Freight wagons.

## BMZ

JSC Bryansk Engineering Works
ulica Ulyanova 26, 241 015 Bryansk, Russian Federation
Tel: (+7 832) 55 86 73/00 30   Fax: (+7 95) 203 33 95

**Key personnel**
See entry in *Locomotives and powered/non-powered passenger vehicles* section.

**Products**
Freight wagons, including grain hoppers and refrigerated wagons. Specialised wagons for the iron and steel industry. Refrigerated containers.

## Bombardier Transportation

1101 Parent Street, Saint-Bruno, Québec J3V 6E6, Canada
Tel: (+1 514) 441 20 20   Fax: (+1 514) 441 15 15
Web: http://www.transportation.bombardier.com

**Key personnel**
Director Sales and Marketing Freight:
   Hans-Rudolf Steinegger
Tel: (+49 3588) 24 31 00

See also main entry in *Locomotives and powered/non-powered passenger vehicles*.

**Products**
Bombardier Transportation develops and produces freight wagons designed for economical loading and

unloading techniques. Among special fields of activity are products for bimodal traffic. Bombardier Transportation's knowledge includes expertise in the area of freight wagons with wide-opening roofs and walls.

Recent orders: In 2001 Bombardier Transportation was awarded orders for 400 sliding wall wagons and 100 units eight-axle roll-on/roll-off wagons from European customers. Through a joint venture, Bombardier Transportation received orders for more than 1,000 box cars from North American customers since 1999 and is currently manufacturing 400 stand-alone double stack wagons called Husky.

*UPDATED*

## Bradken Rail

Maud Street, Waratah, New South Wales 2998, Australia
Tel: (+61 2) 49 41 26 67    Fax: +(61 2) 49 41 26 61
e-mail: rail@bradken.com.au
Web: http://www.bradken.com.au

### Background
Previously ANI Railway Transportation Group, Bradken Rail is a business of Bradken Resources Pty Ltd, which also has interests in minerals, mining and industrial activities.

The company has technology partnerships with Amsted Industries International and Miner Enterprises.

### Products
Freight wagons, including container bogie flats, ballast and cement, fuel tank, coal and bulk grain wagons. Bogies for wagons, locomotives and passenger cars. Drawgear sets, including couplers, draftgear and yokes. Spare and renewed parts for freight wagons, locomotives and passenger cars. Service, maintenance and refurbishment of freight wagons, locomotives and passenger cars.

*UPDATED*

## Braithwaite

Braithwaite & Company Ltd
(A Government of India undertaking and subsidiary of BBUNL)
5 Hide Road, Calcutta 700 043, India
Tel: (+91 33) 439 79 62; 74 13; 74 15; 67 27; 66 13
Fax: (+91 33) 439 56 07; 76 32
e-mail: braith.company@gems.vsnl.net.in

### Branch Office
74 Janpath, New Delhi 110 001
Tel: (+91 11) 372 31 44

*Braithwaite coal hopper wagon for Vietnam Railways*
0002416

*Braithwaite 24-wheel special-purpose wagon with 182 tonnes payload*
0002417

### Works
Clive Works, 5 Hide Road, Calcutta 700 043
Angus Works, PO Angus, Dist Hooghly, West Bengal
Victoria Works, P-61, CGR Road, Calcutta 700 043

### Marketing and Projects Office
59B Chowringhee Road (6th Floor), Calcutta 700 020
Tel: (+91 33) 240 25 73; 287 00 36
Fax: (+91 33) 240 07 67
e-mail: bwtmkt@cal2.vsnl.net.in

### Key personnel
Managing Director: P K Mukherjee
General Manager (Marketing and Projects):
  A K Battacharyya
Manager (Marketing): M K Chakraborty
Deputy Manager Marketing: S K Basu

### Products
Railway wagons of different gauge systems (all types- general or special purpose), fabricated steel structures for railway bridges, cast steel bogies and centre buffer couplers. All products are ISO 9000 certified.

*UPDATED*

## Bratsvo

Ilindenska 46, 24106 Subotica, Federal Republic of Yugoslavia
Tel: +(381 24) 56 62 69    Fax: (+381 24) 56 63 44

### Key personnel
Director General: Nivica Davidovic

### Products
Freight wagons and repair/maintenance.

## BREC

BREC NV
Mol Cy NV, Diksmuidesteenweg 63, B-8830 Hooglede, Belgium
Tel: (+32 51) 70 16 81    Fax: (+32 51) 70 30 38
e-mail: info@molcy.com

### Works
Huysmanslaan 53, B-1651 Lot (Beersel), Belgium
Tel: (+32 2) 378 05 10    Fax: (+32 2) 378 11 09

### Key personnel
General Manager: M Mol

### Products
Freight wagons, bogies for freight wagons and passenger coaches.

## Breda

Breda Costruzioni Ferroviarie SpA
Via Ciliegiole 110b, I-51100 Pistoia, Italy
Tel: (+39 0573) 37 01    Fax: (+39 0573) 37 02 92

### Key personnel
See entry in *Locomotives and powered/non-powered passenger vehicles* section.

### Products
Freight wagons in stainless and carbon steel, including bimodal vehicles.

Recent contracts include supply of freight vehicle shuttle wagons for Eurotunnel; and Type Habillnss covered wagons, Type Tadns hopper wagons, Type Sggnss container flat wagons, Type Saadknns low-floor wagons for intermodal traffic and bimodal road/rail trailers for Italian Railways (FS).

## Burn Standard

Burn Standard Co Ltd
A subsidiary of Bharat Bhari Udyog Nigam Ltd
(A Government of India undertaking)
10-C Hungerford Street, Calcutta 700 017, India
Tel: (+91 33) 247 10 67; 17 62; 17 72
Fax: (+91 33) 247 17 88

### Works
20-22 Nityadhan Mukherjee Road, Howrah 711 101
Burnpur Works, Burnpur 713 325
Tel: (+91 33) 660 26 01; 5    Fax: (+91 341) 20 85 30

### Key personnel
Chairman: Shri A K Mohapatra
Managing Director: R P Singh
Director, Engineering: I C Sinha

### Principal subsidiaries
Bharat Brakes & Valves Ltd
22 Gobra Road, Calcutta 700 014
Reyrolle Burn Ltd
99 Dr Abani Dutta Road, Howrah 711 101

### Products
Freight wagons.

## CAF

Construcciones y Auxiliar de Ferrocarriles SA
Padilla 17, E-28006 Madrid, Spain
Tel: (+34 91) 435 25 00    Fax: (+34 91) 576 62 63

### Key personnel
See entry in *Locomotives and powered/non-powered passenger vehicles* section.

### Products
Freight wagons. Designs according to UIC, AAR or individual specifications.

Contracts include 200 pocket wagons and 223 container wagons for Intercontainer and 53 hopper wagons for Israel.

## Callegari

José Callegari e Hijos
Rivadavia y Peru, 2800 Zarate, Prov Buenos Aires, Argentina
Tel: (+54 1) 328 22 88 00    Fax: (+54 1) 325 06 45

### Key personnel
President: Pablo A A Callegari
Director General: Clara Mandelli Vda de Callegari
Sales and Export Director: Eduardo Rivas

### Products
Freight wagons.

## Cattaneo

Ferriere Cattaneo SA
Via Ferriere 12, CH-6512 Giubiasco, Switzerland
Tel: (+41 91) 857 31 31    Fax: (+41 91) 857 69 55
e-mail: fcsa@ferrierecattaneo.ch

### Key personnel
Managing Director: Aleardo Cattaneo
Technical Director: Hans Tandetzki
Engineering Director: Erik Fregni

### Products
Freight wagons.

Product range includes the Mega Double-Waggon for the transport of intermodal loads up to 92 tonnes, such as two craneable 41-tonne semi-trailers (Jumbo and

## 592 MANUFACTURERS/Freight vehicles and equipment

*Cattaneo freight wagons for transport of 21 tonne ACTS containers* 0023856

Megatrailer types included) or four swapbodies or containers (Types 20, 30 and 40); freight wagons with rotating guideways for conveying three 21 tonne ACTS containers. Steel construction for railway bridges.

*UPDATED*

---

## CCC

Companhia Comércio e Construções
Av Rio Branco 156/22°, Salas 2234-5, Centro, Rio de Janeiro CEP 20043, Brazil
Tel: (+55 21) 282 13 43   Fax: (+55 21) 262 14 39

**Products**
Manufacture and repair of passenger cars and freight wagons. The company's two freight manufacturing plants, in Deodoro and Cruzeiro (São Paulo state), can produce 1,500 vehicles annually.

---

## CFC

Costruzioni Ferroviarie Colleferro SpA
A member of the Fiat Group
Via Sabotino, I-00034 Colleferro Rome, Italy
Tel: (+39 06) 978 12 80   Fax: (+39 06) 978 27 46

**Key personnel**
See entry in *Locomotives and powered/non-powered passenger vehicles* section.

**Products**
Freight wagons, refrigerated wagons with glass fibre-reinforced polyester resin bodies and refrigerated containers.

---

## China National Railway Locomotive and Rolling Stock Industry Corporation (LORIC)

10 Fuxing Road, Beijing 100844
China
Tel: (+86 10) 63 51 16 20; 77 66
Fax: (+86 10) 63 51 16 14; 63 26 08 30

**Works addresses**
Qiqihar Rolling Stock Group Company
10 Changqian Street, Zhonghua East Road, Qiqihar 161002, Heilongjiang
Tel: (+86 452) 293 84 72   Fax: (+86 452) 251 44 64
Zhuzhou Rolling Stock Works
Zhuzhou 412003, Hunan
Tel: (+86 733) 840 34 51   Fax: (+86 733) 840 31 34
Beijing February 7th Rolling Stock Works
1 Zhangguozhuang, Fengtai District, Beijing 100072
Tel: (+86 10) 83 87 77 72   Fax: (+86 10) 83 87 61 84
Dalian Locomotive & Rolling Stock Works
51 Zhingchang Street, Dalian 116022, Liaoning
Tel: (+86 411) 460 20 43   Fax: (+86 411) 460 64 47
Guiyang Rolling Stock Works
Dulaying, Baiyun District, Guiyang 550017, Guizhou
Tel: (+86 851) 447 04 93   Fax: (+86 851) 447 01 41
Harbin Rolling Stock Works
2 Gongmao Street, Daoli District, Harbin 150010, Heilongjiang
Tel: (+86 451) 421 47 86   Fax: (+86 451) 421 10 93
Jinan Locomotive & Rolling Stock Works
73 Huaichun Street, Huaiyin District, Jinan 250022, Shandong
Tel: (+86 531) 795 59 30   Fax: (+86 531) 795 75 48
Meishan Rolling Stock Works
Simeng, Meishan 612162, Sichuan
Tel: (+86 833) 850 21 96   Fax: (+86 833) 850 20 46
Qishuyan Locomotive & Rolling Stock Works
Qishuyan, Changzhou 213011, Jiangsu
Tel: (+86 519) 877 17 11   Fax: (+86 519) 877 03 58
Shenyang Locomotive & Rolling Stock Works
75 Kunshan West Road, Huanggu District, Shenyang 110035
Tel: (+86 24) 86 41 53 60   Fax: (+86 24) 86 40 87 30
Taiyuan Locomotive & Rolling Stock Works
84 Jiefang North Road, Taiyuan 030009, Shanxi
Tel: (+86 351) 795 59 30   Fax: (+86 531) 795 75 48
Tongling Rolling Stock Works
Shizishan District, Toling 244142, Anhui
Tel: (+86 562) 680 30 32   Fax: (+86 562) 680 33 44
Wuchang Rolling Stock Works
820 Heping Avenue, Wuchang District, Wuhan 430062, Hubei
Tel: (+86 27) 86 83 26 21   Fax: (+86 27) 86 81 10 17
Wuhan Jiang'an Rolling Stock Works
1378 Jiefang Avenue, Wuhan 430012, Hubei
Tel: (+86 27) 82 87 21 45   Fax: (+86 27) 82 88 79 32
Xi'an Rolling Stock Works
Sanqiao, Xi'an 710086, Shanxi
Tel: (+86 29) 451 24 07   Fax: (+86 29) 451 23 35

**Key personnel**
See entry in *Locomotives and powered/non-powered passenger vehicles* section.

**Products**
Development, design, sales, production, refurbishment, maintenance and after sales service for freight wagons including covered wagons, open-top wagons for coal, ore, steel and timber, hopper wagons for grain, ore, fertiliser, flat wagons, container flat wagons, depressed centre flat wagons, double-deck flat wagons, poultry wagons, tank wagons of all types, tipper wagons, mechanically refrigerated wagons, ice-cooled wagons, ballast wagons, guards vans, diesel cranes and hoists, refrigerated containers, tank containers and bulk cement containers.

LORIC has supplied 232,032 freight wagons over the period 1990 to 1999 for China Railways. Annual output is over 38,000 vehicles, most of them 1,435 mm gauge. Wagons in various track gauges have been supplied to Botswana, Thailand, Bangladesh, Malaysia, Myanmar, Tanzania, Zambia, Sri Lanka, Vietnam, Albania, Nigeria, Iran, Hong Kong, Australia and Cuba.

Recent deliveries include 80 wagons to Nigeria. 493 grain hopper wagons for Dalian and three container flats for Australia.

Recent contracts include 1,483 grain hoppers for Dalian, 66 open-top wagons for Zimbabwe, and 50 container flats and 44 grain hoppers for Australia.

---

## Cimmco International

A division of Cimmco Birla Ltd
D-180 Okhla Phase 1, New Delhi 110 020, India
Tel: (+91 11) 331 43 83; 84; 85
Fax: (+91 11) 332 07 77; 372 35 20

**Main works**
Wagon Division, Bharatpur 321 001, Rajasthan, India

**Key personnel**
Chairman: S Birla
President: R Upadhaya
General Manager: M P Gupta
Marketing Manager: G Sodhi

**Products**
Design and manufacture of freight wagons. The company manufactures wagons to meet special material handling applications and has supplied over 30,000 wagons in India and abroad. The range includes: covered wagons, bottom and side discharge wagons; tank wagons with heating arrangements for transport of all types of liquid.

*UPDATED*

---

## Cometal

Cometal-Mometal Sarl
PO Box 1401, Maputo, Mozambique
Tel: (+258 1) 75 21 24; 5; 6; 7; 8

**Key personnel**
General Director: Ldos A Kanji Simão

**Products**
Freight wagons; baggage vans; inspection cars; harbour and overhead cranes.

*Model D18A depressed centre wagon by LORIC* 2001/0099148

## Cometarsa

Cometarsa SAIC
LN Alem 1067, Piso 24, 1001 Buenos Aires, Argentina
Tel: (+54 1) 313 89 68

**Products**
Freight wagons.

---

## Costaferroviaria

Costaferroviaria SpA
Viale 4 Novembre, I-22041 Costamasnaga, Como, Italy
Tel: (+39 031) 86 94 11   Fax: (+39 031) 85 53 30

**Key personnel**
See entry in *Locomotives and powered/non-powered passenger vehicles* section.

**Products**
Freight wagons.
Recent orders include 520 BA655/656 23.5 tonne/axle bogies and 400 BD682/683 22.5 tonne/axle bogies and 200 Shimmns wagons for DB Cargo, 475 car transport wagons for STVA and 52 hoppers and 108 flat wagons for Spanish infrastructure operator GIF.

**UPDATED**

---

## Cromweld Steels

Cromweld Steels Ltd
The Old Vicarage, Tittensor, Stoke-on-Trent ST12 9HY, UK
Tel: (+44 1782) 37 41 39   Fax: (+44 1782) 37 33 88
e-mail: enquiries@cromweld.com
Web: http://www.cromweld.com

**Key personnel**
Contacts: Jacqueline Redman, Neil Cooper

**Subsidiary**
Cromweld Steels
PO Box 1500, Cornelius, North Carolina 28031, USA
Tel: (+1 704) 896 81 14   Fax: (+1 704) 896 81 15

**Products**
Supplier of 3CR12, a low-cost stainless steel for wagon construction. Typical applications include structural frames and subframes, flooring, walls and outer skinning/cladding, as well as applications for the construction of rail infrastructure.

**VERIFIED**

---

## Daewoo

Daewoo Heavy Industries Ltd
PO Box 7955, Daewoo Centre Building 22nd Floor, 541, 5-Ga, Namdaemun-Ro, Jung-gu, Seoul, South Korea
Tel: (+82 2) 726 31 79; 31 82
Fax: (+82 2) 726 31 86; 756 26 79

**Key personnel**
See entry in *Locomotives and powered/non-powered passenger vehicles* section.

**Products**
Freight wagons.
Daewoo has supplied more than 10,000 freight wagons to operators in over 30 countries.
Recent contracts include the supply of 117 container flat wagons and 24 ballast hopper wagons for Korean National Railroad.

---

## Dalian Locomotive and Rolling Stock Works

51 Zhong Chang Street, Dalian 116022, People's Republic of China
Tel: (+86 411) 419 93 86; 460 20 43
Fax: (+86 411) 460 30 64

**Key personnel**
See entry in *Locomotives and powered/non-powered passenger vehicles* section.

**Products**
Freight wagons, including Type C64 and C62B gondola wagons.
Recent contracts include the supply of 900 C64 and 100 C62B gondola wagons for Sino Railways Construction Development Centre, People's Republic of China.

---

## W H Davis Ltd

PO Box 3, Langwith Junction, Mansfield NG20 9SA, UK
Tel: (+44 1623) 74 26 21   Fax: (+44 1623) 74 44 74
e-mail: Maco.burg@whdavis.co.uk
Web: http://www.Whdavis.co.uk

**Key personnel**
Chairman: D Sharpe
Sales Director, Wagons: M S Burge
Managing Director: D G Bradley
Commercial Director and Company Secretary: G A Wardle
Sales Director, Containers: D G Bradley

**Products**
Freight wagons, containers and swapbodies.

**Contracts**
Contracts include the supply of rolling stock to Kenya Railways, Bardon London Ltd, Cleveland Potash, Marcon Topmix and Indonesia.

**VERIFIED**

---

## Dorsey

Dorsey Trailers, Inc
100 Paces West, Suite 1200, 2727 Paces Ferry Road, Atlanta, Georgia 30339, USA
Tel: (+1 404) 438 95 95   Fax: (+1 404) 438 81 90

**Key personnel**
President and Chief Executive Officer: Marilyn R Marks
Executive Vice-President, Sales: Hank Carter

**Products**
Trailers, piggyback trailers, platform trailers, reefers, dump, and drop-frame vans.

---

## Duro Daković

Railway Vehicles Factory Ltd
PO Box 94, 55102 Slavonski Brod, Croatia
Tel: (+385 55) 24 19 26; 23 21 89
Fax: (+385 55) 23 24 54

**Products**
Freight wagons.
Contracts include the supply of freight wagons to SLZ Ljubljana and HZ Zagreb.

---

## EKA

Valkyrie House, 38 Packhorse Road, Gerrards Cross SL9 8EB, UK
Tel: (+44 1753) 88 98 18   Fax: (+44 1753) 88 00 04

**Key personnel**
Managing Director: W O Forster
Sales Liaison Manager: J E Fadelle

**Products**
The EKA 'Stevedore' side-loading semi-trailer is ideally suited to handling ISO containers at lightly used road/rail transfer yards where the cost of expensive fixed gantries or heavy forklift trucks cannot be justified. There is also no need for separate vehicles for transporting containers by road. With the 'Stevedore', one man can collect a container at a transfer yard and deliver to a destination where it can be grounded for emptying or stacked for storage. Individually controlled hydraulic stabilisers ensure total stability and ease of levelling. There are versions for 20 and 40 ft long ISO containers weighing up to 28 tonnes.
EKA Simple Rail Transfer Equipment (SRTE), comprises a demountable sideloader which unloads 20 ft ISO containers/flatracks from rail wagons alongside. EKA has supplied 24 SRTE units to the Ministry of Defence, UK, and one Stevedore and one SRTE to the Ministry of Defence, Ireland.

---

## Energomachexport

25A Protopopovsky per, 129010 Moscow, Russian Federation
Tel: (+7 095) 288 84 56; 69 83
Fax: (+7 095) 288 79 90; 69 83
e-mail: in@eme.tsr.ru

**Key personnel**
See entry in *Bogies and suspensions, wheels and axles* section.

**Products**
Freight wagons. The range available includes four- and six-axle freight vehicles for 1,435, 1,520 and 1,676 mm gauges; box wagons, flat wagons for containers; open-top wagons; tank wagons; dumpers; and hopper wagons.

---

## Evans Deakin

Evans Deakin Industries Ltd
PO Box 866, South Brisbane, Queensland 4101, Australia
Tel: (+61 7) 38 40 22 22   Fax: (+61 7) 3840 48 50
e-mail: admin@ede.com.au

**Key personnel**
Evans Deakin Engineering Group General Manager: Robin Taylor
Evans Deakin Engineering (Manufacturing and Construction) General Manager: Mark Greene

*Costaferroviaria four-axle articulated car transporter for STVA*

## MANUFACTURERS/Freight vehicles and equipment

**Products**
Freight wagons.
Contracts include 350 coal freight wagons for Queensland Rail (February 1998).

---

### Ferrostaal AG

PO Box, Hohenzollernstrasse 24, D-45128 Essen, Germany
Tel: (+49 201) 818 01   Fax: (+49 201) 818 28 22

**Key personnel**
See entry in *Locomotives and powered/non-powered passenger vehicles* section.

**Products**
Freight wagons, including special designs; inspection and service trolleys for track and overhead maintenance and track installation; bogies for freight wagons, rail-mounted cranes and special trolleys; rolling stock components such as wheels, axles, assembled wheelsets, bearings, suspensions and couplers.

*UPDATED*

---

### Fiat

Fiat Ferroviaria SpA
Piazza Galateri 4, I-12038 Savigliano (CN), Italy
Tel: (+39 0172) 71 81 11   Fax: (+39 0172) 71 83 06
e-mail: public.relation@fiatferroviaria.it

**Key personnel**
See entry in *Locomotives and powered/non-powered passenger vehicles* section.

**Principal subsidiary companies**
Elettromeccanica Parizzi
FiatSig Schienenfahrzeuge AG®

**Corporate development**
In June 2000, Alstom Transport (qv) acquired a 51 per cent shareholding in Fiat Ferroviaria.

**Products**
Special freight wagons; bogies and components.

---

### Finsam

A/S Finsam International Inc
PO Box 3065 El, N-0207 Oslo 2, Norway
Tel: (+47) 22 44 18 60   Fax: (+47) 22 55 87 05

**Key personnel**
President: P R Samuelsen
Export Director: K E Jensen

**Products**
Refrigerated containers (20 and 40 ft ISO), insulated refrigerated swapbodies (lengths: 7.15, 7.43, 7.82 and 13.6 m; width 2.6 m), woodchip and reefer containers, refrigeration and heating systems.

---

### FIREMA Trasporti SpA

c/o I D P Milano Fiorenza, Via Triboniano, 220 I-20156, Milan, Italy
Tel: (+39 02) 23 02 02 23   Fax: (+39 02) 23 02 02 34
e-mail: firema.com@firema.it
Web: http://www.firema.it

**Key personnel**
See entry in *Locomotives and powered/non-powered passenger vehicles* section.

**Products**
Freight wagons. FIREMA has completed a prototype 'Twist Wagon', designed to simplify the loading and unloading of 'rolling highway' trains. The wagon deck pivots around its centre, and integral end ramps allow lorries to be driven on or off without the need for a special platform.
Recent orders include 110 Type VFaccs bogie hopper wagons, 20 Type DDm double-deck car-carrying wagons for Italian Railways (FS) and 100 bogie hopper wagons for DB Cargo.

*UPDATED*

---

### FM Industries

FM Industries
(a Division of Progress Rail Services)
8600 Will Rogers Blvd, Fort Worth, Texas 76140, USA
Tel: (+1 817) 293 42 20   Fax: (+1 817) 551 58 10

**Key personnel**
President: James Kingerski

**Parent company**
Progress Rail Services (qv)

**Products**
Hydraulic end-of-wagon cushioning devices.

---

### Freudenberg Schwab GmbH

Freudenberg Simrit KG
Höhnerweg 2-4, D-69465 Weinheim, Germany
Tel: (+49 1805) 74 67 48
e-mail: simrit.service@freudenberg.de
Web: http://www.simrit.de

**Key personnel**
See *Bogies and suspension, wheels and axles, bearings* section.

**Products**
Vibration control: rubber/metal elastic elements, standard as well as specially designed. Include resilient bushes, spherical bearings, buffers, conical mountings, V-mountings, machine mountings, rectangular mountings and hydraulic bushes.
Innovative products for vibration control include hydraulic mountings and bushes for speed-dependent stiffness, such as axle guide bearings for rail vehicles on tightly curved track, and systems for reduction of structure-borne noise such as equalisation of vibrations from wheel flats.

*UPDATED*

---

### Fuji Car

Fuji Car Manufacturing Co Ltd
3 Shoho Building, 2-2-3 Nishishinsaibashi, Chuo-ku, Osaka 542, Japan
Tel: (+81 6) 213 27 11   Fax: (+81 6) 213 40 71

**Key personnel**
See entry in *Locomotives and powered/non-powered passenger vehicles* section.

**Products**
Freight wagons, ladle wagons and bogies.

---

### Ganz Vagon Kft

Vajda Péter utca 12, H-1430 Budapest, Hungary
Tel: (+36 1) 210 11 77   Fax: (+36 1) 210 11 75
e-mail: vagon.board@ganz-holding.hu

**Key personnel**
See entry in *Locomotives and powered/non-powered passenger vehicles* section.

**Products**
Specialised freight wagons. Recent deliveries include 22 sliding wall wagons for Delacher & Co, Austria; 20 similar wagons for Györ-Sopron-Ebenfurt Railway (GySEV), Hungary; 30 Type Saadkms ROLA intermodal wagons for Hungarian State Railways (MÁV), manufactured under licence from Waggonfabrik Talbot of Germany; 82 coil transport wagons manufactured for Adtranz-Siegen, Germany with 200 more on order and 60 Type Shimms telescopic roof steel coil transport wagons for MÁV Hungary. Three twin-car covered car transport wagons have been delivered to Austria Car Rail Logistics of Austria, running under the GySEV branding.

---

### Goša

Goša Holding Corporation
Equipment and Vehicle Industries
Kolarčeva 8, 11000 Belgrade, Federal Republic of Yugoslavia
Tel: (+381 11) 63 36 50; 63 30 31
Fax: (+381 11) 63 45 31

**Products**
Tank wagons; refrigerated wagons and special purpose wagons.

---

### Graaff

Graaff Transportsysteme GmbH
Heinrich-Nagel Strasse 1, D-31008 Elze, Germany
Tel: (+49 5068) 182 15   Fax: (+49 5068) 182 81
e-mail: gts.vertrieb@t-online.de

**Key personnel**
Financial Director: Wolfgang Hassepass
Production Director: Günter Homes
Sales Director: Eberhard Miehlke

**Products**
Tank wagons for chemical products; container wagons; coil wagons; insulated and refrigerated wagons with shock-absorbing systems for load protection and electric heating and air ventilation; tarpaulin-covered wagons; 31 m car carriers; insulated and refrigerated containers (including advanced-design Volumax); box wagons; swapbody designs; specialised containers; sandwich panels.
Insulated customised sandwich panels and kits for truck bodies.

*VERIFIED*

---

### The Greenbrier Companies

One Centerpointe Drive, Suite 200, Lake Oswego, Oregon 97035, USA
Tel: (+1 503) 684 70 00   Fax: (+1 503) 684 75 53
Web: http://www.gbrx.com

**Key personnel**
Chairman of the Board: Alan James
President and Chief Executive Officer: William A Furman
Senior Vice-President, Marketing and Sales:
  Robin D Bisson
Senior Vice-President, Chief Financial Officer:
  Larry G Brady

**Worldwide offices**
**Greenbrier Europe Office**
Welterstrasser 60 D-57072, Siegen, Germany
Tel: (+49 271) 70 22 53   Fax: (+49 271) 741 28 94

**Greenbrier London Office**
Bonnie Gillespie Greenbrier Europe
25 Hasker Street, London SW3 2LE, UK
Tel: (+44 20) 75 84 18 98

**Corporate development**
Greenbrier manufactures freight wagons at Gunderson Inc (Portland, Oregon), TrentonWorks Ltd (Nova Scotia, Canada), WagonySwidnica (Poland), Gunderson-Concarril (Mexico) (all qv). In January 2000, Greenbrier acquired the German-based freight wagon manufacturing interests of Adtranz from DaimlerChrysler.
Greenbrier is also a leading provider of leasing and wagon fleet management services (see 'Greenbrier Leasing Corporation' entry in *Rolling stock leasing companies* section) and also provides wagon

Freight vehicles and equipment/**MANUFACTURERS** 595

maintenance, repair and overhaul services via its Gunderson Rail Services subsidiary (see entry in *Vehicle maintenance equipment and services* section).

## The Gregg Company

The Gregg Company Ltd
PO Box 430, 15 Dyatt Place, Hackensack, New Jersey 07602, USA
Tel: (+1 201) 489 24 40   Fax: (+1 201) 592 02 82

**Key personnel**
Chairman: R T Gregg

**Products**
Covered and open wagons, mineral wagons, refrigerator wagons, tank wagons, wagons for transport of road vehicles, container wagons, bulk powder wagons, flat wagons, ballast and aluminium wagons, conventional and self-steering bogies for freight and passenger vehicles.

## Gunderson

Gunderson Inc
A subsidiary of The Greenbrier Companies
4350 Northwest Front Avenue, Portland, Oregon 97210, USA
Tel: (+1 503) 972 57 00   Fax: (+1 503) 972 59 86

**Key personnel**
Chairman: C Bruce Ward
President: L Clark Wood
Chief Engineer: Gary S Kaleta

**Products**
Freight wagons. Conventional freight wagons include box cars, centre-partition lumber cars, flat cars and gondolas. Principal intermodal products are the Maxi-Stack III, the Husky-Stack family.

The Maxi-Stack III uses 125-short ton bogies and can handle 20, 24, 40, 45 or 48 ft containers in all wells, as well as any size container from 20 to 53 ft on the top level. The Husky-Stack is a stand-alone version of the double-stack wagon, designed for very heavy container loads up to 166,000 lb (75,300 kg).

Conventional car types include box car wagons for paper and wood industries, refrigerated wagons for frozen foods, gondolas, covered hopper wagons, woodchip wagons, flat wagons and other speciality cars. Gunderson also repairs and refurbishes freight wagons, wheels and axles.

Other wagon products include the heavy capacity Maxi-Stack® III double-stack wagon, Maxi-Stack® AP (all-purpose) double-stack wagon and the Auto-Max® high-capacity automobile carrier wagon

At its marine facility at the same location in Portland, Oregon, Gunderson builds ocean-going barges.

## Gunderson-Concarril

Gunderson-Concarril SA de CV
A subsidiary of The Greenbrier Companies Inc
Domicilio Conocido, Zona Industrial, Cd Sahagun, Edo de Hgo, CP 43990 Mexico

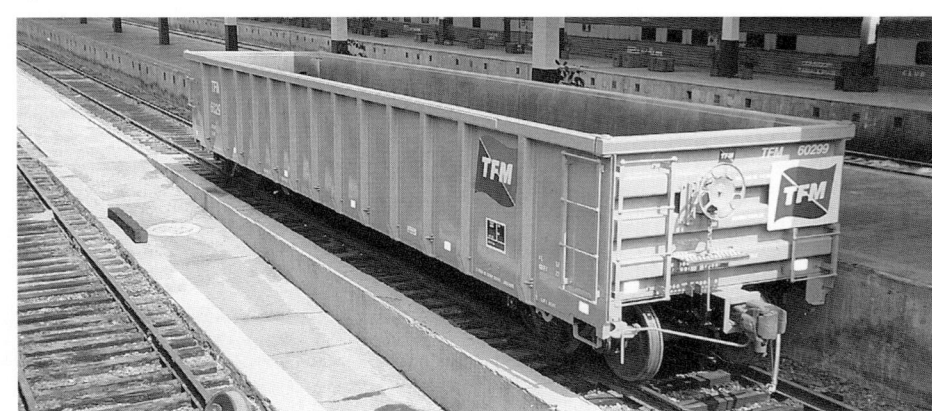

*Gunderson-Concarril mill gondola wagon*  0063721

*Hanjin bulk cement wagon*  0002425

**Mexico sales office**
Greenbrier de Mexico, S de RI de CV
Boulevard Manuel Avila Camacho, 340 Piso 11
Col Lomas de Chapultepec, Mexico, DF 11000
Tel: (+52 5) 202 49 25   Fax: (+52 5) 202 53 87

**Key personnel**
General Manager: Victor Silva

**Corporate development**
Gunderson-Concarril is a joint venture between The Greenbrier Companies and Bombardier Transportation.

**Products**
Freight wagons. Conventional freight wagons include box, flat and gondolas. Gunderson- Concarril's mill gondola car is designed, engineered and built to meet the demands of hauling heavy loads such as steel pipe and steel scrap. It features extra strong ends, covers, side posts, top chords, and steel decking. This car meets AAR specifications for construction and interchange requirements.

## Haacon

Haacon Hebetechnik GmbH
Josef Haaman Strasse 6, D-97896 Freudenberg/Main, Germany
Tel: (+49 9375) 840   Fax: (+49 9375) 84 66
e-mail: haacon@haacon.de
Web: http://www.haacon.de

**Key personnel**
Managing Director: Thomas Lotz
Export Sales Director: Stefan Schulz

**Products**
Winches for platforms of car-transporter wagons; container-handling equipment; jacks for shifting screens inside freight wagons.

*UPDATED*

## Hanjin

Hanjin Heavy Industries Co Ltd
118 Namdaemunro-2-Ga, Chung-ku, Seoul, South Korea
Tel: (+82 2) 728 54 41; 54 20
Fax: (+82 2) 755 09 28; 756 54 55

**Key personnel**
See entry in *Locomotives and powered/non-powered passenger vehicles* section.

**Products**
Freight wagons, including covered wagons, flat wagons, hopper wagons, gondola cars, ore wagons, box cars and tank wagons. Rolling stock components.

Contracts include 22 cement hopper wagons for Thailand in 1997. Deliveries overall have passed the 5,000 mark.

## HEI

Hindusthan Engineering & Industries Ltd
Mody Building, 27 Sir RN Mukherjee Road, Calcutta 700 001, India
Tel: (+91 33) 248 01 66
Fax: (+91 33) 248 19 22; 220 26 07
e-mail: hindus@cal2.vsnl.net.in

**Works**
Santragachi Plant (SP)
PO Box Jagacha 711 311, District Howrah, West Bengal, India

**Key personnel**
President, Engineering Unit: M L Lohia

**Products**
Freight wagons, including open wagons, covered wagons, tank wagons, intermodal wagons, special purpose wagons including container flat wagons and bottom discharge wagons for the transport of cement, coal and fertiliser.

*UPDATED*

## Holland Company LP

1000 Holland Drive, Crete, Illinois 60417-2120, USA
Tel: (+1 708) 672 23 00   Fax: (+1 708) 672 01 19
e-mail: postmaster@hollandco.com
Web: http://www.hollandco.com

**Key personnel**
See entry in *Permanent way components, equipment and services* section.

**Products**
Anti-wear components for wagons; product protection systems for steel coils and paper rolls, load securement

# MANUFACTURERS/Freight vehicles and equipment

systems for commercial and military vehicles; container securement locks for securing intermodal containers to rail wagons and for double-stacking, contract testing of sleeper/rail for rail roll-over and weak areas of track using Holland's Hi-Rail TrackSTAR vehicles.

*NEW ENTRY*

## Hoogovens

Hoogovens Large Extrusion Technology Unit
Friedrich-Wöhler-Strasse 2, D-53117 Bonn, Germany
Tel: (+49 228) 552 02    Fax: (+49 228) 552 22 68

**Key personnel**
See entry in *Locomotives and powered/non-powered passenger vehicles* section.

**Products**
Development and design of aluminium components for freight wagons (sliding sides, side traps, and so on), fabricated from extrusions, rolled sheets or castings as well as the calculation of these parts by means of the finite element method. Supply of bent, machined and/or welded extrusions.

## Hunslet-Barclay

Hunslet-Barclay Ltd
(Incorporating Hunslet Engine Co Ltd and Hunslet-Barclay Rail Ltd), Caledonia Works, West Langlands Street, Kilmarnock KA1 2QD, UK
Tel: (+44 1563) 52 35 73    Fax: (+44 1563) 54 10 76

**Key personnel**
See entry in *Locomotives and powered/non-powered passenger vehicles* section.

**Products**
Freight wagons, special purpose wagons, vehicle conversion.

**Contracts**
Contracts include the supply of ramped tracked tank transporter wagons to the UK Ministry of Defence and the conversion of 44 ex-British Rail Class 307 emu cars to Propelling Control Vehicles (PCVs) for English, Welsh and Scottish Railways Ltd.

*VERIFIED*

## Hyundai

Hyundai Precision & Ind Co Ltd
Hyundai Building, 140-2 Gye-Dong, Chongro-ku, Seoul, South Korea
Tel: (+82 2) 719 06 49    Fax: (+82 2) 719 07 41

**Key personnel**
See entry in *Locomotives and powered/non-powered passenger vehicles* section.

**Products**
General freight wagons; special freight wagons.

## INKA

PT (Persero) Industri Kereta Api (PT INKA)
Jalan Yos Sudarso No 71, Madiun 63122, Indonesia
Tel: (+62 351) 46 23; 46 24; 35 54
Fax: (+62 351) 28 92

**Key personnel**
See entry in *Locomotives and powered/non-powered passenger vehicles* section.

**Products**
Freight wagons. Up to 300 units are produced annually.
Indonesian Railways has taken delivery of 158 coal hopper wagons; 70 ballast hopper wagons have been ordered by State Railways of Thailand.

*INKA ballast hopper wagon for State Railways of Thailand*    0023860

## Intamodal-Eimar

Intamodal-Eimar SA
Poligono Industrial de Malpica 23, E-50057 Zaragoza, Spain
Tel: (+34 976) 57 32 68; 57 17 85
Fax: (+34 976) 57 31 40

**Key personnel**
Director: Angel Tutor

**Products**
Intermodal transport built to CSC, UIC and TIR specifications.

## Jenbacher

Jenbacher Energiesysteme AG
Achenseestrasse 1-3, A-6200 Jenbach, Austria
Tel: (+43 5244) 60 00    Fax: (+43 5244) 611 01
Web: http://www.jenbacher.com

**Key personnel**
See entry in *Locomotives and powered/non-powered passenger vehicles* section.

**Products**
Freight wagons. These include four- and two-axle Type Sgjns flat wagons for containers; Type Shimms four-axle hood wagons, with shock-absorbers; Type DDm four-axle double-deck car transporters (meets UIC 567-4); and the Type Uacs four-axle silo wagon for transporting powdery goods, with a compressed air discharge system.

*UPDATED*

## Jessop

Jessop & Company Ltd, Calcutta
63 Netaji Subhas Road, Calcutta 700 001, India
Tel: (+91 33) 243 20 41; 243 34 20
Fax: (+91 33) 243 16 10

**Key personnel**
See entry in *Locomotives and powered/non-powered passenger vehicles* section.

**Products**
Freight wagons, including tank wagons and covered wagons. Diesel breakdown cranes.

## Johnstown America Corporation

17 Johns Street, Johnstown, Pennsylvania 15901, USA
Tel: (+1 814) 533 50 00    Fax: (+1 814) 533 50 10
e-mail: ewhalen@jacorp.com
Web: http://www.johnstownamerica.com

**Key personnel**
Chairman, President and Chief Executive Officer:
    John E Caroll Jr
Vice-President, Marketing: Edward J Whalen
Vice-President, Engineering: James D Hart

**Background**
Johnstown America Corporation, a freight wagon builder, operates manufacturing facilities in Johnstown, Pennsylvania, and in Danville, Illinois. Its subsidiary, Chicago-based JAIX Leasing Company provides lease financing and rail wagon management for new and rebuilt wagons.

**Products**
Manufacture and repair of freight wagons, including open top aluminium gondola and hopper wagons used for the haulage of coal, spine wagons for intermodal traffic and steel and aluminium, open and covered hopper wagons used for the haulage of grain, fertiliser, iron ore, minerals and other bulk products.
Johnstown America Corporation has also introduced an aluminium vehicle carrier wagon used to haul automobile and small truck as well as a specialised spine wagon used to haul steel slabs and a transverse trough spine wagon used to haul steel coils.

*UPDATED*

*Johnstown America Corporation open top hopper wagon for hauling coal*    2002/0129561

Freight vehicles and equipment/**MANUFACTURERS** 597

## K & M

K & M Industrie Metalmeccaniche srl
Via Ugo La Malfa 6, I-90146 Palermo, Italy
Tel: (+39 091) 16 80 05 11   Fax: (+39 091) 16 80 05 16
e-mail: km@telegest.it

**Corporate background**
The company previously traded as Keller SpA.

**Products**
Freight wagons including high-capacity wagons; wagons with sliding doors; intermodal wagons; infrastructure maintenance vehicles.

---

## Kawasaki

Kawasaki Heavy Industries Ltd
World Trade Center Building, 4-1 Hamamatsu-cho 2-chome, Minato-ku, Tokyo 105, Japan
Tel: (+81 3) 34 35 25 88
Fax: (+81 3) 34 35 21 57; 34 36 30 37

**Key personnel**
See entry in *Locomotives and powered/non-powered passenger vehicles* section.

**Products**
Freight wagons.

*VERIFIED*

---

## Keller Elettromeccanica SpA

Zona Industriale I-09039, Villacidro, Cagliari, Italy
Tel: (+39 070) 933 62 02   Fax: (+39 070) 933 62 44
e-mail: info@keller.it
Web: http:/www.keller.it

**Key personnel**
See entry in *Locomotives and powered/non-powered passenger vehicles* section.

**Products**
Freight wagons including: Type Kgps platform wagons; Type Vfaccs hopper cars; Type Laadkks flat wagons; Type Tadgs hopper wagons; Type Habillss wagons with sliding light alloy walls.

*NEW ENTRY*

---

## Kinki Sharyo

The Kinki Sharyo Co Ltd
3-9-60 Inada-Shinmachi, Higashi-Osaka City, Osaka 577-8511, Japan
Tel: (+81 6) 67 46 52 40   Fax: (+81 6) 67 45 51 35
e-mail: KSRTAN@Kinsha.dp.u-netsurf.ne.jp
Web: http://www.kinkisharyo.co.jp

**Key personnel**
See entry in *Locomotives and powered/non-powered passenger vehicles* section.

**Products**
Refrigerator wagons; freight wagons; industrial wagons and equipment.

---

## Kockums

Kockums Industrier AB
S-205 55 Malmö, Sweden
Tel: (+46 40) 34 80 80   Fax: (+46 40) 34 87 75
e-mail: info.kiab@celsius.se

**Key personnel**
President: Thomas Abrahamsson
Senior Vice-President, Rolling Stock: Björn Widell
Senior Vice-President, Technical Department: Lars-Olof Nilsson
Senior Vice-President, Production: Lennart Ek

*Kockums 25 tonne bogie freight wagon*  0063722

**Corporate background**
Kockums Industrier is owned by the Celsius Group.

**Products**
Kockums has rebuilt a large number of goods wagons for Swedish State Railways. It has developed, designed and produced 72 heavy transport freight wagons equipped with Kockums own design Y25 TTV bogie for a 25 tonne axleload. An option exists for a further 60 wagons.

Other recent contracts include development/design and production of four service vehicles for Swedish National Rail Administration. An option exists for a further 26 vehicles.

---

## Kolmex

Kolmex SA
Grzybowska 80/82, PL-008-44 Warsaw, Poland
Tel: (+48 22) 661 50 00   Fax: (+48 22) 620 93 81
e-mail: kolmexsa@kolmex.com.pl
Web: http://www.komex.com.pl

**Key personnel**
See entry in *Locomotives and powered/non-powered passenger vehicles* section.

**Products**
Two- and four-axle covered wagons including wagons with sliding wall Hbbillns type; four-axle coal wagons; two- and four-axle tank wagons for transportation of liquids (including tank wagons with heating and insulation) and liquefied gas; special tank wagons for transportation of bulk materials; self-discharging wagons; four-axle hopper wagons for transportation of ballast during construction/repair of railway track; four- and six-axle hopper wagons for transportation of crushed materials; four-axle Talbot-type wagons for transportation of ore; flat wagons, two-, four- and six-axle; pocket and special wagons for combined transport (including two-, four- and six-axle articulated wagons for containers and removable tanks); multi-axle low-floor wagons; Shimms type wagons for transportation of sheets in coils; two-axle wagons for palletised loads; special wagons for transportation of ingots and heavy loads.

---

## K T Steel

K T Steel Industries Pvt, Ltd
9 Altamount Road, Bombay 400 026, India
Tel: (+91 22) 386 35 03; 386 04 34
Fax: (+91 22) 363 46 53

**Key personnel**
Chairman: T K Gupta
Executive Director: V R Gupta

**Products**
Rolling stock. In addition to supplying wagons for the home market, K T Steel Industries has built wagons for Iranian State Railways (400 ore wagons); South Korea (120 covered wagons); Sudan (120 covered wagons); and Sri Lanka. The company specialises in the manufacture of special purpose wagons including 21,000- and 40,000-litre milk tank wagons; and pressurised tank wagons.

---

## Kryukovsky

Kryukovsky Railway Car Building Works
139 I Pridhodko Street, Kremenchung 315307, Ukraine
Tel: (+38 5366) 695 05; 697 95; 611 01

*Kolmex Type Faccpps self-discharging ballast wagon*

# 598 MANUFACTURERS/Freight vehicles and equipment

*Bogie hopper wagon with 72 tonne capacity by Kryukovsky*    2000/0087656

*Open wagon with 70 tonne capacity by Kryukovsky*    2000/0087655

Fax: (+38 532) 50 14 21; (+38 5366) 611 01; (+38 44) 295 72 03
e-mail: root@kvsz.poltava.ua

**Products**
Vehicles for 1,435 and 1,520 mm gauge with a cargo capacity of up to 75 tonnes, including: open wagons; hopper wagons; tank wagons; flat wagons for intermodal traffic.

## Lyudinovo Locomotive Works JSC

1 K Liebknecht Street, Lyudinovo, Kaluga region 249400, Russian Federation
Tel: (+7 084 44) 201 20; 252 59
Fax: (+7 084 44) 201 20; 252 59

**Key personnel**
See entry in *Locomotives and powered/non-powered passenger vehicles* section.

**Products**
Tank wagons.

## Manoir Industries

Sambre et Meuse
Railway Division
PO Box 2, rue des Usines, F-59750, Feignies, France
Tel: (+33 3) 21 69 68 82    Fax: (+33 3) 27 69 69 89

**Key personnel**
Managing Director: Daniel Pain
Sales and Marketing Manager: Jean Jomeau

**Products**
RailTrailer bimodal system. The RailTrailer has been designed to be as close to a standard trailer as possible with a profile which can fit in the A loading gauge. The bogie/trailer interface allows for independent roll and pitch movement of two consecutive trailers which reduces the stress on each trailer. Various body versions are available: the prototype is a curtain-sided trailer and other versions under design include a flat bed for containers, plywood or rigid steel walls; refrigerated and a tank configuration.

## Marcroft Engineering Ltd

350 Bournville Lane, Birmingham B30 1QZ, UK
Tel: (+44 121) 475 51 51    Fax: (+44 121) 477 82 86
e-mail: sales@marcroft.co.uk
Web: http://www.marcroft.co.uk

**Key personnel**
Managing Director: Roger Crutchley
Sales and Marketing Director: Byron Murray

**Corporate background**
Marcroft Engineering is part of the European Rail Division of Brambles Industries Ltd.

**Products**
Manufacture, conversion, maintenance and refurbishment of all types of freight wagons.
Recent contracts include orders for 50 102 tonne bogie box wagons for Nacco UK Limited, which leases the vehicles to Mendip Rail Limited (qv). These are the first wagons in the UK to be equipped with TF25 'Track Friendly' bogies.

## Marrel

Division of Bennes Marrel
PO Box 56, F-42161 Andrezieux-Boutheon Cedex, France
Tel: (+33 4) 77 36 29 29    Fax: (+33 4) 77 36 29 19

**Key personnel**
Chairman and Chief Executive Officer: Guy de Narbone
Executive Vice-President: Pierre Faurot
Sales Manager: Emmanuel de Laage de Neux

**Products**
Ampliroll load transfer system. Introduced in 1992, allows containers 5.7 to 7.3 m in length to be transferred from rail to road and vice versa by handling equipment on the road vehicle which is operated by the driver. The system dispenses with the need for independent transfer machines and employs special flat wagons with rotating guideways.

## MÁV

MÁV Debreceni Jármüjavtó kft
Faraktár út 67, H-4034 Debrecen, Hungary
Tel: (+36 52) 34 68 00    Fax: (+36 52) 31 47 25

**Key personnel**
Managing Director: Imre Kerékgyártó

**Associate company**
Dunakeszi Wagon Building & Repair Works
See Adtranz, *Locomotives and powered/non-powered passenger vehicles* section.

**Products**
Freight wagons including 10-axle low-floor large goods vehicle (LGV) carrier and tank wagons.

*MÁV container wagon*    0002427

## Mecanoexportimport

30 Dacia Boulevard, Bucharest, Romania
Tel: (+40 1) 211 98 55    Fax: (+40 1) 210 78 94

**Key personnel**
See entry in *Locomotives and powered/non-powered passenger vehicles* section.

**Products**
Freight wagons, including flat wagons; hopper wagons; covered wagons; tank wagons; and special purpose wagons.

## Meva

SC Meva SA
A Trinity Industries Inc company
3 Dunării Boulevard, 1500 Drobeta Turnu Severin, Romania
Tel: (+40 52) 31 24 14    Fax: (+40 52) 31 51 39
e-mail: meva@expert.ro

**Key personnel**
General Director: Fulger Popescu
Technical Director: Constantin Popescu
Sales and Marketing Director: Gheorghe Pănescu
Head of Export Department: Ionel Mihart

**Products**
Freight wagons. These include two- and four-axle wagons for general applications and tank wagons for oil, chemical and gas transport.
Recent contracts include supply of new and refurbished tank wagons to KVG Germany.

## More Wear Industries

PO Box 2199, 5510 Harare, Zimbabwe
Tel: (+263 4) 62 17 31   Fax: (+263 4) 62 17 37
e-mail: apexcorp@primenetzw.com
Web: http://www.apex.co.zw

**Key personnel**
Chief Executive: R T Nyatsoka
Marketing and Sales Executive: Jonas S Zvemhara

**Products**
Freight wagons, high-sided wagons, tankers, flat-deck container wagons, box wagons, Gloucester-rubber suspension bogies, ride control bogies and railway spares.

## National Steel Car Ltd

PO Box 2450, Hamilton, Ontario L8N 3J4, Canada
Tel: (+1 905) 544 33 11   Fax: (+1 905) 547 40 69
e-mail: alwilson@steelcar.com
Web: http://www.steelcar.com

**Key personnel**
Chairman and Chief Executive Officer: G Aziz
Chief Operating Officer: D Elliott
Executive Vice-President, Marketing and Sales: A Wilson

**Products**
Freight wagons; industrial and mining wagons.

**Contracts**
Recent contracts include the supply of covered hopper wagons for the transport of grain, plastic pellets and potash; centre-beam flat wagons for packaged timber; coil wagons; 53 ft double-stack wells; 60 ft high-cube boxcars; 360 ton heavy duty flat wagons.

*UPDATED*

## Nippon Sharyo

Nippon Sharyo Ltd
Riverside Yomiuri Building, 11th Floor, 36-2 Nihombashi-Hakozaki-cho, Chuo-ku, Tokyo 103-0015, Japan
Tel: (+81 3) 36 68 33 30   Fax: (+81 3) 36 69 02 38

**Key personnel**
See entry in *Locomotives and powered/non-powered passenger vehicles* section.

**Products**
Freight wagons of all types including tank wagons, international and domestic containers and intermodal wagons, heavy-duty carriers and pressure vessels.

*VERIFIED*

## OFV

Officine Ferroviarie Veronesi SpA
Lungadige A Galtarossa 21, I-37133 Verona, Italy
Tel: (+39 045) 806 41 11   Fax: (+39 045) 803 28 76

*National Steel Car covered coil-steel gondola freight wagon*   0063723

**Key personnel**
See entry in *Locomotives and powered/non-powered passenger vehicles* section.

**Products**
Freight wagons.

## Oleo International Ltd

Grovelands, Longford Road, Exhall, Coventry CV7 9NE, UK
Tel: (+44 2476) 64 55 55   Fax: (+44 2476) 36 42 87

**Key personnel**
Managing Director: S B Gelderd
Commercial Director: C C Brown

**Products**
Freight vehicle cushioning units including gas-hydraulic units and polymer; also draw gears. For specialist applications Long Stroke units in wagon chassis. Oleo is IS9001 and ISO14001 accredited.

*UPDATED*

## Orval

Ateliers d'Orval SA
PO Box 64, route de l'Ombrée, F-18202 Saint-Amand-Montrond Cedex, France
Tel: (+33 2) 48 96 07 39   Fax: (+33 2) 48 96 50 97

**Key personnel**
General Manager: Yves Jesset

**Products**
Freight wagons of all types, mobile brake testing equipment.

## Pakistan Railways Carriage Factory

Sector I-11, Khayaban-e-Sir Syed, Islamabad, Pakistan
Tel: (+92 51) 86 02 53; 86 03 49   Fax: (+92 51) 86 15 50

**Key personnel**
See entry in *Locomotives and powered/non-powered passenger vehicles* section.

**Products**
Freight wagons for any gauge.
Contracts include 34 wagons each with a capacity of 67.1 tonnes for Bangladesh.

## PEC

PEC Ltd
A Government of India enterprise
Hansalaya, 15 Barakhamba Road, New Delhi 110 001, India
Tel: (+91 11) 331 63 72; 36 19; 55 08; 33 51; 47 23
Fax: (+91 11) 331 52 79; 36 64
e-mail: burman@peclimited.com

**Key personnel**
See entry in *Locomotives and powered/non-powered passenger vehicles* section.

**Products**
Freight wagons for various gauges; spares. PEC has exported over 9,300 wagons to various countries such as Uganda, Tanzania, Zambia, Hungary, Sri Lanka, Myanmar, Bangladesh, South Korea, Malaysia, Nigeria, Poland, Sudan, Iran, Yugoslavia and Vietnam.

*UPDATED*

## Portec

Portec Rail Products Inc
Shipping Systems Division
122 West 22nd Street, Oak Brook, Illinois 60523, USA
Tel: (+1 630) 573 47 87   Fax: (+1 630) 573 46 59

**Key personnel**
President and General Manager: L J Sieja
Vice-President, Engineering: Richard A Tatina
Sales and Marketing Manager: Clayton S Baker

**Products**
Wagon tie-down systems and intermodal and freight wagon components; standard COFC container pedestals with optional positive locks for transport of hazardous materials; special container locks and pedestals for TOFC/COFC skeleton (spine) rail wagons; portable and permanent bridge plates for TOFC and auto racks; winches, chain, cable and webbing tie-down components for flat wagons and autoracks; securing system for paper rolls.

## Price

A & G Price
Division of CPD Engineering Ltd
Private Bag, Thames, New Zealand
Tel: (+64 7) 868 60 60   Fax: (+64 9) 309 28 19
e-mail: contracts@agprice.co.nz

**Key personnel**
See entry in *Locomotives and powered/non-powered passenger vehicles* section.

**Products**
Freight wagon manufacture, modification and repair, supply of components, points and crossings.

## Procor Ltd

2001 Speers Road, Oakville, Ontario L6J 5E1, Canada
Tel: (+1 905) 827 41 11   Fax: (+1 905) 827 09 13
Web: http://www.procor.com

**Key personnel**
President: Ronald W Wayne
Vice-President, Marketing and Sales: Roger Tipple
Vice-President, Operations: M C Parker
Director of Engineering: J S McKechnie
Fleet Manager: N Dachuk
Director of Marketing: Roger Tipple
Manager, Business Development: Scott Whale
Manager, Communications: Y Amor

**Corporate background**
Procor is a member of the Marmon Group.

**Products**
Tank and special-purpose freight wagons.
Procor designs and manufactures tank wagons and freight wagons for a great variety of products, for lease to shippers in Canada. The company operates and maintains the largest (over 22,000 vehicles) fleet of privately owned freight and tank wagons in Canada.

*UPDATED*

# MANUFACTURERS/Freight vehicles and equipment

## Progress Rail Services

Progress Rail Services Corporation (Mechanical Group)
1600 Progress Drive, PO Box 1037, Albertville, Alabama 35950, USA
Tel: (+1 256) 593 12 60   Fax: (+1 256) 593 12 49

**Key personnel**
Senior Vice-President: Jackie Nesmith
Senior Vice-President, Sales: James W Kingerski

**Subsidiary companies/divisions**
FM Industries (manufacturer of railcar cushioning devices)
Progress Vanguard Corporation (axles)
Railcar Repair Division (wagon repairs)
Wheel Shop Division (wheel reconditioning)
Parts Division (bolsters, sideframes, air cylinders)
Locomotive and Transit Products Division (axles, traction motors, wheelsets)

**Products**
Reconditioned and new wagon parts including wheels, axles, bolsters and bogie sideframes; hydraulic cushioning units, wagon and locomotive repair facilities. Also wagon and locomotive leasing.

*UPDATED*

## Qiqihar

Qiqihar Rolling Stock (Group) Co Ltd
10 Zhonghua East Road, Qiqihar Heilongjiang 161002, People's Republic of China
Tel: (+86 452) 293 91 58   Fax: (+86 452) 251 44 64
e-mail: qrswceo@public.qq.hl.cn
Web: http://www.qrrs.com

**Key personnel**
Chairman of Board of Directors: He Dianchen
General Manager: Liu Hualong
Chief Engineer: Xu Guoming
Sales and Marketing: Liu Dezeng

**Products**
Freight wagons, including P64, Type P64A and P65 covered wagons, Type D38 380-ton special heavy duty wagons, Type C35 grain hoppers and Type C3 container flats for Austalia. Diesel-hydraulic rail-mounted cranes (15, 63, 125 and 160 short tons).
Equipped with rotary couplers and high-capacity draftgear, the Type C63A open wagon is designed for the transport of coal in unit train service.

*UPDATED*

## Qishuyan

Qishuyan Locomotive and Rolling Stock Works
Qishuyan, Changzhou City, Jiangsu Province, People's Republic of China
Tel: (+86 519) 877 17 11   Fax: (+86 519) 877 03 58

**Key personnel**
See entry in *Locomotives and powered/non-powered passenger vehicles* section.

**Products**
Freight wagons and components.

## Reggiane

Officine Meccaniche Italiano SpA
PO Box 431, 27 Via Vasco Agosti, I-42100 Reggio Emilia, Italy
Tel: (+39 0522) 58 81   Fax: (+39 0522) 58 82 43

**Key personnel**
See entry in *Locomotives and powered/non-powered passenger vehicles* section.

**Products**
Freight wagons; rolling stock components.
Capabilities include: construction of special wagons and crane equipment for railborne vehicles and manufacture of machines for removal and laying of track.

## Rolanfer

Rolanfer Matériel Ferroviaire SA
72 route de Thionville, PO Box 629, F-57146 Woippy, Cedex, France
Tel: (+33 3) 87 30 14 85   Fax: (+33 3) 87 31 23 05
e-mail: rolanfer-materiel.ferroviaire@wanadoo.fr

**Key personnel**
Chairman: Y Henry
General Manager: Jean-Claude Schmitz
Export Sales and Marketing Manager: Laurence Courvalet

**Subsidiary**
Rolanfer Deutschland GmbH
Carl-Diem Strasse 11, D-41065 Mönchengladbach, Germany
Tel: (+49 2161) 17 85 05   Fax: (+49 2161) 17 85 05

**Products**
Design and construction of freight wagons.
Construction of six-axle flat wagons for steel industry customers for the transport of heavy and hot products.

*UPDATED*

## Rotem Company

231 Yangjae-Dong, Soecho-ku, Seoul, Korea 137-938
Tel: (+82 2) 34 64 46 45   Fax: (+82 2) 34 64 47 92
Web: http://www.rotem.co.kr

**Key personnel**
See entries in *Locomotives and powered/non-powered passenger vehicles* section.

**Background**
See entry in *Locomotives and powered/non-powered passenger vehicles* section.

**Products**
Rotem manufactures gondola cars, box cars, ore wagons, petroleum tank wagons, ballast hoppers, refrigerated wagons, high-pressure gas containers for ammonia and polypropylene and other specially designed vehicles, including double-deck car-carriers.

*UPDATED*

## RSD

Rolling Stock Division
PO Box 229, Boksburg East 1460, Transvaal, South Africa
Tel: (+27 11) 914 14 00   Fax: (+27 11) 914 38 85
Web: http://www.de.dorbyl.com/rsd

**Key personnel**
See entry in *Locomotives and powered/non-powered passenger vehicles* section.

**Background**
A division of Dorbyl Ltd.

**Products**
Freight wagons, tank wagons including dry bulk and LPG tank wagons.
Contracts include 100 covered wagons for Ghana Railway Corporation and two LPG tank wagons for Hydro-Congo, Brazzaville, Congo.

*UPDATED*

## SABB

SABB SA
Av Bautista Buriasco s/n, 2445 Maria Juana, Santa Fé, Argentina
Tel: (+54 42) 912 14   Fax: (+54 42) 916 82

**Products**
Freight wagons; welded steel bogies.

## Santa Matilde

Cia Industrial Santa Matilde
Rua Frei Caneca 784, São Paulo – SP, CEP 01307-000, Brazil
Tel: (+55 11) 852 24 76   Fax: (+55 11) 30 61 99 15

**Key personnel**
See entry in *Locomotives and powered/non-powered passenger vehicles* section.

**Products**
Freight wagons; bogies.
330 wagons for CVRD were delivered in 1997.

## SCIF

Société Cherifienne du Matériel Industriel et Ferroviaire
PO Box 2604, Allée des Cactus, Aïn-es-Sebaa, Casablanca, Morocco
Tel: (+212 27) 35 39 11   Fax: (+212 27) 35 09 60

**Key personnel**
See entry in *Locomotives and powered/non-powered passenger vehicles* section.

**Products**
Freight wagons.

## SEEC

SEEC Inc
Airport Business Plaza, 1408 Northland Drive, Suite 301, Mendota Heights, Minnesota 55120, USA
Tel: (+1 651) 681 80 00   Fax: (+1 651) 681 84 00
e-mail: seeccic@aol.com
Web: http://www.seec-cic.com

**Key personnel**
Chief Executive Officer and President: Stewart Erickson
Vice-President, Sales and Marketing: Dick Sommerstad

*SEEC's design of full-bottom discharge containers incorporates side-mounted quick-release latches permitting rapid emptying*   0063726

# Freight vehicles and equipment/MANUFACTURERS

**Products**
Reusable full-bottom containers, from 20 to 350 cu ft and with capacities up to 56,000 lbs. The containers are made from high-strength coated fabrics with rubber. The containers are designed for easy repair and can be used up to 2,000 times.

## Ray Smith Group plc

Fengate, Peterborough, PE1 5XG, UK
Tel: (+44 1733) 639 36   Fax: (+44 1733) 34 70 90

**Key personnel**
Group Sales and Joint Managing Director: D Browning

**Products**
Demountable systems for all weights of chassis. Ground loader bodies for police, fire and MoD requirements. Cantilever tail-lifts from 500 to 3,000 kg capacity.

*UPDATED*

## Soma

Soma Equipamentos Industries SA
Parque Industrial Mariano Ferraz, Avenida Soma 700, Sumaré, São Paulo, Brazil
Tel: (+55 11) 73 10 00   Fax: (+55 11) 73 24 72

**Products**
Freight wagons; tank wagons; refrigerator wagons; ore wagons; ingot wagons; hopper wagons; car building, repairing, maintenance and leasing.

## Société Générale Egyptienne de Matériel des Chemins de Fer (SEMAF)

PO Box, Cairo, Egypt
Tel: (+20 2) 556 21 77; 555 00 37
Fax: (+20 2) 556 40 96; 555 00 37

**Key personnel**
See entry in *Locomotives and powered/non-powered passenger vehicles* section.

**Products**
Freight wagons.

*UPDATED*

## Stag AG

Industriestrasse, CH-7304 Maienfeld, Switzerland
Tel: (+41 81) 303 58 00   Fax: (+41 81) 303 58 99
e-mail: mail@stagltd.com
Web: http://www.stagltd.com

**Key personnel**
Managing Director: Christian Gloor
Sales and Marketing: Christian Gloor, Josef Doller

**Principal subsidiaries**
Stag GmbH
D-66740 Saarlouis, Germany
Stag France
F-67320 Drulingen, France

**Products**
Bulk transport wagons with pneumatic discharge and unloading equipment and components.
Contracts include supply of 180 wagons for China, 75 wagons for SBB, Switzerland and 140 wagons for TPI Bangkok, Thailand.

*VERIFIED*

## Strick

Strick Corporation
225 Lincoln Highway, Fairless Hills, Pennsylvania 19030, USA
Tel: (+1 215) 949 36 00   Fax: (+1 215) 949 47 78

**Key personnel**
President, Manufacture: Frank Katz
President, Intermodal Leasing: Charles Willmott

**Products**
Dry freight containers, piggyback trailers and container chassis.

## Tafesa

Tafesa SA
Carretera de Andalucía Km 9, E-28021 Madrid, Spain
Tel: (+34 91) 798 05 50   Fax: (+34 91) 798 09 61

**Key personnel**
See entry in *Locomotives and powered/non-powered passenger vehicles* section.

**Products**
All types of freight rolling stock; special containers; bogies; covered wagons; car transporter wagons; dual-purpose container wagons; piggyback wagons; air discharge cement wagons; ventilated wagons with sliding doors; power line masts; vans.

## Tatravagónka

Tatravagónka AS
Štefánikova 887/53, SK-058 01 Poprad, Slovakia
Tel: (+421 52) 72 32 75   Fax: (+421 52) 72 17 32
e-mail: market@vapop.sk

**Key personnel**
Managing Director: František Králik
Commercial Director: Mikuláš Bobák
Sales Director: Rudolf Fabian

**Products**
Freight wagons, including open, covered, tank, bulk powder, hopper, intermodal, car transporters, coil steel and specialised types including ladle wagons for transporting molten metal.
Contracts in 1997 include 370 four-axle frames with bogies for Habinss wagons and 199 frames with running gear for DWA Niesky Germany; 47 Zacns four-axle tank wagons for EVA Düsseldorf and 75 for VTG, Hamburg; 388 four-axle high-sided open Eanoos wagons for AAE Zug, Switzerland; 80 for ZSR Slovakia with a further 22 four-axle Sdgnss wagons for ZSR and 105 four-axle container flat wagons for ACTS Utrecht, Netherlands.

*UPDATED*

## Texmaco Ltd

6th Floor, Birla Building, 9/1 RN Mukherjee Road, Calcutta 700 001, India
Tel: (+91 33) 22 04 383; 248 01 35
Fax: (+91 33) 220 58 33
e-mail: texmaco@cal.vsnl.net.in

**Main works**
Belgahria, Calcutta 700 056, India
Tel: (+91 33) 539 16 82; 31
Fax: (+91 33) 539 24 52; 26
e-mail: texmaco@cal.vsnl.net.in

**Key personnel**
President: R Maheshwari
Vice-Presidents: S K Agrawal, R C Chopra
Vice-President, Marketing: A K Sinha

**Products**
Freight wagons, bogies and couplers. Also railway points and crossings.

## Thrall

Thrall Car Manufacturing Co
2521 State Street, Chicago Heights, Illinois 60411, USA
Tel: (+1 708) 757 23 14   Fax: (+1 708) 757 41 12

**Key personnel**
Vice-Chairman: Michael E Flannery
Vice-President, Marketing: Chris Schmalbruch

*Thrall International EuroSpine®*

## 602 MANUFACTURERS/Freight vehicles and equipment

Vice-President, International Markets:
 Charles Magolske
Vice-President, Automotive Products: Robert Ortner
Thrall Europa GmbH
Brunngasse 4, CH-8400 Winterthur, Switzerland
Tel: (+41 52) 269 32 42  Fax: (+41 52) 269 32 43
Vice-President, Marketing and Sales – Europe:
 Albert Hartmann

**Works**
Chicago Heights, Harvey, and Clinton, Illinois
Cartersville and Winder, Georgia
York, UK

**Principal subsidiaries**
Thrall North American Rail Car
Thrall Europa/Service Parts
Thrall Rail Project sro
Thrall Vagónka Studénka as
Solimar Pneumatics

**Corporate development**
A wagon building facility opened in 1998 at the former rail vehicle manufacturing plant at York, UK, for the supply of wagons to English, Welsh and Scottish Railways.

In August 1999, Thrall acquired the Slovakian design and engineering company Rail Project, which specialises in bogies and freight wagon components. In March 2000, the company acquired ČKD Vagónka Studénka (formerly MSV) in the Czech Republic and in September of the same year established European headquarters at Winterthur, Switzerland.

**Products**
Thrall designs and manufactures a wide variety of freight wagons, leases equipment and supplies parts for freight wagons. It operates six manufacturing facilities in Europe and the USA.

The EuroSpine® wagon by Thrall International is designed to bring the advantages of pocket wagon operation to the UK. It consists of an articulated four-segment wagon on five two-axle bogies. Trailers and containers can be loaded or off-loaded on average in 2 minutes.

---

## TrentonWorks Ltd

A subsidiary of the Greenbrier Companies Inc
PO Box 130, Trenton, Nova Scotia B0K 1X0, Canada
Tel: (+1 902) 752 15 41  Fax: (+1 902) 755 32 44

**Key personnel**
President: Richard McKay
Engineering Manager: Glenn MacDonald

**Products**
Freight wagons, including box cars for paper and wood, centre partition lumber cars, flat wagons and gondolas.

Conventional wagon types include refrigerated wagons, covered hopper wagons, woodchip wagons, flat wagons and other speciality wagons.

Trenton builds a 27 m intermodal flat wagon in 70 and 100 tonne configurations for auto-rack service according to TTX Company's specification.

---

## Trinity Difco

Trinity Difco Inc
2525 Stemmons Freeway, PO Box 568887, Dallas, Texas 75356-8887, USA
Tel: (+1 214) 631 44 20  Fax: (+1 214) 589 81 71

**Main works**
Bessemer, Alabama

*TrentonWorks 27 m flat wagon* 0063728

*23,000 gallon capacity tank wagon by Union Tank Car for general-purpose service* 0002430

Greenville, Pennsylvania
Mount Orab, Ohio
Oklahoma City and Tulsa, Oklahoma
Beaumont, Dallas, Fort Worth and Longview, Texas

**Key personnel**
President and Chief Executive Officer: W Ray Wallace
Senior Vice-President and Chairman, Railcar Division:
 Tim Wallace
Vice-President, Freight Car Sales and Marketing:
 Duncan Gillies
General Manager, Freight Car Sales: Clay Howard
Vice-President, Tank Car Sales: Tim Schitter
Director, Sales and Marketing: Robert J Ward

**Corporate development**
In 1997, former freight wagon manufacturer Difco merged with Trinity Industries to become Trinity Difco.

**Products**
Freight wagons, including covered hoppers for transporting grain, cement, plastic pellets and chemicals; pressure discharge wagons for transporting dry free-flowing materials; intermodal wagons including spine wagons and well wagons for transporting trailers or double-stack containers; steel and aluminium gondolas for transporting coal, ore, forest products, steel products or scrap; open hoppers including steel or aluminium conventional and rapid discharge wagons for coal, aggregates, woodchips and ore; covered wagons, including insulated wagons constructed from composite materials; tank wagons for chemicals, corn syrup, clay slurry, liquid gases, crude oil and alcohol.

Trinity Industries also has a repair and parts division based in Asheville, North Carolina, specialising in rebody kits and replacement parts for freight wagons.

---

## Tuchschmid AG

Kehlhofstrasse 54, CH-8501 Frauenfeld, Switzerland
Tel: (+41 52) 728 81 11  Fax: (+41 52) 728 81 00
e-mail: info@tuchschmid.ch
Web: http://www.tuchschmid.ch

**Key personnel**
Manager: Richard Nägeli
Manager, Intermodal Transport Systems: Daniel Erni
Manager, High Rack Storage: Urs Kern

**Products**
ACTS system of container transfer, developed in conjunction with Swiss Federal Railways and road hauliers. The system dispenses with independent transfer machines and enables the driver of a road vehicle to achieve a road-rail transfer or vice-versa on his own. The system employs special flat wagons equipped with rotating guideways and road chassis equipped with a tilting frame and chain mechanism to slide the containers on and off the wagons.

Rotating guideways in various configurations to suit customers' needs including 16.5 tonnes for old-type flat wagons and 21/30 tonnes for new-type flat wagons.

***VERIFIED***

---

## Tülomsas

The Locomotive and Motor Corporation of Turkey
Ahmet Kanatli Cad, TR-26490 Eskisehir, Turkey
Tel: (+90 222) 224 00 00  Fax: (+90 222) 225 72 72
e-mail: tulomsas@tulomsas.com.tr
Web: http://www.tulomsas.com.tr

**Key personnel**
See entry in *Locomotives and powered/non-powered passenger vehicles* section.

**Products**
Special-purpose freight wagons including tank wagons, refrigerated hopper wagons and wagons for the transport of ore, tracked tanks and containers.

---

## Union Tank

Union Tank Car Co
A member of The Marmon Group of companies
175 West Jackson Boulevard, Chicago, Illinois 60604, USA
Tel: (+1 312) 431 31 11  Fax: (+1 312) 431 50 03

**Key personnel**
President: Frank D Lester
Senior Vice-President, Marketing and Sales:
 William L Snelgrove
Senior Vice-President and Controller: Mark J Garrette
Operations: Louis A Kulekowskis
Vice-President, Fleet Management:
 Wiliam R Constantino

**Products**
Steel, stainless steel and aluminium tank wagons for liquids and compressed gases; covered hopper wagons for plastic pellets and resins.

***UPDATED***

## United Goninan

PO Box 3300, Hamilton, New South Wales 2303, Australia
Tel: (+61 2) 49 23 50 00  Fax: (+61 2) 49 23 51 12

### Key personnel
See entry in *Locomotives and powered/non-powered passenger vehicles* section.

### Products
Freight wagons, including bulk hoppers, tank wagons, flat wagons and container transport wagons.

### Contracts
Recent contracts include the supply of Type XT aluminium-bodied grain hoppers for Australian Western Railroad and 130 iron ore wagons for Portman Mining.

***UPDATED***

## Unity

Unity Railway Supply Co Inc
805 Golf Lane, Bensenville, Illinois 60106, USA
Tel: (+1 630) 595 45 60  Fax: (+1 630) 595 06 46

### Key personnel
Chairman of the Board: Harold R O'Connor
President: Robert S Grandy
Executive Vice-President, Financial: Robert Holden

### Products
Components for freight wagons including: roller bearing adapters; Adapter 'Plus' adapters with polymer roof liners; airbrake hose supports; batten bars; bolster bowl liners; brake levers, bottom rods, jaws and eyes; brake pins; brake release rods; brake steps; steel castings, centre pins; coupler centering wear plates; draft key retainers; draft lugs; end platforms; camcar fasteners; pipe bracket/dust strainer filters; floor deck plugs; standard and split wedge friction castings; grab irons; handbrakes, handwheels and bell cranks; journal box lids; journal lubricators; ladders; lading anchors; lumber corner protectors; train line pipe anchors; gravity-type outlet gates; plug door guides; running boards; reusable shipping containers; sill steps; striker castings; trainline trolley shackles; blue flag and barricade warning lights; dual-purpose wear plates; and wheel chocks.

***VERIFIED***

## Uralvagonzavod

622006, Nizhny Tagil, Russian Federation
Tel: (+7 83435) 23 17 74; 23 01 97
Fax: (+7 83435) 23 34 92; 23 03 57

### Products
Freight wagons.

*Wabash National Triple Crown Services RoadRailer trailer with DuraPlate® RoadRailer trailers on Mark V intermediate bogies*  0063729

*Sleeper-carrying wagon designed and manufactured for Jarvis Rail by Wabtec Rail*  2000/0084684

## Wabash National

Wabash National Corporation, RoadRailer Division
PO Box 6129, Lafayette, Indiana 47903, USA
Tel: (+1 771) 449 57 45  Fax: (+1 771) 449 54 74
Web: http://www.wabashnational.com

### Key personnel
President and Chief Executive Officer, Wabash National: William P Greubel
President, RoadRailer and Senior Vice-President, Marketing, Wabash National: Lawrence J Gross
Chief Operating Officer: Richard J Giromini
Vice-President and General Manager: Bryan K Langford
Vice-President, Engineering: Rodney Ehrlich

### Products
Design, production, licensing, marketing and sales of the RoadRailer® Mark V intermodal system for both North America and international markets through the RoadRailer division.

The RoadRailer Mark V system consists of a detachable two or three-axle rail bogie supporting specially designed truck trailers. All Mark V rail bogies can be used to carry any RoadRailer trailer, no matter what the length, height or type. All RoadRailer trailers use their air suspension to lower and raise the road wheels, eliminating the need for terminal cranes. RoadRailer trailers are joined together with special couplers to form trains (up to 125 units in length or 4,800 short tons in trailing weight), or at the end of conventional trains. RoadRailer trains are coupled to conventional wagons by means of the CouplerMate® bogie.

For the North American market, DuraPlate® dry vans are available in 48, 53 and 57 ft lengths, in both standard and high-cube versions. The high-cube van uses smaller tyres to provide an interior height of up to 118 in at the nose and 121 in at the rear of the trailer. The AutoRailer® van is a special type of high-cube trailer that has a raisable deck for carrying up to six full-size cars. A new variant of the AutoRailer has a split-deck design, making it possible to carry trucks and cars or light commercial vehicles. Other dry vans are the 48 and 28 ft sheet and post trailers. The 48 ft van is for mail service and has large side doors. The 28 ft van is called a PupRailer trailer, has a single axle, pintle hook and roll-up door.

The ReeferRailer® trailer is a refrigerated RoadRailer and is available in 48 and 53 ft lengths. For the international market, RoadRailer trailers are available in a wide range of configurations and all trailers built for Europe are compatible with each other, permitting co-ordinated service.

Current RoadRailer operators include Triple Crown, Swift Transportation, Schneider National, Amtrak and Burlington Northern Santa Fe. Nearly 6,000 units are in service in the USA. RoadRailer trailers are also in operation in Brazil, Thailand, China, India, Germany, France, Italy and Australia, and prototypes have been tested in the UK, Thailand, China and India.

***UPDATED***

## Wabtec Rail Ltd

PO Box 192, Hexthorpe Road, Doncaster DN1 1PJ, UK
Tel: (+44 1302) 79 00 27  Fax: (+44 1302) 79 00 58
e-mail: probinson@wabtec.com
Web: http://www.wabtec.com

### Key personnel
See entry in *Locomotives and powered/non-powered passenger vehicles* section.

### Corporate development
Wabtec Rail formerly traded as RFS(E), changing its name in March 2000.

### Products
Design, manufacture and supply of freight vehicles and overhaul, refurbishment, conversion, maintenance, field servicing and repairs for freight rolling stock.

Wabtec 'Fleetcare' operates from a network of sites located throughout the UK, providing a 24 hour operational maintenance support service.

Recent contracts include the design and manufacture of 30 sleeper-carrying freight wagons for Jarvis Rail including a comprehensive 'Fleetcare' operational maintenance support package; conversion of over 200 tank wagons to box body wagons for EWS; overhaul of bogies, wheelsets, bearings, air brake equipment, hydraulic buffers, hydraulic dampers; crash damage repairs and repainting.

***UPDATED***

## Wagon Pars

Wagon Pars Company
10 Azarshar Street, South Kheradmand Avenue, Tehran, 15846, Iran
Tel: (+98 21) 884 83 30; 83 39  Fax: (+98 21) 884 83 38

**Works address**
Km 4, Tehran Rd, Arak
Tel: (+98 861) 330 46 50    Fax: (+98 861) 339 99

**Key personnel**
Marketing Executive: Reza Esfahlani

**Products**
Freight wagons including cement and powder wagon, LPG tank wagon, hopper wagon, covered wagon and four-axle wagon.

## WagonySwidnica SA

A subsidiary of The Greenbrier Companies Inc
ul Strzclinska 35, Swidnica, PL-581-00 Poland

**Warsaw sales office**
ul Widok 8, 8th floor, PL-000-23 Warsaw, Poland
Tel: (+48 22) 690 6810    Fax: (+46 22) 690 6811

**Greenbrier Europe office**
Welterstrasser 60 D-57072, Siegen, Germany
Tel: (+49 271) 271 70 22 53    Fax: (+49 271) 741 28 94

**Greenbrier London office**
25 Hasker Street, London SW3 2LE, UK
Tel: (+44 20) 75 84 18 98

**Key personnel**
President: Tom Peczerski
Chief Engineer: Dionizy Studzinski

**Products**
Freight wagons. Conventional freight wagons include tank wagons, gondolas and flat wagons.
WagonySwidnica has gained approval from Deutsche Bahn AG, Germany.
The 105 m³ tank wagon for transport of liquefied hydrocarbons has a maximum load capacity of 56 tons. Tank wagons for transport of products such as mineral oils, LPG and ammonia are also built at the plant.
New products include the East-West Tank Wagon which incorporates both automated and link and pin couplers, in addition to a dual-valve system to cope with differences in load/discharge practice in Russia and West Europe. Also, a lighter weight/increased-volume tank wagon is being designed, based on the US stub sill tank wagon.

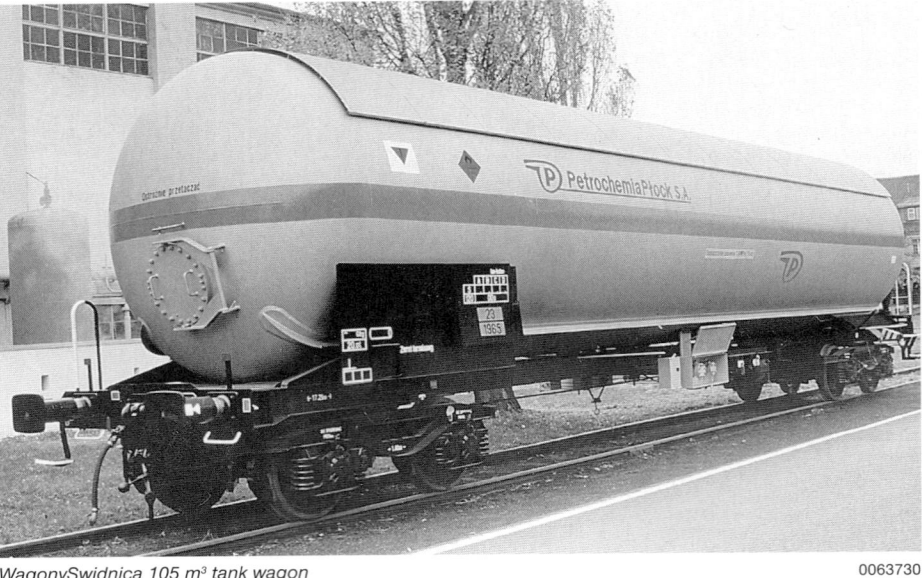

## Wakamatsu Sharyo

Wakamatsu Sharyo Co Ltd
1 Kitaminato machi 6-chome, Wakamatsu-ku,
Kitakyushu 808, Japan
Tel: (+81 93) 761 23 31    Fax: (+81 93) 761 23 35

**Products**
Freight wagons, specialised steelworks vehicles.

*WagonySwidnica 105 m³ tank wagon*

*Zastal Falns self-discharging wagon*

## Zastal

Zastal-Wagony SA (Joint Stock Co)
ul Sulechowska 4a, PL-65-119 Zielona Góra, Poland
Tel: (+48 68) 320 29 07; 328 45 52
Fax: (+48 68) 328 46 40
e-mail: wagony@zastal.pl
Web: http://www.wagony.zastal.pl

**Key personnel**
President: Ryszard Oblęór
Board Members: Mieczyslaw Konwiński, Jadwiga Karapka
Commercial Manager: Janina Król
Technical Manager: Janusz Kapala

**Products**
Freight wagons manufactured according to UIC standards, including: four-axle flat coal wagons and self-discharge wagons for aggregates and ore traffic; two- and four-axle flat and covered wagons for the transport of cereals; and tank wagons. Freight wagons for operation on 1,520 mm (CIS) gauge; wagon main assemblies and spare parts and refurbishment, steel structures and technological equipment.
Contracts include: 500 Shmmns hot-rolled steel coil carriers for SNCB, Belgium, with an option for an additional 200; standard Eanos coal wagons for PKP Poland (1998); self-discharging Falns wagons for PKP; and self-discharging Tanoos wagons for Bombardier Transportation DWA Germany (1998/1999).

## Zeco

Zimbabwe Engineering Ltd
PO Box 1874, Bulawayo, Zimbabwe
Tel: (+263 9) 789 31    Fax: (+263 9) 722 59
e-mail: zeco@acacia.samara.co.zw

**Key personnel**
See entry in *Locomotives and powered/non-powered passenger vehicles* section.

**Products**
Construction, overhaul and rebuilding of freight wagons. Supply of complete bogies, bogie components and all spares for freight wagons.

## Zhuzhou

Rolling Stock Works
Xinhua East Road, Zhuzhou, Hunan, PR China
Tel: (+86 733) 840 32 84    Fax: (+86 733) 840 32 84; 31 34

**Key personnel**
Director: Liu Yuzhou

**Products**
Freight wagons including gondola cars, hopper wagons, flat wagons, heavy-duty wagons, tankers, wagon components and bogies.
Contracts include salt wagons for Botswana Railways, steel gondolas for Tanzania and Zambia and ballast wagons for Hong Kong.

# BRAKES AND DRAWGEAR

## Alphabetical listing

ABC-NACO Inc
Abex Rail
Acieries de Ploërmel
ADES Technologies
Amsted
Anchor Brake Shoe LLC
ASF
Atlas Copco Compressors Ltd
Avon Spencer Moulton
BBA Friction
Bharat
Bradken Rail
Bremskerl
Buckeye
Buffalo Brake Beam Co
Buhlmann SA
Carbone Lorraine
Cardo Rail
Cardwell Westinghouse WABCO
China National Railway Locomotive and Rolling Stock Industry Corporation (LORIC)
Cimmco International
ČKD-Dako as
Cobra Brake Shoes
Cobreq
Comet
Cometna
Conbrako (Pty) Ltd
DAKO-CZ as
Dellner Couplers AB
Delta Rail
Dominion Castings Ltd

Ellcon National Inc
Escorts Ltd
European Friction Industries Ltd
Federal-Mogul (FERODO) Ltd
FMI – FM Industries Inc
Forges de Fresnes
Frenoplast
Frenos Calefaccion y Señales
Freudenberg Schwab GmbH
Futuris
GE Harris
Graham-White
Greysham and Co
Hanning & Kahl GmbH & Co
Honeywell Bremsbelag
ICER Brakes SA
Jarret
Karl Georg
Keystone
Keystone Bahntechnik
Knorr-Bremse
Kovis doo
LAF
Lesjöfors AB
Manoir Industries
Metcalfe Railway Products Ltd
Miner
Mitsubishi Electric Corporation
Multi-Service Supply
MZT HEPOS
NABCO Ltd
Newag

OKE
Oleo
Paulstra SNC
Peddinghaus Group
Poli
Radenton
Réservoir
Saalasti Oy
SAB WABCO
Scharfenbergkupplung
SEE
SGL Carbon Group
SMC
Stabeg
Standard
Stone India Ltd
Sumitomo Metal Industries Ltd
Textar
Thyssen Krupp
Tokyu
Triax-YSD
TSM Inc
Ueda
Unity Railway Supply
WABCO
Wabtec Rail
Westinghouse Brakes Ltd
Westinghouse Saxby Farmer
William Cook Rail
Yutaka Manufacturing Co Ltd

# MANUFACTURERS/Brakes and Drawgear

## Classified listing

### BRAKE PADS AND SHOES
ABC-NACO
Abex Rail
Acieries de Ploërmel
Anchor Brake Shoe
BBA Friction
Bremskerl
BSI
Carbone Lorraine
Cobra Brake Shoes
Cobreq
European Friction Industries Ltd
Federal Mogul (FERODO) Ltd
Frenoplast
Futuris
Honeywell Bremsbelag
ICER
Kovia doo
NABCO
Newag
SGL Carbon Group
Standard
Textar
Thyssen Krupp
Ueda

### BRAKE SYSTEMS AND COMPONENTS
ADES Technologies
Atlas Copco
Bharat
Buffalo Brake Beam
Buhlmann
Cardwell Westinghouse WABCO
Cardo Rail
China National Railway Locomotive and Rolling Stock Industry Corporation (LORIC)
Cimmco International
ČKD-Dako
Comet
Conbrako
Dr Techn Joseph Zelisko*
Ellcon National
Escorts
Forges de Fresnes
Freinrail*
Frenos Calefaccion y Señales
Frensistemi*
Freudenberg Schwab
GE Harris
Graham-White
Greysham International
Hanning & Kahl
Industria Freios Knorr*
Knorr Brake*
Knorr Brake Australia*
Knorr Brake Corporation*
Knorr-Bremse
Knorr-Bremse (Far East)*
Knorr-Bremse GesmbH*
Knorr-Bremse Rail Systems India*
Knorr-Bremse Rail Systems Korea*
Knorr-Bremse SA*
Kolmex
Koshin-Knorr*
Lesjöfors AB
Metcalf Railway Products Ltd
Mitsubishi Electric
Multi-Service Supply
MZT Hepos
NABCO
Oerlikon-Knorr Eisenbahntechnik*
OKE
Poli
Réservoir
SEE
SMC
Stabeg
Stone India
Tokyu
Triax-YSD
TSM
Unity Railway Supply
WABCO
Wabtec Rail
Westinghouse Brakes
Westinghouse Saxby Farmer
William Cook Rail

### COUPLERS AND DRAWGEAR
Acieries de Ploërmel
ALSTOM
ASF
Avon
Bradken Rail
BSI
Buckeye
Buhlmann
Cardwell Westinghouse WABCO
China National Railway Locomotive and Rolling Stock Industry Corporation (LORIC)
Cimmco International
Cometna
Conbrako
Dellner Couplers
Delta Rail
Dominion Castings
Escorts
FMI
Karl Georg
Keystone
Keystone Bahntechnik
LAF
Manoir Industries – Sambre et Meuse
Miner
Oleo
Paulstra
Peddinghaus Group
Radenton
Saalasti
Scharfenbergkupplung
Stabeg
Sumitomo
Textar
WABCO
Wabtec Rail
William Cook Rail
Yutaka Manufacturing Co Ltd

*See Knorr-Bremse

# Brakes and Drawgear/**MANUFACTURERS**

## Company listing by country

**AUSTRALIA**
Bradken Rail
Futuris
SMC

**AUSTRIA**
Stabeg

**BELGIUM**
Buhlmann SA

**BRAZIL**
Cobreq

**CANADA**
Dominion Castings Ltd

**CHINA**
China National Railway Locomotive and Rolling Stock Industry Corporation (LORIC)

**CZECH REPUBLIC**
DAKO-CZ as

**FINLAND**
Saalasti Oy

**FRANCE**
Avon Spencer Moulton
Carbone Lorraine
Delta Rail
Forges de Fresnes
Jarret
LAF
Manoir Industries
Paulstra SNC
Réservoir
SEE

**GERMANY**
Allied Signal Bremsbelag
Bremskerl
Freudenberg Schwab GmbH
Hanning & Kahl GmbH & Co
Karl Georg

Keystone Bahntechnik
Knorr-Bremse
Newag
Peddinghaus Group
Scharfenbergkupplung
SGL Carbon Group
Textar
Thyssen Krupp

**INDIA**
Bharat
Cimmco International
Escorts Ltd
Greysham and Co
Stone India Ltd
Westinghouse Saxby Farmer

**ITALY**
Poli

**JAPAN**
Mitsubishi Electric Corporation
NABCO Ltd
Sumitomo Metal Industries Ltd
Tokyu
Ueda
Yutaka Manufacturing Co Ltd

**MACEDONIA**
MZT HEPOS

**POLAND**
Frenoplast

**PORTUGAL**
Cometna

**SOUTH AFRICA**
Conbrako (Pty) Ltd
Frenos Calefaccion y Señales
ICER Brakes SA

**SLOVENIA**
Kovis doo

**SWEDEN**
Cardo Rail
Dellner Couplers AB
Lesjöfors AB
SAB WABCO

**SWITZERLAND**
OKE

**UNITED KINGDOM**
Atlas Copco Compressors Ltd
BBA Friction
European Friction Industries Ltd
Federal-Mogul (FERODO) Ltd
Metcalfe Railway Products Ltd
Oleo
Radenton
Wabtec Rail
Westinghouse Brakes Ltd
William Cook Rail

**UNITED STATES OF AMERICA**
Amsted
Anchor Brake Shoe LLC
ASF
Buckeye
Buffalo Brake Beam Co
Cardwell Westinghouse WABCO
Cobra Brake Shoes
Comet
Ellcon National Inc
FMI – FM Industries Inc
GE Harris
Graham-White
Keystone
Miner
Multi-Service Supply
Standard
Triax-YSD
TSM Inc
Unity Railway Supply
WABCO

# MANUFACTURERS/Brakes and Drawgear

## ABC-NACO Inc

2001 Butterfield Road, Suite 502, Downers Grove, Ilinois 60515, USA
Tel: (+1 630) 852 13 00   Fax: (+1 630) 852 22 64
Web: http://www.abc-naco.com

**Key personnel**
Chairman and Chief Executive Officer: Donald W Grinter
Vice-President, Planning and Investor Relations:
    Paul E Dunn
Vice-President, Export Sales: David G Kleeshulte

**Products**
Normal and high-phosphorus cast-iron brake shoes; computer systems.

## Abex Rail

Lütticher Strasse 565, D-52074 Aachen, Germany
Tel: (+49 241) 712 83   Fax: (+49 241) 712 52
e-mail: info@abexrail.com

**Key personnel**
Managing Director: K W Kever

**Main works**
Rütgers Rail Italia, Avellino, Italy
Piret SA, Gilly, Belgium

**Products**
Normal and high-phosphorus (patented) cast-iron brake shoes. Composition and sintered brake shoes and disc brake pads.

*UPDATED*

## Acieries de Ploërmel

PO Box 103, F-56804 Ploërmel, France
Tel: (+33 2) 97 73 24 70   Fax: (+33 2) 97 74 03 90
e-mail: ap.ctrochu@wanadoo.fr

**Key personnel**
Managing Director: Jean-Luc Lancelot
Sales Manager: Alain Noblet

**Background**
Acieries de Ploërmel is a member of the Amsted Group.

**Products**
Brake block holders, buffers.

## ADES Technologies

13 rue Edouard Martel, ZI de la Chauvetière, F-42100 St Etienne, France
Tel: (+33 4) 77 59 59 23   Fax: (+33 4) 77 80 95 64
e-mail: business@ades-technologies.com

**Key personnel**
Managing Director: Jean-Louis Modrin
Commercial Director: Jean-Michel Pagnerre

**Products**
Design, manufacture and maintenance of hydraulic and pneumatic systems, including: Auxim cock and isolating valves for compressed air applications; Raflex fittings for metal tubing to SNCF STM 820 A Norm and UIC 803 35 OR standards; and Auxim internal safety devices for tank wagons. The company's Someplan department provides its Systemier concept for the design and assembly of modules and panels from preformed tubes or manifold blocks.
    Organisations supplied include Alstom, Bombardier, Siemens and SNCF.

*UPDATED*

## Amsted

Amsted Rail International (a division of Amsted Industries Inc)
200 West Monroe Street, Chicago, Illinois 60606, USA
Tel: (+1 312) 372 53 84   Fax: (+1 312) 372 82 30

**Key personnel**
President: Glen F Lazar
Vice-President: Charles Spencer

**Products**
Amsted Rail International handles all business, licensing and sales of American Steel Foundries (ASF) and Griffin Wheel Company (see *Bogies and suspension, wheels and axles, bearings* section), which are divisions of Amsted Industries Inc.

*UPDATED*

## Anchor Brake Shoe LLC

1920 Downes Drive, West Chicago, Illinois 60185, USA
Tel: (+1 630) 293 11 10   Fax: (+1 630) 293 71 88

**Key personnel**
Chairman: Richard A Mathes
President: Jack M Payne
Plant Manager: James Quattrone
Field Service Manager: Joseph H Samolowicz
Quality Control Supervisor: Michael Tatera

**Products**
Composition brake shoes for locomotives and freight cars.

## ASF

American Steel Foundries/Amsted Industries International
200 West Monroe Street, Suite 2301, Chicago, Illinois 60606, USA
Tel: (+1 312) 372 53 84   Fax: (+1 312) 372 82 30
See also *Bogies and suspension, wheels and axles, bearings* section.

**Key personnel**
President: Glen F Lazar
Vice-President: Charles Spencer

**Products**
Cast steel freight car components; hot-wound coils; yokes; articulated couplers; snubbing packages; friction shoes. Automatic couplers and yokes. ASF's Articulated Connector provides a means to fully exploit the articulated wagon or train principle.

## Atlas Copco Compressors Ltd

PO Box 79, Swallowdale Lane, Hemel Hempstead HP2 7HA, UK
Tel: (+44 1442) 612 01   Fax: (+44 1442) 23 47 91
e-mail: john.fitzpatrick@atlascopco.com
Web: http://www.atlascopco.com

**Key personnel**
Managing Director: Geert Follers

**Products**
GA series of rotary screw compressors for electric and diesel locomotives, railcars, LRVs and tramcars.

*UPDATED*

## Avon Spencer Moulton

21 rue de la Gare, F-45330 Malesherbes, France
Tel: (+33 2) 38 32 72 29   Fax: (+33 2) 38 34 73 42
e-mail: guy.joly@asm.avon-rubber.com

**Key personnel**
Sales Manager: Guy Joly

**Products**
Drawgear, buffers, rubber-to-metal bonded components and suspension systems.

*VERIFIED*

## BBA Friction

PO Box 18, Cleckheaton, West Yorkshire, UK
Tel: (+44 1274) 85 40 00   Fax: (+44 1274) 85 40 01
e-mail: smorris@bbafriction.com

**Key personnel**
Business Manager, Rail: S Morris
Principal Engineer, Rail: N J Hughes

**Principal subsidiary**
BBA Friction Becorit GmbH
Rumplerstrasse 6-10, D-45659 Recklinghausen, Germany
Tel: (+49 2361) 66 67 14   Fax: (+49 2361) 66 67 79
e-mail: info@bbadecorit.de
Web: http://bbadecorit.de

**Products**
Asbestos-free low- and high-friction composition brake blocks for passenger and freight applications. Asbestos-free disc pads for a variety of applications. BBA Friction supplies railway braking products under the Becorit, TBL and Don brand names.
    Recent contracts include the supply of disc brake pads for Virgin West Coast tilting trains and high-friction brake blocks for the Singapore metro.

## Bharat

BBVL (Bharat Brakes & Valves Ltd) (a Government of India undertaking and subsidiary of Burn Standard Co Ltd)
22 Gobra Road, Calcutta 700 014, India
Tel: (+91 33) 244 48 03; 17 56; 08 57; 08 58; 246 19 63
Fax: (+91 33) 244 08 55
e-mail: bbvlcal@cal2.vsnl.net.in

**Key personnel**
Managing Director: Benu Munshi
Chief Manager, Finance: G C Bardhan
Deputy General Manager (Works): R Sinha
Manager (Commercial): S Das

**Products**
Vacuum brake equipment for wagons and coaches; Northey-rotary positive air-cooled high-vacuum locomotive exhausters; airbrake equipment including distributor valves for wagons; and brake regulators comprising slack adjuster, empty load device and changeover gear for wagons; air compressors.
    Regular supplier to Indian Railways and of equipment for locomotives, coaches and wagons in India. Vacuum brake equipment also supplied to Bangladesh Railways, the UK and to several countries in Africa and Southeast Asia.

## Bradken Rail

PO Box 105, Maud Street, Waratah, New South Wales 2298, Australia
Tel: (+61 2) 49 41 26 00   Fax: (+61 2) 49 41 26 61
e-mail: rail@bradken.com.ay
Web: http//www.bradken.com.au

**Background**
See entry in *Freight vehicles and equipment* section.

**Products**
Drawgear sets, including alliance couplers, articulated connectors, reduced slack couplers, miner draftgear and yokes.

*UPDATED*

## Bremskerl

Bremskerl Reibbelagwerke Emerling & Co KG
D-31629 Estorf-Leeseringen, Germany
Tel: (+49 5025) 97 80   Fax: (+49 5025) 97 81 10
e-mail: bk@bremskerl.de
Web: http://www.bremskerl.de

**Key personnel**
Managing Director: Herr Gramatke
Sales Director: Herr Wolf
Technical Director: Herr Hering

**UK Office**
Bremskerl (UK) Ltd, Unit 2, Stable Yard, Windsor Bridge Road, Bath BA2 3AY, UK
Tel: (+44 1225) 44 28 95   Fax: (+44 1225) 44 28 96
General Manager: Chris Prior

**Products**
Brake linings, disc brake pads, brake blocks.

*VERIFIED*

---

## Buckeye

Buckeye Steel Castings Co
2211 Parsons Avenue, Columbus, Ohio 43207, USA
Tel: (+1 614) 444 21 21   Fax: (+1 614) 445 20 84

**Key personnel**
President and Chief Executive Officer: Joe W Harden
Vice-President, Sales: Jeffrey E Laird
Director, Engineering: J R Downes
Manager, Product Engineering: R Polley

**Principal subsidiary company**
GSI Engineering Inc

**Products**
Reduced slack drawbar system. Automatic couplers, draft yokes, centre plates, sill centrebraces, draft sill ends and transition castings.

*UPDATED*

---

## Buffalo Brake Beam Co

400 Ingham Avenue, Lackawanna, New York 14218-2536, USA
Tel: (+1 716) 823 42 00   Fax: (+1 716) 822 38 23
e-mail: bbb@brakebeam.com
Web: http://www.brakebeam.com

**Key personnel**
Chairman and Chief Executive Officer: Richard G Adams
President and Chief Operating Officer: Garold L Stone Jr
Vice-President, Sales: Christopher F Adams
Director of Engineering: Louis E Bobsein
Director of Sales: Christopher F Adams

**Products**
Wagon brake beams, unit side-frame wear plates (steel or plastic), brake rod connectors, brake shoe keys and coupler carrier wear plates.

---

## S A Buhlmann NV

Leuvensesteenweg 31, B-1932 St Stevens-Woluwe, Belgium
Tel: (+32 2) 711 20 30   Fax: (+32 2) 720 20 64
e-mail: buhlman@skynet.be

**Key personnel**
Chairman: Olivier Buhlmann
Manager, Rolling Stock Department: Frederic Collier

**Products**
Railway, including light rail, for: hydraulic brakes, electric and electromagnetic; automatic couplers.

*UPDATED*

---

## Carbone Lorraine

Brake division
41 rue Jean Jaurès, BP 148, F-92231 Gennevilliers, France
Tel: (+33 1) 41 85 43 65   Fax: (+33 1) 41 85 43 63
e-mail: herve.mace@carbonelorraine.com
Web: http://www.carbonelorraine.com

**Key personnel**
Managing Director: Luc Themelin
Sales and Marketing managers: Hervé Macé, Jean Demay
Plant manager: Loïc Lelièvre

**Principal subsidiaries**
Carbone of America Corp, 400 Myrtle Avenue, Boonton New Jersey 07005, USA
Tel: (+1 973) 334 07 00

Carbono Lorena SA, AV Francisco Monteiro,1701 09400-000, Ribeirao Pires-SP, Brazil
Tel: (+55 112) 46 62 33

Carbone Lorraine, Apollo Building, Room 703, 1440 Yan'An Road, Shangaï 200040, China
Tel: (+86 21) 62 49 68 36

Carbone Lorraine Korea Co, Ltd , Eden Bldg, 4 Fl-1579-1, Seocho Dong, Seocho-Ku, Seoul, South Korea
Tel: (+82 2) 598 00 71

Le Carbone K K, 6 F, Shinkuju Royal Bldg, 7-21-1, Nishi-Shinkuju, Shinkuju-Ku, Tokyo 160-0023, Japan
Tel: (+81 353) 32 53 61

Le Carbone Lorraine Australia Pty Ltd, PO Box 196, 75 Sparks Avenue, Fairfield, Victoria 3078, Australia
Tel: (+61 3) 94 89 24 55

Le Carbone (SA) Pty Ltd
CNr Commando and Wright Street, Industria, West Johannesburg, South Africa
Tel: (+27 11) 474 00 00

**Products**
Low-noise, sintered metal substitutes to cast-iron brake shoes; low-friction coefficients sintered metal brake shoes C10, medium friction coefficients sintered metal brake shoes C17, for hot and wet and icy effective braking; high-friction coefficients sintered metal brake shoes C30, for wagons and locomotives speeding over 100 km/h; sintered metal disc brake pads; dynanometer braking simulations; customised friction material for specific applications.

**Contracts**
Recent contracts include Austrian Railways brake pads supply for 'Rolling Highways', French National Railways brake pads supply for TGV, brake shoes for diesel and electric freight locomotives.

*VERIFIED*

---

## Cardo Rail

Cardo Rail AB
Roskildevägen 1, PO Box 193, SE-201 21 Malmö, Sweden
Tel: (+46 40) 35 04 60   Fax: (+46 40) 30 38 03
e-mail: info@sabwabco.com
Web: http://www.sabwabco.com

**Key personnel**
President: Ingar Jensen
Senior Vice-President, Finance and Administration: Rolf Lundahl
Business Area Director and Contract Management: Mats Svensson

**Corporate development**
A member of the Cardo AB group, Cardo Rail's principal products are rail vehicle brake systems marketed under the SAB WABCO trademark.

**Subsidiaries**
SAB WABCO AB, Sweden
SAB WABCO Nordic AB, Sweden
SAB WABCO International AB, Sweden
SAB WABCO SA, France
SAB WABCO NV, Belgium
SAB IBERICA SA, SAB WABCO SA, Spain
SAB WABCO Products Ltd, UK
SAB WABCO Ltd, UK
SAB WABCO SpA, Italy
SAB WABCO do Brazil SA, Brazil
SAB WABCO CS sro, Czech Republic
SAB WABCO D&M Engineering Ltd, Australia
SAB WABCO BSI Verkehrstechnik Products GmbH, Germany
SAB WABCO BSI Verkehrstechnik GmbH, Germany
Gutehoffnungshütte Radsatz GmbH, Germany
SAB WABCO KP GmbH, Germany
SAB WABCO Korea Ltd, South Korea
SAB WABCO India Ltd, India
SAB WABCO Polska sp zoo, Poland

**Products**
Braking systems for locomotives, passenger and freight vehicles, including LRVs and guided vehicles with rubber tyres; UIC approved automatic airbrakes to the requirements of most railway administrations; electropneumatic, electrohydraulic, electromechanical and all- electric brake systems; vacuum and combined brake systems.

Air generation: air supply equipment, reciprocating and screw compressors, air treatment devices.

Tread brakes/disc brakes: automatic slack adjusters, variable load devices; friction pair devices, tread brakes, brake discs, calliper assemblies, disc brake actuators with spring, hydraulic or mechanically operated parking; friction materials; electromagnetic track brakes.

Wheel products: solid wheels, wheelsets, resilient and low-noise wheels, running gear.

Other: UIC-approved microprocessor-controlled wheelslide protection devices, anti-slip and speed controls; automatic test equipment for brake controls; automatic computer-controlled systems for marshalling yards; transit car coupling systems.

Recent contracts for high-speed trains include supply of complete brake systems for Pendolino trains, TGV South Korea, TGV France, brake equipment for X2000 Sweden and wheels for ICE Germany.

Brake systems and brake equipment for dmus and emus have been supplied to: Australia, Brazil, France, Germany, Hungary, Italy, Netherlands, Spain, Sweden, Taiwan and United Kingdom. Also wheels for ET474 cars, Germany.

Complete brake systems and brake equipment for freight wagons have been supplied to many railways around the world.

Complete brake systems for container wagons among others have been supplied to AAE, RoadRailer and NS.

Electrohydraulic brake systems have been supplied for LRVs and trams for Cologne, Rome, and Grenoble, electrohydraulic brake systems and wheels to Strasbourg, and wheels to Val de Seine. Electromechanical systems have been supplied to Hungary and Czech Republic, and wheels have been supplied for Darmstadt, Nuremberg, Vienna and Manila.

Electropneumatic brake systems have been delivered to the Paris metro, Rome metro, Santiago metro, Teheran metro and Tehran metro and electropneumatic brake systems and wheels to the Stockholm metro.

For locomotives, complete brake systems have gone to Italy, Germany and France.

*UPDATED*

---

## Cardwell Westinghouse WABCO

8400 South Stewart Avenue, Chicago, Illinois 60620-1794, USA
Tel: (+1 708) 655 52 00   Fax: (+1 708) 655 52 02

**Key personnel**
Vice-President and General Manager: Mark Van Cleave

**Corporate developments**
Cardwell Westinghouse has become a subsidiary of WABCO (qv)

**Products**
Friction, rubber-friction and hydraulic friction draftgear; handbrakes; automatic slack adjusters. Vacuum brake equipment and components, Alliance couplers, AAR standard-type Alliance couplers, MCA couplers, automatic centre buffer couplers, enhanced screw couplers, screw couplings.

## MANUFACTURERS/Brakes and Drawgear

### China National Railway Locomotive and Rolling Stock Industry Corporation (LORIC)

10 Fuxing Road, Beijing 100844, China
Tel: (+86 10) 63 51 16 20; 77 66
Fax: (+86 10) 63 51 16 14; 63 26 08 30

**Works address**
See entries in *Locomotives and powered/non-powered passenger vehicles* and *Freight vehicles and equipment* sections.

**Products**
Development, design, engineering, production, sales, installation, refurbishment, maintenance and after-sales services for all types of brakes and drawgear.

*LORIC Model 102 brake system distribution valve* 2001/0099150

### Cimmco International

A division of Cimmco Birla Ltd
Prakash Deep, 7 Tolstoy Marg, New Delhi 110 001, India
Tel: (+91 11) 331 43 83; 84; 85
Fax: (+91 11) 332 07 77; 372 35 20

**Key personnel**
See entry in *Freight vehicles and equipment* section.

**Products**
Vacuum brake equipment and components; automatic centre-buffer couplers, including AAR types E and F, Alliance II and high-tensile couplers; enhanced centre-buffer couplers for freight wagons; ABC couplers for locomotives; and MCA and PH type couplers for coaches.

### Cobra Brake Shoes

Railroad Friction Products Corporation
PO Box 1349, Laurinburg, North Carolina 28353, USA
Tel: (+1 910) 844 97 10   Fax: (+1 910) 844 97 33

**Key personnel**
Vice-President and General Manager: F J Grejda
Director, Sales and Marketing: L R Charity
Product Manager: Michael F Griffin

**Products**
Composition brake shoes and disc pads.

### Cobreq

Cia Brasileira de Equipamentos
Praia do Flamengo 200, 9° Andar, Flamengo 22210, Rio de Janeiro, Brazil
Tel: (+55 21) 285 22 33   Fax: (+55 21) 285 70 60

**Main works**
Rua Tupi 293, Caixa Postal 54, Vila Maria, Indaiatuba, 13300-001 São Paulo, Brazil
Tel: (+55 192) 75 31 33   Fax: (+55 192) 75 71 29

**Key personnel**
Sales Director: R Darigo

**Products**
Non-metallic composition brake shoes and brake pads for railroad vehicles.

### Comet

Comet Industries Inc
4800 Deramus Avenue, Kansas City, Missouri 64120, USA
Tel: (+1 816) 245 54 00   Fax: (+1 816) 245 54 35

**Main works**
2405 Nicholson City, Missouri 64120, USA
4504 Macks Drive, Bossier City, Louisiana 71111

**Key personnel**
President: L J Pagel
Cheif Financial Officer: Mike Klinock
Executive Vice-president: Steve Woodson
Rail Products Operations Manager (Exports Sales): Randall Haan

**Products**
New and used wagon parts; reconditioned and second-hand bolsters/sideframes; distributor of Kohler power equipment; voice date installation and maintenance.

### Cometna

Copanhia Metalurgica Nacionel
Rua Marechel Gomes Dacosta, Famoes P-2675 Odivelas, Lisbon, Portugal
Tel: (+351 1) 933 31 39   Fax: (+351 1) 933 31 43

**Key personnel**
President: Jose Bissaia Barreto

**Products**
Knuckle-type couplers for locomotives and rolling stock.

### Conbrako (Pty) Ltd

PO Box 4018, Luipaardsvlei 1743, Transvaal, South Africa
Tel: (+27 11) 762 24 21   Fax: (+27 11) 762 65 35

**Key personnel**
Managing Director: R G Child

**Products**
Air and vacuum brakes; drawgear; snubbers.

### William Cook Rail

Cross Green, Leeds LS9 0SG, UK
Tel: (+44 113) 249 63 63   Fax: (+44 113) 249 13 76
e-mail: admin@cook-catton.co.uk
Web: http://www.william-cook.co.uk

**Key personnel**
Managing Director: Kevin Grayley
Field Sales Manager: David Walshaw
Also at
Parkway Avenue, Sheffield S9 4WA
Tel: (+44 114) 273 01 21   Fax: (+44 114) 275 25 08
Sales Director: Trevor Stephenson

**Products**
Steel brake discs. Couplers and coupler assemblies, including Drophead Buckeye, Alliance and Tightlock types.

*VERIFIED*

### DAKO-CZ as

Budovatelů 323, CZ-53843 Třemošnice, Czech Republic
Tel: (+420 455) 61 71 11   Fax: (+420 455) 61 71 15
e-mail: ckddako@ckd-dako.cz
Web: http://www.dako-cz.cz

**Corporate background**
DAKO-CZ, previously known as ČKD-DAKO, changed its name in August 2001.

**Products**
Manufacturer of brake devices and components for rail vehicles; development, manufacture and sales of hydraulic and mechanical devices and components for both civil and military equipment.
   Principal products include DAKO complete compressed-air brake systems for both freight wagons, passenger cars and locomotives conforming with UIC standards; compressed-air brake devices for high-speed traffic; brake systems for trams.
   DAKO-CZ is ISO 9001 certified.

*UPDATED*

### Dellner Couplers AB

Vikavägen 144, SE-791 95 Falun, Sweden
Tel: (+46 23) 76 54 00   Fax: (+46 23) 76 54 10
e-mail: info@dellner.se
Web: http://www.dellner.com

**Key personnel**
President: Clas Nicolin
Technical Director: Dieter Ernst
Marketing Director: A Philip Pastouna
General Manager, USA: Tom Tarantino
Sales Manager: Roger Danielsson
After Sales Manager: Tomas Westbom

Dellner Couplers UK
Bickerstaffe, Chester Road, Gayton, Wirral L60 3RZ
Tel: (+44 151) 342 38 52   Fax: (+44 151) 342 70 40
e-mail: dccparuk@aol.com

Marketing Director: A P Pastouna
Dellner Kupplungen GmbH
Stahlstrasse 4a, D-42281 Wuppertal, Germany
Tel: (+49 202) 25 05 10   Fax: (+49 202) 250 51 77
e-mail: dellner@dellner.de

Dellner Couplers Inc
8334-H Arrowridge Blvd, Charlotte, North Carolina 28273, USA
Tel: (+1 704) 527 21 21   Fax: (+1 704) 527 21 25
e-mail: ttaranti@freewwweb.com

Dellner Couplers Sp zoo
Osada Kolejowa 12, 81-220 Gdynia, Poland
Tel: (+48 586) 28 54 81   Fax: (+48 586) 28 54 80
e-mail: dellner@dellner.com.pl

Brakes and Drawgear/**MANUFACTURERS**

**Dellner Couplers France**

10 Passage Ronsin, F-77300 Fontainebleau, France
Tel: (+33 1) 64 69 55 21    Fax: (+33 1) 64 69 55 28
e-mail: dellnercouplers1@hotmail.com

**Products**

Automatic and semi-automatic couplers compatible for all coupler systems and applications. Also supplied are side buffers, semi-trailer joints, adapters, hatches, snow-gaiters and other front-end parts for rail vehicles.

Couplers have recently been supplied for Munich metro, LRVs in Adana, Turkey, XT Norway, Slovenian Railways Pendolinos, Washington metro, Porto metro, Virgin Trains CrossCountry and West Coast fleets, JFK Airport people mover, Regina vehicles in Sweden, Warsaw metro, Catania metro, Vancouver Mark II vehicles, Santa Clara and Halle LRVs.

## Delta Rail

1 Rue Roussel, F-92250 La Garenne Colombes, France
Tel: (+33 1) 42 42 11 44    Fax: (+33 1) 42 42 11 16

**Key personnel**
President: Yves Daunas
Marketing: Maire Collins

**Products**
Rolling stock buffers, shock-absorbers, suspension air springs, platform buffers.

## Dominion Castings Ltd

An ABC-NACO Inc Company
100 Depew Street, PO Box 5010, Hamilton, Ontario L8L 8G1, Canada
Tel: (+1 905) 544 50 00    Fax: (+1 905) 544 12 25

**Key personnel**
Vice-President Canadian and Calera Operations:
 David L Wayne
General Manager: Dale Harper

See also *Bogies and suspension, wheels and axles, bearings* section.

**Products**
Coupler systems; associated parts and drawbars; custom coupler components for manufacturers of automatic couplers for transit systems.

## Ellcon National Inc

50 Beechtree Boulevard, PO Box 9377, Greenville, South Carolina 29604-9377, USA
Tel: (+1 803) 277 50 00    Fax: (+1 803) 277 52 07

**Key personnel**
See entry in *Passenger coach equipment* section.

**Products**
Handbrakes, slack adjusters and bogie-mounted brakes.

## Escorts Ltd

Railway Equipment Division
Plot 115, Sector 24, Faridabad 121 005, India
Tel: (+91 129) 544 22 75; 528 02 86
Fax: (+91 129) 23 21 48; 528 30 69; 526 42 86
e-mail: cgtech.asp-escorts@.gndel.global.net.in

**Key personnel**
Vice-President: Devraj Singh
Associate Vice-President: Krishna Havaldar
Deputy General Manager, Marketing: Naveen Sangari
Chief General Manager, Technical: C Grover

**Products**
Complete airbrake systems for locomotives, freight and passenger vehicles, overhead equipment inspection cars and diesel cranes. Electropneumatic brake systems for metro cars and electric multiple-units. Vacuum control valves. Composite brake blocks. Automatic and semi-permanent centre buffer-couplers for emus and metro cars. Rail fastening systems.

Escorts is the prime supplier to Indian Railways, delivering over 50,000 airbrake sets, 2,000 sets of electropneumatic brake equipment and 12,000 centre buffer-couplers. Products are also exported to over 15 countries.

New products under development or validation include a bogie-mounted brake system for freight wagons.

Escorts is certified to ISO 9002.

## European Friction Industries Ltd

Enterprise House, 6/7 Bonville Road, Brislington, Bristol BS4 5PF, UK
Tel: (+44 117) 971 48 37    Fax: (+44 117) 971 65 78
e-mail: rail@efiltd.co.uk

**Key personnel**
Rail Business Manager: Kevin Alexander
UK Sales and Operations Manager: Pete Higgins

**Products**
Composite friction materials for braking for all types of rail vehicles, including tram, heavy freight, high-speed and mining applications; OE and replacement pads and blocks.

*UPDATED*

## Federal-Mogul (FERODO) Ltd

Chapel-en-le-Frith, High Peak, Derbyshire SK23 0JP, UK
Tel: (+44 1298) 81 15 98    Fax: (+44 1298) 81 15 80
e-mail: fpgrailenquiries@eu.fmo.com

**Key personnel**
Director of Operations: T M Saxby
Commercial Manager: H Lavender

**Products**
High-performance, cost-effective friction brake materials for all types of rail vehicles, including high-speed, passenger and light rail vehicles. Composite disc brake pad materials including Sinter Metal Pads. Low-friction 'L' and 'LL' blocks and high-friction 'K' blocks are supplied, covering a wide spectrum of braking requirements.

*UPDATED*

## FMI – FM Industries Inc

8600 Will Rogers Boulevard, PO Box 40555 Fort Worth, Texas 76140, USA
Tel: (+1 817) 293 42 20    Fax: (+1 817) 551 58 01

**Key personnel**
President: James Kingerski
Senior Vice-President, Operations: M S Dew
Vice-President, Sales and Marketing: T W Howe
Vice-President Engineering: R N Hodges

**Products**
FreightMaster/Freight-Saver/Hydra-Buff brand of end-of-car and centre-of-car hydraulic cushioning devices.

FMI offers new and reconditioned gas return cushioning devices designed to eliminate high in-train forces. FMI's EOC devices are shipped precharged with nitrogen gas and gagged short of full extension for ease of installation. A sight glass to verify the hydraulic fluid level is provided in all new and reconditioned devices.

## Forges de Fresnes

80 rue Pasteur, PO Box 11, F-59970 Fresnes-sur-Escaut, France
Tel: (+33 3) 27 25 92 22    Fax: (+33 3) 27 26 17 27

**Key personnel**
Manager: J M Deramaux

**Products**
Forged brake beam assemblies and other forgings for bogies, passenger coaches and freight wagons.

## Frenoplast

ul Watykanska 15, PL-05-200 Wolomin-Majdan, Poland
Tel: (+48 22) 787 80 04    Fax: (+44 22) 787 94 79
e-mail: info@frenoplast.pl
Web: http://www.frenoplast.pl

**Products**
Disc pads for rail vehicles; centre plate linings and shoes; composition brake inserts; clutch linings for anti-slip devices.

## Frenos Calefacción y Señales

Sociedad Española de Frenos, Calefacción y Señales SA
Calle Nicolás Fúster 2, E-28320 Pinto, Madrid, Spain
Tel: (+34 91) 691 00 54    Fax: (+34 91) 691 01 00
e-mail: sefrenos@frenos.dobytec.es

---

**LAF — LES APPAREILS FERROVIAIRES**

**LLOYD ABC COUPLERS**

Conception, Development and Production of:
- *Automatic couplers,*
- *Drawbars,*
- *Ring springs,*
- *Draft gears,*
- *Specific traction devices.*

Literature on request.

LES APPAREILS FERROVIAIRES - LAF - 55, Rue du Bois Chaland - CE 2928 LISSES - 91029 EVRY CEDEX – FRANCE
Tél. 33.(0) 1.69.11.93.26 - Fax 33. (0)1.69.11.93.27 - E.mail laf@cimgroupe.com

## 612 MANUFACTURERS/Brakes and Drawgear

**Key personnel**
Board Member: Nicolás Fúster Junquera
General Director: Miguel Angel Martín Jiménez
Commercial Director: Agustín Lagartos Ruano
Manufacturing Director: Eugenio Blázquez

**Products**
Airbrake products, vacuum brakes and high-voltage heating; compressed air production and treatment; all types of brake control units; electronic anti-skid, anti-spin and brake control systems (analogue and microprocessor); bogie equipment such as cylinders, discs, block brake units; hydraulic brakes, magnetic track brakes and vacuum toilets.

Contracts include the supply of brake equipment for: 16 emus for Metro Madrid, 33 emus and 154 wagons for RENFE, 80 demus for Belgium and 13 emus for Metro Bilbao.

---

### Freudenberg Schwab GmbH

Freudenberg Simrit KG
Höhnerweg 2-4, D-69465 Weinheim, Germany
Tel: (+49 1805) 74 67 48
e-mail: simrit.service@freudenberg.de
Web: http://www.simrit.de

**Key personnel**
See *Bogies and suspension, wheels and axles, bearings* section.

**Organisation**
See *Bogies and suspension, wheels and axles, bearings* section.

**Products**
Vibration control: rubber/metal elastic elements, standard as well as specially designed. Includes resilient mountings for brake calipers and compressors.

*UPDATED*

---

### Futuris

Futuris Industrial Products Pty Ltd
6 Wenban Street, Wetherill Park, New South Wales 2164, Australia
Tel: (+61 2) 604 11 55   Fax: (+61 2) 604 22 58; 725 27 03

**Key personnel**
Managing Director: Tony Carpani
Marketing Manager: Peter Turner
Business Development Manager: Frank Wren

**Products**
High, medium and low-friction asbestos and lead-free composite brake shoes and railway disc brake pads.

---

### GE Harris

GE Harris Railway Electronics LLC
407 John Rhodes Boulevard, Melbourne, Florida 32934, USA
Tel: (+1 407) 242 51 74   Fax: (+1 407) 242 50 19
e-mail: rjohns@ge-harris.com
Web: http://www.geharris.com

**Key personnel**
See *Signalling and communications systems*.

**Products**
The LOCOTROL® EB integrates the controls of distributed power and locomotive electronic air brake into one package, providing five-fold reliability gain and automated diagnostics. The modular designed LOCOTROL® EB electronic air brake has fewer line-replaceable units and offers higher level diagnostics, enabling fast ready track service. The LOCOTROL EB system provides the performance advantages of distributed power and locomotive electronic braking.

### Graham-White

Graham-White Manufacturing Co
Sales Division, PO Box 1099, 1242 Colorado Street, Salem, Virginia 24153-1099, USA
Tel: (+1 540) 387 56 20   Fax: (+1 540) 387 56 39
e-mail: sbruce@grahamwhite.com

**Key personnel**
President and Chief Executive Officer: James S Frantz
Vice-President, Marketing: W Stewart Bruce Jr
International Customer Service Representative: Sherry Noller

**Corporate development**
The company is now ISO 9001 accredited.

**Products**
Pneumatic and electropneumatic devices for locomotives and powered passenger vehicles such as regenerative air dryers, locomotive sanding systems, air filters, automatic drain valves, air check valves (one- and two-way), solenoid valves, horn valves, coalescing air filters, bell ringers, analogue air gauges, air test fittings for air gauges and pressure switches, electric timers, mirror and windshield wing combinations, locomotive cab awnings and ventilators for locomotive cabs. Combined dirt collector and cut-out cock; electronic bell; new-generation 994 air dryer system, which keeps compressed air clean, dry and oil-free, with 6 year intervals between dryer overhauls. It makes use of Graham-White's patented self-adjusting purge valve and plug-in mounting bracket.

---

### Greysham and Co

7249 (1/1) Roop Nagar, Delhi 110 007, India
Tel: (+91 11) 397 39 89; 38 54; 294 74 32; 40 89; 24 63
Fax: (+91 11) 393 10 21; 294 08 92
e-mail: greysham@nda.vsnl.net.in

**Key personnel**
Managing Director: Mohan Singh
Executive Director: Subodh Singh
Technical Adviser: K B L Wadhwa
General Manager (Commerical): S Anand
General Manager (Operations): Pradeep Kumar Gupta
Export Manager: S T Ghosh

**Associate company**
Greysham Railway Friction Products Pvt Ltd
(Joint Venture Company with Railroad Friction Products Corporation (COBRA), Lauringburg, USA)
2/89 Roop Nagar, Delhi 110 007, India
Tel: (+91 11) 294 24 63; 392 24 39; 397 53 68
Fax: (+91 11) 393 10 21; 294 08 92
Products: Composite low-friction asbestos-free brake blocks (L-type and K-type)

*LOCOTROL EB system*

### Products
The company is ISO 9002 accredited and a member of the Railway Supply Association.

Braking systems – complete air brake systems for freight and passenger vehicles; OHE (overhead inspection) cars, dmu (motor and trailer) cars, C3W distributor valves to SAB WABCO design; EST distributor valve; automatic load sensing device; empty/load change-over valves; bogie-mounted brake systems and brake cylinders; reservoirs and rubber hoses.

Vacuum brake equipment, including 'E' and 'F' type cylinders; Prestall cylinders; QSA valves; couplings; release valves and similar equipment.

Shock-absorbers for passenger coaches, windows for high-speed air conditioned passenger coaches; toilet controller systems; electronic chokes and ceiling fans.

LED signal lights for railway traffic, non-powered water coolers for passenger coaches; semi-automatic locks for flat wagons.

A load-sensing device has been introduced and a shock-absorber range is being developed.

---

### Hanning & Kahl GmbH & Co

Rudolf Diesel Strasse 6, D-33813 Oerlinghausen, Germany
Tel: (+49 5202) 70 76 00   Fax: (+49 5202) 70 76 29
e-mail: Hanning-Kahl@t-online.de
Web: http://www.hanning-kahl.de

**Key personnel**
General Manager: Eckart Dümmer
Brake Division Manager: Dietrich Radtke
LRT Division Manager: W Helas

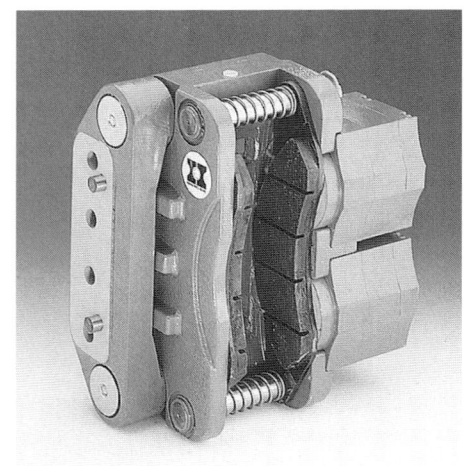

*HYS301 spring-applied actuator*

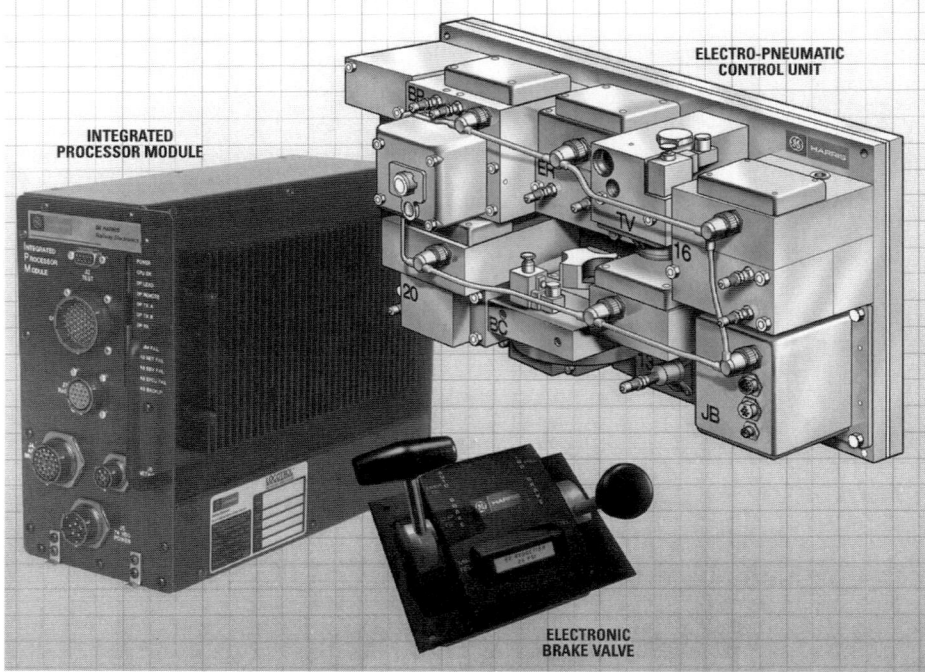

Sales Manager, Brakes: Jürgen Stammier
Sales Manager, LRT: Hans-Joachim Pässler

**Products**
Electrohydraulic brake systems; spring-applied actuators, active calipers, hydraulic-power units, hydraulic emergency release units, electronic brake control systems with slide protection, track brakes, and filter and flushing units.

Contracts include the supply of equipment to operators in Potsdam, Helsinki, Chemnitz, Bielefeld, Kassel, St Etienne, Bucharest and FVG Delijn.

## Honeywell Bremsbelag (Jurid)

Honeywell Bremsbelag GmbH (Jurid Products)
PO Box 1201, D-21504 Glinde, Germany
Tel: (+49 40) 727 10   Fax: (+49 40) 72 71 24 08

**Main works**
Glinder Weg 1, D-21509 Glinde/Hamburg, Germany

**Key personnel**
Managing Director: G Kasper
Sales Director: R Drummond
Sales Manager, Railway Products: Peter Franz

**Products**
Composition brake blocks; disc brake pads; friction plates; sintered brake blocks and disc brake pads for heavy-duty rail brakes; data acquisition equipment and instrumentation for rail brake system evaluation; opto-electronic laser systems for engineering measurement.

*UPDATED*

## ICER Brakes SA

Poligono Industrial Agustinos, C/G, s/n, E-31013 Pamplona, Spain
Tel: (+34 948) 32 16 46; 45 40
Fax: (+34 948) 18 94 79
e-mail: railway@icerbrakes.com
Web: http://www.icerbrakes.com

**Key personnel**
Chairman: Victor Ruiz Rubio
Managing Director: Juan Miguel Sucunza

**Products**
High, medium, low and special friction asbestos-free composition brake blocks, disc brake pads and friction plates, including UIC-approved, for coaches, high-speed coaches, locomotives, freight cars, emus, LRVs and metro cars.

*UPDATED*

## Jarret

198 avenue des Grésillons, F-92602 Asnières Cedex, France
Tel: (+33 1) 46 88 16 20   Fax: (+33 1) 47 90 03 57
e-mail: contact@jarret.fr

**Key personnel**
Chairman and General Manager: Bruno Domange
Managing Director: Antoine Domange

**Products**
Buffers; shock-absorbers for automatic couplers; buffer stops.

*UPDATED*

## Karl Georg

Karl Georg Bantechnik GmbH & Co KG
Rheinstrasse 15, D-57638 Neitersen, Germany
Tel: (+49 26) 81 80 80   Fax: (+49 26) 818 08 21
e-mail: K.Georg.Bahntechnik@T-Online.de

**Key personnel**
Managing Directors: Michael Schnaufer
George W Hoffmann
Sales Manager: Achim Geyer

**Background**
Karl Georg is a member of the Amsted Group.

**Products**
Karl Georg produces buffers using a hot-extruding process. Products include: side buffers in all categories according to UIC 526-1; longstroke buffers according to UIC 526-3; passenger coach buffers according to UIC 528; drawgear; buffers for industrial equipment; parts for automatic couplers; hot-extruded components from 20 to 350 kg.

## Keystone

Keystone Industries Inc
3420 Simpson Ferry Road, PO Box 456, Camp Hill, Pennsylvania 17001-0456, USA
Tel: (+1 717) 761 36 90   Fax: (+1 717) 763 99 17

**Key personnel**
President: G W Hoffman
Vice-President, International Marketing: W T Malinowski
Vice-President and Chief Technical Officer: M P Scott

**Products**
Hydraulic end-of-car and centre-of-car cushioning unit with strokes from 120 to 500 mm for freight wagon, locomotive and passenger coach applications. Friction steel and elastomeric draft gear for freight wagons, locomotives and passenger coaches. KeyGard elastomeric pads for railroad and industrial applications. Keystone hopper outlet sliding gates.

Contracts include the supply of Keystone products to UP, SP, BNSF, CSX, NS, Conrail, CN and CP and railways in Asia, Australia, Africa and South America, in addition to General Motors, GE Transportation Systems, Thrall, TTX, Johnstown America, TrentonWorks, Transcisco Industries, Goninan and Dorbyl.

## Keystone Bahntechnik

Keystone Bahntechnik GmbH
Rheinstrasse 15, D-57638 Neitersen, Germany
Tel: (+49 2681) 80 80   Fax: (+49 2681) 808 21
e-mail: keystone@krec.de
Web: http://www.krec.de

**Key personnel**
Managing Directors: Lothar Gintze, Michael Aherme, Achim Geyer

**Background**
Keystone Bahntechnik is a member of the Amsted Industries Group.

**Products**
Buffers using a hot-extruding process. Includes buffers in all UIC 526-1 categories; longstroke buffers according to UIC 526-3; passenger coach buffers according to UIC 528; drawgear; buffers for industrial equipment; parts for automatic couplers; hot-extruded components from 20 to 350 kg.

*UPDATED*

## Knorr-Bremse AG

Moosacher Strasse 80, D-80809 Munich, Germany
Tel: (+49 89) 354 70   Fax: (+49 89) 35 47 27 67
Web: http://www.knorr-bremse.com

**Key personnel**
Chairman: Heinz Hermann Thiele
Executive Board: H H Thiele, Peter Riedlinger
Marketing and Planning: Jörg Faltin

**Knorr-Bremse Systeme für Schienenfahrzeuge GmbH**
(address as Knorr-Bremse AG)

Management board: Dieter Wilhelm; Albrecht Köhler; Wolfgang Schlosser

**Works**
Berline and Munich

**Subsidiaries**
Knorr-Bremse Electronic GmbH, Munich
Knorr-Bremse GesmbH, Mödling, Austria
Dr Techn Josef Zelisko GesmbH, Mödling, Austria
Oerlikon-Knorr Eisenbahntechnik AG, Zürich, Switzerland
Freinrail SA, Reims, France
Frensistemi Srl, Florence, Italy
Sociedad Espanola de Frenos, Calefaccion y Señales SA, Pinto/Madrid, Spain
Knorr-Bremse Rail Systems India Pvt Ltd, Faridabad, India
Knorr-Bremse SA (Pty) Ltd, Kempton Park, South Africa
Knorr-Brake Australia Pty Ltd, Cardiff, New South Wales, Australia
Knorr-Bremse Rail Systems Japan Ltd, Tokyo, Japan
Knorr-Bremse Rail Systems Korea Ltd, Seoul, South Korea
Knorr-Brake Holding Corp, Watertown, New York, USA
Knorr Brake Corp, PO Box 9300, Westminster, Maryland 21158-9300, USA
Tel: (+1 410) 875 09 00   Fax: (+1 410) 875 90 53
New York Air Brake Corporation, Watertown, USA
Knorr-Brake Ltd, Kingston, Canada
Knorr-Bremse (Far East) Ltd, Hong Kong, PR China
Freios Knorr Sistemas Ferroviários Ltda, São Paulo, Brazil
Westinghouse Brakes (UK) Ltd, Chippenham, Wiltshire, UK
Knorr-Bremse NAF Broms AB, Sweden

**Products**
Rail-based brake systems for rapid transit, tramcars, LRVs, people mover and metro systems; air supply systems; wheel-slip and wheel-slide protection; auxiliary equipment including windscreen washer and wiper, sanding equipment, air suspension, door control, pantograph control and emergency brake systems; bogie brake equipment including slack adjusters, tread brake units and electromagnetic track brakes.

**Knorr-Bremse Systeme für Nutzfahrzeuge GmbH**
(address as Knorr-Bremse AG)
General Management: Dr Rudolph Gerich (Chairman), Oscar Flach, Viktor Kühne

**Subsidiaries**
Knorr-Dahl Freinage SA, Lisieux, France
Knorr-Bremse Systems for Commercial Vehicles Ltd, Douglas Road, Kingswood, Bristol BS15 2NL, UK
Tel: (+44 117) 984 61 00   Fax: (+44 117) 984 61 01
Knorr-Bremse Sistemi per Autoveicoli Commerciali, Milan, Italy
Knorr-Bremse Ungarn GmbH, Kecskemét, Hungary
Knorr-Autobrzdy Sro, Jablonec, Czech Republic
Knorr-Bremse Benelux BVBA, Herentals, Belgium
Knorr-Bremse System för Tunga Fordon AB, Malmö, Sweden
Knorrbrakes Ltd, New Delhi, India
Knorr-Orsan Ticari Arad Sistemleri Ltd, Turkey
Knorr-Bremse Sistemas Para Veiculos Commerciais Brasil Ltda, Brazil
Knorr Brake Truck Systems Co, Watertown, New York, USA
AlliedSignal Truck Brake Systems Co, Elyria, Ohio, USA

**Affiliated companies**
Knorr-Bremse Systems for Rail Vehicles GmbH, took a 49 per cent shareholding in IFE (Industrie-Einrichtungen Fertigungs-Atkiengesellschaft), Austria, in 1997.

Knorr-Bremse Systems for Rail Vehicles GmbH is a 50 per cent shareholder in the Albatros Group, which is the majority shareholder in Stone Ibérica SA and Sepsa SA, Spain.

**Products**
Pneumatic, hydraulic and electric brake systems and brake equipment for railways; air supply systems (compressor, air dryer, oil separator, filter, air reservoir); brake commands (driver's brake valve, electronic brake control system, electropneumatic control, brake manifold); brake controls (brake manifolds, distributor valve, pressure transformer, load brake valve, relay valve, magnet valve, auxiliary pneumatic equipment, pressure reducing valve); wheelslip and wheelslide protection (mechanical wheelslip, electronic wheelslip and wheelslide protection, dump valves, speed sensors);

auxiliary equipment (windscreen washer and wiper, sanding equipment, warning system, air suspension, pantograph control, automatic couplers); bogie brake equipment (brake cylinder, slack adjuster, tread brake unit, disc brake, electromagnetic track brake and eddy current brake), automatic door systems, power converters and toilet systems.

Recent contracts include: brake equipment for Virgin Trains West Coast Main Line (UK); KCRC and MTRC, Hong Kong (China); Vienna metro (Austria); Lisbon metro (Portugal); Long Island Rail Road and Amtrak Acela (USA).

*UPDATED*

## Kovis doo

Velika Dolina 37, SL-8261 Jesenice na Dolenjskem, Slovenia
Tel: (+386 7) 457 31 00   Fax: (+386 7) 495 73 32
e-mail: kovis@siol.net
Web: http://www.kovis.sl

**Products**
Brake discs and brake lining supports for trams and main line rail vehicles. Customers include national operators in Austria, Czech Republic, Germany, Romania and Slovenia.

*NEW ENTRY*

## LAF

Les Appareils Ferroviaires
87 avenue de l'Aérodrome, F-94310 Orly, France
Tel: (+33 1) 49 79 25 26   Fax: (+33 1) 49 79 25 27
e-mail: laf@worldnet.fr

**Key personnel**
General Manager: Alain Lovambac
Sales Department: C Danel
Technical Department: S Franco

**Products**
Couplers and draftgear, including automatic and knuckle couplers, special transition couplers, draw hooks and screw couplings, ring (friction) springs for draft and buffing gear.

## Lesjöfors AB

SE-524 92 Herrljunga, Sweden
Tel: (+46 513) 220 00   Fax: (+46 513) 230 24
e-mail: info@lesjoforsab.com
Web: http://www.lesjofors.com

**Products**
Springs for rail vehicle braking systems. Companies supplied include SAB Wabco.

## Manoir Industries

Sambre et Meuse
Railway Division, PO Box 2, Rue des Usines, F-59750, Feignies, France
Tel: (+33 3) 21 69 68 82   Fax: (+33 3) 27 69 69 89

**Key personnel**
See entry in *Freight vehicles and equipment* section.

**Products**
UIC couplers, buffers.
Manoir Industries – Sambre et Meuse has worked on the development of a European centre buffer coupler which has become the UIC coupler for freight wagons. It is being produced for rolling stock in several countries. US buffer and shock absorber systems.

## Metcalfe Railway Products Ltd

Tolletts Farm, Leek Old Road, Sutton, Macclesfield, Cheshire SK11 0HZ, UK
Tel: (+44 1260) 25 23 29   Fax: (+44 1260) 25 34 13
e-mail: metcalferailprodltd@hotmail.com
Web: http://www.metcalfrailprodltd.co.uk

**Key personnel**
Chairman and Managing Director: R H Metcalfe
Sales Manager: N Pointon

**Products**
UIC-approved Oerlikon-type air brake equipment for locomotives, freight wagons, passenger vehicles and associated equipment. SAB-type slack adjusters, tread brake equipment and weight valves ECT. Brake cylinders, hose couplings, anti-frost devices. UIC- and ISO-approved. Manual and on-site training courses.

*UPDATED*

## Miner

Miner Enterprises Inc
International Sales
PO Box 471, 1200 East State Street, Geneva, Illinois 60134, USA
Tel: (+1 630) 232 30 00   Fax: (+1 630) 232 30 55

**Key personnel**
President: K C Jurasek
Vice-President: M L McGuigan
Marketing Managers: C Vanbutsele

**Foreign Licensees**
Australia: Bradken Rail, Maud Street, Waratah, Newcastle, New South Wales 2298
France: Manoir Industries, Usine de Feignies, PO Box 2, rue des Usines, F-59750 Feignies

**Foreign Sales Agents**
In Argentina; Austria; Brazil; Chile; Colombia; Egypt; Greece; India; Israel; Italy; Mexico; Netherlands; South Africa; Switzerland; Turkey; and Venezuela.

**Products**
Draftgear; constant-contact side bearings; TecsPak buffer and traction springs; buffers; discharge systems for bulk commodities; brake beams.

TecsPak is a heavy-duty elastomeric spring package based on Hytrel.

The Miner TF-880 and SL-76 draftgear, developed for use in 24½ in standard pockets, are approved in accordance with AAR Specification M-901E.

The Crown SE draftgear is an all-steel draftgear engineered for heavy unit train applications.

Miner Constant Contact Side Bearings are engineered to reduce bogie hunting on freight wagons.

The AutoMEC air cylinder-activated door mechanism is designed primarily for coal hopper wagon unloading and is adaptable for 8 to 20 door openings.

The Autolok II discharge gate for hopper wagons features the BackLOK positive locking mechanism, ledgeless clear opening, sealed door and low operating torque. It meeets all AAR S-233 specification requirements.

*UPDATED*

## Mitsubishi Electric Corporation

Mitsubishi Denki Bldg, 2-3 Marunouchi 2-chome, Chiyoda-ku, Tokyo 100, Japan
Tel: (+81 3) 32 18 34 30   Fax: (+81 3) 32 18 90 48

**Key personnel**
See entry in *Locomotives and powered/non-powered passenger vehicles* section.

**Products**
Airbrake equipment for locomotives, electric multiple-units, light rail vehicles, rubber-tyred vehicles and monorails.

## Multi-Service Supply

Multi-Service Supply Division, The Buncher Co
Leetsdale, Pennsylvania 15056, USA
Tel: (+1 412) 741 15 00   Fax: (+1 412) 741 33 20

**Key personnel**
President: Ralph L Coffing
Vice-President and General Manager: Robert Lewis
Director, Marketing: Paul Bittner

**Products**
Airbrake systems and components for locomotives, freight wagons and passenger coaches, repair and reconditioning.

*UPDATED*

## MZT HEPOS

Pero Nakov bb, 91000 Skopje, Macedonia
Tel: (+389 91) 54 97 80; 54 97 91
Fax: (+389 91) 54 98 51; 54 98 48
e-mail: mzthepos@on.net.mk
Web: http://www.hepos.com.mk

**Key personnel**
Managing Director: Vlado Atanasovski
Deputy Managing Director: Stojče Smileski
Sales Director: Dušan Popović

**Products**
Complete pneumatic and brake systems for locomotives, passenger and freight vehicles; brake equipment (UIC approved) including pneumatic, electropneumatic, hydropneumatic systems and electronic components; driver's brake valves, distributors, disc brakes and tread brake actuators, brake cylinders, slack adjusters, load brake valves, auxiliary pneumatic equipment, end cocks, hoses and coupling heads, air dryers, brake panels, windscreen washers, wheelslide protection device, diagnostic and test stands.

MZT HEPOS has designed and developed a new brake accelerator valve designated VBK 100. It has been developed to meet the new regulations introduced in 1989 and 1995 to meet the increasing demands for such devices for service on modern passenger rolling stock. The VBK 100 accelerator valve provides two important features of performance, when compared with earlier designs. First, there is only a limited drop in brake pipe pressure to 2-2.5 bar. This feature reduces the time taken to recharge the complete brake system. It also results in a significant economy in the usage of compressed air. Second, the VBK 100 valve is insensitive to the brake pipe

*VERIFIED*   MZT-HEPOS VBK 100 brake accelerator valve 0063737

pressure, when using a high pressure-releasing surge. The introduction of the VBK 100 brake accelerator valve, together with the UIC-approved AKR pressure controller MH3F distributor makes MZT HEPOS fully compliant with the latest UIC specifications and regulations. The MH3H distributor valve is a further development of the existing MH3F distributor valve. The main functions of MH3F are being retained in the MH3H. They include a main distributor valve, accelerator valve, locking valve, initial admission valve, change-over cock and automatic release valve. However, the stop valve and check valves are being redesigned, the filling and equalising valve is being omitted and a new maximal pressure limiter is inserted. These improvements can be built into the existing housing of the MH3F distributor valve with minimum modifications so allowing a modification of the old types of distributor valves from this series. The MH 3H can be used in all types of railway vehicles.

*UPDATED*

## NABCO Ltd

Railroad Products Division, 9-18 Kaigan 1-chome, Minato-ku, Tokyo 105-0022, Japan
Tel: (+81 3) 54 70 24 01  Fax: (+81 3) 54 70 24 24
e-mail: takashi_koyama@nabco.co.jp

**Works**
3-3, 7-chome, Takatsukadai, Nishi-Ku, Kobe 651-2271, Japan
Tel: (+81 78) 993 03 00   Fax: (+81 78) 993 03 30

**Key personnel**
President: Shigeo Iwatare
Managing Director: Kunio Oshita
Director: Masanori Kawanishi
General Manager, Sales and Marketing:
  Yukiyasu Fujimoto
General Manager, Overseas Marketing:
  Takashi Koyama

**Products**
Airbrake systems; air compressors, composition brake shoes; automatic slack adjusters; air suspension levelling valves and automatic brake testing systems.

Plug and sliding door systems; platform doors (manufactured and supplied by NABCO Building Products division); pressure-sealing systems; windscreen wiper motors.

NABCO brake systems are operating on over 48,000 emu cars of various Japanese operators and on the Shinkansen high-speed trainsets of the JR Group companies.

**Contracts**
Recent contracts include the supply of braking systems to the People's Republic of China for 224 metro cars for Beijing Urban Transit Railway Co Ltd, 116 cars for Tianjin Binhai Mass Transit Development Co Ltd.

*UPDATED*

## Newag GmbH & Co KG

PO Box 120355, D-46117 Oberhausen, Germany
Tel: (+49 208) 86 50 30   Fax: (+49 208) 865 03 20
e-mail: info@newag.de

**Key personnel**
See entry in *Locomotives and powered/non-powered passenger vehicles* section.

**Products**
Composition brake shoes, shoe carriers, disc brake pads. Newag has developed a range of non-asbestos composition brake shoes and can now supply appropriate friction materials with friction coefficients between 0.15 and 0.35 µm for any desired brake shoe. The same applies to Newag disc brake pads, which can be supplied with friction coefficients between 0.25 and 0.35 µm.

*VERIFIED*

## OKE

Oerlikon-Knorr Eisenbahntechnik AG
Mandachstrasse 50, CH-8155 Niederhasli, Switzerland
Tel: (+41 1) 852 31 11   Fax: (+41 1) 852 31 31

**Key personnel**
Managing Director: F Bonetti

**Corporate development**
OKE is a subsidiary of Knorr-Bremse (qv).

**Products**
Screw compressors and air dryers, pneumatic brake control systems (UIC type) for freight wagons and passenger coaches, electropneumatic brake control systems, microprocessor-based electronic brake control systems and anti-wheel slip/spin control. Microprocessor-based driver's brake installation for locomotives and trainsets, disc brakes, actuators and block brake units, electromagnetic and permanent-magnetic track brakes (PMS).

Apart from the development, production and sales of Oerlikon braking equipment, OKE is responsible for marketing all products for railborne vehicles manufactured by Knorr-Bremse AG in Switzerland and in the Netherlands.

Current projects include systems for bilevel Intercity coaches and tilting trains for SBB.

## Oleo International Ltd

Grovelands, Longford Road, Exhall, Coventry CV7 9NE, UK
Tel: (+44 2476) 64 55 55   Fax: (+44 2476) 36 42 87

**Key personnel**
See entry in *Freight vehicles and equipment* section.

**Products**
Supplier of hydraulic side buffers to major European railways. Oleo has introduced specialised long-stroke side buffers to its range. By increasing the stroke from the

---

# PEOPLE'S SAFETY AND COMFORT

**NABCO's Railroad Products Division provides comprehensive safety systems for high-speed railway vehicles.**
electro-pneumatic brake systems,
composition brake shoes,
plug and sliding door systems,
door airtightness devices.

Brake Operating Unit
Electric Automatic Sliding Door
Motor-Driven Air Compressor Unit
Tread Brake Unit and Composition Brake Shoe

SAFE-TECH & AMENI-TECH

**NABCO**
NABCO Ltd.
9-18, KAIGAN-1-CHOME, MINATOKU, TOKYO 105-0022 JAPAN
TEL.+81-3-5470-2401  FAX.+81-3-5470-2424
http://www.nabco.co.jp

# MANUFACTURERS/Brakes and Drawgear

traditional 105 to 150 mm, the energy capacity is increased by up to 50 per cent. The Type 5SC-150 has been developed to meet the requirements of provisional UIC 526-3. Long-stroke hydraulic side buffers give additional protection to delicate goods.

Also available are the standard Type 4EC-80-105 and 5SC-105 (high static resistance) side buffers. The company also offers the Type 3RCA in combination with a friction spring, supplied by Ringfeder.

The Oleo Hydraulic Draftgear Type DA 4463 (Hycon) has an energy absorption capacity of 300,000 ft lb.

Products include the Oleo Hydraulic Drawspring, an adaptation of the Oleo side buffer capsule to protect drawhooks from snatch damage, particularly on long trains.

Energy-absorbing Anticlimber Side Buffers for passenger stock are on the Heathrow Express trainsets and Class 465 emus in the UK.

*UPDATED*

## Paulstra

Railway Department
61 rue Marius Aufan, F-92305 Levallois-Perret, France
Tel: (+33 1) 40 89 53 31   Fax: (+33 1) 47 58 75 16
e-mail: auto.levallois@hutchinson.fr
Web: http://www.hutchinson.fr

**Key personnel**
Sales Director: Laurent Poirier

**Subsidiary companies**
Stop-Choc GmbH
Stop-Choc UK
Vibrachoc España
Paulstra Industries Inc, USA

**Products**
Buffers; elastic couplings; primary springs, air spring secondary suspension, axle bushes, engine mounts, sandwich mounts and pads, chevrons, bogie pivot bushes, rubber/metal secondary suspension, gangway seals, floor tiles and oil seals.

*UPDATED*

## Peddinghaus Group

Carl Dan Peddinghaus GmbH & Co KG
Mittelstrasse 64, D-58256 Ennepetal, Germany
Tel: (+49 2333) 79 60   Fax: (+49 2333) 79 63 88
e-mail: cdp-en@t-online.de
Web: http://www.peddinghaus-group.de

**Products**
A supplier of high quality steel and aluminium forgings and components including screw couplings and hooks.

## Poli

Poli Costruzione Materiali Trazione SpA
Via Fontanella 11, I-26010 Camisano, Cremona, Italy
Tel: (+39 0373) 77 72 50   Fax: (+39 0373) 77 72 29
e-mail: info@polibrakes.com
Web: http://www.polibrakes.com

**Key personnel**
Chief Executive Officer: Francesco Poli
Technical Director: Dott Ing Antonio Poli
Technical Export Sales Manager: Dott Giuseppe Poli
Finance Director: Alessandro Poli
Public Relations Director: Francesco Cappellazzi
Purchasing Manager: Alberto Poli

**Principal subsidiary**
CTE Srl
Corso Concordia 16, I-20129 Milan, Italy

**Products**
Complete pneumatic and electrohydraulic braking systems for high-speed trains, passenger cars, freight wagons, locomotives, dmus, emus, track maintenance vehicles, light rail vehicles and low-floor trams; disc brake units, featuring friction crowns which can be replaced without removing the wheel from the axle; electromagnetic track brakes.

Poli products have been supplied to operators in Austria, France, Germany, Greece, Italy, Japan, Netherlands, Poland, Switzerland, UK and USA. Projects employing Poli products include: FS TAF double-deck emus; FS ETR 500 high-speed trainsets; and FS E402B electric locomotives.

*VERIFIED*

## Radenton

Radenton Scharfenberg Ltd
Unit 7, Silverdale Industrial Centre, Silverdale Road, Hayes UB3 3BP, UK
Tel: (+44 20) 85 89 77 30   Fax: (+44 20) 85 69 07 23
e-mail: andrew.cowell@rdn-voith.co.uk

**Key personnel**
Managing Director: Patrick Keogh
Commercial Manager: Andrew Cowell

**Corporate background**
Radenton Scharfenberg is a Voith Turbo company.

**Products**
'Wedgelock' autocouplers and bar couplers; anticlimbers; Scharfenberg autocouplers and bar couplers; Tightlock autocouplers; Albert couplers; shock-absorbing front hoods.

Recent contracts include the supply of autocouplers for trainsets in use on London Underground Ltd's Northern line. Recent contracts include orders from Great Western Holdings and ScotRail.

*UPDATED*

## Réservoir

Le Réservoir SA
rue Eugène Sue, ZI Blanzat, PO Box 1139, F-03103 Montluçon Cedex, France
Tel: (+33 4) 70 03 47 47   Fax: (+33 4) 70 03 77 03

**Key personnel**
Commercial Director: M Mardele
Export Sales: M Tracol

**Products**
Air vessels for brake and suspension systems.

## Saalasti Oy

Saalasti Oy
Juvan teollisuuskatu 28, FIN-02920 Espoo, Finland
Tel: (+358 9) 251 15 50   Fax: (+358 9) 25 11 55 10
e-mail: info@salaasti.fi
Web: http://www.saalasti.fi

**Key personnel**
See entry in *Locomotives and powered/non-powered passenger vehicles* section.

**Products**
Shunting couplers, multicouplers, drawgears.

Saalasti has delivered over 800 automatic multicouplers to Finnish State Railways and to private industry in Finland and Sweden. With this Vapiti multicoupler it is possible to couple the locomotive to both the drawhook and the central buffer. The latest model, Vapiti 90, is especially suited for hauling passenger coaches due to its patented tensioning method.

A further development is the OTSO-coupler, a semi-automatic locomotive coupling for drawhooks. The design makes it possible to couple the locomotive on curved track.

Contracts include the supply of OTSO-couplers to operators in Sweden and Finland.

*VERIFIED*

## SAB WABCO

See entry for Cardo Rail

*VERIFIED*

## Scharfenbergkupplung

Scharfenbergkupplung GmbH & Co KG
PO Box 311157, D-38239 Salzgitter, Germany
Tel: (+49 5341) 21 40 31   Fax: (+49 5341) 21 42 02
e-mail: info.schaku@voith.de
Web: http://www.schaku.de

**Key personnel**
General Manager: Martin Wawrh
Sales Director: Holgar Costard
Technical Director: Reinhardt Friedow
Commercial Director: Jochen Heine

**Principal licensees and subsidiary companies**
Australia: Scharfenbergkupplung Australia Pty Ltd
PO Box 1215, Osborne Park, Perth WA 6917, Australia
Spain: CAF
UK: Radenton Scharfenberg Ltd (qv)
France: Couplomatic Scharfenberg,
21 rue de Clichy, F-93584 Saint Ouen Cedex, France

**Corporate background**
Scharfenbergkupplung GmbH & Co KG is a Voith Turbo company.

*Scharfenbergkupplung automatic couplers fitted to DB AG ICE 3 high-speed trainsets*   2001/0105888

Brakes and Drawgear/**MANUFACTURERS**

**Products**
Automatic multifunction couplers, semi-permanent couplers and drawgear for light rail, rapid transit, trams, metros, powered and non-powered passenger vehicles, freight wagons, locomotives, automated guideway transit, mountain railways; special couplers for shunting vehicles, ladle cars, cranes; adaptor couplers, electric couplers; safety bumpers with hinged front hoods.

Recent contracts include automatic and semi-permanent couplers for Oresund OTU trains, Sweden, ICE3 trains, Germany, IC2000 RENFE trains, Spain; Shanghai metro Line 2; and Singapore Line 3 metro trains.

*UPDATED*

## SEE

Société Européenne d'Engrenages
5 rue Henri Cavallier, PO Box 716, F-89107 Saint-Denis-les-Sens, France
Tel: (+33 3) 86 95 62 00   Fax: (+33 3) 86 95 62 41

**Key personnel**
President: J P Fontaine
Commercial Director: P Davion

**Products**
Disc brakes, hangers and hydraulic calipers.
SEE designed and manufactured the high-performance disc brake mounted on SNCF's TGV-Atlantique high-speed train (300 km/h speed in service).
The company has introduced a wheel flanged disc brake provided with flexible steel wheel fixation.

## SGL Carbon Group

SGL Technologies GmbH
Werner von Siemens Strasse 18, D-86405 Meitingen, Germany
Tel: (+49 8271) 83 21 60   Fax: (+49 8271) 83 14 27
e-mail: technik@sglcarbon.de
Web: http://www.sglcarbon.com

**Products**
Sigrasic lightweight carbon fibre-reinforced silicon carbide (CSiC) brake discs for high-speed trains.

*UPDATED*

## SMC

SMC Pneumatics
Transport Division, 18 Hudson Avenue, Castle Hill, NSW 2154, Australia
Tel: (+61 2) 935 48 22 22   Fax: (+61 2) 96 34 77 64

**Key personnel**
See entry in *Electric traction equipment* section.

**Products**
Air dryers and filters, drain valves, pressure and flow control valves, EP valves.

## Stabeg

Stabeg Apparatebau GmbH
Reinlgasse 5-9, A-1140 Vienna, Austria
Tel: (+43 1) 92 26 28   Fax: (+43 1) 92 61 66

**Products**
Airbrake equipment for locomotives, coaches, freight wagons; air springs; drawgear; buffer and drawgear; side buffers.

## Standard

Standard Car Truck Co
865 Busse Highway, Park Ridge, Illinois 60068, USA
Tel: (+1 847) 692 60 50   Fax: (+1 847) 692 62 99

**Key personnel**
See entry in *Bogies and suspensions, wheels and axles* section.

**Products**
High and low-friction Anchor composition brake shoes for locomotives and freight wagons.

## Stone India Ltd

16 Taratalla Road, Calcutta 700 088, India
Tel: (+91 33) 401 46 61   Fax: (+91 33) 401 48 86
e-mail: stonein@cal.vsnl.net.in

**Key personnel**
Managing Director: A Ray
Vice-President, Marketing: S L Ahuja

**Products**
Airbrake systems for locomotives, passenger coaches and freight wagons; non-asbestos composite brake blocks, rubber components and slack adjusters; tread brake unit.

*UPDATED*

## Sumitomo Metal Industries Ltd

8-11 Harumi 1-Chome, Tokyo 104-6111, Japan
Tel: (+81 3) 44 16 62 71   Fax: (+81 3) 44 16 67 90
e-mail: skr@sumitomometals.co.jp
Web: http://www.sumitomometals.co.jp

**Works address**
Osaka Steel Works, 1-109 Shimaya 5-chome, Konohana-ku, Osaka 554-0024, Japan

**Key personnel**
Senior Vice President: Yasutaka Toya
Vice President: Kaoru Goto
General Manager, Sales: Y Miyamoto
Manager, Railway Products and Equipment Sales: R Iino

**Products**
Couplers; draftgear and steel castings for the railway industry; bogies (see *Bogies and suspension, wheels and axles, bearings* section).

*UPDATED*

## Textar

Textar Kupplungs-und Industriebeläge GmbH
Industriestrasse 7, D-57577 Hamm/Sieg, Germany
Tel: (+49 2682) 70 82 34   Fax: (+49 2682) 70 81 50

**Products**
Non-asbestos friction materials, mainly based on organic binders.

## Thyssen Krupp

Thyssen Krupp Gleistechnik GmbH
Altendorfer Strasse 104, D-45143 Essen, Germany
Tel: (+49 201) 188 37 10   Fax: (+49 201) 188 37 14

**Works**
Kaiser-Wilhelm-Strasse 100, D-47166 Duisburg, Germany
Tel: (+49 203) 524 06 20   Fax: (+49 203) 522 46 94

**Products**
Brake discs.

## Tokyu Car Corporation

3-1 Ohkawa, Kanazawa-ku, Yokohama 236-0043, Japan
Tel: (+81 45) 785 30 09   Fax: (+81 45) 785 65 50

**Key personnel**
See entry in *Locomotives and powered/non-powered passenger vehicles* section.

**Products**
Disc brakes.

*VERIFIED*

## Triax-YSD

401 North 8th Street, Benton Harbour, Michigan 49022, USA
Tel: (+1 616) 925 00 11   Fax: (+1 616) 925 00 00
e-mail: sales@triax-ysd.com
Web: http://www.triax-ysd.com

**Key personnel**
President: William Mundinger
Vice-President, International Sales: Bob Jackson

**Products**
Solid-truss brake beams and bogie-mounted braking systems including custom designs.

## TSM Inc

10765 Ambassador Drive, Kansas City, Missouri 64153, USA
Tel: (+1 816) 891 65 44   Fax: (+1 816) 891 93 29

**Key personnel**
Vice-President & General Manager: Douglas D Klink
Vice-President, Sales: John H Chionchio
Director, Sales & Marketing: Ron Rudnicki

**Products**
EABS electronic airbrake system for freight wagons.
Recent contracts include the supply of EABS electronic airbrake systems to BNSF and various electric utilities.

## Ueda

Ueda Brake Co Ltd
10-19 Tomobuchi-cho 2-chome, Miyakojima-ku, Osaka, Japan
Tel: (+81 6) 921 29 71   Fax: (+81 6) 921 29 75

**Key personnel**
President: Takafumi Ueda
Marketing Director: Tadayoshi Akiyama
Senior Manager, Engineering: Akio Yoshioka

**Products**
Composite brake shoes to prevent reduction of the adhesion coefficient between wheel and rail during operation in wet weather.

## Unity Railway Supply

Unity Railway Supply Co Inc
805 Golf Lane, Bensenville, Illinois 60106, USA
Tel: (+1 630) 595 45 60   Fax: (+1 630) 595 06 46

**Key personnel**
President and Chairman: Harold R O'Connor
Vice-President, Sales: Robert S Grandy
Executive Vice-President, Financial: Robert Holden

**Products**
Adapter 'PLUS' adapter/polymer roof liner; air brake hose supports; batten bars; bolster bowl liner; box car ends; roller bearing adapters; handbrakes; hand wheels and bell cranks; brake levers and parts; cast steel draft lugs and centre plates; centre pins; draft lugs and centre plates; end platforms (grating type); fasteners, filters, pipe brackets/dust strainers; floor deck plug; friction castings (standard and split wedge); gondola ends; gravity discharge outlet gates; handholds (grab irons); hopper chutes; hopper door frames; hopper slope sheets; journal lubricators; ladders; lumber corner protectors; plug door guides; running boards (grating type); side posts; sill steps; warning lights (blue flag and barricade) wear plate (dual-purpose for narrow pedestal side frames); wheel chocks.

*VERIFIED*

## MANUFACTURERS/Brakes and Drawgear

## WABCO

Westinghouse Air Brake Company
1001 Air Brake Avenue, Wilmerding, Pennsylvania 15148, USA
Tel: (+1 412) 825 10 00   Fax: (+1 412) 825 10 19

### Key personnel
President and Chief Executive Officer: Greg Davies
Chief Financial Officer: Robert J Brooks
Executive Vice-President, Freight Group: Paul Golden
Executive Vice-President, Transit Group: John M Meister
Executive Vice-President, Moulded Products: Tony Carponi
Vice-President, International: Timothy J Logan
Vice-President, Investor Relations: Tim Wesley

### Principal subsidiaries
Cardwell Westinghouse Company
Pulse Electronics Inc
Motive Power
Railroad Friction Products Corp
Universal Railway Devices Inc
Vapor Corporation
Young Touchstone

### Products
Complete brake system components for locomotives, powered and non-powered passenger vehicles and freight wagons; pneumatic, electropneumatic, electrohydraulic, electromechanical and electronic (pneumatic and hydraulic) brake equipment; mechanical and electric reciprocating and rotary air compressors; bogie-mounted brake cylinders (actuators), tread and disc brake units, brake discs, automatic slack adjusters, track brakes; composition (non-metallic, asbestos-free) brake shoes (blocks) and disc brake pads; fully automatic mechanical, pneumatic and electrical couplers for LRVs, metro trainsets and electric multiple-units; friction-type, all-metal and rubber/metal draft gears, draft gears for freight service; geared handbrakes; electronic data recorders, end-of-train units, speed indicators, alertness devices, onboard computers, fault monitors/annunciators, fuel level indicators; electromechanical and electropneumatic door actuators for passenger vehicles; air conditioning equipment for passenger vehicles.

*UPDATED*

## Wabtec Rail

Wabtec Rail Ltd
PO Box 192, Hexthorpe Road, Doncaster DN1 1PJ, UK
Tel: (+44 1302) 79 00 27   Fax: (+44 1302) 79 00 58
e-mail: probinson@wabtec.com
Web: http://www.wabtec.com

### Key personnel
See entry in *Locomotives and powered/non-powered passenger vehicles* section.

### Corporate development
Wabtec Rail formerly traded as RFS(E), changing its name in March 2000.

### Products
Overhaul of hydraulic buffers, air brake equipment and drawgear equipment.

## Westinghouse Brakes (UK) Limited

Foundry Lane, Chippenham SN15 1JB, UK
Tel: (+44 1249) 44 20 00   Fax: (+44 1249) 65 50 40
e-mail: wbl.sales@westbrake.com

### Key personnel
Managing Director: Paul R Johnson
Engineering Director: Jason Abbott
Marketing and Sales Director: Peter Johnson
Projects Director: Danny Lee
Manufacturing Director: Robert H Wagner
Finance Director: Neil Booth
Business Group Manager, Brakes Systems: Ian Palmer
Business Group Manager, Brake Products: Richard Bew
Business Group Manager, Customer Service: David Briers

### Background
Westinghouse Brakes (UK) Limited is a member of Knorr-Bremse group (qv).

### Products
Brake systems comprising air and vacuum brake equipment, electro-pneumatic brake systems with digital or analogue control for metro and commuter passenger trains. Equipment includes rotary and reciprocating air compressors, air treatment equipment, drivers brake and brake/traction controllers, wheelslide protection equipment, sanding systems, warning equipment, air suspension control equipment, brake actuation equipment, tread and disc brake equipment and magnetic track brakes.

A comprehensive after sales service is available providing equipment repair, overhaul and long-term maintenance support in addition to spare parts supply.

### Contracts
Recent contracts include: brake systems for Desiro, Electrostar, Juniper and Coradia multiple-unit vehicle platforms, Arriva Trains Northern trains, 'Voyager' CrossCountry and Midland Main Line 'Meridian' demus, Kuala Lumpur Airport Express trains, Docklands Light Railway, Shanghai Pearl Line and Shanghai Xin Min metro trains, Class 66 locomotives and wheelside equipment for the First Great Western high-speed trains.

*UPDATED*

## Westinghouse Saxby Farmer

Westinghouse Saxby Farmer Ltd
17 Convent Road, Entally, Calcutta 700-014, India
Tel: (+91 33) 244 71 61   Fax: (+91 33) 244 71 65
e-mail: wsfedp@cal2.vsnl.net.in

### Key personnel
Managing Director: A N Dutta
Director, Finance & Marketing: D K De Sarker

### Products
Electro-pneumatic brake system including regenerative brake blending equipment for emus and subway coaches; air and vacuum brake system for locomotives, passenger coaches, wagons, diesel rail cranes, special purpose railway vehicles and trams; semi-permanent type centre buffer couplers for emus; parking brakes for emus.

### Contracts
Recent contracts include the supply of 350 sets of electro-pneumatic brake equipment.

*UPDATED*

## Yutaka Manufacturing Co Ltd

1-18-17 Kitakojiya Ota-ku, Tokyo 144-0032, Japan
Tel: (+81 3) 37 41 41 31   Fax: (+81 3) 57 05 70 65
e-mail: hideo.kamei@yutaka-ss.co.jp
Web: http://www.kutaka-ss.co.jp/

### Products
Automatic electrical couplers to form part of automatic train coupling/uncoupling systems.

# BOGIES AND SUSPENSION, WHEELS AND AXLES, BEARINGS

## Alphabetical listing

ABC-NACO Inc
Acieries de Ploërmel
ALSTOM Transport SA
ALSTOM Schienenfahrzenge AG
American Koyo Corporation
AMPEP plc
Amsted Industries International
Amurrio Ferrocarril
ASF
Astra
Ateliers de Braine-le-Comte et Thiriau Réunis SA
Avon Spencer Moulton
AWS
BHEL
Bochumer Verein
Bombardier Transportation
Bonatrans AS
Bradken Rail
Breda
Buckeye
Bumar Ltd
CAF
Cardo Rail
CFD
China National Railway Locomotive and Rolling Stock Industry Corporation (LORIC)
Cimmco International
ČKD
ČKD Kutná Hora as
Cockerill Forges & Ringmill
Comet Industries Inc
Cometna
ContiTech
Delta Rail
Devol
Dominion Castings Ltd
Energomachexport
Escorts Ltd
FAG
Federal-Mogul Corporation
Ferraz SA
Ferrostaal AG
FIREMA Trasporti SpA
Freudenberg Schwab GmbH

Fuchs Lubricants (UK) plc
Ganz Vagon
GMT
Greysham International
Griffin
Gutenhoffnungshütte Radsatz GmbH
HDA Forgings Ltd
Hindustan Eng & Ind
IBG
IBG Monforts
ICF
IMS UK
Issels
Kinex-KLM
KLW – Wheelco SA
Kockums
Koni BV
Koyo Seiko Co Ltd
Krupp Brüninghaus GmbH
Kryukovsky
Langen & Sondermann
Lesjöfors AB
Lord Corporation
Lubricant Consult GmbH
Lucchini Group
Magnus/Farley Inc
Manoir Industries – Sambre et Meuse
Mecanoexportimport SA
Mediterr Shock-Absorbers Srl
MIBA Gleitlager AG
Multi-Service Supply Division
MWL Brasil Rodas & Eixos Ltda
Nippon Sharyo Ltd
Nizhnedneprovsky
NSK Ltd
NSK-RHP UK
NTN Toyo
OFV
ORX
Peddinghaus Group
Penn
Phoenix AG
Poli
Powell Duffryn Rail

Precima Development AB
Puzhen
Qiqihar
Radsatz Ilsenburg
Railko Ltd
Ringrollers
Rose Bearings Ltd
Rotem
RSD
R W Mac Co
SAB WABCO
Silvertown UK Ltd
SKF
Standard Steel LLC
Steel Authority of India Ltd
Stork RMO BV
Stucki
Sumitomo
Superior Graphite Co
Swasap
Tafesa SA
Talgo
TATRAVAGÓNKA AS
Techlam
Techni-Industrie SA
Tenmat Ltd
Thyssen Krupp
Timken Rail Service
Trelleborg
TSM
Tülomsas
United Goninan
Uralvagonzavod
Valdunes
Vibratech Inc
VSFT
Wabtec Rail Ltd
Walkers
Wheel & Axle
William Cook Rail
Willy Vogel
Woodhead Shock Absorbers
Zeco
ZF Sachs AG

# MANUFACTURERS/Bogies and suspension, wheels and axles, bearings

## Classified listing

### AXLES, TYRES, WHEELS AND WHEELSETS
ABC-NACO
Bochumer Verein
Bonatrans
Bumar Ltd
CAF
Cardo Rail
ČKD Kutná Hora
Cockerill Forges & Ringmill
Energomachexport
Ferrostaal
Fuchs Lubricants
GMT
Griffin
Gutenhoffnungshütte Radsatz
IMS
KLW – Wheelco
Kryukovsky
Lucchini Group
Mecanoexportimport
Nizhnedneprovsky
ORX
Peddinghaus Group
Penn
Poli
Railx
Ringrollers
Standard Steel LLV
Steel Authority of India
Swasap
Thysell Krupp
TSM
Valdunes
Wabtec Rail
Wheel & Axle
Willy Vogel

### BEARINGS
American Koyo Corporation
AMPEP
AWS
Comet Industries
Devol
FAG
Federal-Mogul Corporation
IBG
Kinex-KLM
Koyo Seiko
Magnus/Farley
MIBA
Multi-Service Supply
NSK
NSK-RHP
NTN Toyo
Puzhen
Railko
Railx
Rose Bearings
Rotem
SKF
Stucki
Tenmat
Timken

### BOGIES
Acieries de Ploërmel
ALSTOM
ALSTOM Schienenfahrzenge AG
Amsted Industries International
Amurrio Ferrocarril
ASF
Astra
Ateliers de Braine-le-Comte et Thiriau Réunis
BHEL
Bombardier Transportation
Bradken Rail
Breda
Buckeye
CAF
CFD
China National Railway Locomotive and Rolling Stock Industry Corporation (LORIC)
Cimmco International
ČKD
Cometna
Dominion Castings
Energomachexport
Ferrostaal
Ganz Vagon
HDA Forgings
Hindustan Eng & Ind
ICF
Issels
Kockums
Kryukovsky
Manoir Industries – Sambre et Meuse
Nippon Sharyo
Nizhnedneprovsky
OFV
ORX
Powell Duffryn Rail
Qiqihar
Railx
Rotem
RSD
R W Mac
Siemens SGP
Standard
Stork RMO
Stucki
Sumitomo
Tafesa
TATRAVAGÓNKA
Techni-Industrie
Tülomsas
United Goninan
Uralvagonzavod
VSFT
Wabtec Rail
Walkers
William Cook Rail
Zeco

### SUSPENSION SYSTEMS AND COMPONENTS
ALSTOM
AMSU
Avon
Cardo Rail
ContiTech
Curtiss Wright
Delta Rail
Energomachexport
Escorts
Ferraz
Ferrostaal
Freudenberg Schwab
IBG
Koni
Krupp Brüninghaus
Langen & Sondermann
Lesjöfors AB
Lord
Phoenix
Precima Development AB
R W Mac
SAB WABCO
Silvertown UK
Standard
Stucki
Superior Graphite
Talgo
Techlam
Trelleborg
Vibratech
Woodhead Shock Absorbers

# Company listing by country

**AUSTRALIA**
Amsted Industries International
Bradken Rail
United Goninan
Walkers

**AUSTRIA**
MIBA Gleitlager AG
Siemens SGP

**BELGIUM**
Ateliers de Braine-le-Comte et Thiriau Réunis SA
Cockerill Forges & Ringmill

**BRAZIL**
MWL Brasil Rodas & Eixos Ltda

**CANADA**
Bombardier Transportation
Dominion Castings Ltd

**CHINA, PEOPLE'S REPUBLIC**
China National Railway Locomotive and Rolling Stock Industry Corporation (LORIC)
Puzhen
Qiqihar

**CZECH REPUBLIC**
Bonatrans AS
ČKD
ČKD Kutná Hora as

**FRANCE**
Acieries de Ploërmel
ALSTOM
AMSU SA
Avon Spencer Moulton
CFD
Delta Rail
Ferraz SA
Manoir Industries – Sambre et Meuse
Techlam
Techni-Industrie SA
Valdunes

**GERMANY**
AWS
Bochumer Verein
ContiTech
FAG
Ferrostaal AG
Freudenberg Schwab GmbH
GMT
Gutenhoffnungshütte Radsatz GmbH
IBG
IBG Monforts
Langen & Sondermann
Lubricant Consult GmbH
Peddinghaus Group
Phoenix AG
Radsatz Ilsenburg
Thyssen Krupp
Willy Vogel
ZF Sachs AG

**HUNGARY**
Ganz Vagon

**INDIA**
BHEL
Cimmco International
Escorts Ltd
Greysham International
Hindustan Eng & Ind
ICF
Steel Authority of India Ltd
Wheel & Axle

**ITALY**
Breda
FIREMA Trasporti SpA
Lucchini Group
Mediterr Shock-Absorbers Srl
OFV
Poli

**JAPAN**
Koyo Seiko Co Ltd
Nippon Sharyo Ltd
NSK Ltd
NTN Toyo
Sumitomo

**KOREA (SOUTH)**
Rotem

**NETHERLANDS**
Koni BV
Stork RMO BV

**POLAND**
Bumar Ltd

**PORTUGAL**
Cometna

**ROMANIA**
Astra
Mecanoexportimport SA

**RUSSIAN FEDERATION**
Energomachexport
Uralvagonzavod

**SLOVAKIA**
Kinex-KLM
TATRAVAGÓNKA AS

**SOUTH AFRICA**
Ringrollers
RSD
Swasap

**SPAIN**
Amurrio Ferrocarril
CAF
Tafesa SA
Talgo

**SWEDEN**
Cardo Rail
Kockums
Lesjöfors AB
Precima Development AB
SAB WABCO
SKF

**SWITZERLAND**
ALSTOM Schienenfahrzenge AG
KLW – Wheelco SA

**TURKEY**
Tülomsas

**UKRAINE**
Kryukovsky
Nizhnedneprovsky

**UNITED KINGDOM**
AMPEP plc
Devol
Fuchs Lubricants (UK) plc
HDA Forgings Ltd
IMS UK
NSK-RHP UK
Powell Duffryn Rail
Railko Ltd
Rose Bearings Ltd
Silvertown UK Ltd
Tenmat Ltd
Timken Rail Service
Trelleborg
Wabtec Rail Ltd
William Cook Rail
Woodhead Shock Absorbers

**UNITED STATES OF AMERICA**
ABC-NACO Inc
American Koyo Corporation
ASF
Buckeye
Comet Industries Inc
Federal-Mogul Corporation
Griffin
Lord Corporation
Magnus/Farley Inc
Multi-Service Supply Division
ORX
Penn
Railx
R W Mac Co
Standard Steel LLC
Stucki
Superior Graphite Co
TSM
Vibratech Inc

**ZIMBABWE**
Issels
Zeco

## MANUFACTURERS/Bogies and suspension, wheels and axles, bearings

## ABC-NACO Inc

2001 Butterfield Road, Suite 502, Downers Grove, Illinois 60515, USA
Tel: (+1 630) 852 13 00   Fax: (+1 630) 852 22 64
Web: http://www.abc-naco.com

**Key personnel**
See entry in *Brakes and drawgear* section.

**Products**
Axle motion low track force bogies, cast-steel wheels, wheelsets and metal brake shoes, suspension systems for freight wagons, passenger coaches and locomotives.

## Acieries de Ploërmel

PO Box 103, F-56804 Ploërmel, France
Tel: (+33 2) 97 73 24 70   Fax: (+33 2) 97 74 03 90
e-mail: ap.ctrochu@wanadoo.fr

**Key personnel**
See entry in *Brakes and drawgear* section.

**Background**
Acieries de Ploërmel is a member of the Amsted Group.

**Products**
Bogie components for TGV trainsets, pendular trains, LRVs and metro trains.

Recent contracts include parts for bogies for ALSTOM's UK Juniper emu contract; for Bombardier for the Cologne metro and for Croydon Tramlink, UK; for ALSTOM for the Citadis contract in France and for new ALSTOM projects of Metropolis and MF2000.

## ALSTOM Schienenfahrzeuge AG

CH-8212 Neuhausen am Rheinfall, Switzerland
Tel: (+41 52) 674 61 61   Fax: (+41 52) 674 66 07
e-mail: sales.fss@sig.ch

**Key personnel**
Managing Director: Carlo Venturi
Sales and Marketing Manager: Peter Huber

**Corporate development**
In October 2000, ALSTOM Transport (qv) acquired a 51 per cent shareholding in Fiat Ferroviaria, FiatSig's main shareholder.

**Products**
Powered, motor and trailer bogies for a wide range of applications.

Recent contracts include the supply of motor bogies for mDDM double- deck motor cars for NS Netherlands; trailer bogies for IC double-deck coaches for SBB Switzerland and VR Finland; trailer bogies for IC coaches for SBB Switzerland and DB Germany; tilting bogies for ICN and tilting trains for SBB Switzerland; bogies for Cobra tramcars in Zurich and single-axle bogies for gondolas in Cottbus, Brandenburg, Mulheim, Basle and Gothenberg.

***VERIFIED***

## ALSTOM Transport SA

1 rue Baptiste Marcet, PO Box 42, F-71202 Le Creusot Cedex, France
Tel: (+33 3) 85 73 60 00   Fax: (+33 3) 85 73 67 99
e-mail: bernhard.russell@alstom.transport.com

**Key personnel**
Managing Director: Michel Poisson
Sales and Marketing Manager: Bernhard Russell
DISPEN Dampers Manager: Dominique Martinez

**Joint venture**
ALSTOM Qingdao Railway Equipment Co
231 Ruichang Road, Qingdao 266031, People's Republic of China
Tel: (+86 532) 489 41 05   Fax: (+86 532) 489 41 02
Managing Director: Frank Liu

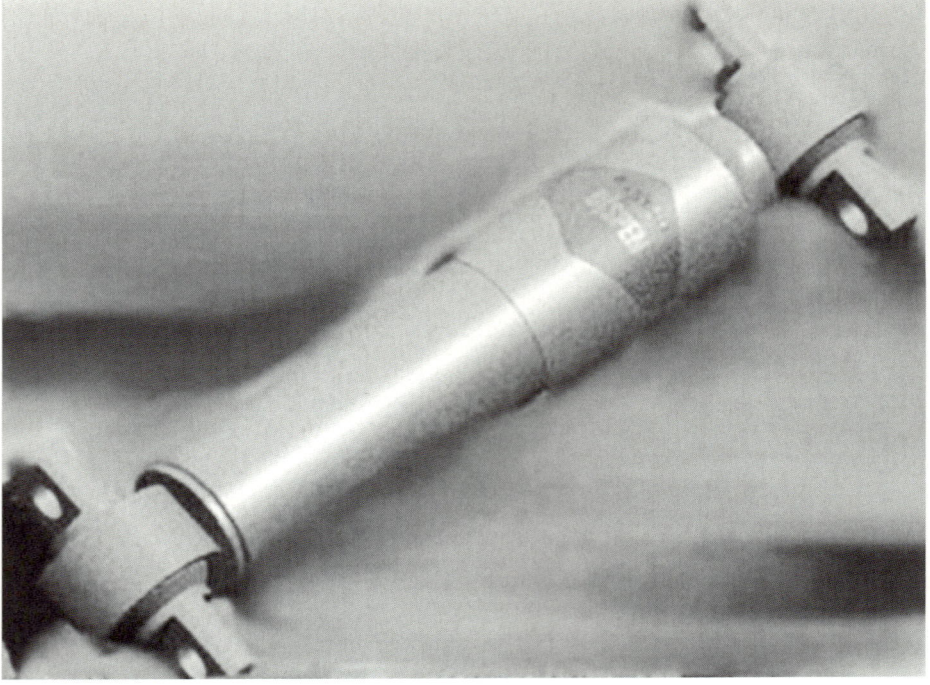

*DISPEN Damper*

**Products**
ALSTOM designs and produces bogies and dampers, for supply through ALSTOM Transport directly to operators or through alternative car builders. These components are accompanied by worldwide service support.

Applications extend from urban tramcars and metros to very-high-speed TGVs. ALSTOM also offers proprietary tilt technology and compact single-axle bogies, and is creating innovative solutions to weight-saving requirements on latest generations of rolling stock.

Bogie axleloads vary from 5 to 25 tonnes, wheel gauges from metre, 1,435 to 1,520 mm, and design speeds from 60 to 80 km/h in trams to over 300 km/h for TGV vehicles.

In 2000, ALSTOM acquired a 51 per cent shareholding in Fiat Ferroviaria SpA, which produces bogies for tractive units and hauled vehicles, including trailer and motor bogies for the Pendolino tilting and non-tilting trainset family.

DISPEN dampers are specifically engineered to railway standards and serve bogie requirements in both primary and secondary suspensions (vertical, horizontal and anti-yaw damping) as well as inter-car applications.

Annual production capacity of bogies and dampers is 2,500 and 40,000 respectively. Plant sites exist across Europe, but also in Asia, and in North and South America. Key orders and deliveries since 1999 include Shanghai, Warsaw, NYCT New York, Metrovías São Paulo and Singapore. Other recent contracts include: 112 1,067 mm gauge bogies for KOROS, South Korea, to equip emus for Taiwan; 46 bogie kits for PT INKA, Indonesia.

DISPEN Damper business was particularly active in 1999, including the largest international order to date (for the Korean TGV), a sharp increase in European and Chinese orders, and strong demand in service support activities. The Korean contract is for 8,702 dampers to equip 34 ALSTOM TGV trainsets to be manufactured in the KOROS manufacturing plant. Delivery is between January 2000 and December 2002. It is the biggest order for DISPEN dampers that ALSTOM has received so far. In 2000 JR West placed an order for 56 DISPEN anti-yaw dampers, with options on additional units.

In mid-1999 a joint venture in China, ALSTOM Qingdao, was established.

***UPDATED***

## American Koyo Corporation

Division of KCU Corporation of USA
29570 Clemens Road, Westlake, Ohio 44145, USA
Tel: (+1 216) 835 10 00   Fax: (+1 216 835) 93 47

**Key personnel**
General Manager: Yoshio Yabuno
Vice-President, Sales: Ray Normandin
OEM Sales Manager: Roger Lewis
After-Sales Manager: Don Kishton
OE Industrial Marketing Manager: Dale Neumann

**Products**
ABU-type journal roller bearings.

*SNCF TGV lateral damper assembly incorporating AMPEP bearings*

## AMPEP plc

Dept R, Strode Road, Clevedon BS21 6QQ, UK
Tel: (+44 1275) 87 60 21   Fax: (+44 1275) 87 84 80
e-mail: mail@ampep.co.uk

**Key personnel**
Technical Sales Director: Fred Rendell

**Background**
The company was formed in 1963 and in 1988 became part of the SKF Group (qv).

**Products**
Self-lubricating PTFE/glass fibre lined plain bearings. AMPEP bearings have been used in rail bogies for over 20 years. Applications include tilt mechanisms, torsion bars, damper attachment points, swing links, brake mechanisms, steering linkages valve linkages, auto-coupler and tailpin linkages.

*VERIFIED*

## Amsted Rail International

200 West Monroe Street, Suite 2301, Chicago, Illinois 60606, USA
Tel: (+1 312) 372 53 84   Fax: (+1 312) 372 82 30
e-mail: lgwood@megsinet.net

**Key personnel**
President: Glen F Lazar
Vice-President: Charles P Spencer
Manager of Engineering: Ronald D Colembiewski

**Products**
American Steel Foundries (ASF) lightweight Ride Control, Super Service Ride Control, Ridemaster, Super Service Ridemaster and AR-1 steerable bogies, all supplied assembled or in kit form; Griffen Wheel Co pressure-poured cast steel low-stress wheels; wagon body centreplates; Brenco taper roller bearings.

*UPDATED*

## Amurrio Ferrocarril y Equipos SA

Maskuribai 10, E-014709 Amurrio, Alava, Spain
Tel: (+34 945) 89 16 00   Fax: (+34 945) 89 24 80
e-mail: aferreq@sea.es
Web: http://www.amufer.es

**Key personnel**
General Manager: J M de Lapatza
Joint Manager: L M de Lapatza
Director of Engineering: V Ruiz
Technical Manager: R Sanabria
Sales Manager: J M Gutierrez
Quality Manager: J A Garcia

**Products**
Bearings and axleboxes for locomotives and wagons; adaptors; wheelsets, bogies, centre pivots; buffing gear, traction motor yokes and frames; frames and bolsters for bogies and other rolling stock parts.

*UPDATED*

## ASF

American Steel Foundries/Amsted Industries International (a division of Amsted Industries Inc)
200 West Monroe Street, Suite 2301, Chicago, Illinois 60606, USA
Tel: (+1 312) 372 53 84   Fax: (+1 312) 372 82 30

**Key personnel**
See entry in *Brakes and drawgear* section.

**Products**
ASF designs, tests, manufactures and markets cast steel components and hot-wound coil products for both the rail and road industry. Freight car components include side frames, bolsters, bogies, draft sill end castings, couplers, rotary couplers, yokes, articulated connectors, slack-free drawbars, AAR and low-profile centre plates, snubbing packages (Ride Control, Super Service Ride Control, Ridemaster, Super Service Ridemaster), AR-1 self-steering trucks, strikers, draft lugs, AAR coils and control coils.

## Astra Vagoane Călători Arad SA/Arad

1-3 Petru Rareş, R-2900 Arad, Romania
Tel: (+40 257) 23 36 51   Fax: (+40 257) 25 81 68
e-mail: astra.calatori@astrac.rdsar.ro

**Key personnel**
See entry in *Locomotive and powered/non-powered passenger vehicles* section.

**Products**
Bogies for metro cars, passenger coaches, freight wagons and special purpose vehicles. Production includes 200 km/h Y32 bogies manufactured under Alstom/De Dietrich licence. Ring-type springs for traction and dumpers.

*UPDATED*

## Ateliers de Braine-le-Comte et Thiriau Réunis SA

Rue des Frères Dulait 14, B-7090 Braine-le-Comte, Belgium
Tel: (+32 67) 56 02 11   Fax: (+32 67) 56 12 17

**Key personnel**
Commercial Manager: A Lejeune
Commercial Manager, Railway Division: R Brohée

**Products**
Welded bogies, three-axle bogies.

---

# Bochumer Verein
## Verkehrstechnik GmbH · seit 1842

### Our product range

- Sound- and weight-optimated solid wheel with wheel brake discs
- Sound-absorbed tyred wheel with double-corrugated lightweight wheel disc 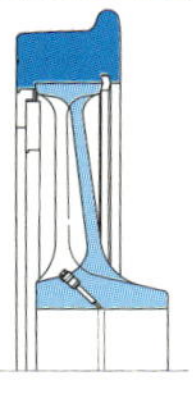
- Sound- and weight-optimated solid wheel with stress balanced wheel disc
- Rubber cushioned wheel Bo 54 in standard arrangement
- Low-floor axle bridge with loose wheel Type Bo 84 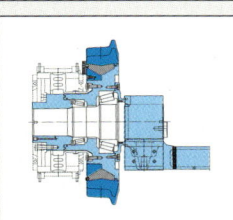
- Rubber cushioned wheel Bo 84 in standard arrangement

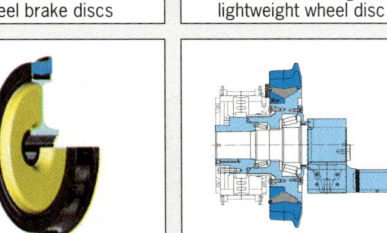

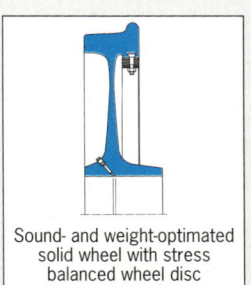

The company's product range is widely orientated to wheelsets and wheelset components for lightrail and heavy rail traffic.

Special products, such as rubber cushioned wheels, noise absorbers and light weight solid wheels are of particular importance.

Bochumer Verein Verkehrstechnik GmbH is also leading in the development of idler axles for new low floor cars.

Clearly defined, distinct product areas are the essential prerequisites to direct dialogue between business partners, efficient product development, high productivity and optimal quality assurance, flexibility and readiness for delivery.

The company is certified to DIN ISO 9001/EN 29001.

**Bochumer Verein Verkehrstechnik GmbH**
Alleestraße 70 · D-44793 Bochum/Germany
Tel.: +49 (0) 2 34/68 91-0
Fax: +49 (0) 2 34/68 91-5 80
E-mail: info@bochumer-verein.de
www.bochumer-verein.de

# MANUFACTURERS/Bogies and suspension, wheels and axles, bearings

## Avon Spencer Moulton

21 rue de la Gare, F-45330 Malesherbes, France
Tel: (+33 2) 38 32 72 29   Fax: (+33 2) 38 34 73 42
e-mail: guy.joly@asm.avon-rubber.com

### Key personnel
See entry in *Brakes and drawgear* section.

### Products
Suspension systems, including safety springs, chevrons and primary/secondary suspension bondings; sealing sections; drawgear packs, buffing springs and rail pads.

**UPDATED**

## AWS

Achslagerwerk Stassfurt GmbH
An der Liethe 5, D-39418 Stassfurt, Germany
Tel: (+49 3925) 96 03   Fax: (+49 3925) 96 04 05
e-mail: info@aws-tec.de
Web: http://www.aws-tec.de

### Key personnel
Managing Director: Heinz-Jürgen Luig
Chief Buyer and Sales Manager: Georg Lohmann

### Works address
PO Box 1153, D-39401 Stassfurt, Germany

### Products
Axlebox housings for rail vehicles including locomotives, railcars, passenger cars and freight wagons to UIC and GOST specification and for the standard Type Y25 freight bogie.

## BHEL

Bharat Heavy Electricals Ltd
Jhansi, India 284129
Tel: (+91 0517) 44 02 40; 44 06 15; 44 09 44
Fax: (+91 0517) 44 31 08; 44 43 66

### Key personnel
See entry in *Locomotives and powered/non-powered passenger vehicles* section.

### Products
Fabricated steel bogies for freight and passenger locomotives.
Contracts include 150 fabricated bogies for Indian Railways.

## Bochumer Verein Verkehrstechnik GmbH

Alleestrasse 70, D-44793 Bochum, Germany
Tel: (+49 234) 689 12 46   Fax: (+49 234) 689 15 80
e-mail: info@bochumer_verein.de
Web: http://www.bochumer_verein.de

### Key personnel
Managing Directors: Dr Ing Götz-Peter Blumbach;
  Dipl Wirt Ing Gerhard Störmer; Dipl Kfm Frank Kahle
Head of Sales and Marketing: Dipl Wirt Ing Olaf Toenjes
Head of Design and Calculation: Dipl Ing Franz Murawa
Head of Quality Management: Dr Martin Gumbiowski
Head of Research and Development: Dr Ingo Poschmann

### Products
Wheel and axle sets and components for light rail, metro and main line railway systems. Rolled steel wheels, tyres and wheel centres. Rubber-cushioned single-ring wheels, vibration absorbers to reduce running noise and curve squeal.

**UPDATED**

## Bombardier Transportation

1101 Parent Street, Saint-Bruno, Québec J3V 6E6, Canada
Tel: (+1 450) 441 20 20   Fax: (+1 450) 441 15 15
Web: http://www.transportation.bombardier.com

### Key personnel
See entry in *Locomotives and powered/non-powered passenger vehicles* section.

### Products
Bombardier Transportation has a full range of bogies for all types of applications. Among the technologies offered is the B5000 type for Virgin Cross Country, which weighs 30 per cent less than equivalent conventional bogies and minimises life cycle costs by reducing energy consumption, wheel and track wear, as well as maintenance. Based on the B5000 design principles, the ICE21 prototype bogies were tested at speeds up to 393 km/h in Germany and Japan using advanced technologies like active damping, lateral suspension and condition monitoring. Another application is the new generation of low-floor diesel tilting trains for Norway, which are equipped with bogies with the ContRoll-system, a unique and straight-forward mechanical interface to the car body without supplementary tilting bolster.

**UPDATED**

*Bombardier Transportation bogie for Talent Multiple Units, Germany*   0065308

*Bombardier Transportation bogie for SNCF Z2N double-deck emu*   2001/0099152

## Bonatrans AS

Bezručova 300, CZ-735 93 Bohumín, Czech Republic
Tel: (+420 69) 708 23 04   Fax: (+420 69) 708 28 05
e-mail: info@bonatrans.cz
Web: http://www.bonatrans.cz

### Key personnel
Managing Director: Pavel Lazar
Commercial Director: Vilém Balcárek

*Bombardier B5000 bogie for Virgin CrossCountry*   2001/0116574

*Bombardier bogie for ICE 21 prototype*   2001/0116573

*Bombardier bogie for low floor tilting trains*   2001/0116571

*Bombardier BM2000 bogie for light rail vehicles*   2001/0116572

## Bogies and suspension, wheels and axles, bearings/MANUFACTURERS

Marketing and Strategy Director: Jaroslav Sedlák
Technical Director: Radim Zima
Production Director: Jan Kusněř

**Corporate development**
The company previously traded as ŽDB AS, changing its name to Bonatrans AS in 1999.

**Products**
Wheelsets, solid wheels, resilient wheels, axles, tyres and wheel centres for locomotives, powered and non-powered passenger vehicles, urban rail vehicles and freight wagons.

*UPDATED*

## Bradken Rail

PO Box 105, Maud Street, Waratah, New South Wales 2298, Australia
Tel: (+61 2) 49 41 26 67   Fax: (+61 2) 49 41 26 61
e-mail: rail@bradken.com.au
Web: http://www.bradken.com.au

**Background**
See entry in *Freight vehicles and equipment* section.

**Products**
Bogies for locomotives, passenger coaches and freight wagons, supplying more than 100,000 bogies to domestic and local markets. ANI offers a wide range of bogies for standard, broad and narrow gauge, including metre gauge railways. Specific designs for high speed, stable ride and reduced track wear are also available.

**Contracts**
Recent contracts include the supply of bogies to India, Israel, Malaysia, New Zealand, Thailand and the USA.

*UPDATED*

## Breda

Breda Costruzioni Ferroviarie SpA
Via Ciliegiole 110/b, I-51100 Pistoia, Italy
Tel: (+39 0573) 37 01   Fax: (+39 0573) 37 02 92

**Key personnel**
See entry in *Locomotives and powered/non-powered pasenger vehicles* section.

**Products**
Motor and trailer bogies for locomotives, high-speed trainsets, metro trainsets, light rail vehicles, passenger coaches and freight wagons.

Contracts include motor and trailer bogies for light rail vehicles for San Francisco and Boston; motor and trailer bogies for metro trainsets for Atlanta, Copenhagen, San Francisco and Los Angeles; motor and trailer bogies for double-deck emus for Italian Railways (FS); motor and trailer bogies for ETR 500 high-speed trainsets for FS; bogies for freight wagons; and motor bogies for E 402B electric locomotives for FS.

## Buckeye

Buckeye Steel Castings Co
2211 Parsons Avenue, Columbus, Ohio 43207, USA
Tel: (+1 614) 444 21 21   Fax: (+1 614) 445 20 84

**Key personnel**
See entry in *Brakes and drawgear* section.

**Products**
Cast-steel four-wheel bogie side frames, bogie bolsters, wagon couplers, draft yokes, centre plates, sill centre braces, draft sill ends, six-wheel bogies, span bolsters, and other castings for railroad wagons. Running gear for railroad passenger cars and mass transit rail vehicles. Buckeye Steel Castings is a major supplier to railroads, railcar builders and railcar repair shops.

*UPDATED*

*Bogie for Los Angeles metro trainset by Breda*

## Bumar Ltd

Al Jana Pawla II, 11, PL-00-828 Warsaw, Poland
Tel: (+48 22) 620 51 30   Fax: (+48 22) 620 46 69
e-mail: phzbumar@phzbumar.com.pl

**Products**
Axles, axle gears and pinions for EMD and GE locomotives, wheel centres, tyres for heavy and light rail vehicles, tyred and monoblock wheelsets with wheels from 360 to 1,130 mm diameters. ISO 9002 and AAR certified.

*UPDATED*

## CAF

Construcciones y Auxiliar de Ferrocarriles SA
Padilla 17, E-28006 Madrid, Spain
Tel: (+34 91) 435 25 00   Fax: (+34 91) 576 62 63

**Key personnel**
See entry in *Locomotives and powered/non-powered pasenger vehicles* section.

**Products**
Bogies, axles and wheel assemblies.

## Cardo Rail

Cardo Rail AB
Roskildevägen 1, PO Box 193, SE-201 21 Malmö, Sweden
Tel: (+46 40) 35 04 60   Fax: (+46 40) 30 38 03
e-mail: info@sabwabco.com
Web: http://www.sabwabco.com

**Key personnel**
See main entry in *Brakes and drawgear* section.

**Products**
SAB WABCO air suspension control equipment; resillient wheels for main line vehicles, noise reducing wheels for LRVs.

*UPDATED*

## CFD

CFD Industrie
9-11 rue Benoît Malon, F-92150 Suresnes, France
Tel: (+33 1) 45 06 44 00   Fax: (+33 1) 47 28 48 84

**Key personnel**
See entry in *Locomotives and powered/non-powered pasenger vehicles* section.

**Products**
Locomotive bogies for axleloads up to 22 tonnes and speeds up to 120 km/h. Passenger-coach bogies for speeds up to 140 km/h.

## China National Railway Locomotive and Rolling Stock Industry Corporation (LORIC)

10 Fuxing Road, Beijing 100844, China
Tel: (+86 10) 63 51 16 20; 77 66
Fax: (+86 10) 63 51 16 14; 63 26 08 30

*Freight wagon bogies for South Korea*

2001/0099153

## 626    MANUFACTURERS/Bogies and suspension, wheels and axles, bearings

**Works addresses**
See entries in *Locomotives and powered/non-powered passenger vehicles* and *Freight vehicles and equipment* sections.

**Products**
Development, design, engineering, production, sales, installation, refurbishment, maintenance and after-sales services for all types of bogies.
    Bogies have been supplied to Egypt, South Korea, Thailand and Vietnam.

---

## Cimmco International

A division of Cimmco Birla Ltd
Prakash Deep (6th Floor), 7 Tolstoy Marg, New Delhi 110,001, India
Tel: (+91 11) 331 43 83; 84; 85
Fax: (+91 11) 332 07 77; 372 35 20

**Key personnel**
See entry in *Freight vehicles and equipment* section.

**Products**
Cast-steel bogies for passenger and freight wagons.

---

## ČKD

ČKD Dopravn Systémi AS
Ringhofferova 115/1, CZ-15500 Praha 5, Czech Republic
Tel: (+420 2) 20 32 28 30    Fax: (+420 2) 20 32 28 33
e-mail: ckddos1@mbox.vol.cz

**Key personnel**
See *Locomotives and powered/non-powered pasenger vehicles* section.

**Products**
Bogies for trams, LRVs, locomotives and multiple units.

---

## ČKD Kutná Hora as

CZ-284 49 Kutná Hora, Czech Republic
Tel: (+420 327) 50 61 11    Fax: (+420 327) 51 36 74
e-mail: ckdkh@pha.pvtnet.cz

**Corporate background**
Founded in 1967, the company was transformed from a state-owned enterprise to a joint stock company in 1995 as part of the Czech Republic's privatisation reforms.

**Products**
Y25, Y33 and TF25 bogies; bogies to special designs for main line and light rail vehicles; cast and welded bogie frames and components.

---

## Cockerill Forges & Ringmill SA

PO Box 65, B-4100 Seraing 1, Belgium
Tel: (+32 4) 330 35 35    Fax: (+32 4) 337 79 02
e-mail: cfr@cfr.be

**Works**
Main Cockerill Site, Seraing, Belgium

**Key personnel**
Chief Executive Officer: Fred Godard
Executive Vice-President, Marketing and Sales: Raymond Rauw
Research and Development Director: Robert Pesch
Commercial Director: Raymond Raw

**Products**
Steel tyres for all types of railway, light rail, tramway and metro rolling stock.

*UPDATED*

---

## Comet Industries Inc

4800 Deramus Avenue, Kansas City, Missouri 64120, USA
Tel: (+1 816) 245 94 00    Fax: (+1 816) 245 94 61

**Key personnel**
See entry in *Brakes and drawgear* section.

**Products**
Rail-associated bearings and components.

---

## Cometna

Companhia Metalurgica Nacionel
Rua Marechal Gomes Dacosta, Famoes P-2675 Odivelas, Lisbon, Portugal
Tel: (+351 1) 933 31 39    Fax: (+351 1) 933 31 43

**Key personnel**
President: Jose Bissaia Barreto

**Products**
Cast-steel bogies for locomotives and freight wagons.

---

## ContiTech Luftfedersysteme GmbH

Vahrenwalder Strasse 9
D-30165 Hannover, Germany
Tel: (+49 511) 938 02    Fax: (+49 511) 938 27 66
e-mail: mailservice@contitech.de
Web: http://www.contitech.de

**Key personnel**
See entry in *Passenger coach equipment* section.

**Corporate background**
See entry in *Passenger coach equipment* section.

**Products**
Suspension products for rail vehicles including primary springs; rubber metal conical springs with integrated hydraulic damping system; rubber metal layer springs; rolling rubber springs for axle suspension; secondary airbags; air spring suspension systems.
    Vehicle programmes employing ContiTech suspension components include: Alstom's LIREX prototype; Amtrak Acela trainsets; DB AG VT605 and ICE 3 trainsets; TGV-Duplex trainsets; and SNCF X-TER emus.
    The ContiTech product range also includes Clouth rolling rubber and combination springs.

*VERIFIED*

---

## Delta Rail

1 Rue Roussel, F-92250 La Garenne Colombes, France
Tel: (+33 1) 42 42 11 44    Fax: (+33 1) 42 42 11 16

**Key personnel**
See entry in *Brakes and drawgear* section.

**Products**
Shock-absorbers, suspension air springs.

---

## Devol

Devol Engineering Limited
Clarence Street, Greenock PA15 1LR, UK
Tel: (+44 1475) 72 53 20    Fax: (+44 1475) 78 78 73
e-mail: sales@devol.com
Web: http://www.devol.com

**Key personnel**
Rail Products Manager: Martin Wainwright
Internal Sales: Mitchell Farquhar
Operations Director: G Stark

**Subsidiary company**
Devol Moulding Services Ltd

**Products**
Polymer bearing materials and components for bearings and bushes applied to disc caliper and clasp brake gear; anti-rollbar spherical and plain bearings; axlebox guides; gangway fascias; drawbar and side bearer pads; coupler support wear plates; dry slide wear plates for turnouts.

*UPDATED*

---

## Dominion Castings Ltd

An ABC-NACO Inc Company
100 Depew Street, PO Box 5010, Hamilton, Ontario L8L 8G1, Canada
Tel: (+1 905) 544 50 00    Fax: (+1 905) 544 12 25

**Key personnel**
See entry in *Brakes and drawgear* section.

**Products**
Standard and high-speed two-axle bogies for AAR 50, 70 or 100 short ton freight applications. Cast-steel locomotive and passenger vehicle bogies.

---

*ContiTech spring systems fitted to a second-generation ICE high-speed trainset bogie*    2001/0103971

## Energomachexport

25A Protopopovsky per, 129010 Moscow, Russian Federation
Tel: (+7 095) 288 84 56; 69 83
Fax: (+7 095) 288 79 90; 69 83
e-mail: in@eme.tsr.ru

**Key personnel**
General Director: M Nosanov
Director, Transenergo Department: G Stepnov

**Products**
Bogies for passenger and freight vehicles; primary and secondary suspension units; rolled-steel wheels, tyres; axles and wheelsets; and Type SA-3 automatic coupling devices.

## Escorts Ltd

Railway Equipment Division
Plot 115, Sector 24, Faridabad 121 005, India
Tel: (+91 129) 544 22 75; 528 02 86
Fax: (+91 129) 23 21 48; 528 30 69; 526 42 86
e-mail: cgtech@asp-escorts@gndel.global.net.in

**Key personnel**
See entry in *Brakes and drawgear* section.

**Products**
Shock-absorbers for locomotives, emus, passenger coaches and diesel cranes. Escorts is the prime supplier to Indian Railways, having supplied over 400,000 shock-absorbers.
New products under development include Uniflow-type shock-absorbers with adjustable damping.

## FAG

FAG OEM und Handel Aktiengesellschaft
PO Box 1260, D-97419 Schweinfurt, Germany
Tel: (+49 9721) 91 39 78   Fax: (+49 9721) 91 37 88
e-mail: rail_transport@fag.de
Web: www.fag.de

**Key personnel**
Division Manager: Dr Raimund Abele

**Works**
Georg-Schäfer Strasse 30, D-97421 Schweinfurt, Germany

**Production facilities**
In Austria, Brazil, Canada, China, Germany, Hungary, India, Korea, Portugal, UK and USA.

**Products and services**
FAG products for rail vehicles include various types of axleboxes (also light alloy housings and axleboxes equipped with speed-temperature and vibration sensors); cartridge units; insulated traction motor bearings; Cronidur steel rings; transmission bearings; specific Arcanol greases and mounting/dismounting devices.
Applications include locomotives, freight and passenger coaches, commuter train vehicles, subways and tramways, chiefly for bearings for axleboxes, traction motors and transmissions.
*UPDATED*

## Federal-Mogul Corporation

Powertrain Systems (formerly known as Glacier Clevite)
5037 North State Route 60, McConnelsville, Ohio 43756, USA
Tel: (+1 740) 962 42 42   Fax: (+1 740) 962 82 02

**Key personnel**
Operations Manager: Ted McConnell
General Manager, Global Marketing: Joseph J Vauter
Manager Railroad Replacement: David A Comer

**Products**
Main, con-rod and flanged main journal bearings, thrust washers, cam bearings and various other shapes for accessory applications. Heavy wall innovations include tri-metal steel-backed cast-copper lead bearings, precision-plated overlays, nickel dam and the delta wall which allows the loading capacity to be raised without increasing the size of the bearing. An OE supplier to the world's locomotive engine PASSENGER COACH EQUIPMENT, Federal-Mogul also produces bearings for other large engine, compressor and aircraft applications.

## Ferraz SA

PO Box 3025, F-69391 Lyon Cedex 03, France
Tel: (+33 4) 72 22 66 11   Fax: (+33 4) 72 22 67 13

**Key personnel**
See entry in *Electric traction equipment* section.

**Products**
Earth current units to prevent current flowing through bearings of axleboxes and associated resistors; current collecting device on live rail and its associated shoe fuse box.

## Ferrostaal AG

Hohenzollernstrasse 24, D-45128 Essen, Germany
Tel: (+49 201) 818 01   Fax: (+49 201) 818 28 22

**Key personnel**
See entry in *Locomotives and powered/non-powered passenger vehicles* section.

**Products**
Motor and trailer bogies for all types of rolling stock; wheels, axles, assembled wheelsets, bearings and suspensions.
*UPDATED*

## FIREMA Trasporti SpA

c/o I D P Milano Fiorenza, Via Triboniano, 220 I-20156, Milan, Italy
Tel: (+39 02) 23 02 02 23   Fax: (+39 02) 23 02 02 34
e-mail: firema.com@firema.it
Web: http://www.firema.it

**Key personnel**
See entry in *Locomotives and powered/non powered passenger vehicles* section.

**Products**
Motor and trailer bogies for high-speed trainsets and locomotives. Contracts include the supply of 70 motor bogies for E402 locomotives; 194 trailer bogies and 30 motor bogies for ETR 500 high-speed trains, all for Italian Railways.
*UPDATED*

## Freudenberg Schwab GmbH

Freudenberg Simrit KG
Höhnerweg 2-4, D-69465 Weinheim, Germany
Tel: (+49 1805) 74 67 48
e-mail: simrit.service@freudenberg.de
Web: http://www.simrit.de

**Key personnel**
Chief Executive Officers: Dr Detlef Cordts; Peter Kofmel; Jörg Sost

**Organisation**
Freudenberg Schwab GmbH is jointly owned by Freudenberg & Co (51 per cent) and Schwab Holding AG (49 per cent). The company collaborates closely with Schwab Schwingungstechnik AG in Switzerland.

**Products**
Vibration control: rubber/metal elastic elements, standard as well as specially designed. Range includes elastic mountings for traction equipment and components for primary and secondary suspension, resilient couplings linking motor, gearbox, axle and other mountings, resilient bushes, spherical bearings, buffers, conical mountings, V-mountings, machine mountings, rectangular mountings and hydraulic bushes.
Innovative products for vibration control include hydraulic mountings and bushes for speed-dependent stiffness, such as axle guide bearings for rail vehicles on tightly curved track, and active absorbers for reduction of structure-borne noise such as equalisation of vibrations from wheel flats.
(See also *Brakes and drawgear* and *Passenger coach equipment* sections.)
*UPDATED*

## Fuchs Lubricants (UK) plc

New Century Street, Hanley, Stoke-on-Trent ST1 5HU, UK
Tel: (+44 8701) 20 04 00   Fax: (+44 1782) 20 20 72
e-mail: contact-uk@fuchs-oil.com
Web: http://www.fuchslubricants.com

**Key personnel**
Managing Director: R Halhead
Automotive Sales Director: S E Cox
Director, Mining Division: F Thornhill

**Products**
Manufacture and supply of a full range of lubricants for the railway industry including: diesel engine oils; transmission fluids; hydraulic oils, special greases for wheel-flange and switch-plate applications; biodegradable products for most applications, including engine oils, gear oils, hydraulic oils and grease. The company is also a supplier of industrial cleaning products, degreasing fluids and hygiene products.
*UPDATED*

## Ganz Vagon

Ganz Mozdony-, és Járműgyártó Kft
PO Box 29, H-1430 Budapest, Hungary
Tel: (+36 1) 210 11 77
Fax: (+36 1) 210 11 80; 303 94 11
Sales office: (+36 1) 303 94 06

**Key personnel**
See entry in *Locomotives and powered/non-powered passenger vehicles* section.

**Products**
Fabricated bolsterless bogies with mechanical or air-sprung secondary suspension for speeds of up to 200 km/h and for 1,000 to 1,676 mm gauges.
Motor bogies for railcars and multiple-unit vehicles with bevel-gear axleboxes or electric traction motor drives.

## Gummi Metall Technik GmbH

5 Liechtersmatten, D-77815 Bühl, Germany
Tel: (+49 23) 80 40   Fax: (+49 23) 210 75
e-mail: info@gmt-gmbh.de
Web: http://www.gmt-gmbh.de

**Key personnel**
See entry in *Passenger coach equipment* section.

**Sales offices**
See entry in *Passenger coach equipment* section.

**Products**
Rubber and rubber-metal elements, such as axle springs, rolling rubber springs, bushes, cone mountings, ball joints and bonded springs. Resilient wheel systems.
*UPDATED*

## Greysham International

2/81 Roop Nagar, Delhi 110 007, India
Tel: (+91 11) 396 52 60; 396 93 81
Fax: (+91 11) 396 11 68; 294 30 68; (+91 575) 471 60 08
e-mail: gipldel@nda.vsnl.net.in
Web: http://www.greysham.com

# 628  MANUFACTURERS/Bogies and suspension, wheels and axles, bearings

**Key personnel**
See entry in *Brakes and drawgear* section.

**Products**
Axlebox assemblies.

## Griffin

Griffin Wheel Co/Amsted Industries International
200 West Monroe Street, Chicago, Illinois 60606, USA
Tel: (+1 312) 372 53 84   Fax: (+1 312) 372 82 30

**Key personnel**
President: Glen F Lazar
Vice-President: Charles Spencer

**Products**
Steel wheels using the unique controlled-pressure pouring system into graphite moulds. These wheels are AAR-approved for locomotive, passenger and freight applications.

## Gutenhoffnungshütte Radsatz GmbH

Postfach 110226, D-46122 Oberhausen, Germany
Tel: (+49 208) 692 43 50   Fax: (+49 208) 692 43 55
e-mail: gr.radsatz@sabwabco.com

**Corporate development**
Gutenhoffnungshütte Radsatz GmbH is an operating company in the Cardo BSI Rail group.

**Products**
Wheelsets for locomotives, dmus, emus, metro cars, light rail vehicles, passenger coaches and freight wagons; running gear and components for low-floor light rail vehicles; resilient wheels. Wheelsets are also manufactured for special vehicles for the rail and steel industries.

## HDA Forgings Ltd

Windsor Road, Redditch B97 6EF, UK
Tel: (+44 1527) 642 11   Fax: (+44 1527) 59 17 60
e-mail: pjrm(CA}hdaf.co.uk

**Key personnel**
Managing Director: A J Scanlon
Financial Director: G A Berry
Operations Manager: Paul R Langston
Sales and Marketing Director: P J R Masters
Commercial Director: D W Smith

**Products**
Forged components in aluminium alloys for railway rolling stock.
Contracts include the supply of aluminium alloy bolster forgings produced on a 12,000 tonne press, for London Underground Northern Line ALSTOM trains.

## HEI

Hindusthan Engineering & Industries Ltd
Mody Building, 27 Sir RN Mukherjee Road, Calcutta 700 001, India
Tel: (+91 33) 248 01 66
Fax: (+91 33) 248 19 22; 220 26 07
e-mail: hindus@cal2.vsnl.net.in

**Works**
Bumunari Plant (BP), National Highway No 2, Bumunari 712 205, District Hooghly, West Bengal, India

**Key personnel**
See entry in *Freight vehicles and equipment* section.

**Products**
Cast steel two and three-axle bogies, locomotive bogies fitted with suspension arrangements, axleboxes, high-tensile coupler and high-capacity draft gear.

*UPDATED*

## IBG

IBG Monforts GmbH & Co
An der Waldesruh 23, D-41238 Mönchengladbach, Germany
Tel: (+49 2166) 868 20   Fax: (+49 2166) 86 82 44
e-mail:: info@ibg-montforts.de

**Products**
Slide bearing systems for applications such as bogie air springs.

*IBG Montforts slide bearing systems*   0063767

## IBG Monforts

An der Waldesruh 23, D-41238 Mönchengladbach, Germany
Tel: (+49 2166) 868 20   Fax: (+49 2166) 86 82 44
e-mail: info@ibg-monforts.de
Web: http://www.ibg-monforts.de

**Products**
Slide bearing systems for applications such as bogie air springs.
Recent contracts include the supply of bearing systems for ICE-2 high-speed trainsets, VT611 tilting dmus and double-deck coaches for DB AG as well as for ICT trainsets.

## ICF

The Integral Coach Factory
Ministry of Railways, Chennai 600 038, India
Tel: (+91 44) 626 01 52; 00 54
Fax: (+91 44) 626 01 52; 00 54
e-mail: coachnet@md2.vsnl.net.in
Web: http://www.icf.gov.in

**Key personnel**
See entry in *Locomotives and powered/non-powered passenger vehicles* section.

**Products**
All-coil all-steel high-speed bogies with bogie-mounted brakes and conventional brakes; bogies with pneumatic suspension system.

*UPDATED*

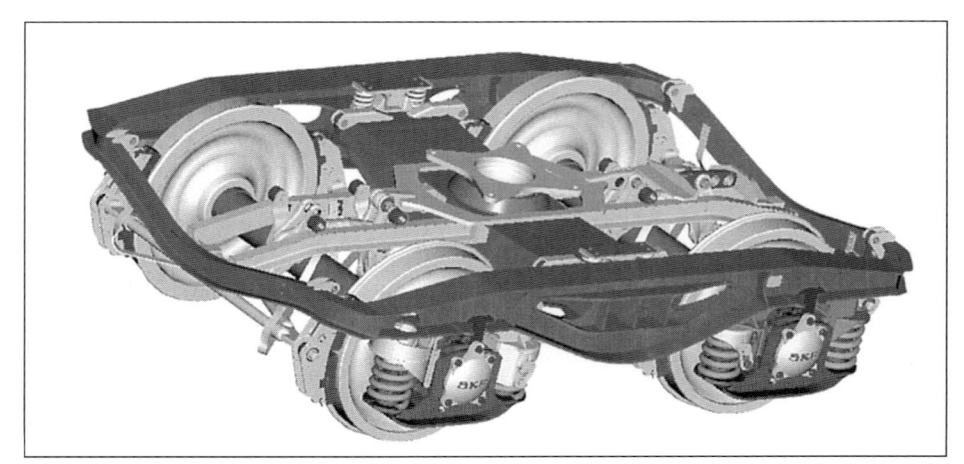

*Kockums Y25 TTV freight wagon bogie*   0063734

## IMS UK

Canklow Meadows Industrial Estate
West Bawtry Road, Rotherham, South Yorkshire S60 2XN, UK
Tel: (+44 1709) 78 80 00   Fax: (+44 1709) 78 80 30
e-mail: imsuk.north@ims-group.com

**Key personnel**
Financial Director: J Christie
Division Directors: C Beal;
   J Conroy; A Hance;
   G Moxham; J Murray
Export Manager: B Christie
Purchasing Manager: M Hole

**Other offices**
Arley Road, Saltley, Birmingham B8 1QX, UK
Tel: (+44 121) 326 10 00   Fax: (+44 121) 326 10 10
e-mail: ims.special steels@imsuk.co.uk

Fyne Avenue
Righead Industrial Estate, Bellshill, Lanarkshire ML4 3JY, UK
Tel: (+44 1698) 74 69 22   Fax: (+44 1698) 74 69 97
e-mail: imsuk.scotland@ims-group.com

**Products**
Stockholding and distribution of speciality steels. Mill representation in the UK for Valdunes railway wheels, axles, brake discs, assembled wheelsets and forged saftety-critical parts, including crane wheels; RTM (Roues et Trains Montes) a subsidiary of Valdunes, offering wheelset overhaul in addition to railway wheels, axles and assembled parts; CFR (Cockerall Forges & Ringmill) tyres for rail vehicles and trams; LAF (Les Appareils Ferroviaires) automatic couplers for freight and passenger vehicles.

*UPDATED*

## Issels

F Issels & Son Ltd
PO Box 2199, Bulawayo, Zimbabwe

**Products**
Bogies including the A3 Ride Control bogie pack for use on railways in Africa, north of the Limpopo.

## Kinex-ZVL A/S

Kukučinova 2346, 024 01 Kysucké Nové Mesto, Slovakia
Tel: (+421 41) 420 10 40   Fax: (+421 41) 420 18 70
e-mail: marketing@kinex-klf.sk
Web: http://www.kinex-klf.sk

**Key personnel**
Managing Director: Igor Kováč
Commercial Director: Ján Čelko
Marketing Manager: František Vilk

**Products**
Single-row cylindrical roller bearings for railway axles, axle boxes, gearbox and transmission bearings, traction motor bearings, ball and roller bearings.

*UPDATED*

Jane's World Railways 2002-2003

Bogies and suspension, wheels and axles, bearings/**MANUFACTURERS** 629

## KLW – Wheelco SA

Via Calloni 1, CH-6900 Lugano, Switzerland
Tel: (+41 91) 986 58 50   Fax: (+41 91) 986 58 51
e-mail: info@asgroup.ch
Web: http://www.klw-wheelco.ch

**Key personnel**
Managing Director: M Staroseletskyy

**Products**
Wheels, tyres, wheelsets, bogies and bogie compartments; rolling stock components.

## Kockums

Kockums Industrier AB
SE-205 55 Malmö, Sweden
Tel: (+46 40) 34 80 80   Fax: (+46 40) 34 87 75
e-mail: info.kiab@celsius.se

**Key personnel**
See entry in *Freight vehicles and equipment* section.

**Corporate background**
Kockums Industrier is owned by the Celsius Group.

**Products**
Kockums Industrier's new products is the Y25 TTV (Lsdl) bogie for 25 tonne axleload which is approved by Swedish State Railways (SJ) and has been in operation since 1986. It has developed, designed and produced 72 heavy transport freight wagons with this bogie.

## Koni BV

Langeweg 1, PO Box 1014, NL-3260AA Oud-Beijerland, Netherlands
Tel: (+31 186) 63 55 00   Fax: (+31 186) 63 56 05
e-mail: pmaarleveld@koni.nl
Web: http://www.koni.com

**Key personnel**
Chairman and Managing Director: C R van der Heyden
Technical Director: R H M Vrenken
Marketing and Sales Director: H C A Wielaard

**Subsidiary company**
Koni-Jim Vance
15279 Alphin Lane, Culpeper, Virginia 22701, USA

**Products**
In-house research, development, engineering and manufacturing of dampers for trains, metros, passenger coaches and freight wagons, locomotives, high-speed trains and pantographs; electrically controlled dampers.
 In addition to the normal range of vertical and horizontal dampers, Koni has developed a yaw damper which is designed to control small amplitude sinusoidal rotational movements and enable vehicles to operate at higher speeds.

***UPDATED***

## Koyo Seiko Co Ltd

5-8 Minamisemba 3-chome, Chuo-ku, Osaka 542, Japan
Tel: (+81 6) 245 60 87   Fax: (+81 6) 244 08 14

**Key personnel**
President: Hiroshi Inoue
Vice-President: Takatoyo Uematsu
Senior Executive Director: Fumio Morishita
Executive Director: Hajime Hori

**Products**
Axlebox cartridge-type cylindrical and tapered sealed journal roller bearings; open-type cylindrical, tapered and spherical roller bearings and ball-bearings.
 Traction motor bearings, including insulated cylindrical roller bearings and ball bearings. Standard bearings are also available.
 Gear bearings, including tapered, cylindrical and spherical roller bearings and ball-bearings.
 Also ball spline-type universal drive bearings.
 Koyo cartridge-type tapered roller bearings with seals are used on the Shinkansen Series 500 Nozomi axle journals.

## Kryukovsky

Kryukovsky Railway Car Building Works
139 I Pridhodko Street, Kremenchung 315307, Ukraine
Tel: (+38 5366) 695 05; 697 95; 611 01
Fax: (+38 532) 50 14 21; (+38 5366) 611 01;
(+38 44) 295 72 03
e-mail: root@kvsz.poltava.ua

**Products**
Two-axle bogies for freight wagons; wheelsets, including products to UIC 812-3 and ISO 1005/3 standards for passenger coaches and freight cars; wheels and axles; equipment for strengthening wheels.

*Two-axle freight wagon bogie by Kryukovsky*
*2000*/0087657

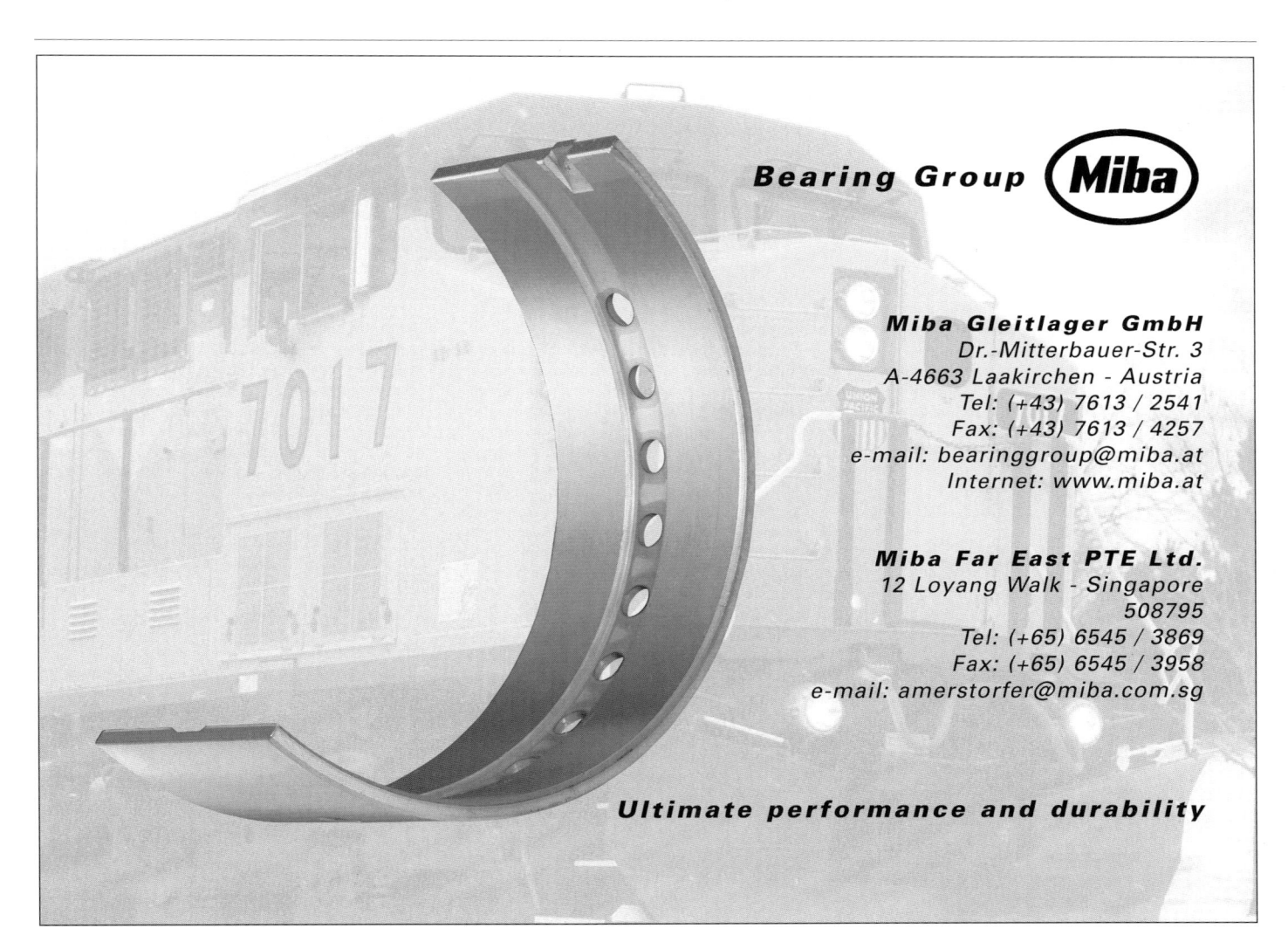

---

**Bearing Group** **Miba**

**Miba Gleitlager GmbH**
*Dr.-Mitterbauer-Str. 3*
*A-4663 Laakirchen - Austria*
*Tel: (+43) 7613 / 2541*
*Fax: (+43) 7613 / 4257*
*e-mail: bearinggroup@miba.at*
*Internet: www.miba.at*

**Miba Far East PTE Ltd.**
*12 Loyang Walk - Singapore*
*508795*
*Tel: (+65) 6545 / 3869*
*Fax: (+65) 6545 / 3958*
*e-mail: amerstorfer@miba.com.sg*

*Ultimate performance and durability*

## MANUFACTURERS/Bogies and suspension, wheels and axles, bearings

## Lesjöfors AB

SE-524 92 Herrljunga, Sweden
Tel: (+46 513) 220 00   Fax: (+46 513) 230 24
e-mail: info@lesjoforsab.com
Web: http://www.lesjofors.com

**Products**
Suspension springs and stabiliser equipment for rail vehicles. Companies supplied include Adtranz and Bombardier Transportation.

## Langen & Sondermann

Langen & Sondermann Federnwerk
Bergkampstrasse 57, D-44534 Lünen, Germany
Tel: (+49 2306) 75 05 70   Fax: (+49 2306) 576 72
e-mail: post@langen-sondermann.de
Web: http://www.langen-sondermann.de

**Key personnel**
Managing Director: J Kohl
Sales Director: Heinz Hermann
Technical Manager: Dipl Ing Dieter Schmidt

**Products**
Conventional (trapezoidal) leaf springs, parabolic springs (also design and development), coil springs (up to metal diameter of 80 mm); TKS-springs® (coil springs with progressive compression characteristics); design and development of steel springs.

*VERIFIED*

## Lord Corporation

Mechanical Products Division, 2000 West Grandview Boulevard, PO Box 10040, Erie, Pennsylvania 16514-0040, USA
Tel: (+1 814) 868 54 24   Fax: (+1 814) 868 31 09

**Key personnel**
President: Charles Hora
Director, International Business: Larry Bindseil
Manager, International Business Development: Eric Ravinowich

**Principal subsidiary**
Lord GmbH
Im Niederfeld 4, D-64293 Darmstadt, Germany
Tel: (+49 6151) 89 71 51   Fax: (+49 6151) 89 71 55

**Products**
LC-Pads for roller bearing adaptors, designed to reduce lateral forces, accommodate motion without wear, reduce rail wear and eliminate adaptor crown wear on self-steering bogies.
V Springs (chevron springs) for the primary suspension system. Applications include primary suspension for rapid transit bogies, locomotive bogies, mining cars and maintenance equipment.
Bolster mounts to accommodate lateral movement of locomotive bolsters.
Dyna-Deck for loading-shock protection. Designed to absorb longitudinal shocks and movements up to 12 in.

## Lubricant Consult GmbH

Gutenbergstrasse 13 D-63477 Maintal, Germany
Tel: (+49 6109) 765 00   Fax: (+49 6109) 76 50 51
e-mail: webmaster@lubcon.com
Web: http://www.lubcon.com

**Subsidiaries**

*Austria*
Büro Linz, Pollheimer Strasse, 16 A-4020, Linz
Tel: (+43 73) 267 16 30   Fax: (+43 73) 267 16 30
e-mail: info-austria@lubcon.com

*Czech Republic/Slovakia*
LUBCON sro
Diouhá 783 CZ-76321, Slavicin
Tel: (+420 636) 34 36 18   Fax: (+420 636) 34 20 09
e-mail: info-czechrepublic@lubcon.com

*France*
LUBCON SARL
Alpespace – La Pyramide F-73800, Montmélian
Tel: (+33 4) 79 84 38 60   Fax: (+33 4) 79 84 38 61
e-mail: france@lubcon.com

*Italy*
LUBCON Italia SRL
Via Trieste, 16 1-21040 Sumirago (VA)
Tel: (+39 0331) 90 87 62   Fax: (+39 0331) 90 87 54
e-mail: info-italy@lubcon.com

*Poland*
LUBCON Polska Sp zoo
Al. Lotników Polskich 1, PL-21-045 Swidnik
Tel: (+48 81) 468 82 60   Fax: (+48 81) 468 82 61
e-mail: lubcon@lubcon.com.pl

*Slovenia*
LUBCON doo
Pod gradom 2 SLO-2380, Slovenj Gradec
Tel: (+386 2) 883 19 86   Fax: (+386 2) 883 19 87
e-mail: info-slovenia@lubcon.com

*Switzerland*
LUBCON Lubricant Consult AG
Im Leisibühl 35 CH-8044, Zurich
Tel: (+41 1) 882 30 37   Fax: (+41 1) 882 30 38
e-mail: lubcon-ch@bluewin.ch

*USA*
TURMO LUBRICATION, Inc
760 36 Street SE, Grand Rapids, Michigan 49548
Tel: (+1 616) 247 01 29   Fax: (+1 616) 247 08 01
e-mail: turmolube@aol.com

**Products**
Lubcon biologically degradable special lubricants for the wheel/rail system to counteract wear and noise.

## Lucchini Group

Headquarters
Lucchini SpA
Via Oberdan 1/a, I-25128 Brescia, Italy
Tel: (+39 030) 399 21   Fax: (+39 030) 338 40 65
e-mail: commerciale@lucchini.it
Web: http://www.lucchini.it

**Key personnel**
President: Giuseppe Lucchini
Vice-Presidents: Severo Bocchio, Loris Fontana
Managing Directors: Michele Bajetti, Piero Nardi
Corporate Commercial Director: Giovanni Bajetti
Business Manager Railway Division: Roberto Boni
Sales Manager, Railway Products: Roberto Forcella

**Background**
In November 2000, Lucchini acquired the shares and assets of the wheel and wheelset manufacturing activities of Adtranz Manchester, UK, and Surahammar, Sweden. Together, the two facilities have capacity annually of 50,000 wheels and 3,200 assembled wheelsets for passenger and freight vehicles and locomotives. The businesses have been renamed Lucchini UK – Wheel Systems Division and Lucchini Sweden respectively.
During 2001 Lucchini began a new activity dedicated to the railway sector in its company, Huta Lucchini Warszawa, Huta L W. This new division produces wheels, forged axles and wheelsets complete with axleboxes and drive units. Since mid-2002 this activity has been owned by a new company, Lucchini Poland.
A new company named Lucchini Sidermeccanica was created on 1 January 2002 following a strategy of business unit diversification. This combines the activities of all group companies dedicated to the production of rolling stock components. The Lovere and the LMF plants have been merged, together with the subsidiary companies of Lucchini UK, Lucchini Sweden and Lucchini Poland to form Lucchini Sidermeccanica SpA.

**Subsidiary companies**
Lucchini Sidermeccanica SpA
I-25128 Brescia, Italy
Tel: (+39 030) 399 25 62   Fax: (+39 030) 338 40 65
e-mail: rollingstock@lucchini.it
President: Giuseppe Lucchini
Managing Director: Michele Bajetti, Piero Nardi
General Manager: Roberto Boni
Sales Manager: Roberto Forcella

Lucchini UK – Wheel Systems Division
Ashburton Road West, Trafford Park, Manchester M17 1GU, UK
Tel: (+44 161) 872 04 92   Fax: (+44 161) 872 28 95
e-mail: salesuk@lucchini.co.uk
Managing Director: Chris Fawdry
Technical Manager: Martin Clarke
Sales Manager: Tim Cornes, Mike Wood

Lucchini Sweden
Bruks Gatan, Box 210, S-73523 Surahammar, Sweden
Tel: (+46 22) 03 47 00   Fax: (+46 22) 03 47 80
e-mail: info@lucchini.se
Managing Director: Lennart Nordhall
Technical Manager: Peter Ekström
Sales Manager: Lennart Nordhall

Lucchini Poland
Ul Kasprowicza, 132, PL-01949 Warsaw, Poland
Tel: (+48 22) 835 89 20   Fax: (+48 22) 835 08 33
e-mail: rodeggi@hutalw.com.pl
Managing Director: Michel Sablonniere
Technical Manager: Adam Osinski
Sales Manager: Piotr Krzyzanowsky

**Products**
Lovere Works (Lucchini SpA): design and manufacture of wheels, tyres, axles and assembly of wheelsets complete with axleboxes, brake discs and drive units.
LMF Works (Lucchini Sidermeccanica SpA): overhaul and full refurbishment of wheelsets including axleboxes, bearings, disc brakes and drive units. Production of axleboxes for railway and mass transit systems.
Lucchini UK – Wheel Systems Division: production of all types of railway wheels and assembly of complete wheelsets for trucks, carriages and locomotives.
Lucchini Sweden: wheels, tyres, axles and wheelsets with axleboxes and drive units.
Lucchini Poland: wheels, forged axles and wheelsets complete with axleboxes and drive units.

*UPDATED*

## Magnus/Farley Inc

PO Box 1029, Fremont, Nebraska 68026-1029, USA
Tel: (+1 402) 721 95 40   Fax: (+1 402) 721 23 77
e-mail: dburns@magnus-farley.com
Web: http://www.magnus-farley.com

**Key personnel**
President: J E Macklin
Sales Manager: David Burns

**Products**
High-leaded bronze bearings for traction motor application; tin bronze bearings and special analysis; solid journal bearings; proprietary centrifugal castings, horizontal and vertical; babbitt bearing linings, centrifugal, static and plated; Statistical Process Control (SPC); robotic material handling and integrated machining; electric induction furnaces and spectrographic analysis.

*VERIFIED*

## Manoir Industries – Sambre et Meuse

Railway Division, PO Box 2, Rue des Usines, F-59750, Feignies, France
Tel: (+33 3) 21 69 68 82   Fax: (+33 3) 27 69 69 89

**Key personnel**
See entry in *Freight vehicles and equipment* section.

**Products**
Design, testing and manufacture of three-piece bogies for gauges from 1,000 mm to 1,600 mm; rigid cast-steel bogies Types Y25, Y33, Y39 and VNH for 1,435 mm and other European gauges, for speeds up to 160 km/h and 25 tonne axleloads. Parts for welded bogies including spring supports, pivots and suspension caps.

# KLW WHEELCO
**A COMPANY OF ALLIED STEEL GROUP**

## Exclusive distributor for
### JSC "Nizhnedneprovsky Tube Rolling Plant" (Dnepropetrovsk, Ukraine) and JSC "Kryukovsky Railway Car Building Works" (Kremenchug, Ukraine)

**Quality**
**Reliability**
**Durability**

KLW-Wheelco S.A. is capable to supply the following railway material:

More than 70 typical sizes of solid rolled wheels from vacuum degassed steel of various shapes with diameters from 730 mm till 1265 mm for freight and passenger cars, locomotives, electro trains. Tyres from vacuum degassed steel with diameters from 690 mm till 1300 mm for locomotives, underground cars, trains, etc.

Ring type products, blank for coupler gears of electro trains, rolled centers for compound wheels etc.

Axles, wheelsets, bogies etc. Rails, turnouts and other related railway items.

The products are supplied to more than 50 countries of the world and are successfully operated in the various climatic zones from Far North to Tropics. High quality, reliability and durability in the operations are guaranteed by Quality Management System, certified by TUV in accordance with DIN EN ISO 9002 and AAR in accordance with M-1003.

Wheels and tyres are supplied to the requirements of the specifications:
UIC 812-3; UIC 812-1; UIC 810-1; UIC 810 - 2, ISO 1005; BN 918277; BS 5892, part 4; BS 5892, part 3:1992; BS 24; IRS R 34-99; IRS R 19 - 93; IRS R 15 - 95; TTS 094; TTS 248; UNI 6102, MOR - M - 2001 - 2; PN - 91/K-91032; PN - 84 H- 4027/06; PN - 92/K-91018; ASTM A551-81; AAR M107/208; JIS E 5402-1989; M4T 2000; UNI 7176 - 73; NF F 01 - 131; NF F 01 - 115; NF F 01- 33.

KLW-WHEELCO S.A. Via Calloni 1, P.O. Box 45, CH-6907, Lugano, Switzerland
Tel.: +41 91 986 5800, Fax +41 91 986 5801/11
E-mail: info@asgroup.ch

## Mecanoexportimport SA

30 Dacia Boulevard, Bucharest, Romania
Tel: (+40 1) 211 98 55   Fax: (+40 1) 210 78 94

**Key personnel**
See entry in *Locomotives and powered/non-powered passenger vehicles* section.

**Products**
Wheels, axles, wheelsets and bogies (including Y25 types) for locomotives, passenger coaches and freight wagons.

## MIBA Gleitlager AG

Dr Mitterbauer Strasse 3, A-4663 Laakirchen, Austria
Tel: (+43 7613) 254 10   Fax: (+43 7613) 42 57

**Key personnel**
President, Sales: Bernd Werkausen
Vice-President, Sales: Johann Jandrasits

**Products**
Engine bearings and bushes for diesel locomotives.

*UPDATED*

## MSA Mediterr Shock-Absorbers SpA

Via G A Valentini 127, I-93100 Caltanissetta, Italy
Tel: (+39 0934) 57 53 60   Fax: (+39 0934) 57 53 73

**Works**
Stada Statale 457 No 37/39, I-14033 Castell' Alfero, AT, Italy
Tel: (+39 0141) 20 47 57   Fax: (+39 0141) 20 46 70

**Products**
Shock-absorbers for rail vehicles, including specialised applications.

*UPDATED*

## Multi-Service Supply Division

The Buncher Co, Leetsdale, Pennsylvania 15056, USA
Tel: (+1 412) 741 15 00   Fax: (+1 412) 741 33 20

**Key personnel**
See entry in *Brakes and drawgear* section.

**Products**
Roller bearings; couplers; yokes, draft gears; wheel and axle assemblies; complete bogie assemblies with or without brake rigging.

*VERIFIED*

## MWL Brasil Rodas & Eixos Ltda

Rodovia Vito Ardito, s/n° Km 1, Caçapava-SP, 12280-000 Brazil
Tel: (+55 12) 253 14 11; 14 65   Fax: (+55 12) 253 12 81
e-mail: mwlbrasil@mwlbrasil.com.br

**Key personnel**
President: Aparecido Nobuo Terazima
Industrial Director: Domingos José Minicucci
Finance Director: João Aquino Carvalho Junior
Commercial Manager: Sandra Lopes

**Products**
Rail vehicle forged wheels and axles, crane wheels, sheave wheels, discs, blanks and ingots.
  Recent contracts executed or obtained have been from: Indian Railways Board; Adtranz (UK); Alstom PATH, ORX (USA); Snim-Sem (Mauritania); Ferrosur Roca, Ferrovías, Siemens, STF UTE, TBA and TMR (Argentina); América Latina Logística do Brasil, Companhia Vale do Rio Doce (Brazil).

## Nippon Sharyo Ltd

Riverside Yomiuri Building, 11th Floor, 36-2 Nihombashi-Hakozaki-cho, Chuo-ku, Tokyo 103-0015, Japan
Tel: (+81 3) 36 68 33 30   Fax: (+81 3) 36 69 02 38

**Key personnel**
See entry in *Locomotives and powered/non-powered passenger vehicles* section.

**Products**
Powered and trailer bogies for all types of rolling stock, including tilting and self-steering bogies.

*VERIFIED*

## Nizhnedneprovsky

Nizhnedneprovsky Tube Rolling Plant
21 Solotov St, Dnepropetrovsk, 320060, Ukraine
Tel: (+380 0562) 20 73 01; 20 73 90
Fax: (+380 0562) 27 16 43; 23 05 45

**Key personnel**
Vice Director of Foreign Economic Relations: Mikhail Staroseletsky
Head of Communications: Svetlana Chernikova

**Background**
Nizhnedneprovsky Tube Rolling Plant has been manufacturing wheels and tyres for over 60 years.

**Products**
Manufacturer and supply of more than 50 sizes of wheels and tyres for emus, LRVs, metrocars, trainsets, locomotives and freight wagons. Steel for the wheels and tyres is produced in the company's open-hearth furnaces and is refined for resistance to fatigue and brittleness.

**Contracts**
Include supply of wheels and tyres to 36 countries including fromer CIS countries, Bangladesh, China, France, Germany, India, Italy and Tanzania.

## NSK Ltd

Nissei Building, 1-6-3 Ohsaki, Shinagawa-ku, Tokyo 141, Japan
Tel: (+81 3) 37 79 71 20   Fax: (+81 3) 37 79 74 33

**Key personnel**
President: T Sekiya
Managing Director: K Moriya

**Products**
Axleboxes, journal bearings, cylindrical and spherical roller bearings, ball-bearings and pillow units.

## NSK-RHP UK

Mere Way, Ruddington Business Park, Ruddington NG11 6JZ, UK
Tel: (+44 115) 936 66 00   Fax: (+44 115) 936 67 02; 3

**Products**
Traction motor bearings, axlebox bearings, ball and roller bearings.

## NTN Toyo

NTN Toyo Bearing Co Ltd
3-17 chome Kyomachibori, Nishi-ku, Osaka, Japan
Tel: (+81 6) 443 50 01

**US office**
American NTN Bearing Manufacturing Corporation
1600 East Bishop Court, Mount Prospect, Illinois 60056, USA
Tel: (+1 708) 298 75 00   Fax: (+1 708) 699 97 44

**Products**
Journal roller bearings of all types.

## OFV

Officine Ferroviarie Veronesi SpA
Lungadige A Galtarossa 21, I-37133 Verona, Italy
Tel: (+39 045) 806 41 11   Fax: (+39 045) 803 28 76

**Products**
Bogies for freight wagons.

## ORX

One Park Avenue, Tipton, Pennsylvania 16684, USA
Tel: (+1 814) 684 84 84   Fax: (+1 814) 684 84 00
e-mail: orx@orxrail.com
Web: http://www.orxrail.com

**Key personnel**
President: Glenn Brandimarte
Sales Manager: Jim Brandimarte

**Products**
Axles, wheelsets and bogies.
  ORX is the OEM (Original Equipment Manufacturer) supplier for GM DD locomotives, Los Angeles Red Line cars, New York City R142 cars and Amtrak's Acela Express trains.

*UPDATED*

## Peddinghaus Group

Carl Dan Peddinghaus GmbH & Co KG
Mittelstrasse 64, D-58256 Ennepetal, Germany
Tel: (+49 2333) 79 60   Fax: (+49 2333) 79 63 88
e-mail: cdp-en@t-online.de
Web: http://www.peddinghaus-group.de

**Products**
A supplier of high quality steel and aluminium forgings and components including railway axles and coupling shafts.

## Penn

Penn Machine Company (a member of the Marmon Group)
106 Station Street, Johnstown, Pennsylvania 15905, USA
Tel: (+1 814) 288 15 47   Fax: (+1 814) 288 22 60
e-mail: richt@internetmci.com

**Key personnel**
Vice-President and General Manager: H Karl Wiegand
Vice-President, Manufacturing and Engineering: Thomas Redvay
Vice-President, Transportation Sales: Richard E Trail
Sales Engineer, Transportation and Export Sales: Paul V Campbell
Sales Engineer, Transportation Sales: Richard Spring

**Principal subsidiary**
Penn Locomotive Gear Company
470 Roberts Avenue, Louisville, Kentucky 40214, USA
Tel: (+1 502) 367 48 58   Fax: (+1 502) 367 49 11

**Sales Office**
210 Pine Street, Carnegie, Pennsylvania 15106, USA
Tel: (+1 412) 279 44 60   Fax: (+1 412) 279 44 65

**Licensing agreements**
Penn Machine Company has agreements with ZF Hurth and Bochumer Verein of Germany to manufacture passenger vehicle gearboxes and resilient wheels in the USA.

**Products**
Resilient wheels; axles; pinions; gears; journal boxes; complete gearboxes; gearbox components; pinions, gears and shafts for diesel-electric locomotives, primarily General Motors, GE Transportation Systems and Alco types.
  Contracts include the supply of resilient wheels and axles to Siemens for LRVs for San Diego, St Louis, Portland and Denver; to Breda for LRVs for San Francisco; and to Kinki Sharyo for LRVs for Dallas and Boston.

*VERIFIED*

## Phoenix AG

PO Box 900854, Hannoversche Strasse 88, D-21048 Hamburg, Germany
Tel: (+49 40) 76 67 22 77   Fax: (+49 40) 76 67 22 11

**Key personnel**
Chief Engineers: Peter Eckworth/Dirk Lambrecht
Export Sales: Angela Büttner
Sales Manager: J Eggers

**Subsidiary companies**
Phoenix (GB) Ltd
Phoenix (GB) Ltd
Timothy Bridge House, Timothy Bridge Road, Stratford upon Avon CV37 9NQ, UK
Tel: (+44 1789) 20 50 90   Fax: (+44 1789) 29 86 38
Phoenix North America Inc
Phoenix North America Inc
1 Minue Street, Carteret, New Jersey 07008-1198, USA
Tel: (+1 908) 969 03 19   Fax: (+1 908) 969 37 51

**Products**
Suspensions for bogies, axle springs, mouldings, primary springs, secondary spring system, air spring bellows.
Primary suspension contracts include layer springs, bushes and buffers for the Adtranz Variotram and primary spring silent blocks for ICEII, DB, and Taiwan metro.

## Poli

Poli Costruzione Materiali Trazione SpA
Via Marconi 3, I-26014 Romanengro (CR), Italy
Tel: (+39 0373) 27 01 26   Fax: (+39 0373) 72 90 97
e-mail: info@polibrakes.com
Web: http://www.polibrakes.com

**Key personnel**
See entry in *Brakes and drawgear* section.

**Products**
Gear reductors, resilient wheels, tyres, manufacture and overhaul of complete wheelsets for traction units and trailers.

*VERIFIED*

## Powell Duffryn Rail Ltd

Cambrian House, Charnwood Court, Parc Nantgarw, Cardiff CF15 7QZ, UK
Tel: (+44 1443) 84 82 50   Fax: (+44 1443) 84 82 51
e-mail: sales@pdrail.com
Web: http://www.pdrail.com

**Key personnel**
Chairman: S C Harris
Managing Director: A B Harding
Sales Director: R Parker
Finance Director: E W Pulman

**Products**
Bogies for freight wagons including the TF (Track Friendly) range of bogies and suspensions. Wheels, axles and wheelsets for freight and passenger stock.

*UPDATED*

## Precima Development AB

Box 51, SE-642 22 Flen, Sweden
Tel: (+46 157) 122 40   Fax: (+46 157) 515 66

**Products**
Dampers for railway rolling stock, including: primary and secondary suspension; roll dampers; yaw dampers; secondary couple dampers; and displacement-sensitive dampers.
Customers supplied include: Adtranz; Alstom; Bombardier Transportation; Dellner Couplers; Siemens; and TGOJ.

## Puzhen

Puzhen Rolling Stock Works of Ministry of Railways
No 5 Longhu Lane, Puzhen, Nanjing, People's Republic of China
Tel: (+86 75) 85 24 24; 85 47 03
Fax: (+86 75) 85 24 24; 85 26 55

**Key personnel**
Factory Director: Song Zu Yu
Chief Engineer: Wang Wui Sheng

**Products**
Roller bearings.
Roller bearings featuring an oblique block frame and solid cage have been introduced. Sections of this bearing can be interchanged with existing bearings.

## Qiqihar

Qiqihar Rolling Stock (Group) Co Ltd
10 Zhonghua East Road, Qiqihar Heilongjiang 161002, People's Republic of China
Tel: (+86 452) 293 91 58   Fax: (+86 452) 251 44 64
e-mail: qrswceo@public.qq.hl.cn
Web: http://www.qrrs.com

**Key personnel**
See entry in *Freight vehicles and equipment* section.

**Products**
Type K2 high-speed bogie (120 km/h) with linkage below bolster; Type K1 high-speed bogie (120 km/h) with linkage passing through centre of bolster; freight bogies for 160 km/h operations.

*NEW ENTRY*

## Radsatz Ilsenburg

Radsatzfabrik Ilsenburg GmbH
Schmiedestr 16/17, D-38871 Ilsenburg, Germany
Tel: (+49 394) 529 30   Fax: (+49 394) 529 32 05
e-mail: info@rafil-gmbh.de
Web: http://www.rafil-gmbh.de

**Key personnel**
General Managers: Dipl Ing Jorg Villmann,
  Dipl Kaufm Müller
Sales Manager: H Böhme

**Products**
Wheels, wheelsets, brake pulleys and axles.
A special development is a lightweight monobloc wheel, proved in German Railways (DB AG) service. It has an axleload from 22.5 to 25 tonnes and is capable of a maximum speed of 350 km/h.
Also available is a wheelset that can change gauge from 1,435 to 1,524 mm and 1,668 mm.
Contracts include the supply of wheelsets to Greenbrier, Bombardier, DB AG, ÖBB, Preussag Stahl, ZF Hurth, Tatra Vagónka Poprad, ALSTOM, Siemens SGP, SBB, SJ, and NeDtrain.

*UPDATED*

## Railko Ltd

Boundary Road, Loudwater, High Wycombe HP10 9QU, UK
Tel: (+44 1628) 52 49 01   Fax: (+44 1628) 81 07 61
e-mail: info@railko.co.uk

**Key personnel**
Managing Director: Dr G D Wells
Sales Director: P J Cumberlidge
Sales Manager, Railways: S G Burdon

**Products**
Composite thermoset bearings and thermoplastic bearings. Applications include centre pivot liners, side bearer liners, torsion bar bearings, friction dampers, brake gear bushes, door slides, sliding gangway liners and axlebox guides.
Contracts in 1999 included the supply of centre pivot liners and side bearer liners for freight bogies to Slovakia; pedestal liners for FS Italy.

*VERIFIED*

## Ringrollers

PO Box 504, Springs 1540, South Africa
Tel: (+27 11) 362 66 70   Fax: (+27 11) 815 28 05
Web: http://www.de.dorbyl.com/ringrollers/index.html

**Key personnel**
General Manager: S Nel
Export Marketing Manager: Roberto Gaspari
Ringrollers USA Manager: T Karshagen
Ringrollers Africa Manager: F Burr-Dixon
Technical Manager: M De Lange

**Background**
A division of Dorbyl Ltd.

**Products**
Forged railway tyres, flanges and rectangular rings

*UPDATED*

## Rose Bearings Ltd

Doddington Road, Lincoln LN6 3RA, UK
Tel: (+44 1522) 50 09 33   Fax (+44 1522) 69 64 85

**Key personnel**
Director and General Manager: Mark Stansfield
Industry Specialist: Dr Paul Smith

**Products**
Self-aligning and spherical bearings including couplers and coupling bearings, suspension and door operating mechanisms, complete assemblies and linkages.

*NEW ENTRY*

## Rotem Company

231 Yangjae-Dong, Soecho-ku, Seoul, Korea 137-938
Tel: (+82 2) 34 64 46 45   Fax: (+82 2) 34 64 47 92
Web: http://www.rotem.co.kr

**Key personnel**
See entry in *Locomotives and powered/non-powered passenger vehicles* section.

**Background**
See entry in *Locomotives and powered/non-powered passenger vehicles* section.

**Organisation**
Rotem manufactures a complete range of bogies suitable for high-speed trainsets, diesel and electric locomotives, emus and dmus, passenger coaches and all types of freight wagons. To verify bogie performance, CAD, CAE and simulation techniques are applied from the first stage of R&D, including: 3-D digital mock-up design, finite element analysis, vehicle dynamic simulation, static and fatigue load testing of bogie frames, roller rig running tests of the complete bogie, riding quality tests and dynamic stress tests.

*UPDATED*

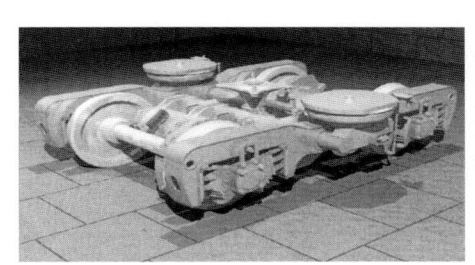

*Rotem bolsterless bogie with air suspension for the Seoul metro*   2001/0099151

## 634 MANUFACTURERS/Bogies and suspension, wheels and axles, bearings

## RSD

Rolling Stock Division
PO Box 229, Boksburg 1460, South Africa
Tel: (+27 11) 914 14 00   Fax: (+27 11) 914 38 85
Web: http://www.de.dorbyl.com/rsd

**Key personnel**
See entry in *Locomotives and powered/non-powered passenger vehicles* section.

**Background**
A division of Dorbyl Ltd.

**Products**
Locomotive, coach and freight wagon bogies, including the Scheffel High Stability bogie.

*UPDATED*

---

## R W Mac Co

PO Box 56, Crete, Illinois 60417, USA
Tel: (+1 708) 672 63 76; 81

**Key personnel**
President: R W MacDonnell
Vice-President, Sales and Exports: J K MacDonnell

**Products**
Car-safe freight wagon bolster supports; locomotive bogie bolster supports; EMD and GE Journal box wear plates (steel); custom-made locomotive and freight wagon parts.

---

## SAB WABCO

See entry for Cardo Rail.

*NEW ENTRY*

---

## Silvertown UK Ltd

Horninglow Road, Burton upon Trent, Staffordshire DE13 0SN, UK
Tel: (+44 1283) 51 05 10   Fax: (+44 1283) 51 00 52
e-mail: sales.enq@silvertown.co.uk
Web: http://www.unipoly.com

**Corporate development**
Silvertown UK Ltd is a member of the Unipoly group.

**Products**
Silentbloc elastomeric components and assemblies including: resilient rubber/metal bushes; ball joints; anti-vibration and shock mountings; flexible couplings; laminated spring and link assemblies; suspension systems and anti-roll bar systems.
Silentbloc also provides a comprehensive re-manufacturing service for products requiring refurbishment during normal service life.

---

## SKF

Aktiebolaget SKF
SE-415 50 Gothenburg, Sweden
Tel: (+46 31) 337 14 32   Fax: (+46 31) 337 10 87
Web: http://www.skf.com

**Key personnel**
Railway Segment Director: Egon Ekdahl

**Products**
Axleboxes with roller bearings (cylindrical, spherical, tapered and double row tapered for all types of railway rolling stock); traction motor bearings; transmission bearings for all types of drive systems and motor suspension units for axle-hung motors; plain bearings for bogie linkages; maintenance equipment for mounting/dismounting and bearing inspection; and bearing lubricants.

*UPDATED*

---

## Standard

Standard Car Truck Co
865 Busse Highway, Park Ridge, Illinois 60068, USA
Tel: (+1 847) 692 60 50   Fax: (+1 847) 692 62 99

**Key personnel**
Chairman and Chief Executive Officer: Richard A Mathes
Chief Operating Officer/President: Michael R Bayles
Vice-President, International: David J Watson
Vice-President, Sales & Service: Mark Pace
Secretary/Treasurer: Donald J Popernik

**Subsidiary companies**
Anchor Brake Shoe Co
Henry Miller Spring
Triangle Engineered Products Co
Sancast Inc
Durox Company

**Products**
Cast steel bogies incorporating load-sensitive Barber Stabilized suspension and control elements.
The Barber Stabilized bogie utilises vertical damping forces directly related to the vehicle's load. A wide range of capacities and track gauges can be accommodated.
The same damping features are offered in self-steering radial bogies. The advantages of self-steering can also be enjoyed with existing bogies through the use of the Barber Frame Bracing retrofit.

*Standard Car Truck frame brake retrofit design*
0003955

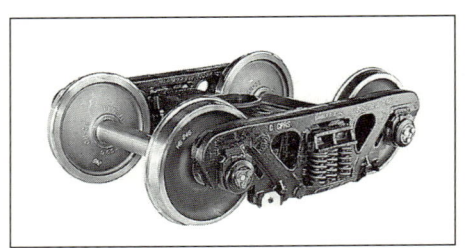

*Standard Car Truck frame brake integral cast design*
0003956

---

## Standard Steel, LLC

500 N Walnut Street, Burnham, Pennsylvania 17009, USA
Tel: (+1 717) 248 49 11   Fax: (+1 717) 248 80 50

**Key personnel**
President and Chief Executive Officer: Michael J Farrell
Senior Vice-President Sales and Operations:
  John M Hilton
Senior Vice-President Finance and Administration:
  Dana L Patterson

**Principal subsidiaries**
Standard Steel, Burnham and Latrobe, Pennsylvania, USA

**Background**
Standard Steel, LLC was previously named Freedom Forge Corporation.

**Products**
Various types of wheels, axles and mounted assemblies (freight, diesel and transit). Box lids.

*UPDATED*

---

## Steel Authority of India Ltd

Durgapur Steel Plant, Durgapur, West Bengal, India
Tel: (+91 343) 830 00   Fax: (+91 343) 823 17

**Key personnel**
See entry in *Permanent way components, equipment and services* section.

**Products**
Forged wheels, axles and wheelsets.
Recent contracts include supply of rails, wheels, axles and wheelsets to Indian Railways and rails to Bangladesh Railways.

---

## Stork RMO BV

PO Box 1250, NL-1000 BG Amsterdam, Netherlands
Tel: (+31 20) 523 37 00   Fax: (+31 20) 622 06 17
e-mail: info.RMO@stork.com

**Key personnel**
Managing Director: Ir J N M Koot

**Works**
Oostenburgervootstraat 181, NL-1018 MP Amsterdam, Netherlands

**Products**
Manufacturing and overhaul of motor and trailer bogies for emus, trainsets, LRVs, metro trainsets and tram cars; motor and trailer bogies with radial adjustable wheelsets for passenger trainsets; overhaul of bogies and components; automatic retractable interconnecting gangways for passenger trainsets.

**Contracts**
Recent contracts include the supply of high-speed bogies to ALSTOM for TGV Thalys trainsets, bogies to Bombardier for RET Rotterdam metro cars and IRM trains for Netherlands Railways.

*UPDATED*

*Stork RMO motor bogie*
0063735

---

Jane's World Railways 2002-2003

www.janes.com

## Stucki

A Stucki Company
2600 Neville Road, Pittsburgh, Pennsylvania 15225-1480, USA
Tel: (+1 412) 771 73 00   Fax: (+1 412) 771 73 08
e-mail: jfaryniak@stucki.com
Web: http://www.stucki.com

**Key personnel**
Chairman: W G Hansen
President: J G Faryniak
Vice-President, Customer Technical Support: D Rhen
Vice-President, International Sales: T Bell

**Products**
Hydraulic bogie stabilisers, HS-7, HS-7-100 and HS-10, designed to control harmonic rocking and vertical bounce in 50, 70 and 100 short ton freight wagons; single and double roller steel bogie side bearings, resilient constant contact side bearings (conventional and metal-capped), to control light bogie hunting; body side bearing wear plates and wedges for 50, 70 and 100 short ton wagons; resilient-padded friction wedges for elimination of bolster wear in Ride Control or Barber bogies.

A new development is a locomotive air dryer, using a membrane drying system to remove moisture in the train air supply.

Supplying bogie and body-side bearings for current Thrall-Europa wagon programmes for EWS, UK.

*UPDATED*

## Sumitomo

Sumitomo Metal Industries Ltd
8-11 Harumi 1-Chome, Tokyo 104-6111, Japan
Tel: (+81 3) 44 16 62 71   Fax: (+81 3) 44 16 67 90
e-mail: skr@sumitomometals.co.jp
Web: http://www.sumitomometals.co.jp

**Key personnel**
See entry in *Brakes and drawgear* section.

**Products**
Bogies, bogie components, wheels and wheelsets, axles and gearboxes.

Sumitomo has developed a bolsterless bogie with 40 per cent fewer components and weighing some15 per cent less than conventional designs. Better running performance through curves is claimed. Based on this experience, SMI has developed several new bogie designs and test equipment. Included are a prototype high-speed test bogie for JR Shinkansen trains, and bogie rotational test equipment. Sumitomo also developed linear induction motors for the Osaka and Tokyo mini-metro systems.

*UPDATED*

## Superior Graphite Co

10 S Riverside Plaza, Suite 1600, Chicago, Ilinois 60606, USA
Tel: (+1 312) 559 29 99   Fax: (+1 312) 559 90 64
Web: http//www.superiorgraphite.com

**Key personnel**
Chairman: Peter R Carney
President and Chief Executive Officer: Edward O Carney
Senior Vice-President Operations, Sales and Marketing: Wesley C Krueger
Senior Vice-President Finance: Ronald G Pawelko

**Overseas offices**

*Sweden*
PO Box 1300, Sundsvall
Tel: (+46 60) 13 41 88   Fax: (+46 60) 13 41 28

*Canada*
PO Box 20015, John Galt Postal Station, Cambridge, Ontario N1R 8C8
Tel: (+1 519) 650 16 08   Fax: (+1 519) 650 18 03

**Products**
Graphite-based rail lubricants.

Lubricants have been supplied to Indian Railways and rail systems in the USA including Burlington Northern Railroad.

*UPDATED*

## Swasap

A division of Baughan (Pty) Ltd
PO Box 366, Germiston 1400, South Africa
Tel: (+27 11) 873 66 66
Fax: (+27 11) 873 76 88; 825 46 72
e-mail: swasap@bongroup.com
Web: http://www.bongroup.com/swasap/index.htm

**Main works**
Rinkhals Street, Industries East, Germiston, Gauteng, South Africa

**Key personnel**
Factory Manager: Mike Braney
Contracts Controller: Gerrie Nel

**Products**
Axles and wheelsets.

**Contracts**
Contracts include supply of 2,676 axles for New York CTA, USA, and a two-year contract for all maintenance and new-build axles for Spoornet.

*UPDATED*

## Tafesa SA

Carretera de Andalucía Km 9, E-28021 Madrid, Spain
Tel: (+34 91) 798 05 50   Fax: (+34 91) 798 09 61

**Key personnel**
See entry in *Locomotives and powered/non-powered passenger vehicles* section.

**Products**

## Talgo

Patentes Talgo SA
C/Gabriel García Márquez 4, E-28230 Las Rozas, Madrid, Spain
Tel: (+34 91) 631 38 00; 27 00   Fax: (+34 91) 631 38 99
e-mail: comercial@talgo.com

**Key personnel**
See entry in *Locomotives and powered non-powered passenger vehicles* section.

**Subsidiary companies**
Talgo America
100 South King Street, Suite 320, Seattle, Washington 98104, USA
Tel: (+1 206) 748 61 40   Fax: (+1 206) 748 61 47
e-mail: info@talgoamerica.com
Talgo Deutschland GmbH
Revaler Strasse 99, D-10245 Berlin, Germany
Tel: (+49 30) 29 72 27 51   Fax: (+49 30) 29 72 11 43
e-mail: talgodeutschland@talgo.com

**Products**
Talgo RD automatic wheelset gauge-changing system, enabling freight wagons and Talgo passenger vehicles to operate between railway networks with track gauges ranging from 1,000 to 1,668 mm. The system comprises two elements: wheelsets in which the position of the wheels on the axles can be unlocked to enable them to be moved to conform to the gauge of the destination railway; fixed gauge-changing installations which include side-bearers to take the weight of each vehicle as wheelset adjustment takes place.

## Tatravagónka AS

Štefánikova 887/53, SK-058 01 Poprad, Slovakia
Tel: (+421 52) 72 32 75   Fax: (+421 52) 72 17 32
e-mail: market@vapop.sk

**Key personnel**
See entry in *Freight vehicles and equipment* section.

**Products**
Y25-type bogies for freight wagons.

Contracts include 68 two-axle bogies for Krupp, Germany; 998 for DWA Niesky, Germany; 170 for LHB, Germany; 300 for DB AG; 200 two-axle Y25 Ls(s)d1 bogies for ZNTK Gniewczyna, Poland; 476 for Zastal-Wagonwy Zelona Góra, Poland; 391 for MSV Studénka; 30 for VTG Hamburg; 600 two-axle Y25Rs bogies for Prema Bratislava, Slovakia.

*UPDATED*

## Techlam

1 rue de l'Industrie, BP 6, F-68701 Cernay Cedex, France
Tel: (+33 3) 89 75 30 82 Fax: (+33 3) 89 39 89 62
e-mail: info@techlam.org

**Products**
Flexible mechanical systems and elastomer/rubber components, including: anti-roll bar components for TGV high-speed trainset motor bogies; Orgal steering system for VAL 208 automated rubber-tyred metro vehicles; and elements for inter-car articulation for low-floor light rail vehicles.

*NEW ENTRY*

## Techni-Industrie SA

ZI de la Chambrouillère, F-53960 Bonchamp-lès-Laval, France
Tel: (+33 2) 43 59 23 80   Fax: (+33 2) 43 59 23 89

**Key personnel**
See entry in *Passenger coach equipment* section.

**Products**
Bogies for metro trainsets and freight wagons.

## Tenmat Ltd

Ashburton Road West, Trafford Park, Manchester M17 1RU, UK
Tel: (+44 161) 872 21 81   Fax: (+44 161) 872 75 96
e-mail: info@tenmat.com
Web: http://www.tenmat.com

**Key personnel**
Marketing Officer: Colin Stansfield
Technical Services Manager: Dave Hill

**Products**
Ferobestos and Feroform wearing and bearing materials for centre pivot liners, side bearer pads, brake pivot bushes and other applications; non-asbestos arc and heat-resistant insulation boards; millboards and intumescents for thermal insulation and fire protection.

*UPDATED*

## Thyssen Krupp

Thyssen Krupp Gleistechnik GmbH
Altendorfer Strasse 104, D-45143 Essen, Germany
Tel: (+49 201) 188 37 10   Fax: (+49 201) 188 37 14

**Works**
Kaiser-Wilhelm-Strasse 100, D-47166 Duisburg, Germany
Tel: (+49 203) 524 06 20   Fax: (+49 203) 522 46 94

**Products**
Wagon components; wheel sets, wheels, axles, wheel tyres.

## Timken Rail Service

16 Quorn Way, Grafton Industrial Estate, Northampton NN1 2PN, UK
Tel: (+44 1604) 62 70 15   Fax: (+44 1604) 63 64 54

**Head office**
The Timken Company
1875 Dueber Avenue, SW, Canton, Ohio 44706, USA
Tel: (+1 330) 471 30 00

**UK head office**
British Timken Ltd
Main Road, Duston, Northampton NN5 6UL, UK
Tel: (+44 1604) 75 23 11
Canton, Ohio 44706, USA

**Key personnel**
President, Rail: Vinnie Dasari (Canton)
General Manager, Duston Bearing Plant:
    William Kelleher (Duston)
Director, European Rail and Passenger Systems:
    Keith P Kruger (Quorn Way)
Manager, Operations and Engineering:
    Christian Moly (Quorn Way)

**Manufacturing plants**
Australia, Brazil, Canada, China, France, Italy, Poland, South Africa, UK and USA.

**Products and services**
Tapered roller bearings; AP and SP tapered roller bearing cartridge units; and complete axleboxes and motor suspension units.

Design, manufacture and supply of tapered roller bearings and ancillary equipment covering transmissions, axleboxes, traction motor suspension units and other equipment, such as cooling fans and screw compressors.

Reconditioning and remanufacturing of tapered roller bearings for rail applications.

## Trelleborg

Trelleborg Industrial AVS (Metalastik)
PO Box 98, Evington Valley Road, Leicester LE5 5LY, UK
Tel: (+44 116) 273 02 81   Fax: (+44 116) 273 56 98
Web: http://www.metalastik.com

**Key personnel**
Sales and Marketing Manager: Keith Croysdale

**Corporate development**
Formerly a subsidiary of Dunlop Ltd, Metalastik was acquired by the Swedish group Trelleborg in March 2000, becoming a subsidiary of Trelleborg Holdings UK Ltd.

**Products**
Chevrons; Metacones; hour-glass springs; bearer springs and air springs; spherilastic bearings; bushes; centre control mountings; centre pivot bearings; control links; drive couplings; auxiliary engine mounts; and air conditioning mounts.

Recent contracts include an order from KOROS for 2,688 chevron sets for bogie primary suspension for metro cars for Pusan, South Korea.

Recent contracts include the supply of 2,000 sidebearer springs to CLW, India, for both new-build and retrofit applications on electric locomotives for Indian Railways.

*UPDATED*

*Primary suspension chevrons supplied by Trelleborg Industrial AVS for Pusan metro* 2001/0103972

## TSM

Technical Service and Marketing Inc
10765 Ambassador Drive, Kansas City, Missouri 64153, USA
Tel: (+1 816) 891 65 44   Fax: (+1 816) 891 93 29

**Key personnel**
See entry in *Diesel engines, transmission and fuelling systems* section.

**Products**
Onboard flange lubricator systems with electronic control.

Contracts include the supply of flange lubricator systems to Burlington Northern Santa Fe, USA, maintained and serviced by TSM Services.

## Tülomsas

The Locomotive & Motor Corporation of Turkey
Ahmet Kanatli Cad, TR-26490 Eskisehir, Turkey
Tel: (+90 222) 224 00 00   Fax: (+90 222) 225 72 72
e-mail: tulomsas@tulomsas.com.tr
Web: http://www.tulomsas.com.tr

**Key personnel**
See entry in *Locomotives and powered/non-powered passenger vehicles* section.

**Products**
Bogies for locomotives and freight wagons.

## United Goninan

PO Box 3300, Hamilton, New South Wales 2303, Australia
Tel: (+61 2) 49 23 50 00   Fax: (+61 2) 49 23 51 12

**Key personnel**
See entry in *Locomotives and powered/non-powered passenger vehicles* section.

**Products**
Bogies for locomotives, passenger vehicles and freight wagons.

**Contracts**
Contracts include the supply of 129 Barber S2HD bogies by Standard Truck, USA, for BHP Iron Ore, Australia; 850 fabricated primary suspension bogies for coal wagons for FreightCorp, Australia; 160 fabricated six-wheel primary suspension locomotive bogies for National Rail Corporation, Australia and 80 fabricated primary suspension locomotive bogies for State Rail of Thailand.

*UPDATED*

## Uralvagonzavod

622006 Nizhny Tagil, Russian Federation
Tel: (+7 83435) 23 17 74; 23 01 97
Fax: (+7 83435) 23 34 92; 23 03 57

**Products**
Bogies.

## Valdunes

Immeuble International, Bâtiment A2, 2 rue Stephenson, F-78180 Montigny-le-Bretonneux, France
Tel: (+33 1) 39 30 84 84   Fax: (+33 1) 39 30 84 75
e-mail: welcome@valdunes.com

**Key personnel**
Chief Executive Officer: Jean-Pierre Auger
Commercial Manager: Christian Pignerol

**Products**
Forged wheels, including low-stress wheels, sound-dampening wheels and wheels for light rail vehicles and heavy-haul applications; axles; powered and trailer wheelsets; brake discs; gear blanks.

Contracts include the supply of wheels and wheelsets to operators, traction and rolling stock builders and private owners in over 60 countries.

*UPDATED*

## Vibratech Inc

11980 Walden Avenue, Alden, New York 14004-9790, USA
Tel: (+1 716) 937 79 03   Fax: (+1 716) 937 46 92
e-mail: dcovelli@vibratech.com
Web: http://www.vibratech.com

**Key personnel**
Sales Manager: Daniel Covelli

**Products**
Vibration and motion damping systems.

Customers include Adtranz, Gevisa, ALSTOM, RSD Dorbyl, General Electric, Kawasaki, Siemens, Sumitomo and Bombardier.

*UPDATED*

*Vibratech telescopic shock-absorbers to control yaw motion in locomotive, freight and passenger rail applications* 0063736

## Vossloh Schienenfahrzeugtechnik GmbH (VSFT)

PO Box 9293, D-24152 Kiel
Falckensteiner Strasse 2, D-24159 Kiel, Germany
Tel: (+49 431) 39 99 30 89   Fax: (+49 1) 39 99 22 74
e-mail: vertrieb.kiel@vsft.vossloh.com
Web: http://www.vsft.de

**Works**
Service-Zentrum Moers, Klever Strasse 48, D-47441 Moers, Germany
Tel: (+49 2841) 140 40   Fax: (+49 2841) 14 04 50

**Key personnel**
See entry in *locomotives and powered/non-powered passenger vehicles* section.

**Products**
Design and manufacturing of two- and three axle bogies for hydraulic and electric drive according to European and US standards.

*NEW ENTRY*

## Wabtec Rail Ltd

PO Box 192, Hexthorpe Road, Doncaster DN1 1PJ, UK
Tel: (+44 1302) 79 00 27   Fax: (+44 1302) 79 00 58
e-mail: probinson@wabtec.com
Web: http://www.wabtec.com

**Key personnel**
See entry in *Locomotives and powered/non-powered passenger vehicles* section

**Corporate development**
Wabtec Rail formerly traded as RFS(E), changing its name in March 2000.

## Bogies and suspension, wheels and axles, bearings/MANUFACTURERS

**Products**
Overhaul of bogies and wheelsets for locomotives, multiple units, coaching stock and freight vehicles; overhaul of bearings and axle boxes.

Recent contracts include the overhaul of over 1,000 bogies for Central Trains including Class 150, 153, 156 and 158 dmu bogies and Class 323 emu bogies.

## Walkers

Walkers Ltd
A member of the Evans Deakin Industries Group
23 Bowen Street, Maryborough, Queensland 4650, Australia
Tel: (+61 71) 20 81 00   Fax: (+61 71) 22 44 00

**Key personnel**
See entry in *Locomotives and powered/non-powered pasenger vehicles* section.

**Products**
Bogies for freight wagons.

## Wheel & Axle

Wheel & Axle Plant (Indian Railways)
Yelahanka, Bangalore 560 064, India
Tel: (+91 80) 846 03 49; 20 45   Fax: (+91 80) 846 03 67

**Key personnel**
General Manager: Gopal Krishna Malhotra
Chief Mechanical Engineer: Rajneesh Dubey

**Products**
Cast-steel wheels, axles and wheelsets.
Contracts include the supply of 948 wheels and 200 axles to Progress Rail Services, USA.

## William Cook Rail

Cross Green, Leeds LS9 0SG, UK
Tel: (+44 113) 249 63 63   Fax: (+44 113) 249 13 76
e-mail: admin@cook-catton.co.uk
Web: http://www.william-cook.co.uk

**Key personnel**
See entry in *Brakes and drawgear* section.

**Products**
Bogie castings, including frame castings, centre castings, brackets, axleboxes, traction motor casings and suspension parts.

## Willy Vogel

Motzener Strasse 35/37, D-12277, Germany
Tel: (+49 30) 72 00 20   Fax: (+49 30) 72 00 21 11
e-mail: info@vogel-berlin-de
Web: http://www.vogel-ag.de

**Key personnel**
Director, International Sales: Vincent F Warnecke

**Products**
Wheel flange lubrication systems for rail vehicles.

## Woodhead Shock Absorbers

Church Street, Ossett WF5 9DL, UK
Tel: (+44 1924) 27 35 21
Fax: (+44 1924) 27 61 57; 26 46 56

**Key personnel**
Chairman: S Beyazit
Director: A C Kart

**Products**
Dampers (primary and secondary) for rolling stock, bogies and door actuating systems. Refurbishment facility for rolling stock and bogie dampers.
*UPDATED*

## Zeco

Zimbabwe Engineering Ltd
PO Box 1874, Bulawayo, Zimbabwe
Tel: (+263 9) 789 31   Fax: (+263 9) 722 59

**Key personnel**
See entry in *Locomotives and powered/non-powered pasenger vehicles* section.

**Products**
Bogies, bogie components and spares for freight wagons.

## ZF Sachs AG

Center of Excellence
Rail Vehicle Damping
Bogestrasse 50, D-53783 Eitorf, Germany
Fax: (+49 2243) 122 80
e-mail: rail.technology@sachs.de

**Key personnel**
General Manager: Matthias Raulf
Key Account Management: Dietmar Clemens

**Subsidiary company**
Sachs Automotive of America
2107 Crooks Road, Troy, Michigan 48084, USA
Tel: (+1 248) 458 36 00   Fax: (+1 248) 458 36 01

**Works**
Schweinfurt, Germany

**Products**
Vehicle suspension components ranging from horizontal and vertical damper for primary and secondary applications to a complete family of yaw dampers. Sachs offers shock absorbers for all rail vehicle applications. Sachs has developed adaptive damping systems such as electrically switchable yaw dampers which achieve maximum safety and comfort even at high speeds and also significantly reduce wear and tear.
Sachs also provides customer support globally.

*UPDATED*

*ZF Sachs dampers for rail vehicles*   2002/0122673

# SIMULATION AND TRAINING SYSTEMS

## Alphabetical listing

Corus Rail Consultancy Ltd
Corys TESS
Dornier GmbH
DST
EBIM SA
Fokker
IIT Research Institute
Kolmex sa
Krauss-Maffei Wegmann
Oktal
Orthstar Inc
PC-Rail Software
STERIA
STN ATLAS
Systra
Tata
Vossloh System-Technik York Ltd

---

## Classified listing

**DRIVING SIMULATORS**
Corus Rail Consultancy
Corys TESS
DST
EBIM
Fokker
IIT Research Institute
Kolmex
Krauss-Maffei Wegmann
Oktal
Orthstar
PC-Rail Software
STERIA
STN ATLAS
Systra
Tata

**OPERATIONS AND SIGNALLING SIMULATION**
DST
Oktal
STERIA
Systra
Vossloh System-Technik York Ltd

**TRAINING SYSTEMS**
EBIM
IIT Research Institute
Kolmex
Oktal
Systra

---

## Company listing by country

**FRANCE**
Corys TESS
EBIM SA
Oktal
STERIA
Systra

**GERMANY**
Dornier GmbH
DST
Krauss-Maffei Wegmann
STN ATLAS

**INDIA**
Tata

**NETHERLANDS**
Fokker

**POLAND**
Kolmex

**UNITED KINGDOM**
Corus Rail Consultancy Ltd
PC-Rail Software
Vossloh System-Technik York Ltd

**UNITED STATES OF AMERICA**
IIT Research Institute
Orthstar Inc

## Corus Rail Consultancy Ltd

PO Box 298, York YO1 6YH, UK
Tel: (+44 1904) 52 21 64  Fax: (+44 1904) 52 38 76
e-mail: info@corusrailconsultancy.com
Web: http://www.corusrailconsultancy.com

### Key personnel
See entry in *Consultancy services* section.

### Products
A route familiarisation package using computer-generated images has been developed to create a three-dimensional view of a new track layout as seen by a train driver. The first application of the system, which is designed to run on a Pentium III or equivalent computer using a Windows 95/98 platform, was developed for Railtrack in the UK to simulate new routes through a remodelled track layout at Leeds station.

### Contracts
Recent contracts include Corus Rail Consultancy being appointed by Railtrack to design a signal sighting simulation package for a proposed new signalling layout at Rugby, UK, as part of the West Coast Route Modernisation.

**VERIFIED**

*Three-dimensional route familiarisation simulator package developed by Corus Rail Consultancy*
2001/0103636

## Corys TESS

74 rue des Martyrs, F-38027 Grenoble,
Cedex 01, France
Tel: (+33 4) 76 28 82 00  Fax: (+33 4) 76 28 82 11
e-mail: coryscom@corys.fr
Web: http://www.corys.com

### Key personnel
Managing Director: Geroges Van Billoen
Transport Simulation Manager: Ralf Gathmann

### Corporate background
Corys TESS (Training & Engineering Support Systems) was formed in 1997 when Tractabel Engineering of Belgium took over the Corys company. All the previous activities of Corys have been continued at Corys TESS.

### Products
Training for train drivers from computer-based training applications to task simulators through to full scope motion replica simulators. Corys TESS has designed and manufactured diesel locomotive, electric locomotive, underground, suburban and high-speed train driving simulators as well as railway traffic control simulators.

Over 150 Corys TESS simulators are installed in 25 countries. Recent contracts include the American Flyer high-speed trainset driving simulator for Amtrak and the Citytrain suburban train driving simulator for Queensland Rail Australia.

## Dornier GmbH

VE7A1, D-88039 Friedrichshafen, Germany
Tel: (+49 89) 60 72 64 81  Fax: (+49 89) 60 70
Web: http://www.dasa.com

### Background
Dornier is a subsidiary of Daimler-Benz Aerospace.

### Products
Simulation and training systems for high-speed, LRV and metro trains.

Customers include DB AG, Germany and Stuttgarter Strassenbahnen AG.

## DST

Deutsche System-Technik GmbH
PO Box 450262, D-28296 Bremen, Germany
Tel: (+49 421) 428 70  Fax: (+49 421) 40 46 60

### Key personnel
Chairmen and Chief Executive Officers: Hans-Jörg Zobel, Bruno Jacobi
Director, International Sales and Marketing: Dr Christian Wetzel

### Products
Driving and signalling simulators.

## EBIM SA

ZI St Joseph, F-04012 Manosque Cedex, France
Tel: (+33 4) 92 72 18 66  Fax: (+33 4) 92 87 31 86

### Key personnel
Chairman: M Giusti
Managing Director: J J Valade
Assistant Managing Director: B Giusti
Business Manager: A Nassif

### Products
Static and dynamic driving simulators; computer-assisted training systems for railway personnel. French National Railways (SNCF) has 42 EBIM multimedia computer-assisted training stations in service at 36 training centres. The training stations are used to familiarise personnel with different types of rolling stock (TGV high-speed trainsets, Corail passenger coaches and suburban trainsets) and train them in operational, safety and fault finding/rectification procedures.

Recent contracts include the supply of a static Eurostar driving simulator and a static Class 92 locomotive driving simulator to EPS, UK; two static driving simulators to Eurotunnel; and three dynamic (Eurostar, Class 92 and TGV-Réseau) driving simulators to SNCF, France.

## Fokker

Fokker Space BV
Newtonweg 1, PO Box 32070,
NL-2303 DB Leiden, Netherlands
Tel: (+31 71) 524 54 55  Fax: (+31 71) 524 54 98
e-mail: J.Hoogstraten@fokkerspace.nl

### Key personnel
Product Manager, Civil Simulators: Jos A Hoogstraten
Marketing Manager: A J de Vries

### Products
Simulators for trains and train drivers. Fokker uses a combination of video and computer-generated images to keep down the production costs of its simulators.

## IIT Research Institute

10 W 35th Street, 8th Floor, Transport Technology Division, Chicago, Illinois 60616, USA
Tel: (+1 312) 567 45 79  Fax: (+1 312) 567 46 08
e-mail: mbrennan@iitri.org
Web: http://www/iitri.org

### Key personnel
President: Bahman Atefi
Senior Vice-President: Lynn Cumberbatch
Division Manager, Transport Technology: Michael R Wozniak

### Products
With over 20 years of experience in providing train simulators, the Transport Technology Division is a worldwide supplier of railroad industry-accepted training products for operations and maintenance. Incorporating the latest advances in rail, and having the most detailed simulator software models, IITRI claims to have provided state-of-the-art technology to more railroads than any other provider. IITRI has helped many of the world's railroads solve their most challenging educational needs, with e-learning products and information management services. Every system is customised with the features and functions to meet user needs. Full customer service is provided for all products.

**UPDATED**

## Kolmex sa

Grzybowska 80/82, PL-00-844 Warsaw, Poland
Tel: (+48 22) 661 50 00  Fax: (+48 22) 620 93 81
e-mail: kolmexsa@kolmex.com.pl
Web: http://www.kolmex.com.pl

### Key personnel
Chairman: Andrzej Nalęcz
Commercial Director: Krystyna Stepaniuk

### Products
Railway simulator for driver training.

## Krauss-Maffei Wegmann GmbH & Co KG

Krauss-Maffei-Strasse 11, D-80997 Munich, Germany
Tel: (+49 89) 81 40 40 67  Fax: (+49 89) 81 40 49 87
e-mail: simulation@kmweg.de
Web: http://www.kmwsim.de

*Corys computer-generated image for rail driving simulator*
0041520

## Simulation and training systems/MANUFACTURERS

*KMW training device with partial simulation as delivered to Luxembourg Railways (together with a full mission simulator and a CBT system)* 2002/0143312

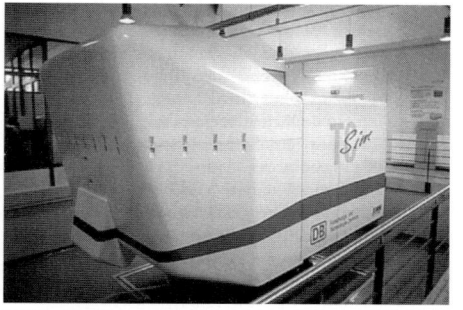

*TCSim system of KMW, at research facilities of German Railways in Munich-Freimann* 2002/0143311

**Key personnel**
Director: Dieter Weber
Sales and Projects: Robert Bodner
Commercial Affairs: Friedemann Neuhäuser
Executive Sales Manager: Hermann J Bidermann

**Products**
Planning, development, manufacturing, integration and marketing of training and simulations for civilian and non-civilian applications. With its leading role in the field of driving simulation, the products in that field cover the complete spectrum for the installation of integrated training concepts including: Computer Based Training (CBT), part task trainers and full mission simulators.

The simulation systems include the complete train model and KMW has modelled locomotives and trains of many of the major locomotive manufacturers worldwide including Siemens, Bombardier and Alstom. The simulation of any track logics, signalling systems or train control systems such as ATO/ATP, the German standard LZB. The simulation of train diagnostic system displays. A sound simulation system which includes the simulation of a train radio system. The simulation of any operational and/or technical malfunctions that can online be released by the instructor (on- or offline) and a highly sophisticated instructor's station software (MMI) which enables the instructor to operate the simulator.

*UPDATED*

## Oktal

Immeuble Aurelien 2, 2 rue Boudeville, F-3100 Toulouse, France
Tel: (+33 5) 62 11 50 10   Fax: (+33 5) 62 11 50 29
e-mail: oktal@oktal.fr
Paris office
55 rue Thiers, F-92100 Boulogne, France
Tel: (+33 1) 46 94 97 80

**Associated company**
Technirail, Belgium

**Products**
Train driving simulators, including visual and motion systems.

## Orthstar Inc

Airport Corporate Park, PO Box 459, Big Flats, New York 14814, USA
Tel: (+1 607) 562 21 00   Fax: (+1 607) 562 21 10
e-mail: info@ORTHSTAR.com
Web: http://www.orthstar.com

**Key personnel**
Chief Executive Officer: James E Orsillo
President: Joseph E Strykowski
Vice-President: Carolyn B Spencer

**Corporate development**
Orthstar Inc, a systems and software engineering organisation, bought Hughes Training rail simulation business in 1997.

**Products**
Locomotive and train simulators, metro car simulators, GPS tracking systems and parts task trainers. Development of real-time on-train and wayside products for the rail industry.

*VERIFIED*

## PC-Rail Software

PO Box 27, Cromer NR27 0HA, UK
Tel: (+44 1263) 51 40 47
e-mail: info@pcrail.co.uk
Web: http://www.pcrail.co.uk

**Key personnel**
Principle Consultant: John D Dennis

**Products**
PC-Rail range of railway signalling simulations for use with Windows 95 or later (including 98, ME, XP, NT and 2000).

*UPDATED*

## STERIA

12 rue Paul Dautier, PO Box 58, F-78142 Velizy Cedex, France
Tel: (+33 1) 34 38 60 00   Fax: (+33 1) 34 88 61 60
Web: http://www.steria.fr

**Key personnel**
See *Signalling and communications systems* section.

**Products**
Traffic control, model networks, scheduling, equipment and power consumption control, passenger information, ticketing, simulation, high-reliability systems (Atelier B).

Recent contracts executed and obtained include SOSIE – metro controller training simulator for RATP Paris.

## STN ATLAS

Sebaldsbrücker Heerstrasse 235, D-28305 Bremen, Germany
Tel: (+49 421) 457 41 98   Fax: (+49 421) 457 38 17

**Key personnel**
Marketing Manager: Uwe Paczula

**Products**
Train traffic simulator, with sound and electric movement of cab.

*UPDATED*

Jackie Clarke

## Systra

Groupe Systra
5 avenue du Coq, F-75009 Paris, France
Tel: (+33 1) 40 16 63 33   Fax: (+33 1) 40 16 64 44
e-mail: systra@systra.com
Web: http://www.systra.com

*STN ATLAS train traffic simulator* 0002462

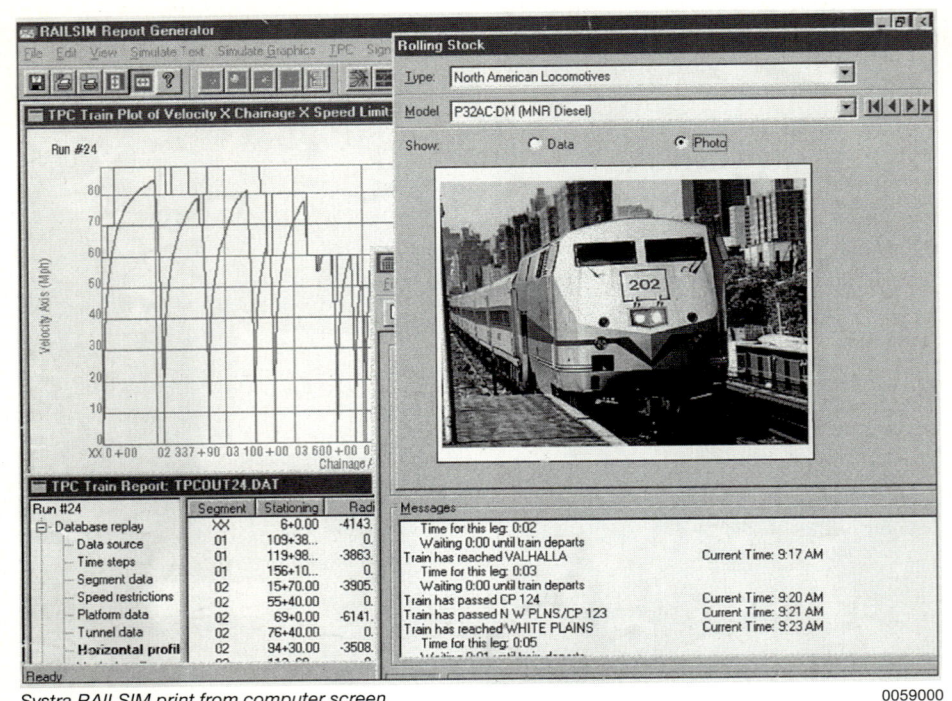

## 642 MANUFACTURERS/Simulation and training systems

*Systra RAILSIM print from computer screen*

#### Key personnel
See *Consultancy* section

#### Products
RAILSIM® Train Performance Calculator (TPC) Version 7. Development of rail simulation software products, RAILSIM TPC can simulate and analyse the performance of any train on any rail system. It can generate travel time predictions, train control attainable speed and safe braking distance analyses, ruling grade and curve analyses, rail alignment alternative analyses, and rolling stock performance evaluations.

Part of the RAILSIM Simulation Software Suite, RAILSIM TPC Version 7 has many new features for additional rail simulation applications, including:

- The ability to select computed or predefined manufacturer curves for tractive, friction, and dynamic/regenerative braking effort and motor efficiency
- The ability to create user-defined rolling stock libraries, with customised performance curves
- An expanded selection of rolling stock libraries and resistance equations
- Support for freight train air brake propagation times through the train, including modelling of mid-train and helper locomotives
- Air brake propagation times which are specific to each locomotive and car in the train
- Support for electronic braking systems
- Support for friction braking and blended braking (combination of friction and dynamic/regenerative braking, with user-specified transition speeds)
- Support for emergency braking (concurrent application of friction, dynamic/regenerative braking and track braking, where applicable)
- An expanded selection of text and graphical output reports, including the new train summary report and energy/power plot

A standard RAILSIM TPC licence package includes the TPC, three rolling stock libraries and two rolling resistance algorithms, plus RAILSIM Database Editor and RAILSIM Report Generator.

### Tata

Tata Electronic Development Services
A division of Tata Electric Companies
Bombay House, 24 Homi Mody Street, Mumbai 400 001, India
Tel: (+91 80) 852 04 09 16   Fax: (+91 80) 852 04 17

#### Key personnel
General Manager, Operations: S Gnyana Sundar
Senior Manager, Projects & Marketing: Col J Banerjee
Senior Manager, Simulators and Manufacturing:
    V Kishore Kumar

#### Products
Replica locomotive driving simulators. Tata simulators feature an exact replica of the locomotive cab, a six-axis motion base, visual display replayed from video discs and sound replay using digitised real sounds stored by computer.

A driver console for the WAG-9 locomotive supplied by Adtranz Sweden is available; also the subsystems of WAG-9 locomotives.

### Vossloh System-Technik York Ltd

St Mary's Court, 39 Blossom Street, York YO24 1AQ, UK
Tel: (+44 1904) 63 90 91   Fax: (+44 1904) 63 90 92
Web: http://www.comreco-rail.co.uk

#### Key personnel
Directors: R A Gough, T A Greaves
Export Sales: J K Hammerton

#### Developments
Vossloh System-Technik, a subsidiary of the Vossloh Group, acquired this company as Comreco Rail Ltd in September 1999, renaming it VST Comreco Rail Ltd. It was further renamed Vossloh System-Technik York in April 2002.

#### Products
RailPlan™ is a simulation modelling system for infrastructure from simple single-track systems through to the most complex rail networks, assessment of real time operational performance impacts of variable train service patterns; PerformancePlan™ is a system which assesses traction performance capability for route profiles; PowerPlan™ is a system which simulates power supply demands for both AC and DC networks; PerformancePlanner™ analyses scheduled service plans to assess timetables and identify potential problems.

VST Comreco Rail achieved ISO 9001 accreditation in February 2002.

#### Contracts
Recent contracts include: supply of TrainPlan™, RailPlan™, ResourcePlan™, Train Manager™ and Resource Manager™ to Norwegian State Railways; supply of UK-wide integrated train planning systems and planning database with RailPlan™ and TrainPlan™ to Railtrack; supply of TrainPlan™ to Swedish State Railways and New Jersey Transit; supply of TrainPlan™ and ResourcePlan™ to Romanian State Railways and to Scotrail (UK); supply of RailPlan™ and PowerPlan™ to Kowloon–Canton Railway Corporation, Hong Kong; supply of TrainPlan™ and ResourcePlan™ to Chiltern Railways, UK.

***UPDATED***

**Nature provides the blueprints for tomorrow's transport systems.**

Signalling and Communications Systems

4 0 1 9 8

**SENSORS**

**INDICATORS**

**INCIDENT RECORDERS**

**IT-SOLUTIONS**

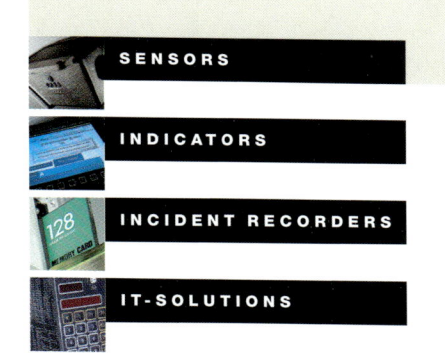

In an increasingly mobile world, people everywhere are entering into a dialogue characterized by common goals. Goals that demand a flexible approach.

DEUTA-WERKE are responding to these global changes. We interact closely with our partners to create customized solutions from standardized designs. Our innovative components technology for safe transport and navigation systems has won us a worldwide reputation – starting with sensors, indicators, man machine interfaces and train protection systems up to IT-solutions. Our quality management system according to DIN EN 9001 and a shared commitment to TQM give our customers additional security.

Individual solutions born of cooperation keep on track to a successful future. We think ahead.

**DEUTA-Werke GmbH**

Postfach 20 02 60
**D-51432 Bergisch Gladbach**

Paffrather Straße 140
**D-51465 Bergisch Gladbach**
Fon 02202 9 58-0
Fax 02202 95 81 45
support@deuta.de
www.deuta.com

**DEUTA-WERKE**

ON TRACK FOR SUCCESS

- LOCOTROL®
- ELECTROCODE 5®
- VITAL HARMON LOGIC CONTROLLER (VHLC)
- HXP-3
- SERVICES
- HAWK® EVENT RECORDER/ANALYZER
- CROSSING & WAYSIDE SIGNALS

## YOUR STRENGTH IN SIGNALING.

Today's railroads rely on a complex integration of systems and products to keep the trains running safely and performing productively. And they count on GE Transportation Systems Global Signaling for the building blocks of this entire infrastructure. From dispatcher to wayside. Wayside to cab. Cab to consist. For solutions that accelerate your control capabilities, contact Global Signaling. **1-800-825-7090**

**GE Transportation Systems**
*Global Signaling*

www.getransportation.com

## CONTROL

### It's never a headache with LockTrac

Managing a network should not be complicated. Alcatel's LockTrac handles the complexity of running thousands of trains easily, reliably and safely. We created our first electronic interlocking in the 80's, before most of our competitors. And since then, Alcatel Transport Automation Solutions has always been on top. From the operations department to the financial department, customers are pleased with LockTrac. If you want long-term cost savings when you invest in an interlocking system, Alcatel can put you on the right track. www.alcatel.com/tas

▶ TRANSPORT AUTOMATION SOLUTIONS

ALCATEL

# MANUFACTURERS/Signalling and communications systems

**Spain**
ALSTOM Transport
Apolonio Morales 13A, E-28036 Madrid, Spain
Tel: (+34 91) 343 17 70   Fax: (+34 91) 350 99 95
Managing Director: Antonio Puyol Gomez

**UK**
ALSTOM Transport
Borehamwood Industrial Park, Rowley Lane, Borehamwood WD6 5PZ, UK
Tel: (+44 20) 89 53 99 22   Fax: (+44 20) 82 07 59 05
Managing Director: Charles Burch

**USA**
ALSTOM Transport
150 Sawgrass Drive, Rochester, New York 14620, USA
Tel: (+1 716) 783 20 00   Fax: (+1 716) 783 20 88
Managing Director: Stephen Navarra

### Products
Covers main line and mass transit. For main line, ALSTOM offers ATLAS for high-speed lines, intercity and regional lines as well as for low-density lines, freight-only lines and single-track operations. This new-generation signalling system applies the latest technologies for train detection, interlocking, route management and speed control. ATLAS implements the new European Rail Traffic Management System (ERTMS) which sets interoperability standards for train control throughout the continent.

ALSTOM claims a leading position in the market for ERTMS projects and products, with more orders in more countries than its competitors. The modular ATLAS system is available at three ERTMS levels, ATLAS 100, 200 and 300, while ATLAS 400 offers a low-cost solution for low- to medium-density lines.

By the end of 2000, ALSTOM was active in seven projects, some involving interoperability, some to provide test tracks:
EMSET test, Spain, involving on-site testing of Eurobalise, BTM-Antenna, Euradio and Eurocab equipment near Madrid;
tests on a section of the Vienna Budapest line, commissioned in November 1999;
tests on a section of line between Tournan and Marles-en-Brie, France;
tests to ERTMS Level 2 on a section between Florence and Arezzo, Italy;
the 300 km/h high-speed line between Rome and Naples, Italy;
the BEV21 project in the Netherlands, involving a redesign of the signalling system based on ERTMS levels 1-3, customised for NS;
the West Coast Main Line in the UK, a joint venture between ALSTOM Signaling/EES and Railtrack to provide an ERTMS-based train control system to Levels 1 and 2 and possibly Level 3 after 2005 over 3,000 track/km.

ALSTOM's ATLAS-based Advanced Civil Speed Enforcement System (ACSES) has been successfully tested on the Transportation Test Center test track in Pueblo, USA and is looked on favourably for installation on Amtrak's Northeast Corridor from Washington BC to Boston. ACSES is designed to control and enforce train movements at various speeds, enforce civil speed restrictions (including curves, bridges and poor track conditions), provide positive train stopping at interlockings and protect work crews with temporary speed restrictions. ACSES generates and enforces profiles for various train types as required by Positive Train Control (PTC) and Communications-based Train Control (CBTC). The system integrates track transponder transmission systems, mobile communication radios and onboard computers, speed sensors and aspect display units.

ACSES will be overlaid on Amtrak's existing nine-aspect cab signalling system to allow Acela high-speed tilting trains to reach speeds of up to 240 km/h (150 mph). ACSES is being provided to Amtrak for 320 km (200 miles) on the Northeast Corridor, which contains 48 interlockings and is served by up to 430 tractive units. The signal system and ACSES are independent systems; each is designed for stand-alone use.

ALSTOM is also supplying 170 MBTA Boston commuter trainsets with ACSES.

For mass transit operations, ALSTOM offers the Urbalis solution for heavy metro and suburban networks as well as for light rail systems.

These systems are modular and adaptable and can be designed to follow changes in railway design.

ALSTOM has developed four product categories:
Smartway: conventional signalling products covering basic needs including train detection, points equipment, level crossing equipment, signals, relays and accessories.
Smartlock: mainly electronic interlocking for railway stations.
Advantik: ATC systems for main line operation.
Mastria: ATC for mass transit operation including ATP, ATO and all attached facilities. The ATC system can be fully integrated with interlocking and train supervision functions.
Iconis: Automatic Train Superversion (ATS) also called Integrated Electronic Control Center System, integrating all activities required for train control, train supervision or monitoring, management functions, SCADA requirements, maintenance or alarm centralisation and supervision.

### Contracts
**Chile:** URBALIS Automatic Train Control equipment features in a turnkey project secured by ALSTOM in July 2002 to equip the 32 km Line 4 of Santiago's metro network.

**China:** The Kowloon-Canton Railway Corporation (KCRC) of Hong Kong awarded ALSTOM a contract for supply of a signalling system for its East Rail line. The order has two aspects: a signalling system for the new 9 km two-station East Rail line extension; and a capacity upgrade of the entire East Rail line to allow up to 27 trains to operate on the line per hour. The East Rail line is already in operation with an ALSTOM signalling system. The upgrade will be made possible by integrating ALSTOM's AXONIS Automatic Train Control and Signalling system. This will increase line capacity and enhance line safety without requiring any major modification to rolling stock or infrastructure.

**Egypt:** Egypt's National Authority for Tunnels (NAT) has awarded ALSTOM, as leader of the INTERINFRA consortium, a turnkey contract for the extension of Line 2 (Phase 2C). The 2.5 km surface line will run south of Giza Suburban station to El Mounib, adding two new stations. The turnkey contract is composed of civil works, electromechanical equipment and power supply and low voltage equipment. ALSTOM's contribution includes power supply, signalling and automatic train operation, and a centralised control system, as well as overall project management of the turnkey contract.

**India:** ALSTOM Transport Ltd (India) has signed a contract with Delhi Metro Rail Corporation for the design and supply of an integrated automatic train control, signalling and telecommunication system for the operator's metro project currently under construction in Delhi.

**Singapore:** Singapore's Land Transport Authority (LTA) has awarded the ALSTOM/STE consortium an order worth €170 million, for the second phase of construction of its automatic Marina metro line. ALSTOM's share of this contract is valued at €123 million. ALSTOM will supply its AXONIS™ automatic metro system for this line.

This order was an extension of the Marina Line Phase 1 project, awarded to ALSTOM on a turnkey basis in December 2000. The first stage covers 5.6 km and has six stations. This second section will extend the Marina line by 5 km and add five new stations. By 2002, contracts for further phases had been subsequently announced for the line, which will eventually cover 34 km and circle the island of Singapore, making it the world's longest automatic metro line.

**Switzerland:** In 2002, ALSTOM secured a contract from Swiss Federal Railways to supply components from its ATLAS system to equip the Mattstetten—Rothrist line according to European Train Control System (ETCS) Levels 1 and 2 standards. Final delivery and commissioning are scheduled for November 2004.

**Turkey:** An ALSTOM-led consortium has been awarded a contract by Istanbul Buyuksehir Belediyesi (the Greater City Municipality of Istanbul) for the Sishane metro extension. This project will be carried out within the framework of a previous contract with the same consortium for Phase 1 of the Istanbul metro. The Sishane extension will add 1.8 km of underground double track and one metro station. ALSTOM will be responsible for design, supply and installation of all electromechanical works. The scope of the works includes ALSTOM's complete signalling system including ATC (Automatic Train Control) and ATS (Automatic Train Supervision), now marketed under the name URBALIS™.

**USA:** ALSTOM has been awarded a contract to supply Providence and Worcester Railroad Company with the ICONIS™ Personal Traffic Master (PTM), a computer-based central control system designed to enhance the safety and efficiency of shortline rail lines. It will go into service in 2002.

*UPDATED*

---

## Ametek

Ametek Panalarm Division
7401 North Hamlin Avenue, Skokie, Illinois 60076, USA
Tel: (+1 312) 675 25 00   Fax: (+1 312) 675 30 11
Web: http://www.panalarm.com

### Key personnel
General Manager: Roger Piegza
Sales Manager: Frank Kay
Export Sales Manager: Ervin Whitfield
Transportation Marketing Manager: Rick Schoneman

### Products
Panalarm mosaic tile graphic displays, available in illuminated and non-illuminated form, and capable of printing with any symbols to customer requirement: incorporating push-button or switch controls, indicator lights, digital readout displays as required; annunciators; event recorders.

Contracts include supply of displays to Union Switch and Signal (1998), Metro North Railroad (1998), Harmon Industries (1998) and Metro Dade Transit (1999).

---

## Andrew

Andrew Kommunikationssysteme AG
Bächliwis 2b, CH-8184 Bachenbülach, Zurich, Switzerland
Tel: (+41 1) 863 73 52   Fax: (+41 1) 863 73 56

### Key personnel
Managing Director: R J Fiedler
Systems Engineering: H H Junge, M Kalt
Operations: T Clachers

### Products
Design, manufacture and installation of radio communications systems for tunnels and buildings; Heliax coaxial cables, Radiax leaky feeder cables, Panel antennas, unidirectional and bidirectional amplifiers, cell extenders for GSM and PCN.

---

## ANSALDOBREDA

Ansaldo Trasporti SpA
An Ansaldo Finnmeccanica company
425 Via Argine, I-80147 Naples, Italy
Tel: (+39 081) 243 11 11   Fax: (+39 081) 243 26 98

### Subsidiary company
Ansaldo Signal NV
This company controls the Ansaldo signalling companies Ansaldo Signalamento Ferroviario, Italy; CSEE Transport, France; AT Signal System, Sweden; Union Switch & Signal, USA; and Union Switch & Signal Pty in Australia.

### Key personnel
See entry in *Locomotives and powered/non-powered passenger vehicles* section.

### Products
Automation and signalling for railway, underground and surface transport systems; components for power and signalling electronics; all-relay and solid-state interlocking; automatic block systems; electronic track circuit and continuous cab signalling equipment; microcomputer-based automatic train operation apparatus; remote-control equipment; train describer and automatic line supervision systems; level crossing automation; traffic control systems for industrial railways;

## Signalling and communications systems/MANUFACTURERS

remote control of electrification networks; signalling and automation systems for marshalling yards.

Contracts include an automatic signalling system for New York CTA; Microlok II control system for the Nuneaton to Peterborough line for Railtrack plc; six CTC systems for FS Italy main lines, including ATC and signalling systems; CTC and signalling systems for emu depot in Seremban, Malaysia; 32 solid state control systems for the Mediterranean TGV line, France; ATC system for urban and suburban railways in Teheran, Iran; advanced speed control system (ASES) for New Jersey Transit Authority, USA; CTC and ATC signalling systems for Lines B, C and D of Metropolitano de Lisboa, Portugal.

## Antenna Specialists

31225 Bainbridge Road, A, Cleveland, Ohio 44139-2281, USA
Tel: (+1 440) 349 84 00   Fax: (+1 440) 349 84 07

### Key personnel
President: F Kim Goryance
Marketing Director: Carol Broniman
International Director: Jo Virant

### Products
Two-way communications antenna systems; cellular equipment.

*UPDATED*

## APD Voyager

16 Shenley Pavilions, Chalkdell Drive, Milton Keynes MK5 6LB, UK
Tel: (+44 1482) 85 59 27   Fax: (+44 1908) 50 74 91
e-mail: marketing@apdcommunications.co.uk
Web: http://www.apdvoyager.co.uk

### Corporate background
APD Voyager is the public transport division of APD Communications Ltd, a member of the IT Communication division of Lynx Group plc.

### Products
APD Voyager specialises in the integration of communications with IT, focusing on the public transport market. Applications include software for telephone and radio call handling in a control room environment and mobile workforce management. APD also manufactures a range of wireless-based solutions with applications including telematics and automatic vehicle location.

Clients for APD Voyager systems include MRTC, Hong Kong, London Underground Ltd and Railtrack, UK.

*NEW ENTRY*

## AREX

PL 80-454 Gdańsk, ul. Nad Stawem 5, Poland
Tel: (+48 58) 344 35 40   Fax: (+48 58) 344 35 39
e-mail: marketing@arex.pl
Web: http://www.arex.pl

### Key personnel
Founder and General Director: D Phil Andrzej Darski
Technical Manager: Krzysztof Lutowicz

### Products
DIMaC-EK control and communications system. The system is provided especially for installation in unstaffed stations and is supervised from one dispatcher's centre. The DIMaC-EK system incorporates systems to control electric switch point heating; light; electric power switch control; hydrotechnical tunnel services and lighting; electrical heating cubicle; electric power measurement; pump service; intruder alarm.

These systems are independent and can operate in automatic mode with full diagnostics of the equipment, with possibility of remote change-over and monitoring. Each is provided with measuring, actuating and control equipment. Microprocessor plant controllers operating in accordance with the preset algorithms are provided as control equipment. The controllers are fitted in switchboards and control cabinets.

*ATSS-equipped train and transponders by ATSS fo SL's Roslagsbanan, Stockholm*   2002/0102883

## ATSS

AT Signal System AB
PO Box 8142, Gunnebogatan 22, SE-163 08 Spånga, Sweden
Tel: (+46 8) 621 95 00   Fax: (+46 8) 621 14 24
e-mail: atss@atss.se

### Key personnel
Managing Director: Paolo Bianchi
Marketing Manager: Lars Wennerholm
Technical Manager: Bertil Sjöbergh
Operations Manager: Mats Bylund
Product Manager: Lucas Orve

### Corporate development
ATSS is a subsidiary of Ansaldo Signal NV.

### Products
L12000 modular Automatic Train Protection (ATP) and Automatic Train Operation (ATO) system. Represents Ansaldo Signal group on the Scandinavian market for Traffic Control Centres (TCC), monitoring devices (including hot box detectors and hot wheel detectors) and general railway signalling products such as point machines, track circuits, interlockings and signals.

Recent contracts include ATP (Intermittent) for KTMB Malaysia, NSB Norway, BV Sweden, SJ Sweden, WAGR Australia and Midland Metro UK; ATP (Integrated) for HI Australia, NJT USA, Øresund link Sweden/Denmark and FS Italy; ATO and radio block for LKAB Sweden; TCC for BV Sweden.

Microlok II® Interlocking for SL Sweden.

*UPDATED*

## AWA

AWA Communications
2-6 Orion Road, Lane Cove, New South Wales, 2066 Australia
Tel: (+61 2) 94 13 63 33   Fax: (+61 2) 94 13 63 00

### Key personnel
Managing Director, Communications: Paul Lowry
Divisional Manager, Communications Projects: Garry Brook
Manager, Sales and Marketing: Ted Nugent

### Main works
23 Harvton Street, Stafford, Queensland, Australia 4053
Tel: (+61 7) 856 48 88   Fax: (+61 7) 356 68 77

### Products
Railway telecommunications: control room consoles and switches; signal post telephone concentrators; ELCPs; signal box communications systems; radio switching network infrastructure; specialised multiplexers; voice and data switching; 2 MBPS digital multiplexers; higher-order multiplexers; fibre optic OLTEs; microwave radio; design, engineering and telecommunications project management.

## Aydin

Aydin Corporation
700 Dresher Road, PO Box 349, Horsham, Pennsylvania 19044, USA
Tel: (+1 215) 657 75 10   Fax: (+1 215) 657 38 30

### Products
Communications systems and equipment.

## AŽD Praha sro

Žirovnická 2, Praha 10, CZ-10617, Czech Republic
Tel: (+420 2) 72 65 61 59   Fax: (+420 2) 72 65 61 42
e-mail: mno.rsp@azd.cz
Web: http://www.azd.cz

### Services
Research, development, design, manufacture, installation, sales and servicing of signalling, shunting, information, telecommunication and automation technologies for railway transport.

### Products
Electronic signalling and interlocking systems, level crossing safeguard systems, ATP and ATO systems, wayside equipment (point machines, locks, track circuits, axle counters, light signals), installation of telecommunications and information networks, cabling (metallic or FO cables).

*UPDATED*

## Bombardier Transportation

1101 Parent Street, Saint-Bruno, Québec, Canada J3V 6E6
Tel: (+1 450) 441 20 20   Fax: (+1 450) 441 15 15
Web: http://www.transportation.bombardier.com

Saatwinkler Damm 43, D-13627 Berlin, Germany
Tel: (+49 30) 383 20   Fax: (+49 30) 38 32 20 00

### Key personnel
See main entry in *Locomotives and powered/non-powered passenger vehicles* section.

# MANUFACTURERS/Signalling and communications systems

*ATC information display on the driver console of a VR multipurpose Sr 2 locomotive, one of 20 supplied by Bombardier* 0021713

## Products

Development, design, engineering, production, sales, installation, maintenance, after-sales service of, and customer support for, rail control and signaling systems:

*ERTMS/ETCS (The European Rail Traffic Management System/European Train Control System)*. Integrated Control Rooms (Traffic Management Systems (MS), for rail traffic. Power and SCADA control are included when the customer requires integration.

*Electronic Systems for Safety Applications*, including wayside and onboard computers with software for interlocking, Automatic Train Protection (ATP) and Automatic Train Operation (ATO).

*Train/Track Communications*: cable and radio transmission, coded track circuits, loops, balises (transponders), with associated wayside and trainborne equipment.

*Wayside Components*: point machines, barriers, signals and also electromechanical interlocking systems.

*Auxiliaries*: train detectors, interference monitoring, GPS-based positioning and velocity systems, and health monitoring systems.

In 1995 European railways unanimously selected Bombardier Transportation magnetic transponder (Balise) technology for track-to-train communication proposed for the Euro-Balise.

## Contracts

**Australia:** A traffic management system for the Melbourne suburban lines for the Public Transport Company of Victoria, supplied in partnership with ABB Signal in Australia, was contracted in 1998. The system covers 215 stations and controls 38,000 departures per day.

**Chile:** Esmeralda copper mine, owned by Codelco, has received a fully automatic radio-based control system for industrial railways. This includes interlocking with control system and radio block centre, ATC and point machines. It controls and supervises 2 km of underground track. Commissioning took place in April 1999.

**Colombia:** Ferrovias de Colombia (Colombian Railway Administration) has received a complete radio signalling system for the 200 km railway line between La Loam and Santa Marta. Commissioning took place in 2000.

**Finland:** Finnish Railways (VR) took delivery of nine electronic interlockings during 1998 for 275 km of main line track with 35 stations.

An integrated Traffic Management System (TMS) has been operating since 1996. The ITM supervises and controls both the power supply and the tracks of the electrified lines in southern Finland.

In 1997, VR received the first delivery from the company of an ATC system from Bombardier Transportation. The Kirkkonummi-Turku coast line was the first to have been equipped with the ATC system. In total, 2,355 km of VR lines will have been equipped with ATC by 2002.

**Germany:** Railway and Ports (Eisenbahn und Häfen GmbH), has acquired industrial railway interlockings and IT systems for train control and for a dispatching centre. An IT system has been developed for Deutsche Bahn (DB) AG for rostering locomotives and drivers, scheduling timetables, train formations and dispatching of coaches.

DB's Business Department network took delivery of a new system for radio-based railway operation in 1999. The fundamental philosophy of the radio concept is decentralisation of the control and safety tasks performed by conventional interlockings. The contract includes a radio centre, nine radio-based level crossings and the intelligence equipment for six vehicles. This will be the first line to meet ERTMS specification requirements.

**Greece:** Hellenic Railway (OSE) has ordered centralised traffic control to increase capacity between Athens and Larissa.

**Italy:** Italian State Railways (FS) operates a TMS system on the Roccasecco-Avezzano line. The Lambrate-Piotello section of the Milan-Venice line is being fitted with an automatic block, relay interblocking and telecommunication system.

The Livorno-Civitavecchia line is operating an automatic block system, relay interlocking and telecommunication.

**Korea:** In 2001 Korean National Railway (KNR) awarded the company a contract to supply track signalling equipment. This followed an earlier contract to supply similar equipment to the Pusan metro which was fulfilled in partnership with South Korea-based Huk Shin Engineering Co Ltd, which participates in production and delivery. The contract covers 510 sets of TI21 track circuits, 510 health monitoring units and 128 impedance bonds. The track circuits were for use primarily on the 444 km Seoul-Pusan high-speed rail link. The TI21 (Traction Immune) circuit is an audio frequency jointless type designed for service on lines with DC or AC power supply and high rates of interference.

**Norway:** In association with the Norwegian Railway Administration (Jernbaneverket), a TMS was introduced to control Oslo central station and adjoining stations. Two electronic interlockings, ATP and point machines were supplied at Asker, and were commissioned at the end of 1998.

Electronic interlocking, ATP and point machines have been installed for the Vestfoldbanan line to control and supervise four stations on a 20 km section between Drammen and Larvik. The signalling system was commissioned in 1999.

**Philippines:** After commissioning at the end of 1999, Manila Light Rail Transit Authority (LRTA) is equipped with a complete signalling system including traffic control, ATP and wayside equipment for its light rail transit system, line 3. It now comprises 13 stations with 14 km of track.

**Poland:** Polish Railways (PKP) has received 12 Bombardier Transportation interlockings. These are installed in Kostrzy, Nekla, Ychlin, Bednary, Szymanów, Ozarów, Strza-kowo, Kodawa, Blonie, Gollbk, Pochocin and Szczecin.

**Romania:** Bucharest Metro System (Metrorex RA) ordered for its Line 2 an ATP and Automatic Train Operation (ATO) system. Line 2 was due to be in operation by the end of 2002. It represents an important part of the comprehensive modernisation programme of the Bucharest Metro, built in 1979. Today it has three lines with a total track length of 60 km and a total of 40 stations. Annual transport volume amounts to 250 million people. This metro has also ordered 108 cars for its system from Bombardier Tranportation.

**Russia:** New electronic interlockings have been supplied for the St Petersburg-Moscow line.

*TMS control centre at Stockholm central station; similar TMS centres are also in operation at Gövle and Hallsberg* 0021715

*Ebiswitch point machines as fitted for the Asker station project and on the Vestfoldbanan line* 0021714

**Slovakia:** Slovakian Railways (ZSR) is operating its first-ever electronic interlocking. It controls 40 km of track and stations. The interlocking is being installed at the Cadca junction, it was commissioned in 1998.

**South Korea:** An ATO system has been supplied for Seoul Metro Lines 5, 7 and 8. Pusan Metro Line 2 received the first stage of a turnkey signalling system including electronic interlockings, ATP, ATO and wayside equipment. Line 2 has 29 km of track, 38 stations and a depot. With a 108-second headway, 49 trains will operate on the line.

**Spain:** Equipment supplied to Metro Madrid Line 10 includes three electronic interlockings at Lago, Plaza del España and Batan stations and double carrier ATP adaptation over 9 km of track and eight stations. Another five interlockings have been delivered. Metro de Bilbao has been supplied with a turnkey signalling system for 25 km track and 24 stations with electronic interlockings, ATP, ATO and wayside equipment.

**Sweden:** Arlanda Link Consortium (ALC) received a turnkey signal installation for the Arlanda airport link. The signalling system includes electronic interlockings, ATC, passenger information system and point machines. The contract also includes the redesign of the Traffic Management System (TMS) control centre at Stockholm central station.

Øresund Consortium was supplied with a signalling system for the Øresund rail link between Sweden and Denmark. The installation includes electronic interlockings, line block, ATC and wayside equipment. The system controls and supervises 15 km of double track. Commissioning took place in 2000. The company also delivered turnkey signalling solutions for the connecting rail link on the Swedish side and the Continental line in Malmö, which has been upgraded to cope with an expected increase in traffic.

Swedish National Rail Administration (Banverket) has taken delivery of two electronic interlockings for the Eskilstuna Flen line. They control six stations and were commissioned in October 1998. The company has also supplied a TMS control centre at Gävle, which controls and supervises 101 stations, a TMS control centre at Hallsberg, which controls and monitors 72 station and has upgrading Malmö freight yard and Arlöv station to meet traffic increases.

SL Roslagsbanan controls 6 km of track including four stations. Another complete signalling system for a new LRT line between Gullmars-plan and Alvik was commissioned in 1999 and 2000. This 11 km line has 12 stations. The turnkey contract, includes design, installation and commissioning and comprises a control system, three electronic interlockings, ATC and wayside equipment. An ATC system for the Saltjobanan LRT line was also included in the contract.

**Switzerland:** The first signalling system to meet the requirements of the ERTMS Level 2 standard was commissioned by the company in April 2002. The project covers 35 km of double track line between Olten and Luzern and between 120 and 140 trains will run, per day, in each direction. The system uses GSM-R radio transmission and some 200 positioning balises in place of conventional signals.

Radio remote-control systems have been supplied to Swiss Federal Railways (SBB) to equip 17 Class 460 locomotives and 30 each of Classes Re 6/6 and Re 4/4 II used as assisting engines on the Gotthard line. These were all commissioned by May 2000. A second phase of the programme was to see an additional 13 Class 460 and 30 of either Re 6/6 or Re 4/4 II types fitted with the system.

**Turkey:** Adana operates a new light rail transit system. The turnkey project included financing, design and construction and installation of a complete system and operation support during its first year of service. The signalling system includes electronic interlockings, traffic control system, ATC and passenger information system. The 13.3 km line has 13 stations. Izmir received a total signalling system for its new light rail line.

**Taiwan:** Bombardier Transportation has been awarded a contract by Taiwan Railway Administration, for a complete Automatic Train Protection System (ATP system) which includes ATP computers for 832 locomotives, 14,000 balises, and 2,000 encoders. The order also includes 13 simulators for driver training and systems for train data presentation including driver panels.

**The Netherlands:** Bombardier Tranportation was awarded a contract by NS Railinfrabeheer for the delivery of ERTMS level 1, 2 and 3. The contract includes Computerized Interlocking, Radio Block Centres, Ebicab 2000 on-board ATP systems, Linside Electronic Units and fixed and controlled Eurobalise.

Bombardier Transportation was awarded a contract by Railinfrabeheer B.V (RIB) in the Netherlands for the delivery of 1,200 Ebiswitch point machines. The deliveries are scheduled to take place during the next five years from May 2002 to May 2007.

**United Kingdom:** Railtrack were supplied with a complete turnkey signalling system for the Woking area, including a new signalling centre. The scheme included new telecommunications, traction power supply system upgrades and permanent way remodelling at Woking and Surbiton stations. Final commissioning took place in 1998.

The company's pilot project in the UK bringing the first installation of the Ebilock Interlocking, is at Horsham. The project involved complete replacement of signalling equipment, including interlocking, signals, cables and location cases. It also involved new train detection. Automatic Warning System (AWS) and Train Protection Warning System (TPWS). All the main installation work was completed by November 2001 with full commercial service in February 2002.

Awarded in 2000, the Thameslink Associated Signalling Works design and development contract for Railtrack's Thameslink 2000.

In 2001 Korean National Railway (KNR) awarded the company a contract to supply track signalling equipment. This followed an earlier contract to supply similar equipment to the Pusan metro which was fulfilled in partnership with South Korea-based Huk Shin Engineering Co Ltd, which participates in production and delivery. The contract covers 510 sets of T121 track circuits, 510 health monitoring units and 128 impedance bonds. The track circuits were for use primarily on the 444 km Seoul Pusan high-speed rail link. The T121 (Traction Immune) circuit is an audio frequency jointless type designed for service on lines with DC or AC power supply and high rates of interference.

*UPDATED*

---

## BP Solar Ltd

PO Box 191, Chertsey Road, Sunbury-on-Thames TW16 7XA, UK
Tel: (+44 1932) 77 95 43   Fax: (+44 1932) 76 26 86
Web: http://www.bpsolar.com

**Key personnel**
Managing Director: Michael Pitcher
Sales Manager, Railway Systems: Peter Carter

**Principal subsidiaries**
BP Solar Arabia, Saudi Arabia
BP Solar Australia, Australia
BP Solar España, Spain
BP Solar Inc, USA
Tata BP Solar, India

**Products**
Solar electric photovoltaic power systems to supply signalling, telecommunications, track circuits and lighting. PV solar cell materials and PV cell materials convert light into electricity.

Contracts include KTM Malaysia, Perumka (Indonesia), Ghana Railways, Indian Railways, Mozambique Railways, Kenya Railways and Saudi Rail and an IMWp multicrystalline roof atria system has been installed into stations for Deutsche Bahn.

*UPDATED*

---

## S A Buhlmann NV

Leuvensesteenweg 31, B-1932 St Stevens-Woluwe, Brussels, Belgium
Tel: (+32 2) 711 20 30   Fax: (+32 2) 720 20 64
e-mail: buhlman@skynet.be

**Key personnel**
See entry in *Brakes and drawgear* section.

**Products**
Point setting and point controllers; track circuit equipment and accessories; level crossing gates, barriers and warning signals.

*UPDATED*

---

## Cadex Electronics Inc

22000 Fraserwood Way, Richmond, British Columbia V6W 1J6, Canada
Tel: (+1 604) 231 77 77   Fax: (+1 604) 231 77 55
e-mail: info@cadex.com
Web: http://www.cadex.com

**Key personnel**
President and Chief Executive Officer: Isidor Buchmann
Accounts Manager, Export: Richard Janzen
Marketing Specialist: Andrew Green

**Products**
Cadex C7000 series battery analysers service and restore batteries as used in portable communications equipment,

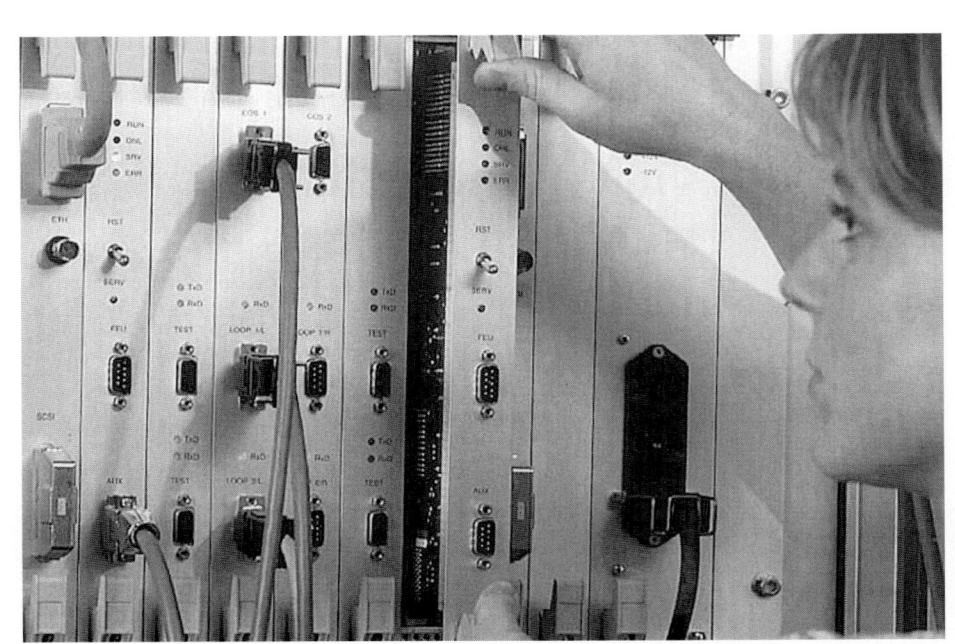

*The Ebilock Computerised Interlocking, installed across Europe. The Horsham pilot project will see its first installation on to Railtrack infrastructure in the UK*   2001/0116577

# MANUFACTURERS/Signalling and communications systems

computers and data acquisition devices; battery-specific adapters for all common batteries; multiple batteries serviced with the FlexArm™; user-selectable programmes for all battery needs such as the QuickTest™ programme which supports all common battery chemistries. Cadex analysers print service reports and battery labels and interfacing with a PC is possible with BatteryShop™.

*UPDATED*

## Cattron Theimeg

58 West Shenango Street, Sharpsville, Pennsylvania 16150-1198, USA
Tel: (+1 412) 962 35 71   Fax: (+1 412) 962 43 10
e-mail: cattron.inc@industry.net
Web: http://www.cattron.com

### Key personnel
President and Chief Executive Officer: James P Cattron
Executive Vice-President: Carl Verholek

### Principal subsidiaries
Cattron-Theimeg (UK) Ltd
Riverdene Industrial Estate, Molesey Road, Hersham, Walton-on-Thames KT12 4RY, UK
Tel: (+44 1932) 24 75 11   Fax: (+44 1932) 22 09 37
Managing Director: Nigel P Day

Cattron Controls Ltd
150 Armstrong Avenue, Units 5-6, Georgetown, Ontario, Canada
Tel: (+1 905) 873 94 40   Fax: (+1 905) 873 94 49
General Manager: Bill Goldie

Cattron Africa (Pty) Ltd
25 O'Rielly Merry Road, Rynfield, Benoni, South Africa
PO Box 15444, Farrarmere, Benoni, Gauteng 1518, South Africa
Tel: (+27 11) 849 57 17   Fax: (+27 11) 425 59 38

### Sales and service representatives
Transportation Product Sales Company (TPSC), USA
Ronsco Inc, Canada
Invent SA de CV, Mexico
Winco Comercio Internacional, Brazil
GEMCO, Australia/New Zealand

### Products
Radio and infra-red portable control systems and related products allowing operators to control equipment from a safe distance. CATTRON® portable remote controls can be used to control overhead cranes, monorails, hoists, shunting locomotives, underground mining locomotives, railcar movers, ballast wagon doors and many other types of equipment.

*UPDATED*

*Cattron Theimeg DR Series portable remote-control system used to control ballast wagon doors* 2002/0114664

## cdsrail

1570 Parkway, Solent Business Park, Fareham PO15 7AG, UK
Tel: (+44 1489) 57 17 71   Fax: (+44 1489) 57 15 55
e-mail: sales@cdsrail.com
Web: http://www.cdsrail.com

### Products
Asset monitoring systems for railways infrastructure. The company's Trackwatch system provides event and condition monitoring for: relay and electronic/solid state signal events; signal interlockings; level crossings; point machines; clamp locks; point heaters; signalling power supplies and UPS systems; flood monitoring; track circuit condition monitoring; hot axlebox detectors; axle counters; and equipment status.

The Pointwatch system has been developed to provide early warning of impending points failure. In a typical installation it uses non-invasive, rugged sensors to monitor motor current, hydraulic air pressure, operating force and changeover time.

Analysis of data and alarms can be monitored from a single workstation using Trackwatch Analysis software or at client workstations attached to a Trackwatch Sentinel master supervisory system database server.

Infrastructure asset monitoring systems have been supplied by cdsrail to railways in India, Netherlands, Poland, Singapore, South Africa and UK.

*UPDATED*

## Channel Electric Equipment

Bath Road, Thatcham RG18 3ST, UK
Tel: (+44 1635) 86 48 66   Fax: (+44 1635) 86 91 78

### Key personnel
Managing Director: George Renshaw
Marketing Manager: Alex Bert
Commercial Director: Chris Antysz

### Background
Channel Electric Equipment is a member of LPA Group plc.

### Products
Terminal junction module assemblies and other components for telecommunications use.

*UPDATED*

## China Railway Signal & Communication Corporation (CRSC)

111 Zao Jia Cun, Fengtai, Beijing, China
Tel: (+86 1) 381 62 89   Fax: (+86 1) 381 62 89

### Key personnel
President: Yu Xiaomang
Chief Engineer: Wang Jinchen
Deputy Chief Engineer: Lu Jiasheng
General Manager, International Co-operation Department: Lu Delian

### Products
All-relay interlockings, automatic and tokenless block, ATC equipment, CTC, cab signalling equipment, track circuits, relays, point machines, communications and telephone systems.

## Chloride Power Protection

George Curl Way, Southampton SO18 2RY, UK
Tel: (+44 23) 80 61 03 11   Fax: (+44 23) 80 61 08 52

### Subsidiary companies
Chloride Hytek Pty Ltd, Australia
Chloride Power Protection, Brazil
Chloride Telecom Systems, France
Chloride Power Protection, France
Chloride Industrial Systems, France
Germany and International Sales, Germany
Chloride Silectron, Italy
Chloride Power Protection, Portugal
Chloride Power Protection, Singapore
Chloride Boar, Spain
Chloride Power Protection, Thailand
Masterguard, Turkey
Chloride Industrial Middle-East, UAE
Chloride Power Protection, USA
Oneac Corporation, USA

### Corporate background
Chloride Power Protection is part of Chloride Group plc.

### Products
Battery-backed Uninterruptible Power Supply (UPS) systems as a means of ensuring stable and continuous power for signalling systems, maintaining reliable continuous operation in the event of breaks and electrical transients affecting the incoming AC supply.

The Chloride Power Protection UPS range extends from 300VA single-phase to 6.4MVA three-phase.

*NEW ENTRY*

## Collis Engineering Ltd

Salcombe Road, Meadow Lane Industrial Estate, Alfreton DE55 7RG, UK
Tel: (+44 1773) 83 32 55   Fax: (+44 1773) 52 06 93
e-mail: sales@colliseng.demon.co.uk
Web: http://www.collis.co.uk

### Key personnel
Chairman: Peter Collis
Managing Director: Peter Roberts
Manufacturing Director: Nigel Gatley

### Products
Mechanical signalling equipment, gantry supplies, advance warning system steelwork, embankment platforms, point fittings, and signal structures. Design, supply and installation, civil engineering.

### Contracts
Contracts include a mechanical signalling contract for National Railway Supplies, renewed until 2003; Railtrack minor works contractor for LNE; and design, supply and installation of gantries for Manchester Victoria resignalling scheme for Tarmac. Supply of gantry for Woking and Surbiton resignalling project (Adtranz Signalling), Manchester Victoria resignalling project (Tarmac), ROSS resignalling project (Westinghouse Signalling) and minor works for signalling of level crossings (Railtrack LNE Region).

*UPDATED*

## Computer Products Professional bv

Biezenvijer 4, NL-3297 GK Puttershoek, Netherlands
Tel: (+31 78) 676 29 99   Fax: (+31 78) 676 52 02
Web: http://www.compprof-RTP.com

**Key personnel**
Director: Ing W G Bouwmeester

**Products**
Remote control units for sensing and control of railway switches and signals for train tracking. Control units for mimic panels. Alpha-numeric indicators.

## Crompton Greaves Ltd

1 Dr V B Gandhi Marg, Mumbai 400 023, India
Tel: (+91 22) 202 80 25

Rail Transportation Systems Division
5G, Vandhna, 11 Tolstoy Marg, 110 001 New Delhi, India
Tel: (+91 11) 331 70 75; 373 04 45
Fax: (+91 11) 331 70 75; 332 43 60
e-mail: dhingra_cgl@mantraonline.com

**Key personnel**
Managing Director: S M Trehan
General Manager, Rail Transportation Systems Division: A K Raina
All India Marketing Manager, Rail Transportation Systems Division: Harsh Dhingra

**Products**
Signalling relays, point machines, axle counters, route relay interlocking systems, solid state signalling and data loggers.

**Developments**
Integrated power supply, AFTC and digital axle counters.

*NEW ENTRY*

## CSEE Transport

4 avenue du Canada, BP 243 Les Ulis, F-91944 Les Ulis, France
Tel: (+33 1) 69 29 65 65   Fax: (+33 1) 69 29 07 07
Web: http://www.csee-transport.fr

**Key personnel**
Chief Executive Officer: Georges Dubot
Chief Financial Officer and Member of the Board: Dominique Athanassiadis
Vice-President, Sales: Gilles Pascault
Vice-President, Marketing: Emmanuel Viollet
Vice-President, Development: Pierre Advani
Vice-President, Manufacturing: Francis Cornet
Purchasing Manager: Dominique Marie

**Main works**
ZAC des Portes de Riom, BP 13, F-63201 Riom Cedex, France

**Principal subsidiaries**
Ecosen – Caracas, Venezuela
CS Transport Hong Kong Ltd, Hong Kong
Beijing CS Signalling Control System Co Ltd, China

**Products**
Signalling, traffic supervision and train monitoring systems. Jointless track circuits, Automatic Train Control (ATC) and track-to-train transmission, Automatic Train Protection (ATP) and Automatic Train Operation (ATO) for railways and metros (TVM SACEM), signalbox mechanisms, electronic treadles, hot box and wheel detectors, electronic point machines and safety relays.
   Computerised safety systems, speed control, solid state interlocking. Passenger Access Control (PAC).

**Contracts**
France: European Train Control System (ERTMS).
France (ERTMS): design and development of the prototype Eurocab.
France (SNCF): supply access control system for RER Line C.
France (SNCF): ATP type TVM 430 and SEI Interlocking – LN05 TGV Méditerranée.
Belgium (SNCB): hot box detectors for various lines.
UK (Railtrack plc): Nuneaton to Peterborough line – Phase 1 and 2.
UK (Railtrack plc): Manchester South.
UK (Railtrack plc):Channel Tunnel Rail Link (TVM/ERTMS – SCADA).
China (SRA): signalling.
Portugal (Metropolitano de Lisboa): turnkey contract for ATP/ATO equipment and signalling for Lisbon Metro.
Thailand (SRT): level crossing signalling (Eastern lines).
Hong Kong (MTRC): CTC of three existing lines and SCADA for Lantau Airport.
Korea (KHRC): Seoul–Pusan line ATP (type TVM 430) and track circuits.

*UPDATED*

## Cubic Transportation Systems Ltd

177 Nutfield Road, Merstham RH1 3HR, UK
Tel: (+44 1737) 64 68 00   Fax: (+44 1737) 64 36 93

**Key personnel**
See entry in *Revenue collection systems and station equipment* section.

**Products**
Communications systems including closed-circuit television, public address systems, passenger help points, radio systems and security systems.

**Contracts**
Contracts for London Underground Ltd include the upgrading of communications systems at stations on the Northern Line and the provision of passenger security systems at stations on the Piccadilly Line.

*UPDATED*

## David Clark Company

360 Franklin Street, Worcester, Massachusetts 01604, USA
Tel: (+1 508) 751 58 00   Fax: (+1 508) 753 58 27
e-mail: sales@davidclark.com
Web: http://www.davidclark.com

**Key personnel**
Vice-President, Sales and Marketing: Robert J Murphy
International Sales Manager: James E Comer
Product Manager: Mark Gardell

**Products**
Locomotive crew intercom systems featuring noise-reducing headsets to provide hands-free intercom, music and radio transmitting and reception with alarms integrated into the intercom system. Noise attenuating headsets and radio interference adapters for mobile and portable radios.

**Contracts**
Recent contracts include supply of equipment to Burlington Northern Santa Fe, Quebec North Shore and Labrador, Canadian Pacific, Canadian National and Amtrak.

*VERIFIED*

## Dialight

Exning Road, Newmarket CB8 0AX, UK
Tel: (+44 1638) 66 23 17   Fax: (+44 1638) 56 04 55

**Key personnel**
See entry in *Passenger coach equipment* section.

**Products**
Level crossing signal lights.

## Dimetronic SA

Avda de Castella 2, Parque Empresarial, E-28830 San Fernando de Henares, Madrid, Spain
Tel: (+34 91) 675 42 12   Fax: (+34 91) 756 21 15
e-mail: marketing@dimetronic.es

**Key personnel**
President: Jose Martinez Gomez
Managing Director: Luis Escribanoiz
Marketing Director: Luis Garcia Sanchez

**Principal subsidiary**
Dimetronic Portugal

**Background**
Dimetronic is an associated company of Westinghouse Rail Systems Ltd (qv).

**Products**
Signalling systems; electronic interlockings, CTC, ATP, ATO, ATC, ERTNS train describer, automatic route setting, cab signalling and traffic regulation equipment.
   Most of the projects are of a turnkey nature.

**Contracts**
Westrace electronic and CTC systems for RENFE and Lisbon metros, ATP/ATO, CTC and Westrace for Madrid metro and Bucharest metro, SSI and CTC for REFER (Portugal). SSI installations for 30 CP stations, signalling for the Valencia metro (including ATP) and Westrace electronic interlocking for FGC Spain.

*UPDATED*

## EFACEC

EFACEC Sistemas de Electrónica SA
Signalling Systems Division, Av Eng Ulrich, PO Box 31, P-4470 Maia, Portugal
Tel: (+351 2) 941 36 66   Fax: (+351 2) 948 54 28

*David Clark locomotive crew intercom system*

## MANUFACTURERS/Signalling and communications systems

**Products**
Signalling and telecommunications systems and components, including electronic interlocking, automatic train speed control, track circuits, level crossing equipment including barrier machines, and ATP panels, encoders, recording and evaluation units. Installation, repair and maintenance of signalling equipment.

## Elektrim SA

ul Chalubinskiego 8, PO Box 638, PL-00-950 Warsaw, Poland
Tel: (+48 22) 830 04 24; 12 54
Fax: (+48 22) 830 04 14; 03 58

**Key personnel**
Publicity Officer: Rita Wrzesniowska

**Products**
Interlockings, signals, automatic block, track circuits, level crossing protection, electromechanical systems, marshalling yard mechanisation and automation. High-speed circuit breakers and contactors for DC. Lightning arresters.

## Elektroimpex

PO Box 296, H-1392 Budapest, Hungary
Tel: (+36 1) 132 83 00   Fax: (+36 1) 131 05 26

**Key personnel**
Managing Director: Dr Miklós Kadala

**Products**
Signalling equipment, CTC, train describers, level crossing apparatus.

## Erico Inc

34600 Solon Road, Solon, Ohio 44139, USA
Tel: (+1 440) 248 01 00   Fax: (+1 440) 309 89 11
e-mail: info@erico.com
Web: http://www.erico.com

**Key personnel**
Division Manager: Dan Johnston
Marketing Manager: Mitchell Bednarek
Export Sales Manager: Phil Graham

**Principal Subsidiary Companies**
In Australia, Brazil, Chile, France, Germany, Hong Kong, Mexico, Netherlands, South Africa and UK.

**Products**
An engineered system of bonding, grounding and electronic protection products: power and signal bonds, track circuit connectors; Cadweld® exothermic bonding process; ground enhancement material; electronic protection panels, electronic protection devices.

*VERIFIED*

## Fiber Options

80 Orville Drive, Suite 102, Bohemia, New York 11716, USA
Tel: (+1 631) 567 83 20   Fax: (+1 631) 567 83 22
e-mail: info@fiberoptions.com
Web: http://www.fiberoptions.com

**Key personnel**
President: John Collins
Founder: Bob Delia
Director of Marketing: Jerry Jacobson

**Products**
Fibre optic communication systems.

## FKI Godwin Warren

Brearley Works, Luddendenfoot, Halifax HX2 6JB, UK
Tel: (+44 1422) 88 23 83   Fax: (+44 1422) 88 40 71

**Key personnel**
General Manager: A D Garrity
Director, Sales and Marketing: M J Brimble
Sales Support Engineer: A J Bailey

**Products**
Level crossing barrier systems.

## Futurit

Swarco Futurit Verkehrssignalsysteme GmbH
Altmannsdorferstrasse 329, A-1230 Vienna, Austria
Tel: (+43 1) 661 30   Fax: (+43 1) 66 13 01

**Key personnel**
Executive Directors: F P Hofstadler, F Silhengst
Sales: K Brünner

**Products**
Lanterns with 200, 160 and 125 mm diameter lens; level crossing signals with 200 and 300 mm diameter lens; fibre optic signs for display of messages, including speed restrictions; and fibre optic signs for tunnels.

## GAI-Tronics Ltd

Brunel Drive, Stretton Business Park, Burton-on-Trent DE13 0BZ, UK
Tel: (+44 1283) 50 05 00   Fax: (+44 1283) 50 04 00
e-mail: sales@gai-tronics.co.uk
Web: http://www.gai-tronics.co.uk

**Key personnel**
See entry in *Passenger coach equipment* section.

**Other offices**
GAI-Tronics Corporation, USA
Tel: (+1 610) 777 13 74   Fax: (+1 610) 775 65 40
Web: http://www.gai-tronics.com

GAI-Tronics Srl, Italy
Tel: (+39 02) 48 60 14 60   Fax: (+39 02) 458 56 25

GAI-Tronics Corporation, Malaysia
Tel: (+60 3) 637 60 91   Fax: (+60 3) 638 60 93

**Background**
GAI-Tronics Limited was established in 1964 to provide communications equipment to the mining industry. It has now expanded into the provision of specialised communications equipment for road and rail transportation industries.

**Products**
Metal-bodied weather-resilient telephones; SMART self-monitoring and reporting telephone systems.

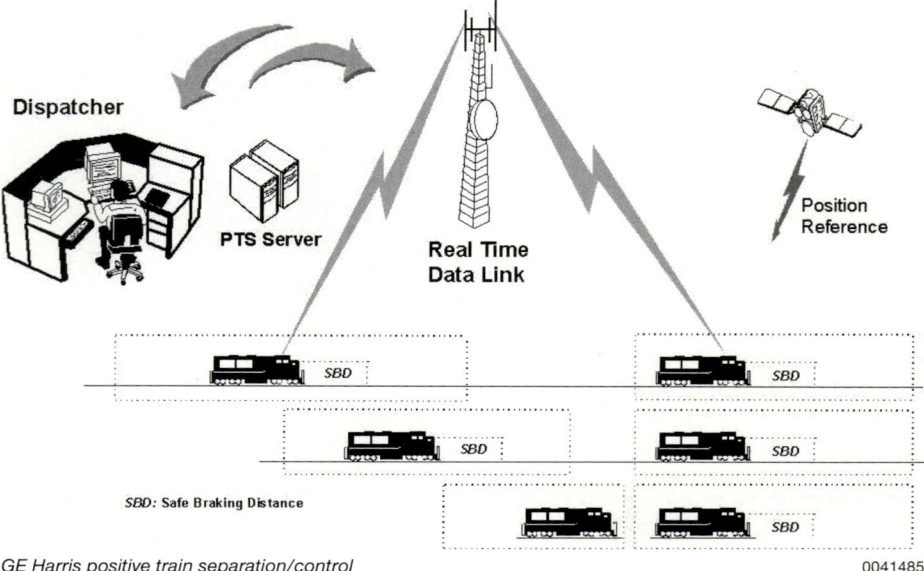

*UPDATED*

## GE Harris

GE Harris Railway Electronics LLC
407 John Rhodes Boulevard, Melbourne, Florida 32934, USA
Tel: (+1 407) 242 51 74   Fax: (+1 407) 242 50 19
e-mail: rjohns@ge-harris.com
Web: http://www.ge-harris.com

**Key personnel**
President: Greg Lucier
Director, Planning Systems: Mark Dash
Vice-President Railcar Systems: Don Herndon
Vice-President Centre Systems: N Holmes
Manager, Service: Amanda Hecht
Vice-President, Locomotive Systems: Dave Ball

**Products**

*TrainTalk Intra-Train Communications*
The TrainTalk®, intra-train communications protocol is a high band width wire-free radio system for data communications of multiple applications along a train, including electronically-controlled pneumatic (ECP) brakes for rail vehicles, onboard sensors and diagnostics, EOT and distributed power. Engineered specifically for the rigorous rail environment, TrainTalk Intra-Train Communications provides a high-data throughput capacity to handle control and reporting of multiple applications along a train.

*Communication systems*
The communication handler antenna combines all locomotive antenna hardware requirements (up to eight separate antennae) into a single radome-protected, cab-roof mounted package. The integrated, maintenance-free antenna was specifically designed to withstand everything from extreme tunnel heat to jet spray washers. The rugged radome is made of Lexan (polycarbonate which eliminates corrosion, water leaks and resists drive-by damage). With just one hole, antenna installation is simplified. Broad frequency coverage of voice, EOT, dual distributed power, data radio, GPS, and cellular radio channels are also included.

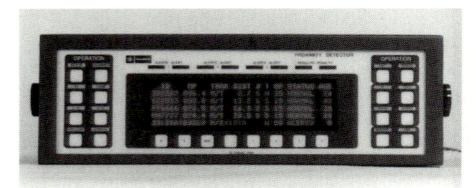

*GE Harris guardian proximity detection device*
0041481

*GE Harris hot box detector*
0021719

*GE Harris positive train separation/control*
0041485

# Signalling and communications systems/MANUFACTURERS

*GE Harris precision dispatch* 0041480

*GE Harris communication test device* 0041478

### Control systems, Divided Locomotive
LOCOTROL remotely controls up to four distributed locomotive consists from the lead for improved hauling capacity, fuel efficiency and throughput. Each LOCOTROL-equipped locomotive may be operated as a lead or a remote, so longer trains can be run in high density corridors. LOCOTROL uses safe RF transmissions to communicate between distributed consists. The LOCOTROL product family has been integrated with a variety of locomotive and brake system types. A performance-guaranteed package is provided with LOCOTROL. Other options include tower control for loading operations, remote shunting control, slow speed control, and message repeaters for rugged terrain environments.

### Positive train separation/control
Positive Train Separation (PTS) is a safety overlay system for both signalled and unsignalled territories that helps prevent collisions and overspeed accidents. The PTS system continuously monitors the position of trains equipped with the location determination system. Following existing wayside signals or track warrants, the PTS system predicts potential authority limit violations and if required, will take action to safely stop a train prior to the violation. This open architecture system can be implemented in either a centralised or decentralised train dispatch configuration and is upgradable to the additional capabilities and productivity gains of Precision Train Control.

### Precision Train Control
Precision Train Control™ (PTC) is an advanced movement planning and control system that is designed to provide train engineers with up-to-the-minute information on the location, speed and acceleration requirements of the train, allowing trains to operate safely and on time. Control schedules are optimised and downloaded over a wireless communication system, in real-time, to onboard locomotive systems. These capabilities allow rail operators to precisely control meet-merge-pass scenarios and communicate schedule changes well in advance, resulting in significantly reduced train delays.

### Precision Dispatch
Precision Dispatch® System is a supervisory control system for railway dispatch centres. Based on the Foresight® movement planner from GE Harris, this open system features the automated routing smart forms in electronic dispatcher notebooks and playback "what-if" capabilities. This movement planner creates train dispatch plans that factor in all necessary inputs such as: train consist data, track grades (inclines) and curvatures, and locomotive capabilities to improve traffic flow. It also can re-schedule plans in the event of a train delay.

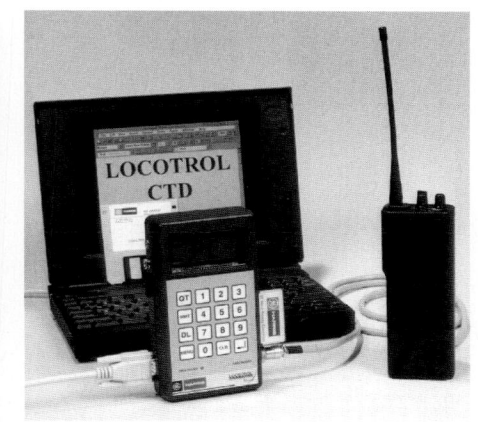

### Navigator Dispatch
The Train Navigator® Dispatch system is a family of computer-aided dispatch (CAD) products that implements traffic control functions for regional and short-line operations. Navigator Dispatch runs under Microsoft Windows NT® (to provide Centralised Traffic Control (CTC) plus integrated Direct Train Control and Track Warrant Control). Train Navigator provides the ability to integrate local and remote networks using off-the-shelf computers with Windows®. Add-on modules for Train Navigator include customised forms blocking, alarm display and control, track layout editor, and historical playback capability among others. GE Harris offers service support and maintenance packages in addition to periodic software upgrades.

### Guardian Proximity Detection Device
The Guardian® Proximity Detection Device (PDD) is a multi-layered warning system that enhances operator awareness of potentially unsafe operating conditions. With use of GPS, the device recognises train location and alerts operators of all trains within a range. If a proximity alarm is ignored, the device will initiate an automatic braking applications. PDD is a vehicle-based system that requires no wayside equipment and is an open-architecture design that accommodates future locomotive electronic systems as well as wayside vehicles and equipment. With a railway's track database PDD can track a train location with 300 foot (100 m) accuracy. It also has an option to relay information to train operators and dispatchers to further improve railroad productivity.

### Remote Shunter System
The Remote Shunter System provides remote control of all throttle and braking functions. The portable remote shunting unit can control any locomotives equipped with the LOCOTROL onboard unit simply by dialling in the locomotive unit number. LOCOTROL remote shunter includes all the safety and reliability features developed over the past 30 years of LOCOTROL Distributed Power Systems. Over 4000 LOCOTROL systems are in use around the world.

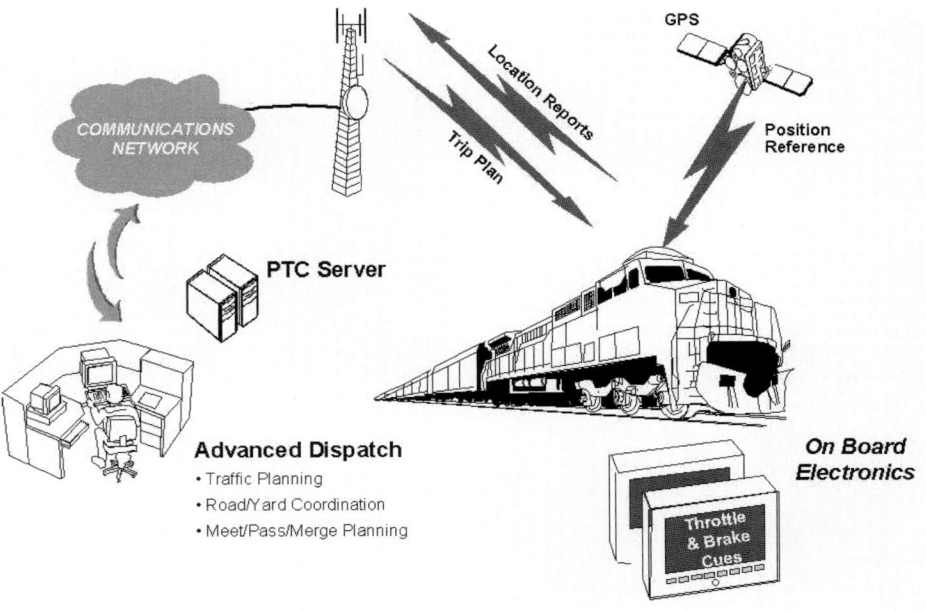

*GE Harris communications handler antenna* 0041479

*GE Harris precision train control* 0041486

# 656 MANUFACTURERS/Signalling and communications systems

*GE Harris icon integrated control system* 0041483

### Tower Control
Tower Control offers rail operators and mines increased productivity by allowing operations to control locomotives equipped with LOCOTROL distributed power remotely from a tower location for loading and unloading operations. Tower Control allows control of complete distributed power trains with up to four remotes on a single locomotive at the head end.

### On Site Advantage Program
The GE Harris On Site Advantage Programme provides field maintenance service over an extended time period on all GE Harris systems. Located on-site at the railways, GE Harris provides support for scheduled and unscheduled maintenance activities and renewal parts logistics for installed GE Harris systems.

### Train Defect Detector
The Hot Bearing Detector is used for hot box and dragging brake detection. The unit detects overheated axle bearings and overheated wheels due to dragging brakes using multi-element IR technology. The unit accurately distinguishes the difference between overheated bearings or wheels and heat generated from environmental factors. This capability sharply reduces the instances of false alarms to less than one per cent. The hot bearing detector requires only annual maintenance.

### Wheel Load Scale Plus
Wheel Load Scale Plus measures the impact of wheels on the rails and excessive lateral force. Problems such as uneven loading, overloaded vehicles and slide flats can be detected. The wheel load scale plus reduces the risk of derailment or damage to wagons, cargo and track.

### Broken Rail Detector
The GE Harris ultrasonic broken rail detector detects broken rails which may result from load impact, fatigue, and acts of sabotage, such as sawing, detonating, leveraging/prying, hammering or acts of natural disaster. The system operates on the principle of sound transmission in the ultrasonic range. Ultrasonic signals are generated from an actuator and received by sensors. Signal processing computers analyse the waveforms and determine the integrity of the track.

### Communication Test Device
the Communication Test Device (CTD) is a hand-held unit used to automate the functional testing of LOCOTROL message repeaters. The CTD supports real time monitoring and storage of LOCOTROL communications sessions and can be used to perform communication surveys and radio coverage analysis. The CTD is offered in an enhanced version called the Commissioner. The commissioner enables a LOCOTROL equipped locomotive to be commissioned and tested without the use of a second locomotive.

### ICON Integrated Control system
ICON Integrated Control system is an open-architecture cab electronics and display system for onboard train control and cab electronics applications. ICON is integrated to improve reliability over current systems, reduce cab and display clutter and allow ease in upgrading. ICON is designed as a vital system so it may incorporate systems like cab signal as well as the new wave of Positive Train Separation and Precision Train Control® applications. The ICON system is based on open VME technology and accommodates all LSI interfaces. GE Harris offers an ICON developer kit and certification services for companies interested in integrating existing or developing new functions.

### Vehicle ID Unit
The GE Harris Vehicle ID is a small enclosed microprocessor unit which is capable of storing all essential parameters about a railway's most valuable assets. It is installed conspicuously on a vehicle. Parameters such as wheel diameter, vehicle number, and maintenance schedules can be stored and available for other computers to read or update as required. The Vehicle ID Unit is equipped with a non-volatile electrically-erasable and re-programmable memory. The device requires no batteries and little power. Now valuable vehicle data can stay with the vehicle when electronic systems are swapped out.

### High Speed Freight Yard Radio System
The High Speed Yard Radio System from GE Harris provides the capability of sustained 1 Mbit/sec upload and download of locomotive information. The system offers IEEE 802.11 compliant wireless LAN (local area network) mobile radios for the locomotives and access components tailored to the marshalling yard environment enabling office applications transparent TCP/IP access to mobile locomotive information. Both frequency hopping and direct sequence spread spectrum radio models are available.

### Cab Display Equipment
The GE Harris Cab Display Unit is a rugged dual-display unit equipped with solid state memory and a 486 or Pentium computer. It is an integral part of GE Harris systems such as TrainTalk® and LOCOTROL® EB. It supports any number of real time operating systems as well as LSI communications.

### Locomotive Display
The GE Harris locomotive display is an integral part of Positive Train Separation and Precision Train Control® systems. It offers a full color display which can be mounted in both console or AAR cab stand applications. This Pentium-based computer with a PCMCIA interface features 250 Mbyte of solid state memory, sunlight readable display, NEMA 12 enclosure and Ethernet. It supports a number of real-time operating systems and LSI communications.

### Pinpoint®
This GE Harris locomotive tracking service provides location, direction, fuel level, and locomotive health status information at a low cost. Using GPS location information, and a low bandwidth satellite communication channel, key information is available wherever the locomotive may travel. This basic information is used for fleet wide application to quickly locate needed power and better manage fuel utilisation. Locomotive equipment is designed for very rapid installation.

*GE Harris Pinpoint train locator* 0021720

## GE Harris Harmon

GE Harris Harmon Railway Technology
1600 NE Coronado Drive, Blue Springs, Missouri 64014, USA
Tel: (+1 816) 229 33 45    Fax: (+1 816) 229 05 56
Web: http://www.geharrisharmon.com

### Key personnel
President and Chief Executive Officer: Gregory Herrema
Vice President, Sales and Marketing: Lloyd T Kaiser
Transit and International Sales: Russell E Taylor

### Subsidiary companies
GE Harris Harmon Control & Information Systems LLC
4553 Glenco Avenue, Suite 100, Marina Del Rey, California 90292, USA
Tel: (+1 310) 751 32 01    Fax: (+1 310) 751 32 02

GE Harris Harmon Control & Information Systems LLC
1840 Hutton Suite 190, Carrolton, Texas 75006, USA
Tel: (+1 972) 488 85 88    Fax: (+1 972) 488 87 88

GE Harris Harmon Railway Technology Ltd
The Maltings, Hoe Lane, Ware SG12 9LR, UK
Tel: (+44 1920) 46 22 82    Fax: (+44 1920) 46 07 02

Industries de Mexico SA de CV
Av Milimex Suite 321, Parque Industrial Milimex, CP6660, Carretera Miguel Almena Km16.5, Apodaca, NL Mexico
Tel: (+52 8) 369 87 17    Fax: (+52 8) 369 87 33

Mid-America School of Railway Technologies
321 SE AA Highway, Blue Springs, Missouri 64014, USA
Tel: (+1 816) 229 60 55    Fax: (+1 816) 229 61 22

GE Harris Harmon SES Co Division
40 Pond Park Road, Hingham, Massachusetts 02043-4371, USA
Tel: (+1 781) 740 02 00    Fax: (+1 781) 740 02 02

GE Harris Harmon Railway Technology Ltd
21 Via Pietro Fanfani, I-50127 Firenze, Italy
Tel: (+39 055) 423 41    Fax: (+39 055) 438 68

GE Harris Harmon Railway Technology Ltd
167 Labrosse Avenue, Pt Claire, (PQ) H9R 1A3, Canada
Tel: (+1 514) 630 61 33    Fax: (+1 514) 683 61 33

GE Harris Harmon DJR Services
3800 Ten Oaks Road, Suite B, PO Box 305, Glenelg, Maryland 21737-0305, USA
Tel: (+1 410) 442 17 06    Fax: (+1 410) 442 29 71

GE Harris Railway Electronics, GmbH & Co KG
Bruchtrasse 79A, D-67098 Bad Durkheim, Germany
Tel: (+49 63) 229 47 80    Fax: (+49 63) 22 94 78 25

### Products
Formerly Harmon Industries Inc, GE Harris Harmon designs and manufactures product and service line, trackside and vehicle-carried components, engineering and railway management services, training, level crossings, transit/commuter signalling and train control, communications, control centres, traction motors and traction power systems.

## GrantRail Ltd

Carolina Court, Lakeside, Doncaster DN4 5RA, UK
Tel: (+44 1302) 79 11 00    Fax: (+44 1302) 79 12 00
e-mail: sales@grantrail.co.uk
Web: http://www.grantrail.co.uk

### Key personnel
See entry in *Permanent way components, equipment and services* section.

### Capabilities
Capabilities cover: support for permanent way renewals, enhancements and maintenance; modifications and renewals of signalling construction; and installation of new signalling.

**VERIFIED**

## Hanning & Kahl

Hanning & Kahl GmbH & Co
Rudolf Diesel Strasse 6, D-33813 Oerlinghausen, Germany
Tel: (+49 5202) 70 76 00    Fax: (+49 5202) 70 76 29
e-mail: Hanning-Kahl@t-online.de
Web: http://www.hanning-kahl.de

*GE Harris cab display unit* 0041477

## Signalling and communications systems/MANUFACTURERS

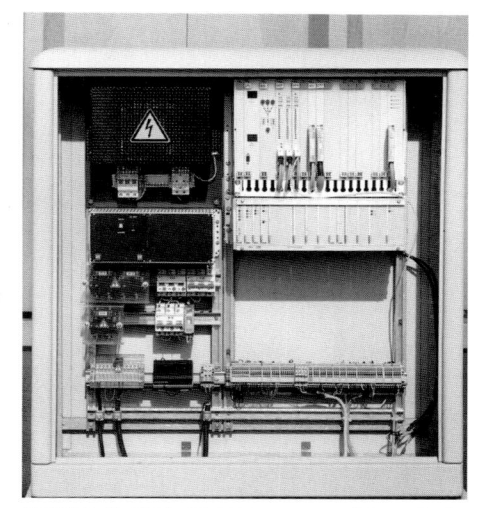

*Hanning & Kahl microprocessor point controller*
0063772

*Hanning & Kahl equipment in a control depot*
0063773

**Key personnel**
See entry in *Brakes and drawgear* section.

**Products**
*LRT Division*
Point controls, signalling systems, level crossing safety devices, single-line track safety devices, track circuits, mass detectors, vehicle reporting system, radio control, electronic data recorder and accessories including insulated guard rail tie bars, rail termination boxes and contact systems.

*Point setting mechanisms*
Point mechanisms for all gauges and types of rail, manual point mechanisms, electric point mechanisms with magnetic, motor, electrohydraulic or central control.

All point mechanisms can also be set manually and are available with a tongue detector and a mechanical double-interlocking device for the tongue in closed and open positions.

Recent contracts include projects in Salt Lake City, Dallas, San Diego, San Jose, Calgary; Manchester, Birmingham, Croydon, Sheffield; Rome, Turin, Milan; cities in Germany, Switzerland, Austria, Belgium and the Netherlands; Norway, Sweden, Finland; Melbourne and Hong Kong.

## Henry Williams Group

Dodsworth Street, Darlington DL1 2NJ, UK
Tel: (+44 1325) 46 27 22   Fax: (+44 1325) 24 52 20
e-mail: sales@hwilliams.co.uk
Web: http://www.hwilliams.co.uk

**Key personnel**
Managing Director: A W D Puddick
Production Director: G R Fenley
Sales Engineer: Bryan Blareau
Sales Co-ordinator: S Thompson

**Products**
Domino mosaic mimic diagrams; sheet steel mimic diagrams; switch heater cubicles; Sagem treadle switches and track-to-train transmission systems; level crossing schemes; light rail point control systems; small signalling schemes.

Recent contracts include Daventry International Railfreight Terminal; WPEP level crossing, BNFL Sellafield; Edinburgh Haymarket Mimic diagram upgrade; KCRC power distribution cubicles (GASL); GE resignalling switch heater cubicles; Tinsley Yard level crossing; Proof House junction REB and location case manufacture.

*UPDATED*

## Hitachi Ltd

Overseas Marketing Department
Transportation Systems Sales Division
6 Kanda Surugadai 4-chome, Chiyoda-ku, Tokyo 101-8010, Japan
Tel: (+81 3) 52 95 55 40   Fax: (+81 3) 32 58 52 30

**Key personnel**
See entry in *Locomotives and powered/non-powered passenger vehicles* section.

**Products**
Systems for operation management and control, traffic control systems, railway supervisory control and data acquisition, Automatic Train Operation (ATO) and Automatic Train Control (ATC), autonomous train integration train communication networks.

*NEW ENTRY*

## Honeywell Control Systems

Zodiac House, Callera Park, Aldermaston, Berkshire RG7 8HW
Tel: (+44 118) 906 26 00   Fax: (+44 118) 981 75 13
Web: http://www.honeywell.com/sensing

**Works**
Newhouse Industrial Estate, Motherwell ML1 5SB, Scotland

**Key personnel**
Director of Aircraft, Transport, Ordnance and Marine: P Murray
European Marketing Manager: R Ventura
European Programme Manager: R Bilbrough

**Products**
Train detection technology: railwheel sensors; train approach and departure systems for level crossings; axle counting modules; profile systems for loading gauge measurement with capability to add proprietary train inspection systems.
Radar technology: onboard train speed systems; trackside train speed and distance systems; radar level crossing obstacle detection systems.
Solid-state sensors and electromechanical components for point machines; train braking systems; heating, ventilation and air conditioning systems; door systems.

## Isolux

Isolux Wat SA
Alcocer 41, E-28021 Madrid, Spain
Tel: (+34 91) 796 30 00   (+34 91) 798 37 70
e-mail: sistemas@isolux.es
Web: http://www.isolux.es

**Key personnel**
Director, Control & Systems Division: Miguel Angel Tapia
Commercial Director Control & Systems Division: José Ignacio Martinez

**Products**
Hot wheel detector; station signalling and operation system; centralised control of installations in stations; video surveillance and control of stations.

Contracts include hot wheel detectors and signalling systems for RENFE, and CTC for RENFE. Video surveillance has been supplied for FGC Barcelona metro and CTC for Madrid metro.

## Kapsch Group

Wagenseilgasse 1, A-1121 Vienna, Austria
Tel: (+43 1) 81 11 10   Fax: (+43 1) 81 11 18 88
Web: http://www.kapsch.headoffice@kapsch.net

**Subsidiaries**
**Austria**
Austria Telecommunication GmbH
Triester Strasse 70, A-1102 Vienna
Tel: (+43 1) 60 50 10   Fax: (+43 1) 605 01 32 01
Web: http://www.austria.telecommunication.at@kapsch.net

**Bulgaria**
Kapsch AG Bulgaria
ul Sitnjakovo N: 5A, BG-1124 Sofia
Tel: (+359 2) 46 82 00   Fax: (+359 2) 46 82 00
e-mail: vvkapsch@mbox.infotel.bg

**Chile**
Combitech Traffic Systems AB
Av Las Condes 11400 Suite 32, 668 0002 Vitacura, Santiago
Tel: (+56 2) 217 53 25   Fax: (+56 2) 217 53 10
e-mail: ctschile@terra.cl

**Croatia**
Kapsch Telecom doo
Kneza Mislava 1, HR-10000 Zagreb
Tel: (+385 1) 466 48 46   Fax: (+385 1) 461 79 32
Web: http://www.kapsch.telecom.hr@kapsch.net

**Czech Republic**
Kapsch Telecom spol sro
Opletalova 1015/55 CZ-110 00 Praha 1
Tel: (+420 2) 21 46 63 11   Fax: (+420 2) 22 24 42 88
Web: http://www.kapsch.telecom.cz@kaptsch.net

**Germany**
Kapsch Telecom GmbH
Stuttgarterstrasse 61, D-71554 Weissach im Tal
Tel: (+49 7191) 355 90   Fax: (+49 7191) 35 59 60 80
Web: http://www.kapsch.telecom.de@kapsch.net

**Hungary**
Kapsch Telecom Kft
Bocskai út 77-79, H-1113 Budapest
Tel: (+36 1) 209 21 10   Fax: (+36 1) 209 21 11
Web: http://www.kapsch.telecom.hu@kapsch.net

**Poland**
Kapsch Telecom Sp zoo
ul Sniadeckich 1, PL-02-785 Warszawa
Tel: (+48 22) 544 60 00   Fax: (+48 22) 544 60 05
Web: http://www.kapsch.telecom.pl@kapsch.net

Koltel Sp zoo
ul Ludwikowo 1, PL-85-502 Bydgoszcz
Tel: (+48 52) 322 86 93   Fax: (+48 52) 322 78 84
Web: http://www.koltel.pl@kapsch.net

**Russia**
OOO Kapsch NIIShA Tel
ul Nizhegorodskaja 27, RF-109029 Moskwa
Tel: (+7 095) 262 82 74   Fax: (+7 095) 262 04 43
Web: http://www.kapsch.niishatel.ru@kapsch.net

**Slovak Republic**
Kapsch Telecom spol sro
Bratislava Business Center, Plynárenská 1, SK-821 09 Bratislava
Tel: (+421 7) 53 41 83 00   Fax: (+421 7) 53 41 83 01
Web: http://www.kapsch.telecom.sk@kapsch.net

**Slovenia**
Kapsch Telecom doo
Kotnikova 12, SI-1000 Ljubljana
Tel: (+386 1) 300 84 70   Fax: (+386 1) 300 84 79
Web: http://www.kapsch.telecom.si@kapsch.net

**Ukraine**
Kapsch Telecom TOV
Bocskai ut 77-79, H-1113 Budapest
Tel: (+36 1) 209 21 10   Fax: (+36 1) 209 21 11
Web: http://www.kapsch.telecom.hu@kapsch.net

**Products**
Closed-circuit radio communication systems for main and ancillary lines, KS2000 closed-circuit telecommunications system and GSM-Railway (GSM-R) for high-speed trains.

## MANUFACTURERS/Signalling and communications systems

GSM-R is a uniform radio communication system developed by Kapsch.

The GSM core network is the dominant mobile communications platform and is the basis for over 20,000 roaming agreements in the world. The multirate codec AMR has recently been developed for GSM and it will also be the standard codec for UMTS.

*UPDATED*

---

### Kenelec Pty Ltd

48 Henderson Road, Clayton, Victoria 3168, Australia
Tel: (+61 3) 95 60 10 11   Fax: (+61 3) 95 60 18 04

**Key personnel**
Engineering Manager: Kevin Donahoo
National Sales Manager: Peter Langley

**Products**
CTC systems, signals, jointless and impulse track circuits.

---

### Kyosan

4-2 Marunouchi 3-chome, Chiyoda-ku, Tokyo 100-0005, Japan
Web: http://www.kyosan.co.jp

**Key personnel**
President: T Nishikawa
Managing Director, Export Sales: T Doi
General Manager, Overseas Department: F Takenouchi

**Subsidiary**
Taiwan Kyosan Co Ltd, Taichung, Taiwan

**Products**
Centralised Traffic Control (CTC) system, Automatic Train Protection (ATP) system, Automatic Train Operation (ATO) system, Automatic Train Stop (ATS) system, automatic block signal equipment, solid-state interlocking equipment, relay interlocking equipment, level crossing signal and gate information display system.

**Contracts**
Contracts include supply of systems for the automated people mover for Hong Kong airport at Lantau.

*UPDATED*

---

### Leach International Europe SA

2 rue Goethe, F-57430 Sarralbe, France
Tel: (+33 3) 87 97 98 97   Fax: (+33 3) 87 97 84 04
e-mail: jmsigaud@leachint.fr
Web: http://www.leachintl2.com

**Key personnel**
Commercial Director: J M Sigaud
Export Sales Manager: P Saunders

**Products**
Relays and relay systems; contactors; time-delay relays and timers; keyboards and panels; indicators; switches.

*UPDATED*

---

### Lincoln Industries

8021 National Tumpike, Louisville, Kentucky 40214, USA
Tel: (+1 502) 368 65 65   Fax: (+1 502) 367 14 84

**Key personnel**
Vice-President, Sales: Eddie Ramer

**Corporate development**
Lincoln Industries is a division of Progress Rail Services Corporation.

**Products and services**
Level crossing safety devices, signalling hardware, relay cases and housings, cantilevers, signal masts and bases, switch layout and accessories, inspection and severe storm damage repair.

---

### Luxram Lighting Ltd

PO Box, Calendariaweg 2A, CH-6405 Immensee, Switzerland
Tel: (+41 41) 854 44 44   Fax: (+41 41) 854 44 50
e-mail: info@luxram.com
Web: http://www.luxram.com

**Key personnel**
General Manager: F J Naegeli
Production Manager: H Ullrich

**Products**
Lamps for railway applications, including signal lamps.

Recent contracts include the supply of lamps to SBB, Luxembourg Railway Company, SNCB, MÁV, Croatian State Railway, KTM, Malaysia, Melio Nedellin and Swedish Rail.

*UPDATED*

---

### Marconi Communications

Marconi Communications Limited
New Century Park, PO Box 53, Coventry CV3 1HJ, UK
Tel: (+44 24) 76 56 55 00   Fax: (+44 24) 76 56 58 88
e-mail: pete.hallard@marconicomms.com
Web: http://www.marconicomms.com

**Key personnel**
Managing Director, Strategic Networks: Neil Sutcliffe
Sales Director, Strategic Networks: Graham Outterside

**Products**
Design, supply, maintenance and management of complex transportation communication networks. Has specialist knowledge in system design, integration, implementation and project management, incorporating the following communication systems: PDH and SDH digital transmission systems, optical fibre, copper distribution and signalling cable systems, telephone systems, PABX, fixed and track-to-train CCTV, analogue and digital public address, passenger information displays, VHF/UHF mobile radio, passenger alarm and help point systems and a comprehensive Station Management System (SiMS) platform.

SiMS includes control of all communications equipment on a station, in addition to tunnel telephone systems, ticketing machines, SCADA and a comprehensive decision support package.

An example of integration capability is the development of an integrated communications system, controlling telecommunications, public address, CCN and passenger information displays via a single screen.

Marconi Communications CNS (Customer Network Services) targets communication networks and control systems in the mass transport sector.

Contracts include London Underground Ltd Jubilee Line Extension (prime contractor for Contract 204); London, Tilbury and Southend resignalling scheme (Railtrack); Docklands Light Railway; Beijing Metro Line 1 modernisation; and London Underground Ltd Northern Line rolling stock communications infrastructure and maintenance.

Strategic Networks is providing communications for Hong Kong's Lantau Airport rail link and for Midland Metro Line 1.

---

### Matra Transport SA

PO Box 531, F-92542 Montrouge Cedex, France
Tel: (+33 1) 49 65 75 00   Fax: (+33 1) 49 65 70 93

**Key personnel**
See entry in *Locomotives and powered/non-powered passenger vehicles* section.

**Corporate background**
Matra is part of the Siemens Group.

**Products**
Electronic signalling and telecommunications, automatic control (ATP-ATO) and safety systems; fail-safe track-to-train/train-to-track transmission systems; train identification systems; design, manufacture and installation of SCADA systems.

---

### Maxon

Maxon America Inc
10828 NW Airworld Drive, Kansas City, Missouri 64153, USA
Tel: (+1 816) 891 63 20   Fax: (+1 816) 891 88 15
e-mail: market@maxonusa.com
Web: http://www.maxonusa.com
Parent company
Maxon Electronics Co Ltd
459-23, Ka-San Dong, Kumchon-Ku, Seoul, South Korea
Tel: (+82 2) 850 11 14   Fax: (+82 2) 864 51 00
e-mail: dyun@maxon.maxon.co.kr

**Key personnel**
President and Chief Executive Officer: M W Sohn
Executive Managing Director: W B Choi
Managing Director: D Y Yang

**Products**
Two-way equipment including VHF, UHF, UHF trunking and 800 MHz two-way radios, personal communication devices, wireless products and paging equipment.

---

### Maxon Europe

Maxon House, Maxted Close, Hemel Hempstead HP2 7EG, UK
Tel: (+44 1442) 26 77 77   Fax: (+44 1442) 21 55 15
e-mail: sales@maxon.co.uk
Web: http://www.maxon.co.uk

**Key personnel**
European Sales: Doug Leigh
Marketing Communications Controller: Penny Waterfall

**Subsidiary companies**
MRSA (Maxon France, Paris)
MISA (Maxon Iberia, Madrid)

**Products**
VHF and UHF hand-held radios, mobile radios, all with a wide area of paging.

Contracts include the supply to Polish Railways of SL70 hand-held portable radios.

---

### Mer Mec SpA

Via Oberdan 70, I-70043 Monopoli (BA), Italy
Tel: (+39 080) 887 65 70   Fax: (+39 080) 887 40 28
e-mail: mermec@tin.it
Web: http://www.mermec.it

**Key personnel**
See entry in *Permanent way components, equipment and services* section.

**Products**
Measuring vehicles and diagnostic systems for the maintenance of railway infrastructure; telecommunication monitoring systems, signalling monitoring systems.

*NEW ENTRY*

---

### Mirror Technology

Craswell Scientific Ltd
Unit 4, Redwood House, Orchard Trading Estate, Toddington GL54 5EB, UK
Tel: (+44 1242) 62 15 34   Fax: (+44 1242) 62 15 29
e-mail: mirtec@aol.com
Web: http://www.mirrortechnology.co.uk

**Key personnel**
Sales Director: G T Poyner
Production Director: R M J Chambers
Sales Executive: M M Robertson

**Products**
Platform mirrors for driver-only operation, surveillance and as an aid to safety by providing rearward visibility from the driver's cab; vandal-resistant polycarbonate pedestrian subway mirrors.

## Signalling and communications systems/MANUFACTURERS

*Mirror Technology platform mirror*

UK train operating companies supplied include Chiltern Railways, Connex South Central, Thames Trains and West Anglia Great Northern.

## Morio Denki Co Ltd

34-1 Tateishi 4-chome, Katsushika-ku, Tokyo 124-0012, Japan
Tel: (+81 3) 36 91 31 81   Fax: (+81 3) 36 92 13 33
Web: http://www.morio.co.jp

**Key personnel**
See entry in *Electric traction equipment* section.

**Products**
Automatic Train Control and Automatic Train Stop units, station override prevention systems, event recorders, monitoring systems and alarm systems.

*UPDATED*

## Mors Smitt Relais

1 Place du Marivel F-92316, Sevres Cedex, France
Tel: (+33 1) 55 64 01 39   Fax: (+33 1) 55 64 01 40
e-mail: sales@MorsSmittRelais.com
Web: http://www.MorsSmittRelais.com

**Works address**
Z A du Pont, 2 rue Mandinière, F-72300 Sablè sur Sarthe

**Key personnel**
Sales Manager: Christian Acard

**Products**
Railway relays, cab panel indicators, relay panels, contactors, traction protection relays.

**Contracts**
Currently installing HVAC control panel on LIRR M3 cars and electro mechanical components for LIRR M7 cars and NJT Comet V.

*UPDATED*

## Motorola

Land Mobile Products Sector
Jays Close, Viables Industrial Estate, Basingstoke RG22 4PD, UK
Tel: (+44 1256) 582 11   Fax: (+44 1256) 46 98 38

**Key personnel**
Director of Operations: Graham Hobbs
UK Sales Director: Mark Ellis

**Parent company**
Motorola (Schweicz) AG
Geweberpark, CH-5506 Mägenwil, Switzerland
Tel: (+41 62) 889 53 60   Fax: (+41 62) 889 55 66

**Corporate background**
Motorola took over the railway communications business of Ascom Radiocom AG in 1999.

**Products**
Railway communications systems, including: track-to-train radio systems; tunnel radio systems; portable, mobile and fixed radio communications systems. Recent products include the MSTR track-to-train mobile station, designed for cross-border rail operations.

Hand-held portable UHF and Band Three trunked radios; base station equipment. Band Three Radio Electronic Token Block (RETB); Field Radio Unit (FRU); Band Three mobile National Rail Network (NRN); Band Three trunked Starnet system.

Recent contracts include the supply of multifunctional track-to-train mobile equipment for PBKA trains, capable of operating on four different radio systems (200 units per year); CF200 – base station for SNCF (50 units per year); SE160E portable shunting radio (700 units per year); BS770CPN base station for Portuguese Railways (75 units per year); Railco 770 modular track-to-train radio system (200 units per year); SX with shunting applications (200 units per year).

## Motorola Canada Ltd

Communications Division
3125 Steeles Avenue East, North York, Ontario M2H 2H6, Canada
Tel: (+1 416) 499 14 41

**Products**
Two-way portable radios; the PHD 5000 Trackside Communications Network, a self-contained and integrated voice and data system, interconnecting management, control offices, field staff and vehicles on the move.

## Nippon Signal

The Nippon Signal Co Ltd
1-1 Higashi-Ikebukuro, 3-chome, Toshima-ku 170-6047 Tokyo, Japan
Tel: (+81 3) 359 54 45 47   Fax: (+81 3) 595 445 51
e-mail: info@signal.co.jp

**Key personnel**
President: K Nishimura

**Products**
Centralised Traffic Control (CTC); electronic interlocking system; relay interlocking system; electronic tokenless block system; automatic block signalling system; level crossing signals and automatic gate; track circuit system; Automatic Train Protection system (ATP); Automatic Train Operating system (ATO); Remote Control equipment (RC); Programmed Route Control system (PRC); automatic announcing system; inductive-type wireless remote-control system; electric point machine; relays for signalling; Integrated Traffic Control system by computer (ITC); coloured signal (bulb, LED); LED route indicator; LED destination indicator; axle counting system; obstruction detector for level crossings; transponders.

## Nortel

Nortel Networks
Business Development GSM-R (ND158), Wilhelm-Runge-Strasse 11, D-89081 Ulm, Germany
Tel: (+49 731) 505 14 10   Fax: (+49 731) 505 1820
e-mail: leonie.geray@nortel-dasa.de
Web: http://www.nortelnetworks.com

**Key personnel**
Assistant Business Development GSM-R: Leonie Geray

**Subsidiary companies**
Offices in Canada, Europe, Asia-Pacific, Caribbean, Latin Amercia, Middle East, Africa and USA.

**Products**
Missioncritical telephony and IP-optimised networks supplied to customers in 150 countries; ASCI (Advanced Speech Call Items) for high-speed trains. GSM-R base transceiver station (BTS) for trackside coverage under adverse evironmental cnditions; specially-adapted radio algorithms to allow error free voice and data communications at train speeds up to 500 km/h. Nortel is a member of the MORANE consortium (Mobile Radio for Railway Networks in Europe).

## NRS

National Railway Supplies
Gresty Road, Crewe CW2 6EH, UK
Tel: (+44 1270) 53 30 00   Fax: (+44 1270) 53 39 56
e-mail: commercial@natrail.demon.co.uk
Web: http://www.natrail.co.uk

**Other offices**
Room 206, Engineering Depot, New England Road, Brighton BN1 3TU
Tel: (+44 1273) 32 62 10   Fax: (+44 1273) 22 81 44
Leeman Road, York Y026 4ZD, UK
Tel: (+44 1904) 52 22 93   Fax: (+44 1904) 52 26 96

**Key personnel**
Managing Director: Cliff Webb
Commercial Director: David A Kierton
Marketing Manager: Dave Tilmouth

**Corporate background**
NRS is a wholly owned subsidiary of the Unipart Group of Companies.

**Products**
Supply chain management service to the rail industry.

**Contracts**
Contracts include Balfour Beatty Rail Maintenance, Serco Rail Maintenance, AMEC Rail, Jarvis Rail and Westinghouse Signals. Manufacture, production, servicing, repair and distribution of signalling, track maintenance and telecoms products, infrastructure and permanent way. Also design and assembly of signalling, TPWS and UPS location cases.

*UPDATED*

## OTP Rail & Transit

Oregon Technical Products
541 Taylor Way 12, Belmont, California 94002, USA
Tel: (+1 415) 594 93 41   Fax: (+1 415) 594 93 42

**Key personnel**
President: John J McCloskey
Chief Engineer: Jesse E Taylor
Marketing Manager: William R Rice

**Products**
Trackside/train integrity management systems; voice digital hot box analysers; voice synthesisers; mini talkers; electronic locomotive and component test meters; locomotive fan control; event recorder/monitor; crossing recorder/monitor.

## Peek Traffic BV

Basicweg 16, PO Box 2542, NL-3800 GB Amersfoort, Netherlands
Tel: (+31 35) 689 17 77   Fax: (+31 35) 689 18 50
e-mail: info@peektraffic.nl
Web: http://www.peektraffic.nl

**Key personnel**
Business Manager, Railway Products: J R Opperman
Export Manager: A Koopmans

**Products**
Train identification and information systems for metros and light rail systems.

*UPDATED*

## MANUFACTURERS/Signalling and communications systems

### Pintsch Bamag Antreibs – und Verkehrstechik GmbH

PO Box 100420, D-46524 Dinslaken, Germany
Tel: (+49 2064) 60 20  Fax: (+49 2064) 60 22 66
e-mail: info@pintschbamag.de
Web: http://www.pintschbamag.de

**Key personnel**
Managing Director: Dr Rolf-Dieter Krächter

**Background**
Pintsch Bamag is a member of the Schaltbau Group (qv).

**Products**
Electrical and electronic power supply, lighting, heating and air conditioning equipment for rail vehicles; level crossing protection equipment (hand-operated or rail-actuated) with flashlights and luminous signals, with barrier guarding and radar obstacle detection; train approach indicator for gang warning; fibre optic luminous signal indicators; electric gas-operated infra-red and oil-fuelled circulation, compact-type point heating equipment; solid-state snow detectors; train preheating equipment; test sets for electrical installations on rail vehicles.

*UPDATED*

---

### Progressive Engineering (AUL) Ltd

Clarke Street, Ashton-under-Lyne OL7 0LJ, UK
Tel: (+44 161) 285 33 22  Fax: (+44 161) 343 26 48
e-mail: johnw@progressive-eng.demon.co.uk
Web: http://www.progressive-eng.demon.co.uk

**Key personnel**
Managing Director: J Williams
Chairman: C Williams
Works Manager: P Moss

**Products**
Hot axlebox detection system.

*UPDATED*

---

### Quest

Quest Corporation
12900 York Road, North Royalton, Ohio 44133, USA
Tel: (+1 440) 230 94 00  Fax: (+1 440) 582 77 65
e-mail: questcor@aol.com

**Key personnel**
President: Kurtis S Wetzel
Sales and Marketing Manager: Daniel J Donovan

**Products**
Hot bearing simulators; hot wheel simulators; hand-held line pressure testers; locomotive warning strobes; locomotive headlight/crossing light controls.

---

### Railroad Signal Inc

15110 East Pine Street, Tulsa, Oklahoma 74116, USA
Tel: (+1 918) 234 15 22  Fax: (+1 918) 234 15 29
e-mail: info@railroadsignal.com
Web: http://www.railroadsignal.com

**Key personnel**
President: Eddie Burns
Vice-President, Marketing: Alan Barker

**Products**
Engineering and signal design, installation and 24-hour maintenance of signal systems, level crossing signals, turnkey capability, manufacture and distribution of signal parts and components; repair of printed circuit cards; remanufacture of switch/point machines, relays, gate mechanisms and other signal equipment, installation and maintenance of hot box detectors, bridge detectors, drag detectors and AEI reader systems, supply of train flashing rear end services.

---

### Railway Products

Railway Products (India) Limited
168 Mount Poonamallee High Road, Porur, Madras 600016, India
Tel: (+91 44) 482 78 64; 83 84; 85  Fax: (+91 43) 44 60 35

**Key personnel**
See entry in *Brakes and drawgear* section.

**Products**
Signalling relays, plug-in and shelf-types; line and track relays for use in 25 kV 50 Hz AC traction areas; electric point machines with ground connections; relay racks, control panels and other accessories for relay interlocking installations; tokenless block instruments; axle counters and radio block equipment; Solid-State Interlocking (SSI) systems; software for SSI and CTC systems.

---

### SAB WABCO do Brasil

Rua Lauriano Fernandes Júnior 10, Vila Leopoldina, 05089-070 São Paulo, Brazil
Tel: (+55 11) 260 31 22  Fax: (+55 11) 831 60 35

**Key personnel**
Managing Director: Eduardo José Gomes Gonçalves
Marketing Manager: Manuel Domingos Dias da Ines

**Products**
Point motors, signals, level crossing barriers. (See also *Brakes and drawgear* section.)

---

### Safetran Systems Corporation

An Invensys company
2400 Nelson Miller Parkway, Louisville, Kentucky 40223, USA
Tel: (+1 800) 626 27 10  Fax: (+1 502) 244 74 44
Web: http://www.safetran.com

**Key personnel**
Vice-President, Marketing, Sales and Service:
  John J Paljug
General Manager, Marketing and Technology:
  John T Sharkey
Sales and Service Engineer: Bob Shaw

**Products**
Signalling, communications, warehouse services and maintenance-of-way equipment for railway and mass transit applications.

Products include: crossing warning products; power supplies; wayside signal products; freight yard products; communications services; maintenance-of-way transit systems housings and foundations.

Safetran's new wayside communications controller/field protocol device (WCC/FPD) maintenance utilities for Windows 98/NT are designed to be used by customers requiring maintenance and diagnostic access to their WCC/FPD equipment from local, remote, or dial-in Windows 98/NT workstations.

---

### SAGEM SA

Terminals and Telecommunications Division, 6 Avenue d'Iéna, F-75783 Paris Cedex 16, France
Tel: (+33 1) 40 70 63 00  Fax: (+33 1) 40 70 84 36

**Projects**
Driver assistance systems: platform and train doorway monitoring, CCTV, onboard repetition of wayside signalling, audio assistance to train guard, onboard GPS positioning and radio links.
(See also *Passenger information systems* section.)

---

### SAIT Systems

Chaussée de Ruisbroek 64, B-1180 Brussels, Belgium
Tel: (+32 2) 370 54 78  Fax: (+32 2) 370 51 11
Web: http://www.saitrh.com

**Key personnel**
Managing Director: P de Groote

**Corporate background**
SAIT-Devlonics is a member of the SAIT-Stento Group.

**Products**
Turnkey implementation of HF, VHF, UHF, SHF fixed and mobile telecommunication networks; communication and control systems for public transport, including use of radio in underground and other difficult environments.

---

### SAT

Network and Telecommunications Division, 11 rue Watt, F-75626 Paris Cedex 13, France
Tel: (+33 1) 55 75 75 75  Fax: (+33 1) 55 75 30 94

**Corporate background**
SAT is part of the SAGEM Group.

**Products**
SDH and asynchronous fibre optic systems, microwave radio systems, wireless subscriber loops, private business networks, multiservice multiplexers, digital television distribution, personal paging systems, engineering and network design and turnkey networks.

---

### SchlumbergerSema Group

Rail Control Systems
143/149 Farringdon Road, London EC1R 3AD, UK
Tel: (+44 20) 78 30 44 44  Fax: (+44 20) 72 78 05 74

**Affiliated and associated companies**

*Belgium*
SchlumbergerSema
Rue de Stalle 96 Stallestraat, B-1180
Tel: (+32 2) 333 55 11  Fax: (+32 2) 333 55 22
e-mail: info-request@be.sema.com

SchlumbergerSema Global Services
Raketstraat 98 rue de la Fusee, B-1130
Tel: (+32 2) 724 92 90  Fax: (+32 2) 724 92 92
e-mail: request@sgs.be.sema.com

*Brazil*
SchlumbergerSema
Rua Alexandre Dumas, 1711, Bloco 12-1, andar Sao Paulo, CEP 04717004
Tel: (+55 11) 34 44 76 00

*Railroad Signal level crossing signals*

# Signalling and communications systems/MANUFACTURERS

*China*
SchlumbergerSema
6th floor, Lido Office Tower, Lido Place, Jichang Road, Beijing 10004

*France*
SchlumbergerSema
50 avenue Jean Jaurès, BP 62012 F-92542 Montrouge
Tel: (+33 1) 46 00 66 67

Schlumberger Limited Paris
42, rue Saint Dominique, F-75007 Paris
Tel: (+33 1) 40 62 10 00

*Netherlands*
SchlumbergerSema Informatica
Van Houten Industriepark 11, PO Box 143, NL-1380, AC Weesp
Tel: (+31 294) 23 95 00   Fax: (+31 294) 23 95 01

*Mexico*
SchlumbergerSema
Ejercito Nacional 425, Colonia Granada, Delegacion, Miguel Hidalgo, CP 11520, Mexico DF
Tel: (+52 55) 52 63 30 00

*Germany*
Dreieich
Otto-Hahn Strasse 36, D-63303 Dreieich
Tel: (+49 69) 23 83 30 00

*Italy*
SchlumbergerSema Rome, Via Riccardo Morandi 36, I-00050
Tel: (+39 6) 83 07 42 01

*Spain*
SchlumbergerSema
Avinguda Diagonal 210-218, Barcelona E-08018
Tel: (+34 93) 486 18 18

SchlumbergerSema
Albarracin 25, E-28037 Madrid
Tel: (+34 914) 40 88 00

*UK*
Schlumberger Cambridge Research
High Cross, Madingly Road, Cambridge CB3 0EL
Tel: (+44 1223) 32 52 00

SchlumbergerSema
4 Triton Square, Regent's Place, London NW1 3HG
Tel: (+44 207) 830 44 47

*Gatwick*
Schlumberger House
Buckingham Gate, Gatwick Airport, West Sussex RH6 0NZ
Tel: (+44 1293) 55 66 55

*USA*
Schlumberger Austin Technology Centre
8311 Ranch Road 620 N, Austin, Texas 78726-4010

SchlumbergerSema
6399 South Fiddler's Green Circle,
Suite 600, Greenwood Village, Colorado 80111
Tel: (+1 303) 741 84 00

Schlumberger iCenter
1325 South Dairy Ashford, Houston, Texas 77077-2307
Tel: (+1 281) 285 13 00

Schlumberger Solutions Center
SchlumbergerSema
5599 San Felipe, Houston, Texas 77056-2724
Tel: (+1 713) 513 20 00

Schlumberger Data Management Center
(in the CMS Energy Building)
5444 Westheimer, Houston, Texeas 77056
Tel: (+1 713) 513 20 00

Schlumberger Limited New York
153 E 53rd Street, 57th Floor, New York NY 10022
Tel: (+1 212) 350 94 00

Schlumberger Doll Research
36 Old Quarry Road, Ridgefield, Connecticut 06877-4108
Tel: (+1 203) 431 50 00

Schlumberger Reservoic Completic Center
14910 Airline Road, Rosharon, Texas 77583-1590
Tel: (+1 281) 285 52 00

Schlumberger Sugar Land Campus
The Forum
210 Schlumberger Drive, Sugar Land, Texas 77478
Tel: (+1 281) 285 85 00

### Background
In 2001, Schlumberger Limited acquired Sema plc and combined it with part of its former transaction business and other acquisitions. The company is now called SchlumbergerSema and is one of two business segments of Schlumberger Limited.

### Products
Design and supply of computer systems; electronic signalling control equipment; automatic route-setting systems; passenger information systems; rail control systems consultancy.

The main product supplied is the Integrated Electronic Control Centre (IECC). SchlumbergerSema Group developed the IECC and it is now the standard control system used for major resignalling schemes in the UK.

**UPDATED**

## SCI
Specialty Concepts Inc
8954 Mason Avenue, Chatsworth, California 91311, USA
Tel: (+1 818) 998 52 38   Fax: (+1 818) 998 52 53

### Products
Charge regulators, load management controllers and other monitoring equipment for photovoltaic and solar-powered equipment.

## Sécheron
Sécheron SA
14 Avenue de Sécheron, CH-1211 Geneva 21, Switzerland
Tel: (+41 22) 739 41 11   Fax: (+41 22) 738 73 05
e-mail: info@secheron.com
Web: http://www.secheron.com

### Key personnel
See entry in *Electric traction equipment* section.

### Products
Microprocessor-controlled On-Train Monitoring and Recording (OTMR) systems, optical pulse generators for axle or gearbox mounting, modular cab display systems for ATC and ATP applications; compact LCD display systems including high-performance LCD displays based on PC architecture.

Recent orders include the supply of on-train monitoring and recording systems, type TELOC 2200 for type X41 rolling stock of SJ Sweden; supply of electronic data recorders type TEL 1000 to Ned Trath in Holland for the upgrade of passenger rolling stock.

**UPDATED**

## SEPSA
Sistemas Electrónicos de Potencia SA
Albatros 7 and 9, (Pol Ind) La Estación, E-28320 Pinto, Madrid, Spain
Tel: (+34 91) 691 52 61   Fax: (+34 91) 691 39 77
Web: http://www.sepsa.es

### Key personnel
See entry in *Passenger coach equipment* section.

### Background
SEPSA is a member of the Albatros Group (qv).

### Products
Automatic train protection (ATP) systems (CESARES).

**UPDATED**

## Siemens Switzerland
Siemens Switzerland Transportation Systems
Industriestrasse 42, CH-8304 Wallisellen, Switzerland
Tel: (+41 1) 832 32 32   Fax: (+41 1) 832 36 00
e-mail: verkehrstechnik@siemens.ch
Web: http://www.siemens.ch/vt

### Key personnel
Managing Director: S Gerlach
Manager, Export Department, South East Asia: V Ritter
Manager, Export Sales, South East Asia: N Vögeli

### Products
Electronic, hybrid and relay interlockings; intermittent and continuous ATP and ATC systems, including vehicle and trackside equipment; CTC and electronic remote-control systems; block and track vacancy proving equipment (axle counters, track circuits, last vehicle detection); point locking equipment including point machines and point locking system; signals and indicators; safety relays.

Swiss Railways (SBB) has awarded Siemens a contract to build and operate a GSM-R (GSM-Railway) pilot system

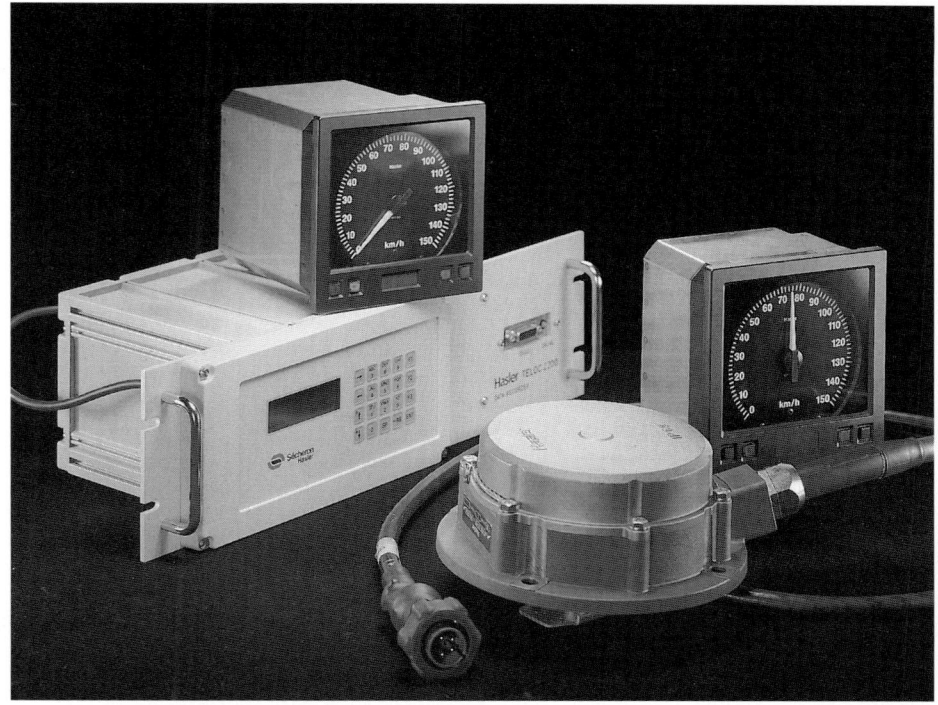

*Hasler TELOC-2200 on-train data recorder from Sécheron*

to provide mobile radio communication on trains. The first test journeys are to be carried out along the 36 km long pilot stretch between Zofingen (Canton Aargau) and Sempach (Canton Lucerne), where the GSM-R technology is being tested in accordance with the European EIRENE requirements. The aim of this pilot project is to test the suitability of the GSM-R system for nationwide implementation in Switzerland. SBB is the second European railway company to implement GSM-R into railway traffic with Siemens as technology supplier. In 1998 Siemens started to install a nationwide turnkey GSM-R system including switching systems and base stations in Sweden for the railway infrastructure company Banverket.

GSM-R was designed to meet the railway-specific communication requirements and is also planned as a communications platform for information services, in the first instance for train personnel and later to provide information for passengers. For safety reasons GSM-R works in a different frequency spectrum from traditional GSM.

## Siemens Transportation Systems

Ackerstrasse 22, D-38126 Braunschweig, Germany
Tel: (+49 531) 22 60   Fax: (+49 531) 226 42 00

### Key personnel
President, Signalling and Control Systems, Main Line & Mass Transit: Thomas Ganswindt
See also main entry in *Locomotives and powered/non-powered passenger vehicles* section.

### Joint venture companies
Siemens Signalling Ltd
SSL, Xian, China
(51 per cent owned by Siemens Transportation Systems)
Railway Signalling Technology SRL
Bucharest, Romania
(81 per cent owned by Siemens Transportation Systems)

### Products
*Portfolio*
Siemens delivers a comprehensive range of integrated systems, products and services for main line signalling applications. This includes CTC systems, microcomputer and relay interlocking systems, intermittent and continuous, ATP, ATC, radio-based operating systems, electric point machines with internal or external locking; colourlight signals and fibre optic route indicators, jointed and jointless track circuits, axle counters and speed-checking equipment, level crossings, block protection and transmission systems, freight management systems, maintenance and consulting activities.

*CTC systems*
Siemens is experienced in CTC systems with widely different requirements and of different extensions. On the basis of products approved and in use worldwide Siemens designs and delivers system solutions in accordance with customers' needs. Different customer requirements can be identified such as improvement of route performance, relieving operation staff from routine tasks, reduction of manpower costs, improvement and centralisation of data transfer, preparation and warehousing, improvement of passenger comfort by train connections and passenger information (see *Passenger information systems* section).

*Siemens level crossing protection system on Brunswick-Magdeburg line, Germany* 0021724

*Siemens track-installed conductor (LZB500 ATC system)* 0021725

In order to meet these requirements, Siemens proposes the Vehicle and Infrastructure Control and Operating System (VICOS). Siemens reports that VICOS is a reliable and robust system with 32 bit multiprocessors and RISC architecture based on standards including the UNIX operating systems, Ethernet/TCP-IP/ISO-OSI network and Oracle database, and is easy to configure.

It provides the following function set: definition/application of operators access rights and control areas, status monitoring (rain tracking, interlocking indication), remote interlocking control (automatic, manual control, command management), automatic train routing (including timetable data management, train sequence calculation), conflict management, messaging, alarms and data logging.

VICOS has recently been installed or is under construction in: Nuremberg, Germany; Tampere, Finland; Copenhagen, Denmark; Berlin and Oslo.

*Interlocking systems*
Based on Intel microprocessors, the SIMIS family of Siemens electronic interlockings has been introduced by many railway companies, fulfils different country-specific operating requirements and is designed to meet the new European CENELEC standards. Available in different configurations, the SIMIS family is built up in modular function units. The in-door equipment is pre-assembled at the Siemens factory and delivered to the site. Interlocking logic and monitoring can be dispatched to several computers that communicate and process the data as a multiprocessor system. Siemens offers SIMIS easy interface to existing train management systems and field elements. Since 1982 more than 100 Siemens electronic interlockings with 25,000 elements have been commissioned worldwide. Recent projects have been carried out in several countries which include Germany, Poland, Hungary, Finland and China.

*ATP/ATC systems*
The ZUB family of intermittent ATC systems offers continuous real-time calculation and onboard monitoring of speeds up to 250 km/h for train protection. The high-performance ZUB 123 employs a fail-safe onboard microcomputer and offers an intermittent ATC function using trackside ZUB beacons and in-fill loops.

Continuous ATC function using track-to-train and train-to-track transmission is provided by the LZB80 system. LZB 80 is currently applied for high-speed lines in European countries.

With experience of transmission and communications-based signalling systems, Siemens has developed innovative and continuous ATP/ATC designed to meet ETCS standards.

New members in the ZUB family have recently been introduced and fulfil the requirements of ETCS Level 1. The new ZUB systems overlay the existing signalling equipment and allow a high safety level in the communication chain between the onboard microcomputers and the interlockings. Moreover, several optional functions can significantly improve train speed and traffic capacity.

Maximised performance is available with the continuous ATP/ATC system according to the specification of ETCS Level 2. The information transmitted to and from the train via a public network is supervised by the onboard microcomputer and displayed to the driver. This system can operate without wayside signals and consequently maintenance costs are reduced. Both systems are upgradable from one to the other as they use the same components and architecture. Three important projects have been carried out in Germany. They are on the Berlin-Halle-Leipzig line, the Frankfurt-Cologne line and the Jüterborg-Leipzig line.

A key component for ETCS is the standardised spot transmission system called Euro-Balise for track-to-train communication. Siemens reports that it is the first company to produce the Euro-Balise system for commercial operation.

*Radio-based Operating System*
Based on the decentralisation of the control and safety tasks performed by today's signalboxes, the recently developed Radio-based Operating System integrates all the main ATP and interlocking systems. This allows reduction in the field elements assigned to a route such as signals or track vacancy indicators.

It incorporates Intelligent onboard equipment including route map, intelligent and centralised control devices for points and level crossings, safe data transmission via radio and Euro-Balise for correcting errors regarding vehicle position.

*Level crossing systems*
The EBÜT80 and NBUE90E level crossing systems have been designed for main lines. The systems can be used on single or double-track lines and activated/deactivated automatically by the train or manually.

The Siemens range of point machines includes the S 700 K with external locking and the BSG-drive 9 with internal locking. More than 150,000 units have been installed. Siemens has introduced switch diagnostics to save the life-cycle costs of point machines and switches. The motor of the point machine is used as a sensor to measure the clutch force, switching force or lock release force.

The Az S family of axle counters has been recently updated with SIMIS technology to provide data transmission and remote diagnostics which offer single and multiple axle counting capability at speeds up to 350 km/h for line sections up to and above 10 km. Over 2,000 Siemens electronic axle counters with more than 5,000 wheel sensors have been installed worldwide.

**Mass Transit Signalling and Control Systems**
Address as for Signalling & Control Systems
Tel: (+49 531) 226 22 30   Fax: (+49 531) 226 42 49

### Key personnel
President: Thomas Ganswindt
Vice-President, Business Administration and Finance: M F Duttenhoffer

### Associate companies
HPW, Hani-Prolectron is a subsidiary of Siemens AG. The organisation is responsible for control systems for buses and trams.
Matra Transport International
This is a joint venture of the Lagardère Group and Siemens Transportation Systems. The organisation is responsible for advanced ATC systems for light rail and mass rapid transit.

### Products
*For LRT and metro systems:*
Include ATC, ATP, ATO (up to fully automated driverless train operation); interlockings (SICAS); signals; track vacancy detection.

*Siemens ZUB ATC system for urban transport* 0021726

*For buses and trams:*
Automatic vehicle control and location (AVM/AVC); onboard information systems; traffic light pre-emption.

Also: passenger information systems (see *Passenger information systems*); telecommunications; train radio and ticketing/fare collection management systems; data communication systems; fire detection and intrusion detection systems.

Recent contracts include ATC systems for Stockholm, Zurich S Bahn, Stuttgart Stadtbahn, Dortmund, Bielefeld, Frankfurt, Mainz, Munich, Berlin, Vienna. Contracts for SICAS have been received from Cologne, Guangzhou, Bangkok and Laubag.

Siemens Transportation Systems commissioned the first electronic interlocking systems to be installed in China in 1999. Located at the Fuyang marshalling yard in Anhui province, the four systems control 180 sets of points and 260 signals, and feature the world's first applications of Siemens. Type SIMIS-W interlocking. SIMIS-W has been developed for international applications from the company's SIMIS-C interlocking. Part of Chinese Railways Beijing-Hong Kong trunk line scheme, the Fuyang facility comprises four yards, each with 120 controlled elements. Each yard is equipped with a SIMIS-W electronic interlocking consisting of an operator workstation system, overhead computers, control area computers, service and diagnostic PCs, as well as relay element interface modules, trackside equipment and cables. The installation follows a 1995 contract award.

Swiss Federal Railways (SBB) has awarded the Information and Communications division of Siemens a contract to install and operate a GSM-R (GSM Railway) pilot system to provide onboard mobile radio communications for its trains. Under this initial project, a 36 km stretch of line between Zofingen, in Aargau canton, and Sempach, Luzern was equipped in 1999. The aim of the pilot scheme, which complies with the requirements of the EIRENE (European Integrated Railway Radio Enhanced Network), is to test the suitability of GSM-R technology for network-wide implementation in Switzerland.

This Siemens contract follows a July 1998 order from Swedish rail infrastructure authority Banverket to install an nationwide turnkey GSM-R system. GSM-R has been designed to meet the specific needs of railway communications, and for safety reasons operates in a different frequency spectrum to traditional GSM.

The Transportation Systems Group (VT) of Siemens AG has been appointed by the Kowloon-Canton Railway Corporation (KCRC), Hong Kong, to be general contractor in charge of planning, supplying and installing the complete communications system for the new metro extension West Rail. The order includes, among other items, the supply and installation of a passenger information system, the service radio and telephone system, the transmission equipment for voice and data communication as well as for image transmissions, and a closed-circuit video surveillance system for the nine stations and depot on the West Rail metro line. When completed by the end of 2003, this new line will link Hong Kong's Kowloon district with the New Territories and Tuen Mun to the northwest of the metropolis. At first some 340,000 passengers will travel on the 30 km long metro line every day, but long-range plans expect ridership to increase to about 500,000 passengers daily. For Guangzhou in southeast China, VT had installed a similarly complex communications system for that city's metro, which was inaugurated in May 2000.

For the mass transit operator MTR (Mass Transit Railway) Siemens is supplying the signalling and control system for the extension of metro line Tseung Kwan O. This order includes the engineering, manufacture, installation and maintenance of the operations control system, which features state-of-the-art rail safety and signalling technology, for the 13 km line. The MTR order is being processed by VT in co-operation with its French subsidiary Matra Transport International (MTI), Paris.

Siemens Transportation Systems has been appointed by MTA New York, USA, to install an automatic train control and operation system based on a technology which was developed by the group's subsidiary Matra Transport International (MTI), Paris, for the latest extension to the Paris Metro. The system – called Meteor – has been operating successfully for Metro Line 14 in the French capital for about a year. It has also been in trial operation on a line section in New York for the past 15 months.

## Siemens Transportation Systems

Rail Automation Division
PO Box 3327, D-38023 Braunschweig, Germany
Tel: (+49 531) 22 60 Fax: (+49 531) 226 42 64
e-mail: internet@ts.siemens.de
Web: http://www.siemens.com/ts

### Corporate headquarters
Siemens AG
Transportation Systems
PO Box 910220, D-12414 Berlin, Germany
Tel: (+49 30) 385 50

### Key personnel
President, Transportation Systems Group:
  Herbert J Steffen
Group Vice Presidents: Hans-Dieter Bott;
  Thomas Ganswindt; Hans M Schabert
Directors: Dr R Alter, M F Duttenhofer, R Grolms, H Hess

### Subsidiary companies
See entry in *Locomotives and powered/non-powered passenger vehicles* section.

### Products and services
Major product categories include:
Signalling: relay-based and electronic interlockings; radio-based train control systems; intermittent and continuous automatic train control (ATC) and automatic train protection (ATP) systems; hump yard systems; level crossing systems; and signalling components.
Operations control systems: centralised train control systems; train describer systems; control centres; man-machine interface (MMI) systems; and marshalling yard equipment.
Major service categories include:
Training; project management; life-cycle costing; systems integration; testing before commissioning using the Braunschweig Test Center; installation, commissioning and maintenance; and financing.

### Developments
In March 2001, Siemens signed an agreement with Kapsch AG covering the joint development and marketing of a new generation GSM-R Mobile Termination (MT) unit and cab radio. The GSM-R MT unit provides the means for cab radio to connect to the GSM-R network. It also includes the latest (General Packet Radio Service) GPRS functionality, enabling railway operators to use GSM-R for data transmission to and from trains for purposes such as passenger information, maintenance information, diagnostics and onboard ticketing.

### Contracts
Recent or current contracts include:

**Canada:** In June 2002, Siemens received an order from Canadian National for an operations control system to handle and monitor all operations on the company's 12,000 km network. Equipped with 46 operator consoles and located in Montreal, the syetem was die to be commissioned by the end of 2005.

**China:** In August 2001, Siemens secured a contract from KCRC, Hong Kong, to supply and install signalling and control equipment and passenger information systems for 4 km of new line and the existing 30 km network of the Tuen Mun light rail system.

Also in August 2001, Siemens won an order to supply a VICOS operations control system, SICAS electronic interlocking and ZUB 200 intermittent automatic train control system for the new 17 km Xinmin Line LRT system in southern Shanghai. Trial operations were scheduled to begin in July 2003.

In October 2000, Siemens was awarded a contract by Guangzhou Metro Corporation and Chinese Railways to plan, supply and commission a complete signalling and operations control system for Line 2 of the Guangzhou metro. The 23 km 20-station line was due to be commissioned in June 2004.

**Germany:** In February 2002, Siemens was awarded a contract by German Rail (DB AG) to supply and install a new interlocking system at Braunschweig main station. To be controlled from an operations centre in Hanover, the Type El S interlocking will be based on Siemens' Simis C microcomputer technology. Work involves renovation of 294 signals and 78 switches, as well as provision of derailers and track vacancy detection sections.

In January 2002, DB AG placed a contract with Siemens to upgrade the main interlocking at Frankfurt. The project also features the use of a Type El S interlocking and Simis computers, and includes renovation of 315 signals, 331 switches, 41 electronically decentralised switches and 306 track vacancy detection sections.

In October 2001, the last of seven operations control centres for DB AG was commissioned in Munich. Supplied by the Siemens-led BZ 2000 consortium, which also included Alcatel SEL AG and Vossloh System Technik GmbH, the seven centres cover some 15,000 km of the DB main line network, monitoring, despatching and controlling train movements. In a second phase of the project, due to be implemented by the end of 2002, the seven centres will be linked together.

In June 2001, Siemens won a contract to modernise the signalling system at Magdeburg, providing SIMIS C interlockings. The project included provision of three

*SICAS computer cabinet for the Cologne—Mülheim interlocking*

# MANUFACTURERS/Signalling and communications systems

sub-centres and eight decentralised control computers, and the modernisation of 418 signals and 320 switches and derailers. Completion of the scheme was scheduled for the end of 2003.

In July 2000, Siemens commissioned the first application of its SIMIS (R) FFB microcomputer-controlled radio-based train control system on a 26 km regional line in the Nordrhein-Westfalia region. The system employs GSM-R digital mobile communications technology.

**Malaysia:** In February 2001, Siemens received an order from Mitsui, acting as general contractor, to supply signalling and train control equipment for the upgraded line between Rawang and Ipoh. Siemens was to be responsible for system engineering, supplying and commissioning the CTC system, signalling and point operating equipment.

**Poland:** In March 2001, Siemens commissioned a SIMIS W interlocking at Zywiec for Polish State Railways.

**Romania:** In November 2001, Siemens commissioned the country's most modern interlocking at Ploiesti. The SIMIS W installation controls over 200 points and signals.

**USA:** In July 2000, Siemens won an order from MTA, New York, to upgrade and expand the communications system used by New York City Transit. A goal of the project is to permit an unrestricted exchange of information among the 188 stations and three traffic control centres of the NYCT system. Additional functions for voice and data communications and a CCTV system were due to be added at later stages of the project. The contract also included maintenance of the system for five years from its commissioning in April 2004.

Other orders for signalling technology form part of turnkey contracts, detailed in the *Turnkey systems contractors* section.

*UPDATED*

## Signal House Ltd

Signal House, Cherrycourt Way, Stanbridge Road, Leighton Buzzard LU7 8UH, UK
Tel: (+44 1525) 37 74 77   Fax: (+44 1525) 85 09 99
e-mail: tech@signalhouse.demon.co.uk
Web: http://www.collis.co.uk

**Key personnel**
Chairman: Peter Collis
Managing Director: Peter Roberts
Operations Director: P Hobbs
Technical Director: J Wareing
Senior Sales Engineer: D Farrington

**Associate company**
Collis Engineering Ltd

**Products**
Fibre optic signalling indicators; trackside enclosures; Planlite 5000 series switch heaters; oil and electric lamps for signalling and other applications; colour light signals; terminal blocks and fuseholders.

*VERIFIED*

## Simoco

Simoco Europe Ltd
57b West Harbour Road, Edinburgh EH5 1PP, UK
Tel: (+44 131) 552 62 92   Fax: (+44 131) 552 97 14

**Key personnel**
European Sales Manager – Transport: David G Giles

**Products**
Hand-held radios and mobile telephones.

## Smith System Engineering Ltd

Surrey Research Park, Guildford GU2 5YP, UK
Tel: (+44 1483) 44 20 00   Fax: (+44 1483) 44 23 04
Web: http://www.smithsys.co.uk

**Key personnel**
Contact: Clive Adams

**Products**
System engineering, integration, research and consulting in transport, telecommunications, defence, public safety, environmental monitoring and utilities.

Contracts include a cab secure radio (CSR) system for Merseyrail Underground metro system on behalf of Railtrack North West.

## Solartron

Victoria Road, Farnborough GU14 7PW, UK
Tel: (+44 1252) 37 66 66   Fax: (+44 1252) 54 49 81
e-mail: support@trackwatch.co.uk
Web: http://www.trackwatch.co.uk

**Products**
Trackwatch range of integrated systems for condition monitoring and fault analysis of key signalling installations.

## Specialty Bulb

The Specialty Bulb Co Inc
80 Orville Grove, Bohemia, New York 11716-0231, USA
Tel: (+1 631) 589 33 93   Fax: (+1 631) 563 30 89
e-mail: info@bulbspecialists.com
Web: http://www.bulbspecialists.com

**Key personnel**
See entry in *Passenger coach equipment* section.

**Products**
Lamps for signal applications.

## Springboard Wireless Networks Inc

5100 Orbitor Drive, Mississauga, Ontario L4W 4Z4, Canada
Tel: (+1 905) 238 52 55   Fax: (+1 905) 212 20 04
e-mail: info@springboardwireless.com
Web: http://www.springboardwireless.com

**Key personnel**
President, Chief Executive Officer:
   Herman Chang
Vice President Marketing and Sales:
   Dave Fisher

**Products**
Communications-based Train Control (CBTC). Springboard can provide train control suppliers and rail operators with a one-stop shopping point for data communications requirements – from R & D to system engineering to installation. Expertise in designing custom radio frequency (RF) modems, routers and protocol converters.

Wireless solutions for rail applications include code line replacement, highway grade crossings and positive train separation. The RailPath system is a wireless network that has been specifically developed for CBTC applications. RailPath has been designed to allow for compatibility with the world's leading train control systems. Springboard's RailPath was field tested in CBTC demonstrations on New York City Transit's Culver Line (January to July 1999). For these NYCT demonstrations, Springboard was partnered with Alcatel Transport Automation, ALSTOM Signaling and Matra Transport International/Union Switch & Signal.

The company also provides integrated radio-dispatch solutions for major rail clients such as CN, CP, and TTC. InterTalk, the company's standards based communication control system, integrates wide area mobile radio and telephone networks.

## Stein

Stein GmbH
Stahlgruberring 36, D-81829 Munich, Germany
Tel: (+49 89) 427 19 00   Fax: (+44 89) 427 190 19
e-mail: office@steingmbh.com
Web: http://www.steingmbh.com

**Products**
bi-control remote radio control system for locomotives. bi-control employs a two-computer system, which monitors itself automatically during operation and processes all commands in fail-safe mode. Up to 23 radio remote controls may work in the same area on one frequency. The system is tested and approved by TÜV Rail and the Eisenbahn-Bundesamt in Germany.

*NEW ENTRY*

## STERIA

12 rue Paul Dautier, PO Box 58, F-78142 Velizy Cedex, France
Tel: (+33 1) 34 38 60 00   Fax: (+33 1) 34 88 61 60
Web: http://www.steria.fr

**Key personnel**
Railway Department Manager: Jean Charles Tarlier
Transportation Sales Manager: Jacques Lafay
Transportation Communication Representative:
   Virginie Cabanes

**Works**
STERIA Services
58 Quai de Jemmapes, F-75010, Paris
STERIA SBT
1467 rue de Courcelles, F-75017, Paris
STERIA
230 rue Frédéric Joliot, PO Box 16000, Pôle d'activités des Milles, F- 13791 Aix en Provence, Cedex 3
STERIA
Bureaux Phénicia, PO Box 3111, F-31026 Toulouse, Cedex 3
STERIA Software Partner GmbH
Juilius Reiber Str 17, D-64293 Darmstadt, Germany
STERIA SA/NV
Avenue Joseph Wybran, 40, Erasmus Technology Center, B-1070 Brussels, Belgium
STERIA Solinsa SA
Chapel les Mestres 9 bis, E-08950 Esplugues de Llobregat, Spain
STERIA Informatic SA/AG
35 rue des Bains, CH-1205 Geneva, Switzerland
STERIA Informatic SA/AG
Militarstrasse 105, CH-8004 Zurich, Switzerland
STERIA Informatic SA/AG
Bahnhofplatz, 10 b, CH-3011 Berne, Switzerland
STERIA London, UK

**Subsidiary companies**
SYSINTER
58 Quai de Jemmapes, F-75010 Paris, France
IAI
Centre Helioparc Bat B, 2 avenue du President Angot, F-64000 Pau, France
BSGL
251 boulevard Pereire, F-75852 Paris, Cedex 17, France

**Products**
Rail Expert computer-aided rail traffic control system, model networks, scheduling, equipment and power consumption control, passenger information, ticketing including clipcards and contactless smartcards, suitable for multimodal transport, simulation, high-reliability systems (Atelier B).

Recent contracts executed and obtained include: automation of Meteor line, Paris, resource planning for RATP, a unified rail traffic regulation system (SURF) for Swiss Federal Railways; computer-aided traffic control (SEPIA) for SNCF; Etape – management of optional or unscheduled trains, for SNCF; statistical analysis of train delays in Paris for SNCF; PCC – central control stations on the Parisian RER rapid transit system for RATP Paris; SOSIE – metro controller training simulator for RATP Paris; PCS – public transportation passenger and staff information system for RATP Paris; 3615 RATP – public teletext information server; RIS – passenger information system for DB AG.

## STS (Intertec)

Space Technology Systems Ltd
Amery House, Steeple Drive, Alton GU34 1TN, UK
Tel: (+44 1420) 886 83   Fax: (+44 1420) 891 90

**Works address**
Unit 2, Stone Lane Industrial Estate, Wimborne BH21 1HD, UK
Tel: (+44 1202) 88 84 02   Fax: (+44 1202) 84 17 17
e-mail: concept32@compuserv.com

**Key personnel**
Managing Director (Alton): D G Evans
Business Manager (Wimborne): B R Bristow
Customer Services Manager (Wimborne): P J Webb

**Products**
Concept 32 Telephone Concentrator – 16 to 512 lines, one or two operators. Over 300 in service with UK and other railways. Approved for connection to the PSTN. Networked version with diverse routing control now available. Operators unit either key and lamp, or monitor and trackerball/touch screen.

Other telephone systems available include dispatcher, party line and block systems. Has designed and supplied these to the railway authorities of Ethiopia, Iraq, Bangladesh, Turkey, Indonesia, Thailand and the Irish Republic. The systems operate over open wire, cable or transmission networks using DTMF or FSK signalling.

Also designs and manufactures miniature signalling relays to BR Spec 930, cab-to-track signalling systems (incuding AWS), key token equipment, colour light signals, circuit controllers and gravity locks. The Company is ISO 9001 registered.

## STS Signals

Doulton Road, Cradley Heath B64 5QB, UK
Tel: (+44 1384) 56 77 55   Fax: (+44 1384) 56 77 10
e-mail: signals@spacetechsys.co.uk

**Key personnel**
Managing Director: D G Evans
Business Manager: T Warrington
Commercial Manager: N Evans

**Products**
Signalling equipment ground-based, including miniature signalling relays, shelf relays, colour light signals, key token instruments, circuit controllers and electric lever locks.

For onboard use, the equipment range covers TPWS and AWS systems, driver safety pedals and wiring assemblies.

*VERIFIED*

## SYSECA Transportation Division

66-68 avenue Pierre Brossolette, Malakoff, Cedex, France
Tel: (+33 1) 41 48 00 00   Fax: (+33 1) 41 48 13 13

**Key personnel**
President/Director General: C Mons
Marketing and Sales Manager: Gérard de Gaye

**Principal subsidiaries**
Syseca Ltd
Southmoor House, Southmoor Road, Wythenshawe, Manchester M23 9SY, UK
Tel: (+44 161) 946 10 01   Fax: (+44 161) 946 70 00
(also at Dalkeith, Scotland)
Syseca Inc
4553 Glencoe Avenue, Suite 100, Marina del Rey, California 90292, USA
Tel: (+1 310) 301 90 40   Fax: (+1 310) 301 33 50

**Key personnel**
President: Philippe Tartavull
Other subsidiaries in Belgium, Germany, Hong Kong, Italy, Mexico, Russia, Singapore, Spain, Venezuela

**Products**
Computerised systems for train control, power control and communications for railway, metro and light rail applications. Management information systems for railways.

Contracts include the supply of a rail control centre for New York City Transit and the construction of Line 3 and the extension of Line 1 of the Singapore Metro, in partnership with Singapore Technologies. Syseca has also been awarded the contract to provide signalling control and ancillary services, including passenger information and CCTV for Croydon Tramlink, London.

## Teknis

Teknis Electronics Pty Ltd
Angas Mews, 75A Angas Street, Adelaide, South Australia 5000, Australia
Tel: (+61 8) 82 23 54 11   Fax: (+61 8) 82 23 54 99
e-mail: info@teknis.net
Web: http://www.teknis.net

**Key personnel**
Managing Director: K Bladon

**Products**
Electronic control systems, SCADA systems. DDU (Driver Display Unit), as in-cab train driver's display for signalling and train orders. WCM (Wheel Condition Monitor) for analysing wheel condition and detecting wheel faults causing damage to track structure. In motion train weighing at line speed. WMS (Wayside Monitoring System) integrating the WCM and other industry standard sensors and instrumentation into a single data/communications system.

*UPDATED*

## Telephonics

Telephonics Corporation
815 Broadhollow Road, Farmingdale, New York 11735, USA
Tel: (+1 516) 549 60 62   Fax: (+1 516) 549 60 18

**Key personnel**
Vice-President Business Development, Commercial Operations: Phil Greco
Manager, Business Development: Norbert Trokki

**Products**
Integrated digital communications systems for rail vehicles, including public address, passenger/crew intercom, automated announcements, radio communications. Other products include integrated wayside communication and central control systems, event recording, CCTV and control centre equipment.

**Contracts**
Train line multiplexer, network controller and vehicle communication systems for MTA New York R142 and R143 212 metro cars, vehicle communication, radio network and CCTV door observation for SEPTA Philadelphia, vehicle communication for MBTA Boston, vehicle communication, health monitoring and vehicle CCTV for Hudson-Bergen LRVs, integrated wayside communication for Newark APM and vehicle communication/passenger entertainment for Caltrans USA.

*UPDATED*

## Telkor Signalling (Pty) Ltd

PO Box 784271, Sandton 2146, South Africa
Tel: (+27 11) 805 44 00   Fax: (+27 11) 805 44 29

**Key personnel**
Director: A D Smith

**Products**
Hot box detectors; dragging equipment detectors; track circuits; interlockings; ticket issuing machines.

## Thales Communications BV

Bestevaer 46, PO Box 88, NL-1271 ZA Huizen, The Netherlands
Tel: (+31 35) 524 83 18   Fax: (+31 35) 524 81 63
e-mail: jw.veltman@signaal.nl

**Key personnel**
Marketing Manager: Jan W Veltman

**Products**
SmartSwitch, a compact, modular and flexible Integrated Access ATM Switching Node, to be used in multimedia network applications.

## Thales Communications Ltd

Newton Road, Crawley RH10 9TS, UK
Tel: (+44 1293) 51 88 55   Fax: (+44 1293) 41 64 00
e-mail: kenm@rmel.com

**Key personnel**
Transport Sales Manager: Ken McFarland

**Background**
Thales Communications Ltd was formerly Redifon MEL.

**Products**
Platform door interface to ensure platform door and train door synchronisation; TPWS, preventing trains going through danger signals; track-to-train, data communications, solutions in a range of technologies; TramCom, a two-way data communication system between trams and trackside equipment.

*NEW ENTRY*

## Thales Translink

Phoenix House, Station Hill, Reading RG1 1NB, UK
Tel: (+44 118) 908 60 00   Fax: (+44 118) 908 64 54
Web: http://www.thales-translink.com

**Key personnel**
Managing Director: David Poole
Marketing Director: Richard Bligh
Director & General Manager: Bryan Visser
Director of Technology: John Edwards

**Corporate development**
Thales Translink is a division of Thales Telecommunications Services Ltd, which is part of the Thales Group formed by the merger of Thomson-CSF and Racal. Formerly trading as Racal Telecom, the company's origins lie in its acquisition of the former BRT private telecommunications network during the privatisation of British Rail in the 1990s.

**Products**
Thales Translink's business principally consists of the provision of operational and business telecommunications services to the railway industry in the UK. Its core network comprised 17,000 km of trunk cable, of which some 4,000 route-km are made up of fibre optic cable. During 1997 the former Racal upgraded the network by creating a resilient SDH backbone network which includes a further 1,200 route-km of fibre optic cable.

Facilities provided include national fixed-line telecommunications systems in support of trackside telephony, signalling control systems, CCTV and mainframe computer connections. The company also provides facilities management for Railtrack's National Radio Network, which provides 'driver-to-shore' communications.

Thales Translink is the leading partner in CityLink Telecommunications Ltd, a special purpose company formed to operate, maintain and renew London Underground's operational radio and transmission systems. The 20-year contract has been let on a Private Finance Initiative (PFI) basis. Thales Translink's contribution to the project includes the design, installation, testing and commissioning of a new network-wide SDH transmission system with CCTV and to manage the implementation of a new digital Tetra radio system.

Also for London Underground, Thales Translink has developed In-Cab CCTV, a system designed to enhance the safety of passengers on station platforms by enabling train drivers to view the platform before arrival, during the stop and after departure, and was contracted to act as project manager for XTP, an advertising medium that uses cross-track digital projection to display advertisments on walls facing station platforms.

*UPDATED*

## Theimeg Elektronikgeräte GmbH & Co

Krefelder Strasse 3, D-41066 Mönchengladbach, Germany
Tel: (+49 2161) 636 30
e-mail: theimeg@theimeg.de
Web: http://www.theimeg.de

### Subsidiaries
Theimeg Elektronic Pty, Johannesburg, South Africa
Theimeg Inc, Stowe, Vermont, USA

### Background
Theimeg locomotive radio remote-control systems have been used for more than 25 years on almost all European rail networks and many outside Europe, both private and public. The company's multiple-use systems enable a one-carrier frequency to control a large number of locomotives simultaneously. Over 6,000 units have been delivered for locomotives in Europe, USA, Canada, Asia, Australia, South America and New Zealand and over 2,500 installed in European national railways and their successors.

### Products
The TH-EC/LO remote-control system is the first remote control in the world which was designed to adhere to the European safety regulations for locomotives (EN 502390). The system enables electric track points to be operated remotely and reduces the need for operators to walk long distances while shunting long trains.

The system comprises two basic types of transmitter houses. The first uses the X-Y joystick. The brake and throttle commands are activated by moving the joystick in the appropriate direction. The second version uses a lever control. Up to five throttle/brake command positions are available on this lever. The first and last step can be set up as a momentary or fixed step.

Both transmitters are light and comfortable and the design includes recessed controls to avoid unintentional commands. Each system comes with a harness.

The receiver also has two versions, the first has an aluminium mould housing and the interface is wired to a multicontact quick-disconnect connector. In the second version, the receiver electronics are housed in a 19 in rack, which has three levels.

Mobi 8000 radio data communications systems with mobile or hand-held terminals are for online data management in railway marshalling yards and container ports.

The company also makes crane radio remote-control systems and data communications systems, the HANDYcontrol, MINIcontrol and EASYcontrol radio systems.

*Theimeg's TH-EC/LO in use*     2000/0085462

## Tiefenbach GmbH

PO Box 911320, D-45538 Sprockhoevel, Germany
Tel: (+49 2324) 70 52 03    Fax: (+49 2324) 70 51 14
e-mail: info@tiefenbach.de
Web: http://www.tiefenbach.de

### Key personnel
Managing Director: Peter Jochums
Sales & Technical Manager: Juergen Burghoff
Export Sales Manager (Contracts): Stefan Peiser

### Corporate development
Tiefenbach is a member of the Hauhinco Group.

### Products
Point control equipment: complete control equipment for automation and signalling of depots and marshalling yards; axle counter systems; track vacancy detection and level crossing switching with axle counter systems based on Tiefenbach's double wheel sensor.

### Contracts
Complete systems design and supply of depot signalling works at Cottbus (DB AG), Cologne (DB AG), Antwerp (SNCB), marshalling yard control and signalling works at Kassel (DB AG), Hamm (DB AG), Gdansk, Poland; complete systems design and supply of axle counter systems for SOB-Sudostbahn, Switzerland (main line); AKN Eisenbahn AG suburban feeder service at Hamburg, Germany.

## Toshiba Corporation

Railway Projects Department
Toshiba Building, 1-1 Shibaura 1-chome, Minato-ku, Tokyo 105, Japan
Tel: (+81 3) 34 57 49 24    Fax: (+81 3) 34 57 83 85

### Products
Automatic train control equipment; automatic train stop equipment; electrical indicating and train describing equipment; centralised traffic control and remote-control systems; marshalling yard equipment, including retarders.

## TransCore, Inc

Emerging Markets
19111 Dallas Parkway, Suite 300, Dallas, Texas 75257-3104, USA
Tel: (+1 972) 733 66 00    Fax: (+1 972) 733 64 86

### Key personnel
President and Chief Executive Officer:
  John Worthington
Chief Operating Officer:
  John Simler
Executive Vice-President Marketing: Dick Blackwell
Executive Vice-President Corporate Development:
  John Foote
Executive Vice-President and Chief Technical Officer:
  Kelly Gravelle
Chief Scientist and Executive Vice-President:
  Dr Jerry Landt

### Products
Automatic equipment identification and monitoring systems; automatic train positioning systems.

*UPDATED*

## Transmitton Ltd

Ashby Park, Ashby-de-la-Zouch LE65 1JD, UK
Tel: (+44 1530) 25 80 00    Fax: (+44 1530) 25 80 05
e-mail: rail@transmitton.co.uk
Web: http://www.transmitton.co.uk

### Key personnel
See entry in *Electrification contractors and equipment suppliers* section.

### Products
The Transmitton Cromos SCADA system provides comprehensive control and monitoring featuring a real-time computer master station with high-resolution full workstation graphics.

Fastflex intelligent electronic control and data gathering services. Supply and system integration for traction power control, communication networks, passenger information systems, public address, passenger help points, fare collection and other intelligent equipment used in rail and mass transit systems.

*NEW ENTRY*

## Transportation Products Sales Co Inc

618 Cepi Drive, Suite B, Chesterfields, Missouri 63005, USA
Tel: (+1 314) 532 11 44    Fax: (+1 314) 532 14 82
e-mail: tpscarms@tpsc-arms.com

### Key personnel
See entry in *Electric traction equipment* section.

### Products
Batteries by GNB Technologies for back-up duties in signalling and telecommunications systems. DC power systems for rail electronics (see *Electric traction equipment* section).

## UniControls AS

Krenickául 2257, CZ-100 00 Praha 10, Czech Republic
Tel: (+420 2) 781 78 85    Fax: (+420 2) 781 44 75
e-mail: unic@unicontrols.cz
Web: http://www.unicontrols.cz

### Products
Communications and control systems for trains and rail vehicles, including: train communication network-wire train bus (TCN-WTB) equipment; multi-vehicle communications equipment; vehicle communications devices; and drivers cab equipment and displays.

*UniControls train communications and control systems are fitted into Prague metro stock*    2000/0089428

## Contracts

Train communications and control systems for refurbished Russian-built Prague metro stock; train communications system for St Petersburg metro stock; train and vehicle communications system and drivers cab equipment for Czech Railways Class 471 emus; automatic train control system for Czech Railways Class 680 tilting trainsets; drivers cab equipment for refurbished Class 772 locomotive.

## Universal Power Systems

Weldon Road, Loughborough LE11 5RN, UK
Tel: (+44 1509) 26 11 00   Fax: (+44 1509) 26 11 48
e-mail: sales@upsltd.com
Web: http://www.upsltd.co.uk

**Key personnel**
General Manager, Rail Division: Chris Smith

**Products**
Uninterruptible power supply systems.

*NEW ENTRY*

## US & S

Union Switch & Signal Inc
An Ansaldo Signal company
1000 Technology Drive, Pittsburgh, Pennsylvania 15219-3120 USA
Tel: (+1 412) 688 24 59   Fax: (+1 412) 688 23 99

**Key personnel**
President and Chief Executive Officer:
   Gary Ryker
Director, International Marketing: Thomas Gibson
Director, Product Marketing: Jeremy Hill
Director, Railroad Sales & Customer Service:
   George Rudge
Director, Transit Marketing: Kean Smith
Director, Communications: Gregory Babicz

**Products**
Design and manufacture of signalling and train control systems for passenger, freight, high- speed and mass transit railways including: vehicle-mounted signalling, positioning and monitoring systems; marshalling yard components and management systems; automation and integration technologies for dedicated and multimodal traffic management.

Contracts include: computerised traffic management systems at Boden for Banverket, Sweden and for Hamersly Iron Ore Railway, Australia; computer-controlled marshalling yards at Xuzhou and Jing Jiu, People's Republic of China; Shanghai Metro control system, China; ATC system for Green Line, Los Angeles, USA; operations control centre for Tri- Met LRT system, Portland, Oregon, USA.

## Wabtec Railway Electronics

21200 Dorsey Mill Road, Germantown, Maryland 20876, USA
Tel: (+1 301) 515 20 00   Fax: (+1 301) 515 21 00
Web: http://www.wabtec.com

**Key personnel**
President: Robert Haag
Vice-President Marketing and Sales: Mark T Kramer

**Background**
Wabtec Railway Electronics formerly Pulse Electronics, is a division of Wabtec Corporation. WRE was founded in 1977 and its first product was the locomotive event recorder, Train Trax, which is currently installed worldwide and is a standard on many US railroads.

**Products**
Train Trax solid-state locomotive even recording system, a flexible, virtually maintenance-free, fully FRA-compliant recording system designed to improve operational safety and performance by monitoring and recording key channels from the locomotive; TrainLink II End of Train Telemetry System, which continuously monitors key conditions on the last car including brake pipe pressure, end of train motion, battery condition and marker light status and communicate the information to the lead locomotive while adding end of train emergency braking capability; locomotive speed indicators with both MPH and KPH models; Iso-Amp Speed Isolation Amplifier an alternative to the Axle Generator or passive sensors mounted on the locomotive drive gear; Train Sentry III Engineman Alertness Device, a solid-state system designed to enhance the safe operation of railway vehicles by monitoring the alertness of the engineman; FuelLink fuel measurement system, which incorporates solid-state electronics and advanced pneumatics for determining locomotive fuel levels accurate to +/- one per cent; Q-Tron's QEG 1000 Electronic autostart system, which reduces engine fuel consumption resulting in significant fuel savings by safely shutting down and restarting the locomotive engine during appropriate idle periods; LocoTemp II cooling system controller, which reliably monitors and controls locomotive coolings systems temperature, providing 'New Locomotive' technology to a non-microprocessor fleet; Q-Tron QTRAC 1000 locomotive traction control system, a standalone unit that monitors and controls locomotive wheel slip by reducing excitation to the main AC (or DC) generator when wheel slip is detected; Wayside Device Monitor (WDM-450) vigilant highway crossing monitoring system, which provides continuous real-time monitoring and event recording of the status of grade crossing installations; electronically controlled pneumatic braking system.

*UPDATED*

*M6W Locomotive event recorder with wireless and memory card download port*

## Wandel & Goltermann

Wandel & Goltermann Kommunikationstechnik GmbH
PO Box 1262, D-72795 Eningen uA, Germany
Tel: (+49 7121) 86 16 16   Fax: (+49 7121) 86 13 33
e-mail: info@wago.de
Web: http://www.wg.com
A member of the Schaltbau Group

**Key personnel**
Managing Director: Fariborz Khavand
Director, Public Transportation Systems:
   Karl-Heinz Bahnmüller
Director, Public Safety Systems: Alex Treffers

**Products**
Onboard computers, next-stop displays, digital announcement equipment, public address systems with integrated passenger alarm intercom for buses and trains; electromagnetic field measurement for personal safety.

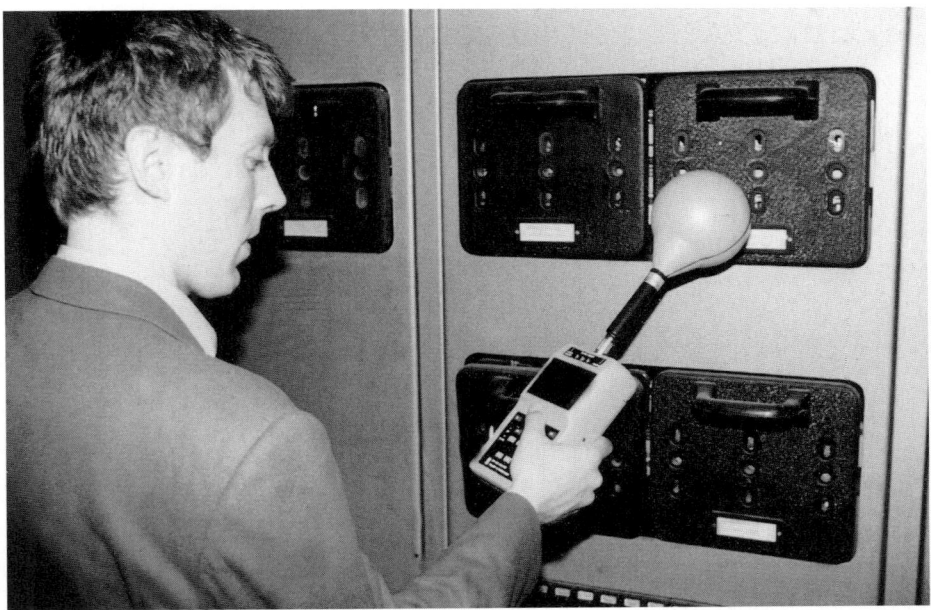

*Wandel & Goltermann offers an electromagnetic field measurement service for personal safety*

## Contracts
Include supply of equipment for Netherlands Railways, Berlin S-Bahn and München transport.

---

## Western-Cullen-Hayes Inc

2700 West 36th Place, Chicago, Illinois 60632-1682, USA
Tel: (+1 773) 254 96 00   Fax: (+1 773) 254 11 10
e-mail: wch@wch.com
Web: http://www.wch.com

### Key personnel
President: Ronald L McDaniel
Vice-President: Barbara Gulick
Sales Manager: Carl J Pambianco
Customer Service Manager: Bill Crain
Systems Application: Rodney Yourist

### Products
Railway safety signals and accessories, gate arms, railway crossing signals, industrial crossing warning systems, flashing light signals: incandescent and LED, bells: AC-DC and electronic, switch lamps, and targets, bumping posts: fixed, sliding and hydraulic; wheel stops, chocks, switch point guards, programmable yard switch machine, track drills, rail benders, rail tongs, journal and hydraulic jacks, derails: sliding, hinged and portable and accessories, derail operators: ELDO, Delectric and solar powered, blue flags, wagon re-railers, locomotive revolving lights and warning bells, and other custom designed equipment for railroad, transit and industrial applications.

---

## Westinghouse Rail Systems Ltd

PO Box 79, Pew Hill, Chippenham SN15 1JD, UK
Tel: (+44 1249) 44 14 41   Fax: (+44 1249) 65 23 22
e-mail: wrsl.marketing@invensys.com
Web: http://www.westinghouserail.co.uk

### Key personnel
Managing Director: J A Cotton
Head of Projects: P Threlfall; A MacKenzio
Head of Technology: C E Riley
Sales & Marketing Director: J E Clark
Operations Director: S Barry
Finance Director: G C J Campion
Head of Human Resources: R Drury
Head of SCADA Group: A MacDonald

### Associated companies
Invensys Rail Systems, Australia
Dimetronic, Spain
Safetran Systems Corporation, USA
Burco Services, USA

### Products
Systems available cover the complete range of railway signalling and control systems. They include electronic interlocking, relay interlocking, automatic train control, cab secure radio, centralised traffic control, electronic control centres, train describers, remote-control telemetry, SCAOA.

Products include colourlight signals, fibre optic signals, electric point machines, jointed and jointless track circuits, apparatus cases, VDUs, control panels, remote control, indication and data acquisition equipment, safety plug-in relays and solid-state interlocking modules.

Control panels and illuminated diagrams (model boards) are supplied to customer requirements in both mosaic and plain forms for a wide variety of applications, ranging from major control centres to monitoring and emergency control panels. VDU displays and workstations are also available either as an alternative to hard-wired panels, or in combination with them.

WESTRACE is a second-generation safety processor which has been developed by Westinghouse Rail Systems and its three associate signalling companies to satisfy a range of safety applications to worldwide standards. Applications range from simple wayside interlockings to complete Centralised Traffic Control (CTC). The equipment can provide trainborne safety processing for ATP systems, or can be configured as a solid-state highway crossing controller.

Westronic System Two is a microprocessor-based data handling and transmission system designed specifically for railway applications. It is a modular system that can be configured to provide any specific combination of signalling, train control or supervisory facilities, such as CTC, train description, traction power telecontrol, station plant supervision and monitoring, panel processing and so on.

The new Transmission-Based Signalling (TBS) system provides operational flexibility in both main line and metro applications. The system can be overlaid on existing signalling allowing minimum disruption to operations during installation. TBS provides greater capacity, better regulation, improves operation and enhances infrastructure performance as well as providing ATP and ATO facilities.

Westinghouse Rail Systems undertakes system design for railway telecommunication facilities including telephone exchanges, transmission systems, public address, closed-circuit television, centralised clock systems, optical fibre transmission and fixed and mobile radio. The company manufactures a high-security train-to-signalbox radio system which provides both voice and data communication between control centre and the driver.

For urban mass transit railways, Westinghouse Rail Systems provides Automatic Train Operation (ATO), fixed and moving-block Automatic Train Protection (ATP) and Automatic Train Supervision (ATS) systems.

Routine maintenance, fault attendance, diagnosis and repair services are provided to suit customer needs. Maintenance and support services include maintenance monitoring, diagnostic and logging systems, control and allocation of spares and maintenance logistic support, together with repair and refurbishment of electronic, electric and electromechanical equipment, including service-exchange facilities.

*UPDATED*

---

## Westinghouse Saxby Farmer

Westinghouse Saxby Farmer Ltd
17 Convent Road, Entally, Calcutta 700-014, India
Tel: (+91 33) 244 71 61   Fax: (+91 33) 244 71 65
e-mail: wsfedp@cal2.vsnl.net.in

### Key personnel
Managing Director: A N Dutta
Director, Finance & Marketing: D K De Sarker

### Products
Signalling equipment including route relay and point interlocking systems.

### Contracts
Recent contracts include the supply of 20,000 signalling relays and other equipment to Indian Railways.

Other contracts include Route Relay Interlocking Project for Patna Junction of the Eastern Railway and others in India.

*NEW ENTRY*

---

## Zelisko Elektrotechnik und Elektronik GesmbH

Steinfeldergasse 12, 43-45, A-2340 Mödling, Austria
Tel: (+43 2236) 40 60   Fax: (+43 2236) 40 62 99
e-mail: info@zelisko.com
Web: http://www.zelisko.com

### Key personnel
Managing Director: Dr Wolfgang Widl
Sales Director: Gerhard Brychta

### Corporate background
Zelisko is a wholly owned subsidiary of the Knorr-Bremse Group.

### Products
Safety equipment for level crossings including half and full barriers, with acoustic signals (the barrier drives are controlled by battery-powered 24 V DC shunt motors powered by nickel-iron batteries with constant charge from the mains electricity); railway signals in fibre optic and LED displays; alphanumeric LED displays for passenger information; telecommunications equipment.

*UPDATED*

# PASSENGER INFORMATION SYSTEMS

## Alphabetical listing

AEG MIS
ALSTOM Transport
Conrac GmbH
CTS
Data Display Co Ltd
DHJ Media AB
ELNO
Ferrograph
Firema
Focon
GAI-Tronics
Gorba AG
Halo
HPW
ICL
Info Systems GmbH
Inova Corporation
Interalia

IVS Insta Visual Solutions
Jasmin Electronics
KRONE-REW GmbH
LTS
Lumino Licht Elektronic GmbH
Mattig-Schauer GmbH
Meister Electronic GmbH
Metra Blansko AS
Mitron Oy
Morio Denki
Net Display Systems bv
Omega
Optech
Page
Philips
Postfield Systems
SAGEM SA
SAIT-Devlonics

ScanAcoustic
Sema Group
SEPSA
Siemens Transportation Systems Ltd
Solari di Udine SpA
STERIA
Sysco Srl
Techspan Systems plc
Thales Translink
Telephonics
Trivector System AB
Vaughan Harmon Systems Ltd
Velec SA
Voice Perfect Ltd
VST
Vultron

## Classified Listing

**ON-TRAIN AUDIO SYSTEMS**
ALSTOM Transport
ELNO
Interalia
Jasmin Simtec
SAGEM
ScanAcoustic
Schauer
SEPSA
Siemens Austria
Telephonics
Velec
Voice Perfect

**ON-TRAIN DISPLAYS**
ALSTOM
EEV
ELNO
Firema
Focon
Gorba
Halo
HPW
InfoSystems
IVS Insta Visual Solutions
Jasmin Simtec
KRONE-REW
Lumino Licht Elektronik GmbH

Meister Electronic
Metra Blansko
Morio Denki
Optech
SAGEM
SEPSA
Siemens Austria
Siemens Transportation Systems
STERIA
Techspan Systems
Telephonics
Velec

**STATION AUDIO SYSTEMS AND DISPLAYS**
Adtranz
AEG MIS
ALSTOM Transport
Conrac GmbH
CTS
Data Display
DHJ Media AB
EEV
Ferrograph
GAI-Tronics
Gorba
ICL
InfoSystems
Inova Corporation

Interalia
Jasmin Simtec
KRONE-REW
LTS
Metra Blansko
Mitron
Net Display Systems bv
Omega
Optech
Page
Philips
Postfield Systems
SAIT-Devlonics
ScanAcoustic
Schauer
Sema Group
Siemens Aktiengesellschaft
Siemens Austria
Solari
STERIA
Sysco
Techspan Systems
Trivector System AB
Vaughan Harmon
Velec
Voice Perfect
VST
Vultron

## Company listing by country

**AUSTRIA**
Mattig-Schauer GmbH
Siemens Austria

**BELGIUM**
SAIT-Devlonics

**CANADA**
Interalia

**CZECH REPUBLIC**
Metra Blansko AS

**DENMARK**
Focon
ScanAcoustic

**FINLAND**
IVS Insta Visual Solutions
Mitron Oy

**FRANCE**
ALSTOM Transport
ELNO
SAGEM SA
Sema Group
STERIA
Velec SA

**GERMANY**
AEG MIS
Conrac GmbH
Info Systems GmbH
KRONE-REW GmbH
Lumino Licht Elektronik GmbH
Meister Electronic GmbH
Siemens
VST

**IRELAND**
Data Display Co Ltd

**ITALY**
Firema
Solari di Udine SpA
Sysco Srl

**JAPAN**
Morio Denki

**NETHERLANDS**
Net Display Systems bv
Philips

**SPAIN**
Page
SEPSA

**SWEDEN**
DHJ Media AB
LTS
Trivector System AB

**SWITZERLAND**
Gorba AG
HPW
Omega

**UNITED KINGDOM**
CTS
EEV
Ferrograph
GAI-Tronics
Halo
ICL
Jasmin Electronics
Optech
Postfield Systems
Siemens Transportation Systems Ltd
Techspan Systems plc
Thales Translink
Vaughan Harmon Systems Ltd
Voice Perfect Ltd
Vultron

**UNITED STATES OF AMERICA**
Inova Corporation
Telephonics

## MANUFACTURERS/Passenger information systems

## AEG MIS

AEG Gesellschaft für moderne Informationssystem mbH
Söflinger Strasse 100, D-89077 Ulm, Germany
Tel: (+49 731) 933 15 61   Fax: (+49 731) 933 16 01
e-mail: info@aegmis.de
Web: http://www.aegmis.de

### Key personnel
Directors: Dr Reiner Bayrle; Peter Mack
Secretary: Antonia Baur

### Corporate development
AEG MIS was formed under a management buyout following the break-up of AEG Corporation.

### Products
High-tech Liquid Crystal Display systems worldwide for mobile and stationary use.

## ALSTOM Transport

### Information Solutions
11-13 avenue du Bel Air, F-69627 Villeurbanne Cedex, France
Tel: (+33 4) 72 81 52 00   Fax: (+33 4) 72 81 52 87
Web: http://www.transport.alstom.com

### Key personnel
Managing Director: Antoine Doutriaux
3330 De Miniac Street, St Laurent, Quebec, Canada H4S 1Y4
Tel: (+1 514) 333 08 88   Fax: (+1 514) 333 04 96
Managing Director: Marshall Moreyne

(See also ALSTOM entry in *Locomotives and powered/non-powered passenger vehicles* section)

### Products
Real-time onboard passenger information systems for rolling stock: AGATE Media passenger information systems for mass transit and railway stations.

ALSTOM acquired Telecite Inc in 1999. The Montreal-based Telecite becomes ALSTOM's worldwide centre of excellence in Advanced Traveller Information Systems (ATIS).

The company specialises in developing, manufacturing and marketing real-time information and communication systems for public transportation and other applications. It has sales of €7.4 million and a nine per cent world market share. The firm now employs nearly 80 people in Montreal, Quebec and Williston, Vermont.

The acquisition of Telecite further strengthens ALSTOM's presence in North America. Recent acquisitions have expanded its rolling stock, traction equipment, signalling systems, field service and turn-key project management capabilities in the US and Canada, complementing its already strong presence in Mexico.

ALSTOM's co-operation with Telecite over the years leading to acquisition has brought orders from Europe, Latin America and Asia. For example, ALSTOM chose Telecite as its partner to supply real-time advanced traveller information systems to the Mass Transit Railway Corporation (MTRC) in Hong Kong. It is being installed on 104 cars (eight trains each 13 cars) and each car will have four displays.

**UPDATED**

## Conrac GmbH

Lindenstrasse 8, D-97990 Weikersheim, Germany
Tel: (+49 7934) 10 10   Fax: (+49 7934) 10 11 02
e-mail: marketing@conrac.de
Web: http://www.conrac.de

### Key personnel
Managing Director: Walter Hammel
Director Sales: Ingo Richter
Marketing Communications: Petra Ollhoff

### Subsidiaries
Conrac France SARL
47 Route de Baillon, F-95270 Chaumontel, France
Tel: (+33 1) 30 35 06 34   Fax: (+33 1) 34 71 29 26
e-mail: pheurtaux@aol.com

*Large-screen plasma displays in special IP protected version at Singapore Changi Airport SMRT station* 2002/0134266

Conrac Asia Display Products Ltd
5 Lorong Bakar Batu #04-05, MacPherson Industrial Complex 348742, Singapore
Tel: (+65) 67 42 79 88   Fax: (+65) 67 47 39 33
e-mail: sales@conrac-asia.com

### Products
Intelligent information display systems for railway applications (hardware and software). Special customised solutions such as IP protection, front access facilities, climate control; large-screen colour plasma displays; large-screen CRT monitors, large-screen multimedia displays; split-flap, LED and LCD boards. Conrac is an ISO 9001 certified company.

New developments include a 60 inch high-resolution colour plasma information display and 23 and 30 inch high-resolution TFT-displays.

**UPDATED**

## CTS

Cubic Transportation Systems Ltd
177 Nutfield Road, Merstham RH1 3HR, UK
Tel: (+44 1737) 64 68 00   Fax: (+44 1737) 64 36 93

### Key personnel
See entry in *Revenue collection systems and station equipment* section.

### Products
Passenger information systems, help points and security systems.

Recent contracts include passenger security and information systems for London Underground Ltd's Piccadilly Line; customer information systems and maintenance support for train operating companies.

## Data Display Co Ltd

Deerpark Industrial Estate, Ennistymon, Co Clare, Ireland
Tel: (+353 65) 707 26 00   Fax: (+353 65) 707 13 11
e-mail: sales@data-display.com
Web: http://www.data-display.com

### Key personnel
Sales Director: Paul Neville
Sales: Lorraine Case
Marketing Manager: Connor McFadden

### Subsidiary companies
Data Display UK
3 The Meadows, Waterberry Drive, Waterlooville PO7 7XX, UK

Tel: (+44 1705) 24 75 00   Fax: (+44 1705) 24 75 19
e-mail: data.display@pipex.com
Web: http://www.data.display.sales@dial.pipex.com

Data Display USA
5004 Veteran's Memorial Highway, Holbrook, New York 11741, USA
Tel: (+1 631) 218 21 30   Fax: (+1 631) 218 21 40
e-mail: salesinfo@ddusa.com

Data Display BV
Het Tasveld 12, NL-3342 GT Hendrik Ido Ambacht, Netherlands
Tel: (+31 78) 684 05 04   Fax: (+31 78) 684 05 08
e-mail: datadisplay@wxs.nl

Data Display Ireland
Unit 21, Sandyford Office Park, Sandyford Industrial Park, Dublin 18, Ireland
Tel: (+353 1) 295 92 66   Fax: (+353 1) 295 92 69
e-mail: dublin@ddisplay.iol.ie

Data Display France (Eridan)
19 Chemin de Bel Air, F-93160 Noisy le Grand, France
Tel: (+33 1) 43 03 75 00   Fax: (+353 1) 43 03 12 58
e-mail: eridan@eridan.fr

Data Display Portugal
Granja Park, 9, Recta da Granja-Campo Raso, P-2710 Sintra, Portugal
Tel: (+351 21) 910 67 60   Fax: (+353 1) 910 67 69
e-mail: datadisplayportugal@mail.telepac.pt

### Products
Data display, passenger information systems using LED, LCD, CRT, plasma and flip dot technologies; comms packages using pagers, telephone modem, radio modem, gsm and sms are now available.

A radio pager information display has been introduced for locations where a system using data cable would be too expensive. It offers two lines of up to 20 characters, 50 mm height and with multicolour characters. The display comes complete with radio pager Motorola J39 series or RS-232 data input for connection to a pager docking station.

Platform indicators have been supplied to Tyne & Wear Metro, Newcastle-on-Tyne, UK, DART (Dublin Area Rapid Transit), London Underground Jubilee Line, Connex Rail Ltd, UK and Eurotunnel.

*Radio pager-controlled information display*   0003957

## Passenger information systems/MANUFACTURERS

*Data Display platform indicator on DART system, Dublin*  0021645

Data Display is offering a range of multicolour graphics displays. The dot size is 5 mm and the dot pitch is 7.62 mm and the displays use one LED per point. The LEDs were specially designed for Data Display and the company is offering pure red rather than orange-red. The displays are available in three levels of brightness, highbright, superbright and ultrabright. Communication is via a standard RS-232/RS-485 interface and the displays are capable of showing 1,200 pages of information in multicolour or 2,400 pages in monocolour. The displays are offered in the new curved silver profile, with hinges on the back of the housing to facilitate easy access to the electronics.

Bitmap format is used throughout the graphics aspect. Windows is used if text is required on the display. Graphic images can be taken from any source which can be saved as a bitmap file including scanned photographs Internet, video and from other Windows- based packages such as CorelDraw® or Paintbrush.

An LED display with 18 mm-high characters is available in modules of five lines of 20 characters, up to a maximum size of 20 lines, 100 characters. Red and green characters are available in high-bright LEDs.

## DHJ Media AB

Box 3422, SE-103 68, Stockholm, Sweden
Tel: (+46 8) 58 77 15 00   Fax: (+46 8) 58 77 15 01
e-mail: info@dhj.com
Web: http://www.dhj.com

**Key personnel**
Chairman: Soren Gyll
Managing Director: Per Johnsson
Director Sales and Marketing: Johan Hård

**Products**
Outdoor Evolution digital information and advertising system.
Recent contracts include the provision of Outdoor Evolution systems for Arlanda Express, Stockholm and London Underground, UK.

## ELNO

ELNO SN
17 rue Jean Pierre Timbaud, F-95100 Argenteuil, France
Tel: (+33 1) 39 98 44 44   Fax: (+33 1) 39 98 44 46
e-mail: sales@elno.fr

**Key personnel**
See entry in *Passenger coach equipment* section.

**Products**
Audio and video systems for passenger vehicles.

## Ferrograph

New York Way, New York Industrial Park, Newcastle upon Tyne NE27 0QF, UK
Tel: (+44 191) 280 88 00   Fax: (+44 191) 280 88 10
e-mail: ferrograph@ferrograph.com
Web: http://www.ferrograph.com

**Key personnel**
Managing Director: Tom Batey
Sales Manager, Ground Transport: Brian Lowing

**Products**
Passenger information displays, LED, LCD, CRT monitor and plasma technologies.
Recent contracts include supply and installation of main departure board at London Marylebone station, 1997; supply of LED platform displays for Thames Trains, UK, 1998, supply, installation and commissioning and maintenance of complete CIS system at London Paddington station comprising over 150 plasma displays, 1998/99; supply of plasma displays for WAGN network (based on London and suburbs) 1999 and supply of 26 plasma and LED displays for London Bridge station to show next train to over 250 destinations, 1999.

*UPDATED*

## Firema Trasporti SpA

c/o I D P Milano Fiorenza, Via Triboniano, 220 I-20156, Milan, Italy
Tel: (+39 02) 23 02 02 23   Fax: (+39 02) 23 02 02 34
e-mail: firema.com@firema.it
Web: http://www.firema.it

**Key personnel**
See entry in *Locomotives and powered/non-powered passenger vehicles* section.

**Products**
Onboard computers; automatic voice announcement of next stop, public address for buses and trains.

*NEW ENTRY*

## Focon Electronic Systems A/S

PO Box 269, Damvang DK-6400 Sønderborg, Denmark
Tel: (+45) 73 42 25 00   Fax: (+45) 73 42 25 01
e-mail: focon@focon,com
Web: http://www.focon.com

**Key personnel**
Managing Director: Henrik Raunkjeer
Senior Managers
   Sales, Marketing and PR: Niels-Henrik Hedegaard
   Purchasing: Birgit E Bader
   Research and Development Manager:
      Per Viggo Rasmussen

**Products**
Audio-visual and communication systems for onboard applications, passenger entertainment systems, public address, alarm, crew communications and talk-back systems, automatic seat reservation systems. Video surveillance and full-colour graphic displays.

**Contracts**
Recent contracts include: internal and external information displays, PA with digital voice announcer, passenger emergency talkback system, cab alarm system and crew communication have been supplied to Alstom for London Underground Jubilee Line trains, to Siemens for 112 Copenhagen S-Bane trains, for Penduloso trains in Lisbon, to SL Stockholm for tramcars and for Copenhagen Öresund Train Unit including GPS positioning, train radio communication and luggage racks.

*UPDATED*

## GAI-Tronics Ltd

Brunel Drive, Stretton Business Park, Burton on Trent DE13 0BZ, UK
Tel: (+44 1283) 50 05 00   Fax: (+44 1283) 50 04 00
e-mail: sales@gai-tronics.co.uk
Web: http://www.gai-tronics.co.uk

**Key personnel**
See entry in *Passenger coach equipment* section.

**Other offices**
GAI-Tronics Corporation, USA
Tel: (+1 610) 777 13 74   Fax: (+1 610) 775 65 40
Web: http://www.gai-tronics.com

GAI-Tronics Srl, Italy
Tel: (+39 02) 48 60 14 60   Fax: (+39 02) 458 56 25

GAI-Tronics Corporation, Malaysia
Tel: (+60 3) 637 60 91   Fax: (+60 3) 638 60 93

**Background**
GAI-Tronics Limited was established in 1964 to provide communications equipment to the mining industry. It has now expanded into the provision of specialised communications equipment for road and rail transportation industries.

**Products**
Help point telephone: hands-free use, weather and vandal resistant. Allows easy access to information or emergency assistance. Option for remote monitoring, programming and maintenance. Information point: column containing both information and emergency line access, and public address facility. Remote programming and monitoring option.

*UPDATED*

## Gorba AG

Sandackerstrasse, CH-9245 Oberbüren, Switzerland
Tel: (+41 71) 955 74 74   Fax: (+44 71) 951 96 74
e-mail: info@gorba.com
Web: http://www.gorba.com

**Key personnel**
Administration: Cornelia Eberli

## MANUFACTURERS/Passenger information systems

**Subsidiary company**
Gorba GmbH
Rauentalerstrasse 22/1, D-76437 Rastatt, Germany
Tel: (+49 7222) 50 66 77   Fax: (+49 7222) 50 66 70
e-mail: kobus@gorba.de
Web: http://www.gorba.de

**Products**
Audio and visual passenger information systems including dot matrix, LED, LCD, roller-blind, Gorbainfo mobile information signs, Gorbastop in-vehicle signs, radio-synchronised clocks, Gorbaplan roller-blind/LCD variable route displays and Gorbaterm variable information indicator systems for stationary applications.

*UPDATED*

## Halo

The Halo Company (Sussex) Ltd
Osborne House, Station Road, Burgess Hill RH15 9EN, UK
Tel: (+44 1444) 24 77 17   Fax: (+44 1444) 87 02 20
e-mail: halo.co@btinternet.com

**Key personnel**
Managing Director: Peter Low
Sales Director: John Veasey
Commercial Director: Bob King

**Products**
Livery for rail rolling stock (passenger and freight), internal and external signs and notices; station nameplates and signing.

Contracts in the UK include manufacture and application of livery to 73 four-car emus for Great Eastern Railway; manufacture and application of livery to 30 four-car emus for Connex South Eastern; manufacture and supply of livery to Connex South Central; manufacture and supply of Thameslink livery for Wessex Traincare; supply of decals and notices for South West Trains; supply of decals for power cars and passenger cars for Great Western; ScotRail decals and notices for Railcare Ltd; supply of Midland Mainline decals to Adtranz; supply of Virgin Decals to Bombardier Transportation; supply of livery for English Welsh & Scottish Railway; supply of livery and notices for Silverlink.

## HPW

Häni-Prolectron AG
Industriestr, CH-9552 Bronschhofen, Switzerland
Tel: (+41 71) 913 73 73   Fax: (+41 71) 913 73 74
e-mail: info@hpw.siemens.ch

**Key personnel**
Chief Executive Officer, Senior Management:
  Hess Hansjörg
Managing Director, Senior Management (sales):
  Schär Hans-Peter
Managing Director, Senior Management:
  Voegeli Beat

**Products**
ALVC systems, integrated planning software, onboard computers, radio and wayside equipment, dynamic passenger information systems, traffic signal pre-emption systems, mobile fare management systems; electronic components for local and long-distance transport.

System consulting, system integration, project management, integration and support, commissioning, maintenance and training/instruction.

## ICL

Eskdale Road, Winnersh, Wokingham RG41 5TT, UK
Tel: (+44 1189) 63 44 96   Fax: (+44 1189) 63 44 07

**Key personnel**
Sales Manager, Rail: Gary Mills

**Products**
Passenger information systems using Fujitsu plasma screen technology.

## Info Systems GmbH

Uellendahler Strasse 437, D-42109 Wuppertal, Germany
Tel: (+49 202) 709 50   Fax: (+49 202) 709 51 02
e-mail: info@wtal.infosystem.de
Web: http://www.infosystems.de

**Key personnel**
Managing Directors: F Khavand, K Bämer
Sales Manager: H Spahn
Export Sales Manager: M Scharowsky

**Background**
Info Systems is a member of the Schaltbau Group.

**Products**
Passenger information systems for buses and trains; components for suburban road and rail traffic systems.

The FZG 400 remote-control unit generates, stores and transmits data for the information of driver, passengers and ground-based central control. It can be operated either as an autonomous control and information system or as part of a computer-controlled central control system. Separate input and output channels are available for data exchange and the vehicle bus for flow of data inside the vehicle.

The company's LED full-matrix indicator for vehicle interior display of stopping points allows 98 items of information with a total of 2,040 letters. The unit is supplied with the names of stopping points via an IBIS remote-control unit.

Units have been supplied to DB AG, Belgium (Brussels metro and De Lijn, Antwerp).

## Inova Corporation

110 Avon Street, Charlottesville Virginia 22902, USA
Tel: (+1 434) 817 80 00   Fax: (+1 434) 817 80 02
e-mail: info@inova.corp.com

**UK office**
City Tower, Level 4, 40 Basinghall Street, London EC2V 5DE, UK

**Products**
Provision of station systems and displays to Metropolitan Transit Authorities in the USA, with installations including Los Angeles, Philadelphia, Boston, St Louis, Atlanta and Washington DC.

*NEW ENTRY*

## Interalia

4110-79th Street NW, Calgary, Alberta, Canada T3B 5C2
Tel: (+1 403) 288 27 06   Fax: (+1 403) 288 59 35
e-mail: bcormack@interalia.ca
Web: http://www.interalia.com

**Key personnel**
President and Chief Executive Officer: John Trester
Chief Financial Officer: Garth Hunter
Chief Operations Officer and Manager Special Products including Transportation Division: Robert Cormack

**Subsidiaries**
Interalia Communications Inc, USA
Interalia Communications Ltd, Europe, Middle East and Africa

**Products**
Passenger information systems including onboard and platform announcers:

*Transit voice* - platform digital voice announcement system
*Trouncer* – onboard and platform announcer/sign controller
*Commander* – platform announcer and sign controller offering full live broadcast and local recording capability.
Vehicle monitoring:
*Transit Owl* - for monitoring train equipment and security in remote waysides.

Contracts include supply of Transit voice to London Underground. Trouncer to Calgary Transit, BC Rapid Transit Company Limited, Ferrograph Signs, Trak Com Wireless, Bombardier Transportation, Geo Focus LLC, Data Display Co Ltd. Commander to London Underground, Oxford Circus and Bank/Monument, Gloucester Road, South Kensington, Russell Square and Embankment and in 2002, Earl's Court, East Ham and Fulham Broadway.

*UPDATED*

## IVS Insta Visual Solutions

Sarankulmankatu 20, FIN-33900 Tampere, Finland
Tel: (+358 3) 265 91 11   Fax: (+358 3) 265 96 20
e-mail: IVS@insta.fi
Web: http://www.insta.fi

**Key personnel**
Business Development Manager: Markku Tapio

**Subsidiary companies**

*UK*
IVS UK
160 High Street, Broadstairs CT10 1JA
Tel: (+44 1843) 86 38 10   Fax: (+44 1843) 86 92 95
e-mail: stephen.king@ivsuk.co.uk
Web: http://www.insta.fi

*Switzerland*
Insta Visual Solutions (Switzerland) GmbH
Schulhausstrasse 21, CH-6318 Walchwil
Tel: (+41 41) 759 02 72   Fax: (+41 41) 759 02 71
e-mail: IVS@insta.fi
Web: http://www.insta.fi

**Background**
Insta Visual Solutions is a member of the Instrumentointi Group.

**Products**
Video and entertainment systems, passenger announcement systems, crew communication systems, internal and external displays.

**Contracts**
Include: bodyside and interior information displays, entertainment system and automatic audio information system for ICS double-deck intercity coaches supplied by Talgo to VR-Group, Finland; exterior bodyside information displays for Virgin UK West Coast Pendolino trainsets supplied by Alstom; entertainment systems for Pendolino trainsets supplied to VR-Group by Fiat/Transtech and by Alstom.

*UPDATED*

## Jasmin Electronics

Sellers Wood Drive, Bulwell, Nottingham NG6 8UX, UK
Tel: (+44 115) 165 165   Fax: (+44 115) 927 86 14
e-mail: enquiry@jasmin.plc.uk

**Products**
Passenger information systems for on and off-train use, including front-of-train and internal information displays, closed-circuit television, audio systems, full train management systems and on-station passenger information systems.

## KRONE-REW GmbH

Knorrstrasse 119, D-80807 Munich, Germany
Tel: (+49 89) 351 80 39   Fax: (+49 89) 354 19 45

**Key personnel**
Board of Directors: Hans-Dieter Grunwald,
  Hans-Karl Mucha, Leo Meyboom

**Principal subsidiaries**
KRONE (Australia) Tech Pty Ltd
POB 335, Wyong, New South Wales 2259, Australia

**KRONE (UK) Tech Ltd**

Runnings Road, Kingsditch Trading Estate, Cheltenham GL51 9NQ, UK
KRONE GmbH
Kroneplatz, A-2521 Truman/NÖ, Austria

**Products**

Passenger information and advertising signage systems, split flaps, video, LCD, automatic control and specialised interfaces. Passenger information systems are installed at railway stations in Austria, Denmark, Finland, Germany, Italy, Netherlands, Norway, Spain, Sweden and the UK. The company developed a liquid crystal transflective display for use on board the DD-IRM and SM 90 trainsets for NS.

## LTS

Linné Trafiksystem AB
FO Petersons gata 28, SE-412 31 Västra Frölanda, Sweden
Tel: (+46 31) 89 69 60  Fax: (+46 31) 49 44 65
Web: http://www.linnedata.se

**Key personnel**

Managing Director: Bengt Rodung
Sales Director: Stefan Bertling

**Products**

Turnkey supplier of intelligent passenger information systems.

The Linaria/Dynamite system has been installed in 30 cities. Passenger information systems have been supplied to SL Stockholm and Gothenberg local operators.

## Lumino Licht Elektronik GmbH

Oppumer Strasse 81, D-47799 Krefeld, Germany
Tel: (+49 2151) 819 60  Fax: (+49 2151) 81 86 59
Web: http://www.lumino.de

**Products**

Dynamic LED-based passenger information systems for station platforms and tram stops. Displays can be configured to show text, graphics and logos and are produced to display images in green, red and yellow and at variable levels of brightness. Formats include single- or double-sided and single- or multiline displays. Dynamic audio announcements and clock systems can also be integrated with the systems, which are supplied with all software and hardware.

*NEW ENTRY*

## Mattig-Schauer GmbH

Matznergasse 34, A-1141 Vienna, Austria
Tel: (+43 1) 78 97 98 90  Fax: (+43 1) 78 97 98 92 39
e-mail: sales@schauer.at

**Key personnel**

International Sales Manager: Ing Larcher Ralf
Deputy Manager: Ing Stockner Karl
General Manager: Dr Mantler

**Works address**

Lutzowgasse 12, A-1140 Vienna, Austria

**Products**

Time display systems, clock systems; automatic announcment systems for stations and trains; voice logging systems for emergency calls.

## Meister Electronic GmbH

Kölner Strasse 37, (PO Box 903160, D-51124, Cologne) D-51149 Cologne, Germany
Tel: (+49 2203) 17 01 20  Fax: (+49 2203) 17 01 30
e-mail: customerrelations@meisterelectronics.com
Web: http://www.meisterelectronics.com

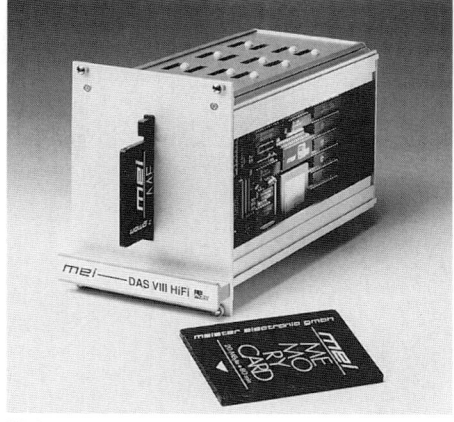

*Meister digital announcement system* 0021646

**Key personnel**

CEO: Fritz E Meister

**Subsidiaries**

Meister Electronic GmbH Systemtechnik, Brieselang, Germany
Meister Electronic Inc, Tampa, Florida, USA

**Products**

On-board information displays; digital announcement systems; video surveillance systems.

## Metra Blansko AS

Hybešova 53, CZ-678 23 Blansko, Czech Republic
Tel: (+420 506) 49 41 15  Fax: (+420 506) 49 41 45
Web: http://www.metra.cz

**Products**

On-train interior and exterior dot matrix and LED display systems.

**Contracts**

Include provision of information systems for Czech Railways Class 471 double-deck emu vehicles and for new metro cars for Prague.

## Mitron Oy

PO Box 113, Tiilenyojankatu 5, FIN-30101 Forssa, Finland
Tel: (+358 3) 424 04 00  Fax: (+358 3) 435 53 21
e-mail: feedback@Mitron.fi
Web: http://www.mitron.fi

**Key personnel**

Director: Heino Ruottinen
Project Manager: Kimmo Ylander

**Products**

Optical information systems for buses and trains including LCD, mosaic, dot-matrix and LCD-mosaic displays; platform and station displays.

Customers include VR Finland, Helsinki City Tram department.

## Morio Denki

Morio Denki Co Ltd
34-1 Tateishi 4-chome, Katsushika-ku, Tokyo 124-0012, Japan
Tel: (+81 3) 36 91 31 81  Fax: (+81 3) 36 92 13 33

**Key personnel**

See entry in *Electric traction equipment* section.

**Products**

Information systems featuring LED, liquid crystal and plasma display. Train destination displays.

Recent contracts include the supply of passenger information systems for JR Central's Series 300 Shinkansen high-speed trainsets.

## Moser-Baer SA

Export Division
Ch du Champ-des-Filles 14, CH-1228 Plan-les-Ouates, Switzerland
Tel: (+41 22) 884 96 11  Fax: (+41 22) 884 96 90
e-mail: export@mobatime.com
Web: http://www.mobatime.com

**Key personnel**

Export Division Manager: J C Zgraggen
Export Sales Manager: T Fric

**Products**

Self-setting and radio-controlled timekeeping equipment and master clocks; secondary clock systems, analogue or digital, for indoor or outdoor use; public address systems; interfaces for time and data recording by computers, ticket printers, traffic control processors and recording equipment.

*NEW ENTRY*

## Net Display Systems bv

Luchthavenweg 31, NL-5657 EA Eindhoven, Netherlands
Tel: (+31 40) 266 11 77  Fax: (+31 40) 266 11 78
e-mail: info@nds-nl.com
Web: http://www.nds-nl.com

**Key personnel**

Managing Director: Louis van Geldrop
Sales Director: Jan Kosters
Product and Marketing Manager: Arthur Damen

**Affiliated company**

Internet Display Services

**Products**

Public Area Display System (PADS). The system supports the following display devices: TVs, VGA monitors or plasma's (4:3 and 16:9), LEDs, LCDs, split-flap board and video walls. Remote Monitor Control (RMC) additional software package for PADS enabling the user to inspect what is actually displayed, obtain information about the operation of the system and install new software from a desktop PC.

*NEW ENTRY*

## Omega

Omega Electronics SA
PO Box 6, CH-2500 Bienne, Switzerland
Tel: (+41 32) 34 31 11  Fax: (+41 32) 343 38 08
e-mail: PIS@omega-electronics.ch
Web: http://www.omega-electronics.ch

**Key personnel**

Managing Director: H Kayal
Sales: A Raffini

**Background**

A member of the Swatch Group.
Web: http://www.swatchgroup.ch

**Products**

Alphanumeric and graphic display boards based on flaps, LCD transflective displays and three-colour LED indicators; video monitor network (CRT, TFT, Plasma 16:9 or 4:3); automatic public address systems; staff information systems and on-line communication with external networks.

*Model Range*
Passenger Information Systems PIS
Designed to supply information for passengers, staff and people waiting for arriving passengers. In a typical situation, the information is displayed in crowded areas by means of large boards, whereas smaller boards supply the same information at a closer range. Announcements initiated by the system are transmitted through the terminal's public address system. A master clock generates the exact time which is distributed to the slave clocks throughout the terminal and other buildings.

## MANUFACTURERS/Passenger information systems

*Omega information display on Leipzig station*    0041390

Controlling equipment is housed in the equipment and control room. Main boards are in the main public areas such as departure hall, while smaller boards are installed on the platforms. Televisions are installed in waiting rooms and other areas. The heart of the system is the central control room where the PC server hardware and software is kept. The PC server insures that the information entered by an operator via the PC network or by direct link from another system is available at all times for transmission to the display devices and other elements as and when required. The software in turn ensures that the display and other devices carry out the functions required by station management.

Omega's proposals for PIS are based on the following products:
PC network for computer centre and operators
Software with standard operating system and data file
Display boards with split flaps or LCD technology
Intelligent colour VGA/SVGA TV monitors or plasma monitors
Transmission network interfaces from RS-485 9,600Bit/s to Fast-Ethernet 100 MBit/s.

Each project is closely monitored, from inception to completion, by a project manager and quality control procedures are applied in accordance with ISO9001 quality accreditation.

Specific and extensive documentation is provided with each project. Each system can be reached at any time via modem link from Omega software engineers.

Recent contracts include supply of systems for Leipzig main station, Germany, Zurich airport main station, Fribourg bus station, several Swiss and German railway stations and many others.

*UPDATED*

---

### Optech

Lee Beesley Deritend plc, Beesley House, 8 Ironmonger Row, Coventry CV1 1ES, UK
Tel: (+44 1204) 38 11 19    Fax: (+44 1204) 38 13 06
e-mail: optech@optech.co.uk
Web: http://www.optech.co.uk

**Works address**
11 Queensbrook, Spa Road, Bolton BL1 4AY, UK

**Key personnel**
General Manager: Andy Devlin
Business Development Manager: Eddie Hayhurst

**Corporate background**
Optech is a trading division of Lee Beesley Deritend plc.

**Products**
Help points: passenger help and information systems enabling passengers to summon assistance, report a fire and ask for information. Help points are monitored by CCTV and exercised by a Man Machine Interface (MMI).
Security and Safety Systems: these are integrated with command, control and transmission systems. Security and safety systems include software-based control, fibre optic transmission and CCTV surveillance.

Voice Announcements: personal computer-driven digital voice announcements which allow pre-recorded public address messages.
Vehicle Number Recognition: recognition and monitoring of vehicles which can be compared with a predefined database.

Recent contracts executed and obtained include:
1999: number recognition system on Metropolitan Line for London Underground Ltd.
1998: number recognition trial system at Royal Oak station on Hammersmith and City Link line for London Underground Ltd; updating existing Optech CCTV security systems at Brixton, Vauxhall and Pimlico stations on the Victoria Line for London Underground Ltd; maintenance contract for Optech help points at Liverpool Street station for London Underground Ltd; number recognition system on Victoria Line for London Underground Ltd.
1997: personnel training for commercial video advertising and distribution system in Hong Kong; supply of spares for existing Optech system for Manchester Metrolink; additional lift alarms on existing Optech CCTV security systems for Docklands Light Railway; fibre optic transmission equipment for Bangkok Elevated Road and Train System.

---

### PAGE

Avda de La Industria, 24, E-28760, Tres Cantos, Madrid, Spain
Tel: (+91 807) 39 99    Fax: (+91 807) 18 04
e-mail: page@pagetelecom.com
Web: http://www.pagetelecom.com

**Products**
Integrated passenger information systems; information displays; automatic centralised public address systems; automatic announcement systems; onboard communications systems, CCTV.

**Contracts**
PAGE has developed and installed an automatic passenger information system for RENFE's Madrid suburban network.

*NEW ENTRY*

*Optech passenger alarm point on Docklands Light Railway, London*    0021647

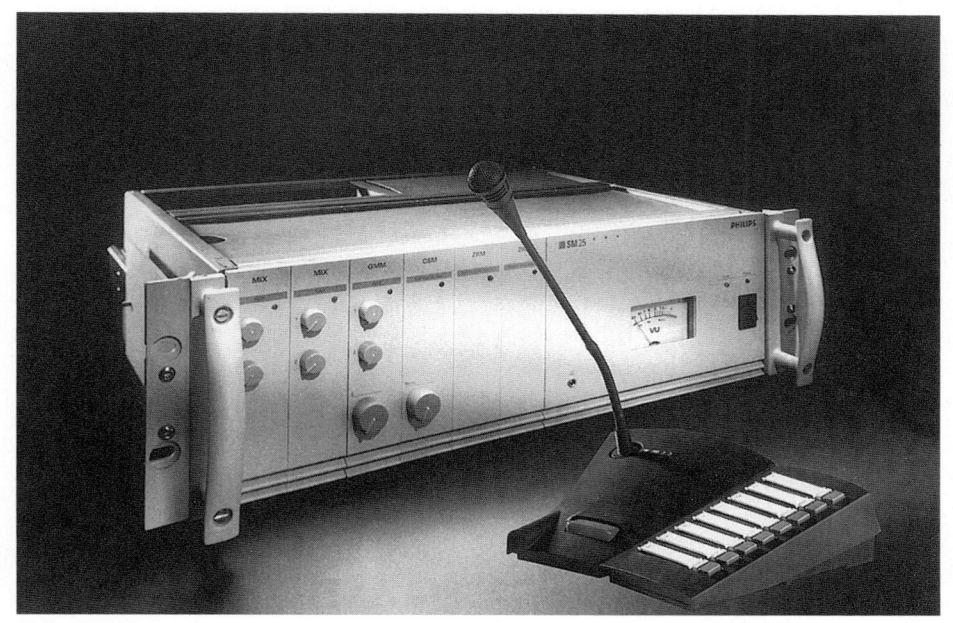

*Philips SM25B sound management system*

## Philips

Philips Industrial Electronic Services
Building TQV5, PO Box 80033, NL-5600, JZ Eindhoven, Netherlands
Tel: (+31 40) 278 86 20; 89 08
Fax: (+31 40) 278 57 36; 81 80

**Subsidiary companies**
Philips Communications and Security Systems
International Business Centre, Brooklands Close, Sunbury on Thames TW16 7DX, UK
Tel: (+44 1932) 76 56 66    Fax: (+44 1932) 78 31 98
Contact: Kevin Vickers
Philips Projects
Cromwell Road, Cambridge CB1 3HE, UK
Tel: (+44 1223) 24 51 91    Fax: (+44 1223) 41 35 51
Contact: David Chapman

**Products**
Passenger information systems
Contracts include supply of a passenger information system for the Gardermoen airport link; Philips Communications and Security Systems is producing a modular public address system, the SM25B, which is designed for railway and other public transport stations. Up to nine individual call stations can be daisy-chained to a single master call station to simplify wiring and installation. Further call stations can be added using call station extension units.

Philips Projects is a supplier of integrated systems and has installed a combined CCTV and PA system for Glasgow Underground. It has also won a contract to install CCTV at London's 19 main line stations and at Waterloo International Terminal.

## Postfield Systems

11 Bushey Close, Old Barn Lane, Kenley CR8 5AU, UK
Tel: (+44 20) 86 45 97 60    Fax: (+44 20) 86 60 18 04
e-mail: carl.littlejohn@postfield.co.uk
Web: http://www.postfield.co.uk

**Key personnel**
Directors: J F Coward; L E Hardy
Sales Contact: Carl Littlejohn

**Products**
Design, supply, installation and maintenance of telecommunication systems within the railway industry.

**Contracts**
A customer information display system has been installed at Paddington station, London. The Postfield Control System may be operated as a stand-alone system (as in Paddington) or alternatively may be operated in a networked environment.

*NEW ENTRY*

## SAGEM SA

Terminals and Telecommunications Division, 6 avenue d'Iéna, F-75783 Paris Cedex 16, France
Tel: (+33 1) 40 70 63 00    Fax: (+33 1) 40 70 84 36

**Projects**
Passenger information systems on railway stations, broadcasting, railway station resources management, real-time management, display systems, public address systems, CCTV systems, information systems in trains, passenger entertainment.

## SAIT-Devlonics

Chaussée de Ruisbroek 66, B-1180 Brussels, Belgium
Tel: (+32 2) 370 54 78    Fax: (+32 2) 370 51 11
Web: http://www.saitrh.com

**Key personnel**
See entry in *Signalling and communications systems* section.

**Corporate background**
SAIT-Devlonics is a member of the SAIT-RadioHolland Group

**Products**
Passenger information display systems under control of central processing units.

## ScanAcoustic

ScanAcoustic AS
Gefionsvej 7, DK-3400 Hillerød, Denmark
Tel: (+45 42) 25 50 22    Fax: (+45 42) 25 20 60
e-mail: mail@scanacoustic.dk
Web: http://www.scanacoustic.dk

**Key personnel**
Managing Director: J V Andersen
Chief Engineer: T Krogh
Sales and Marketing: K Mollenboch

**Products**
PA systems for passenger coaches (UIC and non-UIC standards); train entertainment systems; train intercom, custom designed and UIC standard; PA systems for railway stations, remotely controlled from railway control centres or from trains.
GPS-controlled passenger information systems.

## SEPSA

Sistemas Electrónicas de Potencia SA
Albatros 7 and 9, (Pol Ind) La Estación, E-28320 Pinto, Madrid, Spain
Tel: (+34 91) 691 52 61    Fax: (+34 91) 691 39 77
Web: http://www.sepsa.es

**Key personnel**
See entry in *Passenger coach equipment* section.

**Background**
SEPSA is a member of the Albatros Group (qv).

**Products**
Onboard passenger information systems comprising public address systems, automatic station announcement systems and internal (LED or dot matrix) and external (LED or electromagnetic) information display units.

*UPDATED*

## Siemens Transportation Systems

Rail Automation Division
PO Box 3327, D-38023 Braunschweig, Germany
Tel: (+49 531) 22 60    Fax: (+49 531) 226 42 64
e-mail: internet@ts.siemens.de
Web: http://www.siemens.com/ts

**Corporate headquarters**
Siemens AG
Transportation Systems
PO Box 910220, D-12414 Berlin, Germany
Tel: (+49 30) 385 50

**Key personnel**
President, Transportation Systems Group: Herbert J Steffen
Group Vice Presidents: Hans-Dieter Bott; Thomas Ganswindt; Hans M Schabert
Directors: Dr R Alter, M F Duttenhofer, R Grolms, H Hess

**Subsidiary companies**
See entry in *Locomotives and powered/non-powered passenger vehicles* section.

**Products**
Passenger information systems for mass transit and main line railways, including the VICOS (R) 1 dynamic system.

*UPDATED*

## Solari di Udine SpA

Via Gino Pieri 29, I-33100 Udine, Italy
Tel: (+39 0432) 49 71    Fax: (+39 0432) 48 01 60
e-mail: info.solari@solari.it
Web: http://www.solari.it

**Key personnel**
Chairman: Massimo Paniccia
Vice President: Arduino Paniccia
Marketing Director: Dino Domeneghetti
Systems Sales Director: Alberto Vazzoler
Products Sales Director: Alberto Zuliani
Technical Director: Giorgio Segatto

**Products**
Passenger and staff information display systems using monitors and display boards (flaps: LED; LCD; plasma; 16/9 – 4/3 monitors); master and slave clocks; automatic announcement systems; time and attendance recording systems; advertising display systems; automatic information systems; access control systems. Provision of systems on a turnkey basis; staff training and organisation of maintenance.

Recent contract include projects at 9 Italian railway stations during 1999-2000; Rome Termini St and 22 other stations; Paris Austerlite, Chartres, Plaisir-Grignon (continuing); New York route 128 (continuing); New York, Jamaica Station (1999) and Ancona and Pescara stations (February 2000).

*VERIFIED*

# MANUFACTURERS/Passenger information systems

## STERIA

12 rue Paul Dautier, PO Box 58, F-78142 Velizy Cedex, France
Tel: (+33 1) 34 38 60 00   Fax: (+33 1) 34 88 61 60
Web: http://www.steria.fr

**Key personnel**
See *Signalling and communications systems* section.

**Products**
Include traffic control, model networks, scheduling, equipment and power consumption control, passenger information, ticketing, simulation, high-reliability systems (Atelier B).

Contracts executed and obtained include PCC – central control stations on the Parisian RER rapid transit system for RATP Paris; PCS – public transportation passenger and staff information system for RATP Paris; 3615 RATP – public teletext information server; RIS – passenger information system for DB AG.

## Sysco Srl

Via Monti Sibillini 10, I-00141 Rome, Italy
Tel: (+39 06) 818 81 25   Fax: (+39 06) 818 60 06
e-mail: sysco@tin.it
Web: http://www.tin.it/syscoinfo

**Key personnel**
President and Chief Executive Officer: Vincenzo Manzini
Marketing Manager: Bruno Angius
Technical Manager: Romano Mariani

**Works**
Via Trento 5c, I-00040 Pomezia (Rome), Italy

**Products**
An ISO 9001 certified company, Sysco Srl supplies turnkey passenger information systems and peripheral equipment for railway stations, airports, bus stations and ferry terminals. It makes split-flaps with microprocessor control, stepper motor drive, backplane wired boards in 100, 60, and 35 mm character heights and widths with 1, 2, 4, 6, 8 modules; 40 and 60 flaps available. Standard mechanical assemblies and up to IP65 protection grade enclosures for demanding applications are offered. Vacuum fluorescent displays for concourses and metro stations with character heights from 50 to 20 mm available. Blue-green colour standard characters also available on request for ADA applications; LED and LCD displays integration.

Other products include video display terminals with normal or VGA resolution or 16:9 ratio VGA – SVGA CRT with own graphic generators; digital audio broadcast systems for large terminals or unattended stations; stand-alone or multistation software in Windows NT® or MS-DOS format; unattended remote station controllers with digital audio and CRT or split-flap display control; network master controller; time systems with master clock and slave analogue or digital clocks.

*Sysco's split flap modules for information boards*   *2000*/0092477

Sysco offers design, project management, installation and service of high-technology systems. All displays link to the central controls on serial or Ethernet LAN replacement control units and software is available for any existing PC or minicomputer-based display system.

Recent contracts include the supply of public information systems to FS Italy stations at Casale Minferrato, Chiusi, Civitavecchia, Fiumicino Airport, Genoa Brignole, Messina, Milano Cadorna, Napoli, Reggio Calabria, Roma Ostiense, Trento and Vicenza.

## Techspan Systems plc

Church Lane, Chalfont St Peter SL9 9RF, UK
Tel: (+44 1753) 88 99 11   Fax: (+44 1753) 88 74 96
e-mail: sales@techspan.co.uk
Web: http://www.prismo.co.uk

**Key personnel**
Managing Director: Kevin Lynch
Finance Director: Louise Martin
Sales and Marketing Director: John Phillips
Contracts Manager: John Wintle
Purchasing Manager: Laurence Joseph

**Corporate development**
Techspan is part of the Jarvis Group of companies.

**Products**
Design, supply, installation and maintenance of passenger information systems. Product range includes LED and LCD information signs; plasma flat panel monitors; CRT video monitor; digital clocks; electromechanical signs, stand-alone and networked computer control systems; PA/audio-visual information systems; RhinoCase environmental enclosures for monitors and electronic displays.

Recent contracts include supply and maintenance of passenger information systems for Eurostar (UK) Ltd, Railtrack and Racal Telecom and RhinoCase environmental enclosures for First Great Western Trains.

*UPDATED*

## Telephonics

Telephonics Corporation
815 Broad Hollow Road, Farmingdale, New York 11735, USA
Tel: (+1 631) 549 60 62   Fax: (+1 631) 549 60 18

**Key personnel**
See entry in *Passenger coach equipment* section.

**Products**
Integrated digital communications systems for rail vehicles, including public address, passenger/crew intercom, automated announcements, radio communications. Other products include passenger entertainment, CCTV and control centre equipment.

**Contracts**
Train line multiplexer, network controller and vehicle communication systems for MTA New York R142 and R143 212 metro cars, vehicle communication, radio network and CCTV door observation for SEPTA Philadelphia, vehicle communication for MBTA Boston, vehicle communication, health monitoring and vehicle CCTV for Hudson-Bergen LRVs, integrated wayside communication for Newark APM and vehicle communication/passenger entertainment for Caltrans, USA.

*NEW ENTRY*

## Thales Translink

Phoenix House, Station Hill, Reading RG1 1NB, UK
Tel: (+44 118) 908 60 00 Fax: (+44 118) 908 64 54
Web: http://www.thales-translink.com

**Key personnel**
See entry in *Signalling and communications systems* section.

**Corporate development**
See entry in Signalling and communications systems section.

**Products**
Torus real-time integrated passenger information systems.

Torus (Train Operator Rapid Update System) passenger information systems are in use at more than 700 station in the UK. A contract to equip all stations served by Thames Trains was the country's first networked passenger information system, offering centralised control and public access to real-time train running information via the Internet.

*NEW ENTRY*

## Trivector System AB

Åldermansgatan 13, SE-227 64 Lund, Sweden
Tel: (+46 42) 38 65 00   Fax: (+46 42) 38 65 25
e-mail: info@trivector.se

**Key personnel**
Managing Director: Klas Odelid
Marketing Manager: Ola Fogelberg

**Products**
TriTrans, a module-based information system for public transport which operates in real time and serves all parties

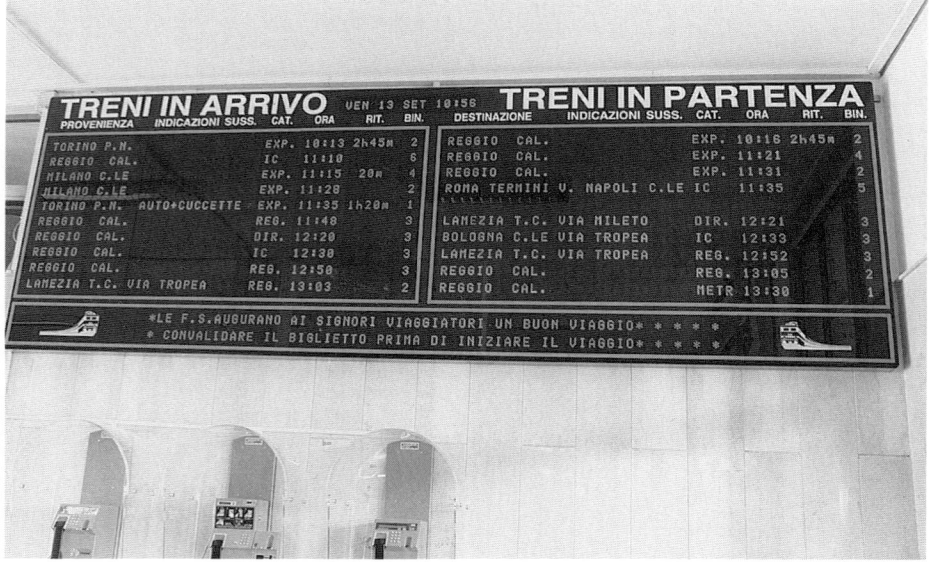

*Sysco vacuum fluorescent technology board*   0021649

involved such as planners, dispatchers, drivers and passengers. TriTrans is based on a network of on-board vehicle computers and a traffic control centre where information is stored and processed to provide the different user group with the most reliable information.

*UPDATED*

## Vaughan Harmon Systems Ltd

The Maltings, Hoe Lane, Ware SG12 9LR, UK
Tel: (+44 1920) 44 33 00    Fax: (+44 1920) 46 07 02
e-mail: sales@vaughanharmon.com
Web: http://www.vaughanharmon.com

**Head office**
Harmon Industries Inc
Blue Springs, Missouri, USA

**Key personnel**
See entry in *Signalling and communications systems* section.

**Products**
Passenger information systems; train reporting systems; staff information systems; timetable creation and control systems.

## Velec SA

278 chaussée Fernand Forest, PO Box 6303, F-59203 Tourcoing, France
Tel: (+33 3) 20 25 77 00    Fax: (+33 3) 20 25 77 55

**Key personnel**
Commercial Director: J Apruzzese
Marketing Manager: D Knockaert
Railway Sales Manager: M A Balut

**Products**
Onboard public address systems, destination indicators, digital announcement systems, LCD and LED signs, video monitoring systems, alarm and service intercoms. Track-to-train transmission by leaky feeder cable. Station video and audio information systems for passengers, platform surveillance video equipment.

## Voice Perfect Ltd

2a High Street, Edlesborough, Dunstable LU6 2HS, UK
Tel: (+44 1525) 22 25 55    Fax: (+44 1525) 22 22 55
e-mail: tech@voiceperfect.co.uk

**Works address**
Units 23-24, D&R Business Centre, 2-8 Fountayne Road, London N15 4QL, UK
Tel: (+44 20) 84 93 84 84    Fax: (+44 20) 83 65 06 50

**Key personnel**
Commercial Director: Nick Hallett
Technical Director: Rufus Potter

**Products**
Digital voice announcer and voice transfer unit.
PC-DCAS broadcasts digitised announcements from the pc hard disk. Windows 3.11, 95, 98 and NT(2000) can be used and an upgraded version, PC-DCAS, can integrate with and broadcast to a timetable. 3-Factors is a software system developed for London Underground, allowing PC-DCAS to be sited at any station and relate messages.
Talk-2 is a voice transfer system which allows a conversation through security glass and it can be customised for a window surround or built in with a gooseneck cashier microphone.
Recent contracts include: PC discrete customer address system for Jubilee Line Extension stations, Waterloo, London Bridge, Canary Wharf and North Greenwich as subcontract for Marconi Strategic Networks; Talk-2 systems for 40 Central Line and 127 Metropolitan Line ticket offices for London Underground.

*VERIFIED*

## VST

Vossloh Systemelektronik GmbH
PO Box 1320, D-85751 Karlsfeld, Germany
Dieselstrasse 8, D-85757 Karlsfeld, Germany
Tel: (+49 8131) 907 53 01    Fax: (+49 8131) 907 53 10
e-mail: info@vstm.vossloh.com
Web: http://www.vst-vossloh.com

**Corporate development**
Vossloh Systemelektronik is a subsidiary of Vossloh System-Technik GmbH (VST), Kiel.

**Products**
Automatic passenger information systems based on train-stop detection. Sensors detecting train stops automatically initiate audio announcements and flap-indicator or plasma information displays. The system's software calculates options for connecting services and announces these automatically, taking into account any delays to services.
VST has installed 52 applications of this system at Hanover's main station and at stations on the local rail network on behalf of DB Netz AG.

*UPDATED*

## Vultron

Vultron International Ltd
City Park Industrial Estate, Gelderd Road, Leeds LS12 6DR, UK
Tel: (+44 113) 263 03 23    Fax: (+44 113) 279 41 27

*Flap-indicator departure display supplied by VST to DB Netz AG as part of a passenger information system for Hanover*   2001/0109478

e-mail: vultronuk@aol.com
Web: http://www.vultron.co.uk

**Subsidiary company**
Vultron Inc
2600 Bond Street, Rochester Hills, Michigan 48309, USA
Web: http://www.vultron.com

**Key personnel**
Managing Director: John Moorhouse
Project Manager: Paul Kiley

**Products**
Passenger information display systems, including 'Clearsign' Liquid Crystal Displays (LCDs), now available with transflective display technology, Digi-Dot electromechanical reflective disc displays now with Diamond Grade reflective film, high-intensity LEDs, Talking Signs, Windows CE-based Talking Information System (TIS) and plasma panels.
Recent contracts include large LED departures/arrivals display boards for Edinburgh Waverley, Scotland.

**Developments**
Vultron has announced the Ventriloquist, a new talking sign system, that translates visual information in airports, bus and rail stations into speech. Called Talking Signs, it receives data communications from the host system in exactly the same way as an electronic sign and converts it into speech using true text to speech conversion software. The Talking Sign can then be activated using devices such as a contactless sensor, a contactless smartcard or an infra-red device.

*UPDATED*

# REVENUE COLLECTION SYSTEMS AND STATION EQUIPMENT

## Alphabetical listing

Abberfield Technology
ADT Security Systems
Alcatel Transport Automation
Almex Information Systems
Ascom Transport Revenue Systems
Atron Electronic GmbH
Automatic Systems
BelBim AS
Burle Industries
BZA
Casas
Comelta SA
CTS
Cubic Nordic
Cubic Transportation Systems
Dassault Automatismes et Télécommunications
DocuSystems Inc
Elgeba
ERG Transit Systems
FG
FIREMA
GFI-Genfare
Guhl & Scheibler
Gunnebo Entrance Control
Höft & Wessel
Henry Booth Group
Hering-Bau
Howe Green Ltd
IBM
ICL
IER
Indra Sistemas SA
Intec Ltd
Italdis
Kaba Gilgen AG
Kier Rail
Klüssendorf Produkte und Vertriebs GmbH
Klein Transport
Laakmann
Logibag
MAEL
Magnadata International Ltd
Magnetic Autocontrol
MEI
Mobile Data Processing
Motorola
Narita
Newbury Data
Nippon Signal
O&K
Omron
Philips Semiconductors
Rand McNally & Co
Sadamel SA
Scheidt & Bachmann GmbH
Schlumberger
Shere Limited
Siemens
Siemens Gebaudetechnik GmbH & Co
Siemens Nixdorf
Sony Corporation
STERIA
Takamisawa Cybernetics Co Ltd
Tecnost Sistemi Spa
The Gates Rubber Co
Toshiba Corporation
Toyo Denki
Westinghouse Brakes
Zelisko Elektrotechnik un Elektronik GesmbH

## Classified listing

### ACCESS CONTROL EQUIPMENT
ADT Security Systems
Ascom
Atron Electronic
Automatic Systems
Burle Industries
CTS
Cubic Transportation Systems
Dassault Automatismes et Télécommunications
GFI-Genfare
Gunnebo
ICL
Indra Sistemas
Intec
Italdis
Kaba Gilgen
Klein
Magnetic Autocontrol
Nippon Signal
Omron
Siemens
Takamisawa Cybernetics
Toshiba
Toyo Denki

### STATION EQUIPMENT
ADT Security Systems
AREP
Casas
Gates Rubber Company, The
Hering-Bau
Howe Green
Kier Rail
Logibag
Narita
Newbury Data
O&K
Trion
Westinghouse Brakes

### TICKET ISSUING EQUIPMENT
Abberfield Technology
Alcatel Transport Automation
Almex Information Systems
Ascom
Atron Electronic
Automatic Systems
Comelta
CTS
CTS Scanpoint
Cubic Transportation Systems
Dassault Automatismes et Télécommunications
Elgeba
ERG Transit Systems
FIREMA Trasporti
GFI-Genfare
Höft & Wessel
IBM
IER
Intec
Klüssendorf
MAEL
MEI
Motorola
Nippon Signal
Omron
Sadamel
Scheidt & Bachmann
Schlumberger
Shere Limited
Siemens
Siemens Nixdorf
Toshiba
Toyo Denki
TTI Systems
Zelisko Elektrotechnik un Elektronic GesmbH

### TICKETS AND SMARTCARDS
Belbim
BZA
CTS
CTS Scanpoint
DocuSystems
Elgeba
ERG Transit Systems
FG
Henry Booth Group
Intec
Laakmann
Magnadata International
Mobile Data Processing
Philips Semiconductors
Rand McNally
Sony
STERIA

# MANUFACTURERS/Revenue collection systems and station equipment

## Company listing by country

**AUSTRALIA**
Abberfield Technology
ERG Transit Systems

**AUSTRIA**
Philips Semiconductors
Zelisko Elektrotechnik un Elektronik GesmbH

**BELGIUM**
Automatic Systems

**DENMARK**
CTS Scanpoint
Cubic Nordic

**FRANCE**
Alcatel Transport Automation
Dassault Automatismes et Télécommunications
IER
Klein Transport
Logibag
Schlumberger
STERIA

**GERMANY**
Atron Electronic GmbH
Elgeba
FG
Höft & Wessel
Hering-Bau
Klüssendorf Produkte und Vertriebs GmbH
Laakmann
O&K
Scheidt & Bachmann GmbH

Siemens
Siemens Gebaudetechnik GmbH & Co
Siemens Nixdorf

**ITALY**
FIREMA
Italdis
MAEL
Mobile Data Processing
Tecnost Sistemi Spa

**JAPAN**
Narita
Nippon Signal
Omron
Sony Corporation
Takamisawa Cybernetics Co Ltd
Toshiba Corporation
Toyo Denki

**KOREA, SOUTH**
Intec Ltd

**SPAIN**
Casas
Comelta SA
Indra Sistemas SA

**SWEDEN**
Gunnebo Entrance Control

**SWITZERLAND**
Ascom Transport Revenue Systems
Guhl & Scheibler

Kaba Gilgen AG
MEI
Sadamel SA

**TURKEY**
BelBim AS

**UNITED KINGDOM**
ADT Security Systems
Almex Information Systems
CTS
Henry Booth Group
Howe Green Ltd
Gates Rubber Co, The
IBM
ICL
Kier Rail
Magnadata International Ltd
Newbury Data
Shere Limited
Westinghouse Brakes

**UNITED STATES OF AMERICA**
Burle Industries
BZA
Cubic Transportation Systems
DocuSystems Inc
GFI-Genfare
Magnetic Autocontrol (ACE)
Motorola
Rand McNally & Co

## Abberfield Technology

Abberfield Technology Pty Ltd
32 Cross Street, Brookvale, New South Wales 2100, Australia
Tel: (+61 2) 99 39 28 44   Fax: (+61 2) 99 38 34 62

**Key personnel**
Managing Director: John M Colyer
Finance Director: John J James

**UK Technical Support Office**
Abberfield (Europe) Ltd
4 Andover Street, Sheffield S3 9EG
Tel: (+44 114) 272 71 08   Fax: (+44 114) 272 71 08

**Products**
Ticket vending machines and ticket validators; design and manufacture of ticketing systems.

---

## ADT Security Systems

Systems Group, Titan House, 184-192 Bermondsey Street, London SE1 3TQ, UK
Tel: (+44 20) 74 07 97 41   Fax: (+44 20) 74 07 16 93

**Key personnel**
Systems Sales Consultant: Pat Meacle
Railway Systems Group
4 Bloomsbury Square, London WC1A 2RL, UK
Tel: (+44 20) 72 42 88 55   Fax: (+44 20) 78 31 45 32

**Products**
Access control, closed circuit system television, fire alarm systems and intruder alarm systems.
Contracts include supply of equipment to the major rail operators in the UK and to operators in other countries.

---

## Alcatel Transport Automation

54, rue Boétie, Paris, France
Tel: (+33 1) 40 76 10 10   Fax: (+33 1) 40 76 59 07
Web: http://www.alcatel.com

**Key personnel**
President: Jean-Pierre Forestier
Vice-Presidents: Friedrich Smaxwil, Gérard Guiho
Director, Marketing and Communications: Renaud Da

**Regional offices and subsidiary companies**
TAS Austria
Scheydgasse 41, A-1210 Vienna
Tel: (+43 127) 722 57 79   Fax: (+43 127) 722 36 24
Managing Director: Thomas Necker
Communications Manager: Christian Studnicka
TAS Canada
1235 Ormont Drive, Weston, Ontario, M9L 2W6, Canada
Tel: (+1 416) 742 39 00   Fax: (+1 416) 742 11 36
Managing Director: Walter Friesen
Communications Manager: Marc Drolet
TAS China
Floor 20, 500 Zhangyang Road, 200122 Shanghai, China
Tel: (+86 21) 58 36 88 00   Fax: (+86 21) 58 36 88 01
Managing Director: Guy Sellier
TAS Denmark
Lautrupvang 2, DK-2750 Ballerup, Denmark
Managing Director: Bent-Aage Hansen
TAS France
Centre du Bois de Bordes, BP 57 F-91229 Brétigny-sur-Orge Cedex
Tel: (+33 1) 69 88 52 00   Fax: (+33 1) 69 88 58 50
Managing Director: Jean-Claude Hue
Communications Manager: Patricia Huc
TAS Germany
Lorenzstrasse 10, D-70435 Stuttgart, Germany
Tel: (+49 711) 82 14 44 92   Fax: (+49 711) 82 14 68 13
Managing Director: Friedrich Smaxwil
Communications Manager: Helmut Uebel
TAS Italy
Via Salaria km 91, I-02015 Cittaducale (Rieti), Italy
Tel: (+39 0746) 60 06 19   Fax: (+39 0746) 60 04 09
Managing Director: Maurizio Polini
Communications Manager: Giuliano Cabrele
TAS Mexico
Avenida Ciencia, 1354730 Mexico City
Tel: (+52 5) 870 90 00   Fax: (+52 5) 870 90 38
Managing Director: Arnaud Lavasier
TAS Netherlands
Burg Elsenlaan NL-1702288 BH Rijswijk, Netherlands
Tel: (+31 70) 307 91 09   Fax: (+31 70) 307 92 15
Managing Director: Erik-Jan Zuil
TAS Portugal
São Gabriel-Cascais, P-2750 Cascais, Portugal
Tel: (+351 1485) 91 52   Fax: (+351 1485) 91 12
Managing Director: João Araujo
Communications Manager: Thomas D'Agostini
TAS Singapore
6 Commonwealth Lane, #04-01/04 GMTI Building, Singapore 149547
Tel: (+65 472) 20 02   Fax: (+65 378) 44 80
Managing Director: Ben Chong
TAS Spain
Avenida de Andalucia, km10, 3 E-28021 Madrid, Spain
Tel: (+34 91) 795 13 13   Fax: (+34 91) 796 78 45
Managing Director: Anastasio Gallego
Communications Manager: Ramon Mayorga
TAS Switzerland
Friesenbergstrasse 75, CH-8055 Zurich, Switzerland
Tel: (+41 1) 465 24 84   Fax: (+41 1) 465 26 98
Managing Director: Kurt Bächli
TAS UK
Suite 6.01, Exchange Tower, 1 Harbour Exchange Square, London E14 9GE, UK
Tel: (+44 20) 79 45 49 00   Fax: (+44 20) 74 10 91 86
Managing Director: John Mills
TAS USA
5700 Corporate Drive, Suite 300, Pittsburgh, Pennsylvania 15237, USA
Tel: (+1 412) 366 88 14   Fax: (+1 412) 366 88 17
Managing Director: John Brohm

**Products**
Fare collection systems for metros, LRTs and buses using magnetic tickets and/or contactless smartcards, incorporating control gates, validators, automatic ticket vending machines, point of sale terminals, portable verifying units and similar equipment; fleet management and passenger information systems for buses and tramways.
Contracts include AFC systems in France (SNCF, Paris, Marseilles, Rouen, Strasbourg), Hong Kong (Island Line), Chile (Santiago metro: Lines 1, 2 and 5), Taiwan (Taipei metro: Mucha, Tamshui and Hsin-Tien lines), Malaysia (Kuala Lumpur LRT Line 1), Venezuela (Caracas metro), Brazil (Rio de Janeiro and São Paulo), Egypt (Cairo metro), Philippines (Manila LRTA); contactless control gates for Singapore (North-East line).

---

## Almex Information Systems

Metric Group
Metric House, Love Lane, Cirencester GL7 1YG, UK
Tel: (+44 1285) 65 14 41   Fax: (+44 1285) 65 06 33
e-mail: info@almex.demon.co.uk

**Key personnel**
Managing Director: Marcus Burton
Sales Team: Ashley Bailey
  Alistair Aitken
  Sophie Fitzpatrick
  Claudia Johnston

**Principal subsidiaries**
Allwood Brighton Office Centre
2 Brighton Road, 3rd Floor, Clifton, New Jersey 0712, USA
Tel: (+1 201) 777 59 69
General Manager: James Meany

Almex GmbH
Kuehnstrasse 71, Haus D-22045 Hamburg, Germany
Tel: (+49 40) 66 99 22 20
Managing Director: Klaus Schiering

**Corporate background**
Almex Information Systems is a member of the Hanover-based Höft & Wessel group.

**Products**
Ticketing and revenue collection systems for railway and light rail applications; ticket issuing machines, portable ticket issuing machines, magnetic ticket validators, automatic vending machines; contact and contactless smartcards.
*UPDATED*

---

## Ascom Transport Revenue Systems

**Key personnel**
Head of Business Unit: Stefan Kalt
Marketing: Daniel Burkhalter

*Associate companies*
Ascom Autelca AG
Wobstrasse 201, CH-3073 Gümligen, Bern, Switzerland
Tel: (+41 31) 999 61 11   Fax: (+41 31) 999 68 11
Head of Unit: Christopher Franzen
Sales: Leo Muff
Marketing: Robert Engel

Ascom Monétel SA
rue Claude Chappe, F-07503 Guilherand-Granges, France
Tel: (+33 4) 75 81 41 41   Fax: (+33 4) 75 81 42 00
Head of Unit: Eric Jean
Sales and Marketing: Robert Coste

**Products**
Automatic revenue collection systems including stationary and onboard ticket vending machines, ticket office machines, driver consoles, access gates and validators for rail, metro, tramway and bus operators. Ascom's fare collection systems are designed for use with magnetic tickets (TFCO and TFC1 formats) or with contactless smartcards (memory type A and microprocessor type B).
Collection and processing of all relevant data, revenue collection in multi-operator transport networks and clearing of cash and cashless payments are covered by customised data management systems.

**Contracts**
Recent contracts include the supply of equipment to DB AG, SBB, ÖBB, NS, MTRC Hong Kong, rail operators in UK, New Jersey Transit, RATP Paris, Mexico City, Meddelin (Colombia), Kuala Lumpur, Brasilia, Toulouse, Goiania (Brazil), Adelaide, Nice, Montpellier, Porto and Malaysia.
*UPDATED*

---

## Atron Electronic GmbH

Landsberger Strasse 509, D-81241 Munich, Germany
Tel: (+49 8121) 50 71   Fax: (+49 8121) 403 33
Web: http://www.atron.de

**Products**
Smartcard terminals; AFC systems; stationary and mobile ticket machines.

---

## Automatic Systems

Avenue Mercator 5, B-1300 Wavre, Belgium
Tel: (+32 10) 23 02 11   Fax: (+32 10) 23 02 02
e-mail: asmail@automaticsystems-group.com

**Key personnel**
President and Chief Executive Group AS: Yves Peuriere
AS Benelux General Manager: Freddy Van Cauter
Financial Manager: Alain Pajot
General Manager Engineering: Jean-Philippe De Groote
Manufacturing Manager: Christophe Tribouillard
Customer Service Manager: Daniel Wautrecht
IT Manager: Jean-Luc Léonard
Human Resources Manager: Odette Ruytinx

**Background**
Automatic Systems is a member of the IER, a subsidiary of the French group Bolloré.

**Subsidiary companies**
**Belgium**
Automatic System sa
Avenue Mercator 5, B-1300 Wavre
Tel: (+32 10) 23 02 11   Fax: (+32 10) 23 02 02
e-mail: asmail@automaticsystems-group.com

**Canada**
Automatic Systems America Inc
1370 Rue Joliot Curie, Suite 712, Boucherville, Québec J4B 7L9

# MANUFACTURERS/Revenue collection systems and station equipment

Tel: (+1 450) 449 65 48   Fax: (+1 450) 449 65 56
e-mail: sales@automatic-systems.ca

Automatic Systems America Inc
180 Traders Blvd, East Mississauga, Ontario L4Z 1W7
Tel: (+1 905) 568 04 49   Fax: (+1 905) 568 99 47
e-mail: sales@automatic-systems.ca

**France – North**
Automatic Systems sa
18 rue de l'Estérel, Silic 518, F-94623 Rungis, Cedex, Paris
Tel: (+33 1) 56 70 07 07   Fax: (+33 1) 56 70 07 08
e-mail: asmail@automatic-systems.fr

**France – South**
Automatic Systems sa
ZID Ière avenue, Le Broc Center BP 309, F-06514 Carros, Nice
Tel: (+33 4) 92 08 01 21   Fax: (+33 4) 92 08 01 26
e-mail: asmail@automatic-systems.fr

**Netherlands**
Automatic Systems sa
Moeder Teresalaan, 100, NL-3527 WB Utrecht
Tel: (+31 30) 298 60 85   Fax: (+31 30) 298 66 66
e-mail: sales.nederland@automatic-systems.be

**Spain**
Automatic Systems Española sa
Calle Antracita, no 7 4a planta, E-28045, Madrid
Tel: (+34 91) 659 07 66   Fax: (+34 91) 654 23 07
e-mail: asemadrid@automatic-systems.net

**UK**
Automatic Systems Equipment UK Ltd
Access House, 58 Kepler Tamworth, Staffordshire B79 7XE
Tel: (+44 1827) 31 35 39   Fax: (+44 1827) 31 35 40
e-mail: sales@automaticsystems.co.uk

**USA**
Automatic Control Systems Inc
14 Vanderventer Avenue, Suite 105, PO Box 1516, Port Washington, New York 11050
Tel: (+1 516) 944 94 98   Fax: (+1 516) 767 34 46
e-mail: mktg@automaticsystems.net

**Products**
Design and manufacture of access control toll and security equipment for vehicles and pedestrians; automatic rising barriers, tripod turnstiles, high security gates, safety rotating drums, unguarded gates, automatic exit doors, high-speed gates, special tripod turnstiles for buses and uni- or bidirectional counting system to count pedestrians in public areas.

**Contracts**
Recent contracts include: the company supplied equipment for fee collection in underground networks in Singapore, Brasilia, Buenos Aires, Warsaw, Barcelona, Stockholm, in railway networks in Portsmouth, Southampton, Epsom, Chelmsford, Romford, UK and in the light rail system of Tunis. The installation of 200 PNG382 in partnership with Sainco Traffico for the Catalan region of Catalogne, Spain; South West Trains, London; Connex, London. The delivery of 70 turnstiles for Irish Rail, Ireland and the delivery of more than 1,200 barriers from 8 to 13.5 m for SNCB Belgian National Railways, Belgium.

*UPDATED*

## BelBim AS

Mahir Iz Cad No 17/A, TR-81190 Altunizade, Istanbul, Turkey
Tel: (+90 216) 343 48 38
Fax: (+90 216) 343 48 38; 391 88 22
e-mail: akazok@be/bim.com.tr
Web: http://www.ibb.gov.tr
http://www.belbim.com.tr

**Key personnel**
General Manager: Ahmet Kazokoglu
Project Co-ordinator: Hatice Gonul

**Background**
BelBim is affiliated to Istanbul Municipalty and was established in 1987.

*AKBIL ticket machine from BelBim*   2000/0085460

**Products**
Advice on design, development, production of electronic and computer automation projects, traffic signalling equipment and other utility issues for both public and private institutions.

A smartcard electronic ticket named AKBIL has been developed for Istanbul. The city has 12 million inhabitants and five million passengers a day, and has a steamship, motorboat, ferry, suburban railway, light rail transport, trams, buses and private minibuses. Until AKBIL was introduced, passengers used over 45 different tickets, tokens, passes and cards. AKBIL stands for Electronic Ticket and Fare Collection System for the Intermodal Public Transport System and the project was started in June 1994.

The system is based on touch-based technology and the electronic ticket is recharged at automatic refilling machines. Each ticket has a coloured plastic handle about 5 cm long with transponder. It has a minimum operational life of six years and is water resistant.

The fare collection system now comprises:
- 3,600 validators, bus type
- 85 validators, tram type
- 752 turnstiles (seabus, steamships, subways, suburban railway system)
- 99 selling/refilling machines for AKBIL
- 68 automatic refilling machines for AKBIL
- 342 vending machines, equipped with AKBIL validators
- various station data collection computers
- transmission equipment
- database management software.

## Burle Industries

Burle Robot Access Control Hardware
7041 Orchard Street, Dearborn, Michigan 48126, USA
Tel: (+1 313) 846 26 23   Fax: (+1 313) 846 35 69

**Key personnel**
General Manager: J Kane
Product Manager: B Sparling

**Products**
Turnstiles, gate operators and barrier gates.

## BZA

BZA
Suite 230, 8466 North Lockwood Ridge, Sarasota, Florida 34243, USA
Tel: (+1 941) 351 67 97   Fax: (+1 941) 351 95 12

**Products**
Stored-value smartcards, mobile ticket-vending unit, smartcard loading terminals, smartcard reader.

## Casas

Casas M, SL
PO Box 1.333, Poligono Santa Rita, E-08755 Castellbisbal, Barcelona, Spain
Tel: (+34 93) 772 46 00   Fax: (+34 93) 772 21 30
e-mail: casas@casas.net
Web: http://www.casas.net

**Key personnel**
Export Manager: Umberto Ferrari Cassina
Marketing: Rosa Maria Casas

**Products**
Compas range of modular seating in aluminium, with or without backs, up to six seats in length. Impact and scratch-resistant material is used. Suma range in steel has seating for up to six. Units can be joined together.
Casas seats are fire, impact and scratch resistant.

**Contracts**
Provision of seating at Barajas Airport in 1997 and 1998, Antaiya International Airport in Turkey, Rio de Janeiro International Airport and Belem International Airport in Brazil in 1998.

*VERIFIED*

## Comelta SA

Avda Parc Tecnológic, 4, E-08290 Cerdanyola del Vallès, Barcelona, Spain
Tel: (+34 91) 582 19 91   Fax: (+34 91) 582 19 92
e-mail: infocom@comelta.es
Web: http://www.comelta.es

**Key personnel**
Technical Director: Mark Rocky
Sales Manager: Maria Delmar Vías

**Background**
Comelta is owned by Avanzit.

**Products**
Ticketing machines: self-service terminals, TIC, Serviticket, Smallticket.

## CTS

Cubic Transportation Systems Ltd
177 Nutfield Road, Merstham RH1 3HR, UK
Tel: (+44 1737) 64 68 00   Fax: (+44 1737) 64 36 93

**Key personnel**
Managing Director: David Rainey
European Business Development Director (Sales/Marketing): Steve Harris
General Manager, Customer Services: Nigel Bryant
Finance Director: Andy Akerman
General Manager, Systems Division: John Annison

**Products**
Automatic fare collection systems (design and manufacture); passenger information systems (design and supply); security systems including CCTV, passenger help points and radio clocks; electrical works, including power and data cables, lighting and power supplies; facilities management, including maintenance, 24 hour fault desk, management reporting and system monitoring.

Recent contracts include the supply of automatic fare collection systems for London Underground Ltd's Jubilee Line Extension, Heathrow Express and other train operating companies; security systems for LUL Northern and Piccadilly Lines, customer information systems for Thameslink and British Airports Authority; trackside cabling for Railtrack.

Currently working on the recently awarded LT Prestige contract as part of the Transys Consortium.

## Cubic Nordic

Priorparken 152, DK-2605 Brøndby, Denmark
Tel: (+45 43) 48 39 99  Fax: (+45 43) 43 38 88
e-mail: sales@scanpoint.dk
Web: http://www.scanpoint.dk

**Key personnel**
Managing Director: Claus Bording
Marketing Manager: Kirsten Joensen

**Subsidiary companies**
France: CTS-Scanpoint SA, Paris
Germany: CTS-Scanpoint GmbH, Bad Soden
Norway: CTS-Scanpoint AS, Trondheim

**Products**
Electronic fare collection systems based on the use of magnetic strip plastic cards (high or low coercivity) or smartcards (contact/contactless) complying with ISO standards.
Mobile, stationary and portable fare computers.

**Contracts**
Recent contracts include the supply of a contactless smartcard system to SüdbadenBus, Germany, in 1998 and a system of Kystpilen ticket vending machines for Swedish Railways in 1998.

*UPDATED*

---

## Cubic Transportation Systems

Cubic Corporation
5650 Kearny Mesa Road, San Diego, California 92111, USA
Tel: (+1 619) 268 31 00  Fax: (+1 619) 571 99 87

**Corporate background**
Transportation Systems is a member of the Cubic Corporation family of companies.

**Key personnel**
Chairman: Raymond L deKozan
President and Chief Executive Officer: John Lincoln

**Principal subsidiaries**
Cubic Transportation Systems Ltd, UK (qv)
Southern Cubic Pty Ltd, Australia
Cubic Transportation Systems Far East Ltd, Hong Kong
CTS Scanpoint Technology A/S, Denmark (qv)

**Products**
Design, manufacture, installation and maintenance of automatic fare collection systems for public transport, including software and systems integration. Products include all components and subsystems such as ticket vending machines, onboard ticket issuing equipment, entry/exit gates, data acquisition and analysis systems, as well as development and implementation of contactless smartcard technology for advanced fare collection applications.

**Contracts**
Contracts include the supply of automatic fare collection equipment to Atlanta, Bangkok, Chicago, Hong Kong, London, Miami, New York, Singapore, Sydney, Washington DC and, recently, to Guangzhou and Shanghai. In 1998 a US$1.7 billion contract was awarded to the TranSys consortium, in which CTS is a major shareholder, for the London Transport Prestige project, LT's upgrade of ticketing and revenue collection systems for both bus and rail. CTS won the contract for the London Underground's first AFC system in 1978.

*VERIFIED*

---

## Dassault Automatismes et Télécommunications

9 rue Elsa Triolet, ZI Les Gâtines, PO Box 13, F-78373 Plaisir Cedex, France
Tel: (+33 1) 30 81 20 00  Fax: (+33 1) 30 55 19 31

**Key personnel**
Director, International Operations: M Gaucher

**Principal subsidiaries**
Dassault Electronique Inc, New York, USA
DAT Telecommunications Equipment (Beijing) Co Ltd
ICS, Madrid, Spain
Business Relations Office, Hong Kong

**Products**
Automatic ticketing and access control systems for transport operators in urban, air, sea and rail applications. Range includes ATB printers, boarding gates and card readers, self-service ticketing and self check-in devices.
The new BPR 640 boarding pass printer is designed for processing magnetic boarding passes for travel agencies or check-in desks. This compact machine allows ticket validation, reading, encoding and printing with the possibility of using three different bins for paper load. The main characteristics of this printer are its size (220 × 220 × 400 mm), plug and play architecture and easy maintenance.
The BGD 320 boarding gate device is capable of decoding/encoding magnetic tickets for all the boarding passes issued from ATB printers.
Dassault AT also offers AFC systems for rail operators including ticket vending and office machines, control gates and validators and central management systems which collect traffic data.
Dassault AT started supplying ticketing systems for RATP/Paris Metro over 30 years ago. Since then, the company has extended its market throughout the world to cities including Madrid, London, Cairo, Los Angeles and Calcutta.
Dassault AT has developed a range of contactless ticketing products which have been implemented in several locations in Europe.

---

## DocuSystems Inc

8700 Waukegan Road, Morton Grove, Illinois 60053, USA
Tel: (+1 800) 833 01 37  Fax: (+1 847) 583 12 40
Web: http://www.docusystems.nct

**Key personnel**
President, Chief Executive Officer: Thomas Breen
Vice-President, Sales: Vince Heaton

**Products**
Machine-readable tickets and tags, plastic and paper cards for transport and related industries.

---

## Elgeba

Elgeba Gerätebau GmbH
PO Box 6140, Eudenbacher Strasse 10-12, D-53604 Bad Honnef, Germany
Tel: (+49 2224) 828 50  Fax: (+49 2224) 802 94
e-mail: info@elgeba.de
Web: http://www.elgeba.de

**Key personnel**
Managing Director: Bodo Faber
Sales Manager: Peter Stegmayer

**Products**
Ticket cancelling, vending and printing machines, information displays, master control units, EDP revenue systems, special purpose machines, cashless payment systems (magnetic or smartcards).

---

## ERG Transit Systems

247 Balcatta Road, Balcatta, Western Australia 6021, Australia
Tel: (+61 8) 92 73 11 00  Fax: (+61 8) 92 73 12 08
ERG Transit Systems: (+61 8) 93 44 36 86
e-mail: info@au.ergtransit.com
Web: http://www.erggroup.com

**Key personnel**
Chief Executive Officer: Peter Fogarty
Chief Financial Officer: Richard Howson
New Business Development Director: Glyn Denison
General Manager: Stephen Waterhouse

**Principal subsidiaries**
ERG Transit Systems (Eur) NV
Leuvensesteenweg 540 bus 2, B-1930 Zaventum
Tel: (+32 2) 722 89 11  Fax: (+32 2) 720 87 94
e-mail: info@be.ergtransit.com
Chief Executive Officer: Franky Carbonez
New Business Development Director: Eddy Van Hecke

ERG Transit Systems (NA)
151 Brunel Road, Suite 18, Mississauga, Ontario L4Z 2H6, Canada
Tel: (+1 905) 890 27 94  Fax: (+1 905) 890 45 90
e-mail: info@na.ergtransit.com
President: Paul Gooderham

**Products**
ERG Transit Systems (formerly AES Prodata) offers design, manufacture and project management of Automated Fare Collection (AFC) systems. The company offers a turnkey approach to the supply and installation of a complete AFC system.
Fare collection products and systems for all modes of transport utilising all types of ticket technology including paper, magnetic stripe and contactless and dual interface smartcards.
Range includes advanced onboard devices such as ticket issuing machines, validators, contactless smartcard readers, portable inspection and ticket issuing devices; on-station equipment such as platform validators, add value machines, gate control units; data communications equipment and software; back-office software for small to medium sized and complex multimodal transit systems; and central clearing house software.
Through its alliance with Motorola's Worldwide Smartcard Solutions Division, ERG Motorola Alliance, ERG Transit Systems won major smartcard-based fare collection contracts in Berlin, the Netherlands, Rome, San Francisco and Singapore. In February 2001 ERG Limited and Motorola Worldwide Smartcard Solutions Division announced that ERG was to acquire Motorola's interest in the alliance.
ERG Transit Systems designed and developed the world's largest integrated contactless smartcard fare collection system in Hong Kong, known as Octopus. In 1997, the Octopus card was launched and at the beginning of 2000, a total of 6.1 million Octopus cards had been issued to a population of 6.8 million. In November 1999, Hong Kong's largest bus operator, The Kowloon Motor Bus Company (KMB), joined the system and in March 2001 ERG Transit Systems was awarded a contract by the Kowloon-Canton Railway Corporation to extend the Octopus System to the new extension to its Light Rail network and to Light Rail interchanges with West Rail.
In France, ERG Transit Systems has implemented over 15 new AFC systems including 1,750 in just 12 months. In April 1999, the company won a contract to provide the Spanish city of Bilbao and the surrounding Bizkaya region with a contactless smartcard-based AFC system which includes over 1,200 ticket issuers and validators. In Tenerife, one of the Canary Islands, ERG has implemented an AFC system for the entire bus fleet of the island, comprising 1,500 units. Apart from the contract win in Rome, ERG won a contract to provide the city of Aosta in northern Italy with a new AFC system comprising ticket issuers, validators and infra-red communication devices. The system is smartcard ready and it is expected that contactless smartcard technology will be implemented in the near future.
ERG Transit Systems has also won several contracts in Australia, Canada, Romania, Sweden and the UK. In September 1999, ERG formed a joint venture company in the UK, Prepayment Cards Limited (PCL), to provide total smartcard solutions for both the transit and non-transit sectors throughout the UK. PCL has exclusive UK rights to ERG's advanced software that enables the issue and management of smartcards in public transport and multi-application smartcard systems. Other members of PCL are Sema Group UK Ltd, Stagecoach Holdings plc, FirstGroup plc and National Express Group plc. These transport companies alone will account for 20,000 buses and over 2 billion passenger journeys per annum.
In February 2000, PCL was granted the right to take a Proton multi-application smartcard technology licence for the UK and Italy. ERG is a shareholder of Proton World and had already obtained licences to the rights of the Proton e-purse technology in Australia and New Zealand.
ERG's multi-application smartcard solution software will allow for millions of smartcard transactions to be settled by users and operators daily on a common platform. The software will be used in the San Francisco and Singapore projects which are being implemented by the ERG Motorola Alliance.

*UPDATED*

## MANUFACTURERS/Revenue collection systems and station equipment

## FG

Fleischhauer-Gizeh GmbH & Co KG
PO Box 100869, Kohlenstrasse 51, D-44795 Bochum, Germany
Tel: (+49 234) 45 90 60   Fax: (+49 234) 459 06 39

**Key personnel**
General Manager: Eike Betzold
Sales and Marketing Director: Wilhelm Königsbüscher
Technical Director: Klaus Hodapp
New Products, Chip- and Smartcards: Ekkehard Klysch

**Products**
Printed tickets for transport applications, including ATB format (SNCF); ISO format (TMB, Barcelona); and Edmondson format (MTT, Tasmania).

## FIREMA Trasporti SpA

c/o I D P Milano Fiorenza, Via Triboniano, 220 I-20156, Milan, Italy
Tel: (+39 02) 23 02 02 23   Fax: (+39 02) 23 02 02 34
e-mail: firema.com@firema.it
Web: http://www.firema.it

**Key personnel**
See entry in *Locomotives and powered/non-powered passenger vehicles* section.

**Products**
Automatic fare collection systems employing magnetic or paper tickets and/or contactless smartcards; integrated ticketing and station automation.

**Contracts**
Contracts include the supply of automatic fare collection systems for eight stations on Rome Metro Line A; 10 stations on the Rome Metro Line B and entry/exit gates for four stations on Milan's Passante Ferroviario.

*UPDATED*

## The Gates Rubber Co

Edinburgh Road, Heathhall, Dumfries DG1 1QA, UK
Tel: (+44 1387) 26 95 51   Fax: (+44 1387) 25 01 87
e-mail: info@floormaster-plus.com
Web: http://www.floormaster-plus.com

**Products**
Fire-safe floor coverings for use in stations, including metro applications.

## GFI-Genfare

751 Pratt Boulevard, Elk Grove Village, Illinois 60007, USA
Tel: (+1 847) 593 88 55   Fax: (+1 847) 593 18 24
e-mail: kim.green@gfi.gensig.com
Web: http://www.gfigenfare.com

**Key personnel**
President: James A Pacelli
Vice-President, Sales and Marketing: Kim Richard Green

**Products**
Design, manufacture, sales, installation and maintenance of Automatic Fare Collection (AFC) systems. GFI's fare collection products include: electronic validating and registering fareboxes; electronic fare gates for underground railways; magnetic card processing systems; electronic smartcard processing systems; passenger processing systems; revenue vaults; ticket and token vending equipment; data collection and reporting systems. GFI's line of audio equipment and systems provide automated stop announcement systems.

Contracts: GFI's fare collection systems are installed in over 200 cities across North America and are in use at more than 85 per cent of the largest North American transit agencies. Over 40,000 electronic registering fareboxes are in service at major transit bus operations; also automatic faregates and vending equipment are installed in many of the largest rail (subway) systems in the US.

GFI has supplied fare collection equipment and systems to major US transit agencies in cities including Atlanta, Boston, Chicago, Cincinnati, Cleveland, Columbus, Dallas, Denver, Detroit, Kansas City, Los Angeles, Louisville, Memphis, Miami, Milwaukee, Minneapolis, New Jersey, New Orleans, New York, Philadelphia, Pittsburgh, Portland and Washington DC. GFI has supplied systems throughout Canada.

GFI Genfare's Odyssey – Revenue Collection Center is now available, a modern transit farebox, providing coin and note validation and smaller than other systems.

*UPDATED*

## Guhl & Scheibler

Pfeffingerring 201, CH-4147 Aesch, Switzerland
Tel: (+41 61) 756 20 20   Fax: (+41 61) 756 21 00
e-mail: mail@guhl-scheibler.ch
Web: http://www.stralfordsgroup.com.ch

**Key personnel**
Innovation Manager: Merckell Patrick
e-mail: mailto:patrik.merckell@guhl-scheibler.ch

**Products**
Various machine-produced tickets and ticket machines.

## Gunnebo Entrance Control

Gunnebo Entrance Control AB
SE-590 03 Gunnebo, Sweden
Tel: (+46) 49 08 90 00   Fax: (+46) 49 02 98 89
e-mail: info@ind.gunnebo.se

**Works**
Gunnebo Italdis SpA
Via A Volta, 15, I-38015 Lavis (Trento), Italy
Tel: (+39 0461) 24 03 57   Fax: (+39 0461) 24 65 23
e-mail: info@italdis.com

Gunnebo Mayor Ltd
Bellbrook Business Park, Uckfield, East Sussex TN22 1QQ, UK
Tel: (+44 1825) 76 10 22   Fax: (+44 1825) 76 38 35
e-mail: marketing@mayor.co.uk

**Key personnel**
Managing Director, Gunnebo Italdis SpA
   Division: Giancosimo Lagamba
International Sales Manager, Gunnebo Metro
   Division: Leo Detassis
Managing Director, Gunnebo Mayor Ltd
   Division: Rob Wheeler

**Principal subsidiaries**
Gunnebo Entrance Control
A/S Gunnebo Protection
Handvaerkervej 10, DK-6800 Varde, Denmark
Tel: (+45 75) 22 46 00   Fax: (+45 75) 22 50 11

Gunnebo Entrance Control SARL
8 rue Jean-Antoine de Baïf, F-75644 Paris Cedex 13, France
Tel: (+33 1) 56 61 93 00   Fax: (+33 1) 56 61 93 09
e-mail: info@gunnebo-ec.fr

Gunnebo Entrance Control
Nortkichenstrasse 57, D-44263 Dortmund, Germany
Tel: (+49 231) 518 14 81   Fax: (+49 231) 518 14 83
e-mail: schirmak@t.online.de

Gunnebo Entrance Control
10/f Allied Capital Resources Building, 32-38 Ice House Street, Central, Hong Kong
Tel: (+852) 28 82 83 37   Fax: (+852) 25 23 78 80
e-mail: gecako@netvigator.com

Gunnebo Troax A/S
Postbox 179, Kalbakken, N-0903 Oslo, Norway
Tel: (+47 22) 80 42 00   Fax: (+47 22) 80 42 01

Gunnebo Entrance Control
Fichet SA, Calle Ribas, 71, E-08013 Barcelona, Spain
Tel: (+34 933) 16 26 54   Fax: (+34 932) 32 66 97

**Products**
Automatic fare collection gates and barriers, access regulation and control systems, including specially designed automatic doors, tripod turnstile and full-height turnstiles.

Contracts include supply of equipment to Lima metro (1996), RATP Paris (1997), Kuala Lumpur metro (1997), Singapore metro (1998), ATM Milan (1997), DART Dublin (1996), Lisbon (1996-1997), Turkish Transit System (1999), Shanghai metro (1999), SNCF French National Railways (1999).

*UPDATED*

## Henry Booth Group

Stockholm Road, Sutton Fields, Hull HU7 0XY, UK
Tel: (+44 1482) 82 63 43   Fax: (+44 1482) 37 13 86
Web: http://www.henrybooth.co.uk

**Key personnel**
Director: Mike Shanley

**Background**
Formerly a division of Bemrose Corporation plc, Henry Booth Group was subject to a management buyout.

**Products**
Printing of specialised tickets and labels for industry, including mass transit.

**Contracts**
Recent contracts include a five-year deal to supply ticketing for the UK's rail network.

*VERIFIED*

## Hering-Bau

Hering GmbH & Co KG
Neuländer 1, D-57299 Burbach, Germany
Tel: (+49 2736) 272 61   Fax: (+49 2736) 272 36
e-mail: gruppe@hering-bau.de
Web: http://www.hering-bau.de

**Key personnel**
Director: Dipl Ing Annette Hering

**Products**
Seating, waiting shelters, permanent and temporary prefabricated station platforms, modular toilets for stations.

## Höft & Wessel

Höft & Wessel AG
Rotenburger Strasse 20, D-30659 Hannover, Germany
Tel: (+49 511) 610 20   Fax: (+49 511) 610 24 11
Web: http://www.hoeft-wessel.de

**Key personnel**
Managing Directors: Michael Höft, Rolf Wessel, Peter Claussen
Marketing Communications Manager: Nicole Funck

**Products**
Development and production of ticketing systems, electronic payment, devices for mobile data acquisition, internet terminals, parking systems and telematics.

*UPDATED*

## Howe Green Ltd

12 Merchant Drive, Mead Lane Industrial Estate, Hertford SG13 7BH, UK
Tel: (+44 1992) 55 43 88   Fax: (+44 1992) 58 46 12
e-mail: info@howegreen.co.uk
Web: http://www.howegreen.co.uk

**Key personnel**
UK Sales Director: Richard Centa

**Products**
Access and duct covers used in concourses, platforms and service areas where sealing and good surface appearance are important. These conform to EN124 where applicable. Also Visedge hatch covers for incorporation in the floors of rolling stock and a patented bonding system for floor covering.

These products are also made under licence by Arden Architectural Specialties Inc, USA.

*VERIFIED*

---

## IBM

IBM Global Travel & Transportation Industry Solutions Unit
1 New Square, Bedfont Lakes, Feltham TWI4 8HB, UK
Tel (+44 20) 88 18 40 00   Fax: (+44 20) 88 18 54 37

**Key personnel**
Marketing and Communications Manager:
 Richard Whitaker
Global Solutions Executive: Chris Guiya
Tel: (+1 303) 689 71 66

**Products**
Self-service kiosks for rail ticketing; internet booking systems for railways.

Amtrak USA has installed 150 self-service multimedia touchscreen kiosks in 43 stations and has an option to install another 50. The kiosks are connected to Amtrak's reservations mainframe using IBM's global network technology. This network of machines is monitored using IBM's Kiosk Manager solution.

*UPDATED*

---

## ICL

West Avenue, Kidsgrove, Stoke-on-Trent ST7 1TL, UK
Tel: (+44 1782) 78 14 44   Fax: (+44 1782) 78 14 55

**Key personnel**
Business Manager, Rail: Richard Betts

**Works**
Eskdale Road, Winnersh, Wokingham RG41 5TT

**Products**
Revenue collection and allocation systems, ATB2 ticket printers, materials and purchasing management systems, hand-held devices for penalty fares issue and other similar uses.

Contracts include London Transport PASS ticketing system Possession Management, London Underground penalty fares, materials and purchasing, strategic consulting and IT operations, Gardermobanen IT ticketing, train movements, personnel, finance and information systems; Eurostar departure control system; Hungarian Rail financial systems.

---

## IER

3 rue Salomon de Rothschild, PO Box 320, F-92156 Suresnes Cedex, France
Tel: (+33 1) 41 38 60 00   Fax: (+33 1) 41 38 62 75

**Key personnel**
Charles Schulman
President and CEO: Jean-Jacques Rochat
Senior Vice-President, Industrial Affairs: Jacques Bouillon
Senior Vice-President, Business Development and Communication: Jean A Salomon
Senior Vice-President, Transportation Industry Division:
 Jean-Pierre Sany

**Subsidiaries**
IER Inc
4004 Beltline Road, Suite 140, Addison, Texas 75001, USA
Tel: (+1 972) 991 22 92   Fax: (+1 972) 991 10 44

IER Pte Ltd
298 Tiong Bahru Road, #02-06 Tiong Bahru Plaza, 68730 Singapore
Tel: (+65) 276 69 66   Fax: (+65) 271 55 63

**Branch office**
IER China
Kuen Yang Plaza 1406, 798 Zhao Jia Bang Road, Xuhui District, Shanghai 200030
Tel: (+86 21) 64 73 83 96   Fax: (+86 21) 64 73 84 07

**Products**
ATB ticketing, E-ticketing and boarding systems.

The range includes the IER 557 ATB ticket printer. It is supplied with up to three input slots and with a front feed insertion slot for revalidation and self-service use. In direct thermal or thermal transfer configuration, the IER 557 combines high speed and printing at 8 dots/min. It accommodates multipass ribbons with self-rewinding in plastic or biodegradable cassettes and is available as a desktop compact unit, a floor stand-alone unit or as an integrated unit.

The IER 801 enhanced gate reader provides a modular and flexible solution to accommodate mixed ATB and contact smartcard boarding applications and goes further in combining both systems with customer convenience.

SNCF has awarded IER a contract for the supply of 2,450 IER 557 ATB printers. Delivery of a first range of 1,000 printers began in October 1997 to replace existing thermal transfer ATB printers. Delivery of the remaining 1,450 printers was due to be completed by the end of 1999.

Eurostar has taken delivery of IER 557 ATB printers and IER 801 enhanced gate readers for its frequent traveller programme with Carlson.

---

## Indra Sistemas SA

C/La Granja, 84 Pol. Industrial, Alcobendas, E-28108 Madrid, Spain
Tel: (+34 91) 396 73 00   Fax: (+34 91) 396 73 33
e-mail: transport@alc.indra.es

**Key personnel**
Commercial Manager: Miguel Ángel Tapia
Export Manager: Alberto Calvo

**Products**
Access control equipment for ISO and Edmonson machines; automatic barriers, gates and turnstiles; automatic ticket machines; ticket office machines; magnetic and contactless smartcard technology; credit card prepayment systems; computerised management and system control; urban, intercity and multimodal software applications; passenger control and flow regulation.

Also radio communications systems for railways.

Contracts include supply of equipment to RENFE: Madrid, Barcelona, Bilbao, Valencia y Málaga; FGC (Barcelona); FGV (Valencia); Euskotren (Bilbao); Trenes de Buenos Aires; Tren de la Costa (Buenos Aires); Metro Santiago de Chile. Also to Madrid, Barcelona and Bilbao metro and bus access control.

---

## Intec Ltd

192 Pang I-Dong, Song Pa-Ku, Seoul, 138-050 South Korea
Tel: (+82 2) 34 34 40 00   Fax: (+82 2) 34 34 41 70
e-mail: jyulbest@unitel.co.kr

**Products**
Ticket machines; access control cards; smartcard and contactless systems and machines; AFC systems.

Contracts include provision of an AFC system for metro and KNR lines in Seoul.

Intec has developed a non-touch prepaid card. It is not a smartcard but contains monetary value and has been developed in conjunction with LG Credit Card Services.

---

## Italdis

Italdis Industria SpA
Piazza Loreto 27, I-38015 Lavis (TN), Italy
Tel: (+39 0461) 24 03 57   Fax: (+39 0461) 24 65 23

**Key personnel**
President and Managing Director: Marco O Detassis
International Sales Director: Leo Detassis

**Subsidiary company**
Italdis France Sarl
82 rue de Paris, F-94220 Charenton, Paris

**Products**
Turnstiles and automatic barriers for passenger access control. Hercules tripod turnstile; security swing doors.

Recent contracts include DART, Dublin (1996) and Lima metro, Peru (1996); Portuguese Railways in Lisbon.

---

## Kaba Gilgen AG

Freiburgstrasse 34, CH-3150 Schwarzenburg, Switzerland
Tel: (+41 31) 734 41 11 Fax: (+41 31) 734 44 75

**Key personnel**
Sales Director: Konrad Zweifel
Project Director, Platform Screen Doors:
 Hans Krähenbühl

**Products**
Platform screen door systems, access control systems, automatic pedestrian doors.

Recent contracts include platform screen door systems for metro and rapid transit projects for Hong Kong, Lille, New York and Toulouse.

---

## Klein Transport

Etablissements Georges Klein
221 avenue du Président Wilson, F-93218 La Plaine, Saint Denis Cedex, France
Tel: (+33 1) 49 17 87 41   Fax: (+33 1) 42 43 99 93
e-mail: g.klein@wanadoo.fr

**Key personnel**
See main entry in *Passenger coach equipment* section.

**Products**
Turnstiles and gates for automatic fare collection systems.

---

## Klüssendorf Produkte und Vertriebs GmbH

Zitadellenweg 20 D-F, D-13599 Berlin, Germany
Tel: (+49 30) 35 48 10   Fax: (+49 30) 35 48 12 59
e-mail: info@kpv.de
Web: http://www.kpv.de

**Key personnel**
Managing Director: F Vandepoele
Manager, Sales Promotion: W Burghausen

**Products**
Ticket machines and validators/cancellers, including microprocessor-based units; counter ticket printers.

---

## Laakmann

Laakmann Karton GmbH
PO Box 110329, D-42531 Velbert, Germany
Tel: (+49 2052) 603 25   Fax: (+49 2052) 603 47

**Key personnel**
Managing Director: D Warsberg
Export Sales Manager: R Mollenkott

**Products**
Railway tickets (30.5 × 57 mm); ticket reels for automatic vending machines.

## Logibag

Centre d'Affaires Paris-Nord Tour Continental, PO Box 200, F-93153 Le Blanc-Mesnil Cedex, France
Tel: (+33 1) 49 39 32 23   Fax: (+33 1) 49 39 33 58
e-mail: mcapn@dialup.francenet.fr

**Works address**
Centre d'Affaires Paris-Nord Tour Continental, PO Box 200, F-93153 Le Blanc-Mesnil Cedex, France

**Products**
Passenger information kiosk; electronic left luggage lockers.

## MAEL

Vicolo Antoniniano 13, I-00153 Rome, Italy
Tel: (+39 06) 70 19 01   Fax: (+39 06) 700 27 11

**Key personnel**
General Manager: Enzo Cisilotto
Marketing Manager: Franco Olearo

**Products**
Automatic ticket issuing systems for ticket office/agency applications with online capability (M402 series); automatic ticket issuing systems for onboard use (M400/N series).

## Magnadata International Ltd

Norfolk Street, Boston PE21 6AF, UK
Tel: (+44 1205) 31 00 31   Fax: (+44 1205) 31 26 12
e-mail: sales@magnadata.co.uk

**Key personnel**
Managing Director: R Colclough
Sales and Marketing Director: A Laidlaw

**Overseas sales offices**
Magnadata USA Inc
Tel: (+1 732) 505 90 69   Fax: (+1 732) 505 20 84

**Products**
Magnetic strip tickets for automatic fare collection systems. These can be supplied in a number of formats (cut single, fan-folded, reel to dimensional requirement) on a variety of materials (paper, plastic, paper/plastic sandwich), including thermally coated materials. Both low- and high-coercivity magnetic striped tickets can be supplied. Numerous security features can be incorporated into the ticket design, including anti-photocopying inks, UV inks and security backgrounds. Magnadata also manufactures ATB tickets, and can supply plastic thermal material for medium- and long-term magnetic transport tickets and also smartcards.

*UPDATED*

## Magnetic Autocontrol

Magnetic Automation Corporation
275 Barnes Boulevard, Rockledge, Florida 32955, USA
Tel: (+1 321) 635 85 85   Fax: (+1 321) 635 94 49
e-mail: info@ac.magnetic-usa.com
Web: http://www.magnetic-autocontrol.com

**Subsidiaries**
Magnetic Automation Pty Ltd
19 Beverage Drive, Tullamarine, Victoria 3043, Australia
Tel: (+61 39) 330 10 33   Fax: (+61 39) 338 13 98
e-mail: info@magnetic-oz.com

Magnetic Autocontrol GmbH
Grienmatt 20, D-79650 Schopfheim, Germany
Tel: (+49 7622) 69 55   Fax: (+49 7622) 69 56 03
e-mail: info@ac.magnetic.de

**Products**
Magnetic Autocontrol access control systems. Barriers can be connected to control systems which include light barriers and readers for code cards, coins, tickets and fingerprints. Barriers are produced in a variety of versions and all models can operate in 'open' mode.

*NEW ENTRY*

## MEI

Mars Electronics International Inc
Geneva Branch
PO Box 2650, CH-1211 Geneva 2, Switzerland
Tel: (+41 22) 884 05 05   Fax: (+41 22) 884 05 04
e-mail: meicustomerservice@effem.com
Web: http://www.meiglobal.com

**Key personnel**
Industry Manager: Reinhard Banasch
Marketing Manager: Serge Guillod
Business Development Manager: Maurice Reber
Sales Manager: Ruedi Lüthi

**Associate companies**
USA
Mars Electronics International, 1301 Wilson Drive, West Chester, Pennsylvania 19380
Tel: (+1 610) 430 25 00   Fax: (+1 610) 430 26 94

UK
Mars Electronics International
Eskdale Road, Winnersh Triangle, Wokingham RG41 5AQ
Tel: (+44 118) 969 77 00   Fax: (+44 118) 99 44 64 12

**Products**
Development and manufacture of banknote validators under the Sodeco® Cash Management Systems brand. These systems are designed for incorporation into ticket vending machines.

The new range of compact high-speed Sodeco® BNA5 validators is now complete and will accept from four to 60 banknotes inserted in all four directions in which it is possible to present them. Three main products are offered.

The Sodeco® BNA 52/54 is a validator with an escrow facility for up to 15 notes, a stacker and a security cash-box with a capacity of 1,000 banknotes or an optional 2,000 note high-capacity cash-box on the latest model. The BNA product has become the standard specification bill acceptor for most mass transit applications worldwide.

The Sodeco® BNA 51/54 is a validator with a stacker and is compatible with the above cash-boxes. The Sodeco® BNA 50 is a validator only, with an optional stainless steel drawer-box with a 100 to 400 note capacity.

All MEI products are designed to offer the highest performance in terms of security against counterfeit notes and fraudulent manipulation.  MEI's specification for these machines includes a high acceptance rate over time, combined with the low jam rate, easy servicing and maintenance. The robust construction is suited for outside use and the units are fully compatible with Windows NT/95® environment for those users who wish to network their TVMs. Money collection is both simple and secure with the principle of cash-box exchange avoiding the need for contact with the cash until the box is emptied. Money is also protected by electronic security measures in addition to the more conventional locks and keys. All Sodeco® validators are CE marked and UL approved.

MEI also manufactures the CashFlow® range of change-givers and coin mechanisms for the acceptance of coins in unattended situations and the provision of coin-based change.

MEI offers a worldwide supply and service operation with 'just-in- time' deliveries and technical back-up, plus a research and development programme that ensures new notes can be accepted as soon as they are issued. MEI states that its manufacturing sites are ISO 9001 certificated.

Recent installations of Sodeco® validators include The Long Island Railroad, New York; Metro North, New York; MTA Baltimore; WMATA, Washington DC; Blue Line, Los Angeles; BC Transit, Vancouver; former British Rail companies, UK; SRA City Rail Sydney; Berliner Verkehrsbetrieb; SBB Switzerland; KCRC/MTRC Hong Kong and KTM Malaysian Railways; STIB; NYCTA; San Diego Trolley among many others.

## Mobile Data Processing

Viale Regione Veneto 26, I-35127 Padua, Italy
Tel: (+39 049) 806 98 11   Fax: (+39 049) 806 98 43
e-mail: 4pmob@iperv.it
Web: http://www.campiello.it/4p

**Key personnel**
Managing Director: Silvano Mansutti

**USA office**
7400 Oxford Avenue, Philadelphia, Pennsylvania 19111-3095

**Product**
Hand-held computer with card reader for outdoor operations.

## Motorola

Motorola Worldwide Smartcard Solutions Division (WSSD)
1301 East Algonquin Road, 5th Floor, Schaumburg, Illinois 60196, USA
Web: http://www.motorola.com
Tel: (+1 847) 576 69 31

**Key personnel**
Vice-President and General Manager: Francois Dutray

**Products**
Motorola Inc provides embedded electronic and integrated communications solutions. Motorola's Worldwide Smartcard Solutions Division (WSSD) provides complete multi-application smartcard system solutions including smartcards, application development, systems integration and operations management. The company's platforms allow organisations quickly to deploy and build value-added smart card applications in areas such as transit, access control, campus, government and healthcare.

Motorola WSSD and Amtrak have developed an Automated Fare Collection System (AFCS), being implemented with Amtrak's Acela Express high-speed rail service between Boston, New York and Washington. In October of 2000, it will be implemented throughout Amtrak's nationwide rail network. The new fare collection system, that Amtrak has begun developing, will replace the current onboard manual ticket collection and payment system. The computerisation of many tasks and the introduction of smartcards will make the system more efficient for customers and conductors. The new system will also give Amtrak more accurate and timely ridership and revenue data and will permit the sale of cancelled reservations or sale of seats of ticketed passengers who do not board the train, as well as giving Amtrak better accounting of passengers on board the train.

On Acela Express, conductors now use a hand-held device (HHD) configured with the train's passenger manifest to read the ticket barcode, process ticket sales using credit cards, cheques, cash or smartcards, and issue a receipt or seat ticket using a separate printer that fits on the belt. The information captured by the HHD will be transmitted to an onboard Computer (OBC) via an HHD docking station. Once the train reaches a designated station, the data will be transmitted to a Station Information Computer (SIC) via wireless LAN technology, which is linked to Amtrak's Arrow reservations system. When operational nationwide in October 2000, data will be transmitted while the train is in motion, not at designated stations, via a wide-area, wireless communications network. The contract also calls for Amtrak and Motorola to test two smartcard applications and eventually roll them out systemwide. In one pilot project, frequent customers of Acela Express' first-class service will be able to use the Motorola M-SmartT smartcard as an e-ticket. In another pilot, the smartcard will be used to track onboard meals on Amtrak's long-distance trains. The results of the pilots will enable Amtrak and Motorola to refine the requirements for the larger scale rollout of smartcards. Smartcards are credit-card sized devices embedded with a computer chip that can accept, store and send up to 100 times more information than traditional magnetic- striped cards. Today under new leadership, Amtrak is turning the corner to become a successful business enterprise. In 1998, Amtrak passenger revenues surpassed US$1 billion for the first time powered by the largest ridership increase in a decade, totalling more than 21 million customers and the best on-time performance in 13 years. Amtrak is focusing on growing public and private business partnerships, improving consistency and quality of service, introducing high-speed rail in the northeast in 2000 and developing other high-speed rail corridors nationwide. Motorola is a provider of integrated communications solutions and embedded electronic solutions such as software-enhanced wireless telephone, two-way radio, messaging and satellite communications products and systems, networking and Internet-access products for consumers, network operators and commercial, government and industrial customers. Sales in 1998 were US$29.4 billion.

## Narita

Narita Manufacturing Ltd
20-12 Hanaomote-cho, Atsuta-ku, Nagoya 456-0033, Japan
Tel: (+81 52) 881 61 91
Fax: (+81 52) 881 67 48 (General Affairs)
e-mail: sinarita@narita.co.jp
Web: http://www.narita.co.jp

**Key personnel**
See entry in *Passenger coach equipment* section.

**Products**
Platform door leaves.

*UPDATED*

## Newbury Data

Newbury Data Recording Ltd
Premier Park, Road 1 Industrial Estate, Winsford, Cheshire CW7 3PT, UK
Tel: (+44 1606) 59 34 24   Fax: (+44 1606) 55 69 69

**Key personnel**
Managing Director: Alan J Phillips
Product General Manager: Ashley Bailey
Marketing Executive: Philippa Molyneux

**Products**
Flexstore is a hand-held AB ticket reader, designed to read and display information held on magnetic stripe tickets and to download that data into a central computer for passenger and ticket analysis purposes. Currently supplied to European Passenger Services for that company's Eurostar trains.

Flexfare is a modular booking office ticketing system, comprising a terminal, receipt printer and ISO-sized card ticket issuer. Fully configurable to customer's requirements.

## Nippon Signal

The Nippon Signal Co Ltd
1-1, Higashi-Ikebukuro 3-chome, Toshima-ku 170 6047, Tokyo, Japan
Tel: (+81 3) 5954 46 78   Fax: (+81 3) 59 54 45 78
e-mail: info@signal.co.jp

**Key personnel**
See entry in *Signalling and communications systems* section.

**Products**
Bill changers; ticket vending machines; gate controllers; automatic passenger gates; automatic fare adjusting machines; season ticket issuing machines; multifunction booking office machines; ticket issuing machines for station staff; data processing machines; station control equipment; remote-control equipment; centralised monitoring equipment; contactless IC card systems; RFID baggage handling systems; RFID material handling systems.

## O&K

O&K Rolltrepen GmbH
Nierenhofer Strasse 10, D-45525 Hattingen/Ruhr, Germany
Tel: (+49 2324) 20 50   Fax: (+49 2324) 20 52 15

**Products**
Escalators and autowalks.

## Omron Corporation

Omron Tokyo Building, 3-4-10 Toranomon, Minato-Ku, Tokyo 105-0001, Japan
Tel: (+81 3) 34 36 72 64   Fax: (+81 3) 34 36 70 54

**Key personnel**
General Manager, Global AFC Systems Sales: H Mitani
Manager, Global AFC Systems Sales: K Yokochi

**Products**
Complete automatic fare collection systems, including ticket issuing machines, barrier equipment, validators/cancellers, and fare adjustment machines.

A contactless smartcard ticket has been developed for opening automatic gates. Lithium batteries are not used – the card has an induction system for its power supply.

*UPDATED*

## Philips Semiconductors

e-mail: info.bli@philips.com
Web: http://www.semiconductors.philips.com

**Key personnel**
Marketing Manager Transport: Walter Dulnigg

**Corporate developments**
With an estimated market share of 80 per cent, billions of card transactions and a total of over 200 million ICs shipped by the end of 2001, Philips Semiconductors MIFARE® interface technology claims to be the defacto industry standard for contactless and dual interface proximity smart card schemes.

An open standard, fully-compliant with ISO 14443 A, MIFARE®-based contactless and dual interface smartcard and reader products are available from a variety of suppliers, with an independent certification authority guaranteeing compatibility. This ensures that supplies will continue to meet the rapidly growing demands and, with its commitment to contactless smartcard IC technology, Philips Semiconductors delivers a complete portfolio of MIFARE® ICs.

**Products**
Philips Semiconductors offers a unique, total capability in IC-based identification with a portfolio covering all smartcard and RFID applications.

With MIFARE®, Philips Semiconductors fully supports an open platform strategy ranging from low to high-end IC products, thus being the first to provide all required components to set up a 100 per cent contactless ticking system. In line with the international standard for contactless smartcards ISO 14443 'A, the MIFARE® Interface Platform covers ICs for smartcards and read/write terminals: Contactless intelligent memory card ICs, such as MIFARE® Classic for contactless multi-application smartcards. Sophisticated high-security contactless microcontroller ICs for dual interface smartcards allow to securely combine contactless applications with contact ones, such as banking, mobile communications and secure network access on a single smartcard. For the reader infrastructure, Philips offers cost-effective single-chip reader ICs for high-volume applications, which are easy to design-in.

MIFARE® has been successfully installed in public transport schemes all over the world. The world's largest contactless ticketing installation in Seoul, Korea has seen more than 15 million MIFARE® cards issued to date and comprises more than 50,000 MIFARE® reader terminals. In China 26 cities run transport systems based on MIFARE® along with other systems established worldwide including: Warsaw, Poland; Izmir, Turkey; Bombay, India; Trondheim, Norway; Santiago, Chile; Sao Paulo, Brazil; Pusan, Korea; and Moscow, Russia.

*UPDATED*

## Rand McNally & Co

8255 North Central Park Avenue, Skokie, Illinois 60076, USA
Tel: (+1 847) 329 81 00   Fax: (+1 847) 673 81 43

**Key personnel**
Vice-President, Sales: M Dawson

**Principal subsidiary**
Rand McNally International
McNally House, Tring Business Park, Tring HP23 4JX, UK
Tel (+44 1442) 82 40 11   Fax: (+44 1442) 82 85 31
Sales Director: A Heseltine

**Products**
Magnetically striped and bar-coded tickets and cards, and other security printed products.

## Sadamel Ticketing Systems

rue du Collège 73, CH-2300 La Chaux-de-Fonds, Switzerland
Tel: (+41 32) 968 07 70   Fax: (+41 32) 968 08 85
e-mail: info@sadamel.ch
Web: http://www.sadamel.ch

**Key personnel**
Chairman: Roger Cattin
Managing Director: Louis-George Lecerf
General Director: Roger Cattin
Development Director: Jerôme Froidevaux
Production Director: Daniel Courtet
Sales Manager: Daniel Eberhard

**Products**
Automatic ticket vending machines suitable for paper and magnetic tickets with payment by coins, banknotes and bank cards. Automatic coin recycling and change giver units.

Automatic fare collection management system including monitoring of networked ticket vending and validating equipment.

Passenger operated automatic ticket vending machines. Onboard or counter-based automatic ticket vending machines, portable ticket machines and ticket cancelling units.

Contracts include Swiss Federal Railways (SBB): 120 ticket vending machines (counter-based with touchscreen facility); Verkehrsbetriebe Luzern (VBL): 230 stationary ticket vending machines and onboard vending machines for 55 buses and six sales points.

Transports Publics Neuchâtelois to fit retrofit stationary ticket vending machines with the Swiss Cash Card (electronic purse).

The latest contract received is from Portugese Railways CP-USGL/USGP for a complete AFC system with 140 ticket vending machines and 250 magnetic card validators.

Representationship for ERG Transit Systems for Switzerland.

*UPDATED*

## Scheidt & Bachmann GmbH

PO Box 201143, D-41211 Mönchengladbach, Germany
Tel: (+49 2166) 26 65 50   Fax: (+49 2166) 26 66 99
e-mail: Fahrausweis@Scheidt-Bachmann.de
Web: http://www.scheidt-bachmann.de

**Key personnel**
Head of Fare Collection Systems Dept: Christoph Poos
Marketing Manager, Europe: Manfred Feiter
Manager Business Development: Frithjof Struye

**Products**
Automatic fare collection and ticket vending machines for stationary and onboard applications; point of sales; central computer systems for accounting; data provision and technical administration of associated fare collection equipment.

Recent products include the FAA-2000/C (cashless) and the FAA-2000/M (cards and coins) ticket vending machines incorporating the main features of the FAA 2000 family of machines. The FAA-2000/C and the FAA 2000/M can be used in onboard or stationary applications, will validate electronic tickets and can serve as an information point. The FAA-2000/M can also encode and distribute smart cards. The FAA 2000 machines can also be used as multimedia terminals, providing advertising and marketing potential, or as an information platform displaying information on unique local events or common local data.

*UPDATED*

# MANUFACTURERS/Revenue collection systems and station equipment

## SchlumbergerSema

50 avenue Jean Jaurès, BP 62012, F-92542 Montrouge Cedex, France
Tel: (+33 1) 47 46 79 50   Fax: (+33 1) 47 46 68 66
e-mail: marand@montrouge.ts.slb.com
Web: http://www.slb.com

**Subsidiary**
SchlumbergerSema Test & Transactions
Ferndown Industrial Estate, Wimborne BH21 7PP
Tel: (+44 1202) 85 09 25   Fax: (+44 1202) 85 09 03

**Asia office**
SchlumbergerSema Singapore
Tel: (+65) 746 63 44
e-mail: schew@singapore.asia.slb.com
Contact: Sally Chew

**Background**
In 2001, Schlumberger Limited acquired Sema plc and combined it with part of its former transaction business and other acquisitions. The company is now called SchlumbergerSema and is one of two business segments of Schlumberger Limited.

**Products**
The range comprises smartcard systems and the Addams, DAC, Discobb and TVM ticket dispensers.

Addams: A multidestination ticket dispenser with an emphasis on security, since it automatically prints a financial control ticket and will not allow any ticket to be issued with the door open. Modular, it provides a choice of destination, 30 possible fare structures and choice of class.

DAC: An automatic ticket book dispenser with a dual application. It receives money which is deposited by drivers (coins, notes and cheques) and also supplies them with tickets 24 hours a day. Security is an important feature as a receipt is issued for each transaction which is performed.

Discobb: A dispenser and validator for single tickets. All parameters can be modified (ticket type, display, fares).

TVM: A ticket vending machine which is fully automated for ticketing and fare collection.

Installation of a complete ticketing solution for Tramtrack Croydon Ltd, the operating company of Croydon Tramlink has been carried out. The automatic fare collection system is based on a remote Java-server and is designed to reduce the average transaction time to less than 15 seconds. This helps to maximise revenues by reducing queuing time and increasing passenger throughput, particularly at peak times.

The Croydon Tramlink project is a light rail public transport system in the south of London linking Croydon with Wimbledon, Beckenham and New Addington. Tickets sold by the ticket vending machines will be magnetically encoded upon issue. This will make them compatible with the ticketing systems used by London Underground and local rail services.

The automatic fare collection system consists of 78 SchlumbergerSema High-Flow traffic ticket vending machines, but also includes a fibre-optic local area network (LAN) with a Java-based server for remote monitoring and control of the whole ticket vending machine network including comprehensive analysis of all passenger traffic and revenue. The LAN feeds a hub supporting communication and application servers, a workstation and printers. This system enables alarms, warnings and transaction details to be sent to the central computer and commands, operational settings and fare variations to the ticket vending machines.

SchlumbergerSema has installed some 90,000 terminals in over 30 countries.

*UPDATED*

## Shere Limited

4 Bridge Park, Merrow Industrial Estate, Guildford, GU4 7BF, UK
Tel: (+44 1483) 55 74 00   Fax: (+44 1483) 55 74 01
e-mail: briscoen@shere.com
Web: http://www.shere.com

**Products**
Kiosk systems integrating ticket printers, card readers, touchscreens, pin pads, scanners, UPS, sensors and alarms.

## Siemens

Siemens Transportation Systems
Dept VT27 Automatic Fare Collection
PO Box 910220, D-12414 Berlin, Germany
Tel: (+49 30) 386 512 46; 510 32; 513 21
Fax: (+49 30) 61 74 10 32

**Key personnel**
General Manager: Volker Rind
Sales (Germany): M Netka
Sales (other countries): J Janssen

**Products**
Automatic fare collection systems; complete turnkey systems for integrated ticketing and fare collection, based on magnetic cards and contact and contactless smartcards; system components, including smartcard readers, ticket vending machines, ticket gates and ticket office machines.

Recent contracts include BTSC Bangkok, Thailand 1997; VRS Cologne/Bonn and BVG Berlin.

CHIPTICKET contactless and dual-interface smartcard system for public transport; secure contactless card terminal.

*VERIFIED*

## Siemens Gebaudetechnik GmbH & Co

Identification Systems Group, CCTV Access Control Systems
Siemensallee 84, D-76187 Karlsruhe, Germany
Tel: (+49 1721) 595 26 04   Fax: (+49 1721) 595 28 25
e-mail: ulrich.krienen@khe.siemens.de

**Key personnel**
Principal: Dr Uerich Krienen

**Products**
Access control systems; CCTV systems for rail applications including passenger control and monitoring; SITRAIL® wireless TV transmission systems.

Contracts include supply of systems to Metro Shanghai (Line 1, Line 1 extension, Line 2); London Underground; Metro Athens (CCTV and Access Control); Hamburger Hochbahn.

*VERIFIED*

## Siemens Nixdorf

Siemens Nixdorf Informationssysteme AG Transportation Division
Lyoner Strasse 27, D-60528 Frankfurt-am-Main, Germany
Tel: (+49 69) 66 82 12 11   Fax: (+49 69) 66 82 10 60

**Munich office**
Transportation Division
Leopold Krenner, Otto-Hahn-Ring 6, D-81739 Frankfurt-am-Main, Germany
Tel: (+49 89) 63 64 48 26   Fax: (+49 89) 63 64 31 60

**Products**
RailVision integrated system for all activities related to information, ticketing and reservations. It is based on XPG4 servers and Windows® software.

## Sony Corporation

Card Systems Development Department, 6-7-35 Kitashinagawa, Shinagawa-ku, Tokyo 141, Japan
Tel: (+81 3) 54 48 68 32   Fax: (+81 3) 54 48 68 33

**Products**
Smartcard systems, including the Felica contactless smartcard system.

## STERIA

12 rue Paul Dautier, PO Box 58, F-78142 Vélizy Cedex, France
Tel: (+33 1) 34 38 60 00   Fax: (+33 1) 34 88 61 60
Web: http://www.steria.fr

**Key personnel**
See *Signalling and communications systems* section.

**Works**
See *Signalling and communications systems* section.

**Products**
Ticketing including clipcards and contactless smartcards, suitable for multimodal transport, simulation, high-reliability systems (Atelier B).

## Takamisawa Cybernetics Co Ltd

Nakano Heiwa Building, 2-48-5 Chuo, Nakano-ku, Tokyo 164-0011, Japan
Tel: (+81 3) 32 27 33 71   Fax: (+81 3) 32 27 33 96
e-mail: export_dept@tacy.co.jp

**Key personnel**
Manager of Trading Department: J Tada

**Works**
Nagano Factory No 1
525-22 Kitagawa, Usuda, Minami-Saku, Nagano, 384-0304, Japan

**Subsidiary companies**
Takamisawa Service Co Ltd
Takamisawa Mex Co Ltd

**Products**
Design and manufacture of automatic fare collection systems and equipment, including automatic ticket vending machines, automatic gates, fare adjustment machines and ticket printers; AFC-related currency and card handling unit.

Customers include all Japan railway companies and some Asian countries.

*UPDATED*

## Tecnost Sistemi Spa

Via Jervis, I-77-10015 Ivrea (TO), Italy

**Key personnel**
President: A Garroni

**Other offices**
Corso D'Azeglio, I-69-10015 Ivrea (TO)
Tel: (+39 0125) 52 00
Via T Tasso, I-19-25080 Molinetto di Mazzano (BS)
Tel: (+39 030) 212 11 11   Fax: (+39 030) 262 96 31
Vicolo Antoniniano, I-13-00153 Rome
Tel: (+39 06) 70 19 01   Fax: (+39 06) 700 27 11

**Corporate developments**
Previously known as Technotour-Eltec SpA.

**Products**
Automatic fare collection systems for rail, metro, urban and extra urban including ticket vending machines for onboard and stationary applications, cancelling machines, booking office machines, driver control units; multimedia kiosk systems and self-service terminals.

The range includes: Tecnotour-Eltec and Mael branded products; HD3 ticket cancelling machines; ECHO, a contactless and smartcard control unit; Mael 400 and Mael 400T ticket and smartcard machines; M2T ticket vending machine.

Recent contracts include: supply to Italian Railways FS and other public and private transport companies; ticket cancelling machines for the transport companies in Turin, Genoa, Bologna.

## Toshiba Corporation

Automation Systems Group: Electronic Systems Department
1-1 Shibaura 1-chome, Minato-ku, Tokyo 105, Japan
Tel: (+81 3) 34 57 25 45  Fax: (+81 3) 54 44 94 09

**Key personnel**
Senior Manager: M Okada
Assistant Senior Manager: T Imamura

**Products**
Automatic fare collection systems.

Products include season ticket renewal machine, which is operated by a passenger by inserting the old season ticket; a ticket vending machine, including change dispenser; multifunction booking office machine; Automatic flap door-type gate, available in three models: entry, exit, and reversible.

A portable ticket issuing machine replaces the time-consuming process of issuing train tickets by hand.

## Toyo Denki

Toyo Denki Seizo KK
Yaesu Mitsui Building, 7-2 Yaesu 2-chome, Chuo-ku, Tokyo 104, Japan
Tel: (+81 3) 32 71 63 74  Fax: (+81 3) 32 71 46 93

**Key personnel**
See entry in *Electric traction equipment* section.

**Products**
Ticket issuing systems for suburban and rapid transit railway systems; automatic ticket issuing machines and fare adjusting equipment.

Toyo Denki's ticket issuing system for suburban and rapid transit systems can issue magnetic tickets for automatic gates. It can also calculate fares for complex urban networks where different routeings are possible and there is much interline traffic between different operators.

## Westinghouse Brakes (UK) Ltd

Foundry Lane, Chippenham SN15 1JB, UK
Tel: (+44 1249) 44 20 00  Fax: (+44 1249) 65 50 40
e-mail: wbl.sales@westbrake.com

**Key personnel**
See entry in *Brakes and drawgear* section.

**Corporate background**
Westinghouse Brakes (UK) Ltd is part of the Knorr-Bremse Group (qv).

**Products**
Platform screen door systems. Projects equipped include: China (Guangzhou Metro, Hong Kong International Airport); Denmark (Copenhagen Metro); Malaysia (Kuala Lumpur LRT2); Singapore (North-South Line, East-West Line, North East Line, Changi Airport Line); UK (Jubilee Line).

*UPDATED*

## Zelisko Elektrotechnik un Elektronik GesmbH

Steinfeldergasse 12, A-2340 Mödling, Austria
Tel: (+43 2236) 40 60 Fax: (+43 2236) 40 62 99
e-mail: info@zelisko.com
Web: http://www.zelisko.com

**Key personnel**
See entry in *Signalling and communications systems* section.

**Products**
Ticket printers; automatic ticket vending machines; fare collection software; technology for the integration of magnetic cards or smartcards.

*NEW ENTRY*

# ELECTRIFICATION CONTRACTORS AND EQUIPMENT SUPPLIERS

## Alphabetical listing

A Kaufmann AG
Allied Insulators (Group) Ltd
ALSTOM
Aluminium Inductors Ltd
Ampcontrol
ANSALDOBREDA
ApATeCh Electro
Adtranz
Balfour Beatty Rail Power Systems GmbH
Balfour Beatty Rail Projects
Balfour Beatty Rail Renewals Ltd
Barclay Mowlem
BEML
Benkler AG
Brecknell, Willis
Brush Transformers Ltd
Cembre SpA
Costaferroviaria SpA
Crompton Greaves Ltd
CTS
Delta
Ebo Systems

EFACEC
Elpro
ENSTO SEKKO OY
Felten & Guilleaume Kabelwerke GmbH
Ferraz SA
FIREMA
Flury
Fuji Electric Co Ltd
Furrer + Frey AG
Galland
Geismar
Greysham International
Hawker Siddeley Switchgear Ltd
Hindustan Eng & Ind
Hitachi Ltd
Hyundai
Insul-8 Corporation
Kershaw Manufacturing
Kummler + Matter AG
Lerc SA
Merlin Gerin Brasil SA
Muromteplovoz

Paul Keller Engineering Ltd
Pfisterer Srl
Plasser & Theurer
Powernetics Ltd
RPG Transmission Ltd
SAE (India) Ltd
SAFT
SDCEM
Sefag AG
Siemens Transportation
Sirti SpA
South Wales Transformers Ltd
SPIE Enertrans
Supertek Enterprise Inc
Toshiba Corporation
Total Power Solutions
Transmitton Ltd
Trend Installation Tooling Ltd
Ultra Electronics Power Magnetics and Electronic Systems Ltd
Whipp & Bourne
Wild & Grunder AG

---

Furrer+Frey AG
Overhead contact line engineering
Design, manufacturing, installation
Thunstrasse 35, P.O. Box 182
CH-3000 Berne 6, Switzerland
Telephone   + 41 31 357 61 11
Fax         + 41 31 357 61 00

www.furrerfrey.ch

**Furrer+Frey**
Overhead contact lines

## MANUFACTURERS / Electrification contractors and equipment suppliers

## Classified listing

**MAINTENANCE VEHICLES AND EQUIPMENT**
BEML
Costaferroviaria
Geismar
Muromteplovoz
Plasser & Theurer

**OVERHEAD LINE AND THIRD RAIL EQUIPMENT**
Allied Insulators
ALSTOM
ApATeCh Electro
Benkler AG
Brecknell, Willis
Cembre
EFACEC
Elpro
ENSTO SEKKO
Felten & Guilleaume Kabelwerke GmbH
Flury
Galland
Geismar
Greysham International
Hindustan Eng & Ind
Insul-8 Corporation
Kaufmann
Kummler + Matter
Lerc
Pfisterer
RPG Transmissiom
SDCEM
Sefag
Siemens
Sirti
Wild & Grunder

**POWER SUPPLY EQUIPMENT**
ALSTOM
Aluminium Inductors
Ampcontrol
ANSALDOBREDA
Balfour Beatty Rail Power Systems GmbH
Brush Transformers
Cembre
Delta
Ebo Systems
EFACEC
Elpro
Ferraz
FIREMA Trasporti
Fuji Electric
Hawker Siddeley Switchgear
Hitachi Ltd
Hundai
Merlin Gerin Brasil
Paul Keller Engineering
Powernetics
RPG Transmission
SAE (India)
SAFT
SDCEM
Sécheron
South Wales Transformers
Toshiba
Transmitton
Trend
Ultra Electronics
Whipp & Bourne

**TURNKEY RAILWAY ELECTRIFICATION**
ALSTOM
ANSALDOBREDA
Balfour Beatty Rail Projects
Balfour Beatty Rail Renewals
Barclay Mowlem
CTS
Furrer + Frey
SAE (India)
Siemens
SPIE Enertrans

## Company listing by country

**AUSTRALIA**
Ampcontrol
Barclay Mowlem

**AUSTRIA**
Plasser & Theurer

**BRAZIL**
Merlin Gerin Brasil SA

**FINLAND**
ENSTO SEKKO OY

**FRANCE**
Ebo Systems
Ferraz SA
Galland
Geismar
Lerc SA
SAFT
SDCEM
SPIE Enertrans

**GERMANY**
Adtranz
Balfour Beatty Rail Power Systems GmbH
Elpro
Felten & Guilleaume Kabelwerke GmbH
Siemens

**INDIA**
BEML
Crompton Greaves
Greysham International
Hindustan Eng & Ind
RPG Transmission Ltd
SAE (India) Ltd

**ITALY**
ANSALDOBREDA
Cembre SpA
Costaferroviaria SpA
FIREMA
Pfisterer Srl
Sirti SpA

**JAPAN**
Fuji Electric Co Ltd
Hitachi Ltd
Toshiba Corporation

**KOREA, SOUTH**
Hyundai

**PORTUGAL**
EFACEC

**RUSSIAN FEDERATION**
ApATeCh Electro
Muromteplovoz

**SWITZERLAND**
A Kaufmann AG
Benkler AG
Flury
Furrer + Frey AG
Kummler + Matter AG
Paul Keller Engineering Ltd
Sécheron
Sefag AG
Wild & Grunder AG

**UNITED KINGDOM**
Allied Insulators (Group) Ltd
ALSTOM
Aluminium Inductors Ltd
Balfour Beatty Rail Projects
Balfour Beatty Rail Renewals Ltd
Brecknell, Willis
Brush Transformers Ltd
CTS
Delta
Hawker Siddeley Switchgear Ltd
Powernetics Ltd
South Wales Transformers Ltd
Total Power Solutions
Transmitton Ltd
Trend Installation Tooling Ltd
Ultra Electronics Power Magnetics and Electronic Systems Ltd
Whipp & Bourne

**UNITED STATES OF AMERICA**
Insul-8 Corporation
Kershaw Manufacturing
Siemens Transportation
Supertek Enterprise Inc

## Allied Insulators (Group) Ltd

PO Box 17, Milton, Stoke-on-Trent ST2 7EE, UK
Tel: (+44 1782) 53 43 21  Fax: (+44 1782) 54 58 04
e-mail: sales@alliedgroup.co.uk
Web: http://www.alliedgroup.com

**Key personnel**
Managing Director: D R Perrin
Commercial Director: R G Shenton
Sales & Marketing Director: M Pettigrew

**Principal subsidary companies**
Allied Insulators Ltd
Doulton Insulators Ltd
Hopyard Foundries Ltd

**Products**
Insulator assemblies for feeder transmission, tracked overhead transmission, third rail systems, pantograph support and switching apparatus.

Current contracts include the supply of overhead catenary insulators to Railtrack, London Underground (third rail). Recent contracts include supply of equipment to Hong Kong, Taiwan and South Africa.

## ALSTOM Transport SA

System Infrastructure Business Unit
3 rue Eugène & Armand Peugeot, F-92508 Rueil-Malmaison Cedex, France
Tel: (+33 1) 47 52 80 00  Fax: (+33 1) 47 52 82 46

**Key personnel**
Director: Alain Goga
Electrification SpA
10 Via Lago dei Tartari, I-00012 Guidonia, Rome, Italy
Tel: (+39 06) 0774 37 74 85  Fax: (+39 06) 0774 35 34 30
Director: Roberto Tazzioli

ALSTOM Transport Service (PanChex)
48 rue Albert Dhalenne, F-93482 Saint-Ouen Cedex, France
Tel: (+33 1) 41 66 86 09  Fax: (+33 1) 41 66 92 70
Contact: Stéphen Guy

**Services**
The Infrastructure Business unit of ALSTOM Transport Systems offers solutions at the system or subsystem level for power generation and distribution including: AC and DC traction substations; overhead facilities; contact lines or catenaries; third-rail or at-level integrated supply system; SCADA; auxiliary power supply; track laying; maintenance workshops; communications; signalling (tramways); electromechanical equipment in station; and electronic guidance systems for buses.

Its scope includes design, procurement, installation, commissioning, technical assistance, maintenance and training.

The electrification activities of ALSTOM cover power supply production, distribution and control of the traction current.

ALSTOM provides AC power distribution networks from high-voltage to medium-voltage conversion to feed traction substations and low-voltage station utilities.

Conversion is to AC single-phase current, primarily for main line railways:
- 25 kV 50 Hz for conventional railways
- 15 kV 16⅔ Hz for Rail Link
- 2 × 25 kV 50 Hz for high-speed trains

Conversion to DC current in six-pulse or 12-pulse rectification:
- 3,000 V for conventional railways
- 1,500 V for suburban trains and urban mass transit systems with overhead catenary
- 750 V for mass rail transit metro systems through third rail
- 750 V for light rail transit systems and trolleybuses through overhead contact wire.

More than 1,100 rectifier units have been supplied by ALSTOM, supplying more than 3.3 million MW.

ALSTOM provides in-line traction current distribution:
- third rail (or fourth rail) for mass transit systems, mainly 750 V.
- Overhead catenary for 25 kV AC high-speed trains, single-phase AC for conventional railways and for DC systems in 3,000, 1,500 and 750 V light rail transit systems. More than 17,000 km of overhead wire has been supplied by ALSTOM. Overhead contact lines have been supplied for urban tramways, trolleybuses or guided buses.

ALSTOM provides innovative power electronics solutions, and control systems for local and remote traction substations. The company has developed a new concept for urban light transit systems (tramways and rubber-tyred vehicles with electric propulsion) to minimise the impact on the environment in the heart of a city and to provide traction power supply avoiding overhead contact wires.

ALISS (At Level Integrated Supply System) is a hidden, reliable, maintenance-free flexible system using static safety-redundant IGBT commutation, to provide vehicles with traction power, only on adequate sectors with dynamic identification under the vehicle assemblies. A diagnostic and monitoring management signalling system ensures communication with the centralised control centre. After successful reliability and performance laboratory tests, on-site demonstration with real loaded vehicles took place from mid-2000 on ALSTOM's Aytré plant's test tracks. PanChex overhead line protection system is a trackside asset protection system that monitors the interaction of each passing train with the overhead line system. PanChex is a licensed technology from AEA Technology Rail Ltd.

**Contracts**
25 kV: TGV France (SNCF) and TGV Korea (KHRC)
25 kV: Algeria (SNTF), Portugal (CP), Costa Rica
16⅔ Hz: Arlanda Express airport rail link
3,000 V: Brazilian railways (Fepasa, CBTU), Morocco (ONCFM), Italy (FS)
1,500 V: Cairo metro line 1 (NAT), La Paz Pantitlan (Covitur, Mexico), Dublin (CIE) for Howth Bray line, Serpong and Tangerang for Indonesia (Jabotabek), Hong Kong Lantau airport rail link
750 V third-rail metros: Caracas lines 1 to 4 (CAMC), Athens lines 2 and 3, Mexico (STC and Covitur), Santiago de Chile (Metro SA), Cairo line 2 (NAT), Istanbul, Ankara, Lyon, Marseille
750 V overhead: tramways and trolleybuses (contact wire): Azteca Xochimilco (Mexico), Manchester Metrolink
Tramways in France: Rouen, Grenoble, Montpellier, Lyon, Nantes, Lille, Bobigny
Trolleybuses: Belo Horizonte, Lyon, Nancy, Grenoble, Marseille, Mexico
600-750 V: London Underground, Manchester, Hong Kong tramways, Mexico trolleybuses, New York, Chicago

**Developments**
*Modular Traction Substations*
To avoid the installation of unsightly metallic shelters in towns, ALSTOM has developed a modular traction substation, the use of which means that storage of materials on site and long construction periods are no longer necessary. Increasing worldwide demand for light metros or tramway systems, the growing trend towards standardisation of substations and the search for the most competitive overall price are all factors which prompted ALSTOM to develop the modular substation.

A complete substation is created, using production distribution and traction current control equipment. This consists of two concrete shelters easy to transport by road, each one comprising premises equipped with access doors for operational personnel as well as for possible handling of equipment. Once the concrete slab is constructed, installation is fast. All cable links are prepared for a quick assembly on site and only an easy connection to the electrical network is required. Tests carried out in factory conditions using reduced voltage, allow immediate commissioning.

**UPDATED**

## Aluminium Inductors Ltd

29 Lower Coombe Street, Croydon CR0 1AA, UK
Tel: (+44 181) 680 21 00  Fax: (+44 181) 681 15 77

**Key personnel**
Managing Director: Barry Martindale

**Products**
Transformers, inverter-based supply systems.

A power conversion system designed by R-R Industrial Controls, Gateshead, UK, has a new design of transformer to cut weight and boost efficiency.

In association with R-R Industrial Controls advanced high-density inverter-based supply systems for trains are being developed to cope with both alterations in rail traction DC supply environment and the provision of reliable power for emergency battery chargers, three-phase fan motors for air conditioning and motors for air compressor braking systems.

The systems make use of IGBT switching circuits.

## Ampcontrol

Ampcontrol Pty Ltd
250 Macquarie Road, Warners Bay, New South Wales 2282, Australia
Tel: (+61 2) 49 56 58 99  Fax: (+61 2) 49 56 59 85
e-mail: info@ampcontrol.com.au
Web: http://www.ampcontrol.com.au

**Key personnel**
National Sales Manager: John Holmquest
Export Manager: Gary Hillier

**Products**
Traction control switchgear; traction power control systems; traction substation switchrooms (AC and DC); specialised transformers and switchgear.

Recent contracts include: 22 kV DC substation for Melbourne Docklands redevelopment tram route; DC substation for trams serving Melbourne Docklands, Colonial Stadium.

## ANSALDOBREDA

Ansaldo Trasporti SpA
425 Via Argine, I-80147 Naples, Italy
Tel: (+39 081) 243 11 11  Fax: (+39 081) 243 26 98

**Key personnel**
See entry in *Locomotives and powered/non-powered passenger vehicles* section.

*Ampcontrol equipment in transit*  2000/0092274

# MANUFACTURERS/Electrification contractors and equipment suppliers

## Products
AC and DC electrification systems with centralised control; high-speed circuit breakers; rectifiers; static converters for AC and DC substations; design, supply and erection of feeder lines and substations; electronic converters and controls, auxiliary apparatus; sales, installation, start-up and servicing.

## ApATeCh Electro

Zhukovsky Street 2, Building 131, Dubna, 141980 Moscow Region, Russian Federation
Tel: (+7 09621) 257 92   Fax: (+7 09621) 234 92
e-mail: electro@dubna.ru

### Products
Plain and ribbed rod insulators in composite materials for overhead contact line systems for main line and urban railways.

## Adtranz

DaimlerChrysler Rail Systems
Group Holding Headquarters and Group Corporate Centre
Saatwinkler Damm 43, D-13627 Berlin
Tel: (+49 303) 83 20   Fax (+49 303) 832 20 00

### Head Office, Fixed Installations Product Unit
Mainzer Landstrasse 349-351, D-60326 Frankfurt, Germany
Tel: (+49 69) 750 75 50   Fax (+49 69) 750 75 84

### Key personnel
Executive, Fixed Installations Group: Manfred Leger

*Other countries* (see full address in *Locomotives and powered/non-powered passenger vehicles* section)

### Products
Development, design, engineering, production, sales, installation, maintenance, aftersales service of — and customer support for — fixed installations of railway systems:
Electrification Systems, AC and DC, for main, regional or city railways and trolleybuses, in turnkey contracts or as subsupplier.
AC or AC/DC substations, including mobile substations, in turnkey contracts or as subsupplier.
Catenaries and conductor rails, with complete networks in turnkey contracts or as subsupplier.
Refurbishment, maintenance and repair services — in turnkey contracts or as subsupplier.
More than 360 Adtranz substations are in use throughout Europe. Recent examples are:
ÖBB Austria: Parnsdorf and Zirl transformer substations — both 110 kV/15 kV and the Enzigerboden station.
Brazil: CPTM São Paulo is taking delivery of overhead line equipment and Adtranz Brazil is supplying the substation.
Bulgaria: Adtranz s in a consortium to electrify 131 km of line between Dupnitza and Kulata.
China: Electrification of the Harbin—Dalian line in North East China began in 2000. It is being carried out by a consortium of Adtranz and Siemens, in association with China National Machinery Import and Export Company (CMTC). A total of 950 km of double-track line is being electrified with overhead contact line based on the system designed for DB AG, Germany. The line is used mainly for heavy freight traffic. Adtranz is supplying pantographs for the Chinese locomotives.
Germany: Adtranz has won an order from Deutsche Bahn AG to provide electrification and train control equipment for the 70 km Nuremburg-Ingolstadt high-speed line. The contract covers: overhead line equipment; switchgear and electrical systems; train safety and control systems; telecommunications equipment; and overall co-ordination of all equipment.The train control system will be based on GSM-R mobile communications technology, and the line will be suitable for 330 km/h operation. Work will start this year and the contract is to be completed by 2003.
Greece: Athens metro, electrification of lines 2 and 3 with DC substations and third rail equipment.
Italy: FS has taken delivery of HV circuit breakers, silicon rectifiers and substations at Le Cave. Silicon rectifiers have been supplied to Magrini Galileo, and Milan metro has taken delivery of a diagnostic system.
Ireland: Iarnród Éireann has placed an order with the Fixed Installation Group for the electrification of the Northern and Southern extensions of the suburban railway network of the Dublin Area Rapid Transit (DART). The Adtranz Fixed Installation Business Group is co-ordinating the whole project. It comprises construction and installation of 15 km of overhead, the electronic equipment for three rectifier substations, one switching substation and the replacement of the existing power control system.
Mexico: Mexico City metro has ordered 19 rectifier substations and a test installation from Adtranz Spain.
Netherlands: Adtranz has won an order from Netherlands Railways to supply trackside power supply equipment for a 27 km section of the new Rotterdam-Duisburg freight line. This initial section of the line, which will provide a link into the port of Rotterdam, will be the first in the Netherlands to be electrified at 25 kV AC 50 Hz, and is being equipped jointly by Adtranz as general contractor, with ABB Systems and Strukton Railinfra as partners. Delivery of the Adtranz equipment was scheduled for late 1999 and the company's contract includes maintenance provision for the first five years.
Spain: RENFE's high-speed line from Madrid to Seville has received AC substations and catenary equipment; Metro de Barcelona and Metro de Bilbao have both taken delivery of substations.
Sweden: The Roslagsbanan has taken delivery of power supply substations and thyristor rectifiers. Banverket has commissioned its largest static power converter station at Boden. It went into service in October 1997; on the Kiruna-Svappavaara line Banverket is testing a new power supply system with 30 kV voltage, together with Adtranz Sweden, which built it. The Svealandsbanan, Eskiltuna, took delivery of a compact Megamac static converter station in early 1998. So far 14 Megamacs have been delivered.

## Balfour Beatty Rail Projects Ltd

7 Mayday Road, Thornton Heath, Surrey CR7 7XA, UK
Tel: (+44 1332) 26 23 08   Fax: (+44 1332) 26 22 95
e-mail: peter.kehoe@bbrail.co.uk
Web: http://www.bbrail.com

### Main works address
B203 Midland House, Nelson Street, Derby DEI 2SA
Tel: (+44 1332) 26 26 66   Fax: (+44 1332) 26 28 46

### Key personnel
Managing Director: Rob Boulger
Engineering Director: Andy Curzon
Operations Director: Paul Copeland
Finance Director: Rory Mitchell
Commercial Director: Keith Hampson
Human Resources Director: Peter Raza
Marketing Manager: Bill Pownall

### Products
Design, supply, installation, testing and commissioning of overhead line and power supplies for high-speed, mixed traffic, heavy haul, light rail and mass transit systems. The company offers multidisciplinary project design and construction.

### Contracts
Recent contracts include: electrification of more than 25,000 km of rail systems throughout the world; track design and electrification of the MTRC Lantau and Airport Railway, Hong Kong (1995-98); electrification of the Guangzhou metro, China (1994-98); track design and construction of the Changi Airport Line, Singapore (1999-2000); design, supply and installation of trackwork, signalling, telecommunications, overhead line, civil works and power supply of the Euston area Alliance remodelling, London, UK (1999-2002); design, supply and installation of overhead line and power distribution for the WCML upgrading, UK (1999-2005).

*UPDATED*

## Balfour Beatty Rail Renewals Ltd

12th Floor, Marlowe House, 109 Station Road, Sidcup, Kent DA15 7AU, UK
Tel: (+44 20) 83 08 71 00   Fax: (+44 20) 83 08 71 01

### Works
Southern Track Renewals, PO Box 272, Croydon CR0 1YW, UK

### Track Systems
12th Floor, Marlowe House, Sidcup DA15 7AU, UK

### Key personnel
Managing Director: Eric Prescott
Commercial Director: Tony Smith
Technical Director: David Watson
Finance Director: John Marlor
HR Director: Terry O'Brien
Signal Systems Manager: Steve Simmonds
Electrification Manager: Kevin Northwood
Track Systems Manager: Graham Eastabrook
Logistics Manager: Will Browning

### Services
Balfour Beatty Rail Renewals brings together track systems, electrification and signal systems. The Track Systems business provides a complete service for large scale track renewals and associated works including signalling and communications, installations, provision of new and remodelled track and track welding. The Signal Systems business offers a design, supply and install test and commission services and can provide the necessary support to signalling and communications activities. The Electrification business carried out both overhead and third rail works.

## Barclay Mowlem

Barclay Mowlem Construction
20 Bridge Street, Pymble, New South Wales 2073, Australia
Tel: (+61 2) 98 55 16 00   Fax: (+61 2) 98 55 16 20

*Four-wheeled overhead equipment inspection car for Indian Railways*   2002/0134279

## Electrification contractors and equipment suppliers/MANUFACTURERS

**Key personnel**
Managing Director: D C Hudson
General Manager, Rail: Bill Killinger
Commercial Manager, Rail: Bob Cooke

**Subsidiary company**
Austrak Pty Ltd

**Products**
Main line and LRT electrification schemes, AC or DC; manufacture of prestressed concrete poles.

*VERIFIED*

---

## BEML

Bharat Earth Movers Ltd
BEML Soudha, 23/1 4th Main, SR Nagar, Bangalore 560 027, India
Tel: (+91 80) 222 44 58   Fax: (+91 80) 229 19 80
e-mail: techrnd@vsnl.com
Web: http://www.bemlindia.com

**Key personnel**
See entry in *Locomotives and powered/non-powered passenger vehicles* section.

**Products**
Overhead equipment inspection cars, in eight-wheeled and four-wheeled versions for periodic inspection and maintenance of overhead equipment on electrified rail routes. These self-propelled cars are self-contained with workshop, storage facilities, staff cabins and elevating platform and are equipped for repairs to overhead equipment and erecting catenary and contact wires.

**Contracts**
Recent contracts include the supply of 30 eight-wheeled cars and 10 four-wheeled cars (1,676 mm gauge) for Indian Railways.

*UPDATED*

---

## Benkler AG

Nordstrasse 1, CH-5612 Willmergen, Switzerland
Tel: (+41 56) 618 72 00   Fax: (+41 56) 618 72 99
e-mail: info@benkler.ch
Web: http://www.benkler.ch

**Corporate background**
Benkler AG is a member of the Sersa Group (qv).

**Services**
Overhead line maintenance and construction equipment and services; cable construction.

*NEW ENTRY*

---

## Brecknell, Willis

Brecknell, Willis & Co Ltd
PO Box 10, Chard TA20 2DE, UK
Tel: (+44 1460) 649 41   Fax: (+44 1460) 661 22

**Key personnel**
See entry in *Electric traction equipment* section.

**Products**
Current collection and power distribution equipment for the transportation sector.
  Includes supply of complete overhead contact and third rail systems for railway and metro applications covering design, manufacture, supply and installation.
  Gas tensioning equipment, spring boxes and ground return units for railways, metro, light rail systems and tramways.
  Projects include systems for LUL Jubilee Line Extension and Northern Line improvement programmes, Ankara and Taipei Metro systems; overhead contact systems for the Midland Metro LRT system and third rail system for Merseyrail.

---

## Brush Transformers Ltd

PO Box 20, Loughborough LE11 1HN, UK
Tel: (+44 1509) 61 14 11   Fax: (+44 1509) 61 05 50
e-mail: sales@btl.fki-eng.com
Web: http://www.fki-eng.com

**Key personnel**
Managing Director: B S Bullock
International Sales and Marketing Director: Luay C Toma
Commercial Director: Stuart Bennet

**Background**
Brush Transformers Limited is part of the Electrical Engineering section of the Engineering Group of FKI plc, an international manufacturing group with over 75 operating units.

**Products**
Distribution, power, dry-type, traction repair and flameproof transformers and flameproof switchgear in the range 2 MVA to 45 MVA (60 MVA OFAF), at up to 145 kV, dry type 100 kVA to 4 MVA 15 kV. Applications include power utilities, major contractors, and the oil and gas, petrochemical, rail, steel and coal industries. The repair and refurbishment of traction transformers, industrial transformers and flameproof equipment.

*UPDATED*

---

## Cembre SpA

Via Serenissima 9, I-25135 Brescia, Italy
Tel: (+39 030) 369 21   Fax: (+39 030) 336 57 66
e-mail: cembre.spa@interbusiness.it
Web: http://www.cembre.com

**Principal subsidiary**
Cembre Ltd
Fairview Industrial Estate, Kingsbury Road, Curdworth, Sutton Coldfield B76 9EE, UK
Tel: (+44 1675) 47 04 40   Fax: (+44 1675) 47 02 20

**Subsidiary companies**
Cembre A/S
Fossner Senter, N-3160 Stokke, Norway
Tel: (+47 33) 36 17 65   Fax: (+47 33) 36 17 66
e-mail: cembre@cembre.no

Cembre España SL
Called Llanos de Jerez,
2 Pol Ind de Coslada, E-28820, Spain
Tel: (+34 91) 485 25 80   Fax: (+34 91) 485 25 81
e-mail: info@cembre.com

Cembre GmbH
Taunusstrasse, 23 D-80807 Munich, Germany
Tel: (+49 89) 358 06 76   Fax: (+49 89) 35 80 67 77
e-mail: info@cembre.com

Cembre Inc
Raritan Center Business Park
70 Campus Plaza II, Edison, New Jersey 08837, USA
Tel: (+1 732) 225 74 15   Fax: (+1 732) 225 74 14
e-mail: salesus@cembre.com

Cembre Sarl
22 avenue Ferdinand de Lesseps, F-91420, Morangis, France
Tel: (+33 1) 60 49 11 90   Fax: (+33 1) 60 49 29 10
e-mail: info@cembre.fr

**Products**
Drilling machines for rail web and wooden sleepers; rail bush contact kits; related accessories

*UPDATED*

---

## Costaferroviaria SpA

Viale 4 Novembre, I-23845 Costamasnaga, Italy
Tel: (+39 031) 86 94 11   Fax: (+39 031) 85 53 30

**Key personnel**
See entry in *Locomotives and powered/non-powered passenger vehicles* section.

**Products**
ASTRIDE road/rail vehicle which is suitable for maintenance of electric overhead lines and is equipped with a platform fitted to a crane providing a wide range of access. The vehicle has a railway system which takes the power from the engine of the road vehicle (modified Iveco 150). The front axle is driven and the rear axle is trailing. The wheels are 500 mm in diameter and are fitted with leaf springs and shock-absorbers in order to obtain good contact with the rail even at high speeds. Traction is hydromechanical and the braking system utilises disc brakes. Also, the vehicle is provided with service, emergency and parking brakes.
  Maximum speed is more than 50 km/h, while at low speeds it is possible to use a remote control from the inspection basket.
  ASTRIDE, fitted by Permaquip, is in service in the UK.

---

## Crompton Greaves Ltd

I Dr V B Gandhi Marg, Mumbai 400 023, India
Tel: (+91 22) 202 80 25

Rail Transportation Systems Division
5-E Vandhna 11, Tolstoy Marg, New Delhi 110 001, India
Tel: (+91 11) 331 70 75; 373 04 45
Fax: (+91 11) 331 70 75; 332 43 60
e-mail: dhingra_cgl@mantraonline.com
Web: http://www.cromptongreaves.com

**Key personnel**
Managing Director: S M Trehan
General Manager, Rail: A K Raina
All India Marketing Manager, Rail Transportration Systems Division: Harsh Dhingra

**Products**
Traction transformers, SF6 gas interrupters/circuit breakers, lightning arrestors, turnkey electrification contracts.

*NEW ENTRY*

---

## CTS

Cubic Transportation Systems Ltd
177 Nutfield Road, Merstham RH1 3HR, UK
Tel: (+44 1737) 64 68 00   Fax: (+44 1737) 64 36 93

**Key personnel**
See entry in *Revenue collection systems and station equipment* section.

**Products**
Electrical installation, cabling, maintenance.
  Contracts include power transformer installation and tunnel relighting for London Underground Ltd, and data cabling and routeing for Railtrack Northwest.

---

## Delta

Delta Crompton Cables (part of Draka UK Ltd)
Millmarsh Lane, Brimsdown, Enfield EN3 7QD, UK
Tel: (+44 20) 88 04 24 68   Fax: (+44 20) 88 04 75 05

**Works**
Alfreton Road, Derby DE2 4AE, UK

**Key personnel**
Commercial Manager: I Imrie
National Sales Manager: G Davies

**Products**
Power, data, control and instrumentation cables insulated with a variety of insulants, including zero halogen, low-smoke compounds.

---

## Ebo Systems

Boulevard d'Europe, PO Box 10 F-67211, Obernai, Cedex, France
Tel: (+33 3) 88 49 50 51   Fax: (+33 3) 88 49 50 14

## MANUFACTURERS/Electrification contractors and equipment suppliers

e-mail: ebosystemsint@yahoo.com
Web: http://www.ebo-systems.com

**Key personnel**
Managing Director: Peter Caldwell

**Products**
FRP/GRP cable management systems; cable trays, ground ducts, cable ladders; fixing and supporting material.

## EFACEC

Sistemas de Electrónica SA
Av Eng Frederico Ulrich, PO Box 31, P-4470 Maia, Portugal
Tel: (+351 2) 941 36 66   Fax: (+351 2) 948 54 28

**Products**
Electrification equipment, including traction substations (1,500 V DC and 25 kV 50 Hz AC) and associated telecontrol systems, catenary systems.

## Elpro

Elpro BahnstromAnlagen GmbH
Marzahner Strasse 34, D-13053 Berlin, Germany
Tel: (+49 30) 98 61 22 53   Fax: (+49 30) 98 61 22 51
Web: http://www.elpro.de

**Products**
Equipment for AC and DC electrification systems, including substations, switchgear, overhead lines, control and distribution systems.

## Ensto Sekko Oy

PO Box 51, FIN-06101 Porvoo, Finland
Tel: (+358) 204 76 21   Fax: (+358) 204 76 25 15
e-mail: utility.networks@ensto.com
Web: http://www.ensto.com

**Key personnel**
Managing Director: Tutu Wegelius-Lehtonen
Product Manager: Veijo Vilenius

**Products**
Aluminium cantilevers and components; composite, ceramic and glass insulators; crimp and screw-type fittings; hot-dipped galvanised steel parts.

**Contracts**
Recent contracts include VR, Finland; Banverket, Sweden; NSB, Norway; DSB, Denmark; BTBBJV, Balfour-Beatty, UK and SNCB, Belgium.

*UPDATED*

## Felten & Guilleaume Kabelwerke GmbH

Schanzenstrasse 6-20, D-51063 Cologne, Germany
Tel: (+49 221) 67 60   Fax: (+49 221) 676 24 60
e-mail: infoservice@nktcables.com

**Products**
Magnesium and silver-alloy contact wires.

## Ferraz SA

PO Box 3025, F-69391 Lyon Cedex 3, France
Tel: (+33 4) 72 22 66 11   Fax: (+33 4) 72 22 67 13

**Products**
AC protistor fuses for the internal protection of the AC/DC and/or AC/DC/AC substation converters, large power filters and auxiliary circuits; disconnectors to isolate substation converters; automatic fast-acting earthing device with large short-circuit capability, which can be either bi- or unidirectional.

## FIREMA

FIREMA Trasporti SpA
Viale Edison 110, I-20099 Sesto S Giovanni (Milano), Italy
Tel: (+39 02) 249 41   Fax: (+39 02) 248 35 08

**Key personnel**
See entry in *Locomotives and powered/non-powered passenger vehicles* section.

**Products**
Converters and feeder substations.
Recent orders include substations for the Rome metro Line A extension and MV/LV equipment for Rome layover areas A Cornelia and Laurentina.

## Firema Trasporti SpA

c/o IDP Milano Fiorenza, Via Triboniano, 220 I-20156 Milan, Italy
Tel: (+39 02) 23 02 02 23   Fax: (+39 02) 23 02 02 34
e-mail: firema.com@firema.it
Web: http://www.firema.it

**Key personnel**
See entry in *Locomotives and powered/non-powered passenger vehicles* section.

**Products**
Substation equipment for AC and DC electrification; converting group and auxiliary transformers; solid-state rectifiers; high/medium-voltage switchgear with high-speed circuit breakers, auxiliary and protection relays; minor parts and maintenance.
Work continues on development of diagnostics and automatic maintenance systems.

*NEW ENTRY*

## Flury

Arthur Flury AG
Fabrikstrasse 4, CH-4543 Deitingen, Switzerland
Tel: (+41 32) 613 33 66   Fax: (+41 32) 613 33 68
e-mail: aflury@bluewin.ch
Web: http://www.aflury.ch

**Key personnel**
President: Adrian Flury
Managing Director: Jürg Zwahlen

**Products**
Components for overhead electrification systems, including section insulators and phase breaks; messenger wire and contact wire insulators; earthing equipment; terminals, suspension clamps, connecting clamps and feeder clamps.

## Fuji Electric Co Ltd

Gate City Ohsaki, East Tower, 11-2, Osaki 1-chome, Shimagawa-ku, Tokyo 141-0032, Japan
Tel: (+81 3) 54 35 70 46   Fax: (+81 3) 54 35 74 23
e-mail: info@fujielectric.co.jp
Web: http://www.fujielectric.co.jp

**Key personnel**
See entry in *Electric traction equipment* section.

**Products**
Power supply equipment: computer-based remote supervisory control equipment; fluorocarbon cooling silicon rectifiers, SF6 gas circuit breakers and mini high-speed circuit breakers; moulded transformers; total control systems including electric power management, station office apparatus control, data management and disaster prevention management.

*VERIFIED*

## Furrer + Frey AG

PO Box 182, Thunstrasse 35, CH-3000 Berne 6, Switzerland
Tel: (+41 31) 357 61 11   Fax: (+41 31) 357 61 00
e-mail: adm@furrerfrey.com
Web: http://www.furrerfrey.com

**Key personnel**
Chief Executive Officer, Export and Marketing: B Furrer
Executive Officer, Construction Department for Railway Electrification: F Friedli
Executive Officer, Electrification and Design Products: U Wili
Executive Officer, Export Department: R D Brodbek

**Works**
PO Box, Eisenbahnstrasse 62-64, CH-3645 Gwatt

**Subsidiary**
UP AG, Berne

**Products**
Design, manufacture and installation of overhead contact lines for railways, up to 25 kV AC. Aerial surveys for electrification projects.
Specialist equipment includes overhead contact lines for rack railways, tram and light rail systems; overhead conductor rails; movable conductor rail for depots and maintenance facilities. Also the provision of software for electrification projects; consultancy; maintenance vehicles.

**Contracts**
1997-2005 catenary planning for a third track of the Geneva—Coppet line; 1999-2000 fixed overhead conductor rail installation in two depots for DB AG, in Erfurt and in Frankfurt; 6 km of conductor rail installation for renewal of urban transport tunnels in central Copenhagen; movable conductor rail installation in maintenance depot Helgoland of Banestyreisen, Copenhagen; movable conductor rail installation in maintenance hall at Arlandabanan, Stockholm; electrification of Zimmerbergtunnel Rail 2000 for Swiss Federal Railways; design and installation of overhead conductor rail in the maintenance hall, Geneva, for SBB Switzerland; movable conductor rail installations on five swing and bascule bridges on the northeast corridor section between Boston and Newhaven for Amtrak; installation of catenary in the 24 km long Vereina tunnel for Rhaetian Railways; supply to Norwegian Rail Administration of 600 supports for use in very narrow tunnels.

*UPDATED*

## Galland

20 rue de l'Insurrection Parisienne, F-94600 Choisy-le-Roi, France
Tel: (+33 1) 46 80 25 72   Fax: (+33 1) 46 80 83 42
e-mail: info@j-galland.com
Web: http://www.j-galland.com

**Key personnel**
Chairman: Denis Galland
Managing Director: Philippe d'Huy
Technical Director: Dominique Bec
Export Manager: Jacques Milhem

**Products**
Overhead line equipment from 750 V to 25 kV, reinforced, normal, flexible, gantry, single, light.
Section insulators from tramway to high-speed, tested up to 270 km/h.
Tensioning device: spring and pulley tensioning device. Isolating and selector switch, with and without earth (new European standard).
Tramway equipment: catenary, anchorages, section insulators, delta suspension, tensioning devices, isolators and selector switches.

## Geismar

113 bis avenue Charles-de-Gaulle, F-92200 Neuilly sur Seine, France
Tel: (+33 1) 41 43 40 40   Fax: (+33 1) 46 40 71 70

**Works**
5 rue d'Altkirch, F-68006 Colmar Cedex, France
Tel: (+33 3) 89 80 22 11   Fax: (+33 3) 89 79 78 45

## Products

Geismar provides equipment to erect or maintain AC and DC catenary lines; a large variety of dedicated tools; a range of overhead line components; overhead line erection/unrolling trains; maintenance and servicing vehicles, catenary inspection/measurement gang cars, trailers.

Geismar also provides tracklaying and maintenance equipment and services.

*VERIFIED*

## Greysham International

Greysham (International) Pvt Ltd
2/81 Roop Nagar, Delhi 110 007, India
Tel: (+91 11) 396 52 60; 93 81
Fax: (+91 11) 396 11 68

### Key personnel
See entry in *Brakes and drawgear* section.

### Products
Overhead fittings for railway electrification projects.

## Hawker Siddeley Switchgear Ltd

Newport Road, Blackwood NP12 2XH, UK
Tel: (+44 1495) 22 31 00   Fax: (+44 1495) 22 56 74
e-mail: sales@hssl.fki-eng.com
Web: http://www.fki-eng.com

### Key personnel
Managing Director: Brian S Bullock

### Parent company
FKI Group of companies
Registered Office: West House, King's Cross Road, Halifax HX1 1EB, UK

### Products
Structure-mounted outdoor 25 kV swtichgear for traction applications.

## HEI

Hindusthan Engineering & Industries Ltd
Mody Building, 27 Sir RN Mukherjee Road, Calcutta 700 001, India
Tel: (+91 33) 248 01 66
Fax: (+91 33) 248 19 22; 220 26 07
e-mail: hindus@cal2.vsnl.net.in

### Works
Insulators & Electrical Company (IEC)
1/8 New Industrial Area, Mandideep 462,046, District Raisen, Madhya Pradesh, India

### Key personnel
President IEC: B D Tulsian

### Products
Manufacture and supply of 25 kV solid core insulators.

*UPDATED*

## Hitachi Ltd

Overseas Marketing Department
Transportation Systems Sales Division
6 Kanda Surugadai 4-chome, Chiyoda-ku, Tokyo 101-8010, Japan
Tel: (+81 3) 52 95 55 40   Fax: (+81 3) 32 58 52 30

### Key personnel
See entry in *Locomotives and powered/non-powered passenger vehicles* section.

### Products
Traction substation equipment for AC and DC electrification projects; diode and thyristor rectifiers; power regenerative inverters; transformers; AC and DC switchgear; control and protection devices; computerised systems – substation supervisory remote-control systems, automatic car diagnosis system, station management system, security system.

*NEW ENTRY*

## Hyundai

Hyundai Heavy Industries Ltd
Electro-Electric Systems
Hyundai Building, 140-2 Kye-dong, Chongro-ku, Seoul 110-793, South Korea
Tel: (+82 2) 746 75 30   Fax: (+82 2) 746 74 79
e-mail: rolling@hhi.co.kr
Web: http://www.hhi.co.kr

### Products
Transformers; rectifiers; switchgear; SCADA systems.

## Insul-8 Corporation

10102 F Street, Omaha, Nebraska 68127, USA
Tel: (+1 402) 339 93 00   Fax: (+1 402) 339 96 27
e-mail: vprell@insul-8.com
Web: http://www.insul-8.com

### Key personnel
President: Lon Miller
Project Manager: Richard Prell

### Other offices
Other offices in Canada, Australia and Manchester, UK.

### Background
Insul-8 is part of the Delachaux Group, Gennevilliers, France.

### Products
Conductor rail systems up to 6,000 A. Specialises in conductor rail with stainless steel on aluminium extrusion.

### Contracts
Las Vegas Monorail and MRTA, Bangkok.

### Developments
Contact rails with choice of amperage range to meet system demands.

*NEW ENTRY*

## A Kaufmann AG

Pilatustrasse 2, CH-6300 Zug, Switzerland
Tel: (+41 41) 711 67 00   Fax: (+41 41) 859 16 01
e-mail: info@kago.ch
Web: http://www.kago.com

### Key personnel
Sales Director: Patrick Kaufman

### Products
KAGO specialist engineering products for railways, including a complete range of non-screwed rail contact clamps, discs and strips for electrical rail connections (return current, signalling circuits, earthing), cable fastenings for rails and sleepers, special welding electrodes for copper welding; complete range of screwing, welding and interlocking fittings; self-tapping sleeper screws for concrete, steel or wooden sleepers; sleeper spring clips; high-voltage insulations.

Recent development: KAGO contract strips and discs for electrical rail connections in complex pathwork.

### Services
Track returns and earthing wires; earthing poles; heavy-duty and special mountings and drillings; suspensions for radiating cables.

*UPDATED*

## Kershaw Manufacturing

PO Box 244100, Montgomery, Alabama 36124, USA
Tel: (+1 334) 387 91 00   Fax: (+1 334) 215 75 51
Web: http://www.kershawusa.com

### Key personnel
Vice-President and COO: G Reg Valley
Vice-President of Sales and International Sales Manager: Phil Brown

### Products and services
Vehicles to cut safely trees or branches growing in the path of overhead lines, power-lines and catenary. Rubber-tyred or rail-mounted, one-man operation, with reach up to 21.2 m.

*UPDATED*

## Kummler + Matter AG

Hohlstrasse 176, CH-8026 Zürich, Switzerland
Tel: (+41 1) 247 47 47   Fax: (+41 1) 247 47 77
e-mail: kuma@kuma.ch
Web: http://www.kuma.ch

### Key personnel
President: Daniel Steiner
Marketing Director: René Kopp
Purchasing Manager: H P Villringer
Export Sales Managers: Rodolfo Middelmann, Reto Hügli, André Eichorn

### Products
Overhead contact line equipment for light rail, branch lines, suburban and main line railways, and trolleybuses. Engineering and feasibility studies.

*UPDATED*

*KAGO rail contact clamps (inset) and cable connection in progress*

# MANUFACTURERS/Electrification contractors and equipment suppliers

## Lerc SA

600 Chemin des Hamaïdes, PO Box 119, F-59732 Saint Amand les Eaux Cedex, France
Tel: (+33 3) 27 22 85 50   Fax: (+33 3) 27 22 85 05
e-mail: commercial@lerc.fr
Web: http://www.lerc.fr

**Key personnel**
Managing Director: J Mourey
Technical Director: Y Foissac
Sales Manager: F Romet
Export Marketing Manager: Vincent Lernoud

**Subsidiary company**
Janssen Engineering

**Products**
A range of insulators with silicon shed shells for railway, tram and metro lines; bushing and insulating systems; composite insulators for energy (transport and distribution). Production and refurbishment of composite bushings.

*UPDATED*

## Merlin Gerin Brasil SA

Av Brigadeiro Faria Lima 2003, 14th andar, 01451-001 São Paulo SP, Brazil
Tel: (+55 11) 816 45 00   Fax: (+55 11) 813 09 43

**Main works**
Av da Saudade s/n, 13171-320, Sumaré, SP, Brazil

**Key personnel**
See entry in *Electric traction equipment* section.

**Products**
Traction chopper control system; high and low-voltage switchboards; self-inductive coils, resistors and static converters, traction rectifiers; control boards; auxiliary switchboards and low-voltage rectifiers; track circuits; power and signalling mimic panels; relay racks; data transmission; boards; low-, medium- and high-tension equipment.

## Mer Mec SpA

Via Oberdan 70, I-70043 Monopoli (BA), Italy
Tel: (+39 080) 887 65 70   Fax: (+39 080) 887 40 28
e-mail: mermec@tin.it
Web: http://www.mermec.it

**Key personnel**
See entry in *Permanent way components, equipment and services* section.

**Services**
Measuring vehicles and diagnostic systems for the maintenance of railway infrastructure; systems for measurement of overhead line geometry, contract wire wear and pantograph interaction, arcing measurement, measurement of electric parameters, video inspection systems, overhead line and way side, positioning systems, analysis software.
Railway vehicles for track and overhead line maintenance, trailers, railway cars equipped with cabins, lifting cranes, caissons, inspection platforms, catenary drums, lifting masts and auxiliary items, rail-road vehicles.

**Contracts**
Overhead line system for MTR Corporation (Hong Kong), Roger 1000 K multi-diagnostic vehicles with integrated monitoring of the track and the overhead line infrastructure for KHRC (Korea).

*NEW ENTRY*

## Muromteplovoz

Murom Diesel Locomotive Works
ulica Filatova 10 602 200 Murom, Vladimir region, Russian Federation

Tel: (+7 095) 291 31 68   Fax: (+7 09234) 443 03
e-mail: mteplo@cl.murom.ru
Web: http://www.cl.murom.ru

**Key personnel**
See entry in *Locomotives and powered/non-powered passenger vehicles* section.

**Products**
Equipment for the erection and maintenance of AC and DC overhead catenary systems.

*Muromteplovoz Type ARV-1 self-propelled overhead line maintenance vehicle with lifting and rotating cradle*
2001/0103973

## Paul Keller Engineering Ltd

Hochbordstrasse 9, CH-8600 Dübendorf, Switzerland
Tel: (+41 1) 821 40 27   Fax: (+41 1) 821 45 40
e-mail: pkag@pkag.ch
Web: http://www.pkag.ch

**Subsidiaries**
Berninastrasse 4, CH-5430 Wettingen, Switzerland
Tel: (+41 56) 438 08 88   Fax: (+41 56) 438 08 89
Bahnhofstrasse 37, CH-7302 Landquart, Switzerland
Tel: (+41 81) 330 66 60   Fax: (+41 81) 33 06 66 10
Huggenberg, CH-8354 Hofstetten, Switzerland
Tel: (+41 52) 364 16 76   Fax: (+41 52) 364 16 56
Via Collina 54, CH-6612 Ascona, Switzerland
Tel: (+41 91) 791 63 01   Fax: (+41 91) 791 58 85
Alte Steinhauserstrasse 33, CH-6330 Cham, Switzerland
Tel: (+41 41) 740 23 33   Fax: (+41 41) 74 06 33 30

**Products**
Power distribution networks; traction power supply for railways; site surveying; corrosion protection; structures and catenaries; control systems; telecommunication systems.

## Pfisterer Srl

I-20094 Corsico, Milan Via Pacinotti 31, Italy
Tel: (+39 02) 448 70 61   Fax: (+39 02) 447 90 08
e-mail: pfisterer@pfisterer.it

**Key personnel**
Managing Director: Dr Ing Osvaldo Nannini
Export Manager: Dip Ing Paolo Zorzan

**Other offices**
Pfisterer
Kontaktsysteme GmbH & Co KG
Inselstrasse 140, D-70327 Stuttgart, Germany
Tel: (+49 711) 301 20   Fax: (+49 711) 301 21 97

Pfisterer GmbH
A-1091 Wien, Augasse 17, Austria
Tel: (+43 1) 31 76 53 10   Fax: (+43 1) 317 65 31 12

Sefag AG
CH-6102 Malters/Luzern, Werkstrasse 7, Switzerland
Tel: (+41 41) 497 19 91   Fax: (+41 41) 497 22 69

Upresa SA
E-08025 Barcelona, Calle Industria 90-92, Spain
Tel: (+34 93) 436 47 01   Fax: (+34 93) 436 77 01

**Products**
Silicon rubber composite insulators for railway, tram and metro lines; clamps and earthing devices; equipotential reversible cable hanger for use on FS high-speed lines electrified at 25 kV 50 Hz AC; voltage detectors, tensioning system TENSOREX®, a mechanical pull regulation system which can handle continuous tension on the contact wire specially designed for narrow spaces like tunnels.
Contracts include the supply of overhead line equipment for the Milan metro, and of silicon rubber arm and tension insulators to SNCB.
Pfisterer has developed TENSOREX®, a patented automatic tensioning device for the overhead line without the need for weights.

## Plasser & Theurer

Johannesgasse 3, A-1010 Vienna, Austria
Tel: (+43 1) 51 57 20   Fax: (+43 1) 513 18 01

**Key personnel**
See entry in *Permanent way components, equipment and services* section.

**Products**
Since 1981 Plasser & Theurer has developed and built machines for the installation and maintenance of overhead wires and the associated equipment. The particular advantage highlighted by Plasser & Theurer catenary renewal machines is that contact wire and carrying cable are installed with the final tension as well as in the correct stagger. The unavoidable post-tensioning necessary when using traditional methods of installation can be dispensed with entirely, which enables a considerable increase in renewal output, reports the company.
The benefits of the system include: immediate use of the reopened line at full speed after renewal; no closure of adjacent tracks; low staff requirements; high-quality work; and renewal of a complete section in one track possession.

*FUM cantenary erector*

With appropriate equipment of the machines, return current circuits on the outer side of the masts or feeders at the top of the masts can be removed and installed.

The FUM 100.051 is equipped with reeling-off devices for installation of one carrying cable and two contact wires in one operation.

From the complete catenary renewal system to a variety of sizes of motor tower car for inspection and maintenance, individual solutions are adapted to meet the requirements of the specific railway administration.

## Powernetics Ltd

Jason Works, Clarence Street, Loughborough, LE11 1DX, UK
Tel: (+44 1509) 21 41 53   Fax: (+44 1509) 26 24 60
e-mail: sales@powernetics.co.uk
Web: http://www.powernetics.co.uk

**Key personnel**
Managing Director: Satish Chada
Financial Controller: Bob Lawson
Sales Office Manager: Jim Goddard
Operations Manager: Konrad Chada
Export Sales Manager: Aran Chada
Project Sales Manager: Andy Vickers
Purchasing Manager: I W Dakin

**Products**
Independent designer and manufacturer of RAIL POWER UPS systems for signalling, telecoms, radio and level crossing applications, trackside, tunnel and signal box locations. The equipment is compliant with Railtrack Group Standards. Clients include GTRM, BBRR, Amey, AMEC, Jarvis, First Engineering.

*VERIFIED*

## RPG Transmissiom Ltd

29&30 Community Commercial Centre, Basant Lok, Vasant Vihar, New Delhi 110057, India
Tel: (+91 11) 614 26 55; 614 58 01
Fax: (+91 11) 614 63 40
e-mail: chari@rpgtl.rpgms.ems.vsnl.net.in

**Main works address**
PO Box 96, Jabalpur-482001, India

**Key personnel**
Executive Director: S C Khanna
General Manager (Projects & Marketing): D Luthra
Chief Manager (Projects & Marketing): A K Das

**Principal subsidiary**
KEC International Ltd, Mumbai, India

**Products**
Design, supply and erection of 3 kV DC and 25 kV 50 HZ AC overhead equipment, sub-stations, booster transformer stations; telecommunication cabling for railway electrification.

Contracts include electrification of 1,050 track km at 25 KV 50 Hz AC for Indian Railways; design, supply and erection of 25 kV 50 HZ AC overhead equipment, booster, transformer stations, switching stations in the Nidadavolu-Annavaram section of SC Railway, India, completed in May 1997. Three contracts obtained for a total of 1,050 track km in the Kharagpur–Bhubaneswar section of the of SE Railway, India, in 1998.

## SAE (India) Ltd

29-30 Community Commercial Centre, Basant Lok, Vasant Vihar, New Delhi 110 057, India
Tel: (+91 11) 688 26 55; 58 01
Fax: (+91 11) 611 11 90; 688 59 58

**Main works**
PO Box 96, Jabalpur 482001, India

**Key personnel**
President: Dr R K Dwivedi
Vice-President, Finance: Y L Madan
General Manager: P Varma
General Manager, Marketing: D Luthra
Chief Manager, Projects: A K Das

**Products**
Design, supply and erection of 3 kV DC and 25 kV 50 Hz AC overhead equipment; substations; booster transformer stations; telecommunications cabling for railway electrification.

Contracts include electrification of 300 track-km at 25 kV 50 Hz AC for Indian Railways.

## SAFT

156 avenue de Metz, F-93230 Romainville, France
Tel: (+33 1) 49 15 36 00   Fax: (+33 1) 49 15 34 00
Web: http://www.saftbatteries.com

**Key personnel**
See entry in *Passenger coach equipment* section.

**Products**
Saft Nife Ni-Cd batteries, with pocket or low maintenance sintered plastic bonded electrodes for supplying energy to all fixed electrification equipment.

Recent contracts include the supply of batteries to Singapore metro, Pakistan Railways, CP Rail.

## SDCEM

Société Dauphinoise de Constructions Electro Mécaniques
10 allée de La Grange, F-38450 Vif, France
Tel: (+33 4) 76 72 76 72   Fax: (+33 4) 76 72 46 26

**Key personnel**
Managers: Claude Yvetot; Alain Plirai; François Mees; Gérard Dubois

**Products**
Catenary and switch disconnectors for 1.5/3 kV DC, 25 kV and 15 kV 16⅔Hz AC with manual and electrical operating mechanisms; 25 to 330 kV disconnectors for substations.

## Sécheron

Sécheron SA
14 Avenue de Sécheron, CH-1211 Geneva 21, Switzerland
Tel: (+41 22) 739 41 11   Fax: (+41 22) 738 73 05
e-mail: info@secheron.com
Web: http://www.secheron.com

**Key personnel**
See entry in *Electric traction equipment* section.

**Products**
DC traction power substations and ancillary equipment including system engineering and network computer simulation; solid-state rectifiers and inverters; harmonic filters; DC switchgear; DC high-speed circuit breakers, isolating and changeover switches; electronic protection relays; microprocessor-based remote-control and protection systems.

See entry in *Signalling and communications systems* section.

Recent contracts include the design, supply and installation of type KMB metal clad DC switchgear for LRT Singapore, Metro Porto and other public transport systems.

*UPDATED*

## Sefag AG

Werkstrasse 7, CH-6102 Malters, Switzerland
Tel: (+41 41) 499 72 72   Fax: (+41 41) 497 22 69
e-mail: connect@sefag.ch

**Key personnel**
Managing Director: Dr K O Papailiou
Technical Director: W Fluri
Sales Director: W Bachmann
Works Director: W Wipfli
Export Director: M Peter
Business Services: H Wicki

**Products**
Silcosil composite insulators with silicon sheds as suspension, dead-end and post insulators, and as special insulators for tunnels and high-speed routes.

Contracts include the supply of insulators to Swiss Federal Railways, Austrian Railways, Bern-Lötschberg-Simplon Railway, and other railways in Switzerland and abroad.

*UPDATED*

## Siemens Transportation Systems

Electrification Division
PO Box 3240, D-91050 Erlangen, Germany
Tel: (+49 9131) 70   Fax: (+49 9131) 72 60 08
e-mail: internet@ts.siemens.de
Web: http://www.siemens.com/ts

**Corporate headquarters**
Siemens AG
Transportation Systems
PO Box 910220, D-12414 Berlin, Germany
Tel: (+49 30) 385 50

## MANUFACTURERS/Electrification contractors and equipment suppliers

**Key personnel**
President, Transportation Systems Group:
 Herbert J Steffen
Group Vice Presidents: Hans-Dieter Bott;
 Thomas Ganswindt; Hans M Schabert
Directors: Dr W Kouckow, L Zagel

**Subsidiary companies**
See entry in *Locomotives and powered/non-powered passenger vehicles* section.

**Products and services**
Supply and installation of traction power supply systems for mass transit and main line railways; supply and installation of contact lines for mass transit and main line railways.

**Contracts**
Recent contracts include:

**China:** In August 2001, a Siemens-led consortium with Barclay Mowlem received a contract covering the electrification of KCRC's East Rail Extension Project in Hong Kong. The contract includes the supply of electrification equipment for the new line and project management.
**Germany:** In February 2001, Siemens was awarded a contract by DB Netz AG to install Germany's first gas-insulated switchgear at Griebnitzsee, near Potsdam. The substation equipment is insulated with inert sulphur hexafluoride.
In January 2001, Siemens-led consortium that includes Elpro BahnstromAnlagen GmbH secured a contract to install complete electrical equipment for 30 rectifier substations on the Berlin S-Bahn system. The contract was scheduled for completion by the end of 2003.
Other orders for electrification technology form part of turnkey contracts, detailed in the *Turnkey systems contractors* section.

*UPDATED*

---

## Sirti SpA

Via Pirelli 20, 20100 Milan, Italy
Tel: (+39 6) 22 54 54 22   Fax: (+39 6) 22 55 54 30

**Key personnel**
Marketing & Sales, Transport Sector: Giuseppe Celli

**Products**
Telecommunication, electrification and signalling systems for railways and metros.

---

## South Wales Transformers Ltd

FKI Transformers Division, Blackwood NP12 2XH, UK
Tel: (+44 1495) 23 21 00   Fax: (+44 1495) 23 21 32
e-mail: sales@swtpans.co.uk
Web: http://www.fki-eng.com

**Key personnel**
Operations Director: Alan Laws
International Sales and Marketing Director: Luay C Toma

**Parent company**
FKI Group of companies
Registered Office: West House, King's Cross Road, Halifax HX1 1EB, UK

**Products**
Booster transformers for overhead railway electrification systems (as supplied to former British Rail companies); ground-mounted transformers for traditional supply systems.

---

## SPIE Enertrans

Parc Saint-Cristophe, F-95861 Cergy-Pontoise Cedex, France
Tel: (+33 1) 34 22 56 08   Fax: (+33 1) 34 22 62 76

**Key personnel**
Operations Director: M Fortuné
Business Development Manager: R Zampieri

**Products**
Design, construction and maintenance of railway infrastructure including: trackwork, catenary systems, power supplies and electromechanical systems for railways including high-speed rail, metros, tramways and other transport systems.
Recent contracts include Channel Tunnel, RATP (Paris metro), TGV Atlantique, TGV Nord, Cairo metro and Heathrow Express.

*UPDATED*

---

## Supertek Enterprise Inc

2231 Colby Avenue, Los Angeles, California 90064, USA
Tel: (+1 310) 444 11 55   Fax: (+1 310) 444 11 64
e-mail: SPKDAVID@aol.com

**Key personnel**
President: David Chang

**Korean address**
Supertek Inc
1070-12 Hwagok Hong, Kangsen Gu, Seoul, South Korea
Tel: (+82 2) 696 19 90   Fax: (+82 2) 698 82 64
e-mail: DollyDoh@hitel.net
Director: J S Doh

**Products**
Complete overhead systems, substation systems, signal systems, communication systems, AFC systems.

---

## Toshiba Corporation

Railway Projects Department, Toshiba Building, 1-1 Shibaura 1-chome, Minato-ku, Tokyo 105, Japan
Tel: (+81 3) 34 57 49 24   Fax: (+81 3) 34 57 83 85

**Products**
DC and AC railway substation equipment; supervisory control systems; transformers; rectifiers; circuit breakers; arresters.

---

## Total Power Solutions

77 Micklegate, York YO1 6LJ, UK
Tel: (+44 1904) 54 15 55 Fax: (+44 1904) 54 15 56

**Corporate background**
Total Power Solutions is a joint venture between GrantRail and Total Power Solutions Ltd.

**Products and services**
Design, supply and installation of 25 kV AC overhead line equipment.
Capabilities include: project planning and management; consultancy services; supply and installation construction works; new works commissioning; isolation planning and implementation services; design and data verification.

*NEW ENTRY*

---

## Transmitton Ltd

Ashby Park, Ashby-de-la-Zouch LE65 1JD, UK
Tel: (+44 1530) 25 80 00   Fax: (+44 1530) 25 80 05
e-mail: rail@transmitton.co.uk
Web: http://www.transmitton.co.uk

**Key personnel**
Managing Director: D Moore
Transport Sales Director: R Burdis
Transport Accounts Manager: E Turnock

**Products**
The Transmitton Cromos SCADA system provides comprehensive control and monitoring featuring a real-time computer master station with high-resolution full workstation graphics.
Fastflex intelligent electronic control and data gathering services. Supply and system integration for traction power control, communication networks, passenger information systems, public address, passenger help points, fare collection and other intelligent equipment used in rail and mass transit systems.

*VERIFIED*

---

## Trend Installation Tooling Ltd

Unit 11, Brindley Road, St Helens WA9 4HY, UK
Tel: (+44 1744) 85 11 00   Fax: (+44 1744) 85 11 22
e-mail: info@trendrail.com;
J.taylor@trendrail.com
Web: http://www.trendrail.com

**Key personnel**
Managing Director: Jack Taylor
Company Secretary: Margaret Taylor
Sales/Marketing: Georgina Oates
Production Manager: Gary Birchall

**Products**
Railway engineering and electrification products/catenary wire fittings; small parts steelwork including arcing horns, angles, fabrications, plates, links and balance weights.
Contracts include West Coast Main Line refurbishment, 2000-2002; spares for maintenance to all regions, Channel Tunnel Rail Link, light rail projects (Hong Kong).

*UPDATED*

---

## Ultra Electronics Power Magnetics and Electronic Systems Ltd

Bridport Road, Greenford UB6 8UA, UK

**Works**
Armitage Road, Rugeley WS15 1DR, UK
Tel: (+44 1889) 50 33 00   Fax: (+44 1889) 57 29 13
e-mail: enquiries@pmes.com
Web: http://www.pmes.com

**Background**
Previously Foster Rectifiers, PMES has over 40 years experience of DC power system design and manufacture of transformer rectifier systems for traction applications.

**Key personnel**
Managing Director: R Sharma
Marketing Director: J S Greenhalgh
Sales and Marketing Manager: K A Mortimer
Sales Manager, Rectifier and Transit Systems:
 T W Boston, D R Huselbee

**Principal subsidiaries**
PMES (Asia) Pte Ltd, Singapore
Ultra Electronics Power Systems, Anapolis USA

**Products**
Traction DC power systems. Equipment supply from stand-alone units to complete DC substations including transformers, rectifiers, AC and DC switchgear, SCADA, auxiliary equipment, power cables and civil works. Also, full system design and co-ordination, project management, installation and commissioning. In-house manufacture of rectifiers voltage controlled rectifiers/inverters, drainage diode cubicles, negative busbar cubicles, earthing contactor cubicles, mimic panels, control and protection panels and depot battery chargers.
Current major projects:
Ansaldo Transporti for Copenhagen Minimetro: System design, equipment supply, integration, project management and site supervision of installation and commissioning of 15 DC substations for the Copenhagen Minimetro Phase 1 and 2a. Equipment supply includes transformer rectifiers, HV and LV switchboards, auxiliary transformers, UPS systems and other associated equipment.
Railtrack Southern: Design, supply and system integration at over 60 DC substations of 33 off, 2,000 kW 750 V DC, indoor air natural rectifiers with outdoor transformers, 60 off Control and Protection Panels, 38 off LVAC Changeover panels and 37 off Battery Chargers.

ABB for London Underground Limited: Design, supply and commissioning of 48 off 1,500 kW and 9 off 2,000 kW 630/750 V DC air natural rectifiers with LNAN transformers complete with Open Circuit Arm Detectors for the Northern Line.

### Developments
Static Signalling Regulator (SSR). A new generation, static power converter which provides a high-quality regulated, single phase, AC output suitable for signalling and other auxiliary equipments. The regulator is designed to be capable of handling the requirements of modern solid state interlocking (SSI) signalling systems. The quality of its output is such that the regulator is suitable for use as the primary power source.

## Whipp & Bourne
A division of FKI Engineering Group
Switchgear Works, Castleton, Rochdale OL11 2SS, UK
Tel: (+44 1706) 63 20 51    Fax: (+44 1706) 34 58 96
e-mail: sales@whipps.fki-eng.com
Web: http://www.fki-eng.com

### Key personnel
Managing Director: B S Bullock
Sales and Marketing Director: L C Toma

### Products
High-speed DC circuit breakers with ratings up to 3 kV, 12,000 A, 255 kA (short-circuit); semi-high-speed DC circuit breakers with ratings up to 1,000 V, 3,150 A, 80 kA (short-circuit); microprocessor-based multifunction overcurrent and impedance/undervoltage protection relays for DC traction systems.

## Wild & Grunder AG
Kelamttstrasse 10, CH-6403 Küssnacht, Switzerland
Tel: (+41 41) 850 60 20   Fax: (+41 41) 850 60 26

### Key personnel
Engineer: Roland Ferrari

### Products
Computer system for mapping information on lineside structures, such as location of overhead support poles and the date on which they were installed.

# CABLES AND CABLE EQUIPMENT

## Alphabetical listing

Adaptaflex
AEI Cables
Agro AG
ALSTOM Transport Electrification SpA
Andrew
ApATeCh Electro
BCM Contracts Ltd
BICC
Brand-Rex
Carrier Khéops Bac
Drallim Telecom
DSG-Canusa UK
Ebo Systems
Ferranti Technologies
Harting Ltd
Hellermann
Hitachi Cable
HPP GmbH
Hypertac
Icore
Litton
LPA
Marconi Communications
Multi-Contact (UK) Ltd
Pirelli Cables Ltd
PMA
Racal Telecom
Simclar International Corporation
Tyco Electronics
Weidmüller Interface GmbH & Co
Yutaka Manufacturing Co Ltd

## Classified listing

### CABLE SYSTEMS
Adaptaflex
AEI Cables
ALSTOM
Andrew
BCM Contracts
BICC
Brand-Rex
DSG-Canusa UK
Ebo Systems
Ferranti Technologies
Hellermann
Hitachi Cable
Marconi Communications
Mettex
Multi-Contact (UK)
Pirelli Cables
Racal Telecom
Raychem

### CONDUIT, CONNECTORS, SEALS, TIES AND ASSOCIATED EQUIPMENT
Agro
ALSTOM
ApATeCh Electro
Carrier Khéops Bac
DSG-Canusa UK
Hellermann
HPP GmbH
Hypertac
Icore
Litton
LPA
PMA
Simclar International Corporation
Tyco Electronics
Weidmüller Interface
Yutaka Manufacturing Co Ltd

## Company listing by country

### FRANCE
Carrier Khéops Bac
Ebo Systems
Hypertac

### GERMANY
HPP GmbH
Weidmüller Interface GmbH & Co

### ITALY
ALSTOM Transport Electrification SpA

### JAPAN
Hitachi Cable
Yutaka Manufacturing Co Ltd

### RUSSIAN FEDERATION
ApATeCh Electro

### SWITZERLAND
Agro AG
Andrew

### UNITED KINGDOM
Adaptaflex
AEI Cables
BCM Contracts Ltd
BICC
Brand-Rex
Drallim Telecom
DSG-Canusa UK Ltd
Ferranti Technologies
Harting Ltd
Hellermann
Icore
Litton
LPA
Marconi Communications
Multi-Contact (UK) Ltd
Pirelli Cables Ltd
PMA
Racal Telecom
Tyco Electronics

### UNITED STATES OF AMERICA
Simclar International Corporation

# MANUFACTURERS/Cables and cable equipment

## Adaptaflex

Station Road, Coleshill, Birmingham B46 1HT, UK
Tel: (+44 1675) 46 82 00   Fax: (+44 1675) 46 49 30
Export: Tel: (+44 1675) 46 82 46
Fax: (+44 1675) 46 49 44
e-mail: sales@adaptaflex.co.uk

**Key personnel**
Marketing Manager: Martyn Turner
UK Sales Manager: Doug Anderson
Export Sales Managers: George Bellanti; Jeremy Curtis

**Products**
Adaptasteel: metallic-based conduit system for cable management applications.
Adaptalok/Adaptaseal: new metallic-based conduit systems.
All products available with approvals from UK railway companies.
Contracts include supply of equipment to London Underground, SNCF, Bombardier and ALSTOM.

*UPDATED*

## AEI Cables

Birtley, Chester-le-Street DH3 2RA, UK
Tel: (+44 191) 410 31 11   Fax: (+44 191) 410 83 12
e-mail: transcab@aeicables.co.uk
Web: http://www.aeicables.co.uk

**Key personnel**
UK Sales Director: Steven Wike
Export Sales Director: David Fraser
Transcab Account Managers:
 Rolling Stock: Mike Bent
 Signalling and Infrastructure: Ray Shields

**Corporate background**
AEI Cables is a subsidiary of TT Electronics plc.

**Products**
Transcab range of cables covers TC12, TC104, TC105 specifications for rolling stock and traction applications. RSE/STD/024 part 6 for LUL contracts, 65/ES 0872 for signalling projects as well as fire performance and high-voltage cables up to 25/44 kV for infrastructure projects.
Customers include Metro Taipei, ALSTOM Transport's Coradia dmu contract and Citadis LRV, London Underground Northern Line, Jubilee Line and CTA Chicago.

*UPDATED*

## Agro AG

Korbackerweg 7, CH-5502 Hunzenschwil, Switzerland
Tel: (+41 62) 889 47 47   Fax: (+41 62) 889 47 50

**Products**
Cable seals for shielded cables which cut out electromagnetic interference.

## ALSTOM Transport Electrification SpA

10 Via Lago dei Tartari, I-00012 Guidonia, Rome, Italy
Tel: (+39 0774) 37 74 85   Fax: (+39 0774) 35 34 30
See also ALSTOM entry in *Locomotives and powered/non-powered passenger vehicles* section.

**Key personnel**
Managing Director: Massimino Colombo

**Products**
Cable, fibre optic and radio communications systems employing base band, FDM and PCM technology.

## Andrew

Andrew Kommunikationssysteme AG
Bächliwis 2b, CH-8184 Bachenbülach, Zurich, Switzerland
Tel: (+41 1) 863 73 52   Fax: (+41 1) 863 73 56

**Key personnel**
See *Signalling and telecommunications* section.

**Products**
Heliax coaxial cables, Radiax leaky feeder cables.

## ApATeCh Electro

Zhukovsky Street 2, Building 131, Dubna, 141980 Moscow Region, Russian Federation
Tel: (+7 09621) 257 92   Fax: (+7 09621) 234 92
e-mail: electro@dubna.ru

**Products**
Ground cable duct systems in composite materials.

## BCM Contracts Ltd

Unit 22, Civic Industrial Park, Whitchurch SY13 1TT, UK
Tel: (+44 1948) 66 53 21; 36 53 22
Fax: (+44 1948) 66 63 81
e-mail: bcmgrc@aol.com

**Key personnel**
Directors: J A Butler, D K Clark, P R Mason

**Products**
A range of lightweight and easily installed cable channel and its accessories – which includes both elevated and ground systems. Complying with UK Railtrack Group standards the glass fibre reinforced concrete (GRC) cable channel system includes not only both new and replacement channel – available in sizes which correspond to the internal dimensions of existing concrete channel – but also a full range of accessories such as channel bends, joint boxes, T-pieces, UTX chambers and junction boxes, point covers and joint bay covers.
Together these allow continuous cable runs to be installed either at ground level, over bridges, or through tunnels, with simple connection to each other or to existing cable troughs.
The elevated cable channel, for example, has been specially designed to be installed above ground level by using tailor-made channel supports, brackets and security clamps. The system also includes easily installed H-piece locking devices which lock the channel lids to the channel to ensure that the system remains tamper-proof.
Apart from being easily installed and maintained, the BCM cable channel system also offers advantages by using GRC as a manufacturing material. These include a high resistance to fire and the emission of toxic fumes, lightweight yet high strength, an ability to be worked with standard hand tooling without damage or breakage, plus other rot-proof, rust-proof, and shatter-proof characteristics.
The material's lightweight characteristics – it weighs approximately one quarter the weight of concrete – plus the channel's ease of installation, mean that a six man team should be able to lay at least 600 m of channel in one day – estimated at least twice that possible using a concrete alternative.

*UPDATED*

## BICC

BICC Cables Ltd
Chester Business Park, Chester CH4 9PZ, UK
Tel: (+44 1244) 68 84 00   Fax: (+44 1244) 68 84 01

**Main works**
Leigh Industrial Cables, Leigh Works, Leigh WN7 4HB, UK
Tel: (+44 1942) 67 24 68   Fax: (+44 1942) 67 99 83

**Key personnel**
Director and General Manager: A C Unsworth
Market Sector Manager, Mining and Railways:
 A Greenwood

**Products**
Signalling and control cables.
Contracts include the supply of signalling cables to London Underground Ltd for the Central Line resignalling scheme.

BICC Components has developed a new connector which eliminates the need for time-consuming trackside crimping of cables. It is produced by the company's Flexo Products unit and has been specially developed for the Flexo Paulve signalling detectors on the Paris express metro RER system and national railways, SNCF. BICC Components is part of BICC Cables.

## Brand-Rex

Viewfield Industrial Estate, Glenrothes KY6 2RS, UK
Tel: (+44 1592) 77 85 19   Fax: (+44 1592) 77 84 29
e-mail: scumiske@brand-rex.com
Web: http://www.brand-rex.com

**Key personnel**
Managing Director: Ian Mack

**Products**
Power, control, data communications cables for rail and mass transit applications. X-Treme range of cable employs irradiation cross-linking technology, offering superior performance, improved electrical performance and reduced fire propagation.

*UPDATED*

## Carrier Khéops Bac

Group Compagnie Deutsch
Z1 Sud, boulevard Pierre Lefaucheux, F-72027 Le Mans, Cedex 2, France
Tel: (+33 2) 43 61 45 45   Fax: (+33 2) 43 61 45 01
e-mail: ckb@compagnie.deutsch.com
Web: http://www.compagnie-deutsch.com

**Key personnel**
Managing Director: Denis Plantey
Finance Director: Jean-Claude Thieury
Marketing Manager: Patrick Roseleur
Public Relations: Agnes Favalelli

**Products**
Electrical connectors for signalling, power and control supply for metro, suburban rail, high-speed trains and LRT systems; fibre optic systems, coaxial connection systems.

**Contracts**
Equipment has been supplied for metro systems in Santiago, Mexico, Caracas and Singapore, and for tramways in Grenoble and St Etienne, M6 cars, for Korean TGV.

*UPDATED*

*Carrier Khéops CMC series of connectors*
2000/0087658

## Drallim Telecom

A division of Drallim Industries Ltd
Brett Drive, Bexhill-on-Sea TN40 2JP, UK
Tel: (+44 1424) 21 66 11   Fax: (+44 1424) 21 66 36
e-mail: email@drallim.com
Web: http://www.drallim.com

**Key personnel**
Chief Executive: R B McBrien
Marketing Director: M F Dawson

## Cables and cable equipment/MANUFACTURERS

### Products
Pressurisation equipment for telephone cables and waveguides; microprocessor telephone network alarm monitoring systems for pressurised cables and security alarm systems.

Contracts include the supply of pressurisation equipment complete with automatic monitoring to the Derby/Birmingham area in the UK and the supply and installation of cable pressurisation units at 11 sites between London Euston and Bletchley for Railtrack, UK, with staff training and continuing spares support.

### DSG-Canusa UK Ltd

Bergstrand House, Parkwood Close, Broadley Industrial Park, Roborough, Plymouth PL6 7EZ, UK
Tel: (+44 1752) 20 98 80   Fax: (+44 1752) 20 98 50
Web: http://www.dsgcanusa.com

#### Key personnel
Managing Director: S Hill
UK Sales Manager: Nigel Westermann

#### Products
Heat-shrinkable products for cable protection, jointing and insulation. Major supplier in the supply of zero halogen heat-shrinkable tubings.

DSG-Canusa products are extensively specified throughout the railway industry.

**UPDATED**

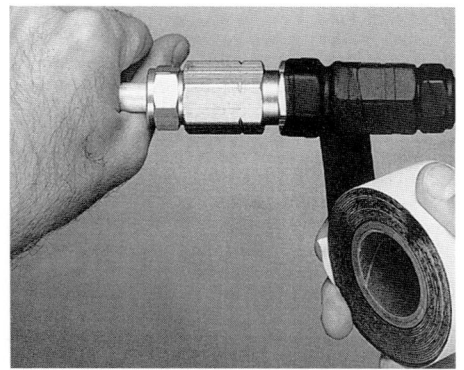

*Canusa Systems self-amalgamating tape being applied to an aluminium connector* 0021681

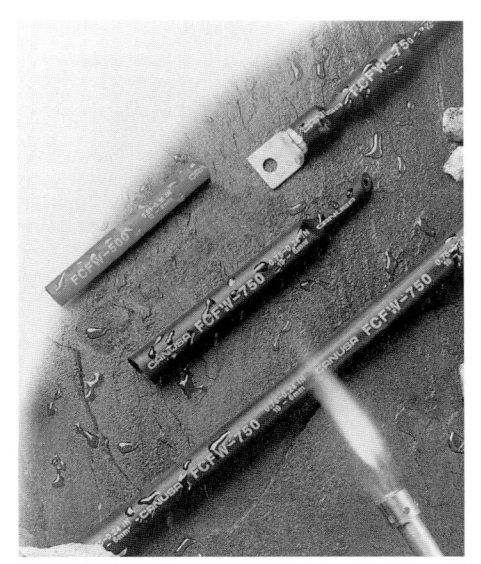

*Canusa Systems flame-retardant heavy wall heatshrink tubing* 0021682

### Ebo Systems

Boulevard d'Europe, PO Box 10, F-67211 Obernai Cedex, France
Tel: (+33 3) 88 49 50 51   Fax: (+33 3) 88 49 50 14
e-mail: ebosystemsint@yahoo.com
Web: http://www.ebo-systems.com

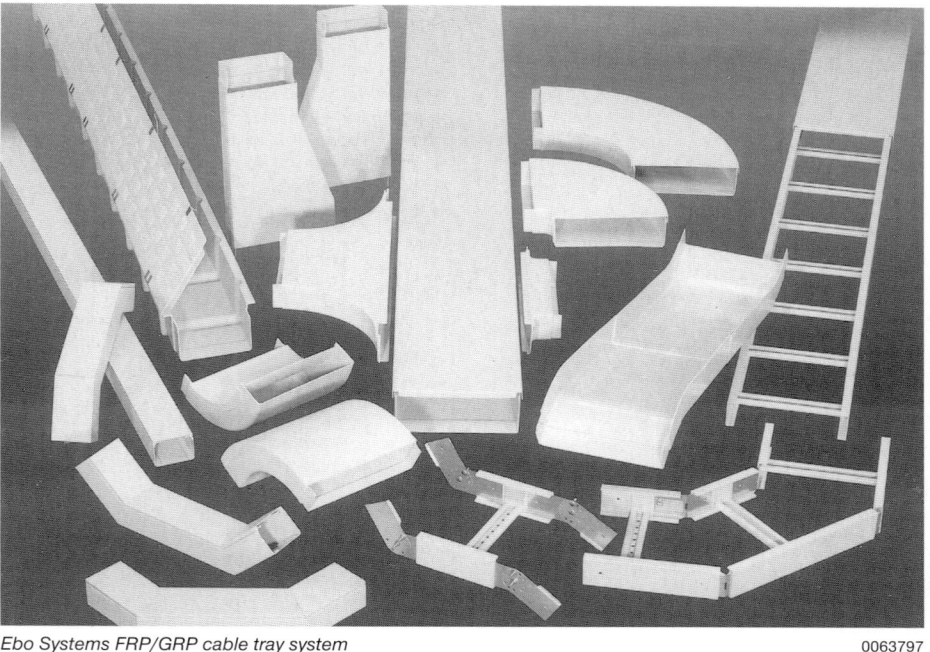

*Ebo Systems FRP/GRP cable tray system* 0063797

#### Key personnel
Manager: Peter Caldwell

#### Contact points

*France, Portugal, Spain, Belgium, Luxembourg, Middle East*
Ebo Systems
32/34 Avenue Salvador Allende, F-93800 Epinay/Seine
Tel: (+33 1) 49 71 55 80   Fax: (+33 1) 49 71 55 85
Contact: Jacques Pouret
e-mail: ebosystemsF@compuserv.com
Web: http://www.ebo-systems.com

*Germany*
Ebo Systems GmbH
Zum Gurrterstal, D-66440 Blieskastel
Tel: (+49 6842) 92 19 10   Fax: (+49 6842) 92 19 19
Contact: Ernst Messenzehl
e-mail: ebosystemsD@t-online.de
Web: http://www.ebo-systems.com

*Italy*
Ebo Systems Srl
Via Guido Rossa 5/7, I-Cumo (BG)
Tel: (+39 035) 46 20 88   Fax: (+33 035) 46 20 89
Contact: Antonio Rondelli
e-mail: ebosystems@cyberg.it
Web: http://www.ebo-systems.com

*Switzerland*
Ebo Systems AG
Tambourstrasse 8, CH-8833 Samstagern
Tel: (+41 1) 78 78 78 7   Fax (+41 1) 78 87 79 9
Contact: René Fontolliet
e-mail: ebo-systems-ch@active.ch
Web: http://www.ebo-systems.com

*United Kingdom*
Ebo Systems c/o Hager Ltd
Hortonwood 50, Telford TF1 4FT
Tel: (+44 1952) 67 68 18   Fax (+44 1952) 67 66 39
Contact: Simon Laugharne
e-mail: ebosystemsint@yahoo.com
Web: http://www.ebo-systems.com

*Head office, other countries*
See main address
Key Account Manager: Pascal Muller

#### Products
FRP/GRP cable management systems: cable trays, ground ducts, cable ladders; supports for trays, ducts and ladders.

FRP/GRP profiles for light structures, gratings, hand rails, stairs and ladders with safety cages.

Contracts include UK-France Channel Tunnel (1999); Vienna metro (1989-97); Berlin metro (1990-95); Swedish Railways (1991-95); Norwegian Railways; Czech Railways (1996); and French Railways.

### Ferranti Technologies Ltd

Cairo House, Waterhead, Oldham OL4 3JA, UK
Tel: (+44 161) 624 02 81   Fax: (+44 161) 624 52 44
e-mail: sales@ferranti-technologies.co.uk
Web: http://www.ferranti-technologies.co.uk

#### Key personnel
See *Passenger coach equipment* section.

#### Products
UV laser cable marking and manufacturer of cable looms.

**UPDATED**

### Harting Ltd

Caswell Road, Brackmills Industrial Estate, Northampton NN4 7PW, UK
Tel: (+44 1604) 76 66 86   Fax: (+44 1604) 70 67 77

#### Key personnel
Managing Director: R Wood

#### Products
Heavy-duty electrical connectors for rail and other transport applications. The range includes hoods, housings, inserts and contacts, all selected to offer environmental resistance and EMI/FRI protection. Fibre optic devices can also be supplied for critical control applications where immunity from electromagnetic interference is required.

**VERIFIED**

### Hellermann

Hellermann Insuloid
Leestone Road, Wythenshawe, Manchester M22 4RH, UK
Tel: (+44 161) 998 85 51   Fax: (+44 161) 945 37 08

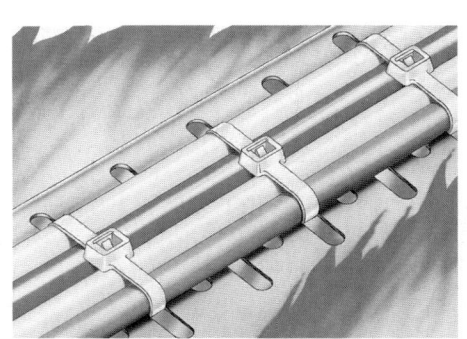

*Hellermann Insuloid flame-retardant and high-temperature cable ties* 0021683

**Key personnel**
European Product Manager: Tony Orme

**Products**
Flame-retardant ties in nylon or stainless steel.
Contracts include the supply of low-toxicity flame-retardant ties to London Underground and SNCF.

## Hitachi Cable

Hitachi Cable Ltd
2-1-2 Marunouchi, Chiyoda-ku, Tokyo 100-8338, Japan
Tel: (+81 3) 52 52 34 52
Fax: (+81 3) 32 13 04 02; 32 01 05 09

**Key personnel**
General Manager Export Dept No 2 Overseas Division:
 Yasuhito Mitomi

**Products**
Leaky coaxial cable and accessories; fibre optic cables and accessories.

## HPP GmbH

Philipp-Müller Strasse 12, D-23966 Wismar, Germany
Tel: (+49 3841) 75 81 50   Fax: (+49 3841) 75 81 51
e-mail: blickehpp@aol.com
Web: http://www.hpp-gmbh.com

**Products**
Plastic cable protection systems, including cable ducts, GRP support systems and cable protection pipes.
*NEW ENTRY*

## Hypertac

31 rue Isidore Maille, F-76410 Saint Aubin lès Elbeuf, France
Tel: (+33 2) 32 96 91 76   Fax: (+33 2) 32 96 91 70
e-mail: marketing@frb-connectron.fr
Web: http://www.frb-connectron.com

**Background**
The Hypertac Interconnect Group is part of Smiths Industries.

**Products**
Design, development and manufacturing of electrical connection systems for the rail traction industry.
All Hypertac Interconnect solutions have machine-turned round pins in the male half and the special Hypertac hyperboloid socket contact in the female half. This socket has a number of spring wires, set at a small angle to the centre line giving the special hyperboloid contact. As the pin enters the socket, the spring wires are deflected within their elastic limit. There is a very smooth wiping action and as result, minimal wear.
Products include rectangular connectors lhs/lhf series including modular connectors, rack and panel connectors and amovable contacts, as approved by SNCF and RATP.
Circular couplers include three-pole connectors, power couplers, car-to-car connection.
The Hypertac group has provided interconnect products for more than 40 years for mass and rapid transit projects throughout the world, including TGV, Eurostar, Mass Transit railway Hong Kong, London Underground and Seoul subway, using its engineering expertise to design connectors for applications such as signalling equipment, power supplies, AC/DC converters, lighting, communications and auxiliary equipment.

## Icore International Ltd

Leigh Road, Slough SL1 4BB, UK
Tel: (+44 1753) 57 41 34   Fax: (+44 1753) 87 36 24
e-mail: information@icore.co.uk
Web: http://www.icoregroup.com

**Key personnel**
European Commercial Manager: Christine Wickings

**Products**
Icore designs, manufactures and supplies wired interconnect systems, including lightweight and heavy duty zero halogen conduit systems, EMC protection for wired harnesses, specialised high power connectors and custom designed solutions. Typical applications include: intercarriage signal and power jumpers and carriage to bogie links; automatic coupling systems, sensors and braking systems.
*UPDATED*

## Litton

Veam
72 Whitecraigs Road, Whitehill Industrial Estate, Glenrothes, Fife KY6 2RX, UK
Tel: (+44 1592) 77 21 23   Fax: (+44 1592) 63 18 08

**Key personnel**
General Manager: Mike Hansen
Product Manager: Eric Cooke
Business Manager: Keith Gordon

**Products**
Circular connectors for power, control, data transmission and fibre optic systems. Intervehicle jumpers and electronic connectors and systems.

## LPA

LPA Industries
PO Box 15, Tudor Works, Debden Road, Saffron Walden CB11 4AN, UK
Tel: (+44 1799) 51 28 00   Fax: (+44 1799) 51 28 28
e-mail: sales@lpa-ind.demin.co.uk

**Key personnel**
Chief Executive Officer: Peter Pollock
Sales Director: Kevin Comfoot
Production Director: Graham Clark
Technical Director: B Simpkin

**Corporate background**
LPA Industries is a member of LPA Group plc.

**Products**
Electrical connectors (intervehicle), underframe assemblies/fabrications, cable glands, clamps, harnesses.
Contracts include supply of equipment to ALSTOM Transport (Juniper), Adtranz (Turbostar), all UK major train building contracts, KCRC Hong Kong and New Zealand Rail.

## Marconi Communications

Marconi Communications Limited
New Century Park, PO Box 53, Coventry CV3 1HJ, UK
Tel: (+44 1203) 56 55 00   Fax: (+44 1203) 56 58 88
e-mail: pete.hallard@marconicoms.com
Web: http://www.marconicomms.com

**Key personnel**
See *Signalling and telecommunications* section.

**Products**
Optical fibre, copper distribution and signalling cable systems.

## Multi-Contact (UK) Ltd

3 Presley Way, Crownhill, Milton Keynes MK8 0ES, UK
Tel: (+44 1908) 26 55 44   Fax: (+44 1908) 26 20 80
e-mail: sales@multi-contact.co.uk
Web: http://www.multi-contact.co.uk

**Key personnel**
Director: Vic Lavell
Commercial Director: Susan Thomson
Technical Manager: Selwyn Corns

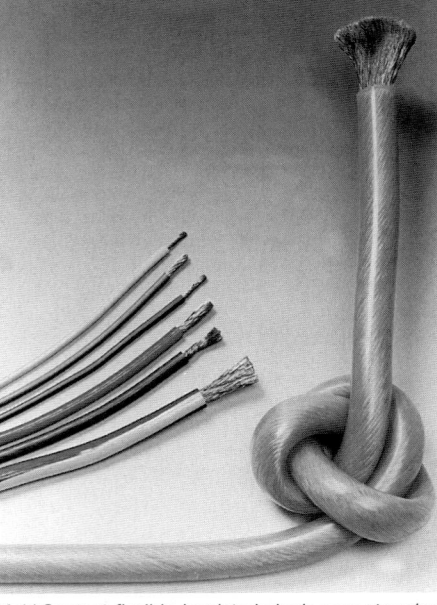

*Multi-Contact flexible insulated single-core stranded cable* 0021684

**Main works**
Multi-Contact AG Basel
Stockbrunnenrain 8, CH-4123 Allschwil 1, Switzerland
Tel: (+41 61) 302 45 45   Fax: (+41 61) 302 45 68

**Products**
Special-purpose high-current connectors. Typical rail applications include: power supply connections for preheating coaches; high-current connectors in modular static converters; automatic train couplers with control leads; plug-in power connector valves; and plug-in magnetic coils for linear maglev systems.
Flexible single-core cables; PVC, silicone, TPE and Teflon-insulated 0.10 to 95 mm$^2$.

## Pirelli Cables Ltd

PO Box 6, Leigh Road, Eastleigh SO50 9YE, UK
Tel: (+44 845) 767 83 45   Fax: (+44 238) 029 54 65

**Key personnel**
Managing Director: Martin Coffey
Business Director, Utilities: Michael Simms
Director, General Market: John Sloam
Operations Director, Energy Cables: Paul Davies
Chief Engineer: Bob Rosevear

**Products**
Power and telecommunications cables. Pirelli Cables makes a wide range of power cables, from track feeder cables to high-voltage cables for track power supplies. The company has introduced low-smoke zero halogen cables for power, signalling and communication purposes. These cables, designated LSOH (Low-Smoke Zero Halogen) are specifically designed for metro systems and were developed in close collaboration with London Transport Ltd. LT has been supplied with optical fibre communication cables sheathed with LSOH material for in-tunnel use, and with X-Flam 15 for use above ground.
Telecommunication cables for railway use include range of multipair designs to Railtrack specifications, specially screened designs for use with 25 kV AC overhead systems and optical fibre cables.
*UPDATED*

## PMA UK Ltd

Unit 4, Imperial Court, Magellan House, Walworth Industrial Estate, Andover SP10 5NT, UK
Tel: (+44 1264) 33 35 27   Fax: (+44 1264) 33 36 43
e-mail: sales@pmauk.co.uk
Web: http://www.pma-info.co.uk

**Key personnel**
Country Manager: Joy Levett

## Cables and cable equipment/**MANUFACTURERS**

*PMAFLEX VAM conduit and PMAfix male connectors with IP68 metal thread for increased mechanical requirements* 0021685

Financial Controller: Leanne Smith
Regional Sales Manager (North): Mark Fletcher
Key Account Manager: Donna Clash, Annabella Webb

**Head office**
PMA-AG
Aathalstrasse 90, CH-8610 Uster, Switzerland
Tel: (+41 1) 905 61 11  Fax: (+41 1) 905 61 22
e-mail: info@pma.ch
Web: http://www.pma.ch

**Key personnel**
Chairman: Ernst Schwarz
Worldwide Sales Manager: Rene Grivaz
Financial Director: Dieter Grabher
Marketing Assistant: Irene Freitag

**Subsidiary companies**
Australia, Austria, Belgium, Denmark, Finland, France, Germany, UK, Hong Kong, Hungary, Israel, Italy, Japan, Netherlands, Norway, Poland, Portugal, Singapore, Spain, Sweden, Taiwan, Turkey, Canada and USA.

**Products**
Nylon-based halogen-free cable protection; PMAfix cable connectors. VAM is a specially modified nylon 6 conduit with self-extinguishing and flammability characteristics particularly for internal carriage zones.

**Developments**
A new product range – Light Line which can be combined with the complete PMA standard product range.

**Contracts**
Contracts include supply of VAM conduit to London Underground Northern line, cable protectors to Siemens, ALSTOM and Bombardier Transportation.

*UPDATED*

## Racal Telecom

Phoenix House, Station Hill, Reading, RG1 1NB, UK
Tel: (+44 118) 908 60 00  Fax: (+44 118) 908 64 54

**Key personnel**
See *Signalling and telecommunications* section.

**Products**
Racal Telecom's business principally consists of the provision of operational and business telecomunications services to the railway industry in the UK. In March 1996, Racal Telecom's core network comprised 11,000 route-km of trunk cable, of which some 4,000 route-km were made up of fibre optic cable. During 1997, Racal upgraded Racal Telecom's network by creating a resilient SDH backbone network which included a further 1,200 route-km of fibre optic cable.

## Simclar International Corporation

9114 58th Place, Suite 500, Kenosha, Wisconsin 53144, USA
Tel: (+1 262) 653 99 99  Fax: (+1 262) 653 95 99
e-mail: simclar@execpc.com
Web: http://www.simclar.com

**Subsidiary company**
Simclar International Ltd
Pitreavie Business Park, Dunfermline KY11 8UN, UK
Tel: (+44 1383) 73 51 61  Fax: (+44 1383) 73 99 86
e-mail: sales@simclar.com

**Products**
Cable harness assemblies for traction equipment, cabs, high- and low-voltage applications, data communications systems and earthing equipment.

## Tyco Electronics

Tyco Electronics UK Ltd
Faraday Road, Dorcan, Swindon SN3 5HH, UK
Tel: (+44 1793) 52 81 71  Fax: (+44 1793) 57 25 16
Web: http://www.tycoelectronics.com

**Key personnel**
Worldwide Market Manager for Rail: Eddie Williams
Worldwide Marketing Communications Manager: Wendy Worger

**Products**
Products based on plastics, metals and chemicals including low fire hazard wire and cable, heat shrinkable zero halogen tubing and moulded parts, wire marking systems, electrical interconnection devices, electrical harness sealing products, electrical connector adaptors.
Lightweight wire and cable meeting low fire hazard criteria. Zerohal 100 wire offers a range of reduced fire hazard properties while retaining good mechanical performance and chemical resistance. The low fire hazard range of products has been expanded with the TMS-ZH-SCE family of heat-shrinkable cable markers.
Contracts: Zerohal 100 wire from Tyco Electronics has been utilised on a number of major rail and mass transit projects around the world – among them the New Jersey Transit Hudson Bergen line, Talent in Germany, the Brussels metro, the Seoul metro, as well as on several other major rolling stock projects in Europe and Asia.

## Weidmüller Interface GmbH & Co

AnderTalle 89, D-33102 Paderborn, Germany
Tel: (+49 5252) 96 00  Fax: (+49 5252) 96 01 16
e-mail: weidmueller@weidmueller.de
Web: http://weidmueller.de

**Key personnel**
Owner: W Schubel
Chief Executive Officer: Thomas Hagan
Managing Director ConNect: Ch. Bönsch
Head of Transportation: Mikhael Hoenig
International Project Manager: Stephen Ward

**Subsidiaries**
Australia, Austria, Bahrain, Belgium, Brazil, Bulgaria, Canada, China, Croatia, Czech Republic, Denmark, Finland, France, Germany, Greece, Hong Kong, Hungary, India, Israel, Italy, Japan, South Korea, Macedonia, Malaysia, Mexico, Netherlands, Norway, Pakistan, Poland, Portugal, Romania, Singapore, Slovakia, Slovenia, South Africa, Spain, Sweden, Switzerland, Taiwan, Thailand, Turkey, UK, Ukraine and USA

**Products**
Connectors and connection equipment including terminal blocks and terminal strips, HD connectors and terminal connectors for printed circuits.
Installation: wire, cables, terminals and instruments, enclosures, manual and automatic tools, ferrules and mounting trails.
Electronic interface modules, relay interface and PLC interfaces, power supply.
I/O components: decentralised I/O, field bus, SCADA and control software, industrial PC.
Customers include ALSTOM, Bombardier and Siemens.

*UPDATED*

## Yutaka Manufacturing Co Ltd

1-18-17 Kitakojiya Ota-ku, Tokyo 144-0032, Japan
Tel: (+81 3) 37 41 41 31  Fax: (+81 3) 57 05 70 65
e-mail: hideo.kamei@yutaka-ss.co.jp
Web: http://www.kutaka-ss.co.jp/

**Products**
Jumper cable connectors; high- and low-voltage connectors; multicontact connectors for power input and output.

# PERMANENT WAY COMPONENTS, EQUIPMENT AND SERVICES

## Alphabetical listing

A & K
A I Welders Ltd
A Kaufmann AG
AB Strängbeton
ABC-NACO Inc
Abetong Teknik
Abtus Ltd
ADMc
Akzo Nobel
Aldon Company Inc
Alfred McAlpine
ALH Systems Ltd
Allegheny
ALSTOM
Amec Rail Ltd
Amec Spie Rail Systems Ltd
American Railroad Curvelining Corporation
Amey Railways Ltd
Amurrio
Angle Plant
ApaTeCh
Apcarom SA
Arbil Ltd
Arcelor
Aspen Aerials
Aspen Equipment Co
Atlantic Track
Atlas Copco
Atlas Copco Berema
Atlas Hydraulic Loaders Ltd
Atlas Weyhausen
Austrak Pty Ltd
Avon Polymers France
BAC Corrosion Control Limited
Balfour Beatty Rail Engineering Ltd
Balfour Beatty Rail Ltd
Balfour Beatty Rail Ltd—Plant Division
Balfour Beatty Rail Maintenance Ltd
Ballast Nedam
Bance
Banestyrelsen Service Division
Banverket
Barclay Mowlem
Beilhack
BEML
Benkler
Benntec Systemtechnik GmbH
Bethlehem Steel Corporation
BHP Steel
Bomag GmbH
Bumar Ltd
Burn Standard
BWG
Caillard Cowans Sheldon
Camlok Lifting
CDM
Cemafer
Cembre SpA
Centrac Ltd
Century Group Inc
CF&I Steel
Chemetron
Chemgrate
Chipman Rail
Cimmco
Clouth
Cogifer
Colbond Geosynthetics
Colebrand Ltd
Collis Engineering Ltd
Comsa SA
Conbrako
Contec GmbH
ContiTech
Cooper & Turner
Corus Foundry
Corus Rail Modular Systems
Corus Rail Switches and Crossings
Cowans Sheldon
Créabéton
CSI Productos Largos SA
CSR Humes Pty Ltd
CXT Inc
Danieli Centro Maskin

Darcy Products Ltd
DBT GB Ltd
Delkor Pty Ltd
Derby Rubber Products
Desec Ltd
D'Huart
DISAB
Donelli DIMAF SpA
Drouard
Durisol Raalte BV
EBS
Ecomeca Fabrication Française
Edgar Allen Ltd
Edilon BV
Eichholtc
Electrologic Pty Ltd
Elektro-Thermit GmbH and Co KG
Energomachexport
Enzesfeld-Caro Metallwerke AG
ESAB Welding Equipment AB
ESCO Equipment Service Co
Eurailscout
Euroswitch
EWEM
Exel Oy
'EXIM' Verkehrs-, Hafen- und Umwelttechnik GmbH & Co Vertriebs KG
FAB-RA-CAST
Fairmont Tamper (Australia)
Fassetta
Faur SA
Ferotrack
Ferrostaal AG
Ferrostaal Corporation
Findlay, Irvine Ltd
First Engineering Ltd
Foster
Framafer
Geismar
Gemco
Getzner
Gleisbaumechanik Brandenburg
Grant Lyon Eagre
GrantRail Ltd
Greenwood Engineering
Grimma GmbH
Grinaker Duraset
GSK GmbH
GTRM
Gummiwerk Kraiburg Elastik GmbH
H J Skelton & Co Ltd
H J Skelton (Canada) Ltd
Hanning & Kahl GmbH & Co
Harsco Track Technologies
Harsco Track Technologies Ltd
Henry Williams Darlington Ltd
Hi-Force Hydraulics Ltd
Hindustan Eng & Ind
Hioma-aine Oy
Holdfast Level Crossing Ltd
Holland
Holland Co
Huck
IAD Rail Systems
ImproRail
Inexa Profil AB
Infra Safety Services
Infrasoft Ltd
INFUNDO GmbH
Interep SA
International Track Systems Inc
IPA
Jackson Eve Infrastructure Services
JAFCO
Jakem Timbers Ltd
Jaraguá
Jarret
Jarvis Rail
J C Bamford Excavators Ltd
JEZ Sistemas Ferroviarios
Kalyn Siebert
Kershaw
KIHN SA
Kirow

Kloos Oving BV
Knox Kershaw Inc
Kockums
Kolmex SA
Krautkrämer GmbH & Co
Künzler
Laser Rail Ltd
Leonhard Weiss GmbH and Co
Lewis Bolt & Nut Co
Lindapter International
Linsinger Maschinenbau GesmbH
Loram Maintenance of Way, Inc
Lord Corporation
Lucchini Group
LUKAS
Lyudinovo Locomotive Works JSC
Mannesmann
Manoir Industries
Matériel de Voie SA
Matisa
Max Bögl
Mecanoexportimport SA
Mer Mec SpA
metronom Gesellschaft für Industrievermessung mbH
Metrum Information Storage
Millbrook Proving Ground
Mitchell Equipment Corporation
Mitsukawa Metal Works Co Ltd
Modern Track Machinery Canada Ltd
Monterrey
Moog GmbH
Moore & Steele
Mossboda Trä AB
MTH Praha AS
Muromteplovoz
NedTrain BV
Newag
Newt International
Nippon Kido Kogyo
NKK
Nordco
Norwest Holst
NRS
ØDS-Caltronic AS
Oleo International Ltd
OLMI SpA
ORTEC
Orton/McCullough
Osmose Railroad Division
Palfinger
Pandrol Rail Fastenings
Parachini SA
Partner Dimas UK
Peddinghaus Group
Permali Gloucester Ltd
Pettibone
Pfleiderer AG
Phoenix AG
Pintsch Bamag GmbH
Plasser & Theurer
Pohl Corporation
Portec
Pouget
Premesa
Presto Products Company
Progress Rail Services Corporation
PS Corporation
Qiqihar
Quest
Racine Railroad Products Inc
Railpro
Railquip Inc
Rails Company
Railtech International
Railtech Schlatter Systems
RailWorks Corporation
Ranalah
Rawie
Response Environmental Services Ltd
Rexquote
RICA
Richardson & Cruddas (1972) Ltd
RMC Concrete Products (UK)
RMS Locotec

# MANUFACTURERS/Permanent way components, equipment and services

Road Rail Equipment
Robel
Rosenqvist Rail Tech AB
Rotabroach
Rotamag Rail Division
Saar-Gummi
Salient Systems Inc
Sateba International
Schlatter AG, HA
Schramm Inc
Schweizer Electronic
Schwihag
SECO-Rail
Semperit
Sersa AG
SGB
Siemens Switzerland
Sika Ltd
SILF Srl
Slab Track Systems International
Sola
Somafel
Sonatest plc
Spefaka
Speno International SA
Sperling Railway Services Inc
Sperry
Spie

Spitzke GmbH
SPX Fluid Power
SRS
Steel Authority of India
Strukton Railinfra BV
Swingmaster Corporation
Sydney Steel Corporation
System Bahnbau International (SBI)
Thermon Manufacturing Co
Tülomsas
Türk + Hillinger GmbH
Tarmac
Technirail
Tectran
Tempered Spring
Templeton
Tensol Rail
Thebra
Thermit Australia Pty
Thermit Welding (GB) Ltd
Thims
Thyssen Krupp
Tiefenbach GmbH
Tiflex Ltd
Tipco Inc
TKL Rail
Tokimec
Trinity Difco Inc

True Temper
TSO
Turkington Precast Concrete
Two-Way Technology Ltd
Tyco Electronics Corporation
Ultra Dynamics
Unit Rail Anchor Company Inc
UniTrac Systems Product Group – IMPulse NC Inc
Upright UK Ltd
VAE Aktiengesellschaft
VAE Nortrak
VAE UK Ltd
Vaia Car
Voest Alpine Schienen
Vortok International
Vossloh Rail Systems GmbH
Wabtec Rail Ltd
Wacker (GB) Ltd
Walter Bau-Aktiengesellschaft
Western-Cullen-Hayes Inc
Wieland
Willy Vogel AG
Windhoff AG
Yamatech
Yamato Kogyo
Zollner GmbH
Zweiweg Schneider GmbH & Co KG
Zwiehoff GmbH

## Classified listing

**TRACK COMPONENTS**

A & K
ABC-NACO
Abetong Teknik
AB Strangbeton
Akzo Nobel
ALH Systems
Allegheny
Amurrio
ApATeCh
Apcarom
Arcelor
Atlantic Track
Austrak
Avon Polymers France
BAC Corrosion Control
Balfour Beatty Rail Engineering
Bance
Barclay Mowlem
Bethlehem Steel
BHP Steel
British Steel Railway & Foundry Products
BUMAR Ltd
Burn Standard
BWG
CDM
Cembre
Century Precast
CF&I Steel
Chemgrate
Cimmco
Clouth
Cogifer
Colebrand Ltd
Collis Engineering
ContiTech
Cooper & Turner
Corus Rail Modular Systems
Créabéton
CSI Productos Largos
CSR Humes
CXT
Daido
Darcy
Delkor
D'Huart
Drouard
Durisol Raalte
Edgar Allen
Edilon
Eichholtc
Eurailscout
EWEM
Exel
EXIM
FAB-RA-CAST

Fassetta
Ferotrack
Ferrostaal
Ferrostaal Corporation
Findlay, Irvine
Foster
Getzner
Grant Lyon Eagre
GrantRail
Grinaker Duraset
GSK
Gummiwerk Kraiburg Elastik
Hanning & Kahl
Hindustan Eng & Ind
Henry Williams Darlington
H J Skelton (Canada) Ltd
Holdfast Level Crossing Ltd
Holland
Huck
IAD Rail Systems
ImproRail
Inexa Prodii AB
Interep
International Track Systems
IPA
Jakem
Jaraguá
Kaufmann
KIHN
Kloos Railway Systems
Lewis Bolt & Nut
Lindapter
Lord
Lucchini
Lukas
Manoir Industries
Matériel de Voie
Max Bögl
Mecanoexportimport
Mitchell Equipment
Mitsukawa
Monterrey
Moore & Steele
Mossboda Trä AB
NARSTCO
Nippon Kido Kogyo
NKK
Norwest Holst
NRS
ØDS Caltronic
Oleo
OLMI
ORTEC
Osmose
Pandrol Rail Fastenings
Peddinghaus Group

Permali UK
Pettibone
Phoenix
Pintsch Bamag
Pohl
Portec
Portec Rail Products (UK)
Pouget
Premesa
Presto Products Company
Progress Rail Services
PS
Qiqihar
Railpro
Rails
Ranalah
Rawie
Raychem
Response Environmental Services
RICA
Richardson & Cruddas
RMC Concrete Products
SaarGummi
Salient
Sateba
SBI
Schwihag
Semperit
Siemens Switzerland
Sika
SILF
H J Skelton
Slab Track Systems International
Sperry
SRS
Steel Authority of India
Sydney Steel
Tarmac
Technirail
Tempered Spring
Tensol Rail
Tetsudo Kiki
Thermon Manufacturing Co
Thyssen Krupp
Tiefenbach
Tiflex
Tipco
TKL Rail
Türk + Hillinger
Turkington Precast
Ultra Dynamics
Unit Rail Anchor
UniTrac Systems
VAE UK Ltd
VAE Nortrak
Voest Alpine Schienen

Vortok
Vossloh Rail Systems
Walter Bau-Aktiengesellschaft
Yamato Kogyo

### TRACK CONSTRUCTION AND MAINTENANCE EQUIPMENT
A & K
Abtus
A I Welders
Aldon
ALH Systems
American Railroad Curvelining
Angle Plant
Arbil
Aspen Aerials
Aspen Equipment
Atlas Copco
Atlas Copco Berema
Atlas Hydraulic Loaders
Atlas Weyhausen
Avon Polymers France
Balfour Beatty Rail Plant
Ballast Nedam
Bance
Banverket
Barclay Mowlem
Beilhack
BEML
Benkler
Bomag
Caillard Cowans Sheldon
Camlok Lifting
Cemafer
Chemetron
Chipman Rail
Conbrako
Contec GmbH
Danieli Centro Maskin
Darcy
DBT GB Ltd
Desec
Donelli
EBS
Electrologic
Elektro-Thermit
Energomachexport
Esab
Eurailscout
Euroswitch
EXIM
Fairmont Tamper
Fairmont Tamper (Australia)
Fassetta
Faur
Framafer
Geismar
Gemco
Henry Williams Darlington
Hi-Force Hydraulics
Holland Co
ImproRail
JAFCO
J C Bamford Excavators Ltd
JEZ Sistemas Ferroviarios
Kalyn Siebert
Kershaw Manufacturing
Kirow
Knox Kershaw
Kockums
Kolmex
Krautkrämer
Künzler
Laser Rail
Leonhard Weiss
Linsinger
Loram
Lord
Lukas
Lyudinovo Locomotive Works JSC
Mannesmann
Matisa
Mer Mec
Millbrook Proving Ground
Mitchell Equipment
Modern Track Machinery
Moss Systems
MTH Praha
Newag
NKK
Nordco
Orton/McCullough
Palfinger
Partner Dimas UK
Permaquip
Pettibone
Plasser & Theurer
Pouget
Progress Rail Services
Quest
Racine
Railpro
Rails
Railtech
Railtech Schlatter Systems
Rexquote
RFS(E)
RMS Locotec
Road Rail Equipment
Robel
Rotabroach
Schlatter
Schramm
Schweizer Electronic
SGB
Siemens Switzerland
SMIS
Sola
Sonatest
Spefaka
Speno
Spie
SPX Fluid Power
SRS
Swingmaster
Templeton
Tensol Rail
Thebra
Thermit Australia
Thermit Welding
TKL Rail
Tokimec
Tooltract
Trinity Difco
True Temper
TSO
Tülomsas
Upright UK
Unit Rail Anchor
VAE Nortrak
Vaia Car
Wacker
Western-Cullen-Hayes
Wieland
Windhoff
Yamatech
Zollner GmbH
Zweiweg Schneider

### TRACK CONSTRUCTION AND MAINTENANCE SERVICES
ALH Systems
ALSTOM
AMEC Rail
AMEC Spie Rail Systems
American Railroad Curvelining
Amey Railways
Balfour Beatty
Balfour Beatty Rail Maintenance
Ballast Nedam
Banestyrelsen Service Division
Banverket
Benntec Systemtechnik
Centrac
Chemetron
Chipman Rail
Cogifer
Comsa
Derby Rubber Products
Desquenne et Giral
Drouard
Fairmont Tamper
First Engineering
Grant Lyon Eagre
GrantRail
Greenwood Engineering
GTRM
Holland Co
IBM
Jackson Eve Infrastructure Services
Jarvis Rail
Kolmex
Laser Rail
Metronom Gessellschaft für Industrievermessung
Metrum
Millbrook Proving Ground
Muromteplovoz
Newt International
NKK
Norwest Holst
OLMI
Osmose
Pandrol Jackson
Parachini SA
Permaquip
PS
Railpro
Relayfast
RMS Locotec
Rosenqvist RailTech
SBI
SECO-Rail
Sersa AG
Slab Track Systems International
Somafel
Southern Track Renewals
Speno
Sperling Railway Services
Sperry
Spie
Spitzke GmbH
SRS
Strukton Railinfra
Technirail
Tectran
TSO
Two-Way Technology
Wacker

## MANUFACTURERS/Permanent way components, equipment and services

### Company listing by country

**AUSTRALIA**
Austrak Pty Ltd
Barclay Mowlem
BHP Steel
CSR Humes Pty Ltd
Delkor Pty Ltd
Derby Rubber Products
Electrologic Pty Ltd
Fairmont Tamper (Australia)
Gemco
Holland
Mitchell Equipment Corporation
Thermit Australia Pty
TKL Rail

**AUSTRIA**
Enzesfeld-Caro Metallwerke AG
Getzner
Linsinger Maschinenbau GesmbH
Palfinger
Plasser & Theurer
Semperit
Sola
VAE Aktiengesellschaft

**BELGIUM**
CDM
Technirail

**BRAZIL**
Jaraguá
Premesa
Tectran
Thebra

**CANADA**
H J Skelton (Canada) Ltd
Modern Track Machinery Canada Ltd
NARSTCO
Sydney Steel Corporation
Tipco Inc
VAE Nortrak

**CHINA, PEOPLE'S REPUBLIC**
Qiqihar

**CZECH REPUBLIC**
MTH Praha AS

**DENMARK**
ØDS-Caltronic AS
Greenwood Engineering

**FINLAND**
Desec Ltd
Exel Oy
Hioma-aine Oy

**FRANCE**
ALSTOM
Avon Polymers France
Caillard Cowans Sheldon
Cogifer
D'Huart
Drouard
Ecomeca Fabrication Française
Fassetta
Framafer
Geismar
Interep SA
Jarret
Manoir Industries
Matériel de Voie SA
Pouget
Railtech International
Railtech Schlatter Systems
Sateba International
SECO-Rail
Spie
TSO

**GERMANY**
Atlas Weyhausen
Beilhack
Benntec Systemtechnik GmbH
Bomag GmbH
BWG
Cemafer

Clouth
Contec GmbH
ContiTech
Elektro-Thermit GmbH and Co KG
'EXIM' Verkehrs-, Hafen- und Umwelttechnik GmbH & Co Vertriebs KG
Ferrostaal AG
Gleisbaumechanik Brandenburg
Grimma GmbH
GSK GmbH
Gummiwerk Kraiburg Elastik GmbH
Hanning & Kahl GmbH & Co
INFUNDO GmbH
Kirow
Krautkrämer GmbH & Co
Leonhard Weiss GmbH and Co
LUKAS
Mannesmann
Max Bögl
metronom Gesellschaft für Industrievermessung mbH
Moog GmbH
Newag
ORTEC
Peddinghaus Group
Pfleiderer AG
Phoenix AG
Pintsch Bamag GmbH
Rawie
Robel
Saar-Gummi
Schweizer Electronic
Slab Track Systems International
Spefaka
Spitzke GmbH
System Bahnbau International (SBI)
Türk + Hillinger GmbH
Thyssen Krupp
Tiefenbach GmbH
Voest Alpine Schienen
Vossloh Rail Systems GmbH
Walter Bau-Aktiengesellschaft
Wieland
Willy Vogel AG
Windhoff AG
Zweiweg Schneider GmbH & Co KG
Zwiehoff GmbH

**INDIA**
BEML
Burn Standard
Cimmco
Hindustan Eng & Ind
Richardson & Cruddas (1972) Ltd
Steel Authority of India

**ITALY**
Cembre SpA
Donelli DIMAF SpA
IPA
Lucchini Group
Mer Mec SpA
OLMI SpA
RICA
SILF Srl
Vaia Car

**JAPAN**
Mitsukawa Metal Works Co Ltd
Nippon Kido Kogyo
NKK
PS Corporation
Tokimec
Yamatech
Yamato Kogyo

**LUXEMBOURG**
KIHN SA

**MEXICO**
Monterrey

**NETHERLANDS**
Akzo Nobel
Ballast Nedam
Colbond Geosynthetics
Durisol Raalte BV
Edilon BV
Eurailscout

ImproRail
Infra Safety Services
Kloos Oving BV
NedTrain BV
Railpro
Strukton Railinfra BV

**POLAND**
Bumar Ltd
Kolmex SA
Somafel

**ROMANIA**
Apcarom SA
Faur SA
Mecanoexportimport SA

**RUSSIAN FEDERATION**
ApaTeCh
Energomachexport
Lyudinovo Locomotive Works JSC
Muromteplovoz

**SOUTH AFRICA**
Conbrako
Grinaker Duraset

**SPAIN**
Arcelor
Amurrio
Comsa SA
CSI Productos Largos SA
JEZ Sistemas Ferroviarios

**SWEDEN**
AB Strängbeton
Abetong Teknik
Atlas Copco Berema
Banverket
Danieli Centro Maskin
DISAB
ESAB Welding Equipment AB
Inexa Profil AB
Kockums
Mossboda Trä AB
Rosenqvist Rail Tech AB
SRS
Thims

**SWITZERLAND**
A Kaufmann AG
Benkler
Créabéton
EBS
Euroswitch
EWEM
Künzler
Matisa
Parachini SA
Schlatter AG, HA
Schwihag
Sersa AG
Siemens Switzerland
Speno International SA
Tensol Rail

**TURKEY**
Tülomsas

**UNITED KINGDOM**
Abtus Ltd
ADMc
A I Welders Ltd
Alfred McAlpine
ALH Systems Ltd
Amec Rail Ltd
Amec Spie Rail Systems Ltd
Amey Railways Ltd
Angle Plant
Arbil Ltd
Atlas Copco
Atlas Hydraulic Loaders Ltd
BAC Corrosion Control Limited
Balfour Beatty Rail Engineering Ltd
Balfour Beatty Rail Ltd
Balfour Beatty Rail Ltd—Plant Division
Balfour Beatty Rail Maintenance Ltd
Bance

Camlok Lifting
Centrac Ltd
Chipman Rail
Colebrand Ltd
Collis Engineering Ltd
Cooper & Turner
Corus Foundry
Corus Rail Modular Systems
Corus Rail Switches and Crossings
Cowans Sheldon
Darcy Products Ltd
DBT GB Ltd
Edgar Allen Ltd
Ferotrack
Findlay, Irvine Ltd
First Engineering Ltd
Grant Lyon Eagre
GrantRail Ltd
GTRM
H J Skelton & Co Ltd
Harsco Track Technologies Ltd
Henry Williams Darlington Ltd
Hi-Force Hydraulics Ltd
Holdfast Level Crossing Ltd
IAD Rail Systems
Infrasoft Ltd
Jackson Eve Infrastructure Services
JAFCO
Jakem Timbers Ltd
Jarvis Rail
JC Bamford Excavators Ltd
Laser Rail Ltd
Lindapter International
Metrum Information Storage
Millbrook Proving Ground
Newt International
Norwest Holst
NRS
Oleo International Ltd
Pandrol Rail Fastenings
Partner Dimas UK

Permali Gloucester Ltd
Ranalah
Response Environmental Services Ltd
RMC Concrete Products (UK)
RMS Locotec
Road Rail Equipment
Rotabroach
Rotamag Rail Division
SGB
Sika Ltd
Sonatest plc
SPX Fluid Power
Tarmac
Tempered Spring
Thermit Welding (GB) Ltd
Tiflex Ltd
Turkington Precast Concrete
Two-Way Technology Ltd
Ultra Dynamics
Upright UK Ltd
VAE UK Ltd
Vortok International
Wabtec Rail Ltd
Wacker (GB) Ltd

**UNITED STATES OF AMERICA**
A & K
ABC-NACO Inc
Aldon Company Inc
Allegheny
American Railroad Curvelining Corporation
Aspen Aerials
Aspen Equipment Co
Atlantic Track
Bethlehem Steel Corporation
Century Group Inc
CF&I Steel
Chemetron
Chemgrate
CXT Inc
ESCO Equipment Service Co

FAB-RA-CAST
Ferrostaal Corporation
Foster
Harsco Track Technologies
Holland Co
Huck
International Track Systems Inc
Kalyn Siebert
Kershaw
Knox Kershaw Inc
Lewis Bolt & Nut Co
Loram Maintenance of Way, Inc
Lord Corporation
Moore & Steele
Nordco
Orton/McCullough
Osmose Railroad Division
Pettibone
Pohl Corporation
Portec
Presto Products Company
Progress Rail Services Corporation
Quest
Racine Railroad Products Inc
Railquip Inc
Rails Company
RailWorks Corporation
Salient Systems Inc
Schramm Inc
Sperling Railway Services Inc
Sperry
Swingmaster Corporation
Templeton
Trinity Difco Inc
True Temper
Tyco Electronics Corporation
Unit Rail Anchor Company Inc
UniTrac Systems Product Group – IMPulse NC Inc
Western-Cullen-Hayes Inc

## MANUFACTURERS/Permanent way components, equipment and services

## A & K

A & K Railroad Materials Inc
1505 South Redwood Road, Salt Lake City, Utah 84104, USA
Tel: (+1 801) 974 54 84    Fax: (+1 801) 972 20 41

**International office**
5206 FM 1960 West Suite 103, Houston, Texas 77069, USA
Tel: (+1 281) 893 39 08    Fax: (+1 281) 893 83 71
Web: http://www.akrailroad.com

**Key personnel**
Chairman: K W Schumacher
President: M H Kulmer
Vice-President, International: Julian Polit
Manager, International Sales: Alfredo Sansores

**Products**
Rail (new and used), rail accessories, track tools, trackwork materials, welding, continuous welded rail, complete switches, frogs, anchors, bolts, spikes, lockwashers, gauge rods, ties, sleepers, hand track tools and other track materials.

## ABC-NACO Inc

2001 Butterfield Road, Suite 502, Downers Grove, Illinois 60515, USA
Tel: (+1 630) 852 13 00    Fax: (+1 630) 852 22 64
Web: http://www.abc-naco.com

**Key personnel**
See entry in *Brakes and drawgear* section.

**Products**
Trackwork products including frogs, switches, points, crossings, guardrails, switch stands, turnouts and turnout components.

## Abetong Teknik

PO Box 24, SE-351 03 Växjö, Sweden
Tel: (+46 470) 965 00    Fax: (+46 470) 160 81
e-mail: abetong@scancem.com
Web: http://www.railway-technology.com

**Main works**
Växjö

**Key personnel**
Managing Director: Stefan Westberg
General Manager: Ulf Malmqvist

**Principal subsidiary**
Swetrak AS, Estonia

**Products**
Prestressed concrete sleepers for main lines and turnouts; prefabricated grade crossings; production equipment and technical services for the manufacture and design of concrete sleepers.

The company has supplied its know-how to some 25 different factories worldwide; together these plants have now produced over 40 million sleepers.

The company has designed concrete sleepers for heavy-duty turnouts to suit traffic specifications of 37 tonnes maximum and 30 tonnes nominal axleloads at up to 80 km/h, and annual gross train tonnages of more than 50 million. Abetong has also developed special sleepers for high-speed lines.

## AB Strängbeton

Box 5074, SE-131 05 Nacka, Sweden
Tel: (+46 8) 615 82 00    Fax: (+46 8) 641 66 70

**Products and services**
Prestressed concrete sleepers. Services provided include: total track construction planning; feasibility studies for sleeper production; supply of complete plant for concrete sleeper manufacture, with technology transfer; project planning, management and control; and technical training.

## Abtus Ltd

Falconer Road, Haverhill CB9 7XU, UK
Tel: (+44 1440) 70 29 38    Fax: (+44 1440) 70 29 61
e-mail: info@abtus.co.uk
Web: http://www.abtus.co.uk

**Key personnel**
Managing Director: Russell Owen
Technical Manager: Ashley May

**Principal subsidiary**
Tereor Electronics Ltd

**Products**
Sighting, void detection, track and overhead line measurement (digital and analogue), bond drilling and track slewing equipment; self-powered track maintenance vehicles; design, consultancy, full repair and recalibration.

**Contracts**
Recent contracts include the supply of standard and purpose-made equipment to Railtrack, London Underground Ltd, Docklands Light Railway, British Rail Infrastructure Services, all major European railway systems and Hong Kong.

*UPDATED*

## Arcelor

Apartado 520, (Edificio Energías 2a P), E-33200 Gijón, Asturias, Spain
Tel: (+34 98) 518 71 67    Fax: (+34 98) 518 75 43
e-mail: fsainzb@aceralia.es
Web: http://www.aceralia.es

**Key personnel**
Marketing Manager: D Fernando Sáinz Varona

**Corporate development**
Arcelor is the result of a merger of three major European steel producers. Aceralia, Arbed and Usinor, claimed to have created the biggest steel company in the world.

**Products**
Arcelor produces rails for all the world markets, especially for high-speed and heavy-haul lines. Arcelor produces a variety of standard types of rail, including RN 45, TR 45/90RA-A, UIC 54, UIC 60, TR 57/11RE, TR 68/136RE, VIGNOLE 46; BS 100A, BS 90A, BS 80A.

*UPDATED*

## A I Welders Ltd

Seafield Road, Longman Industrial Estate, Inverness IV1 1LZ, UK
Tel: (+44 1463) 23 93 81    Fax: (+44 1463) 22 54 45
e-mail: 101364.453@compuserve.com

**Key personnel**
Managing Director: A J Hunter
Production Director: H Cossar
Applications Engineer, Sales: N Sherriffs

**Products**
Rail welding machines for continuous welded rail, switches and crossings; static and mobile rail straightening presses; complete rail welding depot installations, including conveyor systems and gantry cranes; reconditioning and upgrading of rail welding machines and depots.

## A Kaufmann AG

Pilatusstrasse 2, CH-6300 Zug, Switzerland
Tel: (+41 41) 711 67 00    Fax: (+41 41) 859 16 01
e-mail: info@kago.ch
Web: http://www.kago.com

**Products**
KAGO specialist engineering products for railways, including a complete range of non-screwed rail contact clamps, discs and strips for electrical rail connections (return current, signalling circuits, earthing), cable fastenings for rails and sleepers, special welding electrodes for copper welding; complete range of screwing, welding and interlocking fittings; self-tapping sleeper screws for concrete, steel or wooden sleepers; sleeper spring clips; high-voltage insulations.

Recent development: KAGO contract strips and discs for electrical rail connections in complex pathwork.

**Services**
Track returns and earthing wires; earthing poles; heavy-duty and special mountings and drillings; suspensions for radiating cables.

*UPDATED*

*KAGO easily mounted electrical rail contact with vibration-resistant cable fixing*   2000/0093216

*Rail production by Arcelor*   2001/0103967

www.gottwald.com

## Competence on rails

Whatever you need — track-maintenance cranes, breakdown cranes ... — we have the technology and experience to ensure you get the tailored solution you need.

Gottwald railway cranes — throughout the world

**Gottwald Port Technology GmbH:** P.O. Box: 18 03 43 • 40570 Düsseldorf, Germany
Phone: +49 211 7102-0 • Fax: +49 211 7102-651 • info@gottwald.com • www.gottwald.com

**GOTTWALD** port technology

# MANUFACTURERS/Permanent way components, equipment and services

## Akzo Nobel

Akzo Nobel Geosynthetics
PO Box 9300, Westervoortsedijk 73, NL-6800 SB Arnhem, Netherlands
Tel: (+31 26) 366 46 00    Fax: (+31 26) 366 48 30

**Key personnel**
General Manager: Jan van Boldrick
Sales Manager: Blair Rawes
Marketing Manager: Wim Voskamp

**Products**
Enkadrain TP and Colbonddrain, track components.

---

## Aldon Company Inc

3410 Sunset Avenue, Waukegan, Illinois 60087, USA
Tel: (+1 847) 623 88 00    Fax: (+1 847) 623 61 39
e-mail: aldonco@interaccess.com

**Key personnel**
President: J R Ornig
General Manager: J A Shelton

**Products**
Railway safety and maintenance equipment, including lightweight straddle-type rerailers; track levellers; track gauges; track jacks; safety derailers; rail benders and track carts.

---

## Alfred McAlpine

Exchange House, Kelburn Court, Leacroft Road, Birchwood, Warrington WA3 6SY, UK
Tel: (+44 1925) 85 80 00    Fax: (+44 1925) 85 80 99
Web: http://www.alredmcalpine.com

**Key personnel**
General Manager: Jeff Boden

**Organisation**
Alfred McAlpine provides a wide variety of services within the rail sector, from complex major projects to discrete schemes for individual clients. The services include engineering works on the railway, ranging from structures maintenance/renewals and embankment stabilisation through to effective management and delivery of complex multi-discipline schemes.

Through their Assurance Case for works on Railtrack infrastructure, Alfred McAlpine undertakes works both for Railtrack directly and for rail industry clients wishing to carry out construction, renewal or maintenance works on the railway.

*NEW ENTRY*

---

## ALH Rail Coatings Ltd

Carolina Court, Lakeside, Doncaster DN4 5RA, UK
Tel: (+44 1302) 79 11 00    Fax: (+44 1302) 79 12 00

**Works**
Hebden Road, Scunthorpe DN15 8DT, UK
Tel: (+44 1724) 84 87 65    Fax: (+44 1724) 84 87 65

**Key personnel**
Managing Director: Bernard Stell
Technical Director: Malcolm Davies
Sales Director: Robert Venell

**Corporate background**
ALH Rail Coatings is a joint venture between GrantRail and Hyperlast.

**Products**
Using its expertise as a formulator and manufacturer of polyurethane and epoxy resin systems, ALH supplies a patented precoated rail system offering high electrical insulation properties combined with reduced noise and vibration characteristics.

The system was chosen by Laing Civil Engineering and GrantRail Ltd for street running sections of the Midland Metro project and the Phase 2 extension of the Manchester Metrolink light rail system.

*UPDATED*

---

## Allegheny

Allegheny Rail Products
A division of L B Foster Co
415 Holiday Drive, Pittsburgh, Pennsylvania 15220-2793, USA
Tel: (+1 412) 928 35 00    Fax: (+1 412) 928 35 12

**Key personnel**
President: Henry M Ortwein Jr
General Manager, Sales and Engineering: Sidney A Shue
Product Manager: Michelle C Chapin
Director, International Sales: Hakan Eksioglu
Controller: Dennis E Koehler

**Products**
Bonded insulated and bonded standard rail joint kits, 'Toughcoat' polyurethane-encapsulated joint bars; 'Temprange' epoxy bond insulated plug rails; glass fibre and polyurethane end posts; 'bulldog' rail defect/weld protection bars.

---

## ALSTOM Transport SA

System Infrastructure Business Unit
3 rue Eugène & Armand Peugeot, F-92508 Rueil-Malmaison Cedex, France
Tel: (+33 1) 47 52 80 00    Fax: (+33 1) 47 52 82 46

**Key personnel**
Director: Alain Goga

**Services**
The Infrastructure Business unit of ALSTOM Transport offers comprehensive solutions at the system or subsystem level for power generation and distribution including AC and DC traction substations; overhead facilities; contact lines or catenaries; third-rail or at-level integrated supply system; SCADA; auxiliary power supply; track laying; maintenance workshops; communications; signalling (tramways); electromechanical equipment in station; and electronic guidance systems for buses.

Its scope embraces design, procurement, installation, commissioning, technical assistance, maintenance and training.

**Products**
ALSTOM has considerable experience relating to urban track for mass transit and light rail/tramway systems, both for ballasted and concrete-bed applications, and steel-wheeled or rubber-tyred vehicles.

Through its expertise in concrete, ALSTOM has developed a new concept in urban track laying. APPITRACK™ is a new automatic process for the construction of track on a concrete bed which avoids the use of sleepers. The method involves slip-form concreting derived from motorway and airport runway construction.

The track is automatically constructed directly on the project alignment using automatic plate and pin inserts. The process reduces erection time, costs and nuisance impact on the urban environment and allows higher noise and vibration requirements to be met. The APPITRACK™ process uses computerised monitoring aids for accuracy of execution and allows:
- speed of execution and limitation of disturbance (noise, vibrations);
- cost savings combined with a high performance level.

**Contracts**
ALSTOM has taken the responsibility for the track in metro projects including Caracas, Cairo, Athens, and Istanbul (steel wheel) and Lyon, Mexico (rubber tyre).

ALSTOM has also supplied tracks for the Paris and Toulouse VAL systems, and the Saint-Etienne, Rouen, Orleans and Lyon tramway systems.

*VERIFIED*

---

## Amec Rail Ltd

Stephenson House, 2 Cherry Orchard Road, Croydon CR9 6JA, UK
Tel: (+44 20) 86 67 36 66    Fax: (+44 20) 86 67 27 03
e-mail: enquiries.amecrail@amec.com
Web: http://www.amec.com

**Key personnel**
Managing Director: John Moss
Directors
  Business Development: David Hill-Smith
  Commercial: Bob Carter
  Finance: Richard Hunt
  Operations: Kevin Beauchamp
  Personnel: Alan Barnes
  Technical: Bruce Littleword

**Subsidiaries**
Amec Rail Consulting
Yardley Court, 11-12 Frederick Road, Birmingham B15 1JD, UK
Tel: (+44 121) 455 68 99    Fax: (+44 121) 454 58 76

Amec Rail Training
Fairbairn Close, Beaumont Road, Purley CR8 2AT, UK
Tel: (+44 20) 86 66 69 20    Fax: (+44 20) 86 66 64 17

Amec Rail Project Maintenance
West Yard, Dundonald Road, Wimbledon, London SW19 3QJ, UK
Tel: (+44 20) 85 45 58 85    Fax: (+44 20) 85 45 51 60

**Corporate development**
Amec Rail is one of the infrastructure engineering businesses created as part of the privatisation of British Railways. It is now part of Amec Services.

The company specialises in the maintenance and renewal of track and signalling systems and the installation and maintenance of power supplies to electrified track. It also undertakes structural examinations and other civil engineering works for Railtrack, London Underground and a number of other infrastructure owners.

Following the acquisition of 41.6 per cent of Spie SA (France) by Amec plc, a new UK-based railway infrastructure company was formed called Amec Spie Rail Systems Ltd.

**Services**
Infrastructure and track maintenance and upgrading.

*UPDATED*

---

## Amec Spie Rail Systems Ltd

Stephenson House, 2 Cherry Orchard Road, Croydon CR9 6JA, UK
Tel: (+44 20) 86 67 28 36    Fax: (+44 20) 86 67 27 69
e-mail: atkinsonb.amecrail@ems.rail.co.uk
Web: http://www.amec.com

**Key personnel**
General Manager: John Moss
Commercial Director: Ken John
Development Director: Barry Atkinson

**Corporate developments**
Following the acquisition of 41.6 per cent of Spie SA (France) by Amec plc, a UK-based railway infrastructure company was formed called Amec Spie Rail Systems Ltd.

**Services**
Design, supply, installation, testing and commissioning of all types of railway infrastructure, including catenary systems, power supply and electromechanical packages.

AMEC SPIE can draw specialist services from its parent companies to offer a fully integrated railway infrastructure package with a focus on UK rail clients.

Recent contracts include work on French TGV Atlantique and Nord lines, the Seoul-Pusan high-speed route, the Great Belt link in Denmark, Heathrow Express electrification, Queensland Rail electrification and the Caracas metro.

*UPDATED*

---

## American Railroad Curvelining Corporation

137 Hollywood Avenue, Douglaston, Long Island, New York 11363-1110, USA
Tel: (+1 718) 224 11 35    Fax: (+1 718) 631 33 04
e-mail: renef@eruls.com

Permanent way components, equipment and services/**MANUFACTURERS** 717

**Key personnel**
Chief Executive Officer: R A Fichter
President: J M Flechter

**Subsidiaries**
Bondarc Division
Marine Division

**Products**
Track geometry analysis; curvelining computers; roll ordinators; Trakchek; Trakanalyzer. Products include the Archimedes high-memory graphic display curveliner. Archimedes stores practically unlimited volumes of information. Using the latest video technology, it displays the middle ordinate diagram in full size, while identifying the diagram of original ordinates in one colour, the corrected diagram in another and the superelevation in a third colour. The system automatically highlights the area currently being worked on in a fourth colour. It can be supplied in a set of separate components, and can be interfaced with IBM-PC and other systems. The high-capacity built-in memory can give the engineer complete control of all maintenance work. Data is fed directly from the Model ATB Roll-Ordinator to Archimedes or to Archimedes program on PC.

## Amey Railways Ltd

125 House, 1 Gloucester Street, Swindon SN1 1SU, UK
Tel: (+44 1793) 51 54 00   Fax: (+44 1793) 51 55 64

**Key personnel**
Managing Director: Richard Entwhistle
Managing Director, Infrastructure: Stephen Peat
Operations Director: Richard Adams
Marketing Manager: Peter Burton

**Corporate development**
Amey Railways is a subsidiary of Amey plc, previously British Rail Western Infrastructure Maintenance Unit.

**Services**
Amey Railways undertakes rail infrastructure maintenance and construction and renewal work, including permanent way, signalling and civil engineering. Activities also include mechanical and electrical engineering, telecommunications work and planning and project management. The company also provides rail safety training.
Recent Railtrack contracts include infrastructure maintenance in the Bristol, Chilterns, Exeter, Newport, Reading and Thames areas, plain line track renewals in the Great Western Zone, rerailing in the Cardiff Valleys and pointwork renewals at Bristol. Signalling projects include a three-year Great Western Zone renewals programme, Guildford area resignalling and a scheme in the Taff Valley. Civil engineering projects include seven structure renewals, Great Western Zone tunnel repairs and station regeneration schemes.

## Amurrio

Amurrio Ferrocarril y Equipos SA
Maskuribai 10, E-01470 Amurrio, Alava, Spain
Tel: (+34 945) 89 16 00   Fax: (+34 945) 89 24 80
e-mail: afferq@sea.es

**Key personnel**
See entry in *Bogies and suspension, wheels and axles, bearings* section.

**Products**
Points, crossings, movable-frog crossings for high-speed crossovers, turnouts, manganese steel frogs, expansion joints, insulated rail joints, turntables, buffers, height gauges, rerailers.

## Angle Plant

Angle Plant (UK) Ltd
The Mount Buildings, Tunnel Hill, Upton-upon-Severn WR8 0QL, UK
Tel: (+44 1684) 59 30 52   Fax: (+44 1684) 59 22 49
e-mail: angleplant@aol.com
Web: http://www.angleplant.co.uk

*Euromach walking excavator, supplied by Angle Plant* 0021662

**Key personnel**
Director: Doug Guest

**Products**
PowerTilt TT-10 allows the bucket of a road-rail excavator to be tilted up to 70° each way. Powertilt attachments are available to fit excavations from 1 to 35 tonnes and can be used with all buckets and attachments.
Angle Plant is also UK distributor for Euromach walking excavators which are designed to work on very steep terrain or where access for conventional machines is very restricted.

## ApaTeCh

PO Box 388, Zhukovsky City, 140180, Moscow Region, Russian Federation
Tel: (+7 095) 556 42 47   Fax: (+7 095) 911 00 19
e-mail: ushakov@tsagi.rssi.ru

**Key personnel**
Director: Andrey Ushakov

**Products**
Insulating fishplates using metal/composites to provide electrically insulated joints between rails of all types. The fishplates are supplied with a guaranteed service life of three years on lines handling train speeds of up to 200 km/h. They provide electrical resistance of over 100 $\Omega$ and are designed for installation in environments with a temperature range of -60° to +80°C. Fishplates are also produced for use with UIC-60 rail for speeds of up to 300 km/h.

## Apcarom SA

SC Apcarom SA
2 Soseaua Brailei, Buzau R-5100, Romania
Tel: (+40 38) 71 05 11   Fax: (+40 38) 71 02 18

**Key personnel**
General Manager: Vintila Mocanu
Technical Manager: Ion Matei

**Products**
Design and manufacture of points and crossings for railway and metro systems; track compensating devices for bridges; speed regulators; transition rails; glued insulating rail joints.

## Arbil Ltd

Lifting Gear Centre, Foundry Lane, Fishponds Trading Estate, Bristol BS5 7XH, UK
A member of the Raymond Bills group of companies
Tel: (+44 117) 965 31 43   Fax: (+44 117) 965 86 07

**Key personnel**
Manager: Dave Vale

**Products**
Rail thimbles. Four standard models are available with fixed or swivel eye, manual or hydraulically operated.
The MK2 has a working load limit of 3 tonnes on lifting points of vertical roller pins. Features include improved

*Arbil MK2 rail thimble* 0006273

design of tapered rolling pins for ease of replacement, hydraulic cylinder fitted with safety valve in case of hose failure as part of standard specification and heat-treated wearing parts.

## Aspen Aerials

Aspen Aerials Inc
4303 West 1st Street, PO Box 16958, Duluth, Minnesota 55816-0958, USA
Tel: (+1 218) 624 11 11   Fax: (+1 218) 624 17 14

**Key personnel**
Vice-President: John W Stubenvoll

**Products**
UB30 truck-mounted bridge inspection unit. An aerial platform, it operates either side of the truck, within a 2.4 m width when rotated, and does not require outriggers. It features an articulating fourth boom and interchangeable platforms. These can be either a three-person inspection platform with a 272 kg capacity, or a 5.18 m long, 454 kg capacity maintenance platform.

**VERIFIED**

## Aspen Equipment Co

9150 Pillsbury Avenue South, Minneapolis, Minnesota 55420, USA
Tel: (+1 612) 888 25 25   Fax: (+1 612) 888 94 45
Web: http://www.aspen-companies.com
e-mail: jgallo@aspeneq.com

**Key personnel**
President: Steven Sill
Vice-President and General Manager: Tom Cherne
Vice-President, Production: Jerry Neises
Treasurer: Mark Fitzgerald
General Sales Manager, Rail Products: John Gallo

**Principal subsidiary**
Reach Equipment

**Products**
Aspen Equipment supplies hi-rail trucks for infrastructure maintenance purposes. The company specialises in the installation of cranes from manufacturers which include from National, IMT, Autocrane, Prentice and Fassi, and supplies custom-built bodies in steel and aluminium and standard bodies in steel aluminium and glass fibre. Truck-mounted equipment supplied includes bridge inspection units, welders, air compressors and hydraulic and pneumatic tools systems.   Aspen Equipment has recently supplied truck-mounted equipment to major railroads in North America, including Wisconsin Central and Canadian Pacific. Other customers include BNSF and Union Pacific.

## Atlantic Track

Atlantic Track and Turnout Co
270 Broad Street, PO Box 1589, Bloomfield, New Jersey 07003, USA
Tel: (+1 201) 748 58 85   Fax: (+1 201) 748 45 20
e-mail: info@atlantictrack.com
Web: http://www.atlantictrack.com

## MANUFACTURERS/Permanent way components, equipment and services

**Main works**
St Clair Industrial Park, RD No 3, PO Box 360, Pottsville, Pennsylvania 17901, USA

**Key personnel**
President and Chief Executive Officer: R H Dreesen
Export Sales Director: P A Hughes
Domestic Sales Director: T R Jones

**Products**
All new ASCE, AREA, ARA-A, ARA-B rail sections produced; full line of relay rail and special trackwork; track accessories including switch materials, maintenance tools and insulating material. Third-rail transit products including glass fibre insulators, coverboard and brackets.

*VERIFIED*

### Atlas Copco

Atlas Copco Compressors
PO Box 79, Swallowdale Lane, Hemel Hempstead HP2 7HA, UK
Tel: (+44 1442) 612 01   Fax: (+44 1442) 23 44 67

**Key personnel**
Executive: P Haddow

**Products**
Self-contained power tamper/drill and pneumatic equipment, pumps, tampers. Hydraulic breakers. Portable and stationary compressors.

### Atlas Copco Berema

PO Box 767, SE-131 24 Nacka, Sweden
Tel: (+46 8) 743 96 00   Fax: (+46 8) 743 96 50

**Works**
Kalmar Works, PO Box 703, SE-391 27 Kalmar, Sweden

**Key personnel**
Managing Director: Claes Ahrengart
Marketing Manager: Peo Sollerud
Manager, Rail Department: Derek McCool

**Principal subsidiaries**
Atlas Copco Berema Inc, USA
Atlas Copco Berema A/S, Norway

**Products**
Pionjär and Cobra self-contained petrol-powered combination drill, breaker and ballast tamper for construction, maintenance and permanent way work.
Pneumatic breakers and rock drills, as well as heavy-duty boom-mounted hydraulic hammers for bridge deck demolition and pile driving, compressors and pneumatic accessories.

### Atlas Hydraulic Loaders Ltd

Wharfedale Road, Euroway Estate, Bradford BD4 6SE, UK
Tel: (+44 1274) 68 68 27   Fax: (+44 1274) 68 78 89

**Products**
Road/rail excavators.

### Atlas Weyhausen

PO Box 1844, Stedinger Strasse 324, D-27747 Delmenhorst, Germany
Tel: (+49 42) 21 49 10   Fax: (+49 42) 21 49 12 13

**Key personnel**
Chairman: Dipl Oec Carsten Weyhausen
Marketing Director: Gerhard Brünjes
Export Manager: Carl Egbers

**Subsidiary company**
Atlas Hydraulic Loaders Ltd, Blackwood, UK

**Products**
Road/rail excavators from 15.4 to 22 tonnes, with and without stabilisers and a slewing radius from 1,575 to 2,000 mm. Both models have the AWE4 hydraulic system and are equipped with the CARSY computerised rail adhesion regulating system; range of loading cranes from 20 to 600 kNm.

### Austrak Pty Ltd

973 Fairfield Road, Moorooka, Queensland 4105, Australia
Tel: (+61 7) 33 08 78 80   Fax: (+61 7) 33 08 78 81
e-mail: sdouglas@bmcl.com.au

**Key personnel**
Managing Director: D C Hudson
General Manager: S G Douglas
Operations Manager: D J L Priddle

**Products**
Manufacture of concrete sleepers and turnout ties.

### Avon Polymers France

ZI du Prat, PO Box 188, F-56005 Vannes, Cedex, France
Tel: (+33 2) 97 26 70 12   Fax: (+33 2) 97 26 70 26

**Key personnel**
Product Manager: Christian Noël

**Products**
Rubber rail pads (Railtrack and SNCF-approved); rubber base plate pads; rubber sleeper boots; soffit pads; sleeper pads in solid and formed rubber (closed cells).
The company is ISO 9002 approved.

### BAC Corrosion Control Limited

Stafford Park 11, Telford TF3 3AY, UK
Tel: (+44 1952) 29 03 21   Fax: (+44 1952) 29 03 25
e-mail: bac@bacgroup.com
Web: http://www.brightbond.com

**Products**
Bright-Bond pin brazing systems for track bonding for signalling purposes, the connection of heater strips and earth connections to masts carrying overhead power supply lines.
There are two main types of Bright-Bond unit: the BB3, with the capacity to produce approximately 150 connections per charge; and the portable BB2 unit, for service and maintenance operations, giving approximately 50 connections per charge. A wide range of ancillary equipment is also supplied, including several types of brazing gun, specially designed bonds and cables, batteries and accessories.

*Bright-Bond pin brazing system for track bonding*
2001/0109479

### Balfour Beatty Rail Engineering Ltd

Osmaston Street, Sandiacre, Nottingham NG10 5AN, UK
Tel: (+44 115) 921 82 18   Fax: (+44 115) 921 82 19
e-mail: phil.bean@bbrail.co.uk

**Key personnel**
General Manager: Keith Churm
Business Development Manager: Philip Bean

*Balfour Beatty has supplied trackwork for Amtrak's Northeast Corridor in the USA* 2002/0113340

UK Client Account Manager: Gary Elliott
Chief Engineer: Andy Foan
Finance Manager: Keith Ravenscroft

**Subsidiaries**
Midland Foundry, Sandiacre; Balfour Beatty Rail Engineering Ltd, Darlington

**Products**
Design, manufacture and supply of special trackwork to the UK and international market, including switches, crossings, friction buffer stops, cast and fabricated track materials, lever boxes and switch stands.
Recent UK projects include: Leeds remodelling, Manchester South capacity improvement programme and Proof House Junction. Overseas projects include: the Singapore MRT extension to Changi Airport and, in the USA, high-speed turnouts for Metro-North's Hudson River Line and the Grand Central Terminal loop in Manhattan.

*UPDATED*

### Balfour Beatty Rail Ltd

7 Mayday Road, Thornton Heath, CR7 7XA, UK
Tel: (+44 20) 87 10 50 90   Fax: (+44 20) 87 10 53 09
e-mail: customer.service@bbrail.co.uk
Web: http://www.bicc.com

**Key personnel**
Chairman: Jim Cohen
Customer Services Director: Charles Nicholls
Personnel Director: Paul Raby
Finance Director: Peter Hutchinson

**Principal subsidiaries**
Balfour Beatty Rail Engineering Ltd
Balfour Beatty Rail Maintenance Ltd
Balfour Beatty Rail Ltd—Plant Division
Balfour Beatty Rail Projects Ltd
Balfour Beatty Rail Renewals Ltd
Balfour Beatty Rail Ltd – Strategic Development Group

**Services**
Comprising the companies detailed above, Balfour Beatty Rail Ltd provides a complete rail infrastructure and multi-disciplinary service, including consulting, design, manufacture and supply, contracting and maintenance.

### Balfour Beatty Rail Ltd—Plant Division

PO Box 5063, Raynesway, Derby DE21 7ZL, UK
Tel: (+44 1332) 66 14 91   Fax: (+44 1332) 28 82 22

**Key personnel**
*Plant division*
Managing Director: Keith Fidler

## Permanent way components, equipment and services/MANUFACTURERS

Director, Rail Plant Unit: Keith Fidler (Acting)
Director, Raynesway Plant Unit: Ray Reed
Director, Fleet Services Unit: Jeff Bussey
**Rail plant unit**
Operations Manager: Giles Swindley
Development/Reliability Manager: Geoff Brown
Professional Head of Engineering: Dave Elias
Project Manager: Alan Wardle
**Raynesway plant unit**
Road/Rail Vehicles and Rail Portable Tools
Southern Area Manager: Steve MacIver
Northern Area Manager: Alex McCaig
Accommodation Fleet Manager: Ian Morrison

### Services
Balfour Beatty Rail Limited has three operating units: the Rail Plant Unit provides mechanised on-track equipment services, including tampers for plain line and for switches and crossings, trams, rail cranes, tracklayers, ballast regulators, ballast cleaners and gophers.

The Raynesway Plant Unit provides road/rail equipment, general plant maintenance and hire services for portable tools, accommodation, safety equipment, communications and CCTV systems plus design and manufacture of specialised road/rail equipment. The Fleet Services Unit undertakes transport fleet maintenance and fleet management and maintains Balfour Beatty's 7,000-vehicle fleet.

## Balfour Beatty Rail Maintenance Ltd

Grant House, 101 Bourges Boulevard, Peterborough PE1 1NG, UK
Tel: (+44 1733) 55 98 40   Fax: (+44 1733) 55 98 41

### Key personnel
Managing Director: Steve Huxley
Commercial Director: Paul Pethica
Operations Director: Ray Bond
Human Resources Director: Ken Richardson
Proposals Director: David Gardner
General Manager, Wessex: Steve Jagger
Engineering Director: Ken Mee
Finance Director: Dominic Gibb
Performance Director: Steve Hobden
Regional Director, Derby: Brian Counter
Regional Director, ECML: Tony Walker
Regional Director, Anglia: Steve Hooker
Regional Director, South: Chris Rayner

### Services
Infrastructure inspection, maintenance and management services, including track, signalling, telecommunications and power supply, both overhead and third rail.

## Ballast Nedam

Ballast Nedam Grond en Wegen BV
PO Box 2268, NL-1180 EG Amstelveen, Netherlands
Tel: (+31 20) 545 39 07   Fax: (+31 20) 545 39 35

### Key personnel
Project Manager: H J C Masselink

### Services
Implementation and construction of rail infrastructure projects.

Ballast Nedam and Balfour Beatty (qv) have formed a joint venture for carrying out rail infrastructure projects in Holland.

## Bance

R Bance & Co Ltd
Cockcrow Hill House, St Mary's Road, Surbiton KT6 5HE, UK
Tel: (+44 20) 83 98 71 41   Fax: (+44 20) 83 98 47 65
e-mail: sales@bance.co.uk
Web: http://www.bance.com

### Key personnel
Managing Director: R Bance
Marketing and Sales: G Smales
Engineering: B Steel

*2 Diesel with two loaded trailers*     2002/0125198

### Products
Tapered rail joint shims for maintaining jointed track; self-powered impact wrenches and augers; rail disc cutters; rechargeable work lights; emergency standby lights; electric bonding clamps; single rail trolleys; cross level gauges and other track measuring gauges; Alumi-Cart portable rail inspection vehicle and trailer; tie tampers; UTC ultrasonic rail flaw detection vehicle; trolley-train for moving rail to worksite.

**UPDATED**

## Banverket

Banverket Industrial Division
SE-57121 Nässjö, Sweden
Tel: (+46 380) 724 00   Fax: (+46 380) 725 00

### Key personnel
General Manager: Göthe Persson

### Services
Banverket Industrial Division is an offshoot of the Swedish National Rail Administration (see *Systems* section) set up to tender for contract work. It has had some success in obtaining contracts outside its parent company, having undertaken work for NSB Norway.

*Banverket rail-laying machine at work in Norway*     0006276

## Banestyrelsen Service Division

Vanløse Allé 89, DK-2720 Vanløse, Denmark
Tel: (+45) 82 34 45 02
e-mail: service@servicebane.dk

### Services
Maintenance and construction operations within: track works; overhead catenary systems; power systems; interlocking systems; telecommunication.

**NEW ENTRY**

## Barclay Mowlem

20 Bridge Street, Pymble, New South Wales 2073, Australia
Tel: (+61 2) 94 81 13 33   Fax: (+61 2) 94 81 13 69

### Key personnel
Managing Director: D C Hudson
General Manager, Railway Engineering & Construction Group: P W Welley
Business Procurement Manager, Railway Engineering & Construction Group: H J Tarrant

### Subsidiary company
Austrak Pty Ltd (qv)

### Products
Design and construction of track layouts; track upgrading and maintenance; manufacture of prestressed sleepers.

## Beilhack

Beilhack Systemtechnik GmbH
PO Box 100155, D-83001 Rosenheim, Germany
Tel: (+49 8031) 18 06 30   Fax: (+49 8031) 38 07 48
e-mail: infor@beilhack.de

### Key personnel
Managing Partners: W Beilhack, S Potocnik
Project Manager: W Grübler

### Products
Production and supply of self-propelled, propelled and vehicle-mounted snow-clearing equipment and vehicles, including blowers, ploughs, rail sweeping equipment, flangers and ice cutters; multipurpose infrastructure maintenance vehicles, including self-propelled units with tipper, crane and mower equipment; feasibility studies and consultancy.

## BEML

Bharat Earth Movers Ltd
BEML Soudha, 23/1 4th Main, SR Nagar, Bangalore 560 027, India
Tel: (+91 80) 222 44 58   Fax: (+91 80) 229 19 80

*BEML overhead inspection car*     2000/0089077

*Spoil disposal unit supplied to Indian Railways* 2002/0134278

e-mail: techrnd@vsnl.com
Web: http://www.bemlindia.com

**Key personnel**
See entry in *Locomotives and powered/non-powered passenger vehicles* section.

**Products**
Tracklaying equipment, including tracklayers and spoil disposal units. The BEML self-propelled diesel-hydraulic tracklayer is designed to move on an auxiliary track. It has hydraulically operated grippers for handling concrete sleepers and rails from wagons and panel assemblies of concrete sleepers and rails. Maximum lifting capacity is nine tonnes.

BEML's spoil disposal unit is designed for use with ballast cleaning machines for the reception, storage and unloading of spoil generated during ballast screening. Equipped with a hydraulically operated horizontal conveyor inside its hopper and a slew conveyor at one end, the spoil disposal unit can unload itself into similar units coupled together, wagons on an adjacent track or on to the slope of the formation.

Contracts include the supply of 29 tracklayers and five spoil disposal units to Indian Railways.

**UPDATED**

## Benkler AG

Nordstrasse 1, CH-5612 Willmergen, Switzerland
Tel: (+41 56) 618 72 00   Fax: (+41 56) 618 72 99
e-mail: info@benkler.ch
Web: http://www.benkler.ch

**Corporate background**
Benkler AG is a member of the Sersa Group (qv).

**Services**
Rail grinding; track inspection; overhead line maintenance and construction.

**NEW ENTRY**

## Benntec Systemtechnik GmbH

Walter-Geerdes-Strasse, 10-12, D-28307 Bremen, Germany
Tel: (+49 421) 43 84 90   Fax: (+49 421) 438 49 90
e-mail: info@benntec.de
Web: http://www.benntec.de

**Products**
Rail Check, designed to detect anomalies of rail surfaces, missing fastening elements, cracked ties and visible changes of ballast conditions automatically and online at inspection speeds of 160 km/h.

Rail Scan, a multipurpose video inspection of railway track and the corresponding environment, digitally recording information of the track structure for off-line analysis and documentation.

## Bethlehem Steel Corporation

Pennsylvania Steel Technologies Inc
215 South Front Street, Steelton, Pennsylvania 17113, USA
Tel: (+1 717) 986 22 76   Fax: (+1 717) 986 27 00

**Key personnel**
Chairman and Chief Executive Officer: Curtis H Barnette
President: Andrew R Futchko
Vice-President, Commercial: Kirkland H Gibson Jr

**Corporate development**
Pennsylvania Steel Technologies Inc is a subsidiary of Bethlehem Steel Corporation.

**Products**
Rail, including 80 ft long rail in four grades (in-line head hardened, fully heat-treated, medium hardness and standard) T-rail, contact rail and crane rail sections.

## BHP Steel

PO Box 196B, Newcastle, New South Wales 2300, Australia
Tel: (+61 2) 49 40 24 11   Fax: (+61 2) 49 40 25 05

**Key personnel**
Manager, Export Market: Greg Booth

**Sales offices**
Taiwan
Tel: (+886 7) 333 69 00   Fax: (+886 7) 333 69 07
General Manager: John Hunt
China/Hong Kong
Tel: (+852) 284 02 33   Fax: (+852) 284 02 44
General Manager: Manzar Iqbal
Philippines
Tel: (+63 2) 894 01 21   Fax: (+63 2) 894 78 32
General Manager: Mauro Cervames
Singapore/Malaysia
Tel: (+65) 535 06 22   Fax: (+65) 532 71 82
General Manager: Harold Quek
India/Sri Lanka/Bangladesh/Middle East
Tel: (+971 4) 31 48 48   Fax: (+971 4) 31 08 86
General Manager: Barry Gallagher

**Products**
Rolled steel rail (standard carbon and head hardened to UIC and Australian standards), steel sleeper bar, structural steel sections.

## Bomag GmbH

Hellerwald, D-56154 Boppard, Germany
Tel: (+49 6742) 10 00   Fax: (+49 6742) 30 90
e-mail: info@bomag.de
Web: http://www.bomag.de
Part of United Dominion company

**Key personnel**
President: Lothar Wahl
Senior Vice-Presidents
Marketing and Sales: Dr Kay Mayland
  Dr Kay Mayland
  Finance: Martin Ochotta
Vice-President, Sales: Joachim Untiedt

**Principal subsidiaries**
In Austria, Canada, France, Japan, Jordan, Singapore, UK and USA.

**Products**
Tampers, vibrating plates (single direction and reversible), single and double drum rollers (hand guided), trench compactors, tandem rollers, combi rollers, single drum rollers (including asphalt versions), pneumatic tyred rollers, towed vibratory rollers, sanitary landfill compactors, asphalt surface recycler, soil stabiliser, hardware and software for compaction control of permanent way including data processing of all measured data, high-frequency internal vibrator.

## Bumar Ltd

Al Jana Pawa II nr 11, PL-00-828 Warsaw, Poland
Tel: (+48 22) 620 46 65   Fax: (+48 22) 654 70 16

**Products**
Spring rail fastening for heavy and light rail applications; dog spikes.

## Burn Standard

A subsidiary of: Bharat Bhari Udyog Nigam Ltd
10-C Hungerford Street, Calcutta 700 017 India
Tel: (+91 33) 247 10 67; 17 62; 17 72
Fax: (+91 33) 247 17 88

**Key personnel**
See *Freight vehicles and equipment* section.

**Products**
Points and crossings, sleepers, fishplates, bridge girders.

## BWG

Butzbacher Weichenbau Gesellschaft mbH & Co KG
PO Box 305, D-35503 Butzbach, Germany
Tel: (+49 6033) 89 20   Fax: (+49 6033) 89 21 13
e-mail: t.kalkbrenner.bwg-wbg.com

**Key personnel**
Chief Executive Officer: E Bittel
Marketing and Engineering Executive: H Höhne
Export Manager: D Schluck

**Works**
PO Box 305, Wetzlarer Strasse 101, Industriegebiet Nord, D-35510 Butzbach, Germany

**Products**
Points and crossings (semi-welded and monoblock), carbon steel crossings, swing-nose crossings and expansion joints.

Contracts include Amtrak/NJT; DORTS, Taipei; Konkan Railway, India; DB AG, NSB Norway and VR Finland.

## Caillard Cowans Sheldon

Place Caillard, PO Box 1368, F-76065 Le Havre Cedex, France
Tel: (+33 2) 35 25 81 31   Fax: (+33 2) 35 25 11 41

**Key personnel**
Managing Director: K Bayram
Sales Manager: A Beroule
Railway Crane Department Manager: F Elbaroude

**Products**
Breakdown cranes (up to 250 tonnes capacity), railway recovery cranes and multipurpose cranes (tracklaying/bridge construction); rail and pneumatic tyre-mounted

gantries for container handling; mobile cranes; gantry cranes and jib cranes for general, container or bulk cargo; mobile cranes for ports and railways.

Recent contracts include railway breakdown cranes for Algeria (5), Australia (1) and Bangladesh (4).

## Camlock Lifting Clamps Ltd

Knutsford Way, Sealand Industrial Estate,
Chester CH1 4NZ, UK
Tel: (+44 1244) 37 53 75   Fax: (+44 1244) 37 74 03
e-mail: sales@camlok.co.uk
Web: http://www.liftingclamps.com

### Products
Rail handling equipment including: MR multi-rail clamps; MRS multi-rail clamps grabs; CR and SCR rail clamps; RA rail anchors and RP rail pulling clamps.

**VERIFIED**

## CDM

Reutenbeek 9-11, B-3090 Overijse, Belgium
Tel: (+32 2) 687 79 07   Fax: (+32 2) 687 35 52
e-mail: general@cdm.be
Web: http://www.cdm.be

### Products
Elastic materials and systems for track noise and vibration isolation for high-speed, main line, metro and light rail infrastructure. Products include rail support pads and strips, under-baseplate pads and under-sleeper mats, ballast mats and embedded rail systems.

## Cemafer

Cemafer Gleisbaumaschinen und Geräte GmbH
Ihringer Landstrasse 3, PO Box 1327, D-79206 Breisach, Germany
Tel: (+49 7667) 905 90   Fax: (+49 7667) 90 59 59
e-mail: cemafer.breisach@cemafer.com
Web: http://www.cemafer.com

### Key personnel
General Manager: A Wagner

### Products
Power wrenches, coach-screwing machines, rail drills, rail saws, sleeper drills, sleeper adzing and drilling machines, rail grinding equipment, rail benders, light tampers, inspection trolleys, trailers, portal cranes, hand tools, electric generators (portable), gauges, jacks, rail cutting machines, rail stripping machines, sleeper boring machines, sleeper placing machines, spanners, spike drivers and extractors, and tracklaying equipment.

## Cembre SpA

Via Serenissima 9, I-25135 Brescia, Italy
Tel: (+39 030) 369 21   Fax: (+39 030) 336 57 66

**UK subsidiary**
Cembre Ltd Fairview Industrial Estate
Kingsbury Road, Curdworth, Sutton Coldfield B76 9EE
Tel: (+44 1675) 47 04 40   Fax: (+44 1675) 47 02 20

### Subsidiaries
See entry in *Electrification contractors and equipment suppliers* section.

### Products
Rail drilling equipment.

**UPDATED**

## Centrac Ltd

3rd Floor, Quayside Tower, 252-260 Broad Street, Birmingham B1 2HF, UK
Tel: (+44 121) 654 81 03   Fax: (+44 121) 654 83 18

### Key personnel
Director: Ian Webb
Managers:
  Commercial: Chris Helm
  Production: Richard Ladd
  Plant: Angus Selstrom

### Services
Plain line and switch and crossing design, installation and maintenance work.

Recent contracts include Railtrack East Anglia Zone plain line renewals and Midlands and North West Zone switch and crossing renewals over the period 1998-2001.

## Century Group Inc

PO Box 228, Sulphur, Louisiana 70664-0228, USA
Tel: (+1 800) 527 52 32 ext 118   Fax: (+1 800) 887 21 53
e-mail: sales@centurygrp.com
Web: http://www.centurygrp.com

### Key personnel
President/CEO, Railroad Products Division:
  Rusty Vincent
National Director, Sales and Marketing, Railroad Products Division: Robert W Goodner
Vice-President, Sales and Marketing, Railroad Products Division: Jerry McCoombs

### Products
Full-depth concrete grade crossings in North America. Manufactured of high strength reinforced concrete, the Century crossings are durable, safe, economical and simple to install. The versatile concrete grade crossings are manufactured to fit any size rail and are compatible with all major types of rail fastening systems. The crossings are manufactured for curves, turnouts, diamond crossings, devil strips and many other applications and with all crossings comes an innovative elastomeric flangeway filler for the safety of pedestrian and vehicular traffic and also to protect the track structure from contaminants.

The HDPE Enviropan system is a state of the art railroad spill collection system to assist railroads, military facilities, light rail transit and industry to protect the environment. It is a high impact puncture and tear resistant closed drain system which minimised exposure at pan and cross drain connections. The Enviropan modular lightweight construction allows for fast installation, eliminating railroad track downtime.

Recent contracts include: Railroad crossings and spill collection systems for Metropolitan Atlanta Rapid Transit (MARTA) 1999; Burlington/Northern Santa Fe railroad 1999; Union Pacific Railroad 2000; New Jersey Transit 1999; Port of Houston 1999; Illinois Central 2000; Kansas City Southern Railroad 1999; and Dow Chemical 2000.

*HDPE crossing*   2000/0087701

*Century's concrete railroad grade crossing*   2000/0087703

*Century's HDPE Enviropans*   2000/0087702

## CF&I Steel

PO Box 1830, Pueblo, Colorado 81002, USA
Tel: (+1 719) 561 61 30   Fax: (+1 719) 561 69 92

### Key personnel
Vice-President, Sales and Marketing: J E Dionisio
Sales Manager, Railroad Products: M C McLean

### Products
Rails, including T-rails.

## Chemetron

Chemetron Railway Products Inc
8021 National Turnpike, Louisville Kentucky 40214, USA
Tel: (+1 502) 368 65 62   Fax: (+1 502) 367 14 84

**Main works**
5600 Stillwell Street, Kansas City, Missouri 64120, USA

### Key personnel
Assistant Vice-President, Welding and Equipment Sales: Larry J Taylor

### Corporate development
Chemetron Railway Products Inc is a division of Progress Rail Services Corporation.

### Products
Electric flash-butt rail welding plants including rail welders, rail end polishers, base grinders, rail saws, automatic rail straighteners and rail pushers. Rail trains, rail wagons and miscellaneous rail handling equipment including turnkey design of rail welding plants. Contract welding service of rail into continuous welded rail in any of standard, alloy or head-hardened rails. Ergonomically safe manually operated switch stands.

Chemetron rail welding machines operate using AC or DC power. Systems are solid-state and can be controlled with various levels of automation. Production capabilities are in excess of 25 welds/h for all rail sizes. Transportable/mobile flash-butt rail welding plants are also available, including truck-mounted road/rail in-track units.

Chemetron operates plants in Canada and the USA and provides equipment and technical advice to Asia, Australia, Mexico and South America.

## Chemgrate

Chemgrate Corporation
4115 Keller Springs Road, Suite 218 Addison, Texas 75244-3024, USA
Tel: (+1 752) 44 30 24   Fax: (+1 972) 732 80 70

### Products
Anti-slip and corrosion-resistant grating, stair treads and floor plates for rail systems.

## MANUFACTURERS/Permanent way components, equipment and services

### Chipman Rail

Chipman Rail plc
The Goods Yard, Horsham RH12 2NR, UK
Tel: (+44 1403) 26 03 41   Fax: (+44 1403) 26 47 99

**Key personnel**
General Manager: Paul Easton
Head of Engineering: Steve Chambers

**Products**
Equipment and technology for track weed control, drain clearing, leaf jetting and Sandite application.

### Cimmco

Cimmco International
Prakash Deep, 7 Tolstoy Marg, New Delhi 110001, India
Tel: (+91 11) 331 43 83; 84; 85
Fax: (+91 11) 332 077; 372 35 20

**Key personnel**
See entry in *Freight vehicles and equipment* section.

**Products**
Permanent way materials including: cast-iron, pressed steel and concrete sleepers; elastic rail fastening system; rigid fasteners; points and crossings; rail anchors; fishplates, nuts and bolts; track tools and various types of spikes.

### Clouth

Clouth Gummiwerke AG
Conveyor Belt Division, PO Box 600229, Niehler Strasse, D-50682 Cologne, Germany
Tel: (+49 221) 777 36 24; 35 93   Fax: (+49 221) 777 37 00

**Key personnel**
Executive: Norbert Martin
Technical Manager: Dr Wilhelm Engst
Manager, Marketing and Sales: Michael Kottmann

**Products**
Elastic rail fasteners (DFF®); SBM® sub-ballast matting and trackbed matting; RRS resilient primary suspension; MFS® elastomeric bearings for floating slab systems; ASM® protective matting for waterproof coatings of bridges and structures; insulation matting and Oil-EX® oil absorption mats.

### Cogifer

54, avenue Victor Hugo, BP 56606, F-92566 Rueil Malmaison, Cedex, France
Tel: (+33 1) 55 47 73 00   Fax: (+33 1) 55 47 73 92
e-mail: contact@cogifer.fr
Web: http://www.cogifer.com

**Works**
Reichshoffen
BP 1, F-67110 Reichshoffen, France
Tel: (+33 3) 88 80 86 80   Fax: (+33 3) 88 09 67 33
e-mail: contact@cogifer.fr

Reichsoffen
4 rue d'Oberbronn
Reichshoffen BP 02, F-67891 Niederbronn Cedex, France
Tel: (+33 3) 88 80 85 00   Fax: (+33 3) 88 80 85 18
e-mail: system@cogifer.fr

Fére en Tardenois
Zone Industrielle, F-02130 Fère en Tardenois, France
Tel: (+33 3) 23 82 58 88   Fax: (+33 3) 23 82 71 99
e-mail: contact@cogifer.fr

**Key personnel**
President: Régis Bello
Managing Director, Cogifer and Industrie Department:
   Claude Schwartz
Managing Director, Signalling Department:
   Jean-Louis Wagner

International Projects Directors:
   Marc-Antoine de Dietrich, Alain Montgaudon
President of Cogifer TF: Henri Dehe

**Subsidiaries**
Eav-Durieux
138, rue d'Anderlues, B-7141 Carnières, Belgium
Tel: (+32 64) 43 14 00   Fax: (+32 64) 45 86 32
e-mail: durieux-eav@media.be

Cogifer Teijo
Telakkatie 18, FIN-25570, Teijo, Finland
Tel: (+35 8) 27 36 60 10   Fax: (+35 8) 27 36 60 20
e-mail: cogifer.teijo@cogifer.fi

Jacquemard – Avr
389, rue des Frères Lumière, ZI de Molina la Chazotte, France
Tel: (+33 4) 77 47 68 68   Fax: (+33 4) 77 47 68 69
e-mail: michaelcuminetti@cogifer.fr

Weichenbau Laeis GmbH
Ruwerer Strasse, 21 D-54292 Trier, Germany
Tel: (+49) 651 55 80   Fax: (+49) 651 558 15
e-mail: laeis@t-online.de

Cogifer Italia
Uffici di Milano
Via G de Vittorio 20/22, I-20016 Pero, Italy
Tel: (+39 02) 353 57 39   Fax: (+39 02) 358 15 84
e-mail: cogita@tin.it

Kihn SA
17, rue de l'Usine BP 20, L-3701 Rumelange, Luxembourg
Tel: (+352) 564 77 11   Fax: (+352) 56 58 54
e-mail: kihn@pt.lu

Rodelokken Ind
PO Box 292, N-2001 Lilleström, Norway
Tel: (+47 64) 84 35 90   Fax: (+47 64) 84 35 99

Cogifer Polska
UL Ludwikowo 2, PL-85-502 Bydgoszcz, Poland
Tel: (+48 52) 322 52 24   Fax: (+48 52) 322 46 76

Futrifer SA
Praça da Alegria 8 R/C, P-1250-004 Lisbon, Portugal
Tel: (+351 41) 89 77 28; 89 74 51
Fax: (+351 41) 89 00 57
e-mail: lisboa@futrifer.pt

Amurrio Ferrocarriles y Equipos
Maskuribai, 10, E-01470 Amurrio (Alava), Spain
Tel: (+34 945) 89 16 00   Fax: (+34 945) 89 24 80

Cogifer Nordic
Södr Grev Rosengatan 1, Box 1502, SE-70115 Örebro, Sweden
Tel: (+46 19) 17 25 00   Fax: (+46 19) 17 24 50
e-mail: owe.ohrling@cogifer.se

ATO
31st floor, Italtahi Tower, 2034/134 New Petchburi Road, Bangkapi, Huaykwang, Bangkok 10320, Thailand
Tel: (+66 2) 716 14 19   Fax: (+66 2) 716 14 20
e-mail: cofigerthai@ibm.net

Corus Cogifer
Hebden Road, Scunthorpe DN15 8XX, UK
Tel: (+44 1724) 86 21 31   Fax: (+44 1724) 29 52 43
e-mail: tim.bessel@coruscogifer.com

**Background**
In January 2001, the company established a joint venture with Corus Rail, Corus Cogifer Ltd, aimed at meeting UK market needs.

**Products**
Design, manufacture and installation of switches and crossings for high-speed railways, metro systems, light rail systems and main line and suburban rail networks. Products include: moveable manganese frogs; countered switches and crossings; manganese frogs with welded legs; and special forgings for switch rails; switch mechanisms; clamp lock systems; traffic detectors; and the Paulvé mechanically driven points detector. Support services include: diagnostic reports on points in service; inspection; use and maintenance training; technology transfer; and financial services.

*UPDATED*

### Colbond Geosynthetics

PO Box 9600, Werstervoortsedijk, NL-6800 TC Arnhem, Netherlands
Tel: (+31 26) 366 46 00   Fax: (+31 26) 366 58 12
e-mail: geosynthetics@colbond.com
Web: http://www.geosynthetics.colbond.com

**Key personnel**
General Manager: Axel Poscher
Sales Manager: Blair Rawes
Marketing Manager: Wim Voskamp
Research and Development Manager: Willem Gevers

**Products**
The company's products include: track components, Enkadrain® for structural drainage; Enkamat® for erosion control; Armater® for erosion control; Enkagrid® for soil improvement, and Colbonddrain® for soil impovement.

### Colebrand Limited

Colebrand House, 18-20 Warwick Street, London W1B 5ND, UK
Tel: (+44 20) 74 39 10 00   Fax: (+44 20) 77 34 33 58
e-mail: enquiries@colebrand.com
Web: http://www.colebrand.com

**Key personnel**
Managing Director: K N Tusch
General Manager: N R Barnes

**Main Works**
CXL Factory, Goodshawfold Road, Rossendale BB4 8QF, UK

**Products**
The Colebrand Lock Up Device (LUD) is fitted to railway bridges in order to provide a rigid link under short dynamic loads. The device is fitted between the deck and pier, or deck to abutment, or deck to deck, and provides a means of sharing loads within a structure. At the same time the device allows the structure to move freely during normal temperature changes while locking up under dynamic loads.

The LUDs are approved for use on Railtrack UK bridges and by Systra, the French railway consultants. They have been incorporated into railway structures to protect them from braking/traction forces and, in certain parts of the world, earthquakes.

Colebrand LUDs are currently being used in a variety of applications. In Korea, where 500 units are installed they accommodate the high traction and braking loads exerted on the structure. In the UK, LUDs have been installed vertically on a railway bridge to reduce deflections of the deck and at the same time allowing some settlement of the pier. In Taiwan they are installed for both seismic protection and to accommodate traction and braking loads.

*UPDATED*

### Collis Engineering Ltd

Salcombe Road, Meadow Lane Industrial Estate, Alfreton DE55 7RG, UK
Tel: (+44 1773) 83 32 55   Fax: (+44 1773) 52 06 93
e-mail: sales@colliseng.demon.co.uk
Web: http://www.collis.co.uk

**Key personnel**
See entry in *Signalling and communications systems* section.

**Products**
Point fittings, sitework tents for trackside maintenance and cable jointers, rail drilling jigs, permanent way equipment and services and structural steelwork.

*VERIFIED*

## Comsa SA

Edificio Numancia 1, Calle Viriato 47, E-08014 Barcelona, Spain
Tel: (+34 93) 430 15 152   Fax: (+34 93) 405 13 30
Web: http://www.comsa.com

**Subsidiaries**
Intraesa
(address as parent company)
Tel: (+34 93) 430 49 44   Fax: (+34 93) 439 17 69
Travipos SA
Calle Irlanda del Norte s/n, Poligono Industrial Constanti, Sector Norte, E-43120 Constanti, Tarragona, Spain
Tel: (+34 977) 29 65 53   Fax: (+34 977) 29 65 53
Joint venture with Pfleiderer Verkehrstechnik GmbH & Co KG

**Services**
Construction and maintenance of high-speed, conventional and mass transit railway infrastructure including metro and light rail; construction of railway installations such as traction and rolling stock maintenance depots and marshalling yards.

Contracts include infrastructure maintenance for the Madrid-Seville high-speed line, construction and maintenance work on the Alicante-Barcelona Euromed line and construction of the Valencia light rail system. Overseas projects include rolling stock and maintenance facilities for Kuala Lumpur's STAR light rail system.

## Conbrako

PO Box 4018, Luipaardsvlei 1743, Transvaal, South Africa
Tel: (+27 11) 762 24 21   Fax: (+27 11) 762 65 35

**Products**
Track jacks.

## Contec GmbH

In den Eichen, D-56244 Ötzingen-Sainerholz, Germany
Tel: (+49 2666) 952 00   Fax: (+49 2666) 95 20 28
e-mail: info@contec-group.com
Web: http://www.contec-group.com

**Products**
Switch machines; track wiring systems; control systems; lineside cabinets; electrically and petrol-driven rail drilling equipment; rail bonding systems; fastenings.

**Services**
Civil engineering; cable laying; signal gantry assembly; track and signalling planning; depot design; signalling cable installation.

*NEW ENTRY*

## ContiTech

Niehler Strasse 102-116, D-50733 Cologne, Germany
Tel: (+49 221) 777 34 97   Fax: (+49 221) 777 37 00
e-mail: brigitte.krueminel@clouth.contitech.de

**Key personnel**
Divisional Manager: Norbert Martin

**Products**
Bridge supports, rail track supports; sub-ballast mats; Oil-Ex oil-absorbing rubber mats.

## Cooper & Turner

Sheffield Road, Sheffield S9 1RS, UK
Tel: (+44 114) 256 00 57   Fax: (+44 114) 244 55 29
e-mail: sales@cooperandturner.com
Web: http://www.cooperandturner.com

**Key personnel**
Directors: Paul Cook, Alan White

**Products**
Fish-bolts, track-bolts, screwspikes, crossing-bolts, Renlok locknut, insulated fishplate kits, HSFG bolts and nuts.

## Corus Cogifer Switches and Crossings

Hebden Road, Scunthorpe DN15 8XX, UK
Tel: (+44 1724) 86 21 31   Fax: (+44 1724) 29 52 43
e-mail: info@coruscogifer.com
Web: http://www.coruscogifer.com

**Background**
A subsidiary of Corus Rail, previously known as British Steel Railway & Foundry Products, Workington.

**Corporate development**
In January 2001, Corus Rail established a joint venture with Cogifer, Corus Cogifer Ltd, aimed at meeting UK market needs, especially the conversion to CEN60-E1 rail.

**Products**
Design, manufacture and assembly of points, crossings and railway track layout systems for maintenance and renewal. The company can provide short delivery times and produces a wide range of track fittings and accessories for all rail sections, insulated joints, buffer stops, adjustment switches, bridge and crane rails and fittings with on-site prefabrication, if required.

*UPDATED*

## Corus Foundry

New Stevenson Works, Stevenson Street, Motherwell, Lanarkshire ML1 4LS
Tel: (+44 1698) 73 24 88   Fax: (+44 1698) 73 50 90

**Background**
A subsidiary of Corus Rail, previously known as British Steel Railway & Foundry Products, Workington.

**Products**
Railway castings up to 90 tonnes in grey iron and cutile iron, including a wide range of base plates, blocks and washers, mainly for switches and crossings.

*VERIFIED*

## Corus Rail

Moss Bay, Derwent Howe, Workington CA14 5AE, UK
Tel: (+44 1900) 643 21   Fax: (+44 1900) 648 00
e-mail: marketing@corusrail.com
Web: http://www.corusgroup.com

**Key personnel**
Managing Director: Jon Bolton
General Manager UK Railway Businesses: Kevin Lane
Commercial Director: Jean-François Maubert
Operations Director: Kerry Hill
Technology Manager: Mike Poulter
Public Relations Manager: B P Curran
Purchasing Manager: J Allen

**Subsidiary companies**
Corus Rail Consultancy
Corus Rail Modular Systems
Corus Rail Technologies
Corus Cogifer
GrantRail

**International sales**
Parc du Saint-Laurent-le Toronto, 54 route de Sartrouville, F-78232 le Pecq Cedex, France
Tel: (+33 1) 30 15 24 24   Fax: (+33 1) 30 15 24 00
e-mail: corusrail@corusgroup.com

**Products and services**
Track products for high-speed, heavy-haul and rapid transit railways. With its constituent businesses, capabilities include the manufacture of rails, sleepers, switches and crossings and foundry products such as ingot moulds, cast bar and small castings. Services range from design and consulting to track renewal and maintenance.

The company has produced track for Railtrack and supplied railway accessories worldwide and has gained supplier accreditation from Railtrack (Level 2), DB Germany, SNCB, London Underground, SBB, LRQA, SNCF, TML, NSB, SNCFR, MRT Singapore, Tranz Rail, New Zealand and over 60 other customers. During 2001 the first type 560 and 600 steel sleepers were installed on the Railtrack network. Both are able to accept BS113A (or CEN54) and CEN60 rail sections.

Awarded BS 7570 (ISO 14001) environmental accreditation.

*UPDATED*

## Corus Rail Modular Systems

Moss Bay, Workington CA14 5AE, UK
Tel: (+44 1900) 643 21   Fax: (+44 1900) 648 00
e-mail: steven.syddall@corusgroup.com
Web: http://www.corusgroup.com

**Key personnel**
Commercial Manager: Steven Syddall

**Corporate background**
Corus Rail Modular Systems is a division of Corus Rail.

**Capabilities**
Corus Rail Modular Systems is a dedicated new business focused on the delivery of complete, integrated solutions for the design, fabrication, and installation of modular platforms within the railway environment. Drawing upon a wide range of expertise from within the Corus Group, Corus Rail Modular Systems aims to provide the most cost effective and technically advantageous solution for a variety of platform requirements.

**Products**
The Modular system can be applied to new permanent platforms, temporary installation and for the extension of existing platforms. Superficially, the platform can mimic the traditional construction appearance or a more modern, architectural look, whilst still complying with passenger safety requirements.

The adjustable superstructure of the modular solution, can accommodate uneven ground conditions and curved track alignments. As well as being suitable for main line and light passenger station applications, the system can also be used in depots and other railway facilities. The possibility of adjustment in horizontal and vertical planes allows for subsequent regauging. A choice of platform services is offered.

*UPDATED*

## Cowans Sheldon

A subsidiary of Rolls-Royce, Clarke Chapman Ltd
PO Box 9, Saltmeadows Road, Gateshead NE8 1SW, UK
Tel: (+44 191) 477 22 71   Fax: (+44 191) 478 39 51

**Key personnel**
Product Manager: Peter Ball

**Products**
Diesel-electric and diesel-hydraulic railway breakdown, general purpose and tracklaying cranes from 12 tonnes to 250 tonnes lifting capacity.

Refurbishment, life extension and upgrade of existing cranes as well as track maintenance machines.

## Créabéton

Créabéton Matériaux SA
Industrie Nord 2, CH-3225 Müntschemier, Switzerland
Tel: (+41 32) 312 98 50   Fax: (+41 32) 312 98 88
e-mail: muentsche@creabeton.ch
Web: http://www.tribeton.ch

**Corporate background**
Créabéton Matériaux SA is a member of the Vigier group.

**Products**
Tribeton concrete sleepers for standard and narrow gauge railways; concrete products for railway civil engineering applications.

*NEW ENTRY*

## CSI Productos Largos SA

Paseo de Castellana 91, E-28046 Madrid, Spain
Tel: (+34 91) 596 94 26   Fax: (+34 91) 596 95 60

### Corporate development
CSI Productos Largos is a subsidiary of CSI Corporación Siderúrgica.

### Products
Rail for a wide range of applications; accessories, including fishplates and tieplates.

---

## CSR Humes Pty Ltd

Building D, 4th Floor, World Trade Centre, Corner of Flinders and Spencer Streets, Melbourne, Victoria 3005, Australia
Tel: (+61 39) 286 26 66   Fax: (+61 39) 286 26 71

### Key personnel
Technical Services Manager: M Kiefel

### Products
Prestressed concrete railway sleepers, box culverts and pipes.

---

## CXT Inc

2420 N. Pioneer Lane, Spokane, Washington 99216, USA
Tel: (+1 509) 924 63 00   Fax: (+1 509) 927 02 99
e-mail: info@cxtinc.com
Web: http://www.cxtinc.com

### Key personnel
President: Alec Bloem
Vice-President: Dave Millard

### Works
2420 N Pioneer Lane, Spokane, Washington 99216, USA

### Products
Prestressed concrete sleepers for both track and turnouts; prefabricated buildings and precast concrete grade crossing panels.

CXT has developed geometric design capabilities for turnout layouts; for track, with a facility for gauge widening, tangent sleepers development and for standard track sleepers.

### Contracts
Concrete sleepers supplied to Calgary LRT, MTA Baltimore, Vancouver, Utah, Los Angeles, New Jersey, Denver, Portland and Southern California Regional Rail Authority, UP, BNSF and other heavy-haul railways.

Standard and curve concrete level crossing panels supplied to the Union Pacific Railroad, Burlington Northern Santa Fe Railway and other main line railroads a well as light rail transit systems throughout North America.

*UPDATED*

---

## Danieli Centro Maskin

Danish Centri Maskin SpA
Swedish branch office
PO Box 17067, Lilla Munkebäcksg 4, SE-402 61 Gothenburg, Sweden
Tel: (+46 31) 25 03 40   Fax: (+46 31) 25 07 11

### Key personnel
Managing and Marketing: Ove Lein

### Products
Carbide-tipped saws and carbide-tipped drill units for cutting rail to length.

---

## Darcy Products Ltd

Invicta Works, East Malling, West Malling ME19 6BP, UK
Tel: (+44 1732) 84 31 31   Fax: (+44 1732) 87 00 16

### Products
Track Mats, for protection of ballast and sleepers from oil, grease, grit and other rubbish. Darcy reports that the mats improve ballast formation and minimise the risk of run-off from the track flowing into nearby streams and watercourses or polluting ground water.

Track Mats consists of 4 m long 145 cm wide double thicknesses of high-tensile strength Drizit polypropylene oil-absorbent material with a backing to prevent splitting when laid over sharp ballast. They are fitted with tie ribbons for securing to rail holding clips. Sleeper ends can be protected in the same manner using sleeper end mats.

Track Grip is a lightweight plastic grid providing a non-slip surface for foot traffic and to protect the absorbent material from erosion by continual contact with fuel lines, power cables, hose couplings and similar equipment.

---

## DBT GB Ltd

Hallam Fields Road, Ilkeston DE7 4BS, UK
Tel: (+44 115) 951 25 00   Fax: (+44 115) 932 96 83
e-mail: info@dbt-gb.com
Web: http://www.dbt.de

### Products
Developed jointly with Jarvis Fastline Ltd, DBT GB manufactures the RBE-1 rapid ballast excavator, a road-rail crawler-mounted excavator developed primarily to remove spent ballast from the trackbed during renewals and transfer it to rail wagons on an adjacent track via conveyors mounted on the vehicle. Powered by a 150 kW diesel engine, the excavator employs rail wheels to travel to the site of work and is controlled by one operator. The RBE-1 also has bulk material handling applications at freight terminals.

*UPDATED*

---

## Delkor Pty Ltd

75 Hutchinson Street, St Peters, New South Wales 2044, Australia
Tel: (+61 2) 95 50 51 11   Fax: (+61 2) 95 50 56 25
e-mail: delkor@delkor.com.au
Web: http://www.delkor.com.au

### Key personnel
Managing Director: Peter Herbert
Technical Manager: Peter Schonstein
Sales Manager: George Stamboulis

### Products
Elastic rail fasteners, including noise-reducing fasteners for bridges and tunnels; ballast mats for ballasted track; floating slab systems.

### Contracts
The supply of noise-reducing elastic rail fasteners for the Sydney Harbour Bridge, Australia; and rail fasteners for the Tsing Ma Bridge, Hong Kong.

*UPDATED*

*Turnout transport wagon from Desec*

*Desec Tracklayer laying turnouts direct from wagons*

## Derby Rubber Products

84 Derby Street, Silverwater 2128, Australia
Tel: (+61 2) 96 48 49 11    Fax: (+61 2) 96 48 47 83
Web: http://www.derby rubber.com.au

**Key personnel**
Managing Director: Stephen Sheppard

**Products**
Rubber broom elements for ballast regulating machines.

---

## Desec Ltd

FIN-39700 Parkano, Finland
Tel: (+358 3) 448 34 42; (+358 3) 52 60 95 50
Fax: (+358 3) 448 34 43; (+358 3) 52 60 94 48
e-mail: desec@vip.fi
Web: http://www.desec.com

**Key personnel**
Managing Director: Seppo Koivisto
Sales Manager: Einari Venäläinen

**Products**
Track and turnout replacement machines; trolleys for turnout and track laying; lifting devices for track maintenance; supply of turnout transport wagons; railway cranes.

Desec Tracklayers are radio-controlled, straddle carrier-type multipurpose machines for carrying, lifting and assembling very long and heavy track and turnout elements. They are designed to work under catenary and in tunnels; tracklaying and replacement of turnout elements can be carried out without any additional lifting aid.

A Tracklayer unit is transported to the site on a conventional flat wagon or road trailer and is capable of loading and unloading itself using its crawler tracks and four supporting legs. The crawler tracks are driven by hydraulic motors and located on arms that can be horizontally and vertically telescoped in and out. When the crawler tracks are in their widest position, an element of 5 m in width, 32 m in length and 36 tonnes in weight can be lifted, moved and assembled by one TL 50 tracklayer.

The TL 70 Tracklayer can handle elements up to 40 m in length.

Recent contracts include the supply of three TL 50 units to VR Track Ltd, Finland; two TL 70 units to Banverket, Sweden; one TL 50 unit to ZS Praha AS, Czech Republic; one TL 50 unit to NNRA, Norway; one TL 50 unit to TSS Bratislava AS, Slovakia; one TL 70 unit to TECSA SA, Spain, four TL 70 units to SNCFR, Romania; five turnout transport wagons to SNCFR Romania; one TL 50 to Bosnia; one TL 50 to NESCO, Spain; lifting devices to VR Track Ltd, Finland; tracklaying trolleys to NNRA, Norway; and a sleeper assembly beam tracklayer to Bosnia and Herzogovina.

---

## D'Huart

Jean D'Huart et Cie
3 rue de l'Industrie, F-57110 Yutz, France
Tel: (+33 3) 82 56 34 84

**Products**
Rail, steel and timber sleepers, fishplates, other track components.

---

## DISAB

DISAB Vacuum Technology AB
Skiffervägen 44, S-224 78 Lund, Sweden
Tel: (+46 46) 38 42 00    Fax: (+46 46) 38 42 20
e-mail: info@disab-vacuum.se

**Products**
Railvac air-vacuum excavator system for cleaning cable culverts and drainage ditches and other rail infrastructure applications.

---

## Donelli DIMAF SpA

Via Romana 99, I-42028 Poviglio, Reggio Emilia, Italy
Tel: (+39 0522) 96 90 46; 7; 8    Fax: (+39 0522) 96 96 91

**Key personnel**
Managing Director: S Fitoussi

**Products**
Ballast regulators, hydraulic cranes, jacks, sleeper placing machines, track aligners, tracklaying equipment, track lining machines.

Other products: light and heavy-duty gang cars; brushwood cutters; workshop trailers; weedkiller-spreading trailers; overhead catenary line erection; maintenance and servicing vehicles; catenary inspection gang cars; catenary inspection trailers; rail/road loaders; hi-rail cranes.

---

## Drouard

Parc Saint-Christophe, F-95865 Cergy-Pontoise Cedex, France
Tel: (+33 1) 34 22 50 00    Fax: (+33 1) 34 22 62 29

**Key personnel**
Director: D Mallet
General Manager: J Lemercier

**Products**
Tracklaying and associated works (including TGV); manufacture of concrete sleepers; maintenance and renovation of track and ballast for rail, metros and tramways.

*UPDATED*

---

## Durisol Raalte BV

PO Box 40, NL-8100 AA Raalte, Netherlands
Tel: (+31 572) 34 64 00    Fax: (+31 572) 34 64 99

**Products**
Prefabricated wood-fibre concrete elements for track and lineside noise reduction.

---

## EBS

Eisenbahn Sicherung AG
Steinengraben 22, CH-4002 Basle, Switzerland
Tel: (+41 61) 285 14 44    Fax: (+41 61) 285 14 45

**Key personnel**
Sales Manager: Uwe Wunram

**Products**
Warning system for track maintenance teams which economises on look-out personnel. The approach of a train triggers flashing lights.

---

## Ecomeca Fabrication Française

Zone Industrial de Mariage, rue des Bryeres, F-69330 Pusignan, France
Tel: (+33 4) 72 05 18 70    Fax: (+33 4) 72 05 18 71

**Services**
Construction and modification of specialised machinery including hydraulic, hydrostatic transmissions and mechanical engineering.

---

## Edgar Allen Ltd

PO Box 42, Shepcote Lane, Sheffield S9 1QW, UK
Tel: (+44 114) 244 66 21    Fax: (+44 114) 242 68 26
Web: http://www.edgar-allen.co.uk

**Key personnel**
Directors
    Managing: R A Laird
    Financial: C Murphy
    Operations: D Eyre
Managers
    Sales and Technical: T Grindle
    Quality Assurance: I Grant
    Contracts Manager: S Turner

**Background**
Edgar Allen is part of the Mowlem Group.

**Products**
Design and manufacture of trackwork, switches and crossings for railways, mass transit, tramways, docks and harbours and steel works; manganese-steel wearing parts for locomotive and axlebox manufacturers and railway maintenance workshops.

The company is a major supplier to Railtrack of switches and crossings in manganese and other steels. It also supplies trackwork to North America to AREA specifications and to other countries to UIC specifications.

*VERIFIED*

---

## Edilon BV

Nijverheidsweg 23, PO Box 1000, NL-2031 CN Haarlem, Netherlands
Tel: (+31 23) 531 95 19    Fax: (+31 23) 531 07 51
e-mail: mail@edilon.nl
Web: http://www.edilon.com

**Key personnel**
Managing Director: A J Houck
Sales Director: W P Schram

**Principal subsidiaries**
Edilon International BV, St Denis, France
Edilon Corkelast SA, Spain
Edilon GmbH, Munich, Germany

**Products**
Specialised adhesives and elastomers for permanent way applications: Edilon Corkelast, a resilient pourable elastomer for embedded rail and embedded single block systems; Edilon Dex range, specialised epoxy-based products for timber sleeper preservation and glued insulated rail joints; and Edilon acoustic web blocks for noise reduction from track. In co-operation with the Silent Bridge Group, Edilon has introduced the integrated steel Silent Bridge concept with optimal noise and vibration concepts.

*UPDATED*

---

## Eichholz

Eichholz GmbH & Co KG
Bahnhofstrasse 17, D-97922 Lauda-Königshofen, Germany
Tel: (+49 93) 43 50 60
e-mail: info@eichholz.de
Web: http://www.eichholz.de

**Services**
Track building, platforms, large machines, civil engineering, rail grinding and underground construction. Engaged in major new building and extension projects for Deutsche Bahn and also the high-speed railway lines of Hanover–Berlin, Cologne–Frankfurt and Nuremberg–Munich.

*NEW ENTRY*

---

## Electrologic Pty Ltd

Unit 16, 43 College Street, Gladesville, New South Wales 2111, Australia
Tel: (+61 2) 98 16 15 15    Fax: (+61 2) 98 16 59 78
e-mail: info@electrologic.com.au
Web: http://www.electrologic.com.au

**Key personnel**
Managing Director: B Heij

## MANUFACTURERS/Permanent way components, equipment and services

**Products**
Continuous non-contact optical track geometry measurement system; continuous non-contact optical rail-shape measurement system; portable track recording system; rail thermometers; survey database systems; non-contact wheel shape measurement; rail stress monitor; and non-contact overhead wire measurement system.

**Contracts**
Non-contact optical track geometry recording car measurement system and overhead wire geometry measurement system for Queensland Railways; overhead geometry measurement system for SEPTA Philadelphia, USA; non-contact track geometry and third rail recording car for MRTC Singapore; non-contact track geometry for Iarnród Éireann, Ireland; and non-contact overhead and wire wear for China. Non-contact track geometry laser measurement system TRA, Taiwan.

*UPDATED*

---

### Elektro-Thermit GmbH and Co KG

Gerlingstrasse 65, D-45139 Essen, Germany
Tel: (+49 201) 173 03   Fax: (+49 201) 173 18 56
e-mail: info@elektro-thermit.de
Web: http://www.elektro-thermit.de

**Key personnel**
Managing Director, Commercial: Hugo Wortz
Managing Director, Technical: Henri Cohrt

**Subsidiaries**
Elektro-Thermit Dienstleistungs GmbH, Essen, Germany
P C Wagner Elektrothermit Schweissgesellschaft, Vienna, Austria
Form-Thermit spol sro, Brno, Czech Republic
MAV-Thermit, Hegesztö, Erd, Hungary
Thermit Welding (GB) Ltd, Rainham, UK
Thermit Italiana SpA, Milan, Italy
Thermit Australia Pty Ltd, Somersby, New South Wales, Australia
Thermit do Brasil Indústria e Comércio Ltda, Rio de Janeiro, Brazil
Thermitrex Pty Ltd, Gauteng, South Africa
Orgo-Thermit Inc, USA
Hans Goldschmidt Forschungs und Entwicklungs GmbH

**Products**
Thermit rail welding equipment and materials, rail grinding machines, glued insulated rail joints, hydraulic joint shearing device; Vortok coils.

---

### Energomachexport

25A Protopopovsky per, 129010 Moscow, Russia
Tel: (+7 095) 288 84 56; 69 83
Fax: (+7 095) 288 79 90; 69 83
e-mail: in@eme.tsr.ru

**Key personnel**
See entry in *Bogies and suspension, wheels and axles, bearing* section.

**Products**
Ballast cleaning machines; tamper-leveller-liner machines; tracklaying cranes and gantries; snow-plough equipment; rail welding equipment; portable powered machines for tamping, rail cutting, drilling and grinding; maintenance railcars.

---

### Enzesfeld-Caro Metallwerke AG

Fabrikstraße 2, A – 2551 Enzesfeld, Austria
Tel: (+43 2256) 811 45   Fax: (+43 2256) 844 52 25
e-mail: austroroll@caro.at
Web: http://www.austroroll.at

**Products**
Austroroll – switch point rollers.

*UPDATED*

---

### ESAB Welding Equipment AB

SE-695 81 Laxa, Sweden
Tel: (+46 584) 810 00   Fax: (+46 584) 41 17 21
e-mail: johny.sundin@esab.se

**Key personnel**
Divisional Manager: Lars Göran Eriksson
Divisional Manager Engineering: Johny Sundin

**Products**
Fixed and mobile flash-butt welding machines for rail; equipment for welding automation in rolling stock production; equipment for building-up welding of wheels.

*UPDATED*

---

### ESCO Equipment Service Co

117 Garlisch Drive, Elkgrove Village, Illinois 60007, USA
Tel: (+1 847) 750 98 60   Fax: (+1 847) 750 98 61
e-mail: escoequip@aol.com

**Key personnel**
President: T Y Gehr
Executive Vice-President: T E Dickey

**Products**
Abrasive cut-off and grinding stone; rail welding; rail saws and drills, rail ultrasonic testing; hydraulic track tools; magnetic pick-up devices; rail and tie tongs; rail fastening machines and maintenance-of-way machines; solar-powered switch machines, hy-rail cranes.

*UPDATED*

---

### Eurailscout

Eurailscout Inspection and Analysis BV
Postbox 349, NL-3800 AH Amersfoort, Stationsplein 325, NL-3818 LE Amersfoort, Netherlands
Tel: (+31 33) 469 70 00   Fax: (+31 33) 469 70 50
e-mail: info@eurailscout.com
Web: http://www.eurailscout.com

**Key personnel**
Directors: Armin Birkenbeul, Han Smits

**German office**
Büro Berlin, Warschauer Strasse 34-38, D-10243 Berlin, Germany
Tel: (+49 30) 29 33 96 10   Fax: (+49 30) 29 33 96 19

**Services**
A joint venture formed by GSG Knape Gleissanierung (Germany) and Strukton Railinfra (Netherlands), Eurailscout undertakes inspection, measurement and analysis of track geometry, rail profile, rail surface, and overhead line using a Plasser & Theurer UFM 120 Universal Measuring Car. The vehicle is also equipped with video inspection facilities, allowing monitoring of overhead wire and pantograph and of track surroundings, and meets the necessary regulatory conditions to operate on Dutch and German national rail networks.

*UPDATED*

---

### Euroswitch

SBB AG
Mittelstrasse 43, CH-3011 Bern, Switzerland
Tel: (+41 512) 20 47 96   Fax: (+41 512) 20 52 71
e-mail: monica.dumoulin@sbb.ch
Web: http://www.sbb.ch

Sersa AG
Brauerstrasse 126, CH-8004 Zurich, Switzerland
Tel: (+41 1) 242 52 30   Fax: (+41 1) 242 52 61
e-mail: info@sersa-group.com
Web: http://www.sersa-group.com

**Corporate background**
Founded in August 2000, Euroswitch is a joint venture between Swiss Federal Railways (SBB AG) and (66.6 per cent shareholding) Sersa AG (33.3 per cent).

*Euroswitch Type WTW wagon*   2002/0131435

**Services**
Developed and operated jointly by SBB AG and Sersa AG, Euroswitch provides a 'just-in-time' system of delivering switches and crossings by rail to work sites. Trackwork is conveyed on specially designed Matisa-built Type WTW wagons with a carrying capacity of 40 tonnes and a maximum operating speed of 120 km/h. Each wagon is equipped with a 16 kW diesel engine to power the vehicle's hydraulic positioning and handling systems. By the mid-2003, Euroswitch expected to have 20 Type WTW wagons at its disposal.

*NEW ENTRY*

---

### EWEM

Thundorferstrasse 58, CH-8500 Frauenfeld, Switzerland
Tel: (+41 52) 375 20 00   Fax: (+41 52) 375 20 11

**Key personnel**
Managing Director: A A G van Hees

**Principal subsidiaries**
EWEM BV, Den Haag, Netherlands
EWEM Ag Co Ltd, Bangkok, Thailand

**Licence holders for DE Clips:**
Arte Tecnica SA, Porto Alegre, Brazil
Pt Pindad (Persero), Bandung, Indonesia

**Products**
DE elastic rail fastener and DE system, which includes springclip and sleeperplate or shoulder cast in concrete sleeper.

---

### Exel Oy

PO Box 29, FIN-52701 Mäntyharju, Finland
Tel: (+358 15) 346 11   Fax: (+358 15) 346 12 16

**International sales and technical support**
Kolmark Ltd
Irisviksv 34H2, FIN-02230 Esbo, Finland
Tel: (+358 9) 88 15 81 40   Fax: (+358 9) 88 15 81 45
e-mail: jan.kolster@kolmark.fi

**Key personnel**
Managing Director: Jan Kolster

**Products**
Insulated rail joints for jointed and welded track; composite profiles and tubing for power line support.

*VERIFIED*

---

### 'EXIM' Verkehrs-, Hafen- und Umwelttechnik GmbH & Co Vertriebs KG

PO Box 1406, D-35004 Marburg, Germany
Tel: (+49 6421) 810 01; 003   Fax: (+49 6421) 853 53
e-mail: EXIMGmbHuC@aol.com

Permanent way components, equipment and services/**MANUFACTURERS**

**Key personnel**
General Manager: A J Frangoulis
Sales Managers: Jurgen Hofman, Gunter Nolte

**Products**
Sleepers, turnouts, rolling stock materials, fastenings, glued joints, welding equipment for workshops, permanent way equipment, switch point machines.

## FAB-RA-CAST

FAB-RA-CAST is a division of Horizon Manufacturing Inc
23820 Lee Baker Drive, Southfield, Michigan 48075, USA
Tel: (+1 248) 354 71 85   Fax: (+1 248) 354 71 85

**Key personnel**
President: John Cook

**Products**
Concrete railway crossings; rubber flangeway filler material. Contracts include the Tri-Met light rail system in Portland, Oregon.

## Fassetta

Fassetta mécanique
36 boulevard de la Gare, F-13713 La Penne S/Huveaune, France
Tel: (+33 4) 91 87 70 30   Fax: (+33 4) 91 87 70 39
e-mail: fasmec@fassetta.com
Web: http://www.fassetta.com

**Key personnel**
General and Export Manager: Frederic Fassetta
Technical Sales Manager: Bernard Rousset

**Products**
Track construction and maintenance equipment including wooden sleepers, sleeper manufacturing and machining plants. Special machines designed and produced on request.

*UPDATED*

## Faur SA

Basarabia Boulevard 256, Bucharest 3, R-73249, Romania
Tel: (+40 1) 255 15 13   Fax: (+40 1) 255 00 71

**Key personnel**
Development and General Manager: Victor Vieru
Economic Manager: Dumitru Ghinea
Image, Human Resources, Strategy Manager:
  Livia Niculescu
Sales and Purchasing Manager: Vasile Diaconescu
Production Manager: Mihai Baldea

**Products**
Track maintenance machines and spare parts for track maintenance machines.
  Recent contracts include the supply of track maintenance machines to the Russian Federation.
  Together with Plasser & Theurer, Austria, production of eight 09-32CSM track maintenance machines for SNCFR Romania.

## Ferotrack

Ferotrack Engineering Ltd
332 Kilburn High Road, London NW6 2QN, UK
Tel: (+44 20) 76 24 01 03   Fax: (+44 20) 76 24 89 79

**Works**
Willow Vale, Davenham Road, Oakley MK43 7SZ, UK

**Key personnel**
Managing Director, Export Sales: I O Schwarz
Director, Production and Design: K T Birchall

**Products**
Electric pad point and crossing heaters; cartridge heaters; clamp lock heaters; control cabinets; plus a major range of 996 Type Ni/Cd rechargeable batteries with integral electronic charger.

## Ferrostaal AG

PO Box, Hohenzollernstrasse 24, D-45116 Essen, Germany
Tel: (+49 201) 818 01   Fax: (+49 201) 818 28 22
Telex: 897100fsd

**Key personnel**
See entry in *Locomotives and powered/non-powered passenger vehicles* section.

**Products**
Permanent way materials: rail of all grades, light and heavy vignole rail, crane rail, grooved rail; wooden, concrete and steel sleepers; rail fastening systems and individual components for ballasted and slab tracks, resilient and rigid clips, sole plates, sleeper screws, spring washers, anti-creep rail anchors, sleeper anchoring devices; switch and crossing systems of various types, expansion joints, insulated joints; turntables; sliding buffer stops; rail welding materials; plastic components, screw dowels, plastic dowels for reconstruction of wooden and concrete sleepers, rail pads; elastomers for reducing groundborne noise, ballast mats, bearings for floating and slab tracks, resilient pads.

*VERIFIED*

## Ferrostaal Corporation

16510 Northchase Drive, Houston, Texas 77060, USA
Tel: (+1 281) 999 99 95   Fax: (+1 281) 999 41 43
Telex: 857100fsd

**Key personnel**
Vice-President: Dietrich H Seraphin

**Products**
Head-hardened rail and accessories.

## Findlay, Irvine Ltd

Bog Road, Penicuik EH26 9BU, UK
Tel: (+44 1968) 67 12 00   Fax: (+44 1968) 67 12 37
e-mail: sales@findlayirvine.com
Web: http://www.findlayirvine.com

**Key personnel**
Chairman: James S Findlay
Managing Director: Colin Irvine
Marketing Director: Delia Haverson
Sales Manager: Tom Findlay

**Products**
Electronic control systems for railway switch heating and monitoring.
  The Icelert 407M controller is a switch heating controller utilising the latest technology designed specifically for rail switch heating. It uses a variety of sensors to determine the possibility of the formation of ice. These include two rail-mounted temperature sensors (one on an unheated section of rail, one on a heated section), a precipitation (rain or snow) sensor and an optional blown-snow detector.
  The control unit has a digital display readout which indicates all the adjustable parameters such as 'set point' temperatures, 'delay' on switch-off of heating, 'hysteresis' levels and fault conditions. There are also LEDs to indicate when 'set points' have been reached and when precipitation and faults have been detected. Self-testing, manual override facilities and monitoring outputs have also been incorporated.
  The use of two cold rail set points and two hot rail set points (one if precipitation is detected and the other if precipitation is not detected) gives a total of four set points. The Icelert 407M automatically uses the 'wet' set points if precipitation or snow is detected and the 'dry' set points otherwise. This enables considerable cost savings to be made in dry conditions by not switching the heat on until the temperature drops to a lower level than if the precipitation is detected.
  Findlay, Irvine also produces a monitoring data-logger system for use in conjunction with the Icelert 407M accepting analogue, digital and 20 mA loop inputs from a wide range of proprietary sensors.

**Contracts**
Contracts include the supply of Icelert controllers to Polish Railways; and remote switch heating monitoring systems and weather monitoring control units for Railtrack, UK.

*UPDATED*

## First Engineering Ltd

Floor 7, Buchanan House, 58 Port Dundas Road, Glasgow G4 0HG, UK
Tel: (+44 141) 335 30 05   Fax: (+44 141) 335 30 06

**Key personnel**
Managing Director: Tony Smith
Commercial Director: John Cowie

**Corporate development**
Formerly known as Scotland Infrastructure Maintenance Co, First Engineering was one of the British Rail Infrastructure Services Units sold off as part of the British Rail privatisation. The company was sold in 1996 to a management buyout team known as TrackAction.

**Services**
Railway infrastructure construction, maintenance, renewals and consultancy, in addition to property management and maintenance service from its facilities divisions.

## Foster

L B Foster Company
415 Holiday Drive, Pittsburgh, Pennsylvania 15220, USA
Tel: (+1 412) 928 34 00   Fax: (+1 412) 928 78 91

**Key personnel**
Vice-President, Rail Products: Jack Rice

**Products**
New prime rail, relay rail, light rail, crane rail, rail and track accessories, track work, transit products and mass transit systems including rail fasteners, contact rail, catenary systems, coverboards and special testing.

*Plasser & Theurer UNIMAT 08-4X4-4S-RT tamping machine supplied to First Engineering, built in compliance with Railtrack Group Standard GM/RT 2400*  0021667

### Foster Transit Products Division

PO Box 47367, Doraville, Georgia 30362, USA
Tel: (+1 404) 662 77 74   Fax: (+1 404) 662 77 97
Contact: Sid Shue

**Products**
Direct fixation rail fasteners; special trackwork; composite and co-extruded conductor rail; concrete and wood sleepers; resilient rail fasteners for heavy haulage; catenary equipment; test laboratory for track components.

### Framafer

Société Française de Construction de Matériel Ferroviaire
77 rue de la Gare, F-57803 Bening-les-Saint-Avold, France
Tel: (+33 3) 87 29 22 00   Fax: (+33 3) 87 81 50 63

**Key personnel**
Sales Manager: Philippe Crovisier

**Products**
Automatic track levelling, tamping and lining machines, ballast cleaners and ballast regulators, track relaying systems, sleeper changing machines, brush-cutters, ditch-cleaners, track measuring cars, flash-butt welding machines, multipurpose track maintenance machines.

*VERIFIED*

### Geismar

113 bis avenue Charles-de-Gaulle, F-92200 Neuilly sur Seine, France
Tel: (+33 1) 41 43 40 40   Fax: (+33 1) 46 40 71 70

**Works**
5 rue d'Altkirch, F-68006 Colmar Cedex, France
Tel: (+33 3) 89 80 22 11   Fax: (+33 3) 89 79 78 45

**Products and services**
Tracklaying and maintenance equipment and services. Permanent way tools. Hand-held machinery, including rail drills, saws, disc cutters, grinders, benders, weld shears, tensors, pre-heaters, strikers, descalers, lifters, loaders; sleeper drills, adzers, plug drivers; fastening machines, fishbolters, coachscrewers, impact wrenches, elastic clip and spike inserters and extractors.

Heavy equipment, including gantries for laying and replacing track panels and switches, threaders, slewers, sleeper-changers, tampers and regulators.

Transport and maintenance vehicles, including inspection and flying gang trolleys, heavy-duty track cars, shunters, trailers, and railway excavators.

Turnkey plants and workshop machinery for rail welding, reprofiling or machining, timber sleeper machining and impregnation, steel sleeper reclamation.

Measuring instrumentation, including manual gauges and devices, hand-pushed or self-propelled or onboard electronic systems.

Geismar also supplies equipment to install and maintain AC and DC overhead catenary, including dedicated tools; overhead line components; and overhead line erection and wiring trains, maintenance and servicing vehicles, catenary inspection and measurement gang cars and trailers.

*VERIFIED*

### Gemco

Gemco George Moss Ltd
PO Box 136, Mount Hawthorn 6016, 461-465 Scarborough Beach Road, Osborne Park, Western Australia 6017, Australia
Tel: (+61 8) 94 46 88 44   Fax: (+61 8) 94 46 34 04

**Key personnel**
See entry in *Locomotives and powered/non-powered passenger vehicles* section.

**Products**
Track maintenance machinery, such as resleepering machines, rail-handling cranes, sleeper-handling machines, ballast scarifiers (linear), spike pullers, track jacks; tracklayers; rail flash-butt welding equipment.

The company also offers rail flaw detection, track recording equipment and track management systems.

### Getzner

Herrenau 5, PO Box, A-6706 Bürs/Bludenz, Austria
Tel: (+43 5552) 20 10   Fax: (+43 5552) 20 18 99
e-mail: sylomer@getzner.at
Web: http://www.getzner.at/werkstoffe

**Key personnel**
Managing Director: R Pfefferkorn
Sales Director: P Burtscher
Advertising Manager: Wolfgang Erhard

**Associated company**
Getzner Werkstoffe GmbH
Nördliche Münchner Strasse 27a, D-82031 Grünwald, Germany
Tel: (+49 89) 693 50 00   Fax: (+49 89) 69 35 00 11

**Products**
Sylomer® and Sylodyn® elastomers for noise and vibration reduction in track and structure construction, sleeper pads, ballast mats for subways, light rail and main line track; elastic bearings for track slabs; resilient baseplate pads and resilient rail pads.

Getzner Werkstoffe can also supply tailor-made orders to customer's requirements.

*UPDATED*

### Gleisbaumechanik Brandenburg

Am Sudtor, D-14774 Brandenburg-Kirchmoser, Germany
Tel: (+49 3381) 81 24 32   Fax: (+49 3381) 81 23 81

**Products**
GAF 100R and GAF 200 self-propelled rail and catenary maintenance vehicles.

### Grant Lyon Eagre

Hebden Road, Scunthorpe DN15 8XX, UK
Tel: (+44 1724) 86 21 31   Fax: (+44 1724) 29 52 43

**Key personnel**
Chairman: A V L Williams
General Manager: T J Bessel
Works Manager: S Flower
Design Manager: A Lenton

**Products**
The company manufactures switches and crossings to UIC and national standards for high-speed and heavy-load applications. Manufacturing facilities include rail machining shop, foundry, fabrication and assembly shops.

### GrantRail Ltd

Carolina Court, Lakeside, Doncaster DN4 5RA, UK
Tel: (+44 1302) 79 11 00   Fax: (+44 1302) 79 12 00
e-mail: sales@grantrail.co.uk
Web: http://www.grantrail.co.uk

**Key personnel**
Managing Director: J G Edwards
Engineering Director: David Philpott
Light Rail and Freight Director: Ray Rogers
Marketing and Business Development: Wim de Jong
General Manager, London Underground Division: Paul Kyte

**Corporate background**
British Steel (now Corus) and Royal Volker Wessels Stevin formed GrantRail as a jointly owned company. It is now a subsidiary of Corus Rail.

**Associate companies**
ALH Rail Coatings Ltd (50 per cent) (qv)
Total Power Solutions (50 per cent) (qv)

**Capabilities**
Construction, renewal and maintenance of LRT, metro, underground and heavy rail systems. Complete systems are offered for LRT projects, covering planning, supply of rail and installation.

Recent investments in equipment include a Kirow 810 C (UK) crane, three Matisa B45 tamping machines and a Matisa R24 ballast regulator.

**Contracts**
Major customers are Railtrack, London Underground, Manchester Metrolink and Midland Metro. As well as fulfilling numerous industrial and freight facilities contracts, GrantRail has also developed its own signalling and electrification divisions.

*VERIFIED*

### Greenwood Engineering

H J Holst Vej 3-5C, DK-2605 Brøndby, Denmark
Tel: (+45 36) 36 02 00   Fax: (+45 36) 36 00 01
Web: http://www.greenwood.dk

*MiniProf Rail, measuring railhead profile* 2002/0134496

*Sylomer® mass spring system on a main-line bridge in Germany* 2002/0101700

## Products

Development and production of measuring equipment including the MiniProf Rail for measuring railhead profiles.

*UPDATED*

## Grimma GmbH

Prophetenberg 7, D-04668 Grimma, Germany
Tel: (+49 3437) 921 10   Fax: (+49 3437) 92 11 26
e-mail: info@esa-grimma.de
Web: http://www.esa.grimma.de

### Products

Point heating systems, platform lighting, track system lighting, electrical energy distribution systems.

## Grinaker Duraset

PO Box 751752, Gardenview 2047, South Africa
Tel: (+27 11) 454 28 15   Fax: (+27 11) 454 17 13
e-mail: chris@gcl.co.za
Web: http://www.gcl.co.za/branches

### Works

PO Box 365, Brakpan 1540, South Africa
Tel: (+27 11) 813 23 40   Fax: (+27 11) 813 42 22

### Key personnel

Executive Director: J C Havinga
Managing Director: C A Visser
Product Manager: K Burger

### Products

Prestressed concrete railway products including sleepers, level crossing slabs, turnouts and electrification masts.

## GSK GmbH

Emil Rohrmann Strasse 9, D-58239 Schwerte, Germany
Tel: (+49 2304) 99 49 40   Fax: (+49 2304) 46 90 49

### Products

Permanent way materials; rails of all grades, including light and heavy Vignole rail, crane rail and grooved rail; rail fastening systems and individual components; baseplates; fishplates; sleeper screws; clips; nuts and bolts; fishplate bolts; spring washers; anti-creep anchors; plastic components; screw dowels; rail pads; noise- and vibration-reducing elastomers; ballast mats; wood, concrete and steel sleepers; switches and crossings.

## GTRM

GT Railway Maintenance Ltd
252-260 Broad Street, Birmingham B1 2HF, UK
Tel: (+44 121) 654 82 00   Fax: (+44 121) 654 86 51
e-mail: LesDeakin@gtrm.co.uk
Web: http://www.gtrm.com

### Key personnel

General Manager: John Penney
Managing Director: Paul Kirk
Commercial Director: John Hurrel
Director of Projects: John Osborne

### Corporate background

GT Railway Maintenance is a wholly owned subsidiary of Carillion plc following the sale by ALSTOM in September 2001 of its 51 per cent shareholding in the company. Each area director is responsible for both the technical and commercial performance of the Area Business Unit. In order to provide a focus for new projects, outside GTRM's maintenance activities, GTRM's Projects Group has been formed. The Projects Group is responsible for all major new works projects, national schemes and extended arm or managing agency contracts. Within the Projects Group three separate but closely related discipline-based units directly provide or manage resources for projects. These units, Signalling, Electrification and Civil Engineering, are capable of carrying out single discipline projects or combining to expedite multidisciplinary turnkey projects. Overall project and construction management is promoted from within the Projects Group.

### Corporate development

GT Railway Maintenance Ltd is owned by a joint venture between ALSTOM and Carillion plc, formerly Tarmac Construction Ltd. Formerly known as Central Infrastructure Maintenance Co, GT Railway Maintenance Ltd was one of the British Rail Infrastructure Services units sold off as part of the British Rail privatisation to ALSTOM and Carillion in 1996.

### Services

Track maintenance and upgrading; also inspection and renewal of railway infrastructure and buildings. Additional but related products and services, such as training and consultancy, are provided.

GTRM is the main contractor for these core activities on the West Coast Mainline from London Euston to Gretna Green, Scotland and for the Central band of England and Wales, East Coast to West Coast. GTRM also has activities in other parts of the UK railway network. GTRM holds contracts making it responsible for over 15 per cent of UK route-km, and employs around 3,400 multidisciplinary staff.

The activities of GTRM embrace the disciplines of civil engineering, electrical engineering, signals engineering, mechanical engineering, buildings and plant and telecommunications, as well as finance, contracts and personnel specialists.

GTRM has bought two Unimat 0.8 tampers for track maintenance on the UK's West Coast main line. It has also bought a Trakrat utility vehicle for mechanised patrolling and staff transport. Powered by a diesel engine with hydraulic drive it can be used to tow fittings such as access units scissor lifts and stone-blowing equipment.

GTRM and Sonatest, manufacturers of non-destructive testing equipment for the rail industry, have developed an advanced method of detecting breaks or flaws in rails, including dark areas such as tunnels.

Railtrack awarded two of its first tranche of UK Infrastructure Maintenance contracts to GTRM in 1999, for the maintenance of the Great Western Zone's South Wales area. GTRM holds infrastructure maintenance contracts for five Railtrack zones, representing 20 per cent of UK route-km.

*UPDATED*

## Gummiwerk Kraiburg Elastik GmbH

Göllstrasse 8, D-84529 Tittmoning, Germany
Tel: (+49 8683) 70 10   Fax: (+49 8683) 701 26
e-mail: info@kraiburg-elastik.de
Web: http://www.strail.de

### Key personnel

President: Andreas Starnecker
Administration: Georg Stockhammer
Sales and Marketing:
  Agriculture: Tilman Ziegler
  Level Crossing Systems: Andreas Herder
  Engineering: Thomas Passler
Technical Director: Uwe Dahlweg

### Products

STRAIL level crossing system – a full-depth rubber crossing designed for use at locations which experience dense traffic; PedeSTRAIL modular panels for pedestrian crossings; EcoSTRAIL accommodation crossings; and STRAIL-profile. The company has supplied crossings to railway companies in Europe and throughout the world.

Ballast matting: under contract to SL Stockholm Kraiburg is installing approximately 3,000 m² of ballast mats for the new Snabbspårvägen cross-city rail link in Stockholm. In Switzerland, Kraiburg has installed a ballast mat on the Sembrancher Viaduct, on the Martigny-Orsières rail line.

## Hanning & Kahl GmbH & Co

Rudolf Diesel Strasse 6, D-33818 Oerlinghausen, Germany
PO Box 1342, D-33806 Oerlinghausen
Tel: (+49 5202) 70 76 00   Fax: (+49 5202) 70 76 29
e-mail: HANNING-KAHL@t-online.de
Web: http://www.hanning-kahl.de

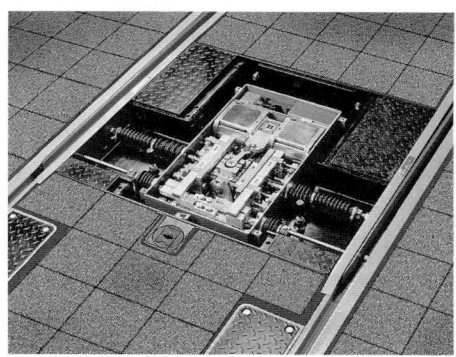

*Hanning & Kahl's point setting mechanism*
*2000/0088387*

### Key personnel

See entry in *Brakes and drawgear section*.

### Products

LRT Division: points mechanisms for all gauges and types of rail with magnetic, motor or electrohydraulic drive; manual point setting mechanisms; point mechanism for grooved rail; point setting mechanisms are also available with a tongue detector and a mechanical double-interlocking device for the point tongue.

Points controller and signalling systems for point controllers, depot controllers, level crossing safety devices, single-line track safety devices, mass detectors, vehicle reporting system, radio control, technical electronic data recorder and accessories like insulated guard rail tie bars, rail termination boxes and contact systems.

Contracts include the supply of point setting mechanisms to Calgary (Canada); Salt Lake City, Dallas, San Diego, San Jose (USA); Manchester, Birmingham, Croydon and Sheffield (UK); Rome, Turin, Milan (Italy); Melbourne (Australia); Hong Kong; and cities in Germany, Switzerland, Austria, Belgium, the Netherlands, Norway, Sweden and Finland.

## Harsco Track Technologies Ltd

Harsco House, Regent Park, 229 Kingston Road, Leatherhead KT22 75G, UK
Tel: (+44 115) 938 70 00/70 05   Fax: (+44 115) 938 70 01
e-mail: permaquip@harsco.com

### Key personnel

Managing Director: Larry Hawker
Director, UK Hy-Rail Operations: L A Withers
Technical Director: Bryce Randall

### Corporate development

Now part of Fairmont Tamper, Harsco Track Technologies previously traded as Permaquip.

### Products

Design and manufacture of tools, plant and vehicles for infrastructure maintenance and construction. Products, including those of Fairmont Tamper, are available for sale, lease or hire.

Sleeper handling: hand tools and plant for moving, machining and changing wooden and concrete sleepers, including a portable sleeper squarer/spacer.

Rail handling: Ironman and powered rail pullers for the mechanised handling of rail and Continuously Welded Rail (CWR) within or outside track possessions; rail threaders, rail joint straighteners and specialised rail carrying vehicles.

Stressing CWR: hydraulic tensors for all-weather control of stressing CWR, including obstructionless types with lightweight power packs; weld trimmers for track welding and accessories; self-contained mobile welding workshops for CWR maintenance.

Track maintenance and construction: tampers, ballast regulators, maintenance grinders, complete track relaying trains; Permaclipper for production rate installation and removal of Pandrol fastenings, including the Mk V Permaclipper adaptable for use with Pandrol Fastclips; slewing machines, lightweight Ironman for manual movement of points and crossings; hydraulic spike extractors.

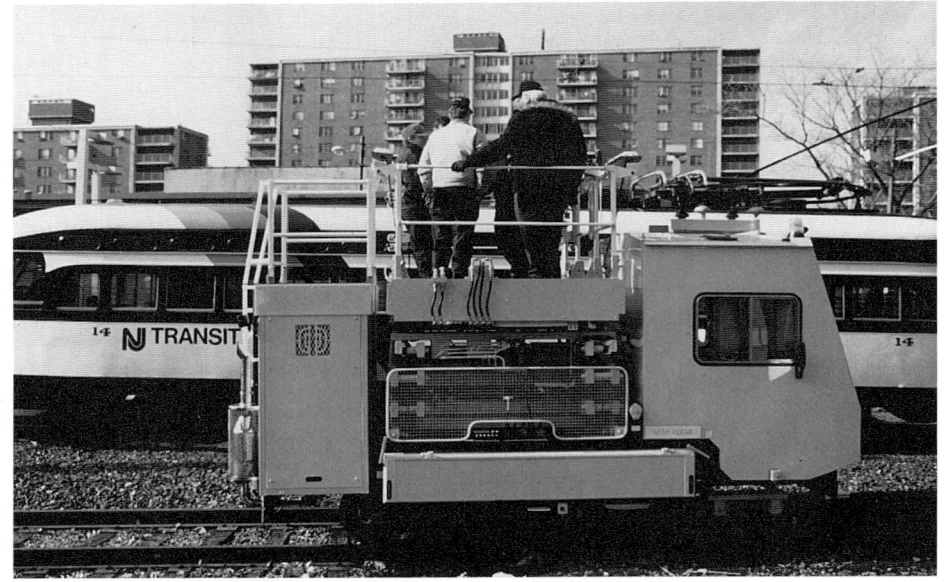

## MANUFACTURERS/Permanent way components, equipment and services

*Harsco Track Technologies high-capacity trolley supplied to New Jersey Transit* 0006290

*Land Rover converted to road/rail by Harsco Track Technologies* 0006291

Materials and personnel transport: a wide range of vehicles ranging from manual trolleys to road/rail trucks; on-track vehicles including tug units and general purpose Tramms; specialist vehicles for metro systems and customised personnel carriers.

Structures and overhead line maintenance: access platforms mounted on road/rail or on-track vehicles, featuring cantilever extension, creep control for driving from the elevated platform, electrical/hydraulic Power Take Off (PTO) and auxiliary lighting.

Road/rail trucks: a wide range of road vehicles can be adapted for road/rail use with the Fairmont hi-rail system of bolt-on rail guidance wheels. Fittings for road/rail trucks include cranes, access platforms, tipper bodies, rail carrying frames, drum carriers, crew cabs and trailers. General purpose road/rail trucks available for hire in the UK, including a 17 tonne GVW unit with crane and rail carrying facility.

Contract support: spares and service support; operator and contract support for specialist contract work such as stressing, joint straightening, weed control, ballast cleaning and sleeper squaring.

*UPDATED*

### Harsco Track Technologies Pty Ltd

PO Box 5287, 4 Strathwyn Street, Brendale, Queensland 4500, Australia
Tel: (+61 7) 32 05 65 00   Fax: (+61 7) 32 05 73 69
e-mail: sales@harscotrack.com.au

**Key personnel**
Managing Director: D K Harley
Sales Manager: G A Twilley
Contract and Service Manager: P R Hibberson

**Products**
The complete range of Fairmont, Tamper and Jackson track maintenance equipment including tamping machines, ballast regulators, ballast undercutters, sleeper renewal equipment, track renewal trains, rail grinders, hi-rail equipment, track and overhead geometry vehicles, utility vehicles and a comprehensive range of support equipment.

*UPDATED*

### Harsco Track Technologies

2401 Edmund Road, Box 20, Cayce-West Columbia, South Carolina 29171-0020, USA
Tel: (+1 803) 822 91 60   Fax: (+1 803) 822 74 71
e-mail: rnewman@harscotrack.com
Web: http://www.harscotrack.com

**Manufacturing and sales facilities**
415 North Main Street, Fairmont, Minnesota 56031-1837, USA
Tel: (+1 507) 235 33 61   Fax: (+1 507) 235 73 70

200 South Jackson Road, Ludington, Michigan 49431, USA
Tel: (+1 231) 843 34 31   Fax: (+1 231) 843 48 30

28 Eagle Road, Danbury, Connecticut 06810, USA
Tel: (+1 203) 778 68 11   Fax: (+1 203) 778 86 70

4 Strathwyn Street, PO Box 5287 Brendale, Queensland 4500, Australia
Tel: (+61 7) 32 05 65 00   Fax: (+61 7) 32 05 73 69

Harsco House, Regent Park 299 Kingston Road, Leatherhead KT22 75G, UK
Tel: (+44 115) 938 70 00   (+44 115) 938 70 01

**Key personnel**
President: G Robert Newman
Vice-President, Sales and Marketing: Donald Benza
Senior Director Sales North/South America: Jon Reilly
Director Sales Western Europe: Nicola Tosto

**Principal subsidiaries**
Harsco Track Technologies (Aus) Pty Ltd
Harsco Track Technologies (UK)

**Products**
Maintenance of way equipment, including Hy-Rail guide wheel attachments to adapt road vehicles for railway applications; automated tamping equipment; rail grinders; tracklaying and renewal machines; sleeper handlers, removers/inserters; spike drivers and pullers; utility track vehicles; track recording vehicles; rail lifters; remanufacturing of track maintenance equipment; and contract provision of new track construction, track renewal, track and turnout undercutting, sleeper laying and rail grinding services, rail flaw detection and snow blowing.

*UPDATED*

### HEI

Hindusthan Engineering & Industries Ltd
Mody Building, 27 Sir RN Mukherjee Road, Calcutta 700 001, India
Tel: (+91 33) 248 01 66
Fax: (+91 33) 248 19 22; 220 26 07
e-mail: hindus@cal2.vsnl.net.in

**Works**
Tiljala Plant (TP)
38 Tiljala Road, Calcutta 700 039, India

Bamunari Plant (BP)
National Highway No 2, Bamunari 712 205, District Hooghly, West Bengal, India

General Engineering Works (GEW)
Industrial Area, Bharatpur 31 001, Rajasthan, India

**Key personnel**
See entry in *Freight vehicles and equipment* section.

**Products**
Turnouts, points and crossings, both fabricated and Cast-Manganese Steel (CMS), explosion-hardened CMS crossings; track components and sleepers.

*UPDATED*

### Henry Williams Group

Dodsworth Street, Darlington DL1 2NJ, UK
Tel: (+44 1325) 46 27 22   Fax: (+44 1325) 38 17 44
e-mail: sales@h.williams.co.uk
Web: http://www.hwilliams.co.uk

**Key personnel**
Managing Director: B Hope
Sales Office Manager: S Todd
Head of Group Marketing: A W D Puddick

**Products**
Forged and fabricated railway equipment including forged, and rolled fishplates; rail anchors and clips; switch clamps; lineside apparatus cases; signalling cranks and rods; switch levers; track tools and gauges; maintenance escalator trolleys; and specialist fabrications and machined parts.

Contracts include the supply of lineside cases to Indonesia, Dartford and Willesden, UK, as well as the infrastructure maintenance market through NRS.

*UPDATED*

### H F Wiebe GmbH & Co KG

Im Finigen 8, D-28832 Achim, Germany
Tel: (+49 4202) 98 70   Fax: (+49 4202) 98 71 00
e-mail: info-wiebe-achim@wiebe.de
Web: http://www.wiebe.de

## Key personnel
Chairman of the Board: Hermann Wiebe, Sen
Managing Directors: Thorsten Bode, Norbert Modersitzki Werner Zitz

## Services
All aspects of new construction, conversion or maintenance whether for rolling stock, platform facilities or stations; GBM track construction machines; SDS safety with latest equipment in FA and AWS (track possession and automatic warning systems) engineering; BLP construction supervision and logistics.
Wiebe also undertakes building engineering, tunnel construction and building construction.

*NEW ENTRY*

---

# Hi-Force Hydraulics Ltd

Bentley Way, Daventry NN11 5QH, UK
Tel: (+44 1327) 301 00 00   Fax: (+44 1327) 70 65 55
e-mail: sales@hi-force.com
Web: http://www.hi-force.com/hi-force

## Key personnel
Directors: Chris Jones, John Taylor
Export Sales Manager: Ronnie Birch

## Products
Petrol-engined hydraulic pumps for rail stressing equipment, hydraulic rail joint pusher for insulated joint maintenance, hydraulic nut splitters, wagon rerailing equipment, low-height telescopic jacks, hydraulic tools, presses, pumps and cylinders.

*UPDATED*

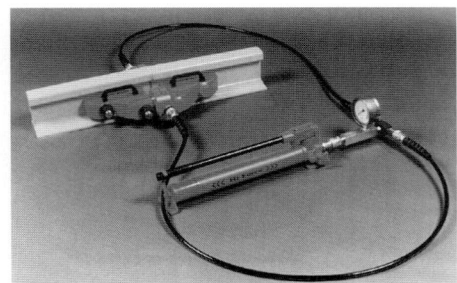

*Hi-Force Hydraulics HRJP65 rail joint pusher* 0064325

---

# Hioma-aine Oy

PO Box 133, FIN-06151 Porvoo, Finland
Tel: (+358 19) 65 40 02   Fax: (+358 19) 65 40 82
e-mail: abrasives@hioma.fi
Web: http://www.hioma.fi

## Key personnel
Managing Director, Exports & Marketing: Stefan Nymark

## Main works office
Jakarintie 451, FIN-07320 Jakari, Finland

## Products
Grinding wheels in resin bond for rail profiling and grinding of rail joint weldings.
Recent contracts include: VR-Rata Oy, Finland, 2000; Banverket, Sweden, 2000; Verktoy og Maskin AS, Norway, 2000.

---

# H J Skelton (Canada) Ltd

165 Oxford Street E, London, Ontario N6A ITA, Canada
Tel: (+1 519) 67 99 18 00
Fax: (+1 519) 679 01 93; 434 47 87

## Key personnel
General Manager: Peter Fraser
Sales Director: Geoffrey Richey

## Associated company
TKL Rail, Australia

---

## Products
Supplier of a wide variety of track components, special trackwork, sliding rail expansion joints, switch machines, sliding rail buffer stops, Icosit polyurethane/cork grout for undersealing grooved rail and injected pads for direct fixation. Specialises in LRT in-street applications, also railway rail (both T and grooved), crane rails and turnouts. Rawie sliding friction buffer stops to suit a range of applications. Range includes high-speed buffer stops bumping posts to stop trains at up to 56 km/h and also for low-floor LRVs. Contec switch machines and track wiring systems. Range of rails, points, crossing and special trackwork.

## Contracts
Five-year supply contract for TTC Toronto for all-manganese frogs, crossing and points for tram tracks; special trackwork for Calgary LRT; Icosit polyurethane grout for Tri-Met Portland, Memphis and Salt Lake City; screw spikes and washers for CN Rail and CP.

*NEW ENTRY*

---

# H J Skelton & Co Ltd

9 The Broadway, Thatcham RG19 3JA, UK
Tel: (+44 1635) 86 52 56   Fax: (+44 1635) 86 57 10
e-mail: info@hjskelton.com
Web: http://www.hjskelton.co.uk

## Key personnel
Director: J W G Smith

## Products
Railway rails and crane rails to British, European and North American BS, UIC and ASTM standards; special trackwork in flat-bottom and grooved rails; Rawie sliding friction buffer stops, fixed stops and wheel stops; Contec in-sleeper switch machines suitable for main line and tramway use.

## Contracts
Recent contracts include the supply of Rawie friction buffer stops for Heuston station, Dublin.

*UPDATED*

---

# Holdfast Level Crossings Ltd

Brockenhurst, Chedworth, Cheltenham, GL54 4AA, UK
Tel: (+44 1242) 57 88 01   Fax: (+44 1285) 72 07 48
e-mail: peter@railcrossings.co.uk
Web: http://www.railcrossings.co.uk

## Key personnel
Managing Director: Peter Coates Smith

## Products
Full depth rubber level crossing systems to suit any rail, sleeper and situation. Features include: very fast and low cost installation; high antiskid values; stable and durable panels.

*UPDATED*

---

# Holland

John Holland Construction & Engineering Pty Ltd
10th Floor, Durack Centre, 263 Adelaide Terrace, Perth, Western Australia 6000, Australia
Tel: (+61 8) 92 25 47 77   Fax: (+61 8) 93 25 70 24
e-mail: ht982@jhg.com.au

## Key personnel
General Manager, Rail Division (Perth): David Tasker
Operations Manager (Perth): Joe Angelucci
Planning Manager (Melbourne): Robb van Toledo
Rail Maintenance Manager (Sydney): Terry Brady

## Products
Manufacture of single-gauge and gauge-convertible concrete sleepers. Track design, construction, rehabilitation, gauge conversion and maintenance, including installation of concrete sleepers under traffic conditions or during temporary line closures.

---

# Holland Company LP

1000 Holland Drive, Crete, Illinois 60417-2120, USA
Tel: (+1 708) 672 23 00   Fax: (+1 708) 672 01 19
e-mail: postmaster@hollandco.com
Web: http://www.hollandco.com

## Key personnel
President: Phil Moeller
Vice-President Rail Mechanical Group: Len O'Kray
General Manager TrackStar®: Robert Madderom
Director, International Sales: E Parker
General Manager: Mod-Mark Rovnyak
Controller: Frank Francis

## Products
Sales and contracting of electric flash-butt welding personnel and equipment; rail and road mobile welders and portable on-site welding plants. Products also include the Intelliweld® fully digitised flash-butt welding control system. Holland can supply all support equipment or provide a turnkey operation.

*UPDATED*

---

# Huck International Inc

Huck Fasteners-HQ
PO Box 27207, Tucson, Arizona 85726, USA

## UK address
Huck International Ltd
Unit C, Stafford Park 7, Telford TF3 3BQ
Tel: (+44 1952) 29 00 11   Fax: (+44 1952) 29 04 59
Vice-President: John Coles

## Key personnel
Executive Vice-President, International Operations: Robert S Levine

## Products
Fastening systems, including lockbolts for use in rail joints and rolling stock.

*UPDATED*

---

# IAD Rail Systems

63 + 64 Gazelle Road, Weston Super Mare, BS24 9ES, UK
Tel: (+44 1934) 42 70 00   Fax: (+44 1934) 42 70 20
e-mail: head-office@iadrailsystems.com
Web: http://www.iadrailsystems.com

## Key personnel
Managing Director: Trevor Brown
Director of Marketing: Mick Ledger

## Background
IAD Rail Systems is part of the Industrial Actuation Division of Claverham Group Ltd, formed in January 1998 following the acquisition of Fairey Hydraulics Ltd from Fairey Group plc.

## Products
Switch and crossing actuation systems. The company has developed its High Performance Switch System (HPSS), which incorporates reliable actuation, locking and detection technologies with proven in-sleeper torsional back-drives and the latest trackwork features. Suitable for line speeds of up to 250 km/h, HPSS is claimed to be easy to install and to require no scheduled maintenance. Through tamping is also possible.

*IAD Rail Systems' HPSS switch actuation system*
2001/0103970

## MANUFACTURERS/Permanent way components, equipment and services

The first production installation of HPSS took place in the UK at a location in south London on Railtrack's Southern Zone late in 2000.

*UPDATED*

---

### ImproRail

Nassau Zuilensteinstraat 4, NL-2596 Den Haag, Netherlands
Tel: (+31 70) 326 89 66   Fax: (+31 70) 324 46 44
e-mail: 101773.300@compuserve.com

**Products**
A joint venture between Gleisunterhaltung mbH (Germany), Houthandel Pieter Ressenaar and Railpro BV (both Netherlands), ImproRail undertakes the treatment, preparation and reinforcement of wooden sleepers, as well as the preparation of wood for other railway applications, such as bridge construction.

---

### Inexa Profil AB

Box 927, SE-971 28 Luleå, Sweden
Tel: (+46 920) 735 00   Fax: (+46 920) 735 99
e-mail: inexa@inexa.se
Web: http://www.inexa.se

**Products**
Rail to S49, S54, BV50, UIC54, 113A and UIC60 specifications in lengths of up to 60 m, or in greater lengths in co-operation with rail welding partners. Production is based in UIC860 standards.

---

### Infra Safety Services

PO Box 1075, NL-3300 BB Dordrecht, Netherlands
Tel: (+31 78) 654 06 55   Fax: (+31 78) 651 44 21

**Key personnel**
Director: C J de Graaff
General Manager: J F A M Weijtmans

**Products**
Infra Safety Services provides a total package for securing the work area. The company draws up and executes safety plans and develops high-standard systems such as ARW 5/2 and Minimel 90 or PWA.

---

### Infrasoft Ltd

North Heath Lane, Horsham, West Sussex RH12 5QE, UK
Tel: (+44 1403) 25 95 11   Fax: (+44 1403) 21 77 46
e-mail: info@infrasoft.civil.com
Web: http://www.infrasoft.civil.com

**Key personnel**
Managing Director: Jim Paton
International Sales Manager: Chris Palfreyman
UK Sales Manager: Robin Akers

**Subsidiary companies**
Infrasoft Ltd – India Branch
Infrasoft BV
Infrasoft North America

**Capabilities**
MXRAIL is a design and analysis system used for high speed to light rail, switch and crossings, alignment matching, cant design, drainage and automated drawing production.

---

### INFUNDO GmbH

Pasteurstrasse 7, D-80999 Munich, Germany
Tel: (+49 89) 892 86 40   Fax: (+49 89) 89 28 64 20
e-mail: feste-fahrban@infundo.de
Web: http://www.infundo.de

**Background**
Infundo GmbH was set up in 1999, with the registered office in Munich, as the joint subsidiary of contractors Leonhard Weiss Gmbh & Co, Göppingen, and Edilon BV, Haarlem, Netherlands.

**Products**
Track components

---

### Interep SA

11 rue de l'Industrie, F-43110 Aurec-sur-Loire, France
Tel: (+33 4) 77 35 20 21   Fax: (+33 4) 77 35 26 17
e-mail: sales@interep.fr

**Key personnel**
Managing Director: Daniel Boffy
Sales and Marketing Director: Philippe Charbonnier
Technical Manager: Joël Hugues

**Products**
Vibration-absorbing microcellular foam rubber for use in ballast/sleeper mats and rail/sleeper/slab pads.

---

### International Track Systems Inc

International Track Systems Inc Railroad Rubber Products
620 West 32nd Street, PO Box 857, Ashtabula, Ohio 44004, USA
Tel: (+1 216) 992 92 06   Fax: (+1 216) 992 67 52

**Key personnel**
Managing Director: Harold L Reiter
Sales Director: Benjamin F Baker

**Products**
Rubber products including tie pads, insulating rubber tie plates, direct fixation fasteners, flangeway filler strips for level crossings, and rubber tie boots. Window and door glazings for passenger cars and rubber sand pipe nozzles for locomotives. Polyethylene shims and tie pads, rubber and plastic extrusions and mouldings.

---

### IPA

Industria Prefabbricati E Affini
Via Provinciale per Trescore, I-24050 Calcinate (BG), Italy
Tel: (+39 035) 442 30 77   Fax: (+39 035) 442 32 05

**Works**
Via Don P Bonetti 45, I-24060 Gorlago (BG), Italy
Tel: (+39 035) 95 10 66   Fax: (+39 035) 95 24 14

**Key personnel**
Executive: Enzo De Biasio

**Principal subsidiary**
Ipabras
Via Oswaldo Pinto Martins 260, 06900 Embú-Guacu, São Paulo, Brazil

**Products**
Prestressed concrete sleepers for track and switches; prestressed concrete slabs for track, switches, bridges, level crossings and tramways; noise barriers.

---

### JacksonEve Infrastructure Services

West Offices, City Business Centre, Station Rise, York YO1 6HT, UK
Tel: (+44 1904) 61 33 61   Fax: (+44 1904) 61 29 36
Web: http://www.jacksoneve.co.uk

**Key personnel**
Managing Director: Graham Reid
Business Development Manager: Chris Buckingham

**Corporate background**
A member of The Peterhouse Group, JacksonEve Infrastructure Services was formed in 2001 by combining the activities of Jackson Rail (civil engineering and permanent way contracting), Eve NCI (cable installation), Eve Rail (signaling and power networks) and Eve Utility Services (utilities infrastructure).

**Services**
Civil engineering, permanent way maintenance and renewal, signalling, traction power supplies, telecommunications and cable installation.

*NEW ENTRY*

---

### JAFCO

JAFCO Tools Ltd
St Paul's Road, Wood Green, Wednesbury WS10 9QX, UK
Tel: (+44 121) 556 77 00   Fax: (+44 121) 556 77 88

**Key personnel**
Managing Director: Jane Antill

**Products**
Track maintenance hand tools, both insulated with fibreglass handles and non-insulated. Supplier to the major UK track operators/contractors. Registered to ISO 9002.

---

### Jakem Timbers Ltd

The Old Malt House, 125 High Street, Uckfield TN22 1EG, UK
Tel: (+44 1825) 76 85 55   Fax: (+44 1825) 76 84 83

**Key personnel**
Director: R A Helyar

**Products**
Hardwood sleepers, crossing and bridge timbers.

---

### Jaraguá

Jaraguá Equipamentos Indústrias Ltda
Av Mofarrej 706, 05311-903 Vila Leopoldina, São Paulo SP, Brazil
Tel: (+55 11) 835 83 55   Fax: (+55 11) 260 15 81; 21 56

**Works**
Av Jaraguá 300, 18087-308 Aparecidinha, Sorocaba SP, Brazil
Tel: (+55 15) 235 53 00   Fax: (+55 15) 225 14 88; 17 05

**Key personnel**
Managing Director: Hans H Klemm
Sales Manager: Pedro Fernandes

**Products**
Turnouts, switches and crossings.

---

### Jarret

198 avenue des Grésillons, F-92602 Asnières Cedex, France
Tel: (+33 1) 46 88 16 20   Fax: (+33 1) 47 90 03 57
e-mail: contact@jarret.fr

**Key personnel**
See entry in *Brakes and drawgear* section.

**Products**
Shock-absorbers for bridge protection; protection against earthquakes for railway bridges, end-of-track buffers.

*UPDATED*

---

### Jarvis Rail

Jarvis House, Toft Green, York YO1 6JZ, UK
Tel: (+44 1904) 71 27 12   Fax: (+44 1904) 71 37 10
e-mail: marketing@jarvis-uk.com

## Permanent way components, equipment and services/**MANUFACTURERS**

**Key personnel**
Managing Director: Tony Cunningham
Human Resource Director: Martin Northard
Commercial Director: Martin Brazier
Finance Director: Steve Hurrell
Managing Director, UK Rail Operations:
  Bob Doyle
Managing Director, Major Projects Delivery:
  Mick McKeever
Managing Director, Operations and Safety:
  Richard Davies

**Services**
Jarvis Rail is the railway engineering arm of Jarvis plc, responsible for the design, construction, renewal and maintenance of all facets of railway infrastructure within nine regional offices, 81 works depots and 12 plant depots throughout the UK.

**Contracts**
Contracts include Railtrack maintenance work contracts for Central, East Coast Main Line and Liverpool, Merseyside and North Wales areas involving some 3,530 km of railway infrastructure and the track upgrading of the West Coast Main Line, valued at £550 million.

*UPDATED*

---

## JC Bamford Excavators Ltd

JCB
Rocester ST14 5JP, UK
Tel: (+44 1889) 59 03 12   Fax: (+44 1889) 59 34 55
e-mail: gordon.henderson@jcb.com
Web: http://www.jcb.com

**Key personnel**
Director, UK Sales: Gordon Henderson

**Products**
JCB JS175W Roadrail road-rail vehicle. The 22 tonne unit features a heavy duty JS200W chassis to support independently driven wheels and four independent stabilisers. Lifting capacity with stabilisers deployed is 4,400 kg at 4.5 m reach and over 3,200 kg without stabilisers. Maximum rail speed is 23 km/h. Attachments which can be fitted to the Roadrail's light duty, triple-articulated boom include: rail 'indig' bucket for excavation between rails; hedge flails; ballast brushes; rail thimbles; hydraulic rail beams; and rail clip insertion and removal machines.

*NEW ENTRY*

---

## JEZ Sistemas Ferroviarios

Arantzar s/n, E-01400 Llodio-Laudio, (Alava), Spain
Tel: (+34 94) 672 12 00   Fax: (+34 94) 672 00 92
e-mail: infor@jez.es
Web: http://www.jez.es

**Key personnel**
President: Txaber de Errazti

**Corporate background**
JEZ Sistemas Ferroviarios is a member of the VAE group of companies.

**Products**
Specialises in points and crossings including high-speed turnouts.

*UPDATED*

---

## Kalyn Siebert

Kalyn Siebert Inc
PO Box 758, Gatesville, Texas 76528, USA
Tel: (+1 817) 865 72 35   Fax: (+1 817) 865 72 34
e-mail: wesc@kalyntx.com
Web: http://www.kalynsiebert.com

**Key personnel**
Sales Manager: Wes Chandler

**Products**
Road trailers for the transport of rail vehicles, with hydraulically operated folding goose-necks for loading and unloading.

*UPDATED*

---

## Kershaw

Kershaw Manufacturing Co
PO Box 244100, Montgomery, Alabama 36124, USA
Tel: (+1 334) 215 10 00   Fax: (+1 334) 215 75 51
Web: http://www.kershawusa.com

**Key personnel**
Vice-President and Chief Operating Officer:
  Greg Valley
Vice-President of Sales and International Sales Manager:
  Phil Brown

**Corporate development**
Kershaw Manufacturing Co is a division of Progress Rail Services Corporation.

**Products and services**
Established in 1944. Design and manufacture of machines for 914; 1,000; 1,067; 1,435; 1,520; 1,600 and 1,676 mm track gauges: ballast regulators (120 to 275 hp); ballast undercutters/cleaners (200 to 750 m$^3$/h); machines for sleeper or rail replacement; snow/ice and sand removers; one-man operated railcar-loading-ramps (20 t/axle); road/rail locomotive cranes (60 to 150 t); on/off-track tree, high branches and brush cutting/clipping vehicles; customised motor cars.

*UPDATED*

---

## Kier Rail

Tempsford Hall, Station Road, Sandy, Bedfordshire SG19 2BD, UK
Tel: (+44 20) 79 22 60 05   Fax: (+44 20) 79 22 69 03
e-mail: rail@euston.kier.co.uk
Web: http://www.kier.co.uk

**Key personnel**
Managing Director: Paul Sheffield
Operations Director: Philip Gray
Business Development Manager: Marcelle Cater

**Works**
Euston Station, Barnby Street, London NW1 2RS, UK

**Background**
Kier Group. Kier Rail is a division of Kier Construction.

**Products**
Management and construction of railway related projects including trackwork, signals, earthworks, mechanical and electrical works, land remediation, catenary works, building and civil engineering and planned maintenance.

**Contracts**
Contracts include: Railtrack station regeneration programme, Southern Zone, in an extended management contract, 1996-2000; West Coast traincare including upgrade of maintenance depots on West Coast Main Line for tilting trains, 2000.

*UPDATED*

---

## KIHN SA

17 rue de l'Usine, L-3701 Rumelange, Luxembourg
Tel: (+352 56) 477 11   Fax: (+352 56) 58 54
e-mail: kihn@pt.lu

**Key personnel**
Manager: Jean Pierre Allegrucci
Export Sales Engineer: Jose Chartier

**Products**
Engineering and supply of turnouts, points and crossings, crossovers and junctions, trackwork combinations, monobloc and welded frogs, diamond crossings, expansion joints, glued insulated joints and special layouts for urban transport systems, main line railways and industrial network.

---

## Kirow

Maschinenbau Kirow Leipzig Rail & Port AG
Spinnereistrasse 13, D-04179 Leipzig, Germany
Tel: (+49 341) 495 30   Fax: (+49 341) 477 32 74
e-mail: vorstand@kirow.de
Web: http://www.kirow.de

**Key personnel**
Managing Director: L Koehne
Technical Director: W Köllner
Marketing Director: J Kühn

**Products**
Cranes for bridge and track construction, breakdowns and accidents. The latest model is the KRC 900 rail-based rescue crane.

Recent contracts include supply of a crane to Tanzania Railways Corporation; Pohang Iron & Steel Co, South Korea; a diesel hydraulic crane for ENR Egypt, a diesel hydraulic crane for Amtrak USA; a diesel hydraulic crane for Vanomag Track Construction Switzerland; 10 diesel hydraulic cranes for Russian Railways; and a 100-tonne diesel hydraulic crane for GrantRail, UK a diesel electric crane for the State Mining Company, Kazakhstan.

*Kirow rail-mounted KRC 900 rescue crane for Tanzania*

## 734 MANUFACTURERS/Permanent way components, equipment and services

## Kloos Oving bv

West-Kinderdijk 24, 2953 XW Alblasserdam, PO Box 3, NL-2960 AA Kinderdijk, Netherlands
Tel: (+31 78) 691 40 00   Fax: (+31 78) 691 45 42
e-mail: info@kloos-oving.s3c.nl

### Key personnel
General Manager: J van Houwelingen

### Products
Design, development, construction and delivery of standard and custom-built track materials for main line, metro, light rail systems and heavy-duty systems including: turnouts, crossings, points, expansion joints and special constructions.

### Contracts
Recent contracts include the supply of track materials to operators in Colombia, Germany, Indonesia, Iran, Netherlands and Singapore.

*UPDATED*

## Knox Kershaw Inc

11211 Trackwork Street, Montgomery, Alabama 36117, USA
Tel: (+1 334) 387 56 69   Fax: (+1 334) 387 45 54
e-mail: sales@knoxkershaw.com
Web: http://www.knoxkershaw.com

### Key personnel
Chairman: J Knox Kershaw
Chief Executive Officer: George Rutland
Marketing: Thomas L Pair

### Products
Ballast regulators, repair kits, improved performance kits, ballast undercutter/cleaners, railway cranes, equipment for sleeper and rail replacement, sanc and snow removal, vegetation control and various other maintenance operations.
Sales are made to many USA railways.

## Kockums

Kockums Industrier AB
SE-205 55 Malmö, Sweden
Tel: (+46 40) 34 80 80   Fax: (+46 40) 34 87 75
e-mail: info.kiab@celsius.se

### Key personnel
See entry in *Freight vehicles and equipment* section.

### Corporate background
Kockums Industrier is owned by the Celsius Group.

### Products
Include the new MPSV-1 multipurpose vehicle for the Swedish Rail Administration. It is a flexible vehicle, equipped with a quick-lock system for interchangeable cargo platforms. It can be adapted for different purposes such as for transportation of materials and staff as well as overhead line work, for clearing activities on or around the track area. A turntable allows 180° rotation, easily controlled by the driver. The MPSV-1 can pull 400 tonnes of wagons with up to 18 axles. It is powered by a diesel engine and has also a hydraulic power unit for other equipment.

## Kolmex SA

Grzybowska 80/82, PL-008-44 Warsaw, Poland
Tel: (+48 22) 661 50 00   Fax: (+48 22) 620 93 81
e-mail: kolmexsa.kolmex.com.pl
Web: http://www.kolmex.com.pl

### Key personnel
Chairman: Andrzej Nalecz
Commercial Director: Krystyna Stepaniuk

### Products
Track construction and maintenance machines and equipment including track-laying trains, tamping machines, snow ploughs, broken-stone cleaning machines, weed-killing trains, auxiliary lorries, ditch cutters, track-measuring devices, electric and diesel drilling machines, electric and diesel saws, electric and diesel bolting machines, hydraulic bending machines, hot box and flats detection devices on trains, points, turnouts and crossings, type SB-3 elastic rail fasteners, screws, nuts, bolts and coil spring washers.

## Krautkrämer GmbH & Co

Robert Bosch Strasse 3, D-50354 Hürth, Germany
Tel: (+49 2233) 60 10   Fax: (+49 2233) 60 14 02
e-mail: hotline@krautkramer.de

### Products
Stationary installations for non-destructive testing of rails and axles using ultra-sonics; portable ultra-sonic flaw detectors for manual inspection of rails, axles and wheels.

## Künzler

Künzler Jav AG, CH-3426 Aefligen, Switzerland
Tel: (+41 34) 445 14 84   Fax: (+41 34) 445 53 42

### Key personnel
Sales Manager: Kurt Beck

### Products
Inspection tower capable of running on rails or highways. The telescopic tower can be used for repairs to overhead catenary, lamps, tunnel roofs and bridges, both under and over the line.

## Laser Rail Ltd

Fitology House, Smedley Street East, Matlock DE4 3GH, UK
Tel: (+44 1629) 76 07 50   Fax: (+44 1629) 76 07 51
e-mail: info@laser-rail.co.uk
Web: http://www.laser-rail.co.uk

### Key personnel
Managing Director: David M Johnson
Operations Director: Alison B Stansfield
Technical Director: Steve Ingleton

### Background
Laser Rail was established in 1989 in response to a rapidly growing need to manage the implementation of new technology into the commercial rail environment.

### Products
ClearRoute, ClearRoute LT, Stress Route and DesignRoute gauging system software for gauging applications; LaserSweep portable structure profile measuring system; Laser gauging road rail measuring vehicle. Track geometry measurement and database systems for track assessment, redesign and monitoring of both track performance and maintenance machinery. Route assessments for existing and new rolling stock feasibility studies for existing and new routes. Design of new rolling stock for existing routes. All of which applies to Network Rail and London Underground.
Laser Rail operates a range of computer facilities as part of its services. It also provides training and certification to various levels of competency and this can be supplied as part of the overall support package. Laser Rail operates in the UK, USA and the Pacific Rim.

*UPDATED*

## Lewis Bolt & Nut Co

15500 Wayzata Blvd, Suite 611, Wayzata, Minnesota 55391, USA
Tel: (+1 612) 449 96 30   Fax: (+1 612) 449 96 07
e-mail: DMBLBN@aol.com

### Key personnel
Chief Executive Officer: Mark Paper
Vice-President: Dave Barry

### Products
Fasteners for track, level crossings and timber structures.

## Lindapter International

Lindsay House, Brackenbeck Road, Bradford BD7 2NF, UK
Tel: (+44 1274) 52 14 44   Fax: (+44 1274) 52 11 30
e-mail: enquiries@lindapter.com
Web: http://www.lindapter.com

### Key personnel
Managing Director: Tod Altman
Export Sales Managers: Ashley Watkins
Technical Support Manager: Michael Knight

### Background
Lindapter International was formed in 1934 by Henry Lindsay to market traditional hook bolt adapters and has been part of the Victulic Group, Glynwed International and in 1999 was taken over by Tyco International Ltd.

### Products
Holdfast adjustable rail clips; the Soft clip holds rails in precise alignment while the Hard clip prevents vertical rail movement. A Spring clip also caters for rail wave while holding the rail down. A Type BR clip suits flat bottom or bridge rails up to an 8° slope. The Temporary Support System supports and insulates running rails while essential repair work is being carried out.

*Kockums MPSV-1 multipurpose vehicle* 0064326

*Lindapter's rail clip* 2000/0092275

Permanent way components, equipment and services/**MANUFACTURERS**

**Contracts**
Manchester Piccadilly station reroofing. Greenwich station transport interchange (connections in roof structure), London Underground rerailing project. Other contracts include Rome metro, Channel Tunnel and the East Coast Main Line, UK.

*UPDATED*

---

## Linsinger Maschinenbau GesmbH

Dr Linsinger Strasse 24, A-4662 Steyrermühl, Austria
Tel: (+43 7613) 88 40  Fax: (+43 7613) 88 40 38
e-mail: maschinenbu@linsinger.com
Web: http://www.linsinger.com

**Key personnel**
Shareholder: F Weingartner
Managing Director: H Knoll
Technical Manager: W Neubauer
Marketing: W Kastinger

**Products**
Mobile rail milling machine with post grinding and measuring equipment, SF03.

---

## Loram Maintenance of Way, Inc

PO Box 188, 3900 Arrowhead Drive, Hamel, Minnesota 55340, USA
Tel: (+1 763) 478 60 14  Fax: (+1 763) 478 22 21
e-mail: sales@loram.com
Web: http://www.loram.com

**Key personnel**
Vice-President, Marketing: P J Homan
Manager, International: T L Smith

**Products**
Manufacture of self-propelled rail grinding, excavator/vacuum, ditching and shoulder ballast cleaning equipment, available for purchase or lease. Contract services for railways, metros and LRT systems.

*VERIFIED*

---

## Lord Corporation

Mechanical Products Division, 2000 West Grandview Blvd, PO Box 10040, Erie, Pennsylvania 16514-0040, USA
Tel: (+1 814) 868 54 24  Fax: (+1 814) 868 31 09

**Key personnel**
See entry in *Bogies and suspension, wheels and axles, bearings* section.

**Products**
Elastomeric direct fixation fasteners. Manufactured in a variety of designs for new and existing transit systems, they are installed at grade, below grade and on elevated structures, and are fully tested and qualified by user transit authorities. The mid-range direct fixation fastener vertical spring rate ranges from 100,000 to 300,000 lb/sq in, the low-range (soft) direct fixation fastener from 60,000 to 90,000 lb/sq in, and the mid-range special trackwork fastener's vertical spring rate is comparable to that of the mid-range direct fixation fastener. Rail clamping systems are available for aerial and rigid installations.

---

## Lucchini Group

Lucchini SpA
Via Oberdan 1/a, I-25128 Brescia, Italy
Tel: (+39 030) 399 24 52  Fax: (+39 030) 39 17 82
e-mail: rails@lucchini.it
Web: http://www.lucchini.it

**Works**
Piombino Works (Lucchini SpA)
V le della Resistenza, 2 I-57025 Piombino (Livorno, Italy

**Key personnel**
See entry in *Bogies and suspension, wheels and axles, bearings* section.

**Subsidiary company**
Bari Fonderie Meridionali – BFM
Via Tommaso Columbo 7, I-70123 Bari, Italy
Tel: (+39 080) 582 71 11  Fax: (+39 080) 534 41 35
Managing Director: Pier Luigi Scetti
Sales Manager: Priamo Priami

**Products**
Piombino Works (Lucchini SpA): Rails from 27 to 70 kg/m in various steel grades. Maximum rail lengths: 108 m for unwelded rails, 144 m for welded.
Bari Fonderie Meridionali (BFM): Manganese cast steel monobloc crossings for switches; mechanical moulded cast steel components.

*UPDATED*

---

## LUKAS

LUKAS Hydraulic GmbH & Co Kg
Weinstrasse 39, D-91058, Erlangen, Germany
Tel: (+49 91) 31 69 80  Fax: (+49 91) 31 69 83 94

**Key personnel**
Sales Manager: Herr U Kirchner

**Products**
Development and manufacture of hydraulic rerailing equipment for rolling stock.
 LUKAS rerailing equipment allows for precise lifting and rerailing to within 1 mm. LUKAS also makes equipment for uprighting overturned rolling stock. It also makes a pulling device for pulling apart rolling stock, either from each other or from tunnel/bridge walls.
 LUKAS rescue tools and pneumatic lifting bags are in worldwide use.

*LUKAS compact rerailer* 0021664

---

## Lyudinovo Locomotive Works JSC

1 K Liebknecht Street, Lyudinovo, Kaluga region 249400, Russia
Tel: (+7 084) 442 01 20; 252 59
Fax: (+7 084) 442 01 20; 252 59

**Key personnel**
See entry in *Locomotives and powered/non-powered passenger vehicles* section.

**Products**
Rail lubricating machines, rotary snow ploughs track maintenance cars.

---

## Mannesmann

Mannesmann Dematic AG Gottwald
PO Box 18 03 43, D-40570 Düsseldorf, Germany
Tel: (+49 211) 710 20  Fax: (+49 211) 710 26 51
e-mail: Michael.Hoberg@dematic.de
 Achim.Baeuckert@dematic.de
Web: http://www.gottwald.com

**Key personnel**
Managing Director: D V Kelp
Sales Manager: M Hoberg

**Products**
Railway cranes for any track and loading gauge and with telescopic or fixed boom. Designed in accordance with maximum permissible axle and wheel loads, they offer SWL ratings up to 300 tonnes, minimum tail radii, hauling speeds up to 120 km/h, self-propelled speeds up to 100 km/h and a range of brake systems and buffers or couplers to suit; road/rail cranes.
 Recent contracts cover track maintenance cranes for private contractors in Japan, Germany and the USA as well as heavy breakdown cranes for India and South Korea.

---

## Manoir Industries

BP119, F-62230 Outreau, France
Tel: (+33 3) 21 99 53 00  Fax: (+33 3) 21 99 53 03

**Key personnel**
Plant Manager: Didier Dages
Sales Manager: Eric Chery
Railway Department: Michel Rommelaere

**Products**
Cast monobloc, manganese steel crossings to AREA and UIC specifications; welded crossings; cast cradles for movable point crossings; cast bodies and tongues for tram systems; track components for metro systems. Recent contracts include equipment supplied to MTRC's Lantau line in Hong Kong, to Balfour Beatty for the MRT Changi airport extension in Singapore and to Cogifer for the Milan-Rome high-speed line.

---

## Matériel de Voie SA

Le Parc du Saint Laurent, Immeuble Toronto,
54 route de Sartrouville, F-78230 Le Pecq, France
Tel: (+33 1) 30 15 24 24  Fax: (+33 1) 30 15 24 00

**Key personnel**
Communications Manager: D Fougeray

**Products**
Rails, fishplates, baseplates, steel sleepers.

---

## Matisa Matériel Industriel SA

Case Postale, CH-1023 Crissier-Lausanne, Switzerland
Tel: (+41 21) 631 21 11  Fax: (+41 21) 631 21 68
e-mail: matisa@matisa.ch

**Key personnel**
Managing Director: Rainer von Schack
Technical Director: Jörg Ganz
Marketing Director: Jörg Marbach

**Principal subsidiaries**
France
Matisa SA
Offices and workshop: 9 rue de l'Industrie, ZI Les Sablons, F-89100 Sens
Tel: (+33 3) 86 95 83 35  Fax: (+33 3) 86 95 36 94
e-mail: matisa.fr@wanadoo.fr
President: Michel Chevrery
Sales of Matisa group products in France, Benelux and French-speaking Africa. After-sales service, spare parts and overhaul of Matisa machines in France.

Germany
Matisa Maschinen GmbH
Kronenstrasse 2, D-78151 Donaueschingen
Tel: (+49 771) 15 80 63  Fax: (+49 771) 15 80 64
e-mail: matisa.donaueschingen@t-online.de
General Manager: F Wernick
Sales of Matisa group products in Germany, after-sales service and spare parts of Matisa machines operating in Germany.

Italy
Matisa SpA
Via Ardeatina km 21, I-00040 Pomezia/Santa Palomba (Rome)
Tel: (+39 06) 91 82 91  Fax: (+39 06) 91 98 45 74
e-mail: matisa.spa@interbusiness.it

## 736 MANUFACTURERS/Permanent way components, equipment and services

General Manager: Eng J Berga
Sales of Matisa group products and after-sales service, spare parts and overhaul of Matisa machines in Italy.

### Japan
Matisa Japan Co Ltd
Shiba Building, 5-16-7 Shiba, J-Minato-Ku, Tokyo 108
Tel: (+81 3) 34 54 75 61   Fax: (+81 3) 34 54 75 63
e-mail: matisajp@tkh.att.ne.jp
General Manager: U E Peter
Sales of Matisa group products and after-sales service, spare parts and overhaul of Matisa machines operating in Japan.

### Spain
Matisa Matériel Industriel SA Española
Sucursal Española
Avda de Brasil 17, Pisa 11F, E-28020, Madrid
Tel: (+34 91) 556 12 80   Fax: (+34 91) 556 68 79
e-mail: matisa@accessnet.es
Works: Estacion de Grinon, E-28970 Grinon Madrid
General Manager: Eng J Sanchez
Sales of Matisa group products in Spain; after-sales service, spare parts and overhaul of Matisa machines operating in Spain and Portugal.

### UK
Matisa (UK) Ltd
PO Box 202, Scunthorpe, DN15 8YH
Tel: (+44 1724) 28 14 85   Fax: (+44 1724) 38 76 61
e-mail: franz.messerli@virgin.net
General Manager: F Messerli
Sales of Matisa group products and after-sales service, spare parts and overhaul of Matisa machines operating in the UK.

### Products
Manufacture and sale of track construction and maintenance machinery, including tamper-leveller-liners (continuous, conventional, combined for points and crossings and plain track); regulators with and without hoppers; tracklaying and track renewal trains; ballast cleaners; track and catenary measuring, recording and analysis vehicles; track and catenary service vehicles.

**UPDATED**

---

## Max Bögl

Industriegebiet Schlierferheide/Bögl
PO Box 11 20, D-92301 Neumarkt, Germany
Tel: (+49 91 81) 90 90   Fax: (+49 91 81) 90 50 61

### Products
Slab track system.

---

## Mecanoexportimport SA

30 Dacia Blvd, Bucharest, Romania
Tel: (+40 1) 211 98 55   Fax: (+40 1) 210 78 94

### Key personnel
See entry in *Locomotives and powered/non-powered passenger vehicles* section.

### Products
Permanent way materials including screws, fishplates, baseplates, steel sleepers, turnouts, switches, points and crossings, guardrails and rail clips.

---

## Mer Mec SpA

Via Oberdan 70, I-70043 Monopoli (BA), Italy
Tel: (+39 080) 887 65 70   Fax: (+39 080) 887 40 28
e-mail: mermec@tin.it
Web: http://www.mermec.it

### Key personnel
Managing Director: Vito Pertosa
Quality Assurance Director: Mauro Simone
International Sales Manager: Carlo Evangelisti
International Sales Dept Diagnostic Systems Manager: Giovanni Pascoschi
Mechanic and Electric Design Manager: P Pirrelli
Research Manager: P Sforza

*Archimede high-speed diagnostic train supplied by Mer Mec to RFI, Italy*   2002/0142176

### Products
Measuring vehicles and diagnostic systems for the maintenance of railway infrastructure; recording cards, high-speed measuring systems, unmanned systems, systems for measurement of track geometry, rail profile and rail corrugation, rail surface defects, systems for measurement of overhead line geometry, contact wire wear and pantograph interaction, arcing measurement, measurement of electric parameters, ride quality measurement, systems for measurement of wheel-rail contact, wheel profile, wheel-rail interaction and vehicle accelerations, video inspection systems of track, overhead line and way side, positioning systems, telecommunication monitoring systems, signalling monitoring systems, analysis software.

Maintenance vehicles: railway vehicles for track and overhead line maintenance, trailers, railway cars equipped with cabins, lifting cranes, caissons, inspection platforms, catenary drums, lifting masts and auxiliary items, rail-road vehicles.

### Contracts
ARCHIMEDE high-speed diagnostic train for RFI (Italy), feasibility study for TGV application of MER MEC track geometry system for SNCF (France), overhead line system for MTR Corporation (Hong Kong), 15 track maintenance cars for RENFE (Spain), Roger 1000 K multi-diagnostic vehicles with integrated monitoring of the track and the overhead line infrastructure for KHRC (Korea), two Type MM 120 SRP road-rail loaders for OSE (Greece).

**UPDATED**

---

## metronom Gesellschaft für Industrievermessung mbH

Hauptstrasse 17-19, D-55120 Mainz, Germany
Tel: (+49 6131) 96 25 70   Fax: (+49 6131) 962 57 18
e-mail: info@metronom.de
Web: http://www.metronom.de

### US office
17672 Laurel Park Drive North, Suite 400, Livonia, Missouri 48152, USA
Tel: (+1 734) 384 59 91   Fax: (+1 734) 384 59 93
e-mail: infor@metronomna.com
Web: http://www.metronomna.com

### Products and services
Railway measuring technology, including: systems for measuring gauge, camber, contact wire height and tunnel profiles; systems for detecting and surveying loading gauge restrictions; systems for inspecting contact wires; video documentation and inspection systems; video measuring systems; stereoscopic measuring systems; testing and calibration software; mobile 3D measuring services. Also undertaken are: studies; training; technical consultancy; individual measuring and evaluation software; contract development of railway measuring systems; development and realisation of complete measuring trains.

Projects include development, integration and support for the measuring technology installed in a complete loading gauge restriction measuring vehicle (LIMEZ II).

---

## Metrum Information Storage Limited

Oxford Street, Long Eaton NG10 1JR, UK
Tel: (+44 115) 972 09 49 Fax: (+44 115) 946 19 53
e-mail: enquiries@metrum.co.uk
Web: http://www.metrum.co.uk

### Products
Measurement and monitoring equipment for the railway industry, covering all aspects of railway track parameter

*The MacKarT multipurpose maintenance vehicle*   2002/0114663

recording and analysis. With equipment ranging from lightweight portable single-operator trolleys to self-propelled measuring frames, Metrum provides a series of instruments that measure ride comfort and monitor vibration. The company also designs and produces a variety of inspection vehicles and trailers for transporting maintenance crews and equipment to site.

A recently developed product is the MacKarT, an easily transported multipurpose maintenance vehicle, which can be lifted on and off the track by four personnel in less than 10 minutes. The cart comprises a main chassis weighing approximately 110 kg, a battery pack comprising 12 70 Ah sealed lead acid traction batteries each weighing 25 kg, and a range of tops which can be specifically designed for a wide range of applications. Two standard tops are available: a nine-man carriage weighing 110 kg and a flat top with a single driving position weighing approximately 60 kg.

*NEW ENTRY*

---

## Mitchell Equipment Corporation

16 Ballantyne Road, Kewdale, Western Australia 6105, Australia
Tel: (+61 8) 93 50 63 63   Fax: (+61 8) 94 51 45 16

**Key personnel**
Managing Director: A G Evans
Marketing Manager: G R Birkbeck
Sales Engineer: P A N Hayes

**Principal subsidiary**
Mitchell Equipment Corporation, Toledo, Ohio, USA

**Products**
All road/rail vehicular conversion equipment; insulated fishplate joints, switchblade slide pads; specialised track insulation.

---

## Mitsukawa Metal Works Co Ltd

21 Harima-cho-nijima, Kako district, Hyogo Pref, Japan
Tel: (+81 794) 35 22 88   Fax: (+81 3) 32 84 03 61

**Key personnel**
Sales Director: K Kukuda

**Products**
Rail fastenings, steel sleepers and forged crossings.

---

## Modern Track Machinery Canada Ltd

5926 Shawson Drive, Mississauga, Ontario L4W 3W5, Canada
Tel: (+1 905) 546 12 11   Fax: (+1 905) 564 12 17
e-mail: mtmcanada@attcanada.net

**Key personnel**
President: Claude Geismar
International and General Sales Manager: M J Byrne

**Corporate development**
MTM Canada is a subsidiary of Geismar Corporation of Paris, France.

**Principal subsidiary**
Modern Track Machinery Inc
1415 Davis Road, Elgin, Illinois 60123-1375, USA
Tel: (+1 847) 697 75 10   Fax: (+1 847) 697 01 36
General Manager: John W Fox

**Products**
Railway maintenance equipment (hydraulics, gas, high frequency including saws, drills, grinders, impact wrenches, spike drivers, pullers, tie inserters).

Recent contracts include: CIDA, Mozambique (completed in March 2000); Ferrosur, Mexico (completed in February 2000).

## Monterrey

Monterrey Industrial Ferroviaria SA de CV
Avenue Insurgentes Sur 2462, CO 01070 Villa Alvaro Obregón, Mexico, DF
Tel: (+52 5) 550 46 05; 83 77; 616 23 82
Fax: (+52 5) 550 69 15
e-mail: meraco@internet.com.mx

**Main works**
Dia del Empresario 999, PO Box 1012, CP 67110, CD Guadalupe, NL, Mexico
Phone: (+52 83) 64 97 66   Fax: (+52 83) 64 97 17
e-mail: ferro@infosel.net.mx

**Key personnel**
President: Felipe Zirion Quijano
Sales Manager: Rafael Carballo Maradiaga
Plant Manager: Adolfo Pérez Murillo

**Principal subsidiaries**
Cia Mexicana de Material para Ferrocarril, SA de CV
Miner y Mendez de Mexico, SA de CV

**Products**
Turnout sets for all rail sections, solid manganese or assembled frogs, switch points, guardrails, plates, heel plates and switch stands (to AREA and European standards).

---

## Moog GmbH

Brückenuntersichtsgeräte + Hocharbeitsbühnen D-88693 Deggenhausertalm Im Gewerbegebeit 8, Germany
Tel: (+49 75) 55 93 30   Fax: (+49 75) 559 33 66
French Office:
Pont Acces, 2 rue de Condant, F-67480 Forstfield (Strasbourg)

**Products**
Bridge inspection equipment for road and railway bridges. The design was originally for electric trains and allows lowering and folding up of the platform without shutting off the electric current in overhead wires. The tower system can be extend above the bridge railing with a telescopic arm.

MOOG 1200 T and 1500 T bridge lifts can be mounted on a vehicle or self-propelled railcar, has two points of rotation for all round mobility, horizontal reach of 12 to 15 m, the bucket arm has a rotation of 2 × 180° with a working area for several people. Also available are dual track version, railway vehicle unit, pier inspection unit.

---

## Moore & Steele

Moore & Steele Corporation
PO Box 189, Oswego, New York 13827, USA
Tel: (+1 607) 687 27 51   Fax: (+1 607) 687 39 14

**Key personnel**
President: S M Lounsberry III

## Products
Rail lubrication systems including hydraulic and electronic wayside lubricators, mobile lubricators mounted on road/rail vehicles and bulk lubricant dispensing systems.

---

## Mossboda Trä AB

SE-718 92 Frövi, Sweden
Tel: (+46 581) 720 30   Fax: (+46 581) 720 36

**Products**
Pressure-treated and unimpregnated pine sleepers. Customers include Banverket and railway construction companies.

---

## MTH Praha AS

Kamdertova 1a/1131, CZ-180 00 Praha 8, Libeň, Czech Republic
Tel: (+420 2) 84 09 32 02   Fax: (+420 2) 84 09 32 81
e-mail: mth@mth.cz
Web: http://www.mth.cz

**Key personnel**
President: Martin Pinl
General Director: Petr Wagenknecht
Director, Sales: Pavel Türk

**Indian joint venture company**
MTH India PVT Ltd
Technip House, D-10/3, Okhla Industrial Area, Phase-1, New Delhi, 110020, India
Tel: (+91 11) 681 17 12; 681 60 49
Fax: (+91 11) 681 63 24
e-mail: arun@technipimpex.com

**Key personnel**
Managing Director: Suresh Kumar Mandal
Marketing Director: Arun Kumar Mandal

**Products**
Manufacture of permanent way maintenance machines and equipment including ballast cleaners, ballast wagons and ballast distribution systems; track stabilisers; catenary maintenance vehicles; ballast compactors; brush cutters; track recording cars; motor cars and power units; hand tools.

**Contracts**
Contracts include the supply of maintenance equipment to Austria, India, Russia, Slovakia and USA.

*UPDATED*

---

## Muromteplovoz

Murom Diesel Locomotive Works
ulica Filatova 10 602 200 Murom, Vladimir region, Russian Federation

*Muromteplovoz Type AGS-1 self-propelled multipurpose infrastructure maintenance vehicle*

# MANUFACTURERS/Permanent way components, equipment and services

*Muromteplovoz Type RN-04 rail-end clearance maker* 2001/0103969

Tel: (+7 095) 291 31 68  Fax: (+7 09234) 443 03
e-mail: mteplo@cl.murom.ru
Web: http://www.cl.murom.ru

### Key personnel
See entry in *Locomotives and powered/non-powered passenger vehicles* section.

### Products
Self-propelled track maintenance vehicles; ballast cleaners; hydraulic jacks; rail straighteners; clearance makers.

## NedTrain Consulting BV

PO Box 2025, NL-3500 Utrecht, Netherlands
Tel: (+31 30) 235 77 72; 47 11  Fax: (+31 30) 235 55 04

### Key personnel
Director: J Kitzen

### Corporate development
NS Materieel Engineering changed its name to NedTrain Consulting in 1999.

### Products
NedTrain Consulting BV is a company employing some 3,500 people working in the field of engineering, maintenance, service, overhaul and refurbishment of rolling stock.

Traditional customers are NS Reizigers and NS Cargo but a growing amount of turnover is now devoted to municipal transport companies and other railway companies.

Contracts include an ultra-sonic testing car, able to record at 140 km/h under own power and at 200 km/h when towed by another vehicle. The measuring system was designed by NS Materieel and based on a grill-express car from SNCF.

**UPDATED**

## Newag GmbH & Co KG

Ripshorster Strasse 321, D-46117 Oberhausen, Germany
Tel: (+49 208) 86 50 30  Fax: (+49 208) 865 03 20

### Key personnel
See entry in *Locomotives and powered/non-powered passenger vehicles* section.

### Products
Track motor cars; personnel and platform trolleys; multipurpose and custom-built cars and trolleys; special purpose trains such as ballast and dirt handling trains for ballast cleaners and wagon-mounted mobile concrete plants for foundation work on bridges, tunnels, and for electrification; hi-rail road/rail vehicles and cranes; remanufacture of tampers, levellers and liners for all gauges; ballast regulators and cleaners; gantries; rail positioners; rail lifters and threaders.

### Developments
Newag is offering the Jumbo 2000, a heavy-duty high-speed road/rail vehicle. It is able to travel at up to 100 km/h as a result of a new suspension system. Two disc brakes per wheelset ensure short stopping distances at high speeds and with large loads. Axleloads of up to 11 tonnes per wheelset allow for a gross vehicle weight of up to 44 tonnes.

**VERIFIED**

*Overhead catenary construction vehicle, based on the Newag Jumbo 2000 high-speed road/railer*  0022579

## Newt International

1 Orion Court, Rodney Road, Portsmouth PO4 8SZ, UK
Tel: (+44 23) 92 73 00 60  Fax: (+44 23) 92 73 00 70
e-mail: sales@lizard.co.uk
Web: http://www.lizard.co.uk

### Products
Rail flaw detection system employing the Lizard® field gradient camera.

Developed as an alternative to ultrasonic testing, the capabilities of the field gradient camera are claimed to include detection of poor surface fusion in welds; high-level accuracy and repeatability; no limitations imposed by any surface geometry or crack size; crack depth and length/indication of high-speed inspection; suitable for use on non-conductive coatings; surface cleaning not required; arrays are able to 'see' through coatings in excess of 8 mm; arrays available in both manual and electronically scanned versions; the 2-D planar array with asymmetric excitation can be configured to inspect almost any 3-D shape; no couplant required; direct contact with the rail is not essential; use of multimode software; database of records; improved asset management planning, for example condition monitoring; detection of defects on new rail; monitoring of growth of existing defects; detection and monitoring of profile changes; detection of changes in the condition of the surface.

**VERIFIED**

## Nippon Kido Kogyo

Meiho Building 21-1 Nishi Shinjuku 1-chome, Shinjuku-ku, Tokyo 160, Japan
Tel: (+81 3) 33 43 83 22  Fax: (+81 3) 33 49 87 05

### Works
Tone Factory, PO 306, 77 Nakatashinden, Koga, Ibaraki, Japan
Tel: (+81 280) 480 73 35  Fax: (+81 280) 48 31 84

### Key personnel
Managing Director: A Nakano

### Products
Precast concrete slab for level crossings, concrete sleepers, rail fastenings.

## NKK

NKK Corporation
1-1-2 Marunouchi, Chiyoda-ku, Tokyo 100, Japan
Tel: (+81 3) 32 17 22 44  Fax: (+81 3) 32 14 84 17

### Key personnel
President: Shunkichi Miyoshi
Export Director: Kiyoshi Kishi

### Products
Rail to meet all internationally recognised specifications including AREA, ASTM, UIC, BS, JIS and others.

NKK produces two types of premium rail, the Thicker Head-Hardened 370N (THH370N) and Thicker Head-Hardened 370A (THH370A) with low alloy, by an online typed heat treatment process. The top surfaces of these rails feature Brinell hardness ($H_B$) values of 341 to 388, and $H_B$ 351 to 405, respectively. The steel is produced by a continuous casting machine including a vacuum degassing process. THH370N and THH370A rails have been supplied to Canada, the USA and other countries. For domestic users, NKK produces 50 m long standard carbon rails.

NKK also has extensive experience in providing rail welding technology, both for hardware and software, and welding services. The enclosed arc welding repair of high-speed Shinkansen track is performed chiefly by NKK. The company has developed an automatic rail welding machine, the Rail Welding Robot, for field welding of rail. This machine has been developed by applying the high-speed rotating arc welding method to enclosed arc welding.

## Nordco

182 W Oklahoma Avenue, Milwaukee, Wisconsin 53207, USA
Tel: (+1 414) 769 46 00  Fax: (+1 414) 769 46 04
e-mail: sales@nordco.com

### Key personnel
President: Don Himes
Marketing Manager: Steve Wiedenfeld

### Products
Self-propelled adzers, rail drills, spike hammers, hydraulic spike pullers, tie drills, gauging machines, hydra-spikers, rail lifters, rail gang spikers, X-level indicators, track inspectors, two-tie screw spikers, anchor removers, anchor applicators. Tie remover/inserter and plate positioner, tie plugger, G2 ballast regulator, brush cutters.

Model NETP-I tie plugging machine is a high-production two-person machine able to fill spike holes while operating in rail or regauging gangs. It has a 400 gallon capacity of non-foam polyurethane compound, known as SpikeFast.

Trailblazer Model BC60 Brushcutter has a 30 ft reach from the track centre on each side, hydrostatic drive, four-speed manual transmission and a speed of 35 mph.

Tie Remover Inserter Plate Positioner (TRIPP) can remove and insert ties from either side of the main frame. The machine will mechanically position tie plates in the

*Nordco G2 ballast regulator*  2000/0093218

**PFLEIDERER**
AKTIENGESELLSCHAFT

# Your objective is our challenge.

**Pfleiderer** track systems

the way to go

**Engineering, Production, Supply, Logistics, Quality Management.**

We provide innovative rail infrastructure for railways and urban traffic, in Germany and worldwide. Our systems enable high load-bearing capacities through decades of no-maintenance operation: with stable track positioning and a maximum of riding comfort. Since your way is our goal, we attach great importance to a close collaboration with you as customers, planners, and business partners.
Take advantage of our extensive railway business experience. We would be pleased to offer you customized solutions.

Pfleiderer track systems · Ingolstaedter Strasse 51 · 92318 Neumarkt · Tel +49 9181 28-136/-648
Fax +49 9181 28-646 · Mail tracksystems@pfleiderer.com · www.pfleiderer-track.com

gauge section of the rail on the first, second or third tie behind the tie being removed and the gripper is adjustable to eliminate damage to new ties being installed.

G2 ballast regulator has a rear-mounted engine, uses a hydraulically positioned ballast plough and can travel at 35 mph using a four-wheel hydrostatic shaft drive system.

*UPDATED*

## Norwest Holst

Norwest Holst Construction Ltd
Astral House, Imperial Way, Watford WD2 4YX, UK
Tel: (+44 1923) 23 34 33   Fax: (+44 1923) 25 64 81

**Key personnel**
Managing Director: D A L Joyce

**Subsidiary companies**
McGregor Paving
87 New Square, Chesterfield S40 1AH, UK
Tel: (+44 1246) 27 69 71   Fax: (+44 1246) 20 76 80
Norwest Holst Rail
address as Norwest-Holst Construction
Tel: (+44 1923) 47 02 32   Fax: (+44 1923) 47 03 34

**Products**
In collaboration with British Rail's Research Division, Robert McGregor developed PACT – the Paved Concrete Track system. PACT is an alternative to conventional ballasted track.

The system, produced by Norwest Holst subsidiary McGregor Paving, consists of a continuously reinforced concrete slab which provides a continuous support to the rails through a resilient rail pad. Main advantages of the system are its shallow depth of construction and it ensures that the track geometry remains within tolerance over long periods. The PACT system has been in service for over 25 years throughout the world.

Contracts involved installation of PACT through the 14 km Rogers Pass Tunnel, the longest rail tunnel in North America; and in Sandling Tunnel, Kent, as part of Channel Tunnel route clearance work for Railtrack.

Norwest Holst Rail, in collaboration with a number of specialist designers and contractors, is providing multi-disciplinary design, procurement, management and construction services for the railway industry. Projects include the provision of new infrastructure works and refurbishment and enhancement of existing infrastructure, structures and property.

Recent contracts involved bridge replacement, station refurbishment, construction of new stations, depot refurbishment, embankment and cutting stabilisation.

## National Railway Supplies (NRS)

Gresty Road, Crewe CW2 6EH, UK
Tel: (+44 1270) 53 30 00   Fax: (+44 1270) 53 39 56
e-mail: enquiries@natrail.com
Web: http://www.natrail.co.uk

**Other offices**
Room 206, Engineering Depot, New England Road, Brighton BN1 3TU
Tel: (+44 1273) 32 62 10   Fax: (+44 1273) 22 81 44
Leeman Road, York Y026 4ZD, UK
Tel: (+44 1904) 52 22 93   Fax: (+44 1904) 52 26 96

**Key personnel**
See entry in *Signalling and communications systems* section.

**Background**
NRS is a wholly owned subsidiary of the Unipart Group of companies.

**Products**
Supply Chain Management Service to the rail industry. Current contracts include AMEC Rail, Balfour Beatty Rail Maintenance, Jarvis Rail, May Gurney, Serco Rail Maintenance and Westinghouse Rail Systems. Manufacture, production, servicing, repair and distribution of electronic, electromechanical and engineering products for railway infrastructure, including permanent way, overhead line and third rail equipment.

*UPDATED*

## ØDS-Caltronic AS

Kroghsgade 1, DK-2100 Copenhagen Ø, Denmark
Tel: (+45) 35 26 60 11   Fax: (+45) 35 26 50 18
Web: http://www.odegaard.dk
e-mail: ods@oedan.dk

**Key personnel**
Managing Director: John Ødegaard
Director: Ulrik Danneskiold-Samsøe
Business Manager: Ove Ramkow-Pedersen

**Product**
Wheel monitoring systems for online detection of train wheel defects such as flats. The system is modular and can be combined with proprietary AVI wagon identification equipment.

## Oleo International Ltd

PO Box 216, Grovelands Estate, Longford Road, Exhall, Coventry CV7 9NE, UK
Tel: (+44 2476) 64 55 55   Fax: (+44 2476) 36 42 87

**Key personnel**
See entry in *Freight vehicles and equipment* section

**Products**
Oleo produces a wide range of long-stroke hydraulic buffers suitable for mounting on fixed or sliding end-stops. Applications include freight yards, steelworks and passenger terminals.

On sliding friction end-stops the need for continual resetting of the friction elements is eliminated, and the hydraulic buffers absorb all of the impact energy at low speeds. Typically a 400 tonne train may be arrested by a pair of 800 mm stroke buffers at 6 km/h without causing the end-stop to slide. Initial and final jerk forces are also eliminated. These buffer units are available for all types of rail operation from LRVs to heavy freight.

*UPDATED*

## OLMI SpA

Viale Europa 29, I-24040 Suisio (Bg), Italy
Tel: (+39 035) 99 91 11   Fax: (+39 035) 99 92 61
e-mail: sleepers@olmi.it

**Key personnel**
Managing Director: Andrea Montagni
Project Manager: Walter Cavadini
Assistant Managing Director: Alessandra Teli

**Products**
Design, construction, installation and after-sales service of concrete sleeper manufacturing plants for both plain track and turnouts.

**Contracts**
Recent contracts include supply of 16 plants for sleepers manufactured in Italy, Spain, Poland, Belgium, Slovenia, China, Germany and Russia. Six production plants for turnout sleepers manufactured in Poland, Czech Republic and Italy.

*UPDATED*

## ORTEC

ORTEC Gesellschaft für Schienentechnische Systeme mbH
Eigelstein 10-12, D-50668 Köln, Germany
Tel: (+49 221) 120 69 60   Fax: (+49 221) 12 06 96 66
e-mail: ORTEC-GmbH@t-online.de
Web: http://www.ORTEC-GmbH.de

**Key personnel**
Managing Director: Hermann Ortwein

**Products**
Vibration-insulating rail fasteners, Whisper Rail continuous elastic rail embedment material, noise insulation material, ISOLast insulating embedment material, Loadmaster for reduction of ground and structure-borne vibrations.

Contracts include reconstruction of 8 km of tramway in Budapest with ISOLast; 26 km of Whisper Rail for the Wuppertal monorail; 1 km of Whisper Rail for Brunswick.

*UPDATED*

## Orton/McCullough

Orton/McCullough Crane Company
1244 East Market Street, PO Box 830, Huntington, Indiana 46750, USA
Tel: (+1 260) 356 79 00   Fax: (+1 260) 356 79 02

**Key personnel**
Chairman: J F McCullough

**Products**
Cranes and heavy lifting gear.

*UPDATED*

## Osmose Railroad Division

PO Box 8276, Madison, Wisconsin 53708, USA
Tel: (+1 608) 221 22 92   Fax: (+1 608) 221 06 18

**Key personnel**
Vice-President: Harry Holekamp
Products Manager: David Ostby

**Products**
TIE-GARD® preservative gel to prevent decay of sleeper plate areas.

**Services**
The engineered repair of concrete, steel and timber railroad bridges.

*UPDATED*

## Palfinger

Palfinger Hebetechnik
Moosmühlstrasse 1, A-5203 Köstendorf/Salzburg, Austria
Tel: (+43 6216) 766 54 05   Fax: (+43 6216) 77 63
e-mail: h.gollegger@palfinger.com

**Key personnel**
Sales and Marketing Manager, Railway Cranes: Heinrich Gollegegger

*Palfinger railway aerial platform*

Permanent way components, equipment and services/**MANUFACTURERS**

## Products

Cranes (1 to 75 tonne/m lifting moment), aerial access platforms for catenary inspection construction and maintenance.

*UPDATED*

## Pandrol Rail Fastenings

63 Station Road, Addlestone, Weybridge KT15 2AR, UK
Tel: (+44 1932) 83 45 00   Fax: (+44 1932) 85 08 58
e-mail: info@pandrol.com
Web: http://www.pandrol.com

### Key personnel
Managing Director: G M Lodge
Chief Operating Officer: J Beal-Preston

### Principal subsidiaries
Pandrol Australia Pty Ltd, Blacktown, Australia
Pandrol Avaux SA, Anderlues, Belgium
Pandrol Canada Ltd, Montréal, Canada
Promorail SA, Paris, France
PT Pandrol Indonesia, Jakarta, Indonesia
Pandrol Italia SpA, Teramo, Italy
Pandrol Daewon Ltd, Seoul, Republic of Korea
Pandrol UK Ltd, Worksop, UK
Pandrol USA LP, Bridgeport, New Jersey, USA
Vortok International Ltd, Addlestone, UK

### Products
Design and manufacture of rail fastening systems and associated installation equipment; resilient rail pads; resiliently supported direct fixation (DF) systems; Vortok Coils for restoring worn screwspike holes (see entry for Vortok International).

Pandrol continues its research into the dynamic behaviour of track to increase understanding of the relationship between forces in track and component performance, and of the generation of noise and vibration. Pandrol has developed a new range of fastening designs for specific applications, including the Pandrol Fastclip® system, which is designed for low-cost installation and maintenance, and the new track support systems designed for application in areas which are sensitive to noise and vibration, including Pandrol VIPA-SP, the latest product in the Pandrol VIPA range incorporating Fastclip® and Pandrol Vanguard, a revolutionary new concept.

*VERIFIED*

*Pandrol VIPA-SP assembly*   2000/0089430

## Partner Dimas UK

Oldends Lane Industrial Estate, Stonedale Road, Stonehouse GL10 3SY, UK
Tel: (+44 1453) 82 03 05; 82 03 06
Fax: (+44 1453) 97 15 77
Web: http://www.partner.industrial.com

### Key personnel
Product Manager: Peter Waldron
Marketing Manager: Shirley Simmons

### Corporate background
Partner Dimas UK is a member of the Electrolux Group.

### Products
Handheld power tools for rail maintenance and installation. The product range includes two petrol powered and one hydraulically powered railsaw with cutting arm attachments as a complete unit for the accurate cutting of rail track sections. The two petrol machines are powered by the Partner K1250-120 cc power cutter, the RA125014 uses a 350 mm blade and the RA125016 uses a 400 mm blade. Both machines can cut through a rail section in one pass and both have a reversible cutting arm to enable the machine to be used either side of the rail. The hydraulically powered RA16A has a 4 kW motor powering a 400 mm blade.

*UPDATED*

## Peddinghaus Group

Carl Dan Peddinghaus GmbH & Co KG
Mittelstrasse 64, D-58256 Ennepetal, Germany
Tel: (+49 2333) 79 60   Fax: (+49 2333) 79 63 88
e-mail: cdp-en@t-online.de
Web: http://www.peddinghaus-group.de

### Products
A supplier of high quality steel and aluminium forgings and components including maintenance-free roller slide plates; lubrication-free clamp lock devices; lubrication-free point locks; valve rods; checkrail plates and fishplates.

## Permali Gloucester Limited

Bristol Road, Gloucester GL1 5TT, UK
Tel: (+44 1452) 52 82 82   Fax: (+44 1452) 50 74 09
Web: http://www.permali.co.uk
e-mail: sales@permali.co.uk

### Key personnel
Managing Director: R B D Cole
Technical Director: M W Mallorie
Sales and Marketing Manager: D E Cahill

### Products
Permaglass MER components include shoebeams and arc boxes/barriers for a range of electrically powered units.

Permaglass COMP E2 is another material developed for use as an insulating rail joint.

*UPDATED*

## Pettibone

Pettibone Corporation
Railroad Products Group
5401 W Grand Avenue, Chicago, Illinois 60639, USA
Tel: (+1 312) 745 94 96   Fax: (+1 312) 237 37 63

### Main works
Pettibone Ohio, 6917 Bessemer Avenue, Cleveland, Ohio 44127, USA

### Key personnel
President: Larry Klumpp
General Manager: T E Hitesman

### Products
Switches, switch-points, frogs, crossings, switch stands, guardrails, rail fasteners, compromise joints, switch plates, mobile maintenance-of-way and material handling equipment.

## Pfleiderer track systems

Ingolstaedter Strasse 51, D-92318 Neumarkt, Germany
Tel: (+49 9181) 281 36   Fax: (+49 9181) 286 46
e-mail: tracksystems@pfleiderer.com
Web: http://www.pfleiderer-track.com

### Products
Pfleiderer track systems is a provider of innovative products for railway and urban traffic worldwide. It has eleven production plants at seven locations and produces concrete sleepers (prestressed and slack-reinforced), and ballasted and non-ballasted rail tracks.

For railways, Pfleiderer track systems provides standard and specialised concrete sleepers, including wide sleepers, elastically-footed sleepers and ballastless track systems such as the RHEDA 2000® and GETRAC®. For urban traffic, the product range includes, in addition to concrete sleepers, non-ballasted track systems such as RHEDA MRT, RHEDA CITY and ATD-G (the 'Green Track').

*UPDATED*

## Phoenix AG

PO Box 900854, D-21048 Hamburg, Germany
Tel: (+49 40) 76 67 26 73   Fax: (+49 40) 76 67 23 55
Web: http://www.phoenix-ag.com

### Key personnel
See entry in *Bogies and suspension, wheels and axles, bearings* section.

### Products
Elastomer trackbed matting: CentriCon and Megiflex rail fasteners; rubber groove-sealing sections for safety of rails in workshops and other pedestrian areas; rubber boots with pads; continuous rail seating; and noise-absorbing material.

## Pintsch Bamag Antriebs – und Verkehrstechik GmbH

PO Box 100420, D-46524 Dinslaken, Germany
Tel: (+49 2064) 60 20   Fax: (+49 2064) 60 22 66
e-mail: info@pintschbamag.de
Web: http://www.pintschbamag.de

### Key personnel
See entry in *Signalling and communications* section.

### Corporate background
Pintsch Bamag is a member of the Schaltbau Group (qv).

### Products
Automatic propane-fuelled infra-red and electric point-heating equipment; solid-state snow detectors.

*UPDATED*

## Plasser & Theurer

Johannesgasse 3, A-1010 Vienna, Austria
Tel: (+43 1) 51 57 20   Fax: (+43 1) 513 18 01

### Main works
Pummererstrasse 5, A-4021 Linz/Donau

### Principal subsidiaries
Australia, Brazil, Canada, Denmark, France, Germany, Hong Kong, India, Italy, Japan, Mexico, Poland, Spain, South Africa, UK and USA.

### Products
Automatic track levelling, lining and tamping machines; universal point (switch) and crossing tamping machines; dynamic track stabilisers; ballast consolidating machines; ballast regulators; ballast cleaning machines; ballast suction machines; formation rehabilitation machines; track laying and relaying machines; gantry cranes; rail grinding and planing machines; track recording cars; railway motor vehicles; catenary maintenance and inspection cars; catenary renewal trains; railway cranes;

## MANUFACTURERS/Permanent way components, equipment and services

*Plasser MDZ 2000 mechanised maintenance train*

special machines and lightweight equipment for track maintenance.

The Plasser & Theurer 08 and 09 Series of tamping machines offers a range of equipment to meet the most varied conditions and requirements.

The 09-32 CSM moves forward in a continuous motion while only 20 per cent of the total mass is accelerated and braked because only the lifting, lining and tamping units (32 tamping tines together), positioned on a separate underframe, are moved in work cycles from sleeper to sleeper. The main frame of the machine, with cabins, power supply and drive for the entire machine, moves forward continuously.

The 09-3X Tamping Express is the result of experience in operation and is based on the 09-CSM Series. New features of the 09-3X are two three-sleeper track tamping units which enable, for the first time, three sleepers to be tamped in one operation. Each tamping unit consists of two separate parts to be able to work on tracks with irregular sleeper spacing, if required.

The 09-90 and 09-Super CAT machines are tamping machines with an integrated ploughing and sweeping device. They can produce exact track geometry in just one work cycle.

The 09-Dynamic is a continuous-action tamping machine with integrated ploughing, sweeping and dynamic track stabilising unit.

The UNIMAT 08-275 is a levelling, lining and tamping machine for plain track, switches and crossings. It is equipped with two heavy-duty, universal tamping units, carrying eight tines each. When tamping plain track, all eight tines of the tamping unit are in action in their basic position. The ballast beneath each rail/sleeper intersection is tamped in one work cycle, that is, the sleeper is tamped both inside and outside the rail simultaneously. The pairs of tines can be tilted up sideways and adapted to the particular configuration of the point or crossing.

A further development is the UNIMAT 08-275 3S, equipped with three-point lifting device for maintenance of heavy design points (for example, with concrete sleepers). The pivoting design of the tamping units permits easy adaptation to slanting sleepers.

The latest development is the ability of the outer tamping units of the UNIMAT 08-475 4S to swing out 3.2 m from the centre of the machine. This means that the departing line at points can be treated simultaneously ('four rail tamping').

The UNIMAT 09-4S machines combine the advantages of a continuous action plain line tamping machine with the features of the latest generation of a switch tamping machine with three-rail lifting and four-rail tamping.

The Unimat Sprinter is a machine for the elimination of spot faults. For this special task, new software was developed for the ALC automatic guidance computer.

Plasser & Theurer states that the range of ballast distributing and grading machines in the PSR, SSP and USP series covers every type of operation.

The BDS Ballast Distribution and Storage system consists of two units, a ploughing and ballast dosage unit and a sweeping and ballast transfer unit. MFS hopper and conveyor units can be coupled between them to increase storage capacity. The BDS can insert ballast precisely on plain track and in points and crossings and collects surplus ballast for added economy.

The DGS 62 N (Dynamic Track Stabiliser) produces stabilisation of the track following tamping work, ballast cleaning or laying track. Using controlled stabilisation it is possible to achieve the correct settlement of the track without altering the track geometry. In this way speed restrictions are eliminated. If required, the DGS can also be fitted with a two-axle measuring trailer. In combination with a multichannel recorder, various parameters can be recorded.

The newly developed AFM 2000 automatic track finishing machine performs the work of a ballast profiling, track stabilising and track acceptance machine. In addition to the maintenance work it performs, the machine documents the quality of work achieved to an extent not previously known (acceptance threshold values, ballast profile, correct consolidation).

The RM series offers various sizes of undercutter cleaners for plain track and points.

The VM 150 Jumbo vacuum scraper/excavator provides an alternative to conventional equipment for removing material such as ballast, soil and dust, particularly where obstacles may be present. Material picked up by the rotating suction nozzle passes through a material separator and a filter chamber, and then on to a transfer conveyor belt.

The EM series offers different sizes of track measuring and recording cars for the most varied working conditions with measuring speeds up to 250 km/h. For measuring speeds over 120 km/h Plasser & Theurer has developed and built vehicles which are equipped with non-contact measuring systems. Various evaluation programs are available. A laser-based non-contact catenary measuring system can also be provided for track measuring cars.

With the APT 500, flash-butt welding, previously restricted to stationary practice, has been mobilised and can now be carried out on track. Microprocessor control guarantees consistent welding quality, even for high-alloy rails. Plasser & Theurer welding machines have been built in a variety of designs (mobile, self-propelled, on-track welding machines, on-/off-track welding machines, stationary and pallet-mounted units). With the 'Super Stretch' accessory final welds below neutral rail temperature can be performed using a high-capacity rail pulling and tensioning device.

The SBM 250 rail rectification (planing) machine reprofiles side and head-worn rails *in situ*. The GWM 250 is a bogie-mounted rail grinding machine with two grinding units per rail and six grinding stones per unit; the GWM 550 is a six-axle machine with five grinding units. Both machines can work on plain track, points and crossings.

The PM 200 formation rehabilitation machine excavates old ballast by excavation chain and transports it to the area ahead of the machine via conveyor belts; inserts sand via conveyor belts; grades the surface of the sand with grading plate; consolidates the sand layer with plate consolidators; and inserts fresh ballast via conveyor belts and chutes. The AHM 800 R is a formation rehabilitation machine with ballast recycling.

The latest highlight is the RPM 2002 – 140.9 m long, weighing 590 tons and with a total engine output of 2,467 kW; Plasser & Theurer says it is the largest formation rehabilitation machine in the world.

Plasser & Theurer applied the assembly line principle to track relaying in 1968 with the development of the SUZ 2000 track relaying train. The SUM-SMD and SVM and HUZ Series (high-speed tracklaying and relaying machines of modular design) are the present day models, which can be adapted for any conditions. The WM system is designed for relaying points and crossings without auxiliary tools, while the WTW system can transport them directly from place of manufacture to the worksite without the need to dismantle them.

In recent years, a number of machines were built for the maintenance, inspection and renewal of catenary. These vehicles in the MSW, MTW and FUM series were specifically designed and equipped to the customer's needs. Continuous operation catenary renewal trains were built for high output.

To meet the demands of customers, a wide range of special machines (for example sand removal machines) for track maintenance and track work is available, including all kinds of motor vehicles and single or twin-jib heavy railway cranes as well as lightweight track maintenance equipment.

*Plasser FUM catenary renewal train*

## Pohl Corporation

PO Box 13613, Reading, Pennsylvania 19612, USA
Tel: (+1 610) 926 54 00   Fax: (+1 610) 926 18 97

**Key personnel**
President: Walter Pohl

**Products**
Rail from 12 lb ASCE to 175 Crane Rail and related accessories; special trackwork and switch components; spikes; steel sleepers (ties) for narrow-gauge track for the mining industry; New Century® switch stands and replacement parts.

## Portec

Portec Rail Products Inc
PO Box 38250, 900 Freeport Road, Pittsburgh, Pennsylvania 15238-8250, USA
Tel: (+1 412) 782 60 00   Fax: (+1 412) 781 10 37
Web: http://www.PortecRail.com

**Key personnel**
President and Chief Executive Officer:
   John S Cooper
Chief Financial Officer: Michael Bornak

**Subsidiaries**
Railway Maintenance Products Division
(address, tel, fax and website as above)

**Canada**
Portec Rail Products Ltd
2044 32nd Avenue, Lachine, Quebec H8T 3H7
Tel: (+1 514) 636 55 90   Fax: (+1 514) 636 57 47
President and General Manager: Richard J Jarosinski
Manager, International Sales: Barbara Petkus

**UK**
Portec Rail Products (UK) Ltd
Vauxhall Industrial Estate, Ruabon, Wrexham LL16 6UY
Tel: (+44 1978) 82 08 20   Fax: (+44 1978) 82 14 39
e-mail: portec@portec.co.uk
Web: http://www.portecrail.com
Managing Director: Graham Tarbuck
Financial Director: Malcolm Lawley
Divisional Director, Rail Projects: Christopher Twigg

**Products and services**
Standard and insulated rail joints, rail and flange lubrication systems; rail friction measuring systems; lubrication consulting and contracting services; geocomposite track materials for environmental protection from rail curve greases; locomotive refuelling point mats; track components including rail anchors, gauge plate insulators, switch rod insulators, rail separation temporary repair devices, switchglides, switch point protectors and rail rollover protection devices.
   In partnership with Environmental Lubricants Manufacturing, Inc (ELM), Portec Rail also supplies Soy Trak™, a new soybean-based high-performance rail curve lubricant, claimed to be safe for the environment.
   Recent contracts include: supply of switchglide to Netherlands Rail; supply of lubricators to Irish Rail and Bulgarian Railways.

*UPDATED*

## Pouget

PO Box 69, 6 allée du Val du Moulin, F-93240 Stains, France
Tel: (+33 1) 48 26 62 12   Fax: (+33 1) 48 22 37 15
e-mail: pouget-rail@wanadoo.fr
Web: http://www.asiaffairs.com—pouget

**Key personnel**
General Manager: Robert Pouget

**Products**
Tracklaying gantry cranes, coach-screwing machines, fishplate-bolting machines, sleeper drills, rail saws, disc rail-cutting machines, rail drills, portable vibrating tampers, rail grinders, rail loaders, sleeper adzing/drilling machines, light ballast cleaners, ballast profiling and regulating equipment, lorries, jacks, hand tools and twin-bloc steel sleepers.

## Premesa

Premesa SA Industrio e Comercio
Av Nossa Senhora do O 565, Limão, São Paulo, Brazil
Tel: (+55 11) 266 81 88   Fax: (+55 11) 210 60 31

**Key personnel**
General Manager: José Luiz Martins
Sales Superintendent: Luiz da Costa

**Products**
Turnouts, crossings, switches, points, frogs, track components.

## Presto Products Company

PO Box 2399, Appleton, Wisconsin 54912-2399, USA
Tel: (+1 920) 738 11 18   Fax: (+1 920) 739 12 22
e-mail: info@prestogeo.com
Web: http://www.prestogeo.com

**Products**
Geoweb® perforated cellular confinement system. Applications include: stabilisation of track sub-base; slope and channel protection; earth retention; and load support in terminal yards and port facilities.

*NEW ENTRY*

## Progress Rail Services

Rail and Trackwork Group
1600 Progress Drive, PO Box 1037, Albertville, Alabama 35950, USA
Tel: (+1 256) 593 12 60   Fax: (+1 256) 593 12 49

**Key personnel**
Senior Vice-President: David Roeder
Vice-President, Sales: Glen Lehmann

**Subsidiary companies/divisions**
The Rail and Trackwork Group of Progress Rail Services Corporation includes:
Rail and Trackwork Division
(rail crossings, turnouts, track components)
Chemetron Railway Products
(rail welding)
Kershaw, DAPCO Rail Services
(ultrasonic rail flaw detection)
True Temper Railway Appliances
(rail anchors)
Lincoln Industries
(level crossing safety devices and signal equipment)
All-Track Equipment
(used maintenance-of-way equipment)

**Products and services**
New and relay rail; rail anchors; custom switches and crossings; rail welding; new and used maintenance-of-way equipment; grade crossing safety devices and signal equipment and mobile rail pick-up crews.

*UPDATED*

## PS Corporation

3-4-1 Marunouchi 3-chome, Chiyoda-ku, Tokyo 100-0005, Japan
Tel: (+81 3) 32 16 18 93   Fax: (+81 3) 32 16 19 16

**Key personnel**
President: Giichi Tanaka
Executive Managing Director, Marketing:
   Toshihiko Kanbara
Executive Managing Director, Export Sales:
   Yasuharu Arakawa

**Subsidiaries**
JUS Consultants Co, Ltd
Hatano Seisakusho Co, Ltd
New Tech Co, Ltd
Dairyo Co, Ltd
PT Komponindo Betonjaya (Indonesia)

**Products**
Prestressed concrete sleepers, track slabs and beams; construction of prestressed concrete railway bridges.
   Recent contracts include the construction of a bridge on the Hokuriku Shinkansen high-speed line; construction of the Kansai new airport connection bridge, Osaka; construction of sections A4, B1 and C1 of the Jabotabek railway project, Indonesia.

## Qiqihar

Qiqihar Rolling Stock (Group) Co Ltd
10 Zhonghua East Road, Qiqihar Heilongjiang 161002, People's Republic of China
Tel: (+86 452) 293 91 58   Fax: (+86 452) 251 44 64
e-mail: qrswceo@public.qq.hl.cn
Web: http://www.qrrs.com

**Key personnel**
See entry in *Freight vehicles and equipment* section.

**Products**
Diesel-hydraulic railway cranes (15, 63, 125 and 160 short tons) equipped with fixed or telescope beam.

*NEW ENTRY*

## Quest

Quest Corporation
950 Keynote Circle, Brooklyn Heights, Cleveland, Ohio 44131, USA
Tel: (+1 216) 398 94 00   Fax: (+1 216) 398 77 65

**Key personnel**
See entry in *Signalling and communications systems* section.

**Products**
Hand-held ultra-sonic rail flaw detectors; electronic weighing systems and controls.

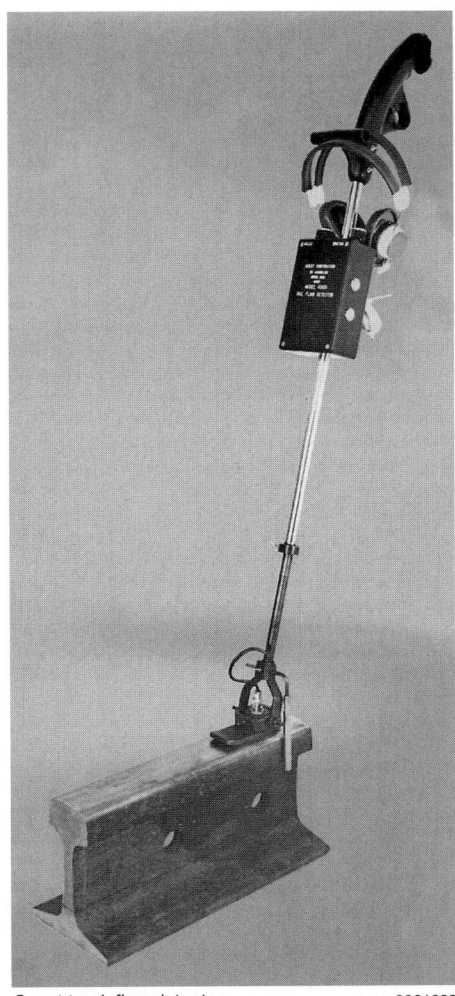

*Quest track flaw detector*   0021668

MANUFACTURERS/Permanent way components, equipment and services

## Racine Railroad Products Inc

PO Box 4029, 1524 Frederick Street, Racine, Wisconsin 53404, USA
Tel: (+1 414) 637 96 81   Fax: (+1 414) 637 90 69

**Key personnel**
President: S J Birkholz
Chief Engineer: D Brenny
Operations Manager: Jim Hilliard
Sales and Marketing Manager: J Syltie
Service Manager: R Rhodes
Controller: G Harmann
Customer Service: L Powell, P Degen

**Products**
Automatic anchor applicators; dual anchor spreaders and adjusters; dual clip applicators; Pandrol Fastclip applicators/removers; anchor removers; clip setters/applicators; abrasive saws; electric and petrol-driven profile grinders; reciprocating hacksaws; rail drills.

## Railpro

Railpro BV
Nieuwe Crailoseweg 8, PO Box 888, NL-1200 AW Hilversum, Netherlands
Tel: (+31 35) 688 96 00   Fax: (+31 35) 688 96 66
e-mail: railinfo@Railpro.nl
Web: http://www.Railpro.nl

**Products**
Railpro supplies all materials required in railway infrastructure work, acting as a stockist for contractors. The company can arrange transport to the worksite by road, water or rail; it operates a fleet of 2,200 rail wagons.

*UPDATED*

## Railquip Inc

3731 Northcrest Road, Suite 6, Atlanta, Georgia 30340, USA
Tel: (+1 770) 458 41 57; (+1 800) 325 02 96
Fax: (+1 770) 458 53 65
e-mail: railquip@aol.com
Web: http://www.railquip.com

**Key personnel**
President: Helmut Schroeder
Sales Manager: Paul Wojcik

**Products**
Maintenance and supply of: hydraulic track jacks; Azobe hardwood ties; road/rail-equipped Unimog multipurpose vehicle; Dematic Gottwald tracklaying cranes with horizontally extendable boom up to 150 tons (capacity) and 250 tons terrain cranes; maintenance-of-way utility cranes with accessories; Hi-rail equipment trailers; track vacuum refuse collector; gasoline-powered vacuum cleaner back-pack-mounted or with two-wheeled refuse container; cable channels; laser track measuring device; rail aligner; gasoline engine impact wrench; tamper machine and rail grinding machines; automatic rail welding machine.

**Contracts**
Recent contracts include: rail grinding of 50 km track of the Metrorrey in Monterrey, Mexico; vacuum trash collector for Dallas Area Rapid Transit, Dallas, Texas; containerised air compresor system for South New Jersey Transit Authority; portable hydraulic rerailing equipment for Washington Metropolitan Area Transit Authority, Massachusetts Bay Transportation Authority - Boston, Utah Transit - Salt Lake City, Utah, Maxi Railcar Mover for John F Kennedy Airport - Airtrain, New York.

*UPDATED*

## Rails Company

101 Newark Way, Maplewood, New Jersey 07040-3393, USA
Tel: (+1 973) 763 43 20   Fax: (+1 973) 763 25 85

e-mail: rails@railsco.com
Web: http://www.railsco.com

**Key personnel**
President: G N Burwell
Vice-President: J Maldonado
Secretary/Treasurer: M Kinda
Sales: J Vertum, L Campos

**Products**
Rail anchors, switch point locks, switch heaters (propane and natural gas), lubricators, compressors, controls, snow detectors, wheel stops and car retarders.

*UPDATED*

## Railtech International

119 avenue Louis Roche – BP 152, F-92231 Gennevilliers Cedex, France
Tel: (+33 1) 46 88 17 00   Fax: (+33 1) 46 88 17 01
e-mail: management@railtech.fr
Web: http://www.railtech.fr

**Key personnel**
Chairman and Chief Executive: Jean-Pierre Colliaut
Engineering Director: Didier Bourdon
Sales and Marketing Manager: Gilles du Fou

**Products**
Aluminothermic rail welding and track maintenance equipment; third rail electrification.

## Railtech Schlatter Systems

119 avenue Louis Roche – BP 152, F-92231 Gennevilliers Cedex, France
Tel: (+33 1) 46 88 17 30   Fax: (+33 1) 46 88 17 40
e-mail: management@railtech.fr
Web: http://www.railtech.fr

**Key personnel**
Managing Director: Didier Bourdon
Product Managers: Jean-Pierre Mornac, Klaus Nebel

**Products**
Stationary and mobile flash-butt welding machines and ancillary equipment.

## RailWorks Corporation

6225 Smith Avenue, Suite 200 Baltimore, Maryland 21209-3613, USA
Tel: (+1 410) 580 60 00

**Key personnel**
Chairman and Chief Executive Officer: Ab Rees
President and Chief Operating Officer: Jim Kimsey

**Subsidiaries**
Railworks Products and Services Group
Tel: (+1 412) 325 02 02
e-mail: wdonley@railworks.com
President: William R Donley
Vice-President of Business Development: George Caric

Railworks Track Systems Group
Tel: (+1 801) 366 93 39
President: Robert D Wolff

Railworks Transit Systems Group
Tel: (+1 914) 323 30 12
President: C William Moore

Pacific Northern Rail Contractors Inc
(a RailWorks Company)
Tel: (+1 604) 850 91 66
President: Henry Braun

**Background**
In September 2001, RailWorks Corporation and its operating subsidiaries in the US voluntarily filed for protection under chapter 11 of the US Bankruptcy Code.

**Services**
Integrated rail system services and products, active in new construction, rehabilitation, track repair and maintenance, signalling, communications, electrical and other track-related systems plus rail products manufacturing and supply.

**Projects**
New York City Transit Authority (NYCTA) White Plains – Phase II signal rehabilitation project, White Plains, New York.
New Jersey Transit (NJT) Morrisville Train Storage Yard, Falls Township Philadelphia: construct 12 new storage yard tracks and to install related crossovers, turnouts, electrical switch heaters and yard lighting. Modification of existing tracks, rehabilitation of two existing yard tracks, yard drainage, accesses roads and paving.
Minnesota Constructors Team, Hiawatha Light Rail Line, Minneapolis: extending from downtown Minneapolis, through Minneapolis, through the Minneapolis—St Paul International Airports to the Mall of America in Bloomington. The completed project will be approximately 11.4 miles long.
TransLink (Vancouver), Millennium Line Expansion of the Vancouver Skytrain, Vancouver, Canada: Linear induction motor and power rail installation, including the installation of 40,000 lineal metres of LIM (Linear Induction Motor) reaction rail and 80,000 linear metres of a side-mounted power rail including thermal expansion joints, power feeds, isolation joints, and coverboard. Also, core drilling and grouting of 120,00 support studs for the LIM rail and core drilling 60,000 holes to anchor the power rail insulator brackets.
New York City Transit Authority (NYCTA) Carnarsie Line, New York: complete installation of a new Communications Based Train Control System (CBTC) for 13 route miles of the Canarsie Line subway in association with Matra Transport International and Union Switch & Signal.
NYCTA, New York: Rehabilitate the train control signal system for 5.1 miles of track on the Flushing Line subway. Also to furnish and install eight escalators at five locations in the boroughs of Brooklyn and Manhattan.
Miami International Airport, Miami, Florida: Electrical and guideway construction services including automatic train control systems and 8,500 ft of concrete guideway in association with Sumitomo.
Panama Canal Railway, a venture between Kansas City Southern Industries and Lanco International: Reconstruction and expansion of track and facilities involving a 44-mile stretch of track, running parallel to the Canal from Colon to Balboa.
Vancouver Wharves, British Columbia, Canada: Rail yard construction services.
Long Island Rail Road, Long Island: Rehabilitation and improvements of the diesel yard.
IPSCO Steel, Mobile: Steel mill expansion project involving 30,000 crossties and additional switch ties.
US Lime and Minteral-Arkansas Lime, Batesville: The design/build project involves the removal and construction of 15,000 ft of track including three turnouts, grade crossing and bridgework.
Tuscola and Saginaw Bay Railroad, Michigan: Refurbishment project involving 20,000 crossties for the 12.5-mile branch line.

*UPDATED*

## Ranalah

Ranalah Moulds Ltd
New Road, Newhaven BN9 0EH, UK
Tel: (+44 1273) 51 46 76   Fax: (+44 1273) 51 65 29

**Key personnel**
Directors: J H Layfield, P F Phillips
Technical Director: P F Phillips
Technical/Design Manager: S Orwin

**Products**
Design of prestressed concrete sleepers, moulds and equipment; design and manufacture of equipment to suit any type of sleeper production; factory layout design, plant supply and commissioning; full operational training, initial management assistance. Turnkey service for supply of sleeper production and manufacturing plant.

## Rawie

Dornierstrasse 11, D-49090 Osnabrück, Germany
Tel: (+49 541) 91 20 70   Fax: (+49 541) 912 07 36
e-mail: info@rawie.com
Web: http://www.rawie.com

**Key personnel**
Managing Director, Marketing: J Fründ
Export Manager: N L C Pratt
Senior Design Engineer: H Klose

**Products**
Fixed and friction buffer stops; fixed and/or friction buffer stops with hydraulic or elastomeric cylinders; friction, fixed and folding wheel stops; specialist track endings to customer requirements, including folding buffer stops and buffer stops with integral loading ramps.

Recent contracts include: LTA, Singapore (1999); MTRC, Hong Kong (1999); DB AG, Hannover Expo (1999); and Atlanta, USA and Toronto, Canada.

*VERIFIED*

**Contracts**
Contracts include supply of sleeper plants to Hong Kong, Philippines, Thailand, Georgia, Turkey, Sudan, Malaysia, Bulgaria, Europe and the UK.

*VERIFIED*

## Response Environmental Services Ltd

Abbeyfield House, Blyth Road, Maltby, South Yorkshire S66 8HX, UK
Tel: (+44 1709) 81 61 04   Fax: (+44 1709) 81 61 12
e-mail: response@netcomuk.co.uk

**Key personnel**
Managing Director: John Phillips
Technical Director: John Bent
Commercial Manager: R W Townsend

**Products and services**
Bioremediation of track ballast, ground and groundwaters; decontamination of diesel and human detritus on the trackbed; Bio-spray for accelerated biodegradation of detritus in stations; Novatrack trackbed protection system to combat constant recontamination of ballast; Novacell automated biological *in situ* interceptor treatment system; 24-hour emergency spill response system throughout the UK.

Recent contracts include a 24-hour call-out contract with the UK train operator, Northern Spirit and bioremediation and laying of Novatrack matting at Manchester Piccadilly station for Railtrack.

*Novatrack trackbed protection matting installed by Response Environmental Services at Manchester Piccadilly station for Railtrack*   0064329

## Rexquote

Requote Limited
Broadgauge Business Park, Bishops Lydeard, Taunton, TA4 3BU, UK
Tel: (+44 1823) 43 33 98   Fax: (+44 1823) 43 37 25
e-mail: sales@rexquote.co.uk
Web: http://www.rexquote.co.uk

**Products**
Road-rail conversions and products including: road-rail hydraulic excavators (roadrailers); road-rail hydraulic crane/excavators (superailers/megarailers); road-rail dumpers and road-rail access platform; road-rail tracked vehicles; trailers.

*NEW ENTRY*

## RICA

Via Podgora 26, I-31029 Vittorio Veneto (TV), Italy
Tel: (+39 0438) 91 01
Fax: (+39 0438) 91 22 36; 91 22 72; 91 03 26
e-mail: rica@zoppas-industries.it
Web: http://www.rica.zoppas-industries.it

**Corporate development**
RICA is a member of the Zoppas Industries group.

**Products**
Switch-point and rail de-icing systems.

## Richardson & Cruddas (1972) Ltd

PO Box 4503, Sir J J Road, Byculla, Bombay 400 008, India
Tel: (+91 22) 37 66 83 28

**Key personnel**
Managing Director: Shri N H Borde

**Products**
Manufacture of points and crossings; pressed-steel turnout sleepers; steel track; sleepers; slide chairs; fabrication of overhead structures for railway electrification.

## RMC Concrete Products (UK)

Aston Church Road, Saltley, Birmingham B8 1QF, UK
Tel: (+44 121) 327 08 44   Fax: (+44 121) 327 75 45
e-mail: sleepers@rmc-concreteproducts.co.uk

**Key personnel**
Commercial and Technical Executive: Tony Darroch

**Other offices**
St Helen Auckland, Bishop Auckland, DL14 9AJ UK
Tel: (+44 1388) 60 39 31   Fax: (+44 1388) 45 00 56

**Products**
Pretensioned concrete monobloc sleepers; reinforced concrete sleepers; concrete cable troughs, crossing bearers, platform units; plus general precast products for station regeneration and building work.

Recent contracts completed include a three-year contract (1998-2001) for Railtrack renewals requiring approximately 200,000 sleepers per year; and sleepers for the remodelling of London's Euston station; supply of 250,000 944 sleepers to Railtrack (2000). Concrete sleepers and cable troughing are currently being supplied for the West Coast main line upgrade.

*UPDATED*

## RMS Locotec

Rail Management Services
Vanguard Works, Bretton Street, Dewsbury WF12 9BJ, UK
Tel: (+44 1924) 46 50 50   Fax: (+44 1924) 46 54 22
e-mail: sales@rmslocotec.com

**Key personnel**
Managing Director: Lawrence Crossan
Commercial Manager: Peter Briddon
Operations Manager: Derek Webb

**Services**
Maintenance of track, structures and fixed equipment; short- and long-term locomotive hire, maintenance and overhaul; safety management and training; engineering consultancy; rail operations and facilities management.

*UPDATED*

## Road Rail Equipment

Road Rail Equipment Ltd
Unit A, Home Farm Industrial Park, Hunsdon Road, Stanstead Abbots, Ware SG12 8LA, UK
Tel: (+44 1920) 87 75 00   Fax: (+44 1920) 87 76 00

**Associate company**
Hiremee Ltd
Marsh Lane, Ware SG12 9QB, UK
Tel: (+44 1920) 41 21 00   Fax: (+44 1920) 41 20 30

**Products**
Road/rail equipment including dumpers, access platforms, Mecalac 14MXT RR crane.

*Road Rail Equipment Mecalac 14MXT RR crane*   0021669

## Robel

Robel Bahnbaumaschinen GmbH
Industriestrasse 31, D-83395 Freilassing, Germany
Tel: (+49 8654) 60 90   Fax: (+49 8654) 60 91 00
e-mail: info@robel-rail.com
Web: http://www.robel-rail.com

**Key personnel**
Managing Director: Erwin Stocker

**Products**
Heavy machinery: powered gangers' trolleys, rail handling vehicles, track laying machines for panels, sleepers and switches, rail loading and transportation equipment, catenary maintenance systems, special wagons and trailers.

Small machinery: rail drills, rail cutters, rail grinders (profile, web and switch), rail lifting devices, rail clamps for temporary joints, rail benders, plain line and switch blade, power wrenches, carrying tongs for sleepers and rail, track jacks, mechanical and hydraulic, track lifting and slewing machines, material transport trolleys (1 and 12 tonnes) lightweight tramping units, site illumination systems, track measuring devices, full range of special railway hand tools.

*UPDATED*

## Rosenqvist Rail Tech AB

Box 334, SE-824 27 Hudiksvall, Sweden
Tel: (+46 650) 165 05   Fax: (+46 650) 165 01
e-mail: anders.rosenqvist@rosenqvist-group.se
Web: http://www.rosenqvistrt.se

**Products**
Rail fastening machines and attachments; sleeper laying and replacement attachments; multifunctional road-rail vehicles; attachments for contact wire work; technical consulting and engineering services; and training.

Contracts include the supply of equipment to permanent way contractors in Poland, Norway, Sweden, the UK and the USA, as well as to railway systems in Japan.

## Rotabroach

Savile Street, Sheffield S4 7UD, UK
Tel: (+44 114) 276 77 95   Fax: (+44 114) 275 33 08
e-mail: info@rotabroach.co.uk
Web: http://www.rotabroach.co.uk

**Key personnel**
Director and General Manager: R Stych
Managing Director: M Duffin
Sales and Marketing: N E Price
Sales Director: P W Dorsett
Technical Director: B Wood

**Products**
Petrol-driven rail drill for remote locations, designed with an integral two-stroke engine and petrol tank. It weighs 18 kg and can be operated and carried by one man.

Micro bonder weighing 12.3 kg for bonding hoe and signal drilling applications. It is ready for use quickly by slipping the clamping unit beneath the rail and locking it with a single lever to produce two bonding holes with either a drill up to 12 mm diameter or a Rotabroach cutter up to 22 mm diameter. The machine indexes from one centre to the other on a horizontal slideway.

*The Rotabroach petrol-driven rail drill in use in many countries*   2000/0089076

Hydraulic rail drill can be used for cutting holes up to 38 mm diameter through rails up to 25 mm thick. It can be used on high tensile steel rails where high torque and low running speeds are required for cutting and because it is quiet when operational can be used at night in urban areas.

High-frequency rail drill with a 135 V or 265 V 200 Hz electric motor; can be used for fish plate holes, stretcher rails and bonding hole applications.

Electric rail drill used by railways around the world. It weighs 21 kg and comes in two variations, the RD 171M 110 V and RD 173M 230 V.

Recent contracts include the supply of equipment to SBB, ČD, Japan, Singapore, Hong Kong and Australian National Railways.

## Rotamag Rail Division

Universal Drilling and Cutting Equipment Ltd
43 Catley Road, Sheffield S9 5JF, UK
Tel: (+44 114) 291 10 20   Fax: (+44 114) 261 31 86
e-mail: dennis@udce.co.uk

**Key personnel**
Managing Directors: Vic Archer, Mike Bryan
Divisional Director: Dennis Learad

**Background**
Rotanag Rail is part of the UDCE Group.

**Products**
Rail drilling machines; rail broaching cutters; rail jacks; rail bonding equipment; permanent way hand tools; third rail shrouds; rail trolleys; weld shears; and track-handling equipment.

Contracts include the supply of rail bonding equipment, drilling machines and pulling tools for London Underground Ltd, UK.

*VERIFIED*

## Saar-Gummi GmbH

D-66687 Wadern-Büschfeld, Germany
Tel: (+49 6874) 691 09   Fax: (+49 6874) 691 59
e-mail: Werner.Koch@saargummi.com
Web: http://www.saargummi.com

**Key personnel**
General Managers: Jan Trommershausen,
   Achim Pietsch, Dr Wolfgang Schneider
Manager Moulded Parts Department:
   Bernhard Lindenmayer
Sales Manager Rail Products: Werner Koch

**Subsidiaries**
SaarGummi Iberica, Madrid, Spain
SaarGummi Czech, Cerveny Kostelec, Czech Republic
SGGS, India
SaarGummi Americas, Ann Arbor, USA
SaarGummi Tennessee, Pulaski, USA
SaarGummi Quebec, Canada
SaarGummi do Brasil, Bahia, Brazil

**Products**
Products for ballasted and ballastless track, including: solid rubber boots and baseplate pads; rail and microcellular pads of foamed synthetic rubber with closed cellular structure.

**Contracts**
Recent contracts include the supply of components to Deutsche Bahn AG, Hannover–Berlin, Hannover–Würzburg and Köln–Frankfurt new high-speed Intercity III line, Leighton RSA (West Rail Hong Kong) and Channel Tunnel Rail Link. ballastless high-speed lines.

*UPDATED*

## Salient Systems Inc

4330 Tuller Road, Dublin, Ohio 43017-5008, USA
Tel: (+1 614) 792 58 00   Fax: (+1 614) 792 58 88
Web: http://www.salientsystems.com

**Key personnel**
President and Chief Executive Officer:
   Harold Harrison
Executive Vice-President and Chief Financial Officer:
   S A Harrison
General Manager and Sales Director: Dana Earl

**Products**
Microprocessor-based wayside inspection and detection instrumentation for monitoring track/train dynamics at selected wayside sites. Salient's Mk II Wheel Impact Load Detector (WILD) will report and identify flat or out-of-round wheels causing excessive impact to track and structures.

*VERIFIED*

## Sateba International

262 boulevard St-Germain, F-75007 Paris, France
Tel: (+33 1) 40 62 26 00   Fax: (+33 1) 40 62 26 01
e-mail: sateba-paris@sateba.com

**Key personnel**
Chief Executive Officer: Claude Cazenave
Deputy Managing Director: Denis Vallet

**Principal subsidiaries**
Sotradest, Charmes Vosges, France

**Products**
Design and manufacture of Vagneux system of twin-block concrete sleepers, and prestressed concrete sleepers for turnouts; Stedef system and S312 sleepers for slab track; PRA system polyurethane sleeper pads; sleeper design and adaptation to all fastening systems; design and commissioning of sleeper manufacturing plants. Also technical studies, assistance and staff training.

*UPDATED*

## Schlatter AG, HA

Brandstrasse 24, CH-8952 Schlieren, Switzerland
Tel: (+41 1) 732 71 11; 72 00   Fax: (+41 1) 732 72 02
e-mail: email@schlatter.ch
Web: http://www.schlatter.ch

**Key personnel**
Product Manager: Klaus Nebel

**Subsidiary companies**
Railtech Schlatter Systems SAS (joint venture) (qv)
Sales and service subsidiaries in: Australia, Brazil, France, Germany, Italy, Netherlands, UK and USA.

**Products**
Stationary and mobile flash-butt welding equipment.

*UPDATED*

## Schramm Inc

800 Virginia Avenue, West Chester, Pennsylvania 19380, USA
Tel: (+1 610) 696 25 00   Fax: (+1 610) 696 69 50
e-mail: Schramm@schramminc.com

**Key personnel**
President: Dick Schramm
Marketing Manager: Robert V Edwards

**Products**
Pneumatractors; high-pressure air compressors; Rotadrills; Pneumagopher. The HT300C Pneumatractor can be fitted with four flanged wheels to permit its use in track maintenance and construction; its 9 m$^3$/min rotary screw compressor can power heavy-duty drills, torque wrenches, spike drivers and tampers.

## Schreck-Mieves GmbH

Krückenweg 113, D-44225 Dortmund (Barop), Germany
Tel: (+49 231) 710 80   Fax: (+49 231) 71 15 88
Web: http://www.schreck-mieves.de

## Permanent way components, equipment and services/MANUFACTURERS

### Products
ESA electronically controlled rail lubrication systems for urban, industrial and main line railways; EKOS® lubrication-free tongue roller devices for existing and new switches and crossings.

*NEW ENTRY*

---

### Schweizer Electronic AG

Industriestrasse 3, CH-6260 Reiden, Switzerland
Tel: (+41 62) 749 07 07   Fax: (+41 62) 749 07 00
e-mail: info@schweizer-electronic.ch
Web: http://www.schweizer-electronic.ch

### Products
Safety equipment and systems for permanent way engineering staff and track workers.

Recent products include the Minimel 95 system in which train movements are detected by hand-held or rail-mounted switches, or from the signalling centre, and relayed by radio a control centre. This then activates devices in the work area, which emit audible and visual warnings.

*NEW ENTRY*

---

### Schwihag

Schwihag Gesellschaft für Eisenbahnoberbau mbH
Lebernstrasse 3, CH-8274 Tägerwilen, Switzerland
Tel: (+41 71) 666 88 00   Fax: (+41 71) 666 88 01
e-mail: schwihag@bluewin.ch
Web: http://www.railway-technology.com

### Key personnel
Managing Director: Dipl Betriebswirt Karl-Heinz Schwiede

### Products
IBSR and IBRR rail anchoring systems for turnouts, including clips, baseplates and slide plates.

Recent developments include a modular sleeper with an integrated switch actuating system and a roller side plate for lubrication-free operation and a boltless check rail support for continuous check rail in curved track and opposite crossings.

Equipment has been supplied to the MTRC Lantau Airport Railway, KCRC Hong Kong, SMRT Singapore, TRC Taipei, TTC Toronto, FS Italy and Railtrack UK, as well as to many other major European national railway systems, including DB, FS, RENFE, SNCB and SNCF.

*VERIFIED*

---

### SECO-Rail

Espace Lumière, Bâtiment 1, 6 rue Emile Pathè, F-78403 Chatou Cedex, France
Tel: (+33 1) 30 09 83 00   Fax: (+33 1) 30 09 83 01
e-mail: info@seco-rail.com

### Corporate background
SECO-Rail is part of the Colas group of companies.

### Services
Tracklaying; track renewal; track maintenance.

*NEW ENTRY*

---

### Semperit

Semperit Technische Produkte GmbH & Co KG
Triester Bundesstrasse 26, A-2632 Wimpassing, Austria
Tel: (+43 1) 26 30 31 04 58   Fax: (+43 1) 26 30 31 04 88
Web: http://www.semperit.at

### Key personnel
Divisional Managers: Ing Manfred Faustmann, Peter Horn

### Products
Rubber and plastic track items, including rail pads, elastic sleeper supports and plastic fastenings. Elastomer profiles, including track trough sealing sections.

---

### Sersa AG

Brauerstrasse 126, CH-8004 Zurich, Switzerland
Tel: (+41 1) 242 52 30   Fax: (+41 1) 242 52 61
e-mail: info@sersa-group.com
Web: http://www.sersa-group.com

### Key personnel
President: Konrad Schnyder

### Subsidiary companies
Sersa SA
Route Jo Siffert 38, CH-1762 Givisiez, Switzerland
Tel: (+41 26) 466 50 60   Fax: (+41 26) 466 50 61
Sersa GmbH
Falkstätterstrasse 10B, D-12621 Berlin, Germany
Tel: (+49 30) 565 46 60   Fax: (+49 30) 56 54 66 15
Sersa bv Utrecht
Fultonbaan 15, NL-3439 NE Nieuwegein, The Netherlands
Tel: (+31 75) 617 23 73   Fax: (+31 75) 617 94 64
Benkler AG (qv)
Eurogleis
Euroswitch (qv)
Gleis- und Bautechnologie AG
Klenk Verwaltungs GmbH
Metrag AG
Parachini SA (qv)
Sersa (UK) Ltd
SIT GmbH

### Services
Track construction; construction of track substructures; planning industrial track systems; track maintenance; operation, hire and maintenance of track construction and maintenance machinery and works locomotives; rail grinding; rail welding; track cleaning; resinification of sleeper screw holes; overhead line construction and maintenance; cable construction.

*NEW ENTRY*

---

### SGB Youngman

Specials Division
1st Floor, Holmwood, Broadlands Business Campus, Langhurstwood Road, Horsham RH12 4SU, UK
Tel: (+44 1403) 22 00 00 Fax: (+44 1403) 22 00 01
e-mail: youngmandirect@sgb.co.uk
Web: http://www.youngmandirect.co.uk

### Products
Access equipment for infrastructure construction and maintenance. Recent products include a link trolley for the BOSS Zone 1 access system, which is non-conductive, non-sparking, non-corrosive and non-oxidising.

*NEW ENTRY*

*Link trolley for the BOSS Zone 1 access system*
2002/0114665

---

### Siemens Switzerland

Siemens Switzerland Transportation Systems
Industriestrasse 42, CH-8304 Wallisellen, Switzerland
Tel: (+41 1) 832 32 32   Fax: (+41 1) 832 36 00
e-mail: verkehrstechnik@siemens.ch
Web: http://www.siemens.ch/vt

### Key personnel
See entry in *Signalling and communications systems* section.

### Products
Block and track vacancy proving equipment (axle counters, track circuits, last vehicle detection); point locking equipment including point machines and point locking system; signals and indicators; safety relays.

---

### Sika Ltd

Watchmead, Welwyn Garden City AL7 1BQ, UK
Tel: (+44 1707) 39 44 44   Fax: (+44 1707) 39 32 96
e-mail: sales@uk.sika.com
Web: http://www.sika.com

### Key personnel
Managing Director: D Bratt
Regional Sales Manager: Steve Dunn

### Products
Sikarail KC330 resilient rail-fixing system is a combination of a tough elastic, polyurethane reaction-curing binder and compressible fillers that absorb vibration, reduce noise and is available in a variety of grades to ensure suitability with differing load-bearing requirements.

Sika also provides admixture designs for high-specification concrete mixes, jointing systems, mortars and grouts, adhesives and bonding agents, waterproofing, corrosion inhibitors, concrete repair and protective coatings for concrete and steel including industrial flooring.

### Contracts
Base-plate bedding material for direct fixation system for London Underground Northern Line; Heathrow Express (track fixation at Paddington station platforms and at Semi-Outside Double Slip (SODS) crossover, Heathrow Airport).

*UPDATED*

---

### SILF Srl

Via Romagnosi 60, I-29100 Piacenza, Italy
Tel: (+39 0523) 33 85 85   Fax: (+39 0523) 38 51 24
e-mail: SILF@writeme.com
Web: http://www.SILFsrl.com

### Works
SS 10, Via Emilia Pavese 2, I-29010 Sarmato Piacenza, Italy
Tel: (+39 0523) 88 62 00   Fax: (+39 0523) 88 78 20
Tx: 530122 rotaia1

### Key personnel
President: Cesare Golzi

### Products
Light and heavy rail sections; crane rail and grooved rail for tramways; guardrail; wooden, concrete and steel sleepers; plates; clips; nuts and bolts; spikes; anchor bolts; screwspikes; fishplates and baseplates; buffer stops; frogs; points and crossings; turnouts.

Contracts include supply of equipment to Fiat, Condo-Metro, Rome, Nova SpA, Milan and MetroRoma SpA.

---

### Slab Track Systems International

Web: http://www.sts-international.com
e-mail: infor@sts-international.com
Germany:
Max Bögl Bauunternehmung GmbH & Co KG
Industriegebiet Schlieferheide/Bögl, PO Box 1120, D-92301 Neumarkt, Germany
Tel: (+49 91) 81 90 90   Fax: (+49 91) 81 90 50 61

**MANUFACTURERS**/Permanent way components, equipment and services

Netherlands:
Grimbergen Engineering & Projects BV
Bedrijfsweg 23-25, PO Box 145, NL-2400 AC Alphen aan den Rijn, Netherlands
Tel: (+31 172) 43 27 21   Fax: (+31 172) 44 42 21

**Products**
The Bögl solid railbed system, comprising prefabricated panels, connected longitudinally and installed on a hydraulically bonded bed.

## SMIS

Surrey Materials Inspection Systems
Alan Turing Road, Surrey Research Park, Guildford, Surrey, GU2 5YF, UK
Tel: (+44 1483) 50 66 11   Fax: (+44 1483) 56 31 14
e-mail: materials@smis.co.uk
Web: http://www.smis.co.uk

**Key personnel**
General Manager: Dr N MacCuaig

**Products**
Automated and manual equipment for railway non-destructive testing and infrastructure monitoring applications; vehicle-based inspection systems for infrastructure monitoring including ultra-sonic track inspection, overhead line inspection, track geometry, structure gauging, as well as a range of depot maintenance equipment. The BR2000 is claimed to be the lowest noise flaw detector available for axle inspection and the only such instrument to be certified by BR. The R56 digital flaw detector for track, wheels and other applications was developed in collaboration with BR for manual inspection of track and is certified by Railtrack.

Recent contracts include the supply to Indian Railways of two sets of instrumentation to monitor the condition of overhead catenary and the installation of a major online ultra-sonic inspection system for the Steel Authority of India Ltd.

**VERIFIED**

## Sola

Ing Guido Scheyer Measuring Instrument GesmbH & Co
Unteres Tobel 25, A-6840 Gotzis, Austria
Tel: (+43 5523) 533 80   Fax: (+43 5523) 533 85

**Key personnel**
Managing Director: Dr Walter Hörburger
Sales and Marketing Manager: Franz Huber

**Products**
Track gauge and superelevation measuring equipment; measuring devices for lower clearance; switch gauge.

## Somafel

Av da República 42-5, P-1050 Lisbon, Portugal
Tel: (+351 1) 799 03 30   Fax: (+351 1) 795 10 38

**Key personnel**
Managing Director: D Serpa Santos
Deputy Managing Director: Fernando S Santos
Equipment Department Directors: Vitor Farrajota, Leaver Costa

**Products**
Track construction, renewal, maintenance and electrification for main line and metro systems.

## Sonatest plc

Dickens Road, Old Wolverton, Milton Keynes MK12 5QQ, UK
Tel: (+44 1908) 31 63 45   Fax: (+44 1908) 32 13 23
e-mail: sales@sonatest-plc.com
Web: http://www.sonatest-plc.com

**Key personnel**
Managing Director: M S Reilly
Sales Director: J Whyte
Sales Administrator: Carol Stevenson

**Principal subsidiary**
Sonatest Inc
4734 Research Drive, San Antonio, Texas, USA
Tel: (+1 210) 697 03 35   Fax: (+1 210) 697 07 67
e-mail: sonartest@flash.net
Vice-President: R Sidney

**Products**
Railscan 125 ultra-sonic portable flaw detector for rail testing; Powerscan 400 ultra-sonic flaw detector for axle testing; ultra-sonic transducers for testing rail, wheels and axles, including special probes used in systems for Thermit weld testing; rail tester trolleys and equipment for the Bance (qv) rail cart.

Equipment has been supplied to Applied Inspection, Balfour Beatty Rail Maintenance, GTRM, London Underground Ltd, MTR Corporation of Hong Kong and Serco Ltd.

**VERIFIED**

## Spefaka

Spezialfahrzeugaufbau und Kabeltechnik GmbH
Verlängerte Apoldaer Strasse 18, D-06116 Halle/Saale, Germany
Tel: (+49 345) 56 99 50   Fax: (+49 345) 569 95 90

**Key personnel**
General Manager: G Hofmann

**Products**
Road/rail vehicles equipped for infrastructure construction, maintenance and inspection duties. Spefaka produces 3, 13, 20 and up to 32 tonne vehicles equipped with light, medium and heavy-duty rail running units and available with a range of body structures including hydraulic lifting platforms; loading platforms, mobile workshops and units for the storage of materials and interchangable tools; cable drum with cable dispensing/tensioning equipment; loading platform with crane with grab, cable drum carrier or working basket; rail cleaning, point maintenance and rail lubrication equipment; high-pressure cleaning and suction units; ballast cleaners and distributors; sweeper and snow clearing units; recovery unit with winch for rerailing and towing. Road/rail trailers equipped with cable drum or as tunnel drive (with a battery-operated electrohydraulic drive unit) are also available.

Developments include specialised road/rail vehicles for erecting overhead electrification systems (including concrete mixer and pile driver units) and for complete rail/roadbed maintenance.

Contracts include the supply of vehicles and components to Siemens, Adtranz, Kummler + Matter and urban transport operators in Brussels, Bratislava, Berlin, Cologne, Chemnitz and Halle/Saale and a recovery unit (32 tonnes, four axles) to DB AG in 1998.

## Speno International SA

PO Box 16, 26 Parc Château-Banquet, CH-1211 Geneva 21, Switzerland
Tel: (+41 22) 906 46 00   Fax: (+41 22) 906 46 01
Tx: 412-775 SPN CH
e-mail: info@speno.ch

**Key personnel**
Managing Director: J J Méroz
Management Representative: J Cooper
Marketing Manager: D Arvet-Thouvet
Finance Manager: G Chignol
Technical Manager: L Palmieri
Purchasing Manager: S Torrequadra
Production Manager: J Neumayer
Maintenance Manager: G Stranczl
Application Manager: W Schöch

**Principal subsidiaries**
Speno Rail Maintenance Australia Pty Ltd
12 Hehir Street, Belmont, Western Australia 6104, Australia
Tel: (+61 9) 479 14 99   Fax: (+61 9) 479 13 49

*US1 ultrasonic rail flaw detection vehicle 2001*/0105690

Nippon Speno KK
Asahi Bank Gotanda Building 5F, 1-23-9 Nishigotanda, Shinagawa-Ku, Tokyo 141-0031, Japan
Tel: (+81 3) 34 95 71 61   Fax: (+81 3) 34 95 71 62

**Products**
Specialised machines for in-track rail rectification, rail surface measurement and rail flaw detection. Speno machines are in service around the world, operated by railway authorities and Speno itself, which provides contract services for more than 50 railway companies.

The new generation of Speno reprofilers are single-suspension carrier vehicles to ensure setting down of units in curves, and to benefit from shorter parking places. They incorporate a cab display of railhead longitudinal and transverse profiles allowing constant monitoring and providing digital documentation of rail condition, including transverse profile, as well as automatic control of grinding angles and pressures to ensure consistent quality of work. Other features include single-command setting of grinding patterns giving instant access to profitable multipass strategies; fully automatic rectification to a given target profile; and a rail protection alarm system. The machines can be fitted with full dust-collection equipment for suburban environments and exhaust gas cleaning for unrestricted underground operation.

Mini 8 M grinders: compact 'green grinders' specially designed for urban networks. In addition to a grinding dust-collection system and a catalytic exhaust gas system, they feature fully developed sound-proofing. Maximum speed 50 km/h, recommended grinding speed is 4 to 6 km/h. Minimum radius when grinding is 100 m. Maximum length 14 m and total working weight is 38 tonnes. On track, available for different gauges.

LRR 8-M/LRR 8 grinders: intended mainly for metro and suburban networks, these are self-propelled units capable of 80 km/h in either direction. LRR 8-M is a two-section vehicle, LRR 8 is single-section. They comply with UIC and Japanese safety and environmental protection standards. Recommended grinding speed is 4 to 6 km/h. Minimum radii when grinding are 60 m for the LRR 8-M and 85 m for the LRR 8. Maximum lengths are 17.6 m and 11 m respectively, with maximum heights of 3.7 m and 3.6 m respectively. Total weights empty/loaded are 33/37 tonnes and 23/25 tonnes respectively.

RR 16 grinders: self-propelled units capable of a maximum speed of 90 km/h in either direction. They comply with UIC and Japanese safety and environmental protection standards. Recommended grinding speed is 4 to 6 km/h. Minimum radius when grinding is 60 m and standard grinding angles are −70° inward to +30° outward. Unit dimensions are: 21 m long; 2.4 m wide, with a maximum height of 3.4 m. Total weight empty/loaded: 52/56 tonnes.

RR 24 grinders: similar to the RR 16 model, but with a unit length of 43 m, width 2.4 m and maximum height 3.4 m. Total weight empty/loaded: 114/119 tonnes.

RR 32 grinders: similar to the other two models but 45 m long, 2.8 m wide and 3.7 m high. Total weight empty/loaded: 115/123 tonnes.

Heavy-duty grinders: unmatched and computer-controlled power per grinding stone ensures maximised metal removal for repair grinding applications.

Self-propelled recording cars: these vehicles measure and record all running surface defects (such as corrugations, short and long waves and rail joint irregularities) at a speed of 80 km/h. The measuring system relies on four accelerometers for each rail and is accurate to within a few hundredths of a millimetre. The chart recorder plots the faults with wavelength and amplitude. The machine is also equipped with a digital analyser which classifies the defects in each section of each rail string according to size. Recently developed measuring of rail cross-profile at 80 km/h enables the classification of rails in track according to their shape.

Currently in production is the SM 775, which is capable of measuring 350 km of track per shift, providing rail longitudinal and cross-sectional data. The 18 m self-propelled unit weighs 40 tonnes empty and 45 tonnes loaded and is equipped with a 250 kW engine.

Ultrasonic flaw detection cars US1 and US6: developed to detect all internal rail flaws by ultrasonic testing. The machine is fitted with a probe carrier containing eight probes for each rail string as follows: one 0° probe to detect horizontal cracks; four 70° probes to detect transverse flaws in the entire railhead section; one 55° probe for longitudinal vertical cracks in the railhead; and two 35° probes to detect bolthole cracks. The vehicle also includes frog detectors (which automatically raise the probe holder) and bolthole detectors. The capacity of the water tank is sufficient for an operating range of 150 km. The information provided by the probes is processed and interpreted by the electronics which convert it into immediately usable data. The incoming signals are continuously displayed on a monitor screen and a pilot lamp lights up each time a flaw is detected. Presumed defect sites are paint-marked by an automatic spray gun. The monitor display is augmented by analogue and digital records. The analogue record is produced by a chart recorder and is also displayed on a video screen. In addition, the probe information is interpreted by a computer which provides a hard-copy printout of the data on an extra high-speed printer, listing the defects according to type, size and kilometric location in the track.

*UPDATED*

---

## Sperling Railway Services Inc

5309 Southway Street SW, Canton, Ohio 44706, USA
Tel: (+1 330) 479 20 04   Fax: (+1 330) 479 20 06
e-mail: info@sperlingrailway.com
Web: http://www.sperlingrailway.com

**Key personnel**
President: Fred Sperling
Vice-President, Sales and Marketing: Warren Stryffeler

**Products**
Maintenance of way equipment, related items and railway track signs.

*UPDATED*

---

## Sperry

Sperry Rail Service Division of Sperry Rail Inc
46 Shelter Rock Road, Danbury, Connecticut 06810, USA
Tel: (+1 203) 791 45 00   Fax: (+1 203) 798 99 47
e-mail: tdejsrs@aol.com; aveitch@sperryrail.com
Web: http://www.sperryrail.com

**Key personnel**
President: T F De Joseph
Director, International Projects: A Veitch
Director of Engineering: R Clark

**Products and services**
Sperry owns and operates a fleet of 55 rail flaw detector cars, as well as rail testing vehicles and portable rail testing systems; the company also supplies track components.

---

## Spie

Société Spie (Service Voies Ferrées)
Parc Saint-Cristophe, Edison 3, F-95861 Cergy-Pontoise Cedex, France
Tel: (+33 1) 34 22 50 02; 3   Fax: (+33 1) 34 22 57 24

**Key personnel**
Operations Director: D Mallet
Export Manager: J Lemercier

**Products**
Track welding and maintenance equipment.

*VERIFIED*

---

## Spitzke GmbH

Warmensteinacher Strasse 60, D-12349 Berlin, Germany
Tel: (+49 30) 762 90 90
Fax: (+49 30) 76 29 09 90; 76 29 09 91
e-mail: berlin@spitzke.de
Web: http://www.spitzke.de

Electrical engineering/contact lines division
Markgrafendamm 24/Haus 16, D-10245 Berlin, Germany
Tel: (+49 30) 293 46 50   Fax: (+49 30) 29 34 65 99

**Key personnel**
Managing Director: Waldemar Münich

**Subsidiary**
Spitzke Spoorbouw BV
NL-3633 CZ Vreeland, Netherlands
Tel: (+31 294) 23 02 45   Fax: (+31 294) 23 02 45

**Services**
Planning, development, construction and maintenance of track facilities for main line, metro and light rail networks, including conductor rail installation and maintenance, cable installation and laying, electrical engineering and the installation and maintenance of overhead power supply lines, and civil engineering work such as the construction of new platforms. A logistics department oversees the planning and implementation of materials supply to track construction sites.

Spitzke equipment includes: four tamping machines; three rapid ballast levelling machines; one 45 tonne crane; two ballast bed cleaning machines; two V100 and two LDK 1250 locomotives; and various excavators, bulldozers and wheel loaders.

---

## SPX Fluid Power

Windrush Park Road, Windrush Industrial Park, Witney OX29 7EZ, UK
Tel: (+44 1993) 77 64 01 Fax: (+44 1993) 77 50 90

**Corporate background**
SPX Fluid Power is the trading name of Smith Industries Hydraulics Company, part of Smiths Industries plc.

**Products**
Condition-monitored in-sleeper Rail Clamp Lock Point system; level crossing barriers; hydraulic power packs for train stops, brakes, passenger welfare devices and permanent way maintenance equipment; and jointing machines for signal cables.
Countries to which equipment has been supplied include Australia, the Czech Republic, Hong Kong, India, Ireland, Malaysia, Singapore and the UK.

*NEW ENTRY*

---

## SRS

Swedish Rail System AB SRS
PO Box 1512, SE-27 100 Ystad, Sweden
Tel: (+46 411) 138 20   Fax: (+46 411) 55 57 42

**Key personnel**
Managing Director: Alf Göransson
Deputy Managing Director: Tommy Andersson
Export Directors: Bertil Öster, Pher Lundgren

**Principal subsidiaries**
Norwegian Rail System AS
SRS America

**Products**
Concrete sleepers; machines developed for the mechanical mounting of sleepers and fastenings; gantry cranes; rail threaders; hydraulic track lifters; switch exchanger; Stormobil hi-rail vehicles; Clicomatic rail lubricators.

---

## Steel Authority of India

Steel Authority of India Ltd
International Trade Division
13th Floor, Hindustan Times House, 18-20 Kasturba Gandhi Marg, New Delhi 110 001, India
Tel: (+91 11) 332 73 16; 335 57 33
Fax: (+91 11) 332 10 18; 371 27 74

**Main works**
Bhilai, Madya Pradesh
Durgapur Steel Plant, West Bengal

**Key personnel**
Chairman: Arvind Pande
Commercial Director: A K Singh
Executive Director, International Trade Division: B N Jha

**Products**
Rails of various types.

*UPDATED*

---

## Strukton Railinfra BV

Westkanaaldijk 2, NL-3542 DA Utrecht
PO Box 1025, NL-3600 BA Maarssen, Netherlands
Tel: (+31 302) 48 69 01   Fax: (+31 302) 48 66 01

**Key personnel**
Managing Directors: Ir A Schoots, Ir G J Vos
Public Relations: B Venema
Marketing: J J Gozens (Strukton Railinfra Development & Technology BV)

**Corporate background**
Strukton Railinfra is part of the construction company, Strukton Groep NV.

**Services**
Innovation, engineering, market monitoring, project management, competence development, maintenance management, product development, breakdown repair, electrical power, underground infrastructure, cabling, telecommunications, rolling stock, production and maintenance of high output equipment and production welding.

*UPDATED*

---

## Swingmaster Corporation

11415 Melrose Avenue, Franklin Park, Illinois 60131, USA
Tel: (+1 708) 451 12 24   Fax: (+1 708) 451 12 47

**Key personnel**
President: Dan A Grammatis
Vice-President: Jerry Rakowski
General Manager, Manufacturing: John Noga

**Products**
On- and off-track, rough terrain loaders, excavators and cranes.

---

## Sydney Steel Corporation

1 Inglis Street, PO Box 1450, Sydney, Nova Scotia B1P 6K5, Canada
Tel: (+1 902) 564 79 00   Fax: (+1 902) 564 79 03

**Key personnel**
President: J A Rudderham
Vice-President, Sales: Steve Didyk
Manager, Sales: John Murphy
Manager, Human Resources: Sam Campbell
Director, QA Assurance: J B MacDonald
Steelmaking: Brian Musgrave

## 750 MANUFACTURERS/Permanent way components, equipment and services

Manager, Rolling Mills: M Morrison
Director, Commercial Services: Y Williams

**Products**
A major supplier to Canadian railways and world markets of various steel rail sections.

Sydney Steel manufactures steel rails to major national and international specifications, including AREA, ASTM, BS, CNR, CPR, ISO and UIC. Sydney Steel produces premium wear-resistant head-hardened rails, standard carbon, intermediate strength and premium alloy grades, all using clean steel practice. Sections range from 45 to 70 kg/m. Rail lengths can be produced up to 26 m.

## System Bahnbau International (SBI)

Bessemerstrasse 42b, D-12103 Berlin, Germany
Tel: (+49 30) 75 48 73 78   Fax: (+49 30) 75 48 73 79
e-mail: wolf@sbi-ffc.de

**Key personnel**
Technical Managing Director: Wolf-Dietrich Rommel
Commercial Managing Director: Roland Österlein
Head of Technical Department: Günther Wolf

**Associate company**
System-Bahnbau International
Brunnenstrasse 36, D-74504 Crailshelm, Germany
Tel: (+49 79) 332 43   Fax: (+49 79) 332 60

**Corporate development**
SBI is a joint venture between Leonard Weiss GmbH & Co and ILBAU Deutschland GmbH.

**Products and services**
Construction of Feste Fahrbahn Crailsheim system ballastless track in the variations: 3.2 m wide for high-speed traffic; 2.4 m wide for conventional rail applications; and a Low Cost Track (LCT) option for speeds of up to 120 km/h. Contracts include the Hannover-Berlin high-speed line (two sections of 17 and 580 km); 4 km of urban track in Munich; and 3 km of urban track in Stuttgart.

## Tarmac

Tarmac Precast Concrete Ltd
Tallington, Stamford PE9 4RL, UK
Tel: (+44 1778) 38 10 00   Fax: (+44 1778) 34 80 41

**Key personnel**
Managing Director: M J Saunders
Technical Director: Dr H P J Taylor
Commercial Director: N D Claxton
Commercial Manager, Rail: A B Moore
UK Sales Manager, Rail: Ian Coates

**Principal subsidiaries**
RCC
Charcon Tunnels
S G Baldwin Ltd

*Tarmac Bomac polymer concrete and reinforced concrete level crossing system*   0021671

*Tectran 25-seat road/rail personnel carrier*   0006307

**Products**
Precast products for the rail industry (BSI approved). The product range includes sleepers, bearers, Bomac polymer concrete and reinforced concrete level crossing systems, cable troughs and other bespoke products. To maintain its position in the market place, Tarmac Precast Concrete is offering technical support and licence agreement for indigenous companies.

Recent contracts include supply of products for the UK Rail Industry, London Underground (tunnel and ballasted track) and supply of prestressed concrete monobloc sleepers to SNCB Belgium.

## Technirail

Rue Ravenstein 60, B 6, B-1000 Brussels, Belgium
Tel: (+32 2) 540 90 40   Fax: (+32 2) 502 09 14

**Corporate development**
Technirail combines the resources of Transurb Consult and Belgian National Railways (SNCB).

**Services**
Services provided by Technirail include: track construction, renewal and maintenance; supply of long welded rail; manufacture of switches and crossings; procurement agency services for infrastructure materials.

## Tectran

Tecnologia em Transporte
Rodovia Presidente Dutra, Km 155/156
São José dos Campos SP CEP 12240-420, Brazil
Tel: (+55 12) 331 82 00
Fax: (+55 12) 322 94 40; 321 18 20

**Products**
Road/rail vehicles including personnel carriers for up to 25 passengers, cranes and tractors.

## Tempered Spring

Tempered Spring Co
Park Works, Foley Street, Sheffield S4 7WS, UK
Tel: (+44 1742) 72 00 31   Fax: (+44 1742) 73 14 13
A unit of T & N plc

**Key personnel**
Sales Manager: M L Martin

**Products**
Elastic rail fastenings, including BTREC system and CS-Springlock for concrete sleepers, KTG for K-type baseplates and KT for switches and crossings.

## Templeton

Templeton, Kenly & Co Inc
2525 Gardner Road, Broadview, Illinois 60153, USA
Tel: (+1 708) 865 15 00   Fax: (+1 708) 865 08 94

**Key personnel**
President and Chief Executive Officer:
Robert Spath
Vice-President, Sales and Marketing: Tom Danza

**Products**
Mechanical trip/track jacks; hydraulic rail puller and expanders; hydraulic rerailing system; portable air/hydraulic jacks for car shop maintenance; hydraulic track jack.

## Tensol Rail

Tensol Rail SA
CH-6776 Piotta, Switzerland
Tel: (+41 91) 873 66 11   Fax: (+41 91) 873 66 10
e-mail: tensolrail@tensolrail.com
Web: http://www.tensolrail.com

**Sales office**
Tensol Rail SA, Glutschbachstrasse 49, CH-3661 Uetendorf
Tel: (+41 33) 346 50 28   Fax: (+41 33) 346 50 29

**Key personnel**
Manager, Railway Maintenance: J Marfurt

**Corporate background**
Tensol Rail is a member of the TrackNet Holding group.

Permanent way components, equipment and services/**MANUFACTURERS**

## Products
Rail fastenings, points, crossings; racks and rack turnouts for cog-wheel railways; turnouts; turntables and transfer tables.

Rail welding and grinding and permanent way equipment.

*UPDATED*

---

## Thebra

Thebra do Brasil
Rua Antonio Austregesilo 360, Rio de Janeiro GB, Brazil
Tel: (+55 21) 28 04 73; 260 42 34

### Products
Aluminothermic in-track welding equipment and rail grinders.

---

## Thermit Australia Pty

170 Somersby Falls Road, Somersby, New South Wales
Australia 2250
Tel: (+61 2) 43 40 49 88   Fax: (+61 2) 43 40 40 04
e-mail: thermit@ozemail.com.au

### Key personnel
Managing Director: Ron Moller
Commercial Manager: Malcolm Beckwith
Marketing Manager: Bryan Pieper
Services Manager: David Harnot

### Subsidiary company
Rail Track Maintenance, New Zealand

### Products
Thermit brand welding materials; hydraulic rail shears; rail weld grinders; glued and mechanical insulated rail joints; training of Thermit welders; removable level crossing systems; Kryorit ballast stabilisation; waterproof bridge membranes.

Recent contracts include welding on the Taipei and Bangkok mass transit systems.

---

## Thermit Welding (GB) Ltd

87 Ferry Lane, Rainham RM13 9YH, UK
Tel: (+44 1708) 52 26 26   Fax: (+44 1708) 55 38 06
e-mail: thermitwelding@demon.co.uk

### Key personnel
General Manager, Technical Sales: R S Johnson
General Manager, Operations: T C Clifton

### Principal subsidiary
Thermitrex (Pty) Ltd, Boksburg, South Africa

### Products
Aluminothermic rail welding products, training and inspection; insulated rail joints; ballast stabilisation.

Recent contracts include Hong Kong Lantau Airport Railway; Heathrow Express; Jubilee Line Extension; Kuala Lumpur LRT and Midland Metro and Croydon Tramlink.

---

## Thermon Manufacturing Co

Commercial Products Division
100 Thermon Drive, PO Box 609, San Marcos, Texas 78667-0609, USA
Tel: (+1 512) 396 58 01   Fax: (+1 512) 754 24 31

### Key personnel
President and Chief Executive Officer: Mark Burdick
Support Services Manager: Sandra Michaewicz

### Worldwide offices
Thermon UK Ltd
Seventh Avenue, Gateshead Tyne and Wear NE11 0JW, UK
Tel: (+44191) 499 49 00

Thermon France
18 rue du Marais, Montreuil F-93100, France
Tel: (+33 1) 48 70 42 90

Thermon Deutschland
Raiffeisenstrasse 45, Olpe D-57462, Germany
Tel: (+49 2761) 938 30

Thermon Far East
3rd Floor, Recruit Yokohama Building, Yokohama 221-0056, Japan
Tel: (+81 45) 461 03 73

Vorkauf Sociedad Anónima, Commandante Franco, 3 Madrid E-28016, Spain
Tel: (+34 91) 359 17 12

### Products
Heat tracing systems for rail infrastructure applications, including: third rail heating systems; point heating systems; including rail web and switch rod heaters; heating systems for people mover and rapid transit guideways; light rail vehicle pantograph heaters; heating systems for station platform surfaces; heating systems for depots and fuelling and servicing installations.

*NEW ENTRY*

---

## Thims

Kvarnen Varetop, SE-360 40 Rottne, Sweden
Tel: (+46 708) 89 65 65   Fax: (+46 470) 966 65
e-mail: thim.s@telia.com

### Main works
Växjö

### Key personnel
Managing Director: Stig Thim

### Products
Prestressed concrete sleepers for main lines and turnouts; prefabricated grade crossings; production equipment and technical services for the manufacture and design of concrete sleepers.

---

## Thyssen Krupp

Thyssen Krupp Gleistechnik GmbH
Altendorfer Strasse 104, D-45143 Essen, Germany
Tel: (+49 201) 188 37 10   Fax: (+49 201) 188 37 14

### Works
Kaiser-Wilhelm-Strasse 100, D-47166 Duisburg, Germany
Tel: (+49 203) 524 06 20   Fax: (+49 203) 522 46 94

### Products
Rails, flat-bottom rails, grooved rails, crane rails, light-railway rails, conductor rails, special rail sections, rails for points and crossings; sleepers, steel sleepers, Y-steel sleepers, concrete sleepers, wooden sleepers, sleepers for points and crossings; trackage/points, points, standard and narrow gauge, points accessories, points replacement parts, crossings, standard and narrow gauge, complete points installations, complete track installation; rail fastening material, ribbed base plates, sole plates, flat plates, fishplates and fishbolts, insulated fishplates, screws and bolts for fastenings, clips, spring washers, elastic fasteners; rail fastening systems, MX-rail fastening system, Krupp Elastic Compact Fastener; special systems, slab track, systems for stations and tunnels, cable ducts DRAE-KA/AU-KA, noise control system; used railway equipment, rails, sleepers, points, buffer stops; technical consulting, planning and engineering; track and points installations, product treatments (bending, sawing and welding of rails), stockkeeping, logistics, maintenance.

---

## Tiefenbach GmbH

PO Box 911320, D-45538 Sprockhoevel, Germany
Tel: (+49 2324) 70 52 03   Fax: (+49 2324) 70 51 14
e-mail: info@tiefenbach.de
Web: http://www.tiefenbach.de

### Key personnel
Managing Director: Peter Jochums
Sales and Technical Manager: Juergen Burghoff
Export Sales Manager (Contracts): Stefan Peiser

### Corporate development
Tiefenbach is a member of the Hauhinco Group.

### Products
Point control equipment: complete control equipment for automation and signalling of depots and marshalling yards; axle counter systems; track vacancy detection and level crossing switching with axle counter systems based on Tiefenbach's double wheel sensor.

### Contracts
Complete systems design and supply of depot signalling works at Cottbus (DB AG), Cologne (DB AG), Antwerp (SNCB), marshalling yard control and signalling works at Kassel (DB AG), Hamm (DB AG), Gdansk, Poland; complete systems design and supply of axle counter systems for SOB-Sudostbahn, Switzerland (main line); AKN Eisenbahn AG suburban feeder service at Hamburg, Germany.

---

## Tiflex Ltd

Tiflex House, Liskeard, PL14 4NB, UK
Tel: (+44 1579) 32 08 08   Fax: (+44 1579) 32 08 02
e-mail: trackelast@tiflex.co.uk
Web: http://www.tiflex.co.uk

### Key personnel
Managing Director: N Spearman
Sales and Marketing Director: P V Stiles
Product Specialist: T R Smith

### Products
Rail pads, baseplate pads, undersleeper pads, ballast mats, floating slab track bearings, anti-vibration track support materials.

Contracts include the supply of trackform bearings for the Tsing Ma Bridge, Hong Kong, floating slab track bearings for the Jubilee Line Extension, London, undersleeper pads for the Sabadell tunnel in Spain and anti-vibration materials for the refurbishment of the Bucharest metro.

*UPDATED*

---

## Tipco Inc

1 Coventry Road, Bramalea, Ontario L6T 4B1, Canada
Tel: (+1 905) 791 98 11   Fax: (+1 905) 791 49 17
Web: http://www.tipcopunch.com

### Key personnel
President: John Ferrone
Manager, Track Bit Department: B Crichton

### Products
Flat beaded track bits.

*UPDATED*

---

## TKL Rail

Thompsons, Kelly & Lewis Pty Ltd
26 Faigh Street, Mulgrave, Victoria 3170, Australia
Tel: (+61 3) 95 62 07 44   Fax: (+61 3) 95 62 28 16

*Thyssen Krupp Y-steel sleeper system*   2001/0105890

## MANUFACTURERS/Permanent way components, equipment and services

**Works**
5 Parker Street, Castlemaine, Victoria 3450, Australia

**Key personnel**
Sales Manager, Railway Products: E A Smith
Manager, Railway Products: W G Kinscher
Manager, Sales and Marketing: A Grage
General Manager: W J Coulter

**Principal subsidiary**
Davies & Baird

**Products**
Trackwork, turnouts, points and crossings, switches; steel turnout sleepers, insulated/non-insulated; and a range of accessories.

Contracts include the supply of tramway trackwork for Hong Kong; crossings for MTRC, Hong Kong; turnouts for the Jabotabek track layout improvement project, Indonesia; turnouts for State Railway Authority of New South Wales, Australia; and points and crossings for Westrail and Victoria Public Transport Corporation, Australia; turnouts for the Sydney LRT system, turnouts for BHP Iron Ore Nelson Point yard and Jimblebar mine, Australia; five-year contract for tramway trackwork for Toronto Canada and turnouts for the State Railway of Thailand Track Rehabilitation Project, Phases 1 and 2; turnouts for upgrading the Forrestfield Yard, Perth, Australia; turnouts for upgrading the Mount Isa line, Queensland, Australia.

---

## Tokimec

Tokimec Inc
2-16 Minami Kamata, Ota-ku, Tokyo 144-8551, Japan
Tel: (+81 3) 37 32 21 11   Fax: (+81 3) 37 36 02 61
Web: http://www.tokimec.co.jp

**Key personnel**
Director and Division Manager: Sodao Fukai
General Sales Manager: Katsuo Saji

**Principal subsidiary**
Tokimec Hong Kong Ltd
Room 903, One Hysan Avenue, Causeway Bay, Hong Kong
Tel: (+852) 28 81 66 79   Fax: (+852) 28 90 55 09

**Products**
Ultra-sonic flaw detectors, Models SM-101, SM-1, UM and SM series; portable rail flaw detectors, PRD series and ultra-sonic thickness meters, Models UTM 101/201 and UTM-1. The company has also supplied an ultra-sonic rail flaw detector car with rail damage detection systems to each JR company and to several private railway companies.

---

## Trinity Difco Inc

PO Box 238, Findlay, Ohio 45839, USA
Tel: (+1 419) 422 05 25   Fax: (+1 419) 422 12 75

**Key personnel**
See entry in *Freight vehicles and equipment* section.

**Products**
Rolling stock for permanent way construction and maintenance duties including air-operated side-dump wagons; air-operated drop-end side-dump wagons; and Ballaster and Auto-Ballaster systems.

The Auto-Ballaster system provides automated ballasting using remote valves located at one end of the wagon to control the gate operation. Radio remote controls are available as an option. Ballast flow, which is adjustable, can be directed to the centre or either side of the track. Power comes from the locomotive air compressor; a separate line provides air to each car in the train. The gates, which open and close with enough power to shear limestone ballast, are made of heavy-steel plates with a shape and motion that tends to push the ballast back into the wagon when closing. The gates can also be operated manually.

---

## True Temper

True Temper Railway Appliances
2081 Bloomingdale Road, Glendal Heights, Illinois 60139-2183, USA
Tel: (+1 941) 627 57 18   Fax: (+1 941) 627 86 99

**Works**
6800 St John Avenue, Kansas City, Missouri 64123, USA

**Key personnel**
President: P J Cunningham
Vice-President, Controller: P A Likus
Vice-President, General Manager, Sales: J A Schebo

**Corporate development**
True Temper is a division of Progress Rail Services Corporation.

**Products**
Channeloc rail anchors for wooden sleepers; Cliploc concrete sleeper fasteners.

---

## TSO

Travaux du Sud-Ouest SA
Chemin du Corps de Garde, Zone Industrielle, PO Box 8, F-77501 Chelles Cedex, France
Tel: (+33 1) 64 72 72 00   Fax: (+33 1) 64 26 30 23
e-mail: info@tso.com

**Key personnel**
President of the Executive Board: Emmanuèle Perron
Export Manager: Claude Petit
Manager, France: Christian Boscher
Equipment: Jean-Marie Delpy

**Products**
Track construction and maintenance for railways, rail transit authorities, light rail and tram systems and private sidings. Contracts include: TGV tracklaying for French Railways; ballastless tracklaying for the Channel Tunnel; dual-gauge track construction for the Jamuna rail link in Bangladesh; track construction for the Orléans light rail system.

---

## Tülomsas

The Locomotive and Motor Corporation of Turkey
Ahmet Kanatli Cad, TR-26490 Eskisehir, Turkey
Tel: (+90 222) 224 00 00
Fax: (+90 222) 225 57 57; 72 72
e-mail: tulomsas@tulomsas.com.tr
Web: http://www.tulomsas.com.tr

**Key personnel**
Managing Director: D Zeki Daloglu
Assistant General Managers: Galip Pala, Cengiz Özan, Fatih Turan, Haluk Akova
Head of Marketing: Erol Çetin

**Products**
Diesel-hydraulic and diesel-electric shunting and main line locomotives (545 to 1,790 kW); electric locomotives (3,200 kW); special purpose freight wagons including tank wagons, refrigerated hopper wagons and wagons for ore transport, tracked tanks and containers; diesel engines with outputs of 1,865, 2,200 and 2,400 hp; traction motors, motor generator sets, control equipment for electric locomotives, maintenance and repair work; bogies for locomotives and freight wagons; self-propelled rail vehicles for infrastructure maintenance including car equipped with hydraulic crane, catenary maintenance and inspection car.

---

## Türk + Hillinger GmbH

PO Box 242, D-78503 Tuttlingen, Germany
Tel: (+49 7461) 701 40   Fax: (+49 7461) 70 14 10

**Key personnel**
President: Erich Hillinger
Managing Director: Eberhard Härter

**Principal subsidiaries**
Türk + Hillinger GmbH
Dorotheenstrasse 22, D-9102 Limbach/Oberfrohna, Germany
Tel: (+49 3722) 718 90   Fax: (+49 3722) 71 89 16

Türk + Hillinger Hungaria Kft
Arany J u 2, H-3350 Kal, Hungary
Tel: (+36 36) 48 70 53   Fax: (+36 36) 48 70 53

**Products**
Electric point-heating systems: these consist of flat, tubular heaters with a chrome-nickel- steel connection housing or a complete watertight connecting cable. All clamps and springs for installation at different rail profiles are available.

Contracts include the supply of point heaters for DB AG, SBB and SNCF.

---

## Turkington Precast Concrete

James Park, Mahon Road, Portadown BT62 3EH, County Armagh, Northern Ireland
Tel: (+44 0283) 833 28 07   Fax: (+44 0283) 836 17 79
e-mail: info@turkington-precast.com

**Key personnel**
Managing Director: Jim McKeag
Executive Director: Trevor Turkington
Sales and Marketing Manager-Precast: David Hamilton

**Products**
Prestressed concrete railway sleepers.

Contracts: supplier to Northern Ireland Railways and Iarnrod Eireann in Ireland, approved supplier to Railtrack.

*UPDATED*

---

## Two-Way Technology Ltd

Unit 4B Barham Road, Forties Campus, Rosyth Europarc, Dunfermline KY11 2XB, UK
Tel: (+44 1383) 41 04 00   Fax: (+44 1383) 42 00 02
e-mail: sales@two-way.co.uk

**Key personnel**
Managing Director: Eric Pryde
Technical Sales Director: Mick Rice
Sales and Marketing Director: Brian Lang

**Products**
Road-rail vehicles for infrastructure maintenance work based on the Mercedes-Benz range of Unimog road vehicles. The latest product is based on the 130 kW Unimog U400, equipped with a centre chassis-mounted hydraulic turntable and a 350 kg access module mounted on a subframe and provided with four stabiliser legs. Rail guidance is via twin articulated 144 mm diameter guide wheels and the vehicle is fitted with rail-use tyres. Gross weight is 11.99 t.

---

## Ultra Dynamics

Upperfield Road, Kingsditch Trading Estate, Cheltenham GL51 9NY, UK
Tel: (+44 1242) 70 79 00   Fax: (+44 1242) 70 79 01
e-mail: sales@ultradynamics.demon.co.uk

**Key personnel**
See entry in *Freight vehicles and equipment*.

**Products**
Spring frog switch dampers for controlling the return of the wing rail on spring frogs. The high-performance and heavy-duty design has applications for both original switch manufacturers and main line retrofit purposes.

The dampers are supplied with fasteners for easy replacement and are double-sealed with low-friction seals with high-speed high-pressure rating.

*VERIFIED*

## UniTrac Systems Product Group – IMPulse NC Inc

PO Box 889, 100 Impulse Way, Mount Olive, North Carolina 28365, USA
Tel: (+1 919) 658 22 00   Fax: (+1 919) 658 22 68
e-mail: Unitrac@mindspring.com

**Key personnel**
UniTrac Systems Product Group
Director of Marketing: Bernard Campbell
Director of Engineering: Kenneth Fitzgibbon
Mechanical Engineering Support: Paul Singla

**Products**
Switch point and third rail heater controls; Calrod heater elements; electric switch machines and controls; overhead electrification equipment for LRT systems.

Recent contracts include the supply of equipment for: Bi-State, St Louis (St Clair County extension); NYCTA (White Plains); Muni, San Francisco (Mid Embarcadero); MVRTA, Dayton (Townview extension); and MBTA Boston (Old Colony & Newburyport).

## Unit Rail Anchor Company Inc

2604 Industrial Street, Atchison, Kansas 66002, USA
Tel: (+1 913) 367 72 00   Fax: (+1 913) 367 05 59
Web: http://www.unitrail.com

**Key personnel**
President: Paul T Ciolino
International Sales: Carol Hale

**Products**
Unit rail anchors, spring and drive-on; reclamation and remanufacture of rail anchors; E-Z Wrench spring anchor applicator tool.

## Upright UK Ltd

Special Products Division, 153 Newton Road, Lowton, Warrington WA3 1EZ, UK
Tel: (+44 1942) 68 01 60   Fax: (+44 1942) 60 19 84
e-mail: specials@upright.co.uk

**Key personnel**
Manager: David Tilsley-Curtis

**Products**
Rail-mounted alloy and glass fibre access towers, carriage roof mobile access and guard-rail systems, alloy pit bridging boards, carriage access steps.

Maintenance platforms have been supplied to the Arlandabanan, Stockholm and to Old Oak Common, London, for Heathrow Express.

## VAE Aktiengesellschaft

Rotenturmstrasse 5-9, A-1010 Vienna, Austria
Tel: (+43 1) 53 11 80   Fax: (+43 1) 53 11 82 22
e-mail: marketing@vae.co.at

**Key personnel**
Board Member, Engineering, Sales, Marketing:
  Josef Mülner
Board Member, Finance Controlling, Internationalisation:
  Mohamed Kaddoura

**Principal subsidiaries**
VAE Eisenbahnsystem & GmbH, Austria
Welchenwerk Wörth GmbH, Austria
VAE Railway Systems Pty Ltd, Australia
VAE Nortrak Ltd, Canada
VAE Nortrak Inc, USA
VAE Nortrak Cheyenne Inc, USA
VAMAV Vasúti Berendezések Kft, Hungary
VAE Riga SIA, Latvia
UAB VAE Legetecha, Lithuania
HBW Light Rail BV, Netherlands
JEZ Sistemas Ferroviarios SL, Spain
Transwerk Perway (Pty) Ltd, South Africa
VAE Africa (Pty) Ltd, South Africa
VAE UK Ltd, UK

VAE Italia Srl, Italy
VAE Sofia OOD, Bulgaria
VAE Apcarom SA, Romania
BWG, Gesellschaft mbH & Co KG, Germany

**Products**
Turnouts and turnout components, crossings, fastening materials, steel sleepers, ballastless track system with plastic sleepers (Zeltweg patent), cast crossings (also welded, Zeltweg patent); VAE Roadmaster 2000 turnout monitoring system; 1S 2000 non-contact monitoring system for tongues; Hydrolink/Hydrostar hydraulic setting devices, HOA/FOA hot box/blocked brake detector.

*UPDATED*

## VAE Nortrak

16160 River Road, Richmond, British Columbia V6V 1L6, Canada
Tel: (+1 604) 273 30 30   Fax: (+1 604) 273 89 27

**Key personnel**
President: Al Tuningley
Chief Financial Officer: Eduard Peinhopf

**Subsidiary company**
VAE Nortrak Cheyenne Inc
1740 Pacific Avenue, Cheyenne, Wyoming 82007-1004, USA
Tel: (+1 307) 778 87 00   Fax: (+1 307) 778 87 77
Vice-President, Sales and Marketing: Gord Weatherly

**Products**
Supply and manufacture of track materials including RBM, SSGM, welded heel manganese frogs, welded spring manganese frogs, jointless and boltless manganese frogs, movable point frogs and vario frogs; AREA and asymmetrical switches, guardrails, transition rails and related components; new relay rail, crane rail, tie plates and joint bars; screwspikes, cut spikes, track-bolts, frog and switch-bolts; track tools. Contract design and engineering services.

*UPDATED*

## VAE UK Ltd

Sir Harry Lauder Road, Portobello, Edinburgh EH15 1DJ, UK
Tel: (+44 131) 550 20 79   Fax: (+44 131) 550 26 60
e-mail: vaeuk@compuserve.com

**Corporate background**
VAE UK is a member of the VAE group of companies.

**Products**
Switch and crossing systems, including trackwork to Railtrack's RT60 specification.

*NEW ENTRY*

## Vaia Car

Via Isorella 24, I-25012 Calvisano (BS), Italy
Tel: (+39 030) 968 62 61   Fax: (+39 030) 968 67 00
e-mail: vaiacar@vaiacar.it
Web: http://www.vaiacar.it

**Products**
Permanent way maintenance equipment, including: road-rail mobile flash butt welders, cranes, excavators and radio-controlled tractive units; cranes; rail, switch, track panel and sleeper handling equipment; tampers; sleeper replacement equipment.

*NEW ENTRY*

## Voest Alpine Schienen

Kerpelystrasse 199, A-8704 Leoben/Donawitz, Austria
Tel: (+43 3842) 202 42 11   Tel: (+43 3842) 254 21
e-mail: sales@va.schienen.at
Web: http://www.va.schienen.at

**Subsidiary company**
Voest Alpine Klöckner Bahntechnik GmbH
Alboinstrasse 96-110, D-12103 Berlin, Germany
Tel: (+49 30) 75 48 40   Fax: (+49 30) 75 48 41 68
e-mail: max.jaeger@kloeckner.de

**Products and services**
Rail products: unwelded rail in lengths of up to 120 m, also produced in mill heat-treated quality; Dobain-grade bainitic rail; mill heat-treated quality bullhead rail; Vignoles rail; pointwork.

Rail Putler handling system for welded and unwelded (up to 120 m in length) rail. The system can be mounted on conventional two-axle flat wagons.

Logistics solutions, including just-in-time delivery to site and unloading of rail products.

## Vortok International

63 Station Road, Addlestone KT15 2AR, UK
Tel: (+44 1932) 82 88 12   Fax: (+44 1932) 82 86 91
e-mail: sales@vortok.co.uk
Web: http://www.vortok.demon.co.uk

**Works**
Units 6-7 Haxter Close, Belliver Industrial Estate, Roborough, Plymouth PL6 7DD, UK

**Key personnel**
Director and General Manager: J R Byles
Technical Director: P Shrubsall

**Principal subsidiary**
Multiclip Company Ltd

*Vortok Universal rigid safety barrier (Jarvis Rail)*

# 754 MANUFACTURERS/Permanent way components, equipment and services

### Products

Permanent way maintenance equipment and components, including: the Vortok Coil, for the rehabilitation of loose screws in wood sleepers; temporary sign board supports for securely and safely placing signs near the rail without ballast penetration; clip-on insulators for the prevention of track circuit signal failure by items passing under both rails; insulated block joint trimmers, portable and self-powered grinders for deburring rail ends at block joints; VERSE, a non-destructive method of measuring stress-free rail temperature; adjustable block spacers, enabling worn check block to be moved without removal from the track; and rigid safety barriers, fitted to the foot of the adjacent open line to enable green zone working at higher train speeds.

Vortok is a supplier to most European railway companies.

## Vossloh Rail Systems GmbH

Vosslohstrasse 4, D-58791 Werdohl, Germany
Tel: (+49 2392) 520   Fax: (+49 2392) 523 75
e-mail: vrs@vrsw.vossloh.com
Web: http://www.vossloh-rail-systems.de

### Key personnel
Managing Director: Ulrich Rieger
Sales Manager: F G Heisler
Regional Sales Managers: J Spors
   Winfried Bösterling
Technical Sales: Dipl Ing Dirk Vorderbrück
Overseas Business Office, Regional Sales Managers,
   Düsseldorf: J Spors; D Pfeiffer

### Works
Vossloh Werdohl GmbH
Vosslohstrasse 4, D-58791, Werdohl
Overseas business office, Düsseldorf
Tel: (+49 2102) 490 90   Fax: (+49 2102) 490 94

### Products
Rail fastening systems for concrete, timber and steel sleepers on ballasted and slab track; directly fixed rail fastenings; sleeper anchors for lateral track stabilisation; rehabilitation systems; noise reduction systems and vibration damping; absorption track mats and web cushioning.

*UPDATED*

## Wabtec Rail Ltd

PO Box 192, Hexthorpe Road, Doncaster DN1 1PJ, UK
Tel: (+44 1302) 79 00 27; 34 07 00
Fax: (+44 1302) 79 00 58; 34 06 93
e-mail: probinson@wabtec.com
Web: http://www.wabtec.com

### Key personnel
See entry in *Locomotives and powered/non-powered passenger vehicles* section.

### Corporate development
Wabtec Rail formerly traded as RFS(E), changing its name in March 2000.

### Products
Special wagons for rail maintenance and construction.
Recent contracts include the design and manufacture of 30 sleeper-carrying wagons for Jarvis and refurbishment of 22 snow-ploughs for Railtrack.

## Wacker (GB) Ltd

Lea Road, Waltham Cross, Hertfordshire EN9 1AW, UK
Tel: (+44 1992) 70 72 00   Fax: (+44 1992) 70 72 01
Web: wacker-machinery.co.uk

### Key personnel
Sales Manager: Andrew Howells

### Products
Petrol-powered tie tamper with remote ignition cut-out system; triple-plate ballast compaction set, comprising three vibrating plates, allowing single passes covering the full width of the track bed up to 2.6 m.

Contracts include supply of Wacker machines to railway operators in Europe.

*Wacker tie tamper*   0021672

## Walter Bau-Aktiengesellschaft

PO Box 102547, Böeheimstrasse 8, D-86153 Augsburg, Germany
Tel: (+49 821) 55 82 00   Fax: (+49 821) 558 23 20
e-mail: walterbau.na@augustanet.de
Web: http://www.walter-bau.de

### Key personnel
Director, International Division: Martin Lommatzsch
Head of Department, Railway Construction and Prestressed Concrete Sleepers: Lothar Geiger

### Products and services
Underground works including metros; bridge construction. Prestressed concrete (monobloc) sleepers suitable for any gauge and for any type of rail fastening.

## Leonhard Weiss GmbH and Co KG

Fabrikstrasse 40, D-73037 Geoppingen, Germany
Tel: (+49 7161) 60 22 96   Fax: (+49 7161) 60 24 18
e-mail: gleisbau@leonhard-weiss.de
Web: http://www.leonhard-weiss.de

### Key personnel
Executive Vice-President, Track Construction:
   Ulrich Weiss

### Products and services
Among other products and services within Leonhard Weiss GmbH and Co the Track Construction department offers a track reconstruction and maintenance programme.

It offers track renewal trains for wood, steel and concrete sleepers, track and bridge construction cranes, computerised track survey systems, tampers and similar equipment on a turnkey rental or lease-to-own basis.

The product and services range also includes the laying of concrete and permanent slab track for commuter, urban and high-speed applications as well as an on-site continuous soil conditioner and tamping system for up to 3 m working depth. All the above can include on-site training and knowledge transfer.

*UPDATED*

*Kirow track-laying crane used by Leonhard Weiss GmbH & Co*   2002/0524953

*Wabtec refurbished snow-plough for Railtrack*   0064330

## Western-Cullen-Hayes Inc

2700 West 36th Place, Chicago, Illinois 60632-1682, USA
Tel: (+1 773) 254 96 00   Fax: (+1 773) 254 11 10
e-mail: wch@wch.com
Web: http://www.wch.com

**Key personnel**
See entry in *Signalling and communications systems* section.

**Principal subsidiary**
Hayes Plant Western-Cullen-Hayes Inc
120 North 3rd Street, Box 756, Richmond, Indiana 47374, USA

**Products**
Railway safety track appliances; bumping posts, fixed, sliding and hydraulic; wheel stops and chocks; switch point guards; yard switch machines; WCHT-72 programmable and Solar Tech switch machines; track drills; rail benders; rail tongs; journal and hydraulic jacks; sliding, hinged and portable derails; derail operators; Eldo, DeLectric and solar-powered derail operators; blue flags; and other custom-designed equipment for railway and industrial applications.

## Wieland

Wieland Lufttechnik GmbH
PO Box 3669, D-91024 Erlangen, Germany
Tel: (+49 9131) 606 70   Fax: (+49 9131) 60 44 01

**Key personnel**
Product Manager: Thomas Fenzel

**Products**
ExcaVac attachment for hydraulic excavators and vehicle-mounted loading booms, suitable for ballast removal, refuse collection and light excavation.

## Willy Vogel AG

Motzener Strasse 35137, D-1227 Berlin, Germany
Tel: (+49 30) 72 00 20   Fax: (+49 30) 72 00 21 11
e-mail: info@vogel-berlin.de
Web: http://www.vogelag.com

**Key personnel**
Director International Sales: Vincent F Warnecke
Press, Marketing: Gotz Mehr
Tel: (+49 30) 72 00 21 09   Fax: (+49 30) 72 00 23 49
e-mail: mehr@vogel-berlin.de

**Main subsidiaries**
VOGEL fluidtec GmbH, Hockenheim, Germany
VOGEL JAPAN LTD, Osaka, Japan
VOGEL LUBRICATION, INC, Newport News, Virginia, USA
VOGEL NEDERLAND BV, Enschede, the Netherlands
WILLY VOGEL BELGIUM BVBA, Kampenhout, Belgium
WILLY VOGEL IBERICA, SA, Spain
VOGEL Ltd, Kenilworth, UK
BERGER VOGEL srl, Milan, Italy
VOGEL MECAFLUID SA, Saumur, France
WILLY VOGEL HUNGARIA Jármütechnika Kft, Budapest, Hungary

**Products**
Wheel flange lubrication systems for rail vehicles.

## Windhoff AG

PO Box 1963, D-48409 Rheine, Germany
Tel: (+49 5971) 580   Fax: (+49 5971) 582 09
e-mail: info@windhoff.de
Web: http://www.windhoff.de

**Key personnel**
Board Members: Dipl Ing Heinz Lörfing, Dr Udo Meyke, Dipl Ing Klaus Muller, Dipl Ing Christoph Wessels
Managers: Dipl Ing Günter Knieper, Dipl Ing Franz-Josef Cramer, Dipl Ing Helmut Pühs, Dipl Ing Peter Ahlers, Dipl Ing Frank Prange, Dipl Ing Martin Limmenschmidt

**Products**
Repair, installation and maintenance vehicles, multipurpose track maintenance machinery with a wide range of attachments, such as tamping units, sleeper changing units and shrub cutters.

The BR 711 catenary maintenance vehicle is built for DB AG (German Railways). It has a six-cylinder diesel engine and a maximum speed of 120 km/h, working platforms, a hydraulically adjustable catenary and messenger wire unit for precise positioning, a video recording facility, a measuring pantograph assessing catenary height and stagger, an automatically operated earthing isolation switch, an observation seat for inspection of catenary and the measuring pantograph, two driver cabins – front and back – with all control and monitoring equipment, and a workshop area with work bench and high-capacity storage facilities as well as a spacious social room for the operating team, with kitchen and sanitary facilities.

Railtrack is taking delivery of 25 MPVs during 2000/2001 for weedspraying, jetting and de-icing duties. They are based on the CargoSprinter design supplied to DB, Germany and Socofer, France and are powered by two Volvo Penta DH10A-360 265 kW diesel engines, driving through a Volvo Powertronic five-speed automatic gearbox. The length of both vehicles over buffers is 20.2 m and they are fitted with snow-ploughs. Train protection Warning System and GPS tracking is fitted. The driving vehicle weighs 50.72 t and the driving trailer weighs 31.6 t. Modules are provided for water jetting, de-icing, Sandite laying, auxiliary power, messing (sink, seats, cooking), weedspray and an insulated water tank. It is not possible to spray if the vehicle is running below a certain speed and safety requirements insist on personnel being in the driving cabs of mess module when the vehicle is in motion.

## Yamatech

Yamakazi Gear Industry Co
674 Toda, Atsugi, Kanagawa 243-0023, Japan
Tel: (+81 462) 28 22 39   Fax: (+81 462) 29 18 90

**Key personnel**
President: Kiyomizu Yamazaki
Director: Toshio Kikuchi
Sales General Manager: Minoru Saito

**Products**
Rail cutters, drills, flow grinders, bolting machines, spike drivers/pullers, gears, conveyors.
Contracts include supply of maintenance equipment to JR East.

## Yamato Kogyo

Yamato Kogyo Co Ltd
380 Kibi Otsu-ku, Himeji, Hyogo Pref, Japan
Tel: (+81 792) 73 10 61

**Key personnel**
Manager: S Ichimura

**Products**
Rail, sleeper plates, fishplates, standard and special turnouts, welded frogs, expansion joints, glued insulated joints, rack rail and steel sleepers.

## Zöllner GmbH

Signal System Technologies
Zur Fähre 1, D-24143 Kiel, Germany
Tel: (+49 431) 702 71 11   Fax: (+49 431) 702 72 02
e-mail: signal@zoellner.de
Web: http://www.zoellner.de

**Key personnel**
General Manager, Operations: Ulrich Matthieson

**Products**
ATWS Autoprowa radio-based warning systems for protecting personnel on track worksites. The modular system typically comprises an SSE2 main control unit, radio remote controls, Type WGL flashing lamp, Type WGH horn, F 300 treadle rail contacts for train detection, and cables and cable remote controls. The system can be configured for bidirectional operation on two tracks. The WGH horn system measures ambient noise levels and adjusts the warning volume level appropriately. An independent rechargeable battery provides power for the system.

Zöllner also produces the Autoprowa Light ZAL warning system for spot worksites. In addition, the company provides inspection and training services related to its systems.

*NEW ENTRY*

## Zweiweg Schneider GmbH & Co KG

Oberbüscherhof, D-42799 Leichlingen, Germany
Tel: (+49 2174) 790 95   Fax: (+49 2174) 79 09 70
e-mail: info@zweiweg.de
Web: http://www.zweiweg.com

**Key personnel**
See entry in *Freight yard and terminal equipment* section.

**Products**
Track-guidance rollers which convert a road vehicle into a rail vehicle. Besides its use in creating a shunting unit (the resultant tractive power equals approximately that of a 20 tonne locomotive), the device also permits use of the Daimler-Benz Unimog truck on rails as a working unit with various supplementary equipment.

A Zweiweg Unimog model ZW 82S provided with a steam-jet can be employed for points cleaning. For example, another unit equipped with a loading crane (and at the same time as a shunting unit) can haul up to 25 loaded wagons. For winter operation a rotary snow-plough or a drum-type snow-plough can be fitted, permitting effective snow removal on rails as well as on the road.

Two special units are available for the construction and maintenance of catenary: a Zweiweg Unimog with hydraulic lifting platform and the Zweiweg road-railer with working platform, which was initially constructed for the Netherlands Railways. The Zweiweg Unimog vehicles are also available for broad-gauge lines.

Recent contracts include: 22 vehicles to Japan; 14 vehicles for Federal German Railways and four ballast ploughs to Amey Fleet Services, UK.

# FREIGHT YARD AND TERMINAL EQUIPMENT

## Alphabetical listing

ABC
Aldon
ANSALDOBREDA
Babcock & Wilcox
Blatchford Transport Equipment
Bosch Telecom
BP-Battioni & Pagani SpA
Caillard Cowans Sheldon
Central Power Products
Control Chief Corp
Hegenscheidt-MFD GmbH & Co KG
Hyster
Jarret
Kalmar
KCI
Kershaw
Kyosan
LeTourneau Inc
Liebherr Container Cranes Ltd
Mannesmann
Mitsubishi
Nelcon BV
Noell
Oleo
Pfister
Railweight
Rautaruukki
Rawie
Saalasti Oy
Safetran Systems Corporation
Siemens Switzerland
Siemens Transportation Systems
Sika Ltd
Steele
Strachan & Henshaw
Swing Thru International Ltd
Taylor
Telemotive
Thyssen
Toshiba
Trackmobile Inc
Tuchschmid
Ultra Dynamics
Unilok
Vollert
Wabtec Rail Ltd
Weighwell
Windhoff AG
YEC
ZAGRO Bahn- und Baumaschinen GmbH
Zweiweg Schneider GmbH & Co KG
Zwiehoff GmbH

## Classified listing

**BUFFERSTOPS AND WHEEL CHOCKS**
Aldon
Jarret
Oleo
Rawie

**CRANES AND CARGO-HANDLING EQUIPMENT**
Babcock & Wilcox
BP-Battioni & Pagani
Blatchford Transport Equipment
Caillard Cowans Sheldon
Herbert Pool (see Blatchford Transport Equipment)
Hyster
Kalmar
KCI
Kershaw
LeTourneau
Liebherr
Mannesmann
Mitsubishi
Nelcon
Noell
Rautaruukki
Stothert & Pitt
Strachan & Henshaw
Swing Thru International Ltd
Taylor
Tuchschmid

**ROAD/RAIL VEHICLES**
Central Power Products
Hegenscheidt-MFD
Steele
Trackmobile®
Unilok
YEC
ZAGRO
Zweiweg Schneider
Zwiehoff

**WAGON-HANDLING EQUIPMENT**
Babcock & Wilcox
Kyosan
Pfister
Railweight
Steele
Strachan & Henshaw
Thyssen
Vollert
Weighwell
Windhoff

**YARD CONTROL EQUIPMENT**
ABC
ANSALDOBREDA
Bosch Telecom
Control Chief
Nippon Signal
Safetran Systems Corporation
Siemens
Siemens Switzerland
Telemotive
Thyssen
Toshiba
Ultra Dynamics
Wabtec Rail

## Company listing by country

**FINLAND**
KCI
Saalasti Oy

**FRANCE**
Caillard Cowans Sheldon
Jarret

**GERMANY**
Bosch Telecom
Hegenscheidt-MFD GmbH & Co KG
Mannesmann
Noell
Pfister
Rawie
Siemens Transportation Systems
Thyssen
Vollert
Windhoff AG
ZAGRO Bahn- und Baumaschinen GmbH
Zweiweg Schneider GmbH & Co KG
Zwiehoff GmbH

**IRELAND**
Liebherr Container Cranes Ltd
Unilok

**ITALY**
ANSALDOBREDA
BP-Battioni & Pagani SpA

**JAPAN**
Kyosan
Mitsubishi
Toshiba

**NETHERLANDS**
Nelcon BV

**NEW ZEALAND**
Swinf Thru International Ltd

**SPAIN**
Babcock & Wilcox

**SWEDEN**
Kalmar

**SWITZERLAND**
Siemens Switzerland
Tuchschmid

**UNITED KINGDOM**
Blatchford Transport Equipment
Hyster
Oleo
Railweight
Sika Ltd
Steele
Strachan & Henshaw
Ultra Dynamics
Wabtec Rail Ltd
Weighwell
YEC

**UNITED STATES OF AMERICA**
ABC
Aldon
Central Power Products
Control Chief Corp
Kershaw
LeTourneau Inc
Rautaruukki
Safetran Systems Corporation
Taylor
Telemotive
Trackmobile Inc

758　**MANUFACTURERS**/Freight yard and terminal equipment

## ABC

ABC Rail Products Corporation
Track Products Division, 200 S Michigan Avenue, Chicago, Illinois 60604, USA
Tel: (+1 312) 322 03 60　Fax: (+1 312) 322 03 77

**Key personnel**
See entry in *Brakes and drawgear* section.

**Products**
Yard control systems.

---

## Aldon

Aldon Company Inc
3410 Sunset Avenue, Waukegan, Illinois 60087, USA
Tel: (+1 847) 623 88 00; 01　Fax: (+1 847) 623 61 39
e-mail: aldonco@interaccess.com

**Key personnel**
See entry in *Permanent way components, equipment and services* section.

**Products**
Wheel blocks, wheel chocks, warning signs, portable friction rail skids, wagon stops, bumping posts, electric and pneumatic wagon shakers, winch-type wagon pullers, electric wagon haulers, power wagon movers, wagon door wrenches and pullers, automatic bulk wagon gate openers and retarders.

---

## ANSALDOBREDA

425 Via Argine, I-80147 Naples, Italy
Tel: (+39 081) 21 11　Fax: (+39 081) 243 26 98

**Key personnel**
See entry in *Locomotives and powered/non-powered passenger vehicles* section

**Products**
Yard control equipment and yard layout design; power signalling apparatus; geographic relay interlocking; remote-control equipment; level crossing automation.
　Recent contracts include the automation of the Marciancise and Orbassano marshalling yards, Italy; and supply of automation systems for two marshalling yards on the new Beijing-Kowloon line, China.

---

## Babcock & Wilcox

Babcock & Wilcox Española SA
PO Box 294, Alameda Recalde 27, E-48009 Bilbao, Spain
Tel: (+34 94) 424 17 61　Fax: (+34 94) 423 70 92

**Key personnel**
See entry in *Locomotives and powered/non-powered passenger vehicles* section.

**Products**
Mechanical handling equipment; container cranes; portal cranes; dockside cranes; shipyard portal cranes; giant shipyard portal cranes; polar cranes for nuclear power facilities; overhead travelling cranes of all kinds; ingot mould stripper and foundry ladle cranes; ship discharging machinery; wagon tipplers.

---

## Blatchford Transport Equipment

A division of Herbert Pool Ltd
95 Fleet Road, Fleet GU51 3PJ, UK
Tel: (+44 1252) 62 04 44　Fax: (+44 1252) 62 22 92

**Key personnel**
Managing Director: Nigel Pool

**Products**
Mechanical handling systems for intermodal transport, including truck/trailer-mounted side loaders; trailer and rail-mounted cranes; self-propelled rail-mounted cranes; heavy-duty cranes for terminal use; low-temperature application container handlers.

　The Blatchford side loader is available for fixed mounting to vehicle chassis or sliding mounting to trailer chassis for handling 20 to 45 ft long ISO containers.
　The Blatchford T-lift trailer and rail-mounted container and swapbody cranes use a patented lifting and cross-transfer system with capacities up to 36 tonnes.
*VERIFIED*

---

## Bosch Telecom

Robert Bosch GmbH
PO Box 106050, D-70049, Stuttgart, Germany
Tel: (+49 711) 81 10　Fax: (+49 711) 811 66 30

**Key personnel**
See *Passenger coach equipment* section.

**Products**
Radio systems for shunting operations.

*Bosch Telecom shunter's yard radio system*　0006306

---

## BP-Battioni & Pagani SpA

Località Croce, I-43058 Sorbolo (Parma), Italy
Tel: (+39 0521) 60 41 40; 200　Fax: (+39 0521) 60 43 59

**Key personnel**
Chairman: Gianfranco Pagani
Vice-President: Amilcare Battioni

**Products**
Side loaders with capacity from 2 to 15 tonnes; electric side loaders with capacity from 2 to 6 tonnes.

---

## Caillard Cowans Sheldon

PO Box 1368, Place Caillard, F-76065 Le Havre Cedex, France
Tel: (+33 2) 35 25 81 31　Fax: (+33 2) 35 25 11 41

e-mail: caillard@caillard.fr
Web: http://www.caillard.fr

**Key personnel**
Managing Director: K Bayram
Head of Railway Cranes Department: F Elbaroudi

**Products**
Diesel-electric and diesel-hydraulic railway breakdown cranes with lifting capacities from 60 tonnes to 250 tonnes. Recent contracts include an oder for four diesel-hydraulic breakdown cranes for Indian Railways.

---

## Cattron Theimeg

58 West Shenango Street, Sharpsville, Pennsylvania 16150-1198, USA
Tel: (+1 724) 962 35 71　Fax: (+1 724) 962 43 10
Web: cattron.com
e-mail: mail@cattron.com

**Key personnel**
See entry in *Signalling and communications systems* section.

**UK subsidiary**
Cattron Theimeg (UK) Ltd
Riverdene Industrial Estate, Molesey Road, Hersham, Walton on Thames KT12 4RY
Tel: (+44 1932) 24 75 11　Fax: (+44 1932) 22 09 37
Operations Manager: Nigel P Day

**Products**
Radio and infra-red cordless control systems for railway equipment including shunting locomotives, overhead cranes, wagon movers and ballast wagon doors.
*UPDATED*

---

## Central Power Products

Central Manufacturing
4116 Dr Greaves Road, PO Box 777, Grandview, Missouri 64030, USA
Tel: (+1 816) 767 03 00　Fax: (+1 816) 763 07 05
e-mail: central@birch.net
Web: http://www.centralmfg.com

**Key personnel**
President and Chief Executive Officer: John L Ying
Vice-President, Sales and Engineering: Jack Highfill
Vice-President, Operations: Ed Harbour
Customer Support: Joe Eaves

**Products**
SHUTTLEWAGON®: mobile road/rail wagon mover of 24,000 to 55,000 lb drawbar pull (eight models are available); maintenance of way equipment; RYD-A-RAIL® road-to-rail conversion units.

**Contracts**
Contracts include supply of mobile wagon movers to Norfolk Southern Railroad, BART San Francisco, Long Island Railroad, Metro North Railroad, CSX, Union Pacific, Amtrak, Chicago Transit Authority and Eurostar, Belgium.
*UPDATED*

*Central Power Products Shuttlewagon road/rail tractor in service with Eurostar, Belgium*　2002/0134161

## Freight yard and terminal equipment/MANUFACTURERS

### Control Chief Corp

PO Box 141, Bradford, Pennsylvania 16701, USA
Tel: (+1 814) 362 68 11   Fax: (+1 814) 368 41 33
Web: http://www.controlchief.com

**Key personnel**
Chief Executive Officer/President: Douglas S Bell

**Products**
Control Chief manufacturers a broad range of industrial wireless remote control systems. Each remote control system is custom-engineered for rail applications.

*UPDATED*

### Hegenscheidt-MFD GmbH & Co KG

PO Box 1652, D-41806 Erkelenz, Germany
Tel: (+49 243) 18 60   Fax: (+49 243) 18 64 66

**Key personnel**
See entry in *Vehicle maintenance equipment and services* section.

**Products**
Portable hydraulic rerailing systems in aluminium alloy; hydraulic equipment for rapid track clearing after serious accidents; road/rail vehicle with rerailing equipment.

### Hyster

Hyster Europe
Flagship House, Reading Road North, Fleet GU13 8HR, UK
Tel: (+44 1252) 81 02 61   Fax: (+44 1252) 77 07 02
e-mail: sales@hyster.co.uk
Web: http://www.hyster.co.uk

**Key personnel**
Managing Director: Timo Luukainen
Area Business Director, North Eastern Europe, Africa, Middle East: Terry Foreman

**Principal subsidiaries**
Hyster France SARL
Hyster GmbH, Germany
Hyster Italia SrL

**Products**
Forklift trucks and reach stackers for container and swapbody handling; counter-balanced forklift trucks, with capacities from 1 short ton upwards, for stuffing/stripping of containers and freight wagons.
  Recent contracts include an agreement with DB for service and support of forklift trucks from 1 to 8 tonnes capacity.

*Hyster RS46-30IH ReachStacker at the DSB railway container terminal in Copenhagen, Denmark*   0006297

### Kalmar

SE-341 81 Ljungby, Sweden
Tel: (+46 372) 260 00   Fax: (+46 372) 263 90

**Key personnel**
Managing Director: Jonas Suaufesson
Vice-President, Corporate Communications: S E Petterson
Subsidiary companies in Austria, France, Germany, Hong Kong, Netherlands, Norway, Spain, Singapore and USA

**UK subsidiary**
Kalmar UK Ltd
Siskin Drive, Coventry CV3 4FJ, UK
Tel: (+44 1203) 83 45 00   Fax: (+44 1203) 83 45 23

**Key personnel**
Managing Director: J Arkell
Financial Controller: E Pook
Parts and Service Director: Keith Snow

**Products**
IC engine and electric counterbalance lift-trucks up to 90 tonnes capacity; IC engine and electric side loaders from 2 to 15 tonnes capacity; IC engine reachstackers for container and intermodal handling.

### Kalmar Industries BV

PO Box 5303, Doklaan 22, NL-3008 AH Rotterdam, Netherlands
Tel: (+31 10) 294 66 66   Fax: (+31 10) 294 67 77
Web: http://www.kalmarind.com

**Key personnel**
Managing Director: J K Lukumaa
Sales Manager: K Derks

**Products**
Container quay cranes; rail-mounted container stacking cranes; automated stacking cranes; rail-mounted harbour cranes; straddle carriers.

*UPDATED*

### KCI

Konecranes VLC Corporation
PO Box 666, FIN-0580 Hyvinkää, Finland
Tel: (+358 14) 427 11   Fax: (+358 14) 427 31 00

**Key personnel**
President: Markku Leinonen
Regional Marketing Manager: Hannu Rossi

**Products**
Railway terminal gantry cranes, container-handling dockside cranes, multipurpose cranes, cargo and container-handling gantry cranes, container storage cranes, overhead travelling cranes for containers and other loads.

### Kershaw

Kershaw Manufacturing Co Inc
PO Box 244100, Montgomery, Alabama 36124-4100, USA
Tel: (+1 334) 387 91 00   Fax: (+1 334) 215 75 51
Web: http://www.kershawusa.com

**Key personnel**
Vice-President and COO: Greg Valley
Vice-President of Sales and International Sales Manager: Phil Brown

**Corporate development**
Kerhsaw Manufacturing is a division of Progress Rail Services Corporation.

**Products and services**
Rail/road yard cleaners; road/rail cranes (60 to 150 t) for handling containers, wagons and locomotives; one-man operated loading ramps for rubber-tyred or rail-mounted vehicles.

*UPDATED*

### Kyosan

Kyosan Electric Mfg Co Ltd
4-2 Marunouchi 3-chome, Chiyoda-ku, Tokyo 100-0005, Japan
Tel: (+81 3) 32 14 81 36   Fax: (+81 3) 32 11 24 50
e-mail: f-takenouchi@kyosan.co.jp
Web: http://www.kyosan.jp

**Main works**
29-1 Heiancho 2-chome, Tsurumi-ku, Yokohama 230-0031, Japan

**Key personnel**
See entry in *Signalling and communications systems* section.

**Products**
Automatic wagon haulage systems.

*UPDATED*

### LeTourneau Inc

PO Box 2307, Longview, Texas 75606, USA

**Key personnel**
President and Chief Executive Officer: Dan C Eckermann
Vice-President, Sales and Marketing: Dwight Baker

**Products**
Gantry cranes and side porters.
  Recent contracts include the supply of five SST-100 gantry cranes to CAST, Montreal.

### Liebherr Container Cranes Ltd

Killarney, Co Kerry, Ireland
Tel: (+353 64) 702 00   Fax: (+353 64) 316 02; 327 35
e-mail: sales@lcc.liebherr.com

**UK sales office**
Liebherr Great Britain Ltd, Travellers Lane, Welham Green, Hatfield AL9 7HW, UK
Tel: (+44 1707) 26 81 61   Fax: (+44 1707) 26 16 95

**Key personnel**
Directors: P O'Leary, R Geiler, J Coffey
Secretary: A Boehm
Sales Manager: G Bunyan

# MANUFACTURERS/Freight yard and terminal equipment

## Products
Liebherr manufactures rail-mounted container handling cranes and RTGs for ship-to-shore terminals, railway and trucking terminals and storage yards. Sizes, speeds and safe working loads to meet all international tenders and customers' specific requirements.

*UPDATED*

## Mannesmann

Mannesmann Dematic AG Gottwald
PO Box 18 03 43, D-40570 Düsseldorf, Germany
Tel: (+49 211) 710 20   Fax: (+49 211) 710 26 51
e-mail: michael.hoberg@dematic.de
    achim.baeuckert@dematic.de
Web: http://www.gottwald.com

### Key personnel
See entry in *Permanent way components, equipment and services* section.

### Products
Railway cranes. Available for any track and loading gauge and designed in accordance with the maximum permissible axle and wheel loads. The cranes offer SWL ratings up to 300 tonnes, minimum tail radii, hauling speeds up to 120 km/h, a range of different brake systems and buffers or couplers to suit.

## Mitsubishi

Mitsubishi Heavy Industries Ltd
5-1 Marunouchi 2-chome, Chiyoda-ku, Tokyo 100, Japan
Tel: (+81 3) 32 12 96 07   Fax: (+81 3) 32 12 97 67

### Key personnel
See entry in *Locomotives and powered/non-powered passenger vehicles* section.

### Products
Straddle carrier and gantry cranes.

## Noell

Noell Stahl-und Machinenbau GmbH
Division NHV, Alfred Nobel Strasse 20, D-97080 Würzburg, Germany
Tel: (+49 931) 903 12 69   Fax: (+49 931) 903 10 16
e-mail: johannc.wu@noelle.de

### Key personnel
Sales and Marketing Director: Bernd Vossnacke
Sales Director: V Schuessler

### Principal subsidiaries
Noell Inc
2411 Dulles Corner Park, Suite 410, Herndorn, Virginia 22071, USA
Manager: Manfred Kohler
e-mail: mkohler@noellcrane.com
Preussag Noell
China Merchants Mechanical Engineering Co Ltd
Floor 16B, Heng Tong Hua Yuan Hubin Bei Lu, Xiamen 361012, People's Republic of China
Tel: (+86 592) 511 28 59   Fax: (+86 592) 511 30 29
e-mail: hessey@pncm.com
Peiner France
124 rue Nationale, Stiring Wendel, F-57600 Forbach, France
Manager: Roger Poliwoda

### Products
Rail-mounted and rubber-tyred container gantry cranes and straddle carriers.
Contracts include the supply of 10 rail-mounted gantry cranes for APL Los Angeles, USA; and additional rubber-tyred gantry crane for Rail Combi, Sweden; and straddle carriers for Portnet, South Africa, Hessenatie Antwerpen, Belgium and VIT Norfolk, USA.

*Mannesman Dematic breakdown crane for a Japanese railway client* 0064333

## Oleo International Ltd

PO Box 216, Grovelands Estate, Longford Road, Exhall, Coventry CV7 9NE, UK
Tel: (+44 2476) 64 55 55   Fax: (+44 2476) 36 42 87

### Key personnel
See entry in *Freight vehicles and equipment* section.

### Products
50 Series, 70 Series and 700 Series long-stroke hydraulic buffers (250-2,400 mm stroke) available for mounting on either rigid or sliding stop structures, providing effective emergency impact protection for railway rolling stock.

*UPDATED*

## Pfister

Pfister Waagen GmbH
Stätzlinger Strasse 70, D-86165 Augsburg, Germany
Tel: (+49 821) 794 90   Fax: (+49 821) 794 92 45
e-mail: marketing@waagen.pfister.de
Web: http://www.pfister.de

### Products
Sirius dynamic in-motion weighrail vehicle weighing system; Pluto modular rail weighbridges.

## Railweight

A trading name of Avery Berkel Ltd
Hurstfield Industrial Estate, Hurst Street, Reddish, Stockport SK5 7BB, UK
Tel: (+44 161) 431 51 55   Fax: (+44 161) 433 13 56
e-mail: sales@railweight.co.uk
Web: http://www.railweight.co.uk

### Key personnel
General Manager: Chris Rason
Sales: G Villalon
Customer Services: R Tyson

### Products
Weighing systems for all types of rolling stock, including locomotives, freight wagons and passenger-carrying vehicles. For general freight weighing applications, Weighline provides in-motion weight data of axles, bogies, full draft or unit train, for many different train combinations. For workshop maintenance weighing applications, Weighline provides static or in-motion weight data for locomotives and rolling stock. It is used for quality control procedures and adjusting wheel/bogies suspensions to ensure balanced loading. Weighline High Speed, the latest version, is capable of in-motion weighing at speeds up to 70 km/h. It can provide valuable data including side-to-side and end-to-end imbalance loading, at main line speeds.

Integrated management systems are available which automatically capture vehicle number and weight data and detect out of balance loads, wheel flats and other characteristics.

### Contracts
Recent contracts include the supply of equipment to: RSA, Australia; Shen Hua Mines, China; POSO Steel, South Korea; and RJB Mining, UK.

*UPDATED*

## Rawie

A Rawie GmbH & Co
Dornierstrasse 11, D-49090 Osnabrück, Germany
Tel: (+49 541) 91 20 70   Fax: (+49 541) 912 07 36
e-mail: info@rawie.com

### Key personnel
See entry in *Permanent way components, equipment and services* section.

### Products
Buffer stops with integral loading ramps; friction, fixed and folding (manual or motorised) wheel stops; fixed and friction buffer stops; specialist track endings to customer requirements.

*UPDATED*

## Saalasti Oy

Juvan teollisuuskatu 28, FIN-02920 Espoo, Finland
Tel: (+358 9) 251 15 50   Fax: (+358 9) 25 11 55 10
e-mail:: info@saalasti.fi

### Key personnel
See entry in *Locomotives and powered/non-powered passenger vehicles* section.

### Products
Snow-ploughs. The patented rolling snow-plough can be converted from the transport to the ploughing position in 2 minutes.
Recent contracts include the supply of snow-ploughs to Finnish State Railways.

*VERIFIED*

## Safetran Systems Corporation

2400 Nelson Miller Parkway, Louisville, Kentucky 40223, USA
Tel: (+1 800) 626 27 10   Fax: (+1 502) 244 74 44
Web: http://www.safetran.com

Freight yard and terminal equipment/**MANUFACTURERS** 761

**Key personnel**
See entry in *Signalling and communications* section.

**Products**
Marshalling yard communication systems; dispatcher communication systems.

---

## Siemens Switzerland

Siemens Switzerland Transportation Systems
Industriestrasse 42, CH-8304 Wallisellen, Switzerland
Tel: (+41 1) 832 32 32   Fax: (+41 1) 832 36 00
e-mail: verkehrstechnik@siemens.ch
Web: http://www.siemens.ch/vt

**Key personnel**
See entry in *Signalling and communications* section.

**Products**
Domino mosaic panels for marshalling yard control systems; alphanumerical keyboard control.

---

## Siemens Transportation Systems

Rail Automation Division
PO Box 3327, D-38023 Braunschweig, Germany
Tel: (+49 531) 22 60   Fax: (+49 531) 226 42 64
e-mail: internet@ts.siemens.de
Web: http://www.siemens.com/ts

**Key personnel**
Divisional Executive Management: J Lochmann
Divisional Technical Manager: Dr F W Hagermeyer
Divisional Commercial Manager: B Weiss

**Products**
Planning, control and monitoring of humping operations in marshalling yards; Automatic Vehicle Identification systems; electrically operated points; freight management and dispatching systems. Marshalling yard operation and freight traffic solutions
Systems for marshalling yard operation (flat type and gravity type); freight management and dispatching systems; identification systems; management and consulting services for freight traffic.

Marshalling yard systems comprise a multicomputer system in hot standby operation that can be extended with locally controlled systems. The marshalling yard system is designed for hump yards (for example with variable hump speed and computer-controlled retarder) and shunting areas. It reduces the time and costs for shunting operations and improves shunting quality. These systems offer high reliability and easy handling in combination with accurate slowing down even on curved tracks.

Freight management and dispatching systems include client server systems with standard relational databases to administer train, wagon and freight data. It reduces the need for shunting manpower. Identification and location systems aid in net-wide optimisation for handling freight wagons and trains.

Marshalling yard systems have been installed in Vienna and Villach (OBB), Bologna and Milan (FS), Munich (DB), Ludwigshafen (industry – BASF), Hamburg Harbour Railway, Antwerp (SNCB), Limmattal (SBB) and Kijfhoek (NS).

Examples for freight management and dispatching systems include Vienna (OBB), Limmattal and Chiasso (SBB), Hamburg Maschen (DB) and Bologna (FS).

*UPDATED*

---

## Sika Ltd

Watchmead, Welwyn Garden City AL7 1BQ, UK
Tel: (+44 1707) 39 44 44   Fax: (+44 1707) 32 91 29
e-mail: sales@uk.sika.com
Web: http://www.sika.com

**Key personnel**
See entry in *Permanent way components, equipment and services* section.

**Products**
Sikarail KC330 elastic rail fixing system is a combination of an elastic durable reaction curing binder and compressible filler that absorbs vibration and redistributes eccentric loading ensuring that no compressive stresses are developed leading to edge failure.

Sika provides admixture designs for high-specification concrete mixes, jointing systems, mortars and grouts, adhesives and bonding agents, waterproofing, corrosion inhibitors, concrete repair and protective coatings for concrete and steel including industrial flooring.

*VERIFIED*

---

## Steele

E G Steele & Co Ltd
25 Dalziel Street, Hamilton ML3 9AU, UK
Tel: (+44 1698) 28 37 65   Fax: (+44 1698) 89 15 50

**Key personnel**
See entry in *Locomotives and powered/non-powered passenger vehicles* section.

**Products**
Locopulsor shunting machine, a single-wheel vehicle capable of moving wagons weighing 160 to 200 tonnes on straight level track. It can also move wagons in curves, split a line of wagons and handle a wagon on a turntable.

The company is UK agent for Trackmobile road/rail shunting equipment. It offers a range of shunters capable of moving loads from 10 to 2,000 tonnes.

---

## Strachan & Henshaw

PO Box 103, Ashton House, Ashton Vale Road, Bristol BS99 7TJ, UK
Tel: (+44 117) 966 46 77   Fax: (+44 117) 975 29 92
e-mail: shmarketing@compuserve.com
Web: http://www.strachan-and-henshaw.com

**Key personnel**
Chairman: Kevin Gamble
Managing Director: Ken Grove
Director, Business Development: P D Brooks
Business Development Manager: Colin Bazeley

**Subsidiaries**
Strachan & Henshaw Australia Pty Ltd
Strachan & Henshaw Inc, USA
Strachan & Henshaw Pty Ltd, South Africa

**Products**
Wagon tipplers (dumpers) for random wagons or rotary-coupled unit trains; train movers (indexers, chargers, positioners) for use with wagon tipplers and at loadout stations; 'Beetle' haulage systems and wagon traversers.

Contracts include the supply of wagon tipplers (dumpers) to Africa, Australia and China. Tandem-unit train dumper for BHP Iron Ore, Australia (1998/99); single-unit train dumper for Sun Metals, Australia (1999); upgrade of tippler for Peru (1999); twin-car crescent dumper (two lines) for Tianjin, China (ongoing); various Rotaside XL dumpers in India via S&H licensee, Larsen & Toubro of Chennai.

---

## Swing Thru International Ltd

PO Box 118, Dunedin, New Zealand
Tel: (+64 3) 471 80 99   Fax: (+64 3) 471 84 60
e-mail: swingthru.nz@paradise.net.nz
Web: http://www.swingthru.com

**Key personnel**
General Manager: Geoff Kidd

**Products**
Diesel-powered double-sided container handling system which can be fitted to most vehicle or trailers fitted with standard 20 ft ISO twistlocks. Lifting capacity of the system ranges from 10 to 35 tonnes and it can handle container lengths from 10 to 45 ft.

Manufacturers in Australia, New Zealand, UK and USA have been licensed to produce either single examples or longer production runs of the design.

*NEW ENTRY*

---

## Taylor

Taylor Machine Works Inc
Louisville, Mississippi 39339, USA
Tel: (+1 601) 773 34 21   Fax: (+1 601) 773 96 46

**Products**
Container and trailer handling trucks, offering a wide range of lift attachments: top pick; side pick; top and bottom pick; bayonet; twistlocks; fork-mounted; carriage-mounted or suspended by chains; for use with 7 to 13 m (20 to 44 ft) empty or laden containers, conventional or refrigerated. Attachments range from 5,670 to 40,820 kg (12,500 to 90,000 lb) capacity. The truck is designed specifically as a container or container/trailer handler.

*Strachan & Henshaw single-cage Triple Rail Car dumper system, capable of unloading three 100 tonne wagons of coal at 90 wagons an hour per line. Commissioned in 1997 for phase IV expansion at Port of Qinhuangdao, China*
0021673

# MANUFACTURERS/Freight yard and terminal equipment

## Telemotive

Telemotive Industrial Controls
175 Wall Street, Glendale Heights, Chicago, Illinois 60139-1985, USA
Tel: (+1 630) 582 11 11   Fax: (+1 630) 582 11 94
e-mail: info@telemotive.com
Web: http://www.telemotive.com

**Key personnel**
Marketing Manager: Ken Bird

**Products**
Radio remote-control systems for locomotives, wagon movers, cranes and other freight handling systems.

*UPDATED*

## Thyssen

Thyssen Umformtechnik & Guss GmbH
PO Box 28 11 44, D-47241 Duisburg, Germany
Tel: (+49 203) 73 22 80   Fax: (+49 203) 73 22 96

**Foreign Sales Agency**
Siemens Aktiengesellschaft
Transportation Systems Group
Goods Transport Division (VT 1C)
Ackerstrasse 22, D-38126 Braunschweig, Germany
Tel: (+49 531) 226 25 50   Fax: (+49 531) 226 41 04

**Products**
Marshalling yard retarders and wagon-moving equipment including the Thyssen TKG multipiston retarder system. The company has supplied retarders for more than 60 German Railways' (DB AG) marshalling yards, and to German industry and railway companies abroad. The Hamburg Maschen shunting yard alone incorporates as many as 136 Thyssen retarders.

Contracts include the supply of seven primary two-rail beam retarders and 40 secondary single-rail beam retarders for Antwerp Noord marshalling yard, Belgium; 10 primary two-rail beam retarders and 43 secondary single-rail beam retarders for Kijfhoek marshalling yard, Netherlands.

## Toshiba

Toshiba Corporation
Railway Projects Department, 1-1, Shibaura 1-chome, Minato-ku, Tokyo 105, Japan
Tel: (+81 3) 34 57 49 24   Fax: (+81 3) 34 57 83 85

**Products**
Yard control equipment including retarders; and Automatic Car Identification (ACI) systems employing vehicle-mounted transponders and track-mounted interrogators. Toshiba ACI showed reliability and performance in a field test at Hokkaido (northern Japan) conducted by JR with 60 transponders and an interrogator under severe environmental conditions such as low temperature (–30°C) and thick snow which covered the interrogator to a depth of 150 mm or more.

*Thyssen TKS multipiston retarder system, left, activated, right, free flow mode* 0021674

## Trackmobile Inc

1602 Executive Drive, La Grange, Georgia 30240-5751, USA
Tel: (+1 706) 884 66 51   Fax: (+1 706) 884 03 90
Web: http://www.trackmobile.com
e-mail: trackmobile@trackmobile.com

**Key personnel**
President: Jack W Kennedy
Executive Vice-President, Worldwide Marketing: James R Codlin

**Products**
Manufacture of bimodal (road/rail) mobile rail vehicle movers. The Trackmobile® range comprises seven different models with tractive effort from 7,076 kg to 25,000 kg. Features include automatic weight transfer couplers. Various gauge and coupler configurations are available.

Recent developments include the introduction of the new 4650TM, 4750TM and 4850TM Trackmobile models; the MAX-TRAN automatic weight transfer system, which ensures maximum weight transfer and tractive effort; and the MAX-TRAC wheelslip control system.

## Tuchschmid

Tuchschmid Enterprises AG
Kehlhofstrasse 54, CH-8501 Frauenfeld, Switzerland
Tel: (+41 52) 728 81 11   Fax: (+41 52) 728 81 00
e-mail: info@tuchschmid.ch

**Key personnel**
See entry in *Freight vehicles and equipment* section.

**Products**
COMPACTTERMINAL is a low-cost intermodal terminal. The system is modular and suitable for all sizes from installations for small throughputs to high-performance freight distribution centres. Hercules power-operated transfer equipment for the ACTS road-rail container handling system.

## Ultra Dynamics

Upperfield Road, Kingsditch Trading Estate, Cheltenham GL51 9NY, UK
Tel: (+44 1242) 70 79 00   Fax: (+44 1242) 70 79 01
e-mail: sales@ultradynamics.demon.co.uk

**Key personnel**
Managing Director: M Lane
Marketing Manager: S Middleton

**Principal subsidiary**
Ultra Dynamics Inc
1110A Claycroft Road, Columbus, Ohio 43230-6625, USA
Tel: (+1 614) 759 90 00   Fax: (+1 614) 759 90 46
e-mail: sales@ultradynamics.com
Web: http://www.ultradynamics.com

*Ultra retarders in Vienna yard, Austria* 0006299

**Products**
Ultra retarders are speed-sensitive units bolted to the inside of rails at strategic intervals along the track and these can be installed on the hump, in the switching area and in the classification tracks to provide the required wagon speed control.

Wagons are retarded accurately from the switching area to a safe buffing speed in the sidings. In the case of automatic couplers, wagon speeds are controlled between the specified bandwidth to ensure coupling takes place. The retarder units are preset during manufacture to the required speed control conditions of a particular marshalling yard. Noise levels are low and no exterior power source is required.

Retarders can be configured as High Capacity or Trackmaster models. Retarders are available with a retraction facility for use in yards where the operations require considerable resorting of trains.

The company also manufactures emergency stopping systems and safety systems and is BS EN ISO9001 approved.

Contracts include installations in Copenhagen and Padborg marshalling yards (DSB); Vienna and Villach in Austria (ÖBB); Nuremberg, Germany (DB); Hallesborg, Sweden (SJ); Limmattal, Switzerland (SBB); Keiyo Railways, Japan, Murata marshalling yard and several yards of the Union Pacific, CP and BNSF rail companies in North America.

*UPDATED*

## Unilok

Unilokomotive Ireland Ltd
Oranmore, Galway, Ireland
Tel: (+353 91) 79 08 90   Fax: (+353 91) 79 08 46
e-mail: sales@unilok.ie

**Key personnel**
See entry in *Locomotives and powered/non-powered passenger vehicles* section.

**Products**
The Unilok range of road/rail wagon movers and shunting locomotives. Models are classified according to maximum drawbar pull up to 12,500 kg. A range of diesel engines may be fitted with outputs from 70 to 150 hp (52 to 112 kW) providing maximum speeds up to 30 km/h on road and rail. All machines are available with hydrostatic drive transmissions and a range of optional equipment including radio remote control, snow-plough, and hydraulic crane.

Uniloks are in service worldwide and are available in all gauges and coupler types.

**Contracts**
The supply of shunting vehicles to Mozambique, Syria and China.

*UPDATED*

# Vollert

Vollert GmbH & Co KG Anlagenbau
D-74185 Weinsberg, Germany
Tel: (+49 7134) 522 29  Fax: (+49 7134) 522 03
e-mail: info@vollert.de
Web: http://www.vollert.de

### Products
Shunting equipment of various types; wagon transfer cars, radio-controlled diesel, battery or electric robot shunters of varying sizes and power including models capable of moving trains of 100 to 10,000 tonnes in temperatures between −50°C and +50°C; remote-controlled functions include disengagement of couplings and an infinitely variable traction speed for accurate wagon positioning at discharge points.

*UPDATED*

# Wabtec Rail Ltd

PO Box 192, Hexthorpe Road, Doncaster DN1 1PJ, UK
Tel: (+44 1302) 79 00 27  Fax: (+44 1302) 79 00 58
e-mail: probinson@wabtec.com
Web: http://www.wabtec.com

### Key personnel
See entry in *Locomotives and powered/non-powered passenger vehicles* section.

### Corporate development
Wabtec Rail formerly traded as RFS(E), changing its name in March 2000.

### Products
Shunting locomotives based on the Sentinel modular range, including hire, and radio control systems for Sentinel range.

# Weighwell

Weighwell Works, Wakefield Commercial Park, Horbury Bridge, Wakefield WF4 5NW, UK
Tel: (+44 1924) 28 33 34 Fax: (+44 1924) 28 33 35

### Products
Train weighing systems. Recent products include the Portable Train Weigher (PTW), which can be carried by two persons to any site. Installation takes a maximum of 15 minutes.

The PTW comprises two convex shoes fitted with strain gauge sensors, which clamp against the inner sides of any conventional rails. When the flanges of the wheel engage the shoes dynamically the tyres of the wheels are raised just clear of the rails. A signal is collected and the wheels are guided back on to the rail. The signals are digitised and processed by the system to give a weight.

*NEW ENTRY*

# Windhoff AG

PO Box 1963, D-48409 Rheine, Germany
Tel: (+49 5971) 580  Fax: (+49 5971) 582 09
e-mail: info@windhoff.de
Web: http://www.windhoff.de

### Key personnel
See entry in *Permanent way components, equipment and services* section.

### Products
Tele-Trac shunting vehicle, diesel or electrohydraulically driven, control of shunting course and coupling operations by radio or by interlinking with loading programme; marshalling yard equipment; turntables and traversers; screw-jacks for lifting locomotives, wagons and other heavy loads; lifting equipment for complete trains.

Contracts include the supply of a Tele-Trac shunter to Netherlands Railways (NS).

*Minilok DH100 four-axle road/rail vehicle from YEC*  0006301

# YEC

Yorkshire Engine Co Ltd
PO Box 66, Rotherham S60 1DD, UK
Tel: (+44 1709) 82 02 02  Fax: (+44 1709) 82 02 06
e-mail: yec@fsbdial.co.uk

### Works
Unit A7, Meadowbank Industrial Estate, Rotherham, UK

### Minilok works
Translok GmbH
D-47608 Geldern, Germany

### Key personnel
See *Locomotives and powered/non-powered passenger vehicles* section.

### Products
YEC is the UK agent for the Minilok road/rail locomotive range. The smallest is the two-axle DH30, which weighs 16 tonnes and the range extends up to the DH340 six-axle vehicle which weighs 75 tonnes.

# ZAGRO Bahn- und Baumaschinen GmbH

Mühlstrasse 11-15, D-74906 Bad Rappenau, Germany
Tel: (+49 7266) 916 80  Fax: (+49 7266) 91 68 25
Web: http://www.zagro.de
e-mail: zagro@t-online.de

### Key personnel
Managing Director and Sales Manager:
  Wolfgang Zappel

### Products
Road vehicles equipped with ZAGRO track guiding equipment for railway operation. A variety of mounted implements ensures multiple use and efficiency. Designed for quick derailing and rerailing. All drive functions can be radio-controlled.

The range of road vehicles equipped with ZAGRO railway guide wheels includes the Mercedes-Benz Unimog for servicing, maintenance and transport duties on standard, broad and narrow-gauge systems; Mercedes-Benz Sprinter-type for use as a personnel carrier and for servicing and maintenance duties; Renault Traffic 4 × 4 for duties including inspection and maintenance from the track or alongside. The ZAGRO forklift shunter is platform-driven, with a haulage capacity of 300 tonnes.

The ZAGRO Mini-Shunter and Maxi-Shunter have a maximum tractive effort of 200 tonnes. Both can be powered by petrol, gas or diesel engines. The required thrust force is transmitted from its wheel flanges to the wagon wheel. This and the continuously controlled hydraulic drive ensure safe braking of wagons. Wagons can be shunted in both directions without removing the machine.

All vehicles can be supplied for use on narrow, standard or broad gauge railways.

# Zweiweg Schneider GmbH & Co KG

Oberbüscherhof, D-42799 Leichlingen, Germany
Tel: (+49 2174) 790 95  Fax: (+49 2174) 79 09 70
e-mail: Zweiweg@t-online.de
Web: http://www.zweiweg.com

### Key personnel
Chief Executive Officer: Josef Wagner
Managing Director: Walter Wagner
Technical Director: Jörge Lange
Chief Engineers: Rashed Jarrar; Michael Meyer
Sales Managers: Werner Gassen; Ingo Vogt

### Products
Daimler-Chrysler Unimog rail/road vehicles with track guidance device. Applications include shunting, maintenance and overhead construction tasks, as well as track cleaning, cleaning grooved rails, tunnel cleaning, rescue, tower work, snow-ploughs, brush cutters, ballast ploughs and cranes. Zweiweg Schneider also supplies a range of trucks with hydrostatic drives (bogie and single-axle) for multiple rail applications.

Clients supplied include BASF, Bayer, Siemens, DB, NS, Schlatter, ATM Milan, GTRM, Amey Fleet Services, STIB, JR Central, JR East and the Tokyo metro.

# Zwiehoff GmbH

Tegernseestrasse 15, D-83022 Rosenheim, Germany
Tel: (+49 8031) 21 96 01  Fax: (+49 8031) 21 96 03
e-mail: info@zwiehoff.com
Web: http://www.zwiehoff.com

**MANUFACTURERS**/Freight yard and terminal equipment

**Key personnel**
Managing Director: Gerd Zwiehoff

**Products**
Road/rail vehicles for shunting loads of up to 3,000 tonnes or equipped as multipurpose vehicles; self-propelled Mini Shunter for loads of up to 150 tonnes; self-propelled Maxi Shunter for loads of up to 200 tonnes; forklift truck-propelled wagon shunter for loads of up to 300 tonnes; motorised one-seat track inspection car.

**UPDATED**

*Zwiehoff Maxi Shunter*
0064334

# VEHICLE MAINTENANCE EQUIPMENT AND SERVICES

## Alphabetical listing

ACC Ingeniere et Maintenance
ALSTOM
Alzmetall
ASC Industries
Atlas
BBM
Bingham Rail
Bombardier Transportation
Bradken
BvL
CAE Cleaning Technologies plc
CAM Industries
Casaire
Cattron Inc
Ceccato
CESPA
Chemirail
Cimmco International
ČMKS Traction Vehicles
Corade
Cragg Railcharger
Crous Chemical GmbH
Davenset
Delaware Car Company
Deutsche Bahn AG
Devonport Royal Dockyard Ltd
EEC
Emanuel srl
Ematech
English Welsh & Scottish Railway Ltd
Environmental Cleaning Services Ltd
Eurogamma srl
EuroMain AB
Eurostar (UK) Ltd

Fraunhofer Institute for Non-Destructive Testing
Gevisa S/A
Gilardoni SpA
Gmeinder
Greenwood Engineering
Gregomatic
Hegenscheidt-MFD GmbH
Hi-Force Hydraulics
Holland Co
Hovair Systems Ltd
HYWEMA Lifting Systems
IBEG
INME
Instron Wolpert GmbH
Kärcher
Kambre i Täby AB
Keller Elettromeccanica
Koncar Elektricne lokomotive
Linsinger-Maschinenbau GesmbH
Maintrain Ltd
Marcroft Engineering Ltd
McConnell Research Enterprises Pty Ltd
Mechan Ltd
MTS
MTS Systems GmbH
Nencki AG
Neuero Technology GmbH
NEU International
Niles-Simmons
NWRZ
Penetone Corporation
Pfaff-silberblau
Portec Rail Products Inc
Proceco Inc

Progressive Engineering
Railquip Inc
Rescar Companies
REW
Rolanfer
Ross & White Company
Rosvagonmash
Rotem
RPL
RSI
SEFAC
Simmons
Smith Bros & Webb Ltd
Somers Railway Engineering
Steril-Koni
SweMaint
Talgo
TGOJ
Thrall
Toshiba Corporation
TraffiCare AB
Trenitalia SpA
Ultrasonic Sciences Ltd
Upright UK Ltd
USF
Vanjax
VIA Rail Canada
Von Roll BETEC
Walter Finkbeiner GmbH
Wesurail Limited
Whiting Corporation
Windhoff AG
YEC

## Classified listing

**CLEANING AND PAINTING EQUIPMENT**
Bingham Rail
BvL
CAE Cleaning Technologies
Ceccato
Chemirail
Crous Chemical GmbH
Environmental Cleaning
Gregomatic
Kambre i Täby
Kärcher
McConnell Research Enterprises
Penetone
Proceco
Railquip
Ross & White
Smith Bros & Webb
USF
Wesurail Limited

**HEATING EQUIPMENT**
Casaire

**LIFTING GEAR AND ACCESS EQUIPMENT**
ASC Industries
Atlas
BBM
Cattron
CESPA
Emanuel srl
Eurogamma srl
Hi-Force Hydraulics
Hovair Systems
HYWEMA
INME
Mechan
Nencki
Neuero Technology
Pfaff-silberblau
Portec Rail Products

Railquip
RPL
SEFAC
Somers Railway Engineering
Stanley
Steril-Koni
Toshiba
Upright UK
Vanjax
Walter Finkbeiner GmbH
Whiting
Windhoff

**MAINTENANCE AND REPAIR SERVICES**
ACC Ingeniere et Maintenance
ALSTOM
Bradken Rail
Bombardier Transportation
Corade
Delaware Car Company
Deutsche Bahn
Ematech
English Welsh & Scottish Railway Ltd
EuroMaint AB
Eurostar
Gevisa
Gmeinder
Holland Co
Keller Elettromeccanica
Koncar Elektricne lokomotive
Maintrain
Marcroft Engineering
NEU International
Rescar
REW
Rolanfer
Rosvagonmash
Rotem
RPL
RSI

SweMaint
TGOJ
Thrall
TraffiCare AB
Trenitalia SpA
VIA Rail Canada
VSFT

**TESTING EQUIPMENT**
Cragg Railcharger
Davenset
ECC
Fraunhofer Institute
Greenwood Engineering
Gilardoni SpA
IBEG
Instron Wolpert
MTS
MTS Systems
Nencki
Proceco
Progressive Engineering
Toshiba
Ultrasonic Sciences

**WHEEL LATHES AND MACHINE TOOLS**
Alzmetall
Atlas
CAM Industries
Cimmco International
Hegenscheidt-MFD
Hi-Force Hydraulics
Linsinger-Maschinenbau
Niles-Simmons
Proceco
Progressive Engineering
Railquip
Simmons
Talgo
Von Roll BETEC

# MANUFACTURERS/Vehicle maintenance equipment and services

## Company listing by country

### AUSTRALIA
Bradken Rail
McConnell Research Enterprises Pty Ltd

### AUSTRIA
Linsinger-Maschinenbau GesmbH

### BRAZIL
Gevisa S/A

### CANADA
Bombardier Transportation
VIA Rail Canada

### CZECH REPUBLIC
ČMKS Traction Vehicles

### DENMARK
Greenwood Engineering

### FRANCE
ACC Ingeniere et Maintenance
ALSTOM
Chemirail
Rolanfer
RSI
SEFAC
USF

### GERMANY
Alzmetall
BvL
Deutsche Bahn AG
Fraunhofer Institute for Non-Destructive Testing
Gmeinder
Hegenscheidt-MFD GmbH
HYWEMA Lifting Systems
IBEG
Instron Wolpert GmbH
Kärcher
MTS Systems GmbH
Neuero Technology GmbH
Niles-Simmons
Pfaff-silberblau
VSFT
Walter Finkbeiner GmbH
Windhoff AG

### INDIA
Cimmco International
EEC
Vanjax

### ITALY
BBM
Ceccato
CESPA
Corade
Emanuel srl
Eurogamma srl
Gilardoni SpA
Keller Elettromeccanica
Trenitalia SpA

### JAPAN
Toshiba Corporation

### KOREA (SOUTH)
Rotem

### NETHERLANDS
Ematech
Steril-Koni

### RUSSIAN FEDERATION
NWRZ
Rosvagonmash

### SPAIN
INME
Talgo

### SWEDEN
EuroMain AB
Kambre i Täby AB
SweMaint
TGOJ
Gregomatic
Nencki AG
Von Roll BETEC

### SWITZERLAND
Crous Chemical GmbH

### UNITED KINGDOM
Atlas
Bingham Rail
CAE Cleaning Technologies plc
Casaire
Davenset
Devonport Royal Dockyard Ltd
English Welsh & Scottish Railway Ltd
Environmental Cleaning Services Ltd
Eurostar (UK) Ltd
Hi-Force Hydraulics
Hovair Systems Ltd
Maintrain Ltd
Marcroft Engineering Ltd
Mechan Ltd
Progressive Engineering
REW
RPL
Smith Bros & Webb Ltd
Somers Railway Engineering
Thrall
Ultrasonic Sciences Ltd
Upright UK Ltd
Wesurail Limited
YEC

### UNITED STATES OF AMERICA
ASC Industries
CAM Industries
Cattron Inc
Cragg Railcharger
Delaware Car Company
Holland Co
MTS
Penetone Corporation
Portec Rail Products Inc
Proceco Inc
Railquip Inc
Rescar Companies
Ross & White Company
Simmons
Whiting Corporation

## ACC Ingeniere et Maintenance

PO Box 93, Rue du Pré-la-Reine, F-63016 Clermont Ferrand, Cedex 1, France
Tel: (+33 4) 73 98 38 38    Fax: (+33 4) 73 98 38 20

### Key personnel
Chairman of the Board: Jean-Marc Couderc
Railway Division Director: Claude Liothin

### Products and services
Maintenance, conversion and refurbishment of railway carriages.

Contracts include supply and installation of equipment to SNCF and RATP Paris.

## ALSTOM Transport

ALSTOM Transport Service
48 rue Albert Dhalenne, F-93482 Saint-Ouen, France
Tel: (+33 1) 41 66 90 00    Fax: (+33 1) 41 66 92 70
Web: http://www.transport.alstom.com
See also ALSTOM entry in *Locomotives and powered/non-powered passenger vehicles* section.

### Key personnel
Senior Vice-President, ALSTOM Transport Service: Hamdi Conger

### Contact addresses

**Australia**
ALSTOM Australia Ltd
373 Horsley Road, Milperra New South Wales 2214
Tel: (+61 2) 97 74 74 48    Fax: (+61 2) 97 74 46 67

ALSTOM Australia Ltd
3 Bridge Street, Pymble New South Wales 2073
Tel: (+61 2) 94 88 48 10    Fax: (+61 2) 94 88 48 11

**Brazil**
ALSTOM Transport do Brazil
Lapa Unit, Avenida Raimundo Pereira de Magalhães, 230, CP 05092-901, São Paulo
Tel: (+55 11) 863 21 31    Fax: (+55 11) 260 02 24

**Canada**
AMF Transport Inc
1830 Le Ber Street, Montréal, Québec H3K 2A4
Tel: (+1 514) 925 39 00    Fax: (+1 514) 925 39 99
(Within North America: (+1 800) 267 00 35)

**France**
ALSTOM Transport
11-13 avenue du Bel Air, F-69627 Villeurbanne
Tel: (+33 4) 72 81 52 00    Fax: (+33 4) 72 81 52 87

ALSTOM Transport
Porte Magenta, 1 rue Baptiste Marcet, BP 42, F-71202 Le Creusot
Tel: (+33 3) 85 73 60 00    Fax: (+ 33 3) 85 73 67 99

**Hong Kong**
ALSTOM Transport Hong Kong Ltd
Room 910/912, New Kowloon Plaza, 38 Tai Kok Tsui Road, Kowloon, Hong Kong
Tel: (+852 26) 94 28 17    Fax: (+852 26) 88 57 94

**Mexico**
ALSTOM Transporte
Norte 45 No 919, Col Industrial Vallejo, 02300 Mexico DF
Tel: (+525) 719 08 70    Fax: (+525) 719 08 96

ALSTOM Transporte
Av Mario Colín s/n, Col. Valle Ceylán, Tlalnepantla, 54150, Estado de Mexico
Tel: (+525) 390 10 03    Fax: (+525) 390 50 32

ALSTOM Transporte SA
Prol. Miguel Alemán s/n, Col Ferrocarrilera, 91120, Xalapa, Veracruz
Tel: (+522 8) 40 01 29    Fax: (+522 8) 40 08 65

ALSTOM Transporte
Av Manuel Barragán #4850, Col Miguel Hidalgo, 64290, San Nicolás, Nuevo León
Tel: (+528) 351 55 56    Fax: (+528) 351 95 69

**Romania**
ALSTOM Transport Bucharest
256 Blvd Basarabia, Sector 3, 73249 Bucharest
Tel: (+401 255) 47 00    Fax: (+401 255) 66 11

**Spain**
ALSTOM Transporte SA
Paseo de la Castellana 257, 5 Plta, E-28046 Madrid
Tel: (+34 91) 334 57 00    Fax: (+34 91) 334 57 21

**UK**
ALSTOM Transport Service UK
PO Box 248, Leigh Road, Washwood Health, Birmingham B8 2YF
Tel: (+44 121) 695 36 00    Fax: (+44 121) 695 39 40

ALSTOM Transport Service UK
Campbell Road, Eastleigh SO50 5ZB
Tel: (+44 23) 80 62 40 01    Fax: (+44 23) 80 62 40 05

ALSTOM Transport Service UK
Channel Way, Preston PR1 8XL
Tel: (+44 1772) 55 35 71    Fax: (+44 1772) 53 33 66

ALSTOM Railcare Ltd
3 Ibstock Road, Coventry CV6 6NL

**USA**
ALSTOM Signaling Inc
150 Sawgrass Drive, Rochester, New York 14620
Tel: (+1 716) 783 20 00    Fax: (+1 716) 274 87 77

ALSTOM Transportation Inc
1 Transit Drive, Hornell, New York 14843
Tel: (+1 607) 324 45 95    Fax: (+1 607) 324 45 68

**Venezuela**
ALSTOM Transport Service
Av Francisco de Miranda, Editico Banco del Orinoco, PH La Floresta, Caracas 1060
Tel: (+58 2) 285 81 81    Fax: (+58 2) 284 98 98

### Background
ALSTOM Transport Service provides a range of service options for passenger and freight rolling stock, track and infrastructure. In addition, ALSTOM researches and develops products, including eService solutions, remote and in-condition monitoring. ALSTOM can also facilitate its customers' business objectives through short- and long-term financing arrangements.

See also Corporate developments in *Locomotives and powered/non-powered passenger vehicles section*.

### Services

**Total TrainLife Management**
ALSTOM Transport Service has created distinct service-product ranges within its Total TrainLife Management concept. These can be provided individually or combined into comprehensive support packages. Principal service-products include:

**Remote monitoring capabilities**
Intelligent, automated, condition monitoring systems collecting information rather than data, thus helping to identify costs and provide a more scientific approach to solving underlying engineering issues. In particular, these systems offer train operators and maintainers opportunities to reduce maintenance costs, manage assets more cost effectively, and monitor the performance and use of train services more closely.

Through the Internet, ALSTOM Transport Service offers its clients diagnostic tools aimed at:
- reducing costs by automating inspection and optimising material usage
- identifying faults before they affect the train service
- focusing maintenance action to get best value
- monitoring train operating and usage to provide a better service for customers.

Depending on the application, diagnostic tools are train-mounted or trackside-installed. Some monitor vehicles, while others monitor the railway infrastructure. These systems are complete solutions, designed to bring raw data from its source, process it, transform it into information and then present it to end-users in a way that allows them to make the decisions they need quickly and easily.

**Railway maintenance**
This provides operators and owners with a maintenance service regardless of the original manufacturer. ALSTOM can take its people and expertise to the operators' premises and assume control and ownership of the facilities and manpower, or it can complement the operator's existing resources through a maintenance management function. ALSTOM also offers the option of maintaining rolling stock at existing ALSTOM depots, where the servicing of 'passing traffic' can be accommodated.

In addition, it provides technical support services where it identifies performance improvements to enhance a network's availability.

*ALSTOM undertakes the maintenance of AVE high-speed trainsets operated by RENFE, Spain* 2002/0525427

## MANUFACTURERS/Vehicle maintenance equipment and services

### Railway renovation
As well as routine, heavy overhaul and repair activities, ALSTOM's renovation service offers interior retrofits and technology upgrades which together deliver 'new vehicle' features, for both ALSTOM-built and other manufacturers' rolling stock.

### Parts and replacement units
ALSTOM offers a worldwide supply chain management service. This is designed to provide a flexible response to different customer needs. ALSTOM has the ability to source replacement parts for all makes of rolling stock, from the latest equipment to vehicles that have been in service for more than 30 years. ALSTOM can also provide turnkey warehousing, procurement and inventory management.

As new features of its service capabilities, ALSTOM Transport has created *Partslink* to manage complex parts and service procurement via the Internet. Partslink is intended to replace the complex process of sourcing parts, enabling train operators easily to track and place orders.

### Asset management
ALSTOM facilitates customers' business objectives through short- and long-term financing arrangements, including operating leases, capital spares pooling and integrated services. It can assist its customers with short- and long-term financial structuring in both freight and transit markets.

ALSTOM facilitates refinancing and new financing of transactions, which offer flexible terms through which customers can build, renew or upgrade their fleets to suit their business objectives. Services offered include:Operating leases
For certain product lines, ALSTOM offers operating leases. These can be combined with various levels of maintenance service, from a single lease through to full service provision or power by the hour. The number of segments covered is expected to grow and currently includes some passenger rolling stock and used and new diesel locomotives. Where the product does not fall into an existing operating lease segment, ALSTOM can arrange financing.Capital spares leasing
Where standard products are used, ALSTOM offers the opportunity for spares pooling. Customers pay a regular monthly fee for access to a pool of spare parts. This avoids the need for expensive spare part purchases by rail operators and offers access to a larger pool than would be available to a single operator.Equipment upgrade
Where operators wish to upgrade or add equipment to existing rolling stock (for example vehicle positioning equipment or passenger information systems), ALSTOM can arrange for such upgrades to be leased with additional services, rather than purchased outright by an operator. This could include, for example, leasing access to a website, which gives the position of a fleet in real time or on-line condition monitoring systems.

### Contracts
Maintenance contracts linked to new train deliveries are listed in the *Locomotives and powered/non-powered passenger vehicles* section. Other recent contracts secured or in progress include:

**China:** ALSTOM secured a contract to refurbish 351 passenger cars for the KCRC, Hong Kong. Work included conversion from three doors per side to five, removal of intermediate cabs within the 12-car configuration and new passenger information systems.

**Ireland:** In May 2002, ALSTOM was awarded a 15-year contract by Ireland's Railway Procurement Agency (RPA) to maintain the fleet of 40 Citadis trams supplied by the company for Dublin's light rail system.

**New Zealand:** In December 2001, ALSTOM secured a contract to undertake maintenance and overhaul of Tranz Rail's fleet of 180 diesel-electric, electric and shunting locomotives for a seven-year period commencing in April 2002. To fulfill its contract, ALSTOM has taken over from Tranz Rail the Hutt workshops in Wellington.

**Spain:** In August 2000, ALSTOM received a contract from Spanish National Railways to refurbish 30 Class 333 diesel-electric locomotives.

**UK:** In July 2001, ALSTOM was awarded a contract by Anglia Railways to renovate 120 Mark 2 locomotive-hauled coaches owned by HSBC Rail (UK) Ltd. Undertaken at ALSTOM's Eastleigh facility between 2001 and 2004, the work includes full bogie overhaul.

ALSTOM holds a long-term maintenance contract with Virgin Trains covering the operator's West Coast Main Line rolling stock. In February 1999, Virgin transferred all its maintenance activities to a dedicated company, West Coast Traincare, since absorbed within ALSTOM Transport Service Ltd. This is responsible for: managing maintenance depots; employing all maintenance staff; and maintaining and cleaning trains. Initial arrangements covered the existing train fleet; as Virgin Trains new fleet of 53 nine-car Pendolino tilting trainsets is progressively delivered, ALSTOM Transport Service is assuming responsibility for their commissioning and maintenance.

**USA:** ALSTOM was awarded an order to refurbish 96 subway cars for the Chicago Transit Authority (CTA). This order represents the first option exercised by the CTA under a base contract signed with ALSTOM in December 1997, which provided for the overhaul of 284 cars, with three options for an additional 314 vehicles. The refurbishment of the cars will extend the operating life of the rolling stock to 30 years. Under the base contract 90 cars were refurbished and shipped to the CTA.

The Board of the Washington Metropolitan Area Transit Authority (WMATA) has awarded ALSTOM a contract valued at €370 million to overhaul 364 cars of its 764-car rapid transit fleet. ALSTOM is completely to refurbish the vehicles, which were built between 1983 and 1988, replacing the existing propulsion systems with its ONIX traction drives, and install an advanced cab signalling system. Work is to be carried out at ALSTOM's Hornell and Rochester, New York, facilities. Deliveries are scheduled from August 2002 to June 2005.

## Alzmetall

Alzmetall Werkzeugmaschinenfabrik und Giesserei Friedrich GmbH & Co
Harald Friedrich Strasse 2-8, D-83352 Altenmarkt/Alz, Germany
Tel: (+49 8621) 880   Fax: (+49 8621) 882 13

### Key personnel
Managing Director: W Schiepek
Export Director: H Christis

### Products
Drilling machines; machining centres; special purpose machines.

*UPDATED*

## ASC Industries

1406 West 175th Street, East Hazelcrest, Illinois 60429-1820, USA
Tel: (+1 708) 647 49 00   Fax: (+1 708) 799 60 71
Web: http://www.ascindustries.com

### Key personnel
Vice-President Sales and Marketing: Tony Fastuca

### Products
The Klaw rail wheel handling device. This features three adjustable arms and is ideal for lifting 36, 40, and 42 inch wheels. Its multiple pick points allow for horizontal to vertical and vertical to horizontal movement. The three-prong system keeps the load steady while lifting and allows it to be manipulated with better control.

*The Klaw rail wheel horizontal lift* 2001/0109480

## Atlas

Atlas Engineering Company
12 Croydon Road, Caterham CR3 6QB, UK
Tel: (+44 1883) 34 76 35   Fax: (+44 1883) 34 56 62
e-mail: atlas.hp@btinternet.com
Web: http://www.atlasengineering.co.uk

### Key personnel
Sales Director: P J Hines
Finance Director: M Prockter

### Products
Mobile railway lifting jack (up to 35 tonnes capacity); wheel profile trueing machines; crank axle turning machines; jacks; screwing machines; underfloor wheel trueing machines; double wheel lathes; hydraulic wheel presses.

Recent contracts include the supply of equipment to: JFK Airport, USA; Railtrack, UK; and Adana metro, Turkey.

## BBM

Officine Mecchaniche BBM SpA
Via Mottinello 141, I-36028 Rossano Veneto (VI), Italy
Tel: (+39 0424) 54 44 00   Fax: (+39 0424) 54 03 72

### Products
Vehicle lifting and handling equipment; wheelset presses; testing equipment. Products comply with ISO 9000 requirements.

## Bingham Rail

Bingham Rail
3 Dunston Place, Dunston Road, Whittington Moor, Chesterfield S41 8XA, UK
Tel: (+44 1246) 26 86 78   Fax: (+44 1246) 26 90 08
e-mail: info@trainwash.co.uk
Web: http://www.trainwash.co.uk

### Products
Flail-based train and locomotive washing systems, designed to wash cab and rear ends, roofs and eaves, skirts and bodysides. Features include Bingham Rail's LonWorks operating system, speed monitoring and management and automatic vehicle type identification. Flails are manufactured from polypropylene.

*NEW ENTRY*

## Bombardier Transportation

1101 Parent Street, Saint-Bruno, Québec, Canada J3V 6E6
Tel: (+1 450) 441 20 20   Fax: (+1 450) 441 15 15
Web: http://www.transportation.bombardier.com

Saatwinkler Damm 43, D-13627 Berlin, Germany
Tel: (+49 30) 383 20   Fax: (+49 30) 38 32 20 00

### Key personnel
See entry in *Locomotives and powered/non-powered passenger vehicles* section.

### Services
Bombardier Transportation's complete range of support services is designed to meet the rapidly changing needs of the rail industry worldwide. The company's portfolio includes full train and fleet maintenance, materials and logistics programmes and both vehicle and component re-engineering and overhaul. Whilst working in partnership with operators, Bombardier Transportation develops long term support packages to meet individual client requirements. This can include customer-supported management information systems,

*Bombardier Transportation maintains GO Transit rolling stock at the Willowbrook, Toronto facility*
2001/0099502

*Bombardier refurbished passenger coaches for Hungary*
2002/0524877

supply and training of staff and consulting services. This comprehensive portfolio and experience offers customers a range of benefits, including increased availability for a given fleet through balanced maintenance, increased reliability through monitoring and upgrades, lower life cycle costs, full support parts management and above all safe trains. Equally, the services are provided whether the vehicles were built by Bombardier or another company.

As examples of providing hands-on support from the beginning of the vehicle life Bombardier has a number of parts supply contracts around the world. These include consignment stock agreements whereby stocks of Bombardier-owned parts are stored at the clients' premises awaiting drawdown: examples include BVG – the Berlin public transport authority and Öresund Trains (OTU) and the Gardemoen Airport Shuttle in Norway. In the UK Bombardier is supplying kits of parts to Thames Trains and other operators: these kits have been developed with the operator to provide the specific self-contained package of parts that are required for specific maintenance operations. For Gardemoen in Norway Bombardier provides a vendor-managed inventory of parts. These different arrangements are optimised to provide maximum availability of parts at minimal cost to the operator. The company is developing Internet parts ordering which will further simplify and lower the costs of operators' ordering processes.

### Contracts

**Australia:** Provision of maintenance for 15 years, including the construction of a maintenance and stabling facility, was a feature of a contract placed in 2002 with a joint venture of Bombardier Transportation and EDI- Rail to supply new emus for Perth area suburban services. From mid-2004, 31 three-car emus, with an option for 10 more, are to be delivered to the Western Australian Government for the southern leg of the Perth Urban Rail Development project.

Bombardier maintains 275 trams in Swanston, Melbourne, on behalf of the National Express Group for 2 years.

Bombardier operates and maintains people mover systems at a number of airports including Tampa, Miami, Pittsburgh, Frankfurt, Newark, and Kuala Lumpur and provides technical support and assistance at others.

Other maintenance examples include locomotives in Italy and a joint venture with Uganda Railways Corporation maintaining about 40 locomotives near Kampala in Uganda.

Bombardier has a range of facilities around the world, where it is modernising vehicles and components.

**Canada:** In Canada, Bombardier is refurbishing 71 bilevel commuter cars (56 intermediate trailers and 15 driving trailers) for GO Transit in Toronto. The work is being performed at Bombardier's Thunder Bay, Ontario plant. In Toronto, Bombardier is performing locomotive and coach maintenance service under a six-year contract with GO Transit. Services include supplying management, labour and materials; managing train movements in the yard; and maintaining over 300 Bombardier-built bi-levels and 40 General Motors F59PH locomotives.

**Germany:** Locomotive re-engineering and modernisation contracts in Germany include: equipping 80 Class 298 diesel locomotives with radio remote control and MICAS-L control technology for DB Cargo; modernising 16 MaK diesel locomotives for HGK Cologne; modernising four Class V100.4 and two Class 60 diesel locomotives for various German operators. Additionally refurbishment of two Class 232 2,460 kW diesel locomotives for Schauffele; and the supply of four Class 293 diesel locomotives for GSG, a rail infrastructure company is being undertaken.

**Hungary:** Bombardier Transportation executes the refurbishment of 136 Bhv type passenger coaches, in Dunakeszi (Hungary) by the order of MÁV. Up to now 41 of the coaches, originally built in Dunakeszi, have been refurbished. The aim of the refurbishment of more than 30 year old coaches is to improve comfort for passengers in suburban traffic, to reduce maintenance time, frequency and costs for the operator and to extend the life span of the vehicles for another 15 years. The refurbishment of the vehicles involves replacing worn and used parts of the coaches and modernising systems. The refurbished vehicles will be equipped with air-heating system, automatic sliding doors, glass-fibre reinforced plastic interior covering, individual seats with textile upholstery, luggage racks with glass pane and fluorescent lamps. The automatic sliding doors ease passengers' access and egress and also significantly increase passengers' safety.

**Mexico:** Bombardier has signed an agreement with Mexico City's transit authority, Sistema de Transporte Colectivo (STC), for the refurbishment of 28 rapid transit trainsets of nine cars each, plus four spare cars, for a total of 256 rubber-tyred MP-68 cars.

**Netherlands:** In 2001 Bombardier was awarded the contract to overhaul and modernise 60 Class SGM-III three-car EMUs for Netherlands Railways (NS Reizigers): this work takes place at Bombardier's Randers facility in Denmark.

**South Africa:** Bombardier won a contract for the modernisation and overhaul of 45 Class 11E electric locomotives for Spoornet: this includes upgrading the control technology with the MITRAC system. The locomotives are used to haul heavy coal trains between the Mpumalanga coalfields and Richards Bay.

**Sweden:** Bombardier has maintenance contracts for approximately 127 emu cars being operated in Sweden.

**UK:** Bombardier Transportation has been awarded a 14-year contract by Virgin Trains to maintain the new Bombardier-manufactured rolling stock, comprising 352 diesel-electric vehicles, and the existing CrossCountry fleet. The new fleet is being maintained at a £30 million purpose-built facility at Central Rivers, near Burton on Trent, UK and at other sites.

The 99-year Croydon Tramlink concession in the UK has been awarded to Tramtrack Croydon – a consortium with Bombardier as a key member. Bombardier was

*SG2 metro cars refurbished for RET Rotterdam (Ken Harris)*
2001/0116288

*Soviet-built Class 232 diesel-electric locomotive, refurbished for private German operator Schauffele (Ken Harris)*
2001/0116287

## MANUFACTURERS/Vehicle maintenance equipment and services

*Bombardier maintenance facility in Central Rivers, UK*                    2002/0524884

awarded the contract to manufacture the 24 trams and is now maintaining them.

Bombardier has built 296 emu cars for c2c, part of the National Express Group. Bombardier is maintaining these vehicles at the East Ham Depot.

Connex South East operates on a number of routes and Bombardier is supplying 438 emus. Bombardier and Connex have a joint venture in which they will jointly maintain the trains, using the Connex depots and the Bombardier Works in Chart Leacon. This joint venture will initially operate for five years but could be extended up to 30 years.

In 2002, Bombardier Transportation secured an initial four-year maintenance contract related to an order for 127 Class 222 diesel-electric multiple-unit cars for Midland Mainline. A new depot is to be built in South Yorkshire, and use will also be made of two other re-commissioned or existing facilities. The contract includes an option to extend it to 15 years.

A 20-year materials supply and technical support agreement was signed in March 2002 by Bombardier Transportation and Govia as part of a contract to supply 700 Class 375/377 Electrostar emu cars for services on the South Central franchise in southern England.

Heavy general repair of 31 Class 91 25 kV AC high-speed electric locomotives owned by HSBC Rail, and operated by Great North Eastern Railway, has been undertaken in Bombardier's UK works.

Bombardier has carried out the complete remanufacture of 522 metro cars for London Underground's Piccadilly Line. The refurbishment includes completely new interiors with many additional features such as passenger information displays, enlarged vestibule areas with perch seats, colour-coded grab poles and longitudinal seating throughout.

**USA:** As a member of the Bombardier Alstom Consortium, Bombardier has developed three maintenance facilities to provide service and inspection for Amtrak's first high-speed rail system along the Northeast Corridor, serving Boston, New York, and Washington DC. The consortium is supplying management services for up to 10 years to meet the demanding performance standards of this service, which uses 20 trainsets each consisting of two power cars and six coaches.

*UPDATED*

### Bradken Rail

Maud Street, Waratah, New South Wales 2998, Australia
Tel: (+61 2) 49 41 26 67   Fax: (+61 2) 49 41 26 61
e-mail: rail@bradken.com.au
Web: http://www.bradken.com.au

**Background**
See entry in *Freight vehicles and equipment* section.

**Services**
Express Parts service based at Mittagong, New South Wales, supplying new and renewed spare parts for locomotives and passenger and freight vehicles, including brake and drawgear equipment and bogie components; rolling stock servicing, maintenance and refurbishment; bogie and drawgear refurbishment. Refurbishment facilities are located at: Mittagong, New South Wales; Karrabin, Queensland; and Bassendean, Western Australia.

*NEW ENTRY*

### BvL

BvL Oberflächentechnik GmbH
Grenzstrasse 16, D-48488 Emsbüren, Germany
Tel:(+49 5903) 951 60   Fax: (+49 5903) 951 34

**Key personnel**
Managing Directors: Wilhelm van Lengerich;
 Bernhard Sievering

**Products**
Cleaning systems for bogies and wheelsets.

### CAE Cleaning Technologies plc

Mount Street, Bradford BD3 9SN, UK
Tel: (+44 1274) 72 93 41   Fax: (+44 1274) 37 07 99
e-mail: sales@cae-ct.co.uk
Web: http://www.caeclean.com

**Key personnel**
Managing Director: David G Holmes
Sales Director: Alan R Holmes
Sales and Marketing Manager: Sakeb Zahoor

**Corporate background**
CAE Cleaning Technologies plc is part of the CAE Cleaning Technologies Group.

**Products**
Bogie washers and wheelset washers (high-pressure aqueous); bearing washers; traction motor washers; axle gear washers; ultrasonic cleaning systems.

Contracts include supply of equipment to DSB Denmark, Adtranz, the Hellenic Railways Organisation and London Underground.

### CAM Industries Inc

215 Philadelphia Street, Hanover, Pennsylvania 17331, USA
Tel: (+1 717) 637 59 88   Fax: (+1 717) 637 93 29
e-mail: sales@camindustries.com
Web: http://www.camindustries.com

**Key personnel**
President: Charles A McGough III

**Products**
Complete equipment for electric traction motor repair workshops including undercutters, handling equipment, test equipment and universal armature machines.

**Contracts**
Bart, California, Toronto Transit.

*UPDATED*

### Casaire

Raebarn House, Northolt Road, Harrow HA2 0DY, UK
Tel: (+44 181) 423 23 23   Fax: (+44 181) 864 29 52
e-mail: enquiries@cas-h.demon.co.uk

**Works**
Dashwood Avenue, High Wycombe HP12 3DP, UK

**Key personnel**
Chairman and Company Secretary: R T Roberts
Managing Director: W M Murdock
Technical and Sales Director: G A Harrison

**Products**
Space heating systems.

### Ceccato

Via Battaglia, I-36041, Alte Di Montecchio Maggiore (VI), Italy
Tel: (+39 0444) 70 84 11   Fax: (+39 0444) 70 85 09
e-mail: info@ceccato-carwash.it
Web: http://www.ceccato.it

**Key personnel**
Managing Director: Piero Rizzon
Technical Director: Piero Pillon
Sales and Marketing Director: Massimo Ghirardi

**Products**
Complete plants for the external washing of surface trains, trams, underground trains and associated rolling stock. Units can be configured with a high number of modular groups; each one designed to perform a specific washing function on different shapes and surfaces of the vehicles.

*UPDATED*

### CESPA

Costruzioni Elettromeccaniche Spavone
Via Luigi Volpicella 145, I-80147 Napoli, Italy
Tel: (+39 081) 752 48 63   Fax: (+39 081) 559 05 61
e-mail: cespaiet@tin.it
Web: http://www.paginegialle.it/cespa-01

**Key personnel**
Technical Director: Massimo Spavone
Managing Director and General Manager: Luigi Spavone

**Products**
Repair and workshop machinery; lifting equipment; workshop bogies for supporting vehicles; mobile lifting jacks for rail and bus applications; testing platforms for bogies; elevated platforms for access to vehicles; rain testing plants; electric motor maintenance equipment; underfloor lifts for bogies and wheelset mounting equipment.

Recent contracts have included the supply of equipment to Ansaldo Trasporti, Adtranz, Breda, Fiat Ferroviaria, Firema and Italian Railways.

### Chemirail

Société des Établissements Roger Brillié SA
25 rue de la Victoire, PO Box 45, F-93155 Blanc Mesnil Cedex, France
Tel: (+33 1) 48 65 20 76   Fax: (+33 1) 48 67 30 18

## Vehicle maintenance equipment and services/MANUFACTURERS

**Key personnel**
Chief Executive Officer: M Vaniscotte
Director, Export Sales: J N Vassilopoulos
Technical Manager: M Lenaert
After-Sales Service: M Da Vinha

**Products**
Design, manufacture and installation of rolling stock washing machines to customer specification. Customers include SNCF (sole supplier, including special apparatus for TGV trainsets), RATP, DB AG, RENFE, SNCFT, CFCO and various metro and light rail systems.

## Cimmco International

Prakash Deep, 7 Tolstoy Marg, New Delhi 110001, India
Tel: (+91 11) 331 43 83; 384; 385
Fax: (+91 11) 332 07 77; 372 35 20

**Key personnel**
See entry in *Freight vehicles and equipment* section.

**Products**
Machinery and equipment for manufacture and maintenance of rolling stock.

## ČMKS Traction Vehicles

ČMKS Kolejová vozidla, Drahelick 2083, CZ-288 03 Nymburk, Czech Republic
Tel: (+420 325) 53 13 35    Fax: (+420 325) 53 13 35
e-mail: cmks@cmks.cz

**Key personnel**
Chief Designer, Rail Vehicles: Ing Bohumil Skála

**Subsidiary companies**
ČMKS Trade as
ČMKS Jihlavská lokomotivní společnost sro (Jihlava)
Zeleznični opravny a strojírny as (Česká Třebová)
Českomoravská železniční oprava sro (Přerov)
Letohradská správkárenskásro (Letohrad)
Lokomont sro
ČMKS Arrow Line as (Ostrava)
ČMKS Polska Sp zoo (Gliwice, Poland)

**Services**
Refurbishment, re-engining and modernisation of diesel and electric main line and shunting locomotives and special rail vehicles; component overhaul and refurbishment. A modular system is employed for modernising Series 740 Bo-Bo diesel-electric locomotives, with the option of a new Caterpillar engine available in outputs from 370 to 1,120 kW.

## Corade

Via P Toselli 81 I-50144, Florence FI, Italy
Tel: (+39 055) 322 71    Fax: (+39 055) 32 27 27

e-mail: info@corade.it
Web: http://www.corade.it

**Products**
Painting booths and under chassis air blowing systems for railways and urban vehicles. Corade also provides a wide range of design and consulting services for developing and supplying equipment for rail vehicle depots and workshops.

## Cragg Railcharger

4972 Highway 169 North, New Hope, Minnesota 55428, USA
Tel: (+1 612) 537 37 02    Fax: (+1 612) 537 37 78

**Key personnel**
See entry in *Signalling and communications systems* section.

**Product**
Cragg ST-2L, a digital display device to verify hot bearings and wheel defects, using a non-contact thermometer.

## Crous Chemicals GmbH

Postfach 174, CH-3800 Interlaken, Switzerland
Tel: (+41 33) 823 19 53    Fax: (+41 33) 823 48 34
e-mail: info@crous-chemicals.com
Web: http://www.crous-chemicals.com
http://www.anti-graffiti.net

*Delaware Car repair shop with an articulated LRV from MTA Los Angeles, a coach from the State of Connecticut, a BART metro car and a lounge car from North Carolina DOT* 0010292

**Products**
Graffiti removal products and systems for rail vehicle exteriors and interiors, as well as for fixed installation; graffiti protection products and systems; graffiti removal services.

*NEW ENTRY*

## Delaware Car Company

2nd and Lombard Streets, Wilmington, Delaware 19899, USA
Tel: (+1 302) 655 66 65    Fax: (+1 302) 655 71 26

**Key personnel**
President: Harry E Hill
Chief Engineer: J Winter
Mechanical Superintendent: L J Reed
Vice-President, General Manager: T J Crowley
Marketing and Special Projects Engineer: S F Rogowski

**Products**
Refurbishment, repair and assembly of passenger rolling stock, including metro, suburban and commuter cars. Specialities include stainless steel parts fabrication and bogie repair and overhaul.

**Contracts**
CTA – structural repair to rapid transit cars numbered 2929, 2401, 2402, 2531; METRA – structural repair to commuter cars numbered 781, 7405; New Jersey Transit – installation of new and upgraded cab signal equipment on the entire fleet of emus, cab cars and locomotives. Long Island Rail Road, Amtrak, PATCO & Metro-North Railroads – blanket order for repair of Pioneer III truck side frames and bolsters; Metropolitan Atlanta Rapid Transit Authority (MARTA) – structural repairs to six rapid transit cars; SEPTA – structural repair of four Silverliner commuter cars; Metro-North commuter railroad – structural repair of one Bombardier commuter car and one M-6 style car.

*UPDATED*

## Davenset

Hunters Lane, Rugby CV21 1EA, UK
Tel: (+44 1788) 54 13 26    Fax: (+44 1788) 54 09 37

**Key personnel**
Railway Products: Keith McNeil

**Products**
Battery chargers for platform, workshop and charge/dischargers for load testing of batteries.

*Series 740 diesel-electric locomotive for a Czech cement manufacturer, refurbished by ČMKS Traction Vehicles and equipped with an 883 kW Caterpillar engine (Milan Šrámek)* 2001/0105892

## Dawson-Aquamatic

Gomersal Works, Gomersal, Cleckheaton BD19 4LQ, UK
Tel: (+44 1274) 87 34 22  Fax: (+44 1274) 87 49 30

**Key personnel**
Managing Director: B J Turner
Divisional Manager: P Barnett

**Products**
Design, manufacture and installation of drive-through washing and brushing systems for railcars, ranging from the simplest detergent/water wash-up to fully automatic installations for daily detergent washing and periodic removal of oxides and staining by acidic solutions; supporting control systems, water storage, effluent treatment and water recycling systems; railway workshop cleaning plant including bogie washing installations.

## Deutsche Bahn AG

Beriech Spezialwerke
Fahrzeugbau Halberstadt, Agustenstrasse, D-38820 Halberstadt, Germany
Tel: (+49 39) 415 20  Fax: (+49 39) 412 41 42
e-mail: Fahrzeugbau-HBS@t-online.de

**Services**
Modernisation and refurbishment of rail vehicles.

## Devonport Royal Dockyard Ltd

Plymouth PL1 4SG, UK
Tel: (+44 1752) 55 29 08  Fax: (+44 1752) 55 41 00
e-mail: john.small@devonport.co.uk
Web: http://www.devonport.co.uk

**Key personnel**
Group Manager, Rail Support: Geoff Buck
Sales and Marketing Manager, Rail Support: John Small

**Services**
Repair of locomotive power units, including turbochargers, pumps and injectors; repair of power and trailer bogies; passenger coach refurbishment and modification; refurbishment of rail infrastructure vehicles; and repair of electrical equipment, including traction motors, alternators and generators.

Contracts include: repair of Class 43 (HST) power cars for UK operators, as well as overhaul of traction motors, generators and alternators; repair of Class 80 power units for Northern Ireland Railways; overhaul of Trac Gopher infrastructure vehicles; conversion work on catering cars; and fitting secondary door locks to HST coaches.

## EEC

Electronic & Engineering Company
EEC House, C-7 Dalia Industrial Estate, New Link Road, Near Laxmi Industrial Estate, Andheri (West), Mumbai 400053, India
Tel: (+91 22) 636 71 48; 636 74 23
Fax: (+91 22) 636 90 09; 633 23 19

**Key personnel**
Managing Director: Ramesh Parikh
Research and Development Production Director: Nikhil Parikh
Sales and Marketing Director: Rajul Parikh

**Products**
Ultrasonic non-destructive testing equipment. The range includes an ultrasonic flaw detector for axles and general railway components; an ultrasonic rail tester, mounted on a trolley complete with probes and water container; a pocket ultrasonic rail tester with LED display for direct reading of defect location; and a multichannel multirail tester to test both rails simultaneously, provided with preset alarm functions and mounted on a lightweight, portable push trolley.

## Emanuel srl

Via G Marconi 3, I-40011 Anzola Emilia (BO), Italy
Tel: (+39 051) 73 26 52  Fax: (+39 051) 73 40 01
e-mail: ema.bo@alinet.it
Web: http://www.emanuel-impianti.it

**Products**
Hydraulic and electro-mechanical lifting systems and equipment for heavy-rail and light-rail vehicles.

## Ematech

PO Box 8093, NL-3503 RB Utrecht, Netherlands
Tel: (+31 30) 246 91 60  Fax: (+31 30) 246 91 76
e-mail: info@ematech.nl
Web: http://www.ematech.nl

**Corporate background**
Ematech has been an autonomous subsidiary of NS (Netherlands Railways) since 1996.

**Key personnel**
General Manager: Ing Joost Kruiswijk
Engineering Manager: Ing Edwin de Groot
Sales and Marketing Manager: Paul Matlung

**Products**
Overhaul, maintenance and upgrade of traction motors, converters, generators and ancillary equipment. Calibration of safety equipment.

Life-cycle management programmes: ISO 9002 qualified.

Recent contracts for clients in the Netherlands include work for NS Reizigers, Railion, RET Rotterdam, Connexxion and GVB Amsterdam. Non-Dutch customers include: Italian Railways; ATM Milan; Docklands Light Railway, London, and HSBC in the UK; MIVB, Brussels; and Essener Verkehrsbetriebe GmbH and Stadtwerke Bielefeld GmbH in Germany. Safety equipment calibration has been undertaken for Railpro in the Netherlands.

## English Welsh & Scottish Railway Ltd

310 Goswell Road, Islington, London EC1V 7LW, UK
Tel: (+44 20) 77 13 23 00  Fax: (+44 20) 77 13 23 11
Web: http://www.ews-railway.co.uk

**Key personnel**
Chief Executive: Philip Mengel
Commercial Engineering Manager: Keith Miller

**Services**
The UK's leading rail freight operator, EWS also offers traction and rolling stock maintenance facilities and expertise for other operators. Under a contract placed by train builder Bombardier Transportation, EWS undertakes routine maintenance on examples of the Class 220 Voyager and Class 221 Super Voyager high-speed diesel-electric multiple-unit fleet operated by Virgin CrossCountry. By early 2002, EWS had established maintenance facilities for these trains within its existing depots in Bristol (Barton Hill), Gatwick (Three Bridges), London (Old Oak Common), Newcastle (Tyne Yard) and Southampton (Eastleigh).

*NEW ENTRY*

## Environmental Cleaning Services Ltd

36-39 Westmoor Street, London SE7 8NR, UK
Tel: (+44 20) 88 58 84 84  Fax: (+41 20) 88 58 19 68

**Key personnel**
Managing Director: J I Charlton

**Products**
Graffiti removal and protection: chemical and mechanical cleaning of stone, concrete and floors, non-slip surfaces. Deep clean and cosmetics for buildings and rolling stock. Paint stripping and degreasing using safe bicarbonate of soda suitable for carriage renovation. Cleaning and protection of subways and stations. Odour destruction products, specialist odour-destroying cleaning products.

## Eurogamma srl

Via di Castelpulci, I-50018 Scandicci (FI), Italy
Tel: (+39 055) 72 20 01  Fax: (+39 055) 722 00 20
e-mail: info@eurogamma.com

**Products**
Mobile lifting jacks for rail vehicles. Jacks can be grouped to lift a single vehicle or an entire train, with a modular design control unit which can be reprogrammed to synchronise the number of jacks in use. Products are ISO 9001-certificated.

## EuroMaint AB

Box 1134, SE-111 81 Stockholm, Sweden
Tel: (+46 8) 762 51 00
Web: http://www.euromaint.com

**Key personnel**
President and Chief Executive Officer: Ragnar Hellstadius

**Corporate background**
Formerly SJ Engineering, the business sector responsible for traction and rolling stock maintenance for Swedish State Railways. EuroMaint AB was established in 2001 as part of the restructuring resulting from the break-up of the state railway company. The group of companies forming EuroMaint includes:
- RPL, based in Örebro, which provides maintenance logistics and spare parts services;
- TGOJ, based in Eskilstuna, which undertakes heavy vehicle and component maintenance and renovates, modifies and repairs rolling stock;
- TrainMaint, which operates 14 vehicle maintenance facilities throughout Sweden;
- TrainTech, based in Solna, which specifies maintenance requirements, devises maintenance programmes, provides documentation and acts as an independent consultant for vehicle procurement;
- EuroMaint also holds a 33 per cent shareholding in SwedeRail AB (qv).

**Services**
Traction and rolling stock maintenance, overhaul, repair, refurbishment, component purchasing, spare parts supply and vehicle procurement.

EuroMaint's principal clients are Green Cargo AB and SJ AB, but the company has also secured contracts from other train operators in Sweden.

*NEW ENTRY*

## Eurostar (UK) Ltd

North Pole International, Mitre Way, London W10 6AT, UK
Tel: (+44 20) 89 64 70 89  Fax: (+44 20) 89 64 70 07

**Key personnel**
Head of Engineering Production: David Bailey

**Services**
Workshop facilities including wheel lathe, bogie drop, vehicle wash, simultaneous lift and LDA (Lavatory Discharge Apron). Services include vehicle approval, technical engineering, technical support, commissioning engineering, safety case, document scrutiny, design scrutiny, training and languages.

Contracts include Eurostar servicing and maintenance.

## Fraunhofer Institute for Non-Destructive Testing

Fraunhofer Institute for Non-Destructive Testing
Fraunhofer Institut Zerstörungsfreie Prüfverfahren
Universität Gebäude 37, D-66123 Saarbrücken, Germany
Tel: (+49 681) 930 20  Fax: (+49 681) 93 02 59 01
e-mail: info@izfp.fhg.de
Web: http://www.izfp.fhg.de

## Vehicle maintenance equipment and services/MANUFACTURERS

**Key personnel**
Managing Director: Prof Dr Michael Kröning
Director, Applications Centre: Dipl-Ing Bernd Rockstroh

**Products and services**
Automated ultrasonic wheelset testing such as test and measurement technology, including specification, design, development and manufacturing and continuing through all service cycles, including operations and maintenance.

Policymakers and the Deutsche Bahn respond to the high density of German business transportation by implementing specific measures to enhance profitability, efficiency, availability and safety of railroad operations, including non-destructive testing of railroad wheels, complete wheelsets and rails.

*UPDATED*

### GE

GE Transportation Systems
2901 East Lake Road, Erie, Pennsylvania 16531, USA
Tel: (+1 814) 875 22 40   Fax: (+1 814) 875 59 11
Web: http://www.getransportation.com

**Key personnel**
See main entry in *Locomotives and powered/non-powered passenger vehicles* section.

**Services**
GE Global locomotive maintenance service maintains several thousand locomotives in comprehensive service programmes. GE Transportation Systems provides customised maintenance solutions ranging from field technical support to full turnkey maintenance facility operations. These services feature high performance through reliability-centred maintenance programmes, continuous training, supply chain integration and dedicated engineering support.

*VERIFIED*

### Gevisa S/A

Praça Papa João XXIII 28, Cidade Industrial, 32210-100 Contangem – MG, Brazil
Tel: (+55 31) 369 33 33   Fax: (+55 31) 369 33 34
e-mail: faleconosco.getrans@trans.ge.com
Web: http://www.getransportation.com.br

**Key personnel**
See entry in *Locomotives and powered/non-powered passenger vehicles* section.

**Services**
Rolling stock overhaul and workshop services, including: refurbishment; repair; remanufacturing and reconstruction; maintenance; painting; supply of spares.

### Gilardoni SpA

Via Arturo Gilardoni 1, I-23826 Mandello del Lario (Lecco), Italy
Tel: (+39 0341) 70 52 82   Fax: (+39 0341) 70 52 83
e-mail: gx@gilardoni.it
Web: http://www.gilardoni.it

**Products**
Non-destructive testing systems for rail applications, including ultrasonic testing of rail vehicle wheels.

*NEW ENTRY*

### Gmeinder

Gmeinder Lokomotiven- und Maschinenfabrik GmbH
PO Box 1355, D-74803 Mosbach, Baden, Germany
Tel: (+49 6261) 80 60   Fax: (+49 6261) 80 61 90
e-mail: info@gmeinder.de
Web: http://www.gmeinder.de

**Key personnel**
See entry in *Locomotives and powered/non-powered passenger vehicles* section.

**Services**
Modernisation and refurbishment, re-engining, general overhaul, maintenance and repair of diesel locomotives.

### Greenwood Engineering

HJ Holst Vej 3-5C, DK-2605 Brøndby, Denmark
Tel: (+45 36) 36 02 00   Fax: (+45 36) 36 00 01
Web: http://www.greenwood.dk

**Products**
Development and production of measuring equipment including MiniProf Wheel for measuring wheel profiles.

*UPDATED*

*MiniProf Wheel measuring wheel profile* 2002/0134497

### Gregomatic

Zwydenweg 14, CH-6052 Hergiswil NW, Switzerland
Tel: (+41 41) 630 32 78   Fax: (+41 41) 630 32 79
e-mail: info@gregomatic.com
Web: http://www.gregomatic.com

**Products**
Vacuum washing system for vehicle interiors.

### Hegenscheidt-MFD GmbH

PO Box 1408, D-41804 Erkelenz, Germany
Tel: (+49 243) 18 60   Fax: (+49 243) 18 64 66

**Key personnel**
Managing Director: Georg Hauschild
Sales Director: Markus Von Reden

**Subsidiaries**
Hegenscheidt Corp, Troy, Michigan, USA
Hegenscheidt Australia, Melbourne
Hegenscheidt Liaison Office, Delhi, India

**Background**
In 1995, the activities of Wilhelm Hegenscheidt GmbH and Hoesch Maschinefabrik Deutschland GmbH were merged as Hegenscheidt-MFD GmbH, a subsidiary of Vossloh AG.

In 2001, a joint venture was established between Niles-Simmons and Hegenscheidt-MFD.

**Products**
Underfloor wheel lathes for machining wheelsets *in situ*; above-floor wheel lathes for universal machining of wheelsets; hydraulic rerailing systems for lifting and repositioning vehicles; special equipment for machining engine crankshafts; wheelset diagnostic systems.

*UPDATED*

### Hi-Force Hydraulics

Bentley Way, Daventry NN11 5QH, UK
Tel: (+44 1327) 30 10 00   Fax: (+44 1327) 70 65 55
e-mail: sales@hi-force.com
Web: http://www.hi-force.com/hi-force

**Key personnel**
See entry in *Permanent way components, equipment and services* section.

**Products**
High-pressure hydraulic tools, including wagon door straighteners; jacks and presses; torque tools and accessories; pumps; crimping tools and nutsplitters.

Recent contracts include the supply of hydraulic jacks to London Underground Ltd.

### Holland Company LP

1000 Holland Drive, Crete, Illinois 60417-2120, USA
Tel: (+1 708) 672 23 00   Fax: (+1 708) 672 01 19
e-mail: postmaster@hollandco.com
Web: http://www.hollandco.com

**Key personnel**
See entry in *Permanent way components, equipment and services* section.

**Services**
Wagon cleaning, light wagon repair, train loading, bulk material transfer. Locomotive fuelling and service are available through its H-BAR-D Rail Tech, Inc division.

*NEW ENTRY*

### Hovair Systems Ltd

Unit 3, Kingstons Industrial Estate, Eastern Road, Aldershot GU12 4TD, UK
Tel: (+44 1252) 31 99 22   Fax: (+44 1252) 34 18 72
e-mail: info@hovair.co.uk
Web: http://www.hovair.co.uk

**Key personnel**
Managing Director: Maurice Ward

**Products**
Air film load-handling equipment. The system, which uses air bearing technology, has a multidirectional capability providing low resistance to motion and no damage to floors. It allows carriages to be moved within the workshop area unconstrained by rails. Complete carriages, with or without bogies, can be manoeuvred throughout the whole workshop, by only two men, allowing for removal of finished stock from a production or repair line.

Carriages or trainsets can be rotated removing the need for turning facilities and, in manufacturing areas, can be used for movement between build, paint and fitting out. Complete carriages can be stored close together and, when required, taken to the single incoming rail for transfer to the rail network.

*UPDATED*

### HYWEMA Lifting Systems

Wuppertaler Strasse 134-148, D-42653 Solingen, Germany
Tel: (+49 212) 257 70   Fax: (+49 212) 257 71 00
Web: http://www.hywema.de

**Key personnel**
General Manager: D Paul
Sales: R Heidtmann
Purchase: G Greupner

**Products**
To optimise operations during manufacture of the German ICE train, HYWEMA developed a mobile Lift-Jack-System with a special ground base. The Type FL-N lift jacks can lift from 40,000 to 80,000 kg. A key feature is mobility on the workshop floor without auxilliary

## 774 MANUFACTURERS/Vehicle maintenance equipment and services

*Mobile lifting system developed by HYWEMA for use during the manufacture of high-speed trainsets*
2002/0129422

rails. Due to a special steering mechanism, the lift jacks can move forwards and backwards.

HYWEMA produces a range of mobile lift jacks to meet the individual requirements of vehicles and operators.

HYWEMA also manufactures lifting systems for rigid (20,000 kg capacity) and articulated (30,000 kg) buses.

*UPDATED*

## IBEG

IBEG Maschinen-und Gerätebau GmbH
Stettiner Strasse 9, D-45770 Marl, Germany
Tel: (+49 2365) 510 30   Fax: (+49 2365) 126 47

### Products
Bogie and wheelset maintenance equipment: axle parallelism measurement systems; rail vehicle load measurement systems; laser wheel profile measurement systems; wheel circumference measurement systems; bogie noise measurement systems.

## INME

Alameda de Urquijo 87, E-48013 Bilbao, Spain
Tel: (+34 94) 442 04 48   Fax: (+34 94) 442 12 21

### Key personnel
Marketing Manager: Pablo Diez
Engineering Manager: Jesus Ferro

### Products
Mobile lifting columns, bogie platforms, overhead cranes, workshop haulage systems.

## Instron

Corporate Headquarters
100 Royall Street, Canton, Massachusetts 02021-1089, USA
Tel: (+1 781) 575 50 00

### Key personnel
General Managers: Malcolm Buchanan, Norman Smith
Marketing Manager: Bernd Schlichtenbrede
Market Services Manager: Brigitte Iffländer-Wiegmann
Technical Manager: Klaus J Vedder

### European Headquarters
Coronation Road, High Wycombe, Buckinghamshire HP12 3SY, UK
Tel: (+44 1494) 46 46 46   Fax: (+44 1494) 45 61 23

### Subsidiaries
Instron Structural Testing Systems
28700 Cabot Drive, Suite 100 Novi, Michigan 48377, USA
Tel: (+1 248) 553 46 30   Fax: (+1 248) 553 68 69

Instron Canada
975 Fraser Drive, Unit 1, Burlington, Ontario L7L 4X8, Canada
Tel: (+1 800) 461 91 23   Fax: (+1 905) 639 86 83

Instron de Mexico
Bulevar V Carranza 4120, Local 20, Col Villa Olimpica, CP 25230 Saltillo, Coah, Mexico
Tel: (+52 84) 44 39 14 19   Fax: (+52 84) 44 39 14 20

Instron Deutschland
Landwehrstrasse 65, D-64293, Germany
Tel: (+49 6151) 39 17-0   Fax: (+49 6151) 391 75 00

Instrumentacion y Servicos Tecsis Ltda
Avenida Holanda 1248, Casilla 50/9 Correo 9, Providencia, Santiago, Chile
Tel: (+56 2) 205 13 13   Fax: (+56 2) 225 07 59

### Products
Testor hardness testing machines, spring testing machines, universal testing machines for tensile, compression, shear and bending tests; pendulum impact testing machines; special purpose testing machines to customer specification, automatic testing machines and installations.

*UPDATED*

## International Technical Services

400 Queens Avenue, London, Ontario N6B 1X9, Canada
Tel: (+1 519) 439 23 62   Fax: (+1 519) 675 18 68
e-mail: info@ITSrail.com
Web: http://www.ITSrail.com

### Key personnel
See entry in *Consultancy services* section.

### Capabilities
EMD locomotive specialists; EMD engine rebuild; locomotives and freight vehicle maintenance; air brake systems specialists; locomotive rebuilding and repowering; welding services (engine repair).

*NEW ENTRY*

## Kambre i Täby AB

PO Box 7221, SE-187 13 Täby, Sweden
Tel: (+46 8) 54 44 04 25   Fax: (+46 8) 54 44 04 29
Web: http://www.kambre.se
e-mail: kambre@alogonet.se

### Key personnel
Chairman: Claes Johansson
Managing Director: Karl-Axel Kambre

### Principal subsidiaries
Styrlogic AB, Täby, Sweden
Brövig A/S, Kristiansand, Norway

### Products
Train washing machines, featuring brush and brushless washing equipment; specialised washing machines for cleaning the upper and lower surfaces of raked train noses; train interior cleaning systems. Bus maintenance systems, including washing and interior cleaning systems.

## Kärcher

Alfred Kärcher GmbH & Co
Alfred-Kärcher-Strasse 28-40, D-71364 Winnenden, Germany
Tel: (+49 7195) 140   Fax: (+49 7195) 14 22 12
e-mail: vertrieb.cin@de.kaercher.com
Web: http://www.kaercher.com

### Key personnel
Managing Directors: Dr Bernhard Graf; Roland Kamm; Hubert Konhäusner
Deputy Managing Directors: Hartmut Jennes, Thomas Schöbinger

### Principal subsidiary
Atlantis International Ltd
18 Weldon Road, Loughborough LE11 5RA, UK
Tel: (+44 1509) 23 37 70   Fax: (+44 1509) 21 05 42

### Products
Kärcher is a supplier of washing systems, waste water treatment, hauling systems and turnkey solutions. With drive-through washing plants, gantries and underbody washes, Kärcher systems wash vehicles from diesel and electric locomotives to entire passenger trains, urban and underground passenger cars and freight wagons.

Recent contracts include: delivery of train washing plant to Zürich/Herdern for Swiss Federal Railways AG (SBB); supply and installation of a type RBR/RBF train washing system at Arnhem for Netherlands Railways; provision of a fully automatic brush-type washing system at Frankfurt/Höchst to clean ICE high-speed trainsets; and the supply to DB AG of a train washing plant at Hof, Bavaria.

### Services
Project planning, architecture, implementation and turnkey handover. Kärcher offers assistance with financing issues.

*UPDATED*

## Keller Elettromeccanica SpA

Zona Industriale I-09039, Villacidro, Cagliari, Italy
Tel: (+39 070) 933 62 02   Fax: (+39 070) 933 62 44
e-mail: info@keller.it
Web: http://www.keller.it

*Fully automated washing plant for DB AG ICE high-speed trainsets installed by Kärcher at Frankfurt/Höchst*
2001/0103637

## Vehicle maintenance equipment and services/MANUFACTURERS

### Key personnel
See entry in *Locomotives and powered/non-powered passenger vehicles* section.

### Services
Maintenance, overhaul, conversion and refurbishment of all types of passenger coaches and freight vehicles. Projects include: conversion of self-service coaches into Ristobar coaches; overhaul of UIC-X coaches into IR trailer coaches; overhaul of Gran Comfort coaches; maintenance of UIC-X coaches; refurbishment of Ale 801-940 Le 108 trains; overhaul of various types of wagons; cyclic overhaul of couchette coaches.

*NEW ENTRY*

---

## Končar – Elecktrične Lokomotive

Končar-Electric Locomotives Inc
Velimira Škorpika 7, HR-10090 Zagreb, Croatia
Tel: (+385 1) 349 69 59   Fax: (+385 1) 349 69 60
e-mail: uprava.ellok@koncar.tel.hr
Web: http://www.koncar.hr/koncar/ellok/

### Key personnel
See entry in *Locomotives and powered/non-powered passenger vehicles* section.

### Services
Repair, reconstruction, refurbishment and modernisation of locomotives, dmus, emus and trains.

*UPDATED*

---

## Linsinger-Maschinenbau GesmbH

Dr Linsinger Strasse 24, A-4662 Steyrermühl, Austria
Tel: (+43 7613) 244 10   Fax: (+43 7613) 24 41 38
e-mail: maschinenbau@linsinger.com
Web: http://www.linsinger.com

### Key personnel
Shareholder and Managing Director: F Weingärtner
Managing Director: F Reisenberger
Technical Manager, Development Department:
  D I J Pomikacsek
Marketing: H Pamminger

### Products
Mobile rail milling machine with post grinding and measuring equipment.

*VERIFIED*

---

## Maintrain Ltd

3rd Floor, Burdett House, Becket Street, Derby DE1 1JB, UK
Tel: (+44 1332) 26 28 38   Fax: (+44 1332) 26 27 44
e-mail: enquiries@maintrain.co.uk

### Key personnel
Managing Director: D W Astill

### Background
Maintrain was created in January 1999 from the train maintenance activities of UK train operator Midland Mainline and is a wholly owned subsidiary of the National Express Group.

### Services
Located at four UK sites, Maintrain provides servicing and maintenance for several train operating and leasing companies, freight operators and a number of the major rolling stock manufacturers. In addition, Maintrain is project manager for the delivery of new trains in Australia for its parent company.

*UPDATED*

---

## Marcroft Engineering Ltd

350 Bournville Lane, Birmingham B30 1QZ, UK
Tel: (+44 121) 475 51 51   Fax: (+44 121) 477 82 86
e-mail: sales@marcroft.co.uk
Web: http://www.marcroft.co.uk

*Class 1061 Bo-Bo-Bo 3 kV DC electric locomotive refurbished for Croatian Railways*   2002/0122620

### Key personnel
See entry in *Freight vehicles and equipment* section.

### Corporate background
See entry in *Freight vehicles and equipment* section.

### Services
Overhaul and refurbishment of freight rolling stock and infrastructure vehicles; vehicle damage repair and modifications; wheelset overhaul; provision of spares for air brake systems; refurbishment, repair and cleaning of tank containers.

*VERIFIED*

---

## Maschinen- und Stahlbau Dresden

Postfach 27 01 45, D-01171 Dresden, Germany
Tel: (+49 351) 423 40   Fax: (+49 351) 423 41 03
e-mail: info@msd-dresden.de
Web: http://www.msd-dresden.de

### Key personnel
Managing Director: Dr Ing Martin Herrenknecht
Managing and Sales Director: Dipl-Ing Jürgen Bialek
Head of Production: Raimund Schäfer

### Corporate background
MSD is a subsidiary of Herrenknecht AG.

### Products
Traversers; locomotive and wagon turntables; vehicle lifting systems; wheelset handling systems.
Customers include: Bombardier Transportation; Deutsche Bahn AG; FGV, Valencia; Volkswagen, Hanover.

*NEW ENTRY*

---

## McConnell Research Enterprises Pty Ltd

68 Bond Street West, Mordialloc, Victoria 3195, Australia
Tel: (+61 3) 95 87 22 66   Fax: (+61 3) 95 80 78 48

### Key personnel
Managing Director: Peter McConnell
Director and Sales Manager: John McConnell

### Products
Maxi-Steam fixed and truck-mounted vehicle interior cleaning systems. Clients supplied include Melbourne's Public Transport Commission, Westrail and KTM in Malaysia.

---

## Mechan Ltd

Thorncliffe Park, Chapeltown, Sheffield S35 2PH, UK
Tel: (+44 114) 257 05 63   Fax: (+44 114) 245 11 24
e-mail: admin@mechan.co.uk
Web: http://www.mechan.co.uk

### Key personnel
See entry in *Passenger coach equipment* section.

### Products
Rail coach jacks; turntables (for wheelsets, bogies and complete vehicles); bogie presses; accommodation bogies; rail coach stands; traversers; wheelset and bogie drops; undercar trolleys; undercar manipulators; overhead cranes; swing jib cranes; lifting and jacking equipment; brackets; lifting beams.

Mechan Micro-Link microprocessor control systems are used for the control, monitoring and synchronisation of rail vehicle jacks. This system allows the jacks to be linked by only two control wires for complete sets of jacks and can be fitted to new equipment or to existing sets of jacks.

Weighing equipment can also be fitted to the jacking systems.

*VERIFIED*

*150 tonne MSD traverser system installed at the Opladen workshops of Deutsche Bahn AG*   2002/0131018

# MANUFACTURERS/Vehicle maintenance equipment and services

## MTS

MTS Systems Corporation
14000 Technology Drive, Eden Prairie, Minnesota 55344-2290, USA
Tel: (+1 612) 937 40 00   Fax: (+1 612) 937 45 15
e-mail: info@mts.com

**Key personnel**
Chairman and Chief Executive Officer: Sidney W Emery Jr
Vice-President, Vehicle Dynamics: Steve Cohoon

**Products**
MTS provides systems, including simulation software, for testing complete rail vehicles, car bodies and components, trains, bolsters, couplings and many other mechanical aspects of the railway industry.
  MTS also makes railcar simulators and software for laboratory fatigue, damage and durability simulation testing of products shipped by rail.

## MTS Systems GmbH

Hohentwielsteig 3, D-14163 Berlin, Germany
Tel: (+49 30) 81 00 20   Fax: (+49 30) 81 00 21 00

**Key personnel**
President and Sales Manager: W Ongyert
Manager, Vehicle Dynamics Division: Sushil K Sharma
Marketing Manager: Dr Thomas W Frank

**Principal subsidiaries**
MTS Systems France, Lognes, France
MTS Systems Srl, Turin, Italy
MTS Systems Norden AB, Askim, Sweden
MTS Systems Ltd, Stroud, UK

**Products**
Servo-hydraulically controlled simulation, static or dynamic testing equipment for the analysis of designs and for the evaluation of performance characteristics of materials, components, subassemblies and entire rail vehicles. Complete test stands for the investigation and improvement of ride comfort, noise, vibration, safety and durability.

## Nencki AG

Gaswerkstrasse 27, CH-4901 Langenthal, Switzerland
Tel: (+41 62) 922 76 76   Fax: (+41 62) 922 29 31
e-mail: info@nencki.ch
Web: http://www.nencki.ch

**Key personnel**
Managing Director: A Schneider
Sales Manager: A Gerber

**Products**
Bogie and axle exchanging facilities, lifting tables, scissor platforms and lifting jacks; hydraulic bogie test stands, working platforms for paint shops and washing plants. Side and front access platforms. Rail handling equipment such as bending and straightening presses. Self-propelled rail cars with working platforms and cranes for catenary wire installation.
  Recent contracts include equipment supplied to: Ministry of Railways, China; DB AG; SBB and Swiss private railways; Israel Railways; MST, Iran; TGV, Korea; and DGT Bützow, Germany.

*UPDATED*

## Neuero Technology GmbH

Buersche Strasse 60, D-49324 Melle, Germany
Tel: (+49 5422) 60 70   Fax: (+49 5422) 21 04
e-mail: info@neuero-tec.de
Web: http://www.neuero-tec.de

**Key personnel**
Managing Director: Bernhard Uhlen
Export Sales Director: Heinrich Wöstefeld

**Products**
Lifting jacks, underfloor lifting plants, bogie lifting stands, lifting trucks and tables, shunting vehicles, dismantling devices for wheelsets and bogies, mobile handling equipment, turntables, maintenance platforms, auxiliary bogies, lifting and turning devices. Measuring and testing equipment including devices for measuring rolling stock, axles and wheelsets; test benches for metal rubber and cylindrical springs, shock-absorber test benches, bogie assembly and test benches; wheel load measuring systems. Air cushion transport systems for rolling stock manufacturers.

**Contracts**
Recent contracts include: underfloor lifting plants, bogie repair hoists, bogie transfer table and electrical bogie tractor for East and West Rail KCRC Hong Kong; underfloor lifting plants for Iris Rail, Dublin; lifting plant for London Underground, UK; lifting plants, turntables, bogie repair hoist for Metro Tapei, Taiwan; lifting jacks for Shanghai Urban Rail, China; turntables, lifting/turning tables, disassembly stands for bogies and lifting tables for Deutsche Bahn AG, Kassel, Germany; lifting jacks for Korean high-speed trainsets; lifting jacks, turntables, road-rail vehicles, train-washing plant, bogie-washing plant, and bogie drop-table for the Sentral project in Kuala Lumpur, Malaysia.

*UPDATED*

## NEU International

PO Box 4039, 70 rue du Collége, F-59704 Marcq en Baroeul, France
Tel: (+33 3) 20 45 64 35   Fax: (+33 3) 20 35 65 99
e-mail: railway@neu-international.com

**Subsidiary companies**
NEU Engineering Ltd
Lion House, Oriental Road, Woking GU22 8AP, UK
Tel: (+44 1483) 75 65 65   Fax: (+44 1483) 75 51 77
e-mail: mail@neu-nel.com

NEU Inc
PO Box 488, Paoli, Pennsylvania 19301-0488, USA
Tel: (+1 610) 725 04 01   Fax: (+1 610) 725 04 02
e-mail: mail@neu-inc.com

NEU Solids Handling Pte Ltd
7 Temasek Boulevard, The Penthouse #44-01, Sunsec Tower One, Singapore 038987
Tel: (+65) 430 66 86   Fax: (+65) 430 66 66
e-mail: mail@neu-pte.com.sg

**Products**
NDS rail vehicle sanding systems for applications from light rail to heavy freight locomotives. Main line systems supplied include: Amtrak, USA; DB AG, Germany; Ferrocarril Mexicano, Mexico; FS, Italy; and SNCF, France. NDS systems have also been supplied to urban operators in Belgium, France, Germany, Netherlands, Norway, Portugal, Sweden, UK and USA.

*NEW ENTRY*

## Niles-Simmons

Niles-Simmons Industrieanlagen GmbH
Zwickauer Strasse 355, D-09117 Chemnitz, Germany
Tel: (+49 371) 80 22 01   Fax: (+49 371) 85 03 28
e-mail: info@niles-simmons.de

**Key personnel**
Chairman and Chief Executive Officer, Simmons Machine Tool Group: Hans J Naumann
President, Simmons Machine Tool Corporation: John O Naumann
Executive Vice-President: Micaela Schoenherr

**Principal subsidiaries**
Simmons Machine Tool Group also includes:
Simmons Machine Tool Corporation, Albany, New York (qv)
Constant Velocity Systems Inc, Albany, New York
International Electronic Machines Inc, Albany, New York (associated company)
Hegenscheidt-MFD GmbH, Erkelenz, Germany

**Products**
Underfloor wheel profiling machines of types UPM-T (turning); UPM-TM (turn-milling); and UPM-M (milling). Types UPM-T and UPM-M machines are supplied in sizes for up to 16 tonnes axle load and up to 40 tonnes axle load. Above-floor wheel lathe and wheel shop equipment and worldwide sales and service.

*UPDATED*

## NWRZ

Novorossiysk Carriage Repair Works
Mihailova 1, 353906 Novorossiysk, Russian Federation
Tel: (+7 861) 345 20 21   Fax: (+7 861) 342 42 93

**Key personnel**
General Manager: Nikolai V Maltsev
Engineering Manager: Anatoliy Naumenko
Marketing Manager: Efim Komskiy
Works Manager: Igor Mosha
Chief Accountant: Raisa Suhorukova

**Products**
Passenger coach refurbishment, including catering vehicles and air conditioning systems. Spare parts manufacture. Manufacture and repair of wheelsets. Repair and refurbishment of refrigerated wagons.
  Contracts include the refurbishment of passenger coaches in conjunction with MÁV and Adtranz Dunakeszi, Hungary.

## Penetone Corporation

74 Hudson Avenue, Tenafly, New Jersey 07670, USA
Tel: (+1 201) 567 30 00   Fax: (+1 201) 569 53 40

**Key personnel**
President: E W Phares II
Vice-President, Sales and Marketing: Mike Bradford
Vice-President, Finance and Administration: Bruce Muretta

**Principal subsidiary**
West Chemical Products of Canada Ltd

**Products**
Cleaning, maintenance and process chemicals.
  The range includes Penetone solvent emulsion degreasers, safety solvents and cleaning products that penetrate tenacious deposits, such as iron pyrites and silica soils, and remove them from exterior rolling stock surfaces. Operations covered include: exterior locomotive body cleaning; bogie cleaning; stainless steel and painted exterior carbody cleaning; interior diesel locomotive cleaning; diesel engine overhaul; journal box cleaning and repair; machine shop, locomotive maintenance; hot and cold tank cleaning; electrical equipment maintenance; steam cleaning operations (both ferrous and non-ferrous metals); pit and ramp maintenance; prepaint treatment; and rust prevention and protective coating application.

## Pfaff-silberblau, Hebezeugfabrik GmbH & Co

Äussere Industriestrasse 18, D-86316 Friedberg, Derching, Germany
Tel: (+49 821) 780 18 40   Fax: (+49 821) 780 12 99
e-mail: contact@pfaff-silberblau.de
Web: http://www.pfaff-silberblau.de

**Key personnel**
Managing Directors: Stefan Pfaff; Guido Bretthauer; Hans-Jürgen Lehmann
Chief Engineer: Xavier Ertl
Export Manager: Peter Zeller

**Principal subsidiaries**
Pfaff-silberblau, Winden und Hebezeuge AG
Furtbachstrasse 32, CH-8107 Buchs ZH, Switzerland
Tel: (+41 1) 844 14 66   Fax: (+41 1) 844 11 71
e-mail: pfaff@pfaff-silberblau.ch
Web: http://www.pfaff-silberblau.ch

## Vehicle maintenance equipment and services/MANUFACTURERS

**Pfaff-silberblau, Winden und Hebezeuge GesmbH**
Enzesfelderstrasse 1, A-2552 Hirtenberg, Austria
Tel: (+43 2256) 815 15   Fax: (+43 2256) 815 80
e-mail: pfaff-silberblau@nextra.at

**Pfaff-silberblau Ltd**
Prenton Way, North Cheshire Trading Estate, Prenton, Wirral CH43 3DU, UK
Tel: (+44 151) 609 00 99   Fax: (+44 151) 609 08 52
e-mail: anyone@pfaff.u-net.com
Web: http://www.pfaff-silberblau.co.uk

**Pfaff-silberblau**
Utilaje de Ridicat si Transportat srl
Sector 1, Turda Strasse, 127 Bloc 2, Scara B, Etaj 1, Ap 41, Bucharest, Romania
Tel: (+40 1) 665 18 21   Fax: (+40 1) 224 16 73
e-mail: italon@freemail.fx.ro

**Pfaff-silberblau Canada Inc**
530 Otto Road, No 22/23, Mississauga, Ontario, Canada L5T 2L5
Tel: (+1 905) 565 96 33   Fax: (+1 905) 565 97 33
e-mail: jsantos@pfaffgroup.com

**Pfaff-silberblau Benelux BV**
Economiestraat 39, NL-6433 KC Hoensbroek, Netherlands
Tel: (+31 45) 523 45 45   Fax: (+31 45) 523 73 45
e-mail: info@pfaff-silberblau.nl
Web: http://www.pfaff-silberblau.nl

**Pfaff-silberblau France SARL**
215 rue Henri Barbusse, F-95100 Argenteuil, France
Tel: (+33 1) 34 34 60 50   Fax: (+33 1) 34 34 00 63
e-mail: pfaff-france@magic.fr

**Pfaff-silberblau South Africa (Pty) Ltd**
Strydom Industrial Park, Hammer Road, Strydom Park Ext 25, Randburg, South Africa
Tel: (+27 11) 791 06 37   Fax: (+27 11) 792 35 73
e-mail: pfaff@icon.co.za

**Pfaff-silberblau Hungária**
Csörlök és Emelöeszközök Kft
Dózsa György u 84, H-2220 Vecsés, Hungary
Tel: (+36 29) 35 64 33   Fax: (+36 29) 35 64 34
e-mail: pfaff@pfaff-silberblau.hu

### Products
Lifting systems and jacks for rail vehicles. Lifting systems are available for rail vehicles (trams, metro, railways) built to the customer's specification and to the loading capacity required. The systems are fully lowerable to below ground level. The lifting of different types of vehicles and various lengths can be achieved by means of one lifting arrangement.

Lifting jacks are produced with capacities from 5,000 to 35,000 kg. Direct drive to the spindle is by a worm gear reduction box with automatic lubrication system.

Also supplied: auxiliary bogies; axle breakage cars; bogie-handling units; bogie disassembly wagons; support stands; turntables; and track jacks.

Pfaff-silberblau is an ISO 9001 accredited company.

*VERIFIED*

## Portec Rail Products Inc

Railway Maintenance Products Division, Box 38250, 900 Freport Road, Pittsburgh, Pennsylvania 15238-8250, USA
Tel: (+1 412) 782 60 00   Fax: (+1 412) 782 10 37
Web: http://www.PortecRail.com

### Key personnel
See entry in *Permanent way equipment* section.

### Products
Portec spot wagon and locomotive repair systems allow for repair of wagons and locomotives in an efficient central area, with wagon-handling achieved by 'rabbits' under push-button control. The systems include integrated jacking, job cranes, hosereels and other accessories. The systems operate on the basic principle of moving the wagons to the men and materials, rather than have men carry materials to wagons needing repairs. Advantages claimed include increased labour efficiency, reduction in wagon hire costs, and savings of 50 to 90 per cent in switch engine hours.

Portec's locomotive drop table is a single-axle hydraulic unit for changing locomotive wheel/axle/traction motor assemblies. The work table is mounted on a transporter.

## Proceco Inc

14790 St Augustine Rd, Jacksonville, Florida 32258, USA
Tel: (+1 904) 886 02 00   Fax: (+1 904) 886 02 32

### Principal subsidiary
Proceco Industrial Machinery Ltd
7300 Tellier Street, Montréal, Québec H1N 3T7, Canada
Tel: (+1 514) 254 84 94   Fax: (+1 514) 254 81 84

### Products
Machinery washers for items such as bogies, engine blocks and cylinder heads.

Locomotive traction motor and main generator (alternator) spray washing and vacuum drying system, vacuum-pressure impregnating devices, traction motor stripping and assembly device, traction motor remanufacturing transfer line.

## Progressive Engineering

Progressive Engineering (AUL) Ltd
Clarke Street, Ashton-under-Lyne OL7 0LJ, UK
Tel: (+44 161) 285 33 22   Fax: (+44 161) 343 26 48
e-mail: johnw@progressive-eng.demon.co.uk
Web: http://www.progressive-eng.demon.co.uk

### Key personnel
See entry in *Signalling and communications systems* section.

### Products
Design and manufacture of valves, mountings and auxiliary fittings, air brake dump valves, anti tow-away interlocks.

*UPDATED*

## Railquip Inc

3731 Northcrest Road, Suite 6, Atlanta, Georgia 30340, USA
Tel: (+1 770) 458 41 57   Fax: (+1 770) 458 53 65
e-mail: railquip@aol.com
Web: http//www.railquip.com

### Key personnel
President: Helmut Schroeder
Sales Manager: Paul Wojcik
Sales Engineer: Jorge Larrache
Treasurer and Office Manager: Debbie Fox

### Products
Maintenance equipment for railcar and locomotive workshops; portable hydraulic rerailing equipment and containers; underfloor and above ground lifting equipment; turntables; emergency truck for locked axles; Demag jib cranes, gantry cranes and bridge cranes; mobile passenger vehicle washing units and drive-through washing systems; power lift bags; compressed air stations; intermodal car lift system; wheel

*Railquip forklift truck-operated wagon mover*

*Railquip mobile brush wash system*

# MANUFACTURERS/Vehicle maintenance equipment and services

presses and wheel lathes; mechanical wheel handlers; rail car movers; forklift truck-operated railcar mover; bogie assembly stands.

### Contracts
20 refrigerant reclamation units for New York CTA; rerailing equipment for San Francisco Muni; hydraulic intermodal car lift for BNSF; four sets of column lifts for Atlanta Airport people mover; shop fleet cleaner mobile train wash for Staten Island Rapid Transit Authority; auxiliary bogie for locked axles for SEPTA; bogie assembly stand for Metro de Valencia, Venezuela; turnkey installations for vehicle maintenance equipment for Tren Urbano, San Juan, Puerto Rico and Metro de Valencia.

*UPDATED*

## Railway Projects Limited (RPL)

Lisbon House, 5-7 St Mary's Gate, Derby DE1 3JA, UK
Tel: (+44 1332) 34 92 55   Fax: (+44 1332) 29 46 88
e-mail: sales@railwayprojects.co.uk
Web: http://www.railwayprojects.co.uk

### Key personnel
Managing Director: Ian Duffy
Financial Director: Sue Llanos
Engineering Director: Jim Thomson
Project Director: Jez Ward
Sales and Marketing Director: Kelvin Roberts

### Services
An engineering services company offering a turnkey approach for rolling stock maintenance, refurbishment, modification and overhaul. RPL specialises in on-site working and is ISO 9002 certified and Link Up approved.

*UPDATED*

## Rescar Companies

Rescar Incorporated
1101 31st Street, Suite 250, Downers Grove, Illinois 60515, USA
Tel: (+1 630) 963 11 14   Fax: (+1 630) 963 63 42
e-mail: marketing@rescar.com

### Key personnel
Chief Executive Officer: Joe Schieszler
President: Gus Schieszler Senior Vice-President and Chief Financial Officer: Joe Schieszler
Senior Vice-Presidents:
  Steven L Brown; Richard P Hoffman; Marvin Hughes

### Principal subsidiaries
Rescar Inc
Rescar Industries Inc
Transtek Solutions Ink

### Products
Repair and maintenance of freight wagons. Rescar operates repair workshops at Longview, Orange and Channelview, Texas; Du Bois, Pennsylvania; Cedar Rapids, Iowa; Gordon, Georgia; Elk Mills, Maryland; Chicago, Illinois; Washington, Indiana; and Hudson, Colorado. Other services include mobile operations, servicing at the customer's plant, wagon shunting services and rail car cleaning facilities; locomotive servicing and fleet management.

## REW (Acton) Ltd

130 Bollo Lane, Acton, London W3 8BZ, UK
Tel: (+44 20) 79 18 66 66   Fax: (+44 20) 79 18 65 99
e-mail: sales@r-e-w.co.uk
Web: http://www.r-e-w.co.uk

### Key personnel
Sales Manager: Chris Darvall
REW Manager: John Copeman

### Background
A subsidiary of Infraco Sub-Surface Limited.

### Services
Overhaul and repair service, on and off site, with capabilities from a variety of railway equipment including wheelsets and bogies, traction motors, compressors and control systems, through to electronics, clocks and passenger seating.

*UPDATED*

## Rolanfer

Rolanfer Matériel Ferroviaire SA
72 Route de Thionville, PO Box 629, F-57146, Woippy, Cedex, France
Tel: (+33 3) 87 30 14 85   Fax: (33 3) 87 31 23 05
e-mail: rolanfer-materiel.ferroviaire@wanadoo.fr

### Key personnel
See entry in *Freight vehicles and equipment* section.

### Services
Overhaul, repair and conversion of freight wagons.

## Ross & White Company

1090 Alexander Court, PO Box 970, Cary, Illinois 60013-0970, USA
Tel: (+1 847) 516 39 00   Fax: (+1 847) 516 39 89
e-mail: sales@rossandwhite.com
Web: http://www.rossandwhite.com

### Key personnel
President: Jeffery A Ross
Vice-President: Roy A Schuetz
Chief Engineer: Richard M Tock

### Products
Design, manufacture and installation of train washing and companion water reclamation systems; sand handling equipment; Buck Cyclone cleaners for passenger coach interiors; brush scrubbing and pressure washing equipment for passenger coach exteriors.

Contracts include the installation of a coach washing facility for Metra, USA; development and installation of a car progression train washing system for Chicago Transit Authority, USA; development and installation of a gantry-type moving washing system for Chicago Transit Authority; design, supply and installation of a three-lane train washing system for MBTA, USA; and design and installation of six-train washing systems for WMATA, USA.

*UPDATED*

## Rosvagonmash

1a Sokoljnicheslij Val, Box 30, 107113 Moscow, Russian Federation
Tel: (+7 095) 269 06 36; 269 20 88
Fax: (+7 095) 269 58 82

### Services
Repair and refurbishment of passenger rail vehicles. Recent contracts include the refurbishment of Russian Railways Class ER1 and ER2 emus.

## Rotem Company

231 Yangjae-Dong, Soecho-ku, Seoul, Korea 137-938
Tel: (+82 2) 34 64 46 45   Fax: (+82 2) 34 64 47 92
Web: http://www.rotem.co.kr

### Key personnel
See entry in *Locomotives and powered/non-powered passenger vehicles* section.

### Background
See entry in *Locomotives and powered/non-powered passenger vehicles* section.

### Services
Systems logistics, including the design and construction of turnkey maintenance and overhaul workshops with E&M facilities and computerised maintenance information systems. Customer support for rolling stock maintenance, including vehicle refurbishment and repair, field service and maintenance, commissioning and warranty and supply of spare parts.

Contracts include selection by MTRC, Hong Kong, for the provision for seven years of maintenance services for 104 new emu cars operating on the Tseun Kwan O line. In 2000, Rotem was also negotiating a contract to provide maintenance facilities and services for 404 cars for the Inchin International Airport Railway in Korea.

*UPDATED*

## RPL

Railway Projects Ltd
Britannic House, 5-7 St Mary's Gate, Derby DE1 3A, UK
Tel: (+44 1332) 34 92 55   Fax: (+44 1332) 29 46 88
e-mail: sales@railwayprojects.co.uk
Web: http://www.railwayprojects.co.uk

### Key personnel
Business Manager: Graham Fairweather

*Ross & White Company pressure washing equipment*

2002/0125199

### Services
Vehicle maintenance and overhaul, bogie overhaul, company branding (vehicle repainting), refurbishment, warranty and maintenance support, modification programmes, project management.

---

## RPS

Rail Passenger Services Inc
PO Box 26381, Tucson, Arizona 85726, USA
Tel: (+1 520) 747 03 46    Fax: (+1 520) 747 03 78

### Key personnel
President: Peter M Robbins
Vice-President and Chief Financial Officer:
  William B Pickeral

### Principal subsidiary
Arizona Rail Car Inc
PO Box 26381, Tucson, Arizona 85726, USA
Tel: (+1 520) 748 17 86    Fax: (+1 520) 747 03 78

### Products
Heavy passenger coach and freight wagon rebuilding and modernisation. The company specialises in one-off customised passenger coach refurbishments.

In addition, the company also operates the 'Sierra Madre Express' tourist train in Mexico. See entry for Fenomex in the Mexico section of Railway Systems.

**VERIFIED**

---

## Rail Services International SA (RSI)

Rue de la Presse, 4, B-1000 Brussels, Belgium
Tel: (+32 2) 227 11 52    Fax: (+32 2) 218 31 41
e-mail: info@railsi.com
Web: http://www.railsi.com

### Key personnel
See entry in *Locomotives and powered/non-powered passenger vehicles* section.

### Subsidiaries
RSI Austria
Domaniggasse, 2, A-1100 Vienna, Austria
Tel: (+43 1) 617 77 71 12    Fax: (+43 1) 617 77 71 28
e-mail: info@railsi.at
Managing Director: Reinhard Rössler

RSI Belgium
Vaartblekersstraat, 29, B-8400 Oostende, Belgium
Tel: (+32 59) 70 09 08    Fax: (+32 59) 70 23 75
e-mail: info@railsi.be
Managing Director: Jan Baert

RSI France
38, rue de la Convention, F-94270 Le Kremlin-Bicêtre, France
Tel: (+33 1) 53 14 17 30    Fax: (+33 1) 53 14 17 49
e-mail: info@railsi.com
Managing Director: Philippe Aloyol

RSI Italia SpA
Via Sesto San Giovanni, 9, I-20126 Milan, Italy
Tel: (+39 02) 66 14 02 01    Fax: (+39 02) 66 10 09 61
e-mail: info@railsi.it
Managing Director: Renato Mantegazza
Unit Manager Milan: Guido Sarzilla
Unit Manager Rome: Pasquale Grieco

RSI Netherlands
Onderhoudpost Watergraafsmeer, Kruislaan, 254, NL-1098 Amsterdam SM
Tel: (+31 6) 15 03 67 70    Fax: (+31 6) 205 57 88 18
e-mail: info@railsi.nl
Managing Director: Jan Baert
Unit Manager: Bart Janssen

### Services
Development, design, engineering and technical assistance for fitting out passenger car interiors. RSI's Study and Design Department works on new projects such as interiors and technical specifications for passenger cars. RSI carries out maintenance, overhaul and major refurbishment of all kinds of rolling stock at its four workshops (Milan, Ostende, Rome and Vienna) or units in 20 European locations.

Customer support for railway operators, day-to-day operations, wheelset maintenance, repair, warranty, mobile operations at customer's plant and supply of spare parts.

### Contracts
RSI has signed maintenance contracts with CFF, FS, NS, ÖBB, SNCB, SNCF, ICF and Eurotunnel.

**UPDATED**

---

## SEFAC

SEFAC
PO Box 101, 1 Rue André Compain, F-08800 Montherme, France
Tel: (+33 3) 24 53 01 82    Fax: (+33 3) 24 53 29 18
e-mail: vjolliot@sefac.fr
Web: http://www.sefac.fr

### Key personnel
Managing Director: Emmanuel de Rohom Chobot
Finance Director: F Pauchet
Sales and Marketing Manager: Vincent Jolliot
Technical Director: O Morlot
Purchasing Manager: J P Fernand

### Principal subsidiaries
SEFAC Inc
7175 Oakland Mills Road, Columbia, Maryland 21046, USA
Tel: (+1 410) 964 08 06    Fax: (+1 410) 964 08 77
Manager: Buck Stork

SEFAC SA
Camino de las Rejas 1, Nave 10, E-28820 Coslada (Madrid), Spain
Tel: (+34 91) 672 36 12    Fax: (+34 91) 672 33 96
Manager: R Serrano

### Products
Electromechanical lifting systems with mobile or fixed columns, partially or totally in ground, capacity per column from 5 to 40 tonnes. SEFAC lifting systems allow the lifting of power cars, LRVs, trainsets and wagons for underfloor maintenance work to be carried out; lifting platforms allow maintenance of bogies and underfloor equipment; bogie drops allow maintenance without uncoupling cars.

### Contracts
Contracts include the supply of lifting systems to railway operators including SNCF, SNTF, FGC, Ferrovías, TRA, SNCB, OCTRA and CP; metro operators in Hong Kong, Baltimore, Lisbon, Paris, Rotterdam and Cairo; and to rolling stock manufacturers including Adtranz, ALSTOM, Bombardier-ANF and Fiat.

**UPDATED**

---

## Siemens Transportation Systems

Integrated Services Division (Infrastructure)
PO Box 3327, D-38023 Braunschweig, Germany
Tel: (+49 531) 22 60    Fax: (+49 531) 226 42 64

Integrated Services Division (Rolling Stock)
PO Box 3240, D-91050 Erlangen, Germany
Tel: (+49 9131) 72 99 35    Fax: (+49 9131) 72 35 31
e-mail: service@ts.siemens.de
Web: http://www.siemens.com/ts

### Corporate headquarters
Siemens AG
Transportation Systems
PO Box 910220, D-12414 Berlin, Germany
Tel: (+49 30) 385 50

### Key personnel
President, Transportation Systems Group:
  Herbert J Steffen
Group Vice Presidents: Hans-Dieter Bott;
  Thomas Ganswindt; Hans M Schabert
Directors: Th Sponholz, L Zimmerman

### Subsidiary companies
See entry in *Locomotives and powered/non-powered passenger vehicles* section.

### Services
Integrated Services was established in December 1999, offering service and maintenance provision for: rolling stock; infrastructure; signalling and communications systems; and power supply systems.

Rolling stock service provision includes: routine vehicle maintenance; refurbishment; spare parts supply; and bogie overhaul. Infrastructure service provision includes: maintenance; spare parts supply; and diagnostic services. The Charter Rail service is based on using the customer's own staff, which are sub-contracted at a fixed price, with Siemens assuming responsibility for maintenance planning, spares provision and services with guaranteed costs and availability.

Integrated Services also offers consulting, training, documentation and financing services.

### Developments
In July 2002, Siemens announced that it had formed a joint venture subsidiary with Spanish National Railways (RENFE) to maintain and repair a fleet of 30 Class 440 and 20 Class 447 emus operating in the greater Barcelona area. Siemens hold a 51 per cent shareholding in the company, Nertus Mantenimiento Feroviario SA. Maintenance activities were to be undertaken at a RENFE-owned facility in Barcelona.

In January 2002, Siemens acquired a 50 per cent shareholding in Leipziger Infrastruktur Betriebe (LIB), which was formerly the infrastructure maintenance subsidiary of Leipzig's transit authority, Leipziger Verkehrsbetriebe (LVB). This followed the earlier acquisition by Siemens of a 50 per cent shareholding in the authority's rolling stock maintenance subsidiary, Leipziger Fahrzeug-Service Betriebe (LFB). Both ventures are regarded as pioneering steps in public-private partnerships in Germany.

Siemens has a shareholding of 51 per cent in ERL Maintenance Support Sdn Bhd (EMAS), which provides repair and maintenance services for the rolling stock and infrastructure of the Express Rail Link airport line in Kuala Lumpur Malaysia. The contract provides for transfer of technology to Siemens' partner, ERL, within three years of the start of operations, which took place in April 2002.

In September 2000, Siemens launched its Internet-based Rail Mall spare parts ordering system, enabling operators of light rail vehicles supplied by the company to obtain parts in most countries in Europe within 24 hours.

### Contracts
Current contracts include:

**Argentina:** rolling stock maintenance for Metrovías, Buenos Aires, providing maintenance and refurbishment of 64 vehicles.
**Egypt:** Siemens is responsible for the maintenance of Egyptian National Railways' 350 km Cairo Baharya freight line, covering track, signalling and communications systems.
**Germany:** Siemens is responsible to DB AG for maintenance of the signalling and operations control system of the upgraded Berlin Magdeburg high-speed line.

Under a five-year contract, Siemens maintains contact line and power supply equipment for the 330 km Laubag Industriebahn mining railway in Brandenburg, and under a 10-year agreement signed in 1995 has maintained and refurbished its signalling and control systems.
**Spain:** Under a five-year agreement with Spanish National Railways, Siemens is responsible for substations serving the 471 km Madrid Seville high-speed line, and for maintenance of the power supply and telecommunications systems.
**Thailand:** having supplied and equipped the 23.1 km BTS mass transit system in Bangkok, Siemens is responsible for maintenance, covering 105 metro vehicles, track, signalling, operations control systems, power supply, safety systems, stations and all technical equipment for a period of five years.
**UK:** Siemens has secured rolling stock maintenance contracts for several urban and main line operators in the UK. These include: Arriva Trains Northern, servicing Class 333 emus supplied by Siemens, using a depot in Leeds; Heathrow Express, for which Siemens constructed and operates a dedicated depot in west London to maintain the operator's fleet of Siemens-supplied Class 332 emus; South Yorkshire Supertram, maintaining 25 trams at a

## 780 MANUFACTURERS/Vehicle maintenance equipment and services

purpose-built depot in Sheffield. In addition, Siemens is to be responsible for the maintenance of a fleet of 785 emu cars being supplied to South West Trains. This was to be undertaken at a depot to completed at Southampton by the end of 2002.

Other orders for infrastructure and rolling stock maintenance services form part of turnkey contracts, detailed in the Turnkey systems contractors section.

**NEW ENTRY**

## Simmons

Simmons Machine Tool Corporation
1700 North Broadway, Albany, New York 12204, USA
Tel: (+1 518) 462 54 31   Fax: (+1 518) 462 03 71
e-mail: smt@smtgroup.com
Web: http://www.smtgroup.com

**Key personnel**
Chairman and Chief Executive: Hans J Naumann
President: John O Naumann
Finance Director: David A Simonian

**Subsidiary**
Simmons-Stanray Wheel Truing Machine Corporation
(address as above)

**Affiliated company**
Niles-Simmons Industrieanlagen GmbH
Zwickauer Strasse 355, D-09117 Chemnitz, Germany

**Products**
Design and manufacture of equipment and machines for manual and automated railway and transit wheel workshops, including: underfloor wheel profiling machines; special machines for wheel, axle and wheelset maintenance; CNC grinding centres; CNC vertical turning and boring centres. Simmons also provides engineering design and layout services for complete wheel shops.

**UPDATED**

## Smith Bros & Webb Ltd

Britannia Works, Arden Forest Industrial Estate, Alcester, Warwickshire B49 6EX, UK
Tel: (+44 1789) 40 00 96   Fax: (+44 1789) 40 02 31
e-mail: sbw@vehicle-washing-systems.co.uk
Web: http://www.vehicle-washing-systems.co.uk

**Key personnel**
Managing Director: John P Bennett
Sales and Marketing Manager: Rob Everton
Service and Installation Manager: Bob Smith
Technical Manager: Tony Appleton

*Smith Bros & Webb train washing system for First Great Western at Bristol, UK* 2000/0087659

**Products**
Britannia automatic washing systems for main line and metro trains. Options available include: detergent or acid application; front, rear, roof, valence and skirt washing; blow-drying; pure water final rinse; train speed indication; water recycling and effluent treatment. After-sales service offered.

Recent contracts include train washing installations for Croydon Tramlink, West Midlands Metro and First Great Western (Bristol, UK) and two systems for MTRC, Hong Kong.

**UPDATED**

## Somers Railway Engineering

Unit 1, Hayes Trading Estate, Folkes Road, Lye, Stourbridge DY9 8RH, UK
Tel: (+44 1384) 42 69 00   Fax: (+44 1384) 42 69 08
e-mail: sgrsomers@aol.com
Web: http://www.somers-handling.com

**Key personnel**
Managing Director: Stephen Reece
Technical Manager: Ian Payne
Service and Repair Manager: James Simms

**Products**
Mobile and fixed rail vehicle lifting jacks; traversers; scissor lift tables; bogie rotators; bogie drop systems; bogie turntables; bogie turning systems; rail drop systems; all types of workshop equipment.

**UPDATED**

*Transit jacking bogie system supplied by Somers Railway Engineering to Alstom* 2001/0105893

## Stertil-Koni

PO Box 23, NL-9288 ZG Kootstertille, Pays-Netherlands
Tel: (+31 512) 33 44 44   Fax: (+31 512) 33 44 30
e-mail: info@stertil.nl
Web: http://www.stertil.nl

**Subsidiary**
Stertil BV
1900 Benhill Avenue, Baltimore, Maryland 21226, USA
Tel: (+1 410) 355 71 00   Fax: (+1 410) 355 71 70
e-mail: lifts@stertil-koni.com
Web: http://www.stertil-koni.com

**Products**
Hydraulic lifting systems for rail vehicles. Systems have been supplied to urban rail systems in Brussels, Calgary, Graz, Innsbruck, Jacksonville (on behalf of Bombardier Transportation) and Linz.

**VERIFIED**

## SweMaint

Utbyvägen 151, SE-415 07 Gothenburg, Sweden
Tel: (+46 31) 10 36 00   Fax: (+46 31) 10 36 69
e-mail: info@swemaint.se
Web: http://www.swemaint.se

**Services**
Freight wagon maintenance, repair and refurbishment.

**VERIFIED**

## Talgo

Patentes Talgo SA
C/Gabriel Garcia Marquez 4, E-28230 Las Rozas, Madrid, Spain
Tel: (+34 91) 631 38 00; 27 00   Fax: (+34 91) 631 38 99
e-mail: comercial@talgo.com

**Key personnel**
See entry in *Locomotives and power/non-powered passenger vehicles section*.

**Subsidiaries**
Talgo America
100 South King Street, Suite 320, Seattle, Washington 98104, USA
Tel: (+1 206) 748 61 40   Fax: (+1 206) 748 61 47
e-mail: info@talgoamerica.com

Talgo Deutschland GmbH
Revaler Strasse 99, D-10245 Berlin, Germany
Tel: (+49 30) 29 72 27 51   Fax: (+49 30) 29 72 11 43
e-mail: talgodeutschland@talgo.com

Talgo-Transtech Oy (qv)

**Products**
Design and manufacture of machinery and equipment for rolling stock wheelset examination and maintenance, including pit lathes with CNC control or a hydraulic copying device for loads of 18, 26 or 30 tonnes per wheelset, with accessories for machining brake discs *in situ;* haulage carts for positioning rolling stock, bogies or wheelsets up to 300 tonnes in weight at speeds up to 5 km/h; and equipment for dynamic measurement of wheel parameters, including diameter, flange height and thickness, to determine turning programmes for CNC-controlled lathes.

Recent contracts include the supply of underfloor wheel lathes to: TBA, Argentina; DB Reise & Touristik, Germany; Lisbon metro, Portugal.

## TGOJ

S-631 92 Eskilstuna, Sweden
Tel: (+46 16) 17 26 00   Fax: (+46 16) 17 26 01
e-mail: contact@tgoj.se

**Services**
Maintenance, repair and refurbishment of freight wagons and passenger coaches.

## Thrall

Thrall Europa Service Parts
Holgate Park, 156 Holgate Road, York YO24 4FJ, UK
Tel: (+44 1904) 75 60 00    Fax: (+44 1904) 75 60 06
e-mail: ServiceParts@ThrallEuropa.co.uk

**Key personnel**
See entry in *Freight vehicles and equipment* section.

**Services**
Supply of spare parts and components for the manufacture, repair, conversion and overhaul of freight wagons, with a capability to distribute products throughout Europe.

## Toshiba Corporation

Railway Projects Department, Toshiba Building, 1-1, Shibaura 1-chome, Minato-ku, Tokyo 105, Japan
Tel: (+81 3) 34 57 49 24    Fax: (+81 3) 34 57 83 85

**Products**
Multipurpose test equipment for traction motors; automatic test equipment for silicon rectifiers; battery trucks for transporting carbodies; battery tractors interchangeable with both steel and rubber-tyred wheelsets for moving carbodies in shops or yards.

## TraffiCare AB

Box 340, SE-101 26 Stockholm, Sweden
Tel: (+46 8) 762 35 00
Web: http://www.trafficare.se

**Key personnel**
Managing Director: Tommie Wikström

**Corporate background**
Formerly SJ Terminal Production, the sector responsible for train and station cleaning and minor rolling stock repairs for Swedish State Railways, TraffiCare AB was established in 2001 as part of the restructuring resulting from the break-up of the state railway company.

**Services**
TraffiCare's 'Ready Train' service covers vehicle cleaning and preparation, train formation, logistics and minor repairs. Clients include SJ AB, A-Train, Tågkompaniet and Linx.

*NEW ENTRY*

## Trenitalia SpA

Italian State Railways
Rolling Stock Technology Department (UTMR)
Viala S Lavagnini 58, I-50129 Florence, Italy
Tel: (+39 055) 47 60 00 Fax: (+39 055) 48 19 05

**Services**
With more than 5,000 employees, UTMR is responsible for the maintenance of Italian State Railways (FS) traction and rolling stock. It also undertakes overhaul, refurbishment and conversion projects using the 13 facilities that form the company's Major Repairs Workshops (OGR) division. These resources and capabilities are offered to other operators.

*NEW ENTRY*

## Ultrasonic Sciences Ltd

Unit 4 Springlakes Industrial Estate, Deadbrook Lane, Aldershot, Hants, GU12 4UH, UK
Tel: (+44 1252) 35 05 50   Fax: (+44 1252) 35 04 45
e-mail: info@ultrasonic-sciences.co.uk
Web: http://www.ultrasonic-sciences.co.uk

**Key personnel**
Chairman: J B Kennelly
Sales Director: C S Gartside

**Products**
Automated and semi-automated ultrasonic testing systems for manufacturing plant and in-service inspection. Applications include testing of machined solid axles and forged or cast wheels, *in situ* inspection of hollow axles from the bore, and inspection of wheeltreads in maintenance or services workshops.

**Contracts**
Supply of systems for Lucchini (1999), SNCF (2000), Bombardier Transportation (2001), Indian Wheel and Axle Plant (2001) and Alstom (2002).

*UPDATED*

## United Goninan

Broadmeadow Road, Broadmeadow, New South Wales 2060, Australia
Tel: (+61 2) 49 23 50 00    Fax: (+61 2) 49 23 50 01
Web: http://www.unitedgroup.com.au

**Key personnel**
See entry in *Locomotives and powered/non-powered passenger vehicles* section.

**Services**
Rail vehicle maintenance; locomotive and passenger vehicle overhaul, upgrading and refurbishment.

**Contracts**
Include: contract maintenance of dmus for TransAdelaide; contract maintenance of sulphuric acid tank wagons for Western Mining Corporation; upgrading 13 Class 2600 diesel-electric locomotives for QR; modernisation of 40 diesel electric locomotives for Pakistan National Railways in a joint venture with General Electric; refurbishment of 767 double-deck passenger coaches for the State Railway Authority of New South Wales; conversion of 472 trams to driver-only operation for PTC, Victoria; refurbishment of 762 metro cars for MTRC, Hong Kong, China.
United Goninan's Maintrain Auburn Service Centre is responsible for contract maintenance of the NWS State Rail Authority's CityRail fleet of approximately 1,450 cars. In 2001, a maintenance facilities improvement programme was under way aimed at increasing the scope and extent of planned maintenance.

*NEW ENTRY*

## Upright UK Ltd

Special Products Division, 153 Newton Road, Lowton, Warrington WA3 1EZ, UK
Tel: (+44 1942) 68 01 60    Fax: (+44 1942) 60 19 84

**Key personnel**
See entry in *Permanent way equipment* section.

**Products**
Supply and rental of access equipment for rolling stock maintenance including powered platforms, glass fibre towers and light-alloy scaffold systems; alloy pit bridging boards; windscreen stands, passenger coach side access platforms, access steps; roof guardrail systems, guardrails for passenger coach doorways, pit bridges. Staff training in the use of work platforms and scaffold systems.

## USF

USF Wheelabrator Sisson Lehmann
24 rue Camille Didier – BP 39, F-08001 Charleville-Mézières, France
Tel: (+33 3) 24 33 63 00    Fax: (+33 3) 24 37 39 37
e-mail: wslcom@aol.com
Web: http://www.traitementdesurface.com

**Key personnel**
Sales and Marketing Manager: Alain Portebois
Operations Director: Dominique Schwab

**Products**
Stripping and surface preparation equipment for rail vehicles and vehicle components, including shot-blasting for vehicle paint-stripping and shot-peening of critical components.

## Vanjax Sales Pvt Ltd

343 Sidco Industrial Estate, Ambattur, Chennai 600 098, India
Tel: (+91 44) 625 46 67; 48 75; 53 00
Fax: (+91 44) 625 97 72
e-mail: vanjax.sales@rmj.sprintrpg.ems.vsnl.net.in
Web: http://www.eepc.gov.in

**Key personnel**
Chairman and Managing Director: Fakhruddin Vanak
Director, Engineering Works: Daniel F Vanak
Director, Commercial: Juzar F Vanak

**Products**
Hydraulic portable floor cranes, workshop presses, trolley jacks, hydraulic jacks and cylinders, hydraulic pullers, pipe benders, bolt tensioners and hydraulic pumps/power packs.

*UPDATED*

## VIA Rail Canada

Equipment Maintenance Business and Maintenance Services
201 Ash Avenue, Montreal, Quebec H3K 3K2, Canada
Tel: (+1 514) 934 75 45    Fax: (+1 514) 934 75 20
e-mail: alan_mackenzie@viarail.ca
Web: http://www.viarail.ca

**Key personnel**
Manager, Planning and Logistics: Alan MacKenzie

**Services**
VIA Rail Canada is the country's national long-distance passenger train operator. It offers the following services to other operators: inspections, maintenance and repair of rolling stock; daily and weekly train servicing; inspection and overhaul of bogies; repair and requalification of dampers and other components; wheel profiling; bearing replacement; automatic train washing; fluid analysis; vibration analysis; testing and calibration of test instruments; assembly of wiring harnesses and equipment storage.
In addition, the following professional services are offered through a skilled management and technical team: operations planning; repair feasibility studies; project management; technical studies and performance specifications; industrial engineering and productivity studies; vehicle performance testing.
VIA has maintenance centres at Montreal, Winnipeg and Vancouver and train servicing locations at Toronto and Halifax.

## Von Roll BETEC

Edenstrasse 20, Post Box, CH-8045 Zurich, Switzerland
Tel: (+41 1) 204 30 41    Fax: (+41 1) 204 30 43
Web: http://www.vonroll.ch

**Key personnel**
Managing Director: Dr Peter Schildknecht
Marketing Manager: Marc Bickel

**Products**
Underfloor wheel profiling equipment including wet grinding machines wheelset measuring systems.

*UPDATED*

## Vossloh Schienenfahrzeugtechnik GmbH (VSFT)

PO Box 9293, D-24152 Kiel
Falckensteiner Strasse 2, D-24159 Kiel, Germany
Tel: (+49 431) 39 99 30 89    Fax: (+49 1) 39 99 22 74

# MANUFACTURERS/Vehicle maintenance equipment and services

e-mail: vertrieb.kiel@vsft.vossloh.com
Web: http://www.vsft.de

**Works**
Service-Zentrum Moers, Klever Strasse 48, D-47441 Moers, Germany
Tel: (+49 2841) 140 40   Fax: (+49 2841) 14 04 50

**Key personnel**
See entry in *Locomotives and powered/non-powered passenger vehicles* section.

**Products**
Fleet management and maintenance. Full service or maintenance programmes adapted to the client's specific needs for VSFT locomotives as well as for diesel freight and shunting locomotives from other provinces.

*NEW ENTRY*

## Walter Finkbeiner GmbH

Alte Poststrasse 9, D-72250 Freudenstadt, Germany
Tel: (+49 7441) 40 31   Fax: (+49 7441) 877 78
e-mail: finkbeiner-lifts@t-online.com
Web: http://www.finkbeiner-lifts.com

**Key personnel**
Managing Director: Gerhard Finkbeiner

**Products**
Mobile lifting equipment including mobile lifting column model ranges:EHB 707K to lift rail vehicles such as streetcars and wagons, with a capacity of 7,200 kg per column (15,000 lbs), equipped with a chassis bracket with direct operation from any column;EHB 710K to lift rail vehicles such as light engines and wagons, with a capacity of 10,000 kg per column (22,000 lbs) equipped with a chassis bracket with direct operation from any column.

*NEW ENTRY*

## Whiting Corporation

26000 Whiting Way, Monee, Illinois 60449, USA
Tel: (+1 708) 596 66 00
e-mail: sales@whitingcorp.com
Web: http://www.whitingcorp.com

**Key personnel**
President: J L Kahn
Vice-President, Sales and Marketing: C J Skorpinski
Manager, Product Systems and Transportation Sales: M N Milligan
Manager, Applications: Ron Koziel

**Principal subsidiary**
Whiting Equipment Canada Inc
PO Box 217, 350 Alexander Street, Welland, Ontario L3B 5P4, Canada
Tel: (+1 905) 732 75 85   Fax: (+1 905) 732 23 66
President: Rudi Kroeker

**Products**
Conventional/shallow pit car hoists, body hoists/supports, bogie repair hoists, transfer tables, bogie/vehicle turntables, portable electric jacks, wagon/train progression systems, drop tables, overhead and gantry cranes.

## Windhoff AG

PO Box 1963, D-48409 Rheine, Germany
Tel: (+49 5971) 580   Fax: (+49 5971) 582 09
e-mail: info@windhoff.de
Web: http://www.windhoff.de

**Key personnel**
See entry in *Permanent way components, equipment and services* section.

**Products**
Bogie lifting plants and rotation installations, transporters, air-cushion vehicles and lifting stands. Windhoff developed 70 vehicles with lifting work platforms for the inspection and maintenance of DB AG ICE high-speed trainsets; these were delivered to the ICE Maintenance and Service Centre in Hamburg-Eidelstedt. The complete eight-track installations mounted on supports, the lifting cars with guiding system and the air-cushion-type bogie and wheelset changing equipment were supplied by Windhoff.

Windhoff has also introduced a mobile wheel scale system for precise measurement of axle load, bogie load and gross weight of rail vehicles. The modular system can be transported easily by road.

## YEC

Yorkshire Engine Company Ltd
PO Box 66, Rotherham, S60 1DD, UK
Tel: (+44 1709) 82 02 02   Fax: (+44 1709) 82 02 06
e-mail: yec@fsbdial.co.uk

**Key personnel**
See *Locomotives and powered/non-powered passenger vehicles* section.

**Products**
Safety Scotch: a device for immobilising rail vehicles during maintenance or engineering work.

# TURNKEY SYSTEMS CONTRACTORS

## Alphabetical listing

(See also *Turnkey railway electrification* in classified listing in *Fixed electrification equipment* section)
Alcatel Canada
ALSTOM
Ansaldo Trasporti Sistemi Ferroviari
Balfour Beatty Rail Projects
Bombardier Transportation
Chemetron
Davy British Rail International
Dimetronic
Fiat
GE
Interinfra
KOROS
Marconi Communications
Mecanoexportimport
Parsons Brinckerhoff
Ranalah
SAGEM
SAIT-Devlonics
SAT
Scitel Telematics
Sema Group
Siemens
Siemens Switzerland
Siemens Transportation Systems
TCI
Temoinsa

## Company listing by country

**AUSTRALIA**
ALSTOM

**BELGIUM**
SAIT-Devlonics

**BRAZIL**
ALSTOM

**CANADA**
Alcatel Canada
Bombardier Transportation

**FRANCE**
ALSTOM
Interinfra
SAGEM
SAT
Sema Group

**GERMANY**
Siemens

**HUNGARY**
Scitel Telematics

**ITALY**
ALSTOM
Ansaldo Trasporti Sistemi Ferroviari
Fiat

**KOREA**
Rotem

**ROMANIA**
Mecanoexportimport

**POLAND**
ALSTOM

**SPAIN**
ALSTOM
Dimetronic
Temoinsa

**SWITZERLAND**
Siemens Switzerland

**UK**
ALSTOM
Balfour Beatty Rail Projects
Davy British Rail International
Marconi Communications
Ranalah
Siemens Transportation Systems
TCI
Telephone Cables
Transintech

**USA**
ALSTOM
Chemetron
GE
Parsons Brinckerhoff
Siemens Transportation Systems

## MANUFACTURERS/Turnkey systems contractors

## Alcatel Canada Inc

Transport Automation
1235 Ormont Drive, Weston, Ontario M9L 2W6, Canada
Tel: (+1 416) 742 39 00   Fax: (+1 416) 742 11 36

**Key personnel**
General Manager: Walter Friesen
Director, Business Development: Kevin D Fitzgerald

**Projects**
Turnkey signalling systems for Stockholm metro, Quebec Cartier Railway, Toronto Transit Commission, Walt Disney World, Hong Kong MTRC and KCRC West Rail and East Rail Extension, San Francisco MUNI, and London Docklands Light Railway.

*UPDATED*

*Metropolis metro trainset supplied as part of a turnkey contract for Singapore's Land Transport Authority*
*2002/0525428*

## ALSTOM Transport SA

Systems Business
48 rue Albert Dhalenne, F-93482 Saint-Ouen Cedex, Paris, France
Tel: (+33 1) 41 66 90 00   Fax: (+33 1) 41 66 96 66
Web: http://www.transport.alstom.com

**Key personnel**
Senior Vice President: C Carlier
See main entry in *Locomotives and powered/non-powered passenger vehicles* section.
Mass Transit Business Unit
Vice President Mass Transit: M Bourboulon
Main Line Business Unit
Vice President Main Lines: D Simmoneau

Concession Business Unit
PO Box 134, Manchester M60 1AH, UK
Tel: (+44 161) 872 24 31   Fax: (+44 161) 875 21 31
Vice President: Jeffrey Done

**Background**
Business Systems in its current form was created in 1998 following the acquisition of Cegelec, the electrical contracting arm of the Alcatel ALSTOM group.

**Services**
The Business Systems of ALSTOM Transport offers global public transportation solutions including turnkey management, execution of infrastructure packages, interfaces with civil works and rolling stock.

The business addresses urban transit systems, interurban lines and main lines, and can be involved in projects at the individual subsystem level, at the full turnkey level, or at the level of an equity investor.

The Mass Transit business acts as main contractor for metro and light rail transit systems, airport rail links, trolleybus systems, guidance systems and cable-driven people movers and houses all the competencies necessary for the development of a project concept, its detailed design, and its delivery.

The Infrastructure Business unit of ALSTOM Transport Systems offers solutions at the system or subsystem level for including power generation and distribution. It includes AC and DC traction substations, overhead lines, surface contact third rail, at-level integrated supply system, SCADA, auxiliary power supply, track laying, maintenance workshops, communications, signalling (tramways), electromechanical equipment in-station and electronic guidance systems for buses.

Its scope embraces design, procurement, installation, commissioning, technical assistance, maintenance and training.

**Contracts**
**Brazil:** ALSTOM won a turnkey order from Metrofor for a metro system in Fortaleza, northeastern Brazil. The 24 km line, which has 17 stations, of which three are underground, links Joao Felipe in the city centre to Villa Das Flores in the suburbs. It was commissioned in 2001. The order covered 10 four-car trainsets, which incorporate the ONIX 3000 drive system, and the signalling system. In addition, ALSTOM was responsible for the management of the project and the integration and installation of the complete electrical and mechanical system. The overall system was manufactured by ALSTOM's factories in São Paulo, with traction equipment supplied by ALSTOM's plant in Tarbes, France.

**Chile:** In July 2002, ALSTOM was selected to supply rolling stock, Urbalis automatic train control equipment and maintenance services for the 32 km north-south Line 4 of Santiago's metro system.

**Egypt:** Egypt's National Authority for Tunnels (NAT) has awarded ALSTOM, as leader of the Interinfra consortium, a turnkey contract for the extension of Line 2 (Phase 2C). The 2.5 km surface line will run south of Giza Suburban station to El Mounib, adding two new stations. The turnkey contract is composed of civil works, electromechanical equipment and power supply and low-voltage equipment. ALSTOM's contribution includes power supply, signalling and Automatic Train Operation (ATO), and a centralised control system, as well as overall project management of the turnkey contract.

**Greece:** Athens metro was inaugurated in 2000. The metro system was built as a turnkey project by the Olympic Metro Consortium, led by Siemens (Germany) and Interinfra (France), of which ALSTOM is the main shareholder, comprising 21 German, French and Greek companies.

**Poland:** ALSTOM has also won an order to upgrade the Bytom to Katowice tramway for the Tramway Communication Company of Katowice in Silesia. As well as provision of new vehicles, the turnkey order includes the refurbishment of the rail infrastructure and stations on the existing 20 km Line 6/41. The trams, which will be supplied by the company's Polish subsidiary ALSTOM Konstal, will be fitted with ONIX traction drives.

**Singapore:** Singapore's Land Transport Authority (LTA) has awarded the ALSTOM/STE consortium an order worth €170 million, for the second phase of construction of its automatic Marina metro line. ALSTOM's share of this contract is valued at €123 million. ALSTOM will supply its AXONIS™ automatic metro system for this line.

This new order is an extension of the Marina Line Phase 1 project, awarded to ALSTOM on a turnkey basis in December 2000. The first stage covers 5.6 km and has six stations. This second section will extend the Marina line by 5 km and add five new stations. Subsequent contracts placed with ALSTOM covered construction of the remainder of the line, which will eventually cover 34 km and circle the island of Singapore, making it the world's longest automatic metro line.

For this second phase, ALSTOM will supply seven three-car Metropolis™ trainsets, the signalling system and related infrastructure and will be responsible for the overall management of the project. The delivery of the first trainsets is scheduled for 2004, with commercial service commencing in 2006.

**Spain:** As part of the TramMet consortium, ALSTOM was awarded contracts to build and equip Lines 1 and 2 of the Barcelona light rail system As well as supplying 19 and 18 Citadis tramsets respectively for the new lines, ALSTOM is responsible for system engineering, traction power supply substations, telecommunications, ticketing, signalling, workshop equipment and project management of the electromechanical package. ALSTOM holds a shareholding of 25 per cent in TramMet, which holds 15-year operating and maintenance concessions on the system. The first phase is due to be commissioned in March 2004.

**Venezuela:** ALSTOM, as part of the FRAMECA consortium, has been awarded a turnkey order from the Caracas metro authority, CAMC, for the 5.5 km Line 4 of the city's metro system, which is scheduled to enter service in 2002. In addition to supplying 44 metro cars and the signalling system, ALSTOM will carry out electrification of the line and provide a complete fire protection system.

*UPDATED*

## Ansaldo Trasporti Sistemi Ferroviari

Via Argine 425, I-80147 Naples, Italy
Fax: (+39 081) 243 25 70
Genoa office
Via dei Pescatori 35, I-16129 Genoa, Italy
Fax: (+39 010) 655 20 28

**Key personnel**
Chief Executive: Sante Roberti

**Background**
Ansaldo Trasporti Sistemi Ferroviari continues the business activities of the former Ansaldo Trasporti SpA System Business Unit following a break-up of the company in April 2001. These cover the design, construction, testing, commissioning, system engineering, project management, maintenance and project financing of subsystems or complete main line and urban electrified mass transit systems as the main contractor or partner. The company employs around 300 staff.

**Projects**
Include: Copenhagen driverless metro, Denmark; Dublin light rail lines A and C, Ireland; Midland Metro, UK; Manchester Metrolink, UK; Lima metro, Peru; Genoa LRT and trolleybus systems, Italy; Sassari LRT, Italy; Naples metro line 6; Rome metro; Circumvesuviana and other regional lines, Italy; Rome Naples high-speed railway, Italy; and Trieste innovative stream system, Italy.

*UPDATED*

## Balfour Beatty Rail Projects Ltd

7 Mayday Road, Thornton Heath, Surrey CR7 7XA, UK
Tel: (+44 1332) 26 20 57   Fax: (+44 1332) 26 22 95
e-mail: bill.pownall@bbrai.com

**Main works**
B203 Midland House, Nelson Street, Derby DEI 2SA
Tel: (+44 1332) 26 26 66   Fax: (+44 1332) 26 28 46

**Key personnel**
Managing Director: Rob Boulger
Tendering and Business Development Director:
  Mike Greenwood
Commercial Director: Keith Hampson
Operations Director: Paul Copeland
Engineering Director: Andy Curzon
Finance Director: Rory Mitchell
Human Resources Director: Peter Raza

Turnkey systems contractors/**MANUFACTURERS** 785

**Principal subsidiaries**
Balfour Beatty Rail Infrastructure Services
Balfour Beatty Rail Track Systems
Balfour Beatty Rail Plant
Balfour Beatty Rail Power Systems
Balfour Beatty Rail Technologies

**Products**
Design, supply, installation, testing and commissioning of railway infrastructure, including track, overhead, power supplies and signalling for high-speed, mixed traffic, heavy haul, light rail and mass transit systems. The company offers multidisciplinary project design and construction capability.

**Contracts**
Recent contracts include: track design and electrification of the MTRC Lantau and Airport Railway, Hong Kong (1995-1998); design and construction of the Changi Airport Line, Singapore; design, supply and install trackwork, signalling, telecomms, overhead line civil works and power supply of the Euston Remodelling, London, UK; design, supply and installation of trackwork and overhead line of the Leeds Remodelling, UK.

Ongoing contracts include the design, supply and installation of the overhead line and power distribution, the upgrade of the WCML, UK; Heathrow Terminal 5 and Watford—Bletchley.

**UPDATED**

*Bombardier automated rapid transit system for New York's JFK International Airport, USA* 2002/0524886

## Bombardier Transportation

Total Transit Systems
PO Box 220, Station A, Kingston, Ontario, Canada K7M 6R2
Tel: (+1 613) 384 31 00   Fax: (+1 613) 384 52 40
Web: http://www.transportation.bombardier.com

**Key personnel**
See main entry in *Locomotives and powered/non-powered passenger vehicles* section.

**Products and Services**
Working in partnership with local civil contractors and suppliers, Bombardier Transportation designs, integrates, installs and delivers the industry's broadest range of technologies – from large-scale urban transit systems to automated people movers.
- Automated people mover systems
- Monorail systems
- Light rail transit systems
- Metro/rapid transit systems
- Operations and maintenance services

**Contracts**
**Canada:** The Millennium Line, an extension to Vancouver's fully automated SkyTrain system, opened in September 2002. Bombardier Transportation completed the design, supply and installation of the Electrical and Mechanical systems for the 20.5-km line. Bombardier's scope of work included automatic train control and communication systems, power supply and distribution system, trackwork, power rail, platform and guideway intrusion detection systems, system engineering and integration, and testing and commissioning for 20.5 km of dual-track guideway. Under a previous contract, Bombardier also supplied 60 ART MK II SkyTrain vehicles, employing Bombardier's LIM technology.

**Malaysia:** In 2001, Bombardier was selected to lead a consortium that will undertake improvements to a 180-km section of Malaysia's state-owned railway line. The project includes upgrading and converting existing single track to double track together with electrification and a new signalling system. Bombardier will integrate and manage the design engineering, supply, installation and commissioning, defects liability period and maintenance support of the project.

**Portugal:** In 1998 Bombardier Transportation, as a member of the Normetro Consortium, is responsible for

*Bombardier Light Rail System for Porto, Portugal* 2002/0524963

the delivery of a full turnkey, 70 km light rail system under contract to the City of Porto, Portugal. Bombardier is supplying all of the electrical and mechanical subsystems including 72 light rail vehicles, signalling and train management systems, the power supply and distribution system, communications systems and depot/workshop machinery and tools. When completed, the system will feature 56 above ground and 10 underground stations. The first line is scheduled to open in November 2003, and the entire network is scheduled to open in 2004.

**Spain:** Bombardier Transportation is supplying the first application of automated people mover technology in Spain at the Barajas Airport in Madrid. The system will connect a new midfield terminal with a new satellite terminal. The project includes the supply of 19 vehicles, 2.5 km of underground guideway running surface, and automatic train control and power distribution systems. The system is scheduled to begin operation in 2004.

**Turkey:** In 2002, a consortium comprised of Bombardier Transportation and engineering group Yapi Merkezi of Turkey, was awarded a contract to supply a 14.2 km LRT system for the City of Eskisehir. Bombardier is responsible for the design, supply and installation of the turnkey system, including power supply, communications, traffic light and switch control systems, as well as operations and maintenance services. Eighteen low-floor trams are also being provided. The network is designed to handle around 170,000 passengers per day and is scheduled to open in 2004.

**UK:** As a member of the Arrow Light Rail Ltd. Concession Company, Bombardier Transportation is responsible for the landmark 30.5 year contract to design, build, operate and maintain the Nottingham Express Transit (NET) Line 1 light rail system. Bombardier's scope for the 14 km

*Bombardier LRT System Mk II car for Kuala Lumpur* 0065306

*Fully automated rapid transit system for Vancouver SkyTrain, Canada* 2002/0524888

*Bombardier Innovia for Dallas/Fort Worth Airport, USA* 2002/0524890

turnkey system includes 15 low-floor light rail vehicles, project management, system engineering and integration, power supply and distribution system, signalling and system control, communications and security systems, ticketing equipment and depot maintenance equipment.

**USA:** At Dallas/Fort Worth International Airport, Bombardier was chosen in 2000 to supply the first application of its new Innovia technology. The system will connect the airport's existing terminals with a new terminal and a new parking garage. The 15 km dual-track guideway system includes 64 vehicles and a five-year operations and maintenance contract. The system is scheduled to open in 2005.

In 2001, Bombardier was awarded the contract to expand its people mover system at George Bush Intercontinental Airport in Houston. The new extension will connect the present system, originally supplied and operated by Bombardier, to the international terminal complex currently under construction. Ten new CX-100 vehicles and 11 new switches are being supplied for the 0.6 km extension as well as a new off-line maintenance facility with carwash, and a new power distribution system. Revenue service is expected to being in 2004. Also in 2001, Bombardier was awarded a contract for the supply of 24 CX-100 people movers and associated equipment for Hartsfield Atlanta International Airport. Bombardier is responsible for production, system integration and testing of the vehicles, which will replace the existing fleet of C-100's that have been operating since 1980.

Bombardier Transportation, as the lead member of the Las Vegas Monorail Team, is supplying its M-VI Monorail System in the heart of the resort corridor. Designed according to urban transit safety standards, the system will link eight major resort properties and the Las Vegas Convention Center. The 36 cars will be operated in nine four-car trains and represent the latest innovation in monorail technology. Bombardier is responsible for providing all the electrical and mechanical elements of the system including design and supply of 36 M-VI monorail cars, overall project management, automatic train control, communications systems, power supply and distribution systems, automatic fare collection systems, guideway and guidance switching systems, system engineering and integration, platform doors for seven stations, testing and commissioning, training and manuals, and up to 15 years of operations and maintenance services. The system is expected to enter revenue service in 2004.

In 1999, Bombardier Transportation, as a member of the Southern New Jersey Rail Group, was awarded a contract to design, build, operate and maintain a unique 55 km (34 mile) turnkey system that will operate between Trenton and Camden. Scheduled to enter revenue service in 2003, this project will be the first application of a diesel light rail transit system on an existing freight corridor in the USA. Bombardier is supplying all of the electrical and mechanical system elements including 20 diesel multiple units and 10 years of operations and maintenance.

Also in 1999, Bombardier was chosen to supply a replacement people mover system to Seattle-Tacoma International Airport. The original system, supplied to Seattle-Tacoma International Airport in 1973, consists of two transit loops connecting the north and south satellites with the main terminal. A separate shuttle system runs the length of the main terminal, linking the satellite loops, serving main terminal ticketing and providing access to the parking garages. For the new system, Bombardier will supply and install 21 CX-100 vehicles, Flexiblok train control, central control equipment, a power distribution system and station doors. Full passenger service is scheduled to open in stages beginning in 2003 and concluding in 2004.

As part of the AirRail Transit Consortium, Bombardier Transportation is supplying a fully automated rapid transit system for the John F. Kennedy International Airport, New York, USA. Under contract to the Port Authority of New York and New Jersey, using a design-build-operate and maintain approach, the consortium is responsible for the turnkey design and construction of the driverless light rail system, including 32 ART MK II LIM-powered vehicles, as well as operations and maintenance for a period of up to 15 years.

Also in 1998, Bombardier was awarded a contract to supply an APM system to the San Francisco International Airport linking a new international terminal with existing domestic terminals, parking garages and the airport's rapid transit station. The system includes 38 CX-100 vehicles, nine stations and 10.2 km of elevated guideway. The contract also includes three years of operations and maintenance services. The system is scheduled to open in summer 2002.

*UPDATED*

## Chemetron Railway Products Inc

177 West Hintz Road, Wheeling, Illinois 60090, USA
Tel: (+1 847) 520 54 54   Fax: (+1 847) 520 63 73
e-mail: cttsales@aol.com

**Key personnel**
See main entry in *Permanent way components, equipment and services* section.

**Projects**
Turnkey design of rail welding plants. Contract welding service of rail into continuous welded rail in any of standard, alloy or head-hardened rails.

## Dimetronic SA

Avda de Castilla 2, Parque Empresarial, E-28830 San Fernando de Henares, Spain
Tel: (+34 91) 675 42 12   Fax: (+34 91) 756 21 15
e-mail: marketing@dimetronic.es

**Key personnel**
See main entry in *Signalling and communications systems* section.

**Projects**
Most of the projects contracted are of a turnkey nature.

**Contracts**
Westrace electronic interlocking and CTC systems for the metros of Madrid and Lisbon, SSI installations for 30 CP (Portugal) stations, signalling for the Valencia metro (including ATP) and Westrace electronic interlocking for FGC (Spain).

*UPDATED*

## Interinfra

2 rue Albert Dhalenne, Parc Dhalenne, F-93400 St Ouen Cedex, France
Tel: (+33 1) 41 66 84 15   Fax: (+33 1) 66 84 62; 84 63
Telex: 230500F

**Key personnel**
Chairman and Chief Executive Officer: Charles Carlier
Deputy Managing Director: Marc Bourboulon
General Secretary: Yann Teissier du Cros
Operations Director: Christophe Lavorel

**Projects**
Turnkey contracts for the supply of railway and rapid transit systems outside France.

## Marconi Communications

Marconi Communications Limited
New Century Park, PO Box 53, Coventry CV3 1HJ, UK
Tel: (+44 24) 76 56 55 00   Fax: (+44 24) 76 56 58 88
e-mail: pete.hallard@marconicoms.com
Web: http://www.marconicomms.com

**Key personnel**
See main entry in *Signalling and communications systems* section.

**Projects**
Marconi Communications Strategic Networks provides communication solutions for the rail, metro and light rail market worldwide. Marconi Communications designs, supplies, maintains and manages complex transportation communication networks.

The business has specialist knowledge in system design, integration, implementation and project management of specialist communication projects.

An example of the company's integration capability is the development of a communications system controlling telecommunications public address, CCTV and passenger information displays via a single screen.

Marconi Communications (Customer Network Services) is a whole life service provision business targetting communication networks and control systems in the transportation sector.

Strategic networks is providing communications for Hong Kong's Lantau Airport rail link, London Underground Ltd Jubilee Line Extension and Northern Line rolling stock communications infrastructure and maintenance, and for Midland Metro Line 1.

## Mecanoexportimport

30 Dacia Boulevard, Bucharest, Romania
Tel: (+40 1) 211 98 55   Fax: (+40 1) 210 78 94

**Key personnel**
See entry in *Locomotives and powered/non-powered passenger vehicles* section.

**Products**
Construction on turnkey basis of industrial units and workshops.

Turnkey systems contractors/**MANUFACTURERS** 787

## Parsons Brinckerhoff Inc

One Penn Plaza, New York, New York 10119, USA
Tel: (+1 212) 465 50 00   Fax: (+1 212) 465 50 96

**Key personnel**
See main entry in *Consultancy services* section.

**Projects**
As a subcontractor for the Tren Urbano system, San Juan, Puerto Rico, Parsons Brinckerhoff is providing programme management and design services for the systems and test track turnkey contract; the company is also involved in the West Coast modernisation project for Railtrack, and Thameslink 2000.

## Ranalah

Ranalah Moulds Ltd
New Road, Newhaven BN9 0EH, UK
Tel: (+44 1273) 51 46 76   Fax: (+44 1273) 51 65 29

**Key personnel**
See main entry in *Permanent way components, equipment and services* section.

**Projects**
Turnkey service for supply of sleeper manufacturing plant.

**Contracts**
Contracts include the supply of sleeper plants to Hong Kong, Philippines, Thailand, Georgia, Turkey, Sudan, Malaysia; also to Bulgaria, Europe and the UK.

**VERIFIED**

## Rotem Company

231 Yangjae-Dong, Soecho-ku, Seoul, Korea 137-938
Tel: (+82 2) 34 64 46 45   Fax: (+82 2) 34 64 47 92
Web: http://www.rotem.co.kr

**Key personnel**
See entry in *Locomotives and powered/non-powered passenger vehicles* section.

**Background**
See entry in *Locomotives and powered/non-powered passenger vehicles* section.

**Products**
Rotem is participating in Inchon International Airport Railway Project, Korea as the E&M supplier including rolling stock. The project is expected to start commercial service by the middle of 2006. KOROS will provide 404 cars, maintenance facilities, signalling, maintenance service and system engineering.

Rotem is now involved in two LRT projects. One is the Kimhae LRT project, the other is the Hanam project, both in Korea. Rotem has submitted the proposal successfully to each project as E&M supplier including vehicles. These projects are expected to start commercial service by the middle of 2006.

**UPDATED**

## SAGEM SA

Terminals and Telecommunications Division
6 avenue d'Iéna, F-75783 Paris Cedex 16, France
Tel: (+33 1) 40 70 63 63   Fax: (+33 1) 40 70 39 46
Web: http://www.sagem.com

**Key personnel**
Chairman and Chief Executive Officer: Pierre Faurre
Executive Vice-President, Managing Director Automotive & Cables Division: Michel Toussan

**Projects**
Project management, including turnkey projects, contracting, subcontracting, local partnerships and co-operative partnerships for passenger information systems, display systems, information systems in trains and driver assistance systems.

## SAT

Part of the SAGEM Group
Network and Telecommunications Division
11 rue Watt, F-75626 Paris Cedex 13, France
Tel: (+33 1) 55 75 75 75   Fax: (+33 1) 55 75 30 94

**Key personnel**
See also main entry in *Signalling and communications systems* section.

**Projects**
Engineering and network design and turnkey networks.

## Scitel Telematics Ltd A

Árbóc u 6, 3rd Floor, H-1133 Budapest, Hungary
Tel: (+361 359) 98 77   Fax: (+361 359) 98 70
e-mail: marketing@transport.alstom.hu

**Key personnel**
See main entry in ALSTOM Signaling *Signalling and communications systems* section.

**Projects**
Turnkey projects comprising design, supply, installation, commissioning and maintenance of signalling, telecommunications and vehicle identification systems, train traffic monitoring and control systems from stations to regions with schedule planning, staff assignment and passenger information.

## Siemens Transportation Systems

Siemens AG
Transportation Systems
PO Box 910220, D-12414 Berlin, Germany
Tel: (+49 30) 385 50
e-mail: internet@ts.siemens.de
Web: http://www.siemens.com/ts

**Key personnel**
President, Transportation Systems Group:
  Herbert J Steffen
Group Vice Presidents: Hans-Dieter Bott;
  Thomas Ganswindt; Hans M Schabert
Directors, Turnkey Systems (TK): K Neubeck/D Roussel,
  Dr U Stock

**Services**
Turnkey projects including: main line systems; intercity and high-speed systems; commuter and express rail links; mass transit systems; light rail systems; and automated guideway transit systems. Capabilities include provision or procurement of: civil engineering; infrastructure; traction power supply; control systems; signalling and safety systems; telecommunications systems; rolling stock; training services; and service and maintenance provision. Project management functions include project planning, project control and project supervision. Siemens can also arrange financing of turnkey projects.

**Projects**
Recent or current projects include:
China: As an equal partner in the Transrapid International consortium, Siemens is participating in the fulfillment of a contract to build and equip a 30 km magnetic levitation line linking Shanghai's Pudong international airport with the city's Lujiazui financial district. The system was due to be commissioned in early 2004, with maglev trains operating at speeds of up to 430 km/h to complete the journey in seven minutes.France: In May 2001, Matra Transport International (now Siemens Transportation Systems SAS) was awarded a contract by SMTC, Toulouse, to supply and equip its second automated metro line, the 16 km 20-station Line B. The contract includes the supply of 35 Type VAL 208 vehicles. The company is working with the Toulouse metro operator, SMAT, as system integrator on the project, which was due to be completed in 2007.Germany: In November 2001, Siemens was awarded a contract by Verkehrs AG (VAG), Nuremberg, to equip the authority's Line U3, then under construction, for automated, driverless operation. In addition, Siemens was to retrofit Line U2 for similar operation. The contract included the supply of 30 two-car Type DT 3 two-car trainsets, 16 for Line U3 and 14 for Line U2. The automatic train protection and operations control system was to be designed and manufactured at Siemens Braunschweig facility.Italy: In November 2001, a Siemens-led consortium was awarded a contract to build two light rail lines in Verona. Together the two lines will total 15 track-km and serve 35 stops. The Siemens portion of the contract was to include the provision of signalling and telecommunications equipment, traction power supply and overhead line system, train control equipment for vehicle control at road intersections, and the provision of 22 three-section Combino bidirectional trams. Other consortium members are Mazzi and CCC, which together were to be responsible for civil engineering and track construction. The two lines were due to be commissioned in mid-2004.

Also in November 2001, as a member of the project company, VAL 208 Torino GEIE, received an order from SATTI, Turin, to supply 46 VAL 208 automated metro trainsets. The followed the award of a contract in July 2000 to Siemens subsidiary Matra Transport International (now Siemens Transportation Systems SAS) to supply and equip a 9.6 km 15-station VAL automatic rapid transit system for the city.Malaysia: In April 2002, the Express Rail Link system connecting Kuala Lumpur with its new airport was commissioned. As leader of the SYZ Consortium, Siemens was responsible to the line's concessionaire, ERL SB, for track, signalling and train

*Siemens TS led a turnkey consortium which built and equipped the Express Rail Link, connecting Kuala Lumpur, Malaysia with its new international airport*    2002/0525408

control systems, traction power supply and overhead line equipment, telecommunications systems, E & M construction, SCADA equipment, depot and workshop facilities and rolling stock. The last-mentioned took the form of 12 articulated four-car Desiro ET emus. Siemens is also the majority partner in EMAS, which is responsible for maintenance of the entire system.Taiwan: In August 2001, Siemens won a contract from the Kaohsiung Rapid Transit Corporation (KRTC) to supply signalling equipment, traction power supply equipment and 42 three-car trainsets for the Red Line (28 km, including 9 km elevated, 23 stations) and Orange Line (14 km, 14 stations) of the city's metro system. Siemens was also to be responsible for project management and systems integration of the electro-mechanical portion of the project. Services were due to commence in 2007.Thailand: In January 2002, Siemens announced that it had signed an agreement with Bangkok Metro Corporation Ltd for the supply and maintenance of the Thai capital's first metro system, a 20 km line with 18 stations. The project entails supply of the line's complete infrastructure, including signalling, power supply, communications and depot equipment, as well as the manufacture of 19 three-car trainsets to serve the line. The contract also covers project management and maintenance of the line over a 10-year period. The line was due to be commissioned in 2004.Turkey: In 2001, operations commenced on a 20.6 km two-line LRT system in Bursa. Construction and fitting out the system was undertaken by the BursaRay consortium, led by Siemens, which was also was responsible for the development and manufacture of the system's 48 B 80 six-axle LRT cars.USA: In March 2001, Siemens was awarded a contract by the Metropolitan Transit Authority of Harris County to construct Houston's first light rail system. Siemens is responsible for project management, planning, delivery, installation and commissioning of the 12 km line, which was due to be commissioned in December 2003. This includes the manufacture and supply of 18 S 70 LRVs, and of the line's signalling, control and traction power supply systems.Venezuela: In July 2000, Siemens announced that it had won a turnkey contract to build the initial phase of the first light rail line in Maracaibo. Siemens was to supply infrastructure equipment, including signalling and communications systems, traction power supply equipment, ticketing systems and a maintenance depot for the 6.9 km line, which will connect the city with its airport and will eventually total 14 km. In addition, the company was to supply 12 LRVs to serve the line.

**UPDATED**

## Temoinsa

Técnicas Modulares e Industriales
Poligono Industrial Congost, Avenida San Julián 100,
E-08400 Granollers, Barcelona, Spain
Tel: (+34 93) 860 92 00   Fax: (+34 93) 860 92 03
e-mail: tmi@termoinsa.com

**Key personnel**
See main entry in *Passenger coach equipment* section.

**Projects**
Turnkey projects for complete interiors of new vehicles and refurbishment.

# INFORMATION TECHNOLOGY SYSTEMS

## Alphabetical listing

Andersen Consulting
Audio Visual Computer
Cadex Electronics
Com-Net Software Specialists Inc
Datastream Systems (UK) Ltd
European Rail Software Applications (ERSA)
Fleet Software
HPW
IBM
ICL
Infodev
InfoVision Systems Ltd
Infrasoft Corporation
Infrasoft Ltd
Innovata
Interautomation
IRFP
Laser Rail
Maxwell Soft Park Ltd
MultiModal Applied Systems
PAFEC Ltd
PC-Soft GmbH
Sabre Inc
Science Systems Group
Siemens Nixdorf
Socratec GmbH
Spear Technologies Inc
STERIA
Systra Consulting Inc
Timera Inc
Unigrid AB
Union Pacific Technologies
VIPS AB
ZT

## Company listing by country

**CANADA**
Cadex Electronics

**FRANCE**
European Rail Software Applications (ERSA)
STERIA

**GERMANY**
Interautomation
PC-Soft GmbH
Siemens Nixdorf
Socratec GmbH

**INDIA**
Maxwell Soft Park Ltd

**SWEDEN**
VIPS AB

**SWITZERLAND**
HPW

**UNITED KINGDOM**
Audio Visual Computer
Datastream Systems (UK) Ltd
Fleet Software
IBM
ICL
InfoVision Systems Ltd
Infrasoft Ltd
Laser Rail
PAFEC Ltd
Science Systems Group

**UNITED STATES OF AMERICA**
Andersen Consulting
Com-Net Software Specialists Inc
Infrasoft Corporation
Innovata
MultiModal Applied Systems
RMI
Sabre Inc
Spear Technologies Inc
Systra Consulting Inc
Timera Inc
Union Pacific Technologies
ZT

## MANUFACTURERS/Information technology systems

### Andersen Consulting

100 S Wacker Drive, Suite 1070, Chicago, Illinois 60606, USA
Tel: (+1 312) 507 29 00   Fax: (+1 312) 507 79 65
Web: http://www.ac.com

**Key personnel**
See main entry in *Consultancy services* section

**Capabilities**
Andersen Consulting Transportation and Travel Services Group services include IT strategy, customer service, network design, information systems, operations, service delivery, service design and financial/accounting systems.

**Projects**
Andersen Consulting Transportation and Travel Services include many of the world's major railway operators.

### Audio Visual Computer plc

Seymour House, 11-13 Mount Ephraim Road, Tunbridge Wells, Kent TN1 1EH, UK
e-mail: enquiries@avcomputer.co.uk
Web: http://www.avcomputer.co.uk

**Key personnel**
Chief Executive: Robin Colclough

**Products**
AVC specialises in audio-visual multimedia computer technology, manufacturing a range of enhanced PC-based computer systems, such as the ePC600 and ePC601.
Clients include international airports, manufacturing industry and scientific facilities.
The ePC and ViewPoint have been installed at the new Heathrow Express terminals to provide rail and flight information.

### Cadex Electronics

22000 Fraserwood Way, Richmond, British Columbia V6W 1J6, Canada
Tel: (+1 604) 231 77 77   Fax: (+1 604) 231 77 55
e-mail: info@cadex.com

**Key personnel**
Marketing Manager: Isider Buchmann
Marketing Specialist: Frank Leffeldar

**Products**
Cadex C7000 battery analyser to test and recharge batteries for portable communications devices, data acquisition units, video cameras and notebook computers. The batteries interface through configured cups or plug-cables which can be programmed with the analyser's menu function. It prints service reports and battery labels.
Windows® application software is available to obtain data from up to 120 C7000 series analysers. Battery test results, inventory status and performance graphs are stored in a database from which print reports can be generated.

### Com-Net Software Specialists Inc

3728 Benner Rd, Miamisburg, Ohio 45342, USA
Tel: (+1 937) 859 63 23   Fax: (+1 937) 859 75 11
Web: http://www.comnet-fids.com

**Key personnel**
Systems Integration Account Executive: Linda Palmer

**Products**
Provision of turnkey integrated information display systems, including real-time information display.
Com-Net's WTI (Windows on Transit Information System) is an integrated information display system based on experience from more than 250 installations.

Other products include video monitors, LED and LCD display systems and outdoor LCD display systems.

*UPDATED*

### Datastream Systems (UK) Ltd

First Floor, 10 Stoke Gardens, Slough SL1 3QQ, UK
Tel: (+44 1753) 89 66 00   Fax: (+44 1753) 89 66 01
e-mail: info@dstm.co.uk
Web: http://www.dstm.com

**Products**
Asset management systems for rail applications, covering both infrastructure and rolling stock. Users of the company's MP5i system include: London Underground Ltd; Glasgow Underground; Angel Trains; FirstGroup; Banestyrelsen, Denmark; EMEF, Portugal; Netherlands Railways; BASF, Germany; and RATP, Paris.
A recent contract with Romanian Railways covered the provision of an MP5i system to manage 250 infrastructure sites on the country's network as part of the World Bank-funded IRIS project.

### Dilax International

Dilax (International) AG
Fidlerstrasse 2, CH-8272 Ermatingen, Switzerland
Tel: (+41 71) 663 75 75   Fax: (+41 71) 663 75 76
e-mail: info@dilax.ch
Web: http://www.dilax.ch

**Key personnel**
Contact: Iris Bährle

**Subsidiary company**
Dilax Intelcom GmbH
Schillerstrasse 3, D-10625 Berlin, Germany
Tel: (+49 30) 77 30 92 40   Fax: (+49 30) 77 30 92 50

**Products**
Design manufacture and supply of automatic systems for passenger counting and operations analysis. Systems are supplied for both fixed and vehicle-mounted applications. Operators supplied with Dilax and automatic passenger counting systems include: Hamburger Hochbalm; S-Bahn Hamburg and AKN-Eisenbahn, Germany; SBB and TPG, Switzerland; and Muni, San Francisco, USA.

*NEW ENTRY*

### European Rail Software Applications (ERSA)

84 route de Strasbourg, BP 273, F-67504 Haguenau Cedex, France
Tel: (+33 3) 88 07 15 50   Fax: (+33 3) 88 07 15 51
e-mail: info@ersa-france.com
Web: http://www.ersa-france.com

**Key personnel**
Technical Director: Patrick Deutsch

**Products**
European Rail Software Applications is a 60 per cent subsidiary of ERS (qv in *International Railway Associations and Agencies* section), specialising in the development and adaptation of simulation software for railway applications. ERSA also maintains and supports other software packages.

### Fleet Software

3 Newton Business Centre, Thorncliffe Park Estate, Chapeltown, Sheffield S30 4PH, UK
Tel: (+44 114) 257 16 00   Fax: (+44 114) 257 16 09

**Key personnel**
Managing Director: John Rands

**Products**
TACT, software for rolling stock maintenance in the UK. It records individual parts performance and management of reliability issues. TACT software has been approved for use across the networks of National Express Group and Prism. TACT was first introduced to Supertram, Gatwick Express and in 1996 to Heathrow Express. It has now been extended to rolling stock manufacturers.
TACT technology was originally developed around the privatised bus industry when engineering costs became an issue.

### HPW

Häni-Prolectron AG
Industriestrasse, CH-9552 Bronschhofen, Switzerland
Tel: (+41 71) 913 73 73   Fax: (+41 71) 913 73 74
e-mail: info@hpw.siemens.ch

**Key personnel**
Chief Executive Officer, Senior Management:
  Schär Hans-Peter

**Corporate background**
HPW is part of the Siemens Transportation Group

**Products**
AVLC systems; Integrated planning software; onboard computers; dynamic passenger information systems, mobile fare management systems; electronic components for local and long-distance transport.
Häni-Prolectron also provides consulting, project management, commissioning, training, after-sales service and customised maintenance services.

### ICL

West Avenue, Kidsgrove, Stoke-on-Trent ST7 1TL, UK
Tel: (+44 1782) 78 14 44   Fax: (+44 1782) 78 14 55

**Key personnel**
Business Manager, Rail: Richard Betts

**Works**
Eskdale Road, Winnersh, Wokingham RG41 5TT

**Products**
Railway journey information systems, revenue collection and allocation systems, ATB2 ticket printers, materials and purchasing management systems, hand-held devices for penalty fares issue and other similar uses, possession management systems, outsourced and managed IT services, IT systems design and build.
Contracts include London Transport PASS ticketing system, London Underground Possession Management, London Underground penalty fares, materials and purchasing, strategic consulting and IT operations, Gardermobanen IT ticketing, train movements, personnel, finance and information systems, Eurostar departure control system.
Train companies in the UK are installing a high-technology journey information system which will provide improved customer service, giving more accurate and up-to-date information on train times, routes and fares. The train companies have signed a contract with ICL to develop a new Rail Journey Information Service (RJIS) which will be at the heart of the integrated transport network of the future.
The system can also supply information about station and other facilities necessary to integrated transport, such as the availability of bus links, cycle facilities, disabled access, taxis and car parking drop-off points and detailed information about other public transport services such as tram and ferry timetables.

### Infodev Inc

PO Box 1222 HV, Quebec QC, Canada G1R 5A7
Tel: (+1 418) 681 35 39   Fax: (+1 418) 681 12 09
e-mail: info@infodev.com

**Key personnel**
Vice-President and Director Research and Development:
  Pierre Deslauriers
Chief Executive Officer: Alain Miville De Chene
Transit Sales: Sandra Howlett

## Information technology systems /**MANUFACTURERS**

**Other office**
Transit Sales
Tel: (+1 418) 681 35 39  Fax: (+1 418) 681 12 09
e-mail: sh@infodev.ca

**Products**
Production of Automatic Passenger Counting systems (APC) and Automatic Vehicle Location Systems (AVL) using directional optical sensors and also a GPS satellite positioning system applied to vehicles in order to identify and track their positions.

*NEW ENTRY*

## InfoVision Systems Ltd

Slack Lane, Derby DE22 3FL, UK
Tel: (+44 1332) 34 71 23  Fax: (+44 1332) 34 51 10
e-mail: info@infovision.co.uk
Web: http://www.infovision.co.uk

**Key personnel**
Chairman and Chief Executive: Peter Crawford
Marketing Manager: Paul Metcalfe
Business Development Manager: Tony Preece
Financial Director: John Stride

**Capabilities**
DRUID™ software enabling fast and intelligent manipulation of complex data which can be delivered on CD-ROM and hard disk or network-based mediums.
On-line systems for publishing data via internet, intranet and worldwide web.
Electronic documentation comprising technical authorship, technical sources and driveline in common formats.
Multiple and bespoke software development services.

**Projects**
Supply of DRUID™ and related documentation services to Midland metro (1999), Siemens/Northern Spirit Class 333 (1999), Bombardier/Virgin Trains Class 220/221 (2000) and Siemens/Heathrow Express (2000).

*VERIFIED*

## Infrasoft Corporation

99 Rosewood Drive, Suite 150, Danvers, Massachusetts 01923, USA
Tel: (+1 978) 777 99 88  Fax: (+1 978) 777 52 59
Web: http://www.infrasoft-civil.com

**Works**
Infrasoft Ltd, North Heath Lane, Horsham RH12 5QE, UK

**Key personnel**
Chief Executive Officer: Rick Fiery
Vice-President, Engineering: Stan Fenton
Managing Director, Infrasoft Ltd/Vice-President of International Channels & Marketing: Jim Paton

**Products**
MXRAIL, an engineer-friendly tool for rapid design of rail projects from new design to infrastructure maintenance and renewal.

*VERIFIED*

## Infrasoft Ltd

North Heath Lane, Horsham, RH12 5QE, UK
Tel: (+44 1403) 25 95 11  Fax: (+44 1403) 21 77 46
e-mail: info@infrasoft.civil.com
Web: http://www.infrasoft-civil.com

**Key personnel**
Managing Director: Jim Paton
International Sales Manager: Chris Palfreyman
UK Sales Manager: Robin Akers

**Subsidiary companies**
Infrasoft Ltd – India Branch
Infrasoft BV
Infrasoft North America

**Products**
MXRAIL is a Microsoft Windows-compliant design and analysis system used for high-speed to light rail, switch and crossings, alignment matching, cant design, drainage, and automated drawing production.

## Innovata

3915 Old Mundy Mill Road, Oakwood, Georgia 30566, USA
Tel: (+1 770) 539 54 78  Fax: (+1 770) 539 50 30
Web: http://www.innovata-LLC.com

**Key personnel**
General Manager, Europe: Sarah Ennis
Tel: (+44 1923) 49 01 38

**Capabilities**
Innovata aggregates and distributes global travel data including passenger rail, airline, hotel, rental car and destination information. It offers content suppliers a single information delivery solution to reach a variety of distribution channels. Innovata's affiliates receive extensive and reliable travel data, industry expertise, and technological solutions. These affiliates and data users include a growing number of rail operators, airlines, airports, and software companies. Innovata provides a data repository and management services downloadable to PCs and PDAs to maximise distribution of database content.

## Interautomation

Interautomation Deutschland GmbH
Ollenhauerstrasse 98, D-13403 Berlin, Germany
Tel: (+49 30) 412 20 87
e-mail: wolfgang.doerks@interautomation.de

**Key personnel**
Sales Manager, Vehicle Technology: Wolfgang Dörks

**Products**
Automatic passenger counting, door controlling, time management and access control systems for urban transit systems, regional and suburban trains, buses and depots. Products were originally developed and marketed by Pronova Elektronik, which was acquired by Interautomation Deutschland on 1 January 2000.

## IRFP

Institut für Regional- und Fernverkehrsplanung
Fasanenweg 12, D-04420 Frankenheim, Germany
Tel: (+49 341) 942 45 08  Fax: (+49 341) 942 45 07
e-mail: leipzig@irfp.de
Web: http://www.irfp.de

Postfach 320123, D-01013 Dresden, Germany
Tel: (+49 352) 476 81 90  Fax: (+49 351) 470 68 19
e-mail: dresden@irfp.de

**Products**
FBS (Fahrplan-Bearbeitiungs-System) PC-based train scheduling and timetable planning software for main line and regional railway networks.

*NEW ENTRY*

## Laser Rail

Jessop House, 39-45 Smedley Street East, Matlock DE4 3FQ, UK
Tel: (+44 1629) 76 07 50  Fax: (+44 1629) 76 07 51
e-mail: HYPERLINKmailto:tech@laser-rail.co.uk
Web: http://www.laser-rail.co.uk

**Key personnel**
Directors: David M Johnson, Alison B Stansfield

**Corporate development**
Laser Rail was established in 1989 by David Johnson in response to a rapidly growing need to manage the implementation of new technology into the commercial rail environment.

**Capabilities**
Interactive track design gauging system software for gauging applications, including route enhancement. Computerised systems for designing track geometry, for both renewal and maintenance. Track geometry measurement and database systems for track assessment, redesign and monitoring of both track performance and maintenance machinery.
Laser Rail operates a range of computer facilities as part of its services. It also provides training and certification to various levels of competency and can be supplied as part of the overall support package.

## Maxwell Soft Park Ltd

1/3/3 Millennium Business Park, MIDC Mahape, Navi Mumbai 400 701, India
Tel: (+91 20) 566 18 50  Fax: (+91 20) 566 18 51
e-mail: pune@maxwell-india.com
Web: http://www.maxwell-india.com

**Key personnel**
Manager, Overseas Marketing: Sudhir Patil

**Products**
TOMIS (Train Operations Management and Information System) covering: movement tracking; freight wagon accounting; passenger coach accounting; locomotive accounting; crew control; fixed assets information; commercial functions; and analytical processing. TOMIS is a consultancy-based system which includes detailed study and solutions based on: preset methods of operations; level of automation; service rules; management perception; evaluation of solutions; improvement sought; existing problems and bottlenecks; and financial commitment.

*UPDATED*

## MultiModal Applied Systems

125 Village Boulevard, Suite 270, Princeton, New Jersey 08540, USA
Tel: (+1 609) 419 98 00  Fax: (+1 609) 419 96 00
Web: http://www.multimodalinc.com

**Products**
MultiRail is an integrated PC software system designed for the development and maintenance of railway operating plans including network design, timetables, equipment planning, crew management, traffic analysis, wagon blocking, and trip planning. MultiRail is available in versions that are optimised for either freight or passenger railways. The product has many graphical tools including a graphical network and track builder, editable string lines, and graphical crew and equipment management. The freight version supports the analysis of train sizes, yard workloads, traffic routings, wagon schedules and provides many types of system level statistics.
MultiRail is used by every Class I railroad in North America and is installed with railways in Europe, Asia, South America, Africa and Australia.

*UPDATED*

## Onerail

Level 1, 263 Liverpool Street, Darlinghurst, Sydney 2010, NSW, Australia
Tel: (+61 02) 93 39 12 22  Fax: (+61 02) 93 26 01 99
e-mail: rail@onerail.com
Web: http://www.onerail.com

**Key personnel**
Chief Executive Officer: Grant Holmes
Chief Operating Officer: Ross Holland
Marketing Director: Matthew Stewart
Director of Professional Services and Support: Darryl Garbutt

**Corporate background**
Onerail has its head office in Sydney Australia and has its technology and development office in Toronto Canada.

## MANUFACTURERS/Information technology systems

### Products

Founded in 1996, Onerail offers rail operators four key products: the Orion Reservation System; Orion Select; Odyssey Distribution Systems and Your Odyssey.

Onerail's Orion reservation system is engineered for high-volume transaction and mission critical reservations and ticketing environments. The system's contemporary architecture fully supports a wide range of functionality, including: reservations, inventory control, pricing and ticketing, train consists, scheduling, seat and berth allocations and feeds to major financial systems. Orion has been developed in a Graphical User Interface (GUI) environment.

In addition to the features of Orion, Orion Select integrates rail, tour and accounting functionality into one system.

The Onerail Odyssey Distribution technology enables travel agents and consumers to make timetable, schedule, seat availability, fare enquiries and reservations on-line. Connection to Odyssey is available via: all travel agent distribution channels; the consumer direct via www.onerail.com; or the rail operator as their online booking engine.

Each client's Odyssey system is a tailored version of the Odyssey Distribution Solution, enabling the rail operator to brand its online booking tool.

In 2002, users of Onerail technology include: Via Rail (Canada), Amtrak (USA), railways of New South Wales (Australia), Queensland Rail (Australia), Venice Simplon Orient Express (Europe), Great Southern Pacific Express (Australia), Eastern & Oriental Express (Singapore), Road to Mandalay (Myanmar), The British Pullman (UK) and the Northern Bell (UK).

*NEW ENTRY*

---

## PAFEC Ltd

Strelley Hall, Nottingham NG8 6PE, UK
Tel: (+44 115) 935 70 55   Fax: (+44 115) 935 70 64
e-mail: peter.roberts@pafec.com
Web: http://www.pafec.com

### Key personnel

Sales Manager: Peter Roberts

### Products

Electronic document management (EDM) for the rail industry including EDM system capable of managing document handling such as archiving, visual browsing, document search techniques, audit trails and document distribution.

---

## PC-Soft GmbH

Adolf Hennecke Strasse 37, D-01968 Senftenberg, Germany
Tel: (+49 3573) 707 50   Fax: (+49 3573) 70 75 19
e-mail: info@pcsoft.de
Web: http://www.pcsoft.de

### Products

VIPS software suite, including VIPS Carsis, developed for fleet management and covering: management planning control; vehicle component history; vehicle monitoring, evaluation, data processing and statistics; and data management. VIPS/Disposition provides solutions for: movements and shunting supervision and planning; vehicle and cargo location data; data import, such as EDIFACT; integration of radio communication for data exchange; and direct invoicing, archives and enquiries. VIPS/Traincar data management handles: automatic mass measuring data entry and processing; interface to accounting systems; and statements, archives and enquiries.

Versions are available to function under various operating systems, including Unix, Windows, Windows NT and Linux.

---

## RMI

Railcar Management Inc, providers of RailConnect
1819 Peachtree Road North East, Suite 303, Atlanta, Georgia 30309, USA

Tel: (+1 404) 355 67 34   Fax: (+1 404) 352 88 14
e-mail: marketing@railcarmgt.com
Web: http://www.railcarmgt.com

### Key personnel

President: Mac Purdy
Vice-President, Business Development: Karl Knauff
Export Marketing: Steve Murray

### Products

Supplier of railway application software, shipper services and RailConnect BSP services. RMI specialises in shippment and freight management information systems for EDI, yard and wagon control, train control, intermodal operations, waybilling, revenue cash management and wagon hire. Assistance, training and implementation services are also provided.

*UPDATED*

---

## Sabre Inc

4255 Amon Carter Boulevard, Fort Worth, Texas 76155, USA
Tel: (+1 817) 963 64 00
Web: http://www.sabre.com

### Subsidiary companies

Sabre Inc, France
11-13 Avenue de Friedland, 75008 Paris, France
Tel: (+33 1) 53 53 55 00   Fax: (+33 1) 53 53 55 00

Sabre UK Marketing Ltd
Trinity Square, 23-59 Staines Road, Hounslow, TW3 3HE, UK
Tel: (+44 20) 88 14 42 00   Fax: (+44 20) 85 77 49 39

### Capabilities

Information technology solutions including customised software development and software products, transaction processing, consulting and information technology outsourcing.

Customers include Amtrak, USA; Belgium Railways (SNCB); Eurostar UK; German Federal Railways (DB AG); London Underground; Société Nationale des Chemins de Fer Français (SNCF); Swiss Rail (SBB); Taipei Rapid Transit.

The SABRE Group has signed a seven-year agreement with London Underground Ltd to modernise and maintain its train and crew scheduling system. The system will streamline the scheduling process for London Underground's 480 trains, 267 stations and 1,250 daily train staff.

---

## Science Systems Group

23 Clothier Road, Brislington, Bristol BS4 5SS, UK
Tel: (+44 117) 971 72 51   Fax: (+44 117) 972 18 46

### Key personnel

Managing Director: Dr M D Love
Operations Director: B T Evans
Business Development Director: Peter J M Turner
Business Development Executive: Richard C Jones

### Capabilities

Software development and project management for train control systems, control centres, simulation, passenger information and automatic fare collection.

### Projects

Work has been carried out on London Underground Central Line and the Jubilee Line Extension; Seoul subway system; trainer's interface software (LUL); Docklands Light Railway, London.

---

## Siemens Nixdorf

Siemens Nixdorf Informationssysteme AG, Transportation Division
Lyoner Str 27, D-60528 Frankfurt-am-Main, Germany
Tel: (+49 69) 66 82 12 11   Fax: (+49 69) 66 82 10 60
See also *Automatic fare systems* section

### Products

Information technology, including allocation and distribution of freight wagons, route and track management systems, timetable design, timetable simulation, resource management, planning of work schedules for crews and passenger coach deployment.

*UPDATED*

---

## Spear Technologies Inc

436 14th Street, Suite 200, Oakland, California 94612, USA
Tel: (+1 510) 267 33 33   Fax: (+1 510) 267 33 44
Web: http://www.speartechnologies.com

### Key personnel

Vice President, Marketing: Ken Voss

### Products

Spear 2000 is an asset management suite of software products designed specifically for rolling stock and rail infrastructure. The software suite is fully integrated and supports maintenance, materials, rebuilds, warranty, imaging, and decision support. Spear 2000 is a web-accessible, multi-tier client server system and supports wireless handheld computers for inspection and materials handling.

*UPDATED*

---

## STERIA

12 rue Paul Dautier, PO Box 58, F-78142 Velizy Cedex, France
Tel: (+33 1) 34 38 60 00   Fax: (+33 1) 34 88 61 60
Web: http://www.steria.fr

### Key personnel/Works

See *Signalling and communications* section.

### Products

Include traffic control, model networks, scheduling, equipment and power consumption control, high reliability systems (Atelier B).

Recent contracts executed and obtained include PCC – central control stations on the Parisian RER rapid transit system for RATP Paris; PCS – public transportation passenger and staff information system for RATP Paris; 3615 RATP – public teletext information server; RIS – passenger information system for DB AG.

---

## Systra Consulting Inc

2 Whipple Place, Suite 302, Lebanon, New Hampshire 03766-1356, USA
Tel: (+1 603) 448 02 00   Fax: (+1 603) 448 17 50
e-mail: info@railsim.com
Web: http://www.systraconsulting.com

### Key personnel

Assistant Vice-President: F William Lipfert, Jr

### Products

Include the Railsim Train Performance Calculator (TPC), which runs on Windows® 95, 98, 2000, XP and NT. It has the following features: libraries of locomotives, coaches, freight wagons and multiple unit vehicles, including photographs; automated calculation of curve maximum speeds based on curvature, super-elevation and curve imbalance; automatic maximum speed limiting; rolling/aerodynamic resistance methodologies; variable calculation time step to support fast processing required for planning analyses and detailed processing required for engineering efforts.

The Railsim TPC package includes the Railsim Database editor and report generator. TPC output includes TPC train plots, text reports, compatibility with any Windows plotter or printer and generation of TPC plots in AutoCAD® DXF file format, ready for incorporation into reports and engineering drawings.

Two Railsim TPC software add-ons, for processing signal system headway (capacity) and safe braking distance computations, are also available for license. The safe braking distance add-on handles both 'forward' and 'reverse' braking curves, as well as both stopping and reducing computations.

The Railsim TPC is part of the Railsim simulation software suite also available from Systra Consulting. The full Railsim suite also includes the Railsim network simulator, Railsim electrical load flow analyser and Railsim signal designer.

*UPDATED*

## Timera Inc

5775 Flatiron Parkway, Suite 110, Boulder, Colorado 80301, USA
Tel: (+1 303) 444 37 58   Fax: (+1 303) 444 97 49
e-mail: lw_tatro@pstechno.com

**Key personnel**
Vice-President, Marketing: L Wayne Tatro Jr

**Corporate background**
Timera is part of the Fenix group of companies, a wholly owned subsidiary of Union Pacific Corporation, which serves as a holding company for four UP technology firms.

**Products**
Formerly PS Technology, Timera supplies System for Crew Assignment Tracking (SCAT) workforce management software. Customers include most Class 1 freight railroads in North America and several commuter lines. The software product suite addresses workforce management needs by minimising time required for scheduling and assigning staff to shifts. Products are designed automatically to fill vacancies with qualified staff, schedule and monitor holiday leave, maintain assignments, rosters, records, details of employee status and history and calculate gross pay.

## Unigrid AB

Box 40, SE-171 11 Solna, Sweden
Tel: (+46 8) 762 50 00
Web: http://www.unigrid.se

**Key personnel**
Managing Director: Björn Nilsson

**Corporate background**
Formerly SJ Data, the sector responsible for data processing and information technology for Swedish State Railways, Unigrid AB was established in 2001 as part of the restructuring resulting from the break-up of the state railway company.

**Services**
Unigrid offers a wide range of data processing and information technology-related services to the transport and travel industries including: systems development; application management; operations and communications services and business development services. The company also provides information technology consultancy services.

*NEW ENTRY*

## Union Pacific Technologies

7930 Clayton Road, St Louis, Missouri 63117, USA
Tel: (+1 314) 768 68 00
e-mail: DABOCK@notes.up.com
Web: http://www.uptweb.com

**Products and services**
A subsidiary of Union Pacific Corporation, Union Pacific Technologies (UPT) specialises in developing computer systems for the transportation industry. It has had a major role in extending communications/data/management systems into former SP territory and in interfacing with BNSF over the 6,400 km of trackage and haulage access. For 1997-1998 the installation of TCS on the SP was a priority. Since 1993 it has installed a yard management programme at the 17 largest yards on the National Railways of Mexico (FNM) system and installed a computer upgrade at the FNM central office in Mexico City.

With the onset of privatisation in Mexico, UPT foresees a large market for systems to connect the several new private properties that are evolving. UPT has taken on a Mexican partner to offer its products in Spanish language versions throughout Latin America. To explore the international market, UPT has joined with an IBM subsidiary, Integrated Systems Solutions Corporation.

Wisconsin Central has also adopted TCS as its primary management tool, and UPT is also implementing a version of the system in the UK for the English, Welsh and Scottish Railway.

## VIPS AB

FO Petersons Gata 28, SE-421 31 Västra Frölunda, Sweden
Tel: (+46 31) 89 69 40   Fax: (+46 31) 47 86 01

**Key personnel**
Managing Director: Bo Sahlström

**Products**
Supplier of PC-based strategic planning systems mainly for public transport but also for private transport.

More than 70 VIPS systems are installed worldwide with bus, tram, metro and heavy rail operators.

## Vossloh System-Technik York Ltd

St Marys Court, 39 Blossom Street, York YO24 1AQ, UK
Tel: (+44 1904) 63 90 91   Fax: (+44 1904) 63 90 92
Web: http://www.comreco-rail.co.uk

**Key personnel**
See *Simulation and training systems*.

**Developments**
See *Simulation and training systems*.

**Products**
TrainPlan™ is a planning, scheduling and timetabling system for scheduling of train services, crew and equipment. TrainPlan ACT™ is a timetabling tool to optimise infrastructure access with a minimum of specialist involvement; ResourceManager™ controls rolling stock at an individual vehicle level ensuring compliance with all necessary maintenance and service commitments; TRACS™ organises train crew work schedules to minimise the number of crew needed for services; TrainManager™ manages everyday operations and contingency planning; PerformancePlan™ is a system which assesses traction performance capability for route profiles; PowerPlan™ is a system which simulates power supply demands for both AC and DC networks; PerformancePlanner™ analyses scheduled service plans to assess timetables and identify potential problems.

VST Comreco achieved ISO 9001 accreditation in February 2002.

**Contracts**
Recent contracts include: supply of TrainPlan™, RailPlan™, ResourcePlan™, TrainManager™ and ResourceManger™ to Norwegian State Railways; supply of UK-wide integrated train planning systems and planning database with RailPlan™ and TrainPlan™ to Railtrack; supply of TrainPlan™ to Swedish State Railways and New Jersey Transit; supply of TrainPlan™ and ResourcePlan™ to Romanian State Railways and to Scotrail (UK); supply of RailPlan™ and PowerPlan™ to Kowloon—Canton Railway Corporation, Hong Kong; supply of TrainPlan™ and ResourcePlan™ to Chiltern Railways (UK).

*UPDATED*

## ZT

Zeta-Tech Associates Inc
900 Kings Highway North, PO Box 8407, Cherry Hill, New Jersey 08002, USA
Tel: (+1 609) 779 77 95   Fax: (+1 609) 779 74 36
e-mail: zetatech@zetatech.com
Web: http://www.zetatech.com

**Key personnel**
President: Dr Allan M Zarembski
Vice-President of Costing and Economic Analysis: Randolph R Resor
Director of Marketing: Jim Blaze
Director of Training and Field Engineering: Donald Holfeld
Director of Engineering Analysis: Joseph W Palese
Senior Engineer: Pradeep K Patel
Manager, Engineering Systems: John Webster
Project Engineers: Sunil Kondapalli, Leonid Katz
Senior Programmers: Nick Forte, Maciej Gorny
Office Administrator: Kim Corrigan
Administrative Assistant: Katy White

**Capabilities**
Zeta-Tech Associates is a technical consulting and applied technology company directed at the railway and transportation industries. Its expertise covers:

Track and track systems covering fasteners and fastener systems; sleepers; track strength; track buckling; track maintenance; and track geometry.

Vehicle/track interaction; freight wagon systems; inspection and measurement systems; fatigue design and analysis of structures; applied economics; technical marketing; computer simulation and modelling; transportation cost analysis.

Operations analysis including train simulation modelling freight and passenger equipment; and benefit analysis of improved operations, equipment, advanced train control systems.

Costing including development of detailed operating costs, cost allocation and life cycle costing.

Technical training for all areas of the railway/transit industry, including needs assessment, training material development, training delivery and training evaluation.

Maintenance management, comprising the development and application of computer software for use in forecasting component failure and planning of maintenance requirements, including database development and track component degradation/failure modelling and prioritisation of maintenance activities.

Custom software development including integrated graphic facilities management, geographical information systems, component failure modelling, clearance simulation and other rail-specific software.

# ROLLING STOCK LEASING COMPANIES

# ROLLING STOCK LEASING COMPANIES

## EUROPE

### AAE

Ahaus Alstätter Eisenbahn Holding AG
Poststrasse 6, PO Box 856, CH-6301 Zug, Switzerland
Tel: (+41 41) 727 20 50    Fax: (+41 41) 727 20 75
e-mail: ole.nygaard@aae.ch
Web: http://www.aae.ch/

**Key personnel**
Managing Director: DR Eckhart Lehmann
Deputy Managing Director, Operations: Markus Vaerst
Deputy Managing Director, Finance: Mark Stevenson
Technical Director: Dr Johannes Nicolin
Sales and Marketing: Ole Nygaard

**Vehicles**
AAE has over 10,000 freight wagons rented to state railway operators and private companies, including DB AG, SBB, NS, SNCB, SJ, DSB, NSB, CFL, ÖBB, ČD, MÁV, ŽSR, Intercontainer/Interfrigo, Hupac, Novotrans, Cemat and Nordwaggon. AAE is a member of UIC, RIV and BCC and its fleet includes covered wagons, flat wagons, pocket wagons and container wagons.

### Algeco SA

16 avenue de l'Opera, F-75040 Paris Cedex 01, France
Tel: (+33 1) 42 86 23 00    Fax: (+33 1) 42 97 41 59

**Key personnel**
Assistant Director, Exploitation: Michel Bernard

**Vehicles**
Tank and special purpose wagons; ISO tank containers for hazardous products.

### Angel Trains

Angel Trains Ltd
22nd Floor, Portland House, Stag Place, London SW1E 5BH, UK
Tel: (+44 20) 75 92 05 00    Fax: (+44 20) 75 92 05 03
e-mail: feedback@angeltrains.com
Web: http://www.angeltrains.com

**Key personnel**
Chairman: Chris Sullivan
Managing Director: Haydn Abbott
Commercial Director: John Vale
Engineering Director: Allan Baker
Finance Director: George Lynn
Legal Director: Louise Oddy
Operations and Sales Director: Peter Rigby
Human Resources Manager: Nick Bratton
International Business Development Manager: Tim Jackson
Corporate Communications: Jane Adley

**Background**
Angel Trains was established in April 1994 within British Rail and in 1995 it was transferred to the UK government in preparation for its sale to the private sector. Angel Trains is now 100 per cent owned by The Royal Bank of Scotland Group plc.

Angel Trains is one of Britain's three train leasing companies. It provides much of Britain's rail industry with rolling stock and is now expanding its business both in the UK and in other countries. It is active in the procurement, financing, ownership, maintenance and asset management of new and used equipment. Its key role is in the introduction of new capital and ideas to railway operations.

**Traction and rolling stock**
Angel Trains is investing £2.3 billion in new trains for UK operators, including: £375 million for 280 new freight locomotives for English, Welsh & Scottish Railway, the UK's largest-ever order for freight traction; £593 million for 53 225 km/h tilting trains for the West Coast Main Line, built by Alstom and to be operated by Virgin Trains; £55 million for new Class 333 emus for Northern Spirit; £78 million for new dmus for First North Western; £75 million for Desiro UK emus to First Great Eastern and £640 million for Desiro UK emus for South West trains.

**Angel Trains Ltd**

| Class | Train operating company | Number of vehicles in service June 2000 |
|---|---|---|
| **Locomotives** | | |
| 43 | GNER, Virgin West Coast, First Great Western | 113 |
| 66 | EWS | 250 |
| 67 | EWS | 26 (part of order for 30) |
| **Multiple-units** | | |
| Various dmus and railcars | First North Western, Silverlink, ScotRail | 69 |
| 142 | First North Western, Northern Spirit, Cardiff Railways | 188 |
| 150/0 | Central Trains | 6 |
| 150/1 | First North Western, Central Trains Silverlink | 100 |
| 150/2 | First North Western, Central Trains | 40 |
| 153 | Northern Spirit, Wales and West | 30 |
| 156 | ScotRail, Northern Spirit | 152 |
| 158 | Central Trains, Wales and West | 150 |
| 165 | Chiltern Railways, Thames Trains | 177 |
| 166 | Thames Trains | 63 |
| 303 | ScotRail | 129 |
| 305/2 | ScotRail, First North Western | 29 |
| 308 | Northern Spirit | 63 |
| 309 | First North Western | 20 |
| 312 | First Great Eastern, LTS | 196 |
| 314 | ScotRail | 48 |
| 317 | WAGN | 288 |
| 421 | Connex South Central | 332 |
| 423 | Connex South Eastern | 264 |
| 442 | South West | 120 |
| 465/2 | Connex South Eastern | 200 |
| 466 | Connex South Eastern | 86 |
| 507 | Merseyrail | 96 |
| 508 | Merseyrail, Connex South Eastern | 129 |
| HST Trailer Cars | GNER, First Great Western, Virgin West Coast | 366 |
| HST Catering Cars | GNER, First Great Western, Virgin West Coast | 54 |

*UPDATED*

### Armita

Armita Nederland BV
Apollolaan 109, NL-1077 AN Amsterdam, Netherlands
Tel: (+31 20) 673 61 17    Fax: (+31 20) 673 58 57

**Key personnel**
Manager: H M Endstra

**Vehicles**
Tank cars: 420.

### ARR Rail Rent

Transportmittel Vermietungs GesmbH
Kunigundbergerstrasse 40, A-2380 Perchtoldsdorf, Austria
Tel: (+43 1) 865 66 85    Fax: (+43 1) 865 66 85 91

**Key personnel**
Managing Directors: Gernot Schwayer, Dr Helmut Breit, Johannes Hansbart

**Vehicles**
Short and long-term leasing of freight wagons. The company owns a fleet of over 1,000 wagons.

### Brambles Italia Srl

Via Lanzone 29/31, I-20123 Milan, Italy
Tel: (+39 02) 80 63 01    Fax: (+39 02) 86 45 53 01

**Key personnel**
Managing Director: Albert Counet
Sales Manager: Maristella Caimi
Technical Manager: Andreá Sangiorgi

**Vehicles**
1,700 double-deck wagons for automotive transport and rail services for the chemical industry with 450 wagons.

### CAIB

CAIB Benelux
Uitbrieustrystraat 60, B-2600 Brussels, Belgium
Tel: (+32 2) 663 75 00    Fax: (+32 2) 663 75 50

**Key personnel**
General Manager: A Margeus
Executive Directors: H Thoumyre, P G L Sudreau

**Vehicles**
Approximately 1,500, of which a quarter are for petroleum products, a quarter for chemicals, a quarter for dry bulk loads and the remainder comprise gas, high-cube and car transporter wagons.

The company belongs to the Brambles Group, a large European private wagon group which owns 35,000 wagons.

### CAIB UK Ltd

Imperial House, 350 Bournville Lane, Birmingham B30 1QZ, UK
Tel: (+44 121) 478 03 30    Fax: (+44 121) 477 83 38 (wagon hiring)
Tel: (+44 121) 475 51 51    Fax: (+44 121) 477 82 86 (Marcroft Engineering)

**Key personnel**
Managing Director (wagon hiring): K Jagger
Managing Director (Marcroft Engineering): R N Crutchley

**Vehicles**
CAIB UK offers a comprehensive rail freight service, including wagon hire, full maintenance package, and domestic and international transit management. The hire fleet numbers just over 2,100 wagons catering for all types of bulk liquids, solids and finished goods. The Marcroft Engineering subsidiary provides nationwide field maintenance service from 40 outstations supported by two principal workshops catering for overhaul, conversion and painting of all wagon types. Intermodal Repairs and Storage based at Widnes offers a similar range of engineering services to tank container users.

## CFCL Australia Pty Limited

PO Box 6406, North Sydney, New South Wales 2060, Australia
Tel: (+61 1) 70 85 99 10 20  Fax: (+61 1) 70 85 99 40 70
e-mail: mcgeemj@aol.com
Web: http://www.crdx.com/cfcl.australia.htm

### Key personnel
Manager: Mike McGee

### Organisation
CFCLA Australia is owned by Chicago Freight Car Leasing Co of USA.

### Services
The company is involved in the leasing and provision of locomotives and rolling stock to the industry.

### Vehicles
The company purchased 13 former Australia National EL Class 2,240 kW locomotives and leases them to others. They were overhauled by Goninans, Western Australia, to Dash 8 technical standards and had gearing altered to improve their suitability for freight work. Five were leased to Austrac (qv) for Sydney–Melbourne freight hauls in 1999 while others are regularly seen on Melbourne–Adelaide freights.

CFCL Australia has also purchased 50 new container flat wagons from China and has rebuilt another 22 locally.

## Convoy

Convoy-Contigas BV
Apollolaan 109, NL-1077 AN Amsterdam, Netherlands
Tel: (+31 20) 673 61 17  Fax: (+31 20) 673 58 57

### Key personnel
Director: W Endstra

### Vehicles
180 tank wagons.

## DEC

Dyrekcja Eksploatacji Cystern Sp zoo
ul Twarda 30, 00-831 Warsaw, Poland
Tel: (+48 22) 622 05 05; 697 91 94
Fax: (+48 22) 697 91 95
e-mail: marketing@decyst.com.pl
Web: decyst.com.pl

### Key personnel
Managing Director: Stefan Garus
Commercial Director: Tadeusz Kościelak

### Products
DEC is the owner of 11,500 tank wagons for the transport of light and heavy petroleum products, liquefied gases, chemicals, molasses, liquid foodstuffs and other products. Facilities are situated all over Poland, mainly on the premises of refineries, fuel and reloading depots, at pipeline terminals and at railway border crossing points.

DEC divisions have been authorised by Polish Railways and the Railway Technical Supervision to carry out repairs. The rolling stock repair plant in Ostróda is the production plant within DEC. Its main responsibility is to provide general overhauls and inspection of wagons. This plant is also adapted to carry out modernisation of existing stock. It handles the assembly of new types of wagons and freight wagon bogies.

## ERMEWA Ltd

38 Station Road, Cambridge CB1 2JH, UK
Tel: (+44 1223) 32 42 61  Fax: (+44 1223) 35 17 84

### Key personnel
Managing Director: R J Head

### Vehicles
Tank wagons for transport of liquefied gases including cryogenics, liquid chemicals and powders, as well as a diversified fleet of specialised wagons for bulk commodities (grains), heavy industrial products (steel coils, steel profiles) and palletised goods.

## EVA

Eisenbahn-Verkehrsmittel GmbH
Schillerstrasse 20, D-40237 Dusseldorf, Germany
Tel: (+49 211) 670 20  Fax: (+49 211) 670 21 10

### Key personnel
Managing Director: Friedrich D Hess

### Vehicles
Tank, powder and high-cube wagons: 9,993 owned and 2,190 managed.

## GE Rail Services

Linden House, 153-155 Masons Hill, Bromley BR2 9HB, UK
Tel: (+44 181) 466 90 45  Fax: (+44 181) 466 90 37

### Key personnel
Managing Director: Stephen Goodwin
Technical/Procurement Director: Christopher Anspack
Marketing Manager: Michael C Houlan

### Services
GE Rail Services' fleet is in excess of 4,600 wagons, of which 2,000 are suitable for Channel Tunnel traffic. Following GE Capital's acquisition of Cargowaggon GmbH and Tiphook Rail Ltd the two businesses have been successfully integrated and the new company has offices in UK, Germany, France, Italy and Sweden.

The fleet covers commodity sectors such as intermodal, automotive, infrastructure, construction, steel, hazardous and general cargoes.

350 new wagons are on order for delivery by the end of 1999 and GE Rail Services is involved in a number of other new wagon build projects.

## HSBC Rail (UK) Ltd

PO Box 29499, London NW1 2ZF, UK
Tel: (+44 20) 73 80 50 40  Fax: (+44 20) 73 80 53 26

### Key personnel
Director and Head General Manager: Peter Aldridge
Head of Finance: David Mead
Heads of Commercial Services: Ellen Harwood, Chris Moss, Bob Marrill
Head of Business Standards: Kevin Kilbey

### Corporate development
Formerly Forward Trust Ltd, HSBC Rail (UK) Ltd is a member of the HSBC Group. It acquired the fleet as well as the leases with the Train Operating Companies created from the privatisation of British Rail.

### Traction and rolling stock
HSBC Rail's portfolio of stock is predominantly electric, and covers some of the more modern types in Britain. The Company owns the Intercity 225 trains in service on the East Coast Main Line and the Class 86 locomotives in use on the West Coast Main Line, as well as over 2,400 electric multiple-unit vehicles.

HSBC Rail has been awarded the contracts to supply new electric multiple units to both Scotrail and Connex and of Class 66 diesel locomotives to Freightliner Ltd and TGOJ Trafik, Sweden.

#### HSBC Rail (UK) Ltd

| Class | Train operating unit(s) | Number of vehicles in service Jan 2000 |
|---|---|---|
| **Locomotives** | | |
| 86/2 | West Coast, CrossCountry, Anglia | 43 |
| 91 | GNER | 31 |
| 66 | Freightliner | 15* |
| 66 | TGOJ Trafik | 2** |
| **Multiple-units** | | |
| 170 | ScotRail | 27 |
| 306 | First Great Eastern | 3 |
| 310 | Central Trains, London Tilbury, Southend | 179 |
| 313 | Silverlink, West Anglia Great Northern | 192 |
| 315 | West Anglia Great Northern, First Great Eastern | 244 |
| 318 | ScotRail | 63 |
| 320 | ScotRail | 66 |
| 321 | Silverlink, Great Eastern | 456 |
| 322 | West Anglia Great Northern | 20 |
| 334 | ScotRail | 120 |
| 365 | WAGN, Connex South Eastern | 164 |
| 421 | Connex South Eastern, South West Trains | 320 |
| 423 | South West Trains, Connex South Central | 308 |
| 455 | Connex South Central | 184 |
| 465/0 | Connex South Eastern | 368 |
| 483 | Isle of Wight | 12 |
| **Coaches** | | |
| Mark 2d/e/f | West Coast, CrossCountry, Anglia, Great Western Trains, ScotRail | 454 |
| Mark 4 | GNER | 314 |
| Mark 2a | First North Western, Cardiff Railway Company | 30 |
| Mark 1 | Anglia, First North Western | 10 |

\* Delivery summer 2000
\*\* Delivery autumn 2000

## Invatra

Industrial de Vagones y Transportes SA
Poligono Industrial Alces, Alcazar de San Juan,
Ciudad Real, Spain
Tel: (+34 926) 51 11 13

### Vehicles
58 tank wagons.

*Tank wagon owned by DEC*

## KVG

KVG Kesselwagen Vermietgesellschaft mbH
Herrengraben 74, D-20459 Hamburg, Germany
Tel: (+49 40) 36 80 40   Fax: (+49 40) 36 80 41 13
e-mail: info@kvg.mhs.compuserv.com

**Key personnel**
Executive Directors: Rainer Baumgarten,
   Gernot Schwayer
Managing Directors: Volker Grahl, Manfred Gürges

**Subsidiary**
Jungenthal-Waggon GmbH
Am Hafen 29, D-30629 Hannover, Germany
Tel: (+49 511) 95 87 70   Fax: (+49 511) 958 77 15
Managing Directors: Volkmar Gassmann, Volker Grahl

**Associated company**
KVG Kesselwagen Vermietgesellschaft mbH
Kunigundbergstrasse 40, A-2380 Perchtoldsdorf, Austria
Tel: (+43 1) 865 66 85   Fax: (+43 1) 86 56 68 59
Executive Directors: Gernot Schwayer,
   Rainer Baumgarten, Johannes Mansbart

**Vehicles**
KVG hires privately owned tank wagons and other specialised vehicles. The company owns a fleet of approximately 10,000 vehicles transporting light and heavy oil products, liquefied petroleum gases, acids, alkalis, solvents and other chemicals, powdered or granular products as well as standard goods wagons.

## NACCO SA

40 rue La Boétie, F-75008 Paris, France
Tel: (+33 1) 45 61 56 20   Fax: (+33 1) 40 74 06 24
e-mail: nacco@nacco.c-si.fr
Web: http://www.naccorail.com

**Key personnel**
Managing Director: David MacNaughton

**Subsidiary companies**
NACCO GmbH (Hamburg, Germany); NACCO UK (Manchester, UK); Representative offices in Prague, Czech Republic and Budapest, Hungary.

**Services**
Founded in 1973, the company has a fleet of 4,000 specialised wagons, in majority tank cars, covered hopper wagons and pressure discharge cars, for the transport of petroleum products, chemicals, LPG and granular or powdered products.

*UPDATED*

## NS Financial Services Company

Behan House, 10 Lower Mount Street, Dublin 2, Ireland
Tel: (+353 1) 638 13 80   Fax: (+353 1) 638 13 99
e-mail: Hans.dejong@nsfinancialservices.ie
Web: http://www.nsfsc.com

**Key personnel**
Managing Director: B van Dijk
Manager, Marketing and Sales: J J M de Jong
Manager, Rolling Stock: F J van der Linden

**Background**
NS Financial Services Company (NSFSCA) is a wholly owned subsidiary of NS Groep (Netherlands Railways). NS Financial Services Company was established as an Irish company and commenced trading in 1999 to manage rolling stock assets both for NS and for new operators, especially in newly liberated markets in European Union countries. The primary focus of the company is to provide equipment on dry lease, working closely with manufacturers and maintenance providers such as sister company Nedtrain to provide other services.

**Vehicles**
In the Netherlands the company owns vehicles operated by NS Reizigers, including 127 dmus, 242 emus and four ICE-3 high-speed trains. The company is also part owner of 37 electric locomotives, 19 diesel locomotives and 531 wagons operated by Railion Benelux.

*UPDATED*

## OEVA

Oesterreichische Eisenbahn-Verkehrs-Anstalt GmbH
Volksgartenstrasse 3, A-1010 Vienna, Austria
Tel: (+43 1) 52 33 62 10   Fax: (+43 1) 523 15 55

**Key personnel**
Managing Director: Gerhard W Schwertmann

**Vehicles**
900 owned and 1,350 managed.

## On Rail

Gesellschaft für Vermietung und Verwaltung von Eisenbahnwaggons mbH
Schwarzbachstrasse 30, D-40822 Mettmann, Germany
Tel: (+49 2104) 929 70   Fax: (+49 2104) 252 54
e-mail: info@on-rail.com

**Key personnel**
Directors: Ulrich Swertz, Nathalie Tastevin

**Vehicles**
On Rail manages and leases a fleet of 2,500 private wagons, of which around 1,100 are tank wagons for the transport of light and heavy petroleum products, chemicals, pressurised gases and powders. On Rail also leases wagons for the transport of bulk goods and steel products.

*UPDATED*

## Porterbrook Leasing Company Ltd

Burdett House, Becket Street, Derby DE1 1JP, UK
Tel: (+44 1332) 26 24 05   Fax: (+44 1332) 26 44 19
e-mail: continental@porterbrook.co.uk
Web: http://www.porterbrook.co.uk

**Key personnel**
Managing Director: Paul Francis
Directors
   Engineering: Tim Gilbert
   Commercial Director: Keith Howard
   International Business Managers: Ken Harper;
      Neil Bennett

**Political background**
Porterbrook is one of three rolling stock companies sold by the British government in January 1996. It was bought by a management buyout group for £527 million.
   The company was sold with leases in place to many of the franchised train operating companies, and in August 1996 was acquired by Stagecoach Holdings, operator of the South West Trains franchise. This acquisition valued the company at £825.5 million.
   In 2000, Stagecoach announced the sale of Porterbrook to Abbey National plc for a cash payment of £773 million and the assumption of £669 million of external debt, valuing the company at £1,442 million.

**Traction and rolling stock**
Porterbrook owns about 3,800 vehicles, which it supplies on operating leases. In early 2000, the fleet comprised: 94 electric locomotives; 90 diesel locomotives and 81 HST power cars; 1,488 emu and 841 dmu vehicles; and 381 freight wagons. Customers include 18 of the 25 UK train operating companies as well as freight operator Freightliner Ltd. Since 1996, the company has ordered 360 new emu vehicles, 240 dmu vehicles and 11 diesel locomotives at a total cost of £600 million.
   Recent contracts include: an additional 10 Turbostar vehicles for Chiltern Railways; an additional six Class 66/5 locomotives for Freightliner; and a purchase, rebuild and lease back deal on 11 Class 57 locomotives for Freightliner.

Porterbrook has recently entered the fare collection equipment market with the lease of automatic ticket barriers and ticket-issuing machines to Chiltern Railways and South West Trains.

*UPDATED*

## SGW

Société de Gerance de Wagons Grande Capacité
163 bis avenue de Clichy, F-75838 Paris Cedex 17, France
Tel: (+33 1) 40 25 37 00   Fax: (+33 1) 40 25 37 60

**Key personnel**
Chairman: Jacques Rolland
General Manager: Bernard Kail

**Products**
SGW caters exclusively for unit train movement of bulk freight suitable for open-wagon conveyance, such as coal, coke, ores, sand, stones and ballast, throughout Europe. It does not own wagons, but markets and manages the deployment of a pool of some 6,500 special purpose vehicles on behalf of wagon manufacturers, national and private industries, and private wagon leasing companies.

## Siemens Dispolok GmbH

PO Box 3240, D-91050 Erlangen, Germany
Tel: (+49 9131) 74 43 68   Fax: (+49 9131) 72 83 42
Web: http://www.dispolok.com

**Key personnel**
Chief Operating Officer: Dr Walter Breinl

**Background**
A wholly owned subsidiary of Siemens, Dispolok initially operated as a division of the company, having been established as a full service supplier in the locomotive leasing and rental market. It became an autonomous company in January 2001. Aiming at the upper end of the market, Dispolok offers modern, high-performance locomotives, including traction for cross-border operations, and can also provide maintenance and repair services, as well as spare parts supply and driver training.

**Vehicles**
In 2002, Dispolok offered four locomotive types: the ES 64 F/ES 64 U2, Siemens 6,400 kW second generation development of the EuroSprinter family of high-performance three-phase electric locomotives, of which the 'F' version was for 15 kV AC operation of freight traffic and the 'U2' variant a dual-voltage (15 kV/25 kV AC) machine; the ES 64 P 6,400 kW EuroSprinter prototype electric locomotive; the ME 26 2,650 kW diesel-electric locomotive; and the MH 05 three-axle 675 kW diesel-hydraulic shunting and trip locomotive. By May 2002, Dispolok had procured or ordered 38 examples of the ES 64 F/ES 64 U2 EuroSprinter type, while the stock of ME 26 locomotives totalled 12.
   Operators using Dispolok locomotives include the Swiss-based intermodal freight company, Hupac, which has leased three ES 64 U2s, and Lokomotion-Gesellschaft für Schienentraktion mbH, which in October 2001 accepted two similar machines. In June 2002, Logistik Service GmbH (LogServ), a subsidiary of Voest-Alpine, took delivery of its first leased ES 64 U2 locomotive. This was to be joined by a second machine by the end of 2002 to haul lime between Steyrling and Linz.
   Type ME 26 diesel-electric locomotives have been leased to Luxembourg Railways.

*NEW ENTRY*

## Simotra SA

A member of the Brambles Group
33 avenue du Maine, PO Box 50, F-75755 Paris Cedex 15, France
Tel: (+33 1) 40 47 33 00   Fax: (+33 1) 40 47 33 67

**Key personnel**
Managing Director: C van Eeden

# ROLLING STOCK LEASING COMPANIES

General Manager: P Boucheteil
Deputy General Manager: P Charbonnier

**Vehicles**
9,641 rail wagons.

## Steele

E G Steele & Co Ltd
25 Dalziel Street, Hamilton ML3 9AU, UK
Tel: (+44 1698) 28 37 65   Fax: (+44 1698) 89 15 50

**Key personnel**
See entry in *Locomotives and powered/non-powered passenger vehicles* section.

**Vehicles**
Ninety-five 45 tonne tank wagons chiefly for petroleum products; seven 45 tonne stainless steel wagons for chemical products (mainly sulphuric and nitric acid).

## STVA

Société de Transports de Véhicules Automobiles
Immeuble Le Cardinet, PO Box 826, F-75828 Paris Cedex 17, France
Tel: (+33 1) 44 85 56 78   Fax: (+33 1) 44 85 57 00
e-mail: stva@stva.com
Web: http://www.stva.com

**Key personnel**
Chairman of the Executive Board: J P Bernadet
Managing Director: J Elissèche
   Finance and Administration: J J Pronzae
      Deputy Managing Director Business Development:
      J Henry
   Advisor to the Chairman: S Charles

**Vehicles**
Automobile transporters; full service (predelivery inspection) throughout Europe.

*UPDATED*

## Touax

Groupe Touax
Tour Arago, 5 rue Bellini, F-92800 Puteaux La Defense, France
Tel: (+33 1) 46 96 18 00   Fax: (+33 1) 46 96 18 18

**Services**
Touax is an operator of rail vehicles in France and USA and is active in the leasing market.

## Transfesa

Transportes Ferroviarios Especiales SA
Musgo 1, Urbanizacion La Florida, Aravaca, E-28023 Madrid, Spain
Tel: (+34 91) 307 65 85   Fax: (+34 91) 372 90 59
e-mail: transfesa@transfesa.es
Web: http://www.transfesa.es

**Key personnel**
President and Executive Director:
   Emilio Fernandez Fernandez
Managing Director: Luis Del Campo Villaplana

**Products**
The company is primarily engaged in activities covering the management of transport, distribution and warehousing of goods and logistic services.

**Vehicles**
The company owns a fleet of over 7,500 wagons, including vehicles with interchangeable axles to run between Spain and other European countries.

## TRG Wagonmarket Spol sro

Ulica Rovná 594/5, PO Box 25, SK-05801 Poprad, Slovakia
Tel: (+421 52) 716 42 01; 716 42 03; 716 42 05
Fax: (+421 52) 716 42 18; 227
e-mail: wagonmarket@trinityraileurope.com

**Key personnel**
General Manager: František Štupák
Commercial Manager: Zuzana Strakova
Technical Manager: Ján Gavlák

**Products**
Freight wagon leasing, purchase and sale of freight wagons, bogies, tank wagons, subassemblies and spare parts for the freight wagons and tanks.

*UPDATED*

## Trinity Chemical Industries Inc

PO Box 701436, Tulsa, Oklahoma 74170
Tel: (+1 918) 495 35 00   (+1 918) 485 35 61
e-mail: info@trinitychem.com
Web: http://www.trinitychem.com

**Key personnel**
President: Richard B Fenimore
Vice-President: Terry L Fisher
Sales: Ryan Edwards

**Services**
Long- and short-term full service leases for tank cars of various sizes and covered hoppers for plastic pellet transport. Lined and unlined tank cars are available and special equipment options include stainless steel tanks, heating coils, insulation and magnetic gauging devices. Trinity Chemical Industries also undertakes vehicle cleaning and fleet management services and undertakes sub-leasing and/or storage for companies with excess cars in their fleet.

*NEW ENTRY*

## VTG Vereinigte Tanklager und Transportmittel GmbH

Nagelsweg 34, D-20097 Hamburg, Germany
Tel: (+49 40) 235 40   Fax: (+49 40) 23 54 11 99

**Key personnel**
Managing Directors: Dr Klaus-Jürgen Juhnke,
   Heribert Becker, Michael Behrendt, Heinrich Sikora

**Principal subsidiaries**
VTG GmbH Vienna; VTG AG, Basel; VTG Benelux BV, Rotterdam; ALGECO SA, Paris; VTG Benelux BV, Brussels; VTG Hungaria Kft, Budapest; VTG Italia, Milan; Transpetrol GmbH; VTG France SA, Paris; VTG Finland Oy, Helsinki; VTG USA Inc, Philadelphia; Lehnkering Montan Transport AG, Duisberg; Transwaggon AG, Zug; ATG Autotransportlogistic GmbH, Eschborn

**Products**
Hiring company for tank wagons and special purpose freight wagons. VTG handles the products of the chemical and petrochemical industries, from liquid chemicals through pressurised gases to dry goods in bulk. VTG Tank-tainers are available for intermodal transportation of chemicals, gases or foodstuffs door-to-door.
   VTG is an independent tank operator, with installations at seaport terminals in Hamburg and Amsterdam. Facilities are available for the temporary or longer term storage of mineral oil and chemical products.
   The activities of the VTG group also cover: forwarding services of tank wagons and special purpose wagons; international forwarding services for freight wagons; inland waterway shipping of liquid and dry products as well as LPG; lorry transport.

**Vehicles**
22,000 tank and special purpose wagons; 5,000 automobile-carrying wagons; 7,000 general purpose freight wagons.

---

# NORTH AMERICA

## CGTX Inc

15th Floor, 1600 Boulevard René Lévesque Ouest, Montréal, Québec H3H 1P9, Canada
Tel: (+1 514) 931 73 43   Fax: (+1 514) 931 55 34

**Key personnel**
President and Chief Executive Officer: J C Leger
Vice-President and Treasurer: Jacques Poulin
Vice-President, Marketing and Sales: R A Podsiadlo
Vice-President, Engineering/Fleet Maintenance:
   G Sinclair
Director, Fleet Maintenance: G Cooper

**Products**
Lessors of railway rolling stock in Canada: tank wagons and freight wagons. The company has maintenance workshops at Montréal, Red Deer and Moose Jaw.

**Vehicles**
8,300.

## Chicago Freight Car Leasing Co

1 O'Hare Centre, Suite 7000, 6250 N River Road, Rosemont, Illinois 60018, USA
Tel: (+1 847) 318 80 00   Fax: (+1 847) 318 80 45
e-mail: tom@crdx.com

**Key personnel**
President: F R Sasser
Senior Vice-President, Marketing and Sales:
   T F Kuklinski

**Products**
New and rebuilt freight wagons of all types; leasing services.

**Vehicles**
7,000.

*VERIFIED*

## First Union Rail

6250 River Road, Suite 5000, Rosemont, Illinois 60018, USA
Tel: (+1 847) 318 75 75   Fax: (+1 847) 318 75 88

**Key personnel**
President: Jack Thomas
Vice-President, Marketing: Rich Seymour
Vice-President, Operations: Rick Grossman
Vice-President, Finance: Lori Heissler

**Products**
Comprehensive fleet management services for railcar owners: approximately 67,000 railcars in fleet. Provides fleet management services, innovative lease packages, railcar portfolio acquisition, sale and lease-back programmes on all types of railroad equipment. First Union Rail also has longer-term financing available through single investor and leverage leases.

# GATX

General American Transportation Corp
500 W Monroe Street, Chicago, Illinois 60661, USA
Tel: (+1 312) 621 62 00   Fax: (+1 312) 621 65 81

### Key personnel
President: D Ward Fuller
Senior Vice-President: D Stephen Menzies
Vice-President and Chief Financial Officer:
   D J Schaffer

### Products
Rail wagon leasing, repair, maintenance and fleet management services. GATX operates 65,000 wagons, 80 per cent of which are tank wagons. Over half of the tank wagon fleet is employed in chemicals traffic. The GATX tank wagon fleet includes the TankTrain system, a series of tank wagons interconnected with flexible hoses that allow the entire string to be loaded and unloaded from one connection.

GATX offers tank wagons of every size for handling any liquid commodity transported by rail. The tank wagon fleet includes general service, pressure, stainless steel, aluminium and commodity-specific tank.

The Airslide wagon is suitable for transporting and unloading finely divided bulk chemical and food products such as talc, flour, sugar, starch and carbon black. For shippers who require pneumatic unloading of their dry bulk commodities, GATX now complements its Airslide wagon by offering the Trinity-designed Power-Flo 15 $lb/in^2$, 5,125 $ft^3$ covered hopper wagon.

Additions to the GATX fleet include 3,000 $ft^3$ covered hopper wagons for the transport of cement and aggregates and jumbo covered hopper cars for grain.

### Vehicles
65,000.

# GE Capital Rail Services

A unit of GE Capital Services
33 West Monroe Street, Chicago, Illinois 60603, USA
Tel: (+1 312) 853 50 00   Fax: (+1 312) 853 51 55

### Key personnel
President and Chief Executive Officer: R W Speetzen
Executive Vice-President, Sales: K Schneider

### Corporate development
GE Capital Services, USA, bought Cargowaggon in 1997. It has become part of GE Capital's Rail Services business, based in Chicago, Illinois.

### Products and services
GE Capital Rail Services offers a range of rail vehicles and leasing solutions worldwide. The fleet spans a variety of railcar equipment, including covered hopper wagons, tank wagons, boxcars and pressure differential wagons and for industries such as agriculture, forest products, utilities, petroleum/chemicals, auto, steel and consumer goods.

Leasing solutions include per-diem, fixed, operating and finance leases, sales/leasebacks and structured financial products. Also repair, maintenance and administrative services through a network of service centres. The European business, GE Rail Services, provides of rail transport services. Through its offices in England, France, Germany, Italy and Sweden, it provides rail vehicle equipment and related services to railways and other transport providers throughout Western and Central Europe.

*Union Pacific intermodal train with TTX-leased wagons en route to Cheyenne and points east* (Tom Harley/TTX)
0064385

# Greenbrier Leasing Corporation

A subsidiary of the Greenbrier Companies Inc
One Centerpointe Drive, Suite 200, Lake Oswego, Oregon 97035, USA
Tel: (+1 503) 684 70 00   Fax: (+1 503) 684 75 53
Web: http://www.gbrx.com

### Products
Greenbrier Leasing Corporation specialises in leasing freight wagons and in managing wagon fleets for third parties. Greenbrier Leasing invests heavily in research and development and since 1985 has sponsored the development of the Gunderson range of double-stack container wagons, centre-partition timber wagons and high-capacity box cars. Since its acquisition of TrentonWorks in 1995, Greenbrier Leasing has also assisted in the development of covered hoppers and box cars produced at the Nova Scotia plant. The company also sponsored development of Autostack, a system for transporting motor vehicles in containers, and more recently Auto-Max, a multilevel vehicle-carrying wagon.

The Greenbrier Intermodal subsidiary claims to be the leading provider of intermodal freight wagons, for which it continually develops the market.

### Vehicles
Greenbrier Leasing's fleet of owned, leased or managed equipment totals more than 37,000 vehicles and includes a full range of types, including: box cars; double-stack wagons; covered and open-top hoppers; centre-partition timber wagons; mechanically and cryogenically refrigerated wagons; gondolas; wood-chip wagons; and the company's new Auto-Max vehicle-carrier.

# Procor Limited

2001 Speers Road, Oakville, Ontario L6J 5E1, Canada
Tel: (+1 905) 827 41 11   Fax: (+1 905) 827 08 00
Web: http://www.procor.com

### Key personnel
See entry in *Freight vehicles and equipment* section.

### Products
Leasing of tank and special-purpose freight wagons.

### Vehicles
Over 22,000.

**VERIFIED**

# TTX Company

101 North Wacker Drive, Chicago, Illinois 60606, USA
Tel: (+1 312) 853 32 23   Fax: (+1 312) 984 37 90
Web: http://www.ttx.com

### Key personnel
President and Chief Executive Officer: R C Burton Jr
Senior Vice-President, Fleet Management: H V Logan
Senior Vice-President, Equipment and Engineering:
   R S Hulick

### Products
TTX owns, maintains and rents to North American railways, including operators in Mexico, a fleet of freight wagons, principally flat wagons, for the movement of containers, road trailers and new automobiles.

# Union Tank

Union Tank Car Co – A member of The Marmon Group of companies
175 West Jackson Boulevard, Chicago, Illinois 60604, USA
Tel: (+1 312) 431 31 11   Fax: (+1 312) 431 50 03

### Main works
151st and Railroad Avenue, East Chicago, Illinois 46312, USA

### Key personnel
See entry in *Freight vehicles and equipment* section.

### Products
Steel, stainless steel and aluminium tank wagons for carrying liquids and compressed gases. Covered hopper wagons for bulk plastics.

### Vehicles
49,000 for lease in the USA and Mexico.

**UPDATED**

# INTERNATIONAL RAILWAY ASSOCIATIONS AND AGENCIES

# INTERNATIONAL RAILWAY ASSOCIATIONS AND AGENCIES

## INTERNATIONAL

### Association of Spanish Manufacturers of Railway Equipment

Asociación Nacional de Constructores Españoles de Material Ferroviario (Cemafe)
Príncipe de Vergara 74, 4a planta, E-28006 Madrid
Tel: (+34 915) 62 15 52   Fax: (+34 915) 62 19 22
e-mail: cemafe@cemafe.com
Web: http://www.cemafe.com

**Organisation**
Established in 1980, Cemafe represents and co-ordinates the interests of Spanish rolling stock and railway equipment manufacturing companies at national and international levels.

*NEW ENTRY*

### Institute of International Container Lessors (IICL)

PO Box 605, 630 Old Post Road, Bedford, New York 10506, USA
Tel: (+1 914) 234 36 96   Fax: (+1 914) 234 36 41
e-mail: info@iicl.org
Web: http://www.iicl.org

**Key personnel**
Chairman: Brian Sondey
President: Henry F White Jr
First Vice-President: Robert S Ward
Second Vice-President: Jeffrey Ski
Treasurer: George Elkas

*UPDATED*

### Intergovernmental Organisation for International Carriage by Rail (OTIF)

Secretariat: Central Office for International Carriage by Rail (OCTI)
Gryphenhübeliweg 30, CH-3006 Berne, Switzerland
Tel: (+41 31) 359 10 10   Fax: (+41 31) 359 10 11
e-mail: otif@otif.ch

**Key personnel**
Chairman of Administrative Committee: H R Isliker (CH)
Director-General: (Vacant)
Deputy Director-General: G E Mutz

### International Air-Rail Organisation (IARO)

Room B217, MacMillan House, Paddington Station, London W2 1FT, UK
Tel: (+44 20) 87 50 66 32   Fax: (+44 20) 87 50 66 47
e-mail: intl_airrail@baa.com
Web: http://www.iaro.com

**Key personnel**
Director-General: Andrew Sharp

The object of IARO is to spread world class best practice and good practical ideas among people interested in rail links to airports. The organisation represents railways, airports, airlines and the supply industry.
Members include: Heathrow Express; Amsterdam Airport Schiphol; Manchester Airport; MTR Corporation Ltd; Hong Kong; Express Rail Link; Kuala Lumpur; Booz Allen Hamilton; the Chicago Transit Authority; and the Port Authority of New York and New Jersey. There is a regular newsletter, 'Air Rail Express' and regular conferences and workshops.

*UPDATED*

### International Association of Public Transport (UITP)

Union Internationale des Transports Publics
rue Sainte Marie 6, B-1080 Brussels, Belgium
Tel: (+32 2) 673 61 00   Fax: (+32 2) 660 10 72
e-mail: communication@uitp.com
Web: http://www.uitp.com

**Key personnel**
President: Jean Paul Bailly (Paris)
Vice-Presidents:
  Caetano Jannini Netto (São Paulo)
  Dmitry Gaev (Moscow)
  Johannes Sloth (Copenhagen)
  Dieter Ludwig (Karlsruhe)
  Jack C K So (Hong Kong)
  Enrico Mingardi (Rome)
  Tom Kaper (Den Haag)
  Ted Hesketh (Belfast)
  Richard J Simonetta (Atlanta)
Secretary-General: Hans Rat

UITP is the worldwide association of urban and regional passenger transport operators' authorities and suppliers. With over 2,000 members from nearly 80 countries, UITP promotes a better understanding of the potential of public transport and acts as the international network for all public transport professionals.
It acts as an international forum for the transport section to exchange information and ideas to further the position of public transport and is a platform for discussion between the industry, operators and authorities.

*UPDATED*

### International Container Bureau (BIC)

Bureau International des Containers
167 rue de Courcelles, F-75017 Paris, France
Tel: (+33 1) 47 66 03 90   Fax: (+33 1) 47 66 08 91

**Key personnel**
General Secretary: J Rey

### International Rail Transport Committee (CIT)

Bahnhofplatz 10A, CH-3000 Bern 65, Switzerland
Tel: (+41 512) 20 29 54   Fax: (+41 512) 20 34 57
e-mail: cit@cit-rail.org
Web: http://www.cit.org

**Key personnel**
Secretary: Thomas Leimgruber

Founded in 1902, the International Rail Transport Committee (CIT) is a non-profit-making association under Swiss law. It has legal personality and has its headquarters in Bern. It is the railway organisation responsible for handling issues of international rail transport law.
Undertakings or associations of undertakings may become members if they provide transport in accordance with the Convention Concerning International Carriage by Rail (COTIF) or manage railway infrastructure on which such transport is carried out.
The CIT currently has as members about 300 railway organisations (carriers and infrastructure managers), shipping companies and road carriers from states that apply COTIF.

*UPDATED*

### International Railway Congress Association (IRCA)

Association Internationale du Congrès des Chemins de Fer
Section 10, 85 Rue de France, B-1060 Brussels, Belgium
Tel: (+32 2) 520 78 31   Fax: (+32 2) 525 40 84

**Key personnel**
President: E Schouppe (Chief Executive, SNCB)
Vice-President: T Mignauw (member of the Executive Committee, SNCF)
Secretary General: A Martens (Deputy Director-General, SNCB)

*UPDATED*

### International Union of Private Railway Wagon Owners' Associations (UIP)

Union Internationale d'Associations de Propriétaires de Wagons de Particuliers
Boulevard du Souverain 53/17, B-1160 Brussels, Belgium
Tel: (+32 2) 672 88 47   Fax: (+32 2) 672 81 14
e-mail: uip@unicall.be
Web: http://uiprail.org

**Key personnel**
Secretary-General: Wolf D Gehrmann

### International Union of Railways (UIC)

Union Internationale des Chemins de Fer
16 rue Jean-Rey, F-75015 Paris, France
Tel: (+33 1) 44 49 20 20   Fax: (+33 1) 44 49 20 29
e-mail: (name)@uic.asso.fr
Web: http://www.uic.asso.fr

**Key personnel**
Chairman: Etienne Schouppe (JNCB)
Vice-Chairmen: Hartmut Mehdorn (DB)
  Masatake Matsuda (JR East)
  Marton Kukely (MÁV)
Chief Executive: Philippe Roumeguère
Deputy Chief Executive: Werner Breitling
Communications Director: Paul Véron

The UIC is the world body for international railway co-operation, with more than 158 members on five continents. Its goals are to promote all forms of co-operation among railway companies, achieve technical harmonisation and interoperability and develop international rail transport at world level.

*UPDATED*

### Organisation for the Collaboration of Railways (OSJD)

Hoza 63/67, Warsaw, Poland
Tel: (+48 22) 621 94 17   Fax: (+48 22) 657 36 54

**Key personnel**
Committee Chairman: Tadeusz Szozda
Secretary: Rastislav Chovan

## CONTINENTS

### Arab Union of Railways (UACF)

PO Box 6599, Aleppo, Syria
Tel: (+963 21) 266 72 70; 56 11   Fax: (+963 21) 268 60 00

**Key personnel**
Chairman of Management Board:
  Eng Omar Mohamed, Mohamed Nour (General Manager, Sudan Railways)
Deputy Chairman of Management Board:
  Eng Jamal Krouyem (President/General Director, Lebanese Railways)
Secretary-General: Eng Mourhaf Sabouni

Formed in 1979, the UACF stimulates co-operation between railways in Arab countries and co-ordinates their activities to ensure exchanges with each other and with international rail networks. Membership comprises railways in Algeria, Egypt, Iraq, Jordan (Aqaba and Hedjaz railways), Lebanon, Libya, Morocco, Syria (CFS and Syrian Hedjaz railways) and Tunisia, as well as a number of manufacturers, associations and railway-related organisations in several Arab countries.

The UACF also produces publications and stages events such as seminars and symposia, including a major biennial congress.

### Latin American Railway Association (ALAF)

Asociación Latinoamericana De Ferrocarriles
Avda Belgrano 863, ler piso, 1092 Buenos Aires, Argentina
Tel: (+54 1) 331 12 98; 343 05 93
Fax: (+54 1) 331 27 47

**Key personnel**
General Secretary: Ing Agustin R Pigliacampo
Technical-Administrative Secretary: Ing Vigder Sletean
International Transport Department: Alberto Paolini
Accounting Department: Cont Rodolfo Cascio
Administrative Co-ordinator: Dr Jorge Gutracht
Standards Department: Atilio Sanguinetti
International Technical Co-operation Department:
  Ing Jorge O Franco

### Pan American Railway Congress Association (ACPF)

Asociación del Congreso Panamericano de Ferrocarriles
Casilla de Correo 129 Suc 1, 1332 Buenos Aires, Argentina
Tel: (+54 11) 49 81 06 25   Fax: (+54 11) 48 14 18 23
e-mail: acpt@nat.com.ar

**Key personnel**
President: Major General Eng Juan Carlos De Marchi
First Vice-President: Arq Eduardo Santos Castillo
General Secretary: Ing Alfredo Fernandez
Treasurer: Dr Ricardo S Tawil
Special Adviser: Dr Adalberto Rodríguez Giavarini
  (Director of International Organisation, Ministry of Foreign Affairs, Argentina)

### Union of African Railways (UAR)

Avenue Tombalbaye 869, PO Box 687, Kinshasa, Zaire
Tel: (+243 12) 238 61   Fax: (+243 12) 251 66

**Key personnel**
President: Hanson Sindowe
Vice-Presidents
  North Africa: Sudan Railway Corporation
  West Africa: Mali
  East Africa: Djibouti-Ethiopia Railways
  Central Africa: Congo
  Southern Africa: Tazara
General Secretariat (staff)
  Secretary-General: Robert G Nkana
  Administration and Finance: Canute Peter Shengena
  Translations: Nsanbu Seke

## EUROPEAN

### Association of Public Transport Operators

Union des Transports Publics (UTP)
5-7 rue d'Aumale, F-75009 Paris, France
Tel: (+33 1) 48 74 63 51   Fax: (+33 1) 40 16 11 72

**Key personnel**
President: Michel Cornil
Director General: T Soupault

The UTP represents the interests in France of domestic public transport operators.

### European Company for the Financing of Railroad Rolling Stock (EUROFIMA)

Rittergasse 20, PO Box 1764, CH-4001 Basel, Switzerland
Tel: (+41 61) 287 33 40   Fax: (+41 61) 287 32 40
e-mail: info@eurofima.org
Web: http://www.eurofima.org

**Key personnel**
General Manager (Chief Executive Officer):
  Andre M Bovet
Senior Vice-Presidents: Bernard de Closset,
  Jean-Pierre Phan
First Vice-Presidents: Jean-Pierre Deriaz,
  Marco Termignone

**Shareholders**
DB AG (24.9%); SNCF (24.9%); FS (13.5%); SNCB (9.8%); NS (5.8%); RENFE (5.22%); SBB (5%); JŽ (Yugoslavia) (2.3%); SJ (2%); CFL (2%); ÖBB (2%); CP (1%); ICH (0.2%); MÁV (0.2%); HŽ (Croatia) (0.2%); SŽ (Slovenia) (0.2%); ŽBH (Bosnia and Herzegovina) (0.2%); BDŽ (Bulgaria) (0.2%); ŽSR (Slovakia) (0.2%); MŽ (Macedonia) (0.1%); TCDD (Turkey) (0.04%); DSB (0.02%); NSB (0.02%).

**Activity**
EUROFIMA finances railway equipment purchases for its shareholder national railways. Railway equipment is supplied to the national railways under equipment financing contracts. These contracts provide for periodical payments by the railways calculated to recover, over the life of a contract, repayments of principal and payments of interest on the funds borrowed, as well as EUROFIMA's expenses.   *UPDATED*

### European Conference of Ministers of Transport (ECMT)

2 rue André Pascal, F-75755 Paris Cedex 16, France
Tel: (+33 1) 45 24 97 10   Fax: (+33 1) 45 24 97 42
e-mail: ecmt.contact@oecd.org
Web: http://www.oecd.org/cem

**Key personnel**
Secretary-General: Jack Short

The European Conference of Ministers of Transport (ECMT) is an intergovernmental organisation established by a Protocol signed in Brussels on 17 October 1953. It is a forum in which ministers responsible for transport, and more specifically the inland transport sector, can co-operate on policy. Within this forum, ministers can openly discuss current problems and agree joint approaches for improving utilisation and rational development of European transport systems of international importance.

**Member countries**
*Founding members (since 1953)*
Austria, Belgium, Denmark, France, Germany, Greece, Ireland, Italy, Luxembourg, Netherlands, Norway, Portugal, Spain, Sweden, Switzerland, Turkey, UK.

*Other members*
Albania, Azerbaijan, Belarus, Bosnia Herzegovina, Bulgaria, Croatia, Czech Republic, Estonia, Finland, FYR Macedonia, Georgia, Hungary, Iceland, Latvia, Lithuania, Moldova, Poland, Romania, Russian Federation, Slovak Republic, Slovenia, Ukraine.

*Associate members*
Australia, Canada, Japan, New Zealand, USA.

*Observer countries*
Armenia, Lichtenstein, Morocco.   *UPDATED*

### Union of European Railways Industries (UNIFE)

Avenue Louise 221 Bte 11, B-1050 Brussels, Belgium
Tel: (+32 2) 626 12 60   Fax: (+32 2) 649 27
e-mail: mail@unife.org
Web: http://www.inife.org

**Key personnel**
General Manager: Drewin Nieuwenhuis
Office and Events Manager: Véronique Friob
Managers of International Affairs: Lara Isasa;
  Loris Di Pietrantonio, Hilary Mc Mahon; Nicola Erb

The Union of European Railway Industries is an industrial organisation representing its member's interest towards the European institutions, rail operator associations and other business relations. It represents 80 of the largest and medium-sized companies of the railway supply industry and a further 800 suppliers of railway equipment are associated members through their national associations.   *UPDATED*

### European Rail Research Institute (ERRI)

Arthur van Schendelstraat 754, NL-3511 MK Utrecht, Netherlands
Tel: (+31 30) 232 42 52   Fax: (+31 30) 236 89 14

# INTERNATIONAL RAILWAY ASSOCIATIONS AND AGENCIES

e-mail: rail_research@erri.nl
Web: http://www.erri.nl

**Key personnel**
Chairman of the Supervisory Board: Rod Muttram
Managing Director: Gunnar Gustafsson
General Manager: I Korpanec
Finance and Administration Director: R Hondelink
Technical Director: H Lagneau

**Services**
The European Rail Research Institute (ERRI) is a foundation under Dutch law within the International Union of Railways (UIC), carrying out research, studies and tests in fields of common interest. In 2000, ERRI had 32 European participants and 10 affiliates from 28 countries.

The Institute carries out collaborative research projects with various partners (railway operators, infrastructure owners and manufacturers, technical research centres, universities and so on) to boost the effectiveness of projects and allow more flexibility and responsiveness to research requirements at a European level.

Research is targeted mainly at improved productivity, reduced operating costs, interoperability and environmental issues. Activities include the co-ordination of long-term research programmes.

Key skills include:
- Management and execution of studies, research programmes and test programes;
- Initiation and drafting of research and development programmes;
- Development and testing of railway equipment;
- Monitoring and application of emerging rail technologies.

ERRI has professional inhouse engineering and project management personnel, some directly employed and some seconded from participating railways under long-term contracts. Personnel for specific projects are also drawn from the engineering divisions of UIC railways, consultancies and universities. Individual specialists are sometimes contracted direct. ERRI uses the laboratories and testing facilities of the European railways for model and full-scale tests and demonstrations.

In 1998, ERRI launched a commercial branch, European Rail Services BV (ERS ) (qv).

**Subsidiaries**
European Rail Services BV (ERS) is a wholly owned subsidiary of ERRI whose primary function is to provide ERRI products and services to non-UIC members.

ERSA (European Rail Software Applications) is a 60 per cent subsidiary of ERS. It specialises in the development and adaptation of simulation software for railway applications and also has the capability to carry out maintenance and support of other software packages.

## European Rail Services BV (ERS)

Arthur van Schendelstraat 754, NL-3511 MK Utrecht, Netherlands
Tel: (+31 30) 232 48 23   Fax: (+31 30) 232 48 15
e-mail: ers@ers.erri.nl
Web: http://www.erri.nl

**Key personnel**
Managing Director: Bert Goote

European Rail Services BV handles all the commercial activities of the European Rail Research Institute's (ERRI), marketing its knowledge and experience in railway technology.

ERS products and services include reports and technical documents, drawings, software and consultancy. The client base is worldwide, encompassing mass transit and light rail authorities, academic institutions, manufacturers, infrastructure suppliers, freight and passenger operating companies, rolling stock leasing companies and consultancies. ERS also organises ERRI Interactive Conferences, promoting ERRI's R&D results to a wider audience.

In 1998, ERS set up a subsidiary, European Rail Software Applications (ERSA) (qv). ERSA's role is to develop software and to provide software services related to ERRI research projects.

## European Wagon Pool (Europ Agreement)

Communauté d'Exploitation des Wagons Europ (Convention Europ)
SNCB, Frankrijkstraat 85, B-1060 Brussels, Belgium
Tel: (+32 2) 525 41 00   Fax: (+32 2) 525 44 97

**Key personnel**
President: A Martens

## Institution of Railway Operators

PO Box 5539, Derby DE1 9FE
Tel: (+44 1332) 26 33 69   Fax: (+44 1332) 26 31 25

**Key personnel**
Chairman: Richard Morris

The Institution was formed in 1999 by representatives of train operating companies in the UK to enable the exchange of technical and professional expertise within the industry.

## International Association of Railway Journalists (AIJF)

3 avenue Hoche, F-75008 Paris, France
Tel: (+33 1) 46 22 53 71   Fax: (+33 1) 40 54 98 93
e-mail: aijf@free.fr
Web: http://aijf.free.fr

**Key personnel**
President: Christian Scasso
Secretary: Jesper Sejl
Treasurer: Nadia Bourakba

The AIJF is a specialist forum for all journalists active in reporting the rail industry, with a worldwide membership.

## Public Transport Association (UTP)

Union des Transports Publics, 5-7 rue d'Aumale, F-75009 Paris, France
Tel: (+33 1) 48 74 63 51   Fax: (+33 1) 40 16 11 72
e-mail: lettre@utp.fr

**Key personnel**
President: Michel Cornil
Vice President: Antoine Frérot; Philippe Segretain
Secretary General: Thierry Soupalt

UTP membership comprises rail and road public transport operators in France. The organisation protects the industry's interests and represents it domestically and at a European level.

*NEW ENTRY*

## UNIFE

Union of European Railway Industries/Union des Industries Ferroviaires Européennes (UNIFE)
221 Avenue Louise, Bte 11, B-1050 Brussels, Belgium
Tel: (+32 2) 626 12 60   Fax: (+33 2) 626 12 61
e-mail: mail@unife.org
Web: http://www.unife.org

**Key personnel**
Chairman: Herbert Steffen
General Manager: Drewin Nieuwenhuis

**Services**
UNIFE's mission is to contribute to the development of the railway supply industry and promote rail transport initiatives aimed at providing for sustainable mobility, economic growth and an improved quality of life. UNIFE represents its members interests and maintains contact with the major European Institutions. Its members cover a wide range of suppliers including system integrators infrastructure and subsystems manufacturers. UNIFE works in partnership with other worldwide Associations to promote rail transport.

---

# NATIONAL

## ARGENTINA

### Chamber of Railway Industries

Cámara de Industriales Ferroviarios
Alsina 1607, Buenos Aires
Tel: (+54 1) 40 49 67; 55 71   Fax: (+54 1) 40 49 09 58

**Key personnel**
President: Eng E G Nottage
Secretary: E R Paduto

**Members**
Active members are Artimsa SA, Est Met A Longo SA, Ferromec SA, Petro Parts SA, Saft Nife Argentina SA, Servotron SA, Siderea SAIC yA and Siemens SA.

## AUSTRALIA

### Australasian Railway Association Inc

PO Box 266, Collins Street West, Melbourne 8007
Tel: (+61 3) 96 14 51 62   Fax: (+61 3) 96 14 55 14
e-mail: ara@access.net.au
Web: http://www.ara.net.au

**Key personnel**
President: P Stephen Bradford (GSR)
Vice-President: Martin Lacome (ARG)
Secretary: Peter Strachan (NEG)
Treasurer: David Gotze (Indec Consulting)
Executive Director: John Kirk
Manager, Programs: Bryan Williams
Manager Research: D Hill

The Australasian Railway Association Inc (ARA) is the leading industry body for the rail sector in Australia and New Zealand. It represents the interests of both private and government-owned rail operators in freight, passenger and tourist/heritage sectors, track owners, manufacturers of locomotives and rolling stock, suppliers of signalling and communications systems, maintenance and construction companies, freight forwarders, investment banks, legal firms, information technology and service providers, consultants and rail unions. Founded in 1994, the ARA currently has 166 members.

*UPDATED*

## INTERNATIONAL RAILWAY ASSOCIATIONS AND AGENCIES

### Rail Track Association of Australia

PO Box 6086, Blacktown, New South Wales 2148, Australia
Tel: (+61 2) 671 65 55   Fax: (+61 2) 671 78 75

**Key personnel**
President: S Maxwell

---

### Railway Technical Society of Australasia

11 National Circuit, Barton, ACT 2600 Australia
Tel: (+61 62) 70 65 55   Fax: (+61 62) 73 14 88
e-mail: jarmstrong@eol.ieaust.org.au

**Key personnel**
National Chairman: Professor Philip Laird
Sydney Chapter Chair: Les McNaughton
Queensland Chapter Chair: Dr Luis Ferreira
Victoria Chapter Chair: D J Ferris
SA Chapter Chair: John Adams
Western Australian Chapter Chair: Shane Hinchliffe
The Society's mission is to provide a learned society and communal functions for individuals and groups in the railway industry and to provide practice-based opinion and advice for The Institution of Engineers, Australia.

---

## AUSTRIA

### Federation of Cable Railways

Fachverband der Seilbahnen
PO Box 172, Wiedner Hauptstrasse 63, A-1045 Vienna
Tel: (+43 1) 501 05 31 65; 31 66
e-mail: wolf@wk.or.at

**Key personnel**
Director: G D Dipl Ing Dr Helmut Draxler
Manager: Dr Erik Wolf

---

### Federation of Private Railways

Fachverband der Schienenbahnen
PO Box 172, Wiedner Hauptstrasse 63, A-1045 Vienna
Tel: (+43 1) 501 05 31 65; 31 66
Fax: (+43 1) 50 20 62 42

**Key personnel**
Director: Dr Helmut Draxler
Manager: Dr Erik Wolf

---

## CANADA

### Canadian Urban Transit Association

55 York Street, Suite 1401, Toronto, Ontario M5J 1R7
Tel: (+1 416) 365 98 00   Fax: (+1 416) 365 12 95
e-mail: transit@cutaactu.ca
Web: http://www.cutaactu.ca

**Key personnel**
President and Chief Executive Officer:
    Michael Roschlau

**Quebec office**
4612 Rue Sainte-Catherine Ouest, Montreal, Quebec, H3Z 1S3

The CUTA membership reflects the predominance of local buses on the public transport scene in Canada. Membership by manufacturers, suppliers and consultants also reflects the predominance of the local bus.

*UPDATED*

---

### The Railway Association of Canada

99 Bank Street, Suite 1401 Ottawa, Ontario K1P 6B9
Tel: (+1 613) 567 85 91   Fax: (+1 613) 567 67 26
e-mail: rac@railcan.ca
Web: http://www.railcan.ca

**Key personnel**
Chairman: R J Ritchie
Vice-Chairman: P M Tellier
President and Chief Executive Officer: W A Rowat

**Services**
The Railway Association of Canada represents 56 freight and passenger railways operating in Canada. They originate six million carloads and containers of freight, and carry 51 million passengers. The RAC conducts research and lobbies key audiences to increase public awareness of the role rail plays in Canada's trade dependent economy, and what it can do to reduce road and airport congestion, pollution and fuel consumption. The RAC develops rules and standards for the industry, public safety campaigns, training, and supplies specialised services to members, customers and municipal governments to ensure safe, secure, reliable transport.

**Member companies**
Agence Métropolitaine de Transport
Alberta Prairie Railway Excursions
Amtrak
Arnaud Railway Company
Athabasca Northern Railway Ltd
Barrie-Collingwood Railway
Burlington Northern and Santa Fe Railway Company
Burlington Northern (Manitoba) Ltd
Canadian American Railway Co
Canadian National Railway
Canadian Pacific Railway
Cape Breton & Central Nova Scotia Railway
Cartier Railway Co
Central Manitoba Railway Inc
Central Western Railway
Chemin de Fer Baie des Chaleurs Inc
Chemin de Fer Charlevoix Inc
Chemin de Fer de la Matapedia et du Golfe Inc
CSX Transportation Inc
E&N Railway Company (1998) Ltd
Essex Terminal Railway Co
FerroEquus Railway Company Ltd
Goderich-Exeter Railway Co Ltd
GO Transit
Great Canadian Railtour Company Ltd
Great Western Railway Ltd
Huron Central Railway Ltd
Kelowna Pacific Railway
Lakeland & Waterways Railway
Mackenzie Northern Railway
New Brunswick East Coast Railway Inc
New Brunswick Southern Railway Co Ltd
Norfolk Southern Corp
Ontario Northland Transportation Commission
Ontario Southland Railway Inc
Ottawa Central Railway Inc
Ottawa Valley Railway
Québec North Shore & Labrador Railway Company Inc
Québec & Gatineau Railway Company
Québec Southern Railway Company Ltd
Roberval and Saguenay Railway Company, The
South Simcoe Railway
Southern Manitoba Railway
Southern Ontario Railway
Southern Railway of British Columbia Ltd
St Lawrence & Atlantic Railroad (Quebec) Inc
Sydney Coal Railway
Sydney Railway Company
Toronto Terminals Railway Company Ltd
Trillium Railway Company Ltd
VIA Rail Canada Inc
Wabush Lake Railway Company, Ltd
West Coast Express Ltd
White Pass & Yukon Route
Windsor & Hantsport Railway
Wisconsin Central Ltd

The Association publishes *Railway Trends*, an annual statistical digest of the Canadian rail industry based on Canadian data; research reports, background and position papers, newsletters, an annual report and produces industry-related videos. The RAC held its first Regional and Short line Railway Conference in Ottawa on 2 November 2001 to identify the challenges facing the industry.

*UPDATED*

---

## FRANCE

### Railway Industries Association

Fédération des Industries Ferroviaires (FIF)
12 rue Bixio, F-75007 Paris
Tel: (+33 1) 45 56 13 53   Fax: (+33 1) 47 05 29 17
Web: http://www.fif.asso.fr

**Key personnel**
President: Jean-Claude Berthod
General Delegate: J P Audoux

*UPDATED*

---

### SYCAFER

Groupement des Installations Ferroviares Fixes (French Track Suppliers and Contractors Association)
12 rue Bixio, F-75007 Paris, France
Tel: (+33 1) 47 77 00 55   Fax: (+33 1) 47 05 52 49
e-mail: yvon.estelle@cofiger.fr

**Key personnel**
President: Jean-Louis Wagner
Vice-President: Gilles du Fou
General Secretary: Yvon Estellé
Deputy General Secretary: Dany Dupont-Weider

*VERIFIED*

---

## GERMANY

### Association of German Transport Undertakings (VDV)

Kamekestrasse 37-39, D-50672 Cologne, Germany
Tel: (+49 221) 57 97 90   Fax: (+49 221) 51 42 72
e-mail: info@vdv.de
Web: http://www.vdv.de

**Subsidiaries**
VDV-Geschäftsstelle Berlin
Strasse des 17 Juni, D-10623 Berlin
Tel: (+49 30) 39 99 32-0   Fax: (+49 30) 39 99 32 15
e-mail: vdv-berlin.t-online.de
Manager: Dr Ing Martin Runkel

VDV-Geschäftsstelle Brüssel
c/o UITP, Brussels
Manager: Klaus J Meyer

**Key personnel**
President: Dr-Ing Eh Dieter Ludwig
Vice-Presidents:
    Dipl Kfm Günter Elste (Passenger Traffic)
    Dr Rolf Bender (Freight Traffic)
General Manager:
    Professor Dr-Ing Adolf Müller-Hellmann
Manager: Dr Thomas Muthesius (Passenger Traffic)
Manager: Dr Martin Henke (Freight Traffic)
Head of Marketing, Press and PR Department:
    Dipl- Volksw Friedhelm Bihn
    Dipl G Stephan Dnemüller (Freight Traffic)

**Services**
Trade association of the German public transport industry. Represents, among others, 51 'private', non-Deutsche Bahn, passenger railways and 147 freight, port and industrial railways. Very few railways still offer both passenger and freight services.

*UPDATED*

## Association of Privately Owned Wagon Operators

Vereinigung der Privatgüterwagen Interessenten (VPI)
Schauenburger Strasse 52, D-20095 Hamburg, Germany
Tel: (+49 40) 450 50 86   Fax: (+49 40) 450 50 90
e-mail: vpihamburg@t-online.de

**Key personnel**
President: Rainer Baumgarten
Vice-Presidents: Heribert Luzar, Dieter Trapp
General Manager: Henning Traumann

*UPDATED*

## Association of the Railway Supply Industry in Germany

Verband der Bahnindustrie in Deutschland eV
Lindenstrasse 30, D-60325 Frankfurt/Main
Tel: (+49 69) 72 72 44   Fax: (+49 69) 72 72 94
e-mail: vdb.schiene@t-online.de

**Key personnel**
President: Dipl Ing Peter Witt
Directors: Dipl Ing Joachim Körber,
  Dipl Wi-Ing Norbert G Liebler

The organisation, which represents the railway supply industry in Germany, was formerly the German Railway Supply Industry Association.

## Rolled Steel Association Long Products Division/Railway Material

Walzstahl Vereinigung Abt Profilstahl
Sohnstrasse 65, D-40237, Düsseldorf
Tel: (+49 211) 670 71 88   Fax: (+49 211) 670 79 32

**Key personnel**
Secretary: H Bauer

## Switch and Crossing Manufacturers Association

Fachverband Weichenbau
PO Box 1020, D-58010 Hagen
Tel: (+49 2331) 20 08; 29   Fax: (+49 2331) 20 08; 28

**Key personnel**
Chairman: Eckhard Bittel

# ITALY

## ANIE

Italian Association of Electrotechnical and Electronics Industries
Via Algardi 2, I-20148 Milan, Italy
Tel: (+39 02) 326 41   Fax: (+39 02) 326 42 12

**Key personnel**
Chairman: Ing Gio Batta Clavarino
General Secretary: Ing Lorenzo Tringali-Casanuova

## College of Italian Railway Engineers

Collegio Ingegneri Ferroviari Italiani
Via G Giolitti 34, I-00185 Rome
Tel: (+39 06) 488 21 29   Fax: (+39 06) 474 29 87
e-mail: mol1958@mclink.it

**Key personnel**
President: Dr Ing E Maestrini
Secretary: Dr Ing B Cirillo

# JAPAN

## Japan Overseas Rolling Stock Association (JORSA)

Tekko Building, 1-8-2 Marunouchi, Chiyoda-ku, Tokyo 100-0005
Tel: (+81 3) 32 01 31 45   Fax: (+81 3) 32 14 47 17
e-mail: infoweb@jorsa.or.jp

**Key personnel**
Senior Managing Director: S Suzuki
Director, Administration: Y Kurasawa
Director, General Affairs: T Amano

Established in 1953 the association is an umbrella organisation of 25 Japanese traders and manufacturers and promotes trading relations between members and railway operators and users.

*UPDATED*

## Japan Railway Engineers' Association

Tani Building, 1-28-6 Kameido, Kohtoh-ku, Tokyo 136-0071
Tel: (+81 3) 56 26 23 21   Fax: (+81 3) 56 26 23 25

**Key personnel**
Chairman: Koichi Sakata
Deputy Chairmen: Masao Kodamd (General Manager, Nippon Steel Corporation), Tatsuyuki Enomoto (President, Nippon Densetsu Kogyo Co Ltd), Dr Eng Misao Sugawara (Tokyo University of Science)
Executive Director: Hiroyuki Yoshiba

*UPDATED*

## Japan Society of Mechanical Engineers

Shinanomachi-Rengakan Building, Shinanomachi 35, Shinjuku-ku, Tokyo 160
Tel: (+81 3) 53 60 35 00   Fax: (+81 3) 53 60 35 08

**Key personnel**
Secretary: Y Takahashi

## Railway Electrical Engineering Association of Japan

Kimigayo Building 4F, 3-20-15 Asakusabashi Taito-ku, Tokyo 111-0053
Tel: (+81 3) 38 61 86 78   Fax: (+81 3) 38 61 85 06
e-mail: info@rail-e.or.jp

**Key personnel**
President: Masanori Ozeki
Vice-Presidents: Nobuaki Maruyama, Tatsuyuki Enomoto, Shinichiro Otsuka
Senior Managing Director: Tatsumi Honda
Managing Directors: Hiroto Yasuhara, Sakuro Tsukuda

# SPAIN

## Institution of Spanish Railways

Fundación de los Ferrocarriles Españoles
Palacio de Fernán Núñez, C/ Santa Isabel 44, E-28012 Madrid, Spain
Tel: (+34 91) 527 61 72
Web: http://www.ffe.es

**Key personnel**
Director: Carlos Zapatero Ponte

The aims of the institution include: increasing the knowledge and use of rail; sponsoring studies into the rail transport mode; promotion of the socio-economic benefits and cultural importance of rail; and the conservation of the heritage of the railway in Spain. The institution's patrons include: RENFE; GIF; FEVE; FGC; and EuskoTren.

## Spanish Private Wagon Owners Association

(Spanish Private Wagon Owners Association)
Asociación de Propietarios de Vagones de España
Juan Alvarez Mendizábal 30, 4° Centro, E-28008 Madrid
Tel: (+34 91) 547 82 86   Fax: (+34 91) 547 82 86

**Key personnel**
President: D Emilio Fernández Fernández
Vice-President: Bruno Torresano Guerreiro
Secretary: D Pablo Rodríguez Mosquera

**Principal member companies**
Cementos Alfa SA
LTF
Saltra
SEmat SA
Transfesa
Tudela Veguin SA

Member companies own 5,811 wagons, predominantly covered vehicles, tank wagons, car transporters and intermodal flat wagons. The association offers integrated transport solutions to meet logistics needs of the industry with interchangeable-axle rolling stock, swap bodies and trucks.

*UPDATED*

# SWITZERLAND

## Swissrail Export Association

Effingerstrasse 8, PO Box 7948, CH-3001 Bern
Tel: (+41 31) 398 50 50   Fax: (+41 31) 398 55 55
e-mail: mail@swissrail.com
Web: http://www.swissrail.com

**Key personnel**
General Manager: Walter Graeppi

**Organisation**
The Swissrail Export Association was founded in 1977. It is a private law-based association with more than 70 member companies active abroad as well as in Switzerland, including leading consultants and industrial companies and a high number of innovative medium and small size enterprises in the field of public transport systems. Swiss Federal Railways, public transport authorities, including associated private railways and urban transport operators, the Federal Office of Transport and the Institute of Transportation, Traffic, Highway and Railway Engineering are supporting Swissrail activities.

*UPDATED*

# UNITED KINGDOM

## The Institute of Logistics and Transport

Earlstrees Court, Earlstrees Road, PO Box 5787, Corby NN17 4XQ
Tel: (+44 1536) 74 10 00   Fax: (+44 1536) 74 01 01
e-mail: enquiry@iolt.org.uk
Web: http://www.iolt.org.uk

*London office*
Supply Chain Centre, PO Box 5787, Corby, NN17 4XQ

**Key personnel**
Acting Director of Policies: John Glover
Transport Policies Executive: Darren Weaver

*UPDATED*

# INTERNATIONAL RAILWAY ASSOCIATIONS AND AGENCIES

## Institution of Civil Engineers

One Great George Street, London SW1P 3AA
Tel: (+44 20) 76 65 21 50   Fax: (+44 20) 72 22 09 73
e-mail: claire.sanders@ice.org.uk
Web: http://www.ice.org.uk

**Key personnel**
President: Mark Whitby
Acting Chief Executive and Secretary: Atmar Bhogal
Marketing Manager: Claire Sanders

*UPDATED*

## Institution of Diesel and Gas Turbine Engineers

PO Box 43, Bedford MK40 4JB
Tel: (+44 1234) 24 13 40   Fax: (+44 1234) 35 54 93
e-mail: secretary@idgte.org
Web: http://www.idgte.org

**Key personnel**
Secretary: K S Edmanson

*UPDATED*

## Institution of Electrical Engineers (IEE)

Savoy Place, London WC2R 0BL
Tel: (+44 20) 72 40 18 71   Fax: (+44 20) 72 40 77 35
e-mail: postmaster@iee.org.uk
Web: http://www.iee.org.uk/

**Key personnel**
Chief Executive: Dr A Roberts

*VERIFIED*

## Institution of Mechanical Engineers Railway Division

1 Birdcage Walk, London SW1H 9JJ
Tel: (+44 20) 79 73 12 80; 12 44
Fax: (+44 20) 79 73 01 82
e-mail: m_pepper@imeche.org.uk
Web: http://www.imeche.org.uk/railway

**Key personnel**
Chairman: Eur Ing J W Nuttall
Executive Officer: Matt Pepper
Executive Assistant: Mike Wilkinson

## Institution of Railway Signal Engineers (IRSE)

Savoy Hill House, Savoy Hill, London WC2R 0BS
Tel: (+44 20) 72 40 32 90   Fax: (+44 20) 72 40 32 81
e-mail: admin@irse.u-net.com
Web: http://www.irse

**Key personnel**
President: P W Stanley
Chief Executive: K W Burrage

*UPDATED*

## Locomotive & Carriage Institution

69 Avondale Close, Horley RH6 8BN, UK
Tel: (+44 1293) 77 32 39
e-mail: loco.carriage@tinyworld.co.uk
Web: http://www.lococarriage.org.uk

**Key personnel**
President: N P Agnew
Chairman: D Kirkland
General Secretary: J E Lunn

**Organisation**
The Institution holds meetings and seminars covering contemporary railways topics and arranges tours of railway installations in the UK and elsewhere in Europe.

*UPDATED*

## Permanent Way Institution

Lucks Cottage, Lucks Lane, Paddock Wood TN12 6OL, UK
Tel: (+44 1892) 83 32 50   (+44 1892) 33 71 99
e-mail: peter.coysten@halliburton.com
Web: http://www.pwi.org.uk

**Key personnel**
President: Rob Boulgen (2001-2002)
The Secretary: Peter Coysten
Membership and Sales Officer: Colin Cowey
Finance Officer: Jack Scott
Education and Technical Officer: John Elliott
Promotions and Publications Officer: Philip Sutcliffe

*UPDATED*

## Private Wagon Federation

Homelea, Westland Green, Little Hadham SG11 2AG
Tel: (+44 1279) 84 34 87   Fax: (+44 1279) 84 23 94

**Key personnel**
Chairman: John Jagger
Secretary-General: G Pratt

## Rail Civil Engineers' Association

One Great George Street, Westminster London SW1P 3AA, UK
Tel: (+44 20) 76 65 22 31   Fax: (+44 20) 77 99 13 25
e-mail: rcea@ice.org.uk

Membership is open to professional engineers who hold positions with responsibility for the development, design, construction or maintenance of infrastructure for railway operators.

*NEW ENTRY*

## The Railway Forum

12 Grosvenor Place, London SWX 7HH
Tel: (+44 20) 72 59 65 43   Fax: (+44 20) 72 59 65 44
e-mail: railinfo@railwayforum.com
Web: http://www.railwayforum.com

**Key personnel**
Chairman: Dr Keith Lloyd
Director-General: Adrian Lyons
Communications Director: John Dennis

The Railway Forum is an industry-wide body sponsored by and paid for by most UK train operating companies, the rolling stock leasing companies, the Passenger Transport Executives, Railtrack, London Underground, Eurotunnel and many manufacturing and infrastructure companies, as well as other business connected with the railways. There are some 60 members.
The organisations key role is to act as a think tank, information exchange and point of contact for those committed to and interested in the UK's rail industry.

*UPDATED*

## Railway Industry Association

22 Headfort Place, London SW1X 7RY
Tel: (+44 20) 72 01 07 77   Fax: (+44 20) 72 35 57 77
e-mail: ria@riagb.org.uk
Web: http://www.riagb.org.uk

**Key personnel**
Chairman: John Cotton
Director General: Jeremy Candfield
Technical Director: Richard Gostling
Director, Communications: Graham Coombs
Administration Manager: Barbara Williams
Research Officer: David Eades

The trade association for UK-based manufacturers, maintainers, contractors, consultants, leasing companies and other providers of specialist services to the worldwide railway industry.

*UPDATED*

## Wagon Building and Repairing Association

'Homelea', Westland Green, Little Hadham SG11 2AG, UK
Tel: (+44 1279) 84 34 87   Fax: (+44 1279) 84 23 94

**Key personnel**
Chairman: M Burge
Vice-Chairman: R Crutchley
Secretary: G Pratt

# UNITED STATES OF AMERICA

## American Association of Railroad Superintendents (AARS)

PO Box 131, Griffith, Illinois 46319, USA
Tel: (+1 219) 922 10 72   Fax: (+1 219) 922 12 26

**Key personnel**
President: K E Haugen
Administrative Manager: Barbara Marlow
Treasurer: G J Ruffing

*UPDATED*

## American Association of State Highway and Transportation Officials (AASHTO)

444 North Capitol Street, NW, Suite 249, Washington DC 20001, USA
Tel: (+1 202) 624 58 13   Fax: (+1 202) 624 58 06
e-mail: penne@aashto.org
Web: http://www.transportation.org

**Key personnel**
Executive Director: John Horsley
Secretary, Standing Committee on Rail Transportation: Leo Penne

AASHTO represents States on safety; state-supported passenger services; high-speed programmes; and industry restructuring, covering both short line and major carriers.

*UPDATED*

## American Public Transportation Association (APTA)

1666 K Street NW, Washington DC 20006, USA
Tel: (+1 202) 496 48 00   Fax: (+1 202) 496 43 24
Web: http://www.apta.com

**Key personnel**
President: William W Millar
Vice-Presidents:
  VP and Chief Counsel: Daniel Duff
  VP, Member Services: Anthony M Kouneski
  VP Financial and Administration: C Samuel Kesna
  VP, Communications and Marketing:
    Rosemary Sheridan

VP, Programme Management and Education Services:
  Pamela Boswell

An industry effort, PRESS (Passenger Rail Equipment Safety Standards) is an APTA task force started in 1995 and chaired by Metra (qv in Railway Systems, USA).

*UPDATED*

---

## American Railway Car Institute

700 N Fairfax Street, Suite 601, Alexandria, Virginia 22314
Tel: (+1 703) 836 23 32   Fax: (+1 703) 548 00 58
e-mail: rpi@rpi.org

**Key personnel**
Chairman: John E Carroll, Jr
  (Johnstown America Corporation)
Executive Director: Thomas D Simpson

*UPDATED*

---

## American Railway Engineering and Maintenance of Way Association (AREMA)

6201 Corporate Drive, Suite 1125, Landover, Maryland 20785
Tel: (+1 301) 459 32 00   Fax: (+1 301) 459 80 77
e-mail: wtayman@arema.org
Web: arema.org

**Key personnel**
Executive Director: Dr Charles H Emely
Director of Finance and Administration: W S Taylor

---

## American Short Line and Regional Railroad Association

1120 G Street, NW, Suite 520, Washington DC 20005-3889
Tel: (+1 202) 628 45 00   Fax: (+1 202) 628 64 30

**Key personnel**
President and Treasurer: Frank E Turner
Vice-President and General Counsel: Alice C Saylor
Executive Director, Membership Services:
  Kathleen M Cassidy
Executive Director, Federal and Industry Programmes:
  Matthew B Reilly
Executive Director, Traffic and Tariff Programmes:
  K Grant Ozburn
Director, Finances and Administration:
  Kenneth P Schoppmann

---

## Association of American Railroads

American Railroads Building, 50 F Street NW, Washington DC 20001
Tel: (+1 202) 639 21 00   Fax: (+1 202) 639 28 06
Web: http://www.aar.org

**Key personnel**
President and Chief Executive Officer:
  Edward R Hamberger
Executive Vice-President, Safety and Operations:
  Charles E Dettmann
Vice-President Administration and Finance:
  Jeff Marsh
Vice-President Communications: Peggy Wilhide
Vice-President Government Affairs:
  Obie O'Bannon
Vice-President Policy and Economics:
  Craig Rockey
Senior Vice-President, Law and General Counsel:
  Louis P Warchot

**Subsidiaries**
Transportation Technology Center Inc (TTCI)
PO Box 11130, Pueblo, Colorado 81001
Tel: (+1 719) 584 05 01   Fax: (+1 719) 584 07 11

President: Roy A Allen
See entry in *Consultancy services* section.

RAILINC
7001 Weston Parkway, Suite 200 Cary, North Carolina 27513
Tel: (+1 800) 544 72 45   Fax: (+1 919) 651 54 10
e-mail: csc@railinc.com
Web: http://www.railinc.com
President: James W Gardner

The AAR is the trade association for the rail industry. On behalf of the industry it engages in lobbying, standard-setting, communications and other public policy initiatives. AAR's subsidiarries, TTCI and RAILINC Corp engage in research and technology activities and information technology activities respectively.

*UPDATED*

---

## The High Speed Ground Transportation Association (HSGTA)

1010 Massachusetts Avenue NW, Suite 110, Washington DC 20001
Tel: (+1 202) 789 81 07   Fax: (+1 702) 789 81 09
e-mail: info@hsgt.org
Web: http://www.hsgt.org

**Key personnel**
Chairman: William C Nevel
President and Chief Executive Officer: Mark R Dysart
Director, Operations and Planning: Patric Anater
Director, Public Affaris: Anne Chettle

The HSGTA has a foundation, the High Speed Rail/Maglev Foundation, at the above address.

The HSGTA advocates the development and implementation of high-speed ground transport in North America. Members include suppliers, engineers, consultants, trade unions, public utilities, public officials and members of the public. The HSGTA produces a quartlery publication, *Speedlines* and hosts an annual conference. Active in the pursuit of federal and state legislation on behalf of its members, with issues of advocacy including: full funding for Amtrak, the continuation of the Maglev Deployment Programme and the expansion of the Next Generation High Speed Rail Programme, particularly in the area of highway-railway grade crossings.

*UPDATED*

---

## National Mediation Board

1301 K Street NW, Suite 250E, Washington DC 20572
Tel: (+1 202) 692 50 00   Fax: (+1 202) 692 50 80

**Key personnel**
Chairman: Ernest W Dubester
Member: Magdalena G Jacobsen
Chief of Staff: Stephen E Crable
Chief Financial Officer: June King
General Counsel: Ronald M Etters
Hearing Officers: Mary L Johnson, Benetta Mansfield, Sean Rogers

---

## The National Railroad Construction and Maintenance Association Inc (NRC)

122 C Street NW, Suite 850, Washington DC 20001
Tel: (+1 202) 638 77 90   Fax: (+1 202) 638 10 45
e-mail: info@nrcma.org
Web: http://www.nrcma.org

**Key personnel**
President: Ray Chambers
Chairman of the Board: Larry Laurello
Vice-Chairman: Richard Sherman

NRC is a non-profit trade association of several hundred companies involved in the railroad construction industry. NRC members perform rail construction and maintenance work on every type of rail property: Class I, II, and III freight railroads, industry and military-owned track, transit, commuter and intercity passenger railroads. NRC companies also perform specialised work in areas such as monorails and port cargo crane rail systems.

*UPDATED*

---

## National Railway Labor Conference

Suite 500, 1901 L Street NW, Washington DC 20036
Tel: (+1 202) 862 72 00

**Key personnel**
Chairman: Robert F Allen

*VERIFIED*

---

## National Transportation Safety Board (NTSB)

490 L'Enfant Plaza SW, Washington DC 20594, USA
Tel: (+1 202) 314 60 00   Fax: (+1 202) 314 64 97
Web: http://www.ntsb.gov

**Key personnel**
Board Members: John J Goglia, Jim Hall,
  John Hammerschmidt, George Black
Director, Office of Railroad Safety: Robert C Lauby

**Regional offices**
Chicago, Dallas, Fort Worth, Atlanta, Miami, Los Angeles, Denver, Seattle, Anchorage and Parsippany, New Jersey. NTSB is an independent federal accident investigation agency created in 1967. It ascertains probable cause, conducts special studies and assists federal agencies with rules and regulations.

---

## Operation Lifesaver

1420 King Street, Suite 401, Alexandria, Virginia 22314
Tel: (+1 800) 537 62 24
e-mail: general@oli.org
Web: http://www.oli.org

**Key personnel**
President: Gerri Hall
Vice-President of Communication: Marmie Edwards

Operation Lifesaver is a national non-profit organisation that promotes public education and awareness, engineering and enforcement, to reduce collisions, injuries and fatalities at level crossings and to prevent railway trespass deaths and injuries on railway property.

---

## Port Terminal Railroad Association

8934 Manchester, Houston, Texas 77012, USA
Tel: (+1 713) 393 65 00   Fax: (+1 713) 393 66 73

**Description**
The Port Terminal Railroad Association is an association comprising any rail carrier that has trackage into Houston, Texas and wishes to be a member and the Port of Houston. Current members are the Burlington Northern Santa Fe, Texas Mexican Railway Company and the Union Pacific. Operating expenses are apportioned by wagons handled. The 51.6 km property includes 14.5 km equipped with CTC. The association leases 24 units of type MK1500D from MK Rail.

In 1998 the Association handled 517,945 wagonloads.

# INTERNATIONAL RAILWAY ASSOCIATIONS AND AGENCIES

## Railroad Human Resource Management Association (RHMA)

c/o Association of American Railroads
50 F Street NW, Room 3901, Washington DC 20001
Tel: (+1 202) 639 21 51   Fax: (+1 202) 639 28 06

**Key personnel**
Chairman: Paul N Austin
Vice-Chairman: Dennis J Cech
Secretary and Treasurer: Penny L Prue

## Railroad Retirement Board

844 North Rush Street, Chicago, Illinois 60611-2092
Tel: (+1 312) 751 47 77   Fax: (+1 312) 751 71 54
Web: http://www.rrb.gov

**Key personnel**
Members: Cherryl T Thomas (Chair); V M Speakman (Labour member), Jerome F Kever (Carrier Member)
Senior Executive Officer and General Counsel: Steven A Bartholow
Director of Programs: Bobby V Ferguson
Director of Administration: Dorothy Isherwood
Director of Public Affairs: William G Poulos
Chief Financial Officer: Kenneth P Boehne
Chief Information Officer: Kenneth J Zoll
Chief Actuary: Frank J Buzzi

*UPDATED*

## Railway Progress Institute

700 N Fairfax Street, Suite 601, Alexandria, Virginia 22314-2098
Tel: (+1 703) 836 23 32   Fax: (+1 703) 548 00 58
e-mail: rpi@rpi.org

**Key personnel**
President: Robert A Matthews
Chairman: Ronald L McDaniel (Western-Cullen-Hayes)
Vice-Chairman: J Craig Rice (Brenco Inc)

## Railway Systems Suppliers, Inc

9304 New LaGrange Road, Suite 200, Louisville, Kentucky 40242
Tel: (+1 502) 327 77 74   Fax: (+1 502) 327 05 41
e-mail: rssi@rssi.org

**Key personnel**
Chairman and President: Phil C Hess
Executive Vice-President: George W Rudge
First Vice-President: Ronald L McDaniel
Second Vice-President: Patti Jon Christensen
Executive Director/Secretary-Treasurer: Donald F Remaley

## Regional Railroads of America

122 C Street, NW, Suite 850, Washington DC 20001
Tel: (+1 202) 638 77 90   Fax: (+1 202) 638 10 45

**Key personnel**
Chairman: Peter Gilbertson, Anacostia & Pacific
Vice-Chairman: Mort Fuller, Genesee & Wyoming
Treasurer: Mike Barron, Ann Arbor RR

# CONSULTANCY SERVICES

# CONSULTANCY SERVICES

## Alphabetical listing

Accent Marketing and Research
Accenture
Advanced Railway Research Centre
AEA Technology Rail
ALK Associates Inc
ANSALDOBREDA
Ardanuy Ingeneria SA
AREP
ARUP
Aspen Burrow Crocker Ltd
A T Kearney Inc
Austria Rail Engineering
Babtie Group
Balfour Beatty Rail
Banverket Consulting
Barton-Aschman Associates, Inc
BCD Consulting Sas
Bechtel Corporation
Best Impressions
Blue Print Rail
BMT Reliability Consultants Ltd
Booz, Allen & Hamilton Inc
Bovis Lend Lease
Brown & Root Services
Cambridge Systematics Inc
CANAC International Inc
Canarail Consultants Inc
Cape Engineering
Carmen Systems AB
CEFRAC
Century Engineering Inc
Chambers, Conlon & Hartwell Inc
CIE Consult
Clough, Harbour & Associates LLP
Cole, Sherman & Associates Limited
Colin Buchanan and Partners
Colston, Budd, Wardrop & Hunt
Corradine Group, The
Corus Rail Consultancy Ltd
Corus Rail Technologies
COWI Consulting Engineers and Planners AS
CPCS Ltd
Cre'active Design
Crown Agents for Oversea Governments and Administrations Ltd
Currie & Brown
Daniel, Mann, Johnson & Mendenhall
DCA Design International Ltd
DE-Consult
Delcan Corporation
De Leuw, Cather & Company
Design and Projects Int Ltd
Design Research Unit
Design Triangle
DHA
DHV Holding BV
EDS
Edwards and Kelcey Inc
EG & G Dynatrend Inc
Electrack
Electrowatt Infra
Engineering Link Ltd, The
ENOTRAC AG
EPV-GIV
ERM Lahmeyer International GmbH
Esveld Consulting Services BV
EurailTest
Eurostation SA
Finnish Railway Engineering Ltd
First Engineering Ltd
Fleet Software

Flow Science Ltd
Fluor Daniel Pty Ltd
Fluor Global Services Consulting
FM Design Ltd
Frazer-Nash Consultancy Ltd
GHD-Transmark Pty Ltd
GIBBRail Ltd
Gotch Consultancy
GRA Incorporated
HaCon Ingenieurgesellschaft mbH
Halcrow Group Ltd
Hanson-Wilson Inc
Harry Weese Associates
Hatch Mott MacDonald Inc
HDR Engineering Inc
High-Point Rendel Ltd
Hill International Inc
Hodgson and Hodgson
Holland Railconsult
HTM-Infra
Hyder Consulting
IBIS Transport Consultants Ltd
IBM Global Travel & Transportation Industry Solutions
ICB
ICF Kaiser Engineers Inc
IIT Research Institute
Infra Safety Services
Interconsult AS
Interfleet Technology Ltd
Intermetric GmbH
International Rail Consultants
Intraplan Consult GmbH
IP-Solutions
Italferr SpA
James Scott
JARTS
Jones Garrard Transport
KAMPSAX International A/S
Lahmeyer International GmbH
Laramore, Douglass and Popham
LEK Consulting Ltd
Lester B Knight & Associates Inc
Lloyds Register MHA Limited
LTK Engineering Services
Maguire Group Inc
Martyn Cornwall Design
Maunsell
MBD Design
Mercer Management Consulting Inc
Metroconsult
Metro Consulting Ltd
Millbrook Proving Ground
Modjeski & Masters Inc
Mott MacDonald Group
Mouchel Consulting Ltd
MTR Corporation Consultancy Services
MVA
NEA Transport Research and Training
NedTrain BV
NEL
New Markets Ltd
Nichols Group, The
NS Railplan bv
Ødegaard & Danneskiold-Samsøe A/S
OMI Logistics Limited
Oscar Faber
Parsons Brinckerhoff Inc
Patrick Engineering Inc
PB Kennedy & Donkin Ltd
Philips Projects BV
PricewaterhouseCoopers

QSS Group, The
Queensland Rail Consulting Services
Radermacher & Partner GmbH
Railcare Ltd
Railmotive GmbH
Rail Sciences Inc
Rail Services Australia
Railway Consultancy, The
Railway Engineering Associates Limited
Railway Systems Consultants Ltd
Railway Technology Strategy Centre
RailWorks Corporation
Ranbury Management Group
Rescar Incorporated
RIQC – Rail Industry Quality Certification Ltd
RITC Ltd
RITES Ltd
R L Banks & Associates Inc
RMS Locotec
Roland Berger & Partner GmbH
Roundel Design Group
ScanRail Consult
SCC Scandiaconsult International
Scott Wilson Railways
Seneca Group LLC, The
Serco Raildata
Serco Railtest Limited
SGTE
SJ International
Solvera Information Services Ltd
Southdowns Environmental Consultants Ltd
Steer Davies Gleave
Steria Transports
Strategic Development Group
STV Group
SwedeRail
Symonds Group
Systra
TAMS Consultants Inc
TDG
TecnEcon Ltd
TERA
Thomas K Dyer Inc
TIFSA
Tilney Shane
TLC
TMG International Pty Ltd
Tractebel Development
Transcorp
Transportation Technology Center Inc
Transport Design International
Transport Research Laboratory (TRL)
TransTec
Transurb
Transurb Technirail SA
Transys Projects Ltd
Trauner
Trenitalia SpA
TUC Rail
Tyréns Infraconsult AB
Uvaterv Engineering Consultants Ltd
Vanness-Brackenridge Group
Vossloh System-Technik York Ltd
Wendell Cox Consultancy
Wilbur Smith Associates
Wilson, Ihrig & Associates
WS Atkins Rail Limited
YTT International Inc
ZGF – Zimmer Gunsul Frasca Partnership

# CONSULTANCY SERVICES

## Company listing by country

### AUSTRALIA
Colston, Budd
Wardrop & Hunt
Fluor Daniel Pty Ltd
GHD-Transmark Pty Ltd
Queensland Rail Consulting Services
Rail Services Australia
Ranbury Management Group
TMG International Pty Ltd

### AUSTRIA
Austria Rail Engineering

### BELGIUM
Tractebel Development
Transurb Technirail SA

### CANADA
CANAC International Inc
Canarail Consultants Inc
Cole, Sherman & Associates Limited
CPCS Ltd
Delcan Corporation
International Rail Consultants
TDG
Transurb

### DENMARK
COWI Consulting Engineers and Planners AS
KAMPSAX International A/S
Ødegaard & Danneskiold-Samsøe A/S
ScanRail Consult

### FINLAND
Finnish Railway Engineering Ltd

### FRANCE
AREP
CEFRAC
EurailTest
MBD Design
SGTE
Steria Transports
Systra
TUC Rail

### GERMANY
DE-Consult
EPV-GIV
ERM Lahmeyer International GmbH
HaCon Ingenieurgesellschaft mbH
ICB
Intermetric GmbH
Intraplan Consult GmbH
Lahmeyer International GmbH
Metroconsult
Radermacher & Partner GmbH
Railmotive GmbH
Roland Berger & Partner GmbH
TLC
TransTec

### HONG KONG
MTR Corporation Consultancy Services

### INDIA
RITES Ltd

### IRELAND
CIE Consult

### ITALY
ANSALDOBREDA
BCD Consulting Sas
Italferr SpA
Transystem SpA
Trenitalia SpA

### JAPAN
JARTS
YTT International Inc

### NETHERLANDS
DHV Holding BV
EDS
Esveld Consulting Services BV
Holland Railconsult
HTM-Infra
Infra Safety Services
IP-Solutions
NEA Transport Research and Training
NedTrain BV
NS Railplan bv
Philips Projects BV

### NORWAY
Interconsult AS

### SPAIN
Ardanuy Ingeneria SA
TIFSA

### SWEDEN
Banverket Consulting
Carmen Systems AB
SCC Scandiaconsult International
SJ International
SwedeRail
Tyréns Infraconsult AB

### SWITZERLAND
Electrowatt Infra
ENOTRAC AG

### UNITED KINGDOM
Accent Marketing and Research
Advanced Railway Research Centre
AEA Technology Rail
ARUP
Aspen Burrow Crocker Ltd
Babtie Group
Balfour Beatty Rail
Best Impressions
Blue Print Rail
BMT Reliability Consultants Ltd
Bovis Lend Lease
Brown & Root Services
Cape Engineering
Colin Buchanan and Partners
Corus Rail Consultancy Ltd
Cre'active Design
Crown Agents for Oversea Governments and Administrations Ltd
Currie & Brown
DCA Design International Ltd
Design and Projects Int Ltd
Design Research Unit
Design Triangle
Engineering Link Ltd, The
First Engineering Ltd
Fleet Software
Flow Science Ltd
Fluor Global Services Consulting
FM Design Ltd
Frazer-Nash Consultancy Ltd
GIBBRail Ltd
Gotch Consultancy
Halcrow Group Ltd
High-Point Rendel Ltd
Hodgson and Hodgson
Hyder Consulting
IBIS Transport Consultants Ltd
IBM Global Travel & Transportation Industry Solutions
Interfleet Technology Ltd
James Scott
Jones Garrard Transport
LEK Consulting Ltd
Lloyds Register MHA Limited
Martyn Cornwall Design
Maunsell
Metro Consulting Ltd
Mott MacDonald Group
Mouchel Consulting Ltd
MVA
NEL
New Markets Ltd
Nichols Group, The
OMI Logistics Limited
Oscar Faber
PB Kennedy & Donkin Ltd
PricewaterhouseCoopers
QSS Group, The
Railcare Ltd
Railway Consultancy Ltd, The
Railway Engineering Associates Limited
Railway Systems Consultants Ltd
Railway Technology Strategy Centre
RIQC – Rail Industry Quality Certification Ltd
RITC Ltd
RMS Locotec
Roundel Design Group
Scott Wilson Railways
Serco Raildata
Serco Railtest Limited
Solvera Information Services Ltd
Southdowns Environmental Consultants Ltd
Steer Davies Gleave
Strategic Development Group
Symonds Group
TecnEcon Ltd
Tilney Shane
TranscorpTransport Design International
Transport Research Laboratory (TRL)
Transys Projects Ltd
Trident Consultants Ltd
Vosper Thornycroft (UK) Ltd
VST Comreco Rail Ltd
WS Atkins Rail Limited

### UNITED STATES OF AMERICA
Accenture
ALK Associates Inc
A T Kearney Inc
Barton-Aschman Associates, Inc
Bechtel Corporation
Booz, Allen & Hamilton Inc
Cambridge Systematics Inc
CAM International Inc
Century Engineering Inc
Chambers, Conlon & Hartwell Inc
Clough, Harbour & Associates LLP
Corradino Group, The
Daniel, Mann, Johnson & Mendenhall
De Leuw, Cather & Company
DHA
Edwards and Kelcey Inc
EG & G Dynatrend Inc
Electrack
GRA Incorporated
Hanson-Wilson Inc
Harry Weese Associates
Hatch Mott MacDonald Inc
HDR Engineering Inc
Hill International Inc
ICF Kaiser Engineers Inc
IIT Research Institute
Laramore, Douglass and Popham
Lester B Knight & Associates Inc
LTK Engineering Services
Maguire Group Inc
Mercer Management Consulting Inc
Modjeski & Masters Inc
Parsons Brinckerhoff Inc
Patrick Engineering Inc
Rail Sciences Inc
RailWorks Corporation
Rescar Incorporated
R L Banks & Associates Inc
Seneca Group LLC, The
STV Group
TAMS Consultants Inc
TERA
Thomas K Dyer Inc
Transportation Technology Center Inc
Trauner
Vanness-Brackenridge Group
Wendell Cox Consultancy
Wilbur Smith Associates
Wilson, Ihrig & Associates
ZGF – Zimmer Gunsul Frasca Partnership

## CONSULTANCY SERVICES

## Accent Marketing and Research

Gable House, 14-16 Turnham Green Terrace, Chiswick, London W4 1QP, UK
Tel: (+44 20) 87 42 22 11    Fax: (+44 20) 87 42 19 91
e-mail: info@accent-mr.com
Web: http://www.accent-mr.com

### Key personnel
Managing Director: Rob Sheldon
Directors: Kate Barber, Chris Heywood, Miranda Mayes

### Capabilities
Accent is a full service research agency, with offices in London, Bristol, Edinburgh and Munich and the resources and equipment to undertake both qualitative and quantitative studies of significant size.

Accent is an expert in research using trade-off techniques and has been instrumental in the introduction and development of the technique in the UK, having conducted many studies using these methods for high-profile clients.

Accent's research in the rail industry includes: customer priorities, estimating demand, real-time information, strategy and policy, ticketing, value of time and vehicle design.

### Contracts
Recent research studies have been commissioned by the following UK-based clients:

- GNER: to undertake research to provide a hierarchy and willingness to pay value for existing and potential features of StandardPlus. Also a study into stakeholder attitudes towards GNER, including a programme of quantitative research of customer usage, awareness and satisfaction with the on-train catering facilities that GNER currently offer. The assessment of customer attitude to GNER following the Hatfield rail crash and the subsequent disruptions. Research to examine the price elasticity between Weekend First ticket prices and standards of service available. Research was also undertaken to help define GNER's smoking policy.
- London & Continental Railways (responsible for building the Channel tunnel Rail Link): commissioned research with local residents, businesses and key opinion formers to determine the most popular name for the new station being built at Ebbsfleet, UK.
- Department of Transport (UK): interviews conducted, relating to the development of Transport Direct, a new transport information service.
- Lancashire County Council (UK): a pre-feasibility study into demand for a station to be located in the town centre of Skelmersdale.
- SRA: as part of a panel led by Mott MacDonald, including Oxera, First Class Partnerships and Line by Line to provide economic and transport forecasting advice and development of solutions to specific issues including project evaluation, statistical advice, financial modelling and regulatory and competition issues.
- Ove Arup & Partners: investigation into the potential of building facilities along a freight line which runs near Liverpool Football Club's new stadium.
- ATOC: market research into the need for a new ticket designed to encourage the use of rail by group of two people travelling together. Also the estimation of passengers' willingness to pay for new and refurbished rolling stock through stated preference and revealed preference analysis techniques.
- First Great Eastern: independent objective assessment of the cleanliness of every First Great East train arriving at Liverpool Street station. Also research was carried out to determine customer priorities with respect to rolling stock.
- OPRAF: with the University of Newcastle, research was undertaken into a number of areas concerned with rail services and infrastructure.
- Northern Spirit, Scotrail and First North Western: the measurement of disbenefits of 'crowdedness' on trains operated by the three operators.
- BAA: research was conducted to establish the price that should be charged to passengers on the Heathrow Express service in First Class and Standard.
- Eurotunnel: a customer profile survey was conducted of Le Shuttle's users. Information was required regarding customers' activities at the terminals.

*UPDATED*

---

## Accenture

100 S Wacker Drive, Suite 1070, Chicago, Illinois 60606, USA
Tel: (+1 312) 507 29 00    Fax: (+1 312) 507 79 65
Web: http://www.ac.com

### Key personnel
Chairman: George T Shaheen

### Contact information

*Americas*
See main address

*Europe/Middle East/Africa/India*
2 Arundel Street, London WC2R 3LT, UK
Tel: (+44 20) 74 38 50 70    Fax: (+44 20) 48 31 11 33

*Asia Pacific*
17th Floor, Menara PJ, Amcorp Trade Centre, No 18 Persiaran Barat, Off Jalan Timur, 46200 Petaling Jaya, Selangor Darul Ehsan, Malaysia
Tel: (+60 3) 756 51 33    Fax: (+60 3) 758 22 10

### Capabilities
Formerly Andersen Consulting, Accenture provides services which include business process management, infrastructure, customer interaction, IT strategy, customer service, network design, information systems, operations, service delivery, service design and financial/accounting systems.

### Projects
Clients include Czech Railways (introduction of market disciplines to change its perspective from cost-centric management to a profit-centric view and, within a few years, to make a profit).

---

## Advanced Railway Research Centre

The Innovation Centre, 217 Portobello, Sheffield S1 4DP, UK
Tel: (+44 114) 222 01 51    Fax: (+44 114) 222 01 55
e-mail: n.farquhar@sheffield.ac.uk

### Key personnel
Director: Dr Mark Robinson
Chairman: Brian Clementson
City Freight Research Manager: Tom Zunder
Composite Research Manager: Dr Joe Carruthers
Rail Freight Research Manager: Phil Mortimer
Administrator: Nicki Farquhar

### Capabilities
Enhancement of contact between industry and academia by an information service and a series of seminars; focal point in UK for European land transport projects by small businesses; funding of a programme of railway-related research; teaching and training modules for students and industry professionals.

### Projects
Hycoprod (2000-2004): the major objective of Hycoprod is to design advanced composite production processes for the systematic manufacture of very large monocoque hybrid composite sandwich structure for the transportation sector.

Bestufs (2000-2004): the aim of Best Practice in Urban Freight Solutions is establishing and maintaining an open European network between urban freight transport experts, user group/association, on-going projects, interested cities, the relevant European Commission Directorates and representatives of national transport administrations in order to identify, describe and disseminate best practices, success criteria and bottlenecks with respect to the movement of goods in urban areas.

IN-HO-TRA (2000-2003): The Innovative Horizontal Transhipment (IN-HOT-RA) project will validate innovative horizontal transhipment technologies, their interoperability and the possibilities to integrate them into current intermodal transport operations, in order to make intermodal transport more effective, more competitive and to decrease the economic break even distance of intermodal transport.

Themis (2000-2004): the prime objective of Thematic Network Intermodal Services (THEMIS) is to co-ordinate on-going activities for research and development in the field of Intermodal Freight Transport (IFT) information systems in Europe, while providing at the same time a forum for dissemination and concertation activities among all parties involved.

Cargospeed (2001-2003): Cargospeed demonstrates new technology to prove intermodal transfer efficiency gains. The project itself includes the design and construction of a modified wagon equipped with movable well-floor, as well as new road/rail interchange technology and economic feasibility calculations.

Trainsafe (2002-2004): the Trainsafe Thematic Network has a remit which will co-ordinate, advise and support the activities necessary to implement the Safety Strand for European Rail Research. Trainsafe will create links to key actors and research emanating from other transport modes. The objective is to set up a network of experts, establish a programme of workshops chaired by leading industry personalities, identify centres of excellence, mobilise a network of excellence and run a website for the benefit of the European railway industry as a whole.

Composit (2001-2003): the focus on The Future Use of Composites In Transport (Composit) is a tool to develop and strengthen the use of composite across the transport modes by identifying the appropriate technologies and solutions, and this is justified by the fact that transport is a key generator of economic growth.

Moldova (2001-2002): the Advanced Railway Research Centre (ARRC) has been successful in securing European Commission TACIS funding to advise on the restructuring of the railway system in Moldova. Moldova achieved independence from the Soviet Union in the early 1990s. It is one of the poorest countries in economic terms in Europe. The railway system will be a vital component in the development of the national economy. The railway system operates on the 5'0' gauge, and mainly with equipment designed and built in the former Soviet Union. The railway operates on very orthodox operational grounds and has lacked investment in equipment, systems and management methods.

City Freight (2002-2005): the City Freight project proposes a comparison of a number of innovations in freight transport in different European Metropolitan Conurbations, taking into account the existing experiences and knowledge regarding urban and inter-urban transport and its effects. The field of research will cover technical aspects and other issues such as: new traffic and parking management methods aiming to dissuade certain categories of goods vehicles to enter the city centre; new urban planning principle aiming to influence positively the freight transport demand patterns.

*UPDATED*

---

## Your Partner for Railway Systems

LAHMEYER INTERNATIONAL GmbH offers a wide range of planning and consultancy services, primarily for complex infrastructure projects.

During the past 25 years the Transportation Division has played a key role in numerous railway projects, including high-speed and upgraded railway lines in Eastern European countries, Central Asia, Indonesia, Greece, Germany, and Korea.

## LAHMEYER INTERNATIONAL

LAHMEYER INTERNATIONAL GmbH
Friedberger Strasse 173 . D-61118 Bad Vilbel
Phone: +49 (6101) 55-1812 . Fax: +49 (6101) 55-1520
E-mail: info@lahmeyer.de
Internet: www.lahmeyer.de

# CONSULTANCY SERVICES

## AEA Technology Rail

PO Box 2, RTC Business Park, London Road, Derby
DE24 8YB, UK
Tel: (+44 1332) 26 32 94  Fax: (+44 1332) 26 31 78
e-mail: aeat.rail@aeat.co.uk
Web: http://www.aeat.co.uk

**Key personnel**
Managing Director: Cliff Perry

**Subsidiary company**
AEA Technology Rail BV
PO Box 8125, 3503 RC Utrecht, Netherlands
Tel: (+31 30) 235 44 18  Fax: (+31 30) 235 73 29
e-mail: kees.aling@nl.aeat.com
Web: http://www.nl.aeat.com

**Capabilities**
AEA bought British Rail Research in 1996 and offers railway solutions, highlighting the identification of root causes rather than symptoms; introduction of innovative approaches to finding solutions and sharing of risk.

It offers condition monitoring, line of route maintenance, signalling and operational control, incident investigation, incident mitigation, modelling, safety cases, environmental management and interfaces.

**Projects**
For trains include fixed-price safety case and on-time adaptation of and delivery of specialist rolling stock.

For infrastructure include improvement of maintenance management and a contribution to reducing dewirement risk.

For operations includes live monitoring of vehicle and infrastructure performance direct to the desktop.

**Corporate development**
AEA Technology has acquired Transportation Consultants International Limited (TCI). Operating from five locations in the UK and one in Hong Kong, TCI specialises in transport economics and planning, signalling design and testing, safety and risk management and railway project management, and was created primarily out of the former BR Projects, which was bought from British Rail by its management in 1996.

TCI is being absorbed into its AEA Technology Rail subsidiary, which was established when BR Research was acquired.

*UPDATED*

## ALK Associates Inc

1000 Herrontown Road, Princeton, New Jersey 08540, USA
Tel: (+1 609) 683 02 20  Fax: (+1 609) 683 02 90
e-mail: hornung@alk.com
Web: http://www.alk.com

**Key personnel**
Senior Vice-President: Mark A Hornung

**Capabilities**
ALK specialises in information technology products and services for the transportation industry. Capabilities include strategic planning, operations control systems, locomotive management, marshalling and scheduling, line capacity analysis, and geographic information systems.

ALK's E-tracker®, not only automatically tracks, locates and provides the status of individual containers or rail cars but can be used with Vendor-managed Inventory software to automatically keep track of supplies on hand and notify suppliers when an inventory falls to a certain level. E-tracker gives a complete overview of shipments in transit, sorted by consignee, carrier or corridor. It rapidly detects bottlenecks or service disruptions and gives carrier performance analyses including dependability and relative cost. E-tracker reduces equipment overheads by shortening cycle times, allowing rail cars to handle more shipments per year and matches incoming and on-hand equipment with upcoming demand, identifying potential equipment shortages in any given area.

**Projects**
ALK has undertaken a number of strategic planning studies for major railways, especially involving mergers, consolidations, and network rationalisation. It has also developed locomotive management systems for Canadian National, Southern Pacific and Union Pacific (USA) and a pricing system for TFM (Mexico). ALK has acted as consultant to Norfolk Southern (USA) on an interline trip planning system, which preplans the marshalling sequence and train assignments for freight wagons before the beginning of their journey. It monitors the progress of each wagon and update connecting railways and the shipper of deviations from plan.

ALK has also undertaken scheduling and line capacity improvement studies for Chinese People's Republic Railways, Pakistan Railways and CSX, DME, MARC and Metra (USA).

*UPDATED*

## ALSTOM

Alstom Transport SA
48 rue Albert Dhalenne, F-93482 Saint-Ouen Cedex, Paris, France
Tel: (+33 1) 41 66 81 35  Fax: (+33 1) 41 66 96 66
Web: http://www.transport.alstom.com

**Key personnel**
Senior Vice-President: Hamdi Conger

**Services**
Caters to operator and maintenance provider needs for rolling stock, equipment, locomotives, track and infrastructure after-sales related services.

ALSTOM offers a range of services to support in-house capabilities or to out-source service and maintenance activities of operators, rolling stock owners or maintenance providers for all makes of transit or freight rolling stock, for track and other infrastructure.

It provides modernisation and upgrade solutions for older applications as well as renovation proficiency to extend product life, enhance performance and increase passenger comfort.

The company also offers parts and repair identification, servicing and distribution for all applications as well as management facilities services.

## ANSALDOBREDA

425 Via Argine, I-80147 Naples, Italy
Tel: (+39 081) 243 11 11  Fax: (+39 081) 243 26 88

**Key personnel**
See entry in *Locomotives and powered/non-powered passenger vehicles* section.

**Capabilities**
Main contractors, project managers and system engineers for long-distance railways, suburban, metro and mass transit systems.

## Ardanuy Ingeneria SA

Avenida Europa 34, Edificio B, E-28023 Madrid, Spain
Tel: (+34 91) 799 45 00  Fax: (+34 91) 799 45 01
e-mail: ardanuy@ardanuy.com
Web: http://www.ardanuy.com

**Key personnel**
General Manager: Josep-Maria Ribes
Projects Manager: Carlos Alonso
Technical Assistances Manager: Felix Ardiaca

**Capabilities**
Studies, projects, works supervision and advice services of railways, metros and tramways (signalling, communications, overhead, power substations, track, rolling stock), tunnels, edification.

**Projects**
Analysis and bid evaluation for the new system of ATP in Bulgaria for BDŽ; project of legalisation and work management of the power and traction substations of the FC Madrid–Arganda; safety facilities, telecommunications, catenary and track project for the Castellbisbal–Mollet section; specialised assistance for the development of basic engineering and technical assistance for the purchasing control of the Valparaiso–Viña del Mar traffic interconnection. Valparaiso Regional underground; Phare cross-border co-operation between Bulgaria and Greece. Dupnitza–Kulata Railways Project; NISA. Gas introduction in the border region; project of modernisation of signalling system on the East-West Corridor in Latvia; basic project for the metro system in Seville; Nudo de Trinidad–Montcada section of the high-speed line between Madrid and the French border.

*UPDATED*

## AREP

163 bis, avenue de Clichy, Impasse Chalabre, F-75017 Paris, France
Tel: (+33 1) 56 33 05 08  Fax: (+33 1) 56 33 04 08
e-mail: contact@arep.fr

**Key personnel**
President: Jean Marie Duthilleul
General Manager: Etienne Tricaud
Director, International Projects: Eric Dussiot

**Background**
AREP is part of the SNCF Group and a subsidiary of SNEF, FRP, SYSTRA and SICF.

**Capabilities**
AREP is a multidisciplinary engineering and consulting firm that designs and builds urban transport centres and exchange hubs and public spaces. It makes its competencies available to carriers, decision-makers and investors in different sectors through nine departments covering: urban planning and layout; design, engineering and site supervision; international projects; programming; interior layouts and design; structures; building engineers; design and installation of utility systems and economic viability studies.

*VERIFIED*

## Aspen Burrow Crocker Ltd

Priory House, 45-51 High Street, Reigate RH2 9RU, UK
Tel: (+44 1737) 24 01 01  Fax: (+44 1737) 22 15 02

**Key personnel**
Chairman: Mike Cottell

**Head office**
Aspen Associates
Dippen Hall, Eastbourne Road, Blindley Heath, Lingfield RH7 6JX, UK
Tel: (+44 1342) 89 38 00  Fax: (+44 1342) 89 37 73

**Capabilities**
Transport consulting engineers.

## A T Kearney Inc

222 West Adams, Chicago, Illinois 60606, USA
Tel: (+1 312) 648 01 11  Fax: (+1 312) 223 62 00

**Key personnel**
Vice-President and Managing Director of
  Transportation: Justin F Zubrod Sr

**Capabilities**
A T Kearney is a rail transportation consulting firm with more than 30 offices in North America, Europe and Asia.

A T Kearney has been conducting management assignments in the industry since 1945. In the past decade it has worked for both passenger and freight rail carriers around the world as well as other industry stakeholders – investment banks, equipment manufacturers, lessors and government agencies.

Over the past few years A T Kearney has been substantially involved in assisting railways throughout the world in repositioning themselves to be more commercial and efficient, and in privatising government-owned railway operations. It has recently worked in Europe, Asia-Pacific and North America on a variety of rail restructuring and privatisation projects.

Its experience in the rail industry includes market entry and strategy, merger/acquisition strategy, new product development, competitive analyses, customer service strategy, value-added logistics services, restructuring and privatisation, strategic resourcing, operations improvement, pricing, cost reduction, and information technology.

A T Kearney has also actively participated in the growth and development of the intermodal sector worldwide. It was involved in the early US Department of Transportation studies on establishing an intermodal network in the United States. More recently, for the President's National Commission on Intermodal Transportation, A T Kearney acted as facilitator to the Commission's deliberations. In addition, for the European Commission (DG-7) A T Kearney developed a blueprint for developing a land-based intermodal system in Europe. Finally A T Kearney has been intimately involved with the recent emergence of intermodalism in China.

## Austria Rail Engineering

Österreichische Eisenbahn, Transport Planungs-und Beratungsgesellschaft mbH
PO Box 54, A-1072 Vienna, Austria
Tel: (+43 1) 526 93 31    Fax: (+43 1) 526 93 31 85
e-mail: are@aon.at

### Key personnel
General Manager: Ing. Friedrich Pichler

### Capabilities
Austria Rail Engineering (ARE), the lead company of the Austrian railway sector for international activities, is a broadly based transportation-management and engineering organisation. Founded in 1979, ARE is transferring tried and tested Austrian railway technology and provides technical and advisory services to governments and private companies worldwide; planning, engineering, operating, marketing and maintenance expertise for rail-bound transportation systems is provided by ARE by using a staff exchange scheme with the Austrian Federal Railways.

In 20 railway co-operations ARE is acting as a co-ordinator.

### Projects
Current work includes projects in Algeria (technical assistance and railway design study); China (technical assistance) and Pakistan (track modernisation).

*UPDATED*

## Babtie Group

Marketing Support, 95 Bothwell Street, Glasgow G2 7HX, UK
Tel: (+44 141) 566 82 57    Fax: (+44 141) 226 31 09
e-mail: marketing@babtie.co.uk

### Railway contacts
Ross Barr (Glasgow)
Tel: (+44 141) 566 82 67

Mike Jenkins (Derby)
Tel: (+44 1332) 28 51 11

### Transportation contacts
Alan Duff (Glasgow)
Tel: (+44 141) 204 25 11
Bob Duff (Glasgow)
Tel: (+44 141) 204 25 11
John Atkins (Maidstone)
Tel: (+44 1189) 88 15 55
John Hopkins (Wakefield)
Tel: (+44 1924) 36 29 15

### International offices
**(Associated companies)**
Babtie BMT Harris & Sutherland (Hong Kong) Ltd
15/F Cornwall House, 28 Tong Chong Street, Quarry Bay, Hong Kong
Tel: (+852 28) 80 97 88    Fax: (+852 25) 65 55 61
Babtie BMT Harris & Sutherland (Singapore) PTE Ltd
#30-06 International Plaza, 10 Anson Road, Singapore 079903
Tel: (+65 2) 23 66 47    Fax: (+65 2) 21 91 73
Babtie BMT Harris & Sutherland Sdn Bhd
22nd Floor, Menara Safuan, 80 Jalan Ampang, (Letter Box 63), 50450 Kuala Lumpur, Malaysia
Tel: (+60 3) 466 01 67    Fax: (+60 3) 466 01 67
Babtie Consultants (India) Private Ltd
83 New York Tower 'A', Thaltej Cross Roads, Thaltej, Ahmedabad 380 054, Gujarat, India
Tel: (+91 79) 744 24 26    Fax: (+91 79) 744 24 27
Babtie International
4th Floor, Meridian Plaza, 6-3-853/1, Ameerper, Hyderabad, 500 016, India
Tel: (+91 40) 330 19 74    Fax: (+91 40) 330 24 60
PPU – Babtie spol s r o
Vyzlovska 2243, Praha 10, 100 000, Czech Republic
Tel: (+42 2) 781 25 37    Fax: (+42 2) 781 24 97
Babtie Pettit
9 Upper Leeson Street, Dublin, D4 Ireland
Tel: (+353 1) 660 60 97    Fax: (+353 1) 281 51 71
Allott & Lomax Polska SP ZO O
PL-04-355 Warszawa ul Kordeckiego 56/58M46, Poland
Tel: (+48 2) 26 33 95 11

### Capabilities
Babtie Group is an independent technical and management consultancy operating from offices, laboratories and training centres across the United Kingdom and from key locations strategically placed for international business.

Together with its associated companies, the Group has over 3,000 professional, technical and support staff.

### Services
*Railways:* include network appraisal, re-establishment of disused lines, extensions to the network, patronage forecasting, refurbishment of existing infrastructure, station developments, operational studies, assessment of freight transport, depot design and refurbishment, workshop plant and machinery, condition surveys, station design and refurbishment, geo-engineering advice, contaminated land, performance indicators, value engineering, asset delivery, procurement and specification, track alignment, freight operations and assessments, rolling stock, bridge inspection, assessment and design, signalling, tunnelling, geotechnical, electrical and mechanical, hydro-geology, environmental, surveying, quantity surveying.

*Transportation:* Babtie's skills cover railways, highways, airports, public transport networks, ports and canals. Planning capability includes market research, strategic transport modelling, economic appraisals, feasibility and procurement strategies, pre-investment financial auditing, environmental impact assessments, training, value engineering and risk assessment, cost and contract consultancy, local transport plans.

Skills in construction methods, programming and value engineering include:
- tunnelling and ground engineering
- bridge design
- docks, ports and harbour design
- highway design, traffic control and telematics
- permanent way and railway depot design
- airports, pavement and ground lighting design
- busways and light rail infrastructure
- project management and cost consultancy.

## Balfour Beatty Rail

Strategic Development Group
Midland House, Nelson Street, Derby DEI 2SA, UK
Tel: (+44 1332) 26 24 24    Fax: (+44 1332) 26 22 95
e-mail: carly.waring@bbrail.co.uk

### Key personnel
Technical Director: Neil Andrew
Manager, Strategic Development Group: Charles Penny

### Services
The Strategic Development Group focuses on the development of new products and working methods to support the business units of Balfour Beatty Rail and external customers in the UK and abroad.

## Banverket Consulting

SE-781 85 Borlänge, Sweden
Tel: (+46 243) 44 61 00    Fax: (+46 243) 44 61 10
e-mail: consulting@hk.banverket.se

### Key personnel
Director: John-Olof Hermanson
Area Directors: Sture Åberg, Rolf Ericsson, Leif Malm, Lars Moberg, Lennart Eldh and Jan Nilsson

### Corporate development
Banverket Consulting is a consultancy unit within Banverket (the Swedish National Rail Administration). Banverket Consulting has run its operation since 1998 and is based in Borlänge, with area offices in six locations throughout Sweden.

### Capabilities
Banverket Consulting offers a range of services and products: services in railway research, project planning, and project and construction management within the railway sector. Its operations are IT-intensive with technical planning tools integrated in common computer

---

TRAINING ■ CONSULTING SERVICES ■ TECHNICAL PUBLICATIONS ■ PROJECT MANAGEMENT ■ PLANNING ■ TECHNICAL ASSISTANCE

# INTERNATIONAL TECHNICAL SERVICES

Technical & Management Training
Technical Publications
Fleet & Facilities Evaluation
Diesel Engine Rebuild
Crane Operator Training
Locomotive & Freight Maintenance
Locomotive Rebuild & Repower
Air Brake Systems Specialists
Production Planning
Worldwide Experience

Railway Consulting Services
Project Management & Supervision
Procurement Planning
Welding Services - Engine Repair
Operator/Driver Training
Needs Assessment /Analysis
Facilities Management
Locomotive Specialists
Car Equipment Specialists

**Railway Technical Training & Consulting Specialists**

400 QUEENS AVENUE LONDON, ONTARIO CANADA N6B 1X9    TEL: 519 439-2362    FAX: 675-1868   e-mail: **info@itsrail.com**
visit our WEB SITE: www@itsrail.com

# CONSULTANCY SERVICES

and CAD environments. Also expertise within the areas of marshalling technology, carrying capacity, power supply simulations and track geometry.

## BCD Consulting Sas

Via Divisione Julia 30, I-33100 Udine, Italy
Tel/Fax: (+39 0432) 50 76 21
e-mail: bchiaranti@iol.it

**Key personnel**
Managing Director: Dr Bruno G Chiaranti

**Capabilities**
Consolidating 25 years of experience in the market, BCD Consulting was recently founded to provide specification design and estimation up to tender evaluation and proposal management services for tendering and project management in passenger information systems for public transport terminals.

Services are offered for main line railway stations, multistation networks, bus and ferry terminals and airports. The company provides consultancy on software functional specifications, system configuration, display and multimedia peripherals design and sourcing research.

## Bechtel Corporation

PO Box 193965, San Francisco, California 94119-3965, USA
Tel: (+1 415) 768 08 35   Fax: (+1 415) 768 45 60
Web: http://www.bechtel.com

**UK office**
11 Pilgrim Street, London EC4V 6RW
Tel: (+44 20) 76 51 77 77   Fax: (+44 20) 76 51 79 60
Web: http://www.bechtel.co.uk

**Capabilities**
Bechtel offers a broad spectrum of services including feasibility and environmental studies, architectural/engineering design, project management, engineering management, construction management, start-up and operations, and financial planning in addition to engineering, procurement and construction.

Bechtel's transportation experience includes over 20 urban rapid transit systems and more than 5,600 miles of railways. The company has been involved in most new transit projects in the USA (Washington metro; Boston rapid transit; San Diego light rail; Sacramento light rail; Atlanta MARTA; San Francisco BART; Baltimore rapid transit; MTA/LIRR East Side Access in New York; and the Los Angeles metro), in domestic main line projects, including the Alameda Corridor-East (ACE) freight corridor upgrade in California, and in key international transit and rail projects, such as the Caracas metro, the São Paulo metro, Taipei rapid transit, Attika Metro in Athens, South Korea high-speed rail, the Western Corridor Railway linking Kowloon (Hong Kong) with northwest New Territories, and the Channel Tunnel Rail Link, Thameslink 2000 and Jubilee Line Extension in the UK.

Bechtel was retained by London Underground Ltd to provide a fast-track push to the commissioning and completion of the Jubilee Line Extension in time to support the official opening of the millennium in Greenwich. The system was commissioned in three phases culminating in the provision of through passenger service from Stanmore to Stratford on 20 November 1999. The final passenger station, Westminster, opened on 22 December 1999.

*UPDATED*

## Best Impressions

15 Starfield Road, Shepherds Bush, London W12 9SN
Tel: (+44 20) 87 40 69 93   Fax: (+44 20) 87 40 91 34
e-mail: talk2us@best-impressions.co.uk

**Key personnel**
Principal: Ray Stening

**Capabilities**
Leaflets, maps, brochures, liveries, branding, corporate identity and vehicle styling.

**Projects**
Nationwide livery for UK bus operator Arriva; brand building for Arriva The Shires 757 Green Line service from London to Luton; brand building for Heathrow Airport-Feltham Railair service in west London; rail liveries for South West Trains, Central Trains and Birmingham Metro trams; publicity for Thameslink services between Brighton, Sutton and Bedford, through central London.

## Blue Print Rail Ltd

Suite 2c, East Mill, Bridgefoot, Belper, Derbyshire DE56 1XG, UK
Tel: (+44 1773) 82 83 59   Fax: (+44 1773) 82 83 49
e-mail: blue—print—rail@compuserv.com

**Key personnel**
Directors: S P Chadwick, R P Gibney

**Capabilities**
Blue Print Rail Ltd specialises in rolling stock design including freight wagons, passenger vehicles and locomotives. The company's client base includes a large number of the major railways in Europe and the southern hemisphere.

Blue Print Rail can make available a broad spectrum of specialised activities to support a client's existing design capability, or to take on the role of a complete design office including design scrutiny and vehicle acceptance in the UK.

To support the design and general consultancy services a number of specialist skills are available in-house including: 3-D CAD modelling; structural analysis using FEA software; rail vehicle gauging including development of Kinematic Envelopes and clearance assessment; rail vehicle dynamics; bogie design; tender response; and preparation of vehicle specifications.

## BMT Reliability Consultants Ltd

12 Little Park Farm Road, Fareham PO15 5SU, UK
Tel: (+44 1489) 55 31 00   Fax: (+44 1489) 55 31 10 01
Web: http://www.bmtrcl.com

**Key personnel**
Managing Director: Jim Lambert
Marketing Director: Stuart Duffin
Commercial Director: Ashley Fookes
Projects Director: Arthur Roberts
Transport and Safety Business Development Manager: Michael Starling (contact)

**Capabilities**
Engineering consultancy services to reduce risk and improve reliability, safety and through-life economics of railway assets and processes. The company develops and applies techniques which assist infrastructure suppliers and operators to assess and optimise rolling stock reliability, maintenance, safety, risk and cost.

**Projects**
Reliability and safety of the Heathrow Express train for Siemens and CAF; independent safety assessment of the Networker Classic for Adtranz; maintenance optimisation of the Swanley Junction switched diamonds for Balfour Beatty Rail Maintenance; through-life cost model development for GEC ALSTOM; risk analysis in support of the East London Line extension private finance initiative application for London Underground; corrosion management of Classes 313 and 321 for Eversholt Leasing.

Other completed projects include: reliability studies for SAB Wabco (Davies and Metcalfe), IFE, Forward Trust (now HSBC Rail) and Radenton Scharfenberg; safety studies and audits for Railtrack and Mannesman.

## Booz, Allen & Hamilton Inc

Transportation Consulting Division
101 California Street, Suite 3300, San Francisco, California 94111, USA
Tel: (+1 415) 391 19 00
Fax: (+1 415) 281 49 12; 627 42 83

**Key personnel**
Principal: William T Reed

**Capabilities**
Booz, Allen & Hamilton conducts assignments for passenger and freight railways spanning a broad range of functional areas and issues: vehicle engineering; operations and productivity improvement; strategic planning and reliability, maintainability and safety systems.

*UPDATED*

## Bovis Construction Group

Bovis House, Northolt Road, Harrow, Middlesex HA2 0EE, UK
Tel: (+44 20) 84 22 34 88   Fax: (+44 20) 84 23 43 56
Web: http://www.bovis.com

**Key personnel**
Chairman: Sir Frank Lampl
Managing Director, Bovis Europe: John Anderson
Business Development Director: Mike Temple
Bovis Rail Divisional Directors: Doug Chalmers
  Nick Crossley
Managing Director, Bovis Asia Pacific, Singapore: Fritz Rehkopf
President & CEO, Bovis Inc, New York: Luther Cochrane

**Capabilities**
Bovis Rail provides professional project management, consultancy and construction management services on main line, suburban and light railway projects worldwide. Working for government agencies, railway operators, developers and commercial entities in the UK, Europe, the Americas and Asia Pacific, Bovis is currently managing over £4,000 million worth of railway projects.

Its services cover feasibility, project development, strategic planning and preconstruction phases, through to developing procurement strategies, cost plans, construction planning, and the tender process; to construction phase management, co-ordination and control, including quality, value, risk, and safety management.

**Projects**
Railtrack, UK: major route resignalling and modernisation projects on the West Anglia, Great Eastern, London-Tilbury-Southend, and SWISS networks; 900 stations on the station regeneration programme throughout Scotland, Midlands and South West regions; structures renewals; Paddington Station improvements for the Heathrow Express services; and investment programme management in the Great Western Zone.

Light rail projects in Dublin, and BOT light rail projects in Sydney, Australia, and Auckland, New Zealand.

Asia Pacific: train maintenance and capital works programme management in Australia; development of the Sydney-Canberra Very High Speed Train BOT project; the new Kuala Lumpur central station in Malaysia; and Boni Station, Manila MRT, Philippines.

The Americas: Grand Central Terminal modernisation, New York; the Newark International Airport automatic monorail system; the San Juan urban railway, Puerto Rico; and Syracuse multimodal terminal.

## Brown & Root Services

Contacts
Americas Region
1550 Wilson Boulevard, Arlington, Virginia 22209, USA
e-mail: Transportation@halliburton.com

Asia Pacific Region
186 Greenhill Road, Parkside South, Australia 5063
e-mail: International@hallliburton.com

# CONSULTANCY SERVICES

Europe/Africa Region
Hill Park Court, Springfield Drive, Leatherhead KT22 7NL, UK
Tel: (+44 1372) 86 35 72   Fax: (+44 1372) 86 33 58
e-mail: Consulting_uk@halliburton.com

**Key personnel**
President: Randy Harl
Director, Transportation, Europe & Africa: Danny Grand
Public Relations: Ken Beedle
Tel: (+44 1372) 86 66 22
e-mail: ken.beedle@halliburton.com
Parent company: Halliburton Company
Web: http://www.Halliburton.com

**Capabilities**
Project management, engineering, life cycle and programme management from conceptual studies through to construction and operations, maintenance and logistics for major railway programmes anywhere in the world. Brown & Root employs 20,000 people around the world. Recently, the company signed an agreement to collaborate with Holland Railconsult BV, of Utrecht, Netherlands, aiming to improve technical capabilities and project management skills in the railway industry.

---

## Cambridge Systematics, Inc

150 Cambridge Park Drive, Suite 4000, Cambridge, Massachusetts 02140, USA
Tel: (+1 617) 354 01 67   Fax: (+1 617) 354 15 42
Web: http://www.camsys.com

**Key personnel**
President: Dr Lance A Neumann
Travel Forecasting/Market Research: Marc R Cutler
    Senior Vice-President: Thomas F Rossi
    Principal: Dr Moshe
    Senior Principal: Ben-Akiva
    Principal: Maren L Outwater
Transportation Planning/Policy Analysis:
    Senior Vice-Presidents: Robert A Lepore, Arlee T Reno
    Vice-President: Steven M Pickrell
    Principals: Dr Vassili Alexiadis, Brad W Wright
Economic/Investment Planning
    Principals: Laurie L Hussey, Christopher Wornum, John G Kaliski
Air Quality/Conformity
    Principal: John H Suhrbier
Intermodal Freight Planning
    Senior Vice-President: Marc R Cutler
    Principal: John G Kaliski
    Senior Associate: Michael J Fisher, PE
Public Transport Service and Policy Planning:
    Principals: Robert G Stanley, Laurie L Hussey, Samuel T Lawton III
    Senior Associate: Stephen D Decker
Information Technology
    Principals: Hyun-A Park, Michael J Markow, Allen R Marshall, Bradford W Wright, Dr Nicholas J Vlahos
    Senior Associate: Dr John C Sutton

**Other offices**
4445 Willard Avenue, Suite 300, Chevy Chase, Maryland 20815, USA
Tel: (+1 301) 347 01 00   Fax: (+1 301) 347 01 01

1300 Clay Street, Suite 1010, Oakland, California 94612
Tel: (+1 510) 873 87 00   Fax: (+1 510) 873 87 01

Civic Opera Building
20 North Wacker Drive, Suite 1475
Chicago, Illinois 60606, USA
Tel: (+1 312) 346 99 07   Fax: (+1 312) 346 99 08

**Capabilities**
In partnership with it's clients, Cambridge Systematics analytical techniques are applied in many areas including transportation planning and management; intelligent transportation systems; information technology; asset management; commercial vehicle operations products, services, and support; travel demand forecasting and modeling; and market research. More specialised work includes new technology assessments, congestion management/air quality planning, traffic and transit planning, multimodal planning, growth management, decision support, and Geographic Information Systems (GIS).

**Contracts**
Work has been undertaken for many federal, state, and local agencies in the United States, Europe, Asia, and other countries, as well as for private clients.
Cambridge Systematics has been awarded two major contracts by the US Department of Transportation (DoT), Federal Highway Administration (FHWA). One is a task order contract with the FHWA's Operations Core Business Unit (CBU) for which it supports the Operations CBU's initiative through technical and policy studies, demonstration projects, evaluations, technical assistance, and technology transfer. It also supports the FHWA's Office of Environment and Planning in the areas of funding, planning, infrastructure management, and environmental provisions under a major, multi-year task order contract.

**Developments**
Development of Intelligent Transport Systems (ITS), Intelligent Deployment Analysis System (IDAS) an ITS sketch planning tool to assist public agencies and consultants with integrating the deployment of ITS into the transport planning process.
Streamlining Commercial Vehicle Operations (CVO) administrative and enforcement activities for developing and integrating computer systems to support CVO activities including development of PERMIT, a computerised permit issuing system; CVIEW the commercial vehicle information exchange window, and IFTA, an interstate fuel tax administration system.

*NEW ENTRY*

---

## CANAC International Inc

Subsidiary of Canadian National Railways
1100 University, Suite 500, Montréal, Québec H3B 3A5, Canada
Tel: (+1 514) 399 57 41   Fax: (+1 514) 399 82 98
e-mail: pubmail@ns.canac.com

**Key personnel**
President and Chief Executive Officer: Frank Trotter
Vice-Presidents:
    North American Sales and Services: John Reoch
    Railroad Technologies Division: Gord Patterson
    International Sales and Services: Réjean Bélanger
    Railroad Transportation Institute: Tom Kingsbury

**Capabilities**
CANAC provides expertise in management (administration, planning, information systems, costing, project control), design and engineering, construction, operation, direct management and maintenance of new or existing railway systems. The company also offers equipment and materials procurement and inspection services and manages the sale of new and used railway supplies around the world.
CANAC's Railway Transportation Institute develops, delivers and evaluates training and performance support for railways and railway-related businesses.
CANAC's Railroad Technologies Division is a research and development facility, employing some 50 scientists and engineering specialists.

---

## Canarail Consultants Inc

1140 de Maisonneuve Boulevard West, Suite 1050, Montreal, Quebec H3A 1M8, Canada
Tel: (+1 514) 985 09 30   Fax: (+1 514) 985 09 29
e-mail: inbox@canarail.com
Web: http://www.canarail.com

**Key personnel**
Chairman: Hovig Bedikian
President: James D Spielman
Vice-President and Chief Engineer: Donald R Gillstrom
Vice-President: Claude Anne Baillargeon
Vice-President, Business Development: Pierre H Fallu

**Subsidiary**
Maintex International Inc

**Capabilities**
Urban and railway transportation services such as engineering including civil, mechanical, signalling and telecommunications, track and infrastructure, electrical supply and electrified overhead power lines. Studies including feasibility, transportation planning, human resources, financial and economic services, asset valuation. Training including needs analysis, programme development, testing and certification, training delivery. Management including re-organisation, railways operations and maintenance, private sector initiatives, Connex services.

**Projects**
*Bangladesh:* construction management of dual gauging works Dhaka–Joydephur for Bangladesh Railways. Feasibility study for the extension of Cox's Bazar-Dohazari railway line.

*Canada:* overhead line maintenance policy for a Montreal suburban electrified line for Agence métropolitaine de transport – AMT. Study of line 4 and 5 for the Montreal metro extension. Optimisation study for the operation of line number 2 of the Montreal metro. Feasibility study for electrification of a suburban line for AMT. Electrical facilities conceptual design for AMT's suburban stabling yard.

*Croatia:* Croatian Railways modernisation and restructuring project, Locomotive Rehabilitation Component.

*Taiwan:* training, operations and management of Taiwan High Speed Rail Corporation Construction Railway.

*Thailand:* preparation of detailed regulatory regime and private participation options for rail business for the Government of Thailand.

*Uganda:* lead a consortium to act as transaction advisor to the Government of Uganda with regard to the privatisation of the Uganda Railways.

*UPDATED*

---

## Cape Engineering

Cape Engineering UK Ltd
Birmingham Road, Warwick CV34 4TX, UK
Tel: (+44 1926) 47 84 10   Fax: (+44 1926) 47 84 11
e-mail: sales@cape-eng.co.uk
Web: http://www.cape-eng.co.uk

**Key personnel**
Managing Director: Steve Meredith
Technical Director: Peter J Moire

**Capabilities**
Cape Engineering offers a full data acquisition, mechanical structural (FEA) and thermal (CFD) computer analysis and environmental test service to meet rail industry needs.
Data acquisition includes measuring strains, accelerations, temperature and atmospheric corrosion, to establish design needs accurately.
Static and dynamic FEA stress analysis establishes the best design, to optimise weight, strength, durability and cost.
Large-scale test facilities qualify equipment to RIA, Continental and North American standards for vibration, shock, temperature, humidity and IP.

---

## Carmen Systems AB

Odinsgatan 9, SE-411 03 Gothenburg, Sweden
Tel: (+46 31) 80 71 00   Fax: (+46 31) 80 71 20
e-mail: carmen@carmen.se
Web: http://www.carmen.se

**Key personnel**
Managing Director: Leif Heidenfors
Manager, Railway Marketing: Mathias Kremer

**Capabilities**
Crew and equipment scheduling systems for railways and airlines.

## CEFRAC

Centre Francais d'accidentologie
18, rue des Moines, F-75017 Paris, France
Tel: (+33 1) 49 21 10 30   Fax: (+33 1) 49 21 10 38

**Key personnel**
Founder: André Kleniewski

**Capabilities**
Determination of origin and cause of accidents such as train derailments, collisions between trains and road vehicles, fires and explosions.

**Projects**
Prepared evidence in court on cause of Italian rail disaster on Rome-Bergamo Eurostar in March 1998 and on several collisions on French TER trains and on derailments in France and Belgium.

## Century Engineering Inc

32 West Road, Towson, Maryland 21204, USA
Tel: (+1 410) 823 80 70   Fax: (+1 410) 823 21 84

**Key personnel**
Assistant Vice-President: Anthony R Frascarella

**Projects**
Baltimore North Corridor Transportation alternative study; Baltimore Mass Transit Systems: Section C; Jones Fork Railroad Extension, Knott County, Kentucky, for CSX; Mass Transit Administration US 301 South Corridor multi-modal transportation study.

## Chambers, Conlon & Hartwell Inc

122 C Street NW, Suite 850, Washington DC 20001, USA
Tel: (+1 202) 638 77 90   Fax: (+1 202) 638 10 45
e-mail: john.roots@cchinc.com
Web: http://www.cchinc.com

**Key personnel**
Chairman: Ray Chambers
President: Keith Hartwell
Principals: Jerry Conlon, Don Norden, John Roots

**Subsidiary**
The Seneca Group (qv)

**Capabilities**
Chambers, Conlon & Hartwell is registered as a lobbyist before the US Congress on behalf of its clients for which a lobbying registration is required by law. Clients include Tri-County Commuter Rail Authority, New York Metropolitan Transportation Authority, Alaska Railroad, Michigan Department of Transportation, City and Borough of Juneau, Alaska, Southern California Regional Rail Authority.

Associations and coalitions include the American Short Line & Regional Railroad Association, National Railroad Construction & Maintenance Association, Rail Supply & Service Coalition, Investment Counsel Association of America and the False Claims Act Legal Center.

Rail companies include Norfolk Southern, Union Pacific, Canadian National, Illinois Central, Florida East Coast, Indiana Rail Road, Delaware Otsego Corporation, RailTex Corporation and Emons Corporation.

Other individual companies include Advanced Power Technologies, Inc, Anacostia & Pacific.

Has long-term relationships with the staff of the key Congressional Committees and US DOT. CC&H provides 'one stop shopping' for its clients by identifying and/or creating funding opportunities and then processing the applications necessary to secure that funding.

**Projects**
CC&H was an active participant in the drafting of the 1991 Intermodal Surface Transportation Act (ISTEA). It is a regular participant at all rail industry group meetings, and is the only Washington transportation firm which is represented at regular Washington Rep meetings at both the American Public Transit Association (APTA) and the Association of American Railroads (AAR). It offers legal drafting, and public relations that provides in- house support for promotional materials, client testimony and technical language for congressional committees or administrative bodies. CC&H works with the national transit and rail unions and has worked co-operatively with them on various rail funding issues.

CC&H specialises in securing federal financial assistance for its railway clients.

## CIE Consult

Grattan Bridge House, 3 Upper Ormond Quay, Dublin 7, Ireland
Tel: (+353 1) 703 47 01   Fax: (+353 1) 703 47 25
e-mail: info@cieconsult.ie
Web: http://www.cieconsult.ie

**Key personnel**
General Manager: Barry Collins
Manager, International Business: Michael Barry

**Capabilities**
CIE Consult draws on the resources and expertise of CIE Group of operating companies Iarnród Éireann (the Irish state rail network), Bus Atha Cliath (the Dublin City bus operator) and Bus Éireann (operator of all other bus services) to provide transport related consultancy services for public transport management, particularly restructuring and commercial orientation, operations and staff training, civil and mechanical engineering, signalling and telecommunications.

**Projects**
Recent contracts include privatisation and concessioning of Tanzania Railways Corporation; conessioning of Zimbabwe Railways; support to Lithuanian Railways for restructuring and privatisation; design of rehabilitation programme for Romanian Railways; study of transport investment needs in Macedonia; supervision and co-ordination of works for interlocking systems in four main railway stations; support to the PMU in Bulgaria and Slovakia; Central Asia Railway restructuring studies; Pakistan Railways corporatisation; rail privatisation study in Georgia; and Russian Railways MIS study.

*UPDATED*

## Clough, Harbour & Associates LLP

111 Winners Circle, Albany, New York 12205, USA
Tel: (+1 518) 453 45 00   Fax: (+1 518) 458 17 35
Web: http://www.cha-llp.com

**Key personnel**
Chief Executive Officer: William A Harbour
Partner: Robert W Badger

**Principal subsidiary**
CHA Technical Services LLC

**Capabilities**
Engineering services, design and building.

**Projects**
In 1998, contracts included a parking garage at Poughkeepsie Station for Metro Northern Railroad, in addition to general engineering work for New Jersey Transit and Amtrak.

## Cole, Sherman & Associates Limited

75 Commerce Valley Drive East, Thornhill, Ontario L3T 7N9, Canada
Tel: (+1 416) 882 44 01   Fax: (+1 416) 882 43 99
e-mail: csa@wcc.com

**Key personnel**
Managing Director and Chief Executive Officer: S R Cole
Executive Vice-President: M Thompson

**Capabilities**
Cole, Sherman & Associates Limited has specialist staff in planning and research, providing services on such subjects as policy analysis, feasibility planning, corporate planning, economic analysis, technology analysis and management systems development.

**Projects**
Development of supervisory central software for Pandrol Jackson stoneblower; contracting of GO Transit locomotive and coach maintenance; design of metro stations for TTC Toronto.

## Colin Buchanan and Partners

59 Queens Gardens, London W2 3AF, UK
Tel: (+44 20) 72 58 37 99   Fax: (+44 20) 72 58 02 99

**Key personnel**
Director, Transportation Engineer: Malcolm Buchanan
Associate Director, Rail Planning: Roland Niblett
Associate, Rail Operations: John Glover

**Capabilities**
CPB is an established firm of transport, planning and economics consultants, who provide advice on rail planning. This includes heavy rail, light rail and intermediate capacity modes, and covers new lines, extensions, new stations, passenger surveys, demand forecasting, service design and economic evaluation.

**Projects**
The firm is retained by Millennium Central Ltd to advise on travel arrangements for the proposed Millennium exhibition at Greenwich, including park-and-ride.

## Colston, Budd, Wardrop & Hunt

Suite 71, Chatswood Village, 47 Neridah Street, Chatswood, New South Wales 2067, Australia
Tel: (+61 2) 94 11 79 22   Fax: (+61 2) 94 11 28 31

**Capabilities**
Railway operating consultancy; modelling of system performance; proving of computerised schedules; traffic optimisation.

## The Corradino Group

200 South Fifth Street, Suite 300 North Louisville, Kentucky 40202, USA
Tel: (+1 502) 587 72 21   Fax: (+1 502) 587 26 36

*Corradino was partner in the joint venture which provided architectural and engineering consultancy for the Miami rapid transit system*

e-mail: corradino@ntr.net
Web: http://www.corradino.com

**Key personnel**
Chief Executive Officer: Joe C Corradino
President: Burt J Deutsch
Executive Vice President: Fred P Pool
Vice Presidents: Joe M Corradino, Steve Sullivan

**Head Office**
First Trust Centre – 300N, 59th Market Street, Louisville, Kentucky 40202, USA
Tel: (+1 502) 587 72 21   Fax: (+1 502) 587 26 36
e-mail: jcorradino@corradino.com
Web: http://www.corradino.com

**Projects**
Recent contracts include: Indianapolis Region Transit Plan; 1-73 Project feasibility study; 1-75 corridor study; Pontire, Michigan downtown plan; Owensboro Airport runway extension; Louisville Airport improvement programme.
Louisville Light Rail Alternatives Analysis, Transitional Study.
Under TARC's 2020 Plan, Corradino developed a long-range plan for transit development in TARC's service area, which helped TARC gain federal approval for a Major Investment Study for light rail transit. Corradino was also a consultant for the US$1.1 billion Miami rail rapid transit system and for the US$4.5 billion Los Angeles Metro rail transit system, for which it developed a computerised public/private development cash flow model.

## Corus Rail Consultancy Ltd

PO Box 298, York YO1 6YH, UK
Tel: (+44 1904) 52 21 64   Fax: (+44 1904) 52 38 76
e-mail: info@corusrailconsultancy.com
Web: http://www.corusrailconsultancy.com

**Key personnel**
Managing Director: Hugh Fenwick
Commercial Director: David Segar
Director, Railway Systems:
 Jim Veitch
Director, Projects: Jeremy Blake
Director, Permanent Way: Kevin Sibson

**Other offices**
5th Floor, Whittles House, 14 Pentonville Road, Islington, London N1 9HF, UK
Tel: (+44 121) 242 12 40   Fax: (+44 121) 246 46 64

6th Floor, Alpha Tower, Crowne Plaza, Suffolk Street, Birmingham B1 1TT, UK
Tel: (+44 121) 242 12 40   Fax: (+44 121) 246 46 64

Room G1, Rail House, Store Street, Manchester M60 1DQ, UK
Tel: (+44 161) 228 46 36   Fax: (+44 161) 228 50 92

3rd Floor, Leeson Court, 88 Lower Leeson Street, Dublin 2, Ireland
Tel: (+353 1) 631 06 11   Fax: (+353 1) 678 54 65

**Capabilities**
A subsidiary of Corus, the company is one of the country's leading multi-disciplinary consultancies providing expertise in track design, bridges, stations and freight depots. Corus Rail Consultancy's services includes the design of new railways, upgrading of existing railways for higher speeds, electrification or heavier axleloads; design and specification of electrical and mechanical equipment/plant for railway operations; signalling and level crossing design; geotechnical services; environmental appraisal, quantity surveying; architecture and design; cost planning and project management; and supervision of site activities and training and advice on safety.

**Projects**
Multifunctional consultancy contract for West Coast Route Modernisation in south Midlands; outline and detailed design to create two new approach tracks for the Leeds First Project; alignments including line speed diversionary routes, structure modifications and renewals at the East Coast Main Line upgrade project design of stations and structure for the extension of the Tyne and Wear Metro to Sunderland; outline design to enhance rail capacity on the Dublin to Cork railway to facilitate a Railway Order application; design of a cost efficient cross bay gantry system for hoists, the whole system being operated through synchronous radio control; work related to Railtrack's National Gauging Project; and a contract to increase speed and provide capacity improvements on the North Trans-Pennine route.

*UPDATED*

## Corus Rail Technologies

Swinden Technology Centre, Moorgate, Rotherham S60 3AR, UK
Tel: (+44 1709) 82 01 66   Fax: (+44 1709) 82 53 37
e-mail: corusrail@corusgroup.com
Web: http://www.corusgroup.com

**Capabilities**
Technical consultancy services related to the in-service performance of railway components and the behaviour of complete track and railways systems, including: rail breakage investigation; rolling contact fatigue sample analysis and test site monitoring; specialist data mining techniques; and the development of a holistic suite of track system models. Much of the company's work is related to gauge corner cracking.

*UPDATED*

## COWI Consulting Engineers and Planners AS

Parallelvej 15, DK-2800 Lyngby, Denmark
Tel: (+45) 45 97 22 11   Fax: (+45) 45 97 22 12
e-mail: cowi@cowi.dk
Web: http://www.cowi.dk

**Key personnel**
Managing Director: Klaus H Ostenfeld
Director, Rail, Metro and Tunnel: Arne Steen Jacobsen

**Other offices**
Also in Norway (Oslo), Germany (Berlin), Belgium (Brussels), Spain (Madrid), Lithuania (Vilnius), Poland (Warsaw), Russia (Moscow), USA (San Francisco), Canada (Vancouver), Tanzania (Dar es Salaam), Nigeria (Lagos), Kenya (Nairobi), Uganda (Kampala), Ghana (Accra), Burkina Faso (Tenkodogo), South Africa (Johannesburg), Bahrain (Manama), United Arab Emirates (Dubai), Oman (Qurum), Qatar (Doha), Saudi Arabia (Dammam), Philippines (Manila), Thailand (Bangkok), China (Beijing) and Vietnam (Hanoi).

**Corporate background**
Since its foundation in 1930, the firm has been involved in more than 25,000 projects in 110 countries. The number of employees totals 2,100.
COWI is privately owned with the COWI Foundation as the majority shareholder.

**Capabilities**
COWI offers consulting services at all stages of multi-disciplinary large-scale railway projects from initial planning and engineering design to construction management and supervision and advice on operation and maintenance. COWI's services range from professional advice on a particular problem to total coverage of services required by public and private clients from idea to realisation of railway systems. Feasibility studies, development of tender solutions and contract documents, managing of tender procedures, contracting, authority approval management, contract administration, environmental management, risk management, system certification management and maintenance management, analysis for the maintenance and reinvestment of railway infrastructure and administration.
Recent contracts include: to develop a maintenance management system for the Danish and Norwegian railway agencies; project management and consultant on civil works design for the 21 km driverless metro system, worth £600 million, being developed in Copenhagen; consultant for the conceptual design and outline design of the 6.5 km Malmo City Railway tunnel linking Malmo Central Station to Copenhagen, worth £550 million; for EU PHARE railway upgrading projects in eastern Europe, and in Denmark, COWI is project manager for the S-train ring line running around the centre of Copenhagen and design of the Flintholm station, the largest in Denmark.

## CPCS Ltd

CPCS Technologies Ltd
740 Notre Dame Street West, Suite 760, Montréal, Québec H3C 3X6, Canada
Tel: (+1 514) 876 19 00   Fax: (+1 514) 875 10 23

**Branch office**
4 Lansing Square, Ontario M2J 1T1, Canada
Tel: (+1 416) 499 26 90   Fax: (+1 416) 499 29 29

**Key personnel**
Chairman and Chief Executive Officer: G T Fisher
President: D H Page

**Capabilities**
CPCS Ltd is a privately owned international consulting firm specialising in transportation, telecommunications and commercialisation/privatisation. It provides technical, advisory and training services to governments and the private sector in the planning, engineering, operating, marketing and maintenance of transportation and telecommunications systems. Since its establishment in 1969, CPCS Ltd has successfully completed over 700 projects in over 60 countries around the world.
CPCS Technologies Ltd is the technology and operating company associated with CPCS Ltd, undertaking procurement and assistance in contract operation of railways and other major transportation projects, including privatisation and commercialisation.

## Creactive Design

22 New Street, Leamington Spa CV31 1HP, UK
Tel: (+44 1926) 83 31 13   Fax: (+44 1926) 83 27 88
e-mail: info@creactive-design.co.uk
Web: http://www.creactive-design.co.uk

**Key personnel**
Directors Sales and Marketing: Neil Bates, Tony Hume

**Other office**
St John's Innovation Centre, Cowley Road, Cambridge CB4 OWS, UK
Tel: (+44 1223) 42 11 41   Fax: (+44 1223) 42 10 36
e-mail: hans@creactive-design.co.uk

**Capabilities**
Specialising in transport projects, Creactive Design provides a design resource for transport design with a

*Anglia Railways train livery*   2000/0087709

*Standard class interior*   2000/0087710

team of designers, rolling stock engineers and ergonomists.

The company offers interior and exterior design for refurbished and new rolling stock, safety and emergency design. Environmental design including seating, street furniture, signage, telephone kiosks, lighting and station/stop design. Creative designs and supplies mock-up models, rigs and prototypes.

**Projects**
Currently the company is assembling a metro car prototype to enter service for customer trial and evaluation.

Other recent contracts include: design of new metro trains, KCRC West Rail, Hong Kong for IKK (Itochu, Kawasaki, Kinki); refurbishment and manufacture of D78 stock for London Underground; new emu rolling stock design for Fiat Ferroviaria; design of Warwick Parkway railway station for Chiltern Railways/Birse Rail, as well as projects for Anglia Railways, Bombardier Transportation, and the Greater Nottingham Rapid Transit.

*UPDATED*

---

## Creadesign Oy

Laivanvarustajankatu 5, FIN-00140 Helsinki, Finland
Tel: (+358 9) 251 21 00   Fax: (+358 9) 60 58 32
e-mail: hannu.kahonen@creadesign.fi
Web: http://www.creadesign.fi

**Key personnel**
Managing Director: Hannu Kähönen

**Capabilities**
Industrial design, including rolling stock styling and interiors, from strategic concept design to product launch; corporate image; marketing communication.

**Projects**
Projects include interior and exterior design of the Variotram built by Bombardier Transportation and Talgo for HKL, Helsinki. Design work has also been undertaken for VR Ltd (Finnish Railways) and Talgo.

*NEW ENTRY*

---

## Crown Agents for Oversea Governments and Administrations Ltd

St Nicholas House, St Nicholas Road, Sutton SM1 1EL
Tel: (+44 20) 86 43 33 11   Fax: (+44 20) 86 43 82 32
e-mail: john.wrighton@crownagents.co.uk
Web: http://www.crownagents.com

**Key personnel**
Executive Chairman: P Berry
Director, Procurement and Consultancy Services:
  D Phillips
Head of Railways: J A Wrighton

**Capabilitites**
Crown Agents specialises in providing consultancy and procurement services associated with locomotives, rolling stock and track renewal and rehabilitation, and the provision of assistance with railway management reforms, restructuring and privatisation. Services are provided internationally with specialist knowledge of international regulations and conditions.

**Projects**
Recent contracts include: feasibility studies for the manufacture of track-grinding trains in Russia (1997); cost verification for track rehabilitation and upgrading in Russia (1999); maintenance management of Class 36 locomotives, Tanzania Railways (1999-2001); and contracts management for Railtrack recovery cranes overhaul and enhancement (1997-2000).

---

## Currie & Brown

The Red House, High Street, Redbourn, St Albans AL3 7LE, UK
Tel: (+44 1582) 79 30 03   Fax: (+44 1582) 79 30 00

e-mail: graham.waring@currieb.co.uk
Web: http://www.currieb.com

**Key personnel**
Chairman: Doug Leedham

**Other offices**
9 King Street, London EC2V 8EA, UK
Tel: (+44 20) 76 00 87 87   Fax: (+44 20) 77 26 23 98

Level 5, 67 Albert Avenue, Chatswood, Sydney New South Wales 2067, Australia
Tel: (+61 2) 94 15 16 00   Fax: (+61 2) 94 15 14 43

TM Hiroo Building, 7th Floor, 1-9-20 Hiroo, Shibuya-ku, Tokyo 150-0012, Japan
Tel: (+81 3) 34 42 66 42   Fax: (+81 3) 34 42 19 58

Suite 200, 45 Rockefeller Plaza, New York, New York 10111-0100, USA
Tel: (+1 212) 332 32 09   Fax: (+1 212) 332 32 09

**Capabilities**
Strategic procurement advice; procurement of works; commercial management; schedule and programme management; risk management; alliance and partnering advice; project management; project performance measurement; value management; and supply chain management.

**Projects**
Include: a range of services for five of the seven zones of Railtrack in the UK; services connected with station reconstruction and refurbishment, health and safety measures, CCTV systems and maintenance works for London Underground Ltd; establishment of a Project Implementation Unit for Azerbaijan Railways; provision of contractor and third party management systems for Irish Rail; and services connected with signalling rehabilitation for Victoria Public Transport Corporation, Australia.

---

## Daniel, Mann, Johnson & Mendenhall

3250 Wilshire Boulevard, Los Angeles, California 90010 USA
Tel: (+1 213) 381 36 63   Fax: (+1 213) 383 36 56

**Key personnel**
Corporate Vice-President and Director, Transportation:
  Gerald W Seelman

**Projects**
Leader since 1967 of joint venture for planning, design, construction and management of Baltimore Metro; design and engineering management, in joint venture, of Los Angeles Metro Red Line (full metro), Green Line (Norwalk-El Segundo light rail), Blue Line (Long Beach-Los Angeles light rail) and Blue Line Pasadena Extension; design, engineering and programme management of Oceanside-San Diego commuter rail service; design of F-10 section of Metro rail system for WMATA, Washington DC; design and construction services, in joint venture, for commuter and heavy-rail systems in Taipei, Taiwan; and principal consultant for all facilities on Vancouver Advanced Light Rail Transit system, Canada.

---

## DCA Design International Ltd

19 Church Street, Warwick CV34 4AB, UK
Tel: (+44 1926) 49 94 61   Fax: (+44 1926) 40 11 34
e-mail: transport@dca-design.com
Web: http://www.dca-design.com/transport

**Key personnel**
Managing Director: Michael Groves
Directors: Rob Bassil, John Daly, Rob Woolston,
  John Sheppard

**Capabilities**
Multidisciplinary design consultancy specialising in visual, ergonomic and component engineering aspects of transport design. Services include exterior styling, interior design, engineering design, electronic design, corporate design, model-making, ergonomics/human factors, CAD, detailed drawing, computer visualising and animation,

'fast track' product design including 3-D CAD. Large in-house workshop facilities enable construction of full-size mockups, prototypes and models. ISO 9001.

**Projects**
These have included designs for new rolling stock for London Underground Ltd's Central Line; visual and driver ergonomic aspects of the British Rail Class 90 and 91 locomotives; design of the Tangara double-deck commuter trainset for the State Rail Authority of New South Wales, Australia; Channel Tunnel shuttle wagons and locomotives for European and Canadian members of the ESCW and ESCL consortia; refurbishment of London Underground Ltd's Metropolitan Line trainsets; design of the British Rail Class 341 emu for the proposed CrossRail line; the Class 365 'Networker Express' trainset; Class 371 Thameslink 2000 trains; train and corporate design work for the new cross-border train services between Belfast and Dublin; new and refurbishment concepts for MTRC in Hong Kong; M6 double-deck cars for SNCB, Belgium; and mockups and detailed design of Virgin CrossCountry demus; TfL PPP ITT support; and Eurostar refurbishment seating design and supply and interior detail design and specification.

*UPDATED*

---

## Delcan Corporation

133 Wynford Drive, Toronto, Ontario M3C 1K1, Canada
Tel: (+1 416) 441 41 11   Fax: (+1 416) 441 41 31
e-mail: info@delcan.com
Web: http://www.delcan.com

**Key personnel**
Chairman and Chief Executive Officer: Peter J Boyd
President, National Engineering Technology: Jim Kerr
Vice-President, Program and Project Management:
  Charles Orolowitz

**Overseas offices**
Barbados, El Salvador, Greece, Hong Kong, Israel, Malawi, Taiwan, USA (Atlanta, Chicago, Los Angeles, Salt Lake City and Virginia) and Venezuela.

**Background**
The DHV Group holds a 40 per cent interest in Delcan Corporation.

**Capabilities**
A full range of consulting services ranging from studies to the overall design and construction supervision of large railway infrastructures. Project management, feasibility studies, engineering, compliance auditing, implementation, operations and maintenance for urban transit, commuter, intercity passenger and freight railways.

*UPDATED*

---

## Deutsche Eisenbahn-Consulting GmbH

A subsidiary of German Railway (DB) and Deutsche Bank AG
Reinhardtstrasse 18, D-10117 Berlin, Germany
Tel: (+49 30) 30 63 43; 11 15
Fax: (+49 30) 30 63 43; 10 51

**Business Department**
International Transportation and Railway Service
Oskar-Sommer-Strasse 15, D-60596 Frankfurt am Main
Tel: (+49 69) 631 90   Fax: (+49 69) 631 92 95
e-mail: ITRS@de-consult.de
Web: http://www.de-consult.de

**Key personnel**
Supervisory Board Chairman: Roland Heinisch
Board of Managing Directors:
  Chair: Dr Hermann Lenke
  Dipl-Kfm Gerd Wiederwald
Head of Business Unit: Thomas Eckart

**Background**
DE-Consult is an independent transport consultancy founded in 1966, whose shareholders are Deutsche Bahn

## CONSULTANCY SERVICES

AG and Deutsche Bank AG. It employs around 1,200 people worldwide.

### Capabilities
Range of advisory services including planning and management of complex infrastructure projects involving long-distance and urban passenger and freight transport, rolling stock and workshops, management consultancy, operations planning, transport economics, finance and marketing, manpower development and training.

### Projects
DE-Consult has been involved in over 1,000 projects internationally. High-speed projects in Germany, Korea, Taiwan, Spain and Italy; suburban transport systems projects in Thailand, Greece, Netherlands and Germany; rehabilitation projects in Eastern Europe, Africa, America and the Far East; freight transport projects in Germany, South America, Eastern Europe and Africa; training projects in South America, Eastern Europe, Africa and Asia.

***UPDATED***

---

## De Leuw, Cather & Company

A Parsons Transportation Group Company
1133 15th Street NW, Washington DC 20005-2701, USA
Tel: (+1 202) 775 33 00   Fax: (+1 202) 775 34 22

### Key personnel
President: R S O'Neil
Executive Vice-Presidents: G M Randich, V P Lamb
Managers:
   International Region: W J Custer Jr
   Eastern Region: A A Patnaude
   Central Region: G M Randich
   Western Region: T E Barron
   Business Development: A Bonds Jr
Sector Manager, Railways: C C De Weese

### Overseas offices
Abu Dhabi, Bandung, Bangkok, Buenos Aires, Dar es Salaam, Dubai, Gaborone, Islamabad, Izmir, Jakarta, Kaohsiung, Karachi, Khartoum, Kuala Lumpur, Llongwe, London, Manila, Mbabane, Mwanza, Shanghai and Taipei.

### Capabilities
Services include: feasibility studies; preliminary and final design; site development, surveys, soil investigations; specifications and cost estimates; environmental analysis/permitting; contract documents, construction supervision, construction management and programme management.

---

## Thomas K Dyer Inc

HNTB Corporation
1762 Massachusetts Avenue, Lexington, Massachusetts 02420, USA
Tel: (+1 781) 862 20 75   Fax: (+1 781) 861 77 66
e-mail: dwoodbury@hntb.com
Web: http://www.hntb.com

### Key personnel
Vice-Presidents: Douglas J Woodbury
Marketing: Kimberly Durkee

### Other offices
Over 60 offices throughout the USA.

### Background
Thomas K Dyer became part of HNTB Corporation in June 2001.

### Capabilities
Architecture, engineering and planning, providing services throughout the USA and worldwide. With nearly 3,000 professional and technical employees, HNTB offers services within the disciplines of surface transportation, aviation, architecture, environmental engineering and construction services.

***UPDATED***

---

## Design and Projects Int Ltd

Wessex House, Upper Market Street, Eastleigh SO50 9FD, UK
Tel: (+44 23) 80 61 60 66   Fax: (+44 23) 80 61 60 68
e-mail: dpil@msn.com
Web: http://www.railwaymaintenance.com

### Key personnel
Managing Director: Colin Brooks
Operations Director: Stuart Blyth

### Capabilities
Design, supply and setting to work of equipment needed to overhaul, maintain, repair and clean rail vehicles and their components for metro, main line and suburban railway systems. This includes all depot/workshop, track and overhead catenary system maintenance equipment.

While the company normally executes contracts on a turnkey basis, projects can also be undertaken for equipment and supplier studies, and the design of one-off specialist equipment. The company can also provide other engineering and management support in relation to railway maintenance facilities, purpose equipment, design and supply of diagnostic test equipment for rail vehicles; supply of maintenance equipment for track work, signalling and all fixed systems.

### Projects
Contracts include the supply of maintenance equipment for a people mover at Chep Lap Kok airport, Hong Kong, for Manila LRT3 and for the Arlanda Airport link.

Nottingham NET (Adtranz, March 2000), London Underground, Victoria Line depot upgrade (March 2000), Singapore Senbang/Punggol (MHI, September 1999) and Tashkent depot rehabilitation (September 1999).

---

## Design Research Unit

The Old School, Exton Street, London SE1 8UE, UK
Tel: (+44 20) 76 33 97 11   Fax (+44 20) 72 61 03 33
e-mail: info@dru.co.uk
Web: http://www.dru.co.uk

### Key personnel
Directors: Hugh Crawford, Irvin Morris, Maurice Green, Chris Ellingham, Paul Cook, Peter Austin, James Rayner

### Other offices
Design Research Unit International
2,103 Universal Trade Centre, 3 Arbuthnot Road, Hong Kong
Tel: (+852) 23 77 47 37   Fax: (+852) 27 36 64 57
e-mail: general@designresearchunit.corn.hk

Design Research Unit Gulf (LLC)
PO Box 4233, Dubai, United Arab Emirates
Tel: (+971) 42 24 65 65   Fax: (+971) 42 28 09 69
e-mail: dru@emirates.net.ae

### Capabilities
Station planning, architecture, interior design, graphic design and building condition surveys.

### Projects
Architectural and planning work has been undertaken for many transport authorities. Current projects include rail/light rail and metro systems in Bangkok, Copenhagen, Hong Kong, London and Nottingham (UK). Completed works includes metro and rail systems in Athens, Baghdad, Birmingham, Kuala Lumpur, Singapore, Taipei and Toronto.

***UPDATED***

---

## Design Triangle

The Maltings, Burwell, Cambridge CB5 0HB, UK
Tel: (+44 1638) 74 30 70   Fax: (+44 1638) 74 34 93
e-mail: mail@designtriangle.co.uk

### Key personnel
Partners: Siep Wijsenbeek, Andrew Crawshaw, Andrew Clark

### Capabilities
Specialist vehicle interior and exterior design for the public transport industry, from the creation of innovative new concepts through to production design. Design Triangle is an independent team of industrial designers, engineers and ergonomists. The integrated services encompasses styling, engineering design and ergonomics for operators and manufacturers of public transport and specialist vehicles; industrial design for manufacturers of transport-related products; and design management consultancy for operators.

Other facilities offered include: textile design, 3-D CAD modelling and walk-through animation, full-size and scale modelling, prototype build, textile design, colour forecasting and trend analysis.

### Projects
Exterior and interior design of the Heathrow Express train including checked luggage facilities; exterior design of the Hong Kong Airport Express and Tung Chung Line train for the MTR Corporation including cab interior and detrainment device; development of exterior styling for the TKE train, also for the MTR Corporation; consultancy for London Underground planning standards; capacity and passenger flow studies for Docklands Light Railways;

---

# SwedeRail

### The Swedish Railway Consultants

## Developing the potential of the railway in a changing world

www.swederail.se     info@swederail.se     tel +46 8 762 37 80     fax +46 8 10 62 43

## CONSULTANCY SERVICES

*CAD design for Heathrow Express by Design Triangle*
0016444

interior design for Alstom; modular seating prototypes for KAB Seating; design and engineering for British Aerospace and Kawasaki for Maryland double-deck cars; interior and exterior design of RET Rotterdam metro; design of new rolling stock for Metro de Madrid and many light rail vehicles.

*UPDATED*

---

## DHA

Delon Hampton & Associates
800 K Street NW, North Lobby, Suite 720,
Washington DC 20001, USA
Tel: (+1 202) 898 19 99  Fax: (+1 202) 371 20 73
e-mail: dhafbeach@aol.com

**Key personnel**
Chairman of the Board and Chief Executive Officer:
  Dr Delon Hampton (President of the American Society of Civil Engineers)
President and Chief Operating Officer: Elijah B Rogers
Executive Vice-President and Principal:
  Foster J Beach III, PE

**Capabilities**
Design, planning and inspection of rapid transit and light rail systems and other transportation structures; programme and construction management services; planning, design and construction support services and construction inspection services.

**Projects**
Projects include Program Management Oversight consultant for the Federal Transit Authority overseeing a five-year (1999-2004) project for New Jersey Transit Corporation, Connecticut Department of Transport, and Metro Northern Railroad; construction management services for the Los Angeles River Bridge for the Almeda Corridor Railroad System completed 1999 and also for the Washington Boulevard/Santa Fe grade separation; design and programme management for the Memphis Area Transit Authority during 1999; and assisting with evaluation of Tren Urbano Transit System in San Juan Puerto Rico.

---

## DHV Holding BV

PO Box 219, NL-3800 AE Amersfoort, Netherlands
Telephone: (+31 33) 468 37 00  Fax: (+31 33) 468 37 48
e-mail: info@dhv.nl
Web: http://www.dhv.com

**Key personnel**
Executive Board: Hans C Huis in't Veld, Renko G Campen
Corporate Communications: Jeannette van Enst
e-mail: corpcomm@beh.dhv.nl

**Background**
DHV Group is an international consultancy and was founded in 1917.

**Capabilities**
Consultancy in market research, economic analysis and public transport planning.

**Projects**
As a partner in the High-Speed Rail Link-South Project Organisation, DHV developed noise barriers which not only limit the noise nuisance for the surrounding area but which can also be used for the sustainable generation of electricity. The company has also been closely involved in the planning and design of the five tunnels required for the high-speed link.
DHV is also conducting research into techniques of laying track beds on the soft terrain found in delta areas.
Other recent projects include a feasibility study for an underground logistics systems for Tilburg.

---

## Doxiadis Associates SA

13 Aegidon & Seneka str, GR-14564 Nea Kifissia, Athens, Greece
Tel: (+30 10) 624 63 00  Fax: (+30 10) 24 63 99
e-mail: doxiadis@doxiadis.com

**Key personnel**
Managing Director: Yiannis Pasgianos
Vice Chairman, Business Development:
  Anastasios C Antonopoulos
Director Transportation and Traffic Planning:
  Emmanuel Constantas

**Background**
Doxiadis Associates SA was established in 1951.

**Capabilities**
Transport planning and engineering design, traffic management, analysis and design, urban planning, project management, highway engineering, construction supervision and maintenance. Also participates in study teams for preparation of comprehensive development, regional and urban plans.

*NEW ENTRY*

---

## EDS

Electronic Data Systems Nederland BV
PO Box 2233, NL-3500 GE Utrecht, Netherlands
Tel: (+31 30) 292 49 05  Fax: (+31 30) 297 03 54

**Key personnel**
Principal: Michiel Deerenberg

**Capabilities**
The travel and transportation division of EDS Northern Europe has established the Rail International Centre of Expertise (RICE) which serves as a database for European railways which are undergoing transformation. RICE also researches new systems, products and services.

---

## Edwards and Kelcey Inc

299 Madison Avenue, PO Box 1936, Morristown, New Jersey 07962-1936, USA
Tel: (+1 973) 267 05 55  Fax: (+1 973) 267 35 55
Web: http://www.ekorp.com

**Key personnel**
Chief Executive Officer: Kevin J McMahon
Executive Vice-Presidents: Kenneth J Garrity;
  Richard M Hallahan
  Mark G Pilla
  Richard E Tangel

**Offices**

*USA*
Amherst, Massachusetts; Baltimore, Maryland; Boston North, Massachusetts; Boston South, Massachusetts; Chicago, Illinois; Dallas, Texas; Florham Park, New Jersey; Houston, Texas; Jacksonville, Florida; Kittery, Maine; Leesburg, Virginia; Londonderry, New Hampshire; Manchester, New Hampshire; Milwaukee, Wisconsin; Minneapolis, Minnesota; Morristown, New Jersey; New Haven, Connecticut; New York, New York; Philadelphia, Pennsylvania; Providence, Rhode Island; Saratoga Springs, New York; Tallahassee, Florida; Tampa, Florida; Tarrytown, New York; West Chester, Pennsylvania.

*International*
Amsterdam, Netherlands; Carolina, Puerto Rico.

**Capabilities**
Environmental, planning, design and construction services for railways, mass transit, highways, airports and ports. Urban transport services include: terminals and stations, railways and metros, tunnels, maintenance shops and yards, track, catenary support structures, bridges, and parking. Other services include alternatives analysis and transport planning, patronage forecasting, ridership surveys, urban freight movement, traffic control systems, traffic impacts, circulation studies, route and corridor selection, busways, cycleways and pedestrianways.

---

## EG & G Dynatrend Inc

24 New England Executive Park, Burlington, Massachusetts 01803, USA
Tel: (+1 617) 272 03 00  Fax: (+1 617) 270 49 99

**Key personnel**
President: Robert Ward

**Capabilities**
Accessibility and related requirements for people with disabilities; project and construction management for rail systems; application of advanced technologies; and transportation planning and analysis.

---

## Electrack

A division of Heery International
8201 Corporate Drive, Landover, Maryland 20785, USA
Tel: (+1 301) 306 01 18  Fax: (+1 301) 577 20 52

**Key personnel**
Vice-President: David Rankin

**Capabilities**
Electrack offers planning, design and construction services for people mover, light rail, monorail, main line and high-speed railway systems. Electrack focuses on the design and construction management of electrification systems, including traction power, operational simulations, catenary and third rail.

*UPDATED*

---

## Electrowatt Infra Ltd

Hardturmstrasse 161, PO Box CH-8037 Zurich, Switzerland
Tel: (+41 1) 355 55 55  Fax: (+41 1) 355 55 56
e-mail: lothar.garbe@ewe.ch

**Key personnel**
Head of Infrastructure Division: Jonathan Schmieder

**Regional offices**
Germany, eastern Europe, UK, Middle East, Asia, Latin America

**Capabilities**
Feasibility studies, environmental studies, modelling and data processing, economic assessment; safety/security consulting, planning and engineering of rail systems; specifications, tender documents, bid evaluations; supervision of manufacture and installation; project management; planning of timetables; consultancy for BOT projects, operation, maintenance and outsourcing.

**Projects**
Switzerland: drawing up of tender documents and supervision of exploratory construction work for the new Gotthard Rail Tunnel.
Germany: construction supervision of sections of the high-speed railway line between Cologne and Frankfurt.
Poland: planning the upgrading of the railway route from Warsaw to Belarus.

*UPDATED*

## Engage

A Shop, Derby Carriage Works, Litchurch Lane DE24 8AD, UK
Tel: (+44 1332) 29 99 88  Fax: (+44 1332) 25 17 64
e-mail: david.peel@engage-kgn.com
Web: http://www.engage-gkn.com

**Key personnel**
Business Development Manager: David Peel

**Capabilities**
Predictive analysis services for rail application including: structural analysis; joint analysis, thermal analysis, modal analysis and crashworthiness.

*NEW ENTRY*

## The Engineering Link Ltd

Trent House, RTC Business Park, London Road, Derby DE24 8UP, UK
Tel: (+44 1332) 26 34 48  Fax: (+41 1332) 26 49 60
e-mail: net@the-engineering-link.co.uk
Web: http://www.the-engineering-link.co.uk

**Key personnel**
Managing Director: Tony Butler
Sales and Marketing Director: Martin Hayhoe
Production Resources Director: Charles Saunders
Finance Director: Chris Wright

**Other offices**
Doncaster, London

**Capabilities**
The Engineering Link is a rail engineering consultancy covering freight and passenger vehicles, special purpose vehicles, ontrack plant and depot equipment. Services include: strategic studies, engineering design, VR modelling and finite element analysis, project management, risk assessment, maintenance support, independent audit, wagon design, refurbishment, safety acceptance, problem solving, specifications and documentation, training and competence assessment, and the company is an authorised rail vehicle acceptance body.

*UPDATED*

## ENOTRAC AG

PO Box 23, CH-3661 Uetendorf, Switzerland
Tel: (+41 33) 345 62 22  Fax: (+41 33) 345 62 25
e-mail: heinz.voegeli@enotrac.com
Web: http://www.enotrac.com

**Key personnel**
Executive: Heinz Voegeli

**Subsidiary**
ENOTRAC UK Ltd
Times House, Throwley Way, Sutton SM1 4AF, UK
Tel: (+44 20) 87 70 35 01  Fax: (+44 20) 87 70 35 02
e-mail: ziad.mouneimne@enotrac.com
Executive: Dr Ziad S Mouneimne

**Capabilities**
ENOTRAC provides consulting services covering systems engineering, feasibility studies, planning, technology evaluation, tender preparation and evaluation, asset replacement strategy, equipment specification, procurement support, software development, field tests, quality assurance, reliability and safety assessments, signalling compatibility studies and operational procedures.
For rolling stock, the services encompass performance evaluation, energy consumption, comparative assessment of traction equipment, rehabilitation and maintenance management.
For fleet management, ENOTRAC provides VIPSCARSIS, the software system for configuration, warranty, maintenance and modification management including LCC- and RAM-calculations, tailor-made for rolling stock and fixed installations. The services include process studies and consulting, workshops, training and full user support.

Power supply services include rating of equipment (substations, catenary), optimum substation spacing, reinforcement requirements, short-circuit calculations and protection, earthing, step and touch voltages, and energy, active and reactive power requirements and magnetic field computation. Optimised design is achieved by a powerful software suite developed in-house for multitrain simulation of complex AC and DC-supplied networks.

*VERIFIED*

## EPV-GIV

Europrojekt Verkehr Gesellschaft für Ingenieurleistungen im Verkehrswesen mbH
Markgrafendamm 24, Haus 16, D-10245 Berlin, Germany
Tel: (+49 30) 29 38 06 20  Fax: (+49 30) 29 38 06 21
e-mail: geschaeftsleistung@epv-giv.de
Web: http://www.epv-giv.de

**Corporate development**
EPV-GIV was created by the amalgamation in 1994 of EPV (Europrojekt Verkehr GmbH & Co) and GIV (Gesellschaft für Ingenieurleistungen im Verkehrswesen GmbH.

**Capabilities**
The company offers consultancy services in: project management; project financing; transport planning and technology; marketing; training and further education; and project co-ordination. These include the preparation and assessment of: analyses and studies for the development of traffic in Europe; strategic concepts for the development of transport; complex transport planning for countries and regions; studies regarding transport planning and analysis; and concepts, traffic streams, market and demand forecasting in the areas of passenger and freight traffic, in particular for railways.
In addition, EPV-GIV organises and co-ordinates: co-operation with partners at location; support during privatisation or company foundation and the formation of joint ventures; processing of offers for planning and construction of transportation routes; preparation of pre-qualification documents; co-operation with other consultancy firms; and participation in fairs and exhibitions.

**Projects**
EPV-GIV is active throughout Europe. Present activities are concentrated on Poland, the Czech Republic, the Baltic republics, Russia and other CIS states.

## ERM Lahmeyer International GmbH

Konrad-Adenauer-Strasse 3, D-63263 Neu-Ilsenburg, Germany
Tel: (+49 6102) 20 60  Fax: (+49 6102) 20 62 02
e-mail: info@erm-li.de
Web: http://www.erm-li.de

**Key personnel**
Consultant: Peter Loose

**Offices**
Düsseldorf, Stuttgart

**Capabilities**
ERM Lahmeyer International specialises in the provision of environmental consulting services, including environmental audits, environmental management, permitting and project management, contaminated site investigation, waste management and engineering services, environmental planning and natural resources management and information technology.

**Projects**
Include: Fehmarn Belt fixed link environmental impact feasibility study; Fehmarn Belt rail and road connections environmental impact feasibility study; Jerusalem light rail environmental impact feasibility study; environmental impact assessment elaboration for S-Bahn extension in Stuttgart.

## Esveld Consulting Services BV

PO Box 331, NL-5300 AH Zaltbommel, Netherlands
Tel: (+31 41) 801 63 69  Fax: (+31 41) 801 63 72

**Key personnel**
Director: Dr C Esveld

**Capabilities**
Consultancy in track technology.

## EurailTest

75, avenue Parmentier, F-75544 Paris Cedex 11, France
Tel: (+33 1) 40 21 11 04  Fax: (+33 1) 40 21 24 21
e-mail: eurailtest@eurailtest.com
Web: http://www.eurailtest.com

**Capabilities**
Established in 1999 by French National Railways (SNCF) and Regie Autonome des Transports Parisiens (RATP), EurailTest undertakes railway testing services including: the characterisation and behaviour of non-metallic materials; analysis and inspection of metal components; environment and protection; railway dynamics; acoustics and aerodynamics; traction and electrical equipment; braking; structural strength; mechanical components; development and measurement, and engineering and test organisation; and track inspection.
Areas of expertise include: active and passive safety; interface management; environmental occupational hygiene; comfort and ride quality; performance; maintenance failure analysis; material and component characterisation; and crime prevention in the railway environment. Consultancy and training services are also provided.

*UPDATED*

## Eurostation SA

Rue Brogniezstraat 54, B-1070 Brussels, Belgium
Tel: (+32 2) 529 09 11 Fax: (+32 2) 522 23 79; 520 99 61
e-mail: eurostation@eurostation.be

**Key personnel**
President: Jean-Pierre Van Wouwe
Managing Director: Herwig Persoons

**Capabilities**
A subsidiary of Belgian National Railways, Eurostation combines architectural and civil engineering expertise with property acquisition, development and facilities management to optimise the commercial potential of stations.

**Projects**
Projects include: the development of properties at the high-speed train terminal at Brussels South (Midi); redevelopment of Antwerp station to create four operational levels, including facilities for the high-speed route to the Netherlands; and a feasibility study into a proposed major new station in the north of Brussels.

*NEW ENTRY*

## Finnish Railway Engineering Ltd

PO Box A51, FIN-01019 IVO, Finland
Tel: (+358 9) 85 61 15 81  Fax: (+358 9) 507 11 63

**Key personnel**
Managing Director: Pekka Salo
Marketing Manager: Raimo Mättö

**Capabilities**
Railway technology consulting.

**Projects**
Finnish Railway Engineering has carried out efficiency-improvement and computerised ticketing and reservation work for Malayan Railway Administration (KTM); and conducted a rail wear study for Saudi Arabia.

## CONSULTANCY SERVICES

### First Engineering Ltd

Floor 7, Buchanan House, 58 Port Dundas Road, Glasgow G4 0HG, UK
Tel: (+44 141) 335 30 05    Fax: (+44 141) 335 30 06

**Key personnel**
Chief Executive Officer: Tony Smith
Commercial Director: John Cowie

**Corporate development**
Formerly known as Scotland Infrastructure Maintenance Co, First Engineering was one of the British Rail Infrastructure Services Units sold off as part of the British Rail privatisation. The company was sold in 1996 to a management buyout team known as TrackAction.

**Capabilities**
Railway infrastructure and civil engineering consultancy.

---

### Fleet Software

3 Newton Business Centre, Thorncliffe Park Estate, Chapeltown, Sheffield S30 4PH, UK
Tel: (+44 114) 257 16 00    Fax: (+44 114) 257 16 09

**Key personnel**
Managing Director: John Rands

**Projects**
Developed TACT, software for rolling stock maintenance in the UK. It records individual parts performance and management of reliability issues. TACT software has been approved for use across the networks of National Express Group and Prism. TACT was first introduced to Supertram, Gatwick Express and in 1996 to Heathrow Express. It has now been extended to rolling stock manufacturers.
  TACT technology was originally developed around the privatised bus industry when engineering costs became an issue.

---

### Flow Science Ltd

Goldstein Research Laboratory, Barton Airport, Eccles, Manchester M30 7RU, UK
Fax: (+44 161) 787 87 49
e-mail: flowsci@fsi.ae.man.ac.uk

**Key personnel**
Operations Director: Dr D J Smith
Windtunnel Managers: A Kennaugh, I Lunnon

**Capabilities**
Flow Science Ltd is a fluid dynamics consultancy, with expertise in windtunnel testing with moving ground to speeds of 60 m/s. Services include general-purpose windtunnel testing for ventilation systems, and so on; earth boundary layer windtunnel for topographic studies, such as cuttings; and investigation of flow around buildings and bridges.

**Projects**
Recent projects include windtunnel testing of the ICE 2 high-speed trainset design for Krauss-Maffei, Germany and preliminary investigations for the Korean high-speed train (August 1998).
  The company has been awarded ISO 9001 1382/9 certification.

---

### Fluor Daniel Pty Ltd

Level 2, the Gateway, 312 St Kilda Road, Melbourne Victoria 3004, Australia
Tel: (+61 3) 92 68 60 00    Fax:(+61 3) 92 68 60 30
e-mail: ron.davison@fluordaniel.com
Web: http://www.fluordaniel.com

**Key personnel**
Vice President, International Maintenance: Byrd Isom
Managing Director: Trevor Stafford
General Manager, Diversified Plant Services: Greg Hocking
Manager, Rail Business: Ron Davison

Rail Operations Manager: Bruce McComas
Senior Manager, Railway Engineering: David O'Grady
Senior Manager, Technical Support: Norm Prince
Manager, Business Development: Bruce Crossley

**Capabilities**
Asset management; track infrastructure maintenance and construction, signals, communications and overhead traction maintenance; design and engineering consultants, simulation services, project development and management.

**Projects**
Ongoing work for Hamersley Iron (Western Australia) since 1968, involving asset management, condition monitoring, maintenance planning, routine and defect maintenance; capital projects. Maintenance of standard gauge railway, including routine caretaker maintenance, cyclic maintenance, asset rehabilitation, upgrading and construction where required and materials purchasing and control. Contractor for routine maintenance, capital works and total asset management on Waterfall-Bomaderry Line railway infrastructure in NSW since July 1997. Routine and periodic maintenance, capital works and total asset management on Rail Access corporation East Hills Line (NSW) since May 1998.

---

### Fluor Global Services Consulting

Newnhams, West Street, Farnham, Surrey GU9 7EQ, UK
Tel: (+44 1252) 74 17 00    Fax: (+44 1252) 73 51 55
e-mail: enquiries@fluorGS.co.uk

**Key personnel**
Market Director: David Angove
Lead Consultant: John Taylor
Principal Consultant: Cathy Hunsley

**Background**
Advantage Business Group was formed in 2001 by the management buy-out from Fluor Corporation of its consulting and information technology elements in transport, defence, energy and manufacturing sectors.

**Capabilities**
Strategic business planning, organisational alignment and development, business process engineering, programme management, information technology and electronic-business, change management, risk management, technical/engineering support, safety management, spares/stockholding optimisation, reliability centred maintenance, business modelling with operational simulations.

---

### FM Design Ltd

1a Lonsdale Square, London N1 1EN, UK
Tel: (+44 20) 77 00 33 33    Fax: (+44 20) 77 00 05 97
e-mail: design@fmgroup.co.uk
Web: http://www.fmdesign.co.uk

**Key personnel**
Directors: Ben Fether, Richard Miles

**Capabilities**
FM undertakes projects from market analysis through concept generation to detailed design development utilising its own CAD systems, model-making and prototyping capabilities to specification and tender documentation. The consultancy works, where appropriate, in collaboration with operators' and/or manufacturers' in-house teams.

---

### Frazer-Nash Consultancy Ltd

Stonebridge House, Dorking Business Park, Dorking RH4 1HJ, UK
Tel: (+44 1306) 88 50 50    Fax: (+44 1306) 88 64 64
e-mail: info@fnc.co.uk
Web: http://www.fnc.co.uk

**Key personnel**
Managing Director: A G Milton
Engineering Director: W T Chester

Business and Information Systems Director: Dr C C H Guyott
Projects Director: P J Best
Financial and Commercial Director: R R Burge
Operations Director: Chris Edwards
Business Manager, Rail: Andy Thompson

**Other offices**
Bristol and Burton on Trent (Midlands)

**Capabilities**
Frazer-Nash Consultancy provides a range of services to the rail industry in the UK and worldwide for the design and assessment of rolling stock structures, equipment and assemblies. Its principal areas of activity are project management services, bodyshell, bogie and underframe equipment design, crashworthiness, noise and vibration, safety reliability and maintainability, integrated logistics support. The company is active in other sectors, enabling leading edge technologies and analytical techniques to be brought to rail projects.

**Projects**
Recent contracts include: design and procurement support to development of rail points machinery; noise consultancy Heathrow Express; expert witness/technical support for litigation on emu brakes, cab, doors and bogies; design and installation of brakes for purpose built test equipment; design of engine and transmission underframe raft for dmu; predictive fire performance analysis for Pendolino vehicles; commercial assistance refurbishment project; gearbox dynamic analysis; brake rig instrumentation; transtop gauging accuracy; emu solebar burn through analysis; drivetrain analysis.
  Support to HM Railways Inspectorate, UK into the effects of low-speed buffer-stop collision at Cannon Street station, London; crashworthiness design of European Nightstock for the former GEC Alsthom Metro Cammell Ltd; safety case development for luggage stowage for European Passenger Services; concept development and assessment to support the procurement specification for London CrossRail project; design support to Thorn Transit Systems International on the thermal performance of automated ticket machines in hostile environments; crashworthiness design and noise consultancy to CAF for the Heathrow Express emu; structural assessment of the refurbished KCRC rolling stock for the former GEC Alsthom Metro Cammell Ltd; infrastructure assessment for MTRC and escalator risk assessment work for London Underground; design of traction and auxiliary equipment rafts and dynamic gauging of train stops.

*UPDATED*

---

### GHD-Transmark Pty Ltd

A joint venture company formed between Gutteridge Haskins & Davey Pty Ltd and Halcrow Transmark
39 Regent Street, Railway Square, New South Wales 2008, Australia
PO Box K839, Haymarket, New South Wales 1238, Australia
Tel: (+61 2) 96 90 70 37    Fax: (+61 2) 96 90 14 64
e-mail: transmarksyd@ghd.com.au

**Projects**
Illawarra electrification: State Rail Authority of New South Wales (value A$200 million).
East Hills-Cambelltown railway link: State Rail Authority of New South Wales (value A$80 million).
Implementation of train radio system: State Rail Authority of New South Wales (value A$80 million).
Automatic train fare collection: State Rail Authority of New South Wales.
VFT Sydney access studies: VFT Consortium.
Ultimo Pyrmont Light Rail Project (value A$100 million)
Bondi Rail Link (ongoing, value A$100 million) New Southern Railway.

---

### GIBBRail Ltd

Gibb House, London Road, Reading RG6 1BL, UK
Tel: (+44 118) 963 50 00    Fax: (+44 118) 949 10 54
e-mail: gibbrail@gibb.co.uk
Web: http://www.gibbltd.com

**Key personnel**
Managing Director, Transportation: Tony King
Director, Rail: Andy Collinson
Director, Transport Consulting: Nigel Ash
Technical Director, International: Brian Green
Technical Director, UK: Paul Dawkins

**Offices**
Reading (UK headquarters), Glasgow, York, Derby, Birmingham, London

**Overseas offices**
Belgium, Botswana, Bulgaria, Ethiopia, Ghana, Greece, Hong Kong, Hungary, Indonesia, Japan, Jordan, Kenya, Lebanon, Lesotho, Malawi, Mauritius, Oman, Poland, Portugal, Romania, Russian Federation, South Africa, Spain, Sudan, Swaziland, Tanzania, Turkey, UAE, Georgia USA, Uganda, Zambia, Zimbabwe.

**Background**
GIBBRail is part of GIBB Ltd (formerly Sir Alexander Gibb & Partners Ltd) and is a specialist team within the LAWGIBB Group. The group includes professional railway system engineers and technical staff experienced in planning, operating engineering, development, procurement, construction and maintenance of high-speed, main line, metro and light rail projects for organisations in the UK and overseas. In-house capability includes project management; civil, structural, mechanical and electrical engineering; architecture; environmental and economic studies; topographical and geological surveys.

**Projects**
GIBBRail can undertake complex and routine maintenance inspections, multidisciplinary detailed designs typified by the remodelling of main line stations in Poland, Leeds station, UK, and the tram project in Croydon, UK. The company has carried out rehabilitation projects in Estonia and Latvia and detailed designs for 12 km of underground alignment, 20 km of tunnelling and 13 underground stations for Line 3 of the Rome metro. Other contracts include: independent engineer at Porto metro, Portugal; works supervision, advisers on EIB contract procedures at Latvia East-West Rail Corridor renewals; engineer for construction work on new rail connection to Ventspils Port Rail Terminal, Latvia; project management and delivery of track renewals at London Underground corporate track alliance project; full multidisciplinary design at Leeds Station remodelling, UK; consultancy services for tunnel under railway at Dublin Port Rail Tunnel, Ireland; engineer for supervision of contracting at St Petersburg Transportation and Commercial Centre, Russian Federation; detailed design at Croydon Tramlink, UK; government technical adviser for the Channel Tunnel Rail Link, UK; feasibility and studies, detailed design on network development for Railtrack IOS, UK; civil engineering and plant engineering design work at Rome Metro Line C, Italy; strategic planning on the West Coast Mainline route modernisation, UK; project management of safety programme for Iarnród Eireann (Irish Railways), Ireland; system design on Thameslink 2000, UK; route modernisation feasibility study on East Coast Mainline, UK.

---

## Gotch Consultancy

21 Alleyn Road, London SE21 8AB, UK
Tel: (+44 20) 87 66 79 99   Fax: (+44 20) 87 66 79 99
e-mail: jeremy@gotchconsultancy.freeserve.co.uk

**Key personnel**
Principal Transport Consultant: Jeremy Gotch

**UPDATED**

---

## GRA Incorporated

115 West Avenue, Suite 201, Jenkintown, Pennsylvania 19046, USA
Tel: (+1 215) 884 75 00   Fax: (+1 215) 884 13 85
e-mail: gramail@gra-inc.com
Web: http://www.gra-inc.com

**Key personnel**
President: Frank Berardino
Executive Vice-Presidents: Richard Golaszewski, John J Grocki, Chris A Frankel
Associates: W Bruce Allen, Geoffrey Zeh

**Capabilities**
Rail economics including: rates and pricing, costing, cost allocation and financial analysis; special studies of operations and maintenance, including short line operations; privatisation; asset valuation, disposition, rehabilitation and financing analysis; traffic analysis; reorganisation planning and economics; high-speed rail feasibility studies; rail economic impact studies, due diligence analysis for mergers and acquisitions.

**Projects**
Include preparation of expert witness testimony before Surface Transportation Board in Conrail-CSX-Norfolk Southern merger proceedings and in Union Pacific-Southern Pacific merger proceedings; financial analysis of a railway acquisition; several valuation studies of transportation assets; analysis of worldwide rail market for new products; economic analysis and feasibility study of various operating scenarios for a rail passenger line; study of freight wagon hire charges; short line railroad operations studies.

**VERIFIED**

---

## HaCon Ingenieurgesellschaft mbH

Königstrasse 53, D-30175 Hannover, Germany
Tel: (+49 511) 33 69 90   Fax: (+49 511) 336 99 99
e-mail: info@hacon.de
Web: http://www.hacon.de

**Capabilities**
HAFAS program system: timetable information on local intercity and air traffic routes and connections; UX-SIMU program system: interactive timetable planning and simulation; RASIM program system: simulation of marshalling operations and Radis program system: online information and scheduling management system.

---

## Halcrow Group Ltd

Vineyard House, 44 Brook Green, Hammersmith, London W6 7BY, UK
Tel: (+44 20) 89 70 18 01   Fax: (+44 20) 89 70 18 11
e-mail: rail@halcrow.com
Web: http://www.halcrow.com

**Key personnel**
Chief Executive: David W Miller
Resources Director: Alan Runacres
Commercial Director: David Watters
Development Director: Mark Brown

**Background**
The principal businesses of the Halcrow Group include:
Halcrow Fox
Contact: Peter Daly
Halcrow Rail
Contact: David AB Walters

International site offices and local representation in Antigua, Argentina, Australia, Austria, Bahamas, Bangladesh, Belarus, Belgium, Belize, Bolivia, Bulgaria, Chile, China, Colombia, Costa Rica, Czech Republic, Denmark, Dominican Republic, Egypt, Eire, Eritrea, Ethiopia, Germany, Greece, Ghana, Guyana, Hong Kong, Hungary, India, Indonesia, Iran, Italy, Jamaica, Korea, Latvia, Lesotho, Lithuania, Malaysia, Moldova, Morocco, Nepal, Netherlands, NIS, Pakistan, Paraguay, Philippines, Poland, Portugal, Qatar, Romania, Russia, Slovak Republic, Slovenia, South Africa, Sri Lanka, St Lucia, Sweden, Syria, Tanzania, Thailand, Trinidad, Tunisia, Turkey, Ukraine, United Arab Emirates, USA, Uzbekistan, Venezuela, Vietnam, West Indies, Yemen.

---

**BEFORE CONSULTING QR FOR A RAIL TRANSPORT SOLUTION, TALK TO ONE OF OUR CLIENTS**

QR has participated in innovative rail solutions in over 25 countries. From complicated signaling problems to the design and management of large construction projects - and everything in between - our team has skillfully completed projects in every aspect of rail transport on time, within budget, and in just about every language. So, whatever your rail transport needs, talk to the team at QR.

QR Consulting Services
GPO Box 1429 Brisbane Qld 4001
Ph +61 7 3235 3390
Fax +61 7 3235 3346
Email: qrcs@qr.com.au

**QR CONSULTING SERVICES**

# CONSULTANCY SERVICES

*Halcrow is involved in the Jubilee Line Extension, London* 0021899

**Principal subsidiaries**
Halcrow Business Solutions
Halcrow Crouch
Halcrow Fox
Halcrow Gilbert
Halcrow Management Sciences
Halcrow Maritime
Halcrow Transportation Infrastructure
Halcrow UK
Halcrow Walter
Halcrow Waterman

**Capabilities**
Professional consultancy, covering all aspects of railway planning, operations, maintenance, design and engineering.
Halcrow Fox offers transportation, development and environmental planning and economics/evaluation.
Halcrow Rail offers consultancy in railway infrastructure, design engineering and services.

**Projects**
Current railway schemes include:
Channel Tunnel Rail Link, UK: engineering, planning and design, procurement, construction supervision, commissioning and testing of CTRL. Founder member of London & Continental Railways.
Recent contracts include: *Railtrack*: 27 structures examination (April 1997–March 2001); examination of 7,000 bridges, tunnels, viaducts, retaining walls, coastal defences and gantries, and 12 km Merseyrail underground system.
Spoornet railway division of Transnet, Republic of South Africa: profitability and performance review of its general freight business.

## Hanson-Wilson Inc

3100 Broadway Suite 900, Kansas City, Missouri 64111, USA
Tel: (+1 816) 561 90 54  Fax: (+1 816) 561 06 54

**Key personnel**
President: James G Gibbs
Vice-President: Gary J Potts

**Capabilities**
Complete railroad services – design, design/build and construction management for freight railways, light rail and commuter rail providers. Includes: intermodal, automotive transfer, and fuelling facilities; capacity improvement programmes; track design, evaluation and inspection; bridge design, evaluation and inspection; environmental/waste management; survey, mapping and photogrammetry; and catenary design.

## Harry Weese Associates

10 W Hubbard Street, Chicago, Illinois 60610, USA
Tel: (+1 312) 467 70 30  Fax: (+1 312) 467 70 51
e-mail: j.torvik@hwachicago.com

**Key personnel**
President: James A Torvik

**Projects**
Washington metro: general architectural consultant for 160 km, 86-station system.

Metra Passenger Terminal, Chicago: 10-year rehabilitation programme in progress, including the replacement of platforms and canopies, lighting, trackwork and mechanical systems and the repair of two classical brick façades.
Main Street station, Richmond, Virginia: three-phase project to design a modern intermodal transportation centre.
Union Station, Worcester, Massachusetts: restoration of this abandoned historic downtown railway station includes commuter rail and bus service, structured parking, travel support facilities and restaurants.
Hamilton Station, Hamilton, New Jersey: design of multi-modal transit station.
Largo and Summerfield Stations, Maryland: two-station extension of the Washington metro's Blue Line.
Potomac Yard, Alexandria, Virginia: planning and design services for the first privately funded station on the Washington metro.

## Hatch Mott MacDonald Inc

6140 Stoneridge Mall Road, Suite 250, Pleasanton, California 94588, USA
Tel: (+1 925) 469 80 10  Fax: (+1 925) 469 80 11
e-mail: corporate@hatchmott.com
Web: http://www.hatchmott.com

**Key personnel**
President and Chief Executive Officer: Gordon A Smith
Director and COO: David P White
Directors: Jan J Feberwee, Peter Wickens, Ronald R Nolan, Timothy J Thirlwell
Secretary and Treasurer: Eric R Hartley

**Canada office**
2955 Speakman Drive, Sheridan Science & Technology Park, Mississauga, Ontario, L5K 1B1
Tel: (+1 905) 855 20 10  Fax: (+1 905) 855 26 07

**Capabilities**
Engineering consulting services, project and construction management and planning and architectural services for rail and transit systems. Services include: planning, route selection and environmental assessment; civil engineering, including alignment, trackwork, structures, bridges and elevated guideways; tunnels in soft ground or rock, including planning, architecture and safety; building services; systems engineering including signalling, telecommunications, traction power and distribution, tunnel ventilation; programme and project management; and construction management.

**Projects**
Recent and current projects include: programme management services for Toronto Transit Commission's Rapid Transit Expansion Programme; design, project management and construction management for CN North America's St Clair River Tunnel between Sarnia, Canada and Port Huron, USA; construction management services for the construction of the Denver LRT system; application engineering services for the installation of an enhanced speed enforcement system at priority locations systemwide for New York City Transit Authority; detailed design of Ocean Parkway interlocking as part of the Brighton Beach Line resignalling programme for New York City Transit Authority; construction management services for the traction power system for the Montréal-Deux Montagnes route modernisation; and consulting and oversight services to Santa Clara County Transportation Agency on the design of trackwork, signals and telecommunications for the 12 mile Tasman Corridor LRT extension.

## HDR Engineering Inc

1101 King Street, Suite 400, Alexandria, Virginia 22314, USA
Tel: (+1 703) 518 86 65  Fax: (+1 703) 518 85 78
e-mail: tsmithbe@hdrinc.com
Web: http://www.hdrinc.com

**Key personnel**
Senior Vice-President & National Director, Rail:
  Tom Smithberger, PE

**Capabilities**
Railway structures design and inspection; trackwork design and inspection; construction administration services; metro (line and station) designs; terminal and transfer facilities design; light rail and peoplemover design; and environmental and security work.

**Projects**
Continuing projects with all North American Class I railroads, Amtrak and various commuter rail and transit agencies.

*UPDATED*

## High-Point Rendel Ltd

61 Southwark Street, London SE1 1SA, UK
Tel: (+44 20) 79 28 89 99  Fax: (+44 20) 79 28 55 66

**Key personnel**
Chief Executive: I W Reeves
Head of Road and Rail Infrastructure: J Falconer
Chief Operating Officer: K W T Hingley
Finance Director: S H Greenwood
Group Strategy and Business Development Director: N Ogunshakin

**Overseas offices**
Bangladesh, Canada, Hong Kong, Indonesia, Libya, Malaysia, Singapore, Turkey, United Arab Emirates, USA

**Capabilities**
High-Point Rendel has experience of railway planning, design and maintenance of metros and LRT systems. Main areas of activity include: feasibility, economic and investment studies; survey, design and construction supervision for freight and urban railways; reconstruction, development and rehabilitation of railway infrastructure; and modernisation programmes for motive power, rolling stock and other equipment. Rendel Palmer & Tritton has also had a broad range of experience in the design and equipping of container and freight terminals; the design and development of loading and unloading installations for bulk transport; and in the development of railway containerisation and rail/port links.

## Hill International Inc

1 Levitt Parkway, Willingboro, New Jersey 08046 USA
Tel: (+1 609) 871 58 00  Fax: (+1 609) 871 12 61
Web: http://www.hillintl.com

**Key personnel**
Chairman: Irvin E Richter

**Capabilities**
Engineering consultancy; project and construction management; project management supervision; construction claims analysis; expert witness testimony; claims prevention and dispute resolution.

**Projects**
Projects include: Istanbul LRT line, Turkey; Frankford Elevated reconstruction, Norristown Line reconstruction and RRD main line improvement programme, Philadelphia, USA; Los Angeles Metro Rail, USA; Tren Urbano rapid transit study, San Juan, Puerto Rico; Kearny rail connection, Kearny, USA; and Long Island Rail Road Richmond Hill improvements, Queens, USA.

## Hodgson and Hodgson

Hodgson and Hodgson Group Ltd
Winnington Hall Mews, Northwich CW8 4DU, UK
Tel: (+44 1606) 765 93  Fax: (+44 1606) 743 15
e-mail: efitzpatrick.hodgsongroup.co.uk

**Key personnel**
Chairman: G Balshaw-Jones
Managing Director: J Roberts
Technical Director: N Grundy
Commercial Director: P Rollinson
Export Sales Manager: E Fitzpatrick
Acoustic Manager: P Eade

## CONSULTANCY SERVICES

**Services**

Acoustic consultancy services for bus and railway traction units, rolling stock and associated buildings.

Recent projects have included Waterloo Eurostar Terminal (buildings), St Petersburg Rail Terminal (buildings), Barratt Housing Project (railside development), Eurotram (complete vehicle), Europa Transrapid (complete vehicle), MTRC Hong Kong (complete vehicle), Arlanda, Stockholm (complete vehicle), Juniper, Turbostar and Electrostar and West Coast Main Line (rolling stock), Brush Engines (traction units), First Bus, Mellor Vancraft, Optare and Marshalls (engine/exhaust jacketing and moulded internal and external lining panels).

*UPDATED*

## Holland Railconsult

Daalseplein 101, NL-3500 GW Utrecht, Netherlands
Tel: (+31 30) 265 42 20   Fax: (+31 30) 265 42 21
e-mail: information@hr.nl
Web: http://www.hr.nl

**Key personnel**

Executive Board Members: Gerrit Disberg; Wim Jol; Jan Moerkerk
Divisional Directors:
  Infrastructure: George Brouwer
  Urban Interchanges: Jan Garvelink
  Major Projects: Peter Otten
  International Consultancy: Rob Brugts

**Overseas offices**

Richard Wagnerstrasse, D-38106, Braunschweig, Germany
Tel: (+49 531) 380 23 95   Fax: (+49 531) 380 23 96

Apartado 239, P-2750 Cascais, Portugal
Tel: (+351 214) 86 98 16   Fax: (+351 214) 86 98 37

Railconsult Éireann & Partners
Arena House, Arena Road, Sandyford, Dublin 8, Ireland
Tel: (+353 1) 294 08 00   Fax: (+353 1) 294 08 20

**Capabilities**

The company is an engineering consultancy specialising in public transport and rail infrastructure, the design and engineering of guided transport systems including interchanges from feasibility studies, to planning, design and execution. The company employs 1,700 staff. Recently, the company signed an agreement to collaborate with Brown & Root Services (a Halliburton Company) aiming to improve their technical capabilities and project management skills in the railway industry.

**Projects**

Include European Railway Traffic Management Systems; Brussels 1997-2002; Xabregas Bridge in Portugal, 1998; pre-design of Trolihättan double track lift bridge in Sweden, 1998; maintenance and renewal assessments of Railtrack, UK, 1998-1999; design of Ranstad light rail system including integration of the Hague Central Station in the Netherlands, 1998; environmental impact study of Betuwe high-capacity cargo railway link from Rotterdam harbour to the German border and Kijfhoek Marshalling Yard including 25kV power supply and design and contract mangement of catenary system, in the Netherlands, 1997-98.

## HTM-Infra

PO Box 28503, NL-2502 KM The Hague, Netherlands
Tel: (+31 70) 384 84 30
e-mail: infra@htm.net
Web: http://www.htm.nl

**Capabilities**

HTM-Infra designs, builds and maintains the tracks for tramways and light rail systems. It also works for other organisations such as transport companies and city operators, both in the Netherlands and abroad.

## Hyder Consulting

2-3 Cornwall Terrace, Regents Park, London NW1 4QP, UK
Tel: (+44 20) 75 44 66 00   Fax: (+44 20) 74 70 00 19

**Key personnel**

Director Rail, UK: David Potter
Marketing Manager: Gwyn Evans

**Other offices**

Aston Cross Bus Village, 50 Rocky Lane, Aston, Birmingham B6 5RO, UK
Tel: (+44 121) 333 44 66   Fax: (+44 121) 333 42 75
Principal Engineer, Bridges and Rail: Nigel Moore
Principal Consultant, Rail: Jeremy Thorne
70 Redcliff Street, Bristol BS1 6AL, UK
Tel: (+44 117) 988 18 81   Fax: (+44 117) 988 16 61
Signalling Group Manager: Ed Gerrard
The Surrey Research Park, Guildord, GU2 5AR, UK
Tel: (+44 1483) 53 50 00   Fax: (+44 1483) 53 50 51
Director Transport Planning: John Mussett
The Genesis Centre, Science Park South, Birchwood, Warrington, WA3 7BH, UK
Tel: (+44 1925) 83 02 06   Fax: (+44 1925) 83 02 07
Rail Group Manager: Mahmoud Alghito

**Capabilities**

Consultancy in civil engineering, signalling systems, infrastructure design, operations and commercial/business strategic management. Areas of activity include mainline regional and suburban railway services, metros and urban transit systems including light rail and people movers; heavy-haul freight, general merchandise, utilised loads, bimodal and intermodal technologies.

**Projects**

Typical rail projects completed or in hand are:
UK GNER, East Coast Main Line upgrade review. Edinburgh Cross – rail feasibility.
Chiltern Railways, infrastructure upgrade feasibility.
Railtrack Midlands – structure design.
Railtrack North West, station improvements. Great Western – signalling design. West Coast Mainline – upgrade geotechnics study. Stratford Station Redevelopment (Western and Eastern Concourse) – structural and services design for new station concourse.
Istanbul metro, Turkey: electrical and mechanical systems design: supervision of implementation: commissioning and acceptance.
Thailand SRT Freight railway proposal: Feasibility study.
LAR Lai King Station, Hong Kong: detailed design of all E&M services and civil and structural aspects for the Lai King station, which is the interchange station of the Tsuen Wan line and Lantau Airport line.
Ankara LRT, Turkey: supervision of supply and installation of rolling stock, E&M subsystems, commissioning and acceptance.
Kuala Lumpur LRT system, Malaysia: checking engineer for the contracting consortium on Line 1, Stage 2.
New Southern Railway, Sydney, Australia: comprehensive review of technical aspects including contractual construction and environmental issues and tunnelling concepts.
Krakow, Poland: project appraisal of the financing and technology option.

## IBIS Transport Consultants Ltd

12 High Street, Chalfont St Giles, Bedfordshire HP8 4QA, UK
Tel: (+44 1494) 87 60 58   Fax: (+44 1494) 87 56 29

**Key personnel**

Managing Director: I M D Barrett

**Capabilities**

Provides consultancy, project and contract management services for public transport to aid agencies, government organisations and planning authorities. Its specialists can offer advice on strategic development and institutional reform, as well as practical technical and managerial assistance and training in all aspects of bus operations. Investment appraisal, and business restructuring and valuation are also covered.

**Projects**

Ireland and Romania: medium-term passenger transport strategy and investment priorities. Bangladesh and Pakistan: feasibility studies for private-sector bus investment. South Africa, Tanzania and Ghana: bus company restructuring and valuation for privatisation. Kyrgystan, Uzbekistan and Mongolia: operations and maintenance analysis of public-sector undertakings, and action plans for commercialisation.

Work has also been undertaken in the passenger transport sector in Barbados, Fiji, Hong Kong, Jamaica, Kenya, Latvia, Malawi, Nigeria, Palestine, Saudi Arabia, Sri Lanka, Uganda, Vietnam, Zimbabwe and the UK.

## IBM Global Travel & Transportation Industry Solutions

South Bank, 76 Upper Ground, London SE1 9PZ, UK
Tel: (+44 20) 72 02 37 44   Fax: (+ 44 20) 72 02 37 92; 93
e-mail: whitaker@uk.ibm.com

**Key personnel**

Global Marketing Executive: Michael O Hulley

**Capabilities**

The unit provides a range of travel services including rail freight logistics.

## ICB

Ingenieur-Consult Verkehrstechnik GmbH
Rudower Chaussee 4, Haus 8, D-12489 Berlin, Germany
Tel: (+49 30) 670 59 90   Fax: (+49 30) 67 05 99 11
e-mail: icb-gmbh.berlin@t-online.de

**Key personnel**

Managers: Dipl Ing Rainer Patzig, Dipl Ing Thomas Just
Ingenieur-Consult fur Bahn und Verkehrstechnik Hamburg GmbH
Teilfeld 5, D-20459 Hamburg
Tel: (+49 40) 374 93 40   Fax: (+49 40) 374 26 23

**Capabilities**

Railway and transport engineering including planning and implementation of railway projects; taking over building supervision from railway organisations; tender preparation; traffic development planning; project co-ordination.

## ICF Consulting

9300 Lee Highway, Fairfax, Virginia 22031, USA
Tel: (+1 703) 934 30 00   Fax: (+1 703) 934 37 40
e-mail: mpeterson@icfconsulting.com

**Key personnel**

President and Chief Executive Officer: Sudhakar Kesavan
Executive Vice-President: Michael Gaffney
Senior Vice-President, Transit: John Bergerson

**Capabilities**

Specialists in addressing issues regarding transport, energy, economic development; also environmental issues such as environmental assessments, oil and gas transport, air quality analysis and the transportation of hazardous materials. Global transport planning services focus on the relationship between transport, land use, energy consumption and sustainable development.

**Projects**

Seattle LRT (Programme management); Manila LRT (design-build); Miami Intermodal Centre (design management, construction management); Bangalore LRT (project management, design management, systems integration); freight railway, Portugal (project management, engineering, construction management); Boston Southwest Corridor freight/passenger line (preliminary engineering, final design, services during construction); Taipei metro (general consultant, technology transfer); Chicago Southwest Corridor (co-ordinating consultant, new rail link to Midway Airport); Park Avenue tunnel rehabilitation, New York (construction management); Jubilee Line Extension, London (electrical and mechanical design); Chicago Circulator (light rail programme management); Los Angeles metro and LRT (programme management and design); Baltimore metro (programme management; design, construction management); Dade County (Miami) Metrorail (programme management, design, construction management); Jacksonville Automated Guideway Express (people mover programme management, design and construction management).

*UPDATED*

## Infra Safety Services

PO Box 1075, NL-3300 BB Dordrecht, Netherlands
Tel: (+31 78) 654 06 55   Fax: (+31 78) 651 44 21

**Key personnel**
Director: C J de Graaff
General Manager: J F A M Weijtmans

**Capabilities**
Infra Safety Services provides a total package for securing the work area. The company draws up and executes safety plans, and develops high-standard systems such as ARW 5/2 and Minimel 90 or PWA.

## Interconsult AS

Grenseveien 90, PO Box 6412 Etterstad, N-0605 Oslo, Norway
Tel: (+47) 22 63 59 00   Fax: (+47) 22 63 59 90

**Key personnel**
Group Managing Director: Thorleif Eriksen
Head of Transport Branch: Ingvar Karlsson
Head of Railway Department: Karstein Søreide
Managing Director, Interconsult International AS:
  Ole K Paulsen

**Principal subsidiary**
Interconsult International AS

**Capabilities**
Planning consultancy services within civil works, tracks, power supply including overhead lines, signalling systems and telecommunications for railway operators.

## Interfleet Technology Ltd

Interfleet House, Pride Parkway, Derby DE24 8HX, UK
Tel: (+44 1332) 22 33 30   Fax: (+44 1332) 22 33 31
e-mail: info@interfleet.co.uk
Web: http://www.interfleet.co.uk

**Key personnel**
Managing Director: David Rollin
International Projects: Jonathan Wragg
Sales & Marketing Director: Peter Dudley
Operations Director: Neil Wilson
Development Director: David Curtis
Finance Director: Richard Tapping
Account Managers: Stephen Pritchard, John Kelly, Nigel Davies, Glen Mackenzie, Rob Armstrong, Chris Baker, Frank Alcock, John O'Flynn, James Rollin, Matt Stimson

**Other offices**
3 Millharbour, London E14 9XP, UK
Tel: (+44 20) 79 87 48 20
Interfleet Technology Pty Ltd
Level 8, 99 York Street, Sydney, New South Wales 2000, Australia
Tel: (+61 2) 92 62 60 11   Fax: (+61 2) 92 62 60 77
e-mail: michaelgrace@interfleet.aust.com
Principal Consultant: Michael Grace

Interfleet Technology SE Asia
Level 40, Tower 2, Petronas Twin Towers, KLCC, Kuala Lumpur, Malaysia
Tel: (+60 3) 21 68 44 06

Interfleet Technology Inc
17761 I Street NW, Washington DC 20006, USA
Tel: (+1 202) 756 47 82
Business Development Manager: Ernie Aftinson

**Capabilities**
Rolling stock consultancy providing independent strategic/technical advice and innovative design and engineering solutions to the international rail industry for 30 years. Capabilities encompass business/change management, engineering consultancy, turnkey project management services and technical support.

**Projects**
UK: the client base encompasses train operators, rolling stock leasing companies, manufacturers, equipment suppliers and infrastructure companies. Interfleet Technology also works closely with the strategic government rail authorities, and is currently retained by the Office of Passenger Rail Franchising (OPRAF) as rolling stock adviser. Other notable projects include supporting Sea Containers Group with tilting train procurement, procurement advice for Connex Rail and project management support for National Express Group. International: projects have included consultancy work for CAF in Spain, Eurotunnel in France, Fiat in Italy, SIG in Switzerland and Union Carriage & Wagon in South Africa. Interfleet Technology has opened an office in Sydney, Australia.

## Intermetric GmbH

Industriestrasse 24, D-70565 Stuttgart, Germany
Tel: (+49 711) 780 03 92   Fax: (+49 711) 780 03 97

**Capabilities**
Track geometry design; surveying; plans; geotechnical measuring.

## International Rail Consultants

1045 Howe Street, Vancouver, British Columbia V6Z 2 A9 Canada.
Tel: (+1 604) 684 93 11
Fax: (+1 604) 688 59 13; 685 79 46
e-mail: IRC@sandwell.com

**Key personnel**
Director: M J C Leeper

**Capabilities**
International Rail Consultants (IRC) was established in 1985 as a joint venture to provide railway consulting services in tracks, bridges, buildings and terminals; operations, motive power and rolling stock; economics, financial and tariff analyses; marketing and cost analyses, training and technical assistance; and strategic planning and commercialisation to industries and governments worldwide. The joint venture has its headquarters in Vancouver, Canada, and can draw on the international transportation consulting experience of Sandwell Engineering Inc.

**Projects**
In 1999, International Rail and Sandwell were involved in projects in Argentina, Australia, Bangladesh, Brazil, Canada, Chile, China, Colombia, India, Indonesia, Peru, Philippines, Russia, Sri Lanka, Thailand, Uruguay, USA and Venezuela.

## International Technical Services

400 Queens Avenue, London, Ontario N6B 1X9, Canada
Tel: (+1 519) 439 23 62   Fax: (+1 519) 675 18 68
e-mail: info@ITSrail.com
Web: http://www.ITSrail.com

**Key personnel**
President: William Graves
Director of Operations: Rick Girvin

**Capabilities**
Railway consulting services; project management and supervision; technical and management training; technical publications; fleet and facilities evaluation; operator/driver training; crane operator training; production planning; procurement planning; needs assessment/analysis; facilities management.
  EMD locomotive specialists; EMD engine rebuild; locomotives and freight vehicle maintenance; air brake systems specialists; locomotive rebuilding and repowering; welding services (engine repair).

*NEW ENTRY*

## Intraplan Consult GmbH

Orleansplatz 5a, D-81667 Munich, Germany
Tel: (+49 89) 45 91 10   Fax: (+49 89) 447 05 93
e-mail: info@intraplan.de

**Key personnel**
Managing Directors: Dipl Ing Hans Ulrich Mann,
  Dipl Ing Utz Senger
Directors: Dipl Ing Reinhard Mück, Dr Markus Schubert

**Capabilities**
Consultancy in local and long-distance transport; models for demand forecasting, demand simulation, operations simulation, evaluation studies, cost and revenue allocation; demand and revenue allocation systems; and software engineering services.

**Projects**
Interplan supply planning model for high-speed rail, used by DB AG since 1997. Consultancy for transport undertakings, government departments, and private investors in Germany and other countries.

## IP-Solutions

Leidseveer 35, Utrecht, Netherlands
PO box 2025, NL-3500 HA Utrecht, Netherlands
Tel: (+31 30) 235 54 62   Fax: (+31 30) 235 63 19
e-mail: ipsol@ns.nl

**Key personnel**
CEO NS Materieel: Ing Tjibbe Stelwagen
Director IP-Solutions: Ing Joost de Graaf
Account Manager/Senior Consultant: Ing Jan Eise de Vries
IP-Solutions is a subsidiary of NS Materieel (rolling stock division of the Netherland Railways)

**Capabilities**
IP-Solutions employs 20 people, working as consultants in the field of design and improvement of facilities for maintenance of rolling stock, focused on increasing availability and decreasing costs for customers in the Netherlands and several other countries including Germany, Israel and Norway.

**Projects**
Masterplan to decrease costs of train washing in the Netherlands; plan to improve competitiveness of freight workshops by decreasing the plant and speeding up the overhaul processes; plan to increase flexibility of maintenance centres and prepare them for light rail; plan and realisation of an overhaul workshop using air-skate technology for internal transport of coaches; evaluation of existing maintenance centres as an aspect of establishing new joint-ventures in the market of rolling stock maintenance.

## Italferr SpA

Via Marsala 53, I-00185 Rome, Italy
Tel: (+39 06) 497 51   Fax: (+39 06) 49 75 24 37
e-mail: itf.com@italferr.it
Web: http://www.italferr.it

**Key personnel**
Chairman and Managing Director: Livio Vido
Vice-Chairman: Carlo Ianniello
General Technical Manager: Massimo Palliccia
General Operations Manager: Pier Ugo
Commercial and Marketing Director: Gaetano Piepoli

**Capabilities**
Italferr SpA is the consulting engineering company of the Italian Railways (FS) and was founded in 1984. Italian Railways is the majority shareholder with 93 per cent (€7.3 billion). Italferr has a turnover of €154 million and has continuing projects worth around €26 billion.
  The company's activities include traditional and high-speed rail as well as metro and non-rail transport systems and, in Italy, it carries out works on high-speed systems, lines and junctions, inter-regional links, alpine crossings, interconnections between main line and metropolitan areas, management and control, maintenance, station/railway freight villages as well as technological and development research for Italian Railways.

Other services include transport development plans; feasibility studies; conceptual design and system definition; environmental impact appraisal; design of mono and multimodal transport systems; preliminary and final design; cost estimates, technological specifications and tender documents; maintenance manuals/construction site safety plans; preparation and evaluation of tenders; project management; supervision of works, testing, inspection, start-up assistance; technical assistance and training; organisation and management studies; BOT and project financing assistance.

### Projects

Italferr is responsible for the development of the US$25 billion high-speed railway system linking Turin with Venice, Milan with Naples and Genoa. The 1,200 km railway system will be an integral part of the European high-speed railway network. The project includes revamping urban junctions in Turin, Milan, Genoa, Verona, Venice, Bologna, Florence, Rome and Naples to enable them to cater for the new high-speed traffic.

Technical assistance to SNCFR — Romanian Railways for management, technical and teacher training and for the reorganisation of existing training centres (1997-99); concession agreement and minimum safety works for the Chemins de fer Djibouto—Ethiopien (1999 to date); study on competitiveness of railway transport on the Casablanca—Rabat—Meknass—Fes axis in Morocco, conducted on behalf of the World Bank; feasibility study, preliminary design and technical assistance for Lima urban electric train service in Peru and technical feasibility study on the Asmara—Massawa railway line in Eritrea.

Other contracts in Italy include doubling the existing railway line between Anconaan Bari (1999 to date); new high-speed stations at Naples, Florence and Bologna (1998 to date); people mover transport system for the city of Monza (1999); preliminary project for light rail metro for Cagliari (1999); upgrading and technical development of the Bologna—Verona—Brennero railway line (1998-99); preliminary and detailed design and works supervision for metropolitan rail of Salerno (1999 to date); and a computer interlocking system for Rome Termini (1995-99).

Current contracts include consultancy services for the rehabilitation of the Matsapha to Phuzumouya and Mpaka to the Mozambique border railway lines (1999 to date); Uzbekistan railways modernisation project (1999 to date) – financed by ADB; feasibility study on the development of railways and combined transport on Corridor IV (1996-99); high-voltage booster 2 (2000); Ispa project preparation support, modernisation of signalling and safety devices on the railway line Divaca—Kopa (2000).

Technical assistance for training: to Ferrocar, Venezuela (1999); to EFE, Chilean railways/Ministerio de Obras Publicas y Telecommunicaciones (2000).

These projects have been carried out: study of the Ukraine section of the Trieste—Budapest—Kiev railway line; the Railway Track training project and the validation of studies for the construction of a test section on the new Moscow—St Petersburg high-speed line. European Railway Traffic Management System pilot installation on the E20 railway line; modernisation of the electric traction system on E20 Kunowice—Warsaw line.

## James Scott

Division of AMEC Mechanical & Electrical Services Ltd
80-110 Finnieston Street, Glasgow G3 8LA, UK
Tel: (+44 141) 221 38 66   Fax: (+44 141) 226 30 68
e-mail: sales@isl.amec.co.uk
Web: http://www.amec.co.uk

### Key personnel

Rail Business Manager: H MacEwan
Business Development: W Baird
Consulting Manager: M Scully
Branch Manager, Doncaster: C Brown
Business Development: D Atkinson

### Other offices

Birmingham, London and Doncaster

### Works address

Room 100, Dension House, PO Box 29 Doncaster DN1 1PD

### Capabilities

James Scott offers a comprehensive electrical, mechanical and instrumentation service to the UK Railway infrastructure, from initial feasibility study through to installation and project management. Principal areas of expertise encompass:

Track infrastructure equipment including points heating, standby signalling supplies, approval of on-track plant and machinery.

Station facilities, including lifts and escalators, lighting design, air conditioning systems.

Infrastructure engineering support, including asset condition surveys, technical support and assistance with standards and legislative requirements.

Heavy workshops and train servicing facilities, including carriage washing facilities, fuel and oil delivery and recovery systems; depot facilities.

### Projects

Include provision of improved stabling facilities on London Underground Northern Line, UK; transformer/rectifier renewals on Merseyrail, UK; various M & E design and installation packages on the Great Eastern resignalling scheme, UK; design and installation of points heating schemes, UK; swing bridge improvements, UK; refurbishment of funicular railway, UK; total renewal of electrical infrastructure on Blackpool Tramway, UK.

Current projects for Railtrack include a £15 million contract to design and install points heating, signalling generators, a control centre, plus signalling installation works and a £3 million design and survey lighting contract (1999-2003).

## Japan Railway Technical Service (JARTS)

Taiyokan Building, 27-8 Hongo 2-chome, Bunkyo-ku, Tokyo 113-0033, Japan
Tel: (+81 3) 56 84 31 71; 31 79
Fax: (+81 3) 56 84 31 70; 31 80
e-mail: jarts@pop02.odn.ne.jp

### Key personnel

President: Sadaaki Kuroda
Senior Executive Vice-President: Naofumi Takashige
Executive Vice-Presidents: Hisashi Koshimizu,
   Kiyoharu Takagi, Hisashi Sato, Takuji Sasaki

### Capabilities

Studies, surveys, design, planning specifications, preparation of contract documents, and project control and supervision of railway, metro, monorail and advanced guided transit; construction of new lines; modernisation and improvement of track; electrification; dieselisation; modernisation of rolling stock; restructuring of railway management.

*UPDATED*

## Jones Garrard Transport

Jones Garrard Ltd, 116 Regent Road, Leicester LE1 7LT, UK
Tel: (+44 116) 254 23 90   Fax: (+44 116) 255 66 58
e-mail: design@jones-garrard.co.uk

### Key personnel

Directors: Michael Rodber, Chris Harris
Director of Projects: Mike Muldoon
Director of Engineering: Dominic Newton

### Capabilities

Jones Garrard is a design consultancy specialising in the translation of design concepts into production. Skills include industrial design, design engineering, engineering analysis, systems integration, safety certification and project management.

### Projects

UK: emu interiors, front-end design, engineering and certification, dmu interiors; customers include Gatwick Express, South West Trains, Scotrail, First North Western, Virgin Rail (cab exterior engineering and interior design, engineering, certification and supply).

Europe: Eurostar; AVE; Stockholm Metro; Arlanda Airport Express.

Hong Kong: MTRC airport trains (TCL and AEL); emu modernisation; TKE consultancy; KCRC emu refurbishment and Kowloon-Guanzhou intercity through train.

## KAMPSAX International A/S

PO Box 1143, Stamholmen 112, DK-2650 Hvidovre, Copenhagen, Denmark
Tel: (+45) 36 39 07 00   Fax: (+45) 36 77 28 29
e-mail: international@kampsax.dk

### Key personnel

Managing Director: Allan Jørgensen
Deputy Managing Director: Søren Nysom
Chief Railway Engineer: Flemming Danielsen

### Subsidiary and associate companies

Denmark, China, Russia, India, Philippines, Poland

### Capabilities

Design and supervision, planning, maintenance and training activities.

## Lahmeyer International GmbH

Friedberger Strasse 173, D-61118 Bad Vilbel, Germany
Tel: (+49 6101) 55 18 11   Fax: (+49 6101) 55 15 20
Web: http://www.lif.de

### Key personnel

Manager Directors: Dr Henning Nothdurft (President),
   Rainer Bothe
Transportation Division: Peter Haaks, Joachim Neumann,
   Heinz Saxer

### Other offices

Berlin, Frankfurt, Munich, Stuttgart.

### Capability

The Lahmeyer International Group, with its 13 associated companies, is an independent engineering consultancy covering a spectrum of planning and consulting services in the fields of transportation, energy, hydropower and water resources, civil engineering and project management, technology and environmental sectors. The transportation division offers engineering services concerning transportation technology, railways and regional transport systems, tunnels and underground installations, bridges, roads, and motorways, airports and specialised transportation facilities. The range of consultancy services encompasses studies, design and planning, tendering, project management, supervision and commissioning for high-speed railways, line-upgrading, stations, marshalling yards, intermodal terminals, depots and workshops, integrated transportation systems, suburban fast trains and feeder systems, underground and metro systems, tramways and light rail systems as well as maglev systems. Lahmeyer International possesses expertise and experience in specialised areas such as Life-Cycle Costing (LCC) in relation to rail traffic through observations and analyses in the RAMS sector (reliability, availability, maintainability and safety). For privately financed projects (BOT, PPP) it offers advisory and consultancy services to prospective owners or bidding consortia.

### Projects

*Bosnia and Herzegovina:* Assistance for the Project Implementation Unit in terms of detailed design, specifications, tender documents, tender evaluation process, construction supervision, and project monitoring for the recovery of two main railway corridors.

*Jones Garrard has carried out projects for Eurostar*
0021900

## 834 CONSULTANCY SERVICES

*Croatia:* Upgrading and rehabilitation of the European Corridor Vc, which runs in the north-south direction through Croatia. The main task of Laymeyer International is to define the upgrading and rehabilitation program, to check the design made available by the Croatian Railways, to participate in the preparation of tender documentation and supervise the awarding of tenders as well as to supervise the construction.

*Central Asia:* Consulting services for feasibility study of new rail links between the Ferghana Valley, Bishkek and lines linking the Chinese rail network with the networks of Europe and Central Asian countries, crossing the Tien Shan and Pamir mountain ranges.

*Indonesia:* Preparation of a feasibility study for the improvement of urban transport in the Jabotabek (Jakarta, Bogor, Tangerang, Bekasi) in Indonesia comprising capacity and condition investigations of the existing Jabotabek rail system and proposing adequate measures to improve quality and performance of urban train operations and rolling stock maintenance including technical and financial viability and the implementation of a program for procurement.

*Germany:* Consultancy services for the new railway connection between the Airport Cologne—Bonn and the German High Speed Railway Line Cologne—Rhine-Main and the metro system of the Cologne/Bonn region. The alignment with a length of about 15 km includes two tunnels and 11 major civil structures. Lahmeyer International's services include the whole spectrum of engineering beginning with surveying and technical design, cost evaluation, design review, document control and ends with site supervision and excavation management.

*Korea:* Construction of a second high-speed railway link of 360 km length in South Korea between Seoul the capital and the south-western province of Honam. Lahmeyer International was commissioned to undertake a technical review and comment upon all existing documentation and in addition to supplement this with information from other projects when necessary.

*NEW ENTRY*

## Laramore, Douglass and Popham

332 South Michigan Ave, Suite 400, Chicago, Illinois 60604, USA
Tel: (+1 312) 427 84 86   Fax: (+1 312) 427 84 74
e-mail: postmaster@ldpgroup.com

**Key personnel**
President: Richard T Harvey
Vice-President: H Saxena

**Capabilities**
Design and project management for electrified rapid transit and electric railway traction power supply and distribution systems.

**Projects**
Recent contracts include Red and Brown Line rehabilitation for Chicago Transit Authority; Kenmore substation rehabilitation for Massachusetts Bay Transportation Authority; Fairgreen substation for Miami Valley Transit Authority.

*UPDATED*

## LEK Consulting LLP

Adelphi Building, 1-11 John Adam Street, London WC2N 6BW, UK
Tel: (+44 20) 79 30 12 44   Fax: (+44 20) 78 39 37 90

**Key personnel**
Directors: A H Allum; J I Goddard; P S Debenham
Principal: C Stokes

**Other offices**
Auckland, Bangkok, Beijing, Boston, Chicago, London, Los Angeles, Melbourne, Milan, Munich, Paris, San Francisco, Shanghai, Singapore, Sydney.

**Capabilities**
LEK is an international strategic consultancy and advises a broad range of transport-related clients worldwide. It has been active in public sector reform in the UK, Europe and Australia, and has advised passenger, freight, infrastructure and rolling stock organisations on key strategic and commercial issues. LEK has advised on a number of prominent European high-speed projects.

It offers advice in strategic and operational areas, including privatisation and commercialisation advice, competition policy, traffic and financial forecasting, mergers and acquisitions and impact assessments of new rail technologies.

*UPDATED*

## Lester B Knight & Associates Inc

549 W Randolph Street, Chicago, Illinois 60606, USA
Tel: (+1 312) 346 21 00   Fax: (+1 312) 648 10 85

**Key personnel**
Vice-Presidents: Dominick J Gatto, Lee A Hoyt

**Capabilities**
Transport and environmental studies; railroads and rapid transit systems planning, design and construction, engineering and management; operations and maintenance.

## Lloyd's Register MHA Ltd

Dukesbridge Chambers, 1 Duke Street, Reading, RG1 4JA, UK
Tel: (+44 118) 955 61 00   Fax: (+44 118) 955 61 01
e-mail: mha@lrmha.com
Web: http://www.lrmha.com

**Key personnel**
Managing Director: M J Hamlyn
Directors: P Cheeseman, G Christmas, R Clutton, P Thomas, C H Porter
Commercial Director: R Evans

**Offices**
Offices also in Derby, Glasgow, Leatherhead, Crewe, Hong Kong and Singapore.

**Corporate background**
Lloyd's Register MHA Ltd is a wholly owned subsidiary of Lloyd's Register of Shipping.

**Capabilities**
A multidisciplinary rail and transit consultancy, with engineering expertise in systems, safety critical systems, signalling, control, communications and rolling stock. The company can carry out feasibility studies, development, design, testing, maintenance support and infrastructure surveys for signalling and communication including strategies, new project and post-design safety engineering, risk assessment, independent assessment and for audit of rolling stock.

**Contracts**
Supply of project management, systems support and engineering services on major resignalling projects for Iarnrod Eireann, and preparation of rail standards for Irish government. Safety case for Virgin CrossCountry tilting rolling stock for the Bombardier Transportation Group. Preparation of safety cases for the Networker fleet of IISBC Rail (UK); development and application of braking deficiency software for Railtrack; technical support and signalling design for Railtrack; technical support to develop new-generation control, train detection and interlocking systems.

*UPDATED*

## Lockheed Martin Rail Systems

55 Charles Lindbergh Boulevard, Mitchel Field, New York 11553-3682, USA
Tel: (+1 516) 228 20 91 Fax: (+1 516) 228 18 97
e-mail: joe.tumbarello@lmco.com
Web: http://www.lockheedmartin.com

**UK office**
Lockheed Martin UK Integrated Systems
PO Box 41, North Harbour, Portsmouth PO6 3AU, UK
Tel: (+44 23) 92 56 54 00 Fax: (+44 23) 92 38 35 46
e-mail: bob.prothero@lmco.com
Web: http://www.lockheedmartin.co.uk

**Capabilities**
Systems integration provision for rail transport systems and projects.

**Projects**
In the USA, Lockheed Martin received a contract from the Illinois Department of Transportation to develop a Positive Train Control (PTC) system incorporating moving block technology to optimise track capacity and safety. The company was charged with managing the design, development, integration and test processes of the scheme by using integrated product teams to promulgate plans, manage and control processes and allocate resources during the project's life cycle.

In the UK, Lockheed Martin was designated Control Systems Integrator (CSI) by Railtrack for its West Coast Route Modernisation (WCRM) project, ensuring the scheme meets key agreed performance indicators and provides a foundation for future deployment of ERTMS technology. Responsibilities include: establishing baseline requirements; managing the development of major system interfaces; defining and implementing a comprehensive human factors integration programme; support for Railtrack safety initiatives; systems level integration and test management; project management; and system level commissioning and integration. The Control Systems Integration of Phase 2 of the WCRM scheme will integrate the following elements into the overall WCRM programme: the Network Management Centre; train control system; conventional signalling; fixed bearer communications; and voice communications.

*NEW ENTRY*

## LTK Engineering Services

A member of the Klauder Group
100 West Butler Avenue, Ambler, Pennsylvania 19002, USA
Tel: (+1 215) 542 07 00   Fax: (+1 215) 542 76 76
Web: http://www.ltk.com

**Key personnel**
President: George N Dorshimer
Vice-President, Midwest Region: John S Gustafson
Vice-President, Eastern Region: Frederick H Landell
Vice-President, Northwest Region: Thomas B. Furmaniak
Vice-President, Southwest Region: F. William Frandsen
Director, Business Development: David H Oglevee

**Capabilities**
LTK offers a wide variety of engineering, managerial and planning services tailored specifically to meet the needs of the rail transport industry. LTK expertise includes: design, specification, manufacture, installation and construction management for rail vehicles of all kinds; traction electrification systems; signalling and train control systems; telecommunications systems; fare collection equipment; and vehicle maintenance facilities.

**Projects**
LTK has provided engineering and managerial support for the following rail vehicle procurement programmes: high-speed trainsets for Amtrak Northeast Corridor services; new-generation metro trainsets for New York City Transit Authority; low-floor LRVs for Portland, Oregon; double-deck push-pull coaches and diesel-electric locomotives for Southern California Regional Rail Authority; and emus for Long Islad Rail road and Metro-North Railroad.

LTK has provided railway and rail transit systems engineering for a variety of projects including: Newark-Elizabeth rail link, New Jersey Transit; Westside and Hillsborough extensions of Portland LRT system; LRT System in Seattle, Washington and signalling modernisation projects for SEPTA's Broad Street metro line and CTA's Green Line.

## Maguire Group Inc

225 Foxborough Blvd, Foxborough, Massachusetts 02035, USA
Tel: (+1 508) 543 17 00    Fax: (+1 508) 543 51 57

**Key personnel**
President: Richard J Repeta

**Projects**
Vermont Avenue Station design (US$30 million) for Los Angeles Metro Wilshire Line; tunnel ventilation shafts (US$9 million) for Massachusetts Bay Transportation Authority (MBTA); Red Line extension tunnel section (US$110 million) with an associate firm, for Massachusetts Bay Transportation Authority (MBTA).

## Martyn Cornwall Design

Unit 15, Swan Court, 9 Tanner Street, London SE1 3LE, UK
Tel: (+44 20) 72 34 06 12    Fax: (+44 20) 74 03 38 68
e-mail: enq@mcdesign.co.uk

**Key personnel**
Director: Martyn Cornwall
Production Director: David French

**Capabilities**
Provision of comprehensive design services; strategic advice and planning of all aspects of design requirements; with a design team qualified to undertake corporate identity, graphic design, multimedia, web and interior design projects.

**Projects**
Include the development and implementation of new corporate identities for train operating companies in the UK, including train liveries and promotional material.

*VERIFIED*

## Faber Maunsell

Malborough House, Upper Malborough Road, St Albans, AC1 3UT, UK
Tel: (+44 20) 87 84 57 84    Fax: (+44 20) 87 84 57 00
Web: http://www.fabermaunsell.com

**Key personnel**
Chief Executive (International): Ken Dalton

**UK offices**
Altrinchon, Beckenham, Belfast, Birmingham, Bristol, Cardiff, Devizes, Edinburgh, Exeter, Glasgow, Leeds, London, Manchester, Norwich, Oxted, St Alban, York, Redhill, Sheffield, Witham.

**International offices**
Athens, Brussels, Budapest, Bulgaria, Denmark, Netherlands, Poland.

**Capability**
Building, engineering, transportation planning, transportation infrastructure.

*UPDATED*

## MBD Design

11 rue Victor Hugo, F-93177 Bagnolet Cedex, France
Tel: (+33 1) 48 57 30 00    Fax: (+33 1) 48 57 41 31

**Key personnel**
Chairman: Yves Domergue
General Manager: Jean-Claude Marbach

**Capabilities**
MBD Design accepts commissions from network authorities and rolling stock manufacturers for both long- and short-term railway transportation projects.

**Projects**
Design studies have been undertaken for: BB 36000 and BB 27000 locomotives for SNCF; Singapore, Shanghai and Warsaw Metros for ALSTOM; TER (regional express train) TER 2N (double-deck regional express train) and AGC single-deck emu/dmu; MI 2N three-door double-deck car for the Paris RER; TRN (National rapid train) for SNCF.

*UPDATED*

## Mercer Management Consulting Inc

1166 Avenue of the Americas, New York, New York 10036, USA

**Transportation Group**
33 Hayden Avenue, Lexington, Massachusetts 02173, USA
Tel: (+1 617) 861 75 80    Fax: (+1 617) 862 39 35

**Key personnel**
Vice-President: Hugh Randall

**UK office**
1 Grosvenor Place, London SW1X 7HJ, UK
Tel: (+44 20) 72 35 54 44    Fax: (+44 20) 72 45 69 33

**Key personnel**
Vice-President: Matthew Vanderbroeck

**Capabilities**
Mercer's Transportation Group assists railways and other transport undertakings in the following areas: strategy development; privatisation and commercialisation planning and implementation; organisational restructuring and management development; process re-engineering; operations enhancement and cost reduction; marketing and market research; information management; acquisition and alliance planning; and litigation support.

## Mer Mec SpA

Via Oberdan 70, I-70043 Monopoli (BA), Italy
Tel: (+39 080) 887 65 70    Fax: (+39 080) 887 40 28
e-mail: mermec@tin.it
Web: http://www.mermec.it

**Key personnel**
See entry in *Permanent way components, equipment and services* section.

**Services**
Technical assistance, maintenance service, infrastructure monitoring, asset data management, engineering assistance, wheel-rail analysis, axle stress and fatigue analysis.

*NEW ENTRY*

## Metroconsult

Helene-Weber-Allee 15, D-80637 Munich, Germany
Tel: (+49 89) 157 68 66    Fax: (+49 89) 157 24 73
e-mail: info@metroconsult.com
Web: http://www.metroconsult.com

**Key personnel**
Managing Director: Dr Ing Jürgen Rauch

**Capabilities**
Design of metro, railway stations and consultancy to designers and architects; methods of increasing capacity of metros and commuter railways systems; design of innovative platform screen door systems for metro stations; planning of buildings for public infrastructure; integration of metro systems into the transportation system of a city, technically and by means of architectural design; design of innovative parking systems in cities and within limited space; design of commuter parking systems; development of materials of fire protection in confined spaces as there are tunnels and underground stations; technology development support to manufacturers; support for innovative concepts of railway vehicle for public transport.

**Projects**
Passenger guidance system for the commuter railway network of Munich, Germany; several metro stations and parking systems in south Germany; vehicle parking related to public transport; development of fire protection materials in confined spaces such as tunnels and underground stations for better orientation in daily operation and emergency situations; consultancy to several city authorities and to manufacturers in the public transport industry; development of platform door systems for metros; development of concepts for a light rail train with energy systems not yet used in railway technology.

*NEW ENTRY*

## Metro Consulting Ltd

17 Queen Anne's Gate, London SW1H 9BU, UK
Tel: (+44 20) 72 22 25 26    Fax: (+44 20) 72 22 25 27
e-mail: metroconsulting@compuserv.com

**Key personnel**
Executive Chairman: W A E Bray
Managing Director: Ron Taylor
General Manager, Commercial: Harvey Robinson
Business Development Manager: Paul Dupeé

**Capabilities**
Core activities include project management services, railway engineering, safety assessment, asset management and information, graphic design, training programmes, signalling, communications, station control and infrastructure management.

In addition, Metro Consulting offers both strategic and operational capabilities to undertake transport planning, feasibility studies and organisational restructuring.

**Projects**
Include management assignments for London Underground, Railtrack and in Hong Kong. These have included assignments in business planning, restructuring and reorganisation, risk assessments, quality and safety management activities, management information systems, engineering and technology strategies.

## Millbrook Proving Ground

Millbrook, Near Ampthill, Bedford MK45 2JQ, UK
Tel: (+44 1525) 40 42 42    Fax: (+44 1525) 40 34 20
Web: http://www.millbrook.co.uk

**Key personnel**
Principal Rail Engineer: Vaughan Phillips

**Products**
Mobile and laboratory testing services for rail vehicles, including whole-vehicle crash testing, emissions development testing, system durability and refinement analysis.

Recent projects include diesel multiple-unit crash testing and Hyge Sled crash simulations on seats and occupants.

*VERIFIED*

## Modjeski & Masters Inc

PO Box 2345, Harrisburg, Pennsylvania 17105, USA
Tel: (+1 717) 790 95 65    Fax: (+1 717) 790 95 64
e-mail: harrisburg@modjeski.com
Web: http://www.modjeski.com

**Key personnel**
President & Chief Engineer: Dr J M Kulicki, PE

**Capabilities**
Rail structures; design and maintenance inspections of fixed and movable bridges.

*VERIFIED*

## Mott MacDonald Group

St Anne House, Wellesley Road, Croydon CR9 2UL, UK
Tel: (+44 20) 87 74 20 00   Fax: (+44 20) 86 81 57 06
e-mail: railways@mottmac.com
Web: http://www.mottmac.com

### Key personnel
Group Board Directors: T J Thirlwall, P M Chesworth, R B Fox, J D Gadd CBE (non-executive), M O Blackburn, A Knight (non-executive)
Main Board Directors: N G Bristow, R E Williams
Divisional Directors, Railways and Transport Systems Division: J D Corrie, R N Dumolo, M D Grounsell, J Hughes, R S Staniforth, M G Simpson, A R Walker, A West, D P White
Railways Divisional Manager: R Williams

### Other offices
Australia, Bahamas, Bangladesh, Bulgaria, Cambodia, Canada, China, Cyprus, Czech Republic, Denmark, Egypt, Ethiopia, Ghana, Greece, Guyana, India, Indonesia, Ireland, Jordan, Kazakstan, Kenya, Korea, Lesotho, Malaysia, Mozambique, Namibia, Nepal, New Zealand, Nigeria, Oman, Pakistan, Philippines, Portugal, Qatar, Romania, Russia, Saudi Arabia, Singapore, Sri Lanka, Syria, Taiwan, Tanzania, Thailand, Turkey, Uganda, United Arab Emirates, Uzbekistan, USA and Vietnam.

### Capabilities
Mott MacDonald is a multidisciplinary engineering consultancy with a worldwide staff resource of over 5,000 including chartered engineers, transportation planners, computer specialists, environmental scientists and support staff.

Capabilities encompass investigations, studies and technical feasibility reports, project definition, financial and environmental appraisal; safety assessment; preliminary and detailed design, contract preparation and tendering supervision, project scheduling, specification and procurement, quality control, cost and budget control, project implementation and construction management. The Group undertakes management and operational planning in the areas of traffic engineering, rail and transit operation and management related to different modes, inspection and testing of equipment during manufacture; investment planning, including development of transport models, traffic forecasting, evaluation techniques on economics, financial, technical and environmental grounds and modal choice techniques.

### Projects
Lantau Airport Railway, Hong Kong: design of Tsing Ma Bridge and design supervision for Kap Shui Mun Bridge.
Great Belt Crossing, Denmark: preliminary and detailed design of 8 km of rail tunnel to link Sprøgo to Zeeland beneath the Eastern Channel of the Great Belt.
Channel Tunnel Rail Link: engineering design for tunnels.
Heathrow Express: civil, mechanical and engineering design for 12 km of tunnel (plus open cut-and-cover works) with two underground stations; provision of an in-house developed geological and Geotechnical Data Management System (GDMS).
Linha do Norte Upgrading, Portugal.
Rolling stock procurement for Royal Mail, UK.
Banverket, Sweden: signalling and ATP design services.
Railtrack, UK: safety of dual-voltage earthing arrangements on the North London line.
London Underground Ltd, UK: asset and condition survey of earth structures.
Taipei Department of Rapid Transit Systems, Taiwan: consultancy services, for mechanical and electrical commissioning.
Railtrack, UK: design and enabling works for Croydon Tramlink.
LTS Rail, UK: procurement of new rolling stock.
OPRAF, UK: tilting train studies and specifications for West Coast Main Line.
Bangkok MRTA, Thailand: project management for 20 km underground metro system.
Department of Transport, UK: project representative for Channel Tunnel Rail Link.
DART Ireland: power supply design for Greystones extension.
North East Line, Singapore: overhead catenary system design.
PowerGen, UK: trackwork, signalling and telecoms design for Hams Hall National Distribution Park.
Railtrack, UK: civil engineering and signalling design for Ivanhoe and Robin Hood lines.
PRaK, Czech Republic: feasibility study for rail link to Prague airport.

Additional projects include Dublin LRT, Ireland (power supply and OHLE design); Jakarta North-South integrated toll road and LRT project, Indonesia (transport planning and conceptual design); LA Metro, USA (construction management for Red Line North Hollywood extension); Railtrack, UK (site manager for Robin Hood line).

Marina Line, Singapore: concept design and performance specifications; Budapest Metro Line 4, Hungary: railway authorisation design; West Coast Modernisation, UK: multi-functional consultant; Kaohsiung Metro, Taiwan: technical audit; Kulala Lumpur monorail, Malaysia: independent checking engineer; Putrajaya Light Rail, Malysia: design and project management; Dorset coast resignalling UK: feasability and safety case development; Virgin Trains, UK: independent assessment of safety case; LUL Power PPP, UK: lenders engineer; Railtrack, UK: Copenhagen Metro, Denmark: tunnel ventilation studies; Sumatra, Indonesia: South Sumatra Railway Study.

### Contracts
Recent contracts include: West Coast Main Line upgrace for Railtrack as consultant for feasibility and detailed design for whole route; Dorset Coast resignalling in partnership with Siemens on Railtrack's £20 million new signalling system; programme manager (in a joint venture with Fluor) for Railtrack's £1 billion East Coast Main Line upgrade; support work on the Infraspeed Consortium's HSL-Zuid railway in Holland; as lead consultant to monitor and audit the design, construction and commissioning of the £10 billion BOT railway for Taiwan High Speed Rail Corporation (as part of the IREG consortium). Orbirail project for SRA; promotor's advisory engineer to GMPTE for Manchester Metro; advisory services to construction joint venture on Croydon Tramlink; railway consultant to Railtrack on Parkside International Terminal.

*UPDATED*

---

## Mouchel Consulting Ltd

West Hall, Parvis Road, West Byfleet KT14 6EZ, UK
Tel: (+44 1932) 33 70 00   Fax: (+44 1932) 35 61 22

### Key personnel
Chairman: Colin Coulson
Deputy Chairman: Jim Harding
Director, Environment: Paul Driver
Director, Transportation: Bill Wyley
Director, Civil and Power: David Thompson

### Capabilities
Mouchel is a multidisciplinary consultancy specialising in transport and civil engineering. Areas of expertise include transport planning, demand forecasting, economic assessment of projects, development impact studies, civil and structural design, communications and signalling systems, project management and environmental consultancy.

Mouchel Asia and Gibb have joined forces to form a new consultancy group, Mouchel-Gibb, to pursue rail-related work in Hong Kong and mainland China. Projects vary from system upgrades – including the installation of platform screen doors and station and rolling stock refurbishments – through to the development and planning of massive new rail extensions, to project financing and privatisation issues.

Mouchel-Gibb believes there is a huge market for the skills the company is offering, especially given current expenditure plans.

About HK$13 billion will be spent in Hong Kong alone over the next five years on rail projects. There are also large schemes proposed in mainland China, where spending on rail is set to top more than HK$6.5 billion this year, and nearly HK$1.3 billion of foreign investment will be required over the next five years.

---

## MTR Corporation Consultancy Services

MTR Tower, Telford Plaza, Kowloon Bay, Hong Kong
Tel: (+852) 29 93; 23 17
Fax: (+852) 29 93 77 74
e-mail: jjdring@mtr.com.hk

### Key personnel
Consultancy Services Manager: Jonathan J Dring

### Capability
With 25 years experience in building and operating a successful metro system, the MTR offers a wide range of consultancy services extending throughout the project life cycle. The key areas of service include: project preliminaries – financial proposals, feasibility studies, project definition and concept planning; project planning, design and construction – detailed plannnog, programming, design, system assurance, system integration, project management, construction management, inspections, testing and commissioning, operational readiness; railway operation and maintenance – station operations, train operations, central control, incident management, revenue services, documentation, infrastructure maintenance, railway system maintenance, asset management, management information system; railway support services – safety management, quality management, environmental management, training, procurement, contract administration, inspection services, performance management; other related services – non-fare revenue, integrated property development, project financing, privatisation.

### Projects
Recent consultancy projects include: O&M services for Kaohsiung Metro; O&M of Automated People Mover in Hong Kong International Airport; O&M, human resources and training service to Bangkok Metro; training for Singapore Bus Services; training for Shenzhen Metro; training for Singapore Bus Services; training for Shenzhen Metro; training for Singapore Bus Services; training for Shenzhen Metro; AFC design advice for Delhi Metro; rail maintenance advice for Taipei Metro; baggage trolley study for Japan Central Airport Authority.

*UPDATED*

---

## MVA

MVA House, Victoria Way, Woking GU21 6DD, UK
Tel: (+44 1483) 72 80 51   Fax: (+44 1483) 75 52 07
e-mail: mail@mva.co.uk
Web: http://www.mva-group.com

### Key personnel
Chairman: Alain Estève
Board Directors: Fred Brown, Vincent Depondt, Jean-Christophe Hugonnard, Michael Roberts
Other Directors: Richard Crossley, Martin Dix, Eileen Hill, Mike Slinn, John Wicks, Steve Williamson, Jonathan Thomas, Carol Riddington, Brian Sheriff

### Other offices
Bangkok, Beijing, Hong Kong, Luxembourg, Lyon, Manila, Paris and Singapore.

### Associated companies
MVA Beijing Consultants Ltd
MVA Hong Kong Ltd
The MVA Consultancy Sdn Bhd

### Background
MVA was established in 1968 and has 350 staff.

### Capabilities
Transport planning, research and related information services. MVA advises on all stages, from strategy through to implementation, in partnership with central and local government, transport operators and private sector interests around the world. It also offers a number of software products.

MVA's transport planning covers land-use and integrated transport studies; air, rail, bus and car modes; passenger and freight movements; road and rail infrastructure schemes. It can improve the performance of existing public transport systems, plan future provision and provide economic and financial appraisal of investment proposals and service provision for bus and rail operators and scheme promoters. MVA also offers the market research and market analysis skills needed to boost patronage and attract finance. It specialises in achieving successful integration within a range of regulatory regimes, through the provision of intermodal interchanges, passenger and management information and fares and ticketing systems. MVA is a UK market leader in integrated ticketing advice and development of smartcard schemes covering all forms of transport.

TRIPS is a suite of programs for highway and public transport planning, while the START model provides a rapid assessment of transport options under different economic and land-use scenarios. The GIS-based accessibility model, ACCMAP, calculates, analyses and displays the detailed effects of varying levels of public service provision on the local community.

### Projects
Recent projects include: the review of high-speed rail terminals and intermodal connections for the Korean high-speed rail line; patronage and revenue forecasts for proposed Shatin—Central line (Hong Kong) for Mass Transit Railway Corporation Limited (MTRCL); research into passenger information displays on Kowloon—Canton railway; the Guangzhou (China) railway development review; advice on network planning to Transitlink, Singapore; traffic and revenue studies for Speedrail, Australia.

### Contracts
UK contracts include appraisal of options for re-opening Stirling-Alloa railway line; options for enhancement of Southport-Wigan rail corridor; the Scottish Borders Railway feasibility study; economic assessment of high-speed rail lines connecting London to the North of England; development of an Appraisal Framework for London's Crossrail; ScotRail customer satisfaction monitor; advice to Translink (Northern Ireland) on procurement and implementation of a smartcard-enabled ticketing system.

*UPDATED*

---

## NEA Transport Research and Training

Sir Winston Churchillaan 297, PO Box 1969, NL-2280 DZ Rijswijk, Netherlands
Tel: (+31 70) 398 83 88  Fax: (+31 70) 395 41 86
e-mail: email@nea.nl
Web: http://www.nea.nl

### Key personnel
Managing Director: Leo C Spaans
Directors: Menno M Menist;
 Arthur L Gleijm
 Pieter B D Hilferink
 Ad Rosenbrand
 Leo G van der Velden

### Capabilities
NEA is an independent organisation specialising in research, consultancy and training services in the field of traffic, transport, infrastructure and logistics. NEA's activities encompass the economic and social aspects of both passenger and freight transport for all modes. In the field of consultancy, NEA has experience in modelling, forecasting and evaluation of international freight flows, including simulation, scenario building, economic impact analysis, socio-economic research, market research and mobility studies. Training experience includes development of course materials and case studies, training needs assessments, institutional strengthening, legal harmonisation and legal reform.

### Projects
Research, training and consultancy assignments have been undertaken for governments, international agencies and organisations. Clients include the World Bank, Asian Development Bank, Commission of the European Communities, the Netherlands government, international branch organisation and the private sector.

*UPDATED*

---

## NedTrain BV

Katreinetoren 9, Stationhal 17, PO Box 2167, NL-3500 GD Utrecht, Netherlands
Tel: (+31 30) 300 46 78  Fax: (+31 30) 300 46 47
e-mail: info@nedtrain.nl
Web: http://www.nedtrain.nl

### Key personnel
Chief Executive Officer: J Huberts
Business Development Director: T Enzing
Financial Director: G Taute

### Principal subsidiary
NedTrain Consulting BV
NedTrain Ematech BV

### Background
NS Materieel changed its name to NedTrain in 1999.

### Capability
NedTrain supports operators and owners during the lifecycle of rolling stock, including refurbishment and overhauling, and has a complete package of in-house integrated services.

Traditional customers are NS Reizigers and NS Cargo but a growing amount of turnover is now devoted to municipal transport companies and other railway companies.

### Contracts
Contracts include an ultrasonic testing car, able to record at 140 km/h under own power and at 200 km/h when towed by another vehicle. The measuring system was designed by NS Materieel and based on a grill-express car from SNCF.

*UPDATED*

---

## NEL

National Engineering Laboratory
Scottish Enterprise Technology Park, East Kilbride, Glasgow G75 0QU, UK
Tel: (+44 1355) 22 02 22  Fax: (+44 1355) 27 29 99
e-mail: info@nel.co.uk

### Key personnel
Managing Director: W Paton
Business Development Manager-Consultancy:
 Stewart Kane

### Capabilities
NEL employs 242 people and offers transport engineering technology; noise engineering; structural analysis and testing; emission reduction, fuel systems, cooling techniques; environmental engineering and testing; quality accreditation.

---

## New Markets Ltd

Theocsbury House, 18-20 Barton Street, Tewkesbury GL20 5PP, UK
Tel: (+44 1684) 29 15 44  Fax: (+44 1684) 29 15 45
e-mail: davidrichman@newmarkets.co.uk

### Key personnel
Director, Rail Industry Projects: David Richman
Director: Andrew Turner

### Background
New Markets Ltd is a sales and marketing company which assists companies to export into all countries in the European rail sector. Activities include product marketing, sales support, sourcing and business development by finding partners for joint ventures or acquisitions.

### Projects
These have been completed for major companies in Australia, Germany, Switzerland and the UK. New Markets acted as a consultant for the Birmingham Chamber of Commerce's Deutsche Bahn Suppliers' Day and SNCF programmes.

Agents for Carl Dan Peddinghaus – lubrication free sliding plates for switches; Delestre Industrie – Brasero infra-red station heating; Ederena Concept – lightweight sandwich composite components; FTD (Fahrzeugtechnik Dessau) – bodyshells, plug and play cabs, powerpacks and engineering design and services; Premaberg Manufacturing – air intake grills and separators; Saira Alluminio SpA – complete interiors, ceiling groups, luggage racks, stacks and tables; Semco Vakuumteknik AS – vacuum toilet systems and modules.

*VERIFIED*

---

## The Nichols Group

2 Savile Row, London W1X 1AF, UK
Tel: (+44 20) 72 92 70 00  Fax: (+44 20) 72 92 50 00
e-mail: info@nichols.co.uk
Web: http://www.nicholsgroup.com

### Key personnel
Chairman and Chief Executive: Mike Nichols
Executive Team: David Waboso (Rail)
 Debra Rymer (Financial Services and Other Services)
 Colin Britt (Unit Management)
 Kathryn Nichols (Company Secretary and Corporate Services)

### Capabilities
The Nichols Group is a project management consultancy which focuses on four main services: managing, consulting, resourcing and training. With offices in London and Hong Kong, the group has over 55 permanent project management professionals and more than 250 senior associates. For 25 years it has supported clients in transportation, utilities and financial services with project resourcing and training of project sponsors and team managers.

Capabilities include major project reviews, project and programme management, systems integration and risk management.

### Projects
Strategic programme reviews for London Underground, Railtrack, power generation and telecoms companies (1990 – present); programme and project management for Strategic Rail Authority, London Underground, Transport for London, ROSCOs and TOCs (1996 – present).

*UPDATED*

---

## NS Railplan bv

PO Box 2025, 3500 HA Utrecht, Netherlands
Tel: (+31 30) 235 64 11  Fax: (+31 30) 235 57 57

### Key personnel
Manager: Ir A J Toet
Senior Consultant: Ing Th van Hessen
Junior Consultant: Dr J Sluijter
Senior Consultants: Hans J A Kartman, Prof H Overeem

### Background
The company is a subsidiary of Netherlands Railways that offers services to governments, railway companies and other transport companies.

Railplan specialises in interactive support to railway companies.

### Services
Advice on privatisation and/or restructuring, on combined transport; cargo handling and transhipment; (intermodal transport development), transport and traffic studies, logistics studies; feasibility studies on rehabilitation and upgrading of railway tracks; information technology and application.

Recent contracts include: management support for HZ (Croatian Railways) to modernise and restructure the organisation, World Bank Trustfund/Senter; telecom services for infrastructure in Lithuania railways, PSO/Senter; preparation of proposals, evaluation and management information for Russian Railways, EC-Tacis; inventory and advice on combined transport operations, timetabling, tracking and tracing, applications and customs procedures in Russia, EC-Phare; technical and operations project for extension of trans-European Rail Freight Freeways through central Europe with special attention to tracking and tracing systems, EC-Phare; design of rail infrastructure in the Port of Poti, Georgia, PSO-Senter; railway restructuring conference for BDZ Management in Bulgaria for Netherlands Ministry of Transport; continuing improvement of information

# CONSULTANCY SERVICES

infrastructure in Lithuania, PSO-Senter; redevelopment study of Zagreb Railway Junction, Croatia, PSO-Senter; feasibility study of an integrated railway transport system in Poland, EC-Phare; upgrading of electric traction motors in Romania, PESP/Senter, and restructuring and commercialisation of Slovenian Railways in Slovenia, PSO/Senter.

## Ødegaard & Danneskiold-Samsøe A/S

Titangade 15, DK-2200 Copenhagen N, Denmark
Tel: (+45) 35 31 10 00   Fax: (+45) 35 31 10 01
e-mail: uds@oedan.dk
Web: http://www.odegaard.dk

**Key personnel**
Managing Director: John Ødegaard
Sales Manager, Chairman of the Board:
  Ulrik Danneskiold-Samsøe
Senior Consultants: Henrik W Thrane, Uffe Degn

**Subsidiary**
Ødegaard & Danneskiold-Samsøe Jylland ApS
Beder Landevej 29, DK-8330 Beder, Denmark

**Capabilities**
Consulting engineers, specialising in noise and vibration control of trains and other modes of transport. The company's services apply to all phases of the life of a train, from design through to operation. Services offered include: design advice, noise and vibration analyses and troubleshooting.

*UPDATED*

## OMI Logistics Limited

2-10 Cawte Road Southampton SO15 3TD, UK
An OMI International plc Company
Tel: (+44 23) 80 90 82 00   Fax: (+44 23) 80 33 61 17
Web: http://www.omi-logistics.co.uk

**Key personnel**
Business Development Manager: John Churchman

**Capabilities**
Production of technical documentation for the major transportation industries.

**Projects**
OMI Logistics has recently delivered the first issue of a full suite of manuals at the end of an initial 21-month contract to the Siemens Transportation Systems consortium for Heathrow Express rolling stock.
  Covering maintenance, operation, operator training and an illustrated parts catalogue, OMI compiled the hard copy manuals with supporting illustrations on CD-ROM from information provided by the pan-European group of manufacturers involved in the project, including CAF of Spain and Faiveley of France, as well as the German and UK arms of Siemens.
  In addition, OMI worked on the signalling system for the Hong Kong Mass Transit System and provided documentation for new trains introduced on the London Underground Central Line.

## Oscar Faber

18 Upper Marlborough Road, St Albans AL1 3UT, UK
Tel: (+44 20) 87 84 57 84   Fax: (+44 20) 87 84 57 00

**Key personnel**
Chairman: Alec Moir

**Capabilities**
Include project identification, planning, design, engineering and management. Resource capabilities cover a wide range of disciplines embracing economics, engineering, financial appraisal, planning, project management, research and statistics, and transportation modelling. The range of services includes: customer and market research; demand forecasting; operation assessment and costing; financial and economic evaluation. The company has a specialist customer survey section whose abilities include revealed and stated preference techniques.

**Projects**
Oscar Faber has been commissioned to carry out a series of studies on the impact of the first line of the new Midland Metro Light Rail System, Birmingham, UK, on passengers. The 20.4 km route with 23 stops was due to open in October 1998 and runs between Birmingham Snow Hill and Wolverhampton St Georges via Handsworth, West Bromwich, Wednesbury and Bilston.
  Centro has commissioned the study on behalf of a steering group which also includes the concessionaire Altram, the Department of Environment, Transport and the Regions and Birmingham, Sandwell, Walsall and Wolverhampton local authorities.
  Line 1, the largest public transport project in the West Midlands for many years, will have a major impact on travel and local development, which needs to be quantified.
  Oscar Faber is identifying users, why they have changed their method of travel, whether they previously made the journey by car, bus or train, what benefits they have gained and the frequency of use. Car and bus journey times along specified routes will be compared with journey time data preceding the introduction of Midland Metro Line 1. Household surveys will also be conducted as too will be the impact of the line on local employers, their employees and specifically on job creation.

## Ove Arup & Partners

13 Fitzroy Street, London W1T 4BQ, UK
Tel: (+44 20) 76 36 15 31   Fax: (+44 20) 77 55 24 51

**Key personnel**
Transport Directors: Gordon Henderson,
  Ed Humphreys

**Capability**
Transport planning, environmental, economics, acoustics, geotechnical, civil, mechanical and electrical engineering, structural and building engineering services. Planning and design of urban and interurban transport systems; business case appraisal, specialists in rail, light rail and bus planning and appraisal, strategic transport planning studies, demand forecasting and modelling, information technology, bus priority and network planning, rail and LRT operations, traffic control systems, feasibility studies, design of infrastructure including bus and rail stations, station capacity, rail and road construction management; traffic engineering including parking control and strategy work; pedestrian movement and flow modelling.

**Projects**
TERFFS extension; gauge corner cracking control strategy development; rail freight grant regime review and industry consultation; King's Cross rail and station planning; Channel Tunnel rail link; rail freight avoidable cost review; Bangkok MRT; LUL PPP technical advisor to LUL; Tyne & Wear Metro Sunderland extension – planning and design; Heathrow new rail services; Dublin suburban rail strategy; Manchester – crewe layout remodelling; level crossing signalling renewals for Railtrack LNE; Sunderland extension Metro-Railtrack signalling interface specification and implementation; Welwyn—Hitchin upgrade feasibility.

*NEW ENTRY*

## Parsons Brinckerhoff Inc

One Penn Plaza, 250 West 34th Street, New York, New York 10119, USA
Tel: (+1 212) 465 50 00   Fax: (+1 212) 465 50 96
e-mail: pbinfo@pbworld.com
Web: http://www.pbworld.com

**Key personnel**
President: Thomas J O'Neill
Chair: Robert Prieto
Controller: Richard A Schrader

**Subsidiaries**
Parsons Brinckerhoff Quade & Douglas Inc
One Penn Plaza, New York, New York 10119, USA
Tel: (+1 212) 465 50 00   Fax: (+1 212) 465 50 96

PB Transit & Rail Systems Inc
Marathon Plaza, 303 Second Avenue, Suite 700N, San Francisco, California 94107-1317, USA
Tel: (+1 415) 243 46 00   Fax: (+1 415) 495 67 32

Parsons Brinckerhoff Construction Services Inc
Spring Park Technology Center, 465 Spring Park Place, Herndon, Virginia 20170, USA
Tel: (+1 703) 742 57 00   Fax: (+1 703) 742 58 00

Parsons Brinckerhoff Ltd (formerly PB Kennedy & Donkin Ltd)
Westbrook Mills, Godalming GU7 2AZ, UK
Tel: (+44 1483) 52 84 00   Fax: (+44 1483) 52 89 89
and
4 Roger Street, London WCIN 2JX, UK
Tel: (+44 20) 72 42 28 98   Fax: (+44 20) 72 42 19 81

Parsons Brinckerhoff Power Inc
Five Penn Plaza New York, New York 1001, USA
Tel: (+1 212) 613 88 90   Fax: (+1 212) 613 88 88

Parsons Brinckerhoff International Pte Ltd
95 South Bridge Road, 08-08 Pidemco Centre, Singapore, 058717
Tel: (+65 533) 95 95   Fax: (+65 536) 95 69

PB Facilities Inc
One Penn Plaza, New York, New York 10119, USA
Tel: (+1 212) 465 50 00   Fax: (+1 212) 465 50 96

PB Telecommunications Inc
One Penn Plaza, New York, New York 10119, USA
Tel: (+1 212) 465 50 29   Fax: (+1 212) 631 37 89

**Major operations managers**
President, Parsons Brinckerhoff Quade & Douglas, Inc:
  Gary E Griggs
Tel: (+1 212) 465 50 20
Chairman, PB Transit & Rail Systems Inc: Anthony Daniels
Tel: (+1 415) 243 46 34
President, Parsons Brinckerhoff Construction Services, Inc: Christopher E Reseigh
Tel: (+1 703) 742 57 01
Parsons Brinckerhoff Ltd
Managing Director: David A McAlister
Tel: (+44 1481) 352 84 00
President, Parsons Brinckerhoff Power Inc:
  Joel Bennett
Tel: (+1 212) 465 57 00
Director of Marketing: John M Bordelon
Tel: (+44 1483) 52 85 05
President, Parsons Brinckerhoff International Pte Ltd:
  Keith J Hawksworth
Tel: (+852) 25 79 87 00
President, PB Facilities Inc: William S Roman
Tel: (+1 212) 465 50 23
President, PB Telecommunications Inc: Robert Bellhouse
Tel: (+1 212) 465 50 29
Program Area Manager, Railroads: Robert C Vanderclute
Tel: (+44 20) 79 04 73 16

**Corporate offices**
Australia, Argentina, Belgium, China, Egypt, Hong Kong, Indonesia, Ireland, Israel, Japan, Lebanon, Malaysia, New Zealand, Philippines, Poland, Singapore, South Africa, South Korea, Spain, Thailand, Turkey, United Arab Emirates, UK and USA.

**Capabilities**
Parsons Brinckerhoff (PB) provides multidisciplinary planning, engineering, programme and construction management, and operations and maintenance services for urban transport – heavy rail and light rail, commuter rail and conventional railroad, automated people mover, and maglev and high-speed rail. PB also specialises in intermodal and multimodal transportation; track, structures and facility design and inspection; tunnels and subsurface structures; bridge design and inspection; signal and communications systems; electrification; equipment analysis; maintenance facilities and management of assets. It provides clients with a support, including alternatives evaluation, systems design, fire/life/safety programmes, operations and maintenance plans, simulations, procurement support, and testing and start-up.

## Projects

Representative project experience includes:

Railtrack Programme Management, UK, providing programme management and implementation services to Railtrack for specifically the upgrading of the West Coast mainline linking London with Birmingham and Manchester in northwest England, as well as Glasgow and Edinburgh in Scotland. Elements of the system slated for modernisation include electrification schemes, resignalling, fibre optic cabling, re-railing programmes, bridge and structure renewals, station rehabilitation, integrated electronic control centres, and other individual projects geared to improving efficiency, economy and, above all, safety.

Metropolitan Atlanta Rapid Transit Authority (MARTA) Transit System, Atlanta, Georgia: For more than 30 years, PB in joint venture has provided planning, design, and construction management services for MARTA, a US$3.6 billion rapid transit system encompassing 96 km of rapid transit lines, one express busway and five branch lines, 45 rail passenger stations, park-and-ride facilities for more than 33,000 vehicles, four rapid transit rail vehicle storage/maintenance facilities and 338 rapid transit rail vehicles.

General on-call services for Class 1 US Railroads: PB is providing on-call services for several major United States freight carriers as well as intercity and commuter carriers. The services encompass all types of engineering and planning as needed by the carriers.

Minnesota Intermodal Rail Terminal Study (19010): PB undertook a three-part study to determine the rail operating parameters, develop an operating plan and conceptual designs of the proposed rail terminal, and create a pro forma business plan for a new intermodal terminal facility to be shared by Burlington Northern Santa Fe, Union Pacific and Canadian Pacific Railroads Minneapolis-St. Paul Twin Cities area.

Vermont State Railway Policy Plan (18660): PB developed a statewide rail policy plan to provide overall direction for public investment in rail transportation.

Northeast Corridor (NEC) Strategic Plan (21006): PB developed a 20-year capital programme by co-ordinating the needs of all users of the NEC which included Amtrak, eight Commuter rail agencies and three freight railroads.

MARC Commuter Rail Master Rail (17819): PB provides railroad planning and operations services to address growth options for the 187-mile system between northern portions of West Virginia and Maryland and the Baltimore and Washington, DC business districts.

Tren Urbano, San Juan, Puerto Rico: As a subcontractor, PB is providing program management and design services for the systems and test track turnkey contract, providing management and interface co-ordination of all systemwide elements, including vehicles, train control, electrification, trackwork and communication systems as they relate to the fixed facilities of the double track heavy rail system.

Greater Cairo Metro, Cairo Egypt: PB is leading the joint venture team responsible for providing management consultancy services for the turnkey design, contraction and commissioning of the 19.2 km heavy rail line. PB's services include evaluation of tender documents; review and co-ordination of design, procurement, installation and commissioning of trackwork, rolling stock, and all electrical/mechanical system; construction inspection; materials/systems testing; budget and schedule development and monitoring; operations and maintenance planning, training and implementation. Phase 1 and Phase 2 have been completed and opened for revenue service; PB is supervising concept design and tender documentation preparation for an extension to Line 2.

Taipei MRT, Taipei, Taiwan: PB's services encompassed the design and construction of a 64 km, 57 station, high-capacity MRT and a 23 km, 23-station MCT line. Additional lines are planned for the future, with an estimated construction value of over US$24 billion.

Bay Area Rapid Transit (BART) Extension, San Francisco, California: PB is a member of the General Engineering Consultant (GEC) joint venture guiding the US$3.2 billion BART Extensions Programme which begun in the 1980s, involving 30 miles of rapid rail line and 10 stations. PB is managing the overall expansion programme in addition to providing design services, managing procurement, installation and construction and assisting with testing and start-up.

Airport Access, New York, New York: As general engineering consultant during this Design-Build-Operate-Maintain (DBOM) programme, PB is providing a wide range of planning, design, environmental analysis, construction management and procurement activities, while also helping to operate a programme office jointly with the client's staff members.

Singapore MRT, Singapore: PB is providing mechanical/electrical consultancy services for the engineer's design of the tunnel ventilation system and station environmental control system for 16 underground stations on the Singapore subway 20 km North East Line. This is PB's second major environmental control/tunnel ventilation contract on the Singapore MRT system.

Atlanta (MARTA): In 2002, PB, in a joint venture with Turner Associates/Architects and Planners (Atlanta), H J Russell & Company (Atlanta) and Parsons Transportation Group, was selected as the General Engineering Consultant for MARTA. The name of the joint venture is Regional Transit Partners (RTP). PB serves as the lead in the joint venture, which was to negotiate an agreement to support MARTA's capital programme, including renovation, transit-oriented development, expansion, improvement and planning of the authority's rapid transit and bus system.

*UPDATED*

## Patrick Engineering Inc

22 W 600 Butterfield Road, Glen Ellyn, Illinois 60137, USA
Tel: (+1 708) 434 70 50   Fax: (+1 708) 434 84 00
e-mail: sheath@patrickengineering.com
Web: http://www.patrickengineering.com

### Key personnel
President: Daniel P Dietzler
Vice-President, Transportation & Design Services: Ted W Lachus
Vice-President: Jeffrey C Schuh
Vice-President: Ron J Darin

### Capabilities
Professional engineering, project management, and architectural services including civil, structural, mechanical, electrical and environmental engineering; architectural and surveying services including GPS; geotechnical investigations and drilling; design/build services for industrial systems and other railway projects. Patrick Engineering has provided services for Class I and short line railways in the USA and Canada and in Central America.

### Projects
Contracts completed recently include embankment stabilisation of triple main line embankment; major rail yard improvement; and emergency bridge replacement.

## PB Kennedy & Donkin Ltd

Westbrook Mills, Godalming GU7 2AZ, UK
Tel: (+44 1483) 42 59 00   Fax: (+44 1483) 42 51 36

### Key personnel
Managing Director: John R Springate
Business Development Director: Suzan Audras
Commercial Director: Rowland R Vye
Transportation Director: Robert A Gray
Sales Director: John Bordelon
Business Development Manager: David Brewerton
Offices in 17 countries
(A Parsons Brinckerhoff company)

### Capabilities
Project management, feasibility studies, system design and engineering, safety and risk management and environmental services. The staff includes project managers, engineers, economists, operators, architects and planners with a wide range of experience in the planning, design, operation and management of railways, LRT and metro systems. Also, signalling, electrification, rolling stock, power supply, tunnel ventilation, stations, civil and structural services covering infrastructure and permanent way, offices and depots; design and supervision of construction geotechnical and environmental engineering.

### Projects
Hong Kong: installation supervision of automatic train protection and bi-directional operation for KCRC; systemwide power supply and distribution review of Hong Kong MTR.
Thailand: specification and tender evaluation and contract supervision for elevated metro developed by Bangkok Transit System Public Company Ltd. Design of tunnel ventilation and E & M systems for the Bangkok MRTA.
Turkey: design, construction, commissioning and initial operation works of the Adana LRT scheme.
Delhi, India: project management and supervision of construction for new metro system.
Bulgaria: EC PHARE-assisted technical assistance for railway restructuring and procurement of US$100 million of improvements.
Cairo, Egypt: construction supervision for Line 2, Cairo metro.
UK: *Railtrack* – Programme Manager for the West Coast Route Modernisation; management of the delivery of the Train Protection and Warning Systems (TPWS) nationwide; Thameslink 2000 – Railtrack's designer for the signalling of the inner core area, permanent way, E&M services and tunnel ventilation; feasibility study for Railtrack and Virgin's proposals to upgrade cross-country routes for tilting trains.

*London Underground Limited* – Joint Engineering Adviser for the Public Private Partnership.

*Department of Transport* – Project Representative for Channel Tunnel Rail Link acting as agent.

*AMEC Spie* – Manchester South systems integration.
Turkey: engineer for the design, construction, commissioning and initial operation works of the Adana LRT Scheme.

Other projects have been carried out in Algeria, Bulgaria, Lithuania, Malaysia, Nigeria, Pakistan, Russia, Singapore, Slovenia and USA.

## Philips Projects BV

Building TAM, PO Box 218, NL-5600 MD Eindhoven, Netherlands
Tel: (+31 40) 278 51 94   Fax: (+31 40) 278 69 14
e-mail: Rene.vanEijkelenburg@nl.ccmail.philips.com
Web: http://www.philips-projects.philips.com

### Key personnel
Regional Director EMEA: René van Eijkelenburg

### Offices
Austria, Belgium, Czech Repiblic, Denamrk, Finland, France, Germany, Greece, Italy, Netherlands, Poland, Portugal, Spain, Switzerland, and UK.

### Capabilities
Railway stations systems overview, including: real time database, security management system; fire alarm system and public address management system, passenger tracking system; information display management system for timetables, baggage information, passengers information, station information and staff information; and media systems.

### Projects
Video transmission system for CCTV on stations and platforms in the UK, including major London stations and Greater Manchester Metrolink; acoustics for PA in stations and platforms in Germany; system integration for PA systems for metros in France, Italy, Norway, and Singapore; public data and video for advertisements in the Netherlands. Philips is involved in station control systems for Italian railways; the new Dortmund railway station project and in the Telsul project in Portugal.

## PricewaterhouseCoopers

1 Embankment Place, London, WC2N 6NN, UK
Tel: (+44 20) 72 13 47 43   Fax: (+44 20) 72 13 24 54
e-mail: chris.j.castles@uk.pwcglobal.com
Web: http://www.pcglobal.com

### Key personnel
Partner, Transport Consultancy Services: Christopher Castles
Director: Hugh Ashton

## 840 CONSULTANCY SERVICES

**Capabilities**
Restructuring and privatisation of railways throughout the world including strategy advice on restructuring options, economic and financial advice and the evaluation and financing of large-scale systems development projects.

PwC provides a range of consulting and financial advisory services to railways and associated organisations covering policy, strategy, economics and financial advice, with extensive international experience in railway business strategy, restructuring, privatisation and regulation and providing detailed analytical support and advice. This covers all the major business issues affecting railways' performance including market analysis and forecasting, railway cost and profitability analysis, subsidy policy, track access charging, design of concessions and other forms of private sector participation, development of regulatory mechanisms, organisation restructuring and performance improvement.

## The QSS Group

PO Box 464, London Road, Derby DE24 8ZL, UK
Tel: (+44 1332) 26 21 80    Fax: (+44 1332) 26 36 92
e-mail: enquiries@theqssgroup.co.uk
Web: http://www.theqssgroup.co.uk

**Key personnel**
Group Managing Director: Kenneth Mee
Director of Safety, Quality and Environmental Services: Peter Abbott
Director, Engineering Services: Tony Levy

**Capabilities**
The QSS Group, with its origins as the in-house specialist arm of the former British Rail, is an international practice. Its divisions embrace the design, audit and implementation of quality, safety and environmental business processes, the measurement of engineering product compliance together with a Vehicle Acceptance Body.

The Group offers full-time consulting engineers and specialist associates and project management of heavy and light rail systems and of integrated transport networks, across the UK, Europe, the Far East.

QSS serves clients including SNCF, Deutsche Bahn, The Kowloon-Canton Railway Corporation and Dopravni Podnik Prahy, Prague.

In the UK, QSS provides safety and quality assurance support on infrastructure-related projects. The QSS Group reports that, as an authority on safety approval and quality control for rolling stock projects, it has been involved in many new rolling stock builds to date (see RIQC).

*UPDATED*

## Queensland Rail Consulting Services

13th Floor, 127 Creek Street, Brisbane, Queensland 4000, Australia
GPO Box 1429, Brisbane, Queensland 4001
Tel: (+61 7) 32 35 33 90    Fax: (+61 7) 32 35 33 46
e-mail: qrcs@qrail.com.au

**Key personnel**
Manager, QR Consulting Services: Mike Garrett
Marketing & Operations Manager: Michael Walsh

**Capabilities**
Queensland Rail Consulting Services (QRCS), the commercial arm of Queensland Rail (QR), provides professional, managerial and technical expertise derived from over 130 years experience in the devlopment and operation of QR. Clients include external organisations both within Australia and overseas.

QRCS is able to access railway expertise derived from the day-to-day operation of QR's modern railway network of over 9,400 km of track. Expertise available includes planning, operations, maintenance, administration, engineering, financial accounting, financial management and information systems.

**Projects**
QRCS has delivered improved technology, management and training systems to railways in Australia, South East, Southern and Central Asia, the Middle East, Europe and Africa.

## Radermacher & Partner GmbH

Elsenheimerstrasse 41, D-80687 Munich, Germany
Tel: (+49 89) 57 00 90    Fax: (+49 89) 57 00 91; 99
e-mail: mail@radermacher.de
Web: http://www.radermacher.de

**Key personnel**
Managing Directors: Hans-Josef Mayer, Erich F Pante e

**Capabilities**
Solution of strategic, operational and organisational tasks within engineering, supply chain management, production, quality. Clients are predominantly businesses with their own development and production. Radermacher has advised the German railway industry for a number of years.

## Railmotive GmbH

Gross-Berliner Damm 73E, D-12487 Berlin, Germany
Tel: (+49 30) 63 94 71 20    Fax: (+49 30) 63 94 71 99
e-mail: info@ivm-railmotive.com
Web: http://www.brunel.de

**Background**
Railmotive GmbH, formerly trading as IVM Railmotive GmbH, is owned by Brunel Group.

**Capabilities**
Engineering services in the development of new rail vehicles including supply of coach body/underframe, bogie, interior fittings and furnishings, ventilation/air conditioning, driver's cab, electrical fittings, circuit diagrams. IVM meets standardised specifications such as UIC Directives, DB AG design directives, customer specifications or documentation tailored to long-distance rail vehicles.

At Görlitz, the company owns and operates test tracks and static vehicle testing facilities.

*UPDATED*

*Type DABpbzf double-deck driving car on the centre of gravity measurement bed at IVM Railmotive's Görlitz test facility*    2001/0103633

## Rail Sciences Inc

3 North Clarendon Avenue, Avondale Estates, Georgia 30002-1151, USA
Tel: (+1 404) 294 53 00    Fax: (+1 404) 294 54 23
e-mail: railsciences@worldnet.att.net
e-mail: info@railsciences.com
Web: http://www.railsciences.com

**Key personnel**
President: Gary P Woolf
Vice-President: Warren B Egan

**Capabilities**
Railway consultancy specialising in the application of advanced analytical techniques to solve operational problems; accident and derailment analysis, rail line capacity simulation modelling, schedule feasibility, vehicle dynamics, operational planning and analysis, computer model development, dispatching control systems, driver training, testing and data acquisition, mechanical inspections.

## Rail Services Australia

Level 13, Pacific Power Building, 201 Elizabeth Street, Sydney New South Wales 2000
Locked Bag A4090 South Sydney, New South Wales 1235
Tel: (+61 2) 92 24 37 02    Fax: (+61 2) 92 24 26 00
e-mail: railservicesaustralia.com.au

**Key personnel**
Chief Executive Officer: Terry Ogg
General Manager Workshops: Michael Peter
General Manager Corporate Services: Irina White
Chief Financial Officer: Frank Morrison
Manager Human Resources: Col Shrubb
General Manager, Business Development: Karl Mociak
General Manager Contracts: Geoff Baxter
General Manager Resources: Colin Andrews
Manager Legal Services: Susi Curtis

**Capabilities**
Asset management; design and investigation; project management; rolling stock; signalling, control and communications; electrical maintenance; bridge examination and maintenance; signalling maintenance; track monitoring and maintenance; railway turnouts and crossings; rail wagon maintenance, repair and modification; railway signalling, electrical and electronic equipment servicing; signal construction; track construction; civil construction; electrical construction. Rail Services Australia has particular skills in rail projects over difficult terrain or through high-density areas.

**Projects**
Contracts include the New South Wales New Southern Railway tunnel fitout; the Blackdown to Richmond (NSW) Infrastructure Works and Maintenance. Provider contract in association with Theiss Contractors. The Homebush Bay Olympic Loop and main line, interface works. Two significant projects for Australian Rail Track Corporation in South Australia and Western Australia; works are under way in Asia and the UK.

## The Railway Consultancy Ltd

43a Palace Square, Crystal Palace, London SE19 2LT, UK
Tel: (+44 20) 86 53 10 97    Fax: (+44 20) 87 71 31 71
e-mail: info@railcons.com
Web: http://www.railcons.com

**Key personnel**
Managing Director: Dr Nigel G Harris
Director: David R McIntosh
Senior Analyst: Ties van Ark

**Capabilities**
Demand, revenue and passenger benefit estimation for both train and station services; operational consultancy (for both train and station services including simulations, timetable preparation, disruption and contingency planning); transport policy and management advice; business planning, including project appraisal and economic assessments; specification and design of IT systems to assist the railway planning process; training courses on railway and transport planning issues.

The GCOST™ model for estimating the passenger demand, revenue and time-saving impacts of new stations and the TRAKA TTK train service simulation is available as part of in-house planning tools.

**Projects**
Franchise bid preparation; economic assessment of different urban transport technologies for UK Department of the Environment, Transport and the Regions; design of database to hold information on operational incidents for London Underground Ltd, UK; fares regulation analysis

for MTRC Hong Kong; service planning for a number of UK operators; Norreport Station Operability study for Danish Ministry of Transport; maintenance of track access rights database for Railtrack (1998 – continuing).

*UPDATED*

---

## Railway Engineering Associates Limited

68-82 Boden Street, Glasgow G40 3PX, UK
Tel: (+44 141) 554 38 68   Fax: (+44 141) 556 50 91
e-mail: henrymaxwell@rea.uk.com

**Key personnel**
Principal Consultants: Henry Maxwell, Donald McCallum

**Capabilities**
Specialist railway engineering consultancy services for companies involved in railway works or works involving encroachment on to operational railway land. Expertise includes permanent way design, bridge/structure design, station and depot design.

---

## Railway Systems Consultants Ltd

Church View, Knockhundred Row, Midhurst GU29 9DQ, UK
Tel: (+44 1730) 81 32 80   Fax: (+44 1730) 81 71 52
e-mail: rscuk@compuserv.com

**Key personnel**
Director: Nico M J Dekker

**Capabilities**
Rapid transit, including guided bus, people movers, light and heavy rail. Feasibility and outline design studies, including systems engineering, power systems, command control and communications, rolling stock, operations and maintenance, highway traffic management and urban design. Systems, subsystems, business and operational specification. Preparation of tender and contract documentation, tender evaluation and negotiation, contract monitoring and supervision.

**Projects**
Cross River Partnership, London: definition and evaluation of rapid transit route alignments between Stockwell, Elephant & Castle, Waterloo, Euston, Kings Cross and Camden, including operational, traffic management and urban design aspects.
Croydon Tramlink, UK: project development, including systemwide performance specification. Evaluation of EMC and stray-current protection options. Overhead line studies to evaluate indicative engineering designs and associated aesthetic qualities. Pre-qualification and tender assessment of technical aspects of bidders. Technical monitoring of the concessionaire on behalf of London Transport.
Docklands Light Railway, London: assessment of performance derogation to be offered to franchisees due to system reliability deficiencies.
Nottingham Express Transit (LRT): overhead line design studies. Track-sharing option evaluation with Railtrack.
Birmingham International Airport, UK: technical and operational advice with regard to upgrading people mover and replacement options. Preparation of tender and contract documents, subsequent tender assessment.
Channel Tunnel Rail Link: preparation of cost estimates for overhead line remodelling at Dollands Moor, Ashford and Euston.

---

## Railway Technology Strategy Centre

Centre for Transport Studies,
University of London Department of Civil Engineering, Imperial College of Science, Technology and Medicine, London SW7 2BU, UK
Tel: (+44 20) 78 23 99 42   Fax: (+44 20) 75 94 61 07
e-mail: w.adeney@ic.ac.uk
Web: http://www.ulcts.cv.ic.ac.uk/~rtsc

**Key personnel**
Chairman: Professor T M Ridley
Director: William R Steinmetz
Senior Associates: Michael Hamlyn, Nigel Harris, Robin Hirsch, Paul Cheesman, Roger Clutton

**Capabilities**
The Railway Technology Strategy Centre (RTSC) was established in 1992 with funding from the former British Rail and now carries out projects on strategic, technology and economic issues for BR successors and railways elsewhere in the world.

**Projects**
The RTSC has developed a programme to assist metros in identifying and implementing the best practice through detailed case studies and benchmarking comparisons. The metros involved in this exercise are Berlin, Hong Kong, London, Mexico City, Moscow, New York, Paris, São Paulo and Tokyo.
A second benchmarking group has now been formed for medium-sized metro systems, the participants being Glasgow, Hong Kong, Lisbon, Madrid, Newcastle, Oslo and Singapore.
The RTSC has been involved in: updating signalling strategy for Railtrack UK; signalling asset modelling for London Underground Limited; and an evaluation of asset planning best practice for Hong Kong's MTRC system. A speciality of the research work is the application of risk analysis techniques to financial, strategic and engineering decisions.

---

## RailWorks Corporation

1104 Kenilworth Drive, Baltimore, Maryland 21204, USA

**Key personnel**
See entry in *Permanent way components, equipment and services* section.

**Subsidiaries**
Railworks Products and Services Group
Tel: (+1 412) 325 02 02
e-mail: wdonley@railworks.com
President: William R Donley
Vice-President of Business Development: George Caric

Railworks Track Systems Group
Tel: (+1 801) 366 93 39
President: Robert D Wolff

Railworks Transit Systems Group
(+1 914) 323 30 12
President: C William Moore

Pacific Northern Rail Contractors Inc
(a RailWorks Company)
Tel: (+1 604) 850 91 66
President: Henry Braun

**Background**
In September 2001, RailWorks Corporation and its operating subsidiaries in the US, voluntarily filed for protection under chapter 11 of the US Bankruptcy Code.

**Capabilities**
Integrated rail system services and products, active in new construction, rehabilitation, track repair and maintenance, signalling, communications, electrical and other track-related systems, and rail products manufacturing and supply.

**Projects**
New York City Transit Authority (NYCTA) White Plains – Phase II signal rehabilitation project, White Plains, New York.
New Jersey Transit (NJT) Morrisville Train Storage Yard, Falls Township Philadelphia: construct 12 new storage yard tracks and to install related crossovers, turnouts, electrical switch heaters and yard lighting. Modification of existing tracks, rehabilitation of two existing yard tracks, yard drainage, accesses roads and paving.
Minnesota Constructors Team, Hiawatha Light Rail Line, Minneapolis: extending from downtown Minneapolis, through Minneapolis, through the Minneapolis–St Paul International Airports to the Mall of America in Bloomington. The completed project will be approximately 11.4 miles long.
TransLink (Vancouver), Millennium Line Expansion of the Vancouver Skytrain, Vancouver, Canada: Linear induction motor and power rail installation, including the installation of 40,000 lineal metres of LIM (Linear Induction Motor) reaction rail and 80,000 lineal metres of a side mounted power rail including thermal expansion joints, power feeds, isolation joints, and coverboard. Also, core drilling and grouting of 120,00 support studs for the LIM rail and core drilling 60,000 holes to anchor the power rail insulator brackets.
New York City Transit Authority (NYCTA) Carnarsie Line, New York: complete installation of a new Communications Based Train Control System (CBTC) for 13 route miles of the Canarsie Line subway in association with Matra Transport International and Union Switch & Signal.
NYCTA, New York: Rehabilitate the train control signal system for 5.1 miles of track on the Flushing Line subway. Also to furnish and install eight escalators at five locations in the boroughs of Brooklyn and Manhattan.
Miami International Airport, Miami, Florida: Electrical and guideway construction services including automatic train control systems and 8,500 feet of concrete guideway in association with Sumitomo.
Panama Canal Railway, a venture between Kansas City Southern Industries and Lanco International: Reconstruction and expansion of track and facilities involving a 44-mile stretch of track, running parallel to the Canal from Colon to Balboa.
Vancouver Wharves, British Columbia, Canada: Rail yard construction services.
Long Island Rail Road, Long Island: Rehabilitation and improvements of the diesel yard.
IPSCO Steel, Mobile: Steel mill expansion project involving 30,000 crossties and additional switch ties.
US Lime and Minteral-Arkansas Lime, Batesville: The design/build project involves the removal and construction of 15,000 ft of track including three turnouts, grade crossing and bridgework.
Tuscola and Saginaw Bay Railroad, Michigan: Refurbishment project involving 20,000 crossties for the 12.5-mile branch line.

*UPDATED*

---

## Ranbury Management Group

PO Box 914, Brisbane, Queensland 4001, Australia
Tel: (+61 7) 32 11 23 00   Fax: (+61 7) 32 11 29 13
e-mail: ranbury@bigpond.com
Web: http://www.ranbury.com.au

**Key personnel**
Executive Director: Nic Tilley
Operations Director: Eric Evans
Rollingstock Director: David Porter

**Capabilities**
A multidisciplinary rail, property and infrastructure consultancy with management and engineering expertise in rolling stock design and manufacture; systems, signalling and communication; and the redevelopment of railway property. Ranbury's services also include business process management of assets including information systems, financial systems, accounting systems, compliance and strategic planning.

**Projects**
Projects include: the management of the Alliance Agreement between Walkers Engineering and Queensland Rail for the design and manufacture of diesel tilt trains to run between Brisbane and Cairns; the management and co-ordination of the design, construction and redevelopment of Roma Street Station, Brisbane; the administration and management of the ATP contract for the Brisbane to Rockhampton electric tilt trains; and the Development and Project Manager roles for the redevelopment of the North Ipswich rail yards and workshops.

---

## Rescar Incorporated

1101 31st Street, Suite 250/Downers Grove, Illinois 60515, USA
Tel: (+1 708) 597 68 00   Fax: (+1 708) 597 68 95

# 842 CONSULTANCY SERVICES

**Key personnel**
Chief Executive Oficer: Joe Schiesler, Sr
Senior Vice-President: Steve Brown
Director: Andy Schaffer

**Capabilities**
New railcare technical consulting and compliance service, fleet management services, training, management and financial consulting.

## RIQC – Rail Industry Quality Certification Ltd

PO Box 464, London Road, Derby DE24 8ZL, UK
Tel: (+44 1332) 26 27 63   Fax: (+44 1332) 26 36 92
e-mail: the-qss-group@compuserve.com

**Key personnel**
Group Managing Director: Michael Winwood
Senior Executive: Laurie Fitch

**Capabilities**
Include supplier auditing and assessment; systems auditing, supervised and accredited by the United Kingdom Accreditation Service (UKAS) on behalf of the Department of Trade and Industry, to ISO 9000 Series standards.

## RITC Ltd

Africa House, 64-78 Kingsway, London WC2B 6AH, UK
Tel: (+44 20) 73 20 04 36   Fax: (+44 20) 73 20 01 93
e-mail: RITC@compuserv.com

**Key personnel**
Chief Executive: Jackie Chappell
Business Development Manager: Angela Byrne
Administration (incl Marketing): Dawn Garden

**Capabilities**
National occupational standards of competence, covering engineering and operations activities; national and Scottish vocational qualifications; advice on compliance with railway safety-critical work regulations; advice on implementation of competence management systems.

The RITC membership list includes Iarnród Éirann, Ireland; in the UK members include Anglia Railways, Central Trains, Chiltern Trains, Connex, Direct Rail Services, Docklands Light Railway, Eurostar, EW&S, GNER, London Transport, Merseyrail Electrics, NEXUS, Tyne & Wear, Northern Spirit (Regional Railways Northeast), Racal Telecommunications, Railtrack, ScotRail, Serco Metrolink, Stagecoach Supertram (Sheffield), South West Trains, Translink (Northern Ireland Railways), Virgin Trains, WAGN.

Engineering companies belonging to RITC include Amec, First Engineering, Centrac, Adtranz, Balfour Beatty Rail Renewals (Track Systems), Jarvis Training Management and Jarvis Fastline.

Associate members are Spoornet (South African Railways) and, in the UK, Heritage Railways, Creative Training Services, Four Counties Training and South Coast Training.

## RITES Ltd

Rail India Technical and Economic Services Ltd
New Delhi House, 27 Barakhamba Road, New Delhi 110001, India
Tel: (+91 11) 335 48 00   Fax: (+91 11) 331 52 86
e-mail: info@rites.com
Web: http://www.rites.com

**Key personnel**
Managing Director: D C Mishra
Technical Director: H R S Tyagi
Finance Director: B L Bagra

**Background**
RITES Ltd is a Government of India Enterprise.

**Capabilities**
Consultancy, engineering and project management services for railways and other transport sectors. Services include: perspective and master planning, techno-economic and Environmental Impact Assessment (EIA) studies, multimodal transport studies, design and detailed engineering, economic and financial evaluation, project management and construction supervision, operation and maintenance, technical and management support, quality management as per ISO 9000, ISO 14000, QS 9000, ISO 17025, material procurement services, workshop management, management information systems, privatisation and concession, human resource development, property development and financial management. RITES has working experience in over 56 countries in Africa, Europe, Middle East, Latin America and South East Asia.

**Projects**
Recent projects include: Overseas: Bangladesh, supply and maintenance of locomotives and conversion of ordinary coaches to air conditioned coaches; Bhutan, preparation of DPR, tender documents and construction supervision of three bridges; Botswana, management accountancy services to Botswana Railway and detailed engineering for improvements on two international airports; Colombia, maintenance management services for rolling stock for Atlantic Railway; Ethiopia, consultancy services for detailed engineering, design review, bid evaluation for Nazreth—Asela—Dodola, Shashemena—Goba (World Bank Project) and Mekenjo—Najao—Mendi (OPEC funded) road upgrading projects; Iran, engineering supervision services for Karadj Locomotive Workshop; Iraq, supply of railways auxiliary equipment with spares for airbrake systems for Iraqi Railways; Malaysia, expert services for track and bridges and technical assistance for maintenance of rolling stock; Malawi, technical management assistance to the Central East African Railways (CEAR); Mozambique, rehabilitation of Sena line of Beira corridor (World Bank funded); financial expertise to Mozambique Ports and Railways; Myanmar, supply of 10 MG locomotives and techno-economic feasibility study for inland waterways, highways, pipeline links along River Kaladan; Nepal detailed project report and construction management for nine bridges and construction supervision of three in-land container terminals; Sri Lanka, supply of BG locos and spares, upgrade and maintenance of diesel electric loco shed and rehabilitation of three coastal bridges; Tanzania, leasing of 10 YDM4 locomotives; UK, design support of railway electrical engineers/CAD operators to M/s WS Atkins at Sharjah; Uganda-Kampala Urban Traffic Improvement Plan (IDA funded); Vanuatu, development studies, detailed design and engineering services for new international airport and rehabilitation of ring road; Vietnam, supply of various loco and coach spares and rolling stock sub-assemblies such as coach bogies with wheel sets; Zambia, construction supervision for rehabilitation of 236 km road and study of valuation of assets for privatisation of Zambian Railways.

In India: key member of the International Consortium commissioned as general consultants for the Mass Rapid Transit System for Delhi; engineering services for rail bridges at Patna, Monghyr and Jubli rail bridge at Calcutta; redevelopment and property development of Sealdah, Metro and Howrah railway stations, Calcutta and New Delhi Railway station and Metro station at Chennai.

*UPDATED*

## R L Banks & Associates Inc

1717 K Street NW, Washington DC 20006-5331, USA
Tel: (+1 202) 296 67 00   Fax: (+1 202) 296 37 00
e-mail: transport@rlbadc.com

**Key personnel**
Chief Executive: Robert L Banks
President: Charles H Banks
Vice-Presidents: William W Delaney, George K Withers
Managing Director: David J Shuman

**Capabilities**
Economic and financial analysis, planning and policy development, privatisation, organisational restructuring, traffic/cost research, feasibility studies, conceptual engineering, trackage/running rights, due diligence.

**Projects**
Recent and current projects include commuter rail feasibility studies at Burlington, Vermont, Columbia, South Carolina, Des Moines, Iowa and Kansas City, Missouri; railroad line, yard, and facility relocations at Cincinnati and Columbus, Ohio; rail accident investigation for principals and insurers at Barre, Vermont and Lima, Ohio; state rail plans for Colorado, Montana, Vermont and West Virginia; Indiana and Iowa passenger rail studies; analyses of proposed rail mergers for The Port Authority of New York and New Jersey.

## RMS Locotec

Rail Management Services
Vanguard Works, Bretton Street, Dewsbury WF12 9BJ, UK
Tel: (+44 1924) 46 50 50   Fax: (+44 1924) 46 54 22
e-mail: sales@rmslocotec.com

**Key personnel**
Managing Director: Lawrence Crossan
Commercial Manager: Peter Briddon
Operations Manager: Derek Webb

**Capabilities**
RMS was established to meet the demand for rail management services due to the impending changes in the UK rail industry, primarily on the freight side. The services offered cover feasibility studies, project management, operations and commercial studies and specialist engineering services.

RMS can provide a full rail operations and maintenance package, including provision of labour and resources, management of rail traffic, provision of an interface with rail operators and other suppliers, and management of fleets of locomotives, wagons or carriages. It can provide safety systems and offers staff training and certification for rail operations.

*UPDATED*

## Roland Berger & Partner GmbH

Arabellastrasse 33, D-81925 Munich, Germany
Tel: (+49 89) 922 30   Fax: (+49 89) 922 32 02

**Key personnel**
Partner: Dipl Ing, Dipl Wirtsch Ing Albrecht Crux
Principal: Dr Detlef Trefzger

**Capabilities**
Strategy development, business process re-engineering, change management and restructuring.

Has assisted rolling stock manufacturers throughout Europe as well as giving strategic advice to European railways and urban transit authorities.

## Roundel Ltd

7 Rosehart Mews, Westbourne Grove, London W11 3TY, UK
Tel: (+44 20) 72 21 19 51   Fax: (+44 20) 72 21 18 43
Web: http://www.roundel.com

**Key personnel**
Directors: Tony Howard, Michael Denny, Ian St John

**Capabilities**
Corporate identity design for transport systems and operators including service branding, livery design, signing and information design, branded environments and corporate communications.

**Projects**
Branding, livery design, environments and passenger information for Kowloon—Canton Railway; livery designs for Royal Train locomotives and Class 92 Channel Tunnel locomotives; branding and livery design for Railfreight, Great Western, Finnish State Railways and Southern; signing and information design for Docklands Light Railway and for all CTRL stations including St Pancras International; Light Rail system brands, environments and information design for Amey/Bechtel; design guidelines for London Underground and corporate communication design for ABB.

*UPDATED*

## CONSULTANCY SERVICES

## ScanRail Consult

Pilestraede 58, DK-1112 Copenhagen, Denmark
Tel: (+45) 33 76 50 05 ext 155555   Fax: (+45) 33 76 50 61
e-mail: info@rdg.bane.dk
Web: http://www.scanrail-consult.dk

**Key personnel**
Chairman of the Board: Jens Andersen
Director: Preben Olesen

**Capabilities**
ScanRail Consult is an independent organisation within the Danish National Railway Agency. With approximately 350 engineers, planners, strategic business consultants, and architects and economists, ScanRail Consult covers strategic planning, transport management and mechanical expertise related to railway systems.

Competence areas include: railway consultancy from planning and design to implementation, supervision and commissioning of all technical systems for the railway, including project management, quality and environmental management, validation and safety assessment.

Transport consultancy from research and development, studies and cost/benefit analyses, capacity analyses, traffic forecast, operation and traffic analyses, risk analyses, technology strategies, maintenance management systems and intermodal transport consultancy.

ScanRail Consult is actively taking part in international research and development within its competence areas. Furthermore, ScanRail Consult assists the European Commission, UIC and ERRI in the development of European codes and standards for railway systems.

**Projects**
Some of ScanRail Consult's current and recent projects are:
OPTIRAILS: for UIC and the European Commission, ScanRail Consult is analysing the OPTIRAILS project (OPTImisation of traffic through the European RAIL traffic management Systems). The objective of the OPTIRAILS project is to specify the functions of a support system for the international railway traffic in Europe. OPTIRAILS is planned to form part of the ERTMS.
CrossRail: The CrossRail project is outlining the standards for the future European Tram Trains. By introducing European standards and reducing the unit costs on the rolling stock, Tram-Train solutions will constitute an economically attractive solution for many European cities. CrossRail is an R&D project financed by the European Commission, 5th Framework Programme. ScanRail Consult is leading the project, which also includes eight European partners.

ScanRail Consult is rendering consultancy services in the Nordic countries, eastern Europe, the Baltics and to the European Commission. In Denmark all planning and engineering for the Danish National Railway Agency and the Danish Ministry of Transport is part of ScanRail Consult's total portfolio of projects. This includes building new and upgrading existing lines in Denmark and construction of high-speed main lines.

ScanRail Consult has also been rendering consultancy services to the building of the Øresund Fixed Link (bridge-tunnel) between Denmark and Sweden.

ScanRail Consult has played a significant role as consultant on the railway part of the Great Belt Link.

## Scandiaconsult International

Box 4205, SE-102 65 Stockholm, Sweden
Tel: (+46 8) 615 60 00   Fax: (+46 8) 702 19 25
e-mail: info@scc.se
Web: http://www.scc.se

**Capabilities**
Initial investigations, environmental studies, and feasibility studies; complete planning and design; preparation of tender documents; tender evaluation; procurement; construction supervision; and, project management and cost control.

**Projects**
Recent projects include: the Arlanda rapid rail link between Arlanda Airport and Stockholm Central; the Öresund Link between Malmö, Sweden and Copenhagen, Denmark; the Stockholm Light Rapid Transit System; and, the 450 km northern extension of the Bodö–Trondheim railway in northern Norway.

*UPDATED*

## Schofield Lothian

1 Swallow Court, Welwyn Garden City, AL7 1SB, UK
Tel: (+44 1707) 39 00 85   Fax: (+44 1707) 39 14 11
e-mail: info@schofields.com
Web: http://www.schofields.com

**Other offices**
Dublin, Ireland
Berlin, Germany
Hong Kong

**Capabilities**
Engineering management, interface management, clash checks, possession management, system integration, safety case and product acceptance, occupational health and safety, Her Majesty's Railways Inspectorate's approvals, Railway Act regulatory regime, train operations and logistics, risk management.

**Projects**
Connex South Eastern Limited: design and installation of CET facilities at Ashford and St Leonards Depots. London Underground's 'Infraco JNP' civils and asset maintenance providing project and construction expertise to senior programme managers. Railtrack, Balfour Beatty Rail, Westinghouse Signal Limited: West Coast Route modernisation, since 1996, supplying key support personnel to the Euston Alliance, delivering design and interface management, risk assessment and logging, handover and handback support, planning management, databases for the control of design and contract administration and more recently construction delivery. Railtrack Southern Zone: Shortlands Junction, providing advice for efficient co-ordination and management of environmental issues relating to the immediate area around Shortlands Junction and grade separation with management of the Transport and Works Order for promotion of this key project associated with the channel tunnel link. Thameslink: Luton Parkway Station, managing all the regulatory approvals necessary under the Access Conditions and the Railways Act.

*NEW ENTRY*

## Scott Wilson Railways

Western House, 1 Holbrook Way, Swindon SN1 1BY, UK
Tel: (+44 1793) 51 59 07   Fax: (+44 1793) 51 54 87
e-mail: lorraine.gee@scottwilson.com
Web: http://www.scottwilson.com

**Key personnel**
Managing Director: Hugh Blackwood
Overseas Projects Director: Alan Brookes
Head of Business Management: Peter Crane
Head of Permanent Way: John Perkin
Head of Civil & Structural Engineering: Jim Dykes
Head of Electrical and Mechanical Engineering:
  Gareth Clarke
Head of Railway Electrification Engineering: Rob Tidbury
Head of Signalling and Telecommunications Engineering:
  David Nye
Regional Director (Midlands): Robin Hawley

**Background**
Scott Wilson Railways is part of the Scott Wilson Kirkpatrick group.

**Principal subsidiaries**
Scott Wilson Kirkpatrick Ltd
Scott Wilson Railways (Scotland) Ltd
SWK Pavement Engineering Ltd
Scott Neale & Partners Ltd
Scott Wilson Kirkpatrick (Mechanical & Engineering) Ltd

**Capabilities**
Study, design and management of contracts for heavy rail, light rail, high speed routes, trams and metros. It has expertise in civil and structural engineering, permanent way engineering; electrification; signalling and telecommunications; railway operations; railway safety; environmental impact; fabrication inspection; construction management and supervision and risk assessment.
Also value management; rolling stock utilisation and remote monitoring.

**Projects**
Current and recent projects include rail access to airports serving London, Manchester, Liverpool, Glasgow UK and Hong Kong; light rail and metro systems in London, Nottingham, Liverpool, Birmingham, Croydon UK, Mauritius, Johannesburg, Delhi and Hong Kong; commuter operations serving London, Nottingham, Swansea, Norfolk, Leicestershire and Glasgow, UK; train maintenance depots in Reading, Plymouth and Aylesbury (UK) and Tanzania; stations in UK and overseas including the St Petersburg high-speed rail terminal; high-speed rail including the Channel Tunnel Rail Link.

*UPDATED*

## Semaly SA

25 Cours Emile Zola, F-69625 Villeurbanne, France
Tel: (+33 4) 72 69 60 00   Fax: (+33 4) 78 89 68 57
e-mail: semaly@semaly.com
Web: http://www.semaly.com

**Key personnel**
General Manager: Hervé Chaine
Managing Director: Philippe Vuaillat
Finance Director: Olivier Bouvart
Sales Director: Philippe Cou
Marketing Director: David Bouchet
Technical Director: Christian Teillon

**Capabilities**
Semaly undertakes financial and economic studies, feasibility studies, preliminary and detail design work, construction management, operational management and training.

*NEW ENTRY*

## The Seneca Group LLC

122 C Street NW, Suite 850, Washington DC 20001, USA
Tel: (+1 202) 783 58 61   Fax: (+1 202) 783 60 96
e-mail: mccarthy@senecagrp.com
Web: http://www.senecagrp.com

**Key personnel**
President: Chris McCarthy
Principals: David Soule, Phil Davila, John Pinto

**Capabilities**
The Seneca Group provides public and private sector clients expertise to manage projects, develop business opportunities, and secure funding and financing sources. In most instances the need for such assistance is short-term, and the client receives the benefit of essential expertise without the commitment to expand overhead costs.

Seneca offers project management, technical writing, financial analysis, product promotion, and public policy development.

## Serco Raildata

Derwent House, rtc Business Park, London Road, Derby DE24 8UP, UK
Tel: (+44 1332) 26 35 84   Fax: (+44 1332) 26 24 38
e-mail: loreilly@serco.railtest.co.uk

**Key personnel**
Business Manager: Kevin Fretwell

**Background**
Serco Raildata is a division of Serco Railtest.

**Capabilities**
Serco Raildata, the data management division of Serco Railtest Limited, offer professional information management services, accredited to ISO 9002 quality assurance levels. These include electronic delivery systems for rapid retrieval of structural text and graphics, database management services, parts cataloguing, document, drawing and parts data management, data packaging, electronic delivery systems, archiving services.

*UPDATED*

## Serco Railtest Limited

Derwent House, rtc Business Park, London Road, Derby DE24 8UP, UK
Tel: (+44 1332) 26 26 26   Fax: (+44 1332) 26 46 08
e-mail: info@serco.railtest.co.uk
Web: http://www.sercorail.com

### Key personnel
Managing Director: Chris Napier
Production Director: David Partridge
Business Development Director: Barry Winchurch
General Manager (Testing): Richard Hobson

### Subsidiary
Serco Raildata

### Background
Serco Railtest Limited is accredited to BS EN ISO 9002 and is a licensed train-operating company with a Railway Safety Case, Track Access and nationwide depot access agreements.

### Capabilities
Condition monitoring of track and infrastructure components, gauging of structures both manually and using the structure-gauging train, route gauge clearance services.

High-speed monitoring of track geometry, track condition and overhead alignment. Radio signal measurement, line video survey.

Testing, development and acceptance of all types of new and modified vehicles. Including on-site engineering support for fault identification, reliablity testing, field engineering and commissioning. Approved by Railtrack to type-test new and modified vehicles including on-track plant.

Special train operations and planning, vegetation control and rail grinding.

Materials Evaluation Service including non-destructive testing and training centre examining personnel to PCN standards, also magnetic particle inspection to PCN standards. Also offered is bearing examination and training plus a full range of metallurgical analysis techniques of failed components.

*UPDATED*

## SGTE

Société Générale de Techniques et d'Etudes
Parc Saint Christophe, 10 avenue de l'Entreprise, Pôle Galilée 3, F-95865 Cergy-Pontoise Cedex, France
Tel: (+33 1) 34 24 44 00   Fax: (+33 1) 34 24 42 90

### Key personnel
Chairman: Olivier Dubois
General Manager: Bernard Bodin
Deputy General Manager: Claude Antoine

### Capabilities
Planning, project design, works supervision and project management of rail and urban transit systems.

### Projects
Systems engineering for the West Rail of the Kowloon Canton Railway Corporation in Hong Kong. Detailed design of the fourth line for the Caracas Metro; support to the Vietnamese Ministry of Planning and investment in the BOT sector; power supply dimensioning studies for metros in Athens and Caracas.

Third line for the Caracas metro: project management on behalf of Frameca Consortium. Athens Mass Transit: member of the Engineering Subgroup of the Franco-German Consortium. Algiers metro: management of the consortium in charge of the supervision of civil work and infrastructure installation.

Maintenance assistance, safety and reliability studies for the Channel Tunnel. Cairo metro: member of the Engineering Subgroup.

Railway upgrading projects in France for the Rennes-Brest, Rennes- Quimper connections, in Germany for the Berlin-Leipzig-Halle-Erfurt link and in Poland for the Katowice-Wisla Most-Zebrzydowice/Zwardon section (E-65 corridor).

Extending and upgrading urban transport in Berlin and Lisbon; detailed design of the TVR (guided light transport system) for the city of Caen, France.

Preliminary design of the fixed equipment of the tunnel for the Lyon- Turin project.

Basic design of the guided light transport system for the city of Clermont-Ferrard, France.

Control systems, scope definition and interfaces for the Tseung Kwan O Extension project for MTRC Hong Kong.

## SJ International

Suite SE-105 50, Stockholm, Sweden
Tel: (+46 8) 762 50 14   Fax: (+46 8) 762 36 06
e-mail: paula.jonsson@int.sj.se

### Corporate background
SJ International is now the consultancy arm of SwedeRail.

### Capabilities
Include project identification, feasibility studies, market survey and analysis, design, cost estimates and cost flow requirements, detailed project engineering, management support, technical support, project monitoring supervision on or off site, implementation and commissioning services, human resources development training in Sweden and abroad, economic and financial evaluation, efficiency development, restructuring, optimisation studies, quality assurance and control, environmental rehabilitation and training.

## Solvera Information Services Ltd

Chadsworth House, Wilmslow Road, Handforth, Wilmslow, Cheshire SK9 3HP, UK
Tel: (+44 1625) 25 60 00   Fax: (+44 1625) 53 62 46
Web: http://www.solvera.inform.com

### Key personnel
Business Development Manager: John Churchman
Processing of technical information into operation and maintenance manuals, training manuals and promotional literature.

Supplier of documentation and training for the rail industry. Recent contracts include supply of training aids and manuals for New York City Transit Authority, Heathrow Express, and London Underground. Also supplier to ALSTOM, Hong Kong Mass Transit Corporation, Kowloon-Canton Rail Corporation and TGV Korea.

## Southdowns Environmental Consultants Ltd

Suite A3, 16 Station Street, Lewes, East Sussex BN7 2DB, UK
Tel: (+44 1273) 48 81 86   Fax: (+44 1273) 48 81 87
e-mail: secl@tcp.co.uk
Web: http://www.tcp.co.uk/~secl

### Key personnel
Directors: Patrick Williams, Dr R Hood, R H Method

### Capabilities
Southdowns Environmental Consultants Ltd specialises in the measurement, calculation, evaluation and mitigation of environmental noise and vibration impacts from railways.

### Projects
Washington Metro (1996); Channel Tunnel Rail Link (1998); West Coast Main Line (1999); London Tilbury Southend Line (1997); Dublin Light Rail (1999); Taiwan High Speed Rail (1998) and Lantan Railway.

*VERIFIED*

## Strategic Development Group

Midland House, Nelson Street, Derby DE1 2SA, UK
Tel: (+44 1332) 26 24 24   Fax: (+44 1332) 26 22 95

### Key personnel
Managing Director: Bob Somerville
Manager SDG: Charles Penny

### Capabilities
The Strategic Development Group is a partnership with Halcrow Transmark, with a focus on the development of new products and working methods. It draws on expertise from within Balfour Beatty, BICC and Halcrow Transmark.

## Steer Davies Gleave

28-32 Upper Ground, London SE1 9PD, UK
Tel: (+44 20) 79 19 85 00
Fax: (+44 20) 78 27 98 50; 1; 2
e-mail: sdginfo@sdgworld.net
Web: http://www.sdgworld.net

### Branch offices
1 York Place, Leeds, West Yorkshire, LS1 2DR, UK
Tel: (+44 113) 242 99 55   Fax: (+44 113) 242 96 89
e-mail: leedsoffice@sdgworld.net
21 Landsdowne Crescent, Edinburgh, EH12 5EH, UK
Tel: (+44 131) 535 11 01   Fax: (+44 131) 337 97 71
e-mail: edinburgh@sdgworld.net
Plaza de España No 18, Torre de Madrid, Of 8-3, Madrid E-28008, Spain
Tel: (+34 91) 541 86 96   Fax: (+34 91)541 39 96
e-mail: madrid@sdgworld.net
Via de Griffoni 8, I-40123, Bologna, Italy
Tel: (+39 051) 656 93 81   Fax: (+39 051) 656 79 52
e-mail: italy@sdgworld.net
Tren Urbano Building, 398 Jesus Pinero Avenue, Hato Rey, San Juan, 00918 Puerto Rico
Tel: (+1 787) 765 09 27 (ext 293)
Fax: (+1 787) 765 38 85
e-mail: sdgpr@caribe.net
Hernando de Aguirre 201, Of 1301, Santiago, Chile
Tel: (+56 2) 244 43 00   Fax: (+56 2) 244 43 43
e-mail: chile@sdg.cl
Lima 369, Piso 5, b, Edificio del World Trade Center, CP1073, Buenos Aires, Argentina
Tel: (+54 11) 43 82 62 10   Fax: (+54 11) 43 82 61 86
e-mail: argentina@sdg.com.ar

*Bombardier Transportation contracted Serco Railtest to undertake acceptance testing of the new Virgin CrossCountry fleet of Voyager trains (Bombardier Transportation)* 2002/0129113

Nivel C2, CCCT, Apartado Postal 64853, Caracas 1064, Venezuela
Tel: (+58 2) 943 06 23

22-26 Vardon Avenue, East End, Adelaide, South Australia 5000
Tel: (+61 8) 82 23 16 77    Fax: (+61 8) 82 23 18 77
e-mail: adelaideinfo@sdgworld.net.au

**Key personnel**
Managing Director: Jim Steer
Directors: Fred Beltrandi, Charles Russell, Luis Willumsen
Deputy Managing Director: Peter Twelvetree
Executive Director: Brian Martin

**Capabilities**
Policy and business development strategy, advice on privatisation and open access regimes, demand and revenue forecasting, feasibility studies for new and/or reopened lines and stations, project finance and public funding case development, operational and engineering advice.

**Projects**
Santiago—Valparaiso high-speed link, Chile; business franchise advice to Virgin Rail Group and Chiltern Railways, UK; track charging systems, EU; Sydney—Canberra high-speed rail, Australia; East West Rail Link, UK; Ebbw Vale rail strategy, Welsh Development Agency, UK.

## Steria Transports

12 rue Paul Dautier, PO Box 58, F-78142 Vélizy, Cedex, France
Tel: (+33 1) 34 88 60 00    Fax: (+33 1) 34 88 62 62
e-mail: jacques.lafay@steria.fr

**Key personnel**
Sales and Marketing Director: Jacques Lafay

**Capabilities**
Traffic management, control and regulation: maintenance management systems; information display systems; ticketing and smartcards.

## Strukton Railinfra BV

Westkanaaldijk 2, NL-3542 DA Utrecht
PO Box 1025, NL-3600 BA Maarssen, Netherlands
Tel: (+31 302) 48 69 01    Fax: (+31 302) 48 66 01

**Key personnel**
See entry in *Permanent way components, equipment and services* section.

**Corporate background**
Strukton Railinfra is part of the construction company, Strukton Groep NV.

**Services**
Innovation, engineering, market monitoring, project management, competence development, maintenance management, product development, breakdown repair, electrical power, underground infrastructure, cabling, telecommunications, rolling stock, production and maintenance of high output equipment and production welding.

*NEW ENTRY*

## STV Group

205 West Welsh Drive, Douglassville, Pennsylvania 19518, USA
Tel: (+1 610) 385 82 00    Fax: (+1 610) 385 85 01
e-mail: info@stvine.com
Web: http://www.stvinc.com

**STV Incorporated**
225 Park Avenue South, New York, New York 10003, USA
Tel: (+1 212) 777 44 00    Fax: (+1 212) 529 52 37

**Key personnel**
President and Chief Executive Officer: D M Servedio

Key Rail Staff: W F Matts, K Bossung, O Allen, M Gagliardi, T Spearing

**Capabilities**
Transport planning; system and facility design; rolling stock engineering; operations and maintenance analysis.

*UPDATED*

## SwedeRail

SwedeRail AB
PO Box 205, SE-101 24 Stockholm, Sweden
Tel: (+46 8) 762 37 80    Fax: (+46 8) 10 62 43
e-mail: info@swederail.se
Web: http://www.swederail.se

**Key personnel**
President: Christer Beijbom
Project Directors: Gunnar Hallert
 Ulf Halloff
 Robert Hallenborg
 Björn Andersson
 Per Ola Strömberg
 Bernt Andersson
 Bo Marklund
 Jan Gullbrandsson

**Corporate development**
SwedeRail is owned by Swedish State Railways (SJ) which operates on a wholly commercial basis and also represents the National Rail Administration (BV), a government agency responsible for the construction and maintenance of state-owned rail infrastructure.

**Capabilities**
SwedeRail markets railway knowledge to operators within the transport sector through qualified railway knowledge and practical experience of restructuring, market orientation and railway operation in a deregulated market.

**Current projects**
Research and development within the EU Frame Programme; international training course 'Railway Safety Management', international training course for the Swedish Agency for Develoment Cooperation (SIDA); management development (for SIDA), railway rehabilitation and a technical study (for the European Bank of Reconstruction and Development) in Bosnia Herzegovina; maintenance and technical support in China and Kosovo; technical support in Croatia; legal reforms in Kazakhstan; technical support in Portugal; seminars on restructuring in Russia; operation of regional railways in Sweden; development of business plans for the Ukrainian National Rail Transport Administration.

## Symonds Group

24-30 Holborn, London EC1N 2LX, UK
Tel: (+44 20) 74 21 20 00    Fax: (+44 20) 74 21 22 22

**Works**
Symonds House, Wood Street, East Grinstead, RH19 1UU, UK
Tel: (+44 1342) 32 71 61
Fax: (+44 1342) 31 35 00; 31 59 27
Web: http://www.symonds-group.com

**International offices**
Australia, Hong Kong, Hungary, India, Indonesia, Malaysia, New Zealand, Oman and the Philippines.

**Key personnel**
Director, Railways & Transit: Roger Sawyers
Associate, Economics and Business Strategy: Andrew Marsay

**Capabilities**
Symonds is responsible for the detail design of the permanent way and structures for Contract 434 which provides the links from the Channel Tunnel Rail Link into Ashford International Station. The company is assisting various train operating companies develop proposals for infrastructure enhancements in respect of their passenger franchise bids. It continues to advise UK and international funders on a wide variety of rail projects, including, Arlandabanan Airport Link, Sweden; Bangkok Metro, Thailand; DLR Lewisham Extension, UK and Chiltern and South Central Franchises, UK. Symonds is also appointed to the SRA's Freight Panel providing assistance on freight facilities grants and other freight related issues. Other projects include a study for the European Commission on single wagonload traffic and strategic planning advise for the Budapest Metro.

*UPDATED*

## Systra

5 avenue du Coq, F-75009 Paris, France
Tel: (+33 1) 40 16 61 00    Fax: (+33 1) 40 16 61 04
e-mail: systra@systra.com
Web: http://www.systra.com

**Key personnel**
Chairman: Michel Cornil
President: Thierry Ossent
Vice-President, Marketing and Business Development:
 Allen Lee
Vice-President, Business Development:
 Jean Christophe Hugonnard
Vice-President, Finance & Legal Affairs: Vincent Depondt
Vice-President, Engineering: Jean-Pierre Orsi
Vice-President, Human Resources and Information
 Systems: Serge Dassonville
Marketing Director: Jean-Francois Bourgeois

**Subsidiaries**
The MVA Group: UK, France, Hong-Kong
Systra Consulting: USA
CANARAIL: Canada
SYSTRA SpA/SOTECNI: Italy
SOTEC Ingénterie: France

**Other subsidiaries and participations:**
Mexistra: Mexico
Sofrecad: Chile
SFCH: China
Eurometuoes: Romania
Semto: Reunion Island
Systra: Philippines

**Corporate development**
Systra is a subsidiary of SNCF and RATP Paris.

**Capabilities**
Systra offers consulting services for high-speed trains, conventional rail, mass transit, metro, light rail, automatic guided transit systems and buses. Capabilities include: feasibility studies; economic and financial analyses; preliminary and detailed design; contract preparation; construction management; testing and commissioning of equipment; planning operations and maintenance.

**Projects**
China: Xinmin LRT.
Taiwan: rail link, Taipei airport.
South Korea: Seoul—Pusan high-speed rail project (1994-2003) – design and design review services.
UK: London/Channel Tunnel High-Speed Link (1996-2003) – leader for the systemwide design and procurement; modification of Eurotunnel railway signalling; final design of the Saint Pancras High-Speed Station in London.
France: Design and construction of Bordeaux LRT network; Orleans LRT Line 1.
Canada: design of the extension of lines four and five of the Montreal metro.
CIS railways restructuring study in Kazakhstan, Uzbekistan, Turkmenistan, Tajikistan, and Kyrgyzstan.
Russia: study for upgrading services on the Moscow St Petersburg—Helsinki corridor.
Bangladesh: supervision of the construction of the Jamuna bridge.
Egypt: feasibility study for the regional Alexandria metro line.

## TAMS Consultants Inc

655 Third Avenue, New York, New York 10017, USA
Tel: (+1 212) 867 17 77    Fax: (+1 212) 697 63 54
e-mail: marketing@tamsconsultants.com
Web: http://www.tamsconsultants.com

## 846 CONSULTANCY SERVICES

**Key personnel**
President: Anthony R Dolcimascolo
Principals: Patrick J McAward Jr, Lyle H Hixenbaugh, Edward C Regan, G Barrie Heinzenknecht, Ronald H Axelrod, Frank A Baragona, Eric Cole, E Patrick Sorensen, Albert DiBernardo, Joseph Fiteni Jr, Kenneth F Standing, Charles F van Cook

**Capabilities**
TAMS offers international services in engineering, architecture, and planning. The firm has worked in more than 100 countries, providing comprehensive services for major ports, highways, railroads, bridges, airports, dams, agricultural and regional development, waste management, and urban planning projects.

TAMS has experience in the planning, design, and inspection of railroad facilities, ranging from the engineering of more than 4,000 km of railroads throughout the world to the design of major tunnels and stations. Projects include planning new lines through jungle or desert and rapid transit systems in US cities. Services provided by TAMS include location and alignment, trackwork, bridges, tunnels, and marshalling yards.

## TDG

Transit Design Group Inc
81 D Brunswick Boulevard, Dollard des Ormeaux, Quebec H9B 2J5, Canada
Tel: (+1 888) 866 18 34   Fax: (+1 514) 685 72 39
Web: http://www.tdgdesign.com

**Key personnel**
Vice-President: Robert J Gagne

**Capabilities**
Design, engineering and manufacture of lighting products for the transportation market, including exterior lighting, interior lighting and a range of illuminated signs.

## TecnEcon Ltd

Glen House, 125 Old Brompton Road, London SW7 3RP, UK
Tel: (+44 20) 73 73 77 55   Fax: (+44 20) 73 70 33 28
e-mail: tecnecon@dial.pipex

**Key personnel**
Managing Director: Jeff Ody
Commercial Director: Alan Power
Director, Transport Planning Services: Philip Bates
International Transport Planning: Stephen Rutherford
Transport Planning, South-East: Eddie Strankalis
Public Transport: Hermann Maier
Traffic and Parking Studies, South-East: David Warriner
European Transport: Jean Pierre Soulie

**Middle East regional office**
PO Box 52750, Dubai, United Arab Emirates

**Capabilities**
Multimodal urban transport planning specialists in modelling and operational studies, economic and financial appraisal; market research into public transport attitudes and product development in relation to real-time passenger information systems; technical assistance and policy advice to international lending agencies, governments and transport operators.

## TERA

Transportation and Economic Research Associates Inc
107 E. Holly Avenue, Suite 12, Sterling, Virginia 20164-5405, USA
Tel: (+1 703) 406 44 00   Fax: (+1 703) 406 15 50
Web: http://www.teraus.com

**Key personnel**
President: Asil Gezen
Vice-President: Lynn Harmon

**Offices**
Beijing; Manila; Sofia

**Capabilities**
TERA is a respected contract research and consulting firm founded in 1976. Capabilities include restructuring, concession, privatisation analyses; socio-economic/poverty impact assessments; management information systems; strategic planning and analyses; infrastructure evaluations; organisational and management reviews; trade/traffic forecasting; operational assessments; freight and passenger tariffs/marketing analyses; accounting and traffic costing; regulatory and institutional analyses.

**Projects**
TERA has successfully completed various projects in railway transportation in the USA, Central and Eastern Europe, Africa, the Middle East, Latin America and Central and Southern Asia. Project experience covers rail car ferry service operations, metro and light rail projects computer simulation of freight and passenger traffic locomotive workshop and other facility evaluations motive power and rolling stock engineering and requirements analysis and intermodal operations, including rail car ferry services on the Caspian Sea, the Black Sea, the Baltic Sea and Lake Michigan. The company has been involved in various evaluations and feasibility studies worldwide, such as regional rail corridor assessments for the Balkans and a regional locomotive rehabilitation facility and centralised parts warehouse in Eastern and Southern Africa for the Union of African Railways.

*UPDATED*

## TIFSA

Tecnología e Investigación Ferroviaria SA
Capitan Haya 1-5 planta, E-28020 Madrid, Spain
Tel: (+34 91) 555 95 62   Fax: (+34 91) 555 10 41
e-mail: TIFSA@tifsa.es

**Key personnel**
President & Chief Executive Officer: José E Seco Domínguez
General Director: A Fernández Gil
Directors: Juan Batanero Bernabeu, José A Hurtado

**Capabilities**
TIFSA is a subsidiary of RENFE and was established in 1983. Its activities were previously restricted to Spain, Europe and Latin America but it is now willing to consider contracts anywhere in the world. Its capabilities include:
Railway engineering: definition of systems, technological development and design of technical specifications.
Railway infrastructure projects, urban transport equipment and logistic nodes.
Railway restructuring, privatisation processes, organisation and human resources, business plans and legal aspects of service contracts.
Technical assistance in the construction of fixed facilities, construction management and site supervision.
High speed engineering: projects, technical assistance, technology transfer and systems development.
Rolling stock engineering: development of specific equipment, factory inspection, test and maintenance programmes, commissioning and acceptance of works, quality control.
Inspection and maintenance audits of permanent way and railway installations: viaducts, bridges, trackworks, traction substations.
Software for the transport sector and communications: systems, remote control, telemetry and GIS (Geographical Information Systems).
Environment: environmental audits, environmental impact, soil contamination and risks assessment.
Transport Consultancy: institutional development, market studies, intermodal planning, investment plans and infrastructure networks, whether urban or interurban.
Training programmes in the transport sector, requalification and updating of personal, management and technical capacitation.
Design of business plans in the transport sector, strategic and action plans; technical assistance to reconversion and adjustment plans.

**Projects**
Updating of RENFE Track Standards. Development of 'optimum rolling profiles' for RENFE powered rolling stock. Quality audits of train production factories in France and Spain. Development of a new computer-assisted system for RENFE for designing station interlocks. High-speed programme in Spain.
Supervision for the installation of signalling on the Bilbao metro.
Freight operation monitoring and control system (Russia).
Technical assistance to Oktober Railways (Russia).
Technical assistance to Belarussian Railways.
Brest Railway Bottleneck (Belarus).
Restructuring support to Slovenian railways.
E 20 trunk railway line (Warsaw-Kunowice section) market study (Poland).
Development of an Integrated Transport Information System (ITIS) Centre in Poland.
Preliminary Coastal Train study (Uruguay).
Feasibility study for the implementation of a light metro system in Tijuana (Mexico).
Design appraisal, inspection of testing services related to the supply of 21 diesel locomotives (Israel).
Monitoring and supervision of the manufacturing of 65 new Talgo coaches (USA).

*UPDATED*

## Tilney Shane

5 Heathmans Road, London SW6 4TJ, UK
Tel: (+44 20) 77 31 69 46   Fax: (+44 20) 77 36 33 56
e-mail: info@tilneyshane.co.uk
Web: http://www.tilneyshane.co.uk

**Key personnel**
Chief Executive: Kathy Tilney
Design Directors: Marvin Shane and Jonathan Wilson
Projects Director: Roger Edey
Financial Director: Heather Shane

**Capabilities**
Design of interiors for transport systems and of environments suitable for high passenger densities; design of specialist rail vehicles including concepts, engineering development and textile design. Rail project design includes passenger flow analysis, CAD drawing production, mockup build supervision, technical and procurement specification.

*UPDATED*

## TLC

Transport, Informatik, und Logistik-Consulting GmbH
Hallesches Ufer 30, D-10963 Berlin, Germany
Tel: (+49 611) 173 45 58   Fax: (+49 611) 173 41 13
e-mail: TLC.Sales@tlc.de

**Key personnel**
Managing Director: Dr Gerhard Pintag
International Sales: Dr Hubert Kreutzmann

**Offices**
TLC has branches in Wiesbaden, Frankfurt, Berlin, Vienna, Sofia and Bucharest.
Established 1988
Staff: 1,050

**Background**
TLC is 100 per cent owned by Deutsche Bahn AG of Germany.

**Capabilities**
Consultancy and logistics services for the transport industry, specialising particularly in business-process re-engineering. The company has been responsible for the design and implementation of computer software solutions, not only for the parent company (German Rail) but also for a large number of other customers in the transport industry. Increased emphasis being placed on contracts with customers outside Germany.

**Projects**
Include rail and local transport ticketing systems, train reservation systems, internet sales (including online ticketing fulfilment), freight management systems, infrastructure and property management systems. TLC is currently implementing the complete restructuring for DB's Cargo (freight) division.

## TMG International Pty Ltd

13th Floor 39-41 York Street, Sydney, New South Wales 2000, Australia
Tel: (+61 2) 92 62 41 11   Fax: (+61 2) 92 62 41 10

**Key personnel**
Group Managing Director: Dale Coleman
Managing Director TMG Australia: Peter Thornton
Director Queensland: Keith Walker
Director Modelling Services: Alex Wardrop
Managing Director TMG International (Asia) Limited: Clive Yep

**Other offices**
98 South Road, Torrensville PO Box 253, Torrensville Plaza South Australia 5031, Australia
Tel: (+61 8) 84 43 41 33   Fax: (+61 8) 84 43 41 55
e-mail: tmgsa@senet.com.au

11/114 Albert Road, South Melbourne Victoria 3205, Australia
Tel: (+61 3) 96 96 01 06   Fax: (+61 3) 96 96 27 78

3rd Floor, 447 Upper Edward Street, Brisbane, Queensland 4000, Australia
Tel: (+61 7) 38 39 14 03   Fax: (+61 7) 38 31 67 11
e-mail: tmgbne@gil.com.au

TMG International Asia
Suite 2501, Golden Centre, 188 Des Voeux Road, Central Hong Kong
Tel: (+852 2) 815 65 99   Fax: (+852 2) 815 65 99
e-mail: tmgasia@nevigator.com

**Capabilities**
System modelling and simulation, timetable planning and development, operational and infrastructure planning, energy efficient train regulation, condition monitoring and dynamic analysis systems, maintenance analysis and planning, safety and risk analysis, operations and infrastructure benchmarking, asset management systems and support.

*UPDATED*

## Tractebel Development

Avenue Ariane 7, B-1200 Brussels, Belgium
Tel: (+32 2) 773 78 62   Fax: (+32 2) 773 79 90
e-mail: development@tractebel.com
Web: http://www.tractebel.com

**Key personnel**
Rail and Road Department Manager: V Wilkin
Projects Manager: M Brismée

**Capabilities**
Tractebel's capabilities in railways, underground and light rail transit systems include: engineering infrastructures, superstructures, rolling stock, electricity supply, signalling, telecommunications, safety, and geotechnology; project management and supervision of works; turnkey projects, and consultancy in town and country planning, freight/passenger transport systems, transport master plans and feasibility studies

## Transcorp

22 New Street, Leamington Spa CV31 1HP, UK
Tel: (+44 1926) 83 31 13   Fax: (+44 1926) 83 27 88
1a Lonsdale Square, London N1 1EN, UK
Tel: (+44 20) 74 66 44 33   Fax: (+44 20) 77 00 05 97
e-mail: tcorp@fmgroup.co.uk

**Key personnel**
Executives: Neil Bates, Tony Hume, David King, Peter Trickett

**Capabilities**
Transcorp is a consortium of companies providing a design resource for passenger-focused transport. This includes total vehicle engineering, exterior and interior design, brand creation, architectural design, ergonomics, customer research, preference and user trials, landscape architecture/environmental design, urban planning, infrastructure design, project management and technical engineering.

**Projects**
Clients include Adtranz, Anglia Railways, Bombardier, CAF, Chiltern Railways, Greater Nottingham Rapid Transit, Grande Lignes, Holec Ridderkerk (now Traxis BV and Transys Projects Ltd), London Underground, Manchester Metrolink, Kinki Sharyo, KCRC Hong Kong, Siemens, SNCF and Virgin Atlantic.

## Transportation Technology Center Inc

A subsidiary of the Association of American Railroads
PO Box 11130, Pueblo, Colorado 81001, USA
Tel: (+1 719) 584 07 50   Fax: (+1 719) 584 06 72
e-mail: marketing@ttci.aar.com
Web: http://www.ttci.com

**Key personnel**
President: Roy A Allen
Vice-President Technology: Keith L Hawthorne
Vice-President Business Development: Dr Albert J Reinschmidt
Vice-President and Chief Financial Officer: Dr Scott B Harvey
Senior Assistant, Vice-President Research and Development: Semih Kalay
Assistant Vice-President Strategic Planning Capabilities: Dr James R Lundgren
Assistant Vice-President Communications and Train Control Technologies: Alan L Polivka

**Background**
TTCI was formed on 1 January 1998 as a wholly owned subsidiary of the Association of American Railroads. About 275 engineers, technicians and support personnel make up the staff of TTCI.

**Capabilities**
Major areas of expertise include: intelligent train systems, communications and train control systems, wheel/rail interface, vehicle/track performance, track condition monitoring, track integrity, special trackwork, bridges, track components, heavy axle loads, hazardous materials safety, and advanced train components. TTCI has extensive modern facilities for testing, training and research, including a leading railroad technology R&D centre, over 50 miles of test tracks, full-scale vehicle and component test equipment, and dynamic modelling programs.

**Projects**
TTCI has a Facility for Accelerated Service Testing (FAST) for evaluating the effects of increased axle loads on track and rolling stock, and also modelling tools such as NUCARS (for vehicle response to railway geometry) and TEM (for energy consumption). TTCI has successfully completed thorough testing of 150 mph passenger trains for the USA and Japan.

*UPDATED*

## Transport Design International

12 Waterloo Park Estate, Bidford-on-Avon B50 4JH, UK
Tel: (+44 1789) 49 03 70   Fax: (+44 1789) 49 05 92
e-mail: designoffice@tdi.uk.com
Web: http://www.tdi.uk.com

**Key personnel**
Executives: Martin Pemberton (UK), John Brown (Australia)

**Joint venture companies**
Warwick Design Consultants Ltd, UK
Design Resource Australia Pty Ltd, Australia
Minitram Systems Ltd, UK

*Japanese-built gauge-convertible emu at Pueblo*

*Amtrak Acela high-speed tilting trainset on TTCI's Pueblo test track*

# 848  CONSULTANCY SERVICES

*London Underground Piccadilly Line refurbishment*
0016446

## Capabilities
Transport design service for the development of new vehicles and products from concept through to production. With offices in the UK and Australia, Transport Design International employs specialist industrial designers, ergonomists and mechanical and electronic engineers and maintains full workshop and prototyping facilities within each studio complex. Typical commissions involve feasibility analysis, layout and design of vehicle interiors including: saloons, driving cabs and control desks, passenger seating, onboard catering, information and entertainment facilities. Exterior styling is also undertaken, and scale models and full-size mockups of complete vehicles are produced in-house and delivered on site.

The group's designers are also experienced in working with architectural teams to create station environments.

## Projects
Current and recent projects include:
London Underground Ltd: design of refurbishment of Piccadilly Line and Northern Line trainsets, including construction of full-size interior mockups; design of metro trainsets for Jubilee Line Extension, including construction of full-size interior mockups.
Queensland Rail: feasibility studies on the design of tilting trainsets for Brisbane—Rockhampton—Cairns service and new designs for emus.
SRA New South Wales: new designs for fourth-generation Tangara emus, XPT seating and suburban rolling stock refurbishment.
PTC Melbourne: emu fleet refurbishment.
KCRC West Rail Hong Kong: concept design and tender specification for rolling stock.
Former GEC ALSTOM: night stock conversion feasibility and mock-up design.
Clyde Engineering: design of new fourth generation double-deck train for SRA New South Wales.
Manchester Metrolink: bid support on phase 3 extension.

***UPDATED***

---

# TRL Limited (Transport Research Laboratory)

Old Wokingham Road, Crowthorne, Berkshire RG45 6AU, UK
Tel: (+44 1344) 77 00 07   Fax: (+44 1344) 77 08 80
e-mail: enquiries@trl.co.uk
Web: http://www.trl.co.uk

## Key personnel
Head of Rail: Peter Lindon
Corporate Market Research Manager: Mary Treen

## Capabilities
TRL employs over 500 people including 380 technical specialists, and operates worldwide. Its capabilities include: transport strategy and scheme appraisal; transport modelling, monitoring and planning; generic safety and environmental consultancy; transport strategy and scheme appraisal, transport modelling, monitoring, planning.

***UPDATED***

---

# TransTec

Transport und Technologie Consult TransTec GmbH
Lister Strasse 15, D-30163 Hannover, Germany
Tel: (+49 511) 399 50   Fax: (+49 511) 39 95 14 99
e-mail: tt-consult@transtec-hannover.de
Web: http://www.transtec-hannover.de

## Offices
Hannover, Hamburg, Berlin, Amsterdam, Chicago

## Capabilities
TransTec-consult is a company in the German TransTec Group. It provides consultancy for organisation and management, public transport and operations technology and innovation.

---

# Transurb

85 Sainte-Catherine St West, Montreal H2X 3P4, Canada
Tel: (+1 514) 287 85 00   Fax: (+1 514) 282 28 08
e-mail: http://www.tecsult.com

## Key personnel
President: Pierre Asselin
Vice President: Michel Larocque

## Capabilities
Undertakes services from initial studies to project management, including demand and traffic surveys, geological inspection, civil engineering design, railway design, procurement and construction management.

## Projects
Transurb is presently completing feasibility studies for the extension of the metro in Montreal.

---

# Transurb Technirail SA

60 Rue Ravenstein, Bte 18, B-1000 Brussels, Belgium
Tel: (+32 2) 512 30 47   Fax: (+32 2) 513 94 19
e-mail: a.willaert@transurb.com
Web: http://www.transurb.com

## Key personnel
Chief Executive: Patrick Steyaert
Finance Director: F Saussez
Commercial Director: E Deblon
Marketing Manager: A Willaert

## Principal subsidiaries
TUC Rail
Transurb Argentina
Transurb Gabon
Transurb Malaysia
Transurb International Ltd Russia

## Capabilities
Transurb Consult was formed in 1973 to bring together the various aspects of Belgian transport technology. Its capital is equally apportioned between Belgian Railways (SNCB), Luxembourg Railways (CFL), the Brussels Public Transport Company (STIB), the public transport companies of the Walloon and Flemish Regions (TEC and De Lijn). The private sector is mainly represented by Tractebel, a major holding company in Belgium, and by specialised private research offices dealing with all aspects of transportation.

---

# Transys Projects Ltd

2 Priestley Wharf, Holt Street, Aston Science Park, Birmingham B7 4BN, UK
Tel: (+44 121) 359 77 77   Fax: (+44 121) 359 18 11
e-mail: info@transysprojects.ltd.uk

## Key personnel
Managing Director: Jeremy J Ashley
Marketing and Sales Director: Kevin Lane
Engineering Director: Karl J Barras

## Corporate structure
Transys Projects Ltd is a member of the Brant Beheer Group.

## Capabilities
Multidisciplined engineering consultancy and project management organisation, covering all aspects of passenger rail vehicles and their related support services. This covers mass transit vehicles, LRVs and tramcars as well as main line dmus, emus, and passenger coaches. Particularly specialising on UK, Railtrack Group Standards, Safety Cases and vehicle acceptance.

Certified to BS EN ISO 9001 with 'Link-Up' accreditation in eight relevant areas. London Underground registered supplier for consultancy services in rolling stock engineering No R45445.

Specific capabilities include:

*Design Engineering*
- design of complete rail vehicles or discrete areas
- concept to production drawings/schedules
- bodyshells, underframes, cabs, interiors
- assembly, component and system design
- mockups, modular design

*Engineering Services*
- optimise design to obtain requisite certification
- FEA, classical calculations, kinematics, coupler movements
- specification and management of structural testing
- tender/tender response documents and purchase specifications

*Electrical and Mechanical Systems, Engineering and Integration*
- ability to project engineer a complete range of equipment, systems and services through design, testing and validation.
- vehicle mechanical equipment, systems, diesel drivelines and so on
- electrical/electronic systems including control and traction auxiliaries
- material choice, fire safety and testing
- vehicle performance, simulation on specified routes
- vehicle acceptance and safety case issues
- fault finding, trouble shooting

*Project Support*
- provide project management and planning
- select/monitor subcontractors and/or product performance
- vehicle maintenance, efficiency and reliability improvement
- developing technical literature and support information
- product support group undertakes modification and upgrade work.

## Projects
Design engineered and project managed Class 323 and Malaysian emus plus Glasgow Underground trailer cars.

Various recent tender support projects for major European vehicle manufacturers, covering emus, dmus and demus, predominantly for the UK but also for the Far East.

Feasibility studies and engineering investigations for UK rail vehicle leasing companies (ROSCOs) as well as turnkey projects. Various proposed design solutions for UK train operating companies (TOCs).

Complex underframe installation designs covering complete diesel drivelines, fuel tanks, brake frames, electric traction drives and auxiliary equipment cases. Interior finish design/engineering for several new multiple unit packages in the UK.

General engineering consultancy, detailed structural design, safety and maintenance support for Fiat Ferroviaria on their joint UK contract with Alstom Transport for Virgin's West Coast high-speed tilting trains.

Design support for Alusuisse Road and Rail. Various other contracts for engineering consultancy and maintenance support activities.

***UPDATED***

---

# Trauner

1617 JFK Boulevard, Suite 600, Philadelphia, Pennsylvania 19103, USA
Tel: (+1 215) 814 64 00

## Key personnel
Vice President, Business Development: Tracy M Doyle

## Capabilities
Most aspects of rail and road consultancy.

## Projects
Trauner has been brought in to assure construction quality for the US$1.9 billion Alameda Corridor Transportation Authority (ACTA) rail project. The Corridor

will be a freight track which runs north from the nation's largest seaports and is the first consolidated railroad link of its kind. The double-tracked Alameda Corridor will begin in the City of Compton before descending into a 10-mile long trench, finally emerging in Los Angeles and dispersing among the railroad mainlines. Construction on this project includes the digging of 33 ft deep trenches, new Los Angeles River crossings, and associated bridge structures. Trauner's professional engineers and consultants will be involved in the evaluation of the Design-Build Contractor's baseline schedules, design review and oversight, claims analysis and dispute resolution, and the preparation and delivery of training/workshops for ACTA personnel.

The Alameda Corridor will reduce traffic delays by eliminating conflicts at nearly 200 street-level railway crossings. The ACTA plan includes new overpasses to separate train and road traffic and the widening of Alameda Street from four lanes to six.

## Trenitalia SpA

Italian State Railways
Rolling Stock Technology Department (UTMR)
Viala S Lavagnini 58, I-50129 Florence, Italy
Tel: (+39 055) 47 60 00 Fax: (+39 055) 48 19 05

### Services

With more than 5,000 employees, UTMR is responsible for the maintenance of Italian State Railways (FS) traction and rolling stock. It also undertakes overhaul, refurbishment and conversion projects using the 13 facilities that form the company's Major Repairs Workshops (OGR) division. These resources and capabilities are offered to other operators.

*NEW ENTRY*

## TUC Rail

TUC Rail SA
Rue de France 91, B-1070 Brussels, Belgium
Tel: (+32 2) 529 78 20   Fax: (+32 2) 529 79 00
e-mail: info@tucrail.be
Web: http://www.tucrail.be

### Capabilities

Preliminary studies for development of railway infrastructures, design of bridges, viaducts and tunnels, tracklaying, signalling, telecommunications, quality control, safety monitoring, validation and testing.

## Tyréns Infraconsult AB

SE-118 86 Stockholm, Sweden
Tel: (+46 8) 429 00 00   Fax: (+46 8) 429 00 60
e-mail: info@tyrens.se
Web: http://www.tyrens.se

### Capabilities

Include: environmental engineering and assessment; ground, water and sewerage planning; geotechnical engineering and rock mechanics; landscape and urban planning; cartography and surveying technology; and civil engineering, including railway, tunnel, street and highway design.

### Projects

Projects on which Tyréns has provided services include: the Swedish National Rail Administration's Sveland Mälar valley, Arlanda and West Coast lines; Malmo City Tunnel; the Öresund Fixed Link; and for Norwegian State Railways, the reconstruction of Skien station, south of Oslo.

## Vanness-Brackenridge Group

9652 Preston Trail W, Ponte Vedra Beach, Florida 32082, USA
Tel: (+1 904) 280 18 98   Fax: (+1 904) 280 18 99
e-mail: vanco@attbi.com
Web: http://www.transmatch.com

### Key personnel

Principals: J Christopher Rooney, T Stephen O'Connor

### Capabilities

Consultancy services for railways, governments and bilateral lending agencies concerning restructuring and strategic planning issues. The Vanness-Brackenridge Group has experience in railway restructuring, strategic planning, financial modelling, market analysis, organisational restructuring and policy development.

### Projects

The Vanness-Brackenridge Group has served clients in 15 countries including Argentina, Australia, Bolivia, Brazil, Canada, Chile, Ecuador, South Korea, Mexico, Myanmar (Burma), New Zealand, Spain, Sri Lanka, Thailand and USA.
Recent projects include:
Advising US Department of Transportation with respect to Amtrak-related issues.
CSX Transportation, USA: advised on post merger strategy, value realisation and network restructuring; and on acquisition of rail properties in north and south America.
Ferrocarriles Metropolitanos, Argentina: supervision of activities of Amtrak and New Zealand Rail advisers in the formulation of business strategies and financial budgets for Buenos Aires suburban passenger services on the Sarmiento and San Martín systems.
Canadian National Railways: advice as part of a continuing assignment to address strategic marketplace, competitive and organisational issues.
Companhia Vale do Rio Doce, Brazil: management of a long-term engagement to transform the Vitória a Minas Railway (EVFM) from an industrial system into a full-service operation offering general freight and passenger services.
Conrail, USA: supervision of technical staff preparing for privatisation.
Chilean State Railways (EFE): analysis for the Inter-American Development Bank of the feasibility of restructuring EFE.
Bolivian National Railways (ENFE): analysis of an open access policy for operating private freight services over ENFE infrastructure.
State Railways of Ecuador (ENFE): advice to the Ecuadorean government and the Inter-American Development Bank concerning the best strategy for ENFE's future development.
National Railways of Mexico (FNM): analysis for the Mexican Secretariat of Transport and Communications of various strategies for FNM privatisation.
New Zealand Rail (NZR): participation in the sale of NZR to a consortium including Wisconsin Central Transportation.
Sri Lanka Railway (SLR): advice to Sri Lanka Ministry of Transport and World Bank on the restructuring of SLR.
State Railway Authority of New South Wales, Australia: study of current operations and proposed reforms.

*UPDATED*

## Vossloh System-Technik York Ltd

St Mary's Court, 39 Blossom Street, York YO24 1AQ, UK
Tel: (+44 1904) 63 90 91 Fax: (+44 1904) 63 90 92
Web: http://www.comreco-rail.co.uk

### Key personnel

See *Simulation and training systems*.

### Developments

See *Simulation and training systems*.

### Capabilities

Trainplan™ complete train planning system including timetabling and crew and vehicle scheduling using Resourceplan™, Railplan™, a multitrain simulation system, Powerplan™ for analysing electrical supply networks and TRACSIII™, a crew optimising system. All are available for licensed use and are used by Comreco Rail in consultancy work worldwide.

### Projects

Provision of consultancy, planning and management of rail operations, exploitation of infrastructure capacity and development of operations planning processes for a wide range of clients including Railtrack, Scotrail, South West Trains, EW&S, Queensland Rail, NSB, SJ, Long Island Railroad, Amtrak, WS Atkins, Parsons Brinckerhoff and Bechtel.

### Contracts

Recent contracts include: supply of TrainPlan™, RailPlan™, ResourcePlan™, TrainManager™ and ResourceManager™ to Norwegian State Railways; supply of UK-wide integrated train planning systems and planning database with RailPlan™ and TrainPlan™ to Railtrack; supply of TrainPlan™ to Swedish State Railways and New Jersey Transit; supply of TrainPlan™ and ResourcePlan™ to Romanian State Railways and to Scotrail (UK); supply of RailPlan™ and PowerPlan™ to Kowloon—Canton Railway Corporation, Hong Kong; supply of TrainPlan™ and ResourcePlan™ to Chiltern Railways, (UK).

*UPDATED*

## Wendell Cox Consultancy

PO Box 841, Belleville, Illinois 62222, USA
Tel: (+1 618) 632 85 07   Fax: (+1 618) 632 85 38
e-mail: policy@publicpwpose.com
Web: http://www.publicpwpose.com

### Key personnel

Principal: Wendell Cox
Associate: Jean Love

### Capabilities

Urban transport organisational design; competitive tendering; feasibility studies; strategic planning; legislation, planning and policy; privatisation; land use; smart growth.

### Projects

Market analysis for US market entry, for UK and Italian companies (1997); review of Atlanta regional plans; review of Florida high-speed rail project; review of Austin regional plan; performance analysis of Texas public transport agencies; review of Charlotte light rail project; analysis of US urban rail analysis in relation to Auckland; New Zealand project; land use and smart growth presentations in the US, Europe, Australia and New Zealand.

*UPDATED*

## Wilbur Smith Associates

1301 Gervais Street, 16th Floor, Columbia, South Carolina 29201-3356, USA
Tel: (+1 803) 758 45 00   Fax: (+1 803) 251 20 64
e-mail: intl@wilbursmith.com; mktg@wilbursmith.com
Web: http://www.wilbursmith.com
Postal address
PO Box 92, Columbia, South Carolina 29202-0092, USA

### Key personnel

President and Chief Executive Officer: Robert J Zuelsdorf
Regional Vice-President: D R Danforth
Regional Vice-President: S W Schar
Vice-President: Gary A Schnelder
Vice-President: M S Smith
Vice-President Marketing Co-ordinator: Jasper Salmond

### Capabilities

Transportation consulting services covering rail, road, air and water systems, extending from planning, pre-feasibility and preliminary engineering through development of final design, contract documents, construction and maintenance services, training and technical assistance and field supervision. Management consultation services include planning, programming, budgeting and supervision of contractors and subcontractors. Services also include transit vehicle/station/facility design, design of architectural graphics and related visual communications systems, and interior space planning.

### Projects

Development of San Francisco County Transportation Plan – WSA is leading a multimodal transportation planning team in developing a 20 year plan for the area.

## CONSULTANCY SERVICES

Total planning of Singapore MRT system plus design of phase IIA (in joint venture with DCIL).
Los Angeles: Santa Barbara rail corridor study, phases I and II for Southern California Association of governments.
Virginia Rail programme needs for Virginia Department of Highways and Transportation.
Washington State on-call freight rail services for Washington State Department of Transport (DOT).
Detroit: Chicago rail passenger demand forecasts in association with URS Consultants and PBQD.
Southeast Florida rail corridor study for Florida DOT.
Metro 12E section design for Washington, DC Metro Area Transit Authority.
Georgia rail system evaluation for GA DOT.
Hong Kong Aberdeen LRT feasibility study.
HSST rail patronage analysis for HSST Nevada Corridor.
Ohio high-speed rail ridership study for Ohio High-Speed Rail Authority.
Florida rail system plan for FDOT.
Passenger train operating speed improvements for North Carolina DOT.
Chicago—Milwaukee high-speed rail, subcontractor to Environdyne Engineers for Illinois and Wisconsin DOTs.
Florida alternative passenger route assessments (all speeds) and update of Florida rail system plan for Florida DOT.
Statewide passenger study for Washington DOT.
Nationwide high-speed rail study, Thailand.
Caracas metro transportation planning services, Venezuela.
Bangkok mass transit master planning study, Thailand.
Sentosa Island LRT system study, Singapore.
Richmond Multimodal Transportation Center for City of Richmond, Virginia.
Inland access to Wilmington and Morehead City terminals for North Carolina Port Authority.
California high-speed rail economic impacts for Caltrans.
On-call services for North Carolina Railroad.

*UPDATED*

## Wilson, Ihrig & Associates

5776 Broadway, Oakland, California 94618 USA
Tel: (+1 510) 658 67 19   Fax: (+1 510) 652 44 41
Web: http://www.wiai.com

### Key personnel
President: George Paul Wilson
Principal: Steven L Wolfe

### Capabilities
Acoustical design of stations, line sections and facilities; vehicle noise, vibration and ride quality evaluation; assessment and prediction of ground-borne vibration; track fastener design, testing and specification; noise and vibration criteria development.

*VERIFIED*

## WS Atkins Rail Limited

Berkshire House, 171 High Holborn, London WC1V 7AA, UK
Tel: (+44 20) 74 97 15 02   Fax: (+44 20) 73 79 85 63
e-mail: rail@wsatkins.com
Web: http://www.wsatkins.com

### Key personnel
Managing Director: Tony Fletcher
Deputy Managing Director: David Marsden
Development/International: Mike Donnelly

### Subsidiary company
Atkins Danmark A/S
Pilestraede 58, DK-1112 Copenhagen K, Denmark
Tel: (+45) 82 33 95 55
e-mail: info-dk@wsatkins.com
Managing Director: Preben Olsen

### Regional offices
WS Atkins Rail UK regional office locations: Belfast, Birmingham, Crewe, Croydon, Derby, Glasgow, Manchester, Swindon and York.

### Overseas offices
WS Atkins office locations: Australia, Belgium, Brunei, Canada, China, Czech Republic, Denmark, France, Gibraltar, Greece, Hong Kong, Hungary, India, Ireland, Japan, Kuwait, Malaysia, Mexico, Oman, Poland, Portugal, Romania, Saudi Arabia, Sharjah, Singapore, Spain, Thailand, UAE and USA.

### Capabilities
WS Atkins Rail can take a project through its complete life-cycle from concept, market and revenue forecasting, through multidiscipline design to life management of the asset. Projects include rolling stock and infrastructure, procured through project teams formed from civil, signalling and telecommunications, electrification, rolling stock and project development groups.

These are supported by specialists in reliability-centred maintenance, safety and risk analysis, vehicle testing and acceptance, quality process and system audit, product testing and acceptance, passenger information and ticketing systems, CCTV security and surveillance, plus the wide range of skills from the WS Atkins plc organisation. Project management service is offered. The company has a successful record of investing in private finance initiatives, including raising project finance from both equity and loans.

### Projects
Successful infrastructure projects in the UK include the Channel Tunnel, West Coast Main Line, Thameslink and Heathrow Express, station design at Waterloo and Ashford International and rebuilding of Paddington, project management of Lisbon—Oporto and North-South lines in Portugal, design of WestRail in Hong Kong in association with Atkins China.

WS Atkins Rail is assisting with the implementation of transmission-based signalling for the West Coast and Main Line project, supporting both Railtrack (infrastructure) and Alstom (rolling stock aspects).

The DRA project has been completed. This involves the design, supply, installation and commissioning of the Drivers' Reminder Appliance, a safety device fitted to the majority of driving cabs of passenger rolling stock in the UK.

Outline design of the East London Line southern extension for London Underground, where the bridges, track, stations, power and signalling systems design is being carried out for London Underground Ltd.

Traction and Rolling stock division working on a series of turnkey projects including refurbishment of Mk III sleeping vehicles, replacement of Halon fire protection systems and the fitting of CCTV surveillance systems.

WS Atkins Rail is undertaking multifunctional engineering design work associated with the upgrade of Thameslink routes. This follows the operational and power system simulation studies providing design parameters to upgrade the routes to carry 24 to 30 trains per hour through the central section under London.

Specialists from each discipline are providing inputs to PHARE sponsored projects in Bulgaria, Czech Republic, Hungary and Romania.

*UPDATED*

## YTT International Inc

2-33-4 Musashi-dai, Fuchu, Tokyo 183-0042, Japan
Tel: (+81 423) 28 15 15   Fax: (+81 423) 28 08 08
e-mail: niadanza@yttinc.co.jp

### Key personnel
President: Yojiro Tawaragi
Vice-President: Shuhei Uchida
Directors: Iwao Yamamoto
General Manager, International Projects:
   Nicholas M Iadanza
Manager: Douglas W Martin
Administration: Sumiko Hanamura

### Capabilities
Engineering, construction supervision and project management for rail vehicle projects; feasibility, planning, technical interface and co-ordination; rail vehicle specifications, inspection, testing, quality control and assurance, rail maintenance equipment, shop equipment, depot management and fare collection.

*UPDATED*

## ZGF – Zimmer Gunsul Frasca Partnership

320 SW Oak, Suite 550, Portland, Oregon 97204, USA
Tel: (+1 503) 224 38 60   Fax: (+1 503) 224 24 82
e-mail: rpackard@zgf.com
Web: http://www.zgf.com

### Key personnel
Managing Partner: Robert G Packard III
Partner: Gregory S Baldwin
Principal: Patrick C Tillett
Principal: Kelly D Davis
Associate Partner: Ronald R Steward

### Branch Offices
1191 Second Avenue, Suite 800, Seattle, Washington 98101, USA
Tel: (+1 206) 623 94 14   Fax: (+1 206) 623 78 68
333 South Grand Avenue, Suite 3600, Los Angeles, California 90071, USA
Tel: (+1 213) 617 19 01   Fax: (+1 213) 617 00 47
7920 Norfolk Avenue, Suite 600, Bethesda, Maryland 20814, USA
Tel: (+1 301) 986 19 54   Fax: (+1 301) 986 18 63

### Capabilities
Zimmer Gunsul Frasca Partnership, recipient of the 1991 AIA Architecture Firm Award, is an architecture, planning and interior design firm with offices in Portland, Seattle, Los Angeles and Washington, DC. With a total staff of 350, ZGF offers a comprehensive range of services in land use planning, site selection and urban design, architectural design, project management, space planning and interior architecture. The firm is managed by 10 partners, supported by 24 principals, 66 associate partners, and 61 associates, technical and clerical staff.

### Projects
In the last 40 years, ZGF has managed and designed nationally recognised projects, representing a broad range of project types. Transportation-related public projects include planning and design for major expansions to the Portland International Airport since 1966; as well as planning studies at Sea-Tac International Airport. The firm has been responsible for architecture and urban design on a number of light rail systems in the USA, including Portland's MAX; Seattle's Sound Transit Link and Commuter Light Rail Systems; the Minneapolis/St Paul International Airport Tunnel Station and Hiawatha Corridor Light Rail Transit System; and the Hudson-Bergen Light Rail Transit System for the New Jersey Transit Authority. Other transit malls, multimodal facilities, street improvements, pedestrian corridors and transit-supportive development have been designed for communities around the country including Portland, Seattle, Denver, Los Angeles, Chicago, Boise, Houston and San Francisco.

# INDEX

# Index

To help users of this title evaluate the published data, *Jane's Information Group* has divided entries into three categories.
[N] NEW ENTRY Information on new equipment and/or systems appearing for the first time in the title.
[V] VERIFIED The editor has made a detailed examination of the entry's content and checked its relevancy and accuracy for publication in the new edition to the best of his ability.
[U] UPDATED During the verification process, significant changes to content have been made to reflect the latest position known to *Jane's* at the time of publication.
Items in italics refer to entries which have been deleted from this edition with the relevant page numbers from last year.


3M Europe SA ..... 562
3M Germany ..... 551

### A

AAE ..... 797
A& K ..... 714
Abberfield Technology Pty ..... 681
ABC-NACO Inc ..... 608, 622,714
ABC Rail Products Corporation ..... 758
Aberdeen & Rockfish Railroad Co ..... 420
Aberdeen, Carolina & Western Railway Co ..... 420 [U]
Abetong Teknik AB ..... 714
Abex Rail ..... 608
ABRF Industries–Atelier Bretons de Réalisations Ferroviaires ..... 590
AB STRängbeton ..... 714
Abtus Co ..... 714
ACC Ingenerie et Maintenance ..... 767
Accent Marketing and Research ..... 817 [U]
Accenture ..... 817
ACF Industries Inc ..... 590
Acieries de Ploërmel ..... 608, 622
ACTS Nederland BV ..... 280 [U]
Adams & Westlake Ltd ..... 562
Adaptaflex ..... 704
ADES Technologies ..... 608 [U]
ADT Security Systems ..... 681
Adtranz ..... 694
Advanced Railway Research Centre ..... 817 [U]
Advanced Structures Corporation ..... 562
AEA Technology Rail ..... 818 [U]
AEG MIS ..... 670
AEG Mobile Communication GmbH ..... 646
AEI Cables ..... 704 [U]
Afghanistan ..... 3
Agro AG ..... 704
A I Welders Ltd ..... 714
Aim Aviation (Henshalls) ..... 562
Air International Transit ..... 562 [U]
Airscrew Ltd ..... 562 [U]
Airtrain Citylink Ltd ..... 19 [U]
A K Fans Ltd ..... 551 [U], 562
AKN Railway ..... 153
Akzo Nobel Geosynthetics ..... 716
Alabama & Florida Railway Co ..... 420 [N]
Alabama & Gulf Coast Railway ..... 420 [N]
Alabama Railroad Co ..... 420 [N]
Alabama/Louisiana/Mississippi ..... 451
Alaska Railroad, The ..... 420
Albania ..... 3
Albanian Railways (HSH) ..... 3 [U]
Albatros Corporation ..... 562 [U]
Alberta RailNet Inc ..... 78 [N]
Albright International ..... 562
Albtalbahn (AVG) ..... 154
Alcan Mass Transportation Systems ..... 478 [U]
Alcatel Canada Inc ..... 784 [U]
Alcatel Transport Automation ..... 646 [U], 681
Alcoa Railroads ..... 221
Aldon Co ..... 716, 758
Alfred County Railway ..... 324
Alfred McAlpine ..... 716 [N]
Algeco SA ..... 797
Algeria ..... 4
Algerian National Railways (SNTF) ..... 4 [U]
Algoma Central Railway ..... 78
ALH Rail Coatings Ltd ..... 716 [U]
Alifana Railway/Benevento-Naples Railway (FABN) ..... 207 [U]
ALK Associates Inc ..... 818 [U]
ALL Central ..... 7
ALL Mesopotamico ..... 8
Allegheny & Eastern Railroad ..... 421
Allegheny Rail Products ..... 716
Allied Insulators ..... 693
Almex ..... 681
Alna Koki Co ..... 478, 563, 590
Alpha Zaicon Technology ..... 646
Alstec Ltd ..... 646
ALSTOM Consultancy ..... 818
ALSTOM Engines, Mirrlees Blackstone ..... 533
ALSTOM Engines, Paxman ..... 533
ALSTOM Konstal ..... 590
ALSTOM Schienenfahrzeuge AG ..... 622
ALSTOM Transport Electrification SpA ..... 704
ALSTOM Transport SA ..... 478 [U], 551 [U], 563 [V], 622 [U], 646 [U], 670 [U], 693 [U], 716 [V], 767, 784 [U]
Altamont Commuter Express Authority ..... 438
Aluminium Inductors Ltd ..... 693
Alzmetall ..... 768 [U]
Amboim Railway ..... 6
AMEC Rail Ltd ..... 716
AMEC Spie Rail Systems Ltd ..... 716
American Koyo Corporation ..... 622
American Railroad Curvelining Corporation ..... 716
Ametek Panalarm ..... 648
Amey Railways Ltd ..... 717
Amherst Industries ..... 590
Ampcontrol ..... 693
AMPEP plc ..... 623 [V]
Amsted Rail International ..... 608, 623 [U]
AMT L'Agence Métropolitain de Transport ..... 77
Amtrak ..... 438
Amurrio Ferrocarril y Equipos SA ..... 623 [U], 717
Anacostia & Pacific Company Inc ..... 421
Anchor Brake Shoe LLC ..... 608
Andersen Consulting ..... 790
Andrew Kommunikationssysteme AG ..... 648, 704
Angel Trains Ltd ..... 797
Angle Plant (UK) Ltd ..... 717
Anglia Railways ..... 382
Angola ..... 5
Angst+Pfister AG ..... 563
ANIE ..... 809
ANSALDOBREDA ..... 483 [U], 552, 648, 693, 758, 818
Ansaldo Trasporti Sistemi Ferroviari ..... 784 [U]
Antenna Specialists ..... 649
Antofagasta (Chile) & Bolivia Railway plc (FCAB) ..... 93 [U]
Apalachicola Northern Railroad Co ..... 421
ApATeCh Electro ..... 563, 694, 704, 717
Apcarom SA ..... 717
APD Voyager ..... 649 [N]
Appenzell Railway (AB) ..... 350
Appulo-Lucane Railway (FAL) ..... 200 [U]
APS Electronic AG ..... 552
Aqaba Railway Corporation (ARC) ..... 246
Arab Union of Railways (UACF) ..... 806
Arbel Fauvet Rail ..... 590
Arbil Ltd ..... 717
Arcelor ..... 714 [U]
Ardanuy Ingenieria SA ..... 818 [U]
AREP ..... 818 [V]
AREX ..... 649
Arezzo Railways (LFI) ..... 208
Argentina ..... 7
Århus-Odder Railway ..... 127
Arizona & California Railroad ..... 421
Arizona Eastern Railway Company ..... 421
Arkansas & Missouri Railway Co ..... 421
Arlanda Express ..... 340 [V]
Armenia ..... 17
Armenian Railways ..... 17
Armita Nederland ..... 797
Arriva plc ..... 383 [U]
Arriva Tog ..... 127 [N]
Arriva Trains Merseyside ..... 383 [U]
Arriva Trains Northern ..... 384 [U]
ARR Rail Rent ..... 797
ASC Industries ..... 768
Ascom Radiocom (see Motorola UK)
Ascom Transport Revenue Systems ..... 681
ASF American Steel Foundries ..... 608, 623
Ashley, Drew & Northern Railway Co ..... 422
Asia Pacific Freight Consortium Pty Ltd ..... 19 [N]
Aspen Aerials Inc ..... 717 [V]
Aspen Burrow Crocker Ltd ..... 818
Aspen Equipment Co ..... 717
Association of German Transport Undertakings ..... 808
Association of Privately Owned Wagon Operators ..... 809
Association of Public Transport Operators ..... 806
Association of Rail Operators (BVS) ..... 279
Association of Spanish Manufacturers of Railway Equipment ..... 805
Association of Train Operating Companies (UK) ..... 382 [U]
Astarsa ..... 484
Astra-SC Astra Vagoane Arad SA ..... 590 [U]
Astra Vagoane Călători SA Arad ..... 484 [U], 563 [U], 623 [U]
AT Kearney Inc ..... 818
Ateliers de Braine-le-Comte et Thiriau Réunis SA (ABC) ..... 623
Atlantic & Gulf Railroad Co ..... 422
Atlantic Track & Turnout Co ..... 717 [V]
Atlas Copco Berema ..... 718
Atlas Copco Compressors ..... 608 [U]
Atlas Engineering Company ..... 768
Atlas Hydraulic Loaders Ltd ..... 718
Atlas International Ltd ..... 563
Atlas Weyhausen GmbH ..... 718
Atron Electronic ..... 681
ATSS ..... 649
Audio Visual Computer plc ..... 790
Augsburger Localbahn ..... 154
Austrac Rail Ltd ..... 20 [V]
Austrak ..... 718
Australasian Railway Association ..... 807
Australia ..... 18
Australia Southern Railroad (ASR) ..... 21 [U]
Australian Northern Railroad ..... 20 [N]
Australian Railroad Group Pty Ltd ..... 20 [N]
Australian Rail Track Corporation Limited (ARTC) ..... 21 [U]
Australian Transport & Energy Corridor Limited (ATEC) ..... 21 [N]
Australian Western Railroad ..... 22 [N]
Austria ..... 43
Austria Rail Engineering ..... 819 [U]
Austrian Federal Railways (ÖBB) ..... 43 [U]
Automatic Systems SA ..... 681
Autoroche Industrie ..... 563
AVE Rail Products ..... 563
Avery Dennison ..... 563
Avon Polymers France ..... 718
Avon Spencer Moulton ..... 608 [V], 624 [U]
AWA Communications ..... 649
AWS ..... 624
Aydin Corporation ..... 649
AZD Praha sro ..... 649
Azerbaijan ..... 50
Azerbaijani Railways (AZR) ..... 50

### B

Babcock & Wilcox Española SA ..... 484, 758
Babcock Rail ..... 484, 590
Babtie Group ..... 819
BAC Corrosion Control Ltd ..... 718
Baier + Käppel GmbH + Co ..... 564 [N]
Balfour Beatty Rail Ltd ..... 718, 819
Balfour Beatty Rail Engineering Ltd ..... 718
Balfour Beatty Rail Maintenance Ltd ..... 719
Balfour Beatty Rail Plant Ltd ..... 718
Balfour Beatty Rail Projects ..... 694 [U], 784 [U]
Balfour Beatty Rail Renewals Ltd ..... 694
Ballast Nedam ..... 719
Bance R & Co ..... 719
Bandegua Railway ..... 181
Banestyrelsen ..... 122
Banestyrelsen Service Division ..... 719 [N]
Bangladesh ..... 51
Bangladesh Railway ..... 51
Bangor & Aroostook Railroad Co ..... 422 [U]
Banverket ..... 341 [V], 719, 819
Barclay Mowlem Construction ..... 694 [V], 719
Bari-Nord Railway (FT) ..... 208 [U]
BASF ..... 154
Bay Colony Railroad Corporation ..... 422 [U]
Bayer AG ..... 154
Bayerische Oberlandbahn (BOB) ..... 155
Bayham Ltd ..... 563
Bayside Trains ..... 22 [U]
BBA Friction Ltd ..... 608
BBM ..... 768
BC Rail ..... 78
BCD Consulting Sas ..... 820
BCM Contracts ..... 704 [U]
Bechtel Corporation ..... 820 [U]
Behala ..... 155
Behr Industrietechnik ..... 533 [U], 563 [U]
Beijing 'Feb 7' Locomotive Works ..... 484
Beilhack Systemtechnik GmbH ..... 719
Bekaert Composites ..... 564 [N]
Belarus ..... 52
Belarussian Railways (BCh) ..... 52
Belbim AS ..... 682
Belgium ..... 53
Belt Railway Company of Chicago ..... 422

854 **INDEX**/B–C


BEML ... 485 [U], 695 [U], 719 [U]
Benguela Railway ... 6
Benin ... 57
Benkler AG ... 695 [N], 720 [N]
Benntec Systemtechnik GmbH ... 720
Bentheimer Eisenbahn (BE) ... 155
Bern-Solothurn Railway (RBS) ... 350 [U]
Bessemer & Lake Erie Railroad Co ... 423
Best Impressions ... 820
Bethlehem Steel Corporation ... 423, 720
Bharat Brakes & Valves Ltd ... 608
Bharat Wagon & Engineering ... 590
BHEL ... 486, 552, 624
BHP Iron Ore Railroad ... 23 [U]
BHP Steel Long Products Division ... 720
BICC Cables ... 704
Bière-Apples-Morges Railway (BAM) ... 350
Bingham Rail ... 768 [N]
Bircher AG ... 564
Birmingham Southern Railroad Co ... 423
BK-Tåg AB ... 341
Blatchford Transport Equipment ... 758 [V]
BLS Lötschbergbahn ... 351
Blue Print Rail ... 820
BMT Reliability Consultants ... 820
BMZ ... 486, 590
Bochumer Verein ... 624
Bode, Gebrüder, & Co GmbH ... 564
Bodensee-Oberschwaben Bahn (BOB) ... 155
Bodensee-Toggenburg Railway (BT) ... 352
Bolivia ... 58
Bolivian National Railways ... 58
Bomag GmbH ... 720
Bombardier Transportation ... 486 [U], 552 [U], 590 [U], 624 [U], 649 [U], 768 [U], 785 [U]
Bonatrans AS ... 624
Bong Mining Company ... 256
Booz, Allen & Hamilton Inc ... 820 [U]
Bosch Telecom ... 564, 758
Bosnia-Herzegovina ... 59
Bosnia-Herzegovina Railways ... 59
Boston & Maine Corporation ... 409
Botniabanan AB ... 341 [N]
Botswana ... 60
Botswana Railways ... 60
Bovis Construction Group ... 820
BP-Battioni & Pagani ... 758
BP Solar ... 651
Bradken Rail ... 591 [U], 608 [U], 625 [U], 770 [N]
Braithwaite & Co ... 591
Brambles Italia ... 797
Brand-Rex ... 704 [U]
Bratsvo ... 591
Brazil ... 61
Brazilian railway projects ... 72
BREC ... 591
Brecknell, Willis & Co ... 553 [U], 695
Breda Costruzioni Ferroviarie SpA ... 491, 591, 625
Bremskerl Reibellagwerke Emerling ... 609 [V]
Brookville Mining Equipment ... 491
Brown & Root Services ... 820
Brush Traction Ltd ... 491, 553
Brush Transformers Ltd ... 695
BSL–Olefinverbund GmbH ... 155
BTZ ... 469
Buckeye Steel Castings ... 609 [U], 625 [U]
Buffalo & Pittsburgh Railroad Inc ... 423
Buffalo Brake Beam Co ... 609
Buhlmann, SA ... 609 [U], 651 [U]
Bulgaria ... 72
Bulgarian State Railways (BDZ) ... 72
Bumar Ltd ... 625 [U], 720
Bumar-Fablok ... 491
Burkina Faso ... 74
Burle Industries ... 682
Burlington Northern Santa Fe (BNSF) ... 409
Burn Standard Co ... 591, 720
Butzbach-Licher Eisenbahn AG (BLE) ... 155
BvL Oberflächentechnik GmbH ... 770
BVZ Zermatt-Bahn ... 352
BWG Butzbacher Weichenbau GmbH ... 720
BZA ... 682


## C


c2c ... 384 [U]
C&H Chemical ... 564
Cadex Electronics Inc ... 651 [U], 790
CAE Cleaning Technologies plc ... 770
CAF ... 491 [U], 591, 625
CAIB Benelux ... 797
CAIB UK ... 797
Caillard Cowans Sheldon ... 720, 758
Calabria Railways (FC) ... 208 [U]
California Northern Railroad ... 423
Callegari, José ... 591
CalTrans ... 451
CAM Industries ... 770 [U]
Camas Prairie Railroad Co ... 423
Cambodia ... 75
Cambridge Systematics Inc ... 821 [N]
Cameroon ... 76
Cameroon Railways (Camrail) ... 70 [U]
Camlock Lifting Clamps Ltd ... 721 [V]
CANAC International Inc ... 821
Canada ... 76
Canadian American Railroad (CARC) ... 79
Canadian National Railway Company ... 80 [U]
Canadian Pacific Railway Company ... 84
Canadian Transport Agency (CTA) ... 77
Canadian Urban Transit Association ... 808 [U]
Canarail Consultants ... 821 [U]
Cando Contracting Ltd ... 86 [N]
Cape Breton & Central Nova Scotia Railway ... 86
Cape Engineering UK Ltd ... 821
Carajás Railway (EFC) ... 61
Carbone Lorraine ... 609 [V]
Cardo Rail ... 609 [U], 625 [U]
Cardwell Westinghouse WABCO ... 609
Carmen Systems ... 821
Caroline Piedmont Railroad ... 423 [N]
Carrier Khéops Bac ... 704 [U]
Carrier Sütrak GmbH ... 564
Carrier Transicold ... 564
Cartier Railway ... 86 [U]
Casaire ... 770
Casalecchio Vignola Railway ... 209
CASAS-M SL ... 565 [U], 682 [V]
Cascade & Columbia River Railboard ... 423 [N]
Catalan Railways (FGC) ... 327
Caterpillar Inc ... 533
Cattaneo SA ... 591
Cattron Theimeg ... 652 [U], 758 [U]
CCC ... 592
CDG Express ... 150 [V]
CDM ... 721
cdsrail ... 652 [U]
Ceccato ... 770 [U]
Cedar Rapids and Iowa City Railway Co ... 423
CEFRAC ... 822
Celsius Communications Systems AB ... 658
Cemafer Gleisbaumaschinen und Geräte GmbH ... 721
Cembre SpA ... 695 [U], 721 [U]
Cementation Railways (see VAE)
Centrac ... 721
Central Japan Railway Co (JR Central) ... 226
Central Michigan Railway Co ... 423
Central Montana Rail Inc ... 423
Central Oregon & Pacific Railroad ... 424
Central Power Products ... 758
Central Railroad of Indiana ... 424 [N]
Central Railroad of Indianapolis ... 424 [N]
Central Railway ... 190
Central Railway (Peru) ... 298
Central Romana Railroad ... 131
Central Trains Ltd ... 385
Central Umbria Railway (FCU) ... 209
Central Western Railway ... 87 [N]
Century Engineering Inc ... 822
Century Group ... 721
CESPA ... 770
CF&I Steel ... 721
CFC ... 492, 592
CFCL Australia Pty Limited ... 798
CFCO ... 106
CFD Industrie ... 150 [U], 492, 534, 625
CFR Calatori SA ... 306 [N]
CFR Marfa ... 307 [N]
CFR SA ... 307 [N]
CFTA ... 150 [V]
CGTX Inc ... 800
Chamber of Railway Industries (Argentina) ... 807
Chambers, Conlon & Hartwell Inc ... 822
Changchun Car Company ... 492
Changzhou Diesel & Mining Locomotive Plant ... 493
Channel Electric Equipment ... 565, 652 [U]
Chapman Seating Ltd ... 565 [U]
Chemetron Railway Products Inc ... 721, 786
Chemgrate Corporation ... 721
Chemin de Fer Congo-Océan (CFCO) ... 108 [U]
Chemin de Fer de la Guinée (ONCFG) ... 182
Chemins de Fer du Mali (RCFM) ... 267
Chemins de Fer Syriens (CFS) ... 365
Chemirail ... 770
Chesapeake & Albemarle Railroad ... 424 [N]
Chicago Central & Pacific Railroad Co ... 424
Chicago Freight Car Leasing Co ... 800 [V]
Chicago Rail Link ... 424
Chicago SouthShore & South Bend Railroad ... 424
Chichibu Railway ... 238
Chile ... 93
Chilean State Railways (EFE) ... 94
Chiltern Railways ... 385
China National Railway Locomotive & Rolling Stock Industry Corporation (LORIC) ... 493, 534, 553, 592, 610, 625
China, People's Republic ... 97
China Railway Signal & Communication Co (CRSC) ... 652
Chinese Railways (CR) ... 97
Chipman Rail ... 722
Chiriquí Land Company Railways ... 296
Chiriquí National Railroad ... 296
Chipman Rail ... 722
Chloride Power Protection ... 652 [N]
Cimarron Valley Railroad ... 424
Cimmco International ... 592 [U], 610, 626, 722, 771
Circumetnea Railway (FCE) ... 209
Circumvesuviana Railway (SFSM) ... 209
Cisalpino AG ... 467 [U]
CityNightLine ... 467
Citypendeln Sverige AB ... 342 [U]
CityRail NSW ... 24 [U]
Citytunneln ... 342 [N]
CKD Dopravni Systémi AS ... 495, 554, 626
CKD VAGONKA as ... 495 [U]
C Kutná Hora as ... 626
Cleff, C W, GmbH & Co ... 565
Clerprem SpA ... 565
Clough, Harbour & Associates ... 822
Clouth Gummiwerke AG ... 722
CLW Chittaranjan Locomotive Works ... 495
Clyde Engineering ... 554
CMC Interiors ... 565 [V]
CMKS Traction Vehicles ... 771
Cobra Brake Shoes ... 610
Cobreq ... 610
Cockerill Forges & Ringmill ... 626 [U]
Cockerill Mechanical Industries SA ... 496 [U], 535 [U]
Cogifer ... 722
Colbond Geosynthetics ... 722
Cole, Malcom, Ltd ... 565
Cole, Sherman & Associates Ltd ... 822
Colebrand Ltd ... 722
Colin Buchanan and Partners ... 822
College of Italian Railway Engineers ... 809
Collis Engineering Ltd ... 652 [U], 722 [V]
Colombia ... 106
Colorado & Wyoming Railway Co ... 424
Colston, Budd, Wardrop & Hunt ... 822
Columbia Basin Railroad, The ... 424 [U]
Comalco Railway ... 25 [U]
Comelta SA ... 682
Comet Industries Inc ... 610, 626
Cometal-Mometal Sarl ... 592
Cometarsa SAIC ... 593
Cometna ... 610, 626
Comilog Railway ... 108
Com-Net Software Specialists ... 790 [U]
Compagnie Togolaise des Mines de Benin (CTMB) ... 373
Companhia Brasileira de Trens Urbanos (CBTU) ... 62
Companhia Ferroviaria do Nordeste (CFN) ... 62
Companhia Paulista de Trens Metropolitanos (CPTM) ... 63
Compin ... 565
Computer Products Professional bv ... 653
Comreco Rail Ltd (see VST Comreco Rail)
Comsa SA ... 723
Conbrako (Pty) Ltd ... 565, 610, 723
Concargo Ltd ... 565 [U]
Congo ... 108
Congo, Democratic Republic ... 108
Connecticut Department of Transportation ... 442
Connecticut Southern Railroad ... 424 [N]
Connei SpA ... 565
Connex South Eastern ... 386 [U]
Connex Trains Melbourne ... 25 [U]
Conrac GmbH ... 670 [U]
Conrail ... 411
Container Corporation of India ... 191
Contec GmbH ... 723 [N]
Continental Components Pvt Ltd ... 554 [V]
ContiTech Holding GmbH ... 565 [U]
ContiTech Luftfedersysteme GmbH ... 626 [V], 723
Control Chief Corporation ... 759 [U]
Convoy-Contigas BV ... 798
Cooper & Turner ... 723
Copper Basin Railway Inc ... 424
Corade ... 771
Corradino Group ... 822
Corus Cogifer Switches and Crossings ... 723 [U]
Corus Foundry ... 723 [V]
Corus Rail ... 723 [U]
Corus Rail Consultancy ... 640 [V], 823 [U]
Corus Rail Modular Systems ... 723 [U]
Corus Rail Technologies ... 823 [U]
Corys TESS ... 640
Costa Rica ... 109
Costa Rica Railways (Incofer) ... 109
Costaferroviaria SpA ... 496 [U], 593 [U], 695
Costruzioni Ferroviarie Colleferro SpA (CFC) ... 494, 596
Cote d'Ivoire ... 110
Countrylink ... 26 [U]
Cowans Sheldon ... 723
COWI Consulting Engineers & Planners AS ... 823
CPCS Technologies Ltd ... 823
Cragg Railcharger ... 771
Craig and Derricott ... 565
Créabéton ... 723 [N]
Cre'active Design ... 823
Creadesign Oy ... 824 [N]
Cressall Resistors ... 566 [U]

|  |  |
|---|---|
| Croatia | 111 |
| Croatian State Railway | 111 U |
| Crompton Greaves Ltd | 554 N, 653, 695 U |
| Cromweld Steels Ltd | 566 V, 593 V |
| Crossrail | 387 N |
| Crous Chemicals GmbH | 771 N |
| Crown Agents for Overseas Governments and Administrations (UK) | 824 |
| CSEE | 653 U |
| CSI Productos Largos | 724 |
| CSR Humes | 724 |
| CSX Intermodal Inc (CSXI) | 412 |
| CSX Transportation Inc (CSXT) | 412 |
| CTE Srl Engineering | 535 |
| CTS | 670 |
| CTS Scanpoint Technology A/S | 682 |
| Cuba | 113 |
| Cuban Railways (UFC) | 113 U |
| Cubic Nordic | 683 |
| Cubic Transportation Systems (CTS) | 653 U, 683 V, 695 |
| Cumana & Circumflegrea Railways (SEPSA) | 209 |
| Cummins Inc | 535 |
| Currie & Brown | 824 |
| CXT | 724 |
| Cytec Fiberite | 566 |
| Czech Railways (CD) | 114 |
| Czech Republic | 114 |

### D

|  |  |
|---|---|
| Daewoo Heavy Industries Ltd | 554, 593 |
| DaimlerChrysler Rail Systems (see Adtranz) | |
| DAKO-CZ as | 610 U |
| Dakota Minnesota & Eastern Railroad Corporation | 425 |
| Dakota Missouri Valley & Western Railroad Inc | 425 |
| Dakota Southern Railroad Co | 425 |
| Dalian Locomotive and Rolling Stock Works | 497, 536, 593 |
| Dakota Southern Railroad Co | 425 |
| Dallas Garland & Northeastern Railroad | 429 N |
| D & I Railroad Co | 425 |
| Daniel, Mann, Johnson & Mendenhall | 824 |
| Danieli Centro Maskin SpA | 724 |
| Danish State Railways (DSB) | 124 U |
| Dansk Dekor-Laminat A/S | 566 |
| Darcy Products Ltd | 724 |
| Dassault Automatismes et Télécommunications | 683 |
| Data Display Co Ltd | 670 |
| Datastreams Systems (UK) Ltd | 790 |
| Datong Locomotive Works | 497 |
| Davenset | 771 |
| David Brown Engineering Ltd | 537 U |
| David Clark Co | 653 V |
| Davis Ltd, W H | 593 V |
| Davy British Rail International (DBRI) | 724, 777 |
| Dawson-Aquamatic | 772 |
| DB Cargo | 165 |
| DB Netz | 162 |
| DB Regio | 166 |
| DB Reise&Touristik AG | 164 |
| DB Station&Service AG | 167 |
| DBT GB Ltd | 724 U |
| DCA Design International Ltd | 824 |
| Deans Powered Doors | 572 |
| De Dietrich Ferroviaire (see ALSTOM) | |
| De Leuw, Cather & Company | 825 |
| Deans Powered Doors | 566 |
| DEC | 798 |
| Decatur Junction Railway Co | 429 N |
| Deco Seating | 566 |
| DEG-Verkhers GmbH | 156 |
| Delaware Car Company | 771 U |
| Delaware Otsego Corporation | 425 |
| Delcan Corporation | 824 |
| Del Fungo Giera (DFG) | 210 U |
| Delkor Pty Ltd | 724 |
| Dellner Couplers AB | 610 |
| Delta Crompton Cables Ltd | 695 |
| Delta Rail | 611, 626 |
| Denmark | 122 |
| Derby Rubber Products | 725 |
| Desec Ltd | 725 |
| Design & Projects International Ltd | 825 |
| Design Research Unit | 825 |
| Design Triangle | 825 |
| Desná Railway (ZD) | 121 |
| Desso Carpets | 566 |
| Detroit Diesel Corporation | 537 U |
| Detroit, Toledo & Ironton Railroad | 425 |
| Deuta-Werke | 566 |
| Deutsch Relays Inc | 572 |
| Deutsche Bahn AG | 772 |
| Deutsche Eisenbahn-Consulting | 824 |
| Devol Engineering | 626 U |
| Devonport Royal Dockyard Ltd | 772 |
| DEVZ | 497 |
| Dewhurst | 567 |
| DHA | 826 |

|  |  |
|---|---|
| DHJ Media AB | 671 |
| D'Huart & Cie | 725 |
| DHV Holding BV | 826 |
| Dialight | 567, 653 |
| Diesel Supply Co Inc | 499 |
| Dilax International | 790 N |
| Dimetronic SA | 653 U, 786 U |
| Direcçao Nacional dos Caminhos de Ferro (Angola) | 5 |
| Direct Rail Services | 387 U |
| DISAB | 725 |
| DL Cargo | 53 |
| DLW | 498 |
| Dnepropetrovsk Electric Locomotive Factory (DEVZ) | 497 |
| DocuSystems Inc | 683 |
| Dominica Government Railway | 131 |
| Dominican Republic | 131 |
| Dominion Castings | 611, 626 |
| Domodossola–Locarno Railway (SSIF) | 210 |
| Donelli DIMAF SpA | 725 |
| Dornier GmbH | 640 |
| Dorsey Trailers Inc | 593 |
| Dortmunder Eisenbahn (DE) | 156 |
| Doxiadis Associates SA | 826 N |
| Drallim Telecom | 704 |
| Driessen Railway Interior Systems | 567 |
| Drouard | 725 |
| DSB S-Train | 126 |
| DSG-Canusa UK Ltd | 705 U |
| DST | 640 |
| Duisburg Häfen AG | 156 |
| Duluth, Missabe & Iron Range Railway Co | 425 |
| Dürener Kreisbahn (DKB) | 156 |
| Durisol Raalte bv | 725 |
| Duro Daković | 499, 593 |
| Dynex Semiconductor | 554 |

### E

|  |  |
|---|---|
| Eagle Ottawa Callow & Maddox | 567 |
| E&N Railway Company (1998) Ltd | 87 N |
| EAO AG | 567 U |
| East Japan Railway Co (JR East) | 223 U |
| Eastern Alabana Railway | 426 N |
| Eastern Railway (IR) | 192 |
| Eastern Railway (SJS) | 127 U |
| Eastern Shore Railroad | 426 |
| Ebac Ltd | 567 |
| EBIM SA | 640 |
| Ebo Systems | 568, 695, 705 |
| EBS | 725 |
| EC Engineering Oy | 568 |
| Ecomeca Fabrication Française | 725 |
| Ecuador | 131 |
| Edelaraudtee AS | 135 U |
| Ederena Concept | 568 V |
| Edgar Allen Ltd | 725 |
| Edilon bv | 725 |
| EDS | 826 |
| Edwards and Kelcey | 826 |
| EEC | 772 |
| EFA | 64 |
| EFACEC Sistemas de Electrónica | 554 V, 568 V, 653, 696 |
| EFC | 61 |
| EFE (Chile) | 94 U |
| EFT/MRN | 65 |
| EFVM | 71 |
| EG & G Dynatrend Inc | 826 |
| EG & G Rotron Inc | 554 |
| EG Steele | 499 V, 761, 800 |
| Egypt | 132 |
| Egyptian National Railways (ENR) | 132 U |
| EH | 156 |
| EIB | 157 |
| Eichholz | 725 N |
| Eisenbahn und Hafen GmbH (EH) | 156 |
| EKA | 593 |
| EKE Electronics | 568 |
| EKO Trans | 157 |
| El Cerrejon Coal Railway | 106 |
| El Salvador | 134 |
| El Salvador National Railways (FENADESAL) | 134 |
| Elbe-Weser Railways (EVB) | 157 |
| Electrack | 826 |
| Electrologic Pty ltd | 725 U |
| Electroputere SA | 499 |
| Electrowatt Infra Ltd | 826 U |
| Elektrim | 654 |
| Elektro-Thermit GmbH | 726 |
| Elettromeccanica Parizza | 568 |
| Elgeba Gerätebau GmbH | 683 |
| Elgin, Joliet & Eastern Railway | 426 |
| ELIN EBG Traction | 554 |
| Elkhart & Western Railroad Co | 426 N |
| Ellcon National Inc | 568 U, 611 |
| ELNO | 569 U, 671 |
| Elpro GmbH | 696 |
| Emanuel srl | 772 |
| Ematech | 772 |

|  |  |
|---|---|
| EMG Elektro-Mechanik GmbH | 537 |
| Emilia Romagna Railway (FER) | 210 U |
| Eminox Ltd | 537 V |
| Emons Transportation Group Inc | 426 |
| Empresa Minera del Centro del Perú | 298 |
| Empresa Nacional de Ferrocarriles (ENFE, Ecuador) | 131 |
| ENAFER-Peru | 297 |
| Energomachexport | 499, 593, 627, 726 |
| ENFE, Ecuador | 131 |
| Engineering Link, The | 827 |
| English, Welsh & Scottish Railway | 387 U, 772 N |
| ENOTRAC AG | 827 V |
| ENR | 132 U |
| Ensto Sekko Oy | 696 U |
| Entrelec (UK) Ltd | 555 |
| Environmental Cleaning Services | 772 |
| Enzesfeld-Caro Metallwerke | 726 U |
| EPV-GIV | 827 |
| Erfurter Industriebahn (EIB) | 157 |
| ERG Transit Systems | 683 |
| Erico Inc | 654 V |
| Eritrea | 135 |
| Eritrean Railways | 135 |
| ERMEWA Ltd | 798 |
| ERM Lahmeyer International GmbH | 827 |
| ERSA | 790 |
| ESAB Welding Equipment AB | 726 |
| Escanaba & Lake Superior Railroad | 426 |
| ESCO Equipment Service | 726 U |
| Escorts Ltd | 611, 627 |
| Essex Terminal Railway Company | 87 N |
| Estonia | 135 |
| Estrada de Ferro do Amapa (EFA) | 64 |
| Estrada de Ferro Trombetas (EFT/MRN) | 65 |
| Esveld Consulting Services BV | 827 |
| Eurailscout Inspection & Analysis | 726 |
| EurailTest | 827 U |
| Eurobahn | 154 |
| Eurogamma srl | 772 |
| EuroLuxCargo SA | 259 U |
| EuroMaint AB | 772 N |
| European Company for the Financing of Railroad Rolling Stock (EUROFIMA) | 806 U |
| European Conference of Ministers of Transport (ECMT) | 806 |
| Eurogamma srl | 772 |
| European Friction Industries Ltd | 611 |
| European Rail Shuttle BV | 469 U |
| European Rail Research Institute (ERRI) | 806 |
| European Wagon Pool (Europ Agreement) | 807 |
| Eurostar Group | 467 |
| Eurostar (UK) Ltd | 389 U, 772 |
| Eurostation SA | 827 N |
| Eurotunnel | 390 U |
| Euroswitch | 726 N |
| Euskotren (ET/FV) | 328 |
| EVA | 798 |
| EVAC GmbH | 569 U |
| Evans Deakin Industries | 499, 593 |
| EVB | 157 |
| EVR (Estonian Railways) | 132 |
| EWEM AG | 726 |
| EWS-EXTEL Systems Wedel | 569 V |
| Excil Electronics | 569 U |
| Exel Oy | 726 V |
| EXIM GmbH | 726 |
| Express Rail Link (Malaysia) | 264 |

### F

|  |  |
|---|---|
| FAB-RA-CAST | 727 |
| Faber Maunsell | 835 U |
| FAF–Ferrocarril Austral Fueguino | 9 |
| FAG OEM & Handel AG | 627 U |
| FAGA-Fahrzeugausrüstung Berlin GmbH | 570 V |
| FAINSA-Fabricacion Asientos Vehiculos Industriales | 570 U |
| Faiveley Transport | 555, 570 |
| Farge-Vegesacker Eisenbahn (FVE) | 157 |
| Farmrail System Inc | 426 |
| FASI Seating Systems | 570 |
| Fassetta & Cie, F | 727 |
| Faur SA (see also ALSTOM) | 538 V, 727 |
| FBC–Ferrocarril Belgrano Cargas SA | 9 |
| FBP | 208 U |
| FC | 208 U |
| FCA | 65 |
| FCAB | 93 U |
| FCC | 11 |
| FCCM | 269 U |
| FCE Circumetnea Railway | 209 U |
| FCPCAL | 296 |
| FCU | 209 U |
| FdeC (Argentina) | 11 |
| FdG | 219 |
| FdS | 219 |
| Federal-Mogul Corporation | 627 |
| Federal-Mogul Limited | 611 |
| Federal Railroad Administration | 408 |

# INDEX/F–H

Federal Railway Administration (EBA) ...... 152
Federal Railways Fund (BEV) ...... 153
Federal Transit Administration ...... 409
Federation of Cable Railways ...... 808
Federation of Private Railways ...... 808
FEGUA ...... 181
Felten & Guilleaume Kabelwerke ...... 696
FENADESAL ...... 134
FEPASA (Chile) ...... 96
FEPSA ...... 11
FER ...... 210 U
Ferotrack Engineering ...... 727
Ferranti Technologies ...... 570 U, 705 U
Ferraz SA ...... 555, 570, 627, 696
Ferro (Great Britain) Ltd ...... 570 U
Ferro International A/S ...... 571
Ferroban ...... 66
Ferrocar (Venezuela) ...... 455
Ferrocarril Austral Fueguino (FAF) ...... 9
Ferrocarril Belgrano Cargas SA (FBC) ...... 9
Ferrocarril de Bolivia al Pacifico ...... 96
Ferrocarril del Istmo de Tehuantepec (FIT) ...... 269
Ferrocarril Coahuila a Durango (LCD) ...... 269
Ferrocarril Córdoba Central (FCC) ...... 11
Ferrocarril Ingenio San Antonio ...... 289
Ferrocarril Presidente Carlos Antonio López (FCPCAL) ...... 296
Ferrocarriles Chiapas-Mayab (FCCM) ...... 269 U
Ferrocarriles del Chubut (FdeC) ...... 11
Ferrocarriles Españoles de Via Estrecha (FEVE) ...... 329
Ferrocarriles Mediterráneos (FeMed) ...... 11
Ferrocarriles Nacionales de México (FNM) ...... 268
Ferrocoop ...... 11
Ferroeste ...... 65
FerroExpreso Pampeano SA (FEPSA) ...... 11
Ferrograph ...... 671
Ferromex ...... 270
Ferrominera Orinoco ...... 457
Ferronor ...... 97
Ferronorte ...... 66
Ferrostaal AG ...... 550 U, 594 U, 627 U, 727 U
Ferrostaal Corp ...... 727
Ferrosur (Mexico) ...... 270
Ferrosur Roca (FR) ...... 12
Ferrovia Centro-Atlantica (FCA) ...... 65
Ferrovia Norte-Sul ...... 68
Ferrovia Novoeste ...... 68
Ferrovia Sul-Atlantico ...... 68
Ferrovia Tereza Cristina (FTC) ...... 68
Ferroviario Urquiza de Paraná ...... 9
Ferrovias (Argentina) ...... 13
Ferrovias (Colombia) ...... 107
Ferrovias Bandeirantes ...... 66
Ferrovís Guatemala (FEGUA) ...... 181
Fersystem ...... 571
FEVE ...... 329
FG (Fleischhauer-Gizeh GmbH) ...... 684
FGC (Italy) ...... 215 U
FGC (Spain) ...... 327
FGV ...... 336
Fiat Ferroviaria SpA ...... 538, 594
Fiber Options ...... 654
Fiberline Composites A/S ...... 571
Findlay, Irvine Ltd ...... 727 U
Fine Products SA ...... 571
Finnish Railway Engineering Ltd ...... 827
Finnyards Materials Technology ...... 571
Finsam A/S ...... 594
FIREMA Trasporti ...... 500, 555, 594 U, 627 N, 671 N, 684 U, 696
First Engineering Ltd ...... 727, 828
First Great Eastern Ltd ...... 391
First Great Western Ltd ...... 392 U
FirstGroup plc ...... 391 U
First North Western ...... 392 U
First Union Rail ...... 800
Fischer Industries ...... 571
FIT ...... 269
FKE ...... 158
FKI Godwin Warren ...... 654
Flachglas Wernberg GmbH ...... 571 U
Fleet Software ...... 790, 828
Florida East Coast Railway Co ...... 426
Florida high-speed transportation program ...... 452
Flow Science Ltd ...... 828
Flumitrens ...... 68
Fluor Daniel Pty Limited ...... 828
Fluor Global Services Consulting ...... 828
Flury, Arthur AG ...... 696
FM Design Ltd ...... 828
FM Industries ...... 594, 611
FNH ...... 182
FNME Ferrovie Nord Milano Esercizio ...... 215
FNM (Mexico) ...... 268
FO ...... 352 U
Focon Electronic Systems A/S ...... 671 U
Fokker Space BV ...... 640
Forges de Fresnes ...... 611
*Forum Train Europe* ...... 767
Forth Smith Railroad Co ...... 427 N
Foster Co, L B ...... 727

Foxboro Transportation Systems ...... 660
FP ...... 216
FR–Ferrosur Roca ...... 12
Framafer ...... 728 V
France ...... 140
France,
  Railway Industries Association ...... 808 U
  Track Suppliers Association (SYCAFER) ...... 808 V
Frankfurt-Königsteiner Eisenbahn (FKE) ...... 158
Franz Kiel GmbH & Co KG ...... 574 U
Fraunhofer Institute for Non-Destructive Testing ...... 772 U
Frazer-Nash Consultancy ...... 828
Freiberger Eisenbahngesellschaft mbH (FE) ...... 158
Freight Australia ...... 26 U
FreightCorp ...... 27 U
Freightliner Ltd ...... 393 U
French National Railways (SNCF) ...... 143 U
French Railways Infrastructure Authority (RFF) ...... 140 U
Frenoplast ...... 611
Frenos Calefaccion y Señales ...... 611
Freudenberg Dichtungs- & Schwingungstechnik KG ...... 571 U
Freudenberg Schwab GmbH ...... 538 U, 571 U, 594 U, 612 U, 627 U
Freudenberg Simrit KG ...... 555 U
FS Holding SpA ...... 210
FSE ...... 220 U
FSF ...... 220 U
FT ...... 207
FTC ...... 68
FTM ...... 220 U
Fuchs Lubricants (UK) plc ...... 627 U
Fuji Car Manufacturing Co ...... 501, 594
Fuji Electric ...... 555 U, 571 U, 696 V
Fuji Heavy Industries ...... 501
Furka-Oberalp Railway (FO) ...... 352
Furrer + Frey ...... 696
Futuris Industrial Products ...... 612
Futurit ...... 654
FVE ...... 157 V
FY-Industries Ltd ...... 571

## G

Gabon ...... 151
Gabon State Railways (OCTRA) ...... 151
GAI-Tronics ...... 572 U, 654 U, 671 U
Galland ...... 696
Ganz-David Brown Transmissions Kft ...... 538
Ganz-Hunslet ...... 501
Ganz Vagon Kft ...... 501, 594, 627
Garden City Western Railway ...... 427 N
Gates Rubber Co Ltd, The ...... 572, 684
Gateway Western Railway ...... 427
Gatwick Express Ltd ...... 394 U
GATX ...... 801
GB Railfreight ...... 394 U
GB Railways ...... 395
GE Capital Railcar Services ...... 801
GE Harris Harmon ...... 656
GE Harris Railway Electronics ...... 612, 654
GE Rail Services ...... 798
GE Transportation Systems ...... 502, 538, 573 V
Geismar ...... 696 V, 728 V
Gemco (George Moss Ltd) ...... 504, 728
General Motors Corporation, Electro-Motive Division ...... 504, 538
General Railway Corporation (Saudi Arabia) ...... 316
Genesee & Wyoming Inc ...... 427
Genesee-Rail-One ...... 87 N
Genoa–Casella Railway (FGC) ...... 215
Georg Eknes Industrier A/S ...... 572 U
Georges Halais SA ...... 572
Georgia Southwestern Railroad ...... 427 U
Georgian Railways ...... 151
Georgsmarienhütte Eisenbahn (GET) ...... 158
German Railways (DB) ...... 158
Germany ...... 152
Germany,
  Association of German Transport Undertakings (VDV) ...... 808
  Association of Privately Owned Wagon Operators (VPI) ...... 809 U
  Railway Supply Industry Association ...... 809
  Rolled Steel Association Long Products Division ...... 809
  Switch & Crossing Manufacturers Association ...... 809
GET ...... 158
Gettysburg & Northern Railraod Co ...... 427 N
Getzner Werkstoffe GesmbH ...... 728
Gevisa SA ...... 505, 773
GEZ ...... 572
Geze GmbH ...... 572 U
GFI-Genfare ...... 684
Ghana ...... 177
Ghana Railway Corporation (GRC) ...... 177
GHD-Transmark Pty Ltd ...... 828
GIBBRail ...... 828
GIF (Spain) ...... 330
Gilardoni SpA ...... 773 N

Giro Engineering Ltd ...... 539 U
Giumma SpA ...... 572 U
Glacier Clevite (see Federal-Mogul)
Gleisbaumechanik Brandenburg ...... 728
GMD ...... 539
Gmeinder ...... 505, 539, 773
GO Transit (Ontario) ...... 87
Go-Ahead Group, The ...... 395
Goderich-Exeter Railway ...... 87
Gorba AG ...... 671 U
Gosa Holding Corporation ...... 594
Gotch Consultancy ...... 829
GRA Inc ...... 829 U
Graaff GmbH ...... 594
Graham-White Manufacturing ...... 612
Grammer AG ...... 572 U
Grand Rapids Eastern ...... 427 N
Grandi Motori Trieste ...... 539
Grandistazioni ...... 215 N
Grant Lyon Eagre Ltd ...... 728
GrantRail Ltd ...... 656 U
Graz-Köflach Railway ...... 48
GRC ...... 177
Great North Eastern Railway ...... 395
Great Northern ...... 28 U
Great Southern Railway (GSR) ...... 29 U
Great Western Railway Co of Colorado ...... 427
Greater Copenhagen Local Railways ...... 127 N
Greater Vancouver Transportation Authority (GVTA)-Translink ...... 88
Greece ...... 178
Green Cargo AB ...... 342 U
Green Mountain Railroad Corporation ...... 428
Greenbrier Companies, The ...... 594
Greenbrier Leasing ...... 801
Greenwood Engineering ...... 728 U, 773 U
Gregg Company Ltd, The ...... 595
Gregomatic ...... 773
Greysham International ...... 612, 627, 697
Gribskov Railway (GDS) ...... 128
Griffin Wheel Co ...... 628
Grimma GmbH ...... 729
Grinaker Duraset ...... 729
GSK GmbH ...... 729
GSR ...... 29 U
GT Railway Maintenance Ltd ...... 729
Guatemala ...... 181
Guhl & Scheibler ...... 684
Guilford Rail System ...... 428
Guinea Republic ...... 182
Gummi Metall Technik GmbH (GMT) ...... 572 U, 627 U
Gummiwerk Kraiburg Elastik ...... 729
Gunderson Inc ...... 595
Gunderson-Concarril SA ...... 595
Gunnebo Entrance Control ...... 684
Gutenhoffnungshütte Radsatz ...... 628
Györ-Sopron-Ebenfurt Railway (GySEV) ...... 183

## H

Haacon Hebetechnik ...... 595
HaCon Ingenieurgesellschaft mbH ...... 829
Hafen und Güterverkehr Köln (HGK) ...... 168
Hagenuk Faiveley GmbH (HFG) ...... 573 U
Halcrow Group Ltd ...... 829
Halo Company (Sussex) Ltd ...... 672
Hamburg Port Railway ...... 168
Hamersley Iron Ore Railway ...... 29 U
Hamworthy Compressor Systems Ltd ...... 555
Hanjin Heavy Industries Co Ltd ...... 505, 595
Hankyu Corporation ...... 239
Hanning & Kahl GmbH ...... 612, 656, 729
Hanshin Electric Railway ...... 239
Hanson-Wilson Inc ...... 830
Harbor Belt Line ...... 428
Harry Weese Associates ...... 830
Harsco Track Technologies (Australia) ...... 730 U
Harsco Track Technologies (UK) ...... 729
Harsco Track Technologies (US) ...... 730
Harting Ltd ...... 705 V
Harz Narrow Gauge Railways ...... 168
Hatch Mott MacDonald Inc ...... 830
Hawker Siddeley Switchgear ...... 697
Haynes Corporation ...... 539
HDA Forgings ...... 628
HDR Engineering Inc ...... 830
Heathrow Express ...... 395
Hedjaz Jordan Railway (HJR) ...... 247
Hegenscheidt-MFD GmbH ...... 759, 773 U
HEI ...... 595 U, 628 U, 697 U, 730 U
Heinrich Helms Metallwarenfabrik ...... 573
Hellenic Railways Organisation (OSE) ...... 178 U
Hellermann Insuloid ...... 706
HellertalBahn ...... 169
Helsingør-Hornbaek-Gilleleje Railway ...... 128
Henry Booth Group ...... 684 V
Henry Williams Group ...... 657 U, 730
Herbert Pool Limited (see Blatchford Transport Equipment)
Hering-Bau ...... 684

Hessische Landesbahn (HLB) ... 169
Hexcel Composites ... 573 [U]
HFG ... 573 [U]
HF Wiebe GmbH ... 730 [N]
HGK ... 168
Hidromecanica ... 539
Hi-Force Hydraulics ... 731, 773
High-Point Rendel Ltd ... 830
Hill International Inc ... 830
Hillerød-Hundested Railway (HFHJ) ... 128
Hioma-aine Oy ... 731
Hitachi Cable Ltd ... 706
Hitachi Ltd ... 505 [U], 540 [U], 556 [U], 657 [N], 697 [N]
H J Skelton & Co Ltd ... 731 [N]
H J Skelton (Canada) ... 731 [N]
Hjørring-Hirsthals Railway (HP) ... 128 [U]
Høng-Tølløse Jernbane A/S (HTJ) ... 126
Hodgson & Hodgson Group ... 573 [U], 830 [U]
Höft & Wessel GmbH ... 684 [U]
Hohenzollerische Landesbahn (HzL) ... 169
Hokkaido Railway Co (JR Hokkaido) ... 231 [U]
Holland Co ... 731 [U]
Holland Co LP ... 595 [N], 773 [N]
Holland Construction & Engineering Pty ... 731
Holland Railconsult ... 831
Honduras ... 182
Honduras National Railway (FNH) ... 182
Honeywell Bramsbelag (Jurid) ... 613 [U]
Honeywell Control Systems ... 657
Honeywell Serck ... 540, 573
H ng-T ll se Railway (HTJ) ... 128 [U]
Hoogovens ... 506, 595
Hörseltalbahn (HTB) ... 170
Housatonic Railroad Co Inc ... 428
Houston Belt & Terminal Railway Co ... 428
Hovair Systems Ltd ... 773 [U]
Howden Buffalo ... 573
Howe Green ... 684
HP Srl ... 573
HPP GmbH ... 706 [N]
HPW ... 672, 790
HSBC Rail (UK) ... 798
HTM-Infra ... 831
Hübner Gummi- & Kunststoff GmbH ... 573
Huck International ... 573, 731 [U]
Hull Trains ... 396 [U]
Hungarian State Railways (MÁV) ... 183
Hungary ... 183
Hunslet-Barclay Ltd ... 506, 596
Hupac SA ... 469 [N]
Huron Central Railway ... 88 [N]
Huron & Eastern Railway ... 428
Hyder Consulting Ltd ... 831
Hygate Transmissions ... 540 [V]
Hypertac ... 706
Hyster Europe Ltd ... 759
Hyundai ... 556, 697
Hyundai Precision & Industry Co Ltd ... 596
Hywema Lifting Systems ... 773 [U]


## I


IAD Rail Systems ... 731 [U]
I&M Rail Link ... 428
Iarnród Éireann (IE) ... 203
IBAB ... 343 [U]
IBEG ... 774
IBG Monforts GmbH ... 628
IBIS Transport Consultants ... 831
IBM Travel & Transportation ... 685 [U], 831
ICB ... 831
ICER Brakes SA ... 613 [U]
ICF Integral Coach Factory ... 507 [U], 628 [U]
ICF Consulting ... 831 [U]
ICL ... 672, 685, 790
Icore International ... 706 [U]
IE Iarnród Éireann ... 203 [U]
IER ... 685
IES Transportation Inc ... 428
IFE ... 574
IIT Research Institute ... 640 [U]
ILEA Rail AB ... 343 [N]
Illinois & Midland Railway Co ... 428 [U]
Illinois Central Railroad ... 414
Illinois Department of Transportation ... 452
Illinois/Wisconsin high-speed route ... 452
Ilo-Toquepala Railway ... 298
IMI Norgren GmbH ... 574 [N]
Impco Products Inc ... 507
ImproRail ... 732
IMS UK ... 628 [U]
Incofer ... 109
India ... 186
Indian Railway Board (IR) ... 186
Indiana & Ohio Rail System ... 428
Indiana Harbor Belt Railroad ... 429
Indiana Hi-Rail Corporation ... 429
Indiana Rail Road Co ... 429
Indiana Southwestern Railroad Co ... 429 [N]
Indonesia ... 197
Indonesian Railways Public Corporation (Perumka) ... 197
Indra Sistemas ... 685
Inexa Profil AB ... 732
Infodev Inc ... 790 [N]
Info Systems GmbH ... 556 [N], 672
InfoVision Systems Ltd ... 791 [V]
Infra Safety Services ... 732, 832
Infrasoft Corp ... 791 [V]
Infrasoft Ltd ... 732, 791
INFUNDO GmbH ... 732
INKA Industri Kereta Api ... 507 [U], 596
Inlandsbanan AB (IBAB) ... 343
Inlandsgods AB ... 344 [U]
INME ... 774
Innovata ... 791
Inova Corporation ... 672 [N]
Institute of International Container Lessors (IICL) ... 805 [U]
Institution of Logistics and Transport ... 809 [U]
Institution of Railway Operators ... 807
Institution of Spanish Railways ... 809
Instron ... 774
Insul-8 Corporation ... 697 [N]
Intamodal-Eimar SA ... 596
Intec Ltd ... 685
Interalia ... 672
Interautomation ... 791
Interconsult AS ... 832
Intercontainer-Interfrigo ... 469
Interep SA ... 732
Interinfra ... 786
Interfleet Technology ... 832
Intergovernmental Organisation for International Carriage by Rail (OTIF) ... 805
Intermetric GmbH ... 832
International Air-Rail Organisation (IARO) ... 805
International Association of Railway Journalists (AIJF) ... 807
International Container Bureau (BIC) ... 805
International Metals Reclamation Co (INMETCO) ... 574 [U]
International Nameplate Supplies Ltd ... 574 [V]
International Rail Consultants ... 832
International Rail Transport Committee (CIT) ... 805
International Railway Congress Association (IRCA) ... 805
International Technical Services ... 774 [N], 832 [N]
International Track Systems Inc ... 732
International Union (Association) of Public Transport (UITP) ... 805
International Union of Private Railway Wagon Owners' Associations (UIP) ... 805
International Union of Railways (UIC) ... 805
Intraplan Consult GmbH ... 832
Invatra ... 798
Iowa Interstate Railroad Ltd ... 429
IP-Solutions ... 832
IPA ... 732
IR (India) ... 186 [U]
IR (Israel) ... 205 [U]
Iran ... 199
Iraq ... 202
Iraqi Republic Railways (IRR) ... 202 [U]
Irausa Loire SA ... 574
Ireland ... 203
Iron Road Railways Inc ... 429
IRR Iraqi Republic Railways ... 202 [U]
Islamic Iranian Republic Railways (RAI) ... 199
Island Line ... 396 [U]
Isolux Wat SA ... 657
Israel ... 205
Israel Railways (IR) ... 205 [U]
Issels & Son Ltd ... 628
Italdis Industria ... 685
Italferr SpA ... 832
Italy ... 207
Italy,
  Association of Electrotechnical & Electronics Industries (ANIE) ... 809
  College of Italian Railway Engineers ... 809
Ivory Coast ... 110
Ivory Coast Railway (SIPF) ... 110
IVS Insta Visual Solutions ... 672 [U]
Iyo Railway ... 239
Izu Hakone Railway ... 239
Izukyu Corporation ... 240


## J


JacksonEve Infrastructure Services ... 732 [N]
JAFCO Tools Ltd ... 732
Jakem Timbers ... 732
Jamaica ... 221
Jamaica Railway Corporation (JRC) ... 222
James Scott ... 833
Japan ... 222
Japan,
  Freight Railway Co ... 235
  Overseas Rolling Stock Association (JORSA) ... 809 [U]
  Railway Construction Corporation (JRCC) ... 222
  Railway Electrical Engineering Association ... 809
  Railway Engineers' Association ... 809 [U]
  Railway Technical Service (JARTS) ... 833
  Railways Group (JR) ... 222
  Society of Mechanical Engineers ... 809
Jaraguá SA ... 732
Jarmuszerelvenyt Guarto RT ... 574
Jarret ... 613 [U], 732 [U]
JARTS ... 833 [U]
Jarvis Rail ... 732 [U]
Jasmin Electronics plc ... 672
JBV ... 290 [U]
JC Bamford Excavators Ltd ... 933 [N]
Jenbacher Energiesysteme AG ... 540 [V], 596 [U]
Jernhusen AB ... 344 [N]
Jessop & Co ... 507, 596
JEZ Sistemas Ferroviarios ... 733
Jindřichův Hradec Local Railways (JHMD) ... 121 [V]
JMA Railroad Supply Company ... 540 [U]
John Holdsworth ... 573 [U]
Johnstown America ... 596
Jones Garrard Ltd ... 833
Jordan ... 246
Joyce Loebl Ltd ... 574
JR (Japan) ... 223 [U]
JR-Central ... 226
JR-East ... 223 [U]
JR-Hokkaido ... 231 [U]
JR-Kyushu ... 232 [U]
JR-Shikoku ... 234
JR-West ... 22 [U]
Jungfraubahnen (BOB/WAB) ... 353
Jupiter Plast ... 574
JZ ... 459 [U]


## K


K & M ... 597
Kaba Gilgen AG ... 574, 685
Kaiser Bauxite Railway ... 222
Kalmar Industries BV ... 759 [U]
Kalmar Sweden ... 759
Kalugaputjmach ... 508
Kalyn Siebert Inc ... 733
Kambre i Täby AB ... 774
KAMPSAX International A/S ... 833
K & M Industrie Metalmeccaniche srl ... 600
Kankakee Beaverville & Southern Railroad Company ... 429
Kansas City Southern Railway Company ... 414
Kansas South Western Railway ... 429
Kapsch Group ... 657 [U]
Kärcher ... 774 [U]
Karl Georg ... 613
Karsdorfer Eisenbahn (KEG) ... 170
Kassel-Numburger Eisenbahn (KNE) ... 170
Kaufmann, A, AG ... 697 [U], 714 [U]
Kawasaki Heavy Industries Ltd ... 508 [U], 597 [V]
Kazakhstan ... 248
Kazakhstan State Railways (KTZ) ... 248
KCI ... 759
Kearney Inc, A T ... 818
Keef, Alan, Limited ... 508 [U]
KEG ... 170
Keifuku Electric Railway ... 240
Keihan Electric Railway Co Ltd ... 240
Keihin Express Electric Railway ... 241 [U]
Keio Teito Electric Railway ... 241
Keisei Electric Railway ... 241
Keller Elettromeccanica SpA ... 508 [N], 774 [N]
Keller SpA ... 597 [N]
Kenelec Pty Ltd ... 658
Kenya ... 249
Kenya Railways (KR) ... 249
Keokuk Junction Railway Co ... 430 [N]
Kershaw Manufacturing Co Inc ... 697 [U], 759 [U]
Keystone Bahntechnik ... 613 [U]
Keystone Industries ... 613
Kiamichi Railroad ... 430
Kidde Fire Protection Ltd ... 574
Kiel, Franz, GmbH ... 574 [U]
Kiepe Elektrik ... 556 [U]
KIHN ... 733
Kim Hotstart ... 540 [U]
Kinex-ZVL A/S ... 628 [U]
Kinki Nippon Railway (Kintetsu) ... 242
Kinki Sharyo Co ... 508 [U], 597
Kirghiz Railways ... 250 [U]
Kirghizia ... 250
Kirow Leipzig GmbH ... 733
Kleeneze Sealtech Ltd ... 575 [V]
Klein, Transport ... 575, 685
Kloos Oving BV ... 734 [U]
Klüssendorf Produkte und Vertriebs GmbH ... 685
KLW-Wheelco SA ... 629
KMT-teknikka Oy ... 556 [N]
KNE ... 170
Knorr-Bremse GmbH ... 613
Knox Kershaw Inc ... 734
KNR ... 252 [U]
Kobe Electric Railway ... 242

858 **INDEX**/K–N


Kockums Industrier AB ... 509, 597, 629, 734
Kolmex ... 509, 597, 640, 734
Kolomna Plant JSC ... 509 [U], 541 [U]
Komatsu Diesel Company ... 541 [V]
Konan Railway ... 242
Koncar-Electric Locomotives Inc ... 510 [U], 556 [U], 775 [U]
Koni BV ... 629 [U]
Konkan Railway Corporation Ltd ... 193 [U]
Konstal (see ALSTOM)
Korea High Speed Rail Construction Authority ... 251
Korea, North ... 250
Korea, South ... 251
Korean National Railroad (KNR) ... 252
Korean State Railway (ZCi) ... 250
Kosovo ... 253
Kosovo Railway Enterprise ... 253
Kovis doo ... 614 [N]
Kowloon-Canton Railway (KCR) ... 104 [U]
Koyo Seiko Co ... 629
KR ... 249 [U]
Krauss-Maffei Wegmann ... 640 [U]
Krautkrämer GmbH ... 734
KRONE-REW ... 672
Kryukovsky Railway Car Building Works ... 597, 629
KTM ... 265
K T Steel Industries Pvt ... 597
KTZ ... 248 [U]
Kummler + Matter ... 697
Künzler Jav AG ... 734
KV Ltd ... 575
KVG Kesselwagen Vermietgesellschaft mbH ... 799
Kyle Railroad Co (Kansas) ... 430
Kyosan Electric Manufacturing Co ... 658 [U], 759 [U]
Kyrgyizia ... 250
Kyrgyizia Railways ... 250 [U]
Kyushu Railway Co (JR Kyushu) ... 232 [U]


## L


L & M Radiator ... 542
Laakmann Karton GmbH ... 685
LAF Les Appareils Ferroviaires ... 614
Lahmeyer International ... 833 [N]
Lake Superior & Ishpeming Railroad Co ... 430
Lakeland & Waterways Railway ... 88 [N]
Lakenden Kylmäkeskus Oy ... 575 [N]
Lamco Railroad ... 256
Langen & Sondermann Ferdenwerk ... 630 [V]
Laos ... 254
Laramore, Douglass and Popham ... 834
Laser Rail Ltd ... 734 [U], 791
Latin American Railway Association (ALAF) ... 806
Latvia ... 254
Latvian Railways (LDZ) ... 254
Laubag ... 170
Laurinburg & Southern Railroad Co ... 430
Lausanne-Echallens-Bercher Railway (LEB) ... 354 [U]
Lazzerini & Co Srl ... 575
LCD ... 269
LDZ ... 254 [U]
Leach International Europe SA ... 658
Lebanon ... 256
Lechmotoren GmbH ... 556
LEK Consulting ... 834 [U]
Lekov AS ... 556 [U]
Lenard Bauer & Co GmbH ... 575 [U]
Leonhard Weiss ... 754
Lerc SA ... 698
Lesjöfors AB ... 614, 630
Lester B Knight & Associates ... 834
LeTourneau Inc ... 759
Leuna ... 170
Lewis Bolt & Nut ... 734
LFI ... 208 [U]
LFU ... 454
LG ... 257
LHB (see ALSTOM)
Liberia ... 256
Libya ... 257
Liebherr Container Cranes Ltd ... 759
Liebherr-Verkehrstechnik Frankfurt ... 575
Lincoln Industries ... 658
Lindapter International ... 734
Lineas Ferreas Uruguayas (LFU) ... 454
Linsinger Maschinenbau ... 735, 775 [V]
Linx AB ... 468 [U]
Lithuania ... 257
Lithuanian Railways (LG) ... 257
Litton ... 706
Lloyd's Register MHA Ltd ... 834 [U]
LM Glasfiber A/S ... 575 [U]
Local Railway, The ... 128 [N]
Lockheed Martin Rail Systems ... 834 [N]
Logibag ... 686
Lolland Railway (LJ) ... 129
London & Continental Railways Ltd ... 396
Long Island Rail Road Co ... 442 [U]
Loram Maintenance of Way Inc ... 735 [V]
Lord Corporation ... 630, 735
LORIC (China National Railway Locomotive & Rolling Stock Industry Corporation) ... 493
Louisiana & Delta Railroad ... 430 [U]
Louisville & Indiana Railroad Co ... 430
Lovers Rail ... 280
LPA Industries ... 706
LTK Engineering Services ... 834
LTS ... 673
Luanda Railway ... 7
Lubricant Consult GmbH ... 630
Lucchini Group ... 630 [U], 735 [U]
Lucerne-Stans-Engelberg Railway (LSE) ... 354
Lugansk Diesel Locomotive Works ... 510
Lukas Hydraulic GmbH ... 735
Lumino Licht Elektronik GmbH ... 673 [N]
Luxembourg ... 259
Luxembourg Railways (CFL) ... 259
Luxram Lighting Ltd ... 658
Lyngby-Naerum Railway ... 129 [U]
Lyria ... 468 [U]
Lyudinovo Locomotive Works ... 510, 598, 735


## M


M & J Diesel Locomotive Filter ... 542
Macedonia ... 261
Macedonian Railways (MZ) ... 261
Mackenzie Northern Railway ... 88 [N]
Madagascar ... 262
MAEL ... 686
Mafelec ... 576 [U]
Magnadata International Ltd ... 686
Magnetic Autocontrol ... 686 [N]
Magnus/Farley Inc ... 630 [V]
Maguire Group Inc ... 835
Maine Central Railroad Company ... 430
Maintrain Ltd ... 775 [U]
Maintrain Ltd ... 775 [U]
Major private and third sector railways (Japan) ... 238
Malawi ... 263
Malawi Railways (1994) Ltd (MR) ... 263
Malayan Railway (KTM) ... 265
Malaysia ... 264
Mali ... 267
Malmtrafik i Kiruna AB (MTAB) ... 344 [U]
MAN Nutzfahrzeuge AG ... 543
Mannesmann Dematic AG Gottwald ... 735, 760
Manoir Industries ... 598, 614, 630, 735
Manufacturers Railway Co ... 430
MARC ... 443
Marconi Communications Ltd ... 658, 706, 786
Marcroft Engineering ... 598, 775 [V]
Marrel ... 598
Mars Electronics International ... 686
Martyn Cornwall Design ... 835 [V]
Maryland & Delaware Railroad Co ... 430
Maryland & Pennsylvania Railroad Co ... 431
Maryland Mass Transit Administration ... 443
Maryland Midland Railway Inc ... 430
Maryland Rail Commuter Service ... 439
Maschinen- und Stahlban Dresden ... 775 [N]
Massachusetts Bay Transportation Authority ... 443
Matériel de Voie SA ... 735
Matisa Matériel Industriel SA ... 735
Matra Transport SA ... 658
Mattig-Schauer ... 673
Maunsell, Faber ... 835 [U]
Mauritania ... 268
Mauritanian National Railways (SNIM) ... 268 [U]
MÁV ... 598
MÁV Debreceni ... 658
Max Bögl ... 736
Maxon America Inc ... 658
Maxon Europe ... 658
Maxwell Soft Park Ltd ... 791 [U]
MBD Design ... 835 [U]
McConnel Research Enterprises ... 775
Mecanoexportimport ... 510, 598, 632, 736, 786
Mechan Ltd ... 576 [V], 775 [V]
Meister Electronic GmbH ... 673
Mendip Rail Ltd ... 397
Mer Mec SpA ... 658 [N], 698 [N], 736 [U], 835 [N]
Merak Sistemas Integrados de Climatizacíon ... 576 [U]
Mercer Management Consulting Inc ... 835
Merlin Gerin Brasil ... 698
Metalastik (see Trelleborg)
Metcalfe Railway Products ... 614 [U]
Metra ... 44 [U]
Metra Blansko AS ... 673
Metro Consulting ... 835
Metroconsult ... 835 [N]
Metrofor ... 69
Metrolink ... 449 [U]
Metronom Gesellschaft für Industrievermessung mbH ... 736
Metro-North Railroad Co ... 445
Metropolitana di Roma SpA (Met.ro) ... 215 [U]
Metropolitano–Buenos Aires ... 13
Metrorec ... 69
Metrovías (Argentina) ... 13
Metrowagonmash ... 510
Meva SA ... 598
Mexico ... 268
MIBA Gleitlager AG ... 632 [U]
Michigan high speed routes ... 452 [U]
Michigan Shore Railroad ... 431 [N]
Michigan Southern Railroad Co ... 431 [N]
Michurinsk Locomotive Works ... 510
Microelettrica Scientifica SpA ... 576 [V]
Microphor Inc ... 576
Midland Mainline ... 397
Mid-Michigan Railroad Inc ... 431
Millbrook Proving Ground Ltd ... 835 [V]
Miner Enterprises Inc ... 614
Minnesota Commercial Railway Co ... 431 [U]
Mirror Technology Ltd ... 658
Mississippi Central Railroad Co ... 431 [N]
Mississippi Export Railroad ... 431
Missouri & Northern Arkansas Railroad ... 431
Mitchell Equipment Corporation ... 737
Mitron Oy ... 673
Mitsubishi Electric Corporation ... 510 [U], 556, 614 [V]
Mitsubishi Heavy Industries Ltd ... 760
Mitsukawa Metal Works ... 737
Mittelland Regional Railways (RM) ... 355
Mittel-Thurgau Railway (MThB) ... 355 [U]
MOB ... 356 [U]
Mobile Climate Control Corp ... 576 [U]
Mobile Data Processing ... 686
Modern Track Machinery Canada Ltd ... 737
Modjeski & Masters ... 835
Moës, Moteurs, SA ... 511
Mohawk Adirondack & Northern Railroad Corporation ... 431
Moldova ... 271
Moldovan Railways (CFM) ... 271
Molli ... 171
Monfer ... 215 [N]
Mongolia ... 272
Mongolian Railway (MTZ) ... 272
Monogram Systems ... 576 [U]
Montana Rail Link Inc ... 431 [U]
Monterrey Industrial Ferroviaria SA ... 737
Montreux-Oberland Bernois Railway (MOB) ... 356
Moog GmbH ... 737
Moore & Steele Corporation ... 737
More Wear Industrial Holdings ... 599
Morio Denki Co Ltd ... 556 [U], 576 [U], 659 [U], 673
Moroccan Railways (ONCFM) ... 273 [U]
Morocco ... 273
Mors Smith Relais ... 659 [U]
Moser-Baer SA ... 673 [N]
Mossboda Trä AB ... 7367
MotivePower Industries ... 511
Motorola Canada ... 659
Motorola UK ... 659
Motorola WSSD ... 686
Mott MacDonald Group ... 836
Mouchel Consulting Ltd ... 836
Mozambique ... 275
Mozambique Ports & Railways (CFM) ... 275
MR (Malawi) ... 263
MR (Myanmar) ... 276
MRS Logistica ... 69
MSA SpA ... 632 [U]
MTB Equipment Ltd ... 576 [N]
MTH Praha as ... 737
MThB ... 355 [U]
MTL Services plc ... 398
MTR Corporation Consultancy Services ... 836
MTS ... 776
MTS Systems GmbH ... 768
MTU ... 542 [U]
MTZ Mongolian Railway ... 272
Multi-Contact (UK) Ltd ... 706
MultiModal Applied Systems ... 791 [U]
Multi-Service Supply ... 614 [U], 632 [V]
Murom Diesel Locomotive Works ... 511, 698
Muromteplovoz ... 737
MVA Consultancy ... 836 [U]
MWL Brasil Rodas & Eixos ... 632
MWM ... 543 [V]
Myanmar (Burma) ... 276
Myanmar Railways (MR) ... 276
MZ ... 261 [U]
MZT HEPOS ... 614


## N


NABCO ... 577 [U], 615 [U]
NACCO SA ... 799 [U]
Nagoya Railroad ... 242
Namibe Railway ... 7
Namibia ... 277
NamRail ... 277 [U]
Nankai Electric Railway ... 243
Narita Manufacturing Ltd ... 577 [U], 687 [U]
Nashville & Eastern Railroad Corporation ... 432
National Electrical Carbon ... 557

National Express Group ... 398 [U]
National Iron Ore Co Ltd (Liberia) ... 256
National Rail Corporation Ltd (NR) ... 30 [U]
National Railway Equipment Company ... 512
National Railway Supplies (NRS) ... 740 [U]
National Railways of Mexico (FNM) ... 268
National Railways of Zimbabwe (NRZ) ... 462
National Steel Car Ltd ... 599
Nationale Maatschappij der Belgische Spoorwegen (NMBS) ... 53
NCA ... 14 [U]
NEA Transport Research & Training ... 837
Nebraska Central Railroad Company ... 432
Nebraska, Kansas & Colorado RailNet Inc ... 432
Nederlandse Spoorwegen NV (NS) ... 280
NedTrain BV ... 738, 837 [U]
NEL ... 837
Nencki AG ... 776 [U]
Nepal ... 278
Nepal Government Railway (NR) ... 278
Net Display Systems bv ... 673 [N]
Netherlands ... 278
Netherlands Railways (NS) ... 280
Network Connection, The ... 577
NEU International ... 776 [N]
Neu Systems Ferroviaires ... 577
Neukölln-Mittenwalder Eisenbahn (NME) ... 171
Neuero Technology GmbH ... 776 [U]
Neusser Eisenbahn ... 171
NEVZ (Novocherkassk Electric Locomotive Works) ... 512
New Brunswick Southern Railway ... 89 [U]
New England Central Railroad ... 432
New England Southern Railroad ... 432
New Jersey Transit Rail ... 446
New Markets Ltd ... 837 [V]
New Orleans Public Belt Railroad ... 432
New York & Atlantic Railway Company ... 432
New York high speed routes ... 452 [U]
New York, Susquehanna & Western Railroad Corporation ... 432
New Zealand ... 286
Newag GmbH & Co KG ... 512 [U], 615 [V], 738 [V]
Newbury Data Recording ... 687
Newt International ... 738 [V]
NFR Northeast Frontier Railway ... 194 [U]
NIAG ... 171
Nicaragua ... 289
Nichols Group ... 837
NICO ... 543
Nieaf-Smitt ... 577
Niederrheinische Verkehrsbetriebe (NIAG) ... 171
Nigeria ... 289
Nigerian Railways Corporation (NRC) ... 289
Niigata Converter Co (NICO) ... 543
Niigata Engineering Co ... 512 [U], 543
Niles-Simmons ... 776 [U]
Nippon Kido Kogyo Co ... 599 [V], 738
Nippon Sharyo Ltd ... 513 [U], 632 [V]
Nippon Signal Co ... 659, 687
NIR ... 398
Nishi Nippon Railroad ... 243
Nizhnedneprovsky Tube Rolling Plant ... 632
Njanji Railways ... 462
NKK Corporation ... 738
NMBS ... 53 [U]
NME ... 171
Noell GmbH ... 760
NoordNed Personenvervoor BV ... 285
Nordco ... 738
Nordfriesische Verkehrsbetriebe (NVAG) ... 171
Nordjyske Jernbaner A/S (NJ) ... 129 [N]
Nord-Ostsee-Bahn (NOB) ... 171
NordWestBahn (NWB) ... 172 [U]
Norfolk Southern Corporation ... 415
Nortel Networks ... 659
North American RailNet Inc ... 432
North Carolina/Virginia high speed route ... 452
North Carolina & Virginia Railroad ... 432 [N]
North Eastern Railway (IR) ... 193 [U]
North Milan Railway (FNME) ... 215 [U]
North San Diego County Transit ... 448 [U]
Northeast Frontier Railway (NFR) ... 194 [U]
Northern Indiana Commuter Transportation ... 448
Northern Ireland Railways Co Ltd (NIR) ... 398
Northern Plains Railroad ... 432 [U]
Northern Railway (IR) ... 194 [U]
Northern Rivers Railroad Pty Ltd (NRR) ... 31 [U]
Northern Rubber Co Ltd ... 577
Northwestern Pacific Railroad ... 432
Nortrade srl ... 577
Norway ... 290
Norwegian National Rail Administration (JBV) ... 290
Norwegian State Railways (NSB) ... 291
Norwest Holst Construction ... 740
Novocherkassk Electric Locomotive Works (NEVZ) ... 512 [U]
NR (Nepal) ... 278
NR (NSW) ... 30 [U]
NRC ... 289
NRR ... 31 [U]
NRS ... 659 [U]
NRZ ... 462
NS Financial Services ... 799
NS Railplan bv ... 837
NSK Ltd ... 632
NSK-RHP UK Ltd ... 632
NTN Toyo Bearing Co ... 632
Nuevo Central Argentino (NCA) ... 14 [U]
NVAG ... 171
NWB ... 172 [U]
NWRZ ... 776


**O**


O&K Rolltrepen GmbH ... 687
ÖBB ... 43 [U]
Oberrheinische Eisenbahn Gesselschaft (OEG) ... 172
OCBN ... 57
OCTRA ... 151
Odakyu Electric Railway ... 243
Ødegaard & Danneskiold-Samse A/S ... 838 [U]
Odsherreds Railway (OHJ) ... 129 [U]
ØDS-Caltronic AS ... 740
OEG ... 172
Oerlikon-Knorr Eisenbahntechnik (OKE) ... 615
OEVA ... 799
Office des Chemins de Fer et du Transport en Commun ... 256 [U]
Officine Ferroviarie Veronesi (OFV) ... 514, 599, 632
OHE ... 172 [U]
Ohio Central Railroad Inc ... 433 [U]
Ohmi Railway ... 244
OKD Doprava ... 122 [U]
OKE ... 615
Oktal ... 641
Oleo International Ltd ... 599 [U], 615 [U], 740 [U], 760 [U]
OLMI SpA ... 740
OME ... 172
Omega Electronics ... 673 [U]
OMI Logistics Ltd ... 838
OmniTRAX Inc ... 433
Omron Corporation ... 687
OMT SpA ... 543 [U]
On Rail GmbH ... 799
ONATRA ... 108
Onerail ... 791 [N]
Ontario Midwestern Railway Company ... 89
Ontario Northland Railway ... 89 [U]
Optech ... 674
Øresund Consortium ... 127 [U], 344 [V]
Organisation Commune Benin-Niger des Chemins de Fer et des Transports (OCBN) ... 57
Organisation for the Collaboration of Railways (OSJD) ... 805
ORTEC ... 740
Orthstar Inc ... 641 [V]
Orton/McCullough Crane Co ... 740
Orval, Ateliers d' ... 599
Orvec International Ltd ... 578 [U]
ORX ... 632
Oscar Faber ... 838
Osmose Railroad Division ... 740
Osthannovesche Eisenbahnen (OHE) ... 172 [U]
O-Train ... 89 [N]
OTP Rail and Transit ... 665
Ottawa Valley Railroad ... 89 [N]
Otter Tail Valley Railroad ... 433 [N]
Ove Arup & Partners ... 838 [N]


**P**


Pacific Harbor Line Inc ... 433
Padane Railways (FP) ... 217
Paducah & Louisville Railway ... 433
Pafawag (see Adtranz)
PAFEC Ltd ... 792
PAGE ... 674 [N]
Pakistan ... 293
Pakistan Railways (PR) ... 293
Pakistan Railways Carriage Factory ... 514, 599
Palfinger Hebetechnik ... 740
Pan American Railway Congress Association (ACPF) ... 806
Panama ... 296
Panama Canal Railroad (PCRC) ... 296
Pandrol Rail Fastenings Ltd ... 741 [V]
Paraguay ... 296
Parizzi ... 557
Parker Pneumatic ... 578
Parsons Brinckerhoff Inc (PB) ... 787, 838 [U]
Pascal International AB ... 578
Patapsco & Black Rivers Railroad ... 433
Patrick Engineering Inc ... 616 [U], 839
Paul Keller Engineering Ltd ... 698
Paulstra ... 543 [U]
PB Kennedy & Donkin Ltd ... 839
PCK Raffinerie ... 173
PCRC ... 296 [U]
PC-Soft GmbH ... 792
Peaker Services Inc (PSI) ... 544 [U]
PEC ... 514 [U], 599 [U]
Peddinghaus Group ... 616, 632, 741
Peek Traffic BV ... 659
Penetone Corporation ... 776
Peninsula Corridor Joint Powers Board ... 448
Penn Machine Co ... 632 [V]
Pennsylvania high speed route ... 452
People Seating Ltd ... 578 [V]
Peoria Locomotive Works ... 514
Peoria & Pekin Union Railway ... 433
Percy Lane Products ... 578
Permali Gloucester Ltd ... 557 [U], 578 [U], 741 [U]
Peru ... 297
Pettibone Corporation ... 741
PFA Partner für Fahrzeug-Ausstattung ... 514
Pfaff-silberblau ... 776 [V]
Pfister Waagen ... 760
Pfisterer Srl ... 698
Pfleiderer track systems ... 741 [U]
Philadelphia, Bethlehem & New England Railroad Co ... 433
Philippine National Railways (PNR) ... 299
Philippines ... 299
Philips Industrial Electronic Services ... 675
Philips Projects BV ... 839
Philips Semiconductors ... 687
Phoenix AG ... 578, 633, 741
Pickersgill-Kaye Ltd ... 578 [U]
Pijiguaos Railway, Los ... 457
Pilkington Aerospace ... 578 [U]
Pinsly Railroad Company ... 433
Pintsch Bamag ... 578 [U], 660 [U], 741 [U]
Pioneer Railcorp ... 433
Pirelli Cables Ltd ... 706 [U]
Pixy AG ... 578 [N]
PKP ... 300
Plasser & Theurer ... 698, 741
PMA UK ... 706 [U]
PNR ... 299
Pohl Corporation ... 743
Poland ... 300
Polarteknik PMC Oy AB ... 578 [U]
Poli Costruzione Materiali Trazione SpA ... 616 [V], 633 [V]
Polish State Railways (PKP) ... 300
Ponce & Guayama Railway ... 306
Port Terminal Railroad Association ... 434
Portaramp ... 579
Portec Rail Products Inc ... 599, 743 [U], 777
Porterbrook Leasing ... 799
Portland & Western Railroad ... 434 [U]
Portugal ... 303
Portuguese National Rail Administration (REFER) ... 305
Portuguese Railways (CP) ... 303
Postfield Systems ... 675 [N]
Pouget ... 743
Powell Duffryn Rail Ltd ... 633
Powernetics Ltd ... 579, 699 [V]
Power-One AG ... 579 [N]
Powertron Ltd ... 579 [U]
PR ... 293
Precima Development Ltd ... 633
Premesa SA ... 743
Price Ltd, A & G ... 514, 599
PricewaterhouseCoopers ... 839
Prignitzer Eisenbahn GmbH (PEG) ... 173 [U]
Prime Manufacturing Corp ... 554
Privatbanen Sønderjylland ApS (PBS) ... 130 [U]
Proceco Inc ... 777
Procor Ltd ... 599 [U], 801 [V]
Progress Rail Services ... 600 [U], 743 [U]
Progressive Engineering (AUL) ... 660 [U], 777 [U]
Protec ... 579
Providence & Worcester Railroad Co ... 434
PS Corporation ... 743
PSI (Peaker Services Inc) ... 544 [U]
Public Transport Association (UTP) ... 807 [N]
Puget Sound & Pacific Railroad ... 434 [N]
Pulse Electronics Inc (see Wabtec Railway Electronics)
Puzhen Rolling Stock Works ... 633


**Q**


Qiqihar Rolling Stock Co Ltd ... 600 [U], 633 [N], 743 [N]
Qishuyan Locomotive & Rolling Stock ... 514, 600
QR ... 31 [U]
QSS Group ... 840 [U]
Qualter Hall & Co Ltd ... 515
Québec-Gatineau Railway ... 90 [N]
Québec North Shore & Labrador Railway ... 90
Québec Railway Corporation ... 90 [U]
Queensland Rail (QR) ... 31 [U]
Queensland Rail Consulting Services ... 840
Quest Corporation ... 660, 743


**R**


Racal Telecom ... 707
Racine Railroad Products Inc ... 744

860 **INDEX**/R–S

Radenton Scharfenberg 616
Radermacher & Partner GmbH 840
Radsatzfabrik Ilsenberg 633 U
RAI 199 U
Rail Access Corporation (NSW) 35 U
Rail Industry Quality Certification Ltd (RIQC) 842 V
Rail Project Ltd 778 U
Rail Sciences Inc 840
Rail Services Australia (RSA) 36 U, 840
Rail Services International SA (RSI) 515 U, 779 U
Rail Track Association of Australia 808
Rail Traction Company (RTC) 217U
RailAmerica Inc 90 U, 434 U
RaiLink Ltd 90
Railion Denmark 130
Railitaly 217 V
Railko Ltd 633 V
Railmotive 840 U
Railpro BV 744
Railquip Inc 744 U, 777 U
Railroad Signal Inc 660
Rails Co 744
Railtech International 744
Railtech Schlatter Systems 744
RailTex Canada Inc 90
Railtrack 399 U
RailTronic AG 579 N
Railway Association of Canada 808
Railway Consultancy 840
Railway Engineering Associates Ltd 841
Railway Industries Association (France) 808
Railway Infrastructure Authority (Spain) 330
Railway Products (India) Ltd 660
Railway Projects Limited (RPL) 778 U
Railway Safety 401 N
Railway Systems Consultants 841
Railway Technical Society of Australasia 808
Railway Technology Strategy Centre 841
Railways Executive Board (Libya) 257 U
Railweight 760
RailWorks Corporation 744 U, 841 U
Raja Passenger Trains 201
Ranalah Moulds 744 V, 787 V
Ranbury Management Group 841
Rand McNally 687
Rarus Railway Company 435
Rawie GmbH 745 V, 760 U
Ray Smith Group 601 U
RBB 174
RBG 173
RBS 350 U
RCFM 267
RDS Technology Ltd 557
Reading & Northern Railroad Co 435
Red River Valley & Western Railroad Co 435 U
Rede Ferroviaria Federal SA (RFFSA) 71
Rede Ferroviaria Nacional (REFER) 305
Rede Nacional de los Ferrocarriles Españoles (RENFE) 331
Regentalbahn (RBG) 173
Reggiane 515, 600
Reggiane Railways (ACT) 217
Regio-Bahn 173
Regiobahn Bitterfeld (RBB) 174
Reidler Decal Corp 579
Relco Locomotives Inc 515
RENFE 331
Republic Locomotive 515
Rescar Inc 778, 841
Réseau National des Chemins de Fer Malagasy (RNCFM) 262
Réservoir, Le 616
Response Environmental Services 745
Rete Ferroviaria Italiana (RFI) 219 N
REW (Acton) Ltd 778 U
Rex Articoli Tecnici SA 579
Rexquote 745 N
RFF 140 U
RFFSA 71
RFIRT 17
RFS(E) (see Wabtec Rail)
Rhaetian Railway (RhB) 356 U
Rheinbraun 174
Rhein-Haardtbahn (RHB) 174
Rhenus Keolis 157 U
RICA 579, 745
Richardson & Cruddas (1972) Ltd 745
Riga Electric Machine Building Works 557 U
Riksrafiken 345 U
Ringrollers of South Africa 633
RIQC 842
RITC 842
RITES 842
RL Banks & Associates 842
RM 355
RMC Concrete Products 745 U
RMI 792 U
RMS Locotec 745 U, 842 U
RNCFM 262
Road Rail Equipment 745
Robe River Iron Associates (Railroad) 36 U
Robel GmbH 746
Rocafort Ingenieros 516
Rochester & Southern Railroad Inc 435 U
Rocky Mountaineer Railtours 91 N
Roland Berger & Partner 842
Rolanfer SA 600 U, 778
Rolled Steel Association 809
Romania 306
Romanian National Railways (CFR) 306 N
Rose Bearings Ltd 633 N
Rosenqvist Rail Tech AB 746
Ross & White Company 778 U
Rosvagonmash 778
Rotabroach 746
Rotamag Rail Division 746 V
Rotem Company 516 U, 557 U, 600 U, 633 U, 778 U, 787 U
Roundel Ltd 842 U
Royal Railway of Cambodia 75
RPG Transmission Ltd 699
RPL 778
RPS Rail Passenger Services Inc 779 V
RSD 516 U, 600 U, 634 U
Rügensche Kleinbahn (RüKB) 174
Ruhrkohle Bergbau AG 174
Ruhr-Lippe Eisenbahn 175
Ruhrthaler Maschinenfabrik 516
Russian Federation 308
Russian Railways (RZhD) 308
RVR Riga Carriage Building Works 517
R W Mac Co 634

## S

Saalasti Oy 517 U, 616 V, 760 V
Saar-Gummiwerk GmbH 746
SAB WABCO AB 616 V, 634 N
SAB WABCO do Brasil SA 660
Sabah State Railways 267
SABB SA 600
Sabre Inc 792
Sadamel Ticketing Systems 687 U
SAE (India) 699
Safenet AB 579
Safetran Systems Corporation 660, 760
SAFT 557, 579, 699
Sagami Railway 244
SAGEM SA 660, 675, 787
Saginaw Valley Railroad 435 N
Saint-Gobain Sully 579 U
Saint-Gobain Sully NA, Inc 579 U
SAIT-Devlonics 675
SAIT-Systems 660
Salient Systems Inc 746 V
San Diego & Imperial Valley Railroad Co 435
SAN Engineering & Locomotive Co 517
San Joaquin Valley Railroad 435 N
San Pedro & Southwestern Railway 435 N
San Severo-Peschici Railway (F&G) 219
Sangritana Railway (FAS) 219
Santa Matilde, Cia Industrial 518, 600
Sanyo Electric Railway 244
SARCC 324
Sardinian Railways (FdS) 219 U
Sassuolo-Modena Railway (ATCM) 219 U
SAT 660, 787
Sateba International 746 U
SATTI 221 U
Saudi Arabia 315
Saudi Railways Organisation 315
SBF 580
SBI 750
ScanAcoustic AS 675
Scania 544
ScanRail Consult 843
Scandiaconsult International 843 U
Schalke Eisenhütte Maschinenfabrik 518
Schaltbau GmbH 580 N
Schaltbau Holding AG 580 N
Scharfenbergkupplung GmbH 616
Schauer Time & Communication (see Mattig-Schauer)
Scheidt & Bachmann GmbH 687
Schlatter AG, HA 746
Schlegel Swiss Standard 580
SchlumbergerSema Group 660 U, 688 U
Schofield Lothian 843 N
Schöma (Christoph Schöttler Maschinenfabrik GmbH) 518 U
Schramm Inc 746
Schreck-Mieves GmbH 746 N
Schunk Bahntechnik 580 N
Schweizer Electronic AG 747 N
Schwihag GmbH 747 N
SCI 661
Science Systems Group 792
SCIF 518, 600
Scitel Telematics 787
ScotRail 401 U
Scott Wilson Railways 843 U
SDCEM 699
Sea Containers Services Ltd 402 U
SECO-Rail 747 N
Sécheron 557 U, 661 U, 699 U
SEE Société Européenne d'Engrenages 617
SEEC Inc 600
SEFAC Equipement 779
Sefag AG 699
SEFECHA 14
SeFePa 14
Seibu Railway 244
Selectron Systems AG 580 N
SEMAF 518
Semaly SA 843 N
Semco Vacuumteknik A/S 580 U
Seminole Gulf Railway 435
Semperit 747
SEMT Pielstick 544 U
Seneca Group 843
Senegal 317
SEPSA (Italy) 209 U
SEPSA (Spain) 580 U, 661 U
SEPTA 449 U
Serco Raildata 843
Serco Railtest Ltd 844 U
SERINOX 581
Sersa AG 747 N
Servicios Ferroviarios Chaqueños (SEFECHA) 14
Servicios Ferroviarios Patagónicos (SeFePa) 15
SFM 331
SFSM 209 U
SGB Youngman 747 N
SGL Carbon Group 617 U
SGTE 844
SGW 799
Shere Limited 688
Shikoku Railway Co (JR Shikoku) 234
Shimabara Railway 245
Shin Keisei Electric Railway 245
Shinkansen network development 236
Shinkansen rolling stock 236
Short Lines BV 285
Shortline Väst AB 345 V
Siemens Dispolok GmbH 799 N
Siemens Gebaudetechnik, CCTV Systems 688 V
Siemens Nixdorf 688, 792 U
Siemens Rolling Stock Electronics 558 U, 581 N
Siemens Switzerland Transportation Systems Ltd 661, 747, 761
Siemens Transportation Systems Group 662, 663, 699 U, 779, 787 U
Siemens Transportation Systems Inc 519 U
Siemens Transportation Systems Ltd 675 U, 688 V, 761 U
Siemens Westinghouse Technical Services 558
Signal House Ltd 664 V
Sihltal-Zurich-Uetliberg Railway (SZU) 357
Sika AG 747 N
Sika Ltd 761 V
SILF Srl 747
SILSAN 545 V
Silverlink Train Services 402
Silverton Tramway Company 37 U
Silvertown UK Ltd 634
Simclar International Corporation 707
Simmons 780 U
Simoco Europe Ltd 664
Simotra SA 799
Sirti SpA 700
Sitarail 110
SJ AB 345
SJ International 844
Skagen Railway 130
Skelton H J 731 U
SKF 634 U
Skoda Dopravni Technika sro 522 U
Slab Track Systems International 747
Slovakia 318
Slovakian Republic Railways (ZSR) 318 U
Slovenia 323
Slovenian Railways (SZ) 323 U
SLR 337 U
SM Strömungsmaschinen GmbH 545
SMA Regelsysteme GmbH 581
SMC Pneumatics 617
SMIS 748 V
Smith Bros & Webb Ltd 780 U
Smith System Engineering 664
SMTC 581
SNCB 53 U
SNCF 143 U
SNCFT 373 U
SNCS 317 U
SNCT 373
SNIM 268 U
SNTF 4 U
SOB 358 U
Sociedad Colombiana de Transporte Ferroviario SA (STF) 107
Sociedad de Transporte Ferreo de Occidente SA (STFO) 108

# S–T/INDEX

Società Trasporto Alto Adige (STA) ... 220 N
Société Européenne d'Engrenages (SEE) ... 622
Société Générale Egyptienne de Matériel des Chemins de Fer (SEMAF) ... 610 U
Société Nationale des Chemins de Fer Belges (SNCB) ... 53 U
Société Nationale des Chemins de Fer Congolais ... 108 U
Société Nationale des Chemins de Fer du Sénégal (SNCS) ... 317 U
Société Nationale des Chemins de Fer Français (SNCF) ... 143 U
Société Nationale des Chemins de Fer Togolais (SNCT) ... 373
Société Nationale des Chemins de Fer Tunisiens (SNCFT) ... 373 U
Sola ... 748
Solari di Udine SpA ... 675 V
Solartron ... 664
Sóller Railway ... 331
Solvera Information Services ... 844
Soma Equipamentos Industrias SA ... 601
Somafel ... 748
Somers Railway Engineering ... 780
Sonatest plc ... 748 V
SOPAFER-B ... 74
Sound Transit Board ... 449
South Africa ... 324
South African Rail Commuter Corporation (SARCC) ... 324
South African Railways ... 325
South Buffalo Railway Co ... 436
South Carolina Central Railroad Inc ... 436
South Central Ltd ... 403 U
South Central Florida Express ... 436
South Central Railway (IR) ... 195
South Eastern Railway (IR) ... 195
South Eastern Railway (FSE) (Italy) ... 220
South Eastern Railway (Peru) ... 298
South Eastern Railway (Switzerland) ... 358 U
South Kansas & Oklahoma Railroad Inc ... 436
South Wales Transformers ... 700
South West Trains ... 403
Southco Europe Ltd ... 581
Southdowns Environmental Consultants ... 844 V
Southeastern Pennsylvania Transportation Authority (SEPTA) ... 449 U
Southern Ontario Railway ... 91 N
Southern Railway (India) ... 196
Southern Railway (Peru) ... 299
Southern Railway of British Columbia ... 91
Southwestern Railroad Co ... 436
Space Technology Systems (STS Intertec) ... 664
Spain ... 327
Spanish National Railways (RENFE) ... 331
Spanish Narrow-Gauge Railways (FEVE) ... 329
Spanish Private Wagon Owners Association ... 809
Spear Technologies Inc ... 792
Specialized Container Transport ... 37 U
Specialty Bulb Co Inc ... 581, 664
Spefaka GmbH ... 748
Speno International SA ... 748
Sperling Railway Services Inc ... 749 U
Sperry Rail Service ... 749 V
Spie ... 749 V
SPIE Enertrans ... 700
SPII SpA ... 558
Spitzke GmbH ... 749
Spoornet ... 325
Springboard Wireless Networks ... 664
SPS Isoclima SpA ... 581
SPX Fluid Power ... 749 N
SR (Swaziland) ... 339 U
SRA ... 381 U
SRC ... 338 U
Sri Lanka ... 337
Sri Lanka Railways (SLR) ... 337
SRS Swedish Rail System ... 749
SRT ... 370 U
SSIF ... 210 U
St Lawrence & Atlantic Railroad Co ... 91 N, 435
Stabeg Apparatebau GmbH ... 617
Stadler Rail Group ... 523 U
Stag AG ... 610 V
Stagecoach ... 404 U
Standard Car Truck Co ... 617, 634
Standard Steel, LLC ... 634 U
State Railway Authority/SRA (New South Wales) ... 37 U
State Railway of Thailand (SRT) ... 370 U
State Railways Administration (Uruguay) (AFE) ... 453
State Railways of Ecuador (ENFE) ... 131
STB ... 175 U
Steel Authority of India ... 634 U, 749 U
Steele & Co, E G ... 499, 761, 800
Steer Davies Gleave ... 844
Stein ... 664 U
Stemmann-Technik GmbH ... 558
STERIA ... 641, 664, 676, 688, 792
Steria Transports ... 845
Steril-Koni ... 780 V
Stern & Hafferl Light Railways ... 49

STF (Colombia) ... 107
STFO (Colombia) ... 108
STN ATLAS Electronik GmbH ... 641 U
Stone India Ltd ... 582 V, 617 U
Stone International ... 582
Stork RMO BV ... 634 U
Strachan & Henshaw Ltd ... 761
Strategic Development Group ... 844
Strategic Rail Authority (SRA) ... 381
Stratiform Industries ... 582
Strick Corporation ... 601
Strukton Railinfra BV ... 749, 845
STS (Intertec) ... 664
STS Signals ... 665 V
Stucki Company ... 635 U
STV Group ... 845
STVA ... 469 U, 800 U
Styrian Provincial Railways ... 49
Sudan ... 338
Sudan Railways (SRC) ... 338 U
SüdThüringenBahn (STB) ... 175 U
Südwestdeutsche Verkehrs AG (SWEG) ... 175
Sumitomo Metal Industries Ltd ... 617 U, 635 U
Superior Graphite Co ... 635 U
Supersine Duramark Ltd ... 582
Supertek Enterprise ... 700
Suzzara-Ferrara Railway (FSF) ... 220
Svedab–Svensk-Danska Broföbindelsen AB ... 346 V
Svenska Tågkompaniet AB ... 346 U
Swasap Works ... 635
Swaziland ... 339
Swaziland Railway (SR) ... 339 U
Sweden ... 340
SwedeRail AB ... 845
Swedish National Rail Administration (BV) ... 347
Swedish Rail System AB (SRS) ... 749
SWEG ... 175
SweMaint ... 780 V
Swing Thru International Ltd ... 761
Swingmaster Corporation ... 749
Swiss Federal Railways ... 359 U
SWISSRAIL Export Association ... 809 U
Switch and Crossing Manufacturers Association ... 809
Switzerland ... 349
SYCAFER ... 808 V
Sydney Steel Corporation ... 749
Symonds Group ... 845
Syntus ... 286
Syria ... 365
Sysco Srl ... 676
SYSECA ... 665
System Bahnbau International ... 750
Systra Consulting Inc ... 792 U, 845
Systra, Groupe ... 641
SŽ ... 323
SZU ... 357

## T

TAB ... 150 N
Tafesa ... 523, 601, 635
Tågåkeriet i Bergslagen (Tågab) ... 348 U
Taiwan ... 366
Taiwan High Speed Railway Corp (THSRC) ... 366
Taiwan Railway Administration (TRA) ... 367
Tajik Railways ... 368
Tajikistan ... 368
Takamisawa Cybernetics ... 688
Talgo ... 523, 635, 780
Talgo-Transtech ... 524 U
TAMS Consultants Inc ... 845
Tanzania ... 369
Tanzanian Railways Corporation (TRC) ... 369
Tanzania-Zambia Railway Authority (TAZARA) ... 370
Tarmac Precast Concrete Ltd ... 750
Tasrail Services Pty Ltd ... 38 U
Tata Electronic Development ... 642
Tatravagónka ... 601 U, 635 U
Taylor Machine Works Inc ... 761
TAZARA ... 370
TBA (Argentina) ... 15
TBA Textiles Ltd ... 582
TCDD ... 375
TDG ... 846
Techlam ... 635 N
Technical Resin Bonders ... 582
Techni-Industrie SA ... 582, 635
Technirail ... 750
Techspan Systems plc ... 676
TecnEcon Ltd ... 846
Tecnologia e Investigacion Ferroviaria SA (TIFSA) ... 846 U
Tecnost Sistemi SpA ... 688
Tectran ... 750
Tehran Urban & Suburban Railway Company ... 201
Teknis Electronics ... 665 U
Teknoware Oy ... 582
Telemotive Industrial Controls ... 762 U
Telephonics Corp ... 582 U, 665 U, 676 N
Telkor Signalling (Pty) Ltd ... 665

Temoinsa (Tecnicas Modulares e Industriales SA) ... 582 V, 788
Tempered Spring Co ... 750
Templeton, Kenly & Co ... 750
Tenmat Ltd ... 635
Tennessee Southern Railroad Co ... 436
Tensol Rail ... 750
TERA ... 846 U
Terminal Ferroviaria del Valle de México (TVFM) ... 270
Terminal Railroad Association of St Louis ... 436
Teutoburger Wald Eisenbahn (TWE) ... 175
Texas high speed route ... 452 U
Texas Mexican Railway Co ... 436
Texas & Northeastern Railroad (TNER) ... 436 N
Texas-New Mexico Railroad ... 436 U
Texmaco Ltd ... 601
Textar Kupplungs- und Industriebeläge GmbH ... 617
TFM (Mexico) ... 271
TFVM ... 270
TFVM-SNIM ... 270
TGOJ ... 348 U, 780
th-contact AG ... 583 N
Thailand ... 370
Thales Communications BV ... 665
Thales Communications Ltd ... 665 N
Thales Translink ... 665 U, 676 N
Thalys International SC ... 468
Thames Trains ... 404 U
Thameslink ... 405
The Local Railway ... 128 N
The Network Connection ... 577
The rump of JNR ... 238
Thebra do Brasil ... 751
Theimeg Elektronikgeräte ... 666
Thermit Australia ... 751
Thermit Welding (GB) Ltd ... 751
Thermo King ... 583
Thermon Manufacturing Co ... 751 N
Thims ... 751
Thomas K Dyer Inc ... 825 U
Thorn Transport Lighting Ltd ... 583
Thrall Car Manufacturing Co ... 601
THSRC ... 366
Thrall Europa Service Parts ... 781
Thurbo AG ... 364 N
Thyssen Krupp ... 617, 635, 751
Thyssen Umformtechnik GmbH ... 762
Tiefenbach GmbH ... 666, 751
Tiflex Ltd ... 583 U, 751 U
TIFSA ... 846 U
Tilney Shane ... 846
Timera Inc ... 793
Timken Co ... 636
Tipco ... 751 U
TKL Rail ... 751
TLC ... 846
TMG International Pty ... 847 U
Tobu Railway ... 245
TODCO Inc ... 583
Togo ... 373
Tokimec ... 752
Tokyo Express Electric Railway ... 245
Tokyu Car Corporation ... 524 U, 617 V
Toledo, Peoria & Western Railroad ... 436
Toll Ltd ... 38 V
Toronto Terminals Railway Company Ltd ... 91 N
Toshiba Corporation ... 525, 558, 584, 666, 689, 700, 762, 781
Total Power Solutions ... 700 N
Touax Groupe ... 800
Toyama Chiho Railway ... 246
Toyo Denki Seizo KK ... 558, 584, 689
TPF ... 364
TRA ... 367
Trackmobile Inc ... 762
Tractebel Development ... 847
TrafficCare AB ... 781 N
TransAdelaide ... 39 U
Transcarpathian Railroads ... 379
Transcore, Inc ... 666 N
Transcorp ... 847
Transferreos Ltda ... 108
Transfesa ... 800
Transit Control Systems ... 584 U
Transit Design Group (TDG) ... 846
Transkentucky Transportation Railroad Inc ... 436
Transmatic Inc ... 584
Transmitton Ltd ... 666 N, 700 V
Transport Design International ... 847
Transport Research Laboratory ... 848 U
Transportacion Ferroviaria Mexicana (TFM) ... 271
Transportation & Economic Research Associates (TERA) ... 846 U
Transportation Products Sales Inc ... 558, 666
Transportation Technology Center ... 847 U
Transports Public Fribourgeois (TPF) ... 364
Transrapid International ... 525 U
Trans Regio ... 175
TransTec ... 848
Transtechnik ... 584
Transurb ... 848

862 **INDEX**/T–Y


Transurb Technical SA 848
Transwerk 526
Transys Projects 848 [U]
Tranz Rail 286 [U]
Tranz Scenic 2001 Ltd 289 [N]
Trauner 848
TraXion 131 [N]
Trend Installation Tooling 700
Trenes de Buenos Aires (TBA) 15
Trenes & Turismo SA 16
Trenitalia SpA 781 [N], 849 [N]
Trensurb 71
Trento-Malè Railway (FTM) 220
TrentonWorks 602
Trevira 584 [V]
TRG Wagonmarket Spol sro 800 [U]
Triax-YSD 617
TriCon Design GmbH 584
Tri-County Commuter Rail Authority (Tri-Rail) 450 [U]
Trinity Chemical Industries Inc 800 [N]
Trinity Difco 602, 752
Trinity Railway Express 451 [U]
Trivector System AB 676 [U]
TRL 848
True Temper 752
TSM Inc 545, 617, 636
TSO 752
TTX Company 801
TUC Rail SA 849
Tuchschmid AG 602 [V], 762
Tucumán Ferrocarriles SA (TuFeSA) 16
Tülomsas 526 [V], 545 [V], 558, 602, 636, 752
Tunisia 373
Tunisian National Railways (SNCFT) 373 [U]
Turbomeca 545
Turin Local Railways (SATTI) 221
Türk + Hillinger 752
Turkey 375
Turkington Precast 752
Turkish State Railways (TCDD) 375
Turkmenistan 377
Turkmenistan State Railway 377
Tuscola & Saginaw Bay Railway 436
TWE 175
Twiflex Ltd 546 [U]
Twin Cities & Western Railroad Co 436
Twin Disc Inc 546 [V]
Two-Way Technology Ltd 752
Tyco Electronics 707
Tyréns Infraconsult AB 849


## U


UBB 175
UCM Reşiţa 546 [U], 617
Ueda Brake Co Ltd 617
UEPFP 17
UFC (Cuban Railways) 113 [U]
Uganda 378
Uganda Railways Corporation (URC) 378
UIRR SC 469 [U]
Ukraine 379
Ukrainian National Rail Transport Administration (UZ) 379
Ultra Dynamics Ltd 752 [V], 762 [U]
Ultra Electronics 700
Ultrasonic Sciences Ltd 781 [U]
Unicel Corporation 584
UniControls AS 584, 666
Unidad Ejecutora del Programa Ferroviario Provincial (UEPFP) 17
UNIFE 807
Unigrid AB 793 [N]
Unilog NV 470 [U]
Unilokomotive Ireland Ltd 526 [U], 762 [U]
Union Carriage & Wagon Co 526
Union of African Railways (UAR) 806
Union of European Railway Industries (UNIFE) 806 [U]
Union Pacific Railroad Co 417
Union Pacific Technologies 793
Union Railroad Co 437
Union Tank Car Co 602 [U], 801 [U]
Unipar Inc 546 [V]
Unit Rail Anchor 753
United Goninan 527 [U], 603 [U], 636 [U], 781 [N]
United Kingdom 381
United Kingdom,
Association of Train Operating Companies 382 [U]
Association of Wagon Building & Repairing 810
Institute of Logistics and Transport 801
Institution of Civil Engineers 810 [U]
Institution of Diesel & Gas Turbine Engineers 810
Institution of Electrical Engineers 810 [V]
Institution of Mechanical Engineers Railway Division 810
Institution of Railway Signal Engineers 810 [U]
Locomotive & Carriage Institution 810
Permanent Way Institution 810 [U]
Private Wagon Federation 810
Rail Civil Engineers' Association 810 [N]
Railway Forum 810 [U]
Railway Industry Association 810 [U]
United States of America 408
United States of America,
Association of American Railroads 811
Association of Railroad Superintendents 810
Association of State Highway & Transportation Officials 810
High Speed Ground Transportation Association 811 [U]
National Mediation Board 811
National Railroad Construction & Maintenance Association 81 [U]
National Railway Labor Conference 811 [V]
National Transportation Safety Board 811
Operation Lifesaver 811
Port Terminal Railroad Association 811
Public Transportation Association (APTA) 810 [U]
Railroad Human Resource Management Association 812
Railroad Retirement Board 812 [U]
Railway Car Institute 811 [U]
Railway Engineering & Maintenance Association 811
Railway Progress Institute 812
Railway Systems Suppliers 812
Regional Railroads of America 812
Short Line Railroad Association 811
UniTrac Systems 753
Unity Railway Supply Co Inc 603 [V], 617 [V]
Universal Power Systems 667 [N]
Upper Merion & Plymouth Railroad Co 437
Upright UK Ltd 753, 781
Uralvagonzavod 603, 636
URC 378
Uruguay 453
US & S 667
USF 781
US Steel Company/Blackstone Partners/Transtar Inc 437
Usedomer Bäderbahn (UBB) 175
USSC Group Inc 585
Utah Railway Co 437
UZ 379
Uzbekistan 454
Uzbekistan Railway 454 [U]


## V


VAE AG 753 [U]
VAE Nortrak 753 [U]
VAE UK Ltd 753 [N]
Vaia Car 753 [N]
Valdunes 636 [U]
Valencia Railways (FGV) 336
Vanjax Sales Pvt Ltd 781 [U]
Vanness-Brackenridge Group 849 [U]
Vapor Corporation 585
Vaughan Harmon Systems 677
VBK Transport Interior 585
Velec SA 677
Vemb-Thyborøn Railway 131 [U]
Venete Railways (FV) 221 [U]
Venezuela 455
Venezuelan State Railways (Ferrocar) 455
Venice-Simplon-Orient-Express Ltd (VSOE) 468
Ventra Locomotives Ltd 527 [U]
Ventura County Railroad 437 [N]
Verkehrsbetriebe Kreis Plön (VKP 176
Verkehrsbetriebe Peine-Salzgitter (VPS) 176
Vermont Railway Inc 437
VIA Rail Canada 91 [U], 781
Viamont 122 [U]
Vibratech Inc 636 [U]
Victoria Public Transport Corporation 40 [U]
Victorian Rail Track Corporation 40 [U]
Vienna-Baden Railway (WLB) 49
Vietnam 457
Vietnam Railways (DSVN) 457
Villares, Equipamentos, SA 527
VIPS AB 793
Virgin CrossCountry 405
Virgin Southern Railroad 437 [N]
Virgin Trains 405 [N]
Virgin West Coast 406
Virginia Railway Express (VRE) 451
Vitoria a Minas Railway (EFVM) 71
VKP Verkehrsberiebe Kreis Plön 176
V/Line Passenger 39 [U]
Voest Alpine Schienen 753
Voice Perfect 677 [V]
Voies Ferrées Locales et Industrielles (VLFI) 150 [U]
Voith Safeset 546 [V]
Voith Turbo GmbH 546
Volkswagen Transport GmbH 176
Vollert 763 [U]
Volvo Penta AB 557 [V]
Von Roll BETEC 781 [U]
Vortok International 753
Vossloh Rail Systems GmbH 754 [U]
Vossloh Schienenfahrzeugtechnik 527 [U], 636 [N], 781 [N]
Vossloh System-Technik YorkLtd 642 [U], 793 [U], 849 [U]
VPS Verkehrsbetriebe Peine-Salzgitter 176
VRE 451
VRT 40 [U]
VSOE Venice-Simplon-Orient-Express Ltd 468
VST 677 [U]
VTG 800
Vultron International Ltd 677 [U]


## W


Wabash National Corporation 603 [U]
WABCO Westinghouse Air Brake Company 585 [N], 618 [U]
Wabtec Rail 528, 586, 603 [U], 618, 636, 754, 763
Wabtec Railway Electronics 667
Wacker GB Ltd 754
Wagon Pars 528, 603
WagonySwidnica SA 604
Wakamatsu Sharyo 604
Wales & Borders Trains 407 [U]
Walkers Ltd 637
Walter Bau-AG 754
Walter Finkbeiner 782 [N]
Walter Mäder Aqualack GmbH 586 [N]
Wandel & Goltermann 667
Wanne-Herner Eisenbahn und Hafen (WHE) 176 [U]
Washington high speed rail project 452
WEBA 176
WEG 177
Weidmüller Interface GmbH 707 [U]
Weighwell 763 [N]
Wendell Cox Consultancy 849 [U]
Wessex Trains 407 [N]
West Anglia Great Northern Railway 408
West Coast Railway (Victoria) 41 [U]
West Japan Railway Co (JR West) 229 [U]
West Michigan Railroad Co 437 [N]
West Texas & Lubbock Railroad 437 [N]
Westcode Inc 586 [N]
Western Australian Government Railways (Westrail) 41 [U]
Western-Cullen-Hayes Inc 668, 755
Western Railway (WR) 197 [U]
Western Railway (VNJ) 131
Westerwaldbahn (WEBA) 176 [U]
Westfälische Landes-Eisenbahn (WLE) 176
Westfälische Verkehrsgesellaft (WVG) 177
Westinghouse Brakes Ltd 618 [U], 689 [U]
Westinghouse Rail Systems Ltd 668 [U]
Westinghouse Saxby Farmer Ltd 618 [U], 668 [N]
WestNet Rail 43 [N]
Wesurail Limited 772
WHE 176 [U]
Wheel & Axle Plant, Indian Railways 637
Wheeling & Lake Erie Railway 437
Whipp & Bourne 700
Whiting Corporation 782
Wichita Tillman & Jackson Railway Co 438 [U]
Widney Transport Components 586
Wieland Lufttechnik GmbH 755
Wilbur Smith Associates 849 [U]
Wild & Grunder 701
Willamette & Pacific Railroad Inc 438 [U]
William Cook Rail 610 [V], 637
Willy Vogel 637, 755
Wilson, Ihrig & Associates 850 [V]
Winchester & Western Railroad Co 438
Windhoff AG 755, 763, 782
Windsor & Hantsport Railway 93
Winstanley & Co (Kings Norton) Ltd 586
Wisconsin & Southern Railroad Co 438
Wisconsin Central Transportation Corporation 420
Wismut 177
WLB 49
WLE 176
Woodhead Shock Absorbers 586 [U], 637 [U]
Woodville Polymer Engineering 586 [U]
WS Atkins Rail Ltd 850 [U]
Württembergische Eisenbahn-Gesellschaft (WEG) 177
WVG 177
Wyoming Colorado Railroad Inc 438


## X


XP plc 586


## Y


Yacimientos Carboniferos Rio Turbio SA (RFIRT) 17
Yadkin Valley Railroad Co 438
Yamatech 755
Yamato Kogyo 755
YEC Yorkshire Engine Co 529, 763, 782
YTT International Inc 850 [U]

Yugoslavia, Federal Republic ......................................... 459
Yugoslav Railways (JZ) 2002 .................................. 459 U
Yutaka Manufacturing Co Ltd ............................... 618, 707

## Z

ZAGRO Bahn- und Baumaschinen GmbH ................... 763
Zambia ............................................................................. 460
Zambia Railways Ltd (ZRL) ...................................... 460 U
Zastal SA ........................................................................ 604
ZCi ................................................................................... 250
ŽD ................................................................................... 121 U
ZDB AS (see Bonatrans AS)
Zeco Zimbabwe Engineering ........................ 529, 604, 637
Železničná spoločnost as (ŽS) .................................. 322 N
Zelisko .......................................................... 668 U, 689 N
Zephir SpA ................................................................. 529 U
ZF Friedrichshafen AG ................................................. 547U
ZF Sachs AG ................................................................. 637U
ZF Padova SpA ............................................................ 547 V
ZGF Zimmer Gunsul Frasca .......................................... 850
Zhuzhou Electric Locomotive Works ........................... 529
Zhuzhou Rolling Stock Works ..................................... 604
Zimbabwe ...................................................................... 462
Zöllner GmbH ........................................................... 755 N
ZRL ............................................................................. 460 U
ZSR ............................................................................. 318 U
ZT Zeta-Tech Associates ............................................... 793
Zweiweg Schneider ................................................. 755, 763
Zwiehoff GmbH .......................................... 529 U, 763 U

# NOTES